CQ's

Politics in America

2002

THE 107TH CONGRESS

By Congressional Quarterly's Staff
Brian Nutting and H. Amy Stern, Editors

★

Congressional Profiles

Contact Information

District Data

Key Votes

★

Robert W. Merry, President and Publisher
David Rapp, Executive Editor, Senior Vice President
Patrick Rockelli, Associate Publisher, Senior Vice President
John A. Jenkins, General Manager, Senior Vice President CQ Press

Published by Congressional Quarterly Inc.
Andrew Barnes, Chairman
Andrew P. Corty, Vice Chairman
Nelson Poynter (1903-1978), Founder

Copyright ©2001 Congressional Quarterly Inc.

All rights reserved. No part of this publication may be reproduced or transmitted in any form or by any means, electronic or mechanical, including
photocopy, recording or any information storage and retrieval system,
without permission in writing from the publisher.

Printed in the United States of America

ISBN 1-56802-655-2 (hard)   ISBN 1-56802-656-0 (paper)

ISSN 1064-6809

The Library of Congress catalogued an earlier edition of this title
as follows:

Congressional Quarterly's Politics in America: 1994, the 103rd
Congress / by CQ's political staff: Phil Duncan, editor.

p.   cm.

Includes index.

1. United States. Congress — Biography.   2. United States.
Congress — Committees. 3. United States. Congress — Election
districts — Handbooks, manuals, etc.   I. Duncan, Phil.   II.
Congressional Quarterly Inc. III. Title: Politics in America.
JK1010.C67 1993   328.73'073'45'0202

R
328.73
P75c
2002

Politics in America 2002
THE 107TH CONGRESS

EDITORS
Brian Nutting, H. Amy Stern

MANAGING EDITOR
Peter Roybal

ASSISTANT MANAGING EDITORS
Suzanne Dougherty, Peter H. King

ASSISTANT EDITORS
David Hawkings, Christine C. Lawrence, Katrina Van Duyn

CONTRIBUTING EDITORS
Martha Angle, Bob Benenson, Mike Christensen, Colette Fraley,
Lara Hearnburg Johnson, Bob Menaker, Scott Montgomery

CONTRIBUTING WRITERS
Rebecca Adams, Sandra Basu, James C. Benton, Adriel Bettelheim,
Mary Agnes Carey, Julie Hirschfeld Davis, Jack Deutsch, Karen Foerstel,
Gregory L. Giroux, Alan Greenblatt, David Hosansky, Mary Clare Jalonick,
Chuck McCutcheon, Barbra Murray, David Nather, Lori Nitschke,
Alan K. Ota, Elizabeth A. Palmer, Daniel J. Parks, Emily Pierce, Jeff Plungis,
Miles A. Pomper, Andrew Taylor, Pat Towell, Matthew Tully, Derek Willis

RESEARCHERS
Arwen Adams, Jonathan Allen, Victoria Allred, Nell Benton,
Mara Caputo, Dana E. King, Kirstyn Leuner, Alecia Marzullo, Steven Patrick,
Michael Phillips, Pam Richardson, Susie Sohn, Nate Teti, Lisa Weintraub

EDITORIAL ASSISTANTS
Karin M. Caifa, Anne M. Nordness

COMMITTEE INFORMATION
Rich Daly, Heather M. Rothman, Adam Graham-Silverman,
Joseph J. Schatz, Jeremy Torobin

INTERNS
Maria Bray, Elizabeth Brown, Katie Dunn, Lisa Licari,
Brianna Piec, Christopher Windham

PHOTOGRAPHY
Scott J. Ferrell

PRODUCTION EDITOR
Yolie Dawson

MEMBERS DATA CONVERSION
George R. Codrea, Kevin Shanley

PRESIDENTIAL VOTE CALCULATION
Gregory L. Giroux

BOOK DESIGN
Robert Sugar and David Fox, Aurus Design; Marilyn Gates-Davis

WEB SITE DESIGN
Sherri Patterson, DKSdesign; Susan Dillingham Shipp

ACQUISITIONS EDITOR
David R. Tarr

WITHDRAWN
OESTERLE LIBRARY NCC
NAPERVILLE, IL 60540

Politics in America

THE 11TH EDITION

Every vote counts. That simple if not always self-evident truth was brought home with a vengeance in the 2000 elections, which produced so many close results that it was difficult to find any other unifying message or meaning in the outcome.

If nothing else, the landmark contests for control of the White House, Senate and House of Representatives at the turn of the millennium suggest that individuals do make the difference in the nation's ongoing political experiment. This book, "Politics in America," is about the individuals who make up the 107th Congress that was elected in 2000.

The House convened on Jan. 3, 2001, with 221 Republicans, only three seats more than the 218 votes needed to win a roll-call vote on the floor. The Senate had an even more problematic situation: a 50-50 split between Republicans and Democrats. The GOP took control of the chamber only after President Bush was sworn into office on Jan. 20. Vice President Dick Cheney, as the constitutionally designated president of the Senate, gave Republicans the tie-breaking vote.

In other words, every vote still counts, and each member of Congress could well hold the balance of power in his or her hands.

What better mission, then, for this 11th biennial edition of "Politics in America" than to give both insiders and concerned citizens the insights they need on the personalities, legislative agendas and driving political ambitions of each of those 535 congressional power brokers?

The staff of Congressional Quarterly, which has been covering Congress since 1945, considers it part and parcel of our journalistic mandate to know the Capitol Hill players. And it is not enough to follow just the party leaders and committee chairmen. The decisive word on one issue or another may well come from a lawmaker who is little-known to most of the nation.

The legwork for this book began more than a year before the 2000 elections and kicked into overdrive when the election results became known. Herein are the results of that endeavor: in-depth profiles of the 100 senators, the 435 House members, and the states and districts that they serve. Each profile constitutes a "chapter" and seeks to give a full, rounded and objective picture of that member.

Our journalistic eye is focused first and foremost on the legislative landscape: What are the member's experiences and accomplishments in crafting and passing bills? This is what we are most qualified to do: The 100 reporters, editors and researchers on the CQ editorial team follow every piece of legislation that moves through Congress. Reporters spend thousands of hours in committee rooms, in House and Senate press galleries, and in Capitol hallway "stakeouts" of backroom meetings, waiting to question members, their aides and lobbyists of all political persuasions.

We present Congressional Quarterly's best assessment of each member of Congress. Is she a leader, follower or maverick? Is he a show horse or workhorse? How well does he relate to the district that elected him?

As we have stated from the first edition of this book 20 years ago, CQ does not care where a politician stands on an issue, but rather how he expresses his views, and how effectively he accomplishes self-proclaimed goals.

We trust that our guiding corporate philosophy is as valuable in the 21st century as it was for the second half of the 20th. When every vote counts, it becomes even more important to have a reliable, objective and impartial understanding of every person who casts a vote in Congress.

David Rapp
Executive Editor

The 107th Congress – A Group Portrait

The first Congress elected in this new century looks very different from the institution of just 10 years earlier. Heavy turnover in the early 1990s, spurred by a surge of retirements and the Republican Party's upswing, has resulted in a 107th Congress that is relatively inexperienced — at least compared with the seniority-worshipping legislature of the past.

Only one in three current House members was on Capitol Hill during the Cold War. A bare majority knew congressional life under the Democratic control that prevailed before the 1995 GOP takeover. Almost two-thirds of the House members were first elected in 1992 or since, meaning George W. Bush is the first Republican president with whom they have served.

In the Senate, the average length of service has not fluctuated much, and four of the six longest-serving senators in American history are now in office. Yet there is a parallel wave of relative Senate newcomers. As the 107th Congress began, 45 senators had been in the chamber for six years or less, a figure not matched since 1981.

This comparative lack of experience was a complication for the congressional leadership and the new Bush administration, as Republicans claimed their first control of both ends of Pennsylvania Avenue in 46 years.

All promised to push for achievements in a Capitol more closely divided along party lines than at any time since the 83rd Congress convened in 1953. The House, as of April 2001, had 220 Republicans, 210 Democrats, two independents and three vacancies. The Senate was evenly divided, 50 Republicans and 50 Democrats, so the nominal GOP control of Congress resided in the tie-breaking vote of Vice President Dick Cheney.

This close party division, and the lingering rancor from partisan warfare during the two-term presidency of Democrat Bill Clinton, would challenge Bush's pledge to "change the tone" of politics in Washington. Norman Ornstein, a political scholar at the American Enterprise Institute, said of the current members, "Their entire experience in Congress has been a period of enormous tumult and sharp partisan acrimony, and sharp partisan division, so they don't have much to fall back on in terms of an example of how the institution can function as a cooperative place."

A growing percentage of the membership of the 107th Congress came of age in the 1970s and 1980s — during the so-called "me" generation, in which national trends pointed to a resurgence of individual-based, rather than community-oriented, thinking.

Some "Old Bull" veterans of the Congresses before the 1990s, especially Democrats, see as the turning point in this regard the GOP takeover of six years ago — a victory engineered by Rep. Newt Gingrich of Georgia, who rose from the back benches to the Speaker's chair by waging a charismatic campaign against the House as an institution.

Possibly exacerbating partisan tension is the fact that the newest members of Congress have less political experience than their predecessors. In the 107th, 73 percent of new House members have held prior elected office, down from 83 percent two years earlier. Only 64 percent of the new senators held prior office, down from 78 percent two years ago.

"It may be that the junior members have had less opportunity to learn that their opponents don't have horns, so to speak," said John R. Hibbing, a political science professor at the University of Nebraska at Lincoln. Hibbing and others are more concerned about the effects of an increasingly junior Congress on the institution's legislative agenda. A less-senior House and Senate

House tenure is continuing a steep decline, so many lawmakers have served only in a period of partisan rancor.

About the Editors

Brian Nutting came to Congressional Quarterly in 1982, joining the staff of the CQ Weekly magazine. He moved to the CQ Daily Monitor in 1984 as a reporter and later became managing editor. He began working on "Politics in America" in 1997. Born in Greeley, Colo., he earned bachelor's and master's degrees from the University of Utah. He worked for the Salt Lake Tribune for 11 years before joining CQ. He lives in Rockville, Md. He and his wife Suzanne have two daughters, Meredith and Christina.

H. Amy Stern came to Congressional Quarterly in 1981 as an editorial assistant for the CQ Weekly magazine. Since then, she has worked as an environmental reporter and an editor on the CQ Daily Monitor, as a managing editor of the New Media Department, and as a recruiter for the CQ News Division. Born in Trenton, N.J., she earned a B.A. in American Government from the University of Virginia and has studied at the Alliance Française in Paris. She gets her affinity for politics from her father, Sam Stern, who took her into the voting booth, introduced her to the local pols, and sparked her interest in the national political scene by helping her memorize all the presidents through Nixon.

might not be as savvy about the intricacies of the legislative process, they say, and might be less likely to produce substantive bills.

But the injection of new blood into Congress has its advocates. While their learning curve may be steep, new members can reinvigorate long-stalled debates, some say, and the approaches of political neophytes can change the legislative dynamic. "It is, in the long term, like hitting the 'refresh' button on your computer — it keeps us in touch," said Jack Horner, director of member services for the House Republican Conference.

Democrats, meanwhile, have had to develop "adapt to survive" strategies as they seek the elusive strategy for reclaiming control of Congress.

Operating from the minority, albeit a sizable one, has prompted House Democratic leaders to invite their centrist members to help develop legislative strategy and policy. Likewise, Democrats who have never been in the majority have learned to forge alliances with moderate Republicans in order to have greater influence over what goes on in the House.

The 107th Congress is notable for the number of women senators. In 2000, all six women nominees were elected, and a seventh — Democrat Jean Carnahan of Missouri — was appointed to the seat to which her late husband, Mel Carnahan, was elected. As a result, 13 women, an all-time record, are in the Senate now. The House gained three women this year, to 59, or 14 percent of the membership. Fifty-three of the 72 women in the 107th Congress (74 percent) have prior experience in elected office.

It is uncertain what effect the arrival of more women on Capitol Hill — most notably in the historically male Senate — might have on the way Congress functions. But few rebut the premise that the increasing number of women will alter an institution that has lagged behind most other venues in reflecting shifts in cultural and workplace norms.

"What we've seen in the past in terms of how the Senate functions, the 'old boy' club ... they just can't operate in the same way," Ornstein said.

Ethnic minorities made no significant electoral gains in 2000 and will again make up about 12 percent of Congress. Racial diversity increased in the 103rd Congress, after House boundaries were redrawn for the 1992 elections because of redistricting, but has since plateaued.

The Senate again has only three minority members, none of them black or Hispanic: Hawaii Democrats Daniel K. Akaka, a native Hawaiian, and Daniel K. Inouye, a Japanese-American; and Colorado Republican Ben Nighthorse Campbell, an American Indian.

Of the 36 black House members (8 percent of the total), only one is a freshman: William Lacy Clay Jr., D-Mo., who succeeded his father. The one freshman among the 19 Hispanics (4 percent) is Hilda Solis, D-Calif.

The range of career backgrounds also has not shifted much since the 106th Congress. The number of members who have served in the military — 133 in the House, 38 in the Senate — continues its decade-long decline. The majority of the 107th Congress has experience in the legal profession, the business world or the public sector. Roman Catholic continues to be the most common religious affiliation, with 149 members claiming it.

The youngest senators are Illinois Republican Peter G. Fitzgerald and Arkansas Democrat Blanche Lincoln, both born in 1960. The oldest, born in 1902, is South Carolina Republican Strom Thurmond, who was first elected in 1954 and holds the record for the longest senatorial service ever. In the House, freshman Florida Republican Adam Putnam, born in 1974, is the youngest, while New York Republican Benjamin A. Gilman, born in 1922, is the oldest.

Table of Contents

Explanation of Statistics

State Profiles

Each state profile contains information on the state's governor, composition of the legislature, and information about major cities. Information about the state legislatures reflect the status as of March 2001. Details about the makeup of the state legislatures, salaries of members and legislative schedule was obtained from state officials.

POPULATION AND URBAN STATISTICS

Demographic information for each state and congressional district was obtained from the Bureau of the Census and the Bureau of Economic Analysis, both within the Department of Commerce.

State population figures come from the 2000 Census. City population figures are 1999 Census Bureau estimates.

Data on median age; the percentage of residents born in the state and born in another country; urban/rural breakdown; and violent crime rate figures are from 1997. Poverty rate, federal workers and military personnel are 1998 figures.

DISTRICT STATISTICS

The chart at the bottom of each state page gives the vote for president in 1992, 1996 and 2000 for each congressional district. In states where significant changes in district maps were made after 1992, some 1992 and 1996 election results cannot be compared to 2000 results.

Greg Giroux of Congressional Quarterly calculated the 2000 district vote for president. Percentages are given for the Democratic and Republican candidate in each election. In addition, the percentage of the vote received by Ross Perot in 1992 and 1996 and by Ralph Nader in 2000 is given.

Polidata of Lake Ridge, Va., calculated the 1996 and 1992 district vote for president data, with the assistance of Congressional Quarterly. The 1992 district vote for president was calculated using data only for the major candidates. Percentages for the 1996 and 2000 district vote for president are calculated using all votes cast for president.

Data on racial composition, Hispanic origin, median household income, age breakdown and percentage of college graduates for each congressional district are from the 1990 Census. The Census Bureau recalculated data for states that redrew district lines in the middle portion of the decade. Some data have been recalculated for Virginia and North Carolina, whose new maps took effect later. Some changes in North Carolina and Virginia were so minor that the data is presented even though it has not been recalculated.

Member Profiles

Committees

Standing and select committees are listed for Senate and House members, as are major joint committees. Full committee and subcommittee chairmanships are noted.

A complete roster of committee and subcommittee assignments is in the back of the book.

Career and Political Highlights

The career entry includes the member's principal occupations before becoming a full-time public official, with the most recent occupation listed first. In many cases, the political offices listed were part-time jobs and the member continued working at his or her "career" job.

Political offices listed include elected positions in government, unsuccessful candidacies for public office, high party posts, and posts requiring legislative confirmation. Dates given cover years of service, not election dates.

Key to Party Abbreviations

21ST	21st Century
AC	American Constitution
ACP	A Connecticut Party
AF	America First
AFE	Anti Federalist
AKI	Alaskan Independence
AM	American
AMH	American Heritage
AMI	American Independent
C	Conservative
CA	Constitutional American
CC	Concerned Citizens
CFC	Conscience for Congress
CITFIRST	Citizens First
CNSTP	Constitution
CONSTL	Constitutional
COPP	Concerns of People
CP	Commonwealth
D	Democratic
DDD	Damn Drug Dealers
EF	Earth Federation
FDM	Freedom
FN	Future Now
FWC	Francis Worley Congress
GCP	Green Coalition
GR	Grassroots
GREEN	Green
I	Independent
IA	Independent American
ICM	Independent Citizens Movement
IF	Independence Fusion
IG	Independent Grassroots
INDC	Independence
IPC	Independent Peoples Coalition
JPR	Jobs, Property Rights
KAF	Keep America First
L	Liberal
LAWR	LaRouche Was Right
LIBERT	Libertarian
LMN	Legal Marijuana Now
LMP	Legalize Marijuana
LU	Liberty Union

continued on next page

Key to Party Abbreviations

continued from previous page

MNTAX	Minnesota Taxpayers
MRF	Marijuana Reform
NA	New Alliance
NJC	N.J. Conservative
NJI	New Jersey Independents
NL	Natural Law
NON	Non-Partisan
NP	New Progressive
P	Prohibition
PAC	Politicians Are Crooks
PACIFIC	Pacific
PAT	Patriot
PF	Protecting Freedom
PFP	Peace and Freedom
PLC	Pro Life Conservative
PLP	Pro Life
POPDEM	Popular Democratic
PRI	Puerto Rican Independence
PRO	Progressive
PS	Protect Seniors
PTC	Property Tax Cut
R	Republican
REF	Reform
RES	Resource
ROP	Running On Principles
RTL	Right to Life
S	Socialist
SE	Socialist Equality
SM	Save Medicare
SSS	Save Social Security
SW	Socialist Workers
TAX	Taxpayers
TCN	Tax Cut Now
TLC	Term Limits Candidate
TLL	Truth, Life, Liberty
UC	United Citizens
USA	Undauntable Stalwart Allegiance
USP	U.S. Pacifist
USTAX	U.S. Taxpayers
VG	Vermont Grassroots
VREF	Virginia Reform
WC	Working Class
WFM	Working Families
WG	Wisconsin Greens
WSN	West Side Neighbors
WW	Workers World
X	Not applicable

Elections

General election returns are listed for House members for 2000 and 1998 and for senators and governors for their most recent election. Returns do not include candidates who received less than 1 percent of the vote. Because percentages have been rounded and some minor candidates have been excluded, election results do not always add up to 100 percent.

Earlier election victories are noted for members of the House and Senate, with the member's percentage of the vote is given. If no percentage is given for a year, the member either did not run or lost the election.

In special elections where a candidate would have won outright if they had received a majority of the votes, two election tallies are given — one for the first election and one for the subsequent runoff election.

PRIMARY ELECTIONS

Primary election procedures in three states deserve special note. Washington and California have "jungle," or open, primaries, in which candidates of all parties appear on the same ballot; the candidate in each party with the most votes advances to the general election. Louisiana holds its primary on Election Day. It is an open primary, with candidates from all parties on the ballot. Any candidate who receives more than half the votes, or who is unopposed, is elected. If no candidate receives more than half the votes, the top two vote-getters, regardless of party, advance to a runoff election later. Since the current procedure has been in place — for the 1998 and 2000 elections — no runoffs have been required, and the November election is labeled as a general election.

Key Votes

CQ editors selected key votes from the roll-call votes taken during the 106th Congress. The following captions give the bill number, a brief description of the matter being voted upon, a breakdown of the vote, the date the vote was taken and the president's position on the issue (if he took one).

Senate Key Votes

2000

HR 833. Bankruptcy Overhaul/Passage. Passage of the bill that would revise bankruptcy laws to make it easier for courts to move debtors from Chapter 7 of the bankruptcy code, which allows most debts to be discharged, to Chapter 13, which requires a reorganization of debts under a repayment plan. It also would increase the minimum wage, currently $5.15 an hour, by $1 over three years. Passed 83-14: R 50-2; D 33-12 (ND 26-11, SD 7-1). Feb. 2, 2000.

H Con Res 290. Fiscal 2001 Budget Resolution/Conference Report. Adoption of the conference report on the fiscal 2001 budget resolution. The resolution calls for cutting taxes by $150 billion over five years and creating a "reserve fund" of $25 billion that could also be used for tax cuts. It also would establish a $40 billion reserve fund for Medicare overhaul and to provide prescription drug coverage for seniors. The plan calls for $600.3 billion in discretionary spending and allows for $310.8 billion in defense appropriations. Adopted 50-48: R 50-4; D 0-44 (ND 0-36, SD 0-8). April 13, 2000.

S 1287. Nuclear Waste Storage/Veto Override. Passage, over President Clinton's April 25, 2000, veto, of the bill that would provide for the completion of siting and licensing activities for a permanent nuclear waste repository at Yucca Mountain, Nev. Rejected 64-35: R 51-3; D 13-32 (ND 5-32, SD 8-0). A two-thirds majority of those present and voting (66 in this case) of both houses is required to override a veto. A "nay" was a vote in support of the president's position. May 2, 2000.

S 2521. Fiscal 2001 Military Construction Appropriations/U.S.

Troops in Kosovo. Levin, D-Mich., amendment to strike the provision that would terminate funding for continued deployment of U.S. ground troops in Kosovo after July 1, 2001, unless Congress authorizes the deployment. Adopted 53-47: R 15-40; D 38-7 (ND 32-5, SD 6-2). A "yea" was a vote in support of the president's position. May 18, 2000.

S 2549. Fiscal 2001 Defense Authorization/Hate Crimes. Kennedy, D-Mass., amendment that would broaden hate crimes to include crimes related to gender, sexual orientation and disability and would make it easier for the federal government to get involved in the investigation and prosecution of hate crimes. Adopted 57-42: R 13-41; D 44-1 (ND 36-1, SD 8-0). A "yea" was a vote in support of the president's position. June 20, 2000.

HR 4577. Fiscal 2001 Labor-HHS-Education Appropriations/Genetic Discrimination. Jeffords, R-Vt., amendment that would prohibit health insurers from using predictive genetic information to discriminate in the health care system. It also would prohibit insurance companies from raising rates or denying patients health coverage based on the results of genetic tests. Adopted 58-40: R 55-0; D 3-40 (ND 3-32, SD 0-8). June 29, 2000.

S 2549. Fiscal 2001 Defense Authorization/Missile Defense System Testing. Cochran, R-Miss., motion to table (kill) the Durbin, D-Ill., amendment that would require the Pentagon to test the national missile defense system against reasonable decoys and countermeasures that the system could encounter in a launch, and establish an independent panel to review the testing. Motion agreed to 52-48: R 52-3; D 0-45 (ND 0-37, SD 0-8). July 13, 2000.

HR 4810. Alleviate "Marriage Penalty" Tax/Conference Report. Adoption of the conference report on the bill that would reduce taxes for married couples by approximately $89.8 billion over five years. The measure would increase the standard deduction claimed by married couples to twice the amount claimed by single taxpayers. The upper boundary of the 15 percent tax bracket would gradually increase to twice the limit for singles. The measure also would make changes affecting couples in the earned income tax credit and the alternative minimum tax. Adopted (thus cleared for the president) 60-34: R 53-1; D 7-33 (ND 5-27, SD 2-6). A "nay" was a vote in support of the president's position. July 21, 2000.

HR 4444. China Trade/Passage. Passage of the bill that would make normal trade relations with the People's Republic of China permanent. The bill includes provisions to protect U.S. businesses and workers from import surges; establish a commission to monitor human rights, labor standards and religious freedom in China; require the administration to report annually on China's compliance with trade agreements; and express the sense of Congress that Taiwan should be admitted to the World Trade Organization.The measure would also authorize $99 million for Radio Free Asia and the Voice of America to expand broadcasts to China and neighboring countries. Passed (thus cleared for the president) 83-15: R 46-8; D 37-7 (ND 29-6, SD 8-1). Sept. 19, 2000. A "yea" was a vote in support of the president's position.

1999

Impeachment of President Clinton/Article II/Obstruction of Justice. Conviction on Article II, which would find President Clinton guilty of obstruction of justice, concealing evidence and delaying proceedings in the Paula Jones federal sexual harassment civil lawsuit. Acquitted 50-50: R 50-5; D 0-45 (ND 0-37, SD 0-8). Feb. 12, 1999. A two-thirds majority of those present and voting (67 in this case) is required to convict the president and remove him from office. A "nay" was a vote in support of the president's position.

S 280. Educational Flexibility/New Teachers. Jeffords, R-Vt., motion to table (kill) the Murray, D-Wash., amendment to the committee substitute

Key Votes

CQ editors selected key votes from roll-call votes taken during the 106th Congress. The following symbols are used:

Y	voted for (yea)
N	voted against (nay)
#	paired for
+	announced for
X	paired against
–	announced against
P	voted "present"
C	voted "present" to avoid possible conflict of interest
?	did not vote or otherwise make a position known.
I	ineligible
S	Speaker exercised his discretion to not vote

amendment. The Murray amendment would authorize $11.4 billion over six years to fund President Clinton's proposal to hire 100,000 new teachers to reduce class size. Motion agreed to 55-44: R 55-0; D 0-44 (ND 0-36, SD 0-8). March 11, 1999. A "nay" was a vote in support of the president's position.

S 254. Juvenile Crime/Gun Show Checks. Lautenberg, D-N.J., amendment to require criminal background checks on all gun sales at gun shows, prohibit non-federal licensees from taking part in gun shows and direct the attorney general to hold background files on gun owners for 90 days. Adopted 51-50: R 6-49; D 44-1 (ND 36-1, SD 8-0), with Vice President Gore casting a "yea" vote, May 20, 1999. A "yea" was a vote in support of the president's position.

S 1344. Managed Care Revisions/Passage. Passage of the bill to provide federal protections, such as access to emergency care, continuing care and approved clinical cancer trials, primarily for the 48 million Americans in self-insured health plans. The bill also would establish an internal and external appeals process, prohibit denials based on predictive genetic information, allow self-employed individuals to deduct the full cost of their health care and expand the availability of medical savings accounts. Passed 53-47: R 52-2; D 0-45 (ND 0-37, SD 0-8); I 1-0. July 15, 1999. A "nay" was a vote in support of the president's position.

S 1233. Fiscal 2000 Agriculture Appropriations/Unilateral Food and Medicine Sanctions. Helms, R-N.C., motion to table (kill) the Ashcroft, R-Mo., amendment to the Daschle, D-S.D., amendment. The Ashcroft amendment would terminate U.S. unilateral sanctions on agricultural and medicinal goods and bar the president from imposing such sanctions against a country without congressional approval, with certain exceptions. Motion rejected 28-70: R 17-36; D 10-34 (ND 8-28, SD 2-6); I 1-0. Aug. 3, 1999.

HR 2084. Fiscal 2000 Transportation Appropriations/Fuel Efficiency Standards. Gorton, R-Wash., amendment to express the sense of the Senate that the Department of Transportation should be allowed to study whether to raise the corporate average fuel economy (CAFE) standard for vehicles. Rejected 40-55: R 6-45; D 34-9 (ND 29-7, SD 5-2); I 0-1. Sept. 15, 1999.

Nuclear Test Ban Treaty/Adoption. Adoption of the resolution of ratification of the Comprehensive Nuclear Test Ban Treaty (Treaty Doc 105-28), which would ban nuclear weapons testing six months after the pact is ratified by the 44 nations that have either nuclear power plants or nuclear research reactors. Rejected 48-51: R 4-50; D 44-0 (ND 36-0, SD 8-0); I 0-1. A two-thirds majority of those present and voting (66 in this case) is required for adoption of resolutions of ratification. Oct. 13, 1999. A "yea" was a vote in support of the president's position.

S 1593. Campaign Finance Revisions/Soft Money Donations and Union Dues/Cloture. Motion to invoke cloture (thus limiting debate) on the Reid, D-Nev., amendment to the Daschle, D-S.D., substitute amendment. The Reid amendment would prohibit national party committees from collecting "soft money" donations, which currently are unlimited and unregulated, and would prohibit unions from using the dues of non-union workers for political purposes without the workers' consent. Motion rejected 53-47: R 8-46; D 45-0 (ND 37-0, SD 8-0); I 0-1. Three-fifths of the total Senate (60) is required to invoke cloture. Oct. 19, 1999.

S 900. Financial Services Overhaul/Conference Report. Adoption of the conference report on the bill that would eliminate current barriers erected by the 1933 Glass-Steagall Act and other laws that impede affiliations between banking, securities, insurance and other firms. The bill also would require that owners of automated teller machines (ATMs) provide notice on the ATM and on-screen of any charges imposed for the use of the terminal. Adopted 90-8: R 52-1; D 38-7 (ND 30-7, SD 8-0). Nov. 4, 1999.

House Key Votes

2000

HR 3846. Minimum Wage/Two-Year Increase. Traficant, D-Ohio, amendment that would increase the minimum wage by $1 over two years. Adopted 246-179: R 42-173; D 203-5 (ND 155-0, SD 48-5); I 1-1. March 9, 2000. A "yea" was a vote in support of the president's position.

HR 4205. Fiscal 2001 Defense Authorization/Kosovo Operations. Kasich, R-Ohio, amendment that would withhold the bill's funding authorization for Kosovo operations, unless extenuating circumstances arise, until the president certifies that European nations are meeting specific burden-sharing targets by April 1, 2001. Kosovo funds could be used only for withdrawing U.S. ground forces from Kosovo if the president failed to provide such certification. Adopted 264-153: R 195-18; D 67-135 (ND 49-100, SD 18-35); I 2-0. May 17, 2000. A "nay" was a vote in support of the president's position.

HR 4205. Fiscal 2001 Defense Authorization/Retiree Health Care. Taylor, D-Miss., amendment that would expand and make permanent the Defense Department Medicare subvention demonstration program. The program would be available to all Medicare-eligible military retirees and their dependents by Jan. 1, 2006. Adopted 406-10: R 207-9; D 197-1 (ND 145-1, SD 52-0); I 2-0. May 18, 2000.

HR 4444. China Trade/Passage. Passage of the bill to make normal trade relations with the People's Republic of China permanent. The bill includes protections for U.S. businesses and workers from import surges; establishes a commission to monitor human rights, labor standards and religious freedom in China; requires the administration to report annually on China's compliance with trade agreements; and expresses the sense of Congress that Taiwan should be admitted to the World Trade Organization. The measure would also authorize $99 million for Radio Free Asia and the Voice of America to expand broadcasts to China and neighboring countries. Passed 237-197: R 164-57; D 73-138 (ND 43-114, SD 30-24); I 0-2. May 24, 2000. A "yea" was a vote in support of the president's position.

HR 8. Estate Tax Repeal/Passage. Passage of the bill that would amend the Internal Revenue Code to phase out the estate and gift taxes, repealing them entirely by 2010. Passed 279-136: R 213-0; D 65-135 (ND 43-104, SD 22-31); I 1-1. June 9, 2000. A "nay" was a vote in support of the president's position.

HR 4578. Fiscal 2001 Interior Appropriations/National Monuments. Hansen, R-Utah, amendment to the Dicks, D-Wash., amendment that would reinstate the bill's provision that would prohibit the Interior Department from using funds to design, plan or manage federal lands as national monuments that have been designated since 1999 under the Antiquities Act. Rejected 187-234: R 177-38; D 9-195 (ND 4-148, SD 5-47); I 1-1. June 15, 2000. A "nay" was a vote in support of the president's position.

HR 4680. Prescription Drugs/Passage. Passage of the bill that would provide prescription drug coverage for Medicare beneficiaries and establish the Medicare Benefits Administration within the Department of Health and Human Services to administer the program. The benefit would be provided by private insurers with a choice between at least two plans. Passed 217-214: R 211-10; D 5-203 (ND 4-150, SD 1-53); I 1-1. June 28, 2000. A "nay" was a vote in support of the president's position.

HR 4811. Fiscal 2001 Foreign Operations Appropriations/Debt Relief. Waters, D-Calif., amendment that would increase funding for the Highly Indebted Poor Countries Trust Fund by $156 million and offset it with cuts to various other programs. The fund was created to help debtor countries write off most of the money owed to multilateral agencies. Adopted 216-211: R 26-194; D 189-16 (ND 142-9, SD 47-7); I 1-1. July 13, 2000.

Key Votes

CQ editors selected key votes from roll-call votes taken during the 106th Congress. The following symbols are used:

Y   voted for (yea)
N   voted against (nay)
\#   paired for
\+   announced for
X   paired against
–   announced against
P   voted "present"
C   voted "present" to avoid possible conflict of interest
?   did not vote or otherwise make a position known.
I   ineligible
S   Speaker exercised his discretion to not vote

Key Votes

CQ editors selected key votes from roll-call votes taken during the 106th Congress. The following symbols are used:

Y	voted for (yea)
N	voted against (nay)
#	paired for
+	announced for
X	paired against
−	announced against
P	voted "present"
C	voted "present" to avoid possible conflict of interest
?	did not vote or otherwise make a position known.
I	ineligible
S	Speaker exercised his discretion to not vote

1999

HR 975. Steel Imports/Passage. Passage of the bill to direct the president, within 60 days of enactment, to take necessary steps — including imposing quotas, tariff surcharges or negotiated enforceable voluntary export restraints — to ensure that the volume of steel products imported into the United States (based on tonnage) during any month does not exceed the average of monthly import volumes during the three years preceding July 1997. Passed 289-141: R 91-128; D 197-13 (ND 146-9, SD 51-4); I 1-0. March 17, 1999. A "nay" was a vote in support of the president's position.

HR 1000. FAA Reauthorization/Off-Budget Funds. Young, R-Fla., amendment to strike the provisions of the bill that would take the Airport and Airway Trust Fund off budget and thereby permit all aviation tax revenue to be spent on aviation programs, exempt from budgetary restrictions but still subject to annual appropriations. Rejected 179-248: R 111-108; D 68-139 (ND 49-106, SD 19-33); I 0-1. June 15, 1999.

HR 2122. Gun Shows/Passage. Passage of the bill to require background checks for purchasers at gun shows, defined as any event with 10 or more vendors and where 50 or more guns are offered for sale; background checks would have to be completed in 24 hours; gun show organizers would be required to destroy purchase records of those who pass background checks. Rejected 147-280: R 137-82; D 10-197 (ND 6-146, SD 4-51); I 0-1. June 18, 1999.

HR 10. Financial Services Overhaul/Passage. Passage of the bill to eliminate barriers against cross ownership among banks, securities firms, insurance companies and other firms. The bill would prohibit banks from selling private customer financial information to telemarketing firms and would allow customers to "opt out"of information-sharing by financial firms with other companies. The bill would allow mutual insurance companies to move their businesses to a different state when reorganizing into a stock company. The bill would prohibit financial companies from conditioning the sale of products on the purchase of other financial products. Passed 343-86: R 205-16; D 138-69 (ND 95-58, SD 43-11); I 0-1, July 1, 1999.

HR 1995. New Teachers and Training Programs/Funding Increases. Martinez, D-Calif., substitute amendment to increase funding for professional development and class-size reduction activities, with a separate authorization for the class-size reduction program. The amendment would authorize $1.5 billion in fiscal 2000 for the class-size reduction program, increasing to $3 billion by fiscal 2005; it would authorize $1.5 billion for teachers' professional development, increasing to $3 billion by fiscal 2004. Rejected 207-217: R 3-215; D 203-2 (ND 151-0, SD 52-2); I 1-0. July 20, 1999. A "yea" was a vote in support of the president's position.

HR 417. Campaign Finance Overhaul/Passage. Passage of the bill to ban all contributions of soft money — money used for party-building activities as opposed to supporting a specific candidate — and impose restrictions on issue advocacy communications. The measure would raise the individual aggregate contribution limit from $25,000 to $30,000 per year and raise the amount that individuals could give to state political parties from $5,000 to $10,000. House candidates who receive coordinated party contributions would be barred from spending more than $50,000 in personal funds. The measure would require labor unions to notify dues-paying nonmembers of any portion of their dues used for political purposes. Passed 252-177: R 54-164; D 197-13 (ND 148-8, SD 49-5); I 1-0. Sept. 14, 1999. A "yea" was a vote in support of the president's position.

HR 2723. Managed Care Patient Protection/Passage. Passage of the bill to require health plans to cover emergency care when a "prudent layperson" could reasonably believe such care was required. Health plans would have to allow direct access to gynecological and pediatric care. The bill would establish an internal and external appeals process to review denial of care. Patients or their estates would have the right to sue their health plan in state courts when the plan makes negligent decisions that result in injury or death of patients. Passed 275-151: R 68-149; D 206-2 (ND 153-1, SD 53-1); I 1-0. Oct. 7, 1999. A "yea" was a vote in support of the president's position.

Voting Studies

Each year, Congressional Quarterly prepares voting studies that represent the percentage of the time a member of Congress has supported or opposed a given position. The votes are listed under two columns — support and oppose. For example, a score of 25 percent under the support column in the presidential support study would indicate that the member supported the president 25 percent of the time on the votes that were used in the study. An explanation of each of the voting studies follows.

PARTY UNITY

Party unity votes are defined as votes in the Senate and House that split the parties, a majority of voting Democrats opposing a majority of voting Republicans. Votes on which the parties agree, or on which either party divides evenly are excluded.

Party unity scores represent the percentage of party unity votes on which a member voted "yea" or "nay" in agreement with a majority of the member's party. Opposition-to-party scores represent the percentage of party unity votes on which a member voted "yea" or "nay" in disagreement with a majority of the member's party.

The score is based only on votes cast; failure to vote did not lower a member's score.

PRESIDENTIAL SUPPORT

CQ tries to determine what the president personally, as distinct from other administration officials, does and does not want in the way of legislative action. This is done by analyzing his messages to Congress, news conference remarks and other public statements and documents.

Occasionally, important measures are so extensively amended that it is impossible to characterize final passage as a victory or a defeat for the president. These votes have been excluded from the study.

Votes on motions to recommit, to reconsider or to table (kill) often are key tests that govern the legislative outcome. Such votes are included in the presidential support tabulations. The score is based only on votes cast; failure to vote did not lower a member's score. All presidential-issue votes have equal statistical weight in the analysis.

Interest Group Ratings

Ratings for members of Congress by four interested groups are chosen to represent liberal, conservative, business and labor viewpoints. Following is a description of each group in the order they appear.

AMERICAN FEDERATION OF LABOR-CONGRESS OF INDUSTRIAL ORGANIZATIONS (AFL-CIO)

The AFL-CIO was formed when the American Federation of Labor and the Congress of Industrial Organizations merged in 1955. With affiliates claiming more than 13 million members, the AFL-CIO accounts for about three-fourths of national union membership. In 1999, the ratings were based on nine House votes and nine Senate votes. In 2000, the AFL-CIO rated 10 House votes and eight Senate votes. (www.aflcio.org)

Congress by the Numbers

Throughout this book, CQ frequently refers to a congressional session by its number. Following is a list of what years are covered within a session.

	YEARS COVERED	ELECTION YEAR
98th Congress	1983-85	1982
99th Congress	1985-87	1984
100th Congress	1987-89	1986
101st Congress	1989-91	1988
102nd Congress	1991-93	1990
103rd Congress	1993-95	1992
104th Congress	1995-97	1994
105th Congress	1997-99	1996
106th Congress	1999-01	1998
107th Congress	2001-03	2000

AMERICANS FOR DEMOCRATIC ACTION (ADA)

Americans for Democratic Action was founded in 1947 by a group of liberal Democrats that included Minnesota Sen. Hubert H. Humphrey and Eleanor Roosevelt. In 1999 and 2000, the ratings were based on 20 votes each year for each chamber of Congress. (www.adaction.org)

CHAMBER OF COMMERCE OF THE UNITED STATES (CCUS)

The Chamber of Commerce of the United States represents local, regional and state chambers as well as trade and professional organizations. It was founded in 1912 to be "a voice for organized business." In 1999, the chamber used 25 House votes and 17 Senate votes to develop its ratings. In 2000, 21 House votes and 15 Senate votes were analysed. (www.uschamber.org)

AMERICAN CONSERVATIVE UNION (ACU)

The American Conservative Union was founded in 1964 "to mobilize resources of responsible conservative thought across the country and further the general cause of conservatism." The organization intends to provide education in political activity, "prejudice in the press," foreign and military policy, domestic economic policy, the arts, professions and sciences. In both 1999 and 2000, the ACU studied 25 votes in each chamber to develop its ratings. (www.conservative.org)

District Descriptions

Most congressional district lines were drawn in 1991 and 1992, and are due to be redrawn for the next decade before the 2002 elections (except in Maine). The description briefly sets forth the economic, sociological, demographic and political forces that are the keys to elections and which influence the legislative agenda of the district's member of Congress.

The population figures given for cities in the district are based on 1999 Census Bureau estimates. In cases in which only part of a city is located within the district, the most recent figures available are from the 1990 Census.

Campaign Finance

Figures are given for all members of Congress and their general election opponents as reported by the Federal Election Commission (FEC). If only one candidate is listed, that candidate was either unopposed or the second-leading vote-getter did not raise at least $5,000.

For House members, figures are given for the 2000 elections. For senators, figures are given for their most recent election.

Except where noted, data cover the receipts and expenditures of each candidate during the two-year election cycle. Data for 2000 cover the period Jan. 1, 1999 to Dec. 31, 2000. Data for 1998 cover the period Jan. 1, 1997 to Dec. 31, 1998. Data for 1996 cover the period Jan. 1, 1995 to Dec. 31, 1996.

Other candidate transactions — such as contributions to other campaigns, loan repayments, purchase and redemption of certificates of deposit, and debts owed to or by the campaign committee at the end of the election year — were not subtracted from the receipts and expenditures totals.

The figures for political action committee (PAC) receipts are based on the FEC summary report for each candidate. Amounts designated include contributions from both PACs and candidate committees but not party committees. PAC contributions received by a candidate but returned within 20 days are not reflected in the FEC compilation. In cases where CQ was able to determine that a member does not accept PAC contributions, a zero appears in the column for PAC contributions.

The FEC updates its information regularly. See the FEC web page at www.fec.gov.

Redistricting Shapes Future Congresses

The disparity in population growth between the boom states of the South and West and slower-growing states of the North and East has been going on for too long to be a phenomenon. It has become a simple fact of American life.

The Census Bureau in December 2000 reported that the 2000 census, conducted the previous April, counted 281.4 million people in the United States, an increase of 13.2 percent over the 248.7 million people enumerated in the 1990 census. There were sharp regional contrasts. The combined population of states in the West increased by 19.7 percent, and Southern states grew by 17.3 percent. Growth in the Midwest (7.9 percent) and East (5.5 percent) lagged behind.

The House of Representatives will reflect that population shift: Beginning with the 108th Congress in 2003, the West will have six more seats in the House, while the South will have a net gain of four. The East and Midwest will each lose five. In all, 12 House seats will be moved from one state to another.

WINNERS AND LOSERS

Nevada's population grew by 66.3 percent in the 10 years leading up to the 2000 census. Arizona's population increased by 40 percent. In percentage terms, California grew more modestly than in recent decades. Yet its 13.8 percent population increase, to a total of 33.9 million, amounted to a gain of more than 4.1 million people — a figure greater than the populations of 26 other states.

The story was different for states in the historic industrial bastions of the Northeast and Midwest. New York — the nation's most populous state from the 1810 census until 1970, when it was passed by California — grew by 5.5 percent and fell to third place behind Texas (which had a 22.8 percent increase). The nation's slowest population growth was in North Dakota (0.5 percent increase) and West Virginia (0.8 percent increase).

REAPPORTIONMENT

As has been the case for decades, the so-called Sunbelt is gaining clout in the U.S. House of Representatives because of its hot population growth.

Congress in 1911 passed a law setting the size of the House at 435 members, where it has stayed despite a tripling of the nation's population in the years since. Thus the need for the decennial reapportionment.

The Constitution guarantees each state at least one House seat. Beyond that, a complex mathematical formula, known as the method of equal proportions, adopted in 1941, is used to apportion the remaining 385 House seats.

All of the states that gained seats were in the South and West: Arizona, Florida, Georgia and Texas each gained two seats, while California, Colorado, Nevada and North Carolina picked up one apiece. California, which already holds the record for the largest state congressional delegation, will have 53 seats in the next Congress.

States that lost seats in the House were mainly in the North and East. New York and Pennsylvania both lost two House seats; Connecticut, Illinois, Indiana, Michigan, Mississippi, Ohio, Oklahoma and Wisconsin saw their House delegations shrink by one.

The new House districts will average about 646,000 people — up from 572,000 people per district based on the 1990 census.

Yet even though the reapportionment formula is designed to provide states with proportional representation, there are anomalies. Montana and Wyoming each will remain at one at-large district, even though the 2000 census found 902,195 people in Montana and 493,782 people in Wyoming.

The Bureau's data is based on an actual head count of the population. Most Democrats and many statisticians argued that the census should be adjusted using a procedure known as statistical sampling to address a per-

Political power continues to shift to the South and West.

Redistricting for the 2002 elections will influence Congress' partisan makeup for the next decade.

Biggest Gainers

Districts that grew fastest in the 1990s, ranked by percentage increase.

STATE, DISTRICT	2000 POPULATION	% INCREASE
Nev. 2	1,062,153	76.8
Ariz. 6	1,001,151	63.6
Ariz. 3	997,565	63.4
Ga. 6	943,373	60.1
Nev. 1	936,104	55.7
Texas 26	845,541	49.7
Colo. 5	810,423	47.5
Texas 3	835,040	47.2
Fla. 19	800,902	42.3
Ga. 11	836,416	41.9
Texas 21	801,078	41.5
Fla. 14	790,852	40.6
Fla. 21	789,742	40.4
Va. 10	792,534	41.0
Texas 10	791,117	39.7
Idaho 1	702,521	39.6
Fla. 20	783,412	39.2
Fla. 8	782,397	39.2
N.C. 4	765,876	38.6
Ga. 9	814,305	38.2
Texas 22	784,759	37.8
Texas 15	780,310	37.7
Texas 8	776,623	37.4
Texas 7	772,147	36.7
Tenn. 6	738,663	36.3

Biggest Losers

Districts that lost the most population in the 1990s, ranked by percentage decrease.

STATE, DISTRICT	2000 POPULATION	% DECREASE
Md. 7	539,439	-9.7
Mo. 1	514,264	-9.5
Pa. 1	515,560	-8.9
Mich. 15	531,634	-8.5
Ohio 11	532,337	-6.8
Wis. 5	507,636	-6.6
Pa. 14	529,299	-6.5
Pa. 2	532,455	-5.8
Ala. 7	544,117	-5.8
Pa. 18	535,432	-5.4
Tenn. 9	512,881	-5.3
Mich. 14	550,599	-5.2
Ohio 1	542,618	-5.0
N.Y. 30	563,256	-3.0
N.Y. 23	563,385	-2.9
Ill. 2	556,482	-2.7
Ohio 3	556,039	-2.6
Ill. 1	560,239	-2.0
La. 2	590,824	-2.0
Ill. 12	560,912	-1.8
N.Y. 25	569,864	-1.8
Pa. 12	556,856	-1.6
Ohio 17	563,164	-1.4
N.Y. 29	572,581	-1.3

sistent undercount of residents in hard-to-count areas, such as inner cities. But most Republicans backed the raw head count, noting that the Constitution requires an "actual enumeration" of the population, and the Supreme Court, in a 1999 decision, agreed with the GOP that the actual head count would be used to determine congressional apportionment.

In March 2001, a 12-member committee of Census Bureau professionals recommended that unadjusted numbers should also be used as the basis for redrawing congressional lines within the states. Donald L. Evans, who oversees the Census Bureau as Commerce secretary to President George W. Bush, accepted the recommendation.

NEXT COMES REDISTRICTING

Now that each state has been assigned its members of the House, and the Census Bureau has provided the states with detailed information about the geographical distribution and the racial and ethnic composition of the populace, it is up to the states to create new congressional districts.

The redistricting dance will take place in each of the 43 states that have more than one congressional district. Few states have statutory deadlines to finish redistricting, but nearly all of them will have new lines in place in time for candidates to file for the 2002 elections.

Even those states whose number of House seats remained the same must alter their district lines, to reflect differences in population growth patterns over the last decade. Since the Supreme Court's 1962 "one man, one vote" decision in the case of *Baker v. Carr*, states have been required to equalize as closely as possible the populations of their congressional districts. Court cases since then have reiterated that standard, with the court ruling in *Karcher v. Daggett* that while it may be impossible to achieve perfect population equality, states should make a "good-faith effort" to do so.

The most common justification accepted by federal courts for any population deviation between congressional districts is preserving "communities of interest." In Iowa and Arkansas, for example, a congressional redistricting plan cannot divide any county between congressional districts.

In many states, an overriding imperative is the Voting Rights Act of 1965, which has been interpreted to require that district lines should be drawn to maximize minority political power. The growing political empowerment of minorities, particularly African-Americans and Hispanics, has resulted in the creation of dozens of congressional districts designed to elect black or Hispanic House members.

Because minorities tended strongly to vote Democratic, officials of that party generally supported efforts to create such districts. But following the 1990 census, the Justice Department of George Bush's Republican administration jumped into the cause with full force. Using its authority under the Voting Rights Act to "pre-clear" certain states' redistricting plans, the Justice Department demanded that states maximize the number of black- and Hispanic-oriented congressional districts.

HOW IT IS DONE

The redistricting process in most states follows the textbook process of how a bill becomes a law. A redistricting plan is introduced as a bill, which is referred to a committee and is subject to amendment. The state legislature votes on the plan, and the governor can sign it into law or veto it.

There are variations. Five states with more than one district — Arizona, Hawaii, Idaho, New Jersey and Washington — empower commissions to handle congressional redistricting. Even redistricting commissions are not immune from political influence, however. In most of those states, appointees are selected by Republican and Democratic leaders of state legislatures.

Iowa's redistricting process may be the most de-politicized of any. The state's nonpartisan Legislative Service Agency has initial responsibility for congressional redistricting and cannot consider election results, most demographic data and incumbents' needs when redrawing lines.

With redistricting looming, the political parties in 2000 concentrated heavily on winning races for governor and state legislative seats that rarely attract national attention. That led some analysts to describe the battle for control of redistricting as the "hidden national election" of 2000.

One party will control redistricting in some of the most populous states: Republicans in Florida, Michigan, Ohio and Pennsylvania; Democrats in California and Georgia.

But most districts in this redistricting round will be redrawn in states where the parties share power or commissions handle redistricting duties.

Moreover, one party's control over the redistricting process in a state does not necessarily translate into a clear-cut victory. Numerous experts predicted that nearly every redistricting plan would wind up in the courts.

POLITICAL IMPLICATIONS

Although redistricting engages the interest of few average voters, it should: How the districts are drawn will define the presence — or lack — of competition for House seats over the next 10 years. Districting is political destiny. According to a Congressional Quarterly analysis, three-fourths of the House seats (328 of 435) were held by the same party throughout the five elections — 1992, 1994, 1996, 1998 and 2000 — that were conducted using the current boundaries.

Because the South and West contain much of the nation's most conservative-voting areas, those regions' accretion of House seats in recent decades has generally benefited the Republican Party. The GOP's rise to dominance in the South, once a solidly Democratic region, contributed greatly to the party's capture of House control in the 1994 elections.

Republican officials contend that the post-2000 reapportionment and congressional redistricting will result in further GOP gains. These partisans noted that most of the states that gained seats voted for Bush in 2000. But Democratic strategists, as expected, are prepared to block Republican efforts to make gains through redistricting.

And the redistricting process is replete with other priorities that sometimes compete with efforts to achieve partisan gains.

For instance, there are House incumbents who zealously resist the slightest alteration of their turf, even if doing so would help elect members of their own party. Meanwhile, state lawmakers eyeing their own runs for Congress seek posts on the legislative committees that draw the lines. Interest groups representing blacks and Latinos advocate greater congressional representation for their constituencies.

As district lines have been drawn in compliance with the Voting Rights Act, GOP political strategists have backed efforts by black and Hispanic groups to draw districts that include large numbers of minorities. That is because the corollary to concentrating minorities in a few districts is that surrounding districts have fewer Democratic-voting minority residents — and thus are more prone to elect Republicans. Many of the majority-minority districts created in the 1990s redistricting had convoluted lines that provoked lawsuits. Eight states — Florida, Georgia, Louisiana, New York, North Carolina, South Carolina, Texas and Virginia — had to redraw their lines during the 1990s after their original district maps were invalidated by courts.

Nonetheless, the Supreme Court, which traditionally has been reluctant to get involved in redistricting, declined to provide definitive guidelines on how districts should be drawn. This virtually ensures that there will be another round of protracted lawsuits over redistricting in the coming decade.

Largest Districts

Twenty of the 25 largest districts are represented by Republicans. The largest districts:

STATE, DISTRICT	2000 POPULATION	MEMBER, PARTY
Nev. 2	1,062,153	Gibbons, R
Ariz. 6	1,001,151	Hayworth, R
Ariz. 3	997,565	Stump, R
Ga. 6	943,373	Isakson, R
Nev. 1	936,104	Berkley, D
Mont. AL	902,195	Rehberg, R
Texas 26	845,541	Armey, R
Ga. 11	836,416	Linder, R
Texas 3	835,040	S. Johnson, R
Ariz. 1	829,492	Flake, R
Ga. 9	814,305	Deal, R
Colo. 5	810,423	Hefley, R
Texas 21	801,078	L. Smith, R
Fla. 19	800,902	Wexler, D
Ariz. 5	793,256	Kolbe, R
Va. 10	792,534	Wolf, R
Texas 10	791,117	Doggett, D
Fla. 14	790,852	Goss, R
Fla. 21	789,742	Diaz-Balart, R
Texas 22	784,759	DeLay, R
Del. AL	783,600	Castle, R
Fla. 20	783,412	Deutsch, D
Fla. 8	782,397	Keller, R
Ga. 3	781,694	Collins, R
Texas 15	780,310	Hinojosa, D

Smallest Districts

Twenty-one of the 25 smallest districts are represented by Democrats. The least populated districts:

STATE, DISTRICT	2000 POPULATION	MEMBER, PARTY
Wyo. AL	493,782	Cubin, R
Wis. 5	507,636	Barrett, D
R.I. 1	510,287	Kennedy, D
Tenn. 9	512,881	Ford, D
Mo. 1	514,264	Clay, D
Pa. 1	515,560	R. Brady, D
Miss. 2	517,345	B. Thompson, D
Pa. 14	529,299	Coyne, D
Miss. 4	530,679	Shows, D
Mich. 15	531,634	Kilpatrick, D
Okla. 6	531,937	F. Lucas, R
Ohio 11	532,337	S. Jones, D
Pa. 2	532,455	Fattah, D
Pa. 18	535,432	Doyle, D
Neb. 3	535,568	Osborne, R
R.I. 2	538,032	Langevin, D
Md. 7	539,439	Cummings, D
Ohio 1	542,618	Chabot, R
Ala. 7	544,117	Hilliard, D
Mich. 14	550,599	Conyers, D
Conn. 1	552,127	Larson, D
Ohio 3	556,039	T. Hall, D
Ill. 2	556,482	Jackson, D
Pa. 12	556,856	Murtha, D
Minn. 5	557,819	Sabo, D

2000 Census and Congressional Apportionment

STATE	2000 POPULATION	1990 POPULATION	PERCENT CHANGE	SEATS IN HOUSE 2003-2013	GAIN/ LOSS
California	33,871,648	29,760,021	13.8	53	+1
Texas	20,851,820	16,986,510	22.8	32	+2
New York	18,976,457	17,990,455	5.5	29	-2
Florida	15,982,378	12,937,926	23.5	25	+2
Illinois	12,419,293	11,430,602	8.6	19	-1
Pennsylvania	12,281,054	11,881,643	3.4	19	-2
Ohio	11,353,140	10,847,115	4.7	18	-1
Michigan	9,938,444	9,295,297	6.9	15	-1
New Jersey	8,414,350	7,730,188	8.9	13	
Georgia	8,186,453	6,478,216	26.4	13	+2
North Carolina	8,049,313	6,628,637	21.4	13	+1
Virginia	7,078,515	6,187,358	14.4	11	
Massachusetts	6,349,097	6,016,425	5.5	10	
Indiana	6,080,485	5,544,159	9.7	9	-1
Washington	5,894,121	4,866,692	21.1	9	
Tennessee	5,689,283	4,877,185	16.7	9	
Missouri	5,595,211	5,117,073	9.3	9	
Wisconsin	5,363,675	4,891,769	9.6	8	-1
Maryland	5,296,486	4,781,468	10.8	8	
Arizona	5,130,632	3,665,228	40.0	8	+2
Minnesota	4,919,479	4,375,099	12.4	8	
Louisiana	4,468,976	4,219,973	5.9	7	
Alabama	4,447,100	4,040,587	10.1	7	
Colorado	4,301,261	3,294,394	30.6	7	+1
Kentucky	4,041,769	3,685,296	9.7	6	
South Carolina	4,012,012	3,486,703	15.1	6	
Oklahoma	3,450,654	3,145,585	9.7	5	-1
Oregon	3,421,399	2,842,321	20.4	5	
Connecticut	3,405,565	3,287,116	3.6	5	-1
Iowa	2,926,324	2,776,755	5.4	5	
Mississippi	2,844,658	2,573,216	10.5	4	-1
Kansas	2,688,418	2,477,574	8.5	4	
Arkansas	2,673,400	2,350,725	13.7	4	
Utah	2,233,169	1,722,850	29.6	3	
Nevada	1,998,257	1,201,833	66.3	3	+1
New Mexico	1,819,046	1,515,069	20.1	3	
West Virginia	1,808,344	1,793,477	0.8	3	
Nebraska	1,711,263	1,578,385	8.4	3	
Idaho	1,293,953	1,006,749	28.5	2	
Maine	1,274,923	1,227,928	3.8	2	
New Hampshire	1,235,786	1,109,252	11.4	2	
Hawaii	1,211,537	1,108,229	9.3	2	
Rhode Island	1,048,319	1,003,464	4.5	2	
Montana	902,195	799,065	12.9	1	
Delaware	783,600	666,168	17.6	1	
South Dakota	754,844	696,004	8.5	1	
North Dakota	642,200	638,800	0.5	1	
Alaska	626,932	550,043	14.0	1	
Vermont	608,827	562,758	8.2	1	
Wyoming	493,782	453,588	8.9	1	
Total	**281,421,906**	**248,709,873**	**13.2**	**435**	

Official 2000 Population Count by District

Population figures are from the Census Bureau. Current representatives are listed. Republicans are in *italics*.

UNITED STATES	2000	1990	PERCENT CHANGE
UNITED STATES	**281,421,906**	**248,709,873**	**13.2**
ALABAMA	**4,447,100**	**4,040,587**	**10.1**
1 *Callahan*	646,181	577,375	11.9
2 *Everett*	650,321	577,203	12.7
3 *Riley*	643,525	577,116	11.5
4 *Aderholt*	643,275	577,058	11.5
5 Cramer	654,886	577,235	13.2
6 *Bachus*	664,795	577,170	15.2
7 Hilliard	544,117	577,430	-5.8
ALASKA	**626,932**	**550,043**	**14.0**
AL *Young*	626,932	550,043	14.0
ARIZONA	**5,130,632**	**3,665,228**	**40.0**
1 *Flake*	829,492	610,817	35.8
2 Pastor	773,824	610,266	26.8
3 *Stump*	997,565	610,424	63.4
4 *Shadegg*	735,344	610,708	20.4
5 *Kolbe*	793,256	611,128	29.8
6 *Hayworth*	1,001,151	611,885	63.6
ARKANSAS	**2,673,400**	**2,350,725**	**13.7**
1 Berry	629,974	588,588	7.0
2 Snyder	666,058	587,412	13.4
3 *Hutchinson*	764,853	589,523	29.7
4 Ross	612,515	585,202	4.7
CALIFORNIA	**33,871,648**	**29,760,021**	**13.8**
1 Thompson	644,525	572,870	12.5
2 *Herger*	633,808	573,226	10.6
3 *Ose*	675,618	571,545	18.2
4 *Doolittle*	725,180	571,027	27.0
5 Matsui	669,412	573,659	16.7
6 Woolsey	644,600	571,360	12.8
7 Miller	636,367	572,857	11.1
8 Pelosi	617,094	573,192	7.7
9 Lee	597,285	573,669	4.1
10 Tauscher	713,341	571,979	24.7
11 *Pombo*	684,178	571,650	19.7
12 Lantos	615,370	571,667	7.6
13 Stark	678,177	572,333	18.5
14 Eshoo	615,917	571,058	7.9
15 Honda	612,416	572,360	7.0
16 Lofgren	689,817	571,460	20.7
17 Farr	653,209	571,077	14.4
18 Condit	683,642	571,358	19.7
19 *Radanovich*	709,622	573,077	23.8
20 Dooley	711,574	573,555	24.1
21 *Thomas*	666,684	571,143	16.7
22 Capps	631,659	572,956	10.2
23 *Gallegly*	642,427	571,562	12.4
24 Sherman	629,832	572,287	10.1
25 *McKeon*	699,526	573,189	22.0
26 Berman	660,224	571,538	15.5
27 Schiff	600,986	572,629	5.0
28 *Dreier*	609,233	572,189	6.5
29 Waxman	584,823	571,386	2.4
30 Becerra	582,745	572,604	1.8
31 Solis	600,376	572,758	4.8
32 Vacant	586,031	572,630	2.3
33 Roybal-Allard	600,695	570,893	5.2
34 Napolitano	617,343	573,456	7.7
35 Waters	607,944	570,697	6.5
36 Harman	591,448	573,665	3.1
37 Millender-McDonald	616,103	572,191	7.7
38 *Horn*	634,392	572,676	10.8
39 *Royce*	622,921	573,941	8.5
40 *Lewis*	674,431	573,939	17.5
41 *Miller*	666,225	572,529	16.4
42 Baca	700,491	571,595	22.6
43 *Calvert*	736,634	571,090	29.0
44 *Bono*	742,718	571,843	29.9
45 *Rohrabacher*	619,092	570,991	8.4
46 Sanchez	663,548	570,963	16.2
47 *Cox*	715,625	571,605	25.2
48 *Issa*	773,292	573,211	34.9
49 Davis	586,882	573,437	2.3
50 Filner	641,790	573,244	12.0
51 *Cunningham*	713,746	572,850	24.6
52 *Hunter*	640,630	573,355	11.7
COLORADO	**4,301,261**	**3,294,394**	**30.6**
1 DeGette	662,711	549,053	20.7
2 Udall	702,336	548,953	27.9
3 *McInnis*	723,533	549,120	31.8
4 *Schaffer*	748,228	549,216	36.2
5 *Hefley*	810,423	549,264	47.5
6 *Tancredo*	654,030	548,788	19.2
CONNECTICUT	**3,405,565**	**3,287,116**	**3.6**
1 Larson	552,127	547,979	0.8
2 *Simmons*	568,007	548,018	3.6
3 DeLauro	561,576	547,904	2.5
4 *Shays*	574,101	547,561	4.8
5 Maloney	581,903	547,907	6.2
6 *Johnson*	567,851	547,747	3.7
DELAWARE	**783,600**	**666,168**	**17.6**
AL *Castle*	783,600	666,168	17.6
FLORIDA	**15,982,378**	**12,937,926**	**23.5**
1 *Scarborough*	683,987	562,575	21.6
2 Boyd	678,025	562,359	20.6
3 Brown	586,694	562,080	4.4
4 *Crenshaw*	734,246	562,459	30.5
5 Thurman	689,672	562,926	22.5
6 *Stearns*	755,939	562,219	34.5
7 *Mica*	722,139	563,552	28.1
8 *Keller*	782,397	562,244	39.2
9 *Bilirakis*	722,068	562,814	28.3
10 *Young*	583,809	562,301	3.8
11 Davis	628,167	562,293	11.7
12 *Putnam*	671,347	562,381	19.4
13 *Miller*	677,666	562,501	20.5
14 *Goss*	790,852	562,489	40.6
15 *Weldon*	718,294	562,542	27.7
16 *Foley*	758,365	561,856	35.0
17 Meek	577,167	563,284	2.5
18 *Ros-Lehtinen*	597,947	562,394	6.3
19 Wexler	800,902	562,978	42.3
20 Deutsch	783,412	562,673	39.2
21 *Diaz-Balart*	789,742	562,402	40.4
22 *Shaw*	630,775	560,959	12.4

	2000	1990	PERCENT CHANGE
23 Hastings	618,766	563,645	9.8
GEORGIA	**8,186,453**	**6,478,216**	**26.4**
1 Kingston	692,199	588,541	17.6
2 Bishop	650,392	587,583	10.7
3 Collins	781,694	589,718	32.6
4 McKinney	744,717	589,431	26.3
5 Lewis	646,184	589,380	9.6
6 Isakson	943,373	589,018	60.1
7 Barr	752,161	589,915	27.5
8 Chambliss	662,811	587,912	12.7
9 Deal	814,305	589,355	38.2
10 Norwood	662,201	588,046	12.6
11 Linder	836,416	589,317	41.9
HAWAII	**1,211,537**	**1,108,229**	**9.3**
1 Abercrombie	568,524	554,174	2.6
2 Mink	643,013	554,055	16.1
IDAHO	**1,293,953**	**1,006,749**	**28.5**
1 Otter	702,521	503,141	39.6
2 Simpson	591,432	503,608	17.4
ILLINOIS	**12,419,293**	**11,430,602**	**8.6**
1 Rush	560,239	571,908	-2.0
2 Jackson	556,482	572,188	-2.7
3 Lipinski	629,597	570,902	10.3
4 Gutierrez	625,941	571,162	9.6
5 Blagojevich	635,824	571,053	11.3
6 Hyde	615,419	572,268	7.5
7 Davis	569,470	572,039	-0.4
8 Crane	699,513	571,464	22.4
9 Schakowsky	593,205	571,611	3.8
10 Kirk	627,793	571,501	9.8
11 Weller	635,653	571,050	11.3
12 Costello	560,912	571,441	-1.8
13 Biggert	759,124	571,344	32.9
14 Hastert	720,663	571,540	26.1
15 Johnson	595,833	571,292	4.3
16 Manzullo	691,356	571,488	21.0
17 Evans	567,712	571,585	-0.7
18 LaHood	597,447	572,238	4.4
19 Phelps	575,769	571,390	0.8
20 Shimkus	601,341	571,138	5.3
INDIANA	**6,080,485**	**5,544,159**	**9.7**
1 Visclosky	571,747	554,514	3.1
2 Pence	567,204	554,321	2.3
3 Roemer	610,182	554,482	10.0
4 Souder	619,891	554,577	11.8
5 Buyer	585,988	554,240	5.7
6 Burton	724,143	553,865	30.7
7 Kerns	633,484	554,500	19.7
8 Hostettler	590,205	554,347	6.5
9 Hill	608,430	554,516	9.7
10 Carson	569,211	554,797	2.6
IOWA	**2,926,324**	**2,776,755**	**5.4**
1 Leach	603,837	555,229	8.8
2 Nussle	568,857	555,494	2.4
3 Boswell	573,674	555,299	3.3
4 Ganske	621,351	555,276	11.9
5 Latham	558,605	555,457	0.6
KANSAS	**2,688,418**	**2,477,574**	**8.5**
1 Moran	637,670	619,371	3.0
2 Ryun	641,387	619,385	3.6
3 Moore	733,606	619,445	18.4
4 Tiahrt	675,755	619,373	9.1

	2000	1990	PERCENT CHANGE
KENTUCKY	**4,041,769**	**3,685,296**	**9.7**
1 Whitfield	652,338	614,265	6.2
2 Lewis	706,978	615,131	14.9
3 Northup	626,676	613,266	2.2
4 Lucas	691,720	602,896	14.7
5 Rogers	648,751	624,837	3.8
6 Fletcher	715,306	614,901	16.3
LOUISIANA	**4,468,976**	**4,219,973**	**5.9**
1 Vitter	666,747	602,867	10.6
2 Jefferson	590,824	602,830	-2.0
3 Tauzin	637,359	602,814	5.7
4 McCrery	616,120	602,692	2.2
5 Cooksey	610,398	602,928	1.2
6 Baker	683,536	602,764	13.4
7 John	663,992	603,078	10.1
MAINE	**1,274,923**	**1,227,928**	**3.8**
1 Allen	666,936	613,960	8.6
2 Baldacci	607,987	613,968	-1.0
MARYLAND	**5,296,486**	**4,781,468**	**10.8**
1 Gilchrest	682,770	597,821	14.2
2 Ehrlich	652,938	597,450	9.3
3 Cardin	643,935	597,712	7.7
4 Wynn	648,764	597,791	8.5
5 Hoyer	714,886	597,573	19.6
6 Bartlett	723,196	597,660	21.0
7 Cummings	539,439	597,701	-9.7
8 Morella	690,558	597,760	15.5
MASSACHUSETTS	**6,349,097**	**6,016,425**	**5.5**
1 Olver	610,522	601,721	1.5
2 Neal	615,557	601,490	2.3
3 McGovern	655,701	601,852	8.9
4 Frank	639,072	601,392	6.3
5 Meehan	644,869	601,527	7.2
6 Tierney	652,455	601,811	8.4
7 Markey	616,542	601,476	2.5
8 Capuano	620,372	602,396	3.0
9 Moakley	630,499	601,250	4.9
10 Delahunt	663,508	601,510	10.3
MICHIGAN	**9,938,444**	**9,295,297**	**6.9**
1 Stupak	639,161	581,006	10.9
2 Hoekstra	686,086	581,017	18.1
3 Ehlers	662,041	580,874	14.0
4 Camp	651,347	580,890	12.1
5 Barcia	587,031	580,981	1.0
6 Upton	610,640	580,973	5.1
7 Smith	620,053	581,005	6.7
8 Rogers	658,695	581,072	13.4
9 Kildee	633,553	580,908	9.1
10 Bonior	671,306	580,974	15.5
11 Knollenberg	640,548	580,934	10.3
12 Levin	574,950	580,987	-1.0
13 Rivers	628,363	580,882	8.2
14 Conyers	550,599	580,977	-5.2
15 Kilpatrick	531,634	580,933	-8.5
16 Dingell	592,437	580,884	2.0
MINNESOTA	**4,919,479**	**4,375,099**	**12.4**
1 Gutknecht	594,864	546,881	8.8
2 Kennedy	613,816	546,890	12.2
3 Ramstad	642,053	546,796	17.4
4 McCollum	577,077	547,061	5.5
5 Sabo	557,819	546,858	2.0
6 Luther	720,995	546,807	31.9

	2000	1990	PERCENT CHANGE
7 Peterson	588,825	547,011	7.6
8 Oberstar	624,030	546,795	14.1
MISSISSIPPI	**2,844,658**	**2,573,216**	**10.5**
1 *Wicker*	607,229	515,196	17.9
2 Thompson	517,345	514,469	0.6
3 *Pickering*	588,915	515,225	14.3
4 Shows	530,679	513,715	3.3
5 Taylor	600,490	514,611	16.7
MISSOURI	**5,595,211**	**5,117,073**	**9.3**
1 Clay	514,264	568,472	-9.5
2 *Akin*	610,984	568,449	7.5
3 Gephardt	596,066	568,105	4.9
4 Skelton	659,533	569,295	15.9
5 McCarthy	577,050	569,289	1.4
6 *Graves*	635,835	568,823	11.8
7 *Blunt*	695,069	568,017	22.4
8 Emerson	611,537	568,385	7.6
9 *Hulshof*	694,873	568,238	22.3
MONTANA	**902,195**	**799,065**	**12.9**
AL *Rehberg*	902,195	799,065	12.9
NEBRASKA	**1,711,263**	**1,578,385**	**8.4**
1 *Bereuter*	581,488	526,291	10.5
2 *Terry*	594,207	526,573	12.8
3 *Osborne*	535,568	525,521	1.9
NEVADA	**1,998,257**	**1,201,833**	**66.3**
1 Berkley	936,104	601,042	55.7
2 *Gibbons*	1,062,153	600,791	76.8
NEW HAMPSHIRE	**1,235,786**	**1,109,252**	**11.4**
1 *Sununu*	625,527	554,303	12.8
2 *Bass*	610,259	554,949	10.0
NEW JERSEY	**8,414,350**	**7,730,188**	**8.9**
1 Andrews	609,847	594,494	2.6
2 *LoBiondo*	652,730	594,723	9.8
3 *Saxton*	647,095	594,667	8.8
4 *Smith*	674,193	594,673	13.4
5 *Roukema*	638,669	594,581	7.4
6 Pallone	632,202	594,650	6.3
7 *Ferguson*	642,715	594,844	8.0
8 Pascrell	640,015	594,912	7.6
9 Rothman	647,240	594,790	8.8
10 Payne	597,384	593,876	0.6
11 *Frelinghuysen*	665,932	594,526	12.0
12 Holt	709,867	594,577	19.4
13 Menendez	656,461	594,875	10.4
NEW MEXICO	**1,819,046**	**1,515,069**	**20.1**
1 *Wilson*	592,911	505,329	17.3
2 *Skeen*	596,790	504,767	18.2
3 Udall	629,345	504,973	24.6
NEW YORK	**18,976,457**	**17,990,455**	**5.5**
1 *Grucci*	642,032	580,076	10.7
2 Israel	612,961	580,303	5.6
3 *King*	588,611	580,468	1.4
4 McCarthy	611,953	580,492	5.4
5 Ackerman	615,731	581,073	6.1
6 Meeks	664,941	581,812	14.3
7 Crowley	684,573	580,116	18.0
8 Nadler	618,987	581,453	6.4
9 Weiner	652,370	579,876	12.5
10 Towns	621,305	581,311	6.9
11 Owens	586,819	582,332	0.8
12 Velázquez	620,677	577,757	7.4

	2000	1990	PERCENT CHANGE
13 *Fossella*	670,006	579,521	15.6
14 Maloney	608,017	578,639	5.1
15 Rangel	607,324	580,354	4.6
16 Serrano	647,437	581,053	11.4
17 Engel	627,566	578,424	8.5
18 Lowey	620,213	581,021	6.7
19 *Kelly*	626,776	580,386	8.0
20 *Gilman*	635,820	580,025	9.6
21 McNulty	573,294	580,320	-1.2
22 *Sweeney*	619,548	580,522	6.7
23 *Boehlert*	563,385	580,259	-2.9
24 *McHugh*	582,371	580,376	0.3
25 *Walsh*	569,864	580,233	-1.8
26 Hinchey	589,237	580,540	1.5
27 *Reynolds*	610,516	580,317	5.2
28 Slaughter	592,533	580,347	2.1
29 LaFalce	572,581	579,831	-1.3
30 *Quinn*	563,256	580,818	-3.0
31 *Houghton*	575,753	580,400	-0.8
NORTH CAROLINA	**8,049,313**	**6,628,637**	**21.4**
1 Clayton	587,830	553,426	6.2
2 Etheridge	730,266	552,529	32.2
3 *Jones*	615,614	551,918	11.5
4 Price	765,876	552,441	38.6
5 *Burr*	637,158	552,337	15.4
6 *Coble*	689,529	552,663	24.8
7 McIntyre	690,054	552,037	25.0
8 *Hayes*	661,112	552,039	19.8
9 *Myrick*	693,042	552,490	25.4
10 *Ballenger*	655,413	552,303	18.7
11 *Taylor*	656,619	552,497	18.8
12 Watt	666,800	551,957	20.8
NORTH DAKOTA	**642,200**	**638,800**	**0.5**
AL Pomeroy	642,200	638,800	0.5
OHIO	**11,353,140**	**10,847,115**	**4.7**
1 *Chabot*	542,618	571,052	-5.0
2 *Portman*	634,061	570,779	11.1
3 Hall	556,039	570,913	-2.6
4 *Oxley*	591,795	570,917	3.7
5 *Gillmor*	589,716	570,946	3.3
6 Strickland	620,901	570,804	8.8
7 *Hobson*	620,156	570,939	8.6
8 *Boehner*	625,445	570,837	9.6
9 Kaptur	569,053	570,911	-0.3
10 Kucinich	573,874	570,530	0.6
11 Jones	532,337	571,295	-6.8
12 *Tiberi*	661,049	571,341	15.7
13 Brown	645,068	570,838	13.0
14 Sawyer	586,402	570,987	2.7
15 *Pryce*	649,980	570,740	13.9
16 *Regula*	605,661	570,705	6.1
17 Traficant	563,164	570,963	-1.4
18 *Ney*	586,247	570,784	2.7
19 *LaTourette*	599,574	570,834	5.0
OKLAHOMA	**3,450,654**	**3,145,585**	**9.7**
1 *Largent*	586,853	524,135	12.0
2 Carson	599,445	524,389	14.3
3 *Watkins*	565,932	524,287	7.9
4 *Watts*	572,589	524,407	9.2
5 *Istook*	593,898	523,729	13.4
6 *Lucas*	531,937	524,638	1.4

	2000	1990	PERCENT CHANGE
OREGON	3,421,399	2,842,321	20.4
1 Wu	743,195	568,501	30.7
2 Walden	701,847	568,437	23.5
3 Blumenauer	650,092	568,276	14.4
4 DeFazio	633,335	568,395	11.4
5 Hooley	692,930	568,712	21.8
PENNSYLVANIA	12,281,054	11,881,643	3.4
1 Brady	515,560	566,133	-8.9
2 Fattah	532,455	565,242	-5.8
3 Borski	572,488	565,884	1.2
4 Hart	582,777	565,809	3.0
5 Peterson	582,083	565,736	2.9
6 Holden	600,437	565,923	6.1
7 Weldon	587,281	565,815	3.8
8 Greenwood	624,248	565,820	10.3
9 Vacant	588,138	565,858	3.9
10 Sherwood	613,459	565,777	8.4
11 Kanjorski	579,470	565,802	2.4
12 Murtha	556,856	565,760	-1.6
13 Hoeffel	628,203	565,663	11.1
14 Coyne	529,299	565,838	-6.5
15 Toomey	612,265	565,818	8.2
16 Pitts	647,575	565,908	14.4
17 Gekas	608,390	565,702	7.5
18 Doyle	535,432	565,771	-5.4
19 Platts	632,862	565,789	11.9
20 Mascara	570,336	565,789	0.8
21 English	581,440	565,806	2.8
RHODE ISLAND	1,048,319	1,003,464	4.5
1 Kennedy	510,287	501,696	1.7
2 Langevin	538,032	501,768	7.2
SOUTH CAROLINA	4,012,012	3,486,703	15.1
1 Brown	684,765	581,195	17.8
2 Spence	731,022	580,636	25.9
3 Graham	670,139	580,861	15.4
4 DeMint	670,335	581,385	15.3
5 Spratt	655,525	581,174	12.8
6 Clyburn	600,226	581,452	3.2
SOUTH DAKOTA	754,844	696,004	8.5
AL Thune	754,844	696,004	8.5
TENNESSEE	5,689,283	4,877,185	16.7
1 Jenkins	628,443	541,978	16.0
2 Duncan	636,383	541,780	17.5
3 Wamp	595,855	542,065	9.9
4 Hilleary	635,355	541,650	17.3
5 Clement	607,853	541,878	12.2
6 Gordon	738,663	542,002	36.3
7 Bryant	728,956	542,270	34.4
8 Tanner	604,894	541,852	11.6
9 Ford	512,881	541,710	-5.3
TEXAS	20,851,820	16,986,510	22.8
1 Sandlin	622,475	565,594	10.1
2 Turner	669,591	565,906	18.3
3 Johnson	835,040	567,383	47.2
4 Hall	707,329	567,231	24.7
5 Sessions	657,495	566,887	16.0
6 Barton	759,418	565,504	34.3
7 Culberson	772,147	565,007	36.7
8 Brady	776,623	565,315	37.4
9 Lampson	636,960	564,287	12.9
10 Doggett	791,117	566,357	39.7
11 Edwards	663,275	566,280	17.1
12 Granger	661,753	565,988	16.9
13 Thornberry	597,401	566,682	5.4
14 Paul	688,604	566,008	21.7
15 Hinojosa	780,310	566,805	37.7
16 Reyes	620,847	566,238	9.6
17 Stenholm	618,958	566,255	9.3
18 Jackson-Lee	606,441	568,146	6.7
19 Combest	607,535	565,925	7.4
20 Gonzalez	624,384	564,865	10.5
21 Smith	801,078	566,105	41.5
22 DeLay	784,759	569,350	37.8
23 Bonilla	762,627	566,736	34.6
24 Frost	680,808	567,791	19.9
25 Bentsen	662,264	563,510	17.5
26 Armey	845,541	564,764	49.7
27 Ortiz	664,428	565,992	17.4
28 Rodriguéz	646,161	566,447	14.1
29 Green	672,591	568,250	18.4
30 Johnson	633,860	564,902	12.2
UTAH	2,233,169	1,722,850	29.6
1 Hansen	765,156	574,205	33.3
2 Matheson	702,102	574,412	22.2
3 Cannon	765,911	574,233	33.4
VERMONT	608,827	562,758	8.2
AL Sanders (I)	608,827	562,758	8.2
VIRGINIA	7,078,515	6,187,358	14.4
1 Davis	709,060	563,486	25.8
2 Schrock	574,058	562,789	2.0
3 Scott	567,683	560,280	1.3
4 Vacant	645,733	563,206	14.7
5 Goode (I)	620,104	562,273	10.3
6 Goodlatte	609,802	562,426	8.4
7 Cantor	699,196	562,729	24.3
8 Moran	627,849	562,808	11.6
9 Boucher	582,943	562,508	3.6
10 Wolf	792,534	562,257	41.0
11 Davis	649,553	562,596	15.5
WASHINGTON	5,894,121	4,866,692	21.1
1 Inslee	632,484	540,315	17.1
2 Larson	719,487	540,861	33.0
3 Baird	698,038	540,658	29.1
4 Hastings	672,059	540,701	24.3
5 Nethercutt	625,971	540,865	15.7
6 Dicks	611,292	540,836	13.0
7 McDermott	590,062	541,202	9.0
8 Dunn	695,277	540,735	28.6
9 Smith	649,451	540,519	20.2
WEST VIRGINIA	1,808,344	1,793,477	0.8
1 Mollohan	595,385	598,056	-0.4
2 Capito	635,965	597,921	6.3
3 Rahall	576,994	597,500	-3.4
WISCONSIN	5,363,675	4,891,769	9.6
1 Ryan	612,814	543,380	12.8
2 Baldwin	624,959	543,625	15.0
3 Kind	600,914	543,447	10.6
4 Kleczka	578,409	543,482	6.4
5 Barrett	507,636	543,607	-6.6
6 Petri	606,416	543,531	11.6
7 Obey	582,884	543,569	7.2
8 Green	617,575	543,526	13.6
9 Sensenbrenner	632,068	543,602	16.3
WYOMING	493,782	453,588	8.9
AL Cubin	493,782	453,588	8.9

Gov. Donald Siegelman (D)

First elected: 1998
Length of term: 4 years
Term expires: 1/03
Salary: $94,654
Phone: (334) 242-7100
Hometown: Montgomery
Born: Feb. 24, 1946, Mobile, Ala.
Religion: Roman Catholic
Family: Wife, Lori Siegelman; two children
Education: U. of Alabama, B.A. 1968; Georgetown U., J.D. 1972
Military Service: Ala. Air National Guard, 1968
Career: Lawyer
Political highlights: Ala. secretary of state, 1979-87; Ala. attorney general, 1987-91; sought Democratic nomination for governor, 1990; lieutenant governor, 1995-99

Election results:

1998 GENERAL

Don Siegelman (D)	760,155	57.7%
Fob James, Jr. (R)	554,746	42.1%

Lt. Gov. Steve Windom (R)

First elected: 1998
Length of term: 4 years
Term expires: 1/03
Salary: $48,620
Phone: (334) 242-7900

STATE LEGISLATURE

Legislature: Meets annually; limited to 30 legislative days within 105 calendar days; special sessions common
House: 105 members, 4-year terms
2001 breakdown: 37R, 68D; 97 men, 8 women
Salary: $10/day, $50 for each 3-day week, plus $2,280/month living expenses
Phone: (334) 242-7600
Senate: 35 members, 4-year terms
2001 breakdown: 11R, 24D; 32 men, 3 women
Salary: $10/day, $50 for each 3-day week, plus $2,280/month living expenses
Phone: (334) 242-7800

STATE TERM LIMITS

Governor: 2 consecutive terms
Senate: No
House: No

URBAN STATISTICS

CITY	POPULATION
Birmingham	249,459
Mobile	200,206
Montgomery	195,690
Huntsville	177,893
Tuscaloosa	85,171

REGISTERED VOTERS

Voters do not register by party.

POPULATION

2000 population	4,447,100
1990 population	4,040,587
Percent change	+10.1%
Rank among states	23
Median age	35.3
Born in state	76%
Foreign born	1%
Urban/rural	60%/40%
Crime rate	565/100,000
Poverty level	14.5%
Federal workers	53,249
Military	42,064

REAPPORTIONMENT

Alabama retained its seven House seats in reapportionment. The state legislature will draw new district lines.

MISCELLANEOUS

Web: www.state.al.us
Capital: Montgomery
Land area: 50,750 sq. miles
Rank among states: 28
STATE ELECTION OFFICIAL
(334) 242-7210
DEMOCRATIC HEADQUARTERS
(334) 262-6477
REPUBLICAN HEADQUARTERS
(256) 536-0518

District Statistics

DIST.	2000 D	2000 R	GREEN	1996 D	1996 R	REF	1992 D	1992 R	I	WHT	BLK	ASIAN	HISP	HOUSEHOLD INCOME	OVER 65+	UNDER 18	COLLEGE EDUCATION
1	38%	60%	1%	39%	53%	7%	37%	52%	12%	70%	29%	1%	1%	$22,881	13%	28%	15%
2	35	63	1	37	56	6	35	53	12	75	24	1	1	$24,374	13	27	17
3	41	57	1	44	49	7	42	48	11	73	26	0	1	$21,594	13	26	12
4	39	59	1	43	48	8	44	45	12	92	7	0	0	$20,877	15	25	8
5	43	55	1	43	49	8	41	44	15	83	15	1	1	$28,364	11	25	20
6	28	70	2	28	67	4	27	64	9	90	9	1	1	$31,864	12	23	26
7	74	25	0	73	24	2	72	24	5	32	67	0	0	$16,560	14	29	11
STATE	42	56	1	43	50	6	41	48	11	74	25	1	1	$23,597	13	26	16

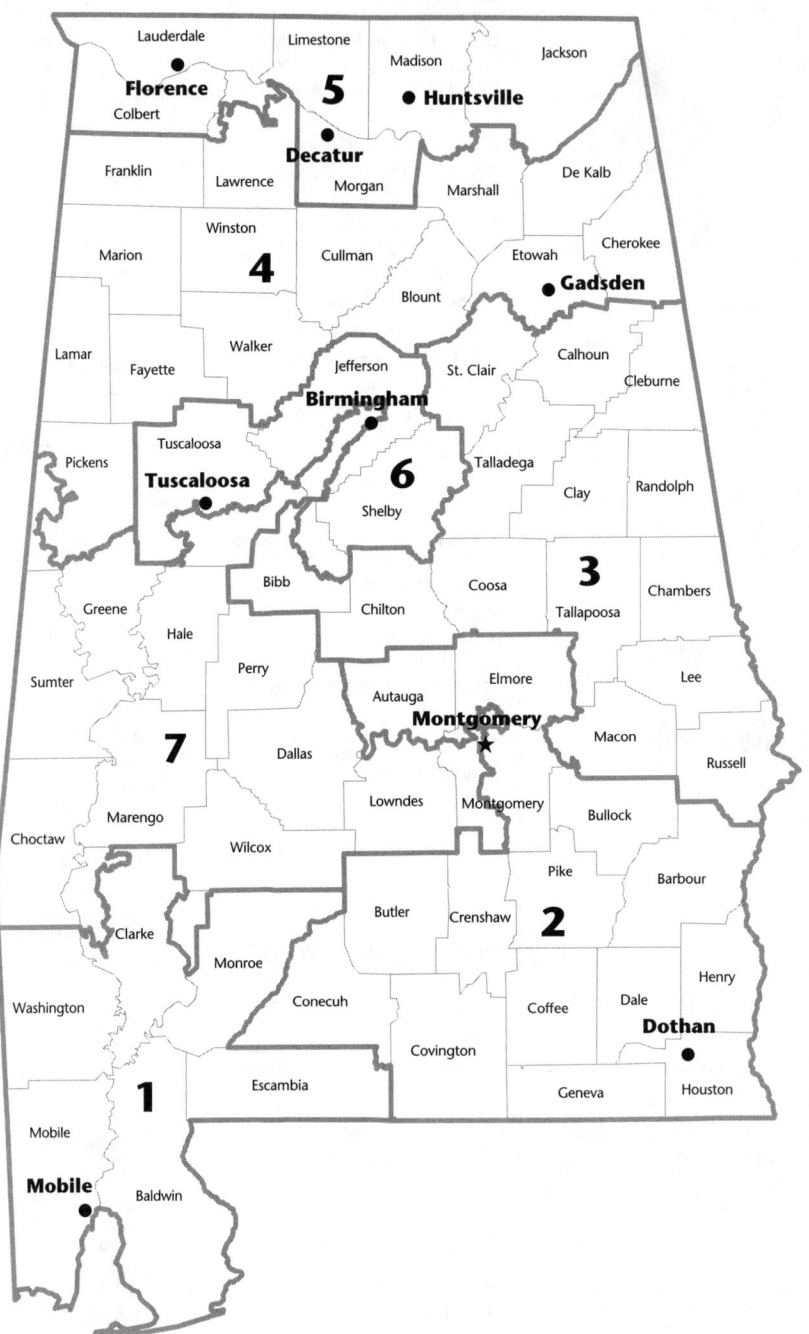

Lauderdale
Limestone
Madison
Jackson
Florence ●
Colbert
5
● **Huntsville**
Franklin
Lawrence
Decatur ●
Morgan
Marshall
De Kalb
Winston
Cullman
Etowah
Cherokee
Marion
4
Blount
● **Gadsden**
Walker
Jefferson
St. Clair
Calhoun
Lamar
Fayette
Birmingham ●
Cleburne
Pickens
Tuscaloosa
Talladega
Clay
Randolph
Tuscaloosa ●
6
Shelby
Bibb
Coosa
Chambers
Greene
Chilton
Tallapoosa
3
Hale
Perry
Elmore
Lee
Sumter
Autauga
Montgomery
Macon
7
Dallas
Montgomery ★
Russell
Marengo
Lowndes
Montgomery
Bullock
Choctaw
Wilcox
Pike
Barbour
Clarke
Butler
Crenshaw
2
Monroe
Henry
Washington
Conecuh
Coffee
Dale
● **Dothan**
1
Covington
Houston
Mobile
Escambia
Geneva
Mobile ●
Baldwin

Sen. Richard C. Shelby (R)

CAPITOL OFFICE
224-5744; fax 224-3416; 110 Hart Bldg. 20510

INTERNET
e-mail: senator@shelby.senate.gov
web: shelby.senate.gov

COMMITTEES
Appropriations
  (Transportation - chairman)
Banking, Housing & Urban Affairs
Energy & Natural Resources
Select Intelligence - chairman
Special Aging

HOMETOWN
Tuscaloosa

BORN
May 6, 1934, Birmingham, Ala.

RELIGION
Presbyterian

FAMILY
Wife, Annette Nevin Shelby; two children

EDUCATION
U. of Alabama, A.B. 1957, LL.B. 1963

CAREER
Lawyer; city prosecutor

POLITICAL HIGHLIGHTS
Ala. Senate, 1971-79 (served as a Democrat); U.S.
House, 1979-87 (served as a Democrat)

ELECTION RESULTS

1998 GENERAL

Richard C. Shelby (R)	817,973	63.2%
Clayton Suddith (D)	474,568	36.7%

1998 PRIMARY

Richard C. Shelby (R)	unopposed

PREVIOUS WINNING PERCENTAGES
1992 (65%); 1986 (50%); 1984 House Election (97%);
1982 House Election (97%); 1980 House Election
(73%); 1978 House Election (94%)
*Elected as a Democrat 1978-92

Elected 1986; 3rd term

When he first ran for Congress in 1978, Shelby was a progressive Democrat known for championing the Equal Rights Amendment. Today, his voting record and criticism of Democratic positions on national security issues put him among the Senate's most conservative Republicans. Despite this political transformation, Shelby has consistently charted an independent course that has sometimes put him at odds with the party to which he has belonged for six years.

Shelby was one of President Clinton's harshest critics, yet in 1999 he voted "not guilty" on one of the two articles of impeachment considered by the Senate. Now the second-most-senior Republican on the Banking Committee, he has been a staunch ally of Chairman Phil Gramm, R-Texas, but he has broken ranks with Gramm and other leading Senate Republicans on a key consumer privacy issue.

As chairman of the Intelligence Committee, Shelby is called on to make the rounds of the Sunday television talk shows during foreign policy crises, but he keeps a low profile around the Senate. Unflappable, with a polite demeanor and a ready smile, his recent work on consumer privacy has done much to raise his visibility.

Shelby opposes allowing banks and their related securities and insurance concerns to exchange information about customers without their permission. By taking this stand, he has emerged as one of the leading congressional advocates of enhancing consumer privacy — an issue expected to resurface in several guises in the 107th Congress, as Capitol Hill weighs its role in regulating an economy fueled by electronic commerce.

Shelby immersed himself in the privacy issue in the 106th Congress, after learning in 1999 that some states were providing information from driver's licenses to marketing firms without motorists' knowledge. He became a founder of the Congressional Privacy Caucus, taking on some of the same lobbying groups that generally supported him as a member of the Banking Committee. The caucus's other leaders are from opposite sides of the House's ideological divide: Democratic Rep. Edward J. Markey of Massachusetts and Republican Rep. Joe L. Barton of Texas.

"I think the American people are just now becoming aware of the extent that their privacy is trampled upon," Shelby said. "As you get into it, you see how broad it is — it's all aspects of your life. This is an issue that's going to be with us, because there's a lot of concern."

Shelby spends about half of his work time on intelligence matters, most of it out of the public eye. But he was aggressive in challenging the Clinton administration on national security and foreign policy matters. He assumed the chairmanship of the Intelligence Committee in 1997 and began by leading the opposition to Clinton's choice of Anthony Lake as CIA director, a stance that angered many Democrats. Shelby questioned Lake's management ability as head of the National Security Council. He and other Republicans said they were troubled about Lake's involvement in the Clinton administration's tacit approval of the shipment of arms from Iran to the Muslim-dominated Bosnian government.

The senator travels frequently on Intelligence Committee business. During one month in 1999, for example, he visited Indonesia, Australia, New Zealand, Papua New Guinea, Singapore, Malaysia, the Philippines, Thailand, Cambodia and Vietnam.

Shelby has said little about the internal conflicts that appear to have plagued the Intelligence panel on his watch. Those conflicts came to light in April 2000, when the staff director left, reportedly fired by Shelby. The departure came six months after one committee aide was fired and another was demoted, reportedly as a result of their handling of controversial legislation to impose sanctions against alleged drug kingpins. The Capitol Hill newspaper Roll Call suggested a cause of the intra-committee conflicts was that senators were departing from the panel's longstanding bipartisan way of doing business.

Shelby said he had worked hard to build bipartisanship on the committee, and that any disgruntlement was because some panel members "don't want us to go back to doing oversight" over such sensitive issues as former CIA Director John Deutch's improper storage of classified information on his home computers.

Shelby also serves on the Appropriations Committee. When he announced his switch from Democrat to Republican — the day after the GOP won control of Congress in 1994 — he not only was rewarded with a seat on Appropriations, something the Democrats had denied him, but he also was given the chairmanship of the Treasury, Postal Service and General Government Subcommittee.

The senator gained additional clout in 1997 when he took the gavel of the Transportation Subcommittee, which he still holds. In that post, Shelby has gotten into his share of scraps. He angered some Texans by pushing to move additional airline service away from Dallas-Fort Worth International Airport to Love Field in inner-city Dallas. (Shelby was seeking to add flights between Love Field and Alabama, Mississippi and Kansas.) Later, Shelby took on New York's congressional delegation by proposing a plan that essentially would have prevented any state from getting more than 12.5 percent of the total federal allocation for mass transit.

On Appropriations, Shelby looks out for federal installations in his home state. He has been of special service to Huntsville, a booming space and defense center. But Shelby downplays his influence, at least publicly. "I tell my people back home that the only reason you will survive is if you're part of the national purpose," he said. "You can only defend [increased spending for Alabama] as part of the national fabric."

Shelby's party-switch struck many as opportunistic. But Shelby said he made the move because of what he saw as the demise of the pro-defense, conservative wing of the Democratic Party. "I'm certainly better off" as a Republican, Shelby said, "and I think the Democrats are better off to have a cohesive body that shares the basic Democrat ideology. There's not a conservative Democrat left in the whole South."

A former prosecutor in Tuscaloosa, Shelby sometimes cites his law-enforcement background in justifying his political flexibility. He entered politics by serving eight years in the state Senate, where he often was at odds with Gov. George C. Wallace. Although Shelby initially was interested in the lieutenant governorship, more than a dozen other Democrats had the same idea. When his former law partner, Democratic Rep. Walter Flowers, gave up his seat in 1978 to run for the Senate, Shelby was easily persuaded to change course and run for Congress.

For eight years, Shelby worked largely behind the scenes in the House, devoting his time to bringing federal projects to his district. But he also became an increasingly reliable ally of the GOP on the Energy and Commerce Committee. In 1986, he won a 1 percentage point victory over Republican Sen. Jeremiah Denton, a former naval officer and Vietnam prisoner of war, who was not as skilled as Shelby at personal politicking. Shelby has had less trouble since then, thanks to the opposing party's inability to recruit top-tier opponents and the senator's prodigious skill at raising money.

KEY VOTES

2000

Yes Overhaul bankruptcy law and increase minimum wage

Yes Limit fiscal 2001 discretionary spending to $600.3 billion

Yes Override veto on nuclear waste disposal at Yucca Mountain site in Nevada

No Oppose effort to terminate Kosovo mission

No Include gender, sexual orientation and disability in federal hate crime protections

Yes Approve GOP plan to restrict use of genetic information by health insurers

Yes Kill amendment delaying implementation of an anti-missile defense system

Yes Cut taxes for married couples

Yes Grant China permanent normal trade status

1999

Yes Remove President Clinton from office for obstruction of justice

Yes Kill amendment authorizing state grants to hire teachers and reduce class size

No Require criminal background checks for purchases at gun shows

Yes Approve GOP proposal to increase rights of patients in managed-care health plans

No Block effort to allow farm and medicine exports to Cuba

No Allow study of tougher automobile fuel efficiency standards

No Ratify nuclear weapons testing treaty

No Prohibit national political parties from collecting "soft money" donations

No Remove barriers among banking, securities and insurance companies

INTEREST GROUPS

	AFL-CIO	ADA	CCUS	ACU
2000	0%	0%	93%	100%
1999	22%	10%	71%	84%
1998	0%	5%	78%	92%
1997	14%	5%	90%	92%
1996	0%	5%	77%	90%
1995	0%	5%	89%	91%
1994	83%	30%	50%	55%
1993	73%	35%	82%	64%
1992	58%	30%	60%	63%
1991	67%	35%	40%	76%

CQ VOTE STUDIES

	PARTY UNITY		PRESIDENTIAL SUPPORT	
	Support	Oppose	Support	Oppose
2000	97%	3%	45%	55%
1999	89%	11%	38%	62%
1998	91%	9%	34%	66%
1997	93%	7%	57%	43%
1996	94%	6%	33%	67%
1995	90%	10%	30%	70%
1994	50%	50%	67%	33%
1993	37%	63%	46%	54%
1992	45%	55%	65%	35%
1991	54%	46%	69%	31%

Sen. Jeff Sessions (R)

CAPITOL OFFICE
224-4124; fax 224-3149; 493 Russell Bldg. 20510

INTERNET
e-mail: senator@sessions.senate.gov
web: sessions.senate.gov

COMMITTEES
Armed Services
  (Seapower - chairman)
Health, Education, Labor & Pensions
Judiciary
  (Administrative Oversight & the Courts -
  chairman)
Joint Economic

HOMETOWN
Mobile

BORN
Dec. 24, 1946, Hybart, Ala.

RELIGION
Methodist

FAMILY
Wife, Mary Blackshear Sessions; three children

EDUCATION
Huntingdon College, B.A. 1969; U. of Alabama, J.D.
1973

MILITARY SERVICE
Army Reserve, 1973-86

CAREER
Lawyer

POLITICAL HIGHLIGHTS
Assistant U.S. attorney, 1975-77; U.S. attorney,
1981-93; Ala. attorney general, 1995-97

ELECTION RESULTS

1996 GENERAL

Jeff Sessions (R)	786,436	52.5%
Roger Bedford (D)	681,651	45.5%

1996 PRIMARY RUNOFF

Jeff Sessions (R)	81,622	59.3%
Sid McDonald (R)	56,131	40.7%

1996 PRIMARY

Jeff Sessions (R)	80,694	37.5%
Sid McDonald (R)	47,320	22.0%
Charles Woods (R)	23,796	11.1%
Frank McRight (R)	21,818	10.1%
Walter D. Clark (R)	18,513	8.6%
Jimmy Blake (R)	15,305	7.1%
Albert Lipscomb (R)	7,600	3.5%

Elected 1996; 1st term

A steadfast conservative with a career rating of 100 percent from the American Conservative Union, Sessions has had to display his pragmatic deal-making side as a key player on several judicial and education issues. In the 106th Congress, for example, he had a central role in negotiations on bankruptcy reform, seizure of assets from criminals and legislation to give states more flexibility in spending federal education dollars.

But, even after four years in office, Sessions has yet to make as much news in the Senate as he did more than a decade ago when senators rejected his nomination to the federal bench.

In 1986, Sessions was only the second judicial nominee in 48 years whose nomination was killed by the Senate Judiciary Committee — which refused even to let the nomination come to the Senate floor for a vote. Sessions' opponents accused him of "gross insensitivity" on racial issues. On a 9-9 vote, the panel killed the nomination. (The nays included the man Sessions replaced in the Senate, Democrat Howell Heflin.)

For his part, Sessions says that the Senate on occasion has been insensitive to the rights and reputation of nominees. Now a member of the Judiciary panel and a subcommittee chairman, he allows that his presence on the committee alongside several of the members who voted against him is a "great irony."

But he has been welcomed even by political opponents who voted against his confirmation, and he is often looked to for guidance on how to handle controversial nominations.

Sessions was serving as chief prosecutor for the Southern District of Alabama and making a name for himself through his prosecution of drug dealers when President Reagan nominated him to be a federal judge. But according to sworn statements by Justice Department lawyers, Sessions called the NAACP and the American Civil Liberties Union "communist-inspired" and said they tried to "force civil rights down the throats of people." Sessions reportedly said of the Ku Klux Klan that he "used to think they're OK" until he learned that some Klan members were "pot smokers." Sessions said his words were in jest or had been misrepresented.

Even though his remarks got him in trouble as a nominee, he is not afraid to speak his mind, even when a little more judicious caution or diplomatic phrasing is called for.

Sessions himself has voted "nay" on at least one judgeship nomination, in both the Judiciary Committee and on the floor, each year since he has been in the Senate. And he has held up nominees to the 9th Circuit Court of Appeals in a long-running battle with other Western conservatives against the court, which he characterized as "the furthest-left circuit in the American judiciary."

Sessions' legislative efforts cut across a wide range of issues. In the 106th Congress, he played a key role in the bipartisan development of legislation to make it more difficult for law enforcement authorities to seize property that may have been linked to a crime. Sessions fought to moderate the bill's provisions and succeeded in protecting the interest of law enforcement officials. And he was in the inner circle of lawmakers who negotiated on a measure to streamline bankruptcy law.

On the Armed Services Committee, he urges increased budgets for the Pentagon and seeks to protect Alabama military bases and the interests of defense contractors. On defense policy, he says the United States "should be an active participant in world affairs, but we must avoid protracted deployments that drain our military budget and capabilities." During the

106th Congress, he made several trips to Kosovo to review the U.S. peace-keeping mission and urged the Clinton administration to pull out U.S. troops as soon as possible.

Sessions and his wife both taught school long ago, and he lists education as his top priority. On the Health, Education, Labor and Pensions Committee in the 106th Congress, he sought changes in the federal program that supports the education of disabled children. The Individuals with Disabilities Act should be amended to give schools greater leeway in dealing with disruptive students, Sessions argued. "Learning is severely affected when students won't behave themselves," he told The Associated Press.

Much of Sessions' energy on Judiciary has been devoted to legislation to toughen punishment of juvenile offenders. He chaired the Judiciary panel's Youth Violence Subcommittee in the 106th Congress and moved to the committee's Administrative Oversight and the Courts panel in the 107th.

He is among those who regularly denounce government programs favored by liberals, whether it is the Endangered Species Act or the National Endowment for the Arts. In 2000, he began an "Integrity Watch" program modeled after former Democratic Sen. William Proxmire's Golden Fleece award, to highlight reports of what he considered inappropriate federal spending.

In 1998, Sessions criticized President Clinton's plan to increase tax credits for parents who send their children to day care but not for stay-at-home parents. He and Mitch McConnell, R-Ky., sought to end preferences in minority contracting as part of the 1998 highway and mass transit law. Also in 1998, Sessions sponsored a resolution in support of displaying the Ten Commandments in public buildings.

Sessions grew up in the tiny towns of Hybart and Camden, southwest of Montgomery. His father owned a general store and then a farm equipment dealership, and Sessions worked around the stores and lived what he describes as an idyllic childhood. A high school teacher introduced him to the National Review magazine, which he says "helped me to appreciate the United States and to develop a political philosophy that respected hard work, faith and country."

His parents were not active politically but urged him to take an interest in government, which he did, as a history and political science student in college. He was active in the Young Republicans and student body president at Huntingdon College in Alabama.

After earning his law degree, Sessions was a lawyer for a firm in Russellville, Ala., becoming assistant U.S. attorney in 1975. He was named U.S. attorney for the Southern District of Alabama in 1981, eventually winning the recognition of the Reagan White House. After the Senate turned back his judgeship nomination, Sessions returned to his work as a federal prosecutor. In 1994, he ran for state attorney general, and with a corruption scandal raging in Montgomery, he rode to victory on a vow to clean up the ethics mess.

Two years later, Sessions was on the move again, lured into the Senate race by Democrat Howell Heflin's retirement after 18 years in Washington. Six other Republicans joined Sessions in the party primary, and he emerged the winner in a runoff. In the general election, Sessions faced Roger Bedford, chairman of the state Senate Judiciary Committee. As was the case with other Alabama GOP candidates in 1996, Sessions gave more prominence to social issues than to fiscal ones. He appealed to Alabama's conservative Christian activists with his advocacy of a constitutional amendment permitting school prayer. In the end, Sessions prevailed over Bedford, 52 percent to 46 percent. Sessions' victory gave Alabama two Republican senators for the first time since Reconstruction.

KEY VOTES

2000

Yes Overhaul bankruptcy law and increase minimum wage

Yes Limit fiscal 2001 discretionary spending to $600.3 billion

Yes Override veto on nuclear waste disposal at Yucca Mountain site in Nevada

No Oppose effort to terminate Kosovo mission

No Include gender, sexual orientation and disability in federal hate crime protections

Yes Approve GOP plan to restrict use of genetic information by health insurers

Yes Kill amendment delaying implementation of an anti-missile defense system

Yes Cut taxes for married couples

Yes Grant China permanent normal trade status

1999

Yes Remove President Clinton from office for obstruction of justice

Yes Kill amendment authorizing state grants to hire teachers and reduce class size

No Require criminal background checks for purchases at gun shows

Yes Approve GOP proposal to increase rights of patients in managed-care health plans

No Block effort to allow farm and medicine exports to Cuba

No Allow study of tougher automobile fuel efficiency standards

No Ratify nuclear weapons testing treaty

No Prohibit national political parties from collecting "soft money" donations

Yes Remove barriers among banking, securities and insurance companies

INTEREST GROUPS

	AFL-CIO	ADA	CCUS	ACU
2000	0%	0%	86%	100%
1999	11%	0%	88%	100%
1998	0%	0%	89%	100%
1997	0%	0%	70%	100%

CQ VOTE STUDIES

	PARTY UNITY		PRESIDENTIAL SUPPORT	
	Support	Oppose	Support	Oppose
2000	97%	3%	42%	58%
1999	94%	6%	24%	76%
1998	98%	2%	28%	72%
1997	99%	1%	56%	44%

Rep. Sonny Callahan (R)

Elected 1984; 9th term

CAPITOL OFFICE
225-4931; fax 225-0562; 2372 Rayburn Bldg. 20515

INTERNET
e-mail: sonny.callahan@mail.house.gov
web: www.house.gov/callahan

COMMITTEES
Appropriations
  (Energy & Water Development - chairman)

HOMETOWN
Mobile

BORN
Sept. 11, 1932, Mobile, Ala.

RELIGION
Roman Catholic

FAMILY
Wife, Karen Callahan; six children (one deceased)

EDUCATION
McGill H.S., graduated 1950; U. of Alabama,
attended 1959-60

MILITARY SERVICE
Navy, 1952-54

CAREER
Moving and storage company executive

POLITICAL HIGHLIGHTS
Ala. House, 1971-79 (served as a Democrat); Ala.
Senate, 1979-83 (served as a Democrat); sought
Democratic nomination for lieutenant governor,
1982

ELECTION RESULTS

2000 GENERAL

Sonny Callahan (R)	151,188	91.3%
Richard M. Coffee (LIBERT)	14,031	8.5%

2000 PRIMARY

Sonny Callahan (R)	unopposed

1998 GENERAL

Sonny Callahan (R)	unopposed

PREVIOUS WINNING PERCENTAGES
1996 (64%); 1994 (67%); 1992 (60%); 1990 (100%);
1988 (59%); 1986 (100%); 1984 (51%)

In an institution with no shortage of self-important people, Callahan stands as an exception. Although a self-made millionaire, the genial Alabamian doesn't take himself too seriously.

A typical example of his self-deprecating style occurred in the wake of the Asian financial crisis of late 1997 and early 1998, when the Clinton administration asked Congress for an $18 billion infusion into the International Monetary Fund (IMF). Callahan, then chairman of the Appropriations subcommittee overseeing foreign aid, declared issues of international finance "far above my pay grade, because my intellect level compared with the average member of Congress is below average."

By leashing his ego, however, Callahan often is able to get his way on substantive issues. The compromise in 2000 that increased U.S. funds to help the world's poorest countries pay their international debts bore Callahan's fingerprints, as did a 1998 agreement on changes in the way the IMF operates. Both deals limited the ability of international financial institutions to make new loans.

In 2000, Callahan showed political smarts and determination in challenging the powerful pro-Israel lobbying group, the American-Israel Public Affairs Committee (AIPAC). Callahan sought to delay some of Israel's foreign aid because of that country's plan to sell China a sophisticated airborne radar system called the Phalcon. Callahan said such aircraft, similar to the U.S. AWACS, might one day endanger U.S. troops if they had to help defend Taiwan. AIPAC and Democrats objected, but in the end Callahan got his way: Israeli Prime Minister Ehud Barak agreed to cancel the sale. "Callahan is someone who leads you to think [he's] just a country hick, but he's a very smart guy," former Israeli Ambassador Itamar Rabinovich told the Jerusalem Post in 1997.

In the 107th Congress, Callahan gave up his chairmanship of Appropriations' Foreign Operations Subcommittee and moved to the helm of the Energy and Water Development Subcommittee — trading a post governed by fiscal restraint for one of financial largess. As a member of the Energy and Water panel, Callahan had steered plenty of projects to his Gulf Coast district. But as he took the subcommittee's chair, he told the Mobile Register, "There's not going to be the pork that was once available back when they had little concern about deficit spending. We're not going to go back to those years."

Relaxed and good-natured, Callahan is comfortable with the personal give-and-take of politics. A former Democrat, he has a colorful way with words that makes him entertaining in committees and on the House floor and has earned him friendships across party lines. Callahan had a moment in the spotlight in the fall of 1998 when Independent Counsel Kenneth W. Starr's report revealed that President Clinton had a sexual encounter with White House intern Monica Lewinsky while he was on the telephone with the congressman. "I was real surprised, as you can imagine," Callahan later told reporters. "I had no knowledge I was sharing the president's time or attention with anyone else."

At other times, though, Callahan's quips have gotten him into trouble, as in 1999 when he complained about Clinton's tendency to announce major foreign aid packages without first talking to Congress. "Every time somebody walks into the White House with a white turban on his head ... the president says, 'Let me give you a little bit of money,' " Callahan said.

Like many of his conservative constituents, Callahan is leery of the federal government in general and of foreign aid in particular. More than once he compared shepherding the foreign spending bill through Congress to the chore of diaper-changing. "It is not a pleasant task to give money to foreign countries politically," he said toward the end of the 105th Congress. "It is not something we like to go home and brag about." He even ended up voting against his own bill in 1999 after House leaders increased its spending levels in response to a White House veto.

Callahan was an unlikely fellow to hold the House purse strings to America's foreign aid programs. Before he became Foreign Operations chairman, Callahan — a high school graduate and a lifelong resident of South Alabama — had taken only one trip outside the United States, and in Congress he had never voted for a foreign aid spending bill. But for six years, he presided over the panel that has a big say in how the billions of U.S. dollars that go to overseas governments are spent — heady stuff for a man who swept warehouse floors and drove 18-wheelers on his way to becoming a moving and storage company executive and elected official.

Callahan took his duties as chairman seriously, regularly leading congressional delegations abroad on fact-finding missions to unglamorous spots such as Azerbaijan and Haiti. While he believes Congress has a constitutional duty to oversee White House foreign policy decisions, he is critical of members who consider themselves "pseudo-secretaries of state." That attitude was evident in the foreign aid bills he crafted, which were light on policy directives and concentrated on fiscal restraint.

Before coming to Congress, Callahan served a dozen years in the Alabama Legislature as a Democrat, but his conservative views earned him friends across the aisle. When GOP Rep. Jack Edwards announced his retirement in late 1983, his endorsement went to Callahan, who had waged a losing bid for lieutenant governor in 1982. The only element of suspense in the race was which party Callahan would choose. He formally joined the GOP in February 1984.

Democrats nominated Frank McRight, a Mobile trial lawyer who won his primary by attacking local government corruption. The issue gained salience in the general-election campaign when it was reported that Callahan had received an illegal campaign contribution two years earlier from a city official later indicted on other charges. In the end, Callahan owed much of his 51 percent victory to President Reagan's resounding win in the 1st District. That was Callahan's last tough campaign. And in three of his re-election races, including the one in 1998, he ran unopposed.

KEY VOTES

2000

No Raise hourly minimum wage by $1 over two years

No Halt funding for U.S. mission in Kosovo unless European nations pay more

Yes Provide Medicare benefits to military retirees and their dependents

Yes Grant China permanent normal trade status

Yes Phase out estate, gift and trust taxes

Yes Prohibit implementation of president's national monument designations

Yes Approve GOP plan to provide prescription drug coverage for Medicare beneficiaries

No Increase help for poor nations indebted to international financial institutions

1999

Yes Impose steel import quotas

Yes Kill proposal to take aviation trust funds off budget

No Require background checks on buyers only at gun shows with 10 or more vendors

Yes Remove barriers among banking, securities and insurance companies

No Authorize state grants to hire teachers and reduce class size

No Overhaul campaign finance law; ban "soft money" and restrict advocacy advertising

Yes Approve bipartisan plan to increase rights of patients in managed-care health plans

INTEREST GROUPS

	AFL-CIO	ADA	CCUS	ACU
2000	0%	0%	85%	69%
1999	33%	10%	84%	91%
1998	0%	0%	100%	96%
1997	14%	5%	90%	88%

CQ VOTE STUDIES

	PARTY UNITY		PRESIDENTIAL SUPPORT	
	Support	Oppose	Support	Oppose
2000	89%	11%	28%	72%
1999	92%	8%	26%	74%
1998	93%	7%	24%	76%
1997	93%	7%	27%	73%

ALABAMA 1
Southwest — Mobile

Crop fields and pine forests merge with Alabama's only Gulf of Mexico coastline to form the 1st. Although Mobile accounts for most of the district's income and population, a symbiotic relationship between the industrial and rural areas keeps the district's economy stable.

Forestry feeds the district's timber mills and shipping companies, despite financial ruin in Southeast Asia in the mid- to late-1990s that forced cutbacks in the local timber industry. Mobile's State Docks, one of the biggest commercial shipping centers in the nation, supports a shipbuilding industry that has stagnated in recent years. But ship repair and other services have kept the ports busy. The overall contraction of timber and ship-related industries forced the district to diversify. Tourism, based around the Gulf Shores, has been the most immediate remedy. Outside Mobile, manufacturing spin-offs have emerged. Textile plants and retail outlets also provide much-needed employment in the rural areas.

While traditionally Republican, the 1st's voters do not always follow the party line. Rural counties tend to favor Democratic candidates, while Mobile residents lean slightly Republican. Local elections can become battles over sensitive issues such as agricultural subsidies and international trade. Republicans have held the congressional seat since 1964, and the district overwhelmingly favored GOP presidential candidates in the 1990s and 2000. But the 1st in 1998 helped elect a Democratic governor.

MAJOR INDUSTRY
Commercial shipping, timber, textiles

CITIES
Mobile, 200,206; Prichard, 31,881; Tillman's Corner (unincorporated), 17,988 (1990); Daphne, 16,305

UNUSUAL FEATURES
Annual National Shrimp Festival at Gulf Shores draws more than 200,000 visitors in October; Wintzell's Oyster House in Mobile has a roomful of pictures of America's Junior Miss contestants – Mobile hosts the competition each summer; Monroeville was home of novelists Truman Capote and Harper Lee.

Rep. Terry Everett (R)

CAPITOL OFFICE
225-2901; fax 225-8913; 2312 Rayburn Bldg. 20515

INTERNET
e-mail: terry.everett@mail.house.gov
web: www.house.gov/everett

COMMITTEES
Agriculture
  (Specialty Crops & Foreign Agriculture -
  chairman)
Armed Services
Veterans' Affairs

HOMETOWN
Enterprise

BORN
Feb. 15, 1937, Dothan, Ala.

RELIGION
Baptist

FAMILY
Wife, Barbara Everett

EDUCATION
Enterprise State Junior College, attended

MILITARY SERVICE
Air Force, 1955-59

CAREER
Newspaper executive; construction company
owner; farm owner; real estate developer;
newspaper reporter

POLITICAL HIGHLIGHTS
No previous office

ELECTION RESULTS

2000 GENERAL

Terry Everett (R)	151,830	68.1%
Charles Woods (D)	64,958	29.2%
Wallace McGahan (LIBERT)	4,111	1.9%

2000 PRIMARY

Terry Everett (R)	unopposed

1998 GENERAL

Terry Everett (R)	131,428	69.3%
Joe Fondren (D)	58,136	30.7%

PREVIOUS WINNING PERCENTAGES
1996 (63%); 1994 (74%); 1992 (49%)

Elected 1992; 5th term

Everett is a self-made millionaire who built a chain of newspapers, owned a home-building company and served as chairman of the board of a local bank. But he also owns a farm and, harking back to his roots as the son of a sharecropper and railroad worker, is still more comfortable wearing boots than wingtips and being known as a regular guy from southeast Alabama than as a member of Congress.

His southeast Alabama roots, his military service right out of high school and his work experience, starting as the farm reporter for the Dothan Eagle, matched his congressional duties perfectly during his first two terms in the House. He held seats on the Agriculture and Armed Services panels and worked hard to protect the 2nd District's peanut farmers, defense contractors and military bases.

In the 107th Congress, Everett takes the reins of the Agriculture panel's Specialty Crops and Foreign Agriculture Programs Subcommittee, whose jurisdiction includes peanuts, sugar and tobacco.

The 2nd District is among the nation's leading peanut producers and has been since the boll weevil wiped out most of the cotton crop in the early 1900s. Everett is the co-chairman of the Congressional Peanut Caucus. When Congress rewrote farm policy in 1996, Everett was a key player in the fight to keep the government price-support system available to peanut farmers. Since then he has had to wage almost annual efforts to defeat congressional bids to reduce price supports.

Everett was outraged in 1998 when the Department of Transportation said it was considering establishing peanut-free buffer zones on commercial airliners to protect passengers with allergies to peanuts. He said the proposal was "an asinine interpretation of federal disability law. ... It is precisely this kind of dumb bureaucratic decision-making which rightly causes Americans to be distrustful of their government." Everett and several other lawmakers from peanut-growing districts blocked the plan. In the 106th Congress, looking to expand the market, Everett urged the Agriculture Department to include peanuts in future food aid packages to Russia.

From the Armed Services Committee, Everett is able to look out for his district's numerous military bases and defense contractors. The 2nd is home to Maxwell Air Force Base and its Gunter Annex and to Fort Rucker, where Army and Air Force helicopter crews train. He carries on the battle begun by his predecessor, Republican Bill Dickinson, to get the Navy's helicopter training mission transferred to Rucker as well. He would like to see private contractors, including several in his district, get more weapons maintenance work.

Everett also has had an assignment on the Veterans' Affairs Committee since he arrived in Washington in 1993. From 1997 through 2000, he chaired the panel's Oversight and Investigations Subcommittee, and he aggressively investigated reported problems within the Department of Veterans Affairs (VA). His probes of favoritism in burial policies, delays in payment of disability claims, complaints about substandard medical care, and the VA's problem-riddled computer modernization program put Everett in the news nationally.

Everett has been a persistent critic of the computer modernization program at the VA. He said he worried that the department's program would ultimately cost taxpayers $1.5 billion without offering faster or better service.

After receiving numerous assurances that the VA was taking the problem seriously, Everett in 2000 blasted the VA for "terrible" service in processing veterans' disability claims. In a hearing of his Oversight Subcommittee, Everett questioned whether the VA had doctored reports to make the problem appear less severe. "I have received a number of letters from veterans who think the VA is waiting for them to die so it will not have to pay them," Everett said, according to an Associated Press account.

Everett's oversight of the VA first made news in 1997 when his subcommittee began looking into allegations that the Clinton administration had traded precious burial plots in Arlington National Cemetery for political donations. Everett ultimately turned up no evidence of presidential wrongdoing, but the inquiry led to House passage in the 106th of legislation cosponsored by Everett to tighten requirements for interment at the cemetery.

The scandal eventually receded from public attention, but Everett's aggressive probing into veterans' affairs, albeit without nearly as much public attention, continued. He investigated reports of sexual harassment and serious mismanagement at veterans hospitals. His subcommittee also looked into allegations that the VA was harassing whistleblower employees and investigated the quality of care in VA hospitals.

Everett's parents died when he was a youth in Midland City, just north of Dothan, and he was largely responsible for his younger siblings when he returned from a four-year hitch in the Air Force, which he had joined right out of high school. He became a newspaper reporter upon his discharge from the Air Force, eventually owned a chain of small weekly and daily newspapers, and became a wealthy man when he sold most of them in the late 1980s. Everett was a home builder for a while and also headed a savings and loan in his birthplace of Dothan. He lives in Enterprise, home of the giant statue to the boll weevil, and owns a 400-acre farm outside Dothan that produces peanuts, among other crops.

He was 55 years old in 1992 and virtually unknown in political circles when Rep. Dickinson decided to retire after 14 terms. An insurgent within his own party, Everett claimed the GOP nomination by defeating a state senator who was the choice of the party establishment.

In the fall campaign against a man with arguably the most famous name in Alabama politics — state Treasurer George C. Wallace Jr., son of the former governor and presidential candidate — Everett proved to have a winning combination of message and means. He spent hundreds of thousands of dollars of his own money blanketing the district in billboards and radio and TV ads blaring: "Send a message, not a politician." Everett won with a bare plurality of 49 percent but has had no trouble winning re-election.

KEY VOTES

2000

No Raise hourly minimum wage by $1 over two years
Yes Halt funding for U.S. mission in Kosovo unless European nations pay more
Yes Provide Medicare benefits to military retirees and their dependents
Yes Grant China permanent normal trade status
Yes Phase out estate, gift and trust taxes
Yes Prohibit implementation of president's national monument designations
Yes Approve GOP plan to provide prescription drug coverage for Medicare beneficiaries
No Increase help for poor nations indebted to international financial institutions

1999

Yes Impose steel import quotas
Yes Kill proposal to take aviation trust funds off budget
No Require background checks on buyers only at gun shows with 10 or more vendors
Yes Remove barriers among banking, securities and insurance companies
No Authorize state grants to hire teachers and reduce class size
No Overhaul campaign finance law; ban "soft money" and restrict advocacy advertising
No Approve bipartisan plan to increase rights of patients in managed-care health plans

INTEREST GROUPS

	AFL-CIO	ADA	CCUS	ACU
2000	0%	0%	78%	90%
1999	33%	5%	80%	91%
1998	11%	5%	89%	100%
1997	0%	0%	80%	96%

CQ VOTE STUDIES

	PARTY UNITY		PRESIDENTIAL SUPPORT	
	Support	Oppose	Support	Oppose
2000	97%	3%	14%	86%
1999	95%	5%	15%	85%
1998	94%	6%	20%	80%
1997	96%	4%	27%	73%

ALABAMA 2
Southeast – Part of Montgomery; Dothan

Besides Dothan and a large portion of the state capital, Montgomery, the 2nd consists of scattered small towns. Farmers have diversified away from cotton since a boll weevil infestation in the early 1900s nearly wiped out their main crop. Poultry farms now complement cotton, peanut and tree farming, but the district's economy is still recouping from losses caused by hurricanes, floods, droughts and ice storms in recent years. Farther south, around Dothan, high-tech and auto parts plants have replaced textile mills that moved overseas.

Defense and state government continue to provide steady employment. Maxwell Air Force Base and its Gunter Annex are responsible for most of the Air Force's computer systems. Tourism also contributes, particularly in Montgomery, where Martin Luther King Jr. launched the civil rights movement from the Dexter Avenue Baptist Church. The Robert Trent Jones Golf Trail, large antebellum homes in Eufaula and fishing at Lake Eufaula also attract visitors from all over the Southeast.

Redistricting in 1992 created the black-majority 7th and left most of Montgomery's white voters in the 2nd. A large military retiree population underscores a conservative constituency that usually votes Republican. On the local level, the 2nd usually sends Democrats to the state legislature.

MAJOR INDUSTRY
Agriculture, military, manufacturing

MILITARY BASES
Fort Rucker (Army), 3,335 military, 1,823 civilian; Maxwell Air Force Base, 5,100 military, 1,129 civilian (2000)

CITIES
Montgomery (pt.), 120,099 (1990); Dothan, 58,383; Prattville, 27,041; Enterprise, 21,562

UNUSUAL FEATURES
Former Gov. George Wallace from Clayton; Hank Williams Sr. Museum in Georgiana.

Rep. Bob Riley (R)

CAPITOL OFFICE
225-3261; fax 225-5827; 322 Cannon Bldg. 20515

INTERNET
e-mail: bob.riley@mail.house.gov
web: www.house.gov/riley

COMMITTEES
Agriculture
Armed Services
Financial Services

HOMETOWN
Ashland

BORN
Oct. 3, 1944, Ashland, Ala.

RELIGION
Baptist

FAMILY
Wife, Patsy Riley; four children

EDUCATION
U. of Alabama, B.A. 1965

CAREER
Auto dealer; trucking company executive; farmer

POLITICAL HIGHLIGHTS
Ashland City Council, 1972-76; candidate for mayor of Ashland, 1976

ELECTION RESULTS

2000 GENERAL

Bob Riley (R)	147,317	86.9%
John P. Sophocleus (LIBERT)	21,119	12.5%

2000 PRIMARY

Bob Riley (R)	unopposed

1998 GENERAL

Bob Riley (R)	101,731	58.1%
Joe Turnham (D)	73,357	41.9%

PREVIOUS WINNING PERCENTAGES
1996 (50%)

Elected 1996; 3rd term

Riley was first elected to the House in 1996, but he feels great affinity with the GOP Class of 1994, and his voting record, rhetoric and agenda bear this out. He is deeply conservative, both on social and fiscal matters, and he told friends that he was "ideologically invigorated" by the elections of 1994 that swept the GOP to control of Congress.

Although Riley served a term in the city council of his small hometown of Ashland (population about 2,000) in the mid-1970s, he regards himself as a businessman, and he says he can identify with the non-governmental, non-political backgrounds that many of the Class of 1994 boast about.

In the 105th Congress, Riley joined with the most fiscally conservative House Republicans to urge their leaders not to be so willing to compromise. He accused Speaker Newt Gingrich of being too timid about pushing a "staunch conservative agenda."

But Riley came to Congress with a wealth of business experience, including selling cars and trucks, and for all his ideological fervor, he can appreciate the art of the deal. So it was that in 1997, when Gingrich and the GOP leadership reached a compromise with President Clinton on balancing the budget, Riley voted for the plan, even as some other conservative Republicans groused that their party should have held out for bigger tax cuts and less new spending. By that fall, Riley was hosting Gingrich for a fundraiser.

Riley is a frequent and ardent proponent of reducing taxes, arguing that such a course will stimulate economic activity. He usually can be counted on as a loyal vote for the party line. But there have been exceptions. He raised a howl as top Republicans pushed through a cost of living salary adjustment for lawmakers in 1997. Citing the mounting national debt, Riley protested, "If my company was $5 trillion in debt and still losing money, the last thing I would do is give management a pay raise." In 1999, he once again tried to block the automatic pay raise but again was thwarted by the GOP leadership's procedural maneuver.

Riley's committee assignments include posts on the Armed Services and Agriculture committees, two panels that deal with issues of importance to the 3rd District.

Fort McClellan, near Anniston, was ordered closed in 1995 and shut down operations in 1999, leaving a large void in the local economy. Riley worked to get the bulk of the base turned over to local authorities, at no cost, for their use in economic development efforts. The nearby town of Lincoln attracted a new Honda automobile assembly plant, to employ 1,500-2,000 workers, and Riley is hopeful that the Fort McClellan facility can attract a number of smaller companies that would provide parts to the Honda plant. In addition, Riley champions the expansion of the Justice Department's Center for Domestic Preparedness, a facility for training local authorities in how to deal with terrorist activities. The center uses a portion of the Fort McClellan property. He also has worked to expand the mission of the Anniston Army Depot.

On the agriculture front, Riley traveled to meetings of the World Trade Organization in Seattle in 1999, to protect U.S. farm exports. Riley told his constituents that "American farmers have taken a back seat in previous global trade talks, so I went to Seattle to make sure that they got a fair deal in this round." Unfortunately, demonstrations that disrupted the talks kept him in his hotel room for three days, preventing him from attending the meetings.

Alabama dairy farmers have been a particular concern of Riley's, as their numbers were cut in half between 1996 and 1999. Although Riley's farmers favor international trade agreements to open new markets, he faces conflicting pressures on the matter, having to weigh the potential effect on textile and other low-wage factories in the district.

Riley has been involved in a long-running battle, waged between Georgia and Alabama, over water. Atlanta's voracious thirst had threatened to reduce the water available for eastern Alabama, and Riley tried to nudge negotiators representing the two states to reach agreement. In the meantime, Riley backed the placement of 11 monitored gauges on the rivers to measure how much water is reaching Alabama.

One highlight for Riley in the 106th Congress was the enactment of his bill to designate 9,200 acres of forest land as the Dugger Mountain Wilderness.

At Christmastime 1999, Riley was one of the first lawmakers to send his constituents a video e-mail. The video clip, which costs less to produce than the traditional taxpayer-financed newsletter, elicited a much higher response from constituents, who were asked to respond to a questionnaire. Riley sent the video greetings only to constituents who previously had e-mailed him.

Riley's family roots go back six generations in Clay County. He earned a degree in business administration from the University of Alabama in 1965 and that same year started a business with his brother selling eggs door-to-door, a venture that grew into a large poultry-and-egg operation. By age 28, Riley was an Ashland city councilman. He held that office for four years, and then, after losing in the 1976 mayoral race, he devoted himself to a variety of business, civic and church pursuits and to raising his four children. He owned a grocery store and pharmacy, sold real estate, and operated an auto dealership, trucking company and cattle farm.

In 1996, inspired by the "Republican revolution" of 1994, and ready for a new direction in his life (his youngest child had just completed school), Riley entered the wide-open race for the 3rd District seat.

Democratic Rep. Glen Browder left his seat in the 3rd to seek his party's 1996 Senate nomination, and Riley joined six other Republicans and four Democrats in the campaign. A devout Baptist who refrained from campaigning on Sundays, Riley drew support from conservative Christian activists, who favored his advocacy of voluntary prayer in schools and his opposition to abortion and to allowing homosexuals in the military. The district, which had elected a Republican to the House only once (in 1964) since Reconstruction, but which consistently had backed the GOP presidential nominee beginning in 1984, liked Riley, by 3 percentage points. Since then, Riley has breezed to re-election, and in 2000, the Democrats did not field a challenger.

KEY VOTES

2000
No Raise hourly minimum wage by $1 over two years
Yes Halt funding for U.S. mission in Kosovo unless European nations pay more
Yes Provide Medicare benefits to military retirees and their dependents
No Grant China permanent normal trade status
Yes Phase out estate, gift and trust taxes
Yes Prohibit implementation of president's national monument designations
Yes Approve GOP plan to provide prescription drug coverage for Medicare beneficiaries
No Increase help for poor nations indebted to international financial institutions

1999
Yes Impose steel import quotas
Yes Kill proposal to take aviation trust funds off budget
No Require background checks on buyers only at gun shows with 10 or more vendors
Yes Remove barriers among banking, securities and insurance companies
No Authorize state grants to hire teachers and reduce class size
No Overhaul campaign finance law; ban "soft money" and restrict advocacy advertising
No Approve bipartisan plan to increase rights of patients in managed-care health plans

INTEREST GROUPS

	AFL-CIO	ADA	CCUS	ACU
2000	10%	5%	75%	91%
1999	33%	5%	79%	91%
1998	10%	5%	89%	100%
1997	0%	0%	78%	95%

CQ VOTE STUDIES

	PARTY UNITY		PRESIDENTIAL SUPPORT	
	Support	Oppose	Support	Oppose
2000	95%	5%	19%	81%
1999	96%	4%	19%	81%
1998	94%	6%	18%	82%
1997	97%	3%	23%	77%

ALABAMA 3
East – Anniston; Auburn

The 3rd can claim to be a microcosm of the entire state. It covers 14 counties and includes chicken farms, a military base, textile plants and universities scattered among mountains and rolling hills.

Anniston, the Calhoun County seat, relies heavily on the military. The Army removed its operations from Fort McClellan in 1999, but the Justice Department turned the base into a training facility for first respondents to chemical, biological and nuclear terrorist attacks. Anniston Army Depot is still located in the city, and local leaders are hoping it does not get targeted in future rounds of base closings.

In the south, Auburn University is one of the state's largest employers and a leading agricultural research center. Although downsized, athletic apparel maker Russell Corp. is a mainstay in Tallapoosa County, where thousands of Birmingham and Montgomery vacationers flock to Lake Martin for recreation. Predominantly black Macon County is one of the nation's poorest.

Most of the 3rd's residents are socially conservative Democrats who have come to favor Republican presidential candidates. Constituents generally want low property taxes and oppose gun control. There are small pockets of liberalism in the university communities of Auburn and Jacksonville.

MAJOR INDUSTRY
Higher education, agriculture, military

MILITARY BASES
Anniston Army Depot Activity, 2,517 civilian (1999)

CITIES
Auburn, 42,601; Phenix City, 27,550; Anniston, 25,622; Opelika, 24,902

UNUSUAL FEATURES
Tuskegee University, founded in 1881 through the efforts of Booker T. Washington, one of the nation's first black colleges.

Rep. Robert B. Aderholt (R)

Elected 1996; 3rd term

CAPITOL OFFICE
225-4876; fax 225-5587
1433 Longworth Bldg. 20515

INTERNET
e-mail: robert.aderholt@mail.house.gov
web: www.house.gov/aderholt

COMMITTEES
Appropriations

HOMETOWN
Haleyville

BORN
July 22, 1965, Haleyville, Ala.

RELIGION
Congregationalist Baptist

FAMILY
Wife, Caroline Aderholt; one child

EDUCATION
Birmingham Southern U., B.A. 1987; Samford U.,
J.D. 1990

CAREER
Lawyer; gubernatorial aide

POLITICAL HIGHLIGHTS
Republican nominee for Ala. House, 1990;
Haleyville municipal judge, 1992-96

ELECTION RESULTS

2000 GENERAL

Robert B. Aderholt (R)	140,009	60.6%
Marsha Folsom (D)	86,400	37.4%
Craig Goodrich (LIBERT)	3,519	1.5%

2000 PRIMARY

Robert B. Aderholt (R)	unopposed

1998 GENERAL

Robert B. Aderholt (R)	106,297	56.4%
Donald Bevill (D)	82,065	43.5%

PREVIOUS WINNING PERCENTAGES
1996 (50%)

Aderholt's congenial and soft-spoken manner does not prevent him from fiercely advocating policies to bring religion into the public sphere and to outlaw abortion. The son of a judge and a Baptist pastor, Aderholt (ADD-er-holt) combines a judicious, strait-laced demeanor with a socially conservative philosophy that was nurtured in a childhood spent in one of the most religiously conservative areas of the nation.

Longtime colleagues cannot recall the last time he raised his voice in anger, and he often comes across as timid. But Aderholt is not shy about taking a stand on some of the most contentious issues before Congress. In fact, he is best known in Washington for his crusade to permit public displays of the Ten Commandments. He became involved in the matter soon after he arrived on Capitol Hill in 1997, when a federal court ordered a judge in Aderholt's district to remove a copy of the Ten Commandments from his courtroom wall. Aderholt sponsored a resolution expressing support for the public display of the Ten Commandments, saying the resolution "is about our national heritage and the role that religion has historically played in our national life. Our nation was founded on Judeo-Christian principles." The House passed the resolution.

In 1999, as the House debated the causes of youth violence in the aftermath of the shootings at Colorado's Columbine High School, he returned to the issue, offering an amendment that would permit states to decide whether to display the Ten Commandments on public property. "Do not kill or steal, obey your parents, do not commit adultery. ... Who can argue with these important rules for any functioning society?" he told reporters.

Once again, the House approved his legislation, disregarding arguments from some that the language would be found unconstitutional. That effort attracted nationwide notice and brought him considerable scorn. Aderholt said he understood that posting of the Ten Commandments "will not change the moral character of our nation overnight." But, he continued, "it is one step that states can take to promote morality and work toward an end of children killing children."

Aderholt's advocacy on behalf of the Ten Commandments is emblematic of his determination to battle what he sees as the official exclusion of religion from public policy. Promoting "traditional values" is of paramount importance to the Alabama Republican.

On social policy issues, he is an unstinting conservative. He favors a constitutional amendment to outlaw abortion, except to save the life of the woman. Aderholt also cosponsored a proposed amendment to the Constitution that would allow prayer on public property and in public schools, arguing that Alabamians overcome their political differences in the act of bowing their heads at the dinner table.

Aderholt was the youngest member of the GOP Class of 1996, and now, in his third term, he is still the seventh-youngest member of the House.

He was one of only two GOP freshmen to receive a prized appointment to the Appropriations Committee in the 105th Congress. The GOP leadership wanted to give Aderholt every opportunity to solidify his hold on the historically Democratic 4th District by giving him a top committee assignment. (District voters had grown used to having representation on the powerful panel — Aderholt succeeded longtime Democratic appropriator Tom Bevill.) From his seat on the Transportation Subcommittee, he has been able to direct a share of federal highway money and other infrastructure spending to the 4th.

On fiscal issues, Aderholt is a believer in the GOP creed that the federal government should tax and spend less. But whatever amount flows from the federal spigot, Aderholt on the Appropriations panel works to see that his district gets its share. To do otherwise might risk the wrath of 4th District voters, who for decades were accustomed to goodies brought in by Bevill. Of particular importance to northern Alabama is funding for Corridor X, a project to upgrade the highway from Birmingham to Memphis. In 2000, Aderholt was able to get $100 million for the ongoing project.

Another top priority is the attempt to replace the 1,800 or so jobs lost when the Gulf States Steel plant in Gadsden closed in 2000. Aderholt backed legislation to provide loan guarantees for steel companies hurt by foreign imports, in hopes of attracting a buyer to reopen the plant. He also cosponsored a bill to impose quotas on steel imports. That, along with his vote against expanded trade ties with China, earned him plaudits from local union leaders.

Aderholt grew up with politics. When he was about five, he wrote a campaign letter touting his father in a local judgeship election, and he recalls meeting Bob Dole when he was about 11.

A month after graduating from law school in 1990, Aderholt was nominated for a state House seat, but he lost in the general election. He was appointed in 1992 to serve as a municipal court judge, and in 1995, he went to work for Republican Gov. Fob James Jr.

When Bevill retired in 1996 after 15 terms, Aderholt said he was encouraged to try for the seat because he felt it shared certain demographic characteristics with the neighboring 1st District of Mississippi, a longtime Democratic bastion that Republican Roger Wicker had won in 1994. In the GOP primary, Aderholt took 49 percent against four others and got the nomination when the second-place finisher declined to demand a runoff. In November, Democrats put up a strong candidate in former state Sen. Robert T. "Bob" Wilson Jr., who was nearly as conservative as Aderholt on social issues. As GOP presidential nominee Bob Dole carried the 4th by 5 percentage points over Bill Clinton, Aderholt prevailed by 2 points.

In Aderholt's next two elections, he had to overcome a Democratic opponent with strong name recognition: In 1998, it was lawyer Donald Bevill, son of the longtime congressman. In 2000, it was Marsha Folsom, wife of former Gov. Jim Folsom Jr. Aderholt beat Bevill by 13 points, and in 2000, although Folsom mounted a creditable campaign, Aderholt prevailed easily, by more than 20 points, with significant support from organized labor.

KEY VOTES

2000

Yes Raise hourly minimum wage by $1 over two years

Yes Halt funding for U.S. mission in Kosovo unless European nations pay more

Yes Provide Medicare benefits to military retirees and their dependents

No Grant China permanent normal trade status

Yes Phase out estate, gift and trust taxes

Yes Prohibit implementation of president's national monument designations

Yes Approve GOP plan to provide prescription drug coverage for Medicare beneficiaries

Yes Increase help for poor nations indebted to international financial institutions

1999

Yes Impose steel import quotas

Yes Kill proposal to take aviation trust funds off budget

No Require background checks on buyers only at gun shows with 10 or more vendors

Yes Remove barriers among banking, securities and insurance companies

No Authorize state grants to hire teachers and reduce class size

No Overhaul campaign finance law; ban "soft money" and restrict advocacy advertising

No Approve bipartisan plan to increase rights of patients in managed-care health plans

INTEREST GROUPS

	AFL-CIO	ADA	CCUS	ACU
2000	30%	15%	71%	88%
1999	33%	5%	80%	84%
1998	30%	10%	83%	96%
1997	0%	0%	80%	96%

CQ VOTE STUDIES

	PARTY UNITY		PRESIDENTIAL SUPPORT	
	Support	Oppose	Support	Oppose
2000	91%	9%	20%	80%
1999	95%	5%	14%	86%
1998	91%	9%	21%	79%
1997	97%	3%	24%	76%

ALABAMA 4
North Central – Gadsden

Encompassing mountains, foothills, flatlands and large waterways, the 4th stretches the width of the state, bordering Georgia and Mississippi. A small black population and a high percentage of unionized workers distinguish it from the rest of the state, but the middle-class inclination that seems to define the state pervades the district as well.

Weakened in part by textile companies moving overseas, the 4th is one of the poorest districts in the state, second only to the majority-black 7th. Coal mining has declined for years. An abundance of relatively new chicken farms provide relief, but the district is still ailing. In Gadsden, the district's only sizable city, national strikes and foreign competition have forced layoffs at rubber and steel plants.

In anticipation of more cutbacks, the area is pushing to attract new, moderate-sized businesses and to work with nearby Birmingham's medical facilities. Large mobile home manufacturing plants fuel Marshall County's economy, and Cullman County profits from an agricultural industry that includes everything from cotton and soybeans to hogs and cattle.

Most of the 4th's population is blue collar and socially conservative, especially on gun control. Although the district originally adhered to Democratic populism, the 4th has voted Republican on recent presidential ballots. In 1996, voters elected a Republican to Congress for just the second time since Reconstruction.

MAJOR INDUSTRY
Chicken farming, timber, manufacturing

CITIES
Gadsden, 42,120; Albertville, 16,795; Jasper, 14,223; Cullman, 14,203

UNUSUAL FEATURES
Winston County briefly became the "free state of Winston" when Alabama seceded from the union; World's longest yard sale, which starts in Gadsden and ends 450 miles later in Covington, Ky., attracts 400,000 bargain shoppers for one weekend in August.

Rep. Robert E. 'Bud' Cramer (D)

Elected 1990; 6th term

CAPITOL OFFICE
225-4801; fax 225-4392; 2367 Rayburn Bldg. 20515

INTERNET
e-mail: budmail@mail.house.gov
web: www.house.gov/cramer

COMMITTEES
Appropriations

HOMETOWN
Huntsville

BORN
Aug. 22, 1947, Huntsville, Ala.

RELIGION
Methodist

FAMILY
Widowed; one child

EDUCATION
U. of Alabama, B.A. 1969, J.D. 1972

MILITARY SERVICE
Army, 1972; Army Reserve, 1976-78

CAREER
Lawyer

POLITICAL HIGHLIGHTS
Madison County district attorney, 1981-91

ELECTION RESULTS

2000 GENERAL

Robert E. "Bud" Cramer (D)	186,059	88.8%
Alan Barksdale (LIBERT)	22,110	10.6%

2000 PRIMARY

Robert E. "Bud" Cramer (D)	unopposed

1998 GENERAL

Robert E. "Bud" Cramer (D)	134,819	69.7%
Gil Aust (R)	58,536	30.3%

PREVIOUS WINNING PERCENTAGES
1996 (56%); 1994 (50%); 1992 (66%); 1990 (67%)

Cramer has adapted himself for political survival over the years. After a surge of Republican voting nearly ousted him in 1994, Cramer (never a liberal) reacted by further distancing himself from Democratic Party stands, and he redoubled his work on district needs. As a result, he has solidified his hold on his conservative-leaning district.

One clear sign of Cramer's efforts to project an independent image has been his diminished rate of agreement with the Democratic position on House floor votes. During the Democratic-controlled 103rd Congress, Cramer backed President Clinton more than 80 percent of the time, and he cast high-profile votes in favor of Clinton's 1993 budget package, which raised taxes, and for the 1994 crime bill. But after 1994, when his party lost the House majority and he nearly lost his seat, Cramer voted with Clinton only about half the time, one of the lowest presidential-support scores for any Democrat. (His presidential-support score in 2000 was just 49 percent.)

That is not to say that Cramer has undergone a metamorphosis. Going back to his first term, he has sided with conservatives on many issues, opposing gun control proposals, for instance, and supporting a balanced-budget constitutional amendment. And Cramer, an approachable, pragmatic man, is a founding member of the "Blue Dogs," a coalition of conservative House Democrats.

In the 106th, Cramer broke with the Clinton administration on tax cuts, gun control and a proposed national missile defense system, voting in 2000 to override Clinton's veto of legislation that would have eliminated the "marriage penalty," a quirk in the tax code that exposes some two-earner married couples to higher income taxes. Similarly, he voted to override Clinton's veto of legislation to cut estate taxes.

But he did not hesitate to work with the Clinton White House when it came to steering federal dollars to his district. In 2000, he voted for an administration-backed measure to grant China permanent normal trade status after the Commerce Department agreed to reconsider a plan to close a national weather station in his tornado-prone district.

Cramer serves on the Appropriations subcommittee that funds the departments of Housing and Veterans Affairs and many independent agencies, including NASA. His fiscal conservatism is tempered by his support for NASA and the Pentagon, both of which have a major presence in the 5th District. Huntsville is home to NASA's Marshall Space Flight Center and the Army's Redstone Arsenal.

Cramer also looks out for programs run by the Tennessee Valley Authority, the massive public works project created to provide low-cost energy, flood control and economic development in a multistate region. In 1998, he sought to convince the Energy Department to choose TVA's never-used nuclear power plant at Bellefonte as the site for producing tritium, a critical element in nuclear explosives. The TVA plant was ultimately selected over the Savannah River nuclear complex site for the multimillion-dollar project.

Acknowledging the risk in relying heavily on federal programs, Cramer has been in the forefront of efforts to encourage the development of private space ventures. In 1996 and 1997, he worked with officials of McDonnell-Douglas (which has since merged with Boeing Corp.) to convince the company to build a $450 million rocket booster plant in Decatur. The plant employed more than 500 workers in early 2001, with plans to expand to as many as 2,000 employees, and has attracted affiliated businesses to the area.

Sharing top billing on Cramer's agenda are children's issues. When he was a district attorney in Huntsville, he founded the Children's Advocacy Center to shelter and counsel abused children. In Congress, he was responsible for legislation in 1992 to provide federal assistance to a growing national network of centers modeled on the Huntsville program. Cramer is a member of the Congressional Missing and Exploited Children's Caucus.

Nevertheless, he advocates a get-tough approach toward youthful offenders. He was one of just six Democrats in the 105th to vote against the party's alternative juvenile crime proposal, which focused on prevention. Instead, he supported the GOP approach, which called for tougher treatment of violent offenders in the courts.

Drawing on his personal experience, Cramer supports abortion rights in general. As his late wife battled cancer (she died in 1987), she needed an abortion to prolong her life. Cramer has voted to permit abortions at overseas military hospitals, to allow federal employees' health care plans to cover abortions, and to retain a requirement that states fund Medicaid abortions for poor women in cases of rape, incest or to save the life of the woman. (He does favor a ban on a procedure its opponents call "partial birth" abortion.) He supports family planning programs and has opposed GOP efforts to require parental notification for teenagers seeking contraceptives.

Before coming to Congress, Cramer served as the Madison County district attorney for 10 years, building a reputation as a nationally recognized expert in child abuse and winning honors from President Reagan in a 1987 White House ceremony. His work on behalf of children, coupled with programs his office instituted to prosecute bad-check cases and spousal abuse, earned Cramer a reputation as a champion of the victim. When seven-term Democratic Rep. Ronnie G. Flippo gave up the 5th District in 1990 to run for governor, Cramer won his seat with two-thirds of the vote.

But in 1994, he was taken to the wire by well-funded and well-connected Wayne Parker, the son-in-law of influential Texas GOP Rep. Bill Archer. Cramer, under attack for supporting Democratic policies, fought back by reminding voters of his efforts to save the space station and to promote job creation. Winning just 50 percent of the vote, Cramer barely survived the Republican tide that virtually wiped out the cadre of white Southern Democrats in the House. (In the 107th Congress, Cramer is one of just five white House Democrats from the five Deep South states — Alabama, Georgia, Louisiana, Mississippi and South Carolina.) In the three elections since that 1994 scare, Cramer has won by comfortable margins.

KEY VOTES

2000

Yes Raise hourly minimum wage by $1 over two years
No Halt funding for U.S. mission in Kosovo unless European nations pay more
Yes Provide Medicare benefits to military retirees and their dependents
Yes Grant China permanent normal trade status
Yes Phase out estate, gift and trust taxes
No Prohibit implementation of president's national monument designations
No Approve GOP plan to provide prescription drug coverage for Medicare beneficiaries
No Increase help for poor nations indebted to international financial institutions

1999

Yes Impose steel import quotas
Yes Kill proposal to take aviation trust funds off budget
No Require background checks on buyers only at gun shows with 10 or more vendors
Yes Remove barriers among banking, securities and insurance companies
Yes Authorize state grants to hire teachers and reduce class size
Yes Overhaul campaign finance law; ban "soft money" and restrict advocacy advertising
Yes Approve bipartisan plan to increase rights of patients in managed-care health plans

INTEREST GROUPS

	AFL-CIO	ADA	CCUS	ACU
2000	40%	35%	80%	40%
1999	78%	55%	72%	41%
1998	70%	65%	78%	44%
1997	75%	45%	80%	48%

CQ VOTE STUDIES

	PARTY UNITY		PRESIDENTIAL SUPPORT	
	Support	Oppose	Support	Oppose
2000	66%	34%	49%	51%
1999	53%	47%	54%	46%
1998	60%	40%	54%	46%
1997	58%	42%	52%	48%

ALABAMA 5

North — Huntsville

A large section of the Tennessee River winds through the 5th, which borders Georgia, Mississippi and Tennessee. Reliant on agriculture before World War II, the 5th now owes its economic well-being to the federal government. Huntsville is best known for hosting the NASA Marshall Space Flight Center, but defense has contributed more to its economy. Redstone Arsenal benefited from base closures in the 1990s, incorporating Army aviation duties to its missile command center and increasing its personnel. Redstone has attracted several high-tech plants.

Tennessee Valley Authority facilities line the river's shores throughout the 5th. Boeing built a satellite rocket booster plant in Decatur in 1999, which provided a boost for the local economy. Jackson County, where the textile industry has all but vanished in the past few years, has lagged. A drywall company recently opened a large facility in Bridgeport, providing initial steps toward economic recovery.

Voters in the 5th have never sent a Republican to Congress, but Republican presidential candidates have enjoyed a slight edge recently. The district generally claims a socially conservative constituency.

MAJOR INDUSTRY
Defense, government, manufacturing

MILITARY BASES
Redstone Arsenal, 809 military, 7,850 civilian (1999)

CITIES
Huntsville, 177,893; Decatur, 54,988; Florence, 39,028; Madison, 27,116; Athens, 20,302

UNUSUAL FEATURES
"Muscle Shoals Sound" originated at Fame Recording Studios, where Aretha Franklin, Otis Redding and Wilson Pickett recorded hit songs.

Rep. Spencer Bachus (R)

Elected 1992; 5th term

CAPITOL OFFICE
225-4921; fax 225-2082; 442 Cannon Bldg. 20515

INTERNET
e-mail: www.house.gov/bachus/citizendirect.htm
web: www.house.gov/bachus

COMMITTEES
Financial Services
 (Financial Institutions & Consumer Credit -
 chairman)
Judiciary
Transportation & Infrastructure

HOMETOWN
Birmingham

BORN
Dec. 28, 1947, Birmingham, Ala.

RELIGION
Baptist

FAMILY
Wife, Linda Bachus; three children, two
stepchildren

EDUCATION
Auburn U., B.A. 1969; U. of Alabama, J.D. 1972

MILITARY SERVICE
Ala. National Guard, 1969-71

CAREER
Lawyer; manufacturer

POLITICAL HIGHLIGHTS
Ala. Senate, 1983; Ala. House, 1983-87; Ala. Board
of Education, 1987-91; candidate for Ala. attorney
general, 1990; Ala. Republican Party chairman,
1991-92

ELECTION RESULTS

2000 GENERAL

Spencer Bachus (R)	212,751	88.0%
Terry Reagin Sr. (LIBERT)	28,129	11.6%

2000 PRIMARY

Spencer Bachus (R)	unopposed

1998 GENERAL

Spencer Bachus (R)	154,761	71.8%
Donna Wesson Smalley (D)	60,657	28.1%

PREVIOUS WINNING PERCENTAGES
1996 (71%); 1994 (79%); 1992 (52%)

A steadfast conservative, Bachus over the years has become identified with popular Republican causes: cutting taxes, restricting abortion, imposing term limits on lawmakers.

So he surprised many political observers by taking on a traditionally liberal cause: forgiving Third World debt. A devout Baptist, Bachus (BACK-us) views debt relief in religious terms. He contends that Americans have a moral obligation to help the less fortunate in poor countries. He even fasted for a day in 1999 to draw attention to a proposal that the United States provide nearly $1 billion in debt relief to dozens of the world's poorest nations.

"We have so much and these countries have so little," he told The Washington Post. "We're all members of the human race, you know." Congress eventually agreed to write off some of the debts of the poorest countries.

Bachus even joined forces in 1998 with his ideological opposite, socialist Independent Bernard Sanders of Vermont, in pushing, unsuccessfully, a proposal to delay the U.S. contribution to the International Monetary Fund until it changed its bylaws to ensure that banks and other lending institutions help provide debt relief to nations in economic crisis.

On most other issues, Bachus is strongly partisan. His style can be confrontational (he is a former trial lawyer) and his criticisms of Democrats sharp (he is a former chairman of the Alabama GOP). But his partisanship seems well-suited to the 6th, one of the most conservative districts in the country.

In person, Bachus is plain-spoken and sometimes acerbic. During one Banking Committee session, Bachus sarcastically asked for the services of an audiologist when he thought Chairman Jim Leach, R-Iowa, called the vote wrong.

Bachus first came to the House in 1992, with a pledge that he would serve no more than eight years. Since then, momentum behind congressional term limits has stalled, and though he continues to support them, he says that unless and until the system changes, there is no need for Republicans such as himself to set an arbitrary limit on how long they will remain in Washington to fight for conservatism.

Bachus favors dismantling the tax code and replacing it with a simpler system. He earns high marks from anti-abortion groups and backs his party on such issues as supporting a constitutional amendment to bar flag desecration.

One of his biggest causes in the 106th Congress was doubling a $5,000 tax credit for people adopting children, thereby seeking to encourage families to open their homes to both American and foreign children. He tried again in the 107th, pointing out that adoption — with medical bills, legal fees, travel expenses and other costs — can be an expensive proposition. Bachus also proposed removing federal taxes on the earnings in prepaid college tuition plans, contending that the government had to make college more affordable.

On another front, he raised concerns that China was using the U.S. bond market to help finance its military buildup, and he proposed a system to better monitor, and even block, such use of the financial markets. He also harshly criticized President Clinton's decision in early 1999 to certify Mexico as "fully cooperating" in the drug war, saying that the certification "defies reality."

The partisan Alabamian gained attention as soon as he entered the House. As a freshman on the Banking Committee in the Democratic-controlled 103rd Congress, he demanded a congressional inquiry into the

Whitewater real estate dealings of the Clintons.

After Republicans took control of the House in 1995, Bachus aggressively pursued alleged White House and administration misdeeds as chairman of the Banking panel's General Oversight and Investigations Subcommittee. In the 106th, he shifted subcommittee posts, taking the chairmanship of the Domestic and International Monetary Policy Subcommittee. In the 107th, he chairs the Financial Institutions and Consumer Credit Subcommittee of the newly named Financial Services panel (formerly Banking).

Bachus operates more quietly on the Transportation Committee, where he devotes much energy to the time-honored pursuit of bringing home the bacon. The massive transportation bill passed in the 105th included about $90 million in funding for various projects Bachus sought, such as local highway and bridge improvements.

Bachus made headlines in the 105th when he criticized a trip that Alabama Democratic Rep. Earl F. Hilliard took to Libya. Although his own destinations aren't so controversial, Bachus has drawn publicity because of his foreign travels. Between January 1996 and May 1997, he ran up a tab topping $30,000 on eight trips financed by special-interest groups. The majority of Bachus' trips were paid for by railroad organizations or other transportation interests. In the 105th, Bachus was a member of the Transportation panel's Railroads Subcommittee, but he said he did not view the trips as a conflict of interest despite his role in overseeing the railroad industry. "I have a special obligation and duty to stay current about the conditions of America's railroads and the railroad industry," he said.

Bachus' wife, Linda, is also active in public life, heading the Cancer Research Foundation's Congressional Families Action for Cancer Awareness — a group comprising spouses of members of Congress, Cabinet officers and Supreme Court justices. In 1999, she testified before a House Appropriations subcommittee, urging a boost in spending on cancer research.

Bachus, who once owned a sawmill and was a practicing criminal trial lawyer for two decades, began his career in elective office in 1983. He served in the state legislature, on the state board of education and as chairman of the Alabama GOP.

In his first House election bid, Bachus benefited handsomely from the post-1990 census remapping of Alabama's congressional districts, which eviscerated the district held for five terms by Democratic Rep. Ben Erdreich, transforming it into a solidly Republican bastion. Bachus won a 52 percent to 45 percent victory in 1992 and has been re-elected with at least 70 percent of the vote since.

KEY VOTES

2000

No   Raise hourly minimum wage by $1 over two years
Yes Halt funding for U.S. mission in Kosovo unless European nations pay more
Yes Provide Medicare benefits to military retirees and their dependents
Yes Grant China permanent normal trade status
Yes Phase out estate, gift and trust taxes
Yes Prohibit implementation of president's national monument designations
Yes Approve GOP plan to provide prescription drug coverage for Medicare beneficiaries
Yes Increase help for poor nations indebted to international financial institutions

1999

Yes Impose steel import quotas
No   Kill proposal to take aviation trust funds off budget
No   Require background checks on buyers only at gun shows with 10 or more vendors
Yes Remove barriers among banking, securities and insurance companies
No   Authorize state grants to hire teachers and reduce class size
Yes Overhaul campaign finance law; ban "soft money" and restrict advocacy advertising
Yes Approve bipartisan plan to increase rights of patients in managed-care health plans

INTEREST GROUPS

	AFL-CIO	ADA	CCUS	ACU
2000	10%	5%	85%	88%
1999	33%	20%	76%	84%
1998	10%	5%	89%	84%
1997	13%	0%	90%	96%

CQ VOTE STUDIES

	PARTY UNITY		PRESIDENTIAL SUPPORT	
	Support	Oppose	Support	Oppose
2000	89%	11%	24%	76%
1999	90%	10%	17%	83%
1998	89%	11%	20%	80%
1997	94%	6%	26%	74%

ALABAMA 6
Part of Birmingham and suburbs

Alabama's smallest but most prosperous district, the 6th is a combination of the whiter and wealthier portions of Birmingham and Tuscaloosa and their suburbs. Rural life still dots the district, but fields and forests are steadily turning into malls. Birmingham's success beginning in the 1980s started with a shift from steel to white-collar business. Banks and medical facilities have made the city a hub for the deep South. Although more than two-thirds of Birmingham's population is in the neighboring 7th, commuters from suburbs in the 6th enjoy most of the city's wealth. Jefferson County's well-to-do, almost exclusively white bedroom communities such as Homewood, Mountain Brook and Hoover are home to people who work in Birmingham's business district.

Tuscaloosa, a medium-size city, is starting to feel the effects of Birmingham's expansion. A new Mercedes plant joins the city's chemical and rubber makers. But the city's signature undoubtedly is

University of Alabama football, which attracts fanatics statewide to watch the "Crimson Tide."

A 1992 redistricting that created the overwhelmingly Democratic, black-majority 7th yielded an equally solid and swelling Republican constituency in the 6th. Congressional and presidential elections since redistricting have favored GOP candidates by an average margin of almost 40 percent. The contrast between the 6th and 7th can lead to conflict, particularly when funds for infrastructure are at stake. Universities in Birmingham and Tuscaloosa account for most of the district's few Democratic votes.

MAJOR INDUSTRY
Banking, manufacturing, higher education

CITIES
Birmingham (pt.), 82,554 (1990); Hoover, 61,406; Tuscaloosa (pt.), 36,622 (1990); Alabaster, 25,950

UNUSUAL FEATURES
A 55-foot cast-iron statue of Vulcan, the Roman god of fire and metalworking, in Birmingham is one of the world's largest iron figures.

Rep. Earl F. Hilliard (D)

CAPITOL OFFICE
225-2665; fax 226-0772
1314 Longworth Bldg. 20515

INTERNET
e-mail: www.house.gov/writerep
web: www.house.gov/hilliard

COMMITTEES
Agriculture
International Relations

HOMETOWN
Birmingham

BORN
April 9, 1942, Birmingham, Ala.

RELIGION
Baptist

FAMILY
Wife, Mary Franklin Hilliard; two children

EDUCATION
Morehouse College, B.A. 1964; Howard U., J.D. 1967; Atlanta U., M.B.A. 1970

CAREER
Lawyer; insurance broker

POLITICAL HIGHLIGHTS
Ala. House, 1975-81; Ala. Senate, 1981-93

ELECTION RESULTS

2000 GENERAL

Earl F. Hilliard (D)	148,243	74.6%
Ed Martin (R)	46,134	23.2%
Kennon H. Hager (LIBERT)	3,829	1.9%

2000 PRIMARY

Earl F. Hilliard (D)	36,249	50.1%
Artur Davis (D)	30,973	42.8%
Wayne Sowell (D)	5,155	7.1%

1998 GENERAL

Earl F. Hilliard (D)	136,431	98.0%
write-ins	2,750	2.0%

PREVIOUS WINNING PERCENTAGES
1996 (71%); 1994 (77%); 1992 (70%)

Elected 1992; 5th term

Hilliard does not hesitate to lash out at policies that he feels could hurt the poor, minorities or farmers, and his 7th District has plenty of all three. He casts a dependably liberal vote and in the 106th Congress was a vice chairman of the Progressive Caucus, the most left-leaning faction of the House Democrats. But he is an equal opportunity critic, and he found plenty to criticize about the Clinton administration over the years.

Hilliard says he is committed to "uplifting the poor, the disenfranchised and the everyday laborer." As a student at Atlanta's Morehouse College in the early 1960s, Hilliard was inspired by a meeting with the Rev. Martin Luther King Jr. and enlisted as "one of Dr. King's foot soldiers in the war for racial equality."

Hilliard, the first black to represent Alabama in Congress since Reconstruction, points out that the 7th is "one of the most economically deprived regions in the nation." His congressional efforts are directed toward rectifying that situation.

In addition to supporting traditional Democratic social programs, Hilliard is willing to try all kinds of economic development ideas to help his district. In the 106th Congress, for example, he offered legislation to add rabbit to the list of federally inspected meats, hoping that a federal seal of approval would help convince consumers to eat rabbit. Hilliard figured that because rabbits reproduce quickly, poor Alabamians could start up a rabbit-producing farm with little investment. "On a small-size city lot, you could have enough rabbits there to make $25,000 a year," he suggested.

Concerns about job security for low-wage factory workers in the 7th District make him wary of lowering international trade barriers.

Hilliard falls in line with conservatives on certain votes. He supported the drive for a constitutional amendment banning flag desecration. On some environmental issues his stance is development-friendly. And he was one of 56 Democrats in 1996 who voted to repeal the ban on certain semiautomatic assault-style weapons; in 2000, however, he announced that he would no longer accept campaign money from the National Rifle Association. He said he supports such measures as gun safety locks and background checks of prospective purchasers of weapons.

Hilliard has used his seat on the Agriculture panel to speak for struggling farmers. In 1995, he lashed out at GOP attempts to reduce the federal role in agriculture, accusing the majority of "treating our farmers like a bunch of ruined chickens, throwing them into the equivalent of the legislative compost heap, to slowly decompose, to rot, to wither and then to simply waste away."

Hilliard's verbal missiles hit Clinton administration targets as well. He had sharp words for the Agriculture and Judiciary departments after media reports publicized the plight of a number of black farmers who had been mired in lengthy, financially ruinous disputes with the federal government over benefits allegedly due them.

In the 106th, Hilliard criticized federal officials who proposed listing the "Alabama sturgeon" as an endangered species. Hilliard called the idea a "precipitous, prejudicial act of bureaucratic arrogance that disregards the economic advancement of people living in Alabama."

He is undaunted by controversies that periodically have swirled around him dating as far back as his days in the Alabama Legislature and as recently as an ongoing House ethics probe. Hilliard's frequent trips overseas at taxpayer expense, for example, have attracted attention. He was declared the

No. 1 congressional traveler in a 1995 NBC News report, part of a feature titled, "The Fleecing of America." But Hilliard says traveling is part of his job on International Relations.

During the August 1997 congressional recess, Hilliard visited Libya, despite a State Department ban on travel to that country. The trip drew a sharply critical reaction from Hilliard's Birmingham-area House colleague, Republican Spencer Bachus, who said it amounted to giving "aid and comfort to the enemy." The House ethics committee eventually dismissed a complaint about the trip.

Born and raised in segregated Birmingham, Hilliard went away for college, earning business and law degrees before returning home to practice law and work in the insurance business. He was first elected to the Alabama Legislature in 1974, earning a reputation as a player of political hardball.

Hilliard won a hard-fought 1992 Democratic contest in the 7th, overcoming accusations of unethical conduct and the opposition of the Birmingham News, which faulted him for what it termed ethical lapses. But Hilliard had the backing of longtime Birmingham Mayor Richard Arrington, one of the state's most powerful black politicians, and he squeaked by to a narrow Democratic primary runoff victory. From there, Hilliard breezed into office, benefiting from the district's overwhelmingly Democratic makeup.

Hilliard is no stranger to controversy. In addition to complaints about his overseas travel and the 1990 state Senate campaign, Hilliard has faced sharp questioning about his 1988 sale of property to the city of Birmingham, his 1991 bankruptcy filing and his 1992 primary campaign. In 1999, the House ethics committee launched a second probe of Hilliard, this time looking into allegations about campaign activities and his business dealings while a member of Congress. That probe was unresolved at the end of the 106th Congress.

Hilliard does not apologize for his actions. Of the 1991 bankruptcy filing, he was quoted by the Associated Press as saying it would make him better able to understand the plight of the poor. He responded to other allegations with affirmations of his innocence.

In 2000, Hilliard faced a serious primary challenge from young Birmingham lawyer Artur Davis. Reminding voters of the 1997 trip to Libya and the ongoing 1999-2000 ethics probe, Davis asked, "Have you noticed that almost everything you hear about Earl Hilliard embarrasses you? We voted for him, but only because we've never had a real choice." At one point, Hilliard's campaign war chest was close to empty, with the money having been spent on attorney's fees, but he posted a 50 percent to 43 percent victory and went on to win by more than 50 points in November.

KEY VOTES

2000

Yes Raise hourly minimum wage by $1 over two years

No Halt funding for U.S. mission in Kosovo unless European nations pay more

Yes Provide Medicare benefits to military retirees and their dependents

No Grant China permanent normal trade status

No Phase out estate, gift and trust taxes

No Prohibit implementation of president's national monument designations

No Approve GOP plan to provide prescription drug coverage for Medicare beneficiaries

Yes Increase help for poor nations indebted to international financial institutions

1999

Yes Impose steel import quotas

No Kill proposal to take aviation trust funds off budget

No Require background checks on buyers only at gun shows with 10 or more vendors

No Remove barriers among banking, securities and insurance companies

Yes Authorize state grants to hire teachers and reduce class size

Yes Overhaul campaign finance law; ban "soft money" and restrict advocacy advertising

Yes Approve bipartisan plan to increase rights of patients in managed-care health plans

INTEREST GROUPS

	AFL-CIO	ADA	CCUS	ACU
2000	100%	90%	52%	12%
1999	89%	80%	24%	4%
1998	100%	100%	28%	8%
1997	100%	80%	44%	10%

CQ VOTE STUDIES

	PARTY UNITY		PRESIDENTIAL SUPPORT	
	Support	Oppose	Support	Oppose
2000	91%	9%	78%	22%
1999	88%	12%	78%	22%
1998	94%	6%	86%	14%
1997	91%	9%	70%	30%

ALABAMA 7
West Central – Parts of Birmingham, Montgomery and Tuscaloosa

The 7th combines the inner-city sections of Birmingham, Montgomery and Tuscaloosa, once the battlegrounds of civil rights, with poor, rural communities. In contrast to its white, well-to-do neighbor, the Republican 6th District, the 7th's residents tend to be lower- to middle-class blacks who vote overwhelmingly Democratic. Redistricting in 1992 solidified a Democratic lock on the 7th and paved the way for Alabama's first black member of Congress since Reconstruction.

While the neighboring 6th's part of Birmingham has prospered, the densely populated downtown portion of the 7th, known as the "finger," has been left behind. Still, there are some signs of revitalization, such as new museums, a theme park and the restoration of old buildings into high-rent apartments. And despite the struggles, several steel plants and communications firms have kept unemployment down.

Near Tuscaloosa, a Mercedes-Benz plant in Vance now tops an industrial sector that complements small- to medium-sized businesses. The 7th also includes state capital buildings in downtown Montgomery, but more and more city residents are moving east, into the 2nd District's part of the city.

The Black Belt, named for the traditionally rich, cotton-growing soil in rural, west-central Alabama, accounts for the rest of the district. This area is in a perpetual state of poverty; it has not known prosperity since before the Civil War, when cotton plantation owners made fortunes from slave labor.

MAJOR INDUSTRY
Agriculture, higher education, manufacturing

CITIES
Birmingham (pt.), 183,414 (1990); Montgomery (pt.), 67,007 (1990); Tuscaloosa (pt.), 41,137 (1990); Selma, 21,774

UNUSUAL FEATURES
"Ghost town" of Cahawba, near Selma, was Alabama's first capital but now is an archaeological site.

Gov. Tony Knowles (D)

First elected: 1994
Length of term: 4 years
Term expires: 12/02
Salary: $81,648
Phone: (907) 465-3500
Hometown: Anchorage
Born: Jan. 1, 1943, Tulsa, Okla.
Religion: Roman Catholic
Family: Wife, Susan Knowles; three children
Education: Yale U., B.A. 1968
Military Service: Army, 1962-65
Career: Restaurateur
Political highlights: Alaska Assembly, 1975-79; Anchorage mayor, 1982-87; Democratic nominee for governor, 1990

Election results:

1998 GENERAL

Tony Knowles (D)	112,879	51.3%
write-ins	43,571	19.8%
Jon Lindauer (R)	39,331	17.9%
Ray Metcalfe (MOD)	13,540	6.1%
Erica L. Jacobsson (GREEN)	6,618	3.0%
Sylvia C. Sullivan (AKI)	4,238	1.9%

Lt. Gov. Fran Ulmer (D)

First elected: 1994
Length of term: 4 years
Term expires: 12/02
Salary: $76,176
Phone: (907) 465-3520

STATE LEGISLATURE

Bicameral Legislature: Meets January to mid-May, with a limit of 121 calendar days
House of Representatives: 40 members, 2-year terms
2001 breakdown: 27R, 13D; 32 men, 8 women
Salary: $2,001/month
Phone: (907) 465-3725
Senate: 20 members, 4-year terms
2001 breakdown: 14R, 6D; 16 men, 4 women
Salary: $2,001/month
Phone: (907) 465-3701

STATE TERM LIMITS

Governor: 2 consecutive terms
Senate: No
House: No

URBAN STATISTICS

CITY	POPULATION
Anchorage	257,808
Fairbanks	32,769
Juneau	30,192

REGISTERED VOTERS

Undeclared	35%
Republican	25%
Democrat	16%
Non-Partisan	15%

POPULATION

2000 population	626,932
1990 population	550,043
Percent change	+14%
Rank among states	48
Median age	31.8
Born in state	34%
Foreign born	5%
Urban/rural	67%/33%
Crime rate	701/100,000
Poverty level	9.4%
Federal workers	17,041
Military	22,707

REAPPORTIONMENT

Alaska retained its one House seat in reapportionment.

MISCELLANEOUS

Web: www.state.ak.us
Capital: Juneau
Land area: 570,374 sq. miles
Rank among states: 1
STATE ELECTION OFFICIAL
(907) 465-4611
DEMOCRATIC HEADQUARTERS
(907) 258-3050
REPUBLICAN HEADQUARTERS
(907) 276-4467

District Statistics

DIST.	VOTE FOR PRESIDENT 2000			1996			1992			WHT	BLK	ASIAN	HISP	HOUSEHOLD INCOME	OVER 65+	UNDER 18	COLLEGE EDUCATION
	D	R	GREEN	D	R	REF	D	R	I								
AL	28%	59%	10%	33%	51%	11%	30%	39%	28%	76%	4%	4%	3%	$41,408	4%	31%	23%

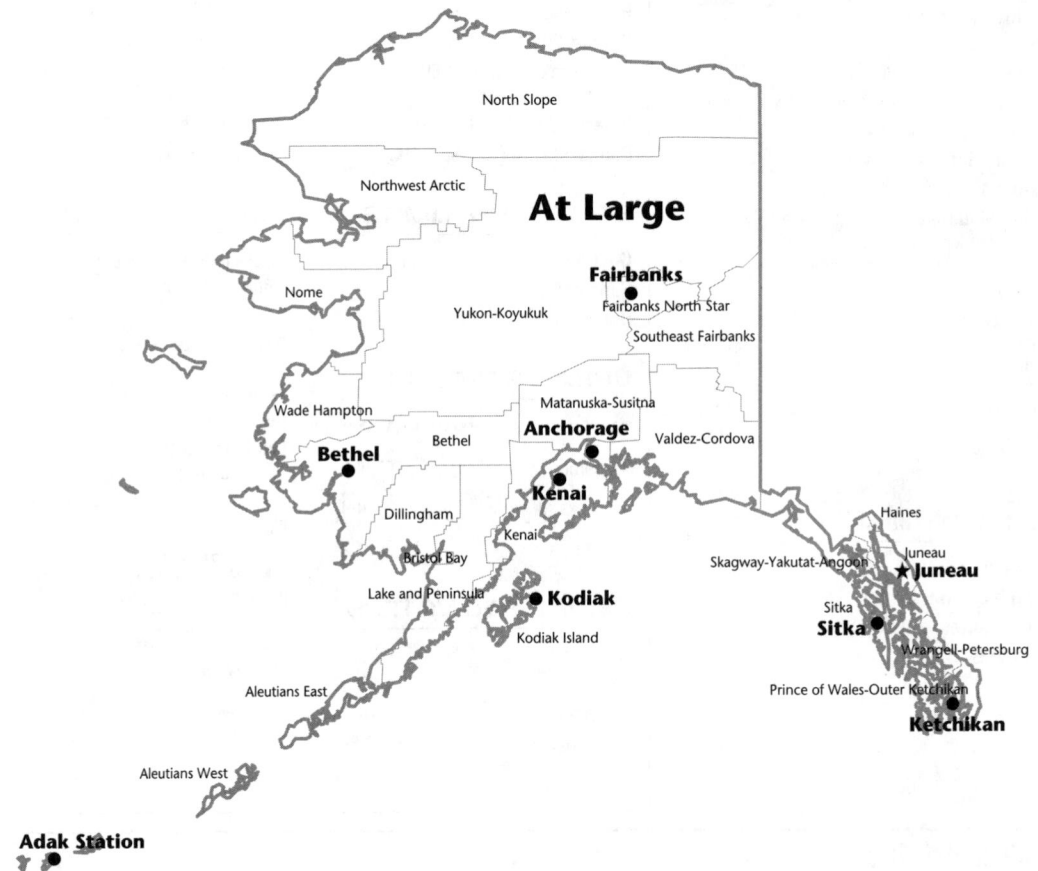

North Slope

Northwest Arctic

At Large

Nome

Fairbanks

Yukon-Koyukuk

Fairbanks North Star

Southeast Fairbanks

Wade Hampton

Matanuska-Susitna

Anchorage

Valdez-Cordova

Bethel

Bethel

Kenai

Haines

Dillingham

Kenai

Juneau

Bristol Bay

Skagway-Yakutat-Angoon

★**Juneau**

Lake and Peninsula

Kodiak

Sitka

Kodiak Island

Sitka

Wrangell-Petersburg

Aleutians East

Prince of Wales-Outer Ketchikan

Ketchikan

Aleutians West

Adak Station

Sen. Ted Stevens (R)

CAPITOL OFFICE
224-3004; fax 224-2354; 522 Hart Bldg. 20510

INTERNET
e-mail: senator_stevens@stevens.senate.gov
web: stevens.senate.gov

COMMITTEES
Appropriations - chairman
  (Defense - chairman)
Commerce, Science & Transportation
Governmental Affairs
Rules & Administration
Joint Library

HOMETOWN
Girdwood

BORN
Nov. 18, 1923, Indianapolis, Ind.

RELIGION
Episcopalian

FAMILY
Wife, Catherine Chandler; six children

EDUCATION
U. of California, Los Angeles, B.A. 1947; Harvard
U., LL.B. 1950

MILITARY SERVICE
Army Air Corps, 1943-46

CAREER
Lawyer

POLITICAL HIGHLIGHTS
U.S. attorney, 1953-56; Republican nominee for
U.S. Senate, 1962; Alaska House, 1965-68 (majority
leader and speaker pro tempore, 1967-68); sought
Republican nomination for U.S. Senate, 1968

ELECTION RESULTS

1996 GENERAL

Ted Stevens (R)	177,893	76.7%
Jed Whittaker (GREEN)	29,037	12.5%
Theresa Obermeyer (D)	23,977	10.3%

1996 PRIMARY (OPEN)

Ted Stevens (R)	71,043	58.9%
Dave W. Cuddy (R)	32,994	27.3%
Theresa Obermeyer (D)	4,072	3.4%
Jed Whittaker (GREEN)	3,751	3.1%

PREVIOUS WINNING PERCENTAGES
1990 (66%); 1984 (71%); 1978 (76%); 1972 (77%);
1970 Special Election (60%)

Elected 1970; 5th full term
Appointed December 1968

Tough, tenacious and unashamedly old school, the 77-year-old Stevens has been blazing his own trail since he was first elected to the Senate three decades ago. He is among the last of the powerful committee barons who typically get their way and don't mind whose feathers they've ruffled.

Soon after Stevens took over the chairmanship of the Appropriations Committee in 1997, he warned colleagues that he was "a mean, miserable SOB." Since then, he has ruled the appropriations process in customary curmudgeonly fashion. Often when working through a difficult jam, he'll don a necktie bearing the likenesses of legendary cartoon tough guys like the Incredible Hulk and the Tasmanian Devil.

But Stevens' bark can be worse than his bite. His frequent explosions are usually short-lived, and offense is rarely taken. Longtime Stevens watchers say they often have seen him throw a fit and then exit the room with a wink. "I believe in using my emotions, not losing my emotions," he says.

He is just as likely to fight with fellow Republicans as he is with Democrats. Since Republicans took control of the Senate and especially after he took the gavel at Appropriations, Stevens has been butting heads with GOP conservatives over budget strategy. He has lost some battles, but in the end appropriators often have gotten their way. And Stevens' beloved Alaska always fares well.

For all his bluster, Stevens remains a throwback to the clubby pragmatism that once permeated the Senate and its spending committee. He works closely with the ranking Democrat on Appropriations, Robert C. Byrd of West Virginia, and other Democrats, a practice necessary to drive the 13 annual appropriations bills through a political and legislative battleground. With Senate membership split evenly between the parties in the 107th Congress, Stevens was among the very few GOP chairmen to support Minority Leader Tom Daschle's push to put an equal number of Democrats and Republicans on Senate committees.

Much to the irritation of the younger GOP conservatives, Stevens has never been one to march in lock step with his party. He has long displayed a moderate streak on a number of issues, from taxes and the budget to abortion and funding for the arts.

In 1999, Stevens voted for the GOP's massive $792 billion tax cut, but he never hid his opposition to the across-the-board spending cuts favored by Majority Leader Trent Lott and other party leaders. And throughout the 106th Congress, Stevens told anyone who would listen that the GOP budget targets would have to be abandoned. "I will live within the number in the budget resolution until the time comes when I can't — and then I'll ask for it to be raised," he said early in 2001, according to Reuters.

At the start of the 107th Congress, Lott turned down Stevens' request for a seat on the Budget Committee, which the Alaskan sought so he could work to change the annual spending guidelines set by that panel.

Stevens' attention to Alaska's parochial needs is legendary. His efforts have been felt in virtually every corner of the state. Most spending bills have something for Alaska: $400 million to subsidize logging in southeastern Alaska, then $132 million in economic aid when the mills closed; $400 million for rural village water and sewer improvements; $265 million for hospital construction; $120 million to help build two ferries.

Stevens is not shy about holding up spending bills to get what he wants, even when it means keeping his colleagues from adjourning for the year. In

2000, he stalled a catchall spending measure at the session's end over a Clinton administration plan to protect Steller sea lions, an endangered species, by limiting fishing of pollock and cod off Alaska's shores.

The Commerce Department said that the new restrictions were necessary to protect the food supply of the sea lion, but Stevens said the plan would cost the state at least $191 million. He insisted that the final spending bill halt the new rules. In the end, he won a partial victory, including $30 million in economic aid to affected fishermen. It is likely he will revisit the matter in 2001.

In 1998, the issue was construction of a road across a wilderness area — a plan bitterly opposed by environmentalists — to provide safe medical transportation for the 700-resident town of King Cove. White House Chief of Staff Erskine Bowles offered Stevens several options: a different road, a new ferry, airport improvements or an upgrade of the town clinic. Without missing a beat, Stevens demanded — and won — the entire $38 million package, at a cost to taxpayers of more than $50,000 per resident.

Under President Bush, Stevens hopes to have more success in rewriting environmental laws to spur timber harvesting in the Tongass National Forest, to open the Arctic National Wildlife Refuge to oil drilling and to make it easier to build roads on federal lands. Such initiatives were blocked by the firm opposition of the Clinton White House.

Stevens once dreamed of becoming majority leader. In 1984, after eight years as Republican whip, he ran a strong race for the top Senate leadership post, losing to Bob Dole of Kansas by only three votes.

With his typical concern for the Senate as an institution, Stevens in early 1999 joined a bipartisan group of six senators in working for an agreement on how to conduct the Senate's impeachment trial of President Clinton in a way that avoided the partisan battles that marked the House proceedings and outraged much of the public. Later, as the trial proceeded, he urged the House "managers" who presented the case against Clinton to avoid a lengthy trial and not to bring witnesses to the Senate floor.

Stevens was one of 10 Republicans to vote against the article of impeachment that accused the president of committing perjury in an attempt to conceal his relationship with former White House intern Monica Lewinsky. (He did, however, vote to convict the president on obstruction of justice charges.)

After flying C-46 transports throughout China during World War II and earning the Distinguished Flying Cross, Stevens earned a law degree and became a federal prosecutor for three years in the mid-1950s. He began his pursuit of a Senate seat not long after Alaska became a state in 1959. He got the party's nomination for the job in 1962 but managed just 41 percent against Democrat Ernest J. Gruening that fall.

Stevens, who went on to serve in the Alaska House, including a stint as majority leader, tried for the Senate nomination again in 1968 but was defeated in the primary. Later that year, however, Democratic Sen. E.L. Bartlett died, and Stevens was appointed to fill the vacancy by GOP Gov. Walter J. Hickel. In the 1970 contest to serve the final two years of Bartlett's term, Stevens bested liberal Democrat Wendell P. Kay, taking 60 percent of the vote. In the campaign, Stevens argued for greater oil and mineral development; Kay was a firm conservationist.

Stevens has cruised to re-election ever since, including in 1978, when he suffered injuries in the plane crash that took the life of his first wife. Since then, only in 1990 has his winning margin dipped below 70 percent; that year, he took 66 percent of the vote.

In 2000, the state legislature named the Anchorage International Airport after him.

KEY VOTES

2000

Yes Overhaul bankruptcy law and increase minimum wage
Yes Limit fiscal 2001 discretionary spending to $600.3 billion
Yes Override veto on nuclear waste disposal at Yucca Mountain site in Nevada
No   Oppose effort to terminate Kosovo mission
Yes Include gender, sexual orientation and disability in federal hate crime protections
Yes Approve GOP plan to restrict use of genetic information by health insurers
Yes Kill amendment delaying implementation of an anti-missile defense system
Yes Cut taxes for married couples
Yes Grant China permanent normal trade status

1999

Yes Remove President Clinton from office for obstruction of justice
Yes Kill amendment authorizing state grants to hire teachers and reduce class size
No   Require criminal background checks for purchases at gun shows
Yes Approve GOP proposal to increase rights of patients in managed-care health plans
Yes Block effort to allow farm and medicine exports to Cuba
No   Allow study of tougher automobile fuel efficiency standards
No   Ratify nuclear weapons testing treaty
No   Prohibit national political parties from collecting "soft money" donations
Yes Remove barriers among banking, securities and insurance companies

INTEREST GROUPS

	AFL-CIO	ADA	CCUS	ACU
2000	0%	5%	100%	92%
1999	33%	10%	88%	84%
1998	25%	20%	94%	56%
1997	14%	30%	80%	58%
1996	29%	20%	85%	80%
1995	8%	5%	94%	73%
1994	43%	25%	67%	77%
1993	55%	25%	91%	80%
1992	33%	20%	80%	74%
1991	42%	10%	60%	76%

CQ VOTE STUDIES

	PARTY UNITY		PRESIDENTIAL SUPPORT	
	Support	Oppose	Support	Oppose
2000	92%	8%	56%	44%
1999	90%	10%	36%	64%
1998	82%	18%	54%	46%
1997	79%	21%	71%	29%
1996	90%	10%	45%	55%
1995	89%	11%	32%	68%
1994	73%	27%	52%	48%
1993	82%	18%	33%	67%
1992	81%	19%	80%	20%
1991	80%	20%	86%	14%

Sen. Frank H. Murkowski (R)

Elected 1980; 4th term

CAPITOL OFFICE
224-6665; fax 224-5301; 322 Hart Bldg. 20510

INTERNET
e-mail: murkowski.senate.gov/webmail.html
web: murkowski.senate.gov

COMMITTEES
Energy & Natural Resources - chairman
Finance
   (Long-Term Growth & Debt Reduction -
   chairman)
Indian Affairs
Veterans' Affairs
Joint Taxation

HOMETOWN
Fairbanks

BORN
March 28, 1933, Seattle, Wash.

RELIGION
Roman Catholic

FAMILY
Wife, Nancy Gore; six children

EDUCATION
U. of Santa Clara, attended 1951-53; Seattle U.,
B.A. 1955

MILITARY SERVICE
Coast Guard, 1955-56

CAREER
Banker

POLITICAL HIGHLIGHTS
Alaska commissioner of economic development,
1966-70; Republican nominee for U.S. House, 1970

ELECTION RESULTS

1998 GENERAL

Frank H. Murkowski (R)	165,227	74.5%
Joseph A. Sonneman (D)	43,743	19.7%
Jeffrey Gottlieb (GREEN)	7,126	3.2%
Scott A. Kohlhaas (LIBERT)	5,046	2.3%

1998 PRIMARY (OPEN)

Frank H. Murkowski (R)	76,649	71.8%
Joseph A. Sonneman (D)	10,721	10.0%
Frank Vondersaar (D)	6,342	5.9%
William L. "Bill" Hale (R)	6,313	5.9%
Jeffrey Gottlieb (GREEN)	4,796	4.5%

PREVIOUS WINNING PERCENTAGES
1992 (53%); 1986 (54%); 1980 (54%)

As popular in Alaska as he is powerful in Washington, Murkowski is known as a stubborn conservative who wages fierce and aggressive battles to defend Alaskan interests. A former banker and a self-made millionaire, he stands with Republicans on budget and tax issues and sides with industry in many energy and natural resources policy disputes. His overarching concern through it all is for his home state.

Like his Alaskan colleagues — Sen. Ted Stevens and Rep. Don Young, both Republicans — Murkowski does not apologize for taking a strong stand. "Every time we give, we lose," he said. Friendly and low-key as he ambles through the hallways of Congress, Murkowski's demeanor can turn gruff when he is arguing to protect his state. It is often through sheer persistence, force of will and experience cutting deals that Murkowski, not known for his attention to legislative detail, prevails.

"Alaska has the most powerful delegation any state has ever enjoyed," Murkowski boasted in a message to constituents in the state's 1998 election pamphlet. "Now is the time to pledge to make 'no little plans' to take advantage of our current clout to fulfill Alaska's biggest needs."

That attitude seems to play well in Alaska, but in Washington it can make for tough sledding. As chairman of the Energy and Natural Resources Committee, Murkowski faces a daunting and often highly charged slate of issues, including energy policy and fuel prices, the disposal of nuclear waste, global warming and electricity deregulation.

Murkowski's views on most matters are in line with that of the GOP: He voted with the party 98 percent of the time in the 106th Congress, and as chairman of the Finance Subcommittee on Long-Term Growth and Debt Reduction, he has been a key architect of Republican budget and tax policies.

Still, his scrupulous devotion to issues of concern to Alaska has at times put him at loggerheads with other Republicans and — on rare occasions — with members of his own delegation. Little comes easily for him, in part because he often is unwilling to change positions. After a particularly brutal fight over a parks bill, Murkowski acknowledged, "It's been kind of a torture chamber around here. I've never given birth, but now I have some idea of how painful the process can be."

That same determination was much in evidence during the 106th, when Murkowski undertook a months-long effort to push a controversial land conservation bill known as the Conservation and Reinvestment Act (CARA) through the Senate. Seeing the huge amount Alaska stood to gain from the measure — an estimated $164 million annually for 15 years — Murkowski worked behind the scenes to reach a bipartisan deal with the Energy Committee's ranking Democrat, Jeff Bingaman of New Mexico.

In doing so, he withstood opposition from two GOP factions in which he normally claims membership: Western senators concerned about private property rights and budget writers defending their prerogatives. A Murkowski aide said the senator was even ready to oppose one of his own long-held goals — opening Alaska's Arctic National Wildlife Refuge to oil and gas drilling — when told a senator opposing CARA would seek to attach to the bill a ban on drilling in the refuge, as a "poison pill." The amendment was not offered.

On at least one occasion, Murkowski's efforts to advance Alaska's interests ran afoul of fellow Alaskan Stevens, chairman of the powerful Appropriations Committee. The two feuded in 1999 over an amendment to allow commercial fishing to continue in Alaska's Glacier Bay National Park, which Murkowski attempted to attach to the Interior appropriations bill. Stevens vowed to oppose the provision as part of an effort to keep spending bills free of policy initiatives, but Murkowski refused to back down. "This issue isn't dead by any means, and I'm going to bring it up every chance I get," he told NBC News' Alaska affiliate. House conferees eventually rejected Murkowski's proposal.

Murkowski, who received a score of 0 in the 106th Congress from the environmental watchdog League of Conservation Voters, is willing to pursue benefits for Alaska at the expense of environmental interests. The state is unique in that local policies — such as increasing logging in a national park, drilling for oil on public land, or setting fishing quotas — quickly achieve national prominence because decisions about managing Alaska's enormous resources are often a model for national standards. "It's always tough because everything in Alaska seems to confront public conflict because we're a public lands state," Murkowski has said.

He also expresses it another way: "Everything in Alaska becomes a cause for the environmental groups to raise money and create membership because it is so far away that people can't see it for themselves," he told The New York Times in September 1998.

Murkowski is no stranger to the cause of cash. The Energy Committee chairman received more than a quarter of a million dollars from electric utilities and about $170,000 from the oil and gas industry between 1995 and 2000, according to the campaign finance watchdog Center for Responsive Politics. He received $29,000 from energy and natural resources political action committees and $18,000 from the nuclear power industry in the 1999-2000 election cycle alone, even though he was not up for re-election.

In the 105th, he helped negotiate a two-year moratorium preventing a federal takeover of fisheries in order to give the Alaska Legislature more time to address the issue. He also boosted Alaska's share of federal highway funding by $1.9 billion over the next six years and was able to include language in the year-end catchall spending bill to increase logging in the Tongass National Forest, a provision that infuriated environmentalists.

Murkowski seemed to relish his fights with President Clinton. He challenged the administration on energy issues by using White House nominees as pawns, delaying for months the confirmation of Federico F. Peña as secretary of energy in response to Clinton's reluctance to open a temporary nuclear waste storage site at Yucca Mountain in Nevada. He also opposed outright the nomination of Sylvia Baca as the Interior Department's assistant secretary for land and minerals management as a "protest vote against the Clinton administration's opposition to oil development nationwide."

Murkowski is a Seattle native who moved to Alaska while in high school. He got his first taste of electoral politics in 1970, when he defeated a member of the John Birch Society in the Republican primary for Alaska's at-large House seat. He lost in the general election to Democratic state Sen. Nick Begich, but the experience made him eager to try again. In 1980, after nine years as a bank president, he announced for the Senate.

His opponent in the general election was Democrat Clark S. Gruening, a popular two-term state legislator and grandson of the legendary Ernest Gruening, a former Alaska senator and governor.

Gruening was an early favorite, but Democratic disunity and the Reagan tide helped Murkowski. He also tied Gruening to the Sierra Club, anathema to Alaska's pro-development voters, who receive an annual check from the state's energy royalties. Murkowski won easily with 54 percent.

His attention to home state issues has helped dissuade big-name Democrats who otherwise might have run against him. He won comfortably in 1986 and 1992 and cemented his hold on the seat in 1998, winning 75 percent of the vote against Democrat Joseph A. Sonneman.

KEY VOTES

2000

Yes Overhaul bankruptcy law and increase minimum wage

Yes Limit fiscal 2001 discretionary spending to $600.3 billion

Yes Override veto on nuclear waste disposal at Yucca Mountain site in Nevada

No Oppose effort to terminate Kosovo mission

No Include gender, sexual orientation and disability in federal hate crime protections

Yes Approve GOP plan to restrict use of genetic information by health insurers

Yes Kill amendment delaying implementation of an anti-missile defense system

Yes Cut taxes for married couples

Yes Grant China permanent normal trade status

1999

Yes Remove President Clinton from office for obstruction of justice

Yes Kill amendment authorizing state grants to hire teachers and reduce class size

No Require criminal background checks for purchases at gun shows

Yes Approve GOP proposal to increase rights of patients in managed-care health plans

Yes Block effort to allow farm and medicine exports to Cuba

No Allow study of tougher automobile fuel efficiency standards

No Ratify nuclear weapons testing treaty

No Prohibit national political parties from collecting "soft money" donations

Yes Remove barriers among banking, securities and insurance companies

INTEREST GROUPS

	AFL-CIO	ADA	CCUS	ACU
2000	0%	0%	100%	100%
1999	11%	5%	88%	92%
1998	13%	5%	100%	78%
1997	0%	10%	100%	68%
1996	29%	15%	92%	95%
1995	0%	0%	100%	91%
1994	0%	10%	90%	96%
1993	20%	20%	100%	86%
1992	30%	25%	100%	70%
1991	42%	5%	60%	86%

CQ VOTE STUDIES

	PARTY UNITY		PRESIDENTIAL SUPPORT	
	Support	Oppose	Support	Oppose
2000	99%	1%	45%	55%
1999	98%	2%	29%	71%
1998	93%	7%	42%	58%
1997	93%	7%	61%	39%
1996	96%	4%	36%	64%
1995	96%	4%	28%	72%
1994	92%	8%	34%	66%
1993	92%	8%	25%	75%
1992	88%	12%	73%	27%
1991	90%	10%	89%	11%

Rep. Don Young (R)

CAPITOL OFFICE
225-5765; fax 225-0425; 2111 Rayburn Bldg. 20515

INTERNET
e-mail: www.house.gov/writerep
web: www.house.gov/donyoung

COMMITTEES
Resources
Transportation & Infrastructure - chairman

HOMETOWN
Fort Yukon

BORN
June 9, 1933, Meridian, Calif.

RELIGION
Episcopalian

FAMILY
Wife, Lula Fredson; two children

EDUCATION
Yuba Junior College, A.A. 1952; California State U.,
Chico, B.A. 1958

MILITARY SERVICE
Army, 1955-57

CAREER
Elementary school teacher; riverboat captain

POLITICAL HIGHLIGHTS
Fort Yukon City Council, 1960-64; mayor of Fort
Yukon, 1964-68; Alaska House, 1967-70; Alaska
Senate, 1971-73; Republican nominee for U.S.
House, 1972

ELECTION RESULTS

2000 GENERAL

Don Young (R)	190,862	69.6%
Clifford Mark Greene (D)	45,372	16.5%
Anna C. Young (GREEN)	22,440	8.2%
Jim Dore (AKI)	10,085	3.7%

2000 PRIMARY

Don Young (R)	unopposed

1998 GENERAL

Don Young (R)	139,676	62.6%
James W. "Jim" Duncan (D)	77,232	34.6%
John J.G. Grames (GREEN)	5,923	2.7%

PREVIOUS WINNING PERCENTAGES
1996 (59%); 1994 (57%); 1992 (47%); 1990 (52%);
1988 (63%); 1986 (57%); 1984 (55%); 1982 (71%);
1980 (74%); 1978 (55%); 1976 (71%); 1974 (54%);
1973 Special Election (51%)

Elected March 1973; 14th full term

Known for his short temper and sharp rhetoric, Young has been a formidable force in shaping natural resources policy and protecting Alaskan interests as the state's only member of the House, working his way up in the chamber's hierarchy even as he offends his critics.

Before taking the helm of the powerful Transportation and Infrastructure Committee in the 107th Congress, Young headed the Resources panel, where the avid sportsman and property rights advocate was never shy about using his perch to promote the economic interests of his state. He has been an advocate of increased logging in national forests — including Alaska's Tongass, the nation's largest — supportive of building roads through wilderness areas and an enthusiastic proponent of efforts to open part of Alaska's Arctic National Wildlife Refuge to oil development.

Like many Western Republicans, Young is an eager ally of energy, mining and timber interests. His zeal for loosening the government's grip on federal lands puts him squarely at odds with environmentalists, who deride him as a blatant exploiter of the nation's most precious resources. Young, in turn, has likened environmentalists to communists. He also clashes frequently with congressional Democrats, federal agencies and moderate Republicans, particularly those from the East.

Far from denying his bombastic reputation, Young seeks to use it to elevate himself. With 57 overdrafts at the unofficial bank for House members and a well-financed, former mayor of Valdez, John E. Devens, as his opponent, Young faced a particularly tough race for re-election in 1992. But he turned his problems to his advantage: He conceded in advertisements that voters found him "abrasive" and "arrogant" and apologized for his style. He also promised to continue fighting for Alaskan interests.

Young is not worried about his opponents. "I have told my enemies as well as my friends, I'm going to outlive you and outlast you," the former riverboat captain told The New York Times in 1998. "I will win these wars. Maybe you won't realize what I am doing, but slowly [and] surely I will win."

Young is aggressively partisan, even though he is a product of Alaska's free-for-all, weak-party politics. As a member of the GOP Steering Committee, the panel that makes Republican committee assignments, he has been known to grill applicants on party loyalty before supporting them for a seat. He votes the party line and supports such conservative causes as a proposed constitutional ban against desecration of the U.S. flag.

While Young has the tact of a raging bull, he has, at times, been able to temper his natural aggression to accomplish a goal. He surprised both his environmentalist enemies and his property rights friends in 1999 when he joined forces with his nemesis, top-ranking Resources panel Democrat George Miller of California, to promote a mammoth environmental bill that would have guaranteed $45 billion in conservation spending over 15 years. "I'm interested in keeping fish and game available, and Miller really wanted full funding for [conservation]," Young told Gannett News Service in March 2000. "So we got together and ... now we've got a broad bill that has something for everyone in every state."

The legislation, known as the Conservation and Reinvestment Act, would have guaranteed about $3 billion annually from oil and gas drilling revenues to pay for land restoration and conservation programs. The bill would have benefited Alaska particularly, steering some $164 million a year to the state. Young became livid when appropriators' budget negotiations with the Clinton administration in 2000 produced a smaller conservation measure subject to yearly appropriations. Young felt he had been rolled and took to the House floor in a rage. He said that congressional appropriators were trying to dictate policy to lawmakers on the House and Senate environmental panels and to the states: "We have to go back to the appropriators and grovel, hold out our hand and beg. ... The natives are getting restless, buddy," he growled.

Young also generated sparks in the Resources Committee during his tenure as chairman from 1995 to 2001, often garnering more publicity for his partisan investigations than for legislative accomplishments. In 1998, as the committee was reviewing the Endangered Species Act, Young outraged environmental groups by writing letters to the Forest Service and the Justice Department demanding a list of agency officials who were members of, or who contributed money to, environmental organizations. He launched investigations during the 106th Congress into political activity by Interior Department officials and later went after the independent watchdog Project on Government Oversight for payments to Interior and Energy department officials for serving as advisers on oil royalty lawsuits.

Young, who came to the House in 1973, is an individualist who regularly demands that Washington stay out of his state's way. But throughout his House career, Young's colleagues have done anything but respect his wishes. After the 1990 enactment of a bill that curbed logging in the Tongass, Young warned: "I may be only one, but they had better not come back at me again. They had better leave my people alone and leave my state alone." While his prominence in Washington has put him in a position to be considered for Cabinet posts — most recently in the Bush administration — he said in 2000 he puts Alaska's interests above his own: "I can do more for the state as chairman," he told The Associated Press.

Born in California, Young moved to Alaska to teach, then became a licensed riverboat captain and a member of the Dog Mushers Association. The only election he has ever lost was his first, in 1972. His opponent, freshman Democratic Rep. Nick Begich, disappeared without a trace along with House Majority Leader Hale Boggs, D-La., during an October airplane flight from Anchorage to Juneau. Begich still beat Young by almost 12,000 votes.

When Begich's seat was declared vacant, Young edged out Emil Notti, the former state Democratic chairman, in a 1973 special election. In 1974, Young weathered a vigorous challenge from state Sen. William L. Hensley; he then enjoyed more comfortable re-elections until two consecutive challenges from Devens in 1990 and 1992 almost toppled him. Against his last four Democratic challengers, Young's winning tally has increased steadily.

KEY VOTES

2000

Yes Raise hourly minimum wage by $1 over two years

Yes Halt funding for U.S. mission in Kosovo unless European nations pay more

Yes Provide Medicare benefits to military retirees and their dependents

No Grant China permanent normal trade status

Yes Phase out estate, gift and trust taxes

Yes Prohibit implementation of president's national monument designations

Yes Approve GOP plan to provide prescription drug coverage for Medicare beneficiaries

No Increase help for poor nations indebted to international financial institutions

1999

Yes Impose steel import quotas

No Kill proposal to take aviation trust funds off budget

No Require background checks on buyers only at gun shows with 10 or more vendors

Yes Remove barriers among banking, securities and insurance companies

No Authorize state grants to hire teachers and reduce class size

No Overhaul campaign finance law; ban "soft money" and restrict advocacy advertising

No Approve bipartisan plan to increase rights of patients in managed-care health plans

INTEREST GROUPS

	AFL-CIO	ADA	CCUS	ACU
2000	22%	10%	78%	73%
1999	33%	10%	88%	86%
1998	44%	20%	78%	84%
1997	38%	5%	80%	86%

CQ VOTE STUDIES

	PARTY UNITY		PRESIDENTIAL SUPPORT	
	Support	Oppose	Support	Oppose
2000	86%	14%	21%	79%
1999	91%	9%	16%	84%
1998	89%	11%	28%	72%
1997	93%	7%	25%	75%

ALASKA

At large

Alaska's remoteness belies its dependence on Washington, D.C. The state's strategic proximity to Russia and the Far East makes it a military stronghold; the federal government is Alaska's largest employer. The state's other economic advantages – oil, minerals and timber – lie mostly on federally owned land. To exploit its natural resources, Alaskan leaders must first lock horns with Congress.

A never-ending battle for control over the local economy has made Alaskan voters hostile to Washington and led them to vote overwhelmingly Republican in national elections. The state hasn't elected a Democrat to Congress since 1974.

Alaska has tried to build a privatized economy by promoting tourism, now a booming industry, but most Alaskans say oil exploration is the best way to independence. The state was able to eliminate its sales and income taxes when it struck black gold near Prudhoe Bay in the '70s.

Internally, the Alaskan vote is less monolithic but still majority Republican. Voters in a few city districts, the panhandle and the sparsely populated tundra vote more Democratic. Third parties proliferate in this frozen frontier state, and the majority of Alaska voters register as either independent or nonpartisan.

MAJOR INDUSTRY
Oil, military, fishing, timber, mining, tourism

MILITARY BASES
Elmendorf Air Force Base, 6,526 military, 2,067 civilian; Fort Wainwright (Army), 4,024 military, 1,307 civilian; Fort Richardson (Army), 1,977 military, 1,321 civilian; Eielson Air Force Base, 3,326 military, 1,251 civilian; Fort Greely (Army), 71 military, 207 civilian; Kodiak Coast Guard Integrated Support Command, 163 military, 88 civilian; Clear Air Force Station, 113 military, 50 civilian (2000); Kulis Air National Guard Base, 183 military, 230 civilian (1997)

CITIES
Anchorage, 257,808; Fairbanks, 32,769; Juneau, 30,192

UNUSUAL FEATURES
Mt. McKinley, highest point in North America at 20,320 feet.

ARIZONA

Gov. Jane Dee Hull (R)

First elected:
Succeeded Fife Symington, R, on Sept. 5, 1997; elected 1998
Length of term: 4 years
Term expires: 1/03
Salary: $75,000
Phone: (602) 542-4331
Hometown: Phoenix
Born: Aug. 8, 1935, Kansas City, Mo.
Religion: Roman Catholic
Family: Husband, Terrace W. Hull; four children
Education: U. of Kansas, B.S. 1957
Career: Public official; teacher
Political highlights: Ariz. House, 1979-93 (speaker, 1989-92); Ariz. secretary of state, 1995-97

Election results:
1998 GENERAL

Jane Dee Hull (R)	620,188	60.9%
Paul Johnson (D)	361,552	35.5%
Katherine Gallant (LIBERT)	27,150	2.7%

Sec. of State Betsey Bayless (R)

(no lieutenant governor)
First elected: Succeeded Jane Dee Hull, R, on Sept. 11, 1997; elected 1998
Length of term: 4 years
Term expires: 1/03
Salary: $70,000
Phone: (602) 542-4285

STATE LEGISLATURE

Bicameral Legislature: Meets January-April, 107 calendar day limit
House: 60 members, 2-year terms
2001 breakdown: 36R, 24D; 38 men, 22 women
Salary: $24,000
Phone: (602) 542-4221
Senate: 30 members, 2-year terms
2001 breakdown: 15R, 15D; 22 men, 8 women
Salary: $24,000
Phone: (602) 542-3559

STATE TERM LIMITS

Governor: 2 consecutive terms
Senate: 4 consecutive terms
House: 4 consecutive terms

URBAN STATISTICS

CITY	POPULATION
Phoenix	1,211,466
Tucson	466,591
Mesa	368,811
Glendale	201,456
Scottsdale	199,943

REGISTERED VOTERS

Republican	41%
Democrat	38%
Other	21%

POPULATION

2000 population	5,130,632
1990 population	3,665,228
Percent change	+40%
Rank among states	20
Median age	34
Born in state	34%
Foreign born	8%
Urban/rural	88%/12%
Crime rate	624/100,000
Poverty level	16.6%
Federal workers	44,070
Military	32,672

REAPPORTIONMENT

Arizona gained two House seats in reapportionment, increasing from six districts to eight. An independent commission will draw new district lines in 2001.

MISCELLANEOUS

Web: www.state.az.us
Capital: Phoenix
Land area: 113,642 sq. miles
  Rank among states: 6
STATE ELECTION OFFICIAL
(602) 542-8683
DEMOCRATIC HEADQUARTERS
(602) 298-4200
REPUBLICAN HEADQUARTERS
(602) 957-7770

District Statistics

DIST.	D	2000 R	GREEN	D	1996 R	REF	D	1992 R	I	WHT	BLK	ASIAN	HISP	HOUSEHOLD INCOME	OVER 65+	UNDER 18	COLLEGE EDUCATION
1	44%	51%	3%	46%	47%	7%	34%	40%	26%	87%	3%	2%	13%	$31,288	9%	25%	28%
2	62	34	3	64	28	7	51	29	20	60	7	1	50	$20,258	10	32	9
3	40	56	3	41	48	10	32	41	27	88	2	1	12	$27,627	20	25	16
4	44	52	3	44	48	7	31	43	26	92	2	2	8	$33,681	11	24	26
5	46	49	4	47	44	8	42	38	20	88	3	2	16	$27,047	15	24	25
6	42	54	2	47	44	8	38.2	38.3	24	70	1	1	13	$25,710	13	30	16
STATE	45	51	3	44	47	8	37	38	24	81	3	2	19	$27,540	13	27	20

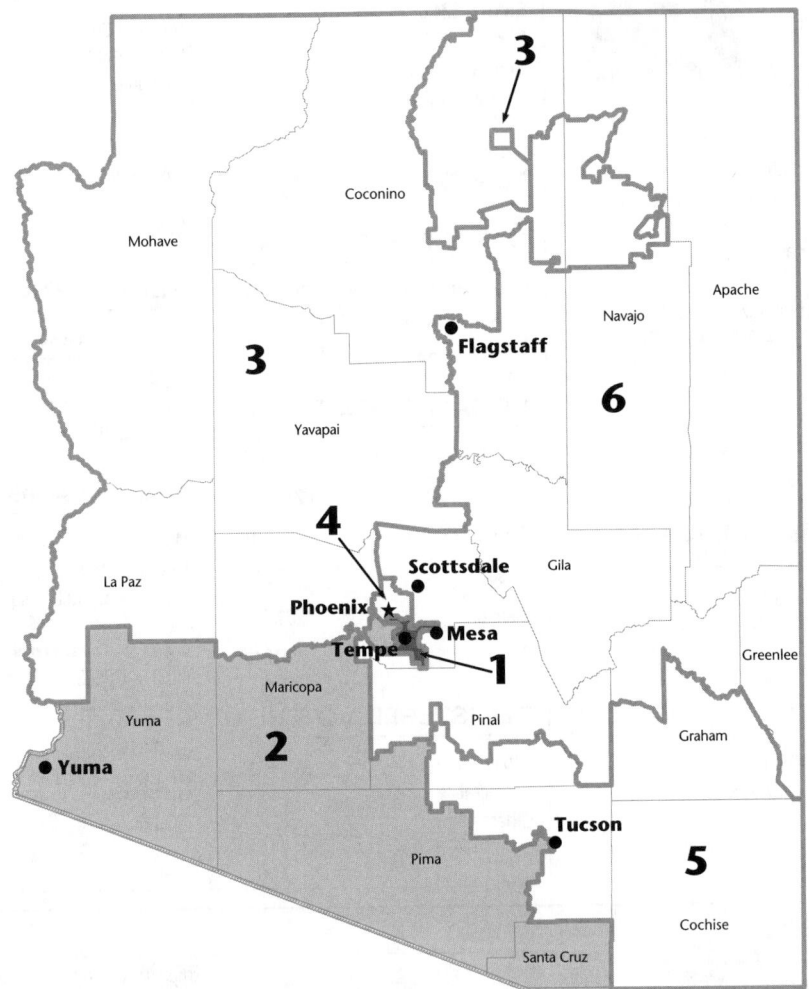

Sen. John McCain (R)

Elected 1986; 3rd term

CAPITOL OFFICE
224-2235; fax 228-2862; 241 Russell Bldg. 20510

INTERNET
e-mail: john_mccain@mccain.senate.gov
web: mccain.senate.gov

COMMITTEES
Armed Services
Commerce, Science & Transportation - chairman
Indian Affairs

HOMETOWN
Phoenix

BORN
Aug. 29, 1936, Panama Canal Zone, Panama

RELIGION
Episcopalian

FAMILY
Wife, Cindy McCain; seven children

EDUCATION
U.S. Naval Academy, B.S. 1958; National War
College, attended 1973-74

MILITARY SERVICE
Navy, 1958-81

CAREER
Navy officer; Senate Navy liaison; beer distributor

POLITICAL HIGHLIGHTS
U.S. House, 1983-87; sought Republican
nomination for president, 2000

ELECTION RESULTS

1998 GENERAL

John McCain (R)	696,577	68.7%
Ed Ranger (D)	275,224	27.2%
John C. Zajac (LIBERT)	23,004	2.3%
Robert "Bob" Park (REF)	18,288	1.8%

1998 PRIMARY

John McCain (R)	unopposed

PREVIOUS WINNING PERCENTAGES
1992 (56%); 1986 (61%); 1984 House Election (78%);
1982 House Election (66%)

Having finished his star political turns of 2000, first as an insurgent presidential candidate and then as a top-draw stump speaker for Republican congressional candidates, McCain faces the challenge of trying to convert his new trove of political capital into a congressional legacy.

At the start of the 107th Congress, McCain continued to champion the cause of comprehensive changes in the campaign finance system, winning early Senate action on the legislation he and Democrat Russell D. Feingold of Wisconsin had been doggedly pushing for years. The measure had been stymied by GOP filibusters.

McCain retained the Commerce, Science and Transportation Committee gavel he has held since 1997, and he can be counted on to use the panel's broad jurisdiction to take a leading role in the congressional oversight of U.S. industry. He has spent his almost two decades in Congress promoting a "reform agenda" — measures aimed not only at taking money out of politics but also at eliminating wasteful federal spending and protecting consumers. Even if his legislative endeavors continue to fall short of the mark, the chairmanship gives him a bully pulpit from which to promote ideas and prod big companies — from automobile makers to Hollywood studios — into, in his view, acting responsibly and dealing fairly with consumers.

McCain's cultivated independent streak has made him broadly popular with voters from both parties. But his brusque style has made him a sometimes despised figure in the Senate, including among fellow Republicans. Even the senators who endorsed his presidential candidacy (four in all) describe him as "in your face." In a chamber where tradition still reigns and members of the club are expected to treat one another with deference, McCain comes off as too eager to use sharp elbows, too quick to discard customary courtesies and not quick enough to hold his legendary temper in check.

Such a reputation might have moved GOP leaders to keep others out of the legislative limelight. But McCain's torrid run on his 2000 GOP presidential campaign bus, the "Straight Talk Express," appears to have ensured that that will not be McCain's fate — at least not anytime soon.

Starting with his upset victory in the New Hampshire primary, he eventually won 5 million Republican primary votes and collected GOP delegates in seven states before being overtaken by George W. Bush. After that, his anti-establishment appeal kept him in demand as a GOP troubleshooter, crossing the country to raise the profiles of candidates. McCain brushed aside talk of the vice presidency or a possible Cabinet post and vowed to turn his popularity with the voters into legislative muscle. "There's no doubt I have more influence," he said. "The question is do I use it appropriately."

During the 106th Congress, he could claim a notable success: enactment in 2000 of a modest change in campaign finance law to close a loophole and require certain political groups, known as 527s for a section of the tax code, to disclose their political activities and who is financing them. Also in the 106th, McCain's long campaign for a more parochial cause paid off with enactment of a law allowing non-stop flights from Washington's Ronald Reagan National Airport to Arizona. And in 1995, he brokered a deal on new Senate rules restricting gifts and meals paid for by lobbyists.

But McCain's ambitious bill to create a comprehensive federal tobacco policy, including a $1.10 per pack increase in cigarette prices over five years, died of its own weight in 1998. And that same year, the Supreme Court struck down a presidential line-item veto law that McCain had championed.

McCain cites the influence of corporate political donations as a force that has undercut his efforts to pass bills. He says he seeks to reduce the sway of money over politics in order to give the practice of politics a better reputation. Some critics see another motive: A desire to repair any damage his own reputation suffered from the "Keating Five" affair. McCain was one of five senators accused of interceding with federal regulators on behalf of wealthy savings and loan operator Charles H. Keating Jr. A protracted Ethics Committee investigation ended with McCain receiving a mild rebuke in 1991.

Despite his maverick image, McCain has been a loyal Republican when voting on the Senate floor. From the GOP takeover of the Senate in 1995 through the 2000 session, McCain's party-unity score — the percentage of times he sided with the GOP in votes that pitted the two parties against each other — is 87.7 percent. The average for all Senate Republicans during the same period is 88.3 percent. Along the way, he has hewed to conservative views on fiscal and social policy issues. He is a defense hawk, opposes abortion rights and has opposed every major gun control measure. His conservationist stance is modeled on that of his hero, Theodore Roosevelt, who was known for his early advocacy of careful stewardship of public lands.

On Commerce, McCain often works closely with ranking Democrat Ernest F. Hollings of South Carolina. They joined forces in the 106th to press entertainment companies to stop marketing graphic violence to children. But the two also have collided on occasion. In 1999, McCain — over Hollings' objection — helped win passage of a bill that limited companies' liability for problems related to the year 2000 computer glitch.

He remains a staunch advocate of cutting government regulation to allow for free competition in business. In 1996, he cast the lone Republican vote against the telecommunications overhaul, arguing that it did not go far enough. He opposes regulation and taxation of Internet commerce. In the 106th, however, his efforts to extend a moratorium on Internet-specific taxes, which expires in October 2001, were stymied when governors sought broader authority to collect sales taxes.

On the Armed Services Committee, he has pushed to increase the salaries of those in uniform. He defends the president's prerogative to guide military policy, but argues against deploying troops unless vital national interests are at stake. "We cannot have 535 commanders in chief," McCain said in the 103rd Congress, when lawmakers were pressing to end the U.S. mission in Somalia. In 1995, McCain backed President Clinton's decision to resume full diplomatic relations with Vietnam.

A key part of McCain's political appeal lies in his personal story. The scion of the first father-and-son admirals in U.S. Navy history, McCain earned his reputation as a rebel by finishing fifth from the bottom in the Class of 1958 at Annapolis. But his countervailing reputation as a hero was cemented nine years later, when his plane was shot down in Vietnam and he spent five and a half years as a prisoner of war, enduring torture and solitary confinement.

McCain's initial opening to Congress came with the 1982 retirement of John J. Rhodes, who had been House minority leader. McCain won the nomination by convincing voters that his post-Vietnam job as the Navy's liaison to the Senate gave him a knowledge of "how Washington works." He won his first term with 66 percent and a second with 78 percent of the vote.

After two terms in the House, McCain easily won his Senate seat in 1986 upon Barry Goldwater's retirement and has not been seriously challenged for re-election. He has long been regarded as a potential candidate for national office. He was considered a possible running mate for George Bush in 1988 and for Bob Dole in 1996, and he relentlessly stumped the country for Dole and GOP House and Senate candidates.

KEY VOTES

2000

? Overhaul bankruptcy law and increase minimum wage
No Limit fiscal 2001 discretionary spending to $600.3 billion
Yes Override veto on nuclear waste disposal at Yucca Mountain site in Nevada
Yes Oppose effort to terminate Kosovo mission
No Include gender, sexual orientation and disability in federal hate crime protections
Yes Approve GOP plan to restrict use of genetic information by health insurers
Yes Kill amendment delaying implementation of an anti-missile defense system
Yes Cut taxes for married couples
Yes Grant China permanent normal trade status

1999

Yes Remove President Clinton from office for obstruction of justice
Yes Kill amendment authorizing state grants to hire teachers and reduce class size
No Require criminal background checks for purchases at gun shows
Yes Approve GOP proposal to increase rights of patients in managed-care health plans
Yes Block effort to allow farm and medicine exports to Cuba
? Allow study of tougher automobile fuel efficiency standards
No Ratify nuclear weapons testing treaty
Yes Prohibit national political parties from collecting "soft money" donations
? Remove barriers among banking, securities and insurance companies

INTEREST GROUPS

	AFL-CIO	ADA	CCUS	ACU
2000	14%	5%	75%	81%
1999	0%	5%	75%	77%
1998	29%	20%	76%	68%
1997	14%	5%	100%	80%
1996	0%	0%	100%	95%
1995	8%	0%	100%	91%
1994	0%	10%	80%	96%
1993	18%	15%	82%	83%
1992	33%	20%	90%	85%
1991	17%	5%	70%	86%

CQ VOTE STUDIES

	PARTY UNITY		PRESIDENTIAL SUPPORT	
	Support	Oppose	Support	Oppose
2000	83%	17%	38%	62%
1999	90%	10%	38%	62%
1998	84%	16%	49%	51%
1997	84%	16%	70%	30%
1996	95%	5%	32%	68%
1995	90%	10%	36%	64%
1994	91%	9%	44%	56%
1993	91%	9%	28%	72%
1992	87%	13%	75%	25%
1991	89%	11%	86%	14%

Sen. Jon Kyl (R)

CAPITOL OFFICE
224-4521; fax 224-2207; 730 Hart Bldg. 20510

INTERNET
e-mail: info@kyl.senate.gov
web: kyl.senate.gov

COMMITTEES
Energy & Natural Resources
Finance
  (Social Security & Family Policy - chairman)
Judiciary
  (Technology, Terrorism & Government
  Information - chairman)
Select Intelligence

HOMETOWN
Phoenix

BORN
April 25, 1942, Oakland, Neb.

RELIGION
Presbyterian

FAMILY
Wife, Caryll Collins; two children

EDUCATION
U. of Arizona, B.A. 1964, LL.B. 1966

CAREER
Lawyer

POLITICAL HIGHLIGHTS
U.S. House, 1987-95

ELECTION RESULTS

2000 GENERAL

Jon Kyl (R)	1,108,196	79.3%
William Toel (I)	109,230	7.8%
Vance Hansen (GREEN)	108,926	7.8%
Barry Hess (LIBERT)	70,724	5.1%

2000 PRIMARY

Jon Kyl (R)	unopposed

PREVIOUS WINNING PERCENTAGES
1994 (54%); 1992 House Election (59%); 1990 House Election (61%); 1988 House Election (87%); 1986 House Election (65%)

Elected 1994; 2nd term

A leading Republican hard-liner on defense, Kyl has amassed one of the most conservative voting records in Congress and works behind the scenes with like-minded colleagues to push an agenda aimed at reducing the role of the federal government.

The son of a former House member, Kyl (pronounced KILE) has an appreciation of institutional process, which gives him the patience to spend several years pursuing passage of his proposals and leads him to join with Democrats occasionally to offer legislation. For instance, he has collaborated with liberal Democrats Dianne Feinstein of California and Charles Schumer of New York on issues such as crime victims' rights, Internet privacy protection and counter-terrorism.

Kyl, who has a reputation as a studious, approachable workhorse, kept a fairly low profile during his first six years in the Senate. In the opening weeks of the Bush presidency, however, the senator took on a more public role as the point man in the battle for confirmation of former Sen. John Ashcroft as attorney general. The two men had forged a close friendship after both came to the Senate in 1995 and joined the Judiciary Committee.

Almost as soon as President Bush tapped Ashcroft for the Justice Department post, Ashcroft asked Kyl to serve as his spokesman to counter the anticipated barrage of criticism from liberal interest groups; Kyl took on the task with enthusiasm. During the Judiciary Committee's confirmation hearings, he methodically rebutted attacks by Massachusetts Democrat Edward M. Kennedy that Kyl said "had the effect of distorting Sen. Ashcroft's record."

In the 106th Congress, Kyl was the first senator to take to the floor to defend Independent Counsel Kenneth W. Starr after Starr released a report calling for the impeachment of President Clinton and detailing Clinton's relationship with a White House intern. Kyl also was a frequent guest on news shows during the Senate impeachment proceedings, arguing the case for removing Clinton from office. His willingness to take on the president so aggressively gave Kyl significant credibility with the conservative House lawmakers presenting the case for impeachment in the Senate and allowed him to persuade the House members to scale back the length of the trial and limit the testimony.

Once the impeachment deliberations were over, Kyl retreated from the spotlight, spending much of his time in the 106th Congress on a range of complex issues, often in a bipartisan role. In 2000, he and Feinstein cosponsored legislation to bolster intelligence gathering against terrorist groups and to block their fundraising efforts. Kyl and Feinstein also worked together in an effort to gain approval of a constitutional amendment granting specific rights to crime victims.

National security is the one policy sphere in which Kyl consistently has taken a leading role. During his four terms in the House, where he was a member of the Armed Services Committee, he was the main advocate of a national missile defense system — a cause he continues to champion in the Senate. As a general proposition, Kyl contends, the United States should rely on its own military means to guarantee its national security rather than on diplomatic agreements such as the 1972 treaty banning nationwide anti-missile defenses.

Kyl favors unilateral steps over negotiated agreements to neutralize emerging military threats; he laid much of the groundwork for the strong

Republican opposition that delayed ratification of the Chemical Weapons Convention for a time in 1997. He contended that the treaty could not be verified, was subject to cheating and would lead to industrial espionage against U.S. private sector chemical plants.

In 1999, aided by the tactical blunders of the Clinton administration and key Democratic senators, Kyl and other conservatives were able to force a vote in which a majority of senators opposed a treaty that would ban nuclear test explosions.

As chairman of the Judiciary Subcommittee on Technology, Terrorism and Government Information, Kyl argued in the 105th Congress that the growing reliance on computers and other information technology could become the most important national security issue facing the country. He cosponsored a measure, which became law in 1998, to make it easier to catch and prosecute so-called identity thieves who steal personal information, often with help from computers, then use it to rack up large bills charged to the victim. He also helped push to passage a law that cracks down on illegal cell phone "cloning," by which thieves make calls that are charged to the unwitting victim.

Kyl's refusal to go along with what he sees as excessive federal spending sometimes has led him to cast the only "no" vote on an appropriations bill, although, typically, he has gotten much less publicity for these stands than his senior state colleague, GOP Sen. John McCain, has gotten for his jeremiads in the Senate against what he terms "pork barrel" spending. On the other hand, Kyl was able to use his seat on the Appropriations Committee to help his state, including securing funds for border patrol and customs personnel and other drug enforcement initiatives.

But in the 107th, Kyl gave up the Appropriations seat and joined two committees that, he said, would help him better serve Arizona: Finance, which has jurisdiction over Social Security and Medicare, so vital to Arizona's large retired population; and Energy, which enables him to focus on local resources issues. One priority for Kyl is ensuring Arizona's access to electric power supplies in the face of the energy crisis that gripped neighboring California in early 2001. He also wants to shepherd through Congress an agreement that would settle the disputed allocation of water from the Gila River among native Indian tribes, farmers and cities.

Kyl remains on the Judiciary and Intelligence panels in the 107th and has become chairman of the Senate Steering Committee, a caucus of Republican conservatives.

Raised in a political family, Kyl had been active in Republican Party affairs before his first House run in 1986. (Kyl's father, John H. Kyl, represented Iowa for 11 years in the 1960s and '70s.) A business-oriented lawyer and former president of the Phoenix Chamber of Commerce, the younger Kyl was able to win strong support from the business community to defeat primary foe John Conlon, a former House member trying for a comeback. Kyl then easily won the general election in the traditionally Republican 4th District, which had been represented by GOP Rep. Eldon Rudd, who retired.

Kyl won three easy re-elections to the House and launched a Senate bid in 1994 even before incumbent Democrat Dennis DeConcini announced his retirement. He breezed through to the GOP nomination while first-term Rep. Sam Coppersmith struggled through a three-way battle to secure the Democratic nomination.

Voters in Arizona were in a mood to hear the themes Kyl had always stressed — too much government, too much taxation and too much regulation. He prevailed over Coppersmith by a 14-point margin. In 2000, the Democrats did not field a candidate.

KEY VOTES

2000

Yes Overhaul bankruptcy law and increase minimum wage
Yes Limit fiscal 2001 discretionary spending to $600.3 billion
Yes Override veto on nuclear waste disposal at Yucca Mountain site in Nevada
No Oppose effort to terminate Kosovo mission
No Include gender, sexual orientation and disability in federal hate crime protections
Yes Approve GOP plan to restrict use of genetic information by health insurers
Yes Kill amendment delaying implementation of an anti-missile defense system
Yes Cut taxes for married couples
Yes Grant China permanent normal trade status

1999

Yes Remove President Clinton from office for obstruction of justice
Yes Kill amendment authorizing state grants to hire teachers and reduce class size
No Require criminal background checks for purchases at gun shows
Yes Approve GOP proposal to increase rights of patients in managed-care health plans
Yes Block effort to allow farm and medicine exports to Cuba
No Allow study of tougher automobile fuel efficiency standards
No Ratify nuclear weapons testing treaty
No Prohibit national political parties from collecting "soft money" donations
Yes Remove barriers among banking, securities and insurance companies

INTEREST GROUPS

	AFL-CIO	ADA	CCUS	ACU
2000	0%	0%	85%	100%
1999	0%	0%	82%	100%
1998	0%	0%	76%	96%
1997	0%	0%	70%	96%
1996	0%	5%	100%	100%
1995	0%	0%	100%	100%
House Service:				
1994	0%	5%	83%	90%
1993	0%	5%	100%	96%
1992	33%	5%	75%	92%
1991	8%	5%	90%	100%

CQ VOTE STUDIES

	PARTY UNITY		PRESIDENTIAL SUPPORT	
	Support	Oppose	Support	Oppose
2000	99%	1%	41%	59%
1999	97%	3%	34%	66%
1998	96%	4%	33%	67%
1997	99%	1%	57%	43%
1996	98%	2%	23%	77%
1995	98%	2%	21%	79%
House Service:				
1994	96%	4%	44%	56%
1993	97%	3%	31%	69%
1992	96%	4%	90%	10%
1991	95%	5%	81%	19%

www.cq.com

Rep. Jeff Flake (R)

CAPITOL OFFICE
225-2635; fax 226-4386; 512 Cannon Bldg. 20515

INTERNET
e-mail: www.house.gov/writerep
web: www.house.gov/flake

COMMITTEES
International Relations
Judiciary
Resources

HOMETOWN
Mesa

BORN
Dec. 31, 1962, Snowflake, Ariz.

RELIGION
Mormon

FAMILY
Wife, Cheryl Flake; five children

EDUCATION
Brigham Young U., B.A. 1986, M.A. 1987

CAREER
Public policy institute director; African business trade representative; lobbyist

POLITICAL HIGHLIGHTS
No previous office

ELECTION RESULTS

2000 GENERAL

Jeff Flake (R)	123,289	53.6%
David Mendoza (D)	97,455	42.4%
Jon Burroughs (LIBERT)	9,227	4.0%

2000 PRIMARY

Jeff Flake (R)	16,745	31.8%
Sal DiCiccio (R)	12,490	23.7%
Susan Bitter Smith (R)	11,763	22.3%
Tom Liddy (R)	10,898	20.7%
Bert Tollefson (R)	764	1.4%

Elected 2000; 1st term

Flake brings to Congress an allegiance to the political philosophy of Arizona's most venerable conservative, Barry Goldwater, as well as an extensive knowledge of world affairs.

Flake's conservative ideology is leavened by real world experience. From 1992 to 1999, he served as executive director of Arizona's Goldwater Institute, a conservative think tank named for the late senator who was the 1964 Republican presidential nominee. But before that, Flake spent much of his time either in Africa or working on behalf of U.S. trade with the continent.

A Mormon missionary in southern Africa from 1982 to 1983, Flake in 1989 moved to Namibia — then recently separated from South Africa — to develop its constitution as director of the Foundation for Democracy. Before and after his stint in Namibia, Flake worked with public relations firms to help educate U.S. localities about trade opportunities with that nation in particular and Africa in general. In the House, his seat on the International Relations panel fits well with that background.

Along with his backing of free-trade agreements with African nations, Flake's priorities include deregulating the electric utility industry, partially privatizing Social Security, and providing what he calls "substantial and significant tax relief."

He also says that Arizona has been getting short shrift in federal transportation dollars and that his state would be better off if the federal gas tax was reduced to just the amount needed to maintain the interstate highway system.

Flake's main challenge in his 2000 campaign was winning the crowded primary in the dependably Republican 1st District. He grabbed a big edge over his four primary opponents by garnering the coveted support of retiring Republican Rep. Matt Salmon, who was stepping down to honor his pledge to serve no more than six years in Congress. Flake also promised to limit himself to three terms.

After winning the GOP nod by a comfortable plurality, Flake bested Democratic labor lobbyist David Mendoza, who also was the Democrats' nominee against Salmon in 1998.

ARIZONA 1
Southeastern Phoenix — Tempe; Mesa

Rooted in the conservative leanings of an affluent, historically Mormon population, the 1st favors Republican candidates. Today the district has a significant population of Mormons, as well as a mix of younger couples living in new developments outside of Phoenix and an established population of retirees. In 1992, redistricting purged the district of two heavily Democratic, minority and lower-income areas. Now nearly half of the district's voters are registered Republicans — compared to 35 percent Democrats.

Despite the 1st's Republican leanings, it showed an independent streak in 1992, throwing 26 percent of the vote in the presidential contest to Ross Perot and sending a Democrat to Congress. The 1st's meager Democratic population is boosted by a small section of minority-rich south Phoenix and northwest Tempe.

The district has grown rapidly since the 1980s, boosted by the arrival of retirees from the West Coast and young professionals employed in the thriving high-tech sector. Chandler, one of the fastest growing cities in the nation, tripled in size in the 1980s, while Mesa grew by 90 percent. Manufacturing also contributes to the economy in Mesa – home to a sizable number of Fortune 500 manufacturing firms – and Tempe, which also relies heavily on Arizona State University for economic sustenance.

MAJOR INDUSTRY
Computer technology, aerospace

CITIES
Mesa (pt.), 169,237 (1990); Tempe, 167,740; Phoenix (pt.), 152,054 (1990)

UNUSUAL FEATURES
Mesa founded by Mormons in 1878 and site of Arizona's Mormon temple; Chandler's Ostrich Festival; 1.2 million-square-foot Arizona Mills Mall in Tempe.

Rep. Ed Pastor (D)

Elected September 1991; 5th full term

CAPITOL OFFICE
225-4065; fax 225-1655; 2465 Rayburn Bldg. 20515

INTERNET
e-mail: ed.pastor@mail.house.gov
web: www.house.gov/pastor

COMMITTEES
Appropriations
Standards of Official Conduct

HOMETOWN
Phoenix

BORN
June 28, 1943, Claypool, Ariz.

RELIGION
Roman Catholic

FAMILY
Wife, Verma Mendez Pastor; two children

EDUCATION
Arizona State U., B.A. 1966, J.D. 1974

CAREER
Teacher; gubernatorial aide; public policy consultant

POLITICAL HIGHLIGHTS
Maricopa County Board of Supervisors, 1977-91

ELECTION RESULTS

2000 GENERAL

Ed Pastor (D)	84,034	68.5%
Bill Barenholtz (R)	32,990	26.9%
Geoffrey Weber (LIBERT)	3,169	2.6%
Barbara Shelor (NL)	2,412	2.0%

2000 PRIMARY

Ed Pastor (D)	unopposed

1998 GENERAL

Ed Pastor (D)	57,178	67.8%
Edward Clyde Barron (R)	23,628	28.0%
Rick Duncan (LIBERT)	2,646	3.1%
Gregory R. Schultz (REF)	911	1.1%

PREVIOUS WINNING PERCENTAGES
1996 (65%); 1994 (62%); 1992 (66%); 1991 Special Election (56%)

A shrewd appropriator and loyal liberal, Pastor enjoys a prominent spot in the House Democratic leadership, earning appointment in 1999 as one of his party's four chief deputy whips. He understands the chemistry of the legislative process as well as chemistry itself: After growing up in a small mining town east of Phoenix, he got a chemistry degree from Arizona State University and taught that subject in high school for a time.

But before long, Pastor (pas-TORE) was back at ASU pursuing a law degree, and that set him on a path in government. He was an aide to former Democratic Gov. Raul Castro, served 14 years on the Board of Supervisors in Maricopa County, and was the establishment's choice in a special election in 1991 to replace veteran Democratic Rep. Morris K. Udall, who was ailing from Parkinson's disease. Pastor won a hard-fought primary over Tucson Mayor Tom Volgy, then easily defeated Republican Pat Conner, a Yuma County supervisor. Since then, he has easily held the district by at least 30 percentage points.

In Washington, Pastor, who is Hispanic, quickly set about becoming an insider, and he was aided in this quest by the Democratic Party's desire to promote promising minority members. He has a seat on the Appropriations Committee, where he has posts on the Transportation and Energy and Water Development subcommittees — two assignments of interest to his district, which is dominated by urban Hispanic populations in Tucson and Phoenix but also includes the dry and sparsely settled southwest corner of Arizona.

In the 106th Congress, Pastor demonstrated his appropriations acumen by capturing funding for a diverse range of initiatives, including transit facilities, water projects, social services, and a program to soundproof homes near Sky Harbor International Airport.

The lone Democrat in the Arizona delegation in recent years, Pastor tends to side with his party rather than his delegation on national and international issues. In the 106th, he opposed GOP tax-cutting efforts, backed a bipartisan plan to allow patients to sue their health maintenance organizations and opposed efforts to restrict the Clinton administration's deployment of troops in Yugoslavia.

Pastor gets high ratings from the League of Conservation Voters and from the AFL-CIO. In keeping with organized labor's views, he voted in 2000 against granting China permanent normal trade status. He also opposed a measure in the 105th Congress that would have given the president fast-track authority to negotiate trade agreements that Congress must approve or reject without amendment.

He supports abortion rights, and his vote against banning a procedure its opponents call "partial birth" abortion drew a rebuke from the Catholic church. A 1998 editorial in a newspaper published by the Roman Catholic Diocese of Phoenix called upon Pastor to change his position. "If not, he ought to disavow his Catholic faith," the editorial said. "He cannot possibly, in good conscience, reconcile his faith and his stance." Nevertheless, Pastor again voted against the ban in 2000.

An active member of the Congressional Hispanic Caucus, he was elected chairman of the group in November 1994, just as the new GOP leadership announced that it was taking away the budgets, staffs and offices of 28 informal caucuses in the House, including the Hispanic Caucus. Although the group could meet, any staff work would have to be done from members' offices. Pastor defended the caucus after his election as chairman, saying, "It is important to have some means to augment or increase the visibility of those groups in Congress which are in the minority."

During his tenure as chairman, which ended at the beginning of 1997, Pastor and his Hispanic colleagues put up a fight against GOP efforts to clamp down on illegal immigration and to bar government services and benefits from being provided to legal immigrants.

In the 105th, Pastor joined most Democrats — and even some Republicans — to try to soften provisions they found objectionable in the 104th's welfare and immigration bills. Their major target was the restriction on legal immigrants receiving Supplemental Security Income, a program for the elderly, blind and disabled. Conservatives yielded ground, and Congress decided that legal immigrants receiving benefits when the welfare law was signed would continue to be eligible. Lawmakers altered another restrictive immigration provision, giving immigrants more time to apply for permanent visas in the United States without first returning to their own countries.

Pastor objected when Republicans in 1996 brought forward a bill to make English the official language of the U.S. government. Proponents said it would save money, citing as one example the extra expense of printing ballots in multiple languages in some areas. And they said that encouraging all U.S. residents to speak English would be a unifying force in society.

Pastor, unmoved, said that the bill was unconstitutional, and that it would not have the unifying impact Republicans intended. "Language minorities want to learn English and participate in American institutions," he said. "But this legislation will further isolate non-native speakers of English and discourage them from fully integrating themselves into society." The Hispanic Caucus introduced its own measure, "English Plus," which expressed the value of multilingualism to the nation, to counter the Republican initiative. Although the GOP measure passed in the House, it got no further.

Pastor has gone to bat on several occasions for native Americans in his state. When the Arizona Legislature in 1997 voted to cut off state funds for charter schools that also receive federal funds — only schools on Indian reservations would be affected — Pastor inserted a provision in an appropriations bill to stop the practice.

In 1997, he was one of 40 lawmakers who successfully fought a proposal by Ways and Means Committee Chairman Bill Archer, R-Texas, to tax revenue from Indian casinos and other tribal businesses. The lawmakers argued that Archer's proposal would infringe on tribal sovereignty.

KEY VOTES

2000

Yes Raise hourly minimum wage by $1 over two years
No Halt funding for U.S. mission in Kosovo unless European nations pay more
Yes Provide Medicare benefits to military retirees and their dependents
No Grant China permanent normal trade status
No Phase out estate, gift and trust taxes
No Prohibit implementation of president's national monument designations
No Approve GOP plan to provide prescription drug coverage for Medicare beneficiaries
Yes Increase help for poor nations indebted to international financial institutions

1999

Yes Impose steel import quotas
Yes Kill proposal to take aviation trust funds off budget
No Require background checks on buyers only at gun shows with 10 or more vendors
Yes Remove barriers among banking, securities and insurance companies
Yes Authorize state grants to hire teachers and reduce class size
Yes Overhaul campaign finance law; ban "soft money" and restrict advocacy advertising
Yes Approve bipartisan plan to increase rights of patients in managed-care health plans

INTEREST GROUPS

	AFL-CIO	ADA	CCUS	ACU
2000	100%	90%	52%	8%
1999	89%	100%	24%	0%
1998	100%	100%	39%	4%
1997	100%	95%	50%	8%

CQ VOTE STUDIES

	PARTY UNITY		PRESIDENTIAL SUPPORT	
	Support	Oppose	Support	Oppose
2000	90%	10%	81%	19%
1999	91%	9%	83%	17%
1998	91%	9%	82%	18%
1997	87%	13%	80%	20%

ARIZONA 2
Southwest – Southwestern Tucson; southern Phoenix; Yuma

Encompassing three-fourths of Arizona's border with Mexico, the 2nd is home to nearly half the state's Hispanic population. South Phoenix, southwestern Tucson and Santa Cruz County – where as much as three-fourths of the population claims Hispanic origin – are some of the state's most faithfully Democratic strongholds. The Tohono O'odham, Pasqua Yaqui and other American Indian reservations within the 2nd also bolster Democratic support.

Although the district incorporates Yuma County's traditionally conservative agricultural producers and ranchers, that county contains only one-fifth of the total district vote and the 2nd remains Arizona's only Democratic bastion.

The 2nd's economy is supported by a large population of seasonal, immigrant workers, who buttress the agriculture and service industries but boost the district's poverty statistics, the highest in the state. The 2nd includes more blue-collar workers and fewer college graduates than Arizona's other districts, although the electronics and technology industries are growing rapidly in the Tucson area.

MAJOR INDUSTRY
Agriculture, technology, manufacturing

MILITARY BASES
Yuma Proving Grounds, 144 military, 661 civilian; Marine Corps Air Station, 4,087 military, 312 civilian (1999)

CITIES
Phoenix (pt.), 226,721 (1990); Tucson (pt.) 140,910 (1990); Yuma 63,059

UNUSUAL FEATURES
Arizona's largest and the nation's westernmost Civil War battle was fought at Picacho Peak; Yuma's Saihati Farm boasts one of the largest camel herds in North America.

Rep. Bob Stump (R)

Elected 1976; 13th term

Stump became chairman of the Armed Services Committee at the beginning of the 107th Congress, continuing an association with the military that began when World War II was raging. In 1943, when he was 16, Stump enlisted in the Navy and served as a combat medic on Luzon, Iwo Jima and Okinawa.

During his previous 12 terms on the Armed Services panel, Stump had quietly backed the committee's high-dollar, conservative consensus. As he assumed the chairmanship of Armed Services, a priority for Stump remained the personnel issues that were his specialty during six years as head of the Veterans' Affairs panel, from 1995 through 2000. Stump believes that military personnel, by virtue of putting their lives on the line every day, have a special claim on the nation's resources. He has been a strong advocate of traditional veterans' benefits, especially health care.

With a Republican in the White House, the Armed Services Committee under Stump likely will be characterized by more pro-Pentagon bipartisanship than during the Clinton administration, when Republicans frequently sniped at the Democratic president's proposed defense cuts.

Stump's passionate advocacy for military men and women was evident during his work on a high-profile initiative in the 105th Congress. Infuriated by the 1997 disclosure that a former ambassador who never served in the military had been buried in Arlington National Cemetery, Stump pushed for passage of legislation the following year to sharply limit the burial of non-veterans at Arlington. The measure died in the Senate.

While he has fought to target health programs to the needs of veterans of World War II and the Korean War, Stump has opposed efforts to expand veterans' benefits in ways that could eat into funds available for basic coverage. For example, he objected to the government's compensating veterans for diseases or deaths traceable to tobacco use that began during their military service.

Stump's career in public office is now in its fifth decade. After the war, he returned to his native Arizona, graduated from Arizona State University, became a cotton farmer and took his place among the state's "pinto Democrats" — the rural, conservative-minded people who were then a dominant force in state politics. Stump's first political victory came in 1958, when he won a state House seat. He went on to serve a decade in the state Senate, rising to become president of that chamber during the 1975 and 1976 sessions. When GOP Rep. Sam Steiger tried for the U.S. Senate in 1976, Stump ran for his House seat.

Over time, much has changed in Arizona. The state's population has grown fivefold, and Republicans have become the dominant political party. Stump himself switched to the GOP in 1981, a not-too-surprising step, since in his first two House terms he had been one of the chamber's more conservative Democrats. Upon taking the Republican label, he said he was breaking off from liberal Democrats who had "created a massive, distant, centralized federal government which overtaxes, overspends and overregulates." The change did not affect Stump's popularity; he has been consistently re-elected by wide margins.

Stump has rarely sought the spotlight during his years in Washington. He eschews press releases, and his office maintains only a bare-bones page on the World Wide Web ("self-promotion crap," he once called such trappings). But he is recognizable on Capitol Hill for his Western-style suits and

CAPITOL OFFICE
225-4576; fax 225-6328; 211 Cannon Bldg. 20515

INTERNET
e-mail: www.house.gov/writerep
web: www.house.gov/stump

COMMITTEES
Armed Services - chairman
Veterans' Affairs

HOMETOWN
Tolleson

BORN
April 4, 1927, Phoenix, Ariz.

RELIGION
Seventh-Day Adventist

FAMILY
Divorced; three children

EDUCATION
Arizona State U., B.S. 1951

MILITARY SERVICE
Navy, 1943-46

CAREER
Cotton and grain farmer

POLITICAL HIGHLIGHTS
Ariz. House, 1959-67 (served as a Democrat);
Ariz. Senate, 1967-77 (president, 1975-77; served as a Democrat)

ELECTION RESULTS

2000 GENERAL

Bob Stump (R)	198,367	65.7%
Gene Scharer (D)	94,676	31.4%
Edward R. Carlson (LIBERT)	8,927	3.0%

2000 PRIMARY

Bob Stump (R)	60,143	82.9%
Dick Hensley (R)	12,427	17.1%

1998 GENERAL

Bob Stump (R)	137,618	67.3%
Stuart Starky (D)	66,979	32.7%

PREVIOUS WINNING PERCENTAGES
1996 (67%); 1994 (70%); 1992 (62%); 1990 (57%);
1988 (69%); 1986 (100%); 1984 (72%); 1982 (63%);
1980 (64%); 1978 (85%); 1976 (48%)
*Elected as a Democrat 1976-80

cowboy boots, and close followers of Congress know him as an ardent proponent of funding for programs and services that benefit veterans.

During his first term as chairman of the Veterans' panel in the 104th Congress, he was working in a climate of spending austerity forced by deficit-reduction pressures. Still, he managed to win approval of a measure to overhaul the veterans' health care system, arguing that the changes would allow the Department of Veterans Affairs to cut costs and use the savings to treat additional veterans. The bill directed the VA away from its traditional emphasis on hospital care, allowing the department to move more veterans out of hospitals and into less-expensive outpatient clinics. He has also pushed efforts to allow the VA to retain payments collected from insurance companies that compensate for VA care, and to require Medicare to pay the VA for treating Medicare-eligible veterans.

The federal budget picture brightened over the course of the 105th, but Stump has shown skepticism toward some proposals to expand veterans' benefits, concerned that they could pinch resources for existing programs.

In the late 1980s, Stump helped slow an effort led by liberal Democrat Lane Evans of Illinois, a Vietnam veteran, to provide compensation for Vietnam veterans who said their exposure to the herbicide Agent Orange had caused them to develop cancer. Stump argued that studies showed no definitive link between certain cancers and Agent Orange; but Evans persisted, and when a compromise measure was enacted in 1991, Stump was a supporter.

Stump and Evans wrangled again in the 105th, this time over how to handle the so-called Persian Gulf syndrome, a range of medical problems that veterans believe may be connected to their exposure to Iraqi chemical agents. Stump emphasized "the absence of any scientific evidence that illnesses experienced by Persian Gulf veterans are linked to exposure known to have occurred in the gulf," and he successfully fought a proposal to allow compensation specifically for Gulf War-related illnesses. However, he did support a compromise allowing the VA to continue treating veterans with undiagnosed illnesses.

Stump's conservatism and history of military service put him at odds with President Clinton more than once. He signed on as a cosponsor of a resolution calling for Clinton's impeachment in November 1997 — months before allegations of an affair between Clinton and a White House intern touched off formal impeachment proceedings. The resolution charged Clinton with a variety of "abuses of office," including campaign finance wrongdoing, bribery and obstruction of justice.

KEY VOTES

2000

No Raise hourly minimum wage by $1 over two years
No Halt funding for U.S. mission in Kosovo unless European nations pay more
No Provide Medicare benefits to military retirees and their dependents
Yes Grant China permanent normal trade status
Yes Phase out estate, gift and trust taxes
Yes Prohibit implementation of president's national monument designations
Yes Approve GOP plan to provide prescription drug coverage for Medicare beneficiaries
No Increase help for poor nations indebted to international financial institutions

1999

No Impose steel import quotas
Yes Kill proposal to take aviation trust funds off budget
No Require background checks on buyers only at gun shows with 10 or more vendors
Yes Remove barriers among banking, securities and insurance companies
No Authorize state grants to hire teachers and reduce class size
No Overhaul campaign finance law; ban "soft money" and restrict advocacy advertising
No Approve bipartisan plan to increase rights of patients in managed-care health plans

INTEREST GROUPS

	AFL-CIO	ADA	CCUS	ACU
2000	10%	0%	76%	92%
1999	11%	0%	84%	92%
1998	0%	0%	78%	96%
1997	0%	5%	90%	100%

CQ VOTE STUDIES

	PARTY UNITY		PRESIDENTIAL SUPPORT	
	Support	Oppose	Support	Oppose
2000	97%	3%	25%	75%
1999	97%	3%	17%	83%
1998	93%	7%	20%	80%
1997	97%	3%	21%	79%

ARIZONA 3
North and West — Glendale; part of Phoenix; Hopi reservation

Although the 3rd spans the entire northwestern third of Arizona, Republicans concentrated in the fast-growing Phoenix suburbs in the southeast corner dominate the district's politics. Places like Peoria, Glendale and the huge retirement community of Sun City are home to the bulk of the 3rd's voters, who compose solid conservative voting blocs.

Democrats maintain isolated areas of influence among American Indians in the northwest corner of the 3rd and in La Paz County, where younger, lower-income and larger minority populations live. Democrats also win support on the Hopi reservation, an appendage added to northeast corner of the 3rd in 1992 after tensions between the Navajo and Hopi prompted a federal court to separate the tribes. Mapmakers went so far as to include in the 3rd the tiny Hopi village of Moenkopi, which is completely surrounded by Navajo lands that are in the 6th.

The 3rd's economy, once grounded in agriculture, has diversified to include manufacturing jobs in the aerospace, electronics, communications and chemical industries. The district also has one of the state's largest copper mines.

MAJOR INDUSTRY
Manufacturing, mining and tourism

MILITARY BASES
Luke Air Force Base, 6,427 military, 800 civilian (1999)

CITIES
Phoenix (pt.), 99,033 (1990); Peoria 94,170; Glendale (pt.) 85,088 (1990)

UNUSUAL FEATURES
Grand Canyon; Lake Havasu City houses the transplanted London Bridge; America's oldest annual rodeo in Prescott; Quartzsite hosts rocks and mineral shows.

Rep. John Shadegg (R)

Elected 1994; 4th term

CAPITOL OFFICE
225-3361; fax 225-3462; 432 Cannon Bldg. 20515

INTERNET
e-mail: j.shadegg@mail.house.gov
web: www.house.gov/shadegg

COMMITTEES
Energy & Commerce
Financial Services

HOMETOWN
Phoenix

BORN
Oct. 22, 1949, Phoenix, Ariz.

RELIGION
Episcopalian

FAMILY
Wife, Shirley Lueck; two children

EDUCATION
U. of Arizona, B.A. 1972, J.D. 1975

MILITARY SERVICE
Ariz. Air National Guard, 1969-75

CAREER
State prosecutor; lawyer

POLITICAL HIGHLIGHTS
No previous office

ELECTION RESULTS

2000 GENERAL

John Shadegg (R)	140,396	64.0%
Ben Jankowski (D)	71,803	32.7%
Ernest Hancock (LIBERT)	7,298	3.3%

2000 PRIMARY

John Shadegg (R)	unopposed

1998 GENERAL

John Shadegg (R)	102,722	64.7%
Eric Ehst (D)	49,538	31.2%
Ernest Hancock (LIBERT)	3,805	2.4%
Doug Quelland (I)	2,757	1.7%

PREVIOUS WINNING PERCENTAGES
1996 (67%); 1994 (60%)

Shadegg has emerged as one of the most influential Republican deal-cutters on an issue at the center of the congressional agenda: what the federal government should do to regulate managed-care medical insurance plans. It is an unexpected role, given the way his Capitol Hill career began. He arrived as a disciple of Newt Gingrich, not only in his conservative philosophy but in his occasionally confrontational political style.

Shadegg (SHAD-egg) won election with the "revolutionary" Class of 1994 and succeeded Gingrich, then the Republican Speaker, as chairman of GOPAC, the political action committee Gingrich created to help engineer his party's takeover. Shadegg put himself firmly in the conservative camp but was not afraid to buck his party's leadership along the way, saying he would prefer to lose on principles rather than win on politics. That attitude led to his chairmanship in the 106th Congress of the Conservative Action Team, or CATs, the caucus of about 60 Republicans whose zeal for reining in the federal government and lack of interest in compromise can give GOP leaders fits, especially in a House with such a narrow majority. (The group has since been renamed the Republican Study Committee, although they are still known informally as the CATs.)

But Shadegg also has proved helpful to his leaders. In the 106th, for example, when a band of GOP mavericks was threatening to join with Democrats to rebuff GOP leaders' health care agenda, Shadegg helped stave off an embarrassing defeat for his leadership by drafting a plan designed to find a middle ground on managed-care reform. Shadegg's proposal, written with Tom Coburn, R-Okla., soared above two other Republican alternatives and came nearest to toppling the largely Democratic measure the House ultimately passed.

Speaker J. Dennis Hastert designated Shadegg and Bill Thomas, R-Calif., then the chairman of the Ways and Means Health Subcommittee, as his representatives to negotiate with Senate leaders on the managed-care issue, talks that came to naught as 2000 ended.

Still, Shadegg secured a reputation as an eloquent spokesman for the Republican view that, with health care costs rising, any move to increase the legal rights of managed-care patients must not lead to a flood of new lawsuits, which ultimately would boost insurance prices even more. At the start of the 107th Congress, with Coburn having retired, Shadegg was one of the most prominent conservative House voices in the medical insurance debate.

Shadegg's health care proposals have a strong market-oriented bent. He champions a range of initiatives aimed at employing private insurance to shrink the ranks of the uninsured. He advocates medical savings accounts; tax credits to help people buy insurance; full tax deductibility for the self-employed; and the creation of new insurance risk pools for small-business workers and others. By contrast, he has criticized Democratic plans to help the uninsured by expanding public programs such as Medicaid.

An energetic man, Shadegg comes across as a patient, detail-oriented lawyer who appears to relish the legislative process. He was one of the lawmakers who benefited from Gingrich's effort to give freshmen a quick chance to exercise influence in the 104th Congress. In addition to the Budget seat, Shadegg was named an assistant party whip and was appointed to the House Republican Policy Committee.

Since 1999, he has been on the Commerce Committee (renamed Energy and Commerce), a consolation prize when he was denied his request for assignment to Ways and Means. In the 107th Congress, when the GOP gave some of the Energy and Commerce panel's jurisdiction to an expanded Banking Committee (renamed Financial Services), Shadegg was one of four members permitted to sit on both panels.

Shadegg's family name is well-known in Arizona GOP circles. His late father, Stephen, was a longtime political adviser to Barry Goldwater, the five-term Arizona senator and 1964 Republican presidential nominee. The younger Shadegg developed his own political connections, working in the state attorney general's office and then serving as counsel to the House Republican caucus in the Arizona Legislature. The election law expertise he garnered in Phoenix was put to prominent use late in 2000, when he wrote a position paper for the House Republican leadership on the application of election law in the disputed 2000 presidential contest. He was a prominent public spokesman for George W. Bush's position.

A ferocious critic of President Clinton, Shadegg boycotted the 1999 State of the Union address, contending that the embattled president should have postponed his annual speech until his Senate impeachment trial was over.

But Shadegg is an equal-opportunity critic, taking aim at his own leaders when he concludes they have strayed too far from conservative policies. In the 105th Congress, he said the House GOP leadership team under Gingrich "sold us out" by cutting deals on spending bills. He gave GOP leaders heartburn during the high-stakes budget showdown in early 1996, joining just 14 other Republicans in voting "no" on a Gingrich-backed agreement that would have ended a partial government shutdown.

On social policy issues, Shadegg is an unyielding conservative voice. He opposes abortion, disapproves of same-sex marriage, supports taxpayer-funded vouchers for private schools and wants to end funding for the National Endowment for the Arts and the National Endowment for the Humanities.

His adamantly anti-tax stance predates his arrival in Congress. In 1992, he led a successful campaign in Arizona for a referendum amending the state constitution to require a two-thirds majority vote of the legislature to raise taxes. In Congress, he backed an unsuccessful version of a balanced-budget constitutional amendment that would have required three-fifths approval in each chamber to raise taxes. "The power of taxation," Shadegg once told the House, "is the power to put a gun at the heads of the American people and take money from them."

Shadegg took 60 percent of the vote in 1994 to win the House seat vacated when Republican Jon Kyl won election to the Senate. He has won about two-thirds of the vote in each of his three subsequent re-election races.

KEY VOTES

2000

No   Raise hourly minimum wage by $1 over two years
Yes   Halt funding for U.S. mission in Kosovo unless European nations pay more
+   Provide Medicare benefits to military retirees and their dependents
Yes   Grant China permanent normal trade status
Yes   Phase out estate, gift and trust taxes
Yes   Prohibit implementation of president's national monument designations
Yes   Approve GOP plan to provide prescription drug coverage for Medicare beneficiaries
No   Increase help for poor nations indebted to international financial institutions

1999

No   Impose steel import quotas
Yes   Kill proposal to take aviation trust funds off budget
No   Require background checks on buyers only at gun shows with 10 or more vendors
Yes   Remove barriers among banking, securities and insurance companies
No   Authorize state grants to hire teachers and reduce class size
No   Overhaul campaign finance law; ban "soft money" and restrict advocacy advertising
No   Approve bipartisan plan to increase rights of patients in managed-care health plans

INTEREST GROUPS

	AFL-CIO	ADA	CCUS	ACU
2000	0%	5%	80%	96%
1999	0%	0%	79%	96%
1998	0%	0%	89%	100%
1997	0%	5%	80%	100%

CQ VOTE STUDIES

	PARTY UNITY		PRESIDENTIAL SUPPORT	
	Support	Oppose	Support	Oppose
2000	96%	4%	22%	78%
1999	95%	5%	15%	85%
1998	97%	3%	22%	78%
1997	96%	4%	24%	76%

ARIZONA 4
Northern Phoenix; Scottsdale

Encompassing the northern half of Phoenix and its suburbs, the 4th is Arizona's most faithfully conservative district. It is also Arizona's least minority-influenced district – 92 percent of its residents are white.

More than half of the district's voters are registered Republicans who consistently support economically and socially conservative candidates at both the local and federal levels. The district supported GOP candidates in presidential contests in the 1990s and 2000.

Democrats have a base of support in the southern part of the 4th, where the district stretches into downtown Phoenix. There, relatively lower-income communities with larger Hispanic and blue-collar populations elect Democrats to state office.

Another portion of Phoenix that lies in the 4th includes wealthy conservatives and retirees. Posh resorts and large homes – where some of the state's most affluent, politically active and conservative

residents live – characterize the eastern communities of Scottsdale and Paradise Valley.

The 4th is one of four Arizona districts centered on Phoenix – the hub of the state's economic activity. More than 4,000 manufacturing companies are in the Phoenix area. To the northwest, Glendale is home to manufacturing, technology and military employers.

MAJOR INDUSTRY
Technology, manufacturing, electronics

CITIES
Phoenix (pt.) 501,883 (1990); Glendale (pt.), 48,362 (1990); Scottsdale (pt.) 48,022 (1990)

UNUSUAL FEATURES
Paradise Valley was home to 1964 GOP presidential nominee Barry Goldwater and is the home to Arizona's current Sens. John McCain and Jon Kyl.

Rep. Jim Kolbe (R)

Elected 1984; 9th term

After almost two decades in the House, Kolbe has developed a reputation as a cool-headed broker who works well with lawmakers of both parties and will occasionally resort to humor to smooth the way for political agreement. At one committee meeting in 2000, he produced a chihuahua doll singing "La Bamba" to ease tension.

In the 107th Congress, as part of a substantial reshuffling of the leadership of the Appropriations Committee, Kolbe moved to the helm of the Foreign Operations Appropriations Subcommittee, giving up the gavel at the Treasury, Postal Service and General Government Subcommittee.

As chairman of the Treasury-Postal spending panel in the 105th and 106th Congresses, Kolbe tried to work out bipartisan compromises, sometimes successfully, sometimes not. In 1997 and 1999, Congress cleared his panel's appropriations bill in time for the new fiscal year. However, in 1998, the measure was stalled by disputes over policy additions, known as "riders," and had to be rolled into an end-of-session package. And in 2000, Kolbe's bill was dragged down by amendments dealing with the trade embargo against Cuba and by disagreements with the administration on funding levels.

Kolbe is generally a reliable Republican vote, standing firmly with the majority of his party on such economic issues as cutting taxes and free trade. But he is a moderate on social issues, supporting abortion rights and legislation to ban hate crimes based on sexual orientation. He supports gun owners' rights but also endorses some gun control measures such as child safety locks. He supported President Clinton 39 percent of the time in the 106th Congress — one of the higher scores among House Republicans.

After the GOP won control of the House in 1994, Kolbe sought the chairmanship of the Republican Policy Committee. He lost by a 2-to-1 margin to Christopher Cox of California, a defeat attributed both to a late-starting campaign and to his moderate views. For example, he opposed legislation to ban a procedure its opponents call "partial birth" abortion, saying the measure did not include an exception allowing the procedure when a woman's life is at risk.

In August 1996, Kolbe's personal life became an issue when he acknowledged his homosexuality after criticism from gay rights activists unhappy with his vote for legislation opposing same-sex marriage. He made his declaration after learning that a magazine was about to break the news. "The fact that I am this way has never, nor will it ever, change my commitment to represent all the people of Arizona's 5th District," Kolbe said at the time. "I am the same person." He said he supported the measure on same-sex marriage because it allowed states to define marriage.

Kolbe's status as the only openly gay Republican in Congress has had little impact on his political career. It briefly became an issue at the 2000 Republican National Convention, when members of the Texas delegation doffed cowboy hats and bowed their heads in prayer to protest Kolbe's selection to deliver a high-profile speech on free trade. Afterward, he told The New York Times that both parties had to do more to open themselves to minorities. "We're not all the way there with our party," Kolbe said.

Kolbe has not endeared himself to Democrats, either. In the 106th Congress, he criticized the use of government travel funds by first lady Hillary Rodham Clinton and insisted that the White House file reports with appropriators on the cost of Air Force flights used to transport the first lady to events for her New York Senate campaign. And in 1997, Kolbe threatened

CAPITOL OFFICE
225-2542; fax 225-0378; 2266 Rayburn Bldg. 20515

INTERNET
e-mail: www.house.gov/writerep
web: www.house.gov/kolbe

COMMITTEES
Appropriations
(Foreign Operations & Export Financing - chairman)

HOMETOWN
Tucson

BORN
June 28, 1942, Evanston, Ill.

RELIGION
Methodist

FAMILY
Divorced

EDUCATION
Northwestern U., B.A. 1965; Stanford U., M.B.A. 1967

MILITARY SERVICE
Navy, 1967-69

CAREER
Real estate consultant

POLITICAL HIGHLIGHTS
Ariz. Senate, 1977-83; Republican nominee for U.S. House, 1982

ELECTION RESULTS

2000 GENERAL
Jim Kolbe (R)	172,986	60.2%
George Cunningham (D)	101,564	35.3%
Michael Jay Green (GR)	9,010	3.1%
Aage Nost (LIBERT)	4,049	1.4%

2000 PRIMARY
Jim Kolbe (R)	35,263	80.1%
Joseph "Joe" Sweeney (R)	9,477	19.9%

1998 GENERAL
Jim Kolbe (R)	103,952	51.6%
Tom Volgy (D)	91,030	45.2%
Phillip W. Murphy (LIBERT)	4,946	2.5%

PREVIOUS WINNING PERCENTAGES
1996 (69%); 1994 (68%); 1992 (67%); 1990 (65%); 1988 (68%); 1986 (65%); 1984 (51%)

to cut the White House's administrative budget unless the administration provided details about overnight guests at the White House.

Kolbe is likely to play a key role in efforts to overhaul Social Security in the 107th. During the 105th, he teamed with Rep. Charles W. Stenholm, D-Texas, and Sens. Judd Gregg, R-N.H., and John B. Breaux, D-La., in chairing a private commission aimed at developing a proposal for shoring up Social Security. The group's report recommended allowing individuals to invest 2 percent of their payroll taxes that now go to Social Security in government-picked investment funds and raising the retirement age to 70 over time. The report was the basis for legislation he introduced in the 106th.

Kolbe favors strong border control policies and has proposed dividing the Immigration and Naturalization Service into two agencies, one focusing on combating illegal immigration and the other on providing services to legal immigrants. In the 106th, he won enactment of his bill to create the Las Cienegas National Conservation Area in southern Arizona, which also allowed for grazing and recreation in the area.

On trade policy, Kolbe was a leading vote-hunter for legislation to grant China permanent normal trade status in 2000. He played the same role in 1993 on the North American Free Trade Agreement. Kolbe also worked unsuccessfully for legislation that would have given Clinton fast-track authority to negotiate trade agreements not subject to revision by Congress.

A former real estate consultant with an MBA from Stanford University, Kolbe first came to Washington as a page to Sen. Barry Goldwater, R-Ariz. He later served two years as a Navy lieutenant on patrol boats in Vietnam. After six years in the Arizona Senate, he won his first House victory in 1984, avenging a loss he had suffered two years earlier at the hands of Democrat James F. McNulty Jr. During his 1984 campaign, Kolbe rode a horse in commercials and reminded voters that he had spent much of his youth on a cattle ranch near the town of Sonoita — while McNulty was born and bred in Boston.

In January 1988, Kolbe was the first Republican in Arizona's congressional delegation to call on embattled GOP Gov. Evan Mecham to resign. Mecham ultimately was removed from office by the GOP-controlled legislature, but his conservative backers vowed revenge against Kolbe. Nonetheless, Kolbe easily won both the primary and general election.

Kolbe's declaration of his homosexuality has not diminished his political standing in the solidly Republican 5th. In 1996, he won re-election with 69 percent of the vote. In 1998, he narrowly held off an aggressive challenge by former Tucson Mayor Tom Volgy; and in 2000, he easily defeated Democratic state Sen. George Cunningham.

KEY VOTES

2000
No   Raise hourly minimum wage by $1 over two years
No   Halt funding for U.S. mission in Kosovo unless European nations pay more
Yes Provide Medicare benefits to military retirees and their dependents
Yes Grant China permanent normal trade status
Yes Phase out estate, gift and trust taxes
Yes Prohibit implementation of president's national monument designations
Yes Approve GOP plan to provide prescription drug coverage for Medicare beneficiaries
No   Increase help for poor nations indebted to international financial institutions

1999
No   Impose steel import quotas
Yes Kill proposal to take aviation trust funds off budget
Yes Require background checks on buyers only at gun shows with 10 or more vendors
Yes Remove barriers among banking, securities and insurance companies
No   Authorize state grants to hire teachers and reduce class size
No   Overhaul campaign finance law; ban "soft money" and restrict advocacy advertising
No   Approve bipartisan plan to increase rights of patients in managed-care health plans

INTEREST GROUPS

	AFL-CIO	ADA	CCUS	ACU
2000	0%	20%	80%	68%
1999	0%	20%	91%	70%
1998	10%	15%	89%	72%
1997	0%	25%	100%	64%

CQ VOTE STUDIES

	PARTY UNITY		PRESIDENTIAL SUPPORT	
	Support	Oppose	Support	Oppose
2000	85%	15%	39%	61%
1999	80%	20%	40%	60%
1998	81%	19%	40%	60%
1997	81%	19%	52%	48%

ARIZONA 5
Southeast – Tucson

Located in the state's southeast corner bordering New Mexico and Mexico, the 5th contains a mix of swing voters and independents who often favor moderates in national elections. Nearly 80 percent of the district's registered voters reside in Pima County, and most of those live in the Tucson metropolitan area.

While Democrats have historically framed the Tucson political scene, which is environmentally focused, Republicans have made significant inroads to the city. Tucson's surrounding communities – dominated by affluent, retired and military populations to the city's northwest and southeast – favor Republicans. Democrats have the majority outside of the metropolitan area, in Graham and Cochise counties.

Tucson hosts a large number of high-tech manufacturing companies, including several large defense contractors and aerospace firms. Tourism, particularly in Tucson, also contributes to the 5th's economic base.

MAJOR INDUSTRY
Manufacturing, aerospace, agriculture

MILITARY BASES
Davis-Monthan Air Force Base, 6,097 military, 1,219 civilian; Fort Huachuca, 4,176 military, 1,984 civilian (1999)

CITIES
Tucson (pt.), 264,480 (1990); Sierra Vista, 38,468; Oro Valley, 22,849; Douglas, 15,717

UNUSUAL FEATURES
The Old West county of Cochise is the home of Tombstone – "the town too tough to die" – notorious for its boomtown lawlessness in the late 1800s.

Rep. J.D. Hayworth (R)

CAPITOL OFFICE
225-2190; fax 225-3263; 2434 Rayburn Bldg. 20515

INTERNET
e-mail: jdhayworth@mail.house.gov
web: www.house.gov/hayworth

COMMITTEES
Veterans' Affairs
(Benefits - chairman)
Ways & Means

HOMETOWN
Scottsdale

BORN
July 12, 1958, High Point, N.C.

RELIGION
Baptist

FAMILY
Wife, Mary Hayworth; three children

EDUCATION
North Carolina State U., B.A. 1980

CAREER
Sports broadcaster; public relations consultant;
insurance agent

POLITICAL HIGHLIGHTS
No previous office

ELECTION RESULTS

2000 GENERAL

J.D. Hayworth (R)	186,687	61.4%
Larry Nelson (D)	108,317	35.6%
Rick Duncan (LIBERT)	9,000	3.0%

2000 PRIMARY

J.D. Hayworth (R)	unopposed

1998 GENERAL

J.D. Hayworth (R)	106,891	53.0%
Steve Owens (D)	88,001	43.7%
Robert Anderson (LIBERT)	6,645	3.3%

PREVIOUS WINNING PERCENTAGES
1996 (48%); 1994 (55%)

Elected 1994; 4th term

A big man with a booming voice and outsize personality, Hayworth is unswervingly devoted to the conservative Republican agenda. His biting criticism of liberal views has irritated more than a few House Democrats and made him a top target in a series of competitive elections, which he has won through energetic campaigning and fundraising prowess.

The former college football player and sports broadcaster can often be heard on the floor of the House extolling the virtues of the latest Republican policy initiative. Thanks to both his membership on the Ways and Means Committee and his smooth script-reading voice, Hayworth in 1999 landed the choice assignment of outlining the GOP's ambitious $1 trillion tax cut in a Fourth of July radio address. In typical barbed fashion, he took aim at the estate tax — the controversial federal levy on a deceased person's assets — by declaring, "There should be no taxation without respiration."

In 2000, he once again was tapped to deliver a GOP radio address, this time focusing on the Republican plan to eliminate the "marriage penalty," a quirk in the tax code that results in some two-earner married couples paying higher taxes than they would if each partner were single.

And in the 107th Congress, Hayworth was named chairman of the Veterans' Affairs Committee's Benefits Subcommittee.

A North Carolina native who attended North Carolina State University on a football scholarship, Hayworth held sports broadcasting jobs in Cincinnati and Greenville, S.C., before landing in Phoenix. He moved into political commentary, an outgrowth of his longstanding interest in government. A political history buff (he is an aficionado of the presidency of Dwight D. Eisenhower), he can readily recount anecdotes from Arizona's colorful past.

His 1997 appointment to Ways and Means provoked some grumbling by his Arizona GOP colleagues John Shadegg and Matt Salmon. Many had assumed that if an Arizonan got on Ways and Means, it would be Shadegg, who seemed more savvy than Hayworth. Salmon called Hayworth "Foghorn Leghorn," the bumbling blowhard rooster of cartoon fame, though he later said he meant nothing by the description.

While some House Republicans can become jittery about their party's strongly conservative image, Hayworth has rewarded GOP leaders by staying the course. "I've done everything I said I would do," Hayworth said. "I have not deviated from that one iota."

Hayworth wants to give the legislative branch of government more control over the federal bureaucracy. He sponsors a bill every Congress to require both congressional and presidential approval of all future regulations issued by government agencies. "In practice ... Congress routinely delegates its lawmaking duties to politically unaccountable bureaucrats who craft regulations with the full force of law," Hayworth wrote his colleagues.

He regularly participates in the "one-minute speeches" that often come at the start of a House session, and his rhetoric usually is designed to provoke his Democratic listeners. During appropriations battles in 1996, veteran Wisconsin Democratic Rep. David R. Obey set his sights on Hayworth. "To the gentleman from Arizona, every time somebody says something you don't like, you open your mouth and you start shouting from your seat," Obey said. "You are one of the most impolite members I have ever seen in my service in this House."

Hayworth seems to take such criticism in stride. He says he was prepared for people to have lower expectations of him when he entered politics because of his reputation as a "somewhat irreverent, gregarious" TV personality. Washingtonian magazine, in its annual anonymous survey of Capitol Hill staffers, reported in 2000 that Hayworth had been singled out as one of the House's "biggest windbags."

Hayworth also drew fire in Arizona when he sent out a fundraising letter in July 1998 that called President Clinton an "unprincipled, philandering president" and claimed that Clinton had presided over "the most corrupt administration in U.S. history." Local Democrats accused Hayworth of lowering himself to mean-spirited name-calling. They also claimed that Hayworth had abused his congressional privilege to send mail at public expense, noting that in 1997 he spent more than $128,000 on constituent mailings, the most among lawmakers in the Arizona delegation.

Attentive to his district's economy, Hayworth tries to promote the interests of the mining industry (copper mining is a big business in the 6th District). He favors ending a moratorium on low-cost sales of federal lands to miners prospecting for hard-rock minerals. Hayworth and many other Westerners stress the benefits of encouraging mining. "The nation as a whole prospers when the mining industry and those working in it can earn a decent, living wage," he has said. He also sponsored a bill to allow transfers of Forest Service land to school districts for construction or other uses for a minimal cost — an important benefit for small school districts.

Hayworth's district is more than 20 percent American Indian, and he has responded by backing tribal issues. In 1999, he sponsored a bill to override laws in California that would require tribes to recognize labor unions in their casinos. "Essentially [the state] is trying to blackmail the tribes of California into coerced unionism," he said.

Although Hayworth's 1994 House bid was his first political campaign, he was already a familiar figure to voters thanks to his seven years doing reporting and commentary on Phoenix's CBS affiliate. A jovial presence on TV and a prominent participant in area charitable events off the air, he entered the campaign with a reservoir of good will. Hayworth defeated freshman Democratic Rep. Karan English by 14 points. But, in a district that narrowly voted for George Bush in 1992 and then backed Bill Clinton by 3 points in 1996, Democrats placed Hayworth high on their target list in both 1996 and 1998.

Hayworth eked out a 1 percentage point win over former state Democratic Party Chairman Steve Owens in 1996 and broadened his advantage to about 9 points in 1998. In 2000, he expanded his tally again, capturing more than 60 percent of the vote.

KEY VOTES

2000
No Raise hourly minimum wage by $1 over two years

Yes Halt funding for U.S. mission in Kosovo unless European nations pay more

Yes Provide Medicare benefits to military retirees and their dependents

No Grant China permanent normal trade status

Yes Phase out estate, gift and trust taxes

Yes Prohibit implementation of president's national monument designations

Yes Approve GOP plan to provide prescription drug coverage for Medicare beneficiaries

No Increase help for poor nations indebted to international financial institutions

1999
No Impose steel import quotas

Yes Kill proposal to take aviation trust funds off budget

No Require background checks on buyers only at gun shows with 10 or more vendors

Yes Remove barriers among banking, securities and insurance companies

No Authorize state grants to hire teachers and reduce class size

No Overhaul campaign finance law; ban "soft money" and restrict advocacy advertising

No Approve bipartisan plan to increase rights of patients in managed-care health plans

INTEREST GROUPS

	AFL-CIO	ADA	CCUS	ACU
2000	11%	5%	84%	100%
1999	11%	10%	80%	100%
1998	0%	0%	89%	100%
1997	0%	5%	90%	96%

CQ VOTE STUDIES

	PARTY UNITY		PRESIDENTIAL SUPPORT	
	Support	Oppose	Support	Oppose
2000	96%	4%	20%	80%
1999	96%	4%	15%	85%
1998	94%	6%	23%	77%
1997	97%	3%	29%	71%

ARIZONA 6
Northeast — Flagstaff; Navajo reservation

The 6th rivals the western 3rd in size, with American Indian reservations occupying much of its territory. However, only a small portion of the district's population comes from this expansive area. The great majority of the people and the political weight are located in the growing metropolitan areas in the southwestern section of the district.

From the Navajo reservation, which occupies all of the northeastern corner of the state except for the Hopi reservation, the district runs southward through the San Carlos and Fort Apache reservations, then takes in Greenlee County and parts of Graham and Pinal counties. The eastern border of the 6th is the Arizona-New Mexico line; the western side of the district includes the cities of Gilbert and part of Mesa, in the Phoenix suburbs, as well as the Gila reservation south of Phoenix and the Salt River north of the city.

The 6th is home to the state's most racially, geographically and economically diverse populations, as well as its most competitive politics. A classic swing district, the 6th's voter registration is split, with

43 percent of the voters in each of the two dominant parties. More than half of the 6th's voters live in white, affluent and rapidly growing population centers surrounding Phoenix in Maricopa County. Members of these communities — in Gilbert, Scottsdale and Mesa — vote overwhelmingly Republican.

The 6th's rural voters tend to vote Democratic, although some voters in the agricultural, logging and ranching industries have conservative viewpoints. Environmental activism has significantly shrunk the 6th's logging industry, but high-tech growth in the Phoenix area and copper mining and agriculture throughout the 6th continue to bolster the economy.

MAJOR INDUSTRY
Agriculture, mining, technology

CITIES
Gilbert, 97,590; Flagstaff (pt.) 45,745 (1990); Scottsdale (pt.), 29,686 (1990); Mesa (pt.) 28,244 (1990)

UNUSUAL FEATURES
Lowell Observatory in Flagstaff, where Clyde Tombaugh discovered Pluto in 1930.

Gov. Mike Huckabee (R)

First elected: Succeeded Jim Guy Tucker on July 15, 1996; elected 1998
Length of term: 4 years
Term expires: 1/03
Salary: $69,920
Phone: (501) 682-2345
Hometown: Little Rock
Born: Aug. 24, 1955, Hope, Ark.
Religion: Baptist
Family: Wife, Janet Huckabee; three children
Education: Ouachita Baptist U., B.A. 1976; Southwestern Baptist Theological Seminary, attended 1976-77
Career: Television talk show host; television documentary producer; pastor
Political highlights: Lieutenant governor, 1993-96

Election results:

1998 GENERAL

Mike Huckabee (R)	421,989	59.8%
Bill Bristow (D)	272,923	39.7%
Keith Carle (REF)	11,099	1.6%

Lt. Gov. Winthrop P. Rockefeller (R)

First elected: 1996
Length of term: 4 years
Term expires: 1/03
Salary: $29,000
Phone: (501) 682-2144

STATE LEGISLATURE

General Assembly: Meets 60 calendar days, January-March, in odd-numbered years
House: 100 members, 2-year terms
2001 breakdown: 30R, 70D; 86 men, 14 women
Salary: $12,769
Phone: (501) 682-7771
Senate: 35 members, 4-year terms
2001 breakdown: 7R, 28D; 31 men, 4 women
Salary: $12,769
Phone: (501) 682-6107

STATE TERM LIMITS

Governor: 2 terms
Senate: 2 terms
House: 3 terms

URBAN STATISTICS

CITY	POPULATION
Little Rock	176,136
Fort Smith	74,947
North Little Rock	59,543
Fayetteville	58,163
Jonesboro	52,558

REGISTERED VOTERS

Voters do not register by party.

POPULATION

2000 population	2,673,400
1990 population	2,350,725
Percent change	+13.7%
Rank among states	33
Median age	35.4
Born in state	67%
Foreign born	1%
Urban/rural	54%/46%
Crime rate	527/100,000
Poverty level	14.8%
Federal workers	20,728
Military	19,178

REAPPORTIONMENT

Arkansas retained its four House seats in reapportionment. The state legislature approved a new map on April 12, 2001.

MISCELLANEOUS

Web: www.state.ar.us
Capital: Little Rock
Land area: 52,075 sq. miles
  Rank among states: 27
STATE ELECTION OFFICIAL
(501) 682-5070
DEMOCRATIC HEADQUARTERS
(501) 374-2361
REPUBLICAN HEADQUARTERS
(501) 372-7301

District Statistics

DIST.	VOTE FOR PRESIDENT 2000 D	R	GREEN	1996 D	R	REF	1992 D	R	I	WHT	BLK	ASIAN	HISP	HOUSEHOLD INCOME	OVER 65+	UNDER 18	COLLEGE EDUCATION
1	50%	47%	1%	58%	33%	8%	59%	32%	9%	81%	18%	0%	1%	$18,180	15%	28%	10%
2	48	49	1	55	37	7	56	36	8	81	18	1	1	$25,142	12	26	19
3	37	59	2	44	45	9	43.2	42.5	14	96	2	1	1	$21,903	16	25	13
4	50	47	1	60	31	8	58	32	10	72	27	0	1	$19,621	16	27	11
STATE	46	51	1	54	37	8	53	35	10	83	16	1	1	$21,147	15	27	13

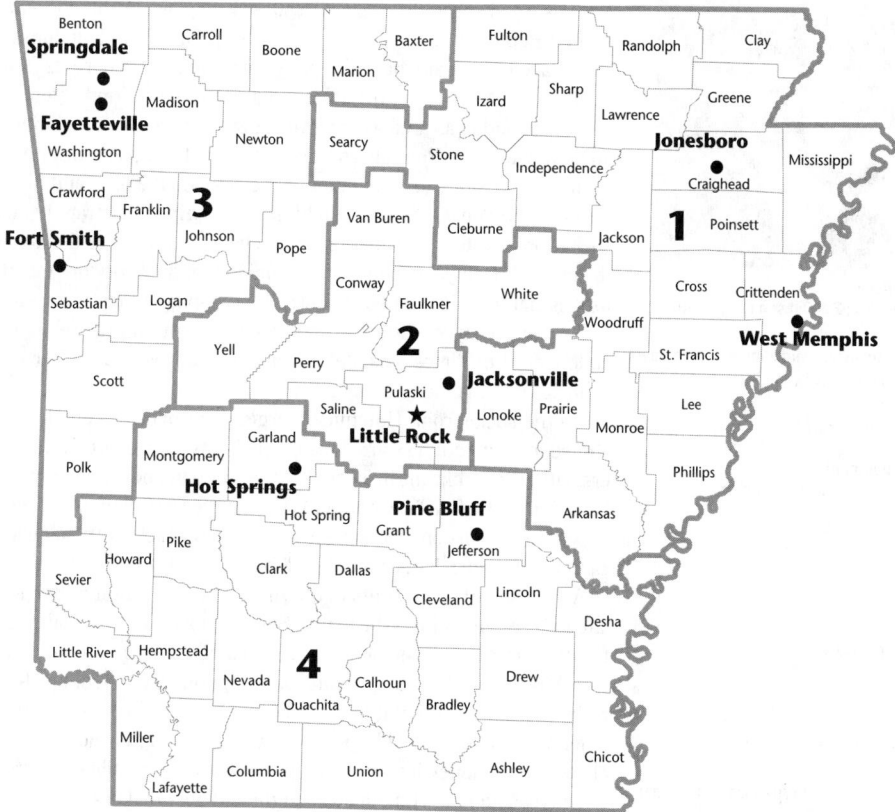

Sen. Tim Hutchinson (R)

Elected 1996; 1st term

CAPITOL OFFICE
224-2353; fax 228-3973; 239 Dirksen Bldg. 20510

INTERNET
e-mail: senator.hutchinson@hutchinson.senate.gov
web: hutchinson.senate.gov

COMMITTEES
Agriculture, Nutrition & Forestry
Armed Services
   (Personnel - chairman)
Health, Education, Labor & Pensions
   (Aging - chairman)
Veterans' Affairs
Special Aging

HOMETOWN
Rogers

BORN
Aug. 11, 1949, Bentonville, Ark.

RELIGION
Baptist

FAMILY
Wife, Randi Fredholm; three children

EDUCATION
Bob Jones U., B.A. 1971; U. of Arkansas, M.A. 1990

CAREER
Minister; college instructor; radio station
executive

POLITICAL HIGHLIGHTS
Ark. House, 1985-93; U.S. House, 1993-97

ELECTION RESULTS

1996 GENERAL
Tim Hutchinson (R)   445,942   52.7%
Winston Bryant (D)   400,241   47.3%

1996 PRIMARY
Tim Hutchinson (R)   unopposed

PREVIOUS WINNING PERCENTAGES
1994 House Election (68%); 1992 House Election
(50%)

Hutchinson was born and raised in the hill country of extreme northwest Arkansas, where Republicans had a foothold long before they gained strength in the rest of the state. He shares his party's longstanding concerns about federal spending and the relationship between government and the private sector and supports the GOP's more recent focus on social policy issues.

Conservative stands on social issues have played well in the South and earned Republicans their majorities on Capitol Hill, in Hutchinson's view. "You have to look at where the party's growing and where its future is. In the Northeast, it's pretty bleak," he said. "It would be kind of foolish for the party to abandon an area which gives us strength and our majority to please an area where the Republican message isn't playing as well."

In his four years as a member of the House (1993-97) and his first four years in the Senate, two of Hutchinson's priorities illustrate his fiscal and social conservatism. He is the sponsor every year of legislation to terminate the tax code four years hence, complaining that the code "has mutated from its original form into an 800,000-word, 7,500-page monster preying on the American taxpayer." Hutchinson reacted to criticism that eliminating the code would be "irresponsible" by saying that it would be "far more irresponsible" to maintain the status quo.

On the social front, Hutchinson urged Republicans when he was in the House to push tough restrictions on eligibility for welfare for unwed mothers. Other Republicans insisted that the language be toned down before its inclusion in the GOP's "Contract With America." Hutchinson is also a vocal opponent of abortion, declaring it "an issue on which we, who believe in the sanctity of human life, cannot bend, buckle or bow."

As a result of some shifts in the Armed Services Committee leadership late in 1999, Hutchinson became a Senate subcommittee chairman in 2000 for the first time. As head of the panel's Personnel Subcommittee, Hutchinson worked to provide prescription drug benefits to military retirees who are eligible for Medicare. He also included in the annual defense authorization bill a provision calling for high schools to lose federal education money if they do not provide access to military recruiters.

Of local interest, Hutchinson sought and obtained assurances that Little Rock Air Force Base, and its C-130 training facility, would remain in the Pentagon's future plans. And he moved the Pentagon toward the construction of a facility at Pine Bluff Arsenal to produce vaccines to defend against biological warfare.

Hutchinson also serves on the Health, Education, Labor and Pensions Committee. In the 106th Congress, he was a conferee on the bill to give patients more clout in dealing with their managed health care providers, and he tried to get more money for the Drug Enforcement Agency to clean up illegal methamphetamine laboratories. Arkansas is among the nation's leaders in the per capita level of meth activity. Hundreds of labs are closed down by authorities each year in the state, but the chemicals remain dangerous without an expensive cleanup effort.

Hutchinson also has had a longstanding interest in legislation directing that more federal education dollars be spent in the classroom, rather than in numerous levels of bureaucracy.

The senator has emerged as a leading critic of China, opposing legislation to grant China permanent normal trade status. "I think that multinational corporations have too much influence in the China debate," he said. "There has been an unholy alliance between big business, the Clinton administration and certain Republicans who have adopted the trade-at-any-price approach."

Hutchinson grew up on a livestock and poultry farm just a few miles from where Arkansas, Oklahoma and Missouri meet. Back then, residents of that part of Arkansas read the Tulsa newspaper, listened to Tulsa and Joplin, Mo., television and favored Republicans much more than the rest of Arkansas.

Hutchinson recalls that he was fascinated with politics at an early age: When he was in junior high school, he went down to Fayetteville and picked up some Barry Goldwater presidential campaign literature to distribute back home in Gravette.

He went to college at Bob Jones University, a bastion of evangelicalism, where he decided to become a minister. Back home in Arkansas, Hutchinson, the father of twin boys, opened a Christian school when he discovered there wasn't one in the area. Later, he co-owned and managed a local radio station for seven years and then taught history at nearby John Brown University. He served eight years in the Arkansas House, gaining a reputation as a friend of law enforcement.

Hutchinson is the elder half of one of two brother teams in Congress (the other pair is the Levin brothers, from Michigan). Tim is older, by just 16 months, than Asa, who now holds the 3rd District House seat that Tim had represented. In their joint tenure in Congress, Asa has often gotten the more favorable reviews. The two were in the limelight early in 1999 when Asa was one of the House "prosecutors" who presented the case for removing President Clinton from office and Tim was one of the Senate's 100 "jurors." Tim voted to remove Clinton. (It was not the first Clinton-Hutchinson conflict. In 1991, when Clinton was governor of Arkansas, Hutchinson sought to dock Clinton's pay for being out of the state so often campaigning for president.)

The two brothers roomed together in Washington for a while, and they still ride to work together from suburban Virginia. Because of the closeness of their ages, they have always been competitive, but also supportive. Asa actually ran for public office first — as city attorney of Bentonville in the 1970s; but in 1992, when veteran GOP Rep. John Paul Hammerschmidt announced his retirement from the 3rd District after 13 terms, it was agreed that Tim, as the older brother, would get first crack at running. Tim ran a grass-roots campaign, managed by Asa, that benefited from redistricting that had made the GOP-leaning 3rd even more so. He was outspent by Democrat John VanWinkle but was able to win election, 50 percent to 47 percent.

Hutchinson was initially reluctant to run for the Senate in 1996. When Arkansas Republicans came calling for a candidate, he turned them down. The state GOP persisted. Arkansas' other House Republican, Jay Dickey, threw his support to Hutchinson. Party officials kept the pressure on and Hutchinson finally agreed.

The draft-Hutchinson effort stemmed from a chain reaction touched off by a failed Arkansas land investment deal, known as the Whitewater scandal. In May 1996, Democratic Gov. Jim Guy Tucker announced he would resign after being convicted of two felonies in a bank fraud case related to Whitewater. Tucker's conviction prompted Lt. Gov. Mike Huckabee to drop his unopposed bid for the GOP Senate nomination and ascend instead to the governor's office. That created the opening for Hutchinson, and he became the first-ever Arkansas Republican elected to the Senate by popular vote.

The Hutchinson family political dynasty includes not only Tim and Asa, but also Tim's son, Jeremy, who was elected to the state legislature in a 2000 special election. Hutchinson says he did not encourage Jeremy to run but supported him when he did.

KEY VOTES

2000

Yes Overhaul bankruptcy law and increase minimum wage

Yes Limit fiscal 2001 discretionary spending to $600.3 billion

Yes Override veto on nuclear waste disposal at Yucca Mountain site in Nevada

No Oppose effort to terminate Kosovo mission

No Include gender, sexual orientation and disability in federal hate crime protections

Yes Approve GOP plan to restrict use of genetic information by health insurers

Yes Kill amendment delaying implementation of an anti-missile defense system

Yes Cut taxes for married couples

No Grant China permanent normal trade status

1999

Yes Remove President Clinton from office for obstruction of justice

Yes Kill amendment authorizing state grants to hire teachers and reduce class size

No Require criminal background checks for purchases at gun shows

Yes Approve GOP proposal to increase rights of patients in managed-care health plans

No Block effort to allow farm and medicine exports to Cuba

No Allow study of tougher automobile fuel efficiency standards

No Ratify nuclear weapons testing treaty

Yes Prohibit national political parties from collecting "soft money" donations

Yes Remove barriers among banking, securities and insurance companies

INTEREST GROUPS

	AFL-CIO	ADA	CCUS	ACU
2000	14%	5%	85%	91%
1999	0%	5%	94%	100%
1998	13%	5%	89%	100%
1997	0%	0%	80%	100%
House Service:				
1996	9%	5%	94%	100%
1995	0%	0%	96%	92%
1994	22%	5%	75%	95%
1993	0%	5%	100%	100%

CQ VOTE STUDIES

	PARTY UNITY		PRESIDENTIAL SUPPORT	
	Support	Oppose	Support	Oppose
2000	98%	2%	38%	62%
1999	95%	5%	24%	76%
1998	98%	2%	26%	74%
1997	95%	5%	60%	40%
House Service:				
1996	95%	5%	31%	69%
1995	96%	4%	18%	82%
1994	95%	5%	38%	62%
1993	92%	8%	31%	69%

Sen. Blanche Lincoln (D)

CAPITOL OFFICE
224-4843; fax 228-1371; 359 Dirksen Bldg. 20510

INTERNET
e-mail: blanche_lincoln@lincoln.senate.gov
web: lincoln.senate.gov

COMMITTEES
Agriculture, Nutrition & Forestry
Finance
Select Ethics
Special Aging

HOMETOWN
Hughes

BORN
Sept. 30, 1960, Helena, Ark.

RELIGION
Episcopalian

FAMILY
Husband, Steve Lincoln; two children

EDUCATION
Randolph-Macon Woman's College, B.A. 1982

CAREER
Lobbyist; congressional aide

POLITICAL HIGHLIGHTS
U.S. House, 1993-97

ELECTION RESULTS

1998 GENERAL

Blanche Lincoln (D)	385,878	55.1%
Fay Boozman (R)	292,906	41.8%
Charley E. Heffley (REF)	21,860	3.1%

1998 PRIMARY RUNOFF

Blanche Lincoln (D)	134,203	62.4%
Winston Bryant (D)	80,889	37.6%

1998 PRIMARY

Blanche Lincoln (D)	145,009	45.5%
Winston Bryant (D)	87,183	27.4%
Scott Ferguson (D)	44,761	14.0%
Nate Coulter (D)	41,848	13.1%

PREVIOUS WINNING PERCENTAGES
1994 House Election (53%); 1992 House Election (70%)

Elected 1998; 1st term

Lincoln didn't come to the Senate with any grand ambitions for hustling up the institutional ladder to become a major power in the chamber. For the time being, she is content to build some legislative victories for Arkansas, look out for the interests of women and children, and keep as many of her nights free as possible.

That may sound odd in a chamber filled with outsize egos and workaholics. But with twin sons born in 1996, Lincoln is a working mother who is determined to balance her public and private responsibilities. That means limiting business-related trips on weekends and Senate breakfasts on weekdays. It means constantly pleading with Senate leaders to allow members time for their families.

And it means making clear that her family life is in Washington, not her native Arkansas. Lincoln has said it was important to let her constituents know early on "that I'm moving my family with me because I want to watch my family grow up. I want to see their school plays. We'll be back here every holiday and every chance I get, but I'm not going to sacrifice my family for this job."

Nonetheless, in the 107th Congress Lincoln landed a plum committee assignment — a seat on the Finance panel — along with a post on Ethics, indicating good prospects for upward mobility in the Democratic ranks.

A farmer's daughter whose Arkansas roots go back seven generations, Lincoln is a moderate and a founding member of the centrist Senate New Democrats. She is likely to be wooed by Republicans when they seek Democratic support on major legislation. But Lincoln was a loyal backer of President Clinton, her fellow Arkansas Democrat, whose impeachment trial confronted her the moment she joined the Senate in 1999. She consistently voted in his favor on procedural issues, then joined with other Democrats to acquit him on both articles of impeachment.

Arkansas was the first state to send a popularly elected woman to the Senate — Hattie Carraway in 1932. According to the Arkansas Democrat-Gazette, Lincoln carried a quote from Carraway's 1932 campaign with her when she ran in 1998: "If I can hold on to my sense of humor and a modicum of dignity, I shall have a wonderful time running for office whether I get there or not." When she won, Lincoln became the youngest woman ever elected to the Senate and the only one from Arkansas since Carraway.

She got her start on Capitol Hill in 1983, when she worked as a receptionist for Democratic Rep. Bill Alexander. She left after two years for a series of research positions with lobbying firms and then decided in late 1991 to head home to challenge Alexander in 1992. Her race attracted little notice until news broke that Alexander was among the top 10 abusers in the House bank overdraft scandal.

The young Blanche Lambert — she was single then — took 61 percent in the primary and coasted to victory in November. She married obstetrician-gynecologist Steve Lincoln in 1993 and won re-election the following year.

Seen as a rising star among Arkansas Democrats, Lincoln put it all aside when she decided not to seek a third House term in 1996 after becoming pregnant with twins. In the book "Nine and Counting," a collaboration of the nine women serving in the Senate in 2000, Lincoln said, "I just didn't see myself riding around on flatbed trucks being eight months pregnant with twins."

But the career interruption did not last long: When Democratic Sen. Dale Bumpers announced that he would not seek a fifth term in 1998, Lincoln jumped at the opportunity to return to politics. She has scripted an entire political narrative around her family life, saying that she re-entered politics to make the nation better for her children — and everyone else's.

Lincoln's outgoing personality and ability to relate to constituents via such connections as her love of duck hunting have made her a popular politician in Arkansas. And she has just enough of a conservative streak to keep her constituents comfortable. The federal government, she said tartly in response to one candidate questionnaire, "grew too large and moves too slowly in response to citizen needs." In the House, she supported GOP tax cut proposals and a balanced-budget amendment to the Constitution. She helped craft an alternative budget put forward by the conservative coalition of House Democrats known as the "Blue Dogs."

But Lincoln is in the Democratic Party mainstream on other issues. She supports abortion rights, although she voted in the House to ban a procedure its opponents call "partial birth" abortion; and she backs more money for teacher pay and improvements to school buildings, while opposing vouchers to cover private school tuition.

In the Senate, in addition to her Finance Committee assignment, Lincoln serves on the Agriculture Committee — an important post from which to look out for home state interests. She spent much of her first two years in the Senate focusing on issues important to Arkansas farmers and other residents. She entered the debate over crop insurance and has worked on legislation dealing with flooding. "Agriculture is really my base, not only for my state's economy but also for my heritage," she says. "I come from a farm family."

Lincoln brings a rural lawmaker's perspective to nearly all the major issues Congress addresses. When it comes to education and health care, for instance, she says the nation's rural areas have unique problems that can't be fixed with a "one size fits all" approach.

But she also seeks to address problems of women in general and working mothers in particular. She says working mothers who have read about her often offer "a wink and a nod" about her daily hassles. "My perspective is a little different, since I'm a working mom and understand what other working mothers are going through," she said in 2001. "I woke up this morning and I thought, 'Oh no, I've exhausted my menu. What am I going to have for dinner tonight?'"

Lincoln says she wants to make sure that a woman's perspective is heard if and when Congress tackles a Social Security overhaul. "I'm doing a lot of work on Social Security, especially in regard to women," she said in 2001, "because it's a program that women are more dependent on than men. It doesn't really focus on our needs. We are in and out of the workplace more often, we make less and we live longer. So we depend on it."

Lincoln's own return to politics was a shot in the arm for her home state Democratic Party, which had been struggling in the 1990s, losing the governorship to Republican Mike Huckabee and a Senate seat to Republican Tim Hutchinson in 1996.

Conservative state Sen. Fay Boozman was hoping to ride that Republican surge in 1998. Hutchinson and Boozman, an eye doctor, were similar in many ways — both were Baptist ministers from the same town and both attended the same church. But that led some voters to question whether they wanted two senators who were that much alike.

Lincoln benefited politically from an embarrassing stumble by Boozman, who was describing his reasons for supporting an exception to a ban on abortion when rape or incest was involved. Boozman reportedly said that a woman was unlikely to become pregnant when she is raped because of hormonal responses in her body he referred to as "God's little protective shield." Lincoln accused Boozman of being insensitive. He later apologized, but the damage was done; Lincoln won by 13 percentage points.

KEY VOTES

2000

Yes Overhaul bankruptcy law and increase minimum wage

No Limit fiscal 2001 discretionary spending to $600.3 billion

Yes Override veto on nuclear waste disposal at Yucca Mountain site in Nevada

Yes Oppose effort to terminate Kosovo mission

Yes Include gender, sexual orientation and disability in federal hate crime protections

No Approve GOP plan to restrict use of genetic information by health insurers

No Kill amendment delaying implementation of an anti-missile defense system

No Cut taxes for married couples

Yes Grant China permanent normal trade status

1999

No Remove President Clinton from office for obstruction of justice

No Kill amendment authorizing state grants to hire teachers and reduce class size

Yes Require criminal background checks for purchases at gun shows

No Approve GOP proposal to increase rights of patients in managed-care health plans

No Block effort to allow farm and medicine exports to Cuba

No Allow study of tougher automobile fuel efficiency standards

Yes Ratify nuclear weapons testing treaty

Yes Prohibit national political parties from collecting "soft money" donations

Yes Remove barriers among banking, securities and insurance companies

INTEREST GROUPS

	AFL-CIO	ADA	CCUS	ACU
2000	50%	70%	86%	20%
1999	89%	95%	65%	12%
House Service:				
1996	57%	30%	64%	36%
1995	58%	60%	63%	20%
1994	33%	60%	83%	10%
1993	75%	65%	45%	25%

CQ VOTE STUDIES

	PARTY UNITY		PRESIDENTIAL SUPPORT	
	Support	Oppose	Support	Oppose
2000	80%	20%	84%	16%
1999	83%	17%	80%	20%
House Service:				
1996	66%	34%	63%	37%
1995	64%	36%	63%	37%
1994	79%	21%	73%	27%
1993	87%	13%	72%	28%

Rep. Marion Berry (D)

Elected 1996; 3rd term

Berry's focus for more than three decades has been farming — running the family farm in southeast Arkansas, holding posts in the state and federal agriculture bureaucracy and, since coming to Capitol Hill in 1997, serving on the House Agriculture Committee.

So it is a bit unusual that his work in the 106th Congress was dominated by health care issues — a circumstance that can be traced back to Berry's training and brief work experience as a pharmacist just out of college in the mid-1960s. He has not worked as a pharmacist since then, although he has retained his license.

Berry was front and center in the 106th on a number of key health issues. He was a conferee on the major health care bill — a measure to give patients more clout in their dealings with their managed health care providers. He also was a co-chairman of the Democratic Caucus Health Task Force and one of three co-chairmen of the group of Democrats who sought to develop a plan to deal with the high cost of prescription drugs.

All that came about because Berry had a pharmacy background to offer the "Blue Dogs," a coalition of conservative Democrats who were looking for lawmakers to take the lead in their work on health care matters. He became the co-chairman of the Blue Dog Health Task Force. Later, when Democratic leaders were fashioning their patients' rights bill, they made sure that the views of the Blue Dogs — a key bloc of votes — were considered.

With the backing of the Democratic leadership, Berry worked closely with Democrat John D. Dingell of Michigan and Republican Charlie Norwood of Georgia in developing a bill that eventually won House approval. When the measure went to a House-Senate conference, Berry was the only Democrat named as a conferee who was not a member of one of the major committees of jurisdiction.

Berry sometimes seemed a bit out of his element in dealing with the details of the managed-care debate. Part of that impression may be ascribed to his demeanor — his easygoing manner and his slow, Southern drawl.

He plays up his rural background, telling an audience back home that he is just a simple "farmer who got more involved in politics than maybe I should have," according to The Jonesboro Sun.

On the prescription drug front, Berry makes it clear that the local pharmacist is not to blame for the cost of drugs for senior citizens, most of whom do not have insurance coverage to help pay for their prescriptions. Drug manufacturers are the bad guys, according to Berry. "Their whole objective is to maintain their extreme profit margins. We think it's just basic greed."

Arkansas is particularly affected by the matter, as the state has a high percentage of elderly people living in poverty. Berry worked on legislation that would permit pharmacies to import drugs from Canada and other countries where prices are lower.

Berry's voting record shows him to be a middle-of-the-road Blue Dog. Although his ties with President Clinton go back almost two decades, he supported Clinton only about three-fifths of the time in key House votes. And Berry strays from the Democratic Party position about a third of the time on contentious issues such as gun control and constitutional amendments mandating a balanced budget, requiring a two-thirds majority vote to raise taxes, and permitting prayer in schools.

Despite his conservative leanings, Berry nevertheless is quick to herald federal spending on behalf of residents of his low-income district. His office

CAPITOL OFFICE
225-4076; fax 225-5602
1113 Longworth Bldg. 20515

INTERNET
e-mail: www.house.gov/writerep
web: www.house.gov/berry

COMMITTEES
Agriculture
Transportation & Infrastructure

HOMETOWN
Gillett

BORN
Aug. 27, 1942, Stuttgart, Ark.

RELIGION
Methodist

FAMILY
Wife, Carolyn Berry; two children

EDUCATION
U. of Arkansas, attended 1960-62; U. of Arkansas, Little Rock, B.S. 1965

CAREER
Farmer; White House aide; pharmacist

POLITICAL HIGHLIGHTS
Gillett City Council, 1976-80; Ark. Soil and Water Conservation Commission, 1986-94 (chairman, 1992)

ELECTION RESULTS

2000 GENERAL

Marion Berry (D)	120,266	60.2%
Susan Myshka (R)	79,437	39.7%

2000 PRIMARY

Marion Berry (D)	unopposed

1998 GENERAL

Marion Berry (D)	unopposed

PREVIOUS WINNING PERCENTAGES
1996 (53%)

churns out two or three news releases every week to announce the award of grants to local schools and law enforcement agencies or funding for local road-building projects.

The demographics of Berry's district are evident in his priorities: The 1st District is the poorest in a state that is one of the poorest in the nation, and Berry's interests are economic development — particularly in the Mississippi Delta region, which includes much of his district; improving rural and children's health care; making education more affordable; and keeping Medicare premiums low. Berry took to the House floor in the 105th to denounce a GOP-drafted budget bill, saying that its children's health provisions represented a "fiscally irresponsible, $16 billion, no strings attached, giveaway of the taxpayers' dollars." He said the children's health insurance plan he developed as co-chairman of the House Democratic Caucus' Health Task Force would cover 10 times as many children for the same cost.

Berry has not ignored his Agriculture panel post, urging increased export opportunities, removal of some sanctions that bar farm exports to some nations, higher loan rates for cotton farmers and expansion of the Conservation Reserve Program. He is also on the Transportation panel, where in the 106th he sought funding for more than a dozen small airports in his district.

After working in a Little Rock pharmacy for two years after college, Berry managed the family's soybean, rice, corn and wheat farm in Gillett. He began his political career in 1976, when he was elected to the Gillett City Council. In 1982, he became Clinton's gubernatorial campaign coordinator in Arkansas County, a post he also held in 1986 and 1990.

In 1986, Gov. Bill Clinton named him to the Arkansas Soil and Water Conservation Commission, where he served for eight years, chairing the panel in 1992. He moved to Washington when Clinton appointed him special assistant to the president for agricultural trade and food assistance issues.

When Democratic Rep. Blanche Lincoln became pregnant with twins and unexpectedly announced her retirement from her 1st District seat, Berry entered the 1996 House race and won a close contest against Republican Warren Dupwe, who had given Lincoln a tough battle in 1994 — a good year for the GOP nationwide.

In a district that has not elected a Republican since Reconstruction, Berry has easily sailed through two re-election campaigns.

Berry's staff reports that one unusual problem that plagued him earlier in his Washington tenure has diminished but still crops up now and then: He is confused occasionally with another Marion Barry (different spelling, same pronunciation), the former mayor of the District of Columbia.

KEY VOTES

2000

Yes Raise hourly minimum wage by $1 over two years
Yes Halt funding for U.S. mission in Kosovo unless European nations pay more
Yes Provide Medicare benefits to military retirees and their dependents
Yes Grant China permanent normal trade status
Yes Phase out estate, gift and trust taxes
No Prohibit implementation of president's national monument designations
No Approve GOP plan to provide prescription drug coverage for Medicare beneficiaries
Yes Increase help for poor nations indebted to international financial institutions

1999

Yes Impose steel import quotas
No Kill proposal to take aviation trust funds off budget
No Require background checks on buyers only at gun shows with 10 or more vendors
Yes Remove barriers among banking, securities and insurance companies
Yes Authorize state grants to hire teachers and reduce class size
Yes Overhaul campaign finance law; ban "soft money" and restrict advocacy advertising
Yes Approve bipartisan plan to increase rights of patients in managed-care health plans

INTEREST GROUPS

	AFL-CIO	ADA	CCUS	ACU
2000	60%	35%	76%	48%
1999	78%	60%	58%	29%
1998	80%	70%	67%	28%
1997	100%	75%	60%	44%

CQ VOTE STUDIES

	PARTY UNITY		PRESIDENTIAL SUPPORT	
	Support	Oppose	Support	Oppose
2000	67%	33%	55%	45%
1999	67%	33%	60%	40%
1998	70%	30%	63%	37%
1997	72%	28%	59%	41%

ARKANSAS 1
Northeast — Jonesboro; West Memphis

One of the nation's poorest districts, the 1st stretches across Arkansas' northeastern third, reaching from the Mississippi Delta through fertile plains and into the hilly north, where the Ozark Mountains begin.

Poverty is most notably present within the largely white, older populations in the northwest and the former sharecropping communities in the Democratic Delta. In the mid-1990s, the predominately black Delta communities began working with Arkansas State University in Jonesboro to attract tourism and manufacturing.

Some of the nation's largest rice and cotton producers farm the Delta and house their corporate headquarters in the 1st. Cattle and poultry businesses are prosperous in the north. Manufacturing is strong in several cities, including Stuttgart, Batesville and Jonesboro. One of the nation's largest steel production plants bolsters Blytheville, where the population and economy sagged after Eaker Air Force Base closed in the early 1990s.

The 1st elects very few Republicans at the state or federal level. In presidential contests in the 1990s and 2000, the district supported Democratic candidates. Western Lonoke County — where Little Rock suburbanites are migrating and some military personnel make their homes — leans Republican, as do some of the 1st's northwestern counties. The heavily Christian district is socially conservative in many areas.

MAJOR INDUSTRY
Agriculture, steel production, manufacturing

CITIES
Jonesboro, 52,558; West Memphis, 26,894; Paragould, 22,311; Blytheville, 18,921

UNUSUAL FEATURES
Author John Grisham born in Jonesboro; Country singer Conway Twitty born and raised in Helena; World duck calling championship in Stuttgart.

Rep. Vic Snyder (D)

Elected 1996; 3rd term

CAPITOL OFFICE
225-2506; fax 225-5903
1319 Longworth Bldg. 20515

INTERNET
e-mail: snyder.congress@mail.house.gov
web: www.house.gov/snyder

COMMITTEES
Armed Services
Veterans' Affairs

HOMETOWN
Little Rock

BORN
Sept. 27, 1947, Medford, Ore.

RELIGION
Presbyterian

FAMILY
Single

EDUCATION
Willamette U., B.A. 1975; U. of Oregon, M.D. 1979;
U. of Arkansas, Little Rock, J.D. 1988

MILITARY SERVICE
Marine Corps, 1967-69

CAREER
Physician; lawyer

POLITICAL HIGHLIGHTS
Ark. Senate, 1991-96

ELECTION RESULTS

2000 GENERAL

Vic Snyder (D)	126,957	57.5%
Bob Thomas (R)	93,692	42.5%

2000 PRIMARY

Vic Snyder (D)	unopposed

1998 GENERAL

Vic Snyder (D)	100,334	58.0%
Phil Wyrick (R)	72,737	42.0%

PREVIOUS WINNING PERCENTAGES
1996 (52%)

Snyder spent more than 15 years as a family physician, and his contemplative manner seems to reflect his medical training, where he was taught to listen attentively to a patient's complaints before proposing a remedy.

He does not introduce a lot of bills — only five in his four years in Congress — or make a lot of speeches. Some of Snyder's most successful ventures in the House have occurred behind the scenes, such as rounding up more than 100 cosponsors for a bill that someone else had introduced.

Snyder occasionally refers to his background as a doctor, relating personal experiences when the topic is prescription drug coverage for seniors or patients' relationships with their health maintenance organizations. On one occasion, he told the House: "I am well aware that doctors and nurses do not know everything about health policy. But one thing I do know is that, in a doctor's office in America today, arguments and shouting matches with insurance companies occur on a regular basis."

But even though health care has become a high-profile issue on Capitol Hill, Snyder generally has remained in the background.

He keeps current in the medical field by occasionally working at a Little Rock health clinic during visits to his district. But, as the Arkansas Democrat-Gazette observed in 1999, "don't look for ... Snyder, the Little Rock family practice doctor-turned-legislator, in the headlines." The newspaper reported that even when Snyder introduced his own bill — to ensure that people know their rights under their health insurance coverage — he "didn't bother to tell the press about his plan."

Snyder is a member of the centrist New Democrat Coalition and his priorities have included balancing the budget while ensuring a strong federal role in education, health care and national defense.

A Vietnam War veteran (he dropped out of college to join the Marines, without telling his mother beforehand), Snyder holds seats on the Armed Services and Veterans' Affairs committees and devotes much of his attention in the House to the work of those panels. He has been wary of any moves to diminish the funding or purpose of Little Rock Air Force Base, which has been threatened by the raiding efforts of Southern Republican lawmakers who want more money directed to their own military bases.

In 2000, Snyder was named to the top Democratic slot on an ad hoc Armed Services panel to assess terrorist threats facing U.S. armed forces and American interests abroad. He also focuses on training, equipment, health care, and other "quality of life" issues facing military personnel and veterans.

On the Veterans' Affairs Subcommittee on Health, he pressured the Defense and Veterans Affairs departments to do more to address the problems of Gulf War syndrome, a mysterious range of ailments reported by veterans of the 1991 military campaign in the Persian Gulf.

Snyder also has been persistent in his efforts to get veterans tested and treated for a serious type of hepatitis, a liver disease that affects about one-tenth of all veterans in central Arkansas, according to a Department of Veterans Affairs study. On that issue, he has a personal as well as a professional perspective — the husband of a 1998 campaign adviser died of the disease.

In addition to his work on veterans' health issues, Snyder played a key role in the 106th Congress in overturning a Medicare regulation that halted coverage for immunosuppressive drugs after less than four years. When some organ transplant recipients stopped taking the drugs because they found they could not pay for them, it sometimes led to organ rejection and the need for another costly transplant — which Medicare covered. Snyder made a major effort to round up cosponsors for a bill to adjust the regulation.

On the home front, Snyder makes periodic radio reports to his constituents, his engaging manner that of a regular guy. He chats about what he's been doing in Washington and ends with the signoff line, "I'm looking forward to seeing you in Arkansas this weekend." With his constituents in mind, in 2000 he directed $3 million home to extend a streetcar line in Little Rock.

Born and raised in Oregon, Snyder as a young man spent much of his time in libraries — he has degrees in both medicine and law, though he has never practiced the latter discipline. After earning his medical degree at the University of Oregon, he came to Arkansas in 1979 to do his medical residency. Snyder remained in his adoptive state after his training, working as a family doctor. He went on medical missions to Asia, Central America and Africa, where he said he realized that many medical problems are solved or created by political decisions.

Snyder served six years in the state Senate, where his priorities included support for small business, increased jail time for violent criminals, a crackdown on underage drinking, and a repeal of the state sales tax on food.

When Democratic incumbent Ray Thornton announced his retirement in 1996, Snyder entered the 2nd District race as an underdog, facing two tough opponents in the primary — prosecuting attorney Mark Stodola and John Edwards, a former aide to retiring U.S. Sen. David Pryor. Snyder finished second to Stodola in the primary but surged in the runoff campaign to narrowly edge out his foe.

Snyder embraced the national Democratic themes in the fall campaign, pledging to oppose GOP initiatives on Medicare, education and the environment. He posted a 52 percent to 48 percent victory over Republican Bud Cummins, a businessman and lawyer, while President Clinton carried the 2nd District by 18 percentage points.

In his re-election campaigns, Snyder has won more comfortably, racking up a 15-point margin in 2000.

In all three of his House campaigns, Snyder has refused to begin fundraising until much later than is traditional — sometimes just a few months before the election. He acknowledges that his approach can be risky — particularly in his first campaign, where he was the underdog, and in his second campaign, where he was coming off a narrow victory. But he told the Arkansas Democrat-Gazette: "If it helps shorten the campaign ... that's an improvement."

KEY VOTES

2000
Yes Raise hourly minimum wage by $1 over two years
No   Halt funding for U.S. mission in Kosovo unless European nations pay more
Yes Provide Medicare benefits to military retirees and their dependents
Yes Grant China permanent normal trade status
No   Phase out estate, gift and trust taxes
No   Prohibit implementation of president's national monument designations
No   Approve GOP plan to provide prescription drug coverage for Medicare beneficiaries
Yes Increase help for poor nations indebted to international financial institutions

1999
Yes Impose steel import quotas
Yes Kill proposal to take aviation trust funds off budget
No   Require background checks on buyers only at gun shows with 10 or more vendors
Yes Remove barriers among banking, securities and insurance companies
Yes Authorize state grants to hire teachers and reduce class size
Yes Overhaul campaign finance law; ban "soft money" and restrict advocacy advertising
Yes Approve bipartisan plan to increase rights of patients in managed-care health plans

INTEREST GROUPS

	AFL-CIO	ADA	CCUS	ACU
2000	90%	70%	55%	4%
1999	78%	85%	29%	4%
1998	90%	85%	61%	16%
1997	88%	80%	60%	20%

CQ VOTE STUDIES

	PARTY UNITY		PRESIDENTIAL SUPPORT	
	Support	Oppose	Support	Oppose
2000	89%	11%	90%	10%
1999	84%	16%	78%	22%
1998	80%	20%	81%	19%
1997	87%	13%	84%	16%

ARKANSAS 2
Central — Little Rock

Encompassing Little Rock and eight surrounding counties, the 2nd is Arkansas' axis of government activity. More than half of the 2nd's population is focused in the Little Rock area, where strong black, union and university populations offer solid support to Democrats in most elections. The district includes the state's largest white-collar population and has the highest median income. While the district supported former Gov. Bill Clinton heavily in 1992 and '96, President Bush narrowly carried the 2nd in 2000.

Democratic support is concentrated in poor and working-class neighborhoods in east Little Rock, where populations are up to 81 percent black. Rural agriculture and mining communities in outlying areas also tend to support Democrats, although social conservatism is more common.

Affluent neighborhoods in north and west Little Rock are more likely to vote for Republicans. The GOP has gained popularity within rapidly

growing suburbs in Faulkner, Saline and Pulaski counties, which are fed by affluent whites leaving Little Rock. Republicans also fare well in White County, where Church of Christ-affiliated Harding University is located.

MAJOR INDUSTRY
Government, higher education, military

MILITARY BASES
Little Rock Air Force Base, 4,942 military, 852 civilian (2000)

CITIES
Little Rock, 176,136; North Little Rock, 59,543; Conway, 42,412; Jacksonville, 28,682

UNUSUAL FEATURES
Site of William J. Clinton Presidential Center, along the south bank of the Arkansas River in Little Rock; Gen. Douglas MacArthur born in Little Rock; North Little Rock's "Old Mill" was seen in the opening credits of "Gone with the Wind;" Little Rock Air Force Base has the largest C-130 training and airlift facility in the world.

Rep. Asa Hutchinson (R)

Elected 1996; 3rd term

CAPITOL OFFICE
225-4301; fax 225-5713
1421 Longworth Bldg. 20515

INTERNET
e-mail: asa.hutchinson@mail.house.gov
web: www.house.gov/hutchinson

COMMITTEES
Judiciary
Standards of Official Conduct
Transportation & Infrastructure
Select Intelligence

HOMETOWN
Fort Smith

BORN
Dec. 3, 1950, Bentonville, Ark.

RELIGION
Baptist

FAMILY
Wife, Susan Hutchinson; four children

EDUCATION
Bob Jones U., B.S. 1972; U. of Arkansas, J.D. 1975

CAREER
Lawyer

POLITICAL HIGHLIGHTS
Bentonville city attorney, 1977-78; U.S. attorney,
1982-85; Republican nominee for U.S. Senate,
1986; Republican nominee for Ark. attorney
general, 1990; Ark. Republican Party chairman,
1990-95

ELECTION RESULTS

2000 GENERAL

Asa Hutchinson (R)		unopposed

2000 PRIMARY

Asa Hutchinson (R)		unopposed

1998 GENERAL

Asa Hutchinson (R)	154,780	80.7%
Ralph Forbes (REF)	36,917	19.3%

PREVIOUS WINNING PERCENTAGES
1996 (56%)

Hutchinson is probably best known for his fight to impeach President Clinton. A member of the Judiciary Committee, he was one of the 13 House "managers" who argued the case against Clinton before the Senate in 1999. But despite his sharp partisanship on impeachment and his solid party establishment credentials, the former federal prosecutor is willing to work across party lines to address broad policy dilemmas. The three-term lawmaker has teamed with Democrats, sometimes over the objections of GOP leaders, to develop privacy standards and to overhaul the nation's campaign finance laws.

Still, Hutchinson has a solid record as a fiscal and social policy conservative. Well-liked within his party, he has contemplated running for the House Republican Conference chairmanship, and the Bush administration considered him for the post of deputy attorney general, the No. 2 position at the Justice Department.

In the 107th Congress, he gave up a slot on the Government Reform panel to serve on the higher-profile Intelligence Committee. He retained his seats on Judiciary and Transportation.

Hutchinson's straightforward and factual approach has won him much attention and praise, even in highly charged situations such as Clinton's impeachment. He helped draw up the four articles of impeachment related to Clinton's efforts to cover up his affair with a White House intern, giving him plenty of exposure on the television talk-show circuit. But on the floor of the Senate, his presentations were devoid of the sweeping rhetoric that permeated the statements of the other managers. A former U.S. attorney — who once prosecuted Clinton's brother, Roger, on drug charges — Hutchinson's deliberative style during the impeachment proceedings earned him high marks.

Despite his lawyerly manner, Hutchinson will bring up personal experience to make a point, as he did in 2000. As the House considered enacting federal hate crimes legislation, Hutchinson recalled his own encounter with a hate group while he was a U.S. attorney. The organization, which had harassed minorities and blown up a synagogue in Missouri, targeted Hutchinson's family for assassination while he was prosecuting the group. Yet he opposed the hate crimes bill, arguing that most state laws were tough enough to deal with hate groups.

Hutchinson co-chaired a bipartisan group of 12 House freshmen who drew up a proposal to overhaul the campaign finance system in the 105th Congress — and he criticized his party's leaders when they scuttled the plan. His stand on campaign financing had some political consequences: In late 1997, the National Right to Life Committee, an anti-abortion group, had its Arkansas affiliate run advertisements in the 3rd District that criticized Hutchinson's efforts to curtail "soft money" contributions, used by advocacy groups to run campaign ads. The group's opposition raised eyebrows because of Hutchinson's staunch anti-abortion views. "I wasn't intimidated by my enemies, and I won't be intimidated by my friends," he responded.

Campaign finance reform remains a priority for Hutchinson. He also has turned his attention to legislation to address the vote tabulation problems in Florida in the 2000 elections. At the start of the 107th, he proposed a bill to authorize $1.5 billion in grants to help states and localities improve the administration of elections by repairing or replacing outdated voting equipment and streamlining the tabulation and reporting of election results.

Hutchinson also considers legislation governing privacy matters a top priority for the 107th. He and Democratic Rep. Jim Moran of Virginia introduced a bill creating a bipartisan commission to conduct a comprehensive study of privacy issues and make recommendations to Congress. The commission would examine privacy regulations governing medical records, financial statements, and the gathering and use of information on the Internet. It would also explore the collection and use of personal information by government agencies. Hutchinson and Moran made a similar proposal in the 106th Congress.

Some people still confuse Asa Hutchinson with his older brother, Sen. Tim Hutchinson, who held the 3rd District seat for four years before running for the Senate in 1996. While the brothers are both Republicans, they do not always agree on legislation. Asa, for example, favored granting China permanent normal trade status in 2000, while Tim opposed such a move. Both expressed concerns about China's human rights record, but Asa said that China's behavior was best influenced by engagement with the United States.

A graduate of the fundamentalist Christian Bob Jones University, Hutchinson has voted to ban a procedure its opponents call "partial birth" abortion, to end federal funding for the arts, and to amend the Constitution to outlaw desecration of the U.S. flag. He supports IRA-style accounts to help families meet education expenses and voted to deny federal funding for national education testing.

Hutchinson got his start in government right after graduating from the University of Arkansas law school when he became Bentonville city attorney. In 1982, President Reagan named him U.S. attorney for the Western District of Arkansas. He left that post to make a bid to unseat Democratic Sen. Dale Bumpers in 1986, but lost.

In 1996, Hutchinson considered trying for the seat being vacated by retiring Democratic Sen. David Pryor. But he decided not to challenge then-Lt. Gov. Mike Huckabee for the GOP nomination. When Huckabee dropped out of the race in order to succeed Gov. Jim Guy Tucker — who resigned after his conviction in a Whitewater-related case — Hutchinson again thought about running. He stepped aside, however, when GOP leaders persuaded his older brother, Tim, to give up his safe House seat to run for the Senate.

Asa then was tapped to replace Tim as the GOP nominee in the 3rd District, the most Republican of Arkansas' four congressional districts. He prevailed over Democrat Ann Henry, a University of Arkansas business professor, by 14 percentage points. Democrats did not bother to field a candidate in 1998 or 2000.

KEY VOTES

2000

No Raise hourly minimum wage by $1 over two years
Yes Halt funding for U.S. mission in Kosovo unless European nations pay more
Yes Provide Medicare benefits to military retirees and their dependents
Yes Grant China permanent normal trade status
Yes Phase out estate, gift and trust taxes
Yes Prohibit implementation of president's national monument designations
Yes Approve GOP plan to provide prescription drug coverage for Medicare beneficiaries
No Increase help for poor nations indebted to international financial institutions

1999

No Impose steel import quotas
No Kill proposal to take aviation trust funds off budget
Yes Require background checks on buyers only at gun shows with 10 or more vendors
Yes Remove barriers among banking, securities and insurance companies
No Authorize state grants to hire teachers and reduce class size
No Overhaul campaign finance law; ban "soft money" and restrict advocacy advertising
No Approve bipartisan plan to increase rights of patients in managed-care health plans

INTEREST GROUPS

	AFL-CIO	ADA	CCUS	ACU
2000	0%	0%	85%	83%
1999	11%	10%	91%	72%
1998	11%	5%	94%	92%
1997	25%	10%	90%	88%

CQ VOTE STUDIES

	PARTY UNITY		PRESIDENTIAL SUPPORT	
	Support	Oppose	Support	Oppose
2000	94%	6%	24%	76%
1999	90%	10%	24%	76%
1998	90%	10%	26%	74%
1997	94%	6%	27%	73%

ARKANSAS 3
Northwest – Fort Smith; Fayetteville

Arkansas' hilly northwest subscribes to a rugged conservatism unique in this heavily Democratic state and, despite an influx of newcomers, this brand of Republicanism still characterizes the 3rd. It voted heavily in favor of President Bush in 2000 and was the state's only district to withhold hearty support from native son Bill Clinton in 1996. The 3rd has sent a Republican to Congress since 1967.

Median household income for the 3rd ranks in the bottom third of congressional districts nationwide, reflecting the district's population of poor, sparsely educated whites who reside in the Ozark hills and farming communities.

Homegrown corporations like Tyson Foods in Springdale and Wal-Mart in Bentonville sustain the 3rd's economy and attract white-collar workers, as does Clinton's one-time employer, the University of Arkansas in Fayetteville. The closure of Fort Chaffee Army Base in the late 1990s hit the district hard, but the city of Fort Smith hopes to redevelop the property in the coming years.

The district's Republican core resides with conservatives in the northwest, where history, religious tradition and an influx of retirees have created a solid GOP base. The remainder of the 3rd – particularly farming communities and population centers Fayetteville, Fort Smith and Springdale – is more open to electing Democrats at the state level, but the northwest sets the overall political tone.

MAJOR INDUSTRY
Agriculture, livestock, retail

CITIES
Fort Smith, 74,947; Fayetteville, 58,163; Springdale, 42,339; Rogers, 39,130

UNUSUAL FEATURES
Sen. J. William Fulbright, who established the Fulbright fellowships, lived in Fayetteville; Seven-story Christ of the Ozarks statue in Eureka Springs.

Rep. Mike Ross (D)

Elected 2000; 1st term

Ross, a pharmacy owner from the small southwest Arkansas town of Prescott, describes himself as "just a country boy." But his modest self-assessment belies his experience in business and politics, which includes a decade in the state Senate, where in 1990 he became the youngest person ever elected to the body.

Farming is important in the mainly rural 4th District, and Ross has a seat on the Agriculture Committee from which to look out for local mainstays, including rice, cotton and soybeans as well as livestock and timber. Saying that he plans to be Arkansas' "economic ambassador," Ross speaks of attracting new industries to his economically lagging area.

The 4th is socially conservative, and Ross says he plans to walk a centrist path in representing it. He at times breaks with Democrats on abortion and denounces gun control legislation, although he supports laws designed to keep weapons out of schools.

Ross' agenda on economic issues, though, is more aligned with most of his Democratic colleagues. He advocates improving schools by increasing teacher pay and reducing class size, and he supports a Medicare-controlled prescription drug program.

Ross' election victory over four-term GOP Rep. Jay Dickey was the Democrats' only victory over an incumbent outside California in 2000, and he had to work hard to get the win. His status as the widely regarded front-runner for the Democratic nomination made him the target of attacks by his three opponents in the party's bitter primary; two of his primary foes later endorsed Dickey. He then endured a hard-fought campaign against Dickey, whose folksy manner had previously kept him popular despite the 4th's traditional Democratic leanings.

Some Republicans explained away Dickey's defeat as the revenge of President Clinton, the 4th District native whose impeachment Dickey had supported in 1998; Clinton made an 11th-hour campaign stop in the district on Ross' behalf, but Ross insisted that his 2-point win was the result of his own constituent-tailored message.

CAPITOL OFFICE
225-3772; fax 225-1314; 514 Cannon Bldg. 20515

INTERNET
e-mail: www.house.gov/writerep
web: www.house.gov/ross

COMMITTEES
Agriculture
Financial Services
Small Business

HOMETOWN
Prescott

BORN
August 2, 1961, Texarkana, Ark.

RELIGION
Methodist

FAMILY
Wife, Holly Ross; two children

EDUCATION
U. of Arkansas, Little Rock, B.A. 1987

CAREER
Pharmacy owner; wholesale drug and medical supply company field representative; aide to lieutenant governor

POLITICAL HIGHLIGHTS
Nevada County Quorum Court, 1983-85; Ark. Senate, 1991-2001

ELECTION RESULTS

2000 GENERAL

Mike Ross (D)	108,143	51.0%
Jay Dickey (R)	104,017	49.0%

2000 PRIMARY RUNOFF

Mike Ross (D)	28,286	58.1%
DeWayne Graham (D)	20,392	41.9%

2000 PRIMARY

Mike Ross (D)	41,668	44.8%
DeWayne Graham (D)	20,575	22.1%
Judy Smith (D)	20,341	21.8%
Bruce Harris (D)	10,539	11.3%

ARKANSAS 4
South – Pine Bluff; Hot Springs

Covering Arkansas' southern half, from the Mississippi River to the Texas border, the 4th is traditionally a socially conservative, but Democratic district that took a Republican swing in the 1990s. In 1992, the district narrowly elected its first Republican representative in the 20th century, but at the same time overwhelmingly supported Hope-born and Hot Springs-raised Bill Clinton in both his presidential bids. However, the district might be returning to its Democratic roots. In 2000, the 4th not only supported Al Gore in the presidential race, but also elected a Democrat to the House. State legislators in the 4th are almost exclusively Democrats.

Rice, soybeans, cotton and rural poverty characterize the eastern edge of the 4th, where many Mississippi River communities have black-majority populations. Democrats receive their most faithful support from these areas and from blue-collar and minority populations in Little River and Lafayette counties to the west.

Republican candidates find communities supported by oil and chemical production in the district's south, as well as military and white-collar communities near Pine Bluff and Hot Springs, to be receptive to their politics.

MAJOR INDUSTRY
Agriculture, timber, livestock

MILITARY BASES
Pine Bluff Arsenal (Army), 409 military, 982 civilian (1999)

CITIES
Pine Bluff, 52,249; Hot Springs, 38,778; Texarkana, 24,014; El Dorado, 21,545

UNUSUAL FEATURES
Author Maya Angelou raised in Stamps; Football coach Paul "Bear" Bryant got his nickname by wrestling a bear in Fordyce.

CALIFORNIA

Gov. Gray Davis (D)

First elected: 1998
Length of term: 4 years
Term expires: 1/03
Salary: $165,000
Phone: (916) 445-2841
Hometown: Los Angeles
Born: Dec. 26, 1942, Bronx, N.Y.
Religion: Roman Catholic
Family: Wife, Sharon Davis
Education: Stanford U., B.A. 1964; Columbia U., J.D. 1967
Military Service: Army, 1967-69
Career: Lawyer
Political highlights: Candidate for Calif. treasurer, 1974; Calif. governor's chief of staff, 1974-81; Calif. Assembly, 1983-87; Calif. controller, 1987-95; lieutenant governor, 1995-99

Election results:
1998 GENERAL
Gray Davis (D)	4,858,817	58.0%
Dan Lungren (R)	3,216,749	38.4%

Lt. Gov. Cruz M. Bustamante (D)

First elected: 1998
Length of term: 4 years
Term expires: 1/03
Salary: $123,750
Phone: (916) 445-8994

STATE LEGISLATURE

Bicameral Legislature: Session meets year-round, with recess
Assembly: 80 members, 2-year terms
2001 breakdown: 28R, 51D; 55 men, 24 women, 1 vacant
Salary: $99,000, $121/day in session
Phone: (916) 445-3614
Senate: 40 members, 4-year terms
2001 breakdown: 14R, 26D; 30 men, 10 women
Salary: $99,000, $121/day in session
Phone: (916) 445-4251

STATE TERM LIMITS

Governor: 2 terms
Senate: 2 terms
Assembly: 3 terms

URBAN STATISTICS

CITY	POPULATION
Los Angeles	3,633,591
San Diego	1,238,974
San Jose	867,675
San Francisco	746,777
Long Beach	435,027

REGISTERED VOTERS

Democrat	45%
Republican	35%
Unaffiliated	14%
Other	5%

POPULATION

2000 population	33,871,648
1990 population	29,760,021
Percent change	+13.8%
Rank among states	1
Median age	33
Born in state	46%
Foreign born	22%
Urban/rural	93%/7%
Crime rate	798/100,000
Poverty level	15.4%
Federal workers	268,568
Military	230,324

REAPPORTIONMENT

California gained one House seat in reapportionment, increasing from 52 districts to 53. The state legislature will draw new district lines in 2001.

MISCELLANEOUS

Web: www.state.ca.us
Capital: Sacramento
Land area: 155,973 sq. miles
Rank among states: 3
STATE ELECTION OFFICIAL
(916) 657-2166
DEMOCRATIC HEADQUARTERS
(916) 442-5707
REPUBLICAN HEADQUARTERS
(818) 841-5210

District Statistics

DIST.	D	2000 R	GREEN	D	1996 R	REF	D	1992 R	I	WHT	BLK	ASIAN	HISP	HOUSEHOLD INCOME	OVER 65+	UNDER 18	COLLEGE EDUCATION
1	50%	41%	8%	48%	35%	10%	47%	29%	24%	85%	4%	4%	11%	$30,943	13%	26%	18%
2	34	59	5	36	51	9	36	39	26	92	1	2	6	$24,807	16	26	16
3	44	51	4	45	44	7	41	37	22	82	3	6	14	$30,296	11	27	20
4	37	58	4	38	51	8	34	41	25	93	2	2	7	$35,772	12	25	21
5	57	37	5	57	34	5	51	31	18	66	13	13	14	$29,974	11	26	24
6	62	30	7	57	29	7	56	24	20	90	2	3	9	$40,564	13	22	33
7	69	27	4	65	25	6	61	22	17	63	17	14	13	$38,608	10	26	23
8	77	15	8	74	14	3	76	16	9	52	13	28	15	$31,659	14	16	34
9	79	12	9	75	13	3	79	12	9	45	32	16	11	$30,067	12	22	35
10	51	45	3	48	43	6	42	36	22	88	2	6	9	$52,378	10	25	36
11	47	50	3	46	45	7	41	39	21	75	6	12	20	$31,605	11	29	15
12	67	27	5	64	26	5	58	27	16	65	4	26	14	$44,720	14	20	32
13	66	30	3	62	28	7	54	26	20	64	7	19	18	$43,877	9	26	22
14	62	32	4	58	31	6	54	27	20	78	5	12	13	$50,078	11	20	44
15	57	38	4	53	35	7	46	30	23	82	2	11	10	$50,823	9	22	35

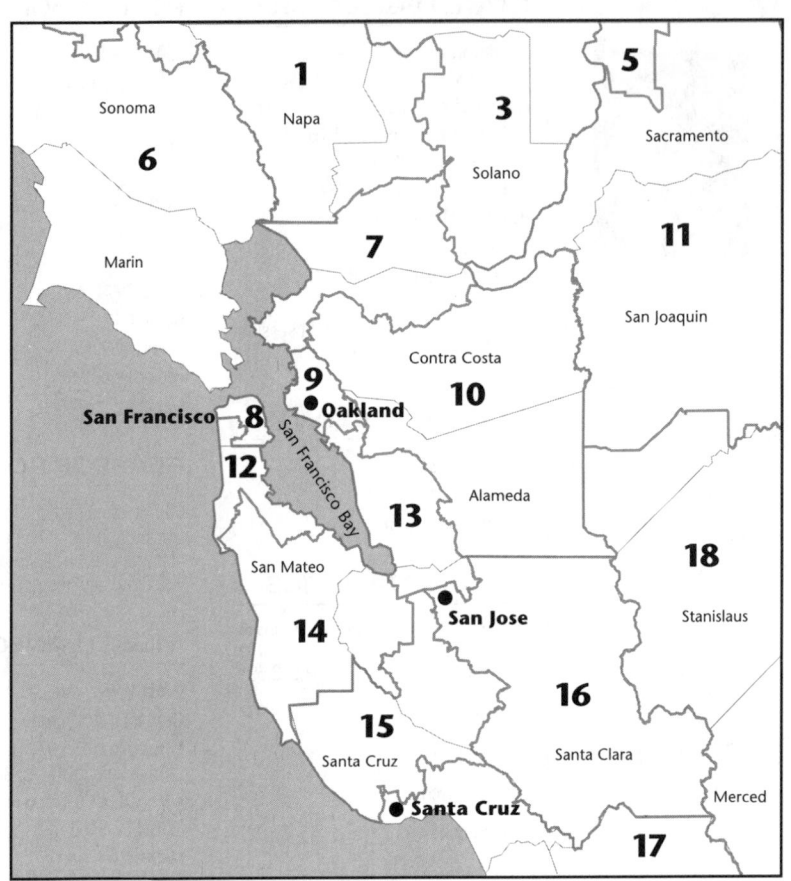

District Statistics

DIST.	VOTE FOR PRESIDENT									WHT	BLK	ASIAN	HISP	HOUSEHOLD INCOME	OVER 65+	UNDER 18	COLLEGE EDUCATION
	D	2000 R	GREEN	D	1996 R	REF	D	1992 R	I								
16	64%	32%	3%	61%	29%	6%	52%	27%	21%	55%	5%	21%	36%	$42,223	7%	28%	19%
17	60	33	6	55	32	6	53	27	20	70	4	6	31	$33,911	10	26	23
18	44	53	3	46	45	7	41	37	22	76	3	6	26	$28,324	10	32	12
19	38	58	3	40	52	6	38	44	18	74	3	7	23	$29,153	11	29	20
20	50	48	2	52	41	6	47	38	16	49	6	6	55	$21,140	9	35	6
21	33	64	2	34	56	8	33	46	21	78	4	3	20	$29,943	11	30	15
22	45	49	6	44.2	44.4	7	41	35	24	82	3	4	21	$33,680	13	23	25
23	48	47	4	46	42	9	38	35	27	77	3	5	30	$42,989	9	28	21
24	58	38	3	52	37	7	48	30	22	85	2	6	13	$48,433	11	21	33
25	45	51	3	41	47	9	36	39	25	80	5	6	16	$46,480	8	28	23
26	70	25	3	65	25	7	57	24	19	54	6	7	52	$32,134	8	28	15
27	53	41	4	49	41	7	44	37	19	71	8	11	20	$37,929	13	22	31
28	49	47	3	45	44	8	38	41	21	71	6	13	24	$43,508	11	26	26
29	72	22	5	67	24	5	66	20	14	84	3	8	13	$37,540	16	13	44
30	75	19	5	71	20	5	63	24	13	44	3	21	60	$23,435	8	27	16
31	69	27	2	65	26	7	52	32	16	48	2	23	58	$30,667	9	29	13
32	83	13	3	81	12	4	78	13	9	32	40	8	30	$28,332	11	24	23
33	83	15	2	80	14	5	63	24	13	36	4	4	83	$20,708	6	33	5
34	67	30	2	64	27	7	51	31	18	57	2	9	62	$36,224	9	30	12

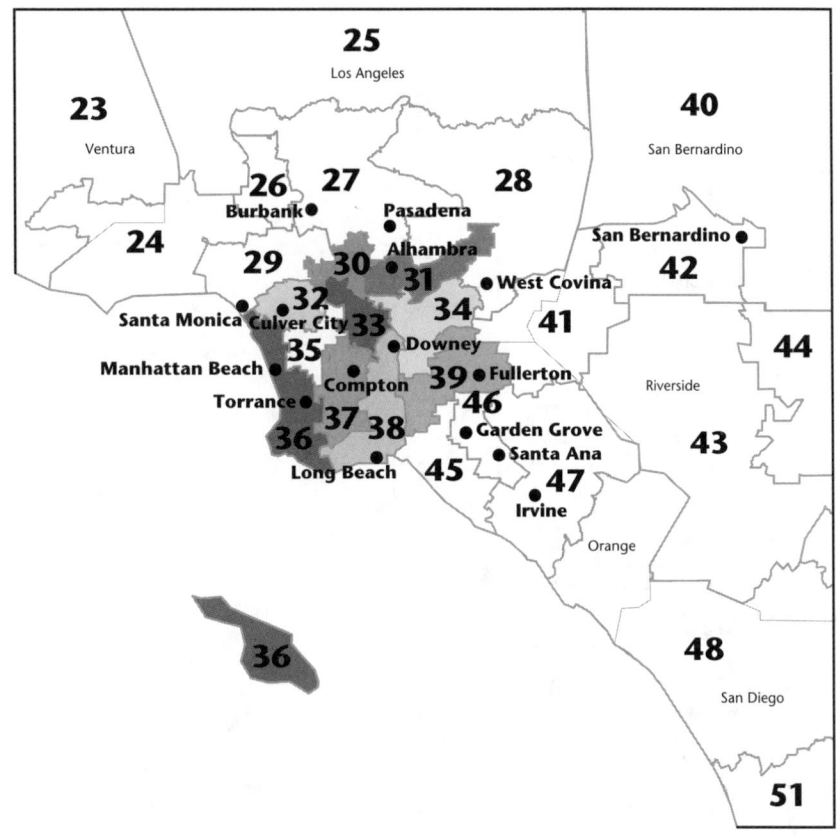

District Statistics

DIST.	D	2000 R	GREEN	D	1996 R	REF	D	1992 R	I	WHT	BLK	ASIAN	HISP	HOUSEHOLD INCOME	OVER 65+	UNDER 18	COLLEGE EDUCATION
35	86%	12%	1%	84%	11%	4%	78%	13%	9%	21%	43%	6%	42%	$25,481	7%	32%	10%
36	51	44	4	47	41	8	41	36	23	78	3	13	15	$48,522	10	19	37
37	83	15	1	82	13	4	74	16	11	26	34	11	44	$27,127	7	34	9
38	58	37	4	53	36	8	45	34	22	69	8	9	25	$34,364	12	24	21
39	43	53	3	41	48	8	34	44	22	73	3	14	22	$46,196	9	25	25
40	39	56	3	38	49	11	35	40	25	82	5	4	16	$30,408	12	29	16
41	47	50	2	43	47	8	35	43	22	68	7	10	31	$44,607	6	30	21
42	57	39	2	54	36	9	46	33	21	66	11	4	34	$33,737	7	33	13
43	44	52	3	43	46	9	37.8	38.2	24	76	6	4	25	$37,806	8	30	16
44	47	49	3	44	45	9	41	36	24	77	5	3	28	$29,049	18	27	13
45	40	56	3	38	51	8	32	42	25	82	1	11	15	$45,074	10	21	28
46	54	42	2	49	41	8	37	40	23	67	2	12	49	$35,416	7	29	12
47	39	57	3	36	54	7	31	46	23	84	2	10	13	$51,554	11	23	37
48	36	60	3	34	56	8	29	44	27	83	4	5	17	$42,389	10	26	28
49	53	41	5	49	40	7	43	32	25	82	5	7	12	$32,562	12	16	34
50	59	37	3	60	32	6	49	30	21	47	14	15	40	$27,655	8	30	14
51	41	55	3	39	52	7	32	40	27	85	2	8	13	$45,186	11	25	35
52	41	54	3	41	48	8	34	37	29	84	3	3	22	$33,046	11	27	17
STATE	53	42	4	51	38	7	46	33	21	69	7	10	26	$35,798	11	26	23

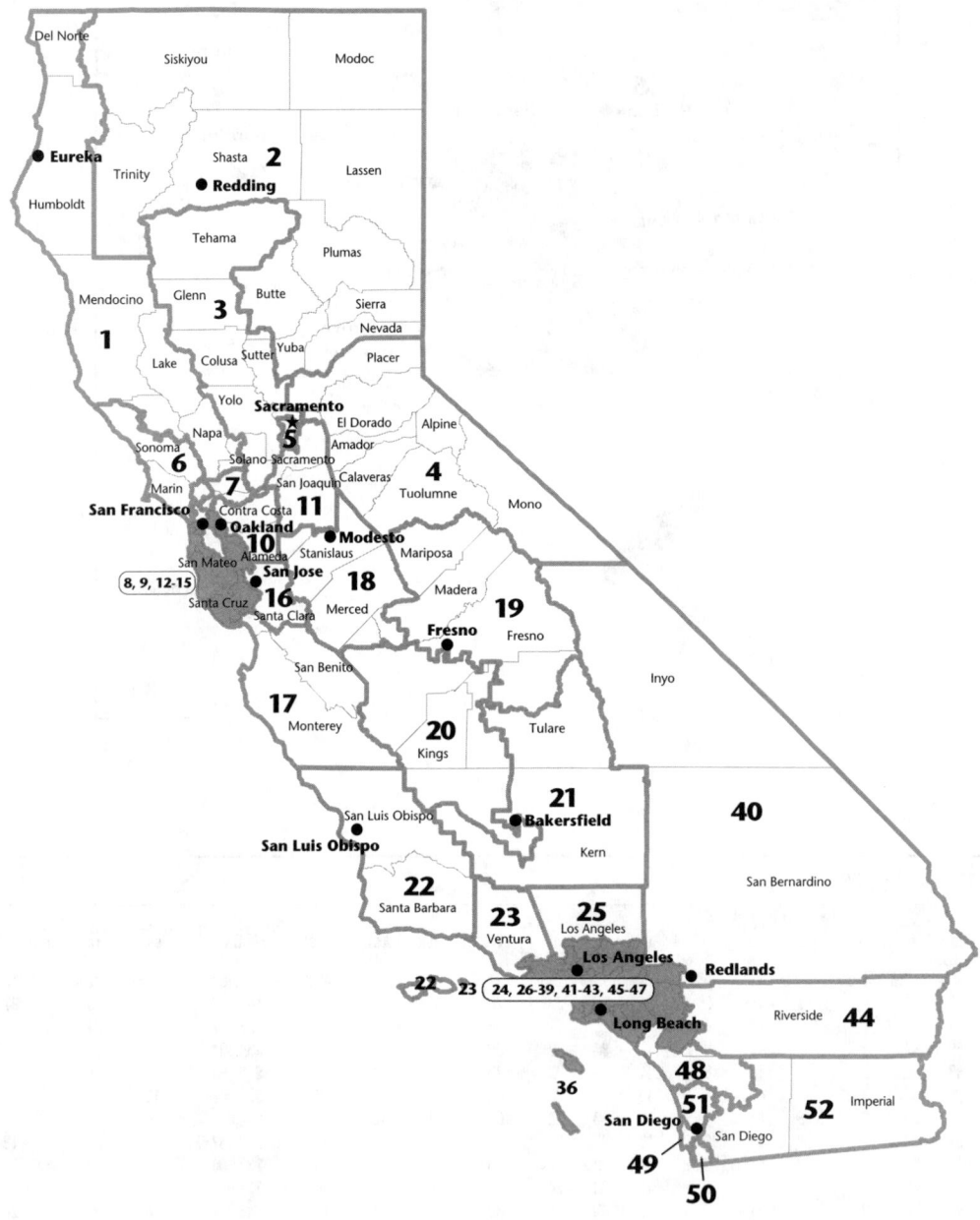

Sen. Dianne **Feinstein** (D)

Elected 1992; 2nd full term

CAPITOL OFFICE
224-3841; fax 228-3954; 331 Hart Bldg. 20510

INTERNET
e-mail: senator@feinstein.senate.gov
web: feinstein.senate.gov

COMMITTEES
Appropriations
Energy & Natural Resources
Judiciary
Rules & Administration
Select Intelligence
Joint Printing

HOMETOWN
San Francisco

BORN
June 22, 1933, San Francisco, Calif.

RELIGION
Jewish

FAMILY
Husband, Richard Blum; one child, three
stepchildren

EDUCATION
Stanford U., A.B. 1955

CAREER
Public official

POLITICAL HIGHLIGHTS
San Francisco Board of Supervisors, 1970-78
(president, 1970-71, 1974-75, 1978); mayor of San
Francisco, 1978-89; Democratic nominee for
governor, 1990

ELECTION RESULTS

2000 GENERAL

Dianne Feinstein (D)	5,932,522	55.8%
Tom Campbell (R)	3,886,853	36.6%
Medea Benjamin (GREEN)	326,828	3.1%
Gail Lightfoot (LIBERT)	187,718	1.8%
Diane Beall Templin (AMI)	134,598	1.3%

2000 PRIMARY (OPEN)

Dianne Feinstein (D)	3,759,560	51.2%
Tom Campbell (R)	1,697,208	23.1%
Ray Haynes (R)	679,034	9.2%
Bill Horn (R)	453,630	6.2%
Michael Schmier (D)	181,104	2.5%

PREVIOUS WINNING PERCENTAGES
1994 (47%); 1992 Special Election (54%)

Feinstein has long been able to straddle the ideological gulf between the two parties without seeming indecisive. While she first gained national prominence as San Francisco's mayor from 1978 to 1989, she has never quite fit the stereotype of the liberal, soft-hearted "San Francisco Democrat." She is tough on crime and supportive of business interests in many instances; her annual ratings from the U.S. Chamber of Commerce are typically higher than the average Senate Democrat's.

Feinstein (FINE-stine) says she developed her political mantra — "govern from the center" — while serving as mayor and trying to work out solutions that the diverse political forces in her city could accept. Feinstein's moderation, personal appeal and high name recognition have made her one of California's most enduring political figures.

A member of the moderate Senate New Democrats and the Centrist Coalition, she is popular in the Senate, and unlike her home state Democratic colleague Barbara Boxer, Feinstein does not infuriate Republicans with stinging verbal assaults. While Boxer comes across as a scrappy liberal, the reserved Feinstein seems more like a corporate executive, determined to get things done, even if it means compromising.

Despite her somewhat restrained manner, Feinstein is not unfriendly. An amateur artist, she often gives signed sketches of birds and flowers to friends and colleagues. And she attempts to put a human face on the issue of the day. Whatever the topic under debate, she tries to find someone who is affected personally to illustrate her points.

In the 107th Congress, Feinstein first sought to shift from the Appropriations Committee to the Finance Committee. But she backed off when party leaders would not guarantee Boxer her seat on Appropriations. Instead, Feinstein added assignments on the Energy and Intelligence committees while continuing to serve on the Appropriations, Judiciary and Rules committees.

With California mired in an electricity crisis in early 2001, Feinstein dug into energy issues immediately. She introduced a bill giving the secretary of energy authority to impose temporary wholesale price caps if the government finds that rates are unjust and unreasonable.

Feinstein has worked with Judiciary Committee Republicans on crime issues. She joined with Arizona Republican Jon Kyl, for instance, in promoting a constitutional amendment to secure crime victims' rights, and the two also worked on the issues of Internet gambling, identity theft and export controls on encryption software, which allows digital information to be scrambled during computer transmission. Unlike many in her party, she has backed a constitutional amendment to ban desecration of the U.S. flag.

Feinstein parts ways with Republicans on gun control, which she strongly supports. "I've lived a life that has been impacted by weapons," she wrote in the book "Nine and Counting," a collaboration of the nine female senators serving in 2000. "So this is not an esoteric, academic exercise for me. Nor is it a political exercise. I come to this issue because of real-life experience."

In November 1978, while serving on the San Francisco Board of Supervisors, Feinstein discovered the body of San Francisco Mayor George Moscone after he and Harvey Milk, the city's first openly gay supervisor, were shot to death in City Hall by former Supervisor Dan White.

Feinstein succeeded Moscone as mayor and won plaudits for the dignified manner in which she held the city together in the wake of the killings. Feinstein's role, which was recalled in the documentary "The Life and Times of Harvey Milk," has given her credibility in the gun debate. When GOP Sen. Larry E. Craig of Idaho, a board member of the National Rifle Association, once hinted that Feinstein didn't have much weapons knowledge, she recounted how she had tried to find Milk's pulse after he was shot.

Although she was supportive of President Clinton's positions on legislation, Feinstein felt personally betrayed by the president's repeated denials of his affair with former White House intern Monica Lewinsky. Feinstein happened to be in the room when Clinton solemnly declared, "I did not have sexual relations with that woman, Miss Lewinsky."

When the president later admitted his deceit, Feinstein pulled no punches. "My trust in his credibility has been badly shattered," she said in August 1998. And so, for a time, she was featured prominently in the media as a symbol of Clinton's damaged relations with his party. But like most Democrats, Feinstein quickly decided that the better part of wisdom was not to hound him. "There's nothing ... so far that's come out to say that this reaches the level of impeachment," she said in September 1998. She ended up voting to acquit Clinton on both impeachment counts brought by the House.

Feinstein has fought hard on various women's issues. She was a prominent skeptic during the Senate Rules Committee's investigation of a GOP challenge to Louisiana Democrat Mary L. Landrieu's narrow 1996 Senate victory. "Hell hath no fury like a man beaten by a woman," Feinstein said. "Women have to fight our way in this process all the way up. No one hands us anything."

Certainly, no one handed her the Senate seat, which she first won in a special election in 1992 against Republican John Seymour, appointed to the seat after Republican Sen. Pete Wilson was elected governor in 1990. Boxer was also running in 1992, and the two — despite their differences in personality and political philosophy — campaigned as "Thelma and Louise," the leading ladies of politics' much-ballyhooed "Year of the Woman."

In 1994, Feinstein faced a tough challenge from millionaire GOP Rep. Michael Huffington, who outspent her by slightly more than a 2-to-1 ratio in what was at the time the most expensive Senate contest in history. Not until she and other Democrats turned attack ads against him — and it was revealed that Huffington had hired an illegal immigrant as a household employee — did Feinstein begin pulling ahead.

In 1997 and early 1998, Feinstein, who had run unsuccessfully for governor in 1990, pondered another gubernatorial campaign but passed in the end, saying no decision had "given me more angst."

Feinstein spent the 2000 election season hobbled by an accident that left her on crutches for months. But the injury, caused by a fall in Aspen, Colo., did not hobble her politically.

Her opponent, former Rep. Tom Campbell, had trouble raising money and did little to inspire GOP conservatives, offering centrist views and even calling Feinstein an effective senator at one point in the campaign. Seen as a pragmatist with a consensus-building approach to politics, Feinstein cruised to re-election.

The larger question in 2000 was whether Vice President Al Gore would tap her as his running mate. In the end, Feinstein was once again a political bridesmaid. In 1984, Democratic presidential nominee Walter F. Mondale gave her strong consideration before selecting former New York Democratic Rep. Geraldine A. Ferraro as the first female vice-presidential candidate from a major political party. In 2000, Connecticut Sen. Joseph I. Lieberman, not Feinstein, became the first Jewish vice-presidential candidate from a major political party.

KEY VOTES

2000
Yes Overhaul bankruptcy law and increase minimum wage
No Limit fiscal 2001 discretionary spending to $600.3 billion
No Override veto on nuclear waste disposal at Yucca Mountain site in Nevada
Yes Oppose effort to terminate Kosovo mission
Yes Include gender, sexual orientation and disability in federal hate crime protections
Yes Approve GOP plan to restrict use of genetic information by health insurers
No Kill amendment delaying implementation of an anti-missile defense system
Yes Cut taxes for married couples
Yes Grant China permanent normal trade status

1999
No Remove President Clinton from office for obstruction of justice
No Kill amendment authorizing state grants to hire teachers and reduce class size
Yes Require criminal background checks for purchases at gun shows
No Approve GOP proposal to increase rights of patients in managed-care health plans
No Block effort to allow farm and medicine exports to Cuba
Yes Allow study of tougher automobile fuel efficiency standards
Yes Ratify nuclear weapons testing treaty
Yes Prohibit national political parties from collecting "soft money" donations
Yes Remove barriers among banking, securities and insurance companies

INTEREST GROUPS

	AFL-CIO	ADA	CCUS	ACU
2000	50%	70%	54%	28%
1999	78%	100%	53%	4%
1998	88%	90%	61%	4%
1997	57%	85%	50%	4%
1996	86%	95%	38%	20%
1995	100%	95%	37%	13%
1994	63%	70%	40%	8%
1993	100%	85%	9%	13%

CQ VOTE STUDIES

	PARTY UNITY		PRESIDENTIAL SUPPORT	
	Support	Oppose	Support	Oppose
2000	88%	12%	84%	16%
1999	91%	9%	87%	13%
1998	87%	13%	88%	12%
1997	86%	14%	89%	11%
1996	81%	19%	90%	10%
1995	80%	20%	84%	16%
1994	89%	11%	92%	8%
1993	90%	10%	92%	8%

Sen. Barbara Boxer (D)

Elected 1992; 2nd term

CAPITOL OFFICE
224-3553; fax 228-1338; 112 Hart Bldg. 20510

INTERNET
e-mail: senator@boxer.senate.gov
web: boxer.senate.gov

COMMITTEES
Commerce, Science & Transportation
Environment & Public Works
Foreign Relations

HOMETOWN
Greenbrae

BORN
Nov. 11, 1940, Brooklyn, N.Y.

RELIGION
Jewish

FAMILY
Husband, Stewart Boxer; two children

EDUCATION
Brooklyn College, B.A. 1962

CAREER
Congressional aide; journalist; stockbroker

POLITICAL HIGHLIGHTS
Candidate for Marin County Board of Supervisors, 1972; Marin County Board of Supervisors, 1977-83; U.S. House, 1983-93

ELECTION RESULTS

1998 GENERAL

Barbara Boxer (D)	4,410,056	53.1%
Matt Fong (R)	3,575,078	43.0%
Ted Brown (LIBERT)	93,926	1.1%

1998 PRIMARY (OPEN)

Barbara Boxer (D)	2,574,284	43.9%
Matt Fong (R)	1,292,662	22.1%
Darrell Issa (R)	1,143,107	19.5%
Frank Riggs (R)	295,886	5.0%
John Pinkerton (D)	219,250	3.7%
Ted Brown (LIBERT)	67,408	1.2%

PREVIOUS WINNING PERCENTAGES
1992 (48%); 1990 House Election (68%); 1988 House Election (73%); 1986 House Election (74%); 1984 House Election (68%); 1982 House Election (52%)

When Boxer's political opponents call her "feisty," as they often do, they usually mean it as a negative attribute. But the liberal feminist, who names abortion rights, environmental protection and gun control among her top priorities, makes no apologies for her partisan positions and bold style.

"My political style is to be extremely candid and straight from the shoulders, and not to be mealy-mouthed or waffle," she said in 2000. "When I believe in something, I believe in it strongly."

That aggressive nature — which often brings her to the Senate floor for impassioned speeches and legislative efforts that can be more symbolic than effective — has been much in evidence throughout Boxer's career. On the wall of her Capitol Hill office hangs a picture of Boxer, then a member of the House, leading six other female representatives up the steps of the U.S. Senate in 1991 to demand public hearings on law professor Anita Hill's allegations of sexual harassment against Supreme Court nominee Clarence Thomas.

Boxer now says that move — remembered by some as an attention-grabbing stunt and by others as a strong show of solidarity — effected a widespread backlash against the overwhelmingly white, male makeup of the Senate, which ultimately led to the 1992 elections being termed the "Year of the Woman." Boxer, who had represented California's 6th District in the House for 10 years, was elected to the Senate that year along with Democrats Dianne Feinstein, also from California, Patty Murray of Washington and Carol Moseley-Braun of Illinois.

"Women saw what happened and realized they still weren't receiving anything approaching a full measure of representation," Boxer wrote in the book "Nine and Counting," which she co-authored in 2000 with the eight other women who were in the Senate in the 106th Congress. "And so they voted to ensure that they might at least have a chance to be heard."

Boxer, on the other hand, has never had a hard time making herself heard. Armed with her "Boxer box," a platform to elevate her 5-foot-tall frame to television camera level, she has spoken out on issues ranging from questionable Pentagon procurement practices to women's health issues to former Sen. Bob Packwood's sexual dalliances.

In the 107th Congress, aiming to capitalize on her outspokenness, Senate Democratic leaders placed Boxer in the newly created post of chief deputy for strategic outreach.

Supporters and opponents say Boxer's relentless style sets her apart. Even when The Sacramento Bee endorsed her in a tough 1998 Senate re-election race against California GOP State Treasurer Matt Fong, the editorial board called her "a high-profile, high-energy politician with a bent for partisanship and self-promotion." Former Senate Majority Leader Bob Dole put it another way, once calling Boxer "the most partisan senator I've ever known."

A passionate legislator who has a reputation for working hard, she was described in a 1998 Associated Press report as "a formidable combination of dervish and policy wonk." While some politicians pride themselves on their ability to horse-trade and compromise in pursuit of their goals, Boxer usually operates as an unremitting activist, often offering proposals that have no chance of adoption, just to make a point about how she feels things ought to be. "I'm very consistent on the issues," says Boxer. "I'm not the type of person that changes views based on polls or ... the way the wind is blowing."

If Boxer's absolutism makes her visible, it can also hurt her chances of success. Her unfashionable adherence to liberal tenets often doesn't play well in the clubby Senate, where deliberation and bipartisan cooperation can be vital. Her dogged persistence and refusal to compromise often mean she doesn't get the backing she needs to get her proposals written into law. She frequently introduces hard-line amendments unlikely to win support from Republicans or even garner much Democratic backing. For example, her attempt in 2000 to forbid the armed forces from using executive jets to transport top military officials failed, with just 32 senators supporting it.

During the 105th Congress, Boxer joined with Feinstein to propose an alternative to a ban on a procedure its opponents call "partial birth" abortion. Their proposal, which would have banned post-viability abortions except to save the woman's life or protect her health, garnered only 28 votes. When the Senate revisited the issue during the 106th, Boxer was more successful, but with a purely symbolic measure. The Senate adopted her amendment stating Congress' support for the 1974 *Roe v. Wade* decision legalizing abortion.

Sometimes Boxer's hard-charging endeavors have an impact. She fought hard in the 106th against an attempt by oil-state senators to delay new Interior Department rules that effectively increased oil royalties. While her attempts — including a filibuster — to block the proposal were ultimately unsuccessful, she gave oil-state senators the battle of their lives. "It was one of the hardest fights I've had," said Texas Republican Kay Bailey Hutchison.

Boxer occasionally partners with more moderate Republicans on lower-profile health and environmental issues, such as efforts with Arlen Specter of Pennsylvania to increase health research funding; with Senate Environment Committee Chairman Robert C. Smith of New Hampshire to ban the gasoline additive MTBE, a suspected carcinogen; with James M. Jeffords of Vermont to promote alternative fuels; and with Olympia J. Snowe of Maine to allow women to choose obstetrician-gynecologists as a primary care doctor.

Boxer also spends much of her time tending to California matters large and small, from finding funding for highways and helping secure national park status for San Francisco's Presidio (a former Army base), to pressuring the Agriculture Department to hold up imports of Argentine lemons that have worried Ventura County growers.

Boxer, a former stockbroker, was drawn into politics because of her vehement opposition to the Vietnam War. A Brooklyn native and child of immigrants who is a product of public schools — all the way from kindergarten through Brooklyn College — Boxer sees herself as a defender of the middle class. "You can't hand anybody anything; it doesn't work that way. But you can give them a chance," Boxer said in 2000.

After six years on the Marin County Board of Supervisors, Boxer was elected to the House in 1982 as the beneficiary of one of the decade's more creative acts of district line-drawing. But after nearly a decade in Washington, Boxer tired of the nastiness she felt permeated the House. "I saw the meanness running through the House, the mean-spiritedness," she said in 2000.

Encouraged by women senators, including Democrat Barbara A. Mikulski of Maryland, Boxer made a bid for the Senate in 1992. She got a boost from the national Democratic ticket and from the dynamism of her pairing with Feinstein, who was seeking California's other Senate seat. Boxer beat out fellow House Democrat Mel Levine and Lt. Gov. Leo T. McCarthy in the primary; in November, she held off the GOP nominee, conservative TV commentator Bruce Herschensohn, by 5 percentage points.

She was in a weak position going into the 1998 election against State Treasurer Fong, who sought to paint her as a liberal extremist with ties to President Clinton — who was weathering the Monica Lewinsky scandal at the time. Boxer turned things around with a last-minute negative TV advertising campaign depicting Fong as a right-wing zealot.

KEY VOTES

2000

No Overhaul bankruptcy law and increase minimum wage

No Limit fiscal 2001 discretionary spending to $600.3 billion

No Override veto on nuclear waste disposal at Yucca Mountain site in Nevada

Yes Oppose effort to terminate Kosovo mission

Yes Include gender, sexual orientation and disability in federal hate crime protections

No Approve GOP plan to restrict use of genetic information by health insurers

No Kill amendment delaying implementation of an anti-missile defense system

? Cut taxes for married couples

Yes Grant China permanent normal trade status

1999

No Remove President Clinton from office for obstruction of justice

No Kill amendment authorizing state grants to hire teachers and reduce class size

Yes Require criminal background checks for purchases at gun shows

No Approve GOP proposal to increase rights of patients in managed-care health plans

No Block effort to allow farm and medicine exports to Cuba

Yes Allow study of tougher automobile fuel efficiency standards

Yes Ratify nuclear weapons testing treaty

Yes Prohibit national political parties from collecting "soft money" donations

No Remove barriers among banking, securities and insurance companies

INTEREST GROUPS

	AFL-CIO	ADA	CCUS	ACU
2000	67%	85%	41%	4%
1999	100%	100%	47%	4%
1998	88%	95%	59%	4%
1997	86%	100%	50%	0%
1996	100%	100%	23%	5%
1995	100%	100%	26%	0%
1994	88%	95%	20%	0%
1993	91%	90%	9%	8%
House Service:				
1992	100%	60%	33%	0%
1991	100%	80%	25%	0%

CQ VOTE STUDIES

	PARTY UNITY		PRESIDENTIAL SUPPORT	
	Support	Oppose	Support	Oppose
2000	100%	0%	92%	8%
1999	97%	3%	84%	16%
1998	90%	10%	90%	10%
1997	97%	3%	89%	11%
1996	94%	6%	90%	10%
1995	95%	5%	90%	10%
1994	92%	8%	87%	13%
1993	95%	5%	91%	9%
House Service:				
1992	92%	8%	8%	92%
1991	98%	2%	24%	76%

Rep. Mike Thompson (D)

Elected 1998; 2nd term

Ambitious but pleasant, Thompson is a member for whom election to Congress was perhaps a bit of a step backward. He represented more people and held more power as chairman of the California Senate Budget Committee, but Thompson fully intends to stick around Capitol Hill long enough to gain renewed stature and seniority — enough for this former vintner to help his beloved wine industry.

As a freshman, Thompson focused largely on issues of parochial concern, such as a disease threatening wine grapes and a local zip code dispute. On national issues, he shares the same priorities as most of the Democratic Caucus: education, health care and the environment. He sounds like an old-fashioned Democrat when he says, "I really believe in public service and I really believe in government." Thompson told a Healdsburg town hall meeting in 1999 that Social Security "is without question the most important government program we have. In addition to that, it's probably the most successful government program we've got."

But he is no rubber stamp for old-fashioned big government programs; he is friendly toward business and is a member of the "Blue Dogs," a coalition of conservative Democrats. Thompson defines leadership as "finding what people can live with." Thus, sharing the plaint of many moderates in a polarized Congress, he said toward the end of his first term, "This institution frustrates me a lot."

Thompson became interested in public service as a young man working as a maintenance supervisor at the Beringer Vineyard in Napa Valley. "I was the guy the Hispanic field laborer would come to with their problems," he said. Seeking to intervene on behalf of one Hispanic worker who had been cheated by a mechanic, Thompson recalls, "The guy in the repair shop said what do you care — the guy's just a Mexican."

Outraged, Thompson said he realized that in order to be able to help people effectively, he would have to complete his education. He had dropped out of high school and joined the Army — he served as a staff sergeant in Vietnam — but in his late 20s and early 30s he got his high school diploma and earned a college degree.

A political science professor suggested that he apply for a fellowship working with the state legislature, which in turn led to a second career as a staff aide. Thompson ran for elective office himself in 1990, winning a seat in the state Senate.

During his tenure in the California Senate, Thompson built coalitions across party lines on budget and other matters. He sponsored a welfare overhaul bill that provided recipients with day care aid, job training and education to move them off the public assistance rolls. He also won passage of a measure that cut the salaries of some state officials and another that required health insurance companies to cover preventive health care for children.

Because of California's legislative term limits, Thompson moved quickly up the ladder in Sacramento. But those same limits meant that he would be out of a job following the 1998 elections, and he set his eyes on Congress. The prospect of facing the popular Thompson, it was widely speculated, was the reason Republican Rep. Frank Riggs abandoned his seat in favor of a quixotic, late bid for the Senate.

Riggs had represented the 1st District for two of the previous three terms; his turnstile career was emblematic of the district, which had sent

CAPITOL OFFICE
225-3311; fax 225-4335; 119 Cannon Bldg. 20515

INTERNET
e-mail: m.thompson@mail.house.gov
web: www.house.gov/mthompson

COMMITTEES
Agriculture
Armed Services

HOMETOWN
St. Helena

BORN
Jan. 24, 1951, St. Helena, Calif.

RELIGION
Roman Catholic

FAMILY
Wife, Janet Thompson; two children

EDUCATION
California State U., Chico, B.A. 1982, M.A. 1996

MILITARY SERVICE
Army, 1969-73

CAREER
Vintner; winery maintenance supervisor; Calif. Assembly aide; college instructor

POLITICAL HIGHLIGHTS
Calif. Senate, 1990-99

ELECTION RESULTS

2000 GENERAL

Mike Thompson (D)	155,638	65.0%
Russell J. "Jim" Chase (R)	66,987	28.0%
Cheryl Kreier (NL)	7,173	3.0%
Emil Rossi (LIBERT)	6,376	2.7%
Pamela Elizondo (REF)	3,161	1.3%

2000 PRIMARY (OPEN)

Mike Thompson (D)	112,185	64.6%
Russell J. "Jim" Chase (R)	21,456	12.4%
Kenneth Hitt (R)	14,489	8.4%
Lawrence Wiesner (R)	14,351	8.3%
Emil Rossi (LIBERT)	4,394	2.5%
Cheryl Kreier (NL)	4,375	2.5%
Pamela Elizondo (REF)	2,327	1.3%

1998 GENERAL

Mike Thompson (D)	121,710	61.9%
Mark Luce (R)	64,622	32.8%
Emil Rossi (LIBERT)	5,404	2.7%
Ernest K. Jones Jr. (PFP)	4,996	2.5%

four different men to Congress since 1988. "The 1st Congressional District has been inadequately represented because of the constant turnover," said Thompson, who is confident that he can hold the seat for the foreseeable future. "The district is a safe district for me, but I think history has shown it's not safe for Democrats." He has handily won both his House elections, and in 2000 he cruised to victory by a ratio of better than 2-to-1.

In his Agriculture Committee post, Thompson devotes much of his energy to protecting California's $33 billion wine industry. He keeps a full rack of wine on display in his office and hosts "Cooking with Mike" fundraisers featuring wine-flavored dishes. When he met Charles W. Stenholm of Texas, the ranking Democrat on the Agriculture Committee, he made a gift of a bottle of wine carrying his personal label. Thompson told a gathering of the American Vintners Association that when Stenholm asked him what his agricultural priorities were, he said: "I just gave you my priorities."

Thompson has not been able to outmaneuver Republican Sen. Strom Thurmond of South Carolina, however, on the issue of allowing wine sales over the Internet, which Thompson favors.

Thompson wavered long enough about supporting a bill to grant China permanent normal trade status that he won some attention from the White House for his pet projects. He received a long-sought separate ZIP code for American Canyon residents and brought Pierce's disease, a grape-destroying disease carried by the glassy-winged sharpshooter, to the attention of Agriculture Secretary Dan Glickman, who pledged federal funding for eradication.

Public Citizen's Global Trade Watch blasted Thompson for "a vile display of vote trading"; he countered, however, that he hadn't traded his vote, but merely used the attention the China vote had brought as an opportunity to raise other concerns. "They've been working with me on it," Thompson told the San Francisco Chronicle. "I'm hopeful they would have done it without this vote. I don't think anybody brought that sharpshooter from Florida to coincide with this vote." By the summer of 2000, Thompson was able to boast that thanks to emergency government funds, wineries had "turned the corner" on fighting the disease.

Thompson's interests on the Armed Services Committee are also largely parochial — looking out for Travis Air Force Base and its more than 11,000 military and civilian employees.

His highest-profile legislation may be the Congressional Gold Medal he and Sen. Dianne Feinstein, D-Calif., sponsored for "Peanuts" creator Charles Schulz, a longtime resident of Santa Rosa.

KEY VOTES

2000

Yes Raise hourly minimum wage by $1 over two years
Yes Halt funding for U.S. mission in Kosovo unless European nations pay more
Yes Provide Medicare benefits to military retirees and their dependents
Yes Grant China permanent normal trade status
Yes Phase out estate, gift and trust taxes
No   Prohibit implementation of president's national monument designations
No   Approve GOP plan to provide prescription drug coverage for Medicare beneficiaries
Yes Increase help for poor nations indebted to international financial institutions

1999

Yes Impose steel import quotas
No   Kill proposal to take aviation trust funds off budget
No   Require background checks on buyers only at gun shows with 10 or more vendors
Yes Remove barriers among banking, securities and insurance companies
Yes Authorize state grants to hire teachers and reduce class size
Yes Overhaul campaign finance law; ban "soft money" and restrict advocacy advertising
Yes Approve bipartisan plan to increase rights of patients in managed-care health plans

INTEREST GROUPS

	AFL-CIO	ADA	CCUS	ACU
2000	70%	75%	66%	8%
1999	78%	95%	44%	4%

CQ VOTE STUDIES

	PARTY UNITY		PRESIDENTIAL SUPPORT	
	Support	Oppose	Support	Oppose
2000	89%	11%	81%	19%
1999	85%	15%	76%	24%

CALIFORNIA 1
Northern Coast — Eureka

It takes about six hours to travel the length of the 1st, a journey that starts in Solano County, about an hour drive north of San Francisco, and ends at the Oregon border in Del Norte County, one of the district's three coastal counties. In between are wineries and majestic Redwoods, which make the Northern Coast famous.

To the north, Mendocino, Humboldt and Del Norte counties have long been ground zero in the battle between environmentalists and the timber industry. East of Mendocino, Lake County's economy is a mix of ranching, farming and tourism. South of Mendocino, the 1st takes in part of Sonoma County and its wine-producing land. Neighboring Napa County is a pre-eminent wine-making region. The district's most urban region, in its far south, includes Fairfield and Vacaville.

Conflicts between economic and environmental interests – particularly off-shore drilling and preserving ancient redwoods – have made the 1st extremely competitive politically, despite a Democratic voter

registration advantage. In the 2000 presidential contest, Ralph Nader received 15 percent of the vote in Mendocino County and 13 percent in Humboldt County.

A Republican represented the 1st for most of the 1990s, but in 1998 voters went for a Democrat, who was re-elected in 2000. The district voted Democratic in presidential contests in the 1990s and 2000. The only county in the district to support President Bush in 2000 was Del Norte.

MAJOR INDUSTRY
Timber, agriculture, tourism

MILITARY BASES
Travis Air Force Base, 10,336 military, 1,110 civilian (2000)

CITIES
Fairfield (pt.), 73,787 (1990); Napa, 67,811 (1990); Vacaville (pt.), 39,926 (1990)

UNUSUAL FEATURES
Niebaum-Coppola, winery owned by film director Francis Ford Coppola.

Rep. Wally Herger (R)

Elected 1986; 8th term

CAPITOL OFFICE
225-3076; fax 225-1740; 2268 Rayburn Bldg. 20515

INTERNET
e-mail: www.house.gov/writerep
web: www.house.gov/herger

COMMITTEES
Ways & Means
 (Human Resources - chairman)

HOMETOWN
Marysville

BORN
May 20, 1945, Sutter County, Calif.

RELIGION
Mormon

FAMILY
Wife, Pamela Herger; eight children

EDUCATION
American River College, A.A. 1967; California State
U., Sacramento, attended 1969

CAREER
Rancher; gas company executive

POLITICAL HIGHLIGHTS
Calif. Assembly, 1981-87

ELECTION RESULTS

2000 GENERAL
Wally Herger (R)	168,172	65.7%
Stan Morgan (D)	72,075	28.2%
John McDermott (NL)	8,910	3.5%
Charles Martin (LIBERT)	6,699	2.6%

2000 PRIMARY (OPEN)
Wally Herger (R)	120,375	64.9%
Stan Morgan (D)	48,858	26.3%
John McDermott (NL)	11,647	6.3%
Charles Martin (LIBERT)	4,634	2.5%

1998 GENERAL
Wally Herger (R)	128,372	62.5%
Roberts A. Braden (D)	70,837	34.5%
Patrice Thiessen (NL)	6,138	3.0%

PREVIOUS WINNING PERCENTAGES
1996 (61%); 1994 (64%); 1992 (65%); 1990 (64%);
1988 (59%); 1986 (58%)

A resolutely conservative rancher and small-business man, Herger sits on a panel with great sway over fiscal policy — Ways and Means. But it is often on natural resources issues that he is most visible. One of Herger's main missions in Congress is to prevent environmentalists from encroaching on the rights of loggers, ranchers and private property owners in his Northern California district.

In the 107th Congress, Herger wields the gavel as chairman of the Ways and Means panel's Human Resources Subcommittee.

Herger's voting record is solidly in the conservative camp of House Republicans. He chafes at what he calls "more extreme elements of the environmental community," and he saw their hand in a number of Clinton administration policies that he said had a negative impact on the 2nd District. When the Clinton administration unveiled an initiative in late 1999 to ban logging and other commercial activities in more than 40 million acres of national forests, Herger accused government officials of creating "de facto" wilderness areas and jeopardizing forests as well as logging interests.

Herger grew up on his family's 200-acre cattle ranch and plum farm in Rio Oso and worked in the family's oil and gas business. He draws heavily on that background in his work on Capitol Hill.

Herger aims much of his fire at environmental regulations. After mammoth flooding and a major levee break on the Feather River north of Sacramento, Herger and fellow California Republican Richard W. Pombo sponsored legislation in the 105th Congress intended to ensure that enforcement of the Endangered Species Act would not block critical levee repairs. Herger argued that levee repairs recommended by a 1990 study had been deferred to protect the habitat of the threatened elderberry beetle.

"We're literally wasting millions of dollars in terms of environmental hoops we're jumping through," he said. His proposal was killed by moderate Republicans who sided with environmentalists on the need to stand by the Endangered Species Act, but Herger continued to warn that the law was getting in the way of saving property and even human lives.

Herger's district includes all or parts of eight national forests, and he has been an outspoken critic of Forest Service management. During the 105th, Herger contended that under President Clinton, timber sales from national forest land had become a money-losing proposition. Despite increased overhead spending, a $300 million annual profit had turned into tens of millions of dollars of annual losses, he said.

In a later interview, he added: "Because of the government bureaucracy in Washington, we are seeing our forests go unmanaged and be lost to catastrophic fires." In the 104th Congress, Herger had played a leading role when the GOP passed legislation allowing more aggressive clearing of dead and dying trees from federal lands, a policy he said would provide jobs and leave forests less vulnerable to fire.

With other House Westerners, Herger fought Clinton administration proposals to raise the fees that ranchers pay to graze their livestock on federal lands. Critics of the existing fees said they were unreasonably low, but Herger argued that what the administration "counts as reform is nothing more than a thinly veiled attempt to stop grazing on public lands."

In 1993, Herger opposed a proposal that the government conduct a National Biological Survey, an inventory of all plant and animal species in the country. He said the survey would do "nothing more than further restrict private property rights and diminish the value of lands for families that depend on natural resources for their existence." Later, he cheered on GOP efforts to gut the biological survey.

On the Ways and Means Trade Subcommittee, Herger generally is in step with the GOP leadership's support for lowering international trade barriers, noting that trade plays a big part in his district's economy. On occasion, however, he has sought to use trade as a weapon, such as his unsuccessful attempt to cut off foreign aid and trading privileges to India in protest of alleged human rights abuses against the Sikh minority in Punjab.

One of Herger's causes in the 106th Congress was to cut down on Social Security payments to prisoners in state and local jails. To build on a provision he authored in the sweeping 1996 welfare law that authorized inmates to inform on other inmates who were fraudulently collecting Social Security disability checks, Herger in 1999 won House passage of a measure to extend the program to other Social Security benefits. "Taxpayers already pay for inmates' food, clothing and shelter," Herger said. "It's unacceptable that prisoners have also been receiving fraudulent benefit checks as bonuses every month."

Herger's 1996 legislation, which authorized payments of as much as $400 to state and local prisons when they report an inmate who fraudulently receives Supplemental Security Income payments, was inspired by a sheriff in Herger's district who noted that prisoners had extra money around the first of the month to spend at the prison commissary. Regulations already outlawed prisoners from receiving such payments, but there was little enforcement.

Herger also aided efforts in the 106th to pass legislation that would reserve Social Security taxes for the Social Security trust fund, preventing their use for general spending purposes.

Herger won election to the state Assembly in 1980 and was in his third term there when GOP Rep. Gene Chappie announced his retirement from the House in 1986. Linking himself to President Reagan and California's Republican governor, George Deukmejian, Herger won the general election with 58 percent of the vote and has had little electoral difficulty since then.

Legislative work aside, Herger scored a personal best in Washington in 1997. He delivered a game-tying double in the last inning of the annual congressional baseball game. The GOP won the game, and Herger told a reporter for Roll Call newspaper: "That was one of the best feelings I've had in my life. It doesn't get any sweeter than that." But the annual baseball game can be humbling as well. In the 1999 game, Herger was best remembered for a face-planting tumble between home plate and first base as he tried to leg out a hit.

KEY VOTES

2000

No Raise hourly minimum wage by $1 over two years
? Halt funding for U.S. mission in Kosovo unless European nations pay more
Yes Provide Medicare benefits to military retirees and their dependents
Yes Grant China permanent normal trade status
Yes Phase out estate, gift and trust taxes
Yes Prohibit implementation of president's national monument designations
Yes Approve GOP plan to provide prescription drug coverage for Medicare beneficiaries
No Increase help for poor nations indebted to international financial institutions

1999

No Impose steel import quotas
Yes Kill proposal to take aviation trust funds off budget
No Require background checks on buyers only at gun shows with 10 or more vendors
Yes Remove barriers among banking, securities and insurance companies
No Authorize state grants to hire teachers and reduce class size
No Overhaul campaign finance law; ban "soft money" and restrict advocacy advertising
No Approve bipartisan plan to increase rights of patients in managed-care health plans

INTEREST GROUPS

	AFL-CIO	ADA	CCUS	ACU
2000	0%	0%	85%	95%
1999	0%	5%	88%	92%
1998	0%	0%	88%	100%
1997	0%	5%	90%	96%

CQ VOTE STUDIES

	PARTY UNITY		PRESIDENTIAL SUPPORT	
	Support	Oppose	Support	Oppose
2000	96%	4%	21%	79%
1999	97%	3%	22%	78%
1998	96%	4%	23%	77%
1997	97%	3%	28%	72%

CALIFORNIA 2
North and East – Chico; Redding

The 2nd is one of the largest districts in the state, encompassing California's northeast corner. The district borders Oregon to the north and Nevada to the east and is California's least densely populated district. Two of its counties, Sierra and Nevada, are named for the mountain range that runs through them.

Only a couple of population centers dot this timber-heavy district, which is largely white and Republican. A large, rural Mormon population in the northern part of the district helps solidify the Republican vote. Two counties, Siskiyou and Plumas, have a noticeable Democratic tilt. Redding, the largest city in the district, sits in Shasta County, about 160 miles north of Sacramento. To the south in Butte County is Chico, home to a California State University campus.

The 2nd has looked for ways to boost tourism and recreation in recent years as the major industry, timber, fell in a steady decline in the 1990s. It also had to fight to save its agriculture industry from harsh weather –

after flooding in 1997, all of the district's 10 counties were declared disaster areas.

MAJOR INDUSTRY
Timber, agriculture, tourism, health care

MILITARY BASES
Beale Air Force Base, 3,442 military, 662 civilian; Sierra Army Depot, 1 military, 500 civilian (1998)

CITIES
Redding, 79,742; Chico, 51,91; Paradise, 25,813

UNUSUAL FEATURES
Dormant Mount Shasta volcano is the southernmost peak of the Cascade Mountains; Sierra Nevada Brewing Co. in Chico; Republican presidential nominee Bob Dole fell from a stage onto a group of photographers at a rally in Chico in 1996.

Rep. Doug Ose (R)

CAPITOL OFFICE
225-5716; fax 226-1298; 215 Cannon Bldg. 20515

INTERNET
e-mail: doug.ose@mail.house.gov
web: www.house.gov/ose

COMMITTEES
Agriculture
Financial Services
Government Reform
  (Energy Policy, Natural Resources &
  Regulatory Affairs - chairman)

HOMETOWN
Sacramento

BORN
June 27, 1955, Sacramento, Calif.

RELIGION
Lutheran

FAMILY
Wife, Lynnda Ose; two children

EDUCATION
U. of California, Berkeley, B.S. 1977

CAREER
Real estate developer

POLITICAL HIGHLIGHTS
No previous office

ELECTION RESULTS

2000 GENERAL

Doug Ose (R)	129,254	56.2%
Bob Kent (D)	93,067	40.4%
Douglas Tuma (LIBERT)	5,227	2.3%
Channing Jones (NL)	2,634	1.1%

2000 PRIMARY (OPEN)

Doug Ose (R)	101,571	61.2%
Bob Kent (D)	58,250	35.1%
Douglas Tuma (LIBERT)	4,222	2.5%
Channing Jones (NL)	2,048	1.2%

1998 GENERAL

Doug Ose (R)	100,621	52.4%
Sandie Dunn (D)	86,471	45.0%
Ross Crain (LIBERT)	4,914	2.6%

Elected 1998; 2nd term

A commercial real estate developer, Ose is a pro-business, moderate Republican who emphasizes his political independence on social issues while taking a more conservative tack on taxes, spending and efforts to reduce the size of government.

During his first term, Ose (OH-see) tried to build bipartisan relationships with his colleagues on the Agriculture and Banking (now Financial Services) committees and within the California delegation. Although he did not hold elective office before coming to Washington, Ose learned about grass-roots politics by leading a successful campaign in the early 1990s to organize and incorporate a new city, Citrus Heights, in a suburban area near Sacramento.

Ose says he hopes to emulate the long service of his predecessor, Democrat Vic Fazio, who represented the district for two decades. While he did not win a long-shot bid for a spot in the 107th Congress on the Appropriations Committee, where Fazio served, Ose has been laying the groundwork to move up in the GOP ranks. Though only in his second term, Ose chairs the Government Reform panel's Energy Policy, Natural Resources and Regulatory Affairs Subcommittee.

Soon after his initial election to Congress, Ose launched a political action committee, the Sacramento Valley Leadership Fund, which aided pro-business candidates. He said he hoped his largess would assist in electing more lawmakers with business acumen while building support among Republican leaders for choice committee appointments.

Ose fits into the mainstream of his party by backing proposals to reduce government waste and cut taxes. (He is a member of a coalition of moderate Republicans known as the Republican Main Street Partnership.) He advocates elimination of the "marriage penalty," a quirk in the tax code that results in some two-earner married couples paying higher taxes than they would if each partner were single. He argues that debt reduction is needed to help promote lower interest rates.

But Ose has strayed from the GOP and sided with Democrats on some social issues, supporting abortion rights and some gun control measures, including child safety locks and instant background checks. And he has taken moderate stands on environmental issues, including backing measures to restrict mining, preserve waterways and bar clear-cutting unless new trees are planted. Such independence is key to attracting voters in a diverse district that encompasses farmland, suburbs and the environmentally conscious college town of Davis.

The plain-spoken Ose has a laid-back style and says his approach is one of consensus building. A soccer ball given to him by friends carries a stress-relieving suggestion: "Something to kick when things get tough."

In 1999, he joined with other California lawmakers to resolve a dispute between two neighboring congressmen, Republican John T. Doolittle and Democrat Robert T. Matsui, over how to protect the Sacramento area from flooding. Ose took a neutral stance initially and encouraged negotiations to work out differences. "I wanted to make sure everyone kept communicating. We needed to settle this," he said. The Californians eventually agreed on a plan to boost water diversion for farmers from two rivers, while providing funds to raise the Folsom Dam and improve levees to prevent flooding.

Ose also worked with area farmers grappling with low commodity prices, lobbying the Agriculture Department to provide aid to a farmer's cooperative in his district that had declared bankruptcy. He said it was important for

Congress to "do what is necessary with the tools already at hand" to help farmers, stopping well short of advocating new programs from his seat on the Agriculture Committee.

Citing his experience as a developer, Ose stresses the importance of increased federal spending on programs aimed at nurturing economic development. He is well-versed in the relationship between banks and local businesses and builders, and on the Financial Services Committee he is a staunch advocate of policies designed to ensure the availability of credit for small businesses and consumers. He has supported efforts to target block grants to help middle-class families buy homes.

To underscore his desire to reduce government waste, Ose cut spending in his own congressional office — he reported that he returned about $198,000 in unspent administrative funds to the Treasury in 1999. On the Government Reform Committee, he has urged agencies to conduct more audits of government contracts.

On foreign policy, Ose joined the Clinton administration in backing permanent normal trade status for China. But he took issue with U.S. policy in Kosovo: Although he supported funding for U.S. peacekeeping troops, he opposed U.S. military intervention in the region. He was part of a bipartisan group of lawmakers who visited U.S. soldiers in Kosovo and toured refugee camps in Albania in 1999.

To aid his district, Ose has backed proposals to find civilian uses for McClellan Air Force Base, which is scheduled for closure in 2001. He pushed for funding to retrain workers and supported a plan calling for the base to be redeveloped with the help of local government. And he has helped win increased federal spending for joint state and federal programs to fight drug trafficking along the Interstate 5 corridor stretching from California to the Pacific Northwest.

Ose entered politics after a long career as a builder. He gained experience in residential housing projects while working for his family's development business, and in 1985 he started his own company, specializing in storage warehouse development. Before coming to Congress, he was active in civic affairs as a member of the Citrus Heights Chamber of Commerce and Sacramento Housing and Redevelopment Commission.

When Fazio announced plans to retire, Ose jumped at the chance to succeed him. He upset a socially conservative GOP state legislator in the 1998 primary and defeated Democratic lawyer Sandie Dunn by 7 points in the general election. Ose spent $2.1 million, including $1.4 million of his own money. In 2000, he cruised to victory, defeating Bob Kent, a local businessman.

KEY VOTES

2000
No Raise hourly minimum wage by $1 over two years
Yes Halt funding for U.S. mission in Kosovo unless European nations pay more
Yes Provide Medicare benefits to military retirees and their dependents
Yes Grant China permanent normal trade status
Yes Phase out estate, gift and trust taxes
Yes Prohibit implementation of president's national monument designations
Yes Approve GOP plan to provide prescription drug coverage for Medicare beneficiaries
No Increase help for poor nations indebted to international financial institutions

1999
No Impose steel import quotas
Yes Kill proposal to take aviation trust funds off budget
No Require background checks on buyers only at gun shows with 10 or more vendors
Yes Remove barriers among banking, securities and insurance companies
No Authorize state grants to hire teachers and reduce class size
Yes Overhaul campaign finance law; ban "soft money" and restrict advocacy advertising
No Approve bipartisan plan to increase rights of patients in managed-care health plans

INTEREST GROUPS

	AFL-CIO	ADA	CCUS	ACU
2000	0%	15%	85%	76%
1999	0%	30%	92%	68%

CQ VOTE STUDIES

	PARTY UNITY		PRESIDENTIAL SUPPORT	
	Support	Oppose	Support	Oppose
2000	89%	11%	33%	67%
1999	78%	22%	37%	63%

CALIFORNIA 3
North Central Valley

The 3rd stretches from Sacramento's urban, southwestern suburbs to the spacious northern county of Tehama, serving as a bridge between the flat agricultural lands of the upper Sacramento River Valley and the state's northern, timber-rich highlands. Politically competitive, the 3rd went Republican in 1998, ending a decades-long Democratic reign. President Bush carried the district with 51 percent of the vote in 2000.

Sacramento County accounts for more than a third of the district's vote. It is the 3rd's most populous county and includes the affluent Sacramento suburbs of Citrus Heights and Rio Linda. The county is politically mixed, and residents tend to work in high-tech industries or state government. Eastern Solano and Yolo counties are more Democratic-leaning. Davis, Yolo's largest city, is home to a campus of the U. of California system.

The slated July 2001 closure of McClellan Air Force Base — formerly the second-largest Air Force community outside of San Antonio — has hurt the 3rd's economy. The area has attempted to lessen the impact by converting the base into an industrial center. North of Sacramento, agriculture drives the economy, and local issues revolve around water and flood control.

MAJOR INDUSTRY
Agriculture, computers, aerospace

MILITARY BASES
McClellan Air Force Base, 1,985 military, 7,042 civilian (1998)

CITIES
Davis, 56,336; Citrus Heights (pt.), 45,036 (1990); Woodland, 44,131; North Highlands (unincorporated) (pt.), 42,105 (1990)

UNUSUAL FEATURES
Thompson Seedless Grapes named after a Sutter County farmer who grew them in 1873; Yuba City, home to the world's largest prune-packing plant.

Rep. John T. Doolittle (R)

Elected 1990; 6th term

CAPITOL OFFICE
225-2511; fax 225-5444; 2410 Rayburn Bldg. 20515

INTERNET
e-mail: doolittle@mail.house.gov
web: www.house.gov/doolittle

COMMITTEES
Appropriations
Budget
House Administration

HOMETOWN
Rocklin

BORN
Oct. 30, 1950, Glendale, Calif.

RELIGION
Mormon

FAMILY
Wife, Julia Harlow; two children

EDUCATION
U. of California, Santa Cruz, B.A. 1972; U. of the Pacific, J.D. 1978

CAREER
Lawyer; state legislature aide

POLITICAL HIGHLIGHTS
Calif. Senate, 1981-91

ELECTION RESULTS

2000 GENERAL

John T. Doolittle (R)	197,503	63.4%
Mark Norberg (D)	97,974	31.5%
William Frey (LIBERT)	9,494	3.1%
Robert Ray (NL)	6,452	2.1%

2000 PRIMARY (OPEN)

John T. Doolittle (R)	149,735	66.2%
Mark Norberg (D)	63,130	27.9%
William Frey (LIBERT)	7,020	3.1%
Robert Ray (NL)	6,393	2.8%

1998 GENERAL

John T. Doolittle (R)	155,306	62.6%
David Shapiro (D)	85,394	34.4%
Dan Winterrowd (LIBERT)	7,524	3.0%

PREVIOUS WINNING PERCENTAGES
1996 (61%); 1994 (61%); 1992 (50%); 1990 (51%)

After a decade on Capitol Hill, Doolittle is still the impassioned conservative, pushing zealously for a diminished federal government role in people's lives. He decries what he sees as threats to personal freedom — sometimes even by some members of his own party — in the name of a well-meaning public policy goal. "Our freedom is at stake, and too many people are willing to give it away," Doolittle warns.

Doolittle is enough of an old hand to understand that things happen slowly in Washington. But that doesn't mean he likes it or is willing to adopt less-ambitious goals. He believes that conservatives should be aggressive in advancing their principles rather than passively playing defense against the barrage of "big government" proposals offered up by liberals. "When you're on the defensive, the best you can expect is keeping the status quo — and that's not nearly good enough," he argues.

Doolittle's website lays out clearly where he stands. He lists ratings of his voting record from 65 different interest groups. Doolittle scores either less than 10 percent or more than 90 percent in most of the rankings, according to the groups' political bent. He also posts a tally of the "number of people killed by their own government" and a "liberal declarations of dependence" creed written by House Republicans.

Doolittle approaches his work with the same serious-minded zeal that he evinced as a Mormon missionary in Argentina just after college, and he does not mind if he ruffles a few feathers. In his first term, as a member of the minority party, he affiliated with the "Gang of Seven," a group of GOP freshmen who forced the disclosure of the names of lawmakers who had overdrawn their accounts at the private bank for members of the House.

In 1997, Doolittle was one of a band of conservative Republicans who felt that top party leaders were giving in too readily to President Clinton, forsaking bedrock conservative principles instead of continuing to press aggressively for the GOP's "Contract With America" legislative agenda.

In an effort to hold his party's leadership to a firm conservative line on economic and social policy issues, he co-founded the Conservative Action Team, known as the CATs, a band of about 70 lawmakers that anchors the Republican Party's right wing in the House.

Doolittle says that in recent years he has come to a better understanding of the way Congress, particularly the Senate, operates. "It's frustrating. I understand that the system is certainly set up for incremental change." He says he still chafes at the pace, "but I'm not going to get frustrated and quit. It will take time, but if we don't keep pushing, it will take even longer."

He points to Republican victories in changing the welfare system and achieving a federal budget surplus. In the 106th Congress, Doolittle gained clout when he was named as a deputy whip on Speaker J. Dennis Hastert's leadership team. And in the 107th, Doolittle won a seat on the Appropriations Committee, along with assignments to the Budget and House Administration panels.

Nevertheless, on several issues dear to him, he has yet to translate his views into legislative victories. After serving his first two House terms in the minority, Doolittle brought an ambitious agenda into the GOP-controlled 104th Congress. As chairman of the Resources Committee's Water and Power Subcommittee, Doolittle promoted a pro-development agenda that often put him at loggerheads with advocates of environmental protection. he had to contend not only with Democratic opposition, but also with organized resistance from the pro-environment wing of his own party.

Despite his enhanced power as subcommittee chairman, he was unable to garner enough GOP support to achieve a sell-off of federal power agencies, to get action on a costly dam project in his district, or to overhaul the laws governing water use in the vast Sacramento Valley. Doolittle has long supported completing the huge Auburn Dam, which lies in his district.

Doolittle was raised in a conservative household in Southern California; his first taste of politics came when he was 9 and got involved, in a small way, in the Nixon-Kennedy 1960 presidential race. Four years later, Republican presidential nominee Barry Goldwater captured Doolittle's imagination. By then, the family had moved to Northern California, where "I think I was the only Goldwater supporter in my freshman class" at Cupertino High School.

For college, he chose the Santa Cruz campus of the University of California over Brigham Young University. Although Doolittle's politics would have fit in nicely at BYU, he says he's glad he went to Santa Cruz, even though he says the liberal campus was too much in tune with the "free love, lawlessness and drugs" of the era. Doolittle was one of only 15 Young Republicans at Santa Cruz, requiring him to learn how to take independent stances and think for himself. "It was a fabulous experience," he says.

Goldwater had inspired in Doolittle the desire to seek office himself, and after the two-year church mission to Argentina and law school, Doolittle took his résumé to Sacramento in search of a job with the state legislature.

He hooked up with state Sen. H.L. Richardson, who not only was an influential conservative lawmaker but also a mentor and adviser when Doolittle launched his own bid for the state Senate in 1980. Richardson convinced Doolittle to run against an entrenched Democratic incumbent, and with California favorite son Ronald Reagan heading the GOP ticket that year, Doolittle emerged with a narrow upset victory.

He quickly made himself well-known in Sacramento, particularly as a dogged proponent of expanded testing for AIDS. He was described in a McClatchy News Service article as "morally self-righteous, passionately conservative and coldly political."

In 1990, Doolittle inherited what had been a safe district for his retiring six-term predecessor, Republican Norman D. Shumway, who also had positioned himself on the GOP's right flank. Doolittle narrowly beat Democrat Patricia Malberg in 1990 and 1992.

Since then, aided by a 1992 remapping that made the district more Republican, he has coasted to re-election.

KEY VOTES

2000

No Raise hourly minimum wage by $1 over two years
Yes Halt funding for U.S. mission in Kosovo unless European nations pay more
Yes Provide Medicare benefits to military retirees and their dependents
Yes Grant China permanent normal trade status
Yes Phase out estate, gift and trust taxes
Yes Prohibit implementation of president's national monument designations
Yes Approve GOP plan to provide prescription drug coverage for Medicare beneficiaries
No Increase help for poor nations indebted to international financial institutions

1999

No Impose steel import quotas
No Kill proposal to take aviation trust funds off budget
No Require background checks on buyers only at gun shows with 10 or more vendors
Yes Remove barriers among banking, securities and insurance companies
No Authorize state grants to hire teachers and reduce class size
No Overhaul campaign finance law; ban "soft money" and restrict advocacy advertising
No Approve bipartisan plan to increase rights of patients in managed-care health plans

INTEREST GROUPS

	AFL-CIO	ADA	CCUS	ACU
2000	0%	5%	76%	88%
1999	11%	5%	80%	91%
1998	10%	5%	89%	100%
1997	0%	0%	80%	96%

CQ VOTE STUDIES

	PARTY UNITY		PRESIDENTIAL SUPPORT	
	Support	Oppose	Support	Oppose
2000	96%	4%	23%	77%
1999	93%	7%	17%	83%
1998	94%	6%	17%	83%
1997	94%	6%	25%	75%

CALIFORNIA 4

Northeast Central

The Mother Lode country, which once drew gold seekers to its mountains and rivers, now attracts those who want to leave the state's crowded cities but still work in a burgeoning high-tech economy. This is safe Republican territory, and the new arrivals have only added to the pool of GOP voters.

The 4th encompasses seven counties between Sacramento and the Nevada state line – and a small slice of northern Sacramento County – and is home to nine federally designated wilderness areas. While the southern portion remains rural, the northern, faster-growing area has become more suburban.

Seventy percent of district residents live in Placer, El Dorado and Sacramento counties, where high-tech companies are attracting transplants from the San Francisco area.

The remaining counties – Amador, Alpine, Calaveras, Tuolumne and Mono – have not fared as well, due to a slowdown in the area's natural resources-based economy.

The district also is a popular vacation destination, with numerous ski resorts dotting the Sierra Nevada mountain range, as well as Lake Tahoe in eastern El Dorado County and Yosemite National Park at the southern end of the district.

MAJOR INDUSTRY
Computers, tourism, aerospace

CITIES
Roseville, 77,048; Citrus Heights (pt.), 62,403 (1990); Folsom, 47,947; Fair Oaks (unincorporated), 26,867 (1990)

UNUSUAL FEATURES
Angels Camp in Calaveras County hosts the annual jumping frog contest made famous by Mark Twain; Squaw Valley hosted the 1960 Winter Olympics; Folsom State Prison, which was immortalized in song by Johnny Cash.

Rep. Robert T. Matsui (D)

Elected 1978; 12th term

CAPITOL OFFICE
225-7163; fax 225-0566; 2308 Rayburn Bldg. 20515

INTERNET
e-mail: www.house.gov/writerep
web: www.house.gov/matsui

COMMITTEES
Ways & Means

HOMETOWN
Sacramento

BORN
Sept. 17, 1941, Sacramento, Calif.

RELIGION
Methodist

FAMILY
Wife, Doris Matsui; one child

EDUCATION
U. of California, Berkeley, A.B. 1963; U. of
California, Hastings College of the Law, J.D. 1966

CAREER
Lawyer

POLITICAL HIGHLIGHTS
Sacramento City Council, 1971-78 (vice mayor, 1977)

ELECTION RESULTS

2000 GENERAL

Robert T. Matsui (D)	147,025	68.7%
Ken Payne (R)	55,945	26.1%
Ken Adams (GREEN)	6,195	2.9%
Cullene Lang (LIBERT)	2,919	1.4%

2000 PRIMARY (OPEN)

Robert T. Matsui (D)	112,132	70.8%
Ken Payne (R)	38,158	24.1%
Ken Adams (GREEN)	3,428	2.2%
Cullene Lang (LIBERT)	2,815	1.8%
Charles Kersey (NL)	1,838	1.2%

1998 GENERAL

Robert T. Matsui (D)	130,715	71.9%
Robert S. Dinsmore (R)	47,307	26.0%
Douglas Tuma (LIBERT)	3,746	2.1%

PREVIOUS WINNING PERCENTAGES
1996 (70%); 1994 (69%); 1992 (69%); 1990 (60%);
1988 (71%); 1986 (76%); 1984 (100%); 1982 (90%);
1980 (71%); 1978 (53%)

While the label of "pragmatist" fits Matsui, it is a bit of a simplification. He may be the most ardently pro-trade Democrat in the House, a member who works in friendly fashion with business interests as well as Republicans. But Matsui is also one of the most socially liberal members of Congress.

Matsui, who has a mild mien, comes across as knowledgeable without seeming like a know-it-all. He is as patient as he is persistent, leading not by intimidation but by listening. "Everybody has to give a little to find the center of gravity in the country," he said in 2000.

Matsui was the White House's point person in 2000 on the legislation that granted permanent normal trade status to China — perhaps the most important foreign policy question before the 106th Congress — and it was a role he accepted with some reluctance. At the start of 1999, he had given up his position as the ranking Democrat on the Ways and Means Trade Subcommittee (which he had chaired during the twilight of the Democratic majority) in favor of taking his party's top position on Ways and Means' Social Security Subcommittee. And although his new subcommittee seemed fairly quiet during the 106th, Matsui fought a constant rear-guard action against the GOP's hopes of privatizing Social Security accounts.

At the close of 2000, however, Matsui was still in the role of leading House Democratic cheerleader for the expansion of international commerce.

He had headed the effort to deliver to President Clinton the Democratic votes he needed to pass a law approving the North American Free Trade Agreement in 1993, a role he would reprise with the China trade bill seven years later. In the meantime, however, he voted against a 1998 bill to extend the president's fast-track trade negotiating authority, concluding that the GOP's decision to bring the issue to the floor as the 105th Congress wound down was a blatant attempt to embarrass Democratic opponents of the policy before the election. Matsui later said he did not want his vote on trade — or any other issue — to become predictable, which he thought would weaken his hand in bargaining on any future legislation.

By 2000, Matsui had decided that Democrats would have to line up in some numbers behind the China trade bill. Actively raising funds for other Democratic candidates, he said his party needed to show businesses that it would not work against corporate interests if it were to regain control of the House.

Matsui stepped into a leadership role on the China bill that might have belonged to Michigander Sander M. Levin, the ranking Democrat on the Trade Subcommittee. But Levin was struggling with how to address concerns from labor unions, human rights activists and others while still increasing trade with China. As a result, the daily duty of counting votes, cajoling undecided Democrats and staying in touch with Republican whips fell to Matsui, an old hand at such matters. Though he consistently maintained a patient countenance in public, he sometimes privately lamented having become so deeply involved in the issue.

Matsui says his sense of social justice stems from his incarceration as a child. At 5 months old, he was sent with his family to an internment camp with other Americans of Japanese ancestry during World War II; he lived there for more than three years. His father had been forced to give up his wholesale produce business, and his mother had nightmares about the camp until she died in 1984. At a 1998 news conference, Matsui recalled how deeply the experience was burned in his memory. When, as a child, he was asked by a schoolteacher whether he had been interned, he had denied it. "The mere fact that I was incarcerated would've raised the specter that ... perhaps I was a spy, that I was an enemy alien," Matsui said. "That still lives with me."

Matsui's mother did not live to see the enactment, in the 100th Congress, of a law to provide federal redress to the surviving Japanese-Americans who were interned. Matsui called the measure "one of the most monumental legislative feats that has occurred" in recent decades. "It is not often when a government is willing to say to its own citizens, 'We made mistakes, and we want to provide an apology and some minor token redress to you.'"

Matsui remains a committed supporter of affirmative action programs, although he says he is not certain whether his personal experience colors that point of view. "I look upon myself as a member who happens to be Japanese-American," he says.

Matsui had planned to become an architect. But he says he felt summoned to a life of public service by President Kennedy's appeal, in the early 1960s, for a new generation of leaders.

He established his political career locally, winning two elections to the Sacramento City Council. In 1972, he chaired Rep. John E. Moss Jr.'s re-election campaign. Six years later, Matsui was preparing to run for the county Board of Supervisors when Moss announced his retirement after 26 years; two other prominent Democrats also filed for the seat, but Matsui's $225,000 primary campaign budget gave him a clear advantage. The 5th District has grown more liberal as it has shrunk geographically during his tenure, and Matsui consistently draws about 70 percent of the vote. He passed up statewide races in 1988, 1990 and 1992 and now says, "I have no plans to leave the Congress."

He and Republican John T. Doolittle, who represents the neighboring 4th District, have clashed over the best approach to bolstering flood control in the Central Valley. Doolittle favors a major new Auburn Dam, while Matsui wants to upgrade Folsom Dam and raise levees along the American River. During the 106th, Matsui succeeded in pushing through legislation to protect Sacramento from a flood of a magnitude likely to occur once every 135 years, up from a once-in-95-years protection level. Describing flood control as his "legacy issue," Matsui vows to increase the protection to a once-in-200-years level.

In a move that would help the many high-tech firms in his district, Matsui during the 106th cosponsored a repeal of the century-old telephone excise tax.

KEY VOTES

2000

Yes Raise hourly minimum wage by $1 over two years
No Halt funding for U.S. mission in Kosovo unless European nations pay more
Yes Provide Medicare benefits to military retirees and their dependents
Yes Grant China permanent normal trade status
No Phase out estate, gift and trust taxes
No Prohibit implementation of president's national monument designations
No Approve GOP plan to provide prescription drug coverage for Medicare beneficiaries
Yes Increase help for poor nations indebted to international financial institutions

1999

Yes Impose steel import quotas
No Kill proposal to take aviation trust funds off budget
No Require background checks on buyers only at gun shows with 10 or more vendors
Yes Remove barriers among banking, securities and insurance companies
Yes Authorize state grants to hire teachers and reduce class size
Yes Overhaul campaign finance law; ban "soft money" and restrict advocacy advertising
Yes Approve bipartisan plan to increase rights of patients in managed-care health plans

INTEREST GROUPS

	AFL-CIO	ADA	CCUS	ACU
2000	90%	85%	47%	4%
1999	78%	100%	29%	0%
1998	90%	95%	39%	4%
1997	100%	90%	40%	20%

CQ VOTE STUDIES

	PARTY UNITY		PRESIDENTIAL SUPPORT	
	Support	Oppose	Support	Oppose
2000	97%	3%	91%	9%
1999	94%	6%	88%	12%
1998	92%	8%	82%	18%
1997	92%	8%	75%	25%

CALIFORNIA 5

Sacramento

Two things tend to dominate the 5th – state politics and triple digit temperatures that send air conditioners into overdrive. Located in California's often hot Central Valley, the 5th is home to most of the state capital, Sacramento, and reaches east and south to include a few upper middle-class suburbs, such as Arden-Arcade and Elk Grove.

Sacramento first attracted fortune seekers as the starting point of the Gold Rush of 1849 and still draws people, although these days it's for government jobs. State government is by far the largest employer. While the city's economy has improved since the recession of the early 1990s, the pace of growth lagged behind the rest of the state until recently. Several big-name technology companies are now major employers in the 5th.

Overall, Democrats hold a substantial edge in voter registration. Democrats gained strength in the 1992 redistricting when mapmakers removed some more affluent suburbs. The city itself is more diverse than neighboring communities, with significant Hispanic and Asian populations, and more likely to vote Democratic, as reflected in the makeup of the local government. In the 2000 presidential contest, Al Gore carried the district with 57 percent of the vote.

MAJOR INDUSTRY
State government, health care, finance

CITIES
Sacramento (pt.), 368,909 (1990); Arden-Arcade (unincorporated) (pt.), 67,437 (1990); Parkway-South Sacramento (unincorporated), 31,903 (1990)

UNUSUAL FEATURES
Sutter's Fort in Sacramento, where John Sutter made the discovery that started the Gold Rush of 1849; Sacramento is the oldest incorporated city in California.

Rep. Lynn Woolsey (D)

Elected 1992; 5th term

CAPITOL OFFICE
225-5161; fax 225-5163; 2263 Rayburn Bldg. 20515

INTERNET
e-mail: lynn.woolsey@mail.house.gov
web: www.house.gov/woolsey

COMMITTEES
Education & Workforce
Science

HOMETOWN
Petaluma

BORN
Nov. 3, 1937, Seattle, Wash.

RELIGION
Presbyterian

FAMILY
Divorced; four children

EDUCATION
U. of Washington, attended 1955-57; U. of San
Francisco, B.S. 1980

CAREER
Personnel service owner

POLITICAL HIGHLIGHTS
Petaluma City Council, 1985-93

ELECTION RESULTS

2000 GENERAL

Lynn Woolsey (D)	182,116	64.3%
Ken McAuliffe (R)	80,169	28.3%
Justin Moscoso (GREEN)	13,248	4.7%
Richard Barton (LIBERT)	4,691	1.7%
Alan Barreca (NL)	2,894	1.0%

2000 PRIMARY (OPEN)

Lynn Woolsey (D)	135,941	66.4%
Ken McAuliffe (R)	57,478	28.1%
Justin Moscoso (GREEN)	4,781	2.3%
Richard Barton (LIBERT)	4,043	2.0%
Alan Barreca (NL)	2,591	1.3%

1998 GENERAL

Lynn Woolsey (D)	158,446	68.0%
Ken McAuliffe (R)	69,295	29.7%
Alan Barreca (NL)	5,240	2.2%

PREVIOUS WINNING PERCENTAGES
1996 (62%); 1994 (58%); 1992 (65%)

No one as liberal as Woolsey will ever make much headway passing legislation in today's House, but in an earnest and occasionally forceful manner she raises her voice for liberal causes or to protest the Republican agenda on a range of issues. She made headlines in 2000 when she offered a measure to revoke the federal charter of the Boy Scouts of America, in protest of their decision to ban avowed homosexuals from membership. She got just 12 votes.

And in 1999, Woolsey and other Democratic congresswomen swept into a Senate Foreign Relations Committee hearing to protest the panel's inaction on a treaty. Chairman Jesse Helms, R-N.C., ordered the women to leave, complaining that they were disrupting the hearing.

On a few occasions, Woolsey has been able to line up some GOP backing for her proposals, such as a school breakfast program that became law late in the 105th Congress. She is a member of both the Education and the Workforce and the Science committees, and one of her top priorities is to expand science and technology education opportunities for women.

Woolsey and her allies on the left cringe as conservatives push for new education policies and labor law changes that are anathema to liberals. While her main focus is on education, she defends the interests of low-income people on a variety of social issues. Protesting House GOP efforts to bar the District of Columbia from providing intravenous drug users with clean needles to cut down on the spread of infectious diseases, she said in 1999: "Some on the Republican side treat D.C. like their own conservative petri dish."

Woolsey has a unique perspective on the federal safety net, since she was once a single mother on welfare. Divorced from her stockbroker husband at age 29, she had no house and no job skills. She says that she lied about her circumstances to land her first job and supported herself and three children for three years on various forms of government aid that supplemented her wages. Woolsey eventually went back to college to get her degree and started her own human resources consulting company. In 1984, she was elected to the Petaluma City Council.

She cited her insider's view of the welfare system to explain her unswerving opposition to sweeping legislation in the 104th Congress that overhauled that program by instituting work requirements and setting limits on benefits. Even after Republicans made compromises to win the reluctant support of President Clinton and many congressional Democrats, Woolsey warned her colleagues that their vote on the compromise bill was "a matter of life and death for millions and millions of children."

Woolsey has introduced legislation to expand child care services to welfare recipients. Also, she wants to alter the welfare law's definition of permissible work activity so that welfare recipients will get credit for being employed when they are working to complete their high school and college degrees.

Woolsey has been able to convince some members of the GOP to support her proposals. In the 104th Congress, she collaborated with Judiciary Committee Chairman Henry J. Hyde, R-Ill., in proposing legislation to enlist the Internal Revenue Service in efforts to track down parents who fail to make child-support payments. Similarly, on the Education panel, she attracted bipartisan backing for her proposal to expand the school breakfast program and provide more funds for after-school snack programs.

She has sided with California Republicans on local issues, such as increasing funds for Highway 101, protecting the Golden Gate Bridge from earthquake damage, and winning federal support for California agricultural products, such as wine.

But Woolsey is better known for her clashes with conservatives. In 1999, she helped lead the delegation of 10 congresswomen who went to the Senate to protest its failure to act on an international treaty against sexual discrimination. They tried to present Helms with a letter supporting the treaty during a Foreign Relations Committee hearing. Helms asked the women to "please act like ladies," then ordered Capitol police officers to escort them from the hearing room. "I'll tell you what we got," Woolsey said of the much-publicized incident. "We got his attention." But the Senate did not act on the treaty.

Woolsey's district is a liberal redoubt that includes all of Marin County and much of Sonoma County, and she has relished her role as a liberal scold. She took a dig at Speaker Newt Gingrich during the late-1995 budget standoff after he complained that Clinton had slighted him during an overseas flight on Air Force One. "Why doesn't the crybaby Speaker cry about real babies?" she asked.

And when a conservative Republican chaplain prominent in the anti-abortion movement was invited to offer the House's morning prayer, Woolsey protested. The mother of a gay man, she has criticized what she calls a "shameful, discriminatory policy toward gays in the military." Of her resolution to revoke the Boy Scouts' charter, she said, "We are not saying the Boy Scouts are bad; we are saying intolerance is bad."

Woolsey served six years on the Budget Committee, rotating off in the 106th Congress. Her last four years on the panel were under GOP control, and the minority's role was usually limited to speaking against the majority's fiscal proposals. A proponent of strong environmental protections, she has sponsored legislation to expand the protected area around the Point Reyes National Seashore, and she opposes offshore oil and gas drilling.

Her pro-labor bent often put her at odds with the Clinton administration on high-profile trade issues such as granting China permanent normal trade status.

The 6th District seat came open in 1992 when Democratic Rep. Barbara Boxer left to run for the Senate. To win the party nomination, Woolsey, who was in her eighth year on the Petaluma City Council, overcame a field of eight other Democrats, using gender as an asset and running well in her populous Sonoma County home base. She won the November election when the favorite, liberal GOP state Rep. Bill Filante, fell ill with brain cancer and could not continue. Since then, Woolsey has won re-election by healthy margins.

KEY VOTES

2000

Yes Raise hourly minimum wage by $1 over two years

Yes Halt funding for U.S. mission in Kosovo unless European nations pay more

+   Provide Medicare benefits to military retirees and their dependents

No Grant China permanent normal trade status

No Phase out estate, gift and trust taxes

No Prohibit implementation of president's national monument designations

No Approve GOP plan to provide prescription drug coverage for Medicare beneficiaries

Yes Increase help for poor nations indebted to international financial institutions

1999

Yes Impose steel import quotas

No Kill proposal to take aviation trust funds off budget

No Require background checks on buyers only at gun shows with 10 or more vendors

No Remove barriers among banking, securities and insurance companies

Yes Authorize state grants to hire teachers and reduce class size

Yes Overhaul campaign finance law; ban "soft money" and restrict advocacy advertising

Yes Approve bipartisan plan to increase rights of patients in managed-care health plans

INTEREST GROUPS

	AFL-CIO	ADA	CCUS	ACU
2000	100%	100%	40%	8%
1999	100%	95%	12%	4%
1998	100%	100%	28%	8%
1997	100%	100%	30%	0%

CQ VOTE STUDIES

	PARTY UNITY		PRESIDENTIAL SUPPORT	
	Support	Oppose	Support	Oppose
2000	98%	2%	79%	21%
1999	97%	3%	78%	22%
1998	95%	5%	85%	15%
1997	98%	2%	81%	19%

CALIFORNIA 6
Northern Bay Area; Sonoma and Marin counties

Drive north across the Golden Gate Bridge and the scenery changes from the cityscape of San Francisco to the Pacific coastline and inland hills of the 6th. This area north of the city is home to upper middle-class suburbs that seem a long way from the city, although the area has grown significantly since the bridge opened in 1937. In recent years, migration from the city has created a tight housing market.

The 6th includes all of Marin County and most of Sonoma County. Marin is home to San Quentin prison, the suburbs of Kentfield, Ross, San Anselmo and San Rafael, the largest city in the county. Some of the county's popular getaway spots include Point Reyes National Seashore, Stinson Beach and Mount Tamalpais.

To the north, Sonoma County is home to a California State University campus and Santa Rosa, the largest city in the district. Wine and dairy ranching dominate the economy here, although

high-tech companies have begun making inroads. Petaluma, with Victorian architecture left untouched by the 1906 earthquake, is near the Sonoma-Marin county line.

The 6th's affluent residents think of themselves as progressive and tolerant of diverse views. After flirting with Republicanism in the late 1970s and early '80s, the 6th turned solidly Democratic.

MAJOR INDUSTRY
Telecommunications, agriculture, tourism

CITIES
Santa Rosa (pt.), 109,826 (1990); Petaluma, 52,799; San Rafael, 51,046; Novato, 48,978; Rohnert Park, 41,082

UNUSUAL FEATURES
San Rafael home to film producer and director George Lucas' companies, Industrial Light & Magic, Lucasfilm Ltd. and Skywalker Sound; Sen. Barbara Boxer represented the 6th from 1983-93.

Rep. George Miller (D)

Elected 1974; 14th term

CAPITOL OFFICE
225-2095; fax 225-5609; 2205 Rayburn Bldg. 20515

INTERNET
e-mail: George.Miller@mail.house.gov
web: www.house.gov/georgemiller

COMMITTEES
Education & Workforce - ranking member
Resources

HOMETOWN
Martinez

BORN
May 17, 1945, Richmond, Calif.

RELIGION
Roman Catholic

FAMILY
Wife, Cynthia Miller; two children

EDUCATION
San Francisco State U., B.A. 1968; U. of California, Davis, J.D. 1972

CAREER
Lawyer; state legislature aide

POLITICAL HIGHLIGHTS
Democratic nominee for Calif. Senate, 1969

ELECTION RESULTS

2000 GENERAL

George Miller (D)	159,692	76.5%
Christopher Hoffman (R)	44,154	21.2%
Martin Sproul (NL)	4,943	2.4%

2000 PRIMARY (OPEN)

George Miller (D)	98,451	75.3%
Christopher Hoffman (R)	18,926	14.5%
Nicolas "Nick" Mraovich (R)	10,503	8.0%
Martin Sproul (NL)	2,792	2.1%

1998 GENERAL

George Miller (D)	125,842	76.7%
Norman H. Reece (R)	38,290	23.3%

PREVIOUS WINNING PERCENTAGES
1996 (72%); 1994 (70%); 1992 (70%); 1990 (61%);
1988 (68%); 1986 (67%); 1984 (66%); 1982 (67%);
1980 (63%); 1978 (63%); 1976 (75%); 1974 (56%)

A true liberal firebrand who was born into a political family and came of age — and to Congress — in the wake of Watergate, Miller has spent his career as a passionate advocate for the left and an increasingly powerful voice on the environment and education.

He routinely grabs attention and headlines with vitriolic speeches about Republican policies and priorities, but he is not one to toe the party line without question. He has been willing to break with Democratic administrations when he felt their positions strayed too far to the center, and he knows the value of working with Republicans to accomplish his goals. Still, President Bush will learn that it takes more than calling Miller "Big George" — a moniker the president came up with in meetings with key lawmakers early in his administration — to win the Californian over.

When Democrats ran the House, Miller sat at the helm of what was then called the Natural Resources Committee; he had to turn over the gavel with the GOP takeover of Congress in 1995 and assumed the post of ranking Democrat on the renamed Resources panel. In 2001, he gave up his ranking spot on Resources to become the senior Democrat on the Education and the Workforce panel. Miller says he has followed the advice of the late California Democratic Rep. Phillip Burton, who told him in 1974 as Miller was headed to the House: "You get on a committee and stay on that committee. That's how you accumulate the power to do what you want to do."

If GOP congressional control has made it difficult for Miller to translate that power into legislative victories, he has made up for it in high-profile policy brawls. For six years, he did constant battle with the equally blustery and rough-edged Resources chairman, Republican Don Young of Alaska, arguing vociferously against Young's attempts to scale back the Endangered Species Act, limit the creation of new wilderness areas, and accelerate timber harvests on federal lands. Miller also complained bitterly that Young was not moving Democrats' environmental bills, sometimes blocking non-controversial GOP measures from passage just to get that point across.

Nevertheless, with Young's term as chairman ending in late 2000, Miller showed his ability to put aside the bickering and compliment his adversary. "Under that grizzly-bear exterior is a very, very caring individual about the other members of this body," Miller said during a Resources meeting, quickly adding, "It's been a real pain in the rear because of your outlook on some of these issues."

That conciliatory tone is rarely in evidence, however. During a debate in 2000 over GOP efforts to halt Clinton administration ergonomics rules, which sought to regulate workplace conditions to avoid repetitive-stress injuries, Miller lashed out at GOP lawmakers. "Maybe the Republicans would recognize ergonomics rules if we applied them to tennis and golf," he said. He earned a place in House lore in 1995 when he and Virginia Democrat James P. Moran got into a shoving match with California Republicans Robert K. Dornan and Randy "Duke" Cunningham over a bill to bar the use of funds for deploying troops in Bosnia without prior congressional approval.

Despite his staunch liberal views, Miller has been in the business of legislating long enough to know that compromise is the price of progress, and behind closed doors he can chuck the fiery rhetoric and cut a deal. He joined his nemesis Young during the 106th Congress to push the Conservation and Reinvestment Act (CARA), which would have guaranteed that $45 billion in oil royalties be spent over 15 years for land conservation programs. The legislation ultimately stalled, but the efforts of the bipartisan coalition Miller helped assemble weren't in vain: The bill ultimately was replaced by a $12 billion, six-year conservation plan hatched by the White House and congressional appropriators, which Miller called "a magnificent start."

The debate over CARA was not the only time Miller found himself opposing the Clinton White House. In the 1999 battle over reauthorizing the Elementary and Secondary Education Act, Miller joined Republican Bill Goodling of Pennsylvania, then chairman of the Education Committee, to support a bill creating a block grant for teacher training. The White House lobbied hard against the measure, preferring to push its plan to reduce class size by hiring 100,000 new teachers. Miller said school districts should be able to use federal funds to ensure teacher quality as well as quantity.

Miller has expressed reservations about Democratic Leader Richard A. Gephardt's all-inclusive leadership style. "When you're trying to lead the opposition by consensus, there's a risk of losing the edge of your message," Miller said in the 105th Congress. And he frequently took the Clinton administration to task for doing just that. He endorsed former Sen. Bill Bradley of New Jersey over Vice President Al Gore for the Democratic nomination for president in 2000, criticizing Gore's education plans as nothing more than "a Washington-style laundry list of 30 different education proposals."

Sought out by Bush after the election as a key Democratic voice on education policy, Miller sounded a note of compromise while warning against a wholesale abandonment of liberal ideals. "We all feel that the country is not interested in any of us just being obstructionists," he told the San Francisco Chronicle, after a luncheon with Bush and other Democrats. But, he added, "we have to hold on to our principles; we have to be careful where we plant our flag. There just can't be two Republican Parties."

He is the third George Miller in his family to earn a living in government. His grandfather, George Miller Sr., was the assistant civil engineer in Richmond; his father, George Jr., was a state senator for 20 years. George Miller III was a law student when his father died. In 1969, he won the Democratic nomination to succeed his father in the state Senate but lost the election.

Miller went to work as a legislative aide to state Sen. George Moscone, the Democratic floor leader. In 1974, when Democratic Rep. Jerome Waldie decided to run for governor, Miller sought his seat in Congress. He won a tough, three-way Democratic primary. In the general election, he exploited the Watergate scandal, which was fresh in voters' minds, disclosing his campaign finances twice a month and chiding his opponent for not doing the same. He won 56 percent of the vote and has since won re-election easily.

KEY VOTES

2000

Yes Raise hourly minimum wage by $1 over two years
Yes Halt funding for U.S. mission in Kosovo unless European nations pay more
Yes Provide Medicare benefits to military retirees and their dependents
No   Grant China permanent normal trade status
No   Phase out estate, gift and trust taxes
No   Prohibit implementation of president's national monument designations
No   Approve GOP plan to provide prescription drug coverage for Medicare beneficiaries
Yes Increase help for poor nations indebted to international financial institutions

1999

Yes Impose steel import quotas
Yes Kill proposal to take aviation trust funds off budget
No   Require background checks on buyers only at gun shows with 10 or more vendors
No   Remove barriers among banking, securities and insurance companies
Yes Authorize state grants to hire teachers and reduce class size
Yes Overhaul campaign finance law; ban "soft money" and restrict advocacy advertising
Yes Approve bipartisan plan to increase rights of patients in managed-care health plans

INTEREST GROUPS

	AFL-CIO	ADA	CCUS	ACU
2000	100%	95%	38%	12%
1999	89%	100%	4%	8%
1998	100%	100%	19%	8%
1997	100%	95%	11%	4%

CQ VOTE STUDIES

	PARTY UNITY		PRESIDENTIAL SUPPORT	
	Support	Oppose	Support	Oppose
2000	96%	4%	76%	24%
1999	93%	7%	74%	26%
1998	97%	3%	84%	16%
1997	97%	3%	80%	20%

CALIFORNIA 7
Northeastern Bay Area

Situated along the San Pablo Bay and home to extensive marshes and wetlands where the Sacramento and San Joaquin Deltas feed into the bay, the 7th combines industrial and suburban areas of Contra Costa County with the southern third of the more rural Solano County.

In Contra Costa County, the district takes in middle-class Concord and the industrial cities of Richmond and Martinez along San Pablo Bay, home to oil terminals and factories. Richmond was home to one of the largest World War II shipbuilding operations.

Vallejo, the largest city in Solano County, was the site of Mare Island Naval Shipyard, which employed about 15,000 people and closed in the mid-1990s after 140 years of operation. The city converted the island to private-sector business property. Vallejo and other Solano County communities, traditionally Democratic, also are home to farm-support services and industry.

Democrats were put in a stronger position in 1992 after redistricting moved some of the more Republican-leaning suburbs south and east of Concord to the neighboring 10th District. With the GOP areas gone, the 7th is a safe Democratic seat.

MAJOR INDUSTRY
Petrochemicals, agriculture, health care

MILITARY BASES
Seal Beach Naval Weapons Station Detachment, 200 military, 500 civilian (2001)

CITIES
Vallejo, 114,204; Concord (pt.), 98,608 (1990); Richmond (pt.), 86,780 (1990); Pittsburg (pt.), 47,559 (1990)

UNUSUAL FEATURES
The forerunner to the Martini, the "Martinez Special," became popular in the city of Martinez during the Gold Rush; Actor Tom Hanks born in Concord; Vallejo twice served as state capital in the 1850s.

Rep. Nancy Pelosi (D)

Elected June 1987; 7th full term

CAPITOL OFFICE
225-4965; fax 225-8259; 2457 Rayburn Bldg. 20515

INTERNET
e-mail: sf.nancy@mail.house.gov
web: www.house.gov/pelosi

COMMITTEES
Appropriations
Select Intelligence - ranking member

HOMETOWN
San Francisco

BORN
March 26, 1940, Baltimore, Md.

RELIGION
Roman Catholic

FAMILY
Husband, Paul Pelosi; five children

EDUCATION
Trinity College, A.B. 1962

CAREER
Public relations consultant

POLITICAL HIGHLIGHTS
Calif. Democratic Party chairman, 1981-83

ELECTION RESULTS

2000 GENERAL

Nancy Pelosi (D)	181,847	84.4%
Adam Sparks (R)	25,298	11.7%
Erik Bauman (LIBERT)	5,645	2.6%
David Smithstein (NL)	2,638	1.2%

2000 PRIMARY (OPEN)

Nancy Pelosi (D)	109,246	85.5%
Adam Sparks (R)	13,501	10.6%
Erik Bauman (LIBERT)	3,575	2.8%
David Smithstein (NL)	1,389	1.1%

1998 GENERAL

Nancy Pelosi (D)	148,027	85.8%
David Martz (R)	20,781	12.0%
David Smithstein (NL)	3,654	2.1%

PREVIOUS WINNING PERCENTAGES
1996 (84%); 1994 (82%); 1992 (83%); 1990 (77%);
1988 (76%); 1987 Special Runoff Election (63%);
1987 Special Election (36%)

As one of the most liberal members, Pelosi has long fought losing battles on a range of issues, including education, abortion, health care and crime. But she perseveres, returning each year with undiminished enthusiasm to fight for the same causes — human rights abroad and social programs at home, with particular attention to the needs of San Francisco's large homosexual population. She wages the battles with such grace and seriousness of purpose that even her foes think kindly of her.

Pelosi (pa-LOH-see) takes solace in a number of quiet successes, and she maintains that her long fight for a tougher trade stance against China, while ultimately unsuccessful, helped focus the international spotlight on that nation's human rights and trade practices. Pelosi — whose San Francisco district includes thousands of Chinese-Americans — argued that Congress should condition normal trade relations with China on "significant progress" in human rights there, such as releasing political prisoners and halting the use of prison laborers to make goods for export to the United States.

When the House voted in 2000 to grant China permanent normal trade status, Pelosi struck back at both her colleagues and President Clinton, who pushed for the change. "The burden is now on members of Congress who voted for this legislation and on the president of the United States to produce some results," she said.

Despite her differences with Clinton on China policy, Pelosi has been a loyal and successful fundraiser for the Democratic Party, raking in more than $3 million for Democratic candidates in the 2000 elections. She is credited with helping the party pick up five seats. Her name was mentioned when Democrats chose a new leader of their campaign arm, the Democratic Congressional Campaign Committee, at the start of the 107th Congress — a post that eventually went to Nita M. Lowey of New York.

In the 106th Congress, Pelosi and Steny H. Hoyer of Maryland each waged a campaign to become Democratic whip in the event the Democrats won control of the House in 2000 and a leadership position came open. The jockeying between Pelosi and Hoyer continued in the 107th amid rumors that the current whip, David E. Bonior of Michigan, might leave to run for governor.

In the 107th, Pelosi landed an assignment as the ranking Democrat on the Intelligence Committee, replacing Julian C. Dixon of California, who died late in 2000. To assume the ranking role on Intelligence, she had to take a leave of absence from her post as the top Democrat on the Foreign Operations Appropriations Subcommittee.

Since the 102nd Congress, Pelosi has been on the Appropriations Committee, which has given her a venue to secure funding for AIDS and breast cancer research, housing for people with AIDS, repair and maintenance work at the Presidio (a former San Francisco Army base that was turned over to the National Park Service in 1996 after a long legislative struggle), and an expansion of the Bay Area's subway system to the San Francisco airport. In June 2000, for example, Pelosi announced a $63.7 million grant from the Federal Transit Administration to help fund the system, dubbed BART, for Bay Area Rapid Transit.

AIDS issues — funding for research to find a cure and money for treatment and support for patients — have long been a priority. In the 105th Congress, she was outraged when the House voted to prohibit the use of federal funds to support needle-exchange programs, which offer clean needles to drug users in an effort to stop the spread of the HIV virus that causes AIDS. Backers of the prohibition argued that the program condoned illegal drug use, but Pelosi argued that it was successful in reducing HIV transmission. She fought, ultimately with success, to prevent Congress from withholding about $67 million from San Francisco because it had passed an ordinance requiring city contractors to offer benefits to their workers' unmarried partners.

She has signaled she will be a strong opponent of President Bush on abortion rights. At a retreat of House Democrats early in 2001, she challenged the president's decision to issue an executive order prohibiting international family planning groups from receiving U.S. aid if they promote or perform abortions, even with their own money. Pelosi said Bush was using a "double standard," because at the same time, he was pushing an initiative to funnel federal funding to faith-based organizations for social services.

Pelosi's political education began early: Her father, Thomas J. D'Alesandro Jr., was a member of the House when she was born in 1940 and, after serving four terms, he went on to become mayor of Baltimore for 12 years. Pelosi, who moved to California, married, and raised five children, became a Democratic Party activist, work that led her to seek public office.

She made her first bid for the House in 1987, running in the special election to succeed Democratic Rep. Sala Burton, who died that February. At the time, Pelosi was more familiar to national Democratic activists than to San Francisco voters. She was a member of the Democratic National Committee and chaired the state party, helping to lure the 1984 Democratic National Convention to San Francisco.

In the campaign, Pelosi was backed by much of the city and state party establishment and carried the endorsement of Burton, offered just a few days before she died. That support was crucial because the district had long been dominated by the organization loyal to Sala Burton and her late husband, Rep. Phillip Burton.

Pelosi's last real hurdle was a vigorous challenge from San Francisco Supervisor Harry Britt, a Democrat and a leading homosexual politician. In a district where the gay vote was roughly 15 percent of the electorate, Britt started with a large base. He also aimed his campaign at a wider audience, citing his efforts on rent control and his opposition to new real estate development.

Pelosi ultimately defeated Britt and easily prevailed over her Republican opponent in June. Since then, she has had easy re-elections in the heavily Democratic district.

KEY VOTES

2000
Yes Raise hourly minimum wage by $1 over two years
Yes Halt funding for U.S. mission in Kosovo unless European nations pay more
Yes Provide Medicare benefits to military retirees and their dependents
No Grant China permanent normal trade status
No Phase out estate, gift and trust taxes
No Prohibit implementation of president's national monument designations
No Approve GOP plan to provide prescription drug coverage for Medicare beneficiaries
Yes Increase help for poor nations indebted to international financial institutions

1999
Yes Impose steel import quotas
Yes Kill proposal to take aviation trust funds off budget
No Require background checks on buyers only at gun shows with 10 or more vendors
? Remove barriers among banking, securities and insurance companies
Yes Authorize state grants to hire teachers and reduce class size
Yes Overhaul campaign finance law; ban "soft money" and restrict advocacy advertising
Yes Approve bipartisan plan to increase rights of patients in managed-care health plans

INTEREST GROUPS

	AFL-CIO	ADA	CCUS	ACU
2000	100%	100%	42%	8%
1999	88%	95%	12%	0%
1998	100%	95%	33%	12%
1997	100%	100%	20%	4%

CQ VOTE STUDIES

	PARTY UNITY		PRESIDENTIAL SUPPORT	
	Support	Oppose	Support	Oppose
2000	96%	4%	79%	21%
1999	96%	4%	81%	19%
1998	97%	3%	84%	16%
1997	96%	4%	81%	19%

CALIFORNIA 8
San Francisco

Since the Gold Rush in the mid-19th century, San Francisco has attracted visitors, new residents and fortune-seekers from around the globe. "The City," as its known to natives, is famous for its landmarks, food and a diverse collection of neighborhoods, from the Italian and Hispanic centers of North Beach and the Mission District to Chinatown.

More than 75 percent of the city's residents live within the 8th. Redistricting in 1992 enlarged the district's share of the city by 50,000 people, while placing neighborhoods south of Golden Gate Park and west of Twin Peaks into the adjacent 12th District.

The first city in California to elect an openly gay official (he and the mayor were killed by a city supervisor in 1978, opening the way for current Sen. Dianne Feinstein to become mayor), the 8th is safe Democratic territory. A center for protest during the Vietnam War, the city also forbade police from arresting illegal immigrants fleeing

Central American bloodshed in the 1980s, in opposition to federal immigration officials. More recently, the city has helped fund the largest needle exchange program in the nation and has voiced support for medical marijuana.

MAJOR INDUSTRY
Tourism, financial services, health care

CITIES
San Francisco (pt.), 573,192 (1990)

UNUSUAL FEATURES
San Francisco was home to the nation's only declared monarch, Norton I, who named himself Emperor of the United States and Protector of Mexico in 1859; Throughout his "reign," Norton issued various proclamations, including an order that a bridge be constructed between San Francisco and Oakland — more than 50 years before the actual construction of the Bay Bridge.

Rep. Barbara Lee (D)

Elected April 1998; 2nd full term

CAPITOL OFFICE
225-2661; fax 225-9817; 426 Cannon Bldg. 20515

INTERNET
e-mail: Barbara.Lee@mail.house.gov
web: www.house.gov/lee

COMMITTEES
Financial Services
International Relations

HOMETOWN
Oakland

BORN
July 16, 1946, El Paso, Texas

RELIGION
Baptist

FAMILY
Husband, Michael Millben; two children

EDUCATION
Mills College, B.A. 1973; U. of California, Berkeley, M.S.W. 1975

CAREER
Congressional aide

POLITICAL HIGHLIGHTS
Calif. Assembly, 1991-97; Calif. Senate, 1997-98

ELECTION RESULTS

2000 GENERAL

Barbara Lee (D)	182,352	85.0%
Arneze Washington (R)	21,033	9.8%
Fred Foldvary (LIBERT)	7,051	3.3%
Ellen Jefferds (NL)	4,214	2.0%

2000 PRIMARY (OPEN)

Barbara Lee (D)	117,173	85.1%
Arneze Washington (R)	13,563	9.9%
Fred Foldvary (LIBERT)	4,565	3.3%
Ellen Jefferds (NL)	2,333	1.7%

1998 GENERAL

Barbara Lee (D)	140,722	82.8%
Claiborne "Clay" Sanders (R)	22,431	13.2%
Gerald Sanders (PFP)	4,767	2.8%
Walter Ruehlig (NL)	1,975	1.2%

PREVIOUS WINNING PERCENTAGES
1998 Special Election (67%)

Lee's voting record shows her to be one of the most liberal members of Congress, and her priorities mesh with the economic, health care and education needs of her liberal and racially diverse constituents in Oakland and Berkeley. Some of the needs are urgent, she argues, such as recognizing the devastation AIDS has wrought on the African-American community in her district.

But she is also a throwback to an earlier era in Congress, when most newcomers to the House quietly focused on learning the ropes — attending committee meetings, casting floor votes, seldom speaking out and, above all, practicing patience. She promised her constituents in 1998 that she would "be a long-distance runner for economic, social and political justice."

When she arrived on Capitol Hill in April 1998, chosen in a special election to succeed the legendary Ronald V. Dellums, a Democrat, Lee's style was in great contrast to that of her predecessor, who came to Washington almost three decades earlier bristling with impatience and raring to stir things up. With a full term under her belt, Lee is not so much a newcomer any more, and she has gone about building a name for herself as comparisons with Dellums, her mentor and former boss, are made less frequently.

But her "long-distance runner" promise is still apt. "I understand that oftentimes the legislative process is slow and cumbersome. Yet, if you have a vision and strong beliefs that you can make this a better world as a member of Congress, you must be willing to hang in there for the long haul," she says.

Employing a straightforward, conversational speaking style, she argues for affirmative action and needle-exchange programs, as well as child care and economic development in poor neighborhoods. She is vice chairwoman of the Progressive Caucus, the most liberal faction of House Democrats.

Lee has been outspoken on a number of issues — the AIDS crisis, both domestic and in Africa; U.S.-Cuba relations; and U.S. military involvement abroad — and she says that confrontational tactics are sometimes called for, such as when she joined other female lawmakers in 1999 in barging into a Senate Foreign Relations Committee hearing to demand that Chairman Jesse Helms, R-N.C., permit action on an international treaty against sexual discrimination.

But she says she must act like a "legislator" when appropriate: "My paradigm is to blend confrontational tactics to confront injustice head-on and to use legislation whenever possible to solve the less-pressing problems."

Lee serves on the Financial Services and International Relations committees, and she focuses much of her efforts on matters of interest to those panels. In the 106th Congress, she voted against legislation to overhaul the financial services industry, in part because the bill did not include her amendment, narrowly approved by the Banking panel (as Financial Services was known then), to bar insurance companies from "redlining" — refusing to sell insurance in certain geographic areas.

As the House considered legislation to overhaul the bankruptcy code, Lee blasted credit card companies for "targeting vulnerable potential new customers," many of whom quickly built up charges far beyond their ability to pay.

In 1999, Lee was the only member of the House to vote against a resolution of support for U.S. troops involved in military operations against Yugoslavia, saying that she deplored U.S.-led air strikes on Yugoslavia. "It is my strong conviction that bombing is the crudest of military instruments, a tactic that has caused and will continue to cause innocent civilian deaths."

Lee urged Alameda County officials to declare a state of emergency in the battle against AIDS, and she authored legislation to greatly increase U.S. support for combating the disease through an "AIDS Marshall Plan for Africa" — an idea championed by Dellums before he left Congress. She also wants to increase U.S. trade ties with Africa, an issue she has been working on since her days in the California Legislature. However, in 2000, she was one of only five black lawmakers to vote against a bill to lift trade restrictions between sub-Saharan Africa and the United States, arguing that the measure did not go far enough in dealing with long-range solutions to African economic development and did not address such issues as workers' rights and the environment.

Lee shares many of Dellums' priorities — not surprising because she was a key Dellums staffer for 12 years and promised in her 1998 special election campaign to "carry the baton" handed to her by Dellums.

Lee's politics are shaped by early-life recollections of discrimination. Her mother initially was refused treatment at an El Paso hospital when in labor with her. She attended a segregated school, and later, she says, a riot was touched off when she was chosen the first black cheerleader at her high school in Southern California. She says that many of her experiences with discrimination "are relatively common with the general experiences of blacks of my generation" — experiences that she says "have shaped my life and fueled my disdain for injustices."

Lee's introduction to politics came as a student at Oakland's Mills College, where she majored in psychology. She had never even registered to vote when she was faced with a course requirement to work for a political campaign during the presidential election year of 1972. She signed on with Democratic Rep. Shirley Chisholm of New York, the nation's first notable black candidate for president. Lee rose quickly through the ranks, eventually running Chisholm's Northern California campaign and, as she proudly recalled a quarter-century later, receiving an "A" in the course.

Lee went on to earn a master's degree in social work at the University of California at Berkeley (as had Dellums) and was a co-founder of a community health center in Berkeley before going to work for Dellums in 1975. She worked for him in both California and Washington, D.C., before running for the California Legislature, where she served six years in the Assembly and one year in the Senate.

When Dellums revealed his plans to resign from the House in early 1998, he endorsed Lee to succeed him. She easily won the special election and has cruised to re-election since then in the heavily Democratic district.

KEY VOTES

2000

Yes   Raise hourly minimum wage by $1 over two years

Yes   Halt funding for U.S. mission in Kosovo unless European nations pay more

Yes   Provide Medicare benefits to military retirees and their dependents

No   Grant China permanent normal trade status

No   Phase out estate, gift and trust taxes

No   Prohibit implementation of president's national monument designations

No   Approve GOP plan to provide prescription drug coverage for Medicare beneficiaries

Yes   Increase help for poor nations indebted to international financial institutions

1999

Yes   Impose steel import quotas

No   Kill proposal to take aviation trust funds off budget

No   Require background checks on buyers only at gun shows with 10 or more vendors

No   Remove barriers among banking, securities and insurance companies

Yes   Authorize state grants to hire teachers and reduce class size

Yes   Overhaul campaign finance law; ban "soft money" and restrict advocacy advertising

Yes   Approve bipartisan plan to increase rights of patients in managed-care health plans

INTEREST GROUPS

	AFL-CIO	ADA	CCUS	ACU
2000	100%	90%	33%	4%
1999	100%	100%	16%	8%
1998	100%	75%	14%	5%

CQ VOTE STUDIES

	PARTY UNITY		PRESIDENTIAL SUPPORT	
	Support	Oppose	Support	Oppose
2000	97%	3%	82%	18%
1999	94%	6%	76%	24%
1998	99%	1%	85%	15%

CALIFORNIA 9
Alameda County — Oakland; Berkeley

Across the Bay from San Francisco, the 9th is anchored by two racially diverse and liberal communities, Oakland and Berkeley, that gained national attention for their political activism in the 1960s.

Most district residents live in Oakland, which is 43 percent black. The city's unemployment rate is slightly above the national average, but revitalization efforts have kept the area in good health, despite the closing of several military facilities. In the city's eastern hills, the neighborhoods tend to be wealthy and less diverse. Tension between blacks and police gave birth to the Black Panther Party in 1966.

Just north of Oakland, Berkeley, home to the flagship campus of the University of California system, looks out over the Bay from the Berkeley Hills. Home to student protests in the 1960s, Berkeley still looks much the way it did then. The remainder of the district includes smaller communities such as Alameda, an industrial port

city, and Albany, a suburb at the north end of the district.

With a core constituency in the left-leaning cities of Oakland and Berkeley, the 9th is a Democratic stronghold. Republicans account for only 12 percent of registered voters.

MAJOR INDUSTRY
Biotechnology, shipping

CITIES
Oakland (pt.), 361,584 (1990); Berkeley, 108,319; Alameda (pt.), 76,457 (1990)

UNUSUAL FEATURES
Author Jack London lived in Oakland for nearly 20 years, ran for mayor twice, and the cabin he lived in during the Yukon Gold Rush of 1897 was moved to Jack London Square, a waterfront shopping center in Oakland, in 1970; West Oakland train station – a terminus for the Transcontinental Railroad – was home to the Union of Sleeping Car Porters, the first integrated union in the country.

Rep. Ellen O. Tauscher (D)

Elected 1996; 3rd term

CAPITOL OFFICE
225-1880; fax 225-5914;
1122 Longworth Bldg. 20515

INTERNET
e-mail: ellen.tauscher@mail.house.gov
web: www.house.gov/tauscher

COMMITTEES
Armed Services
Transportation & Infrastructure

HOMETOWN
Pleasanton

BORN
Nov. 15, 1951, Newark, N.J.

RELIGION
Roman Catholic

FAMILY
Divorced; one child

EDUCATION
Seton Hall U., B.A. 1974

CAREER
Child care screening executive; marketing
executive; investment banker

POLITICAL HIGHLIGHTS
No previous office

ELECTION RESULTS

2000 GENERAL

Ellen O. Tauscher (D)	160,429	52.6%
Claude B. Hutchison Jr. (R)	134,863	44.2%
Valerie Janlois (NL)	9,527	3.1%

2000 PRIMARY (OPEN)

Ellen O. Tauscher (D)	110,702	54.3%
Claude B. Hutchison Jr. (R)	36,257	17.8%
Gordon Thomas Blake (R)	30,532	15.0%
Dennis Kilian (R)	21,039	10.3%
Valerie Janlois (NL)	5,324	2.6%

1998 GENERAL

Ellen O. Tauscher (D)	127,134	53.5%
Charles Ball (R)	103,299	43.4%
Valerie Janlois (NL)	3,941	1.7%
John Place (REF)	3,435	1.4%

PREVIOUS WINNING PERCENTAGES
1996 (49%)

A pro-business Democrat, Tauscher calls herself a centrist. She tends diligently to the needs of her affluent commuter district, which is the most Republican district in the Bay Area.

A successful businesswoman with an eye for the bottom line, Tauscher will tax and spend carefully while investing in programs for the young, the old and the poor. She breaks with labor unions over the issue of expanding international trade, and she battles her own party over providing tax cuts. In wresting the 10th District from GOP control in 1996, Tauscher broadened the definition of the term "Bay Area Democrat," which in the minds of many had been equivalent to "liberal."

Tauscher (rhymes with how-sher) founded three companies that register and screen child care providers, and in 1996 she published a child care reference guide. Earlier, she was one of the first women to hold a seat on the New York Stock Exchange. "Because of my business background, I understand the art of the deal," she said. "Compromise is not a dirty word."

When Tauscher arrived in Washington, she was immediately recruited to join the "Blue Dogs," a coalition of conservative Democrats hailing mainly from the South and West that favors conservative fiscal policies. She also has been active in an organization of centrist House Democrats — the New Democrat Coalition. Early in 2001, she was named national vice chairwoman of the Democratic Leadership Council, the nationwide policy organization that includes New Democrats both in and out of Congress.

In the 106th Congress, party leaders named Tauscher one of three co-chairmen of the Democratic Congressional Campaign Committee, the fundraising arm for House Democrats, to serve under Chairman Patrick J. Kennedy. Her name was mentioned in the 107th Congress as House Democrats sought a successor for Kennedy, who relinquished the post. But the job eventually went to Nita M. Lowey of New York.

Tauscher is a strong advocate of cutting taxes, particularly the estate tax, which affects many in her district who profit from soaring home prices and stock portfolios. She voted to override President Clinton's veto of an estate tax repeal in 2000 and also pressed for other tax reductions, such as cutting capital gains taxes and eliminating the "marriage penalty," a quirk in the tax code that results in some two-earner married couples paying higher income taxes than they would if each partner were single. In 1998, she was one of just 19 Democrats who voted for an $80 billion GOP tax cut plan.

But she balked at a Republican effort in the 106th to cut taxes by $792 billion. "Everybody wants tax cuts," she said. "The difference is that some of us want tax cuts that are irresponsible and will wreak havoc upon the economy ... and some of us know that we still have a little spinach to eat before we go crazy at the dessert cart," the San Francisco Chronicle reported.

Tauscher has pursued fiscally conservative policies since arriving in Congress. One of her first acts was to cosponsor the balanced-budget constitutional amendment, and she joined her Blue Dog colleagues in lending early moral support to efforts by Clinton and congressional Republicans to work out a balanced-budget agreement.

She does not hesitate, however, to press for more federal funds for her district, such as a $199 million funding package for Lawrence Livermore National Laboratory's superlaser project and more than $75 million for Bay Area coastal habitats. The strong high-technology presence in her district has led her to take the lead on such initiatives as pressing the Clinton administration to lift export restrictions on encryption technology, used to scramble telephone calls and online communications. In 2000, Tauscher sided with businesses and voted to grant China permanent normal trade status. "I know that we grow jobs when we export," she said.

She also looks out for her constituents' interests on the Transportation Committee. In the 105th Congress, she was able to secure $31 million for a variety of East Bay highway and transit projects as part of a major transportation authorization bill. In the 106th, she pressed to speed up the federal permit process so new transportation projects could be built more quickly.

Tauscher also emerged as an important voice on energy policy after being chosen as the top Democrat on a panel overseeing the Department of Energy (DOE) reorganization. The shake-up, spurred by concerns over agency mismanagement and security lapses, is an important issue in the 10th District, home to two DOE weapons laboratories. "We are there to make sure that it [the reorganization] not only happens the way we want it to, but that it happens on time," Tauscher said, according to Knight-Ridder. Also, early in the 107th, with California suffering electricity shortages and high prices, she joined with several other California Democrats to propose temporary federal caps on energy prices.

On most issues in the social policy arena, Tauscher is a traditional Democrat, favoring abortion rights, robust environmental protections, federal arts funding and active federal involvement in improving education. An advocate of gun control, she is nevertheless willing to compromise on the issue, and in 1999, she said she would vote for a scaled-back gun control bill if that were the only alternative. "I want to move the ball forward, whether that's inches or whether we get the score," she told the Los Angeles Times. "Ultimately, my job is to get things done."

The 10th District had been represented by Republican Bill Baker since 1992. But by 1996, Baker had taken a hard enough line against abortion and for gun owners' rights that he had alienated a portion of district voters, and Tauscher took aim at his seat. Baker became a national target of Democrats, who argued in ads that his conservative views were out of line with the district. Tauscher gave herself a decisive advantage, contributing $1.7 million of her own money to her campaign and outspending her opponent by almost 2-to-1. By warning that GOP policies would harm senior citizens, students and others of modest means, Tauscher edged Baker by less than 2 percentage points. In 1998, she easily outdistanced a political novice, Charles Ball. She won another competitive race in 2000, fending off an aggressive challenge from GOP banker Claude B. Hutchison Jr.

KEY VOTES

2000

Yes Raise hourly minimum wage by $1 over two years

No Halt funding for U.S. mission in Kosovo unless European nations pay more

Yes Provide Medicare benefits to military retirees and their dependents

Yes Grant China permanent normal trade status

Yes Phase out estate, gift and trust taxes

No Prohibit implementation of president's national monument designations

No Approve GOP plan to provide prescription drug coverage for Medicare beneficiaries

Yes Increase help for poor nations indebted to international financial institutions

1999

Yes Impose steel import quotas

No Kill proposal to take aviation trust funds off budget

No Require background checks on buyers only at gun shows with 10 or more vendors

Yes Remove barriers among banking, securities and insurance companies

Yes Authorize state grants to hire teachers and reduce class size

Yes Overhaul campaign finance law; ban "soft money" and restrict advocacy advertising

Yes Approve bipartisan plan to increase rights of patients in managed-care health plans

INTEREST GROUPS

	AFL-CIO	ADA	CCUS	ACU
2000	50%	70%	71%	20%
1999	67%	100%	68%	8%
1998	60%	75%	72%	12%
1997	88%	85%	50%	20%

CQ VOTE STUDIES

	PARTY UNITY		PRESIDENTIAL SUPPORT	
	Support	Oppose	Support	Oppose
2000	85%	15%	78%	22%
1999	84%	16%	77%	23%
1998	81%	19%	77%	23%
1997	87%	13%	80%	20%

CALIFORNIA 10
Eastern Contra Costa and Alameda counties

Anyone driving through the Caldecott Tunnel or on Interstate 680 during rush hour will probably be surrounded by 10th District residents on their way to and from work in San Francisco or San Jose. Separated from the rest of the Bay Area by the hills east of Oakland, the 10th's residents are mainly well-educated, well-paid professionals who work outside the district.

The landscape features hills and hidden valleys, and the long dry months leave the slopes golden brown. More than two-thirds of the district's residents live in Contra Costa County (although the 10th excludes most of Concord and all of Richmond, the county's two largest cities), and the rest live in Alameda County. The 10th has managed to fend off overdevelopment while keeping pace with the rest of the area economically, giving it a feel significantly different from its more urban neighbors to the west. But the area is at a point where choices will have to be made regarding the future of development.

Despite its Democratic representative, voter registration is almost evenly split and the 10th is the most Republican district in the Bay Area. Some of the residents here represent white flight from Oakland that is now generations old. But many of the newer commuters are younger and may still identify with San Francisco or Berkeley. The district retains a moderate political character – residents tend to be conscious of pocketbook issues but also share their Bay Area neighbor's views on the environment and other quality of life issues.

MAJOR INDUSTRY
Research, utilities, health care

CITIES
Antioch, 84,040; Livermore, 75,515; Pleasanton, 66,482; Walnut Creek, 65,401

UNUSUAL FEATURES
Lawrence Livermore National Laboratory, one of the country's leading centers of experimental physics research and defense analysis.

Rep. Richard W. Pombo (R)

Elected 1992; 5th term

A fourth-generation rancher with a deep-seated suspicion of the federal government, Pombo is in the front ranks of Western House Republicans who want dramatic change in federal environmental regulations, which they say infringe too much on private property rights. He is a forthright and persistent advocate for such conservative causes as "regulatory relief" and tax cuts, and he cuts a noticeable figure in the oversize cowboy hat and boots he sports with his dark suits.

When the Republicans took control of the House in 1995, Pombo, even though he had just two years' experience, was given a key role in their efforts to scale back federal environmental regulations. Successes were few and far between; contributing to the difficulty was the fact that Pombo and fellow Republican Sherwood Boehlert of New York — the co-chairmen of a GOP environmental task force — clashed often and were unable to bridge the gap between the environmental views of Western and Eastern Republicans.

Now older and wiser in the ways of legislating, Pombo says he and his conservative GOP allies are focusing on legislation that is "more targeted, a lot simpler, and we're doing a lot more groundwork than we were doing."

When he fails in legislative efforts, Pombo is willing to battle the government in court: He joined, for example, in an unsuccessful lawsuit against the Clinton administration for its plan to designate certain waterways as American Heritage Rivers. Pombo argued that the program, which singled out rivers for cleanup and preservation or expansion of their waterfronts, was another attempt by the federal government to usurp local control over land use.

He made his feelings about the environmental movement clear when, in 1996, he co-authored "This Land Is Our Land," a book that warned of an "eco-federal coalition" of government regulators and environmental groups with an agenda "that owes more to communism than to any other philosophy."

Pombo is the grandson of a Portuguese immigrant who came to the Central Valley early in the 20th century. The huge Pombo clan is well-known in the area, and one longtime neighbor told the San Francisco Examiner that he remembers young Richard as a "clean-cut young man from a strict family."

Pombo had served only two years on the Tracy City Council when he was convinced to run for the House in 1992 in the newly drawn 11th District. He was a big underdog in the primary against Sacramento County Supervisor Sandra Smoley. He won by branding her a liberal, then fended off negative ads in the general election by saying he was a rancher out to defend his neighbors rather than an ambitious politician. Pombo prevailed by 2 percentage points and has since won re-election comfortably.

Pombo serves on the Agriculture Committee, which is of great importance to his heavily agricultural Central Valley district. He chairs its Livestock and Horticulture Subcommittee, which puts him at the center of regional battles over dairy subsidies.

In the 106th Congress, Pombo took the lead in efforts to slow the Environmental Protection Agency's move to ban the use of some common pesticides. He sponsored a bill, backed by many farmers, that he said would "direct the EPA to use sound science, not a whim of the Washington bureaucracy."

Sometimes Pombo stands to the right of his Republican colleagues. In the 106th, he added an amendment to a popular coast management grant program to restrict the government's acquisition of private property, even

CAPITOL OFFICE
225-1947; fax 226-0861; 2411 Rayburn Bldg. 20515

INTERNET
e-mail: rpombo@mail.house.gov
web: www.house.gov/pombo

COMMITTEES
Agriculture
 (Livestock & Horticulture - chairman)
Resources
Transportation & Infrastructure

HOMETOWN
Tracy

BORN
Jan. 8, 1961, Tracy, Calif.

RELIGION
Roman Catholic

FAMILY
Wife, Annette Pombo; three children

EDUCATION
California State Polytechnic U., Pomona, attended 1979-81

CAREER
Rancher

POLITICAL HIGHLIGHTS
Tracy City Council, 1990-92

ELECTION RESULTS

2000 GENERAL
Richard W. Pombo (R)	120,635	57.8%
Tom Santos (D)	79,539	38.1%
Kathryn Russow (LIBERT)	5,036	2.4%
Jon Kurey (NL)	3,397	1.6%

2000 PRIMARY (OPEN)
Richard W. Pombo (R)	87,160	61.0%
Tom Santos (D)	30,817	21.6%
Robert L. Figueroa (D)	19,152	13.4%
Kathryn Russow (LIBERT)	3,273	2.3%
Jon Kurey (NL)	2,388	1.7%

1998 GENERAL
Richard W. Pombo (R)	95,496	61.4%
Robert L. Figueroa (D)	56,345	36.2%
Jesse Baird (LIBERT)	3,608	2.3%

PREVIOUS WINNING PERCENTAGES
1996 (59%); 1994 (62%); 1992 (48%)

though bill sponsor H. James Saxton, R-N.J., said such a provision was like "rolling a hand grenade" under the bill. In 1997, Pombo went against his own leadership by voting against the spending portion of a balanced-budget agreement that top Republicans had negotiated with President Clinton. He told the Sacramento Bee that one of its components — a $24 billion program to provide health care for poor children — "could end up being quite a weight on the federal government."

But the rancher is best known for his efforts on the Resources Committee, where he has been an important player in the Republican effort to overhaul major environmental statutes, including the 1973 Endangered Species Act. Pombo says the law puts preservation of plants and animals ahead of the well-being of people and treads on the rights of private property owners. "Over 20 years, the law has lost its purpose," Pombo argues. "It is being used for things other than saving endangered species, such as growth control, gaining control of mining, timber, agriculture, private property."

Environmental groups contend that Pombo's strong views are related to his family's large landholdings in the San Joaquin Valley, an assertion Pombo dismisses. In fact, he argues that promises to tame the federal bureaucracy were instrumental in the GOP's winning a House majority in 1994.

After Republican efforts to scale back the Endangered Species Act stalled in the 104th Congress, Pombo introduced a more incremental rewrite of the law in the 105th but continued to use strong rhetoric. In a 1997 letter to his constituents, Pombo took aim at the "extremist environmental movement who will do anything to save bugs and rodents." Moderate Eastern Republicans greatly amended Pombo's measure, and he withdrew it amid considerable intraparty tensions.

In an effort to ensure that Central Valley farmers have enough workers to harvest their crops, Pombo has pushed to loosen immigration requirements — a position that is well-received in his district but that differs from Republican Party doctrine favoring tighter restrictions on immigration. During consideration of a broad immigration bill in the 104th, he offered a guest-worker plan that would have created a new migrant worker program permitting the admission of up to 250,000 foreigners per year to harvest U.S. crops. He called his plan "an insurance policy against unharvested food, closed farms and higher food costs." But the House rejected it as too lenient. In the 105th, the House passed his plan to loosen slightly the eligibility requirements for participation in a program that allows foreigners to visit the country for up to three months without a visa.

KEY VOTES

2000
No Raise hourly minimum wage by $1 over two years
Yes Halt funding for U.S. mission in Kosovo unless European nations pay more
Yes Provide Medicare benefits to military retirees and their dependents
No Grant China permanent normal trade status
Yes Phase out estate, gift and trust taxes
Yes Prohibit implementation of president's national monument designations
Yes Approve GOP plan to provide prescription drug coverage for Medicare beneficiaries
No Increase help for poor nations indebted to international financial institutions

1999
Yes Impose steel import quotas
No Kill proposal to take aviation trust funds off budget
No Require background checks on buyers only at gun shows with 10 or more vendors
Yes Remove barriers among banking, securities and insurance companies
No Authorize state grants to hire teachers and reduce class size
No Overhaul campaign finance law; ban "soft money" and restrict advocacy advertising
No Approve bipartisan plan to increase rights of patients in managed-care health plans

INTEREST GROUPS

	AFL-CIO	ADA	CCUS	ACU
2000	10%	5%	76%	100%
1999	22%	5%	88%	100%
1998	10%	10%	89%	96%
1997	0%	0%	60%	92%

CQ VOTE STUDIES

	PARTY UNITY		PRESIDENTIAL SUPPORT	
	Support	Oppose	Support	Oppose
2000	95%	5%	19%	81%
1999	93%	7%	12%	88%
1998	93%	7%	23%	77%
1997	95%	5%	23%	77%

CALIFORNIA 11

Parts of San Joaquin and Sacramento counties; Stockton

While Sacramento itself has been a source of liberal votes for many years, politics take a more conservative path south of the city and in the rural portion of Sacramento and San Joaquin counties.

The 11th is an agricultural district, and nearly all communities in the district can be found near Interstate 5, the main trucking route in this part of the state. Lodi, about 30 miles south of Sacramento, and Tracy, at the southern end of the district, are two main trucking centers through which the district's agricultural products travel. Woodbridge, to the north, and Lodi produce 40 percent of the state's premium wine grapes.

South of Lodi is Stockton, a port city on the San Joaquin River. A large number of goods find their way to and from the San Francisco Bay through Stockton. It is by far the largest city in the district, home to

about 40 percent of district residents.

Democrats hold a slight edge in voter registration, but these are mostly conservative Democrats. The district as a whole tends to vote Republican, largely because voters have become increasingly distrustful of federal environmental regulations.

MAJOR INDUSTRY
Agriculture, state government, service

MILITARY BASES
Defense Distribution Depot San Joaquin, 3 military; 1,644 civilian (2001)

CITIES
Stockton, 245,020; Lodi, 56,995; Manteca, 49,645; Rancho Cordova (unincorporated), 48,731 (1990)

UNUSUAL FEATURES
Stockton named for Robert Stockton, the second military governor of California, who captured Santa Barbara and Los Angeles from Mexico and proclaimed California U.S. territory in 1847; San Francisco 49er's summer training camp in Stockton at the U. of the Pacific.

Rep. Tom Lantos (D)

Elected 1980; 11th term

A strong-minded partisan, the Hungarian-born Lantos demonstrates many of the traits that made him a fighter in the Nazi resistance in Budapest. Resolute and self-assured, he is determined to defeat his opponents. He is given plenty of opportunity in the Republican-controlled House to practice his verbal warfare.

Lantos is also eloquent and intellectual — some say haughty —with the highbrow air of a man bred in prewar Central European culture who went on to earn a doctorate in economics from the University of California at Berkeley.

His acid rhetoric was on display in the 106th Congress when he blasted a bipartisan group of 11 lawmakers who tried to negotiate a deal with members of Russia's Duma to end the bombing campaign in Kosovo. "You have not been elected to the State Department," Lantos told the delegation at an International Relations Committee hearing. "I know a lot of people in this Congress who would call it treason."

A 1997 comment by a Lantos aide characterizes his confrontational style. Refuting accusations that Lantos had punched a British cameraman, the aide told the San Francisco Chronicle, "He has a tongue that, under the right circumstances, can be as sharp as any sword. But he doesn't resort to physical violence."

Lantos is the top Democrat on the International Relations panel, a post he assumed in the 107th Congress. The congressman, who is Jewish, is an enthusiastic supporter of Israel and a critic of its Arab adversaries. A frequent foreign traveler, he works hard to convince his colleagues that foreign policy deserves more congressional attention. He has called for a tough line against Iraq but urged the Clinton administration and congressional leaders to open a dialogue with Iran.

Lantos was one of the first in Congress to call for a firm U.S. response to what he called Serbia's aggression against other Yugoslavian republics. In 1999, he supported the NATO air campaign against Kosovo. However, he urged against intervening in a 1999 Indonesian crackdown in East Timor. "There is a world of difference because, with respect to Kosovo, we have NATO," he said. East Timor "is not a place where either the United States or Australia or anybody else will begin a war."

Lantos' concern with human rights abuses led him to break with President Clinton and oppose granting China permanent normal trade status. On the eve of a 1997 visit to the United States by Chinese President Jiang Zemin, Lantos said Zemin was seeking "a cynical photo opportunity ... that will not suffice to cover up the shameful record of the Chinese government." Lantos, who is co-chairman of the Congressional Human Rights Caucus, held an event in the 105th Congress to welcome to the United States the Tibetan Dalai Lama, an adversary of the Chinese government.

The California Democrat also has concerns about animals that are abused. He has urged federal research into the link between violence against humans and cruelty to animals. And in 1998, he blasted the Air Force for sending chimpanzees that had been used for the space program to a private research laboratory that had been accused of animal abuse. "Chimps have died and will continue to die at that facility," he warned.

As the No. 2 Democrat on the Government Reform Committee, Lantos was irked in the 105th Congress by Chairman Dan Burton's conduct of an investigation that focused on fundraising practices in Clinton's 1996 cam-

CAPITOL OFFICE
225-3531; fax 225-7900; 2217 Rayburn Bldg. 20515

INTERNET
e-mail: www.house.gov/writerep
web: www.house.gov/lantos

COMMITTEES
Government Reform
International Relations - ranking member

HOMETOWN
San Mateo

BORN
Feb. 1, 1928, Budapest, Hungary

RELIGION
Jewish

FAMILY
Wife, Annette Tillemann Lantos; two children

EDUCATION
U. of Washington, B.A. 1949, M.A. 1950; U. of California, Berkeley, Ph.D. 1953

CAREER
Professor; congressional aide

POLITICAL HIGHLIGHTS
Millbrae School District Board of Trustees, 1959-66 (president, 1960-61, 1965-66)

ELECTION RESULTS

2000 GENERAL

Tom Lantos (D)	158,404	74.5%
Mike Garza (R)	44,162	20.8%
Barbara Less (LIBERT)	6,431	3.0%
Rifkin Young (NL)	3,559	1.7%

2000 PRIMARY (OPEN)

Tom Lantos (D)	103,807	74.2%
Mike Garza (R)	14,165	10.1%
Robert H. Evans Jr. (R)	8,274	5.9%
James Williams Jr. (R)	7,694	5.5%
Barbara Less (LIBERT)	4,098	2.9%
Rifkin Young (NL)	1,788	1.3%

1998 GENERAL

Tom Lantos (D)	128,135	74.0%
Robert H. Evans Jr. (R)	36,562	21.1%
Michael Moloney (LIBERT)	8,515	4.9%

PREVIOUS WINNING PERCENTAGES
1996 (72%); 1994 (67%); 1992 (69%); 1990 (66%); 1988 (71%); 1986 (74%); 1984 (70%); 1982 (57%); 1980 (46%)

paign. At one 1997 committee meeting, Lantos continually interrupted Indiana Republican Burton, so much so that the Los Angeles Times reported that Lantos "became a focal point of the proceedings." The paper also reported that Democrats "concede that they are occasionally uncomfortable with Lantos' sharp tongue."

In that session, Lantos took aim at Independent Counsel Donald C. Smaltz for neglecting to declare his GOP affiliation. The congressman compared Smaltz to U.N. Secretary General Kurt Waldheim, who, Lantos said, "also had a lapse in memory. He conveniently forgot several years when he was a Nazi." The comment provoked Republicans to demand that Lantos apologize, but he did not back down. On other occasions, Lantos has stirred the GOP to anger by using Hitlerian imagery. In a 1995 interview with the San Francisco Chronicle, Lantos described the Republican Party as "goose-stepping" along on its agenda. Later, Lantos said he hadn't intended to label Republicans as Nazis, but added, "I'm glad I used it."

In 1997, Lantos ripped into Oklahoma Republican Tom Coburn for comments he made about an NBC broadcast of "Schindler's List," a film about the Holocaust. Coburn said network television had reached "an all-time low with full frontal nudity, violence and profanity being shown in our homes." Lantos, who was incarcerated in a Hungarian Nazi work camp in 1944 and then escaped, held a news conference at which he condemned Coburn's remarks. "I find it far less discouraging that some child may have learned a four-letter word. ... I am more concerned about the 1.5 million children killed in the Holocaust," he said. Coburn apologized the next day.

It took Lantos two difficult and expensive campaigns before he could settle securely into his 12th District seat. He was working on Capitol Hill as a consultant to the Senate Foreign Relations Committee when Republican Bill Royer won a 1979 special election to replace Democratic Rep. Leo J. Ryan, who had been assassinated the year before in Jonestown, Guyana. Well-known within loyal Democratic circles, Lantos left his job right after Royer's victory and began preparing for a challenge in 1980.

The one-time economics professor at San Francisco State University had held elective office only as a school board president in suburban Millbrae, but he took advantage of the incumbent's overconfidence and won by 3 percentage points. Knowing that Royer would challenge him in the 1982 election, Lantos pursued contributions not only at home, but also among Jewish communities in districts of other members — leading to some hard feelings among his colleagues. He put down Royer's comeback attempt and has topped 65 percent in every election since.

KEY VOTES

2000
Yes Raise hourly minimum wage by $1 over two years
No   Halt funding for U.S. mission in Kosovo unless European nations pay more
Yes Provide Medicare benefits to military retirees and their dependents
No   Grant China permanent normal trade status
Yes Phase out estate, gift and trust taxes
No   Prohibit implementation of president's national monument designations
No   Approve GOP plan to provide prescription drug coverage for Medicare beneficiaries
Yes Increase help for poor nations indebted to international financial institutions

1999
Yes Impose steel import quotas
No   Kill proposal to take aviation trust funds off budget
No   Require background checks on buyers only at gun shows with 10 or more vendors
No   Remove barriers among banking, securities and insurance companies
Yes Authorize state grants to hire teachers and reduce class size
Yes Overhaul campaign finance law; ban "soft money" and restrict advocacy advertising
Yes Approve bipartisan plan to increase rights of patients in managed-care health plans

INTEREST GROUPS

	AFL-CIO	ADA	CCUS	ACU
2000	100%	85%	47%	4%
1999	100%	85%	14%	0%
1998	100%	100%	33%	8%
1997	100%	95%	33%	8%

CQ VOTE STUDIES

	PARTY UNITY		PRESIDENTIAL SUPPORT	
	Support	Oppose	Support	Oppose
2000	98%	2%	87%	13%
1999	96%	4%	83%	17%
1998	95%	5%	81%	19%
1997	94%	6%	80%	20%

CALIFORNIA 12

Most of San Mateo County; southwest San Francisco

A mix of scenic coastal mountains and bayside commuter traffic jams, the 12th lies between its two well-known neighbors of San Francisco and Silicon Valley. The district includes a southwestern section of San Francisco, but most residents live in heavily populated suburbs in San Mateo County between two main commuter routes – the Junipero Serra Freeway (Interstate 280) and Bayshore Freeway (U.S. Highway 101). The district also covers a portion of Pacific coastline between Pacifica and Moss Beach.

While Silicon Valley to the south continues its high-tech success, the 12th is seeing a growth in technology companies itself. A number of biotechnology firms have set up shop in the South San Francisco area, making biotechnology one of the area's leading industries. But the district's largest employer remains the San Francisco International Airport. Just over one-fourth of the district's residents are Asian, with Daly City home to the district's highest concentration, about 42 percent.

Overall, district residents cover a wide range of the political spectrum but have tended to vote Democratic as a whole. At the southern end of the district, residents of the affluent communities of Burlingame and Hillsborough are more conservative, while voters in the San Francisco area are more Democratic.

MAJOR INDUSTRY
Biotechnology, airport, software

CITIES
San Francisco (pt.), 150,712 (1990); Daly City, 99,206; San Mateo, 91,799; South San Francisco, 59,059

UNUSUAL FEATURES
Museum of Pez Memorabilia in Burlingame; 3Com Park (formerly Candlestick Park), home of the San Francisco 49ers and former home of the Giants; Daly City has the largest concentration of Filipinos outside the Philippines.

Rep. Pete Stark (D)

Elected 1972; 15th term

CAPITOL OFFICE
225-5065; fax 226-3805; 239 Cannon Bldg. 20515

INTERNET
e-mail: www.house.gov/writerep
web: www.house.gov/stark

COMMITTEES
Ways & Means
Joint Economic
Joint Taxation

HOMETOWN
Hayward

BORN
Nov. 11, 1931, Milwaukee, Wis.

RELIGION
Unitarian

FAMILY
Wife, Deborah Roderick Stark; five children

EDUCATION
Massachusetts Institute of Technology, B.S. 1953;
U. of California, Berkeley, M.B.A. 1960

MILITARY SERVICE
Air Force, 1955-57

CAREER
Banker

POLITICAL HIGHLIGHTS
Sought Democratic nomination for Calif. Senate,
1969

ELECTION RESULTS

2000 GENERAL

Pete Stark (D)	129,012	70.4%
James Goetz (R)	44,499	24.3%
Howard Mora (LIBERT)	4,623	2.5%

2000 PRIMARY (OPEN)

Pete Stark (D)	77,905	68.8%
James Goetz (R)	22,488	19.8%
Saundra Duffy (R)	7,736	6.8%
Howard Mora (LIBERT)	2,421	2.1%

1998 GENERAL

Pete Stark (D)	101,671	71.2%
James Goetz (R)	38,050	26.6%

PREVIOUS WINNING PERCENTAGES
1996 (65%); 1994 (65%); 1992 (60%); 1990 (58%);
1988 (73%); 1986 (70%); 1984 (70%); 1982 (61%);
1980 (55%); 1978 (65%); 1976 (71%); 1974 (71%);
1972 (53%)

During his three decades in Congress, Stark has pursued a decidedly liberal track, fighting for better medical care for the elderly and coverage for the millions of Americans without health insurance, favoring gun control and pushing for strict environmental laws. While he has had some success, Stark's efforts are constantly undercut by his confrontational and abrasive personality.

Like some other successful businessmen in Congress, Stark occasionally seems to chafe at the collaboration and concessions necessary in politics. He made big money in banking as a young man, and when he wanted to put an 8-foot neon peace symbol over one of his banks in the 1960s, he didn't have to broker a compromise. He just issued the order, and it happened. Crafting legislation is seldom so direct.

Still, as chairman of the Ways and Means Health Subcommittee for 10 years and now as the panel's ranking Democrat, Stark has built a reputation as one of Congress' premier experts on health care issues, even though his sometimes barbed tongue can make him a less-than-charming committee-mate.

In the 106th Congress, Stark's liberal stripes were on display in the debate over providing prescription drug coverage for senior citizens and giving patients more power over their managed-care plans. Stark was a leading critic of a GOP plan calling on insurance companies to develop and sell prescription drug policies to Medicare recipients. Instead, he advocated a Democratic-backed plan that would have had the government develop and administer drug coverage to Medicare's nearly 40 million elderly and disabled beneficiaries. Lawmakers could not reach agreement and the issue remained a key battleground in the 107th Congress.

Stark also pushed his Republican and Democratic colleagues to embrace legislation, backed by a bipartisan coalition but opposed by GOP leaders, that would have expanded patients' ability to sue their health insurers in disputes over the delivery or denial of medical care. Conservative Republicans argued that the legislation would escalate health care costs and force millions of workers to lose their insurance. After struggling over the patients' rights issue in the 105th and 106th Congresses, lawmakers continued to work toward a resolution in the 107th.

Despite his unwanted minority status after Republicans took control of the House in 1995, Stark has had some legislative successes. For example, he helped win new preventive care benefits for Medicare beneficiaries, such as better coverage for mammograms and colorectal screening. Stark also pushed Congress to reduce Medicare beneficiaries' out-of-pocket expenses for hospital outpatient services. But he failed to block more funding to Medicare HMOs, which he said were poorly managed.

Stark may be best known for two laws enacted in 1989 and 1993, known as "Stark I" and "Stark II," that prohibit physician referrals under Medicare for a variety of services, such as laboratory tests and physical therapy, when the referring physician has a financial relationship with the facility, unless certain conditions are met.

Throughout his Capitol Hill career, Stark has shown that he can have a sharp and sarcastic tongue, and he has had harsh words for conservatives' social policy initiatives. In a 1997 floor speech, Stark lampooned an effort to deny federal benefits to legal immigrants as part of welfare overhaul legislation and a move to display the Ten Commandments in public buildings.

"Mr. Speaker, it's a day of Biblical proportions," he began. "I walk through the valley of congressional hypocrisy and take spiritual inventory of the less-than-holy works of my colleagues on welfare. Without trying to upstage Moses, I offer the following principles for consideration." He followed with a list of "commandments" to conservatives, including: "Thou shalt not take the status of legal immigrants in vain."

Nor does Stark mince words when it comes to the high-technology industry, a major force in California. In 1998, he was one of three Bay Area legislators to vote against legislation sought by the industry to increase the number of visas available for temporary foreign workers. "High-tech has been among the selfish and least helpful corporations in the country," Stark told the San Francisco Chronicle. "All they've ever done is come to us and ask for tax breaks and free trade. They're all take and no give."

Stark's rhetoric can take an even more personal turn, as in 1995, when he called Republican Nancy L. Johnson of Connecticut a "whore for the insurance industry." The insult created an uproar, with a group of 32 female House members demanding that Stark apologize, which he did in a letter to Johnson. A year earlier, as the Health Subcommittee under Stark's gavel considered a proposal to remove price limits on prescription drugs, Stark interrupted Johnson to observe, "The gentle lady got her degree from pillow talk," a reference to her physician husband.

Stark grew up in Wisconsin, went to college in Massachusetts and then served in the Air Force before going West for business school and a career in banking. At age 31 he had already founded two banks, but he really made a name for himself by raising the big neon peace symbol over one of them in suburban Walnut Creek.

In 1969, he made his first bid for public office, losing a primary race for a state legislative seat to George Miller, then a young law school student and now a House colleague. Three years later, Stark decided to take on another George Miller — this one a crusty, old-school conservative who had represented Oakland in Congress as a Democrat for 28 years. Stark spent his money generously and made Miller's support of the Vietnam War a major issue on the way to a primary win. The November election was competitive, as Republicans were dominating most of the races that fall. But Stark managed 53 percent.

Only once since then has Stark had a close call. Lulled by years of easy re-elections, he made only a token effort in the 1980 election. But conservative Republican William J. Kennedy, a tireless campaigner, galvanized a host of volunteers in the midst of Ronald Reagan's first presidential landslide and held Stark to 55 percent.

KEY VOTES

2000
Yes Raise hourly minimum wage by $1 over two years
Yes Halt funding for U.S. mission in Kosovo unless European nations pay more
No Provide Medicare benefits to military retirees and their dependents
No Grant China permanent normal trade status
No Phase out estate, gift and trust taxes
No Prohibit implementation of president's national monument designations
No Approve GOP plan to provide prescription drug coverage for Medicare beneficiaries
Yes Increase help for poor nations indebted to international financial institutions

1999
Yes Impose steel import quotas
No Kill proposal to take aviation trust funds off budget
No Require background checks on buyers only at gun shows with 10 or more vendors
No Remove barriers among banking, securities and insurance companies
? Authorize state grants to hire teachers and reduce class size
Yes Overhaul campaign finance law; ban "soft money" and restrict advocacy advertising
Yes Approve bipartisan plan to increase rights of patients in managed-care health plans

INTEREST GROUPS

	AFL-CIO	ADA	CCUS	ACU
2000	100%	95%	25%	4%
1999	100%	85%	8%	8%
1998	100%	90%	6%	8%
1997	100%	100%	10%	4%

CQ VOTE STUDIES

	PARTY UNITY		PRESIDENTIAL SUPPORT	
	Support	Oppose	Support	Oppose
2000	96%	4%	81%	19%
1999	95%	5%	75%	25%
1998	98%	2%	87%	13%
1997	96%	4%	76%	24%

CALIFORNIA 13
East Bay — Fremont, Hayward

In contrast to its neighbors across the Bay, the 13th is dotted with many working-class communities, along with closed naval bases to the north and mud flats to the south. It is often described as the less glamorous side of the San Francisco Bay area. A large minority population and sizable industrial presence have given Democrats a solid base of support.

Fremont and Hayward are the two largest cities in the district. Hayward is home to a campus of the California State U. system, while Fremont hosts an auto plant run by General Motors and Toyota. Both cities have become more oriented toward high-tech industries than the rest of the district as Silicon Valley has extended its influence to the East Bay.

The Oakland portion of the district includes very little of that city's population but does take in the Oakland International Airport and Network Associates Coliseum – home of Major League Baseball's

Athletics and National Football League's Raiders – as well as industrial and storage facilities, many no longer in operation. Just south of Oakland is San Leandro, originally settled by the Portuguese, which has a significant manufacturing presence and contributes many blue-collar votes to the Democratic Party.

MAJOR INDUSTRY
Industrial machinery, electronic equipment, food product processing

CITIES
Fremont, 208,620; Hayward (pt.), 111,495 (1990); San Leandro (pt.), 68,108 (1990); Union City, 66,012

UNUSUAL FEATURES
Fremont, birthplace of the McDonald's Quarter Pounder; Daniel Best, one of the co-founders of Caterpillar Inc., was from San Leandro; Figure skater and Olympic gold medalist Kristi Yamaguchi born in Hayward and resides in Fremont.

Rep. Anna G. Eshoo (D)

Elected 1992; 5th term

CAPITOL OFFICE
225-8104; fax 225-8890; 205 Cannon Bldg. 20515

INTERNET
e-mail: annagram@mail.house.gov
web: www.house.gov/eshoo

COMMITTEES
Energy & Commerce

HOMETOWN
Atherton

BORN
Dec. 13, 1942, New Britain, Conn.

RELIGION
Roman Catholic

FAMILY
Divorced; two children

EDUCATION
Canada College, A.A. 1975

CAREER
Legislative aide

POLITICAL HIGHLIGHTS
Democratic National Committee, 1980-92; San Mateo County Board of Supervisors, 1982-92; Democratic nominee for U.S. House, 1988

ELECTION RESULTS

2000 GENERAL

Anna G. Eshoo (D)	161,720	70.2%
Bill Quraishi (R)	59,338	25.8%
Joseph W. Dehn III (LIBERT)	4,715	2.1%
John H. Black (NL)	4,489	2.0%

2000 PRIMARY (OPEN)

Anna G. Eshoo (D)	111,136	70.6%
Bill Quraishi (R)	17,817	11.3%
Craig DeLue (R)	11,662	7.4%
Henry E. "Bud" Manzler (R)	11,453	7.3%
Joseph W. Dehn III (LIBERT)	3,193	2.0%
John H. Black (NL)	2,121	1.4%

1998 GENERAL

Anna G. Eshoo (D)	129,663	68.6%
John C. "Chris" Haugen (R)	53,719	28.4%
Joseph W. Dehn III (LIBERT)	3,166	1.7%
Anna Currivan (NL)	2,362	1.3%

PREVIOUS WINNING PERCENTAGES
1996 (65%); 1994 (61%); 1992 (57%)

Eshoo is the daughter of immigrants who instilled in her a deep appreciation of the privileges and obligations of living in the United States. Her childhood was preparation for her adult life in public office, although she did not realize it at the time and did not take that route until she was well into her 30s.

Eshoo (EH-shoo), whose mother is of Armenian descent and whose father is Assyrian, recalls that "in our prayers at dinner, we thanked God for the food and also thanked God for this country." She remembers, "My parents very much shaped a sense of obligation to give and to do."

She followed the path of civic involvement, even as a full-time homemaker and mother of young children, and then moved into the realm of electoral politics as her children got older.

Now in her fifth term representing the high-technology hotbed of Silicon Valley, Eshoo is a New Democrat centrist — liberal on many issues but a firm believer in business development and the type of risk-taking entrepreneurship for which Silicon Valley is noted. Her plum assignment on the Energy and Commerce Committee puts her in a good position to look out for Silicon Valley employers and other businesses.

Eshoo has sided with the high-tech industry in trying to lessen restrictions on exports of encryption software and in shielding companies from class-action lawsuits filed by shareholders complaining about the performance of their stocks — a particular problem for high-tech firms that are venturing into new business frontiers and whose stocks are often volatile.

In 1995, Eshoo helped lead the House effort to override President Clinton's veto of a bill giving companies a "safe harbor" from liability for distributing erroneous earnings projections. She and nearly half of the chamber's Democrats deserted the president, marking the first time a Clinton veto was overridden by the House.

Eshoo also battled with Clinton administration officials over easing restrictions on the export of encryption software, which allows digital information to be scrambled during computer transmission.

And in the 106th Congress, Eshoo initially joined with Republicans in voting to end the estate tax, but she rejoined the party fold later in voting to sustain Clinton's veto of the measure.

In the 105th Congress, Eshoo was successful in her bid to require federal agencies to make their forms available online and to allow people to sign the forms using digital signatures. In the 106th, she championed legislation to authorize the use of "electronic signatures" to seal online contracts with the touch of a mouse or a name scrawled on a touch-sensitive computer screen.

When the 1996 Telecommunications Act made it illegal to transmit "indecent" materials to children over the Internet, the California Democrat sought to broker a compromise by introducing a measure to increase parental control over material available online to children without limiting free speech.

From her seat on Commerce, Eshoo also got involved in legislation overhauling the Food and Drug Administration. She was largely credited with brokering a compromise on a bill that reduced the approval time for new medical devices and allowed doctors to use experimental devices in certain life-threatening circumstances.

She has sought to require insurance companies that pay for breast cancer-related mastectomies also to pay for reconstructive breast surgery. And she pushed for Medicaid coverage for treatment of breast and cervical cancers detected in Medicaid-covered screening programs.

Eshoo has faced some tough calls on trade issues. Despite her business-minded views on trade, Eshoo did not come easily to her final conclusion to support the North American Free Trade Agreement in 1993. Many of the 14th District's core Democratic constituencies — organized labor, environmentalists and human rights activists — opposed her decision. In 2000, she voted to grant China permanent normal trade status.

When Eshoo was a child, her father, a jeweler and watchmaker, took the family to political rallies, and portraits of Franklin D. Roosevelt and Harry S. Truman were displayed in their home. One day, as she was walking home from elementary school, a man in a big car drove by, tipped his hat and asked whether she wanted a ride home. Even though Eshoo had been taught not to accept rides from strangers, there were many police officers around, and so she accepted the lift — from President Truman.

Later, in the 1960 presidential campaign, Eshoo, a high school senior, organized more than 800 students in her Connecticut hometown to work for John F. Kennedy. "Back then, I really thought that I was the one who put [Kennedy] over the top."

The family moved to California, and Eshoo married young and devoted herself mostly to raising her two children. She was active in the PTA and civic groups such as the League of Women Voters, earned a two-year associate degree in English literature, and then, at 34, sought elective office — to the San Mateo Community College Board of Trustees — but lost that race.

She got an internship with Leo McCarthy, the Speaker of the California Assembly, then worked for him as chief of staff. She became active in local party politics and won appointment to the Democratic National Committee. When in 1982 McCarthy urged her to run for the San Mateo County Board of Supervisors, she did so, though reluctantly at first. That post, which she held for a decade, shaped her legislative philosophy. Mindful that it was a nonpartisan position, Eshoo learned the value of seeking consensus.

In 1988, she ran unsuccessfully for the House against Republican Tom Campbell, taking a solid 46 percent. Four years later, she tried again, boosted by redistricting that added more Democratic voters and the departure of Campbell to run for the Senate. Her name recognition and campaign experience propelled her to the Democratic nomination against six male candidates, and she won in November by 18 points. With her high-tech interests and her energy, she has co-opted much of the district's business support for the GOP, and her subsequent elections have come without major difficulty.

Eshoo never got around to finishing her college education, but she still dreams of doing so. "I think it would be a hoot to be a student again."

KEY VOTES

2000
Yes Raise hourly minimum wage by $1 over two years
Yes Halt funding for U.S. mission in Kosovo unless European nations pay more
Yes Provide Medicare benefits to military retirees and their dependents
Yes Grant China permanent normal trade status
Yes Phase out estate, gift and trust taxes
No   Prohibit implementation of president's national monument designations
No   Approve GOP plan to provide prescription drug coverage for Medicare beneficiaries
Yes Increase help for poor nations indebted to international financial institutions

1999
No   Impose steel import quotas
Yes Kill proposal to take aviation trust funds off budget
No   Require background checks on buyers only at gun shows with 10 or more vendors
No   Remove barriers among banking, securities and insurance companies
Yes Authorize state grants to hire teachers and reduce class size
Yes Overhaul campaign finance law; ban "soft money" and restrict advocacy advertising
Yes Approve bipartisan plan to increase rights of patients in managed-care health plans

INTEREST GROUPS

	AFL-CIO	ADA	CCUS	ACU
2000	70%	75%	55%	8%
1999	56%	95%	28%	4%
1998	89%	90%	39%	0%
1997	100%	100%	40%	8%

CQ VOTE STUDIES

	PARTY UNITY		PRESIDENTIAL SUPPORT	
	Support	Oppose	Support	Oppose
2000	89%	11%	82%	18%
1999	90%	10%	85%	15%
1998	95%	5%	90%	10%
1997	92%	8%	88%	12%

CALIFORNIA 14
Southern San Mateo and northern Santa Clara counties

With boundaries mirroring those of Silicon Valley, the 14th is known for high-tech innovation. The region has undergone tremendous economic growth since the 1980s. The change in landscape is most evident at the Santa Clara County end of the district, in cities such as Cupertino, Mountain View and Sunnyvale, where apricot and cherry orchards once were common.

Most of the district's residents live in cities at the geographical center of the district, between Interstate 280 and U.S. Route 101, including Redwood City, Mountain View and Palo Alto. Sixty percent of the district lives in Santa Clara County. As a new major metropolitan center, the region is dealing with the consequences of a sustained boom. Traffic congestion is common and real estate prices are among the highest in the nation. The economic fortunes of the area have put growth issues and education at the top of the district's agenda.

The 14th's voters traditionally have been pragmatic, favoring solution-seeking, moderate Republican candidates. Democrats have a significant edge in voter registration, but 1992 marked the first time in nearly six decades that a Democrat was chosen to represent the region, thanks to the successful Clinton campaign and the "Year of the Woman." The district supported the Democratic presidential candidate in 1992, '96 and 2000.

MAJOR INDUSTRY
Computers, biotechnology, defense, aerospace

MILITARY BASES
Onizuka Air Station, 200 military, 347 civilian (2001)

CITIES
Sunnyvale (pt.), 105,736 (1990); Mountain View, 71,470; Redwood City (pt.), 59,707 (1990); Palo Alto, 58,843

UNUSUAL FEATURES
Apple Computer founded in a Cupertino garage; Water tower painted as a Libby's fruit cocktail can, where the cannery operated in Sunnyvale.

Rep. Michael M. Honda (D)

Elected 2000; 1st term

Representing a district that includes much of California's Silicon Valley, Honda has a congressional agenda that is appropriately centered on the high-tech industry. Yet his focus is not solely on business issues.

Honda — a former teacher, principal and school board member — prefers to talk about computer education, which he says will help train the next generation of high-tech workers. He supports expanding the "e-rate" program that provides federal money to help wire schools and libraries to the Internet. And he sees advantages for Silicon Valley companies in increased federal funding for training adult workers in technology skills.

Honda portrays free-trade legislation, such as the measure enacted in 2000 that granted China permanent normal trade status, as the key to continued growth in the computer industry.

He also is concerned with finding regional solutions and perhaps federal funding to deal with the downside of his district's recent economic boom, such as traffic congestion and high housing costs. "Because this is the economic engine of the country, if we don't solve the problems here, the efficiency of the economy will come down," he said.

The 2000 open-seat race in California's 15th District was a ripe opportunity for the Democrats. But it took a phone call from President Clinton just before the candidate filing deadline to persuade Honda to make the race.

Honda wanted to make sure the national party would provide necessary backing for his bid to capture the Democratic-leaning district, which moderate Republican Rep. Tom Campbell had left open for an ultimately unsuccessful challenge to Democratic Sen. Dianne Feinstein.

The 59-year-old Honda presented an impressive résumé to voters. Imprisoned as a youth in a Japanese-American internment camp during World War II, he later volunteered with the Peace Corps in El Salvador, worked as an educator, and served nearly 20 years as an elected official, giving up a state Assembly seat to run for the U.S. House.

Honda was only slightly favored over GOP state Rep. Jim Cunneen, a Campbell protégé, but he defeated the Republican by 12 percentage points.

CAPITOL OFFICE
225-2631; fax 225-2699; 503 Cannon Bldg. 20515

INTERNET
e-mail: mike.honda@mail.house.gov
web: www.house.gov/honda

COMMITTEES
Budget
Science
Transportation & Infrastructure

HOMETOWN
San Jose

BORN
June 27, 1941, Stockton, Calif.

RELIGION
Protestant

FAMILY
Wife, Jeanne Honda; two children

EDUCATION
San Jose State U., B.S. 1969, B.A. 1970, M.A. 1973

CAREER
Teacher; principal; Peace Corps volunteer

POLITICAL HIGHLIGHTS
San Jose School Board, 1981-90; Santa Clara County Board of Supervisors, 1990-96; Calif. Assembly, 1997-2000

ELECTION RESULTS

2000 GENERAL

Michael M. Honda (D)	128,545	54.3%
Jim Cunneen (R)	99,866	42.2%
Ed Wimmers (LIBERT)	4,820	2.0%
Douglas Gorney (NL)	3,591	1.5%

2000 PRIMARY (OPEN)

Michael M. Honda (D)	62,876	39.2%
Jim Cunneen (R)	53,282	33.2%
Bill Peacock (D)	22,499	14.0%
Dale Mead (R)	8,638	5.4%
Dick Lane (D)	3,968	2.5%
Robin Parker (D)	3,646	2.3%
Ed Wimmers (LIBERT)	2,566	1.6%

CALIFORNIA 15

Santa Clara and Santa Cruz counties

With the Pacific Ocean on one side and Silicon Valley on the other, the 15th is home to a diverse landscape and a growing number of high-tech companies. Located at the southern end of the San Francisco Bay area, the district encompasses the mountains of northern Santa Cruz County and the suburban communities around the west side of San Jose.

The northernmost point of the district includes the city of Santa Clara and part of Sunnyvale. South of Santa Clara and west of San Jose are some affluent suburbs, including Campbell, Saratoga and Los Gatos. The bulk of the district's land is in Santa Cruz County, a drive south on state Highway 17 from San Jose. But less than 10 percent of district residents reside in this area.

Most district residents are clustered around San Jose and Santa Clara. Located at the southern end of Silicon Valley, Santa Clara, a Spanish mission in the late 1700s, is now home to large high-tech companies.

Although Democrats hold a 10 percentage point edge in voter registration, the 15th's residents are willing to elect moderate candidates of either party whom they think will address quality-of-life issues, such as traffic and housing. Generally, rural Santa Cruz County has been more liberal than the more affluent Santa Clara County.

MAJOR INDUSTRY
Computers, biotechnology

CITIES
San Jose (pt.), 307,791 (1990); Santa Clara (pt.), 87,319 (1990); Campbell, 38,214

UNUSUAL FEATURES
Santa Clara University, founded in 1851, California's first institution of higher learning; Winchester Mystery House in San Jose – a 160-room Victorian mansion famous for staircases that lead nowhere.

Rep. Zoe Lofgren (D)

Elected 1994; 4th term

CAPITOL OFFICE
225-3072; fax 225-3336; 227 Cannon Bldg. 20515

INTERNET
e-mail: zoe@lofgren.house.gov
web: www.house.gov/lofgren

COMMITTEES
Judiciary
Science
Standards of Official Conduct

HOMETOWN
San Jose

BORN
Dec. 21, 1947, San Mateo, Calif.

RELIGION
Unspecified

FAMILY
Husband, John Marshall Collins; two children

EDUCATION
Stanford U., B.A. 1970; U. of Santa Clara, J.D. 1975

CAREER
Lawyer; professor; congressional aide

POLITICAL HIGHLIGHTS
San Jose-Evergreen Community College District
Board of Trustees, 1979-81; Santa Clara County
Board of Supervisors, 1981-95

ELECTION RESULTS

2000 GENERAL

Zoe Lofgren (D)	115,118	72.1%
Horace Thayn (R)	37,213	23.3%
Dennis Umphress (LIBERT)	4,742	3.0%
Edward Klein (NL)	2,673	1.7%

2000 PRIMARY (OPEN)

Zoe Lofgren (D)	72,515	71.9%
Horace Thayn (R)	23,652	23.5%
Dennis Umphress (LIBERT)	2,914	2.9%
Edward Klein (NL)	1,764	1.8%

1998 GENERAL

Zoe Lofgren (D)	85,503	72.8%
Horace Thayn (R)	27,494	23.4%
John H. Black (NL)	4,417	3.8%

PREVIOUS WINNING PERCENTAGES
1996 (66%); 1994 (65%)

Lofgren's training and background as a lawyer and her district's status as a leading high-technology center shape her views and her legislative agenda in the House.

Silicon Valley is just to the west of Lofgren's 16th District, and many of her constituents work in the high-technology sector. Lofgren (her first name is pronounced ZO) makes no pretense that she is an expert in computer technology — she was a political science major in college — but she says that representing a high-tech district requires elected officials to educate themselves about the industry as much as they can.

Many of her House colleagues and government officials are still coming to grips with the new technology of communications and commerce, and Lofgren sees one of her roles as assisting in the high-tech education of decision-makers.

And as the mother of two teenage children, Lofgren views education in a broader perspective as well. She says that her primary focus as a public official is to see that all children "at least have the same opportunity that I had — and right now not all of them do." She introduced legislation in the 106th Congress urging high school officials to consider starting school later in the day, citing some evidence that teenagers are not fully alert early in the morning. She never expected the House to act on her "Z's to A's Act" — such decisions are the prerogative of local officials — but she did raise awareness of scientific research into teenagers' biological rhythms.

Lofgren sometimes sees virtue in a go-slow approach on Capitol Hill, particularly on high-tech matters. Some government decisions have been made without full appreciation of the new technology or the implications of the decisions, Lofgren argues. "Sometimes the best idea is not to do anything," she says. "It's not always bad that Congress-time and Internet-time don't mesh."

She opposed the 1996 Communications Decency Act, which would have banned Internet and other online dissemination of "indecent" or "patently offensive" material to minors, arguing that it was unconstitutional. The Supreme Court in 1997 agreed and struck it down. Lofgren said that supporters of the legislation were well-meaning but did not understand the Internet, which she says is more like publishing in print than broadcasting over the public airwaves. Keeping minors away from indecent printed material is done not by stopping publication, but by limiting their access to it, Lofgren contends.

Another technology issue that Lofgren says has not been fully understood by decision-makers is computer encryption, which allows digital information to be scrambled during computer transmission. The Clinton administration, urged on by the law enforcement and intelligence communities, long opposed the export of state-of-the-art forms of encryption technology, which is designed to prevent unauthorized access to electronic communications. But U.S. makers of encryption software argued that the restrictions placed them at a competitive disadvantage with foreign firms. Lofgren was pleased in 1999 when the administration changed its policy.

Lofgren is typically a strong supporter of the liberal Democratic line. Commenting on the work of the House in 1995 under the new GOP majority, she said, "I'm frustrated by the sheer volume of the stupid things we've done."

But that outlook does not prevent Lofgren from working in a quieter way to influence the content of bills that Republicans are pushing. She has sought common ground on some issues, especially in the technology arena.

Immigration law was Lofgren's specialty as a lawyer, and it is also an area of concern to high-tech businesses, which say they are having trouble filling skilled jobs without looking to foreign workers. Lofgren and other lawmakers from high-tech districts have worked to increase the quota of skilled foreign workers given special H1-B visas, while emphasizing that the long-term solution is to equip more American schoolchildren with the skills needed for high-tech work. She also favors a new category of visa that would permit foreign students who earn a U.S. postgraduate degree in science or engineering to remain in the country if they take a high-paying job.

Lofgren grew up in a blue-collar neighborhood in south Palo Alto. Her father was a truck driver and her mother was a secretary and later a school cafeteria cook. "I didn't meet a Republican until I went to junior high school," she recalls. While other mothers went door-to-door collecting money for the March of Dimes, Lofgren's mother went after "dollars for Democrats." Lofgren would spend long hours talking politics with her Swedish immigrant grandfather, and she recalls that, instead of dating or going to dances, she and her friends went to political rallies.

Lofgren went to Stanford on a scholarship and then headed to Washington, D.C., landing an internship with Democratic Rep. Don Edwards. Convinced that she needed to go to law school when the House's legislative counsel "ripped to shreds — and for good reason" a draft of a bill she had written, she returned to California and got a law degree.

She served as the first executive director of San Jose's Community Housing Developers, a nonprofit involved in creating low-income housing. In 1979, one of Lofgren's colleagues urged her to run for the local community college board of trustees. She did and won. A year later, she was elected to the Santa Clara County Board of Supervisors, where she served 14 years. Often her efforts placed her in conflict with San Jose's Democratic mayor, Tom McEnery, who pushed redevelopment of downtown San Jose. Lofgren frequently argued that downtown redevelopment funds would have been better spent on education and human services.

When Edwards retired after 32 years, the Democratic primary saw a face-off between Lofgren and McEnery, who was no longer mayor. Lofgren launched her campaign while standing on a kitchen breadbox in the living room of her house in San Jose. She benefited from an uproar that ensued when state election officials barred her from describing herself as "county supervisor/mother" on the ballot. The flap drew national attention to Lofgren's candidacy, and she went on to upset McEnery. She won handily that November and has coasted to re-election since.

KEY VOTES

2000

Yes Raise hourly minimum wage by $1 over two years
Yes Halt funding for U.S. mission in Kosovo unless European nations pay more
Yes Provide Medicare benefits to military retirees and their dependents
Yes Grant China permanent normal trade status
Yes Phase out estate, gift and trust taxes
- Prohibit implementation of president's national monument designations
No Approve GOP plan to provide prescription drug coverage for Medicare beneficiaries
Yes Increase help for poor nations indebted to international financial institutions

1999

No Impose steel import quotas
Yes Kill proposal to take aviation trust funds off budget
No Require background checks on buyers only at gun shows with 10 or more vendors
No Remove barriers among banking, securities and insurance companies
Yes Authorize state grants to hire teachers and reduce class size
Yes Overhaul campaign finance law; ban "soft money" and restrict advocacy advertising
Yes Approve bipartisan plan to increase rights of patients in managed-care health plans

INTEREST GROUPS

	AFL-CIO	ADA	CCUS	ACU
2000	80%	85%	52%	4%
1999	67%	95%	29%	4%
1998	90%	95%	47%	0%
1997	100%	95%	40%	8%

CQ VOTE STUDIES

	PARTY UNITY		PRESIDENTIAL SUPPORT	
	Support	Oppose	Support	Oppose
2000	90%	10%	82%	18%
1999	87%	13%	84%	16%
1998	92%	8%	88%	12%
1997	92%	8%	89%	11%

CALIFORNIA 16
Santa Clara County — San Jose

San Jose has long lived in San Francisco's shadow. But as the city's size and economic stature grew in the 1980s and '90s, so did its reputation as a major metropolitan area.

The district includes two-thirds of Santa Clara County, but 80 percent of the 16th's residents live in San Jose. Silicon Valley's tremendous growth has rubbed off on the city, creating a white-collar workforce and helping to establish San Jose as a leading exporter of high-tech goods.

The 16th is one of the most ethnically diverse districts in the Bay Area. The district's Asian population includes a large Vietnamese community, but Hispanics represent the 16th's largest minority group.

The district becomes more rural as U.S. Route 101 heads south into the foothills and ranchland of Santa Clara County. Wineries in Morgan Hill and nearby San Martin attract tourists into the scenic area, while

Gilroy is known for its annual Garlic Festival.

The 16th has been solidly liberal and Democratic for many years and a recent influx of Hispanics has helped continue that trend. However, white-collar workers are becoming more common residents of the 16th and could begin to make the district's politics slightly more conservative.

MAJOR INDUSTRY
Computers, health care, agriculture

CITIES
San Jose (pt.), 454,705 (1990); Gilroy, 38,470; Morgan Hill, 31,903

UNUSUAL FEATURES
Known today as the "Garlic Capital of the World," Gilroy was the tobacco capital of the United States in the 1870s and home to what was then the world's largest cigar factory, producing more than 1 million cigars each month; San Jose served as the state capital for a short time after California's annexation by the United States.

Rep. Sam Farr (D)

Elected June 1993; 4th full term

Farr heeded President John F. Kennedy's appeal to "ask what you can do for your country" and upon graduation from college joined the early wave of volunteers in Kennedy's newly formed Peace Corps. He says the experience led him to a career in public service.

In Congress, Farr combines an earnestness about public service with a focus on the economy of California's Central Coast and his long-abiding interest in environmental issues (he was a biology major in college). Conveniently for him, those interests often converge. The 17th District's economy depends on its natural resources for farming, fishing and tourism, and sustaining those resources in the long run is key to the area's economic viability. The district boasts rich soil, bountiful fisheries and some of the most beautiful vistas in the world.

Across the spectrum of issues, Farr is generally a dependable vote for the Democratic leadership. He does not emphasize his partisanship, although some GOP positions on environmental issues can elicit a sharp retort, such as the time he said at a Resources Committee hearing, "There is 100 percent agreement in this room that we all love forests. The difficulty is that 50 percent of them love it vertical, and 50 percent of them love [forests] horizontal."

Normally, though, confrontation is not a significant part of Farr's style. He prefers to work unobtrusively, concentrating on his roster of priority matters. In 1999, after quietly lobbying Democratic leaders for months, Farr won a seat on the Appropriations panel, where he serves on two subcommittees of importance to the 17th: Military Construction and Agriculture.

Farr also was elected chairman of the California Democratic delegation for the 106th Congress, a post he used to build consensus among members of the huge, often fractious group. Key concerns for the Golden Staters include securing more federal funding to cover the cost of incarcerating illegal aliens, boosting California's share of Title I education programs for disadvantaged children and protecting the defense and aerospace industries in the state.

The 17th includes fertile inland regions, where Salinas serves as a marketing center for such produce as lettuce, avocados and artichokes from surrounding farms in the nation's "salad bowl." In the 105th, Farr looked out for those farming interests from his seat on the Agriculture Committee. He gave up the Agriculture panel when he was named to Appropriations but continues to focus on farm matters from his seat on the Appropriations panel's Agriculture and Rural Development Subcommittee.

The district is the nation's largest grower of commercial flowers, but business has been weak in recent years, due largely to competition from duty-free imports from Colombia. Farr criticized the Clinton administration for doing nothing about the problem, which arose due to a trade agreement that gives preferential treatment to Latin American flower exporters in hopes they will develop legal alternatives to the cultivation of coca, the raw material used to make cocaine. But Farr notes that coca production has continued to increase, and in the 106th he arranged meetings between Colombian and Californian flower-growers to seek a solution.

The 17th was dealt a blow in 1994 when Fort Ord was ordered closed. Farr has worked hard to ease the base's transition from military to civilian use; he helped secure $51 million in defense spending to open the Monterey Bay campus of California State University at the old base. The base also houses a Defense Department Finance Center, a veterans clinic and an environ-

CAPITOL OFFICE
225-2861; fax 225-6791
1221 Longworth Bldg. 20515

INTERNET
e-mail: samfarr@mail.house.gov
web: www.house.gov/farr

COMMITTEES
Appropriations

HOMETOWN
Carmel

BORN
July 4, 1941, San Francisco, Calif.

RELIGION
Episcopalian

FAMILY
Wife, Shary Baldwin Farr; one child

EDUCATION
Willamette U., B.S. 1963

CAREER
State legislative aide; Peace Corps volunteer

POLITICAL HIGHLIGHTS
Monterey County Board of Supervisors, 1975-81; Calif. Assembly, 1981-93

ELECTION RESULTS

2000 GENERAL

Sam Farr (D)	143,219	68.6%
Clint Engler (R)	51,557	24.7%
E. Craig Coffin (GREEN)	8,215	3.9%
Rick Garrett (LIBERT)	2,510	1.2%
Lawrence Fenton (REF)	2,263	1.1%

2000 PRIMARY (OPEN)

Sam Farr (D)	83,275	56.7%
Clint Engler (R)	21,258	14.5%
Rob Roberts (R)	11,467	7.8%
Joe Grossman (D)	8,104	5.5%
Debra Whitmore (D)	7,661	5.2%
Carole Dooley (R)	6,495	4.4%

1998 GENERAL

Sam Farr (D)	103,719	64.5%
Bill McCampbell (R)	52,470	32.7%
Rick Garrett (LIBERT)	2,791	1.7%
Scott Hartley (NL)	1,710	1.1%

PREVIOUS WINNING PERCENTAGES
1996 (59%); 1994 (52%); 1993 Special Runoff Election (54%); 1993 Special Election (26%)

mental research center for the University of California at Santa Cruz.

In the 105th, Farr sat on the Resources panel, where he worked on ocean issues, urging Congress and the administration to initiate a comprehensive review of the nation's policies on maritime and coastal matters. In 2000, after Republicans had blocked his proposals to expand environmental protections for California offshore islands that are home to seabirds and marine mammals and to expand the Pinnacles National Monument in the coastal range, Farr was able to achieve his goals when President Clinton used Farr's bill as the basis for an executive order creating new national monuments.

Farr's keen interest in environmental issues was manifest in 1998 when, frustrated with the lackluster recycling effort in congressional offices, he got the House to dictate that $100,000 be set aside for implementation of an aggressive recycling program on the Hill. Farr said he was not trying to "fulfill some sort of ecowarrior's dream to save trees," but rather aiming to earn money, reduce landfill costs and "make the House a good corporate citizen." That goal may be a while in coming; in the 106th Congress, Farr observed that the recycling effort had struggled with continued half-hearted participation and improper mixing of recyclables during pickup.

Farr's father was a longtime California state legislator and played a key role in the highway beautification effort of Lady Bird Johnson. Now, the younger Farr is the co-chairman of the Congressional Travel and Tourism Caucus. He is also the co-chairman of the Oceans Caucus and a member of the House Sustainable Development Caucus, which weighs in on a range of issues with environmental implications, including electricity deregulation, fisheries regulation and the development of alternative fuels.

Farr, who was born on July 4, is proud of his work on the 1996 immigration bill to encourage mass naturalization ceremonies around the country on that date. He makes a habit of participating in such a ceremony each year as he celebrates his birthday.

After spending what he calls two "character-forming" years with the Peace Corps in Colombia, Farr returned home and went to work as a staffer in the California Assembly. He later won election to the Monterey County Board of Supervisors. After five years there, he was elected to the California Assembly, where he served 12 years.

In 1993, he won a House special election to replace Democrat Leon E. Panetta, who had been named director of the Office of Management and Budget, winning by 9 percentage points over Republican Bill McCampbell. After winning a 1994 rematch with McCampbell by 8 points, he has won by increasingly comfortable margins, reaching 44 points in 2000.

KEY VOTES

2000

Yes Raise hourly minimum wage by $1 over two years
Yes Halt funding for U.S. mission in Kosovo unless European nations pay more
Yes Provide Medicare benefits to military retirees and their dependents
No   Grant China permanent normal trade status
Yes Phase out estate, gift and trust taxes
No   Prohibit implementation of president's national monument designations
No   Approve GOP plan to provide prescription drug coverage for Medicare beneficiaries
Yes Increase help for poor nations indebted to international financial institutions

1999

Yes Impose steel import quotas
Yes Kill proposal to take aviation trust funds off budget
No   Require background checks on buyers only at gun shows with 10 or more vendors
No   Remove barriers among banking, securities and insurance companies
Yes Authorize state grants to hire teachers and reduce class size
Yes Overhaul campaign finance law; ban "soft money" and restrict advocacy advertising
Yes Approve bipartisan plan to increase rights of patients in managed-care health plans

INTEREST GROUPS

	AFL-CIO	ADA	CCUS	ACU
2000	90%	95%	45%	8%
1999	78%	100%	17%	0%
1998	100%	100%	44%	0%
1997	100%	95%	40%	4%

CQ VOTE STUDIES

	PARTY UNITY		PRESIDENTIAL SUPPORT	
	Support	Oppose	Support	Oppose
2000	95%	5%	82%	18%
1999	96%	4%	85%	15%
1998	95%	5%	87%	13%
1997	93%	7%	83%	17%

CALIFORNIA 17
Monterey, San Benito and Santa Cruz counties — Salinas

The 17th includes the most populated part of upscale Santa Cruz County, along with its namesake city and several sizable seaside communities. Further south, in Monterey County, exclusive Pebble Beach is home to celebrities and Silicon Valley executives. While Santa Cruz County is a Democratic stronghold, the district remains competitive because of its Republican-leaning farmers and retirees.

South of populous Santa Cruz County, agriculture drives the economy. Major wineries and vineyards also dot the landscape. Salinas, the seat of Monterey County, is known as the "nation's salad bowl" for its fresh vegetables. The district's one-third Hispanic population is concentrated here, and Hispanics are beginning to win local offices.

Residents in the 17th expected to suffer economically when they lost their military base, the huge Fort Ord, in 1994. But California State University Monterey Bay has since located there, and the influx of students and related jobs is expected to help replace 17,000 military jobs.

MAJOR INDUSTRY
Agriculture, tourism, higher education

MILITARY BASES
Presidio of Monterey (Army), 3,395 military (includes 3,097 students), 1,282 civilian (1997); Fleet Numerical Meteorology and Oceanography Center, 94 military, 162 civilians; Naval Postgraduate School, 1,400 military, 1,300 civilian (2001)

CITIES
Salinas, 123,607; Santa Cruz (pt.), 49,905 (1990); Watsonville, 36,783; Monterey, 31,804; Seaside, 28,404

UNUSUAL FEATURES
Clint Eastwood was mayor of Carmel; Former White House Chief of Staff Leon E. Panetta represented the 17th from 1977-93; Monterey known for its language institutes; The Big Sur coastline, along U.S. Highway 1, a favorite location for filming car commercials; Author John Steinbeck grew up in Salinas.

Rep. Gary A. Condit (D)

Elected September 1989; 6th full term

CAPITOL OFFICE
225-6131; fax 225-0819; 2234 Rayburn Bldg. 20515

INTERNET
e-mail: www.house.gov/writerep
web: www.house.gov/gcondit

COMMITTEES
Agriculture
Select Intelligence

HOMETOWN
Ceres

BORN
April 21, 1948, Salina, Okla.

RELIGION
Baptist

FAMILY
Wife, Carolyn Berry; two children

EDUCATION
California State U., Stanislaus, B.A. 1972

CAREER
Health care company executive

POLITICAL HIGHLIGHTS
Ceres City Council, 1972-76 (mayor, 1974-76);
Stanislaus County Board of Supervisors, 1976-82
(chairman, 1980); Calif. Assembly, 1983-89

ELECTION RESULTS

2000 GENERAL

Gary A. Condit (D)	121,003	67.1%
Steve Wilson (R)	56,465	31.3%
Page Roth Riskin (NL)	2,860	1.6%

2000 PRIMARY (OPEN)

Gary A. Condit (D)	80,543	65.3%
Steve Wilson (R)	35,335	28.7%
Rodger McAfee (D)	6,142	5.0%
Page Roth Riskin (NL)	1,262	1.0%

1998 GENERAL

Gary A. Condit (D)	118,842	86.8%
Linda M. DeGroat (LIBERT)	18,089	13.2%

PREVIOUS WINNING PERCENTAGES
1996 (66%); 1994 (66%); 1992 (85%); 1990 (66%);
1989 Special Election (57%)

Condit is not afraid to confront his party leadership and to try to push the Democratic Party toward a more centrist path. He has had his share of successes in recent years, and now he has a seat at the table when Democratic leaders meet to discuss the policy agenda.

It is a significant change from Condit's early years in the House when, with the Democrats in control by a large margin, he strayed often from the party line and felt ignored. Once, after the Democrats lost control of the House in 1995, Condit was named a negotiator on an important regulatory bill by Republican Speaker Newt Gingrich when his own leader, Richard A. Gephardt, declined to make the appointment.

In the 106th Congress, however, Condit was chosen to represent the "Blue Dog" coalition of conservative Democrats at Gephardt's leadership meetings. Other factions — including the Progressive Caucus, New Democrat Coalition and the Congressional Black Caucus — were given a formal role in the decision-making process as well.

Condit's voting record is well to the right on the Democratic spectrum. He supported his party's position only about two-thirds of the time in the 106th Congress, but that figure represents a substantial increase in party loyalty since 1995, when his party-unity score was 45 percent. (The average score is about 85 percent.)

Condit was one of the founders of the Blue Dogs in early 1995, as he and a handful of other like-minded Democrats sought to force the party brass to take into account conservative and moderate views. The effort was not aimed at toppling the leadership, perhaps in some measure because of a lesson Condit had learned as a member of the California Assembly.

In 1988, he was one of the "Gang of Five" moderate Democrats who bridled at Assembly Speaker Willie L. Brown Jr.'s ironhanded rule and tried to remove Brown. The effort failed and Condit lost a leadership post and choice committee assignments. (Condit bears no grudge from that confrontation, and in 1999 he worked to help re-elect Brown as mayor of San Francisco.)

The Blue Dogs now number more than 30 and have won praise from both sides of the aisle for work, particularly on the budget, that has fostered an environment in the House in which compromises are possible. Condit argues that bipartisanship is essential. "If we're going to have Social Security reform, it is going to have to be bipartisan. If we're going to have tax cuts, it has to be bipartisan. ... Somebody will be penalized at the voting booth in a couple of years if these things don't get done, and I couldn't tell you with any certainty who voters are going to take that out on."

Condit's association with the Blue Dogs has been a political plus in the 18th District, where many voters see the national Democratic Party as too liberal. He was one of five Democrats to vote with Republicans on 94 percent of the GOP's "Contract With America" agenda in 1995. He takes a conservative stand on fiscal, regulatory and environmental matters.

But on several other issues, Condit lines up with the bulk of his House Democratic colleagues: He backs abortion rights in most cases, has sided with organized labor on some high-profile floor votes and opposed a GOP attempt to repeal the ban on semiautomatic assault-style weapons.

Condit's top legislative priorities include a longstanding effort to rein in unfunded mandates — federal requirements on local governments and businesses that are not accompanied by additional funds. He has worked with California Republican David Dreier to move the federal government to a two-year budget cycle. He also was involved in a bipartisan effort to safe-guard the privacy of personal medical information.

Beyond the work on budget issues that has earned Condit much notice, he spends a lot of time doing less-visible trench work on the Agriculture Committee, an important post for someone who represents the Central Valley, the leading agricultural region of the country.

Although he has never been shy about confrontation on policy matters, Condit has an easygoing, down-to-earth manner. And while he's polished and perfectly coifed on the job, he prefers wearing jeans and cowboy boots and says riding his Harley-Davidson motorcycle is therapeutic.

Through his work on budget policy, Condit developed a friendship with Republican John R. Kasich, who was chairman of the Budget Committee for six years before he retired in 2000. Condit said their friendship had more to do with interests outside of work — they were known to go to rock con-certs together and they chat often via e-mail — but Condit did support Kasich on a number of key budget votes; in 2000, he was one of just two Democrats who voted for the Kasich-drafted budget blueprint. Condit asked Kasich to appear at a California fundraiser for him in 1997, and Kasich agreed. But objections from GOP partisans squelched the event, prompting Condit to complain to the San Francisco Chronicle that his friend was being "vilified by narrow-minded zealots ... [who] believe the sun rises and sets according to partisan affiliation."

The son of a Baptist minister, Condit was in college during the Vietnam War protests, and he recalls thinking that he wanted to put a more con-structive, positive face on the political involvement of college youth. At age 24, he ran for the city council in Ceres, a small city south of Modesto, and to his surprise he won, going on to serve four years.

Condit spent six years on the Stanislaus County Board of Supervisors while working as an executive with a growing local health care company. He then won election to the state Assembly.

In 1989, he seized the opportunity to run for the House when Democrat-ic Rep. Tony Coelho resigned amid questions about his personal finances. Condit's brand of independent, conservative Democratic philosophy appealed to voters and he was an easy winner. He has won handily ever since.

Condit was one of the earliest backers of Gray Davis when the lieutenant governor ran for governor of California in 1998, and he now has the gov-ernor's ear on a number of policy matters, including water issues. Both of Condit's children, who were already in the political arena in Sacramento, are key Davis staffers.

KEY VOTES

2000

Yes	Raise hourly minimum wage by $1 over two years
Yes	Halt funding for U.S. mission in Kosovo unless European nations pay more
Yes	Provide Medicare benefits to military retirees and their dependents
No	Grant China permanent normal trade status
Yes	Phase out estate, gift and trust taxes
No	Prohibit implementation of president's national monument designations
No	Approve GOP plan to provide prescription drug coverage for Medicare beneficiaries
No	Increase help for poor nations indebted to international financial institutions

1999

Yes	Impose steel import quotas
Yes	Kill proposal to take aviation trust funds off budget
No	Require background checks on buyers only at gun shows with 10 or more vendors
No	Remove barriers among banking, securities and insurance companies
Yes	Authorize state grants to hire teachers and reduce class size
Yes	Overhaul campaign finance law; ban "soft money" and restrict advocacy advertising
Yes	Approve bipartisan plan to increase rights of patients in managed-care health plans

INTEREST GROUPS

	AFL-CIO	ADA	CCUS	ACU
2000	60%	50%	57%	44%
1999	67%	70%	64%	44%
1998	80%	60%	67%	56%
1997	75%	60%	60%	52%

CQ VOTE STUDIES

	PARTY UNITY		PRESIDENTIAL SUPPORT	
	Support	Oppose	Support	Oppose
2000	72%	28%	58%	42%
1999	61%	39%	55%	45%
1998	63%	37%	51%	49%
1997	60%	40%	54%	46%

CALIFORNIA 18
Central Valley — Modesto; Merced

The 18th includes central California's Stanislaus and Merced counties, which together account for roughly 95 percent of its vote, and also slivers of San Joaquin, Madera and Fresno counties. Politically, the district is highly competitive, but Democrats hold a slight voter registration edge. While Hispanics and Asians have been moving into the 18th in large numbers, they have yet to exercise commensurate influence in the voting booth.

Modesto, the Stanislaus County seat, lies near the midpoint of the state on the north bank of the Tuolumne River. Highway 99 passes through, and Interstate 5, the only other major artery through the Central Valley, passes a few miles to the west. The city has grown substantially over the years, spurred both by businesses fleeing California's congested coastal cities and by the Central Valley's successful agricultural industry. The 18th includes some of the world's most varied and productive farming. Modesto also has its own canning and food

processing industry, as well as the Gallo Winery, which is responsible for about one-fourth of the domestic wine market.

The 18th also takes in the southwest corners of San Joaquin County (the city of Ripon) and Madera County (stopping short of Chowchilla). It also slices off the northeastern tip of Fresno County. But these are sparsely populated areas; all three together cast about 5 percent of the district vote.

In this agricultural district, local issues tend to revolve around water availability and the preservation of farmland. The seasonal economy and the early-1990s closure of Castle Air Force Base in Merced have contributed to higher unemployment rates than in other parts of California, but the area expects an economic boost with the planned opening of the University of California Merced in 2004.

MAJOR INDUSTRY
Agriculture, wine, food processing

CITIES
Modesto, 188,253; Merced, 60,551; Turlock, 52,429; Ceres, 33,355

UNUSUAL FEATURES
Modesto depicted in the George Lucas film, "American Graffiti."

Rep. George P. Radanovich (R)

Elected 1994; 4th term

CAPITOL OFFICE
225-4540; fax 225-3402; 123 Cannon Bldg. 20515

INTERNET
e-mail: george.radanovich@mail.house.gov
web: www.house.gov/radanovich

COMMITTEES
Energy & Commerce
Resources

HOMETOWN
Mariposa

BORN
June 20, 1955, Mariposa, Calif.

RELIGION
Roman Catholic

FAMILY
Wife, Ethie Radanovich; one child

EDUCATION
California State Polytechnic U., B.S. 1978

CAREER
Vintner; bank manager; carpenter

POLITICAL HIGHLIGHTS
Mariposa County Board of Supervisors, 1989-92
(chairman, 1991); sought Republican nomination
for U.S. House, 1992

ELECTION RESULTS

2000 GENERAL

George P. Radanovich (R)	144,517	64.9%
Daniel Rosenberg (D)	70,578	31.7%
Elizabeth Taylor (LIBERT)	4,264	1.9%

2000 PRIMARY (OPEN)

George P. Radanovich (R)	109,723	66.5%
Daniel Rosenberg (D)	33,921	20.6%
John Hernandez (D)	15,647	9.5%
Elizabeth Taylor (LIBERT)	3,256	2.0%

1998 GENERAL

George P. Radanovich (R)	131,105	79.4%
Jonathan Richter (LIBERT)	34,044	20.6%

PREVIOUS WINNING PERCENTAGES
1996 (67%); 1994 (57%)

Six years after the Republicans swept into power in the House, Radanovich still works to keep alive the message of that 1994 "Republican revolution" — reduce the size and scope of government, shift authority from the federal government to the state and local levels, eliminate regulations that stifle business, and emphasize personal responsibility.

But, applying the lessons of patience he learned as the founder of a winery in Mariposa County ("It takes a long time for the grapes to grow and mature"), Radanovich (ruh-DON-o-vitch) acknowledges that it can take a while to achieve the kind of changes he seeks.

In the 104th Congress, as the president of the 74-member GOP freshman Class of 1994, Radanovich authored a "New America" vision statement that calls for a smaller federal government while at the same time increasing the role of the private sector in American society. Radanovich took to holding up a misshapen chair to illustrate his point. According to his model, one leg, representing government, had grown too long, threatening the balance of the chair, whose family, business and religious-civic legs were much shorter.

He doesn't use the prop much anymore, but he remains firm in his belief that the three non-governmental legs must be lengthened while the government leg should be whittled down. One way to strengthen non-governmental institutions, Radanovich says, is to greatly expand charitable contributions, and he champions a proposal to institute a 100 percent tax credit for each dollar contributed to charity.

In the aftermath of the disappointing GOP showing in the 1998 elections, Radanovich briefly considered a challenge to the party's leadership, saying that "the Republican Party lacks a coherent and comprehensive message. It is time to change the party's message as well as its messengers." Radanovich announced he was running for the party's No. 4 leadership post, but he dropped out before the vote.

With the GOP's slim margin of control in the House, Radanovich, a member of the Conservative Action Team band of House Republicans (known as the CATs), has tempered his conservatism somewhat to help the leadership. A larger GOP margin would afford him the freedom to stray from the party line more often. To that end, Radanovich, safely ensconced in his 19th District seat, has been active in the House GOP's campaign arm, the National Republican Congressional Committee.

That effort on behalf of the GOP was rewarded in the 107th when he won a sought-after seat on the Energy and Commerce panel.

Radanovich also has devoted his time to advancing the agenda advocated by the Western Caucus, which he chaired in the 106th Congress. The group's roughly 60 lawmakers, mostly Republicans, share the same views on property rights and water issues. The Westerners say that lawmakers from other parts of the country do not understand the unique needs of the West, where the federal government owns huge tracts of land and where water is precious. The group espouses a "new environmentalism," which holds that private property owners and local governments should be given incentives and authority to ensure that land and water are well cared for and efficiently used.

In the 106th, Radanovich charged that regulators were willing to be more lenient with environmental problems stemming from building a new bridge across the Potomac River than with projects in California, where the Endangered Species Act was being strictly enforced.

The 19th District contains part of Yosemite National Park, and Radanovich is wary of proposals to deal with park overcrowding that might hurt tourist-dependent towns and businesses near the park.

Radanovich has been criticized for his legislative efforts on behalf of the domestic wine industry, including his work to lower Mexican tariffs on wine, and his opposition to a move to ban alcohol sales on the Internet. He and fellow California lawmaker (and former vineyard owner) Mike Thompson formed the Congressional Wine Caucus. They argue that the move to ban Internet sales, though couched in terms of keeping underage drinkers from buying alcohol, has more to do with wholesalers trying to maintain their distribution monopoly. "What teen steals a credit card, places an order online, and waits two weeks to receive fine wines?" Radanovich asked.

Armenian-Americans make up one of Radanovich's key constituencies, and he offers amendments or bills annually to restrict U.S. aid to Turkey until Ankara formally acknowledges the Armenian genocide that took place between 1915 and 1923. He also has been active in looking out for the interests of his district's substantial Hmong population.

One of eight children of a Croatian immigrant who owned and operated a clothing store in Mariposa, Radanovich spent much of his teenage years on the family's small ranch just outside of town. He earned a college degree in agricultural business management and, after working a few years as a banker, a carpenter and a substitute teacher, Radanovich pursued his first love, farming.

Although the wines for which California is famous are produced primarily in the valleys of Napa, Sonoma and Santa Clara, 150 miles to the west, Radanovich's dream was to establish a winery in the Mariposa County foothills of the Sierra Nevada, where livestock grazing generally takes precedence over farming. He persisted, and Radanovich Winery now ships about 4,000 cases annually of sauvignon blanc, merlot and other wines.

In building his business, the vintner gained firsthand familiarity with the issues of water allocation, farm labor, taxes and regulation.

That led him to a seat on the Mariposa County Board of Supervisors in 1989. In 1992, he made his first bid for Congress. Mariposa is far from the district's population center in Fresno County, where he was largely unknown, but Radanovich acquitted himself well that year, losing a close race to eventual GOP nominee Tal Cloud. Two years later, Cloud decided not to run, and Radanovich took advantage of the GOP tilt in the district caused by the post-1990 census remapping. He cruised to victory over incumbent Democratic Rep. Richard H. Lehman and has racked up formidable margins of victory since then.

KEY VOTES

2000

No Raise hourly minimum wage by $1 over two years
Yes Halt funding for U.S. mission in Kosovo unless European nations pay more
Yes Provide Medicare benefits to military retirees and their dependents
Yes Grant China permanent normal trade status
Yes Phase out estate, gift and trust taxes
Yes Prohibit implementation of president's national monument designations
Yes Approve GOP plan to provide prescription drug coverage for Medicare beneficiaries
No Increase help for poor nations indebted to international financial institutions

1999

No Impose steel import quotas
No Kill proposal to take aviation trust funds off budget
Yes Require background checks on buyers only at gun shows with 10 or more vendors
Yes Remove barriers among banking, securities and insurance companies
No Authorize state grants to hire teachers and reduce class size
No Overhaul campaign finance law; ban "soft money" and restrict advocacy advertising
No Approve bipartisan plan to increase rights of patients in managed-care health plans

INTEREST GROUPS

	AFL-CIO	ADA	CCUS	ACU
2000	0%	5%	90%	100%
1999	0%	5%	96%	88%
1998	0%	0%	94%	100%
1997	0%	0%	80%	96%

CQ VOTE STUDIES

	PARTY UNITY		PRESIDENTIAL SUPPORT	
	Support	Oppose	Support	Oppose
2000	96%	4%	22%	78%
1999	95%	5%	18%	82%
1998	96%	4%	20%	80%
1997	95%	5%	27%	73%

CALIFORNIA 19
Central Valley — Fresno; Madera

The 19th is a fertile farm district that includes the heart of Central California's San Joaquin Valley. It includes all of Madera County and most of the city of Fresno, home to large numbers of Hispanics, Hmong and Armenians.

A Democratic district before 1992 redistricting, the 19th is now more rural and more Republican. The district sends a Republican to Congress and supported GOP presidential candidates in 1992, '96 and 2000. Farmers and senior citizens, leery of government regulations and environmental protection laws, tend to be moderate conservatives. Farming and water issues are perpetual hot topics and are becoming more significant as population growth means less water for agricultural use.

Fresno County, known as the "agribusiness capital of the world," produces about $4 billion in agricultural projects a year, more than any other county in the nation. Tourism at Yosemite National Park also helps keep the 19th's economy afloat, although the district suffers from high unemployment due to the seasonal nature of its driving industries.

MAJOR INDUSTRY
Agriculture, dairy, tourism

MILITARY BASES
Fresno Yosemite International Airport Air National Guard Base, 939 military, 18 civilian (2001)

CITIES
Fresno (pt.), 273,792 (1990); Clovis, 65,737; Madera, 37,384

UNUSUAL FEATURES
During World War II, more than 5,000 Japanese Americans were interned at the Fresno fairgrounds; Yosemite National Park; Crashup Gas Station in Easton, where a two-seat prop plane crashed through the roof of a gas pump island and is still there.

Rep. Cal Dooley (D)

Elected 1990; 6th term

CAPITOL OFFICE
225-3341; fax 225-9308
1201 Longworth Bldg. 20515

INTERNET
e-mail: www.house.gov/writerep
web: www.house.gov/dooley

COMMITTEES
Agriculture
Resources

HOMETOWN
Visalia

BORN
Jan. 11, 1954, Visalia, Calif.

RELIGION
Protestant

FAMILY
Wife, Linda Phillips Dooley; two children

EDUCATION
U. of California, Davis, B.S. 1977; Stanford U., M.A. 1987

CAREER
Farmer

POLITICAL HIGHLIGHTS
No previous office

ELECTION RESULTS

2000 GENERAL

Cal Dooley (D)	66,235	52.4%
Rich Rodriguez (R)	57,563	45.5%
Walter Ruehlig (NL)	1,416	1.1%
Arnold Kriegbaum (LIBERT)	1,320	1.0%

2000 PRIMARY (OPEN)

Cal Dooley (D)	43,608	51.7%
Rich Rodriguez (R)	38,661	45.8%
Arnold Kriegbaum (LIBERT)	1,144	1.4%
Walter Ruehlig (NL)	999	1.2%

1998 GENERAL

Cal Dooley (D)	60,599	60.7%
Cliff Unruh (R)	39,183	39.3%

PREVIOUS WINNING PERCENTAGES
1996 (57%); 1994 (57%); 1992 (65%); 1990 (55%)

It is a measure of Dooley's reputation as a leader of centrist Democrats that his name was floated — during the disputed 2000 presidential election — as a potential appointee to either a Bush or a Gore administration.

The fourth-generation farmer from the Central Valley is one of the principals in the New Democrat Coalition, a group of about 70 House Democrats that depicts itself as a response to "the public's demand for non-bureaucratic but activist government." Ideologically, Dooley and his colleagues in the group fall between the right-of-center "Blue Dog" Democrats and the party's unreconstructed liberals.

Dooley's appeal to both sides of the aisle is necessary in a district with a large Hispanic population that is trending Republican. During his tough 2000 re-election race against Republican Rich Rodriguez, a former television anchorman waging his first political campaign, Dooley picked up endorsements from such traditionally GOP-leaning groups as the U.S. Chamber of Commerce and the Business Roundtable.

He earned his stripes with the pro-business constituency during tough legislative battles in the 106th Congress over expanding trade with China, the Caribbean and Africa, serving with fellow California Democrat Robert T. Matsui as the White House's chief vote-counters during the intense maneuvering in the House before the vote to grant China permanent normal trade status.

Dooley is a loyal Democrat, more apt to reach out to like-minded Republicans on trade or natural resources issues than to openly defy his party's leadership. He supported the "patients' bill of rights" measure passed in 1999, has voted for gun control initiatives and in 2000 opposed GOP legislation to end the "marriage penalty," a quirk in the tax code that exposes some married couples to higher income taxes. And he fulminated against Green Party candidate Ralph Nader for eating into Vice President Al Gore's support in pivotal states during the presidential race, calling Nader a "sanctimonious ass."

Dooley has been rebuffed in his efforts to join the leadership, however. He failed in a 1998 bid to become vice chairman of the Democratic Caucus, losing out to New Jersey's Robert Menendez, 124-81.

In the debate over federal regulation of natural resources, Dooley is strongly involved, in part, because the issue looms so large in the 20th District, which covers portions of the San Joaquin Valley from Fresno to Bakersfield. As a top Democrat on the Resources and Agriculture committees, he brings to policy debates the experiences of a large-scale agribusinessman who, like many of his constituents, makes arid land bloom using water from the Central Valley Project, a network of government-subsidized dams and canals.

Dooley is always on guard against proposals to phase out the irrigation subsidies, as a congressionally appointed panel recommended in 1998. "The Central Valley Project has made the valley the most productive agricultural region in the world," he says, "providing a stable, abundant supply of high-quality food and fiber for the entire nation and for our trading partners."

Since the turn of the century, Dooley's family has tried to coax from the ground a range of crops that includes cotton, alfalfa and walnuts. President of the California Future Farmers of America at age 18, Dooley went on to earn an undergraduate degree in agriculture economics at the University of California-Davis and a master's in management from Stanford University — all good preparation for a supervisory role in the family's San Joaquin Valley business, Dooley Farms.

www.cq.com

In 2000, he worked with California's Democratic Gov. Gray Davis on a joint federal and state master plan for use of Central Valley water. Known as "CALFED," the plan envisions spending more than $8 billion over the next seven years to parcel out water to farmers and city dwellers. Dooley will be instrumental in drafting authorizing language for the plan in the 107th Congress and in securing funding for the plan's full implementation.

Exports are vital to agricultural producers in the Central Valley, a point Dooley has underscored in advocating major trade expansion initiatives. This has put him at odds with Minority Leader Richard A. Gephardt and other Democrats who are close to organized labor.

On fiscal policy, Dooley is more in sync with conservatives than with his fellow Democrats. He voted against President Clinton's landmark 1993 budget, which reduced the deficit with the aid of a healthy tax increase. In 1997, as Congress struggled to reach a balanced-budget agreement with the White House, he voted for an interim Republican plan on taxing and spending that most Democrats rejected.

In votes on environmental policy and worker-management relations, Dooley sometimes sides with the GOP. He has sharp words for Democrats who feel "that employers are evil, that they are mean-spirited people who will use any means to take advantage of their employees."

In the 105th, for example, he was in the minority of Democrats who supported a GOP proposal allowing companies to offer employees compensatory time in lieu of pay for overtime work. Critics of the measure said workers would be coerced into taking whatever form of compensation the company preferred, an assertion Dooley rejected. "I am a private-sector employer, and I take personal offense and find it insulting that so many of my colleagues would contend that we are going to take advantage of the people that work for us."

Dooley was drawn early into not only his family's farming concern but also into politics, another field in which his family had some expertise: His brother and sister-in-law were senior aides to former Gov. Edmund G. "Jerry" Brown Jr. Dooley went to work in 1987 for state Sen. Rose Ann Vuich, a legendary Fresno Democrat. Dooley's association with Vuich helped him temper the more-liberal flavor of his relatives' politics. In 1990, Dooley won the 20th District seat with 55 percent, toppling six-term GOP Rep. Charles "Chip" Pashayan Jr., who was tainted by the 1989 savings and loan scandal. After an easy victory in 1992, Dooley's winning margin slipped a bit in the big GOP year of 1994, leading Republicans to keep him in their sights in future races. In 2000, GOP candidate Rodriguez held Dooley to a 7-point victory margin.

KEY VOTES

2000
Yes Raise hourly minimum wage by $1 over two years
No   Halt funding for U.S. mission in Kosovo unless European nations pay more
Yes Provide Medicare benefits to military retirees and their dependents
Yes Grant China permanent normal trade status
Yes Phase out estate, gift and trust taxes
Yes Prohibit implementation of president's national monument designations
No   Approve GOP plan to provide prescription drug coverage for Medicare beneficiaries
Yes Increase help for poor nations indebted to international financial institutions

1999
No   Impose steel import quotas
Yes Kill proposal to take aviation trust funds off budget
No   Require background checks on buyers only at gun shows with 10 or more vendors
Yes Remove barriers among banking, securities and insurance companies
Yes Authorize state grants to hire teachers and reduce class size
Yes Overhaul campaign finance law; ban "soft money" and restrict advocacy advertising
Yes Approve bipartisan plan to increase rights of patients in managed-care health plans

INTEREST GROUPS

	AFL-CIO	ADA	CCUS	ACU
2000	60%	70%	90%	20%
1999	44%	80%	80%	8%
1998	80%	85%	67%	4%
1997	50%	65%	90%	12%

CQ VOTE STUDIES

	PARTY UNITY		PRESIDENTIAL SUPPORT	
	Support	Oppose	Support	Oppose
2000	82%	18%	71%	29%
1999	77%	23%	72%	28%
1998	80%	20%	80%	20%
1997	77%	23%	76%	24%

CALIFORNIA 20
Parts of Kern, Kings and Fresno counties

The 20th reaches from Fresno to Bakersfield, through portions of Fresno, Kings and Kern counties. It picks up Fresno's southeastern neighborhoods, which are home to many blacks and Hispanics who reliably support Democratic candidates.

The 20th still bears much of the burden of the San Joaquin Valley's urban and rural poor and is beset by crime and high unemployment. It also is one of California's most rural districts and has some of the state's poorest and least-educated residents, many of whom are Hispanic and Hmong immigrants who work in the district's farming community.

The district takes in the portions of Fresno, Kings and Kern counties known as the Westlands. Here, federal water projects have spawned vast farms with battalions of workers. Motorists on Interstate 5 see nary a town while they pass fields filled with a wide variety of products, including alfalfa, cotton, fruits, sugar beets, wheat and nuts.

To assist the area's shaky economy, the 20th has attracted 19 state and privately run prisons. The area is now in the process of building a new baseball stadium in downtown Fresno, which is set to open in early 2002. Local leaders hope it will provide an economic boost to the city.

MAJOR INDUSTRY
Agriculture, dairy, prisons

MILITARY BASES
Lemoore Naval Air Station, 5,500 military, 1,300 civilian (2001)

CITIES
Fresno (pt.), 80,410 (1990); Hanford, 37,819; Delano, 35,085; Bakersfield (pt.), 19,904 (1990)

UNUSUAL FEATURES
Fresno resident Mike Reynolds, whose daughter was murdered, was the catalyst behind California's "three strikes" ballot initiative; The 20th's ethnic population includes many migrants from the Dust Bowl era whose ancestors were farm workers; Murderer Charles Manson in jail at Corcoran State Prison in Kings County.

Rep. Bill Thomas (R)

CAPITOL OFFICE
225-2915; fax 225-8798; 2208 Rayburn Bldg. 20515

INTERNET
e-mail: www.house.gov/writerep
web: www.house.gov/billthomas

COMMITTEES
Ways & Means - chairman
Joint Taxation - chairman

HOMETOWN
Bakersfield

BORN
Dec. 6, 1941, Wallace, Idaho

RELIGION
Baptist

FAMILY
Wife, Sharon Thomas; two children

EDUCATION
Santa Ana Community College, A.A. 1961; San Francisco State U., B.A. 1963, M.A. 1965

CAREER
Professor

POLITICAL HIGHLIGHTS
Calif. Assembly, 1975-79

ELECTION RESULTS

2000 GENERAL

Bill Thomas (R)	142,539	71.6%
Pedro Martinez (D)	49,318	24.8%
James Manion (LIBERT)	7,243	3.6%

2000 PRIMARY (OPEN)

Bill Thomas (R)	98,088	73.7%
Pedro Martinez (D)	29,511	22.2%
James Manion (LIBERT)	5,430	4.1%

1998 GENERAL

Bill Thomas (R)	115,989	78.9%
John Evans (REF)	30,994	21.1%

PREVIOUS WINNING PERCENTAGES
1996 (66%); 1994 (68%); 1992 (65%); 1990 (60%); 1988 (71%); 1986 (73%); 1984 (71%); 1982 (68%); 1980 (71%); 1978 (59%)

Elected 1978; 12th term

Thomas' command of the intricacies of policy — health care, first and foremost — and his fierce negotiating abilities have won him the respect and trust of other Republicans. But his abrasive personality, which Thomas attributes to "a very big inferiority complex," can sometimes grate on Republicans and Democrats alike.

Thomas says he is working to control his caustic temper, which he will want to keep in check now that he has taken the reins of the Ways and Means Committee, arguably the most powerful panel in the House because it writes tax, trade, health care, welfare and Social Security legislation. "The reaction people see in me is not ego-driven, it's inferiority-driven," Thomas said in a June 2000 interview. To compensate, he says, he intentionally tries to work harder than his peers, a strategy he says that some of his colleagues find bothersome: "People get mad because you work so hard it shows them up a little bit."

However, even people who dislike Thomas admire his ability to cut deals and move legislation, skills sure to be tested as he works to turn into law several of the most important pieces of President Bush's agenda — and to ensure that he and other members of the House have at least some say-so along the way.

As chairman of the Ways and Means Subcommittee on Health for the first six years of GOP control, Thomas helped rewrite medical insurance law and was the party's point man on a variety of other health care issues. In the 106th Congress, he played a major role in developing and passing GOP legislation to add prescription drug coverage to Medicare and in formulating the Republican positions on patients' rights and managed-care proposals. He was also involved in negotiations between House and Senate Republicans on tax legislation in recent years but was not viewed as a top-tier player. As Ways and Means chairman, however, he can be expected to wade into the arcana of the IRS code with zeal.

That penchant for detail — and his eagerness to mix it up on both policy and politics — propelled Thomas to the chairmanship upon the retirement of Republican Bill Archer of Texas, who had held the gavel since 1995. Thomas bested Philip M. Crane of Illinois, who had almost 10 years more tenure on the panel but was viewed as a much less energetic lawmaker, and E. Clay Shaw Jr. of Florida, who offered himself as a compromise candidate. The GOP Steering Committee vote that elected Thomas chairman was secret, but participants characterized it as ultimately unanimous.

When he became the ranking minority member on the Health Subcommittee in 1993, Thomas said he immersed himself in its issues. Every day for six months, he rose at 4 a.m. to read background material. "Basically I got a medical degree," he said. He became a master of issues great and small, able to discuss the sweeping political ramifications of policy as well as the intricacies of Medicare reimbursements in thousands of counties. But he was unable to advance his proposal to move consumers away from the employer-based health insurance system to one based on a tax credit that individuals could spend as they wish to purchase coverage.

He did, however, help develop legislation in 1997 that made the most changes to Medicare since its creation in 1965. The result, which was part of that year's budget-balancing package, was widely viewed as a short-term fix. But Thomas said the legislation was significant — "We have broken the logjam. ... We can adjust Medicare," he declared — and at the time he won accolades from Democrats for crafting his program as a bipartisan initiative.

In both 1999 and 2000, however, Congress enacted payment increases to hospitals, HMOs, doctors and other health care providers whose Medicare reimbursements were reduced by the 1997 measure. Thomas said such adjustments are inevitable whenever Congress alters a program as comprehensive as Medicare, which provides health care benefits to nearly 40 million elderly and disabled people. Health care providers' complaints — especially from the vocal and well-financed hospitals lobby — are likely to continue, with Congress possibly facing yearly payment adjustments to silence such outcries.

In 1997, Speaker Newt Gingrich made Thomas one of his four appointees to a 17-member commission studying long-term changes to ensure the viability of Medicare. Gingrich asked his appointees to promise not to vote for any proposal that called for a tax increase. Given those constraints, the panel could not produce a plan that could muster the 11 votes needed for a recommendation to Congress.

Thomas' detail-oriented approach came in handy when he was chairman of the House Administration Committee from 1995 through 2000, as he dealt with the majority's housekeeping tasks, from privatizing congressional parking lots to investigating contested elections. He also was deeply involved in a re-examination of Capitol security measures after two U.S. Capitol Police officers were fatally shot in 1998.

Thomas oversaw the privatization of several House services and slashed committee staffing by about one-third. He also presided over the first-ever outside audit of House finances, which offered Republican leaders hard evidence of what they had long contended: Under the Democrats, the House was in financial shambles, funds were poorly accounted for and frequently overspent, and lawmakers themselves were sometimes the culprits. A 1999 audit gave the House a clean bill of health for the first time. But in typical Thomas style, the news conference he held to announce the results turned into an attack on the way Democrats ran the House.

Thomas was a political science professor before he ran, successfully, for the state Assembly in 1974 as a staunch conservative. In 1978, when GOP Rep. William Ketchum died after the June primary, Thomas positioned himself as the moderate GOP alternative. He was the area's ranking Republican legislator, but it took him seven ballots at a nominating convention to beat two conservative opponents. He went on to easily defeat Democrat Bob Sogge, a former state Senate aide. Thomas has often described himself as a pragmatic conservative, a label that has worked for him at the polls. While he has faced some primary challenges, his seat has been secure.

KEY VOTES

2000
No Raise hourly minimum wage by $1 over two years
Yes Halt funding for U.S. mission in Kosovo unless European nations pay more
No Provide Medicare benefits to military retirees and their dependents
Yes Grant China permanent normal trade status
Yes Phase out estate, gift and trust taxes
Yes Prohibit implementation of president's national monument designations
Yes Approve GOP plan to provide prescription drug coverage for Medicare beneficiaries
No Increase help for poor nations indebted to international financial institutions

1999
No Impose steel import quotas
Yes Kill proposal to take aviation trust funds off budget
? Require background checks on buyers only at gun shows with 10 or more vendors
Yes Remove barriers among banking, securities and insurance companies
No Authorize state grants to hire teachers and reduce class size
No Overhaul campaign finance law; ban "soft money" and restrict advocacy advertising
No Approve bipartisan plan to increase rights of patients in managed-care health plans

INTEREST GROUPS

	AFL-CIO	ADA	CCUS	ACU
2000	0%	10%	90%	80%
1999	0%	10%	96%	66%
1998	10%	0%	100%	92%
1997	13%	10%	100%	80%

CQ VOTE STUDIES

	PARTY UNITY		PRESIDENTIAL SUPPORT	
	Support	Oppose	Support	Oppose
2000	92%	8%	32%	68%
1999	89%	11%	31%	69%
1998	89%	11%	28%	72%
1997	90%	10%	35%	65%

CALIFORNIA 21
Kern and Tulare counties — Bakersfield

The 21st lies between Fresno and Los Angeles, in California's inland core. The district votes consistently Republican, and about three-fourths of its vote comes from Kern County in the southern half of the district. The rest comes from new territory pulled in from Tulare County to the north, added during 1992 redistricting.

Both Kern and Tulare counties have a strong agricultural base and together produce billions of dollars in crops such as grapes, citrus, cotton and nuts. Tulare County also is among the nation's largest dairy producing regions, while Kern is known for its oil production.

Bakersfield, in the southern end of the San Joaquin Valley, is Kern County's largest city. Here, oil and agriculture dominate the economy, although the city is trying to diversify by promoting its growing telecommunications, financial and light manufacturing sectors.

People moving from the Los Angeles Basin and the San Francisco Bay have led to growth that could eventually mean the loss of prime agricultural land, a major political issue in the 21st.

MAJOR INDUSTRY
Agriculture, oil, military

MILITARY BASES
Naval Air Warfare Center Weapons Division, China Lake (shared with 40th District), 889 military, 3,003 civilian; Edwards Air Force Base (shared with 25th District), 3,800 military, 7,400 civilian (2000)

CITIES
Bakersfield (pt.), 154,916 (1990); Visalia (pt.), 49,090 (1990); Tulare (pt.), 32,935 (1990)

UNUSUAL FEATURES
Bakersfield known as the country music capital of the West; Country music star Buck Owens has his Crystal Palace, museum and theater in Bakersfield; Nation's first jet- and rocket-powered flights took off from Edwards Air Force Base; World's largest novelty ice cream plant, Nestle Ice Cream Co., in Bakersfield.

Rep. Lois Capps (D)

CAPITOL OFFICE
225-3601; fax 225-5632
1118 Longworth Bldg. 20515

INTERNET
e-mail: www.house.gov/writerep
web: www.house.gov/capps

COMMITTEES
Energy & Commerce

HOMETOWN
Santa Barbara

BORN
Jan. 10, 1938, Ladysmith, Wis.

RELIGION
Lutheran

FAMILY
Widowed; three children (one deceased)

EDUCATION
Pacific Lutheran U., B.S. 1959; Yale U., M.A. 1964;
U. of California, Santa Barbara, M.A. 1990

CAREER
Elementary school nurse; college instructor

POLITICAL HIGHLIGHTS
No previous office

ELECTION RESULTS

2000 GENERAL

Lois Capps (D)	135,538	53.1%
Mike Stoker (R)	113,094	44.3%

2000 PRIMARY (OPEN)

Lois Capps (D)	105,850	55.3%
Mike Stoker (R)	73,256	38.3%
Allen Rowe (R)	8,385	4.4%

1998 GENERAL

Lois Capps (D)	109,517	55.0%
Tom Bordonaro Jr. (R)	85,927	43.1%
Robert Bakhaus (LIBERT)	2,579	1.3%

PREVIOUS WINNING PERCENTAGES
1998 Special Runoff Election (54%); 1998 Special
Election (45%)

Elected March 1998; 2nd full term

The daughter and granddaughter of Lutheran ministers and with a religion degree herself, Capps' personal faith has been sorely tested in recent years. Her husband, Walter, a philosophy professor before he was elected to Congress in 1996, died suddenly of a heart attack in October 1997. Then early in 2000, her eldest daughter, a psychology professor at the University of California at Berkeley, died of cancer.

Capps says the support from her staff and House colleagues was tremendous — she is particularly close to GOP Rep. Deborah Pryce of Ohio, who also lost a daughter to cancer. Capps says the House is not the place envisioned by some of her friends back home, who wondered when Capps first ran for Congress how she would fare in the competitive environment of Capitol Hill. But Capps, a former school nurse, laughs and says, "I reminded them that I had to deal with a school board all those years."

Capps' personal and professional background seem to have prepared her for a life in public service. Growing up in small towns in Wisconsin and Montana where her father had parishes, she recalls that ministering to people's needs was a central part of her upbringing.

Before her election to Congress, Capps had a history of political activism and civic involvement. She had a long career as an elementary school nurse in the Santa Barbara School District, where she also headed up the county's teenage pregnancy counseling project and served on the boards of various service and political organizations, including the American Red Cross, the American Heart Association and the Santa Barbara Women's Political Committee.

When she arrived in the House in 1998, Capps was given her husband's committee assignments — International Relations and Science.

But she left those in the 106th Congress when she won an assignment to the Commerce Committee (now called Energy and Commerce), which plays a key role in health care matters. To get on the powerful panel, Capps told the Democratic leadership that they needed a nurse or other health professional on the panel. She also served on a Democratic health care task force, which focused on Medicare reform, patients' rights and the cost of prescription drugs.

Capps generally votes the Democratic line. But mindful of the partisan split in her district, she will at times strike a moderate stance. She affiliates with the New Democrat Coalition, a growing faction of moderate House Democrats. She says the group's philosophy is a great match for her district, in which there are environmental concerns about offshore drilling and preservation of fragile land areas as well as support for international trade and high-technology businesses (the area is sometimes referred to as "Silicon Beach"). Many of the New Democrats' centrist themes resonate with the 22nd District's moderate Republican voters.

In the 105th Congress, Capps parted ways with a majority of Democrats in voting for a Republican proposal to make it more difficult for Congress to impose on businesses new regulations that carry a substantial cost. She also backed a Republican plan to revamp federal bankruptcy laws and was one of only 19 Democrats who voted for the GOP's 1998 tax cut bill. In 2000, Capps was among the minority of Democrats who supported repeal of the estate tax.

Capps teamed up with California Republican Mary Bono (who also succeeded her husband) in introducing legislation to block collection of user fees in national forests and on other public lands. "Maybe Congress needs to bite the bullet, with the economy we have, and allocate more money for the forests," she told the Los Angeles Times. She also pushed for a feasibility study on preserving a particular pristine stretch of coastline in her district.

Capps' religious background gives weight to her argument for the separation of church and state. Based on the perspective gained during her years in the public schools, Capps says she believes children should have their religious views instilled in them at home.

The 22nd District is a competitive one — Republicans had held the seat for a half-century before Walter Capps' 1996 victory — and the 1998 special election attracted national attention. But Capps was no novice at campaigning: She had stumped alongside her husband, even standing in for him in his 1996 race while he was recuperating from injuries sustained in a car accident involving a drunken driver.

In a January 1998 all-party special primary, Capps, the only Democrat in the race, ran first with 45 percent of the vote, short of the majority required to win the seat. In second place was conservative Republican state Rep. Tom Bordonaro with 29 percent, followed by moderate Republican state Rep. Brooks Firestone with 25 percent. Bordonaro and Firestone had split on abortion policy and other issues.

By the time of the March special election, outside groups poured hundreds of thousands of dollars into various ad campaigns about term limits and taxes as well as abortion. But Capps made a mantra of the statement that the race turned on "local issues." She consistently talked of how her husband had secured funds for local projects involving bay dredging, space technology and community policing, and she promised to maintain that home district focus.

In a race seen as a possible bellwether of the congressional elections that fall, Capps scored a 9-point victory over Bordonaro by stressing the cornerstone Democratic Party themes of protecting the environment and improving education and health care. Her victory made her the 35th widow to win a House seat left vacant because of the death of her husband.

Capps served out the remaining months of her husband's term and then won re-election in November 1998 to a full term, again besting Bordonaro, this time by 12 percentage points. In 2000, Republicans targeted her district for extra effort, but she turned back Republican Mike Stoker, a former Santa Barbara County supervisor and ex-chairman of the California Agricultural Labor Relations Board, by 9 points.

KEY VOTES

2000

Yes	Raise hourly minimum wage by $1 over two years
No	Halt funding for U.S. mission in Kosovo unless European nations pay more
Yes	Provide Medicare benefits to military retirees and their dependents
Yes	Grant China permanent normal trade status
Yes	Phase out estate, gift and trust taxes
No	Prohibit implementation of president's national monument designations
No	Approve GOP plan to provide prescription drug coverage for Medicare beneficiaries
Yes	Increase help for poor nations indebted to international financial institutions

1999

Yes	Impose steel import quotas
No	Kill proposal to take aviation trust funds off budget
No	Require background checks on buyers only at gun shows with 10 or more vendors
No	Remove barriers among banking, securities and insurance companies
Yes	Authorize state grants to hire teachers and reduce class size
Yes	Overhaul campaign finance law; ban "soft money" and restrict advocacy advertising
Yes	Approve bipartisan plan to increase rights of patients in managed-care health plans

INTEREST GROUPS

	AFL-CIO	ADA	CCUS	ACU
2000	70%	70%	75%	16%
1999	78%	100%	44%	8%
1998	78%	85%	71%	18%

CQ VOTE STUDIES

	PARTY UNITY		PRESIDENTIAL SUPPORT	
	Support	Oppose	Support	Oppose
2000	89%	11%	73%	27%
1999	90%	10%	80%	20%
1998	91%	9%	73%	27%

CALIFORNIA 22
Santa Barbara; Santa Maria; San Luis Obispo

The 22nd is a beach-front, palm tree-laden district that lies on California's Central Coast, just beyond the northern fringe of metropolitan Los Angeles. Redistricting in 1992 stripped the old district of Ventura County and brought the coastal counties of San Luis Obispo and Santa Barbara together to form the new 22nd.

A politically competitive district, the 22nd's evenly split constituency is much more liberal on social issues than on economic matters. Of its three main cities, Santa Maria is the most Republican, with San Luis Obispo and Santa Barbara registering high numbers of Democrats. Wealthy members of Hollywood's elite in Santa Barbara County and thousands of students at California Polytechnic State U. in San Luis Obispo and the U. of California Santa Barbara contribute to Democratic voter rolls.

About 60 percent of the district's vote is cast in Santa Barbara County, its population centered on Vandenberg Air Force Base and the cities of

Lompoc and Santa Maria. Agriculture, including a scattering of cattle ranches, along with a high-tech space industry and a strong service sector, carry the 22nd's healthy economy. In this ecologically concerned area, public opinion has largely turned against on- and offshore oil drilling.

MAJOR INDUSTRY
Agriculture, aerospace, oil

MILITARY BASES
Vandenberg Air Force Base, 3,152 military, 4,162 civilian (1998)

CITIES
Santa Barbara, 86,290; Santa Maria, 69,000; San Luis Obispo, 42,891; Lompoc, 41,295

UNUSUAL FEATURES
Michael Jackson's Neverland Valley Ranch and the 688-acre Reagan Ranch; Santa Barbara, birthplace of the Egg McMuffin; Celebrities, including Bo Derek, Jackson Browne, Jeff Bridges, Rob Lowe, Michael Douglas and Kathy Ireland, live in Santa Barbara County.

Rep. Elton Gallegly (R)

Elected 1986; 8th term

CAPITOL OFFICE
225-5811; fax 225-1100; 2427 Rayburn Bldg. 20515

INTERNET
e-mail: www.house.gov/writerep
web: www.house.gov/gallegly

COMMITTEES
International Relations
  (Europe - chairman)
Judiciary
Resources

HOMETOWN
Simi Valley

BORN
March 7, 1944, Huntington Park, Calif.

RELIGION
Protestant

FAMILY
Wife, Janice Gallegly; four children

EDUCATION
California State U., Los Angeles, attended 1962-63

CAREER
Real estate broker

POLITICAL HIGHLIGHTS
Simi Valley City Council, 1979-86; mayor of Simi Valley, 1980-86

ELECTION RESULTS

2000 GENERAL

Elton Gallegly (R)	119,479	54.1%
Michael Case (D)	89,918	40.7%
Cary Savitch (REF)	6,473	2.9%
Roger Peebles (LIBERT)	3,708	1.7%

2000 PRIMARY (OPEN)

Elton Gallegly (R)	92,010	63.2%
Michael Case (D)	36,221	24.9%
Albert Goldberg (D)	8,786	6.0%
Cary Savitch (REF)	4,306	3.0%
Roger Peebles (LIBERT)	2,994	2.1%

1998 GENERAL

Elton Gallegly (R)	96,322	60.1%
Daniel Gonzalez (D)	64,032	39.9%

PREVIOUS WINNING PERCENTAGES
1996 (60%); 1994 (66%); 1992 (54%); 1990 (58%); 1988 (69%); 1986 (68%)

Gallegly is best known on Capitol Hill for his hard-line stand on illegal immigration, and he casts a conservative vote on most issues, but his alliance with Democrats on a few high-profile measures hints at a more complex political philosophy.

The California Republican has an easygoing demeanor with a touch of self-deprecation. He is one of the few non-lawyers on the Judiciary Committee. In fact, he is a college dropout — something he neither trumpets nor apologizes for — although he notes that he seems to have done all right in building a successful real estate brokerage business and then a political career that is now in its third decade.

Gallegly (GAL-uh-glee) is predominantly known in Washington for his unsuccessful 1996 effort to deny a public school education to the children of illegal immigrants. He argued that states such as California could no longer afford to educate children of illegal aliens and that the promise of free schooling was a magnet drawing unauthorized immigrants into the country. "We're not penalizing children," he said. "We're merely not rewarding them."

Gallegly still argues for aggressive efforts to combat illegal immigration, and he opposes proposals to expand the number of skilled high-technology workers admitted to the country, but he softens his stance with calls for better performance from the Immigration and Naturalization Service in dealing with the routine needs of legal immigrants. In the 106th Congress, he raised eyebrows when he joined Judiciary panel Democrats in backing a proposal to require landowners to provide housing for migrant farm workers temporarily admitted into the United States.

In the 106th Congress, while continuing to build a conservative voting record overall, Gallegly cast his lot with the Democratic majority in backing an overhaul of the campaign finance system and regulation of health maintenance organizations.

As the former mayor of Simi Valley, a community close enough to Los Angeles that many of its residents are concerned about the spread of urban crime, Gallegly in the 103rd Congress supported a five-day waiting period for handgun purchases. He was one of 42 Republicans who voted for the 1994 crime bill sought by President Clinton, even though it included a ban on certain semiautomatic assault-style weapons.

Growing up, Gallegly followed the political persuasions of his father, a lifelong Democrat. But he notes, "He was an FDR Democrat, and they're much different from the Democrats of today. He believed in government helping people who couldn't help themselves, but not those who could," Gallegly told the Los Angeles Times. In high school, the younger Gallegly's Democratic views earned him the nickname "Walter Reuther" — a reference to the long-tenured president of the United Auto Workers union.

After dropping out of college for financial reasons, Gallegly went into the real estate business (his initial investment was $45) and built a successful brokerage. Frustrated in his dealings with local government, he decided to run for office himself in 1979, urged on by his business colleagues.

Gallegly won a seat on the Simi Valley City Council and served concurrently as mayor for six years before running for Congress. In 1986, looking for a new challenge, he made a bid for the House seat being vacated by GOP Rep. Bobbi Fiedler, who ran, unsuccessfully, for the Senate. Gallegly touted his record as mayor of Simi Valley, where he was well-known for having boosted economic development, and won comfortably in November.

Even though the district is competitive politically, Gallegly has had relatively easy re-election contests in recent years. In 2000, his victory by 13 percentage points over a political newcomer, real estate lawyer Michael Case, was his closest House race yet.

Gallegly has a seat on the International Relations Committee, and in the 107th Congress he became chairman of the Europe Subcommittee. He had chaired the Western Hemisphere Subcommittee, which in the 105th Congress looked into ways to reduce the availability of illegal drugs — including boosting efforts to decrease the flow of cocaine and heroin into the United States, eradicating crops that supply the raw materials, and providing incentives for drug-producing countries to grow different crops.

Gallegly is also a member of the Resources Committee, where he buttresses the ranks of Western conservatives who take a dim view of federal involvement in land-use matters.

But his highest-profile initiative in that area came out of the Judiciary Committee in the 105th Congress. His legislation was designed to give landowners and business developers more clout in challenging local zoning laws that prevent them from building on their property. The measure, pushed by property rights advocates, drew opposition from environmentalists, historic preservationists, governors and local officials. It passed in the House but died in the Senate.

In the 106th Congress, Gallegly pressed for special attention to the needs of gifted and talented students in low-income schools. "We have very intelligent kids in street gangs who are tearing down society instead of contributing to its success. We need to reach them early and challenge them so that they, too, can succeed. They are uncut diamonds, and nobody notices," he said.

Also in the 106th, Gallegly won enactment of legislation authorizing the placement of a plaque at the Vietnam Veterans Memorial honoring veterans who died after their service in Vietnam but as a result of injuries from the war.

The congressman is normally a staunch fiscal conservative. In the 103rd Congress, after severe flooding along the Mississippi River destroyed many homes and ruined crops, Gallegly argued that any federal flood relief must be paid for by making cuts elsewhere in the budget. But when parts of Simi Valley were damaged by a California earthquake in 1994, he supported Clinton's disaster relief legislation, even though its cost added to the federal deficit.

KEY VOTES

2000

No	Raise hourly minimum wage by $1 over two years
Yes	Halt funding for U.S. mission in Kosovo unless European nations pay more
Yes	Provide Medicare benefits to military retirees and their dependents
Yes	Grant China permanent normal trade status
Yes	Phase out estate, gift and trust taxes
Yes	Prohibit implementation of president's national monument designations
Yes	Approve GOP plan to provide prescription drug coverage for Medicare beneficiaries
No	Increase help for poor nations indebted to international financial institutions

1999

Yes	Impose steel import quotas
No	Kill proposal to take aviation trust funds off budget
Yes	Require background checks on buyers only at gun shows with 10 or more vendors
Yes	Remove barriers among banking, securities and insurance companies
No	Authorize state grants to hire teachers and reduce class size
Yes	Overhaul campaign finance law; ban "soft money" and restrict advocacy advertising
Yes	Approve bipartisan plan to increase rights of patients in managed-care health plans

INTEREST GROUPS

	AFL-CIO	ADA	CCUS	ACU
2000	0%	5%	85%	72%
1999	33%	25%	84%	79%
1998	20%	15%	83%	76%
1997	0%	5%	100%	80%

CQ VOTE STUDIES

	PARTY UNITY		PRESIDENTIAL SUPPORT	
	Support	Oppose	Support	Oppose
2000	85%	15%	35%	65%
1999	88%	12%	24%	76%
1998	90%	10%	21%	79%
1997	93%	7%	30%	70%

CALIFORNIA 23

Most of Ventura County; Oxnard; Ventura; Simi Valley

The 23rd includes nearly all of Ventura County, where a boom of people arriving from the Los Angeles Basin in the 1980s created a new congressional district in 1992. The district is a mix of lower-income farming communities and more upscale residential neighborhoods, such as Moorepark in the southeast, a small but fast-growing city.

The district is politically split, with Democrats and Republicans virtually even in voter registration, making national elections unpredictable. Oxnard, the largest city in Ventura County, is considered a Democratic pocket and has a large Latino population employed in the area's fertile agricultural industry. Overall, the district is nearly one-third Hispanic.

Ventura County, which absorbed much of the destruction of the 1994 Northridge earthquake, is seeing strong growth in its electronics, finance and insurance sectors. The county grew so much that it passed a slow-growth ballot initiative in 1998 in an effort to stave off urban sprawl. The 23rd benefited from base closures in other areas that transferred military personnel and operations to its two military bases.

MAJOR INDUSTRY
Agriculture, military, electronics

MILITARY BASES
Naval Air Warfare Center Weapons Division and Naval Construction Battalion Center, 8,562 military, 6,605 civilian (2000); California Air National Guard, 1,215 military, 230 civilian (1998)

CITIES
Oxnard, 156,372; Simi Valley, 114,247; San Buenaventura, 100,152; Camarillo, 60,951

UNUSUAL FEATURES
Simi Valley hosted five U.S. presidents in 1991 to dedicate the Ronald Reagan Presidential Library, largest gathering of presidents in 202 years; All-white Simi Valley jury acquitted the police officers accused of beating Rodney King.

Rep. Brad Sherman (D)

Elected 1996; 3rd term

CAPITOL OFFICE
225-5911; fax 225-5879; 1524 Longworth Bldg.
20515

INTERNET
e-mail: www.house.gov/writerep
web: www.house.gov/sherman

COMMITTEES
Financial Services
International Relations

HOMETOWN
Sherman Oaks

BORN
Oct. 24, 1954, Los Angeles, Calif.

RELIGION
Jewish

FAMILY
Single

EDUCATION
U. of California, Los Angeles, B.A. 1974; Harvard
U., J.D. 1979

CAREER
Accountant; lawyer

POLITICAL HIGHLIGHTS
Calif. State Board of Equalization, 1991-97

ELECTION RESULTS

2000 GENERAL

Brad Sherman (D)	155,398	66.0%
Jerry Doyle (R)	70,169	29.8%
Juan Ros (LIBERT)	6,966	3.0%
Michael Cuddehe (NL)	2,911	1.2%

2000 PRIMARY (OPEN)

Brad Sherman (D)	99,236	66.2%
Jerry Doyle (R)	43,762	29.2%
Juan Ros (LIBERT)	4,961	3.3%
Michael Cuddehe (NL)	1,884	1.3%

1998 GENERAL

Brad Sherman (D)	103,491	57.3%
Randy Hoffman (R)	69,501	38.5%
Catherine Carter (NL)	3,033	1.7%
Erich Miller (LIBERT)	2,695	1.5%
Ralph Shroyer (PFP)	1,860	1.0%

PREVIOUS WINNING PERCENTAGES
1996 (50%)

A traditional Democrat when it comes to labor and social issues, Sherman will occasionally slide to the right when the House is considering immigration policy. Smart and funny, he describes himself as a "recovering nerd." He likes to joke that he only seeks jobs held in the lowest possible public esteem. That's the reason, he says, that his career evolved from CPA to lawyer to tax collector.

But now that his job title is Congressman, he has been able to garner several accomplishments that should raise his standing in his party and at home. Sherman cosponsored numerous gun control bill provisions in the 106th Congress that would have required background checks for firearms purchased at gun shows and safety locks on guns. "The absence of a perfect solution shouldn't prevent this Congress from doing the right thing, right now," he wrote in a May 1999 Los Angeles Times column. "Congress needs to make passing reasonable gun control measures the first order of business."

Sherman also tries to be a realist about the limited effect of well-intentioned laws. After a much-publicized shooting at a Southern California Jewish Community Center in 1999, he promised to press for legislation expanding the definition of hate crimes. But, he warned demonstrators: "Changing the culture is more important than changing the law. ... Community involvement may be more important than what we can do in Sacramento or Washington."

Sherman will stray from the Democratic fold on occasion. A member of the moderate New Democrat Coalition, he was among the minority of Democrats who voted for GOP bills to encourage states to prosecute violent juveniles as adults and to overhaul the nation's public housing programs.

On immigration issues, Sherman has been in alliance with such conservative Republicans as Bill McCollum of Florida and Ron Packard and Elton Gallegly of California in support of tamper-proof worker identification cards as well as legislation to tighten restrictions on government benefits for illegal aliens and to track down illegal immigrants. This is an issue that resonates with many in the Los Angeles area, as the city is often the gateway for illegal immigrants.

Sherman's district is home to many Jews and Armenians. From his seat on the International Relations Committee, he backed continued aid to Israel in the face of "the greatest security threat of any country in the world." Sherman would like to see more pressure on Turkey to acknowledge what Armenians call a Turkish campaign of "genocide" against Armenians early in the 20th century. He was unable, however, to win the backing of International Relations members for an amendment that would have explicitly authorized humanitarian aid to an Armenian enclave in Azerbaijan.

He also urged realistic expectations about the impact of the 1999 NATO bombing campaign to help Kosovo. "A ... fact that we are perhaps unwilling or at least reluctant to recognize is that our goal — creating a multiethnic, autonomous Kosovo, multiethnic and harmonious, may be beyond reach," he said in a 1999 floor speech. Although he supported the Clinton administration's military campaign, Sherman noted that the United States should also focus attention on atrocities in areas outside Europe.

Sherman also wants China to clean up its human rights record in return for normal trade relations. In 2000, he voted against a measure to grant China permanent normal trade status. And he believes the United States should be tougher with other trading partners. Noting that France restricts

U.S. television and movie offerings in the name of preserving its culture, Sherman suggested that "we should use ... exaggerated cultural sensitivity" in shielding the Northern California wine industry from French imports.

Drawing on his accounting background, Sherman has repeatedly urged Congress to authorize permanently a popular tax credit for corporate research and development activities, instead of renewing the credit for one year at a time and allowing it to expire periodically. "How can a company count on getting a tax credit for a multi-year, large research and development project if by its very terms the R&D credit is supposed to expire at the end of this year or the end of next year?" he said. "The R&D tax credit can achieve its purpose, and that purpose is to expand the amount of research done in our country, only if companies can count on it."

A hard-liner on eliminating the budget deficit — he had a seat on the Budget Committee in his first term — Sherman campaigned in 1996 on the idea that the "lower interest rates we can achieve from balancing the federal budget will do more for economic growth than any Republican proposal and more for the low-income working families than any Democratic program." He backed the 1997 budget deal (although he refused to support it until President Clinton won concessions from the GOP), and he was one of just 25 Democrats who supported a constitutional amendment to require a two-thirds majority vote of Congress to raise taxes.

Sherman scored a significant victory in his first term by shepherding to enactment a $700 million proposal to buy environmentally sensitive lands. The funding was part of the initial White House-Capitol Hill budget agreement, but it took an amendment by Sherman in the Budget Committee to get it included in the congressional budget blueprint and ensure that the money was actually appropriated. Included in the total was money to buy lands to augment the Santa Monica Mountains National Recreation Area, located in the 24th District.

Sherman got his start in politics as a child, stuffing envelopes for Democratic Rep. George E. Brown Jr., a longtime family friend. He was elected to the five-member California Board of Equalization in 1990 and re-elected in 1994.

In his 1996 House race, before the primary, Sherman sewed up the backing of most area Democrats, including Democratic Rep. Anthony C. Beilenson, who was retiring after holding the seat for 10 terms. He won the 1996 contest by 8 percentage points, and the margin has grown substantially in each of his two re-elections.

KEY VOTES

2000
Yes Raise hourly minimum wage by $1 over two years
Yes Halt funding for U.S. mission in Kosovo unless European nations pay more
Yes Provide Medicare benefits to military retirees and their dependents
No Grant China permanent normal trade status
No Phase out estate, gift and trust taxes
No Prohibit implementation of president's national monument designations
No Approve GOP plan to provide prescription drug coverage for Medicare beneficiaries
Yes Increase help for poor nations indebted to international financial institutions

1999
Yes Impose steel import quotas
No Kill proposal to take aviation trust funds off budget
No Require background checks on buyers only at gun shows with 10 or more vendors
Yes Remove barriers among banking, securities and insurance companies
Yes Authorize state grants to hire teachers and reduce class size
Yes Overhaul campaign finance law; ban "soft money" and restrict advocacy advertising
Yes Approve bipartisan plan to increase rights of patients in managed-care health plans

INTEREST GROUPS

	AFL-CIO	ADA	CCUS	ACU
2000	100%	90%	47%	20%
1999	89%	95%	32%	8%
1998	80%	95%	61%	20%
1997	88%	75%	50%	32%

CQ VOTE STUDIES

	PARTY UNITY		PRESIDENTIAL SUPPORT	
	Support	Oppose	Support	Oppose
2000	93%	7%	83%	17%
1999	87%	13%	78%	22%
1998	83%	17%	72%	28%
1997	80%	20%	77%	23%

CALIFORNIA 24
Northwest Los Angeles County suburbs

While most of the 24th is in Los Angeles, few of the district's mostly white, upper-middle-class residents identify themselves as "Angelenos." Instead, they see themselves as part of the region's fast-growing communities: the Van Nuys, Encino and Sherman Oaks areas of Los Angeles in the San Fernando Valley and – outside Los Angeles – Thousand Oaks and Westlake Village in the Conejo Valley, and Malibu on the coast.

The 24th leans Democratic but becomes more Republican as one heads west on Route 101, away from Los Angeles. Westlake Village, Thousand Oaks and Malibu are the district's wealthy areas, and Malibu tends to be less Democratic than other towns south of the Santa Monica Mountains.

The 24th's commercial district, centered on financial services, is just south of Route 101, along Ventura Boulevard, where bank branch offices compete with miles of fast-food outlets and strip malls. Heavy

industry is limited to a few aerospace contractors. The 24th also has biotechnology companies, located in the west around Agoura Hills.

Malibu is reached most easily by the Pacific Coast Highway, with canyon roads wandering off to connect smaller communities in the hills. While many San Fernando Valley residents worry about traffic congestion, residents in Malibu's controlled residential areas are free to focus on the environment.

MAJOR INDUSTRY
Biotechnology, aerospace, service

CITIES
Los Angeles (pt.), 386,333 (1990); Thousand Oaks (pt.), 96,339 (1990); Agoura Hills, 21,092

UNUSUAL FEATURES
Santa Monica Mountains National Recreation Area, one of world's largest urban parks; San Fernando Valley known as pornography capital of the world; Sherman Oaks Galleria mall considered ground zero for the Valley Girls.

Rep. Howard P. 'Buck' McKeon (R)

Elected 1992; 5th term

A soft-spoken, genial man, McKeon came to Congress, as he tells it, to get off the Santa Clarita City Council. He had been a member of the council for two terms and was reluctantly gearing up to run for a third in 1991 when redistricting created a new House seat around his Santa Clarita base. He jumped at the chance to run for something else and was the surprise victor of the GOP primary, which largely determined the race in the heavily Republican 25th District.

While he is one of the most reliably conservative votes in the House, he works to advance his agenda in less visible and less confrontational ways than many of his colleagues, particularly those from the activist GOP Class of 1994, who came to Washington two years after he did.

McKeon has had experience being in the minority: He arrived in Congress when House Republicans had no real power and minimal input into legislation. Perhaps that is one reason why he has been able to work well with Democrats on two hotly contested and partisan issues: education and job training, which were under his purview as chairman of the Education panel's Postsecondary Education, Training and Life-Long Learning Subcommittee for six years.

In the 107th Congress, forced by GOP-imposed term limits to give up the Postsecondary Education gavel, McKeon took on the chairmanship of Education's Subcommittee on 21st Century Competitiveness.

McKeon acknowledges that education is a difficult area politically for many Republicans. "Our base does not want us to do anything because it's not a federal role. So, if we do something, it makes the base mad," he said. But he points out, "I don't think they're ever going to eliminate student loans or Pell grants; I can't see us killing the Department of Education, so we ought to face up to what's real," he said in 1998.

In the 105th, McKeon worked with his panel's ranking Democrat, Dale E. Kildee of Michigan, to craft legislation to keep banks in the business of making loans to college students. The issue was urgent; without action, the interest rates that banks could charge would drop so low as to discourage lenders from continuing to participate. The student loan language was a key feature of a five-year renewal of federal higher education programs that also contained a teacher training initiative and expansion of college grants.

McKeon also scored another major victory in the 105th: enactment of a plan to overhaul and condense job training programs. His bill consolidated more than 60 federal job training and adult education programs into three state block grants. He began the effort in the 104th, focusing attention on the complex network of more than 100 programs that cost about $20 billion a year. Each chamber passed a bill, but before legislation could reach President Clinton it fell prey to partisan bickering and died.

In 2000, he bucked conservative members of his party and helped win reauthorization of the Older Americans Act, the program that supports nutrition and job programs for the elderly. The act had come under criticism from some Republicans, who argued that it provided too much money for liberal nonprofit groups (which manage many of the jobs programs) without sufficient oversight. The opponents wanted to send the money to the states and let them decide where it should be used.

Groups such as AARP (formerly known as the American Association of Retired Persons) fought back and charged Republicans with wanting to gut the act. The fight nearly killed the bill, but McKeon helped negotiate a com-

CAPITOL OFFICE
225-1956; fax 226-0683; 2242 Rayburn Bldg. 20515

INTERNET
e-mail: tellbuck@mail.house.gov
web: www.house.gov/mckeon

COMMITTEES
Armed Services
Education & Workforce
(21st Century Competitiveness - chairman)
Veterans' Affairs

HOMETOWN
Santa Clarita

BORN
Sept. 9, 1939, Los Angeles, Calif.

RELIGION
Mormon

FAMILY
Wife, Patricia McKeon; six children

EDUCATION
Brigham Young U., B.S. 1985

CAREER
Clothing store owner

POLITICAL HIGHLIGHTS
William S. Hart School Board, 1978-87; Santa Clarita City Council, 1987-92 (mayor, 1987-88)

ELECTION RESULTS

2000 GENERAL

Howard "Buck" McKeon (R)	138,628	62.2%
Sid Gold (D)	73,921	33.2%
Bruce Acker (LIBERT)	7,219	3.2%
Mews Small (NL)	3,010	1.4%

2000 PRIMARY (OPEN)

Howard "Buck" McKeon (R)	92,342	63.3%
Sid Gold (D)	39,748	27.2%
Hal Meyers (R)	7,842	5.4%
Bruce Acker (LIBERT)	4,103	2.8%
Mews Small (NL)	1,896	1.3%

1998 GENERAL

Howard "Buck" McKeon (R)	114,013	74.7%
Bruce Acker (LIBERT)	38,669	25.3%

PREVIOUS WINNING PERCENTAGES
1996 (62%); 1994 (65%); 1992 (52%)

promise between the states and the nonprofits and won Clinton's signature.

Late in the 105th, McKeon was a key supporter of Robert L. Livingston of Louisiana as he waged a campaign for the speakership. When Speaker Newt Gingrich stepped down after the disappointing GOP showing at the polls in November 1998, and Livingston won his party's nomination to succeed Gingrich, McKeon seemed headed for a role in Livingston's inner councils. But that never came to pass, as Livingston, revealing that he had engaged in extramarital affairs, stepped down before the election for Speaker.

McKeon once observed that in his constituency, "most people would just as soon the government went away." But even in the conservative-dominated 25th District, there are some federal expenditures the locals embrace — particularly for military projects. With many aerospace plants in his district, McKeon continually pushes for increased defense spending from his perch on the Armed Services Committee. In the 107th, he sought an assignment to the Appropriations Committee, but lost his battle for the post to fellow Californian John T. Doolittle.

The 25th District hosts a Lockheed Martin plant and a NASA facility that prepares space shuttles for flights. McKeon wants NASA to move all its shuttle landings and preparation work to Palmdale, Calif. He champions the development of the next generation of space vehicle, the X-33; the next generation of fighter, the Joint Strike Fighter; and the F-22 fighter. Manufacturers in his district have thousands of jobs at stake on all three projects.

Upon arriving in Washington, McKeon, a millionaire owner of a chain of Western-wear stores, organized the Congressional Boot Caucus, where footwear aficionados from both sides of the aisle could meet, talk boots and hear presentations from manufacturers on new boot fashions.

McKeon's initial political involvement was with his local school board; he was the first mayor of Santa Clarita after it incorporated in 1987. His move to Congress in 1992 was the result of a razor-thin victory margin — 705 votes out of nearly 62,000 ballots cast — in the GOP primary over Phillip D. Wyman, a 14-year state Assembly veteran. McKeon got the support of GOP Rep. Bill Thomas, who had represented much of what is now the 25th before the redistricting.

In November, Democrat James H. "Gil" Gilmartin, a lawyer and rancher, and Independent Rick Pamplin, a screenwriter who tied his campaign to Ross Perot, tried to make a race of it. But McKeon had a sizable spending advantage and took 52 percent of the vote, finishing 19 points ahead of Gilmartin. Since then, he has won re-election with ease.

KEY VOTES

2000
No Raise hourly minimum wage by $1 over two years
Yes Halt funding for U.S. mission in Kosovo unless European nations pay more
Yes Provide Medicare benefits to military retirees and their dependents
Yes Grant China permanent normal trade status
Yes Phase out estate, gift and trust taxes
Yes Prohibit implementation of president's national monument designations
Yes Approve GOP plan to provide prescription drug coverage for Medicare beneficiaries
No Increase help for poor nations indebted to international financial institutions

1999
No Impose steel import quotas
Yes Kill proposal to take aviation trust funds off budget
Yes Require background checks on buyers only at gun shows with 10 or more vendors
Yes Remove barriers among banking, securities and insurance companies
No Authorize state grants to hire teachers and reduce class size
No Overhaul campaign finance law; ban "soft money" and restrict advocacy advertising
No Approve bipartisan plan to increase rights of patients in managed-care health plans

INTEREST GROUPS

	AFL-CIO	ADA	CCUS	ACU
2000	0%	5%	85%	92%
1999	0%	5%	96%	79%
1998	0%	5%	100%	96%
1997	0%	0%	90%	92%

CQ VOTE STUDIES

	PARTY UNITY		PRESIDENTIAL SUPPORT	
	Support	Oppose	Support	Oppose
2000	95%	5%	30%	70%
1999	93%	7%	22%	78%
1998	95%	5%	24%	76%
1997	97%	3%	29%	71%

CALIFORNIA 25

Northern Los Angeles County; Lancaster; Palmdale

The 25th takes in roughly the northern half of Los Angeles County. Its population is divided into the northeastern Antelope Valley, the western Santa Clarita Valley and the upper San Fernando Valley in the far southwest, including a portion of Los Angeles. The district leans Republican and has a large, upper-middle class, white majority.

Compared to the rest of the district, the San Fernando Valley is more affluent but votes more moderately. This is primarily a residential area, with electronics and aerospace manufacturing on the west side. More conservative Santa Clarita Valley is also suburban, but attracts manufacturing that cannot afford to locate in Los Angeles proper. The 25th's fastest-growing area is the Antelope Valley in the desert, home to Lancaster and Palmdale.

Economically, the 25th has suffered more from the dwindling aerospace industry than from the 1994 earthquake that collapsed buildings and a major freeway. The B-2 bomber program in Palmdale has been phased out, and the district has been recruiting non-defense manufacturing jobs in an effort to replace it.

MAJOR INDUSTRY
Aerospace, manufacturing, construction

MILITARY BASES
Edwards Air Force Base (shared with 21st District), 3,800 military, 7,400 civilian (2000)

CITIES
Los Angeles (pt.), 180,546 (1990); Santa Clarita, 133,887; Lancaster, 123,962; Palmdale, 111,272

UNUSUAL FEATURES
Northridge section of Los Angeles, epicenter of a major earthquake (6.6 on the Richter scale) on Jan. 17, 1994; Vasquez Rock formations in Agua Dulce, named for the famous bandit Tiburcio Vasquez, who used the rocks as a hideout, also served as the town of Bedrock in the movie "The Flintstones."

Rep. Howard L. Berman (D)

Elected 1982; 10th term

CAPITOL OFFICE
225-4695; fax 225-3196; 2330 Rayburn Bldg. 20515

INTERNET
e-mail: howard.berman@mail.house.gov
web: www.house.gov/berman

COMMITTEES
International Relations
Judiciary
Standards of Official Conduct - ranking member

HOMETOWN
North Hollywood

BORN
April 15, 1941, Los Angeles, Calif.

RELIGION
Jewish

FAMILY
Wife, Janis Berman; one child, one stepchild

EDUCATION
U. of California, Los Angeles, B.A. 1962, LL.B. 1965

CAREER
Lawyer

POLITICAL HIGHLIGHTS
Calif. Assembly, 1973-83

ELECTION RESULTS

2000 GENERAL
Howard L. Berman (D)	96,500	84.1%
Bill Farley (LIBERT)	13,052	11.4%
David Cossak (NL)	5,229	4.6%

2000 PRIMARY (OPEN)
Howard L. Berman (D)	60,896	84.6%
Bill Farley (LIBERT)	8,190	11.4%
David Cossak (NL)	2,887	4.0%

1998 GENERAL
Howard L. Berman (D)	69,000	82.5%
Juan Ros (LIBERT)	6,556	7.8%
Maria Armoudian (GREEN)	4,858	5.8%
David Cossak (NL)	3,248	3.9%

PREVIOUS WINNING PERCENTAGES
1996 (66%); 1994 (63%); 1992 (61%); 1990 (61%);
1988 (70%); 1986 (65%); 1984 (63%); 1982 (60%)

A low-key liberal who avoids the spotlight, Berman during his nine terms in Congress has built a solid reputation as an institutionalist and a serious-minded legislator. He does the bulk of his legislative work from his seats on the Judiciary and International Relations committees, while also weighing in on ethics matters as the ranking Democrat on the Committee on Standards of Official Conduct.

Berman's interest in Democratic politics dates back to his student days at UCLA. He succeeded Henry A. Waxman as president of the school's Federation of Young Democrats and in 1968 helped his friend win a seat in the state Assembly. This marked the start of the Berman-Waxman political organization, a network of like-minded politicians and activists who pooled resources to back preferred candidates with money and organizational assistance, thereby influencing western Los Angeles County politics for years.

From his seat on the Judiciary Committee in the 106th Congress, Berman cautioned lawmakers not to outpace the movement toward the electronic conduct of business. On legislation that would make so-called electronic signatures legally binding, Berman offered an amendment to allow states to require written records for such purposes as court orders and medical records, thereby preserving the right of states to set recordkeeping standards and enforce consumer protections. "This is important for the 75 percent of Americans who do not have access to online computing," said Berman, the ranking Democrat on the Courts, the Internet and Intellectual Property Subcommittee. "We must be careful to carry over consumer protections into the new electronic environment."

When Judiciary deals with immigration issues, Berman finds himself in a delicate position. He disagrees with conservatives who target legal immigrants, as in the 104th Congress with a measure to deny them welfare benefits. But he is more accepting of GOP efforts to crack down on illegal immigrants, a stance reflective of the fact that California is hard-pressed financially to solve problems caused by an influx of illegal aliens.

In the 104th, Berman teamed up with one of the most conservative House Republicans, Californian Elton Gallegly, to pass a bill requiring the federal government to screen jails for illegal immigrants with criminal records and deport them before they are arraigned, freeing localities from the costs of their incarceration.

In the 105th, Berman fought hard to ensure that illegal immigrants who come to the United States hoping to become legal through family or employment sponsorship do not have to return to their home countries to apply for permanent resident visas. He also cautioned that a move to increase the number of immigrants with needed job skills should not squeeze out other immigrants seeking to reunite with their families.

Berman's work on the intellectual property subcommittee is important to Southern California's many writers, composers and other artists with a stake in guarding copyrights. He lobbies to protect copyright owners from piracy of their works, an increasing threat as Internet use has grown.

At times, he meets resistance on this issue from other liberal Democrats, who worry that increased piracy protections will prevent materials from reaching the public domain, where they can be used by nonprofit educational institutions and libraries. But Berman draws a hard line. "Copyright owners' exclusive rights of public performance, distribution and reproduction must be protected no less from the grad student who thinks content on the Internet should be free than from the pirate who reaps a fortune from his counterfeiting operation."

In the politically charged days of 1998, as the Judiciary Committee considered the impeachment of President Clinton, Berman sought in a low-key manner to find areas on which Democrats and Republicans could agree. He then quietly explained why he judged that Clinton's actions in covering up an affair with a White House intern did not constitute an impeachable offense. "The impeachment process should not be used as a legislative vote of 'no confidence' on the president's conduct or policies."

Though he usually sided with Clinton, Berman opposed the president's call to grant China permanent normal trade status. Amid increasingly bellicose rhetoric directed by Chinese leaders toward Taiwan, Berman stressed in 1999 that the United States must honor its ties with Taiwan. "I'm very interested in making it clear that if we accord China permanent NTR [normal trade relations], there will be no doubt whatsoever that we will revoke NTR status and the access they now enjoy to our markets if they invade, attack or blockade Taiwan."

On the International Relations Committee, Berman backs foreign aid and opposes conservatives' efforts to attach ideological strings to U.S. money that goes abroad, such as abortion-related restrictions on international family planning aid.

Impressed by Berman's steady hand, party leaders chose him to be the top Democrat on the House ethics committee in 1997. Berman said the ethics committee should be "neither a member protection agency nor a forum for deciding partisan and ideological battles." When the House approved new procedures for the committee, he successfully fought a proposal that would have allowed complaints against members to expire if the committee was deadlocked on the issue for more than 180 days.

After graduating from college, Berman spent a year as a VISTA volunteer before practicing labor relations law in Los Angeles. In 1972, after working behind the scenes to help other Democrats win elections, it was Berman's turn to run, and he won a seat in the California Assembly. A consummate facilitator and tactician with a relaxed style, Berman soon rose to Assembly majority leader but lost in a bid to become Speaker.

He won his seat in Congress in 1982 after the new California House Speaker, Willie L. Brown Jr., helped pass a congressional redistricting plan that included a perfect district for Berman. Since then, he has easily won re-election, never dropping below 60 percent of the vote.

KEY VOTES

2000

Yes	Raise hourly minimum wage by $1 over two years
No	Halt funding for U.S. mission in Kosovo unless European nations pay more
Yes	Provide Medicare benefits to military retirees and their dependents
No	Grant China permanent normal trade status
No	Phase out estate, gift and trust taxes
No	Prohibit implementation of president's national monument designations
No	Approve GOP plan to provide prescription drug coverage for Medicare beneficiaries
Yes	Increase help for poor nations indebted to international financial institutions

1999

No	Impose steel import quotas
Yes	Kill proposal to take aviation trust funds off budget
-	Require background checks on buyers only at gun shows with 10 or more vendors
Yes	Remove barriers among banking, securities and insurance companies
Yes	Authorize state grants to hire teachers and reduce class size
Yes	Overhaul campaign finance law; ban "soft money" and restrict advocacy advertising
Yes	Approve bipartisan plan to increase rights of patients in managed-care health plans

INTEREST GROUPS

	AFL-CIO	ADA	CCUS	ACU
2000	100%	100%	50%	4%
1999	67%	95%	26%	0%
1998	100%	90%	36%	5%
1997	100%	80%	33%	9%

CQ VOTE STUDIES

	PARTY UNITY		PRESIDENTIAL SUPPORT	
	Support	Oppose	Support	Oppose
2000	96%	4%	94%	6%
1999	94%	6%	90%	10%
1998	95%	5%	85%	15%
1997	90%	10%	86%	14%

CALIFORNIA 26
San Fernando Valley

The lower- to middle-class 26th sits in the northeastern San Fernando Valley and encompasses a large portion of Los Angeles. It also takes in the small city of San Fernando in the north, and North Hollywood in the south.

Once composed of predominately white, suburban Los Angeles communities, the area has attracted blacks and large numbers of Hispanics who are bolstering the 26th's already hefty Democratic voter registration edge and are being elected to state and local offices. The district reliably supports Democratic presidential candidates. In 2000, Al Gore captured the 26th with 70 percent of the vote.

The Northridge earthquake in 1994 destroyed many homes in Sylmar, one of the few L.A. communities that still has room for growth. Also hit was San Fernando, a middle-class city where 83 percent of residents are Hispanic. Sun Valley, an industrial and

predominately white working-class area, is on the 26th's eastern edge.

The 26th has not seen as much economic recovery as other parts of the San Fernando Valley. It has some manufacturing plants, but Van Nuys lost its General Motors plant in 1992, and most industry is based in the northern communities of Pacomia and Sylmar. Residents are hoping for an economic boost from the new retail center and industrial park that was built at the old GM site in 2000.

MAJOR INDUSTRY
Service, manufacturing, health care

CITIES
Los Angeles (pt.), 548,419 (1990); San Fernando, 23,010

UNUSUAL FEATURES
The Academy of Television Arts and Sciences, which presents the annual Emmy Awards, based in North Hollywood; Rodney King videotaped being beaten by police in Lake View Terrace; Actor Robert Redford attended Van Nuys High School.

Rep. Adam B. Schiff (D)

Elected 2000; 1st term

CAPITOL OFFICE
225-4176; fax 225-5828; 437 Cannon Bldg. 20515

INTERNET
e-mail: www.house.gov/writerep
web: www.house.gov/schiff

COMMITTEES
International Relations
Judiciary

HOMETOWN
Burbank

BORN
June 22, 1960, Framingham, Mass.

RELIGION
Jewish

FAMILY
Wife, Eve Schiff; one child

EDUCATION
Stanford U., B.A. 1982; Harvard U., J.D. 1985

CAREER
Federal prosecutor; lawyer

POLITICAL HIGHLIGHTS
Assistant U.S. attorney, 1987-93; Democratic nominee for Calif. Assembly (special election), 1994; Democratic nominee for Calif. Assembly, 1994; Calif. Senate, 1997-2000

ELECTION RESULTS

2000 GENERAL

Adam B. Schiff (D)	113,708	52.7%
James E. Rogan (R)	94,518	43.8%
Miriam Hospodar (NL)	3,873	1.8%
Ted Brown (LIBERT)	3,675	1.7%

2000 PRIMARY (OPEN)

Adam B. Schiff (D)	70,449	48.8%
James E. Rogan (R)	68,179	47.2%
Ted Brown (LIBERT)	2,938	2.0%
Miriam Hospodar (NL)	2,799	1.9%

Though his style is hardly flashy, Schiff came to Congress as something of a celebrity: His 2000 campaign for the 27th District against two-term Republican Rep. James E. Rogan — arguably the most hotly contested race in the country — drew even more attention, and campaign money, than many of the year's Senate races.

Schiff, then a state senator, and Rogan raised in all more than $10 million, a House record. Outside groups spent millions more on television ads that sought to influence the outcome. Upon arriving in Washington, Schiff announced that campaign finance overhaul was a top priority.

Schiff won a seat on the Judiciary Committee, a nice fit for the former federal prosecutor, who has made fighting juvenile crime a centerpiece of his political career. As a state senator, Schiff chaired both the Judiciary Committee and a select committee on juvenile justice. He advocates larger investment in early childhood education, from pre-school through third grade — a policy that has been proven to reduce crime, he says.

Also topping Schiff's priorities are a number of Democratic health care proposals, including bills to make prescription drugs available under Medicare and to give patients more control over their managed-care plans.

The 27th has a large Armenian population. As a state senator, Schiff helped secure state funds for a documentary on what some call the Armenian genocide that began in 1915 at the hands of the Ottoman Empire (present-day Turkey). Schiff ran Armenian-language ads in the 2000 campaign; in the 107th Congress, he won a post on the International Relations panel.

Though touted as a GOP rising star, Rogan had won his previous House races by slim margins, as the 27th tilted slightly Democratic. And he had made himself a target with his role as one of 13 House "managers" who presented the case against President Clinton during the 1999 Senate impeachment trial.

Schiff had lost to Rogan twice in 1994, in special and general elections for the state Assembly. He rebounded in 1996, winning a state Senate district that encompassed the 27th Congressional District. In 2000, Schiff's third race against Rogan proved the charm, and he prevailed by 9 percentage points.

CALIFORNIA 27

Northeastern Los Angles County; Pasadena; Burbank

The 27th is set in the rolling San Gabriel Mountains, which form the eastern border of the Los Angeles Basin. The Angeles National Forest dominates the district's northeast, and suburbs are spread evenly throughout. Over the years, immigration has transformed the ethnic composition of once-WASPish neighborhoods, and this previously Republican district now has a Democratic lean. Al Gore won the district by 12 percentage points in 2000 — an improvement over Bill Clinton's 8-point victory in the district in 1996.

The 27th's major cities include suburban Glendale, Burbank and Pasadena. Glendale is the district's largest city, and about 60,000 Armenians have settled there since 1985, joined by large numbers of Asians and

Latinos. Southern Glendale has a largely immigrant population and is staunchly Democratic. About 60 different languages are spoken in Glendale's public schools.

During redistricting in 1992, the 27th gained the heavily black and Hispanic half of Pasadena, a city that includes NASA's Jet Propulsion Laboratory and many high-tech engineering firms attracted by Caltech. In Burbank, television and movie production studios drive the economy.

MAJOR INDUSTRY
Entertainment, high-tech, engineering

CITIES
Glendale, 186,903; Pasadena (pt.), 126,228 (1990); Burbank, 99,039

UNUSUAL FEATURES
Pasadena is home of the Rose Bowl and hosts the Tournament of the Roses Parade; The Tonight Show with Jay Leno filmed at the NBC studio in Burbank; "Father of the Bride," starring Steve Martin, was filmed in exclusive San Marino.

Rep. David Dreier (R)

Elected 1980; 11th term

CAPITOL OFFICE
225-2305; fax 225-7018; 237 Cannon Bldg. 20515

INTERNET
e-mail: www.house.gov/writerep
web: www.house.gov/dreier

COMMITTEES
Rules - chairman

HOMETOWN
San Dimas

BORN
July 5, 1952, Kansas City, Mo.

RELIGION
Christian Scientist

FAMILY
Single

EDUCATION
Claremont McKenna College, B.A. 1975; Claremont Graduate U., M.A. 1976

CAREER
Real estate developer and property manager

POLITICAL HIGHLIGHTS
Republican nominee for U.S. House, 1978

ELECTION RESULTS

2000 GENERAL

David Dreier (R)	116,557	56.8%
Janice M. Nelson (D)	81,804	39.9%
Randall Weissbuch (LIBERT)	2,823	1.4%
M. Lawrence Allison (NL)	2,083	1.0%

2000 PRIMARY (OPEN)

David Dreier (R)	88,837	62.5%
Janice M. Nelson (D)	47,971	33.7%
Randall Weissbuch (LIBERT)	2,327	1.6%
Joe Haytas (AMI)	1,759	1.2%

1998 GENERAL

David Dreier (R)	90,607	57.6%
Janice M. Nelson (D)	61,721	39.3%
Jerry R. Douglas (LIBERT)	2,099	1.3%
Walt C. Sheasby (GREEN)	1,954	1.2%

PREVIOUS WINNING PERCENTAGES
1996 (61%); 1994 (67%); 1992 (58%); 1990 (64%);
1988 (69%); 1986 (72%); 1984 (71%); 1982 (65%);
1980 (52%)

With every step of his smooth ascent to the Republican leadership ranks, the conservative and polished Dreier has worn a smile, an impeccably pressed suit and a handkerchief in his breast pocket. As chairman of the Rules Committee, he specializes in transforming — with a firm hand and a charming manner — the often contentious dictates of the GOP high command into ground rules for floor debates.

The Rules chairmanship keeps Dreier in the middle of legislative fights because his job is to leverage the House's parliamentary procedures to ensure that GOP leaders get their way on legislation. The stressful position, which Dreier took in 1999, does not appear to have worn him down a bit: He has found time to play a leading role in trade and technology issues, serve as a prolific fundraiser and California co-chairman for George W. Bush's presidential campaign, and run GOPAC, the Republican Party's political action committee for state and local candidates.

In many ways, Dreier is the quintessential college Republican all grown up — except he does not look as if he has aged much since he first ran for Congress at age 26 from a room at Claremont Men's College (now Claremont McKenna), where he worked after obtaining his undergraduate and graduate degrees there.

The son of a Marine Corps drill sergeant, Dreier's energy is legendary, from his brisk morning runs to his long sessions — often into the wee hours — in an office filled with cigar smoke, crafting complex floor rules for difficult bills. And his idealism seems unfailing: He is a self-described Reagan Republican who believes in the primacy of the free market and free trade, wants government to stay out of the way of technological innovation and says the GOP "offers the best hope for the future of the country."

Dreier does not make a show of his ambition; in fact, he wants to seem as if he's never trying too hard. Asked about his Rules chairmanship and his top spot at GOPAC, Dreier begins in each case by insisting, "It's not something I really sought." And though chairing Rules makes him one of the most powerful Republicans in the House, Dreier says he is not interested in higher office. "The difference between the House and the Senate," he said, "is that on the floor of the Senate, it's like you're in a living room; and the floor of the House of Representatives is like an arena — it's intense."

The telegenic Dreier is at his best when playing to an audience, whether on the talk-show circuit, in the well of the House or in the small but elegant Capitol room where his Rules panel decides which legislative proposals are voted on by the House. He frequently can be spotted in the press gallery with radio and television crews, and his website has featured a "Media Alert" pop-up box announcing his upcoming appearances. But though he is often in the limelight, Dreier also has been known to disappear into his private hideaway in the depths of the Capitol for a quick game of pinball on his own vintage "Voltan Woman" machine.

In his first five years on Rules, Dreier chafed under Democratic control. But with the GOP in charge — the ratio on the panel is nine Republicans to four Democrats — he now says: "I think it's kind of tough for [Democrats] in good conscience to criticize us for things that they understood have to be done in the majority, that frankly, as a minority member I did not understand."

Though Dreier says fairness is a goal on the panel, he has no qualms about sticking to the party line. "My first priority is to move our agenda," he said. But in so doing, he remains polite and composed. He almost always identifies colleagues on the floor and in committee not only by their home state but also by their hometown, even when he is preparing to tell them their amendment will never see the light of day.

Dreier has an abiding interest in the history and well-being of the House. He says that a relative, Richard Bland Lee of Virginia, served on the first Rules panel near the end of the 18th century. But Dreier is by no means stuck in the past. In 1996, he spearheaded the "21st Century Congress" project, which uses new technologies to enliven the political process. He has since planned online and fully interactive congressional hearings, using e-mail, video conferencing, television and the Internet to create a virtual hearing room for witnesses across the country.

Technology has been central to his work at GOPAC, where he has set up a Web portal with a two-way chat capability that can allow candidates across the nation to communicate about policy and campaigns. In Congress, Dreier has won approval from the technology industry for his work on legislation to limit computer companies' liability for year 2000 glitches and to increase the number of special visas issued to foreign workers with high-tech skills.

Dreier uses his fundraising prowess to reward Republican candidates who support free trade and globalization as strongly as he does. Through his political action committee, the American Success PAC, Dreier gave $120,500 to candidates in the 1998 cycle and delivered $450,000 to candidates before the 2000 election.

So certain is Dreier that free and open trade is "the right thing" that he devoted much of his time during the first half of 2000 whipping up Republican support for granting China permanent normal trade status. Calling it "probably the most important vote that we will face in this session of Congress," Dreier argued that securing open markets in China would help U.S. businesses, workers and even Chinese citizens. "China is in the midst of great and dynamic change, and free market reform is the primary engine pushing that change," he said.

Underfinanced and only 26 years old in 1978, Dreier came within 12,000 votes of defeating Democratic Rep. James F. Lloyd. Two years later, he ran against Lloyd again, this time echoing the national Republican agenda and supporting Ronald Reagan's presidential bid. GOP strategists saw Lloyd as vulnerable, and they helped Dreier outspend the incumbent, 2-to-1. Dreier won with 52 percent. Because of redistricting, Dreier found himself in another fight in 1982, this time against a fellow Republican, Wayne Grisham. Dreier's energy, organization and fundraising brought him a solid victory, and he has won comfortably since.

KEY VOTES

2000

No	Raise hourly minimum wage by $1 over two years
Yes	Halt funding for U.S. mission in Kosovo unless European nations pay more
Yes	Provide Medicare benefits to military retirees and their dependents
Yes	Grant China permanent normal trade status
Yes	Phase out estate, gift and trust taxes
Yes	Prohibit implementation of president's national monument designations
Yes	Approve GOP plan to provide prescription drug coverage for Medicare beneficiaries
No	Increase help for poor nations indebted to international financial institutions

1999

No	Impose steel import quotas
Yes	Kill proposal to take aviation trust funds off budget
Yes	Require background checks on buyers only at gun shows with 10 or more vendors
Yes	Remove barriers among banking, securities and insurance companies
No	Authorize state grants to hire teachers and reduce class size
No	Overhaul campaign finance law; ban "soft money" and restrict advocacy advertising
No	Approve bipartisan plan to increase rights of patients in managed-care health plans

INTEREST GROUPS

	AFL-CIO	ADA	CCUS	ACU
2000	0%	5%	90%	92%
1999	0%	10%	96%	80%
1998	10%	0%	100%	92%
1997	0%	0%	100%	88%

CQ VOTE STUDIES

	PARTY UNITY		PRESIDENTIAL SUPPORT	
	Support	Oppose	Support	Oppose
2000	94%	6%	30%	70%
1999	91%	9%	30%	70%
1998	91%	9%	26%	74%
1997	95%	5%	27%	73%

CALIFORNIA 28

Northeastern Los Angeles suburbs

The 28th is a mix of Los Angeles bedroom communities and the mountainous Angeles National Forest, which runs through its northern half. The district takes in a sliver of eastern Pasadena and the middle- to upper-class cities of Sierra Madre, Arcadia, Monrovia, Covina and San Dimas. While not as ethnically diverse as some of its neighbors, the district's Hispanic and Asian populations are growing steadily.

Like many Los Angeles suburbanites, residents here tend to be socially moderate and economically conservative. West Covina and blue-collar Pomona are more liberal, but the district is politically split. On the national level, the district narrowly supported Al Gore in the 2000 presidential contest and gave the edge to Bill Clinton in 1996, but in 1992 George Bush carried the district by 3 percent.

Many of the 28th's residents commute to work in downtown Los Angeles or have high-tech manufacturing jobs just outside the district. The City of Industry (shared with the 34th and 41st districts) is a heavy

manufacturing area where some 75,000 people work every day.

Most other industry is confined to small defense subcontractors and service industries, although the area has seen some growth in trade-related import and export businesses. The city of Duarte, south of Monrovia, is known for its City of Hope National Medical Center, a nonprofit treatment and research hospital specializing in rare medical problems.

MAJOR INDUSTRY
Service, manufacturing, health care

CITIES
West Covina (pt.), 96,126 (1990); Arcadia (pt.), 48,283 (1990); Glendora (pt.), 47,295 (1990); Covina, 44,803

UNUSUAL FEATURES
Arcadia is home to the Santa Anita Park thoroughbred racetrack; Pomona hosts the Los Angeles County Fair.

Rep. Henry A. Waxman (D)

Elected 1974; 14th term

CAPITOL OFFICE
225-3976; fax 225-4099; 2204 Rayburn Bldg. 20515

INTERNET
e-mail: www.house.gov/writerep
web: www.house.gov/waxman

COMMITTEES
Energy & Commerce
Government Reform - ranking member

HOMETOWN
Los Angeles

BORN
Sept. 12, 1939, Los Angeles, Calif.

RELIGION
Jewish

FAMILY
Wife, Janet Waxman; two children

EDUCATION
U. of California, Los Angeles, B.A. 1961, J.D. 1964

CAREER
Lawyer

POLITICAL HIGHLIGHTS
Calif. Assembly, 1969-75

ELECTION RESULTS

2000 GENERAL

Henry A. Waxman (D)	180,295	75.7%
Jim Scileppi (R)	45,784	19.2%
J. C. Anderson (LIBERT)	7,944	3.3%
Bruce Currivan (NL)	4,178	1.8%

2000 PRIMARY (OPEN)

Henry A. Waxman (D)	114,147	76.3%
Jim Scileppi (R)	27,870	18.6%
J. C. Anderson (LIBERT)	5,419	3.6%
Bruce Currivan (NL)	2,135	1.4%

1998 GENERAL

Henry A. Waxman (D)	131,561	73.9%
Mike Gottlieb (R)	40,282	22.6%
Mike Binkley (LIBERT)	3,534	2.0%
Karen Blasdell-Wilkinson (NL)	2,717	1.5%

PREVIOUS WINNING PERCENTAGES
1996 (68%); 1994 (68%); 1992 (61%); 1990 (69%);
1988 (72%); 1986 (88%); 1984 (63%); 1982 (65%);
1980 (64%); 1978 (63%); 1976 (68%); 1974 (64%)

He has seen the fortunes of liberalism rise and fall during his quarter-century in Washington. But no matter which party holds Congress or the presidency, Waxman always seems to find a way to advance his agenda, which includes protecting the environment, expanding access to health care and putting the screws to tobacco manufacturers.

Born in Los Angeles during the Depression, Waxman grew up in an apartment above the family grocery store. His Russian immigrant father passed on his appreciation of the New Deal aspirations of President Franklin D. Roosevelt. In the House, Waxman can set some similarly ambitious policy goals, but more often he is maneuvering persistently to secure one small objective at a time.

He is among Congress' most adroit political practitioners. He brings extensive policy knowledge into behind-the-scenes negotiations and can be a forceful presence in front of the television cameras. Most of all, he is patient and willing to settle for half a loaf when necessary. Contrasting his legislative philosophy with that of the Republicans who charged into control of the House in 1995, Waxman said, "They think compromise is a dirty word, even though compromise can further your ideas and even help you improve your ideas."

Waxman is aggressive but usually controlled, a style that can bedevil adversaries. And he is a precise, persistent questioner. "Even when Henry Waxman is being unreasonable, he comes across as reasonable," says Mark Souder of Indiana, a senior Republican on the Government Reform Committee, where Waxman has been the ranking Democrat since 1997.

It is Waxman's Government Reform post that has put him in the national spotlight most often during the years of GOP control. In a series of inquiries into alleged Clinton administration malfeasance, he served as the chief foil to the committee's often histrionic chairman, Republican Dan Burton of Indiana.

Calling the panel's investigation into Democratic fundraising in the 1996 election cycle a "subpoena party," Waxman urged that the committee look into the fundraising practices of both parties, not just the Democrats. He said later that the two-year inquiry was "the most partisan, unfair and abusive investigation since the McCarthy hearings in the 1950s."

But even Waxman allowed some exasperation with Bill Clinton's behavior to show through in 2001, when the panel held hearings on the departing president's last-minute pardon of fugitive financier Marc Rich. In the 107th Congress, Waxman has continued to battle the GOP majority, objecting when the committee approved continued broad subpoena powers for Burton and when Burton eliminated the Postal Service Subcommittee without Democratic consultation.

Waxman's chief base of operations for pursuing his progressive agenda has been the Energy and Commerce Committee, where he is the No. 2 Democrat and where he chaired the Health and the Environment Subcommittee from 1979 to 1995. He compiled an impressive record of legislative victories by going after problems bit by bit, year after year, rather than launching a broad frontal assault.

One of his most significant accomplishments came in 1990 with enactment of clean air legislation. For nearly a decade, Waxman had battled fellow Democrat John D. Dingell of Michigan (then chairman of the committee) and the Reagan administration over air pollution standards. Waxman sought tougher measures against acid rain and smog, and Dingell fought to protect Detroit's auto industry and the interests of Midwestern states with coal-burning power plants.

Waxman did not hesitate to go up against Dingell on the powerful chairman's own turf. While many Democrats walked on eggshells around Dingell, Waxman would gavel him down if, during subcommittee deliberations, Dingell spoke beyond the fixed time limit. Waxman skillfully targeted members to build winning coalitions on several motor vehicle pollution provisions Dingell opposed. The compromise ultimately enacted in 1990 was not as tough on pollution as Waxman would have liked but was still considered landmark environmental legislation, more stringent than the GOP administration had proposed.

A one-time smoker, Waxman has persistently pressed on with his crusade to discourage smoking, most memorably during his inquiry into allegations of manipulation of nicotine levels in cigarettes. He convened the unprecedented 1994 hearing during which the chief executives of the nation's seven largest tobacco companies testified, under oath, that they did not believe nicotine was addictive. In 1995, he devoted 36 pages of the Congressional Record to a reprint of apparent Philip Morris research on the addictive effects of nicotine on third-graders, college students and others.

Waxman's political career began at UCLA in the 1960s, when he and fellow student Howard L. Berman became active in California's Federation of Young Democrats. In 1968, after a term as chairman of the state federation, Waxman, with Berman's support, challenged Democratic state Assemblyman Lester McMillan in a primary. McMillan had been in office 26 years and was nearing retirement. Waxman beat him with 64 percent of the vote.

It was the beginning of the so-called Waxman-Berman machine, an informal network of like-minded politicians who pooled their resources to back candidates, with money, organization, computerized mailings and political savvy.

The "machine" was functioning so smoothly in 1974 that Waxman had little trouble winning a new House seat created with him in mind. Not only are his constituents politically involved, no small number of them also are wealthy, giving him the campaign treasury with which to expand his political influence. With his own re-election campaigns mere formalities since then — he has never captured less than 61 percent of the vote — Waxman has helped others win elections, notably Berman, who joined him in the House in 1983.

KEY VOTES

2000

Yes Raise hourly minimum wage by $1 over two years
No Halt funding for U.S. mission in Kosovo unless European nations pay more
Yes Provide Medicare benefits to military retirees and their dependents
Yes Grant China permanent normal trade status
No Phase out estate, gift and trust taxes
No Prohibit implementation of president's national monument designations
No Approve GOP plan to provide prescription drug coverage for Medicare beneficiaries
Yes Increase help for poor nations indebted to international financial institutions

1999

Yes Impose steel import quotas
Yes Kill proposal to take aviation trust funds off budget
No Require background checks on buyers only at gun shows with 10 or more vendors
No Remove barriers among banking, securities and insurance companies
Yes Authorize state grants to hire teachers and reduce class size
Yes Overhaul campaign finance law; ban "soft money" and restrict advocacy advertising
Yes Approve bipartisan plan to increase rights of patients in managed-care health plans

INTEREST GROUPS

	AFL-CIO	ADA	CCUS	ACU
2000	89%	90%	45%	4%
1999	88%	95%	17%	0%
1998	100%	100%	18%	4%
1997	100%	95%	20%	0%

CQ VOTE STUDIES

	PARTY UNITY		PRESIDENTIAL SUPPORT	
	Support	Oppose	Support	Oppose
2000	98%	2%	87%	13%
1999	96%	4%	86%	14%
1998	97%	3%	85%	15%
1997	97%	3%	86%	14%

CALIFORNIA 29
West Los Angeles County; Santa Monica; West Hollywood

The 29th lays claim to the real-life Beverly Hills, 90210. More than just entertainment glitz and coastal affluence, the district is home of the second-largest Jewish population in the nation, the University of California, Los Angeles and the activist gay community of West Hollywood.

Eclectic, wealthy and Democratic describe many of the district's residents. In elections at all levels, the district has rewarded Democratic candidates, usually with more than 60 percent of the vote.

The urban district stretches northeast from Santa Monica and Malibu beaches to the Hollywood Hills and the Los Angeles River. It takes in the suburban southern edges of the San Fernando Valley, on the northern side of the Santa Monica Mountains.

The district's borders edge out many of the Hispanic, Asian and black communities to the east and south, leaving the 29th the "whitest" of the Los Angeles City districts. The economy is overwhelmingly white-collar. Entertainment executives lunch with financial advisers and real estate developers. Tourism brings in copious dollars. A robust health services community is based on the area's seven medical centers. The district also has several successful commercial-industrial parks and shopping malls.

MAJOR INDUSTRY
Entertainment, higher education, health care

CITIES
Los Angeles (pt.), 415,442 (1990); Santa Monica, 91,084; West Hollywood, 36,294

UNUSUAL FEATURES
Former President Ronald Reagan's retirement home in Bel Air.

Rep. Xavier Becerra (D)

Elected 1992; 5th term

CAPITOL OFFICE
225-6235; fax 225-2202
1119 Longworth Bldg. 20515

INTERNET
e-mail: www.house.gov/writerep
web: www.house.gov/becerra

COMMITTEES
Ways & Means

HOMETOWN
Los Angeles

BORN
Jan. 26, 1958, Sacramento, Calif.

RELIGION
Roman Catholic

FAMILY
Wife, Carolina Reyes; three children

EDUCATION
Stanford U., A.B. 1980, J.D. 1984

CAREER
Lawyer; state prosecutor

POLITICAL HIGHLIGHTS
Calif. Assembly, 1990-92; candidate for mayor of Los Angeles, 2001

ELECTION RESULTS

2000 GENERAL

Xavier Becerra (D)	83,223	83.3%
Tony Goss (R)	11,788	11.8%
Jason Heath (LIBERT)	2,858	2.9%
Gary Hearne (NL)	2,051	2.1%

2000 PRIMARY (OPEN)

Xavier Becerra (D)	53,145	83.4%
Tony Goss (R)	6,919	10.9%
Jason Heath (LIBERT)	1,922	3.0%
Gary Hearne (NL)	1,718	2.7%

1998 GENERAL

Xavier Becerra (D)	58,230	81.2%
Patricia Jean Parker (R)	13,441	18.8%

PREVIOUS WINNING PERCENTAGES
1996 (72%); 1994 (66%); 1992 (58%)

Once described by the Los Angeles Times as "the Golden Boy of Latino politics," Becerra is smart, liberal and ambitious. He is the first Hispanic lawmaker to get a seat on the House Ways and Means Committee.

His ambitions led him to wage an uphill struggle early in 2001 to become the first Latino mayor in the modern history of Los Angeles. But, hampered by low name recognition, Becerra failed to make it past the April 10 primary in a 14-candidate field.

An assertive proponent of many liberal causes, Becerra (pronounced HAH-vee-air beh-SEH-ra) has donned the mantle of advocate for the nation's immigrants. With Republicans running Congress, he has had his hands full battling a GOP legislative agenda that he sees as anti-immigrant and anti-Hispanic. But he says he wants to be viewed as more than just a representative of Latino views. "I want folks to know I can be influential and not just on immigration policy," he told the Los Angeles Times. "I still want to be identified as a Latino, but that's not all I do."

Becerra had a disagreement with powerful Ways and Means Chairman Dan Rostenkowski, a fellow Democrat, in a 1993 discussion about welfare benefits for some legal immigrants. Observers thought that the California freshman did not show proper deference to the chairman and had blown his chance of ever winning a seat on the panel. But Rostenkowski was defeated in 1994, and House Democratic leaders, eager to add diversity to top-tier committees, put Becerra on Ways and Means two years later.

During his first two House terms, Becerra's seat on the Judiciary Committee gave him an outlet for his work on immigration issues. In his third term, he left Judiciary to take the Ways and Means post, a switch that concerned many Hispanic leaders who believed they were losing an effective advocate for immigration matters. But Becerra was then elected chairman of the Congressional Hispanic Caucus, which made immigration policy a top priority.

Becerra argued for the use of statistical sampling to augment the 2000 census head count, which he said would fail to include many minority residents. He decried what he characterized as GOP attempts to intimidate Hispanic voters in the contested 1996 election of Loretta Sanchez over Republican Robert K. Dornan in California's 46th District. And he worked to permit Central Americans who sought asylum from civil unrest to stay in the United States.

Becerra can count some successes on behalf of his immigrant constituents. In 1997, he played a lead role in negotiations that restored to many elderly and disabled legal immigrants Social Security benefits that had been eliminated in the 1996 welfare overhaul law. In 1998, Becerra and his Hispanic Caucus colleagues led the effort to defeat legislation that would have turned funding for federal bilingual and immigrant education programs into block grants, giving states and localities more latitude in spending the money.

Proponents argued that states should be free to try alternative approaches such as English immersion. Becerra disagreed: "How can the child master science or math or social studies while they are trying to learn a language at the same time?" Becerra and his allies won that fight; in fact, funding for bilingual education programs was increased. The lawmaker left the Hispanic Caucus chair after his two-year term, saying that many of the group's goals had been achieved.

Becerra remains convinced that the Immigration and Naturalization Service (INS) cannot properly perform its two roles — combating illegal immigration and providing services to legal immigrants. He favors splitting the INS into two agencies. Although legislation to split the service stalled in the 106th Congress, Becerra and his allies won increased funding for the INS to reduce a huge backlog in naturalization applications.

Los Angeles is a leading center for trade with Asia, and Becerra generally has been a proponent of lowering trade barriers. But he was conflicted in 2000 over the proposal to broaden trade ties with China, mainly because of labor's opposition. He wound up supporting the measure.

Becerra's interest in immigration matters is logical, from both a personal and a constituent perspective. The 30th District is a way station for many new immigrants. According to the 1990 census, 46 percent of the residents of the 30th were not citizens. Becerra's father, although born in the United States, spent much of his early life in Mexico, moving back and forth across the border many times. Becerra's mother was born in Mexico. Becerra says he wears his father's wedding ring to remind himself of his humble roots.

Becerra worked his way through Stanford and was the first member of his family to earn a college degree, majoring in economics. He did a yearlong fellowship with the California Senate after graduation. His interest in community advocacy work led him to Stanford law school. Becerra's first job as a lawyer was with a legal services office in Worcester, Mass., helping mentally ill clients. When he returned to California, Becerra worked briefly for state Sen. Art Torres and then for the state attorney general's office.

The congressman says he never envisioned a life in electoral politics. But in 1990, urged on by friends and colleagues, he waged and won a campaign for the California Assembly. Becerra had not yet completed his first term there when he was recruited in 1992 for the newly drawn, overwhelmingly Hispanic 30th District seat. He overcame nine other candidates in the primary, including school board member Leticia Quezada, another rising star in the Latino community. Becerra won nomination with less than a third of the vote.

He won the general election with 58 percent of the vote against Republican Morry Waksberg and three minor-party candidates. His subsequent re-elections have come with steadily increasing shares of the vote — 66 percent, 72 percent, 81 percent and, in 2000, 83 percent. In the 2000 race, despite facing no real challenge, Becerra spent hundreds of thousands of dollars, an investment in reinforcing his political base with an eye on the looming mayoral race.

KEY VOTES

2000
Yes Raise hourly minimum wage by $1 over two years
Yes Halt funding for U.S. mission in Kosovo unless European nations pay more
Yes Provide Medicare benefits to military retirees and their dependents
Yes Grant China permanent normal trade status
No   Phase out estate, gift and trust taxes
-    Prohibit implementation of president's national monument designations
No   Approve GOP plan to provide prescription drug coverage for Medicare beneficiaries
Yes Increase help for poor nations indebted to international financial institutions

1999
Yes Impose steel import quotas
Yes Kill proposal to take aviation trust funds off budget
No   Require background checks on buyers only at gun shows with 10 or more vendors
Yes Remove barriers among banking, securities and insurance companies
Yes Authorize state grants to hire teachers and reduce class size
Yes Overhaul campaign finance law; ban "soft money" and restrict advocacy advertising
Yes Approve bipartisan plan to increase rights of patients in managed-care health plans

INTEREST GROUPS

	AFL-CIO	ADA	CCUS	ACU
2000	90%	90%	45%	8%
1999	78%	100%	22%	0%
1998	100%	90%	35%	0%
1997	100%	90%	30%	0%

CQ VOTE STUDIES

	PARTY UNITY		PRESIDENTIAL SUPPORT	
	Support	Oppose	Support	Oppose
2000	95%	5%	92%	8%
1999	96%	4%	85%	15%
1998	99%	1%	88%	12%
1997	99%	1%	86%	14%

CALIFORNIA 30
Central, East and Southeast Los Angeles

Completely contained within the city of Los Angeles, the 30th is a densely populated, staunchly Democratic district. It starts just west of downtown Los Angeles, swings up and around, and comes down on downtown's eastern side. It has one of the state's largest Hispanic populations. Voter turnout is usually low, although a 1996 ballot initiative to end affirmative action helped energize voters.

Asians, Armenians, Russians and Hispanics have been moving to the 30th, with many settling in the district's western side. This area, which includes East Hollywood, the mid-Wilshire area and Koreatown, was hit hard by the 1992 riots.

Dodger Stadium, north of downtown, serves as the 30th's centerpiece. Elysian Park is a blue-collar neighborhood with a moderate number of Hispanics. Directly west are the "artsy" and largely gay Silver Lake and Echo Park communities. To the northeast sits Eagle Rock, a hilly, middle-class pocket of relative affluence that votes Democratic but leans more toward the political center than other parts of the 30th. The eastern side leads to Highland Park, a heavily Hispanic, blue-collar area with a significant Mexican immigrant presence.

While poor, the 30th is not as economically troubled as some of its southern neighbors and falls mostly outside federal empowerment zone boundaries drawn after the riots. Entertainment studios and a slew of hospitals contribute to the local economy, as do the white-collar, high-rise businesses along Wilshire Boulevard, a central business corridor.

MAJOR INDUSTRY
Service, entertainment, health care

CITIES
Los Angeles (pt.), 572,403 (1990)

UNUSUAL FEATURES
Paramount Pictures, the only major motion picture studio based in Hollywood; Dodger Stadium along Elysian Park.

Rep. Hilda L. Solis (D)

Elected 2000; 1st term

Solis became a new House member the hard way, taking on 18-year Democratic incumbent Matthew G. Martinez in the March 2000 primary. But Solis, an activist state senator, rallied support from 31st District Democratic regulars and trounced Martinez, 62 percent to 29 percent.

That win guaranteed Solis' enrollment in the 107th Congress. No Republican candidate filed to run in the eastern Los Angeles County Hispanic-majority district, a Democratic stronghold, and Solis coasted to victory in the general election over three minor-party candidates.

On her arrival in Washington, Solis won assignment to the Resources and the Education and the Workforce panels, and she was selected as freshman class whip.

Solis brought to the Hill a record of 15 years in elected office — first as a community college trustee, then as a state assemblywoman and state senator. In Sacramento, she served as chairwoman of the state Senate Budget Subcommittee on Labor, on which she helped raise the state's minimum wage requirements. This position helped Solis capture support from organized labor officials who had previously backed Martinez.

Solis also won favor in the Democratic primary by contending that she supported abortion rights and gun control more strongly than Martinez.

The 31st has suffered from high unemployment and crime; Solis believes the district would be helped by passing tougher restrictions on gun ownership, which she hopes would stem violence among gangs. Solis also has said that preventing domestic violence is one of her top priorities.

Solis began talking to local Democratic officials in late 1998 about taking on Martinez. With a dynamic personality that contrasted with Martinez' low-key manner, Solis was at least as well-known as he in the 31st; her state Senate district encompassed most of the congressional district.

Solis drew support from prominent California Democrats such as Rep. Loretta Sanchez, Sen. Barbara Boxer and former Rep. Esteban E. Torres. Feeling abandoned by his party, Martinez later in 2000 switched to the GOP, but Solis' win that November ended the Republicans' brief lease on the seat.

CAPITOL OFFICE
225-5464; fax 225-5467
1641 Longworth Bldg. 20515

INTERNET
e-mail: www.house.gov/writerep
web: www.house.gov/solis

COMMITTEES
Education & Workforce
Resources

HOMETOWN
El Monte

BORN
Oct. 20, 1957, Los Angeles, Calif.

RELIGION
Roman Catholic

FAMILY
Husband, Sam H. Sayyad

EDUCATION
California State Polytechnic U., Pomona, B.A. 1979; U. of Southern California, M.P.A. 1981

CAREER
White House aide

POLITICAL HIGHLIGHTS
Rio Hondo Community College Board of Trustees, 1985-92; Calif. Assembly, 1993-95; Calif. Senate, 1995-2000

ELECTION RESULTS

2000 GENERAL

Hilda L. Solis (D)	89,600	79.4%
Krista Lieberg-Wong (GREEN)	10,294	9.1%
Michael McGuire (LIBERT)	7,138	6.3%
Richard Griffin (NL)	5,882	5.2%

2000 PRIMARY (OPEN)

Hilda L. Solis (D)	48,531	62.2%
Matthew G. Martinez (D)	22,241	28.5%
Krista Lieberg-Wong (GREEN)	3,296	4.2%
Michael McGuire (LIBERT)	2,277	2.9%
Richard Griffin (NL)	1,630	2.1%

CALIFORNIA 31

Eastern Los Angeles County; El Monte; Alhambra; Azusa

The densely populated 31st sits just east of the city of Los Angeles. It takes in the southern San Gabriel Valley and stretches northeast to Azusa, with several good-size cities in between. Once a largely white community, the 31st has evolved into a majority-Latino area where Hispanics leaving L.A. for the suburbs are transforming once-Republican enclaves into solid Democratic domains.

The district's shrinking Republican pockets are in blue-collar Azusa and upscale San Gabriel, which belonged to the solidly Republican 26th before redistricting in 1992. El Monte, in the heart of the San Gabriel Valley, and Baldwin Park to the east are middle-income, blue-collar cities and the 31st's Democratic base. Monterey Park is upper middle class and known as "Little

Taipei" for its Taiwanese and other Asian immigrants.

The 31st lacks a dominant industry, and the San Gabriel Valley has suffered from higher unemployment rates than the rest of the nation. Previously a small farming town, El Monte used to house small aerospace factories. It is now a light manufacturing area with a new retail auto complex. The district's industrial hub is Irwindale, where industrial and commercial building is under way.

MAJOR INDUSTRY
Service, light manufacturing

CITIES
El Monte (pt), 105,444 (1990); Alhambra, 84,896; Baldwin Park (pt.), 68,300 (1990); Monterey Park, 63,060

UNUSUAL FEATURES
El Monte former site of Gay's Lion Farm where Charles Gay trained African lions – the MGM "Lion Logo" features one of Gay's roaring lions; El Monte's original settlers were drawn by the California Gold Rush.

Vacant Seat

Rep. Julian C. Dixon, D
Died Dec. 8, 2000

Julian C. Dixon, who represented the 32nd District for almost 22 years, died of a heart attack Dec. 8, 2000, a month after winning election to a 12th term. Voters in this overwhelmingly Democratic district had sent Dixon to Washington by huge margins. He never dropped below 73 percent of the vote.

A June 5, 2001, special election was scheduled to fill the vacancy. Democrat Diane Watson became the prohibitive favorite by winning an April 10 primary. She was to face Republican Noel Irwin Hentschel and two third-party candidates in the June contest.

Dixon was known for his hard work, low-key diplomacy and steadfastly liberal views. Democratic leader Richard A. Gephardt, Mo., reacting to Dixon's death, said he was "a gentle, conciliatory, wonderful human being."

Dixon won the appreciation of Democratic leaders for his willingness to take on tasks that presented little in the way of hometown benefits. He chaired the House ethics committee for six years. For 18 years, he was the top Democrat on the Appropriations subcommittee that oversees the District of Columbia.

The latter job, although it offered no benefits to his constituents, was important to him personally: Dixon, born and reared in a black, middle-class D.C. neighborhood, was an advocate for greater "home rule" for the city.

In the 106th Congress, Dixon was the top-ranking Democrat on the Intelligence Committee.

In recent years, he had focused more of his energy on Appropriations on national security matters and other issues important to his own California district. In 1997, he showed his liberal colors by being the only member of the Defense Appropriations Subcommittee to join with 108 other House Democrats in an effort to restrain defense spending. However, Dixon parted ways with many liberals and GOP budget-cutters who took aim at a defense program that has been big business in California: the B-2 stealth bomber.

Dixon also promoted California's interests from his seat on the Appropriations subcommittee that funds the Commerce, Justice and State departments, backing more money for the Border Patrol and additional funding for community policing and efforts to combat the manufacture of methamphetamine, a big part of California's illegal drug problem.

Also from his Appropriations post, Dixon helped secure federal funds for Los Angeles' Metro Rail subway, and he pushed for greater access to the subway system for inner-city residents. He was a key player on a supplemental spending bill to aid victims of the January 1994 Northridge earthquake in Southern California.

In her special-election bid to succeed Dixon, Watson put a lifetime of political activism among Los Angeles' African-American population to good use. Born Nov. 12, 1933, Watson was elected in 1978 as the first black woman to serve in the California Senate, where she stayed for 20 years. She later served as President Clinton's ambassador to Micronesia.

Watson took 33 percent of the vote to defeat 10 other Democrats in the April primary. Democratic State Sen. Kevin Murray finished second, with 26 percent. Hentschel, a wealthy tour company owner and philanthropist, defeated two other Republicans for her party's nomination, but took just 5 percent of the overall vote in the open primary.

CALIFORNIA 32
West Los Angeles; Culver City

The 32nd is an ethnically diverse, Democratic district that begins about a mile inland from Venice Beach, runs east through Culver City and ends up in south-central Los Angeles. Blacks, Hispanics and Asians account for more than three-fourths of the population, but the 32nd has no single ethnic majority. Nearly three-fourths of the district's registered voters are Democrats.

Several major demographic shifts have dramatically changed the makeup of the 32nd. The first was in the 1960s when the district's Jewish population migrated to the area's now more upscale northwest end and the district's center became predominantly black. Now, a wave of Hispanic immigrants is settling into the 32nd and whites are moving back into parts of downtown L.A., drawn by the area's affordable housing.

The 32nd has a solid middle class, as well as some sharply contrasting areas like wealthy Rancho Park in the north and poor South Central L.A., which was battered by the 1992 riots. The district is no longer the film production hub it used to be, although some movies are still made here. The service industry drives the economy, but there are also a few oil wells in Baldwin Hills.

MAJOR INDUSTRY
Service, entertainment, health care

CITIES
Los Angeles (pt.) 514,832 (1990); Culver City, 40,137

UNUSUAL FEATURES
The Los Angeles Coliseum, which has hosted two Olympiads, two Super Bowls and a World Series; MGM Studios (now part of Sony Picture Studios), where "Gone with the Wind" was filmed – the burning of Atlanta was really the burning of old King Kong sets; Academy Awards presented at L.A.'s Shrine Auditorium.

RECENT ELECTION RESULTS

2000 GENERAL		
Julian C. Dixon (D)	137,447	83.5%
Kathy Williamson (R)	19,924	12.1%
Bob Weber (LIBERT)	3,875	2.4%
Rashied Jibri (NL)	3,281	2.0%
1998 GENERAL		
Julian C. Dixon (D)	112,253	86.7%
Laurence Ardito (R)	14,622	11.3%
Velko Milosevich (LIBERT)	2,617	2.0%
1996 GENERAL		
Julian C. Dixon (D)	124,712	82.4%
Laurence Ardito (R)	18,768	12.4%
Neal Donner (LIBERT)	6,390	4.2%
Rashied Jibri (NL)	1,557	1.0%
1994 GENERAL		
Julian C. Dixon (D)	98,017	78%
Ernie A. Farhat (R)	22,190	18%
John Honigsfeld (PFP)	6,099	5%
1992 GENERAL		
Julian C. Dixon (D)	150,644	87%
Bob Weber (LIBERT)	12,384	7%
William R. Williams (PFP)	9,782	6%

Rep. Lucille Roybal-Allard (D)

Elected 1992; 5th term

Roybal-Allard has been a pioneer for Latinas. She is the second Hispanic woman ever elected to Congress (Ileana Ros-Lehtinen of Florida was the first), the first woman to head the Congressional Hispanic Caucus and the first Latina to serve on the Appropriations Committee, posts she achieved in the 106th Congress.

But, even as her accomplishments help to change society's expectations for female Hispanics, she has had to alter some attitudes within her own family. Despite her father's trailblazing career in politics, Roybal-Allard was not encouraged to pursue the same vocation. Edward R. Roybal was one of three Hispanic members of the House when he came to Capitol Hill in 1963, serving 30 years in Congress and helping to secure political clout for Hispanics in Southern California.

But when Roybal-Allard was a youth, her father's relatives derided him for sending his daughters to college, saying all that was expected of them was marriage and children. Later, her siblings discouraged her from entering politics after seeing what their father had gone through.

Roybal-Allard grew up hearing about the importance of being involved in the community, but it took the example of another pioneer — a former state representative and the current Los Angeles County supervisor, Gloria Molina — to inspire Roybal-Allard to seek office. She went on to serve six years in the state Assembly before running for the House in 1992, the same year her father retired.

Roybal-Allard realizes that she, in turn, is a role model for young Hispanic women. "We really have to succeed. We're evaluated more harshly than men. ... We have to show that we're capable of doing the job."

Roybal-Allard's Appropriations and Hispanic Caucus assignments, her leadership of the California Democratic delegation in the 105th and her work on behalf of women have helped her make a name for herself apart from the recognition that came to her automatically as Edward Roybal's daughter.

In the 105th, Roybal-Allard drew plaudits for her role in awakening the power of the 52-member California delegation, which had been fractious and unable to wield the clout that such a large delegation should have been able to boast. As the first elected chairman of the California Democratic delegation, she worked with her GOP counterpart Jerry Lewis to find issues on which the majority of the delegation could agree.

Her membership on the Treasury, Postal Service Appropriations Subcommittee in the 106th had particular meaning for her; her father chaired that subcommittee for 12 years. In the 107th, she moved to the Energy and Water Subcommittee, adding it to her post on the Commerce, Justice, State panel.

In the 106th, she became the first woman ever elected to head the Hispanic Caucus. She had been vice chairman of the group in the 104th and directed a task force on the census in the 105th. Priorities for the caucus include increasing the number of Hispanic judges, ensuring fair treatment of immigrants (the 33rd District has one of the highest proportions of non-citizens of any congressional district), and reducing school dropout rates for Hispanic youth. Roybal-Allard also has been active in efforts to boost Latino involvement in the arts and entertainment industries.

One priority she brought with her from her service in the California Assembly has been to improve the lot of women who have been abused or are in unfavorable domestic situations. In Congress, she has chaired the Violence Against Women Task Force. As a member of the Budget Committee

CAPITOL OFFICE
225-1766; fax 226-0350; 2435 Rayburn Bldg. 20515

INTERNET
e-mail: www.house.gov/writerep
web: www.house.gov/roybal-allard

COMMITTEES
Appropriations

HOMETOWN
East Los Angeles

BORN
June 12, 1941, Boyle Heights, Calif.

RELIGION
Roman Catholic

FAMILY
Husband, Edward T. Allard III; two children, two stepchildren

EDUCATION
California State U., Los Angeles, B.A. 1965

CAREER
Nonprofit worker

POLITICAL HIGHLIGHTS
Calif. Assembly, 1987-93

ELECTION RESULTS

2000 GENERAL

Lucille Roybal-Allard (D)	60,510	84.6%
Wayne Miller (R)	8,260	11.5%
Nathan Craddock (LIBERT)	1,601	2.2%
William Harpur (NL)	1,200	1.7%

2000 PRIMARY (OPEN)

Lucille Roybal-Allard (D)	37,618	84.6%
Wayne Miller (R)	5,364	12.1%
Nathan Craddock (LIBERT)	810	1.8%
William Harpur (NL)	655	1.5%

1998 GENERAL

Lucille Roybal-Allard (D)	43,310	87.2%
Wayne Miller (R)	6,364	12.8%

PREVIOUS WINNING PERCENTAGES
1996 (82%); 1994 (82%); 1992 (63%)

in the 104th Congress, she got language into a budget resolution in 1996 to ensure that changes in the welfare system would not exacerbate domestic violence problems faced by low-income women, who might have to choose between staying with an abusive husband for economic support or facing homelessness and hunger.

Roybal-Allard sponsored a bill that aimed to give unemployment insurance benefits to women forced to leave jobs because of domestic violence. The measure also proposed that employers be required to allow domestic violence victims reasonable leave without penalty to seek medical assistance, counseling, safety planning and legal assistance, and to make court appearances.

In her legislative work, she tries to balance the related but not always overlapping needs of the two chief components of her constituency: the minority "underclass" mired in chronic poverty and a substantial Latino working class of laborers and shop owners who have grabbed a low rung on the economic ladder. In recent years, Roybal-Allard and other community leaders have been working hard to encourage citizenship applications and to speed the process.

Roybal-Allard generally has been a dependable supporter of Democratic Party positions and often has won 100 percent favorable ratings from the AFL-CIO. However, after considerable soul-searching, she opposed her allies in organized labor in 1993 to support the North American Free Trade Agreement. But she voted against another labor-opposed trade measure in 2000 to grant China permanent normal trade status.

She diverged from President Clinton in 1997 when he proposed instituting a voluntary program of national testing in the schools, arguing that students who speak English as a second language might find themselves at a disadvantage. That issue may have reminded her of unpleasant experiences in her youth. She recalls being punished for speaking Spanish in school and facing questioning when she and her family went to places such as hotels and the Hollywood Bowl. And her father warned Lucille and her siblings to be careful around the police, against whom he was waging a campaign over what he charged were brutal and racist practices. He told the Los Angeles Times that he was afraid the police would abduct the children.

Roybal-Allard jumped at the chance to run for her father's seat in 1992. Redistricting had given the 33rd an 83 percent Hispanic population, even more favorable turf than the old 25th District in which her father had served. She drew insubstantial opposition in the Democratic primary and won in November by a 2-to-1 margin against Republican Robert Guzman, an education consultant. She has won re-election easily.

KEY VOTES

2000

Yes Raise hourly minimum wage by $1 over two years

No Halt funding for U.S. mission in Kosovo unless European nations pay more

Yes Provide Medicare benefits to military retirees and their dependents

No Grant China permanent normal trade status

No Phase out estate, gift and trust taxes

No Prohibit implementation of president's national monument designations

No Approve GOP plan to provide prescription drug coverage for Medicare beneficiaries

Yes Increase help for poor nations indebted to international financial institutions

1999

Yes Impose steel import quotas

Yes Kill proposal to take aviation trust funds off budget

No Require background checks on buyers only at gun shows with 10 or more vendors

No Remove barriers among banking, securities and insurance companies

Yes Authorize state grants to hire teachers and reduce class size

Yes Overhaul campaign finance law; ban "soft money" and restrict advocacy advertising

Yes Approve bipartisan plan to increase rights of patients in managed-care health plans

INTEREST GROUPS

	AFL-CIO	ADA	CCUS	ACU
2000	100%	90%	35%	8%
1999	89%	95%	16%	0%
1998	100%	100%	29%	0%
1997	100%	100%	30%	8%

CQ VOTE STUDIES

	PARTY UNITY		PRESIDENTIAL SUPPORT	
	Support	Oppose	Support	Oppose
2000	98%	2%	90%	10%
1999	97%	3%	86%	14%
1998	99%	1%	86%	14%
1997	98%	2%	84%	16%

CALIFORNIA 33
East-Central Los Angeles

The Democratic 33rd takes in the heart and eastern part of Los Angeles and is distinguished by its huge Hispanic majority, the largest in the state. One of California's poorest and least-educated districts, the 33rd had the lowest voter turnout of any district in the nation in 2000.

The district's northwest corner reaches into the busy downtown Los Angeles financial center. To the west is Pico Union, an entry port for new immigrants and one of the area's poorest and most populated communities. Conditions improve in the district's southeast portion, where those who have emerged from the ranks of the working poor are settling into middle-class residential areas like South Gate, which is less Democratic than the rest of the district and home to small businesses and a light manufacturing sector.

While much of the 33rd is economically depressed, the cities of Vernon and Commerce in the district's midsection house much of the 33rd's

industry, with facilities including food processing plants and metal-plating operations. The district also is attracting new "green" industries, such as recycling companies.

Other bright spots include construction of the Walt Disney Concert Hall, which is scheduled to open in 2002 and become home to the Los Angeles Phiharmonic; the Alameda Corridor project, an effort to connect manufacturing and distribution sites by rail; and the Staples Center, home for the National Basketball Association's Lakers and the National Hockey League's Kings.

MAJOR INDUSTRY
Government, manufacturing, service

CITIES
Los Angeles (pt.), 214,359 (1990); South Gate, 88,956; Huntington Park, 59,000; Bell Gardens, 44,703

UNUSUAL FEATURES
Site of the 2000 Democratic National Convention at the Staples Center; Downtown's Olvera Street considered L.A.'s birthplace; Angels Flight, trolley used before escalators to move people to the next street level.

Rep. Grace F. Napolitano (D)

Elected 1998; 2nd term

CAPITOL OFFICE
225-5256; fax 225-0027
1609 Longworth Bldg. 20515

INTERNET
e-mail: grace@mail.house.gov
web: www.house.gov/napolitano

COMMITTEES
International Relations
Resources
Small Business

HOMETOWN
Norwalk

BORN
Dec. 4, 1936, Brownsville, Texas

RELIGION
Roman Catholic

FAMILY
Husband, Frank Napolitano; five children

EDUCATION
Brownsville H.S., graduated 1954

CAREER
Regional transportation claims agent

POLITICAL HIGHLIGHTS
Norwalk City Council, 1986-92 (mayor, 1989-90);
Calif. Assembly, 1993-99

ELECTION RESULTS

2000 GENERAL

Grace F. Napolitano (D)	105,980	71.3%
Robert Canales (R)	33,445	22.5%
Julia F. Simon (NL)	9,262	6.2%

2000 PRIMARY (OPEN)

Grace F. Napolitano (D)	68,631	69.5%
Robert Canales (R)	24,140	24.4%
Julia F. Simon (NL)	6,053	6.1%

1998 GENERAL

Grace F. Napolitano (D)	76,471	67.6%
Ed Perez (R)	32,321	28.6%
Jason Heath (LIBERT)	2,195	1.9%
J. Walter Scott (AMI)	2,088	1.8%

Representing the suburbs and bedroom communities east of Los Angeles, first in the California Assembly and now in the House, has been a second calling for Napolitano.

Her first began early. Married at age 18, Napolitano had five children by 23, and attending to their needs, while also working at the Ford Motor Co., was her focus for decades. With her children now grown — and the parents to 13 children of their own — Napolitano directs her attention to Congress, where she is in her second term. There, she has often used the same manner with which she once tended to her family to address the needs of constituents and colleagues alike.

She has looked out for the well-being of her mostly Hispanic constituency by winning funds in 2000 for a pilot program to address the mental health problems of teenage Latinas and convincing the Federal Emergency Management Agency to abandon a plan to raise flood-insurance rates for the residents of southeastern Los Angeles County.

At the Capitol, she has tried to win over her political opponents in much the way she and her husband, Frank, won customers to their Italian restaurant — through their stomachs. During her time in Sacramento, Napolitano's contribution to bipartisan civility was to feed her colleagues at the statehouse. One of them, Republican Gary Miller, who now represents an adjacent congressional district, was a big fan of her green chili enchiladas, tacos and refried beans. Napolitano has kept up her ways of culinary wooing in Congress. She prides herself in catering her own fundraisers with homemade Mexican molés, guacamole and other dishes. She says such personal involvement is the best way to express her thankfulness to her supporters. "I treat them like I would my family," she says.

Still, Napolitano's grandmotherly image, enhanced by her silvery hair, can be deceptive. She can be a fierce political fighter and had to overcome a number of political slights to make it to Washington.

Though she had been a member of the legislature for six years and was mayor and councilwoman in Norwalk — the 34th District's biggest municipality — during the six years before that, Napolitano was overlooked when the district's long-term incumbent, Democrat Esteban E. Torres, announced his retirement in 1997. Torres threw his support to his top aide and son-in-law, James Casso. But Napolitano won by 618 votes in the primary, then won two-thirds of the vote in November. She increased her winning percentage to 71 percent in 2000 against little-known Republican Robert Canales.

Napolitano's initial House race was reminiscent of her first run for office, when she challenged the Norwalk establishment and won a seat on the city council by 28 votes. She capitalized on outrage over an expensive city council trip to Palm Springs and campaigned with $35,000 borrowed using her home as collateral.

She had caught the political bug years earlier as a volunteer in Norwalk's efforts to cultivate a sister-city relationship with Hermosillo, Mexico. While she initially joined the group to show her children and "other youngsters on this side how lucky they were" compared to Mexican children, she became enmeshed in the efforts and managed the organization's budget.

Napolitano grew up in Brownsville, Texas, the daughter of a Mexican immigrant who raised her two children on a shoestring budget. Napolitano has cultivated a strong connection to her mother's homeland as a public official. She accompanied President Clinton on a trip to Mexico in early 1999 and discussed international trade issues with Ernesto Zedillo, then Mexico's president. She had met with Zedillo many times earlier, when she traveled to Mexico as the chairman of the state Assembly's International Trade and Development Committee. In the 107th Congress, she added the International Relations Committee to her portfolio, a post she had sought.

Napolitano had been deeply immersed in the details of the North American Free Trade Agreement, which Clinton signed in 1993, and she believed in the value of open commerce. Still, she represented a district with double-digit unemployment and a prevailing sense that it had been left behind in the economic boom.

Those conflicting pressures placed her in a difficult situation in her first term, when the Clinton administration and big businesses pushed to grant China permanent normal trade status. Labor unions, environmentalists and other groups vociferously opposed the proposal, and many members, such as Napolitano, were caught in the middle. In her second year in office, she was summoned to the White House three times so Clinton could make his case for the measure. Secretary of State Madeleine K. Albright, National Security Adviser Samuel R. Berger, U.S. Trade Representative Charlene Barshefsky and Small Business Administrator Aida Alvarez all visited her office as well. So did Teamsters President James P. Hoffa, to argue that Napolitano should oppose the bill; AFL-CIO President John Sweeney telephoned with the same message.

Through it all, Napolitano did not say how she would vote and turned down an administration-sponsored trip to China. She eventually voted against the bill. "I know trade is good," she said afterward. "I know it's where we are going, but it's not good for the district."

Napolitano had also been thrust into the spotlight earlier in her congressional career when three U.S. servicemen were taken prisoner as part of the military intervention in Kosovo. The family of one — Staff Sgt. Andrew Ramirez — lived in her district. The House passed a resolution Napolitano sponsored calling on the government of Slobodan Milosevic to treat the soldiers humanely, as required under the Geneva Convention.

The committee assignments Napolitano received when she entered the House — Small Business and Resources — reflect her interests in economic development and environmental issues. She spent much of her time in the 106th Congress pushing the Energy Department to clean up a 10-million-ton pile of waste left over from 30 years of uranium mining. The waste, near Moab, Utah, threatened the Colorado River, which provides much of the West's drinking water.

KEY VOTES

2000
Yes   Raise hourly minimum wage by $1 over two years
No   Halt funding for U.S. mission in Kosovo unless European nations pay more
Yes   Provide Medicare benefits to military retirees and their dependents
No   Grant China permanent normal trade status
No   Phase out estate, gift and trust taxes
No   Prohibit implementation of president's national monument designations
No   Approve GOP plan to provide prescription drug coverage for Medicare beneficiaries
Yes   Increase help for poor nations indebted to international financial institutions

1999
Yes   Impose steel import quotas
No   Kill proposal to take aviation trust funds off budget
No   Require background checks on buyers only at gun shows with 10 or more vendors
Yes   Remove barriers among banking, securities and insurance companies
Yes   Authorize state grants to hire teachers and reduce class size
Yes   Overhaul campaign finance law; ban "soft money" and restrict advocacy advertising
Yes   Approve bipartisan plan to increase rights of patients in managed-care health plans

INTEREST GROUPS

	AFL-CIO	ADA	CCUS	ACU
2000	100%	95%	47%	4%
1999	89%	90%	45%	0%

CQ VOTE STUDIES

	PARTY UNITY		PRESIDENTIAL SUPPORT	
	Support	Oppose	Support	Oppose
2000	95%	5%	94%	6%
1999	92%	8%	77%	23%

CALIFORNIA 34
East Los Angeles County suburbs; West Covina

This Democratic stronghold, once a predominately white area, is emerging as a middle-class Hispanic district. It includes more than one-third of East Los Angeles, runs east through Montebello and Pico Rivera, goes up north a bit to La Puente and drops down to pick up most of affluent Whittier and Hacienda Heights, which has the district's largest Republican constituency.

The section of East Los Angeles in the 34th is the heart of East L.A.'s business district. Stores and other businesses are generally owned or operated by Hispanics. The area just to the north, around the 60 Freeway, is populated by what used to be called "Muppies" – Mexican yuppies who have moved in and fixed up old homes.

Montebello is an upper middle-class Hispanic area, with a lot of home-grown residents. It lies to the east of the small city of East Los Angeles and is bordered by four freeways, making it convenient for commuters.

Pico Rivera has been called pure Middle America, Hispanic-style. The city received a major blow in August 2000 with the closure of the district's Northrop Grumman plant. Norwalk, the 34th's largest city, is a bedroom town with a large number of Democratic voters. The district also includes the city of Santa Fe Springs, an industrial area with light manufacturing and oil wells.

The district is reliably Democratic on all levels. Bill Clinton carried the district in 1992 and '96 and in 2000 Al Gore received 67 percent of the vote.

MAJOR INDUSTRY
Manufacturing, oil

CITIES
Norwalk, 98,325; Pico Rivera, 61,498; Montebello, 60,989; Whittier (pt.), 56,997 (1990); East Los Angeles (pt.), 52,103 (1990)

UNUSUAL FEATURES
Whittier, where Richard Nixon lived and attended college, was the epicenter of L.A.'s massive 1987 earthquake.

Rep. Maxine Waters (D)

Elected 1990; 6th term

CAPITOL OFFICE
225-2201; fax 225-7854; 2344 Rayburn Bldg. 20515

INTERNET
e-mail: www.house.gov/writerep
web: www.house.gov/waters

COMMITTEES
Financial Services
Judiciary

HOMETOWN
Los Angeles

BORN
Aug. 15, 1938, St. Louis, Mo.

RELIGION
Christian

FAMILY
Husband, Sidney Williams; two children

EDUCATION
California State U., Los Angeles, B.A. 1970

CAREER
Head Start official

POLITICAL HIGHLIGHTS
Calif. Assembly, 1977-91

ELECTION RESULTS

2000 GENERAL

Maxine Waters (D)	100,569	86.5%
Carl McGill (R)	12,582	10.8%
Gordon Michael Mego (AMI)	1,911	1.6%

2000 PRIMARY (OPEN)

Maxine Waters (D)	64,176	85.4%
Carl McGill (R)	8,898	11.8%
Gordon Michael Mego (AMI)	1,247	1.7%
Rick Dunstan (NL)	861	1.2%

1998 GENERAL

Maxine Waters (D)	78,732	89.3%
Gordon Michael Mego (AMI)	9,413	10.7%

PREVIOUS WINNING PERCENTAGES
1996 (86%); 1994 (78%); 1992 (83%); 1990 (79%)

A combative, liberal Democrat, Waters is outspoken and fearless in defending the interests of her poor, minority-dominated district in south-central Los Angeles. With Republicans running the House, Waters seldom finds sympathy for her pleas for assistance to the inner cities, but she is at her rhetorical best as an insurgent.

"Being in the minority means you don't get your legislation heard, you don't get to chair a committee, and you don't influence policies in other parts of the world," she says.

Whether Waters lacks influence is arguable, however, as her high-profile involvement in such issues as economic and political developments in Africa and Cuba and the battle against AIDS have assured that those matters are not ignored. In the 105th Congress, her post as chairman of the Congressional Black Caucus provided her with a megaphone. Since then, she has remained active in Black Caucus affairs while also serving as one of four appointed chief deputy whips and as a member of the Democratic Steering Committee, which makes committee assignments.

In late 2000 and early 2001, Waters was among the most outspoken lawmakers in protesting the validity of George W. Bush's victory in Florida presidential voting. And, in testimony before the Senate Judiciary Committee, she delivered an impassioned speech against the nomination of John Ashcroft as attorney general, telling senators that Ashcroft's earlier opposition to the confirmation of a black man to the federal bench was beyond insensitivity. "You don't destroy human beings simply because you have the power to do it," Waters said.

A virtual lock for re-election every two years in her 90 percent minority district, Waters is under no electoral pressure to trim her liberal sails or to heed the calls for civility and cooperation in the House. When quarreling with a colleague, she has been known to tell an adversary to "shut up," and she once suggested in a news conference that a conservative member of the California delegation seek psychiatric treatment. No one doubts the depth and sincerity of Waters' feelings, but many members of Congress — in both parties — are put off by her temper and by her unrelenting sense of the rightness of her decidedly liberal opinions.

Waters says that if she softens her stance and engages in the give-and-take typical of Washington politics, her constituents will feel let down. She bristles with anger at the Republican notion that volunteer programs and self-reliance are suitable substitutes for massive government assistance: "Volunteers are great. But volunteers cannot be relied on. Anybody who wants to run a real business does not say, I'm going to run this business with volunteers."

Waters serves on the Financial Services (formerly Banking) and Judiciary committees. On the latter panel in 1998, she was an outspoken critic of Kenneth W. Starr's investigation of President Clinton and of the GOP's move to impeach the president. Waters brings her advocacy for minorities and the poor to the Financial Services panel; she has worked, for example, to stop banks from charging transaction fees to small depositors.

In the 106th, she called for an investigation of mortgage lending practices to low-income blacks. And she blasted the credit card industry for the meteoric rise of personal bankruptcies. Republicans also drew her wrath in crafting a bill to overhaul the bankruptcy system. "It is absolutely outrageous that you can't take a little step down for the consumer in this bill. ... They may not have fancy lobbyists, but what harm is it in extending yourself?" she asked.

Over the years, Waters has been able to win a few battles to obtain job training and community development funding for her district, and for the fight against AIDS, which she argues has become an epidemic in Los Angeles County, particularly among blacks. Waters advocates increased U.S. trade with Africa, but she opposed a bill in the 106th that aimed to boost trade, arguing that the legislation would help large multinational corporations more than the countries in the region. "We're not going to support the rape of Africa a second time in a more sophisticated way," she argued.

During the 104th and 105th Congresses, Waters made a crusade of trying to determine the validity of news reports that the CIA had been complicit in inner-city crack cocaine dealing, with cash proceeds going to the Nicaraguan contras. Waters pressed for hearings and when one took place under the auspices of the Senate Intelligence Committee, she was in the front row. Intelligence Chairman Arlen Specter, R-Pa., allowed Waters — who told Specter he was not asking the "right questions" — to grill the witnesses herself.

Waters comes from modest circumstances. She was born in St. Louis as one of 13 children in a welfare family and was raised in public housing projects. As a teenager, she bused tables in a segregated restaurant. Married just after high school, she moved in 1961 with her first husband and two children to Los Angeles, where she worked in a clothing factory and for the telephone company.

Waters' public career began in 1966, when she volunteered as an assistant teacher in the new Head Start program while attending college. From Head Start she got into community-organizing activities and then politics. After working as a volunteer and a consultant to several candidates, she won an upset election in 1976 to the state Assembly, representing many of the same neighborhoods that she now serves in Congress.

She rose to become majority whip in the Assembly, and Speaker Willie Brown Jr. gave her free rein to pursue projects of personal interest such as divesting state assets from South Africa.

Waters got her chance to run for Congress in 1990, with the retirement of 28-year Democratic Rep. Augustus F. Hawkins. She had been preparing for the move for years. During debates in the legislature over redistricting in 1982, Waters maneuvered to remove from Hawkins' district a blue-collar, mainly white suburb she saw as unfriendly territory. Waters' 1990 election to the House was never in doubt, and she has won handily since.

KEY VOTES

2000

Yes	Raise hourly minimum wage by $1 over two years
No	Halt funding for U.S. mission in Kosovo unless European nations pay more
?	Provide Medicare benefits to military retirees and their dependents
No	Grant China permanent normal trade status
No	Phase out estate, gift and trust taxes
No	Prohibit implementation of president's national monument designations
No	Approve GOP plan to provide prescription drug coverage for Medicare beneficiaries
Yes	Increase help for poor nations indebted to international financial institutions

1999

Yes	Impose steel import quotas
No	Kill proposal to take aviation trust funds off budget
No	Require background checks on buyers only at gun shows with 10 or more vendors
No	Remove barriers among banking, securities and insurance companies
Yes	Authorize state grants to hire teachers and reduce class size
Yes	Overhaul campaign finance law; ban "soft money" and restrict advocacy advertising
Yes	Approve bipartisan plan to increase rights of patients in managed-care health plans

INTEREST GROUPS

	AFL-CIO	ADA	CCUS	ACU
2000	100%	85%	26%	0%
1999	100%	100%	12%	0%
1998	100%	80%	21%	0%
1997	100%	95%	20%	8%

CQ VOTE STUDIES

	PARTY UNITY		PRESIDENTIAL SUPPORT	
	Support	Oppose	Support	Oppose
2000	96%	4%	85%	15%
1999	97%	3%	87%	13%
1998	94%	6%	85%	15%
1997	94%	6%	75%	25%

CALIFORNIA 35
South Central Los Angeles

South Central Los Angeles' 35th is the most secure Democratic district in the state, with almost 75 percent of its voters registered as Democrats. Once predominately black, the 35th is seeing a huge influx of Hispanics, who are beginning to outnumber blacks. The district is set between downtown Los Angeles to the north, Los Angeles International Airport to the west, the Alameda Corridor to the east, and Long Beach to the south. The 35th is mostly poor, but there are some middle-class areas in the southeast cities of Gardena, Inglewood and Hawthorne. Gardena also has a large and politically influential Japanese community.

Riots put the 35th in the headlines in 1992 when a white truck driver was dragged from his vehicle and beaten by a group of blacks at the intersection of Normandie and Florence avenues in the wake of a verdict acquitting four white police officers accused of beating black motorist Rodney King.

The economically depressed 35th has been trying to lure new businesses through loan guarantees and other incentives. In 1994 it became part of a federal empowerment zone established to help areas affected by the riots. For years, Gardena received a strong revenue stream as the only city in Los Angeles County that allowed poker parlors, which account for about 13 percent of the city's budget. In 2000, the Los Angeles Lakers and Kings moved from the Great Western Forum in Inglewood to the new Staples Center in the nearby 33rd, a disappointment for the 35th.

MAJOR INDUSTRY
Service, manufacturing

CITIES
Los Angeles (pt.), 244,712 (1990); Inglewood (pt.), 109,229 (1990); Hawthorne (pt.), 71,330 (1990); Gardena, 55,374

UNUSUAL FEATURES
Hollywood Park racetrack in Inglewood; Hawthorne was the birthplace of the Beach Boys and Northrop Corp., before it became aerospace giant Northrop Grumman Corp.

Rep. Jane Harman (D)

CAPITOL OFFICE
225-8220; fax 226-7290; 229 Cannon Bldg. 20515

INTERNET
e-mail: jane.harman@mail.house.gov
web: www.house.gov/harman

COMMITTEES
Energy & Commerce
Select Intelligence

HOMETOWN
Rolling Hills

BORN
June 28, 1945, Queens, N.Y.

RELIGION
Jewish

FAMILY
Husband, Sidney Harman; four children

EDUCATION
Smith College, B.A. 1966; Harvard U., J.D. 1969

CAREER
Lawyer; White House aide; congressional aide

POLITICAL HIGHLIGHTS
U.S. House, 1993-99; sought Democratic nomination for governor, 1998

ELECTION RESULTS

2000 GENERAL

Jane Harman (D)	115,651	48.4%
Steven T. Kuykendall (R)	111,199	46.6%
Daniel Sherman (LIBERT)	6,073	2.5%
John Konopka (REF)	3,549	1.5%

2000 PRIMARY (OPEN)

Steven T. Kuykendall (R)	66,520	42.7%
Jane Harman (D)	63,013	40.5%
Robert Pegram (R)	12,653	8.1%
James Cavuoto (D)	6,423	4.1%
Daniel Sherman (LIBERT)	2,635	1.7%
Farshad Rastegar (D)	2,508	1.6%

1996 GENERAL

Jane Harman (D)	117,752	52.5%
Susan Brooks (R)	98,538	43.9%
Bruce Dovner (LIBERT)	4,933	2.2%
Bradley McManus (NL)	3,236	1.4%

PREVIOUS WINNING PERCENTAGES
1994 (48%); 1992 (48%)

Elected 1992; 4th term
Did not serve 1999-2001

Harman pulled off a rare short-turnaround comeback in California's 36th District: After leaving the House seat she had held for three terms to run for governor in 1998, Harman narrowly won the seat back in 2000 — ousting the Republican, Steven T. Kuykendall, who had succeeded her.

Reflecting on her return to Washington, Harman said she was "dismayed at how dysfunctional Congress has become." The level of partisanship is intolerable, she said. "We need to change the leadership, but also the culture."

Harman's approach to budget issues is similar to that of other moderate Democrats, including those in the "Blue Dog" coalition, of which she is a member. "I want to take the Blue Dog approach, whereby 50 percent of the surplus goes to debt reduction, 25 percent goes to targeted tax cuts and the other 25 percent goes to building up the nation's defense system."

Representing the mainly upscale, highly educated residents of the suburban Los Angeles district, Harman appeals to swing voters with her fiscal moderation, liberal views on social issues such as abortion, and her pro-defense stance —the 36th has a large defense-related industry.

Harman was the only freshman to win a spot on the Energy and Commerce panel. She also got a seat on the Intelligence Committee.

In 1998, Harman left Congress to seek the Democratic nomination for California governor, but fell short in a tight three-way primary won by Lt. Gov. Gray Davis, who went on to win the governorship.

In 2000, despite some hesitation, she agreed to run for the 36th District seat just two days before the late-1999 candidate filing deadline, after being assured by Democratic congressional leaders that she would regain her past seniority.

The contest was touch-and-go, largely because Harman and Kuykendall appeared to agree on many major issues — Kuykendall, too, touted his support for abortion rights and defense spending. In a contest where both candidates focused on issues and avoided mudslinging, Harman eked out a win by fewer than 2 percentage points.

CALIFORNIA 36
West Los Angeles County; Manhattan Beach; Torrance

The 36th hugs the Pacific coast, running south from Venice to San Pedro and the port of Los Angeles. A swing district where party registration runs even overall, the 36th includes some of the most intensely Democratic and Republican areas in the state. On the presidential level, the 36th supported the Democratic candidate in 1992, '96 and 2000.

While Venice is considered the state's most liberal haven outside of Berkeley, the Palos Verdes Peninsula is home to some of the most exclusive Republican enclaves in the Los Angeles region. Torrance, the district's largest city, is split politically.

A number of major companies maintain headquarters in the 36th, and aerospace firms in El Segundo and Redondo Beach

drive the economy. The 36th has some of the state's most educated residents, but in the early 1990s, it wasn't unusual to see people with doctorates collecting unemployment compensation due to shrinking defense and aerospace spending.

In the 1990s, an effort to diversify the economy and encourage dual-use technology resulted in an economic boost as military and defense contractors converted their technologies to non-defense purposes.

MAJOR INDUSTRY
Aerospace, high-tech, manufacturing

MILITARY BASES
Los Angeles Air Force Base, 13,034 military, 1,000 civilian (1999)

CITIES
Los Angeles (pt.), 163,650 (1990); Torrance, 138,999; Redondo Beach, 64,804

UNUSUAL FEATURES
Orson Welles used Venice as the location for the seedy town in "Touch of Evil" in 1958; Los Angeles International Airport.

Rep. Juanita Millender-McDonald (D)

Elected March 1996; 3rd full term

CAPITOL OFFICE
225-7924; fax 225-7926; 125 Cannon Bldg. 20515

INTERNET
e-mail: millender.mcdonald@mail.house.gov
web: www.house.gov/millender-mcdonald

COMMITTEES
Small Business
Transportation & Infrastructure

HOMETOWN
Carson

BORN
Sept. 7, 1938, Birmingham, Ala.

RELIGION
Baptist

FAMILY
Husband, James McDonald Jr.; five children

EDUCATION
U. of Redlands, B.S. 1981; California State U., Los
Angeles, M.A. 1988; U. of Southern California,
attending

CAREER
Teacher; school program administrator

POLITICAL HIGHLIGHTS
Carson City Council, 1990-92 (mayor pro tempore,
1991-92); Calif. Assembly, 1992-96

ELECTION RESULTS

2000 GENERAL

J. Millender-McDonald (D)	93,269	82.3%
Vernon Van (R)	12,762	11.3%
Margaret Glazer (NL)	4,094	3.6%
Herb Peters (LIBERT)	3,150	2.8%

2000 PRIMARY (OPEN)

J. Millender-McDonald (D)	58,646	81.8%
Vernon Van (R)	8,048	11.2%
Margaret Glazer (NL)	2,751	3.8%
Herb Peters (LIBERT)	2,248	3.1%

1998 GENERAL

J. Millender-McDonald (D)	70,026	85.1%
Saul Lankster (R)	12,301	14.9%

PREVIOUS WINNING PERCENTAGES
1996 (85%); 1996 Special Election (27%)

A dependable Democratic vote and one of President Clinton's staunchest supporters throughout her first five years in Congress, Millender-McDonald is a forceful voice for her constituents, in one of California's poorest districts.

Her interests range from local transportation needs to child care, education, illegal drug use, job training and women's issues. There is a hard edge to her rhetoric when it serves her purposes, particularly when she detects what she views as GOP indifference toward the plight of the poor.

Elected in 1996, Millender-McDonald is in her third career, and she draws liberally from all of her previous experiences.

She is the daughter of a minister who taught her the importance of self-respect and a good education. She married early and had five children by the time she was 26. At the age of 42, with her children older, she got her college degree and embarked on a career as a math and English teacher, and then as an administrator, in the Los Angeles school system.

She was active in local Democratic Party politics, serving as a delegate at the 1984 and 1988 Democratic National Conventions. Then, at age 51, she entered elective politics, winning a city council seat in Carson — a low-income city between Los Angeles and Long Beach.

At each step of her professional life, Millender-McDonald's forceful self-confidence has enabled her to become a powerful and noticeable presence. (She was named one of the best-dressed members of Congress in a poll of Capitol Hill lobbyists conducted by Washingtonian magazine.)

She has a host of ideas that she thinks would make the world a better place, and although many of them look like a tough sell in a conservative-run Congress, she persists. "I am here for the fight and the long haul to ensure ... fairness to my constituents," she said during one floor debate.

Millender-McDonald is by any measure a liberal, but not an inflexible one. If cooperating with Republicans offers a chance of boosting the struggling economy in the 37th District, she'll do it. This is most evident on the Transportation Committee, where she was a backer of the ambitious infrastructure development agenda of former Republican Chairman Bud Shuster of Pennsylvania — a man with whom she agreed on few other issues.

Her top transportation priority is completion of the Alameda Corridor project, a high-capacity throughway running the length of her district and linking Los Angeles' rail yards with the ports of that city and Long Beach. Funding for work on the corridor was included in the 1998 transportation bill, in which Millender-McDonald secured a total of $31 million for projects in her district. She also worked to include funding to help former welfare recipients pay for travel to work.

One of Millender-McDonald's posts with the Los Angeles Unified School District was as director of gender-equity programs, and a couple of her legislative endeavors deal specifically with discrimination against women. She calls for specific assurances that women will get a fair share of federal vocational education training dollars. And from her Aviation Subcommittee seat on the Transportation and Infrastructure panel, she has pressed to find out why female air traffic controllers have leveled allegations of sexual harassment and sexual discrimination at the Federal Aviation Administration.

In the 107th Congress, she is the co-chairwoman of the Congressional Caucus for Women's Issues.

Millender-McDonald also sits on the Small Business Committee, where she has risen rapidly to rank second in seniority among Democrats. In the

106th Congress, she took the ranking Democratic spot on the Empowerment Subcommittee, reorganized as Workforce, Empowerment and Government Programs in the 107th.

In 1997, she called GOP opposition to additional funds for the Women, Infants and Children's feeding program "cruel and without reason." She said it was "preposterous" for some Republicans to propose that employers be exempt from paying the minimum wage to people moving off welfare into the work force. A critic of tuition vouchers and other such ideas advanced by conservatives to improve the quality of education, she said the GOP first should recognize the "deplorable" physical condition of many public schools and commit billions of federal dollars to repair and renovate crumbling buildings.

During both the 105th and 106th Congresses, Millender-McDonald sought to require that all firearms manufactured or sold in the United States be fitted with child safety locks. Hand-in-hand with gun safety, she says, is her effort to end the sale of alcohol to minors through the Internet.

She has worked to increase the number of minority and mixed-race individuals who register as bone marrow donors and was able to win approval of funding for outreach programs to encourage minority participation.

Also in 1999, she won House passage of a measure, cosponsored by the entire California delegation, to rename a post office in Compton, Calif., after former Democratic Rep. Mervyn M. Dymally. It was a small measure of thanks from Millender-McDonald, whose first ventures into elective politics were greatly aided by Dymally, who represented much of what is now the 37th District from 1981 until he retired in 1993.

Dymally put his campaign organization to work for her in 1990 when she sought the Carson City Council seat. Two years later, McDonald (as she was known until she arrived in Congress), to the annoyance of some who thought she should stay longer in city government and pay her political dues, once again drew on the Dymally organization to win an upset victory over two veteran assemblymen for a seat in the state Assembly.

Little more than three years later, she won another promotion, capturing the 37th District seat in a March 1996 special election, held after the exit of Democratic Rep. Walter R. Tucker III. Tucker resigned from Congress on Dec. 15, 1995, a week after a federal jury convicted him on felony charges of extortion and tax evasion. The charges stemmed from actions he took as mayor of Compton, before his election to Congress. In each of her three re-elections, Millender-McDonald has captured more than 80 percent of the vote.

KEY VOTES

2000

Yes Raise hourly minimum wage by $1 over two years
No Halt funding for U.S. mission in Kosovo unless European nations pay more
Yes Provide Medicare benefits to military retirees and their dependents
No Grant China permanent normal trade status
No Phase out estate, gift and trust taxes
No Prohibit implementation of president's national monument designations
No Approve GOP plan to provide prescription drug coverage for Medicare beneficiaries
Yes Increase help for poor nations indebted to international financial institutions

1999

Yes Impose steel import quotas
No Kill proposal to take aviation trust funds off budget
No Require background checks on buyers only at gun shows with 10 or more vendors
Yes Remove barriers among banking, securities and insurance companies
Yes Authorize state grants to hire teachers and reduce class size
Yes Overhaul campaign finance law; ban "soft money" and restrict advocacy advertising
Yes Approve bipartisan plan to increase rights of patients in managed-care health plans

INTEREST GROUPS

	AFL-CIO	ADA	CCUS	ACU
2000	100%	90%	50%	8%
1999	78%	100%	30%	0%
1998	100%	95%	31%	4%
1997	100%	90%	30%	12%

CQ VOTE STUDIES

	PARTY UNITY		PRESIDENTIAL SUPPORT	
	Support	Oppose	Support	Oppose
2000	98%	2%	91%	9%
1999	97%	3%	88%	12%
1998	96%	4%	84%	16%
1997	95%	5%	81%	19%

CALIFORNIA 37

Southern Los Angeles County; Compton; Carson

The 37th includes some of the poorest and most Democratic communities in Los Angeles and the state. Hispanics are the dominant minority group, and minorities represent more than 80 percent of the population. Most of the district's residents are concentrated in the lower- and middle-class cities of Compton, Carson and Lynwood just south of Los Angeles. Democratic presidential candidates secure high margins of victory in the 37th; Al Gore captured 83 percent of the district's vote in 2000.

The 37th's troubled economy suffered in the 1992 riots when fires ravaged parts of Compton and Lynwood. Despite recent development, Compton has still yet to fully recover. It has blocks-long stretches of abandoned buildings and vacant lots. Overall, crime is down, but the district still has many of the violent crime and gang problems found throughout the Los Angeles area. There are some bright spots. Several national retailers and fast-food chains

have moved into communities once considered undevelopable and home sales have increased.

The district also is home to a few major factories, such as Nissan and Toyota. The multibillion-dollar Alameda Corridor project, which will create a rail link between Long Beach docks and distribution areas in Los Angeles, is scheduled to be completed in 2002, and local leaders are hoping it will help the area's economy.

MAJOR INDUSTRY
Service, manufacturing, oil

CITIES
Compton 92,864; Carson 89,089; Lynwood 63,935

UNUSUAL FEATURES
Tennis pro Venus Williams born in Lynwood; Director and actor Forest Whitaker and actress and recording artist Brandy Norwood both longtime residents of Carson.

Rep. Steve Horn (R)

Elected 1992; 5th term

When the topic of debate is abortion, guns, government support for the arts, or other issues in the social policy realm, Horn rates as one of the most liberal Republicans in the House. His support for many traditionally liberal social causes reflects the prevailing sentiment of his Democratic-leaning district, which he barely held onto in 2000.

He is a strong advocate of gun control, campaign finance reform, and gay and abortion rights, and he was one of just eight House Republicans in the 106th Congress to oppose a ban on a procedure its opponents call "partial birth" abortion. In 1999, he backed a bipartisan bill, opposed by GOP leaders, that would have overhauled health care regulations and given managed-care patients the right to sue their health care plans.

Despite such positions, Horn does not go out of his way to provoke Republican leaders. Indeed, on the Government Reform Committee he was every bit as critical of the Clinton administration as the GOP's hard-core right wing. In the 105th, he fumed that the White House had engaged in "a broad and remarkably consistent effort to delay, obstruct, confuse, divert and derail" the committee from getting to the bottom of irregularities in financing the 1996 presidential campaign. Like most Republicans, he voted to impeach President Clinton in 1998.

A lifelong "policy wonk" with decades of experience watching and working in Congress, Horn has a library of books on the institution that runs into the thousands. A former congressional fellow, a Senate aide, and a political science professor, he has written books himself on the Senate Appropriations Committee, ethics and campaign financing.

As chairman of Government Reform's Subcommittee on Government Efficiency, Financial Management and Intergovernmental Relations, Horn likes to play the part of professor, giving government agencies "report cards" that rate their performance in such areas as financial management and computer modernization. No elected official was more persistent than Horn in pushing Washington bureaucrats to come to grips with the federal government's potential year 2000 problem — the glitch that some warned could cause many computers to fail at the turn of the century unless they were reprogrammed.

Horn also has worked to reduce federal agency travel expenses. In the 105th, he won enactment of a bill requiring most federal employees to use a government charge card while on official business, crediting frequent flyer miles and other benefits to the government, rather than to the employee.

Horn serves on the Transportation and Infrastructure Committee as well, where he has kept his district happy by securing funds for a number of big-ticket projects, including the Alameda Corridor, an intermodal link between the ports of Long Beach and Los Angeles (both in his district) and the L.A. rail yards.

He is a steadfast defender of the C-17 transport plane, which is built in the 38th District. In 2000, he criticized Defense Department plans to cut back on the plane's production. "It's a great plane, and we ought to stick with the production schedule," he told Knight-Ridder.

Horn is often uneasy with some of the proposals advanced by conservative House Republicans from more homogeneous, Bible Belt constituencies. The 38th's diverse population includes working-class whites and large communities of Hispanics and Cambodians.

When the House voted in 1997 to express its support for the public dis-

CAPITOL OFFICE
225-6676; fax 226-1012; 2331 Rayburn Bldg. 20515

INTERNET
e-mail: steve.horn@mail.house.gov
web: www.house.gov/horn

COMMITTEES
Government Reform
  (Government Efficiency, Financial Management & Intergovernmental Relations - chairman)
Transportation & Infrastructure

HOMETOWN
Long Beach

BORN
May 31, 1931, San Juan Bautista, Calif.

RELIGION
Protestant

FAMILY
Wife, Nini Horn; two children

EDUCATION
Stanford U., A.B. 1953; Harvard U., M.P.A. 1955; Stanford U., Ph.D. 1958

MILITARY SERVICE
Army Reserve, 1954-62

CAREER
Professor; college president; congressional aide

POLITICAL HIGHLIGHTS
U.S. Commission on Civil Rights vice chairman/member, 1969-82; sought Republican nomination for U.S. House, 1988

ELECTION RESULTS

2000 GENERAL

Steve Horn (R)	87,266	48.5%
Gerrie Schipske (D)	85,498	47.5%
Karen Blasdell-Wilkinson (NL)	3,744	2.1%
Jack Neglia (LIBERT)	3,614	2.0%

2000 PRIMARY (OPEN)

Steve Horn (R)	59,209	50.5%
Gerrie Schipske (D)	17,676	15.1%
Erin Gruwell (D)	16,062	13.7%
Peter Mathews (D)	13,937	11.9%

1998 GENERAL

Steve Horn (R)	71,386	52.9%
Peter Mathews (D)	59,767	44.3%

WINNING PERCENTAGES
1996 (53%); 1994 (59%); 1992 (49%)

play of the Ten Commandments in government buildings, Horn objected to giving special status to that Judeo-Christian code. "There are many great religions in this world — Buddhism, Christianity, Confucianism, Judaism and Islam. ... It is wrong to single out two religions and carve what they believe on the walls," he said.

Horn has been a bulwark against conservatives bent on killing the National Endowment for the Arts. He traces his positive view of federal support for the arts to a memorable childhood experience during the Great Depression, when a touring symphony orchestra funded by the federal Works Progress Administration played in the high school gym of his small California town. The event led him toward a serious pursuit of the French horn. Government-financed exposure to culture, he says, "made a difference in my life, and ... has made a difference in millions of young people's lives."

In his 20s, Horn worked for President Eisenhower's secretary of labor, James P. Mitchell. Later, as an aide to GOP Sen. Thomas H. Kuchel of California, he was on the Senate floor when the Tonkin Gulf Resolution passed in 1964, and he helped draft the Voting Rights Act of 1965. Horn was vice chairman of the U.S. Commission on Civil Rights for 11 years and a political scientist at California State University in Long Beach, where he was president from 1970 to 1988.

Horn made his first bid for the House in 1988, running third in the GOP primary in the old 42nd, just south of the district he holds now. In 1992, however, he eked out a victory over seven other entrants in the GOP primary for the open seat in the 38th. He faced a tough battle in the general election against Long Beach City Councilman Evan Anderson Braude, stepson of Democratic Rep. Glenn M. Anderson, the retiring 12-term incumbent. But Horn overcame the district's heavily Democratic voter registration by mobilizing the GOP base and reaching out to some progressives, and he won the general election by 6 percentage points.

By keeping a close eye on the local economy and taking moderate stands, Horn won re-election three times by margins ranging from 9 to 21 percentage points despite refusing contributions from political action committees. But in 2000, he almost succumbed to a challenge by Democrat Gerrie Schipske. The nurse practitioner and health care policy attorney criticized him for voting to impeach Clinton in 1998 and for not aggressively addressing the problems of health care. Refusing to deviate from his unconventional campaigning style, which included mailing out wordy political pamphlets that stressed issue discussions over photos, Horn kept his seat, but won by fewer than 1,800 votes.

KEY VOTES

2000
Yes Raise hourly minimum wage by $1 over two years
Yes Halt funding for U.S. mission in Kosovo unless European nations pay more
Yes Provide Medicare benefits to military retirees and their dependents
No Grant China permanent normal trade status
Yes Phase out estate, gift and trust taxes
No Prohibit implementation of president's national monument designations
Yes Approve GOP plan to provide prescription drug coverage for Medicare beneficiaries
Yes Increase help for poor nations indebted to international financial institutions

1999
Yes Impose steel import quotas
No Kill proposal to take aviation trust funds off budget
Yes Require background checks on buyers only at gun shows with 10 or more vendors
Yes Remove barriers among banking, securities and insurance companies
No Authorize state grants to hire teachers and reduce class size
Yes Overhaul campaign finance law; ban "soft money" and restrict advocacy advertising
Yes Approve bipartisan plan to increase rights of patients in managed-care health plans

INTEREST GROUPS

	AFL-CIO	ADA	CCUS	ACU
2000	40%	35%	66%	56%
1999	56%	55%	72%	44%
1998	30%	20%	83%	56%
1997	50%	50%	60%	44%

CQ VOTE STUDIES

	PARTY UNITY		PRESIDENTIAL SUPPORT	
	Support	Oppose	Support	Oppose
2000	71%	29%	46%	54%
1999	68%	32%	39%	61%
1998	73%	27%	35%	65%
1997	71%	29%	47%	53%

CALIFORNIA 38

Long Beach; Downey; Lakewood

Largely middle class and residential, the 38th takes in about two-thirds of the coastal city of Long Beach and stretches north to include the inland cities of Paramount, Downey and Bellflower.

While Downey is middle- to upper-class and leans Republican, Paramount is a blue-collar, Democratic city and about 60 percent Hispanic. Politically mixed Long Beach is the district's largest city and has the nation's busiest container port. The city's Cambodian population in the southwest is said to be the largest outside of Cambodia. Schoolchildren in Long Beach speak more than four dozen languages.

Moderate Republicans with liberal social views can be elected in this district, despite a strong Democratic voter registration advantage. On the national level, the district supported the Democratic candidate in presidential contests in the 1990s and 2000.

Defense cuts, coming on the heels of the 1980s depression, seriously hurt the district; it lost 58,000 jobs when its naval station, hospital and shipyard closed in the 1990s. Since then, the economy has been clawing its way back. At the beginning of 2001, Long Beach leased the naval station property to Hanjin, a South Korean shipping line, which is operating a newly constructed terminal.

MAJOR INDUSTRY
Service, aerospace, high-tech

CITIES
Long Beach (pt.), 296,670 (1990); Downey, 94,459; Bellflower, 64,239; Lakewood (pt.), 49,714 (1990)

UNUSUAL FEATURES
Long Beach known as "The Sinking City" in the 1950s and is still pumping water into the ground to replace oil lost to drilling; The Queen Mary docked at Long Beach; Long Beach home to the Aquarium of the Pacific, the Toyota Grand Prix of Long Beach, and former home of the Hughes Flying Boat, or HK-1 "Spruce Goose," the world's biggest wooden airplane, flown by Howard Hughes.

Rep. Ed Royce (R)

CAPITOL OFFICE
225-4111; fax 226-0335; 2202 Rayburn Bldg. 20515

INTERNET
e-mail: www.house.gov/writerep
web: www.house.gov/royce

COMMITTEES
Financial Services
International Relations
  (Africa - chairman)

HOMETOWN
Fullerton

BORN
Oct. 12, 1951, Los Angeles, Calif.

RELIGION
Roman Catholic

FAMILY
Wife, Marie Royce

EDUCATION
California State U., Fullerton, B.A. 1977

CAREER
Tax manager

POLITICAL HIGHLIGHTS
Calif. Senate, 1983-93

ELECTION RESULTS

2000 GENERAL
Ed Royce (R)	129,294	62.7%
Gill G. Kanel (D)	64,938	31.5%
Ron Jevning (NL)	6,597	3.2%
Keith Gann (LIBERT)	5,275	2.6%

2000 PRIMARY (OPEN)
Ed Royce (R)	91,626	67.9%
Gill G. Kanel (D)	35,816	26.6%
Ron Jevning (NL)	3,865	2.9%
Keith Gann (LIBERT)	3,576	2.7%

1998 GENERAL
Ed Royce (R)	97,366	62.6%
A. R. "Cecy" Groom (D)	52,815	34.0%
Jack Dean (LIBERT)	3,347	2.2%
Ron Jevning (NL)	1,937	1.2%

PREVIOUS WINNING PERCENTAGES
1996 (63%); 1994 (66%); 1992 (57%)

Elected 1992; 5th term

In high school, Royce read "Economics in One Lesson." The book, by Henry Hazlitt, challenged the prevailing economic thinking that accorded government a central role, and it intrigued Royce, who was growing up in a blue-collar Democratic household.

He read other books on similar economic theory, drawn to their free-market message, growing more convinced of the ideas, and often finding himself defending their unorthodox viewpoints not only to fellow students but to his teachers as well.

Royce remains an enthusiastic proponent of that economic message, promoting a smaller central government. He wants to abolish the departments of Energy and Commerce, and he targets examples of wasteful federal spending to focus attention on his view that government must be scaled back. Royce is so adamant in his budget-cutting zeal that at times he gives heartburn even to some in his own party. As the longtime co-chairman of the Congressional Porkbusters Coalition and an activist in the Stop Corporate Welfare Coalition, Royce seeks to cut projects and programs that are dear to Republicans and Democrats alike.

The congressman acknowledges that his task is now more difficult since there is no longer the need to balance the budget. He believes that convening a private-sector panel, along the lines of President Reagan's Grace Commission, to propose ways to trim the federal government would be a good idea. Such a commission would take the politically difficult job away from Congress in much the same way the military base-closing commission did in the 1990s.

Royce also finds reason to be optimistic about the eventual ascendency of the free-market, capitalistic system throughout the world, from Uganda to Nigeria, Vietnam to South Korea. He has visited those countries in his role as chairman of International Relations' Africa Subcommittee.

On social issues, Royce casts a dependably conservative vote, but as head of the Africa Subcommittee, he found some common ground with President Clinton in supporting increased U.S. trade and business investment in Africa. The Africa trade bill that emerged from his subcommittee and was passed in the 106th Congress contains language encouraging more African nations to make substantial progress toward free, market-based economies. "For too long, our African policy has been based on foreign aid," Royce said in 1998. "The United States needs to encourage African nations to move toward the free market and steer them in the direction of self-sufficiency. Markets work and subsidies don't."

He recalls meeting a young lawmaker in Uganda who was named after Ronald Reagan and notes that the United States "really should leverage the incredible amount of goodwill toward the United States" that exists throughout the world.

Royce is also interested in U.S. relations with Asia. More trade will result in less poverty, he says, adding that the grip that totalitarian nations have over their people is possible only because of poverty. He credits Radio Free Asia with inspiring young people and dissidents in countries such as North Korea and Vietnam.

Royce said he is glad that he was drawn to unconventional economic views. "The real advantage was that people would argue with me," he said, which gave him plenty of practice in articulating his positions.

The congressman recalls a run-in he had in college with three young men who caused a minor disruption over the presence of a recruiting table for the College Republicans. Royce came to the assistance of the young woman staffing the table and wound up joining the local chapter of the College Republicans. He chaired the California State University-Fullerton chapter and also became a leader of the Young Americans for Freedom in Southern California.

In a college career that stretched over six and a half years because he had to work his way through school, Royce majored in accounting and finance, never anticipating that his college political activities would later lead to involvement in national politics.

Royce regarded President Reagan as a master in articulating the same economic views he holds, with an ability to explain, in a way that made sense to people, why government should be limited. After Reagan was elected president in 1980, Royce decided to give politics a try himself, and in 1982 he won election to the state Senate.

In Sacramento, he authored the nation's first anti-stalking bill, which made it a felony to stalk or threaten someone with injury — giving the police recourse when a stalker has not yet attacked an intended victim. He also was the guiding force behind a 1990 ballot proposition, approved by voters, setting forth rights for victims of crimes.

After 10 years in the state legislature, Royce jumped at the chance to run for the House in 1992 when longtime GOP Rep. William E. Dannemeyer gave up his seat to run for the Senate. Royce had represented a sizable slice of the 39th District's territory in the state Senate, and he drew no primary opposition. His Democratic opponent, Molly McClanahan, proved too liberal for the conservative Republican bastion of Orange County and Royce prevailed by almost 20 percentage points. He has had no trouble winning re-election.

In Washington, Royce continued his anti-stalking campaign, pushing through to enactment a measure similar to the one he had sponsored in the California Senate. The legislation, signed in 1996, made it a federal crime to cross state lines with the intent to stalk or harass someone. And in 1999, Royce and other lawmakers won approval of a bill expanding the kind of behavior that constitutes stalking.

Although Royce says he was thrilled that his 1996 measure made it into law, he was less pleased with his treatment at the White House bill-signing ceremony. He told The Orange County Register that when he arrived at the Oval Office, he was told to stand to Clinton's far right, well out of camera range. And when it came time to thank the anti-stalking bill's sponsors, the president left him out, Royce told the newspaper.

KEY VOTES

2000
No Raise hourly minimum wage by $1 over two years
Yes Halt funding for U.S. mission in Kosovo unless European nations pay more
Yes Provide Medicare benefits to military retirees and their dependents
Yes Grant China permanent normal trade status
Yes Phase out estate, gift and trust taxes
Yes Prohibit implementation of president's national monument designations
Yes Approve GOP plan to provide prescription drug coverage for Medicare beneficiaries
No Increase help for poor nations indebted to international financial institutions

1999
No Impose steel import quotas
Yes Kill proposal to take aviation trust funds off budget
Yes Require background checks on buyers only at gun shows with 10 or more vendors
Yes Remove barriers among banking, securities and insurance companies
No Authorize state grants to hire teachers and reduce class size
No Overhaul campaign finance law; ban "soft money" and restrict advocacy advertising
No Approve bipartisan plan to increase rights of patients in managed-care health plans

INTEREST GROUPS

	AFL-CIO	ADA	CCUS	ACU
2000	0%	0%	80%	100%
1999	11%	5%	76%	96%
1998	13%	5%	71%	100%
1997	0%	10%	80%	100%

CQ VOTE STUDIES

	PARTY UNITY		PRESIDENTIAL SUPPORT	
	Support	Oppose	Support	Oppose
2000	93%	7%	25%	75%
1999	92%	8%	16%	84%
1998	90%	10%	21%	79%
1997	91%	9%	24%	76%

CALIFORNIA 39
Parts of Orange and Los Angeles counties — Fullerton

The 39th straddles the line between Orange and Los Angeles counties – the area where the more affluent parts of Los Angeles County's suburbs meet the less affluent, yet still strongly Republican, sections of Orange County. Los Angeles County's piece of the district gives the 39th a more moderate bent than some of its neighbors but, overall, Republicans dominate.

Like most of the 39th, Fullerton, the district's largest city, is suburban and upper-middle-class. La Habra Heights and the eastern half of Whittier are affluent areas in the 39th's northern Los Angeles County region, while Hawaiian Gardens is a working-class, Democratic pocket with a large Hispanic population. To the north, Cerritos is heavily Asian.

Before massive growth in the 1960s and '70s, Orange County consisted largely of orange and lemon groves, and cities like Cerritos and Artesia

were dairy farm communities. Now the economy centers on aerospace and defense. New high-tech firms also have sprung up in the district.

MAJOR INDUSTRY
Aerospace, defense, manufacturing

CITIES
Fullerton (pt.), 113,983 (1990); Buena Park (pt.), 62,674 (1990); La Habra, 54,942; Cerritos, 54,326; La Mirada, 45,677

UNUSUAL FEATURES
Buena Park home to Knott's Berry Farm, the first amusement park in the United States; Along Beach Boulevard sit the Movieland Wax Museum, Ripley's Believe It Or Not, Wild Bill's Wild West Dinner and the Medieval Times Dinner and Tournament, where Jim Carrey jousted with Matthew Broderick in the movie, "The Cable Guy."

Rep. Jerry Lewis (R)

Elected 1978; 12th term

CAPITOL OFFICE
225-5861; fax 225-6498; 2112 Rayburn Bldg. 20515

INTERNET
e-mail: www.house.gov/writerep
web: www.house.gov/jerrylewis

COMMITTEES
Appropriations
(Defense - chairman)

HOMETOWN
Redlands

BORN
Oct. 21, 1934, Seattle, Wash.

RELIGION
Presbyterian

FAMILY
Wife, Arlene Lewis; four children, three
stepchildren

EDUCATION
U. of California, Los Angeles, B.A. 1956

CAREER
Insurance executive

POLITICAL HIGHLIGHTS
San Bernardino School Board, 1965-68; Calif.
Assembly, 1969-79; Republican nominee for Calif.
Senate, 1973

ELECTION RESULTS

2000 GENERAL

Jerry Lewis (R)	151,069	79.9%
Frank Schmit (NL)	19,029	10.1%
Jay Lindberg (LIBERT)	18,924	10.0%

2000 PRIMARY (OPEN)

Jerry Lewis (R)	86,315	83.7%
Frank Schmit (NL)	8,687	8.4%
Jay Lindberg (LIBERT)	8,155	7.9%

1998 GENERAL

Jerry Lewis (R)	97,406	64.9%
Robert "Bob" Conaway (D)	47,897	31.9%
Maurice Mayben (LIBERT)	4,822	3.2%

PREVIOUS WINNING PERCENTAGES
1996 (65%); 1994 (71%); 1992 (63%); 1990 (61%);
1988 (70%); 1986 (77%); 1984 (85%); 1982 (68%);
1980 (72%); 1978 (61%)

An amiable fellow with a 200-watt smile, Lewis is a throwback as a legislator — an old-fashioned deal-maker who works at putting all the pieces together. With the House closely divided between the two parties, he says: "We as a Republican majority have got to demonstrate, not only a willingness to lead, but a capability of leading, and we can't do that unless we show a willingness to work across the aisle."

In the 107th Congress, Lewis is again being called upon to put several hundred billion dollars where that bipartisan rhetoric is. He is chairman of the Appropriations Subcommittee on Defense, which each year writes the first draft of legislation that allocates more discretionary spending than any of the other 12 appropriations measures.

Lewis dates his interest in government to a trip he made to Washington in 1955. Some of his fellow UCLA students were forced to ride on a separate tourist boat on the Potomac because they were black, and this planted in Lewis the idea that he would have to participate actively in public service if he expected to effect changes in the country. Today he speaks of using his post to make the world safer and more peaceful for his grandchildren.

For more than a decade, Lewis rose steadily through the ranks of a fairly congenial Republican minority, but in 1992 he was elbowed out of his job as third-ranking Republican in the House by Dick Armey, now the majority leader. Lewis still does not have much use for Armey, but he is a fan of Speaker J. Dennis Hastert and gets along well enough with Majority Whip Tom DeLay of Texas, even if he believes that DeLay sometimes gives too much rope to harder-edged conservatives.

Lewis' star has risen again, mostly because of his reputation for frugality. From 1995 to 1999, as head of the Veterans Affairs, Housing and Urban Development, and Independent Agencies Subcommittee, Lewis cut spending more than any other Appropriations chairman. He has been less thrifty on the Defense Subcommittee, however. "I now happen to be in the one job where I think we have to increase spending," he said. In the 106th Congress, Lewis presided over the first big military spending spikes (in inflation-adjusted dollars) in more than a decade.

With the Bush administration, Lewis looks to the White House for allies in his effort to build a fighting force capable of meeting present and future defense needs, rather than one still designed to fight the Cold War. In 2000, Lewis won approval of roughly double the amount sought by the Clinton administration for an Army plan to develop a mobile fighting force that would be able to deploy much more quickly.

But Lewis is skeptical of the Pentagon's $340 billion proposal to build three new tactical planes, a plan that threatens to wipe out the Defense Department's procurement budget over the next 20 years. His purposeful leadership style as chairman was fully on view in 1999, when he pressed to halt spending for production of the F-22 fighter, the least-developed of the new tactical planes. Having consulted with his wide network of informal advisers within the Pentagon and at think tanks, Lewis brought his entire subcommittee — Democrats included — in line behind the idea that it would be wiser to spend the $2 billion requested for the year on more mundane but useful items the Air Force needed, such as spare parts and pilot retention.

Lewis won the battle in the House in the face of heavy lobbying for the plane. And although the F-22 eventually was funded, the congressman claimed a victory anyway, saying that his other priorities for the Air Force had been funded and that the service and its contractors had been put on notice to keep the fighter plane's cost under control.

Lewis took over the Defense Subcommittee in 1999, just before NATO began its war against Yugoslavia, and he looked on the conflict as an object lesson in how current military equipment, including the F-15 fighter jet, was adequate to meet the challenge. But he noted that the military services neglected such issues as maintenance and quality of life for the rank and file. He used the supplemental spending bill that funded the war as an opportunity to attach $5 billion in additional money for the Pentagon and kept the tap flowing the following year. The defense spending bill in 2000 included $5 billion more than the Pentagon had requested, including enhanced prescription drug benefits, a 3.7 percent pay raise and increased housing allowances for soldiers and sailors living off base.

Lewis does not hesitate to funnel federal dollars to the 40th District. His staff points with pride to a July 2000 study by the Chronicle of Higher Education that listed Loma Linda University as the biggest recipient of "pork barrel" spending in fiscal 2000, pulling in $36 million. The school keeps the lawmaker's portrait hanging in a research building. In 1999, Lewis also secured $10 million in seismic retrofitting projects in his district.

In 2000, as chairman of the California GOP delegation, he led a bipartisan effort by California's lawmakers to kill a Senate proposal that would have required public buildings to carry hazard insurance, arguing that the plan would have been prohibitively expensive.

But the parochial issue that perhaps has taken up most of Lewis' time in recent years has been the so-called tanks versus turtles war. Fort Irwin has been trying since the mid-1980s to expand its training grounds into an area that is home to desert tortoises, an endangered species. Lewis and Sen. Dianne Feinstein, D-Calif., worked for two years hammering out a compromise to allow the Army to expand into 131,000 acres while setting aside other environmentally sensitive land.

Lewis is safe in the 40th District, having won each of his 12 terms with at least 61 percent of the vote. He left the insurance business to enter GOP politics in the early 1960s, winning a seat on the San Bernardino School Board. After three years there, he won a state Assembly seat that he held for a decade.

Perhaps Lewis' proudest honor during the 106th Congress came when a swimming pool where he had worked as a lifeguard in his youth was named after him.

KEY VOTES

2000

No	Raise hourly minimum wage by $1 over two years
No	Halt funding for U.S. mission in Kosovo unless European nations pay more
Yes	Provide Medicare benefits to military retirees and their dependents
Yes	Grant China permanent normal trade status
Yes	Phase out estate, gift and trust taxes
Yes	Prohibit implementation of president's national monument designations
Yes	Approve GOP plan to provide prescription drug coverage for Medicare beneficiaries
No	Increase help for poor nations indebted to international financial institutions

1999

No	Impose steel import quotas
Yes	Kill proposal to take aviation trust funds off budget
?	Require background checks on buyers only at gun shows with 10 or more vendors
Yes	Remove barriers among banking, securities and insurance companies
No	Authorize state grants to hire teachers and reduce class size
No	Overhaul campaign finance law; ban "soft money" and restrict advocacy advertising
No	Approve bipartisan plan to increase rights of patients in managed-care health plans

INTEREST GROUPS

	AFL-CIO	ADA	CCUS	ACU
2000	0%	0%	80%	64%
1999	11%	20%	92%	73%
1998	22%	10%	100%	75%
1997	38%	20%	80%	63%

CQ VOTE STUDIES

	PARTY UNITY		PRESIDENTIAL SUPPORT	
	Support	Oppose	Support	Oppose
2000	87%	13%	36%	64%
1999	85%	15%	33%	67%
1998	88%	12%	33%	67%
1997	87%	13%	35%	65%

CALIFORNIA 40
San Bernardino County — Redlands

The 40th covers an enormous desert that includes nearly one-fifth of California and takes in most of San Bernardino County – the nation's largest county – and Inyo County. Nearly everyone lives in the southwestern corner, which includes part of the Inland Empire, Victor Valley and Morongo Basin communities. Republicans enjoy a solid edge in registration.

The Inland Empire grew so much in the 1980s that it gained two new congressional districts in 1992. Such growth continued in the 1990s, especially in Victor Valley, where affordable land and housing have made the area a magnet for Los Angeles workers.

The 40th's economy was hit hard by base closures – it lost close to half of its military population when George and Norton Air Force bases closed in 1992 and '94. Redevelopment has been slow since the two bases were not turned over to local control until 2000. Little has been done with Norton Air Force Base, but the city of San Bernardino has secured a contract to serve as a shipping hub for Swissair at George Air Force Base.

MAJOR INDUSTRY
Military, service, manufacturing

MILITARY BASES
Marine Corps Air Ground Combat Center, 11,008 military, 1,597 civilian; Fort Irwin (Army), 4,784 military, 3,619 civilian; Marine Corps Logistics Base, 284 military, 1,548 civilian; Naval Air Warfare Center Weapons Division, China Lake, 889 military, 3,003 civilian (shared with 21st District) (2000)

CITIES
Victorville, 70,386; Redlands, 68,326; Hesperia, 63,983; Apple Valley, 58,063

UNUSUAL FEATURES
Lowest (Death Valley), and highest (Mt. Whitney) points in California; Roy Rogers Museum in Victorville; Fort Irwin, where the Army trained Desert Storm troops for desert maneuvers; World War II Japanese internment camp at Manzanar in Owens Valley.

Rep. Gary G. Miller (R)

Elected 1998; 2nd term

CAPITOL OFFICE
225-3201; fax 226-6926
1037 Longworth Bldg. 20515

INTERNET
e-mail: PublicCA41@mail.house.gov
web: www.house.gov/garymiller

COMMITTEES
Budget
Financial Services
Science

HOMETOWN
Diamond Bar

BORN
Oct. 16, 1948, Huntsville, Ark.

RELIGION
Protestant

FAMILY
Wife, Cathy Miller; four children

EDUCATION
Mt. San Antonio Community College, attended
1968-70

MILITARY SERVICE
Army, 1967-68

CAREER
Real estate developer

POLITICAL HIGHLIGHTS
Diamond Bar City Council, 1989-90, 1991-95
(mayor, 1993-94); Calif. Assembly, 1995-99

ELECTION RESULTS

2000 GENERAL

Gary G. Miller (R)	104,695	58.9%
Rudy Favila (D)	66,361	37.4%
David F. Kramer (NL)	6,560	3.7%

2000 PRIMARY (OPEN)

Gary G. Miller (R)	60,953	58.5%
Rudy Favila (D)	32,528	31.2%
Anthony Ma (R)	7,140	6.9%
David F. Kramer (NL)	3,519	3.4%

1998 GENERAL

Gary G. Miller (R)	68,310	53.2%
Eileen Ansari (D)	52,264	40.7%
Cynthia Allaire (GREEN)	3,597	2.8%
Kenneth Valentine (LIBERT)	2,529	2.0%
David F. Kramer (NL)	1,714	1.3%

The travails of others have been the stepping stones for Miller's political rise. He was elected to the California General Assembly in 1995 after his predecessor, also a Republican, was recalled by the voters for backing the liberal Democrat Willie Brown as Speaker. He won a seat in Congress in 1998 by ousting three-term Republican Rep. Jay C. Kim, who had been convicted of breaking campaign finance laws. Even Miller's 2000 Democratic challenger had troubles — Rudy Favila was once demoted at the California Youth Authority for offering inmate labor to a contractor in exchange for a free gazebo.

Miller, who dropped out of college when his career as a real estate developer began to take off, is now one of the wealthiest members of the California delegation. He paid for most of his race against Kim out of his own pocket.

Miller considers himself a fiscal and social conservative, and his first foray into public life was as the board member of a Christian school. He subscribes to Republican tenets of shrinking the federal government, overhauling the tax code and advancing a pro-family agenda. And he has criticized House GOP leaders for allowing President Clinton to take credit for legislative successes, such as the 1997 balanced-budget agreement that helped to end the deficit era, which Miller says should be ascribed to the Republican Party.

The congressman has been a reliable supporter of the Republican tax cut agenda, and he voted against the Democrats' efforts in 2000 to boost the minimum wage by $1 an hour over two years. He generally sides with his party on defense issues, and he backed a move in the House to halt U.S. involvement in Kosovo in the absence of increased European involvement. He joined his leadership in support of Clinton's successful push to grant China permanent normal trade status.

In 2000, Miller opposed legislation to guarantee nearly $3 billion a year in spending to buy parks, protect environmentally sensitive lands, prevent urban sprawl and restore historic buildings. He argued that the government already owns too much property. "We are purchasing lands at such a high rate that we cannot even keep up with the maintenance," he said on the House floor. "How can that be considered good land stewardship?"

Miller has a solid anti-abortion record. He has backed prohibitions on federal health plans paying for abortion. And he has voted to restrict U.S. foreign assistance to international organizations that perform or promote abortions as a means of family planning, even if the groups use their own funds.

He supported a 1999 measure making it a federal crime for anyone, other than a parent, to transport a child across state lines for an abortion. "No one should be able to make a mockery of a legal state parental consent law," Miller said. He opposed a Democratic-backed alternative that would have exempted other family members or clergy from prosecution; he said the proposal would have punched a huge loophole in the bill. "Many want us to believe this is about a nice little grandmother," he said. "It is not. It is about an employee of an abortion industry or a sexual predator who wants to cover the rape of a young girl under the age of 18."

In 1999, Miller voted to block states from allowing physician-assisted suicide, and he supported a resolution calling for a "National Day of Prayer" aimed at preventing violence and cultural divisions. He also backed a measure intended to crack down on the sale of violent or sexu-

www.cq.com

ally explicit material to minors.

Miller generally opposes gun control measures. In 1999, he sided with gun owners' rights advocates in supporting a bill that would have required background checks for firearms sales at gun shows, but only at shows with 10 vendors or more. Gun control proponents called the legislation, which was defeated, insufficiently weak and in some cases regressive.

In 2000, Miller again stood for gun owners' rights in voting to block the Justice Department from implementing an agreement with gun manufacturer Smith & Wesson that called for the company to make several design changes to improve gun safety in exchange for local and federal governments dropping lawsuits against the manufacturer.

Miller has bucked his party leadership on occasion. He went against GOP leaders in backing a proposal in 2000 to ease economic sanctions against Cuba. Also in 2000, he supported the enactment of a law, initially opposed by the GOP leadership, to shed light on the activities of certain political action committees. The measure requires the groups, known as 527s for a section of the tax code, to disclose their political activities and who is financing them. Miller, however, opposed more sweeping campaign finance overhaul.

One of his top priorities in both Sacramento and Washington has been to rein in the unsolicited e-mail of businesses and marketers that is known as "spam."

Miller's assignment to the Budget Committee in his first term was reminiscent of his days in the California Legislature. He made history in the Assembly in 1995 when he became the first freshman to be named chairman of the chamber's Budget Committee. In that position, he presided over the state's high-stakes, highly partisan budget battles.

In addition to Budget, Miller now sits on the Financial Services Committee and the Science panel; he gave up his seat on the Transportation Committee that he held in the 106th Congress.

Miller began his political career as a member of Diamond Bar's first city council after the city was incorporated in 1989. He became mayor in 1993 and in 1995 moved to the state Assembly. He served four years before his successful bid for the House.

In beating GOP Rep. Kim in 1998, he was the only challenger to defeat an incumbent in a primary that year. The Republican-leaning 41st District then handed Miller a 13-point general-election victory.

In 2000, his margin of victory increased to 22 percentage points with his win over Democrat Favila.

KEY VOTES

2000

No	Raise hourly minimum wage by $1 over two years
Yes	Halt funding for U.S. mission in Kosovo unless European nations pay more
Yes	Provide Medicare benefits to military retirees and their dependents
Yes	Grant China permanent normal trade status
Yes	Phase out estate, gift and trust taxes
Yes	Prohibit implementation of president's national monument designations
Yes	Approve GOP plan to provide prescription drug coverage for Medicare beneficiaries
No	Increase help for poor nations indebted to international financial institutions

1999

No	Impose steel import quotas
No	Kill proposal to take aviation trust funds off budget
Yes	Require background checks on buyers only at gun shows with 10 or more vendors
Yes	Remove barriers among banking, securities and insurance companies
No	Authorize state grants to hire teachers and reduce class size
No	Overhaul campaign finance law; ban "soft money" and restrict advocacy advertising
No	Approve bipartisan plan to increase rights of patients in managed-care health plans

INTEREST GROUPS

	AFL-CIO	ADA	CCUS	ACU
2000	0%	0%	95%	100%
1999	0%	5%	96%	88%

CQ VOTE STUDIES

	PARTY UNITY		PRESIDENTIAL SUPPORT	
	Support	Oppose	Support	Oppose
2000	97%	3%	25%	75%
1999	96%	4%	21%	79%

CALIFORNIA 41

Parts of Orange, Los Angeles and San Bernardino counties

The 41st is carved from three counties, with its center where Los Angeles, Orange and San Bernardino counties meet. A district with a slight Republican voter registration edge, the 41st is solidly middle and upper class and has the state's highest percentage of married couples and lowest percentage of senior citizens.

The district contains the most Republican portion of affluent, white-collar Orange County and a less affluent and more Democratic section of Los Angeles. Politically mixed San Bernardino County, called the Inland Empire's West End, has the bulk of the district's voters and is a prime political battleground.

The 41st tends to be a reliable vote for Republican presidential candidates, albeit rarely by a large margin. It gave the edge to George Bush in 1992, Bob Dole in 1996 and President Bush in 2000.

Dairy drives the economy in the 41st's western cities of Chino and Chino Hills. In the late 1990s, other businesses got a boost from the expansion of Ontario's regional airport and the construction of the Ontario Convention Center.

MAJOR INDUSTRY
Service, dairy, manufacturing

CITIES
Pomona (pt.), 106,647; Ontario (pt.), 81,708 (1990); Upland, 68,030; Chino, 66,138; Chino Hills, 59,070

UNUSUAL FEATURES
Yorba Linda, birthplace and burial site of Richard Nixon, home of the Nixon Library.

Rep. Joe Baca (D)

Elected November 1999; 1st full term

CAPITOL OFFICE
225-6161; fax 225-8671
1133 Longworth Bldg. 20515

INTERNET
e-mail: www.house.gov/writerep
web: www.house.gov/baca

COMMITTEES
Agriculture
Science

HOMETOWN
San Bernardino

BORN
Jan. 23, 1947, Belen, N.M.

RELIGION
Roman Catholic

FAMILY
Wife, Barbara Baca; four children

EDUCATION
California State U., Los Angeles, B.A. 1971

MILITARY SERVICE
Army, 1966-68

CAREER
Travel agency owner; corporate community relations executive

POLITICAL HIGHLIGHTS
San Bernardino Valley College District trustee, 1979-93; sought Democratic nomination for Calif. Assembly, 1988, 1990; Calif. Assembly, 1993-99 (Speaker pro tempore, 1995); Calif. Senate, 1999

ELECTION RESULTS

2000 GENERAL

Joe Baca (D)	90,585	59.8%
Elia Pirozzi (R)	53,239	35.1%
John "Scott" Ballard (LIBERT)	4,059	2.7%

2000 PRIMARY (OPEN)

Joe Baca (D)	49,234	55.8%
Elia Pirozzi (R)	27,947	31.7%
Jay C. Kim (R)	7,119	8.1%
John "Scott" Ballard (LIBERT)	2,066	2.3%

1999 SPECIAL RUNOFF ELECTION

Joe Baca (D)	23,690	50.6%
Elia Pirozzi (R)	21,018	44.9%

PREVIOUS WINNING PERCENTAGES
1999 Special Election (32%)

The first Latino congressman from the part of Southern California known as the Inland Empire, Baca has catapulted himself with single-minded ambition from shoeshine boy to congressman, where he has set out to fill the shoes of 18-term Democratic Rep. George E. Brown Jr., whom Baca succeeded after Brown's death in 1999.

Baca has moved forcefully to become involved in a wide array of issues, ranging from increased funding for education to benefits for teachers and public safety workers to his proposal that a Congressional Gold Medal be awarded to champion golfer Tiger Woods.

Baca is the first to acknowledge that he is aggressive: "I'm a fighter because I know what it's like to struggle," he says.

In the 107th Congress, Baca secured an appointment as the Hispanic Caucus' representative on the House Democrats' Leadership Council. He also was named to the Democratic Steering Committee, which makes Democratic committee assignments, and chosen as a regional whip. He made no secret of the fact that he wanted a seat on the Rules Committee, which he did not get.

Baca's ambition and drive, which propelled him from humble beginnings to the halls of Congress, can sometimes rub people the wrong way. He has ruffled more than a few feathers during his political ascent. Some colleagues say he is pushy and will take the lion's share of credit for joint projects. And Brown's widow and her supporters said it was inappropriate for him to enter the special-election race against her a short time after the party had helped him win an expensive contest for the state Senate.

The Inland Valley Daily Bulletin, while endorsing Baca in the 1999 special election, also noted, "We harbor some reservations about his tendency at times to put political considerations — especially his own political welfare — ahead of the interests of those he represents."

The congressman refers to himself as "working Joe Baca," a reference not only to his reputation for hard work, but also to his strong support for organized labor. He has counted on the backing of labor groups in all of his elections, and campaign help from union members played a key role in his narrow special-election primary win over Brown's widow, Marta Macias Brown. His election night victory rally was at a local Teamsters union hall.

Mindful of the needs of his working-class constituents, Baca in 2000 authored an amendment directing the secretary of housing and urban development to increase the number of federally owned properties in a special program aimed at helping teachers, firefighters and police officers buy a home.

But Baca's politics tend to be more conservative than those of his predecessor, and his support for gun owners' rights was a major issue in his race against Marta Brown. He affiliates himself with the "Blue Dogs," a coalition of conservative Democrats.

Baca supports a constitutional amendment to ban desecration of the flag, a different view from most in his party. He also voted with the GOP majority to repeal the estate tax, although he returned to the Democratic fold later to uphold President Clinton's veto of the bill.

For all his focused determination, however, Baca sometimes reveals a more humorous, self-deprecating side. When he made his first remarks to the House after his swearing-in and the microphone had to be lowered for him, Baca joked, "I used to be 6 foot 5 as a paratrooper, but I made a lot of jumps; that is why I am only 5 foot 6." He is a spark plug on the Democrats' baseball team. In the 2000 charity game against the GOP team, third baseman Baca's glasses were smashed in a collision with Republican Steve Buyer. The glasses were taped together, and Baca stayed in the game.

Baca was born in tiny Belen, N.M., just south of Albuquerque. The son of a railroad laborer and the youngest of 15 children in a house where little English was spoken, Baca as a boy moved with his family to Barstow, Calif. He shined shoes starting at age 10, delivered newspapers and worked as a janitor as a teenager, and labored for the Santa Fe Railroad between his high school graduation and the arrival of his draft notice in 1966. He spent two years as an Army paratrooper.

After earning a college degree in sociology, Baca entered the white-collar world as a community affairs representative for a local phone company.

His political career began in 1979 with election to the San Bernardino Community College District Board, where he served 14 years. After unsuccessful attempts to oust Democratic state Rep. Jerry Eaves in the 1988 and 1990 primaries, he easily won the Assembly seat when Eaves departed. As speaker pro tempore of the Assembly, Baca was able to get many of his pet projects passed, including a bill extending property tax exemptions for veterans and a measure allowing utility shareholders to profit from utility mergers.

He coasted to re-election twice, then trounced his GOP opponent to win a state Senate seat in 1998. But the state Senate was not Baca's preferred goal for 1998, and he was threatening to challenge Brown in the 1998 primary. Baca, whose state Senate district encompassed most of the 42nd District, boasted that he could beat the 34-year incumbent in every precinct. Some party stalwarts took this challenge as an affront to the state's senior Democrat in Washington, as they had when Baca tried twice to oust fellow Democrat Eaves from the Assembly.

And they were provoked yet again when Baca chose to run in the special election against Brown's widow. Baca narrowly outpolled her by 518 votes in September to advance to the November 1999 runoff. In the Democratic-leaning 42nd, and with a well-organized political apparatus still in place, Baca easily prevailed, 51 percent to 45 percent over GOP businessman Elia Pirozzi.

He was sworn in two days later, just in time to participate in the final, hectic day of the first session of the 106th Congress. Upon his arrival in Washington, Baca was assigned to the Agriculture and Science committees — the same panels on which Brown had served. In 2000, Pirozzi was back for a rematch, but Baca crushed him by 25 points.

KEY VOTES

2000

Yes Raise hourly minimum wage by $1 over two years

No Halt funding for U.S. mission in Kosovo unless European nations pay more

Yes Provide Medicare benefits to military retirees and their dependents

No Grant China permanent normal trade status

Yes Phase out estate, gift and trust taxes

No Prohibit implementation of president's national monument designations

No Approve GOP plan to provide prescription drug coverage for Medicare beneficiaries

Yes Increase help for poor nations indebted to international financial institutions

INTEREST GROUPS

	AFL-CIO	ADA	CCUS	ACU
2000	100%	80%	44%	16%

CQ VOTE STUDIES

	PARTY UNITY		PRESIDENTIAL SUPPORT	
	Support	Oppose	Support	Oppose
2000	83%	17%	75%	25%
1999	100%	0%	100%	0%

CALIFORNIA 42

San Bernardino County — San Bernardino

The city of San Bernardino forms the base of the 42nd, which is located in the heart of the Inland Empire and borders Los Angeles and Orange counties.

The western part of the 42nd rejects the "Inland Empire" label. Many of Rancho Cucamonga's residents identify with Los Angeles, a half-hour west on Interstate 10. Rancho Cucamonga has seen explosive growth, as have the more eastern cities of Fontana and Rialto, adding to the area's reputation as California's fastest growing region.

The 42nd is about one-third Hispanic, and registered Democratic voters have a substantial majority over Republicans. Ethnically diverse San Bernardino and Colton consistently vote Democratic, but other parts of the district are beginning to follow areas like the more upscale Rancho Cucamonga in voting Republican. The district voted for Al Gore in the 2000 presidential contest by a safe margin

and the 42nd tends to vote Democratic on the local level.

This area was a fruit-packing center in the 1930s. Today, its citrus industry shares space with electronics and aerospace firms. A steel mill bankruptcy in the 1980s and the 1994 closing of Norton Air Force base in the neighboring 40th District hurt the 42nd's job base, but new government jobs and growing high-tech and manufacturing industries prove the economy is recovering steadily. Local leaders are trying to redevelop the site of the former base into a commercial zone anchored by the San Bernardino International Airport.

MAJOR INDUSTRY
Manufacturing, electronics, construction

CITIES
San Bernardino (pt.), 127,675 (1990); Rancho Cucamonga, 123,724; Fontana, 114,882; Rialto, 85,436

UNUSUAL FEATURES
Wyatt Earp's brother, Virgil, was the first sheriff of Colton; Fontana is the birthplace of the Hell's Angels.

Rep. Ken Calvert (R)

CAPITOL OFFICE
225-1986; fax 225-2004; 2201 Rayburn Bldg. 20515

INTERNET
e-mail: www.house.gov/writerep
web: www.house.gov/calvert

COMMITTEES
Armed Services
Resources
(Water & Power - chairman)
Science

HOMETOWN
Riverside

BORN
June 8, 1953, Corona, Calif.

RELIGION
Protestant

FAMILY
Divorced

EDUCATION
Chaffey College, A.A. 1973; San Diego State U., B.A. 1975

CAREER
Real estate executive; restaurant business manager

POLITICAL HIGHLIGHTS
Sought Republican nomination for U.S. House, 1982; Riverside County Republican Party chairman, 1984-88

ELECTION RESULTS

2000 GENERAL

Ken Calvert (R)	140,201	73.7%
Bill Reed (LIBERT)	29,755	15.6%
Nathaniel Adam (NL)	20,376	10.7%

2000 PRIMARY (OPEN)

Ken Calvert (R)	73,660	58.2%
Martin Collen (R)	31,907	25.2%
Bill Reed (LIBERT)	9,627	7.6%
Nathaniel Adam (NL)	6,956	5.5%
Khalid Jafri (R)	4,448	3.5%

1998 GENERAL

Ken Calvert (R)	83,012	55.7%
Mike Rayburn (D)	56,373	37.8%
Phill Courtney (GREEN)	5,508	3.7%

PREVIOUS WINNING PERCENTAGES
1996 (55%); 1994 (55%); 1992 (47%)

Elected 1992; 5th term

Calvert's voting record is well to the right on the political spectrum — in his eight years in Congress he has never received a score of more than 5 percent from the liberal Americans for Democratic Action. Calvert has endeared himself to the House GOP leadership by faithfully voting with them more than 90 percent of the time. He says he favors "a smaller, less invasive government."

Calvert represents an area with a diverse economy, one where agriculture, manufacturing, urban sprawl, the military, tourism, land use and the environment all are important issues. From his seats on three committees — Science, Resources and Armed Services — he is able to have a hand in policies that affect the 43rd District. He is new to the Armed Services Committee in the 107th Congress, having left the Agriculture panel, which also dealt with locally important issues such as the avocado and citrus crops and the area's struggling wine industry, which has been decimated by disease.

Calvert also is a member of more than two dozen informal congressional organizations that reflect the varied concerns of his constituents, ranging from the Manufactured Housing Caucus (an industry leader, Fleetwood Enterprises, is headquartered in the 43rd) to the Real Estate Caucus (Calvert's occupation before coming to Congress) to the Native American Caucus (he is one-eighth Cherokee).

Calvert's conservative view of government makes him wary of tougher environmental regulations. As chairman of the Science panel's Energy and Environment Subcommittee, from 1997 to 2001, he questioned the Environmental Protection Agency's scientific justification for imposing stricter air quality standards. He credits the Clean Air Act with helping abate his region's infamous smog problem, but he warns that people will balk at increased standards if they seem "unachievable."

He says enforcement of the Endangered Species Act must be tempered with common sense. He once said that when Democrats ran the House, "rats, bugs and even weeds were more important than people. Certain bureaucrats have become so eager to list new species as endangered, they have lost sight of the intent of the Endangered Species Act and ignored human concerns."

On the Resources Committee, where in the 107th Congress he took the gavel of the Water and Power Subcommittee, he joins other Western lawmakers who say the federal government tramples on landowners' rights in the name of environmental preservation, and he advocates legislation to protect private property owners.

He is skeptical of environmentalists who warn of the impact of pollution on the Earth's weather. He criticized Vice President Al Gore's "apocalypse theory of global warming" in the lead-up to the 1997 Kyoto summit on global warming and said that a U.S. commitment to cut greenhouse gas emissions would require imposing higher taxes on energy sources to reduce consumption.

Calvert's district has a large population of veterans, and in the 106th Congress, he authored legislation designating a site at the Riverside Cemetery as a memorial honoring the nation's Medal of Honor recipients. He also won the transfer of surplus land at the downsized March Air Force Base to be used as a local law enforcement training facility.

In both the 105th and 106th Congresses, Calvert weighed in on the debate over campaign financing, offering an amendment, which was handily defeated both times, to require candidates to raise at least 50 percent of their campaign contributions from within their home districts.

Calvert is a native son of the area he now represents — not all that common in the rapidly growing region that now finds itself part of the sprawling Los Angeles megalopolis. He was born just west of Riverside, in the city of Corona. His family was in the restaurant business. Later, his father, who had changed party affiliation to become a Republican in the mid-1960s, turned to politics, winning election to the city council and then as mayor of Corona.

The younger Calvert remembers working on Richard Nixon's 1968 presidential campaign as a youth. Later, as a college student, he interned in the Capitol Hill office of Republican Rep. Victor Veysey.

After graduation, Calvert used his economics degree and interest in business to go into the restaurant business. He handled the business side of the Jolly Fox restaurant in Corona, while his brother was the chef. He expanded into other ventures — a motel, a bowling alley, other restaurants — before going into the real estate business.

In 1982, with "lots of time and not much money," the 28-year-old Calvert jumped into an open seat race for Congress, in the old 37th District, which contained most of Riverside County. Relying on door-to-door campaigning, Calvert did surprisingly well against a large field headed by Riverside County Supervisor Al McCandless, losing the GOP nomination by just 868 votes.

Calvert stayed active in local party affairs, significantly increasing GOP registration in Riverside County and helping run gubernatorial campaigns for Republicans George Deukmejian and Pete Wilson. In 1992, when reapportionment created a new 43rd District for the western part of Riverside County, Calvert was positioned to run again, and this time he emerged from a tough GOP primary and won a hard-fought victory in November.

Calvert's congressional tenure got off to a rough start. In his freshman term, his tryst with a prostitute drew widespread notice. He was forced to admit that he had engaged in sexual activity with a prostitute, contradicting the story he had told after the incident was first reported. Calvert eventually said his behavior was "inappropriate" and said he had been depressed over his recent divorce and his father's suicide. He said he did not know the woman was a prostitute and did not pay her for sex.

Following the negative publicity, Calvert won the 1994 GOP primary by just 2 percentage points. But the national surge that delivered the House to the GOP carried him to victory. Since then, Calvert's toughest challenges have come from his own party. In 2000, even with no Democrat on the open primary ballot, he still struggled to win the nomination, with just 58 percent. In November, he crushed two minor-party candidates.

KEY VOTES

2000

No	Raise hourly minimum wage by $1 over two years
Yes	Halt funding for U.S. mission in Kosovo unless European nations pay more
Yes	Provide Medicare benefits to military retirees and their dependents
Yes	Grant China permanent normal trade status
Yes	Phase out estate, gift and trust taxes
Yes	Prohibit implementation of president's national monument designations
Yes	Approve GOP plan to provide prescription drug coverage for Medicare beneficiaries
No	Increase help for poor nations indebted to international financial institutions

1999

No	Impose steel import quotas
Yes	Kill proposal to take aviation trust funds off budget
Yes	Require background checks on buyers only at gun shows with 10 or more vendors
Yes	Remove barriers among banking, securities and insurance companies
No	Authorize state grants to hire teachers and reduce class size
No	Overhaul campaign finance law; ban "soft money" and restrict advocacy advertising
No	Approve bipartisan plan to increase rights of patients in managed-care health plans

INTEREST GROUPS

	AFL-CIO	ADA	CCUS	ACU
2000	0%	0%	80%	84%
1999	0%	5%	96%	80%
1998	0%	0%	100%	92%
1997	0%	0%	100%	92%

CQ VOTE STUDIES

	PARTY UNITY		PRESIDENTIAL SUPPORT	
	Support	Oppose	Support	Oppose
2000	94%	6%	31%	69%
1999	92%	8%	30%	70%
1998	94%	6%	24%	76%
1997	95%	5%	27%	73%

CALIFORNIA 43
Riverside County — western suburbs

The 43rd is a fast-growing district that lies east of Los Angeles and north of San Diego. It takes in the city of Riverside and the burgeoning western edge of Riverside County. While the 43rd has become increasingly Republican overall, the more blue-collar Riverside communities and the areas around the University of California at Riverside lean Democratic.

The district is seeing major growth as young, white-collar families move into its southern and western cities. The trend is especially true in Corona, where low real estate prices have produced attractive bedroom communities for Orange County and Los Angeles County commuters. Despite the influx, manufacturing and agriculture (including dairy, citrus, grapes, dates and avocados) continue to drive the economy.

Riverside is the 43rd's largest city and county seat. Established as a silk-worm breeding center around 1870, it soon jumped into the business of growing navel oranges – still one of the area's major crops.

Riverside and San Bernardino counties, which the 43rd shares with other districts, are trying to rein in methamphetamine production. This area, known as the Inland Empire, is believed to be one of the nation's largest producers of the drug.

MAJOR INDUSTRY
Manufacturing, agriculture, health care

CITIES
Riverside, 265,721; Corona, 119,594; Lake Elsinore, 28,942; Norco, 26,543

UNUSUAL FEATURES
Riverside established as a silkworm breeding center; Richard and Pat Nixon were married in Riverside's Mission Inn, and the Reagans also honeymooned there; The district has the highest concentration of endangered species in the nation.

Rep. Mary Bono (R)

Elected April 1998; 2nd full term

CAPITOL OFFICE
225-5330; fax 225-2961; 404 Cannon Bldg. 20515

INTERNET
e-mail: www.house.gov/writerep
web: www.house.gov/bono

COMMITTEES
Energy & Commerce

HOMETOWN
Palm Springs

BORN
Oct. 24, 1961, Cleveland, Ohio

RELIGION
Protestant

FAMILY
Widowed; two children

EDUCATION
U. of Southern California, B.F.A. 1984

CAREER
Homemaker; restaurateur

POLITICAL HIGHLIGHTS
No previous office

ELECTION RESULTS

2000 GENERAL

Mary Bono (R)	123,738	59.2%
Ron Oden (D)	79,302	37.9%
Gene Smith (REF)	4,135	2.0%
Jim Meuer (NL)	2,012	1.0%

2000 PRIMARY (OPEN)

Mary Bono (R)	79,365	56.4%
Ron Oden (D)	20,079	14.3%
Tom Harney (D)	13,170	9.4%
Bud Mathewson (R)	9,800	7.0%
Jon Gordon (D)	9,765	6.9%
Doug Wofford (D)	6,124	4.4%
Gene Smith (REF)	1,628	1.2%

1998 GENERAL

Mary Bono (R)	97,013	60.1%
Ralph Waite (D)	57,697	35.7%
Jim Meuer (NL)	6,818	4.2%

PREVIOUS WINNING PERCENTAGES
1998 Special Election (64%)

Though Bono's athletic good looks and her celebrity as the young widow of Sonny Bono continue to garner her more ink than most members of Congress will ever get, she maintains her focus on matters of local interest, such as the salinity level of the Salton Sea and the threat to grape vines posed by Pierce's disease.

The latest developments in Bono's clothing and hair style and her relationship with a country music drummer fill columns in popular magazines, but on Capitol Hill she cultivates the image of an average person, plain-speaking, unpretentious and interested in rolling up her sleeves and mastering the details of her job.

Bono's GOP colleagues take advantage of her popular appeal, making her one of the most sought-after guests on the campaign fundraising circuit. "She has a freshness and common-sense approach that is rather unusual in people like us," Majority Whip Tom DeLay of Texas told Gannett News Service. And Lindsay Graham, R-S.C., said that "a lot of people admire" the fact that "she got knocked down and got back up and succeeded." She accommodates as many requests as she can, while trying to ensure time with her two elementary school children, who now live in Palm Springs with a nanny.

Bono came to Capitol Hill with little preparation for the job — and in the middle of the session, without benefit of the orientation meetings that freshmen normally get. Nevertheless, she says she brings an appreciation for the challenges faced by a working single mother and that she has small-business experience as the manager of a restaurant she and Sonny owned. Bono also points out that she was the first lady of Palm Springs when her husband was mayor and that she was active in a number of civic groups.

Still, life has changed dramatically for Mary Bono. At the beginning of 1998, she was a stay-at-home mom in Washington, D.C., driving her children to school and working on her martial arts skills while Sonny went off to Capitol Hill every morning. After Sonny's January 1998 death in a skiing accident, she emerged as a public figure in her own right. Urged to run for her husband's seat by GOP leaders who worried that the seat might fall into Democratic hands, Bono won a special election in April.

She was given her husband's old committee assignments, including a post on the Judiciary Committee, which became center stage for the impeachment of President Clinton. Bono, whose college degree is in art history, won generally positive reviews for her work on the Judiciary panel. Initially, she was reserved in her statements about the matter, and at times she even seemed a bit disengaged from the committee's impeachment hearings, bypassing turns to ask questions. But she later won plaudits for her efforts to cut through the legalese and ask the questions that were uppermost in people's minds.

When Bono first arrived in Congress, her goal was to continue her husband's work — notably, saving the Salton Sea, a Southern California lake that is threatened by increasing salinity and pollution from agricultural and industrial runoff. By the end of 1998, Congress had agreed to fund a study to determine the extent of the problem and to begin the lake's rehabilitation. Bono also helped shepherd through the House a copyright extension bill, championed by and named after Sonny.

After she won election to a full term, Bono in the 106th began branching out, working on projects of her own. She kept her husband's Judiciary and Armed Services assignments and added a Small Business post. In the 107th

Congress, she won a coveted seat on the Energy and Commerce Committee, which required her to drop her other assignments.

She has continued, however, to work on cleanup of the Salton Sea and protection of intellectual property rights, another of her husband's projects. In the 106th Congress, she also turned her attention to protecting the Santa Rosa Mountains and saving California vineyards from the scourge of Pierce's disease, which is spread by a small flying insect known as the glassy-winged sharpshooter. The disease has seriously damaged grapevines in Riverside County's Temecula Valley and threatened to spread north to other California wine regions.

Bono drew criticism from homosexual rights groups after she voted to bar San Francisco from using federal funds to enforce a domestic partners benefits law. She said small businesses might be unable to afford benefits for unmarried couples. She favors allowing abortions to remain legal but opposes federal funding of abortions for poor women. "I am neither pro-choice nor pro-life and I am also both pro-choice and pro-life," she told the California Riverside Press-Enterprise. "I believe that's the way most Americans truly are."

Bono found an ally among House Democrats to join her in sponsoring legislation barring national forests from charging fees to recreational users — California Rep. Lois Capps, who also succeeded her late husband in the House. "To tax the great outdoors is offensive to the concept of the national forest system," Bono said.

Bono, whose father was a surgeon and whose mother was a chemist, grew up in South Pasadena, Calif. She worked her way through college and was celebrating her graduation at Sonny Bono's restaurant when she met the owner. They hit it off and married two years later, in 1986.

Her years as the spouse of a celebrity prepared her, to some extent, for the level of attention she now receives. She shares her husband's self-deprecating manner and says she understands that the public can be overly fascinated with such matters as the shoe and hair styles of powerful women, while men in similar roles are not similarly scrutinized.

"The tabloids are having quite a time with me, oh yeah," Bono told The Washington Post during the impeachment inquiry (and after her former mother-in-law complained publicly about Bono going to Washington when faced with the responsibility of bringing up two young children alone). But, she said, "I've learned so much from my years with Sonny," who was sometimes the subject of unflattering publicity. "I watched his reaction to it, watched him take it in stride, and I realize it comes with the territory."

KEY VOTES

2000
No Raise hourly minimum wage by $1 over two years
Yes Halt funding for U.S. mission in Kosovo unless European nations pay more
Yes Provide Medicare benefits to military retirees and their dependents
Yes Grant China permanent normal trade status
Yes Phase out estate, gift and trust taxes
Yes Prohibit implementation of president's national monument designations
Yes Approve GOP plan to provide prescription drug coverage for Medicare beneficiaries
No Increase help for poor nations indebted to international financial institutions

1999
No Impose steel import quotas
No Kill proposal to take aviation trust funds off budget
Yes Require background checks on buyers only at gun shows with 10 or more vendors
Yes Remove barriers among banking, securities and insurance companies
No Authorize state grants to hire teachers and reduce class size
No Overhaul campaign finance law; ban "soft money" and restrict advocacy advertising
Yes Approve bipartisan plan to increase rights of patients in managed-care health plans

INTEREST GROUPS

	AFL-CIO	ADA	CCUS	ACU
2000	0%	5%	100%	68%
1999	22%	15%	79%	76%
1998	29%	0%	93%	95%

CQ VOTE STUDIES

	PARTY UNITY		PRESIDENTIAL SUPPORT	
	Support	Oppose	Support	Oppose
2000	86%	14%	30%	70%
1999	85%	15%	25%	75%
1998	92%	8%	23%	77%

CALIFORNIA 44
Eastern Riverside County

Ritzy desert resorts and large, irrigated farms fueled a growing economy in the area known as California's Inland Empire during the 1990s. The 44th's population base is split into two regions: the upscale, resort-filled Coachella Valley to the east, and Hemet and the rapidly growing Los Angeles Basin and Riverside bedroom communities in Moreno Valley to the west.

Although the 44th is a reliably Republican district, pockets in Rancho Mirage and Palm Springs tend to vote Democratic. Once known as playgrounds for the rich and retired, the resorts have seen a massive influx of younger, middle-class families. Still, the 44th has the highest percentage of senior citizens in California.

On the national level, the district tends to vote Republican, but rarely by large margins. The 44th supported the GOP presidential candidate by only 1 percent in 1996 and by just over 2 percent in 2000.

The Salton Sea – the largest man-made body of water in California, which sits between Palm Springs and the Mexican border (and is shared with the 52nd District) – attracted attention in the 1990s as one of the nation's most polluted bodies of water. Congress voted in 1998 to fund a cleanup effort in honor of the late Rep. Sonny Bono, who represented the 44th from 1995 until his death in January 1998.

MAJOR INDUSTRIES
Tourism, agriculture, manufacturing

CITIES
Moreno Valley (pt.), 111,488 (1990); Hemet, 60,697; Indio, 46,768; Palm Springs, 44,223

UNUSUAL FEATURES
Palm Springs known as the Golf Capital of the world; Presidents Gerald R. Ford and Dwight D. Eisenhower retired to Rancho Mirage and Palm Desert respectively.

Rep. Dana Rohrabacher (R)

Elected 1988; 7th term

CAPITOL OFFICE
225-2415; fax 225-0145; 2338 Rayburn Bldg. 20515

INTERNET
e-mail: dana@mail.house.gov
web: www.house.gov/rohrabacher

COMMITTEES
International Relations
Science
    (Space & Aeronautics - chairman)

HOMETOWN
Huntington Beach

BORN
June 21, 1947, Coronado, Calif.

RELIGION
Baptist

FAMILY
Wife, Rhonda Carmony

EDUCATION
Los Angeles Harbor College, attended 1965-67;
California State U., Long Beach, B.A. 1969; U. of
Southern California, M.A. 1971

CAREER
White House speechwriter; journalist

POLITICAL HIGHLIGHTS
No previous office

ELECTION RESULTS

2000 GENERAL

Dana Rohrabacher (R)	136,275	62.1%
Ted Crisell (D)	71,066	32.4%
Don Hull (LIBERT)	8,409	3.8%
Constance Betton (NL)	3,635	1.7%

2000 PRIMARY (OPEN)

Dana Rohrabacher (R)	89,174	61.5%
Ted Crisell (D)	37,755	26.0%
Long K. Pham (R)	10,942	7.6%
Don Hull (LIBERT)	4,901	3.4%
Constance Betton (NL)	2,208	1.5%

1998 GENERAL

Dana Rohrabacher (R)	94,296	58.7%
Patricia Neal (D)	60,022	37.3%
Don Hull (LIBERT)	4,337	2.7%
William Verkamp Jr. (NL)	2,115	1.3%

PREVIOUS WINNING PERCENTAGES
1996 (61%); 1994 (69%); 1992 (55%); 1990 (59%);
1988 (64%)

A fervent conservative and one of the few public figures in Washington who still refers to the People's Republic of China as "Red China," Rohrabacher promotes an "America first" brand of foreign policy, argues for stricter immigration controls, lobbies to extend patent protections to small inventors and pushes for completion of NASA's space station.

However, he is hardly a conventional right-winger. Rohrabacher (ROAR-ah-BAH-ker) counts writers, artists and musicians such as heavy metal vocalist Sammy Hagar and folk singer Joan Baez as friends and occasionally frequents punk rock clubs in Washington. His congressional website features a photo of him surfing in a black wet suit.

Rohrabacher, who served as assistant press secretary for Ronald Reagan's 1976 and 1980 presidential campaigns and as a speechwriter for President Reagan, thinks there are a lot of things the federal government should not spend money on, such as the United Nations and public services for illegal aliens. But he does want Uncle Sam to open the checkbook for the big-ticket space station, parts of which are built in the 45th District.

Beyond his legislative interests, Rohrabacher finds time to get deeply involved in California politics. He initiated an effort to recall a GOP assemblywoman who had been elected Speaker with Democrats' support, and he recruited the candidate who replaced her. During his state's energy crisis in early 2001, he criticized fellow California conservative GOP Rep. Duncan Hunter's efforts to persuade Congress to support temporary price caps on wholesale power supplies. "The proposal is consistent with the type of liberal nonsense that got us into this trouble in the first place," Rohrabacher told the Los Angeles Times. He believes price caps would discourage construction of new power plants.

In the House, Rohrabacher uses his seat on the International Relations Committee to voice skepticism about the United States getting into entanglements abroad. He has no use for the United Nations, once calling it "a collection of tin-pot dictatorships and corrupt regimes."

Rohrabacher was a critic of U.S. policy toward China during both the senior Bush and Clinton administrations. He has criticized China for its suppression of a student-led democracy movement and its threats against Taiwan, and he opposed legislation letting Chinese goods enter the United States under the same low tariffs afforded most countries.

In 1998, Rohrabacher reacted swiftly to reports that scientists working for two U.S. space satellite companies helped the Chinese government develop missile guidance systems that may have been used to advance Beijing's nuclear missile program. When allegations arose that President Clinton had disregarded advisers' objections and allowed the companies — which had contributed to the Democratic Party — to transfer the technology, he called the reports "the most serious scandal that I have ever heard."

He used similar fiery rhetoric when Clinton, in the last days of his administration, pushed for blanket amnesty for undocumented aliens who arrived in the United States before 1986. Rohrabacher called the proposal "an insult" to legal immigrants and "a betrayal of our country and our people." Rohrabacher also fought efforts during the 106th Congress to allow high-tech companies to bring in hundreds of thousands of skilled foreign workers. "There are enough Americans to do these jobs," he said. "The only thing lacking is the pay levels and the training."

On the Science Committee, Rohrabacher usually eschews liberal-bashing in favor of building support for policies and projects important to aerospace interests that have a big economic impact in his district. Boeing Co., a prime contractor on NASA's space station, is a major employer in the 45th. As chairman of the Space and Aeronautics Subcommittee, Rohrabacher defends the space station against critics who say it is a costly boondoggle. However, in the face of delays and cost overruns linked to Russia's participation in the project, he added language to a 2000 NASA reauthorization bill requiring the space agency to regularly report on Russia's performance.

Rohrabacher also has been dogged in his defense of patent rights for small inventors. In 1997, he opposed a measure offered by Republican Howard Coble of North Carolina that called for publication of patents 18 months after they are filed, even if they have not yet been granted. Many small inventors worried that news of their innovations would no longer remain secret while they waited for their patents to be reviewed. Rohrabacher said Coble's bill favored big corporations at the expense of small investors, and he warned that it would allow foreign competitors to steal U.S. technology. The House eventually approved a patent bill that did not include the 18-month language. Rohrabacher called that a victory of the "little guy over the big guy."

A former reporter and editorial writer for the conservative Orange County Register, Rohrabacher has said he patterns his life on that of Ernest Hemingway, a "man's man." The congressman, who says that John Wayne taught him how to drink tequila, has shown a softer side since marrying his former campaign manager, Rhonda Carmony, in 1997. The couple regularly attends church, and Rohrabacher, in a 1999 interview with The Hill newspaper, gushed about his new lifestyle.

In his first bid for elective office in 1988, Rohrabacher ran for the House seat being vacated by GOP Rep. Dan Lungren, who had been nominated to be state treasurer. The field of primary contenders included an Orange County supervisor who had Lungren's support and Cal State-Long Beach President Steve Horn (who would run and win in a neighboring district in 1992).

Despite the competition, Rohrabacher found a way to win. A campaign fundraiser featuring retired Marine Lt. Col. Oliver L. North of Iran-contra fame raised Rohrabacher's standing among conservatives while adding $100,000 to his coffers. He ended up with 35 percent of the primary vote, well ahead of his nearest rival. He has encountered little difficulty in his general-election contests, although he and Carmony were fined for campaign finance irregularities in connection with their 1995 effort to replace Assemblywoman Doris Allen.

KEY VOTES

2000
No   Raise hourly minimum wage by $1 over two years
Yes   Halt funding for U.S. mission in Kosovo unless European nations pay more
Yes   Provide Medicare benefits to military retirees and their dependents
No   Grant China permanent normal trade status
Yes   Phase out estate, gift and trust taxes
Yes   Prohibit implementation of president's national monument designations
Yes   Approve GOP plan to provide prescription drug coverage for Medicare beneficiaries
No   Increase help for poor nations indebted to international financial institutions

1999
No   Impose steel import quotas
Yes   Kill proposal to take aviation trust funds off budget
Yes   Require background checks on buyers only at gun shows with 10 or more vendors
Yes   Remove barriers among banking, securities and insurance companies
No   Authorize state grants to hire teachers and reduce class size
No   Overhaul campaign finance law; ban "soft money" and restrict advocacy advertising
No   Approve bipartisan plan to increase rights of patients in managed-care health plans

INTEREST GROUPS

	AFL-CIO	ADA	CCUS	ACU
2000	10%	10%	61%	96%
1999	22%	5%	76%	96%
1998	20%	5%	67%	100%
1997	0%	10%	80%	92%

CQ VOTE STUDIES

	PARTY UNITY		PRESIDENTIAL SUPPORT	
	Support	Oppose	Support	Oppose
2000	94%	6%	16%	84%
1999	94%	6%	12%	88%
1998	90%	10%	26%	74%
1997	92%	8%	20%	80%

CALIFORNIA 45
Coastal Orange County

The 45th is a comfortably Republican district with an eclectic mix of senior citizens, surfers and aerospace workers. It has two distinct communities: the coastal region, which has many affluent areas, and the interior, which is more blue-collar, with a slightly higher number of Democrats.

At Seal Beach, which anchors the coastal section, two-thirds of the city's residents are 65 or older and about a third live in Leisure World – a seniors-only community. Down the coast is Huntington Beach, or "Surf City," a hub for both surfers and aerospace workers, many of whom work at the Boeing plant that is the prime design and manufacturing facility for the space station and Delta rocket.

Newport Beach resembles the other coastal communities – more bedrooms for aerospace white-collar workers – but looks a little different. Its terrain lifts into some rolling hills, and Newport Bay runs right up its middle.

The 45th's interior, which includes Westminster, Fountain Valley and parts of Garden Grove and Costa Mesa, tends to be less affluent than the coastal cities and the communities tend to have a higher number of Democrats. These towns are solidly middle-class residential areas. Many of the interior's blue-collar workers are employed by aerospace companies within the district or in Anaheim, Torrance or Long Beach.

MAJOR INDUSTRY
Aerospace, high-tech, manufacturing

MILITARY BASES
Naval Weapons Station Seal Beach, 108 military, 430 civilian (2001)

CITIES
Huntington Beach, 199,618; Costa Mesa (pt.), 95,126 (1990); Westminster (pt.), 77,694; Fountain Valley (pt.), 52,491 (1990)

UNUSUAL FEATURES
Seal Beach known for its seals and sea lions; Surfing is the major recreation activity in Huntington Beach, which hosts the G-Shock U.S. Open of Surfing, the OP Pro of Surfing and the Katin Team Challenge.

Rep. Loretta Sanchez (D)

Elected 1996; 3rd term

CAPITOL OFFICE
225-2965; fax 225-5859
1230 Longworth Bldg. 20515

INTERNET
e-mail: loretta@mail.house.gov
web: www.house.gov/sanchez

COMMITTEES
Armed Services
Education & Workforce

HOMETOWN
Anaheim

BORN
Jan. 7, 1960, Lynwood, Calif.

RELIGION
Roman Catholic

FAMILY
Husband, Stephen Simmons Brixey III

EDUCATION
Chapman U., B.S. 1982; American U., M.B.A. 1984

CAREER
Financial adviser; strategic management associate

POLITICAL HIGHLIGHTS
Candidate for Anaheim City Council, 1994

ELECTION RESULTS

2000 GENERAL

Loretta Sanchez (D)	70,381	60.2%
Gloria Matta Tuchman (R)	40,928	35.0%
Richard B. Boddie (LIBERT)	3,159	2.7%
Larry G. Engwall (NL)	2,440	2.1%

2000 PRIMARY (OPEN)

Loretta Sanchez (D)	40,031	57.7%
Gloria Matta Tuchman (R)	16,606	23.9%
Howard Garber (R)	9,518	13.7%
Richard B. Boddie (LIBERT)	1,769	2.6%
Larry G. Engwall (NL)	1,431	2.1%

1998 GENERAL

Loretta Sanchez (D)	47,964	56.4%
Robert K. Dornan (R)	33,388	39.3%
Thomas E. Reimer (LIBERT)	2,316	2.7%
Larry G. Engwall (NL)	1,334	1.6%

PREVIOUS WINNING PERCENTAGES
1996 (47%)

A daughter of working-class Mexican immigrants, Sanchez evolved from a "shy, quiet girl" who did not speak English into a businesswoman with an M.B.A. Since scoring an upset victory in 1996 against veteran GOP Rep. Robert K. Dornan, she has been hailed as a new Democratic star and a symbol of the rising political aspirations of Hispanic-Americans.

Media-savvy and energetic, Sanchez has a magnetic aura, appearing on the cover of Latino magazines and sought out for autographs. But the sometimes stubborn lawmaker insists on charting her own course, and she has drawn some criticism — most memorably in 2000 when she initially insisted on holding a political fundraiser at the Playboy mansion just before the Democratic National Convention.

Sanchez can trace her ambitions to her first-grade catechism class. According to an account in The Orange County Register, a nun asked her what she wanted to be when she grew up. "I answered, 'The pope. He's the head of everyone, the one making the rules,'" Sanchez told the newspaper. "The nun went on to tell me because I was a woman I could never be pope. I didn't think that was very fair."

Sanchez was so shy as a child that her mother took her to doctors to make sure she was all right and enrolled her in the government's Head Start program. Her father forced her to take speech and drama classes in school. Acutely aware of her parents' limited income, she worked her way through college and earned a master's degree in business administration. Feeling isolated as a Hispanic woman in the investment world, she made her first foray into politics in 1994, losing a race for an Anaheim City Council seat.

Two years later, she brazenly took on Dornan, one of the most conservative and controversial members of the House and a long-shot candidate for the 1996 GOP presidential nomination. After Sanchez won a four-way Democratic primary with 35 percent of the vote, she drew attention from liberal groups who played a hunch that their archenemy Dornan might not have his guard up. Teachers' unions and abortion rights groups helped her build a treasury that topped Dornan's. Thanks to the increasing number of Hispanic voters in the 46th District and a backlash against a ballot initiative to end most state affirmative action programs, Sanchez appeared to score a stunning upset, beating Dornan by 984 votes.

Dornan, however, blamed his defeat on illegal voting by non-citizens. "It was stolen from me, and I have the evidence," he said. The House established a three-member task force to look into the allegations. After considerable partisan battling that went on for more than a year, the task force in early 1998 announced that it had uncovered widespread voting by non-citizens but could not document enough such votes to overturn the election. Dornan got a 1998 rematch with Sanchez, raising $3.7 million but losing this time by a 17-point margin. Sanchez, who spends virtually every weekend in the district and tends carefully to her constituents, won re-election easily in 2000.

Sanchez credits government with much of her success. "I am a Head Start child, a public school kid, a Pell Grant recipient," she once said in a House floor speech. "I think some federal programs do work for our children."

As a member of the Education and the Workforce Committee, she is in the chorus of liberals who complain that conservative Republicans are not committed to improving public education. "It saddens me that during a time when our public schools are facing their most challenging times, we are encouraging American people to turn to private schools to teach their children," Sanchez said in response to a GOP proposal to give low-income parents vouchers to spend at the school of their choice.

On the "workforce" side of the Education and the Workforce Committee agenda, Sanchez has even harsher words for proposals by Republicans, who she once said "are trying, through any means necessary, to destroy American labor unions." In 1998, she resigned from the panel's Oversight Subcommittee to protest the "extreme partisan direction" of its probe into allegations of fraud in the 1996 Teamsters Union presidential election.

Sanchez has family roots in organized labor: Her parents both worked at a manufacturing plant, where her father was a machinist and her mother was a secretary who helped organize plant workers into a union. Sanchez herself joined the United Food and Commercial Workers when she scooped ice cream in high school, and she went to college on a union scholarship.

Because of those union ties, she broke with the Clinton administration on trade issues, siding with organized labor in opposing fast-track authority for the president to negotiate trade deals that Congress cannot amend. She also voted against granting China permanent normal trade status, saying that the Chinese "[do] not reciprocate the trade benefits that we grant them."

Sanchez also sits on the Armed Services panel. Despite her reservations about some military spending, she has backed continued production of fighter planes, such as the F-22, that are important to the California economy. An abortion rights supporter, Sanchez has taken aim at the ban on overseas military abortions. "If a woman is willing to put her life on the line in the military, she should have the same rights she would enjoy if she were stationed in the United States," she told The Orange County Register.

But if debates on education, labor policy, the environment and abortion find Sanchez allied with the Democratic left, she hews to a center-right course on fiscal policy matters, as a member of the "Blue Dogs," a group of about 30 like-minded House Democrats. Conservatives also have found Sanchez on their side on such issues as backing a constitutional amendment to outlaw desecration of the American flag and encouraging states to prosecute violent juvenile offenders as adults.

Sanchez, a talented fundraiser, landed in the center of a controversy in the summer of 2000 when she scheduled a political event at the Playboy mansion. Furious Democrats crossed her name off a list of speakers at the national convention and even considered removing her as the party's general co-chairman. Sanchez initially refused to back down, but eventually moved the venue. "It's never been about the Playboy mansion," she said on NBC's "Today" show. "It's been about putting on a good event and raising money."

KEY VOTES

2000
Yes Raise hourly minimum wage by $1 over two years
No   Halt funding for U.S. mission in Kosovo unless European nations pay more
Yes Provide Medicare benefits to military retirees and their dependents
No   Grant China permanent normal trade status
Yes Phase out estate, gift and trust taxes
No   Prohibit implementation of president's national monument designations
No   Approve GOP plan to provide prescription drug coverage for Medicare beneficiaries
Yes Increase help for poor nations indebted to international financial institutions

1999
Yes Impose steel import quotas
No   Kill proposal to take aviation trust funds off budget
No   Require background checks on buyers only at gun shows with 10 or more vendors
Yes Remove barriers among banking, securities and insurance companies
Yes Authorize state grants to hire teachers and reduce class size
Yes Overhaul campaign finance law; ban "soft money" and restrict advocacy advertising
Yes Approve bipartisan plan to increase rights of patients in managed-care health plans

INTEREST GROUPS

	AFL-CIO	ADA	CCUS	ACU
2000	89%	65%	63%	17%
1999	89%	95%	36%	4%
1998	100%	95%	44%	8%
1997	75%	65%	60%	28%

CQ VOTE STUDIES

	PARTY UNITY		PRESIDENTIAL SUPPORT	
	Support	Oppose	Support	Oppose
2000	94%	6%	75%	25%
1999	90%	10%	75%	25%
1998	90%	10%	78%	22%
1997	84%	16%	69%	31%

CALIFORNIA 46
Part of Orange County; Santa Ana; Garden Grove

A blue-collar district full of older suburban homes and younger families, the 46th is unlike its mostly affluent, Republican neighbors. It takes in parts of Santa Ana and Garden Grove, about 30 miles southeast of Los Angeles, where a growing number of Hispanics and other ethnic minorities are changing its demographics, resulting in an even stronger Democratic voter base.

Almost half of the district's population is in Santa Ana – the seat of Orange County – which has higher unemployment and more blue-collar jobs than surrounding areas.

Garden Grove is more residential and is divided into roughly three sections: the western, more affluent part; the center, a mix of Vietnamese, Koreans and Hispanics; and the eastern, heavily Hispanic area. Little Saigon sits just south of the district in Westminster. An influx of Southeast Asian refugees into Garden Grove has spurred a conservative backlash from some of the city's white, blue-collar

workers.

The 46th has had one of the lowest education rates in California and has been plagued by gangs and high crime rates, however, the area has recently seen a dramatic reduction in crime. Apart from Disneyland, no one employer drives the area's economy. Defense subcontractors and small businesses are scattered throughout the district.

MAJOR INDUSTRY
Small business, service, defense

CITIES
Santa Ana (pt.), 271,662 (1990); Anaheim (pt.), 151,589 (1990); Garden Grove (pt.), 124,182 (1990)

UNUSUAL FEATURES
Disneyland in Anaheim; Garden Grove known for the "positive thinking" television ministry of Robert Schuller and his Crystal Cathedral.

Rep. Christopher Cox (R)

Elected 1988; 7th term

CAPITOL OFFICE
225-5611; fax 225-9177; 2402 Rayburn Bldg. 20515

INTERNET
e-mail: christopher.cox@mail.house.gov
web: www.house.gov/chriscox

COMMITTEES
Energy & Commerce
Financial Services

HOMETOWN
Newport Beach

BORN
Oct. 16, 1952, St. Paul, Minn.

RELIGION
Roman Catholic

FAMILY
Wife, Rebecca Cox; three children

EDUCATION
U. of Southern California, B.A. 1973; Harvard U.,
M.B.A. 1977, J.D. 1977

CAREER
White House counsel; lawyer; professor

POLITICAL HIGHLIGHTS
No previous office

ELECTION RESULTS

2000 GENERAL

Christopher Cox (R)	181,365	65.6%
John L. Graham (D)	83,186	30.1%
David Nolan (LIBERT)	8,081	2.9%
Iris Adam (NL)	3,769	1.4%

2000 PRIMARY (OPEN)

Christopher Cox (R)	134,959	68.6%
John L. Graham (D)	18,913	9.6%
Donald Irvine (D)	16,510	8.4%
Jim Keysor (D)	10,010	5.1%
Maziar Mafi (D)	8,953	4.6%
David Nolan (LIBERT)	4,892	2.5%
Iris Adam (NL)	2,619	1.3%

1998 GENERAL

Christopher Cox (R)	132,711	67.6%
Christina Avalos (D)	57,938	29.5%
Victor A. Wagner Jr. (LIBERT)	2,991	1.5%

PREVIOUS WINNING PERCENTAGES
1996 (66%); 1994 (72%); 1992 (65%); 1990 (68%);
1988 (67%)

His cool, erudite manner and his grasp of legislative detail have given Cox a level of bipartisan respectability usually reserved for more centrist members. And his low-key, methodical style suggests he is a legislator driven more by his own intellectual ruminations than by party loyalty.

Nevertheless, his record as a conservative is rock solid. He once told The Wall Street Journal that President Reagan's assault on non-defense government spending was not aggressive enough. He has endorsed the elimination of both the Energy and Education departments and the consolidation of others. And he has never met a tax cut he didn't like; he left a hospital bed after an appendectomy in 1997 so he could cast a vote in the House for a tax cut measure.

Cox has been Congress' definition of "policy wonk" since his arrival on Capitol Hill in 1989. He turns aside clubby political gossip with a polite but distant smile, preferring to focus on legislation. He has a ready command of facts and figures — his wife, Rebecca, an airline lobbyist, says that her husband reads mathematics texts for fun. In the mid-1980s, Cox and his father published an English version of the official Soviet newspaper Pravda, a labor-intensive effort intended to highlight Soviet propaganda.

Intensely ambitious, Cox has been chairman of the House Republican Policy Committee since his party's takeover of Congress in 1995. He twice considered running for Speaker when the post came up for grabs late in 1998 — after the resignations of Speaker Newt Gingrich and then of the man the GOP had picked as his successor, Robert L. Livingston — but he backed away quickly when it became clear he didn't have much support.

Yet Cox's galloping ambition is bridled by his caution and disdain for the back-slapping, deal-making, vote-counting chumminess that is helpful for one to become Speaker. He once told The Orange County Register that, instead of being Speaker, he would rather have 50 bills with his stamp on them during his House career. Early in 2001, he was reportedly being considered for an appointment to the 9th U.S. Circuit Court of Appeals.

Cox's intellect and calm demeanor made him the natural choice of Republican leaders in 1998 to head a select committee on China's alleged theft of U.S. nuclear and military technology secrets. The assignment vaulted him onto a higher political stage. The conduct of the handpicked committee and its unanimous conclusions bore the mark of Cox's cautious nature. Laboring secretively, methodically and relentlessly, Cox and the panel's ranking Democrat, Norm Dicks of Washington, made sure there were no leaks to the media.

The panel produced a harsh assessment of the Clinton administration's policies toward China but managed to do so with bipartisan credibility and support, including strong words of praise from Dicks. The findings were nonetheless frustrating to some Republicans, who had hoped for a more stinging report condemning the Clinton administration.

Cox has been a longtime critic of China's human rights record, and he consistently voted against granting China normal trading status when the issue came up for annual review. He had an opportunity to underscore those concerns — and his criticisms of U.S. policies toward China — in 2000, when President Clinton pushed for permanent normal trade status with that country. Cox could have used his bipartisan credibility on U.S.-China relations to rally support against the measure, but his high standing in the party leadership made it awkward for him to do so. The China trade bill was one of the few instances when GOP leaders were on Clinton's side and were willing to work with him to overcome the opposition in both parties that sprang from concerns over the potential loss of U.S. jobs and China's human rights violations. Cox worked for inclusion of language requiring annual reviews of China's record on human rights but contributed little else to the debate. He ended up voting for the bill.

It was not the first time Cox backed off a stand in deference to GOP leaders. In 1997, he was one of just 26 Republicans who opposed a balanced-budget deal between congressional Republicans and Clinton, complaining that too much had been given away in the GOP lawmakers' hunger for compromise. However, he eventually voted for the spending and tax bills to implement the deal.

Cox reinforced his commitment to smaller government in 1998, when he was in the minority of Republicans who voted against the massive transportation bill that contained a sizable share of projects for California. Cox said he preferred that states be permitted to keep gas tax receipts and deal with their own road-building and other transportation projects. He also has pushed for changes in the budget process that would boost fiscal discipline and make it more difficult for appropriators to exceed the caps set in the annual budget.

Cox led the effort to enact a bill in 1995 making it more difficult for shareholders to sue when they are disgruntled with a company's performance — one of just two measures that became law over a Clinton veto. He was part of the negotiations that led to enactment of the 1996 telecommunications deregulation law.

And in 1998, he was a prime force behind a law establishing a moratorium on new Internet taxes, which he will seek to extend in the 107th Congress. "Right now, the Internet is not burdened with discriminatory and excessive taxes," he said. "[But] this may change very rapidly. Tax collectors around the country and globe are eyeing the 'Net."

After obtaining simultaneous graduate degrees from Harvard in business and law, Cox clerked with judges on federal appeals courts in San Francisco and Honolulu and practiced law with a Newport Beach firm until 1986, when he became a senior associate counsel in the Reagan White House.

He stayed until 1988, when GOP Rep. Robert E. Badham announced plans to retire from his Orange County seat. In a crowded primary field, Cox separated himself by using his Washington connections. He distributed literature picturing him with President Reagan and Vice President George Bush in the White House. He took 67 percent of the vote in the general election, and he has won with similar ease since then.

KEY VOTES

2000

No   Raise hourly minimum wage by $1 over two years
Yes Halt funding for U.S. mission in Kosovo unless European nations pay more
Yes Provide Medicare benefits to military retirees and their dependents
Yes Grant China permanent normal trade status
Yes Phase out estate, gift and trust taxes
Yes Prohibit implementation of president's national monument designations
Yes Approve GOP plan to provide prescription drug coverage for Medicare beneficiaries
No   Increase help for poor nations indebted to international financial institutions

1999

No   Impose steel import quotas
Yes Kill proposal to take aviation trust funds off budget
Yes Require background checks on buyers only at gun shows with 10 or more vendors
Yes Remove barriers among banking, securities and insurance companies
No   Authorize state grants to hire teachers and reduce class size
No   Overhaul campaign finance law; ban "soft money" and restrict advocacy advertising
No   Approve bipartisan plan to increase rights of patients in managed-care health plans

INTEREST GROUPS

	AFL-CIO	ADA	CCUS	ACU
2000	0%	0%	80%	100%
1999	11%	0%	75%	95%
1998	10%	0%	89%	100%
1997	0%	10%	75%	96%

CQ VOTE STUDIES

	PARTY UNITY		PRESIDENTIAL SUPPORT	
	Support	Oppose	Support	Oppose
2000	95%	5%	19%	81%
1999	93%	7%	18%	82%
1998	92%	8%	27%	73%
1997	94%	6%	25%	75%

CALIFORNIA 47
Coastal — Central Orange County; Irvine

The 47th is a safe Republican district where registered Republicans outnumber Democrats almost 2-to-1. It includes a portion of the coast, the bulk of central Orange County and suburban portions of Anaheim. The district is distinguished by its large white-collar labor force and its high household income.

The 47th's coastal area encompasses part of upscale Newport Beach to the north, as well as Laguna Beach to the south. Newport Beach is a wealthy enclave noted for its beautiful sandy beaches and luxurious housing. Laguna Beach attracts more scuba divers than swimmers and is a more liberal enclave known as "the arts colony." To the east is Laguna Woods, where a large number of senior citizens live. Between them is Crystal Cove State Park, which covers about half of the district's coastline.

While Republicans dominate the 47th, pockets of Democratic strength can be found in the district's northern, suburban Santa Ana territory

and in the more liberal-leaning community surrounding the University of California Irvine. The university's engineering and biomedical research programs have attracted a sizable number of thriving high-tech and biotechnology firms, especially in the growing Irvine Spectrum area, which is beginning to rival Silicon Valley.

While the 1999 closures of the El Toro and Tustin Marine Corps Air stations did not have a huge impact on the economy, much of the area's politics revolve around a proposed commercial airport on the site of the former El Toro base. Local residents are opposed to the airport for environmental and quaility of life reasons.

MAJOR INDUSTRY
High-tech, biomedical, tourism

CITIES
Irvine (pt.), 109,774 (1990); Orange (pt.), 105,200 (1990); El Toro (pt.), 61,604 (1990); Anaheim (pt.), 51,668 (1990)

UNUSUAL FEATURES
Laguna Woods is home to one of the nation's largest senior populations.

Rep. Darrell Issa (R)

Elected 2000; 1st term

Issa voices conservative views on both economic and social issues. This suggests no great change from his predecessor, Republican Ron Packard, who for 18 years represented the 48th District — a GOP stronghold that bridges the outskirts of the Los Angeles and San Diego metropolitan areas.

Issa's interests lie primarily in the high-tech arena. After his stint in the Army ended in 1980, Issa (EYE-sah) used his $7,000 life savings to invest in a Cleveland-based car alarm business, eventually taking full control of the firm (now called Directed Electronics Inc.) and moving it to San Diego in 1985.

Issa is able to pursue his interest in business-related issues with his assignment to the Small Business Committee. He also is on the Judiciary panel, which gives him a say on legislation affecting government regulation of the electronics and telecommunications industries.

His third committee assignment, to the International Relations Committee, also plays to a personal interest. A Lebanese-American, he has been president of the American Task Force for Lebanon, which advocates a role for that nation in the Middle East peace process.

Issa's six-year Army career (two years after high school and four years after college) and his eight years in the Army Reserve certainly do not hurt his appeal in the 48th District, which includes the Camp Pendleton Marine Corps Base.

In the reliably Republican district, which was home to the late President Richard M. Nixon, Issa weathered a nine-candidate primary. His foremost foe, state Sen. Bill Morrow, attacked Issa's lack of legislative experience and questioned his business dealings. But Issa won with 35 percent of the vote.

Issa's wealth may have provided him the essential edge: He sank $2 million into his primary campaign. The general election was routine by comparison, with Issa taking 61 percent to defeat Democrat Peter Kouvelis, a retired Marine officer.

The 2000 race was Issa's first political win, but not his first run. He spent $11 million on a bid for the 1998 Republican nomination to challenge Democratic Sen. Barbara Boxer, but lost to state Treasurer Matt Fong.

CAPITOL OFFICE
225-3906; fax 225-3303
1725 Longworth Bldg. 20515

INTERNET
e-mail: www.house.gov/writerep
web: www.house.gov/issa

COMMITTEES
International Relations
Judiciary
Small Business

HOMETOWN
Vista

BORN
Nov. 1, 1953, Cleveland, Ohio

RELIGION
Antioch Orthodox Christian Church

FAMILY
Wife, Kathy Issa; one child

EDUCATION
Kent State U., A.A. 1976; Siena Heights College, B.A. 1976

MILITARY SERVICE
Army, 1970-72, 1976-80; Army Reserve, 1980-88

CAREER
Car alarm company owner; electronics manufacturing company executive

POLITICAL HIGHLIGHTS
Sought Republican nomination for U.S. Senate, 1998

ELECTION RESULTS

2000 GENERAL

Darrell Issa (R)	160,627	61.4%
Peter Kouvelis (D)	74,073	28.3%
Eddie Rose (REF)	11,240	4.3%
Sharon K. Miles (NL)	8,269	3.2%
Joe Cobb (LIBERT)	7,269	2.8%

2000 PRIMARY (OPEN)

Darrell Issa (R)	67,732	35.3%
Bill Morrow (R)	45,223	23.6%
Peter Kouvelis (D)	20,789	10.8%
Richard Maguire (D)	13,704	7.1%
Mark Dornan (R)	9,534	5.0%
Joe Snyder (R)	8,480	4.4%
William Griffith (R)	5,362	2.8%
Don Udall (R)	5,258	2.7%

CALIFORNIA 48

Part of Orange, San Diego and Riverside counties

Registered Republicans outnumber Democrats nearly 2-to-1 in this GOP stronghold, which includes San Diego and Orange County bedroom communities. Only the neighboring 47th District is considered more Republican. The typical district resident has been described as conservative, white, upper-middle-class and well-educated, with 2.5 children and two cars. To the south and east, the areas of north San Diego County and Vista are a bit more blue-collar.

Although Camp Pendleton Marine Corps Base sits squarely in the middle of the district, the local economy relies less on military contracts than the neighboring 47th. A steady stream of visitors to the 48th's beach communities provides an economic cushion to the 48th's economy, which also relies on the service industry.

Several areas in the district have seen prodigious growth since the 1980s, especially wine-producing Temecula in Riverside County, and San Diego County's San Marcos, where young families, as well as a growing number of military retirees, are settling.

MAJOR INDUSTRY
Tourism, defense, service, health care

MILITARY BASES
Camp Pendleton Marine Corps Base, Air Station, Naval Hospital; 33,000 military, 6,500 civilian (2000)

CITIES
Oceanside (pt.), 118,192 (1990); Vista (pt.), 66,944 (1990); Mission Viejo (pt.), 56,292 (1990); Laguna Niguel, 54,582

UNUSUAL FEATURES
San Clemente, home of Richard Nixon; Swallows flock to Spanish mission in San Juan Capistrano; Fallbrook's famous avocado groves.

Rep. Susan A. Davis (D)

Elected 2000; 1st term

A California term-limit law barred Davis from running again for her San Diego-based Assembly seat in 2000. But the political vulnerability of the 49th District's GOP incumbent, Brian P. Bilbray, provided her with a window of opportunity, and she took full advantage, capturing a narrow victory.

A former school board member who says education should be the nation's top priority, Davis landed a spot on the Education and the Workforce panel from which to advance that cause. In the Assembly, she had authored a bill to reduce eighth-grade class size to 20 students per teacher. She also had sponsored legislation to reward nationally certified teachers for demonstrated teaching skills and to raise minimum standards for retaining teachers. Davis opposes school vouchers, saying tax dollars should not be used for private school education when 90 percent of children attend public schools.

Before entering politics, Davis was a social worker and executive director of the Aaron Price Fellowship Program, an organization designed to teach multi-ethnic high school students leadership and citizenship skills.

On other issues, Davis believes that any budget surpluses should be used first for debt reduction, preservation of Social Security, and health and education programs. She supports targeted tax cuts for child care and higher education and to promote small-business growth.

As the 2000 campaign began, Bilbray was viewed as vulnerable: He had won in the politically competitive 49th with less than 50 percent of the vote twice in his three House victories. Davis did not disappoint.

In the middle of the campaign, a state electricity crisis sent consumer bills in the San Diego area skyrocketing. Bilbray criticized Davis for her support in the Assembly of a 1996 law that opened up the state's electric utilities to competition. But the Davis campaign produced a letter signed by members of the California congressional delegation — including Bilbray — supporting that law. And Davis acted quickly to get legislation passed that retroactively instituted price caps on utility bills in the area. She pulled off the win, 50 percent to 46 percent.

CAPITOL OFFICE
225-2040; fax 225-2948; 1517 Longworth Bldg. 20515

INTERNET
e-mail: susan.davis@mail.house.gov
web: www.house.gov/susandavis

COMMITTEES
Armed Services
Education & Workforce

HOMETOWN
San Diego

BORN
April 13, 1944, Cambridge, Mass.

RELIGION
Jewish

FAMILY
Husband, Steve Davis; two children

EDUCATION
U. of California, Berkeley, B.A. 1965; U. of North Carolina, M.A. 1968

CAREER
High school leadership program director; public television producer; social worker

POLITICAL HIGHLIGHTS
San Diego Board of Education, 1983-92 (president, 1989-92); Calif. Assembly, 1995-2000

ELECTION RESULTS

2000 GENERAL
Susan A. Davis (D)	113,400	49.6%
Brian P. Bilbray (R)	105,515	46.2%
Doris Ball (LIBERT)	6,526	2.9%
Tahir Bhatti (NL)	3,048	1.3%

2000 PRIMARY (OPEN)
Brian P. Bilbray (R)	79,473	50.9%
Susan A. Davis (D)	71,443	45.8%
Doris Ball (LIBERT)	3,505	2.2%
Tahir Bhatti (NL)	1,738	1.1%

CALIFORNIA 49
North San Diego; Coronado; Imperial Beach

The coastal 49th is the economic engine that drives surrounding districts. It includes San Diego's downtown, large employers, coastline and most of its military bases. Upscale La Jolla, Point Loma, Coronado and Del Cerro are part of the district as are more blue-collar Imperial Beach and Clairmont.

The 49th is a marginal seat with a large number of moderates and Reagan Democrats. In recent years, the numbers of registered Democrats and Republicans have been neck and neck. One of the area's most liberal and Democratic places is Hillcrest, which includes a large part of San Diego's gay community.

The 49th's economy has benefited from its large telecommunications and biotech industries. Three rounds of military base closings in the 1990s did not hurt the district – San Diego actually saw a net gain of about 6,000 defense jobs. One-ninth of the city's gross regional product depends on military procurement, retirement benefits and salaries.

MAJOR INDUSTRY
Telecommunications, defense, biotechnology

MILITARY BASES
Naval Air Station North Island/Naval Amphibious Base Coronado, 17,968 military, 9,211 civilian; Naval Station San Diego, 43,160 military, 5,400 civilian; Naval Submarine Base Pt. Loma/SPAWAR, 3,500 military, 5,500 civilian; Naval Regional Medical Center, 3,400 military, 1,200 civilian; Marine Corps Recruitment Depot, 1,725 military, 825 civilian (2000)

CITIES
San Diego (pt.), 520,257 (1990); Imperial Beach, 28,881; Coronado, 28,168

UNUSUAL FEATURES
San Diego Zoo; Marilyn Monroe filmed "Some Like It Hot" at the historic Hotel Del Coronado.

Rep. Bob Filner (D)

CAPITOL OFFICE
225-8045; fax 225-9073; 2463 Rayburn Bldg. 20515

INTERNET
e-mail: www.house.gov/writerep
web: www.house.gov/filner

COMMITTEES
Transportation & Infrastructure
Veterans' Affairs

HOMETOWN
San Diego

BORN
Sept. 4, 1942, Pittsburgh, Pa.

RELIGION
Jewish

FAMILY
Wife, Jane Merrill; two children

EDUCATION
Cornell U., B.A. 1963; U. of Delaware, M.A. 1969;
Cornell U., Ph.D. 1973

CAREER
Public official; college professor

POLITICAL HIGHLIGHTS
San Diego School Board, 1979-83 (president,
1982); candidate for San Diego City Council, 1983;
San Diego City Council, 1987-92 (deputy mayor,
1991)

ELECTION RESULTS

2000 GENERAL

Bob Filner (D)	95,191	68.3%
Bob Divine (R)	38,526	27.6%
David Willoughby (LIBERT)	3,472	2.5%
Leeann Kendall (NL)	2,283	1.6%

2000 PRIMARY (OPEN)

Bob Filner (D)	61,742	67.4%
Bob Divine (R)	18,339	20.0%
Alexander Sorongon (R)	5,420	5.9%
James Good (R)	3,044	3.3%
David Willoughby (LIBERT)	1,934	2.1%
Leeann Kendall (NL)	1,187	1.3%

1998 GENERAL

Bob Filner (D)	unopposed

PREVIOUS WINNING PERCENTAGES
1996 (62%); 1994 (57%); 1992 (57%)

Elected 1992; 5th term

Filner has a large portrait of former Democratic Sen. and Vice President Hubert H. Humphrey in his Capitol Hill office, and like him, Filner is an irrepressible liberal. A one-time aide to the "happy warrior," Filner has recovered from the brief funk that overcame him in the mid-1990s when Republicans took control of the House, and he has emerged as an outspoken advocate on veterans issues.

As the ranking Democrat on the Veterans' Affairs panel's Benefits Subcommittee in the 105th and 106th Congresses, Filner worked for funds to help homeless veterans and sponsored legislation to ensure that veterans can reclaim their state government jobs when they return from military service. In 1999, he offered a series of amendments on the House floor that would have boosted funding for veterans' benefits. Although none won approval, Filner was satisfied that he had drawn attention to the needs of veterans. "I wanted to make the case that we are not doing for our veterans what we should be doing," he told The San Diego Union-Tribune. In the 107th Congress, he became the top Democrat on the Veterans' Affairs Health Subcommittee.

Filner has made a name for himself as far away as the Philippines for his repeated efforts to win benefits for Filipino veterans who served with U.S. forces in World War II. His efforts, inspired by the large Filipino community in the 50th District, have brought the issue to the attention of U.S. decision-makers and won him the gratitude of the Philippine government, particularly when he was arrested with Filipino-American protesters who had chained themselves to the White House fence.

A native of Pennsylvania, Filner became involved in the civil rights movement while in college. He was arrested at a Mississippi civil rights lunch counter sit-in and spent several months in prison. After his release, he earned higher degrees in history and the history of science.

Filner moved to California in 1970 to teach history at San Diego State University. After a congressional fellowship in which he worked for Humphrey and Rep. Don Fraser, both Minnesota Democrats, in the mid-1970s, he served four years on the San Diego School Board and five years on the city council before his successful run for Congress in 1992.

Filner struggled with disillusionment when Republicans took control of Congress after the 1994 election, making it apparent to Filner that he would not be able to achieve many of the goals in the Humphrey tradition that he had set to work on when he came to the Capitol. He told USA Today in 1995: "My friends in San Diego ... say they have never seen me so depressed."

Unlike some Democrats who voted to scale back government social programs, he remained true to his more liberal beliefs. He was among the minority of Democrats who voted against the White House-Capitol Hill budget deal in 1997, which he said "put on a down-slope all the programs I care about," such as housing, health care and education.

In many of his endeavors, Filner uses a community-organizing style — raising public awareness through speeches or publicity gimmicks, building coalitions of like-minded colleagues, and finding influential allies — that has origins in his civil rights work in the 1960s. In 1999, he told The San Diego Union-Tribune that he had advised veterans to surround the Capitol and refuse to leave until they got better benefits. "After all, if anyone knows how to pitch tents, veterans do," he said.

Finding non-legislative answers to problems is also important in helping economic development in the low-income 50th District. Filner has arranged small-business workshops and publicized sources of microloans and other government help for entrepreneurs in the district.

Filner also sits on the Transportation Committee, where in the 105th Congress, he worked with other Californians to get as much money as possible for local projects in the massive reauthorization of federal transportation programs. Of particular importance to Filner was funding for transportation projects along the Mexican border. Facilities there have been strained by increased trade traffic spurred by approval in 1993 of the North American Free Trade Agreement, which he opposed.

Filner also has devoted his energy to environmental protection, another area of local concern. In the 106th Congress, for example, he pushed for legislation to help provide secondary sewage treatment in the Tijuana area of Mexico, thereby reducing the effect of sewage on the southern California coast. "This bill would allow for the technology and the capacity necessary to protect our beaches," he said.

Border crossings by illegal immigrants are a problem in Filner's district, so he has supported more funding and enhanced stature for the Border Patrol. But he objects to what he says is the hostile tone of many who decry illegal immigration.

Filner has been a leading opponent of the placement of a nuclear waste dump in Ward Valley, in the 40th District, and, along with Democratic Sen. Barbara Boxer, fought the Marine Corps' plan to move more than 100 giant helicopters to Miramar Naval Air Base in the 51st District, whose congressman is Republican Randy "Duke" Cunningham. The two men do not get along, and there was a physical confrontation once when Filner showed up to "greet" then-House Speaker Newt Gingrich as he arrived in town for a Cunningham fundraiser.

Filner's appearance with a placard protesting the GOP's policies toward senior citizens was just one example of the stunts he uses to publicize his views. When the Republican National Convention was in San Diego in 1996, Filner attracted considerable attention outside GOP gatherings by setting up a makeshift booth labeled "The Democrat Is In," modeled after the one used by Lucy in the comic strip "Peanuts."

California gained seven seats in the 1992 reapportionment, and with single-minded devotion to fundraising and tireless campaigning, Filner overcame five foes in the Democratic primary for the new 50th District. He had little trouble dispatching Republican Tony Valencia to win his initial election to Congress. In subsequent elections, he has handily defeated his GOP challengers.

KEY VOTES

2000
Yes Raise hourly minimum wage by $1 over two years
No   Halt funding for U.S. mission in Kosovo unless European nations pay more
Yes Provide Medicare benefits to military retirees and their dependents
No   Grant China permanent normal trade status
No   Phase out estate, gift and trust taxes
No   Prohibit implementation of president's national monument designations
-    Approve GOP plan to provide prescription drug coverage for Medicare beneficiaries
Yes Increase help for poor nations indebted to international financial institutions

1999
Yes Impose steel import quotas
No   Kill proposal to take aviation trust funds off budget
No   Require background checks on buyers only at gun shows with 10 or more vendors
No   Remove barriers among banking, securities and insurance companies
Yes Authorize state grants to hire teachers and reduce class size
Yes Overhaul campaign finance law; ban "soft money" and restrict advocacy advertising
Yes Approve bipartisan plan to increase rights of patients in managed-care health plans

INTEREST GROUPS

	AFL-CIO	ADA	CCUS	ACU
2000	100%	95%	27%	0%
1999	89%	100%	20%	0%
1998	100%	100%	22%	4%
1997	100%	95%	30%	8%

CQ VOTE STUDIES

	PARTY UNITY		PRESIDENTIAL SUPPORT	
	Support	Oppose	Support	Oppose
2000	99%	1%	88%	12%
1999	98%	2%	85%	15%
1998	97%	3%	85%	15%
1997	95%	5%	76%	24%

CALIFORNIA 50
Central and south San Diego; Chula Vista; National City

Known as the most ethnically diverse of the San Diego area districts, the 50th is drastically different from the districts that surround it. It has a large Hispanic population and is one of six California districts where no single ethnic group has a majority. While the large minority population and the large number of working-class and low-income residents put the 50th in the Democratic camp, a sizable military and veteran population has produced a more even party split in the booming residential suburb of Chula Vista.

The northern part of the district, just south of San Diego's downtown, houses the worst of the city's urban problems. It is built up with rows of two-story apartment complexes, and while certain parts are being gentrified by "urban pioneers," much of the area is downtrodden.

The 50th has been largely left out of the rapid growth around it, and

small businesses have been hit hard by NAFTA. In an area where unemployment is high and most jobs are located outside the district, the loss of General Dynamics in the neighboring 49th District devastated the economy.

While much of the district is either stagnant or built out, there is some room for expansion in the industrial Otay Mesa area south of Chula Vista. Economic development activities are under way in San Diego's Mid City area and parts of National City.

MAJOR INDUSTRY
Retail, manufacturing, service

CITIES
San Diego (pt.), 360,331 (1990); Chula Vista, 164,914; National City, 55,284

UNUSUAL FEATURES
San Diego-Tijuana border crossing at San Ysidro is the world's busiest; Otay Mesa known as the television capital of the world for its consumer electronics manufacturing.

Rep. Randy 'Duke' Cunningham (R)

Elected 1990; 6th term

CAPITOL OFFICE
225-5452; fax 225-2558; 2350 Rayburn Bldg. 20515

INTERNET
web: www.house.gov/cunningham

COMMITTEES
Appropriations
Select Intelligence

HOMETOWN
San Diego

BORN
Dec. 8, 1941, Los Angeles, Calif.

RELIGION
Christian

FAMILY
Wife, Nancy Cunningham; three children

EDUCATION
U. of Missouri, B.A. 1964, M.A. 1965; National U., M.B.A. 1985

MILITARY SERVICE
Navy, 1966-87

CAREER
Computer software executive; Navy pilot and instructor; teacher and coach

POLITICAL HIGHLIGHTS
No previous office

ELECTION RESULTS

2000 GENERAL

Randy "Duke" Cunningham (R)	172,291	64.3%
George "Jorge" Barraza (D)	81,408	30.4%
Daniel L. Muhe (LIBERT)	7,159	2.7%
Eric Hunter Bourdette (NL)	6,941	2.6%

2000 PRIMARY (OPEN)

Randy "Duke" Cunningham (R)	126,038	67.7%
George "Jorge" Barraza (D)	50,245	27.0%
Daniel L. Muhe (LIBERT)	5,103	2.7%
Eric Hunter Bourdette (NL)	4,858	2.6%

1998 GENERAL

Randy "Duke" Cunningham (R)	126,229	61.0%
Dan Kripke (D)	71,706	34.7%
J. C. "Jack" Anderson (LIBERT)	5,411	2.6%
Eric Hunter Bourdette (NL)	3,532	1.7%

PREVIOUS WINNING PERCENTAGES
1996 (65%); 1994 (67%); 1992 (56%); 1990 (46%)

A "Top Gun" flight instructor during his 20-year Navy career, Cunningham is a hard-charging conservative whose blunt talk in Congress has gotten him into more than a few scrapes with Democrats, independents and administration officials.

Cunningham has a gruff demeanor and disdain for "politically correct" views, all part of his "man of action" image. He has said that "my passions are national security and education," and most of his verbal outbursts have been directed at those who disagree with him on those matters.

Loyal to the Republican leadership and committed to conservative causes, Cunningham landed a seat on the Appropriations Committee in the 105th Congress, his fourth term. As a member of the Defense Subcommittee, he strongly supports GOP efforts to hike military spending while deriding President Clinton in personal terms for avoiding military service when he was younger. "Too many of our defenses are still underfunded, overstretched and on the verge of collapse," he said in 1999. In the 107th Congress, he also got a seat on the Intelligence Committee.

Cunningham has used his experience to successfully advance military spending. In 1998, he test-flew the latest version of the F-18 Navy fighter that had faced some criticism and declared it "head and shoulders above other aircraft I've tested and flown." He also focuses on projects sought by San Diego manufacturers, winning hundreds of millions of dollars in funding in the fiscal 2000 budget for advanced sea-lift and cargo ships. But he reluctantly agreed in the 106th to delay production of the troubled F-22 stealth fighter, parts of which were to have been manufactured in San Diego.

After prostate cancer surgery in 1998, Cunningham has urged his colleagues to boost prostate cancer research funding. He told constituents that the fear he felt when he was diagnosed was like his fear when he was shot down in Vietnam. "You just can't believe it's happening. It's, 'Oh, my God, what is the rest of my life going to be like?'" he told The San Diego Union-Tribune.

But the experience did not seem to make him less caustic. On several occasions he has made disparaging remarks about homosexuals. During 1995 House debate on a clean water bill, Cunningham assailed an amendment that would have regulated discharges from naval nuclear propulsion facilities as pollution. He said it was supported by "the same people that would vote to cut defense $177 billion, the same ones that would put homos in the military."

When independent Rep. Bernard Sanders of Vermont demanded that Cunningham yield for a response, Cunningham said, "No, I will not. Sit down, you socialist." Cunningham half-heartedly apologized for the "homos" reference: "I used the shorthand term, and it should have been homosexuals instead of homos. We do misspeak sometimes."

He has also chided the Pentagon for what he terms its "politically correct" moves to combat sexual harassment and discrimination in the military.

Despite his aggressive talk, Cunningham has an emotional side. He appeared to fight back tears in 1999 when urging his colleagues to support a constitutional amendment outlawing flag desecration. "This is not a matter of freedom of speech. There is free speech," he said. "There is nothing in this amendment that prevents someone from speaking or writing or doing any of the other things, but just the radical burning of the symbol that we hold dear."

Cunningham also is passionate about education initiatives. A former chairman of an Economic and Educational Opportunities subcommittee, he presses for more local authority over spending federal dollars. Cunningham, whose wife is a school administrator and former principal in the San Diego area, argues that billions of dollars in government spending on education are wasted by federal bureaucrats and never make it down to the "zip code," where he says teachers and administrators can use the money wisely. He is proud of his legislation, signed into law in 1997, that provides a tax deduction for corporations that donate computers to schools.

In the 105th, Cunningham was a prime advocate of legislation to implement an international agreement to protect dolphins from inadvertent catch by tuna fishermen. The "dolphin-safe" bill, which did not have universal approval from environmental groups, was important to the San Diego tuna fishing industry because fishermen could then use more efficient methods.

It irks Cunningham that Californians must foot a bigger tax bill for such services as health care, schools and law enforcement in part because of illegal immigration. In 1996, he hailed as "a victory for San Diegans" an immigration bill that increased border patrols and denied certain federal benefits to immigrants. Cunningham calls English a "unifying force" in America and favors making English the official language of the U.S. government.

A member of the Congressional Sportsmen's Caucus (which goes on hunting trips and other outdoor ventures), Cunningham has pushed bills to make military recreation areas accessible to disabled veterans and to require a federal agency to justify actions that significantly diminish fishing and hunting on federal land.

Cunningham began his career as an Illinois high school teacher and swim coach, training two athletes to Olympic medals. He joined the Navy at the age of 25 and became the first ace — a combat pilot who shoots down five enemy planes — in the Vietnam War, winning a barrel of medals, including the Navy Cross, and narrowly avoiding capture after his F-4 fighter was shot down over North Vietnam. He returned to the United States to train pilots at Miramar Naval Air Station just north of San Diego.

After he left the military for a business career, his background caught the eye of GOP Rep. Duncan Hunter, who represents an adjoining district. Cunningham agreed to leave his beach home in exclusive Del Mar and move to the older, middle-class suburb of Chula Vista to challenge Democratic Rep. Jim Bates in 1990 in the old 44th District. Targeting evangelical Christians and conservative Democrats to supplement the small GOP vote, Cunningham eked out a narrow victory. Since redistricting in 1992, he has run from the solidly Republican 51st and has been re-elected by comfortable margins.

KEY VOTES

2000
No Raise hourly minimum wage by $1 over two years
Yes Halt funding for U.S. mission in Kosovo unless European nations pay more
Yes Provide Medicare benefits to military retirees and their dependents
Yes Grant China permanent normal trade status
? Phase out estate, gift and trust taxes
Yes Prohibit implementation of president's national monument designations
Yes Approve GOP plan to provide prescription drug coverage for Medicare beneficiaries
No Increase help for poor nations indebted to international financial institutions

1999
No Impose steel import quotas
Yes Kill proposal to take aviation trust funds off budget
Yes Require background checks on buyers only at gun shows with 10 or more vendors
Yes Remove barriers among banking, securities and insurance companies
No Authorize state grants to hire teachers and reduce class size
No Overhaul campaign finance law; ban "soft money" and restrict advocacy advertising
No Approve bipartisan plan to increase rights of patients in managed-care health plans

INTEREST GROUPS

	AFL-CIO	ADA	CCUS	ACU
2000	0%	5%	95%	92%
1999	0%	10%	92%	88%
1998	0%	0%	100%	100%
1997	0%	0%	100%	92%

CQ VOTE STUDIES

	PARTY UNITY		PRESIDENTIAL SUPPORT	
	Support	Oppose	Support	Oppose
2000	94%	6%	26%	74%
1999	95%	5%	20%	80%
1998	93%	7%	25%	75%
1997	96%	4%	28%	72%

CALIFORNIA 51
San Diego area – Northern county suburbs

With its beautiful beach communities and upper-middle-class suburbs, the 51st is a steadily growing GOP stronghold. Registered Republicans outnumber Democrats by almost 20 percent. More liberal-leaning voters dominate the coast, where beach replenishment and the environment are issues in upscale Del Mar and Encinitas and less affluent Carlsbad.

The 51st's conservative corridor, along Interstate 15, includes the Marine base in Miramar, which until 1996 was home to the Navy's famed "Top Gun" fighter school. As part of downsizing, the Naval Air Station moved to Nevada, and Marines from the closing El Toro and Tustin bases (in the 46th and 47th districts) have been moving to Miramar.

Heading north up Interstate 15 is Poway, an independent city surrounded by San Diego. Poway has more of a rural feel to it than the surrounding suburban sprawl. Just north of Poway is an

expanse of evenly developed suburbs that includes Rancho Bernardo, an area within San Diego's city limits that has attracted many retirees. In the 51st's piece of San Diego, the growing presence of cellular technology companies has contributed to its image as a mini-Silicon Valley.

MAJOR INDUSTRY
High-tech, defense, manufacturing

MILITARY BASES
Marine Corps Air Station Miramar, 10,000 military, 1,500 civilian (2000)

CITIES
San Diego (pt.), 204,554 (1990); Escondido, 122,544; Encinitas, 61,263; Poway, 50,075; Carlsbad (pt.), 48,833

UNUSUAL FEATURES
Del Mar Race Track; Carlsbad grows and distributes most of the West Coast's fresh-cut flowers and is home to several major golf club manufacturers; Rancho Santa Fe, former home of the Heaven's Gate cult, which committed mass suicide in 1997.

Rep. Duncan Hunter (R)

Elected 1980; 11th term

CAPITOL OFFICE
225-5672; fax 225-0235; 2265 Rayburn Bldg. 20515

INTERNET
e-mail: www.house.gov/writerep
web: www.house.gov/hunter

COMMITTEES
Armed Services
(Military Research & Development - chairman;
Merchant Marine panel - chairman)

HOMETOWN
El Cajon

BORN
May 31, 1948, Riverside, Calif.

RELIGION
Baptist

FAMILY
Wife, Lynne Hunter; two children

EDUCATION
U. of Montana, attended 1966-67; U. of California,
Santa Barbara, attended 1967-68; Western State
U., B.S.L. 1976, J.D. 1976

MILITARY SERVICE
Army, 1969-71

CAREER
Lawyer

POLITICAL HIGHLIGHTS
No previous office

ELECTION RESULTS

2000 GENERAL

Duncan Hunter (R)	131,345	64.7%
Craig B. Barkacs (D)	63,537	31.3%
Michael Benoit (LIBERT)	5,995	3.0%
Robert Sherman (NL)	2,117	1.0%

2000 PRIMARY (OPEN)

Duncan Hunter (R)	103,667	70.9%
Craig B. Barkacs (D)	36,715	25.1%
Michael Benoit (LIBERT)	4,408	3.0%

1998 GENERAL

Duncan Hunter (R)	116,251	75.7%
Lynn Badler (LIBERT)	21,933	14.3%
Adrienne Pelton (NL)	15,380	10.0%

PREVIOUS WINNING PERCENTAGES
1996 (66%); 1994 (64%); 1992 (53%); 1990 (73%);
1988 (74%); 1986 (77%); 1984 (75%); 1982 (69%);
1980 (53%)

A decorated Vietnam War veteran representing an area with a large military presence, Hunter is the embodiment of a defense hawk. He takes a blunt, no-holds-barred approach to seeking more money for the Pentagon, telling Navy officials in 2000: "We've gotten almost to the point where you gentlemen need to be pounding the tables with your leadership and with the commander in chief, and I think we in Congress should be doing exactly the same thing."

A steadfast supporter of President Reagan's military buildup in the 1980s, Hunter regularly was among the harshest critics of President Clinton's defense budgets and voted against the 1997 balanced-budget agreement, saying it contained too little defense money. His views should gain more currency as President Bush's administration seeks to shore up the armed forces' readiness for combat and to modernize weapons systems.

Hunter has been on the Armed Services Committee since he joined the House in 1981, and now, still at a relatively young age, he is one of the panel's most influential members. At the start of the 107th Congress, he sought to chair the committee, but emphasized he would do so only if the more-senior Bob Stump of Arizona was rejected for some reason. Stump eventually got the chairmanship, and Hunter settled for chairing the Military Research and Development Subcommittee. (He had been forced to give up his chairmanship of the Procurement Subcommittee because of GOP-imposed term limits on committee chairmanships.)

On broader national matters — including fiscal and social issues — Hunter casts a reliably conservative vote. A leader of the Conservative Opportunity Society, founded by Newt Gingrich in the early 1980s, Hunter was elected chairman of the House Republican Research Committee in 1989, the same year Gingrich became minority whip. In voting to do away with the National Endowment for the Arts, Hunter once lamented that federal arts money had been handed over to "aging hippies ... to desecrate the crucifix."

Hunter's chance at a leadership spot came in 1994 when he ran for chairman of the Republican Conference. He lost, 102-122, to Ohio Republican John A. Boehner, who came to Congress 10 years after Hunter. Boehner had established himself as a leader of junior Republicans when he spearheaded an effort to force Democrats to disclose the names of those with overdrafts at the unofficial bank for House members. One of them was Hunter, with 399 overdrafts.

On trade matters, Hunter holds isolationist views similar to those of political commentator and perennial presidential candidate Patrick Buchanan. When the House voted in 2000 to grant China permanent normal trade status, Hunter led a band of Republicans who warned that the vote would help Beijing rebuild its military to threaten the United States. "If the cemeteries of this country one day hold the bodies of Americans in uniform killed with weapons purchased by American trade dollars, that will be the greatest tragedy of this new 21st century," he said.

Hunter also opposed the 1993 North American Free Trade Agreement and aid to Mexico after the devaluation of the peso in 1994. He has actively worked to upgrade fences along the U.S.-Mexico border and to hire more Border Patrol agents to reduce the flow of illegal immigrants from that country.

His positions have prompted some San Diego business executives to question whether he is attuned to the needs of the area's growing economy, which has expanded beyond defense into high technology and telecommunications and is seeking greater cooperation with the Mexican government. Some of those executives began supporting Hunter's Democratic opponent in the 2000 election, Craig Barkacs, a local attorney and college business professor who told The San Diego Union-Tribune that he found Hunter's views on Mexico "offensive."

Hunter, however, said his support for strengthening the border and opposing increased trade with Mexico has not hurt his relations with that country. He pointed to his work in delivering more than $700,000 worth of food and medical equipment to Mexico. "I don't think you have to agree with their trade agreement to have a good relationship with a country," he told the Union-Tribune.

Hunter overwhelmingly outspent Barkacs, who had trouble getting name recognition; the Union-Tribune even referred to him in a headline as "what's-his-name." Hunter ended up winning easily.

For the three years before his initial House campaign in the late 1970s, Hunter lived and worked in the Hispanic section of San Diego. Running his own storefront law office, he often gave free legal advice to poor people. Later, when President Reagan called for abolition of the Legal Services Corporation, Hunter was one of the dissenters.

Hunter's work in the usually Democratic inner city and his tireless campaigning helped produce his 1980 upset victory over Democrat Lionel Van Deerlin, a nine-term House veteran. Hunter, who won a Bronze Star for participating in 25 helicopter combat assaults in Vietnam, blasted away at what he called Van Deerlin's "anti-defense" record. He promised that his pro-Pentagon stance would keep jobs in the San Diego area, which boasts the nation's largest naval base and numerous defense industries. The message helped propel Hunter to a 53 percent majority.

Before Democrats had a chance to prove that win a fluke, the redistricting plan for 1982 gave Hunter a safely Republican seat. He won re-election with 69 percent that year and did better yet through the remainder of the decade.

Life got more complicated in 1992. Redistricting made Hunter move his home, but it left his base relatively intact. Hunter's real problems stemmed from his House bank overdrafts. Janet M. Gastil, a former school board member, kept Hunter on the defensive and held him to 53 percent. Gastil was back in 1994 but the timing was no longer right; Hunter outpolled her 2-to-1. Since then, he has coasted to re-election.

KEY VOTES

2000

No	Raise hourly minimum wage by $1 over two years
No	Halt funding for U.S. mission in Kosovo unless European nations pay more
Yes	Provide Medicare benefits to military retirees and their dependents
No	Grant China permanent normal trade status
Yes	Phase out estate, gift and trust taxes
Yes	Prohibit implementation of president's national monument designations
Yes	Approve GOP plan to provide prescription drug coverage for Medicare beneficiaries
No	Increase help for poor nations indebted to international financial institutions

1999

Yes	Impose steel import quotas
Yes	Kill proposal to take aviation trust funds off budget
Yes	Require background checks on buyers only at gun shows with 10 or more vendors
Yes	Remove barriers among banking, securities and insurance companies
No	Authorize state grants to hire teachers and reduce class size
No	Overhaul campaign finance law; ban "soft money" and restrict advocacy advertising
Yes	Approve bipartisan plan to increase rights of patients in managed-care health plans

INTEREST GROUPS

	AFL-CIO	ADA	CCUS	ACU
2000	10%	10%	71%	76%
1999	44%	15%	70%	84%
1998	11%	5%	71%	100%
1997	0%	0%	80%	88%

CQ VOTE STUDIES

	PARTY UNITY		PRESIDENTIAL SUPPORT	
	Support	Oppose	Support	Oppose
2000	94%	6%	19%	81%
1999	91%	9%	21%	79%
1998	93%	7%	20%	80%
1997	96%	4%	25%	75%

CALIFORNIA 52
Inland San Diego and Imperial counties

The 52nd is located in the state's far southeastern corner, which borders Mexico and Arizona. It includes agricultural Imperial County and about half of suburban San Diego County, about 10 miles east of San Diego. The population includes a mix of blue- and white-collar employees who vote predominantly Republican. San Diego's large military and defense-related workforce also contributes to the district's conservative personality.

The bulk of the district's San Diego County residents are in three suburban cities on the western edge of the 52nd: El Cajon, the largest of the three, La Mesa and Spring Valley. Economically, La Mesa is a bit better off than the other two, and votes a bit more Democratic, though heavily Republican San Diego continues to make the 52nd a GOP stronghold.

Border issues, particularly illegal immigration, drugs and wastewater treatment, are key with constituents. In the district's agricultural area,

east of El Centro, irrigation is an issue for wheat growers and other farmers, who produce nearly $1 billion in crops annually and depend on the Colorado River. San Diego imports about 90 percent of its water.

After years of slow economic growth, the late 1990s marked a turnaround, particularly in the city of El Cajon, where property values and home sales rose dramatically. Three casinos also have helped some of the 52nd's dozen Indian reservations.

MAJOR INDUSTRY
Technology, manufacturing, agriculture

MILITARY BASES
El Centro Naval Air Facility, 318 military, 198 civilian (2000)

CITIES
El Cajon, 94,578; Santee, 57,915; La Mesa (pt.), 52,893 (1990); Spring Valley (pt.), 51,197 (1990)

UNUSUAL FEATURES
Salton Sea, state's largest man-made body of water (shared with 44th); Glamis Sand Dunes.

COLORADO

Gov. Bill Owens (R)

First elected: 1998
Length of term: 4 years
Term expires: 1/03
Salary: $90,000
Phone: (303) 866-2471
Hometown: Denver
Born: Oct. 22, 1950, Fort Worth, Texas
Religion: Roman Catholic
Family: Wife, Frances Owens; three children
Education: Stephen F. Austin State U., B.S. 1973; U. of Texas, M.P.A. 1975
Career: Management consultant; petroleum association director
Political highlights: Colo. House, 1983-89; Colo. Senate, 1989-95; Colo. treasurer, 1995-99

Election results:

1998 GENERAL
Bill Owens (R)	648,202	49.1%
Gail Schoettler (D)	639,905	48.4%
Sandra D. Johnson (LIBERT)	22,202	1.7%

Lt. Gov. Joe Rogers (R)

First elected: 1998
Length of term: 4 years
Term expires: 1/03
Salary: $68,500
Phone: (303) 866-2087

STATE LEGISLATURE

General Assembly: Meets 120 days, January-May
House: 65 members, 2-year terms
2001 breakdown: 38R, 27D; 43 men, 22 women
Salary: $30,000
Phone: (303) 866-2904
Senate: 35 members, 4-year terms
2001 breakdown: 17R, 18D; 24 men, 11 women
Salary: $30,000
Phone: (303) 866-2316

STATE TERM LIMITS

Governor: 2 terms
Senate: 2 consecutive terms
House: 4 consecutive terms

URBAN STATISTICS

CITY	POPULATION
Denver	499,775
Colorado Springs	350,199
Aurora	252,956
Lakewood	137,916
Fort Collins	113,432

REGISTERED VOTERS

Republican	36%
Unaffiliated	34%
Democrat	30%

POPULATION

2000 population	4,301,261
1990 population	3,294,394
Percent change	+30.6%
Rank among states	24

Median age	35.3
Born in state	43%
Foreign born	4%
Urban/rural	82%/18%
Crime rate	363/100,000
Poverty level	9.2%
Federal workers	53,973
Military	42,580

REAPPORTIONMENT

Colorado gained one House seat in reapportionment, increasing from six districts to seven. The state legislature will draw new district lines.

MISCELLANEOUS

Web: www.state.co.us
Capital: Denver
Land area: 103,729 sq. miles
Rank among states: 8
STATE ELECTION OFFICIAL
(303) 894-2680
DEMOCRATIC HEADQUARTERS
(303) 830-8989
REPUBLICAN HEADQUARTERS
(303) 758-3333

District Statistics

DIST.	2000 D	2000 R	GREEN	1996 D	1996 R	REF	1992 D	1992 R	I	WHT	BLK	ASIAN	HISP	HOUSEHOLD INCOME	OVER 65+	UNDER 18	COLLEGE EDUCATION
1	61%	32%	6%	61%	31%	5%	56%	26%	18%	73%	13%	2%	22%	$24,870	13%	23%	27%
2	48	42	8	49	40	6	45	30	24	93	1	2	9	$35,117	8	26	29
3	39	53	6	43	45	9	40	35	25	92	1	0	17	$24,521	13	26	20
4	37	56	5	41	49	7	37	38	25	91	1	1	15	$26,577	11	28	21
5	32	63	3	33	59	6	28	50	23	89	6	2	7	$33,348	7	28	30
6	44	51	4	43	49	6	37	38	25	92	3	2	6	$37,333	8	26	33
STATE	42	51	5	46	44	7	40	36	23	88	4	2	13	$30,140	10	26	27

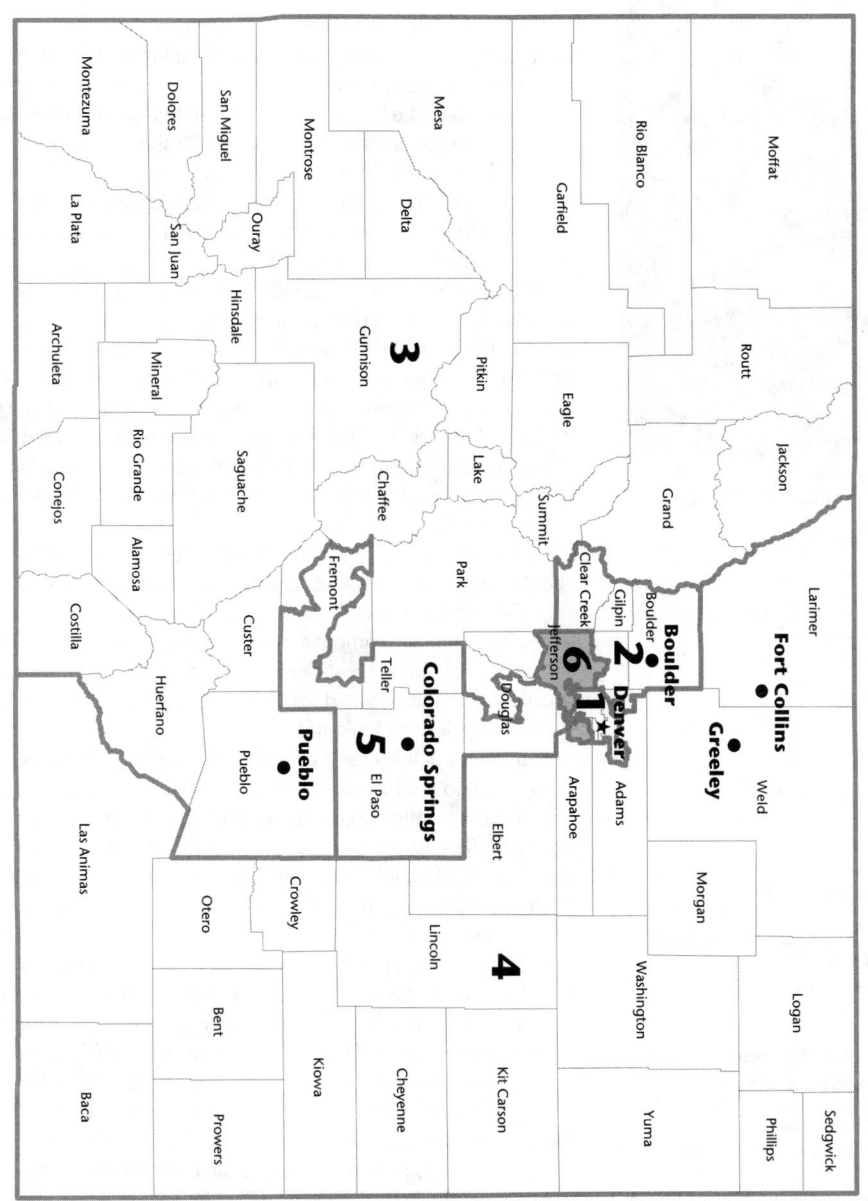

Sen. Ben Nighthorse Campbell (R)

Elected 1992; 2nd term

CAPITOL OFFICE
224-5852; fax 224-1933; 380 Russell Bldg. 20510

INTERNET
web: campbell.senate.gov

COMMITTEES
Appropriations
   (Treasury & General Government - chairman)
Energy & Natural Resources
Environment & Public Works
Indian Affairs - chairman
Veterans' Affairs

HOMETOWN
Ignacio

BORN
April 13, 1933, Auburn, Calif.

RELIGION
Unspecified

FAMILY
Wife, Linda Campbell; two children

EDUCATION
San Jose State U., B.A. 1957; Meiji U. (Tokyo, Japan), attended 1960-64

MILITARY SERVICE
Air Force, 1951-53

CAREER
Jewelry designer; rancher; horse trainer; teacher

POLITICAL HIGHLIGHTS
Colo. House, 1983-87 (served as a Democrat); U.S. House, 1987-93 (served as a Democrat)

ELECTION RESULTS

1998 GENERAL
Ben Nighthorse Campbell (R)	829,370	62.5%
Dottie Lamm (D)	464,754	35.0%
David S. Segal (LIBERT)	14,024	1.1%

1998 PRIMARY
Ben Nighthorse Campbell (R)	154,702	70.6%
William Eggert (R)	64,347	29.4%

PREVIOUS WINNING PERCENTAGES
1992 (52%); 1990 House Election (70%); 1988 House Election (78%); 1986 House Election (52%)
*Elected as a Democrat 1986-92

There have been and always will be senators with a particular style, and then there is Campbell. A motorcycle-riding cattle rancher, Campbell designs and makes his own Southwestern jewelry. His ponytail, jeans and cowboy boots make him instantly recognizable on the Senate floor — while his unusual style earned him a spot on Washingtonian magazine's worst-dressed list in the 106th Congress.

"I don't see why, just 'cause you get elected, you have to drop your whole lifestyle and suddenly buy into this Potomac look," Campbell told The Denver Post in 2000. "To heck with it."

The Senate's lone American Indian, Campbell at times seems to view the formal atmosphere of the Senate with some disdain. A former judo champion, he works out at a Washington gym used by law enforcement officials rather than the Senate health club, remarking to the Denver Rocky Mountain News that "too many overweight guys sitting around in a sauna is not my idea of a workout." He renewed his commercial truck driver's license in 1999 because "I enjoy meeting people who do this for a living." In 2000, he helped drive an 18-wheeler containing the Capitol Christmas tree from Colorado to Washington, D.C.

He told the Rocky Mountain News in 1995 that he had mixed feelings about being in Congress, adding that if any senators talk about liking the job, "they're damn liars." The day after winning re-election in 1998, he pulled on his biker leathers for a long-distance motorcycle trip instead of engaging in traditional post-election analysis. "Ben said the first staff person to call him dies," said Stuart Roy, his campaign manager. "He just loaded up the motorcycles and took off."

Campbell's politics have drifted to the right since his switch from the Democratic to the Republican Party in 1995, and he backs such conservative causes as cutting taxes and regulations and barring desecration of the American flag. An advocate of gun owners' rights, he announced after a shooting at Colorado's Columbine High School in 1999 that he intended to rejoin the National Rifle Association to protest congressional attempts to restrict gun ownership.

But he is hardly in lock step with Senate conservatives. Instead, he tends to look out for the interests of his home state as well as for American Indians.

In the 106th Congress, Campbell, a member of the Northern Cheyenne tribe, won enactment of legislation creating a national historic site at Sand Creek in Colorado, where more than 150 Cheyennes and Arapahos were massacred in 1864. He also focused on other American Indian priorities, such as improving health care for Indians, establishing an office within the Department of Agriculture to help Indians market products overseas, and streamlining the federal system under which Indians bequeath land to their heirs. "If we are serious about [Indian] self-determination, then we have to roll back arcane laws and put tribes in a position where they can compete for jobs and investment," he said.

Campbell scored a win for environmentalists with legislation designating Colorado's Black Canyon of the Gunnison as a national park. But he has clashed with the environmental community more often than not, opposing President Clinton's plans during the 106th to restrict development on federal lands and assailing a bipartisan proposal to spend billions of dollars to preserve open space, saying it "reeks of socialism." His conservative views and support for private property rights helped make him a leading candidate in late 2000 for secretary of interior in the Bush administration, but the job ultimately went to another Coloradan, Gale A. Norton.

As a member of the Appropriations Committee, Campbell has snagged tens of millions of dollars in federal funding for Colorado programs ranging from anti-drug initiatives to military base projects. His appointment to the Environment and Public Works panel in the 107th Congress should help him gain federal money for transportation projects as well as for his state.

The Coloradan is not shy about reminding his colleagues of his heritage when fighting for a share of the federal pie. In 1997, he defended a $6 million appropriation for the controversial Animas-La Plata water project in Southwestern Colorado, despite opposition from fiscal conservatives worried about wasting money and environmentalists concerned about ecological damage. The project was backed by the Ute Indians, who saw it as the fulfillment of a century-old government promise to ensure water supplies to the Southern Ute Reservation.

In a powerful floor speech, Campbell said: "We do not intentionally kill Indians with bullets or disease anymore. But it seems clear that some of our brothers want to kill their livelihood, kill their opportunity, kill their future, kill their culture and kill the natural resources that we promised them in every one of the 472 treaties that we then broke as an arm of the U.S. government."

But true to his general doubts about government, Campbell wants to encourage Indians to gradually wean themselves of their reliance on the federal government. "The movement has been toward self-determination, but it was limited self-determination," Campbell told The Washington Post. "If they could handle it, they could do it. That's the kind of thing I support."

Campbell had a moment in the national limelight when he announced his decision to join the GOP in March 1995, shortly after Republicans took over Congress. His statement came the day after he voted for a balanced-budget constitutional amendment that failed to win Senate passage; he decided he no longer was comfortable calling himself a Democrat.

The switch infuriated Democrats. But on announcing his new party affiliation, Campbell underscored that he would continue on an independent course. "I have always been considered a moderate, much to the consternation of the Democratic Party," Campbell said. "My moderacy will now be to the consternation of the right wing of the Republican Party."

Raised by an alcoholic father and a mother with tuberculosis, Campbell was a high-school dropout and a gang member before turning his life around. He served in the Air Force, worked his way through college driving a truck, and then found success as an Olympian — he was on the U.S. judo team at the 1964 Games.

Campbell began his political career in 1982, winning a state House seat and amassing a record as a conservative Democrat. He prevailed over GOP Rep. Mike Strang in 1986, saying: "People are sick and tired of plastic politicians — professional politicians who have done nothing else with their lives." Campbell easily won re-election to the House twice before making his move for the Senate.

In 1992, he won his Senate seat by 9 points over GOP businessman and former state Sen. Terry Considine, even though Campbell had to correct a statement in his campaign literature that said he had been trapped behind enemy lines in Korea for five weeks. He acknowledged that such an incident never happened while he served in Korea with the Air Force police.

Publicly ambivalent about staying in the Senate, Campbell in 1997 delayed an announcement of his re-election bid for months — and then faced opposition in both parties. But he confounded his critics by appealing to the individualistic leanings of the Colorado electorate and swamped challengers from both the right and the left.

KEY VOTES

2000

Yes   Overhaul bankruptcy law and increase minimum wage

Yes   Limit fiscal 2001 discretionary spending to $600.3 billion

No   Override veto on nuclear waste disposal at Yucca Mountain site in Nevada

No   Oppose effort to terminate Kosovo mission

No   Include gender, sexual orientation and disability in federal hate crime protections

Yes   Approve GOP plan to restrict use of genetic information by health insurers

Yes   Kill amendment delaying implementation of an anti-missile defense system

Yes   Cut taxes for married couples

No   Grant China permanent normal trade status

1999

Yes   Remove President Clinton from office for obstruction of justice

Yes   Kill amendment authorizing state grants to hire teachers and reduce class size

No   Require criminal background checks for purchases at gun shows

Yes   Approve GOP proposal to increase rights of patients in managed-care health plans

No   Block effort to allow farm and medicine exports to Cuba

No   Allow study of tougher automobile fuel efficiency standards

No   Ratify nuclear weapons testing treaty

No   Prohibit national political parties from collecting "soft money" donations

Yes   Remove barriers among banking, securities and insurance companies

INTEREST GROUPS

	AFL-CIO	ADA	CCUS	ACU
2000	14%	5%	84%	96%
1999	22%	15%	94%	88%
1998	38%	25%	83%	76%
1997	29%	25%	60%	72%
1996	80%	45%	82%	78%
1995	22%	30%	94%	59%
1994	88%	55%	50%	25%
1993	80%	75%	18%	12%
House Service:				
1992	71%	55%	43%	38%
1991	92%	55%	40%	45%

CQ VOTE STUDIES

	PARTY UNITY		PRESIDENTIAL SUPPORT	
	Support	Oppose	Support	Oppose
2000	97%	3%	50%	50%
1999	88%	12%	32%	68%
1998	82%	18%	47%	53%
1997	83%	17%	66%	34%
1996	82%	18%	48%	52%
1995	80%	20%	38%	62%
1994	78%	22%	83%	17%
1993	80%	20%	83%	17%
House Service:				
1992	79%	21%	37%	63%
1991	78%	22%	38%	62%

Sen. Wayne Allard (R)

Elected 1996; 1st term

A stalwart conservative who tends to stay in the background, Allard focuses on defense and housing issues while weighing in on Western land conservation plans. He's a strong believer in states' rights and reducing the federal debt, and his anti-tax and anti-regulatory views put him solidly in step with his Western constituents.

A fifth-generation Coloradan raised on a ranch in one of the state's most isolated areas, Allard (AL-ard) is an amiable man with a plodding speaking style whose resolve often is underestimated by his political foes.

He began the 106th Congress on a strong note, winning appointments to chair two subcommittees. As a new member of the Armed Services Committee and newly appointed chairman of the panel's Personnel Subcommittee, Allard had an opportunity to score points with Colorado's large military community. But in keeping with his laid-back legislative approach, his first official action in his new position was to pass up an opportunity to consider a plan to boost military pay and retirement benefits, which he supported. He ceded his authority to the full committee, which approved the bill in January 1999. He explained, "I felt it would only delay the process [to hold] a subcommittee hearing on the bill."

At the end of 1999, Allard gave up the Personnel chairmanship to take over the gavel of Armed Services' Strategic Forces Subcommittee, which oversees ballistic missile programs and nuclear policies, as well as the North American Aerospace Defense Command in Colorado Springs. The senator strongly supports creating an anti-missile defense system. He downplayed the failure of a test missile launch in 2000, saying, "To ultimately achieve success, one must expect some failure."

Allard also chairs Banking's Housing and Transportation Subcommittee. At the end of the 106th, he floated a plan to scale back significantly the Department of Housing and Urban Development (HUD), transferring funds for housing and homeless programs to individual states while putting the agency more tightly under the control of Congress. Although his proposal drew a cool response from the administration, it was in keeping with the senator's philosophy that states, rather than the federal government, should take the lead on many government programs. "The one-size-fits-all approach that HUD currently uses no longer works," he said.

For Allard, a top priority is to pay down the national debt. He touts his own frugality as a lawmaker, saying he has returned more than $2 million in unspent office funds to the Treasury during his congressional tenure. But his plan to eliminate the national debt over two decades by using large amounts of the budget surplus for debt repayment was soundly defeated in the Senate in the 106th. Some fellow Republicans faulted the measure for diverting money from tax cuts. But Allard, who likened the approach to making a regular mortgage payment, indicated he would continue pursuing the plan, and he won a seat on the Budget Committee in the 107th Congress to advance his proposal.

On fiscal issues, Allard usually sides with the most-conservative members of his party. In 1998, he voted against a half-trillion-dollar appropriations bill that had been negotiated by the White House and top lawmakers of both parties, because he felt it spent too much money. He hews to the right on other issues as well. In the 105th Congress, he killed a provision in a banking bill that would have required banks to establish low-cost accounts for low-income people.

CAPITOL OFFICE
224-5941; fax 224-6471; 525 Dirksen Bldg. 20510

INTERNET
e-mail: www.senate.gov/~allard/webform.html
web: allard.senate.gov

COMMITTEES
Agriculture, Nutrition & Forestry
Armed Services
 (Strategic Forces - chairman)
Banking, Housing & Urban Affairs
 (Housing & Transportation - chairman)
Budget

HOMETOWN
Loveland

BORN
Dec. 2, 1943, Fort Collins, Colo.

RELIGION
Protestant

FAMILY
Wife, Joan Malcolm; two children

EDUCATION
Colorado State U., D.V.M. 1968

CAREER
Veterinarian

POLITICAL HIGHLIGHTS
Colo. Senate, 1983-91; U.S. House, 1991-97

ELECTION RESULTS

1996 GENERAL

Wayne Allard (R)	750,325	51.1%
Tom Strickland (D)	677,600	46.1%
Randy MacKenzie (NL)	41,620	2.8%

1996 PRIMARY

Wayne Allard (R)	115,064	56.8%
Gale A. Norton (R)	87,394	43.2%

PREVIOUS WINNING PERCENTAGES
1994 House Election (72%); 1992 House Election (58%); 1990 House Election (54%)

Like other Western Republicans, Allard is a staunch advocate of private property rights and a foe of environmental regulations. As a result, he earned a zero score for several years from the League of Conservation Voters. But in 2000, he agreed to a compromise with the Clinton administration on water rights in an effort to expand Great Sand Dunes National Monument in Colorado and upgrade its status to a national park. He also won praise from environmentalists for backing a permanent ban on commercial flights over Rocky Mountain National Park and for proposing that Rocky Flats, a former nuclear weapons facility outside Denver, be converted into a national wildlife refuge.

After the 1999 shootings at Columbine High School in Colorado, Allard joined other Republicans in criticizing the Clinton administration's advocacy of new gun control measures and arguing for vigorous enforcement of existing gun laws instead. He led a Republican task force that proposed toughening criminal penalties on youths who commit crimes with guns. He and other task force members also advocated a proposal to ask movie, music and computer game manufacturers to tone down the violence in their products.

Allard scored a triumph in the 105th Congress in the area of public transportation. He successfully negotiated a plan to divide a $250 million share of funding for fixed guideway modernization — including light rail — between 10 cities with established systems, such as New York, and a group of 34 cities with new transportation projects, including Denver.

In his three terms in the House, Allard also compiled a solidly conservative record. He advocated eliminating the departments of Education, Energy and Commerce; he spoke up for gun owners' rights; and he supported a constitutional amendment banning abortion under most circumstances. He also pushed to curb "unfunded mandates" — requirements handed down by the federal government without providing states the funds to meet them.

A member of the Resources Committee when he served in the House, Allard in 1994 and 1995 tried unsuccessfully to eliminate funding for the National Biological Survey, a field census intended to help scientists protect threatened species. He feared that the survey would expand the scope of the Endangered Species Act, and he objected to letting government officials prowl on private land.

In 1990, after eight years of dividing his time between the Colorado Senate and his Loveland veterinary practice, Allard seemed on the verge of retiring from politics. But when Republican Hank Brown, who was then representing the 4th District in the House, decided to run for the Senate, Allard successfully ran for Brown's seat and won re-election in 1992 and 1994.

Brown gave Allard another opening by retiring from the Senate after just one term. The August 1996 GOP primary became a showdown between Allard and state Attorney General Gale A. Norton. Norton had better statewide name recognition, but Allard had better fundraising.

Both touted their conservative views. Norton hoped to attract moderates with her support for abortion rights. Allard portrayed himself as a down-to-earth, common-sense lawmaker who kept his political career in perspective, maintaining his veterinary license even though he had sold his practice in the early 1990s. Allard easily won the primary. (Norton went on to become secretary of interior in 2001 under President Bush.)

Allard created a stir in the 1996 general election when, during a televised debate with Democratic nominee Tom Strickland, a Denver lawyer, he responded affirmatively to a hypothetical question about whether he would support public hanging to deter crime. Allard, who drew vigorous opposition from environmentalists but won strong support from conservative Christian groups, won by almost 5 percentage points.

KEY VOTES

2000
Yes Overhaul bankruptcy law and increase minimum wage
Yes Limit fiscal 2001 discretionary spending to $600.3 billion
Yes Override veto on nuclear waste disposal at Yucca Mountain site in Nevada
No Oppose effort to terminate Kosovo mission
No Include gender, sexual orientation and disability in federal hate crime protections
Yes Approve GOP plan to restrict use of genetic information by health insurers
Yes Kill amendment delaying implementation of an anti-missile defense system
Yes Cut taxes for married couples
Yes Grant China permanent normal trade status

1999
Yes Remove President Clinton from office for obstruction of justice
Yes Kill amendment authorizing state grants to hire teachers and reduce class size
No Require criminal background checks for purchases at gun shows
Yes Approve GOP proposal to increase rights of patients in managed-care health plans
No Block effort to allow farm and medicine exports to Cuba
No Allow study of tougher automobile fuel efficiency standards
No Ratify nuclear weapons testing treaty
No Prohibit national political parties from collecting "soft money" donations
Yes Remove barriers among banking, securities and insurance companies

INTEREST GROUPS

	AFL-CIO	ADA	CCUS	ACU
2000	0%	0%	93%	100%
1999	0%	0%	100%	95%
1998	0%	5%	83%	100%
1997	0%	0%	80%	100%
House Service:				
1996	9%	10%	100%	100%
1995	0%	0%	96%	88%
1994	0%	5%	83%	95%
1993	0%	15%	91%	96%
1992	10%	5%	75%	92%
1991	0%	0%	100%	95%

CQ VOTE STUDIES

	PARTY UNITY		PRESIDENTIAL SUPPORT	
	Support	Oppose	Support	Oppose
2000	98%	2%	35%	65%
1999	97%	3%	23%	77%
1998	97%	3%	28%	72%
1997	98%	2%	48%	52%
House Service:				
1996	94%	6%	36%	64%
1995	95%	5%	20%	80%
1994	97%	3%	40%	60%
1993	93%	7%	20%	80%
1992	96%	4%	85%	15%
1991	94%	6%	80%	20%

Rep. Diana DeGette (D)

CAPITOL OFFICE
225-4431; fax 225-5657
1530 Longworth Bldg. 20515

INTERNET
e-mail: degette@mail.house.gov
web: www.house.gov/degette

COMMITTEES
Energy & Commerce

HOMETOWN
Denver

BORN
July 29, 1957, Tachikawa, Japan

RELIGION
Presbyterian

FAMILY
Husband, Lino Lipinsky; two children

EDUCATION
Colorado College, B.A. 1979; New York U., J.D. 1982

CAREER
Lawyer

POLITICAL HIGHLIGHTS
Colo. House, 1993-96

ELECTION RESULTS

2000 GENERAL

Diana DeGette (D)	141,831	68.7%
Jesse L. Thomas (R)	56,291	27.3%
Richard Combs (LIBERT)	5,852	2.8%
Lyle L. Nasser (REF)	2,452	1.2%

2000 PRIMARY

Diana DeGette (D)	unopposed

1998 GENERAL

Diana DeGette (D)	116,628	66.9%
Nancy McClanahan (R)	52,452	30.1%
Richard Combs (LIBERT)	5,225	3.0%

PREVIOUS WINNING PERCENTAGES
1996 (57%)

Elected 1996; 3rd term

DeGette made an auspicious arrival on Capitol Hill in 1997, winning a much-sought-after appointment to the Commerce Committee and making her presence felt during that first term in debates on the budget, public housing, tobacco and abortion policy. In her second term, DeGette continued to be active on those issues, as well as on gun control and a wide range of health care topics, winning a few battles and occasionally catching the limelight as Democrats showcased an effective liberal spokeswoman.

DeGette (de-GET) posts a dependably liberal voting record, and the tone of her public statements is in the same vein, but she insists that she is ready to seek out bipartisan cooperation as circumstances warrant. "It's no secret I don't work well with the far right, but with moderate representatives and thoughtful legislators, I get along well," she told the Rocky Mountain News during the 1996 campaign.

DeGette, who has two young daughters, has devoted much of her attention to children's needs, determining that few other lawmakers were focusing on those issues or could bring to the task the personal perspective of a mother of young children.

In the 105th Congress, for example, she played a part in seeing that the budget package expanded coverage under Medicaid for about 3 million uninsured children. Also in the 105th she won approval of an amendment to a housing bill allowing local housing authorities to use their federal funds to provide child care services for public housing tenants.

In the 106th Congress, DeGette pushed for legislation in the Commerce Committee (now known as Energy and Commerce) to improve children's health insurance coverage through Medicare and the State Children's Health Insurance Program. She also authored legislation to give children priority on organ transplant lists. DeGette, whose youngest daughter has diabetes, has served as co-chairman of the Congressional Diabetes Caucus.

The tobacco industry is a frequent target of DeGette's. In a 1998 Commerce Committee hearing, she got tobacco executives to acknowledge that nicotine is addictive. DeGette's mother died of lung cancer in 1989 after smoking for 38 years, starting at the age of 16. In the 105th Congress, DeGette tried to end the federal crop insurance subsidy for tobacco farmers, losing by seven votes. She offered legislation in the 106th to raise the legal smoking age from 18 to 21.

DeGette is an outspoken supporter of abortion rights. She offers an amendment annually to lift a ban on federal funding for abortions for women in federal prisons. She also speaks out against efforts to ban a procedure its opponents call "partial birth" abortion, urging colleagues to "think rationally." She says, "To assume that any woman would choose this tragic procedure after carrying a healthy fetus for 8 or 9 months is offensive to the women who are facing this gruesome decision and it is offensive to all women."

DeGette has been heavily involved in gun control efforts, particularly in the aftermath of the 1999 mass shootings at Columbine High School, just outside her district. She won House approval later that year of her legislative proposal to ban the import of large-capacity ammunition clips.

She laments what she believes continues to be a double standard for assessing women politicians. She complains that no one asks a male politician with young children how he would cope with the dual roles of career and parenting. DeGette says she would be working full-time even if she weren't in politics, telling The Denver Post, "I'm one of those women for whom maternity leave is difficult."

DeGette's father was serving in the Air Force and stationed in Japan when she was born, but most of her childhood was spent in the Denver area. After her parents divorced, DeGette, the eldest of five children, assumed more household responsibilities and took some after-school jobs to help pay the bills. She recalls being profoundly affected, at age 10, by the news coverage of the assassination of the Rev. Martin Luther King Jr., which broadened her horizons and instilled in her an interest in the civil rights movement.

She worked her way through Colorado College, then went off to New York University to get a law degree, serving an internship with the Environmental Defense Fund. Upon returning to Denver, DeGette was a public defender before going into private law practice, where she specialized in cases of discrimination based on disability, sex and age.

She was active in local party politics and won a seat in the Colorado House in 1992. As a freshman, DeGette won enactment of a law (upheld by the Supreme Court in 2000) requiring protesters to stay 8 feet away from anyone within 100 feet of the entrance to a clinic where abortions are performed. She quickly rose to a party leadership position but early in 1996 resigned from the state House to run for Congress, after 12-term Democratic Rep. Patricia Schroeder announced she would not seek re-election.

DeGette won a highly publicized battle with Joe Rogers, a lawyer and former aide to Colorado GOP Sen. Hank Brown. Rogers, who is black, got the endorsement of a group of black ministers, but DeGette was backed by Denver Mayor Wellington Webb, a black Democrat, and she outspent Rogers 2-to-1, winning by almost 17 percentage points.

In 2000, DeGette's vote in favor of expanded trade with China and her support of Bill Bradley for the Democratic presidential nomination upset many of her Democratic constituents. She faced a short-lived intraparty challenge from Denver City Council member Ramona Martinez, who complained that DeGette was not responsive to constituents, particularly on labor matters and issues of importance to minorities. Martinez mounted her effort too late to win a spot on a primary ballot, but the challenge may presage future rumblings of discontent.

DeGette is not as beloved as Schroeder. While DeGette is sharp and champions many of the same liberal causes as her well-liked predecessor, she does not have Schroeder's personal popularity. DeGette told the Denver Rocky Mountain News that she is resigned to having primary challenges for the rest of her career. Nevertheless, she was re-elected in 2000 with 69 percent of the vote in the overwhelmingly Democratic district.

KEY VOTES

2000
Yes Raise hourly minimum wage by $1 over two years
No   Halt funding for U.S. mission in Kosovo unless European nations pay more
Yes Provide Medicare benefits to military retirees and their dependents
Yes Grant China permanent normal trade status
No   Phase out estate, gift and trust taxes
No   Prohibit implementation of president's national monument designations
No   Approve GOP plan to provide prescription drug coverage for Medicare beneficiaries
Yes Increase help for poor nations indebted to international financial institutions

1999
Yes Impose steel import quotas
No   Kill proposal to take aviation trust funds off budget
No   Require background checks on buyers only at gun shows with 10 or more vendors
No   Remove barriers among banking, securities and insurance companies
Yes Authorize state grants to hire teachers and reduce class size
Yes Overhaul campaign finance law; ban "soft money" and restrict advocacy advertising
Yes Approve bipartisan plan to increase rights of patients in managed-care health plans

INTEREST GROUPS

	AFL-CIO	ADA	CCUS	ACU
2000	90%	75%	47%	8%
1999	78%	100%	24%	0%
1998	100%	95%	22%	4%
1997	100%	100%	22%	13%

CQ VOTE STUDIES

	PARTY UNITY		PRESIDENTIAL SUPPORT	
	Support	Oppose	Support	Oppose
2000	93%	7%	88%	12%
1999	95%	5%	84%	16%
1998	97%	3%	86%	14%
1997	98%	2%	82%	18%

COLORADO 1

Denver

While most of Colorado swings to the right, the 1st remains an enclave of liberalism. Democrats haven't lost this capital district since 1970. In 1996 and 2000, the district voted Democratic in the presidential contest while the state as a whole gave the edge to the GOP candidate.

Many residents of the Mile High City tend to be young, single and culturally liberal. North Denver, historically home to Scottish and Irish immigrants, now has large Hispanic and black populations. The 1st also takes in some blue-collar portions of Aurora and Commerce City, including the $4.9 billion Denver International Airport, engineered by former Mayor Federico Peña (later President Clinton's secretary of Transportation, then Energy). While the pricetag helped make the airport controversial, it has sparked a boom in overseas exports.

After suffering an economic bust in the 1980s, Denver boomed in the 1990s. The economy became more diversified as rapid development in the city's high-tech and telecommunications industries revitalized downtown and mitigated both the loss of Lowry Air Force Base and the shutdown of Fitzsimons Army Medical Center, which closed in 1999. Lowry has become a high-tech education center, and Fitzsimons has become home to the University of Colorado's medical school and a bioscience research park. Denver also is home to two young professional sports teams – the Colorado Rockies (baseball) and the Colorado Avalanche (hockey) – to go along with the Denver Broncos (football) and the Denver Nuggets (basketball).

MAJOR INDUSTRY
Telecommunications, computers, health care

CITIES
Denver, 499,775; Aurora (pt.), 55,504 (1990); Commerce City (pt.), 15,424 (1990)

UNUSUAL FEATURES
Great American Beer Festival, the nation's largest and oldest annual brewing competition; U.S. Mint coin production facility; Rocky Mountain Arsenal near Commerce City, a former chemical weapons storage site that is being converted into a wildlife preserve.

Rep. Mark Udall (D)

Elected 1998; 2nd term

An accomplished mountaineer who came within a few thousand feet of scaling Mount Everest in 1994, Udall epitomizes the outdoorsy, can-do spirit of Colorado's 2nd District, which is anchored by the granola belt haven of Boulder. But Udall also has deep and emotional ties to Congress. In 1961, at the age of 10, he was rousted out of bed to celebrate the first of many House election victories enjoyed by his father, Arizona Democrat Morris K. Udall.

Udall and his cousin Tom — whose father, Stewart Udall, represented Arizona in the late 1950s — achieved a rare double feat in 1998 by winning House seats and perpetuating the family dynasty. Mark Udall pledged to follow his father's example as a staunch environmentalist and Democratic loyalist — a vow that became more poignant when the elder Udall died a month after his son's election, following a long battle with Parkinson's disease.

In addressing issues such as urban sprawl and prescription drug pricing, Mark Udall also has built a following among independents clustered in the working-class suburbs of Denver, who make up the largest percentage of voters in his district. Many believe Udall has higher aspirations and could be a likely U.S. Senate candidate in 2002, when first-term Republican Sen. Wayne Allard faces re-election. Udall has done little to discourage such speculation.

Udall plays up his experience as a mountain climber and former executive director of the Colorado Outward Bound School, saying people have to take risks and believe in causes to be true leaders. In his first term, he criticized pharmaceutical manufacturers for "gouging" senior citizens and subsequently was targeted in a series of critical ads by the industry-backed Citizens for Better Medicare. He chastised the administration of Colorado Republican Gov. Bill Owens for not being aggressive enough in preserving open space in the fast-growing state. He also questioned the environmental effects of a local highway project proposed by the Federal Highway Administration, even though it would have brought jobs to his district.

Reflecting on his first session in Congress, Udall complained that lawmakers tiptoed around big issues such as gun control, campaign finance reform and HMO regulation. On these and other social issues, Udall has stuck close to the Democratic Party line, supporting a proposed Medicare prescription drug benefit and a "patients' bill of rights" that would boost patients' clout in dealing with HMOs. But Udall also has shown an independent streak: He broke with Democrats to support a measure that would have required President Clinton to seek congressional approval before ordering ground troops into Kosovo.

Despite his outspokenness and liberal-leaning record, the tall, telegenic lawmaker is popular with colleagues from both parties and regarded as thoughtful, principled and deliberative. During his one term in the Republican-controlled Colorado House, from 1997 to 1999, Udall crafted an anti-poaching bill that increased fines for bagging trophy-sized wildlife — and then won over reluctant GOP lawmakers, who had viewed the measure as anti-hunting. His popularity among House Democrats in Congress won him posts as deputy regional whip and vice president of his freshman class. Indeed, his appeal is so wide within the caucus that lawmakers are said to go out of their way to get Udall as a cosponsor on their bills.

No issue strikes a chord with Udall more than the environment. His father and his uncle Stewart — who was secretary of interior in the Kennedy and Johnson administrations — were instrumental in crafting major land preservation policies in the West, and his wife, Maggie Fox, is

CAPITOL OFFICE
225-2161; fax 226-7840; 115 Cannon Bldg. 20515

INTERNET
e-mail: www.house.gov/writerep
web: www.house.gov/markudall

COMMITTEES
Resources
Science
Small Business

HOMETOWN
Boulder

BORN
July 18, 1950, Tucson, Ariz.

RELIGION
Unspecified

FAMILY
Wife, Maggie Fox; two children

EDUCATION
Williams College, B.A. 1972

CAREER
Colo. Outward Bound School executive director

POLITICAL HIGHLIGHTS
Colo. House, 1997-99

ELECTION RESULTS

2000 GENERAL

Mark Udall (D)	155,725	55.0%
Carolyn Cox (R)	109,338	38.6%
Ron Forthofer (GREEN)	12,398	4.4%
David Baker (LIBERT)	5,655	2.0%

2000 PRIMARY

Mark Udall (D)	unopposed

1998 GENERAL

Mark Udall (D)	113,946	49.9%
Bob Greenlee (R)	108,385	47.4%
Patrick C. West (NL)	6,111	2.7%

a lawyer with the Sierra Club in Colorado. During Resources Committee hearings, Udall can lift his eyes a few feet above the witness chair and gaze upon a portrait of his father. The elder Udall chaired the panel from 1977 to 1991, when it was known as the Interior Committee.

During his first term, Udall sponsored a variety of environmental initiatives, including bills designating two new wilderness areas in Colorado. He and his cousin also sponsored legislation to create a national environmental stewardship program that would encourage volunteers to help federal land agencies preserve parks, forests and other sensitive tracts of land. Udall also proposed a plan to keep undeveloped a 6,000-acre buffer zone around the contaminated and decommissioned Rocky Flats nuclear weapons plant in his district.

Udall has been a vocal advocate of gun control, particularly in the wake of the April 1999 massacre at Columbine High School in a neighboring congressional district. He again demonstrated his independence on the eve of the first anniversary of the shootings, when he declined an invitation from President Clinton to fly on Air Force One to Denver for a gun control rally. Udall said he preferred to remain in Washington so he could vote on legislation instructing a House-Senate conference committee to begin negotiation on a bill with gun control provisions.

In 2000, Udall drew on personal experience when he opposed granting China permanent normal trade status — a move that seemed at odds with his district's robust high-tech business sector but firmed up his credentials with organized labor, which opposes improving ties. Udall recalled his experiences climbing mountains and running Outward Bound programs in Tibet as he criticized China for human rights repression in that country.

While Udall has been an outspoken advocate of campaign finance reform, he also has been among the Colorado House delegation's leaders in fundraising, according to Federal Election Commission filings. His hefty war chest has increased speculation that Udall has his eye on the Senate.

Udall can be an aggressive campaigner. In his first House race, he hammered his well-funded Republican opponent, former Boulder Mayor Bob Greenlee, after Greenlee questioned the scientific validity of global warming. Udall also spent hours campaigning door-to-door in an effort, he said, to prove he was a "legitimate Coloradan" and not just trying to capitalize on his family name. Udall and Greenlee spent at least $2.5 million on advertising, with Greenlee spending about $1 million of his own fortune. Udall won with just less than 50 percent of the tally, edging out Greenlee by about 5,500 votes. In 2000, Udall's margin was a more comfortable 16 percentage points.

KEY VOTES

2000
Yes Raise hourly minimum wage by $1 over two years
Yes Halt funding for U.S. mission in Kosovo unless European nations pay more
Yes Provide Medicare benefits to military retirees and their dependents
No Grant China permanent normal trade status
Yes Phase out estate, gift and trust taxes
No Prohibit implementation of president's national monument designations
No Approve GOP plan to provide prescription drug coverage for Medicare beneficiaries
Yes Increase help for poor nations indebted to international financial institutions

1999
Yes Impose steel import quotas
No Kill proposal to take aviation trust funds off budget
No Require background checks on buyers only at gun shows with 10 or more vendors
Yes Remove barriers among banking, securities and insurance companies
Yes Authorize state grants to hire teachers and reduce class size
Yes Overhaul campaign finance law; ban "soft money" and restrict advocacy advertising
Yes Approve bipartisan plan to increase rights of patients in managed-care health plans

INTEREST GROUPS

	AFL-CIO	ADA	CCUS	ACU
2000	90%	85%	47%	12%
1999	100%	100%	28%	4%

CQ VOTE STUDIES

	PARTY UNITY		PRESIDENTIAL SUPPORT	
	Support	Oppose	Support	Oppose
2000	93%	7%	77%	23%
1999	93%	7%	80%	20%

COLORADO 2
Northwest Denver suburbs; Boulder

The conservative trend that swept the West has infiltrated the 2nd, where Boulder's liberal granola culture permeates much of the community. Once solidly Democratic, the 2nd is now the most contentious battleground in the state.

The change can be traced to new residents who have poured into Boulder County and Denver's northern suburbs, many of them more conservative than Colorado natives. Registered Democrats now have only a slight edge over Republicans.

Slightly more than 40 percent of the district's residents live in Boulder County. Most of the rest live closer to Denver in portions of two suburban counties, Adams and Jefferson: each has nearly 30 percent of the people in the 2nd. Adams has a more blue-collar flavor; Jefferson is historically Republican. Nearly half the district's land area, but only a fraction of its voters, is a short drive west in the mountain counties of Clear Creek and Gilpin.

Traditional liberal issues, such as the environment, still play heavily here. And since Boulder has been one of the fastest growing cities in the state, urban sprawl has gained attention. Rocky Flats Arsenal plutonium plant, located near the Boulder-Jefferson county line, also provokes concern; it is in a decontamination and cleanup phase and is scheduled to close in 2006.

Education ranks as a high priority for the 2nd, home to the state's flagship university and several federal research labs. But newcomers – and anyone who can afford home in Boulder's high-priced real estate market – tend to be more fiscally conservative than voters past.

MAJOR INDUSTRY
Information technology, government laboratories

CITIES
Boulder, 91,238; Arvada (pt.), 89,229 (1990); Westminster (pt.), 73,342 (1990); Longmont, 64,551

UNUSUAL FEATURES
Robin Williams' 1970s TV series, "Mork and Mindy," set in Boulder; Stephen King's "The Stand" was filmed in the district.

Rep. Scott McInnis (R)

CAPITOL OFFICE
225-4761; fax 226-0622; 320 Cannon Bldg. 20515

INTERNET
e-mail: www.house.gov/writerep
web: www.house.gov/mcinnis

COMMITTEES
Resources
   (Forests & Forest Health - chairman)
Ways & Means

HOMETOWN
Grand Junction

BORN
May 9, 1953, Glenwood Springs, Colo.

RELIGION
Roman Catholic

FAMILY
Wife, Lori McInnis; three children

EDUCATION
Fort Lewis College, B.A. 1975; St. Mary's U. of San Antonio, J.D. 1980

CAREER
Lawyer; police officer; firefighter

POLITICAL HIGHLIGHTS
Colo. House, 1983-93 (majority leader, 1991-93)

ELECTION RESULTS

2000 GENERAL

Scott McInnis (R)	199,204	65.8%
Curtis Imrie (D)	87,921	29.1%
Drew Sakson (LIBERT)	9,982	3.3%
Victor A. Good (REF)	5,433	1.8%

2000 PRIMARY

Scott McInnis (R)	unopposed

1998 GENERAL

Scott McInnis (R)	156,501	66.1%
Robert Reed Kelley (D)	74,479	31.5%
Barry Maggert (LIBERT)	5,673	2.4%

PREVIOUS WINNING PERCENTAGES
1996 (69%); 1994 (70%); 1992 (55%)

Elected 1992; 5th term

McInnis was honored in 2000 by his hometown newspaper, the Glenwood Post, as "Person of the Decade." The Post acknowledged that McInnis isn't universally liked and that his hard-edged views do not make him a favorite with Democrats or environmentalists, but the editors wrote: "Yet, love McInnis or hate him, there's no denying the power he has come to wield in Washington."

Indeed, the House GOP leadership has given McInnis ample opportunities to wield some power. He won a seat on the powerful Rules Committee, which sets the guidelines for consideration of bills on the House floor, in only his second term. In his fourth term, he moved to take a spot on the tax-writing Ways and Means Committee. And, when he considered a run for the Senate in 1998, Speaker Newt Gingrich made a personal plea for McInnis to stay in the House.

But for all the encouragement, McInnis still lets it be known that he is not interested in a long House career. Although he has changed his mind about term limits — he came to the House in 1993 vowing to serve only eight years — the congressman has made it clear he would like to be a senator.

In late 2000, McInnis' name was briefly floated as a possible Bush administration appointee to head a federal agency. "With the committees I'm on and with the seniority I have, I'm not much interested," he told the Denver Rocky Mountain News. "But to leave the House for the Senate, sure," he continued.

In 1998, he had geared up for a Senate race on the assumption that Republican Sen. Ben Nighthorse Campbell would run for governor. When Campbell decided instead to seek re-election, McInnis was irate. He contended that Campbell had reneged on a promise; Campbell retorted that McInnis should "stop whining." Ultimately, McInnis decided to seek re-election to his current job, pleasing Gingrich, who had sent him flowers with an entreaty: "We want you to stay in the House."

Since then, McInnis and Campbell have patched up their differences, and they have teamed up to work on a number of public lands bills. But McInnis also has had a testy relationship with 5th District Rep. Joel Hefley, who has six more years seniority and is viewed by many Colorado political observers as a rival for higher office.

McInnis is not shy about engaging Democrats in partisan rhetorical battles. He is a dependable vote for his party, and he was an early supporter of George W. Bush for president. He is also an outspoken advocate for tax-cutting measures, including the repeal of the estate tax.

Like other Western lawmakers, land-use issues are major concern. When he joined the House, McInnis got a seat on the Natural Resources Committee (now called Resources), which has jurisdiction over federal lands policy and water-rights matters of vital importance to the sprawling 3rd District. McInnis knew the issues well, having served in the Colorado House as chairman of the Agriculture, Livestock and Natural Resources Committee.

Though he gave up his Resources seat when he joined the Rules Committee in 1995, McInnis remained active on public lands issues. In the 107th Congress, he was permitted to rejoin the panel while still keeping his seat on Ways and Means. On Resources, he assumed the chairmanship of the Forests and Forest Health Subcommittee. McInnis says he will work for a reduced federal role in land-use policy, particularly as it affects Colorado's wide-open Western Slope.

In the 106th Congress, McInnis pushed a number of measures establishing wilderness, conservation and park areas on federally owned land in western Colorado, often in cooperation with the Clinton administration. The congressman favors multiple uses for much of the land — including development and recreation as well as preservation. Many of his proposals were designed to pre-empt more stringent protection plans offered by the administration and favored by environmentalists.

McInnis projects a serious, and sometimes even angry, image, but he can be a practical joker. He has been known to place non-working telephones in meeting rooms just to watch his fellow lawmakers get frustrated when they cannot make calls. And he sometimes sends his lunch or dinner bill to colleagues in the members' dining room to see their reaction when asked to pay.

McInnis likes to tout the virtues of common sense, which he finds lacking in many aspects of government and modern-day life. When the House was considering legislation to make it harder for people to escape their financial obligations by declaring bankruptcy, McInnis declared that the current system offers "the easy way out." The answer, he said, is simple: "If you can't afford it, don't buy it."

When he arrived on Capitol Hill, McInnis was one of a number of young Republicans who decided to save money by sleeping in their congressional offices while they were in Washington. He still sleeps in his office, rising early to work out in the House gym or go for a jog along the Mall.

It was a Democrat who sparked McInnis' interest in politics. He was in grade school when he met the legendary Rep. Wayne Aspinall, the longtime chairman of the House Interior Committee, at the dedication of a tree farm. "I didn't know what a congressman was. I knew it was something important, I guess," he says. Aspinall gave McInnis a donkey pin from his lapel.

As a young man, McInnis worked as a police officer, a volunteer firefighter and a lawyer before winning a seat in the Colorado House at age 29. He moved through the ranks, and at age 37, became majority leader of the chamber.

In 1992, when Campbell, then a Democrat, left the 3rd District to run for the Senate, McInnis was ready to make a bid for Congress. He had no Republican primary opposition and battled Democratic Lt. Gov. Mike Callihan in the fall campaign. Callihan had become known to more voters in the vast, rural district, but organizational problems plagued his campaign. McInnis touted his 10 years of legislative experience, stressing the work he had done for local agricultural interests.

McInnis scored a solid 11-point victory, even though Bill Clinton carried the 3rd. He has since won easily, with more than 65 percent of the vote.

KEY VOTES

2000

No	Raise hourly minimum wage by $1 over two years
Yes	Halt funding for U.S. mission in Kosovo unless European nations pay more
Yes	Provide Medicare benefits to military retirees and their dependents
Yes	Grant China permanent normal trade status
Yes	Phase out estate, gift and trust taxes
No	Prohibit implementation of president's national monument designations
Yes	Approve GOP plan to provide prescription drug coverage for Medicare beneficiaries
No	Increase help for poor nations indebted to international financial institutions

1999

Yes	Impose steel import quotas
Yes	Kill proposal to take aviation trust funds off budget
No	Require background checks on buyers only at gun shows with 10 or more vendors
Yes	Remove barriers among banking, securities and insurance companies
No	Authorize state grants to hire teachers and reduce class size
No	Overhaul campaign finance law; ban "soft money" and restrict advocacy advertising
No	Approve bipartisan plan to increase rights of patients in managed-care health plans

INTEREST GROUPS

	AFL-CIO	ADA	CCUS	ACU
2000	0%	10%	84%	95%
1999	13%	20%	88%	92%
1998	0%	5%	100%	96%
1997	0%	0%	90%	91%

CQ VOTE STUDIES

	PARTY UNITY		PRESIDENTIAL SUPPORT	
	Support	Oppose	Support	Oppose
2000	93%	7%	25%	75%
1999	93%	7%	20%	80%
1998	92%	8%	26%	74%
1997	94%	6%	27%	73%

COLORADO 3
Western Slope; Pueblo

A century of boom-and-bust mineral speculation – in gold, silver, uranium and shale oil – has left the Western Slope dotted with small, struggling towns. Profits also have shrunk in the 3rd's other economic mainstays, namely cattle ranching in the west and steel production in Pueblo. But with nine national parks and dozens of ski resorts, tourism has quickly filled the void.

Some tourists come to stay. Residential Colorado has spilled over the Continental Divide onto the Western Slope, pushing the 3rd from a swing district to GOP territory. The newcomers, many of whom migrated to the area to build rustic retirement homes, tend to vote Republican. But pockets of Democratic voters remain and the party overall still remains strong. In unionized Pueblo, Democrats outnumber Republicans more than 2-to-1. And affluent liberals dominate the posh ski communities west and south of Boulder, a swath of land known as

the "granola belt," which includes Aspen, Vail and Breckenridge. This region was a cornerstone of opposition to limiting gay rights in a November 1992 ballot initiative that passed easily in this increasingly conservative state.

Residential growth and a substantial agricultural constituency have made water and land two of the 3rd's hottest issues. Most of the state's rivers flow down the Western Slope to Nevada and California. Farmers in the 3rd would like to see more of that water stored for local usage. Meanwhile, residential development has driven up property values.

MAJOR INDUSTRY
Tourism, skiing, agriculture

CITIES
Pueblo, 103,852; Grand Junction, 40,876; Durango, 13,759

UNUSUAL FEATURES
U.S. Government Consumer Information Center in Pueblo; Mesa Verde plateau, home to the Anasazi Native American civilization for 1,300 years; Ute Mountain and Southern Ute Indian Reservations.

Rep. Bob Schaffer (R)

Elected 1996; 3rd term

CAPITOL OFFICE
225-4676; fax 225-5870; 212 Cannon Bldg. 20515

INTERNET
e-mail: rep.schaffer@mail.house.gov
web: www.house.gov/schaffer

COMMITTEES
Agriculture
Education & Workforce
Resources

HOMETOWN
Fort Collins

BORN
July 24, 1962, Cincinnati, Ohio

RELIGION
Roman Catholic

FAMILY
Wife, Maureen Schaffer; five children

EDUCATION
U. of Dayton, B.A. 1984

CAREER
Property manager; marketing executive;
congressional aide

POLITICAL HIGHLIGHTS
Colo. Senate, 1987-97; Republican nominee for
lieutenant governor, 1994

ELECTION RESULTS

2000 GENERAL

Bob Schaffer (R)	209,078	79.5%
Dan Sewell Ward (NL)	19,721	7.5%
Kordon Baker (LIBERT)	19,713	7.5%
Leslie Hanks (AC)	9,955	3.8%
David A. Swartz (X)	4,539	1.7%

2000 PRIMARY

Bob Schaffer (R)	unopposed

1998 GENERAL

Bob Schaffer (R)	131,318	59.3%
Susan Kirkpatrick (D)	89,973	40.7%

PREVIOUS WINNING PERCENTAGES
1996 (56%)

Schaffer likes to joke that he got interested in politics when he was about four years old and his schoolteacher parents described the concept of taxation to him. "I became an activist," he says. "I decided immediately that I didn't like Democrats and I liked Republicans."

Just 20 years after that childhood epiphany, Schaffer carried his conservative convictions to the Colorado Senate, where he served for a decade. When Schaffer entered Congress in 1997, he still was relatively young, but he drew notice from the GOP leadership as a lawmaker well-versed in legislative politics and eager to take on liberal Democrats. A staunch conservative, he is a reliable vote for tax cuts, gun owners' rights and anti-abortion measures, and a harsh critic of federal land conservation programs.

A member of the Agriculture Committee, Schaffer (SHAY-fer) is a fierce defender of his district's farmers and ranchers. One of his most difficult votes in the 106th Congress was in support of permanent normal trade status for China. Even though he expressed concern about China's human rights record, he said that the trade bill would open up much-needed markets for agricultural interests. "I'm persuaded the 51 percent of this bill that [benefits Colorado] outweighs the 49 percent that stinks," he told reporters after voting.

Schaffer is an unswerving opponent of gun control. Although some members on the right tempered their views after the 1999 shootings at Colorado's Columbine High School, Schaffer remained firm in his opposition to gun restrictions and laid blame for the assault on the moral decay of society. "Our children are confronted daily with the glorification of violence," he told his House colleagues.

From his seat on the Resources Committee, Schaffer criticized President Clinton's environmental agenda as an undue federal infringement on private property rights. He joined with other conservatives in 2000 in an unsuccessful bid to cut off funding for national monuments that Clinton had created by decree. Preserving property owners' water rights is a big concern for Schaffer, whose vast 4th District stretches over the eastern third of Colorado and includes many ranches and farms that rely on irrigation.

Schaffer does not hesitate to go to court to make a political statement. During the 106th, he was a party in lawsuits to block an automatic cost of living increase for members of Congress, to stop Clinton from designating "American Heritage Rivers" for special federal assistance, and to challenge the constitutionality of U.S. involvement in the NATO bombing campaign in the former Yugoslavia. Schaffer lost each time.

The congressman also acknowledged refusing to complete portions of the Census Bureau's 52-question form, a technical violation of the law. "Americans have to use their own prudent judgment to figure out what questions are appropriate or not," he told Denver's Rocky Mountain News.

Schaffer takes pride in being named the House's "most frugal spender" in 1999 by the National Taxpayers Union. (In 1997, he spent $583,733 on staffing and other expenses, more than $280,000 below the average.) He is a leading advocate of cutting taxes, dismissing the estate tax as "taxation without respiration." In 1998, he drew attention as one of the few lawmakers who refused to seek funding for district projects in the massive transportation authorization bill. "I asked for zero ... largely because I thought the practice of pork spending ... was unethical and is exactly what's sick about Washington," he said.

Schaffer's outspoken conservatism helped him win election as GOP freshman class president in 1998. In the 105th, Republican leaders gave Schaffer the honor of being lead sponsor of one of the party's top legislative priorities: a bill that would require labor unions to get written permission from their members before using their union dues for political purposes. Schaffer said it was wrong for unions to "use other people's money — including conservative Republicans' — to support liberal candidates."

On the rare occasions when Schaffer departs from the GOP leadership line, it is to stake out an even more conservative position. In 1997, he was one of only nine House Republicans to vote against a bill aimed at encouraging states to prosecute violent juvenile offenders as adults, saying that Colorado already "did everything in the bill" and that federal "meddling" in local law enforcement would only create "more paperwork and more hassles for Colorado."

Schaffer grew up in Cincinnati and attended the same high school that earlier had produced Ohio GOP Rep. John A. Boehner. Schaffer headed west to Colorado after graduating from the University of Dayton in 1984 and won election to the Colorado Senate just two years after moving. In 1994, he was the GOP candidate for lieutenant governor on the ticket that lost to popular Democratic Gov. Roy Romer.

When the 4th came open in 1996 with the Senate candidacy of Republican incumbent Wayne Allard, Schaffer won a tough primary battle by positioning himself to the right of two other GOP state legislators. He prevailed in the general election and has easily won re-election since. In 2000, Democrats did not field a candidate.

Even though Schaffer pledged during his first congressional campaign to step down after three terms, he has begun to raise the prospect of running for a fourth term in 2002. Some state GOP officials, worried about the delegation's lack of seniority in the House, have urged him to stay on. However, others (including former Colorado Republican Sen. William Armstrong, one of Schaffer's political heroes) say he should stick to his pledge.

Despite the demands of politics, Schaffer tries to take every Sunday off to spend time with his wife and five children in Fort Collins, Colo. "When I decided to run for Congress, I told my campaign manager, 'Block Sundays off,'" Schaffer said in a profile in The Denver Post. "He thought I was nuts. There are a lot of picnics, parades, meet-and-greet type events on Sunday. But I said we're not doing that." To compensate, Schaffer says he works at least until midnight — and sometimes well into the morning — when in Washington.

KEY VOTES

2000

? Raise hourly minimum wage by $1 over two years
Yes Halt funding for U.S. mission in Kosovo unless European nations pay more
Yes Provide Medicare benefits to military retirees and their dependents
Yes Grant China permanent normal trade status
Yes Phase out estate, gift and trust taxes
Yes Prohibit implementation of president's national monument designations
No Approve GOP plan to provide prescription drug coverage for Medicare beneficiaries
Yes Increase help for poor nations indebted to international financial institutions

1999

No Impose steel import quotas
Yes Kill proposal to take aviation trust funds off budget
No Require background checks on buyers only at gun shows with 10 or more vendors
Yes Remove barriers among banking, securities and insurance companies
No Authorize state grants to hire teachers and reduce class size
No Overhaul campaign finance law; ban "soft money" and restrict advocacy advertising
No Approve bipartisan plan to increase rights of patients in managed-care health plans

INTEREST GROUPS

	AFL-CIO	ADA	CCUS	ACU
2000	38%	15%	84%	100%
1999	11%	15%	80%	100%
1998	10%	5%	78%	100%
1997	0%	5%	90%	96%

CQ VOTE STUDIES

	PARTY UNITY		PRESIDENTIAL SUPPORT	
	Support	Oppose	Support	Oppose
2000	90%	10%	20%	80%
1999	91%	9%	21%	79%
1998	89%	11%	18%	82%
1997	93%	7%	28%	72%

COLORADO 4

North and east – Fort Collins; Greeley

The 4th, covering the eastern plains, looks more like Kansas than Colorado. Intensive irrigation has turned these prairies where buffalo roamed into productive wheat and corn fields. Cattle production in Colorado's eastern counties ranks among the highest in the nation. But as demand for beef has fallen and wheat prices have declined, ranchers and farmers have faced hard times.

Fort Collins – the district's largest city and home to Colorado State University – sits more than 50 miles from Boulder and Denver, but it's been able to cash in on the recent economic boom in the Front Range. Some high-tech industry has moved into the city, and the relatively low cost of living has attracted new residents.

The 4th has a long history of supporting GOP House members, and most of the 4th includes rural Republican territory. An exception is Fort Collins, which tends to support Democrats in local elections. Registered Democrats outnumber Republicans in nearby Adams

County, with its generally blue-collar workforce. And the sparsely populated southeastern counties closer to New Mexico also tend to lean away from the GOP.

MAJOR INDUSTRY
Agriculture, meat packing, higher education, manufacturing

CITIES
Fort Collins, 113,432; Greeley, 72,778; Loveland, 48,385

UNUSUAL FEATURES
Greeley Independence Stampede, rodeo and country music festival held annually during the week of July 4th; Koshare Indian Museum; Comanche National Grassland.

Rep. Joel Hefley (R)

CAPITOL OFFICE
225-4422; fax 225-1942; 2230 Rayburn Bldg. 20515

INTERNET
e-mail: www.house.gov/writerep

COMMITTEES
Armed Services
Resources
   (National Parks, Recreation & Public Lands -
   chairman)
Small Business
Standards of Official Conduct - chairman

HOMETOWN
Colorado Springs

BORN
April 18, 1935, Ardmore, Okla.

RELIGION
Presbyterian

FAMILY
Wife, Lynn Hefley; three children

EDUCATION
Oklahoma Baptist U., B.A. 1957; Oklahoma State
U., M.S. 1962

CAREER
Community planner; management consultant

POLITICAL HIGHLIGHTS
Colo. House, 1977-79; Colo. Senate, 1979-87
(assistant majority leader, 1981-86)

ELECTION RESULTS

2000 GENERAL

Joel Hefley (R)	253,330	82.7%
Kerry Kantor (LIBERT)	37,719	12.3%
Randy MacKenzie (NL)	15,260	5.0%

2000 PRIMARY

Joel Hefley (R)	unopposed

1998 GENERAL

Joel Hefley (R)	155,790	72.7%
Ken Alford (D)	55,609	26.0%
Mark A. Mellott (NL)	2,871	1.3%

PREVIOUS WINNING PERCENTAGES
1996 (72%); 1994 (100%); 1992 (71%); 1990 (66%);
1988 (75%); 1986 (70%)

Elected 1986; 8th term

Long before political conservatism was au courant on Capitol Hill, Hefley was offering budget-cutting amendments to annual appropriations bills and staking out generally rightward positions on such social issues as abortion, school prayer and gay rights in the Democratic-controlled House. Those positions have played well in the 5th District, home to Colorado's staunch, rock-ribbed Republican voters as well as the Air Force Academy, Fort Carson, a large population of military retirees and the conservative ministry Focus on the Family.

Hefley, a former community planner and management consultant, is something of a loner, not given to back slapping behavior. He does boast an unusual set of hobbies, however. In his youth, the Oklahoma native acquired roping skills and participated in rodeos. He still counts calf-roping as one of his pastimes. Hefley also is an accomplished, if decidedly partisan, political cartoonist and says that he plans to assemble a book of his favorite caricatures. His talents were first noticed by congressional staffers, who came across his doodlings while cleaning up hearing rooms after long committee sessions.

One area where Hefley has taken a high-profile role is defense spending. In contrast to his stands on most other parts of the budget, Hefley has unabashedly fought for increased defense appropriations and against military downsizing. In one memorable 1998 incident, he pointedly told Pentagon officials they should not seek congressional approval for another round of base closings. "Does 'over my dead body' make it clear enough?" he asked.

As chairman for six years of the Armed Services Subcommittee on Military Installations and Facilities, Hefley regularly won approval for substantially more money for defense facilities and family housing projects than requested by the Clinton administration. He frequently berated the White House for making inadequate budget requests for military infrastructure.

In the 107th Congress, he holds a post with potential for keeping him in the spotlight: He was named chairman of the Committee on Standards of Official Conduct, informally known as the ethics committee.

Hefley has not been afraid to stake out controversial positions. From his seat on the Resources Committee, where in the 107th he took the gavel of the National Parks, Recreation and Public Lands Subcommittee, he has argued that Congress has been too eager to designate new national parks while failing to maintain existing facilities.

In the 103rd Congress, he proposed creating a National Park Service review commission that would develop a list of insignificant or undesirable park sites that could be turned over to local officials or private entities. Hefley said the move would save more money for "crown jewel" parks such as Yosemite and Yellowstone. Environmentalists derided the effort as a "park closing" and lobbied to defeat the measure. Hefley tried again in the 105th Congress with a scaled-back version that focused on future park designations, and the plan was approved.

In 1998, Hefley drew considerable notice — and much criticism — when he authored a controversial proposal to overturn President Clinton's executive order prohibiting federal agencies from discriminating against homosexuals. Hefley said he was not targeting homosexuals but rather objecting to "misuse of the executive order process," which, he said, "is not designed to circumvent Congress." He said Clinton's order could lead to hiring quotas and special privileges for homosexuals. Hefley's proposal was denounced by many people as gay-bashing and was soundly defeated, with many of Hefley's conservative colleagues refusing to support him.

Hefley joined the ethics panel in 1997 and soon was named to head a four-member task force weighing an ethics complaint against Bud Shuster, R-Pa., the powerful chairman of the House Transportation and Infrastructure Committee. The complaint centered on a massive 1998 transportation bill Shuster's panel was drafting — a measure that would award special projects to almost every lawmaker.

Hefley rebuffed suggestions that he appoint an independent counsel to run the Shuster probe, saying Congress was fully capable of investigating the matter — a decision that drew considerable criticism.

The ethics probe extended late into the 106th Congress, with the panel granting Shuster limited immunity. It issued a harshly worded report detailing Shuster's violations of House rules, but meted out a mild form of punishment — sending Shuster a letter of reproval.

Hefley had announced he would not press Shuster to include Colorado highway projects in the generous transportation bill. Nonetheless, Hefley, who voted "present" on the bill, got the projects he originally had sought: some $13 million for a new truck lane on Interstate 25 and work on a major road in Colorado Springs.

Hefley had served a decade in the state legislature when GOP Rep. Ken Kramer vacated the 5th District seat to run for the Senate in 1986. Hefley and a colleague from the legislature sought to avoid a primary battle by flipping a coin to determine which of them would make the House bid. Hefley won the toss but drew a primary challenge anyway from millionaire Harold A. Krause, a Republican national committeeman, who attacked Hefley as being too moderate because he was not consistently allied with the GOP's right wing. Hefley ultimately prevailed in the hard-fought primary and breezed past Democratic businessman Bill Story in November.

Hefley's future plans are the object of periodic speculation because of the abundance of potential GOP candidates in his district. Possible challengers include a number of former legislators who left the statehouse because of a voter-initiated term-limits law. Given the solidly Republican makeup of his district, Hefley's biggest threat would be a primary challenge. However, no serious rivals have emerged in recent years, allowing the veteran lawmaker to sweep to re-election with 70 percent or more of the vote.

Hefley has even seen his family's political domain expand. In 1998, GOP leaders chose his wife Lynn to fill a vacancy in the Colorado House — the same seat he had once held. Later that fall, Mrs. Hefley won the seat in her own right.

KEY VOTES

2000

No Raise hourly minimum wage by $1 over two years

Yes Halt funding for U.S. mission in Kosovo unless European nations pay more

Yes Provide Medicare benefits to military retirees and their dependents

No Grant China permanent normal trade status

Yes Phase out estate, gift and trust taxes

Yes Prohibit implementation of president's national monument designations

Yes Approve GOP plan to provide prescription drug coverage for Medicare beneficiaries

No Increase help for poor nations indebted to international financial institutions

1999

Yes Impose steel import quotas

Yes Kill proposal to take aviation trust funds off budget

No Require background checks on buyers only at gun shows with 10 or more vendors

No Remove barriers among banking, securities and insurance companies

No Authorize state grants to hire teachers and reduce class size

No Overhaul campaign finance law; ban "soft money" and restrict advocacy advertising

Yes Approve bipartisan plan to increase rights of patients in managed-care health plans

INTEREST GROUPS

	AFL-CIO	ADA	CCUS	ACU
2000	10%	10%	84%	100%
1999	38%	20%	79%	100%
1998	0%	0%	75%	100%
1997	0%	5%	80%	96%

CQ VOTE STUDIES

	PARTY UNITY		PRESIDENTIAL SUPPORT	
	Support	Oppose	Support	Oppose
2000	93%	7%	15%	85%
1999	90%	10%	17%	83%
1998	92%	8%	21%	79%
1997	95%	5%	25%	75%

COLORADO 5

South Central – Colorado Springs

God and country dominate the 5th, an overwhelmingly conservative district where Republicans outnumber Democrats more than 2-to-1. Military installations employ more than 30,000 people in the Colorado Springs area. The popular resort town is a prime destination for retired military personnel, who come to enjoy the scenery and find like-minded neighbors. James Dobson's Focus on the Family also makes its home in the 5th, along with other evangelical organizations. High housing prices on the West Coast have resulted in an influx of Californians, especially to Douglas County, one of the state's fastest growing areas.

Defense cutbacks threatened the district in the early 1990s when Congress tried but failed to put Fort Carson on its list of closures. Since then, the district has made itself an indispensable arm of the modern military. Colorado Springs now houses the U.S. Space Command, the North American Aerospace Defense Command and a good portion of

the country's satellite defense research.

The city also has broadened its economic base – only 40 percent of the city's jobs are directly tied to the military, down from 70 percent. But much of the new industry, including superconductor and computer development, depends on the defense industry. Like much of Colorado's Front Range, the city attracts lots of money from tourists, many of whom come to make the 14,110-foot ascent up Pikes Peak.

MAJOR INDUSTRY
Military, tourism, semiconductors

MILITARY BASES
Fort Carson (Army), 15,773 military, 1,839 civilian; Peterson Air Force Base, 4,559 military, 1,495 civilian; U.S. Air Force Academy, 1,987 military, 1,905 civilian; Schriever Air Force Base, 2,151 military, 458 civilian; Cheyenne Mountain Air Station, 977 military, 111 civilian (1999)

CITIES
Colorado Springs, 350,199; Castlewood (unincorporated), 24,392 (1990); Southglenn (unincorporated) (pt.), 24,147 (1990)

UNUSUAL FEATURES
U.S. Olympic Headquarters in Colorado Springs.

Rep. Tom Tancredo (R)

Elected 1998; 2nd term

CAPITOL OFFICE
225-7882; fax 226-4623; 418 Cannon Bldg. 20515

INTERNET
e-mail: tom.tancredo@mail.house.gov
web: www.house.gov/tancredo

COMMITTEES
Education & Workforce
International Relations
Resources

HOMETOWN
Littleton

BORN
Dec. 20, 1945, North Denver, Colo.

RELIGION
Presbyterian

FAMILY
Wife, Jackie Tancredo; two children

EDUCATION
U. of North Colorado, B.A. 1968

CAREER
Think tank president; teacher

POLITICAL HIGHLIGHTS
Colo. House, 1977-81; U.S. Education Department
regional representative, 1981-93

ELECTION RESULTS

2000 GENERAL

Tom Tancredo (R)	141,410	53.9%
Ken Toltz (D)	110,568	42.1%
Adam D. Katz (LIBERT)	6,885	2.6%
John Heckman (COPP)	3,614	1.4%

2000 PRIMARY

Tom Tancredo (R)	unopposed

1998 GENERAL

Tom Tancredo (R)	111,374	55.9%
Henry L. Strauss (D)	82,662	41.5%
George E. Newman (NL)	5,152	2.6%

The former president of a Libertarian think tank, Tancredo did not flinch from staking out controversial positions during his first term. He signed a California group's pledge to eliminate all public schools, saying that "separation of school and state is essential to restore parental responsibility." Tancredo (tan-CRAY-doe) also endorsed measures to repeal all types of income taxes, allow the public display of the Ten Commandments and impose tougher sentences for juvenile offenders.

Tancredo's association with staunchly conservative causes was tested by the events of April 20, 1999, the day two students went on a shooting rampage at Columbine High School — just blocks from his suburban Denver home — killing 12 classmates and a teacher before turning their guns on themselves. In an interview with the Capitol Hill newspaper The Hill, the evangelical Presbyterian and self-proclaimed Second Amendment advocate attributed the killings to Satan, but he later endorsed some gun controls, including a Colorado ballot initiative that required background checks for all firearms sales at gun shows. By doing so, he prompted protests from some gun owners groups but largely inoculated himself against charges from Colorado Democrats that he was on the political fringe and out of touch with his constituents.

Tancredo's record on guns is, in fact, a mixed bag. He cosponsored 1999 legislation by Bob Barr, R-Ga., that protected gun manufacturers from civil lawsuits. He also voted that year for an amendment to a juvenile crime bill offered by John D. Dingell, D-Mich., and backed by the National Rifle Association (NRA) that would have required background checks at gun shows to be completed within 24 hours. Tancredo said inclusion of the provision, opposed by most gun control advocates, was necessary to win support from gun control opponents for another measure that mandated trigger locks and safe-storage devices.

He also endorsed gun control provisions, including SAFE, the Colorado initiative that closes a perceived loophole that allows vendors who are not federally licensed to sell weapons at gun shows without performing background checks on buyers. He also announced that he would not accept campaign contributions from the NRA or other groups on either side of the gun control issue. He had received $9,500 from the NRA during his 1998 campaign.

While some national Republican leaders worried that Tancredo was politically vulnerable entering the 2000 election cycle, his record did not create a significant stir in the 6th District, where Republicans outnumber Democrats 38 percent to 28 percent and constituents tend to be skeptical about new federal tax and social policy initiatives. Indeed, polls suggested that while a majority of Coloradans supported new initiatives such as background checks at gun shows, a majority also believed the new laws would not be necessary if the government better enforced existing laws.

A former public school teacher and regional official in President Reagan's Education Department, Tancredo favors school vouchers and opposes bilingual education, issues he has pursued from his seat on the Education and the Workforce Committee.

He also has pressed the Education Department to make good on funding promises on special education. On another education matter closely related to Columbine, Tancredo worked with local law enforcement and telecommunications companies to launch a toll-free school-safety hotline that gives students, parents and teachers the opportunity to report threats of violence. He has advocated creating a national program modeled on the Colorado effort.

Tancredo also sits on the International Relations Committee, where he criticized U.S. intervention against Yugoslavian aggression in Kosovo in 1999 as "unjust and ill-advised." He has questioned the extent to which the United States should get involved in overseas disputes and opposes NATO involvement in quelling flare-ups within the borders of sovereign states.

On the environment, Tancredo supports using royalties from offshore drilling to protect wildlife habitats and promote more outdoor recreational opportunities. And on an issue that split Colorado's congressional delegation, he endorsed upgrading the 39,000-acre Great Sand Dunes National Monument to a national park, despite protests from some conservatives that the site was not worthy of the special protected status.

Tancredo's political career began with a challenge to the junior high school class he was teaching in the 1970s: He told his 32 students that he would run for public office if each of them volunteered with a campaign. To his surprise, all of them called his bluff. The class then decided that Tancredo should run for the Colorado House.

During his four years in the state legislature more than two decades ago, Tancredo was one of the conservatives dubbed the "House crazies" by the press and Democratic Gov. Richard Lamm for their efforts to overhaul the state's tax system. In 1981, Tancredo began a 12-year tenure as the Education Department's regional representative. He advocated dismantling the department and downsized his own regional staff by 75 percent. The congressman says he has since learned to work within the system for change and realizes the department will not go away anytime soon.

Though he had not held elective office since 1981, Tancredo — most recently the president of the Independence Institute think tank — edged out four other Republicans for the 1998 nomination to succeed retiring GOP Rep. Dan Schaefer in the 6th, which represents most of Denver's southern suburbs. He breezed to victory in November.

In 2000, he fought off a spirited challenge from dry cleaning executive Ken Toltz and two lesser candidates, capturing 54 percent of the vote. Spending in the campaign exceeded $2 million. He has said he will serve no more than six years, telling the term-limits advocacy organization, U.S. Term Limits, "It doesn't take seniority" to be a successful legislator. "It takes tenacity, it takes courage, it takes devotion to an idea that is not 'I want to be re-elected.'"

KEY VOTES

2000
No   Raise hourly minimum wage by $1 over two years
Yes Halt funding for U.S. mission in Kosovo unless European nations pay more
Yes Provide Medicare benefits to military retirees and their dependents
No   Grant China permanent normal trade status
Yes Phase out estate, gift and trust taxes
Yes Prohibit implementation of president's national monument designations
Yes Approve GOP plan to provide prescription drug coverage for Medicare beneficiaries
No   Increase help for poor nations indebted to international financial institutions

1999
No   Impose steel import quotas
Yes Kill proposal to take aviation trust funds off budget
Yes Require background checks on buyers only at gun shows with 10 or more vendors
No   Remove barriers among banking, securities and insurance companies
No   Authorize state grants to hire teachers and reduce class size
No   Overhaul campaign finance law; ban "soft money" and restrict advocacy advertising
No   Approve bipartisan plan to increase rights of patients in managed-care health plans

INTEREST GROUPS

	AFL-CIO	ADA	CCUS	ACU
2000	10%	5%	71%	96%
1999	11%	10%	88%	100%

CQ VOTE STUDIES

	PARTY UNITY		PRESIDENTIAL SUPPORT	
	Support	Oppose	Support	Oppose
2000	93%	7%	17%	83%
1999	94%	6%	18%	82%

COLORADO 6
Denver suburbs — Aurora; Lakewood

Managing growth is a top priority for the affluent, white-collar suburbs that lie south and west of Denver, making up the 6th District. Highway congestion has become a serious problem as commuters living in suburban bedroom communities head into Denver every morning.

Aurora, the state's third largest city, has become a prosperous employment center in its own right. High-tech growth in the suburbs has made the 6th one of the most highly educated districts in the nation. Buckley Air Force Base, a key link in the U.S. Air Force Space Command satellite tracking system, has attracted aerospace firms. Telecommunications is a strong industry in Englewood, home to several national cable companies.

The 6th has been represented by a Republican since its creation in 1982. Colorado's Republican leaders get solid support from Golden-based Coors Brewing Co., the nation's third largest brewer and a frequent contributor to GOP candidates. Still, the 6th has a large constituency of independent voters and presidential candidate Ross Perot captured 25 percent of the district's vote 1992.

On social issues, the district has been trending more moderate. The 6th includes most of Littleton — site of the Columbine High School shootings that left 15 dead in 1999 — thrusting gun control into the spotlight for many voters.

MAJOR INDUSTRY
Telecommunications, aerospace, manufacturing

MILITARY BASES
Buckley Air Force Base, 1,935 military, 306 civilian (1999)

CITIES
Aurora (pt.), 166,137 (1990); Lakewood, 137,916; Englewood, 31,844

UNUSUAL FEATURES
"Buffalo Bill" Cody Memorial; Troublesome Gulch, where the media staked out Democratic presidential candidate Gary Hart's home in 1987.

Gov. John G. Rowland (R)

First elected: 1994
Length of term: 4 years
Term expires: 1/03
Salary: $78,000
Phone: (860) 566-4840
Hometown: Waterbury
Born: May 24, 1957, Waterbury, Conn.
Religion: Roman Catholic
Family: Wife, Patricia Rowland; five children
Education: Villanova U., B.S. 1979
Career: Insurance broker; business consultant
Political highlights: Conn. House, 1981-85; U.S. House, 1985-91; Republican nominee for governor, 1990

Election results:

1998 GENERAL

John G. Rowland (R)	628,707	62.9%
Barbara B. Kennelly (D)	354,187	35.4%

Lt. Gov. M. Jodi Rell (R)

First elected: 1994
Length of term: 4 years
Term expires: 1/03
Salary: $71,500
Phone: (860) 524-7384

STATE LEGISLATURE

General Assembly: Meets January to June in odd numbered years; February to May in even number years

House: 151 members, 2-year terms
2001 breakdown: 51R, 100D; 104 men, 47 women
Salary: $32,500
Phone: (860) 240-0400
Senate: 36 members, 2-year terms
2001 breakdown: 15R, 21D; 28 men, 8 women
Salary: $33,500
Phone: (860) 240-0400

STATE TERM LIMITS

Governor: No
Senate: No
House: No

URBAN STATISTICS

CITY	POPULATION
Bridgeport	137,040
Hartford	128,367
New Haven	122,195
Stamford	110,802

REGISTERED VOTERS

Unaffiliated	41%
Democrat	35%
Republican	24%

POPULATION

2000 population	3,405,565
1990 population	3,287,116
Percent change	+3.6%
Rank among states	29
Median age	36.6
Born in state	57%
Foreign born	4%
Urban/rural	82%/18%
Crime rate	391/100,000
Poverty level	9.5%
Federal workers	22,175
Military	16,986

REAPPORTIONMENT

Connecticut lost one House seat in reapportionment, dropping from six districts to five. The state legislature will draw new district lines in 2001.

MISCELLANEOUS

Web: www.state.ct.us
Capital: Hartford
Land area: 4,845 sq. miles
  Rank among states: 48
STATE ELECTION OFFICIAL
(860) 509-6100
DEMOCRATIC HEADQUARTERS
(860) 296-1775
REPUBLICAN HEADQUARTERS
(860) 388-5402

District Statistics

DIST.	2000 D	2000 R	GREEN	1996 D	1996 R	REF	1992 D	1992 R	I	WHT	BLK	ASIAN	HISP	HOUSEHOLD INCOME	OVER 65+	UNDER 18	COLLEGE EDUCATION
1	62%	32%	4%	59%	30%	9%	50%	31%	20%	78%	14%	2%	10%	$39,961	14%	23%	27%
2	55	38	6	53	32	13	43	30	27	93	4	1	3	$38,524	12	23	23
3	60	34	5	57	31	10	45	35	20	84	12	1	5	$39,815	15	22	27
4	55	41	3	51	40	7	42.0	42.3	16	80	13	2	11	$47,636	14	22	34
5	51	44	4	48	40	11	35	42	23	91	5	1	6	$44,056	13	24	27
6	52	42	5	50	37	11	40	36	24	95	2	1	3	$42,817	14	23	25
STATE	56	38	4	53	35	10	42	36	22	87	8	2	7	$41,721	14	23	27

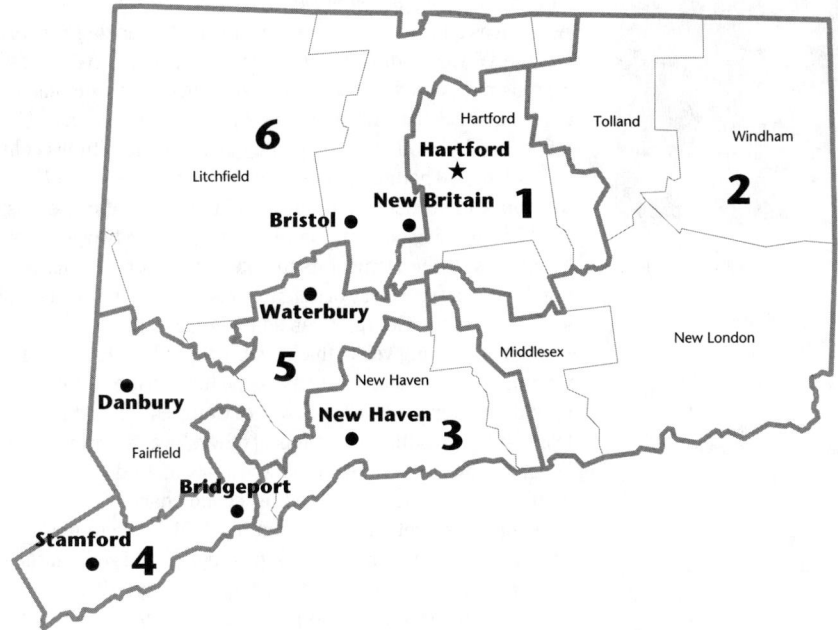

Sen. Christopher J. Dodd (D)

Elected 1980; 4th term

CAPITOL OFFICE
224-2823; fax 224-1083; 448 Russell Bldg. 20510

INTERNET
e-mail: senator@dodd.senate.gov
web: dodd.senate.gov

COMMITTEES
Banking, Housing & Urban Affairs
Foreign Relations
Health, Education, Labor & Pensions
Rules & Administration - ranking member
Joint Library

HOMETOWN
East Haddam

BORN
May 27, 1944, Willimantic, Conn.

RELIGION
Roman Catholic

FAMILY
Wife, Jackie Marie Clegg

EDUCATION
Providence College, B.A. 1966; U. of Louisville, J.D. 1972

MILITARY SERVICE
Army Reserve, 1969-75

CAREER
Lawyer; Peace Corps volunteer

POLITICAL HIGHLIGHTS
U.S. House, 1975-81

ELECTION RESULTS

1998 GENERAL

Christopher J. Dodd (D)	628,306	65.2%
Gary Franks (R)	312,177	32.4%
William Kozak (CC)	12,261	1.3%

1998 PRIMARY

Christopher J. Dodd (D)	unopposed

PREVIOUS WINNING PERCENTAGES
1992 (59%); 1986 (65%); 1980 (56%); 1978 House Election (70%); 1976 House Election (65%); 1974 House Election (59%)

Dodd can be an inscrutable study in contrasts. He is a partisan bulldog but a pragmatist in the legislative clinches, a liberal who often sides with business interests, a leader on children's issues even though he has no sons or daughters of his own. He came of age in the 1960s and describes Bob Dylan as "the finest poet of my generation," but he is also literally a child of the Senate.

The complexities of the man were on view as the 107th Congress began. Dodd was among just eight Democratic senators who voted to confirm John Ashcroft as attorney general, ending the first polarizing Senate debate of the George W. Bush administration. On the one hand, Ashcroft's cultural conservatism appeared anathema to Dodd. But on the other hand, Ashcroft had served in the Senate the previous six years, and the course of Dodd's life was influenced by another senator who got in trouble with his colleagues.

His father, Thomas J. Dodd, saw his own career as a Democratic senator from Connecticut wind down ignominiously after he was censured in 1967 for misusing political contributions. (Twenty-two years later, Dodd was among just three Democrats to vote for former Sen. John Tower, whose nomination as secretary of defense was rejected in the first polarizing Senate debate of the George Bush administration.)

With a booming voice, thick eyebrows and white mane, Dodd excels at waging partisan rhetorical battle — he headed the Democratic Party in the dark days after the GOP takeover of Congress in 1995. "Acting with reckless disregard to the reputations of others" was a serious offense for a public servant and one that Ashcroft was guilty of, Dodd told the Senate, but the nominee nonetheless deserved "a second chance."

When President Bush unveiled his 2001 budget outline several weeks later, Dodd commended the new president for his emphasis on bipartisanship and federal aid to education, a top Dodd priority as well, but said that Bush nonetheless needs "to go back to the drawing board and hone his math skills because this budget just doesn't add up."

And when Senate Republicans called up a bill to name the Peace Corps' headquarters after the late GOP Sen. Paul Coverdell, a former agency director who was one of the Senate's most popular figures when he died in 2000, Dodd unexpectedly held it up. The only Peace Corps volunteer in the Senate (Dominican Republic, 1966-68), he questioned whether it was right to name the building after one person, and he gave a speech extolling the agency's creation in a Democratic administration. He allowed the bill to move forward, however, after some Republicans complained that Dodd was threatening early deadlock in the 50-50 Senate.

After spending the 1980s becoming known mostly as a leading Senate spokesman for liberal causes, in the 1990s Dodd became much more of a full-fledged player in policymaking. He is an active legislator, seen as capable of forging coalitions with members of both parties and delving into a range of issues through his assignments on the Banking, Foreign Relations, Rules, and Health, Education, Labor and Pensions committees. Already the only person in Connecticut history to have been popularly elected to four Senate terms, he would become one of the chamber's most-senior members in the middle of this decade if he wins in 2004.

But his chance of attaining higher office appears to have passed him by. He was an 11th-hour entrant in the race for Senate Democratic leader in 1994 and lost by just one vote to Tom Daschle. He was on the long list of potential vice-presidential candidates in 2000, but Al Gore picked Sen. Joseph I. Lieberman instead, marking the first time in many years that Dodd was no longer the first name on the lips of those talking politics in Connecticut.

For a while, much of that chatter was about Dodd's personal life, including a period of well-publicized carousing in the 1980s with Edward M. Kennedy, D-Mass. (Both senators were divorced at the time.) After a decade-long courtship, in 1999 Dodd married Jackie Marie Clegg, an Export-Import Bank official. One of his Senate friends, Orrin G. Hatch, R-Utah, had long urged the Catholic Dodd to marry Clegg, who like Hatch is a Mormon.

In the halls of the Senate, Dodd still comes off as something akin to a class clown. A quip constantly at the ready, he can be seen joking with everyone from fellow senators to reporters to the Capitol elevator operators.

Dodd's ability to be a true-blue Democrat one day and a bipartisan negotiator the next is nothing new. The Hartford Courant once wrote that "Dodd believes reasonable people can disagree, but it's important not to cross the line and develop enemies; in fact, you seek ways to keep them as friends." Dodd himself warned graduating seniors of the University of Connecticut in 2000 against holding grudges. "Resist the temptation to retaliate," he told the students. "Revenge may be sweet but it leaves a bitter aftertaste."

Dodd walks a tightrope between his own liberal leanings and the needs of industries vital to Connecticut's economy. He was an ardent advocate for the state's insurance industries during the debate that led to the 1999 overhaul of the laws regulating financial services. And throughout the 1990s he doggedly fought for funding for the *Seawolf* class of submarines, three of which will ultimately be built in Groton, Conn.

A prime sponsor of the 1993 law requiring businesses to grant workers time to address their family or medical needs, Dodd pushed legislation in the 106th to improve child care safety and quality, and to make it more affordable. He also has been a leader in the effort to require safety locks on handguns.

Dodd has taken a big interest in one of the emerging hot-button issues of the "new economy" — trying to find ways to heighten consumers' protection of their own financial, medical and genetic information. He said people should be able to "deadbolt" such information just as they lock their homes.

Foreign policy is another priority. As ranking Democrat on Foreign Relations' Western Hemisphere Subcommittee, Dodd has paid particularly close attention to Central America. He has fought tougher sanctions against Cuba and worked to increase international cooperation in the fight against drug trafficking.

Though he was general chairman of the Democratic National Committee in 1995-96, his fellow senators declined to call him to testify before the Senate committee investigating campaign finance irregularities in the 1996 presidential campaign. But Dodd has had his own fundraising controversies. In 1997, he raised $40,000 in a single day from high-technology and securities firms, just before he introduced legislation to make it harder for shareholders to sue in state courts. High-tech firms, whose stock can be volatile, strongly supported the bill.

Despite the end to his father's congressional career, the family name still resonated with voters when Dodd, at age 30, won an open House seat that had been held by a Republican in the post-Watergate election of 1974. Six years later, when Democratic Sen. Abraham Ribicoff retired, Dodd became the youngest person ever elected to the Senate from Connecticut. He took 56 percent against former Sen. James L. Buckley of New York, who carried the standard of the newly resurgent conservative wing of the state GOP and whose family homestead is in Connecticut. Dodd won his subsequent three elections more easily, taking almost two-thirds of the vote in 1998 against Gary A. Franks, who had lost re-election to the House two years before.

KEY VOTES

2000
No Overhaul bankruptcy law and increase minimum wage
No Limit fiscal 2001 discretionary spending to $600.3 billion
No Override veto on nuclear waste disposal at Yucca Mountain site in Nevada
Yes Oppose effort to terminate Kosovo mission
Yes Include gender, sexual orientation and disability in federal hate crime protections
No Approve GOP plan to restrict use of genetic information by health insurers
No Kill amendment delaying implementation of an anti-missile defense system
No Cut taxes for married couples
Yes Grant China permanent normal trade status

1999
No Remove President Clinton from office for obstruction of justice
No Kill amendment authorizing state grants to hire teachers and reduce class size
Yes Require criminal background checks for purchases at gun shows
No Approve GOP proposal to increase rights of patients in managed-care health plans
No Block effort to allow farm and medicine exports to Cuba
Yes Allow study of tougher automobile fuel efficiency standards
Yes Ratify nuclear weapons testing treaty
Yes Prohibit national political parties from collecting "soft money" donations
Yes Remove barriers among banking, securities and insurance companies

INTEREST GROUPS

	AFL-CIO	ADA	CCUS	ACU
2000	75%	95%	53%	13%
1999	88%	95%	53%	0%
1998	88%	95%	61%	4%
1997	57%	90%	50%	4%
1996	100%	85%	38%	10%
1995	92%	95%	32%	4%
1994	75%	80%	38%	0%
1993	82%	75%	36%	12%
1992	92%	75%	30%	11%
1991	92%	75%	20%	24%

CQ VOTE STUDIES

	PARTY UNITY		PRESIDENTIAL SUPPORT	
	Support	Oppose	Support	Oppose
2000	95%	5%	98%	2%
1999	90%	10%	86%	14%
1998	91%	9%	93%	7%
1997	87%	13%	94%	6%
1996	89%	11%	81%	19%
1995	87%	13%	92%	8%
1994	90%	10%	95%	5%
1993	92%	8%	98%	2%
1992	83%	17%	32%	68%
1991	84%	16%	50%	50%

Sen. Joseph I. Lieberman (D)

Elected 1988; 3rd term

CAPITOL OFFICE
224-4041; fax 224-9750; 706 Hart Bldg. 20510

INTERNET
e-mail: senator_lieberman@lieberman.senate.gov
web: lieberman.senate.gov

COMMITTEES
Armed Services
Environment & Public Works
Governmental Affairs - ranking member
Small Business

HOMETOWN
New Haven

BORN
Feb. 24, 1942, Stamford, Conn.

RELIGION
Jewish

FAMILY
Wife, Hadassah Lieberman; four children

EDUCATION
Yale U., B.A. 1964, LL.B. 1967

CAREER
Lawyer

POLITICAL HIGHLIGHTS
Conn. Senate, 1971-81 (majority leader, 1975-81);
Democratic nominee for U.S. House, 1980; Conn.
attorney general, 1983-89; Democratic nominee for
vice president, 2000

ELECTION RESULTS

2000 GENERAL

Joseph I. Lieberman (D)	828,902	63.2%
Philip A. Giordano (R)	448,077	34.2%
William Kozak (CC)	25,509	2.0%

2000 PRIMARY

Joseph I. Lieberman (D)	unopposed

PREVIOUS WINNING PERCENTAGES
1994 (67%); 1988 (50%)

The day after Al Gore conceded the 2000 presidential election, Lieberman told home state reporters he was returning to the Senate "the same person I've always been." Maybe so, but his four-month stint as Gore's running mate radically transformed his political persona.

On the plus side, Lieberman, who had been most widely known for his niche role as a sometimes lonely, moral crusader against Hollywood, "gangsta" rappers and even his own Democratic White House, established himself during the campaign as one of his party's leading national figures, a dynamic campaigner with a puckish wit.

As the first Jew on the national ticket of a major party — indeed, a religiously observant Orthodox Jew who would not campaign on the Sabbath — Lieberman brushed aside what had been assumed to be a taboo and did so at no apparent political cost. "While my faith was the focus of the earliest reactions to my candidacy, it was not even mentioned at the end of the campaign," he told the Senate. "That is good news for all Americans."

On the other hand, Republican critics contended that Lieberman had seriously tarnished his image as a principled centrist and bipartisan bridge builder by, they said, knuckling under to powerful liberal interest groups and backing away from some middle-of-the-road positions. They said he had abandoned his support for school vouchers and for limited privatization of Social Security and soft-pedaled his condemnation of Hollywood in order to help Gore raise money from entertainment moguls.

The campaign highlighted the combativeness and ambition that have propelled Lieberman's career, but that have been obscured by his warm, low-key demeanor. By all accounts, he was one of the hard-liners in the Gore campaign's inner circle who argued for carrying the fight over Florida's electoral votes into the courts. And it was Lieberman, not Gore, who took the lead in publicly denouncing Republican demonstrators who stopped a recount in Dade County.

Lieberman insisted that he had returned to the Senate with his centrist views and his bipartisan style intact: "You get things done when you work from the middle out," he told the Hartford Courant in December 2000. "Campaigns are partisan. ... Governing should not be."

In the opening weeks of the 107th Congress, Lieberman reasserted his centrist stance. He urged new Defense Secretary Donald H. Rumsfeld to drum up public support for higher defense budgets. And he also announced that along with other senators, including conservative Republican Sam Brownback of Kansas, he was drafting a bill that would penalize entertainment companies that market violent or sexually explicit movies, music and electronic games to children.

Education policy provides a test of Lieberman's ability to regain his role as a bridge-builder in the 107th. When the Senate debated Republican school legislation in the 106th, Lieberman and other centrist Democrats offered an alternative strikingly similar to the education overhaul plan proposed by then-candidate George W. Bush, though it did not include private school vouchers. Lieberman's amendment, which would have consolidated more than 50 federal education programs into five "performance-based grants," received only 13 votes. Although President Bush and Lieberman differ on some specifics, their idea is the same: To outline goals, let states decide how to achieve them, reward states for their successes and penalize them for their failures.

As a member of the Armed Services Committee, Lieberman looks out for Connecticut's defense-related industries and has more enthusiasm for a robust defense budget than do many Democrats. But he also has staked out some innovative stands that have no obvious parochial connection. He is among the minority of Democrats on the committee who supported moving ahead with a national missile defense system as soon as it is technologically feasible. In 1996, he was a leading proponent of a blue-ribbon panel to review long-range defense plans. He became a staunch proponent of large-scale war games to test novel ways of organizing U.S. forces to deal with post-Soviet threats.

Despite all that, Lieberman sticks to party positions most of the time. He is solidly in favor of abortion rights and gun control and consistently supported President Clinton on budget and tax issues. He has good relations with labor, gay rights advocates and environmentalists.

His centrist reputation stems from his stand on such issues as education. In 2000, he was one of nine Senate Democrats supporting a bill to create tax-deferred education savings accounts that parents could use for tutoring, supplies or private school tuition. He also sided with some Republicans against trial lawyers, another Democratic constituency, in a 1996 vote for a bill to limit damages in product liability cases. The measure was strongly backed by insurance companies — a major industry in Connecticut.

Lieberman had spoken in favor of the idea of partially "privatizing" Social Security — a concept roundly opposed by Clinton and Gore under which individuals could invest all or a portion of their Social Security payroll tax in the securities markets. Gore and many other leading Democrats said such a plan could undermine the financial structure of Social Security. After his vice-presidential nomination was announced, Lieberman reversed course, and his office distributed a previously unpublished essay titled "My Private Journey Away From Privatization," in which he said, "the promises and the numbers" of privatization advocates "don't add up."

Lieberman is perhaps best known to voters for a September 1998 speech that criticized Clinton's behavior in the Monica Lewinsky scandal as "not just inappropriate. It is immoral. And it is harmful, for it sends a message of what is acceptable behavior to the larger American family — particularly to our children."

The senator never called for the president's resignation, nor did he advocate the lesser penalty of censure. By condemning Clinton's behavior but also declaring "that talk of impeachment and resignation now is unwise," he may have bucked up the prospects of the man he was rebuking.

Lieberman has always been politically ambitious. He won a state Senate seat in 1970 — helped by a 24-year-old campaign aide named Bill Clinton, who was then at Yale Law School — and soon rose to majority leader. He lost a race for the U.S. House in the Reagan landslide of 1980, but rebounded in 1982 to become Connecticut attorney general, where he earned positive reviews.

In 1988, Lieberman ran against three-term GOP Sen. Lowell P. Weicker Jr., mounting a tough, sometimes negative campaign in which he scored a narrow upset. In that race he rallied his Democratic base while running to the right of the often-liberal Weicker on school prayer, Cuba and the 1983 invasion of Grenada.

Even though 1994 was a big year for Republicans in state after state, Lieberman was untouchable. Rated "safe" for re-election in all pre-election forecasts, he rolled up 67 percent of the vote against former GOP state Sen. Jerry Labriola. In 2000, he cruised to re-election in a Senate campaign that basically ran on autopilot while he campaigned for vice president.

KEY VOTES

2000

Yes Overhaul bankruptcy law and increase minimum wage

No Limit fiscal 2001 discretionary spending to $600.3 billion

No Override veto on nuclear waste disposal at Yucca Mountain site in Nevada

Yes Oppose effort to terminate Kosovo mission

Yes Include gender, sexual orientation and disability in federal hate crime protections

Yes Approve GOP plan to restrict use of genetic information by health insurers

No Kill amendment delaying implementation of an anti-missile defense system

No Cut taxes for married couples

? Grant China permanent normal trade status

1999

No Remove President Clinton from office for obstruction of justice

No Kill amendment authorizing state grants to hire teachers and reduce class size

Yes Require criminal background checks for purchases at gun shows

No Approve GOP proposal to increase rights of patients in managed-care health plans

Yes Block effort to allow farm and medicine exports to Cuba

Yes Allow study of tougher automobile fuel efficiency standards

Yes Ratify nuclear weapons testing treaty

Yes Prohibit national political parties from collecting "soft money" donations

Yes Remove barriers among banking, securities and insurance companies

INTEREST GROUPS

	AFL-CIO	ADA	CCUS	ACU
2000	80%	75%	33%	20%
1999	78%	95%	47%	0%
1998	75%	80%	56%	16%
1997	29%	75%	60%	20%
1996	86%	75%	54%	35%
1995	100%	95%	33%	10%
1994	71%	65%	30%	8%
1993	82%	65%	45%	20%
1992	83%	70%	50%	22%
1991	83%	65%	30%	25%

CQ VOTE STUDIES

	PARTY UNITY		PRESIDENTIAL SUPPORT	
	Support	Oppose	Support	Oppose
2000	88%	12%	94%	6%
1999	87%	13%	89%	11%
1998	80%	20%	83%	17%
1997	77%	23%	93%	7%
1996	76%	24%	90%	10%
1995	72%	28%	82%	18%
1994	76%	24%	88%	12%
1993	83%	17%	95%	5%
1992	77%	23%	37%	63%
1991	81%	19%	52%	48%

Rep. John B. Larson (D)

Elected 1998; 2nd term

CAPITOL OFFICE
225-2265; fax 225-1031
1419 Longworth Bldg. 20515

INTERNET
e-mail: www.house.gov/writerep
web: www.house.gov/larson

COMMITTEES
Armed Services
Science

HOMETOWN
East Hartford

BORN
July 22, 1948, Hartford, Conn.

RELIGION
Roman Catholic

FAMILY
Wife, Leslie Larson; three children

EDUCATION
Central Connecticut State U., B.S. 1971

CAREER
Insurance company owner; high school teacher

POLITICAL HIGHLIGHTS
East Hartford Board of Education, 1978-79; East Hartford Town Council, 1979-83; Conn. Senate, 1983-95 (president pro tempore, 1987-95); sought Democratic nomination for governor, 1994

ELECTION RESULTS

2000 GENERAL

John B. Larson (D)	151,932	71.9%
Bob Backlund (R)	59,331	28.1%

2000 PRIMARY

John B. Larson (D)	unopposed

1998 GENERAL

John B. Larson (D)	97,681	58.1%
Kevin O'Connor (R)	69,668	41.4%

A dozen years in the Connecticut Senate and a 1994 run as Democratic gubernatorial nominee did not prepare Larson for the sharp partisanship he encountered as a freshman congressman in the minority party. An affable former high school teacher accustomed to the familiar give-and-take of state politics, Larson expressed dismay at the post-impeachment bitterness that often pervaded House floor debates in the 106th Congress.

To try to focus colleagues on the dignity of the chamber, he sponsored legislation directing the Librarian of Congress to prepare a history of the House, heading off potential partisan bickering by signing on both Speaker J. Dennis Hastert and Minority Leader Richard A. Gephardt as cosponsors. He also suggested that lawmakers limit their one-minute floor speeches at the beginning of each day to "constructive comments" about goings-on in their districts.

Still, Larson has not shied away from tough fights when his district's interests are at stake. During his first year, he strenuously fought proposed cuts to the Air Force's F-22 jet fighter, whose engines are made by East Hartford-based Pratt & Whitney. Critics said the aircraft was too expensive and draining money for other Pentagon projects. Larson and other backers of the next-generation stealth fighter failed to stop the House from initially voting to deny the $1.9 billion the Clinton administration had requested to build six of the aircraft. (Supporters of the plane said the move was tantamount to killing the program.)

Larson's interpersonal skills with other lawmakers helped forge a House-Senate compromise that restored $1 billion of the funding but required the Air Force to conduct additional testing before committing to full-scale production. Additional funding was secured in 2000 to continue testing the F-22 and to buy 10 more of the planes.

In the 106th Congress, Larson weighed in on a range of bedrock Democratic issues, advocating Medicare coverage of prescription drugs for senior citizens and backing efforts to shore up the Social Security trust fund. From his seat on the Science Committee, the former educator pressed for expanded Internet service for poor and minority neighborhoods and schools as a way of narrowing the so-called digital divide.

Such positions speak well to economic conditions in a district that has a significant number of poor black and Hispanic neighborhoods but that is best known as a state capital and insurance center with a host of well-paying jobs. Larson also called for tax incentives so teachers could obtain more training and sought federal backing for a high-tech business incubator at Pratt & Whitney's East Hartford plant.

In the 106th, Larson also voted against granting China permanent normal trade status, explaining he was keeping a campaign promise he had made to organized labor in his heavily Democratic district, even while acknowledging that the trade pact would likely help Connecticut exports. The Hartford Courant noted that it was not the first time Larson had made "rash promises," pointing out that in 1991 he voted against the state income tax in order to keep a campaign promise, even while admitting that the tax would help Connecticut grapple with budget problems. Nonetheless, the newspaper endorsed Larson for a second term, praising his energy and work ethic on behalf of a district so solidly liberal that "a Democrat could probably take a two-year nap and be re-elected."

Although the 1st District has sent a Democrat to Congress in every election but one since 1948, Larson is the first in decades to hail from outside the Hartford city limits. But Larson was no stranger to Hartford-area voters when he ran in 1998 to succeed veteran Democratic Rep. Barbara B. Kennelly, who gave up her 1st District seat in an unsuccessful bid for governor. He had served in the East Hartford city government for four years and then in the state Senate from 1983 until 1994, rising to the post of president pro tem.

Larson, who grew up with seven siblings in a public housing project, has long been a supporter of activist government. While in the state Senate, he authored Connecticut's Family and Medical Leave Act — the first such law enacted in the country. He also pushed for "family resource centers," public school buildings that are used to offer child care and family support services.

Larson has shown, though, that he can work in bipartisan coalitions. In 1984, when Republicans took control of the state Senate, Larson was the only Democrat allowed to chair a committee — the Energy and Technology panel. Two years later, when the Democrats won back a majority, he was named Senate president pro tem, the state's third-highest office. He continued to serve in that post for the next eight years — making him the longest-serving president pro tem in state history — before staging an unsuccessful bid for governor in 1994. In the gubernatorial contest, he won party leaders' endorsement but lost the primary to state Comptroller Bill Curry.

The lawmaker said his loss in the gubernatorial race taught him the necessity of establishing a solid network of grass-roots supporters, and he has taken pains to reach out to urban constituents, particularly the elderly. His district staff helps localities write applications for federal grants and generally deal with Washington's bureaucrats. He also has proved effective at bringing home federal dollars, winning $3 million to reduce lead exposure in Hartford neighborhoods. To establish some continuity with his predecessor, Larson hired several members of Kennelly's staff and even moved into the Washington apartment the veteran lawmaker was leaving.

During the 2000 election cycle, Larson faced an unusual challenge from Republican Bob Backlund, a charismatic former professional wrestler with no prior political experience. Larson refrained from negative campaigning, saying only that his opponent did not appear to have a full grasp of the issues. Larson was also helped by a war chest of more than $600,000 and the presence of vice-presidential candidate Connecticut Sen. Joseph I. Lieberman at the top of his party's ticket.

KEY VOTES

2000

Yes	Raise hourly minimum wage by $1 over two years
No	Halt funding for U.S. mission in Kosovo unless European nations pay more
Yes	Provide Medicare benefits to military retirees and their dependents
No	Grant China permanent normal trade status
No	Phase out estate, gift and trust taxes
No	Prohibit implementation of president's national monument designations
No	Approve GOP plan to provide prescription drug coverage for Medicare beneficiaries
Yes	Increase help for poor nations indebted to international financial institutions

1999

Yes	Impose steel import quotas
No	Kill proposal to take aviation trust funds off budget
No	Require background checks on buyers only at gun shows with 10 or more vendors
Yes	Remove barriers among banking, securities and insurance companies
Yes	Authorize state grants to hire teachers and reduce class size
Yes	Overhaul campaign finance law; ban "soft money" and restrict advocacy advertising
Yes	Approve bipartisan plan to increase rights of patients in managed-care health plans

INTEREST GROUPS

	AFL-CIO	ADA	CCUS	ACU
2000	90%	95%	57%	12%
1999	78%	100%	38%	4%

CQ VOTE STUDIES

	PARTY UNITY		PRESIDENTIAL SUPPORT	
	Support	Oppose	Support	Oppose
2000	93%	7%	85%	15%
1999	93%	7%	83%	17%

CONNECTICUT 1
Central — Hartford

Situated midway between Boston and New York – roughly 100 miles from each – the 1st is an attractive commercial center for businesses straddling the Northeast Corridor. Insurance companies, banks and state government are the lifeblood of Hartford and its well-off suburbs. The metropolitan region boasts seven major insurance firms.

The 1st is rebounding from the 1980s stock market gyrations, sagging real estate prices and dwindling defense contracts. Hartford saw a renewal in the 1990s, cleaning up its downtown and attracting several high-tech manufacturing firms.

Like most of the state, the 1st is solidly liberal, with Democrats outnumbering Republicans by more than 2-to-1. But the 1st has seen a rise in the number of unaffiliated voters, which can be traced to the economic problems of the 1980s and the long-term decline of its traditional, blue-collar voting bloc. Voters hold onto socially liberal views from the past but have become dissatisfied with some

Democrats and are willing to vote for socially moderate candidates of either party. Bill Clinton won majorities in 1992 and '96 and, in 2000, the district gave Al Gore his largest vote margin in Connecticut.

MAJOR INDUSTRY
Insurance, banking, defense

CITIES
Hartford, 128,367; West Hartford (unincorporated), 60,110 (1990); East Hartford (unincorporated), 50,452 (1990)

UNUSUAL FEATURES
Hartford Courant (founded 1764), nation's oldest newspaper in continuous circulation; Noah Webster, author of the first American dictionary, born in West Hartford; Hartford's Wadsworth Antheneum, the nation's oldest public art museum.

Rep. Rob Simmons (R)

CAPITOL OFFICE
225-2076; fax 225-4977; 511 Cannon Bldg. 20515

INTERNET
e-mail: www.house.gov/writerep
web: www.house.gov/simmons

COMMITTEES
Armed Services
Transportation & Infrastructure
Veterans' Affairs

HOMETOWN
Stonington

BORN
Feb. 11, 1943, New York, N.Y.

RELIGION
Episcopalian

FAMILY
Wife, Heidi Simmons; two children

EDUCATION
Haverford College, B.A. 1965; Harvard U., M.P.A. 1979; U. of Connecticut, attended 1988-92

MILITARY SERVICE
Army, 1965-68; Army Reserve, 1970-2000

CAREER
Professor; congressional aide; CIA agent

POLITICAL HIGHLIGHTS
Candidate for Stonington Board of Selectmen, 1985; Stonington Republican Town Committee, 1986-90 (chairman, 1988-92); Conn. House, 1991-2001

ELECTION RESULTS

2000 GENERAL

Rob Simmons (R)	114,380	50.6%
Sam Gejdenson (D)	111,520	49.4%

2000 PRIMARY

Rob Simmons (R)	unopposed

Elected 2000; 1st term

After winning a come-from-behind 2000 race in Connecticut's 2nd District — which helped ensure continued Republican control of the House — Simmons entered Congress with a wealth of personal and political experience. He served in Vietnam, earning two Bronze stars; did stints as an overseas CIA officer and as a top-level congressional aide; and served for 10 years in the Connecticut House.

Every ounce of that gold-plated résumé came in handy for Simmons in 2000, when he narrowly defeated 10-term Democratic Rep. Sam Gejdenson in one of the year's biggest congressional upsets.

Simmons' military background helped him land seats on the Armed Services and Veterans' Affairs committees. Simmons has taken a special interest in submarine projects at General Dynamics' Electric Boat Corp., which is headquartered in Connecticut's 2nd District and is one of the largest employers in southern New England. He also won a seat on the Transportation and Infrastructure Committee.

Indian land claims are a key local issue for Simmons. He contended that Gejdenson did not work to get Congress to hold hearings on tribe recognition in eastern Connecticut, where the Mashantucket Pequot tribe operates the huge Foxwoods Resort Casino.

Simmons' ideological profile stood him in good stead in his bid to win the swing 2nd District. Simmons calls himself a fiscal conservative, opposing the estate tax, the "marriage penalty" tax and any measure that diverts Social Security funds to other initiatives. But he is fairly moderate on social issues, supporting abortion rights and certain gun control measures.

When Connecticut Sen. Joseph I. Lieberman was chosen as the Democratic vice-presidential nominee, it was thought that his presence would boost Democrats across the state — including Gejdenson, who had won easily in 1998 but had some very close races earlier in his career.

But Simmons tapped into local issues and contended that Gejdenson's voting record was too liberal for the district. Simmons' late-surging campaign enabled him to win by 2,860 votes — about 1 percentage point.

CONNECTICUT 2
East — New London

The state's largest and most working-class district, the 2nd runs from the Groton waterfront north to the Massachusetts border. The district leads the state in tourism, with attractions such as such as Mystic Seaport and the huge American Indian-owned Foxwoods and Mohegan Sun casinos.

At the beginning of the 1990s, the 2nd's economy was highly dependent on defense work — until some of the submarine contracts in New London and Groton were sent to Newport News, Va. By the middle of the decade, nuclear technicians became blackjack dealers, finding jobs in the suddenly huge gaming industry along the Interstate 95 corridor. The decade ended without any dramatic shift in employment levels, although the stability of union jobs was gone.

If the 1990s economy was hardly placid, the politics of the district were even more shaken – a political system once built on defense patronage had to learn a whole new set of rules built around a service economy. Democrats were quick to respond to the new issues and were able to hold onto their lock on the 2nd until 2000, when Rep. Simmons became the first Republican elected since 1972.

MAJOR INDUSTRY
Gambling, defense, health care

MILITARY BASES
New London Naval Submarine Base, 8,339 military, 1,293 civilian (1995)

CITIES
Middletown, 44,001; Norwich, 34,852; New London, 25,903; Storrs (unincorporated), 12,198 (1990)

UNUSUAL FEATURES
Foxwoods Resorts Casino, owned by the Mashantucket Pequot Indian Tribe, is the largest casino in the Northern Hemisphere, taking in more than $5 billion annually from slot machines alone.

Rep. Rosa DeLauro (D)

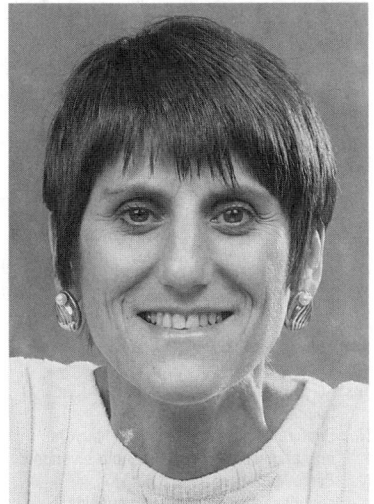

CAPITOL OFFICE
225-3661; fax 225-4890; 2262 Rayburn Bldg. 20515

INTERNET
e-mail: www.house.gov/writerep
web: www.house.gov/delauro

COMMITTEES
Appropriations

HOMETOWN
New Haven

BORN
March 2, 1943, New Haven, Conn.

RELIGION
Roman Catholic

FAMILY
Husband, Stanley Greenberg; three stepchildren

EDUCATION
London School of Economics, attended 1962-63;
Marymount College, B.A. 1964; Columbia U., M.A.
1966

CAREER
Political activist; congressional and mayoral aide

POLITICAL HIGHLIGHTS
No previous office

ELECTION RESULTS

2000 GENERAL

Rosa DeLauro (D)	156,910	71.9%
June Gold (R)	60,037	27.5%

2000 PRIMARY

Rosa DeLauro (D)	unopposed

1998 GENERAL

Rosa DeLauro (D)	109,726	71.3%
Martin Reust (R)	42,090	27.4%

PREVIOUS WINNING PERCENTAGES
1996 (71%); 1994 (63%); 1992 (66%); 1990 (52%)

Elected 1990; 6th term

DeLauro has mastered the role of the outspoken Democratic partisan, one who can rally the party faithful with a rousing speech or a well-crafted, pithy sound bite. But she also has a track record as someone who can bring women's issues to the forefront, giving voice to concerns on everything from child care to health care to equal pay protections. Her bills have not fared well under Republican majorities in Congress, but she has attracted enough attention to win a spot in the Democratic leadership — and a chance to make sure her party does not take for granted the women voters who are one of its strongest constituencies.

In the 106th Congress, DeLauro (da-LAUR-o), who had served as one of her party's four chief deputy whips, ran for the Democratic Caucus chairmanship. But she was defeated by Martin Frost of Texas, who had served as chairman of the Democratic Congressional Campaign Committee. That outcome, in combination with other contests, left Democrats with no women in leadership posts. So Minority Leader Richard A. Gephardt appointed DeLauro to a new position in the party leadership: assistant to the Democratic leader. In this role, she oversees coordination of policy, communications, and research and serves as a liaison to freshmen; she also has a seat on the Steering Committee, which makes Democratic committee assignments.

DeLauro's leadership post gives her more visibility than she might have had otherwise, but she was never in danger of disappearing from the stage. She is too good at the finger-in-the-eye politics Democrats have used to compete against the GOP majority.

On the House floor, she speaks with a verve and intensity that attracts as much attention as her unconventional garb of tunics, flowing skirts and funky jewelry. A typical DeLauro broadside came in 1999, when Republicans ran ads that accused the Democrats of raiding Social Security — at a time when the Congressional Budget Office said the Republicans themselves were tapping the Social Security trust fund to finance their spending bills. "The Republican leadership reminds me of the little boy who denies eating cookies even though his mouth is smeared with chocolate and his shirt is covered with crumbs," she said.

DeLauro developed her liberal views and political smarts growing up in an activist family — both her parents were New Haven aldermen — and later as a senior staff member on Capitol Hill; she worked for seven years as Democratic Sen. Christopher Dodd's chief of staff.

DeLauro adds to the rhetorical volleys on bread-and-butter Democratic issues, including school construction and Medicare prescription drug coverage for seniors, but her own legislative agenda is shaped to throw a spotlight on women's issues. In the 106th, she sponsored a bill to require that managed-care plans and health insurers pay for at least 48 hours of hospital care after a mastectomy — ending a practice commonly known as "drive-through mastectomies." She also introduced measures to make child care more readily available and to toughen the penalties against employers who do not pay women and men equally for doing the same kind of work.

Her legislative interests are linked, in part, to personal experience. During debate on a 1993 reauthorization bill for the National Institutes of Health, DeLauro noted her own battle with ovarian cancer, which she said was diagnosed only "by chance." She said, "For years, women's health concerns have been systematically ignored by the federal government."

A staunch proponent of abortion rights, DeLauro has worked to remove a restriction that prevents health insurance programs for federal workers from covering abortion costs. She argues that the ban discriminates against female civil service workers by constraining their legal right to end a pregnancy.

Though she is best known for her fiercely partisan floor rhetoric, DeLauro also can play the inside game. On the Appropriations Committee, she works to secure federal dollars for home state interests, particularly Connecticut companies that do defense-related work. In the 105th Congress, she successfully lobbied defense appropriators to increase funding for Black Hawk and Comanche helicopters, products of the Stratford, Conn.-based Sikorsky Aircraft Corp.

Also with an eye toward her state, DeLauro in 2000 tried to boost special-education funding in the annual Labor, Health and Human Services, and Education appropriations bill, arguing that Congress has not lived up to its promise to reimburse 40 percent of states' costs. Congress, she said, was "putting an unfunded mandate on our communities" — one of the few issues on which she and Republicans agree.

Mostly DeLauro sees little to like in what the GOP majority proposes, and in her zeal to denounce conservatives, she has been known to ignore the customs and courtesies of the House. Once, during floor debate in the 105th, she pressed on so far beyond her allotted speaking time that Speaker Newt Gingrich pounded the gavel to command her to sit down. "I don't speak to the gavel. I speak to the people who put me here," she said later.

DeLauro's political instincts are rooted in her upbringing in Wooster Square, a tight-knit Italian neighborhood in New Haven. Her father was an Italian immigrant and her mother a factory worker. She was a community organizer in President Johnson's War on Poverty program and later served as executive assistant to the mayor of New Haven. She also married into politics: Her husband is Stanley Greenberg, a prominent Democratic pollster.

In 1990, DeLauro left her job running EMILY's List, an organization that raises funds for women candidates, to try for the House herself when Democratic Rep. Bruce Morrison gave up his 3rd District seat to run for governor. DeLauro's political contacts enabled her to raise money quickly and shoo away intraparty competition. Republicans put up state Sen. Thomas Scott, an energetic conservative opposed to gun control and abortion rights. He pulled close by painting her as a far-left radical, but she forged a coalition of activist liberals and blue-collar voters, and they helped give her a 4-point victory.

Scott came back for a rematch in 1992, but DeLauro was ready with a healthy campaign chest and won with 66 percent of the vote. Since then, she has been easily re-elected.

KEY VOTES

2000

Yes Raise hourly minimum wage by $1 over two years
No Halt funding for U.S. mission in Kosovo unless European nations pay more
Yes Provide Medicare benefits to military retirees and their dependents
No Grant China permanent normal trade status
No Phase out estate, gift and trust taxes
No Prohibit implementation of president's national monument designations
No Approve GOP plan to provide prescription drug coverage for Medicare beneficiaries
Yes Increase help for poor nations indebted to international financial institutions

1999

Yes Impose steel import quotas
Yes Kill proposal to take aviation trust funds off budget
No Require background checks on buyers only at gun shows with 10 or more vendors
No Remove barriers among banking, securities and insurance companies
Yes Authorize state grants to hire teachers and reduce class size
Yes Overhaul campaign finance law; ban "soft money" and restrict advocacy advertising
Yes Approve bipartisan plan to increase rights of patients in managed-care health plans

INTEREST GROUPS

	AFL-CIO	ADA	CCUS	ACU
2000	100%	90%	42%	8%
1999	100%	100%	16%	0%
1998	100%	100%	28%	8%
1997	100%	95%	30%	13%

CQ VOTE STUDIES

	PARTY UNITY		PRESIDENTIAL SUPPORT	
	Support	Oppose	Support	Oppose
2000	97%	3%	87%	13%
1999	97%	3%	82%	18%
1998	97%	3%	82%	18%
1997	96%	4%	84%	16%

CONNECTICUT 3
South – New Haven

Working-class, bedrock constituents of the Democratic Party mix with the liberal elite of the ivory tower in the 3rd. Situated on the state's southern coast, it encompasses both the working-class elements of New Haven, a busy blue-collar port, and prestigious Yale University. Yale might be the city's largest employer, but there is tension between the university and the town surrounding it. Flashpoints include unionization, a big issue for any blue-collar city. Still, Yale has made increasing efforts to support the community, encouraging workers and professors alike to live within city limits.

New Haven is solidly Democratic, with outlying towns leaning slightly to the right. The 3rd is home to many minority groups that traditionally support Democrats. Hispanics are the fastest growing minority, and the district also has a high percentage of Italian-Americans. This mix may create tensions within the Democratic Party, but it keeps the district solidly liberal.

The defense industry plays a large role in the 3rd. Sikorsky Aircraft, a helicopter manufacturer, depends on the military for survival. The 3rd was dealt a blow when Stratford Army Engine Plant was shut down in 1995. Local leaders are hoping that the town will be given local control of the abandoned plant for redevelopment. Plans include a waterfront park. Legislators in the area know the importance of making jobs available, and employment has remained stable, if not spectacular.

MAJOR INDUSTRY
Trade, manufacturing, defense

CITIES
New Haven, 122,195; West Haven, 51,622; Stratford (unincorporated), 49,389 (1990); Milford, 48,231

UNUSUAL FEATURES
Trial resulting from the slave revolt that inspired the movie "Amistad" took place in New Haven; Frisbee invented at Yale University in 1920 when students discovered that empty pie plates from the Frisbee Baking Co. of nearby Bridgeport were fun to toss around on New Haven Green.

Rep. Christopher Shays (R)

Elected August 1987; 7th full term

CAPITOL OFFICE
225-5541; fax 225-9629
1126 Longworth Bldg. 20515

INTERNET
e-mail: rep.shays@mail.house.gov
web: www.house.gov/shays

COMMITTEES
Financial Services
Government Reform
  (National Security & Veterans Affairs -
  chairman)
Science

HOMETOWN
Stamford

BORN
Oct. 18, 1945, Darien, Conn.

RELIGION
Christian Scientist

FAMILY
Wife, Betsi de Raismes; one child

EDUCATION
Principia College, B.A. 1968; New York U., M.B.A.
1974, M.P.A. 1978

CAREER
Real estate broker; public official; Peace Corps
volunteer

POLITICAL HIGHLIGHTS
Conn. House, 1975-87; Republican candidate for
mayor of Stamford, 1983

ELECTION RESULTS

2000 GENERAL

Christopher Shays (R)	119,155	57.6%
Stephanie Sanchez (D)	84,472	40.9%

2000 PRIMARY

Christopher Shays (R)	unopposed

1998 GENERAL

Christopher Shays (R)	94,767	69.1%
Jonathan Kantrowitz (D)	40,988	29.9%
Marshall C. Harrison (LIBERT)	1,449	1.1%

PREVIOUS WINNING PERCENTAGES
1996 (61%); 1994 (74%); 1992 (67%); 1990 (77%);
1988 (72%); 1987 Special Election (57%)

Shays, who has an interest in martial arts, directs his rhetorical punches at fellow Republicans almost as often as he jabs at Democrats. He proudly touts a long list of issues on which he routinely goes against the prevailing winds of his party.

He supports environmental protections, gun control and abortion rights, and he has opposed efforts to eliminate family planning funds from both domestic and foreign spending bills. He is particularly proud of his environmental positions. "That's what really defines me as a moderate," Shays says. "I believe we're not going to have a world to live in if we neglect it." In 2000, he was one of 10 Republicans endorsed by the Sierra Club.

Shays, a Peace Corps alumnus who served in the Fiji Islands, accepts the need to work for change incrementally in Congress. He is deliberate and patient when making his case. Although not shy about challenging his opponents, he usually does so without appearing strident.

But Shays is not afraid occasionally to take a more bold, confrontational approach. As a state legislator in 1985, he served several days in jail on a contempt citation after he attempted to make a courtroom statement accusing a judge of going easy on an attorney charged with misconduct. The incident prompted an outpouring of positive press portraying Shays as a man challenging the establishment to demand high ethical standards.

Such instincts perhaps are not surprising given that most of Shays' adult life has focused on politics. He was elected to Congress in 1987 at age 41 after serving in the state legislature for 12 years.

Shays' signature legislative effort in recent years has been his partnership with a Democrat — Martin T. Meehan of Massachusetts. In both 1998 and 1999, their bill to overhaul campaign finance laws drew 58 percent of the House vote despite opposition by the GOP leadership. The legislation aimed to bar national parties from receiving or spending "soft money" — unlimited contributions used for party-building activities and issue ads. A similar bill pushed in the Senate by Republican John McCain of Arizona and Democrat Russell D. Feingold of Wisconsin failed to get any traction.

Shays was one of only four House Republicans who opposed all four articles of impeachment against President Clinton. In total, he has voted more frequently with Clinton than all but a handful of his GOP colleagues; in the 106th Congress, he backed Clinton almost half the time — ranking him as one of the president's top 10 Republican allies.

Shays was one of a sizable minority of Republicans who bucked their leadership and sided with Democrats in 1996 and in 2000 in support of increasing the minimum wage. He also was in the minority of Republicans who supported Clinton's 1994 anti-crime bill, which included a ban on certain semiautomatic, assault-style weapons.

Still, he has managed to avoid completely alienating the GOP hierarchy. There was no mistaking Shays' Republican stripes in his votes on the Budget Committee, where party leaders first gave him a seat in 1991 and on which he served until he left in 2001 to take a spot on the Financial Services panel.

On Budget, he was a consistent scold about reining in spending. Shays notes that he advocates spending restraint even on defense and transportation, areas in which many of his conservative colleagues are inclined to be generous.

He has earned his GOP credentials in other ways as well. Republican leaders chose him to be the lead sponsor of the Congressional Accountability

Act, the first major piece of legislation to become law after the GOP took control of Congress in 1995. The act put Congress under some of the labor, civil rights and health laws that apply to the private sector.

In 1997, Shays joined with close friend and Budget Committee Chairman John R. Kasich, R-Ohio, to craft a plan to balance the budget by 2002. And in the spring of 1998, he again teamed with Kasich in objecting to the House's passage of the $218 billion transportation reauthorization bill. Shays said the bill had "more pork in it than the Democrats would ever have tried."

Shays also put up a fuss in the waning days of the 105th, when GOP leaders made numerous concessions to Democrats on a huge, catchall spending bill. "This bill represents everything I fought against as a fiscal conservative in this House," he said. In 2000, he voted against a $13.2 billion supplemental spending bill pushed by House GOP leaders. Most of the money was for defense spending, and Shays said he was appalled by the size of the package.

Shays, a veteran member of the Government Reform Committee, was a prime mover of two House-passed "reform" measures — one prohibiting members from receiving gifts other than those from close friends and family and one requiring thorough lobbying disclosure.

As chairman of the Government Reform Subcommittee on Human Resources, Shays in 1997 conducted an investigation into reports of illnesses suffered by veterans of the Persian Gulf War. He faulted the Pentagon and the Department of Veterans Affairs for not paying enough attention to so-called Persian Gulf syndrome ailments.

In the 106th, Shays took over a new Government Reform subcommittee — National Security, Veterans Affairs and International Relations — where he aggressively investigated the military's policy of requiring anthrax vaccines for soldiers. The military required its personnel to use the vaccine as protection from biological attacks, but Shays' panel issued a report in 2000 saying the vaccines were ineffective and challenging the military's claim that they have been proven safe.

Shays came to Congress by winning a 1987 special election held after GOP Rep. Stewart B. McKinney died. With an extensive grass-roots network and tireless campaigning, Shays won the primary with a 38 percent plurality. The 4th District is a bastion of moderate Republicanism, and Shays, campaigning from the center, beat Democrat Christine M. Niedermeier with 57 percent of the vote.

Since handily winning his seat, Shays has never faced a substantial electoral challenge. In 1999, he told the Connecticut Post that he would "love to be governor of Connecticut one day."

KEY VOTES

2000

Yes Raise hourly minimum wage by $1 over two years
Yes Halt funding for U.S. mission in Kosovo unless European nations pay more
No   Provide Medicare benefits to military retirees and their dependents
Yes Grant China permanent normal trade status
Yes Phase out estate, gift and trust taxes
No   Prohibit implementation of president's national monument designations
Yes Approve GOP plan to provide prescription drug coverage for Medicare beneficiaries
Yes Increase help for poor nations indebted to international financial institutions

1999

No   Impose steel import quotas
Yes Kill proposal to take aviation trust funds off budget
No   Require background checks on buyers only at gun shows with 10 or more vendors
Yes Remove barriers among banking, securities and insurance companies
No   Authorize state grants to hire teachers and reduce class size
Yes Overhaul campaign finance law; ban "soft money" and restrict advocacy advertising
Yes Approve bipartisan plan to increase rights of patients in managed-care health plans

INTEREST GROUPS

	AFL-CIO	ADA	CCUS	ACU
2000	30%	40%	76%	60%
1999	11%	55%	60%	44%
1998	40%	45%	56%	40%
1997	38%	55%	70%	56%

CQ VOTE STUDIES

	PARTY UNITY		PRESIDENTIAL SUPPORT	
	Support	Oppose	Support	Oppose
2000	71%	29%	49%	51%
1999	66%	34%	48%	52%
1998	58%	42%	57%	43%
1997	66%	34%	55%	45%

CONNECTICUT 4
Southwest — Stamford; Bridgeport

The sparkling "Gold Coast" of Connecticut, bordering Long Island Sound and New York City, is a wealthy enclave surrounding the working-class city of Bridgeport. This contrast creates a complex world for politicians to navigate. Polo clubs rub elbows with the decayed city of Bridgeport.

Many district residents travel to jobs in New York City and Stamford, causing severe traffic problems on Interstate 95, already a congested route. Traffic issues permeate the public debate. Welfare-to-work programs also have become an issue as poor Bridgeport residents seek jobs in the suburbs. Having failed to place welfare recipients in good jobs in the city, the government has alarmed some suburbanites by making moves to place workers in the affluent suburbs.

The suburban elite are the driving force of the 4th's political landscape, giving the district more registered Republicans than any

other in Connecticut. Still, the 4th gave the edge to the Democratic presidential candidate in 1996 and 2000. There is an uneasy mix between the wealthy, homogenous villages and the poor, urban areas where a majority of the population generally votes Democratic. Republican mayors dominate local politics and have been responsive to the large businesses headquartered in the district.

MAJOR INDUSTRY
Manufacturing, banking, medical

CITIES
Bridgeport, 137,040, Stamford, 110,802, Norwalk, 78,083

UNUSUAL FEATURES
P.T. Barnum, founder of the Ringling Bros., Barnum & Bailey Circus, made his home in Bridgeport; During both World Wars I and II, Bridgeport was the largest producer of ammunition for the Allied forces.

Rep. Jim Maloney (D)

CAPITOL OFFICE
225-3822; fax 225-5746
1427 Longworth Bldg. 20515

INTERNET
e-mail: www.house.gov/writerep
web: www.house.gov/jimmaloney

COMMITTEES
Armed Services
Financial Services

HOMETOWN
Danbury

BORN
Sept. 17, 1948, Quincy, Mass.

RELIGION
Roman Catholic

FAMILY
Wife, Mary Maloney; three children

EDUCATION
Harvard U., B.A. 1972; Boston U., J.D. 1980

CAREER
Lawyer; anti-poverty organization director

POLITICAL HIGHLIGHTS
Conn. Senate, 1987-95; Democratic nominee for
U.S. House, 1994

ELECTION RESULTS

2000 GENERAL

Jim Maloney (D)	118,932	53.6%
Mark D. Nielsen (R)	98,229	44.3%
Joseph A. Zdonczyk (CC)	4,653	2.1%

2000 PRIMARY

Jim Maloney (D)	unopposed

1998 GENERAL

Jim Maloney (D)	78,394	49.9%
Mark D. Nielsen (R)	76,051	48.4%
Robert V. Strasdauskas (CC)	2,712	1.7%

PREVIOUS WINNING PERCENTAGES
1996 (52%)

Elected 1996; 3rd term

Maloney is a New Democrat, a moderate in the tradition of his state's junior senator, Joseph I. Lieberman, and his legislative agenda in Washington reflects that. He is not afraid to break with his party now and then on issues such as taxes, and his ratings from various interest groups confirm a centrist voting record.

Thus, Maloney's background may come as somewhat of a surprise: In 1968, midway through Harvard, he put his college education on hold for two years to work in Gary, Ind., as a VISTA anti-poverty volunteer, a seminal experience that started him down the path of public life. After graduating from college, Maloney became executive director of Danbury's anti-poverty agency, overseeing initiatives such as the Women, Infants and Children nutrition program, Meals on Wheels for the elderly and the Head Start program for preschool children.

One might expect a person with those experiences to be a proponent of activist government. But Maloney has been involved in western Connecticut politics since 1986, and his stands reflect the views of his constituents. Still, he has remained true to the beliefs that spurred him to volunteer for VISTA: In 2000, Maloney joined a number of other lawmakers in a symbolic walk across the Edmund Pettus Bridge in Selma, Ala., to commemorate the 35th anniversary of the famous civil rights march.

The 5th District, which includes some of the nation's wealthiest people but also a fair number of blue-collar workers, is just about evenly divided politically. Recent congressional elections have reflected that split: The 54 percent that Maloney captured in 2000 was the most for any winner since Republican John G. Rowland won the 5th by a landslide in 1988.

Maloney himself had to wage two hard-fought campaigns to wrest the 5th from the GOP, and every day in Congress he wakes up knowing that Republicans are bent on taking back the seat.

His strategy for surviving in a competitive district is twofold: Vote carefully, giving both conservatives and liberals some of what they want, and keep up a high profile at home (something his predecessor, Republican Gary A. Franks, neglected to do). Maloney, a burly, back-slapping man, quick with a laugh or a joke, wins praise for his constituent service.

The Democratic leadership put Maloney on committees that give him a chance to boost his district and state. He sits on Armed Services, where he looks out for the interests of Connecticut's defense-related industries, whose output for the Pentagon includes Black Hawk and Comanche helicopters, engines for the F-22 jet fighter, nuclear submarines and high-tech electronics.

Maloney also serves on the Financial Services panel, which brings him in contact with businesses and individuals whose investment decisions could benefit his 5th District as it struggles to generate new economic activity to replace declining or defunct manufacturing.

He is a reliable supporter of strong environmental protections, particularly steps to clean up "brownfields" — idle and contaminated industrial sites — so they can attract private investment. Such sites in the district's Naugatuck Valley are a drag on local economic recovery. Maloney backs organized labor, voting no in 2000 on a bill to expand trade ties with China.

In the education arena, he calls for more investment in public schools and opposes conservatives' efforts to give parents vouchers they could use to pay private school tuition. He argues that schools must have high standards and be accountable for the success or failure of students. He authored a bill in the 106th Congress to give local schools more federal money if they end the practice of "social promotion" — advancing students to the next grade regardless of their academic achievement. And in his first term, he sponsored a bill to put specially trained police — "school resource officers" — in schools.

As a freshman, he was one of only 25 Democrats to vote for a constitutional amendment requiring a two-thirds vote in Congress to raise federal taxes. He backed constitutional amendments to limit congressional service and to allow Congress to outlaw desecration of the U.S. flag, and he voted to ban a procedure its opponents call "partial birth" abortion. Maloney was a start-to-finish supporter of the 1997 drive for a balanced-budget agreement.

In the 106th Congress, he was in the minority of Democrats who voted to repeal the estate tax and to end the "marriage penalty," a quirk in the tax code that results in some two-earner married couples paying higher taxes than they would if each partner were single.

Maloney grew up in Massachusetts, the oldest of 10 children. He recalls admiring Robert F. Kennedy and Martin Luther King Jr., and it was in 1968, the year both were assassinated, that he interrupted college to become a VISTA volunteer. After a half decade as Danbury's anti-poverty director, Maloney became a lawyer. He won four two-year terms in the state Senate, where he focused on tax reduction and economic development.

He gave up his state Senate seat to run for Congress in 1994 and ended up losing by only 6 points to Republican Franks. Despite that creditable showing in a strong GOP year, Maloney was regarded as a long shot when he returned to challenge Franks in 1996. But the incumbent, one of only two black Republicans in Congress at the time, was so confident of re-election that he dedicated several weeks in the summer to a national tour promoting a book he had written about his experiences as a conservative black Republican.

Maloney assembled a strong grass-roots organization and a solid fundraising machine that made him a more formidable candidate than he had been in 1994, and he ousted Franks, 52 percent to 46 percent.

In 1998, the national Republican Party had Maloney in its sights. But in a year in which only six incumbents were defeated in November, Maloney narrowly eked out another victory, 50 percent to 48 percent. His 2,343-vote margin of victory made it the second-closest House race in the nation.

In a 2000 rematch with his 1998 foe, former state Sen. Mark D. Nielsen, a campaign that sometimes got nasty, Maloney prevailed by 10 points, benefiting from Lieberman's presence on the ballot as the vice-presidential candidate.

KEY VOTES

2000
Yes Raise hourly minimum wage by $1 over two years
No Halt funding for U.S. mission in Kosovo unless European nations pay more
Yes Provide Medicare benefits to military retirees and their dependents
No Grant China permanent normal trade status
Yes Phase out estate, gift and trust taxes
No Prohibit implementation of president's national monument designations
Yes Approve GOP plan to provide prescription drug coverage for Medicare beneficiaries
No Increase help for poor nations indebted to international financial institutions

1999
Yes Impose steel import quotas
No Kill proposal to take aviation trust funds off budget
No Require background checks on buyers only at gun shows with 10 or more vendors
Yes Remove barriers among banking, securities and insurance companies
Yes Authorize state grants to hire teachers and reduce class size
Yes Overhaul campaign finance law; ban "soft money" and restrict advocacy advertising
Yes Approve bipartisan plan to increase rights of patients in managed-care health plans

INTEREST GROUPS

	AFL-CIO	ADA	CCUS	ACU
2000	60%	55%	52%	36%
1999	89%	85%	44%	28%
1998	90%	85%	56%	32%
1997	75%	75%	60%	32%

CQ VOTE STUDIES

	PARTY UNITY		PRESIDENTIAL SUPPORT	
	Support	Oppose	Support	Oppose
2000	78%	22%	62%	38%
1999	80%	20%	72%	28%
1998	79%	21%	68%	32%
1997	85%	15%	68%	32%

CONNECTICUT 5
West – Waterbury; Danbury

Some of the nation's richest residents make their home in exclusive small towns in the 5th, but their business and social lives are centered in New York City. Fairfield County, in the southern part of the district, empties out each morning as residents head for New York on commuter trains, in luxury sedans.

Heading into the central part of the state, the other half of the 5th's residents live less-charmed lives. As in much of New England, the economy fell apart in the 1980s with the almost complete loss of defense and manufacturing jobs. New Haven County managed to climb out of the hole in the 1990s, attracting some high-tech businesses and starting to clean up the area's brownfields, created by brass and hat manufacturing plants. Solving environmental problems is seen as a key to making New Haven County as livable as its genteel neighbor.

Compromise is a politician's best friend in the 5th, a competitive district

where neither county can be ignored. Fairfield County is focused on maintaining its high standard of living and keeping out crime, but will support socially liberal candidates who attract voters in New Haven County. And New Haven County voters will support moderate Republicans who recognize the needs of their cities.

The district swings in presidential contests. It gave a 7 percent edge to George Bush in 1992. But it gave Bill Clinton an 8-point win in 1996. While President Bush did not capture any Connecticut district in the 2000 presidential election, his highest vote percentage came from the 5th, where he garnered 44 percent.

MAJOR INDUSTRY
Manufacturing, defense, health care

CITIES
Waterbury, 104,263; Danbury, 66,965; Meriden, 56,365

UNUSUAL FEATURES
The Wiffle Ball Inc. makes the original Wiffle Ball in Shelton; The official Congressional Pin, a lapel pin worn by all members of Congress, is manufactured in Waterbury.

Rep. Nancy L. Johnson (R)

Elected 1982; 10th term

CAPITOL OFFICE
225-4476; fax 225-4488; 2113 Rayburn Bldg. 20515

INTERNET
e-mail: njohnson@mail.house.gov
web: www.house.gov/nancyjohnson

COMMITTEES
Ways & Means
(Health - chairwoman)

HOMETOWN
New Britain

BORN
Jan. 5, 1935, Chicago, Ill.

RELIGION
Unitarian

FAMILY
Husband, Theodore Johnson; three children

EDUCATION
Radcliffe College, B.A. 1957; U. of London,
attended 1957-58

CAREER
Civic leader

POLITICAL HIGHLIGHTS
Republican candidate for New Britain Common
Council, 1975; Conn. Senate, 1977-83

ELECTION RESULTS

2000 GENERAL

Nancy L. Johnson (R)	143,698	62.6%
Paul Vincent Valenti (D)	75,471	32.9%
Audrey A. Cole (GREEN)	7,303	3.2%
Timothy A. Knibbs (CC)	3,071	1.3%

2000 PRIMARY
Nancy L. Johnson (R) — unopposed

1998 GENERAL

Nancy L. Johnson (R)	101,630	58.1%
Charlotte Koskoff (D)	69,201	39.6%
Timothy A. Knibbs (CC)	3,217	1.8%

PREVIOUS WINNING PERCENTAGES
1996 (50%); 1994 (64%); 1992 (70%); 1990 (74%);
1988 (66%); 1986 (64%); 1984 (64%); 1982 (52%)

Johnson is a classic moderate. She can be a thorn in her party's side, openly working with lawmakers from across the aisle, coaxing her own Republican colleagues along, and forcing them to confront issues they might have preferred to avoid. She also compromises easily — sometimes too easily, her allies have complained. Often it is hard for either side to predict which way she will go and for what reason.

Perhaps that is because of the difficult balance Johnson strives for as she tries to hold the congressional center on social issues — where she has significant influence as Ways and Means Health Subcommittee chairman in the 107th Congress — while throwing enough fiscal conservatism into the mix to remind Republicans that she is one of them. That would explain why the same Johnson who cosponsored a school construction bill favored by Democrats also received an award from the National Federation of Independent Business for supporting so many of the tax-cutting bills favored by small businesses.

Both parties have an uneasy relationship with their moderates, but Johnson has had enough influence and drawn enough attention to be considered Senate material — a possibility had Connecticut's Democratic senator, Joseph I. Lieberman, won the vice presidency in 2000. If nothing else, she is well-positioned to keep House Republicans on their toes in the 107th.

In the 106th, she made a name for herself as a champion of federal aid to build new schools. She and Charles B. Rangel of New York, who is the ranking Democrat on Ways and Means, teamed up on legislation that would have used federal money to indirectly help build new schools, by creating tax credits to pay the interest on $24.8 billion in construction bonds over two years.

It was not an easy position for a Republican to take, as the bill was similar to a proposal in President Clinton's budget and her support for the idea gave him lots of political mileage. House GOP leaders had to pull one of their highest legislative priorities from the floor — a bill to let parents save money in tax-free accounts for education expenses — when Johnson and Rangel appeared to have enough votes to pass their plan as an alternative. In public, Republican leaders opposed the Johnson-Rangel bill as an inappropriate expansion of the federal role in education. But they also were under tremendous pressure from business lobbyists because the measure would have required the projects to pay the local prevailing wage to construction workers under the Davis-Bacon Act — a poison pill for business groups.

That issue showed two sides of Johnson: the rebellious Republican willing to challenge GOP conventional wisdom and the cautious Republican anxious not to isolate herself completely. The rebellious Johnson wrote a letter to her colleagues insisting that paying prevailing wages for construction projects built with federal funds is "nothing new" and would not inflate construction costs. But when Republicans countered with a milder, narrower proposal that did not include the prevailing wage requirement, the cautious Johnson immediately jumped on board.

The congresswoman is used to being squeezed by both sides. During her first three terms, her ambition to land a prestigious committee assignment was thwarted by GOP conservatives, who took a dim view of her high-profile support for abortion rights and her calls for more diversity in the Republican Party. She joined the Ways and Means Committee in 1989, but she was soundly beaten in a bid for a low-level leadership post three years later.

Johnson chaired the House ethics committee in the 104th Congress, and the post almost cost her her House seat. The marquee case before the panel involved the political fundraising activities of Speaker Newt Gingrich, and her handling of the matter displeased lawmakers and constituents in both parties. Democrats said she was dragging the case out to help her Speaker; Republicans said her actions played into the Democrats' hands. She won her eighth term in 1996 by just 1,587 votes.

Johnson's closest allies in the House are other moderate Republicans, but the Connecticut lawmaker is clearly willing to push the envelope only so far. She must, for example, look out for the insurance companies that are a major presence in her state — making it hard for Johnson to endorse any significant regulation of medical insurance. She voted against the bipartisan managed-care overhaul bill passed by the House in 1999 in favor of the more limited alternative endorsed by the GOP leadership.

Still, Johnson earns high marks from Democrats for her willingness to listen and her ability to work with both parties. Under pressure from Democrats, she agreed to beef up a child support bill by allowing states to pass along up to $400 a month in child support payments to poor families while they were still on welfare. In doing so, Johnson had to persuade many GOP conservatives to abandon their position that single mothers should receive as little public aid as possible and that welfare payments should be cut if child support money is available.

Born in Chicago, Johnson came East to go to college, married an obstetrician, raised three children and got involved in community affairs in New Britain. Her civic activism led Republicans to recruit her into politics, and after losing a city council election in 1975, she won a state Senate seat the next year, waging a frenetic door-to-door campaign to defeat a complacent Democratic incumbent by 150 votes. By 1980, her winning percentage was up to 62 percent.

When Democratic Rep. Toby Moffett announced that he was giving up the 6th District seat to run for the Senate in 1982, Johnson moved eagerly to take his place. She quickly captured the backing of the party establishment and GOP donors, and she overwhelmed a conservative opponent in the primary. In November, she defeated the badly underfunded Democratic candidate, state Sen. Bill Curry, by 4 percentage points. She won easily until her close call in 1996.

Since that scare, Johnson has more than recovered politically; she won with 63 percent in 2000. Still, her long-term future is uncertain: Connecticut lost a House seat in reapportionment and her district could be split up.

KEY VOTES

2000
Yes Raise hourly minimum wage by $1 over two years
Yes Halt funding for U.S. mission in Kosovo unless European nations pay more
Yes Provide Medicare benefits to military retirees and their dependents
Yes Grant China permanent normal trade status
Yes Phase out estate, gift and trust taxes
Yes Prohibit implementation of president's national monument designations
Yes Approve GOP plan to provide prescription drug coverage for Medicare beneficiaries
No Increase help for poor nations indebted to international financial institutions

1999
No Impose steel import quotas
Yes Kill proposal to take aviation trust funds off budget
No Require background checks on buyers only at gun shows with 10 or more vendors
Yes Remove barriers among banking, securities and insurance companies
No Authorize state grants to hire teachers and reduce class size
Yes Overhaul campaign finance law; ban "soft money" and restrict advocacy advertising
No Approve bipartisan plan to increase rights of patients in managed-care health plans

INTEREST GROUPS

	AFL-CIO	ADA	CCUS	ACU
2000	10%	35%	90%	56%
1999	22%	55%	83%	36%
1998	50%	55%	83%	16%
1997	50%	55%	80%	36%

CQ VOTE STUDIES

	PARTY UNITY		PRESIDENTIAL SUPPORT	
	Support	Oppose	Support	Oppose
2000	71%	29%	51%	49%
1999	67%	33%	54%	46%
1998	62%	38%	57%	43%
1997	68%	32%	60%	40%

CONNECTICUT 6
Northwest – New Britain

Located in northwest corner of the state, the 6th is a model of small-town New England living. Towns still have commons, greens and town hall meetings. The Berkshire Mountains roll into the district's edges. Still, there are many pockets of industry, and several cities border the rural farmland. This blended landscape attracts New Yorkers looking to escape city life while maintaining their standard of living.

The 6th's economy has been slowly improving since the recession of the late 1980s. Once affluent, the 6th bore the brunt of the downturn in Connecticut, shrinking in population after losing manufacturing jobs. Once famed for its ball bearing plants and specialized precision work, the district's economic turnaround is being aided by a rise in the health care industry.

The area has been considered Democratic since the late 1980s because of its economic instability, although Republicans have a solid presence in the smaller towns and a moderate Republican holds the

House seat. Republican presidential candidates did well in the 1980s. But that began to change when the recession hit in the late '80s and early '90s, and Democratic presidential candidates scored easier victories. In 2000, Al Gore clinched the district by 10 percentage points over President Bush.

Legislators have to be attuned to social concerns, including regenerating the district's cities. In an area that was used to affluence, maintaining the standard of living is a big issue for both parties.

MAJOR INDUSTRY
Health care, insurance, manufacturing

CITIES
New Britain, 70,010; Bristol, 59,145; Torrington, 34,583

UNUSUAL FEATURES
Bill Rasmussen, the founder of ESPN, dreamed up the idea for a cable sports network in Bristol; Pulitzer Prize-winning author Philip Roth resides in the district.

Gov. Ruth Ann Minner (D)

First elected: 2000
Length of term: 4 years
Term expires: 1/05
Salary: $114,000
Phone: (302) 739-4101
Hometown: Milford
Born: Jan. 17, 1935; Milford, Del.
Religion: Methodist
Family: Widowed; three children
Education: Delaware Technical and Community College, G.E.D. 1968
Career: Towing company owner; state legislature aide
Political highlights: Del. House, 1975-83; Del. Senate, 1983-93; lieutenant governor, 1993-2001

Election results:

2000 GENERAL

Ruth Ann Minner (D)	191,695	59.2%
John Burris (R)	128,603	39.8%
Floyd E. McDowell Sr. (IP)	3,271	1.0%

Lt. Gov. John Carney (D)

First elected: 2000
Length of term: 4 years
Term expires: 1/05
Salary: $60,000
Phone: (302) 739-4151

STATE LEGISLATURE

General Assembly: Meets January-June
House: 41 members, 2-year terms
2001 breakdown: 26R, 15D; 31 men, 10 women
Salary: $33,400
Phone: (302) 739-4087
Senate: 21 members, 4-year terms
2001 breakdown: 8R, 13D; 15 men, 6 women
Salary: $33,400
Phone: (302) 739-4129

STATE TERM LIMITS

Governor: 2 terms
Senate: No
House: No

URBAN STATISTICS

CITY	POPULATION
Wilmington	71,491
Dover	32,099
Newark	28,318

REGISTERED VOTERS

Democrat	42%
Republican	34%
Other	23%

POPULATION

2000 population	783,600
1990 population	666,168
Percent change	+17.6%
Rank among states	45
Median age	35.3
Born in state	50%
Foreign born	3%
Urban/rural	73%/27%
Crime rate	678/100,000
Poverty level	10.3%
Federal workers	5,407
Military	8,946

REAPPORTIONMENT

Delaware retained its one House seat in reapportionment.

MISCELLANEOUS

Web: www.state.de.us
Capital: Dover
Land area: 1,955 sq. miles
Rank among states: 49
STATE ELECTION OFFICIAL
(302) 739-4277
DEMOCRATIC HEADQUARTERS
(302) 996-9458
REPUBLICAN HEADQUARTERS
(302) 651-0260

District Statistics

DIST.	2000 D	2000 R	GREEN	1996 D	1996 R	REF	1992 D	1992 R	I	WHT	BLK	ASIAN	HISP	HOUSEHOLD INCOME	OVER 65+	UNDER 18	COLLEGE EDUCATION
AL	55%	42%	3%	52%	37%	11%	44%	35%	20%	80%	17%	1%	2%	$34,875	12%	25%	21%

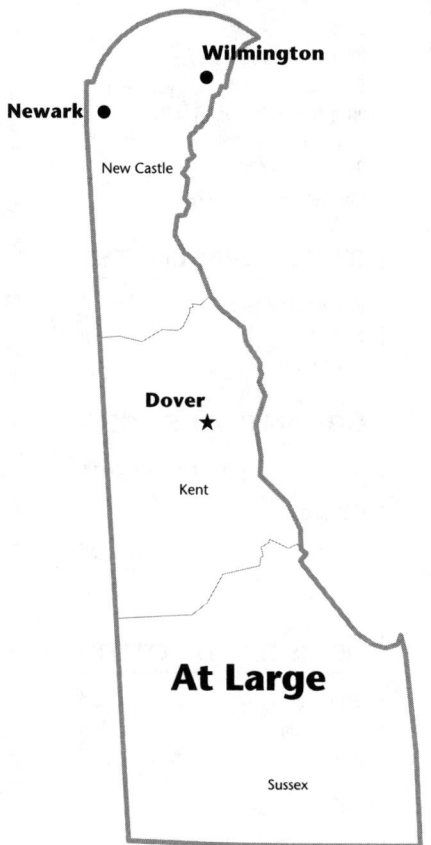

Sen. Joseph R. Biden Jr. (D)

Elected 1972; 5th term

CAPITOL OFFICE
224-5042; fax 224-0139; 221 Russell Bldg. 20510

INTERNET
e-mail: senator@biden.senate.gov
web: biden.senate.gov

COMMITTEES
Foreign Relations - ranking member
Judiciary

HOMETOWN
Wilmington

BORN
Nov. 20, 1942, Scranton, Pa.

RELIGION
Roman Catholic

FAMILY
Wife, Jill Biden; four children (one deceased)

EDUCATION
U. of Delaware, B.A. 1965; Syracuse U., J.D. 1968

CAREER
Lawyer

POLITICAL HIGHLIGHTS
New Castle County Council, 1970-72

ELECTION RESULTS

1996 GENERAL

Joseph R. Biden Jr. (D)	165,465	60.0%
Raymond J. Clatworthy (R)	105,088	38.1%
Mark Jones (LIBERT)	3,340	1.2%

1996 PRIMARY

Joseph R. Biden Jr. (D)	unopposed

PREVIOUS WINNING PERCENTAGES
1990 (63%); 1984 (60%); 1978 (58%); 1972 (50%)

Nearing the end of his third decade in the Senate, Biden is far removed from the 30-year-old wunderkind he was when he first arrived, but he still exhibits the intelligence, drive and passion of his youth. He can be eloquent at times, yet even in a chamber known for its long-winded speakers, Biden's loquaciousness stands out.

He remains a large figure on the domestic and international scene, where he brings his wide-ranging expertise to bear on a variety of issues. And, even though his run at the presidency in 1987 was cut short by a flap over plagiarized speeches, aides say that Biden has not abandoned his presidential ambitions and could seek the Democratic nomination again in 2004, when he will be 61.

Many senators look to Biden, a constitutional law expert, during such highly publicized events as President Clinton's 1999 impeachment trial. But his most important words in recent years may have been spoken behind closed doors — in conversations with North Carolina Republican Jesse Helms, chairman of the Foreign Relations Committee, where Biden has been the top Democrat since 1997.

The two come from sharply different political backgrounds — one is a Southern conservative, the other a Northern liberal — but they share a long history of serving together (both became senators in 1973), a pragmatic streak and a determination to return the panel to a key role in shaping foreign policy. That common interest has led to landmark legislation to repay the U.S. debt to the United Nations, reorganize the foreign affairs bureaucracy, ratify the Chemical Weapons Convention and authorize many foreign aid programs for the first time in 15 years.

Biden and Helms hardly see eye to eye every time. But Biden's ability to maintain lines of communication with all groups often has made him, rather than Helms, the key vote on Foreign Relations. He has held together Democrats who frequently had splintered under the panel's previous ranking Democrat, Claiborne Pell of Rhode Island. And despite being in the minority, Biden often managed to make common cause with enough panel Republicans to assemble majorities on the committee for some of Clinton's priorities, from debt relief for the world's poorest countries to increased assistance to combat HIV and AIDS overseas.

Indeed, the Clinton administration pushed foreign affairs priorities without Biden at its peril, such as when it enlisted Byron L. Dorgan, D-N.D., to lead what was ultimately a failed fight in 1999 to approve the ratification of the Comprehensive Test Ban Treaty.

Biden chaired the Judiciary Committee from 1987 to 1995 and still exerts considerable influence in that arena. During the hearings in early 2001 on the nomination of former Sen. John Ashcroft to be attorney general, Biden was especially outspoken in his criticism of the nominee. He said he wished Ashcroft had been picked for "secretary of anything but this single job." In questioning that centered on Ashcroft's record on racial issues, Biden said that the Justice Department is an institution African-Americans rely on for protection.

Biden suggested that because of Ashcroft's decisions, from appearing at Bob Jones University, which until recently prohibited interracial dating, to giving an interview to Southern Partisan magazine, blacks wondered if they would get a fair hearing from his Justice Department. When Ashcroft said that those actions did not constitute endorsements, Biden countered:

"This matters to people, John. Words matter. Words matter. And the less you have, the more distraught you are; the less you think you can get representation, the more the words matter."

Biden's stewardship at Judiciary will probably be best remembered for his handling of the 1991 nomination of conservative Clarence Thomas for the Supreme Court. The nationally televised committee hearings at which law professor Anita F. Hill accused Thomas of sexual harassment were an acute embarrassment to Biden, whose committee had not conducted more than a cursory investigation of Hill's charges until after they were leaked to the media.

As Judiciary chairman in the 103rd Congress, Biden shepherded to passage a comprehensive, $30.2 billion anti-crime package. In the 104th Congress, he helped craft an anti-terrorism law that was enacted after the 1995 bombing of a federal building in Oklahoma City. He also has played a key role in consideration of juvenile justice legislation.

Over the years, Biden has taken more moderate stands on foreign policy. While he opposed the use of military force in the Persian Gulf in 1991 and insisted that Congress be a full partner with the White House in decisions to send U.S. forces to hostile areas, he shifted toward a more hawkish stance at the start of the 103rd Congress. From his post at the time as chairman of Foreign Relations' European Affairs Subcommittee, he urged Clinton to consider air strikes against the artillery positions of Bosnian Serbs.

Biden loves to talk, as reporters, aides and his fellow lawmakers can attest. While other senators are in private meetings or secluded in their offices, he often spends hour after hour in the halls and hideaways of Congress, holding court with reporters, twisting the arms of his colleagues and chatting with his constituents.

The Irish Catholic son of a Scranton, Pa., automobile dealer, Biden — who overcome a childhood stutter — often speaks with a self-deprecation that is part of his charm. But part of what has made the senator such a compelling political figure are the tragedies and dramas of his private life.

Biden was the underdog when, as a 29-year-old county councilman, he summoned his celebrated brashness to challenge Republican Sen. J. Caleb Boggs in 1972. Running on a dovish Vietnam platform, advocating more spending on mass transit and health services, and accusing the incumbent of being a do-nothing, he won by 3,162 votes.

Five weeks after his election, Biden's wife, Neilia, and their infant daughter, Amy, were killed and their two sons seriously injured in an automobile accident. Biden said at first that he did not want to take the job he had just won. Persuaded by Majority Leader Mike Mansfield, D-Mont., to assume his seat, Biden was sworn in at the bedside of one of his sons. He has won re-election easily ever since.

After 15 years building his Senate credentials and rebuilding his life — he remarried and commutes by train from Wilmington every day — Biden launched a campaign for the presidency. He withdrew in September 1987 amid reports that he had plagiarized passages in his speeches and in a 1965 law school paper and that he had exaggerated his résumé.

No sooner did that presidential campaign end than a brush with death put Biden back in the news. In 1988, he had a near-fatal brain aneurysm. By early 1989, he was back in action but looked potentially vulnerable to a GOP challenge in 1990. Conservatives were eager to avenge the 1987 defeat of the Supreme Court nomination of Robert H. Bork, which failed during Biden's watch as Judiciary chairman. Biden's triumph over his health problems bolstered the affections of supporters, however, and he won his fourth term with 63 percent. He won his fifth term with 60 percent in 1996.

KEY VOTES

2000
Yes Overhaul bankruptcy law and increase minimum wage
No Limit fiscal 2001 discretionary spending to $600.3 billion
No Override veto on nuclear waste disposal at Yucca Mountain site in Nevada
Yes Oppose effort to terminate Kosovo mission
Yes Include gender, sexual orientation and disability in federal hate crime protections
No Approve GOP plan to restrict use of genetic information by health insurers
No Kill amendment delaying implementation of an anti-missile defense system
Yes Cut taxes for married couples
Yes Grant China permanent normal trade status

1999
No Remove President Clinton from office for obstruction of justice
No Kill amendment authorizing state grants to hire teachers and reduce class size
Yes Require criminal background checks for purchases at gun shows
No Approve GOP proposal to increase rights of patients in managed-care health plans
No Block effort to allow farm and medicine exports to Cuba
No Allow study of tougher automobile fuel efficiency standards
Yes Ratify nuclear weapons testing treaty
Yes Prohibit national political parties from collecting "soft money" donations
Yes Remove barriers among banking, securities and insurance companies

INTEREST GROUPS

	AFL-CIO	ADA	CCUS	ACU
2000	63%	80%	60%	16%
1999	89%	95%	47%	4%
1998	88%	85%	56%	4%
1997	57%	70%	70%	16%
1996	86%	80%	46%	20%
1995	92%	95%	37%	17%
1994	86%	80%	20%	0%
1993	91%	80%	33%	21%
1992	100%	100%	20%	0%
1991	83%	90%	20%	5%

CQ VOTE STUDIES

	PARTY UNITY		PRESIDENTIAL SUPPORT	
	Support	Oppose	Support	Oppose
2000	88%	12%	91%	9%
1999	93%	7%	89%	11%
1998	87%	13%	91%	9%
1997	82%	18%	84%	16%
1996	79%	21%	92%	8%
1995	87%	13%	85%	15%
1994	92%	8%	89%	11%
1993	92%	8%	97%	3%
1992	92%	8%	29%	71%
1991	92%	8%	34%	66%

Sen. Thomas R. Carper (D)

Elected 2000; 1st term

CAPITOL OFFICE
224-2441; fax 228-2190; 513 Hart Bldg. 20510

INTERNET
e-mail: carper.senate.gov/email
web: carper.senate.gov

COMMITTEES
Banking, Housing & Urban Affairs
Environment & Public Works
Governmental Affairs
Special Aging

HOMETOWN
Wilmington

BORN
Jan. 23, 1947, Beckley, W.Va.

RELIGION
Presbyterian

FAMILY
Wife, Martha Carper; two children

EDUCATION
Ohio State U., B.A. 1968; U. of Delaware, M.B.A. 1975

MILITARY SERVICE
Navy, 1968-73; Naval Reserve, 1973-92

CAREER
State economic development official

POLITICAL HIGHLIGHTS
Del. treasurer, 1977-83; U.S. House, 1983-93; governor, 1993-2001

ELECTION RESULTS

2000 GENERAL

Thomas R. Carper (D)	181,566	55.5%
William V. Roth Jr. (R)	142,891	43.7%

2000 PRIMARY

Thomas R. Carper (D)	unopposed

PREVIOUS WINNING PERCENTAGES
1990 House Election (66%); 1988 House Election (68%); 1986 House Election (66%); 1984 House Election (59%); 1982 House Election (52%)

Carper became a Delaware political star in 1976 at age 29, and his rise has continued unbroken in the nearly quarter-century since.

Elected first as state treasurer, then to five terms in the state's sole U.S. House seat, then to two terms as governor, Carper holds the Delaware record for most wins for statewide office — 10 — after accomplishing his biggest feat yet — his victory, by a comfortable margin, over popular five-term Republican Sen. William V. Roth Jr.

Carper is a centrist, pro-business Democrat, a posture that has helped him maintain his popularity in a state that generally eschews ideological politics and in which Democrats and Republicans share power to an extent unusual among the states. "I was a New Democrat before it was fashionable," he says. "I really think that we need more people in Congress who think like governors — who are result-oriented, who are not so ideologically driven, people who are impatient with gridlock, and maybe a little less partisan."

Carper has applied his bipartisan approach to addressing problems and, in doing so, has raised his profile nationally. As a member of the National Governors' Association (NGA), he was a chief negotiator in developing the group's federal welfare overhaul proposals that provided the basis for the law enacted in 1996. He served as NGA chairman in 1998.

Carper's ability to work across party lines helped him enact sweeping changes to Delaware's education system, perhaps his top priority as governor. After years of trying to get a legislative package passed, he agreed to a compromise measure, enacted in 2000, that set teacher accountability standards and authorized many programs that he advocated.

During his 10 years in the House, Carper was known as likable and polite, yet as someone who was not shy about defying his party's leadership. In the 100th Congress, for instance, Carper predicted that a surge of bankruptcies in the savings and loan industry would grow unless lawmakers approved enough financial assistance to rectify the problem. He backed a $15 billion package even though House Speaker Jim Wright of Texas and other Democratic leaders supported a much smaller plan. Wright eventually supported the $15 billion measure, but it was rejected by the House and a compromise bill cleared Congress; the industry's problems grew.

Born in West Virginia, Carper came to Delaware in 1973 to get his M.B.A. He has said that he had no master plan for politics — that he decided to enter the arena when he was lying on a beach in 1976 and heard a radio report that his party could not find a candidate for state treasurer. He got into the race and beat a strongly favored Republican.

In 1982, he made a late decision to challenge Republican Rep. Thomas B. Evans, but Carper's burgeoning campaign succeeded, returning the state's House seat to Democratic control for the first time since 1966.

The ambition, energy and hard work that have been Carper trademarks throughout his career were evident in his "battle of the titans" win over Roth, the Senate Finance Committee chairman who was well-known as the architect of the Roth IRA retirement plan. Carper found ways to distinguish himself from Roth, on health care and in other policy areas. He criticized Roth for not supporting bipartisan patients' rights legislation and for stalled efforts on a prescription drug benefit for seniors, an issue before Roth's Finance panel.

Carper dismisses suggestions that Delaware would be better served by someone with Roth's clout. Because of his experience and friends in Washington, he says: "I hit the ground running."

Rep. Michael N. Castle (R)

Elected 1992; 5th term

CAPITOL OFFICE
225-4165; fax 225-2291
1233 Longworth Bldg. 20515

INTERNET
e-mail: delaware@mail.house.gov
web: www.house.gov/castle

COMMITTEES
Education & Workforce
(Education Reform - chairman)
Financial Services
Select Intelligence
(Technical & Tactical Intelligence - chairman)

HOMETOWN
Wilmington

BORN
July 2, 1939, Wilmington, Del.

RELIGION
Roman Catholic

FAMILY
Wife, Jane DiSabatino

EDUCATION
Hamilton College, B.A. 1961; Georgetown U., LL.B.
1964

CAREER
Lawyer; state prosecutor

POLITICAL HIGHLIGHTS
Del. House, 1967-69; Del. Senate, 1969-77 (minority
leader, 1976-77); lieutenant governor, 1981-85;
governor, 1985-93

ELECTION RESULTS

2000 GENERAL

Michael N. Castle (R)	211,797	67.6%
Mike Miller (D)	96,488	30.8%

2000 PRIMARY

Michael N. Castle (R)	unopposed

1998 GENERAL

Michael N. Castle (R)	119,811	66.4%
Dennis E. Williams (D)	57,446	31.8%
James P. Webster (USTAX)	2,411	1.3%

PREVIOUS WINNING PERCENTAGES
1996 (70%); 1994 (71%); 1992 (55%)

The phrase "Castle, a GOP moderate" is so often used to describe the Delaware lawmaker in news reports and biographies that it might seem as if the words are part of his name. Castle, whose views on key social issues are to the left of much of his party, is indeed a centrist politically. But he is more likely to label himself a "pragmatist," believing that being a social moderate with fiscally conservative views is the only way to get things done in Congress.

"People look at Washington and say, 'Why are they fighting all the time?' " Castle told the Boston Globe in 1999. "We're here to get things done, not to carry out political wars."

Castle's emphasis on consensus has positioned him as a leading force in Congress, earning him key allies in the GOP leadership and among moderates in both parties, and landing him in the middle of some of the most contentious debates on Capitol Hill. In the 107th Congress, he is a leader of three centrist coalitions: the Tuesday Group of moderate Republicans, the Republican Main Street Partnership and the bipartisan House Centrist Coalition, formed in 2000. So it is no surprise that on major issues, Castle often carries a substantial bloc of moderate votes behind his positions.

Amiable and relatively quiet, Castle is nonetheless forceful in his opinions and bold about confronting the GOP leadership when he feels it is pursuing an overly conservative course. His role as a moderate leader has rankled some top Republicans. In 2000, Castle enraged Majority Whip Tom DeLay by yielding speaking time on the House floor to Democrat Harold E. Ford Jr. of Tennessee, who went on to excoriate the GOP leadership for threatening to draw out budget battles with President Clinton.

Castle's drive to find the middle ground also has won him an ally in Speaker J. Dennis Hastert, who consults with him regularly about the mood and positions of GOP moderates. In November 1998, Castle helped push Hastert as a rival to conservative Texan Dick Armey for majority leader of the 106th. Armey kept his job, but a month later when Republicans were scrambling to fill the gap left by the abrupt exit of Speaker-designate Robert L. Livingston, the consensus-building qualities Castle had praised in Hastert made him the party's unanimous choice for Speaker.

Being a friend of the Speaker hardly prevents Castle from actively challenging the Republican leadership on matters such as gun control, campaign finance overhaul and environmental policy. In 1999 and 2000, he supported Clinton's position almost half the time and readily admits that he votes "a little more independently than most members of Congress."

He was one of six Republicans in 1999 who signed a petition to force Hastert to bring campaign finance legislation to the House floor. But his rebellious ways can also be useful to Hastert: Caught in a dispute between GOP conservatives, who would not support a minimum wage increase unless states were allowed to opt out, and Republican moderates, who opposed such a provision, Castle provided a way out for the Speaker by being the Republican to propose the amendment eliminating the opt-out provision, which ultimately succeeded.

As chairman of the Education and the Workforce panel's Education Reform Subcommittee, Castle is considered an authority on education issues, even though some conservatives, fearing his moderate bent, have sought to prevent major bills, such as reauthorization of the Elementary and Secondary Education Act, from going through his panel. In 1999, he threw a wrench into House consideration of a bill known as "Straight A's" —

which would have allowed states to convert targeted federal education aid into block grants — after he decided that approach might not work. He led a successful effort to scale back the original bill to a 10-state pilot program.

Although his social policy stances are to the left of most Republicans, Castle also advocates fiscally conservative positions that often call for more frugality than some Republicans might like. In the 106th, he fought bitterly with GOP tax writers to reduce the leadership's cherished $792 billion tax cut, pushing his own smaller plan and ultimately securing a commitment that future cuts be conditioned on reductions in the interest on the national debt. In the end, he still joined three other Republicans in voting against the bill, which he said was "going too far too fast."

Castle's seat on the Financial Services Committee (formerly Banking) is important to Delaware's large corporate constituency. From that post he has sought to raise federal revenues by overhauling the commemorative coin program. In the 105th, he sponsored the measure — which he estimated would raise $3.4 billion for the government — creating a new program to put an image from each of the 50 states on the "tails" side of new quarters. The coins are being minted in the order each state entered the Union, which made Delaware's first out of the gate.

Castle combined his desire for fiscal restraint with his support for pro-environment initiatives in 1999 when he released a "dirty dozen" list of wasteful federal programs that also pose a risk to the environment. The move recalled his unsuccessful attempt in 1998 to cut about $9 billion in member-specific projects from a mammoth, $218 billion transportation bill that he said was fiscally irresponsible. He describes his compulsion to trim fat from the federal budget as an ongoing struggle. "You fail in this as much as you succeed," he told The Associated Press in 1999. "I don't want to suggest this is simple; it requires persistence."

He has been learning such lessons for virtually his entire adult life. Castle got a law degree from Georgetown University in 1964; the following year, at age 26, he became Delaware's deputy attorney general. Two years later, he began a 10-year career in the Delaware General Assembly and went on to serve as lieutenant governor and then governor for eight years.

With his gubernatorial term ending, Castle decided to try for the state's at-large congressional seat in 1992. He won a tough, four-way GOP primary and in November managed 55 percent against a former lieutenant governor, Democrat S.B. Woo. (Castle swapped jobs with Democrat Thomas R. Carper, who won the governorship that year and is now a senator.) With two-thirds of voters backing him every two years, Castle has coasted to re-election.

KEY VOTES

2000
Yes Raise hourly minimum wage by $1 over two years
Yes Halt funding for U.S. mission in Kosovo unless European nations pay more
Yes Provide Medicare benefits to military retirees and their dependents
Yes Grant China permanent normal trade status
Yes Phase out estate, gift and trust taxes
No   Prohibit implementation of president's national monument designations
Yes Approve GOP plan to provide prescription drug coverage for Medicare beneficiaries
Yes Increase help for poor nations indebted to international financial institutions

1999
No   Impose steel import quotas
Yes Kill proposal to take aviation trust funds off budget
No   Require background checks on buyers only at gun shows with 10 or more vendors
Yes Remove barriers among banking, securities and insurance companies
No   Authorize state grants to hire teachers and reduce class size
Yes Overhaul campaign finance law; ban "soft money" and restrict advocacy advertising
Yes Approve bipartisan plan to increase rights of patients in managed-care health plans

INTEREST GROUPS

	AFL-CIO	ADA	CCUS	ACU
2000	20%	30%	80%	68%
1999	33%	55%	72%	44%
1998	40%	30%	67%	42%
1997	38%	50%	90%	56%

CQ VOTE STUDIES

	PARTY UNITY		PRESIDENTIAL SUPPORT	
	Support	Oppose	Support	Oppose
2000	74%	26%	49%	51%
1999	69%	31%	49%	51%
1998	63%	37%	51%	49%
1997	72%	28%	55%	45%

DELAWARE

At large

Long considered a bellwether in national elections, Delaware went for Al Gore in 2000, ending the state's streak of supporting the winning presidential ticket at 12 straight. Voters pursue ticket-splitting with rare relish at all levels, but the state is generally incumbent-friendly and has embraced Republican Rep. Castle with large majorities.

Democrats are strong in Wilmington, the state's largest city. Fifty years ago, almost half the state's residents lived here, but the city's 72,000 residents now cast only about 10 percent of Delaware's vote, largely because of migration to the booming suburbs. Dover, the capital, is set in the state's midsection, in Kent County. It, too, has a strong Democratic constituency.

The GOP's strength lies in Wilmington's suburbs and south of the Chesapeake and Delaware canal, in the poultry farms and coastal marshes of the Delmarva Peninsula. A string of beach resorts at the state's far southeast corner draws hundreds of thousands of tourists each year. The growing number of retirees in these beach communities has made rural Sussex County one of the state's fastest-growing areas and increased the county's conservative tenor.

Delaware enjoys relatively low unemployment, and its favorable tax rates attract the headquarters of many financial services companies, especially credit card firms. Thanks to liberal incorporation rules, Delaware is the on-paper home to half of the Fortune 500, which keeps the state's specialized business court busy. Wilmington is the very real home to the DuPont Company, one of Delaware's largest private employers.

MAJOR INDUSTRY
Financial services, manufacturing, tourism

MILITARY BASES
Dover Air Force Base, 5,444 military, 695 civilian (1999)

CITIES
Wilmington, 71,491; Dover, 32,099; Newark, 28,318

UNUSUAL FEATURES
Ralph Nader wrote "The Company State" (1971) describing the du Pont family's influence on Delaware; the family once owned the newspaper and held the governor's mansion.

Gov. Jeb Bush (R)

First elected: 1998
Length of term: 4 years
Term expires: 1/03
Salary: $120,171
Phone: (850) 488-4441
Hometown: Coral Gables
Born: Feb. 11, 1953, Midland, Texas
Religion: Roman Catholic
Family: Wife, Columba Bush; three children
Education: U. of Texas, B.A. 1973
Career: Real estate developer; nonprofit chairman
Political highlights: Fla. secretary of commerce, 1987-89; Republican nominee for governor, 1994

Election results:
1998 GENERAL
Jeb Bush (R)	2,191,105	55.3%
Buddy MacKay (D)	1,773,054	44.7%

Lt. Gov. Frank T. Brogan (R)

First elected: 1998
Length of term: 4 years
Term expires: 1/03
Salary: $115,112
Phone: (850) 488-4711

STATE LEGISLATURE

Legislature: Meets March-May for 60 days; session often extended
House: 120 members, 2-year terms
2001 breakdown: 77R, 43D; 88 men, 32 women
Salary: $27,900
Phone: (850) 488-1157
Senate: 40 members, 4-year terms
2001 breakdown: 25R, 15D; 34 men, 6 women
Salary: $27,900
Phone: (850) 487-5270

STATE TERM LIMITS

Governor: 2 terms
Senate: 2 terms
House: 4 terms

URBAN STATISTICS

CITY	POPULATION
Jacksonville	695,877
Miami	369,253
Tampa	290,973
St. Petersburg	234,647
Hialeah	212,547

REGISTERED VOTERS

Democrat	43%
Republican	39%
No Party	15%

POPULATION

2000 population	15,982,378
1990 population	12,937,926
Percent change	+23.5%
Rank among states	4
Median age	38
Born in state	31%
Foreign born	13%
Urban/rural	85%/15%
Crime rate	1,024/100,000
Poverty level	13.1%
Federal workers	119,348
Military	111,309

REAPPORTIONMENT

Florida gained two House seats in reapportionment, increasing from 23 districts to 25. The state legislature will draw new district lines in 2001.

MISCELLANEOUS

Web: www.state.fl.us
Capital: Tallahassee
Land area: 53,937 sq.miles
Rank among states: 26
STATE ELECTION OFFICIAL
(850) 488-7690
DEMOCRATIC HEADQUARTERS
(850) 222-3411
REPUBLICAN HEADQUARTERS
(850) 222-7920

District Statistics

DIST.	VOTE FOR PRESIDENT 2000 D	R	GREEN	1996 D	R	REF	1992 D	R	I	WHT	BLK	ASIAN	HISP	HOUSEHOLD INCOME	OVER 65+	UNDER 18	COLLEGE EDUCATION
1	30%	68%	1%	31%	59%	10%	26%	51%	23%	84%	13%	2%	2%	$25,866	11%	25%	18%
2	48	49	1	48	41	11	42	38	20	74	24	1	2	$22,839	12	25	19
3	62	37	1	60	32	8	51	35	14	50	47	1	3	$21,306	13	28	10
4	35	63	1	37	56	7	30	53	17	91	6	2	3	$31,676	14	23	23
5	50	46	3	50	37	13	42	34	24	90	8	1	3	$21,434	25	19	16
6	38	59	1	39	50	11	33	46	22	87	11	1	3	$25,036	18	24	12
7	48	50	2	44	47	9	34	45	21	93	4	1	5	$30,921	16	22	20
8	48	50	1	43	48	9	33	47	20	89	5	2	11	$31,251	11	22	23
9	45	52	2	44.8	45.0	10	34	41	25	95	3	1	4	$29,293	22	20	20
10	53	44	3	51	38	10	40	36	24	89	9	1	2	$25,145	26	18	17
11	53	44	2	52	40	8	41	39	20	79	17	1	14	$26,166	12	23	19
12	43	55	1	43	46	10	35	45	20	84	13	1	6	$25,315	17	25	13
13	45	52	2	43	46	10	35	43	22	93	5	1	4	$27,616	31	17	18
14	38	59	2	38	51	11	31	46	22	92	6	0	6	$29,620	26	19	18
15	44	53	2	41	46	13	31	43	26	90	8	1	3	$29,755	19	22	19

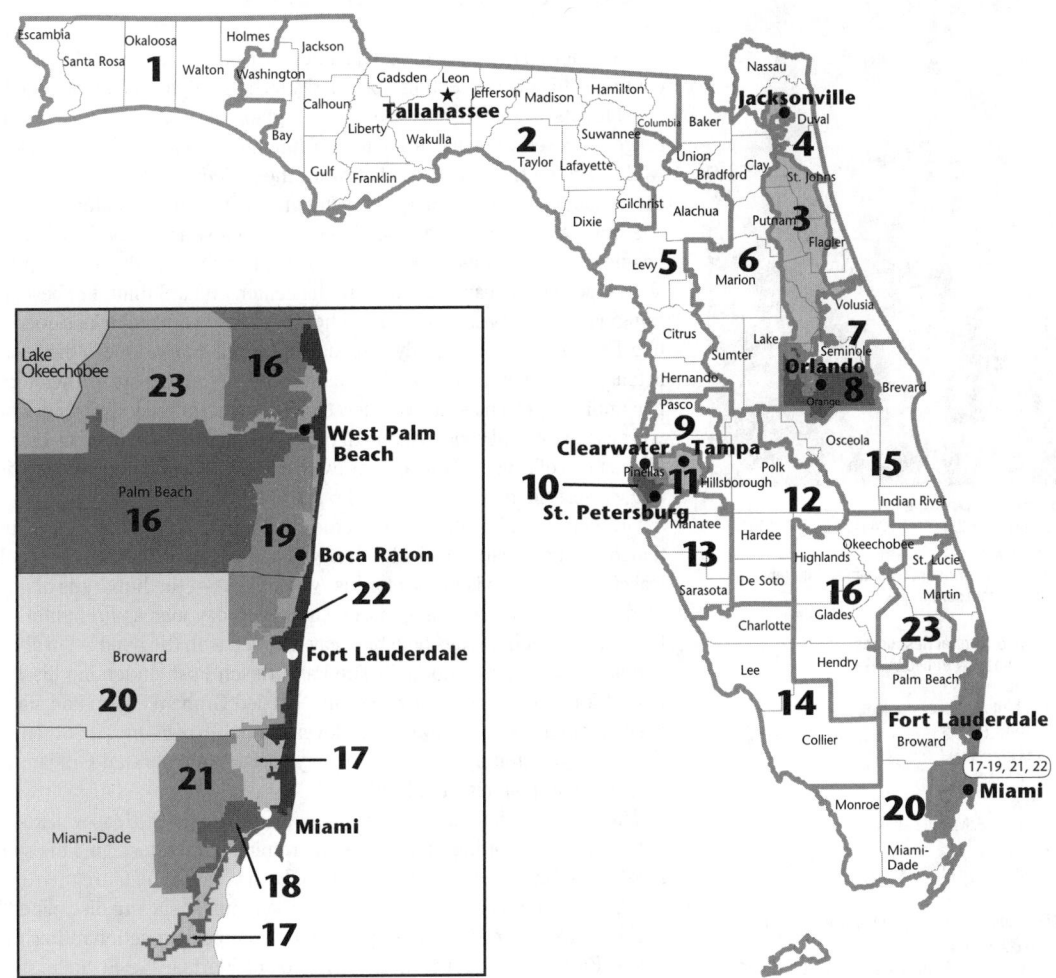

District Statistics

	VOTE FOR PRESIDENT																
DIST.	2000 D	2000 R	GREEN	1996 D	1996 R	REF	1992 D	1992 R	I	WHT	BLK	ASIAN	HISP	HOUSEHOLD INCOME	OVER 65+	UNDER 18	COLLEGE EDUCATION
16	50%	47%	2%	47%	42%	10%	36%	39%	25%	93%	4%	1%	6%	$30,582	24%	20%	18%
17	84	15	1	85	12	3	73	20	7	37	59	1	23	$21,899	10	30	11
18	38	61	1	43	52	5	34	56	10	89	4	1	67	$25,537	17	20	21
19	69	29	1	65	28	7	53	31	16	95	3	1	6	$34,396	28	18	23
20	62	36	1	59	31	9	47	33	20	92	4	2	12	$35,378	16	22	22
21	37	62	1	45	50	5	32	58	11	88	4	1	70	$32,043	10	25	19
22	59	39	2	54	38	8	45	37	17	94	3	1	13	$29,595	31	13	24
23	79	19	1	75	18	6	61	24	15	45	52	1	9	$23,039	13	28	11
STATE	48.8	48.9	2	48	42	9	41	39	20	83	14	1	12	$27,483	18	22	18

Sen. Bob Graham (D)

Elected 1986; 3rd term

Even though these are uncertain times for Democrats in Florida, Graham continues to enjoy exceptional popularity as he pays careful attention to his constituents' needs. He focuses on such high-profile issues as Medicare coverage of prescription drugs and federal funding to clean up the Everglades, while working to bring his party toward the political center as a founder of the Senate New Democrats, a growing group of centrist senators.

A quiet man, Graham can sometimes come across as curt or detached. He has never emerged as a spokesman for his party on Sunday morning talk shows, perhaps because he hews to the center. "What I think I'm best at is bringing people together around an honorable and reasonable position," he told The Tampa Tribune. "My approach to getting things done in the Senate is that you start at the 50-yard line and you begin to build out in each direction until you get a majority. Very few things happen, get accomplished, when you start in the end zone." Although not as well-known nationally as many of his Senate colleagues, Graham has twice come under serious consideration as a vice-presidential candidate — first in 1992 and then in 2000.

Graham's careful attention to home state issues, coupled with a reputation for bridging partisan divides, has won him near-icon status in local political circles. He also is known for his "work days" — the hundreds of days, beginning in 1974, he has spent on such everyday jobs as firefighter and teacher — which he says help him stay in touch with the needs of ordinary people. A laudatory editorial in The Palm Beach Post, endorsing his 1998 re-election in unusually effusive terms, labeled Graham a gem and stated, "Sen. Graham is a hard-working, level-headed grown-up. How many of those will you find in Congress?" One year later, a poll rated Graham the most popular politician in Florida.

There is a studied quality to everything Graham does. He is well-known for methodically jotting down notes and reminders to himself in little spiral notebooks that go everywhere with him. He has saved the more than 2,000 notebooks, which he says is "my greatest attempt at staying disciplined."

If he makes a mistake, it is apt to stem from belated action rather than haste. Early in his first term as governor of Florida, the St. Petersburg Times called him Governor Jell-O. But by his fourth year in office, he was seen as a competent manager.

While he is more conservative than many Democrats, Graham is not viewed as a maverick. He is a strong supporter of environmental safeguards and programs that benefit Florida's large elderly population. He has voted to raise the minimum wage, to prohibit job discrimination against homosexuals, and to uphold President Clinton's veto of a ban on a procedure its opponents call "partial birth" abortion. But he also has backed the death penalty and constitutional amendments outlawing flag burning. And while he supported banning job discrimination based on sexual orientation, he also voted to allow states to ignore same-sex marriages.

Graham sought to expand trade arrangements with Caribbean nations in the 106th Congress. Reminding colleagues that he is a former governor, he also backed legislation to block the federal government from receiving any money from state legal settlements with the tobacco industry. "Many states are using their settlements to achieve responsible, health-conscious goals, and the administration's Johnny-come-lately attempt to share in the spoils of their victories puts these initiatives at risk," he said.

In 1999, Graham and his Florida GOP colleague, Connie Mack, intro-

CAPITOL OFFICE
224-3041; fax 224-2237; 524 Hart Bldg. 20510

INTERNET
e-mail: bob_graham@graham.senate.gov
web: graham.senate.gov

COMMITTEES
Energy & Natural Resources
Environment & Public Works
Finance
Select Intelligence - ranking member
Veterans' Affairs

HOMETOWN
Miami Lakes

BORN
Nov. 9, 1936, Miami Lakes, Fla.

RELIGION
United Church of Christ

FAMILY
Wife, Adele Khoury Graham; four children

EDUCATION
U. of Florida, B.A. 1959; Harvard U., LL.B. 1962

CAREER
Real estate developer; cattle rancher

POLITICAL HIGHLIGHTS
Fla. House, 1967-71; Fla. Senate, 1971-79; governor, 1979-87

ELECTION RESULTS

1998 GENERAL

Bob Graham (D)	2,436,407	62.5%
Charlie Crist (R)	1,463,755	37.5%

1998 PRIMARY

Bob Graham (D)	unopposed

PREVIOUS WINNING PERCENTAGES
1992 (65%); 1986 (55%)

duced legislation to help restore the Florida Everglades, whose natural condition had been drastically changed by earlier federal government flood control projects. In 2000, Congress authorized the first $1.4 billion of the $7.8 billion federal-state project.

Mindful of Florida's large senior population, Graham helped lead efforts in the 106th to expand Medicare benefits to cover prescription drugs. "Medicare won't be relevant in the 21st century if we don't cover the treatments that physicians use and patients require," he warned. He also sponsored a measure to prohibit nursing homes from evicting patients on Medicaid and worked with a bipartisan group of senators for a series of measures that would expand pension coverage for small businesses and strengthen pension security for a variety of workers.

In 1999, Graham became unusually combative during debate over his proposal to prevent health insurance plans from requiring prior authorization for policyholders seeking help in emergency situations. When Tim Hutchinson, R-Ark., abruptly cut him off and charged that Graham's plan would be a "blank check" that would force managed-care companies to pay for virtually any medical service provided in an emergency room, Graham retorted: "The first call that goes out when someone has chest pains, or experiences shortness of breath, or feels extreme pain should be to a doctor — not a health insurance administrator."

During the much publicized 1999-2000 battle over whether 6-year-old Cuban refugee Elián González should remain in the United States or be returned to his father in Cuba, Graham sided with Florida's Cuban population.

Belying his usually serious mien, Graham has a penchant for wearing ties that show the outline of Florida, and he pays assiduous attention to Floridians' parochial concerns. Perhaps the biggest coup in the 105th for Graham, a member of the Environment and Public Works Committee, was to help rewrite highway legislation to steer hundreds of millions of dollars annually to Florida. He also won additional funding for military construction and anti-drug efforts in his home state. At the same time, he sought to bolster his claim of fiscal conservatism by suggesting that the Senate change its rules to make it more difficult for lawmakers to designate funding for various programs as "emergency" spending.

In 1996, Graham broke with some Democrats and supported the landmark welfare overhaul legislation, saying, "I believe that it's time to take that leap of faith," although he was concerned about the elimination of some benefits to legal immigrants, a sizable constituency in South Florida.

Graham inherited an interest in politics from his father, a wealthy dairy farmer who was a state senator in the 1930s and 1940s and an unsuccessful candidate for governor in 1944. After graduating from Harvard Law School, Graham joined his father in the real estate business. His projects, including development of the new town of Miami Lakes, helped him amass a fortune. He was eased into politics by his half-brother Phil, publisher of The Washington Post. Before his suicide in 1963, Phil Graham had introduced Bob to many influential Democrats, including Lyndon B. Johnson, for whom Bob Graham worked at the 1960 Democratic National Convention.

Graham's victory in a 1966 state House campaign began his unbroken string of electoral successes. He moved up to the state Senate in 1970 and succeeded Democratic Gov. Reubin Askew in 1978. In 1986, he won the Senate campaign against Republican incumbent Paula Hawkins.

In 1992, Graham was on Clinton's final list of six contenders for vice president; reportedly, it came down to Graham and Tennesseean Al Gore. Clinton decided on Gore just in time to allow Graham to file for re-election to his Senate seat. In 2000, he was again considered, with many pundits believing his presence on the ballot would give Al Gore a big boost in Florida.

KEY VOTES

2000

No Overhaul bankruptcy law and increase minimum wage
No Limit fiscal 2001 discretionary spending to $600.3 billion
Yes Override veto on nuclear waste disposal at Yucca Mountain site in Nevada
Yes Oppose effort to terminate Kosovo mission
Yes Include gender, sexual orientation and disability in federal hate crime protections
No Approve GOP plan to restrict use of genetic information by health insurers
No Kill amendment delaying implementation of an anti-missile defense system
No Cut taxes for married couples
Yes Grant China permanent normal trade status

1999

No Remove President Clinton from office for obstruction of justice
No Kill amendment authorizing state grants to hire teachers and reduce class size
Yes Require criminal background checks for purchases at gun shows
No Approve GOP proposal to increase rights of patients in managed-care health plans
Yes Block effort to allow farm and medicine exports to Cuba
Yes Allow study of tougher automobile fuel efficiency standards
Yes Ratify nuclear weapons testing treaty
Yes Prohibit national political parties from collecting "soft money" donations
Yes Remove barriers among banking, securities and insurance companies

INTEREST GROUPS

	AFL-CIO	ADA	CCUS	ACU
2000	75%	80%	60%	16%
1999	78%	100%	35%	4%
1998	50%	85%	61%	4%
1997	29%	60%	80%	8%
1996	71%	85%	46%	15%
1995	92%	95%	47%	13%
1994	75%	75%	30%	8%
1993	82%	65%	36%	16%
1992	75%	75%	20%	15%
1991	75%	65%	20%	38%

CQ VOTE STUDIES

	PARTY UNITY		PRESIDENTIAL SUPPORT	
	Support	Oppose	Support	Oppose
2000	91%	9%	95%	5%
1999	88%	12%	93%	7%
1998	85%	15%	83%	17%
1997	71%	29%	84%	16%
1996	81%	19%	86%	14%
1995	80%	20%	84%	16%
1994	85%	15%	92%	8%
1993	85%	15%	90%	10%
1992	73%	27%	35%	65%
1991	82%	18%	48%	52%

Sen. Bill Nelson (D)

Elected 2000; 1st term

The furor over the 2000 presidential vote count in Florida overshadowed the outcome of the state's U.S. Senate contest, in which Nelson scored a signal victory for Florida's Democrats in that open-seat contest.

Nelson's win over Republican Rep. Bill McCollum for the seat vacated by retired two-term Republican Sen. Connie Mack stemmed a political trend in the Sunshine State that had given the GOP control of the governorship, the state legislature and most of Florida's U.S. House seats.

Nelson prevailed by projecting a moderate image similar to that of the state's senior senator, Bob Graham, the Democrats' star performer during the period of Republican upsurge in Florida.

Florida's insurance commissioner when elected to the Senate, Nelson previously served 12 years in the House. But he returned to Washington with different priorities than he held when he left in 1991.

As a House member, he focused on the nation's space program, in large part because his district included the Kennedy Space Center at Cape Canaveral. Nelson chaired the Science panel's Space Subcommittee, and he journeyed into orbit aboard the space shuttle Columbia in 1986.

He pledged to devote himself as a senator to broader issues, including Social Security and health care concerns that are paramount to Florida's large elderly population.

Nelson, who was born in Miami, calls himself a fifth-generation Floridian: his great-great-grandfather came to Florida's Panhandle from Denmark in 1829. Nelson represented Brevard County in the state legislature.

He ran for an open House seat in 1978, taking conservative stands on economic issues and advocating more military spending. Nelson was an early member of the moderate Democratic Leadership Council, and his House voting record confirmed his self-description as a "New Democrat."

Critics contended that aside from his involvement in space issues, Nelson's House service was unremarkable. A Florida business magazine once labeled him an "empty suit" on its cover. Despite the glowing publicity attending his adventure as an astronaut, Nelson lost in the 1990 Democratic primary for governor — his only electoral defeat.

Four years later, though, he was elected insurance commissioner, a high-profile position that gave him a launching pad for his Senate race. Nelson dealt with the aftermath of Hurricane Andrew, which ravaged South Florida and the state's insurance market in 1992. He also helped obtain a $206 million settlement for African-Americans who had been overcharged for life insurance and burial policies, bolstering his image as a consumer watchdog.

From the time he announced his intention to run, Nelson was the frontrunner for the Senate seat left open by Mack. An advocate of fiscal restraint, he supported using budget surpluses to shore up Social Security, a popular position in Florida. He also pledged to add money to the federal education budget for smaller class sizes and modernized schools.

McCollum, a 10-term congressman, appeared a formidable foe. But his strongly conservative views on social issues and his role as a House "manager" in President Clinton's 1999 impeachment trial enabled Nelson and other Democrats to cast him as too far to the right, giving Nelson a lead among the state's crucial bloc of swing voters that he never relinquished.

Democratic leaders rewarded Nelson for his success by naming him vice chairman of the party's Senate campaign arm, the Democratic Senatorial Campaign Committee.

CAPITOL OFFICE
224-5274; fax 228-2183; 716 Hart Bldg. 20510

INTERNET
e-mail: senator@billnelson.senate.gov
web: billnelson.senate.gov

COMMITTEES
Armed Services
Budget
Foreign Relations

HOMETOWN
Tallahassee

BORN
Sept. 29, 1942, Miami, Fla.

RELIGION
Episcopalian

FAMILY
Wife, Grace Cavert; two children

EDUCATION
Yale U., B.A. 1965; U. of Virginia, J.D. 1968

MILITARY SERVICE
Army, 1968-70; Army Reserve, 1965-71

CAREER
Lawyer

POLITICAL HIGHLIGHTS
Fla. House, 1973-79; U.S. House, 1979-91; sought Democratic nomination for governor, 1990; Fla. treasurer and insurance commissioner, 1995-2001

ELECTION RESULTS

2000 GENERAL

Bill Nelson (D)	2,989,487	51.0%
Bill McCollum (R)	2,705,348	46.2%
Willie Logan (I)	80,830	1.4%

2000 PRIMARY

Bill Nelson (D)	692,147	77.5%
Newall J. Daughtrey (D)	105,650	11.8%
David B. Higginbottom (D)	95,492	10.7%

PREVIOUS WINNING PERCENTAGES
1988 House Election (61%); 1986 House Election (73%); 1984 House Election (61%); 1982 House Election (71%); 1980 House Election (70%); 1978 House Election (62%)

Rep. Joe **Scarborough** (R)

Elected 1994; 4th term

CAPITOL OFFICE
225-4136; fax 225-3414; 127 Cannon Bldg. 20515

INTERNET
e-mail: www.house.gov/writerep
web: www.house.gov/scarborough

COMMITTEES
Armed Services
Government Reform
  (Civil Service - chairman)
Judiciary

HOMETOWN
Pensacola

BORN
April 9, 1963, Doraville, Ga.

RELIGION
Baptist

FAMILY
Divorced; two children

EDUCATION
U. of Alabama, B.A. 1985; U. of Florida, J.D. 1990

CAREER
Lawyer

POLITICAL HIGHLIGHTS
No previous office

ELECTION RESULTS

2000 GENERAL

Joe Scarborough (R)		unopposed

2000 PRIMARY

Joe Scarborough (R)	54,032	77.4%
Bob Condon (R)	15,808	22.6%

1998 GENERAL

Joe Scarborough (R)		unopposed

PREVIOUS WINNING PERCENTAGES
1996 (73%); 1994 (62%)

Scarborough is a versatile man whose interests extend far beyond writing laws. An ardent conservative who came to Washington to battle for fiscal restraint and smaller government, he is also a rock musician who keeps guitars in his office and writes biting lyrics about politics. He launched a weekly newspaper in 1999, the Florida Sun, to give voice to his conservative beliefs, but he shocked his staff when he also gave voice in the paper to his ambivalent feelings about being in politics.

As a young lawyer, Scarborough (SCAR-burro) led a protest in 1993 against a tax increase sought by the Pensacola City Council. He soon decided to run for the House — and his prospects for election improved greatly when, on his 31st birthday in April 1994, veteran Democratic Rep. Earl Hutto announced plans to retire.

Scarborough ran to the right of his GOP opponents in a five-way primary for the 1st District seat, pushing his states' rights message on a local cable TV talk show and seeking out churchgoing voters. He overcame former Pensacola City Council member Lois Benson in a runoff before handily dispatching the Democratic nominee, lawyer and car dealer Vince Whibbs Jr.

As a member of the GOP Class of 1994, Scarborough argued for strict fealty to the principles of the "Republican revolution" and was impatient for dramatic change. His steadfast conservative views on fiscal policy precluded compromise with President Clinton on a GOP balanced-budget plan in the 104th Congress. "I have yet to apologize for anything we've done because we were right," Scarborough said at the time. "We're not to be loved. We're to be respected. ... I care more about the future of this country than I do about being loved."

He and several colleagues criticized the GOP leadership for compromising with the Democrats. But after an attempt to overthrow Speaker Newt Gingrich failed in 1997, Scarborough backed off a bit. "Impatience still boils beneath the surface," he says, but he understands better that it can take time to get things done. He told a reporter, "I've learned it is important to realize there is more than one way to reach a goal. ... We've got to recognize that within the American form of government, change doesn't come overnight."

Scarborough has continued to cast a reliably conservative vote on fiscal matters. In 1997, he was one of 26 Republicans who voted against a bipartisan balanced-budget deal negotiated with the White House, saying it did not provide enough in spending cuts and tax relief. He also voted against continued price supports for tobacco farmers and sugar growers in 1997, and he opposed a massive highway authorization measure in 1998, citing the need for spending restraint. In the 106th and 107th Congresses, he sought a seat on the Appropriations Committee from which to continue his efforts to curb spending but failed to win assignment to the panel.

But on the Armed Services panel, Scarborough is a stout defender of Pentagon spending and a supporter of NASA's space station project. In the 104th Congress, he worked to fend off preliminary plans to close or consolidate some military bases in his area.

In the 106th, he won House passage of a bill to use the government's purchasing power to give federal workers and military personnel access to discounted long-term care insurance offered by private companies. Scarborough, chairman of the Government Reform panel's Civil Service Subcommittee, said he was drawn to the issue after his grandmother had to turn to Medicaid for assistance. He said he hopes the federal program will persuade more private employers to offer similar coverage.

Like many conservatives, Scarborough adamantly opposes gun control laws as a way to curb youth violence. But in the 106th, he also argued against a Republican initiative to curb sales of sexually explicit or violent materials to youths. "I've got a problem with the federal government setting up and passing new regulations and new bureaucracies to try to tell me and other parents what is and what is not acceptable for my two boys," he told Gannett News Service.

Scarborough won passage of a measure in the 106th to limit wine sales over the Internet. Although vintners contended that the plan amounted to an attack on electronic commerce, the congressman said the law was necessary to prevent minors from purchasing alcohol. "The new black market is dangerous," he said.

Off the floor, Scarborough is casual in both dress and speech, lacing his conversations with references to contemporary music or entertainment that often escape older colleagues. Given his musical background — he formed a band named "Joe" with some Pensacola friends — it was no surprise in 1998 when Scarborough opposed legislation that would exempt small businesses from paying music licensing fees. He contended that the measure trampled on the property rights of musicians. "For us to just gut their ability to earn a living ... is absolutely ridiculous," he said.

Scarborough is publicly ambivalent about serving in the House. After a series of personal struggles, including a divorce and a severe back injury that cost him numerous year-end House votes in 1999, he hinted that his 2000 campaign might be his last. "I promised myself I would not put up with this life much longer," he wrote in a newspaper column that stunned his aides.

His rock lyrics also reflect his misgivings about politics. A St. Petersburg Times profile of Scarborough quoted one of his stanzas: "So I guess I'll be a congressman/ Where bad acting is rewarded every day/ It's as easy as can be/ If you give your cash to me."

But a surprise primary challenge from Republican lawyer Bob Condon appeared to reinvigorate Scarborough in 2000 — at least temporarily. "This campaign has re-energized me and got me reconnected with a lot of the volunteers and people that helped me in 1994 and reminded me why I ran in the first place," Scarborough said in an interview with Gannett. He easily dispatched Condon and was unopposed on the ballot in November. Some Florida Republicans even have touted Scarborough as a possible Senate candidate in 2002.

KEY VOTES

2000
?	Raise hourly minimum wage by $1 over two years
Yes	Halt funding for U.S. mission in Kosovo unless European nations pay more
Yes	Provide Medicare benefits to military retirees and their dependents
?	Grant China permanent normal trade status
Yes	Phase out estate, gift and trust taxes
No	Prohibit implementation of president's national monument designations
Yes	Approve GOP plan to provide prescription drug coverage for Medicare beneficiaries
No	Increase help for poor nations indebted to international financial institutions

1999
No	Impose steel import quotas
Yes	Kill proposal to take aviation trust funds off budget
No	Require background checks on buyers only at gun shows with 10 or more vendors
Yes	Remove barriers among banking, securities and insurance companies
No	Authorize state grants to hire teachers and reduce class size
No	Overhaul campaign finance law; ban "soft money" and restrict advocacy advertising
?	Approve bipartisan plan to increase rights of patients in managed-care health plans

INTEREST GROUPS

	AFL-CIO	ADA	CCUS	ACU
2000	0%	5%	66%	95%
1999	14%	15%	74%	85%
1998	10%	10%	78%	96%
1997	0%	10%	70%	100%

CQ VOTE STUDIES

	PARTY UNITY		PRESIDENTIAL SUPPORT	
	Support	Oppose	Support	Oppose
2000	90%	10%	26%	74%
1999	88%	12%	11%	89%
1998	91%	9%	26%	74%
1997	91%	9%	23%	77%

FLORIDA 1
Panhandle — Pensacola; Fort Walton Beach

Some residents of the 1st refer to the area as "Lower Alabama," and in spirit the area is much closer to the Old South than to, say, Miami. The district, which stretches from west of Panama City to Pensacola, has several large military bases and a mostly white population. Its Gulf Coast beaches and open spaces attract both tourists and residents seeking a small-town feel. The 1st widens at its eastern edge to include some of Bay County's pristine beaches.

Although voter registration is split between the parties, the 1st is a rock-solid conservative district. Its Democrats are more "Dixiecrats" than liberal, and several local and state officials from the area have switched to the GOP after decades as Democrats. The military presence also plays a significant role in politics; nearly one in seven residents of Okaloosa County is a military employee.

Tourism, health care and retirement communities have helped boost an economy slowed by manufacturing losses during the 1980s and early

'90s. Growth here is slower than Florida's southern regions but could accelerate with the development of waterfront land held by St. Joe's Corp., a paper and real estate giant.

MAJOR INDUSTRY
Defense, health care, tourism

MILITARY BASES
Pensacola Naval Air Station, 11,192 military, 4,438 civilian (1998); Eglin Air Force Base, 7,073 military, 3,243 civilian; Whiting Field Naval Air Station, 2,000 military, 962 civilian; Naval Technical Training Center Corry Station, 2,030 military, 268 civilian (1999); Hurlburt Field, 7,322 military, 853 civilian (2000)

CITIES
Pensacola, 57,112; West Pensacola, 22,107 (unincorporated) (1990); Fort Walton Beach, 20,924

UNUSUAL FEATURES
Famous "Blue Angels" flight group housed at Pensacola Naval Air Station; Setting for the movie "The Truman Show" in the Walton County town of Seaside.

Rep. Allen Boyd (D)

Elected 1996; 3rd term

CAPITOL OFFICE
225-5235; fax 225-5615; 107 Cannon Bldg. 20515

INTERNET
e-mail: rep.boyd@mail.house.gov
web: www.house.gov/boyd

COMMITTEES
Appropriations

HOMETOWN
Monticello

BORN
June 6, 1945, Valdosta, Ga.

RELIGION
Methodist

FAMILY
Wife, Stephanie A. Roush; three children

EDUCATION
North Florida Junior College, A.A. 1966; Florida
State U., B.S. 1969

MILITARY SERVICE
Army, 1969-71

CAREER
Farmer

POLITICAL HIGHLIGHTS
Sought Democratic nomination for Jefferson
County Commission, 1972; Fla. House, 1989-97

ELECTION RESULTS

2000 GENERAL
Allen Boyd (D)	185,579	72.1%
Doug Dodd (R)	71,754	27.9%

2000 PRIMARY
Allen Boyd (D)	unopposed

1998 GENERAL
Allen Boyd (D)	138,440	95.2%
Timothy W. Stein – write-in	6,980	4.8%

PREVIOUS WINNING PERCENTAGES
1996 (60%)

A fifth-generation farmer in the mostly rural Florida Panhandle, Boyd's conservatism on a broad array of fiscal and social issues has enabled him to entrench himself in the 2nd District while many other similar Southern districts have elected Republicans in recent years.

He is a member of the "Blue Dogs," a group of House Democrats who try to exert a center-right pull on the party. Boyd not only augmented the coalition's roster when he arrived in Washington in the 105th Congress, but his work as head of the Blue Dogs' campaign fundraising operation in the past two election cycles contributed to the growth of the group.

The Blue Dogs quickly came to be viewed as a key faction in the narrowly divided House in the 105th and 106th Congresses, and Democratic leaders began putting the coalition's members on key committees. That is how Boyd won a coveted spot on the Appropriations Committee in the 106th, giving up seats on the Armed Services and Small Business panels.

Boyd is a fiscal conservative and favors paying down the national debt rather than approving major tax cuts. He is not willing to spend as generously on the military as some. Nevertheless, Boyd, a Vietnam veteran, looks out for the 2nd District's Tyndall Air Force Base from his seat on the Military Construction Subcommittee.

He is particularly concerned that the U.S. military retain air superiority over potential foes. Once in a subcommittee hearing, he reflected on his ground-combat duty in Vietnam, recalling the morale boost of getting support from U.S. aircraft: "One of the greatest moments in an infantryman's life [was] when he saw those fast movers coming across" the sky, Boyd said.

On Appropriations, Boyd also fights for various agricultural interests, including farmers who have been hurt by the citrus canker, which has devastated the lime crop.

He is on the Rural Caucus, which was rejuvenated in the 106th Congress, and joins many other farm district lawmakers in pressing for changes in the 1996 farm law, which sought to replace New Deal-era crop subsidies with a system more in line with free-market principles. He complains that farmers, in exchange for giving up a safety net, were promised more accessible export markets for their crops and loosened federal regulations. Neither promise has been kept, he argues.

Boyd backed legislation to prevent the Environmental Protection Agency from banning certain pesticides unless it could prove that the decision was based on thorough scientific study. He also was a key player in an effort in the 106th to boost federal payments to rural counties that have large tracts of Forest Service land. Federal payments have dropped in recent years because revenues from timber cutting on federal land have fallen.

Boyd's conservative side has been evident on a range of domestic issues. In 1997, he was one of only six Democrats voting to eliminate the National Endowment for the Arts, and in 2000 he was one of just five Democrats who voted against legislation to increase the minimum wage. For those stands, and for his vote to grant China permanent normal trade status, Boyd was one of a small group of Democrats to receive the endorsement of the U.S. Chamber of Commerce. During his four years in Congress, his ratings from the chamber have averaged close to 70 percent, about the same score he gets from the AFL-CIO (although his rating from the group plummeted in 2000, influenced in part by his China trade vote).

He supports a constitutional amendment banning flag desecration and favors banning a procedure its opponents call "partial birth" abortion.

Boyd, a lifelong hunter, opposed Democratic gun control legislation in the 106th, reflecting not only his own views but those of most of his constituents. Boyd and his sister-in-law, Janegale Boyd, who replaced him in the state legislature, are the hosts of an annual charity fundraising dove hunt and dinner, which in recent years has come under criticism from both animal-rights protesters and from those who object to the fact that lobbyists help pay the food and drink tab.

A product of rural Jefferson County, just east of Tallahassee, Boyd was raised on the family farm. He went to Florida State University just down the road, where he majored in accounting, and he always intended to return to the family farm. After a two-year stint in the Army, including a tour as a junior infantry officer in Vietnam, he returned home to the farm operation, which raises cattle, cotton, sod and peanuts. There, he became involved in a variety of agricultural organizations and civic groups. (He remains active in running the farm during congressional breaks.)

A failed bid in 1972 for an open county commission seat seemed to have rid Boyd of whatever inclination he had for elective office, but more than a decade later, another open seat beckoned him — this time in the state legislature. He won a 1989 special election and served eight years in the legislature, where he cultivated good relations with business and chaired several important committees. He was chairman of the Democratic Conservative Caucus in the Florida House, a group similar to the Blue Dogs.

In his bid for the 2nd District seat in 1996 upon the retirement of popular three-term Democrat Pete Peterson, Boyd demonstrated that he could hold together the 2nd's traditional Democratic coalition: Tallahassee-area voters with jobs in state and local government and higher education; blacks, who make up about one-fourth of the district's population; and the portion of the white electorate still clinging to an inherited aversion to the GOP, which in that region was the party of the enemy in the Civil War.

In 1998, no challenger filed against him, giving him time to devote to fundraising activities on behalf of the Blue Dogs' political action committee. Boyd headed the PAC, which raised more than a quarter million dollars and made contributions to about a dozen incumbent members of the group and a similar number of would-be newcomers. All of the Blue Dogs seeking re-election won, as did seven new members. In 2000, with his own re-election assured, Boyd once again played a key role in fundraising efforts to benefit would-be Blue Dogs, and their ranks were augmented by the election of five freshmen who joined the coalition.

KEY VOTES

2000

No	Raise hourly minimum wage by $1 over two years
Yes	Halt funding for U.S. mission in Kosovo unless European nations pay more
Yes	Provide Medicare benefits to military retirees and their dependents
Yes	Grant China permanent normal trade status
Yes	Phase out estate, gift and trust taxes
No	Prohibit implementation of president's national monument designations
No	Approve GOP plan to provide prescription drug coverage for Medicare beneficiaries
No	Increase help for poor nations indebted to international financial institutions

1999

Yes	Impose steel import quotas
Yes	Kill proposal to take aviation trust funds off budget
No	Require background checks on buyers only at gun shows with 10 or more vendors
Yes	Remove barriers among banking, securities and insurance companies
Yes	Authorize state grants to hire teachers and reduce class size
Yes	Overhaul campaign finance law; ban "soft money" and restrict advocacy advertising
Yes	Approve bipartisan plan to increase rights of patients in managed-care health plans

INTEREST GROUPS

	AFL-CIO	ADA	CCUS	ACU
2000	30%	50%	80%	40%
1999	67%	70%	68%	20%
1998	89%	65%	65%	32%
1997	75%	55%	80%	44%

CQ VOTE STUDIES

	PARTY UNITY		PRESIDENTIAL SUPPORT	
	Support	Oppose	Support	Oppose
2000	68%	32%	57%	43%
1999	70%	30%	67%	33%
1998	69%	31%	62%	38%
1997	68%	32%	61%	39%

FLORIDA 2

Panhandle – Tallahassee; part of Panama City

The 2nd stretches around Florida's Big Bend, joining the Panhandle with state capital Tallahassee and the north central part of the state. Taking in all or part of 19 counties, the district features tobacco and peanut farms, forests and uncongested towns. While safely Democratic, the 2nd isn't as liberal as districts in southeast Florida.

Democrats outnumber Republicans in the district nearly 3-to-1, but many have conservative views on fiscal and social issues. The exception is the Tallahassee area, home to Florida State U. and Florida A&M University, where a more liberal sentiment exists. Panama City has a stronger conservative element, as do the smaller communities that ring the Gulf Coast. One-fourth of the district's population is black, most near Tallahassee and Gadsden County.

The 2nd's economy is driven by its land – from the Gulf Coast beaches where oysters are harvested to farms stocked with soybeans and peanuts. Agriculture has struggled occasionally due to weather and

low prices, but a steady base of government employees buffers any long-term economic effects. Florida's forestry industry has suffered some setbacks but maintains a strong presence. Panama City relies on tourism and the military community around Tyndall Air Force Base.

MAJOR INDUSTRY
Agriculture, government, manufacturing

MILITARY BASES
Tyndall Air Force Base, 3,367 military, 615 civilian (1999)

CITIES
Tallahassee, 135,938; Panama City (pt.), 32,321 (1990); Callaway, 14,610

UNUSUAL FEATURES
The Suwanee River, made famous by Stephen Foster's song "Old Folks at Home;" Liberty County has the fewest registered Republicans of any county in the state – 166 in 2000.

Rep. Corrine Brown (D)

Elected 1992; 5th term

CAPITOL OFFICE
225-0123; fax 225-2256; 2444 Rayburn Bldg. 20515

INTERNET
e-mail: www.house.gov/writerep
web: www.house.gov/corrinebrown

COMMITTEES
Transportation & Infrastructure
Veterans' Affairs

HOMETOWN
Jacksonville

BORN
Nov. 11, 1946, Jacksonville, Fla.

RELIGION
Baptist

FAMILY
Divorced; one child

EDUCATION
Florida A&M U., B.S. 1969, M.A. 1971; U. of Florida,
Ed.S. 1974

CAREER
College guidance counselor; travel agency owner

POLITICAL HIGHLIGHTS
Candidate for Fla. House, 1980; Fla. House, 1983-93

ELECTION RESULTS

2000 GENERAL

Corrine Brown (D)	102,143	57.6%
Jennifer Carroll (R)	75,228	42.4%

2000 PRIMARY

Corrine Brown (D)	unopposed

1998 GENERAL

Corrine Brown (D)	66,621	55.4%
Bill Randall (R)	53,530	44.6%

PREVIOUS WINNING PERCENTAGES
1996 (61%); 1994 (58%); 1992 (59%)

Brown is liberal and staunchly partisan, often employing rhetorical bludgeons to advance Democratic policies and to attack GOP initiatives. But she also has to speak out regularly to defend herself against a long string of allegations of ethical lapses.

She faced questions about her integrity in her first House campaign in 1992 and ran most of her 1998 and 2000 re-election campaigns under the cloud of a House ethics inquiry. Brown has had to work hard to win re-election every two years, but the district's voters do not seem overly concerned with the scandal allegations, returning her to office by double-digit margins.

One reason may be her close attention to the needs of the 3rd District, which is the poorest and least-educated of Florida's 23 House districts. Brown works to protect the military installations around North Florida and, from her seat on the Transportation Committee, has been able to direct a goodly share of federal funding to her district and state. During the 1998 reauthorization of federal transportation programs, Florida received a 57 percent increase. She also won money for Orlando's airport and light rail for Orlando and suburbs and $86 million for a new courthouse in Jacksonville. In the 107th Congress, she is the ranking Democrat on the Transportation panel's Coast Guard and Maritime Transportation Subcommittee.

On the Veterans' Affairs panel, Brown's focus has been on the health care needs of female veterans. She also has sought a new national cemetery for veterans in Florida.

There are several military installations in and around Brown's North Florida district, including the Jacksonville Naval Air Station. Jacksonville is also home to many retired military personnel. Brown would like to see more emphasis placed on the military's human resources, such as increasing training. She sees the military as a place where families, particularly poor families, can find opportunities and learn self-discipline.

On the national legislative front, Brown has watched the House GOP advance its ambitious conservative agenda over her strong, and occasionally voluble, opposition. She voted against efforts to lower tax rates, ban a procedure its opponents call "partial birth" abortion, and limit congressional terms.

Brown is a vocal defender of affirmative action. In 2000, she led protests against Florida GOP Gov. Jed Bush's decision to end affirmative action in state government jobs and at state universities. Brown said that under Bush's "One Florida" executive order, "many minority children will not get the breaks they need to get a college education," according to the Orlando Sentinel.

But she also stresses self-reliance, telling an audience at a black heritage festival, "We are responsible for everything that has happened to us" politically in recent years. After the 2000 presidential election controversy in Florida — with voters, including many minorities, turned away from some polling places and miscast and uncounted ballots — Brown led the volley of criticism and began working to overhaul the election process.

Brown took direct action in 1999 when she and several other female House members twice trooped across Capitol Hill to pay unannounced visits on the Senate Foreign Relations Committee. They urged Chairman Jesse Helms, R-N.C., to act on a treaty against sexual discrimination and on the nomination of former Sen. Carol Moseley-Braun to be ambassador to New Zealand. Helms said the women were disruptive and he had the Capitol Police remove them. Brown called Helms a "rude, mean man." Helms soon scheduled a vote on Moseley-Braun, but took no action on the treaty.

Brown has a long history of having to fend off allegations of ethical lapses. Her 1992 primary opponent, former state Rep. Andrew E. Johnson, filed charges with the Florida Commission on Ethics claiming that Brown received illegal campaign donations and made a staff member from her state representative's office work in her private travel agency.

The St. Petersburg Times in 1998 published a story alleging that Brown had personally benefited from a $10,000 check she received from the Rev. Henry J. Lyons, president of the National Baptist Convention USA Inc. Lyons had been charged in federal and state court with crimes including extortion, theft and conspiracy. Brown denied the allegation.

Fresh allegations of misusing her office for personal gain dogged Brown later that summer. The House ethics committee launched a probe relating to her financial dealings with a West African businessman. The inquiry did not conclude until September 2000, when the panel ruled that she "demonstrated, at the least, poor judgment." But the panel decided not to take disciplinary action, "due in large part to the fact that key witnesses ... were beyond the reach of the committee's subpoena power."

Brown was steered into politics by a woman from her sorority at Florida A&M University, Gwendolyn Sawyer Cherry, who went on to become the first black Florida state representative. Although Brown lost her first state House race in 1980, Cherry kept after her to try again, and Brown won a seat in 1982. She served in the state House for a decade.

After the black-majority 3rd District was created in 1992 redistricting, Brown was one of four candidates in the district's Democratic primary. She emerged from a runoff with a 64 percent to 36 percent victory. She was the beneficiary of financial and organizational support from a number of women's organizations, and when she won the Democratic nomination, she declared, "This is the Year of the Woman, so get out of the way, men." She prevailed in November by an 18 percentage point margin.

Ethical complaints against Brown — often brought by Democratic foes — have dogged her in each of her re-election victories. The district was redrawn by federal court order in 1996, reducing the black population from 55 percent to a still-significant 47 percent. The GOP has run a black candidate against her in three of her re-election campaigns, seeking to eliminate race as a factor. In 2000, the Republican candidate was Jennifer Carroll, a retired Navy lieutenant who had made a name for herself as a Jacksonville area community activist. Brown emerged from the balloting with a comfortable 15-point victory.

KEY VOTES

2000

Yes Raise hourly minimum wage by $1 over two years
Yes Halt funding for U.S. mission in Kosovo unless European nations pay more
Yes Provide Medicare benefits to military retirees and their dependents
No Grant China permanent normal trade status
No Phase out estate, gift and trust taxes
No Prohibit implementation of president's national monument designations
No Approve GOP plan to provide prescription drug coverage for Medicare beneficiaries
Yes Increase help for poor nations indebted to international financial institutions

1999

Yes Impose steel import quotas
No Kill proposal to take aviation trust funds off budget
No Require background checks on buyers only at gun shows with 10 or more vendors
Yes Remove barriers among banking, securities and insurance companies
Yes Authorize state grants to hire teachers and reduce class size
Yes Overhaul campaign finance law; ban "soft money" and restrict advocacy advertising
Yes Approve bipartisan plan to increase rights of patients in managed-care health plans

INTEREST GROUPS

	AFL-CIO	ADA	CCUS	ACU
2000	100%	80%	50%	9%
1999	89%	100%	28%	0%
1998	100%	95%	31%	4%
1997	100%	90%	44%	17%

CQ VOTE STUDIES

	PARTY UNITY		PRESIDENTIAL SUPPORT	
	Support	Oppose	Support	Oppose
2000	92%	8%	82%	18%
1999	93%	7%	83%	17%
1998	95%	5%	84%	16%
1997	88%	12%	71%	29%

FLORIDA 3
North – parts of Jacksonville and Orlando

Split nearly 50-50 between black and white residents, the 3rd roughly follows the St. Johns River from Jacksonville and winds south to take in part of Orlando. A black-majority district prior to a 1996 redistricting, the 3rd is Florida's poorest and just 10 percent of its residents were college-educated as of 1990. Although its population is mostly urban, the 3rd contains miles of swamps and lakes in its rural areas.

Democrats dominate the 3rd – they make up almost 75 percent of registered voters. Slightly more than half of the 3rd's population lives around Jacksonville, a Democratic stronghold. The rural areas of the district have more Republicans and conservative Democrats, but not enough to counter the Democratic majority. The eastern half of Putnam County is included in the 3rd. Often referred to as the "Bass Fishing Capital of the World," Putnam is a blue-collar region. The 3rd does contain some tinges of conservatism, particularly in Clay

County and in the Palatka area (Putnam County) on the St. Johns River.

Mostly a blue-collar area, the district relies on Naval Air Station Jacksonville and other area government facilities for jobs. Jacksonville's emergence as a banking and financial center has helped the economic outlook, while Orlando residents work in tourism jobs at locations like Epcot Center (in the 8th). But most of the areas in between have agricultural land and lack major private employers, contributing to the 3rd's poor economic profile.

MAJOR INDUSTRY
Defense, government, transportation

MILITARY BASES
Naval Air Station Jacksonville, 10,086 military, 7,261 civilian (1999)

CITIES
Jacksonville (pt.), 287,352 (1990); Orlando (pt.), 45,963 (1990)

UNUSUAL FEATURES
Eatonville, hometown of Harlem Renaissance author Zora Neale Hurston; Ocoee, site of the first citrus nursery in the United States.

Rep. Ander Crenshaw (R)

CAPITOL OFFICE
225-2501; fax 225-2504; 510 Cannon Bldg. 20515

INTERNET
e-mail: www.house.gov/writerep
web: www.house.gov/crenshaw

COMMITTEES
Armed Services
Budget
Veterans' Affairs

HOMETOWN
Jacksonville

BORN
Sept. 1, 1944, Jacksonville, Fla.

RELIGION
Episcopalian

FAMILY
Wife, Kitty Crenshaw; two children

EDUCATION
U. of Georgia, A.B. 1966; U. of Florida, J.D. 1969

CAREER
Investment bank executive; lawyer

POLITICAL HIGHLIGHTS
Fla. House, 1972-78; sought Republican nomination
for U.S. Senate, 1980; Fla. Senate, 1986-95
(president, 1993); sought Republican nomination
for governor, 1994

ELECTION RESULTS

2000 GENERAL

Ander Crenshaw (R)	203,090	67.0%
Tom Sullivan (D)	94,587	31.2%
Deborah Katz Pueschel (I)	5,609	1.9%

2000 PRIMARY

Ander Crenshaw (R)	47,588	69.6%
Dan Quiggle (R)	20,816	30.4%

Elected 2000; 1st term

Crenshaw's past experience is an asset as he spends his first term in a House that Republicans control narrowly. In 1993, Crenshaw became the first Republican to be elected president of the Florida Senate, leading a chamber then split evenly between Republicans and Democrats. "What I tried to do was involve everybody in the process," he says.

An investment banker and longtime state lawmaker, Crenshaw left office after a failed 1994 primary bid for governor. But he returned in 2000, at age 56, running to succeed four-term GOP Rep. Tillie Fowler. Crenshaw's easy primary win guaranteed victory in Florida's solidly Republican 4th District.

Fowler stepped aside to observe a term-limit pledge she took when she first ran for the House in 1992; Crenshaw, however, has placed no such limit on his service. But that is one of the few differences between Crenshaw and his conservative Republican predecessor.

Crenshaw effectively opposed a series of tax increases during his tenure in the Florida Legislature. Although he is not outspoken on social issues, in many of his campaigns Crenshaw emphasized a decline in moral values that he has called "problems of the soul."

But he tends to focus on finding pragmatic solutions rather than taking ideological stands. Crenshaw is most interested in military and transportation issues: Northeast Florida is home to several military bases and a constituency, centered in Jacksonville, faced with sprawl and clogged roadways.

The Jacksonville native got part of his committee wish list, with assignments to Armed Services and Veterans' Affairs. He also had sought a seat on the Transportation and Infrastructure Committee, but instead was given a place on the Budget panel.

Crenshaw is a familiar face to his home state colleagues, some of whom served with him in the state legislature. "I'll have the benefit of having a good relationship with some of the Republican leadership," he observed.

Perhaps recognizing this, his fellow GOP freshmen named him their liaison to the House GOP leadership. Crenshaw also has political family ties: His father-in-law is a former Florida Republican governor, Claude R. Kirk Jr.

FLORIDA 4

Northeast – part of Jacksonville

One of the state's more well-to-do districts, the 4th wraps around Jacksonville from the Georgia line to Daytona Beach. Familiar Republican territory, the "First Coast" region is defined by seaside villages, golf courses and white-collar workers. Although only part of Jacksonville lies within the 4th, it is easily the largest population center and has significant military, banking and shipping employers. The surrounding areas have beach resorts and some timber industry facilities.

The 1996 redistricting that carved out a black-majority district in the neighboring 3rd made the 4th a mostly white, safely Republican district. Even though only two of the district's five counties have GOP majorities, an elected Democrat is rare. Voters backed Republican presidential

candidates in 1992, '96 and 2000.

The 4th has some of Florida's oldest cities, which helps boost tourism and keeps a curb on the rapid growth in most areas. Flagler County, just north of Daytona Beach, has been one of the fastest-growing in the nation. Predictably, residents of the district's barrier islands and "mainlanders" don't always see eye-to-eye, especially on development issues.

MAJOR INDUSTRY
Financial services, tourism, defense

MILITARY BASES
Naval Air Station Mayport, 12,254 military, 1,260 civilian (1999)

CITIES
Jacksonville (pt.), 306,235 (1990); Ormond Beach, 35,321; Daytona Beach (pt.), 19,183 (1990)

UNUSUAL FEATURES
Fernandina Beach, the only part of the current United States to have existed under eight flags: Spain (twice), France, England, Mexico, the U.S., Confederate and Union.

Rep. Karen L. Thurman (D)

Elected 1992; 5th term

CAPITOL OFFICE
225-1002; fax 226-0329; 201 Cannon Bldg. 20515

INTERNET
e-mail: thurman@mail.house.gov
web: www.house.gov/thurman

COMMITTEES
Ways & Means

HOMETOWN
Dunnellon

BORN
Jan. 12, 1951, Rapid City, S.D.

RELIGION
Episcopalian

FAMILY
Husband, John Thurman; two children

EDUCATION
Santa Fe Community College, A.A. 1970; U. of Florida, B.A. 1973

CAREER
Teacher

POLITICAL HIGHLIGHTS
Dunnellon City Council, 1975-83 (mayor, 1979-81);
Fla. Senate, 1983-93

ELECTION RESULTS

2000 GENERAL

Karen L. Thurman (D)	180,338	64.3%
Peter C.K. "Pete" Enwall (R)	100,244	35.7%

2000 PRIMARY

Karen L. Thurman (D)	unopposed

1998 GENERAL

Karen L. Thurman (D)	132,005	66.3%
Jack "Thro" Gargan (REF)	67,147	33.7%

PREVIOUS WINNING PERCENTAGES
1996 (62%); 1994 (57%); 1992 (49%)

An outgoing personality and a carefully calibrated voting record have enabled Thurman to thrive in her district and in Congress — where she sits on the powerful Ways and Means Committee. A seasoned politician, Thurman is mostly faithful to her party's liberal line, but she casts enough conservative votes to give her appeal beyond the district's Democratic base.

Environmentalists, proponents of abortion rights, unions and senior citizens typically can count on Thurman to side with them on high-profile issues. In the 106th Congress, she championed such popular Democratic issues as reducing prescription drug costs for senior citizens. But balancing Thurman's ledger are votes to support defense spending, protect gun owners' rights and limit federal regulations, which are popular causes with the more conservative elements in the 5th District.

A former middle school math teacher, Thurman's first brush with politics came when she encouraged students upset about plans to close a nearby beach to take their case to the city council. Then she got involved, eventually winning a seat on the council at the age of 24. She continued teaching while she served as councilwoman and as mayor of Dunnellon, but she gave up the classroom when she was elected to the Florida Senate in 1982.

Thurman spends much of her time on health care, education and environmental issues. In the 106th, she supported a measure to require drug companies to make their products available for Medicare recipients at the same prices that they sell their products to HMOs and other favored customers, which could save seniors as much as 40 percent.

Thurman wants to encourage living organ donation, and she sponsored a measure in the 106th to compensate organ donors for some costs related to the procedures, such as child care and transportation, and make it easier for them to take time off from work. After attending the picnic of a kidney disease support group, she also introduced legislation to enable organ recipients to use Medicare for drugs that could prevent their bodies from rejecting the transplanted organs.

Thurman followed the Clinton administration on education issues, supporting national testing standards and opposing conservatives' calls for taxpayer-financed vouchers to help parents pay private school tuition. In struggles between organized labor and business interests, she usually takes the pro-union side, as when she opposed letting employers offer compensatory time instead of pay for overtime work.

She scored an environmental victory in 2000 when Congress passed a version of her plan to provide communities with $75 million over three years for alternative water projects. By using seawater, wastewater and other water sources, and developing new methods to store water, Thurman said communities could better meet the growing demand for water. "Without alternative water sources, many states may find themselves hunting for water for drinking, agricultural, industrial and commercial uses," she said.

Thurman has not always been liberal in her decisions. She opposed two gun control bills that President Clinton pushed during the 103rd Congress, and in 1996, she supported repeal of the ban on certain semiautomatic assault-style weapons. In the 106th, she opposed efforts to tighten gun control laws, saying such restrictions should be left up to counties.

She also has supported continued production of the B-2 stealth bomber and a constitutional amendment to ban desecration of the U.S. flag. She cast her vote with Republicans in the 104th for a measure that would have overhauled the federal regulatory process and limited the ability of agencies to impose new rules. "The American people want their government to produce necessary and meaningful regulations and not burden them with unnecessary ones," she said. Thurman joined a coalition of Republicans and moderate Democrats that passed welfare overhaul legislation in the 104th and a balanced-budget agreement in the 105th.

Thurman, who came to Congress after 10 years in the state legislature, is patient with the sometimes slow pace of the legislative process. She is willing to pursue incremental change, whether in the form of modest spending increases or targeted tax cuts. In 1997, she helped add $5 million to nutrition programs for the elderly, arguing that the relatively small sum was a prudent investment. "This $5 million will save $15 million in Medicare, Medicaid and VA [Department of Veterans Affairs] health costs because malnourished patients stay in the hospital nearly twice as long," she said.

In 1998, she persuaded the Ways and Means Committee to include a representative for the disabled on a national commission on the future of Social Security.

As a freshman in the 103rd Congress, Thurman took a risk by supporting Clinton's 1993 deficit-reduction package, which included tax increases. She said it would make businesses stronger, provide jobs, and "do some things that this country has needed over the last 12 years" of Republican presidencies. After Republicans took over Congress in 1995, she assailed their deficit-reduction bill, which she characterized as cutting taxes for the wealthy at the expense of older Americans. And in the 106th, she criticized GOP efforts to cut income taxes for married couples as "over-reaching," according to the Tampa Tribune.

Thurman had built a reputation as an astute, hard-working state legislator identified with such issues as education, consumer protection and the environment when she ran for Congress in 1992. As chairwoman of the state Senate's Subcommittee on Congressional Reapportionment during redistricting, critics said she tried to carve out a new congressional district for herself that included much of her state Senate district. If that were the case, her victory in the 1992 contest was not impressive: She beat the Republican candidate, lawyer and former prosecutor Tom Hogan, by just 6 percentage points.

Thurman's lackluster showing emboldened Florida Republicans for the 1994 race, and they did their flamboyant best that year to unseat her, recruiting drag-racing champion "Big Daddy" Don Garlits as her opponent. But Garlits proved a maladroit campaigner, and Thurman dismissed him with relative ease. She has run strongly since.

KEY VOTES

2000
Yes Raise hourly minimum wage by $1 over two years
Yes Halt funding for U.S. mission in Kosovo unless European nations pay more
Yes Provide Medicare benefits to military retirees and their dependents
Yes Grant China permanent normal trade status
No   Phase out estate, gift and trust taxes
No   Prohibit implementation of president's national monument designations
No   Approve GOP plan to provide prescription drug coverage for Medicare beneficiaries
Yes Increase help for poor nations indebted to international financial institutions

1999
Yes Impose steel import quotas
Yes Kill proposal to take aviation trust funds off budget
No   Require background checks on buyers only at gun shows with 10 or more vendors
No   Remove barriers among banking, securities and insurance companies
Yes Authorize state grants to hire teachers and reduce class size
Yes Overhaul campaign finance law; ban "soft money" and restrict advocacy advertising
Yes Approve bipartisan plan to increase rights of patients in managed-care health plans

INTEREST GROUPS

	AFL-CIO	ADA	CCUS	ACU
2000	90%	80%	57%	20%
1999	88%	85%	29%	4%
1998	90%	100%	39%	8%
1997	88%	75%	60%	24%

CQ VOTE STUDIES

	PARTY UNITY		PRESIDENTIAL SUPPORT	
	Support	Oppose	Support	Oppose
2000	88%	12%	78%	22%
1999	87%	13%	78%	22%
1998	87%	13%	77%	23%
1997	84%	16%	79%	21%

FLORIDA 5
Northern West Coast – Gainesville; Spring Hill

The 5th extends through much of North Central Florida, touching Lake City in the north and the Gulf Coast beaches of Pasco County to the south. The district takes in Gainesville (Alachua County), home of the state's largest university, and Hernando County, one of the state's fastest-growing. The other areas feature a mix of newer retirement developments and old Florida towns trying to attract tourism. A combination of ideologies, ages and incomes, the 5th leans Democratic but became more competitive in the 1990s.

Although Democrats hold a sizable advantage in voter registration, mostly thanks to Gainesville's academic community, Republicans are making inroads at the local and state levels. The retirement strongholds around New Port Richey and Spring Hill consistently deliver GOP votes, and some Democrats native to the area count themselves as conservatives.

The University of Florida and surrounding hospitals provide much of the economic activity for the 5th, which generally benefited from a strong economy during the 1990s. Although a motivated populace often has fought development, the southern areas of the district have seen a spark of home-building since the 1980s as more retirees come to the area. Most of Pasco County's population lives in the 5th, which roughly follows U.S. Route 19 north from Holiday to Hernando County.

MAJOR INDUSTRY
Education, health care, agriculture

CITIES
Gainesville, 92,291; Spring Hill (unincorporated), 31,117 (1990)

UNUSUAL FEATURES
Researchers at the University of Florida developed the sports drink Gatorade during the 1960s; Since 1947, tourists have watched "mermaids" perform underwater at the Hernando County resort of Weeki Wachee.

Rep. Cliff Stearns (R)

CAPITOL OFFICE
225-5744; fax 225-3973; 2227 Rayburn Bldg. 20515

INTERNET
e-mail: www.house.gov/writerep
web: www.house.gov/stearns

COMMITTEES
Energy & Commerce
(Commerce, Trade & Consumer Protection - chairman)
Veterans' Affairs

HOMETOWN
Ocala

BORN
April 16, 1941, Washington, D.C.

RELIGION
Presbyterian

FAMILY
Wife, Joan Moore; three children

EDUCATION
George Washington U., B.S. 1963

MILITARY SERVICE
Air Force, 1963-67

CAREER
Hotel executive

POLITICAL HIGHLIGHTS
No previous office

ELECTION RESULTS

2000 GENERAL

Cliff Stearns (R)	unopposed

2000 PRIMARY

Cliff Stearns (R)	unopposed

1998 GENERAL

Cliff Stearns (R)	unopposed

PREVIOUS WINNING PERCENTAGES
1996 (67%); 1994 (99%); 1992 (65%); 1990 (59%); 1988 (53%)

Elected 1988; 7th term

Stearns, who joined the House in 1989, was a forerunner of the tough-talking fiscal and social conservatives who came to Congress in droves in the 1990s, lambasting liberal Democrats and propelling the GOP to a congressional majority. Although he remains a committed conservative, in recent years Stearns has made a mark as an advocate for veterans.

As chairman of the Veterans' Affairs panel's Health Subcommittee, Stearns won passage in the 106th Congress of a plan to expand health care benefits for veterans and a bill aimed at retaining staff at Department of Veterans Affairs (VA) health care facilities. He also focused on legislation to authorize the department to operate a national program of extended-care services. Although some lawmakers worried that the measure could allow the VA to close some less-used facilities, Stearns hailed it as a blueprint for enhancing and expanding health care for veterans. The measure, which passed the House overwhelmingly and was signed into law in 1999, also provided for new veterans cemeteries and speedier construction of the national World War II Memorial.

In past years, Stearns used his subcommittee chairmanship to press for more federal attention to Gulf War syndrome, a mysterious group of health problems plaguing some who served in the Persian Gulf War. He authored legislation to establish a research center to study all war-related afflictions and to educate doctors about treatment of the ailments.

But on a broader health issue in the 106th, he refused to sign on to a "patients' bill of rights" measure — which had the support of a bipartisan majority in the House — that would have allowed patients to sue their health maintenance organizations. Instead, Stearns voted for a GOP alternative that allowed lawsuits under much more limited circumstances.

Stearns, who was tapped in the 105th to head the Task Force on Genetic Privacy and Health Records, has pressed for legislation restricting insurance companies from exchanging information about an individual's health, medical and genetic background. Stearns also authored a measure, which was enacted, aimed at increasing the availability and use of defibrillators in public places.

He took his usual conservative line on most policy issues debated in the 106th. He supported a constitutional amendment requiring that any tax increase be approved by a two-thirds majority in Congress and proposed legislation to allow gun owners with concealed weapons to acquire permits to transport concealed firearms across state lines. He also sponsored an amendment that attempted to move about $2 million from the National Endowment for the Arts into wildfire suppression efforts. "I believe our money would be better spent protecting Americans than being used to promote art that is many times anti-religious," he argued.

Many of his speeches and votes on the floor reflect his strong support for "traditional values," and he minces no words in making his points. In debate on a constitutional amendment banning flag desecration, he said, "Burning the flag is not a method of speech or expression. It is ... a clear measure of hatred for our country."

As a member of the Energy and Commerce Committee (formerly Commerce), Stearns in the 107th Congress took the gavel of the Commerce, Trade and Consumer Protection Subcommittee, which handles privacy issues. On the committee, Stearns has focused on deregulation, most recently of the electric utility industry and the satellite communications business. He has floated the idea of encouraging states to move forward with their own electricity deregulation plans rather than passing a federal bill mandating a timetable for competition. Stearns has also used his post on Commerce to battle pornography on the Internet and violent and sexually explicit TV programs — another indication of his support for traditional values and his strong conservative stance.

In debates on international affairs, Stearns speaks out for an "America First" doctrine, taking stands of the sort popularized by presidential aspirants H. Ross Perot and Patrick J. Buchanan. He voted against granting China permanent normal trade status in 2000, denouncing China as "a communist regime where the government and business sectors are controlled by military generals and political dictators. ... Where President Clinton sees a strategic partner, I see a potential [military] adversary."

Stearns wants other nations to share more of the cost of defending Europe. He pilloried the Clinton-initiated U.S. peacekeeping mission in Bosnia as an "unauthorized operation" that Congress should end. "The United States military is not the private army of the president," he said.

A staunch ally of Christian conservatives, Stearns wants to post the Ten Commandments in public buildings, including the House and Senate chambers, and he supports allowing schools to observe a moment of silence for prayer. Stearns fired off a letter to leading Florida state legislators after learning that a male worker in the Florida state government was appearing at the office dressed as a woman. "It's antithetical to our morals ... to have a man reporting for work with artificial breasts and makeup," he complained. "It sends the wrong signals to our children and people of this county if we tolerate these cultural values."

Before entering politics, Stearns developed some valuable contacts in the process of turning an investment in a dilapidated motel into a successful motel and restaurant management company (called Stearns House, Inc.). He was a chamber of commerce director, served on the board of a major local hospital, and was involved in church and civic groups. With those alliances and instinctive political savvy, Stearns in 1988 was able to beat two better-connected candidates for the Republican nomination for an open House seat.

Although he was a heavy underdog in the general election to Democratic state House Speaker Jon Mills, Stearns' limited political background gave him a salient, populist theme. He stressed that "the time has come for a citizen congressman," and he went on to out-hustle an overconfident Mills for the seat. Since a competitive race in 1990, Stearns' re-elections have been romps. The Democrats didn't even field a candidate against him in 1998 or 2000.

KEY VOTES

2000
No	Raise hourly minimum wage by $1 over two years
Yes	Halt funding for U.S. mission in Kosovo unless European nations pay more
Yes	Provide Medicare benefits to military retirees and their dependents
No	Grant China permanent normal trade status
Yes	Phase out estate, gift and trust taxes
Yes	Prohibit implementation of president's national monument designations
Yes	Approve GOP plan to provide prescription drug coverage for Medicare beneficiaries
No	Increase help for poor nations indebted to international financial institutions

1999
Yes	Impose steel import quotas
Yes	Kill proposal to take aviation trust funds off budget
Yes	Require background checks on buyers only at gun shows with 10 or more vendors
Yes	Remove barriers among banking, securities and insurance companies
No	Authorize state grants to hire teachers and reduce class size
No	Overhaul campaign finance law; ban "soft money" and restrict advocacy advertising
No	Approve bipartisan plan to increase rights of patients in managed-care health plans

INTEREST GROUPS

	AFL-CIO	ADA	CCUS	ACU
2000	10%	5%	80%	100%
1999	33%	10%	72%	92%
1998	10%	5%	83%	96%
1997	13%	10%	70%	100%

CQ VOTE STUDIES

	PARTY UNITY		PRESIDENTIAL SUPPORT	
	Support	Oppose	Support	Oppose
2000	96%	4%	17%	83%
1999	93%	7%	18%	82%
1998	92%	8%	18%	82%
1997	95%	5%	25%	75%

FLORIDA 6

North Central — Lake and Marion counties; part of Jacksonville

A mostly rural district, the 6th covers North Central Florida from the Georgia line to Clermont, west of Orlando. Nearly half of the district's population lives around Ocala, a retirement center known for its horse farms, and Sumter County, where Interstate 75 and Florida's Turnpike meet. The remainder of the district is dotted with rolling hills, dozens of lakes and acres of forest, often passed over by tourists on their way to Tampa and Orlando.

Home to many blue-collar workers, the 6th went Republican at the national level in 1994 and has stayed that way despite a voting population split between the two parties. Much of the 6th had been prime territory for Southern Democrats, but conservatism has outweighed party allegiance since the early 1990s.

The district includes parts of nine counties from Jacksonville to near

Gainesville, benefiting from both cities' employers. The southern part of the 6th saw rapid population growth during the 1980s and '90s, with many of the newcomers moving into the growing number of trailer parks. The prevalence of retirees and blue-collar jobs at prisons and factories held down economic growth during the 1990s. Cecil Field Naval Air Station, outside Jacksonville, closed in 1999 and was converted to a civilian airport. The base employed about 8,000 people before it closed.

MAJOR INDUSTRY
Health care, agriculture/forestry, defense

CITIES
Ocala, 47,926; Jacksonville (pt.), 41,643 (1990); Lakeside (unincorporated), 29,137 (1990)

UNUSUAL FEATURES
Glass-bottomed boat invented for tourists viewing Silver Springs, an aquifer east of Ocala; Citrus Tower in Clermont, a 22-story structure that looks out over Lake County's orange groves.

Rep. John L. Mica (R)

CAPITOL OFFICE
225-4035; fax 226-0821; 2445 Rayburn Bldg. 20515

INTERNET
e-mail: john.mica@mail.house.gov
web: www.house.gov/mica

COMMITTEES
Government Reform
House Administration
Transportation & Infrastructure
(Aviation - chairman)

HOMETOWN
Winter Park

BORN
Jan. 27, 1943, Binghamton, N.Y.

RELIGION
Episcopalian

FAMILY
Wife, Pat Mica; two children

EDUCATION
Miami-Dade Community College, A.A. 1965; U. of
Florida, B.A. 1967

CAREER
Government consultant; real estate investor;
congressional aide

POLITICAL HIGHLIGHTS
Fla. House, 1977-81; Republican nominee for Fla.
Senate, 1980

ELECTION RESULTS

2000 GENERAL

John L. Mica (R)	171,018	63.2%
Daniel Vaughen (D)	99,531	36.8%

2000 PRIMARY

John L. Mica (R)	unopposed

1998 GENERAL

John L. Mica (R)	unopposed

PREVIOUS WINNING PERCENTAGES
1996 (62%); 1994 (73%); 1992 (56%)

Elected 1992; 5th term

Mica seeks out Democratic cosponsors for his legislation, largely eschews incendiary "one-minute" speeches on the House floor and takes his subcommittee to the districts of Democratic panel members for field hearings.

Can this be the same man who was denounced several years ago as "the most dangerous man in history to chair" the Government Reform panel's Civil Service Subcommittee and whose tactics were compared to those of Attila the Hun? "I've tempered a bit," Mica acknowledges. He says he picks his battles more carefully now and concentrates on getting things done, as a leader in the ruling party must do — rather than venting his frustrations, as a member of a minority party is free to do.

Mica once said that he has "the inclination of Newt Gingrich," referring to when Gingrich was a confrontational agitator in the House minority, "but I hope I have the political wisdom of Bob Michel," a pragmatist who was the House GOP leader from 1981 to 1995. "You want to get things done, but sometimes you need to throw bombs," Mica says. In recent years, the Bob Michel side of Mica's personality has been gaining the edge.

Mica's mellowing has been in process for several years now. When he ascended to the Civil Service Subcommittee chairmanship in the 104th Congress, his eagerness to downsize the government, overhaul federal regulations, and change federal employee policies elicited the "Attila the Hun" denunciation from the president of a federal employees union.

By the end of his tenure in that subcommittee — he became chairman of the Criminal Justice Subcommittee in the 106th Congress — the animosity between Mica and government employees groups had eased somewhat. In the 105th, for example, Mica worked to increase federal workers' choices in life insurance and health coverage.

That is not to say that Mica's politics have changed. He remains a dependable vote for the GOP leadership, with a strong pro-business rating for his votes in Congress, and he continued to express his dislike for the legislative policies and the ethical behavior of President Clinton throughout his tenure. One area in which Mica departs from the expected GOP norm is environmental protection — he fights for restoration of the Everglades and preservation of lands and waters in central and northern Florida.

In the 106th, his Government Reform subcommittee was one of the most active panels on Capitol Hill, holding dozens of hearings, most of them focused on the war against drugs — an issue that ranked high on his priority list even before he took over the subcommittee.

Mica was one of several dozen GOP lawmakers appointed in 1998 to a task force to develop a GOP anti-drug strategy. In 1999, Speaker J. Dennis Hastert, who preceded Mica as chairman of the Criminal Justice Subcommittee, named him one of three co-chairmen of a new GOP anti-drug working group.

Mica was disdainful of the Clinton administration's effort to fight drugs, particularly Clinton's certification that Mexico was cooperating in the anti-drug war. Mexico may be a friend of the United States, he said, "but friends are not accomplices in the painful deaths of our children." He said that the administration was "sabotaging" the anti-drug effort by cutting back on Defense Department naval and aerial interdiction efforts. At a 1999 hearing, the Orlando Sentinel reported that administration drug czar Barry McCaffrey complained that Mica was guilty of "unprecedented oversight and interference" and had inundated the drug office with requests for 12,000 documents. In response, showing how much he had mellowed, Mica simply said he wanted to know whether taxpayer money was being spent effectively.

He often displays a huge poster with the phrase "Drugs Destroy Lives," which he hopes to make the slogan of the war against drugs.

Mica sits on the Transportation and Infrastructure Committee, where he has engaged in a long and frustrating crusade to provide upgraded transit service to his district in the Orlando suburbs. He came to Congress hoping eventually to land a chairmanship on that panel and actually had an opportunity to grab one of its less glamorous subcommittee gavels at the beginning of the 106th, but he elected to stay with his meatier job at the helm of the Government Reform subcommittee. In the 107th Congress, however, he leapt at the chance to chair the Transportation Committee's Aviation Subcommittee.

Mica has been able to win approval of highway, airport and bridge funding, but lack of consensus among local officials has stymied his plans for a 52-mile commuter rail project.

He has taken the lead in pressuring the State Department to pursue the 1993 kidnapping in Panama of three missionaries affiliated with the 7th District-based New Tribes Mission. The families of the three men believe they are still alive, and they and Mica want the State Department to demand more forcefully an accounting of the kidnapping and seek the missionaries' release.

A history buff, Mica has long pushed for approval of a visitors center at the Capitol. The shooting incident in July 1998 that left two police officers dead provided new impetus for the visitors center, which will be built largely underground. Mica sits on the Capitol Preservation Commission, which is overseeing the project.

Mica is the older brother of Daniel A. Mica, a Democrat who represented Florida in Congress from 1979 to 1989. Another Mica brother was an aide to Democratic Gov. Lawton Chiles. However, John Mica became a Republican in high school, when he was a member of Youth for Nixon.

Mica served in the state legislature from 1977 to 1981 and was chief of staff and administrative assistant for Florida GOP Sen. Paula Hawkins from 1981 to 1985. He then turned to private business ventures, including international trade consulting and the cellular telephone business, and became a millionaire.

Redistricting and a retirement gave Mica an opening to run for Congress in 1992. GOP Rep. Craig T. James decided not to seek a third House term, and the new Florida map for the 1990s gave the 7th a clear Republican tilt. George Bush carried the 7th by 11 points in presidential voting, and Mica won by 13 points. He has been re-elected with ease since then.

KEY VOTES

2000

No   Raise hourly minimum wage by $1 over two years
Yes Halt funding for U.S. mission in Kosovo unless European nations pay more
Yes Provide Medicare benefits to military retirees and their dependents
No   Grant China permanent normal trade status
Yes Phase out estate, gift and trust taxes
Yes Prohibit implementation of president's national monument designations
Yes Approve GOP plan to provide prescription drug coverage for Medicare beneficiaries
No   Increase help for poor nations indebted to international financial institutions

1999

Yes Impose steel import quotas
No   Kill proposal to take aviation trust funds off budget
No   Require background checks on buyers only at gun shows with 10 or more vendors
No   Remove barriers among banking, securities and insurance companies
No   Authorize state grants to hire teachers and reduce class size
No   Overhaul campaign finance law; ban "soft money" and restrict advocacy advertising
No   Approve bipartisan plan to increase rights of patients in managed-care health plans

INTEREST GROUPS

	AFL-CIO	ADA	CCUS	ACU
2000	10%	5%	80%	88%
1999	22%	10%	88%	80%
1998	10%	10%	89%	92%
1997	0%	0%	100%	100%

CQ VOTE STUDIES

	PARTY UNITY		PRESIDENTIAL SUPPORT	
	Support	Oppose	Support	Oppose
2000	96%	4%	19%	81%
1999	91%	9%	18%	82%
1998	92%	8%	23%	77%
1997	96%	4%	26%	74%

FLORIDA 7

Central – Southern Seminole and Volusia counties; Deltona; Port Orange

The 7th follows Interstate 4 from the southern end of Daytona Beach to the outskirts of Orlando and includes most of Seminole County in between. Dominated by suburban bedroom communities, it is reliably Republican, having shaken off the longtime control by Southern Democrats.

Once a major agricultural area, Seminole County now serves as a suburban home to middle- and upper-class Orlando commuters and their families. The middle of the district maintains its mostly agrarian feel. The 7th contains one-third of Daytona Beach, which continues to attract college students, bikers and race car fans with its beaches and sporting events. But inland Volusia County also has farmers, a more diverse population and voters who rarely fail to predict winners in statewide and national races – even if that means electing a Democrat.

The steady influx of people has meant a sustained economic boom in the district, but also has pushed growth-management issues to the top of the local agenda. Retirees have packed once-small towns closer to the ocean, drawing retail shops but not as many larger employers. A growing aerospace industry near Daytona Beach, helped by pilot trainees at Embry-Riddle University, helps to broaden the base. Sanford, in Seminole County, has been able to attract package delivery distribution centers and other service-oriented businesses.

MAJOR INDUSTRY
Tourism, service, electronics

CITIES
Deltona, 59,169; Port Orange, 45,452; Altamonte Springs (pt.), 34,352 (1990); Winter Springs, 29,334

UNUSUAL FEATURES
Southernmost point of Amtrak's "car-train," which carries vehicles and passengers from Lorton, Va. to Sanford; World's largest fernery from 1912 to 1940 in Altamonte Springs.

Rep. Ric Keller (R)

Elected 2000; 1st term

Succeeding in 2000 as a first-time candidate, Keller hammered home conservative themes on issues such as abortion, gun control and taxes. He was backed by the Club for Growth, a group of fiscally conservative Republicans.

So it appears fitting that Keller describes himself as the ideological heir to the man he replaced, 10-term Republican Bill McCollum, a conservative who left the seat open for a Senate bid that failed.

Keller has a strong pro-business bent and frequently describes himself as a Republican in the mold of Ronald Reagan. His goals include cutting federal taxes across the board and shrinking the size of the federal government.

Yet he also has involved himself in issues that defy ideological categorization. Though Keller had not held elective office before coming to Congress, he had helped author two state constitutional amendments concerning cleanup of the Florida Everglades. One, dubbed "Polluter Pays" and passed by a wide margin, held that sugar companies should contribute to Everglades restoration. Keller has said he favors eliminating federal subsidies to U.S. sugar companies.

Active with a local mentoring program for high school students, Keller got a seat on the Education and the Workforce Committee. He was the first freshman to introduce a bill in the 107th Congress — a measure aimed at increasing funding for higher education Pell Grants. Keller, an employment and liability lawyer, also sits on the Judiciary Committee.

Though Keller's vigorous style and conservative politics earned him attention, he finished second in the GOP primary and came from behind to win an October runoff. Democrats made a strong bid to capture the normally Republican 8th District seat by running a well-known local figure, former Orange County Commission Chairman Linda Chapin.

But Chapin saw her once-comfortable lead in the polls shrink in the face of Keller's campaign sprint, which was bolstered by support from Republican strategists striving to keep the seat in GOP hands. Keller won by fewer than 4,000 votes.

He has pledged to serve no more than eight years in the House.

CAPITOL OFFICE
225-2176; fax 225-0999; 419 Cannon Bldg. 20515

INTERNET
e-mail: www.house.gov/writerep
web: www.house.gov/keller

COMMITTEES
Education & Workforce
Judiciary

HOMETOWN
Orlando

BORN
Sept. 5, 1964, Johnson City, Tenn.

RELIGION
Methodist

FAMILY
Wife, Cathy Keller; two children

EDUCATION
East Tennessee State U., B.S. 1986; Vanderbilt U., J.D. 1992

CAREER
Lawyer

POLITICAL HIGHLIGHTS
No previous office

ELECTION RESULTS

2000 GENERAL

Ric Keller (R)	125,253	50.8%
Linda Chapin (D)	121,295	49.2%

2000 PRIMARY RUNOFF

Ric Keller (R)	16,292	51.9%
Bill Sublette (R)	15,077	48.1%

2000 PRIMARY

Bill Sublette (R)	18,196	43.4%
Ric Keller (R)	12,981	31.0%
Robert Nelson Hering Jr. (R)	10,736	25.6%

FLORIDA 8

Central – Orange County; part of Orlando

The 8th surrounds Orlando and includes most of the upscale suburban areas in Orange County, as well as a portion of Kissimmee, in Osceola County.

Whittled by growth-fueled redistricting, the 8th is a land-locked district powered by the presence of Walt Disney World and the tourism industry in the Orlando area, the world's leading vacation destination. The more rural eastern edge of the district, near coastal Brevard County, hasn't kept pace with Orlando's boom.

Residents of Orlando's suburbs – from middle-class areas near the city to well-heeled Windermere – support conservative Republicans on social and economic issues. The population is younger, wealthier and more educated than most Florida districts. Local officials tend to be

Republicans or conservative Democrats and favor business and development.

Although tourism leads the economy, the district also relies on a growing technology sector headed by defense and aerospace contractor Lockheed Martin and Oracle Corp. Technology and research have replaced the dwindling military presence in the district – Orlando's Naval Training Center was shut down in 1999, costing about 4,000 full-time jobs. The base is being converted into a self-contained community in northeast Orlando.

MAJOR INDUSTRY
Tourism, aerospace, TV production

CITIES
Orlando (pt.), 122,010 (1990); Kissimmee (pt.), 35,876 (1990); Ocoee, 21,839; Winter Park (pt.), 19,343 (1990)

UNUSUAL FEATURES
Golfers Tiger Woods and Mark O'Meara live in Windermere; Costumed Disney World employees are members of the Teamsters Union.

Rep. Michael Bilirakis (R)

Elected 1982; 10th term

CAPITOL OFFICE
225-5755; fax 225-4085; 2269 Rayburn Bldg. 20515

INTERNET
e-mail: www.house.gov/writerep
web: www.house.gov/bilirakis

COMMITTEES
Energy & Commerce
(Health - chairman)
Veterans' Affairs

HOMETOWN
Palm Harbor

BORN
July 16, 1930, Tarpon Springs, Fla.

RELIGION
Greek Orthodox

FAMILY
Wife, Evelyn Miaoulis; two children

EDUCATION
U. of Pittsburgh, B.S. 1959; George Washington U.,
attended 1959-60; U. of Florida, J.D. 1963

MILITARY SERVICE
Air Force, 1951-55

CAREER
Lawyer; county judge; restaurateur; engineer

POLITICAL HIGHLIGHTS
No previous office

ELECTION RESULTS

2000 GENERAL
Michael Bilirakis (R)	210,318	81.9%
Jon Scott Duffey (REF)	46,474	18.1%

2000 PRIMARY
Michael Bilirakis (R)	unopposed

1998 GENERAL
Michael Bilirakis (R)	unopposed

PREVIOUS WINNING PERCENTAGES
1996 (69%); 1994 (100%); 1992 (59%); 1990 (58%);
1988 (100%); 1986 (71%); 1984 (79%); 1982 (51%)

Bilirakis has enjoyed a front-row seat at deliberations on most of the important health care issues before Congress. With more than 18 years of congressional service, he can point to his efforts in drafting bills to provide health insurance "portability," overhaul Food and Drug Administration procedures, and reduce the growth in spending on federal health care programs.

For six years, Bilirakis (bil-li-RACK-us) was chairman of the Commerce Committee's Health and Environment Subcommittee. He was expected to lose the chair at the start of the 107th Congress because of GOP rules that limit chairmanships to three terms. But the Republican leadership decided instead to reorganize Commerce (renamed Energy and Commerce) and the Health and Environment Subcommittee was split, permitting Bilirakis to take the helm of the new Health Subcommittee. This panel has jurisdiction over health insurance regulation, Medicaid, and food and drugs.

On most health issues, however, Bilirakis must share the praise, or the blame, with a number of other lawmakers: Health care has become a partisan battleground, and many decisions in that area are made by leaders above Bilirakis' pay grade. Although he works well with Democrats, he also prides himself as a party loyalist.

But he faces competing pressures: He wants to support his party's efforts to restrain the growth in Medicare spending, but he also must consider the views of the 9th District's many older residents, who are wary of any tampering with their health care benefits. Conscientious and congenial, Bilirakis is known for being accessible to constituents, and he is particularly sensitive to the needs of senior citizens, who make up almost a quarter of the 9th's population — one of the highest percentages in the nation.

With Congress deadlocked in the 106th over plans to change Medicare, Bilirakis turned a cold shoulder to Democratic proposals to greatly expand the program by providing seniors with prescription drug coverage. "Absent fundamental reform, a major expansion of Medicare spending on prescription drugs would seriously threaten the solvency of this vital program," he said. Instead, he says the federal government should help low-income beneficiaries by bolstering state prescription drug assistance programs.

Bilirakis also found himself embroiled in a major battle with the Clinton administration, which proposed revising the nation's organ transplant system to make medical urgency the primary factor in deciding who receives organs. Instead, the congressman introduced legislation that would have retained the current system, under which organ allocation is done at the local and regional levels — and those living nearest the donor are given preference. The administration criticized the existing system as unfair, but Bilirakis insisted that local medical authorities should determine organ transplants, not a federal formula. (A compromise was reached between the administration and the private group that manages the transplant system.)

As often as not, however, Bilirakis successfully teams up with Democrats. He and Florida Democrat Jim Davis, for example, worked together on a measure in 1999, signed by President Clinton, to protect low-income nursing home residents from being evicted.

A pragmatist, Bilirakis has pushed for bipartisan agreement on contentious legislation since his days as ranking minority member of the Health and the Environment Subcommittee. He continued that practice as subcommittee chairman, sometimes to the consternation of more combative conservative members of his own party. Yet his moderate reputation has proved beneficial to the GOP on occasion. For example, with Bilirakis in the Health Subcommittee chair, Republican leaders in the 104th Congress had a useful symbol for their argument that the party's plan to rein in the cost of Medicaid and Medicare would save the programs, not hurt older people. Why else, they asked, would Bilirakis agree to lead the charge?

Bilirakis also faced criticism for his support of the tobacco industry. On one occasion, he told the Tampa Tribune, "I don't think there's a single man or woman in America who doesn't know cigarettes are bad for them — so why do we need hearings?" His subcommittee eventually conducted hearings on the proposed nationwide tobacco settlement.

Bilirakis serves on the Veterans' Affairs panel, where he has worked to increase benefits for widows of veterans and pressed for hearings to probe allegations of sexual harassment, mismanagement and poor care at Department of Veterans Affairs medical facilities. He sought the chairmanship of the panel in the 107th but lost out to the more-senior Christopher H. Smith of New Jersey.

A champion of Greek causes, Bilirakis often delivers floor speeches commemorating special events in Greece; he doesn't lose an opportunity to criticize the Turks, who continue to control northern Cyprus. His wife also is of Greek ancestry, and her homemade Greek food is a big hit at community gatherings.

Bilirakis brings a broad variety of experience to his job. Born in Florida and raised in Pennsylvania, he worked in the Pittsburgh steel mills, entered the Air Force and eventually earned an engineering degree. After working for the Federal Power Commission in Washington, D.C., he returned to Florida to attend law school and stayed in the state, working in the aerospace industry and then opening his own law practice just a few miles from his birthplace. He got involved in several small businesses, taught at area community colleges and served stints as an appointed local judge.

A Democrat until 1970, Bilirakis was intermittently involved in local GOP campaigns before entering the 1982 GOP primary in the newly drawn 9th District. The favorite, state House GOP leader Curt Kiser, made the mistake of taking his nomination for granted, while Bilirakis blanketed the district with signs saying that his was "a hard name to spell but an easy one to remember."

After an upset victory in the primary, Bilirakis narrowly edged out Democratic state Rep. George Sheldon by espousing conservative positions — defending President Reagan's economic program and arguing for a constitutional ban on abortions. He has won re-election since then by comfortable margins and has been unopposed in three elections.

KEY VOTES

2000

No Raise hourly minimum wage by $1 over two years
Yes Halt funding for U.S. mission in Kosovo unless European nations pay more
Yes Provide Medicare benefits to military retirees and their dependents
No Grant China permanent normal trade status
Yes Phase out estate, gift and trust taxes
Yes Prohibit implementation of president's national monument designations
Yes Approve GOP plan to provide prescription drug coverage for Medicare beneficiaries
No Increase help for poor nations indebted to international financial institutions

1999

Yes Impose steel import quotas
Yes Kill proposal to take aviation trust funds off budget
Yes Require background checks on buyers only at gun shows with 10 or more vendors
Yes Remove barriers among banking, securities and insurance companies
No Authorize state grants to hire teachers and reduce class size
No Overhaul campaign finance law; ban "soft money" and restrict advocacy advertising
Yes Approve bipartisan plan to increase rights of patients in managed-care health plans

INTEREST GROUPS

	AFL-CIO	ADA	CCUS	ACU
2000	10%	5%	71%	80%
1999	38%	20%	88%	84%
1998	10%	5%	89%	92%
1997	14%	10%	100%	84%

CQ VOTE STUDIES

	PARTY UNITY		PRESIDENTIAL SUPPORT	
	Support	Oppose	Support	Oppose
2000	91%	9%	24%	76%
1999	90%	10%	17%	83%
1998	91%	9%	20%	80%
1997	94%	6%	28%	72%

FLORIDA 9

West — Northern Pinellas and Hillsborough counties; central Pasco County; Clearwater

Suburban and rural areas north of Tampa and St. Petersburg form the bulk of the 9th, which encompasses northern Pinellas and Hillsborough and central Pasco counties. A 1992 redistricting stripped the district of coastal Pasco, but the Republican Party still has an edge because of its dominance in the communities around Clearwater. The 9th has long been a home for mostly Republican retirees, but Democrats have done well in Pasco County.

The 9th is now an older, mostly residential area. Clearwater, the largest city, is best known as a beach resort and the home of the Church of Scientology, with which the city maintains an uneasy relationship. Palm Harbor and Tarpon Springs have many Greek Orthodox residents, descendants of the area's earliest settlers.

The 9th's economy is driven by tourism, and many residents commute

to Tampa and St. Petersburg. Service-oriented industries add to the mix, but the predominance of shopping centers and strip malls has created growth problems in the coastal areas. The 9th's economy has grown along with its population, although its northeast portions have lagged behind the Clearwater area. The Hillsborough County portion of the district is mostly suburban. Inland Pasco County, which is bisected by Interstate 75, lacks major industry, although it has several sources of spring water.

MAJOR INDUSTRY
Tourism, health care, technology

CITIES
Clearwater (pt.), 96,886 (1990); Palm Harbor (unincorporated), 50,256 (1990); Dunedin, 35,680; Tarpon Springs, 20,311

UNUSUAL FEATURES
Tarpon Springs' waters were a major source of sea sponges before red tides killed them during the 1940s; Clearwater, site of the first Eckerd Drug Store, founded by Jack Eckerd, who once ran for governor.

Rep. C.W. Bill Young (R)

Elected 1970; 16th term

CAPITOL OFFICE
225-5961; fax 225-9764; 2407 Rayburn Bldg. 20515

INTERNET
web: www.house.gov/young

COMMITTEES
Appropriations - chairman

HOMETOWN
Indian Rocks Beach

BORN
Dec. 16, 1930, Harmarville, Pa.

RELIGION
Methodist

FAMILY
Wife, Beverly Young; three children

EDUCATION
Pennsylvania public schools, attended

MILITARY SERVICE
Fla. National Guard, 1948-57

CAREER
Insurance executive; public official

POLITICAL HIGHLIGHTS
Fla. Senate, 1961-71 (minority leader, 1967-71)

ELECTION RESULTS

2000 GENERAL

C.W. Bill Young (R)	146,799	75.7%
Josette Green (NL)	26,908	13.9%
Randy Heine (NP)	20,296	10.5%

2000 PRIMARY

C.W. Bill Young (R)	unopposed

1998 GENERAL

C.W. Bill Young (R)	unopposed

PREVIOUS WINNING PERCENTAGES
1996 (67%); 1994 (100%); 1992 (57%); 1990 (100%);
1988 (73%); 1986 (100%); 1984 (80%); 1982 (100%);
1980 (100%); 1978 (79%); 1976 (65%); 1974 (76%);
1972 (76%); 1970 (67%)

Young has at least one character trait perfectly suited to his often-rocky tenure at the helm of the powerful Appropriations Committee: patience.

His non-confrontational style personifies the go-along, get-along ethos that pervades the pragmatic culture of Appropriations. But it is also a product of a legislative mind-set forged by serving 24 years in what seemed like a permanent House GOP minority, when working with Democrats was a prerequisite for accomplishing anything.

Like most appropriators, Young approaches his job with a bipartisan, get-the-bills-done mind-set, a practice that often runs counter to the wishes of the right, the driving force in the House GOP. Rather than battle conservatives bent on imposing strict fiscal discipline in the 106th Congress, Young let the process play out until legislative reality — the need to gain President Clinton's signature in order to adjourn — tilted the playing field in appropriators' favor.

Time and again, Young's efforts in the 106th to establish a bipartisan appropriations process were overruled by GOP leaders, especially Majority Whip Tom DeLay of Texas, who insisted that the spending bills closely reflect GOP priorities. Often, Republican leaders would rewrite bipartisan, committee-approved bills to placate conservatives. Young protested, correctly as it turned out, that a partisan appropriations process would only ensure a year-end showdown that would maximize Clinton's leverage. Young tried hard not to let his frustrations show — a particular challenge in 2000, when 21 stopgap spending laws were required to complete an appropriations cycle that lasted until mid-December, five weeks after Election Day.

Ever the GOP loyalist, Young has been hesitant to publicly criticize his leadership, even when its strategies leave him at wits' end. But he has had no such hesitation when it comes to his rivals on the Budget Committee, who in recent years drafted annual budgets with such strictures on spending that they handcuffed appropriators, ensuring that at some point the bills would stall because of lack of money to fund a variety of programs.

When Republicans took control of the House in 1995, GOP leaders skipped over Young and two other more-senior members and picked Robert L. Livingston of Louisiana to chair the Appropriations panel. Young insists that Speaker Newt Gingrich did offer him the chair in late 1994 and that he declined. It is a mark of Young's reputation for decency that no one doubts that story's literal truth, but it is taken for granted that the offer was a pro forma gesture to cloak the affront to a loyal partisan and yeoman legislator. The move turned out for the best for Young, whose serious cardiac problems led to triple bypass surgery in 1996. "If I'd taken on a schedule like Bob Livingston, I'd be dead," Young said later. (He appears to have made a full recovery.)

Instead, Young spent four years chairing the Defense Appropriations Subcommittee, a choice consolation prize that gave him great influence in a policy arena that long had been a prime focus of his attention. Like other defense hawks in both parties, Young decried the steady decline in the Pentagon budget and warned that Clinton was undermining the combat readiness of U.S. forces with budgets that were too small.

Young was able to protect most of his defense spending bills from the dogfights that repeatedly stalled final passage of the companion defense authorization measures. Indeed, in a couple of key instances, when negotiations over the defense authorization bill bogged down, Young and Republican Ted Stevens of Alaska, then chairman of the Senate Defense Appropriations Subcommittee (and now full committee chairman), simply settled issues such as the future of the B-2 bomber in the negotiations on the defense spending bill.

As is natural for a senior appropriator, Young has done much for his district, adding funding for such local projects as work on robot minisubmarines conducted by the University of South Florida. But the legislative initiative that seems closest to Young's heart is one that is not targeted at his district. For years, he has added to the annual defense bill several million dollars for research on bone marrow transplants, a treatment for leukemia, and for a federally sponsored bone marrow donor registry funded through the defense budget. Young became interested in the issue in the 1980s after he met a 10-year-old cancer patient from his district who could not find the bone marrow donor she needed. After adopting the cause, Young learned in late 1990 that his eldest daughter had a form of leukemia treatable only through a marrow transplant. She received a transplant that restored her health.

On some issues other than defense, Young shows a moderate streak. He has broken from the party line to support a minimum wage increase, for example, and a ban on semiautomatic assault-style weapons.

He approaches environmental issues from the perspective of a district that places a premium on the condition of its coastal waters. He helped environmentalists kill an attempt to lift a moratorium on oil and gas drilling off large portions of the U.S. coast. He has also used his Appropriations position to fund efforts to replenish the sand on shrinking beaches in his district. In 1999, he rebuffed a request by local utilities to add language to a spending bill that would have allowed the companies to duck a federal lawsuit accusing them of deliberately polluting the environment.

Young was born into hardscrabble poverty in Pennsylvania's coal country during the Depression. His father, an alcoholic, abandoned his family when Young was a boy, and after his mother became ill, the family stayed with relatives in St. Petersburg. Young worked his way to success in the insurance business before going into politics in 1960, when he was elected as the sole Republican in the Florida Senate. By 1967, there were 20 others, and Young was minority leader.

In 1970, he inherited Florida's most dependable Republican House seat from William C. Cramer, who ran for the Senate. The 10th District has tilted Democratic — Al Gore took 53 percent there in 2000 — but more often than not, Young has been re-elected with little or no opposition.

KEY VOTES

2000

Yes Raise hourly minimum wage by $1 over two years
Yes Halt funding for U.S. mission in Kosovo unless European nations pay more
Yes Provide Medicare benefits to military retirees and their dependents
Yes Grant China permanent normal trade status
Yes Phase out estate, gift and trust taxes
?   Prohibit implementation of president's national monument designations
Yes Approve GOP plan to provide prescription drug coverage for Medicare beneficiaries
No   Increase help for poor nations indebted to international financial institutions

1999

Yes Impose steel import quotas
Yes Kill proposal to take aviation trust funds off budget
Yes Require background checks on buyers only at gun shows with 10 or more vendors
Yes Remove barriers among banking, securities and insurance companies
?   Authorize state grants to hire teachers and reduce class size
No   Overhaul campaign finance law; ban "soft money" and restrict advocacy advertising
Yes Approve bipartisan plan to increase rights of patients in managed-care health plans

INTEREST GROUPS

	AFL-CIO	ADA	CCUS	ACU
2000	11%	5%	84%	72%
1999	38%	20%	86%	73%
1998	0%	0%	93%	90%
1997	38%	10%	100%	79%

CQ VOTE STUDIES

	PARTY UNITY		PRESIDENTIAL SUPPORT	
	Support	Oppose	Support	Oppose
2000	90%	10%	33%	67%
1999	89%	11%	31%	69%
1998	92%	8%	24%	76%
1997	89%	11%	27%	73%

FLORIDA 10

West – Southern Pinellas County; St. Petersburg

The 10th takes in the southern portion of Pinellas County, including St. Petersburg and surrounding beachfront communities to the west and south. One of Florida's first Republican areas, the 10th has since achieved more of a political balance; it frequently elects Republicans at the local and state level while opting for Democratic presidential candidates. Democrats also have a narrow voter registration edge.

Although many retirees reside in Largo and the Gulf Coast towns, younger residents live in St. Petersburg and Pinellas Park, closer to major employers and nearby Tampa. Tourism has been an economic mainstay for the district, accounting for about $2 billion a year from area hotels and attractions. But high-tech manufacturers, financial services companies and a new Major League Baseball franchise have added to the 10th's economic strength.

Unlike many areas in Florida, the 10th's population remained stagnant during much of the 1990s, a result of the already crowded conditions in most of the district. But the area continues to add more attractions, including the Florida Aquarium and Tropicana Field, which hosted the 1999 NCAA men's college basketball championship.

MAJOR INDUSTRY
Tourism, health care, retail

CITIES
St. Petersburg (pt.), 234,550 (1990); Largo (pt.), 66,868 (1990); Pinellas Park, 44,388

UNUSUAL FEATURES
Birthplace of Major League Baseball spring training in St. Petersburg; the city also operates the largest recycled water system in the United States, dispensing 20 million gallons per day for lawn irrigation.

Rep. Jim Davis (D)

CAPITOL OFFICE
225-3376; fax 225-5652; 424 Cannon Bldg. 20515

INTERNET
e-mail: www.house.gov/writerep
web: www.house.gov/jimdavis

COMMITTEES
Budget
House Administration
International Relations
Joint Library

HOMETOWN
Tampa

BORN
Oct. 11, 1957, Tampa, Fla.

RELIGION
Episcopalian

FAMILY
Wife, Peggy Bessent Davis; two children

EDUCATION
Washington and Lee U., B.A. 1979; U. of Florida, J.D. 1982

CAREER
Lawyer

POLITICAL HIGHLIGHTS
Fla. House, 1988-97 (majority leader, 1994-97)

ELECTION RESULTS

2000 GENERAL

Jim Davis (D)	149,465	84.6%
Charlie Westlake (LIBERT)	27,197	15.4%

2000 PRIMARY

Jim Davis (D)	unopposed

1998 GENERAL

Jim Davis (D)	85,262	64.9%
Joe Chillura (R)	46,176	35.1%

PREVIOUS WINNING PERCENTAGES
1996 (58%)

Elected 1996; 3rd term

Davis, who sees himself as "a problem-solver and a peacemaker" in the legislative tussle, has been a respected voice on contentious matters since coming to Washington. In his first term, his 42 freshman Democratic colleagues elected him one of four class officers, and his party elders assigned him to the Budget Committee.

In both jobs, he struck a cooperative stance, joining with GOP freshmen interested in changing the campaign finance system and urging his Budget panel colleagues to seek compromise on fiscal policy. "We do some of our best work when we ... try to look very carefully at what we have in common and how we can work together towards the common goal," Davis said at one point in the budget-drafting process.

Calm and deliberative in manner, Davis honed his conciliation skills during eight years in the Florida House, the last two as majority leader. Early in his first term in Congress he aligned with a group of moderate House colleagues called the New Democrat Coalition.

New Democrats lobbied hard to get Davis a seat on the Energy and Commerce Committee in the 107th Congress. He didn't get the post, however, and Davis' allies complained that he was blocked by too many senior Democrats who had been exempted from a rule requiring members who got a seat on the panel to give up all other assignments.

Frugal when it comes to spending bills, Davis generally tends to side with liberals on social issues. Like Florida's senior senator, Democrat Bob Graham, the detail-oriented Davis uses small colored notebooks to scribble both personal and business reminders to himself.

In the 106th Congress, Davis focused on budget and international issues, as well as education and campaign finance revisions. He voted against five appropriations bills at the end of 1999, arguing, "There's a lot of indefensible pork in here. It sets a bad precedent." For the same reason, he voted against a $13 billion emergency supplemental spending bill in 2000.

A longtime fiscal conservative, Davis annually ranks high on the Concord Coalition's "tough choices" scorecard. The coalition is a nonpartisan, grassroots organization that advocates fiscal responsibility. Davis voted against a politically popular 1998 transportation bill that authorized significant increases in spending on highway and transit programs beyond what the 1997 budget agreement allowed.

Davis is as critical of tax cuts as he is of spending increases. In the 106th, he voted against a popular GOP-backed measure that would have reduced taxes on married couples, echoing the arguments of other Democrats that Congress should first reduce the national debt and bolster Medicare and Social Security. "To pass a $182 billion tax break before we pass a budget that makes paying down the debt our highest priority is totally irresponsible," he said.

As a member of the International Relations panel, Davis has been a strong advocate for trade liberalization. Although he is generally a supporter of organized labor, Davis in 2000 broke ranks with labor, voting to grant China permanent trade status — the Port of Tampa's largest trading partner.

Education issues are a major concern for Davis, and in the 106th Congress he proposed solving chronic teacher shortages by providing mid-career professionals with up to $5,000 in grants to pay for teacher training. The plan won backing in 2000 from the Clinton White House, which included $25 million in the budget for it. "This is a very prudent investment," Davis said. "I think the three years of teaching we will get from people will more than pay for the grant we give them to make the mid-life career change."

An opponent of school vouchers, Davis believes that the government instead should boost spending on charter schools. Charter schools, he argues, are public schools that are open to everyone, whereas vouchers would be used to help parents send their children to private schools.

When he joined the Budget Committee, Davis said his priority was "finding a way to balance the budget while protecting our seniors" — always a concern of Florida politicians because of the state's large contingent of elderly voters.

During Congress' protracted debate in 1997 on a long-term blueprint for spending and taxation, Davis remained upbeat about members' ability "to strike the balance between protecting our nation's priorities and securing a reasonable approach toward a balanced budget." He grumbled some about the GOP's tax-cutting agenda, warning that the cost of "some of the proposed tax cuts ... could explode in [later] years."

Davis also sits on the House Administration panel, and he is a strong supporter of campaign finance revisions. "These fat cats aren't pouring money into the system because they're interested in good government."

Although he generally casts a liberal-leaning vote on social policy issues, Davis was one of just two Florida House Democrats voting in 1997 to ban a procedure its opponents call "partial birth" abortion. Also, he backed a constitutional amendment to ban desecration of the U.S. flag.

Davis was born into a Tampa family active in local politics: His father was a judge, and his grandfather a mayor. Davis followed in the family tradition in 1988 when, as a lawyer and civic activist, he won the first of four terms in the state House.

When veteran Democratic Rep. Sam M. Gibbons announced plans to retire from the 11th in 1996, Davis was the least-known of four Democrats who campaigned to succeed him. But with prolific fundraising, Davis was able to air television ads during the primary campaign — the only Democrat to do so — and he played up his endorsements from local teacher, police and firefighter unions.

After beating former Tampa Mayor Sandy Warshaw Freedman in a runoff, Davis turned his attention to Republican Mark Sharpe, who was making his third try for the 11th after losing to Gibbons in 1992 and 1994. Buoyed by a treasury that topped $935,000 for the entire campaign and by an easy Bill Clinton victory in the district's presidential voting, Davis won by 16 percentage points and has continued to post easy victories.

KEY VOTES

2000
Yes Raise hourly minimum wage by $1 over two years
No Halt funding for U.S. mission in Kosovo unless European nations pay more
Yes Provide Medicare benefits to military retirees and their dependents
Yes Grant China permanent normal trade status
No Phase out estate, gift and trust taxes
No Prohibit implementation of president's national monument designations
No Approve GOP plan to provide prescription drug coverage for Medicare beneficiaries
Yes Increase help for poor nations indebted to international financial institutions

1999
No Impose steel import quotas
Yes Kill proposal to take aviation trust funds off budget
No Require background checks on buyers only at gun shows with 10 or more vendors
Yes Remove barriers among banking, securities and insurance companies
Yes Authorize state grants to hire teachers and reduce class size
Yes Overhaul campaign finance law; ban "soft money" and restrict advocacy advertising
Yes Approve bipartisan plan to increase rights of patients in managed-care health plans

INTEREST GROUPS

	AFL-CIO	ADA	CCUS	ACU
2000	70%	75%	57%	16%
1999	56%	80%	44%	12%
1998	80%	85%	67%	16%
1997	88%	75%	60%	16%

CQ VOTE STUDIES

	PARTY UNITY		PRESIDENTIAL SUPPORT	
	Support	Oppose	Support	Oppose
2000	85%	15%	82%	18%
1999	81%	19%	79%	21%
1998	81%	19%	74%	26%
1997	84%	16%	81%	19%

FLORIDA 11
West – Southern Hillsborough County; Tampa

The 11th lies within Hillsborough County and includes most of Tampa and the surrounding Tampa Bay area. One of the younger and more racially diverse districts in the state, the 11th combines a traditional blue-collar manufacturing base with newer high-tech and service industries that have transformed Tampa into a major Southern city.

Like the neighboring 10th, the 11th has seen its traditional one-party dominance fade as Hispanic immigrants and white-collar jobs have moved in. Although the number of Republicans has risen, Democrats continue to do well, but they tend to be more conservative to meet the changing population. In this swing district, issues like urban sprawl and the environment are important to voters, but recent tax hike proposals have been soundly defeated.

As its economy continues to evolve, the Tampa area has attracted professional sports franchises and a steady military presence at MacDill Air Force Base. Tampa's airport and seaport make it a major

shipping and transportation hub, while its traditional cigar industry is attempting a comeback from harder years. The University of South Florida, one of the state's largest schools, is on the city's northern end.

The influence of Cuban and Spanish culture is most pronounced in Ybor City, a downtown Tampa neighborhood named after the man who brought the first cigar factory to Tampa. The neighborhood's success in reinventing itself as a nighttime hot spot has given the area new life.

MAJOR INDUSTRY
Retail, health care, finance

MILITARY BASES
MacDill Air Force Base, 3,975 military, 820 civilian (1999)

CITIES
Tampa (pt.), 281,018 (1990); Town 'n' Country (unincorporated), 60,946 (1990); Brandon (unincorporated) (pt.), 43,864 (1990)

UNUSUAL FEATURES
Hideout for the pirate Jose Gaspar, better known as Gasparilla, in Tampa; Native tribes named the area Tampa, which means "sticks of fire."

Rep. Adam H. Putnam (R)

CAPITOL OFFICE
225-1252; fax 226-0585; 506 Cannon Bldg. 20515

INTERNET
e-mail: ask.adam@mail.house.gov
web: www.house.gov/putnam

COMMITTEES
Agriculture
Budget
Government Reform

HOMETOWN
Bartow

BORN
July 31, 1974, Bartow, Fla.

RELIGION
Episcopalian

FAMILY
Wife, Melissa Putnam

EDUCATION
U. of Florida, B.S. 1995

CAREER
State legislator; citrus and cattle rancher

POLITICAL HIGHLIGHTS
Fla. House, 1997-2000

ELECTION RESULTS

2000 GENERAL

Adam H. Putnam (R)	125,224	57.0%
Michael Stedem (D)	94,395	43.0%

2000 PRIMARY

Adam H. Putnam (R)	unopposed

Elected 2000; 1st term

Putnam was 26 years old when he won the contest to succeed retiring GOP Rep. Charles T. Canady in the 12th District, making him the youngest member of the House Class of 2000 and one of the youngest congressmen ever. With his youthful looks, he could be mistaken for a staff member if he ventures out of his office without wearing the lapel pin identifying him as a member of Congress.

Yet Putnam's résumé reveals that he already is a political veteran. Elected to the Florida House in 1996, just a year out of college, Putnam chaired that chamber's Agriculture Committee — an assignment that played well in his Central Florida district.

After his arrival in Washington, GOP leaders accommodated Putnam's political needs back home by putting him on the Agriculture Committee — replacing Canady — as well as on the Budget and Government Reform panels. Citrus farmers and ranchers find a natural ally in Putnam, a fifth-generation Floridian who comes from a prominent agribusiness family. Among his priorities is international trade, especially opening foreign markets for Florida produce.

When political opponents sought to portray Putnam as inexperienced, he pointed to his tenure in Tallahassee, where he espoused solidly conservative stands on most issues. His state legislative record includes efforts to protect Florida farmers from low commodity prices and to restrict government regulation; he drew the ire of environmentalists by supporting a move to return hundreds of thousands of protected wetlands acreage to private landowners.

Putnam made his mark on a non-farm issue, sponsoring a bill that reduced state prisoners' opportunities for parole from every two years to every five years.

An avid hunter, Putnam is a member of the National Rifle Association.

During college, Putnam interned in the Washington office of his predecessor. Canady made way for Putnam in 2000 when he observed a pledge to limit his service to four terms. Putnam easily defeated Democratic auto dealer Michael Stedem, who sought to make Putnam's youth an issue.

FLORIDA 12

Central – Polk County; Lakeland; parts of Hillsborough County

Florida's 12th has plenty of land but much of it is covered by citrus groves and lakes, not beaches and developments. Wedged between Tampa and Orlando, it includes most of Polk County and all of Hardee and DeSoto counties. The 12th also touches portions of eastern Hillsborough and Pasco counties, mostly rural areas like the rest of the district.

Although Democrats outnumber Republicans, most residents are conservative on social and economic issues. The 12th backed Republican presidential candidates in 1992, '96 and 2000. But for state and local elections, traditional Southern Democrats make this a competitive area.

The 12th's economy grew steadily during the 1990s, despite some weather-related dips among citrus crops. Florida's phosphate mining industry has its home around Bartow and Mulberry, while Publix Supermarkets has its headquarters in Lakeland. These industries provide consistent economic support, while citrus crops are more prone to ups and downs.

Retirees and spring baseball fans are attracted to the district's several stadiums and inexpensive housing, especially mobile home parks.

MAJOR INDUSTRY
Agriculture, mining, utilities

CITIES
Lakeland, 75,177; Winter Haven, 27,366; Plant City (pt.), 22,952 (1990)

UNUSUAL FEATURES
Spook Hill, in Lake Wales, a local oddity where cars parked in neutral at the base of the hill will roll up, defying gravity.

Rep. Dan Miller (R)

Elected 1992; 5th term

CAPITOL OFFICE
225-5015; fax 226-0828; 102 Cannon Bldg. 20515

INTERNET
e-mail: www.house.gov/writerep
web: www.house.gov/danmiller

COMMITTEES
Appropriations
Government Reform
(Census - chairman)

HOMETOWN
Bradenton

BORN
May 30, 1942, Highland Park, Mich.

RELIGION
Episcopalian

FAMILY
Wife, Glenda Miller; two children

EDUCATION
U. of Florida, B.S. 1964; Emory U., M.B.A. 1965;
Louisiana State U., Ph.D. 1970

CAREER
Shopping center and restaurant owner; professor

POLITICAL HIGHLIGHTS
No previous office

ELECTION RESULTS

2000 GENERAL

Dan Miller (R)	175,918	63.8%
Daniel E. Dunn (D)	99,568	36.1%

2000 PRIMARY

Dan Miller (R)	unopposed

1998 GENERAL

Dan Miller (R)	unopposed

PREVIOUS WINNING PERCENTAGES
1996 (64%); 1994 (100%); 1992 (58%)

Miller was the point man for congressional Republicans in the debate with Democrats over whether the Census Bureau could use statistical sampling techniques to augment the traditional head count in the 2000 census. But he also has been an irritant to the GOP leadership with his charges of "pork barrel" spending and "corporate welfare" on fiscal matters.

Republicans adamantly opposed sampling, arguing that Democrats running the Commerce Department would bend the results to their advantage. In Miller, they found an expert to bring a scientific rationale to the debate.

A statistician, Miller knows how to take a sample from a small group and extrapolate the findings over a larger group. Mathematicians view sampling as a legitimate tool, but Miller says that is only "when you do not have enough time or money." He argued that the Constitution mandates an enumeration of the population, and he warned that sampling could be conducted and manipulated for political purposes. "You can prove anything with statistics," he says.

The former college professor thrust himself into the sampling debate in September 1997 in a House floor speech during which he brandished a book he once used in his classes, "How to Lie With Statistics." GOP leaders latched on to Miller, creating a Census Subcommittee a few weeks later and naming him chairman. There, he led the Republican charge against sampling and served as the principal Republican watchdog throughout the preparation and execution of the 2000 census, engaging in a series of partisan battles and winning points with the Republican leadership.

But on other issues important to party leaders, Miller is not always so helpful. On fiscal policy, for example, he says senior Republicans should do more to prevent what he sees as "pork barrel" and "corporate welfare" spending.

Miller, a member of the Appropriations Committee, voted against two landmark bills of the 105th Congress: a $218 billion transportation authorization measure, and a catchall appropriations bill at session's end with a price tag topping $500 billion. Of the transportation bill, he said it contained "more pork than a Memphis barbecue," and he called it shortsighted to spend so freely on members' pet projects just as a balanced budget was being achieved. "The future of our children is more important to me than the federal government picking up the tab for a 'Dan Miller Expressway,'" he quipped.

In the 106th Congress, he voted against numerous programs that he considered to be inappropriate expenditures of federal funds, including money to dredge the Chesapeake Bay and to boost sales of U.S. agricultural products abroad. (Miller and other critics term the export promotion program "corporate welfare" because agribusinesses are among the beneficiaries.)

But Miller's No. 1 crusade during his congressional tenure has been to eliminate the government's sugar subsidy program. Sugar cane growers are a force in Florida politics, and his criticism of price supports irks agriculture lobbies and some Florida lawmakers. But he says Republicans must cut close to home if they are serious about scaling back the scope and cost of the federal government. "I'm willing to take on a powerful interest in my home state," he said. "It's the symbolism of being willing to go after corporate welfare."

Miller annually wages a losing battle to end or reduce the government's sugar subsidies, arguing that the subsidies not only cost the taxpayer, but they raise consumer costs by more than a billion dollars annually. In addition, he says that phosphorus-laden runoff from sugar plantations damages the Florida Everglades.

Another cause for Miller in the 106th Congress was his effort, ultimately successful, to win extradition back to Florida of a man who had fled to Mexico to escape a murder arrest. As an outgrowth of that, Miller drafted a bill to withhold foreign aid and military assistance from countries that do not cooperate with the United States on extradition matters.

Despite objections from advocates for the elderly — an important voting bloc in Florida — Miller has suggested that comparatively well-off senior citizens pay higher Medicare premiums.

Miller's voting record on social policy issues is conservative overall, although he has in some instances supported restrictions on gun owners' rights and voted with proponents of abortion rights.

Florida's West Coast is populated with many who migrated from the Midwest, and Miller fits that pattern. Many of his constituents retired to the Sunshine State, but Miller arrived earlier in life — as a high schooler, when his family moved from Michigan to Bradenton.

He earned a Ph.D. in marketing and statistics, then taught at Georgia State and the University of South Florida. Miller also holds an M.B.A. and has entrepreneurial experience, as co-founder of Miller Enterprises, which operates several Sarasota-area businesses, including a restaurant, a nursing home and retirement residences.

He phased himself out of the teaching profession in the early 1980s, devoting all his time to business and involvement in civic affairs. He was chairman of the local chamber of commerce, headed the hospital board and the local economic development council, and served on the boards of numerous other organizations, including the Manatee County Mental Health Center, the county's Council on Aging and the local symphony.

In 1992, he was lured into politics in the newly drawn 13th District when the lawmaker who had represented much of the area, Republican Andy Ireland, retired. Miller was well-known from his community involvement, and an endorsement from Ireland helped him prevail in a five-way GOP primary. In the general election, the district's GOP registration advantage enabled him to post an easy 16-point victory. His re-election contests have been a breeze.

Miller has already announced he will not seek re-election in 2002, deciding 10 years in the House is enough. "I feel pretty good about where we're going as a country," he told the Sarasota Herald-Tribune. "When I first ran in 1992, I was mad at the government. It was fiscally irresponsible, and I was frustrated as a private citizen."

KEY VOTES

2000

No	Raise hourly minimum wage by $1 over two years
Yes	Halt funding for U.S. mission in Kosovo unless European nations pay more
Yes	Provide Medicare benefits to military retirees and their dependents
Yes	Grant China permanent normal trade status
Yes	Phase out estate, gift and trust taxes
Yes	Prohibit implementation of president's national monument designations
Yes	Approve GOP plan to provide prescription drug coverage for Medicare beneficiaries
No	Increase help for poor nations indebted to international financial institutions

1999

No	Impose steel import quotas
Yes	Kill proposal to take aviation trust funds off budget
Yes	Require background checks on buyers only at gun shows with 10 or more vendors
Yes	Remove barriers among banking, securities and insurance companies
No	Authorize state grants to hire teachers and reduce class size
No	Overhaul campaign finance law; ban "soft money" and restrict advocacy advertising
No	Approve bipartisan plan to increase rights of patients in managed-care health plans

INTEREST GROUPS

	AFL-CIO	ADA	CCUS	ACU
2000	0%	10%	75%	88%
1999	13%	15%	83%	68%
1998	11%	10%	76%	88%
1997	25%	20%	100%	84%

CQ VOTE STUDIES

	PARTY UNITY		PRESIDENTIAL SUPPORT	
	Support	Oppose	Support	Oppose
2000	93%	7%	29%	71%
1999	87%	13%	30%	70%
1998	90%	10%	32%	68%
1997	90%	10%	33%	67%

FLORIDA 13

Southwest — Sarasota and Manatee counties, Sarasota

Midwestern retirees flock to the Gulf Coast cities of Sarasota and Bradenton, making the 13th a reliably Republican district. Sarasota and Manatee counties have nearly 90 percent of the district's population; the more affluent tend to live near Sarasota while middle-class residents are more prevalent around Bradenton. The 13th also takes in residential portions of Charlotte and Hillsborough counties.

Most residents live near the coast, while farmland and citrus groves occupy the inland. Sarasota County cultivates a refined image with its art museums, theater and symphony performances. It generally draws a more highly educated and wealthier class of retirees than most other west coast communities in Florida. Leading private employers include tourism, retail, heath care and banking. Bradenton, the county seat and retail center of Manatee County, has a more noticeable mix of incomes and ethnic groups. The 13th's high proportion of people 65 years and

older makes it a popular home for older part-time residents.

The area grew during the 1990s. Service industries, including investment companies, and trade make up much of the labor force. The district's proximity to Gulf beaches, barrier islands and a large state park makes the environment a bipartisan concern, with residents attuned to the problems of beach erosion and the effects of rapid population growth. The district has one of the highest GOP registrations in the state, ensuring Republican dominance in nearly every election.

MAJOR INDUSTRY
Health care, financial services, marine

CITIES
Sarasota, 50,763; Bradenton, 47,140; Port Charlotte (unincorporated) (pt.), 30,731 (1990)

UNUSUAL FEATURES
Sarasota's Ringling Museum of Art established by circus owner John Ringling, who brought his circus to the area each winter.

Rep. Porter J. Goss (R)

Elected 1988; 7th term

CAPITOL OFFICE
225-2536; fax 225-6820; 108 Cannon Bldg. 20515

INTERNET
e-mail: porter.goss@mail.house.gov
web: www.house.gov/goss

COMMITTEES
Rules
Select Intelligence - chairman

HOMETOWN
Sanibel

BORN
Nov. 26, 1938, Waterbury, Conn.

RELIGION
Presbyterian

FAMILY
Wife, Mariel Goss; four children

EDUCATION
Yale U., B.A. 1960

MILITARY SERVICE
Army, 1960-62

CAREER
Newspaper founder; CIA agent

POLITICAL HIGHLIGHTS
Sanibel City Council, 1974-82 (mayor, 1975-77, 1982); Lee County Commission, 1983-88 (chairman, 1985-86)

ELECTION RESULTS

2000 GENERAL

Porter J. Goss (R)	242,614	85.2%
Sam Farling (NL)	41,988	14.8%

2000 PRIMARY

Porter J. Goss (R)	unopposed

1998 GENERAL

Porter J. Goss (R)	unopposed

PREVIOUS WINNING PERCENTAGES
1996 (74%); 1994 (82%); 1992 (82%); 1990 (100%); 1988 (71%)

Goss' knowledge of intelligence matters and devotion to detail — derived from a decade as a clandestine services officer for the CIA — have earned him respect from members of both parties and led to an assortment of difficult behind-the-scenes assignments on Capitol Hill.

But Goss is far from secretive or aloof with colleagues. Approachable, straight-talking and pragmatic, he has worked actively, if quietly, on a bipartisan basis on a range of issues. In his final two years in Congress, he continues as chairman of the Select Intelligence Committee, with a desire to cooperate with Democrats and Bush administration officials to reshape the nation's spying community for the post-Cold War era.

A comfortable victor in seven House elections, Goss seems well-suited for his district. He won his first bid for Congress with 71 percent of the vote in 1988. As a term-limits supporter, he had considered leaving after winning re-election in 1998 but concluded he could still play a useful role on national security issues. After the 2000 election, however, he decided he had had enough of Congress and announced he would not run in 2002.

Goss was often mentioned as a potential director of the Central Intelligence Agency after George W. Bush won the presidency. Although he said he was interested in the job, Goss denied actively seeking it. He encouraged Bush to take his time in finding a director and to retain President Clinton's director, George J. Tenet, on at least a temporary basis.

Goss is solidly conservative on social and economic issues but follows an independent course. He does not see himself as tied to partisan ideology, noting that he did not come to politics through the traditional party ranks. After leaving the CIA and moving to Florida in 1971, he helped found a weekly newspaper, amassed a fortune — in 1999 he listed assets of at least $20 million — and became immersed in civic issues. "I was a citizen-activist upset about zoning," he recalled. "I was so appalled by the arrogance and contrariness of the local government."

After being named to the Lee County Commission by then-Gov. Bob Graham, a Democrat, Goss — tagged as the commission's environmentalist — got involved in controversial debates about managing growth countywide. He easily won a full term, which positioned him to compete for the House seat in 1988 when GOP Rep. Connie Mack decided to run for the Senate.

Goss has continued to veer from GOP orthodoxy on the environment, an important issue for his tourist-dependent Gulf Coast district. He is strongly opposed to oil and gas development on the continental shelf off Florida. He introduced a bill to halt drilling while a federal-state task force develops a permanent policy. "I believe it's one of the areas where government can make a difference in terms of appropriate regulation," he said.

Goss' background as a community activist also led him to become a strong advocate of congressional reforms. He has supported term limits and joined the fight to enact changes in lobbying and gift-giving rules. He also is in a position to push for institutional changes as the No. 2 Republican on the Rules Committee.

Because of the number of elderly retirees in his district, Goss has been active on Social Security and health issues. He served on Nebraska Democratic Sen. Bob Kerrey's 1994 entitlements commission, as well as on several GOP health task forces. He sponsored legislation signed into law in 1998 to establish a $750 million fund to compensate hemophiliacs who contract the AIDS virus because of contaminated blood products.

On Intelligence, Goss wasted little time taking a hands-on approach, becoming the first chairman to keep an office at the committee's quarters. He organizes and leads briefings for non-committee members who want to keep abreast of international developments, something he said has helped instill confidence in his judgment.

"I do a lot of advocacy work for the intelligence community," he said. "Primarily it's because we're dealing almost totally with classified information. When I go to my colleagues on the House floor and say, 'Look, I can't tell you how much it is,' or 'These terms, I can't tell you what they are, but trust me, it's okay,' that's asking a lot."

Goss' expectations for the CIA and other intelligence agencies are high. He sees information-gathering as playing a crucial role in the 21st century and wants the agencies to begin developing a strategic vision for the next 50 years. "We have a problem where it's very difficult to design capabilities if you don't know what you want to do," he said.

One of his most satisfying accomplishments as a lawmaker, he says, was his involvement in securing more than $1 billion for intelligence activities in 1998 as part of a year-end supplemental spending bill. That extra money, combined with an increase in funding in the fiscal 1999 intelligence authorization bill, was intended to help address some of the structural weaknesses identified by an independent panel that investigated the CIA's inability to warn of India's nuclear tests in May 1998.

But Goss says still more needs to be spent on intelligence. He wants the government to recruit more spies, saying the CIA could double the number of agents on its payroll and still not have enough. He also advocates a greater focus on data analysis, increased investment in cutting-edge technologies and a stepping up of covert actions. Regarding the latter, he said, "I don't mean Bay of Pigs. But how do you create things that happen that you want to have happen where you may not want to identify the American flag, or you have a reason to keep your fingerprints off it?"

In addition to leading the Intelligence panel, Goss was named to a bipartisan nine-member House committee that in 1998 began investigating the transfer of missile technology to China and its impact on national security. Later, he co-chaired a commission that looked at the National Reconnaissance Office, the super-secret arm of the intelligence community that launches spy satellites.

Goss took on the Intelligence chairmanship in 1997, just as he finished his work as chairman of an ethics subcommittee that studied charges of alleged improprieties in the political fundraising activities of Speaker Newt Gingrich.

KEY VOTES

2000
No Raise hourly minimum wage by $1 over two years
Yes Halt funding for U.S. mission in Kosovo unless European nations pay more
Yes Provide Medicare benefits to military retirees and their dependents
Yes Grant China permanent normal trade status
Yes Phase out estate, gift and trust taxes
Yes Prohibit implementation of president's national monument designations
Yes Approve GOP plan to provide prescription drug coverage for Medicare beneficiaries
No Increase help for poor nations indebted to international financial institutions

1999
No Impose steel import quotas
Yes Kill proposal to take aviation trust funds off budget
Yes Require background checks on buyers only at gun shows with 10 or more vendors
Yes Remove barriers among banking, securities and insurance companies
No Authorize state grants to hire teachers and reduce class size
No Overhaul campaign finance law; ban "soft money" and restrict advocacy advertising
No Approve bipartisan plan to increase rights of patients in managed-care health plans

INTEREST GROUPS

	AFL-CIO	ADA	CCUS	ACU
2000	0%	0%	80%	96%
1999	0%	10%	92%	80%
1998	13%	5%	86%	91%
1997	0%	10%	80%	88%

CQ VOTE STUDIES

	PARTY UNITY		PRESIDENTIAL SUPPORT	
	Support	Oppose	Support	Oppose
2000	95%	5%	26%	74%
1999	91%	9%	28%	72%
1998	93%	7%	32%	68%
1997	94%	6%	31%	69%

FLORIDA 14

Southwest – Lee and Collier counties, Cape Coral, Fort Myers

A haven for retirees, the solidly Republican 14th features Gulf Coast beaches and a rapidly expanding population centered in Lee County. Most residents live near Interstate 75, which runs through the entire district before heading into the Everglades.

The population in Collier County grew by more than 65 percent during the 1990s, while neighboring Lee expanded by almost a third. The increase in Lee County was pushed by Cape Coral, whose population has swelled in recent years. Originally a retirement community, Cape Coral has been attracting young professionals, service industries and land developers. Wealthier retirees live around Naples, where golf courses and high-rise condominiums are plentiful and new construction helps put the area among the top 10 in the state in taxable property value.

The eastern part of the district has remained largely agricultural and relies on migrant workers. In Collier County, citrus growers are increasingly attracted to the availability of open land and low risk of freezes. New universities in Lee County and the nearby Everglades help promote eco-tourism and marine biology.

Small Democratic pockets exist within Fort Myers and Port Charlotte, but the 14th has one of the highest Republican concentrations of any Florida district. It voted solidly for GOP presidential candidates in 1992, '96 and 2000.

MAJOR INDUSTRY
Tourism, health care, agriculture

CITIES
Cape Coral, 93,518; Fort Myers, 46,254; Naples, 19,604

UNUSUAL FEATURES
Nation's smallest post office (once a tool shed) in Ochopee, near the edge of Everglades National Park; Collier County created as a favor to land baron Barron G. Collier, who helped build the Tamiami Trail, which stretches from Tampa to Miami.

Rep. Dave Weldon (R)

Elected 1994; 4th term

CAPITOL OFFICE
225-3671; fax 225-3516; 332 Cannon Bldg. 20515

INTERNET
e-mail: www.house.gov/writerep
web: www.house.gov/weldon

COMMITTEES
Financial Services
Government Reform
Science

HOMETOWN
Palm Bay

BORN
Aug. 31, 1953, Amityville, N.Y.

RELIGION
Christian

FAMILY
Wife, Nancy Weldon; two children

EDUCATION
State U. of New York, Stony Brook, B.S. 1978; State U. of New York, Buffalo, M.D. 1981

MILITARY SERVICE
Army Medical Corps, 1981-87; Army Reserve, 1987-92

CAREER
Physician

POLITICAL HIGHLIGHTS
No previous office

ELECTION RESULTS

2000 GENERAL
Dave Weldon (R)	176,189	58.8%
Patsy Kurth (D)	117,511	39.2%
Gerry Newby (I)	5,744	1.9%

2000 PRIMARY
Dave Weldon (R)	unopposed

1998 GENERAL
Dave Weldon (R)	129,278	63.1%
David R. Golding (D)	75,654	36.9%

PREVIOUS WINNING PERCENTAGES
1996 (51%); 1994 (54%)

A staunch conservative, Weldon arrived in Washington as part of the revolutionary GOP Class of 1994, and he takes a back seat to no one in his defense of conservative social values. He began his involvement in politics in the late 1980s as the co-founder of a conservative group, the Space Coast Family Forum, that endorsed candidates based on their stances on abortion, sex education and other social issues.

He has continued along that path in Washington, as a member of a GOP group known as the Values Action Team, which urges GOP leaders to press for action on conservative pro-family policies. Weldon took the American Psychological Association to task for permitting publication in its professional bulletin of an article on pedophilia that suggested that children who had sex with adults did not necessarily suffer psychological harm. And he was among a group of lawmakers who pledged to post a copy of the Ten Commandments in their offices to show support for such displays in schools and other public places.

But Weldon has another passion as well: His "Space Coast" district includes the Kennedy Space Center, and the area economy depends greatly on NASA and private companies attracted there by space-related work. His seat on the Science Committee provides a platform from which he can promote the space program. He calls the space station and space shuttle programs "essential to our nation's continued international leadership in space." A physician, Weldon cites the scientific potential offered by a permanent outpost in space. It would "give researchers a fundamentally new tool to explore fields such as medicine, materials sciences, biology and astronomy," Weldon said in a letter to his House colleagues.

The lawmaker also is a co-chairman of the congressional Space and Aeronautics Caucus. Looking to a future when private industry will play a larger role in space, he wants to make sure the United States and, specifically, Florida's Space Coast, plays a key role in that development.

Weldon adamantly opposes one NASA project, however — the Triana project to send a camera-equipped satellite aloft that would, among other tasks, beam back a full-color image of Earth to be posted on the Internet. The project, proposed in 1998 by Vice President Al Gore, "saps NASA's precious resources and should be terminated post haste," Weldon argues.

Another local priority for Weldon has been to secure funds for a medical facility for veterans. He originally supported building a new hospital but lowered his sights when prospects for that appeared uncertain. Instead, he won approval for a $25 million outpatient clinic and for a pilot project that permits the Department of Veterans Affairs (VA) to contract with local hospitals for inpatient care for veterans. Weldon's decision not to press for a hospital left him open to criticism from political foes in the district.

To stay current in his medical field, Weldon, an internist, does volunteer work when he gets the chance, usually at the new VA clinic in Brevard County. He did not play a high-profile role in the House debate over managed health care in the 106th Congress but was not reluctant to criticize health maintenance organizations. "If someone asked me what is the real solution to the problem ... it is to open up insurance companies and HMOs to litigation because they are practicing medicine," he told Florida Today.

In the social policy arena, Weldon prescribes remedies that sit well with the culturally conservative voters whose influence is growing along central Florida's East Coast.

Weldon has been a passionate proponent of congressional efforts to ban a procedure its opponents call "partial birth" abortion. He says he became a staunch abortion foe after he and his wife, unable to have children of their own, decided to adopt. He said they faced a lengthy wait and were told that such a delay would not have occurred before the U.S. Supreme Court's 1973 *Roe v. Wade* decision legalizing abortion.

Religion plays an important part in Weldon's life. He says he tries to read the Bible and pray every day, and he lists among his political influences his "idol ... Jesus Christ."

In the 106th Congress, Weldon authored a bill, which passed the House, to force those formally accused of rape to submit to a test for the HIV virus — even before going to trial. Weldon argued that time is of the essence in beginning treatment to lower the risk of contracting AIDS.

Weldon casts every bit as conservative a vote as those within the brash element of the GOP Class of 1994, but he was more reserved in his public pronouncements than some of his classmates who said Speaker Newt Gingrich and other GOP leaders were too willing to compromise. He has served on the Republican Policy Committee since he arrived on Capitol Hill.

Like many Floridians, Weldon is a transplant from the North. He grew up on Long Island, the son of a postal clerk. He worked his way through his undergraduate days as an X-ray technician, and the Army paid his way through medical school. After a three-year stint as an Army doctor, he moved to Florida in 1987 and joined an internal medicine group.

Other than his involvement in the Family Forum, Weldon's only taste of political life before 1994 came when he was president of his local home-owners association. But in 1994, when two-term Democratic Rep. Jim Bacchus unexpectedly retired, Weldon entered the race, overcoming criticism that he was too conservative for the district. Weldon's Family Forum ties gave him a ready-made base of support among conservatives, and he won the GOP nomination, capturing 54 percent of the vote in a runoff.

That year found the district's voters in a conservative mood, and Weldon emphasized his support for mainstream GOP fare: tax cuts, welfare reform and other aspects of the House GOP's "Contract With America." Aided by an extensive get-out-the-vote effort conducted by groups such as the Christian Coalition, Weldon defeated Democrat Sue Munsey, also with 54 percent.

Weldon dealt House Democratic leader Richard A. Gephardt a double defeat in 2000: Not only did he win re-election to a seat Democrats had a slim hope of grabbing, his unexpectedly large 20 percentage point victory came over Gephardt's cousin, state Sen. Patsy Kurth.

KEY VOTES

2000

No Raise hourly minimum wage by $1 over two years
Yes Halt funding for U.S. mission in Kosovo unless European nations pay more
Yes Provide Medicare benefits to military retirees and their dependents
No Grant China permanent normal trade status
Yes Phase out estate, gift and trust taxes
Yes Prohibit implementation of president's national monument designations
Yes Approve GOP plan to provide prescription drug coverage for Medicare beneficiaries
No Increase help for poor nations indebted to international financial institutions

1999

No Impose steel import quotas
No Kill proposal to take aviation trust funds off budget
Yes Require background checks on buyers only at gun shows with 10 or more vendors
Yes Remove barriers among banking, securities and insurance companies
No Authorize state grants to hire teachers and reduce class size
No Overhaul campaign finance law; ban "soft money" and restrict advocacy advertising
Yes Approve bipartisan plan to increase rights of patients in managed-care health plans

INTEREST GROUPS

	AFL-CIO	ADA	CCUS	ACU
2000	10%	5%	76%	92%
1999	22%	10%	88%	92%
1998	0%	0%	89%	92%
1997	0%	0%	67%	92%

CQ VOTE STUDIES

	PARTY UNITY		PRESIDENTIAL SUPPORT	
	Support	Oppose	Support	Oppose
2000	96%	4%	19%	81%
1999	95%	5%	16%	84%
1998	94%	6%	16%	84%
1997	96%	4%	19%	81%

FLORIDA 15

Central — Brevard, Osceola and Indian River counties; Palm Bay

The 15th is dominated by Florida's Space Coast, home to space shuttle launches and numerous NASA employees and retirees. Most of the population lives along the Atlantic Coast between Titusville and Vero Beach, although the 15th also contains most of inland Osceola County, except Kissimmee, its largest city. A sliver of northeast Polk County and most of Indian River County round out the 15th.

Republicans have a solid voter registration advantage in the 15th. The coastal areas, especially upscale Merritt Island and Vero Beach, hold some of the strongest GOP contingents in the state. Still, the surest way to be elected is to promote the space industry, something members of both parties have done.

Cape Canaveral, the Kennedy Space Center and Patrick Air Force Base are the economic engines for the district and help to insulate it

from downturns. But when NASA spending falls, the impact can be dramatic. A growing high-tech industry has set up around the space operations and attracts engineers to Brevard County. The area's other attraction is its waterfront. Most cities in the 15th have seen steady growth and a Disney vacation complex near Vero Beach is helping to change that sleepy town into a high-profile resort.

MAJOR INDUSTRY
Aerospace, tourism, agriculture

MILITARY BASES
Patrick Air Force Base, 2,312 military, 942 civilian (1999)

CITIES
Palm Bay, 78,649; Melbourne, 69,779; Titusville, 41,586

UNUSUAL FEATURES
The Merritt Island National Wildlife Refuge has more endangered species than any other in the nation; More than 50 companies have searched for silver and gold lost where the Spanish Plate Fleet sank off Sebastian Inlet in 1715.

Rep. Mark Foley (R)

Elected 1994; 4th term

Thanks to an approachable demeanor and several trappings of power on Capitol Hill, Foley is a visible figure in Congress. He sits on the Ways and Means Committee; he is chairman of an entertainment industry task force that lets him hob-nob with Hollywood celebrities; and he has a job in the House GOP leadership, as a deputy whip.

Foley served in local and state offices before coming to Congress. That legislative experience sets him a bit apart from the ideological conservatives elected with him in the GOP sweep of 1994. He comes across as more patient and less dogmatic, and he is willing to buck his party's line from time to time. Foley's mastery of the legislative dance and his fundraising skills have earned him mention as a possible candidate for statewide office in Florida.

On most issues Foley is a conservative vote, although he has tendencies that mark him as a moderate among his Southern Republican peers, most notably on the environment and abortion. He supported the Clinton administration in House votes about one-third of the time.

In the 106th Congress, a major Foley priority was passing legislation to require people to give businesses 90 days' notice before suing them over non-compliance with accessibility standards in the Americans with Disabilities Act. Foley said that in many cases, businesses would comply with the law if given a chance. "All we're saying is, let's not start active litigation until they've been notified of the problem." In arguing his case, Foley lined up a star witness in actor Clint Eastwood, owner of a Carmel, Calif., hotel that was the target of just such a lawsuit.

Foley's first brush with the entertainment business came in 1980 when the makers of the film "Body Heat" set up shop in Lake Worth, Fla., where he ran a restaurant, the Lettuce Patch. He got a walk-on part — most of which ended up on the cutting room floor, he recalls — but he remembers what a boost the movie crew's business gave to the local economy. (He also snagged a bit part in a 2000 movie, "The Librarians.")

The entire state of Florida benefits from entertainment industry dollars; Disney and Universal are powerful economic players, and Miami is to Latin music what Nashville is to country music.

Foley was co-founder of the Palm Beach County Film and Television Commission. When he came to Congress, he joined the House Entertainment Industry Task Force; he succeeded the late Rep. Sonny Bono as its chairman in 1998. As a leading GOP emissary to Hollywood, he has sought to assure the entertainment industry that Republicans share many of their concerns.

Not only does Foley get to squire around famous Hollywood personalities when they visit Washington, but he also has sought to protect intellectual property rights and to stop the exodus of movie production to cheaper locations abroad, such as Canada. In the 106th, Foley worked hard to defeat a proposal to outlaw the distribution of sexually explicit or violent materials to minors. "There is no stopping once you start this kind of heavy-handed government interference," he said.

Foley, who is fiscally frugal, has played a leading role in fights to eliminate some big-ticket federal expenditures he deems wasteful, such as the Pentagon's B-2 stealth bomber and a host of energy research and water projects.

But at the same time, Foley looks out for the needs of his district, including its sugar cane and citrus industries. On the Agriculture Committee (where he served until he moved to Ways and Means in the 106th), Foley summoned all his polish and persuasiveness in a series of battles over fed-

CAPITOL OFFICE
225-5792; fax 225-3132; 104 Cannon Bldg. 20515

INTERNET
e-mail: mark.foley@mail.house.gov
web: www.house.gov/foley

COMMITTEES
Ways & Means

HOMETOWN
West Palm Beach

BORN
Sept. 8, 1954, Newton, Mass.

RELIGION
Roman Catholic

FAMILY
Single

EDUCATION
Palm Beach Community College, attended 1973-75

CAREER
Catering company founder; real estate broker; restaurant chain owner

POLITICAL HIGHLIGHTS
Lake Worth City Council, 1977-79; sought Democratic nomination for Fla. House, 1980; Lake Worth city commissioner, 1982-84; sought Democratic nomination for Palm Beach County Commission, 1984; Republican nominee for Fla. House, 1986; Fla. House, 1991-93; Fla. Senate, 1993-95

ELECTION RESULTS

2000 GENERAL

Mark Foley (R)	176,153	60.2%
Jean Elliott Brown (D)	108,782	37.2%
John Michael McGuire (REF)	7,556	2.6%

2000 PRIMARY

Mark Foley (R)	unopposed

1998 GENERAL

Mark Foley (R)	unopposed

PREVIOUS WINNING PERCENTAGES
1996 (64%); 1994 (58%)

eral support for sugar. On this issue, he has been at odds with some fellow Floridians, who see the sugar industry as a leading villain in the demise of the Everglades. But Foley also was instrumental in winning $200 million for Everglades restoration as part of the 1996 farm bill.

In the 105th Congress, Foley worked on behalf of the more than 5,000 Floridians who were survivors of the Holocaust, supporting their effort to recover as many of their lost assets as possible. In the 106th, he followed up with seminars to help the survivors with the nuts-and-bolts of filing insurance claims for benefits long denied them.

The congressman also worked to give volunteer organizations access to FBI background checks, so the groups could identify sexual predators seeking to work with children. He was one of the few GOP champions of legislation to expand the federal role in prosecuting hate crimes, including crimes based on the victim's sexual orientation. He sponsored legislation to open college records to determine the extent of crime on campus, and he backed a bill to protect health care workers from retaliation when they report unsafe conditions.

Born into an Irish-Catholic family on the outskirts of Boston, Foley moved to Florida as a child and says he began his political career at age 5, distributing fliers for a local candidate. In 1975, he opened the Lettuce Patch with his mother and later became a real estate broker.

He got involved in government at an early age, gaining a seat on the Lake Worth City Council at age 23 and serving a stint as the city's vice mayor before he turned 30. Foley won election to the Florida House in 1990. Two years later, he moved to the state Senate, where he chaired the Agriculture panel.

In 1994, he was ready for the next step: a bid for Congress, to replace retiring GOP Rep. Tom Lewis. Foley's image as a moderate generated some acrimony from conservatives in the GOP primary, but he easily defeated two other Republicans. His fundraising apparatus was impressive, and he won easily in November. His re-election contests have been uneventful.

Though his re-election competition has been feeble, Foley takes fundraising seriously. He formed a political action committee and made an estimated $200,000 in contributions to other GOP candidates in the 1998 election cycle. One byproduct of that effort was his appointment to the Ways and Means Committee in the 106th. In 2000, he flirted with running for the Senate seat being vacated by Republican Connie Mack. Foley quickly ruled himself out of that race; but with an eye toward a possible bid for the Senate in 2004, he spread his considerable campaign treasury around to support a number of Republicans running for state office.

KEY VOTES

2000

No   Raise hourly minimum wage by $1 over two years

Yes Halt funding for U.S. mission in Kosovo unless European nations pay more

Yes Provide Medicare benefits to military retirees and their dependents

Yes Grant China permanent normal trade status

Yes Phase out estate, gift and trust taxes

No   Prohibit implementation of president's national monument designations

Yes Approve GOP plan to provide prescription drug coverage for Medicare beneficiaries

No   Increase help for poor nations indebted to international financial institutions

1999

No   Impose steel import quotas

Yes Kill proposal to take aviation trust funds off budget

Yes Require background checks on buyers only at gun shows with 10 or more vendors

Yes Remove barriers among banking, securities and insurance companies

No   Authorize state grants to hire teachers and reduce class size

Yes Overhaul campaign finance law; ban "soft money" and restrict advocacy advertising

Yes Approve bipartisan plan to increase rights of patients in managed-care health plans

INTEREST GROUPS

	AFL-CIO	ADA	CCUS	ACU
2000	0%	20%	80%	68%
1999	11%	35%	72%	64%
1998	20%	20%	100%	80%
1997	25%	30%	100%	84%

CQ VOTE STUDIES

	PARTY UNITY		PRESIDENTIAL SUPPORT	
	Support	Oppose	Support	Oppose
2000	81%	19%	39%	61%
1999	78%	22%	32%	68%
1998	84%	16%	38%	62%
1997	90%	10%	36%	64%

FLORIDA 16

Central – Coastal Martin, Palm Beach and St. Lucie counties

The sprawling 16th connects rural Floridians who grow citrus crops and sugar cane with booming cities near the Gold Coast. The district surrounds the western side of Lake Okeechobee and includes most of the white population near the ocean, from Lake Worth to Port St. Lucie.

More than half of the district's population resides in fast-expanding Palm Beach County, where Palm Beach Gardens and Greenacres have grown rapidly since 1990. New residents are coming from the Miami-Fort Lauderdale area or other parts of the nation, drawn by a strong economy and good weather.

Pratt & Whitney, located west of Palm Beach Gardens in the neighboring 23rd District, also is a major employer of the 16th's residents. The company recently moved its military engines business to Connecticut, although the firm maintains a rocket propulsion facility

in Palm Beach County. Agricultural jobs, mainly producing sugar near the lake, also employ several thousand workers.

The longtime Democratic dominance around West Palm Beach has ebbed, and Republicans now outnumber Democrats in the 16th. Democratic pockets can be found among the condominium communities near Lake Worth. Martin County, to the north, has a long tradition of supporting Republicans.

MAJOR INDUSTRY
Aerospace, agriculture, health care

CITIES
Port St. Lucie, 81,845; Jupiter, 32,740; Fort Pierce (pt.), 16,166 (1990)

UNUSUAL FEATURES
Headquarters of the Professional Golfers Association in Palm Beach Gardens; Clewiston, home to U.S. Sugar Corp., bills itself as "America's Sweetest Town."

Rep. Carrie P. Meek (D)

Elected 1992; 5th term

Meek often chooses the pragmatic path of a deal-maker, an effective trait for her seat on Appropriations, where she has a say over directing billions of dollars in federal spending. In that role, she is frequently the compromiser, cooperating with colleagues in the majority to win funds for programs and projects she holds dear.

The oldest member of the freshman Class of 1992, Meek has a disarming, down-home, grandmotherly manner that can persuade even an opponent to go along with her proposals. But she can play it tough, too. Occasionally, when faced with a proposal she abhors, she will urge her colleagues to kill it "Black Flag dead," a reference to the insecticide.

Meek landed the Appropriations assignment in her freshman term after heavily lobbying party leaders. The only freshman Democrat named to the panel, she succeeded in part because Democrats wanted diversity on Appropriations, traditionally a white male preserve. Furthermore, the leadership could count on her to cast a reliably liberal vote.

When she first arrived on Capitol Hill, the task immediately before her was to help her district recover from the ravages of Hurricane Andrew. Now, economic development, health care, education and housing —the litany of basic needs in a poor district such as the 17th — are the focus of her attention. The federal government must play a significant role in addressing those needs, she says, and poor areas must fight to get their share of the money.

That is why the 2000 census became an important issue for her, affecting, as it does, representation in the House and the distribution of federal aid. But while Meek advocated using a method called statistical sampling to adjust census figures to correct for undercounts of minorities, she also worked with Republican Dan Miller — one of sampling's leading foes — to make the head count more accurate.

In the 106th Congress, she sponsored legislation to permit welfare recipients to take census jobs without reducing their government benefits. The bill, which won the approval of Government Reform's Census Subcommittee, which Miller heads, was designed to bolster the Census Bureau's efforts in low-income and immigrant communities, where history has shown there is a substantial undercount.

Meek has shown in other ways that she can cooperate with Republicans. In 1998, she won bipartisan backing to add a new warning label to cigarette packs. Citing studies that found that African-Americans absorb more nicotine than other smokers, which may be one reason they are more likely to develop lung cancer, Meek convinced her Appropriations colleagues that a new warning label should be added to the existing four labels stating, "Surgeon General's Warning: African-Americans suffer the highest death rates from several diseases caused by smoking."

Meek and Appropriations GOP colleague Anne M. Northup of Kentucky have sought federal grants to help colleges aid students who do not read well because of learning disabilities. They also have pushed for funding for the National Institutes of Health to research lupus, a disease causing abnormalities in blood vessels and connective tissue that disproportionately affects minority women. Meek lost a sister and a close friend to lupus.

The more-partisan Meek was on display when Republicans pushed their spending and tax cut proposals through the House on successive days in June 1997. "The spending cuts that the House approved today fall mainly on the weakest members of our society, on the sick and on the elderly,"

CAPITOL OFFICE
225-4506; fax 226-0777; 2433 Rayburn Bldg. 20515

INTERNET
e-mail: cpm@mail.house.gov
web: www.house.gov/meek

COMMITTEES
Appropriations

HOMETOWN
Miami

BORN
April 29, 1926, Tallahassee, Fla.

RELIGION
Baptist

FAMILY
Divorced; three children

EDUCATION
Florida A&M U., B.S. 1946; U. of Michigan, M.S. 1948; Florida Atlantic U., attended 1979

CAREER
Educational administrator; teacher

POLITICAL HIGHLIGHTS
Fla. House, 1979-82; Fla. Senate, 1982-93

ELECTION RESULTS

2000 GENERAL
Carrie P. Meek (D)	unopposed

2000 PRIMARY
Carrie P. Meek (D)	unopposed

1998 GENERAL
Carrie P. Meek (D)	unopposed

PREVIOUS WINNING PERCENTAGES
1996 (89%); 1994 (100%); 1992 (100%)

Meek said. "Tomorrow we will be voting on tax cuts that mainly favor the wealthy. ... Today, the House voted to rob from the poor so that tomorrow the majority can help the rich."

But in July, when the final version of the budget package came up for approval, Meek parted ways with many liberals and supported it, satisfied with concessions that President Clinton had wrung from the GOP.

As is typical for a House member from South Florida, where the Cuban-American community is politically potent, Meek is a critic of Cuban leader Fidel Castro. Meek's district also includes large numbers of Haitian refugees — their neighborhood in Miami is known as Little Haiti — and she has been a strong supporter of efforts to promote democracy in that island nation. And because of concerns about China's human rights record, Meek broke with the Clinton administration in 2000 and voted against granting China permanent normal trade status.

Representing a district that was the scene of a major riot in 1980 and has seen more than its share of violence, Meek is a strong supporter of gun control. In 1996, toward the end of House floor debate on repealing the ban on certain semiautomatic weapons, Meek delivered a brief and angry speech denouncing proponents of repeal. She said retaining the assault weapons ban was the very least Congress should do to deter gun violence. "I want to see every gun controlled because some of these people do not even need to have a gun in their hands," she said. "They are already bad enough without that."

The granddaughter of slaves and daughter of sharecroppers, Meek grew up in a poor area of Tallahassee called Black Bottom when segregation was the norm. She graduated from historically black Florida A & M and went to the University of Michigan for a master's degree.

Meek got involved in politics while working as a teacher and later a college administrator, and in 1978, she won a seat in the state House. She moved to the state Senate in 1982 and was serving there when congressional redistricting created the 17th, the most heavily black and reliably Democratic of Florida's House districts.

In her first congressional campaign in 1992, Meek heard some criticism that at age 66, she would not be able to provide the district with vigorous, long-term representation. The age issue did not resonate with voters: She won the primary with 83 percent of the vote and had no trouble in the general election. (That year, Meek and Democrats Alcee L. Hastings and Corrine Brown became the first blacks elected to Congress from Florida since Reconstruction.) Meek has won re-election easily and was unopposed in 2000.

KEY VOTES

2000

Yes Raise hourly minimum wage by $1 over two years
Yes Halt funding for U.S. mission in Kosovo unless European nations pay more
Yes Provide Medicare benefits to military retirees and their dependents
No Grant China permanent normal trade status
No Phase out estate, gift and trust taxes
No Prohibit implementation of president's national monument designations
No Approve GOP plan to provide prescription drug coverage for Medicare beneficiaries
Yes Increase help for poor nations indebted to international financial institutions

1999

Yes Impose steel import quotas
No Kill proposal to take aviation trust funds off budget
No Require background checks on buyers only at gun shows with 10 or more vendors
Yes Remove barriers among banking, securities and insurance companies
Yes Authorize state grants to hire teachers and reduce class size
Yes Overhaul campaign finance law; ban "soft money" and restrict advocacy advertising
Yes Approve bipartisan plan to increase rights of patients in managed-care health plans

INTEREST GROUPS

	AFL-CIO	ADA	CCUS	ACU
2000	100%	80%	52%	8%
1999	89%	90%	25%	0%
1998	100%	95%	28%	4%
1997	100%	80%	40%	17%

CQ VOTE STUDIES

	PARTY UNITY		PRESIDENTIAL SUPPORT	
	Support	Oppose	Support	Oppose
2000	92%	8%	77%	23%
1999	95%	5%	86%	14%
1998	93%	7%	87%	13%
1997	88%	12%	71%	29%

FLORIDA 17

Southeast – Part of north Miami-Dade County; part of Miami; Carol City

One of the state's poorest districts, the 17th takes in portions of Miami and stretches from Homestead to near the Broward County line. Despite having the lowest voter registration in the state, the district routinely delivers the highest percentages for Democratic candidates in statewide and national elections.

The 17th has the highest percentage of blacks in the state. Residents live in a range of neighborhoods, from the more affluent northern suburbs to the economically depressed Liberty City and Overtown sections of Miami. Most of the district straddles U.S. Highway 1 and the Florida East Coast railroad, taking in small portions of Little Haiti and several Hispanic areas. Many of the district's white residents live closer to the beach north of Miami and tend to add to the 17th's Democratic base. The southern portions of the district come close to the edge of the Everglades and have more agricultural activity.

Aviation is a big part of the 17th: Miami International Airport is located just outside the district and another airport in Opa-Locka serves as a base for civilian pilots. But the district, never an economic powerhouse, lost its major employer when Homestead Air Force Base was shuttered after Hurricane Andrew struck in 1992. A small reserve station and a NASCAR auto racing track now occupy much of the former base.

MAJOR INDUSTRY
Transportation, health care, state and local government

CITIES
Miami (pt.), 132,471 (1990); Carol City (unincorporated) (pt.), 43,858 (1990); North Miami (pt.), 42,308 (1990)

UNUSUAL FEATURES
Opa-Locka's architecture based on an Arabian theme, and the city holds an Arabian festival each year.

Rep. Ileana Ros-Lehtinen (R)

Elected August 1989; 6th full term

CAPITOL OFFICE
225-3931; fax 225-5620; 2160 Rayburn Bldg. 20515

INTERNET
e-mail: www.house.gov/writerep
web: www.house.gov/ros-lehtinen

COMMITTEES
Government Reform
International Relations
  (International Operations & Human Rights -
  chairwoman)

HOMETOWN
Miami

BORN
July 15, 1952, Havana, Cuba

RELIGION
Roman Catholic

FAMILY
Husband, Dexter Lehtinen; two children, two
stepchildren

EDUCATION
Miami-Dade Community College, A.A. 1972; Florida
International U., B.A. 1975, M.S. 1986; U. of Miami,
attending

CAREER
Teacher; private school administrator

POLITICAL HIGHLIGHTS
Fla. House, 1983-87; Fla. Senate, 1987-89

ELECTION RESULTS

2000 GENERAL
Ileana Ros-Lehtinen (R)	unopposed

2000 PRIMARY
Ileana Ros-Lehtinen (R)	unopposed

1998 GENERAL
Ileana Ros-Lehtinen (R)	unopposed

PREVIOUS WINNING PERCENTAGES
1996 (100%); 1994 (100%); 1992 (67%); 1990 (60%);
1989 Special Election (53%)

The first Cuban-American and the first Hispanic woman elected to Congress, Ros-Lehtinen is well-known in Congress and across the country for her devotion to three children: her teenage daughters, Amanda and Patricia, and Cuban-born Elián González. Ros-Lehtinen's daughters can often be spotted sitting beside her in a committee hearing, accompanying her to press conferences or joining her for meals on Capitol Hill.

In the case of Elián, his U.S. relatives sought Ros-Lehtinen's help in keeping the boy in this country after the 5-year-old was rescued from the ocean as he and his mother tried to reach U.S. shores on Thanksgiving Day, 1999. (Elián's mother drowned during the attempt.) The child's situation had particular resonance with Ros-Lehtinen, who arrived in Florida in 1959 with her family as a 7-year-old refugee after Fidel Castro took power. In addition to speaking out on behalf of Elián's U.S. relatives, drawing national attention, Ros-Lehtinen (pronounced il-ee-AH-na ross-LAY-tin-nen) visited the boy several times while he was in the United States, even attending his birthday party and bringing him a monster truck for Christmas.

Her efforts received the ultimate accolade for a Cuban-American legislator: a direct personal attack from Cuba's state-run newspaper, Granma, which called her a "ferocious wolf disguised as a woman." She was so proud that she had "loba feroz" (shortened to "loba frz") stamped on a vanity license plate.

But as with a number of issues in recent years, Ros-Lehtinen's efforts did not sit well with all of her Republican colleagues. Many GOP social conservatives were angered by her attempts to keep Elián in the United States, saying that the boy should not be separated from his father.

Indeed, ever since Republicans took control of Congress in 1995 and made it a priority to push restrictive policies on immigration, Ros-Lehtinen has had a fair share of high-profile disagreements with the party line. She opposed measures to overhaul the welfare system, curb illegal immigration and designate English as the official U.S. language. In the 105th Congress, she worked to restore some benefits to immigrants that had been eliminated in the 104th. She also stands apart from the GOP right in her sympathy for gun control and for some labor-backed positions.

When the House considered the GOP's first welfare overhaul bill in 1995, Ros-Lehtinen expressed concern about an "anti-immigrant sentiment" that is "growing from an unreal perception that immigrants only come to the United States to take advantage of our generous society and become a burden on the state while never integrating nor becoming productive citizens." When the final welfare bill passed the House in 1996, Ros-Lehtinen and fellow Floridian Lincoln Diaz-Balart were the only Republicans voting against it. She also pushed for Congress to exempt from sweeping new deportation rules thousands of refugees fleeing civil wars in Central America.

Ros-Lehtinen and Diaz-Balart were so unhappy with the welfare and immigration bills passed in the 104th that in March 1996 they rejoined the Congressional Hispanic Caucus, which is dominated by House Democrats, as a show of unity against anti-immigrant feelings. The two Republicans had left the caucus at the start of the 104th to comply with the spirit of a GOP move to do away with such organizations. But another issue — Cuba — prompted Ros-Lehtinen and Diaz-Balart to resign again from the caucus early in 1997. They dropped out to protest that caucus Chairman Xavier Becerra, a California Democrat, had taken a trip to Cuba in December 1996.

Ros-Lehtinen takes an absolutist stance toward Castro, fiercely opposing any suggestion that the United States ease its economic embargo against Cuba. "The only embargo that has to be lifted is the embargo on freedom, human rights and democracy that the Cuban dictator has imposed on the people of Cuba," she said in 1998. Ros-Lehtinen's stature in the Cuban-American community has grown in recent years as Cuban-American lawmakers have filled a political vacuum left by the death of Jorge Mas Canosa, the founder of the Cuban American National Foundation.

In her four years as chairwoman of the International Relations Subcommittee on International Economic Policy and Trade, Ros-Lehtinen was little more than a bit player on international business issues. Most of the heavy lifting on those bills has been left to more powerful committees such as Ways and Means and Banking (now Financial Services). In the 107th Congress, with trade issues on the International Relations panel being handled at the full committee level, she took the gavel of a newly constituted International Operations and Human Rights Subcommittee.

Ros-Lehtinen often has been cold to lowering trade barriers. The Clinton administration in the 105th lobbied her rigorously to support fast-track trade negotiating authority for the president, in order to strike trade deals in Latin America — but to no avail. After opposing the North American Free Trade Agreement and the General Agreement on Tariffs and Trade in previous years, Ros-Lehtinen said that past trade initiatives had a questionable impact and "the threshold of trust is therefore very low." Her anti-communism also led her to oppose granting China permanent normal trade status in 2000.

Educated in Miami, Ros-Lehtinen became a teacher and ran a bilingual private school in South Florida. In 1982, at age 30, she was the first Hispanic elected to the state legislature. Although not a major power broker in Tallahassee, she was an articulate campaigner and leading member of South Florida's Cuban-American community.

In a 1989 special-election race to replace the late Democratic Rep. Claude Pepper, Ros-Lehtinen easily defeated three other candidates for the Republican nomination. With generous support from the national Republican Party, she beat Democrat Gerald Richman, a Jewish Miami Beach lawyer with limited political experience. Stressing her support for Israel, she traveled there during the campaign, but the race was close and Ros-Lehtinen's victory margin was less than expected.

Richman's showing led some to believe Ros-Lehtinen's re-election was uncertain. But she prepared well, and several formidable Democrats skipped the 1990 race; she won with 60 percent that year and by a 2-to-1 ratio in a new, overwhelmingly Hispanic district in 1992. Since then, she has run unopposed.

KEY VOTES

2000

Yes Raise hourly minimum wage by $1 over two years
Yes Halt funding for U.S. mission in Kosovo unless European nations pay more
Yes Provide Medicare benefits to military retirees and their dependents
No Grant China permanent normal trade status
Yes Phase out estate, gift and trust taxes
Yes Prohibit implementation of president's national monument designations
Yes Approve GOP plan to provide prescription drug coverage for Medicare beneficiaries
No Increase help for poor nations indebted to international financial institutions

1999

Yes Impose steel import quotas
No Kill proposal to take aviation trust funds off budget
Yes Require background checks on buyers only at gun shows with 10 or more vendors
Yes Remove barriers among banking, securities and insurance companies
No Authorize state grants to hire teachers and reduce class size
? Overhaul campaign finance law; ban "soft money" and restrict advocacy advertising
Yes Approve bipartisan plan to increase rights of patients in managed-care health plans

INTEREST GROUPS

	AFL-CIO	ADA	CCUS	ACU
2000	30%	15%	71%	64%
1999	33%	25%	71%	73%
1998	67%	15%	67%	80%
1997	38%	20%	90%	76%

CQ VOTE STUDIES

	PARTY UNITY		PRESIDENTIAL SUPPORT	
	Support	Oppose	Support	Oppose
2000	86%	14%	30%	70%
1999	83%	17%	27%	73%
1998	81%	19%	29%	71%
1997	88%	12%	32%	68%

FLORIDA 18

Southeast – Parts of Miami-Dade County; part of Miami

The 18th features the glitz of downtown Miami and Miami Beach, but its political base comes from the Latin-dominated areas west of downtown. From downtown Miami, the 18th winds its way around black-majority areas grouped into the 17th District. Two-thirds of the residents claim Hispanic origin and many are stridently anti-Castro, helping make the 18th among the safest Republican districts in the nation.

The district has a wide mix of neighborhoods, from the downtrodden areas of Little Havana to wealthy Pinecrest and more middle-class Kendall and Westchester. Residents tend to be conservative on foreign policy issues but more in line with Democrats on welfare reform and other social issues. A strong economy that doesn't rely solely on tourism has translated into little opposition for incumbents.

International commerce and transportation, including Miami International Airport and several cruise lines, are important parts of the 18th's economy and have been bolstered by increased trade with Latin America. Two large universities – the University of Miami in upscale Coral Gables and Florida International University – attract an international student body.

The United States Southern Command, which oversees military operations in Central and South America, moved from Panama to a location just west of Miami International Airport in September 1997.

MAJOR INDUSTRY
Transportation, trade, higher education

CITIES
Miami (pt.), 238,128 (1990); Coral Gables (pt.), 39,612 (1990); Miami Beach (pt.), 32,811 (1990)

UNUSUAL FEATURES
Richard M. Nixon vacationed regularly on Key Biscayne.

Rep. Robert Wexler (D)

Elected 1996; 3rd term

An outspoken and media-savvy member of the Judiciary Committee, Wexler came to national prominence in 1998 as one of President Clinton's most visible defenders during the panel's impeachment deliberations. Since then, he has emerged as a highly vocal advocate for such liberal causes as abortion rights, environmental protection and federal funding for the arts.

Late in 2000, he once again was on the talk-show circuit, making the Democratic case in the Florida presidential election dispute, arguing for a full recount and complaining about voting procedures that, Democrats said, left many black voters disenfranchised.

But there is another aspect of Wexler's congressional persona, which is demonstrated by his membership in the moderate group of lawmakers known as the New Democrat Coalition. And in the midst of the Florida election dispute, Wexler declared that once it was resolved, "We ought to be big enough people to join behind the new president."

Despite his low seniority on the Judiciary Committee, Wexler rocketed to prominence as a freshman during the panel's 1998 impeachment proceedings against Clinton, which stemmed from his efforts to cover up a relationship with former White House intern Monica Lewinsky. Impeachment, Wexler contended, "is not about adultery. ... It is about subversion of government. The president had an affair. He lied about it. He didn't want anyone to know about it. Does anyone reasonably believe that this amounts to subversion of government? ... Is this where we want to set the bar for future presidents?"

Wexler's staff estimates that he was interviewed on television about 100 times during the six months when the impeachment wars raged in Congress — more time on TV than many lawmakers get in a lifetime. "I got to do in one term what it might have taken 10 terms to do," said Wexler, who rated it an almost entirely positive experience.

But his extroverted and sometimes emotional persona won mixed reviews, with political writer Ronald Brownstein of the Los Angeles Times labeling Wexler "the human advertisement for the mute button."

Having established himself with those who determine the guest lists for TV programs, Wexler, who also serves on the International Relations Committee, was invited back to discuss intervention in Kosovo and other foreign policy topics. "That is the stuff I love talking about," he said, adding that in his district — which includes the heavily Jewish communities of Boca Raton and Palm Beach — Middle East policy is virtually local politics.

Not surprisingly, Wexler became a favorite of the Clinton administration. The president spoke at a May 2000 fundraiser for him that netted an estimated $175,000, hailing the congressman as a man who "stands up and fights for what he believes in," according to The Associated Press. The administration repaid Wexler in other ways as well, allowing the congressman to travel with Secretary of State Madeleine K. Albright on a peace mission to Israel and inviting him to the signing ceremony of the 1998 Wye River peace agreement between Israel and the Palestinian Authority.

In the 106th Congress, Wexler joined forces with one of his foes during the impeachment proceedings, Republican Lindsey Graham of South Carolina, to promote a moderate tax cut targeting the middle class. He urged Democrats and Republicans to set aside their differences on fiscal policy and "concentrate our energies where we find common ground."

As often as not, however, Wexler aimed rhetorical salvos at Republicans.

CAPITOL OFFICE
225-3001; fax 225-5974; 213 Cannon Bldg. 20515

INTERNET
e-mail: www.house.gov/writerep
web: www.house.gov/wexler

COMMITTEES
International Relations
Judiciary

HOMETOWN
Boca Raton

BORN
Jan. 2, 1961, Queens, N.Y.

RELIGION
Jewish

FAMILY
Wife, Laurie Wexler; three children

EDUCATION
Emory U., attended 1978-79; U. of Florida, B.A. 1982; George Washington U., J.D. 1985

CAREER
Lawyer

POLITICAL HIGHLIGHTS
Fla. Senate, 1990-97

ELECTION RESULTS

2000 GENERAL

Robert Wexler (D)	171,080	71.6%
Morris Kent Thompson (R)	67,789	28.4%

2000 PRIMARY

Robert Wexler (D)	unopposed

1998 GENERAL

Robert Wexler (D)	unopposed

PREVIOUS WINNING PERCENTAGES
1996 (66%)

During House debate on a juvenile crime bill in 1999, Wexler, a proponent of gun control, accused Republicans of muddying the waters on the issue by focusing on violence in the entertainment industry. Waving a cardboard cutout of a gun in one hand and a television remote control in the other, he said: "Instead of gun control, we are doing remote control. ... Instead of going after the NRA [the National Rifle Association], Congress is going after NBC." He proposed a bill in the 106th that would have limited handgun purchases to one a month.

Despite such outspoken rhetoric, Wexler often positions himself as a moderate. In 1997, he was one of only two Democrats on Judiciary who joined 18 of the panel's Republicans in voting for a constitutional amendment to ban desecration of the U.S. flag. And he backed a GOP proposal in 1997 to give states financial incentives to prosecute violent juvenile criminals as adults instead of handling their cases through the juvenile justice system.

He was also one of only 37 House Democrats who voted for a constitutional amendment imposing a 12-year service limit on members of Congress.

Wexler gained attention in 1997 for sharply criticizing the performance of the FBI's crime lab, which came under fire for mishandling reports on evidence involved in criminal investigations. In response to what he called a "deepening crisis at the FBI," Wexler introduced legislation aimed at breaking down the agency's "institutional resistance to independent oversight." Wexler's bill sought to make it easier for the Justice Department's inspector general to investigate the FBI.

He has also worked to increase penalties for money laundering, a big concern in South Florida, which is on the front lines in the battle against drug trafficking.

Born in Queens, Wexler was 10 when his family moved to South Florida. While Wexler was chairman of the Florida Senate's Criminal Justice Committee, four-term Democratic Rep. Harry A. Johnston in late 1995 announced he was retiring from his 19th District seat. In the ensuing four-way primary, Wexler won a plurality of the vote, handily defeated state Senate Majority Leader Peter Weinstein in the runoff, and rolled up two-thirds of the general-election vote against Republican Beverly Kennedy, a Pompano Beach financial consultant. He has easily won re-election since.

Wexler jokes that he represents more former New Yorkers than any other member of the House, and he takes that role seriously. In April 1997, as Passover approached, he asked the Florida attorney general to investigate the rising cost of matzo, which was selling in Florida for more than twice its price in Manhattan.

KEY VOTES

2000
Yes Raise hourly minimum wage by $1 over two years
No Halt funding for U.S. mission in Kosovo unless European nations pay more
Yes Provide Medicare benefits to military retirees and their dependents
No Grant China permanent normal trade status
No Phase out estate, gift and trust taxes
No Prohibit implementation of president's national monument designations
No Approve GOP plan to provide prescription drug coverage for Medicare beneficiaries
Yes Increase help for poor nations indebted to international financial institutions

1999
Yes Impose steel import quotas
No Kill proposal to take aviation trust funds off budget
No Require background checks on buyers only at gun shows with 10 or more vendors
Yes Remove barriers among banking, securities and insurance companies
Yes Authorize state grants to hire teachers and reduce class size
Yes Overhaul campaign finance law; ban "soft money" and restrict advocacy advertising
Yes Approve bipartisan plan to increase rights of patients in managed-care health plans

INTEREST GROUPS

	AFL-CIO	ADA	CCUS	ACU
2000	100%	85%	52%	17%
1999	89%	100%	20%	8%
1998	100%	100%	18%	0%
1997	100%	90%	40%	17%

CQ VOTE STUDIES

	PARTY UNITY		PRESIDENTIAL SUPPORT	
	Support	Oppose	Support	Oppose
2000	91%	9%	79%	21%
1999	93%	7%	84%	16%
1998	92%	8%	90%	10%
1997	90%	10%	79%	21%

FLORIDA 19
Southeast — Parts of Palm Beach and northern Broward counties; Boca Raton

Heavily Democratic, the 19th is split between Palm Beach and Broward counties, mostly west of Interstate 95 where subdivisions dot the landscape. Older, upper-middle-class residents make it one of the most-educated and white-collar districts in the state.

Almost exclusively white, the 19th supports Democrats by overwhelming margins at the state and national levels. Retirees, including many Jewish condominium residents who provide a consistent base, live in Boynton Beach and Deerfield Beach. The "condo commandos" who run condominium associations serve as local power-brokers. The GOP has its strength in Boca Raton, which features gated communities and upscale residents, and in fast-growing Coral Springs in Broward County.

High-tech manufacturers, including Motorola Inc. and Sensormatic

Electronics Corp., have facilities in the district, which has long been a home to various corporate headquarters. Lake Worth and Lantana in mid-Palm Beach County have a more blue-collar tilt. Job cuts during the late 1980s and early '90s removed some corporate residents from the district, but most have since been replaced, thanks to a growing workforce.

MAJOR INDUSTRY
Manufacturing, electronics, financial services

CITIES
Coral Springs, 116,136; Margate (pt.), 46,432 (1990); Boca Raton (pt.), 38,962 (1990)

UNUSUAL FEATURES
Headquarters for the tabloid National Enquirer in Lantana; Boca Raton, known for its pink municipal buildings and the Spanish revival architecture of Addison Mizner.

Rep. Peter Deutsch (D)

Elected 1992; 5th term

CAPITOL OFFICE
225-7931; fax 225-8456; 2421 Rayburn Bldg. 20515

INTERNET
e-mail: www.house.gov/writerep
web: www.house.gov/deutsch

COMMITTEES
Energy & Commerce

HOMETOWN
Fort Lauderdale

BORN
April 1, 1957, Bronx, N.Y.

RELIGION
Jewish

FAMILY
Wife, Lori Ann Coffino; two children

EDUCATION
Swarthmore College, B.A. 1979; Yale U., J.D. 1982

CAREER
Lawyer; nonprofit executive

POLITICAL HIGHLIGHTS
Fla. House, 1983-93

ELECTION RESULTS

2000 GENERAL
Peter Deutsch (D)   unopposed
2000 PRIMARY
Peter Deutsch (D)   unopposed
1998 GENERAL
Peter Deutsch (D)   unopposed

PREVIOUS WINNING PERCENTAGES
1996 (65%); 1994 (61%); 1992 (55%)

Hard-charging and tenacious, Deutsch is extremely aggressive in advancing the causes he holds dear, which include preserving the Everglades, defending government programs for senior citizens, agitating for a hard-line U.S. stance against Cuban leader Fidel Castro and fostering a close U.S. relationship with Israel.

"Team player" is not the first phrase that comes to mind in describing Deutsch (DOYCH). In fact, he is such an ardent pursuer of his causes that even natural allies sometimes keep their distance from him, fearful that his sharp elbows and strong rhetoric will complicate the process of building bipartisan coalitions.

In 2000, Deutsch was a key financial supporter of Al Gore's presidential campaign in Florida, and he was a tenacious and vociferous advocate of Gore's position during the state's post-election ballot-counting controversy.

Deutsch makes no apologies for his hard-driving style. With an eye toward expanding his influence, and possibly running statewide someday, he has amassed a sizable war chest. He formed his own political action committee and, in addition to contributing to Gore's campaign, he used the funds to support fellow centrist Democrats. "I'm at a point in my career where I don't want to say I'm just another member of Congress. I want to influence the direction of the party."

Deutsch considered running for the vacant Senate seat of retiring Republican Connie Mack in 2000. But he said family responsibilities and the task of representing the 20th District did not allow time to campaign for the Senate.

Deutsch's voting record places him slightly to the left of the average Southern Democrat and slightly to the right of his party's leadership — positions one would expect from a member of the New Democrat Coalition, which says it works to find "mainstream, bipartisan" solutions. He has sided with conservatives on proposals to overhaul the public housing system, to give property owners a better chance of challenging adverse land-use decisions, and to crack down on violent youths. In the 106th Congress, he teamed up with Republican Michael Bilirakis of Florida to try to ease Clinton administration regulations on Medicare HMOs.

In 2000, his strong anti-Castro views made news when he traveled to Cuba with U.S. permission, but without the consent of Cuban authorities. Deutsch made unscheduled house calls on dissidents and, upon returning to the United States, backed the continuation of the trade embargo against Cuba. He criticized his anti-embargo colleagues in Congress, many of whom were Democrats, as "either naive or crazy," reported the Ft. Lauderdale Sun-Sentinel.

Despite intense White House lobbying in 2000, he voted against legislation granting China permanent normal trade status. "Our goal is to change China to a country that has a rule of law, has worker rights, human rights," he said.

On a range of issues, though, Deutsch votes a liberal line. He supports abortion rights, backs gun control and generally sides with organized labor. Deutsch takes a dim view of GOP efforts to greatly increase defense spending. And he opposes Republicans seeking to limit the regulatory authority of the Environmental Protection Agency.

Much of the land in Deutsch's district is in the Everglades, whose restoration is one of his top priorities. Deutsch calls the Everglades "America's most threatened ecosystem" and contends it is vital to South Florida's economy as well as the environment. "The Everglades sells itself," he said, according to the Sun-Sentinel. "In Florida, the economy is the environment. If there was ever an example of the need to manage both, this is where we have to do it," Deutsch continued. In 2000, Congress authorized the first $1.4 billion of a $7.8 billion federal-state Everglades restoration project.

Deutsch represents a large population of elderly residents and is an outspoken advocate of granting prescription drug benefits to Medicare recipients. In 2000, he surveyed his constituents by mail on the issue and said he was astounded to get back 10,000 replies. "This is an issue that people get," he told the Fort Lauderdale Sun-Sentinel. "It doesn't just affect Medicare beneficiaries. It affects the children of the people on Medicare, and even their grandchildren." He also champions legislation to permit reimportation of U.S. drugs from other countries, at lower cost.

Deutsch is a strong supporter of Israel, and in the 105th, he blasted Palestinian leader Yassir Arafat for statements in which Arafat reportedly said that selling property to a Jew should warrant the death penalty.

Many of his other crusades are inspired by events in his district, such as the murder of a 9-year-old boy who lived in the 20th. The boy was last seen walking home from school; a handyman later was arrested and confessed to killing the boy. Deutsch successfully lobbied Clinton to issue an executive order in 1996 allowing photographs of missing children to be displayed in federal buildings. And at Deutsch's urgings, recent appropriations bills have included funds to teach law enforcement officials how to handle cases involving missing children.

When Deutsch entered Congress at age 35, he had a decade of experience in the Florida Legislature under his belt. He started gearing up for a congressional run when he became chairman of the state House's congressional reapportionment subcommittee in 1990; the Florida district map eventually was drawn by a federal court. When Deutsch learned that the new map placed him in the same district with Democrat Dante B. Fascell, a 38-year House veteran, Deutsch decided to run in 1992 anyway, saying, "He's going to have to beat me." Fascell retired instead, but he and two other departing Florida Democrats, Lawrence J. Smith and William Lehman, issued a letter of support for Deutsch's primary opponent, Broward County Commissioner Nicki Englander Grossman.

The ensuing campaign turned highly personal. Deutsch, who had a big financial advantage, waged a late blitz of TV ads and fliers. He won the nomination with surprising ease, taking 63 percent of the vote, and handily bested GOP nominee Beverly "Bev" Kennedy in the general election. He has won with ease since then; in 1998 and 2000, the GOP did not field a candidate.

KEY VOTES

2000

Yes   Raise hourly minimum wage by $1 over two years

Yes   Halt funding for U.S. mission in Kosovo unless European nations pay more

Yes   Provide Medicare benefits to military retirees and their dependents

No   Grant China permanent normal trade status

Yes   Phase out estate, gift and trust taxes

No   Prohibit implementation of president's national monument designations

No   Approve GOP plan to provide prescription drug coverage for Medicare beneficiaries

Yes   Increase help for poor nations indebted to international financial institutions

1999

Yes   Impose steel import quotas

No   Kill proposal to take aviation trust funds off budget

No   Require background checks on buyers only at gun shows with 10 or more vendors

Yes   Remove barriers among banking, securities and insurance companies

Yes   Authorize state grants to hire teachers and reduce class size

Yes   Overhaul campaign finance law; ban "soft money" and restrict advocacy advertising

Yes   Approve bipartisan plan to increase rights of patients in managed-care health plans

INTEREST GROUPS

	AFL-CIO	ADA	CCUS	ACU
2000	100%	65%	57%	28%
1999	78%	95%	40%	8%
1998	90%	95%	35%	4%
1997	100%	80%	60%	21%

CQ VOTE STUDIES

	PARTY UNITY		PRESIDENTIAL SUPPORT	
	Support	Oppose	Support	Oppose
2000	87%	13%	71%	29%
1999	88%	12%	80%	20%
1998	88%	12%	82%	18%
1997	88%	12%	78%	22%

FLORIDA 20

South – Parts of Broward County; Hollywood; the Keys

The 20th includes some of Florida's most environmentally sensitive land, from the Everglades in western Broward and Dade counties to the Florida Keys, ending in Key West. The mostly Democratic population centers around fast-growing suburbs of Pembroke Pines (which grew by almost 85 percent in the 1990s), Plantation and Davie. The district has the highest median income in the state, thanks to wealthy Keys residents and upscale suburbanites.

The district wraps around the Miami area, but includes many former Miami residents who headed north to Broward County seeking suburban life. The Keys have a significant gay and lesbian population in addition to older natives who adhere to the independence and environmentalism of the "Conch Republic." Tourism and fishing represent the bulk of business in the Keys, while western Broward teems with shopping centers and suburban development.

Davie, closer to the Everglades, has retained a rural feel and is known for its cattle ranches. Plantation has more upscale homes and light industry. Jewish retirees help give the district its overall Democratic bent, but Republicans have been competitive in local and state elections.

MILITARY BASES
Key West Naval Air Station, 1,056 military, 713 civilian (1999)

MAJOR INDUSTRY
Tourism, business services, retail

CITIES
Pembroke Pines, 121,279; Hollywood (pt.), 73,441 (1990); Davie, 69,589; Plantation (pt.), 68,590 (1990)

UNUSUAL FEATURES
The dozens of cats that live at Ernest Hemingway's former home in Key West have six toes on each paw; The city of Sunrise attracted its first residents in 1961 by building an upside-down house complete with garage and car.

Rep. Lincoln Diaz-Balart (R)

Elected 1992; 5th term

CAPITOL OFFICE
225-4211; fax 225-8576; 2244 Rayburn Bldg. 20515

INTERNET
e-mail: www.house.gov/writerep
web: www.house.gov/diaz-balart

COMMITTEES
Rules

HOMETOWN
Miami

BORN
Aug. 13, 1954, Havana, Cuba

RELIGION
Roman Catholic

FAMILY
Wife, Cristina Diaz-Balart; two children

EDUCATION
U. of South Florida, B.A. 1976; Case Western
Reserve U., J.D. 1979

CAREER
Lawyer; state prosecutor

POLITICAL HIGHLIGHTS
Democratic nominee for Fla. House, 1982; Fla.
House, 1987-89; Fla. Senate, 1989-92

ELECTION RESULTS

2000 GENERAL
Lincoln Diaz-Balart (R)	unopposed	

2000 PRIMARY
Lincoln Diaz-Balart (R)	unopposed	

1998 GENERAL
Lincoln Diaz-Balart (R)	84,018	74.8%
Patrick Cusack (D)	28,378	25.2%

PREVIOUS WINNING PERCENTAGES
1996 (100%); 1994 (100%); 1992 (100%)

About half the residents of Florida's 21st District, including Diaz-Balart himself, are of Cuban descent, so it follows that U.S.-Cuba relations are the congressman's top priority. Diaz-Balart's principal goal in Congress has been to keep economic pressure on the government of Cuba, in hopes of ultimately overthrowing President Fidel Castro.

He and the two other Cuban-born members of the House — Ileana Ros-Lehtinen of the nearby 18th District and Democrat Robert Menendez of New Jersey — often urge a hard line against Castro. Diaz-Balart (DEE-az buh-LART) has called for Castro's arrest if he visits the United States.

Diaz-Balart is a skillful inside player and, drawing on his background as a prosecutor, can be persuasive in face-to-face meetings. His Florida House colleagues named him "best in debate" during his first term in the legislature.

As one of only three Hispanic Republicans in the House, Diaz-Balart's assignment to the Rules Committee, a leadership plum he was awarded in just his second term, reflects the GOP's eagerness to showcase the party's minority members. In 2000, a nationwide poll published in Hispanic Magazine cited Diaz-Balart as one of the 10 most influential Hispanics in the nation.

Some of his political opponents claim that he is so obsessed with toppling Castro that he ignores other pressing matters. Diaz-Balart bristles at the notion that he is a one-issue member, but the fact remains that matters involving Cuba are of high import in his district.

Diaz-Balart was a steadfast opponent of the Clinton administration's Cuba policy. He played a high-profile role in the debates on Capitol Hill as the saga of the custody battle over Cuban youngster Elián González grabbed the nation's attention in the 106th Congress, and as the broader issue of U.S.-Cuba relations came to the fore. He argued that Elián, rescued from the ocean after his mother drowned while attempting to defect to the United States, should have remained in this country. When federal agents seized the boy from the home of his Miami relatives, Diaz-Balart was outraged.

In the 106th Congress, Diaz-Balart pressed for the continuation of tough economic sanctions against Castro's regime, even as more lawmakers on Capitol Hill questioned the longstanding U.S. policy. Farm state legislators — led by Washington's George Nethercutt and Missouri's Jo Ann Emerson, both Republicans — pressed for an end to prohibitions on the export of food to Cuba, arguing that the restrictions hurt only American farmers. Diaz-Balart failed to prevent the removal of food export restrictions, but he declared a victory when the pro-sanctions forces were able to write into law existing prohibitions on travel to Cuba by U.S. citizens.

In the 104th Congress, Diaz-Balart had been a key player in drafting a bill that codified sanctions against Cuba. But the law gave the president power to postpone indefinitely a key section that gave U.S. citizens the right to sue foreign companies that own confiscated property in Cuba; and when Clinton did so, Diaz-Balart charged that Clinton had caved in to pressure from foreign interests. "Character of Jell-O, backbone of Jell-O," said Diaz-Balart.

His outrage extends to fellow lawmakers who visit Cuba and fail — in his view — to declare sufficiently their opposition to Castro's regime. In 2000, he supported the Cuban American National Foundation when it aimed campaign advertisements against lawmakers — including some Republicans — whom it regarded as not sufficiently anti-Castro.

While acknowledging that Cuba-related matters are his priority, Diaz-Balart argues that his range is broader than that. He touts his involvement in immigration and refugee policy, including work in 1997 to restore Social Security benefits and food stamps for legal immigrants and to forestall deportation from the United States of thousands of refugees from Central America and the Eastern Bloc. In the 106th Congress, he sought to provide the same immigration help for citizens of Colombia and Peru.

Florida's Cuban community is heavily Republican, but the working-class nature of his district leads him to stray from the GOP line on matters such as welfare and labor-management relations. He was one of the few Republicans who declined to sign the House GOP's 1994 "Contract With America" legislative platform; and he has bucked his party on a number of social programs, including the GOP's welfare overhaul bill in the 104th, which called for denying federal programs to legal immigrants.

In 1997, Diaz-Balart led a successful drive for nationwide application of Florida's tough law against the stalking of children. His proposal was based on the Florida statute, known as the Jennifer Act, that permits law enforcement agencies to arrest child stalkers before they can harm or kidnap their victims. In the 106th, he authored a bill to increase the punishment for child stalkers.

Diaz-Balart was born in Havana to a politically active family. His grandfather, father and uncle served in Cuba's House before the family fled to the United States in 1959. His father's sister was married to Castro in the late 1940s and early 1950s, but they divorced and there was a political falling-out between the families long before Castro took control.

After law school, Diaz-Balart worked for a Miami legal services organization that provided free legal help for the poor. He served as a Dade County prosecutor in the early 1980s under Janet Reno, who was the top county prosecutor.

Diaz-Balart was a Democrat when he first ran, unsuccessfully, in 1982 for the Florida House. He was a co-chairman of the Democrats for Reagan campaign in Florida in 1984 and switched to the GOP in 1985, easily winning a state House seat in 1986. He served three years in the House and three in the state Senate. (His younger brother, Mario, also served in the state Senate. In 2000, required by state term limits to give up that post, Mario won election to the state House.)

When the courts redrew Florida's congressional maps after the 1990 census, a second Hispanic-majority district, the 21st, was created. Diaz-Balart filed and easily bested a fellow Cuban-American state senator in a two-way Republican primary. He drew no Democratic foe that November and since then has been re-elected with little or no contest.

KEY VOTES

2000

Yes	Raise hourly minimum wage by $1 over two years
No	Halt funding for U.S. mission in Kosovo unless European nations pay more
Yes	Provide Medicare benefits to military retirees and their dependents
No	Grant China permanent normal trade status
Yes	Phase out estate, gift and trust taxes
Yes	Prohibit implementation of president's national monument designations
Yes	Approve GOP plan to provide prescription drug coverage for Medicare beneficiaries
No	Increase help for poor nations indebted to international financial institutions

1999

Yes	Impose steel import quotas
No	Kill proposal to take aviation trust funds off budget
Yes	Require background checks on buyers only at gun shows with 10 or more vendors
Yes	Remove barriers among banking, securities and insurance companies
No	Authorize state grants to hire teachers and reduce class size
No	Overhaul campaign finance law; ban "soft money" and restrict advocacy advertising
Yes	Approve bipartisan plan to increase rights of patients in managed-care health plans

INTEREST GROUPS

	AFL-CIO	ADA	CCUS	ACU
2000	40%	20%	65%	56%
1999	44%	25%	60%	64%
1998	70%	25%	72%	68%
1997	63%	20%	70%	72%

CQ VOTE STUDIES

	PARTY UNITY		PRESIDENTIAL SUPPORT	
	Support	Oppose	Support	Oppose
2000	84%	16%	35%	65%
1999	78%	22%	33%	67%
1998	80%	20%	33%	67%
1997	87%	13%	31%	69%

FLORIDA 21

Southeast – Parts of Miami-Dade County; Hialeah

A safe Republican district, the Hispanic-dominated 21st includes suburbs west of Miami, from Miami Lakes in the north through Hialeah and Kendall to the south. The district's politics center around opposition to Fidel Castro. But economic and foreign policy conservatism are balanced by residents' more moderate views on social policy matters.

Hialeah, filled with Cuban-Americans who commute to jobs in Miami, accounts for about one-third of the district's residents. Transportation-related businesses, including Carnival Cruise Lines, have set up facilities close to Miami International Airport, which lies just outside the district's boundaries in the 18th.

The remainder of the district consists of planned developments like Miami Lakes and suburban communities like Kendall, which has more

Democrats. South Florida's healthy economic scene during the 1990s meant more jobs and homes for the 21st and neighboring districts.

Although it borders some of the state's poorer districts, the 21st has one of the highest median incomes and lowest percentages of elderly residents in the state. While Hialeah continued to expand during the 1990s, several other towns saw relatively small changes in population during that time.

MAJOR INDUSTRY
Manufacturing, retail, transportation

CITIES
Hialeah (pt.), 189,280 (1990); Kendall Lakes (unincorporated), 48,524 (1990); Kendall (unincorporated), 43,393 (1990)

UNUSUAL FEATURES
Hialeah boasts 15,000 multilingual businesses; Amelia Earhart's final trip began in 1937 in Hialeah.

Rep. E. Clay Shaw Jr. (R)

Elected 1980; 11th term

CAPITOL OFFICE
225-3026; fax 225-8398; 2408 Rayburn Bldg. 20515

INTERNET
e-mail: www.house.gov/writerep
web: www.house.gov/shaw

COMMITTEES
Ways & Means
 (Social Security - chairman)
Joint Taxation

HOMETOWN
Fort Lauderdale

BORN
April 19, 1939, Miami, Fla.

RELIGION
Roman Catholic

FAMILY
Wife, Emilie Shaw; four children

EDUCATION
Stetson U., B.S. 1961; U. of Alabama, M.B.A. 1963; Stetson U., J.D. 1966

CAREER
Nurseryman; lawyer; city prosecutor

POLITICAL HIGHLIGHTS
Fort Lauderdale associate municipal judge, 1969-71; Fort Lauderdale City Commission, 1971-73; vice mayor of Fort Lauderdale, 1973-75; mayor of Fort Lauderdale, 1975-81

ELECTION RESULTS

2000 GENERAL

E. Clay Shaw Jr. (R)	105,855	50.1%
Elaine Bloom (D)	105,256	49.9%

2000 PRIMARY

E. Clay Shaw Jr. (R)	unopposed

1998 GENERAL

E. Clay Shaw Jr. (R)	unopposed

PREVIOUS WINNING PERCENTAGES
1996 (62%); 1994 (63%); 1992 (52%); 1990 (98%); 1988 (66%); 1986 (100%); 1984 (66%); 1982 (57%); 1980 (55%)

Shaw is no stranger to the political dangers of overhauling federal entitlement programs such as welfare and Social Security. In 2000, he learned firsthand the risks of trying to change Social Security, when he nearly lost his bid for re-election a year after proposing a plan to create individual investment accounts as a partial replacement for Social Security benefits. After a history of easy re-elections, senior citizens got nervous and gave Shaw a scare at the polls: He won by just 599 votes.

Despite his close call, Shaw, as chairman of the Ways and Means Subcommittee on Social Security, remains a central figure in Republican efforts to modify the nation's social safety net. His Social Security plan bore similarities to President Bush's campaign proposal for making individual savings accounts a feature of the federal retirement system, and he will play a crucial role in maneuvering any GOP plan through Congress.

Shaw holds much of the GOP's institutional memory on another major social policy change: the 1996 rewrite of the welfare system. He was one of the key players who molded President Clinton's 1992 promise to "end welfare as we know it" into legislation that Republicans and many Democrats could support. Although Shaw no longer heads the Ways and Means subcommittee that oversees the revamped welfare system, he is an important behind-the-scenes force in preserving those changes as the 107th Congress reconsiders the 1996 law, which expires in October 2002.

Shaw's work on welfare was in keeping with his reputation in Congress for trying to craft legislation that can attract bipartisan backing. During the lengthy and often contentious debate on welfare overhaul in the 104th Congress, Shaw made sure that Democrats' viewpoints got a fair hearing. But he also helped advance the GOP position that localities and states should have more authority over welfare policy, a view anchored in his 13 years' experience in municipal government, including six years as Fort Lauderdale's mayor. Shaw's hope was to make welfare "not a way of life, but simply a short-term bridge over tough times."

As chairman of the Ways and Means Subcommittee on Human Resources, Shaw worked throughout the 104th to craft a welfare plan acceptable to both conservative Republicans and the White House. The final product set a lifetime limit of five years for federal welfare benefits, ending the practice of paying benefits to any family poor enough to be eligible. It cleared the House with nearly unanimous support from Republicans and with consent from exactly half the Democrats.

Since the legislation was enacted, Shaw has argued against those to his right who want to clamp down further on welfare recipients and those to his left who want to undo aspects of the measure they regard as punitive. He notes with satisfaction the declining number of people on welfare, and he credits the law with instilling a sense of greater "personal responsibility" in low-income parents. "There are some people who have fallen through the cracks," Shaw said in 2001. "But the vast majority have really found a life, and they've found that there's a better way than welfare. And they're proud. They're role models for their kids."

Shaw did cooperate in one Democratic-inspired effort to fine-tune the welfare law in 1998, working with Michigan Rep. Sander M. Levin, then the ranking Democrat on the Human Resources Subcommittee, to restore some benefits to most disabled and elderly legal immigrants. The 1996 law had cut an array of federal benefits, including food stamps and Supplemental Security Income, to most legal immigrants.

Shaw may take risks trying to rein in entitlement spending, but he also knows the political value of increasing benefits for senior citizens in an election year. Facing a tough re-election race in 2000, Shaw presided over a repeal of Social Security's so-called earnings penalty. His bill, enacted in April, ended a Depression-era policy that reduced benefits for seniors age 65 through 69 whose wages exceeded an annual limit. He also sponsored legislation requiring Medicare to pay for annual mammograms and pap exams to help elderly women detect the early signs of breast or cervical cancer. That bill was signed into law as part of a larger package reversing some of the 1997 cuts in Medicare payments to hospitals and other health care providers.

Closer to home, Shaw made much of his sponsorship of a massive project to restore the Everglades, pushed through Congress days before the election by an anxious GOP leadership that feared the loss of his seat. He also sponsored a school construction bill that would have allowed a certain type of private bond to be used to build new schools. The measure was too limited for Democratic tastes in the 106th, but Shaw has reintroduced the bill for further consideration in the 107th.

Ranking high on the list of Shaw's other concerns is illegal drugs, a clear threat in his coastal South Florida district. To combat the flow of drugs through South Florida ports, Shaw sponsored a bill in the 105th Congress that would have required criminal background checks of Customs Service officers. The measure won House approval but was left out of a catchall spending bill at the end of the 105th.

Shaw, who was a Fort Lauderdale city official for 10 years, was unopposed for the GOP nomination when he ran for the House in 1980. He capitalized on Democratic squabbling to secure what was then the 12th District: Democratic primary voters dumped 70-year-old Rep. Edward J. Stack for a younger candidate, former state Rep. Alan Becker. Shaw denounced Becker as a liberal carpetbagger — the Democrat had moved into the district just the year before. Shaw bragged that during his tenure as mayor, he had cut spending, broadened the economic base and helped give Fort Lauderdale a more cosmopolitan image.

He won with 55 percent of the vote and was re-elected easily through the 1980s. His district became the 15th in 1982 after the decennial remapping; 10 years later it became the 22nd. His only scare came in 2000, when Democratic state Rep. Elaine Bloom pounced on his plan for revising Social Security and raised fears that Shaw was trying to privatize the program.

KEY VOTES

2000

No   Raise hourly minimum wage by $1 over two years

Yes   Halt funding for U.S. mission in Kosovo unless European nations pay more

Yes   Provide Medicare benefits to military retirees and their dependents

Yes   Grant China permanent normal trade status

Yes   Phase out estate, gift and trust taxes

Yes   Prohibit implementation of president's national monument designations

Yes   Approve GOP plan to provide prescription drug coverage for Medicare beneficiaries

No   Increase help for poor nations indebted to international financial institutions

1999

No   Impose steel import quotas

Yes   Kill proposal to take aviation trust funds off budget

Yes   Require background checks on buyers only at gun shows with 10 or more vendors

Yes   Remove barriers among banking, securities and insurance companies

No   Authorize state grants to hire teachers and reduce class size

?   Overhaul campaign finance law; ban "soft money" and restrict advocacy advertising

Yes   Approve bipartisan plan to increase rights of patients in managed-care health plans

INTEREST GROUPS

	AFL-CIO	ADA	CCUS	ACU
2000	0%	10%	80%	68%
1999	11%	20%	88%	60%
1998	10%	10%	100%	72%
1997	25%	10%	100%	80%

CQ VOTE STUDIES

	PARTY UNITY		PRESIDENTIAL SUPPORT	
	Support	Oppose	Support	Oppose
2000	87%	13%	31%	69%
1999	86%	14%	37%	63%
1998	88%	12%	34%	66%
1997	87%	13%	36%	64%

FLORIDA 22

Southeast – Coastal Broward, Miami-Dade and Palm Beach counties; Fort Lauderdale

The 22nd follows picturesque Route A1A down the Southeast coast from northern Palm Beach County to Miami Beach. Never more than three miles wide, the district takes in upscale beachfront cities and towns while excluding minority areas to the west. It has the highest percentage of elderly residents in the state.

The districts' residents are mostly well-off and overwhelmingly white. Republicans count Palm Beach, Pompano Beach and Fort Lauderdale as their base, while Democrats rely on Hallandale and North Miami Beach condominium residents.

Democrats got more than two-thirds of the presidential vote in 1996 and 2000 in the Miami-Dade County portion of the 22nd, which has a high proportion of Jewish and Hispanic residents. The district overall leans Democratic; in the 1992, '96 and 2000 presidential contests, the

22nd supported the Democratic candidate.

Exclusive hotels and shopping centers lie within the district, while the ports of Palm Beach and Fort Lauderdale attract shipping and cruise line business. The port of Miami is just outside the 22nd's boundaries. The area's elderly population has also made it the home of several large hospitals. The wealth of many district residents helps insulate them from economic pressures, but the area depends heavily on tourism.

MAJOR INDUSTRY
Health care, tourism, shipping

CITIES
Fort Lauderdale (pt.), 76,541 (1990); Miami Beach (pt.), 57,327 (1990); Pompano Beach (pt.), 35,025 (1990); Aventura, 20,121

UNUSUAL FEATURES
Kennedy family's former compound on Palm Beach; Other celebrity residents include singers Rod Stewart and Jimmy Buffett.

Rep. Alcee L. Hastings (D)

Elected 1992; 5th term

CAPITOL OFFICE
225-1313; fax 226-0690; 2235 Rayburn Bldg. 20515

INTERNET
e-mail: alcee.pubhastings@mail.house.gov
web: www.house.gov/alceehastings

COMMITTEES
International Relations
Select Intelligence

HOMETOWN
Miramar

BORN
Sept. 5, 1936, Altamonte Springs, Fla.

RELIGION
African Methodist Episcopal

FAMILY
Divorced; three children

EDUCATION
Fisk U., B.A. 1958; Howard U., attended 1958-60;
Florida A&M U., J.D. 1963

CAREER
Judge; lawyer

POLITICAL HIGHLIGHTS
Sought Democratic nomination for U.S. Senate,
1970; U.S. District Court judge, 1979-89;
Democratic nominee for Fla. secretary of state,
1990

ELECTION RESULTS

2000 GENERAL

Alcee L. Hastings (D)	89,179	76.3%
Bill Lambert (R)	27,630	23.7%

2000 PRIMARY

Alcee L. Hastings (D)	unopposed

1998 GENERAL

Alcee L. Hastings (D)	unopposed

PREVIOUS WINNING PERCENTAGES
1996 (74%); 1994 (100%); 1992 (59%)

As the House went through impeachment proceedings against President Clinton in late 1998, Hastings had a unique perspective on the matter because he had once been through the same ordeal. In 1988, the House impeached him, and in 1989, the Senate convicted him and removed him from his federal judgeship.

But voters in the black-majority 23rd District don't hold that against him. He was elected to the House in 1992 and has breezed to re-election since then.

By the end of the 1990s, with Hastings' impeachment largely faded from public memory, Clinton's saga rekindled interest. Hastings was often asked to give his perspective on the matter. He left no doubt that he thought that Independent Counsel Kenneth W. Starr's probe of the president was out of bounds. He offered a resolution asking the House to impeach Starr for "gross prosecutorial misconduct." And in the 106th Congress, he offered legislation to repeal the law establishing the independent counsel.

But Hastings says he has left behind the residue of his own impeachment, preferring instead to develop an expertise in foreign affairs and work on the needs of his congressional district. He surprised skeptics by getting along with the House members who had voted in 1988 to impeach him. Indeed, he arrived on Capitol Hill determined to be courteous, respectful and hard-working. "Succeeding is the best revenge," Hastings once said. "My goal was to get beyond people viewing me as an impeached judge."

He seems to have succeeded. "Quite a few people here have told me that if they knew then what they know now about me, they would never have voted against me," he told the Palm Beach Post. Republican Tom Campbell, a former colleague on the International Relations Committee, told the newspaper that he regards Hastings as one of the panel's foremost experts on the countries of the former Soviet Union. Of Hastings' impeachment, Campbell said: "It's not a factor. No one ever talks about it." In the 107th Congress, Hastings is the top Democrat on International Relations' Europe Subcommittee.

Hastings has wide-ranging interests in the international arena. He is a frequent participant in congressional fact-finding trips abroad and has traveled to more than two dozen countries on official business, including a half-dozen trips to Africa. Although his district is 52 percent African-American, Hastings says he sees little political gain from his work on matters such as peace between Ethiopia and Eritrea or the African AIDS epidemic. He told The Washington Post that some people in his district "are as interested in day-to-day survival as the people in Sudan are. Therefore, they don't make any connection to Africa."

Clinton's foreign policies did not always suit Hastings. In 1994, he was one of three lawmakers arrested for demonstrating in front of the White House against the U.S. policy of returning Haitian refugees to their country. In the 106th Congress, noting the efforts by many lawmakers to keep youthful Cuban refugee Elián González from being sent back to Cuba, Hastings objected that refugees from other countries were not afforded similar attention. He introduced a bill to permit a 6-year-old girl from Haiti, Sophonie Telcy, to stay and receive medical treatment. And he also offered broader legislation aimed at guarding the rights of unaccompanied refugees under 18.

In addition to his work on International Relations, Hastings involves himself in issues such as funding for Medicare, job training, Head Start and sugar subsidies, all important concerns in his district. Early in 2000, he spearheaded a local referendum to change the governing structure of the school board, making it easier to elect minority members to the board.

He also spends much of his time resisting what he sees as efforts by some white Florida Democrats to shift the state party to a right-of-center stance, diminishing the influence of black voters. He has feuded with white Democratic leaders and has several times urged blacks to consider voting for Republicans as a means of sending the party a signal that it should not take black support for granted.

Hastings was in the forefront of the protests over Florida's handling of the state's ballots in the 2000 presidential election, joining the Democratic protests about miscast and uncounted ballots. He also contended that many black voters were turned away from the polls.

Hastings grew up in a working-class household, the only child of parents who mostly toiled as domestic workers. Although neither of his parents graduated from high school, they pushed Hastings to get an education. He says he still often seeks advice from his mother. After graduating from historically black Fisk University with a zoology degree, he was accepted to medical school but chose to pursue a law career instead.

During the 1960s and 1970s, he ran for a number of offices, in the city council, the state legislature and the U.S. Senate. He lost all those races. In 1979, he was appointed to the federal bench by President Carter, becoming the first black federal judge in Florida.

He lost his lifetime seat over charges that he solicited a $150,000 bribe in exchange for granting a lenient sentence. Although he was acquitted of that charge in a trial, the House voted 426-3 to impeach him in 1988, and the Senate voted 69-26 to remove him from office. In 1997, allegations arose in the media that the FBI had misled Congress and the courts on forensic tests used as evidence in the legal proceedings against Hastings.

Hastings ran unsuccessfully for Florida secretary of state in 1990, but he won a majority of the votes in the areas that subsequently constituted the new 23rd District. Remappers designed the 23rd as a "minority access" district, giving it just a slight black majority — enough to offer African-Americans a chance, but no guarantee, of electing one of their own to the seat.

Hastings tried for the seat in 1992, believing a black candidate with high name recognition could beat front-running state Rep. Lois Frankel, a liberal white Democrat. Frankel took 35 percent to Hastings' 28 percent in the primary. But he surged past her in the runoff to win nomination with 58 percent. In November, against GOP real estate developer Ed Fielding, Hastings won with 59 percent.

KEY VOTES

2000
Yes Raise hourly minimum wage by $1 over two years
No Halt funding for U.S. mission in Kosovo unless European nations pay more
Yes Provide Medicare benefits to military retirees and their dependents
No Grant China permanent normal trade status
No Phase out estate, gift and trust taxes
No Prohibit implementation of president's national monument designations
No Approve GOP plan to provide prescription drug coverage for Medicare beneficiaries
Yes Increase help for poor nations indebted to international financial institutions

1999
Yes Impose steel import quotas
No Kill proposal to take aviation trust funds off budget
No Require background checks on buyers only at gun shows with 10 or more vendors
Yes Remove barriers among banking, securities and insurance companies
Yes Authorize state grants to hire teachers and reduce class size
? Overhaul campaign finance law; ban "soft money" and restrict advocacy advertising
Yes Approve bipartisan plan to increase rights of patients in managed-care health plans

INTEREST GROUPS

	AFL-CIO	ADA	CCUS	ACU
2000	100%	80%	55%	4%
1999	100%	80%	22%	0%
1998	100%	80%	22%	5%
1997	100%	80%	20%	19%

CQ VOTE STUDIES

	PARTY UNITY		PRESIDENTIAL SUPPORT	
	Support	Oppose	Support	Oppose
2000	95%	5%	82%	18%
1999	97%	3%	82%	18%
1998	95%	5%	90%	10%
1997	92%	8%	71%	29%

FLORIDA 23

Southeast – Parts of St. Lucie, Martin, Broward and Palm Beach counties

One of two black-majority districts in the state, the heavily Democratic 23rd stretches from Fort Pierce to the eastern shores of Lake Okeechobee and then through neighborhoods between the Intracoastal Waterway and Interstate 95. Half of the district's residents live in Broward County and a small portion live in Miami-Dade County's northern tip.

Most of the urban areas of the 23rd – Riviera Beach, West Palm Beach and Deerfield Beach – are black neighborhoods, attracting local government employees and other middle-class professionals. Boca Raton, Lauderdale Lakes and Okeechobee have more white residents than the other communities.

Citrus and sugar cane growers work the large but sparsely populated rural portions of the district. Boating and marine companies and other midsize businesses mix with homes along U.S. Highway 1 in the southern section of the district. The district lacks of a major employment sector, and the vulnerability of citrus crops to bad weather makes the 23rd one of the poorest districts in the state. One of the district's primary employers, Pratt & Whitney, recently moved its military engine business from Palm Beach County to Connecticut but still maintains its rocket propulsion facility here.

Voters routinely give Democratic candidates wide margins of victory over GOP opponents, making the Democratic primary the most important race. In close primaries, election results often have split along racial lines.

MAJOR INDUSTRY
Agriculture, local government, marine & boating

CITIES
Fort Lauderdale (pt.), 64,972 (1990); West Palm Beach (pt.), 39,677 (1990); Lauderhill (pt.), 30,873 (1990)

UNUSUAL FEATURES
Lauderdale Lakes has 22 churches within its four square miles.

GEORGIA

Gov. Roy Barnes (D)

First elected: 1998
Length of term: 4 years
Term expires: 1/03
Salary: $118,546
Phone: (404) 656-1776
Hometown: Mableton
Born: March 11, 1948, Atlanta, Ga.
Religion: Methodist
Family: Wife, Marie Barnes; three children
Education: U. of Georgia, A.B. 1969, J.D. 1972
Military service: Army Reserve, 1972-79
Career: Lawyer; banker
Political highlights: Ga. Senate, 1975-91 (Democratic floor leader, 1983-89); sought Democratic nomination for governor, 1990; Ga. House, 1993-99

Election results:
1998 GENERAL

Roy Barnes (D)	941,076	52.5%
Guy Millner (R)	790,201	44.1%

Lt. Gov. Mark Taylor (D)

First elected: 1998
Length of term: 4 years
Term expires: 1/03
Salary: $80,336
Phone: (404) 656-5030

STATE LEGISLATURE

General Assembly: Meets January to mid-March
House: 180 members, 2-year terms
2001 breakdown: 73R, 106D, 1I; 141 men, 39 women
Salary: $16,002
Phone: (404) 656-5082
Senate: 56 members, 2-year terms
2001 breakdown: 24R, 32D; 46 men, 10 women
Salary: $16,002
Phone: (404) 656-0028

STATE TERM LIMITS

Governor: 2 terms
Senate: No
House: No

URBAN STATISTICS

CITY	POPULATION
Atlanta	401,726
Augusta-Richmond County	186,206
Columbus	181,547
Savannah	129,556
Macon	113,336

REGISTERED VOTERS

Voters do not register by party.

POPULATION

2000 population	8,186,453
1990 population	6,478,216
Percent change	+26.4%
Rank among states	10
Median age	33.5
Born in state	65%
Foreign born	3%
Urban/rural	63%/37%
Crime rate	607/100,000
Poverty level	13.6%
Federal workers	93,207
Military	94,817

REAPPORTIONMENT

Georgia gained two House seats in reapportionment, increasing from 11 districts to 13. The state legislature will draw new district lines in 2002.

MISCELLANEOUS

Web: www.state.ga.us
Capital: Atlanta
Land area: 57,919 sq. miles
Rank among states: 21
STATE ELECTION OFFICIAL
(404) 656-2871
DEMOCRATIC HEADQUARTERS
(404) 885-1998
REPUBLICAN HEADQUARTERS
(404) 257-5559

District Statistics

	VOTE FOR PRESIDENT																
	2000			1996			1992							HOUSEHOLD	OVER	UNDER	COLLEGE
DIST.	D	R	GREEN	D	R	REF	D	R	I	WHT	BLK	ASIAN	HISP	INCOME	65+	18	EDUCATION
1	42%	57%	0%	45%	48%	6%	42%	44%	14%	68%	31%	1%	2%	$24,779	11%	28%	15%
2	45	54	0	49	44	7	46	40	13	59	39	0	2	$20,938	12	29	12
3	41	57	0	43	50	7	40	46	14	73	25	1	2	$30,672	9	28	15
4	69	29	0	64	32	4	55	35	10	58	37	4	3	$36,523	8	24	33
5	75	23	0	74	23	3	70	23	7	36	62	1	2	$25,547	10	25	25
6	32	66	0	33	61	5	30	55	15	91	6	2	2	$46,148	5	25	39
7	38	60	0	40	51	9	38	47	15	86	13	1	1	$28,898	11	27	12
8	42	57	0	47	45	8	39	47	15	68	31	0	1	$23,577	12	28	12
9	28	70	0	35	55	10	35	49	16	95	4	0	1	$26,631	12	26	11
10	44	55	0	48	46	6	46	42	13	61	38	1	1	$24,666	11	28	14
11	34	64	0	37	54	8	36	49	15	87	12	1	1	$32,761	9	27	21
STATE	43	55	<1	46	47	6	44	43	13	71	27	1	2	$29,021	10	27	19

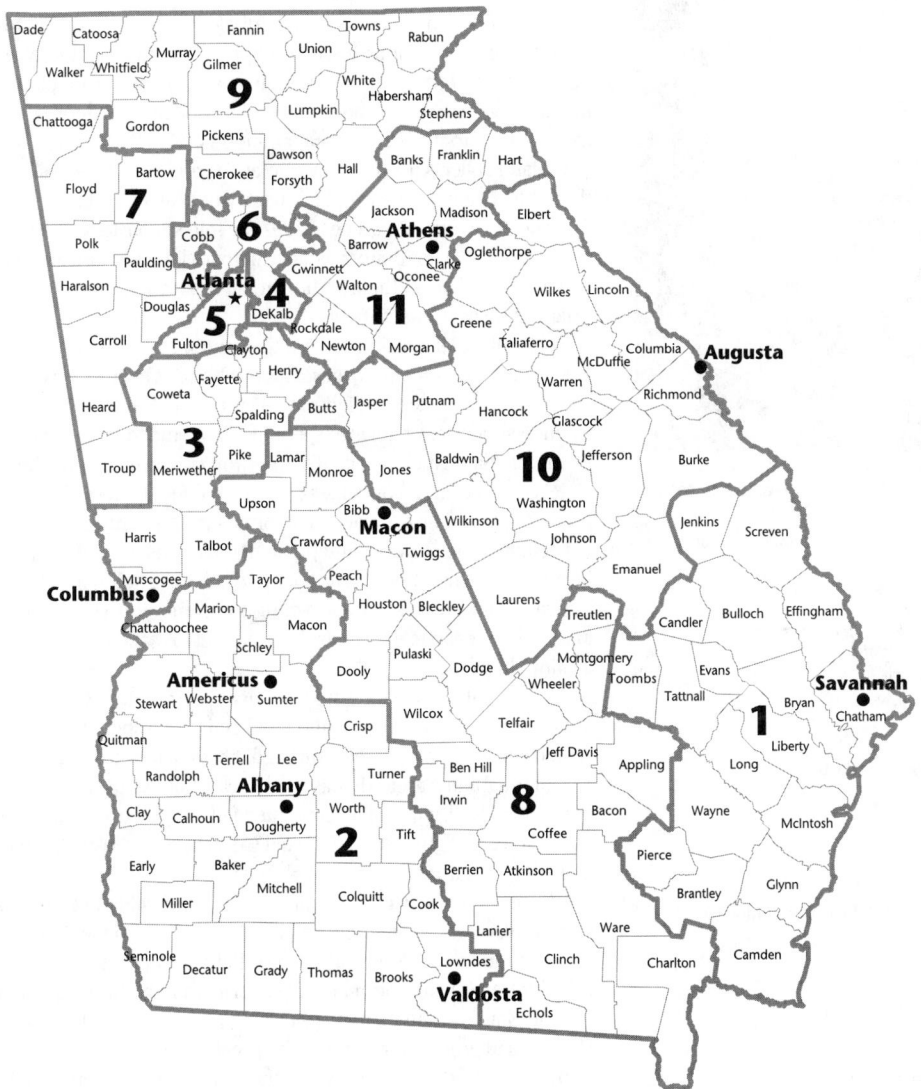

Sen. Max Cleland (D)

Elected 1996; 1st term

CAPITOL OFFICE
224-3521; fax 224-0072; 461 Dirksen Bldg. 20510

INTERNET
e-mail: senator_max_cleland@cleland.senate.gov
web: cleland.senate.gov

COMMITTEES
Armed Services
Commerce, Science & Transportation
Governmental Affairs
Small Business

HOMETOWN
Lithonia

BORN
Aug. 24, 1942, Atlanta, Ga.

RELIGION
Methodist

FAMILY
Single

EDUCATION
Stetson U., B.A. 1964; Emory U., M.A. 1968

MILITARY SERVICE
Army, 1965-68

CAREER
Veterans administration official; congressional aide

POLITICAL HIGHLIGHTS
Ga. Senate, 1971-75; sought Democratic nomination for lieutenant governor, 1974; U.S. administrator of Veterans Affairs, 1977-81; Ga. secretary of state, 1983-96

ELECTION RESULTS

1996 GENERAL

Max Cleland (D)	1,103,993	48.8%
Guy Millner (R)	1,073,969	47.6%
Jack Cashin (LIBERT)	81,262	3.6%

1996 PRIMARY

Max Cleland (D)	unopposed

A legislative moderate who steers clear of partisan disputes, Cleland focuses on overcoming his own physical limitations and serving as an inspiration for others. He lost both legs and an arm in Vietnam, which left him struggling with episodes of health problems and depression for years even as he pursued his political ambitions.

Cleland collects inspirational quotations and anecdotes, and also turns to the Bible, country music and the poetry of William Butler Yeats for solace. After being sworn into office in 1997, he told supporters: "Your dreams can come true if you continue to believe in them long enough and hard enough and never give up on them." Then he broke down in tears, according to the Atlanta Journal-Constitution.

Politically, Cleland aims toward the center. He is a member of the Senate New Democrats — a group of senators who seek to pull the party toward the center. Adroit at steering federal dollars to Georgia, he casts himself as a staunch supporter of defense spending in the mode of the man he replaced, Democrat Sam Nunn. Cleland's other top concerns include improving his state's transportation options, providing aid for small-business owners and protecting southern Appalachian forests from logging.

Cleland took several independent positions in the 106th Congress, becoming the first Senate Democrat to call for a halt to the U.S.-led bombing campaign in Kosovo and voting for some gun restrictions despite a longtime aversion to gun control. He has yet to make his mark on major legislation, however.

As a member of the Armed Services Committee, Cleland focuses on improving health care, education and retirement benefits for those in the armed services. In 1999, he won $125,000 for a new national military cemetery in the Atlanta area. He has tended carefully to his state's other military interests as well, supporting continued federal procurement of such aircraft as F-22 tactical fighters and C-17 and C-130 transport planes, which are built at plants in Georgia.

But he is more cautious than many of his colleagues on committing troops overseas. Cleland broke party ranks over the 1999 bombing campaign in the former Yugoslavia. After initially supporting the bombing, he called for a ceasefire because of concerns that the fighting could lead to a ground war. The situation, he said, "began to smell and look like Vietnam." He has also proposed requiring the president to submit a strategic plan to Congress before committing more than 500 troops to a foreign land. In 1998, he worked to tighten a nonbinding resolution on Iraq, saying the wording reminded him of the 1964 Gulf of Tonkin resolution that led to the military escalation in Vietnam.

Cleland has also struggled with the politically charged issue of gun control. Just one week after helping to kill a Democratic proposal that would have required background checks on firearms sales at gun shows, he voted in 1999 for a similar Democratic plan to require mandatory background checks on gun purchasers at gun shows and pawn shops. He was jolted into changing his position after a Georgia high school shooting that left six students injured. "Our high schools are turning into mini-Vietnams and we can't have that," he said, according to The Associated Press.

The senator is very protective of his home state interests. A defender of Georgia's textile industry, he voted in the 106th against trade pacts with Caribbean and sub-Saharan African nations that he fears could undermine

www.cq.com

domestic textile manufacturers. He cosponsored legislation to establish an inspectors general training academy at the Federal Law Enforcement Training Center at Glynco, Ga.

Cleland also wants to use his position on the Commerce Committee to expand commuter rail systems in Atlanta and other Georgia cities and to fund port and airport improvements. In the 107th Congress, he cosponsored legislation to permit Amtrak to sell bonds to equip most major regions of the country with high-speed trains. Routes connecting Atlanta to Birmingham and to Savannah would be among those served.

Cleland has sought logging restrictions in the southern Appalachians, which are being used increasingly for recreation. He also backed a controversial Clinton administration plan in 1999 to preserve roadless areas in national forests. "We need to take steps to save these delicate lands before we lose them forever," he said.

In the 105th, Cleland stayed mostly in the legislative background. He was a reliable supporter of Democratic positions on social issues but weighed in toward the right on fiscal matters. He supports abortion rights and joined fellow Democrats in opposing a ban on a procedure its opponents call "partial birth" abortion. One of his most notable votes in 1997 was to split with many Democrats and support a balanced-budget constitutional amendment. He also broke party ranks to support some GOP tax cuts.

Cleland is generally uncomfortable around partisan disputes. He took part in Senate hearings into alleged White House campaign finance abuses in the 105th but gradually lost interest. "I don't try to be an attack dog," he said.

Cleland's résumé is unique in the Senate. Fascinated by politics ever since his college days, he determinedly entered the profession just two years after the 1968 grenade explosion in Vietnam that cost him his limbs. He became Georgia's youngest state senator at the age of 28. His tenure in that job coincided with the governorship of Jimmy Carter who, after winning the presidency in 1976, appointed Cleland to head the Veterans Administration. Cleland was back on the campaign trail in Georgia in 1982, when he won the first of four terms as secretary of state.

He gave up that post in 1996 to run for the Senate seat of retiring four-term Democrat Nunn. Although he faced a strong opponent in Republican Guy Millner, a conservative businessman who had nearly won the governorship two years earlier, Cleland portrayed himself as a centrist Democrat in the mold of Nunn and eked out a win by slightly more than 30,000 votes out of more than 2.2 million cast.

His victory forced the Senate to scramble to accommodate Cleland's wheelchair and led to some embarrassing moments. When Vice President Al Gore swore in new senators on Jan. 7, 1997, he asked them to raise their right hands — "or your left hand, as the case may be."

Cleland struggled at first to adjust to Washington, gaining weight and developing sleep apnea, a debilitating sleep disorder that robbed him of rest at night and caused him to fall asleep in committee meetings in the beginning of the 105th. Speaking at a Senate Thanksgiving prayer service at the end of 1997, Cleland said: "It's been a tough year for me, but I'm winding up in a very positive mode. ... Life breaks you. If life hasn't broken you yet, stick around a while."

Since then, Cleland lost 60 pounds. He exercises regularly, engages in daily meditation and prayer, and takes large doses of vitamins. Deeply religious, he frequently ends conversations by saying "May God hold you in the palm of his hand," according to the Atlanta Journal-Constitution. In 1999, he published his second book, "Going for the Max: 12 Principles for Living Life to the Fullest," about people who have overcome injury or disease. His first book was an autobiography: "Strong at the Broken Places."

KEY VOTES

2000

Yes Overhaul bankruptcy law and increase minimum wage

No Limit fiscal 2001 discretionary spending to $600.3 billion

Yes Override veto on nuclear waste disposal at Yucca Mountain site in Nevada

No Oppose effort to terminate Kosovo mission

Yes Include gender, sexual orientation and disability in federal hate crime protections

No Approve GOP plan to restrict use of genetic information by health insurers

No Kill amendment delaying implementation of an anti-missile defense system

Yes Cut taxes for married couples

Yes Grant China permanent normal trade status

1999

No Remove President Clinton from office for obstruction of justice

No Kill amendment authorizing state grants to hire teachers and reduce class size

Yes Require criminal background checks for purchases at gun shows

No Approve GOP proposal to increase rights of patients in managed-care health plans

No Block effort to allow farm and medicine exports to Cuba

Yes Allow study of tougher automobile fuel efficiency standards

Yes Ratify nuclear weapons testing treaty

Yes Prohibit national political parties from collecting "soft money" donations

Yes Remove barriers among banking, securities and insurance companies

INTEREST GROUPS

	AFL-CIO	ADA	CCUS	ACU
2000	50%	70%	73%	24%
1999	78%	100%	47%	0%
1998	75%	85%	56%	0%
1997	57%	75%	80%	8%

CQ VOTE STUDIES

	PARTY UNITY		PRESIDENTIAL SUPPORT	
	Support	Oppose	Support	Oppose
2000	84%	16%	78%	22%
1999	92%	8%	84%	16%
1998	87%	13%	87%	13%
1997	84%	16%	87%	13%

Sen. Zell Miller (D)

CAPITOL OFFICE
224-3643; fax 228-2090; 257 Dirksen Bldg. 20510

INTERNET
e-mail: zell_miller@miller.senate.gov
web: miller.senate.gov

COMMITTEES
Agriculture, Nutrition & Forestry
Banking, Housing & Urban Affairs
Veterans' Affairs

HOMETOWN
Young Harris

BORN
Feb. 24, 1932, Young Harris, Ga.

RELIGION
Methodist

FAMILY
Wife, Shirley Ann Carver; two children

EDUCATION
Young Harris College, A.A. 1951; U. of Georgia,
A.B. 1957, M.A. 1958

MILITARY SERVICE
Marine Corps, 1953-56

CAREER
Professor; state government official

POLITICAL HIGHLIGHTS
Mayor of Young Harris, 1959-60; Ga. Senate, 1961-
65; sought Democratic nomination for U.S. House,
1964, 1966; lieutenant governor, 1975-91; sought
Democratic nomination for U.S. Senate, 1980;
governor, 1991-99

ELECTION RESULTS

2000 SPECIAL

Zell Miller (D)	1,413,224	58.1%
Mack Mattingly (R)	920,478	37.9%
Paul R. MacGregor (LIBERT)	25,942	1.1%

Elected 2000; 1st term
Appointed July 2000

Senate Democrats probably thought they had an ally when Miller, one of Georgia's most popular politicians, was appointed to replace Paul Coverdell after the Georgia Republican died suddenly in July 2000 of a cerebral hemorrhage. But as Democrats have discovered, Miller, who sports cowboy boots with his well-tailored suits, is full of surprises.

Just weeks into the 107th Congress, he signed on as a cosponsor of President Bush's tax cut plan, which many Democrats had attacked as favoring the rich at the expense of the working class.

"Remember that old Elvis Presley song, 'Return to Sender'? Well, that's what we want to do with this overpayment of taxes," said Miller. The combination of high tax rates, record budget surpluses and a possible economic downturn were "an opportunity to reach across party lines and really practice bipartisanship, not just talk about it," he said.

Miller's announcement of support for the tax cuts blindsided Senate Democratic Leader Tom Daschle and Georgia's senior senator, Max Cleland, also a Democrat. "It's my hope that I'll have an opportunity to make my case prior to the time people make their decisions on issues," said Daschle. Miller said he was shocked by the reaction on Capitol Hill and by people asking him whether he was going to switch parties.

His support of the Bush tax plan was in keeping with his philosophy on taxes: Miller had campaigned in 2000 on the evils of high taxes, and as Georgia's governor, he had eliminated the sales tax on groceries and cut the state income tax.

Miller is a member of the Senate New Democrats, a group of about 20 moderate senators. "I hear a lot about this nation being deeply divided. I don't believe this nation is deeply divided, but it is evenly divided. I believe that we will have to look for the middle ground on issues that come before us," he said after his swearing-in at the start of the 107th.

Since coming to Washington, Miller has voted with Republicans much more often than he has with Democrats. But he also has a strong partisan side: His support helped Bill Clinton win Georgia's 1992 presidential primary, and he was rewarded with the role of keynote speaker at that year's Democratic National Convention in New York.

Despite a severe case of strep throat, Miller excoriated then-President George Bush. "If the 'education president' gets another term, even our kids won't be able to spell potato. If the 'law and order president' gets another term, the criminals will run wild, because our commander-in-chief talks like Dirty Harry but acts like Barney Fife," he said. Before his Senate appointment, Miller had been mentioned as a potential vice-presidential running mate for 2000 Democratic presidential nominee Al Gore.

Miller has said he wants to make education one of his top priorities in the 107th Congress, in particular, measures to improve teacher pay and training. In the 106th, he backed several education bills, including legislation to create a tax deduction for college tuition and an expansion of the HOPE scholarship program that he started in Georgia. Miller reports that the program, which pays college tuition for Georgia high school students with a "B" or higher average, has helped more than 500,000 students. It is funded by state lottery revenues.

Miller also created a voluntary pre-kindergarten program for four-year-olds — also funded by the lottery — to give children an early start in their education. He says that more than 372,000 children have been enrolled.

Agriculture is Georgia's top industry, and as a member of the Agriculture Committee, Miller is able to focus on state concerns such as low commodity prices, high production costs and coping with drought conditions. He also plans to play an active role in the rewrite of the 1996 farm law, known as the "Freedom to Farm" act, which replaced crop subsidies with a seven-year schedule of fixed payments.

The 1996 law "left many Georgia farmers guessing about their future," Miller says. "Unfortunately, freedom to farm also provided opportunity to fail." The senator would like to find ways to help Georgia expand its exports, and he wants to develop a better foreign "guest worker" program to aid the state's farmers.

Miller's father, a college dean, died when Miller was 17 days old. After a couple of years of college, Miller joined the Marine Corps. He often cites lessons he learned in the Marines, and his 1997 autobiography is titled, "Corp Values: Everything You Need to Know, I Learned in the Marines."

Miller entered politics in 1959 with a term as mayor of his small North Georgia hometown of Young Harris. In 1960, at age 28, he was elected to the Georgia Senate; in 1974, he won the first of four terms as lieutenant governor; and in 1990, Miller won election as governor.

He inherited a budget crisis, with state revenue shrinking and the state reserve fund depleted, so he cut hundreds of millions of dollars from the budget and axed thousands of state jobs. Once the financial crisis abated, Miller pushed for passage of stronger drunken driving laws and the imposition of a "two strikes and you're out" law that mandates life in prison for any second conviction involving such violent crimes as murder, rape or armed robbery.

Miller's approval rating at the end of his second term was 85 percent, but term limits barred him from seeking another four years as governor. When he concluded his tenure in 1999, Miller said he had no aspirations for higher office. (He had unsuccessfully sought a Senate seat 20 years earlier.) "I've had my hour and more upon the stage," he told the Atlanta Journal-Constitution. Miller and his wife Shirley moved back to the stone house his mother had built 60 years earlier, and he taught history and politics to students at three colleges.

Miller also sought financial security, serving on the boards of seven companies and as board chairman of the U.S. subsidiary of German real estate developer Kollmann AG. And he had more time for his hobbies, which include baseball and music. Miller's fondness for country music is well-known; his parties at the governor's mansion were raucous affairs featuring an array of country music singers.

"I'm doing exactly what I planned to do all along," Miller said in early 1999. "No melancholy. No nostalgia. I've always known I was going back home," he told the Atlanta Journal-Constitution.

When Coverdell, Georgia's senior senator, died unexpectedly, Miller initially rebuffed Democratic Gov. Roy Barnes' offer of an appointment to the Senate, suggesting instead former Democratic Sen. Sam Nunn. The decision to accept the appointment was not an easy one for Miller, who had spent almost 40 years in public service and was enjoying his private life.

But he agreed and promised to take the same kind of bipartisan approach for which Coverdell was noted. "I accept this commission with a heavy heart and a profound sense of duty," he said.

A little more than three months after his appointment to the Senate, Miller was elected to a four-year Senate term in November, beating his closest opponent in a seven-candidate field by 20 percentage points. "In hindsight, he was virtually unbeatable, unless we'd gotten a lot of money," Georgia Senate Minority Leader Eric Johnson told the Journal-Constitution. He said Georgians were inclined to go with the fellow they'd known for 24 years.

KEY VOTES

2000

Yes Grant China permanent normal trade status

INTEREST GROUPS

	AFL-CIO	ADA	CCUS	ACU
2000	33%	0%	100%	n/a%

CQ VOTE STUDIES

	PARTY UNITY		PRESIDENTIAL SUPPORT	
	Support	Oppose	Support	Oppose
2000	25%	75%	100%	0%

Rep. Jack Kingston (R)

Elected 1992; 5th term

CAPITOL OFFICE
225-5831; fax 226-2269
1034 Longworth Bldg. 20515

INTERNET
e-mail: jack.kingston@mail.house.gov
web: www.house.gov/kingston

COMMITTEES
Appropriations

HOMETOWN
Savannah

BORN
April 24, 1955, Bryan, Texas

RELIGION
Episcopalian

FAMILY
Wife, Libby Kingston; four children

EDUCATION
U. of Georgia, B.A. 1978

CAREER
Insurance broker

POLITICAL HIGHLIGHTS
Ga. House, 1984-92

ELECTION RESULTS

2000 GENERAL

Jack Kingston (R)	131,684	69.1%
Joyce Marie Griggs (D)	58,776	30.9%

2000 PRIMARY

Jack Kingston (R)	unopposed

1998 GENERAL

Jack Kingston (R)	unopposed

PREVIOUS WINNING PERCENTAGES
1996 (68%); 1994 (77%); 1992 (58%)

Kingston is a pithy and partisan participant in House floor debates, where he frequently rises to zing liberals as tax-and-spend bad guys. Since 1997, he has headed the GOP's "theme team," which helps develop the party's message to the public and advises lawmakers on how to get that message across to their constituents. He tells his colleagues to keep it short and simple. "It's not lofty or esoteric, it's understandable," he says.

Kingston plays a less-public role on the Appropriations Committee, where he caters to his district's needs by seeking funding for government programs that support agriculture and defense, two pillars of the South Georgia economy. As Georgia's only appropriator in the 106th Congress, he also worked to secure funds for transportation and other statewide needs.

At the same time, he has tried hard to cultivate an image as a frugal guardian of the federal purse. He cuts his personal cost of living by using his Capitol Hill office as a bedroom when he is in Washington. And he cast a high-profile dissenting vote in 1997 on the spending component of a balanced-budget agreement between the Clinton administration and congressional Republicans, arguing that it included too much money for new, liberal-backed programs. He was among just 32 House Republicans to buck the party line.

But he also took some heat in the 106th from the watchdog group, Citizens Against Government Waste — which generally praises Kingston — for winning federal funding for such 1st District projects as onion disease research, a new national peanut competitiveness center, and a water taxi service. Kingston, according to an account in the Atlanta Constitution, fired back at his critics: "Every project in the budget has been through the constitutional process and has been voted on by subcommittees, full committees and by the full House. If these groups have problems with democracy and constitutional procedures, maybe they should study Cuba's government."

He was sharply critical of President Clinton's last-minute executive orders just before he left office. While some of the orders may have had merit, he said, they bypassed the legislative process. "It's like Cinderella looking up at the clock and realizing in 15 minutes the carriage turns back into a pumpkin," he said.

As a member of the Appropriations Subcommittee on Agriculture and Rural Development, Kingston has been especially protective of his district's peanut and cotton farmers. This position has sometimes put him at odds with powerful Republicans such as Majority Leader Dick Armey, who view federal crop subsidy and price-support programs as antithetical to free enterprise. In 1995, Kingston explained: "When we talk about farm subsidies ... we need to keep in mind that the people who are being subsidized are not necessarily the farmers. They are the American consumers."

Kingston, however, will take on other agricultural interests on occasion to help his constituents. During debate on farm legislation in the 104th, he assailed price supports for sugar farmers as "the sweetest deal of all" and said they benefit only wealthy growers while costing consumers. The supports were costly to the nation's largest sugar refiner, Savannah Foods, which is based in Kingston's district.

On many issues, Kingston weighs in with a solidly conservative vote. In addition to supporting GOP tax cut plans, he backed a controversial measure that would have scrapped income taxes altogether. He criticized efforts in 1999 to tighten gun regulations in the wake of a much-publicized mass shooting at Colorado's Columbine High School. "What outrages me as a father of four kids, including two teenagers, is that it's [the legislation] being done on the blood of innocent children in Colorado and it will do nothing to prevent another Colorado from happening," he said.

In the 105th, Kingston and other social conservatives chastised federal judges whom they regarded as too interested in advancing liberal agendas rather than administering the law. During debate in 1998 over a proposed constitutional amendment to expand and clarify the rights of religious expression, Kingston declared, "There is no doubt in my mind that there is a special place in hell for a number of federal court judges."

One of Kingston's main interests is health care, and he has worked to draw attention to the problem of postpartum depression. In the 106th, he supported efforts to include a provision in an appropriations measure to allow the import of lower-cost prescription drugs into the United States.

Kingston disagreed with the Clinton administration on some international trade issues. Breaking with many in his own party, he voted in the 106th against granting China permanent normal trade status, citing that country's record of human rights violations. Concern about job losses in the textile industry and other factories in the 1st District led him to vote in 1993 against the North American Free Trade Agreement.

Kingston's sharp tongue has landed him in trouble on occasion. He rose on the House floor in 1995 to lambaste the Equal Employment Opportunity Commission for pressing the restaurant chain Hooters, known for its shapely and scantily clad waitresses, to hire more male waiters. "There's nothing that men like more than an abundance of buffalo wings and breasts," Kingston said, angering several women lawmakers. He clarified that he was referring to chicken breasts.

Born in Texas, Kingston spent much of his childhood in Athens, Ga. After graduating from the University of Georgia, he moved to Savannah to sell insurance. He won his first election in 1984 to a state House seat, and when Democrat Lindsay Thomas retired from the 1st District in 1992, Kingston was well-positioned to woo voters into the Republican column for a House election; many of them already had been voting Republican for president.

Kingston drew minor primary opposition, while his eventual Democratic opponent, Barbara Christmas, a school principal in rural Camden County, struggled through a crowded primary and a runoff. The Republican emphasized his eight years in the state House and portrayed Christmas as lacking legislative know-how. Kingston took 58 percent in the 1992 race and has had the district securely in hand since.

KEY VOTES

2000

No	Raise hourly minimum wage by $1 over two years
Yes	Halt funding for U.S. mission in Kosovo unless European nations pay more
Yes	Provide Medicare benefits to military retirees and their dependents
No	Grant China permanent normal trade status
Yes	Phase out estate, gift and trust taxes
Yes	Prohibit implementation of president's national monument designations
Yes	Approve GOP plan to provide prescription drug coverage for Medicare beneficiaries
No	Increase help for poor nations indebted to international financial institutions

1999

No	Impose steel import quotas
Yes	Kill proposal to take aviation trust funds off budget
Yes	Require background checks on buyers only at gun shows with 10 or more vendors
Yes	Remove barriers among banking, securities and insurance companies
No	Authorize state grants to hire teachers and reduce class size
?	Overhaul campaign finance law; ban "soft money" and restrict advocacy advertising
No	Approve bipartisan plan to increase rights of patients in managed-care health plans

INTEREST GROUPS

	AFL-CIO	ADA	CCUS	ACU
2000	10%	5%	80%	100%
1999	22%	0%	75%	95%
1998	0%	0%	82%	100%
1997	0%	5%	80%	96%

CQ VOTE STUDIES

	PARTY UNITY		PRESIDENTIAL SUPPORT	
	Support	Oppose	Support	Oppose
2000	95%	5%	17%	83%
1999	93%	7%	14%	86%
1998	94%	6%	20%	80%
1997	93%	7%	23%	77%

GEORGIA 1

Southeast – Savannah; Brunswick

The 1st takes in a swath of southeast Georgia and its entire coastline, stretching from South Carolina to Florida. Like much of the rest of Georgia, the district is ancestrally Democratic but occasionally receptive to Republicans.

The district also is racially mixed, with demographics that make it a microcosm of the state. Among its constituents are a substantial number of white Southern Democrats who tend to vote Republican. Redistricting in 1995 added the predominantly black areas around Savannah, increasing the number of blacks in the district by nearly a third and giving the 1st a 30 percent black population.

Despite a stinging drought and various storms and hurricanes that severely hurt the area's farmers in 1998, peanuts, onions, cotton, tobacco and other crops help sustain the 1st's economy, as do defense, shrimping and tourism. The 1st also has two ports that rely heavily on the international economy, and coastal conservation is a dominant issue. The area is becoming a popular destination for retirees and is seeing an influx of new residents settling between Hilton Head, S.C., and Florida.

MAJOR INDUSTRY
Agriculture, military, manufacturing

MILITARY BASES
Fort Stewart (Army), 15,020 military, 1,844 civilian; Kings Bay Naval Submarine Base, 5,334 military, 2,801 civilian; Hunter Army Airfield, 4,201 military, 78 civilian (1999)

CITIES
Savannah, 129,556; Hinesville, 26,933; Statesboro, 21,812; Brunswick, 17,303

UNUSUAL FEATURES
Parts of the movie "Forrest Gump" filmed at Chippewa Square in Savannah; Vidalia known worldwide for its sweet Vidalia onions; Claxton known as the "Fruitcake Capital of the World" for the Claxton Bakery, which produces and ships between 3 million and 4 million pounds of fruitcake yearly.

Rep. Sanford D. Bishop Jr. (D)

Elected 1992; 5th term

CAPITOL OFFICE
225-3631; fax 225-2203; 2429 Rayburn Bldg. 20515

INTERNET
e-mail: bishop.email@mail.house.gov
web: www.house.gov/bishop

COMMITTEES
Agriculture
Select Intelligence

HOMETOWN
Albany

BORN
Feb. 4, 1947, Mobile, Ala.

RELIGION
Baptist

FAMILY
Divorced

EDUCATION
Morehouse College, B.A. 1968; Emory U., J.D. 1971

MILITARY SERVICE
Army, 1971

CAREER
Lawyer

POLITICAL HIGHLIGHTS
Ga. House, 1977-91; Ga. Senate, 1991-93

ELECTION RESULTS

2000 GENERAL

Sanford D. Bishop Jr. (D)	96,430	53.5%
Dylan Glenn (R)	83,870	46.5%

2000 PRIMARY

Sanford D. Bishop Jr. (D)	unopposed

1998 GENERAL

Sanford D. Bishop Jr. (D)	77,953	56.8%
Joe McCormick (R)	59,305	43.2%

PREVIOUS WINNING PERCENTAGES
1996 (54%); 1994 (66%); 1992 (64%)

Bishop is the most conservative member of the Congressional Black Caucus, and he fits in comfortably with the "Blue Dogs," a coalition of conservative Democrats, where he is one of only two black lawmakers. That reflects not only his political philosophy but it is also smart politics in a district that is about 60 percent white and that has posed tough re-election fights for him in the past three campaigns.

Bishop often works with Republicans — on social as well as fiscal issues — and in the 106th Congress he opposed his party and President Clinton far more often than any other black Democrat. With his independent voting record, he has resisted racial pigeonholing throughout his congressional career. And his attention to the 2nd District's agriculture and military interests and to its veterans' needs has enabled Bishop to build a base beyond the black community.

He serves on the Agriculture Committee, where he played a major role, along with Republican Saxby Chambliss of the neighboring 8th District, in protecting the peanut price-support program when Congress overhauled federal farm policy in 1996. Bishop's district grows more peanuts than any other — considerably more than a quarter of the nation's total output — and he is on the front lines during efforts by budget-cutters to scale back or eliminate the peanut program.

Bishop also sits on the Intelligence Committee, where he works well with members of both parties. To assume the Intelligence post, he took a leave from the Veterans' Affairs panel. He says he will return to that committee when his eight-year term on Intelligence expires in 2005.

The southwest Georgia district hosts several large military installations, including Fort Benning (which also is in the 3rd District), and they are key components of the area's economy. Bishop in 1999 was one of only two Democrats to vote for a foreign operations appropriations bill. He said he backed the bill because it contained funding for the Army's School of the Americas, at Fort Benning.

He defends that school against regular attacks from other lawmakers, who argue that it has trained South and Central American military officers who have been implicated in allegations of human rights abuses. Bishop says that the school does not teach or condone such actions. The school was reorganized and renamed (the Defense Institute for Hemispheric Security Cooperation) in the 106th Congress but will remain in business at Fort Benning.

Bishop's middle-of-the-road politics is evident across a wide spectrum. For instance, he approved of the GOP-inspired get-tough approach to get people off the welfare rolls, but he also insisted that social programs be provided to help recipients work their way off welfare and to support their families while they did so. He was one of only two members of the Black Caucus to back the final version of the 1996 welfare overhaul bill. Bishop casts a skeptical eye on gun control efforts.

Bishop was the lead Democratic cosponsor of a constitutional amendment proposed by Republican Ernest Istook of Oklahoma to guarantee freedom of religious expression in public places, including prayer in schools. He backs legislation to prohibit desecration of the flag.

In the 106th, he was a leading player in an overhaul of the crop insurance program and sponsored legislation to give federal help to upgrade crime labs.

On the fiscal front, when the Black Caucus presented its alternative budget for fiscal 1998, Bishop voted "present," saying that the plan had "noble goals" but that he could not support its cuts in defense spending. He also was among the minority of Democrats who supported the GOP's unsuccessful 1999 tax cut bill. In 2000, he joined with Republicans to back measures to repeal the estate tax and end the "marriage penalty," a quirk in the tax code that results in some two-earner married couples paying higher taxes than they would if each partner were single.

Despite his departures from liberal dogma, Bishop votes a loyally Democratic line on most issues. He supports abortion rights and has taken labor's side in its legislative disputes with the business-oriented GOP majority.

Bishop grew up in Mobile, Ala., where his parents were both educators (his father, Sanford Sr., was the president of a community college that is now named for him — Bishop State Community College — and his mother was the college librarian). The younger Bishop made a name for himself as a civil rights lawyer in Columbus, Ga., before winning election to the state legislature in 1976, where he served for 16 years.

He was on the Reapportionment Committee that, with stern urgings from the Justice Department, drew new congressional district maps that made the 2nd District Georgia's third black-majority district.

Columbus business leaders persuaded Bishop to seek the newly drawn seat in 1992 and helped finance his challenge to white Democratic Rep. Charles Hatcher, who earlier in the year had been identified as one of the chief abusers of the House's private bank, with 819 overdrafts. In a runoff with Hatcher, Bishop won the nomination, 53 percent to 47 percent; and in November, he coasted past Republican physician Jim Dudley, taking 64 percent of the vote.

Bishop now represents a district quite different from the one to which he was first elected. His original district boundaries were ruled an unconstitutional "racial gerrymander" and federal judges handed down a new map in 1995, altering the racial composition of his constituency from 51 percent to 39 percent black; his past three elections have been under the new map.

After the remap, Bishop found that his longtime home in Columbus had been placed in the 3rd District. Although he could have stayed and still sought re-election to the 2nd, which contained 28 of the 35 counties he had previously represented, Bishop moved about 90 miles southeast to Albany, in the center of the 2nd. The redrawn district presents a better opportunity for Republicans than the district that had first elected Bishop in 1992, and he has faced stiff tests every two years. In his closest battle, in 2000, Bishop narrowly defeated former Senate aide Dylan Glenn, who is also black.

KEY VOTES

2000
Yes Raise hourly minimum wage by $1 over two years
Yes Halt funding for U.S. mission in Kosovo unless European nations pay more
Yes Provide Medicare benefits to military retirees and their dependents
Yes Grant China permanent normal trade status
Yes Phase out estate, gift and trust taxes
No   Prohibit implementation of president's national monument designations
No   Approve GOP plan to provide prescription drug coverage for Medicare beneficiaries
Yes Increase help for poor nations indebted to international financial institutions

1999
Yes Impose steel import quotas
No   Kill proposal to take aviation trust funds off budget
No   Require background checks on buyers only at gun shows with 10 or more vendors
Yes Remove barriers among banking, securities and insurance companies
Yes Authorize state grants to hire teachers and reduce class size
No   Overhaul campaign finance law; ban "soft money" and restrict advocacy advertising
Yes Approve bipartisan plan to increase rights of patients in managed-care health plans

INTEREST GROUPS

	AFL-CIO	ADA	CCUS	ACU
2000	60%	50%	78%	43%
1999	89%	65%	56%	28%
1998	70%	70%	61%	44%
1997	88%	75%	60%	29%

CQ VOTE STUDIES

	PARTY UNITY		PRESIDENTIAL SUPPORT	
	Support	Oppose	Support	Oppose
2000	65%	35%	55%	45%
1999	73%	27%	64%	36%
1998	71%	29%	58%	42%
1997	77%	23%	58%	42%

GEORGIA 2
Southwest – Albany; Valdosta

Georgia's 2nd takes in the state's entire southwestern corner and extends from just south of Columbus to the Florida border. Once a black-majority district, redistricting in 1995 reduced its black population from 57 percent to 39 percent, changing the district from a strongly Democratic area to one in which Republicans are competitive.

Democrats, however, still hold most local offices and are strong in the northwestern counties that have higher black populations. Pockets of GOP strength exist in Lee County, in the central part of the district, as well as in Thomasville and other southern parts of the district. Dougherty County, where Albany is the county seat, is the district's most populous county and is reliably Democratic. The 2nd also is attracting growing numbers of retirees and military veterans.

The 2nd's largely rural and heavily agricultural regions have struggled economically for decades and are heavily dependent on farm loan assistance. Farming and livestock are key to the economy, and the district grows more peanuts than any other place in the United States.

MAJOR INDUSTRY
Agriculture, military, manufacturing, health care

MILITARY BASES
Fort Benning (Army), 28,132 military, 13,542 civilian (shared with the 3rd) (2001); Moody Air Force Base, 4,110 military, 365 civilian; Marine Corp Logistics Base, 1,095 military, 2,269 civilian (1999)

CITIES
Albany, 75,929; Valdosta, 42,462; Thomasville, 17,800

UNUSUAL FEATURES
Cairo, the birthplace of Jackie Robinson, who broke baseball's color barrier a half-century ago; Plains, hometown of former President Jimmy Carter; Annual Pecan Harvest Festival in Baconton.

Rep. Mac Collins (R)

CAPITOL OFFICE
225-5901; fax 225-2515
1131 Longworth Bldg. 20515

INTERNET
e-mail: mac.collins@mail.house.gov
web: www.house.gov/maccollins

COMMITTEES
Budget
Ways & Means

HOMETOWN
Hampton

BORN
Oct. 15, 1944, Jackson, Ga.

RELIGION
Methodist

FAMILY
Wife, Julie Collins; four children

EDUCATION
Jackson H.S., graduated 1962

MILITARY SERVICE
Ga. National Guard, 1964-70

CAREER
Trucking company owner

POLITICAL HIGHLIGHTS
Butts County Commission, 1977-81 (chairman);
candidate for Ga. Senate, 1984, 1986; Ga. Senate,
1989-93

ELECTION RESULTS

2000 GENERAL

Mac Collins (R)	150,200	63.5%
Gail Notti (D)	86,309	36.5%

2000 PRIMARY

Mac Collins (R)	39,153	89.2%
Herbie Galloway (R)	4,744	10.8%

1998 GENERAL

Mac Collins (R)	unopposed

PREVIOUS WINNING PERCENTAGES
1996 (61%); 1994 (66%); 1992 (55%)

Elected 1992; 5th term

Since winning his seat in 1992 — on the slogan "Send a Working Man to Congress" — Collins has worked himself onto the Ways and Means and Budget committees, where he follows a conservative, anti-tax line. He still maintains his plain-speaking, "regular guy" persona. The high school-educated trucking company owner likes to say he is a "representative," not a "politician."

A member of the unofficial congressional Boot Caucus, Collins occasionally laces his comments with allusions to his trucking background. Once when he took a tightly scheduled fact-finding trip to Bosnia that involved 20 hours of flying in less than two days, he described the experience as "kind of like a West Coast turnaround in an 18-wheeler."

But one should not be fooled by Collins' speech; he has long been wise in the ways of government. As a boy in Flovilla, Ga., politics was family table talk, and his mother was the first woman elected to the city council there. Collins himself served eight years in public office — four as a Butts County commissioner and four as a Georgia state senator — before coming to Washington.

In the House, GOP leaders have come to appreciate not only his votes — particularly on taxes and defense spending — but also his rhetoric. On Ways and Means, his rough-cut style shows in debates. After a Democrat accused Republicans of crafting a welfare bill that was "radical ... cruel ... and mean to children," Collins shot back, "That is bull, and you know it."

He was equally blunt in rejecting an increase in cigarette taxes in the 106th Congress. Although he does not represent a tobacco-growing district, he is philosophically opposed to new taxes on smokers. "So what does the Clinton-Gore administration do? It finds a captive group of taxpayers, who are a sitting duck for a tax increase," he told Knight-Ridder news service.

Consistently anti-tax, Collins introduced legislation in 2000 to suspend temporarily the federal gasoline tax, to help consumers faced with soaring prices at the pump. He contended that the government had a responsibility to keep fuel affordable. Like most Republicans, Collins supports major tax cut bills, including the elimination of the estate tax and the "marriage penalty," a quirk in the tax code that results in some two-earner married couples paying higher income taxes.

In the 106th, Collins sided with conservatives in blocking Clinton administration attempts to beef up gun regulations. Despite nationwide concern over school shootings, he said in 1999: "I'm going to have to take a real close look at all these gun control provisions because I just don't believe in taking away people's rights," according to the Atlanta Journal-Constitution.

Collins also takes a conservative stand when it comes to environmental regulations. In 2000, he worked with fellow Georgia Republican John Linder to add language to an appropriations measure barring the Environmental Protection Agency from imposing new air quality standards that were being challenged in federal court as exceeding the EPA's authority. However, Collins invests a fair amount of energy in talking about poor air quality in Atlanta and its environs, a problem exacerbated by the region's rapid growth. "I spend a lot of time outdoors and, like most Georgians, value a clean environment. However, I believe that we have to use common sense to balance the need for a clean environment with the need for good jobs and economic growth."

The congressman has introduced legislation offering a $4,000 tax credit for the purchase of an electric vehicle, and he lobbied for funding of an

Atlanta-to-Macon rail line and other mass transit programs aimed at reducing solo commuting by car.

As is typical for a Southern Republican, Collins strongly supports robust spending on the U.S. military. Just outside the city of Columbus in the 3rd District is Fort Benning, the largest military base in Georgia. Collins lambasted some of the Clinton administration's Pentagon budget requests as "indefensible," saying they "downsize our forces, jeopardize our combat readiness and demoralize our soldiers." In the 106th, Collins won passage of a measure directing the government to pay restitution to the families of 15 Americans killed by friendly fire in Iraq in 1994 when U.S. fighter pilots mistakenly shot down two U.S. helicopters.

There is one major policy area in which Collins veers away from the line laid down by the GOP leadership: trade. Concerned about the potential loss of jobs in Georgia's textile industry, Collins voted against a succession of measures aimed at lowering trade barriers, including the 1993 North American Free Trade Agreement and the 1994 General Agreement on Tariffs and Trade. He initially opposed a bill promoting trade with sub-Saharan African countries, but then added provisions in the 106th that were aimed at regulating the trade to protect U.S. textile companies.

Collins voted against a high-profile measure in 2000 granting China permanent normal trade status, contending it would cost U.S. jobs. "The workers and businesses of this country need fair trade, not necessarily free trade," he said. Collins tried unsuccessfully to amend the legislation to require annual reviews of the impact of Chinese trade on U.S. textile companies and of China's progress in distributing U.S. products.

The first round of post-1990 census redistricting in Georgia gave Collins an opening to run for Congress because it dramatically altered Democratic Rep. Richard Ray's 3rd District, giving it a mixture of independent voters, Reagan Democrats and GOP suburbanites who did not know the incumbent. Collins won the 1992 GOP primary, then attacked five-termer Ray as a politician who had lost touch with the folks back home.

Both men touted conservative policies, but Ray, competing on ground now largely unfamiliar to him, could not overcome voters' anti-Congress mood. George Bush carried the 3rd by 11 percentage points in presidential voting, and Collins, who often stumped in jeans and cowboy boots and spent less than $250,000, won with 55 percent.

Collins has flirted with statewide runs for senator or governor. But he has opted to stay in the House, easily winning re-election every two years and drawing no Democratic opposition in 1998.

KEY VOTES

2000

No	Raise hourly minimum wage by $1 over two years
Yes	Halt funding for U.S. mission in Kosovo unless European nations pay more
Yes	Provide Medicare benefits to military retirees and their dependents
No	Grant China permanent normal trade status
Yes	Phase out estate, gift and trust taxes
Yes	Prohibit implementation of president's national monument designations
Yes	Approve GOP plan to provide prescription drug coverage for Medicare beneficiaries
No	Increase help for poor nations indebted to international financial institutions

1999

Yes	Impose steel import quotas
No	Kill proposal to take aviation trust funds off budget
No	Require background checks on buyers only at gun shows with 10 or more vendors
Yes	Remove barriers among banking, securities and insurance companies
No	Authorize state grants to hire teachers and reduce class size
Yes	Overhaul campaign finance law; ban "soft money" and restrict advocacy advertising
No	Approve bipartisan plan to increase rights of patients in managed-care health plans

INTEREST GROUPS

	AFL-CIO	ADA	CCUS	ACU
2000	10%	5%	76%	96%
1999	33%	15%	80%	92%
1998	0%	0%	83%	100%
1997	13%	5%	80%	83%

CQ VOTE STUDIES

	PARTY UNITY		PRESIDENTIAL SUPPORT	
	Support	Oppose	Support	Oppose
2000	96%	4%	19%	81%
1999	95%	5%	14%	86%
1998	95%	5%	12%	88%
1997	96%	4%	27%	73%

GEORGIA 3
West Central — Columbus; Atlanta suburbs

Extending from the suburbs south of Atlanta to the Alabama border, the 3rd is an eclectic mix of urban, suburban and rural counties. It takes in 10 counties, with Muscogee, Clayton (which is shared with the 5th), and Fayette among the largest. Muscogee, which includes the city of Columbus, at the district's southern tip, was added in 1995 redistricting and boosted the district's black population to 25 percent. Henry County, in the northern portion of the district, is moving away from becoming a mere bedroom community to a center of business in its own right.

The most loyal support for Democratic candidates comes from counties at the district's northern and southern ends, Muscogee and Clayton, and in some rural areas to the south. But the Democratic tendency in these areas is offset by the overwhelming Republican trend in southern Atlanta suburbs such as Fayette and the increasingly Republican middle of the district.

The 3rd's military facilities provide sustenance for the area's diverse economy. The district is home to two bases and another, Fort McPherson, is nearby in the 5th. Also in the 5th is the sprawling and ever-bustling Hartsfield Atlanta International Airport, which helps bolster the 3rd's economy, as do textile, manufacturing and health care facilities to the north.

MAJOR INDUSTRY
Transportation, service, military

MILITARY BASES
Fort Benning (Army), 28,132 military, 13,542 civilian (shared with the 2nd) (2001); Fort Gillem (Army), 1,766 military, 543 civilian (1999)

CITIES
Columbus, 181,547; Peachtree City, 32,321; Griffin, 21,550

UNUSUAL FEATURES
Jonesboro, in Clayton County, provided the literary setting for Margaret Mitchell's "Gone With the Wind;" President Franklin D. Roosevelt found the therapeutic waters of Warm Springs soothing for his polio and in 1932 built the cottage now known as "Little White House," where he died in 1945.

Rep. Cynthia A. McKinney (D)

Elected 1992; 5th term

An outspoken liberal who is willing to castigate Democrats and Republicans alike when they disagree with her, McKinney at times finds her capacity for legislative success limited in a House that emphasizes more conservative politics. But McKinney has also displayed a talent for building alliances across the aisle, and she is an influential voice on human rights.

The first black woman elected to the House from Georgia, McKinney is a national symbol and spokeswoman in Congress for the civil rights movement. She also keeps up a high profile at home, wading into Atlanta-area transportation issues, local labor disputes and other matters of specific concern to her constituents.

McKinney has little patience with button-down conservatism, and even the way she dresses — in flamboyant attire, often including gold tennis shoes — underscores her distance from more traditional colleagues.

Notwithstanding her often strident rhetoric and fierce independence, McKinney at times has scored legislative victories on the International Relations and Armed Services committees. In 1999, she worked with Republican Christopher H. Smith of New Jersey to put together a State Department reauthorization bill that incorporated one of her top legislative priorities: permitting U.S. arms sales only to democratic countries that do not engage in human rights abuses or international aggression. She also teamed with another staunch conservative, Republican Dana Rohrabacher of California, on a measure to cancel debts that poor countries owed to the United States and the International Monetary Fund.

Although such liberal-conservative alliances are unusual, McKinney told The Associated Press: "We are all committed to democratization. ... When you operate with these guys on the extreme right, you know that they are compelled to act, from a gut reaction."

McKinney's focus on human rights abuses has sometimes led to clashes with Democrats. In 2000, she broke with the Clinton administration and voted against granting China permanent normal trade status, protesting that country's human rights record. "It is obvious now to me that by negotiating agreements like this that are devoid of moral content, my country has completely abdicated its professed concern for human rights," she said. She also criticized the 1999 NATO bombing campaign against Yugoslavia as causing unnecessary suffering and called for an end to U.S. sanctions against Iraq, which she blamed for harming children and other civilians rather than weakening Iraqi leader Saddam Hussein.

McKinney set off a political furor in 2000 when her office faxed news organizations a statement blasting Al Gore, the Democratic presidential nominee, for having a low "Negro tolerance level" and accusing him of seldom having more than one black in his presence. McKinney later disavowed the remarks as being part of a draft news release never meant for public distribution. But she urged the Clinton administration to investigate allegations of discrimination against African-American Secret Service agents.

Early in the 107th Congress, McKinney complained about not being invited when President Bush visited military bases in Georgia, reminding the White House of her membership on Armed Services and of the president's promise to be racially inclusive. The White House apologized.

That was not her first White House apology: Partly because of her youthful face, trademark braids and unconventional garb, McKinney is not always recognized around Washington as a member of Congress. In 1998, she

CAPITOL OFFICE
225-1605; fax 226-0691; 124 Cannon Bldg. 20515

INTERNET
e-mail: cymck@mail.house.gov
web: www.house.gov/mckinney

COMMITTEES
Armed Services
International Relations

HOMETOWN
Lithonia

BORN
March 17, 1955, Atlanta, Ga.

RELIGION
Roman Catholic

FAMILY
Divorced; one child

EDUCATION
U. of Southern California, B.A. 1978; Tufts U., attending

CAREER
Professor

POLITICAL HIGHLIGHTS
Democratic nominee for Ga. House, 1986; Ga. House, 1989-93

ELECTION RESULTS

2000 GENERAL

Cynthia A. McKinney (D)	139,579	60.7%
Sunny Warren (R)	90,277	39.3%

2000 PRIMARY

Cynthia A. McKinney (D)	unopposed

1998 GENERAL

Cynthia A. McKinney (D)	100,622	61.1%
Sunny Warren (R)	64,146	38.9%

PREVIOUS WINNING PERCENTAGES
1996 (58%); 1994 (66%); 1992 (73%)

demanded — and got — an apology from the Clinton White House after she and two Pakistani-American guests were denied entry to a reception for the prime minister of Italy, while her 23-year-old white staff aide was allowed in. "I don't need to be stopped and questioned because I look like the hired help," she fumed.

Despite her differences with the Clinton administration, McKinney was one of only five lawmakers to vote in 1998 against any form of impeachment inquiry of President Clinton, although she noted that the president has "squandered an historic opportunity, disgracing himself in the eyes of the world and his family. ... Bill Clinton's greatest punishment will be that he has to face that reality every morning for the rest of his life."

McKinney drew headlines in 1997 for a fling at diplomacy when she traveled to Lubumbashi, Zaire, to urge rebel leader Laurent Kabila to overthrow the authoritarian regime of President Mobutu Sese Seko. She said she hoped Kabila could bring democracy to the war-torn country. But in 1998, after Kabila installed himself as president of the renamed Republic of Congo, allegations surfaced that he was ordering the detention and execution of political foes. McKinney condemned Kabila's actions and urged the Clinton administration to "take quick action to save innocent lives."

Born in Atlanta, McKinney went to California for college but returned home to teach. She got an unusual start in politics when her father, a veteran civil rights activist and state representative, decided to get back at a political rival by putting her name on the ballot against the other man. But Billy McKinney did not tell his daughter, and she lost by a wide margin, she recalled in an interview with The Associated Press.

The unauthorized campaign piqued her interest in politics. She successfully ran for the state House two years later. When Georgia got a map for the 1992 election that included three black-majority seats, McKinney sought one, the 11th. She ran a low-cost but aggressive primary campaign and bested two better-financed, better-connected black legislators; she then handily won the runoff and general election.

But in June 1995, the Supreme Court invalidated Georgia's congressional district map as a "racial gerrymander" that violated the Constitution's guarantee of equal protection under the law, citing McKinney's district as the offending black-majority seat. After the remapping by a three-judge federal panel, McKinney's southern DeKalb County base was in the 4th, and blacks made up only one-third of the district's voting-age population, compared with 64 percent in her old district. Nevertheless, McKinney easily won re-election in a particularly nasty 1996 campaign and has prevailed comfortably since.

KEY VOTES

2000

Yes	Raise hourly minimum wage by $1 over two years
?	Halt funding for U.S. mission in Kosovo unless European nations pay more
Yes	Provide Medicare benefits to military retirees and their dependents
No	Grant China permanent normal trade status
No	Phase out estate, gift and trust taxes
No	Prohibit implementation of president's national monument designations
No	Approve GOP plan to provide prescription drug coverage for Medicare beneficiaries
Yes	Increase help for poor nations indebted to international financial institutions

1999

Yes	Impose steel import quotas
No	Kill proposal to take aviation trust funds off budget
No	Require background checks on buyers only at gun shows with 10 or more vendors
No	Remove barriers among banking, securities and insurance companies
Yes	Authorize state grants to hire teachers and reduce class size
Yes	Overhaul campaign finance law; ban "soft money" and restrict advocacy advertising
Yes	Approve bipartisan plan to increase rights of patients in managed-care health plans

INTEREST GROUPS

	AFL-CIO	ADA	CCUS	ACU
2000	100%	95%	23%	12%
1999	100%	95%	8%	8%
1998	100%	100%	22%	8%
1997	100%	100%	30%	13%

CQ VOTE STUDIES

	PARTY UNITY		PRESIDENTIAL SUPPORT	
	Support	Oppose	Support	Oppose
2000	91%	9%	72%	28%
1999	92%	8%	71%	29%
1998	92%	8%	87%	13%
1997	90%	10%	82%	18%

GEORGIA 4

Atlanta suburbs — Parts of DeKalb and Gwinnett counties

The strong Democratic tendencies of the 4th were a good fit for Rep. McKinney, who decided to run in this DeKalb County-based district after a federal court ruled in 1995 that her black-majority, Atlanta-to-Savannah 11th District was an unconstitutional racial gerrymander.

DeKalb County, which sits just east of Atlanta, accounts for 87 percent of the district's population and is Georgia's second most-populous county. Democratic candidates get a warm reception in the county's racially diverse central and western portions, while Republicans run well in northern DeKalb's more white, affluent neighborhoods. The district also takes in a portion of burgeoning Gwinnett County and its growing minority population.

Jobs in the 4th center around health care and higher education. Emory University, home to 11,300 students and a university hospital are major employers. The Centers for Disease Control and Prevention also employs a sizable number of the area's health care workers. Decatur was a 19th century commercial hub until it lost out as a railroad center to Atlanta, but still has many government-related jobs. South DeKalb, which has one of the nation's most affluent concentrations of African-Americans, is seeing rapid growth.

MAJOR INDUSTRY
Retail, health care, government

CITIES
Decatur, 17,247; Doraville, 8,454; Chamblee, 7,382

UNUSUAL FEATURES
Stone Mountain Park features a huge granite outcropping into which a sculpture of Robert E. Lee and other Confederate heroes is carved; Stone Mountain's first African-American mayor lives in the home built by the former Grand Dragon of the Georgia Ku Klux Klan.

Rep. John Lewis (D)

CAPITOL OFFICE
225-3801; fax 225-0351; 343 Cannon Bldg. 20515

INTERNET
e-mail: www.house.gov/writerep
web: www.house.gov/johnlewis

COMMITTEES
Ways & Means

HOMETOWN
Atlanta

BORN
Feb. 21, 1940, Troy, Ala.

RELIGION
Baptist

FAMILY
Wife, Lillian Lewis; one child

EDUCATION
American Baptist Theological Seminary, B.A. 1961;
Fisk U., B.A. 1963

CAREER
Civil rights activist

POLITICAL HIGHLIGHTS
Sought Democratic nomination for U.S. House
(special election), 1977; Atlanta City Council, 1982-
86

ELECTION RESULTS

2000 GENERAL
John Lewis (D)	137,333	77.2%
Hank Schwab (R)	40,606	22.8%

2000 PRIMARY
John Lewis (D)	unopposed

1998 GENERAL
John Lewis (D)	109,177	78.5%
John H. Lewis Sr. (R)	29,877	21.5%

PREVIOUS WINNING PERCENTAGES
1996 (100%); 1994 (69%); 1992 (72%); 1990 (76%);
1988 (78%); 1986 (75%)

Elected 1986; 8th term

As a young, up-and-coming civil rights leader in the summer of 1963, Lewis was scolded by a black journalist who saw a newspaper photo that showed him standing at the edge of a group of civil rights leaders, barely in the frame. "You've got to get out front," the journalist told Lewis. At the time, that was not a comfortable position for the shy, awkward student activist to be in.

"I've never been the kind of person who naturally attracts the limelight," Lewis wrote in his autobiography, "Walking With the Wind." "I'm not a handsome guy. I'm not flamboyant. I'm not what you would call elegant. ... I simply have never been the kind of guy who draws attention."

Somehow, Lewis learned to be a leader. He became chairman of the Student Nonviolent Coordinating Committee in 1963 and spoke at the March on Washington. In fact, his original speech was so fiery that other civil rights leaders made him tone it down. The most famous speaker that day, the Rev. Martin Luther King Jr., simply said, "John, that doesn't sound like you."

By March 1965, he had found enough steel to stand at the front of hundreds of marchers on the Edmund Pettus Bridge in Selma, Ala., facing down charging state troopers without moving a muscle. The images from the "Bloody Sunday" march that day, in which Lewis suffered a severe concussion from the crack of a trooper's billy club, helped jolt Congress into passing the Voting Rights Act.

Now, Lewis is a leader in a different arena. For more than 14 years he has represented Georgia's 5th District, which takes in downtown Atlanta and is the state's only black-majority district. Anyone who hears his booming, thundering preacher's voice on the House floor — with a cadence that sounds eerily like King's — knows Lewis found the confidence he needed to make it in politics.

Lewis still considers himself a shy person. But he says that as a young man at the heart of the civil rights movement, he was "forced to grow up" as he and others took responsibility for the groups of people who sat in at lunch counters and for the Freedom Riders, who took dangerous, integrated bus rides through the Deep South. These days, Lewis says, the act of campaigning in his district draws him out, and the political battles in Congress embolden him by spurring him to "get in the way" — a civil rights expression for physically placing one's self in the way of injustice and forcing the perpetrators to change. "I think the movement liberated me," Lewis says, "and I think being in Congress liberated me more."

Lewis has risen to the ranks of the Democratic leadership, serving as one of four chief deputy whips who make it their business to censure the conservatism of the GOP majority. He sits on the Ways and Means Committee, which gives him a chance to sound off about health care for poor people and the uninsured. And he serves on Democratic task forces on health care, education and Social Security, helping to solidify the party's positions on those bread-and-butter social issues.

Lewis is not the kind of legislator who puts out 15-point policy initiatives. Instead, he works as the motivator — rallying other lawmakers to recognize a problem and work up the will to solve it. For example, Lewis believes that health care is "a basic, fundamental right," and despite the failure of President Clinton's health care overhaul effort in 1994, he argues that Congress needs to keep pushing for universal health coverage. Growing up in rural Alabama, Lewis says he saw firsthand the inadequacy of health care for the poor — black and white. Even today, he says, too many people cannot afford health insurance and wait until they are severely ill to go to the emergency room. Rather than spell out a detailed solution, the congressman says the current challenge is simply to create the political environment to address the issue — much as Congress had to do when it launched Social Security and Medicare in earlier eras.

There are some specific projects on Lewis' plate; in the 106th Congress, for example, he cosponsored legislation to reduce racial disparities in health care, joining forces with a diverse group of lawmakers led by Democratic Rep. Bennie Thompson of Mississippi and Democratic Sen. Edward M. Kennedy of Massachusetts. But generally, Lewis does not spend a lot of time writing legislation; rather, he seeks to be a voice of conscience, using his office as a bully pulpit to speak for racial reconciliation and healing.

In 1995, Lewis announced he would not attend the Million Man March in Washington that was so important to many African-Americans. He explained that while he supported the ideas and goals of the march, he could not condone organizer Louis Farrakhan's history of "hateful, divisive words and ideas." At the same time, Lewis is not afraid to push his fellow lawmakers to confront the racial injustices of the past. He and GOP Rep. J.C. Watts Jr. of Oklahoma cosponsored a resolution in the 106th that officially recognized the contributions of slaves who helped build the Capitol.

In addition, Lewis and GOP Rep. Amo Houghton of New York have organized a discussion group of sorts with House members from both parties in which the lawmakers visit each other's districts and hold community forums on racial issues. They have heard from such speakers as retired Gen. Colin F. Powell, now secretary of state, and Jim Lawson, Lewis' mentor in the non-violent protest tactics that drove the civil rights movement. The idea, Lewis says, is to "humanize American politics" and create a dialogue on race. "What we're saying [is], don't be afraid of it, don't sweep it under the rug, but deal with it as individual members, as a group."

Lewis' constituents seem likely to let him continue in his role as long as he wants; he received 77 percent of the vote in his 2000 contest against Republican Hank Schwab. Moreover, Lewis' message of forgiveness and understanding has won over some of his former adversaries. Joe Smitherman, who served as mayor of Selma at the time of the Bloody Sunday march and held the office until September 2000, used to protect himself politically by uttering racial slurs against King. Now, one of the most prized decorations in Lewis' congressional office is a 1996 award naming him "honorary mayor" of Selma — an award signed by Smitherman.

KEY VOTES

2000

Yes	Raise hourly minimum wage by $1 over two years
No	Halt funding for U.S. mission in Kosovo unless European nations pay more
?	Provide Medicare benefits to military retirees and their dependents
No	Grant China permanent normal trade status
No	Phase out estate, gift and trust taxes
No	Prohibit implementation of president's national monument designations
No	Approve GOP plan to provide prescription drug coverage for Medicare beneficiaries
Yes	Increase help for poor nations indebted to international financial institutions

1999

Yes	Impose steel import quotas
?	Kill proposal to take aviation trust funds off budget
No	Require background checks on buyers only at gun shows with 10 or more vendors
No	Remove barriers among banking, securities and insurance companies
?	Authorize state grants to hire teachers and reduce class size
Yes	Overhaul campaign finance law; ban "soft money" and restrict advocacy advertising
Yes	Approve bipartisan plan to increase rights of patients in managed-care health plans

INTEREST GROUPS

	AFL-CIO	ADA	CCUS	ACU
2000	100%	95%	42%	4%
1999	100%	95%	9%	0%
1998	100%	90%	13%	0%
1997	100%	95%	20%	4%

CQ VOTE STUDIES

	PARTY UNITY		PRESIDENTIAL SUPPORT	
	Support	Oppose	Support	Oppose
2000	96%	4%	80%	20%
1999	96%	4%	84%	16%
1998	99%	1%	87%	13%
1997	97%	3%	79%	21%

GEORGIA 5

Atlanta

The heart of the 5th lies in downtown Atlanta, the symbolic capital of the New South and the commercial center of the Southeast. The district takes in all of the city of Atlanta and most of surrounding Fulton County, where the majority of the district's population is based. Fulton, the largest county in Georgia, is reliably Democratic, save a few pockets of GOP strength in its wealthier northern suburbs.

The 5th is Georgia's only black-majority district after a three-judge federal panel dismantled two others in 1995. Its 61 percent black population helps keep it a Democratic bastion, although the latest census figures show whites moving back into the city after years of flight. Over the course of the 1990s, Atlanta saw a 13 percent increase in the number of white residents, while the black population declined by 3 percent. Overall, Atlanta's population grew by about 6 percent.

Along with Atlanta's downtown business district, the major economic generator in the 5th is the Hartsfield Atlanta International Airport in

Clayton County, which employs more than 44,000 people. The 5th's strategic location also has made it the headquarters for transportation-related industries, distribution companies and other major firms. At the same time, air pollution, gridlock and urban sprawl from the expanding economy is a concern for local residents.

MAJOR INDUSTRY
Transportation, distribution

MILITARY BASES
Fort McPherson (Army), 3,573 military; 1,721 civilian (1999)

CITIES
Atlanta, 401,726; East Point, 33,066; College Park, 19,083; Sandy Springs (unincorporated) (pt.), 17,465 (1990)

UNUSUAL FEATURES
Martin Luther King Jr., born in Atlanta, served as a pastor of Ebenezer Baptist Church; Atlanta hosted the 1996 Summer Olympics; Headquarters for Coca-Cola and CNN.

Rep. Johnny Isakson (R)

Elected February 1999; 1st full term

CAPITOL OFFICE
225-4501; fax 225-4656; 132 Cannon Bldg. 20515

INTERNET
e-mail: ga06@mail.house.gov
web: www.house.gov/isakson

COMMITTEES
Education & Workforce
Transportation & Infrastructure

HOMETOWN
Marietta

BORN
Dec. 28, 1944, Atlanta, Ga.

RELIGION
Methodist

FAMILY
Wife, Dianne Isakson; three children

EDUCATION
U. of Georgia, B.B.A. 1966

MILITARY SERVICE
Ga. Air National Guard, 1966-72

CAREER
Real estate company president

POLITICAL HIGHLIGHTS
Candidate for Cobb County Commission, 1974;
Ga. House, 1977-90 (Republican leader, 1983-90);
Republican nominee for governor, 1990; Ga.
Senate, 1994-96; sought Republican nomination for
U.S. Senate, 1996; Ga. Board of Education
chairman, 1996-99

ELECTION RESULTS

2000 GENERAL

Johnny Isakson (R)	256,595	74.8%
Brett DeHart (D)	86,666	25.3%

2000 PRIMARY

Johnny Isakson (R)	unopposed

1999 SPECIAL

Johnny Isakson (R)	51,548	65.1%
Christina Jeffrey (R)	20,115	25.4%
Gary "Bats" Pelphrey (D)	4,014	5.1%
Barry Doublestein (R)	1,593	2.0%
Alan Baier (R)	1,459	1.8%

When Isakson came to Capitol Hill in February 1999, the only thing most Washingtonians knew about him was that he was not Newt Gingrich.

The Speaker of the House had resigned as the 6th District's congressman, embarrassed and under fire from his Republican colleagues after the party's loss of five seats in the midterm elections. When Isakson won the ensuing special election, word quickly spread that the suburban Atlanta district had picked a stylistically opposite successor: moderate, humble, conciliatory, even-tempered — and pleasant.

Now in his second term, Isakson has successfully emerged from Gingrich's shadow. He still draws remarks from House colleagues about his un-Newtness — mainly from Democrats who cannot resist the comparisons — but he also has been gaining influence among House Republicans because of his detailed knowledge of education policy, developed as chairman of the Georgia Board of Education from 1996 through 1998.

At a time when President Bush and congressional Republicans are challenging Democrats more seriously for the mantle of the party of education — and when the House Education and the Workforce Committee has a new chairman, John A. Boehner of Ohio — Isakson's expertise in education matters should make him a valuable player in House GOP circles.

Though he was the lowest-ranking Education Committee Republican in the 106th Congress, Isakson took the lead on a major piece of legislation. GOP colleagues say he was the driving force behind a party proposal to help states pay for such federally mandated school modernization costs as asbestos removal and physical modifications to accommodate students with disabilities. It was a Republican answer to an increasingly powerful Democratic effort to unleash federal funds for emergency school repairs. The Democratic proposal was resisted by most Republicans — including Bill Goodling, R-Pa., then the Education panel's chairman — who said the federal government could never come close to paying for the nation's school construction needs.

Isakson saw the political power of the school construction issue and convinced Goodling that the Republicans could never win the debate without a proposal of their own. Instead of refusing to back any federal role in fixing the schools, Isakson said, the GOP should counter with a more-limited approach. He advocated a plan to help states comply with federal mandates while recognizing that if voters knew the federal government would step in every time they declined to pay for broader school repairs, "they'd never pass a bond issue again."

That kind of thinking has given Isakson an unusual amount of influence. Goodling was so impressed he bypassed more-senior committee Republicans and secured a slot for Isakson on Congress' Web-Based Education Commission, formed to advise the president and Congress on how to use the Internet to improve student achievement. Isakson was vice chairman and worked closely with Sen. Bob Kerrey, D-Neb., who was chairman.

At the same time, Isakson used his other committee assignment — Transportation and Infrastructure — to prod the Transportation Department to restore highway funds for traffic-clogged Atlanta. He also badgered Georgia officials to bring Atlanta into compliance with the Clean Air Act, a condition it must meet before the flow of highway funds may be restored.

Politically, Isakson considers himself a fiscal conservative — he wants a 10 percent across-the-board tax cut and has sided faithfully with his GOP colleagues on other tax-cutting bills — but he does not argue with those who call him a social moderate. "I like to call myself pragmatic," he said. "I like to look at each issue and do what I think is right, and when you do that, you run the risk of failing someone's litmus test."

Isakson is opposed to a constitutional amendment to ban abortion and is wary of adding the option of private savings accounts to the Social Security program, a Bush proposal. Still, he is in little danger of being mistaken for a Democrat. He opposes gun control and supports a ban on a procedure its opponents call "partial birth" abortion. On education, Isakson backs GOP calls for greater state and local authority in spending federal money and says his view is based on years of practical experience: "I've seen top-down fail over and over again because it tends to breed mediocrity."

Isakson fell in line with Republican leaders on some of the biggest issues in the 106th. He voted against the sweeping managed-care bill the House passed in 1999 — its GOP sponsor was fellow Georgian Charlie Norwood — and in favor of the leadership-backed alternative, which would have allowed customers to sue their managed-care plans under more limited conditions than the Norwood bill. Patients should be able to challenge bad coverage decisions, Isakson said, but he concluded that the Norwood bill would insufficiently protect employers who offer the plans from lawsuits.

During 17 years as a state lawmaker — 14 years in the Georgia House and three in the Senate — Isakson developed a reputation as a skillful arbitrator who was more practical than ideological, a combination that allowed him to bridge gaps within the Republican Party and forge links with state Democrats. "He figured out early on that if you wanted to leave any kind of fingerprint on public policy, you have to be able to work with people," said Charles Bullock, a University of Georgia political scientist.

Still, positioning himself as a relatively moderate voice in the conservative Georgia Republican Party was not always a successful formula for Isakson. In 1990, the real estate developer lost a race for governor as the GOP nominee against Democrat Zell Miller. In 1996, he ran for the Republican Senate nomination and lost in a runoff to conservative businessman Guy Millner. His reputation for bipartisanship eventually paid off, however, when Miller, as governor, appointed Isakson chairman of Georgia's Board of Education in 1996. (Miller is now Georgia's junior senator.)

When Gingrich resigned, Isakson was immediately labeled the front-runner to succeed him. With huge advantages in name identification and campaign funds, he took 65 percent against five opponents in the special election and cruised to an easy re-election victory in 2000.

KEY VOTES

2000

No Raise hourly minimum wage by $1 over two years
Yes Halt funding for U.S. mission in Kosovo unless European nations pay more
Yes Provide Medicare benefits to military retirees and their dependents
Yes Grant China permanent normal trade status
Yes Phase out estate, gift and trust taxes
Yes Prohibit implementation of president's national monument designations
Yes Approve GOP plan to provide prescription drug coverage for Medicare beneficiaries
No Increase help for poor nations indebted to international financial institutions

1999

No Impose steel import quotas
No Kill proposal to take aviation trust funds off budget
Yes Require background checks on buyers only at gun shows with 10 or more vendors
Yes Remove barriers among banking, securities and insurance companies
No Authorize state grants to hire teachers and reduce class size
No Overhaul campaign finance law; ban "soft money" and restrict advocacy advertising
No Approve bipartisan plan to increase rights of patients in managed-care health plans

INTEREST GROUPS

	AFL-CIO	ADA	CCUS	ACU
2000	0%	5%	85%	72%
1999	13%	10%	91%	66%

CQ VOTE STUDIES

	PARTY UNITY		PRESIDENTIAL SUPPORT	
	Support	Oppose	Support	Oppose
2000	91%	9%	30%	70%
1999	87%	13%	29%	71%

GEORGIA 6
Atlanta suburbs — Roswell; part of Marietta

Anchored in Atlanta's burgeoning northern suburbs, the 6th covers parts of four counties that are laden with Republican voters who work in high-technology and other white-collar occupations. The district became an even stronger Republican enclave in 1995 when remapping added portions of fast-growing and reliably Republican Gwinnett County.

This area is referred to as the Golden Crescent; it is sandwiched between three of the state's major interstate highways – Interstates 75, 85, and the 285 perimeter highway. The mostly white 6th remains Georgia's most affluent and educated district. Cobb County, northwest of Atlanta, accounts for more than 50 percent of the district's vote, and many of its residents work at Lockheed Martin, across the district line in the 7th.

Along with its defense industry, Marietta (shared with the 7th) provides Cobb County with its own thriving commercial center. Numerous corporations have office space in the "Platinum Triangle," a huge employment center that has begun to overshadow Atlanta's business district. But the growth and prospering economy also have brought traffic gridlock and air pollution, causing some businesses to reconsider locating here.

In the central part of the 6th are solidly GOP suburbs in northern Fulton County. Alpharetta was once home to a number of large farms that since have been converted into suburban developments. Roswell, formerly a cotton-milling center, is now a booming bedroom community in Fulton County.

MAJOR INDUSTRY
Communications, aerospace, finance

CITIES
Roswell, 57,952; Smyrna, 37,685; Alpharetta, 27,302; Marietta (pt.), 20,144 (1990)

UNUSUAL FEATURES
Former Speaker Newt Gingrich, R, represented the 6th from 1979-99; The "big chicken," a 56-foot-tall sign in Marietta.

Rep. Bob Barr (R)

CAPITOL OFFICE
225-2931; fax 225-2944
1207 Longworth Bldg. 20515

INTERNET
e-mail: barr.ga@mail.house.gov
web: www.house.gov/barr

COMMITTEES
Financial Services
Government Reform
Judiciary
(Commercial & Administrative Law - chairman)

HOMETOWN
Smyrna

BORN
Nov. 5, 1948, Iowa City, Iowa

RELIGION
Wesleyan Fellowship Church

FAMILY
Wife, Jeri Barr; four children

EDUCATION
U. of Southern California, B.A. 1970; George
Washington U., M.A. 1972; Georgetown U., J.D.
1977

CAREER
Lawyer; CIA analyst

POLITICAL HIGHLIGHTS
Sought Republican nomination for Ga. House,
1984; U.S. attorney, 1986-90; sought Republican
nomination for U.S. Senate, 1992

ELECTION RESULTS

2000 GENERAL

Bob Barr (R)	126,312	55.3%
Roger Kahn (D)	102,272	44.7%

2000 PRIMARY

Bob Barr (R)	unopposed

1998 GENERAL

Bob Barr (R)	85,982	55.4%
James F. Williams (D)	69,293	44.6%

PREVIOUS WINNING PERCENTAGES
1996 (58%); 1994 (52%)

Elected 1994; 4th term

With the arrival of the Bush administration and its emphasis on bipartisanship and civility, the cantankerous Barr has been trying to lighten his image. His attempt at transformation should be made easier by the departure of President Clinton, his main nemesis.

Barr and his wife spent much of his campaign in 2000 trying to convince voters that the poker-faced congressman has a softer side. In contrast to his bombastic campaign style of the past, Barr took time to read to children and conduct other "feel-good" activities on the campaign trail. In one television advertisement, Jeri Barr even explained that her husband did not have time for niceties because he was so busy taking care of the 7th District's interests in Washington.

Indeed, Barr generally has not been one to temper his language. For instance, in 2000, during a lengthy and technical Judiciary subcommittee debate over which communities should qualify for federal help in fighting violence against women, Barr expressed his frustration sharply. "This is the most ludicrous debate I've ever heard," he said. "This is an asinine discussion."

While he always seems to be itching for a fight, increasingly the conflict is not only with the liberals he so antagonizes but with those in his own party who do not feel as strongly about privacy or free speech as he does. While best known for his prominent role in pressing for Clinton's impeachment and for his unyielding defense of gun owners' rights, Barr focuses much of his energy these days on trying to prevent government, businesses and other third parties from gathering information on individuals. He has a forum in which to press his views, as chairman of the Judiciary Subcommittee on Commercial and Administrative Law in the 107th Congress.

Barr often is joined in these efforts by lawmakers and groups who find the rest of his right-wing agenda appalling. In the 106th, for example, he teamed up with the American Civil Liberties Union in winning repeal of a 1996 law that he argued would lead to the creation of a national identification card. (The law had required states either to include Social Security numbers on driver's licenses or to keep each driver's Social Security number on file.) Barr and the ACLU also squelched a move that would have eased search warrant restrictions.

Arguing against limiting free speech, he and liberal Democrat Tammy Baldwin of Wisconsin worked together to kill a proposal that would have made it a crime to teach others how to make methamphetamine, better known as "speed," and other drugs, including by posting recipes on the Internet. Also in the 106th, he joined liberal Sen. Charles E. Schumer, D-N.Y., in proposing legislation requiring companies to give notice when they scan employees' e-mail, monitor their Web use or listen to telephone conversations.

Despite such bipartisan efforts, the hard-nosed Barr is still among the members of Congress that liberals most love to hate, and that conservatives most revere. He serves on the board of the National Rifle Association and has received accolades from various conservative groups, including the Christian Coalition and the Conservative Political Action Committee.

His unwavering defense of many conservative causes won him a warm but private reception at the 2000 Republican National Convention. With GOP candidate George W. Bush touting a theme of bipartisan cooperation, outspoken conservatives such as Barr were seen only behind the scenes in Philadelphia. At such gatherings the mood was not one of conciliation. "Sic 'em, Bob," one partygoer shouted to Barr, according to the Los Angeles Times.

The congressman's renown on the GOP right comes, as much as anything, from his standing as one of the first in Congress to push for Clinton's impeachment. In November 1997, he introduced legislation to start an impeachment inquiry focused on financing irregularities in the president's 1996 re-election campaign. Barr was an active participant in the Judiciary Committee's drafting of four articles of impeachment against Clinton in 1998, although the one for which he was most responsible — accusing Clinton of abuse of power for giving "evasive" answers in the House's inquiry — was rejected by the House. Barr was one of the 13 House lawmakers chosen to present the case against Clinton before the Senate in 1999. He was a fixture on national television, and he castigated the Senate for not having the "stomach" to convict and remove Clinton.

The unending and heated nature of his attacks made the twice-divorced Barr a target for cartoonists and comedians as well as for Hustler magazine publisher Larry Flynt, who sought to tar Barr as a hypocrite, saying he lied about extra-marital affairs and an ex-wife's abortion. Barr denied the allegations and also said that he was unaware that a group he had once addressed, the Council of Conservative Citizens, was a white supremacist organization.

He also got into hot water in 1999 when he amended a housing bill to give a group headed by his wife a better chance at getting federal funding.

While Barr's backers have overlooked such infringements, he has not always gotten a free ride from those closest to him. His mother, Beatrice Barr, once threatened to cut him off financially when he flirted with becoming a Democrat as a college freshman. She still considers him a "flaming liberal."

Barr was born in Iowa but traveled around the world as a child because his father was a civil engineer who took jobs in various locales. He has said that the experience left him with a greater love of freedom and the rule of law. He did not move to Georgia until he was close to 30.

Before running for Congress, he worked as a lobbyist for the CIA and served as the U.S. attorney in Atlanta for four years. He was named to the post in 1986 by President Reagan. (Barr was the sponsor of the 1998 law renaming Washington National Airport for Reagan.)

Barr won election to the House in 1994 by unseating Democratic Rep. George "Buddy" Darden. The conservative swing evident nationwide that year was especially pronounced in Georgia, and Barr captured the 7th District with 52 percent of the vote. Barr's partisan image and his role in the Clinton impeachment process have made him a top target of Democrats, but Barr has survived by solid if not comfortable margins. He won by virtually identical 11-point margins in 1998 and 2000.

KEY VOTES

2000
No Raise hourly minimum wage by $1 over two years
Yes Halt funding for U.S. mission in Kosovo unless European nations pay more
Yes Provide Medicare benefits to military retirees and their dependents
No Grant China permanent normal trade status
Yes Phase out estate, gift and trust taxes
Yes Prohibit implementation of president's national monument designations
Yes Approve GOP plan to provide prescription drug coverage for Medicare beneficiaries
No Increase help for poor nations indebted to international financial institutions

1999
Yes Impose steel import quotas
No Kill proposal to take aviation trust funds off budget
Yes Require background checks on buyers only at gun shows with 10 or more vendors
Yes Remove barriers among banking, securities and insurance companies
No Authorize state grants to hire teachers and reduce class size
No Overhaul campaign finance law; ban "soft money" and restrict advocacy advertising
Yes Approve bipartisan plan to increase rights of patients in managed-care health plans

INTEREST GROUPS

	AFL-CIO	ADA	CCUS	ACU
2000	20%	10%	71%	100%
1999	44%	15%	76%	100%
1998	11%	5%	72%	100%
1997	0%	5%	80%	96%

CQ VOTE STUDIES

	PARTY UNITY		PRESIDENTIAL SUPPORT	
	Support	Oppose	Support	Oppose
2000	94%	6%	18%	82%
1999	91%	9%	16%	84%
1998	93%	7%	20%	80%
1997	98%	2%	21%	79%

GEORGIA 7
Northwest — Rome; part of Marietta

The 7th runs alongside the Alabama border, stretching east to take in Atlanta's northwestern suburbs. While the district includes 10 full counties and part of another, nearly half of its voters live in three counties – Cobb, Douglas and Carroll – which are adjacent to Atlanta's Fulton County.

The historically Democratic 7th has been heading Republican. It supported the Republican presidential nominee in the 1990s and 2000, and has elected a Republican congressman since 1994. The district's portion of Cobb County is not as Republican as the neighboring 6th's, but even the 7th's Democrats tend to be socially conservative and supportive of Republican candidates and issues such as gun ownership.

The district takes in the southwestern portion of Cobb County, a collection of largely white-collar, middle-income suburbs, and much of the county seat, Marietta. Moving beyong the metropolitan Atlanta orbit, the land is given over to agricultural pursuits, and there are a number of small towns reliant on textile trades. The beef and timber industries and a few manufacturers provide jobs for residents of counties along the Alabama border.

The district's economy benefits from small businesses, corporate headquarters and military- and aerospace-related employment in Marietta (shared with the 6th). Lockheed Martin is one of the district's top employers. Other big industries include electrical wire in Carroll County and carpet manufacturing in the north.

MAJOR INDUSTRY
Defense, carpet manufacturing, electronics

MILITARY BASES
Naval Air Station Atlanta, 3,703 military, 214 civilian (1999)

CITIES
Rome, 32,677; Marietta (pt.), 30,163 (1990); La Grange, 24,973

UNUSUAL FEATURES
Home to Thomas B. Murphy, Speaker of the Georgia House since 1974; Actress Susan Hayward buried in Carrollton; Kennesaw Mountain National Battlefield Park.

Rep. Saxby Chambliss (R)

Elected 1994; 4th term

CAPITOL OFFICE
225-6531; fax 225-3013
1019 Longworth Bldg. 20515

INTERNET
e-mail: rep.saxby.chambliss@mail.house.gov
web: www.house.gov/chambliss

COMMITTEES
Agriculture
(General Farm Commodities - chairman)
Armed Services
Select Intelligence

HOMETOWN
Moultrie

BORN
Nov. 10, 1943, Warrenton, N.C.

RELIGION
Episcopalian

FAMILY
Wife, Julianne Chambliss; two children

EDUCATION
Louisiana Tech U., attended 1961-62; U. of Georgia,
B.B.A. 1966; U. of Tennessee, J.D. 1968

CAREER
Lawyer; hotel owner

POLITICAL HIGHLIGHTS
Sought Republican nomination for U.S. House,
1992

ELECTION RESULTS

2000 GENERAL

Saxby Chambliss (R)	113,380	58.9%
Jim Marshall (D)	79,051	41.1%

2000 PRIMARY

Saxby Chambliss (R)	unopposed

1998 GENERAL

Saxby Chambliss (R)	87,993	62.4%
Ronald L. Cain (D)	53,079	37.6%

PREVIOUS WINNING PERCENTAGES
1996 (53%); 1994 (63%)

Chambliss is a member of the GOP Class of 1994 who brings business experience and a reputation as a champion of farmers in the Southeast to his position as chairman of the Agriculture Subcommittee on General Farm Commodities and Risk Management.

A small-town lawyer and former motel owner, Chambliss (CHAM-bliss) is a fiscal and social conservative who takes a pragmatic approach to legislation involving farm and defense programs, which are vital to Georgia's economy. "I never was somebody way off on the right-hand side. My district dictates you work in a bipartisan manner on defense and farm issues," he said in 2000.

Chambliss, who was named to the Budget Committee in the 106th Congress, sought the panel chairmanship in the 107th. He had forgone the 2000 Senate race to succeed the late Paul Coverdell with the intent of winning the Budget gavel. To further his cause, he had raised funds through his political action committee, the Common Sense Leadership Fund, to dole out to GOP candidates. Nevertheless, Chambliss lost to Jim Nussle of Iowa in a four-person race that also included Nick Smith of Michigan and John E. Sununu of New Hampshire.

After his defeat, Chambliss won two different prizes: chairmanship of the Agriculture subcommittee that oversees crop insurance and the commodity exchanges, and an appointment to the Intelligence Committee. His Agriculture chairmanship and the choice of another Southerner, Republican Terry Everett of Alabama, to be chairman of the Specialty Crops and Foreign Agriculture Programs Subcommittee will likely raise the profile of farm programs important to Southeastern states in the 107th.

Chambliss echoes GOP calls for lean budgets, but he is not afraid to mix it up with party leaders where the interests of his district's peanut, cotton and tobacco growers are concerned. In 1995, after less than a month in the House, he took on Majority Leader Dick Armey, who had co-authored a "Dear Colleague" letter that denounced the federal peanut-support program as artificially restricting production and suggested that it be eliminated. Chambliss promptly issued a news release calling Armey's suggestion "abominable" and later joined with four other GOP lawmakers on the Agriculture Committee in opposing the 1995 farm bill. The final legislation modified, but did not kill, the peanut program, and Chambliss voted for it.

Chambliss defended peanut growers again in 1998, when the Transportation Department said it was considering the establishment of peanut-free zones on commercial airline flights to protect passengers who were allergic to peanuts. "I cannot understand why the Big Brother Clinton administration insists on taking away another thing America loves," he said. The proposal was scrapped.

In the 106th, Chambliss backed temporary visas for foreign "guest workers" to meet farmers' labor needs and helped win enactment of a law that encourages growers to buy crop insurance by subsidizing a greater share of the annual premium. He also looked out for the interests of Brown and Williamson, which employs more than 2,000 workers at its tobacco plant in his district.

On Armed Services, Chambliss looks out for Robins Air Force Base, a center for aircraft maintenance, in his district and for the F-22 fighter and C-17 and C-130J cargo planes. The C-17 is built by Boeing Co. at a Macon plant, and the F-22 and C-130J are built by Lockheed Martin in Marietta. A co-founder of the Congressional Air Power Caucus, Chambliss tussled in 1997 with Armey and President Clinton over a proposal to keep Texas and California bases functioning as "privatized" maintenance facilities instead of closing them entirely and relocating the work. Armey's role in the talks angered Chambliss. According to the White House Bulletin newsletter, he called Armey a "liar" and the two almost got into a fight on the House floor.

In most areas, Chambliss follows the party line. He favored granting China permanent normal trade status in 2000 and was a strong supporter of the House GOP's "Contract With America," voting for legislation linked to it 98 percent of the time in 1995. And he benefited from a push by then-Speaker Newt Gingrich to promote fellow Georgians: In the 105th and 106th, he served on the Republican Steering Committee, which makes GOP committee assignments.

Chambliss worked with lawmakers of both parties when he chaired a Budget task force on health care in 2000 that sought to reduce paperwork and Medicare fraud. He claims a bond with the Budget Committee's ranking Democrat, John M. Spratt Jr. of South Carolina: As a boy, Chambliss spent summers in Sumter, S.C., which lies in Spratt's district.

Growing up, Chambliss had lived all over the South. His father was an Episcopal minister and moved the family often. Chambliss says he learned how to make friends quickly, which helped him in his political career.

An avid hunter of quail, duck and dove, Chambliss co-chaired the Congressional Sportsmen's Caucus in the 106th and sponsored legislation to establish a federal policy to promote hunting.

Before his first race for Congress, Chambliss was active in business and civic affairs in Moultrie for more than two decades, working on local development and coaching YMCA basketball and Little League baseball. (He had played on the University of Georgia baseball team.)

In his first run for elective office in 1992, he lost the GOP primary, and the district re-elected Democratic Rep. J. Roy Rowland. In 1994, Rowland retired and Chambliss won the seat by defeating Democrat Craig Mathis, a lawyer and the son of former Rep. Dawson Mathis.

In 1996, after a court-ordered redistricting plan put Moultrie in the 2nd District, Chambliss narrowly beat his Democratic challenger, former U.S. Attorney Jim Wiggins. Chambliss and his wife moved to the 8th — to blunt any criticism about not living in the district — but returned to Moultrie after the election. After briefly weighing a run for governor, Chambliss easily won re-election in 1998. In 2000, he defeated Democrat Jim Marshall, the former mayor of Macon, with 59 percent of the vote.

KEY VOTES

2000

No   Raise hourly minimum wage by $1 over two years
Yes   Halt funding for U.S. mission in Kosovo unless European nations pay more
Yes   Provide Medicare benefits to military retirees and their dependents
Yes   Grant China permanent normal trade status
Yes   Phase out estate, gift and trust taxes
Yes   Prohibit implementation of president's national monument designations
Yes   Approve GOP plan to provide prescription drug coverage for Medicare beneficiaries
No   Increase help for poor nations indebted to international financial institutions

1999

No   Impose steel import quotas
Yes   Kill proposal to take aviation trust funds off budget
No   Require background checks on buyers only at gun shows with 10 or more vendors
Yes   Remove barriers among banking, securities and insurance companies
No   Authorize state grants to hire teachers and reduce class size
No   Overhaul campaign finance law; ban "soft money" and restrict advocacy advertising
Yes   Approve bipartisan plan to increase rights of patients in managed-care health plans

INTEREST GROUPS

	AFL-CIO	ADA	CCUS	ACU
2000	0%	0%	90%	91%
1999	33%	10%	80%	80%
1998	0%	0%	94%	96%
1997	0%	5%	88%	88%

CQ VOTE STUDIES

	PARTY UNITY		PRESIDENTIAL SUPPORT	
	Support	Oppose	Support	Oppose
2000	95%	5%	24%	76%
1999	94%	6%	26%	74%
1998	95%	5%	22%	78%
1997	96%	4%	26%	74%

GEORGIA 8

South Central – Macon; Warner Robins

The 8th begins as a narrow strip of territory in the middle of the state and stretches diagonally to the Florida line at Georgia's southeast corner. To the north, Macon and Warner Robins, its two largest cities, recently have seen an influx of residents and a growing white-collar job base. The southern part of the district is more rural and sparsely populated.

Despite the 8th's Republican representative, the district leans Democratic – partly because redistricting in 1995 bolstered the district's black population and partly because of the area's history as a Democratic stronghold. Bibb, the 8th's largest county and home to Macon, has a large black population and is considerably more Democratic than the rest of the district. But as much of the South has embraced the Republican Party, the 8th has become politically competitive.

The 8th is heavily agricultural and has faced hard times. In the late 1990s, cotton and tobacco farmers struggled to overcome the effects of bad weather that had seriously damaged their crops. But aerospace jobs and textile manufacturing in the north, as well as the timber industry in the south, have helped sustain the economy.

MAJOR INDUSTRY
Agriculture, defense, timber

MILITARY BASES
Robins Air Force Base, 7,020 military, 11,082 civilian (1999)

CITIES
Macon (pt.), 108,016 (1990); Warner Robins, 49,396; Waycross (pt.), 17,395 (1990)

UNUSUAL FEATURES
Brown and Williamson Tobacco factory near Macon believed to be the world's largest cigarette plant; Harriet Tubman Historical and Cultural Museum; Georgia Music Hall of Fame; Lanier Cottage, birthplace of famed Georgia poet Sidney Lanier.

Rep. Nathan Deal (R)

Elected 1992; 5th term

Deal was the first of five House Democrats to switch to the Republican Party in 1995, and now, after three terms, he is comfortable in his GOP skin, backing the party more than 90 percent of the time and proudly noting that the growth of the GOP in Southern states such as Georgia has spread from the national level down to the state and local levels.

Twenty years ago, only about an eighth of the Georgia General Assembly was Republican, and now more than 40 percent is. Deal says the principal reason for the shift is that local voters, who grew up with ancestral ties to the Democratic Party, have come to realize that the national party does not reflect their views. Deal says he came to the same conclusion after 12 years as a Democrat in the state Senate and after winning election to Congress as a Democrat in 1992.

When he saw the Democratic response to the House Republican "Contract With America," which he supported, he concluded that "the Democratic Party's attitude wasn't in tune with me or my constituents' beliefs." The party "showed it was unwilling to change their liberal philosophy," Deal said, and so he jumped ship, to the delight of the new GOP majority, which showed its gratitude by giving him a seat on the Commerce Committee.

Deal says his party switch has mattered little to his constituents: "I voted like a Republican even when I was a Democrat," he says. Although Democratic Party officials vowed to make him regret his move, the voters of the 9th District re-elected him by a 31 percent margin in 1996, and Democrats did not even mount a challenge in 1998. In 2000, Deal won more than three-fourths of the votes cast.

With less to complain about these days as a lawmaker comfortably in sync with his party, Deal is seldom seen on the House floor, and many of his relatively few appearances are as the presiding officer. Deal's demeanor is low-key and approachable, a regular-guy persona that dates at least as far back as his street-level, walk-in law practice back home in Gainesville, Ga.

He is fiscally frugal, as he was in his first term when he and about 20 other freshman Democrats formed the Fiscal Caucus to pressure the Clinton administration to cut spending. That caucus was one of the forerunners of the "Blue Dog" coalition of conservative Democrats, which Deal helped found just before he jumped parties.

He has long served on a GOP immigration task force. His particular interest lies in beefing up enforcement against illegal aliens — including those who enter the United States legally but stay longer than permitted — in interior parts of the country, such as North Georgia's 9th District.

At first glance, the landlocked, mostly rural district might seem an unlikely hot spot for concern about immigration. But a closer look reveals that two major industries in the district — poultry processing and carpet manufacturing — are attracting a wave of foreign workers, some of them legal immigrants, some not. The Latino population in the district jumped by an estimated 80 percent in the 1990s, an increase dramatic enough to provoke local concerns and to spur Deal into action to discourage illegal immigration.

Portions of the 9th are now part of the rapidly growing greater Atlanta suburbs and exurbs, but the district still retains some rural areas, where issues such as logging and satellite television access is important. In the 106th Congress, Deal was a leader on legislation to help local counties whose revenues from timber harvesting on federal lands have dwindled. He

CAPITOL OFFICE
225-5211; fax 225-8272; 2437 Rayburn Bldg. 20515

INTERNET
e-mail: www.house.gov/writerep
web: www.house.gov/deal

COMMITTEES
Energy & Commerce

HOMETOWN
Gainesville

BORN
Aug. 25, 1942, Millen, Ga.

RELIGION
Baptist

FAMILY
Wife, Sandra Dunagan Deal; four children

EDUCATION
Mercer U., B.A. 1964, J.D. 1966

MILITARY SERVICE
Army, 1966-68

CAREER
Lawyer; state prosecutor

POLITICAL HIGHLIGHTS
Hall County juvenile court judge, 1971-72; Hall County attorney, 1977-79; Ga. Senate, 1981-93 (served as a Democrat; president pro tempore, 1991-93)

ELECTION RESULTS

2000 GENERAL

Nathan Deal (R)	183,171	75.2%
James Harrington (D)	60,360	24.8%

2000 PRIMARY

Nathan Deal (R)	unopposed

1998 GENERAL

Nathan Deal (R)	unopposed

PREVIOUS WINNING PERCENTAGES
1996 (66%); 1994 (58%); 1992 (59%)
* Elected as a Democrat 1992-94

also authored legislation, which became law, to expand the Chattahoochee River National Recreation Area.

Although the 9th is booming, some backwoods stereotypes remain — it was the setting for "Deliverance" and "Smokey and the Bandit." That may explain why Deal reacted so strongly in 1998 to a perceived slight from actress and Atlanta resident Jane Fonda. She reportedly told a United Nations panel that living conditions in parts of North Georgia are akin to those in some Third World countries. "If Fonda believes there are starving children in North Georgia," Deal said, "she should start feeding them instead of feeding buffalo in Montana [where Fonda has a ranch]. Or maybe she could persuade her husband [media mogul Ted Turner] to redirect his $1 billion pledge to the U.N. and spend it in America."

Deal's views on most national issues are in line with the GOP, including his opposition to gun control and abortion and his support of a healthy defense budget and a constitutional amendment to ban flag desecration.

Deal is the only child of two public school teachers (his wife is a teacher as well), and although his parents were not active in politics, they impressed on him the importance of being active in public life. "After all, teaching is a type of public service," he says.

He was a successful high school and college debater, and he went on to law school. Fulfilling a commitment he made as a four-year member of the ROTC during college, Deal joined the Army, where he served two years in the Judge Advocate General's corps, before opening a law practice in Gainesville.

Deal served as a prosecutor and a juvenile court judge and then, at the urging of friends, ran for an open state Senate seat in 1980. He put together a string of effortless re-elections by the time Democratic Rep. Ed Jenkins announced in 1992 that he was retiring from the House. Deal's GOP opponent that year was Daniel Becker, who made abortion the focus of a "morality in government" campaign; he aired anti-abortion TV ads featuring graphic photos of allegedly aborted fetuses. Becker's appeal proved to be limited. Though George Bush carried the 9th with 49 percent of the vote, Becker managed only 41 percent against Deal's 59 percent.

Deal's conservative first-term voting record helped protect him from the Republican electoral tide in 1994. He won re-election by a solid margin, even as Democratic incumbents lost in the neighboring 7th and 10th districts. Just a few months later, Deal himself contributed to the GOP tide in Georgia, where the party now holds eight of the 11 House seats.

KEY VOTES

2000

No Raise hourly minimum wage by $1 over two years
Yes Halt funding for U.S. mission in Kosovo unless European nations pay more
Yes Provide Medicare benefits to military retirees and their dependents
No Grant China permanent normal trade status
Yes Phase out estate, gift and trust taxes
Yes Prohibit implementation of president's national monument designations
Yes Approve GOP plan to provide prescription drug coverage for Medicare beneficiaries
No Increase help for poor nations indebted to international financial institutions

1999

No Impose steel import quotas
No Kill proposal to take aviation trust funds off budget
No Require background checks on buyers only at gun shows with 10 or more vendors
Yes Remove barriers among banking, securities and insurance companies
No Authorize state grants to hire teachers and reduce class size
Yes Overhaul campaign finance law; ban "soft money" and restrict advocacy advertising
No Approve bipartisan plan to increase rights of patients in managed-care health plans

INTEREST GROUPS

	AFL-CIO	ADA	CCUS	ACU
2000	10%	5%	71%	96%
1999	22%	10%	84%	80%
1998	10%	10%	67%	88%
1997	0%	0%	90%	96%

CQ VOTE STUDIES

	PARTY UNITY		PRESIDENTIAL SUPPORT	
	Support	Oppose	Support	Oppose
2000	95%	5%	15%	85%
1999	92%	8%	16%	84%
1998	94%	6%	16%	84%
1997	96%	4%	23%	77%

GEORGIA 9

North — Dalton; Gainesville; Toccoa

The 9th is anchored by North Georgia's mountains, and runs across the top of the state, from Alabama to South Carolina. Georgia's most rural district, the 9th includes the Cloudland Canyon, the man-made Lake Lanier and several growing Atlanta suburbs.

Residents of the 9th are overwhelmingly white and strongly Republican. Redistricting in 1995 kept the 9th's black population at 4 percent. While Democrats have long dominated local politics, the GOP allegiance in some north-central counties is unwavering and dates to the Civil War. In fast-growing Cherokee, Forsyth and Hall counties, Republicans are becoming even more prevalent as Atlanta suburbanites move to the area.

Economically, the 9th has benefited from a population boom. A surge of new residents in the south has brought new white-collar and service-sector jobs to the district but is straining local water resources. Many of those new residents are Latino immigrants who work in the district's

poultry processing and carpet-making industries in Hall and Whitfield counties. Tourist dollars also play a crucial role in the district's economy.

MAJOR INDUSTRY
Poultry processing, carpet manufacturing, textiles

CITIES
Dalton, 24,048; Gainesville, 20,470; Toccoa 9,635

UNUSUAL FEATURES
Gainesville known as the "poultry capital of the world" – in the center of town is the Georgia Poultry Federation's monument to the industry: an obelisk with a chicken statue on top; Movies "Deliverance" and "Smokey and the Bandit" set in Rabun County; Helen, a hamlet in White County, is a replica of a Swiss village.

Rep. Charlie Norwood (R)

Elected 1994; 4th term

CAPITOL OFFICE
225-4101; fax 225-0279
1707 Longworth Bldg. 20515

INTERNET
e-mail: www.house.gov/writerep
web: www.house.gov/norwood

COMMITTEES
Education & Workforce
(Workforce Protections - chairman)
Energy & Commerce

HOMETOWN
Evans

BORN
July 27, 1941, Valdosta, Ga.

RELIGION
Methodist

FAMILY
Wife, Gloria Norwood; two children

EDUCATION
Georgia Southern U., B.S. 1964; Georgetown U.,
D.D.S. 1967

MILITARY SERVICE
Army, 1967-69

CAREER
Dentist

POLITICAL HIGHLIGHTS
No previous office

ELECTION RESULTS

2000 GENERAL
Charlie Norwood (R)	122,590	63.2%
Marion "Denise" Freeman (D)	71,309	36.8%

2000 PRIMARY
Charlie Norwood (R)	unopposed

1998 GENERAL
Charlie Norwood (R)	88,527	59.6%
Marion "Denise" Freeman (D)	60,004	40.4%

PREVIOUS WINNING PERCENTAGES
1996 (52%); 1994 (65%)

His down-home and folksy public persona belies the political acumen and bull-headedness that made Norwood a constant thorn in the side of his Republican leadership through most of the 106th Congress.

A tobacco-chewing, duck-hunting fisherman with a strong Southern drawl, Norwood is also a dentist, whose preparation for Congress was running his own small practice. His lack of political experience made him a prototypical member of the "revolutionary" GOP Class of 1994; since then, his professional and business experience has led him to take a pivotal role in the debate over how the federal government should regulate the rights of patients whose health care is provided by HMOs.

In 1999, the generally conservative Norwood worked behind the scenes with one of the House's most socially liberal members, Democrat John D. Dingell of Michigan, to craft a broad bill that rebuffed the GOP leadership's view on the central issue of liability. Under the measure, patients would have been allowed to sue their health plans over coverage decisions, a change that the insurance industry said would result in skyrocketing health care costs. But despite constant pressure from his leadership, and in the face of intense lobbying from traditionally Republican business and insurance constituencies, Norwood helped round up 68 Republican votes for the legislation, which the House then passed with a resounding 275 votes.

As punishment for his disobedience, Speaker J. Dennis Hastert refused to appoint Norwood to the conference committee with the Senate, which had passed a narrower bill that Norwood opposed. But Norwood continued to work behind the scenes in hopes of influencing the final legislation, and House leaders, uncomfortably aware of Norwood's pull among his fellow Republicans, allowed him to sit in on conference meetings. While 2000 ended with no deal, Norwood has resumed the fight in the 107th Congress.

In the 105th, Norwood had worked more closely with his leadership on the health care issue. He attracted more than 200 cosponsors for legislation he wrote to strengthen the hand of patients and practitioners in their dealings with managed-care providers. But he abandoned the bill at the request of GOP leaders, who were worried they were losing control of the debate. In a nod to party loyalty, Norwood agreed instead to sit on a special task force to write a consensus House Republican measure. When it was done, he described the task force effort as containing "75 percent" of what he sought, and he vowed to push for its passage. The House did pass a bill in 1998, largely along party lines, but it died in the Senate.

It was that outcome that prompted Norwood to take a more aggressive stance in the 106th. From his seat on the Commerce Committee, he initially tried to work within the system and compromise with top Republicans. But "when the leadership just refused to work with us, after trying all year, I made a personal decision," he said, to reach out to Democrats.

Norwood seemed unperturbed by both his party leaders' anger and the national media attention that followed his rebellious tack. And he reprised his contrarian ways on another top-tier issue in 2000 — trade with China. Along with Bob Ney of Ohio, he led a group of House Republicans who worked against the GOP leadership — and President Clinton — to oppose a measure to grant China permanent normal trade status. The two lawmakers initiated a series of classified briefings for undecided colleagues at which the Central Intelligence Agency laid bare the details of China's growing military strength. This time, Norwood was on the losing end: On its way to becoming law, the China bill was overwhelmingly passed by the House; only 57 Republicans voted "no."

Despite these defections, Norwood is more often than not a loyal foot soldier for the GOP cause. He first ran for Congress on the platform that many problems are better solved at the local and state levels than by federal bureaucrats. Citing his experience as a dentist, he groused about federal regulations that he saw as onerous to small-business owners like himself and promised to work to reduce the federal government's role in people's lives.

Norwood also toes the conservative line on social policy issues. He strongly opposes abortion, supports school choice and school prayer, and is a staunch advocate for the rights of gun owners.

After a 1999 school shooting in Georgia, Norwood called for an emergency vote in the House to allow school prayer. "We took God out of our schools in 1962. Now we're seeing that something else has moved in," he said. "If we want these shootings to stop, we have to take on the U.S. Supreme Court ruling that banned our children and teachers from praying in the classroom."

Norwood says his support of gun owners' rights is deepened by an incident he was involved in when he was 16 years old. He and a high school friend were playing with a .22 caliber pistol when it discharged while in Norwood's hands, killing the other boy. Norwood said the experience had convinced him that no amount of gun control could have prevented such an accident. His position has won him strong backing from the National Rifle Association and helped him solidify a friendship with Dingell, with whom he shares not only an alliance on health care but also an opposition to gun control and a fondness for hunting fowl.

In the 107th Congress, Norwood became a subcommittee chairman for the first time, heading the Education and the Workforce panel's Workforce Protections Subcommittee, which oversees labor, wages and worker safety.

After graduating from dental school and serving as a combat medic in Vietnam, Norwood opened a dental practice. By winning his 1994 campaign, in which he marketed himself as a citizen-legislator willing to take on Washington, he became the first Republican to represent the Augusta area in the House since Reconstruction.

His bid for a second term in 1996 proved more difficult after a Supreme Court ruling led to a remapping that increased his district's African-American population from about one-fifth to almost one-third. Norwood just survived with 52 percent, but he has rebounded since, posting a 19-point victory in 1998 and a 26-point victory in 2000.

KEY VOTES

2000
No Raise hourly minimum wage by $1 over two years
Yes Halt funding for U.S. mission in Kosovo unless European nations pay more
Yes Provide Medicare benefits to military retirees and their dependents
No Grant China permanent normal trade status
Yes Phase out estate, gift and trust taxes
? Prohibit implementation of president's national monument designations
Yes Approve GOP plan to provide prescription drug coverage for Medicare beneficiaries
No Increase help for poor nations indebted to international financial institutions

1999
Yes Impose steel import quotas
No Kill proposal to take aviation trust funds off budget
Yes Require background checks on buyers only at gun shows with 10 or more vendors
Yes Remove barriers among banking, securities and insurance companies
No Authorize state grants to hire teachers and reduce class size
No Overhaul campaign finance law; ban "soft money" and restrict advocacy advertising
Yes Approve bipartisan plan to increase rights of patients in managed-care health plans

INTEREST GROUPS

	AFL-CIO	ADA	CCUS	ACU
2000	10%	5%	71%	100%
1999	44%	10%	71%	88%
1998	10%	5%	83%	100%
1997	0%	0%	90%	96%

CQ VOTE STUDIES

	PARTY UNITY		PRESIDENTIAL SUPPORT	
	Support	Oppose	Support	Oppose
2000	97%	3%	17%	83%
1999	94%	6%	14%	86%
1998	96%	4%	18%	82%
1997	96%	4%	24%	76%

GEORGIA 10

Northeast – Augusta

The 10th includes a large section of east-central Georgia, as well as the city of Augusta on the banks of the Savannah River along the South Carolina border. After the Supreme Court invalidated Georgia's congressional district map as an unconstitutional racial gerrymander in 1995, the 10th was redrawn and made substantially more black and Democratic.

District politics are in a state of flux as longtime Yellow Dog Democrats, who never would have considered voting for a Republican in the past, are beginning to split their tickets. Fast-growing Columbia County is staunchly Republican, and Richmond County – which includes Augusta and casts about 30 percent of the 10th's votes – has been politically split in the past but is trending Republican. In the center of the district, black-majority Hancock County is consistently loyal to Democrats.

Despite the loss of some 13,000 jobs at the Savannah River Site nuclear facility across the river from Augusta, diversity has helped keep the economy robust. Augusta is a regional medical center, and the city's hospitals are major employers. To the south, oats, soybeans, corn, cotton and peanuts are major crops, and dairy production is also a staple. The district also supplies most of the word's top-grade kaolin, the white clay mineral used by paper, paint and rubber manufacturers, and is one of the nation's largest suppliers of granite.

MAJOR INDUSTRY
Health care, agriculture, defense

MILITARY BASES
Fort Gordon (Army), 7,262 military, 1,848 civilian (1999)

CITIES
Augusta, 186,206; Milledgeville, 18,034; Dublin, 17,473

UNUSUAL FEATURES
Augusta National golf course hosts the annual Master's golf tournament; Eatonton is the birthplace of Joel Chandler Harris, author of the Uncle Remus stories, and Alice Walker, whose book, "The Color Purple," won the 1983 Pulitzer Prize.

Rep. John Linder (R)

Elected 1992; 5th term

Although Linder started the 106th Congress on a down note, his fortunes rebounded by the end of the 106th as he became the Republican Party's choice to sell the nation on the idea of a national sales tax.

At the start of 1999, GOP colleagues rebuffed his bid for a second term as chairman of the House Republicans' campaign organization, electing Virginian Thomas M. Davis III instead; and Linder's mentor, Newt Gingrich, a fellow Georgian and the Speaker, had resigned from the House — both events the result of the disappointing GOP showing at the polls in the 1998 elections.

But Linder still had a high-ranking seat on the influential Rules Committee, an arm of the leadership that sets the ground rules for floor action. And with the responsibilities of the campaign committee position gone, he turned his attention in a new direction. With the blessing of Ways and Means Committee Chairman Bill Archer of Texas, Linder assumed a leadership role in building support for a major overhaul of the nation's tax code based on a national retail sales tax — an idea long championed by Archer.

Linder became the point man for the sales tax plan. He traveled around the country, focusing on the home districts of Ways and Means members, offering himself to hundreds of radio talk shows and working with a group called the Americans for Fair Taxation to build grass-roots backing for the proposal — all in preparation for a well-funded legislative push in the 107th Congress. In the 106th, he was the principal sponsor of a bill that called for scrapping the current tax code — eliminating the income tax, payroll tax, self-employment tax, capital gains tax, estate tax — and replacing it with a 23 percent sales tax.

Linder says he is not bitter about his repudiation by fellow Republicans for his leadership of their 1998 campaign effort. Acknowledging a "buck stops here" responsibility, he says that as chairman of the National Republican Congressional Committee (NRCC) for the 1998 campaign cycle, he should be held accountable for the outcome. But he says that without his efforts, and particularly without a last-minute campaign push made possible by the large amounts of money his committee raised, the GOP showing would have been even worse than the five-seat loss that cost him and Gingrich their jobs.

Linder, whose district is next to the one Gingrich represented, was in tune with Gingrich's conservative philosophy and challenge-the-Democrats style. The Speaker rewarded his friend and adviser after the 1996 election by naming him to the NRCC chair. In that post, he not only was responsible for raising campaign money (he says the NRCC poured $45 million into congressional races); he also urged the GOP to shape its 1998 legislative agenda with the elections in mind, by focusing on issues that would energize the Republican base.

Asked whether he would continue to use his expertise in fundraising even though he no longer held an official campaign post, Linder said, "You don't need expertise, you just need to know how to grovel." Linder did remain active in GOP fundraising efforts during the 106th. With no Democratic challenger of his own, he was able to write a sizable check to the NRCC. And along with the other seven Republicans in the Georgia House delegation, he formed the G-8 PAC to raise money for state legislative races, in hopes of winning Republican control of the state General Assembly.

In addition to his efforts to build support for the national sales tax plan, Linder in the 106th Congress worked on a number of local issues. Key

CAPITOL OFFICE
225-4272; fax 225-4696
1727 Longworth Bldg. 20515

INTERNET
e-mail: john.linder@mail.house.gov
web: linder.house.gov

COMMITTEES
House Administration
Rules
(Technology & the House - chairman)

HOMETOWN
Tucker

BORN
Sept. 9, 1942, Deer River, Minn.

RELIGION
Presbyterian

FAMILY
Wife, Lynne Linder; two children

EDUCATION
U. of Minnesota, Duluth, B.S. 1963;
U. of Minnesota, D.D.S. 1967

MILITARY SERVICE
Air Force, 1967-69

CAREER
Financial executive; dentist

POLITICAL HIGHLIGHTS
Ga. House, 1975-81; Republican nominee for Ga. Senate, 1980; Ga. House, 1983-91; Republican nominee for U.S. House, 1990

ELECTION RESULTS

2000 GENERAL

John Linder (R)		unopposed

2000 PRIMARY

John Linder (R)	43,563	86.6%
Vincent Littman (R)	6,717	13.4%

1998 GENERAL

John Linder (R)	120,909	69.3%
Vincent Littman (D)	53,510	30.7%

PREVIOUS WINNING PERCENTAGES
1996 (64%); 1994 (58%); 1992 (51%)

among them is development of a high-technology corridor between Atlanta and Athens, which he envisions as specializing in agricultural research. Linder also worked to upgrade state Highway 316 to be a limited-access highway and sought to speed the permitting process for a commuter rail line that would link Athens, Atlanta and Macon.

Linder grew up in a small Minnesota town. His father was a car salesman who never made more than $7,500 a year, but Linder says he and his brother always thought the family well-off. Linder says his father, though never politically active, was interested in government and public affairs. He recalls listening with his father to the 1952 election returns on the family's huge Philco radio set.

Linder worked his way through college at the University of Minnesota's Duluth campus, where he took pre-med classes and intended to become a doctor. But one day he observed some dentists at a speech clinic, working with children who had cleft palates, and he was hooked on dentistry.

After graduating from dental school, Linder joined the Air Force, where he practiced dentistry in San Antonio for two years. Instead of returning to the upper Midwest, Linder and his wife moved south, where he set up a practice in suburban Atlanta. Linder had remained interested in politics, and his dental office had a subscription to the Congressional Record. Linder says he was most fascinated with the breadth of ideas and good writing he found in the Record's Extension of Remarks section.

A state House seat opened in 1974, and he entered the race, avoiding a GOP primary runoff by just 5 votes and winning in November.

Linder continued to practice dentistry for a while, but in 1977 he founded a lending institution that specialized in providing financial assistance to small businesses. By 1982, he had phased himself out of his dental practice.

Linder served 14 years in the state legislature, earning a reputation for battling the Democratic leadership. He first ran for Congress in 1990, losing a tight battle with Democratic Rep. Ben Jones in the 4th District. After 1992 redistricting gave the 4th a more Republican tilt, Linder tried again. He narrowly edged state Sen. Cathey Steinberg, 51 percent to 49 percent. (Jones ran in the 10th District, losing in the primary.)

The 11th District Linder now serves was drawn in 1995, after a Supreme Court decision invalidated Georgia's congressional map as a "racial gerrymander." The remapping left Linder with a chunk of the Atlanta suburbs, but he also gained much new rural territory. The new territory has proved friendly, and he has rolled up increasingly large re-election margins. He was unopposed in 2000.

KEY VOTES

2000

No Raise hourly minimum wage by $1 over two years
Yes Halt funding for U.S. mission in Kosovo unless European nations pay more
Yes Provide Medicare benefits to military retirees and their dependents
Yes Grant China permanent normal trade status
Yes Phase out estate, gift and trust taxes
Yes Prohibit implementation of president's national monument designations
Yes Approve GOP plan to provide prescription drug coverage for Medicare beneficiaries
No Increase help for poor nations indebted to international financial institutions

1999

No Impose steel import quotas
Yes Kill proposal to take aviation trust funds off budget
Yes Require background checks on buyers only at gun shows with 10 or more vendors
Yes Remove barriers among banking, securities and insurance companies
No Authorize state grants to hire teachers and reduce class size
No Overhaul campaign finance law; ban "soft money" and restrict advocacy advertising
No Approve bipartisan plan to increase rights of patients in managed-care health plans

INTEREST GROUPS

	AFL-CIO	ADA	CCUS	ACU
2000	0%	0%	90%	87%
1999	0%	10%	92%	87%
1998	0%	0%	100%	100%
1997	0%	0%	100%	87%

CQ VOTE STUDIES

	PARTY UNITY		PRESIDENTIAL SUPPORT	
	Support	Oppose	Support	Oppose
2000	96%	4%	22%	78%
1999	95%	5%	18%	82%
1998	96%	4%	21%	79%
1997	94%	6%	32%	68%

GEORGIA 11
Northeast – Part of Gwinnett County; Athens

The strongly Republican 11th takes in a slice of northeastern Georgia, stretching from Atlanta's suburbs to the South Carolina line. Given a vastly new shape in 1995 redistricting, the 11th previously swooped from Atlanta to Savannah but was ruled an unconstitutional racial gerrymander. Redistricting gave the 11th a more rustic, small-town feel compared to its former predominantly urban and suburban constituency. Reps. McKinney and Linder switched district numbers in the 1996 election.

Gwinnett County, in Atlanta's northeastern suburbs, is Georgia's fourth-most-populous county and growing rapidly. Its median household income is higher than the metro Atlanta average, and its residents, including a large number of young suburban professionals, generally vote Republican. To the south, more rural Rockdale County is another expanding region with strong Republican leanings.

Democrats find their strongest support in Clarke County, home to a large number of blacks and the University of Georgia, a major employer. Several large manufacturers and a concentration of high-tech companies in Gwinnett, shared with the 6th, help sustain the district's stable economy.

MAJOR INDUSTRY
Manufacturing, high-tech, education

MILITARY BASES
Navy Supply Corps School, 75 military, 140 civilian (2001)

CITIES
Athens, 89,458; Lawrenceville (pt.), 17,249; Snellville, 16,245

UNUSUAL FEATURES
Famous native Ty Cobb, a baseball player nicknamed "The Georgia Peach," starred for the Detroit Tigers in the early 20th century; Braselton, town formerly owned by actress Kim Basinger, who bought it for $12 million.

HAWAII

Gov. Benjamin J. Cayetano (D)

First elected: 1994
Length of term: 4 years
Term expires: 12/02
Salary: $94,780
Phone: (808) 586-0034
Hometown: Mililani
Born: Nov. 14, 1939, Honolulu, Hawaii
Religion: Unspecified
Family: Wife, Vicki Cayetano; five children
Education: Los Angeles Harbor College, A.A. 1966; U. of California, Los Angeles, B.A. 1968; Loyola Marymount U., J.D. 1971
Career: Lawyer
Political highlights: Hawaii House, 1975-78; Hawaii Senate, 1979-86; lieutenant governor, 1987-95

Election results:
1998 GENERAL
Benjamin Cayetano (D)	204,206	50.1%
Linda Lingle (R)	198,952	48.8%

Lt. Gov. Mazie Hirono (D)

First elected: 1994
Length of term: 4 years
Term expires: 12/02
Salary: $90,041
Phone: (808) 586-0255

STATE LEGISLATURE

Legislature: Meets January-April
House: 51 members, 2-year terms
2001 breakdown: 19R, 32D; 40 men, 11 women
Salary: $32,000
Phone: (808) 586-6400
Senate: 25 members, 4-year terms
2001 breakdown: 3R, 22D; 19 men, 6 women
Salary: $32,000
Phone: (808) 586-6720

STATE TERM LIMITS

Governor: 2 consecutive terms
Senate: No
House: No

URBAN STATISTICS

CITY	POPULATION
Honolulu	395,327
Hilo	37,808 (1990)
Kailua	36,818 (1990)
Kaneohe	35,448 (1990)
Waipahu	31,435 (1990)

REGISTERED VOTERS

Voters do not register by party.

POPULATION

2000 population	1,211,537
1990 population	1,108,229
Percent change	+9.3%
Rank among states	42
Median age	35.7
Born in state	56%
Foreign born	15%
Urban/rural	89%/11%
Crime rate	278/100,000
Poverty level	10.9%
Federal workers	30,127
Military	55,253

REAPPORTIONMENT

Hawaii retained its two House seats in reapportionment. An independent commission will draw new district lines in 2001.

MISCELLANEOUS

Web: www.state.hi.us
Capital: Honolulu
Land area: 6,423 sq. miles
  Rank among states: 47
STATE ELECTION OFFICIAL
(808) 453-8683
DEMOCRATIC HEADQUARTERS
(808) 596-2980
REPUBLICAN HEADQUARTERS
(808) 593-8180

District Statistics

DIST.	2000 D	2000 R	GREEN	1996 D	1996 R	REF	1992 D	1992 R	I	WHT	BLK	ASIAN	HISP	HOUSEHOLD INCOME	OVER 65+	UNDER 18	COLLEGE EDUCATION
1	55%	39%	5%	57%	34%	6%	48%	39%	13%	29%	2%	67%	5%	$40,257	12%	22%	27%
2	56	36	7	57	30	9	49	35	16	38	2	57	9	$37,247	10	28	19
STATE	56	37	6	57	32	8	48	37	14	33	2	62	7	$38,829	11	25	23

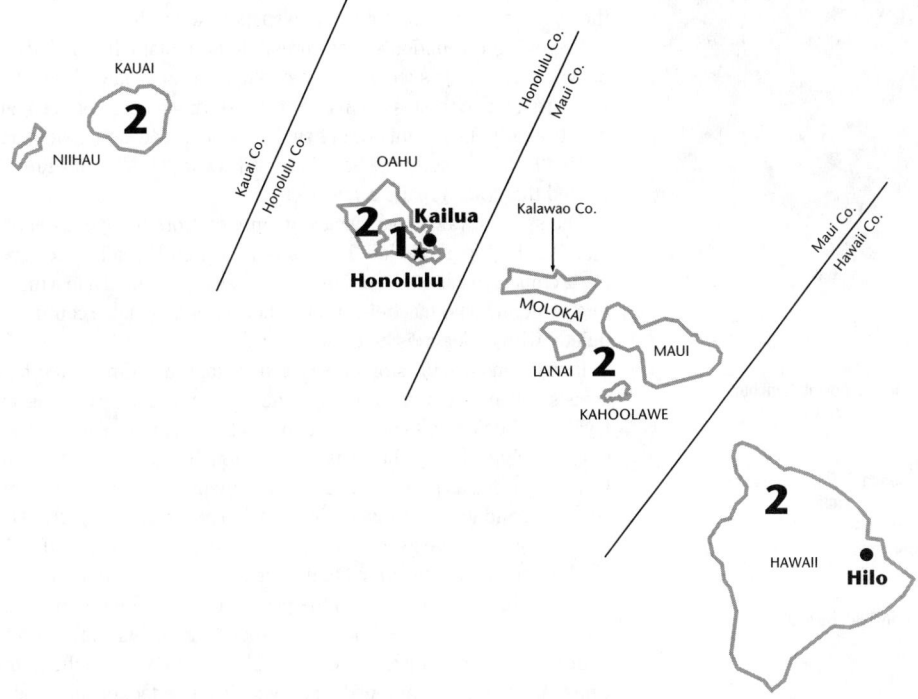

Sen. Daniel K. Inouye (D)

CAPITOL OFFICE
224-3934; fax 224-6747; 722 Hart Bldg. 20510

INTERNET
e-mail: inouye.senate.gov/abtform.html
web: inouye.senate.gov

COMMITTEES
Appropriations
Commerce, Science & Transportation
Indian Affairs - ranking member
Rules & Administration

HOMETOWN
Honolulu

BORN
Sept. 7, 1924, Honolulu, Hawaii

RELIGION
Methodist

FAMILY
Wife, Margaret Shinobu Awamura; one child

EDUCATION
U. of Hawaii, A.B. 1950; George Washington U.,
J.D. 1952

MILITARY SERVICE
Army, 1943-47

CAREER
Lawyer; city prosecutor

POLITICAL HIGHLIGHTS
Hawaii Territorial House, 1954-58 (majority leader);
Hawaii Territorial Senate, 1958-59; U.S. House,
1959-63

ELECTION RESULTS

1998 GENERAL
Daniel K. Inouye (D)	315,252	79.2%
Crystal Young (R)	70,964	17.8%
Lloyd J. Mallan (LIBERT)	11,908	3.0%

1998 PRIMARY
Daniel K. Inouye (D)	105,130	92.8%
Richard H. Thompson (D)	8,105	7.2%

PREVIOUS WINNING PERCENTAGES
1992 (57%); 1986 (74%); 1980 (78%); 1974 (83%);
1968 (83%); 1962 (69%); 1960 House Election (74%);
1959 House Special Election (68%)

Elected 1962; 7th term

When Inouye was awarded a belated Congressional Medal of Honor in 2000 in recognition of his bravery during World War II, he promised himself he would remain stoic. "I thought I could, as a tough politician, receive the medal from the president without batting an eye," he recalled. "But I must confess that when you're standing there, you think about how you got there," he told the Capitol Hill newspaper, Roll Call.

Receiving the nation's most prestigious military honor led Inouye to deliver a stunning speech at a reception the next day about the experiences that led to the loss of his right arm during a fierce battle against German troops in the mountains of Italy. Many of his colleagues wept upon hearing it. "I was choked up," Sen. Patrick J. Leahy, D-Vt., told Roll Call. "He earned that award many times over."

The speech was a rare display of emotion from Inouye, a deeply private man in a highly public job. He has represented Hawaii in Congress since the archipelago joined the union, and he has represented it in a manner befitting someone who has held public office for almost half a century: working quietly with colleagues he calls friends.

Inouye (in-NO-ay) is of an earlier political era, a time when behind-the-scenes collegiality was more important than public appearances, and when loyalty to the Senate as an institution was the norm. Bred in Hawaii's Democratic machine, Inouye has mastered the touch of being a party man without being regarded as partisan. In 1999, he lamented "the changes ... in the way senators conduct themselves" since he first arrived in Congress. "I think it's too bad that we have forgotten some of the courtesies of the office," he said.

The second-most-senior Democrat on the Appropriations Committee and long the top Democrat on the panel's Defense Subcommittee, Inouye secures billions of dollars in federal spending for his state each year. His efforts have made him a prime target of the nonprofit watchdog group Citizens Against Government Waste, which has attacked him for annually adding to appropriations legislation money for his state not sought by the White House. Inouye, however, is unapologetic about helping to boost Hawaii's economy. "The criticism I have received ... is to me an indication that I am doing the job I was elected to do," he said in 2000.

Inouye has spent four decades — more than half his life — on Capitol Hill cultivating an image as a judicious and fair-minded legislator, tending to his committee work and answering when called to serve on special panels. He has usually been all but fanatical in his loyalty to colleagues; he even taped a radio advertisement for Oregon Republican Sen. Mark O. Hatfield, a former colleague on Appropriations, when Hatfield had a tough race in 1990.

Despite his popularity and longevity, Inouye has had trouble ascending the Senate's leadership ladder. The intensely political, impersonal tactics that now dominate Senate action and the need to communicate the party's agenda outside the chamber are contrary to Inouye's style. This helps explain why his 1989 bid for majority leader attracted only 14 of the Senate's 55 Democratic votes. Seniority helped him little. Inouye never expanded his base beyond old hands and colleagues on the Appropriations Committee.

Inouye shares with Republican Ted Stevens of Alaska, chairman of Appropriations and its Defense Subcommittee, an interest in shifting military priorities away from the longstanding concentration on Europe — and toward the Pacific. He has been among the handful of Senate Democrats to support a Republican effort to create a national missile defense system, citing his state's relative proximity to Asian nations.

Inouye secured in excess of $200 million in defense spending for Hawaii in 2000, building on equally successful efforts in previous years. Some of Inouye's efforts have benefited his alma mater, the University of Hawaii.

He touched off a storm of protest that arose from a measure he put in a 1987 appropriations bill that would have spent $8 million to build schools in France for North African Jews. Unfortunately for Inouye, the endeavor became a symbol of the kind of special-interest projects members favor. The Senate rescinded the money in early 1988 at Inouye's request, after news accounts linked the money to a campaign contribution to Inouye. In an emotional speech, Inouye conceded no impropriety, only an error in judgment, and he said he feared he had embarrassed his colleagues.

Inouye has a longstanding relationship with Hawaii's tiny Jewish community, dating back to his recovery from his war wounds. "The man in the next bed told me about the concentration camps," Inouye recalled in 1999. Inouye helped raise the money for the islands' first synagogue.

Another longtime focus of Inouye's energies has been the Senate Indian Affairs panel, which he chaired from 1987 until 1995, and where he remains the ranking Democrat. "This committee has been known as the scrap heap of the Senate," he once said. "I'm going to do everything in my power to change that." Inouye has pushed legislation to allow native Hawaiians housing aid similar to that received by American Indians and native Alaskans.

If Inouye has not been closely associated with many national legislative achievements, he did take center stage during two congressional investigations of executive branch misdeeds. His 1987 appointment to chair the select Senate committee investigating the Iran-contra affair stemmed not only from his impartial manner but also from the esteem accorded him 14 years earlier during hearings on the illegal activities that led to the downfall of the Nixon administration. During the 1973 Watergate hearings, Inouye earned a reputation as a tough but judicious interrogator of President Nixon's aides and associates.

As the first Japanese-American in Congress, Inouye's stature in Hawaii's Japanese community approaches reverence. During World War II, he fought in Europe in the all-Japanese-American 442nd Regiment. When the loss of his arm denied Inouye his ambition to be a surgeon, he went first into law and then into politics. He won his first election in 1954, to Hawaii's territorial House, and helped guide Hawaii to statehood in 1959. He also was a founder of the Democratic organization that has dominated state politics.

In 1959, he was elected Hawaii's first House member and in 1963 became the first Japanese-American in the Senate. He scored four more landslide wins over modest, mainly polite GOP opposition. But in 1992, Inouye's pedestal was shaken by a pair of maverick challengers: Democratic Maui County Commissioner Wayne K. Nishiki and Republican state Sen. Rick Reed.

Reed ran a radio ad featuring claims by Inouye's barber that Inouye had forced sex on her 17 years earlier and had made unwanted advances toward her since. The allegation prompted nine other women to make similar accusations in the news media. Inouye called the accusations "unmitigated lies." The Senate Ethics Committee dropped a review of the charges when the accusers declined to participate in its investigation. Yet the allegation smudged Inouye's reputation and likely contributed to his diminished showing at the polls (57 percent): Never before had he won less than two-thirds of the vote.

Inouye's political decline proved short-lived, however. His re-election numbers returned to form in 1998, when he ran against Crystal Young, a candidate practically unknown even to the state Republican Party, and drew more than 79 percent of the vote.

KEY VOTES

2000

Yes Overhaul bankruptcy law and increase minimum wage
No Limit fiscal 2001 discretionary spending to $600.3 billion
No Override veto on nuclear waste disposal at Yucca Mountain site in Nevada
No Oppose effort to terminate Kosovo mission
Yes Include gender, sexual orientation and disability in federal hate crime protections
? Approve GOP plan to restrict use of genetic information by health insurers
No Kill amendment delaying implementation of an anti-missile defense system
? Cut taxes for married couples
Yes Grant China permanent normal trade status

1999

No Remove President Clinton from office for obstruction of justice
No Kill amendment authorizing state grants to hire teachers and reduce class size
Yes Require criminal background checks for purchases at gun shows
No Approve GOP proposal to increase rights of patients in managed-care health plans
No Block effort to allow farm and medicine exports to Cuba
Yes Allow study of tougher automobile fuel efficiency standards
Yes Ratify nuclear weapons testing treaty
Yes Prohibit national political parties from collecting "soft money" donations
Yes Remove barriers among banking, securities and insurance companies

INTEREST GROUPS

	AFL-CIO	ADA	CCUS	ACU
2000	60%	60%	69%	23%
1999	88%	95%	50%	0%
1998	88%	80%	44%	9%
1997	83%	75%	50%	4%
1996	86%	85%	33%	11%
1995	100%	95%	41%	0%
1994	88%	75%	20%	0%
1993	100%	85%	20%	13%
1992	92%	65%	10%	4%
1991	92%	80%	20%	14%

CQ VOTE STUDIES

	PARTY UNITY		PRESIDENTIAL SUPPORT	
	Support	Oppose	Support	Oppose
2000	91%	9%	94%	6%
1999	91%	9%	86%	14%
1998	93%	7%	87%	13%
1997	91%	9%	87%	13%
1996	87%	13%	86%	14%
1995	84%	16%	85%	15%
1994	92%	8%	95%	5%
1993	92%	8%	95%	5%
1992	87%	13%	41%	59%
1991	80%	20%	52%	48%

Sen. Daniel K. Akaka (D)

CAPITOL OFFICE
224-6361; fax 224-2126; 141 Hart Bldg. 20510

INTERNET
e-mail: senator@akaka.senate.gov
web: akaka.senate.gov

COMMITTEES
Armed Services
Energy & Natural Resources
Governmental Affairs
Indian Affairs
Veterans' Affairs
Select Ethics

HOMETOWN
Honolulu

BORN
Sept. 11, 1924, Honolulu, Hawaii

RELIGION
Congregationalist

FAMILY
Wife, Mary Mildred Chong; five children

EDUCATION
U. of Hawaii, B.Ed. 1952, M.Ed. 1966

MILITARY SERVICE
Army Corps of Engineers, 1945-47

CAREER
State economic grants official; elementary school
teacher and principal

POLITICAL HIGHLIGHTS
Sought Democratic nomination for lieutenant
governor, 1974; U.S. House, 1977-90

ELECTION RESULTS

2000 GENERAL

Daniel K. Akaka (D)	251,215	72.7%
John S. Carroll (R)	84,701	24.5%
Lauri A. Clegg (NL)	4,220	1.2%

2000 PRIMARY

Daniel K. Akaka (D)	150,507	90.2%
Arturo P. Reyes (D)	16,312	9.8%

PREVIOUS WINNING PERCENTAGES
1994 (72%); 1990 Special Election (54%); 1988
House Election (89%); 1986 House Election (76%);
1984 House Election (82%); 1982 House Election
(89%); 1980 House Election (90%); 1978 House
Election (86%); 1976 House Election (80%)

Elected 1990; 2nd full term
Appointed April 1990

In a legislative body known for oversize personalities and powerful egos, Akaka makes his mark by being thoroughly unassuming. While this low-key style means that Akaka is among the least-known senators in Washington, at home he is seen as an active member of a cohesive state delegation that protects Hawaii's interests. In 2000, for instance, he and Hawaii's senior senator, Democrat Daniel K. Inouye, agreed on more than 96 percent of roll call votes.

The only native Hawaiian (his mother is Hawaiian and his father is of Chinese and Hawaiian ancestry) to ever serve in Congress, Akaka (uh-KAH-kuh) gets involved in the nitty-gritty of the issues important to his state. Meeting first with scientists and local officials to gather information, he then uses his position as a senator to build a case among federal officials and fellow lawmakers that helps move legislation. It's a quiet, deliberative way of working — more in tune with traditional Hawaiian ways — that contrasts with the modern media operations run by many in the Senate. One Pacific islander official describes it as "island-style."

He helped craft a landmark measure in 2000 to recognize native Hawaiians as a distinct indigenous group with federally guaranteed rights. The legislation establishes a process for native Hawaiians to create a governing body with rights similar to those of Indian tribes. "This is a question of fundamental fairness," Akaka said.

He also worked with other members of the state delegation in the 106th Congress to pass a measure directing special federal housing aid to thousands of low-income Hawaiians. And he sponsored a bill to designate the Big Island's Ala Kahakai Trail a national historic trail, thereby providing federal protection for what he called "a unique indigenous resource."

The senator has long promoted the rights of indigenous peoples, especially native Hawaiians. An Akaka law enacted during the 104th Congress compensates native Hawaiians by transferring federal land to a trust in return for lands seized by the United States during the state's territorial period. The law builds on a measure that Akaka helped steer through the Senate in 1992: an apology to Hawaiians for the 1893 U.S. overthrow of the native government. But when that apology helped fuel an independence movement in Hawaii, Akaka the conciliator was quick to clarify that his intention was quite the opposite. "I look at the apology resolution as the first step toward healing, not creating new barriers," he said in 1998.

Like most Democrats, Akaka voted "no" on both articles of impeachment against President Clinton early in 1999, but only after he tried to play conciliator when the matter came before the Senate. As all 100 senators gathered together behind closed doors in the old Senate chamber to search for a bipartisan plan for conducting the impeachment proceedings, it was Akaka who delivered the opening prayer. "I prayed we would work through this with dignity and respect and that we would reach a fair agreement on how to handle this gravest of matters," Akaka recalled. "At first there were a lot of sullen faces. ... Finally we reached common ground. It was a great relief."

A reliable liberal vote, Akaka was one of 11 Democrats to vote against the GOP's welfare overhaul plan in 1996. He also opposes a balanced-budget constitutional amendment, the line-item veto and a ban on a procedure its opponents call "partial birth" abortion. He backed the Clinton administration on granting China permanent normal trade status.

Akaka has made some waves in foreign policy. In 2000, he joined two other senators — Democrat Max Baucus of Montana and Republican Pat Roberts of Kansas — on a trip to Cuba that culminated in a 10-hour meeting with Cuban leader Fidel Castro. The senators said it was time to improve relations with the communist nation and ease U.S. trade sanctions. Akaka in particular stressed the importance of increasing educational exchanges between the two countries. "Cooperation in education could create a dialogue," he said.

Akaka steered a measure through the Senate in 2000 to impose federal immigration laws on the Northern Mariana Islands, a U.S. territory. Congress had granted the territory local control over immigration laws in 1976, but the Pacific islands since then had become a haven for clothing industry sweatshops where workers were paid less than the federal minimum wage. "I speak as a friend and neighbor when I say that this policy cannot continue," Akaka said on the Senate floor. "The ... system of indentured immigrant labor is morally wrong and violates basic democratic principles."

Akaka made a rare foray into the national spotlight in 1997 to criticize fellow members of the Governmental Affairs panel for focusing too intently on Asian-Americans as a group during its probe into alleged campaign finance irregularities by the Clinton administration. As the hearings went on, Akaka, the only senator of Chinese ancestry, became distressed over the committee's almost exclusive focus on Asian- and Pacific-American networks — in particular, the fundraising of former Commerce Department official John Huang. "I am seriously concerned with the negative impact that the allegations of fundraising abuses have had on the Asian/Pacific-American community," Akaka said.

A protector of Hawaii's sugar industry, Akaka successfully fought an effort in 1996 by Judd Gregg, R-N.H., to cap sugar prices and loosen import quotas. That vote echoed a similar battle on sugar subsidies that Akaka won against Sen. Bill Bradley, D-N.J., in 1990. Of that fight with Bradley, a former basketball star, Akaka told a newspaper, "I'm only 5-feet-7, but I slam-dunked him."

The remark recalls an incident earlier in Akaka's career. In 1984, the House Democratic leadership was one vote short on a crucial roll call as it sought to block President Reagan's request for production of the MX missile. With time running out, Illinois Democrat Marty Russo located Akaka, who had been recorded as a pro-MX vote, lifted him out of a phone booth and escorted — some witnesses said carried — him into the chamber. Akaka then changed his vote, giving the anti-MX forces a key victory.

Akaka's career is a study in the quiet but steady perseverance of a quintessential team player. From teacher to assistant principal, principal, union official, state bureaucrat, U.S. representative and on to the Senate, he climbed the ladder one rung at a time.

Akaka rose through the Honolulu education bureaucracy before entering politics in 1971 as appointed head of the state Office of Economic Opportunity. In 1976, he captured the 2nd District seat after a difficult primary contest.

When Democratic Sen. Spark M. Matsunaga died in April 1990, Akaka was a logical choice to fill the vacancy. Not only was he on good terms with Democratic Gov. John Waihee III, who made the appointment, he was also close to the leadership of the state Democratic Party and had received support throughout his career from Japanese-Americans, a crucial voting bloc.

However, with Akaka facing a special election in November 1990 to fill the remaining four years of Matsunaga's term, there was a degree of trepidation about his ability to hold the seat in the face of a challenge by 1st District GOP Rep. Patricia F. Saiki. Akaka had been a rather sedate figure during his House career and was not readily identifiable to many Hawaiians. But by playing to his strengths — his low-key personality and his ability to deliver federal largess to Hawaii — he won with a surprisingly solid 54 percent. In 2000, he improved upon that showing, beating his GOP foe by a 3-to-1 margin.

KEY VOTES

2000

- Yes Overhaul bankruptcy law and increase minimum wage
- No Limit fiscal 2001 discretionary spending to $600.3 billion
- No Override veto on nuclear waste disposal at Yucca Mountain site in Nevada
- Yes Oppose effort to terminate Kosovo mission
- Yes Include gender, sexual orientation and disability in federal hate crime protections
- No Approve GOP plan to restrict use of genetic information by health insurers
- No Kill amendment delaying implementation of an anti-missile defense system
- No Cut taxes for married couples
- ? Grant China permanent normal trade status

1999

- No Remove President Clinton from office for obstruction of justice
- No Kill amendment authorizing state grants to hire teachers and reduce class size
- Yes Require criminal background checks for purchases at gun shows
- No Approve GOP proposal to increase rights of patients in managed-care health plans
- No Block effort to allow farm and medicine exports to Cuba
- Yes Allow study of tougher automobile fuel efficiency standards
- Yes Ratify nuclear weapons testing treaty
- Yes Prohibit national political parties from collecting "soft money" donations
- Yes Remove barriers among banking, securities and insurance companies

INTEREST GROUPS

	AFL-CIO	ADA	CCUS	ACU
2000	86%	85%	46%	12%
1999	89%	100%	41%	4%
1998	100%	85%	41%	10%
1997	71%	95%	60%	4%
1996	100%	95%	31%	5%
1995	100%	95%	24%	0%
1994	88%	85%	20%	0%
1993	91%	90%	18%	4%
1992	92%	90%	20%	0%
1991	92%	90%	20%	5%

CQ VOTE STUDIES

	PARTY UNITY		PRESIDENTIAL SUPPORT	
	Support	Oppose	Support	Oppose
2000	98%	2%	97%	3%
1999	96%	4%	89%	11%
1998	96%	4%	91%	9%
1997	97%	3%	90%	10%
1996	95%	5%	88%	12%
1995	95%	5%	89%	11%
1994	94%	6%	97%	3%
1993	95%	5%	94%	6%
1992	92%	8%	30%	70%
1991	91%	9%	35%	65%

Rep. Neil Abercrombie (D)

CAPITOL OFFICE
225-2726; fax 225-4580
1502 Longworth Bldg. 20515

INTERNET
e-mail: neil.abercrombie@mail.house.gov
web: www.house.gov/abercrombie

COMMITTEES
Armed Services
Resources

HOMETOWN
Honolulu

BORN
June 26, 1938, Buffalo, N.Y.

RELIGION
Unspecified

FAMILY
Wife, Nancie Caraway

EDUCATION
Union College, B.A. 1959; U. of Hawaii, M.A. 1964,
Ph.D. 1974

CAREER
Educator

POLITICAL HIGHLIGHTS
Sought Democratic nomination for U.S. Senate,
1970; Hawaii House, 1974-78; Hawaii Senate, 1978-
86; U.S. House, 1986-87; defeated in primary for
re-election to U.S. House, 1986; Honolulu City
Council, 1988-90

ELECTION RESULTS

2000 GENERAL

Neil Abercrombie (D)	108,517	69.0%
Philip L. Meyers (R)	44,989	28.6%
Gerard Murphy (LIBERT)	3,688	2.4%

2000 PRIMARY

Neil Abercrombie (D)	72,289	84.6%
David L. Bourgoin (D)	13,115	15.4%

1998 GENERAL

Neil Abercrombie (D)	116,693	61.6%
Gene Ward (R)	68,905	36.3%
Nicholas Bedworth (NL)	3,973	2.1%

PREVIOUS WINNING PERCENTAGES
1996 (50%); 1994 (54%); 1992 (73%); 1990 (61%);
1986 Special Election (30%)

Elected 1990; 6th full term
Also served September 1986-January 1987

Abercrombie arrived in Congress as a long-haired former war protester backing liberal causes, but both his outward appearance and his politics have edged somewhat closer to congressional norms. He cut off his pony-tail in 1997, conceding that "it was getting in the way of getting the job done," and he has sided with conservatives on some issues, most notably cutting the unpopular estate tax and beefing up defense spending, particularly for Hawaii's military installations.

But Abercrombie still sports the long hair and bushy beard that call to mind his days as a Vietnam War opponent, and he is still a friendly, intense and burly fellow — he bench-pressed 260 pounds in the House gym on his 60th birth-day to set a Hawaii state record for his age group. And he is a proud member of the Progressive Caucus, the most liberal faction of House Democrats.

He greatly impressed a group of machinists visiting the capital from St. Louis in 2000. Filling in at the last minute for House Democratic Leader Richard A. Gephardt, Abercrombie delivered an impassioned tribute to the American worker. The St. Louis Post-Dispatch reported that "Abercrombie, a full-bearded Karl Marx look-alike ... launched into fire-and-brimstone remarks about American prosperity being forged by the sweat of workers, while Wall Street simply plays with the results."

The man who now represents sunny Waikiki got his start in a much cold-er clime. Abercrombie was born in Buffalo, went to Union College in Schenectady, N.Y., taught school for a time and then headed west — way west. He earned a master's degree at the University of Hawaii in 1964 and 10 years later added a doctorate in American studies. In between, Abercrombie became a veteran of protest politics in Hawaii's 1970 Democratic Senate primary, where he drew 13 percent of the vote as an anti-Vietnam War candidate. And in 1974, he won election to the state House.

In the 106th Congress, Abercrombie scored a legislative victory with the enactment of his legislation to recognize native Hawaiians as a distinct indigenous group with the right to self-determination. "This is the biggest thing that has ever happened to me in my legislative career," Abercrombie told the Gannett News Service.

A member of Armed Services, Abercrombie also successfully added pro-visions to a defense bill in 2000 to expand health benefits for military per-sonnel and retirees. The bill "acknowledges and upholds the obligation we have to provide quality health care" to those in the military, he said.

Abercrombie has become adept at steering money toward Hawaii's mil-itary installations. In 2000, he helped land more than $300 million for home state military projects, and he supported efforts for joint military-private development of Ford Island, which is in Pearl Harbor. In the 105th, he had a hand in shaping a military construction spending bill that included $226 million for Hawaii projects.

Even though he protested the Vietnam War, Abercrombie said his views on the military have not changed. "I never opposed the military," he told Gannett News Service in 2000. "It's not about pro-war or anti-war, but how do you keep the peace." He also said he takes a skeptical view toward spending on military projects except for those that benefit his district and improve the quality of life of personnel. He opposed military intervention in Bosnia and Kosovo, pleading for a greater focus on diplomatic efforts.

While Abercrombie has opposed funding some big-ticket defense items such as the B-2 stealth bomber and a space-based nationwide missile defense system, in 1996 he was one of 58 Democrats who voted against an attempt by liberals and budget-cutters to freeze military spending at the previous year's level.

Abercrombie has also steered an independent course on tax measures. He drew some attention by appearing with Republican lawmakers at a news conference in 2000 to urge passage of legislation abolishing the estate tax. Democrats generally opposed the measure, arguing that most of the benefits would go to the wealthy, but Abercrombie contended that family-owned small businesses in Hawaii would otherwise face heavy taxes when the owner died. When President Clinton vetoed the bill, Abercrombie broke party ranks and joined an unsuccessful attempt to override the veto.

Abercrombie also opposed the Clinton administration in 2000 by voting against granting China permanent normal trade status, partly for security reasons. "Some people want to push trade because they think it will make money, and they don't care about the consequences of doing business with a dictatorship," he said.

As a member of the Resources Committee, Abercrombie has a conventionally liberal record, favoring environmental and wildlife protections. Generally speaking, he is opposed to conservatives' views on land-use and resource-management issues. He also sides with liberals on social policy issues, favoring abortion rights and gun control. He voted against a landmark GOP-drafted overhaul of the welfare system in 1996 and opposed GOP efforts to limit legal and illegal immigrants' access to public benefits.

Abercrombie jumps into the fray when state interests are threatened. In the 105th, he led the charge against a plan by budget-cutters to reduce the federal price support on sugar by one cent per pound, a move that would have cost Hawaii sugar producers more than $7 million a year.

After 11 years in the state legislature, Abercrombie briefly served in the House when he won a special election in 1986 to fill the vacant 1st District seat. But he lost the primary, making him ineligible to run for a full term. He got a second chance when the seat opened up in 1990, winning the Democratic primary with 46 percent of the vote and cruising to an easy victory in the general election. But he faced difficult re-election battles in 1994 and 1996 and struggled to fend off charges that he was an extreme liberal.

Abercrombie can claim a literary byline as one of his accomplishments. In 1996, he co-wrote a mystery thriller called "Blood of Patriots." The book opens with a man and woman disguised as Capitol Hill staff members walking into the House during a vote, drawing Uzi submachine guns and killing 125 members of Congress, including the Republican Speaker.

KEY VOTES

2000

Yes	Raise hourly minimum wage by $1 over two years
No	Halt funding for U.S. mission in Kosovo unless European nations pay more
Yes	Provide Medicare benefits to military retirees and their dependents
No	Grant China permanent normal trade status
Yes	Phase out estate, gift and trust taxes
No	Prohibit implementation of president's national monument designations
No	Approve GOP plan to provide prescription drug coverage for Medicare beneficiaries
Yes	Increase help for poor nations indebted to international financial institutions

1999

Yes	Impose steel import quotas
No	Kill proposal to take aviation trust funds off budget
No	Require background checks on buyers only at gun shows with 10 or more vendors
No	Remove barriers among banking, securities and insurance companies
Yes	Authorize state grants to hire teachers and reduce class size
Yes	Overhaul campaign finance law; ban "soft money" and restrict advocacy advertising
Yes	Approve bipartisan plan to increase rights of patients in managed-care health plans

INTEREST GROUPS

	AFL-CIO	ADA	CCUS	ACU
2000	90%	80%	42%	12%
1999	100%	100%	17%	4%
1998	100%	95%	22%	12%
1997	100%	95%	30%	20%

CQ VOTE STUDIES

	PARTY UNITY		PRESIDENTIAL SUPPORT	
	Support	Oppose	Support	Oppose
2000	86%	14%	72%	28%
1999	89%	11%	71%	29%
1998	92%	8%	82%	18%
1997	87%	13%	73%	27%

HAWAII 1

Honolulu – Pearl City

Located on the southern coast of Oahu Island, the compact 1st takes in the narrow plain south of the Koolau mountain range, encompassing the tourist-rich city of Honolulu – the engine that drives all of Hawaii. But Pearl Harbor is the district's unforgettable trademark.

Honolulu is Hawaii's capital, home to most of its business and about one-third of its people. To the east lies Waikiki, heart of Hawaii's leading industry: tourism. But tourism suffered beginning in the mid-1990s as Asia's economic problems meant fewer Japanese visitors. Fortunately, the district's other major economic plank – the military – managed to escape major cuts and is expected to hold steady.

The 1st is a Democratic stronghold and has elected only one Republican to Congress in its history. Japanese-Americans dominate the Democratic Party and are joined by many other non-white constituents who form the majority of the 1st's residents. Locally, Democrats do very well in elections, although some moderate

Republican enclaves exist in the suburbs of East Honolulu and Waikiki. But even in traditionally Republican areas, longtime Democratic Rep. Abercrombie does not fail to muster support.

MAJOR INDUSTRY
Tourism, military, construction

MILITARY BASES
Hickam Air Force Base, 6,984 military, 2,889 civilian; Pearl Harbor Naval Shipyard and Intermediate Maintenance Facility, 610 military, 3,673 civilian; Camp H.M. Smith, 3,550 military, 463 civilian; Pearl Harbor Naval Submarine Base, 2,830 military, 63 civilian; Tripler Army Medical Center, 1,250 military, 1,250 civilian; Fort Shafter, 1,290 military, 700 civilian; Pearl Harbor Naval Station, 567 military, 440 civilian (2000)

CITIES
Honolulu, 395,327; Pearl City, 30,993 (1990); Waimalu, 29,967 (1990)

UNUSUAL FEATURES
Iolani Palace, located in Honolulu, believed to be the only palace in the United States.

Rep. Patsy T. Mink (D)

CAPITOL OFFICE
225-4906; fax 225-4987; 2210 Rayburn Bldg. 20515

INTERNET
e-mail: www.house.gov/writerep
web: www.house.gov/mink

COMMITTEES
Education & Workforce
Government Reform

HOMETOWN
Honolulu

BORN
Dec. 6, 1927, Paia, Maui, Hawaii

RELIGION
Protestant

FAMILY
Husband, John Francis Mink; one child

EDUCATION
U. of Hawaii, B.A. 1948; U. of Chicago, J.D. 1951

CAREER
Lawyer; State Department official

POLITICAL HIGHLIGHTS
Hawaii Territorial House, 1956-58; Hawaii Territorial Senate, 1959; Hawaii Senate, 1962-64; U.S. House, 1965-77; sought Democratic nomination for president, 1972; sought Democratic nomination for U.S. Senate, 1976; Honolulu City Council, 1983-87; sought Democratic nomination for governor, 1986; sought Democratic nomination for mayor of Honolulu, 1988

ELECTION RESULTS

2000 GENERAL

Patsy T. Mink (D)	112,856	61.6%
Russell R. Francis (R)	65,906	36.0%
Lawrence Duquesne (LIBERT)	4,468	2.4%

2000 PRIMARY

Patsy T. Mink (D)	66,255	86.1%
Charles "Lucky" Collins (D)	10,663	13.9%

1998 GENERAL

Patsy T. Mink (D)	144,254	69.4%
Carol J. Douglass (R)	50,423	24.3%
Noreen L. Chun (LIBERT)	13,194	6.3%

PREVIOUS WINNING PERCENTAGES
1996 (60%); 1994 (70%); 1992 (73%); 1990 (66%); 1990 Special Election (35%); 1974 (63%); 1972 (57%); 1970 (100%); 1964-68 (elected at large)

Elected September 1990; 12th full term
Also served 1965-77

Mink is one of only three House lawmakers still serving who were in Congress during the creation in the 1960s of President Johnson's "Great Society" social programs. Almost four decades later, even as political circumstances have changed, she is still an aggressive advocate of progressive politics and a staunch defender of those "big government" civil rights, anti-poverty, health and education programs.

Mink has a gold-plated liberal résumé. She is a member of the Progressive Caucus, a faction of left-leaning House Democrats. She is a past president of the liberal Americans for Democratic Action, and she has been on the board of Planned Parenthood of America and on the American Civil Liberties Union's national advisory panel.

With 22-plus years in the House, Mink has served longer than all but 18 other Democrats, most of whom are either in the party's elected leadership or hold top-ranking committee posts. But because of a lengthy break in her service, she had to start her seniority climb all over again when she returned to Capitol Hill in late 1990 after an absence of almost 14 years.

She sits on the Education and the Workforce and Government Reform committees, which fit well with Mink's interest in education. In the 106th Congress, she co-chaired the House Democrats' education task force.

She was the first non-Caucasian woman elected to Congress. She says she remembers well the roadblocks she faced as she set about getting an education and entering the work force. Mink majored in zoology and chemistry at the University of Hawaii, with the idea of going to medical school. But as a woman, that path was effectively closed to her, and she eventually earned a law degree from the University of Chicago. (Even there, she was one of only two women in a class of 180.)

When she returned to Hawaii looking for a job, she says she ran into men who believed women had no place in the work force. One "liberal white male said to me he didn't think I should work. He wanted me to stay home and take care of my baby," she told The Detroit News years later.

With that experience as a backdrop, Mink is a strong supporter of affirmative action programs such as Title IX, which prohibits sex discrimination in education funding and has required colleges and universities to provide equal funding for women's athletic programs. "In this century, there has not been a law that has had as much dramatic impact on opportunities in education as Title IX. ... That is why we have to be very vigilant" against moves to scale it back, she said in 1999.

True to her commitment to equal opportunity, Mink even protested the fact that Mattel Inc. did not produce an Asian-American version of a "Barbie for President 2000" doll. "It's just such an outrage. How are these girls supposed to buy Asian dolls if there are none to buy?" she complained to The Boston Globe. (Mink herself sought the Democratic presidential nomination in 1972.)

Another crusade for Mink is to retain funding for the Women's Educational Equity Act, which she authored in 1974 to authorize funds for programs to remedy past inequities between the education that girls and boys receive. A longtime defender of a federal role in education policy, Mink has more than once toted pie charts onto the House floor to rebut Republican claims that the Education Department is a wasteful enterprise of meddling bureaucrats and that federal money should be handed over to the states and localities to make their own education decisions without federal mandates.

Mink can be impatient with her staff and her floor speeches can get quite hot, particularly for Republican, and even Democratic, policies she deems unfair, intolerant or shortsighted. She was opposed to the welfare overhaul bill that the Republican Congress and President Clinton agreed to in 1996, and she has worked diligently to restore the welfare safety net. "Throwing people off welfare and forcing them to take the lowest-paying jobs in the community has created a misery index for millions," she told the Hawaii Tribune-Herald in 2000.

To protect a major cash crop and job provider in her state, Mink has steadfastly opposed conservatives' efforts to kill or cut crop subsidies for sugar cane and sugar beets. If the sugar subsidy program were discontinued, U.S. sugar producers would be driven out of business, she said in 1999, and that would put consumers at the mercy of foreign producers. Eventually, sugar prices would go up, she added.

Throughout her career, Mink has pressed for more funding for ovarian cancer research. Her interest in the issue was sparked by a constituent's battle with the disease. Mink has also had her own health scares. In 1994 testimony before the Senate Judiciary Committee, she spoke about having been given an experimental drug during pregnancy known as DES, which proved to be a carcinogen.

Mink first became active in politics when Hawaii was not yet a state. As a young lawyer, she held a number of local Democratic Party posts. In 1956, she won a seat in the Territorial House, and three years later she moved to the Territorial Senate. After Hawaii became a state, she won a 1962 election to the state Senate.

Mink was first elected to Congress in 1964 and established herself as a liberal activist. In 1976, she made a bid for the seat of retiring Republican Sen. Hiram L. Fong. Her Democratic primary rival, House colleague Spark M. Matsunaga, contrasted his image as a conciliator with Mink's more ideological bearing, and he won the election handily.

Mink served briefly as an assistant secretary of state in the Carter administration and then signed on with Americans for Democratic Action, serving as president from 1978 to 1981. She returned to electoral politics, but found the road bumpy: She won two terms on the Honolulu City Council but lost primary bids for governor in 1986 and for Honolulu mayor in 1988.

In 1990, Matsunaga died and Democratic Rep. Daniel K. Akaka (who had succeeded Mink in the House 14 years earlier) was appointed to fill the vacancy. Mink narrowly won a September 1990 special election to return to the House and has been re-elected with ease ever since.

KEY VOTES

2000
Yes Raise hourly minimum wage by $1 over two years
Yes Halt funding for U.S. mission in Kosovo unless European nations pay more
Yes Provide Medicare benefits to military retirees and their dependents
No Grant China permanent normal trade status
Yes Phase out estate, gift and trust taxes
No Prohibit implementation of president's national monument designations
No Approve GOP plan to provide prescription drug coverage for Medicare beneficiaries
Yes Increase help for poor nations indebted to international financial institutions

1999
Yes Impose steel import quotas
No Kill proposal to take aviation trust funds off budget
No Require background checks on buyers only at gun shows with 10 or more vendors
No Remove barriers among banking, securities and insurance companies
Yes Authorize state grants to hire teachers and reduce class size
No Overhaul campaign finance law; ban "soft money" and restrict advocacy advertising
Yes Approve bipartisan plan to increase rights of patients in managed-care health plans

INTEREST GROUPS

	AFL-CIO	ADA	CCUS	ACU
2000	90%	85%	52%	16%
1999	89%	95%	28%	8%
1998	100%	95%	22%	8%
1997	100%	100%	20%	12%

CQ VOTE STUDIES

	PARTY UNITY		PRESIDENTIAL SUPPORT	
	Support	Oppose	Support	Oppose
2000	89%	11%	67%	33%
1999	92%	8%	74%	26%
1998	95%	5%	85%	15%
1997	94%	6%	73%	27%

HAWAII 2
Suburban and Outer Oahu — 'Neighbor Islands'

Some visitors might call these Pacific islands paradise. With sandy beaches, volcanoes, tropical rain forests and deserts, the 2nd is an amazing array of geographic diversity. The district includes part of Oahu and all of the other seven islands that comprise the state. Although the 2nd has an Asian majority, it has a higher percentage of whites than the 1st.

The 2nd's economy struggled through rough times in the 1990s with both of its major industries, tourism and agriculture, in crisis. The Japanese yen's depreciation and Asia's economic woes translated into Asian visitors spending less in the latter part of the decade – a worrisome development in a state that welcomes about 30 percent of its tourists from Japan. A wave of 1990s sugar plantation closures also shook the economy, but efforts are being made to diversify by growing more coffee, macadamia nuts and bananas.

The 2nd is heavily Democratic, and while there are some

predominately white, conservative-leaning communities on Oahu and Maui, these areas barely make a dent. While some observers speculated that economic problems might give the GOP some local wins, the liberal 2nd has kept Democrats in office at all levels.

MAJOR INDUSTRY
Tourism, agriculture, military

MILITARY BASES
Schofield Barracks (Army), 12,005 military, 2,673 civilian (2000); Marine Corps Base Hawaii, 6,970 military, 1,650 civilian; Naval Computer and Telecommunications Area Master Station Pacific, 584 military, 224 civilian (1998); Lualualei Naval Magazine, 232 military, 403 civilian (2000)

CITIES
Hilo (unincorporated), 37,808 (1990); Kailua (unincorporated), 36,818 (1990); Kaneohe (unincorporated), 35,448 (1990)

UNUSUAL FEATURES
Waialeale, on Kauai, the wettest spot on earth, with an average of 300 inches of rain each year.

Gov. Dirk Kempthorne (R)

First elected: 1998
Length of term: 4 years
Term expires: 1/03
Salary: $98,500
Phone: (208) 334-2100
Hometown: Boise
Born: Oct. 29, 1951; San Diego, Calif.
Religion: Methodist
Family: Wife, Patricia Kempthorne; two children
Education: U. of Idaho, B.A. 1975
Career: Public affairs manager; securities representative; political consultant; building association executive
Political highlights: Mayor of Boise, 1986-92; U.S. Senate, 1993-99

Election results:

1998 GENERAL

Dirk Kempthorne (R)	258,095	67.7%
Robert C. Huntley (D)	110,815	29.1%
Patrick Rickards (I)	12,338	3.2%

Lt. Gov. Jack Riggs (R)

First elected: Succeeded C.L. "Butch" Otter, R, on Jan. 31, 2001
Length of term: 4 years
Term expires: 1/03
Salary: $26,000
Phone: (208) 334-2200

STATE LEGISLATURE

Bicameral Legislature: Meets January to March
House: 70 members, 2-year terms
2001 breakdown: 61R, 9D; 50 men, 20 women
Salary: $15,646, $1,700/year in expenses
Phone: (208) 332-1140
Senate: 35 members, 2-year terms
2001 breakdown: 32R, 3D; 28 men, 7 women
Salary: $15,646, $1,700/year in expenses
Phone: (208) 332-1309

STATE TERM LIMITS

Governor: 2 terms; can run again 8 years later
Senate: 4 terms in a 15-year period
House: 4 terms in a 15-year period

URBAN STATISTICS

CITY	POPULATION
Boise	168,370
Pocatello	52,781
Idaho Falls	48,627
Nampa	46,125
Twin Falls	34,316

REGISTERED VOTERS

Voters do not register by party.

POPULATION

2000 population	1,293,953
1990 population	1,006,749
Percent change	+28.5%
Rank among states	39

Median age	33.1
Born in state	51%
Foreign born	3%
Urban/rural	57%/43%
Crime rate	257/100,000
Poverty level	13%
Federal workers	12,728
Military	9,768

REAPPORTIONMENT

Idaho retained its two House seats in reapportionment. An independent commission will draw new district lines.

MISCELLANEOUS

Web: www.state.id.us
Capital: Boise
Land area: 82,751 sq. miles
Rank among states: 11
STATE ELECTION OFFICIAL
(208) 334-2300
DEMOCRATIC HEADQUARTERS
(208) 336-1815
REPUBLICAN HEADQUARTERS
(208) 343-6405

District Statistics

DIST.	D	2000 R	GREEN	D	1996 R	REF	D	1992 R	I	WHT	BLK	ASIAN	HISP	HOUSEHOLD INCOME	OVER 65+	UNDER 18	COLLEGE EDUCATION
					VOTE FOR PRESIDENT												
1	29%	67%	3%	35%	51%	13%	31%	42%	28%	95%	0%	1%	5%	$25,086	13%	29%	17%
2	27	68	2	33	53	13	27	45	28	94	0	1	6	$25,446	11	32	19
STATE	28	67	2	34	52	13	29	43	28	94	<1	1	5	$25,257	12	31	18

www.cq.com

Boundary

Bonner

Coeur d'Alene
●

Kootenai

Benewah   Shoshone

Moscow ● Latah

Clearwater

Nez Perce

Lewiston ●

Lewis

Idaho

1

Adams   Valley   Lemhi

Washington

Custer   Clark   Fremont

Payette

Gem   Boise   **2**

Jefferson Madison Teton

Canyon

Butte

★

Camas   Blaine   ● **Idaho Falls**

Boise

Ada   Elmore   Bingham   Bonneville

Gooding Lincoln

Jerome Minidoka   Power   Caribou

Owyhee   Bannock

●   Bear Lake

Twin Falls

Twin Falls   Cassia   Oneida   Franklin

Sen. Larry E. Craig (R)

Elected 1990; 2nd term

CAPITOL OFFICE
224-2752; fax 228-1067; 520 Hart Bldg. 20510

INTERNET
web: craig.senate.gov

COMMITTEES
Appropriations
Energy & Natural Resources
(Forests & Public Land Management -
chairman)
Veterans' Affairs
Special Aging - chairman

HOMETOWN
Payette

BORN
July 20, 1945, Council, Idaho

RELIGION
Methodist

FAMILY
Wife, Suzanne Craig; three children

EDUCATION
U. of Idaho, B.A. 1969; George Washington U.,
attended 1969-70

MILITARY SERVICE
Idaho National Guard, 1970-71

CAREER
Farmer; rancher

POLITICAL HIGHLIGHTS
Idaho Senate, 1975-81; U.S. House, 1981-91

ELECTION RESULTS

1996 GENERAL

Larry E. Craig (R)	283,532	57.0%
Walt Minnick (D)	198,422	39.9%
Mary J. Charbonneau (I)	10,137	2.0%
Susan Vegors (NL)	5,142	1.0%

1996 PRIMARY

Larry E. Craig (R)	unopposed

PREVIOUS WINNING PERCENTAGES
1990 (61%); 1988 House Election (66%); 1986 House
Election (65%); 1984 House Election (69%); 1982
House Election (54%); 1980 House Election (54%)

Through hard work, loyalty and an unwavering adherence to staunch conservative principles, Craig has risen to the fourth-ranking position in the GOP leadership, and he is a force for conservatives, who sometimes disagree with their leaders' course. Methodical, with flawless diction and a knack for unrehearsed debating, Craig is most passionate when defending the interests of gun owners, Western landowners and the mining and timber industries.

At the start of the 107th Congress, Craig nearly lost his post as Republican Policy Committee chairman to Pete V. Domenici of New Mexico, in a narrow vote that demonstrated the clout of the GOP moderates. With the 50-50 partisan split in the Senate, Craig and his conservative brethren must find a way to forge agreement on key issues with centrist Republicans. The new reality requires a change of operation for Craig, who has been among those helping steer Majority Leader Trent Lott on a rightward course.

Craig, who serves on the board of the National Rifle Association, stands as a sentinel guarding the rights of gun owners. In 1999, Lott handed him an enormous headache: gun control. In the wake of an April 20 massacre at Colorado's Columbine High School, Lott sped a juvenile justice bill to the floor, where it became a vehicle for gun control-related amendments. Craig was the GOP point man on the divisive issue of handgun sales at gun shows.

When Republicans initially defeated a Democratic amendment to require background checks for purchases at guns shows, Craig pushed through a less-restrictive proposal making such checks voluntary. The move was an attempt to provide Republicans political cover, but some GOP senators griped that Craig's proposal was sold as more stringent than in fact it was. In a blow to Craig's standing among his colleagues, the stricter Democratic proposal was ultimately approved, though the bill was never enacted. In the 107th, he will have even more trouble corralling support on issues he holds dear.

Craig has been in Washington 20 years, first as a House member and now in his second term in the Senate, but the passage of time has not tempered his staunch conservatism. He entered the House in 1981, in the first blush of the "Reagan revolution," and he helped move that chamber far enough to the right to pass President Reagan's tax and spending plans. A decade later Craig moved to the Senate, where he has helped pull the GOP membership to the right.

He relishes rhetorical skirmishes, especially when they involve the interests of Westerners affected by federal policies governing mining, timber and grazing operations on public lands. Throughout his career in the House and Senate, Craig has taken aim at environmental laws, most notably the Endangered Species Act, which he says trample on private property rights and inhibit job growth. In 1994, he told an Idaho audience: "Easterners should stop interfering with environmental issues. ... The only endangered species in New York City is probably a free white human being." (He later apologized for a "poor choice of words" after his comments created an uproar among New York political leaders.)

Craig joined the Appropriations Committee in 1997 and used the post, with limited success, to fight the Clinton administration's penchant for regulatory changes affecting public lands. In the 107th Congress, the Appropriations seat became more valuable to his state and region with the 2000 defeat of Northwest powerhouse Slade Gorton, R-Wash., an appropriator.

In the 106th, Craig scored a big win for his state by helping push to enactment a bill to compensate rural counties that had lost revenue because of decreased timber sales from public lands.

He had little sympathy for California's plight in 2001 as it struggled with electricity shortages. He urged Idaho's GOP Gov. Dirk Kempthorne, a former Senate colleague, to defy an Energy Department order to open Northwest dams to generate hydropower for California's use. Craig said he was concerned that the move might jeopardize Idaho's power-generating resources. The state gets about half its power from hydroelectric sources.

Craig's positions and tone reflect a considerable skepticism — bordering on contempt at times — for the work of some federal agencies. His undercurrent of distrust of the federal bureaucracy was evident during floor remarks in 1998 on a bill to overhaul the management of the Internal Revenue Service.

"There is a culture of big government, growing like a cancer on the body politic for two generations, that says the money you earn isn't yours, it's the government's; that says freedom isn't the individual's unalienable right, it's the government's to give or take away; that promises compassion and support, but demands control and dependence," Craig said. "It's becoming more like Big Brother and less like Uncle Sam."

Before the federal budget was balanced in 1997, Craig was perhaps the Senate's most active advocate of a constitutional amendment requiring a balanced budget. He was one of the first Republicans to call for such a change in the Constitution, even urging state legislatures to convene a constitutional convention to draft a balanced-budget amendment.

Craig enjoys a broad base of support from voters in a fairly homogeneous state where conservative politicians are warmly received. Idaho's small population also allows him to cement bonds with voters in person and to respond to constituent concerns rapidly.

Craig's early life seemed to point him toward politics. He was the national vice president of the Future Farmers of America and head of Idaho Young Republicans before running for the state Senate in 1974. In the legislature, he was known as something of a moderate.

But in his initial House campaign in 1980, he tied himself to Steve Symms, the district's conservative incumbent then campaigning for the Senate. After winning a tough primary, Craig was rated a solid favorite against Democrat Glenn W. Nichols. Craig outspent Nichols 3-to-1, but Nichols drew attention by walking the length of the district, from Canada to Nevada, and held Craig to 54 percent.

Craig's unspectacular showing in a strong Republican year guaranteed a tough challenge in 1982. Democrats chose Larry LaRocco, who had worked as northern Idaho field representative for Democratic Sen. Frank Church. But Craig won with 54 percent of the vote and hasn't faced a difficult campaign since. (In 1990, LaRocco succeeded Craig and held the 1st District for two terms.)

The retirement of GOP Sen. James A. McClure gave Craig an opportunity to advance to the Senate. He got into the 1990 race early and easily bested state Attorney General Jim Jones, winning 59 percent of the vote in the GOP primary. In the general election, Craig's popularity in the 1st District, coupled with support in the more conservative 2nd, propelled him past Democrat Ron Twilegar, a former state legislator and Boise City Council member, in a 61 percent to 39 percent victory.

In 1996, Craig's opponent was Walt Minnick, who ran as a Democrat but had strong GOP credentials. Minnick was a one-time White House aide to President Nixon and a former executive at a Boise lumber company. Democrats had a brief flurry of hope, but Craig returned home from Washington, campaigned vigorously and ended up winning easily, capturing 57 percent to Minnick's 40 percent.

KEY VOTES

2000
Yes	Overhaul bankruptcy law and increase minimum wage
Yes	Limit fiscal 2001 discretionary spending to $600.3 billion
Yes	Override veto on nuclear waste disposal at Yucca Mountain site in Nevada
No	Oppose effort to terminate Kosovo mission
No	Include gender, sexual orientation and disability in federal hate crime protections
Yes	Approve GOP plan to restrict use of genetic information by health insurers
Yes	Kill amendment delaying implementation of an anti-missile defense system
Yes	Cut taxes for married couples
Yes	Grant China permanent normal trade status

1999
Yes	Remove President Clinton from office for obstruction of justice
Yes	Kill amendment authorizing state grants to hire teachers and reduce class size
No	Require criminal background checks for purchases at gun shows
Yes	Approve GOP proposal to increase rights of patients in managed-care health plans
No	Block effort to allow farm and medicine exports to Cuba
No	Allow study of tougher automobile fuel efficiency standards
No	Ratify nuclear weapons testing treaty
No	Prohibit national political parties from collecting "soft money" donations
Yes	Remove barriers among banking, securities and insurance companies

INTEREST GROUPS

	AFL-CIO	ADA	CCUS	ACU
2000	0%	0%	93%	100%
1999	0%	0%	88%	96%
1998	0%	5%	100%	84%
1997	0%	5%	100%	84%
1996	0%	0%	100%	95%
1995	0%	0%	100%	96%
1994	13%	0%	80%	100%
1993	18%	5%	91%	100%
1992	17%	0%	90%	100%
1991	25%	5%	100%	86%

CQ VOTE STUDIES

	PARTY UNITY		PRESIDENTIAL SUPPORT	
	Support	Oppose	Support	Oppose
2000	100%	0%	40%	60%
1999	97%	3%	29%	71%
1998	99%	1%	29%	71%
1997	97%	3%	54%	46%
1996	98%	2%	32%	68%
1995	98%	2%	20%	80%
1994	98%	2%	30%	70%
1993	97%	3%	15%	85%
1992	99%	1%	85%	15%
1991	97%	3%	91%	9%

Sen. Michael D. Crapo (R)

Elected 1998; 1st term

In Washington, where the loudest voice often gets the most attention, Crapo is comfortable in the shadows. A devout Mormon who has dedicated much of his life's work to a deceased brother, Crapo needs little of the back-slapping ways of Washington to bolster his self-image.

His mild manner belies a persistent desire to climb the political ladder. Crapo's advancement, like his nature, has been steady. A cum laude graduate of Harvard Law School, Crapo (CRAY-poe) was elected to the Idaho state Senate at age 34 and chosen its president pro tempore four years later. He won the 2nd District's House seat four years after that and was tapped to be the freshman class representative in the councils of the GOP leadership. He breezed to victory for the open Senate seat six years later, in 1998. In the 107th Congress, he was named one of four GOP assistant whips.

Throughout his public life, Crapo has been guided by his desire to fulfill dreams his oldest brother Terry could not. An Idaho state legislator and wunderkind, Terry Crapo died just two weeks after he was diagnosed with leukemia in 1982. In a written response to an Idaho newspaper's question about the motivations of political candidates in 1996, Crapo said, "I began to reflect on how Terry might face this battle if the roles were reversed. I knew without a doubt that he would be in there fighting until the very last moment."

Crapo wrote that the death caused him to consider his goals in public life. He would later boil them down to two guiding principles: compassion and perseverance.

He faced his own trial with cancer in 2000, when doctors diagnosed prostate cancer and operated. He recovered quickly and made cancer prevention a topic in Idaho town hall meetings.

The guiding principles he developed through his family's trials were much in evidence when Crapo first came to Congress. Elected to the House just two years before his Republican Party won control, he aligned himself with a reformist GOP group known as the "Gang of Seven," which badgered the majority Democrats about the manner in which they ran the House. While Crapo was persistent in his criticism of Democrats, he was not as confrontational as others, playing an important although generally low-profile role in the "Republican revolution."

His good relationship with GOP leaders was evidenced by his House committee assignments. He got a seat on the powerful Energy and Commerce panel in his first term and was later awarded a second assignment — to the Resources Committee, which deals with a broad range of Western concerns: mining regulation, grazing fees, timber harvesting, water rights and the balance between property owners' rights and the federal effort to protect endangered species.

As a senator, Crapo is well-placed to continue his work on these issues. He assumed the seat of his predecessor — Republican Dirk Kempthorne, now Idaho's governor — on the Environment and Public Works Committee and chairs its Fisheries, Wildlife and Water Subcommittee. In the 107th, he added a seat on the Agriculture panel, where he chairs the Forestry Subcommittee, and a post on the Joint Economic Committee.

In 2000, Environment Committee Chairman Robert C. Smith, R-N.H., gave Crapo's subcommittee jurisdiction over plans to revamp the Clean Water Act, in addition to its oversight of the Endangered Species Act. The move gave Crapo more leverage with the Environmental Protection Agency, which often tangles with Idahoans and other Westerners over pro-

CAPITOL OFFICE
224-6142; fax 228-1375; 111 Russell Bldg. 20510

INTERNET
e-mail: crapo.senate.gov/~crapo/webform.html
web: crapo.senate.gov

COMMITTEES
Agriculture, Nutrition & Forestry
(Forestry, Conservation & Rural Revitalization - chairman)
Banking, Housing & Urban Affairs
Environment & Public Works
(Fisheries, Wildlife & Water - chairman)
Small Business
Joint Economic

HOMETOWN
Idaho Falls

BORN
May 20, 1951, Idaho Falls, Idaho

RELIGION
Mormon

FAMILY
Wife, Susan Crapo; five children

EDUCATION
Brigham Young U., B.A. 1973; Harvard U., J.D. 1977

CAREER
Lawyer

POLITICAL HIGHLIGHTS
Idaho Senate, 1985-93 (president pro tempore, 1989-93); U.S. House, 1993-99

ELECTION RESULTS

1998 GENERAL

Michael D. Crapo (R)	262,966	69.5%
Bill Mauk (D)	107,375	28.4%
George J. Mansfeld (NL)	7,833	2.1%

1998 PRIMARY

Michael D. Crapo (R)	110,205	87.3%
Matt Alan Lambert (R)	16,075	12.7%

PREVIOUS WINNING PERCENTAGES
1996 House Election (69%); 1994 House Election (75%); 1992 House Election (61%)

tection of land, water and animals.

While Crapo often has been on the other side of EPA administrators on issues such as listing the Canada Lynx as a threatened species and reintroducing wolves into Central Idaho, he has been willing to sit down and talk with agency leaders one-on-one. His efforts seemed to be paying at least small dividends. Under pressure from Crapo and other Idaho officials, the EPA said it would rethink a controversial cleanup plan for a mining waste site in the state and would remove Idaho from a list that, under the Clean Water Act, limited the state's ability to pursue some waterway plans.

Crapo said his efforts in overseeing the EPA's implementation of the Clean Water Act would focus on "giving local and regional voices a place at the table." He introduced legislation to help small communities comply with federal, state and local environmental regulations.

On environmental issues and most others, Crapo is a vote GOP leaders can count on, although in the House he bucked his party's majority on trade issues by opposing legislation to implement both the 1993 North American Free Trade Agreement and the 1994 General Agreement on Tariffs and Trade. In the Senate, he mitigated that position by supporting the permanent normalization of trade relations with China in 2000 — in large part because that could greatly benefit wheat growers, cattle ranchers and other Idaho farmers. He attended the protest-plagued 1999 World Trade Organization meeting in Seattle to ensure that farmers were not given short shrift in trade negotiations.

The senator often seems unlike those in his party who view political opposites as enemies. He worked with Oregon Democrat Ron Wyden in attempting to re-establish an Amtrak route between Boise and Portland. And several education measures he introduced were endorsed by the National Education Association, often at odds with the GOP. The bills aim to improve rural education, technology and teacher training and to increase federal Impact Aid rates for children of military workers who live off-base.

Crapo announced in 2000 that his website would be the first among those of Idaho lawmakers to have text in both English and Spanish —to give Idaho's "growing Hispanic population" better access to Congress.

Crapo has served in high-level positions in his church. He is a devout Mormon and the father of a Mormon missionary. Still, in 2000 he spurned the entreaties of Democratic Whip Harry Reid of Nevada, also a Mormon, to support a controversial nominee of President Clinton's for the U.S. Court of Appeals for the 9th Circuit, which covers Idaho and other Western states. Although three other Republican Mormons voted for the liberal Richard A. Paez, who is also a Mormon, Crapo did not.

The son of an Idaho Falls postmaster and his homemaker wife, Crapo practiced law before and during his tenure in the Idaho Legislature. In 1992, he ran for the 2nd District seat being vacated by Democrat Richard Stallings, who was running for the Senate. In the GOP-leaning 2nd, Crapo was aided by George Bush's top-of-the-ticket presence as the GOP presidential candidate, and he defeated Democrat J.D. Williams by 26 points.

Crapo never had a difficult time winning re-election, and when GOP Sen. Dick Kempthorne retired in 1998, Crapo became the ordained frontrunner. Following a relatively effortless primary, he faced a similarly smooth general election. He campaigned on traditional GOP issues, including overhauling the tax code, scaling back the federal government and paying off the national debt. His Democratic opponent, Bill Mauk, a lawyer and former state Democratic chairman, could counter neither the state's Republican tide nor Crapo's general popularity.

Friends and colleagues would not be surprised if Crapo returns to Idaho to seek the governorship.

KEY VOTES

2000
Yes Overhaul bankruptcy law and increase minimum wage
Yes Limit fiscal 2001 discretionary spending to $600.3 billion
Yes Override veto on nuclear waste disposal at Yucca Mountain site in Nevada
No   Oppose effort to terminate Kosovo mission
No   Include gender, sexual orientation and disability in federal hate crime protections
Yes Approve GOP plan to restrict use of genetic information by health insurers
Yes Kill amendment delaying implementation of an anti-missile defense system
Yes Cut taxes for married couples
Yes Grant China permanent normal trade status

1999
Yes Remove President Clinton from office for obstruction of justice
Yes Kill amendment authorizing state grants to hire teachers and reduce class size
No   Require criminal background checks for purchases at gun shows
Yes Approve GOP proposal to increase rights of patients in managed-care health plans
No   Block effort to allow farm and medicine exports to Cuba
No   Allow study of tougher automobile fuel efficiency standards
No   Ratify nuclear weapons testing treaty
No   Prohibit national political parties from collecting "soft money" donations
Yes Remove barriers among banking, securities and insurance companies

INTEREST GROUPS

	AFL-CIO	ADA	CCUS	ACU
2000	0%	0%	93%	100%
1999	0%	0%	88%	100%
House Service:				
1998	22%	10%	94%	83%
1997	13%	0%	70%	92%
1996	0%	0%	100%	95%
1995	0%	5%	100%	92%
1994	11%	5%	83%	90%
1993	8%	5%	91%	96%

CQ VOTE STUDIES

	PARTY UNITY		PRESIDENTIAL SUPPORT	
	Support	Oppose	Support	Oppose
2000	100%	0%	41%	59%
1999	97%	3%	30%	70%
House Service:				
1998	89%	11%	30%	70%
1997	94%	6%	20%	80%
1996	95%	5%	30%	70%
1995	97%	3%	21%	79%
1994	96%	4%	40%	60%
1993	96%	4%	33%	67%

Rep. C. L. 'Butch' Otter (R)

Elected 2000; 1st term

Idaho's lieutenant governor for 14 years before his 2000 House election victory, Otter is one of the more seasoned freshmen in the 107th Congress.

He came to Washington as an advocate for a limited federal role on almost all issues. While he may stand out as one of the most conservative House newcomers, his views are in line with many residents of Idaho — which has a claim to a distinction as the nation's most Republican-dominated state.

Otter is unlikely to stray far from the voting record of his outspoken predecessor, retired GOP Rep. Helen Chenoweth-Hage. Otter's assignment to the Resources Committee, on which Chenoweth-Hage had served, enables him to pursue his interest in scaling back environmental regulations on businesses and private landowners.

Much of Idaho's land is under federal control; like many Western lawmakers, Otter is an ardent advocate of private property rights and state management of federal lands.

Otter also believes in reducing the federal government's role in education. He favors block grants to the states "with no strings attached" and supports federally funded school vouchers for private school education.

Social Security is an area in which Otter believes government involvement is warranted, but he supports allowing individuals to invest part of their payroll tax money.

Otter's advocacy of government at the most local level possible caused a flap during his 2000 House primary, when he had to defend a "no" vote he cast as a state House member in 1976 on a measure to set state standards for pornography. An out-of-state group aired an ad contending that Otter was soft on pornography, and his GOP rivals sought to use that vote against him. Otter, however, argued that he voted against the bill because he believes decisions on such standards should be left to local communities.

A millionaire businessman and rancher, Otter's biggest House race hurdle came in the 2000 GOP primary: He had to overcome seven competitors, and his primary victory made his November election over Democrat Linda Pall almost a given.

CAPITOL OFFICE
225-6611; fax 225-3029
1711 Longworth Bldg. 20515

INTERNET
e-mail: www.house.gov/otter/email.htm
web: www.house.gov/otter

COMMITTEES
Government Reform
Resources
Transportation & Infrastructure

HOMETOWN
Star

BORN
May 3, 1942, Caldwell, Idaho

RELIGION
Roman Catholic

FAMILY
Divorced; four children

EDUCATION
College of Idaho, B.A. 1967

MILITARY SERVICE
Idaho National Guard, 1967-73

CAREER
Agribusiness company executive; oil company partner

POLITICAL HIGHLIGHTS
Idaho House, 1973-77; lieutenant governor, 1987-2001

ELECTION RESULTS

2000 GENERAL

C. L. "Butch" Otter (R)	173,743	64.8%
Linda Pall (D)	84,080	31.4%
Ronald G. Wittig (LIBERT)	6,093	2.3%
Kevin Philip Hambsch (REF)	4,200	1.6%

2000 PRIMARY

C. L. "Butch" Otter (R)	41,516	47.6%
Dennis Mansfield (R)	23,559	27.0%
Ron McMurray (R)	14,434	16.6%
Craig Benjamin (R)	2,966	3.4%
Jim A. "Big Jim" Pratt (R)	1,281	1.5%
Gene Summa (R)	1,240	1.4%
David W. Shepherd (R)	1,181	1.4%
Harley D. Brown (R)	983	1.1%

IDAHO 1

West – Boise; Nampa; Panhandle

Stretching the 500-mile length of western Idaho, from British Columbia in the north to Nevada in the south, the 1st is mostly rural, punctuated by urban pockets. White-collar workers in Idaho's state capital, Boise (shared with the 2nd), combine with agricultural voters to give it a GOP base.

Boise and its surroundings, home to the headquarters of many lumber, paper, food processing, electronics and construction companies, contain about 20 percent of the district's population. A long history of timber and metal mining make voters in the panhandle and around Coeur d'Alene the strongest Democratic bloc, but they are too few to sway the district.

The 1st's midsize cities have attracted new high-tech businesses, such as Hewlett-Packard, and created new white-collar jobs. In the 1990s, employment in high-tech businesses increased about 70 percent. The district's small towns have not fared as well, suffering ups and downs in their agriculture, timber and mining industries.

The 1st spent a four-year hiatus in the Democratic camp, but returned to its traditional Republican ways in 1994. Republicans now dominate the district. Only three counties – Latah, Shoshone and Nez Perce – supported Bill Clinton in his two elections. President Bush fared even better in 2000, winning all of the counties in the 1st.

MAJOR INDUSTRY
Manufacturing, agriculture, tourism

CITIES
Boise City (pt.), 61,564 (1990); Nampa, 46,125; Coeur d'Alene, 33,659; Lewiston, 30,597

UNUSUAL FEATURES
Sunshine Mine Memorial, site of the 1972 Sunshine Mine fire that killed 91 miners.

Rep. Mike Simpson (R)

Elected 1998; 2nd term

CAPITOL OFFICE
225-5531; fax 225-8216
1440 Longworth Bldg. 20515

INTERNET
e-mail: www.house.gov/writerep
web: www.house.gov/simpson

COMMITTEES
Agriculture
Resources
Transportation & Infrastructure
Veterans' Affairs

HOMETOWN
Blackfoot

BORN
Sept. 8, 1950, Burley, Idaho

RELIGION
Mormon

FAMILY
Wife, Kathy Simpson

EDUCATION
Utah State U., attended 1968-72; Washington U. (Mo.), D.D.S. 1977

CAREER
Dentist

POLITICAL HIGHLIGHTS
Blackfoot City Council, 1980-84; Idaho House, 1985-99 (Speaker, 1993-99)

ELECTION RESULTS

2000 GENERAL

Mike Simpson (R)	158,912	70.7%
Craig Williams (D)	58,265	25.9%
Donovan Bramwell (LIBERT)	7,542	3.4%

2000 PRIMARY

Mike Simpson (R)	unopposed

1998 GENERAL

Mike Simpson (R)	91,337	52.5%
Richard Stallings (D)	77,736	44.7%
Jonathan B. Ratner (NL)	4,854	2.8%

A conservative, small-town dentist elected in 1998, Simpson set out to meet every one of his 434 House colleagues during his first term — he estimates he came up short, at around 350 — and says he has liked every member he has met, even liberal Democrats with whom he disagrees on most policy issues.

"A legislative body functions on relationships," Simpson says. "You may have the best idea in the world, but if you can't convince 218 people to agree with you, you're out of luck," he told the Boise Idaho Statesman soon after he arrived on Capitol Hill. He says he set up appointments to visit his colleagues in their offices and to chat for a while about personal matters, not legislation. Simpson says that two rules he brought with him to Congress, after serving in the Idaho state House for 14 years, are "hear both sides before judging" and "never, never make an enemy needlessly."

Simpson has followed the same philosophy back home, briefly joining the American Civil Liberties Union (ACLU) and the Idaho Conservation League (ICL) and regularly attending meetings with environmental groups with whom he often disagrees. "I agree with the ACLU on some things, and a lot of things I disagree with them on. But I'm glad they're there, just like I'm glad the ICL is there, just like I'm glad the NRA (National Rifle Association) is there," he told the Boise newspaper. "Somebody needs to represent those points of view."

In Washington, Simpson says he represents the views of rural Western lawmakers, whose perspectives on water and land-use issues are often misunderstood by Easterners. He says that Westerners "must resist the temptation to turn local decision-making power over to the federal government in return for assistance in funding."

Simpson received appropriate committee assignments from which to raise those issues — Resources and Agriculture. He takes his committee work seriously, spending hours listening to witnesses during legislative hearings. He also was given seats on the Transportation and Veterans' Affairs panels, giving him one of the heaviest committee workloads in the House. And he was a finalist for an appointment on the Appropriations panel in the 107th Congress, losing out to Donald L. Sherwood of Pennsylvania.

In the 106th, Simpson won enactment of a bill to increase funding for southern Idaho's Minidoka Water Project and another measure to expand the City of Rocks National Reserve. He opposes breaching the four Snake River dams as a method of restoring the region's salmon population, but he was able to win $40 million for other resource restoration efforts in Idaho.

He also proposed legislation to reintroduce the eastern timber wolf into New York's Catskill Mountains. Some members viewed the measure as a tit-for-tat in response to the release of Canadian wolves in Idaho, but Simpson insists that he is serious about applying the Endangered Species Act nationwide and is willing to work with Eastern environmentalists to make the plan work.

A co-chairman of a bipartisan congressional caucus to advance the interests of farmers and ranchers in World Trade Organization (WTO) negotiations, Simpson attended WTO talks in Seattle in 1999. He watches out for his district's sugar beet growers, who are concerned about subsidized competition from abroad. Simpson also favors expanded trade ties with China, which is a promising market for Northwest wheat sales.

Simpson casts conservative votes on most issues, but he broke ranks with most Republicans in supporting mandatory trigger locks for guns. He also was critical of GOP leaders for not negotiating more seriously with President Clinton on a number of tax proposals.

Upon his arrival in Washington, Simpson had intended to work for free in inner-city dental clinics, but he found that licensing requirements made that too complicated. He also discovered that he didn't have time to see patients during his visits back home, so he reluctantly sold his share of the dental practice. Simpson's wife is employed as a public affairs officer with Lockheed Martin, which oversees operations at the Idaho National Engineering and Environmental Laboratory, a part of the Energy Department's nuclear weapons complex.

Simpson grew up in the eastern Idaho town of Blackfoot, where his father and uncle had a dental practice. He met his wife in high school, and they both attended Utah State University. He attended dental school at Washington University in St. Louis.

Simpson returned to Blackfoot to join the family dental practice and soon became involved in local politics, winning election to the city council, a non-partisan post. He says that his interest in politics was first sparked by a high school teacher, who was a staunch Democrat.

After four years on the city council, a seat in the state legislature opened up, and he finally had to choose a party affiliation. "I had never been active in the party, but I figured I was a Republican," he told the Idaho Statesman.

Simpson started out with a reputation as an occasionally angry maverick, but he mellowed and made a name for himself in Boise, rising through the ranks and serving as Speaker of the House during his last six years there.

He had given some thought to running for governor, but Republican Sen. Dirk Kempthorne ran for the job in 1998. Second District GOP Rep. Michael D. Crapo decided to run for Kempthorne's Senate seat, opening up Crapo's House seat. Simpson entered the race, winning a hard-fought four-way GOP primary in which he faced some criticism from social conservatives about whether he was ardent enough on their issues.

During the campaign, Simpson was more worried about voters learning of his recent memberships in the ACLU and the ICL than the fact that he had smoked marijuana in college 30 years before. And he made no effort to hide the fact that he is a lapsed Mormon who once smoked and still drinks occasionally. But these revelations seemed to have little effect on the heavily Mormon, but also heavily GOP, electorate. He went on to defeat conservative Democrat Richard Stallings, who had held the seat from 1985 to 1993, by 8 percentage points. A run for governor may be still be in Simpson's future.

KEY VOTES

2000

No Raise hourly minimum wage by $1 over two years

Yes Halt funding for U.S. mission in Kosovo unless European nations pay more

Yes Provide Medicare benefits to military retirees and their dependents

Yes Grant China permanent normal trade status

Yes Phase out estate, gift and trust taxes

Yes Prohibit implementation of president's national monument designations

Yes Approve GOP plan to provide prescription drug coverage for Medicare beneficiaries

No Increase help for poor nations indebted to international financial institutions

1999

No Impose steel import quotas

No Kill proposal to take aviation trust funds off budget

Yes Require background checks on buyers only at gun shows with 10 or more vendors

Yes Remove barriers among banking, securities and insurance companies

No Authorize state grants to hire teachers and reduce class size

No Overhaul campaign finance law; ban "soft money" and restrict advocacy advertising

No Approve bipartisan plan to increase rights of patients in managed-care health plans

INTEREST GROUPS

	AFL-CIO	ADA	CCUS	ACU
2000	0%	0%	90%	88%
1999	11%	10%	100%	84%

CQ VOTE STUDIES

	PARTY UNITY		PRESIDENTIAL SUPPORT	
	Support	Oppose	Support	Oppose
2000	94%	6%	29%	71%
1999	91%	9%	24%	76%

IDAHO 2

East – Pocatello; Idaho Falls; Twin Falls

Covering the eastern half of Idaho, the 2nd includes part of Boise, a few midsize towns and a vast swath of agricultural land irrigated by the Snake River. On the western side of the district, in Elmore County, is the Mountain Home Air Force Base. But most of the district subsists on agriculture, with potatoes, sugar beets and grain as the major products.

The 2nd's manufacturing economy revolves around food processing (including Ore-Ida's frozen french fries). But farms are faring poorly. To replace crops that have declining market value, farmers have expanded into dairy and cheese processing, especially in Twin Falls and Jerome counties.

Tourism is the district's third-leading industry. With natural wonders like Shoshone Falls and ski resorts like Sun Valley, the 2nd attracts a steady stream of vacationers.

Politically, the district consistently votes Republican on the state and national level. Members of the Church of Jesus Christ of Latter-Day Saints make up the largest religious group; like most Mormon areas, the district is strongly conservative. Since 1992, only Blaine County, with its resorts, has voted Democratic in presidential elections.

MAJOR INDUSTRY
Agriculture, food processing, tourism

MILITARY BASES
Mountain Home Air Force Base, 4,464 military, 425 civilian; Boise Air Terminal Air Guard Station, 1,253 military, 149 civilian (1999)

CITIES
Boise (pt.), 64,174 (1990); Pocatello, 52,781; Idaho Falls, 48,627; Twin Falls, 34,316

UNUSUAL FEATURES
Nearly 85 percent of all commercial trout sold in the United States are produced in the Hagerman Valley near Twin Falls; Sun Valley, America's first ski resort.

Gov. George Ryan (R)

First elected: 1998
Length of term: 4 years
Term expires: 1/03
Salary: $145,877
Phone: (217) 782-0244
Hometown: Kankakee
Born: Feb. 24, 1934; Manquoketa, Iowa
Religion: Methodist
Family: Wife, Lura Lynn Ryan; six children
Education: Butler U., attended 1952-54; Ferris State College, B.S. 1961
Military service: Army, 1954-56
Career: Pharmacist; pharmacy owner
Political highlights: Kankakee County Board, 1966-72; Ill. House, 1973-83 (Republican leader, 1977-81; Speaker, 1981-83); lieutenant governor, 1983-91; Ill. secretary of state, 1991-99

Election results:
1998 GENERAL

George Ryan (R)	1,714,094	51.0%
Glenn Poshard (D)	1,594,191	47.5%
Lawrence Redmond (REF)	50,372	1.5%

Lt. Gov. Corrine Wood (R)

First elected: 1998
Length of term: 4 years
Term expires: 1/03
Salary: $111,554
Phone: (217) 782-7884

STATE LEGISLATURE

General Assembly: Meets January to June
House: 118 members, 2-year terms
2001 breakdown: 56R, 62D; 83 men, 35 women
Salary: $55,778
Phone: (217) 782-8223
Senate: 59 members, rotates between 2 and 4-year terms
2001 breakdown: 32R, 27D; 47 men, 12 women
Salary: $55,778
Phone: (217) 782-5715

STATE TERM LIMITS

Governor: No
Senate: No
House: No

URBAN STATISTICS

CITY	POPULATION
Chicago	2,799,050
Rockford	143,831
Aurora	129,371
Naperville	122,993
Springfield	117,876

REGISTERED VOTERS

Voters do not register by party.

POPULATION

2000 population	12,419,293
1990 population	11,430,602
Percent change	+8.6%
Rank among states	5

Median age	34.6
Born in state	69%
Foreign born	8%
Urban/rural	85%/15%
Crime rate	861/100,000
Poverty level	10.1%
Federal workers	95,718
Military	58,239

REAPPORTIONMENT

Illinois lost one House seat in reapportionment, dropping from 20 districts to 19. The state legislature will draw new district lines in 2001.

MISCELLANEOUS

Web: www.state.il.us
Capital: Springfield
Land area: 55,593 sq. miles
 Rank among states: 24
STATE ELECTION OFFICIAL
(217) 782-4141
DEMOCRATIC HEADQUARTERS
(217) 528-3471
REPUBLICAN HEADQUARTERS
(217) 525-0011

District Statistics

	VOTE FOR PRESIDENT																	
	2000			1996			1992							HOUSEHOLD	OVER	UNDER	COLLEGE
DIST.	D	R	GREEN	D	R	REF	D	R	I	WHT	BLK	ASIAN	HISP	INCOME	65+	18	EDUCATION
1	87%	11%	1%	85%	11%	3%	81%	12%	7%	27%	70%	1%	4%	$24,140	14%	27%	18%
2	88	11	1	85	11	3	80	13	7	27	68	1	6	$30,217	10	30	13
3	55	41	3	53	37	9	41	39	20	93	2	1	7	$36,250	16	23	16
4	78	18	4	80	14	5	65	23	12	49	6	3	64	$23,083	8	33	8
5	63	33	3	63	30	7	51	33	16	87	1	6	13	$33,262	15	18	26
6	45	52	2	43	48	9	33	47	20	92	1	5	5	$44,216	12	23	29
7	83	15	2	82	14	3	78	15	7	29	66	3	4	$25,220	10	29	21
8	42	55	2	41	50	9	31	48	22	92	2	4	5	$47,374	7	26	30
9	70	26	3	69	26	5	61	27	12	73	12	10	9	$32,183	16	18	37
10	53	45	2	50	43	6	41	43	16	87	6	4	7	$50,355	10	26	40
11	53	45	2	51	38	11	44	36	20	87	8	1	6	$33,632	13	27	13
12	55	42	2	56	34	9	54	29	17	82	17	1	1	$25,032	14	26	14
13	42	55	2	41	50	9	32	47	21	92	3	4	3	$50,087	8	28	35
14	42	55	2	41	48	10	34	44	22	89	4	2	10	$39,815	9	29	23
15	44	52	3	46	45	9	43	39	19	90	7	2	1	$26,760	13	24	21

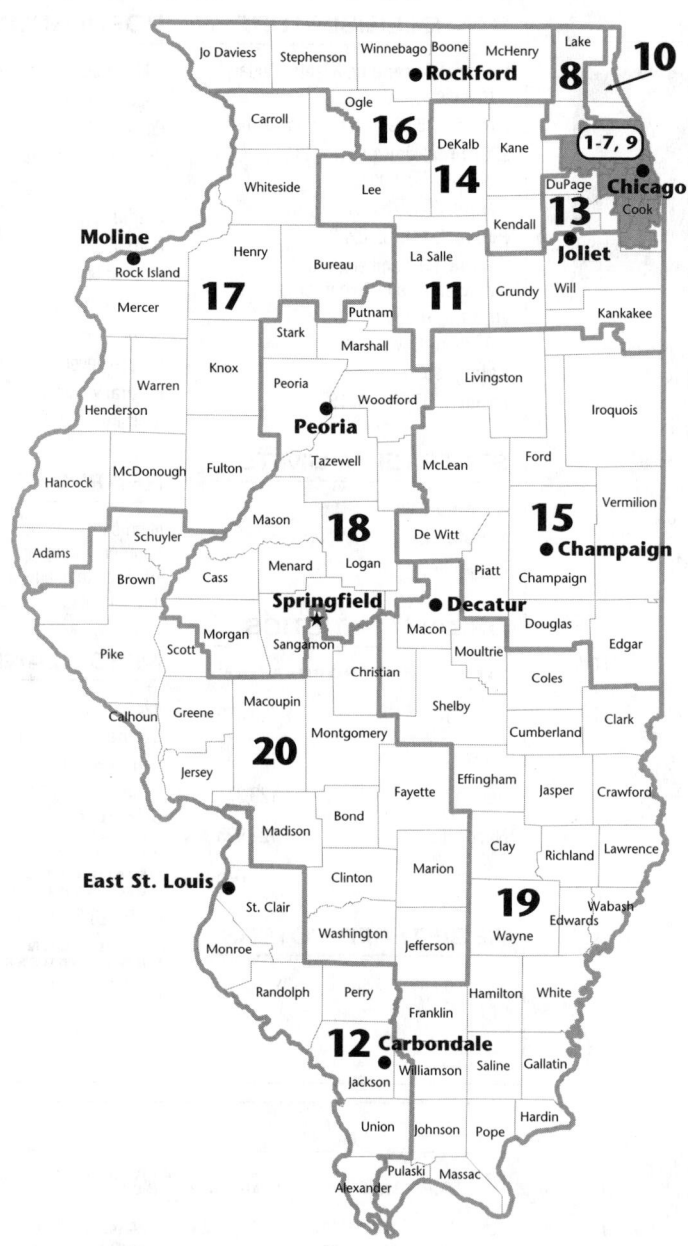

District Statistics

DIST.	VOTE FOR PRESIDENT									WHT	BLK	ASIAN	HISP	HOUSEHOLD INCOME	OVER 65+	UNDER 18	COLLEGE EDUCATION
	D	2000 R	GREEN	D	1996 R	REF	D	1992 R	I								
16	43%	54%	2%	42%	47%	10%	37%	42%	22%	93%	5%	1%	3%	$34,668	12%	27%	17%
17	51	46	2	51	38	10	47	36	17	95	3	1	3	$25,195	17	25	13
18	43	55	2	44	47	8	42	41	17	94	5	1	1	$30,189	14	26	17
19	43	54	2	47	41	12	47	34	18	96	4	0	0	$22,979	17	25	11
20	45	52	2	48	41	11	46	34	20	95	4	0	1	$26,173	16	26	13
STATE	55	43	2	54	37	8	49	34	17	78	15	2	8	$32,252	13	26	21

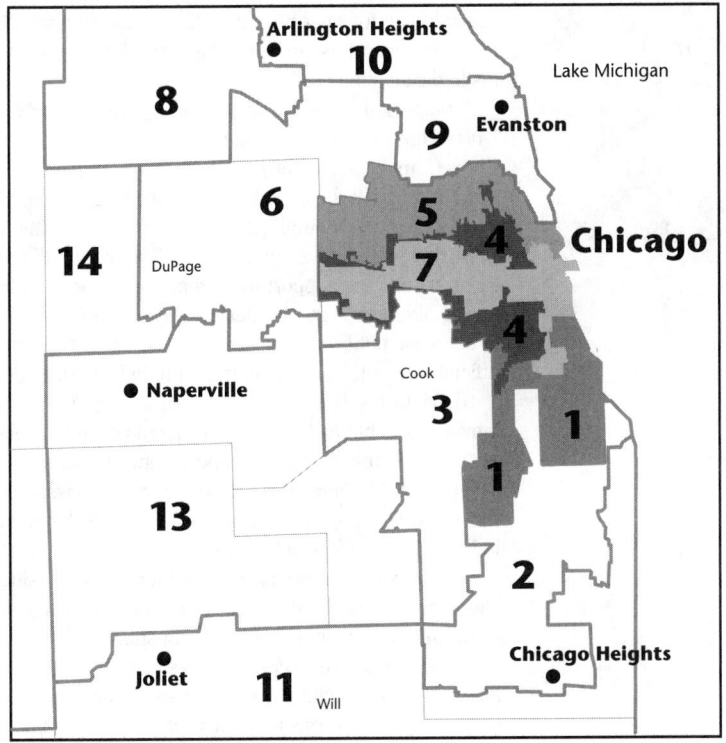

Sen. Richard J. Durbin (D)

Elected 1996; 1st term

CAPITOL OFFICE
224-2152; fax 228-0400; 332 Dirksen Bldg. 20510

INTERNET
e-mail: dick@durbin.senate.gov
web: durbin.senate.gov

COMMITTEES
Appropriations
Governmental Affairs
Judiciary
Select Intelligence

HOMETOWN
Springfield

BORN
Nov. 21, 1944, East St. Louis, Ill.

RELIGION
Roman Catholic

FAMILY
Wife, Loretta Schaefer Durbin; three children

EDUCATION
Georgetown U., B.S.F.S. 1966, J.D. 1969

CAREER
Lawyer; congressional and legislative aide

POLITICAL HIGHLIGHTS
Democratic nominee for Ill. Senate, 1976;
Democratic nominee for lieutenant governor, 1978;
U.S. House, 1983-97

ELECTION RESULTS

1996 GENERAL

Richard J. Durbin (D)	2,384,028	56.1%
Al Salvi (R)	1,728,824	40.7%
Steven H. Perry (REF)	61,023	1.4%

1996 PRIMARY

Richard J. Durbin (D)	512,520	64.9%
Pat Quinn (D)	233,138	29.5%
Ronald F. Gibbs (D)	17,681	2.2%
J. Ahmad (D)	17,211	2.2%
Paul Park (D)	9,505	1.2%

PREVIOUS WINNING PERCENTAGES
1994 House Election (55%); 1992 House Election (57%); 1990 House Election (66%); 1988 House Election (69%); 1986 House Election (68%); 1984 House Election (61%); 1982 House Election (50%)

An eloquent speaker at ease in the oratorical arena of the Senate, Durbin is emerging as a rising Democratic star. He gained national attention in 2000 when Democratic presidential nominee Al Gore considered him as a running mate, and he is the focus of considerable speculation in Illinois over a possible run for governor in 2002. But Durbin, who is a leading voice on issues as diverse as gun control and smoking restrictions, insists he enjoys his legislative duties.

A respected House appropriator before he won a Senate seat in 1996, Durbin has gotten plum assignments in the Senate: a seat on the Appropriations Committee and the position of assistant floor leader for the Democrats. Although he has struggled to pass major legislation, he has made his presence felt on issues ranging from bankruptcy to aviation safety.

Durbin's legislative skills — he was once the Illinois Senate parliamentarian — and his support for anti-poverty programs have given a boost to Senate liberals. An acerbic debater, he belittled a Republican attempt in 2000 to decrease public lands protection, saying, "The party of Teddy Roosevelt officially abandons its commitment to his environmental legacy."

His victories, however, have been limited under the GOP majority. He introduced a bill in 1999 to hold parents criminally liable if their children got hold of guns stored improperly, but the Senate took no action. When a 6-year-old Michigan girl was killed by her classmate in 2000, he said: "If the gun that was used ... was stored safely, perhaps that beautiful little girl in Michigan would still be alive."

Durbin, who has pressed for tighter gun laws since 1991, helped lead Democrats in the 106th Congress on other gun control measures, such as requiring background checks at gun shows.

The Illinoisan has become increasingly supportive of abortion rights during his career, switching from an anti-abortion stance to eventually back public funding of abortions for poor women. In the 106th, he tried to forestall a conservative attempt to ban a procedure its opponents call "partial birth" abortion by introducing an alternative proposal that would have allowed the procedure if two independent doctors certified it was necessary to protect a woman's health. Arguing that it would be wrong for the Senate to substitute its judgment for that of the medical community, he said: "I am not a doctor and I'm not going to play one in the Senate." But his measure failed.

Durbin has been a prominent player in bankruptcy reform. In the 105th Congress, he worked with Republican Charles E. Grassley of Iowa on a major rewrite of bankruptcy laws, but the legislation failed amid disputes over consumer protections. But in the 106th, Durbin joined other liberals in raising objections to a bankruptcy overhaul bill, contending it was overly harsh on debtors. The bill's sponsors "cast the net too large, and it will drag too many unsuspecting people into it," he said. Durbin also unsuccessfully tried to attach an amendment to the measure that would have denied bankruptcy protection to firearms manufacturers and distributors trying to evade wrongful death and personal-injury lawsuits.

Durbin has been active on other consumer safety issues as well. He is a leading advocate of stepping up food safety inspection, proposing to combine federal inspection efforts into one agency. After U.S. aviation officials raised concerns that a copilot on an EgyptAir flight deliberately crashed the plane in 1999, Durbin proposed mandating video cameras in airplane cockpits.

Although Durbin relies on support from organized labor and usually takes up its cause, he has gotten some heat from unions for supporting trade legislation such as the 1993 North American Free Trade Agreement. In 2000, he again broke with unions by supporting the Clinton administration on granting China permanent normal trade status. Although he acknowledged that labor leaders would be displeased, he said he would work with them on better enforcement of trade agreements and boosting worker retraining programs.

Like some other lawmakers with large agricultural constituencies, Durbin supported efforts in the 106th to lift the U.S. food embargo against Cuba. "This has not worked in Cuba," he argued. "For almost 40 years, [Cuban leader] Fidel Castro has been in power. I've seen photographs of him. He's never appeared malnourished to me."

Durbin was 14 when his chain-smoking father died of lung cancer, and Durbin has dedicated much of his congressional career to crusading against tobacco companies. But he downplays that personal aspect of the debate. "I am not unique," he said of the loss of his father. "I know it's a big issue to millions of Americans and their families who have lost loved ones to tobacco."

As a member of the House, Durbin led the successful effort in the late 1980s to ban smoking on most domestic airline flights. Later, as chairman and then ranking member on the House Appropriations' Agriculture Subcommittee, he tried to scale back government support for tobacco farmers, falling just two votes short in a floor vote in 1996. In the 105th, he scored a victory of sorts by getting the Senate to agree to increase fines that companies would have to pay if they failed to reduce tobacco use among minors. Durbin also pressed to make Senate office buildings smoke-free, a proposal that drew a cool response from senators from tobacco states.

Although Durbin has established a close working relationship with Illinois' other senator, Republican Peter G. Fitzgerald, he can engage in partisan battles. Durbin vigorously defended President Clinton and urged investigation of Independent Counsel Kenneth W. Starr months before the House took up formal impeachment proceedings against the president late in 1998. "I don't think Mr. Starr is independent at all," Durbin said, criticizing him for doing outside legal work while investigating the White House.

As a member of the Governmental Affairs Committee, Durbin also raised concerns about the fairness of its chairman, Republican Fred Thompson of Tennessee, who led the panel's investigation into campaign fundraising during the 1996 congressional and presidential races. "The real test will be whether the investigation will be fair and bipartisan," he said.

Durbin earned a law degree from Georgetown University and then went to work for Illinois' lieutenant governor, Democrat Paul Simon (who later went on to a 22-year career in Congress). Durbin spent a decade as an aide in the Illinois legislature. In 1982, he unseated 11-term GOP Rep. Paul N. Findley in the 20th District by a mere 1,410 votes. By his second term, Durbin had a seat on Appropriations and began a string of mostly comfortable, if not overwhelming, re-election victories.

When his old mentor, Simon, announced that he would not seek re-election to the Senate in 1996, Durbin, who had been booted from his post as an Appropriations subcommittee chairman after the House GOP takeover, jumped at the chance to succeed Simon. With endorsements from Simon and Illinois' other Democratic senator, Carol Moseley-Braun, Durbin had little trouble winning the primary. In the general election, he faced off against state Rep. Al Salvi, a little-known conservative with firm anti-abortion and gun owners' rights views. Durbin characterized him as an extreme conservative and won the election by 15 percentage points.

KEY VOTES

2000
Yes Overhaul bankruptcy law and increase minimum wage
No   Limit fiscal 2001 discretionary spending to $600.3 billion
No   Override veto on nuclear waste disposal at Yucca Mountain site in Nevada
Yes Oppose effort to terminate Kosovo mission
Yes Include gender, sexual orientation and disability in federal hate crime protections
No   Approve GOP plan to restrict use of genetic information by health insurers
No   Kill amendment delaying implementation of an anti-missile defense system
No   Cut taxes for married couples
Yes Grant China permanent normal trade status

1999
No   Remove President Clinton from office for obstruction of justice
No   Kill amendment authorizing state grants to hire teachers and reduce class size
Yes Require criminal background checks for purchases at gun shows
No   Approve GOP proposal to increase rights of patients in managed-care health plans
No   Block effort to allow farm and medicine exports to Cuba
Yes Allow study of tougher automobile fuel efficiency standards
Yes Ratify nuclear weapons testing treaty
Yes Prohibit national political parties from collecting "soft money" donations
Yes Remove barriers among banking, securities and insurance companies

INTEREST GROUPS

	AFL-CIO	ADA	CCUS	ACU
2000	75%	95%	50%	4%
1999	89%	100%	35%	4%
1998	100%	95%	50%	8%
1997	100%	100%	40%	4%
House Service:				
1996	91%	80%	27%	0%
1995	100%	85%	25%	8%
1994	78%	95%	25%	0%
1993	92%	90%	27%	13%
1992	83%	90%	13%	4%
1991	92%	95%	30%	5%

CQ VOTE STUDIES

	PARTY UNITY		PRESIDENTIAL SUPPORT	
	Support	Oppose	Support	Oppose
2000	99%	1%	97%	3%
1999	95%	5%	87%	13%
1998	95%	5%	90%	10%
1997	97%	3%	92%	8%
House Service:				
1996	91%	9%	82%	18%
1995	93%	7%	83%	17%
1994	98%	2%	78%	22%
1993	94%	6%	78%	22%
1992	95%	5%	13%	87%
1991	94%	6%	26%	74%

Sen. Peter G. Fitzgerald (R)

Elected 1998; 1st term

CAPITOL OFFICE
224-2854; fax 228-1372; 555 Dirksen Bldg. 20510

INTERNET
e-mail: senator_fitzgerald@fitzgerald.senate.gov
web: fitzgerald.senate.gov

COMMITTEES
Agriculture, Nutrition & Forestry
(Marketing, Inspection & Product Promotion - chairman)
Commerce, Science & Transportation
(Consumer Affairs, Foreign Commerce & Tourism - chairman)
Small Business
Special Aging

HOMETOWN
Inverness

BORN
Oct. 20, 1960, Elgin, Ill.

RELIGION
Roman Catholic

FAMILY
Wife, Nina Fitzgerald; one child

EDUCATION
Dartmouth College, A.B. 1982; Aristotelian U. (Greece), attended 1983; U. of Michigan, J.D. 1986

CAREER
Lawyer

POLITICAL HIGHLIGHTS
Ill. Senate, 1993-99; sought Republican nomination for U.S. House, 1994

ELECTION RESULTS

1998 GENERAL

Peter G. Fitzgerald (R)	1,709,041	50.3%
Carol Moseley-Braun (D)	1,610,496	47.4%
Don A. Torgersen (REF)	74,704	2.2%

1998 PRIMARY

Peter G. Fitzgerald (R)	372,916	51.8%
Loleta Didrickson (R)	346,606	48.2%

Almost from the day he arrived on Capitol Hill, Fitzgerald has been a case study in the danger of false assumptions. Labeled an unbending conservative by his critics, he has startled friend and foe alike with some glaring departures from Republican orthodoxy. Initially seen as aloof, Fitzgerald will chat at length about anything, from arcane budget rules to the Chicago Cubs.

A rumpled, balding and brainy lawyer, Fitzgerald is one of the wealthiest senators, though he is said to be sensitive about being called rich. Spending $7 million of his own money on his 1998 primary campaign, Fitzgerald edged past the GOP establishment's preferred candidate by 4 percentage points and went on to oust Democratic Sen. Carol Moseley-Braun. Overall, Fitzgerald spent $14.6 million, much of it his own money, to win his Senate seat. But that was only a modest bite out of his share of the fortune amassed by his father, Gerald, who developed a chain of suburban banks that were sold in 1994 to the Bank of Montreal for $246 million.

Fitzgerald is indeed a staunch conservative, both on fiscal and social issues, but he is not always a dependable Republican vote. That was never more evident than in 1999, when he bucked his party leaders on patients' rights and gun control — he supported legislation to allow patients to sue their HMOs for denial of coverage and backed an amendment that sought to place new controls on the sale of firearms at gun shows.

Fitzgerald also has proved to be a legislative rabble-rouser when it comes to consideration of Illinois issues. In his first two years in the Senate, he took on some of the most powerful, and popular, GOP politicians in the country — including his home state's top man in Washington, House Speaker J. Dennis Hastert, and the Senate's ultimate maverick, Arizona Republican John McCain.

In 1999, Fitzgerald waged an unwavering fight against McCain's bill reauthorizing the Federal Aviation Administration, forcing McCain to rewrite a key provision involving flight restrictions at O'Hare and three other major airports. Fitzgerald and other Illinois legislators were adamant about retaining some limits on the number of flights permitted at O'Hare, and Fitzgerald eventually succeeded in keeping the restrictions in place, while permitting a few additional flights. To win the concession, his aides drafted 304 amendments that he said he was prepared to offer.

The fight led to a testy exchange between McCain and Fitzgerald, with McCain saying the delay in approval of the aviation measure could jeopardize "the safety of airline passengers across the country, perhaps throughout the world."

Fitzgerald made clear he was not about to back down and infuriated McCain by suggesting that his "dual responsibilities" as a senator and presidential candidate had made it hard to negotiate with him. McCain missed dozens of votes as he campaigned across the country and embarked on a national tour in support of his best-selling book, "Faith of My Fathers," but none of his other colleagues had been willing to take the popular senator to task on the Senate floor. In the 107th Congress, the two men will have plenty of opportunities for interaction, as Fitzgerald won a seat on the Commerce Committee, chaired by McCain.

In 2000, Fitzgerald waged an all-day filibuster of a spending bill to protest $50 million included for the Abraham Lincoln Library in Springfield, Ill. Fitzgerald said the provision, supported by Hastert, could allow Republican

Gov. George Ryan to award contracts to friends and political allies. "There would be no worse or uglier irony than to have a monument for Honest Abe wind up being a gigantic public works project on which a bunch of political insiders wind up lining their pockets at taxpayer expense," Fitzgerald said, according to the Chicago Tribune.

To solve the dilemma, he recommended that language be attached to the bill requiring that federal competitive bidding rules be imposed on the library construction. In the end, he lost his fight.

Time will tell whether Fitzgerald's independent streak will help him as his legislative career progresses. He has sometimes irritated Senate GOP leaders, but they understood why he strayed from the party line on patients' rights and gun control, as he had made his positions clear long before he defeated Moseley-Braun. As for the filibuster, he did not block all action on the floor; he allowed others to speak and permitted unrelated bills to move forward. It was a "targeted filibuster," Fitzgerald said.

Senate Majority Leader Trent Lott says it is clear that Fitzgerald is not one who likes to be told what to do. "He's shown that he's not anybody's tool and that he's going to aggressively look at his state's interests," Lott said in 2000.

Illinois' Democratic senator, Richard J. Durbin, says Fitzgerald will "ruffle some feathers" but also win praise for sticking up for his beliefs. Despite their partisan and philosophical differences, Fitzgerald and Durbin have teamed up to hold weekly "town halls" in Washington for visiting constituents.

Also of parochial interest to his constituents, Fitzgerald sits on the Agriculture Committee, where he keeps tabs on issues relevant to Illinois' many farmers and Chicago's commodity exchanges.

Back home, Fitzgerald has received mixed reviews. In an editorial in 2000, the Chicago Tribune said the senator's "anti-insiders crusade ... was his hallmark as a state legislator." But if he does not continue to complain about pork, the paper warned, his "donnybrook over the library will look like a cheap slap against [Gov.] Ryan," whom some believe Fitzgerald will challenge in 2002.

A devout Roman Catholic, Fitzgerald fervently opposes abortion, even in cases of rape or incest, although he would allow it to save the life of the woman. He sponsored an Illinois law that prohibits same-sex marriages, and he wants to exclude homosexuals from military service.

Those positions, and others of a decidedly conservative bent, might seem out of step with the voters of a generally centrist Midwestern state. But Fitzgerald had the good fortune to take on an incumbent who was dogged throughout her one-term tenure by a string of ethics accusations. The focus on Moseley-Braun's many personal and professional problems enabled Fitzgerald to run a cautious, low-key campaign.

In his first year in the Senate, Fitzgerald was one of only two senators — along with Jesse Helms of North Carolina — to vote against Moseley-Braun's nomination to serve as U.S. ambassador to New Zealand.

Fitzgerald was educated at the Portsmouth Abbey School in Rhode Island, which is run by an order of Benedictine monks. He graduated from Dartmouth College, where he majored in the classics, and he is fluent in Greek. He received his law degree from the University of Michigan and has practiced law in the corporate arena.

By many accounts, one of his closest political advisers is his wife Nina, a Harvard Law School graduate. The two met at a Georgetown reception while Fitzgerald was interning with Rep. Philip M. Crane, R-Ill., whom he later challenged unsuccessfully in 1994. After coming to Capitol Hill, Fitzgerald said all staff hirings would first have to be cleared by Nina.

Fitzgerald is affected by Bell's palsy, a condition that causes a paralysis of facial muscles. The symptoms come and go, and Fitzgerald says he takes no medication or treatment for the condition.

KEY VOTES

2000
C	Overhaul bankruptcy law and increase minimum wage
Yes	Limit fiscal 2001 discretionary spending to $600.3 billion
Yes	Override veto on nuclear waste disposal at Yucca Mountain site in Nevada
No	Oppose effort to terminate Kosovo mission
No	Include gender, sexual orientation and disability in federal hate crime protections
Yes	Approve GOP plan to restrict use of genetic information by health insurers
Yes	Kill amendment delaying implementation of an anti-missile defense system
Yes	Cut taxes for married couples
Yes	Grant China permanent normal trade status

1999
Yes	Remove President Clinton from office for obstruction of justice
Yes	Kill amendment authorizing state grants to hire teachers and reduce class size
Yes	Require criminal background checks for purchases at gun shows
No	Approve GOP proposal to increase rights of patients in managed-care health plans
No	Block effort to allow farm and medicine exports to Cuba
No	Allow study of tougher automobile fuel efficiency standards
No	Ratify nuclear weapons testing treaty
No	Prohibit national political parties from collecting "soft money" donations
C	Remove barriers among banking, securities and insurance companies

INTEREST GROUPS

	AFL-CIO	ADA	CCUS	ACU
2000	25%	25%	71%	95%
1999	33%	15%	88%	92%

CQ VOTE STUDIES

	PARTY UNITY		PRESIDENTIAL SUPPORT	
	Support	Oppose	Support	Oppose
2000	81%	19%	51%	49%
1999	87%	13%	37%	63%

Rep. Bobby L. Rush (D)

Elected 1992; 5th term

CAPITOL OFFICE
225-4372; fax 226-0333; 2416 Rayburn Bldg. 20515

INTERNET
e-mail: bobby.rush@mail.house.gov
web: www.house.gov/rush

COMMITTEES
Energy & Commerce

HOMETOWN
Chicago

BORN
Nov. 23, 1946, Albany, Ga.

RELIGION
Protestant

FAMILY
Wife, Carolyn Rush; five children (one deceased)

EDUCATION
Roosevelt U., B.A. 1973; U. of Illinois, Chicago,
attended 1975-77, M.A. 1994; McCormick
Seminary, M.A. 1998

MILITARY SERVICE
Army, 1963-68

CAREER
Insurance broker; political aide

POLITICAL HIGHLIGHTS
Candidate for Chicago City Council, 1975; sought
Democratic nomination for Ill. House, 1978;
Chicago City Council, 1983-93; candidate for mayor
of Chicago, 1999

ELECTION RESULTS

2000 GENERAL

Bobby L. Rush (D)	172,271	87.8%
Raymond G. Wardingley (R)	23,915	12.2%

2000 PRIMARY

Bobby L. Rush (D)	59,599	61.0%
Barack Obama (D)	29,649	30.4%
Donne Trotter (D)	6,915	7.1%
George C. Roby (D)	1,501	1.5%

1998 GENERAL

Bobby L. Rush (D)	151,890	87.1%
Marlene White Ahimaz (R)	18,429	10.6%
Marjorie Kohls (LIBERT)	4,046	2.3%

PREVIOUS WINNING PERCENTAGES
1996 (86%); 1994 (76%); 1992 (83%)

Rush's life has been evolutionary and, at times, revolutionary, taking many twists and turns before landing him in Congress, where he has a seat on the Energy and Commerce Committee, a place in the party's whip organization and a platform for his work on behalf of his low-income South Side Chicago constituents.

Born in southern Georgia, Rush grew up in Chicago, where his mother moved when he was 7 after her marriage broke up. She worked as a GOP activist because whites dominated the Democratic machine. Rush was in an integrated Boy Scout troop and volunteered for the Army, but, disillusioned by a racist commanding officer, he joined the Student Non-Violent Coordinating Committee.

He soon founded the Illinois chapter of the militant Black Panthers organization. Belying the Panthers' violent image, Rush coordinated a Panthers-run program that provided free breakfast for children and a medical clinic that developed a mass screening effort for sickle cell anemia.

When he was in his 20s, Rush was imprisoned for six months for illegal possession of weapons. He acknowledges that his methods and his views have changed, but he also says that society has changed. In 1999, his son Huey (named after Black Panther Huey Newton) was shot and killed in a Chicago sidewalk robbery. "We've got to rid our communities of guns. Violence and guns don't belong in a civilized society," Rush declared.

Long before his son's death, Rush favored restrictions on guns. He has sponsored a number of gun control measures, including one in the 106th Congress to regulate firearms transactions over the Internet. But he says that legislation is only one small part of the solution. "I believe the black community has a moral responsibility ... to raise the consciousness ... around the issues of guns and violence," he told the Chicago Tribune. He continued, "Nowadays, we've got a spectator community, not an active community. What we've got to do is create opportunities to take those spectators onto the field and say, 'Look, you do have power. You can do something about solving a problem.'"

That is what Rush has tried to do, in a variety of ways, since he organized the Black Panthers chapter in 1968. After graduating from college, he quit the Panthers, sold insurance, and then entered local politics, challenging the party machinery and losing two races. In 1983, however, he won election to the Chicago City Council, riding the coattails of 1st District Democratic Rep. Harold Washington, who was elected in an upset as Chicago's first black mayor.

Rush was elected to Congress in 1992, ousting Democrat Charles A. Hayes, who had replaced Washington in the House, but who was susceptible to Rush's charge that he was not providing aggressive leadership. A gifted political organizer, Rush quickly impressed his party leaders; by his second term, he had a seat on the coveted Commerce Committee and a spot in the Democratic whip organization. In the 107th, he is one of 12 deputy whips.

But if Rush had in mind becoming mostly an inside player, the GOP takeover of Congress in 1995 seems to have altered his agenda. Now he devotes much energy to the oratory of frustration, lashing out at Republican efforts to cut spending for social programs and fuming at those in his own party whom he sees as giving up too much ground to the GOP.

The primary focus of Rush's legislative work is to help his economically struggling urban constituents. Upon his arrival in Washington in the 103rd

Congress, he pursued urban economic revitalization. He maintains that "massive disinvestment" by establishment lenders has caused economic abandonment in many urban areas, bringing high unemployment that spawns a host of social problems.

He was instrumental in legislation to require bankers to do business in poor areas, and in the 106th offered a measure to regulate so-called payday loan companies that provide short-term loans at exorbitant interest rates.

Rush can work with colleagues who stand nowhere near him on the ideological spectrum. In addressing the shortage of health care workers in urban hospitals, for example, Rush allied himself with a prominent conservative, Henry J. Hyde, R-Ill., on a bill to establish a special visa classification for foreign nurses. Rush made the case that the personnel shortage at inner-city hospitals was severe enough to encourage immigration from nurses abroad. And conservative Democrat Ralph M. Hall of Texas told the Chicago Tribune that Rush has "... never written me off saying, 'he's just a damn conservative.' Even though we don't often vote together, I can get on his dance card."

Rush is active in the Congressional Urban Caucus (he was its chairman in the 105th) and pressed for federal help for community redevelopment programs in Chicago and for efforts to reduce health risks, particularly asthma, in inner-city areas.

Because of his past association with the radical Black Panthers, the media instantly plucked Rush from the freshman horde after the 1992 election, making him a TV celebrity before his first term even began. But Rush seldom mentioned his Panther past until the 104th Congress, when the GOP sought to allow a "good faith" exemption for illegal police searches. Rush — who said he had cried at a 1995 movie dramatizing the early days of the Panthers organization — said he was the only member of Congress "ever to have been victimized by illegal search and seizure."

In the 2000 election, Rush, who had successfully challenged a fellow Democrat to win his first election to the House in 1992, was in danger of tasting some of his own medicine. Rush had fared poorly in his 1999 challenge to the re-election of Democratic Richard M. Daley as mayor, receiving just 28 percent in the Democratic primary. Emboldened by that showing, three Democrats lined up to challenge Rush's own re-election bid. The leading contender, state Sen. Barack Obama, tried a tack that must have seemed familiar to Rush — accusing the congressman of not providing vigorous leadership. But voters were not persuaded, and Rush was renominated with 61 percent of the vote, tantamount to re-election in the overwhelmingly Democratic district.

KEY VOTES

2000
Yes Raise hourly minimum wage by $1 over two years
No Halt funding for U.S. mission in Kosovo unless European nations pay more
Yes Provide Medicare benefits to military retirees and their dependents
No Grant China permanent normal trade status
No Phase out estate, gift and trust taxes
No Prohibit implementation of president's national monument designations
No Approve GOP plan to provide prescription drug coverage for Medicare beneficiaries
Yes Increase help for poor nations indebted to international financial institutions

1999
Yes Impose steel import quotas
No Kill proposal to take aviation trust funds off budget
No Require background checks on buyers only at gun shows with 10 or more vendors
Yes Remove barriers among banking, securities and insurance companies
Yes Authorize state grants to hire teachers and reduce class size
Yes Overhaul campaign finance law; ban "soft money" and restrict advocacy advertising
Yes Approve bipartisan plan to increase rights of patients in managed-care health plans

INTEREST GROUPS

	AFL-CIO	ADA	CCUS	ACU
2000	100%	90%	36%	0%
1999	89%	100%	23%	0%
1998	100%	95%	33%	8%
1997	100%	100%	40%	4%

CQ VOTE STUDIES

	PARTY UNITY		PRESIDENTIAL SUPPORT	
	Support	Oppose	Support	Oppose
2000	98%	2%	91%	9%
1999	97%	3%	86%	14%
1998	95%	5%	84%	16%
1997	95%	5%	79%	21%

ILLINOIS 1
Chicago — South Side and southwest

The nation's first black-majority district, the 1st covers the South Side of Chicago. It begins at 26th Street in the historic black hub, then moves south through mainly residential neighborhoods to 103rd Street, at the edge of a once thriving industrial belt. At its midsection, the district swings west through inner-city communities. It also reaches an arm into Chicago's southwest side and close-in suburbs, home to most of the 1st's white residents and much of its spare Republican vote. The 1st has been a relatively compact district since its creation, but the district's boundaries have gradually expanded in the past few decades to adjust for declining populations in some of the area's most economically distressed neighborhoods.

When the steel industry left the South Side in the 1970s, it decimated the district's middle class and many black-owned businesses. Now the 1st is home to some of the city's largest subsidized housing projects, and more than 20 percent of the population lives in poverty.

The district still has several solidly middle-class black neighborhoods, including Chatham and Avalon Park. The north end takes in Bronzeville, which has seen young black professionals move in and rehabilitate old houses instead of leaving for the suburbs.

The 1st has been represented by black congressmen since 1929. Its few white voters live outside the city or in a few historically Irish neighborhoods in the southwest. The district has a powerful Democratic voting bloc that often battles the Daley Democrats.

MAJOR INDUSTRY
Hospitals, higher education, manufacturing

CITIES
Chicago (pt.), 516,419 (1990); Evergreen Park, 20,348; Alsip (pt.), 13,485 (1990)

UNUSUAL FEATURES
National headquarters of Jesse Jackson's Rainbow/PUSH Coalition; Comiskey Park, home of the Chicago White Sox; University of Chicago.

Rep. Jesse L. Jackson Jr. (D)

Elected December 1995; 3rd full term

CAPITOL OFFICE
225-0773; fax 225-0899; 313 Cannon Bldg. 20515

INTERNET
e-mail: comments@jessejacksonjr.org
web: www.jessejacksonjr.org

COMMITTEES
Appropriations

HOMETOWN
Chicago

BORN
March 11, 1965, Greenville, S.C.

RELIGION
Baptist

FAMILY
Wife, Sandi Jackson; one child

EDUCATION
North Carolina A&T U., B.S. 1987; Chicago
Theological Seminary, M.A. 1990; U. of Illinois,
J.D. 1993

CAREER
Lawyer

POLITICAL HIGHLIGHTS
No previous office

ELECTION RESULTS

2000 GENERAL

Jesse L. Jackson Jr. (D)	175,995	89.8%
Robert Gordon III (R)	19,906	10.2%

2000 PRIMARY

Jesse L. Jackson Jr. (D)	unopposed

1998 GENERAL

Jesse L. Jackson Jr. (D)	148,985	89.4%
Robert Gordon III (R)	16,075	9.6%

PREVIOUS WINNING PERCENTAGES
1996 (94%); 1995 Special Election (76%)

Brimming with energy and benefiting from a universally known name, Jackson has gained more notice than is typical for a junior member of the minority party. He has worked to bring the benefits of the nation's fiscal well-being to his South Side and suburban Chicago constituents, while at the same time involving himself in social issues such as the death penalty and health care — areas in which minorities fare poorly in comparison with whites, he says.

Jackson does not have his father's looming physical presence nor the pulpit cadences of his oratory. But the son of the famous civil rights leader is becoming a key player in his own right in black leadership circles.

In just his second full term, he won a seat on the Appropriations Committee, and in 2000 he was named to a small group of lawmakers who met periodically to make contingency plans for a Democratic return to power in the House in 2001. He often is asked to make speeches or to comment on current events that have a race relations aspect. While he turns down many of them, there is no doubt he sees one of his roles as that of spreading his liberal message to a wider audience than just the House.

Though Jackson is unquestionably a liberal, he can work with even the most conservative Republican if he sees benefits for his district. He joined with a fellow Chicagoan, Republican Henry J. Hyde, to form the Partnership for Metropolitan Chicago's Airport Future, a group that wants to use rural land just south of the 2nd District to build the region a third major airport. The venture has the potential to provide thousands of jobs for Jackson's many unemployed constituents.

Jackson is not afraid to break ranks with his allies upon occasion. In the 106th Congress, he was one of only five members of the Congressional Black Caucus to vote against the final version of legislation designed to expand trade with sub-Saharan Africa. The extent of his opposition rankled one of the bill's cosponsors, black Democrat Charles B. Rangel of New York, who said that Jackson had been unprofessional, particularly when some of Jackson's supporters picketed Rangel's office. Jackson apologized but did not change his opposition, arguing that the bill did not go far enough to address important issues such as the AIDS epidemic and the crushing international debt owed by many African nations. "Passage of this bad bill is worse than no bill at all," he said.

Jackson's rhetoric sounds less passionate than his father's — one observer characterizes the congressman as the "accountant for the Rainbow Coalition" — and his message generally centers on economic issues. "In our district there are 60 people for every one job. ... That explains why we're stuck on the Dan Ryan Expressway in traffic, why we pay higher prices for gas ... why we're away from our children before and after school longer," he told a reporter for the Chicago Defender.

To spread his message in narrower, personal terms, he co-authored "It's About the Money" with his father, a book that offers practical advice on personal financial matters, such as credit card use and various strategies for investing and saving money.

Jackson often found himself criticizing the Clinton administration for compromising with the GOP, such as on legislation to significantly overhaul the nation's welfare system. Jackson argues that forcing people off the welfare rolls cannot be successful unless it is accompanied by the creation of plentiful jobs and the availability of affordable child care.

In 2000, in response to Republican Gov. George Ryan's decision to order a moratorium on executions in Illinois after more than a dozen death row inmates were determined to be innocent, Jackson introduced legislation calling for a seven-year halt on all executions, with none permitted after that unless the U.S. attorney general certified that the inmate was given full opportunity to present genetic evidence to establish his or her innocence. Jackson also wrote a bill in the 106th Congress to establish a new research center to look into health care disparities between whites and minorities.

He frequently takes to the House floor to talk about civil rights and other social policy topics. In 1996, for example, Jackson pointed out that many poor people have a better chance of getting an education in prison than they do in free society. "My father always says that it is a real sad day in our country when jails are becoming a step up," he said.

Jackson and his wife, Sandi, became first-time parents in 2000, giving him another outlet for his domestic tendencies. Shortly after the birth of his daughter, the Chicago Tribune reported that Jackson drove all around the Chicago area looking for special lactose-free baby formula. CBS News once filmed Jackson vacuuming the carpet in his Capitol Hill office, and Jackson confessed he does it all the time. "It's relaxing for me. It's a way for me to think and reflect," he said. In 1999, according to the Chicago Sun-Times, Jackson helped out angry airline travelers who were swamping the ticket counter because of flight delays at O'Hare Airport. The congressman, who was mistaken for an airline employee, directed passengers to the proper line.

A lawyer who graduated from Washington's elite St. Alban's School, Jackson presents himself as a vibrant member of a new generation of black leadership. He followed in his father's footsteps, serving as vice president at-large of Operation PUSH (People United to Serve Humanity) and as national field director for the Rainbow Coalition. But unlike his father, he parlayed those activities into an inside role in the national Democratic Party organization, serving as secretary of the Democratic National Committee's Black Caucus. He shared the podium with his father at the 1996 Democratic National Convention in Chicago.

Jackson first sought a seat in Congress in a 1995 special election to replace Democrat Mel Reynolds, who had resigned after being convicted of sexual misconduct. Jackson countered criticism that he was too young for the job of congressman by arguing that being the son of Jesse Jackson amounted to a lifetime of political experience. After winning the Democratic nomination in that first campaign in a hard-fought battle against longtime state Sen. Emil Jones Jr., Jackson has had no difficulty in subsequent elections.

KEY VOTES

2000

Yes Raise hourly minimum wage by $1 over two years
Yes Halt funding for U.S. mission in Kosovo unless European nations pay more
Yes Provide Medicare benefits to military retirees and their dependents
No Grant China permanent normal trade status
No Phase out estate, gift and trust taxes
No Prohibit implementation of president's national monument designations
No Approve GOP plan to provide prescription drug coverage for Medicare beneficiaries
Yes Increase help for poor nations indebted to international financial institutions

1999

Yes Impose steel import quotas
Yes Kill proposal to take aviation trust funds off budget
No Require background checks on buyers only at gun shows with 10 or more vendors
No Remove barriers among banking, securities and insurance companies
Yes Authorize state grants to hire teachers and reduce class size
Yes Overhaul campaign finance law; ban "soft money" and restrict advocacy advertising
Yes Approve bipartisan plan to increase rights of patients in managed-care health plans

INTEREST GROUPS

	AFL-CIO	ADA	CCUS	ACU
2000	100%	100%	23%	4%
1999	100%	100%	8%	8%
1998	100%	100%	22%	8%
1997	100%	100%	20%	4%

CQ VOTE STUDIES

	PARTY UNITY		PRESIDENTIAL SUPPORT	
	Support	Oppose	Support	Oppose
2000	96%	4%	83%	17%
1999	95%	5%	82%	18%
1998	96%	4%	83%	17%
1997	95%	5%	79%	21%

ILLINOIS 2

Chicago – Far South Side; south suburbs; Chicago Heights

U.S. Steel once employed 20,000 people in the 2nd, a roughly U-shaped district that covers Chicago's South Side through the south suburbs to Chicago Heights. When the steel industry collapsed in the late 1970s, it devastated the district's industrial-based economy. Now, Ford Motor Co. is one of the only large manufacturing businesses in the district.

A plan to build a new airport in neighboring Peotone could rejuvenate the 2nd's economy. Advocates hope a new airport would bring in corporate headquarters, hotels, distributors and other new business. In the meantime, unemployment remains high and many residents have some of the longest commutes in the nation, traveling downtown or to the northwest suburbs to work. Ultimately, many former residents have left the South Side to find jobs, draining the district of voters.

The 2nd's predominantly black population and working-class base shape a consistently Democratic district, even though only about half of the district's population lives within Chicago city limits. Democratic candidates need to make a strong appeal to suburban voters, including white ethnic groups that tend to be more socially moderate than city voters. The 2nd's suburbs include pockets of historically Republican communities and newer Hispanic enclaves, as well as the relatively affluent, historically Jewish suburbs of Homewood, Flossmoor and Olympia Fields.

MAJOR INDUSTRY
Automotive and wire manufacturing, steel production, health care

CITIES
Chicago (pt.), 295,554 (1990); Chicago Heights (pt.), 33,048 (1990); Harvey, 29,167

UNUSUAL FEATURES
Pullman, factory town built by the Pullman Place Car Co., maker of Pullman sleepers.

Rep. William O. Lipinski (D)

Elected 1982; 10th term

CAPITOL OFFICE
225-5701; fax 225-1012; 2470 Rayburn Bldg. 20515

INTERNET
e-mail: www.house.gov/writerep
web: www.house.gov/lipinski

COMMITTEES
Transportation & Infrastructure

HOMETOWN
Chicago

BORN
Dec. 22, 1937, Chicago, Ill.

RELIGION
Roman Catholic

FAMILY
Wife, Rose Marie Lipinski; two children

EDUCATION
Loras College, attended 1956-57

MILITARY SERVICE
Army Reserve, 1961-67

CAREER
Parks supervisor

POLITICAL HIGHLIGHTS
Chicago City Council, 1975-83

ELECTION RESULTS

2000 GENERAL

William O. Lipinski (D)	145,498	75.6%
Karl Groth (R)	47,005	24.4%

2000 PRIMARY

William O. Lipinski (D)	46,459	90.3%
R. Benedict Mayers (D)	5,009	9.7%

1998 GENERAL

William O. Lipinski (D)	115,887	72.5%
Robert Marshall (R)	44,012	27.5%

PREVIOUS WINNING PERCENTAGES
1996 (65%); 1994 (54%); 1992 (64%); 1990 (66%);
1988 (61%); 1986 (70%); 1984 (64%); 1982 (75%)

Wiry and fast-talking, Lipinski is the picture of an old-style urban pol. He seems more comfortable negotiating deals in backrooms than touting the party line on television talk shows. A Catholic of Polish and Irish lineage from working-class roots, he sees his job as sticking up for the "little guy" against monied interests.

"I have nothing against people in this economy becoming millionaires, becoming billionaires," he once said. "But I believe that it is really the duty and the responsibility of the ... government to try to create an economy that improves the standard of living of all the citizens of this country."

Like the middle-class white ethnic groups that dominate his suburban Chicago district, Lipinski holds conservative views on social issues and is firmly convinced that U.S. trade policies are a calamity for American industrial workers.

Often a thorn in the side of liberals, Lipinski opposes abortion, wants to outlaw desecration of the flag and supports the Republican call for tuition vouchers and medical savings accounts. Although he consistently sides with labor, he disagreed with President Clinton's position almost half the time in the 105th and 106th Congresses, one of the highest opposition scores of any Democrat.

Lipinski is a member of the "Blue Dogs," a coalition of conservative Democrats. He was one of the few Democrats who gave early support to Republican welfare overhaul plans in the 104th Congress, and in the 105th, he backed GOP legislation to revamp the federal housing program and to encourage states to treat violent juvenile offenders as adults.

Throughout his House career, Lipinski has focused chiefly on matters of parochial interest to Chicago. He has a seat on the Transportation Committee, a good place to look out for a range of Chicago concerns, including the welfare of O'Hare Airport, the fate of aging Midway Airport (in Lipinski's district), and flooding and erosion along the city's 24-mile Lake Michigan shoreline. Lipinski opposes efforts by other Chicago lawmakers to get federal funding for a third metropolitan airport.

Lipinski is the ranking Democrat on the Transportation panel's Aviation Subcommittee, and in the 106th Congress he won House passage of a plan to lift air traffic restrictions at O'Hare Airport.

While he works closely with Republicans on such issues as funding for airports and other transportation projects, he turns on the GOP when debate shifts to worker-management matters. He led the opposition to a Republican measure making it harder for Federal Express employees to unionize. And he opposed a GOP push to allow businesses to offer workers compensatory time off in lieu of pay for overtime work.

Lipinski is also an unyielding foe of lowering international trade barriers. In 1997, he called the North American Free Trade Agreement "a complete and utter failure for working Americans," saying it had "sacrificed 400,000 American jobs at the altar of free trade." In 1999, he won House approval of a provision to increase penalties on Mexican trucks that travel throughout the United States illegally.

When Clinton and GOP leaders sought to grant China permanent normal trade status, Lipinski balked: "We should treat China as a totalitarian regime. ... We must not coddle them. We must not appease them. We must not assist them." He also opposed the free-traders' push in the 105th Congress to renew the president's fast-track authority to request expedited congressional approval of trade agreements that Congress cannot revise. "Fast-track," he said, "will continue the downward slide of the standard of living of all American working people."

Earlier in his career, Lipinski opposed the 1991 civil rights bill, denouncing its "quotas," and he says that special treatment for minorities can disadvantage people of other ethnic backgrounds. "My constituents suffer discrimination," he told the Chicago Sun-Times. "They had nothing to do with slavery." He says that the Democratic left has "tried to make it unfashionable to exhibit many of [the] beliefs real ethnics hold, implying that it's immoral to oppose all abortions, racist to support capital punishment."

He works to secure funding for highway and mass transit projects sought by his colleagues, dismissing critics who decry such spending as "pork." "Who knows better where a certain amount of federal money should be spent locally than the congressman?" he asks. Early in the 107th, Lipinski took a leading role in drafting a wish list of 247 local projects members of the Illinois delegation wanted to ask President Bush for help in funding.

Lipinski broke with the Clinton administration in 1999 by opposing the NATO bombing campaign in Kosovo. He told the Chicago Tribune that Clinton "doesn't have credibility on military issues. ... The American people feel Clinton is unsure. They don't trust him in Kosovo." That same year, he endorsed former Sen. Bill Bradley for president rather than Vice President Al Gore, saying he trusted Bradley more. "There are not an awful lot of people in politics I trust," he said.

A lifelong Chicago resident, Lipinski dropped out of college after hurting his back. Beginning as a weekend athletic instructor, he spent 17 years in the Parks Department and rose to an administrative position. In 1975, Lipinski was elected to the city council, where he lobbied for the establishment of the Southwest Rapid Transit Line. As chairman of the Education Committee, he opposed mandatory busing, a hot-button issue for his heavily ethnic constituency.

Lipinski successfully challenged Democratic Rep. John G. Fary in 1982 during an intraparty split. In 1992, he once again had to survive an intraparty battle, when redistricting forced him into a primary race with fellow Democratic Rep. Marty Russo. He called on the muscle of the city's Democratic organization, as he has throughout the years when necessary, and defeated Russo with 58 percent of the vote. (Lipinski still leads the party's 23rd Ward organization.) In his general-election victories, Lipinski has never gotten less than 54 percent of the vote and on several occasions has won with more than 70 percent.

KEY VOTES

2000

Yes Raise hourly minimum wage by $1 over two years
Yes Halt funding for U.S. mission in Kosovo unless European nations pay more
?   Provide Medicare benefits to military retirees and their dependents
No   Grant China permanent normal trade status
Yes Phase out estate, gift and trust taxes
No   Prohibit implementation of president's national monument designations
No   Approve GOP plan to provide prescription drug coverage for Medicare beneficiaries
Yes Increase help for poor nations indebted to international financial institutions

1999

Yes Impose steel import quotas
No   Kill proposal to take aviation trust funds off budget
Yes Require background checks on buyers only at gun shows with 10 or more vendors
?   Remove barriers among banking, securities and insurance companies
Yes Authorize state grants to hire teachers and reduce class size
Yes Overhaul campaign finance law; ban "soft money" and restrict advocacy advertising
Yes Approve bipartisan plan to increase rights of patients in managed-care health plans

INTEREST GROUPS

	AFL-CIO	ADA	CCUS	ACU
2000	90%	45%	40%	37%
1999	78%	55%	28%	45%
1998	50%	45%	50%	48%
1997	75%	40%	40%	46%

CQ VOTE STUDIES

	PARTY UNITY		PRESIDENTIAL SUPPORT	
	Support	Oppose	Support	Oppose
2000	73%	27%	52%	48%
1999	66%	34%	58%	42%
1998	58%	42%	50%	50%
1997	64%	36%	42%	58%

ILLINOIS 3

Chicago — Southwest side; south and west suburbs

The 3rd covers the southwest corner of Chicago and adjacent suburbs, part of a working-class region known as the "Bungalow Belt" that is stocked with voters of Eastern European, Italian and Irish descent. Only one-fourth of the district's voters live within city limits. The remainder live in neighboring suburbs, including Cicero, a town infamous for being the center of operations for Al Capone's mob and the site of a 1966 race riot.

Crisscrossed by highways, railroads and the Chicago Sanitary and Ship Canal, the 3rd remains a center of manufacturing and distribution. Expansion projects at Midway Airport have broadened the district's retail and service base, which has created new jobs for district residents.

Although the 3rd routinely re-elects its Democratic representative,

its working- and middle-class voters hold conservative views on many social issues. Redistricting shifted this once urban-machine district west into suburban territory when a new Hispanic-majority district was created to its north. The change inserted a significant Republican vote in the district's more affluent suburbs, especially in western Cook County.

In national elections, the 3rd typically votes Democratic, but not by the same wide margins as in other Chicago-based districts. Bill Clinton carried the district easily in 1996, but in '92, he won the 3rd by a slim plurality. In 2000, Al Gore secured the district by 14 percent.

MAJOR INDUSTRY
Metals and other heavy manufacturing, trucking, warehouses

CITIES
Chicago (pt.), 147,861 (1990); Oak Lawn (pt.), 46,540 (1990); Berwyn, 42,894; Cicero (pt.), 39,480 (1990); Burbank, 27,834

UNUSUAL FEATURES
Houby Festival celebrating Czech heritage, named after the Czech word for mushroom.

Rep. Luis V. Gutierrez (D)

Elected 1992; 5th term

CAPITOL OFFICE
225-8203; fax 225-7810; 2452 Rayburn Bldg. 20515

INTERNET
e-mail: luis.gutierrez@mail.house.gov
web: www.house.gov/gutierrez

COMMITTEES
Financial Services
Veterans' Affairs

HOMETOWN
Chicago

BORN
Dec. 10, 1953, Chicago, Ill.

RELIGION
Roman Catholic

FAMILY
Wife, Soraida Arocho Gutierrez; two children

EDUCATION
Northeastern Illinois U., B.A. 1975

CAREER
Teacher; social worker

POLITICAL HIGHLIGHTS
Chicago City Council, 1986-93

ELECTION RESULTS

2000 GENERAL

Luis V. Gutierrez (D)	89,487	88.6%
Stephanie Sailor (LIBERT)	11,476	11.4%

2000 PRIMARY

Luis V. Gutierrez (D)	35,593	82.3%
Joseph L. Pagan (D)	7,663	17.7%

1998 GENERAL

Luis V. Gutierrez (D)	54,244	81.7%
John Birch (R)	10,529	15.9%
William Passmore (LIBERT)	1,583	2.4%

PREVIOUS WINNING PERCENTAGES
1996 (94%); 1994 (75%); 1992 (78%)

Gutierrez is used to waging lonely battles, as a liberal member of a conservative-run House, the first Hispanic member of Congress from Illinois, one of just three members of Puerto Rican descent and a representative of one of the poorest, least-educated districts in the nation. If he can seldom expect to taste legislative victory, at least he makes sure that his views are heard.

Rhetorical barbs have been a favorite weapon of Gutierrez since his earliest days in Congress, bringing him attention, if not always the results he desires. When he was a freshman, his nationally televised criticisms of Congress drew an icy response from his Democratic colleagues, probably ensuring that he will never ascend to a committee with top-drawer prestige.

In more recent years, his targets have ranged from conservative Republicans in the House to the U.S. Navy and the Immigration and Naturalization Service to President and Mrs. Clinton, leaving some colleagues to wonder who might be next.

Since the GOP took control of the House in 1995, Gutierrez (goo-tee-AIR-ez) has fashioned a role for himself as a critic of the majority party and defender of liberal values. In 1997, just before Congress passed the budget plan worked out between the Clinton administration and congressional Republicans, Gutierrez gave his verdict on the agreement: "A low-income veteran who took a bullet or two at Iwo Jima or Vietnam has to make another sacrifice to help an investor who wants to take a profit on Wall Street."

On issues such as the environment, education, labor-management relations and abortion, Gutierrez sees the GOP agenda as detrimental to his district, which has a Hispanic majority and many lower-income people. It is among the top dozen or so districts with the highest percentage of non-citizens and one of the poorest dozen districts in terms of per capita income.

As chairman of the Congressional Hispanic Caucus' Task Force on Immigration and Citizenship, Gutierrez has devoted much rhetorical energy to accusing Republicans of shabby treatment of immigrants. One target was the welfare overhaul bill enacted in the 104th Congress, which barred, temporarily as it turned out, legal immigrants from receiving benefits such as Supplemental Security Income, a program for the elderly, blind and disabled.

Gutierrez's fellow Democrats do not escape his wrath. He complained in a letter to President Clinton that "the trust we placed in you regarding immigration issues was unwarranted and ill-advised."

In 1999 and 2000, he was outspoken in his insistence that the U.S. Navy abandon its training facility on the small island of Vieques, just off the coast of Puerto Rico, after a civilian was killed in a bombing accident. In May 2000, he was among a group of more than 100 protesters, including New York Democratic Rep. Nydia M. Velázquez, who were forcibly removed from the bombing range. He was arrested in another protest in April 2001.

Gutierrez also had a high profile during House debate in the 105th on a bill to let Puerto Rico choose either statehood, independence or continued status as a U.S. commonwealth. Gutierrez, who went to high school in Puerto Rico and says he first registered to vote there, plainly states his preference: "I want Puerto Rico to be a free and independent nation."

Gutierrez's legislative goals include a number of proposals aimed at improving mass transit and making it more affordable for poor people, a bill to outlaw handguns known as Saturday night specials, and legislation to require insurance and securities affiliates of large financial services firms to do business in poor neighborhoods.

Gutierrez sits on the same committees he got when he first came to Congress: Financial Services (formerly Banking) and Veterans' Affairs.

His chances of higher-profile assignments dimmed in 1994, just a year into his tenure in the House, when he denounced Congress' shortcomings on the widely watched CBS program "60 Minutes." Gutierrez's mocking of the ways of Washington drew raves from critics of Congress: After the show, his office reported receiving more than 500 phone calls and faxes praising his integrity and candor. But many of Gutierrez's House colleagues reacted with sneers, calling him a self-serving phony who had cut his political teeth in the rough-and-tumble of the Chicago City Council and then pronounced himself a great congressional reformer.

In the 107th, Gutierrez claimed the top Democratic post on the Financial Services panel's Oversight and Investigations Subcommittee. In the 106th, as the ranking Democrat on the Veterans' Affairs Health Subcommittee, Gutierrez warned that "accountant-driven policy-making" threatened to reduce the quality of health care provided to veterans.

He got into a verbal scuffle with Republicans in 1999 during a Veterans' Affairs Committee meeting on the budget for veterans programs. Gutierrez accused Chairman Bob Stump, R-Ariz., of "acting in an arbitrary and dictatorial manner" and then got into a shouting match with Steve Buyer of Indiana that degenerated into an exchange of "you grow up. ... no, YOU grow up."

Gutierrez's ethnic background put him in the middle of an unusual Capitol Hill incident in 1996. Returning to his office from a reception with his daughter and niece, Gutierrez was confronted by a security officer who questioned his assertion that he was a member of Congress and then said, according to Gutierrez, "Everything would be all right if you and your people would go back to the country you come from."

Gutierrez, who was born in Chicago, returned there after high school in Puerto Rico to attend college. He worked for more than a decade as a teacher, social worker and community activist, backing the 1983 insurgent mayoral bid of Democrat Harold Washington over Democrat Richard M. Daley. He was elected as a Chicago alderman in 1986.

After Washington died and Daley became mayor, Gutierrez and Daley reconciled. When the oddly shaped Hispanic-majority 4th District was created for the 1992 election (incumbent Democratic Rep. George E. Sangmeister was moved to the 11th District), Daley backed Gutierrez for the post. Daley's support practically guaranteed Gutierrez the non-Hispanic white vote, and he won easily in the heavily Democratic district. Since then, he generally has faced a primary challenge and then breezed past any opposition in the fall.

KEY VOTES

2000
Yes Raise hourly minimum wage by $1 over two years
Yes Halt funding for U.S. mission in Kosovo unless European nations pay more
Yes Provide Medicare benefits to military retirees and their dependents
No Grant China permanent normal trade status
No Phase out estate, gift and trust taxes
No Prohibit implementation of president's national monument designations
No Approve GOP plan to provide prescription drug coverage for Medicare beneficiaries
Yes Increase help for poor nations indebted to international financial institutions

1999
Yes Impose steel import quotas
No Kill proposal to take aviation trust funds off budget
No Require background checks on buyers only at gun shows with 10 or more vendors
Yes Remove barriers among banking, securities and insurance companies
Yes Authorize state grants to hire teachers and reduce class size
Yes Overhaul campaign finance law; ban "soft money" and restrict advocacy advertising
Yes Approve bipartisan plan to increase rights of patients in managed-care health plans

INTEREST GROUPS

	AFL-CIO	ADA	CCUS	ACU
2000	100%	90%	38%	9%
1999	100%	95%	16%	0%
1998	100%	90%	28%	16%
1997	100%	95%	13%	13%

CQ VOTE STUDIES

	PARTY UNITY		PRESIDENTIAL SUPPORT	
	Support	Oppose	Support	Oppose
2000	96%	4%	84%	16%
1999	93%	7%	76%	24%
1998	93%	7%	83%	17%
1997	91%	9%	75%	25%

ILLINOIS 4
Chicago — Parts of North Side, southwest side

Surrounding a black-majority district in the center of Chicago, the horseshoe-shaped 4th was drawn to unite the city's Hispanic neighborhoods into one voting bloc. The district was created after the 1990 census showed that Chicago's Hispanic population had boomed to more than 500,000 people.

A narrow strip of land — about 10 miles in length and running along railroad tracks, forest preserves and cemeteries — attaches the Puerto Rican neighborhood of Logan Square to the Mexican-American communities in Little Village and Pilsen. In 1998, the Supreme Court declined to hear a suit alleging that the district had been unconstitutionally drawn with race as the major factor.

The 4th has significant immigrant populations in both its Hispanic communities and adjacent Ukrainian and Polish neighborhoods. It includes the historically Irish neighborhood of Bridgeport, the former home and political base of the Daley machine. It also includes parts

of Back of the Yards, an area that declined when the city's famed stockyards closed in the early 1970s.

With more blue-collar workers than any other district north of the Mason-Dixon line, the 4th is solidly Democratic. It has been plagued by low voter turnout, and many of the district's Hispanic immigrants are ineligible to vote. But success in preserving the district's boundaries has helped mobilize nonpartisan Hispanic organizations to get out the vote.

MAJOR INDUSTRY
Light manufacturing, county administration, electronics

CITIES
Chicago (pt.), 527,492 (1990); Cicero (pt.), 27,956 (1990)

UNUSUAL FEATURES
Mexican Fine Arts Center Museum.

Rep. Rod R. Blagojevich (D)

Elected 1996; 3rd term

CAPITOL OFFICE
225-4061; fax 225-5603; 331 Cannon Bldg. 20515

INTERNET
e-mail: rod.blagojevich@mail.house.gov
web: www.house.gov/blagojevich

COMMITTEES
Armed Services
Government Reform

HOMETOWN
Chicago

BORN
Dec. 10, 1956, Chicago, Ill.

RELIGION
Eastern Orthodox

FAMILY
Wife, Patricia Blagojevich; one child

EDUCATION
Northwestern U., B.A. 1979; Pepperdine U., J.D. 1983

CAREER
Lawyer

POLITICAL HIGHLIGHTS
Assistant Cook County state's attorney, 1986-88; Ill. House, 1993-97

ELECTION RESULTS

2000 GENERAL

Rod R. Blagojevich (D)	142,161	87.3%
Matt Beauchamp (LIBERT)	20,728	12.7%

2000 PRIMARY

Rod R. Blagojevich (D)	unopposed

1998 GENERAL

Rod R. Blagojevich (D)	95,738	74.0%
Alan Spitz (R)	33,687	26.0%

PREVIOUS WINNING PERCENTAGES
1996 (64%)

Growing up in an apartment on Chicago's northwest side, Blagojevich learned to speak his father's native Serbian language and grew to appreciate his parents' Balkan heritage and culture. Four decades later, Blagojevich — the only member of Congress of Serbian extraction — put that unique background to use when he joined the Rev. Jesse L. Jackson on an unofficial trip to Belgrade in early 1999. There, as American bombs rained down, Blagojevich and Jackson negotiated the release of three U.S. servicemen who had been captured during the U.S.-led bombing offensive against Yugoslavian strongman Slobodan Milosevic.

Blagojevich (bla-GOY-a-vich) won a seat in the House in 1996 by defeating Republican Michael Patrick Flanagan, who had upset longtime Democratic war horse Dan Rostenkowski in 1994. Flanagan's win had helped the GOP gain control of the House. In winning back the seat Rostenkowski had held for 36 years, Blagojevich proclaimed, "This vote sends a clear message to Newt Gingrich and the radical right: Your revolution is over. Common sense has prevailed."

Those sounded like fighting words from an ardent liberal, and Blagojevich — a former Golden Gloves boxer who now runs marathons — does stand far to the left of the conservative House GOP majority on numerous high-profile issues, such as abortion and gun control.

But Blagojevich sometimes parts ways with members of his own party. His meeting with Milosevic drew criticism from some Democrats as inappropriate meddling outside official channels. Blagojevich maintains that he had offered his assistance to the Clinton administration in working to obtain the release of the three U.S. servicemen. When the White House did not respond, he hooked up with Jackson.

Blagojevich makes an effort to reach out to the disparate elements of his constituency, which includes upscale "lakefront liberals" in Chicago, more-conservative working-class white ethnic Democrats in the city, and Republican-leaning suburban voters. In the 106th Congress, he was among the minority of Democrats who backed the GOP-drafted bill to ease the "marriage penalty," a quirk in the tax code that results in some two-earner married couples paying higher taxes than they would if each partner were single.

In addition to supporting abortion rights and advocating a ban on handgun ownership by anyone under 21, Blagojevich talks a lot about "working middle-class Americans struggling to pay their bills, send their kids to school and save for their retirement."

A former prosecutor in Chicago's Cook County, Blagojevich decries the "lethal mix of kids and guns." He cites a study by the Centers for Disease Control and Prevention that found that "children in the United States are 12 times more likely to die because of a firearm than children in other industrial countries." Exposure to urban violence — he says he has been robbed at gunpoint twice — motivates his effort to prohibit handgun possession by young people and to limit adults to one handgun purchase per month. Blagojevich says that some gun owners' rights advocates "love their guns more than they love their wives," the Chicago Sun-Times reported.

The lawmaker is associated with a wide range of gun control plans. In the 106th Congress, Blagojevich pressed for background checks on prospective purchasers at gun shows, tough restrictions on armor-piercing .50-caliber sniper rifles and ammunition and a ban on police departments making old police guns and seized weapons available for purchase in the secondhand market.

He joined many Republicans in insisting that part of the blame for an increase in violence among young people should be laid on the entertainment industry. "These people who purvey violence and desensitize violence on the Internet and the video games and so forth are as socially irresponsible as the NRA [National Rifle Association]," he told NBC news.

Blagojevich has attended to a number of district needs, including finding federal money to repair crumbling schools and to supply books for school and public libraries, getting funds for Lake Michigan shoreline protection, and backing the city's fight against drugs and street crime. In the 105th Congress, he raised an alarm over a Navy plan to ship millions of pounds of Vietnam War-era napalm by rail from California, through the Chicago area, to a disposal site in Indiana. Blagojevich was criticized for his concern by those who said he greatly overstated the risks, but the plan was scrapped.

Blagojevich's father was an officer in the Yugoslavian Army during World War II. He was a prisoner of the Nazis for four years and eventually made his way to Chicago, where he met a woman whose parents had come from Bosnia-Herzegovina. Blagojevich's father took a job as a machinist in a factory. At home, Blagojevich learned Serbian music and folklore.

After graduating from Northwestern University with a degree in history, Blagojevich got a law degree from Pepperdine, worked as a neighborhood lawyer back home in Chicago and then served as an assistant state's attorney. In 1992, aided by his father-in-law — powerful Chicago Alderman Richard Mell — Blagojevich entered politics, winning election to the state House. He won re-election in 1994.

In 1996, Alderman Mell mobilized his ward organization for his son-in-law. Blagojevich won the 5th District Democratic primary in a three-way race and took on Flanagan in the general election. The district's Democratic roots showed, and Blagojevich eased to victory, 64 percent to 36 percent. His winning margin was even larger in 1998, and the GOP did not bother to field a challenger in 2000.

In late 1999, Blagojevich moved into the 5th District; he had been living in the nearby 4th District, even though he had represented the 5th in Congress since his 1996 victory. He joked that he was "tired of going to the polls and voting for [Luis] Gutierrez. ... I want to be able to vote for myself," he told the Chicago Tribune.

KEY VOTES

2000

Yes Raise hourly minimum wage by $1 over two years
Yes Halt funding for U.S. mission in Kosovo unless European nations pay more
Yes Provide Medicare benefits to military retirees and their dependents
No   Grant China permanent normal trade status
Yes Phase out estate, gift and trust taxes
No   Prohibit implementation of president's national monument designations
No   Approve GOP plan to provide prescription drug coverage for Medicare beneficiaries
Yes Increase help for poor nations indebted to international financial institutions

1999

Yes Impose steel import quotas
No   Kill proposal to take aviation trust funds off budget
No   Require background checks on buyers only at gun shows with 10 or more vendors
Yes Remove barriers among banking, securities and insurance companies
Yes Authorize state grants to hire teachers and reduce class size
Yes Overhaul campaign finance law; ban "soft money" and restrict advocacy advertising
Yes Approve bipartisan plan to increase rights of patients in managed-care health plans

INTEREST GROUPS

	AFL-CIO	ADA	CCUS	ACU
2000	89%	80%	52%	25%
1999	89%	100%	30%	8%
1998	100%	100%	39%	8%
1997	100%	90%	40%	16%

CQ VOTE STUDIES

	PARTY UNITY		PRESIDENTIAL SUPPORT	
	Support	Oppose	Support	Oppose
2000	86%	14%	74%	26%
1999	91%	9%	81%	19%
1998	88%	12%	77%	23%
1997	89%	11%	82%	18%

ILLINOIS 5
Chicago – North Side

The 5th spans the North Side of Chicago, from Lake Michigan to near O'Hare International Airport (in the 6th District). One of the city's few remaining active industrial sectors runs through the middle of the district, along the north branch of the Chicago River.

On the east side, the 5th includes most of Lincoln Park and the Gold Coast, two wealthy neighborhoods of "lakefront liberals," known for their opposition to the Democratic machine. Voters here rarely support candidates from the local Democratic organization in the primary but then vote Democratic in general elections.

The west side of the district covers part of the "Bungalow Belt," a strip of 1930s brick homes built by Central and Eastern European families. Although still dominated by middle- and working-class German and Polish neighborhoods, this section of town has seen an increasing number of black and Hispanic newcomers. Voters here also lean Democratic, generally supporting the organization's primary

candidates but sometimes voting for Republicans in the general election.

The combination of these voting habits makes for a constituency that leans Democratic. The west's working-class base routinely supports candidates trumpeting populist-style economic causes. But far-west side neighborhoods also have been known to elect a few Republicans to local offices. On the federal level, the district votes Democratic, with Bill Clinton carrying the 5th in the 1990s and Al Gore securing a comfortable victory in 2000.

MAJOR INDUSTRY
Warehousing and storage, electronics, manufacturing, health care

CITIES
Chicago (pt.) 460,009 (1990); Elmwood Park, 22,379; Franklin Park, 17,900

UNUSUAL FEATURES
Famous gangster death sites: S.M.C. Cartage Co. garage, where Al Capone ordered rival "Bugs" Moran's gangsters shot in the 1929 St. Valentine's Day Massacre; Biograph Theatre, where federal agents gunned down outlaw John Dillinger in 1934.

Rep. Henry J. Hyde (R)

CAPITOL OFFICE
225-4561; fax 225-1166; 2110 Rayburn Bldg. 20515

INTERNET
e-mail: www.house.gov/writerep
web: www.house.gov/hyde

COMMITTEES
International Relations - chairman
Judiciary

HOMETOWN
Bensenville

BORN
April 18, 1924, Chicago, Ill.

RELIGION
Roman Catholic

FAMILY
Widowed; four children

EDUCATION
Duke U., attended 1943-44; Georgetown U., B.S. 1947; Loyola U., J.D. 1949

MILITARY SERVICE
Navy, 1944-46; Naval Reserve, 1946-68

CAREER
Lawyer

POLITICAL HIGHLIGHTS
Republican nominee for U.S. House, 1962; Ill. House, 1967-75 (majority leader, 1971-73)

ELECTION RESULTS

2000 GENERAL

Henry J. Hyde (R)	133,327	58.9%
Brent Christensen (D)	92,880	41.1%

2000 PRIMARY

Henry J. Hyde (R)	unopposed

1998 GENERAL

Henry J. Hyde (R)	111,603	67.3%
Thomas A. Cramer (D)	49,906	30.1%
George Meyers (LIBERT)	4,199	2.5%

PREVIOUS WINNING PERCENTAGES
1996 (64%); 1994 (74%); 1992 (66%); 1990 (67%); 1988 (74%); 1986 (75%); 1984 (75%); 1982 (68%); 1980 (67%); 1978 (66%); 1976 (61%); 1974 (53%)

Elected 1974; 14th term

Like Robert Louis Stevenson's fictional character, the House's Mr. Hyde has two different personalities — or at least a pair of distinct public images.

Among his colleagues, Hyde is respected as an old-fashioned wit, one of the sharpest legal minds on Capitol Hill and a genuinely nice man. As staunch a liberal as fellow Chicagoland Rep. Jesse L. Jackson Jr. once called Hyde "a voice of moderation." At the same time, his detractors condemn Hyde as the implacable leader of the drive to impeach President Clinton. An icon of the anti-abortion movement, his legislative legacy is a measure blocking federal funding of abortions for poor women — an accomplishment he is proud to claim but that his opponents decry.

The biggest riddle surrounding Hyde is which of his personalities will be dominant in the twilight of his career, when he is taking on an important new assignment in the House. Forced by GOP-imposed term limits to give up the gavel of the Judiciary Committee, in 2001 Hyde leveraged his seniority and his stature to secure the chairmanship of the International Relations Committee, something of a legislative backwater in recent years. Hyde has not been heavily involved in foreign policy for more than a decade, although during the Reagan administration he had a significant role on arms control issues and in the debate over Central America. He also served on the committee investigating the Iran-contra affair and was ranking Republican on the Intelligence Committee from 1987 through 1990.

Most of his own foreign policy views fall within mainstream Republican thinking, although he says he would like to build support for the further incremental expansion of NATO and write legislation that would condition U.S. aid to the Palestinian Authority on an end to violence and a return to peace negotiations with Israel. Given his status as a hero of the anti-abortion movement, he also can be expected to take a hard line in the annual battle over funds for international family planning groups.

Hyde, who attended Georgetown University on a basketball scholarship, is a hulk of a man whose imposing physical presence is paired with a rousing oratorical style. He is often the most impressive spokesman in legislative battles, pouncing on flaws in foes' arguments with all the wit and sarcasm he once used as a Chicago trial lawyer. He clearly loves the institution of Congress.

Hyde performed yeoman's service in the "Republican revolution," swiftly adapting himself to the influx of conservatives elected in the 1990s — and also helping them adapt to the House. Still, he has had some high-profile differences with the party's right wing. He gave a pivotal speech on the House floor in 1990 in favor of what later became the Family and Medical Leave Act. He voted to ban certain assault-style weapons in 1994 and 1996. And he adamantly opposes term limits, although he allowed proposed constitutional amendments on the issue to pass through his committee.

While now viewed as something of an elder statesman among House Republicans, he has never found the time right to bid for a spot in the party leadership. His highest position, in the early 1990s, was chairman of the Republican Policy Committee. He is still mentioned as a possible candidate for Speaker if the GOP rank-and-file lose faith in the current leadership.

On the legislative front, he is best known for the "Hyde amendment," written in 1976 during his first term, which blocked federal funding of abortions, and remains a source of controversy during debates over appropriations for social services.

Hyde also will always be remembered for leading the impeachment trial of Clinton. When the House voted to institute an impeachment inquiry by the Judiciary Committee in 1998, Hyde, the panel's chairman, approached the process with unswerving determination. He said that Clinton, as the nation's chief law enforcement officer, had undermined "the rule of law" by lying to a federal grand jury about his affair with former White House intern Monica Lewinsky.

Hyde was a ready target of critics of the proceedings. He even had to endure revelations by the Internet magazine Salon that he had engaged in an affair with a married woman when he was in his early 40s — which he dismissed as a "youthful indiscretion."

Hyde was able to win nearly unanimous support among House Republicans to impeach Clinton. But when the impeachment matter went before the Senate in 1999, Hyde hit a brick wall. Senate GOP leaders sought to dispose quickly of the politically unpopular impeachment proceedings when it became clear that they did not have the votes to remove Clinton from office. Hyde was blocked from mounting the far-reaching case he wanted to make.

As the trial in the Senate progressed, Hyde conceded that he and his 12 fellow House "managers" chosen to prosecute the case were an annoyance. "But," he added, "we are a constitutional annoyance." Clinton was acquitted on both impeachment articles brought by the House.

The imbroglio did not completely hamper Hyde's efforts to lead the politically riven Judiciary Committee. In 2000, he scored a personal triumph with enactment of a law, which he had been pushing since 1993, to make it more difficult for federal agents to seize private property that they suspect is linked to a crime. He said that the previous system had been abused by law enforcement agencies and that not enough protections existed for the innocent.

While Hyde has no great reputation for championing parochial concerns, he puts much importance on seeing to the construction of a third airport to serve the Chicago area. His website declares the issue to be his highest priority in Congress. He opposed the reauthorization of federal aviation law in 2000 because it called for more flights at O'Hare, which is in his district.

Hyde grew up in Chicago as an Irish Catholic Democrat. He began having doubts about the Democratic Party in the late 1940s; by 1952, he had switched parties and backed Dwight D. Eisenhower for president.

Elected to the Illinois House in 1966, Hyde was one of its most outspoken and articulate debaters, rising to majority leader, but losing a bid for Speaker. In 1974, longtime GOP Rep. Harold Collier retired from the suburban Chicago 6th District. Capitalizing on his fundraising prowess and his army of precinct workers, Hyde won 53 percent and has been invincible ever since.

KEY VOTES

2000

Yes	Raise hourly minimum wage by $1 over two years
Yes	Halt funding for U.S. mission in Kosovo unless European nations pay more
Yes	Provide Medicare benefits to military retirees and their dependents
Yes	Grant China permanent normal trade status
Yes	Phase out estate, gift and trust taxes
Yes	Prohibit implementation of president's national monument designations
Yes	Approve GOP plan to provide prescription drug coverage for Medicare beneficiaries
No	Increase help for poor nations indebted to international financial institutions

1999

No	Impose steel import quotas
Yes	Kill proposal to take aviation trust funds off budget
Yes	Require background checks on buyers only at gun shows with 10 or more vendors
Yes	Remove barriers among banking, securities and insurance companies
No	Authorize state grants to hire teachers and reduce class size
No	Overhaul campaign finance law; ban "soft money" and restrict advocacy advertising
Yes	Approve bipartisan plan to increase rights of patients in managed-care health plans

INTEREST GROUPS

	AFL-CIO	ADA	CCUS	ACU
2000	20%	10%	71%	76%
1999	22%	15%	75%	72%
1998	0%	0%	88%	92%
1997	25%	20%	70%	68%

CQ VOTE STUDIES

	PARTY UNITY		PRESIDENTIAL SUPPORT	
	Support	Oppose	Support	Oppose
2000	89%	11%	35%	65%
1999	89%	11%	31%	69%
1998	92%	8%	20%	80%
1997	91%	9%	28%	72%

ILLINOIS 6

Northwest and west Chicago suburbs

Adjacent to the north half of Chicago, the 6th includes northern DuPage County and northwest suburban Cook County. It's full of older, mostly built-out bedroom communities along commuter rail lines running into the city. Many of these towns have been revitalizing their downtown districts.

Most residents of the 6th have traditionally commuted to Chicago, but some now travel to booming northwest satellite cities like Shaumburg and Naperville. The 6th's commercial district is concentrated on the far north side near one of the world's busiest airports, O'Hare International (an extension of the city of Chicago). Rosemont, a suburb just east of the airport, has few residents but houses thousands of businesses and hotels for people who use O'Hare as a commuter hub.

The 6th has a reputation as a Republican machine, historically working in opposition to Chicago's Democrats. DuPage County, where two-thirds of the district's population lives, is solidly Republican in both the

6th and 13th districts. The county does have a number of Hispanics who came when agriculture dominated the landscape. Many stayed as Chicago's suburbs began to creep west and take over farmland during the 1970s and '80s. Suburban Cook County's population, including quite a few empty-nesters, is also traditionally conservative.

MAJOR INDUSTRY
Airport, health care, light manufacturing

CITIES
Des Plains (pt.), 52,639 (1990); Elmhurst, 44,153; Wheaton (pt.), 38,464 (1990); Lombard (pt.), 38,032 (1990); Park Ridge, 37,866; Addison, 34,259

UNUSUAL FEATURES
Donald E. Stephens Museum of Hummels, collectible ceramic figurines; Sen. and former First Lady Hillary Rodham Clinton, native of Park Ridge.

Rep. Danny K. Davis (D)

Elected 1996; 3rd term

CAPITOL OFFICE
225-5006; fax 225-5641
1222 Longworth Bldg. 20515

INTERNET
e-mail: www.house.gov/writerep
web: www.house.gov/davis

COMMITTEES
Government Reform
Small Business

HOMETOWN
Chicago

BORN
Sept. 6, 1941, Parkdale, Ark.

RELIGION
Baptist

FAMILY
Wife, Vera Davis; two children

EDUCATION
Arkansas A.M.&N. College, B.A. 1961; Chicago
State U., M.A. 1968; Union Institute, Ph.D. 1977

CAREER
Health care consultant; teacher

POLITICAL HIGHLIGHTS
Chicago City Council, 1979-90; sought Democratic
nomination for U.S. House, 1984, 1986; Cook
County Commission, 1990-97; candidate for mayor
of Chicago, 1991

ELECTION RESULTS

2000 GENERAL

Danny K. Davis (D)	164,155	85.9%
Robert Dallas (R)	26,872	14.1%

2000 PRIMARY

Danny K. Davis (D)	unopposed

1998 GENERAL

Danny K. Davis (D)	130,984	92.9%
Dorn Van Cleave III (LIBERT)	9,984	7.1%

PREVIOUS WINNING PERCENTAGES
1996 (82%)

As a liberal Democrat in a Republican-run institution, Davis' crusades are often lonely ones. He knows that legislative victories can be hard to come by, and he takes pleasure in the occasional triumphs. "We're always climbing up the rough side of the mountain," he says. "When you're on the losing side so often and you finally win, you say to yourself, 'yeah, we got one.'"

One such victory came in 2000, when Davis was a principal mover behind a package of anti-poverty initiatives to revitalize poor neighborhoods. Another was the 1998 House vote in favor of his proposal to increase funding in a massive transportation authorization bill for a program to help low-income people commute to their jobs.

Davis' liberal views make him a natural for the Congressional Progressive Caucus, a group of about 50 members that anchors the left side of the chamber's ideological spectrum. Serving on the caucus' executive committee, he is pragmatic enough to know they will never get enough votes for their legislative agenda, but he dauntlessly keeps pushing. "If you're facing south, you may eventually get to Richmond, even if it's only an inch at a time," he says. "But if you're facing Baltimore, you're not going to make it."

Though his liberal views are strongly held and freely expressed, Davis often sprinkles his arguments with humorous stories and light asides. A gregarious, enthusiastic man with a deep, melodious voice, Davis laces his talk with tidbits of personal philosophy, drawing heavily on his childhood as one of 11 children born to sharecroppers who picked cotton in southeastern Arkansas — one of the poorest regions of the country.

He says he and his brothers and sisters went to a segregated school only four or five months of the year, spending the rest of the time in the fields. Davis recalls how his parents told their children: go to school, do your chores, put in an honest day's work. "We had no money, but we never felt we were poor," he says.

Representing a district in the heart of Chicago is different in many ways from his rural upbringing, but Davis says he sees many of the same problems, a result of the disparity in wealth in American society. He pleads for "economic policies that will also create jobs for which people can actually work and earn a decent wage, a livable wage." His legislative efforts include work to improve transportation, housing, health care and education for his heterogeneous district, which includes not only huge public housing projects but also some well-to-do suburbs, plush "Gold Coast" high rises and the downtown Loop.

He joined in a bipartisan bill to require local and state governments to reduce taxes and regulatory requirements on companies operating in designated urban and rural renewal areas, in addition to tax-advantaged savings accounts for low-income families living in the designated communities.

In the Congressional Black Caucus, Davis has pushed for a serious look at police brutality and racial profiling, seeking "equal application of the law" — which he sees as a major focus in the future of the ongoing civil rights struggle.

A member of the Government Reform Committee, Davis worked to increase participation in the 2000 census, particularly in low-income areas. He also pressed the U.S. Postal Service (where he once worked as a clerk) to move more minorities into the ranks of management.

He offered legislation to give ex-felons the right to vote, explaining that some states reinstate felons' voting rights after they have completed their sentence but that 10 states do not. "Once individuals have paid their debts to society ... then they should have the right to participate," he explained.

Participation in community life is something that Davis is trying to encourage. "People are very cynical and not involved usually ... and it's often the folks who are most affected by public programs who are the least involved," he argues, citing the census as an example.

Davis says he learned perseverance, or maybe stubbornness, from his father and empathy for others from his mother. He recalls times when his mother put him on a mule to deliver a pot of stew to a neighbor in need. "They instilled whatever drive and desire I may have had," he notes.

Davis says he went off to college in Arkansas with the idea of becoming a teacher. After graduation, with $50 given to him by his father, Davis set off for California where a job awaited. But his money ran out, and he got no farther than Chicago. He stayed with an older sister for a time and worked in the post office and at other jobs before landing a teaching position.

The teaching post in a tough Chicago neighborhood was a real education, Davis said. He soon realized he wanted to be more involved in the community, and his activism eventually led to work in the health care field, where he rose to become president of the National Association of Community Health Centers. In 1979, Davis headed a committee of neighborhood leaders looking for a candidate to challenge the Democratic political machine in a city council race, but he failed to turn up anyone. "So I said, 'what the hell,' and decided to run myself," he said.

Davis won — the first black alderman who was not part of the regular party machinery — and served there until 1990, when he became a Cook County commissioner. On the city council, Davis was a close associate of Harold Washington, the city's first black mayor, who also had challenged the Democratic machine.

In 1984, Davis tried for the 7th District seat, waging a Democratic primary challenge to Rep. Cardiss Collins. Davis lost by 10 points but held Collins to less than a majority of the vote. Davis opposed Collins again in 1986 but lost decisively. And in 1991, Davis was the decided underdog in a Democratic primary campaign for mayor against the incumbent, Richard M. Daley.

When Collins announced plans to retire from the House in 1996, Davis jumped into the race to succeed her. He again faced a crowded primary field, as well as opposition from some elements of the party machine, but he cleared those hurdles and won the election in November with ease. He has not been seriously challenged since.

KEY VOTES

2000

Yes Raise hourly minimum wage by $1 over two years
Yes Halt funding for U.S. mission in Kosovo unless European nations pay more
Yes Provide Medicare benefits to military retirees and their dependents
No   Grant China permanent normal trade status
No   Phase out estate, gift and trust taxes
No   Prohibit implementation of president's national monument designations
No   Approve GOP plan to provide prescription drug coverage for Medicare beneficiaries
Yes Increase help for poor nations indebted to international financial institutions

1999

Yes Impose steel import quotas
No   Kill proposal to take aviation trust funds off budget
No   Require background checks on buyers only at gun shows with 10 or more vendors
Yes Remove barriers among banking, securities and insurance companies
Yes Authorize state grants to hire teachers and reduce class size
Yes Overhaul campaign finance law; ban "soft money" and restrict advocacy advertising
Yes Approve bipartisan plan to increase rights of patients in managed-care health plans

INTEREST GROUPS

	AFL-CIO	ADA	CCUS	ACU
2000	100%	100%	33%	4%
1999	100%	100%	17%	0%
1998	100%	95%	28%	8%
1997	100%	100%	10%	8%

CQ VOTE STUDIES

	PARTY UNITY		PRESIDENTIAL SUPPORT	
	Support	Oppose	Support	Oppose
2000	97%	3%	88%	12%
1999	97%	3%	84%	16%
1998	95%	5%	85%	15%
1997	95%	5%	77%	23%

ILLINOIS 7
Chicago — Downtown; West Side

The 7th stretches from the Loop, Chicago's downtown business district, to the DuPage County line, taking in the well-to-do western suburbs of Oak Park and River Forest. The eastern end houses some of Chicago's gems, including the Sears Tower, the plush high rises of River North, several museums, and 12 colleges and universities. But most of the district lives in the poverty-stricken neighborhoods that stretch from the western Loop to the edge of the county.

Except for a few communities of middle-class blacks, the West Side has had problems with gang violence, unemployment and crumbling infrastructure. The situation is beginning to change in the West Loop, once dominated by the Cabrini-Green housing project, where young couples and development companies have rehabilitated old apartment buildings and warehouses, turning them into condos and lofts.

The district fills with white commuters during the day, but two-thirds of the district's permanent residents are black. A reliably Democratic district across the ballot, the only geniune political contests in the 7th are the Democratic primaries. The exception is the far western suburbs, where Republicans are often elected to local offices.

MAJOR INDUSTRY
Insurance, banking, accounting

CITIES
Chicago (pt.), 424,013 (1990); Oak Park (pt.), 45,049 (1990)

UNUSUAL FEATURES
United Center, arena for the Chicago Bulls and Blackhawks; Soldier Field, stadium for the Chicago Bears; Ernest Hemingway's birthplace and home in Oak Park; Oprah Winfrey's Harpo Productions in Chicago; Architect Frank Lloyd Wright's home and studio in Oak Park.

Rep. Philip M. Crane (R)

Elected November 1969; 16th full term

At the start of the 107th Congress, Crane lost a battle for what would have been the biggest prize of his 30-year political career — the chairmanship of the powerful Ways and Means Committee, where he has served for 25 years.

The defeat was made all the more bitter by the fact that the man who won the top post, Republican Bill Thomas of California, had 10 years less seniority than Crane. And the vote of the Republican Steering Committee, the leadership panel that selects chairmen, was unanimous for Thomas.

As a consolation prize, Crane was granted a waiver from the six-year term limits imposed on committee chairmen and allowed to remain at the helm of the Ways and Means Trade Subcommittee. But that only softened the blow after Crane had spent months lobbying GOP leaders and raising campaign funds for other Republican lawmakers in hopes of winning support for the committee chairmanship.

Although Crane is respected for his intelligence — he holds a doctorate in history and has written three books on politics — he has never established himself as a party insider. The House GOP agenda is generally set by leaders who are a decade or two younger than Crane.

Crane's loss of the chairmanship concluded what had been a rollercoaster year for the most-senior member of the House GOP and the only House Republican whose service began in the 1960s.

In March 2000, Crane checked himself into a Maryland rehabilitation clinic where he underwent treatment for alcoholism. He entered the facility after a group of friends confronted him in his House office and urged him to seek help. Crane said he was drinking as many as 10 beers a night. Although he plays down the drinking problem, calling it a bad "habit" similar to smoking and even boasting that he left the clinic several days ahead of schedule, many of his colleagues said the drinking had caused him to lose any effectiveness as a legislator.

Immediately after his treatment, Crane made a quick comeback in the House. On April 12, one day after returning to work following rehabilitation, he did something he had never done in his 32 years in office: He presided over the House in the Speaker's chair. His office said it was just a coincidence that such a visible honor should occur upon his return to Capitol Hill, but it kicked off a series of high-profile events for Crane.

In May, the House passed a bill, written by Crane, to increase imports from the Caribbean, Central America and sub-Saharan Africa. It was similar to legislation Crane had first introduced in 1995. Even months later, Crane proudly kept in his breast pocket a blue pen inscribed with President Clinton's signature given to him by Clinton after he had signed the bill into law.

Three weeks after passage of the Caribbean legislation, the House approved another bill Crane had pushed for, granting China permanent normal trade status. The measure did not go through Crane's Trade Subcommittee, but he served as floor manager during the debate. "In order to protect our national security interests, the United States must develop a policy that encourages China to be a friend and a valued trading partner, rather than an isolated adversary," he said.

With the passage of the two trade bills, Crane can take partial credit for expanding U.S. trade to about 40 percent of the world's population — China, Africa, the Caribbean, and Central America. He does not share the skepticism about lowering trade barriers that is harbored by some on the GOP

CAPITOL OFFICE
225-3711; fax 225-7830; 233 Cannon Bldg. 20515

INTERNET
web: www.house.gov/crane

COMMITTEES
Ways & Means
(Trade - chairman)
Joint Taxation

HOMETOWN
Wauconda

BORN
Nov. 3, 1930, Chicago, Ill.

RELIGION
Protestant

FAMILY
Wife, Arlene Catherine Crane; eight children (one deceased)

EDUCATION
DePauw U., attended 1948-50; Hillsdale College, B.A. 1952; U. of Michigan, attended 1952-54; U. of Vienna (Austria), attended 1953, attended 1956; Indiana U., M.A. 1961, Ph.D. 1963

MILITARY SERVICE
Army, 1954-56

CAREER
Professor; author; advertising executive

POLITICAL HIGHLIGHTS
Sought Republican nomination for president, 1980

ELECTION RESULTS

2000 GENERAL

Philip M. Crane (R)	141,918	61.0%
Lance Pressl (D)	90,777	39.0%

2000 PRIMARY

Philip M. Crane (R)	unopposed

1998 GENERAL

Philip M. Crane (R)	104,242	68.6%
Mike Rothman (D)	47,614	31.4%

PREVIOUS WINNING PERCENTAGES
1996 (62%); 1994 (65%); 1992 (56%); 1990 (82%); 1988 (75%); 1986 (78%); 1984 (78%); 1982 (66%); 1980 (74%); 1978 (80%); 1976 (73%); 1974 (61%); 1972 (74%); 1970 (58%); 1969 Special Election (58%)

right. In the 104th and 105th Congresses, he supported renewing the president's fast-track authority to negotiate trade agreements that Congress must approve or reject without amendment.

A conservative purist — he is a former chairman of the American Conservative Union — Crane has been criticized by some GOP colleagues for pursuing unrealistic legislative goals and failing to assemble a record of legislative accomplishment. "There are four functions of government that we should fund: Defense, State, Justice and the Treasury," Crane told the Chicago Sun-Times in 1995. "Even the Department of Agriculture, which was created in the 1850s, is not essential."

An ardent tax foe, Crane has proposed plans to create a 10 percent flat tax and eliminate all other taxes, such as the income tax. Immediately after losing his bid for the Ways and Means chairmanship, Crane urged Thomas to pursue large tax cuts from his post as leader of the committee. "I strongly believe that we must reduce the tax burden to keep our economy strong and improve Americans' lives," he said. "I believe it would be a grave mistake for our country and the Republican Party not to do so."

For more than three decades, Crane's political career has thrived in the conservative environment of the affluent northwest Chicago suburbs. In 1969, Crane entered the GOP primary in a special election that followed President Nixon's appointment of GOP Rep. Donald Rumsfeld to head the Office of Economic Opportunity. Crane topped a seven-candidate field with 22 percent of the vote. His Democratic opponent tried to paint him as an ideological extremist, but Crane's soft-spoken and articulate manner helped him win with 58 percent.

In the 1970s, Crane was a wunderkind among conservatives. After Jimmy Carter won the presidency in 1976, Crane aspired to lead the national conservative Republican counterattack. Dashingly handsome, well-spoken and still shy of 50, Crane launched a bid for the 1980 GOP presidential nomination.

But after he spent a year trying to organize support for the New Hampshire primary, William Loeb, then the acerbic Manchester Union Leader publisher and political baron, ran articles accusing Crane of heavy drinking and womanizing. By the time New Hampshire voted, Crane was a minor candidate and received just 1.8 percent of the vote. He won five convention delegates but withdrew and instead endorsed Ronald Reagan.

From 1972 through 1990, he won re-election easily, never dropping below 60 percent. In the early 1990s, however, he began to draw serious intraparty challenges from more-moderate Republicans. But Crane survived the primary challenges by relying on his conservative base. His seat has been safe since.

KEY VOTES

2000

No Raise hourly minimum wage by $1 over two years

Yes Halt funding for U.S. mission in Kosovo unless European nations pay more

Yes Provide Medicare benefits to military retirees and their dependents

Yes Grant China permanent normal trade status

Yes Phase out estate, gift and trust taxes

Yes Prohibit implementation of president's national monument designations

Yes Approve GOP plan to provide prescription drug coverage for Medicare beneficiaries

No Increase help for poor nations indebted to international financial institutions

1999

No Impose steel import quotas

No Kill proposal to take aviation trust funds off budget

Yes Require background checks on buyers only at gun shows with 10 or more vendors

Yes Remove barriers among banking, securities and insurance companies

No Authorize state grants to hire teachers and reduce class size

No Overhaul campaign finance law; ban "soft money" and restrict advocacy advertising

No Approve bipartisan plan to increase rights of patients in managed-care health plans

INTEREST GROUPS

	AFL-CIO	ADA	CCUS	ACU
2000	0%	0%	85%	100%
1999	0%	5%	91%	100%
1998	0%	0%	81%	96%
1997	0%	5%	80%	96%

CQ VOTE STUDIES

	PARTY UNITY		PRESIDENTIAL SUPPORT	
	Support	Oppose	Support	Oppose
2000	94%	6%	24%	76%
1999	96%	4%	16%	84%
1998	96%	4%	24%	76%
1997	96%	4%	23%	77%

ILLINOIS 8

Northwest Cook County — Schaumburg; Palatine

Most of the 8th's population lies in the affluent, well-established suburbs of northwest Cook County, about 30 miles from Chicago, west of the North Shore suburbs. Population growth has spurred new developments through western Lake County and into the "chain o' lakes" vacation communities near the Wisconsin border.

The district became a huge employment center in the late 1980s, drawing commuters away from Chicago and causing serious traffic problems. Like other suburban areas, the 8th is struggling with problems that come with rapid development and suburban sprawl. As in other northwestern suburban districts, some of the 8th's cities, such as Schaumburg and Palatine, have attracted corporate headquarters. Motorola has set up shop in Schaumburg.

The district has some well-established suburbs in its southeast corner, the nearest part to Chicago, including Mount Prospect and the southern part of Arlington Heights (the rest is in the 10th District). The

biggest boom has been farther west; development has been abetted by access to Interstates 90 and 290 and proximity to O'Hare International Airport (in the 6th District).

Unlike other staunchly Republican suburban districts, voters in the 8th tend to be socially, as well as fiscally, conservative. The 8th's Republican tradition has been moderated only slightly by newcomers and a small but growing minority population.

MAJOR INDUSTRY
Health care, insurance, retail

CITIES
Schaumburg, 75,242; Palatine, 53,768; Hoffman Estates, 48,521; Streamwood, 35,746

UNUSUAL FEATURES
Arlington International Racecourse; Six Flags Great America amusement park.

Rep. Jan Schakowsky (D)

CAPITOL OFFICE
225-2111; fax 226-6890; 515 Cannon Bldg. 20515

INTERNET
e-mail: jan.schakowsky@mail.house.gov
web: www.house.gov/schakowsky

COMMITTEES
Financial Services
Government Reform

HOMETOWN
Evanston

BORN
May 26, 1944, Chicago, Ill.

RELIGION
Jewish

FAMILY
Husband, Robert Creamer; three children

EDUCATION
U. of Illinois, B.S. 1965

CAREER
Senior citizens council director; consumer
advocate; teacher

POLITICAL HIGHLIGHTS
Candidate for Cook County Commission, 1986; Ill.
House, 1991-99 (floor leader, 1994-99)

ELECTION RESULTS

2000 GENERAL

Jan Schakowsky (D)	147,002	76.4%
Dennis J. Driscoll (R)	45,344	23.6%

2000 PRIMARY

Jan Schakowsky (D)	unopposed

1998 GENERAL

Jan Schakowsky (D)	107,878	74.6%
Herbert Sohn (R)	33,448	23.1%
Michael D. Ray (LIBERT)	3,284	2.3%

Elected 1998; 2nd term

When Schakowsky began hearing horror stories about long lines and poor service at the Immigration and Naturalization Service's downtown Chicago office, she decided to look into it. So she traveled to the office one morning and — without identifying herself as a member of Congress — stood in line for more than three-and-a-half hours before being told to go home. When she didn't leave fast enough, she said a worker told her to "move or go to jail." When the worker asked who she was, she replied, "First of all, I'm a human being."

The incident led to a House subcommittee hearing and subsequent improvements in the office — and cemented Schakowsky's growing reputation among Democrats as a tough-minded and ambitious activist who is willing to roll up her sleeves to get results.

Schakowsky (shuh-KOW-ski) is a firm believer in using the power of government to enhance citizens' lives. She describes Medicare as a "spectacular success" and wants to expand it to pay the medical bills of all Americans. As befits a former elementary school teacher, she is a staunch ally of organized labor and clamors for a stronger federal investment in public education. She supports gun control and a new approach to fighting drug abuse, telling one political columnist that "there is a growing acknowledgment that the drug war hasn't worked."

Amid the post-2000 election talk about the need for both parties to govern from the center, Schakowsky remained an outspoken advocate of pushing the agenda to the left. "It's more important than ever for there to be a very clear, unapologetic progressive voice," she said. "We need to correctly define what the middle of America is; I believe the progressive position is the middle position."

Schakowsky is not satisfied with simply espousing such causes, however. A veteran of more than 25 years of liberal and political activism, she seeks to teach organizing skills to others pushing the progressive cause. "I believe that progressives need to develop a 'winning, not whining' strategy for the new millennium that systematically works to empower us inside and outside legislative bodies," she wrote in The Nation in February 2000.

Indeed, Schakowsky was doing leadership work even before she won her seat in Congress. With her husband, a longtime Chicago political organizer, she set up a training program for political advocates that has become a model for the party and was replicated nationwide. The program used newspaper advertisements and word of mouth to draw volunteers — many of them college students — to Chicago, where a "campaign school" gave them instruction and political tools and then put them in the field to work on several House races.

During her first term in the House, Schakowsky was in the thick of debate over such issues as Medicare, immigration and predatory lending practices by banks. Her dedication and drive earned widespread praise from Democrats and prompted early speculation in the Chicago news media that she would challenge Illinois Republican Sen. Peter G. Fitzgerald in 2004. "She's hitting on all cylinders," one leadership aide told Roll Call, a Capitol Hill newspaper. "Everywhere you look, she's doing something."

Schakowsky said she has been pleasantly surprised that her lack of seniority has not prevented her from contributing to her party. Before coming to Congress, "I still had this notion that freshmen were consigned to being backbenchers — seen but not heard," she said. "What I found was that participation was encouraged at every level."

Schakowsky's activist approach began as a stay-at-home mother in the early 1970s, when she helped launch a successful nationwide campaign to require freshness dates on food products. Following her work for consumer and senior citizen advocacy groups, she was elected to the state House, where she fought for labor unions, family leave benefits and changes in medical insurance law sought by consumer groups. She worked on toughening Illinois' hate crimes law and guaranteeing homeless people the right to vote. Her work earned her the chairmanship of the state House's Labor and Commerce Committee and the position of Democratic floor leader.

In seeking to replace Sidney R. Yates, a liberal Democrat who held the 9th District seat for 48 years before retiring, Schakowsky easily won the staunchly Democratic district in 1998 after besting state Sen. Howard W. Carroll and Hyatt hotel heir Jay "J.B." Pritzker, both more centrist politically, in the primary. She had little trouble sweeping to re-election in 2000, capturing more than 76 percent of the vote.

Schakowsky is a member of the Financial Services Committee, a position that has enabled her to continue her efforts on behalf of consumers. She introduced a comprehensive bill to end automatic-teller surcharges and exorbitant bank fees. At the behest of Chicago Mayor Richard M. Daley, who cited a growing problem with city lending practices, she proposed a bill to crack down on lenders that prey on the poor and elderly by charging high rates and fees for mortgage loans.

For all of her work on such issues, however, Schakowsky has drawn more attention within Democratic circles for her fundraising prowess. Her contacts with donors interested in women's issues, including female business executives, paid off when feminist organizations adopted her during her congressional primary.

Without any serious challengers in 2000, she was able to devote substantial effort to her party's attempt to regain control of the House. She was by far the biggest party fundraiser among first-term House members and one of the highest among all Democrats. "She spends every free moment dialing for dollars," one admiring House aide told the Chicago Tribune.

Schakowsky intends to continue such efforts. "The 2002 election is going to provide some new opportunities," she said. "There will be more open seats because of redistricting, and traditionally, the party out of power has had an advantage in midterm elections. We'll have a good opportunity. I'm going to focus on some more fundraising for the progressive effort."

KEY VOTES

2000
Yes   Raise hourly minimum wage by $1 over two years

No   Halt funding for U.S. mission in Kosovo unless European nations pay more

Yes   Provide Medicare benefits to military retirees and their dependents

No   Grant China permanent normal trade status

No   Phase out estate, gift and trust taxes

No   Prohibit implementation of president's national monument designations

No   Approve GOP plan to provide prescription drug coverage for Medicare beneficiaries

Yes   Increase help for poor nations indebted to international financial institutions

1999
Yes   Impose steel import quotas

No   Kill proposal to take aviation trust funds off budget

No   Require background checks on buyers only at gun shows with 10 or more vendors

No   Remove barriers among banking, securities and insurance companies

Yes   Authorize state grants to hire teachers and reduce class size

Yes   Overhaul campaign finance law; ban "soft money" and restrict advocacy advertising

Yes   Approve bipartisan plan to increase rights of patients in managed-care health plans

INTEREST GROUPS

	AFL-CIO	ADA	CCUS	ACU
2000	100%	85%	40%	4%
1999	100%	100%	20%	4%

CQ VOTE STUDIES

	PARTY UNITY		PRESIDENTIAL SUPPORT	
	Support	Oppose	Support	Oppose
2000	97%	3%	85%	15%
1999	95%	5%	82%	18%

ILLINOIS 9

Chicago – North Side lakefront and suburbs; Evanston

The 9th starts in the liberal suburbs of Evanston and Skokie and runs south through Chicago's multi-ethnic North Side, into one of the city's most prosperous lakefront neighborhoods. More than 70 percent of the district's population is white, with the remainder evenly divided among blacks, Hispanics and Asians.

Two-thirds of the district's population lives in Chicago. The neighborhoods of Rogers Park, Edgewater and Uptown are an eclectic mix of Asian, European and African immigrants. Rogers Park, tucked in the city's northeast corner, takes in the campus of Loyola University. The community of Uptown is mainly working-class, with some low-income areas. Southeast Asians, the area's newest arrivals, have opened shops and restaurants, revitalizing the area's economy.

Lakeview, the district's southernmost point, includes the city's largest gay population. The area around Wrigley Field, home of baseball's Cubs, has become a mecca for affluent young professionals and is home to a hot real estate market.

The mix of immigrants, affluent urbanites and Northwestern U. students makes the 9th solidly Democratic. Although the "lakefront liberals" tend not to vote for machine candidates, they vote reliably Democratic. The district also contains a sizable Jewish population in the suburbs that candidates court, although issues such as aid to Israel rarely decide elections.

MAJOR INDUSTRY
Health care, insurance, light manufacturing

CITIES
Chicago (pt.), 377,262 (1990); Evanston, 71,679; Skokie, 58,573

UNUSUAL FEATURES
Wrigley Field, home of the Chicago Cubs; North Shore Center for the Performing Arts

Rep. Mark Steven Kirk (R)

CAPITOL OFFICE
225-4835; fax 225-0837
1531 Longworth Bldg. 20515

INTERNET
e-mail: www.house.gov/writerep
web: www.house.gov/kirk

COMMITTEES
Armed Services
Budget
Transportation & Infrastructure

HOMETOWN
Wilmette

BORN
Sept. 15, 1959, Champaign, Ill.

RELIGION
Congregationalist

FAMILY
Engaged to Kimberly Vertolli

EDUCATION
Cornell U., B.A. 1981; London School of
Economics, M.S. 1982; Georgetown U., J.D. 1992

MILITARY SERVICE
Naval Reserve, 1989-present

CAREER
Congressional committee counsel; congressional
aide; lawyer; State Department aide; World Bank
officer

POLITICAL HIGHLIGHTS
No previous office

ELECTION RESULTS

2000 GENERAL

Mark Steven Kirk (R)	121,582	51.2%
Lauren Beth Gash (D)	115,924	48.8%

2000 PRIMARY

Mark Steven Kirk (R)	19,717	31.4%
Shawn M. Donnelley (R)	9,585	15.3%
Mark Damisch (R)	9,016	14.4%
Andrew Hochberg (R)	7,480	11.9%
John H. Cox (R)	6,339	10.1%
Scott Phelps (R)	3,712	5.9%
Thomas Lachner (R)	2,555	4.1%
Terry Gladman (R)	2,172	3.5%
James E. Goulka (R)	1,469	2.3%

Elected 2000; 1st term

Kirk once served as chief of staff to the man he succeeded — popular longtime GOP Rep. John Edward Porter, whose "thoughtful, independent leadership" Kirk has often cited and promised to uphold. Like Porter, Kirk is a GOP centrist who supports abortion rights, international family planning programs, gun control and environmental protection efforts. He even shares Porter's penchant to be known by his full name.

A decorated Naval Reserve officer — who twice was called to active duty during the 2000 campaign — and a former official with the State Department and the World Bank, Kirk has experience in foreign and military policy. The congressman, who took a leave from his job as counsel to the House International Relations Committee to run for the 10th District seat, says that foreign policy "matters on Main Street."

Kirk won assignment to the Armed Services Committee, which allows him to look out for the interests of the district's Great Lakes Naval Training Center. He also sits on the Budget Committee and the Transportation and Infrastructure panel. One of his priorities is working to ease local traffic congestion. During the campaign, he referred to clogged Half Day Road in Lincolnshire, a Chicago suburb, as "Full Day Road."

Kirk was not the front-runner when he entered the race to replace Porter, who was retiring. Though a native of the 10th District, he had lived in Washington, D.C., most of his adult life; he also lacked the personal wealth enjoyed by others in the 11-candidate GOP primary field. But Kirk impressed voters with his grasp of policy and his ties to Porter, who endorsed him. He beat his closest competitor, printing company heiress Shawn Margaret Donnelley, by 16 percentage points.

In the general election, Kirk faced a formidable opponent in state Rep. Lauren Beth Gash, a Democratic moderate who had no primary opposition. The suburban Chicago district has switched in recent years from Republican stronghold to partisan battleground and voters backed Al Gore in the presidential race, but Kirk was able to prevail over Gash by 2 percentage points.

ILLINOIS 10
North and northwest Chicago suburbs — Waukegan

The 10th, on the shore of Lake Michigan at the Wisconsin border, includes the eastern half of Lake County and northern edge of Cook County. Along the lakefront, Chicagoland's old-money elite live in exclusive towns like Kenilworth, Wilmette and Winnetka, where homes routinely sell for $500,000 or more.

To the north, the district's industrial sector, Waukegan and North Chicago, found new life in 1994 when nearby Great Lakes Naval Training Center became the nation's only naval recruit training facility. Most of the district's minorities live in Waukegan, which is about 40 percent black and Hispanic.

Suburban and working-class residents combine to make the 10th a moderately Republican district — fiscally conservative but socially liberal, especially on abortion rights and gun control. Cook County tends to be more solidly Republican than the Lake County part of the district. The 10th was a swing district until redistricting in 1992 cut out several working-class neighborhoods to the south.

MAJOR INDUSTRY
Pharmaceutical research, insurance, military

MILITARY BASES
Great Lakes Naval Training Center, 4,945 military, 4,226 civilian (2000); Fort Sheridan Reserve Base (Army), 350 total (2000)

CITIES
Waukegan (pt.), 66,179 (1990); Buffalo Grove, 42,624; Arlington Heights (pt.), 41,120 (1990); North Chicago, 36,097; Northbrook, 33,645

UNUSUAL FEATURES
Halas Hall, Chicago Bears' training facility; Chicago Botanic Garden.

Rep. Jerry Weller (R)

CAPITOL OFFICE
225-3635; fax 225-3521
1210 Longworth Bldg. 20515

INTERNET
e-mail: www.house.gov/writerep
web: www.house.gov/weller

COMMITTEES
Ways & Means

HOMETOWN
Morris

BORN
July 7, 1957, Streator, Ill.

RELIGION
Christian

FAMILY
Single

EDUCATION
Joliet Junior College, attended 1977; U. of Illinois, B.S. 1979

CAREER
Congressional aide; state and federal official; hog farmer; sales representative

POLITICAL HIGHLIGHTS
Ill. House, 1989-95

ELECTION RESULTS

2000 GENERAL

Jerry Weller (R)	132,384	56.4%
James P. Stevenson (D)	102,485	43.6%

2000 PRIMARY

Jerry Weller (R)	unopposed

1998 GENERAL

Jerry Weller (R)	100,597	58.8%
Gary S. Mueller (D)	70,458	41.2%

PREVIOUS WINNING PERCENTAGES
1996 (52%); 1994 (61%)

Elected 1994; 4th term

Mention the catch phrase "marriage penalty" and people think of Jerry Weller, whose frequent speeches on the issue showcase the dogged perseverance of the Illinois lawmaker.

Weller's top legislative priority in the 105th and 106th Congresses was elimination of the so-called marriage penalty, a quirk in the tax code that results in some two-earner married couples paying higher taxes than they would if each partner were single. He made more than 100 floor speeches on the topic in the 105th and 106th and, to put a human face on the issue, introduced the country to the Hallihans of Joliet, two school teachers who wrote him to complain of the unfairness of the marriage penalty.

In more than two dozen floor statements in the 106th, Weller chronicled the Hallihans' lives through the birth of their first child and reminded his colleagues that the couple could have bought thousands of diapers with the extra money they were sending to Uncle Sam. "It is wrong that our tax code punishes society's most basic institution," he argued. "It is time that we stop punishing marriage." Legislation cutting taxes for married couples cleared Congress in the 106th but was vetoed by President Clinton. Weller continued the effort in the 107th.

Weller is persistent on other bills, such as the elimination of the estate tax and a tax break for filmmakers who refrain from taking their business to Canada, and also in his efforts to move up in the House GOP hierarchy. His tenacity makes him a good man to have on one's side, but he is sometimes unwilling to let go, running the risk of annoying even his allies.

An ambitious, serious-minded man not much given to back-slapping, Weller has done well in his short time in Washington, with help from his Illinois neighbor, Speaker J. Dennis Hastert, and boosted by a savvy of the Hill gained from his time as a congressional aide.

With the backing of Hastert, then chief deputy whip, Weller as a freshman was named to the Republican Steering Committee, the panel that makes committee assignments. Two years later, he got a seat on the Ways and Means panel. At the start of his second term, Weller was elected president of the GOP Class of 1994. But his bid to join the ranks of the GOP leadership failed when he ran for secretary of the Republican Conference in 1997 and finished last in a field of four. In the 106th, however, he was appointed to the Republican Policy Committee.

Weller came to Congress as part of the large, conservative-dominated GOP Class of 1994, many of whom portrayed themselves as political outsiders. His philosophy and voting record are indeed conservative, but the "outsider" label doesn't fit: He is an inside operator, and not just because he has an extensive inside-the-Beltway background. Instead of joining many of his classmates in publicly partisan skirmishes with Democrats, Weller is more apt to spend his time on Ways and Means delving into the details of proposals to change the tax code to achieve goals he deems socially beneficial.

Weller grew up on a farm and even though there is substantial rural turf in the 11th District, he often introduces himself in speeches as being from the "South Side of Chicago." That label connects him to the more densely populated parts of his district — areas in the city of Chicago and its southern suburbs where blue-collar voters and other Democrats wield significant political clout. Their influence plays a part in Weller's votes on some issues. In 1996, for instance, he was among 43 Republicans who bucked GOP leaders when they tried to exempt small businesses from having to pay a minimum wage hike. Weller also backed a minimum wage increase in 2000.

Weller usually has voted with GOP leaders in support of lowering international trade barriers. But in the 105th, he and Pennsylvanian Phil English were the only two Republicans on Ways and Means to oppose granting the president fast-track authority to negotiate trade agreements that Congress cannot amend. Another trade issue — the loss of moviemaking jobs abroad, particularly to Canada — has drawn Weller's attention. He tried to win approval of a tax credit for makers of films with budgets of less than $10 million. The effort failed; some critics claimed that it would largely benefit the makers of pornographic films.

He has been active in the debate over establishment of a third airport for Chicago in the south suburbs and was able to win funding for construction of nursing homes for veterans. Another priority for Weller was the conversion of the site of the former Joliet Arsenal into an industrial park, a veterans cemetery and a tallgrass prairie preserve.

In his first term, when he sat on the Banking Committee, Weller gave voice to concerns in his district about an influx of low-income residents. When the committee considered a bill in 1995 to overhaul the nation's public housing system, Weller offered an amendment barring Chicago public housing tenants from using federal rent vouchers to move to the southern Cook County suburbs in the 11th. The amendment provoked lengthy debate, with some outraged Democrats arguing that Weller's motive was that "we don't want those people moving into our towns." The congressman said his amendment was needed because southern Cook County already had absorbed 70 percent of Chicago housing assistance recipients.

Weller, whose family ran a hog farm, majored in agriculture at the University of Illinois. He went to Washington to work for GOP Rep. Thomas J. Corcoran, whose district included part of what is now the 11th. He gained experience in the executive branch working for President Reagan's agriculture secretary, John R. Block.

In 1988, Weller won election to the Illinois House, serving six years in the legislature. In 1994, he ran for Congress when Democratic Rep. George E. Sangmeister decided to retire. The 11th, which had been made significantly more Republican in the 1990s round of redistricting, included about 30 percent of the district Weller had represented in the state House. He easily captured the seat in 1994. However, two years later Democratic challenger Clem Balanoff gave Weller a tough battle in the politically competitive district. Weller prevailed, 52 percent to 48 percent, but the battle showed that he must take care to reach out to voters from both parties.

KEY VOTES

2000
Yes Raise hourly minimum wage by $1 over two years
Yes Halt funding for U.S. mission in Kosovo unless European nations pay more
Yes Provide Medicare benefits to military retirees and their dependents
Yes Grant China permanent normal trade status
Yes Phase out estate, gift and trust taxes
Yes Prohibit implementation of president's national monument designations
Yes Approve GOP plan to provide prescription drug coverage for Medicare beneficiaries
No Increase help for poor nations indebted to international financial institutions

1999
Yes Impose steel import quotas
Yes Kill proposal to take aviation trust funds off budget
Yes Require background checks on buyers only at gun shows with 10 or more vendors
Yes Remove barriers among banking, securities and insurance companies
No Authorize state grants to hire teachers and reduce class size
No Overhaul campaign finance law; ban "soft money" and restrict advocacy advertising
No Approve bipartisan plan to increase rights of patients in managed-care health plans

INTEREST GROUPS

	AFL-CIO	ADA	CCUS	ACU
2000	22%	15%	68%	66%
1999	22%	15%	88%	80%
1998	40%	15%	88%	92%
1997	50%	5%	80%	84%

CQ VOTE STUDIES

	PARTY UNITY		PRESIDENTIAL SUPPORT	
	Support	Oppose	Support	Oppose
2000	86%	14%	41%	59%
1999	88%	12%	24%	76%
1998	88%	12%	26%	74%
1997	92%	8%	28%	72%

ILLINOIS 11
South Chicago suburbs and exurbs — Joliet

The 11th is arguably the most eclectic district in Illinois. The far east side, abutting the Indiana border, includes Chicago's 10th Ward, the working-class neighborhoods south of the city, and part of rural Kankakee County. The district then runs west through the old industrial city of Joliet and into the farming center of the state.

The district's politics are caught up in a plan to build a third Chicago metro-area airport in Peotone. Residents in the 11th's northern reaches and the nearby 2nd District believe that a new airport would boost the ailing suburbs. But the 11th's rural residents worry that the airport would disrupt their way of life.

A mix of white working-class, minority and rural constituents makes the 11th a classic swing district. Parts are becoming more Democratic as black Chicagoans move into the south suburbs. But neighboring Will County, which has seen an influx of young suburban families, leans Republican.

The 11th has the potential to be competitive, but Rep. Weller has been re-elected by solid margins. Bill Clinton won the district in 1992 with only 44 percent as 20 percent of the voters opted for Reform candidate Ross Perot. But the Democratic margin of victory increased in the 1996 and 2000 presidential contests.

MAJOR INDUSTRY
Farm equipment manufacturing, riverboat gambling, agriculture

CITIES
Joliet (pt.), 76,291 (1990); Chicago (pt.), 34,829 (1990); Lansing, 28,612

UNUSUAL FEATURES
Midewin National Tallgrass Prairie; Joliet once known as the wallpaper capital of the world.

Rep. Jerry F. Costello (D)

Elected August 1988; 7th full term

CAPITOL OFFICE
225-5661; fax 225-0285; 2454 Rayburn Bldg. 20515

INTERNET
e-mail: jfc.il12@mail.house.gov
web: www.house.gov/costello

COMMITTEES
Science
Transportation & Infrastructure

HOMETOWN
Belleville

BORN
Sept. 25, 1949, East St. Louis, Ill.

RELIGION
Roman Catholic

FAMILY
Wife, Georgia Cockrum Costello; three children

EDUCATION
Belleville Area College, A.A. 1971; Maryville
College of the Sacred Heart, B.A. 1973

CAREER
Law enforcement official

POLITICAL HIGHLIGHTS
St. Clair County Board chairman, 1980-88

ELECTION RESULTS

2000 GENERAL

Jerry F. Costello (D)		unopposed

2000 PRIMARY

Jerry F. Costello (D)	37,234	89.9%
Kenneth Charles Wiezer (D)	4,189	10.1%

1998 GENERAL

Jerry F. Costello (D)	99,605	60.4%
Bill Price (R)	65,409	39.6%

PREVIOUS WINNING PERCENTAGES
1996 (72%); 1994 (66%); 1992 (71%); 1990 (66%);
1988 (53%); 1988 Special Election (51%)

An elected official who has represented the struggling industrial communities of southwest Illinois for 20 years, first as a county chief executive and then as a member of Congress, Costello long ago decided that the dwindling steel mill, stockyard and coal mining jobs that were the backbone of the economy for many years were not likely to return. Instead, he believes that improving the region's transportation infrastructure will retain and attract new jobs. From his posts on the Transportation and Science committees, Costello has set about to do that, with some success.

Costello has brought millions of federal dollars to his district and the region for industrial parks, visitors centers and transportation projects. His focus has been on funding for expanding MetroLink light rail, which connects the "Metro East" area of Illinois with St. Louis; upgrading and replacing bridges across the Mississippi River; and developing MidAmerica Airport just north of Scott Air Force Base.

Such tangible evidence of his work, despite the difficulty MidAmerica has had attracting commercial airlines, has kept him strong politically, even when tainted by an ethics problem back home. Costello was named an "unindicted co-conspirator" in the 1997 trial of his childhood friend and former business partner Amiel Cueto, who was convicted of trying to block the federal investigation of a convicted racketeer. Republicans have never tired of reminding voters of the connection, but to no avail. Costello won a sixth full term in 1998 by 20 percentage points, and the GOP did not even field a candidate against him in 2000.

Costello denied wrongdoing in the Cueto matter. At the trial, government witnesses testified that Costello was a silent partner in two casino deals and that he helped pass a bill in Congress to aid an Indian tribe that owned the land where one of the casinos was to be built. Costello was not implicated in any crime and said that being named an unindicted co-conspirator was merely a prosecutorial tool to ensure that certain testimony was admissible.

Costello, who rarely speaks on the floor, is a regular but not completely steady vote for Democrats. He supports the party line about three-fourths of the time. He is a staunch labor ally, opposing overseas trade agreements that he says will cost U.S. jobs. He opposes the Clean Air Act, complaining that it was "grossly unfair to the Midwest and has devastated the coal industry in southern Illinois."

On social policy issues, Costello reflects his constituency's cultural conservatism. He was one of 10 House members who lobbied to add language expressing tolerance of anti-abortion views to the 1996 Democratic Party platform. He supports gun owners' rights — in 1998, he backed legislation to exempt retired police officers from state laws restricting concealed weapons. And he voted against lifting the ban on homosexuals in the military.

Costello was a member of the Budget Committee until the 106th Congress, when he had to leave the panel because he had served the allotted three terms. From his Budget post in the 104th, he objected to GOP budget plans that would have reduced or limited the growth of domestic programs of interest to his core constituents, such as Medicare and the Legal Services Corporation. In a rare rhetorical flourish, he said, "This [tax cut] bill has been called the 'crown jewel' of the Republican 'Contract With America,' but it appears most of the crown jewels will only go to the rich."

For his part, Costello keeps working to direct as many baubles to his 12th District as he can. In addition to his work on infrastructure needs, in the

106th Costello won approval of legislation to set aside federal land for a visitor center devoted to the journey of explorers Lewis and Clark, near the site where the expedition departed on its westward journey. Earlier, he had obtained federal funding for the center.

Costello got a rare moment in the spotlight in 1991. With his son preparing for action near the Kuwait-Iraq border, he voted against authorizing the use of military force against Iraq. He was one of only two members with a son or daughter in the Persian Gulf.

Costello grew up in East St. Louis in a politically active family; his father was in the Illinois legislature and served as St. Clair County sheriff and county treasurer. In 1960, when he was 11, the young Irish Catholic Costello was intrigued by the campaign appearance in his home town of another Irish Catholic — John F. Kennedy, who was running for president.

While attending a local community college, Costello began a career in law enforcement during which he served as a court bailiff, street cop, investigator and then administrator of the region's court system. In 1980, he was elected chairman of the St. Clair County Board. He became well-known in his heavily Democratic region, serving at one point as chairman of the metropolitan St. Louis Council of Governments.

His high profile earned him status as heir apparent to Democrat Melvin Price, an elderly House veteran who did not seek re-election in 1988. But in the primary, Madison County Auditor Pete Fields portrayed Costello as an old-style, hardball "boss" in the St. Clair County Democratic machine. A huge financial advantage helped Costello survive, but with only a 46 percent plurality.

Then Price died in April, forcing a special election to fill out his term. Costello's Republican opponent was college official Robert H. Gaffner, who suggested voters call Costello and quiz him about his ethics. Costello barely won the special election in the overwhelmingly Democratic district. He went on to win in November, taking 53 percent of the vote. He was not seriously challenged again until 1998.

That is when he faced Republican Bill Price, an orthopedic surgeon and the son of Melvin Price. The younger Price had been friendly with Costello over the years and had even made campaign donations to Costello. But neither Price nor the National Republican Congressional Committee missed an opportunity to take Costello to task for his connections with Cueto. However, the incumbent's defense of his effectiveness in office and his charges that Price represented a threat to Social Security and Medicare carried the day. Costello took 60 percent of the vote.

KEY VOTES

2000

Yes Raise hourly minimum wage by $1 over two years
Yes Halt funding for U.S. mission in Kosovo unless European nations pay more
Yes Provide Medicare benefits to military retirees and their dependents
No Grant China permanent normal trade status
Yes Phase out estate, gift and trust taxes
No Prohibit implementation of president's national monument designations
No Approve GOP plan to provide prescription drug coverage for Medicare beneficiaries
Yes Increase help for poor nations indebted to international financial institutions

1999

Yes Impose steel import quotas
No Kill proposal to take aviation trust funds off budget
No Require background checks on buyers only at gun shows with 10 or more vendors
No Remove barriers among banking, securities and insurance companies
Yes Authorize state grants to hire teachers and reduce class size
Yes Overhaul campaign finance law; ban "soft money" and restrict advocacy advertising
Yes Approve bipartisan plan to increase rights of patients in managed-care health plans

INTEREST GROUPS

	AFL-CIO	ADA	CCUS	ACU
2000	90%	55%	47%	33%
1999	100%	65%	24%	24%
1998	100%	90%	28%	25%
1997	100%	85%	40%	25%

CQ VOTE STUDIES

	PARTY UNITY		PRESIDENTIAL SUPPORT	
	Support	Oppose	Support	Oppose
2000	76%	24%	52%	48%
1999	73%	27%	63%	37%
1998	76%	24%	68%	32%
1997	76%	24%	60%	40%

ILLINOIS 12

Southwest — Carbondale; East St. Louis

Illinois' worst urban blight isn't in Chicago — it's 300 miles southwest in East St. Louis, where severe white flight and industrial decay nearly bankrupted the city. In the late 1980s, the city cut off most municipal services, including trash collection. Federal and state intervention, coupled with new revenue from casino gambling, restored most city services by the mid-1990s, but residents still face high unemployment and poverty.

Other cities in the 12th also stand on precarious ground. Alton has had to bolster its industrial base with riverboat gambling. Belleville, where Scott Air Force Base is the largest employer, worries about defense cutbacks. And coal mining has almost completely disappeared from the hilly, southern end of the district with the mechanization of the industry and enactment of the 1990 Clean Air Act.

Higher education remains one of the few steadfast employers; Jackson County's economy is bolstered by Southern Illinois University

in Carbondale, which has 22,000 students.

The district's economic anxiety and relatively large minority population make it solidly Democratic turf. A few corn and hog farmers in western counties lean toward the GOP, but they are too few to sway the district.

MAJOR INDUSTRY
Manufacturing, higher education, riverboat gambling, agriculture

MILITARY BASES
Scott Air Force Base, 7,634 military, 2,199 civilian (1999)

CITIES
Belleville, 40,429; East St. Louis, 36,656; Alton, 31,072; Granite City, 31,041; Carbondale, 27,228

UNUSUAL FEATURES
Cahokia Mounds prehistoric civilization, a United Nations-designated World Heritage Site; Alton-native Robert Pershing Wadlow, Guinness Book of World Record's tallest man at 8 feet, 11.1 inches.

Rep. Judy Biggert (R)

Elected 1998; 2nd term

As the only woman in her GOP class — and one of only two women in the 20-member Illinois delegation — Biggert says she is well aware of the obstacles her gender faces in the professional world. As a law school student in the early 1960s, Biggert was told by a professor that she was taking the place of a man. "We're held to an awfully high standard," Biggert says. "We have to work three times as hard."

Biggert was named by Fortune magazine in 1999 as one of the congressional newcomers most likely to become a star, and she has tried to prove the magazine's prophecy: She ran for Republican Conference secretary at the start of the 107th Congress, reminding her colleagues that she had advanced to the leadership of the Illinois House in just her second term there and telling the Capitol Hill newspaper Roll Call, "I think I've really taken a role as a freshman that has been pretty exemplary." Also, she was a prolific fundraiser for the National Republican Congressional Committee in the 2000 campaign cycle. But Biggert lost the leadership post to Wyoming's Barbara Cubin, 123-76.

During her first term, Biggert was invited to the White House twice. She chaired the Women's Caucus subcommittee on education and regularly presided over the House. She is a fiscal conservative and a self-proclaimed social liberal who has made women and children's issues among her top priorities. In the 107th Congress, she is the co-chairwoman of the Congressional Caucus for Women's Issues and she sits on the Education and the Workforce Committee.

Her interest in children's issues stems from her years as a member of the Board of Education in Hinsdale Township, Ill., including a stint as its president from 1983 to 1985. That experience has led her to support reauthorization of the 1994 Violence Against Women Act. She says that as a school board member she learned that children from homes with abused mothers miss out on important early education programs.

In 1999, during her first year in Congress, Biggert helped push through legislation to make it easier for homeless children to enroll and remain in school. She also drafted legislation that would allow local school districts to use federal grants for programs to help students with eating disorders.

She describes herself as a negotiator and consensus builder and says she likes to work across party lines to pass legislation. She counts among her best friends on Capitol Hill the "moderates and women." In the 107th Congress, she and conservative Mark Souder of Indiana are co-chairmen of weekly House GOP "unity dinners" designed to bring disparate factions of the party together.

Biggert supports abortion rights but has opposed most gun control measures, in part because she is a skeet shooter who owns several guns. Her stance also reflects the conservative bent of the 13th District.

Skeet shooting is just one of many athletic activities Biggert pursues. She also skis, sails, golfs and is avid about step aerobics. As a child, Biggert studied ballet for years, and after she became the mother of four, she volunteered as the assistant soccer coach for her daughter's team.

Biggert's interest in women's sports quickly became apparent when she arrived in Washington. The first bill she managed on the House floor was a resolution praising the U.S. Women's Soccer Team for winning the Women's World Cup competition in 1999.

"Looking back on my own childhood ... the sports that we had were bal-

CAPITOL OFFICE
225-3515; fax 225-9420
1213 Longworth Bldg. 20515

INTERNET
e-mail: www.house.gov/writerep
web: www.house.gov/biggert

COMMITTEES
Education & Workforce
Financial Services
Science
Standards of Official Conduct

HOMETOWN
Hinsdale

BORN
Aug. 15, 1937, Chicago, Ill.

RELIGION
Episcopalian

FAMILY
Husband, Rody Biggert; four children

EDUCATION
Stanford U., B.A. 1959; Northwestern U., J.D. 1963

CAREER
Lawyer

POLITICAL HIGHLIGHTS
Hinsdale Board of Education, 1982-85 (president, 1983-85); Ill. House, 1993-99

ELECTION RESULTS

2000 GENERAL

Judy Biggert (R)	193,250	66.2%
Thomas Mason (D)	98,768	33.8%

2000 PRIMARY

Judy Biggert (R)	unopposed

1998 GENERAL

Judy Biggert (R)	121,889	61.0%
Susan W. Hynes (D)	77,878	39.0%

let and music lessons," Biggert said during floor debate. She said the exploding popularity of women's sports now allows young girls "to learn the value of teamwork and competition and to gain the self-confidence and skills that are so valuable in business and in other future careers."

Biggert proudly states that she was the first member of her class asked to preside over the House during her freshman year. The only problem was that the orientation session, in which as a new member she would learn the parliamentary procedures she needed to preside, was not to be held until the following day. Biggert took the assignment anyway and is now a regular at the Speaker's rostrum.

Elected to Congress at age 61, Biggert took the oath of office with her 10-month-old grandson balanced on her hip. She ran for president of her GOP freshman class, attributing her loss, in part, to being the only woman in her class. And as the GOP chose its leaders for the 106th Congress, Biggert made the politically risky move of campaigning for Rep. Jennifer Dunn of Washington in her failed challenge to House Majority Leader Dick Armey of Texas.

Biggert says women bring a special perspective to politics and she hopes to be a role model for other women with political aspirations. She openly laments that women make up a small percentage (only about 14 percent) of the congressional membership, compared with 25 percent in the Illinois state legislature during her time there. In Illinois, she had a relatively easier time moving up the leadership hierarchy, becoming the assistant majority leader in the state House after just one term.

Biggert was the handpicked successor of Republican Harris W. Fawell, who retired in 1998 after holding the seat for 14 years. Biggert's daughter, Adrienne, worked for Fawell as a legislative assistant during his time in Congress. During that first run for Congress, Biggert defeated five men vying for the GOP nomination and went on to soundly win the seat with 61 percent.

Her early success in the Illinois House led Biggert to pledge to observe a six-year term limit when she first ran for Congress. But after arriving in Washington, she retracted the pledge, saying it was a mistake and she had not been aware of the powerful seniority system in Congress. "In the Illinois state legislature, I had accomplished so much in a little period of time," Biggert said. "But [in Congress] I was cut off from so many committees because of seniority."

Biggert represents a strong Republican district and is expected to safely win re-election for years to come. In 2000, she cruised to an easy victory, by a ratio of almost 2-to-1.

KEY VOTES

2000

No   Raise hourly minimum wage by $1 over two years

Yes Halt funding for U.S. mission in Kosovo unless European nations pay more

Yes Provide Medicare benefits to military retirees and their dependents

Yes Grant China permanent normal trade status

Yes Phase out estate, gift and trust taxes

No   Prohibit implementation of president's national monument designations

Yes Approve GOP plan to provide prescription drug coverage for Medicare beneficiaries

No   Increase help for poor nations indebted to international financial institutions

1999

No   Impose steel import quotas

Yes Kill proposal to take aviation trust funds off budget

Yes Require background checks on buyers only at gun shows with 10 or more vendors

Yes Remove barriers among banking, securities and insurance companies

No   Authorize state grants to hire teachers and reduce class size

No   Overhaul campaign finance law; ban "soft money" and restrict advocacy advertising

No   Approve bipartisan plan to increase rights of patients in managed-care health plans

INTEREST GROUPS

	AFL-CIO	ADA	CCUS	ACU
2000	0%	20%	100%	68%
1999	11%	30%	96%	60%

CQ VOTE STUDIES

	PARTY UNITY		PRESIDENTIAL SUPPORT	
	Support	Oppose	Support	Oppose
2000	82%	18%	43%	57%
1999	78%	22%	37%	63%

ILLINOIS 13
Southwest Chicago suburbs — Naperville

More than half of the 13th's population lives in the southern part of booming DuPage County. The district's biggest city, Naperville, has seen its population almost triple since 1980. Sprawling subdivisions and a newly refurbished downtown characterize this fairly young suburb. The 13th also incorporates the residential southwestern corner of Cook County and a mostly rural slice of northern Will County.

Argonne National Laboratory, in southeast DuPage, and Fermi National Accelerator Laboratory, just over the border in the 14th District, have made the area a hub of scientific research and provides a prime source of jobs for district residents.

Both Naperville and Oak Brook, home to a growing number of corporate headquarters, have become leading business centers outside Chicago. Oak Brook, while not especially populous, sits near the nexus of Interstates 88, 294 and 290, which has abetted its

development. These cities increasingly draw in commuters, creating serious traffic problems in suburban communities.

Voters in the 13th tend to be white-collar executive types, loyal to free enterprise. DuPage has gained a national reputation as a Republican stronghold, and the 13th is a reliably Republican district. Some residents, however, hold more liberal opinions on family and women's issues (such as equal pay and child care), as well as environmental protection. In the 2000 presidential contest, the district supported George W. Bush.

MAJOR INDUSTRY
Scientific research, health care, insurance

CITIES
Naperville, 122,933; Bolingbrook, 56,156; Downers Grove (pt.), 43,365 (1990); Woodridge, 29,836

UNUSUAL FEATURE
McDonald's Hamburger University.

Rep. J. Dennis Hastert (R)

CAPITOL OFFICE
225-2976; fax 225-0697; 2369 Rayburn Bldg. 20515

INTERNET
e-mail: dhastert@mail.house.gov
web: www.speaker.gov and
www.house.gov/hastert

COMMITTEES
Speaker of the House — no committee
assignments

HOMETOWN
Yorkville

BORN
Jan. 2, 1942, Aurora, Ill.

RELIGION
Methodist

FAMILY
Wife, Jean Hastert; two children

EDUCATION
Wheaton College, A.B. 1964; Northern Illinois U.,
M.A. 1967

CAREER
Teacher; restaurateur

POLITICAL HIGHLIGHTS
Ill. House, 1981-86

ELECTION RESULTS

2000 GENERAL

J. Dennis Hastert (R)	188,597	74.0%
Vern Deljonson (D)	66,309	26.0%

2000 PRIMARY

J. Dennis Hastert (R)	unopposed

1998 GENERAL

J. Dennis Hastert (R)	117,304	69.8%
Robert A. Cozzi Jr. (D)	50,844	30.2%

PREVIOUS WINNING PERCENTAGES
1996 (64%); 1994 (77%); 1992 (67%); 1990 (67%);
1988 (74%); 1986 (52%)

Elected 1986; 8th term

Call it toughness, persistence or just uncanny luck, but Hastert is a survivor. Anyone who doubts that should consider how close he came to strolling into the office of Majority Whip Tom DeLay of Texas on the afternoon of July 24, 1998, at the exact moment a gunman was firing fatal shots at the Capitol Police detective stationed there. Hastert, then the chief deputy whip, had just steered a GOP managed-care overhaul bill to narrow passage. As he prepared to join up with DeLay, he was waylaid by a reporter for a few crucial minutes.

Hastert's luck that day can serve as a metaphor for his political career. The Illinois Republican does not have a spectacular legislative track record to show for his first two years as the 51st Speaker of the House. He was tarred by some embarrassing failures, most Americans still do not know who he is, and he got caught in an election-eve budget battle that easily could have doomed the House GOP majority — and with it his own career. But on Election Day, the GOP survived. A week later, Republicans nominated Hastert for a second term without the faintest hint of opposition, and he began the 107th Congress unencumbered.

Hastert attained the most powerful legislative office under the Constitution after just 12 years in the House — the fastest rise to the job since 1891 — mostly by being a genial guy who cultivated his legislative skills without drawing much attention. He is also the first Speaker in 80 years not to have previously held an elected leadership job. But, appointed as chief deputy whip, he showed a knack during the first four years of GOP control for pushing the party line without making colleagues feel pressured. To many, he was just "Denny," the amiable, laid-back, former high school wrestling coach. (He also taught government and history.)

So when the Republicans needed a new Speaker in a hurry in December 1998, the dogged if uncharismatic Hastert emerged as the consensus choice in one whirlwind afternoon. Unexpected GOP losses at the polls that fall had prompted Newt Gingrich of Georgia to resign. Then the Republicans' choice as successor, Robert L. Livingston of Louisiana, said he, too, would resign after revelations of his extramarital affairs. DeLay quickly helped his protégé Hastert to secure the post. While many have assumed ever since then that the combative DeLay is the true power behind the throne, the nature of their relationship appears more symbiotic, with Hastert generally working as the soft-spoken and affable "good cop" and DeLay operating most often as the blunt and hard-charging "bad cop."

Hastert is considered a good listener who can take in a range of views, handle lawmakers with difficult egos and persuade reluctant members that voting a certain way is in the party's best interests. He claims he does not threaten waverers — "that's not my style," he says — and Republicans who have received the Hastert treatment generally agree. "You've got to lay out the reasons for us staying together and what happens when we don't," Hastert says of his approach.

He gets less credit from Democrats for reaching across the aisle. In the 106th Congress, he was barely on speaking terms with Minority Leader Richard A. Gephardt, which Hastert says was not his fault: "It kind of limits your ability to negotiate and work with somebody whose sole purpose is to try to make this House fail." Conservative "Blue Dog" Democrats, meanwhile, say Hastert made little effort to work with them — a luxury he may not be able to afford with the GOP majority even narrower than in the

106th. Still, supporters note that, during Bill Clinton's final year in office, Hastert tried to work with the president to find a compromise on a minimum wage increase (a gesture not popular with other GOP leaders) and worked with Clinton to develop and then enact a community renewal package to revive the sinking economies of inner cities and rural areas.

Hastert at times may be laid-back to a fault. When Charlie Norwood, R-Ga., and John D. Dingell, D-Mich., assembled a clear House majority in 1999 for a bill that would have given patients broad new rights to sue their managed-care plans, Hastert took weeks before endorsing a more limited GOP alternative. By the time he did, it was too late to prevent the Norwood-Dingell bill from passing — with 68 Republican votes.

In general, though, Hastert appears to succeed often by inoculating his party against attacks. In 1998, he assembled an earlier managed-care bill designed mainly to compete with a broader, more ambitious version supported by Democrats and some Republicans. House Democrats who wanted to use the managed-care issue against Republicans found it difficult to accuse the GOP of blocking all action. The worst they could say was that the Republican bill was weaker than theirs — not the knockout punch they hoped for.

As Speaker, Hastert elevated the inoculation strategy to an art form. When a $792 billion GOP tax bill was stopped by a Clinton veto in 1999, he championed the idea of breaking the package into pieces, hoping to raise public awareness of the GOP's push to cut estate taxes and taxes for married couples. Clinton vetoed the separate measures, too, but they did gain unexpectedly large numbers of Democratic votes in the election year.

And even though the 2000 budget debate between Clinton and the GOP dragged into a lame-duck session, Hastert could note that at least the House had done its main duty by producing all 13 appropriations bills early in the year. The fact that Clinton had threatened to veto most of them seemed not to register with the electorate. Hastert's supporters gave him credit for recognizing the changes in the political environment — detecting that Republicans were unlikely to be punished for staying in session so late — and for refusing to make the kinds of last-minute concessions the GOP had given Clinton in previous years as the price for getting out of town.

A product of the historically Republican swath of northern Illinois, Hastert taught and coached in high school for 16 years before gaining an appointment to the state legislature to fill a vacancy. When GOP Rep. John E. Grotberg retired because of illness in 1986, Hastert entered and won his first House race, with just 52 percent of the vote; he has since been re-elected easily.

KEY VOTES

2000
S   Raise hourly minimum wage by $1 over two years
S   Halt funding for U.S. mission in Kosovo unless European nations pay more
S   Provide Medicare benefits to military retirees and their dependents
Yes Grant China permanent normal trade status
Yes Phase out estate, gift and trust taxes
S   Prohibit implementation of president's national monument designations
Yes Approve GOP plan to provide prescription drug coverage for Medicare beneficiaries
No   Increase help for poor nations indebted to international financial institutions

1999
S   Impose steel import quotas
S   Kill proposal to take aviation trust funds off budget
Yes Require background checks on buyers only at gun shows with 10 or more vendors
Yes Remove barriers among banking, securities and insurance companies
S   Authorize state grants to hire teachers and reduce class size
No   Overhaul campaign finance law; ban "soft money" and restrict advocacy advertising
No   Approve bipartisan plan to increase rights of patients in managed-care health plans

INTEREST GROUPS

	AFL-CIO	ADA	CCUS	ACU
2000	0%	0%	81%	100%
1999	0%	0%	100%	90%
1998	0%	0%	100%	100%
1997	0%	0%	100%	88%

CQ VOTE STUDIES

	PARTY UNITY		PRESIDENTIAL SUPPORT	
	Support	Oppose	Support	Oppose
2000	100%	0%	28%	72%
1999	95%	5%	17%	83%
1998	96%	4%	21%	79%
1997	96%	4%	32%	68%

ILLINOIS 14
North Central — Aurora; Elgin; DeKalb

Most people in the 14th live on the district's eastern side, in established towns along the Fox River valley. West of the river, prairies and farms stretch to the district's end in Lee County. Rich in hay, soybeans and corn, the flat landscape is interrupted only by Northern Illinois University in DeKalb.

The district's largest cities, Aurora and Elgin, suffered a period of heavy manufacturing decline in the 1980s but have recovered by promoting industrial parks and opening riverboat casinos. But the industrial economy is still important to these cities, with Caterpillar a major employer in Aurora. The cities also have benefited from job growth in nearby Naperville and Schaumburg, suburban cities that have emerged as business centers outside Chicago.

Both Elgin and Aurora have Hispanic populations approaching 25 percent, a vestige of the days when DuPage County farms were cultivated by migrant labor. Those farms have now been paved over

and built upon, but many of the migrant workers remained in the area. Suburban and rural voters who back the GOP far outnumber the cities' blue-collar and minority Democrats. The district votes solidly Republican. Bob Dole narrowly won the district in 1996 with 48 percent of the vote. And George W. Bush carried the 14th with 55 percent of the vote in 2000.

MAJOR INDUSTRY
Farm machinery and other manufacturing, riverboat gambling, agriculture

CITIES
Aurora (pt.), 85,543 (1990); Elgin (pt.), 61,610 (1990); DeKalb, 39,329; Carpentersville, 28,411; St. Charles, 27,957

UNUSUAL FEATURES
Former President Ronald Reagan's birthplace and boyhood home in Dixon and the site of 6-foot-tall portrait of Reagan made of 14,000 jelly beans; Aurora used as the setting for the Wayne's World television skit and movies; Mary Todd Lincoln went insane after Abraham Lincoln's assassination and was sent to Bellevue in Batavia in 1875.

Rep. Timothy V. Johnson (R)

Elected 2000; 1st term

CAPITOL OFFICE
225-2371; fax 226-0791
1541 Longworth Bldg. 20515

INTERNET
e-mail: www.house.gov/writerep
web: www.house.gov/timjohnson

COMMITTEES
Agriculture
Science
Transportation & Infrastructure

HOMETOWN
Sidney

BORN
July 23, 1946, Champaign, Ill.

RELIGION
Assemblies of God

FAMILY
Divorced; nine children

EDUCATION
U.S. Military Academy, attended 1964; U. of Illinois,
B.A. 1969, J.D. 1972

CAREER
Lawyer; realtor

POLITICAL HIGHLIGHTS
Urbana City Council, 1971-75; Ill. House, 1977-2000

ELECTION RESULTS

2000 GENERAL

Timothy V. Johnson (R)	125,943	53.2%
Mike Kelleher (D)	110,679	46.8%

2000 PRIMARY

Timothy V. Johnson (R)	31,485	43.6%
Bill Brady (R)	26,004	36.0%
Sam Ewing (R)	12,526	17.4%
Jeffrey Jones (R)	2,155	3.0%

Johnson has a ready explanation for his long career in politics, which included a city council stint and 24 years in the state House before his 2000 victory for Illinois' open 15th District seat. Public service "has always been in my blood," says Johnson, whose father was a city councilman and whose grandfathers were politically active.

Despite his long tenure in Springfield, Johnson has pledged to keep it short in Washington: Elected to Congress at age 54, he has promised to limit his congressional service to no more than three terms.

Though the 15th has midsize cities, such as Champaign, Bloomington and Kankakee, it is mainly farm country. Agriculture policy is Johnson's primary focus, as it was for his retired GOP predecessor, Thomas W. Ewing. Johnson landed a seat on the Agriculture Committee, replacing Ewing, and says his political philosophy is similar to Ewing's.

"We've both been strong supporters of a free enterprise system. Both of us have an acute awareness of the importance of agriculture and small business within the district," Johnson told the Bloomington Pantagraph in early 2001.

Johnson, who also won seats on the Science and Transportation committees, votes a conservative line on most issues. But he deviates from party orthodoxy in his opposition to federally funded vouchers for private school education.

Known as an indefatigable campaigner, Johnson won a primary in which three of the most influential Illinois Republicans backed different candidates: Gov. George Ryan endorsed Johnson, House Speaker J. Dennis Hastert backed state Rep. Bill Brady and incumbent Ewing supported his son, Sam Ewing. Johnson, running on high name recognition and ample personal funds, won the contest with 44 percent of the vote.

The 15th leans Republican and Johnson entered the general-election race a strong favorite. But he faced a tougher-than-expected battle with his Democratic foe, university instructor Mike Kelleher, a first-time candidate and former Capitol Hill aide. Johnson prevailed, though with a modest 53 percent.

ILLINOIS 15

East Central – Champaign; Kankakee

Corn and soybean fields cover the 11 east-central Illinois counties that make up the 15th. Farmers produce both feed and raw material for food products manufactured just over the district's border at Decatur-based Archer Daniels Midland Co.

Scattered amid the farms are several midsize towns, including Danville and Kankakee, that grew up around agribusiness and manufacturing. These communities struggled with double-digit unemployment in the early 1990s. Higher education is big business in this district, with five colleges in Bloomington-Normal and 37,000 students at the University of Illinois flagship campus in Champaign-Urbana. Bloomington and Normal combine to create the district's largest urban area, one of only a few in downstate Illinois.

Bloomington, home to State Farm insurance, leads downstate Illinois in insurance and finance.

In general, the district votes Republican, although the 15th's urban centers tend to lean more Democratic than rural voters. In 1992 and '96, voters in the more liberal university towns helped swing the district in Bill Clinton's favor, but he did not get more than 46 percent of the vote in either election. The 15th went Republican in 2000, giving 52 percent of the vote to George W. Bush.

MAJOR INDUSTRY
Higher education, food processing, agriculture

CITIES
Champaign, 65,226; Bloomington, 60,872; Normal (pt.), 40,018 (1990); Urbana, 36,744; Danville, 32,938; Kankakee, 26,717

UNUSUAL FEATURES
Famous natives: Vice President Adlai Stevenson of Bloomington, film critic Roger Ebert of Urbana.

Rep. Donald Manzullo (R)

Elected 1992; 5th term

CAPITOL OFFICE
225-5676; fax 225-5284; 409 Cannon Bldg. 20515

INTERNET
e-mail: www.house.gov/writerep
web: www.house.gov/manzullo

COMMITTEES
Financial Services
Small Business - chairman

HOMETOWN
Egan

BORN
March 24, 1944, Rockford, Ill.

RELIGION
Baptist

FAMILY
Wife, Freda Manzullo; three children

EDUCATION
American U., B.A. 1967; Marquette U., J.D. 1970

CAREER
Lawyer

POLITICAL HIGHLIGHTS
Sought Republican nomination for U.S. House, 1990

ELECTION RESULTS

2000 GENERAL

Donald Manzullo (R)	178,174	66.7%
Charles W. Hendrickson (D)	88,781	33.2%

2000 PRIMARY

Donald Manzullo (R)	unopposed

1998 GENERAL

Donald Manzullo (R)	unopposed

PREVIOUS WINNING PERCENTAGES
1996 (60%); 1994 (71%); 1992 (56%)

Manzullo said when he first ran for Congress, "we didn't know anything about running a campaign," so he and his wife bought $110 worth of how-to books. Rejecting as impractical the advice of one book, to get many people to contribute $1,000 each to the campaign, he found another book more helpful with its suggestion to "Take your message to the people." His message: "Government is too big and people are taxed too much."

A decade later, with four terms under his belt, Manzullo's philosophy is the same, both at home and on Capitol Hill, where he has built a solid, pro-business, socially conservative record based on the idea that private enterprise plays a key role in the social and economic well-being of the community. In the 107th Congress, Manzullo (man-ZOO-low) won the gavel of the Small Business Committee, besting Sue W. Kelly of New York.

Manzullo's views are shaped by the example set by his father, who as a struggling grocery store owner in post-war Rockford was generous in extending credit to new arrivals from displaced persons camps in Europe and from rural Arkansas. The Manzullos themselves were not well-off — they lived in a one-room apartment above the store — but Manzullo's father served as a "one man social services agency," helping the newcomers insulate their homes with cardboard and organizing community activities such as boxing tournaments.

Northern Illinois' 16th District today has many small businesses that form the backbone of community life. The district boasts dairy and corn farms and hundreds of mostly small manufacturing companies — Rockford has variously billed itself as a furniture-making center and later as the tool-and-die capital of the world. Exports of agricultural crops, processed foods and manufactured goods have been an important economic factor as the area has pulled itself out of the serious downturn of the 1980s that saw 20 percent unemployment or more.

Manzullo has two broad objectives in Congress: encouraging federal efforts to help U.S. businesses export goods abroad and promoting a domestic agenda of lower taxes and conservative social policies. Manzullo's committee assignments — he sits on Financial Services in addition to Small Business — are good fits for the district's needs.

He strongly supports federal funding for the Export-Import Bank and the Overseas Private Investment Corporation, which assist businesses in expanding exports. Manzullo steadfastly defends the trade agencies, arguing that they are an essential counterbalance to foreign governments that invest much more heavily than the United States in helping their businesses increase exports.

He is one of the biggest Republican boosters of the view that the United States should keep up good commercial relations with emerging markets, especially China. This stance separates Manzullo from GOP conservatives who would restrict U.S. trade with China in hopes of pressuring its government to halt human rights abuses and other unacceptable practices.

Manzullo is a pillar of the Republican right on a range of domestic issues, including taxation, education, the environment and abortion. He belongs to the Conservative Action Team (known as the CATs), a faction of the most conservative House GOP members. For years, he has pushed legislation that would limit federal judges' power to require a state or municipality to raise taxes to enforce a court judgment. In Rockford, a federal judge issued an order that had the effect of raising property taxes to pay for past school desegregation injustices. Manzullo's view: "Allowing appointed federal judges to order or levy taxes goes against the very fabric of our nation's founding."

In the 105th Congress, Manzullo teamed with another socially conservative Republican, Ernest Istook of Oklahoma, to propose that federally funded family planning clinics be required to get parental notification before they provide contraceptives to minors. Manzullo, who helped start crisis pregnancy centers in Rockford and picketed clinics that performed abortions, said he proposed the requirement after learning of an incident in Illinois in which a 37-year-old schoolteacher allegedly brought one of his 14-year-old students to the county health department for birth control injections, which were given without notifying the girl's parents or local authorities.

Manzullo's family lives more than half the year in Washington, where the three children are home-schooled by their mother, who is trained as a microbiologist. He says that home-schooling is not for everyone, but that his family decided it was the best way to keep everyone together under the circumstances of a congressional work schedule. He has nothing against the local school system in Illinois, where the family spends about five months a year on a small beef cattle farm outside Rockford.

Manzullo recalls deciding, at age 4, to become a lawyer when he grew up. At age 10, he also decided that it would be nice to be a member of Congress.

He followed through on the first vow, spending 20 years in law practice, most of them as a small-town lawyer who handled many family cases. But, although he worked three years as an aide to Illinois' independent-minded GOP Rep. John Anderson while an undergraduate at American University, Manzullo never really got involved politically — until 1989 when 16th District GOP Rep. Lynn Martin announced she would run for the Senate the next year. Manzullo jumped into the House race and, with a door-to-door campaign, made a highly respectable 46 percent showing in the GOP primary.

The Republican nominee, John W. Hallock Jr., had the dubious distinction of losing the general election to John W. Cox Jr. — the first Democratic victory in the district in the 20th century — and Manzullo decided to keep right on campaigning. It was expected that Republicans would challenge Cox in 1992 with state Sen. Jack Schaffer, a contender with party establishment backing and more money than Manzullo. But Manzullo and his corps of volunteers, many from families helped by his father years before, went hard after Schaffer, accusing him of supporting increased taxes and a legislative pay raise. Manzullo won the primary with 56 percent of the vote. In November, the district reverted to its traditional GOP form, electing Manzullo with 56 percent, and he has not been seriously challenged since.

KEY VOTES

2000

No	Raise hourly minimum wage by $1 over two years
Yes	Halt funding for U.S. mission in Kosovo unless European nations pay more
Yes	Provide Medicare benefits to military retirees and their dependents
Yes	Grant China permanent normal trade status
Yes	Phase out estate, gift and trust taxes
Yes	Prohibit implementation of president's national monument designations
Yes	Approve GOP plan to provide prescription drug coverage for Medicare beneficiaries
No	Increase help for poor nations indebted to international financial institutions

1999

No	Impose steel import quotas
No	Kill proposal to take aviation trust funds off budget
Yes	Require background checks on buyers only at gun shows with 10 or more vendors
Yes	Remove barriers among banking, securities and insurance companies
No	Authorize state grants to hire teachers and reduce class size
No	Overhaul campaign finance law; ban "soft money" and restrict advocacy advertising
No	Approve bipartisan plan to increase rights of patients in managed-care health plans

INTEREST GROUPS

	AFL-CIO	ADA	CCUS	ACU
2000	0%	5%	90%	95%
1999	0%	15%	96%	92%
1998	0%	0%	94%	92%
1997	0%	5%	90%	100%

CQ VOTE STUDIES

	PARTY UNITY		PRESIDENTIAL SUPPORT	
	Support	Oppose	Support	Oppose
2000	95%	5%	22%	78%
1999	92%	8%	15%	85%
1998	95%	5%	21%	79%
1997	96%	4%	23%	77%

ILLINOIS 16
Northwest – Rockford; McHenry

The 16th spans most of the Illinois-Wisconsin border, covering the rolling northern prairie where family farmers grow corn and raise dairy cows. At its eastern end, the 16th includes McHenry County, the fastest-growing county in Illinois. Located at the edge of Chicago's flourishing northwest counties, McHenry is quickly filling with new suburban bedroom communities.

A fourth of the district's voters live in Rockford, an industrial hub and Illinois' second-largest city. In the 1980s, Rockford became a poster child of Rust Belt decline, with unemployment often exceeding 20 percent. The city recovered by upgrading to high-tech manufacturing and expanding its exports to the NAFTA countries and China. Now, unemployment rates hover around the national average.

Other counties in the 16th are among Illinois' leading dairy producers. Jo Daviess County, in the northwest corner, is a leader in the state in raising beef cattle. Galena, in rolling hills near the Mississippi River, has a tourist-based economy.

More than 90 percent of the district's black population lives in Rockford, giving the city a base of loyal Democrats, but the rest of the 16th covers conservative, Republican territory. Voters elected a Democrat to the House only once in the 20th century – in 1990 when John W. Cox beat a Republican candidate dogged by ethical questions and bad publicity. In 1992, the district reverted to its Republican ways.

MAJOR INDUSTRY
Automotive, aircraft and machine parts, agriculture

CITIES
Rockford, 143,831; Crystal Lake, 34,661; Freeport, 26,031; Lake in the Hills, 21,228

UNUSUAL FEATURES
Ulysses S. Grant, native of Galena; Rockford known as the world's largest producer of fasteners.

Rep. Lane Evans (D)

Elected 1982; 10th term

Evans represents a district of family farms, market towns and small cities that used to vote solidly Republican. Well aware of this, he pays close attention to his constituents, and they have elected him 10 times.

Evans has also received unwavering support from labor unions and from veterans, who appreciate his work on their behalf as the ranking Democrat on the Veterans' Affairs Committee. A veteran himself, Evans is perhaps best known among his colleagues for his tireless work to beef up benefits for others who have served in uniform. Of the 22 bills that he introduced in 2000, only five were not related to the military or veterans' needs.

In 1998, concerns arose about his ability to keep up with the rigorous House schedule when he revealed that he had suffered for three years from Parkinson's disease. Although his walk is visibly slower and shakier these days, the former Marine insists that he is well enough to continue serving his district.

Evans is the first Vietnam-era veteran to hold the ranking slot on Veterans' Affairs. Although he was not assigned to Vietnam during his 1969 to 1971 service in the Marine Corps, he emerged a few years ago as a leading proponent of federal programs benefiting veterans of that conflict.

The congressman touted his work on veterans issues in his 2000 campaign, citing several bills that were signed into law in the 106th Congress. One comprehensive measure established a four-year plan requiring the Department of Veterans Affairs (VA) to provide institutional care — mostly nursing home service — to certain veterans with service-connected disabilities. Previously, the VA could, but was not required to, provide such care. The measure also allowed greater coverage of non-institutional care, including home- and community-based care, for all veterans and authorized the VA to pay for emergency treatment for veterans at non-VA health care facilities.

Evans also pushed through legislation that supports veteran-owned small businesses by creating new assistance programs within the Small Business Administration and requiring the federal government to seek out veteran-owned businesses for contracting projects.

He has long been a crusader for veterans suffering from diseases linked to Agent Orange, a defoliant used during the Vietnam War. His four-year effort to gain medical compensation for these veterans paid off when his bill was enacted in the 102nd Congress.

Evans first made a splash on Veterans' Affairs in December 1992 when he bid for the committee chairmanship, a position held for 12 years by venerable Mississippi Democrat G.V. "Sonny" Montgomery. Evans fell four votes short of taking the chair, and many assumed that his strong showing presaged success against Montgomery in a 1994 rematch. But fate intervened as Republicans seized the House majority that year, and Evans decided against challenging Montgomery for the ranking spot. Later, Montgomery announced that the 104th Congress would be his last.

Evans' attempt to wrest the chairmanship from Montgomery came after years of locking horns with his older colleague over the handling of issues important to Vietnam-era veterans. Younger veterans, who believed Montgomery was dragging his feet on compensation for Agent Orange-related diseases, saw the World War II and Korean War veteran as intent on protecting his own generation's programs at the expense of Vietnam veterans. But Montgomery eventually yielded to the demands of the Vietnam

CAPITOL OFFICE
225-5905; fax 225-5396; 2211 Rayburn Bldg. 20515

INTERNET
e-mail: lane.evans@mail.house.gov
web: www.house.gov/evans

COMMITTEES
Armed Services
Veterans' Affairs - ranking member

HOMETOWN
Rock Island

BORN
Aug. 4, 1951, Rock Island, Ill.

RELIGION
Roman Catholic

FAMILY
Single

EDUCATION
Augustana College (Ill.), B.A. 1974; Georgetown U., J.D. 1978

MILITARY SERVICE
Marine Corps, 1969-71

CAREER
Lawyer

POLITICAL HIGHLIGHTS
No previous office

ELECTION RESULTS

2000 GENERAL

Lane Evans (D)	132,494	54.9%
Mark Baker (R)	108,853	45.1%

2000 PRIMARY

Lane Evans (D)	unopposed

1998 GENERAL

Lane Evans (D)	100,128	51.6%
Mark Baker (R)	94,072	48.4%

PREVIOUS WINNING PERCENTAGES
1996 (52%); 1994 (55%); 1992 (60%); 1990 (67%); 1988 (65%); 1986 (56%); 1984 (57%); 1982 (53%)

vets and allowed Evans' Agent Orange legislation to pass.

Evans also serves on the Armed Services Committee, where he criticized Republican efforts to increase defense spending above levels proposed by the Clinton administration. Since 1992, he and Sen. Patrick J. Leahy, D-Vt., have tried to mobilize U.S. government support for an international agreement to ban the use of land mines.

Evans has consistently opposed Republican proposals, including an overhaul of the welfare and Medicare systems, a repeal of the assault weapons ban and efforts to curb government regulations. He supports abortion rights and opposed a ban on a procedure its opponents call "partial birth" abortion.

He backs Democratic efforts to raise the minimum wage and supports labor in other votes. In 1998, he opposed a proposal to curb "salting," a practice in which union organizers seek employment at non-union firms with the goal of organizing workers. And in 1997, he opposed a Republican measure that would have limited labor protections for Amtrak workers.

Evans points to his parents — his father was a firefighter and his mother a nurse — as the inspiration for his liberal views, saying, "They saved people's lives. I fight for ordinary people and I identify with ordinary people. I think there is something real in my ability to connect with working families."

In 1982, Evans emerged from his community legal clinic in Rock Island to make his first run for public office. It was an effort that seemed futile until the March primary that year, when former state Sen. Kenneth G. McMillan, a New Right stalwart, defeated Rep. Tom Railsback, a moderate eight-term Republican. Railsback's defeat set up a clear ideological choice, one that benefited Evans in the recession year of 1982. Evans urged voters in the economically troubled district to "send Reagan a message." McMillan defended President Reagan's economic program, not a winning tack in that year. Evans won with 53 percent of the vote.

Evans' 1982 capture of this Republican district was regarded as stunning, but with his hard work, engaging manner and constituent service he soon ensconced himself. John Linder, R-Ga., who chaired the National Republican Congressional Committee during the 1998 election cycle, commented, "Lane Evans has a huge constituent service effort. About two-thirds of the senior citizens in his district think he signs their Social Security checks."

Still, district Republicans try every election to convince voters that Evans is too liberal. So far, he has deflected the charge, but the battles have become closer in recent years, holding Evans to 55 percent or lower. For the past three elections, he has faced the same Republican challenger — Mark Baker, a Quincy TV newsman.

KEY VOTES

2000
Yes Raise hourly minimum wage by $1 over two years
Yes Halt funding for U.S. mission in Kosovo unless European nations pay more
Yes Provide Medicare benefits to military retirees and their dependents
No   Grant China permanent normal trade status
No   Phase out estate, gift and trust taxes
No   Prohibit implementation of president's national monument designations
No   Approve GOP plan to provide prescription drug coverage for Medicare beneficiaries
Yes Increase help for poor nations indebted to international financial institutions

1999
Yes Impose steel import quotas
No   Kill proposal to take aviation trust funds off budget
No   Require background checks on buyers only at gun shows with 10 or more vendors
No   Remove barriers among banking, securities and insurance companies
Yes Authorize state grants to hire teachers and reduce class size
Yes Overhaul campaign finance law; ban "soft money" and restrict advocacy advertising
Yes Approve bipartisan plan to increase rights of patients in managed-care health plans

INTEREST GROUPS

	AFL-CIO	ADA	CCUS	ACU
2000	100%	95%	38%	8%
1999	100%	100%	16%	0%
1998	100%	90%	22%	16%
1997	100%	100%	20%	16%

CQ VOTE STUDIES

	PARTY UNITY		PRESIDENTIAL SUPPORT	
	Support	Oppose	Support	Oppose
2000	94%	6%	76%	24%
1999	94%	6%	80%	20%
1998	92%	8%	83%	17%
1997	93%	7%	73%	27%

ILLINOIS 17
West – Rock Island; Moline

The 17th, where John Deere developed the first self-cleaning steel plow in 1837, includes the rich farm lands along the Mississippi River and Rock Island and Moline, two of the four industrial Quad Cities that straddle the river into Iowa.

Defense cutbacks have drained jobs from one of the district's industrial mainstays, the Rock Island Arsenal. Corn, soybeans and hogs fuel most of the rest of the district's economy. Even the industrial sector depends on agriculture: it's dominated by the nation's two largest farm equipment manufacturers. Sliding farm profits have forced the Quad Cities to recruit new types of manufacturing.

The 17th is one of the most politically competitive districts in the state. It used to vote solidly Republican, despite heavily unionized constituencies in Rock Island and Moline that routinely back Democrats. The 17th swung Democratic in the early 1980s when the farm economy went south – not just in western Illinois, but also in

previously rock-ribbed Republican areas like Iowa and other Plains regions. Since then, most of the district has been gradually returning to its Republican roots – albeit slowly. In 1996, Bill Clinton won the district by 13 points and in 2000 Al Gore carried the district, but only by 5 points. A Democrat like Rep. Evans can still carry the district with a strong turnout in Rock Island County and a respectable showing in the more rural and Republican counties.

MAJOR INDUSTRY
Farm equipment manufacturing, agriculture, defense

MILITARY BASES
Rock Island Arsenal, 133 military, 3,719 civilian (1999)

CITIES
Moline, 42,720; Quincy, 40,108; Rock Island, 38,389; Galesburg, 32,888

UNUSUAL FEATURES
Bishop Hill, established in 1846 by Swedish religious dissidents searching for a "utopia on the prairie;" Galesburg, hometown of Illinois' late poet laureate, Carl Sandburg.

Rep. Ray LaHood (R)

Elected 1994; 4th term

While many of LaHood's colleagues in the Republican Class of 1994 revel in their outsider background and routinely blast Congress as an institution, LaHood makes use of the parliamentary knowledge he gained as the chief of staff of former House Republican Leader Robert H. Michel and he plays the role of conciliator, working to narrow the differences between the two parties.

When the House convened in December 1998 to debate whether to impeach President Clinton, LaHood presided over the floor, wielding the Speaker's gavel. He was chosen to oversee the impeachment deliberations because of his reputation as forceful and evenhanded — and someone whom Democrats viewed as fair.

He has had plenty of practice in the Speaker's chair: His office estimates that he probably has presided over House debate on legislation more frequently than any other member since he came to Congress in 1995. The GOP leadership knows that LaHood's rulings, which are confident and quick, help maintain order during complicated or emotionally charged debates. He keeps the legislative process humming along, giving opponents fewer opportunities for making complaints.

LaHood says he learned House rules "almost by osmosis" during his 12 years as a top aide in Michel's district and Capitol Hill office. He first declared his candidacy for Congress the day after Michel announced his retirement in 1993. After easily winning the election with 60 percent of the vote, LaHood actually returned to work in Michel's office for the remaining weeks of the session. He has easily won re-election ever since.

LaHood is among the GOP members who constitute a small, informal group of advisers to Speaker J. Dennis Hastert of Illinois, another Michel protégé. Although LaHood is often described as a moderate, that label applies more to his unflappable manner than to his voting record, which places him in the conservative mainstream of the party.

During the 106th Congress, LaHood voted for the immediate deployment of an anti-missile defense system, against bipartisan legislation to allow patients to sue their health plans, and in favor of a measure to recognize unborn fetuses as entities distinct from pregnant women under federal law.

Yet at times, LaHood has split from his leadership. He has criticized GOP leaders for their resistance to increasing the minimum wage and their efforts to put tax cuts before a balanced budget. And in 2000, LaHood cosponsored legislation to improve prisoners' access to DNA testing when Illinois GOP Gov. George Ryan declared a moratorium on executions in his state after 13 people on death row were found to be innocent.

In the 107th Congress, LaHood won a sought-after seat on the Appropriations Committee; he is also one of three Appropriations members designated to serve on the Budget Committee. With his assignment to Appropriations' Agriculture Subcommittee, he remains in a good position to look out for his district's corn and soybean growers and grain dealers. In the 106th, he sought to broaden the use of ethanol — a clean-burning fuel made from corn and other agricultural products. In 2000, LaHood and Illinois Sen. Richard J. Durbin, a Democrat, sent a letter to the White House touting the benefits of ethanol and calling for its use as a fuel additive. In the 105th Congress, he was a key player in retaining the tax credit for ethanol producers, which Ways and Means Chairman Bill Archer of Texas had sought to eliminate.

As a member of the Agriculture Committee in the 106th, he won enactment of legislation allowing farmers to download and file government forms

CAPITOL OFFICE
225-6201; fax 225-9249
1424 Longworth Bldg. 20515

INTERNET
e-mail: www.house.gov/writerep
web: www.house.gov/lahood

COMMITTEES
Appropriations
Budget
Select Intelligence

HOMETOWN
Peoria

BORN
Dec. 6, 1945, Peoria, Ill.

RELIGION
Roman Catholic

FAMILY
Wife, Kathleen LaHood; four children

EDUCATION
Spoon River Community College, attended 1963-65; Bradley U., B.S. 1971

CAREER
Congressional aide; youth bureau director; urban planning commission director; teacher

POLITICAL HIGHLIGHTS
Ill. House, 1982-83

ELECTION RESULTS

2000 GENERAL

Ray LaHood (R)	173,706	67.1%
Joyce Harant (D)	85,317	32.9%

2000 PRIMARY

Ray LaHood (R)	unopposed

1998 GENERAL

Ray LaHood (R)	unopposed

PREVIOUS WINNING PERCENTAGES
1996 (59%); 1994 (60%)

with the U.S. Department of Agriculture via the Internet. "This bill is a reasonable, sensible way to help farmers spend less time filling out paperwork and spend more time doing what they do best — farming," he said.

LaHood's record on environmental matters is varied. He was an outspoken critic of the stricter clean air standards issued by the Environmental Protection Agency in 1997. But he was a strong backer of Clinton's American Heritage Rivers initiative to preserve waterways, and he obtained funds to maintain and improve the Illinois River. In the 104th, he endorsed efforts to limit the Environmental Protection Agency's authority. But in the 105th, he opposed an attempt to limit enforcement of the Endangered Species Act.

LaHood was one of only three Republicans in the Class of 1994 who did not sign the "Contract With America," which helped the GOP win House control that year. He voiced concern that the Contract's advocacy of tax cuts and defense spending would worsen the federal deficit. He expressed similar concern in 2000 over the tax cut plan promoted by then-candidate George W. Bush during the presidential campaign, but he ended up supporting the Bush plan in early 2001.

LaHood proved prescient on one issue: the Electoral College. Beginning in the 105th Congress, he has sponsored legislation to abolish the Electoral College and allow the president to be chosen by direct election. "The existence of the college needs to be addressed before we are embroiled in a crisis in which a president is elected without winning the popular vote," he said in 1997.

LaHood's respect for the House as an institution prompted him to organize a bipartisan retreat during the 105th Congress to promote understanding, if not harmony, between lawmakers of both parties. He and Colorado Democrat David E. Skaggs began planning the weekend gathering for House members and their families after witnessing a particularly heated floor debate in 1996. "It's not a panacea," LaHood said. "This is the beginning of people building friendships and building relationships."

The retreat in March 1997 drew about 220 members, including both the Democratic and Republican leadership. After the gathering, Congress still had plenty of nasty exchanges, but LaHood maintained that the retreat's influence helped smooth negotiations on the balanced-budget package in 1997. He helped organize the follow-on retreats in 1999 and 2001.

LaHood chose civility as a major theme in his commencement address, in the spring of 1999, to graduates of the American University in Dubai. He told graduates, "It is hard to demonize a political opponent if you have held his 2-year-old daughter on your knee."

KEY VOTES

2000

Yes Raise hourly minimum wage by $1 over two years
Yes Halt funding for U.S. mission in Kosovo unless European nations pay more
Yes Provide Medicare benefits to military retirees and their dependents
Yes Grant China permanent normal trade status
Yes Phase out estate, gift and trust taxes
Yes Prohibit implementation of president's national monument designations
Yes Approve GOP plan to provide prescription drug coverage for Medicare beneficiaries
No Increase help for poor nations indebted to international financial institutions

1999

No Impose steel import quotas
No Kill proposal to take aviation trust funds off budget
Yes Require background checks on buyers only at gun shows with 10 or more vendors
No Remove barriers among banking, securities and insurance companies
No Authorize state grants to hire teachers and reduce class size
No Overhaul campaign finance law; ban "soft money" and restrict advocacy advertising
No Approve bipartisan plan to increase rights of patients in managed-care health plans

INTEREST GROUPS

	AFL-CIO	ADA	CCUS	ACU
2000	10%	15%	95%	72%
1999	22%	15%	84%	66%
1998	40%	20%	83%	60%
1997	38%	20%	80%	64%

CQ VOTE STUDIES

	PARTY UNITY		PRESIDENTIAL SUPPORT	
	Support	Oppose	Support	Oppose
2000	87%	13%	32%	68%
1999	83%	17%	26%	74%
1998	83%	17%	28%	72%
1997	91%	9%	31%	69%

ILLINOIS 18

Central — Peoria; part of Springfield

When Richard Nixon spoke to the silent majority, his message hit home in Peoria, an American Everytown filled with hard-working, conservative, middle-class folks. Thirty years later, Peoria is a Democratic-leaning anomaly in a sea of rural Republicans. The famous city has a substantial union constituency that is consistently outvoted by conservative farmers.

At its far southern reaches, the 18th District also includes a number of Republican suburbanites at the outskirts of Springfield, the state's centrally located capital. The district narrowly supported Bill Clinton in 1992, but backed Republican presidential candidates in 1996 and 2000.

In much of this predominantly agricultural district, voters worry about crop prices, ethanol, free trade and estate taxes. But the district's economic health still depends largely on Caterpillar Inc. Based in Peoria, the company manufactures earth-moving

equipment and other heavy machinery.

After Caterpillar hit rough times in the 1980s, laying off workers and closing factories, the region tried to reduce its economic dependence on the company. The company has since rebounded, much to the relief of the Peoria economy. The city and its neighboring towns have also successfully started to diversify their manufacturing and a few companies have ventured into ethanol and other grain byproducts.

MAJOR INDUSTRY
Construction machinery, ethanol and grain products, agriculture

CITIES
Peoria, 111,127; Springfield (pt.), 35,244 (1990); Pekin, 33,261

UNUSUAL FEATURES
Peoria lays claim to the nation's longest-running Santa Claus Parade; Beardstown Ladies' Investment Club, publisher of the best-selling Beardstown Ladies' Common Sense Investment Guide.

Rep. David Phelps (D)

Elected 1998; 2nd term

CAPITOL OFFICE
225-5201; fax 225-1541
1523 Longworth Bldg. 20515

INTERNET
e-mail: david.phelps@mail.house.gov
web: www.house.gov/phelps

COMMITTEES
Agriculture
Small Business

HOMETOWN
Eldorado

BORN
Oct. 26, 1947, Eldorado, Ill.

RELIGION
Baptist

FAMILY
Wife, Leslie Phelps; four children

EDUCATION
Southern Illinois U., B.S. 1969

CAREER
Retail business owner; teacher; musician

POLITICAL HIGHLIGHTS
Saline County clerk and recorder, 1980-85; Ill.
House, 1985-99

ELECTION RESULTS

2000 GENERAL

David Phelps (D)	155,101	64.6%
James E. "Jim" Eatherly (R)	85,137	35.4%

2000 PRIMARY

David Phelps (D)	unopposed

1998 GENERAL

David Phelps (D)	122,430	58.3%
Brent Winters (R)	87,614	41.7%

Hailing as he does from the Bible Belt, Phelps' political career has been bolstered by his talent for performing gospel music. He and his brothers will often pull into one of the small southern Illinois towns he represents and begin singing from the back of a pick-up truck. Phelps then tops off the act with a speech to the constituents who have gathered.

Yet in Congress, the second-term Democrat comes across as quiet and unassuming, hardly the type who would stage an impromptu concert or sing before a stadium packed with 15,000 people, as the Phelps Brothers Quartet did when Southern Illinois University hosted a Christian-music concert in 2000. Phelps and his brothers made their living from their music in the 1970s and early 1980s, both through their performances and from the proceeds of selling songs written by the future congressman. His work has been recorded by major country-and-Western groups, including the Oak Ridge Boys.

While Phelps' musical skills help him communicate with the voters today, before he could launch his second career he had to overcome his parents' concerns that politics might not mix well with their Baptist beliefs. Democratic Party officials approached the family in 1980 about one of the brothers filling an open position as the Saline County clerk and recorder. When David expressed interest, his mother began to cry. Phelps' parents considered a political life "taboo" and told him as much: "You don't want to get in the backroom, smoke-filled, deal-making atmosphere because it can corrupt you." But Phelps was undeterred and accepted an appointment to the Saline County post.

After four years in county office, he ousted a veteran Republican to win election to the Illinois House. He went on to serve 14 years, and in 1998, he sought the 19th District seat vacated by Democratic Rep. Glenn Poshard, whose blend of social conservatism and union loyalty he shared. While Poshard lost the 1998 governor's race, Phelps won election to the House with 58 percent of the vote. Phelps took 65 percent in 2000 and would seemingly be secure for the future, but with Illinois losing one of its House seats due to reapportionment, the picture is muddied. (A decade ago, Illinois lost two seats, and Poshard was pitted against, and defeated, another Democratic incumbent in the process.)

So far, Phelps has bolstered his electoral prospects by following Poshard's political formula. He mixes conservative stands on social issues and a tendency to cut taxes with strong efforts to bring federal dollars to the financially struggling 19th District. Such a political philosophy has prompted Phelps to join the group of conservative Democrats known as the "Blue Dogs," whose emphasis is on budget and tax issues, and the centrist New Democrats, whose focus is on technology and education.

In 2000, Phelps was one of a handful of Democrats who voted to override President Clinton's vetoes of both of the year's big tax measures, one to cut taxes for married couples and the other to eliminate taxes on estates, gifts and trust funds.

For a low-key freshman, Phelps showed surprising adeptness at inserting his pet projects into spending and authorizing bills. On the appropriations side, he won $1.2 million in transportation funding to expand Highway 51 south of Decatur. He also attached language to restore federally subsidized airline service between Decatur and Chicago's O'Hare Airport to the law that reauthorized the Federal Aviation Administration for three years.

The most difficult issue Phelps faced in his first term was international trade. With the Clinton administration and big business pushing to permanently allow China the same low tariff rates of almost all other countries, Phelps found himself pulled in two directions.

His district is home to one of the nation's largest agriculture processors, Archer Daniels Midland Co., which bills itself as the "supermarket to the world." The company pressured him to vote for the permanent normal trade relations legislation, as did Caterpillar Inc., the Illinois-based large machinery manufacturer and one of the country's most prolific exporters.

On the other side, many of his pro-union and socially conservative constituents worried that China would not keep the promises it had made to open up its market and that life would not improve for political protesters and others who went up against the communist government.

Though the district had benefited from trade through the presence of ADM, the 19th had suffered as smaller manufacturers moved their operations to other countries or closed altogether because they could not compete globally. Phelps had helped secure government-provided training assistance to workers who lost their jobs in a bicycle factory in Olney and at a lavatory and toilet manufacturer in Robinson.

The congressman's well-defined quandary gained him national attention as newspaper reporters traveled to his district. After a lengthy decision process he described as "agonizing," he opposed the China measure. In a statement, he said that he did not want to cede Congress' annual review of China's trade status. "Given the grave concerns I have not been able to reconcile, I am simply not prepared to support the irrevocable sacrifice of America's leverage and oversight," he said. Phelps also stressed that he did not believe trade with China was "the answer to agriculture's problems," either in his district or outside of it.

Southern Illinois remains worlds away from Chicago. It is made up mostly of farms and small towns. Not surprisingly, Phelps sought and won seats on the Agriculture and Small Business committees.

He lists economic development as his main objective but also wants to be a participant when Congress revisits the crop insurance and subsidy provisions of the 1996 farm law. Though he voted against the China measure, Phelps generally backs opening markets, and he is a strong supporter of lifting the trade embargo with Cuba.

In addition, Phelps has sought to raise wages for many in his district by leading efforts in the 106th Congress to increase the minimum wage. The husband of a teacher, Phelps is strongly supportive of the party's positions on increased funding for public education.

KEY VOTES

2000
Yes Raise hourly minimum wage by $1 over two years
Yes Halt funding for U.S. mission in Kosovo unless European nations pay more
Yes Provide Medicare benefits to military retirees and their dependents
No Grant China permanent normal trade status
Yes Phase out estate, gift and trust taxes
No Prohibit implementation of president's national monument designations
No Approve GOP plan to provide prescription drug coverage for Medicare beneficiaries
Yes Increase help for poor nations indebted to international financial institutions

1999
Yes Impose steel import quotas
No Kill proposal to take aviation trust funds off budget
Yes Require background checks on buyers only at gun shows with 10 or more vendors
No Remove barriers among banking, securities and insurance companies
Yes Authorize state grants to hire teachers and reduce class size
Yes Overhaul campaign finance law; ban "soft money" and restrict advocacy advertising
Yes Approve bipartisan plan to increase rights of patients in managed-care health plans

INTEREST GROUPS

	AFL-CIO	ADA	CCUS	ACU
2000	90%	50%	57%	32%
1999	89%	60%	28%	32%

CQ VOTE STUDIES

	PARTY UNITY		PRESIDENTIAL SUPPORT	
	Support	Oppose	Support	Oppose
2000	74%	26%	43%	57%
1999	68%	32%	63%	37%

ILLINOIS 19

Rural – Southern counties; Decatur

The 19th's inclination to vote Democratic masks its split personality. The northern counties cover typical Midwestern country – acres of corn and soybean fields, dotted by small towns. Its conservative, rural voters elect Republicans to local offices.

That's less true in the district's largest and northernmost city, Decatur, which has yet to fully rebound from 1980s industrial downsizing. Grain processing by Archer Daniels Midland Co. and other heavy manufacturing drive the economy of this midsize city, giving it a substantial blue-collar population. Decatur is home to most of the district's small minority population, and it leans slightly Democratic.

The southern half of the district looks more like Appalachia than Midwestern prairie. Its hilly, forested counties depend on timber and coal mining. Unemployment is an endemic problem in much of the region. In recent years, mechanization of mining has caused job losses, along with the passage of the 1990 Clean Air Act, which greatly

reduced demand for the region's high sulfur coal. The area's voters are socially conservative but don't trust Republican politicians to take their economic interests to heart. As a result, they enthusiastically support conservative Democrats with populist platforms.

At the southern tip of the 19th, Pope County, Illinois' least populous, is almost entirely within the Shawnee National Forest. In nearby Massac and Pulaski counties, river towns near the confluence of the Ohio and Mississippi have seen more prosperous days. Williamson County, at the district's western edge, benefits from its proximity to Southern Illinois U. (in the 12th District).

MAJOR INDUSTRY
Agriculture, coal mining, manufacturing, food products

CITIES
Decatur (pt.), 80,458 (1990); Charleston, 21,523; Mattoon, 18,124

UNUSUAL FEATURES
Metropolis, the official Hometown of Superman since 1972; Chicago Bears got their start as the Decatur Staleys in 1918.

Rep. John Shimkus (R)

CAPITOL OFFICE
225-5271; fax 225-5880; 513 Cannon Bldg. 20515

INTERNET
e-mail: www.house.gov/writerep
web: www.house.gov/shimkus

COMMITTEES
Energy & Commerce

HOMETOWN
Collinsville

BORN
Feb. 21, 1958, Collinsville, Ill.

RELIGION
Lutheran

FAMILY
Wife, Karen Shimkus; three children

EDUCATION
U.S. Military Academy, B.S. 1980; Southern Illinois U., M.B.A. 1997

MILITARY SERVICE
Army, 1980-86; Army Reserve, 1986-present

CAREER
High school teacher; Army officer

POLITICAL HIGHLIGHTS
Candidate for Madison County Board, 1988; Collinsville Township Board of Trustees, 1989-93; Madison County treasurer, 1990-97; Republican nominee for U.S. House, 1992

ELECTION RESULTS

2000 GENERAL

John Shimkus (R)	161,393	63.1%
Jeffrey Cooper (D)	94,382	36.9%

2000 PRIMARY

John Shimkus (R)	unopposed

1998 GENERAL

John Shimkus (R)	121,103	61.3%
Rick Verticchio (D)	76,475	38.7%

PREVIOUS WINNING PERCENTAGES
1996 (50%)

Elected 1996; 3rd term

An affable man who will reach across party lines, Shimkus has played a key role on such politically charged proposals as pairing tax cuts with a minimum wage increase. But when asked about his accomplishments in office, he likes to focus on what he has done for individual constituents, such as getting a birth certificate for an elderly woman or disability payments for a former nurse. "This is the part of public service in Congress you never hear about — helping our neighbors," he told the St. Louis Post-Dispatch.

Shimkus has good reason to tend to his constituents. Many Republicans in the House share his conservative voting record, but most of them do not share the same number of Democrats in their districts. He lost his first bid to represent the solidly Democratic 20th District in 1992 and won an open seat in 1996 by only 1,238 votes.

Shimkus is an old hand at thriving in a tough political environment, however. As Madison County treasurer before coming to Congress, he was the only Republican elected countywide. And since his narrow victory in 1996, he has strengthened his grip on the district, cruising to re-election in 1998 and 2000 by more than 20 percentage points.

Shimkus is a pragmatic conservative in the same mold as another Illinois Republican, Speaker J. Dennis Hastert. In the 106th Congress, he played a central role in efforts to craft a bipartisan package that would pair a Democratic-backed minimum wage hike with Republican-backed tax cuts. As the 107th began, he listed an increase in the minimum wage as one of his top legislative priorities. He joined other Republicans in the 106th in voting against gun control initiatives and opposing the military intervention in Kosovo. "The bombing has only made things worse," Shimkus told The State Journal-Register in Springfield, Ill. "It has not made the region and the lives of Kosovo Albanians any better," he said.

Republican leaders had Shimkus' narrow 1996 victory in mind when they awarded him a choice committee seat — Commerce — in the 105th Congress. The panel's broad jurisdiction gives its members contacts with lobbying interests eager to contribute to incumbents' re-election campaigns.

Shimkus landed the Commerce prize with help from Hastert, who used his status as a member of the GOP leadership and as a senior member of the Commerce panel to champion Shimkus' cause. As the lone Illinois Republican in the Class of 1996, Shimkus was a special project of Hastert's.

On one key Commerce issue — deregulation of the electric utility industry — Shimkus aims to protect the interests of his home state, which already has enacted a law deregulating the utility industry. "I am inclined to see that the new Illinois regulations hold in place," he said.

From his Commerce seat (renamed Energy and Commerce in the 107th Congress), Shimkus pursues legislation to promote an alternative fuel called biodiesel, which is refined from soybeans, a crop grown in the 20th. "Biodiesel is good for the environment, good for family farmers and good for the economy," he says. "Meanwhile, soybean farmers are given a new market in which to sell their product." Related to that is Shimkus' effort to promote ethanol (made from corn) and to ban the fuel additive MTBE, which competes with ethanol as a gasoline additive to reduce emissions. MTBE has been found to have contaminated groundwater supplies.

With an eye to his farming constituency, Shimkus voted for an $8.7 billion spending bill in 1999 providing emergency drought assistance to farmers. And he backed $12 billion in Medicare spending to aid rural hospitals.

Shimkus repays his leadership's kind treatment by voting a reliably Republican line even on trade, a tough issue in the 20th. The district has a large population of factory workers wary of foreign competition. He supported a measure granting China permanent normal trade status, and he voted for a bill to give the president fast-track authority to negotiate trade agreements Congress cannot amend. His advocacy for free trade flows in part from his desire to promote agricultural exports from his district and state. Illinois ranks among the top 10 states in agricultural exports.

In 2000, Shimkus joined Georgia Democratic Rep. John Lewis, a former civil rights leader, in a march commemorating the 35th anniversary of civil rights demonstrations in Selma, Ala. "I want to appreciate what the founding fathers of the civil-rights movement experienced," Shimkus told the Chicago Tribune. "I am a former high school history teacher. I believe those who fail to learn from history are doomed to repeat it."

Shimkus' outgoing personality has made an impression on his House colleagues. At a 1997 members retreat organized to foster more collegiality in the House, Shimkus was surprised to learn that some lawmakers had served in the chamber for a number of years without ever speaking to each other. He vowed to meet every member, and to track his progress he carries with him at all times an autograph book for his colleagues to sign. By the end of his first year in Congress, he had collected signatures from every House member, and he had all the senators by the end of the 105th.

Shimkus graduated from West Point, served in the Army from 1980 to 1986, and then returned to his Illinois hometown of Collinsville. (He still serves in the Army Reserve, with the rank of major.) After teaching high school history and government, he entered local politics in 1989, winning election to the Collinsville Township Board of Trustees. The next year, he won the post of Madison County treasurer, and he was easily re-elected in 1994.

He also trained his eye on Congress. In 1992, he challenged Democratic Rep. Richard J. Durbin, who had represented the 20th for the past 10 years. Shimkus took 44 percent of the vote in a losing effort. When Durbin made a move for the Senate in 1996, Shimkus again mounted a House campaign. He won the primary with a majority of the vote.

In the general election, he faced state Rep. Jay C. Hoffman, who emphasized his work on anti-crime legislation in the state legislature. Shimkus portrayed Hoffman as an opponent of tax relief and billed himself as a pro-business voice who would roll back taxes and government regulations. Although Bill Clinton carried the district by 7 percentage points, Shimkus pulled off a narrow victory.

KEY VOTES

2000
Yes Raise hourly minimum wage by $1 over two years
Yes Halt funding for U.S. mission in Kosovo unless European nations pay more
Yes Provide Medicare benefits to military retirees and their dependents
Yes Grant China permanent normal trade status
Yes Phase out estate, gift and trust taxes
Yes Prohibit implementation of president's national monument designations
Yes Approve GOP plan to provide prescription drug coverage for Medicare beneficiaries
No   Increase help for poor nations indebted to international financial institutions

1999
Yes Impose steel import quotas
No   Kill proposal to take aviation trust funds off budget
No   Require background checks on buyers only at gun shows with 10 or more vendors
Yes Remove barriers among banking, securities and insurance companies
No   Authorize state grants to hire teachers and reduce class size
Yes Overhaul campaign finance law; ban "soft money" and restrict advocacy advertising
No   Approve bipartisan plan to increase rights of patients in managed-care health plans

INTEREST GROUPS

	AFL-CIO	ADA	CCUS	ACU
2000	20%	10%	80%	80%
1999	22%	15%	96%	80%
1998	30%	10%	94%	88%
1997	38%	10%	80%	88%

CQ VOTE STUDIES

	PARTY UNITY		PRESIDENTIAL SUPPORT	
	Support	Oppose	Support	Oppose
2000	93%	7%	29%	71%
1999	92%	8%	21%	79%
1998	93%	7%	25%	75%
1997	94%	6%	28%	72%

ILLINOIS 20
West Central – Part of Springfield; Collinsville

In the Land of Lincoln, the 20th is hallowed ground – the district where "Honest Abe" Lincoln was appointed postmaster, elected to the Illinois General Assembly and admitted to practice law in the 8th Circuit Court. The western edge of the district runs along the Mississippi River, and the district extends east into the center of the state.

The 20th also includes the state's modest, Republican capital, which has the highest concentration of people in the 20th and is steeped in historical memorabilia from Lincoln's tenure in Illinois and his presidency. Springfield's state government and health care centers drive the economy of this otherwise rural district. The rest of the 20th's population is dispersed over 19 counties of family farms and tiny towns.

Social conservatism prevails throughout the 20th. Democrats, including state government workers in Springfield and blue-collar

workers in highly unionized manufacturing towns east of St. Louis and mining towns to the south, used to carry the district. The GOP, however, has a stronghold in the farming counties in the northern part of the district and recently has carried congressional races.

MAJOR INDUSTRY
State government, agriculture, manufacturing, mining

MILITARY BASES
Capital Airport Air National Guard Station, Springfield, 1,151 military, 6 civilian (2001)

CITIES
Springfield (pt.), 69,983 (1990); Collinsville, 23,614; Mount Vernon, 17,483

UNUSUAL FEATURES
World's largest ketchup bottle (water tower) in Collinsville; Frank Lloyd Wright's Dana-Thomas House; Two smallest incorporated towns in Illinois: Valley City, population 23, and Time, population 36; Principia College, in Elsah, the only Christian Science college in the nation.

Gov. Frank L. O'Bannon (D)

First elected: 1996
Length of term: 4 years
Term expires: 1/05
Salary: $95,000 (accepts part)
Phone: (317) 232-4567
Hometown: Indianapolis
Born: Jan. 30, 1930; Louisville, Ky.
Religion: Methodist
Family: Wife, Judy O'Bannon; three children
Education: Indiana U., B.A. 1952, J.D. 1957
Military Service: Air Force, 1952-54
Career: Lawyer; publisher
Political highlights: Ind. Senate, 1971-89; lieutenant governor, 1989-97

Election results:
2000 GENERAL
Frank L. O'Bannon (D)	1,232,525	56.6%
David M. McIntosh (R)	908,285	41.7%
Andrew Horning (LIBERT)	38,458	1.8%

Lt. Gov. Joe Kernan (D)

First elected: 1996
Length of term: 4 years
Term expires: 1/05
Salary: $76,000
Phone: (317) 232-4545

STATE LEGISLATURE

General Assembly: First session meets for 90 days between January and April; second session meets for 30 days between January and March
House: 100 members, 2-year terms
2001 breakdown: 47R, 53D; 86 men, 14 women
Salary: $11,600
Phone: (317) 232-9600
Senate: 50 members, 4-year terms
2001 breakdown: 32R, 18D; 38 men, 12 women
Salary: $11,600
Phone: (317) 232-9400

STATE TERM LIMITS

Governor: 2 terms
Senate: No
House: No

URBAN STATISTICS

CITY	POPULATION
Indianapolis	738,907
Fort Wayne	196,708
Evansville	121,864
Gary	110,271
South Bend	98,941

REGISTERED VOTERS

Voters do not register by party.

POPULATION

2000 population	6,080,485
1990 population	5,544,159
Percent change	+9.7%
Rank among states	14

Median age	35.1
Born in state	71%
Foreign born	2%
Urban/rural	65%/35%
Crime rate	515/100,000
Poverty level	9.4%
Federal workers	38,659
Military	21,888

REAPPORTIONMENT

Indiana lost one House seat in reapportionment, dropping from 10 districts to nine. The state legislature will draw new district lines in 2001.

MISCELLANEOUS

Web: www.state.in.us
Capital: Indianapolis
Land area: 35,870 sq. miles
  Rank among states: 38
STATE ELECTION OFFICIAL
(317) 232-3939
DEMOCRATIC HEADQUARTERS
(317) 231-7100
REPUBLICAN HEADQUARTERS
(317) 635-7561

District Statistics

DIST.	VOTE FOR PRESIDENT 2000 D	2000 R	GREEN	1996 D	1996 R	REF	1992 D	1992 R	I	WHT	BLK	ASIAN	HISP	HOUSEHOLD INCOME	OVER 65+	UNDER 18	COLLEGE EDUCATION
1	59%	39%	0%	58%	31%	10%	53%	31%	17%	74%	21%	1%	8%	$31,300	12%	28%	14%
2	42	57	0	42	45	12	35	43	22	95	4	0	1	$26,185	14	25	12
3	42	56	0	43	46	10	38	43	19	91	7	1	2	$29,470	13	26	16
4	35	64	0	36	53	10	31	46	22	93	5	1	2	$30,859	12	29	15
5	37	62	0	37	50	13	31	46	23	97	2	0	1	$27,893	13	27	11
6	29	69	0	28	63	8	23	57	20	98	1	1	1	$38,644	11	26	27
7	36	62	0	35	52	12	32	46	22	96	2	1	1	$28,080	12	25	17
8	41	56	0	45	43	11	43	40	18	96	3	1	1	$25,242	14	24	16
9	40	58	0	45	44	11	40.8	40.5	19	98	2	0	0	$26,900	13	27	10
10	59	38	0	54	37	8	47	36	17	69	30	1	1	$25,304	11	26	17
STATE	41	57	1	42	47	11	37	43	20	91	8	1	2	$28,797	13	26	16

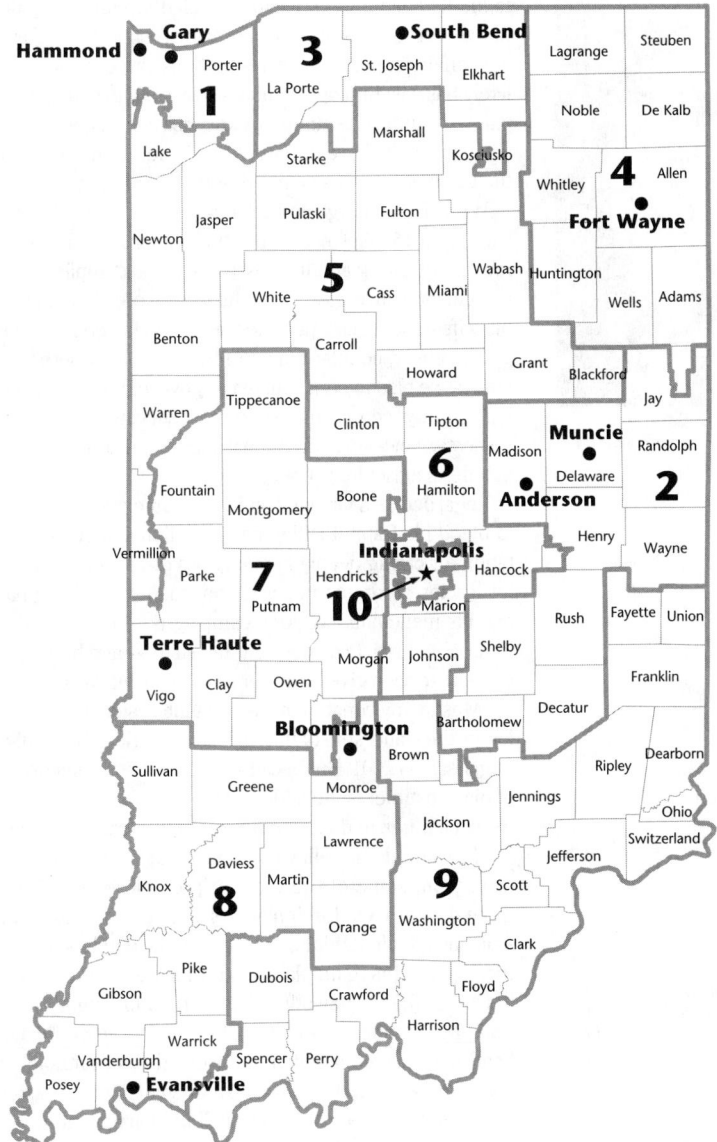

Sen. Richard G. Lugar (R)

Elected 1976; 5th term

CAPITOL OFFICE
224-4814; fax 228-0360; 306 Hart Bldg. 20510

INTERNET
e-mail: senator_lugar@lugar.senate.gov
web: lugar.senate.gov

COMMITTEES
Agriculture, Nutrition & Forestry - chairman
Foreign Relations
Select Intelligence

HOMETOWN
Indianapolis

BORN
April 4, 1932, Indianapolis, Ind.

RELIGION
Methodist

FAMILY
Wife, Charlene Lugar; four children

EDUCATION
Denison U., B.A. 1954; Oxford U., B.A. 1956, M.A. 1956

MILITARY SERVICE
Navy, 1957-60

CAREER
Farm manager; manufacturing executive

POLITICAL HIGHLIGHTS
Indianapolis School Board, 1964-67; mayor of Indianapolis, 1968-75; Republican nominee for U.S. Senate, 1974; sought Republican nomination for president, 1996

ELECTION RESULTS

2000 GENERAL

Richard G. Lugar (R)	1,427,944	66.6%
David L. Johnson (D)	683,273	31.9%
Paul Hager (LIBERT)	33,992	1.6%

2000 PRIMARY

Richard G. Lugar (R)	unopposed

1994 GENERAL

Richard G. Lugar (R)	1,039,625	67.4%
Jim Jontz (D)	470,799	30.5%
Barbara Bourland (LIBERT)	17,343	1.1%
Mary Catherine Barton (NA)	15,801	1.0%

PREVIOUS WINNING PERCENTAGES
1988 (68%); 1982 (54%); 1976 (59%)

Politics is an intellectual calling for Lugar, who cites his unlimited access to intelligence briefings and classified foreign policy documents as one of his favorite aspects of being a senator. A sophisticated and accomplished foreign affairs expert, Lugar has built his career on a serious, sober style that likely has cost him opportunities to ascend to national office. While his gold-plated résumé, international expertise and a seemingly unending supply of navy blue suits have not propelled Lugar to the White House — or even to the Cabinet — he has earned high regard in the Senate.

With all the energy and self-discipline of a long-distance runner — he still runs 12 to 15 miles each week as he approaches 70 years of age — he has racked up a long and impressive list of accomplishments: Phi Beta Kappa at Denison University, where he was co-president of the student body with his wife-to-be, Charlene Smeltzer; Rhodes Scholar at Oxford; naval intelligence officer; popular mayor of Indianapolis, where he pushed through an innovative plan to consolidate the governments of the city and nearby Marion County communities; longest-serving senator in Indiana history; respected voice on international affairs; and architect of a landmark overhaul in federal agriculture policy.

Regarded as a virtual icon in his home state of Indiana, Lugar manages to blend his Capitol Hill image as a dignified elder statesman with a reputation for caring deeply about issues back home. While he admits that the intricacies of foreign policy do not capture the imagination of Indiana voters, his meticulous work on campaigns — he sets specific vote targets for himself in districts throughout the state — and his diligent attention to constituent service give him license to steer his own course in Washington.

"Most of my constituents are not interested in the specifics of foreign policy, or the leadership of the various countries ... or really how policies flow," Lugar said in 2001. But because he places equal importance on the concerns of his constituents, he added, "they have been prepared to give me a great deal of latitude to do the things that I think are important and interest me."

That latitude has allowed Lugar to be a witness to, and often a vital participant in, some of the most gripping foreign policy events of the past three decades. On foreign affairs and other issues, Lugar has a reputation as an independent thinker who studies at length before taking a position and then speaks his mind plainly, if rather woodenly.

During the Reagan administration, when Lugar was the chairman of the Foreign Relations Committee, he was President Reagan's pick in 1986 to head a U.S. delegation monitoring the tumultuous Philippine election between Ferdinand E. Marcos and challenger Corazon C. Aquino. Lugar was an influential force in persuading Reagan that Marcos was stealing the election and should step down.

Lugar scored one of the most heralded U.S. foreign policy victories of the decade in 1991, when he and Sen. Sam Nunn, D-Ga., sponsored an initiative to dismantle thousands of nuclear weapons in the former Soviet Union. During its first 10 years, the program eliminated more than 5,000 Soviet nuclear warheads, rid countries regarded as major nuclear powers of all their nuclear weapons, and earned Lugar and Nunn a nomination for the Nobel Peace Prize.

An unabashed proponent of a strong U.S. global presence, Lugar has advocated bold actions to bring about stable conditions around the world. During the Persian Gulf crisis of 1990-91, he gained national attention for suggesting that Iraqi leader Saddam Hussein "must either leave or be removed" and has since pushed for Hussein's elimination.

But his accomplishments and high-profile role in the foreign policy arena have come about in spite of political setbacks that have cost him chances to run for national office, and to lead the Senate's Foreign Relations panel for more than the two-year period in the mid-1980s. Briefly considered as a vice-presidential prospect in 1980, and later passed over in favor of his junior counterpart, then-Sen. Dan Quayle, R-Ind., as the 1988 pick, Lugar also ran an abbreviated presidential campaign in 1996 in which he was praised as a substantive candidate but ultimately doomed by his dry manner, complex policy speeches and insistence on highlighting international, rather than domestic, issues.

In the Senate, too, the goal of being the GOP's top foreign policy legislator has eluded Lugar. On the Foreign Relations panel, he ranks just below Jesse Helms, R-N.C., who asserted his seniority over Lugar in 1987 to become the ranking Republican on the panel and has been chairman since Republicans recaptured the Senate in 1995. The two have radically different philosophies on foreign policy and have clashed on important issues ranging from U.S. payment of United Nations dues — Lugar says "a great power doesn't renege," while Helms cosponsored a solution that conditioned the funds on U.N. reforms — to the use of unilateral sanctions, which Helms supports and Lugar, an avid free-trader, says can cost America jobs and export dollars.

Lugar does, however, have the top slot on the Agriculture Committee, where he uses his own experience as an Indiana farmer — for 44 years he has run a 604-acre corn, soybean and timber farm that belonged to his father — to shape national agriculture policy. The high point of his tenure there came in 1996, when he won approval of a sweeping farm bill that replaced New Deal-era crop subsidies with a seven-year schedule of fixed payments, moving farmers toward a free-market system.

Lugar, who finds government agriculture programs too confining, worked with Democrats for months to overcome their opposition to the "Freedom to Farm" bill and has since fought hard to keep the new farm policy intact when bad weather, falling commodity prices and weak exports spur farmers to appeal to Washington for financial help.

Lugar is not averse to breaking from the GOP line. His environmental record is more moderate than that of many Senate Republicans, and he has supported some gun control legislation. The senator also has pushed to protect nutrition programs such as food stamps and school lunches. But he rates as a solid conservative on most issues, favoring tax cuts and military spending and opposing abortion except in cases of rape, incest or threat to the life of the woman. His rating from the liberal group Americans for Democratic Action has averaged about 10 percent over his Senate career.

Lugar's long record of electoral success is remarkable given his modest gifts as a campaigner. He meets crowds rather stiffly, and his style borders on lecturing. But he has always impressed Indiana voters as a man of substance. After graduating from Oxford in 1956, Lugar spent three years in the Navy, serving as a briefing officer at the Pentagon. He then returned home to run the family tool business. He won his first election in 1964, to the Indianapolis School Board. Three years later, he won election as mayor.

Even in 1974, running for the Senate in a Watergate-dominated year with a reputation as "Richard Nixon's favorite mayor," he came within a respectable 75,000 votes of Democrat Birch Bayh (whose son Evan is now Indiana's junior senator).

In 1976, against a much weaker Democrat, Sen. Vance Hartke, Lugar won handily, and he has been re-elected four times — the most in Indiana history.

KEY VOTES

2000

Yes Overhaul bankruptcy law and increase minimum wage
Yes Limit fiscal 2001 discretionary spending to $600.3 billion
Yes Override veto on nuclear waste disposal at Yucca Mountain site in Nevada
Yes Oppose effort to terminate Kosovo mission
Yes Include gender, sexual orientation and disability in federal hate crime protections
Yes Approve GOP plan to restrict use of genetic information by health insurers
Yes Kill amendment delaying implementation of an anti-missile defense system
Yes Cut taxes for married couples
Yes Grant China permanent normal trade status

1999

Yes Remove President Clinton from office for obstruction of justice
Yes Kill amendment authorizing state grants to hire teachers and reduce class size
Yes Require criminal background checks for purchases at gun shows
Yes Approve GOP proposal to increase rights of patients in managed-care health plans
No   Block effort to allow farm and medicine exports to Cuba
No   Allow study of tougher automobile fuel efficiency standards
No   Ratify nuclear weapons testing treaty
No   Prohibit national political parties from collecting "soft money" donations
Yes Remove barriers among banking, securities and insurance companies

INTEREST GROUPS

	AFL-CIO	ADA	CCUS	ACU
2000	0%	10%	100%	84%
1999	0%	5%	100%	88%
1998	0%	0%	94%	68%
1997	0%	30%	90%	64%
1996	0%	5%	85%	95%
1995	0%	5%	100%	77%
1994	0%	10%	90%	76%
1993	0%	10%	100%	72%
1992	17%	10%	100%	85%
1991	17%	10%	90%	76%

CQ VOTE STUDIES

	PARTY UNITY		PRESIDENTIAL SUPPORT	
	Support	Oppose	Support	Oppose
2000	86%	14%	65%	35%
1999	88%	12%	40%	60%
1998	84%	16%	54%	46%
1997	83%	17%	62%	38%
1996	90%	10%	31%	69%
1995	92%	8%	28%	72%
1994	78%	22%	45%	55%
1993	88%	12%	34%	66%
1992	88%	12%	90%	10%
1991	89%	11%	93%	7%

Sen. Evan Bayh (D)

CAPITOL OFFICE
224-5623; fax 228-1377; 463 Russell Bldg. 20510

INTERNET
e-mail: bayh.senate.gov/webmail.html
web: bayh.senate.gov

COMMITTEES
Banking, Housing & Urban Affairs
Energy & Natural Resources
Select Intelligence
Special Aging

HOMETOWN
Indianapolis

BORN
Dec. 26, 1955, Shirkieville, Ind.

RELIGION
Episcopalian

FAMILY
Wife, Susan Bayh; two children

EDUCATION
Indiana U., B.S. 1978; U. of Virginia, J.D. 1982

CAREER
Lawyer

POLITICAL HIGHLIGHTS
Ind. secretary of state, 1986-89; governor, 1989-97

ELECTION RESULTS

1998 GENERAL

Evan Bayh (D)	1,012,244	63.7%
Paul Helmke (R)	552,732	34.8%
Rebecca Sink-Burris (LIBERT)	23,641	1.5%

1998 PRIMARY

Evan Bayh (D)	unopposed

Elected 1998; 1st term

Bayh has occupied his father's old desk on the far left side of the Senate chamber since he first arrived in 1999. It would perhaps be more fitting if the desk were moved to the center aisle.

Both before and after his election to the Senate, Bayh (BY) has played the role of political moderate to the hilt. He has aligned himself with other centrists from both parties, introduced legislation that made some fellow Democrats uncomfortable and made a point of seeking compromises that blurred party lines — and partisan credit. Though his father, Birch Bayh, who served from 1963 to 1981, was one of the Senate's great liberals, the younger Bayh is much more in tune with the Hoosier State's conservative bent.

He is clearly trying to carve his niche in the middle. He says he always looks for the center because that's where deals are made. Bayh is a leader of the moderate Senate New Democrats, a group formed in 2000 out of frustration with the chamber's partisan gridlock, and he affiliates with the Centrist Coalition, a bipartisan group of about 30 senators who seek middle-ground solutions to legislative issues.

In 2001, he became chairman of the Democratic Leadership Council, succeeding Connecticut Democratic Sen. Joseph I. Lieberman. In the post, Bayh is the leader and a chief spokesman for the national New Democrat movement, which includes the New Democrat Coalition in the House and the Senate New Democrats, and which advertises itself as the "vital center of American politics."

Bayh has little to worry about back home. His family name is golden there, and he has coasted to victory in each election he has entered since he ran successfully for Indiana secretary of state in 1986. With his movie-star looks, twin sons and cross-party appeal, he maintains enviably high poll ratings, generating predictions that he could someday go all the way to 1600 Pennsylvania Avenue.

It is that very popularity, however, that infuriates some within his own party. Critics say he is too bent on accumulating political capital to risk it on bold substantive initiatives. "I'll never have the political capital or popularity of Evan Bayh," Indiana state Rep. Mark Kruzan, a Democrat, told The Indianapolis Star in 1996. "But I've often sensed that polling information and pressure from advisers was helping to steer the ship."

Bayh is definitely cautious. He tends to inch ahead, rather than rush forward, preferring to examine all sides of an issue carefully before taking a stand. His floor speeches are pallid affairs, filled with calls for compromise and a reliance on "Hoosier values." While many fellow senators gave impassioned speeches just before voting on President Clinton's fate in the 1999 impeachment trial, Bayh, who voted to acquit, delivered remarks crafted like a legal brief.

But he took a couple high-profile stands early in 2001 that put him clearly in line with traditional Democratic constituencies. He was one of the first to oppose the nomination of Attorney General John Ashcroft, saying, "He will bring some of his more strident views to bear in that office in ways that will cause great confrontation and controversy." Bayh was also an early critic of President Bush's tax cut plan.

Though he arrived in the Senate to considerable fanfare, Bayh spent much of his first year well away from the microphones and television cameras, watching as other Democratic freshmen, such as John Edwards of North Carolina and Charles E. Schumer of New York, made a greater splash in the media and party caucus meetings. "I don't think you have to yell and scream, or jump up and down, to have an influence in the United States Senate," Bayh says.

He acknowledges that it was difficult to make the transition from the executive to the legislative branch, saying that he enjoyed the day-to-day accomplishments during his two terms as Indiana governor that are missing from life in the Senate.

His senior colleague, Indiana Republican Richard G. Lugar, says Bayh is easy to work with, in part because the lawmakers' politics are not all that far apart. In fact, in Indiana, Bayh's moderate-to-conservative positions earned him the informal title of "Republicrat." After a Bayh State of the State address in 1995, Indiana Republicans held a press conference and offered to waive the admission fee to allow him to become a card-carrying member of the GOP.

In the Senate, Bayh's conservative views have been most noticeable on votes to ban a procedure its opponents call "partial birth" abortion and to approve a constitutional amendment to allow Congress to outlaw flag desecration — votes that pitted him against a majority of his party.

After a quiet first year, Bayh came out more forcefully in 2000 in support of two legislative priorities: an education plan that would increase federal spending but tie the funding to performance and a bill to promote fatherhood. "Hundreds of thousands of young men ... bring children into the world and walk away from one of the most profound responsibilities that anyone could ever take on," he said in 2001.

He also championed legislation, which became law, aimed at protecting senior citizens from fraud — including deceptive sweepstakes offers, investment schemes and telemarketing come-ons.

Bayh arrived on Capitol Hill already friendly with many lawmakers, including Senate Minority Leader Tom Daschle, and with Clinton and Vice President Al Gore. It was Clinton who selected Bayh to deliver the keynote address at the 1996 Democratic convention in Chicago, a lackluster presentation that left one of the few blots on Bayh's otherwise shiny political image.

Many say Bayh's path to the Senate had been charted for years. He was born in the small town of Shirkieville, Ind., in 1955 and moved to Washington when his father was elected to the Senate in 1962. Like Gore, who also was a senator's son, Bayh attended the elite St. Albans School for boys. Among his babysitters was President Johnson's daughter, Lynda. (Two-term senator Charles S. Robb, who married Lynda, later wrote the young Bayh a recommendation for law school.) The Bayhs also became friends with Sen. Edward M. Kennedy, D-Mass., who was first elected to the Senate in the same year as Birch Bayh.

Before graduating from law school in 1982, Bayh had a defining political moment. In 1980, with Ronald Reagan carrying the Republican banner in the presidential race, Birch Bayh lost his bid for a fourth term to Dan Quayle, who later served as George Bush's vice president. The younger Bayh had managed his father's campaign.

In 1986, at the age of 30, Bayh ran for Indiana secretary of state and won. Then, at 32, he became the youngest governor in the nation. In 1992, he was re-elected in a landslide.

Barred from seeking a third term, Bayh left office in 1996, spending less than two years in the private sector before making his Senate bid in 1998. Statehouse wags had long predicted that Bayh would in 1998 seek the seat once held by his father, challenging Sen. Dan Coats. Coats, however, decided to retire. Bayh faced no primary opponent for the Democratic nomination and trounced Fort Wayne Mayor Paul Helmke in the fall. He raised $4 million to Helmke's $600,000 and won by 29 percentage points.

KEY VOTES

2000
Yes Overhaul bankruptcy law and increase minimum wage
No   Limit fiscal 2001 discretionary spending to $600.3 billion
No   Override veto on nuclear waste disposal at Yucca Mountain site in Nevada
Yes Oppose effort to terminate Kosovo mission
Yes Include gender, sexual orientation and disability in federal hate crime protections
No   Approve GOP plan to restrict use of genetic information by health insurers
No   Kill amendment delaying implementation of an anti-missile defense system
No   Cut taxes for married couples
Yes Grant China permanent normal trade status

1999
No   Remove President Clinton from office for obstruction of justice
No   Kill amendment authorizing state grants to hire teachers and reduce class size
Yes Require criminal background checks for purchases at gun shows
No   Approve GOP proposal to increase rights of patients in managed-care health plans
No   Block effort to allow farm and medicine exports to Cuba
No   Allow study of tougher automobile fuel efficiency standards
Yes Ratify nuclear weapons testing treaty
Yes Prohibit national political parties from collecting "soft money" donations
Yes Remove barriers among banking, securities and insurance companies

INTEREST GROUPS

	AFL-CIO	ADA	CCUS	ACU
2000	75%	80%	60%	16%
1999	89%	90%	59%	12%

CQ VOTE STUDIES

	PARTY UNITY		PRESIDENTIAL SUPPORT	
	Support	Oppose	Support	Oppose
2000	92%	8%	98%	2%
1999	88%	12%	89%	11%

Rep. Peter J. Visclosky (D)

Elected 1984; 9th term

Visclosky sees himself as a man of steel.

Nothing so stirs the passion of the otherwise low-key congressman as issues related to the main economic force in his area, the steel industry. As vice chairman of the Congressional Steel Caucus, the nine-term congressman criticized the Clinton administration for failing to do enough to protect the beleaguered steel industry from aggressive imports. "It is outrageous that the president will allow foreign corporations to break our trade laws," Visclosky (vis-KLOSS-key) said. And now he has taken the lead in pressuring the Bush administration to be more responsive to steelworkers' troubles.

The industry is vital to the local economy. Even though steel-making jobs have plummeted from about 70,000 two decades ago to fewer than half as many now, Visclosky's blue-collar district produces more steel than any other area in the nation.

Not surprisingly, given his concern about imports, Visclosky opposed many of the Clinton administration's trade agreements — including the 1993 North American Free Trade Agreement and the 2000 law that granted China permanent normal trade status.

Beyond protecting the steel industry, Visclosky has other interests: using his position on the Appropriations Committee to bring home funds for his northwest Indiana district, supporting crime-fighting efforts, and pushing to pay down the nation's debt.

Visclosky has spent most of his adult life in politics. After finishing law school in 1973, he linked his fortunes to Adam Benjamin Jr., then a state senator and rising political star. Visclosky coordinated Benjamin's successful campaign for Congress in 1976 and served as his aide in Washington for the next six years.

When Benjamin died in September 1982, Democrats were suddenly without a candidate for the November election. As the 1st District Democratic chairman, Richard G. Hatcher — the longtime mayor of Gary, Ind. — was in a position to choose the Democratic nominee, and he picked Katie Hall, a state senator and loyal ally. Hall won easily but when she sought renomination in 1984, Visclosky and another candidate challenged her.

Visclosky put on dozens of $2 "dog and bean" dinners to attract the young, the elderly and the unemployed. His "Slovak kid" background also helped him, and older voters responded favorably because they remembered his father, John, who had served as Gary's comptroller in the 1950s and as the city's mayor in 1962 and 1963. Visclosky eked out a 35 percent to 33 percent primary victory over the incumbent, and in November, he swamped the GOP candidate. He has had little trouble ever since and appears to be settled in for the long haul.

Visclosky's low-key approach and sharp focus on a shortlist of issues keeps him out of the spotlight. He is a member of just one committee, Appropriations, which generally works in a bipartisan fashion. A detail-minded legislator, he is devoted to the idea that politics is about resolving disputes through discussion and compromise. And he is an unassuming man whose infrequent floor speeches are likely to be tributes to people back home or to a civic organization.

But while Visclosky may be unrecognized, he is not unimportant. He is the only Hoosier on Appropriations, so state colleagues of both parties look to him to carry water for them. Visclosky does so assiduously, snagging

CAPITOL OFFICE
225-2461; fax 225-2493; 2313 Rayburn Bldg. 20515

INTERNET
e-mail: www.house.gov/writerep
web: www.house.gov/visclosky

COMMITTEES
Appropriations

HOMETOWN
Merrillville

BORN
Aug. 13, 1949, Gary, Ind.

RELIGION
Roman Catholic

FAMILY
Divorced; two children

EDUCATION
Indiana U. Northwest, B.S. 1970; U. of Notre Dame, J.D. 1973; Georgetown U., LL.M. 1982

CAREER
Lawyer; congressional aide

POLITICAL HIGHLIGHTS
No previous office

ELECTION RESULTS

2000 GENERAL

Peter J. Visclosky (D)	148,683	71.6%
Jack Reynolds (R)	56,200	27.1%
Christopher Nelson (LIBERT)	2,907	1.4%

2000 PRIMARY

Peter J. Visclosky (D)	31,507	81.1%
Sandra Kay Smith (D)	6,098	15.7%
Cyril B. "Cy" Huerter (D)	1,229	3.2%

1998 GENERAL

Peter J. Visclosky (D)	92,634	72.5%
Michael Petyo (R)	33,503	26.2%
Michael Crass (LIBERT)	1,617	1.3%

PREVIOUS WINNING PERCENTAGES
1996 (69%); 1994 (57%); 1992 (69%); 1990 (66%); 1988 (77%); 1986 (73%); 1984 (71%)

funding for local needs, including the Indiana Dunes National Lakeshore along Lake Michigan, local transit projects, economic development, flood control projects and crime-fighting initiatives.

From his first day in the House, a slot on Appropriations was Visclosky's goal, as he sought to follow in Benjamin's footsteps. Visclosky made it onto the panel in October 1991, filling a vacancy. "It took six years, nine months, and nine days to get to the committee," Visclosky told a newspaper interviewer years later, revealing just how focused he was on the goal.

In 2000, Visclosky claimed credit for winning Appropriations allocations worth tens of millions of dollars for projects in his district. He also added language to an appropriations bill requiring monthly U.S. Census Bureau reports to include more detailed descriptions of data affecting the steel industry.

In his quest to deter crime in the 1st District, historically known as one of the most dangerous areas in the Midwest, Visclosky got northwest Indiana designated as a High Intensity Drug Trafficking Area. He obtained funds to fight the flow of drugs and gang violence in Gary, Hammond and East Chicago. He worked to arrange for the Indiana National Guard to help tear down neighborhood crack houses.

In the 104th Congress, Visclosky secured funds to provide 600 bulletproof vests to northwest Indiana law enforcement officers. Then, learning the problem was a national one — an estimated 25 percent of U.S. police officers do not have access to vests — Visclosky in 1998 joined with New Jersey Republican Frank A. LoBiondo to authorize a new Justice Department grant program and got the House to approve $25 million to help buy vests. In 2000, Visclosky won enactment of reauthorizing legislation allowing the program to continue at the higher level of $50 million per year for four years.

In representing his reliably Democratic district, Visclosky generally votes the party line. But he is a fiscal conservative who breaks with his leadership on some budgetary matters. He supported a balanced-budget constitutional amendment and was among the few lawmakers who pressed for strict enforcement mechanisms to ensure that the 1997 balanced-budget agreement was faithfully implemented. He declares that the government has "a moral responsibility" to balance the budget.

Visclosky also has shown a conservative bent on some social issues, such as his support of a ban on a procedure its opponents call "partial birth" abortion (though earlier he had voted against the ban). He opposed the GOP's initial welfare overhaul legislation but backed the final compromise President Clinton signed in 1996 over some liberal Democrats' objections.

KEY VOTES

2000
Yes Raise hourly minimum wage by $1 over two years
No   Halt funding for U.S. mission in Kosovo unless European nations pay more
Yes Provide Medicare benefits to military retirees and their dependents
No   Grant China permanent normal trade status
No   Phase out estate, gift and trust taxes
No   Prohibit implementation of president's national monument designations
No   Approve GOP plan to provide prescription drug coverage for Medicare beneficiaries
Yes Increase help for poor nations indebted to international financial institutions

1999
Yes Impose steel import quotas
Yes Kill proposal to take aviation trust funds off budget
No   Require background checks on buyers only at gun shows with 10 or more vendors
Yes Remove barriers among banking, securities and insurance companies
Yes Authorize state grants to hire teachers and reduce class size
Yes Overhaul campaign finance law; ban "soft money" and restrict advocacy advertising
Yes Approve bipartisan plan to increase rights of patients in managed-care health plans

INTEREST GROUPS

	AFL-CIO	ADA	CCUS	ACU
2000	100%	75%	33%	12%
1999	100%	95%	4%	12%
1998	100%	80%	28%	12%
1997	88%	65%	50%	29%

CQ VOTE STUDIES

	PARTY UNITY		PRESIDENTIAL SUPPORT	
	Support	Oppose	Support	Oppose
2000	92%	8%	75%	25%
1999	87%	13%	77%	23%
1998	83%	17%	79%	21%
1997	81%	19%	66%	34%

INDIANA 1

Northwest — Gary; Hammond

Bordered to the north by Lake Michigan and to the west by Illinois, the 1st is home to steel workers and large union and minority populations that offer Democrats solid support. More steel is produced here than in any other district in the country, and more than 30,000 steel workers reside in Gary, Hammond and East Chicago. Most of the 1st's population lives in the far northwestern corner, where more than 80 percent of Gary residents are black and more than 25 percent of East Chicago residents are Hispanic. The 1st also is home to many Eastern European ethnic neighborhoods.

Residents around Gary still struggle with the effects of unemployment, suburban flight and urban decay that began when the steel industry took a dive in the early 1980s. Another crisis hit in 1998 when cheap, imported steel flooded the U.S. market in record amounts. At least one steel company went out of business and there were thousands of layoffs.

The district has attracted some lake boat gambling, but so far it is not a replacement for steel's place in the economy.

While Democrats carry congressional and presidential elections by strong margins, Republicans in the 1st have a meager base in growing Porter County and in Lake County suburbs such as Crown Point and Merrillville, where an influx of white Chicago commuters has raised incomes.

MAJOR INDUSTRY
Steel, manufacturing, gaming

CITIES
Gary, 110,271; Hammond, 77,363; Portage, 33,477; Merrillville, 31,290; East Chicago, 30,457

UNUSUAL FEATURES
Michael Jackson raised in Gary; Indiana Dunes National Park; John Dillinger's infamous jailbreak occurred in Crown Point; Popcorn magnate Orville Redenbacher born in Valparaiso.

Rep. Mike Pence (R)

CAPITOL OFFICE
225-3021; fax 225-3382
1605 Longworth Bldg. 20515

INTERNET
e-mail: mike.pence@mail.house.gov
web: www.house.gov/pence

COMMITTEES
Agriculture
Science
Small Business
(Regulatory Reform & Oversight - chairman)

HOMETOWN
Edinburgh

BORN
June 7, 1959, Columbus, Ind.

RELIGION
Christian

FAMILY
Wife, Karen Pence; three children

EDUCATION
Hanover College, B.A. 1981; Indiana U., J.D. 1986

CAREER
Radio broadcasting consultant; radio broadcaster;
think tank president; lawyer

POLITICAL HIGHLIGHTS
Republican nominee for U.S. House, 1988, 1990

ELECTION RESULTS

2000 GENERAL

Mike Pence (R)	106,023	50.9%
Bob Rock (D)	80,885	38.8%
William G. Frazier (I)	19,077	9.2%
Michael Anderson (LIBERT)	2,422	1.2%

2000 PRIMARY

Mike Pence (R)	21,582	44.5%
Jeff Linder (R)	11,615	23.9%
Luke Messer (R)	10,075	20.8%
Brad Steele (R)	2,819	5.8%
David M. Campbell (R)	1,913	3.9%
Cliff Federle (R)	513	1.1%

Elected 2000; 1st term

Like his predecessor, Republican David M. McIntosh, Pence is a strong advocate for fiscal conservatism on Capitol Hill. Early in the 107th Congress, he threw his support behind a much larger tax cut than the $1.6 trillion cut proposed by President Bush, saying tax reductions would enable families, small businesses and family farms to exercise their entrepreneurial spirit.

Pence is also an ardent supporter of socially conservative principles — he cited "morality" as a key campaign issue. Despite his zeal in promoting his viewpoints, he has a soft-spoken, placid manner.

The 2nd District has a large rural constituency, and Pence tends to the interests of his district's farmers from his seat on the Agriculture Committee. He also sits on the Science and Small Business panels. On Small Business, he advanced straight to a chairmanship — of the Regulatory Reform and Oversight Subcommittee.

A Democrat until the early 1980s, Pence worked as a lawyer, the president of a conservative foundation and host of a radio talk show before making his bid to succeed three-term Rep. McIntosh, who left the seat to mount an ultimately unsuccessful campaign for governor.

The 2000 race was Pence's third attempt: In 1988, he ran for the House at age 29 — coming surprisingly close to upsetting Democratic Rep. Philip R. Sharp; and he again ran against Sharp two years later.

Pence, in the latter race, ran a harshly negative campaign against Sharp and ended up losing badly. The following year, Pence wrote an article entitled "Confessions of a Negative Campaigner." "Negative campaigning, I now know, is wrong," Pence wrote, adding, "It is wrong, quite simply, to squander a candidate's priceless moment in history ... on partisan bickering."

Although Pence spent a decade in exile from politics, his years as a radio broadcaster kept his name before the public. When his third chance came, he easily beat state Rep. Jeff Linder and four other opponents in the GOP primary, then topped Democratic lawyer Bob Rock by 12 percentage points — even though former state Sen. William G. Frazier, who ran several times for the 2nd District seat as a Republican, took 9 percent as an independent.

INDIANA 2

East Central – Muncie; Anderson; Richmond; Columbus

Covering the middle third of Indiana's eastern border with Ohio, the 2nd is a mix of farm and suburban populations surrounding Muncie, Anderson and Richmond.

In the 1920s Muncie was the model for "Middletown," a study of small-town American life. Today, it is the 2nd's largest city, and home to Ball State U., as well as a large automotive manufacturing plant. But the city's economy has been unsteady. Through most of the 1990s unemployment was two to three times the state average. A General Motors plant and Ball Corp.'s headquarters closed in 1998, and although some jobs were replaced, the city is still struggling (although unemployment did fall somewhat at the end of the decade). To the southwest, Anderson, another former auto

manufacturing hub, also has seen industrial decline, although a new magnesium plant has created some jobs.

The 2nd is a conservative, Republican-voting district with a Democratic past. In 1992, it was one of 51 districts with a Democratic representative that did not vote for Bill Clinton. Republicans dominate the district's rural areas and pick up a good number of votes around the Indianapolis suburbs. Large Quaker communities and non-union manufacturing towns also supply GOP voters, while the far south is home to political centrists who tend to elect candidates from both parties.

MAJOR INDUSTRY
Auto manufacturing, agriculture

CITIES
Muncie, 66,916; Anderson, 58,317; Richmond, 38,282

UNUSUAL FEATURES
David Letterman attended Ball State U. in Muncie.

Rep. Tim Roemer (D)

CAPITOL OFFICE
225-3915; fax 225-6798; 2352 Rayburn Bldg. 20515

INTERNET
e-mail: tim.roemer@mail.house.gov
web: www.house.gov/roemer

COMMITTEES
Education & Workforce
Select Intelligence

HOMETOWN
South Bend

BORN
Oct. 30, 1956, South Bend, Ind.

RELIGION
Roman Catholic

FAMILY
Wife, Sally Roemer; four children

EDUCATION
U. of California, San Diego, B.A. 1979; U. of Notre Dame, M.A. 1981, Ph.D. 1985

CAREER
Congressional aide; adjunct professor

POLITICAL HIGHLIGHTS
No previous office

ELECTION RESULTS

2000 GENERAL

Tim Roemer (D)	107,438	51.6%
Chris Chocola (R)	98,822	47.4%

2000 PRIMARY

Tim Roemer (D)	22,823	88.4%
Steven W. Osborn (D)	3,008	11.6%

1998 GENERAL

Tim Roemer (D)	84,625	58.1%
Daniel A. Holtz (R)	61,041	41.9%

PREVIOUS WINNING PERCENTAGES
1996 (58%); 1994 (55%); 1992 (57%); 1990 (51%)

Elected 1990; 6th term

A political moderate with the ability to reach across the aisle, Roemer operates comfortably in the legislative arena. He draws on his prior experience as a congressional aide and on lessons about political horse-trading learned from his father-in-law, former Democratic Sen. J. Bennett Johnston of Louisiana.

The 107th Congress will be his last, however, as he announced early in 2001 that he would not seek re-election. Roemer, who has been a leader in urging congressional leaders to adopt a more "family-friendly" schedule, said that he could not do a good job of both serving in Congress and being a husband and father to his four young children.

His interest in spending more time with his family was not new. During the 104th Congress, when the new Republican majority kept the House in session for long hours week after week, Roemer complained that "the only time we see our families is when we take a picture of them out of our wallets." He said the House needed to be run more efficiently, with fewer late-night votes.

Roemer maintains an ideological balancing act because of his politically competitive district, which elected a GOP House member through the 1980s. He is active on a range of issues — advocating charter schools in public education, battling against college sports gambling, crusading against NASA's space station project, and pushing for restrictions on abortion. A fiscal conservative, he has served as a co-chairman of the moderate New Democrat Coalition — a group that says it favors "non-bureaucratic but activist government."

In the 106th Congress, he supported GOP tax-cutting efforts, and he voted to override President Clinton's vetoes of bills designed to reduce taxes on married couples and estates. "Hoosiers that work hard, pay taxes, and build up a business should not be taxed again when a loved one dies," he said about the estate tax. Roemer supports a constitutional amendment requiring a two-thirds majority vote in Congress to raise taxes, and he says that he has never supported legislation to increase taxes. Conservative on spending issues as well, Roemer was one of just 110 House members who voted against a supplemental appropriations bill in 2000.

Roemer's fiscally thrifty image is rooted in a dogged (and so far futile) battle that he has waged against NASA's International Space Station. In the 102nd Congress, when Roemer was a freshman and his party held the House majority, he emerged as a prominent critic of the station, citing cost overruns brought on by schedule slips and design changes. He and his allies failed by just one vote in 1993 to eliminate funding for the station.

After the 1999 failure of NASA's Mars Polar Lander mission, Roemer made a renewed plea to do away with the space station because he blamed it for diverting resources for other space initiatives. "One of my concerns all along has been that the space station is squeezing other programs out the door and makes them run on budgets that might be too tight, makes oversight difficult and creativity a little more overwhelming," he said. But as a member of the Science Committe in the 106th, Roemer added, "I don't think we should give up on Mars," according to Gannett News Service.

Roemer's effort to plot a legislative middle course is especially evident in his work on the Education and the Workforce Committee. Like many conservatives, he supports the establishment of charter schools, which typically operate under the rubric of the public school system but are given more leeway to adopt innovative curricula and teaching methods. But like most liberals, Roemer vehemently opposes tuition voucher plans, which allow parents to use public funds to pay for the cost of a private education.

In 1999, Roemer won passage of an educational flexibility measure that allows state and local officials to waive certain federal regulations, provided that they adhere to certain academic standards. He teamed up with California Republican Frank Riggs in the 105th to sponsor a bill authorizing $100 million in federal funds for a charter school start-up fund. Calling charter schools "cradles of invention and innovation," Roemer asserted that "public school choice is the way we should try to move in this country."

Roemer made a stir in Nevada in the 106th Congress when he tried to bar gambling on college sports. "We have gambling on dogs, you can gamble in casinos, on boats, in lotteries," he said in an interview with The Associated Press. "Let's not gamble on teenage kids in college sports." The National Collegiate Athletic Association, which is based in Indiana, supported his efforts.

Roemer's conservative side is most evident on social policy issues, particularly abortion. He is a high-profile foe of a procedure its opponents call "partial birth" abortion, saying it is "a moral blind spot that this nation can no longer allow." After Congress voted to ban the procedure and Clinton vetoed the bill in 1998, Roemer, who is Roman Catholic, joined most Republicans in voting to override the veto.

On trade issues, Roemer reflects the skepticism that many labor union officials and blue-collar workers have about lowering international trade barriers. He opposed granting the president fast-track authority to negotiate trade agreements that Congress may not amend, but in 2000 he voted to grant China permanent normal trade status.

Roemer's arrival in Congress in 1991 was a homecoming of sorts. He had served as an aide to both Democratic House Majority Whip John Brademas of Indiana and Democratic Sen. Dennis DeConcini of Arizona, and he had taught at American University in Washington, D.C.

In 1990, Roemer took aim at GOP Rep. John Hiler, a veteran of several hard-fought re-elections in the 3rd District. As Johnston's son-in-law, Roemer was able to shake the Washington money tree, and he ran a sophisticated campaign with help from Johnston's research and media consultants. He mixed traditional populism with occasional dashes of conservatism, calling attention to plant closings and the plight of the middle class while also demanding a balanced budget and tax cuts. The strategy was successful, and he ousted Hiler by 2 percentage points. He went on to rack up re-election victory margins of between 10 and 16 percentage points before struggling in 2000 against GOP businessman Chris Chocola, who held Roemer to a 4-point win.

KEY VOTES

2000

Yes Raise hourly minimum wage by $1 over two years

Yes Halt funding for U.S. mission in Kosovo unless European nations pay more

Yes Provide Medicare benefits to military retirees and their dependents

Yes Grant China permanent normal trade status

Yes Phase out estate, gift and trust taxes

No Prohibit implementation of president's national monument designations

No Approve GOP plan to provide prescription drug coverage for Medicare beneficiaries

No Increase help for poor nations indebted to international financial institutions

1999

Yes Impose steel import quotas

Yes Kill proposal to take aviation trust funds off budget

No Require background checks on buyers only at gun shows with 10 or more vendors

Yes Remove barriers among banking, securities and insurance companies

Yes Authorize state grants to hire teachers and reduce class size

Yes Overhaul campaign finance law; ban "soft money" and restrict advocacy advertising

Yes Approve bipartisan plan to increase rights of patients in managed-care health plans

INTEREST GROUPS

	AFL-CIO	ADA	CCUS	ACU
2000	44%	45%	68%	37%
1999	67%	80%	60%	36%
1998	80%	65%	78%	44%
1997	75%	55%	70%	32%

CQ VOTE STUDIES

	PARTY UNITY		PRESIDENTIAL SUPPORT	
	Support	Oppose	Support	Oppose
2000	69%	31%	52%	48%
1999	66%	34%	62%	38%
1998	66%	34%	61%	39%
1997	69%	31%	55%	45%

INDIANA 3
Northern Tier – South Bend; Elkhart

The 3rd touches an eastern corner of Lake Michigan and stretches across the middle third of Indiana's northern border. Traditionally a politically competitive district, the 3rd has long been considered a barometer of national political trends.

It went for a GOP representative at the onset of the "Reagan Revolution" in 1980, and then voted for a Democrat 10 years later when the Reagan-Bush era was drawing to a close. Since then, Rep. Roemer's moderate ideology has helped him survive GOP challengers. In 1996 he was re-elected even as Bob Dole barely carried the district at 46 percent. In 2000, Roemer did it again as George W. Bush carried the district a bit more handily with 56 percent of the vote.

The district's population center, South Bend, is home to an ideologically diverse and economically disparate population. Here, the wealthy, Catholic Notre Dame community is joined by low-income, minority populations downtown, as well as Eastern European, blue-collar communities east of the city. Most support Democrats on the local level. Michigan City's steel-producing areas and blue-collar La Porte also provide solid Democratic support.

To the east, Elkhart County's farming and business community – a national center for the manufactured housing industry – creates a faithful conservative contingency. Elkhart's large Amish population also makes it the state's leading milk producer. The wealthy, white Granger community to South Bend's northeast and affluent portions of La Porte County vote Republican as well.

MAJOR INDUSTRY
Manufacturing, higher education, agriculture

CITIES
South Bend, 98,941; Mishawaka, 46,096; Elkhart, 43,336; Michigan City, 32,752

UNUSUAL FEATURES
Golden Dome at Notre Dame, the signature landmark from which alumni get the name "Domers;" Studebaker family mansion and College Football Hall of Fame in South Bend.

Rep. Mark Souder (R)

CAPITOL OFFICE
225-4436; fax 225-3479
1227 Longworth Bldg. 20515

INTERNET
e-mail: souder@mail.house.gov
web: www.house.gov/souder

COMMITTEES
Education & Workforce
Government Reform
   (Criminal Justice, Drug Policy & Human
   Resources - chairman)
Resources

HOMETOWN
Fort Wayne

BORN
July 18, 1950, Fort Wayne, Ind.

RELIGION
Evangelical

FAMILY
Wife, Diane Souder; three children

EDUCATION
Indiana U., B.S. 1972; Notre Dame, M.B.A. 1974

CAREER
Congressional aide; furniture company executive;
general store owner

POLITICAL HIGHLIGHTS
No previous office

ELECTION RESULTS

2000 GENERAL

Mark Souder (R)	131,051	62.3%
Mike Foster (D)	74,492	35.4%
Michael Donlan (LIBERT)	4,887	2.3%

2000 PRIMARY

Mark Souder (R)	28,710	61.8%
Michael Loomis (R)	17,768	38.2%

1998 GENERAL

Mark Souder (R)	93,671	63.3%
Mark J. Wehrle (D)	54,286	36.7%

PREVIOUS WINNING PERCENTAGES
1996 (58%); 1994 (55%)

Elected 1994; 4th term

Souder has impeccable conservative credentials. He was inspired to enter the realm of politics as a teenager by Ronald Reagan's famous speech in support of Sen. Barry Goldwater's presidential bid in 1964. He is well-placed in the 107th Congress to put into practice his long-held beliefs, including his promotion of faith-based charities, as the new chairman of the Government Reform Subcommittee on Criminal Justice, Drug Policy and Human Resources.

Souder's great-great-grandfather was one of the first Amish settlers in Allen County, in 1846. The family's original harness shop grew into a series of family businesses in Grabill that made the Souder name well-known. His family members are religious conservatives who questioned whether they should have any involvement at all in temporal politics. "If you scratch behind any of my positions, you find my religious beliefs," Souder says.

He adds that such beliefs explain his occasional straying from the orthodox Republican path. He maintains, for example, that support of natural resources conservation fits in with political conservatism, a stance that makes him a Midwest Republican anomaly on the Resources Committee. "As a Christian, part of what you do is be a steward of all creation," he says.

He also believes the government has a role in helping the less fortunate, and he is a committed opponent of abortion. He has pledged to back any bill that includes aid to Israel, even though he shares his constituents' skepticism about foreign aid in general.

Souder is among the leading voices urging the House Republican majority to hew to a conservative line. He was a constant agitator under Speaker Newt Gingrich and participated in the abortive 1997 coup attempt against him. Souder enjoys friendlier relations with Speaker J. Dennis Hastert, whom he credits with listening to the conservative viewpoint before modifying legislation to attract moderate support. "He's straight with us," Souder says. "If it's gonna change, he's gonna tell us."

Although Souder has often stressed the importance of presenting a clear ideological difference with Democrats, he says he recognizes that because of the GOP's narrow majority in the House, Hastert has to do what it takes "to get to 218" — the number of votes needed to guarantee passage of legislation.

As chairman of the Criminal Justice Subcommittee, Souder has oversight authority over federal anti-drug efforts. He has long been active in the anti-drug fight, dating from his days as a staff member on the now-defunct House Select Committee on Children, Youth and Families. Souder supports interdiction efforts — early in 2001, he made his sixth trip to Colombia in as many years — but he also believes the federal government has to back prevention programs. He says "the people growing coca aren't evil" and need help finding alternatives to growing their illegal crop.

Souder also serves on the Education and the Workforce Committee, where he has worked with Philadelphia Democrat Chaka Fattah on higher education legislation. He has tried to impress upon Fattah and other Democrats that his commitment to faith-based charitable programs, including his efforts to help Catholic-school students do volunteer work in public schools, is based more on his concern for the needy than his desire to build up the religious institutions themselves.

Souder was not an early or vocal supporter of George W. Bush's presidential bid, but Bush invited him to ride in the presidential limousine just before the president unveiled his faith-based initiative in 2001.

Souder supports vouchers for private schools but recognizes that there isn't enough political support to pass such legislation. "Parents are concerned every time a voucher referendum comes up that it's going to cost them more money ... and that it's going to take money from the public schools. We, as a conservative movement, have not done a very good job of satisfying those concerns."

Souder was an active member of conservative youth groups. He recalls that, in the 1960s, "While everybody else was protesting, guys like me were wearing buttons that said, 'I'm proud to be a square.' " Still, as a young man he showed more inclination to work the family business than to join the political circuit. He was drawn to Capitol Hill by Republican Daniel R. Coats, who, Souder said, had bought furniture from him. Souder served as district director when Coats was in the House and later worked in Coats' Senate office in Washington. He ran for Coats' old House seat in 1994.

Souder is no rousing orator; his demeanor and interest in the details of his work often make him seem more like the congressional staffer he once was than the House member he now is.

He has an approachable manner and a reputation for being candid. He says it's better to get the bad news out and let people know where you stand. The major political gaffe of his career may have been his declaration that he would oppose the articles of impeachment brought against President Clinton. Souder urged the president to resign and said he preferred that Clinton be prosecuted as a private citizen rather than impeached. Ultimately, he backed one of the four articles of impeachment.

Souder's wavering on Clinton's impeachment rattled his ideological base and earned him a serious primary opponent in 2000. He eventually bested Allen County chief deputy prosecutor Michael Loomis with 62 percent of the vote; he garnered 62 percent in the general election as well.

In Souder's first House race in 1994, he faced a tough, six-candidate primary. All the major contenders in the GOP field that year had strong conservative credentials, but Souder's low-key demeanor during the campaign made him appear less hard-line. He was helped by concerns among many Republicans that, as in past years, the GOP nomination would go to a candidate with limited appeal to the general electorate in November.

After winning the primary, Souder went on the attack early, starting with summer radio ads that portrayed his Democratic opponent, Rep. Jill L. Long, as a Washington insider beholden to special interests. Souder made every attempt to tie Long to the Clinton administration. The strategy paid off; Souder beat Long by 10 points, the closest that Democrats have come.

KEY VOTES

2000

No Raise hourly minimum wage by $1 over two years
Yes Halt funding for U.S. mission in Kosovo unless European nations pay more
Yes Provide Medicare benefits to military retirees and their dependents
No Grant China permanent normal trade status
Yes Phase out estate, gift and trust taxes
Yes Prohibit implementation of president's national monument designations
Yes Approve GOP plan to provide prescription drug coverage for Medicare beneficiaries
No Increase help for poor nations indebted to international financial institutions

1999

Yes Impose steel import quotas
No Kill proposal to take aviation trust funds off budget
No Require background checks on buyers only at gun shows with 10 or more vendors
Yes Remove barriers among banking, securities and insurance companies
No Authorize state grants to hire teachers and reduce class size
No Overhaul campaign finance law; ban "soft money" and restrict advocacy advertising
No Approve bipartisan plan to increase rights of patients in managed-care health plans

INTEREST GROUPS

	AFL-CIO	ADA	CCUS	ACU
2000	10%	10%	71%	88%
1999	33%	5%	80%	80%
1998	20%	15%	76%	83%
1997	0%	5%	80%	100%

CQ VOTE STUDIES

	PARTY UNITY		PRESIDENTIAL SUPPORT	
	Support	Oppose	Support	Oppose
2000	91%	9%	19%	81%
1999	94%	6%	16%	84%
1998	90%	10%	25%	75%
1997	95%	5%	25%	75%

INDIANA 4

Northeast – Fort Wayne

Agricultural communities rooted in strong religious beliefs shape the character of the 4th, a solidly Republican district in Indiana's northeast corner.

The district's long tradition of social conservatism begins in the large Amish communities to the northwest, which are not overtly politically active but both form and reflect the area's traditional values. Rural voters, on farms that lead the state in wheat, oats and soybeans, bolster the state's Republican leanings.

Fort Wayne, the district's largest city and Indiana's second-largest, has white-collar suburban neighborhoods and German-Americans that cement the 4th's conservative loyalties. Like many midsize Midwestern cities, Fort Wayne has a substantial manufacturing sector. But it has been protected from industrial decline by a strong white-collar, service sector. Technology and financial-service jobs have attracted white, wealthy professionals into the city, as Fort

Wayne's population grew by almost 20 percent in the 1990s.

Democrats find support in minority and blue-collar neighborhoods in Fort Wayne, where manufacturing plays a key economic role. Rural Steuben, Noble and DeKalb counties also attract some Democratic support, although these farming and small-business communities lean conservative overall. In the 2000 presidential contest, George W. Bush handily carried the district with 64 percent.

MAJOR INDUSTRY
Manufacturing, agriculture, health care

CITIES
Fort Wayne 196,708; Huntington, 16,101

UNUSUAL FEATURES
Dan Quayle Commemorative Museum in the former vice president's hometown of Huntington; The movie, "In the Company of Men," filmed in Fort Wayne.

Rep. Steve Buyer (R)

CAPITOL OFFICE
225-5037; fax 225-2267; 2443 Rayburn Bldg. 20515

INTERNET
e-mail: www.house.gov/writerep
web: www.house.gov/buyer

COMMITTEES
Energy & Commerce
Veterans' Affairs
(Oversight & Investigations - chairman)

HOMETOWN
Monticello

BORN
Nov. 26, 1958, Rensselaer, Ind.

RELIGION
Methodist

FAMILY
Wife, Joni Buyer; two children

EDUCATION
The Citadel, B.S. 1980; Valparaiso U., J.D. 1984

MILITARY SERVICE
Army Reserve, 1980-84; Army, 1984-87; Army Reserve, 1987-present

CAREER
Lawyer; Army prosecutor

POLITICAL HIGHLIGHTS
No previous office

ELECTION RESULTS

2000 GENERAL

Steve Buyer (R)	132,051	60.9%
Greg Goodnight (D)	81,427	37.5%
Scott Benson (LIBERT)	3,507	1.6%

2000 PRIMARY

Steve Buyer (R)	unopposed

1998 GENERAL

Steve Buyer (R)	101,567	62.5%
David F. Steele III (D)	58,504	36.0%
Carl D. Waters (LIBERT)	2,317	1.4%

PREVIOUS WINNING PERCENTAGES
1996 (65%); 1994 (70%); 1992 (51%)

Elected 1992; 5th term

Buyer's intensity is the hallmark of his political life. He is one of the most pugnacious of Republican partisans, picked in 1998 by House Speaker Newt Gingrich to whip up the troops at the start of the impeachment crusade against President Clinton, and defiant when the effort failed, condemning senators for not following their consciences.

But within a few weeks of the impeachment effort's collapse in 1999, Buyer (BOO-yer) was channeling the same high energy into legislative oversight of a complex policy issue: how to change military pay and benefits to bolster sagging enlistments and retention. As chairman of the Armed Services Subcommittee on Military Personnel, Buyer in the 106th Congress played a pivotal role — with bipartisan support — in the enactment of pay raises, a more generous retirement system and a much-expanded health care system for military retirees. The package not only boosted military morale but was one of the few significant changes in military procedure to win passage.

As if to underscore that his partisan pedigree was unsullied, Buyer closed out the 106th in the same combative type of role he had played in impeachment: With Florida's presidential vote hanging in the balance, Buyer spent nine days in the Sunshine State pressing local officials to count military ballots mailed from overseas, most of which were presumed to be Republican and many of which had been ruled invalid on technical grounds.

As the 107th Congress opened, Buyer took the unusual step of giving up his seniority on the Armed Services Committee and starting over at the bottom of the ladder on the Energy and Commerce Committee. With characteristic chutzpah, he asked Republican leaders to let him transfer his seniority to the new panel, but they declined. But Buyer did win permission to keep his seat on the Veterans' Affairs panel, where in the 107th he chairs the panel's Oversight and Investigations Subcommittee.

In switching committees, Buyer explained that he wanted to use his experience in drafting a prescription drug benefit for military retirees — enacted in 2000 — to help write a prescription drug benefit for Medicare recipients.

An alumnus of The Citadel, the military college of South Carolina, Buyer earned a law degree in his native Indiana and became an Army lawyer, first on active duty and then as a reservist. He was called to serve in the Persian Gulf War, and in 1992, his status as a veteran helped him wrest the traditionally Republican 5th District from a Democratic incumbent who had voted against authorizing the use of military force in the gulf.

Buyer was near several explosions of Scud missiles in 1991 and suffered ill health for years afterward. He told a Capitol Hill hearing and news conference in 1993 that a month after he returned home from the Gulf War, he noticed he could not jog short distances "without feeling exhausted." He also had kidney problems, two cases of pneumonia and spent much of the last month of the 1992 campaign in bed. Late in 2000, Buyer was notified by the Defense Department that he likely had been exposed to chemical agents that drifted in the smoke cloud caused by the missile explosions.

Buyer's initial committee assignments fit his background — Armed Services, Judiciary and Veterans' Affairs — and even before he gained national attention during impeachment proceedings as one of Clinton's harshest critics, he was known in Washington as a tough-talking conservative who sparred with liberals on many issues, including abortion and gun control.

(With characteristic hyperbole, he once argued for a bill that loosened restrictions on concealed weapons, decrying the measure's opponents as "liberal pacifists that live in a fantasy world.")

In the spring of 1998, after the Monica Lewinsky scandal broke, Buyer got a running start in the GOP attack on Clinton, offering an amendment to the annual defense authorization bill that he said was aimed at holding the commander in chief to the same moral and ethical standards as military officers, one of which is a prohibition on even consensual sexual relations between a superior and a subordinate.

"Military leaders are required to provide a good example to these young recruits, yet when they look up the chain of command, they see a double standard at the very top," said Buyer. He later hammered at the same theme as one of the 13 "managers" who took the House's impeachment case to the Senate.

In 1996, Buyer helped lead an inquiry by the National Security Committee (now Armed Services) into allegations that Army drill sergeants at several training bases had pressured female recruits for sex. The congressman distanced himself from those conservatives who maintained the alleged incidents were evidence of the peril of having women in the military. "Let's not give any excuses for these thugs to somehow justify their indecent actions," he said.

The capstone of Buyer's tenure on the Military Personnel Subcommittee was the enactment late in 2000 of an expansion of medical benefits for military retirees expected to cost $60 billion in the first 10 years. In final negotiations on the measure, Buyer broke with the Armed Services tradition of keeping conference negotiations confidential, briefing several military retiree organizations and reporters on his plan, and generating enough outside support to guarantee that the new benefits would be included.

Soon after he returned from the gulf, Buyer took to the campaign stump against three-term Democratic Rep. Jim Jontz, displaying his combat boots at some stops and criticizing Jontz's vote against giving President George Bush authority to commit troops to the gulf. He also drew attention to Jontz's four overdrafts at the private bank for House members.

Bill Clinton took a dismal 31 percent in the district's presidential voting, and a strong local showing by Independent Ross Perot (23 percent) brought to the polls reform-minded voters who found Buyer's pitch appealing. He took 51 percent in one of the biggest upsets of 1992. The 5th District was traditionally Republican before Jontz's tenure, and Buyer has been reelected easily.

KEY VOTES

2000

No   Raise hourly minimum wage by $1 over two years
Yes Halt funding for U.S. mission in Kosovo unless European nations pay more
No   Provide Medicare benefits to military retirees and their dependents
No   Grant China permanent normal trade status
Yes Phase out estate, gift and trust taxes
Yes Prohibit implementation of president's national monument designations
Yes Approve GOP plan to provide prescription drug coverage for Medicare beneficiaries
No   Increase help for poor nations indebted to international financial institutions

1999

Yes Impose steel import quotas
No   Kill proposal to take aviation trust funds off budget
No   Require background checks on buyers only at gun shows with 10 or more vendors
Yes Remove barriers among banking, securities and insurance companies
No   Authorize state grants to hire teachers and reduce class size
No   Overhaul campaign finance law; ban "soft money" and restrict advocacy advertising
No   Approve bipartisan plan to increase rights of patients in managed-care health plans

INTEREST GROUPS

	AFL-CIO	ADA	CCUS	ACU
2000	10%	5%	85%	84%
1999	22%	10%	88%	91%
1998	22%	15%	94%	88%
1997	0%	0%	100%	83%

CQ VOTE STUDIES

	PARTY UNITY		PRESIDENTIAL SUPPORT	
	Support	Oppose	Support	Oppose
2000	94%	6%	22%	78%
1999	92%	8%	24%	76%
1998	91%	9%	24%	76%
1997	93%	7%	24%	76%

INDIANA 5
Northern Rural – Kokomo

Occupying most of the northwestern quadrant of the state, an area that calls itself the "Hoosier Heartland," the largely rural 5th is supported chiefly by auto parts manufacturing in its cities and soybean, corn and hog farming in its countryside.

At the district's southwestern extreme, the terrain turns to coal mining and becomes heavily Democratic. Although the district has a relatively high percentage of blue-collar workers, it tends to favor Republicans for federal office.

Economic downturns in the early 1980s caused problems in the district's smaller, industrial cities. Kokomo, as the site where gasoline-powered cars and stainless steel were invented, has become known as a site for manufacturing innovation.

The auto industry and other manufacturing still drive the city's economy, but the mid-1990s closure of Grissom Air Force Base near Kokomo presented some challenges. The district steadied as Grissom was converted to a combination reserve base, air refueling depot, prison and private office complex. Chrysler also sank $1 billion into its Kokomo facility in the mid-1990s.

The 5th's residents are willing to vote a split ticket but are rooted in Midwestern conservatism. Democrats receive most of their support in local and state races. Working-class communities in Logansport, Wabash and Kokomo and mining towns in Vermillion County, on the Illinois border, provide consistent Democratic support.

MAJOR INDUSTRY
Auto parts manufacturing, agriculture

CITIES
Kokomo, 45,218; Marion, 30,046; Logansport, 16,588

UNUSUAL FEATURES
Cole Porter born in Peru; Kokomo claims the world's largest steer – 4,700-pound Old Ben, stuffed and on display; James Dean Memorial Gallery in his hometown of Fairmount; Circus Hall of Fame in Peru.

Rep. Dan Burton (R)

CAPITOL OFFICE
225-2276; fax 225-0016; 2185 Rayburn Bldg. 20515

INTERNET
e-mail: www.house.gov/writerep
web: www.house.gov/burton

COMMITTEES
Government Reform - chairman
International Relations

HOMETOWN
Indianapolis

BORN
June 21, 1938, Indianapolis, Ind.

RELIGION
Christian

FAMILY
Wife, Barbara Logan Burton; three children

EDUCATION
Indiana U., attended 1958-59; Cincinnati Bible
College, attended 1959-60

MILITARY SERVICE
Army, 1956-57; Army Reserve, 1957-62

CAREER
Real estate and insurance agent

POLITICAL HIGHLIGHTS
Ind. House, 1967-69; Ind. Senate, 1969-71;
Republican nominee for U.S. House, 1970; sought
Republican nomination for U.S. House, 1972; Ind.
House, 1977-81; Ind. Senate, 1981-83

ELECTION RESULTS

2000 GENERAL

Dan Burton (R)	199,207	70.4%
Darin Patrick Griesey (D)	74,881	26.4%
Joe Hauptmann (LIBERT)	9,087	3.2%

2000 PRIMARY

Dan Burton (R)	54,399	79.4%
George Thomas Holland (R)	14,106	20.6%

1998 GENERAL

Dan Burton (R)	135,250	72.0%
Bob Kern (D)	31,472	16.8%
Joe Hauptmann (LIBERT)	21,032	11.2%

PREVIOUS WINNING PERCENTAGES
1996 (75%); 1994 (77%); 1992 (72%); 1990 (64%);
1988 (73%); 1986 (68%); 1984 (73%); 1982 (65%)

Elected 1982; 10th term

Burton is a founder of the House's Conservative Action Team — a group of several dozen conservative Republicans better known as the CATs — and a self-described "pit bull" of the House GOP. He does little to cover his fierce partisanship: He once called President Clinton a "scum bag" and described his Democratic critics as "squealing pigs."

While most Hill Republicans reined in their political attacks on the White House after the Senate acquitted Clinton in the Monica Lewinsky scandal, Burton was not deterred. As chairman of the Government Reform Committee, Burton continued to use his leadership position to pummel the administration throughout the 106th Congress with subpoenas and investigations into such issues as campaign fundraising abuses; the deadly 1993 shootout in Waco, Texas, between federal agents and Branch Davidians; and Clinton's 1999 pardon of 16 Puerto Rican militants.

But Burton's zealous pursuit of alleged Democratic wrongdoing has opened him to similar political attacks. In the middle of the Lewinsky scandal, he was forced to admit that he fathered a son out of wedlock in the early 1980s. Burton, who termed his mistakes "mine and mine alone," said he had accepted his financial responsibility for the cost of raising the child. And as he probed Democratic fundraising, reports surfaced in 1997 that he improperly raised money for his own campaign. "I know of only one person who was perfect, and he was nailed to a cross," Burton said of the charges. "They are just trying to attack me to deflect attention from the investigation."

In 1998, Burton told The Indianapolis Star that he believed his undaunted pursuit of Democratic wrongdoing had made him a target of surveillance and potential physical harm. "When I make phone calls, I assume somebody's listening. I assume every activity I undertake is being checked. If they go as far as they've gone to attack me, anything can happen," he told the newspaper.

Burton's tenacity and combativeness developed early in life. His 6-foot, 8-inch father regularly beat him and his mother and was eventually jailed for abuse. His family lived in hotels and trailer parks, and by the time he was 12, Burton had lived in 38 states, Mexico and Canada.

"I never stopped worrying that Dad would come back after he got out of jail," he told People magazine in 1994. "One day, when I was 13, he did. I was baby-sitting my younger brother and sister when I saw him come up the front walk. I was petrified and yelled, 'Don't come up here.' ... I grabbed a shotgun we kept beside the front door. When he saw the gun, he turned around. I'm glad he did because I might have shot him."

Burton enlisted in the Army at age 18 and later attended Cincinnati Bible College. He worked as an insurance agent and says he entered politics after seeing an interview in 1964 with Norman Thomas, a socialist who had run for president six times. Thomas was telling a reporter, according to Burton, that Americans would never "accept socialism from a socialist" but that socialist philosophy would be accepted under the label of the Democratic Party.

Burton, who until that point had been an independent who largely voted Democratic, said he took off from work the next day, went to the local library and read issues of the Congressional Record to see what legislation Democrats supported. Burton said he was shocked by what he said were bills to expand government control and spending. He immediately called the local GOP and volunteered. Two years later, at age 28, he won a seat in the state legislature as a Republican.

Burton cited his abusive upbringing when he tried to keep 6-year-old shipwreck survivor Elián González in the United States in 2000 rather than allow him to be reunited with his father in Cuba. A longtime opponent of Cuba's communist government, Burton even subpoenaed Elián to testify before his committee to try to delay his possible deportation, although the boy never appeared before the panel.

In the 104th Congress, Burton co-authored anti-Cuba legislation that allows U.S. nationals whose properties have been confiscated by Fidel Castro's government to sue foreign companies that knowingly "traffic" in such properties. The law also bars executives (and their families) who work for companies trading in expropriated properties from obtaining U.S. visas.

In 1999, Burton revealed another personal situation when he held hearings on the risks of childhood vaccines and spoke publicly about his grandson, who is autistic. Burton said the child had exhibited no developmental problems as a toddler, but shortly after receiving a slew of vaccines, the child lost his language skills and exhibited other symptoms of autism. "There have been huge increases in cases of autism and other developmental delays in the last few years — many linked to vaccines," he said.

Burton first made national headlines in 1987 when he proposed mandatory blood tests for everyone in the United States to track the AIDS virus. Associates of Burton have said he has a phobia about AIDS. One former colleague, ex-Rep. Andy Jacobs, D-Ind., told reporters that Burton refuses to eat soup in restaurants for fear of catching the deadly disease.

But the Indiana Republican is best known for his exuberant attacks on the Clinton administration. He infuriated Democrats and shocked some Republicans with his 1994 floor speech questioning presidential counsel Vincent W. Foster Jr.'s apparent suicide and proposing that Foster was murdered. Burton contended that, regardless of how Foster died, his body had been secretly moved to the spot where U.S. Park Police discovered it.

In the course of his investigation, Burton said, he re-enacted Foster's death in his backyard. With the help of a homicide detective, Burton fired a gun into a head-like object — reportedly a pumpkin or a watermelon — to see if the sound could be heard at a distance.

Burton's flamboyant conservatism is a good fit for his wealthy suburban district. He has won his past five elections with more than 70 percent of the vote. In 1998, local Democrats had hoped to exploit some of the negative publicity Burton had received during the Lewinsky scandal. But they were disappointed when the Democratic primary was won by Bob Kern, a crossdressing felon. The Indiana Democratic Party sued unsuccessfully to get Kern's name off the ballot. Burton easily won with 72 percent of the vote.

KEY VOTES

2000

No	Raise hourly minimum wage by $1 over two years
Yes	Halt funding for U.S. mission in Kosovo unless European nations pay more
Yes	Provide Medicare benefits to military retirees and their dependents
No	Grant China permanent normal trade status
Yes	Phase out estate, gift and trust taxes
Yes	Prohibit implementation of president's national monument designations
Yes	Approve GOP plan to provide prescription drug coverage for Medicare beneficiaries
No	Increase help for poor nations indebted to international financial institutions

1999

Yes	Impose steel import quotas
No	Kill proposal to take aviation trust funds off budget
Yes	Require background checks on buyers only at gun shows with 10 or more vendors
Yes	Remove barriers among banking, securities and insurance companies
No	Authorize state grants to hire teachers and reduce class size
No	Overhaul campaign finance law; ban "soft money" and restrict advocacy advertising
No	Approve bipartisan plan to increase rights of patients in managed-care health plans

INTEREST GROUPS

	AFL-CIO	ADA	CCUS	ACU
2000	13%	5%	89%	91%
1999	33%	5%	83%	95%
1998	0%	5%	93%	96%
1997	13%	5%	80%	96%

CQ VOTE STUDIES

	PARTY UNITY		PRESIDENTIAL SUPPORT	
	Support	Oppose	Support	Oppose
2000	98%	2%	17%	83%
1999	94%	6%	13%	87%
1998	93%	7%	21%	79%
1997	95%	5%	26%	74%

INDIANA 6
Central – Suburban Indianapolis

Home to Indianapolis suburbanites and rural farmers, the 6th is Indiana's wealthiest district and is solidly Republican territory. President Bush in 2000 and Bob Dole in 1996 received their best support in the state from 6th District voters. The trend might well continue; the area's suburbanites, who are rapidly taking the region's countryside, have been a largely Republican constituency.

The district's most affluent residents and its few minorities live in northern Indianapolis and in the Hamilton County suburbs of Carmel, Fishers and Noblesville. Here, rapidly growing populations of white-collar workers in electronics and financial services bring median incomes up to $60,000.

Fort Benjamin Harrison (shared with the 10th District) was closed in 1991, but local officials successfully converted it for corporate, military finance, residential and state government use. The base is now the centerpiece of a revitalized downtown Lawrence.

The 6th's rural communities in Clinton, Tipton, eastern Hancock and southern Johnson counties rely on farming and the agricultural products industry – corn, livestock, snack chips and seed are staples of the economy. Suburbs are starting to encroach somewhat on Hancock County. The rural communities are slightly less affluent but just as conservative as their suburban counterparts.

MAJOR INDUSTRY
Agriculture, electronics, financial services

CITIES
Indianapolis (pt.), 213,373 (1990); Carmel, 46,274; Greenwood, 34,951; Fishers, 30,328

UNUSUAL FEATURES
The Indianapolis 500 is run in Speedway; Lawrence hosts one of the nation's largest annual veteran reunions at Fort Benjamin Harrison.

Rep. Brian Kerns (R)

Elected 2000; 1st term

CAPITOL OFFICE
225-5805; 226 Cannon Bldg. 20515

COMMITTEES
International Relations
Transportation & Infrastructure

HOMETOWN
Prairieton

BORN
May 22, 1957, Terre Haute, Ind.

RELIGION
Episcopalian

FAMILY
Wife, Lori Myers; five children

EDUCATION
Indiana State U., B.S. 1991, M.P.A. 1992

CAREER
Congressional aide; university public relations director; state natural resources department spokesman; television reporter and photographer

POLITICAL HIGHLIGHTS
No previous office

ELECTION RESULTS

2000 GENERAL

Brian Kerns (R)	135,869	64.8%
Michael Graf (D)	66,764	31.8%
Bob Thayer (LIBERT)	7,032	3.4%

2000 PRIMARY

Brian Kerns (R)	22,766	39.1%
Bob Griffiths (R)	18,792	32.2%
Alex Gatzimos (R)	7,233	12.4%
Bryan L. Donaldson (R)	2,869	4.9%
Matt Branam (R)	2,156	3.7%
Anthony W. Duncan (R)	2,079	3.6%
Douglas E. Hess (R)	1,458	2.5%
John W. Timm (R)	933	1.6%

Kerns' election to the open 7th District seat is testimony to the benefit of strong political and personal connections. He was chief of staff to his predecessor, retired two-term Republican Ed Pease. And Kerns is married to a daughter of Pease's predecessor, Republican Rep. John T. Myers, who had held the seat for 30 years.

Kerns' background in public relations could help him sharpen his message and tout his efforts. Before joining Pease's staff, Kerns was a reporter and photographer for a TV station in Terre Haute (the 7th District's largest city) and a public relations director for a small Indiana college.

Like most of his GOP House colleagues, Kerns advocates tax reductions. He supports across-the-board income tax cuts and elimination of the estate tax, which he has called "the theft tax" (a play on the Republican label of the levy as the "death tax"). Kerns also plans to continue the strong constituent service that district residents grew accustomed to under Myers and Pease. He was assigned to the Transportation and Infrastructure Committee, on which Pease also sat, as well as the International Relations panel.

When Myers announced his retirement plans early in 1996, Kerns first saw his wife, Lori — Myers' daughter — as the logical candidate, but she had no interest in running. So when Pease revealed his retirement in 2000, Kerns decided to make a run.

His chief competitor in the eight-candidate 2000 Republican primary was Bob Griffiths, a financial executive and first-time candidate. Kerns lost Tippecanoe — the district's largest county and Griffiths' home base — but won the district's other 12 counties, enough to give him a 7 percentage point victory margin. Kerns had some bumpy moments in the race. Shortly before the May primary, several female former Pease staffers told The Indianapolis Star that Kerns was verbally abusive to them and compelled one aide to perform campaign work from a government office. Kerns denied breaking any laws and questioned the timing of the allegations.

Kerns' primary win sealed his election in the heavily Republican district: He trounced Democrat Michael Graf, a United Parcel Service employee.

INDIANA 7

West — Terre Haute; Lafayette

Rural farmland stretching west from Indianapolis to the Illinois border occupies the bulk of the 7th's land and serves as the base for the district's Republican leanings. Lafayette and Terre Haute, the district's two urban centers, grew up along the Wabash River. Lafayette adds to the district's conservative base with engineering-centered Purdue University. A few Democrats are elected locally in Lafayette, bolstered by blue-collar manufacturing workers, but those candidates generally win by downplaying party affiliation.

Terre Haute, the district's largest city and its only source of union strength, is the real source of power for Democrats. Once a hotbed of populist activism, Terre Haute's Democratic leanings have been cemented by economic hard times. At the northern end of Indiana's coal country, the city suffered as the coal industry went under.

Although the economy is steadied somewhat by Indiana State University and Rose-Hulman Institute of Technology, an engineering college, Terre Haute continues to struggle with chronic industrial decline that began in the early 1980s.

A third population center is growing as Indianapolis suburbs continue to spread across once-rural Hendricks, Boone and Morgan counties, depositing wealthy suburbanites who are faithful GOP voters.

MAJOR INDUSTRY
Higher education, manufacturing, agriculture

CITIES
Terre Haute, 52,664; Lafayette, 49,104; West Lafayette, 30,406

UNUSUAL FEATURES
Amelia Earhart taught at Purdue University and helped establish its school of aeronautical engineering; Terre Haute was home to five-time Socialist presidential candidate Eugene V. Debs; Kermit the Frog named after a Purdue philosophy professor.

Rep. John Hostettler (R)

Elected 1994; 4th term

CAPITOL OFFICE
225-4636; fax 225-3284
1507 Longworth Bldg. 20515

INTERNET
e-mail: john.hostettler@mail.house.gov
web: www.house.gov/hostettler

COMMITTEES
Armed Services
Judiciary

HOMETOWN
Wadesville

BORN
July 19, 1961, Evansville, Ind.

RELIGION
General Baptist

FAMILY
Wife, Elizabeth Ann Hamman; four children

EDUCATION
Rose-Hulman Institute of Technology, B.S.M.E.
1983

CAREER
Mechanical engineer

POLITICAL HIGHLIGHTS
No previous office

ELECTION RESULTS

2000 GENERAL

John Hostettler (R)	116,879	52.7%
Paul Perry (D)	100,488	45.3%
Thomas Tindle (LIBERT)	4,342	2.0%

2000 PRIMARY

John Hostettler (R)	unopposed

1998 GENERAL

John Hostettler (R)	92,785	52.1%
Gail Riecken (D)	81,871	46.0%
Paul Hager (LIBERT)	3,401	1.9%

PREVIOUS WINNING PERCENTAGES
1996 (50%); 1994 (52%)

Before coming to Congress, Hostettler's chief experience in the public arena was as a member of the board of deacons at the Twelfth Avenue General Baptist Church in Evansville, where he taught Bible study and led prayer meetings. His strongly held religious beliefs translate into conservative views on most social policy issues, and he is one of Congress' most unyielding opponents of gun control.

Hostettler (HO-stet-lur) votes with the GOP majority about 90 percent of the time. When he strays from the party line, it is generally to take a more conservative stance than his party leaders want, particularly on budget issues. However, he has sided with the Democrats in opposing constitutional amendments requiring a balanced budget and imposing term limits, citing reluctance to make major changes to the Constitution.

Like many conservatives, Hostettler says guns are not the cause of violence in America, and he told the Louisville Courier-Journal he doubts that tougher gun control laws "would have any impact on the moral decay that we see in our youth culture." He led efforts in the 106th Congress to block enforcement of an agreement reached in March 2000 between the nation's largest gun manufacturer, Smith & Wesson, and federal, state and local officials. The company promised to install safety locks, demand background checks at gun shows and develop guns that can only be fired by their owners. In exchange, the Clinton administration and some states and municipalities agreed to drop Smith & Wesson from gun lawsuits.

Hostettler is a firm opponent of abortion. In the 104th, he took aim at an amendment that would have allowed abortions at overseas military facilities if the government were reimbursed for the cost of the procedure. "The Supreme Court has told us that we have to allow the killings of preborn children," he said. "It has not, however, told us that government has an obligation to provide this service." In the 107th Congress, Hostettler won a platform from which to wage his fights on social issues as he swapped a seat on the Agriculture Committee for one on Judiciary.

Hostettler is also one of the most fiscally conservative members of the House, arguing strongly that the government should cut taxes rather than hold onto budget surpluses. "If you overpaid a utility company, you wouldn't allow it to keep this overcharge, would you?" he asked. "You would demand and deserve a refund. ... If you overpay the government, it is only fair that you get a refund in the form of tax relief."

His frugality has caused some headaches for GOP leaders. Joining with other conservative rebels, he tried repeatedly in 1997 to cut spending from appropriations bills, and he initially voted against the Republican budget plan in 2000, one of only five Republicans to vote "no." (Later, he returned to the GOP fold on the budget plan.)

When it comes to transportation and defense, however, Hostettler does back some spending initiatives — especially if it means more funding for Indiana. He helped secure money in the massive 1998 transportation authorization for Interstate 69, one of the highways envisioned for carrying goods between Canada and Mexico. Hostettler said "the benefits of constructing the highway are overwhelming and cannot be emphasized enough." But he particularly touted the estimated 4,500 new jobs that would be created between 2005 and 2034. Hostettler's former employer, Southern Indiana Gas & Electric Co., lobbied for the interstate.

From his seat on the Armed Services Committee, he supported Republican efforts to give more money to the Pentagon than was requested by the Clinton administration.

In the 105th Congress, Hostettler split openly with former Speaker Newt Gingrich, contending early and often that Gingrich's ethics woes and general unpopularity made him a hindrance in spreading the GOP gospel. In January 1997, Hostettler was among five Republican lawmakers to vote "present" in the election of Gingrich to be Speaker, and he later participated in an abortive plan to oust Gingrich from his leadership post.

Democrats regarded Hostettler's 1994 election over Democratic incumbent Frank McCloskey as something of a fluke, and they have repeatedly tried to oust him. But Hostettler has doggedly fended off the challenges in a series of contests so close that his district is sometimes referred to as the "bloody Eighth."

In his first race, in 1994, Hostettler did not gear up for a full-time run until July, at which time his campaign reported a negative bank balance. He overcame those impediments and several campaign gaffes to ultimately defeat the six-term incumbent.

Relying on a grass-roots organization drawn primarily from area churches, Hostettler emerged the top vote-getter in a six-candidate primary field. Some in the GOP establishment said privately that he was too conservative, and others were turned off by comments he made during a Kiwanis Club speech that were criticized as anti-Semitic. Hostettler ran into further trouble when, at a meeting of high school students, he appeared to suggest that citizens have the right to the same weapons as the government — including nuclear arms. (He later denied that that was his meaning.)

Such difficulties probably would have sunk Hostettler's candidacy in other years. But McCloskey was doomed by a voter backlash against the unpopular Clinton administration. As the GOP swept into control of Congress for the first time in 40 years, Hostettler prevailed in the 8th District, 52 percent to 48 percent. The cake at his victory celebration read, "To God Give the Glory."

Hostettler had an even more difficult time in 1996, edging out a former McCloskey aide by just 2 percentage points. In 1998, he enjoyed his widest margin of victory — 6 percentage points — but was still held to just 52 percent of the vote. The Democrats again targeted him in 2000, fielding a conservative Evansville surgeon named Paul Perry, who denounced Hostettler for failing to support health care revisions. But the incumbent touted his stands on gun owners' rights and abortion restrictions, and he won reelection by 7 percentage points, his largest margin to date.

KEY VOTES

2000
No Raise hourly minimum wage by $1 over two years
Yes Halt funding for U.S. mission in Kosovo unless European nations pay more
Yes Provide Medicare benefits to military retirees and their dependents
No Grant China permanent normal trade status
Yes Phase out estate, gift and trust taxes
Yes Prohibit implementation of president's national monument designations
No Approve GOP plan to provide prescription drug coverage for Medicare beneficiaries
No Increase help for poor nations indebted to international financial institutions

1999
Yes Impose steel import quotas
?   Kill proposal to take aviation trust funds off budget
No Require background checks on buyers only at gun shows with 10 or more vendors
Yes Remove barriers among banking, securities and insurance companies
No Authorize state grants to hire teachers and reduce class size
No Overhaul campaign finance law; ban "soft money" and restrict advocacy advertising
No Approve bipartisan plan to increase rights of patients in managed-care health plans

INTEREST GROUPS

	AFL-CIO	ADA	CCUS	ACU
2000	30%	15%	76%	88%
1999	44%	15%	83%	96%
1998	10%	10%	78%	92%
1997	0%	5%	80%	88%

CQ VOTE STUDIES

	PARTY UNITY		PRESIDENTIAL SUPPORT	
	Support	Oppose	Support	Oppose
2000	92%	8%	17%	83%
1999	91%	9%	11%	89%
1998	91%	9%	24%	76%
1997	96%	4%	25%	75%

INDIANA 8
Southwest — Evansville; Bloomington

Indiana's southwest corner, formed by the converging Wabash and Ohio rivers, houses the 8th District, characterized by a sometimes shaky coexistence of academics, laborers and social conservatives. In 1984, the district hosted the most competitive congressional race in the century, in which a margin of only four hotly contested votes separated the candidates. With a tendency to unseat incumbents, the 8th often has displayed a revolving-door policy toward its congressional representatives.

The 8th's manufacturing base and history as a mining center have given Democrats an edge for several decades. But both parties hold a competitive share of an electorate with a strong independent streak. The 8th chose moderate Democratic candidates in most tight federal and state races in the 1990s but also narrowly elected a socially conservative Republican representative.

Bloomington and Evansville are home to the 8th's only substantial minority and liberal populations. While Evansville hosts two small colleges, the University of Southern Indiana and the University of Evansville, it is Bloomington – home of Indiana University – that is the district's college town. Evansville, an Ohio River port and the state's third largest city, is southern Indiana's industrial center.

Past the limestone quarries of Monroe and Lawrence counties is the Naval Surface Warfare Center in Crane (Martin County), one of the district's major employers.

MAJOR INDUSTRY
Higher education, manufacturing, agriculture

MILITARY BASES
Naval Surface Warfare Center, 50 military; 3,141 civilian (1999)

CITIES
Evansville, 121,864; Bloomington (pt.), 58,116 (1990); Vincennes, 18,338

UNUSUAL FEATURES
Boyhood home of comedian Red Skelton in Vincennes; French Lick, hometown of basketball star Larry Bird; Movie "Breaking Away" filmed in Bloomington.

Rep. Baron P. Hill (D)

Elected 1998; 2nd term

CAPITOL OFFICE
225-5315; fax 226-6866
1208 Longworth Bldg. 20515

INTERNET
e-mail: www.house.gov/writerep
web: www.house.gov/baronhill

COMMITTEES
Agriculture
Armed Services
Veterans' Affairs

HOMETOWN
Seymour

BORN
June 23, 1953, Seymour, Ind.

RELIGION
Christian Church

FAMILY
Wife, Betty Hill; three children

EDUCATION
Furman U., B.A. 1975

CAREER
Financial adviser; state student aid commission
director; insurance company manager

POLITICAL HIGHLIGHTS
Ind. House, 1983-91; Democratic nominee for U.S.
Senate, 1990

ELECTION RESULTS

2000 GENERAL

Baron P. Hill (D)	126,420	54.2%
Michael Everett Bailey (R)	102,219	43.8%
Sara Chambers (LIBERT)	4,644	2.0%

2000 PRIMARY

Baron P. Hill (D)	42,235	85.5%
James R. McClure Jr. (D)	5,264	10.7%
Lendall B. Terry (D)	1,921	3.9%

1998 GENERAL

Baron P. Hill (D)	92,973	50.8%
Jean Leising (R)	87,797	47.9%
Diane Feeney (LIBERT)	2,406	1.3%

Politics was not Hill's first love. A basketball star at Seymour High School, he was inducted into the Indiana Basketball Hall of Fame in 2000, along with NBA legend Larry Bird. "When I was growing up in Seymour, all I could think of was basketball and girls. Politics was the furthest thing from my mind," he recalls.

Hill picked up the political bug while in college, watching the Watergate hearings on television and becoming fascinated by the process of government. He first ran for office after a friend of his from the Jaycees retired from his state House seat. Hill ended up serving there for eight years. He says he likes the competitive aspect of politics, which reminds him of sports.

Like many other junior members, Hill's focus has been local, as he seeks to use his office to help his district. Hill learned the importance of personal contact in his 1990 Senate campaign, when he walked across Indiana during his unsuccessful bid to unseat Republican Daniel R. Coats. "I was outspent 4-to-1, so I was looking for ways to garner attention," Hill recalled a decade later. "But what started as a campaign gimmick turned out to be useful. When you walk into a town, you get a different perspective." He still sometimes walks near-marathon lengths between meetings in his district and says that constituent service work is "what gets me juiced in the morning."

He is also interested in helping the folks back home financially. Hill found federal funding for a seven-mile riverfront preservation project between New Albany and Jeffersonville, on part of the Army's shuttered Jefferson Proving Ground. He has been involved in further negotiations to turn the proving ground into a national wildlife refuge. And he was proud to announce in 2000 a $2.5 million Economic Development Administration grant to upgrade Charlestown's sewage treatment plant.

The Indiana Farm Bureau had opposed Hill in 1998, but he won the group's endorsement for his 2000 re-election bid, in part because of his support for granting China permanent normal trade status. The policy was backed by farmers pushing for broader access to markets overseas.

Hill had received much of his campaign money in 1998 from labor unions, which adamantly opposed the Chinese trade measure. But Hill explained to the labor groups that many of his constituents are employed by United Parcel Service at its hub facility just across the Ohio River in Louisville, Ky., and that the shipping company stood to increase employment with more access to the Chinese market.

Hill, who serves on the Agriculture Committee, notes the irony that farmers in his district sometimes will tell him they want to be left alone by the government — but in the next breath will complain about the low price of corn, saying: "You've got to do something about it." He joined with Republican John Thune of South Dakota in sponsoring a bill that would create a position within the Justice Department to investigate agriculture company mergers.

Hill also serves on Armed Services, where, like many members, he speaks regularly about the need to protect the pay and benefits of servicemen and -women. But he is intrigued by the findings of a commission headed by the 9th District's former representative, Democrat Lee H. Hamilton, and former Sen. Warren B. Rudman, R-N.H., that the military should rethink its policy of maintaining readiness for fighting two large regional wars simultaneously. Hill would like to open a dialogue in Congress about whether the "two wars" strategy is the best way to meet the nation's long-term security needs.

A member of the "Blue Dogs," a coalition of conservative Democrats, Hill reflects the social conservatism of Indiana's southeastern hill country on issues such as gun owners' rights. But he votes a reliably Democratic line on fiscal matters, including taxes.

Hill is married to a school teacher, and he has weighed in on education issues. He believes schools would be safer if they were smaller. He says social scientists have found that students perform better and feel more comfortable when in a smaller school. After the massacre at Colorado's Columbine High School, Hill asked fellow Class of 1998 Democrat Brian Baird of Washington what he thought had been the cause. "Our schools are too big," Baird told him. Hill subsequently wrote a bill to provide $100 million to encourage local districts to shrink their schools; he applauded when a similar initiative was funded in an appropriations bill in 1999.

Hill is a former director of Indiana's State Student Assistance Commission and worked for an Indiana Assembly Speaker after losing the 1990 Senate race. He said that he thought he had sworn off politics for good after Democrats in the Indiana House, like their national colleagues, lost control of the chamber in 1994. He went to work as a financial analyst for Merrill Lynch but did not hesitate for long when Hamilton let him know he'd be vacating the 9th District seat after 17 terms.

The 9th is shaky territory for a Democrat, but Hill has been lucky, so far, in his opponents. He won the seat in 1998 by beating former state Sen. Jean Leising, who had run against Hamilton in 1994 and 1996. After coming close the first time, Leising made many enemies within the state GOP and found many fundraising avenues closed to her. Hill was remembered by many voters for his high school basketball exploits nearly three decades before, and he was able to outspend Leising, $1 million to $650,000, to win by about 3 percentage points.

Hill was initially a target for Republicans in 2000, who lined up behind Kevin Kellems, a former aide to Sen. Richard G. Lugar, R-Ind. But Kellems lost the primary to Michael Everett Bailey, who had gained notoriety in 1992 by running graphic TV ads about abortion during his campaign against Hamilton. Bailey ran the same ads against Hill, to no better effect.

Hill enjoyed a large fundraising lead, as Bailey found Republican wallets largely closed to his effort. By contrast, Hill benefited from a May 2000 fundraiser, featuring President Clinton, that raised $100,000. The event was held at the Maryland home of Joe Andrew, chairman of the Democratic National Committee and the former head of the Indiana Democratic Party.

KEY VOTES

2000

Yes Raise hourly minimum wage by $1 over two years
No Halt funding for U.S. mission in Kosovo unless European nations pay more
Yes Provide Medicare benefits to military retirees and their dependents
Yes Grant China permanent normal trade status
No Phase out estate, gift and trust taxes
No Prohibit implementation of president's national monument designations
No Approve GOP plan to provide prescription drug coverage for Medicare beneficiaries
No Increase help for poor nations indebted to international financial institutions

1999

Yes Impose steel import quotas
No Kill proposal to take aviation trust funds off budget
No Require background checks on buyers only at gun shows with 10 or more vendors
Yes Remove barriers among banking, securities and insurance companies
Yes Authorize state grants to hire teachers and reduce class size
Yes Overhaul campaign finance law; ban "soft money" and restrict advocacy advertising
Yes Approve bipartisan plan to increase rights of patients in managed-care health plans

INTEREST GROUPS

	AFL-CIO	ADA	CCUS	ACU
2000	70%	70%	60%	16%
1999	78%	75%	56%	16%

CQ VOTE STUDIES

	PARTY UNITY		PRESIDENTIAL SUPPORT	
	Support	Oppose	Support	Oppose
2000	81%	19%	76%	24%
1999	74%	26%	65%	35%

INDIANA 9
Southeast Hill Country – New Albany

The 9th borders the Ohio River to the south and shares its social conservative roots and, more recently, its competitive politics with other river valley districts. Manufacturing forms the economic foundation of the 9th, although agriculture and retail trade are also prevalent in Indiana's southeastern quadrant.

With the largest blue-collar workforce of Indiana's districts and one of the lowest percentages of college graduates in the nation, the 9th has a long tradition of sending Democrats to Congress and the state legislature.

The district split its presidential vote almost evenly between parties in the 1990s, with almost 20 percent of voters supporting Ross Perot in 1992. However, in the 2000 presidential contest, President Bush easily carried the district with 58 percent.

The 9th's northeastern counties are seeing an influx of Cincinnati migrants which has started to change the district from rural to slightly more suburban. To the south, Clark and Floyd counties are growing rapidly due to Louisville metropolitan area growth and the arrival of several new steel businesses.

Unemployment in some rural communities can run two to three times Indiana's otherwise low average, and rural poverty is an observable fact of life here. The loss of Jefferson Proving Grounds Army installation in the mid-1990s and disastrous floods in 1997 contributed to the area's economic struggles.

MAJOR INDUSTRY
Manufacturing, agriculture, retail

CITIES
New Albany, 40,273; Jeffersonville, 27,057; Clarksville, 20,273

UNUSUAL FEATURES
World's largest casket producer in Batesville.

Rep. Julia Carson (D)

CAPITOL OFFICE
225-4011; fax 225-5633
1339 Longworth Bldg. 20515

INTERNET
e-mail: rep.carson@mail.house.gov
web: www.house.gov/carson

COMMITTEES
Financial Services
Veterans' Affairs

HOMETOWN
Indianapolis

BORN
July 8, 1938, Louisville, Ky.

RELIGION
Baptist

FAMILY
Divorced; two children

EDUCATION
Martin U., attended 1994-95

CAREER
Clothing store owner; human resources manager;
congressional aide

POLITICAL HIGHLIGHTS
Ind. House, 1973-77; Ind. Senate, 1977-91;
Center Township trustee, 1991-97

ELECTION RESULTS

2000 GENERAL

Julia Carson (D)	91,689	58.5%
Marvin B. Scott (R)	62,233	39.7%
Na'llah Ali (LIBERT)	2,780	1.8%

2000 PRIMARY

Julia Carson (D)	22,891	89.8%
Ralph Spelbring (D)	1,639	6.4%
Bobby Hidalgo (D)	956	3.8%

1998 GENERAL

Julia Carson (D)	69,682	58.3%
Gary A. Hofmeister (R)	47,017	39.4%
Fred C. Peterson (LIBERT)	2,719	2.3%

PREVIOUS WINNING PERCENTAGES
1996 (53%)

Elected 1996; 3rd term

When Carson urges people in poverty to find a way to support themselves, she can offer her own life as an example. Born to a teenage single mother, she waited tables, delivered newspapers and did farm labor to generate income as a youth. Later, as a divorced young mother of two, she pinched every penny.

Carson's doctrine of self-reliance might seem to fit right in with the philosophy of Congress' conservative Republicans, but in fact her experiences have led her to very different conclusions about how to help the poor. She used to head the Center Township Trustee's Office, which administered aid to the city's low-income residents. "We got people off of welfare and put them into jobs and into training and into educational experiences," Carson recalled. "We did not do that by being cruel." She typically takes a dim view of the GOP's legislative proposals, using adjectives like "cruel" and "regressive" to describe them.

In her speeches and votes on the House floor, Carson generally aligns with fellow members of the Progressive Caucus, the most liberal faction of the House Democrats. She is a reliable supporter of organized labor, environmental protections, abortion rights, gun control and health care programs. From her seat on the Financial Services Committee (formerly Banking), she has resisted such GOP initiatives as an overhaul of the federal public housing program, which included a requirement that unemployed tenants perform eight hours of community service per month.

Carson occasionally breaks ranks with her allies in unions and other traditionally liberal organizations, however. In 2000, after the Clinton White House lobbied her, she put aside her concerns about human rights violations and reluctantly supported granting China permanent normal trade status. "I feel like I have been put in a Maytag washer and put on the spin cycle," she said before the vote. "I realize it is a no-win situation. Regardless how I vote, someone will be upset."

Similarly, in 1997 Carson was not among the several dozen House Democratic liberals who opposed the bipartisan balanced-budget agreement when it won final House passage in July. Breaking from others on the left who felt President Clinton had yielded too much ground to congressional Republicans, she voted for both the tax and spending components of the budget.

Carson worked with Republicans on several measures in the 106th Congress to expand the reach of social programs. She and fellow Indianan, Republican Sen. Richard G. Lugar, introduced legislation in the House and Senate to encourage schools, child care facilities and federal nutrition programs to share efforts to identify children who could qualify for Medicaid or for the newer Children's Health Insurance Program. Carson said that federal and state governments should be "more creative and aggressive in our outreach efforts."

Similarly, she backed a bipartisan measure that sought to get more low-income fathers to play a larger role in the lives of their children, including taking greater financial responsibility. "I know firsthand what a lonesome feeling it is" not to have a father, she said. "Father absenteeism is a national problem that must be addressed."

More often, however, Carson has sharply criticized GOP initiatives. Responding to Majority Leader Dick Armey's call for abolishing the Legal Services Corporation in the 105th Congress, the congresswoman wrote that it is "incomprehensible" to argue "that the private sector alone can provide for the legal needs of the poor." As for Armey's assertion that Legal Services pursues a political agenda instead of helping those in poverty, Carson called that a "Washington perspective" not in keeping with her experience in Indianapolis.

When the GOP offered a bill in the 105th to provide low-income families with vouchers to cover tuition at any local school, including private and religious institutions, Carson called the measure a "cruel hoax." Citing "record enrollments, crumbling buildings, and the growing threats of crime and drugs that our public schools did not create," she said that "diverting resources to private schools is not the answer. Surely we can put the money to better use."

In the 106th Congress, Carson introduced legislation to award the Congressional Gold Medal to civil rights figure Rosa Parks. The bill initially won little support beyond members of the Congressional Black Caucus, but Carson stirred up media coverage and eventually enlisted more than 300 cosponsors in a successful campaign to pass the measure. When the medal was presented to Parks in a ceremony at the Capitol, Carson said, "It is a celebration of the life of Rosa Parks — receiving this medal while she can still see it, still feel it, still hold it."

Carson began her congressional career as a secretary, and then a district aide, for Indiana Democratic Rep. Andrew Jacobs Jr. In 1972, she won the first of two state House terms; she moved up to the state Senate in 1976, where she served until 1991 and sat on the Finance Committee. During her years in the legislature, she worked as human resources director at Cummins Engine and later opened a dress shop in Indianapolis that failed and left her saddled with debt. (She had her state Senate wages garnished to partially pay off the debts.)

Carson won election as Center Township trustee in 1990 and held that post until 1997. The administrative costs for the Center Township Trustee's Office increased during her tenure, but she improved the agency's financial standing overall, while reducing taxes and lowering the number of people receiving financial assistance from 77,000 to fewer than 38,000.

When Jacobs retired in 1996 after 15 terms, he endorsed Carson to succeed him, helping her win a tough nomination battle and hold off a vigorous Republican attempt to capture the 10th District. Carson's 8-point victory over former state Sen. Virginia Blankenbaker made her one of five black members in the 105th Congress to represent white-majority districts. She has won her two re-election contests by comfortable margins.

KEY VOTES

2000

Yes	Raise hourly minimum wage by $1 over two years
Yes	Halt funding for U.S. mission in Kosovo unless European nations pay more
Yes	Provide Medicare benefits to military retirees and their dependents
Yes	Grant China permanent normal trade status
No	Phase out estate, gift and trust taxes
No	Prohibit implementation of president's national monument designations
No	Approve GOP plan to provide prescription drug coverage for Medicare beneficiaries
Yes	Increase help for poor nations indebted to international financial institutions

1999

Yes	Impose steel import quotas
No	Kill proposal to take aviation trust funds off budget
No	Require background checks on buyers only at gun shows with 10 or more vendors
Yes	Remove barriers among banking, securities and insurance companies
Yes	Authorize state grants to hire teachers and reduce class size
Yes	Overhaul campaign finance law; ban "soft money" and restrict advocacy advertising
Yes	Approve bipartisan plan to increase rights of patients in managed-care health plans

INTEREST GROUPS

	AFL-CIO	ADA	CCUS	ACU
2000	90%	90%	40%	4%
1999	100%	95%	18%	0%
1998	100%	95%	22%	0%
1997	100%	90%	30%	9%

CQ VOTE STUDIES

	PARTY UNITY		PRESIDENTIAL SUPPORT	
	Support	Oppose	Support	Oppose
2000	96%	4%	84%	16%
1999	97%	3%	81%	19%
1998	96%	4%	89%	11%
1997	92%	8%	82%	18%

INDIANA 10

Central – Indianapolis

Indiana's largest concentration of minorities lives in the urban 10th, which houses one of the state's largest white-collar workforces but also has one of its lowest median incomes.

Four times bigger than Fort Wayne, the state's next-largest city, Indianapolis is the state's capital as well as its banking and commercial center. Heavy industry also plays a role in the city's economy, with a few automotive plants hanging on despite industry downturns.

Indianapolis has a reputation for being one of the nation's most conservative metropolitan areas – although Democratic, the 10th tends to support moderate candidates. But in 2000, the 10th elected Indiana's most socially liberal Democratic representative to a third term. The district also threw strong support to Bill Clinton in 1992 and '96 and to Al Gore in 2000.

Large minority populations in central Indianapolis form the 10th's Democratic core. The joint Indiana University-Purdue University campus is here, and some communities are up to 65 percent black. In the city's northern tier, white-collar residents are some of the wealthiest in the state. These communities are more receptive to Republican candidates and supported them heavily for state office in the 1990s.

In the southern part of the district, blue-collar, mostly white populations built around the city's manufacturing industry are more socially conservative and generally supported Republicans on the local level in the 1990s.

MAJOR INDUSTRY
Manufacturing, health care, higher education, financial services

CITIES
Indianapolis (pt.), 517,954 (1990); Lawrence (pt.), 20,008 (1990); Beech Grove (pt.), 10,434 (1990)

UNUSUAL FEATURES
President Benjamin Harrison's family home; John Dillinger's gravesite.

IOWA

Gov. Tom Vilsack (D)

First elected: 1998
Length of term: 4 years
Term expires: 1/03
Salary: $104,352
Phone: (515) 281-5211
Hometown: Mt. Pleasant
Born: Dec. 13, 1950, Pittsburgh, Pa.
Religion: Roman Catholic
Family: Wife, Christie Vilsack; two children
Education: Hamilton College (N.Y.), A.B. 1972; Albany Law School, J.D. 1975
Career: Lawyer
Political highlights: Mayor of Mt. Pleasant, 1987-92; Iowa Senate, 1993-99

Election results:

1998 GENERAL

Tom Vilsack (D)	500,231	52.3%
Jim Ross Lightfoot (R)	444,787	46.5%

Lt. Gov. Sally Pederson (D)

First elected: 1998
Length of term: 4 years
Term expires: 1/03
Salary: $76,698
Phone: (515) 281-0225

STATE LEGISLATURE

General Assembly: Meets January-May
House: 100 members, 2-year terms
2001 breakdown: 56R, 44D; 78 men, 22 women
Salary: $21,380
Phone: (515) 281-3221
Senate: 50 members, 4-year terms
2001 breakdown: 30R, 20D; 39 men, 11 women
Salary: $21,380
Phone: (515) 281-3371

STATE TERM LIMITS

Governor: No
Senate: No
House: No

URBAN STATISTICS

CITY	POPULATION
Des Moines	190,958
Cedar Rapids	115,777
Davenport	98,256
Sioux City	82,843
Waterloo	62,800

REGISTERED VOTERS

Nonaffiliated	38%
Republican	32%
Democrat	30%

POPULATION

2000 population	2,926,324
1990 population	2,776,755
Percent change	+5.4%
Rank among states	30
Median age	36.3
Born in state	78%
Foreign born	2%
Urban/rural	61%/39%
Crime rate	310/100,000
Poverty level	9.1%
Federal workers	20,040
Military	13,979

REAPPORTIONMENT

Iowa retained its five House seats in reapportionment. The state legislature will draw new district lines in 2001.

MISCELLANEOUS

Web: www.state.ia.us
Capital: Des Moines
Land area: 55,875 sq. miles
  Rank among states: 23
STATE ELECTION OFFICIAL
(515) 281-5865
DEMOCRATIC HEADQUARTERS
(515) 244-7292
REPUBLICAN HEADQUARTERS
(515) 282-8105

District Statistics

DIST.	VOTE FOR PRESIDENT 2000 D	2000 R	GREEN	1996 D	1996 R	REF	1992 D	1992 R	I	WHT	BLK	ASIAN	HISP	HOUSEHOLD INCOME	OVER 65+	UNDER 18	COLLEGE EDUCATION
1	53%	43%	3%	54%	37%	8%	46%	35%	19%	95%	3%	1%	2%	$29,544	12%	25%	23%
2	51	45	2	53	37	9	44	35	20	97	2	0	1	$25,010	16	26	14
3	47	49	2	50	39	9	46	37	18	98	1	1	1	$24,767	16	25	16
4	48	50	2	49	42	8	43	39	18	95	3	1	2	$28,591	14	26	19
5	42	55	2	44	45	10	38	42	19	98	1	1	1	$24,150	18	27	13
STATE	49	48	2	50	40	9	43	37	19	97	2	1	1	$26,229	15	26	17

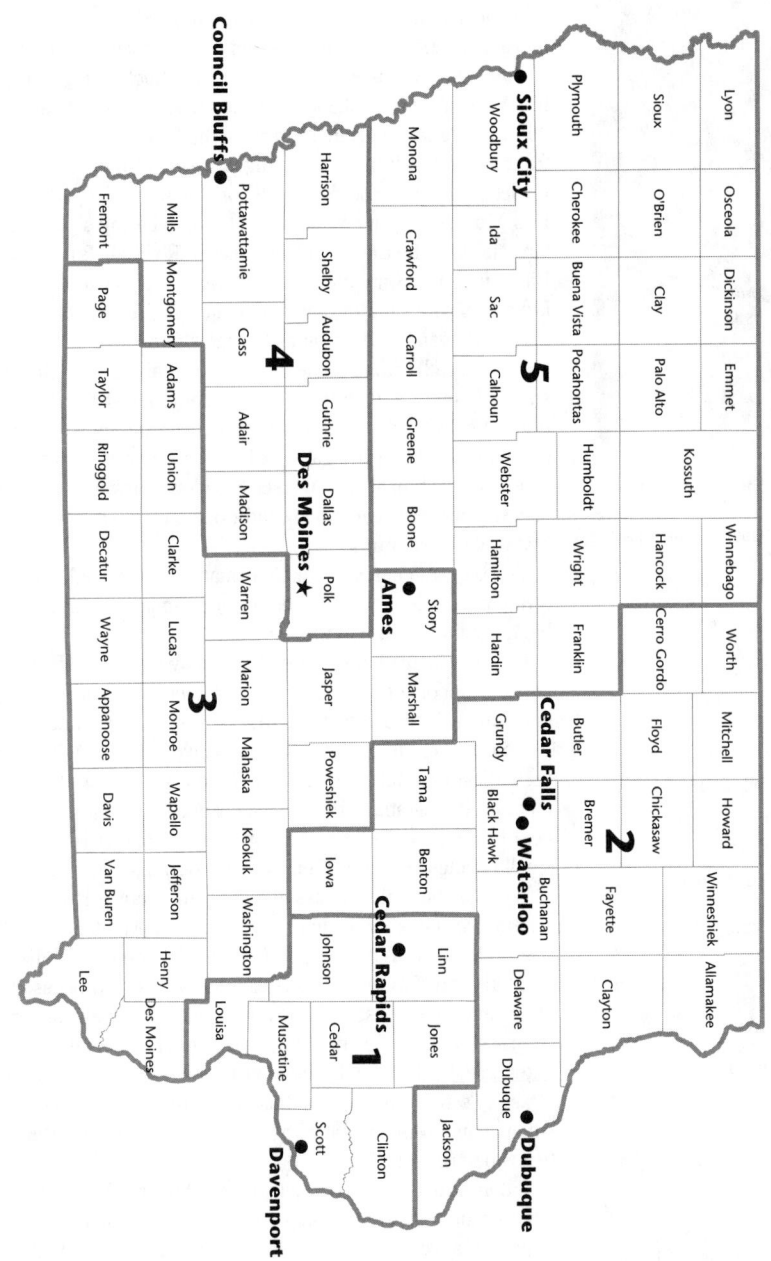

Sen. Charles E. Grassley (R)

Elected 1980; 4th term

CAPITOL OFFICE
224-3744; fax 224-6020; 135 Hart Bldg. 20510

INTERNET
e-mail: chuck_grassley@grassley.senate.gov
web: grassley.senate.gov

COMMITTEES
Budget
Finance - chairman
Judiciary
  (Youth Violence - chairman)
Joint Taxation

HOMETOWN
New Hartford

BORN
Sept. 17, 1933, New Hartford, Iowa

RELIGION
Baptist

FAMILY
Wife, Barbara Grassley; five children

EDUCATION
U. of Northern Iowa, B.A. 1955, M.A. 1956; U. of
Iowa, attended 1957-58

CAREER
Farmer

POLITICAL HIGHLIGHTS
Republican nominee for Iowa House, 1956; Iowa
House, 1959-75; U.S. House, 1975-81

ELECTION RESULTS

1998 GENERAL

Charles E. Grassley (R)	648,480	68.4%
David Osterberg (D)	289,049	30.5%

1998 PRIMARY

Charles E. Grassley (R)	unopposed

PREVIOUS WINNING PERCENTAGES
1992 (70%); 1986 (66%); 1980 (54%); 1978 House
Election (75%); 1976 House Election (57%);
1974 House Election (51%)

Some in Congress may have a smoother delivery, and some may make more sophisticated arguments, but few can match Grassley's persistence.

The Iowa lawmaker may project an aw-shucks image, but underneath he has the tenacity of a bulldog. Once he sinks his teeth into an issue — whether it is stemming procurement waste at the Pentagon, improving medical care for disabled children or protecting farmers in any number of ways — he will not let go. He is the person "for whom the word 'dogged' was invented," the Des Moines Register wrote in 1999. "Maybe my style is a lack of style," Grassley told the Capitol Hill newspaper, Roll Call. But Democrat Joseph R. Biden Jr. of Delaware counsels observers not to be fooled: "Chuck Grassley is a hell of a lot smarter than you think he is," Biden told Roll Call.

As he began his 21st year as a senator, Grassley's persistence paid off. He became the chairman of the Finance Committee, a position from which he should be able to guarantee at least some legislative action on the many trade, health and tax issues that are paramount to his farm-state constituents. Wielding the gavel at Finance (after 16 years of service on the panel) allows him also to oversee broader issues such as shoring up Social Security and Medicare and reauthorizing the 1996 law that revamped federal welfare programs.

The biggest challenge for Chairman Grassley could be dealing with his own party leaders, who will be trying to manage with the slimmest possible margin of control in the Senate.

Grassley is much more open than many top Senate Republicans to seeking the support of Democrats — and liberal ones at that — in an effort to get things done. He teamed with Edward M. Kennedy, D-Mass., in the 106th Congress to push a proposal to give parents Medicaid assistance for their disabled children. He also joined with fellow Finance Committee member Bob Graham, D-Fla., to sponsor a bill that would have taken a number of steps to make pensions more portable and increase the incentives for small businesses to offer retirement programs.

With his farm ties, Grassley's most frequent partners have been from other rural states and include Max Baucus of Montana, now the top Democrat on Finance. With Baucus, Grassley has pressured the administration to open more foreign markets to food grown or processed in the United States and to increase support for hospitals in remote areas.

Grassley is the Senate's only working farmer, a distinction in which he takes great pride. Such devotion to the land is revered in Iowa, where Grassley's share of the vote has not dipped below 66 percent since 1980, when he first won his seat with 54 percent. He served in the House for three terms before that.

When, as a teenager, he was quizzed about his future plans, Grassley told a high school instructor that he would run for a seat in the Iowa House of Representatives when he was legally able to do so at age 21. He was not far off. He first ran when he was 22 and earned a seat three years later.

The son of thrifty Waterloo-area farmers, Grassley was not consumed with political ambitions alone. Upon graduation from the University of Northern Iowa, he did graduate work at two Iowa universities, working the night shift at a factory — where he was a union member — to make ends meet. A few years later, he and his wife, Barbara, took over his family's grain and livestock operation.

Though his schedule is less blistering than it was in his younger years,

Grassley still returns to work the farm on weekends and when the Senate is in recess. He views himself as one of the few farmer-statesmen left in a country founded by them and is not one to put on airs or attempt to spin. "I'm just a farmer from Butler County," he once said. "What you see is what you get."

While he has a consistently conservative voting record, Grassley is not always a friend of business. He does not mind defending the Davids of Iowa against corporate Goliaths.

In a heated floor speech in 2000, Grassley charged that the meatpacking industry had secretly scuttled his efforts to fund an agricultural grant program that would have helped upstart partnerships build pork-processing plants. The American Meat Institute denied it had lobbied against Grassley's proposal. Grassley lambasted the group, saying, "While some may believe the truth is no longer relevant in Washington, that attitude will be given no quarter in dealings with me."

Grassley has expressed alarm at the rate of mergers in the meat-processing industry, and he has pushed the Agriculture Department to take a more aggressive role in investigating anti-competitive practices. He also has teamed with Iowa's other senator, Democrat Tom Harkin, to spur more airline competition in the state. At their behest, the 2000 law reauthorizing the Federal Aviation Administration contained language opening two slots at Washington's crowded Ronald Reagan National Airport to a carrier that would offer nonstop service to Des Moines.

During his career, Grassley has served on a wide range of committees, and in the 107th he holds seats on Judiciary, Budget and Joint Taxation in addition to Finance. But to make room for a junior GOP senator, he was compelled to relinquish the seat he had held on Agriculture since 1991. He also has left the Special Committee on Aging, which he chaired in the 105th and 106th. The panel has no legislative jurisdiction, but it gave Grassley a forum for discussing nursing home abuse, Medicare fraud and other issues pertinent to Iowa's rapidly aging population.

Perhaps Grassley's biggest legislative effort in the past three Congresses came out of his role as chairman of a Judiciary subcommittee, where he pressed for an overhaul of personal bankruptcy laws. Despite some heavy lifting by the industries involved and Grassley's persistent attempts at compromise, each of his bills ended up dying.

Grassley's most active role on Finance has come in the area of international trade. He chaired the Trade Subcommittee beginning in 1995 and pushed hard for bills to further open trade. He traveled to the 1999 World Trade Organization meeting in Seattle and was sorely disappointed when, after days of violent protests, the fledgling trade body was left without a clear agenda.

When Iowa cannot go to the world, Grassley is happy to bring the world to Iowa. Every other year since 1986, about 50 foreign officials have taken part in Grassley's "Ambassador's Tour," spending five days in his home state, visiting with farmers and business people, and staying in local residents' homes.

With his new post as Finance chairman, Grassley's presence on the national scene will grow, with attention likely to be focused on his penchant for homing in on government waste. In the 1980s, he was the senator who ferreted out outrageous purchases at the Pentagon, such as a $7,600 coffee maker. He also worked on overhauling the IRS, trimming the federal judiciary and cleaning up the Congress itself, both by making sure it is not exempted from the laws it passes and by trying to get senators to make public any "holds" they placed to block legislation. With scandal-prone agencies such as the IRS and the Health Care Financing Administration under the Finance Committee's jurisdiction, Grassley will have plenty of opportunities to expose government waste.

KEY VOTES

2000

Yes Overhaul bankruptcy law and increase minimum wage

Yes Limit fiscal 2001 discretionary spending to $600.3 billion

Yes Override veto on nuclear waste disposal at Yucca Mountain site in Nevada

No Oppose effort to terminate Kosovo mission

No Include gender, sexual orientation and disability in federal hate crime protections

Yes Approve GOP plan to restrict use of genetic information by health insurers

Yes Kill amendment delaying implementation of an anti-missile defense system

Yes Cut taxes for married couples

Yes Grant China permanent normal trade status

1999

Yes Remove President Clinton from office for obstruction of justice

Yes Kill amendment authorizing state grants to hire teachers and reduce class size

No Require criminal background checks for purchases at gun shows

Yes Approve GOP proposal to increase rights of patients in managed-care health plans

No Block effort to allow farm and medicine exports to Cuba

No Allow study of tougher automobile fuel efficiency standards

No Ratify nuclear weapons testing treaty

No Prohibit national political parties from collecting "soft money" donations

Yes Remove barriers among banking, securities and insurance companies

INTEREST GROUPS

	AFL-CIO	ADA	CCUS	ACU
2000	0%	0%	100%	96%
1999	0%	0%	94%	92%
1998	0%	5%	83%	80%
1997	0%	5%	100%	80%
1996	0%	15%	92%	90%
1995	0%	5%	100%	91%
1994	0%	15%	90%	92%
1993	0%	20%	91%	88%
1992	17%	30%	90%	74%
1991	17%	15%	60%	81%

CQ VOTE STUDIES

	PARTY UNITY		PRESIDENTIAL SUPPORT	
	Support	Oppose	Support	Oppose
2000	94%	6%	42%	58%
1999	90%	10%	33%	67%
1998	86%	14%	39%	61%
1997	91%	9%	60%	40%
1996	92%	8%	32%	68%
1995	92%	8%	26%	74%
1994	87%	13%	34%	66%
1993	91%	9%	25%	75%
1992	81%	19%	70%	30%
1991	83%	17%	75%	25%

Sen. Tom Harkin (D)

CAPITOL OFFICE
224-3254; fax 224-9369; 731 Hart Bldg. 20510

INTERNET
e-mail: tom_harkin@harkin.senate.gov
web: harkin.senate.gov

COMMITTEES
Agriculture, Nutrition & Forestry - ranking member
Appropriations
Health, Education, Labor & Pensions
Small Business

HOMETOWN
Cumming

BORN
Nov. 19, 1939, Cumming, Iowa

RELIGION
Roman Catholic

FAMILY
Wife, Ruth Harkin; two children

EDUCATION
Iowa State U., B.S. 1962; Catholic U., J.D. 1972

MILITARY SERVICE
Navy, 1962-67; Naval Reserve, 1968-74

CAREER
Lawyer; congressional aide

POLITICAL HIGHLIGHTS
Democratic nominee for U.S. House, 1972; U.S.
House, 1975-85; sought Democratic nomination for
president, 1992

ELECTION RESULTS

1996 GENERAL
Tom Harkin (D)	634,166	51.8%
Jim Lightfoot (R)	571,807	46.7%

1996 PRIMARY
Tom Harkin (D)	unopposed

PREVIOUS WINNING PERCENTAGES
1990 (54%); 1984 (56%); 1982 House Election (59%);
1980 House Election (60%); 1978 House Election
(59%); 1976 House Election (65%); 1974 House
Election (51%)

Elected 1984; 3rd term

Harkin may be a consistently liberal, populist voice in the Senate, but he knows when it is time to put the partisan rhetoric aside to get things done. Every year, Harkin, the top Democrat on the Labor, Health and Human Services, and Education Appropriations Subcommittee, joins forces with the panel's chairman, Republican Arlen Specter of Pennsylvania, to craft the subcommittee's annual spending bill. Harkin's goal: to get funds for the social programs he cherishes.

That is why he often sits out the annual Democratic attacks on GOP spending priorities for education and health care. In 2000, Harkin went so far as to criticize President Clinton for issuing a veto threat against the subcommittee version of the bill two days after the panel approved it. He said Clinton should have "at least waited until the ink was dry." To keep up an image of solidarity, Harkin even appeared with Specter at a press conference a couple months later as the chairman released a revised version of the bill supported only by Republicans. Harkin then went to work behind the scenes to get what he, and Clinton, had wanted all along.

In the end, no Senate Democrat questions Harkin's loyalty. He fights for the same causes — smaller class sizes, repairs for aging schools and more money for job training programs — and will not sign off on bills that ignore Democratic priorities. That is one reason the final version of the Labor-HHS spending bill in 2000 included $1.3 billion for emergency school repairs, a cause he had championed.

Take Harkin out of the Labor-HHS appropriations arena and you get a different man. The populist speeches bashing big business come out — the kind of talk that defines Harkin's public image and shaped his short-lived 1992 run for the presidency. He caters to longtime constituencies, such as labor and agriculture, and has been an outspoken liberal voice on education, welfare and foreign policy matters.

Intense and seemingly hyperactive, Harkin channels his energy into multiple fronts. In the 106th Congress, his legislative causes included funding to repair the nation's oldest schools, authority for the Food and Drug Administration to regulate tobacco products, and grants to help states prevent medical errors. He collaborated with Specter on the medical errors legislation, and the two fought together for huge funding increases for biomedical research. Their hope is to double the budget for the National Institutes of Health over a five-year period.

Harkin got right to work at the start of the 107th Congress. He reintroduced the tobacco regulation bill, proposed a measure to expand a tax credit that helps families pay for child care, and signed on to a Democratic bill to ban the use of genetic information in employment and health insurance coverage decisions. He also has teamed up with Specter on new issues: The two lawmakers have proposed a commission to recommend changes to the voting procedures that attracted so much attention in the 2000 presidential election.

Harkin has a reputation for being tough on staffers and sometimes argumentative with other lawmakers, but by all accounts, those qualities make him more effective in the appropriations process, not less.

It is a personal story, however, that inspired Harkin's most notable success. He was the sponsor of the 1990 Americans with Disabilities Act, which extends broad civil rights protections to an estimated 54 million Americans with mental and physical disabilities. Harkin has said his work on the legislation was inspired by his deaf brother, Frank. When the Senate passed the measure in 1990, Harkin gave part of his floor speech in sign language in Frank's honor — a gesture he repeated in 2000 when he commemorated the law's anniversary. "Many times he told me, 'Gosh, I wish I'd had this when I started out,'" Harkin said in an interview. (Frank Harkin died in June 2000, shortly before the 10th anniversary of the law's signing.)

In 2000, Harkin cosponsored a bill with Republicans Charles E. Grassley of Iowa and James M. Jeffords of Vermont and Democrat Edward M. Kennedy of Massachusetts to allow the parents of children with special health care needs to buy Medicaid coverage. He also has been a successful activist for increased funding for breast cancer research; two of his sisters died of breast cancer.

Farm policy is another subject that ignites his passion; he has been the top Democrat on the Agriculture Committee since 1997. Harkin was a vocal opponent of a sweeping overhaul of farm law in 1996, known as the "Freedom to Farm" act, which replaced farm subsidies with a seven-year schedule of fixed federal payments. By setting lower fixed payments in the law's later years even if market prices dropped, Harkin said during the Senate debate, the farm legislation "has it exactly backward." Lately, he has been hammering at the payments for another reason: He says they have been skewed toward corporate farms at the expense of family farms.

When Congress passed its third farm assistance package in as many years in early 2000 — increasing the annual payments, which are to be phased out — Harkin noted the irony. "Every year we keep doing the same thing over and over, and we expect some different result," he said, "and we do not get a different result."

Harkin has spent much time defending organized labor. After the Republicans took control of Congress in 1995, he made generous use of the filibuster to block what he considered to be anti-labor proposals, which were backed by the GOP. In the 105th Congress, he stalled, for a time, a bill to increase the number of visas for skilled foreign workers, a measure opposed by labor unions fearful of job losses.

The Iowan was also a central figure in a labor-related debate at the end of 1996. He and Kennedy brought the Senate to a standstill as they fought unsuccessfully to kill legislation that they said would make it more difficult for employees of Federal Express Corp. to unionize.

The son of a coal miner, Harkin grew up in a small, crowded house in the town of Cumming. His mother died when he was 10. After graduation from college, Harkin worked for a while as an aide to Democratic Rep. Neal Smith, then as a Legal Aid lawyer in Ames.

Harkin first ran for Congress in 1972 against entrenched GOP incumbent William Scherle and attracted publicity with his gimmick of "work days," toiling alongside farmers, teachers and welfare caseworkers. He lost narrowly and immediately geared up for another run against Scherle in 1974, building a stronger organization and raising more money. Harkin won by a slim margin and quickly secured his hold on the seat, capturing about 60 percent of the vote in his four House re-elections.

The next campaigns were tougher. In his 1984 run for the Senate, Harkin faced a tight race against GOP Sen. Roger W. Jepsen; he took 56 percent of the vote. In 1990, Harkin was considered highly vulnerable, and GOP Rep. Tom Tauke pecked away at him on a variety of issues, accusing him of abusing congressional mailing privileges and voting for excessive spending. None of the attacks truly took hold, and Harkin eventually won by 9 percentage points. In 1996, he became the first Democrat in Iowa history to win a third Senate term, defeating GOP Rep. Jim Ross Lightfoot by 5 percentage points. Republicans are expected to mount another strong challenge in 2002, with GOP Rep. Greg Ganske announcing his candidacy early in 2001.

KEY VOTES

2000

No Overhaul bankruptcy law and increase minimum wage
No Limit fiscal 2001 discretionary spending to $600.3 billion
No Override veto on nuclear waste disposal at Yucca Mountain site in Nevada
Yes Oppose effort to terminate Kosovo mission
Yes Include gender, sexual orientation and disability in federal hate crime protections
No Approve GOP plan to restrict use of genetic information by health insurers
No Kill amendment delaying implementation of an anti-missile defense system
No Cut taxes for married couples
Yes Grant China permanent normal trade status

1999

No Remove President Clinton from office for obstruction of justice
No Kill amendment authorizing state grants to hire teachers and reduce class size
Yes Require criminal background checks for purchases at gun shows
No Approve GOP proposal to increase rights of patients in managed-care health plans
No Block effort to allow farm and medicine exports to Cuba
Yes Allow study of tougher automobile fuel efficiency standards
Yes Ratify nuclear weapons testing treaty
Yes Prohibit national political parties from collecting "soft money" donations
No Remove barriers among banking, securities and insurance companies

INTEREST GROUPS

	AFL-CIO	ADA	CCUS	ACU
2000	75%	95%	57%	4%
1999	89%	100%	47%	4%
1998	100%	95%	50%	5%
1997	71%	85%	70%	12%
1996	86%	80%	38%	10%
1995	92%	95%	44%	9%
1994	88%	100%	30%	0%
1993	73%	90%	27%	0%
1992	91%	85%	17%	0%
1991	90%	100%	14%	0%

CQ VOTE STUDIES

	PARTY UNITY		PRESIDENTIAL SUPPORT	
	Support	Oppose	Support	Oppose
2000	97%	3%	92%	8%
1999	97%	3%	91%	9%
1998	98%	2%	88%	12%
1997	92%	8%	87%	13%
1996	91%	9%	85%	15%
1995	91%	9%	90%	10%
1994	97%	3%	92%	8%
1993	93%	7%	93%	7%
1992	95%	5%	23%	77%
1991	96%	4%	23%	77%

Rep. Jim Leach (R)

CAPITOL OFFICE
225-6576; fax 226-1278; 2186 Rayburn Bldg. 20515

INTERNET
e-mail: talk2jim@mail.house.gov
web: www.house.gov/leach

COMMITTEES
Financial Services
International Relations
(East Asia & the Pacific - chairman)

HOMETOWN
Davenport

BORN
Oct. 15, 1942, Davenport, Iowa

RELIGION
Episcopalian

FAMILY
Wife, Elisabeth Ann "Deba" Leach; two children

EDUCATION
Princeton U., B.A. 1964; Johns Hopkins U., M.A.
1966; London School of Economics, attended
1966-68

CAREER
Propane gas company executive; foreign service
officer; congressional aide

POLITICAL HIGHLIGHTS
Republican nominee for U.S. House, 1974

ELECTION RESULTS

2000 GENERAL

Jim Leach (R)	164,972	61.8%
Bob Simpson (D)	96,283	36.1%
Russ Madden (LIBERT)	5,564	2.1%

2000 PRIMARY

Jim Leach (R)	unopposed

1998 GENERAL

Jim Leach (R)	106,419	56.5%
Bob Rush (D)	79,529	42.3%

PREVIOUS WINNING PERCENTAGES
1996 (53%); 1994 (60%); 1992 (68%); 1990 (100%);
1988 (61%); 1986 (66%); 1984 (67%); 1982 (59%);
1980 (64%); 1978 (64%); 1976 (52%)

Elected 1976; 13th term

Leach was a principal architect of landmark legislation in the 106th Congress overhauling the financial services industry. The law's enactment was notoriously complicated until the end — the affected industries squabbled as they vied for competitive advantage, the Federal Reserve and the Treasury fought over regulatory power — yet Leach managed to succeed where many others had failed in decades of previous attempts.

Yet, in the 107th Congress, he wields no full committee gavel and has no official leadership role. The snub is emblematic of Leach's situation after a quarter-century in the House. He has rarely shied away from bucking the Republican leadership when he disagrees with its course, and his striving for bipartisanship has sometimes come at the expense of the GOP agenda. In the 106th, he voted with most Democrats and against a majority of Republicans 29 percent of the time; only seven others in the House GOP had lower party-unity scores. He also backed President Clinton's position 41 percent of the time, 14th among House Republicans.

Furthermore, his erudite manner makes Leach a bit of an oddity in the House. He shuns the party circuit, makes comparatively few floor statements and does not seek media publicity. One of the Capitol's gentler souls, he treats friend and foe in the same measured, polite way and approaches issues with much introspection. In his six years chairing the Banking Committee — renamed Financial Services in 2001 — Leach went out of his way to be fair in dealing with Democrats on his panel, even when that occasionally put his legislative wishes in jeopardy.

At age 31, he resigned from the Foreign Service to protest President Nixon's "Saturday night massacre" firing of Archibald Cox, the Watergate special prosecutor. In the House, Leach joined nine other Republicans in January 1997 in casting their votes for Speaker for people other than Newt Gingrich, the GOP incumbent whose conduct was then the subject of a House ethics committee investigation. Leach voted for retired House Minority Leader Robert H. Michel of Illinois. (Two of the other dissidents voted for Leach.)

Leach has broken with the Republican leadership on domestic policy on numerous occasions. He has favored minimum wage hikes they opposed, voted to retain a ban on semiautomatic assault-style weapons that they wanted to repeal, opposed their bill to terminate the federal tax code and opposed their school voucher programs.

Though he split his vote on the two articles of impeachment against President Clinton adopted by the House in 1998 — voting for the perjury charge but against the obstruction of justice charge — Leach played a lead role in an earlier GOP attack on Clinton. In the 103rd, when Democrats controlled the House, Leach was the ranking Republican on the Banking Committee and the party's chief Whitewater inquisitor. And in the 104th, Leach chaired a series of hearings into that failed land deal involving the Clintons and the owner of a now-defunct Arkansas thrift. "Whitewater is about the arrogance of power, conflicts of interest that are self-evidently unseemly," he said.

Leach's knowledge of economic theory, developed at Princeton, Johns Hopkins and the London School of Economics, was reflected in his careful stewardship of the financial services overhaul. His committee meetings were drawn-out, repetitive affairs because of his refusal to cut off Democrats, but his accommodating style yielded a bill with strong bipartisan support. The measure repealed New Deal-era barriers among banks, securities firms and insurance concerns, allowing them to be consolidated into conglomerates that might be more competitive globally.

GOP term limits for chairmen required Leach to hand over the committee gavel in 2001. He had hoped to take the chairmanship of the International Relations Committee, where he was second in GOP seniority, but the post went to Henry J. Hyde of Illinois, who was No. 3 in seniority but was bitter at being forced by term limits to step down as Judiciary Committee chairman. In the 107th, Leach's top assignment will be to chair the East Asia and the Pacific Subcommittee.

The outcome did not surprise Leach. "I am not, to put it mildly, a confidant of the Texas leadership," he told The Des Moines Register late in 2000, referring to Majority Leader Dick Armey and Majority Whip Tom DeLay. Leach later said he regretted the remarks, and as an alternative rationale for being passed over, he cited his views on a number of important foreign affairs issues — he backs international family planning efforts and the work of international financial institutions, for example — as out of step with the majority of his party.

Leach's moderate views and his background might have made him a viable candidate for a top State or Treasury post in the Bush administration, but any chances for an appointment were hurt by the Democratic nature of his district. (Al Gore carried the 1st District by 10 percentage points over George W. Bush in 2000, and Clinton handily carried it twice.)

Leach says he remains enthusiastic about his work in Congress. "I don't view chairmanships as the be-all and end-all," he says. "I view them as instrumentalities that can be useful."

Leach was a star wrestler at Davenport High School, where he graduated in 1960, and at Princeton, where he graduated cum laude in 1964. He also played football in high school and rugby in college.

His first job in Congress was as an aide to Rep. Donald H. Rumsfeld, R-Ill., now secretary of defense. Working for the Arms Control and Disarmament Agency, he played a high-level role in negotiating several treaties, including the Biological and Toxic Weapons Convention of 1972.

Leach lost his first bid for the House, against Democratic incumbent Edward Mezvinsky in 1974. He won a rematch in 1976 and was easily re-elected until 1996, when Democratic former state Sen. Bob Rush — charging that Leach had become more partisan and less moderate with the GOP takeover of the House — held the Republican to a 7-point margin of victory.

In 2000, Leach romped to a 26-point win over Democrat Bob Simpson, a state party official and advocate for the disabled.

KEY VOTES

2000

Yes Raise hourly minimum wage by $1 over two years
Yes Halt funding for U.S. mission in Kosovo unless European nations pay more
Yes Provide Medicare benefits to military retirees and their dependents
Yes Grant China permanent normal trade status
Yes Phase out estate, gift and trust taxes
No Prohibit implementation of president's national monument designations
Yes Approve GOP plan to provide prescription drug coverage for Medicare beneficiaries
Yes Increase help for poor nations indebted to international financial institutions

1999

No Impose steel import quotas
No Kill proposal to take aviation trust funds off budget
No Require background checks on buyers only at gun shows with 10 or more vendors
Yes Remove barriers among banking, securities and insurance companies
No Authorize state grants to hire teachers and reduce class size
Yes Overhaul campaign finance law; ban "soft money" and restrict advocacy advertising
Yes Approve bipartisan plan to increase rights of patients in managed-care health plans

INTEREST GROUPS

	AFL-CIO	ADA	CCUS	ACU
2000	20%	30%	80%	58%
1999	22%	55%	76%	48%
1998	44%	45%	89%	32%
1997	50%	45%	100%	60%

CQ VOTE STUDIES

	PARTY UNITY		PRESIDENTIAL SUPPORT	
	Support	Oppose	Support	Oppose
2000	73%	27%	45%	55%
1999	70%	30%	38%	62%
1998	63%	37%	53%	47%
1997	72%	28%	48%	52%

IOWA 1

East – Cedar Rapids; Davenport; Iowa City

One of Iowa's two urban districts, the 1st contains half of the state's six biggest cities: Cedar Rapids and Davenport, which grew up around heavy industry, and Iowa City, home to the University of Iowa and a growing number of high-tech companies.

Long a center for grain processing, Cedar Rapids has weathered hard economic times of late with help from telecommunication equipment firms. Davenport and neighboring Bettendorf are old, industrial, Mississippi River cities whose economies suffered badly during the 1980s but are recovering by capitalizing on tourists drawn to riverboat gambling.

The rest of the district is predominantly rural; its economy relies on exporting agricultural products, including corn, tomatoes, soybeans and pork.

The presence of three urban centers gives the 1st a somewhat

Democratic tilt. In the 1992, '96 and 2000 presidential elections, the district gave the edge to the Democratic candidate. With the influence of a predominantly liberal university, Iowa City and the surrounding area remains a Democratic bastion. But Republican Rep. Leach has held onto the district by mixing fiscal conservatism with moderate social views. Locally, the district sends mostly moderate Democrats to the state legislature.

MAJOR INDUSTRY
Electronics, telecommunications, health care, grain processing

CITIES
Cedar Rapids, 115,777; Davenport, 98,256; Iowa City, 61,298; Bettendorf, 31,552

UNUSUAL FEATURES
U. of Iowa Hospital and Clinics, the largest teaching hospital in the world; Ronald Reagan had his first radio announcing job in Davenport; Besides Paris, France, Cedar Rapids is the only other city in the world that has its government buildings on an island in the center of the city.

Rep. Jim Nussle (R)

Elected 1990; 6th term

In a career filled with more than its share of ups and downs, Nussle began the 107th Congress on a high: He was elected chairman of the Budget Committee, besting three other contenders, including two who had more seniority on the panel.

Nussle's campaign for the Budget chairmanship was just the latest twist in a decade-long career that has seen him aggressively challenge the Democratic leaders who ran Congress when he first arrived, and then, several years later, turn against his own leadership when he and Speaker Newt Gingrich had a falling out.

In between, there was a period when Nussle was a confidant of Gingrich and at the forefront in planning the details of the transition from Democratic to Republican power after the 1994 elections. More recently, he has been back in the good graces of the GOP hierarchy.

Nussle has even feuded with his home state's largest newspaper, the Des Moines Register. And while at times he has lobbed insults at Democratic members, he has also worked in a bipartisan fashion. In fact, Nussle has played a significant role on issues such as the budget process, tax cuts, rural health care and agriculture policy due to his seats on two important committees — Ways and Means and Budget.

He was one of the "Gang of Seven" in the 102nd Congress — a group of Republican freshmen who agitated for changes in the way the Democratic-run House operated. In 1991, he made a speech on the House floor with a paper bag over his head to decry the secrecy surrounding a scandal involving overdrawn accounts at the private bank for House members. The moment — telecast by C-SPAN and reproduced by the national media — seemed to symbolize Congress' public image problems and Nussle's outspoken reform efforts. Nussle told The Wall Street Journal in 1998, "The bag I wore on the House floor is six feet from my desk and ready for action."

As an advocate of institutional reform, after the 1994 elections Nussle became the point man for incoming Speaker Gingrich's plan to remake the House, which included cutting committee staffs and eliminating such institutional traditions as ice deliveries to members' offices. Time magazine named him one of the top 50 rising political leaders in the United States. But once the 104th Congress got under way, Nussle faded from view, becoming just one of many foot soldiers in the Republican "revolution."

Nussle, who was vice chairman of the National Republican Congressional Committee in the 104th Congress, had been rumored to be a contender to head the committee in the 105th, but the job went to John Linder, Gingrich's neighbor in Georgia. A few months later, Nussle lost a contest against another Gingrich-backed candidate —Washington's Jennifer Dunn — for the House Republican Conference vice chairmanship. He had framed his run as a referendum on the party's leadership.

Nussle's bid overlapped with the news that about two dozen rank-and-file Republican lawmakers had plotted to oust Gingrich from his post as Speaker. Nussle was not involved in the unsuccessful plot, and as Gingrich moved to shore up his support, Nussle found himself back in the Speaker's inner circle as part of Gingrich's "Kitchen Cabinet" in the final months of his tenure.

Nussle and Speaker J. Dennis Hastert seem to get along. (The two occasionally refer to each other as "cousin" — Hastert's mother's maiden name is Nussle.)

CAPITOL OFFICE
225-2911; fax 225-9129; 303 Cannon Bldg. 20515

INTERNET
e-mail: nussleia@mail.house.gov
web: www.house.gov/nussle

COMMITTEES
Budget - chairman
Ways & Means

HOMETOWN
Manchester

BORN
June 27, 1960, Des Moines, Iowa

RELIGION
Lutheran

FAMILY
Divorced; two children

EDUCATION
Luther College, B.A. 1983; Drake U., J.D. 1985

CAREER
Lawyer

POLITICAL HIGHLIGHTS
Delaware County attorney, 1986-90

ELECTION RESULTS

2000 GENERAL

Jim Nussle (R)	139,906	55.4%
Donna L. Smith (D)	110,327	43.7%

2000 PRIMARY

Jim Nussle (R)	unopposed

1998 GENERAL

Jim Nussle (R)	104,613	55.2%
Rob Tully (D)	83,405	44.0%

PREVIOUS WINNING PERCENTAGES
1996 (53%); 1994 (56%); 1992 (50%); 1990 (50%)

In the 106th Congress, Nussle headed a bipartisan task force to recommend changes in the federal budget process. The group, co-chaired by Democrat Benjamin L. Cardin of Maryland, proposed that the annual budget resolution be a binding measure sent to the president for his signature or veto, instead of a non-binding document stating Congress' views on taxing and spending. "It makes the opening play of the budget process negotiation rather than confrontation," Nussle explained. The proposal went down to a crushing defeat, but the Iowa lawmaker nevertheless won plaudits for his willingness to work with Cardin and other Democrats.

He normally is a ready vote for his party on social and environmental issues, but as a proponent of reduced government spending across the board, Nussle has broken with the leadership at times to oppose big-ticket military items. He regularly pushes for offsetting spending cuts to cover the cost of emergency spending, even including flood relief aid for Iowa.

Like many of his colleagues, however, Nussle has learned to fight for items of clear interest to his constituents. As a representative of farm country, Nussle favors increasing agricultural exports and has worked to expand domestic markets for ethanol, an alternate fuel source made from corn. Iowa leads the nation in hog farming, and in recent years, Nussle has been particularly concerned about financial difficulties plaguing hog farmers.

Nussle's eldest child has Down's syndrome, and he is a strong supporter of federal special education programs and the Special Olympics. He proudly notes that his daughter won a bronze medal in a soccer skills competition.

Nussle was interested in government and politics from an early age; he was a 30-year-old lawyer with just one term as a county attorney under his belt when he saw the chance to run for the House. Nussle entered the 2nd District race in 1990 when GOP Rep. Tom Tauke (for whom he once interned) decided to run for the Senate.

Nussle won a tense, 1,642-vote victory, and two years later, had to run against another incumbent — Democrat Dave Nagle — when reapportionment cost Iowa a House seat and the redrawn district lines threw the two together in the new 2nd District. Nussle again squeaked by, winning by 2,966 votes.

Nussle's 1994 rematch with Nagle was spirited, but Nussle finally managed to separate himself somewhat from his Democratic foe, winning by 13 percentage points. Since then, Democrats have continued to mount serious challenges every two years, with Nussle winning by margins of about 10 percentage points.

KEY VOTES

2000

No Raise hourly minimum wage by $1 over two years
Yes Halt funding for U.S. mission in Kosovo unless European nations pay more
Yes Provide Medicare benefits to military retirees and their dependents
Yes Grant China permanent normal trade status
Yes Phase out estate, gift and trust taxes
Yes Prohibit implementation of president's national monument designations
Yes Approve GOP plan to provide prescription drug coverage for Medicare beneficiaries
Yes Increase help for poor nations indebted to international financial institutions

1999

Yes Impose steel import quotas
No Kill proposal to take aviation trust funds off budget
Yes Require background checks on buyers only at gun shows with 10 or more vendors
Yes Remove barriers among banking, securities and insurance companies
No Authorize state grants to hire teachers and reduce class size
No Overhaul campaign finance law; ban "soft money" and restrict advocacy advertising
No Approve bipartisan plan to increase rights of patients in managed-care health plans

INTEREST GROUPS

	AFL-CIO	ADA	CCUS	ACU
2000	10%	15%	95%	84%
1999	11%	20%	100%	80%
1998	10%	10%	100%	84%
1997	0%	10%	100%	92%

CQ VOTE STUDIES

	PARTY UNITY		PRESIDENTIAL SUPPORT	
	Support	Oppose	Support	Oppose
2000	93%	7%	25%	75%
1999	87%	13%	22%	78%
1998	89%	11%	27%	73%
1997	94%	6%	28%	72%

IOWA 2

Northeast — Waterloo; Dubuque

The 2nd is dominated by two mid-size industrial cities, Waterloo and Dubuque, and a university town, Cedar Falls. But nearly two-thirds of the district's voters come from these towns' rural surroundings.

Waterloo grew up around the farm-implement and meat-packing industries. While hogs still are slaughtered here in the world's largest pork plant, the economy diversified in the 1990s to include finance and insurance. Neighboring Cedar Falls relies on the influence of the U. of Northern Iowa.

Dubuque, built against the bluffs facing the Mississippi River, is Iowa's oldest city. Its economic base shifted in the 1990s from manufacturing and meat-packing to service, including insurance, finance and telecommunications. City leaders also have been working to lure tourists with riverboat gambling.

Democrats outnumber Republicans in the 2nd, but voters have tended to demonstrate their independence at the polls in recent years. Black Hawk County, with Cedar Falls and Waterloo, has a strong Democratic base from its labor and academic communities. Dubuque is predominantly Democratic by registration, but this heavily Catholic city has a strong conservative outlook on social issues. Voters in Dubuque and the district's rural counties have helped elect a Republican congressman.

MAJOR INDUSTRY
Farm machinery, meat packing, health care, agriculture

CITIES
Waterloo, 62,800; Dubuque, 56,742; Cedar Falls, 34,542; Mason City, 28,690

UNUSUAL FEATURES
Dyersville, home to the baseball field featured in the movie "Field of Dreams;" World's largest pork plant in Waterloo; Mason City inspired native son Meredith Willson to compose the song, "The Music Man."

Rep. Leonard L. Boswell (D)

Elected 1996; 3rd term

CAPITOL OFFICE
225-3806; fax 225-5608
1039 Longworth Bldg. 20515

INTERNET
e-mail: rep.boswell.ia03@mail.house.gov
web: www.house.gov/boswell

COMMITTEES
Agriculture
Transportation & Infrastructure
Select Intelligence

HOMETOWN
Davis City

BORN
Jan. 10, 1934, Harrison County, Mo.

RELIGION
Reorganized Church of Jesus Christ of Latter Day Saints

FAMILY
Wife, Dody Boswell; three children

EDUCATION
Graceland College, B.A. 1969

MILITARY SERVICE
Army, 1956-76

CAREER
Farmer

POLITICAL HIGHLIGHTS
Iowa Senate, 1985-97 (president, 1992-97); sought Democratic nomination for U.S. House, 1986; Iowa Democratic Central Committee, 1992-96; Democratic nominee for lieutenant governor, 1994

ELECTION RESULTS

2000 GENERAL

Leonard L. Boswell (D)	156,327	62.8%
Jay B. Marcus (R)	83,810	33.7%
Sue Atkinson (INDC)	5,563	2.2%

2000 PRIMARY

Leonard L. Boswell (D)	unopposed

1998 GENERAL

Leonard L. Boswell (D)	107,947	56.9%
Larry McKibben (R)	78,063	41.1%
Charles Connolly (REF)	2,180	1.1%

PREVIOUS WINNING PERCENTAGES
1996 (49%)

Boswell's voting record puts him squarely in the ranks of moderate-to-conservative Democrats, and in the 107th Congress he joined the "Blue Dogs," a coalition of like-minded House lawmakers. But Boswell intends to remain open to any and all alliances that may develop on the range of issues on his agenda, which helps explain why he had eschewed an affiliation with the Blue Dogs during his first two terms in the House.

Indicative of his appeal to a wide range of legislative coalitions is the fact that both the AFL-CIO and the U.S. Chamber of Commerce, in their ratings of members, give Boswell good marks — about 75 percent in each case.

His varied background enables him to offer expertise in a number of fields, including military affairs, agriculture and the appropriations process. Boswell is well into his third career — legislator — after spending 20 years in the military and another two decades as a farmer.

His legislative career began in 1985 in the Iowa state Senate, where he chaired the Appropriations Committee and eventually became president. Before that, he had served as an Army pilot, including two tours as a helicopter pilot in Vietnam. He earned two Distinguished Flying Crosses and two Bronze Stars. Upon his retirement from the military, Boswell returned home to become a farmer.

That breadth and depth of experience set him apart from his colleagues when he arrived in Washington as a freshman in 1997, the oldest first-term member. Boswell's age, easygoing and steady demeanor, and military and legislative credentials brought him early respect from his younger colleagues and from Democratic leaders as well, who put him on the party panel that makes committee assignments.

He seldom speaks on the House floor, and when he does it is usually on a matter that has emerged from one of his committees. The Des Moines Register describes his conversational style as giving "quick, short responses ... followed by more detailed explanations." And U.S. News & World Report once described him as "a farmer who looks like Archie Bunker, only more rumpled."

In his role as a steadying influence and wise counsel to younger colleagues, Boswell has found much in common with his neighbor on the ground floor of the Longworth House Office Building — Republican Sam Johnson of Texas, who also is older than many of his colleagues and has an extensive military background, and who offers quiet and dependable leadership to conservative Republicans. Early in the 107th, Boswell rebuffed overtures from the GOP to switch parties.

Boswell joins with the GOP about a third of the time. He voted for several Republican spending and tax proposals in his first term and has strayed from the Democratic Party to support bills that would ban flag desecration, eliminate the "marriage penalty" and outlaw a procedure its opponents call "partial birth" abortion. In 1999, however, Boswell took issue with the GOP's proposed $792 billion tax cut, and he voted against a number of appropriations bills that were drafted on the premise of the big tax cut.

Boswell's legislative agenda is focused on the matters before the committees on which he serves — Agriculture (an essential assignment for someone representing such a farm-oriented district) and Transportation.

In the 106th Congress, Boswell was a tireless advocate of ethanol, an alternative fuel source made from corn. He championed research efforts in Iowa to develop alternative fuels from other crops as well. He backs liberalization of foreign trade — including the normalization of trade relations with China, which his farm constituents favored as a means of opening that huge market to farm exports. That stance was a key factor in winning a re-election endorsement from the Chamber of Commerce.

On the Transportation panel, Boswell works to improve passenger aviation service to Des Moines, which like many medium-size cities must deal with limited service options and high air fares. He was a conferee in 2000 on an aviation bill that authorized funds for airport construction projects, including funding for more than a dozen airports in the 3rd District.

Illegal production of methamphetamines is a serious problem in his district, as it is in many agricultural areas where key ingredients are readily available. He urged the Clinton administration to provide emergency funds to help clean up meth labs and track down dealers of the drug.

Boswell grew up in southern Iowa. He was drafted into the Army in 1956 and spent two decades in the service before returning to his childhood home in Decatur County to become a farmer.

His involvement in community affairs spurred his neighbors to urge him to enter politics, first as a member of the local farmers' co-op and grain elevator board and then in the state Senate. He continued to farm during his tenure in the legislature, and he continues to lend a hand while in Congress, doing chores around his 475-acre cattle spread during congressional breaks.

As chairman of the Iowa Senate Appropriations Committee, Boswell played a key role in the state's move from a deficit to a budget surplus, giving him valuable experience years later as Congress did the same.

In 1996, Boswell gave in to the urging of supporters and entered the race for the 3rd District seat just two days before the filing deadline. That was after the district's GOP incumbent, Jim Ross Lightfoot, announced he would run for the Senate rather than seek re-election.

Capitalizing on his name recognition from years in the legislature and previous bids for Congress (he lost the Democratic primary in 1986) and for lieutenant governor (in 1994), he won the primary easily. In the general election against Republican Mike Mahaffey, Boswell received the endorsement of the Iowa Farm Bureau, unusual for a Democrat. Boswell eked out a thin margin of victory, winning 49 percent to 48 percent.

He had barely arrived in Congress in 1997 when talk back home turned to whether Boswell should run for governor in 1998. Although some observers said the well-liked and middle-of-the-road lawmaker represented the Democrats' best chance to win the governorship, Boswell decided to stay in Congress to continue the work he had just begun.

KEY VOTES

2000

Yes Raise hourly minimum wage by $1 over two years

Yes Halt funding for U.S. mission in Kosovo unless European nations pay more

Yes Provide Medicare benefits to military retirees and their dependents

Yes Grant China permanent normal trade status

Yes Phase out estate, gift and trust taxes

No Prohibit implementation of president's national monument designations

No Approve GOP plan to provide prescription drug coverage for Medicare beneficiaries

Yes Increase help for poor nations indebted to international financial institutions

1999

Yes Impose steel import quotas

No Kill proposal to take aviation trust funds off budget

No Require background checks on buyers only at gun shows with 10 or more vendors

Yes Remove barriers among banking, securities and insurance companies

Yes Authorize state grants to hire teachers and reduce class size

Yes Overhaul campaign finance law; ban "soft money" and restrict advocacy advertising

Yes Approve bipartisan plan to increase rights of patients in managed-care health plans

INTEREST GROUPS

	AFL-CIO	ADA	CCUS	ACU
2000	70%	55%	65%	41%
1999	88%	70%	50%	32%
1998	70%	65%	83%	36%
1997	75%	65%	70%	28%

CQ VOTE STUDIES

	PARTY UNITY		PRESIDENTIAL SUPPORT	
	Support	Oppose	Support	Oppose
2000	69%	31%	60%	40%
1999	69%	31%	67%	33%
1998	65%	35%	65%	35%
1997	72%	28%	73%	27%

IOWA 3
South Central — Ames; Burlington

Taking in 27 counties, nearly 14,000 square miles and six media markets, the 3rd gives a fair picture of Iowa. It includes relatively well-off urban and suburban areas, as well as rural counties, industrial cities and scattered towns with hopes for economic development.

Ames is the district's largest city and is home to Iowa State U., about 30 miles north of Des Moines (in the neighboring 4th District). About one-fourth of the district's residents live in the counties near Des Moines.

The 3rd's other population center is along the Mississippi River in the district's southeast, in Des Moines and Lee counties. Unions still have influence in the area, but an economy once centered on manufacturing is headed toward tourism and riverboat gambling. The rest of the district's residents are spread across Iowa's agriculture-based southern tier.

While the 3rd has leaned Democratic historically, it has turned into a swing district in recent years. Democrats do well in blue-collar communities along the Mississippi River, as well as in Ames and surrounding Story County, although the latter is willing to split tickets. The GOP is strong in the district's vast, rural southern tier. The district supported Bill Clinton in the 1992 and '96 presidential contests, but gave a 1 percent edge to George W. Bush in 2000.

MAJOR INDUSTRY
Manufacturing, textiles, tourism

CITIES
Ames, 48,777; Burlington, 26,585; Marshalltown, 25,941; Ottumwa, 24,259

UNUSUAL FEATURES
F.L. Maytag built the first mechanized washer in 1909 in Newton; Wyatt Earp, the famous Western lawman and gunfighter, grew up in Pella.

Rep. Greg Ganske (R)

CAPITOL OFFICE
225-4426; fax 225-3193
1108 Longworth Bldg. 20515

INTERNET
e-mail: rep.ganske@mail.house.gov
web: www.house.gov/ganske

COMMITTEES
Energy & Commerce

HOMETOWN
Des Moines

BORN
March 31, 1949, New Hampton, Iowa

RELIGION
Roman Catholic

FAMILY
Wife, Corrine Ganske; three children

EDUCATION
U. of Iowa, B.A. 1972, M.D. 1976

MILITARY SERVICE
Army Reserve, 1986-2001

CAREER
Plastic surgeon

POLITICAL HIGHLIGHTS
No previous office

ELECTION RESULTS

2000 GENERAL

Greg Ganske (R)	169,267	61.4%
Michael L. Huston (D)	101,112	36.7%
Steve Zimmerman (LIBERT)	4,552	1.7%

2000 PRIMARY

Greg Ganske (R)	unopposed

1998 GENERAL

Greg Ganske (R)	129,942	65.2%
Jon Dvorak (D)	67,550	33.9%

PREVIOUS WINNING PERCENTAGES
1996 (52%); 1994 (53%)

Elected 1994; 4th term

As a first-year medical resident in the emergency room of Denver General Hospital, Ganske had to inform a family that their 15-year-old son had just died from a bullet to the head. That experience — along with hundreds of other similarly stressful events during nearly two decades as a doctor — helped shape the maverick legislating style and moderate political philosophy that Ganske now exhibits in Congress. "It's more than sufficient experience to handle the stress of political life," he says. "It helps put it into perspective."

Ganske, a soft-spoken physician specializing in plastic and reconstructive surgery, credits the teen's violent death with leading him to support gun control legislation — just one of the many issues on which Ganske has split from the GOP leadership. He is not afraid of a fight and has earned a reputation as a rebel. On several high-profile issues, he has stood apart from most of his colleagues in the conservative GOP Class of 1994.

Throughout the 106th Congress, for example, Ganske (GAN-skee) bucked the leadership on overhauling the country's managed-care system. In 1999, Ganske, a member of the Commerce Committee, joined Democrat John D. Dingell of Michigan and fellow Republican Charlie Norwood of Georgia, a former dentist, to draft a bill that would allow patients to sue their health plans if they were harmed by denial of treatment. House GOP leaders argued that such liability would raise the cost of health insurance.

In the 105th, concerns about inadequate Medicare financing led Ganske to cast one of only 26 GOP votes against the 1997 balanced-budget agreement between the Clinton White House and congressional Republicans. Also, when Republicans pushed a ban on federal funding of needle-exchange programs, Ganske was one of only 11 in his party to oppose the ban. Citing medical evidence that such programs could help slow the spread of AIDS among illegal drug users, Ganske said the ban "may be popular ... but it is not enlightened public policy."

Ganske's hands-on knowledge of Medicare issues — he treated about 1,000 Medicare beneficiaries — led Speaker Newt Gingrich in 1997 to select him as one of his four appointees to a 17-member commission to study long-term changes in Medicare. The appointment came with a requirement that Ganske promise not to vote for a tax increase to rescue the program. But the leadership never asked for a pledge not to join with Democrats to promote a patients' rights bill. In late July 1998, Ganske stood at a news conference with President Clinton and House Democratic Leader Richard A. Gephardt of Missouri to do just that. Ganske resigned from the Medicare panel the same week.

The Iowa lawmaker shut down his private practice when he arrived on Capitol Hill, but he continues to volunteer as a surgeon for charity groups. He has traveled to Peru, Mexico, Guatemala, Armenia and Vietnam to perform surgery on needy children and adults.

Ganske says he opposes abortion rights, but he supports federal family planning programs and occasionally finds himself on the same side as abortion rights supporters.

Ganske's knack for upsetting the leadership began early in his congressional career. Months after being elected in 1994, Ganske joined with Republican Rep. Pat Roberts of Kansas to oppose a GOP effort to give a $500-per-child tax credit to families earning up to $200,000 annually. Roberts and Ganske thought it was extravagant and fought to lower the income cap to $95,000 a year. They were called into a meeting with Gingrich and Majority Leader Dick Armey to discuss the issue. "Armey was literally jumping up and down screaming how could we do this. I thought to myself, 'I've seen chiefs of staffs of surgery angrier than this,' " Ganske said. "I reached over and opened a sack of peanuts and ate my peanuts and watched Dick. Whereupon Newt winks at me."

Ganske also attributes his competitive nature to his wrestling days in high school and college. "It allows the smaller person to compete," said Ganske, who is 5-feet, 7-inches tall.

In the 104th, Ganske voted for most elements of the House GOP's "Contract With America," including a balanced-budget constitutional amendment, welfare overhaul, congressional term limits and easing of federal regulations. Despite his concerns in 1995 about how GOP leaders wanted to target tax reductions, he eventually supported the tax cut bill.

Ganske served in the student senate in college and was a political science major before switching to pre-med in his junior year. He said he decided to re-enter the political world after seeing dozens of teenage mothers bring their children to his medical practice. "There were 13- and 14-year-old mothers, with no fathers around," Ganske said. "The welfare system was one of the main reasons I ran for Congress."

In 1996, he joined the majority of his party in supporting a sweeping overhaul that ended the 61-year-old federal guarantee of cash welfare to low-income mothers and children and replaced the system with block grants giving states almost complete control over eligibility and benefits. The new law required recipients to work within two years of receiving benefits and placed a five-year cap on benefits.

Ganske represents a traditionally Democratic district where he risks electoral trouble if he tilts too far to the right. He first won election to Congress in 1994 by defeating 18-term Democratic Rep. Neal Smith. To underscore his theme that Smith had stayed too long in Congress, Ganske stumped for votes with an antique DeSoto dubbed the Nealmobile. It was a model from 1958, the year Smith was first elected. Ganske spent nearly $1.2 million to Smith's more than $1 million, and he defeated Smith by 7 percentage points.

In 1996, Ganske faced former Des Moines TV weather reporter Connie McBurney. Ganske missed weeks of campaigning while recovering from encephalitis, which he contracted on a medical mission to Peru, but won re-election by 5 percentage points. Since then, he has breezed to re-election.

Early in 2001, Ganske launched a campaign for the Senate seat held by Democrat Tom Harkin, who is up for re-election in 2002.

KEY VOTES

2000
Yes Raise hourly minimum wage by $1 over two years
Yes Halt funding for U.S. mission in Kosovo unless European nations pay more
Yes Provide Medicare benefits to military retirees and their dependents
Yes Grant China permanent normal trade status
Yes Phase out estate, gift and trust taxes
No Prohibit implementation of president's national monument designations
No Approve GOP plan to provide prescription drug coverage for Medicare beneficiaries
Yes Increase help for poor nations indebted to international financial institutions

1999
Yes Impose steel import quotas
No Kill proposal to take aviation trust funds off budget
No Require background checks on buyers only at gun shows with 10 or more vendors
Yes Remove barriers among banking, securities and insurance companies
No Authorize state grants to hire teachers and reduce class size
Yes Overhaul campaign finance law; ban "soft money" and restrict advocacy advertising
Yes Approve bipartisan plan to increase rights of patients in managed-care health plans

INTEREST GROUPS

	AFL-CIO	ADA	CCUS	ACU
2000	30%	15%	80%	73%
1999	63%	35%	45%	44%
1998	20%	5%	81%	64%
1997	13%	30%	70%	76%

CQ VOTE STUDIES

	PARTY UNITY		PRESIDENTIAL SUPPORT	
	Support	Oppose	Support	Oppose
2000	77%	23%	39%	61%
1999	72%	28%	39%	61%
1998	76%	24%	34%	66%
1997	88%	12%	32%	68%

IOWA 4

Southwest – Des Moines; Council Bluffs

Although the 4th sprawls from central Iowa west to the Missouri River, it's anchored in Des Moines, the region's commercial, financial and governmental center. Nearly 60 percent of the 4th's voters live in Des Moines and the surrounding towns in Polk County. The capital has flourished since the 1980s, partly because of its diverse, white-collar employment base and its partial independence from agriculture.

The district's second largest city, Council Bluffs, is located on the western border of the state. Built against bluffs, the city was a bustling crossroads for three westward trails in the early 1800s, and five railroads later met there. Today, many workers cross the Missouri River to work in Omaha businesses that have been lured to Nebraska by lower tax rates.

Harrison and Shelby counties, in the northwest corner of the district, have benefited from a relatively prosperous farming industry. To the south and east, land is rough and relatively dry, more suitable for grazing than farming.

Due almost entirely to the influence of Des Moines and surrounding Polk County, the 4th leans Democratic. Polk has been more reliably Democratic than many parts of the nation, supporting Democratic presidential candidates in the 1980s and '90s. However, in 2000, President Bush narrowly won the district by 2 percentage points. Council Bluffs is a GOP stronghold, but its influence is minimized because of its size relative to Des Moines. The rest of the district generally votes Republican in local and national elections.

MAJOR INDUSTRY
Insurance, meat packing, health care

CITIES
Des Moines, 190,958; Council Bluffs, 57,365; West Des Moines, 44,636; Urbandale, 28,100

UNUSUAL FEATURES
Largest Danish settlement in the United States in Elk Horn; Film star John Wayne born in Winterset.

Rep. Tom Latham (R)

Elected 1994; 4th term

Latham jokes that he lives in the suburbs — his north-central Iowa home is a mile outside a town that has fewer than 200 people. He and his brothers own a seed company and three farms. The land — and what can be grown on it — shape a large part of Latham's life and his work in Congress.

Latham grew up on a farm doing the usual chores and helping in his father's seed business. He stayed close to home in his first 20 years — attending Wartburg College about 50 miles east of his hometown of Alexander, and then going to Iowa State University, about 60 miles south in Ames.

Two out-of-state journeys played key roles in his life. When he was turning 22, he headed to Colorado, spurred in large measure by his father's admonition that his children had to do something on their own before they could take their place in the family business. In Colorado, Latham worked as a bank teller, a bookkeeper, and finally, as an insurance agent. The insurance firm transferred him to Des Moines, Iowa; two years later, Latham moved back to Alexander to take his place at Latham Seed Co. and began dabbling in politics.

The second trip came in 1990, when Latham was a member of a farm delegation that visited Russia and Poland. What he saw there affected him profoundly and focused his interest in politics. Latham says he was appalled at the primitive agricultural methods and machinery, and he blames much of that on the totalitarian governments that he says not only mismanaged the economy, but "destroyed individual freedom and dignity." He remembers one Polish farmer who tearfully told him that farmers hadn't owned their land since the Nazis seized it in World War II.

Latham decided that a government that so profoundly intruded in individuals' lives and controlled what they did with their land was something to be feared and resisted. He can date his resolve to run for public office to that realization. A decade later, one of his top priorities in Congress is to resist and roll back federal regulations.

Since his arrival in Congress, Latham has had committee assignments that play to his background and the interests of his 5th District, home to some of the nation's most productive farmland. As a freshman in the 104th Congress, he got a seat on the Agriculture Committee, which was then wrestling with fashioning a major overhaul of farm programs to bring them more in line with free-market principles. Latham was a strong backer of the "Freedom to Farm" bill, enacted in 1996, which he said would give farmers greater planting flexibility.

In the 105th Congress, he moved to the Appropriations panel, where he has posts on the Agriculture, Energy and Water Development, and Commerce, Justice, State subcommittees.

In the 106th, Latham won approval of an amendment adding $110 million for federally guaranteed farm loans to an emergency spending bill. He also sought funding for a new livestock health research facility in Ames and fought to lift U.S. embargoes on the export of food and medicine to countries, such as Cuba, that are under U.S. economic sanctions. "Embargoes have always destroyed the farmers and never really punished the people they were aimed at," he argues.

On the Commerce, Justice, State Subcommittee, Latham's priority has been the war against illegal drugs. He is proud of his efforts to win funding for a methamphetamine center in Sioux City, which provides training in the region for local law enforcement officials who must cope with the epidem-

CAPITOL OFFICE
225-5476; fax 225-3301; 440 Cannon Bldg. 20515

INTERNET
e-mail: latham.ia05@mail.house.gov
web: www.house.gov/latham

COMMITTEES
Appropriations

HOMETOWN
Alexander

BORN
July 14, 1948, Hampton, Iowa

RELIGION
Lutheran

FAMILY
Wife, Kathy Latham; three children

EDUCATION
Wartburg College, attended 1967; Iowa State U., attended 1967-70

CAREER
Seed company executive; insurance agency marketing representative; insurance agent; bank teller

POLITICAL HIGHLIGHTS
Franklin County Republican chairman, 1984-91

ELECTION RESULTS

2000 GENERAL
Tom Latham (R)	159,367	68.8%
Mike Palecek (D)	67,593	29.2%
Ben L. Olson (LIBERT)	2,875	1.2%

2000 PRIMARY
Tom Latham (R)	22,516	90.1%
Thomas D. Hall (R)	2,458	9.8%

1998 GENERAL
Tom Latham (R)	unopposed

PREVIOUS WINNING PERCENTAGES
1996 (65%); 1994 (61%)

ic of meth labs in rural areas. In 2000, he won House approval of a bill to make convicted drug dealers subject to civil suits seeking damages.

Responding to the plummeting prices hog farmers were getting in 1998 and 1999, Latham won approval of a new system of mandatory reporting of livestock prices nationally, aimed at helping producers match supply and demand. "I've got neighbors — third- or fourth-generation pork producers — who have lost virtually all their equity in the last four months," Latham reported in early 1999. The situation has since improved.

Harking back to his trip to Eastern Europe, Latham also fights environmental regulations and property rights infringements that he says do economic harm to farmers. In 1997, he joined a bipartisan coalition of members to give landowners greater recourse to challenge state and local zoning regulations that prevent them from developing their property.

Latham likes to recount that he and his brothers had to spend $12,000 in 1993 to measure dust microns on their small soybean farm outside Alexander to comply with the Clean Air Act. "It is exactly why any small-business person today is much more concerned about someone from the government walking in and saying they want to help than [about] any competitor down the street."

Latham takes a staunchly conservative position on most issues. He supported all the major items of the House GOP's "Contract With America," favoring a balanced-budget constitutional amendment, overhaul of the welfare system, and tax and spending cuts. His congressional website once provided a link to a "debt clock" that displayed "The Public Debt to the Penny." But in 2000, he proudly announced that, because the "fiscal responsibility and restraint by the Republican Congress" had produced a budget surplus, the clock, located in New York's Times Square, had been turned off.

Defense spending has never been very popular in Iowa because of the combined influence of the state's isolationists and doves, and Latham has sometimes been willing to swing the budget-cutting ax at the Pentagon.

Latham was chairman of the Franklin County Republican Party for seven years, but he resisted entreaties to run for the legislature: The seasonal nature of his seed business conflicted with state legislative sessions. In 1994, however, when GOP Rep. Fred Grandy gave up the 5th District seat to seek the governorship, Latham decided to run. Before Grandy's eight-year tenure, a Democrat had held the seat, and the party's 1994 nominee, Sheila McGuire, waged an aggressive campaign. But Latham was a good fit for the district in a strong GOP year, and he breezed to election. The district is now regarded as the most Republican in the state, and Latham has won re-election easily.

KEY VOTES

2000

No Raise hourly minimum wage by $1 over two years

Yes Halt funding for U.S. mission in Kosovo unless European nations pay more

Yes Provide Medicare benefits to military retirees and their dependents

Yes Grant China permanent normal trade status

Yes Phase out estate, gift and trust taxes

Yes Prohibit implementation of president's national monument designations

Yes Approve GOP plan to provide prescription drug coverage for Medicare beneficiaries

Yes Increase help for poor nations indebted to international financial institutions

1999

No Impose steel import quotas

Yes Kill proposal to take aviation trust funds off budget

Yes Require background checks on buyers only at gun shows with 10 or more vendors

Yes Remove barriers among banking, securities and insurance companies

No Authorize state grants to hire teachers and reduce class size

No Overhaul campaign finance law; ban "soft money" and restrict advocacy advertising

No Approve bipartisan plan to increase rights of patients in managed-care health plans

INTEREST GROUPS

	AFL-CIO	ADA	CCUS	ACU
2000	10%	5%	95%	88%
1999	0%	5%	96%	88%
1998	0%	0%	100%	92%
1997	0%	10%	100%	76%

CQ VOTE STUDIES

	PARTY UNITY		PRESIDENTIAL SUPPORT	
	Support	Oppose	Support	Oppose
2000	94%	6%	26%	74%
1999	91%	9%	23%	77%
1998	94%	6%	24%	76%
1997	93%	7%	28%	72%

IOWA 5

Northwest – Sioux City; Fort Dodge

The 5th takes in nearly 18,000 square miles of fertile soil and gently undulating hills. The bountiful land has allowed the region to remain more like the Iowa of old than any other part of the state.

Sioux City, the district's largest city, accounts for about 15 percent of the 5th's population. Located on the western border of the state, it has developed into a service center for a region that includes part of South Dakota and Nebraska. Some Sioux City businesses have moved across the Missouri River to take advantage of more favorable tax laws in bordering states, but Woodbury County has sprouted numerous bedroom communities to house their employees.

The 5th's only other urban center is Fort Dodge, an industrial center that has relied on gypsum factories to support the area's economy for close to a century. The city also emerged as a leader in veterinary pharmaceuticals.

The 5th is the only Iowa district in which registered Republicans outnumber Democrats; to win statewide, GOP candidates need lopsided margins here. Sioux City has long leaned Republican. The surrounding rural towns are home to many independent farmers who tend to vote Republican in both local and national elections. The few Democratic voters are mostly Irish Catholics in Fort Dodge and surrounding Webster County.

MAJOR INDUSTRY
Meat packing, veterinary pharmaceuticals, agriculture

CITIES
Sioux City, 82,843; Fort Dodge, 25,593; Boone, 12,857

UNUSUAL FEATURES
Annual Donna Reed Festival held in the actress' hometown of Denison; Nation's second-largest county fair in Clay County; Fort Dodge called world's "Gypsum Mining Capital."

KANSAS

Gov. Bill Graves (R)

First elected: 1994
Length of term: 4 years
Term expires: 1/03
Salary: $91,700
Phone: (785) 296-3232
Hometown: Topeka
Born: Jan. 9, 1953; Salina, Kan.
Religion: Methodist
Family: Wife, Linda Graves; one child
Education: Kansas Wesleyan College, B.B.A. 1975; U. of Kansas, attended 1976-79
Career: Trucking company manager
Political highlights: Kan. secretary of state, 1987-95

Election results:
1998 GENERAL

Bill Graves (R)	544,882	73.4%
Tom Sawyer (D)	168,243	22.7%
Kirt Poovey (TAX)	21,710	2.9%

Lt. Gov. Gary Sherrer (R)

First elected: 1998; appointed July 18, 1996
Length of term: 4 years
Term expires: 1/03
Salary: $25,071 (also serves as Kansas' secretary of Commerce and Housing and receives a total salary of $106,646)
Phone: (785) 296-2214

STATE LEGISLATURE

Bicameral Legislature: Meets January-June
House: 125 members, 2-year terms
2001 breakdown: 79R, 46D; 84 men, 41 women
Salary: $76.44/day while in session or working; $85/day expenses; $5,400/year allowance
Phone: (785) 296-7633
Senate: 40 members, 4-year terms
2001 breakdown: 30R, 10D; 27 men, 13 women
Salary: $76.44/day while in session or working; $85/day expenses; $5,400/year allowance
Phone: (785) 296-7344

STATE TERM LIMITS

Governor: 2 terms
Senate: No
House: No

URBAN STATISTICS

CITY	POPULATION
Wichita	335,562
Overland Park	142,783
Kansas City	139,971
Topeka	124,529

REGISTERED VOTERS

Republican	45%
Democrat	28%
Unaffiliated	26%

POPULATION

2000 population	2,688,418
1990 population	2,477,574
Percent change	+8.5%
Rank among states	32
Median age	35
Born in state	61%
Foreign born	3%
Urban/rural	69%/31%
Crime rate	409/100,000
Poverty level	9.6%
Federal workers	26,060
Military	29,108

REAPPORTIONMENT

Kansas retained its four House seats in reapportionment. The state legislature will draw new district lines in 2002.

MISCELLANEOUS

Web: www.state.ks.us
Capital: Topeka
Land area: 81,823 sq. miles
Rank among states: 13
STATE ELECTION OFFICIAL
(785) 296-4561
DEMOCRATIC HEADQUARTERS
(785) 234-0425
REPUBLICAN HEADQUARTERS
(785) 234-3416

District Statistics

DIST.	2000 D	2000 R	GREEN	1996 D	1996 R	REF	1992 D	1992 R	I	WHT	BLK	ASIAN	HISP	HOUSEHOLD INCOME	OVER 65+	UNDER 18	COLLEGE EDUCATION
						VOTE FOR PRESIDENT											
1	28%	67%	3%	28%	62%	9%	28%	42%	29%	94%	1%	1%	5%	$23,433	17%	27%	15%
2	40	55	3	39	49	11	36.1	36.3	28	90	6	1	3	$24,903	14	26	18
3	42	53	4	42	50	6	38	37	25	87	9	2	3	$34,275	10	26	31
4	37	59	3	35	56	8	33	40	27	89	7	2	3	$28,308	14	27	20
STATE	37	58	3	36	54	9	34	39	27	90	6	1	4	$27,291	14	27	21

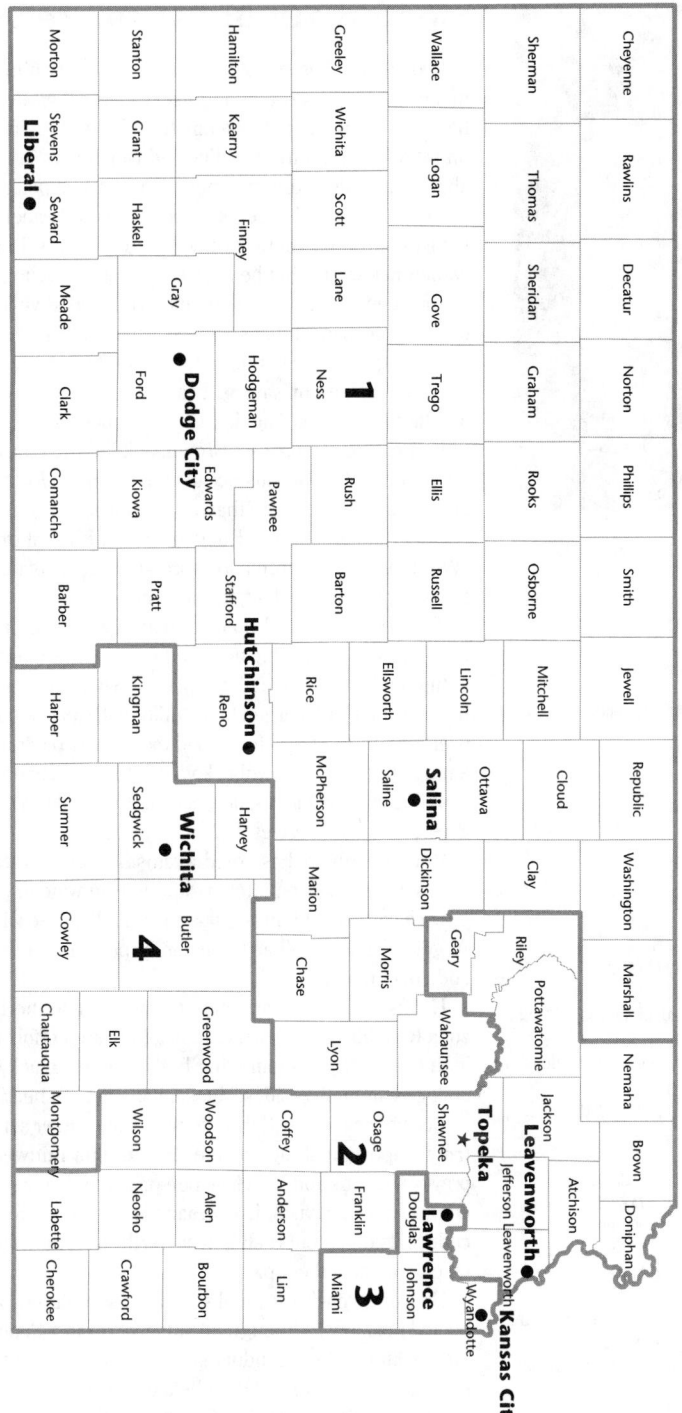

Sen. Sam Brownback (R)

CAPITOL OFFICE
224-6521; fax 228-1265; 303 Hart Bldg. 20510

INTERNET
e-mail: sam_brownback@brownback.senate.gov
web: brownback.senate.gov

COMMITTEES
Commerce, Science & Transportation
Foreign Relations
   (Near Eastern & South Asian Affairs - chairman)
Judiciary
   (Immigration - chairman)
Joint Economic

HOMETOWN
Topeka

BORN
Sept. 12, 1956, Garnett, Kan.

RELIGION
Methodist

FAMILY
Wife, Mary Brownback; five children

EDUCATION
Kansas State U., B.S. 1979; U. of Kansas, J.D. 1982

CAREER
Teacher; lawyer; White House fellow; broadcaster

POLITICAL HIGHLIGHTS
Kan. secretary of agriculture, 1986-93; U.S. House,
1995-96

ELECTION RESULTS

1998 GENERAL

Sam Brownback (R)	474,639	65.3%
Paul Feleciano Jr. (D)	229,718	31.6%
Thomas L. Oyler (LIBERT)	11,545	1.6%
Alvin Bauman (REF)	11,334	1.6%

1998 PRIMARY

Sam Brownback (R)	unopposed

PREVIOUS WINNING PERCENTAGES
1996 Special Election (54%); 1994 House Election
(66%)

Elected 1996; 1st full term

Brownback has quickly made a name for himself as a maverick lawmaker and a supporter of conservative religious causes. An affable but hard-driving man, he has an instinct for getting in the center of the action on issues ranging from Hollywood violence to international human rights abuses, usually taking the most conservative positions.

In contrast to his predecessor, Majority Leader Bob Dole, Brownback focuses more on moral principles than political pragmatism. Colleagues sometimes worry that he goes too far, as when he showed tapes of graphic movie scenes in 2000 to denounce Hollywood violence. But Brownback, a skillful politician who has built occasional alliances with Democrats, makes no apologies. "Parents used to feel buttressed by the popular culture — George Washington saying, 'I cannot tell a lie.' Now culture attacks the family," he told the Los Angeles Times in 2000.

In the 106th Congress, Brownback led the conservative charge against Hollywood, blaming violence in entertainment for many societal ills. "There are more social workers than serial murderers in America. There are more pastors than prostitutes. But you'd never know it from TV," he said in 1999. "When we watch more and more violence, profanity and sleaze, we eventually grow more violent, profane and coarse."

The senator scored political points when he urged the Federal Trade Commission to investigate whether the entertainment industry was marketing violent and sexually explicit movies and songs to young teenagers. In 2000, the FTC charged film studios with marketing R-rated movies to children under 17. With Hollywood executives pledging to change their marketing strategies, Brownback vowed to keep the pressure on. If the studios continue targeting teens, he warned, "they will invite further probing by Congress," the Los Angeles Times reported.

But Brownback has voted against limiting violent TV programming to hours when children likely would not be watching. "I think that starts us down a path of content regulation and I disagree with that," he told the Los Angeles Times. "What I constantly push is the industry setting its own code of conduct."

He also turned his attention to gambling in the 106th, teaming with Arizona Republican John McCain in a long-shot effort to ban gambling on college sports. "Sports gambling has become a black eye on too many of our colleges and universities," he said at a Senate hearing.

Brownback says a 1995 bout with skin cancer served to focus him on the truly important things in life. He attends midweek Bible readings and prayer sessions and has close personal and political connections to religious conservative activists. Brownback is a leading advocate of banning a procedure its opponents call "partial birth" abortion and a supporter of cutting taxes on married couples.

His concern with societal standards sometimes causes him to take unexpected positions. Although he voted with most Republicans to convict President Clinton of misconduct stemming from his affair with a White House intern, he urged his GOP colleagues to show Clinton respect during the 1999 impeachment trial and to attend the president's State of the Union address. "The country will forgive a lot, but not bad manners," he said.

On the Foreign Relations panel, Brownback in 1999 won approval of legislation giving the president the authority to lift sanctions against India and Pakistan. He also voted in 2000 to grant China permanent normal trade status. Grain exports to those countries are important to Midwestern farmers.

As chairman of the Near Eastern and South Asian Affairs Subcommittee, Brownback has been forced to deal with some of the world's intractable conflicts. In concert with Clinton administration officials, he met with Pakistani and Indian leaders to try to defuse tensions on the Asian subcontinent. He has also pressed for a tougher policy against Iraq's Saddam Hussein, saying in 1999, "I don't want to see Saddam outlast another U.S. president." One of his top priorities is to crack down on religious persecution in such countries as Sudan.

Brownback has taken aim at the growing international sex trade, which has often led to young girls being enticed across borders and forced into prostitution. Branding such sex trafficking "the new slavery," Brownback sponsored legislation in the 106th giving expanded legal protections to girls in such situations, stiffening penalties on those who entice someone into sexual slavery and directing the State Department to monitor sex trafficking.

The senator has adopted children from China and Guatemala. But in the 106th, he came under criticism from some adoption advocates for opposing Senate ratification of the Hague Convention on Intercountry Adoption, a treaty designed to impose standards on the often chaotic international adoption process. The treaty, Brownback contended, would create an unwieldy and costly adoption bureaucracy.

A critic of what he terms corporate welfare, Brownback will reach across the aisle if the goal is to reduce spending. Liberal Democrats Edward M. Kennedy and John Kerry of Massachusetts were among a group Brownback joined in 1997 to ask for a bipartisan panel to evaluate tax breaks and other federal largess to corporations.

One of Brownback's lowest moments in Congress came in 1997 during Senate investigations into Democratic National Committee fundraising practices. Describing a bonus pay scheme that Democrats had arranged with fundraiser John Huang, Brownback mimicked a Chinese accent and said: "No raise money, no get bonus." A moment later, he added that he meant "no slight by my statement" — but it was too late. He came under sharp criticism from Asian-American groups, as well as from Sen. Dianne Feinstein, D-Calif., who said: "The United States Senate is no place for racial stereotyping."

Brownback appears to have had politics in his blood since he was president of his eighth-grade class. He was also student body president at Kansas State University, a national officer of the Future Farmers of America, the Kansas secretary of agriculture for six years and a White House fellow in the administration of President George Bush.

He entered the race for Kansas' 2nd District in 1994 upon learning of the retirement of Democratic Rep. Jim Slattery. He easily defeated the state's two-term Democratic governor, John Carlin, whose lengthy public record and two divorces while in office gave Brownback plenty of targets.

When Dole announced in spring 1996 that he would resign his Senate seat to run for president, Brownback acted quickly — even though he was only part-way through his first term in the House. Republican Gov. Bill Graves appointed Lt. Gov. Sheila Frahm to fill the seat until a special election could be held, but Brownback challenged the more-moderate Frahm by reaching out aggressively to business groups and social conservatives. He took the primary by 13 percentage points and won a tough general-election campaign against stockbroker Jill Docking, part of a well-known Kansas political family, with 54 percent of the vote.

In 1998, Brownback easily won election to a full term, besting Democratic state Sen. Paul Feleciano Jr. Some local GOP officials have urged him to consider running for governor in 2002.

KEY VOTES

2000
No Overhaul bankruptcy law and increase minimum wage
Yes Limit fiscal 2001 discretionary spending to $600.3 billion
Yes Override veto on nuclear waste disposal at Yucca Mountain site in Nevada
No Oppose effort to terminate Kosovo mission
No Include gender, sexual orientation and disability in federal hate crime protections
Yes Approve GOP plan to restrict use of genetic information by health insurers
Yes Kill amendment delaying implementation of an anti-missile defense system
Yes Cut taxes for married couples
Yes Grant China permanent normal trade status

1999
Yes Remove President Clinton from office for obstruction of justice
Yes Kill amendment authorizing state grants to hire teachers and reduce class size
No Require criminal background checks for purchases at gun shows
Yes Approve GOP proposal to increase rights of patients in managed-care health plans
No Block effort to allow farm and medicine exports to Cuba
No Allow study of tougher automobile fuel efficiency standards
No Ratify nuclear weapons testing treaty
Yes Prohibit national political parties from collecting "soft money" donations
Yes Remove barriers among banking, securities and insurance companies

INTEREST GROUPS

	AFL-CIO	ADA	CCUS	ACU
2000	0%	0%	100%	100%
1999	0%	5%	94%	95%
1998	0%	0%	94%	92%
1997	0%	0%	100%	100%
House Service:				
1996	0%	5%	93%	100%
1995	8%	0%	100%	92%

CQ VOTE STUDIES

	PARTY UNITY		PRESIDENTIAL SUPPORT	
	Support	Oppose	Support	Oppose
2000	98%	2%	40%	60%
1999	95%	5%	31%	69%
1998	96%	4%	37%	63%
1997	96%	4%	56%	44%
House Service:				
1996	92%	8%	32%	68%
1995	96%	4%	22%	78%

Sen. Pat Roberts (R)

CAPITOL OFFICE
224-4774; fax 224-3514; 302 Hart Bldg. 20510

INTERNET
e-mail: pat_roberts@roberts.senate.gov
web: roberts.senate.gov

COMMITTEES
Agriculture, Nutrition & Forestry
 (Production & Price Competitiveness - chairman)
Armed Services
 (Emerging Threats & Capabilities - chairman)
Health, Education, Labor & Pensions
Select Ethics - chairman
Select Intelligence

HOMETOWN
Dodge City

BORN
April 20, 1936, Topeka, Kan.

RELIGION
Methodist

FAMILY
Wife, Franki Roberts; three children

EDUCATION
Kansas State U., B.A. 1958; Arizona State U.,
attended 1962-64

MILITARY SERVICE
Marine Corps, 1958-62

CAREER
Journalist; congressional aide

POLITICAL HIGHLIGHTS
U.S. House, 1981-97

ELECTION RESULTS

1996 GENERAL
Pat Roberts (R)	652,677	62.0%
Sally Thompson (D)	362,380	34.4%
Mark S. Marney (REF)	24,145	2.3%
Steven A. Rosile (LIBERT)	13,098	1.2%

1996 PRIMARY
Pat Roberts (R)	245,411	78.2%
Tom Little (R)	25,052	8.0%

PREVIOUS WINNING PERCENTAGES
1994 House Election (77%); 1992 House Election
(68%); 1990 House Election (63%); 1988 House
Election (100%); 1986 House Election (77%); 1984
House Election (76%); 1982 House Election (68%);
1980 House Election (62%)

Elected 1996; 1st term

Roberts is one of the Senate's most sharp-spoken lawmakers, but the former House Agriculture chairman is learning to tone down his sarcasm in the more buttoned-down atmosphere of the Senate. "I'm not near as bushy-tailed as I used to be," he said in 1999.

Still, the zingers are never far from the surface. In 2000, he dismissed anti-trade organizations as "the representatives of Ralph Nader, Ross Perot, Pat Buchanan and other various wackos," the Kansas City Star reported. And early in 2001, he said that asking the Health Care Financing Administration, which administers Medicare and Medicaid, for help is like "asking the Boston Strangler for a necklace."

Roberts typically follows traditional Midwestern Republican policies, favoring strong government support of farmers and increased international trade. In addition to his assignments on the Agriculture and Armed Services committees, he drew the difficult task in late 1999 of chairing the Select Ethics Committee, putting him in the uncomfortable position of sitting in judgment on his colleagues.

Although he is a reliable Republican vote on such issues as restricting abortion and cutting government regulations and taxes, he is less confrontational than some of the younger GOP lawmakers, such as fellow Kansan Sam Brownback. Instead, Roberts focuses on economic and national security issues, often building alliances with Democrats who have similar concerns.

Roberts is an outspoken advocate of free trade, and he worries that U.S. economic sanctions against other countries are hurting the farm economy. He pressed for legislation in the 106th Congress that would generally require a president to get congressional approval before imposing embargoes on food or medicine. "Food and medicine should not be used as a foreign policy weapon," he said. "While it is important to maintain pressure on totalitarian countries, we cannot turn our backs on the basic humanitarian needs of the citizens." In 2000, Roberts traveled with two other senators to Cuba to meet with President Fidel Castro and discuss lifting U.S. sanctions against that communist country.

Roberts helped lead efforts in 2000 to pass legislation granting China permanent normal trade status. Although opponents warned that China could emerge as a military threat to the United States, Roberts countered, according to the Topeka Capital-Journal, that "the more two nations trade and invest economically in each other, the less likely they are to engage in military conflict." Roberts also backed legislation lifting sanctions against Pakistan and India, saying it would open the way for millions of dollars of wheat, corn and soybean sales.

Much of the reason for Roberts' concern about sanctions can be traced to landmark farm legislation, known as the "Freedom to Farm" bill, that he crafted in the 104th as chairman of the House Agriculture Committee. The measure, which remains his best-known legislative achievement, replaced traditional farm subsidies with a seven-year system of fixed but declining federal payments to farmers, and it also gave farmers more leeway in their planting decisions. Rural lawmakers who supported it believed that farmers would be able to take advantage of strong overseas markets, especially in Asia, to offset lower federal payments.

By 2000, however, farmers were losing money because prices slumped worldwide. Roberts supported a series of emergency bills in the 105th and

106th that pumped billions of dollars into the ailing farm economy. Critics said the government bailouts were proof that the farm law was flawed, but Roberts blamed the Clinton administration and some in Congress for not doing enough to open overseas markets, pare back regulations, and strengthen crop insurance policies. "It's like 'Freedom to Farm' was the horse you wanted to ride in the Derby, but you hobbled him first — there's no jockey, no saddle and all the rest," he said.

Accordingly, Roberts pressed for legislation in the 106th to reduce the premiums that farmers pay for federally subsidized crop insurance. This would encourage farmers to buy higher levels of insurance and reduce their need for emergency assistance and other forms of federal aid, he said.

A member of the Armed Services Committee, Roberts chairs the Emerging Threats and Capabilities Subcommittee, which oversees security threats ranging from terrorism to illegal drugs. Working with Max Cleland, D-Ga., he urged policymakers to better define the nation's security priorities. "We tend to define members of Congress in certain groups, but on this question we're all over the lot," Roberts said. "We range from humanitarian interventionists to people who want America's involvement to end at the border. But our military is stressed, strained and hollow, and we need to focus our attention," The Associated Press quoted him as saying.

In the 105th, Roberts won passage of a measure requiring President Clinton to detail the objectives and costs of U.S. military missions in Eastern Europe. In 1999, he denounced the NATO bombing campaign in Yugoslavia as failing to deter Yugoslav President Slobodan Milosevic. "U.S. policy and our involvement in Kosovo is spinning out of control and endangering vital national security interests with repercussions for future generations," he said.

Roberts has supported efforts to increase the military's 20-year retirement benefits to encourage personnel to stay on the job longer. Congress cut military retirement benefits in 1986, and commanders are raising concerns that qualified service men and women will begin leaving for more lucrative opportunities. Roberts introduced a bill at the end of the 105th to repeal the 1986 cut and said the Pentagon should also study the best features of other retirement plans.

A former Marine captain and newspaper reporter and editor, Roberts earned legislative experience by working as a House aide for 12 years. When his boss, GOP Rep. Keith G. Sebelius, announced his retirement in 1980, Roberts was ready. He cruised to victory in the general election, capitalizing on Sebelius' popularity and referring to "our record" so frequently that he sounded like an incumbent.

As he became one of the most popular politicians in Kansas, Roberts was often likened to former Majority Leader Bob Dole, another state Republican with a caustic wit and conservative views. Roberts was widely expected to run for the Senate seat of retiring Republican Nancy Landon Kassebaum in 1996. But after months of raising money for a potential Senate bid, Roberts in 1995 stunned many observers by saying he wanted to focus instead on shepherding farm legislation through Congress. Two months later, he reversed course and declared that he would indeed seek Kassebaum's seat.

After easily defeating three little-known opponents in the GOP primary, Roberts faced Democratic state Treasurer Sally Thompson in the general election. Although his friends view Roberts as pleasantly irascible, the pressures of his House chairmanship in the 104th seemed to make him more testy, both in Washington and on the campaign trail. He had to publicly apologize after referring to Thompson during the campaign as a "bitch." Nevertheless, he rolled up a big victory in the heavily Republican state, taking 62 percent of the vote.

KEY VOTES

2000

Yes Overhaul bankruptcy law and increase minimum wage

Yes Limit fiscal 2001 discretionary spending to $600.3 billion

Yes Override veto on nuclear waste disposal at Yucca Mountain site in Nevada

No Oppose effort to terminate Kosovo mission

No Include gender, sexual orientation and disability in federal hate crime protections

Yes Approve GOP plan to restrict use of genetic information by health insurers

Yes Kill amendment delaying implementation of an anti-missile defense system

Yes Cut taxes for married couples

Yes Grant China permanent normal trade status

1999

Yes Remove President Clinton from office for obstruction of justice

Yes Kill amendment authorizing state grants to hire teachers and reduce class size

No Require criminal background checks for purchases at gun shows

Yes Approve GOP proposal to increase rights of patients in managed-care health plans

No Block effort to allow farm and medicine exports to Cuba

No Allow study of tougher automobile fuel efficiency standards

No Ratify nuclear weapons testing treaty

No Prohibit national political parties from collecting "soft money" donations

Yes Remove barriers among banking, securities and insurance companies

INTEREST GROUPS

	AFL-CIO	ADA	CCUS	ACU
2000	0%	0%	100%	92%
1999	0%	0%	94%	88%
1998	0%	0%	100%	84%
1997	0%	15%	90%	68%
House Service:				
1996	0%	5%	94%	95%
1995	0%	0%	96%	80%
1994	0%	0%	92%	100%
1993	0%	0%	100%	100%
1992	17%	10%	88%	88%
1991	0%	5%	90%	83%

CQ VOTE STUDIES

	PARTY UNITY		PRESIDENTIAL SUPPORT	
	Support	Oppose	Support	Oppose
2000	97%	3%	38%	62%
1999	94%	6%	29%	71%
1998	95%	5%	35%	65%
1997	90%	10%	59%	41%
House Service:				
1996	92%	8%	37%	63%
1995	96%	4%	19%	81%
1994	96%	4%	40%	60%
1993	94%	6%	34%	66%
1992	96%	4%	88%	12%
1991	93%	7%	83%	17%

Rep. Jerry Moran (R)

CAPITOL OFFICE
225-2715; fax 225-5124
1519 Longworth Bldg. 20515

INTERNET
e-mail: jerry.moran@mail.house.gov
web: www.house.gov/moranks01

COMMITTEES
Agriculture
Transportation & Infrastructure
Veterans' Affairs
(Health - chairman)

HOMETOWN
Hays

BORN
May 29, 1954, Great Bend, Kan.

RELIGION
Protestant

FAMILY
Wife, Robba Moran; two children

EDUCATION
U. of Kansas, B.S. 1976, J.D. 1982

CAREER
Lawyer; banker

POLITICAL HIGHLIGHTS
Kan. Senate, 1989-97 (vice president, 1993-95;
majority leader, 1995-97)

ELECTION RESULTS

2000 GENERAL

Jerry Moran (R)	214,328	89.3%
Jack W. Warner (LIBERT)	25,581	10.7%

2000 PRIMARY

Jerry Moran (R)	unopposed

1998 GENERAL

Jerry Moran (R)	152,775	80.7%
Jim Phillips (D)	36,618	19.3%

PREVIOUS WINNING PERCENTAGES
1996 (74%)

Elected 1996; 3rd term

Every summer Moran goes on a "listening tour" of the sprawling 1st District, holding town meetings in each of the 66 counties in the Big First, as the district is called. The tour, begun years ago by GOP Rep. Keith G. Sebelius, has been getting more far-flung, as the size of the district has grown, and the meetings much smaller, as population losses on the farms and small communities of western and central Kansas continue, unabated.

The factors that have led to the emptying of the rural Midwest are very much on the minds of Moran's constituents as he drives through his district, stopping to hear what they think at Daylight Doughnuts in Hugoton, the Beecher Bible and Rifle Church in Wabaunsee, and the Blue Bird Cafe in Bird City. During his 2000 tour, the main topics were low agriculture prices and high fuel prices, Moran reported. "It's very frustrating for Kansans to hear about the great economy while they struggle to make ends meet," he told The Topeka Capital-Journal earlier.

From his seat on the Agriculture Committee, Moran tries to help his constituents by pushing for more foreign markets for U.S. farm goods and working to strengthen the federal safety net to shelter farmers from the effects of droughts or plummeting wheat prices. "Ninety-eight percent of the mouths to feed are outside the United States, and many of them are hungry," Moran told the Topeka newspaper. "So if there is going to be profitability on the farm, in large part it's going to come about as the result of the United States getting aggressive about exports."

Moran concedes that Congress can do little about many of the factors that threaten farmers' solvency. "It's like you beat your head against a wall most every day, and sometimes you make a little difference, and sometimes you don't feel like you accomplished anything," he told the Capital-Journal in 1999.

Moran is one of the leaders of the bipartisan Rural Caucus, which was revitalized in 2000 after a period of dormancy to advance the causes of rural America, which many rural lawmakers believe has been slighted when it comes to federal dollars.

He also is active in the Rural Health Care Coalition, which has warned against congressional money-saving moves to cut Medicare reimbursements to health care providers, a step that could have dire consequences for rural hospitals. Moran assumed the chairmanship of the Veterans' Affairs Subcommittee on Health in the 107th Congress, and he is expected to work to improve health care access for veterans who live far from Department of Veterans Affairs facilities.

In 2000, he backed a measure to promote the use of communications technology in medicine. The "telemedicine" legislation called for Medicare reimbursement for care and consultation performed via interactive television hookups, so that patients could receive medical attention without having to travel to a doctor. Because modern communications technology is important in rural areas, Moran says that farmers were among the first groups to embrace computer technology. He wants to be certain that rural America is not left behind when it comes to access to high-speed Internet connections.

Moran also sits on the Transportation Committee, where he works to help Kansans stay connected via more traditional modes — highways, railroads and aviation.

In 2000, Moran was named to a 12-member commission created to make plans for a Washington, D.C., memorial to President Eisenhower, who grew up in Abeline, which is in the 1st District.

The Big First is geographically one of the nation's largest congressional districts, and representing the 1st involves a lot of time spent in and between small towns. In the 1980s, when Kansas had five House members, the district comprised 58 counties. In the 1990s reapportionment, Kansas lost one House seat, and the 1st was redrawn to include 66 counties. Over the past decade, the district has continued to lose population, and redistricting for the 2002 elections will undoubtedly add even more counties and more square miles to the 1st.

Moran grew up in this vast, rural area, where his father worked in the western Kansas oil fields and his mother was a secretary with the electric utility. As a high school student body officer, Moran was in charge of inviting the local congressman — Rep. Sebelius — to speak at a fundraising dinner. They kept in touch and several years later Moran went off to Washington for an internship with Sebelius. It was the summer of 1974, and Moran remembers being an eyewitness to history as the Judiciary Committee held impeachment hearings on President Nixon.

Moran graduated from the University of Kansas with a degree in economics, took a job as a small-town banker, and eventually got a law degree and opened his own practice. In 1988, Moran entered a long-shot race for state Senate against an 18-year incumbent, regarding it as an extension of his other civic involvements. He won by just a few hundred votes. He was unopposed for a second term in 1992.

Moran's state Senate service included a stint as chairman of the Judiciary Committee, and he became majority leader in 1995, demonstrating a knack for appealing to both wings of the Kansas GOP, which has been sharply split between conservatives and moderates.

Moran ran for Congress in 1996 when Republican Rep. Pat Roberts decided to seek the seat of GOP Sen. Nancy Landon Kassebaum, who was retiring. Moran quickly became the front-runner, portraying himself as a pragmatic conservative. In a district with a long Republican tradition — Bob Dole was its congressman during the 1960s — and with Dole topping the GOP ticket as its presidential nominee, Moran rolled to an easy victory, with 74 percent of the vote. That was his closest election. In 2000, the Democrats declined to field a candidate.

The 1st District seems to breed candidates for higher office — Dole and Roberts are examples — and Moran's name is frequently mentioned as a potential candidate for governor in 2002.

KEY VOTES

2000
No Raise hourly minimum wage by $1 over two years
Yes Halt funding for U.S. mission in Kosovo unless European nations pay more
Yes Provide Medicare benefits to military retirees and their dependents
Yes Grant China permanent normal trade status
Yes Phase out estate, gift and trust taxes
Yes Prohibit implementation of president's national monument designations
Yes Approve GOP plan to provide prescription drug coverage for Medicare beneficiaries
No Increase help for poor nations indebted to international financial institutions

1999
No Impose steel import quotas
No Kill proposal to take aviation trust funds off budget
No Require background checks on buyers only at gun shows with 10 or more vendors
No Remove barriers among banking, securities and insurance companies
No Authorize state grants to hire teachers and reduce class size
No Overhaul campaign finance law; ban "soft money" and restrict advocacy advertising
Yes Approve bipartisan plan to increase rights of patients in managed-care health plans

INTEREST GROUPS

	AFL-CIO	ADA	CCUS	ACU
2000	0%	0%	90%	92%
1999	33%	20%	88%	84%
1998	10%	10%	100%	92%
1997	25%	10%	90%	96%

CQ VOTE STUDIES

	PARTY UNITY		PRESIDENTIAL SUPPORT	
	Support	Oppose	Support	Oppose
2000	93%	7%	25%	75%
1999	86%	14%	18%	82%
1998	90%	10%	29%	71%
1997	95%	5%	27%	73%

KANSAS 1

Rural West – Salina; Hutchinson; Dodge City

Stretching across 66 counties, the fiscally conservative 1st covers most of rural Kansas. Starting in east central Kansas, where cattle graze in the nearly treeless prairie of Flint Hills, the 1st takes in farmland and ends at the western Kansas border. In land area, it covers two-thirds of Kansas and is bigger than most U.S. states (including 23 of the 26 states east of the Mississippi River).

The 1st's economy is wedded to agriculture, an industry that suffered from weather disasters in the 1980s and falling commodity prices in the '90s. More and more rural residents have packed their bags for the cities to escape the tough farming life.

The district's largest population center is in the 1st's eastern reaches. Salina (Saline County) is a traditional farm-market town, but has an industrial element – Raytheon has a factory here. In the eastern part of the 1st, the district's second largest city, Hutchinson, is dominated by farm- and food-related business and is also the site of the annual

Kansas State Fair. In the west, towns such as Garden City and Dodge City rely on meat-packing and tourism. Thriving beef-processing plants continue to draw Mexican and Asian immigrants.

Home to former Sen. Bob Dole, the district is comfortably Republican, although it did exhibit an independent streak in the 1992 presidential election, giving Ross Perot 29 percent of the vote. In the 2000 presidential contest the district overwhelmingly voted for President Bush – giving him a 38 point margin over Al Gore. The GOP also dominates local offices, except in Hutchinson and Hays, where Fort Hays State University helps to elect a few Democrats.

MAJOR INDUSTRY
Agriculture, manufacturing, oil and gas

CITIES
Salina, 44,077; Hutchinson, 39,561; Garden City, 25,043; Emporia, 24,897; Dodge City, 22,869

UNUSUAL FEATURES
President Dwight D. Eisenhower's burial place and presidential library in Abilene; Film actor and director Dennis Hopper from Dodge City.

Rep. Jim Ryun (R)

CAPITOL OFFICE
225-6601; fax 225-7986; 330 Cannon Bldg. 20515

INTERNET
e-mail: jim.ryun@mail.house.gov
web: www.house.gov/ryun

COMMITTEES
Armed Services
Budget
Financial Services

HOMETOWN
Jefferson County

BORN
April 29, 1947, Wichita, Kan.

RELIGION
Presbyterian

FAMILY
Wife, Anne Ryun; four children

EDUCATION
U. of Kansas, B.A. 1970

CAREER
Motivational speaker; author; product consultant;
Olympic athlete

POLITICAL HIGHLIGHTS
No previous office

ELECTION RESULTS

2000 GENERAL

Jim Ryun (R)	164,951	67.4%
Stanley Wiles (D)	71,709	29.3%
Ira Dennis Hawver (LIBERT)	8,099	3.3%

2000 PRIMARY

Jim Ryun (R)	unopposed

1998 GENERAL

Jim Ryun (R)	108,527	61.0%
Jim Clark (D)	69,521	39.0%

PREVIOUS WINNING PERCENTAGES
1996 (52%)

Elected 1996; 3rd term

Ryun may be the only member of Congress who was more famous when he was in high school than he is now. But that does not seem to bother the Kansan, who has a low-key manner and a staunchly conservative outlook.

Ryun had held no elective office before his 1996 House campaign, but voters in the 2nd knew his name well. He first achieved notice when he was in high school as the first prep miler to break the four-minute barrier. He was on the cover of Sports Illustrated as its Sportsman of the Year in 1966, won the Sullivan Award as the nation's top amateur athlete in 1967, was named one of the top 10 young men in the country by the Jaycees in 1968, held the world record for the mile for seven years, and was on three U.S. Olympic teams — all by the age of 25.

In the quarter-century after his competitive athletic career ended, Ryun worked with sports camps, founded a public relations firm, gave motivational speeches drawing on athletic and religious themes, and worked with a hearing aid manufacturer to help hearing-impaired children. (He has a hearing impairment himself.) Ryun also dabbled in politics, mostly working on behalf of other candidates who shared his conservative views.

Then, in 1996, Senate Majority Leader Bob Dole left the Senate to campaign full time for the presidency, and the 2nd District's freshman representative, Republican Sam Brownback, decided to seek Dole's Senate seat. That opened up the 2nd, and Ryun, who had been thinking of eventually running for office, decided the time was at hand. With the backing of the conservative wing of Kansas' divided GOP, he prevailed easily in a three-way primary against two more-moderate Republicans.

Democrats tried to focus attention on an article written by Ryun and his wife, Anne, in which they advocated a "courtship" style of dating for young people. They suggested that a boy should seek permission from a girl's father before asking her out and that there should be no dating unless the couple's ultimate intention is to marry — rules the Ryuns say they follow with their children. Ryun's response to the Democrats was that his family should be off-limits.

Despite lukewarm support from moderate Republicans, Ryun held on to beat the Democratic candidate, lawyer John Frieden, in the general election, and his margins have steadily increased.

Although Ryun does not often find himself in the limelight, he stirred some controversy in 1999 when he proposed barring foreign scientists from nuclear weapons labs. His plan was prompted by reports that China stole U.S. nuclear secrets. The Clinton administration sharply objected, contending that the measure would undermine international cooperation on improving the security at nuclear facilities overseas, but Ryun told The Associated Press, "I'm not interested in compromising the basic principle that we need to ensure better security at our labs."

Although that proposal failed, Ryun had more success in 2000 with an amendment to an annual spending bill barring federal employees from drawing salaries from both the Energy Department and a semiautonomous agency intended to combat security lapses at the department. His amendment was prompted by concerns that the Clinton administration was skirting the intent of Congress by giving high-level managers the same jobs within the new National Nuclear Security Administration that they held in the Department of Energy. "Until DOE complies with the existing law, the nuclear secrets of the United States will continue to be in danger of being compromised," Ryun warned. After the amendment won House approval, Ryun's chief of staff told The Associated Press that the vote represented Ryun's biggest victory to date. (The language eventually became law.)

On national issues, Ryun's priorities and philosophy generally mirror those of the House GOP leadership — balancing the federal budget, reducing the role of government in the affairs of individuals and small businesses, maintaining a strong national defense and opposing abortion. He has affiliated himself with a group of the most conservative House Republicans: the Conservative Action Team, known as the CATs.

On the few occasions that Ryun has been at odds with the majority of his party, his position was more conservative than the party's. In 1997, he was one of just 32 Republicans who voted against the spending cut bill implementing the White House-Capitol Hill balanced-budget agreement. He argued that the bill, while reducing overall spending, also included substantial increases in some federal spending.

Also in 1997, Ryun was in the minority of Republicans to vote against eliminating the National Endowment for the Arts and providing arts money to states via block grants. Ryun's vote was not in support of the NEA, but rather in opposition to any federal spending on the arts.

On the Armed Services Committee, Ryun looks out for troops from Fort Riley and Fort Leavenworth in the 2nd District who are sent overseas. Ryun says the committee should deal with the broader issue of whether the United States should act as the world's peacekeeper.

One local issue of interest to Ryun is an effort to amend the "rails-to-trails" act to give the former owners of land under abandoned railroad tracks a crack at getting the land back or receiving compensation. Currently, many unused railbeds are converted to recreational trails for bicyclists, horseback riders, walkers, joggers and inline skaters. Ryun says he has made good use of trails in his running career but argues that the original landowners deserve help against the "Goliath that's denying them all their rights."

Ryun's high school mile record has stood for more than 30 years, and his exploits are still mentioned periodically when a high school phenom appears ready to challenge the mark. Ryun never regarded himself as a phenom. He had failed to make the basketball and baseball teams, he recalled in a 1999 Washington Post interview. "I was a nerd. ... I began running because I was searching for acceptance," he said.

Ryun continues to run — recreationally, but still faster than most. In an annual Washington, D.C., fundraising race that attracts many lawmakers, Ryun covered the three-mile course in less than 20 minutes.

KEY VOTES

2000

No	Raise hourly minimum wage by $1 over two years
Yes	Halt funding for U.S. mission in Kosovo unless European nations pay more
Yes	Provide Medicare benefits to military retirees and their dependents
Yes	Grant China permanent normal trade status
Yes	Phase out estate, gift and trust taxes
Yes	Prohibit implementation of president's national monument designations
Yes	Approve GOP plan to provide prescription drug coverage for Medicare beneficiaries
No	Increase help for poor nations indebted to international financial institutions

1999

No	Impose steel import quotas
Yes	Kill proposal to take aviation trust funds off budget
No	Require background checks on buyers only at gun shows with 10 or more vendors
Yes	Remove barriers among banking, securities and insurance companies
No	Authorize state grants to hire teachers and reduce class size
No	Overhaul campaign finance law; ban "soft money" and restrict advocacy advertising
No	Approve bipartisan plan to increase rights of patients in managed-care health plans

INTEREST GROUPS

	AFL-CIO	ADA	CCUS	ACU
2000	0%	0%	90%	100%
1999	0%	0%	84%	96%
1998	0%	0%	100%	100%
1997	0%	5%	100%	100%

CQ VOTE STUDIES

	PARTY UNITY		PRESIDENTIAL SUPPORT	
	Support	Oppose	Support	Oppose
2000	98%	2%	25%	75%
1999	97%	3%	17%	83%
1998	96%	4%	21%	79%
1997	98%	2%	24%	76%

KANSAS 2
East — Topeka; Manhattan; Leavenworth

Located in the eastern part of Kansas, the 2nd contains 25 counties and runs the entire length of the state from Nebraska to Oklahoma. The moderately conservative district is a combination of rural farm communities and urbanized areas, including the state capital, Topeka. One fourth of district residents live in the Topeka area.

Republicans do well in the district's rural regions, while Democrats are more successful in Topeka and the state's blue-collar southeast corner. Although the 2nd is described as conservative, it is not overwhelmingly Republican; the 2nd was the only congressional district in Kansas where native son Bob Dole failed to win 50 percent or more of the vote in the 1996 presidential election. In 2000, however, President Bush won the district with 55 percent of the vote.

The 2nd's economy has experienced slow but steady growth, and unemployment is low. Most of the district's jobs revolve around agriculture, particularly wheat. State government is Topeka's largest

employer. Fort Riley, in Riley County, and Fort Leavenworth also add to the 2nd's economy, although Fort Riley suffered a round of cutbacks in the mid-1990s.

MAJOR INDUSTRY
Agriculture, defense, manufacturing

MILITARY BASES
Fort Riley (Army) 10,057 military, 3,606 civilian; Fort Leavenworth (Army) 3,152 military, 2,204 civilian (1999)

CITIES
Topeka, 124,529; Manhattan, 41,499; Leavenworth, 39,123; Pittsburg, 18,534

UNUSUAL FEATURES
Boxer Rocky Graziano got his start while at the federal penitentiary in Leavenworth; Cowboy and Old West stage show proprietor William "Buffalo Bill" Cody from Leavenworth.

Rep. Dennis Moore (D)

Elected 1998; 2nd term

CAPITOL OFFICE
225-2865; fax 225-2807; 431 Cannon Bldg. 20515

INTERNET
e-mail: dennis.moore@mail.house.gov
web: www.house.gov/moore

COMMITTEES
Budget
Financial Services
Science

HOMETOWN
Lenexa

BORN
Nov. 8, 1945, Anthony, Kan.

RELIGION
Protestant

FAMILY
Wife, Stephene Moore; seven children

EDUCATION
Southern Methodist U., attended 1965; U. of
Kansas, B.A. 1967; Washburn U., J.D. 1970

MILITARY SERVICE
Army, 1970

CAREER
Lawyer

POLITICAL HIGHLIGHTS
Johnson County district attorney, 1977-89;
Democratic nominee for Kan. attorney general,
1986

ELECTION RESULTS

2000 GENERAL

Dennis Moore (D)	154,505	50.1%
Phill Kline (R)	144,672	46.9%
Chris Mina (LIBERT)	9,533	3.1%

2000 PRIMARY

Dennis Moore (D)	unopposed

1998 GENERAL

Dennis Moore (D)	103,376	52.4%
Vince Snowbarger (R)	93,938	47.6%

Moore is the first Democrat to win a second term from this suburban Kansas City district since 1936. He has succeeded on largely Republican turf because of his credibility on crime as a former county prosecutor and his willingness to go along with the GOP on some issues, such as a tax break for married couples.

Still, he is a reliable vote for Democratic party leaders on certain core issues, supporting, for example, abortion rights and gun control measures such as trigger locks and background checks. He also has stuck with his party during major fights over providing Medicare coverage of prescription drugs for senior citizens and protecting the Social Security surplus. His wife is a nurse, and Moore favors legislation to allow patients to sue their managed-care providers for denial of coverage. In 2000, he voted with House Democrats about three-quarters of the time.

Moore affiliates with both the moderate New Democrat Coalition and the "Blue Dogs," a coalition of conservative Democrats. In the 107th Congress, as part of a concerted effort by moderate and conservative Democrats to win places on top-rank committees, Moore got a seat on the Budget panel.

He took on a tough issue in his first term: overhaul of the campaign finance system. He was a leading voice urging regulation of certain political organizations — called 527 groups after a section of the tax code — that were not required to disclose their fundraising or spending activities as long as they did not express support or opposition to a federal candidate. Lawmakers passed a disclosure requirement in 2000. Moore called the new law "just a down payment on real campaign reform."

Moore served as the Johnson County district attorney for a dozen years, and he was known for the personal approach he took. Barbara Daniels, the mother of a teenager who had been murdered by three men, would call on Moore to testify whenever one of the killers came up for parole. "If I call, he answers," Daniels told The Kansas City Star. "He's really been a good friend." Moore also took the lead in creating a victims assistance program for the county.

In his first term, the congressman sought to direct federal money to Kansas. During his 2000 re-election campaign, Moore made appearances with oversize checks totaling $13.7 million for highway improvements in Wyandotte County. He helped secure other federal funding for his district, including nearly $26 million in flood control assistance along the Turkey Creek basin; $3 million for renovation of the Turner Diagonal Bridge; $2.8 million for buses and equipment; $3 million for Lawrence Airport improvements; and $1.1 million for a program that provides transportation for workers leaving the welfare rolls.

Moore has played guitar since high school, favoring country rock, the blues and classical music, and he once shared the stage at a Farm Aid concert with Willie Nelson and David Crosby. He made a memorable campaign commercial during his 1998 race in which he humorously interspersed his positions on issues with a few guitar licks.

Like many of his generation, Moore was drawn to politics in the 1960s by the issues of race and the war in Vietnam. In 1965, he was inspired by Sen. William Fulbright's convocation speech at Southern Methodist University on the arrogance of the U.S. position in Vietnam. That same year, some friends visiting his dorm room told him they were driving to Selma, Ala., to take part in a civil rights march. To his chagrin, Moore took his father's advice and skipped the trip. He says he is glad that later as a congressman he was able to return to the scene with civil rights pioneer and now House colleague John Lewis, D-Ga., to participate in a re-enactment of the march.

Moore compares his own political career with that of his father, who served as a three-term county prosecutor and ran unsuccessfully for Congress in 1958 and 1960. A framed "Walter Moore for Congress" poster hangs in Dennis Moore's Capitol Hill office. But campaigning in support of his father's congressional bids 40 years ago "did not give me the bug," he recalls. "In fact, if anything, going door-to-door handing out cards for my dad was not something I enjoyed that much." But he adds, "If you're going to be successful in politics, gradually you have to overcome that."

Moore benefited in both his congressional races from a schism within the Kansas Republican Party. The 3rd District had long been represented by moderate Republicans, but in 1998 Moore was able to unseat the more-conservative first-term Rep. Republican Vince Snowbarger. Moore entered the race when he saw that Snowbarger had not raised much money during his first year in office, a mistake Moore was careful not to repeat.

He raised more than $1.5 million for his 2000 re-election bid. His opponent, state Sen. Phill Kline, was another conservative; the moderate Republican president of the Kansas Senate referred to Kline as a "poster boy for the religious right." Moore said, "The division in the Republican Party still is alive and well. And I would not have been elected two years ago if that were not the case — and it's still the case."

Kline tried to portray Moore as being too liberal for the district, saying he had opposed GOP tax-cutting efforts. Moore said he was against a $792 billion tax package pushed by Republicans during the 106th Congress because of his concern for reducing the national debt. Like many Democrats, he did support pieces of the package when they were put forward separately, including elimination of estate and gift taxes and the "marriage penalty," a quirk in the tax code that results in some two-earner married couples paying higher taxes. Moore won by 3 percentage points.

But the congressman is ill at ease with the amount of money needed to win a modern congressional campaign. Late in the 2000 campaign, Moore called his own heavy fundraising "obscene," adding, "I never thought I'd raise as much as I have."

"I always give credit publicly to John McCain," he said, referring to the Arizona Republican who has been the Senate's leading advocate for a campaign finance overhaul. Nonetheless, McCain made a campaign appearance for Kline.

KEY VOTES

2000

Yes Raise hourly minimum wage by $1 over two years
Yes Halt funding for U.S. mission in Kosovo unless European nations pay more
Yes Provide Medicare benefits to military retirees and their dependents
Yes Grant China permanent normal trade status
Yes Phase out estate, gift and trust taxes
No   Prohibit implementation of president's national monument designations
No   Approve GOP plan to provide prescription drug coverage for Medicare beneficiaries
Yes Increase help for poor nations indebted to international financial institutions

1999

Yes Impose steel import quotas
No   Kill proposal to take aviation trust funds off budget
No   Require background checks on buyers only at gun shows with 10 or more vendors
Yes Remove barriers among banking, securities and insurance companies
Yes Authorize state grants to hire teachers and reduce class size
Yes Overhaul campaign finance law; ban "soft money" and restrict advocacy advertising
Yes Approve bipartisan plan to increase rights of patients in managed-care health plans

INTEREST GROUPS

	AFL-CIO	ADA	CCUS	ACU
2000	50%	65%	66%	24%
1999	78%	100%	52%	12%

CQ VOTE STUDIES

	PARTY UNITY		PRESIDENTIAL SUPPORT	
	Support	Oppose	Support	Oppose
2000	76%	24%	68%	32%
1999	82%	18%	77%	23%

KANSAS 3

Kansas City region — Overland Park; Lawrence

Bordering Missouri in eastern Kansas, the 3rd differs markedly from the state's other districts. Geographically compact, it is almost entirely within the metropolitan sphere of Kansas City, Mo. Most of its population lives in the suburbs of Johnson County, Kansas City, Kan., and Lawrence (home to the University of Kansas).

The district is hardly uniform in its economic character. Johnson County is one of the state's richest, with company headquarters, suburban developments and a strong service sector. But poverty and unemployment are prevalent in Wyandotte County and Kansas City itself. Overshadowed by its namesake across the Missouri River, Kansas City, Kan., is an industrial town that has had its share of Rust Belt blues due to factory closures and the long-term decline of urban stockyards. But Kansas City maintains a large industrial base and has attracted some growth in its biotechnology sector.

Heading west, the 3rd takes in Lawrence and most of Douglas County.

The county's eastern portions along state Route 10 are becoming increasingly suburban. University-centered Lawrence has some liberal activists, but the outlying farm areas lean Republican. At the district's southern end is Miami County, which is lightly populated and has a Republican tilt.

The 3rd is a swing district, and many of its counties contrast politically. Wealthy Johnson County is a Republican stronghold, and with more than 400,000 residents, a dominant force in the 3rd. Democrats are strong in Wyandotte County, outnumbering Republicans, and in parts of Douglas County around the University of Kansas.

MAJOR INDUSTRY

Long-distance phone service, auto manufacturing, accounting

CITIES

Overland Park, 142,783; Kansas City, 139,971; Olathe, 88,192; Lawrence, 78,911; Shawnee, 46,364

UNUSUAL FEATURES

Actor Edward Asner from Kansas City; James Naismith, inventor of basketball, University of Kansas' first coach and the only one with a losing record.

Rep. Todd Tiahrt (R)

Elected 1994; 4th term

A staunchly conservative and deeply religious man, Tiahrt is one of the leading practitioners of the art of offering policy amendments to appropriations bills, as he tries to end government backing of needle-exchange programs, funding of abortion-related activities abroad and adoptions by gay couples.

From his Appropriations seat, Tiahrt's insistence on using the spending bills as the battleground for contentious social issues has often given his own leadership a headache, particularly when the fight throws the legislative calendar off schedule. But Tiahrt is unrepentant. As The Wichita Eagle observed, "Tiahrt has turned out to be just as advertised. A fiscal conservative, a social conservative, a religious conservative."

Tiahrt (TEE-hart) says his inspiration for the use of appropriations "riders" was a former colleague and fellow conservative member of the GOP Class of 1994, Mark W. Neumann of Wisconsin.

In the 106th Congress, Tiahrt continued his efforts to bar the District of Columbia from supporting needle-exchange programs aimed at reducing the risk of drug abusers contracting AIDS. "What we're doing through a needle-exchange program is to enable people to drive the coffin nails in," he said. "By handing out needles, we encourage drug abuse," he explained to The Kansas City Star.

He has also offered amendments to abolish AmeriCorps, President Clinton's public service program; to force the withdrawal of U.S. troops from Bosnia; to block a requirement that federal health insurance plans that pay for prescriptions also cover contraceptives; to stop the District of Columbia government from paying for abortions; to place restrictions on U.S. support for foreign family planning programs; and to bar homosexuals from adopting children.

In addition to offering his social policy amendments, Tiahrt also uses his Appropriations seat in a more traditional fashion — winning an array of federal grants for his district, particularly for transportation and water development projects. He also watches out for McConnell Air Force Base, just south of Wichita.

Tiahrt touts his work to ease traffic congestion in Wichita caused by lengthy coal trains winding their way south from the Dakota coal fields. He secured $35 million to improve railroad crossings in the city, proving to his constituents that he could deliver for them — an important question in the minds of some Kansans who wondered whether the departure of GOP Sen. Bob Dole in 1996 would leave Kansas without clout in such money matters.

Tiahrt is a member of the Republican Study Group, formerly known as the Conservative Action Team, a group of the most conservative House Republicans. He says his religious views do not completely define his House agenda. He reminds anti-abortion activists, for instance, that only a handful of the hundreds of votes he casts each year deal with that issue.

He was criticized by some conservatives in 2000 when he declined to attend a gathering of the conservative Kansas Republican Assembly. "I think it's a mistake to have these splinter groups. I think it's important that we pull the party together," he told the Lawrence Journal-World. And he says he refuses to base his relations with colleagues solely on their views on political and social issues.

Born in South Dakota, Tiahrt grew up on the family farm in the southeast part of the state. His father served on the local school board. Tiahrt was an

CAPITOL OFFICE
225-6216; fax 225-3489; 401 Cannon Bldg. 20515

INTERNET
e-mail: tiahrt@mail.house.gov
web: www.house.gov/tiahrt

COMMITTEES
Appropriations

HOMETOWN
Goddard

BORN
June 15, 1951, Vermillion, S.D.

RELIGION
Assemblies of God

FAMILY
Wife, Vicki Tiahrt; three children

EDUCATION
Evangel College, B.A. 1975; Southwest Missouri State U., M.B.A. 1989

CAREER
College instructor; airplane manufacturing company contract manager

POLITICAL HIGHLIGHTS
Republican nominee for Kan. House, 1990; Kan. Senate, 1993-95

ELECTION RESULTS

2000 GENERAL

Todd Tiahrt (R)	131,871	54.4%
Carlos Nolla (D)	101,980	42.0%
Steven A. Rosile (LIBERT)	8,732	3.6%

2000 PRIMARY

Todd Tiahrt (R)	unopposed

1998 GENERAL

Todd Tiahrt (R)	94,785	58.3%
Jim Lawing (D)	62,737	38.6%
Craig Newland (TAX)	5,171	3.2%

PREVIOUS WINNING PERCENTAGES
1996 (50%); 1994 (53%)

all-around athlete. He played football in college and is one of the stars of the annual congressional charity baseball and basketball games.

He enrolled at the South Dakota School of Mines and Technology but transferred to Evangel College in Springfield, Mo., which describes itself as a Christian liberal-arts university. It is run by the Assembly of God church, of which Tiahrt is a member.

After college, Tiahrt embarked on a career in the aerospace industry with Boeing. As a contract manager, he was involved in talks between Boeing and the federal government on a number of projects, including NASA's space station, Air Force One and many military aircraft. His experience is useful in representing the 4th District, home to a number of aviation and defense firms that play a key role in the area's economy.

Tiahrt was originally a registered Democrat because of his grandfather, who had impressed him with the story of how the federal government had helped with the purchase of the family farm during the Depression. Tiahrt says he didn't give his party affiliation much thought until he set out to run for the Kansas House in 1990. He decided then that the Republican Party was a closer match for his strong religious views, and he switched parties.

Tiahrt lost that race for the state House, succumbing in a recount after initial tallies showed him with a 24-vote lead. He remained active in local party politics, and two years later he was elected to the state Senate, where he was best known for pushing legislation allowing people to carry concealed weapons.

In 1994, Tiahrt decided to wage a long-shot challenge to popular nine-term Democratic Rep. Dan Glickman. Glickman's polls throughout the summer showed him with a lead in the 30-point range; but Tiahrt mobilized a grass-roots network that drew heavily from the ranks of the anti-abortion movement, in which his wife was active, and which had engaged in protests and blockades in Wichita.

Tiahrt said he "moved below the radar and kept low-key" and chipped away at Glickman, linking him to the unpopular Clinton administration. He ended up winning by 6 percentage points. In celebrating on election night, his supporters sang, "What a Mighty God We Serve." (A few months later, Glickman became secretary of agriculture.)

Tiahrt had a serious re-election battle in 1996, eventually defeating moderate Democrat Randy Rathbun by just 3 percentage points. Democrats harbor some hope of capturing the district again, but Tiahrt has won his subsequent re-elections by 20 and 12 percentage points, respectively.

Tiahrt is also mentioned as a possible candidate for governor in 2002.

KEY VOTES

2000

No	Raise hourly minimum wage by $1 over two years
Yes	Halt funding for U.S. mission in Kosovo unless European nations pay more
Yes	Provide Medicare benefits to military retirees and their dependents
Yes	Grant China permanent normal trade status
Yes	Phase out estate, gift and trust taxes
Yes	Prohibit implementation of president's national monument designations
Yes	Approve GOP plan to provide prescription drug coverage for Medicare beneficiaries
No	Increase help for poor nations indebted to international financial institutions

1999

No	Impose steel import quotas
Yes	Kill proposal to take aviation trust funds off budget
No	Require background checks on buyers only at gun shows with 10 or more vendors
Yes	Remove barriers among banking, securities and insurance companies
No	Authorize state grants to hire teachers and reduce class size
No	Overhaul campaign finance law; ban "soft money" and restrict advocacy advertising
No	Approve bipartisan plan to increase rights of patients in managed-care health plans

INTEREST GROUPS

	AFL-CIO	ADA	CCUS	ACU
2000	0%	0%	95%	91%
1999	11%	5%	88%	95%
1998	0%	0%	94%	100%
1997	13%	5%	90%	100%

CQ VOTE STUDIES

	PARTY UNITY		PRESIDENTIAL SUPPORT	
	Support	Oppose	Support	Oppose
2000	94%	6%	24%	76%
1999	95%	5%	18%	82%
1998	96%	4%	20%	80%
1997	97%	3%	23%	77%

KANSAS 4
South central — Wichita

In these parts, seeing an airplane is about as commonplace as seeing a bird. The moderately conservative 4th is centered around its largest city, Wichita, with its thriving aviation industry. Farmland stretches throughout the district and surrounds the city.

Wichita's aviation industry keeps the 4th healthy. Boeing, which produces two-thirds of the world's commercial airliners, has a plant here alongside other aviation heavyweights. Even so, with a regional medical center and a university, Wichita can hardly be called just an airplane town.

Much of the rest of the 4th is farmland. Sumner County, on the Oklahoma border, is one of Kansas' leading wheat-growing counties. Wheat is also important to Harper and Kingman counties to the west. Cattle graze in sparsely populated Greenwood, Elk and Chautauqua counties to the east.

Redistricting in 1992 made the politically marginal 4th more favorable to Republicans by taking out Democrat-leaning Reno County and bringing in Republican-oriented Montgomery County. This change helped Republicans win the district in 1994 and keep it since then. Locally, Republicans do best here, but Democrats do win some offices. Cowley County, in the east, tilts more Democratic.

MAJOR INDUSTRY
Aviation, defense, agriculture

MILITARY BASES
McConnell Air Force Base, 2,609 military, 881 civilian (2000)

CITIES
Wichita, 335,562; Derby, 18,855; Newton, 17,742

UNUSUAL FEATURES
Almon Strowger of El Dorado invented the dial telephone in 1889; David Blanton of Wichita invented the airplane autopilot in 1954; Omar Knedlik of Coffeyville invented the first frozen carbonated drink machine in 1961.

Gov. Paul E. Patton (D)

First elected: 1995
Length of term: 4 years
Term expires: 12/03
Salary: $99,657
Phone: (502) 564-2611
Hometown: Pikeville
Born: May 26, 1937; Fallsburg, Ky.
Religion: Presbyterian
Family: Wife, Judi Patton; four children
Education: U. of Kentucky, B.S. 1959
Career: Coal company executive
Political highlights: Ky. deputy transportation secretary, 1979; Ky. Democratic Party chairman, 1981-83; Pike County judge-executive, 1982-91; lieutenant governor, 1991-95

Election results:

1999 GENERAL

Paul E. Patton (D)	349,798	61.5%
Wanda "Peppy" Martin (R)	133,485	23.5%

Lt. Gov. Stephen L. Henry (D)

First elected: 1995
Length of term: 4 years
Term expires: 12/03
Salary: $87,579
Phone: (502) 564-7562

STATE LEGISLATURE

General Assembly: Meets January to mid-April in even years; January-March in odd years
House: 100 members, 2-year terms
2001 breakdown: 34R, 66D; 89 men, 11 women
Salary: $158.18/day while in session; $93.53/day expenses; $1,503/month while out of session
Phone: (502) 564-8100
Senate: 38 members, 4-year terms
2001 breakdown: 20R, 18D; 34 men, 4 women
Salary: $158.18/day while in session; $93.53/day expenses; $1,503/month while out of session
Phone: (502) 564-8100

STATE TERM LIMITS

Governor: 2 terms
Senate: No
House: No

URBAN STATISTICS

CITY	POPULATION
Louisville	253,128
Lexington/Fayette	243,785
Owensboro	54,010
Bowling Green	45,550

REGISTERED VOTERS

Democrat	60%
Republican	33%
Other	7%

POPULATION

2000 population	4,041,769
1990 population	3,685,296
Percent change	+9.7%
Rank among states	25
Median age	35.5
Born in state	77%
Foreign born	1%
Urban/rural	52%/48%
Crime rate	317/100,000
Poverty level	13.5%
Federal workers	36,894
Military	47,221

REAPPORTIONMENT

Kentucky retained its six House seats in reapportionment. The state legislature will draw new district lines.

MISCELLANEOUS

Web: www.state.ky.us
Capital: Frankfort
Land area: 39,732 sq. miles
Rank among states: 36
STATE ELECTION OFFICIAL
(502) 573-7100
DEMOCRATIC HEADQUARTERS
(502) 695-4828
REPUBLICAN HEADQUARTERS
(502) 875-5130

District Statistics

DIST.	VOTE FOR PRESIDENT									WHT	BLK	ASIAN	HISP	HOUSEHOLD INCOME	OVER 65+	UNDER 18	COLLEGE EDUCATION
	2000			**1996**			**1992**										
	D	R	GREEN	D	R	REF	D	R	I								
1	41%	58%	1%	47%	43%	10%	48%	40%	13%	91%	8%	0%	1%	$20,331	15%	25%	9%
2	36	62	1	41	49	10	41	45	14	93	5	1	1	$23,212	11	27	11
3	51	46	2	53	40	7	51	37	13	81	18	1	1	$26,614	14	24	20
4	37	61	2	41	50	9	39	44	17	97	2	0	0	$26,569	12	27	14
5	42	57	1	47	43	9	48	42	10	99	1	0	0	$15,061	12	28	8
6	42	56	2	46	45	8	41	43	16	91	8	1	1	$25,364	11	24	20
STATE	41	57	2	46	45	9	45	41	14	92	7	<1	1	$22,534	13	26	14

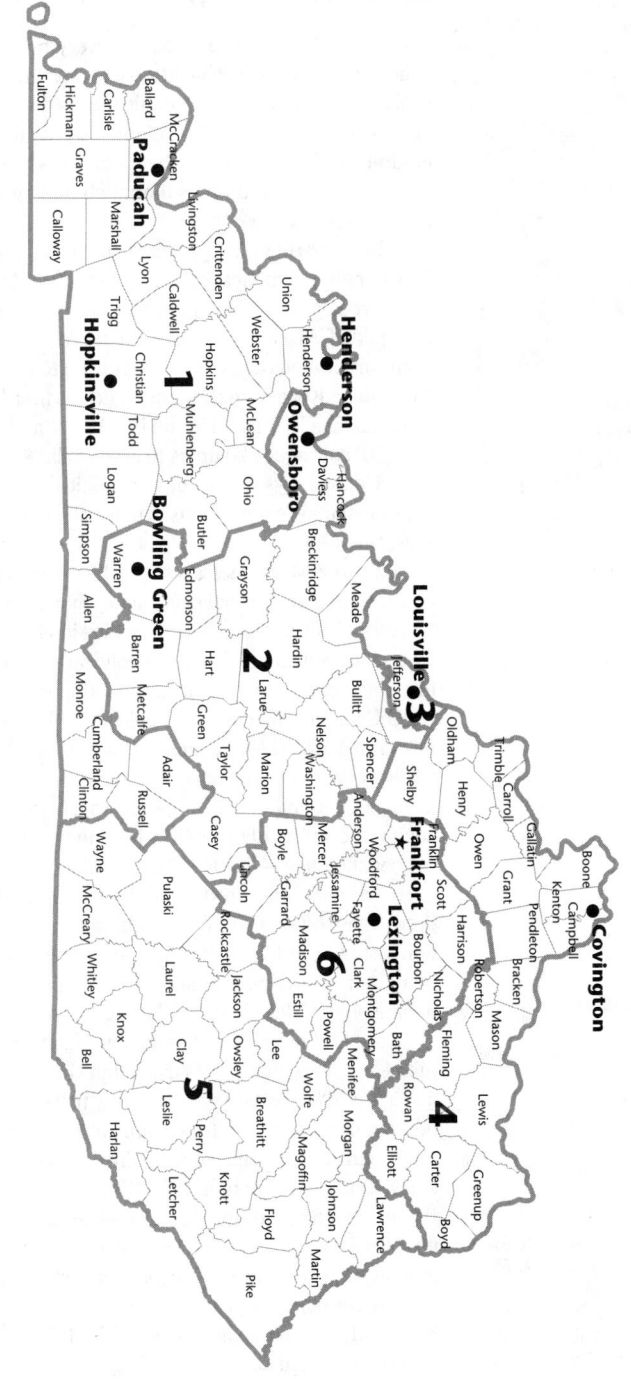

Sen. Mitch McConnell (R)

CAPITOL OFFICE
224-2541; fax 224-2499; 361A Russell Bldg. 20510

INTERNET
e-mail: senator@mcconnell.senate.gov
web: mcconnell.senate.gov

COMMITTEES
Agriculture, Nutrition & Forestry
  (Research, Nutrition & General Legislation - chairman)
Appropriations
  (Foreign Operations - chairman)
Judiciary
Rules & Administration - chairman
Joint Library
Joint Printing – chairman

HOMETOWN
Louisville

BORN
Feb. 20, 1942, Sheffield, Ala.

RELIGION
Baptist

FAMILY
Wife, Elaine L. Chao; three children

EDUCATION
U. of Louisville, B.A. 1964; U. of Kentucky, J.D. 1967

CAREER
Lawyer; Justice Department official;
congressional aide

POLITICAL HIGHLIGHTS
Jefferson County judge/executive, 1978-85

ELECTION RESULTS

1996 GENERAL

Mitch McConnell (R)	724,794	55.5%
Steven L. Beshear (D)	560,012	42.8%

1996 PRIMARY

Mitch McConnell (R)	88,620	88.6%
Tommy Klein (R)	11,410	11.4%

PREVIOUS WINNING PERCENTAGES
1990 (52%); 1984 (50%)

Elected 1984; 3rd term

In a city where titles mean almost everything, McConnell has one that few politicians aspire to: archenemy of campaign finance reform. But the soft-spoken senator has reveled in his role as the Darth Vader of the campaign finance debate, crusading relentlessly against restrictions on political fundraising for years. Few other politicians would dare to intone: "The real problem is not that there is too much money in politics; there is too little money in politics."

In his long-running fight against overhauling campaign funding rules, McConnell was the leader of filibusters that for years stymied legislation, sponsored by Republican John McCain of Arizona and Democrat Russell D. Feingold of Wisconsin, to ban "soft money" — the unlimited contributions from corporations and labor unions used to finance party-building activities and issue advocacy ads. He mounted his first successful filibuster of campaign finance legislation in the late 1980s, and by his count, he marshaled his GOP colleagues 20 times to stop a bill.

McConnell says restrictions on political funding amount to an assault on the Constitution's protections of political speech. Donating to campaigns, he says, "is as American as apple pie."

Moreover, McConnell says that the effect of such limits would not be to end the influence of political money but to restrict political parties, and potential challengers, in favor of outside interest groups and incumbents. "Of what value is it, in our American political system, to weaken the parties, the one entity out there that will always support challengers, no matter what?"

McConnell, who overcame polio as a child, has never lacked for toughness or tenacity. His bare-knuckles tactics in blocking campaign finance legislation have made him the target of critics that range from advocacy groups such as Common Cause to the editorial page of The New York Times. But such criticism hardly worries McConnell, who has his eye on a far different constituency — his Republican colleagues.

He has openly acknowledged that the GOP would be in a bad way if Congress bans soft money. "We Republicans have to spend millions every election just to get a fair shake and counter the liberal bias so prevalent in the news and entertainment media," McConnell said during the March 2001 debate on the McCain-Feingold bill.

Under McConnell's leadership, the National Republican Senatorial Committee — the Senate GOP's campaign committee — raised nearly $93 million in the 2000 election cycle, roughly half of it in soft money. The elections, nevertheless, were a bitter disappointment for Republicans, who lost four seats, leaving the Senate evenly divided. The 1998 elections told a similar story. Under McConnell, the NRSC raised more than $80 million, but Republicans failed to add to their majority in Congress. (McConnell has contemplated a run for Republican whip in 2002, but his chances for such a promotion have been hurt by the party's performance at the ballot box.)

After serving four years as chairman of the Republican campaign committee, McConnell stepped down in the 107th Congress. In that role he had become a trusted ally of Senate Majority Leader Trent Lott.

McConnell has risen through the ranks of the Republican leadership, at least in part because he takes on unpopular jobs. In 1995, for example, he chaired the Ethics Committee when it voted to expel Republican Sen. Bob Packwood of Oregon over charges of sexual misconduct. Packwood subsequently resigned.

For his efforts, McConnell has been awarded an unusually broad portfolio. He chairs the Rules Committee, whose jurisdiction includes campaign funding issues, and he plays a key role in determining levels of U.S. foreign aid from his perch at the helm of the Appropriations Subcommittee on Foreign Operations. He chairs an Agriculture subcommittee, and in the 107th Congress, he added a seat on the Judiciary Committee.

As Foreign Operations chairman, McConnell has focused on a handful of lower-profile international matters. He has been a leading advocate for increased U.S. aid to Ukraine, Georgia and Armenia — seeing them as bulwarks against a potentially resurgent Russia. As a result of McConnell's efforts, for 1999 through 2001, Georgia and Armenia, whose combined population is about 8 million, received as much economic aid as Russia, which has 20 times as many people. And he has championed tough economic sanctions against the military dictatorship in Myanmar.

Though a fierce partisan, McConnell has at times displayed a pragmatic streak. He voted to remove President Clinton from office, backing both impeachment counts brought by the House in 1999, but he was hardly an impeachment enthusiast. Indeed, from the start of the Senate trial, McConnell's primary interest was in supporting Lott's efforts to bring the proceedings to a quick conclusion.

He shares more than his Republican ideology with the Bush administration: His wife, Elaine L. Chao, is the secretary of labor.

Three things brought McConnell to Congress: bloodhounds, Ronald Reagan and dogged persistence in the face of daunting odds. McConnell had long been interested in politics. He was the student body president in high school and college and president of his law school class. After earning his law degree in 1967, McConnell worked for Sen. Marlow Cook, R-Ky., and then served as a deputy assistant U.S. attorney general in the Ford administration. He won two terms as Jefferson County judge, the county's top administrative post, where he was serving when he entered the 1984 Senate race.

Few people believed McConnell had much chance of defeating two-term Democratic Sen. Walter D. Huddleston, and his campaign struggled for quite a while. Then McConnell hit upon a clever, homey gimmick to get across his claim that Huddleston had limited influence and was often absent from committee meetings. McConnell aired TV ads showing bloodhounds sniffing frantically around Washington in search of the incumbent.

That got people talking about a race they had ignored, and many concluded that McConnell had a point — they were not exactly sure what Huddleston had been doing since he went to Congress in 1973. With President Reagan crushing Walter F. Mondale by more than 280,000 votes in Kentucky, McConnell had long coattails to latch onto. He won by four-tenths of a percentage point.

In 1990, McConnell was tabbed as one of the most vulnerable Republicans up for re-election. But he came out early and tough. He brought back the TV bloodhounds, this time to bark up the fact that he had made 99 percent of the votes cast during his first term. McConnell won that race with 52 percent of the vote.

He had his easiest race in 1996, defeating former Lt. Gov. Steven L. Beshear, 55 percent to 43 percent, to win a third term in the Democratic state. Beshear tried to paint McConnell as a dangerous ideologue for opposing campaign finance legislation while supporting much of the conservative Republican congressional agenda.

McConnell countered that Beshear was beholden to special interests because he had accepted sizable campaign contributions from political action committees. McConnell also spent in excess of $4.5 million, more than twice what Beshear spent.

KEY VOTES

2000
Yes Overhaul bankruptcy law and increase minimum wage
Yes Limit fiscal 2001 discretionary spending to $600.3 billion
Yes Override veto on nuclear waste disposal at Yucca Mountain site in Nevada
No Oppose effort to terminate Kosovo mission
No Include gender, sexual orientation and disability in federal hate crime protections
Yes Approve GOP plan to restrict use of genetic information by health insurers
Yes Kill amendment delaying implementation of an anti-missile defense system
Yes Cut taxes for married couples
Yes Grant China permanent normal trade status

1999
Yes Remove President Clinton from office for obstruction of justice
Yes Kill amendment authorizing state grants to hire teachers and reduce class size
No Require criminal background checks for purchases at gun shows
Yes Approve GOP proposal to increase rights of patients in managed-care health plans
Yes Block effort to allow farm and medicine exports to Cuba
No Allow study of tougher automobile fuel efficiency standards
No Ratify nuclear weapons testing treaty
No Prohibit national political parties from collecting "soft money" donations
Yes Remove barriers among banking, securities and insurance companies

INTEREST GROUPS

	AFL-CIO	ADA	CCUS	ACU
2000	0%	5%	92%	100%
1999	0%	0%	88%	84%
1998	0%	0%	94%	92%
1997	0%	5%	100%	88%
1996	14%	10%	85%	95%
1995	0%	0%	100%	91%
1994	0%	5%	90%	92%
1993	0%	15%	100%	79%
1992	18%	15%	100%	89%
1991	17%	0%	90%	90%

CQ VOTE STUDIES

	PARTY UNITY		PRESIDENTIAL SUPPORT	
	Support	Oppose	Support	Oppose
2000	99%	1%	42%	58%
1999	95%	5%	33%	67%
1998	95%	5%	39%	61%
1997	97%	3%	59%	41%
1996	95%	5%	39%	61%
1995	95%	5%	24%	76%
1994	92%	8%	37%	63%
1993	94%	6%	28%	72%
1992	92%	8%	77%	23%
1991	95%	5%	93%	7%

Sen. Jim Bunning (R)

Elected 1998; 1st term

Bunning received two honors at the start of the 107th Congress. The Philadelphia Phillies baseball team announced they would retire his No. 14 at their home opener in April 2001. Bunning, a former pitcher who was inducted into the Baseball Hall of Fame in 1996, won 19 games for the Phillies in each of his first three seasons there and pitched a perfect game for the team against the New York Mets in 1964.

But the senator seemed more excited about the second honor — appointment to the Armed Services Committee. While he let the Phillies announcement pass without comment, he released a statement on the committee assignment touting the fact that he will be the first Kentucky senator to serve on the panel in nearly a half century.

Bunning said he would use his Armed Services seat to protect and enhance the mission of the state's military complexes, including Fort Knox and Fort Campbell, and to work on behalf of the state's tens of thousands of military personnel. He said he would support increased spending for missile defense programs.

Bunning also exercises his interest in economic issues from his seat on the Banking Committee, where in the 107th Congress he ascended to the chairmanship of the Economic Policy Subcommittee, whose jurisdiction includes the monetary policies of the Federal Reserve. He told Kentucky reporters that the post "will enable me to keep a close eye" on the Fed's long-time chairman, Alan Greenspan. A former stockbroker who holds a degree in economics, Bunning has had his disagreements with the Fed chairman, and he told the reporters, "I will continue to keep Alan Greenspan's feet to the fire."

The lawmaker has challenged the Fed's timing of interest rate cuts in 2000 and 2001, arguing that Greenspan should have acted sooner. "Doing so would have helped to reignite the nation's fizzling economy," Bunning told The Cincinnati Enquirer. Challenging someone of Greenspan's stature is not unusual for Bunning, who can be argumentative and acerbic.

A strong opponent of abortion and gun control, Bunning fits in comfortably with the Senate's ideological conservatives. His voting record typically rates 90 percent-plus scores from the American Conservative Union and 10 percent or less from the liberal Americans for Democratic Action.

But he has occasionally displayed a populist streak, particularly on trade. A consistent opponent of normal trade relations with China, he split with most of his Republican colleagues in 2000 in opposing legislation permanently allowing China the same low tariff rates as most other nations. Bunning, who criticized China's human rights record and military history, said the bill put "profits over people," and he joined just seven other Republican senators in voting against the measure, which became law. He also opposed the 1993 North American Free Trade Agreement as a member of the House.

Bunning guards the interests of the state's bread-and-butter industries — tobacco and horse racing. He introduced legislation in the 106th Congress to exempt from federal taxes all payments made to tobacco farmers under a 1997 settlement between states and the tobacco industry. The payments were meant to compensate farmers for reduced sales to cigarette companies forced to cut back on production and distribution under the settlement.

"Tobacco farmers in Kentucky are in desperate need of relief," Bunning said. "Between the Clinton administration's war against tobacco, the recent

CAPITOL OFFICE
224-4343; fax 228-1373; 316 Hart Bldg. 20510

INTERNET
e-mail: jim_bunning@bunning.senate.gov
web: bunning.senate.gov

COMMITTEES
Armed Services
Banking, Housing & Urban Affairs
  (Economic Policy - chairman)

HOMETOWN
Southgate

BORN
Oct. 23, 1931, Southgate, Ky.

RELIGION
Roman Catholic

FAMILY
Wife, Mary Bunning; nine children

EDUCATION
Xavier U., B.S. 1953

CAREER
Investment broker; sports agent; professional baseball player

POLITICAL HIGHLIGHTS
Fort Thomas City Council, 1977-79; Ky. Senate, 1979-83; Republican nominee for governor, 1983; U.S. House, 1987-99

ELECTION RESULTS

1998 GENERAL

Jim Bunning (R)	569,817	49.7%
Scotty Baesler (D)	563,051	49.2%
Charles R. Arbegust (REF)	12,546	1.1%

1998 PRIMARY

Jim Bunning (R)	152,493	74.3%
Barry Metcalf (R)	52,798	25.7%

PREVIOUS WINNING PERCENTAGES
1996 House Election (68%); 1994 House Election (74%); 1992 House Election (62%); 1990 House Election (69%); 1988 House Election (74%); 1986 House Election (55%)

drought, and quota loss due to less domestic demand and shrinking foreign markets, the morale of Kentucky's farm families is at an all-time low."

Another top priority for Bunning is Social Security reform. As a member of the House, Bunning chaired the Ways and Means Subcommittee on Social Security for four years. During his tenure, he championed legislation to raise the amount senior citizens could earn annually without their Social Security benefits being reduced. A bill eliminating the Social Security earnings limit ultimately became law in 2000, and he backed it as a senator.

Bunning's most memorable triumph in the House dealt with the subject he probably knows better than any other member — baseball. He played a leading role in the enactment of legislation in 1998 that partially lifted baseball's exemption from antitrust laws, which he said could improve relations between players and owners.

But he was less successful in the Senate pushing another sports-related measure. During the 106th Congress, Bunning introduced legislation to award a Congressional Gold Medal to boxer Muhammad Ali, a native of Louisville, Ky. The bill never received any action. Veterans opposed the measure because Ali refused to be drafted in 1967.

Bunning was born and raised in the Kentucky suburbs of Cincinnati. He retired from baseball in 1971, ending a 17-year career in which he played primarily for the Detroit Tigers and the Philadelphia Phillies. He was the second pitcher in history — after Cy Young — to record 1,000 strikeouts and 100 wins in both the National and American Leagues. When he retired, he was No. 2 on the all-time strikeout list, second only to Walter Johnson.

After returning home, Bunning won a seat on the Fort Thomas City Council in 1977. Just two years later, he unseated a longtime Democratic state senator. In 1983, in the last year of his four-year Senate term, he challenged the Republican floor leader and won the leadership post by one vote.

Later that year he ran for governor, but lost to Democratic Lt. Gov. Martha Layne Collins, 54 to 44 percent — a respectable showing in a state that usually elects Democratic governors by large margins.

In 1986, GOP officials enlisted Bunning to run for the House after veteran GOP Rep. Gene Snyder announced his retirement. Bunning won that November with 55 percent of the vote and then began a streak of five re-election wins in which he averaged 69 percent of the vote.

The 1998 Senate election to succeed Democrat Wendell H. Ford, who was retiring after 24 years, pitted Bunning against Democrat Scotty Baesler, also a member of the House. Baesler, too, was a sports star — a University of Kentucky basketball captain during the early 1960s. A former mayor of Lexington, he had represented the 6th District, adjacent to Bunning's 4th, for three terms.

In baseball, Bunning was a fierce competitor whose hard, inside fastballs seldom gave ground to opposing batters. His aggressive style in the campaign provoked comparisons to his former occupation. Bunning tried to take advantage of trade issues with an ad that upbraided Baesler for supporting the North American Free Trade Agreement — which Bunning said had resulted in an exodus of jobs to Mexico. "Muchas gracias, Señor Baesler" was the ad's tag line, voiced by an actor with a Mexican accent.

The race was a magnet for spending from outside groups. Campaign for America, a group supporting campaign finance overhaul, and the AFL-CIO spent hundreds of thousands of dollars on television ads praising Baesler or criticizing Bunning. The Christian Coalition and the Campaign for Working Families intervened to attack Baesler's support of abortion rights. Bunning ultimately won the general election by 6,766 votes out of more than 1.1 million cast. His victory margin was the second-smallest of any 1998 Senate race.

KEY VOTES

2000

Yes	Overhaul bankruptcy law and increase minimum wage
Yes	Limit fiscal 2001 discretionary spending to $600.3 billion
Yes	Override veto on nuclear waste disposal at Yucca Mountain site in Nevada
No	Oppose effort to terminate Kosovo mission
No	Include gender, sexual orientation and disability in federal hate crime protections
Yes	Approve GOP plan to restrict use of genetic information by health insurers
Yes	Kill amendment delaying implementation of an anti-missile defense system
Yes	Cut taxes for married couples
No	Grant China permanent normal trade status

1999

Yes	Remove President Clinton from office for obstruction of justice
Yes	Kill amendment authorizing state grants to hire teachers and reduce class size
No	Require criminal background checks for purchases at gun shows
Yes	Approve GOP proposal to increase rights of patients in managed-care health plans
Yes	Block effort to allow farm and medicine exports to Cuba
No	Allow study of tougher automobile fuel efficiency standards
No	Ratify nuclear weapons testing treaty
No	Prohibit national political parties from collecting "soft money" donations
Yes	Remove barriers among banking, securities and insurance companies

INTEREST GROUPS

	AFL-CIO	ADA	CCUS	ACU
2000	13%	5%	78%	100%
1999	11%	0%	82%	100%
House Service:				
1998	0%	0%	94%	92%
1997	0%	0%	90%	92%
1996	9%	5%	81%	100%
1995	0%	0%	96%	92%
1994	11%	5%	83%	95%
1993	8%	10%	91%	100%
1992	27%	10%	71%	90%
1991	8%	10%	90%	100%

CQ VOTE STUDIES

	PARTY UNITY		PRESIDENTIAL SUPPORT	
	Support	Oppose	Support	Oppose
2000	98%	2%	33%	67%
1999	95%	5%	24%	76%
House Service:				
1998	92%	8%	20%	80%
1997	95%	5%	27%	73%
1996	96%	4%	33%	67%
1995	98%	2%	19%	81%
1994	96%	4%	31%	69%
1993	96%	4%	27%	73%
1992	94%	6%	79%	21%
1991	96%	4%	77%	23%

Rep. Edward Whitfield (R)

Elected 1994; 4th term

Whitfield's personal political history is illustrative of the realignment of political power in the South. Elected to the state legislature as a Democrat in the mid-1970s, his early mentor in political life was Democrat Edward Breathitt, who served a term as Kentucky's governor in the 1960s and was a longtime family friend. After being out of elective office for almost 20 years, Whitfield was convinced to run again in 1994, this time as a Republican, by Kentucky GOP Sen. Mitch McConnell.

McConnell, who told Whitfield at the time that he was "the damnedest excuse for a Democrat I've ever seen," played a key role in Whitfield's successful campaign to unseat Democratic Rep. Tom Barlow. The Louisville Courier-Journal wrote that McConnell was "chief strategist, media buyer and liaison with national Republican leaders" for Whitfield's campaign. Whitfield is the first Republican ever to represent western Kentucky in the House.

During the two decades between his elected offices, Whitfield lived mostly in Florida and Washington, D.C., where he was a top railroad executive, a job he initially landed with some help from Breathitt. For a few years in the early 1990s, he served as a lawyer for the Interstate Commerce Commission.

Whitfield's political views are generally quite conservative, but he is seldom partisan in public. The Louisville newspaper quoted a political science professor as saying, "Ed is a No. 1 nice guy." On Capitol Hill, he is low-key and formal.

He usually votes with the GOP majority but has deviated on occasion, such as when he opposed a Republican plan to provide education vouchers. He is also protective of 1st District needs. He was the only Republican on the Commerce Committee's Energy and Power Subcommittee to vote against legislation to deregulate the electric utility industry in the 106th Congress. He disagreed with his party leaders on that measure and another to provide millions of federal dollars in compensation to ailing workers who once worked in nuclear fuel plants.

Whitfield's constituents benefit from low-cost power from the Tennessee Valley Authority (TVA), and he looks with skepticism at any legislation that might endanger the area's low electric rates. And he supported the legislation compensating the nuclear plant workers because it would help employees at the uranium enrichment plant at Paducah, in the 1st District.

Although GOP leaders were initially reluctant to act because of the compensation bill's price tag, Whitfield and his allies were eventually able to win a $150,000 lump sum payment and lifetime medical benefits for ailing workers, with the government forced to bear the burden of proof to show that workers were not eligible. The package also included $78 million for cleanup at the Paducah facility.

Among Whitfield's local legislative accomplishments was money for a new lock at the Kentucky Dam to accommodate barge traffic and funds for the U.S. Forest Service to manage the popular Land Between the Lakes recreation area. Land Between the Lakes had been managed by TVA, but Whitfield, McConnell and other area lawmakers were able to ease the transition to Forest Service management.

Whitfield was also a key player on a 1997 overhaul of the Food and Drug Administration, concentrating on the regulation of food products. Deregulating margarine was a pet concern, he said. The 1950s regulation of the butter substitute was outdated, he argued, because it was a relic of protectionist

CAPITOL OFFICE
225-3115; fax 225-3547; 236 Cannon Bldg. 20515

INTERNET
e-mail: www.house.gov/writerep
web: www.house.gov/whitfield

COMMITTEES
Energy & Commerce

HOMETOWN
Hopkinsville

BORN
May 25, 1943, Hopkinsville, Ky.

RELIGION
Methodist

FAMILY
Wife, Constance Whitfield; one child

EDUCATION
U. of Kentucky, B.S. 1965; Wesley Theological Seminary, attended 1966; U. of Kentucky, J.D. 1969

MILITARY SERVICE
Army Reserve, 1967-73

CAREER
Lawyer; oil distributor; railroad executive

POLITICAL HIGHLIGHTS
Ky. House, 1974-75

ELECTION RESULTS

2000 GENERAL

Edward Whitfield (R)	132,115	58.0%
Brian Roy (D)	95,806	42.0%

2000 PRIMARY

Edward Whitfield (R)	12,013	83.8%
David Lynn Williams (R)	2,317	16.2%

1998 GENERAL

Edward Whitfield (R)	95,308	55.2%
Tom Barlow (D)	77,402	44.8%

PREVIOUS WINNING PERCENTAGES
1996 (54%); 1994 (51%)

laws erected by dairy interests to protect butter. He represents an area that produces soybeans, a key ingredient in margarine.

Whitfield won a slot on the Commerce Committee (now called Energy and Commerce) in his first term. Chairman Thomas J. Bliley Jr. of Virginia was looking to bring friends of the tobacco industry on board, and tobacco is an important crop in the 1st District. When the Clinton administration filed a lawsuit against tobacco companies, Whitfield objected to what he called the administration's "punitive and vindictive pursuit of a legal business and farmers who grow a legal crop." Later, he said that expecting the Democratic administration "to help tobacco growers is akin to a patient seeking a cure from Dr. Kevorkian."

Born in Hopkinsville, Whitfield practiced law and ran an oil distribution company in western Kentucky. He declined to seek re-election to the state House after just one term and soon moved east, where he spent 12 years as a railroad official, including several years as a lobbyist for railroad giant CSX Corp. After leaving his post at the Interstate Commerce Commission, he briefly practiced law in Florida but soon decided to move back to Kentucky to run for the House.

Whitfield's challenge to Barlow looked like an uphill battle, even to McConnell, given that most of the district's 31 counties are at least 80 percent Democratic in registration. The Courier-Journal described Whitfield on the campaign trail in 1994 as looking like the Washington lobbyist he once was. "On the stump, he wears tailored suits and French cuffs. He doesn't hide his urbanity or his intellect." Indeed, Whitfield has acknowledged that often his opponent is a better campaigner, but he argues that he is a better congressman.

In the 1994 race, Whitfield found that his recent conversion to Republicanism did not sit well with some party faithful, nor did the fact that he had recently moved back to Kentucky. But Barlow became a national GOP target and Whitfield was able to tie him to the increasingly unpopular President Clinton. The climate was right for the 1st to chuck its Democratic traditions, and Whitfield managed to win with 51 percent.

Given the district's deep Democratic roots, Whitfield can never rest easily. He was a Democratic target in 1996, but he prevailed, again narrowly, with 54 percent of the vote. Barlow sought a rematch in 1998, but his underfunded campaign failed to win serious support from national Democrats or their allied interest groups. Whitfield won by 10 percentage points. In 2000, he prevailed by his largest margin of victory, besting former U.S. Marshal Brian Roy by 16 points.

KEY VOTES

2000

No	Raise hourly minimum wage by $1 over two years
Yes	Halt funding for U.S. mission in Kosovo unless European nations pay more
Yes	Provide Medicare benefits to military retirees and their dependents
Yes	Grant China permanent normal trade status
+	Phase out estate, gift and trust taxes
Yes	Prohibit implementation of president's national monument designations
Yes	Approve GOP plan to provide prescription drug coverage for Medicare beneficiaries
No	Increase help for poor nations indebted to international financial institutions

1999

Yes	Impose steel import quotas
No	Kill proposal to take aviation trust funds off budget
No	Require background checks on buyers only at gun shows with 10 or more vendors
Yes	Remove barriers among banking, securities and insurance companies
No	Authorize state grants to hire teachers and reduce class size
No	Overhaul campaign finance law; ban "soft money" and restrict advocacy advertising
No	Approve bipartisan plan to increase rights of patients in managed-care health plans

INTEREST GROUPS

	AFL-CIO	ADA	CCUS	ACU
2000	0%	0%	90%	87%
1999	22%	10%	100%	80%
1998	20%	5%	88%	96%
1997	13%	0%	100%	96%

CQ VOTE STUDIES

	PARTY UNITY		PRESIDENTIAL SUPPORT	
	Support	Oppose	Support	Oppose
2000	90%	10%	29%	71%
1999	89%	11%	24%	76%
1998	90%	10%	24%	76%
1997	93%	7%	31%	69%

KENTUCKY 1

West – Paducah

Located in the far western part of the Blue Grass state, Kentucky's rural 1st is a hub of agricultural activity. Here, slaves once helped cultivate cotton and tobacco crops, and tobacco still dominates the economy, although its future is uncertain. The 1st also has seen a steady decline in its coal industry to the north.

The Ohio River port of Paducah (McCracken County) traditionally has been the political and population center of western Kentucky, but its population has been surpassed by Hopkinsville (Christian County), an agricultural market center dependent on nearby Fort Campbell, and by Henderson.

While the 1st has seen its coal and mining industries decline precipitously, Hopkins County has weathered the loss by evolving into a regional industrial and medical center. Tourism and recreation also play a role in the economy, especially near the Land Between the Lakes recreation area, where the Tennessee Valley Authority

maintains a major presence.

The mostly white 1st is a political anomaly. Its Confederate legacy has traditionally translated into Democratic votes, but in the 1994 GOP wave that swelled nationwide, the 1st sent its first Republican to Congress by a small margin and has re-elected him ever since. Most of western Kentucky is dominated by conservative Democrats. The 1st voted for President Bush by a 17 percent margin in 2000 after Bill Clinton carried the district in 1992 and '96.

MAJOR INDUSTRY
Agriculture, manufacturing

MILITARY BASES
Fort Campbell, 25,719 military, 2,802 civilian (2001)

CITIES
Hopkinsville 32,270; Henderson 26,566; Paducah 25,777; Madisonville, 19,768

UNUSUAL FEATURE
In 1861, Confederate areas in the 1st plotted unsuccessfully to secede from Kentucky.

Rep. Ron Lewis (R)

Elected May 1994; 4th full term

CAPITOL OFFICE
225-3501; fax 226-2019; 2418 Rayburn Bldg. 20515

INTERNET
e-mail: www.house.gov/writerep
web: www.house.gov/ronlewis

COMMITTEES
Government Reform
Ways & Means

HOMETOWN
Cecilia

BORN
Sept. 14, 1946, Greenup County, Ky.

RELIGION
Baptist

FAMILY
Wife, Kayi Lewis; two children

EDUCATION
Morehead State U., attended; U. of Kentucky, B.A.
1969; Morehead State U., M.A. 1981

MILITARY SERVICE
Navy, 1972

CAREER
Christian bookstore owner; minister; college instructor

POLITICAL HIGHLIGHTS
Sought Republican nomination for Ky. House, 1971

ELECTION RESULTS

2000 GENERAL

Ron Lewis (R)	160,800	67.7%
Brian Pedigo (D)	74,537	31.4%

2000 PRIMARY

Ron Lewis (R)	unopposed

1998 GENERAL

Ron Lewis (R)	113,285	63.7%
Bob Evans (D)	62,848	35.3%
Jim Ketchel (REF)	1,833	1.0%

PREVIOUS WINNING PERCENTAGES
1996 (58%); 1994 (60%); 1994 Special Election (55%)

A former minister and owner of a Christian bookstore, Lewis often uses his current pulpit — the House floor — to sermonize about the decline of moral values in contemporary America. He decries the primacy of personal gratification and the lack of personal responsibility, and he blasts "a morally corrupt culture" that fosters teenage pregnancy, abortion and drug use.

When two schoolchildren killed four classmates and a teacher with rifles in Jonesboro, Ark., in March 1998, Lewis was outraged that some commentators blamed the incident on the widespread acceptance of guns in Southern culture. "If we want to start placing the blame ... why not start with the TV networks, where our children are exposed to assault, murder, rape, drugs, sex, deviant lifestyles, cheating, stealing and uncivilized gutter language? ... What goes in our children eventually comes out," he said.

Lewis echoed the same themes in the 106th Congress, after shootings at a Colorado high school sparked a nationwide debate over tightening gun regulations. He told the Louisville Courier-Journal he didn't think "one more gun law is going to help," pointing out that the "young men at Columbine broke anywhere from 19 to 23 gun laws. ... The laws on the books aren't being enforced now."

Lewis is a relentless critic of Democratic Party social policies. But his partisan attacks have not hurt him in his district, which leans Republican despite the Democrats' advantage in party registration. Part of the reason for Lewis' popularity is that he tends carefully to home state concerns, fiercely protecting the interests of tobacco farmers, directing federal funds to district projects, and often aligning himself with Democrats on labor issues.

Lewis' dependably conservative voting record and his campaign work for other GOP candidates helped him win an assignment to the Ways and Means Committee in the 106th. He introduced legislation to give tax breaks to foster parents and to small business franchises, but failed to win passage of the bills. In the 107th, he added a seat on the Government Reform panel.

The 2nd District's many tobacco growers have an unflinching advocate in Lewis. The congressman — himself the son of a tobacco farmer — opposed efforts to give the Food and Drug Administration authority to regulate tobacco, saying the issue is best handled at the state and local levels. He also denounced a Clinton administration plan in 1999 to sue the nation's tobacco companies for billions of dollars in smoking-related health care costs. "The tobacco companies already have been hit through the state lawsuits [and] they're hanging on," Lewis said, according to The Courier-Journal in Louisville, Ky. "If there's another big hit, I'm not sure the tobacco companies can continue to do business in this country."

However, Lewis has recognized that political support for federal tobacco programs has dwindled, and he urged farmers to take advantage of any buyout offer that might be part of a tobacco bill, rather than insisting on fighting for continued federal price supports. He was criticized for that stance by some tobacco farmers and some pro-tobacco colleagues.

Concern about the tobacco industry was one reason Lewis backed permanent normal trade status for China in 2000, even though he has opposed some other trade agreements. "Our tobacco farmers, as well as our livestock and grain producers, need new markets in order to stay in business, and China's market will be large once we get this new access to it," he said.

Lewis votes with the right on most social issues. He lays a large share of the blame for the decline in values on the Democratic Party: "For 40 years we had a tax-and-spend Congress ... for 30 years there has been a war on poverty, $5 trillion has been spent. And what have we got?" he asked. "We have more in poverty, we have more welfare, more illegitimacy, lower education, higher crime, more poverty, more drugs."

His conservative social agenda places him on the front lines whenever Congress debates a procedure its opponents call "partial birth" abortion. He has been prominent in the GOP effort to prohibit U.S. aid to international family planning programs unless the legislation includes abortion restrictions. Lewis also has been vocal in opposing government funding for the arts. In the 105th, he pressed for legislation that would have required federal agencies to assess whether proposed regulations strengthen or erode family values.

Although he is a fiscal conservative on most issues, Lewis opposed a GOP proposal in 1995 to kill all funding for the Appalachian Regional Commission, a Great Society program to build roads and spur economic development in 13 Appalachian states. Lewis grew up in Appalachia, and he told colleagues, "I remember the little one-lane roads, the dusty dirt roads, the lack of utilities, the small one-room schools." Because of the commission, he said, there has been "tremendous improvement" in Eastern Kentucky and "now there are nice highways, nice schools, utilities reaching into the homes, paved highways."

Lewis had already filed for the 2nd District race when longtime Democratic Rep. William H. Natcher died in March 1994. Party officials chose Lewis to run in the May special election to replace Natcher, also giving him clear sailing for the GOP nomination for the full-term election in November.

Democrats had represented the district for more than a century, and Natcher had been in office for four decades. But the typical Democratic voter in the 2nd did not have to make a big ideological leap to support Lewis, because the culturally conservative views he espouses had long been the local norm. In the special election, Lewis tied his Democratic opponent, former state Sen. Joseph Prather, to the unpopular Clinton White House. With about $200,000 in funding from the national GOP, Lewis won with 55 percent. Riding on momentum in the strongly Republican year, Lewis won the fall contest with 60 percent of the vote and has easily won re-election since.

Lewis had pledged to serve no more than four terms, but in 1998 he said the promise had been a "mistake. ... It's not fair for people to invest six or eight years in a representative who would be a lame duck his last two years and could not be as effective as he should be or could be." He has left open the possibility that he will leave after four full terms.

KEY VOTES

2000

No   Raise hourly minimum wage by $1 over two years

Yes   Halt funding for U.S. mission in Kosovo unless European nations pay more

Yes   Provide Medicare benefits to military retirees and their dependents

Yes   Grant China permanent normal trade status

Yes   Phase out estate, gift and trust taxes

Yes   Prohibit implementation of president's national monument designations

Yes   Approve GOP plan to provide prescription drug coverage for Medicare beneficiaries

No   Increase help for poor nations indebted to international financial institutions

1999

Yes   Impose steel import quotas

No   Kill proposal to take aviation trust funds off budget

No   Require background checks on buyers only at gun shows with 10 or more vendors

Yes   Remove barriers among banking, securities and insurance companies

No   Authorize state grants to hire teachers and reduce class size

No   Overhaul campaign finance law; ban "soft money" and restrict advocacy advertising

No   Approve bipartisan plan to increase rights of patients in managed-care health plans

INTEREST GROUPS

	AFL-CIO	ADA	CCUS	ACU
2000	0%	0%	90%	96%
1999	11%	5%	100%	92%
1998	0%	0%	100%	100%
1997	0%	0%	78%	95%

CQ VOTE STUDIES

	PARTY UNITY		PRESIDENTIAL SUPPORT	
	Support	Oppose	Support	Oppose
2000	94%	6%	25%	75%
1999	95%	5%	17%	83%
1998	94%	6%	20%	80%
1997	97%	3%	26%	74%

KENTUCKY 2

West Central – Owensboro

The mostly rural 2nd takes in suburban areas near Louisville and runs through rolling tobacco country, ending in the western coal field region. One claim to fame is that Abraham Lincoln was born in the area.

While tobacco remains the district's dominant crop, the 2nd's economy relies on more than agriculture. Oil and coal help make Owensboro, the district's largest city, western Kentucky's leading trade center, while the General Motors Corvette plant in Bowling Green also provides jobs. Away from the main population areas, the economic picture has been somewhat grim. In Taylor County, the closing of a textile plant in the late 1990s helped ratchet its unemployment rate above 20 percent at one point. A new Amazon.com facility has helped steady the area since, however.

While Democratic voters traditionally dominate the 2nd, it has an independent streak and a penchant for backing Republicans for

federal office, making it politically competitive. In 1994, Republicans won the congressional seat for the first time and have managed to retain it since. In 1992, '96 and 2000, the district gave the edge to Republican presidential candidates. Although Democrats are still generally favored in local elections, the Jefferson suburbs and areas around Owensboro lean Republican.

MAJOR INDUSTRY
Tobacco, tourism, manufacturing

MILITARY BASES
Fort Knox, 6,015 military, 6,155 civilian; Port Hueneme Attachment Louisville, 5 military, 180 civilian (1998)

CITIES
Owensboro, 54,010; Bowling Green, 45,550; Elizabethtown, 20,760

UNUSUAL FEATURES
Owensboro is home to the world's largest sassafras tree – a 250- to 300-year-old tree with a circumference of about 16 feet; The U.S. bullion depository at Fort Knox, or "Gold Vault," houses the largest portion of the U.S. gold reserve.

Rep. Anne M. Northup (R)

Elected 1996; 3rd term

Northup is a Republican campaign strategist's dream: a telegenic mother of six, a seasoned legislator and an articulate proponent of pragmatic conservatism. She is just what the doctor ordered for a party that often has image problems with women voters.

As a freshman, she was given a seat on the Appropriations Committee, where she can counter the Democrats' argument that only they know what is important to women. "All soccer moms don't think alike," she told The Christian Science Monitor. "I do not believe the Republican philosophy and perspective is in general anti-minority, anti-women," she says. "But it is certainly portrayed that way."

Northup is pro-business and reliably conservative, but not unwilling to compromise — a characteristic she acquired, she says, from her upbringing in a large family. Her willingness to moderate her stands has helped her survive in a House district that had been represented by Democrats for 26 years. "I call myself conservative, but I'm not extreme," she told the Louisville Courier-Journal in 2000.

Republican leaders make sure she is front and center at party news conferences where priority legislation is discussed, and she is often tapped to give the "working mother" perspective. A quick study, she will speak on the House floor on an array of issues, often citing lessons learned in the Kentucky House and in her own house.

Northup brings what she calls a "family ethic" to policy debates, often prefacing her remarks with the phrase, "As a mother of six children ... ." When adding her support to GOP education overhaul proposals, she has talked about how she sold quilts to pay for special tutoring programs for several of her children, who had learning disabilities. She is the co-founder of the House Reading Caucus, and she often reads to students during school visits back home in Louisville.

During House consideration of a measure to promote adoption, Northup spoke of her own family's experience adopting two children — one African-American and one of mixed race. Northup argues that Democrats do not have all the answers for the African-American community. "Look what they've created — a zillion programs and more hopelessness than ever," she told Insight magazine.

On Appropriations, she tries to balance her interest in fiscal conservatism with her desire to make sure Louisville gets its share of federal spending. Some of her successes include money for two bridges across the Ohio River, medical research grants for local hospitals and the University of Louisville, social service programs for black churches, and research and recording work done by the American Printing House for the Blind in Louisville, which was in dire financial straits.

Northup played a lead role in the 2000 battle over whether the Occupational Safety and Health Administration could issue a new rule requiring businesses to set up programs to prevent repetitive motion injuries. She argued that the new ergonomics rule would be too expensive for most businesses and "simply isn't feasible." Everyone gets repetitive motion injuries in and out of the workplace, she said, adding that the proposed rule would make it easy for workers to take any ache or pain and claim it was related to ergonomic factors.

The rule was of particular interest to United Parcel Service (UPS), which has a large distribution hub in Louisville and has many workers who per-

CAPITOL OFFICE
225-5401; fax 225-5776
1004 Longworth Bldg. 20515

INTERNET
e-mail: rep.northup@mail.house.gov
web: www.house.gov/northup

COMMITTEES
Appropriations

HOMETOWN
Louisville

BORN
Jan. 22, 1948, Louisville, Ky.

RELIGION
Roman Catholic

FAMILY
Husband, Robert Wood Northup; six children

EDUCATION
St. Mary's College, B.A. 1970

CAREER
Teacher

POLITICAL HIGHLIGHTS
Ky. House, 1987-96

ELECTION RESULTS

2000 GENERAL

Anne M. Northup (R)	142,106	52.9%
Eleanor Jordan (D)	118,785	44.2%
Donna W. Mancini (LIBERT)	7,804	2.9%

2000 PRIMARY

Anne M. Northup (R)	unopposed

1998 GENERAL

Anne M. Northup (R)	100,690	51.5%
Chris Gorman (D)	92,865	47.5%

PREVIOUS WINNING PERCENTAGES
1996 (50%)

form repetitive tasks. Northup has also displayed her pro-business bent in opposing an increase in the minimum wage, arguing against legislation permitting doctors to bargain collectively and working to delay changes in health insurance claims procedures.

Northup sought to move into the party leadership ranks in 1998 as vice chairman of the Republican Conference, but she finished second in a field of four to Florida's Tillie Fowler. She did win appointment, however, as one of six vice chairmen of the National Republican Congressional Committee, the organization that seeks to elect Republicans to the House.

In 2000, with Fowler retiring, Northup at first planned to run again for the conference vice chairmanship. But when Deborah Pryce of Ohio entered the race, Northup deferred to her more-senior colleague. Northup ran for conference secretary instead but dropped out a day before the balloting, saying she had had to focus on winning re-election to the House.

Northup comes from a family of 11 children, 10 of them girls (including Olympic champion swimmer Mary T. Meagher). She says that growing up in a large family taught her valuable lessons about compromise: "None of us got our way all the time," she once told her House colleagues.

Northup's father was involved in local Republican politics, and she told The Washington Post that, "Election Day was the second-most-important day to Christmas."

When her youngest child started school, Northup, who had been active in student government in high school and college, rekindled her interest in politics, taking a job at the state legislature. She was elected to the state House in 1987. Her record there was conservative but with an independent streak. For example, even though tobacco is key to Kentucky's economy, Northup led an effort to impose stricter laws against the sale of tobacco to children.

In launching her 1996 House bid against first-term Democratic Rep. Mike Ward, Northup, who opposes abortion, had the backing of some religious conservatives and was able to outspend Ward by more than $300,000. Northup prevailed by just 1,299 votes, becoming the only GOP challenger in the country to oust a Democrat in a district that President Clinton carried.

In 1998 and 2000, Democrats viewed the 3rd District as a key battleground in their effort to retake the House, but Northup was able to amass a campaign war chest of about $2 million in both elections. She prevailed narrowly in 1998 over former state Attorney General Chris Gorman and by a slightly more comfortable 9-point margin in 2000 against state Rep. Eleanor Jordan, the only black woman in the state legislature.

KEY VOTES

2000

No	Raise hourly minimum wage by $1 over two years
Yes	Halt funding for U.S. mission in Kosovo unless European nations pay more
Yes	Provide Medicare benefits to military retirees and their dependents
Yes	Grant China permanent normal trade status
Yes	Phase out estate, gift and trust taxes
Yes	Prohibit implementation of president's national monument designations
Yes	Approve GOP plan to provide prescription drug coverage for Medicare beneficiaries
No	Increase help for poor nations indebted to international financial institutions

1999

No	Impose steel import quotas
No	Kill proposal to take aviation trust funds off budget
Yes	Require background checks on buyers only at gun shows with 10 or more vendors
Yes	Remove barriers among banking, securities and insurance companies
No	Authorize state grants to hire teachers and reduce class size
No	Overhaul campaign finance law; ban "soft money" and restrict advocacy advertising
No	Approve bipartisan plan to increase rights of patients in managed-care health plans

INTEREST GROUPS

	AFL-CIO	ADA	CCUS	ACU
2000	0%	0%	95%	72%
1999	0%	5%	100%	68%
1998	10%	0%	100%	88%
1997	0%	5%	100%	88%

CQ VOTE STUDIES

	PARTY UNITY		PRESIDENTIAL SUPPORT	
	Support	Oppose	Support	Oppose
2000	89%	11%	32%	68%
1999	89%	11%	28%	72%
1998	91%	9%	25%	75%
1997	92%	8%	25%	75%

KENTUCKY 3

Louisville and suburbs

With the Ohio River running along its northern border, the moderate 3rd sprawls across ethnically and economically diverse neighborhoods, taking in thriving Louisville. Compared with the rest of the state, the city has a sizable black population, as well as a large Catholic following, a legacy of a massive German immigration in the mid-19th century.

Despite some job losses from industrial decline, labor strength runs deep among the blue-collar, white residents of the South End. Blacks, who live near downtown in the West End also make up a strong Democratic voting bloc. Republicans live in the affluent East End by the Ohio River.

Although tobacco is an important part of the 3rd's hearty economy, other sectors, such as the service industry, have rivaled it. Louisville claims a booming health care industry, and the United Parcel Service operates an air-freight hub out of Standiford Airport.

Tourism, already big, was boosted by the 1998 opening of a massive floating casino on the Indiana bank of the Ohio River.

A politically competitive district, the 3rd ousted a Democrat in 1996 and has held onto her Republican replacement. Democrats are still favored at the local level, especially in downtown Louisville. But more upscale areas favor Republicans, and the increasing muscle of white-collar suburbanites appears to be swinging the 3rd closer to the GOP.

MAJOR INDUSTRY
Service, manufacturing, trade, tobacco

CITIES
Louisville, 253,128; Pleasure Ridge Park (unincorporated), 25,131 (1990); Jeffersontown (pt.), 24,283 (1990); Shively, 16,757

UNUSUAL FEATURES
Kentucky Derby; Birthplace of Muhammad Ali (1942) and the cheeseburger (1934); Louisville was known as "Strike City" for fractious labor-management relations in the 1980s.

Rep. Ken Lucas (D)

CAPITOL OFFICE
225-3465; fax 225-8698
1237 Longworth Bldg. 20515

INTERNET
e-mail: write.kenlucas@mail.house.gov
web: www.house.gov/kenlucas

COMMITTEES
Agriculture
Financial Services

HOMETOWN
Richwood

BORN
Aug. 22, 1933, Covington, Ky.

RELIGION
Christian Church

FAMILY
Wife, Mary Lucas; five children

EDUCATION
U. of Kentucky, B.S. 1955; Xavier U., M.B.A. 1970

MILITARY SERVICE
Air Force, 1955-57; Ky. Air National Guard, 1957-67

CAREER
Banking executive; university regent; financial planner

POLITICAL HIGHLIGHTS
Florence City Council, 1967-74; Boone County Commission, 1974-82; Boone County judge-executive, 1992-98

ELECTION RESULTS

2000 GENERAL

Ken Lucas (D)	125,872	54.3%
Don Bell (R)	100,943	43.5%
Ken Sain (GR)	3,662	1.6%

2000 PRIMARY

Ken Lucas (D)	unopposed

1998 GENERAL

Ken Lucas (D)	93,485	53.4%
Gex "Jay" Williams (R)	81,547	46.6%

Elected 1998; 2nd term

The day Lucas was sworn into office in 1999, he joined only four other Democrats in voting to approve the 13 House "managers" who would present the case for impeachment against President Clinton in the Senate. That first vote spoke volumes about the Kentucky financial planner's political style. Unafraid to buck his party, Lucas — the first Democrat to represent the 4th District in 32 years — reflects the conservative values and views of his constituency. In an era of slim House majorities and tight voting margins, Lucas' independence makes him a valuable commodity to both parties.

"It's a little frustrating to me that it's been so contentious here and so partisan," Lucas said early in 2001, looking back at his first term in the 106th Congress. "I think you could send a machine up here to vote the party line — that's not why I'm here."

Lucas counts himself among the group of conservative Democrats known as the "Blue Dogs," whose emphasis is on budget and tax issues, and the centrist New Democrats, whose focus is on technology and education. His independence is apparent in his voting record. During the 106th Congress, Lucas, who is anti-abortion, anti-gun control and pro-tobacco, supported the GOP-proposed $792 billion tax cut, a measure to require the support of a two-thirds majority in Congress to increase taxes, a provision in the District of Columbia spending measure that banned adoptions by gay couples, and a bill that would have allowed states to post the Ten Commandments in state government buildings. In all, he bucked the party line exactly half the time in the 106th; only two Democrats voted against the party more often.

Elected at age 65, Lucas was the oldest member of the freshman Class of 1998. He makes no secret of his lack of political ambition or devotion to a monolithic Democratic position. In fact, he frequently attributes his maverick style as a lawmaker to his age. He is a member of the Citizen Legislators' Caucus, a group that supports congressional term limits. He has said he would serve no more than six years.

"Age allows you to maybe be more independent than you might be," Lucas said at the beginning of the 107th Congress. "It allows me to vote my conscience and the will of my district, and not worry too much about the consequences."

A prominent figure in northern Kentucky business and local political circles, Lucas says running for Congress was "an offshoot, really, of my civic work." Throughout his career in finance, Lucas involved himself in various aspects of his community, including serving as a city councilman, a county commissioner, a county executive and a regent at his alma mater, the University of Kentucky — where there is a building named after him and he received an honorary doctorate. His emphasis in Congress on public education and economic development can be traced back to his roots in Florence, just south of Cincinnati, where he founded and led several economic development organizations.

It was at the University of Kentucky that Lucas met the person who ultimately persuaded him to run for Congress, he says. Paul Patton, a fraternity brother of Lucas' in college, would go on to become Kentucky's Democratic governor — with plenty of campaign help from Lucas — and later persuade his friend to pursue a seat in the House.

A self-described "common-sense conservative" who grew up on a dairy and tobacco farm in the 4th District's Grant County, Lucas says his work in

Congress is guided in large part by the characteristics of the area. "I came to Congress not as a partisan politician, but as a person who was just interested in my community," he says. As a freshman serving on the Agriculture Committee, he used his seat to look out for the interests of the district's many tobacco farmers, cosponsoring a bill with fellow Kentuckian Ernie Fletcher, that would have provided tax relief for tobacco farmers hurt by lawsuits against their industry.

He also has pushed measures to protect dairy farmers, including a bill that would have blocked a Clinton administration plan to overhaul federal dairy pricing that opponents said would reduce milk prices paid to farmers by nearly $200 million annually, and one that would create a dairy compact for Southeastern states — including Kentucky — to set minimum milk prices above the federally established level.

In the 107th Congress, Lucas traded his seat on the Budget Committee for one on the Financial Services panel, with the aim of enhancing economic development and homeownership opportunities in his district, as well as bolstering privacy laws.

While his votes on some issues have been to the right of most Democrats, Lucas shares some key positions with his party colleagues. He backs efforts to allow patients to sue their managed-care plans for denial of coverage, he favors Democratic proposals to protect Social Security, and he opposes federally funded vouchers for low-income families to send their children to private schools. But while he is a proponent of public education, he believes there should be more local control over education spending.

But Lucas drew the line in 2000 at supporting a presidential candidate whose views on many issues were diametrically opposed to his own. He made national news the week before the Democratic National Convention by announcing that, as a delegate, he would not vote to nominate Vice President Al Gore as the party's presidential candidate. "I'm pro-life and he's pro-choice; I'm very much for tobacco farmers in Kentucky, and he is not. I'm a Second Amendment rights guy, and he is not," Lucas told reporters.

Lucas was a well-known local figure when he decided to run for the seat being vacated by six-term Republican Jim Bunning, who won a Senate bid in 1998. Lucas' stature in the community and close ties with Gov. Patton allowed him to run a well-financed campaign, raising more than $1 million, and he got past the GOP nominee, state Sen. Gex "Jay" Williams, by roughly a 7-point margin.

In 2000, he prevailed over Republican Don Bell, a retired Secret Service agent, by almost 11 percentage points.

KEY VOTES

2000

No Raise hourly minimum wage by $1 over two years
No Halt funding for U.S. mission in Kosovo unless European nations pay more
Yes Provide Medicare benefits to military retirees and their dependents
Yes Grant China permanent normal trade status
Yes Phase out estate, gift and trust taxes
No Prohibit implementation of president's national monument designations
No Approve GOP plan to provide prescription drug coverage for Medicare beneficiaries
Yes Increase help for poor nations indebted to international financial institutions

1999

Yes Impose steel import quotas
No Kill proposal to take aviation trust funds off budget
No Require background checks on buyers only at gun shows with 10 or more vendors
Yes Remove barriers among banking, securities and insurance companies
Yes Authorize state grants to hire teachers and reduce class size
Yes Overhaul campaign finance law; ban "soft money" and restrict advocacy advertising
Yes Approve bipartisan plan to increase rights of patients in managed-care health plans

INTEREST GROUPS

	AFL-CIO	ADA	CCUS	ACU
2000	40%	25%	80%	60%
1999	63%	40%	88%	64%

CQ VOTE STUDIES

	PARTY UNITY		PRESIDENTIAL SUPPORT	
	Support	Oppose	Support	Oppose
2000	54%	46%	41%	59%
1999	46%	54%	41%	59%

KENTUCKY 4

North and East — Covington; Ashland

Almost half of the 4th's residents live in Cincinnati's suburbs, which helps explain the district's dual economic personality and its competitive, but consistently conservative, politics. Starting near the industrial city of Ashland along the Ohio River, the 4th picks up tobacco farms and small towns, passes through the Ohio commuters region in Boone, Campbell and Kenton counties, and eventually reaches suburbs near Louisville.

The 4th's economy has two drastically different sides. Covington and the northern part of the district have enjoyed steady economic growth, due partly to the Cincinnati-Northern Kentucky International Airport located in Kentucky. The city also serves as a regional center of the Internal Revenue Service, a major employer.

Ashland's economic picture is gloomier. Struggling to cope with the relocation of Ashland Inc. and downsizing of other businesses, the city has become a declining industrial hub.

The 4th also has two dissonant political personalities. While most of its rural counties are Democratic, Oldham County, near Louisville, and areas surrounding Covington and Ashland are becoming more Republican with the decline in blue-collar jobs.

While a Republican had held the 4th since the 1966 election, the Democratic win in 1998 and 2000 demonstrated that conservative Democrats can be competitive. The district gave healthy margins of victory to GOP presidential candidates in 1992, '96 and 2000.

MAJOR INDUSTRY
Service, manufacturing, health care

CITIES
Covington, 40,099; Ashland, 22,057; Florence, 20,171; Erlanger, 16,990

UNUSUAL FEATURES
Underground Railroad went through the 4th.

Rep. Harold Rogers (R)

Elected 1980; 11th term

For more than a dozen years, Rogers played a leadership role on the Appropriations subcommittee that funds the Commerce, Justice and State departments, serving eight years as the ranking Republican and six years as chairman. At the start of the 107th Congress, he left the post, reluctantly, and took the gavel of the Transportation Subcommittee, forced to switch because of GOP-imposed term limits on chairmanships.

Adapting to his new role should not pose a problem for Rogers, who tends toward a pragmatic conservatism. Rogers is an easygoing, old-style pol who understands the art of cutting a legislative deal, honing his skills during almost two decades on the Appropriations Committee, the panel most committed to deal-making.

And while the appropriations bill funding the Commerce, Justice and State departments tends to be one of the more controversial and problematic of the 13 annual spending measures, Rogers seemed to thrive on the challenge. His patience and legislative skill were regularly tested as the panel wrestled with proposals to eliminate the Commerce Department and to change the way the decennial census was conducted. Each year, resistance from congressional Democrats or the White House threatened to stall Rogers' bill in legislative gridlock.

While Rogers firmly agrees with the GOP on the need to shrink the federal bureaucracy, he does not always share some of the younger House Republicans' zeal for slashing the budget. He opposed conservatives' efforts to kill the Commerce Department and instead sought to reduce spending for Commerce programs in order to provide more money for Justice Department anti-crime activities.

He has supported cutting the budget of the Legal Services Corporation, which provides legal aid to the poor, but objects to eliminating the agency entirely, as some have proposed. He defended the Economic Development Administration, which funds public works and technical aid to states and localities, and the Appalachian Regional Commission, a Depression-era development agency whose service area includes Rogers' predominantly rural 5th District.

The 5th is the poorest district in Kentucky and one of the poorest in the country, with many residents struggling to adapt to the long-term decline in coal mining and tobacco farming. These economic conditions help explain why Rogers' votes sometimes differ from those cast by his GOP colleagues representing upscale suburban districts. "I think most of the people I represent are conservative in their personal beliefs, but we must be practical," he told the Louisville Courier-Journal in 1998.

He does not, for instance, concur with his party leadership on trade issues, reflecting the concern among his constituents that lowering international trade barriers may send factory jobs to low-wage foreign employers. In the 106th Congress, he was one of 57 Republicans who voted against the bill to grant China permanent normal trade status. In 1998, he voted against granting the president fast-track authority to negotiate trade agreements that Congress cannot amend. Rogers also split with his party to oppose the 1993 North American Free Trade Agreement.

And because Rogers comes from such a poor area, a good deal of his attention has been focused on making life better for those back home. He helped create a cleanup program in his district in 1997 called PRIDE, standing for Personal Responsibility In a Desirable Environment. Benefiting

CAPITOL OFFICE
225-4601; fax 225-0940; 2406 Rayburn Bldg. 20515

INTERNET
e-mail: Talk2Hal@mail.house.gov
web: www.house.gov/rogers

COMMITTEES
Appropriations
(Transportation - chairman)

HOMETOWN
Somerset

BORN
Dec. 31, 1937, Barrier, Ky.

RELIGION
Baptist

FAMILY
Wife, Cynthia Doyle Rogers; three children

EDUCATION
Western Kentucky U., attended 1956-57;
U. of Kentucky, B.A. 1962, LL.B. 1964

MILITARY SERVICE
Ky. National Guard, 1957-64

CAREER
Lawyer

POLITICAL HIGHLIGHTS
Pulaski and Rockcastle counties commonwealth attorney, 1969-79; Republican nominee for lieutenant governor, 1979

ELECTION RESULTS

2000 GENERAL
Harold Rogers (R)	145,980	73.6%
Jane Bailey-Bamer (D)	52,495	26.5%

2000 PRIMARY
Harold Rogers (R)	unopposed

1998 GENERAL
Harold Rogers (R)	142,215	78.2%
Jane Bailey-Bamer (D)	39,585	21.8%

PREVIOUS WINNING PERCENTAGES
1996 (100%); 1994 (79%); 1992 (55%); 1990 (100%); 1988 (100%); 1986 (100%); 1984 (76%); 1982 (65%); 1980 (68%)

from his position on the Appropriations panel, the congressman has secured about $76 million in three years for PRIDE, a project staffed largely by volunteers to clean up litter and dumps in southeast Kentucky.

Rogers has been at the forefront of a perennial debate involving the Immigration and Naturalization Service (INS), a branch of the Justice Department whose tasks include combating illegal immigration and helping legal resident aliens become part of American society by acquiring language and citizenship skills. Critics, including Rogers, say the agency does a poor job at both of its duties. They contend that the INS is ineffective in enforcing deportation of illegal immigrants and too slow in approving paperwork for new legal residents.

Rogers proposed separating the enforcement and citizenship functions of the agency, a plan considered by the Judiciary Committee in both the 105th and 106th, but which went no further. In arguing for his proposal, Rogers said: "By implementing these changes, we can end the three-year backlog in benefits processings, end the granting of citizenship to criminals and other undeserving individuals, and end the mismanagement of our entire immigration system."

Tobacco is another subject that stirs Rogers. He is a smoker and views the right to smoke as an issue of personal liberty. He fought the Clinton administration's plan to sue the major tobacco companies by not appropriating any money for the Justice Department to pursue the suit.

After earning undergraduate and law degrees at the University of Kentucky, Rogers made a name for himself in the southeastern part of the state as a civic activist, promoting industrial development. In 1969, he took over as the commonwealth's attorney in that part of the state and continued to play a conspicuous role in politics as the prosecutor for Pulaski and Rockcastle counties. Although he lost a 1979 campaign for lieutenant governor, the name recognition he earned paid off when he ran for the House in 1980. He prevailed over 10 other candidates in the GOP primary to succeed retiring GOP Rep. Tim Lee Carter in the historically Republican 5th District.

From 1986 to 1990, Rogers never even drew a Democratic opponent. But in 1992, remapping merged Rogers' district with the 7th District of Democratic Rep. Carl C. Perkins, who decided to retire. Rogers amassed a hefty treasury and made contacts in counties new to him while a crowded field of Democratic aspirants bickered. Rogers prevailed by 10 percentage points.

Recent years have brought Rogers easy re-elections but some personal upheaval. His wife died of cancer in 1995. (He has since remarried.) Then, the week after the 1996 election, a blaze destroyed part of Rogers' home.

KEY VOTES

2000
No Raise hourly minimum wage by $1 over two years
Yes Halt funding for U.S. mission in Kosovo unless European nations pay more
Yes Provide Medicare benefits to military retirees and their dependents
No Grant China permanent normal trade status
Yes Phase out estate, gift and trust taxes
Yes Prohibit implementation of president's national monument designations
Yes Approve GOP plan to provide prescription drug coverage for Medicare beneficiaries
No Increase help for poor nations indebted to international financial institutions

1999
Yes Impose steel import quotas
Yes Kill proposal to take aviation trust funds off budget
Yes Require background checks on buyers only at gun shows with 10 or more vendors
Yes Remove barriers among banking, securities and insurance companies
No Authorize state grants to hire teachers and reduce class size
No Overhaul campaign finance law; ban "soft money" and restrict advocacy advertising
No Approve bipartisan plan to increase rights of patients in managed-care health plans

INTEREST GROUPS

	AFL-CIO	ADA	CCUS	ACU
2000	10%	5%	76%	80%
1999	33%	5%	88%	80%
1998	11%	5%	88%	92%
1997	0%	5%	90%	80%

CQ VOTE STUDIES

	PARTY UNITY		PRESIDENTIAL SUPPORT	
	Support	Oppose	Support	Oppose
2000	91%	9%	23%	77%
1999	93%	7%	21%	79%
1998	92%	8%	23%	77%
1997	92%	8%	27%	73%

KENTUCKY 5

Southeast – Somerset; Middlesboro

The poorest and least-educated population in Kentucky lives in the moderately conservative 5th. Starting in central Kentucky, the 5th reaches northeast into heavy coal territory bordering Virginia and West Virginia. Most of Democratic Eastern Kentucky is within its confines, along with the state's Republican southeastern region, which lies along the Tennessee border.

Coal mining once was a thriving industry in this sparsely populated, Appalachian region, but its decline – which cost the state 20,000 mining jobs in the 1980s and continued to decrease in the 1990s – has brought even harder times to the region's mountain people, who never had it easy to begin with. In 1990, about one in five households lacked a telephone and about the same percentage earned less than $5,000 per year.

Devastated by the waning coal industry, eastern counties have struggled to diversify their economies. Some community leaders have been trying to attract tourists by highlighting the area's country music heritage, building new arts centers and showcasing the area's coal history.

Population in the western section is concentrated in Pulaski and Laurel counties. Like the rest of the west, Somerset relies heavily on tourism and recreation. Lake Cumberland is nearby, as is the Big South Fork National River and Recreation Area.

The 5th is secure GOP territory, and has been held by the same Republican since 1980. Locally, Republicans do well in races in the central and western part of the district. But Democrats maintain a strong presence in the far eastern coal counties where the United Mine Workers union represents a legion of former miners.

MAJOR INDUSTRY
Health care, service, tourism, coal

CITIES
Somerset, 13,203; Middlesboro, 10,358

UNUSUAL FEATURES
Daniel Boone's original trail through Cumberland Gap National Park.

Rep. Ernie Fletcher (R)

Elected 1998; 2nd term

CAPITOL OFFICE
225-4706; fax 225-2122
1117 Longworth Bldg. 20515

INTERNET
e-mail: www.house.gov/writerep
web: www.house.gov/fletcher

COMMITTEES
Agriculture
Budget
Education & Workforce

HOMETOWN
Lexington

BORN
Nov. 12, 1952, Mount Sterling, Ky.

RELIGION
Baptist

FAMILY
Wife, Glenna Fletcher; two children

EDUCATION
U. of Kentucky, B.S 1974, M.D. 1984

MILITARY SERVICE
Air Force, 1974-80

CAREER
Physician

POLITICAL HIGHLIGHTS
Ky. House, 1995-96; Republican nominee for U.S. House, 1996

ELECTION RESULTS

2000 GENERAL

Ernie Fletcher (R)	142,971	52.8%
Scotty Baesler (D)	94,167	34.8%
Gatewood Galbraith (I)	32,436	12.0%

2000 PRIMARY

Ernie Fletcher (R)	unopposed

1998 GENERAL

Ernie Fletcher (R)	104,046	53.1%
Ernesto Scorsone (D)	90,033	46.0%

Fletcher, a family physician, took a high-profile stand in the 106th Congress against popular bipartisan legislation to overhaul the system of managed health care. He also opposed a Democratic plan to provide Medicare coverage of prescription drugs. Those positions put him at odds with two powerful lobbying groups that can make or break a candidate — the American Medical Association and the AFL-CIO.

While both organizations targeted Fletcher during his re-election campaign, he survived handily and vowed to continue his efforts on health care legislation in the 107th Congress.

Just as Senate Republicans look to Bill Frist, a Tennessee surgeon who has become the party's public face on health care, House Republicans turned to Fletcher, hoping he could give them credibility on the politically sensitive subject of patients' rights. At issue: how to allow patients more power with their HMOs while protecting the interests of two key Republican constituencies — health insurers and employers.

As the managed-care debate began to heat up in the summer of 1999, Fletcher emerged as a leading spokesman for House GOP leaders, who were working feverishly to quash the growing momentum behind legislation sponsored by Republican Charlie Norwood of Georgia and Democrat John D. Dingell of Michigan.

Fletcher argued that the Norwood-Dingell plan could wreak the same kind of havoc on the nation as a 1994 health insurance overhaul measure passed by the Kentucky legislature. A number of insurers left the state after the bill became law, claiming that it drove health care costs skyward.

Fletcher was particularly opposed to a provision in the Norwood-Dingell bill that would permit workers to sue their HMOs over denial of coverage. He and many other Republicans warned that employers — fearing they could also be sued — would drop health insurance for their employees. Proponents of the bill said that such charges were unfounded and that employers could be sued only if they made the decision to deny care.

As Fletcher's profile rose, the AMA — which had spent nearly $400,000 in 1998 to help him get elected — retaliated. The powerful doctors group faxed letters to every physician in Fletcher's central Kentucky district, accusing him of choosing "to ignore the concerns of local patients and physicians." Fletcher quickly took a less visible role in the managed-care debate, although he was later named to a House-Senate conference committee that failed to reconcile the two chambers' versions of patients' rights legislation.

On another health matter — prescription drug coverage — the AFL-CIO criticized Fletcher's support of the House GOP plan calling on insurance companies to develop and sell prescription drug policies to Medicare recipients. The group argued that the proposal would have left "millions without coverage." Fletcher disagreed.

The congressman remains a vocal advocate of improving health care. He wants to foster more preventive care and competition, rein in health care costs and enact a patients' rights measure, but he wants to achieve these goals the Republican way: He supports medical savings accounts and frowns on government-run health care programs.

A former Air Force pilot, Fletcher takes a low-key approach to attaining his priorities, which have included federal funding for a cancer prevention center in his district. "Some people want to scream in your face, which I don't think is very effective," he said in 2000, according to The Washington Post.

"I'm one who works by sitting down with people to make a consensus and compromise."

While health care was somewhat of a losing issue for Fletcher during his first term in Washington, he has gained a bit more ground on tobacco, as a member of the Agriculture Committee.

Although he is a physician, Fletcher makes no apologies for defending tobacco farmers, whom he sees as an important constituency that must be protected, and he opposes requiring the tobacco industry to bear the costs of smoking-related illnesses. In early 1999, he criticized President Clinton's proposal to increase tobacco taxes by 55 cents a pack. By mid-2000, however, he was quick to give Kentucky Democratic Gov. Paul E. Patton suggestions on how the state could spend its share from the landmark settlement, reached by the states and the tobacco industry in 1997, awarding compensation for smoking-related health care costs.

Fletcher sent Patton a three-page list of 87 projects in his district, including $6 million for a courthouse museum in Lexington, $4.5 million for communications equipment for the Lexington police, $2.5 million for a Camp Nelson Civil War museum in Jessamine County and $2 million for a bypass in Berea. He later blamed the missive on "aggressive" staff.

The conservative Fletcher, who also holds a seat on the Budget panel, supports a "fairer, flatter" tax and favors allocating half of all budget surpluses to reducing the national debt. His seat on the Education and the Workforce Committee gives him a natural podium to speak out in favor of home schooling and such school-choice issues as vouchers for low-income students.

After taking a respectable 44 percent of the vote in 1996 as the Republican challenger to Democratic Rep. Scotty Baesler, Fletcher tried again in 1998. He was the runaway winner in the GOP primary. When Baesler gave up his House seat for an ultimately unsuccessful run for the Senate, Fletcher wound up facing Democratic state Sen. Ernesto Scorsone.

Scorsone emerged from a bruising six-candidate primary with a reputation as the most liberal candidate the Democrats could have nominated. He tried to paint Fletcher as too extreme, but Fletcher pounded Scorsone as a liberal on crime and taxes. He outspent Scorsone and captured 17 of 19 counties, winning by 7 percentage points.

The 2000 showdown between Baesler and Fletcher became one of the year's most closely watched contests, with House Speaker J. Dennis Hastert and House Minority Leader Richard A. Gephardt visiting the district on behalf of their parties' candidates. Fletcher took advantage of some missteps by Baesler and swamped the Democrat by 18 points.

KEY VOTES

2000

No   Raise hourly minimum wage by $1 over two years
Yes   Halt funding for U.S. mission in Kosovo unless European nations pay more
Yes   Provide Medicare benefits to military retirees and their dependents
Yes   Grant China permanent normal trade status
Yes   Phase out estate, gift and trust taxes
Yes   Prohibit implementation of president's national monument designations
Yes   Approve GOP plan to provide prescription drug coverage for Medicare beneficiaries
No   Increase help for poor nations indebted to international financial institutions

1999

No   Impose steel import quotas
No   Kill proposal to take aviation trust funds off budget
Yes   Require background checks on buyers only at gun shows with 10 or more vendors
Yes   Remove barriers among banking, securities and insurance companies
No   Authorize state grants to hire teachers and reduce class size
No   Overhaul campaign finance law; ban "soft money" and restrict advocacy advertising
No   Approve bipartisan plan to increase rights of patients in managed-care health plans

INTEREST GROUPS

	AFL-CIO	ADA	CCUS	ACU
2000	0%	5%	80%	84%
1999	0%	0%	96%	84%

CQ VOTE STUDIES

	PARTY UNITY		PRESIDENTIAL SUPPORT	
	Support	Oppose	Support	Oppose
2000	92%	8%	22%	78%
1999	93%	7%	19%	81%

KENTUCKY 6
East Central — Lexington; Frankfort

The 6th embodies the culture and economic pursuits that most outsiders associate with the state of Kentucky. This is the heart of the Bluegrass region, which spawns Kentucky Derby champions and is host to considerable tobacco and liquor interests.

A patchwork of urban, suburban and rural areas, the 6th experienced steady economic growth in the 1990s. Lexington, the district's largest city, continues to have a strong equine industry and is known as the thoroughbred capital of the world.

Lexington also boasts a university and Toyota plant. Tobacco, always a highly charged subject in these parts, held strong in the 1990s despite mounting concerns about its future.

The 6th is a swing district and, although it welcomed the GOP with a Republican congressman elected in 1998, Democrats generally have been successful at the local level. District voters tend to be socially conservative, especially on the issue of gun control. On the federal level, the district flirted with Democratic presidential candidate Bill Clinton in 1996, giving him a 1 point edge, but backed Bush tickets in 1992 and 2000.

Government workers in Frankfort favor local Democratic officials, as do voters in most of the farmland around Lexington. Republicans have some strength in the farmland south of Lexington.

MAJOR INDUSTRY
Manufacturing, service, tobacco, retail

MILITARY BASES
Bluegrass Army Depot, 394 military, 643 civilian (1999)

CITIES
Lexington-Fayette, 243,785; Richmond, 28,658; Frankfort, 26,762

UNUSUAL FEATURES
The whiskey Bourbon was named after Bourbon County.

Gov. Mike Foster (R)

First elected: 1995
Length of term: 4 years
Term expires: 1/04
Salary: $95,000
Phone: (225) 342-7015
Hometown: Franklin
Born: July 11, 1930; Shreveport, La.

Religion: Episcopalian
Family: Wife, Alice Foster; two children, two stepchildren
Education: Louisiana State U., B.S. 1952
Military service: Air Force, 1952-55
Career: Sugar cane farmer; contracting business owner; sugar company executive
Political highlights: La. Senate, 1988-96
Election results:
1999 GENERAL

Mike Foster (R)	805,203	62.2%
William J. Jefferson (D)	382,445	29.5%

Lt. Gov. Kathleen Babineaux Blanco (D)

First elected: 1995
Length of term: 4 years
Term expires: 1/04
Salary: $85,000
Phone: (225) 342-7009

STATE LEGISLATURE

Legislature: Meets March-June yearly
House: 105 members, 4-year terms
2001 breakdown: 34R, 70D, 1 vacancy; 84 men, 20 women
Salary: $16,800
Phone: (225) 342-6945
Senate: 39 members, 4-year terms
2001 breakdown: 13R, 26D; 36 men, 3 women
Salary: $16,800
Phone: (225) 342-2040

STATE TERM LIMITS

Governor: 2 terms
Senate: 3 terms
House: 3 terms

URBAN STATISTICS

CITY	POPULATION
New Orleans	460,913
Baton Rouge	210,667
Shreveport	187,393
Lafayette	116,806
Lake Charles	72,173

REGISTERED VOTERS

Democrat	60%
Republican	22%
Other	18%

POPULATION

2000 population	4,468,976
1990 population	4,219,973
Percent change	+5.9%
Rank among states	22

Median age	33.6
Born in state	79%
Foreign born	2%
Urban/rural	68%/32%
Crime rate	856/100,000
Poverty level	19.1%
Federal workers	35,309
Military	41,812

REAPPORTIONMENT

Louisiana retained its seven House seats in reapportionment. The state legislature will draw new district lines in 2001.

MISCELLANEOUS

Web: www.state.la.us
Capital: Baton Rouge
Land area: 43,566 sq. miles
Rank among states: 33
STATE ELECTION OFFICIAL
(225) 342-4971
DEMOCRATIC HEADQUARTERS
(225) 336-4155
REPUBLICAN HEADQUARTERS
(225) 928-2998

District Statistics

DIST.	D	2000 R	GREEN	D	1996 R	REF	D	1992 R	I	WHT	BLK	ASIAN	HISP	HOUSEHOLD INCOME	OVER 65+	UNDER 18	COLLEGE EDUCATION
1	31%	66%	1%	37%	56%	6%	31%	56%	13%	86%	12%	1%	4%	$27,413	12%	26%	22%
2	79	19	1	78	19	3	69	25	6	36	61	2	3	$18,585	11	29	18
3	45	52	1	53	38	8	45	41	14	74	23	1	2	$22,948	9	31	9
4	44	54	1	52	39	7	68	25	8	66	32	1	2	$20,920	12	29	15
5	38	59	1	47	43	9	37	49	14	68	31	0	1	$18,258	13	29	14
6	44	54	1	50	43	7	35	52	14	67	32	1	1	$26,001	9	29	21
7	42	55	1	51	39	9	47	38	15	75	24	0	1	$20,595	11	30	14
STATE	45	53	1	52	40	7	46	41	12	67	31	1	2	$21,949	11	29	16

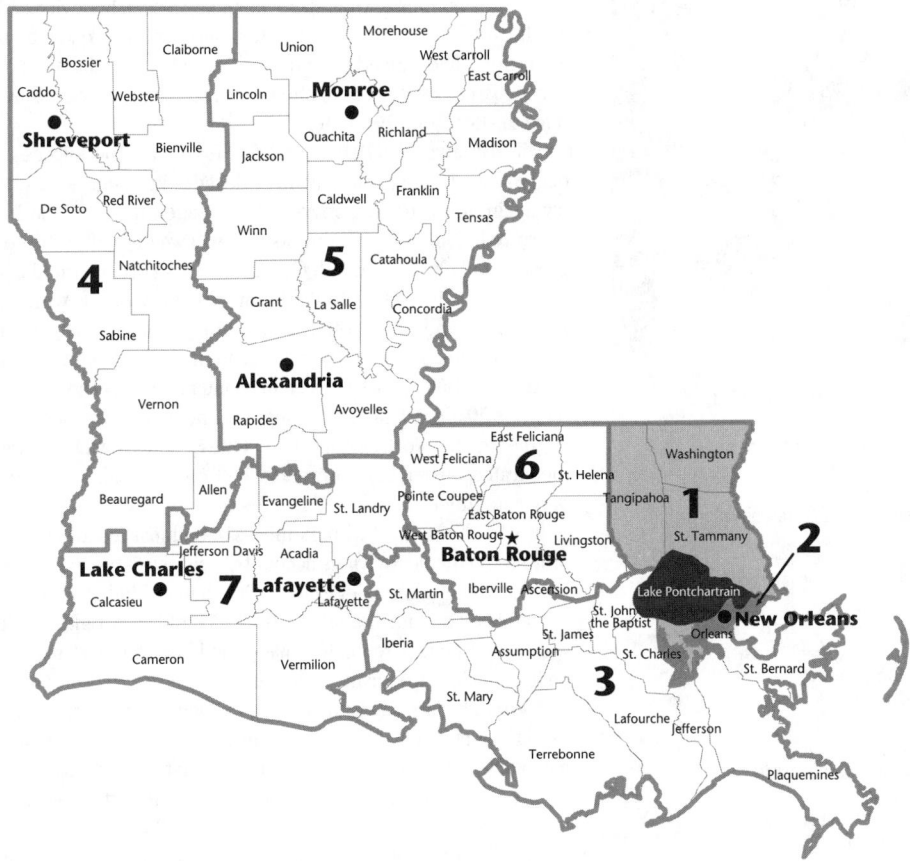

Sen. John B. Breaux (D)

CAPITOL OFFICE
224-4623; fax 228-2577; 503 Hart Bldg. 20510

INTERNET
e-mail: senator@breaux.senate.gov
web: breaux.senate.gov

COMMITTEES
Commerce, Science & Transportation
Finance
Rules & Administration
Special Aging - ranking member

HOMETOWN
Crowley

BORN
March 1, 1944, Crowley, La.

RELIGION
Roman Catholic

FAMILY
Wife, Lois Breaux; four children

EDUCATION
U. of Southwestern Louisiana, B.A. 1964; Louisiana
State U., J.D. 1967

CAREER
Lawyer; congressional aide

POLITICAL HIGHLIGHTS
U.S. House, 1972-87

ELECTION RESULTS

1998 GENERAL

John B. Breaux (D)	620,502	64.0%
Jim Donelon (R)	306,616	31.6%
Raymond Brown (X)	12,203	1.3%
Sam Houston Melton Jr. (D)	9,893	1.0%

PREVIOUS WINNING PERCENTAGES
1992 (72%); 1986 (53%); 1984 House Election (86%);
1982 House Election (79%); 1980 House Election
(100%); 1978 House Election (60%); 1976 House
Election (83%); 1974 House Election (89%); 1972
House Election (100%); 1972 House Special
Election (55%)

Elected 1986; 3rd term

Even at a time when party allegiances and ideologies are irrelevant to many Americans, Breaux has had little luck selling his brand of centrism in an increasingly partisan Senate. In the 106th Congress, he tried to break stalemates on four of the top social policy issues bedeviling the Capitol — Medicare, Social Security, education and health care for the uninsured — with carefully balanced and non-ideological proposals. All his efforts failed, leaving Breaux with little to show for his often-stated view that "all solutions have to start from the center."

Still, Breaux (BRO) has occasionally had some success as a centrist deal-maker during his nearly three decades in Congress, and he is eager to try again in the 107th Congress — so eager, he says, that he spurned an overture to join the new administration. Two days after the contested 2000 presidential election ended, George W. Bush orchestrated a meeting with Breaux as a means to tout his interest in working with congressional Democrats, and also to offer Breaux the job of secretary of energy.

"Both sides have the ability in divided government to block each other from doing things," Breaux said in an interview after the election yielded the Senate's 50-50 partisan split, "but that's not why we're here." Soon after, he augmented his work as chairman of the Senate New Democrats, a group of moderates, by helping to organize the Centrist Coalition, a bipartisan group of Senate moderates as well.

In 1996, he worked with members of both parties to reach a Senate compromise on medical savings accounts, a divisive issue that had stalled health insurance "portability" legislation. Practicing a kind of shuttle diplomacy, he moved back and forth between the office of Majority Leader Trent Lott — with whom he is personally close — and key Democrats. He pitched ideas on how to allow the savings accounts to go forward, as Republicans wanted, with enough safeguards to address Democrats' concerns that the accounts would attract mostly healthy and well-off consumers and wreak havoc on the managed-care system. The fact that the result was a classic Washington compromise — an object lesson on how to get things done — makes it easy to forget how difficult the negotiations were at the time.

Not all of his centrist efforts have been so timely. Breaux teamed up with John H. Chafee, the late Republican moderate from Rhode Island, to develop alternative proposals during the health care overhaul debate of the 103rd Congress and the budget-balancing debates of the 104th. In both cases, however, the plans were rolled out long after the parties were hopelessly deadlocked and essentially had given up for the year.

Breaux's centrist voice has not always won favor with his fellow Democrats. Some think he is too quick to split the difference, more interested in compromise than in pushing legislation built on values. But, Breaux sees himself as a bridge to independent voters. And in his view, pragmatic politics is exactly what they want. "That is the balance of power in the country politically," he said. "They look to the ideas more than the party."

Combining shrewd pragmatism with a droll sense of humor can sometimes land Breaux in trouble, but it also makes him more colorful and personable than the average lawmaker. In 1981, he declared memorably that while his vote could not be bought, "it can be rented." A House member at the time, he explained that he was supporting President Reagan's proposed social spending cuts in return for concessions on natural gas policy and sugar subsidies. Two years later, the Democrats took Breaux to task for having broken so prominently from the ranks and denied him the Budget Committee assignment he wanted.

Since then, he has served Democrats well, helping them add to their majority in 1990 as head of the Democratic Senatorial Campaign Committee, and currently corralling votes as the chief deputy whip. "I've never felt inclined to switch parties," Breaux said. "I'd rather try to change the party from within." He says he has reached an understanding with his Democratic colleagues: "I think they realize that I'm a conservative Democrat, which means I'd be a moderate to the rest of the country. I think that's where most of the country is."

For all his efforts to convince his Democratic colleagues of the wisdom of negotiating from the center, Breaux concentrates his considerable bargaining ability on working with Republicans. In 1998-99, he chaired the National Bipartisan Commission on the Future of Medicare. He was jointly appointed by President Clinton and GOP congressional leaders after he agreed to share some of the leadership duties with Rep. Bill Thomas, R-Calif., an appointee of House Speaker Newt Gingrich. The agreement ended months of negotiation over who would chair the influential panel.

A longtime advocate of structural changes to Medicare, Breaux said he is driven by the program's impending insolvency. "We have a real drop-dead date in 2010. That's when the 77 million Baby Boomers walk in the door saying, 'Here I am. Where's my checks?' "

Breaux's solution was to give senior citizens a fixed contribution toward the purchase of private insurance or fee-for-service coverage from the government. But he was able to muster only 10 of the 11 votes required to forward the plan to Congress with the commission's official stamp of approval. Breaux, who sits on the Finance Committee, and Bill Frist, R-Tenn., introduced a revised version in the Senate, but it attracted little attention at a time when Congress was more interested in adding prescription drug coverage to Medicare than in making fundamental changes to the program.

In 1999, Breaux jumped into the Social Security debate by cosponsoring an overhaul plan with Judd Gregg, R-N.H., and Bob Kerrey, D-Neb., that would have created private savings accounts. In 2000, he teamed up with Joseph I. Lieberman, D-Conn., on an education overhaul plan that would have consolidated more than 50 education assistance programs into five goal-oriented grants that were similar to block grants Republicans proposed but that included accountability standards favored by Democrats. Neither effort bridged the divide between Republicans and Democrats, however, and both were quietly shelved.

Breaux learned the art of the deal from one of Louisiana's masters, former Gov. Edwin W. Edwards. Breaux served for four years as one of Edwards' top congressional aides. When Edwards first won the governorship in 1972, he pushed for Breaux to be his successor in the House. With Edwards' organization, Breaux defeated five other candidates to win a special election. He had no GOP opposition in November in winning a full term, and he was easily re-elected to the House six times.

Breaux had a tougher time in his 1986 bid to replace retiring Democratic Sen. Russell B. Long: Louisiana's oil industry was foundering and Edwards' image had suffered during two corruption trials. Those circumstances gave the GOP one of its best openings in years, and GOP Rep. W. Henson Moore began airing ads charging that Democrats had squandered the state's resources and prostituted the political system to their own advantage.

Ultimately, however, the national political situation helped to bail out Breaux: He warned voters that Moore's first allegiance was to his party and to President Reagan, not to Louisiana. Breaux won 42 of 64 parishes, taking 53 percent of the vote. Since then, his seat has been safe.

KEY VOTES

2000

Yes Overhaul bankruptcy law and increase minimum wage

No Limit fiscal 2001 discretionary spending to $600.3 billion

Yes Override veto on nuclear waste disposal at Yucca Mountain site in Nevada

Yes Oppose effort to terminate Kosovo mission

Yes Include gender, sexual orientation and disability in federal hate crime protections

No Approve GOP plan to restrict use of genetic information by health insurers

No Kill amendment delaying implementation of an anti-missile defense system

No Cut taxes for married couples

Yes Grant China permanent normal trade status

1999

No Remove President Clinton from office for obstruction of justice

No Kill amendment authorizing state grants to hire teachers and reduce class size

Yes Require criminal background checks for purchases at gun shows

No Approve GOP proposal to increase rights of patients in managed-care health plans

No Block effort to allow farm and medicine exports to Cuba

? Allow study of tougher automobile fuel efficiency standards

Yes Ratify nuclear weapons testing treaty

Yes Prohibit national political parties from collecting "soft money" donations

Yes Remove barriers among banking, securities and insurance companies

INTEREST GROUPS

	AFL-CIO	ADA	CCUS	ACU
2000	25%	50%	86%	40%
1999	67%	80%	56%	17%
1998	63%	75%	59%	20%
1997	14%	55%	70%	20%
1996	71%	60%	62%	20%
1995	75%	70%	56%	22%
1994	63%	55%	44%	17%
1993	82%	40%	27%	24%
1992	67%	60%	10%	30%
1991	67%	30%	40%	57%

CQ VOTE STUDIES

	PARTY UNITY		PRESIDENTIAL SUPPORT	
	Support	Oppose	Support	Oppose
2000	73%	27%	85%	15%
1999	75%	25%	77%	23%
1998	73%	27%	79%	21%
1997	65%	35%	81%	19%
1996	70%	30%	78%	22%
1995	73%	27%	77%	23%
1994	78%	22%	85%	15%
1993	80%	20%	86%	14%
1992	70%	30%	42%	58%
1991	61%	39%	66%	34%

Sen. Mary L. Landrieu (D)

Elected 1996; 1st term

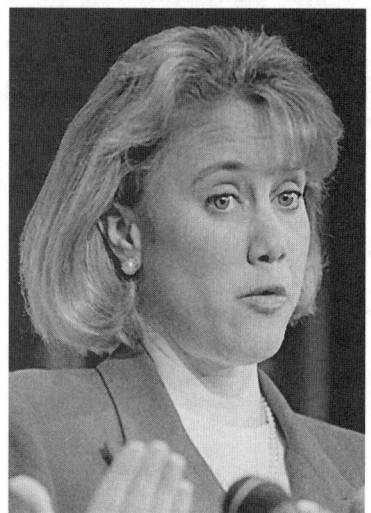

CAPITOL OFFICE
224-5824; fax 224-9735; 724 Hart Bldg. 20510

INTERNET
e-mail: senator@landrieu.senate.gov
web: landrieu.senate.gov

COMMITTEES
Appropriations
Armed Services
Energy & Natural Resources
Small Business

HOMETOWN
Baton Rouge

BORN
Nov. 23, 1955, Arlington, Va.

RELIGION
Roman Catholic

FAMILY
Husband, Frank Snellings; two children

EDUCATION
Louisiana State U., B.A. 1977

CAREER
Realtor

POLITICAL HIGHLIGHTS
La. House, 1980-88; La. treasurer, 1988-96;
candidate for governor, 1995

ELECTION RESULTS

1996 GENERAL RUNOFF

Mary L. Landrieu (D)	852,945	50.2%
Louis "Woody" Jenkins (R)	847,157	49.8%

1996 GENERAL

Louis "Woody" Jenkins (R)	322,244	26.7%
Mary L. Landrieu (D)	264,268	21.9%
Richard P. Ieyoub (D)	250,682	20.8%
David Ernest Duke (R)	141,489	11.7%
Jimmy Hayes (R)	71,699	5.9%
Bill Linder (R)	58,243	4.8%
Chuck McMains (R)	45,164	3.7%
Peggy Wilson (R)	31,877	2.6%
Troyce Guice (D)	15,277	1.3%

After Landrieu ousted an incumbent to claim a state House seat in 1979 at age 23, she was taunted by some of her new colleagues, who called her "Little Mary." When she ran for the Senate in 1996, her opponent was asked in a televised debate to make one positive statement about her. He paused, then said, "She's nice-looking." By the end of the 106th Congress, however, the name-calling had taken on a whole new tone.

"I have been described in many different ways — my favorite one: a pit bull with Louisiana charm," says Landrieu. "At least they threw the charm part in there."

In the 106th, Landrieu (LAN-drew) used both her persistence and her charm in the first major legislative effort of her Senate career — the Conservation and Reinvestment Act (CARA), which sought to guarantee some $3 billion annually for 15 years in offshore drilling revenues to a host of federal and state conservation programs. In a key move, Landrieu won over Energy and Natural Resources Chairman Frank H. Murkowski, R-Alaska, after taking him to dinner at New Orleans' famed Commander's Palace.

In the end, Landrieu and other CARA supporters had to settle for a smaller conservation measure subject to annual appropriations, but even the partial victory was more than some had expected when the legislative battle was at its fiercest. "It's been an exhilarating challenge and extremely tiring, mentally, spiritually and physically," she said of the effort to enact the bill. With her victory only a partial one, she says she intends to pursue the issue again in the 107th Congress.

Landrieu will have an excellent chance to press for full funding for the conservation measure enacted by the last Congress. She won a coveted seat on the Appropriations Committee for the 107th, a plum that should help her in what could be a difficult 2002 re-election bid.

She affiliates with both the Senate New Democrats and the bipartisan Centrist Caucus. "Too often here in Washington, the loudest voices are the ones on the far left and far right," she said in 2000 as the New Democrat group (dubbed the "mod squad" by Landrieu) was organized. "That is why this group was formed, to give voice to those in the sensible center."

The senator has tried to balance her support of traditionally liberal programs such as child care with careful attention to Louisiana's parochial interests. In 1998, she cosponsored a bill to boost protection of private property rights, to the dismay of environmentalists and the applause of her state's real estate interests. She and fellow Louisiana Democratic Sen. John B. Breaux frequently issue joint press releases touting federal dollars they have secured for Louisiana projects. And both vote to promote the interests of their state's big oil and gas industry.

Landrieu voted with President Clinton and fellow Senate Democrats more than 85 percent of the time in 2000, and in early 2001, she joined her party's majority in opposing the nomination of Attorney General John Ashcroft, a staunch conservative. But over the years she has strayed from the party line on a number of high-profile issues. She has supported a cut in the capital gains tax rate and a constitutional amendment to prevent desecration of the flag, while opposing gay marriage. She also backed a GOP plan to give school vouchers to some District of Columbia residents to help them pay for private school tuition or tutoring for their children.

Landrieu featured prominently in the 1997 Senate debate on a GOP-drafted constitutional amendment to require a federal balanced budget.

She had pledged her support for the proposal during her campaign and was one of four freshman Democrats under close scrutiny as the vote approached. In the end, she voted for the amendment, as it fell just one vote short of the necessary two-thirds majority needed for approval.

The senator is well-known in her state as a supporter of abortion rights; retired New Orleans Archbishop Philip Hannan said in the closing days of her 1996 race that it would be a sin for voters to support her or Clinton. But in 1998, she was one of 13 Democrats who voted to overturn Clinton's veto of a ban on a procedure its opponents call "partial birth" abortion. (The effort fell three votes short of the two-thirds majority required.)

Landrieu is acutely aware of the gender gap in the Senate. In 2000, she collaborated on a book, "Nine and Counting," with her eight female Senate colleagues in the 106th Congress. And during the 2000 campaign season, she announced that she would not campaign against any of the women then serving in the Senate, whether they were Democrats or Republicans. "I don't mind saying it here that if my leadership asked me to go campaign against one of these women, I would have told them I won't go," she told CNN's Larry King in July 2000.

Landrieu is no stranger to politics. Her father, Moon Landrieu, served as mayor of New Orleans and as secretary of housing and urban development in the Carter administration. But the younger Landrieu's own political road has hardly been a smooth one. After serving in the state legislature and as Louisiana treasurer, she made an unsuccessful run for governor in 1995. Despite that loss, she was back in the arena a year later, this time seeking the seat of retiring Democratic Sen. J. Bennett Johnston.

Landrieu won by the slimmest margin ever in a Louisiana Senate race — just 5,788 votes out of 1.7 million cast — then spent much of her first year in office fighting a challenge to her election brought by the loser, conservative Louis "Woody" Jenkins, who alleged voter fraud.

Republicans on the Rules Committee, led by Chairman John W. Warner of Virginia, voted for a broad investigation of the election — a bitter, divisive probe that dragged on until October before the panel voted to end it. "Never again should a legally certified senator be held hostage by wild, reckless and unproven allegations from a disgruntled loser," Landrieu said afterward.

She later had to work with Warner when she dropped her Agriculture Committee seat in 1999 to join the Armed Services panel, which he now chairs. Whatever ill feelings she may harbor, she has kept them to herself. The assignment is an important one for her, allowing her to keep a close watch on policies that can mean big money for Louisiana's military contractors, such as Avondale shipyards and Northrop Grumman Corp. Also helpful in that regard is Landrieu's seat, new in the 107th Congress, on the Military Construction Appropriations Subcommittee.

Landrieu is a working mother. She and her husband, Frank Snellings, have two adopted children, and her experience both frames her political perspective and shapes her daily life as a senator. She co-chairs the Congressional Coalition on Adoption with GOP Sen. Larry E. Craig of Idaho. In 1998, she penned a column entitled, "Mothers Make Good Senators Too," after getting angry at a newspaper column that criticized a fellow senator, Democrat Blanche Lincoln of Arkansas, who is the mother of twins.

Landrieu's children often trail her around the Senate. She and her husband have a standing rule: Neither of them can work more than two evenings a week. "I've missed press conferences, I've missed committee hearings, I actually one time missed a vote," Landrieu said, explaining that she was accompanying her son on a field trip when a procedural vote came up. "I just wasn't going to leave my son and come back."

KEY VOTES

2000

Yes	Overhaul bankruptcy law and increase minimum wage
No	Limit fiscal 2001 discretionary spending to $600.3 billion
Yes	Override veto on nuclear waste disposal at Yucca Mountain site in Nevada
Yes	Oppose effort to terminate Kosovo mission
Yes	Include gender, sexual orientation and disability in federal hate crime protections
No	Approve GOP plan to restrict use of genetic information by health insurers
No	Kill amendment delaying implementation of an anti-missile defense system
Yes	Cut taxes for married couples
Yes	Grant China permanent normal trade status

1999

No	Remove President Clinton from office for obstruction of justice
No	Kill amendment authorizing state grants to hire teachers and reduce class size
Yes	Require criminal background checks for purchases at gun shows
No	Approve GOP proposal to increase rights of patients in managed-care health plans
No	Block effort to allow farm and medicine exports to Cuba
No	Allow study of tougher automobile fuel efficiency standards
Yes	Ratify nuclear weapons testing treaty
Yes	Prohibit national political parties from collecting "soft money" donations
Yes	Remove barriers among banking, securities and insurance companies

INTEREST GROUPS

	AFL-CIO	ADA	CCUS	ACU
2000	63%	80%	73%	16%
1999	67%	95%	59%	4%
1998	88%	90%	67%	8%
1997	29%	70%	70%	16%

CQ VOTE STUDIES

	PARTY UNITY		PRESIDENTIAL SUPPORT	
	Support	Oppose	Support	Oppose
2000	88%	12%	85%	15%
1999	81%	19%	86%	14%
1998	89%	11%	86%	14%
1997	77%	23%	87%	13%

Rep. David Vitter (R)

Elected May 1999; 1st full term

CAPITOL OFFICE
225-3015; fax 225-0739; 414 Cannon Bldg. 20515

INTERNET
e-mail: david.vitter@mail.house.gov
web: www.house.gov/vitter

COMMITTEES
Appropriations

HOMETOWN
Metairie

BORN
May 3, 1961, New Orleans, La.

RELIGION
Roman Catholic

FAMILY
Wife, Wendy Vitter; three children

EDUCATION
Harvard U., A.B. 1983; Oxford U., B.A. 1985; Tulane U., J.D. 1988

CAREER
Business lawyer; adjunct law professor

POLITICAL HIGHLIGHTS
La. House, 1992-99

ELECTION RESULTS

2000 GENERAL

David Vitter (R)	191,379	80.5%
Michael A. Armato (D)	29,935	12.6%
Cary J. Deaton (D)	10,982	4.6%
Martin A. Rosenthal (NL)	3,129	1.3%

1999 SPECIAL RUNOFF

David Vitter (R)	61,661	50.8%
David C. Treen (R)	59,849	49.3%

1999 SPECIAL

David C. Treen (R)	36,719	25.1%
David Vitter (R)	31,741	21.7%
David Duke (R)	28,059	19.2%
Monica L. Monica (R)	22,928	15.7%
R.H. "Bill" Strain (D)	16,446	11.2%
Rob Couhig (R)	9,295	6.3%

Known back home as an aggressive politician who is not afraid to challenge party leaders, Vitter has taken a somewhat quieter approach in Washington while laying the groundwork to gain stature and responsibility as he gains tenure.

"People will judge me by the job I do," he told The New Orleans Times Picayune shortly before he took office in 1999. "If they are expecting some grand confrontational style, they will be sorely disappointed."

Vitter had big shoes to fill when he came to Congress. His predecessor, former Appropriations Committee Chairman Robert L. Livingston, had been one of the House's most powerful lawmakers before renouncing his party's nomination to be Speaker in the 106th Congress. That action came after Livingston admitted publicly that he had engaged in extramarital affairs, and eventually resigned.

Vitter moved quickly to make his name known on Capitol Hill. Upon his arrival in Washington, he got the prime office space that had belonged to Livingston — rarified territory for a freshman — and used the location to chat up his next-door neighbor, Armed Services Committee Chairman Floyd D. Spence, R-S.C., in hopes of gaining a spot on that panel.

Defense issues have been a key interest of Vitter's — in the 106th, he introduced legislation to speed development of a national missile defense system — as have other items on the GOP agenda, such as giving local school districts more control over classrooms, banning a procedure its opponents call "partial birth" abortion, lowering federal taxes and barring Social Security revenues from being used to fund other items in the general budget.

Instead of a seat on the Armed Services panel, Vitter won a spot on the Transportation Committee, giving him the opportunity to secure highway, bridge and port improvement projects for his Metairie district outside New Orleans. Vitter also was assigned to the Judiciary and Government Reform panels, where he focused on ferreting out waste just as he had done as a Louisiana state legislator. In the 107th Congress, he dropped those committees to take a plum assignment on the Appropriations panel.

Vitter has generally demonstrated a strong allegiance to the Republican leadership's agenda, voting with the GOP more than 90 percent of the time on issues that pit one party against the other. But he took an activist role when the chamber debated legislation to give patients more clout with their managed-care plans. Vitter joined 67 other Republicans to support a bipartisan measure that would give the federal government a far broader role in governing the nation's health care system.

In the 106th, Vitter tried to use his Washington clout and his seat on the Transportation Committee to settle a struggle back home over possible expansion of the New Orleans International Airport. According to news reports, Vitter pushed a proposal that would have allowed the Federal Aviation Administration to direct all local airport financing to a regional authority, bypassing the aviation board appointed by New Orleans Mayor Marc Morial. Morial characterized Vitter's actions as an "ambush," while Vitter, whose district abuts the airport, said Morial had not advised him and other members of the Louisiana delegation about the possible runway expansion, which would affect their constituents.

Such dust-ups are not unknown to Vitter. During his seven years in the Louisiana statehouse, he was more than willing to ruffle some feathers. The Harvard graduate and Rhodes scholar points with pride to his clashes with the state's political establishment, his success in winning passage of term limits for state lawmakers and his opposition to a pay raise for legislators.

Vitter led a high-profile — and ultimately successful — fight to end a Tulane University scholarship program that allowed state legislators to choose recipients, denouncing the program as an abuse of power.

Just two months after he was elected to the state House, Vitter filed a complaint with the state Board of Ethics charging that Louisiana Gov. Edwin Edwards' friend Bob D'Hemecourt was part of the administration and thus should not be permitted to lobby for casino giant Caesars World. While the ethics panel ruled for D'Hemecourt, Vitter said he was victorious as well because he had focused attention on the issue. Vitter's other priorities in Baton Rouge included repeal of the inheritance tax and tougher prison sentences for serious juvenile offenders.

Some Louisiana political observers have labeled Vitter's actions as political grandstanding, and the smart, brash young conservative has been dubbed a pariah in some circles. State House Speaker Pro Tempore C.E. "Peppi" Bruneau Jr. called him "incapable of working with anybody." But Vitter does not seem to mind the reputation. "I've rocked the boat, and that's caused some resentment," he said, "but that's only in the political establishment."

Despite his statehouse career, Vitter was still able to portray himself as an outsider in his May 1999 special-election campaign against former House member and governor David Treen.

When Livingston announced he would leave office in late February 1999, Vitter was one of nine candidates who jumped into the special-election campaign to replace him. Treen, who had the support of most of the political establishment — including Livingston and GOP Gov. Mike Foster — came in first, with 25 percent. Vitter, who resigned his state House seat, was second with 22 percent, edging out former Ku Klux Klan leader David Duke, who was third with 19 percent.

The runoff campaign between Treen and Vitter gave voters little to choose between: Both are conservative Republicans. Instead, the race was largely about political style and the benefits of the immediate seniority that the 70-year-old Treen would offer from his House tenure (1973-1980) versus the 38-year-old Vitter's prospects for accumulating even more seniority in the future. Vitter was more than able to hold his own against Treen in the fundraising battle and emerged with a narrow, 2 percentage point victory.

In 2000, Vitter coasted to an easy win, by 68 percentage points.

KEY VOTES

2000

No	Raise hourly minimum wage by $1 over two years
Yes	Halt funding for U.S. mission in Kosovo unless European nations pay more
Yes	Provide Medicare benefits to military retirees and their dependents
Yes	Grant China permanent normal trade status
Yes	Phase out estate, gift and trust taxes
Yes	Prohibit implementation of president's national monument designations
Yes	Approve GOP plan to provide prescription drug coverage for Medicare beneficiaries
No	Increase help for poor nations indebted to international financial institutions

1999

No	Kill proposal to take aviation trust funds off budget
No	Require background checks on buyers only at gun shows with 10 or more vendors
Yes	Remove barriers among banking, securities and insurance companies
No	Authorize state grants to hire teachers and reduce class size
No	Overhaul campaign finance law; ban "soft money" and restrict advocacy advertising
Yes	Approve bipartisan plan to increase rights of patients in managed-care health plans

INTEREST GROUPS

	AFL-CIO	ADA	CCUS	ACU
2000	0%	0%	85%	88%
1999	14%	5%	88%	83%

CQ VOTE STUDIES

	PARTY UNITY		PRESIDENTIAL SUPPORT	
	Support	Oppose	Support	Oppose
2000	92%	8%	25%	75%
1999	92%	8%	20%	80%

LOUISIANA 1
East – Metairie; part of Florida Parishes

Away from festive downtown New Orleans, the 1st skims the edges of the city and reaches north across Lake Pontchartrain to the Mississippi border. Despite haggling over redistricting that finally ended in 1996, the 1st remained conservative, with no major boundary changes. The mostly white-collar population that lives in these parts is among the wealthiest and most educated in the state.

The 1st's population center is on the south side of Lake Pontchartrain and includes the upscale Metairie suburbs. The area is packed with white-collar conservatives who generally vote Republican.

North of the lake, the 1st includes three of the "Florida Parishes," so named because they were part of Spanish Florida until 1810. St. Tammany Parish was the fastest growing area in the 1st during the 1990s. Once an isolated vacation area for residents escaping the heat and humidity of New Orleans, St. Tammany now is a booming suburban haven, replete with suburbanites who commute across Lake Pontchartrain Causeway to their jobs in New Orleans. The area is developing more industry of its own, and leaders hope to attract high-tech firms related to the Avondale Shipyard in the 2nd.

Democrats held the 1st for a little more than a century before it became a Republican possession in 1977. Now, the mostly white residents warmly welcome Republicans on the local and federal level. Democrats manage to win a few local offices in the far northern, rural reaches of the district.

MAJOR INDUSTRY
Service, agriculture, health care

CITIES
Metairie (unincorporated), 146,321 (1990); Kenner (pt.), 52,192 (1990); New Orleans (pt.), 38,727 (1990); Slidell, 27,138; Hammond, 18,593

UNUSUAL FEATURES
Lake Pontchartrain Causeway, the longest highway bridge over water in the world at 23.9 miles; Former Ku Klux Klansman David Duke held the Metairie state House seat from 1989 to 1993.

Rep. William J. Jefferson (D)

Elected 1990; 6th term

Raised in poverty in rural northeast Louisiana in a family of 10 children, Jefferson has made his way to a seat on the powerful Ways and Means Committee. He usually votes a liberal line, espousing views shaped by growing up poor and black in the Deep South.

Jefferson has accumulated impressive "insider" credentials over the years. He was student body president at Southern University in Baton Rouge, winner of a scholarship to Harvard Law School, law clerk for a federal judge, congressional aide, successful New Orleans lawyer and a prominent, 11-year member of the Louisiana Senate before winning election to the House in 1990 as Louisiana's first black representative since Reconstruction.

Along the way, Jefferson earned a reputation for moving with ease among blacks and whites. He got into the state Senate by winning a racially mixed New Orleans district that included much of the affluent Uptown area. In Washington, he made a good early impression on Democratic leaders, and their desire to diversify the membership of key committees helped him earn a seat on the Ways and Means panel in his second term.

Jefferson, who has a calm, understated manner, rarely speaks in the House chamber. But during debate on the Republican tax cut bill in 1997, he took to the floor to criticize the GOP and ended his remarks with a rare zinger: "Like we used to say in the Louisiana Legislature, the Republican tax plan is a snake and we ought to kill it."

Jefferson has opposed most conservative initiatives, voting against GOP plans to overhaul the welfare and Medicare systems and rejecting most efforts to cut taxes and reduce spending on social programs. In the 106th Congress, however, he backed a Republican plan to repeal estate taxes. Although many viewed the estate tax as a levy on the wealthy, Jefferson said he was concerned about its impact on the ability of minorities to pass along their earnings to their children. He said the levy was "an anti-wealth-building tax in a time when African-Americans and Hispanics are trying to build wealth," according to The Associated Press.

Most of the time, Jefferson works behind the scenes, often with an eye toward improving economic conditions in his district. In 2000, he supported legislation granting China permanent normal trade status, contending that it would help create jobs. In the 105th, he was one of only four Democrats on Ways and Means to support President Clinton's request for fast-track authority to negotiate trade agreements that Congress cannot revise, saying that New Orleans "stands to greatly benefit from expanded trade, especially with Central and South America."

Jefferson also has actively supported another trade initiative: opening new avenues of commerce with nations in Africa. He was a major proponent of a bill (signed into law in the 105th) to promote economic development and U.S. investment in sub-Saharan Africa. After some House members expressed concern about whether African nations could become reliable partners in trade and investment, Jefferson rose on the House floor in rebuttal. "The African nations ... ought to be insulted by the way we are approaching them," he said. "What we are saying is that we trust them less than we trust the rest of the world." He also voted for legislation in the 106th Congress to lower tariffs on imports from sub-Saharan Africa, Central America and the Caribbean.

Jefferson's views of Africa's potential as a trading partner are informed by

CAPITOL OFFICE
225-6636; fax 225-1988; 240 Cannon Bldg. 20515

INTERNET
e-mail: jeffersonmc@mail.house.gov
web: www.house.gov/jefferson

COMMITTEES
Ways & Means

HOMETOWN
New Orleans

BORN
March 14, 1947, Lake Providence, La.

RELIGION
Baptist

FAMILY
Wife, Andrea Green Jefferson; five children

EDUCATION
Southern U. and A&M College, B.A. 1969; Harvard U., J.D. 1972; Georgetown U., LL.M. 1996

MILITARY SERVICE
Army, 1969-75

CAREER
Lawyer; congressional aide

POLITICAL HIGHLIGHTS
La. Senate, 1980-91; candidate for mayor of New Orleans, 1982, 1986; candidate for governor, 1999

ELECTION RESULTS

2000 GENERAL

William J. Jefferson (D)		unopposed

1998 GENERAL

William J. Jefferson (D)	102,247	86.0%
David Reed (D)	10,803	9.1%
Don-Terry Veal (D)	5,899	5.0%

PREVIOUS WINNING PERCENTAGES
1996 (100%); 1994 (75%); 1992 (73%); 1990 (53%)

several visits he has made to the continent, one as part of a congressional delegation accompanying Clinton on his tour of Africa in 1998.

Jefferson ruffled some feathers even in the Congressional Black Caucus when in the 105th he announced his support for resuming trade relations with Nigeria. That nation's repressive dictatorship provoked U.S. trade sanctions and worldwide condemnation. But, as with China, Jefferson believes that isolating a rogue nation only worsens problems there. "We took the approach that the government was bad to talk to," he told The Times-Picayune, when "instead we should have engaged that government, trying to push them toward democracy."

Jefferson's concerns for local economic prosperity account for an alliance with the GOP on defense spending. Two big employers in his district do a good deal of defense work: Trinity Marine Industries and Avondale Industries. Jefferson has generally echoed calls by Republicans to spend more money on the U.S. military.

Jefferson has also joined with Republicans in backing a constitutional amendment to ban flag burning. And while generally supporting abortion rights, he has voted with conservatives who want to ban the procedure opponents call "partial birth" abortion.

With his constituents in mind, Jefferson proposed a tax deduction in 1999 to help homeowners combat damage caused by infestations of Formosan termites. The destructive insects, which are native to Southern China, are believed to have been inadvertently introduced to Southern port cities at the end of World War II by the military, and Jefferson said the federal government had a responsibility to help control the pests.

Jefferson was well-positioned to succeed Democratic Rep. Lindy (Mrs. Hale) Boggs in 1990 when she announced her retirement from the House. He was a major player in the state Senate, focusing on economic development and budget matters and chairing the Governmental Affairs Committee.

Jefferson finished first in the crowded primary and then, in a bitterly fought November runoff, defeated lawyer Marc Morial, the son of New Orleans' first black mayor, Ernest N. "Dutch" Morial. (The younger Morial was later elected as mayor in 1994.) Since then, Jefferson has won re-election handily.

In 1999, he ran for governor against the GOP incumbent, Mike Foster. He garnered 30 percent of the vote — enough for a second-place finish in the 12-person field, but far behind Foster's 62 percent. Jefferson did not have to relinquish his House seat to run, but he curtailed his House work schedule in the months leading up to the October election.

KEY VOTES

2000
Yes	Raise hourly minimum wage by $1 over two years
No	Halt funding for U.S. mission in Kosovo unless European nations pay more
Yes	Provide Medicare benefits to military retirees and their dependents
Yes	Grant China permanent normal trade status
Yes	Phase out estate, gift and trust taxes
No	Prohibit implementation of president's national monument designations
No	Approve GOP plan to provide prescription drug coverage for Medicare beneficiaries
Yes	Increase help for poor nations indebted to international financial institutions

1999
Yes	Impose steel import quotas
?	Kill proposal to take aviation trust funds off budget
No	Require background checks on buyers only at gun shows with 10 or more vendors
Yes	Remove barriers among banking, securities and insurance companies
Yes	Authorize state grants to hire teachers and reduce class size
Yes	Overhaul campaign finance law; ban "soft money" and restrict advocacy advertising
Yes	Approve bipartisan plan to increase rights of patients in managed-care health plans

INTEREST GROUPS

	AFL-CIO	ADA	CCUS	ACU
2000	89%	70%	66%	13%
1999	71%	75%	40%	4%
1998	100%	80%	43%	13%
1997	100%	75%	50%	17%

CQ VOTE STUDIES

	PARTY UNITY		PRESIDENTIAL SUPPORT	
	Support	Oppose	Support	Oppose
2000	90%	10%	80%	20%
1999	91%	9%	85%	15%
1998	91%	9%	83%	17%
1997	89%	11%	72%	28%

LOUISIANA 2
East – New Orleans

French street names, fortune tellers and voodoo dolls in store windows add to New Orleans' unique cultural mix. But beyond Mardi Gras, the comfortably Democratic 2nd, which takes in most of the city and some middle-class suburbs, has dealt with serious issues. Crime, which encouraged flight from the city, continued to be a problem in the 1990s, although statistics showed a drop at the end of the decade.

The staples of the 2nd's economic diet, the New Orleans Port, shipbuilding and tourism, held strong in the 1990s. The publicly traded Avondale Industries shipyard, which relies heavily on military contracts, built a new technology center that has created jobs and drawn businesses to the area. Meanwhile, the oil and gas industry was the comeback kid of the 1990s. After declining in the 1980s, the industry experienced a resurgence that leveled off toward the end of the 1990s.

Court-ordered redistricting forced the state through three sets of maps during the 1990s. In the final plan, adopted in 1996, the 2nd emerged as Louisiana's only black-majority district. It is safely Democratic. The district routinely gives Democratic presidential candidates more than 60 percent of the vote. In 2000, Al Gore received 79 percent.

MAJOR INDUSTRY
Tourism, shipbuilding, oil and gas

MILITARY BASES
New Orleans Naval Support Activity, 3,865 military, 2,700 civilian (1999); several Coast Guard stations, 684 military, 118 civilian (1998)

CITIES
New Orleans (pt.), 445,290 (1990); Marrero (pt.), 28,077 (1990); Kenner (pt.), 20,706 (1990)

UNUSUAL FEATURES
Opera first performed in the United States in New Orleans in 1796; Lindy Boggs, mother of newscaster Cokie Roberts, elected to the U.S. House in 1973 and served until Rep. Jefferson was elected in 1990.

Rep. Billy Tauzin (R)

Elected May 1980; 11th full term

CAPITOL OFFICE
225-4031; fax 225-0563; 2183 Rayburn Bldg. 20515

INTERNET
e-mail: www.house.gov/writerep
web: www.house.gov/tauzin

COMMITTEES
Energy & Commerce - chairman
Resources

HOMETOWN
Thibodaux

BORN
June 14, 1943, Chackbay, La.

RELIGION
Roman Catholic

FAMILY
Wife, Cecile Tauzin; five children

EDUCATION
Nicholls State U., B.A. 1964; Louisiana State U., J.D. 1967

CAREER
Lawyer

POLITICAL HIGHLIGHTS
La. House, 1971-80 (served as a Democrat); candidate for governor, 1987

ELECTION RESULTS

2000 GENERAL

Billy Tauzin (R)	143,446	78.0%
Edwin J. "Eddie" Albares (I)	16,908	9.2%
Anita Rosenthal (NL)	13,488	7.3%
Dion Bourque (LIBERT)	10,118	5.5%

1998 GENERAL

Billy Tauzin (R)	unopposed

PREVIOUS WINNING PERCENTAGES
1996 (100%); 1994 (76%); 1992 (82%); 1990 (88%); 1988 (89%); 1986 (100%); 1984 (100%); 1982 (100%); 1980 (85%); 1980 Special Election (53%)
*Elected as a Democrat 1980-94

As the new chairman of the Energy and Commerce Committee, Tauzin has been delivering a simple message — "I want to move bills" — to risk-averse business lobbyists, who often think the best legislation on Capitol Hill is dead legislation.

The panel is the oldest legislative committee in Congress, and under Tauzin's direction it is expected to be a very different place than during the previous six years of GOP control. The Louisianan is seen as much more activist than his predecessor, Thomas J. Bliley Jr., R-Va., who retired in 2000. Tauzin, who craves the limelight, appears eager to use his shrewdness, policy acumen and zest for deal-making to enact legislation.

Once known primarily as a fierce champion of his state's oil and gas industry, a mainstay of the "old" economy, Tauzin (TOE-zan) has been positioning himself to take a pivotal role on issues central to the "new" economy. He sees himself as a principal decision-maker in the 107th Congress in the debate over balancing competition and regulation in the e-commerce arena.

Tauzin began his chairmanship aspiring to act on the many fronts within his panel's expansive jurisdiction, including telecommunications, health care, energy, consumer protection and the environment. His approach is rooted in the view that the Republican Party should at times embrace, rather than fear, legislation to shape the behavior of American industry.

In his more than two decades in Congress, Tauzin has increasingly taken a deregulatory approach. But his career has been marked by a desire to be a playmaker, building coalitions to win support for his point of view — and often shifting his point of view in the process.

To the consternation of some conservatives, for example, he responded to the 2000 Firestone tire recall by persuading GOP leaders to work for enactment of his legislation setting new rules for the disclosure of product safety information. In typical fashion, Tauzin sought to trump the philosophical case against the bill, advanced by deregulatory purists, with two arguments. To the auto industry, he said his proposal was far preferable to more stringent alternatives then gathering steam in the Senate. To fellow Republicans, he argued that a failure to legislate would be politically tone deaf in an election year.

Critics suggest that Tauzin's zeal to cut deals could lead him either to regularly ruffle GOP conservatives or to lose control of the size and shape of whatever legislation he is trying to shepherd. Tauzin responds by saying he will make sure that whatever deals he strikes are acceptable to Republican leaders. In the 107th Congress, he is deputy whip.

Since quitting the Democratic Party for the GOP in 1995, Tauzin has displayed that he can work easily with both parties, neither casting doubt on his new fealty to the Republican leadership nor angering his old colleagues across the aisle. Beneath the surface of his animated, back-slapping style lie an intense competitiveness and a diligence when it comes to learning the nuances of policy.

He calls himself the Cajun ambassador to Congress, while his constituents call him the "Swamp Fox." He shifts effortlessly from French to English, and his website is bilingual, too. He makes recipes from his book, "Cook and Tell," a centerpiece of the fundraisers that helped him raise $8 million for the GOP in 1999-2000. An avid deer hunter, he operates a hunt club — actually, a mobile home near a wildlife preserve on Maryland's Eastern Shore — to which several of his longtime lobbyist friends belong.

His office is decorated with hunting trophies, one of them an alligator head with its jaw stuffed with Mardi Gras beads.

A founding member of the conservative "Blue Dog" coalition of House Democrats in 1995, he switched to the GOP seven months after Republicans took control of Congress — but only after he was promised he could keep the seniority he had accrued as a Democrat on the Energy and Commerce Committee. That set the stage for his fierce rivalry with Michael G. Oxley of Ohio, a lifelong Republican with comparable seniority. In their initial face-off, in 1997, a subcommittee both lawmakers wanted to chair was split; the two then began maneuvering to chair the full committee in the 107th.

In 2001, instead of cinching the victory outright — through a vote of all House Republicans — GOP leaders awarded Tauzin the committee chairmanship, but at a higher-than-expected price: Some of Energy and Commerce's most highly prized jurisdiction, over securities and insurance, was transferred to a new Financial Services Committee, with Oxley as chairman.

Still, Tauzin moved quickly to establish an ambitious agenda that will include a new look at ways to regulate the rights of patients in managed-care health plans and to encourage domestic energy production as a remedy to spikes in retail utility bills. He vowed to push for a proposal to revise the 1996 telecommunications overhaul to allow the Baby Bells to carry high-speed data on long-distance telephone lines.

He sought legislation early in the 107th to protect the privacy of online shoppers. He planned to move a rewrite of the superfund law that would limit landowners' liability for hazardous waste problems they inherit from others. And he planned to push for a nationally uniform poll closing time in presidential elections.

Tauzin is reliably conservative on fiscal and social matters. In 1997-98, he gained national exposure on a 40-city tour with Majority Leader Dick Armey to debate the best alternative to the current tax code. Tauzin favors a national sales tax, Armey a flat income tax.

A native of south Louisiana's Cajun country, Tauzin had a law practice in the bayou towns of Houma and Thibodaux. He won a state legislative seat in 1971, and during eight years in the post, he emerged as Gov. Edwin W. Edwards' protégé, serving as floor leader in the state House. Tauzin came to Washington in a 1980 special election to replace GOP Rep. David C. Treen, who had been elected governor. In 1987, he finished fourth in his one bid for higher office — governor of Louisiana. But he has never had a problem holding his House seat — in either party. In 1996, he became the first member of Congress to win re-election without opposition after switching parties.

KEY VOTES

2000
No	Raise hourly minimum wage by $1 over two years
Yes	Halt funding for U.S. mission in Kosovo unless European nations pay more
Yes	Provide Medicare benefits to military retirees and their dependents
Yes	Grant China permanent normal trade status
Yes	Phase out estate, gift and trust taxes
Yes	Prohibit implementation of president's national monument designations
Yes	Approve GOP plan to provide prescription drug coverage for Medicare beneficiaries
No	Increase help for poor nations indebted to international financial institutions

1999
No	Impose steel import quotas
No	Kill proposal to take aviation trust funds off budget
Yes	Require background checks on buyers only at gun shows with 10 or more vendors
Yes	Remove barriers among banking, securities and insurance companies
No	Authorize state grants to hire teachers and reduce class size
No	Overhaul campaign finance law; ban "soft money" and restrict advocacy advertising
No	Approve bipartisan plan to increase rights of patients in managed-care health plans

INTEREST GROUPS

	AFL-CIO	ADA	CCUS	ACU
2000	0%	0%	85%	84%
1999	0%	5%	100%	84%
1998	0%	5%	100%	88%
1997	0%	15%	100%	83%

CQ VOTE STUDIES

	PARTY UNITY		PRESIDENTIAL SUPPORT	
	Support	Oppose	Support	Oppose
2000	92%	8%	26%	74%
1999	93%	7%	21%	79%
1998	92%	8%	23%	77%
1997	93%	7%	31%	69%

LOUISIANA 3

South Central – Houma; New Iberia

Located in southern Louisiana, running along the marshy coast of the Gulf of Mexico, the socially conservative 3rd is Cajun country. Folks here know the intricate details of preparing fish, a major industry in the 3rd, and are well trained in the ways of hurricanes.

After a rough decade in the 1980s, the 3rd enjoyed a stable economy in the 1990s, due in large part to a rebounding oil and gas industry, which is especially big in Terrebonne Parish, along the Gulf. The 3rd also helps the state lead the nation in crawfish, blue crab and shrimp production. Further inland, chemical plants along the Mississippi River are faring better than they did in the 1980s but are concerned about declining demand overseas. Sugar cane also grows well in the 3rd's wet environment.

Although redistricting in 1996 changed the 3rd's boundaries, the district didn't change much politically. Democrats dominated for nearly a century, with a few forays toward the Progressive Party, but the Catholic 3rd now has turned to Republicans. Rep. Tauzin has been re-elected three times since he switched parties to join the GOP. Conservative Democrats do well in local elections.

MAJOR INDUSTRY
Oil and gas, petrochemicals, shipping, sugar cane; fishing

MILITARY BASES
New Orleans Naval Air Station, 2,100 military, 900 civilian (1999)

CITIES
New Iberia, 33,317; Houma, 32,541; Chalmette (unincorporated), 31,860 (1990); Thibodaux, 15,163

UNUSUAL FEATURES
Shrimp & Petroleum Festival every Labor Day in Morgan City; Konriko rice mill, founded in New Iberia in 1912, the oldest rice mill in the United States.

Rep. Jim McCrery (R)

Elected April 1988; 7th full term

Soft-spoken and knowledgeable, McCrery has carved out a position of influence on such politically contentious issues as health care, welfare and tax policy. His views on these matters are strictly Republican, yet his even-tempered demeanor has made him someone with whom Democrats are willing to deal.

His seat on the Ways and Means Committee puts him front and center on these issues, and he has a close relationship with California Republican Bill Thomas, the panel's new chairman. In the 106th Congress, McCrery and Thomas teamed up on an effort to decouple the link between a person's job and his medical insurance. In the 107th, Thomas put McCrery in charge of a new Ways and Means subcommittee, called Select Revenue Measures, to tackle broad tax issues.

GOP leaders have confidence in McCrery, and they have made sure he is included in negotiations on key bills and as a member of GOP task forces on Social Security, managed health care or prescription drugs.

In 2000, at the request of The Atlantic Monthly magazine, McCrery agreed to a lengthy on-the-record discussion with Washington Democratic Rep. Jim McDermott on whether the two philosophically opposed lawmakers could agree on a plan to provide health insurance coverage for every American. Throughout the discussion, which showcased each man's grasp of the complex subject, McCrery made it clear that he realizes significant compromises are needed to achieve better health coverage.

"If we want to save the private health care system, Republicans are going to have to accept some things that normally would be contrary to our basic philosophy," McCrery told the author of the article, Matthew Miller. He said he would require everyone to purchase insurance and would equalize premiums, regardless of a person's age, sex or medical history, to spread the risks broadly.

In both 1999 and 2000, McCrery helped develop legislation to increase Medicare funding in key areas by restoring some of the cuts Congress made in 1997 as it worked to balance the budget. After agreement on the 1999 Medicare spending package was reached, the Clinton White House singled out McCrery for praise.

As vice chairman of the National Republican Congressional Committee, the organization that seeks to elect Republicans to the House, McCrery was in charge of making sure incumbent GOP lawmakers had the resources needed for their re-election bids. Facing no re-election challenge himself in 1998, McCrery was able to pour proceeds from his fundraising efforts into a political action committee — which he called the Committee for the Preservation of Capitalism — to aid fellow Republicans.

McCrery had a key role in the 104th Congress as the GOP pushed through legislation overhauling the nation's welfare system. He was prominent on Ways and Means in challenging some traditional views of the nation's "social safety net" programs, such as welfare and the Supplemental Security Income (SSI) program for the disabled. His most significant achievement was enactment of a plan to tighten eligibility for disabled children to receive benefits from the SSI program. McCrery set his sights on the eligibility requirement after educators in his district said that some parents were encouraging their children to misbehave regularly so they could be classified as "disabled" and receive a monthly SSI benefit.

In 1998, McCrery was given a thankless task — serving as one of four

CAPITOL OFFICE
225-2777; fax 225-8039; 2104 Rayburn Bldg. 20515

INTERNET
e-mail: jim.mccrery@mail.house.gov
web: www.house.gov/mccrery

COMMITTEES
Ways & Means
(Select Revenue Measures - chairman)

HOMETOWN
Shreveport

BORN
Sept. 18, 1949, Shreveport, La.

RELIGION
Methodist

FAMILY
Wife, Johnette McCrery; two children

EDUCATION
Louisiana Tech U., B.A. 1971; Louisiana State U., J.D. 1975

CAREER
Lawyer; congressional aide; government relations executive

POLITICAL HIGHLIGHTS
Candidate for Leesville City Council, 1978

ELECTION RESULTS

2000 GENERAL

Jim McCrery (R)	122,678	70.5%
Phillip R. Green (D)	43,600	25.1%
Michael "Mike" Taylor (I)	4,059	2.3%
James Ronals Skains (I)	3,630	2.1%

1998 GENERAL

Jim McCrery (R)	unopposed

PREVIOUS WINNING PERCENTAGES
1996 (71%); 1994 (80%); 1992 (63%); 1990 (55%); 1988 (69%); 1988 Special Election (51%)

members of an ad hoc ethics panel looking into allegations that the chairman of the Transportation Committee, Republican Bud Shuster of Pennsylvania, had inappropriately accepted gifts from lobbyists. The panel did not complete its work until late 2000, issuing a letter of reproval but calling for no further punishment.

McCrery served on the Armed Services Committee during his first two full House terms, and he still looks out for Barksdale Air Force Base near Shreveport and Fort Polk in the southern part of the 4th District.

In the 106th Congress, he authored a bill, which became law, to create the Red River National Wildlife Refuge in the 4th. He also presses for continued funding for Interstate 69, a newly designated Michigan-to-Mexico highway that would traverse northwestern Louisiana.

Following graduation from law school at Louisiana State University, McCrery joined a law firm in Leesville, where he had grown up, and then moved on to a two-year stint as an assistant city attorney for Shreveport. As a Democrat in 1981, he signed on with Democratic Rep. Buddy Roemer, working first in the district office in Shreveport and then as Roemer's legislative director in Washington. McCrery returned to Louisiana in 1984 to work for Georgia-Pacific Corp., in the state capital of Baton Rouge.

He switched to the GOP in late 1987 just before Roemer was elected governor of Louisiana. Although not well-known in the district, McCrery stood out in the 1988 special election to replace Roemer in the House: He was the only Republican, and he impressed many with his knowledge of legislative issues. He finished first in the primary and narrowly defeated Democratic state Sen. Foster L. Campbell Jr. in the April runoff. After the special election, McCrery had little time to prepare for November. Fortunately for him, the Democratic effort in the 4th District fizzled. Potential challengers stopped in their tracks when Roemer's mother, Adeline, entered the race. She lost heavily.

McCrery's most significant re-election challenge came in 1992, after redistricting matched him against fellow incumbent Jerry Huckaby, an eight-term Democrat. Although Huckaby chaired the Agriculture Subcommittee on Cotton, Rice and Sugar — commodities of great importance to Louisiana — he was at a disadvantage in the new district, with its smaller black population, and he had 88 overdrafts at the private bank for House members. McCrery breezed past Huckaby, winning with 63 percent.

In 1996, another round of remapping was ordered after federal judges rejected earlier maps as "racial gerrymanders," and McCrery ran in a newly drawn 4th District. He won easily and has had little trouble since.

KEY VOTES

2000
No   Raise hourly minimum wage by $1 over two years
Yes Halt funding for U.S. mission in Kosovo unless European nations pay more
Yes Provide Medicare benefits to military retirees and their dependents
Yes Grant China permanent normal trade status
Yes Phase out estate, gift and trust taxes
Yes Prohibit implementation of president's national monument designations
Yes Approve GOP plan to provide prescription drug coverage for Medicare beneficiaries
No   Increase help for poor nations indebted to international financial institutions

1999
No   Impose steel import quotas
Yes Kill proposal to take aviation trust funds off budget
Yes Require background checks on buyers only at gun shows with 10 or more vendors
Yes Remove barriers among banking, securities and insurance companies
No   Authorize state grants to hire teachers and reduce class size
No   Overhaul campaign finance law; ban "soft money" and restrict advocacy advertising
No   Approve bipartisan plan to increase rights of patients in managed-care health plans

INTEREST GROUPS

	AFL-CIO	ADA	CCUS	ACU
2000	0%	5%	95%	83%
1999	0%	0%	96%	80%
1998	10%	5%	100%	96%
1997	0%	20%	100%	83%

CQ VOTE STUDIES

	PARTY UNITY		PRESIDENTIAL SUPPORT	
	Support	Oppose	Support	Oppose
2000	90%	10%	27%	73%
1999	92%	8%	25%	75%
1998	94%	6%	26%	74%
1997	94%	6%	30%	70%

LOUISIANA 4
Northwest and west — Shreveport; Bossier City

Removed from the Cajun influence that characterizes much of southern Louisiana, the mostly white-collar 4th looks more toward Dallas than New Orleans. Covering most of western Louisiana, the conservative 4th takes in Shreveport at its north end and wanders down into agriculture country in Beauregard Parish at its south.

Shreveport, the district's largest city, lost white residents to nearby Bossier City in the 1990s. Although a booming oil industry near Shreveport once brought prosperity to the area, it fizzled in the 1980s. Nowadays, a growing riverboat gambling industry along the Shreveport and Bossier City river fronts gives the economy steam. General Motors is building a new facility in Shreveport, which is expected to attract automotive suppliers to the area. The Barksdale Air Force Base in nearby Bossier City is a major employer for both cities. The forestry industry throughout the 4th and Fort Polk, to the south, add to the economy.

Traditionally, the mostly Protestant 4th sent conservative Democrats to Congress, but the seat went to a Republican in a 1988 special election. Redistricted several times in the 1990s, the 4th had a black majority from 1992-96 but is now only about one-third black. Locally, the 4th favors Democrats, although the suburbs around Shreveport and Bossier City elected some Republicans in the 1990s.

MAJOR INDUSTRY
Military, riverboat gambling, agriculture

MILITARY BASES
Barksdale Air Force Base, 7,217 military, 541 civilian; Fort Polk (Army), 8,911 military, 1,867 civilian (1999)

CITIES
Shreveport, 187,393; Bossier City, 56,413; Natchitoches, 16,834

UNUSUAL FEATURES
Bank robbers Bonnie and Clyde gunned down eight miles south of Gibsland in 1934; the town re-enacts the shooting every year.

Rep. John Cooksey (R)

CAPITOL OFFICE
225-8490; fax 225-5639; 113 Cannon Bldg. 20515

INTERNET
e-mail: congressman.cooksey@mail.house.gov
web: www.house.gov/cooksey

COMMITTEES
Agriculture
International Relations
Transportation & Infrastructure

HOMETOWN
Monroe

BORN
Aug. 20, 1941, Alexandria, La.

RELIGION
Methodist

FAMILY
Wife, Ann Cooksey; three children

EDUCATION
Louisiana State U., B.A. 1962, M.D. 1966; U. of
Texas, M.B.A. 1994

MILITARY SERVICE
Air Force, 1967-69; La. Air National Guard, 1969-72

CAREER
Physician

POLITICAL HIGHLIGHTS
No previous office

ELECTION RESULTS

2000 GENERAL

John Cooksey (R)	123,975	69.1%
Roger Beall (D)	42,977	24.0%
Sam Houston Melton Jr. (D)	7,186	4.0%
Raymond A. Dumas (LIBERT)	5,335	3.0%

1998 GENERAL

John Cooksey (R)	unopposed

PREVIOUS WINNING PERCENTAGES
1996 General Runoff (58%)

Elected 1996; 3rd term

A wealthy ophthalmologist, Cooksey has a mostly conservative voting record, although his background as a physician sometimes puts him at odds with the GOP leadership on such matters as abortion and the rights of patients in disputes with their health maintenance organizations.

Cooksey is generally content to work behind the scenes, just as he did for years in local politics when he helped GOP candidates raise money to mount their campaigns. He has voluntarily given himself a term limit, saying he will not seek re-election to the House in 2002. His work on behalf of other Republicans has not gone unnoticed by party leaders, and Cooksey has found considerable support for a potential Senate bid in 2002 against Democrat Mary L. Landrieu.

In the 106th Congress, Cooksey joined with several other GOP physicians to urge Republican leaders to address the growing issue of patients' complaints about their managed-care plans. The two parties drafted competing proposals. When the Senate passed GOP-authored legislation, Cooksey and some physicians said the measure was not a patients' bill of rights, but rather an "HMO bill of rights." When the legislation came before the House, Cooksey was among 68 Republicans who voted for a Democratic-drafted plan allowing people to sue their health plans for denial of coverage.

Louisiana has one of the highest percentages of uninsured people in the nation, and Cooksey was among a number of lawmakers who sought to develop legislation in the 106th Congress to alleviate that problem. "I want everybody to have the same health care choices that we have in Congress," he said. He drafted a bill to provide tax credits for purchasing medical insurance. Majority Leader Dick Armey was among those who signed on as cosponsors. The bill saw no action, but Cooksey said he would continue his effort in the 107th Congress.

Cooksey, who continues to see patients occasionally during congressional breaks, also worked to increase Medicare and Medicaid payments to rural hospitals by organizing a petition drive that collected 3,000 signatures urging Congress to restore cuts it had made in 1997.

Cooksey's moderate stance on some social issues has contributed to a feud with Louisiana's Republican leaders, as the lawmaker argues that the GOP message should be "economic conservatism and reasonableness on the social issues. But the people running the state party want to pass federal laws to basically dictate every part of everyday life," he told the Baton Rouge Sunday Advocate in 2000.

Cooksey cites his medical experience in supporting, along with a group of mostly liberal lawmakers, a worldwide ban on the use of anti-personnel land mines. He said he came to the cause while treating victims of land mine blasts in Africa during the late 1980s and early 1990s. He made five medical missions to Kenya, to perform free eye surgery and later to establish an eye clinic with money he raised in the United States.

When he could not find other lawmakers to join him on a trip to Sierra Leone in 2000, Cooksey traveled with aides to the war-torn country, in the throes of a brutal civil conflict. According to the New Orleans Times-Picayune, he visited health care facilities, where he saw children who had been maimed. He told the newspaper he blamed U.S. inaction in ending the war there on the cowardice of the Clinton administration and the "callousness" of congressional Republicans, who, he said, didn't seem to care much about the country's human suffering.

While other Republican physicians have been leaders in the anti-abortion movement, Cooksey has not been front and center on that issue. He opposes abortion but says he does not support a constitutional amendment banning the procedure. He argues that the federal government should not get too involved in the matter.

The substantially rural 5th District is the state's poorest, and Cooksey's top priority has been economic development. One of the best ways to create a better climate for business, he says, is to upgrade the region's transportation system. In the 105th Congress, he sought federal funding to widen U.S. 165, the major north-south highway in the district, which connects the two largest cities, Monroe and Alexandria. From his post on the Transportation Committee, he won $30 million to make the highway four lanes wide. In the 106th Congress, Cooksey developed a detailed plan to greatly expand the Monroe airport to bring the airline, bus, Amtrak and cargo terminals under the same roof.

Cooksey's profitable medical practice and his ownership of a 300-acre working farm have given him a net worth of nearly $3 million, making him one of the wealthiest members of Congress. He grew up in the small town of Olla, north of Alexandria, where his father ran a sawmill and his mother was a teacher. He earned his undergraduate and medical degrees from Louisiana State University (he was named alumnus of the year by the medical school in 1999). Fulfilling his college ROTC obligation, he served as an Air Force flight surgeon in Thailand during the Vietnam War.

Returning home, he built a prosperous medical practice and became involved in community affairs and Republican politics, serving as the finance manager for several GOP campaigns. In 1975, he helped lead an effort to pass legislation capping medical malpractice awards in Louisiana at $500,000. But he did not run for office himself until 1996, when court-ordered redrawing of Louisiana's House districts left the 5th District without an incumbent.

Cooksey was the top vote-getter in a six-candidate all-party primary, with 34 percent of the vote. In the runoff, against veteran Democratic state Rep. Francis Thompson, Cooksey parried the charge that he was a rich man out of touch with the district's many lower-income residents. Instead, he traded on his image as a pillar of the community who had volunteered his time in various civic, humanitarian and political endeavors.

President Clinton carried the district, but Cooksey won election easily, with 58 percent. In 1998, he was unopposed, and in 2000 he cruised to victory by 45 percentage points.

KEY VOTES

2000
?	Raise hourly minimum wage by $1 over two years
Yes	Halt funding for U.S. mission in Kosovo unless European nations pay more
Yes	Provide Medicare benefits to military retirees and their dependents
Yes	Grant China permanent normal trade status
Yes	Phase out estate, gift and trust taxes
Yes	Prohibit implementation of president's national monument designations
Yes	Approve GOP plan to provide prescription drug coverage for Medicare beneficiaries
No	Increase help for poor nations indebted to international financial institutions

1999
No	Impose steel import quotas
No	Kill proposal to take aviation trust funds off budget
No	Require background checks on buyers only at gun shows with 10 or more vendors
Yes	Remove barriers among banking, securities and insurance companies
No	Authorize state grants to hire teachers and reduce class size
No	Overhaul campaign finance law; ban "soft money" and restrict advocacy advertising
Yes	Approve bipartisan plan to increase rights of patients in managed-care health plans

INTEREST GROUPS

	AFL-CIO	ADA	CCUS	ACU
2000	0%	0%	87%	73%
1999	13%	15%	91%	62%
1998	14%	0%	100%	96%
1997	0%	10%	100%	91%

CQ VOTE STUDIES

	PARTY UNITY		PRESIDENTIAL SUPPORT	
	Support	Oppose	Support	Oppose
2000	88%	12%	33%	67%
1999	81%	19%	24%	76%
1998	95%	5%	25%	75%
1997	95%	5%	28%	72%

LOUISIANA 5
Northeast and central — Monroe; Alexandria

Stamped with pockets of poverty, the 5th is a picture of economic gloom. The district starts with East Carroll, a poverty-stricken parish at the Arkansas and Mississippi border, and runs south through poor farming towns along the Mississippi River into Cajun country. A conservative district throughout, Baptists and Pentecostals dominate the northern and central parts of the 5th, while Catholics are more common in the south.

Agriculture is abundant but not able to keep the economy from lagging. Along the black, rich land on the Mississippi River, farmers grow cotton, soybeans and corn. Although most of the state's cotton comes from this area, unemployment is high.

Monroe, in Ouachita Parish, is the district's largest city. A longtime trading hub of northeast Louisiana, Monroe is an agricultural center that falls squarely between the forest section and the fertile delta region. To the west of Monroe lie thick pine forests that fuel the timber industry. Union, Lincoln, Jackson and Caldwell parishes are dotted with small lumber and paper mills. In the state's center and the district's southwestern corner lies Rapides Parish, which contains Alexandria, the 5th's second-largest city. Alexandria lies on the west bank of the Red River and is nearly equidistant to Shreveport and Baton Rouge. One bright spot in the 5th was the 1992 transformation of the closed England Air Force Base outside of Alexandria into an industrial park that brought in about 1,500 jobs.

Three rounds of redistricting in the 1990s dramatically changed the shape of the 5th, adding to the district's black population while retaining its conservative, religious character. The longtime conservative Democratic seat became Republican in the 1992 election. Democrats hold most local offices.

MAJOR INDUSTRY
Agriculture, health care

CITIES
Monroe, 52,114; Alexandria, 45,959; Ruston, 20,241

UNUSUAL FEATURES
Gov. and Sen. Huey Long born in Winn Parish in 1893.

Rep. Richard H. Baker (R)

Elected 1986; 8th term

CAPITOL OFFICE
225-3901; fax 225-7313; 341 Cannon Bldg. 20515

INTERNET
e-mail: www.house.gov/writerep
web: www.house.gov/baker

COMMITTEES
Financial Services
  (Capital Markets, Insurance & GSEs - chairman)
Transportation & Infrastructure
Veterans' Affairs

HOMETOWN
Baton Rouge

BORN
May 22, 1948, New Orleans, La.

RELIGION
Methodist

FAMILY
Wife, Kay Baker; two children

EDUCATION
Louisiana State U., B.A. 1971

CAREER
Real estate broker

POLITICAL HIGHLIGHTS
La. House, 1972-86 (served as a Democrat, 1972-85)

ELECTION RESULTS

2000 GENERAL

Richard H. Baker (R)	165,637	68.0%
Kathy J. Rogillio (D)	72,192	29.7%
Michael S. Wolf (LIBERT)	5,649	2.3%

1998 GENERAL

Richard H. Baker (R)	97,044	50.7%
Marjorie McKeithen (D)	94,201	49.3%

PREVIOUS WINNING PERCENTAGES
1996 (69%); 1994 (81%); 1992 (51%); 1990 (100%); 1988 (100%); 1986 (51%)

The son of a minister, Baker gives the lie to the popular perception of the back-slapping, flamboyant Louisiana politician. As a profile in The Financial Services Roundtable put it, "You'd be hard-pressed to catch Richard Baker, were he a football player, dancing in the end zone after scoring a touchdown. It's just not his style."

Disinclined to toot his own horn, Baker declined to employ a press secretary for several years until a 1998 election scare convinced him he needed someone to publicize his legislative accomplishments. Baker has since given his press secretary a number of victories to tout.

He played a key role in the 1999 enactment of legislation to overhaul the financial services industry, even though he didn't get everything he wanted. From his Banking Committee seat, he took on powerful forces in the mortgage loan industry, seeking increased regulation of Fannie Mae and Freddie Mac, the giant government-sponsored housing and loan enterprises, in a battle that also pitted him and his allies at large banks against consumer groups, the real estate industry and small banks.

At the start of the 107th Congress, there was speculation that Baker or fellow veteran Banking Committee member Marge Roukema of New Jersey might be in line to chair the panel, but both lost out to Michael G. Oxley of Ohio. The Republican leadership decided to expand the committee's jurisdiction (an idea that Baker himself had advanced), adding securities and insurance issues. Oxley had dealt with both those policy areas as chairman of Commerce's Finance and Hazardous Materials Subcommittee. The Banking panel was then renamed the Financial Services Committee. In the 107th, Baker chairs the panel's Capital Markets, Insurance and Government-Sponsored-Enterprises Subcommittee.

The Louisiana lawmaker is a solid friend of the business community and conservative down the line — he has had a rating of 0 from the liberal Americans for Democratic Action for 11 consecutive years.

Baker's top priority is to make sure that taxpayers never again have to bail out a segment of the economy, as they did with the savings and loan industry in the late 1980s and early 1990s. "How much risk does the taxpayer have?" Baker wants to know. "We don't share in the profits, we only share in the risk," he told the Baton Rouge Advocate.

That concern was the basis for his probe in the 106th Congress of the demise of the giant hedge fund, Long-Term Capital Management, which had the potential of damaging the financial stability of some of the nation's largest banks. Hedge funds are unregulated and potentially risky investment pools that seek to exploit temporary differences in the market prices of securities, commodities or currencies.

Concern about taxpayer risk also fuels Baker's battle to bring Fannie Mae and Freddie Mac under tighter government scrutiny. At the end of 2000, the two financial entities agreed to move toward Baker's position, by increasing their reserves and offering greater public disclosure about their financial operations; but Baker was not entirely appeased and vowed to continue to pursue legislation to tighten federal regulations.

Baker says he realizes that "99.9 percent of what I do is of no interest to people in the district." But, he says, although his legislative focus is hard to understand and harder to explain, it is important. "My concern is that taxpayers not be called upon to pay off a bill they didn't create."

Baker does look out for the 6th District. His avocation as an amateur astronomer led to a new science research facility, known as a gravity wave observatory, in his district. Baker read about the concept in a science journal, contacted the government agencies involved and suggested the project be located in the 6th District. He also authored legislation that created a 36,500-acre Cat Island National Wildlife Refuge in the 6th, and he campaigned for voter approval of a local tax levy to match the government's contribution for a $100 million-plus Comite River flood-control project.

Baker was the driving force behind the creation of a training camp for at-risk youngsters and a health facility for veterans — both of which are located on the grounds of an old federal leprosarium that he had transferred to state control.

After his graduation from Louisiana State University with a degree in political science, Baker started his own real estate business and won election to the state legislature by the time he was 23.

He made a name for himself in the state Capitol by authoring a major change in the way state highway funds were doled out, establishing objective criteria for allocating money rather than leaving it to the governor's whim. He was a Democrat back then, but he switched parties in 1985 at the urging of GOP leaders who saw in him their best chance to retain the House seat being vacated by Republican W. Henson Moore, who ran for the Senate. Baker put together an unusual coalition of country club Republicans and blue-collar Democrats to defeat a better-financed Democrat.

In 1992, redistricting cost Louisiana a House seat, and Baker wound up running against GOP Rep. Clyde C. Holloway, a conservative who had won three terms in a district that was roughly 85 percent Democratic. In the first round of voting, Holloway came in first, and Baker barely qualified for the runoff, finishing just ahead of Democrat Ned Randolph, the popular conservative mayor of Alexandria. Going head-to-head with Holloway, Baker carried only two parishes (out of 17), but that was enough to offset his losses across the rest of the 6th, and he prevailed with 51 percent.

After easy re-election contests in 1994 and 1996, Baker had formidable Democratic opposition in 1998 from Marjorie McKeithen, who bore a name well-known to voters: Her father and grandfather were both big players in Louisiana politics. McKeithen beat Baker in six of the nine parishes in the redrawn district, but Baker's advantage in the three more-populous parishes enabled him to come out ahead, by less than 3,000 votes out of almost 200,000 cast. Observers expected another tough Baker-McKeithen race in 2000, but she announced early on that she was not interested in a rematch. Democrats could not find another competitive candidate, and Baker cruised to victory.

KEY VOTES

2000
No Raise hourly minimum wage by $1 over two years
Yes Halt funding for U.S. mission in Kosovo unless European nations pay more
Yes Provide Medicare benefits to military retirees and their dependents
Yes Grant China permanent normal trade status
Yes Phase out estate, gift and trust taxes
Yes Prohibit implementation of president's national monument designations
Yes Approve GOP plan to provide prescription drug coverage for Medicare beneficiaries
No Increase help for poor nations indebted to international financial institutions

1999
No Impose steel import quotas
No Kill proposal to take aviation trust funds off budget
Yes Require background checks on buyers only at gun shows with 10 or more vendors
Yes Remove barriers among banking, securities and insurance companies
No Authorize state grants to hire teachers and reduce class size
No Overhaul campaign finance law; ban "soft money" and restrict advocacy advertising
No Approve bipartisan plan to increase rights of patients in managed-care health plans

INTEREST GROUPS

	AFL-CIO	ADA	CCUS	ACU
2000	0%	0%	85%	75%
1999	0%	0%	96%	80%
1998	0%	0%	100%	100%
1997	0%	0%	100%	92%

CQ VOTE STUDIES

	PARTY UNITY		PRESIDENTIAL SUPPORT	
	Support	Oppose	Support	Oppose
2000	90%	10%	26%	74%
1999	94%	6%	17%	83%
1998	94%	6%	20%	80%
1997	97%	3%	25%	75%

LOUISIANA 6
South Central — Baton Rouge

The socially conservative 6th is centered on the state capital, Baton Rouge, and takes in a swath of the Mississippi River that supports a slew of chemical plants. Its rural north hosts farming, while the parishes ringing Baton Rouge have become increasingly suburban, drawing capital commuters.

As in most of the South, socially conservative suburban and rural voters have made a shift toward the GOP. But Baton Rouge retains minority and blue-collar populations that still vote Democratic. Three redistrictings in the 1990s gave the 6th more and more of Baton Rouge, transforming it into a politically competitive district. For local offices, East Baton Rouge, Livingston and Ascension parishes are the most Republican areas.

Because much of the oil refined in the 6th comes from overseas, the 1980s decline of the U.S. oil industry impacted but never crushed the 6th's vast petrochemical industry. Baton Rouge remains a petrochemical hub but also teems with Louisiana State University and Southern University students and government workers. To the west of the city, the Port of Greater Baton Rouge ranks as one of the nation's largest ports but experienced some tough times at the end of the 1990s.

The district's economy also benefits from Catfish Town, a retail development center along the Mississippi River where tourists come for riverboat gambling and the nearby Naval War Museum. The 6th also takes in the sugar cane fields of Point Coupee Parish and much of the timber- and potato-producing parishes of St. Helena and West and East Feliciana.

MAJOR INDUSTRY
Petrochemicals, government, higher education

CITIES
Baton Rouge, 210,667; Baker, 13,648; Zachary, 11,924

UNUSUAL FEATURES
Democratic political consultant James Carville born in Carville, La. (named after his grandfather).

Rep. Chris John (D)

CAPITOL OFFICE
225-2031; fax 225-5724
1504 Longworth Bldg. 20515

INTERNET
e-mail: chrisjohn@mail.house.gov
web: www.house.gov/john

COMMITTEES
Energy & Commerce

HOMETOWN
Crowley

BORN
Jan. 5, 1960, Crowley, La.

RELIGION
Roman Catholic

FAMILY
Wife, Payton John; two children

EDUCATION
Louisiana State U., B.A. 1982

CAREER
Trucking company owner

POLITICAL HIGHLIGHTS
Crowley City Council, 1984-88; La. House, 1988-96;
candidate for lieutenant governor, 1995

ELECTION RESULTS

2000 GENERAL

Chris John (D)	152,796	83.3%
Michael P. Harris (LIBERT)	30,687	16.7%

1998 GENERAL

Chris John (D)	unopposed

PREVIOUS WINNING PERCENTAGES
1996 General Runoff (53%)

Elected 1996; 3rd term

One of the most conservative Democrats in the House, John turned to his own advantage Republican pleas to switch parties and won a coveted seat on the Energy and Commerce Committee in the 107th Congress.

Two years earlier, House GOP members had promised him a seat on the committee — then called Commerce — if he would change parties. "They had some nice offers ... but the fact is, philosophically I'm a Democrat and will always be one," he told the New Orleans Times-Picayune. Democratic leader Richard A. Gephardt promised John a seat on the panel in the 107th and then made good on that pledge.

Even though he remains in the minority party, John figures that his leadership role in a key centrist group — the "Blue Dogs," a coalition of conservative Democrats hailing mainly from the South and West — gives him a position of influence. His affiliation with the Blue Dogs fits in well with his political philosophy and legislative style: John puts a premium on building coalitions.

In his four years in Congress, he has authored just six bills. "I prefer to sit and compromise and to lobby my colleagues," John told the Baton Rouge Advocate when he was first elected. He had a similar track record in the state legislature, where he developed a reputation as someone who was a willing listener, a hard worker and a legislator well-versed on a few key issues, particularly oil and gas matters.

He says his focus on bridge-building across party lines is "what people want — moderates who can be effective, and not someone hellbent on a dogmatic line from which they cannot vary. They don't want to see a lot of fights between donkeys and elephants," he told The Advocate.

John's voting record puts him firmly in the middle of the political spectrum. He has backed the Democratic position on party-line votes slightly more than half the time; and he supported President Clinton about as often. He sides more often with business interests than with organized labor. And, perhaps most telling, his vote ratings from the Americans for Democratic Action and the American Conservative Union are similar — about 40 percent from the liberals and 50 percent from the conservatives.

When he arrived in the House in 1997 with a background in business and politics, John joined up with the Blue Dogs and was soon given a prominent role in announcing the group's plan for achieving a balanced budget. Later that year, he applauded the settlement reached between the Clinton administration and GOP congressional leaders. "It is not a perfect resolution to the problem," John said of the agreement on spending and taxes. "There are some Republican victories. ... There are some Democratic victories. ... But it balances the budget in five years."

In the 106th Congress, he was one of three co-chairmen of the group and presented Blue Dog proposals on prescription drugs, campaign finance and the budget.

To take the Energy and Commerce post, John had to give up seats on the Agriculture and Resources panels, which were good fits for his district, where farming, oil and gas development, and coastal preservation are important issues. He is concerned with developing new markets abroad for the district's soybean and rice growers, and he has gone to bat for Louisiana's crawfish farmers, who said their livelihood was threatened by China "dumping" crawfish meat into the U.S. market at less than fair value. (John and his brothers own two rice and crawfish farms they inherited from their grandparents.)

The state's cyclical oil and gas industry is now thriving, and John says his job is "to make sure that the federal government does not do anything to jeopardize that prosperity." He is mindful of the conflicting interests of energy development and environmental protection. The petroleum industry "is vital to my district, but not at the expense of our environment," he told The Advocate.

In the 106th, John played a prominent role in a bipartisan effort to increase funding for federal land acquisition and conservation programs, with coastal states such as Louisiana in line to receive hefty increases devoted to combating coastal erosion and marsh destruction and to dealing with the impact of offshore drilling.

Before coming to Washington, John helped run his family's trucking company, and he has sought to promote highway improvements that would benefit the 7th District. He was able to win high-priority designation for a project to upgrade U.S. 90 from Lafayette to New Orleans, making it an extension of Interstate 49.

Although the thrust of the Blue Dog effort is fiscal conservatism, John also votes a conservative social line, including opposing gun control and abortion and supporting the display of the Ten Commandments in schools.

The conservative tilt of John's voting record has earned him some criticism from the AFL-CIO, and Democratic Party stalwarts took note when John was endorsed in 1996 by a Republican — the man he was seeking to succeed, Rep. Jimmy Hayes. In 2000, for the second consecutive election, he was endorsed by the U.S. Chamber of Commerce, partly on the basis of his support for a bill to expand trade ties with China.

After earning a degree in business administration from Louisiana State University, John returned to his native Crowley and got into the family's businesses — trucking and politics. He spent four years on the Crowley City Council and in 1987 won the state House seat his father had once held. He served eight years in Baton Rouge. In 1995, he gave up the seat to run, unsuccessfully, for lieutenant governor; but a year later he was back on the ballot.

In 1996, with Hayes leaving the House to run for the Senate, the race for the 7th District drew a crowded field, including John and seven others. As the only legislator on the ballot, and with his run for lieutenant governor fresh in voters' minds, John was the best-known candidate. He emerged from the all-party primary in first place, but fell far short of a majority. He then beat the second-place finisher, another Democrat, lawyer Hunter Lundy, to win the election by 6 percentage points. He had no opposition in 1998 and only a third-party foe in 2000.

KEY VOTES

2000
Yes Raise hourly minimum wage by $1 over two years
No   Halt funding for U.S. mission in Kosovo unless European nations pay more
Yes Provide Medicare benefits to military retirees and their dependents
Yes Grant China permanent normal trade status
Yes Phase out estate, gift and trust taxes
No   Prohibit implementation of president's national monument designations
No   Approve GOP plan to provide prescription drug coverage for Medicare beneficiaries
Yes Increase help for poor nations indebted to international financial institutions

1999
No   Impose steel import quotas
No   Kill proposal to take aviation trust funds off budget
No   Require background checks on buyers only at gun shows with 10 or more vendors
Yes Remove barriers among banking, securities and insurance companies
Yes Authorize state grants to hire teachers and reduce class size
No   Overhaul campaign finance law; ban "soft money" and restrict advocacy advertising
Yes Approve bipartisan plan to increase rights of patients in managed-care health plans

INTEREST GROUPS

	AFL-CIO	ADA	CCUS	ACU
2000	50%	30%	90%	41%
1999	63%	45%	83%	50%
1998	60%	50%	76%	45%
1997	38%	40%	100%	64%

CQ VOTE STUDIES

	PARTY UNITY		PRESIDENTIAL SUPPORT	
	Support	Oppose	Support	Oppose
2000	65%	35%	49%	51%
1999	53%	47%	58%	42%
1998	56%	44%	50%	50%
1997	60%	40%	52%	48%

LOUISIANA 7
Southwest – Lake Charles; Lafayette

Anchored by blue-collar Lake Charles in the west, the white-collar Cajun hub of Lafayette in the east, and the Gulf of Mexico in the south, the 7th takes in both coastal and city life. A sizable French-Catholic citizenry reinforces the district's socially conservative leanings.

Still, Democrats are so firmly in control of the area that is now the 7th that it has remained in their hands since 1885. Lafayette Parish, in the eastern part of the district, is the most Republican-leaning area. Three stabs at redistricting in the 1990s did little to change the 7th. In the final round, in 1996, the 7th regained some black neighborhoods in Lafayette Parish that it had lost in 1992.

Dotted with waterfowl and wildlife refuges, the 7th's Gulf edge serves sports and commercial fishermen. Menhaden, which is ground into feed and industrial oil, accounts for much of the commercial catch. Back on land, some of the farms north and west of Crowley (Acadia Parish) that grow rice now also raise crawfish in fallow rice fields.

Lake Charles (Calcasieu Parish), a refining and chemical-producing hub in the southwestern corner of the district, offers a sharp industrial contrast to the 7th's rural areas. Oil, a weighty part of the economy, nose-dived in the 1980s and then rebounded in the 1990s, helping the petrochemical industry in Lafayette and union stronghold Lake Charles.

On U.S. Highway 165 in Allen Parish lies the small town of Kinder, which houses the one of the state's largest land-based casinos, Grand Casino Coushatta, a 105,000 square foot gaming floor operated by the Coushatta Indians.

MAJOR INDUSTRY
Oil and gas, petrochemicals, agriculture, fishing

CITIES
Lafayette, 116,806; Lake Charles, 72,173; Sulphur, 21,151

UNUSUAL FEATURES
Former Gov. Edwin W. Edwards and Sen. John B. Breaux represented the 7th; Dr. Michael DeBakey, born in Lake Charles, was the first person to successfully use an artificial heart in a patient; Rayne hosts an annual frog festival.

Gov. Angus King (I)

First elected: 1994
Length of term: 4 years
Term expires: 1/03
Salary: $70,000
Phone: (207) 287-3531
Hometown: Brunswick
Born: March 31, 1944; Alexandria, Va.
Religion: Episcopalian
Family: Wife, Mary J. Herman; five children
Education: Dartmouth College, A.B. 1966; U. of Virginia, J.D. 1969
Career: Energy conservation company owner; television program host; alternative energy company executive; lawyer; congressional aide
Political highlights: No previous office

Election results:

1998 GENERAL

Angus King (I)	246,772	58.6%
James B. Longley Jr. (R)	79,716	18.9%
Thomas J. Connolly (D)	50,506	12.0%
Patricia H. Lamarche (I)	28,722	6.8%
Willian P. Clarke (I)	15,293	3.6%

Senate President Michael Michaud (D)

(no lieutenant governor)
Phone: (207) 287-1500

STATE LEGISLATURE

Legislature: Meets January-June in even years; January-April in odd years
House: 151 members, 2-year terms
2001 breakdown: 61R, 89D, 1I; 110 men, 41 women
Salary: $18,730
Phone: (207) 287-1400
Senate: 35 members, 2-year terms
2001 breakdown: 17R, 17D, 1I; 20 men, 15 women
Salary: $18,730
Phone: (207) 287-1540

STATE TERM LIMITS

Governor: 2 consecutive terms
Senate: 4 terms
House: 4 terms

URBAN STATISTICS

CITY	POPULATION
Portland	61,925
Lewiston	36,193
Bangor	32,662

REGISTERED VOTERS

Unenrolled	38%
Democrat	31%
Republican	29%

POPULATION

2000 population	1,274,923
1990 population	1,227,928
Percent change	+3.8%
Rank among states	40
Median age	36.9
Born in state	69%
Foreign born	3%
Urban/rural	45%/55%
Crime rate	121/100,000
Poverty level	10.4%
Federal workers	13,021
Military	10,838

REAPPORTIONMENT

Maine retained its two House seats in reapportionment. A state reapportionment committee will draw new district lines in 2003.

MISCELLANEOUS

Web: www.state.me.us
Capital: Augusta
Land area: 30,865 sq. miles
Rank among states: 39

STATE ELECTION OFFICIAL
(207) 287-4186

DEMOCRATIC HEADQUARTERS
(207) 622-6233

REPUBLICAN HEADQUARTERS
(207) 622-6247

District Statistics

DIST.	VOTE FOR PRESIDENT 2000 D	R	GREEN	1996 D	R	REF	1992 D	R	I	WHT	BLK	ASIAN	HISP	HOUSEHOLD INCOME	OVER 65+	UNDER 18	COLLEGE EDUCATION
1	51%	43%	6%	52%	32%	13%	40%	32%	28%	98%	0%	1%	1%	$31,124	13%	25%	23%
2	48	46	5	51	30	16	38	29	33	98	0	0	1	$24,718	13	26	15
STATE	49	44	6	52	31	14	39	30	30	98	<1	1	1	$27,854	13	25	19

Sen. Olympia J. Snowe (R)

Elected 1994; 2nd term

CAPITOL OFFICE
224-5344; fax 224-1946; 154 Russell Bldg. 20510

INTERNET
e-mail: olympia@snowe.senate.gov
web: snowe.senate.gov

COMMITTEES
Budget
Commerce, Science & Transportation
(Oceans & Fisheries - chairwoman)
Finance
(Health Care - chairwoman)
Small Business

HOMETOWN
Falmouth

BORN
Feb. 21, 1947, Augusta, Maine

RELIGION
Greek Orthodox

FAMILY
Husband, John R. McKernan Jr.

EDUCATION
U. of Maine, B.A. 1969

CAREER
City employee

POLITICAL HIGHLIGHTS
Maine House, 1973-77; Maine Senate, 1977-79;
U.S. House, 1979-95

ELECTION RESULTS

2000 GENERAL

Olympia J. Snowe (R)	437,689	68.9%
Mark Lawrence (D)	197,183	31.1%

2000 PRIMARY

Olympia J. Snowe (R)	unopposed

PREVIOUS WINNING PERCENTAGES
1994 (60%); 1992 House Election (49%); 1990 House
Election (51%); 1988 House Election (66%); 1986
House Election (77%); 1984 House Election (76%);
1982 House Election (67%); 1980 House Election
(79%); 1978 House Election (51%)

Snowe spends her days in Washington searching for the middle ground. On issues ranging from the impeachment of President Clinton to the fight for prescription drug coverage under Medicare, Snowe has sought solutions somewhere between the Republican and Democratic party stances. But on those matters, as on others, Snowe has found leaders of both parties unwilling to budge.

With an evenly split Senate, and President Bush vowing to be a "uniter, not a divider," centrists such as Snowe are in a position to play a critical role in the 107th Congress. And she has made clear to her party leaders that they need to do a better job of reaching across the aisle. "Some changes are in order in the way they approach trying to run the Senate," she said in late 2000. "If there was any mandate" from the election, she said, it was that "people wanted us to end the partisan bickering."

She is a leader of the Centrist Coalition, a group of about 30 senators who hope to find common ground on issues such as tax policy and campaign finance reform. She has championed improved disclosure of the financing of "issue ads" that have played vital roles in many political campaigns.

Snowe's influence should increase in the 107th with her appointment to the Finance Committee. She signaled her reluctance to back Bush's tax cut proposal without assurances that long-term cuts would be dependent on continued budget surpluses. She gave up her Armed Services seat for Finance only when it became clear that her home state GOP colleague Susan Collins would fill her spot, defending Maine's defense industry interests.

With a casual, approachable style, Snowe is known as a modest senator in a chamber filled with big egos. She is popular with her colleagues, and both parties court her heavily on big issues, knowing she is well-regarded. She enjoys preparing for committee hearings, often spending hours at the task, and aides describe her as tough but fair. "She doesn't suffer fools gladly," said one longtime staff member. "But she appreciates us."

Snowe arrived in the Senate in the 1994 electoral sweep that gave control of Congress to the Republicans, and she was notable as the only newly elected Senate GOP moderate. But she also stood out for having a personal story as compelling as many of the military heroes who have come to the Senate.

The daughter of first- and second-generation Greek immigrants, Snowe was orphaned at age 9 and raised by an aunt and uncle in blue-collar surroundings. Snowe was married to state Rep. Peter Snowe and working as an aide to then-U.S. Rep. William S. Cohen in 1973 when Peter was killed in an automobile accident. A month later, she was elected to succeed him in the state House. She won election to the state Senate in 1976, and just two years later, she won a close House race to succeed Cohen, who had moved on to the Senate.

While Snowe was representing the northern 2nd District, another personable moderate Republican, John R. McKernan Jr., won the 1st District seat in 1982. Four years later, he was elected to the first of two terms as governor of Maine. But he won Snowe's heart along the way, and the two were married in 1989.

In the book "Nine and Counting," a collaboration of the nine women serving in the Senate in 2000, Snowe said her personal story shaped her political outlook. "With the devastation of Peter's death came a sensitivity to the tremendous difficulties that other women in similar situations face — such as raising children alone," she wrote. "Later that was brought to bear on issues such as pension reform, child care and displaced homemakers."

Although she finds few ideological soul mates among the Senate's Republicans, Snowe works with those like-minded senators to try to restrain what she sees as the excesses of party conservatives. After seeking to strike a compromise, Snowe will generally support GOP legislation in its final form, although she was more likely to vote in support of Clinton's position than the vast majority of her colleagues.

Early in 1999, Snowe was one of five Republican senators, all from the Northeast, who voted to acquit Clinton on both articles of impeachment brought against him by the House. But in typical fashion, she spent days before the votes trying to work out a bipartisan deal on a punishment for Clinton that would fall short of conviction and removal from office but ensure that he did not walk away scot-free.

Her efforts did not produce a compromise and in the end, as with just about everyone else in the Senate, Snowe's vote came with a message. "Make no mistake about it. I find the president's behavior deplorable and indefensible," she said. "If I were a supporter, I would abandon him."

During the 106th Congress, Snowe worked with Democrat Ron Wyden of Oregon on a plan to provide Medicare coverage of prescription drugs. She split from most in her party to oppose efforts to allow oil drilling in the Arctic National Wildlife Refuge in Alaska — one of Bush's top energy proposals in 2001. And she fought unsuccessfully to force the GOP to include in its convention platform a dissenting opinion on the party's anti-abortion position.

Despite her moderate views, Snowe is an ally of Majority Leader Trent Lott, having served as his deputy during his days as House whip. She holds the appointive post of counsel to the assistant majority leader.

Snowe voted for the Senate's massive $792 billion tax cut in 1999, although she made it clear she preferred a less costly plan. "Over the last few days," she warned just before the vote, "we have heard comments from the administration and from members of this body, saying, 'There is no room for compromise. There is zero room for consensus.' I think that kind of intransigence is unacceptable, because ultimately it will result in no tax cut at all." She was right.

Even though she is a strong supporter of abortion rights, Snowe has tried to broker a compromise, joining with Democrats in seeking an alternative to the GOP's desired absolute ban on a procedure its opponents call "partial birth" abortion. She joined with Democrats on a proposal to require health insurance plans of federal workers to pay for contraceptives, and she was among the few Senate Republicans who in early 2001 vowed to try to overturn President Bush's ban on federal aid to international family-planning organizations that perform or promote abortions. And Snowe sponsored legislation to prohibit insurance providers from denying or canceling coverage on the basis of genetic information.

On the home front, she is a strong advocate for her state's potato farmers in trade disputes with Canada.

After winning election to the House in 1978, Snowe enjoyed a series of easy victories until 1990, when a deepening recession led to restlessness among voters. She eventually defeated Democratic state Rep. Patrick K. McGowan, 51 percent to 49 percent, after a series of heated exchanges between the two. A 1992 rematch was even closer; she won with a 49 percent plurality.

Despite her back-to-back House re-election struggles, Snowe was the presumed GOP nominee when Senate Majority Leader George J. Mitchell, a Democrat, announced his surprise retirement early in 1994. Snowe prevailed with 60 percent of the vote. In 2000, she overwhelmed state Senate President Mark Lawrence with nearly 69 percent of the vote.

KEY VOTES

2000

Yes Overhaul bankruptcy law and increase minimum wage
Yes Limit fiscal 2001 discretionary spending to $600.3 billion
Yes Override veto on nuclear waste disposal at Yucca Mountain site in Nevada
No Oppose effort to terminate Kosovo mission
Yes Include gender, sexual orientation and disability in federal hate crime protections
Yes Approve GOP plan to restrict use of genetic information by health insurers
No Kill amendment delaying implementation of an anti-missile defense system
Yes Cut taxes for married couples
Yes Grant China permanent normal trade status

1999

No Remove President Clinton from office for obstruction of justice
Yes Kill amendment authorizing state grants to hire teachers and reduce class size
No Require criminal background checks for purchases at gun shows
Yes Approve GOP proposal to increase rights of patients in managed-care health plans
Yes Block effort to allow farm and medicine exports to Cuba
Yes Allow study of tougher automobile fuel efficiency standards
No Ratify nuclear weapons testing treaty
Yes Prohibit national political parties from collecting "soft money" donations
Yes Remove barriers among banking, securities and insurance companies

INTEREST GROUPS

	AFL-CIO	ADA	CCUS	ACU
2000	0%	30%	73%	80%
1999	33%	45%	59%	60%
1998	38%	35%	78%	40%
1997	43%	55%	70%	44%
1996	29%	35%	77%	70%
1995	25%	40%	84%	39%
House Service:				
1994	56%	30%	67%	57%
1993	42%	40%	64%	67%
1992	58%	50%	50%	60%
1991	67%	35%	40%	55%

CQ VOTE STUDIES

	PARTY UNITY		PRESIDENTIAL SUPPORT	
	Support	Oppose	Support	Oppose
2000	71%	29%	62%	38%
1999	69%	31%	49%	51%
1998	65%	35%	55%	45%
1997	59%	41%	78%	22%
1996	72%	28%	53%	47%
1995	70%	30%	42%	58%
House Service:				
1994	67%	33%	60%	40%
1993	68%	32%	41%	59%
1992	59%	41%	41%	59%
1991	53%	47%	50%	50%

Sen. Susan Collins (R)

CAPITOL OFFICE
224-2523; fax 224-2693; 172 Russell Bldg. 20510

INTERNET
e-mail: senator@collins.senate.gov
web: collins.senate.gov

COMMITTEES
Armed Services
Governmental Affairs
  (Investigations - chairwoman)
Health, Education, Labor & Pensions
Special Aging

HOMETOWN
Bangor

BORN
Dec. 7, 1952, Caribou, Maine

RELIGION
Roman Catholic

FAMILY
Single

EDUCATION
St. Lawrence U., B.A. 1975

CAREER
Business center director; congressional aide

POLITICAL HIGHLIGHTS
Maine commissioner of financial regulation, 1987-91; Small Business Administration official, 1992-93; Maine deputy treasurer, 1993; Republican nominee for governor, 1994

ELECTION RESULTS

1996 GENERAL

Susan Collins (R)	298,422	49.2%
Joseph E. Brennan (D)	266,226	43.9%
John C. Rensenbrink (I)	23,441	3.9%
William P. Clarke Jr. (TAX)	18,618	3.1%

1996 PRIMARY

Susan Collins (R)	53,339	55.5%
W. John Hathaway (R)	29,792	31.0%
Robert A.G. Monks (R)	12,943	13.5%

Elected 1996; 1st term

In a Congress narrowly divided between feuding parties, Collins tries to stay above the fray. The fiscally conservative Republican values bipartisanship and focuses on such traditional Democratic issues as education and consumer protection. Even though she is a first-term senator, she has quickly established herself as a respected voice on national issues, and she gave the GOP response to President Clinton's 2000 State of the Union address.

The unassuming Collins operates in a low-key manner and likes to move cautiously, studying an issue before proposing a remedy. Soft-spoken and courteous, she joins fellow Maine Republican Olympia J. Snowe in the party's moderate wing, whose members urge a go-slow approach on such politically charged issues as tax cuts.

Since her arrival in Washington, Collins has been an influential voice on health care issues. In the 106th Congress, she spearheaded efforts to block a Democratic bill that would have allowed patients to sue their health care providers, arguing, "You can't just sue your way to quality health care." Instead, Collins won GOP backing for a four-part plan that aimed to strengthen long-term and emergency room care and improve patient access to medical specialists. But her plan died in the face of opposition from Democrats who contended that the right to sue was critical to overhauling the health care system.

Collins has also taken on more modest health care initiatives. In 1999, she won unanimous backing for a measure urging the National Institutes of Health to put greater emphasis on diabetes research. Provoked by funding cuts in health care, she told The Boston Globe, "I can't stand it when government directly creates harm," and teamed up with Democrats to find more money. She also introduced a measure to toughen government inspection of imported food, contending, "We need to make sure that our systems are in place to make sure that we're not allowing tainted foods to get to the tables of American families."

Collins sides with conservatives on several high-profile issues. She resists gun control initiatives, voting in 1999 against a proposal that would have required background checks on buyers at gun shows. On fiscal policy, too, she generally is in line with party conservatives, supporting a balanced-budget constitutional amendment and requiring a two-thirds majority vote of Congress to increase taxes. She backs a constitutional amendment to limit congressional terms and promises to serve no more than 12 years in the Senate.

However, she has turned a cold shoulder to some of the more ambitious GOP tax-cutting proposals. When Republican leaders in the 106th pressed for a $792 billion tax cut, she warned that the plan could throw the federal budget into the red. "We're really taking quite a gamble," she told The Associated Press. "It's like we haven't learned from our past. We've got to target some to paying down our debt. Otherwise, we leave an enormous legacy of unpaid bills for the next generation." As an alternative, she worked with a bipartisan group of moderates on a plan that would have limited the tax cuts.

She also breaks with conservatives on abortion. Criticizing a proposal to ban the procedure opponents call "partial birth" abortion, she told The Boston Globe in 1999: "Everybody knows these laws are unconstitutional on their face." Instead, Collins, Snowe and other moderates have proposed restricting late-term abortions except to prevent "grievous injury" to the woman's health. But the Mainers have come under heavy criticism from abortion opponents, who say the plan would permit any sort of abortion as long as a woman was uneasy about her pregnancy.

Collins also is a leading advocate of campaign finance revisions, again breaking with GOP leaders over the issue.

During the 1999 impeachment trial of Clinton, Collins proposed that the Senate adopt "findings of fact," detailing Clinton's alleged misconduct in matters surrounding his affair with White House intern Monica Lewinsky, thereby allowing those who did not want to remove Clinton from office to nevertheless indicate their disapproval of his conduct. Her idea won wide support from Republicans but could not gain enough backing from Democrats. Eventually, Collins was one of five GOP senators to vote "not guilty" on both articles of impeachment.

Collins chairs the Governmental Affairs Committee's Permanent Subcommittee on Investigations, and she has made a name for herself as a staunch advocate for consumers. In the 106th, she won passage of bipartisan legislation cracking down on the deceptive practices of small sweepstakes companies. "Many of these smaller companies tend to be fly-by-night operations that use multiple trade names to hide their identities and to confuse consumers," she said in Senate debate. "Often their mailings are designed to deceive even the most cautious consumer."

In 2000, Collins obtained a string of fake ID cards to draw attention to Internet sites that provide bogus credentials. "The wide-scale availability of false identifications and credentials on the Internet poses a serious new threat to government and the integrity of government operations," she said. She also pressed for tougher regulations of long-distance telephone companies that impose unauthorized charges on consumers.

Collins, a member of the Health, Education, Labor and Pensions Committee, points to her work on a higher education bill as her proudest accomplishment of the 105th Congress. The bill reauthorized federal education programs for five years and, in a reversal of 1995 GOP proposals, expanded federal assistance to college students. Collins helped author several provisions, including those increasing the amount of money a working student could earn before losing eligibility for Pell Grant higher education assistance. She also worked successfully to expand the State Student Incentive Grant program, a joint federal-state effort to award grants to needy students.

Politics is in Collins' blood: Both her parents served terms as mayor of the small northern Maine town of Caribou. Collins visited the U.S. Capitol as a high school senior and was amazed when Maine's highly regarded senator, Margaret Chase Smith, spent two hours talking with her. After graduating from college, Collins returned to Washington to work for a dozen years, starting in the mid-1970s, for GOP Sen. William S. Cohen as an adviser on business issues. She then served as commissioner of Maine's Department of Professional and Financial Regulation.

Collins' first venture into politics was a disappointment. She won the GOP nomination for governor in 1994 but ran a poor third behind both Democrat Joseph E. Brennan and independent Angus King, who won the race. Many GOP conservatives abandoned Collins in favor of King, because of her support for abortion rights and other moderate positions.

But after Cohen announced that he would not seek a fourth term in 1996, Collins climbed back into the ring. A clearly improved campaigner, she won the GOP primary handily when her two opponents assailed each other with charges of personal improprieties. In the general-election contest, she faced Brennan, who was suffering intraparty troubles after losses in both the 1990 and 1994 gubernatorial elections. Despite a tide in Maine that carried Democrats to victory in both of the state's House districts and in the presidential contest, Collins defeated Brennan by 5 percentage points.

KEY VOTES

2000
Yes Overhaul bankruptcy law and increase minimum wage
Yes Limit fiscal 2001 discretionary spending to $600.3 billion
Yes Override veto on nuclear waste disposal at Yucca Mountain site in Nevada
No Oppose effort to terminate Kosovo mission
Yes Include gender, sexual orientation and disability in federal hate crime protections
Yes Approve GOP plan to restrict use of genetic information by health insurers
No Kill amendment delaying implementation of an anti-missile defense system
Yes Cut taxes for married couples
Yes Grant China permanent normal trade status

1999
No Remove President Clinton from office for obstruction of justice
Yes Kill amendment authorizing state grants to hire teachers and reduce class size
No Require criminal background checks for purchases at gun shows
Yes Approve GOP proposal to increase rights of patients in managed-care health plans
No Block effort to allow farm and medicine exports to Cuba
Yes Allow study of tougher automobile fuel efficiency standards
No Ratify nuclear weapons testing treaty
Yes Prohibit national political parties from collecting "soft money" donations
Yes Remove barriers among banking, securities and insurance companies

INTEREST GROUPS

	AFL-CIO	ADA	CCUS	ACU
2000	0%	25%	80%	76%
1999	11%	25%	76%	64%
1998	38%	35%	78%	36%
1997	14%	50%	80%	48%

CQ VOTE STUDIES

	PARTY UNITY		PRESIDENTIAL SUPPORT	
	Support	Oppose	Support	Oppose
2000	74%	26%	57%	42%
1999	74%	26%	49%	51%
1998	67%	33%	63%	37%
1997	61%	39%	76%	24%

Rep. Tom Allen (D)

CAPITOL OFFICE
225-6116; fax 225-5590
1717 Longworth Bldg. 20515

INTERNET
e-mail: rep.tomallen@mail.house.gov
web: www.house.gov/allen

COMMITTEES
Armed Services
Government Reform

HOMETOWN
Portland

BORN
April 16, 1945, Portland, Maine

RELIGION
Protestant

FAMILY
Wife, Diana Allen; two children

EDUCATION
Bowdoin College, B.A. 1967; Oxford U., B.Phil.
1970; Harvard U., J.D. 1974

CAREER
Policy consultant; lawyer; congressional aide

POLITICAL HIGHLIGHTS
Portland City Council, 1989-95 (mayor, 1991-92);
sought Democratic nomination for governor, 1994

ELECTION RESULTS

2000 GENERAL

Tom Allen (D)	202,823	59.8%
Jane Amero (R)	123,915	36.5%
J. Frederic Staples (I)	12,356	3.6%

2000 PRIMARY

Tom Allen (D)	unopposed

1998 GENERAL

Tom Allen (D)	134,335	60.3%
Ross J. Connelly (R)	79,160	35.5%
Eric R. Greiner (I)	9,182	4.1%

PREVIOUS WINNING PERCENTAGES
1996 (55%)

Elected 1996; 3rd term

A visible and vocal presence on the House floor, Allen has been a prominent player on high-profile issues since his early days as a freshman in the 105th Congress. In his first term, his priority was campaign finance reform, and he charged that the amount of money spent in modern politics has led voters to believe that lawmakers respond only to contributors.

In the 106th Congress, he was in the middle of another hot congressional debate — what to do about the high price of prescription drugs. Allen was one of the first lawmakers to discover the potency of the issue. A series of studies, done at his behest by the Democratic staff of the Government Reform Committee, buttressed his arguments that senior citizens who do not have prescription drug coverage to supplement Medicare are often forced to spend large chunks of their income on medicine.

Allen was tapped for prominent roles as soon as he landed on Capitol Hill. His fellow freshmen picked him as their representative to the Democratic Steering Committee, which determines the party's committee assignments. He was chosen to be the Democratic co-chairman of a bipartisan task force of 12 freshmen formed to develop campaign finance legislation.

In the 106th, he joined the Democratic whip organization and was named to the Democratic prescription drug task force. Allen drafted one of a number of competing bills to address the prescription drug issue. His solution was to require drug companies to make prescription drugs available to Medicare beneficiaries at the lowest price offered to any other purchaser — often a federal agency, such as the Department of Veterans Affairs, which can negotiate lower prices because of bulk purchases.

Allen says the importance of the issue became clear to him at a town meeting, late in 1997 or early in 1998, when a retired firefighter — somebody he knew from an earlier campaign — talked about his $300 per month bill for prescription drugs. Allen enlisted the staff of the Government Reform panel to investigate the matter. Their reports included the finding that drugs for people cost more than the same drugs prescribed for animals.

To counter drug company-sponsored television ads featuring an actress named Flo who said she wanted to keep the government out of her medicine cabinet, Allen arranged for a 78-year-old Augusta, Maine, woman, Florence Dube — whom he dubbed the "real Flo" — to appear at a press conference. There, Allen declared that "without the government in her medicine cabinet, it would be empty."

Allen is thoughtful and deliberate. He was among a dozen freshman lawmakers recruited by PBS to participate in an online presentation, "Freshmen Forums," in which new members answered Internet questions about issues before Congress. Allen invariably gave the longest, most detailed answers, much like the responses to public policy questions usually offered up by one of his contemporaries as a Rhodes Scholar in England in 1970 — Bill Clinton.

In addition to his post on Government Reform, Allen serves on the Armed Services Committee. There, he must balance the need to look out for the 1st District's several naval installations and its defense contractors, such as Bath Iron Works, with his desire to restrain defense spending. In the 106th, Allen was among those lawmakers most skeptical of the GOP push to develop and deploy a missile defense system.

But Allen's interests range far beyond the confines of his committee assignments. He drafted legislation aimed at phasing out old, polluting power plants that did not have to meet stringent clean air standards set in 1970. He sought to reduce mercury emissions, which contaminate lakes and streams, posing a threat not only to birds such as loons, a Maine icon, and fish, but also to people who consume the fish. And he was a co-founder in the 106th of the Oceans Caucus, which he hopes will be the springboard for legislation to protect Maine's fisheries and coastline.

As co-chairman of the freshman task force on campaign finance in the 105th, Allen pushed legislation to ban "soft money," the unlimited contributions used for party-building activities and issue ads; require more timely reporting of donations and expenditures; and raise limits on donations. Most Republicans rejected the recommendations, and the proposal foundered.

But Allen kept fighting for action, and pressure from rank-and-file House members eventually forced the House leadership to bring campaign finance legislation to the floor in 1998. The freshman plan was defeated, however, as many lawmakers backed an alternative measure drafted by Christopher Shays, R-Conn., and Martin T. Meehan, D-Mass.

In the 106th, Allen remained active on the campaign finance front as the debate shifted to regulation of certain political groups that were not required to disclose their fundraising or spending activities as long as they did not express support or opposition to a federal candidate. Lawmakers passed a disclosure requirement in 2000.

Allen comes from a political family: His father and grandfather were both on the Portland City Council, and his mother was active in politics as well. On returning from his studies in England in 1970, Allen worked a short time for Democratic Sen. Edmund S. Muskie, both in an election campaign in Maine and on Muskie's Senate staff.

After practicing law for almost 20 years in Portland, Allen's first elective office was as a member of the Portland City Council, where he served for six years, including one year as the council-elected mayor. Allen chaired Clinton's Maine campaign in 1992 and was an adviser on agriculture issues during the presidential transition.

Following an unsuccessful bid for the Democratic gubernatorial nomination in 1994, Allen in 1996 challenged freshman GOP Rep. James B. Longley Jr. With a million-dollar assist from the AFL-CIO, the Sierra Club and other groups, which ran campaign ads on his behalf, Allen mobilized key elements of his party's base while successfully tying Longley to the "extreme" Republican "Contract With America" agenda. Allen has easily won re-election since then. He is often mentioned as a possible senatorial candidate against Republican Susan Collins in 2002.

KEY VOTES

2000
Yes Raise hourly minimum wage by $1 over two years
No Halt funding for U.S. mission in Kosovo unless European nations pay more
Yes Provide Medicare benefits to military retirees and their dependents
Yes Grant China permanent normal trade status
No Phase out estate, gift and trust taxes
No Prohibit implementation of president's national monument designations
No Approve GOP plan to provide prescription drug coverage for Medicare beneficiaries
Yes Increase help for poor nations indebted to international financial institutions

1999
Yes Impose steel import quotas
No Kill proposal to take aviation trust funds off budget
No Require background checks on buyers only at gun shows with 10 or more vendors
Yes Remove barriers among banking, securities and insurance companies
Yes Authorize state grants to hire teachers and reduce class size
Yes Overhaul campaign finance law; ban "soft money" and restrict advocacy advertising
Yes Approve bipartisan plan to increase rights of patients in managed-care health plans

INTEREST GROUPS

	AFL-CIO	ADA	CCUS	ACU
2000	90%	85%	52%	4%
1999	78%	95%	28%	0%
1998	100%	100%	39%	0%
1997	100%	95%	50%	8%

CQ VOTE STUDIES

	PARTY UNITY		PRESIDENTIAL SUPPORT	
	Support	Oppose	Support	Oppose
2000	94%	6%	84%	16%
1999	96%	4%	86%	14%
1998	93%	7%	84%	16%
1997	94%	6%	82%	18%

MAINE 1
South — Portland; Augusta

Rural oceanfront property draws seasonal residents to the 1st, a district incorporating the southern reaches of Maine that are also bustling with new high-tech jobs. Residents of Maine's largest city, Portland, are moving into outlying areas, replacing farmland and uninterrupted forests with single-family homes.

Although textile- and shoe-manufacturing plants have been downsized or closed, a high-tech boom has kept unemployment low. Companies seeking a strong infrastructure and a high quality of life have moved to southern Maine, where Interstate 95 offers a straight shot to Boston. Well-to-do and largely seasonal residents live on the coast, where former President George Bush travels for retreats at his Kennebunkport estate.

In a state with one of the weakest party systems in the nation, personalities play the largest role in elections; little difference exists between Democrats and Republicans in many local elections. A plurality of the state's voters register as "unenrolled" or independent. Grounded in Maine's strong communities, the state's voting participation is second only to Minnesota — 67 percent in 2000.

MAJOR INDUSTRY
Military shipbuilding, fishing, high-tech

MILITARY BASES
Portsmouth Naval Shipyard, 50 military, 3,315 civilian (2000); Brunswick Naval Air Station, 4,206 military, 657 civilian (1998)

CITIES
Portland, 61,925; South Portland, 23,923; Biddeford, 21,277; Augusta, 19,722

UNUSUAL FEATURES
The 1st helped lead the Prohibition crusade when a mid-19th century Portland businessman, Neal Dow, discontinued the traditional "rum break" for his tannery workers because it interfered with productivity; Dow was the Prohibition Party's presidential candidate in 1880.

Rep. John Baldacci (D)

Elected 1994; 4th term

CAPITOL OFFICE
225-6306; fax 225-2943
1740 Longworth Bldg. 20515

INTERNET
e-mail: baldacci@me02.house.gov
web: www.house.gov/baldacci

COMMITTEES
Agriculture
Transportation & Infrastructure

HOMETOWN
Bangor

BORN
Jan. 30, 1955, Bangor, Maine

RELIGION
Roman Catholic

FAMILY
Wife, Karen Baldacci; one child

EDUCATION
U. of Maine, B.A. 1986

CAREER
Restaraunt operator

POLITICAL HIGHLIGHTS
Bangor City Council, 1978-81; Maine Senate, 1982-94

ELECTION RESULTS

2000 GENERAL

John Baldacci (D)	219,783	73.4%
Richard Campbell (R)	79,522	26.6%

2000 PRIMARY

John Baldacci (D)	unopposed

1998 GENERAL

John Baldacci (D)	146,202	76.2%
Jonathan Reisman (R)	45,674	23.8%

PREVIOUS WINNING PERCENTAGES
1996 (72%); 1994 (46%)

Low-key, thoughtful and deliberate, Baldacci served his first three terms in relative anonymity, voting a dependable Democratic line and concentrating almost exclusively on the bread-and-butter issues affecting his 2nd District. That tack suits Baldacci's constituents, who have re-elected him by wide margins three times since his initial narrow victory in 1994.

Baldacci, who had pledged to serve no more than four terms in the House, making the 107th Congress his last, announced in early 2001 that he will run for governor in 2002.

The Maine lawmaker's quiet presence in the House is in keeping with the reputation he established in local and state government as a moderate, cautious legislator. As Baldacci (ball-DA-chee) told the Bangor Daily News, "The reason I ran for office was not to get up and give speeches."

Instead of holding forth, he quietly tends to his work on an array of local issues — seeking federal economic development aid for the district; guarding against the import of government-subsidized potatoes from Canada; trying to hold on to, or even beef up, airline service to Bangor and Presque Isle; and protecting Maine's fish stocks and its independent fishermen.

Baldacci also has worked to retain the state's veterans hospital. And he wants an east-west highway through the district, which he says is essential to opening Maine's markets to Canada. He has been able to gain federal funds to study the feasibility of the highway.

His seat on the Agriculture Committee provides him some opportunity to assist local farmers, by obtaining disaster relief for the state's potato and apple growers and backing research into the commercial production of wild blueberries.

On the Transportation Committee, Baldacci in the 106th Congress made sure that aviation funds were directed to small airports to finance improvements, and he sought a study of the effects of airline deregulation on rural markets. He also urged congressional leaders to provide additional funds for drug interdiction by the Coast Guard, which he says faces a difficult challenge in patrolling Maine's thousands of miles of coastline and thousands of small offshore islands.

Among the proposals Baldacci advances to meet the 2nd District's economic needs are certain improvements to local infrastructure, including roads and bridges, that could make it easier for the district's farmers and fishermen to transport their products to markets. He also champions the establishment of a federal home heating oil reserve to help even out the swings in the price and supply of the essential fuel during the long Maine winters.

Although he usually tends to business behind the scenes, Baldacci has occasionally played a prominent part on Capitol Hill — such as when he took a leading role in 1998 in mobilizing lawmakers from areas hit by natural disasters to work for federal relief aid.

Baldacci's thoughtful consideration, early in 2000, of a bill to grant permanent normal trade status to China illustrates his deliberate style. Although he did not engage in a lot of public hand-wringing, he was genuinely conflicted by the pros and cons in the matter. He acknowledged that he found the issue a tough one on which persuasive arguments could be made on each side. In the end, despite the one-on-one entreaties of President Clinton in a meeting at the White House, Baldacci voted against the bill, telling his constituents that it did not offer enough protections for Maine workers in rural manufacturing industries.

"I tried to be straightforward [in discussions with the administration]," he told the Bangor Daily News. "Deals were never a part of my discussions."

Baldacci seldom engages in partisan rhetoric. He lives in a Capitol Hill group house with lawmakers from both parties and participates in an informal weekly fellowship meeting. He has authored a resolution directing House and Senate clerks to compile a list of congressional candidates who have agreed to abide by a "code of election ethics" that includes a promise to avoid demeaning references to the opponent and to eschew "subtle deceptions, half-truths, falsifications."

In the aftermath of the 1999 shootings at Columbine High School in Colorado, Baldacci rethought his position on gun control. He had supported GOP efforts in 1996 to repeal a ban on certain semi-automatic weapons and had received backing from the National Rifle Association. After the high school shootings, Baldacci told States News Service: "We have a responsibility to tighten these controls so young people are not able to get possession of a firearm."

Baldacci comes from a large family (his younger brother, Joe, is on the Bangor City Council and took a turn as mayor in the late 1990s), whose standing in Bangor stems in large part from the family's longtime Italian restaurant, Momma Baldacci's, founded by his grandparents.

Baldacci was first elected to the city council at age 23. He moved on to serve 12 years in the state Senate, earning his living by managing the family restaurant. Even now, he still lends a hand at the restaurant, and one of his favorite pastimes is hosting spaghetti dinners to help civic organizations in their fundraising efforts.

In 1994, Democratic Sen. George J. Mitchell unexpectedly announced his retirement, and the 2nd District's Republican Rep. Olympia J. Snowe launched a bid to succeed him. Baldacci grabbed the Democratic nomination for the open-seat race in the 2nd by defeating six other Democrats — one of whom was Mitchell's nephew, James F. Mitchell, a former state party official. Baldacci took 27 percent of the vote to Mitchell's 23 percent. (Baldacci may have benefited from the endorsement of author Stephen King, a Bangor resident known more for his horror stories than his political stances.)

In the general election, Baldacci's base of support in the populous Bangor area helped him defeat Republican state Rep. Richard A. Bennett (who had represented a less-populous inland county), 46 percent to 41 percent. He won his next three elections easily, with more than 70 percent of the vote.

KEY VOTES

2000

Yes Raise hourly minimum wage by $1 over two years
-    Halt funding for U.S. mission in Kosovo unless European nations pay more
Yes Provide Medicare benefits to military retirees and their dependents
No   Grant China permanent normal trade status
No   Phase out estate, gift and trust taxes
No   Prohibit implementation of president's national monument designations
No   Approve GOP plan to provide prescription drug coverage for Medicare beneficiaries
Yes Increase help for poor nations indebted to international financial institutions

1999

Yes Impose steel import quotas
No   Kill proposal to take aviation trust funds off budget
No   Require background checks on buyers only at gun shows with 10 or more vendors
Yes Remove barriers among banking, securities and insurance companies
Yes Authorize state grants to hire teachers and reduce class size
Yes Overhaul campaign finance law; ban "soft money" and restrict advocacy advertising
Yes Approve bipartisan plan to increase rights of patients in managed-care health plans

INTEREST GROUPS

	AFL-CIO	ADA	CCUS	ACU
2000	100%	85%	40%	8%
1999	89%	100%	24%	4%
1998	100%	95%	39%	4%
1997	100%	95%	60%	8%

CQ VOTE STUDIES

	PARTY UNITY		PRESIDENTIAL SUPPORT	
	Support	Oppose	Support	Oppose
2000	89%	11%	79%	21%
1999	91%	9%	82%	18%
1998	92%	8%	80%	20%
1997	90%	10%	84%	16%

MAINE 2

North — Lewiston; Auburn; Bangor

Millions of acres of trees surround the small towns of the 2nd in northern Maine, one of the most politically independent districts in the nation. The largest district east of the Mississippi, the 2nd attracts millions of visitors to Acadia National Park in the southeast.

A billion-dollar lobster industry dominates the east coast, and the timber industry reigns in the rest of the 2nd. Overall, the region is far less wealthy than the 1st. Aroostook County, in the far north, lost more than 10,000 people – 15 percent of its population – after Loring Air Force Base closed in the mid-1990s. As the national economy has become more service-based, the 2nd has felt the pinch. Manufacturing jobs, especially in textiles, have gone overseas, and residents are heading toward Maine's southern end for jobs. The 2nd's Waldo County has benefited from the migration, attracting credit card giant MBNA. The next round of redistricting will have to move the 2nd's border south to pick up more people.

Democrats and Yankee Republicans here often vote across party lines in a state with weak parties. In 1992, Ross Perot lost to Bill Clinton but received one-third of the vote, more than George Bush. A tradition of active participation in town activities helps encourage one of the highest voter turnouts in the nation.

MAJOR INDUSTRY
Logging, fishing, textile manufacturing, tourism

MILITARY BASES
Winter Harbor Naval Security Group Activity, 250 military, 100 civilian (2000); Bangor Air Force Guard station, Bangor, 963 military, 85 civilian (1998)

CITIES
Lewiston 36,193; Bangor, 32,662; Auburn, 22,467

UNUSUAL FEATURES
Chester Greenwood of Farmington invented earmuffs in the 1880s; Francis Edgar Stanley, inventor of the first steam-powered automobile – known as the "Stanley Steamer" – from Kingfield; Author Stephen King lives in Bangor; Abraham Lincoln's first vice president, Hannibal Hamlin, born in Paris Hill.

MARYLAND

Gov. Parris N. Glendening (D)

First elected: 1994
Length of term: 4 years
Term expires: 1/03
Salary: $120,000
Phone: (410) 974-3901
Hometown: University Park
Born: June 11, 1942; Bronx, N.Y.
Religion: Roman Catholic
Family: Wife, Frances Hughes Glendening; one child
Education: Junior College of Broward County, A.A. 1962; Florida State U., B.A. 1964, M.A. 1965, Ph.D. 1967
Career: Professor
Political highlights: Hyattsville City Council, 1973-74; Prince George's County Council, 1974-82 (chairman, 1979-81); Prince George's County executive, 1982-94

Election results:

1998 GENERAL

Parris N. Glendening (D)	846,972	55.1%
Ellen Sauerbrey (R)	688,357	44.8%

Lt. Gov. Kathleen Kennedy Townsend (D)

First elected: 1994
Length of term: 4 years
Term expires: 1/03
Salary: $100,000
Phone: (410) 974-2804

STATE LEGISLATURE

General Assembly: Meets January-April
House: 141 members, 4-year terms
2001 breakdown: 35R, 106D; 95 men, 46 women
Salary: $30,000
Phone: (410) 841-3100
Senate: 47 members, 4-year terms
2001 breakdown: 14R, 33D; 38 men, 9 women
Salary: $30,000
Phone: (410) 841-3100

STATE TERM LIMITS

Governor: 2 terms
Senate: No
House: No

URBAN STATISTICS

CITY	POPULATION
Baltimore	632,681
Frederick	48,710
Gaithersburg	48,395
Rockville	48,160
Bowie	41,091

REGISTERED VOTERS

Democrat	57%
Republican	30%
Other	13%

POPULATION

2000 population	5,296,486
1990 population	4,781,468
Percent change	+10.8%
Rank among states	19
Median age	35.3
Born in state	50%
Foreign born	7%
Urban/rural	81%/19%
Crime rate	847/100,000
Poverty level	7.2%
Federal workers	153,567
Military	51,984

REAPPORTIONMENT

Maryland retained its eight House seats in reapportionment. The state legislature will draw new district lines in 2002.

MISCELLANEOUS

Web: www.state.md.us
Capital: Annapolis
Land area: 9,775 sq. miles
Rank among states: 42
STATE ELECTION OFFICIAL
(410) 269-2840
DEMOCRATIC HEADQUARTERS
(410) 280-8818
REPUBLICAN HEADQUARTERS
(410) 269-0113

District Statistics

DIST.	D	2000 R	GREEN	D	1996 R	REF	D	1992 R	I	WHT	BLK	ASIAN	HISP	HOUSEHOLD INCOME	OVER 65+	UNDER 18	COLLEGE EDUCATION
1	44%	53%	3%	43%	47%	9%	37%	44%	19%	83%	15%	1%	1%	$35,115	12%	24%	20%
2	41	55	3	40	50	9	36	45	19	92	6	2	1	$40,120	12	24	22
3	63	34	3	58	34	7	54	32	14	80	17	2	2	$35,970	13	23	27
4	84	13	2	80	16	3	74	19	7	33	58	5	6	$41,081	7	25	28
5	55	42	2	52	42	6	45	40	16	77	19	3	2	$46,936	8	25	25
6	38	58	3	38	52	9	34	48	18	94	4	1	1	$36,883	11	25	21
7	84	14	2	81	15	3	78	16	6	27	71	1	1	$25,684	12	25	16
8	60	36	3	57	38	4	53	35	12	82	8	8	6	$56,789	10	24	51
STATE	56	40	3	54	38	7	50	36	14	71	25	3	3	$39,386	11	24	27

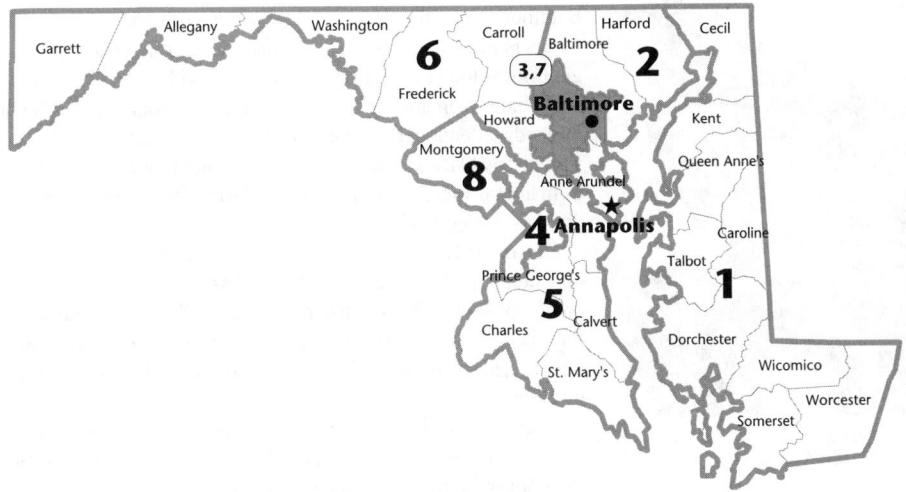

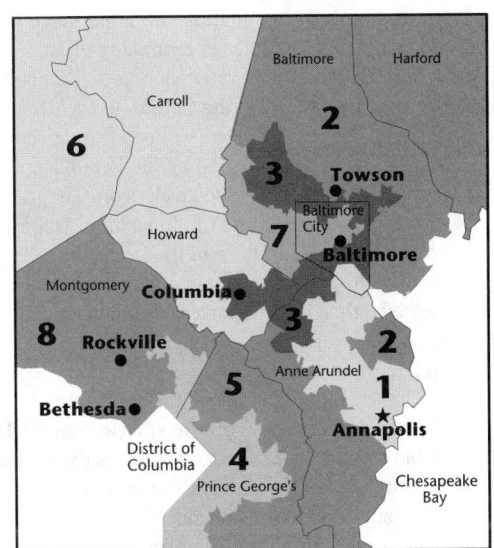

Sen. Paul S. Sarbanes (D)

Elected 1976; 5th term

CAPITOL OFFICE
224-4524; fax 224-1651; 309 Hart Bldg. 20510

INTERNET
e-mail: senator@sarbanes.senate.gov
web: sarbanes.senate.gov

COMMITTEES
Banking, Housing & Urban Affairs - ranking member
Budget
Foreign Relations
Joint Economic

HOMETOWN
Baltimore

BORN
Feb. 3, 1933, Salisbury, Md.

RELIGION
Greek Orthodox

FAMILY
Wife, Christine Dunbar; three children

EDUCATION
Princeton U., A.B. 1954; Oxford U., B.A. 1957; Harvard U., LL.B. 1960

CAREER
Lawyer

POLITICAL HIGHLIGHTS
Md. House, 1967-71; U.S. House, 1971-77

ELECTION RESULTS

2000 GENERAL

Paul S. Sarbanes (D)	1,230,013	63.2%
Paul Rappaport (R)	715,178	36.7%

2000 PRIMARY

Paul S. Sarbanes (D)	384,748	83.2%
George English (D)	45,984	10.0%
Sidney Altman (D)	31,502	6.8%

PREVIOUS WINNING PERCENTAGES
1994 (59%); 1988 (62%); 1982 (64%); 1976 (57%); 1974 House Election (84%); 1972 House Election (70%); 1970 House Election (70%)

As Sarbanes began his Senate campaign in 2000 for a fifth term, a Baltimore Sun editorial described him as the "silver fox," a cautious man who has managed to hold his Senate seat for 24 years by learning how to get things done in Congress "quietly but with shrewd skillfulness."

Sarbanes can appear disinterested in campaigning, and he has little use for media attention. But he is a reliable Democratic vote, representing a state with nearly twice as many Democrats as Republicans, who gets high marks from liberal interest groups. And so, despite his reserved personality, he easily wins re-election.

One of the Senate's most penetrating intellects, he has the skills to leave opponents sputtering, but he is not a provocateur. And Maryland voters seem comfortable with his detached manner while responding to his efforts on their behalf — to keep federal jobs in Maryland, to protect the Chesapeake Bay, to transform public housing programs and to keep personal financial information private.

Nevertheless, his painstaking approach to analyzing issues and his reticent style have frustrated some of his admirers, who feel that such a senior member of Congress should be more of a leader. Sarbanes often vexes colleagues by targeting minor issues for zealous attention, leading some to conclude that his judgment on the importance of subjects does not always equal his thoroughness in examining them.

But he can count some successes, particularly in his role as ranking Democrat on the Banking Committee. His hopes of taking the reins of the panel in the 104th Congress, upon the retirement of Donald W. Riegle Jr. of Michigan, were dashed by the Republican takeover of the Senate, but Sarbanes has fought effectively from his perch as the ranking minority member. He helped the Clinton administration win key concessions from the GOP in the drafting of the sweeping 1999 overhaul of the laws governing the nation's financial services industry. In particular, Sarbanes helped fight a Republican-led attempt to exempt small rural banks from the Community Reinvestment Act, a law aimed at forcing banks to make loans in poor neighborhoods.

One example of Sarbanes' mastery of detail came during a floor duel over the reinvestment law with Republican Sen. Phil Gramm of Texas, a formidable rhetorical opponent, in which Sarbanes mathematically undermined Gramm's claim that the law's impact on bank lending exceeded the gross domestic product of Canada. "When we start probing these figures, we discover it is not there; it is Alice in Wonderland," Sarbanes told Gramm.

Sarbanes also has won praise for taking principled but politically unpopular stands. While members of both parties gush their support for Federal Reserve Chairman Alan Greenspan, Sarbanes has accused the Fed under Greenspan's stewardship of hurting job growth by keeping interest rates unnecessarily high. The senator also has fought a lonely battle to speed up overdue payments owed to the United Nations.

In the 105th Congress, he helped steer to enactment a law allowing credit unions to continue expanding their membership bases, despite opposition from many bank lobbyists. Sarbanes also played a pivotal role on bipartisan public housing legislation that transformed federal programs into block grants, giving local housing authorities greater leeway to set rents and choose tenants. While Republican Sen. Connie Mack of Florida worked to garner GOP support, Sarbanes kept Democrats on board.

Politically, Democratic leaders turn to Sarbanes when they need a spokesman who can hold up against partisan attack: In 1987, he was selected for the panel investigating the Iran-contra arms-for-hostages scandal. In 1995, he was the ranking Democrat on the Senate Whitewater Committee, where he challenged Republican Alfonse M. D'Amato of New York at every opportunity. He argued that the committee hearings into the death of Deputy White House Counsel Vincent W. Foster Jr. and the conduct of the White House staff produced no evidence of wrongdoing.

He also played a critical role in the 1974 proceedings on the impeachment of President Nixon. Then a member of the House Judiciary Committee, Sarbanes drafted the most important article of impeachment, charging the president with obstruction of justice.

For a man who has made politics his life's work, Sarbanes has a strong distaste for publicity. When he does make headlines, it is generally because he has unearthed a detail offensive to his good-government sensibilities. This was the case in 1989, when Sarbanes held up the consideration of ambassadorial nominees who were major contributors to the GOP. While he acknowledged that the practice of rewarding political supporters with ambassadorships has a long bipartisan history, he argued that the administration of President George Bush had pursued the practice to excess.

In 1986, Sarbanes launched the first filibuster of his career over legislation that would have transferred control over two of the major airports serving Washington, D.C, from the federal government to a regional authority. Marylanders saw the bill as an economic threat to their state's major airport, Baltimore-Washington International. Sarbanes talked for five days, with an uncharacteristic enthusiasm that won concessions aimed at providing some protection for Maryland's interests.

Sarbanes has been attentive to his constituency on other fronts. In the 105th Congress, for example, he won passage of a bill to boost efforts to clean up the Chesapeake Bay and create a network of water trails, building on legislation he sponsored in the 101st Congress.

The son of Greek immigrant parents, Sarbanes grew up on Maryland's Eastern Shore, attended Princeton and won a Rhodes scholarship to Oxford. After graduating from Harvard Law School in 1960 — where he befriended Michael S. Dukakis, the 1988 Democratic presidential nominee — Sarbanes practiced law briefly before jumping into public life as an administrative assistant in President Kennedy's Council of Economic Advisers in 1962 and 1963. He practiced law again and won a state House seat in 1966.

In 1970, he challenged veteran Democratic Rep. George H. Fallon for the U.S. House. Running as an anti-war, anti-Democratic-machine insurgent, Sarbanes defeated the aging chairman of the Public Works Committee for the Democratic nomination in Baltimore's multiethnic 4th District. With Democrats enjoying nearly a 4-to-1 registration advantage, Sarbanes won the seat with ease in the fall.

Sarbanes moved to the Senate by unseating one-term Republican J. Glenn Beall Jr. in 1976. Emboldened by their capture of the presidency and control of the Senate in 1980, Republicans put Sarbanes on their 1982 target list. But he raised money aggressively, and state GOP leaders failed to enlist a big-name challenger. In 1988, he trounced Alan L. Keyes, a former State Department official and more recently a presidential candidate. In 1994, he defeated national GOP chairman Bill Brock, a former Tennessee senator for a term in the 1970s, a member of the Cabinet under President Reagan and a wealthy member of the famous candy family. In 2000, Sarbanes triumphed easily over Republican Paul Rappaport, an attorney who also had a lengthy career in law enforcement.

KEY VOTES

2000

No Overhaul bankruptcy law and increase minimum wage

No Limit fiscal 2001 discretionary spending to $600.3 billion

No Override veto on nuclear waste disposal at Yucca Mountain site in Nevada

Yes Oppose effort to terminate Kosovo mission

Yes Include gender, sexual orientation and disability in federal hate crime protections

No Approve GOP plan to restrict use of genetic information by health insurers

No Kill amendment delaying implementation of an anti-missile defense system

No Cut taxes for married couples

No Grant China permanent normal trade status

1999

No Remove President Clinton from office for obstruction of justice

No Kill amendment authorizing state grants to hire teachers and reduce class size

Yes Require criminal background checks for purchases at gun shows

No Approve GOP proposal to increase rights of patients in managed-care health plans

Yes Block effort to allow farm and medicine exports to Cuba

Yes Allow study of tougher automobile fuel efficiency standards

Yes Ratify nuclear weapons testing treaty

Yes Prohibit national political parties from collecting "soft money" donations

Yes Remove barriers among banking, securities and insurance companies

INTEREST GROUPS

	AFL-CIO	ADA	CCUS	ACU
2000	88%	95%	40%	12%
1999	100%	100%	35%	4%
1998	100%	95%	44%	4%
1997	100%	100%	30%	0%
1996	100%	95%	23%	0%
1995	100%	100%	21%	0%
1994	88%	95%	20%	0%
1993	91%	95%	18%	0%
1992	92%	100%	10%	0%
1991	92%	100%	10%	0%

CQ VOTE STUDIES

	PARTY UNITY		PRESIDENTIAL SUPPORT	
	Support	Oppose	Support	Oppose
2000	99%	1%	95%	5%
1999	97%	3%	86%	14%
1998	99%	1%	92%	8%
1997	98%	2%	87%	13%
1996	94%	6%	90%	10%
1995	96%	4%	90%	10%
1994	98%	2%	95%	5%
1993	98%	2%	96%	4%
1992	96%	4%	27%	73%
1991	96%	4%	30%	70%

Sen. Barbara A. Mikulski (D)

Elected 1986; 3rd term

CAPITOL OFFICE
224-4654; fax 224-8858; 709 Hart Bldg. 20510

INTERNET
e-mail: senator@mikulski.senate.gov
web: mikulski.senate.gov

COMMITTEES
Appropriations
Health, Education, Labor & Pensions

HOMETOWN
Baltimore

BORN
July 20, 1936, Baltimore, Md.

RELIGION
Roman Catholic

FAMILY
Single

EDUCATION
Mount Saint Agnes College, B.A. 1958; U. of
Maryland, M.S.W. 1965

CAREER
Social worker

POLITICAL HIGHLIGHTS
Baltimore City Council, 1971-77; Democratic
nominee for U.S. Senate, 1974; U.S. House, 1977-87

ELECTION RESULTS

1998 GENERAL

Barbara A. Mikulski (D)	1,062,810	70.5%
Ross Z. Pierpont (R)	444,637	29.5%

1998 PRIMARY

Barbara A. Mikulski (D)	349,382	84.4%
Ann L. Mallory (D)	43,120	10.4%
Kauko H. Kokkonen (D)	21,658	5.2%

PREVIOUS WINNING PERCENTAGES
1992 (71%); 1986 (61%); 1984 House Election (68%);
1982 House Election (74%); 1980 House Election
(76%); 1978 House Election (100%); 1976 House
Election (75%)

Mikulski was one of just two women in the Senate on her arrival in 1987. Now, midway through her third term, she is one of a record 13 female senators. As the senior woman in the chamber and the secretary of the Democratic Conference, she takes pride in her efforts to mentor the other women, in both parties, helping them develop the skills necessary to thrive in the Senate.

In the book "Nine and Counting," a collaboration of the nine women serving in the Senate in 2000, Mikulski recalls: "I didn't come to politics by the traditional male route, being in a nice law firm or belonging to the right clubs. Like most of the women I've known in politics, I got involved because I saw a community need."

Mikulski remains an unabashed "blue collar" liberal who rarely shies away from the straightforward approach for which she is noted. While her gritty demeanor often comes across as brusque, she defends her blunt style as effective in winning results for her constituents and action on her initiatives. A small but tangible example exists a few miles outside Washington, at the Census Bureau headquarters in Suitland, Md.

After hearing complaints from the complex's residents about the ugliness of a chain-link and barbed-wire fence erected around the facility for security purposes, Mikulski threatened to tear the fence down with her own hands if it were not replaced. After collaborating with residents, labor unions and businesses, she and fellow Democrat Paul S. Sarbanes, Maryland's senior senator, secured federal funding for a brick and wrought-iron replacement, dedicated in 2000.

That results-oriented approach has helped her rise through the ranks in the Senate, and her aggressive pursuit of issues that affect working people — such as medical insurance and retirement benefits — has earned her the high regard of her constituents. So, too, has her success in funneling federal dollars to Maryland, where she has won her past two elections with 71 percent of the vote.

Mikulski's main conduit for directing government money to her constituents has been the Appropriations subcommittee that governs spending on veterans, housing, environmental and space programs. She chaired the panel from 1989 through 1994 and has been its ranking Democrat since. It has been said that she looks for a compelling human need for the special projects she chooses to insert in the annual spending bill, and those run from housing and community development projects to protection of the Chesapeake Bay, which is of vital economic interest to the state.

In 2000, she won inclusion of grants for housing rehabilitation projects in Baltimore, for NASA's Goddard Space Flight Center in Greenbelt and for revitalization along U.S. Route 1, an older commercial corridor between Baltimore and Washington. She was again an ardent defender of the AmeriCorps national service program pushed to enactment by President Clinton, which Republicans wanted to shut down. And she led the Democratic fight, along with the Clinton administration, to add $453 million to fund an additional 79,000 new housing vouchers for low-income residents.

Her style in crafting her panel's spending bill in 2000 was typical. She and subcommittee Chairman Christopher S. Bond, R-Mo., another senator known for a quick temper and an eagerness to deliver federal money back home, declined to even consider a measure until GOP leaders freed up more money for them to spend. When the bill threatened to bog down in the fall — over three House Republican provisions to restrict the activities of the Environmental Protection Agency, which the Clinton administration opposed — Mikulski and Bond found a compromise.

Once the deal was cut, she defended it emphatically, even against criticism from her Democratic colleagues. "You may think we wimped out," she told Democrat Barbara Boxer of California. "We think we had a victory."

Mikulski's record has rarely disappointed women's groups. She is a strong supporter of abortion rights and has tried to ensure that federal health care plans provide abortion coverage. She helped push to enactment the 1990 law that created the women's health research office at the National Institutes of Health. And in 1995, she was the first member of the Senate Ethics Committee to call for public hearings on the sexual harassment allegations against Republican Sen. Bob Packwood of Oregon, a turning point in a three-year case that ultimately led to Packwood's resignation.

Mikulski joined the Democratic leadership as an assistant floor leader after the 1992 elections, when the all-male party hierarchy decided it was time to make their ranks somewhat diverse.

She first gained a following as a community activist in Baltimore by discussing the plight of the "forgotten" ethnic residents of America's cities. With these people in mind, she voted in the 106th Congress against enacting the law lowering regulatory barriers among banking, insurance and securities concerns and worked with federal housing officials to protect Baltimore residents from property "flipping," in which speculators buy homes, often in distressed neighborhoods, make cosmetic repairs, and quickly sell the houses to unsuspecting buyers at inflated prices.

Her parents ran a grocery store across the street from their Baltimore row house; her Polish immigrant grandparents operated a bakery legendary for its jelly doughnuts and raisin bread. (The family no longer owns the bakery but has the rights to the bread recipe.) Parts of the neighborhood were torched after the 1968 assassination of the Rev. Martin Luther King Jr. As a social worker, Mikulski delivered food to the needy during the riots, sometimes by riding a tank. Shortly thereafter, she participated in what later became a multiethnic, multiracial fight against a freeway that would have leveled several city neighborhoods. A brick wall today marks the abrupt end of the road, a reminder of the community-organizing skills that the senator still relies upon.

Building on that effort, Mikulski won a city council seat in 1971 and became prominent in the feminist movement. In 1974, she took 43 percent in a challenge to heavily favored GOP Sen. Charles McC. Mathias Jr. That race positioned her well for 1976, when Sarbanes, then a House member, left to run for the Senate. Mikulski had no trouble winning the Democratic primary for Sarbanes' House seat, and she breezed through five general elections. She sat on the Energy and Commerce Committee in the House, where she was known as a champion of consumer causes.

In 1986, Mikulski ran to succeed the retiring Mathias. She easily defeated Rep. Michael D. Barnes and outgoing Gov. Harry R. Hughes in the Senate Democratic primary. Republicans nominated conservative Linda Chavez, a staff director of the U.S. Commission on Civil Rights under President Reagan. Mikulski coasted to victory.

Bolstered by high approval ratings and a large campaign treasury, Mikulski deterred the most prominent Maryland Republicans in 1992. The GOP nomination went to black conservative activist Alan L. Keyes, a State Department official in the Reagan administration who gained attention for his eloquent opposition to the liberal orthodoxy of most black leaders. Mikulski carried all but one of the state's counties. In 1998, she had little trouble beating Republican challenger Ross Z. Pierpont, a retired surgeon.

KEY VOTES

2000
Yes Overhaul bankruptcy law and increase minimum wage
No Limit fiscal 2001 discretionary spending to $600.3 billion
No Override veto on nuclear waste disposal at Yucca Mountain site in Nevada
Yes Oppose effort to terminate Kosovo mission
Yes Include gender, sexual orientation and disability in federal hate crime protections
No Approve GOP plan to restrict use of genetic information by health insurers
No Kill amendment delaying implementation of an anti-missile defense system
No Cut taxes for married couples
No Grant China permanent normal trade status

1999
No Remove President Clinton from office for obstruction of justice
No Kill amendment authorizing state grants to hire teachers and reduce class size
Yes Require criminal background checks for purchases at gun shows
No Approve GOP proposal to increase rights of patients in managed-care health plans
No Block effort to allow farm and medicine exports to Cuba
No Allow study of tougher automobile fuel efficiency standards
Yes Ratify nuclear weapons testing treaty
Yes Prohibit national political parties from collecting "soft money" donations
No Remove barriers among banking, securities and insurance companies

INTEREST GROUPS

	AFL-CIO	ADA	CCUS	ACU
2000	88%	95%	46%	8%
1999	89%	100%	59%	4%
1998	100%	90%	53%	4%
1997	86%	95%	44%	4%
1996	86%	95%	23%	0%
1995	100%	90%	39%	4%
1994	75%	85%	33%	0%
1993	100%	85%	27%	4%
1992	92%	100%	0%	0%
1991	83%	90%	20%	10%

CQ VOTE STUDIES

	PARTY UNITY		PRESIDENTIAL SUPPORT	
	Support	Oppose	Support	Oppose
2000	97%	3%	92%	8%
1999	96%	4%	86%	14%
1998	97%	3%	91%	9%
1997	92%	8%	91%	9%
1996	92%	8%	90%	10%
1995	87%	13%	89%	11%
1994	90%	10%	93%	7%
1993	92%	8%	95%	5%
1992	90%	10%	23%	77%
1991	92%	8%	33%	67%

Rep. Wayne T. Gilchrest (R)

Elected 1990; 6th term

CAPITOL OFFICE
225-5311; fax 225-0254; 2245 Rayburn Bldg. 20515

INTERNET
e-mail: www.house.gov/writerep
web: www.house.gov/gilchrest

COMMITTEES
Resources
(Fisheries Conservation, Wildlife & Oceans - chairman)
Transportation & Infrastructure

HOMETOWN
Kennedyville

BORN
April 15, 1946, Rahway, N.J.

RELIGION
Methodist

FAMILY
Wife, Barbara Gilchrest; three children

EDUCATION
Wesley College, A.A. 1971; Delaware State U., B.A. 1973; Loyola College (Md.), attended 1990

MILITARY SERVICE
Marine Corps, 1964-68

CAREER
High school teacher

POLITICAL HIGHLIGHTS
Republican nominee for U.S. House, 1988

ELECTION RESULTS

2000 GENERAL

Wayne T. Gilchrest (R)	165,293	64.4%
Bennett Bozman (D)	91,022	35.5%

2000 PRIMARY

Wayne T. Gilchrest (R)	unopposed

1998 GENERAL

Wayne T. Gilchrest (R)	135,771	69.2%
Irving Pinder (D)	60,450	30.8%

PREVIOUS WINNING PERCENTAGES
1996 (62%); 1994 (68%); 1992 (51%); 1990 (57%)

Gilchrest represents a district that wraps around the Chesapeake Bay, and preservation of its wetlands and waterways is the top priority of this quiet, unassuming man, who approaches his work with the same sense of wonder and curiosity that he tried to instill in students when he was a public school teacher.

Gilchrest has a decade of service in the House, and seniority has given him a Resources subcommittee chairmanship, but he never seems impressed with himself. Low-key and slightly disheveled, he still refers to himself as an "accidental" congressman.

Despite his approachable and at times wide-eyed demeanor, Gilchrest is not afraid to challenge GOP leaders. He was one of only about two dozen House Republicans who initially signed on to a bipartisan health care initiative in 1999 allowing patients to sue their health plans. Breaking with many national party leaders, he also backed the long-shot presidential bid of Sen. John McCain, R-Ariz., in 2000, chairing the candidate's Maryland campaign. Both men are Vietnam War veterans, and Gilchrest lauded the senator for "serving his country and standing on principle."

Born in New Jersey, Gilchrest joined the Marine Corps right out of high school. He downplays the 1967 battle that won him the Bronze Star and the chest and shoulder wound that earned him a Purple Heart, claiming that he was more foolhardy than brave. He attended several colleges, mixing in a job as a chicken plucker in Maine and studying rural poverty in Kentucky. After graduating from Delaware State University, he held a series of teaching jobs, ending up at Kent County High School on Maryland's Eastern Shore in 1979.

Gilchrest did two stints with the Forest Service in Idaho and supplemented his teacher's income by moonlighting as a house painter. When he first ran for the House in 1988, he rushed to Annapolis in paint-covered clothes to file for election after he read in a newspaper that the GOP was having trouble finding a candidate.

Gilchrest's pro-environment views place him in the ranks of the moderate Northeastern Republicans who compete with their anti-regulatory colleagues from the West to define the GOP's stance on the environment. "Somebody has to stand up for the critters," he once told the Baltimore Sun. He contends that House Republicans have not built up enough credibility on environmental issues to earn voters' trust in this area. On military and business matters, he says, the GOP has many experts. But, he asks, "Who here has an expertise in the environmental area? The answer is, very few people."

A member of the Resources Committee, where he took the reins of the Fisheries Conservation, Wildlife and Oceans Subcommittee in the 107th Congress, he has won a few battles on the environmental front. In the previous two Congresses, Gilchrest chaired the Transportation Committee's Coast Guard and Maritime Transportation Subcommittee, a job that fit in well with his agenda to preserve the Chesapeake and its watershed; to increase maritime trade in Maryland, particularly at the port of Baltimore; and to preserve the substantial Coast Guard presence in the area.

He scored a victory in the 106th by winning approval of legislation to restore 1 million acres of habitat in estuaries such as the Chesapeake. "Fish catches are at their lowest, shellfish beds have been closed, and the livelihoods of watermen and others are threatened," he said.

He has fought efforts by GOP conservatives to scale back substantially the 1973 Endangered Species Act, but instead of constantly supporting

www.cq.com

environmental controls, Gilchrest says he likes to seek practical solutions that take economic interests into account.

He was the chief sponsor of a bill in the 105th to implement an international agreement lifting the U.S. embargo on Latin American tuna after the tuna industry had agreed to take steps to protect dolphins, which were being caught up in the tuna harvest and killed.

Gilchrest focuses on rural issues because of the heavy agricultural presence in his 1st District. In 1999, he proposed legislation to increase reimbursement rates for health maintenance organizations that provide Medicare benefits to seniors in rural areas. Gilchrest also had his district's needs in mind when he voted against the annual agriculture spending bill in 1999, saying it did not contain enough money for drought-stricken Maryland farmers.

In addition to his moderate environmental views, Gilchrest has voted for gun control measures on a number of occasions, and he supports abortion rights. He backed campaign finance legislation opposed by most Republicans. And he opposed a constitutional amendment to outlaw desecration of the U.S. flag, saying the measure "puts the work of Betsy Ross above the work of Madison and Jefferson." Veterans groups criticized him for that stance in spite of his valor in Vietnam.

But Gilchrest votes with the conservative majority on labor issues, and despite his background as a public school teacher, he supports conservatives' push to give parents taxpayer-financed vouchers to pay for private school education. He says competition will force public schools to improve.

Gilchrest lost his first bid for Congress against Rep. Roy Dyson, a conservative Democrat. But in a 1990 rematch, Gilchrest won a solid 57 percent against Dyson, who had been weakened by reports of ties to a Pentagon procurement scandal and revelations that, despite his hawkish stance on military matters, he had been a conscientious objector during the Vietnam War.

Redistricting in 1992 put Gilchrest in a contest with Democratic Rep. Tom McMillen in the redrawn 1st District. Gilchrest drew on his average-guy appeal, portraying McMillen, a former University of Maryland and Washington Bullets basketball star, as a rich Washington insider. Gilchrest won with 51 percent of the vote; it was his last tough campaign.

Gilchrest's culinary tastes might be called a bit unusual. He told an Annapolis deli owner that his favorite sandwich is peanut butter and mayonnaise on rye. The deli, which names sandwiches after politicians, declined to create the peanut butter and mayonnaise concoction, coming up with another offering to call the "Gilchrest." The congressman was not offended, recognizing that the deli needed to offer sandwiches that people would eat.

KEY VOTES

2000
Yes Raise hourly minimum wage by $1 over two years
Yes Halt funding for U.S. mission in Kosovo unless European nations pay more
Yes Provide Medicare benefits to military retirees and their dependents
Yes Grant China permanent normal trade status
Yes Phase out estate, gift and trust taxes
No   Prohibit implementation of president's national monument designations
Yes Approve GOP plan to provide prescription drug coverage for Medicare beneficiaries
Yes Increase help for poor nations indebted to international financial institutions

1999
Yes Impose steel import quotas
No   Kill proposal to take aviation trust funds off budget
Yes Require background checks on buyers only at gun shows with 10 or more vendors
Yes Remove barriers among banking, securities and insurance companies
No   Authorize state grants to hire teachers and reduce class size
Yes Overhaul campaign finance law; ban "soft money" and restrict advocacy advertising
Yes Approve bipartisan plan to increase rights of patients in managed-care health plans

INTEREST GROUPS

	AFL-CIO	ADA	CCUS	ACU
2000	20%	15%	80%	58%
1999	22%	50%	72%	52%
1998	20%	35%	89%	44%
1997	0%	20%	90%	71%

CQ VOTE STUDIES

	PARTY UNITY		PRESIDENTIAL SUPPORT	
	Support	Oppose	Support	Oppose
2000	79%	21%	50%	50%
1999	72%	28%	41%	59%
1998	71%	29%	38%	62%
1997	81%	19%	45%	55%

MARYLAND 1

Cross Bay – Eastern Shore; Annapolis; Glen Burnie

The 1st includes the rural counties of the Eastern Shore and, across the Chesapeake Bay, the fast-growing suburbs of Anne Arundel County. Although the areas are different in many ways, they share a conservative leaning that often benefits Republicans. The 1st supported the Republican presidential candidate in 1992, '96 and 2000.

The Eastern Shore, which holds about three-fifths of the district's population, has a steady economic grounding in agriculture. The central, more rural part of the Eastern Shore is GOP heartland. The northern counties, closer to Baltimore and Philadelphia, and the southern counties, with larger black and working-class populations, are more Democratic.

Across the Bay in Anne Arundel County, Annapolis, the state capital and the district's urban center, is one-third black and leans Democratic. Party preference in the suburban areas of Anne Arundel

County varies, yet the county votes overwhelmingly conservative in national elections. The 1st also covers a small, blue-collar part of Baltimore that is heavily Democratic.

Anne Arundel County experienced significant economic growth starting in the mid-1990s due to refurbished highways to Washington and Baltimore, increased tourism in Annapolis and the relocation of small businesses to the area. The suburbs of Glen Burnie and Odenton are the fastest-growing areas in the district.

MAJOR INDUSTRY
Agriculture, manufacturing, tourism

MILITARY BASES
U.S. Naval Academy/Annapolis Naval Station, 1,010 military, 1,599 civilian (1999)

CITIES
Glen Burnie (unincorporated), 37,305 (1990); Annapolis, 33,125; South Gate (unincorporated), 27,564 (1990); Salisbury, 21,123

UNUSUAL FEATURES
Oldest state house in continuous legislative use nationwide (since 1779); Tomb of hero John Paul Jones in the Naval Academy Chapel crypt.

Rep. Robert L. Ehrlich Jr. (R)

Elected 1994; 4th term

CAPITOL OFFICE
225-3061; fax 225-3094; 315 Cannon Bldg. 20515

INTERNET
e-mail: ehrlich@mail.house.gov
web: www.house.gov/ehrlich

COMMITTEES
Energy & Commerce

HOMETOWN
Timonium

BORN
Nov. 25, 1957, Baltimore, Md.

RELIGION
Methodist

FAMILY
Wife, Kendel Sibiski Ehrlich; one child

EDUCATION
Princeton U., B.A. 1979; Wake Forest U., J.D. 1982

CAREER
Lawyer

POLITICAL HIGHLIGHTS
Md. House, 1987-95

ELECTION RESULTS

2000 GENERAL

Robert L. Ehrlich Jr. (R)	178,556	68.6%
Kenneth T. Bosley (D)	81,591	31.3%

2000 PRIMARY

Robert L. Ehrlich Jr. (R)	unopposed

1998 GENERAL

Robert L. Ehrlich Jr. (R)	145,711	69.3%
Kenneth T. Bosley (D)	64,474	30.7%

PREVIOUS WINNING PERCENTAGES
1996 (62%); 1994 (63%)

Ehrlich faces a critical career decision in his fourth term: Whether to take his appealing life story statewide in a run for governor in 2002 or to continue his climb in the House, where he has earned a reputation as a solid, reliable member of the GOP's Class of 1994.

Ehrlich (ER-lick) did not plan a long House career when he arrived in Washington, but life in Congress improved when his close friend J. Dennis Hastert became Speaker in January 1999. Ehrlich was rewarded with Hastert's seat on the powerful Commerce Committee (now Energy and Commerce),where he began to carve a niche for himself on complex issues such as the environment, electricity deregulation and telecommunications.

Ehrlich, a skilled campaigner, also has emerged as a top player in Maryland GOP circles. He has several things going for him as a potential statewide candidate in heavily Democratic Maryland: a working-class-kid-makes-good background, a largely pro-abortion rights record, strong fundraising skills and a likable demeanor.

The only child of a car salesman and a legal secretary, Ehrlich grew up in a row house in the suburban Baltimore town of Arbutus. A good student and athlete, he won scholarships to prep school and to Princeton. After graduating from law school, beginning a legal career in Baltimore and becoming active in local GOP politics, Ehrlich won a seat in the Maryland House at age 28. He spent eight years there, earning a reputation as a serious, pragmatic, moderate lawmaker. When Rep. Helen Delich Bentley left the House for an unsuccessful bid for the 1994 GOP gubernatorial nomination, Ehrlich easily bested state Rep. Gerry L. Brewster to keep the 2nd District in Republican hands.

In Congress, he has compiled a more conservative record. His reputation as a GOP leadership loyalist prompted the hometown Baltimore Sun in 1998 to term him a "disappointment." Although The Sun endorsed him for re-election that year, it editorialized: "He squandered a chance to show independence ... and instead carried water for [Speaker] Newt Gingrich."

As he did in Annapolis, Ehrlich gravitated to older, more experienced legislators, such as Hastert, to learn the ropes. When Speaker-designate Robert L. Livingston, R-La., announced in late 1998 that he would step down, Ehrlich rushed to the floor to exhort Hastert to try for the post. Then he helped round up the votes.

Unlike his more confrontational colleagues, many of whom lacked earlier legislative experience, Ehrlich has been content to pay his dues and develop personal ties. He does not seek the limelight in Washington; he is far more likely to celebrate a legislative win by hanging out in Hastert's office than by joining the Speaker before the cameras.

In Maryland, however, Ehrlich has worked to raise his profile, putting much effort into rebuilding the GOP after the drubbing it took in 1998. Ehrlich had energetically campaigned for gubernatorial nominee Ellen Sauerbrey and hoped the party would capture a statewide office for the first time since 1980. But even as Ehrlich coasted to re-election with 69 percent of the vote, Sauerbrey's weak showing against Democratic Gov. Parris N. Glendening made Ehrlich rethink his statewide aspirations.

Ehrlich decided against a long-shot try for the Senate against Democrat Paul S. Sarbanes in 2000 and won an easy re-election to the House. But he is weighing a race for governor, especially if Lt. Gov. Kathleen Kennedy Townsend runs.

www.cq.com

Ehrlich is a frequent visitor to Annapolis, where he advises outnumbered — and sometimes unpolished — GOP state lawmakers on tactics and strategy. But his influence has its limits. He unsuccessfully opposed a controversial 2000 gun raffle fundraiser by Carroll County Republicans and was frustrated that the raffle took attention away from what he regarded as an extremist Democratic anti-gun agenda in Annapolis.

In late 2000, Ehrlich supported a short-lived coup attempt combining Republicans and disgruntled Annapolis Democrats against Maryland Senate President Mike Miller. The attempt unraveled, and Miller vowed to take revenge against Ehrlich when the legislature redrew Maryland's congressional district lines.

"Politics is as close to athletics as you're going to find in life," Ehrlich told The Washington Post in 1999. "I'm competitive and I like to win." Ehrlich captained the football team at Princeton and is an avid golfer and tennis player.

He is solidly conservative but not inflexible. He once told The Washington Post that he is "right of center, but not on the far right of the party." He breaks away from the conservative GOP mold on matters such as abortion rights, family planning and other social issues. In the 105th Congress, he strayed from the party line to oppose mandatory drug testing for federal employees and a constitutional amendment on religious freedom. And he supported an executive order by President Clinton prohibiting federal agencies from discriminating against homosexuals in hiring.

But on major 106th Congress votes on gun control, a "patients' bill of rights" and overhaul of the campaign finance system — on which numerous Republicans defected — Ehrlich was a leadership loyalist, opposing each Democratic initiative.

After several prominent Republicans signed a petition in 1998 that forced the GOP to bring a campaign finance overhaul bill to the floor, Ehrlich circulated a petition urging leaders to discipline committee chairmen and vice chairmen who frequently dissented from the party line. He proposed depriving them of their chairmanships when the party selected leaders for the 106th Congress. "It had almost nothing to do with philosophy, but it does have everything to do with the responsibility of being the governing party," Ehrlich told The Sun. But he did not push his idea when GOP lawmakers organized, in the wake of the leadership upheaval that saw Gingrich quit as Speaker.

Ehrlich said he had little respect for Clinton, calling him dishonest. Even before Clinton's impeachment in 1998 — which he supported — Ehrlich had a policy of not visiting the White House while Clinton was in office.

KEY VOTES

2000

No	Raise hourly minimum wage by $1 over two years
Yes	Halt funding for U.S. mission in Kosovo unless European nations pay more
Yes	Provide Medicare benefits to military retirees and their dependents
No	Grant China permanent normal trade status
Yes	Phase out estate, gift and trust taxes
Yes	Prohibit implementation of president's national monument designations
Yes	Approve GOP plan to provide prescription drug coverage for Medicare beneficiaries
No	Increase help for poor nations indebted to international financial institutions

1999

Yes	Impose steel import quotas
Yes	Kill proposal to take aviation trust funds off budget
Yes	Require background checks on buyers only at gun shows with 10 or more vendors
Yes	Remove barriers among banking, securities and insurance companies
No	Authorize state grants to hire teachers and reduce class size
No	Overhaul campaign finance law; ban "soft money" and restrict advocacy advertising
No	Approve bipartisan plan to increase rights of patients in managed-care health plans

INTEREST GROUPS

	AFL-CIO	ADA	CCUS	ACU
2000	10%	20%	85%	88%
1999	22%	20%	83%	83%
1998	10%	5%	94%	92%
1997	0%	0%	90%	72%

CQ VOTE STUDIES

	PARTY UNITY		PRESIDENTIAL SUPPORT	
	Support	Oppose	Support	Oppose
2000	89%	11%	29%	71%
1999	86%	14%	26%	74%
1998	87%	13%	25%	75%
1997	89%	11%	33%	67%

MARYLAND 2
Baltimore and Harford counties

The 2nd includes Baltimore's northeastern suburbs, the northern and eastern sections of Baltimore County, Harford County to the east and a small portion of Anne Arundel County to the south. Although Democrats hold a 3-2 registration advantage, a mix of conservative Democrats and moderate Republicans has made the district winnable for Republicans.

The district has enjoyed a fair amount of economic growth, aside from eastern Baltimore County's industrial sector, which has struggled with unemployment during the transition from an industrial to a service-based economy. Bethlehem Steel, one of the county's major employers, opened a new mill in 2000 at its Sparrows Point complex that is expected to benefit the economy.

Baltimore's northern suburbs, the most affluent and fastest-growing area of the district, have led the 2nd's trend toward the GOP in national elections. Republican presidential candidates carried the district in

1992, '96 and 2000. Along Interstate 95 is Harford County, a residential area that grew 20 percent in the 1990s. A mix of conservative Democrats and socially conscious Republicans has led the county to support Republicans on the local and national level in recent elections.

In the northern and more agricultural parts of the county, there are more old-line, conservative Democrats and moderate Republicans. The district is Democratic in the small communities along Route 40, which are mostly working-class and military – the district includes Aberdeen Proving Ground, where dozens of the Army's women recruits reported being sexually harassed by drill instructors in 1996.

MAJOR INDUSTRY
Manufacturing, military, agriculture

MILITARY BASES
Aberdeen Proving Ground (Army), 7,500 military, 3,900 civilian (2000)

CITIES
Dundalk (unincorporated), 65,800 (1990); Essex (unincorporated), 40,872 (1990); Towson (unincorporated) (pt.), 37,864 (1990)

UNUSUAL FEATURES
Cal Ripken Jr. Museum; Ladew Topiary Gardens.

Rep. Benjamin L. Cardin (D)

Elected 1986; 8th term

CAPITOL OFFICE
225-4016; fax 225-9219; 2267 Rayburn Bldg. 20515

INTERNET
e-mail: rep.cardin@mail.house.gov
web: www.house.gov/cardin

COMMITTEES
Ways & Means

HOMETOWN
Baltimore

BORN
Oct. 5, 1943, Baltimore, Md.

RELIGION
Jewish

FAMILY
Wife, Myrna Edelman Cardin; two children

EDUCATION
U. of Pittsburgh, B.A. 1964; U. of Maryland, LL.B. 1967

CAREER
Lawyer

POLITICAL HIGHLIGHTS
Md. House, 1967-87 (Speaker, 1979-87)

ELECTION RESULTS

2000 GENERAL
Benjamin L. Cardin (D)	169,347	75.7%
Colin Harby (R)	53,827	24.1%

2000 PRIMARY
Benjamin L. Cardin (D)	unopposed

1998 GENERAL
Benjamin L. Cardin (D)	137,501	77.6%
Colin Harby (R)	39,667	22.4%

PREVIOUS WINNING PERCENTAGES
1996 (67%); 1994 (71%); 1992 (74%); 1990 (70%);
1988 (73%); 1986 (79%)

Since coming to Congress in 1987, Cardin has voted a loyally Democratic line. But he also has shown an increasing willingness to work with Republicans on a range of contentious issues — including taxes, health care and budget matters. His disregard for the consequences of zealous bipartisanship cause fellow Democrats to occasionally label him politically tone-deaf.

Cardin's alliance on Social Security legislation late in the 106th Congress with Florida Republican E. Clay Shaw Jr., a Ways and Means Committee colleague, irked fellow Democrats clamoring to regain their House majority, for example. Some in the party saw the partnership as aiding Shaw, who ultimately won re-election by one of the narrowest margins nationwide.

The friction was all the more notable because Cardin has played key roles trying to extract Democrats from the minority. As transition team leader at the start of the 104th Congress, he helped his colleagues adjust to their diminished status. And he suggested a highly successful Democratic fundraiser in 1995 at Baltimore's Oriole Park at Camden Yards the night Cal Ripken Jr. set a new record for playing in consecutive major league baseball games. By 2000, he had been put in charge of another transition effort, chairing a 36-member group to plan how the Democratic Party would put its stamp on the House if it returned to power.

Cardin says focusing on policy rather than politics is the way to bridge differences between the parties. And his collaborations with GOP colleagues have yielded tangible results, such as the overhaul of the IRS and a revision of Medicare. Cardin also has worked effectively with Republicans to craft compromises on welfare overhaul — including one to provide more child support money to poor mothers — and on pension and retirement legislation.

His vast trove of knowledge leads him to be cast as a Capitol Hill policy wonk, but Cardin remains a potent figure on the Maryland political stage. His flirtation with a 1998 gubernatorial candidacy had both the incumbent Democrat and his leading GOP challenger on edge. It was not the first time Cardin pondered a statewide campaign and, considering he was only 57 as the 107th Congress began, it is not likely to be the last.

For now, Cardin keeps plowing the legislative ground. He teamed up on Ways and Means in the 105th Congress with Rob Portman, R-Ohio, to draft the proposal that became the basis of the 1998 IRS overhaul law; their plan called for creating an independent board to oversee the IRS and instituting new taxpayer rights, including shifting the burden of proof from the taxpayer to the IRS during Tax Court proceedings.

In the 106th, Cardin and Portman joined forces on legislation to boost retirement savings options and revamp pension law; the House passed the measure but it foundered at the end of the year. On Ways and Means' Health Subcommittee, Cardin worked in 1997 with California Republican Bill Thomas, then the subcommittee chairman, to add language to that year's budget-balancing package that provided more benefits to Medicare beneficiaries. One such change is a requirement that managed-care plans pay for treatment that a "prudent layperson" would consider an emergency.

Though he can compromise with Republicans, there are many issues on which Cardin strongly disagrees with the conservative line. On Ways and Means, for example, he has argued against efforts to terminate the tax code, and he opposes establishing tax-sheltered education savings accounts that parents could use for private school expenses.

Organized labor has long been a force in Baltimore politics, but international commerce also plays a key role in the port city's economy. So Cardin walks a careful line on trade issues, trying to promote trade while guarding against the loss of U.S. jobs to lower-cost operations overseas. He voted to implement the North American Free Trade Agreement in 1993 and backed legislation in 2000 to promote U.S. trade with Africa and the Caribbean. However, in 1998 he opposed reviving fast-track authority allowing the president to negotiate trade agreements that Congress cannot amend. And in 2000, he initially opposed a measure granting China permanent normal trade status but eventually came on board, saying his concerns about that country's human rights record had been addressed.

As a House ethics committee member in the 104th, Cardin was the lead Democrat on a four-member panel that investigated alleged ethics violations against Speaker Newt Gingrich. His service on the panel concluded after the 1997 vote to reprimand Gingrich, but later that year Cardin co-chaired of a 12-member task force that recommended changes to the ethics process. Cardin voted against the package the House ultimately adopted because it included elements he had not proposed, among them a ban on allowing those outside Congress to file an ethics complaint unless they could obtain the sponsorship of a member. "By closing the door, we tell the public we do not want to hear from them," he said.

Cardin keeps a close eye on home state interests. He opposed a major rewrite of farm law in 1996 because it did not abolish sugar subsidies that hurt a major refinery in his district. He supported a luxury tax repeal in 1993 because it aided the boat industry, which is critical to Maryland's Chesapeake Bay economy. In his time on Capitol Hill, he has had a hand in preserving the Coast Guard base at Curtis Bay and restoring Fort McHenry in Baltimore. He helped secure funding for Amtrak and development assistance for a light rail system in Baltimore.

Cardin has been a legislator for nearly all his adult years, and by every account he is an extremely skilled practitioner of the political trade. As a 24-year-old in 1967, he already held a seat in the Maryland House when he graduated first in his class at the University of Maryland Law School. By age 32, he was chairman of the state House Ways and Means Committee, and four years later he became the youngest Speaker in the chamber's history, calling the legislative shots for nearly a decade.

In 1986, he cruised into the 3rd District seat vacated when Democrat Barbara A. Mikulski was elected to the Senate. He has easily won re-election since then.

KEY VOTES

2000
Yes Raise hourly minimum wage by $1 over two years
No Halt funding for U.S. mission in Kosovo unless European nations pay more
Yes Provide Medicare benefits to military retirees and their dependents
Yes Grant China permanent normal trade status
No Phase out estate, gift and trust taxes
No Prohibit implementation of president's national monument designations
No Approve GOP plan to provide prescription drug coverage for Medicare beneficiaries
Yes Increase help for poor nations indebted to international financial institutions

1999
Yes Impose steel import quotas
Yes Kill proposal to take aviation trust funds off budget
No Require background checks on buyers only at gun shows with 10 or more vendors
Yes Remove barriers among banking, securities and insurance companies
Yes Authorize state grants to hire teachers and reduce class size
Yes Overhaul campaign finance law; ban "soft money" and restrict advocacy advertising
Yes Approve bipartisan plan to increase rights of patients in managed-care health plans

INTEREST GROUPS

	AFL-CIO	ADA	CCUS	ACU
2000	90%	90%	42%	8%
1999	89%	100%	28%	0%
1998	100%	95%	25%	8%
1997	88%	85%	40%	12%

CQ VOTE STUDIES

	PARTY UNITY		PRESIDENTIAL SUPPORT	
	Support	Oppose	Support	Oppose
2000	92%	8%	94%	6%
1999	92%	8%	83%	17%
1998	91%	9%	78%	22%
1997	85%	15%	83%	17%

MARYLAND 3
Downtown and ethnic Baltimore; Columbia

A reverse-C shape, the 3rd winds in and out of the city of Baltimore, covering the city's downtown, ethnic neighborhoods and northern and southwestern suburbs. The district's mixture of affluent and middle-class suburbanites and ethnic working-class and poor city residents gives Democrats a tight hold in national elections.

In the city, the district includes the downtown and its adjacent gentrified areas, which have enjoyed prosperity due to the Harborplace retail and entertainment complex and the growth of hotels and office buildings. The district then moves east into ethnic, blue-collar neighborhoods whose Italian, Greek and Polish voters gave Democratic Sen. Barbara Mikulski her start in this district.

Along the city's northwest edge, the district picks up Baltimore's wealthiest communities and follows the path of Jewish migration northwest into the wealthy suburbs of Baltimore County. The suburbs further north and west contain larger working-class and black populations, while the suburbs directly north of the city are less Democratic.

To the south of the city, the district includes the liberal-leaning communities of eastern Howard County, including the planned community of Columbia and the middle-class suburbs of northwest Anne Arundel County. Both of these areas, in the corridor between Baltimore and Washington, have experienced heavy growth.

MAJOR INDUSTRY
Manufacturing, military, biotechnology

MILITARY BASES
Fort George G. Meade (Army), 9,925 military, 25,000 civilian (1998)

CITIES
Baltimore (pt.), 251,647 (1990); Columbia (unincorporated) (pt.), 68,184 (1990); Parkville (unincorporated) (pt.), 26,285 (1990)

UNUSUAL FEATURES
Babe Ruth birthplace and museum; Columbia, a planned community designed in 1967 by James Rouse, actor Edward Norton's grandfather.

Rep. Albert R. Wynn (D)

Elected 1992; 5th term

CAPITOL OFFICE
225-8699; fax 225-8714; 434 Cannon Bldg. 20515

INTERNET
e-mail: albert.wynn@mail.house.gov
web: www.house.gov/wynn

COMMITTEES
Energy & Commerce

HOMETOWN
Largo

BORN
Sept. 10, 1951, Philadelphia, Pa.

RELIGION
Baptist

FAMILY
Divorced; one child

EDUCATION
U. of Pittsburgh, B.S. 1973; Howard U., attended 1973-74; Georgetown U., J.D. 1977

CAREER
Lawyer

POLITICAL HIGHLIGHTS
Md. House, 1983-87; Md. Senate, 1987-93

ELECTION RESULTS

2000 GENERAL
Albert R. Wynn (D)	172,624	87.2%
John B. Kimble (R)	24,973	12.6%

2000 PRIMARY
Albert R. Wynn (D)	60,873	88.1%
E. Richard Rosenthal (D)	8,217	11.9%

1998 GENERAL
Albert R. Wynn (D)	129,139	85.7%
John B. Kimble (R)	21,518	14.3%

PREVIOUS WINNING PERCENTAGES
1996 (85%); 1994 (75%); 1992 (75%)

A staunch party loyalist, Wynn gravitated to politics early in life. He won his first elective office when he was in seventh grade and followed that with other student government posts; after college, he entered Democratic Party politics and spent 10 years in the state legislature before coming to Congress in 1993.

He is an intense, high-energy politician, who enhanced his stature in Maryland politics and gained national attention with his backing of Democrat Parris N. Glendening for a second term as governor in 1998. Glendening had party-unity problems, losing the support of two top black politicians — the Baltimore mayor and the Prince George's county executive. Wynn, however, stood by the governor, criticizing the defectors as well as the challenger, GOP candidate Ellen R. Sauerbrey. The congressman organized a massive get-out-the-vote campaign in Prince George's County on Election Day, which helped Glendening score a surprisingly decisive victory.

Wynn's loyalty was rewarded by national Democrats in his own re-election bid in 2000: President Clinton made a public school visit with him in the 4th District and Vice President Al Gore came to an October fundraiser for the congressman.

Wynn has a much-sought-after seat on the Energy and Commerce Committee, and he chairs the Congressional Black Caucus' minority business task force. In the 106th Congress, he was the Black Caucus representative to the Democratic Leadership Council — an extended leadership group that includes representatives of Democratic groups such as the conservative "Blue Dogs," the liberal Progressive Caucus and the Women's Caucus. He also is one of 10 deputy whips and serves on the Message Group, a collection of Democrats who meet frequently to develop a cohesive Democratic strategy to present to voters.

Wynn ran for vice chairman of the Democratic Caucus in the 106th Congress but was unable to broaden his base of support much beyond the Black Caucus; his 50 votes placed him third, behind Robert Menendez of New Jersey and Cal Dooley of California.

On the Commerce panel, Wynn got involved in the 106th in the debate over electricity regulation, offering a bill to ensure the continued reliability of the nation's electric power grid in the context of deregulation. He also took part in the effort to win funds for a new Interstate 95 bridge over the Potomac River, seeking to speed up the resolution of environmental concerns. And Wynn worked on efforts to aid minority-owned small businesses.

The 4th District is the first black-majority district to be dominated by middle-class suburbanites. Because the 4th ranks in the top 20 percent of all districts in terms of college graduates and per capita income, Wynn's constituents' priorities differ from those of the residents of many other black-majority districts. Many of his constituents are small-businessmen whose firms do business with the federal government, and Wynn finds that he is more pro-business than many of his Black Caucus colleagues.

Wynn's district, which surrounds the nation's capital to the north, east and south, is home to more federal employees than any other congressional district in the nation — many of them working in well-paying managerial positions. When congressional Republicans and President Clinton failed to agree on budget priorities in 1995, the resulting partial federal government shutdown had a big impact in the 4th, keeping thousands of Wynn's constituents from reporting for work. He laid the blame at the Republicans' feet.

"My constituents ... are being treated to a sorry spectacle — a bunch of opinionated stuffed shirts sitting around bickering while they are getting paid, while people's lives are being disrupted, and while federal employees are losing their paychecks."

Mindful of the 4th's high concentration of minorities and federal workers, Wynn stresses the importance of enforcing anti-discrimination laws in the federal workplace. He has called discrimination in federal agencies "a long-festering sore," and says, "Corporate America cannot be expected to integrate until the federal government does."

Wynn's desire to protect federal workers led him to join with Republican George W. Gekas , R-Pa., to press, unsuccessfully, for passage of legislation to automatically provide funds to keep the government running if Congress and the president failed to enact spending bills by the start of the fiscal year. Wynn was one of only eight Democrats to vote for the proposal in 2000.

Born in Philadelphia, Wynn spent his early years in North Carolina, where his father farmed and his mother taught school. When his father got a job with the Department of Agriculture, the family moved to the District of Columbia, when Wynn was 7, later settling in the Maryland suburbs in Prince George's County. Wynn went to segregated schools until he was in ninth grade. By his senior year, he was elected class president. "I have always been pretty good at mobilizing" a base of support, Wynn recalls.

Wynn excelled at the trombone and was a debater during his college days at the University of Pittsburgh. After getting a law degree from Georgetown, Wynn went back to the old neighborhood and found a job running the Prince George's County Consumer Protection Commission. He immersed himself in local politics, gaining experience by working on other candidates' campaigns.

In 1982, he entered a race for the state legislature. His door-to-door campaigning skills and his party contacts helped him defeat the incumbent.

With 10 years' experience in Annapolis, he was ready to move up. After redistricting created a black-majority district anchored in Prince George's County, Wynn in 1992 moved to take the seat. He focused on the Montgomery County portion of the district, where he was not well-known, and won the Democratic primary with a 1,300-vote margin in crowded field of 13. That was his last big test in the overwhelmingly Democratic 4th.

In 2000, perennial GOP challenger John B. Kimble won the support of Wynn's estranged wife, who tape recorded a message to voters: "Albert Wynn does not respect black women. He left me for a white woman. Please help us defeat Albert Wynn." Wynn nonetheless prevailed, with a hefty 87 percent.

KEY VOTES

2000
Yes Raise hourly minimum wage by $1 over two years
No Halt funding for U.S. mission in Kosovo unless European nations pay more
Yes Provide Medicare benefits to military retirees and their dependents
No Grant China permanent normal trade status
Yes Phase out estate, gift and trust taxes
No Prohibit implementation of president's national monument designations
No Approve GOP plan to provide prescription drug coverage for Medicare beneficiaries
Yes Increase help for poor nations indebted to international financial institutions

1999
Yes Impose steel import quotas
No Kill proposal to take aviation trust funds off budget
No Require background checks on buyers only at gun shows with 10 or more vendors
Yes Remove barriers among banking, securities and insurance companies
Yes Authorize state grants to hire teachers and reduce class size
Yes Overhaul campaign finance law; ban "soft money" and restrict advocacy advertising
Yes Approve bipartisan plan to increase rights of patients in managed-care health plans

INTEREST GROUPS

	AFL-CIO	ADA	CCUS	ACU
2000	100%	85%	57%	12%
1999	89%	100%	22%	4%
1998	100%	100%	33%	4%
1997	100%	90%	40%	4%

CQ VOTE STUDIES

	PARTY UNITY		PRESIDENTIAL SUPPORT	
	Support	Oppose	Support	Oppose
2000	95%	5%	84%	16%
1999	91%	9%	82%	18%
1998	93%	7%	83%	17%
1997	88%	12%	75%	25%

MARYLAND 4

Inner Prince George's County; Silver Spring

The only suburban district in the nation with a black majority, the 4th includes Washington's eastern suburbs in Prince George's County and the southeastern corner of Montgomery County, north of the city. Democrats have a strong hold on the district's largely middle-class, black population.

The 4th's thriving economy is built on small business and the spillover of high-tech firms from Montgomery County and Northern Virginia. The district includes major parts of the Prince George's County High Tech Triangle, home to companies such as Raytheon and anchored by the University of Maryland and NASA (both in the 5th). Prince George's County is one of the leading areas in the nation for black business formation, home ownership and education. Many of its residents are federal employees who have made the exodus from the city.

Along with hosting FedEx Field, home of the professional football Washington Redskins, the district shares the city's problems of drug trafficking and violent crime in many of its low-income areas, located inside the Capital Beltway that surrounds Washington.

The district's black-majority population in Prince George's County votes mostly Democratic. Thirty percent of the 4th resides in southeastern Montgomery County, stretching north from Silver Spring, which contains a larger white and Hispanic population.

MAJOR INDUSTRY
Retail grocery, computers, recreation

MILITARY BASES
Andrews Air Force Base, 4,400 military, 1,300 civilian; Adelphi Army Research Laboratory, 20 military, 880 civilian (2001)

CITIES
Silver Spring (unincorporated) (pt.) 52,068 (1990); Oxon Hill-Glassmanor (unincorporated) 35,794 (1990); Suitland-Silver Hill (unincorporated) 35,111 (1990); Fort Washington (unincorporated), 24,032; Takoma Park, 19,012

UNUSUAL FEATURES
Air Force One kept at Andrews Air Force Base.

Rep. Steny H. Hoyer (D)

Elected May 1981; 10th full term

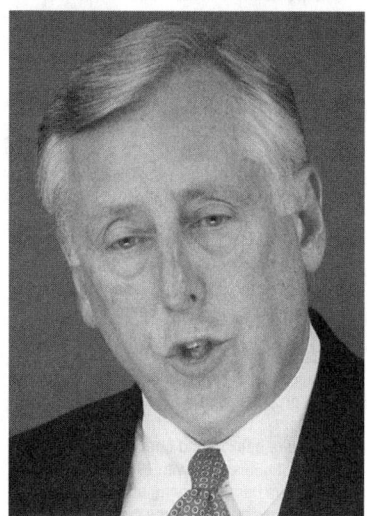

CAPITOL OFFICE
225-4131; fax 225-4300
1705 Longworth Bldg. 20515

INTERNET
e-mail: www.house.gov/writerep
web: www.house.gov/hoyer

COMMITTEES
Appropriations
House Administration - ranking member
Joint Printing

HOMETOWN
Mechanicsville

BORN
June 14, 1939, Manhattan, N.Y.

RELIGION
Baptist

FAMILY
Widowed; three children

EDUCATION
U. of Maryland, B.S. 1963; Georgetown U., J.D. 1966

CAREER
Lawyer

POLITICAL HIGHLIGHTS
Md. Senate, 1967-79 (president, 1975-79); sought Democratic nomination for lieutenant governor, 1978; Md. Board of Higher Education, 1978-81

ELECTION RESULTS

2000 GENERAL
Steny H. Hoyer (D)	166,231	65.1%
Thomas E. Hutchins (R)	89,019	34.9%

2000 PRIMARY
Steny H. Hoyer (D)	46,599	80.7%
Bruce M. Ross (D)	11,163	19.3%

1998 GENERAL
Steny H. Hoyer (D)	126,792	65.4%
Robert B. Ostrom (R)	67,176	34.6%

PREVIOUS WINNING PERCENTAGES
1996 (57%); 1994 (59%); 1992 (53%); 1990 (81%); 1988 (79%); 1986 (82%); 1984 (72%); 1982 (80%); 1981 Special Election (55%)

A polished and experienced legislator whose smoothly coiffed hair falls as neatly as his immaculate business suits, Hoyer looks and acts the part of the natural-born politician, and he knows how to work the legislative system to maximum advantage. Always ready with a handshake and a broad smile, Hoyer can nonetheless be a tough negotiator and has a reputation for working across party lines both publicly and privately to accomplish parochial and broad policy goals.

For most of his life, Hoyer has been tagged as a "rising star," and even though he is now in his 60s and has taken on a variety of legislative, institutional and party duties in the House, he still has the energetic, confident and ambitious manner of somebody who is on his way somewhere. Selected in 1963 as the University of Maryland's "Outstanding Male Graduate," he went on to prove his mettle shortly after he graduated from Georgetown Law School with his election at age 27 to the Maryland Senate, where he later served as its youngest-ever president.

After a brief stumble in a statewide bid in 1978, Hoyer rebounded in 1981 to win a special election to replace Democratic Rep. Gladys Noon Spellman, who had suffered a heart attack that left her in a coma. Hoyer's political acumen soon earned him the respect of Democratic leaders, who made him the only freshman member featured in their response to President Reagan's 1982 State of the Union address and awarded him a coveted seat on the powerful Appropriations Committee. By the early 1990s, his skills as an inside operator and his smoothness before the cameras led to talk that Hoyer might be Speaker someday.

Hoyer is still far from that goal, and he has undergone important changes during that meteoric rise. A self-described "John Kennedy Democrat," who came to Congress representing the mostly liberal, heavily Democratic Prince George's County, he began moderating his views after the redistricting of the 1990s, when he was forced to swap a liberal portion of his district for conservative Southern Maryland. Since then, reaching out to moderates both in his own party and among Republican ranks has become a hallmark of Hoyer's style.

He is both an insider who can work backrooms and a consummate politician who can translate his goals into stark terms that make good sound bites. As the highest-ranking Democrat on Appropriations' Treasury, Postal Service and General Government Subcommittee, he fights relentlessly for the federal workers who make up a large voting bloc in his district. He has won pay raises and lower retirement contribution rates for them in recent years.

A strong proponent of abortion rights, Hoyer has argued vigorously against the conservative-backed policy that prohibits federal employees' health care plans from providing coverage for most abortions.

Hoyer's sometimes passionate, podium-thumping style can draw criticism from opponents, but supporters praise his meticulous attention to legislation and his talent for communicating his message. Those latter qualities have endeared him to House Democrats, whom he has represented as a deputy whip, as Democratic Caucus chairman and currently as a member of the Democratic Steering Committee, which makes the party's committee assignments. In the 2000 campaign cycle, Hoyer's political action committee, AmeriPAC, contributed more than $600,000 to the campaigns of fellow Democrats.

He waged a race against California Democrat Nancy Pelosi in 2000 for the chance to be majority whip if the Democrats took back the House in the

107th Congress and the whip position came open. Hoyer displayed his characteristic political drive in early 2001, as he continued campaigning for the post of Democratic whip amid rumors that David E. Bonior of Michigan — who beat Hoyer for the spot in 1991 — might leave to run for governor.

Hoyer works hard to distance himself from the stereotype that Democrats favor big government and bloated spending, faulting that philosophy for his party's loss of the House in 1994. "Too many Americans believed that our party had become weak on crime and national defense, incapable of making hard decisions on welfare reform and fiscal policy, and irrevocably wedded to the idea that all of our problems could be solved by government and more spending," Hoyer told a gathering of the centrist Democratic Leadership Council in 2000. Instead, he said, he favors "a streamlined but activist government ... that works with the private sector to create opportunities and solve problems."

Hoyer, who often partners with Republicans on the Appropriations panel to secure funding for his highest priorities, also reached out to the GOP during the 106th Congress on such issues as education, where he supported an "Ed-Flex" bill, which returned to states some discretion over spending federal education funds, and legislation to increase the number of H1-B visas available for foreign workers, especially in the technology field.

But for all his enthusiasm for bipartisanship and free trade, Hoyer takes liberal stances on many social issues, making him popular with organized labor and environmental advocates. He uses his rhetorical skills to throw verbal daggers at Republican proposals he feels ignore core social needs.

"This bill deserves an F, for failure to fund," he said in 2000 of a GOP-crafted education, labor and health spending bill that fell some $1.8 billion short of President Clinton's request. "It does not even begin to address the priorities of this nation." Hoyer sought to add funds for programs such as after-school care, Head Start, and child care and educational services for disadvantaged children, but Republicans did not permit a vote on the proposal.

As the ranking Democrat on the House Administration Committee, Hoyer also spends considerable time and energy looking out for general House operations. He was instrumental in 2000 in bringing to light continuing fire safety violations in the Capitol complex.

After a string of easy general-election victories in the 1980s, Hoyer became the target of strong Republican challenges when the 1990s remapping gave the 5th District a more conservative tilt. Beginning in 1992, he got less than 60 percent of the vote three times, but in 1998 and 2000, he returned to comfortable victory margins.

KEY VOTES

2000
Yes Raise hourly minimum wage by $1 over two years
No   Halt funding for U.S. mission in Kosovo unless European nations pay more
Yes Provide Medicare benefits to military retirees and their dependents
Yes Grant China permanent normal trade status
No   Phase out estate, gift and trust taxes
No   Prohibit implementation of president's national monument designations
No   Approve GOP plan to provide prescription drug coverage for Medicare beneficiaries
Yes Increase help for poor nations indebted to international financial institutions

1999
Yes Impose steel import quotas
Yes Kill proposal to take aviation trust funds off budget
No   Require background checks on buyers only at gun shows with 10 or more vendors
Yes Remove barriers among banking, securities and insurance companies
Yes Authorize state grants to hire teachers and reduce class size
Yes Overhaul campaign finance law; ban "soft money" and restrict advocacy advertising
Yes Approve bipartisan plan to increase rights of patients in managed-care health plans

INTEREST GROUPS

	AFL-CIO	ADA	CCUS	ACU
2000	90%	80%	47%	12%
1999	89%	90%	20%	8%
1998	100%	95%	28%	4%
1997	100%	85%	40%	12%

CQ VOTE STUDIES

	PARTY UNITY		PRESIDENTIAL SUPPORT	
	Support	Oppose	Support	Oppose
2000	93%	7%	90%	10%
1999	89%	11%	82%	18%
1998	89%	11%	81%	19%
1997	85%	15%	76%	24%

MARYLAND 5
Outer Prince George's County; Southern Maryland

The 5th includes the less urban parts of Prince George's County, southern Anne Arundel County and the three rapidly growing southern counties of Charles, Calvert and St. Mary's. The mix of liberals in Prince George's County and conservatives throughout the rest of the district sometimes makes the 5th a competitive seat.

Prince George's County, which accounts for almost half of the district's population, includes many liberal black communities and College Park, home of the University of Maryland's main campus. "P.G." County, as some locals call it, was the only county in the district to back Bill Clinton in 1996, allowing Democrats to carry the district. In 2000, Al Gore won both Prince George's County and Charles County, taking the district by 13 percentage points.

The 5th is enjoying a moderate amount of success due to the technology boom. Middle-class residents and technology companies are leaving the Washington metropolitan area for the southern

counties, attracted by the abundance of land and the military presence. The Tri-County area retains its Southern rural character, however, with tobacco as its major crop and a conservative Democratic tradition.

Southern Anne Arundel County, which is mostly rural, contains a mostly upper-class, Republican constituency, yet the longtime Democratic House incumbent, Rep. Hoyer, won this county for the first time in 1998 and repeated that win in 2000.

MAJOR INDUSTRY
Agriculture, high-tech, defense

MILITARY BASES
Patuxent River Naval Air Station, 2,670 military, 6,640 civilian; Naval Surface Warfare Center, 500 military, 2,500 civilian (2000)

CITIES
Bowie, 41,091; St. Charles (unincorporated), 28,717 (1990); College Park, 27,467; Greenbelt, 22,154

UNUSUAL FEATURES
NASA Goddard Space Flight Center.

Rep. Roscoe G. Bartlett (R)

Elected 1992; 5th term

A self-styled citizen-legislator, Bartlett is proud of the calluses on his hands from farm work. He commutes about 50 miles every day from his sheep and goat farm near Frederick to Capitol Hill.

He is also proud of his conservative voting record — he opposed President Clinton more than any member of the House in 1999 — and of his efforts to scale back government and reduce taxes.

The congressman's political philosophy is informed by his strongly held religious beliefs and by his Depression-era upbringing, which leads him to extol self-reliance and personal initiative and denounce the intrusiveness of the federal government.

A former research scientist, teacher and real estate developer, Bartlett says he takes positions based on his experience with the day-to-day challenges of life and not on what others think or whether his views have a chance to prevail. (He backed three candidates for the 2000 GOP presidential nomination, first supporting Dan Quayle, then Steve Forbes and finally George W. Bush after the others had quit the race.)

He teamed with liberal Democrat Edward J. Markey of Massachusetts on a proposal to permit people to invest some of their Social Security money in the stock market. And he is friendly with colorful Ohio Democrat James A. Traficant Jr., who once agreed to appear at a Bartlett campaign fundraiser.

But even though Bartlett sometimes crosses party lines, his overall voting record pleases party leaders — he typically backs the GOP position on about 95 percent of the votes on which the two parties disagree. The septuagenarian is considerably older than many of the conservative young Republican firebrands who joined the House in the 1990s, but he is every bit their equal in ideological fervor. In the 104th Congress, he voted for every item in the House GOP's "Contract With America" legislative agenda.

In the 107th, Bartlett assumed the chairmanship of the Science Committee's Subcommittee on Energy. In the 106th, he chaired the Small Business panel's Government Programs and Oversight Subcommittee, where he sought to reduce regulatory requirements on business and ensure that small firms are able to compete for federal contracts.

On Small Business and on the Armed Services panel, Bartlett pays particular attention to the interests of veterans, including future veterans whose decisions about whether to join or stay in the military are influenced by the benefits that will be available to them when they retire.

A mid-ranking member of Armed Services, Bartlett spent much of the 105th Congress fighting a 1994 Pentagon policy to integrate men and women in housing and basic training. He blamed several high-profile military sex scandals and sexual harassment cases in part on a policy of allowing the sexes to live and train together. He introduced a bill to ban the practice, telling the Hagerstown Herald Mail he would fight against a "powder puff" military.

His support for gun owners' rights leads him to introduce a measure every Congress stipulating in federal law that Americans have the right to use firearms to defend their families and homes. He said his bill is necessary to overturn oppressive state gun control laws and to prevent prosecutors from bringing charges against law-abiding citizens who use guns to defend themselves against criminals. In 2000, he backed the controversial decision by GOP officials in Carroll County, in his district, to raffle off a handgun as a fundraising device. "Crime has nothing to do with guns," he said. "If strict gun control made a place safe, the District of Columbia should be

CAPITOL OFFICE
225-2721; fax 225-2193; 2412 Rayburn Bldg. 20515

INTERNET
e-mail: www.house.gov/writerep
web: www.house.gov/bartlett

COMMITTEES
Armed Services
   (Morale, Welfare & Recreation panel - chairman)
Science
   (Energy - chairman)
Small Business

HOMETOWN
Frederick

BORN
June 3, 1926, Moreland, Ky.

RELIGION
Seventh-Day Adventist

FAMILY
Wife, Ellen Louise Baldwin; 10 children

EDUCATION
Columbia Union College, B.S. 1947; U. of Maryland, M.S. 1948, Ph.D. 1952

CAREER
Real estate developer; scientific research company owner; farmer; biomedical engineer

POLITICAL HIGHLIGHTS
Sought Republican nomination for U.S. Senate, 1980; Republican nominee for U.S. House, 1982

ELECTION RESULTS

2000 GENERAL

Roscoe G. Bartlett (R)	168,624	60.7%
Donald DeArmon (D)	109,136	39.3%

2000 PRIMARY

Roscoe G. Bartlett (R)	57,977	77.8%
Timothy R. Mayberry (R)	16,539	22.2%

1998 GENERAL

Roscoe G. Bartlett (R)	127,802	63.4%
Timothy D. McCown (D)	73,728	36.6%

PREVIOUS WINNING PERCENTAGES
1996 (57%); 1994 (66%); 1992 (54%)

the safest place on the planet," he told The Washington Post.

From his seat on Armed Services, Bartlett has latched onto some attention-grabbing issues. He authored a proposal in 1996 that he said would end the practice of "Uncle Sam subsidizing smut at defense facilities." The measure to bar the sale of "lascivious" magazines or videotapes on military bases was enacted into law as part of that year's defense authorization bill but was later found to be unconstitutional.

Bartlett makes a habit of defending military personnel who run into trouble when they insist on holding out for a principle. He took up the cause of Army Specialist Michael New, a medic who was court-martialed in 1996 for refusing to alter his U.S. Army uniform by wearing a United Nations blue beret and insignia as part of a U.N. peacekeeping mission in Macedonia.

In 1999, he defended an Air Force lieutenant who, citing his religious beliefs, asked not to be teamed with a woman in an isolated missile silo. "Religion is not politically correct. If you are not politically correct, you have no place and no future in today's military," Bartlett observed.

Born on his grandfather's farm in Kentucky, Bartlett saw his father work as a tenant farmer in western Pennsylvania during the Depression era. He originally intended to become a minister but instead pursued a graduate education in physiology at the University of Maryland, eventually earning a master's degree and doctorate.

He taught in both California and Washington, D.C., and did research for the Navy and the National Institutes of Health. He holds 20 patents for his invention of respiratory support and safety devices used by pilots, astronauts and rescue workers and in 1999 was honored for his lifetime services by the American Institute of Aeronautics and Astronautics.

In 1961, Bartlett moved to a dairy farm in Frederick County and continued to work at the Johns Hopkins Applied Physics Laboratory and teach in Frederick. He later entered the home-building business.

He ran unsuccessfully for the House in 1982 but was back a decade later, after closing his home-building firm and leaving his teaching career. He narrowly won a quiet, three-way GOP primary in 1992 and was expecting to face an uphill general-election battle against conservative Democrat Beverly B. Byron, a seven-term incumbent, who had held Bartlett to just 26 percent in 1982. But Byron was upset in the primary by challenger Thomas H. Hattery, and in November, Bartlett capitalized on confusion in Democratic ranks to beat Hattery by 8 points.

He won easy re-election contests in 1996 and 1998 and handily turned back an intraparty challenge in 2000.

KEY VOTES

2000

No	Raise hourly minimum wage by $1 over two years
Yes	Halt funding for U.S. mission in Kosovo unless European nations pay more
Yes	Provide Medicare benefits to military retirees and their dependents
No	Grant China permanent normal trade status
Yes	Phase out estate, gift and trust taxes
Yes	Prohibit implementation of president's national monument designations
Yes	Approve GOP plan to provide prescription drug coverage for Medicare beneficiaries
No	Increase help for poor nations indebted to international financial institutions

1999

Yes	Impose steel import quotas
No	Kill proposal to take aviation trust funds off budget
Yes	Require background checks on buyers only at gun shows with 10 or more vendors
Yes	Remove barriers among banking, securities and insurance companies
No	Authorize state grants to hire teachers and reduce class size
No	Overhaul campaign finance law; ban "soft money" and restrict advocacy advertising
No	Approve bipartisan plan to increase rights of patients in managed-care health plans

INTEREST GROUPS

	AFL-CIO	ADA	CCUS	ACU
2000	10%	5%	71%	100%
1999	33%	10%	84%	96%
1998	10%	5%	78%	100%
1997	0%	5%	90%	100%

CQ VOTE STUDIES

	PARTY UNITY		PRESIDENTIAL SUPPORT	
	Support	Oppose	Support	Oppose
2000	97%	3%	17%	83%
1999	94%	6%	9%	91%
1998	95%	5%	19%	81%
1997	96%	4%	27%	73%

MARYLAND 6

Central and West — Frederick; Hagerstown

The 6th includes the state's five western counties — Garrett, Allegany, Washington, Frederick and Carroll — and more than half the population of Howard County. The 6th has a rural tradition and a conservative bent that often benefit the GOP. Although its eastern counties are thriving economically, the demise of old-line industry has left the Appalachian Mountain area struggling.

Frederick, Carroll and Howard counties are experiencing rapid growth from new residents escaping the city and inner suburbs and commuting to Baltimore and Washington. Carroll County, however, still has an agricultural economy and remains a Republican stronghold.

Howard County has experienced a large influx of technology firms, attracting younger voters who have begun to displace old-line conservative Democrats. Republican Rep. Bartlett won the 6th in 1992 after a conservative Democrat who had represented the district for 14 years was defeated in his primary.

The three western counties are less populous but solidly conservative. Washington County, with its strong manufacturing base, is the only one experiencing economic prosperity. With companies such as Kelly-Springfield closing their operations, Allegany and Garrett counties are both struggling and are now dependent on tourism for the bulk of their jobs.

MAJOR INDUSTRY
Manufacturing, high-tech, agriculture

MILITARY BASES
Fort Detrick (Army), 1,280 military, 4,981 civilian (2000)

CITIES
Frederick, 48,710; Ellicott City (unincorporated) (pt.), 41,233 (1990); Hagerstown, 34,611; Cumberland, 22,615

UNUSUAL FEATURES
Presidential retreat Camp David; Whittaker Chambers' pumpkin patch produced evidence for Richard Nixon during the Alger Hiss trial.

Rep. Elijah E. Cummings (D)

Elected April 1996; 3rd full term

CAPITOL OFFICE
225-4741; fax 225-3178
1632 Longworth Bldg. 20515

INTERNET
e-mail: www.house.gov/writerep
web: www.house.gov/cummings

COMMITTEES
Government Reform
Transportation & Infrastructure

HOMETOWN
Baltimore

BORN
Jan. 18, 1951, Baltimore, Md.

RELIGION
Baptist

FAMILY
Separated; three children

EDUCATION
Howard U., B.A. 1973; U. of Maryland, J.D. 1976

CAREER
Lawyer

POLITICAL HIGHLIGHTS
Md. House, 1983-96 (speaker pro tempore, 1995)

ELECTION RESULTS

2000 GENERAL
Elijah E. Cummings (D)	134,066	87.1%
Kenneth Kondner (R)	19,773	12.8%

2000 PRIMARY
Elijah E. Cummings (D)	unopposed

1998 GENERAL
Elijah E. Cummings (D)	112,699	85.7%
Kenneth Kondner (R)	18,742	14.3%

PREVIOUS WINNING PERCENTAGES
1996 (84%); 1996 Special Election (81%)

Cummings works against difficult odds to help his constituents in Baltimore's black-majority and overwhelmingly Democratic 7th District hold their inner-city neighborhoods together. And along with his attention to his constituents' needs, Cummings has faced his own difficulties.

He has been a public official for almost two decades, but his political successes have been marred by economic hardships. Owing thousands of dollars in back taxes and other debts when he arrived at the Capitol, the congressman warded off foreclosure proceedings on his house and spent two winters without heat because he couldn't afford to fix his furnace.

He blamed his shaky financial condition on a number of reasons that dated back many years — starting his own law firm, trying to support three children, lacking car insurance when he got into an accident — but he told the Baltimore Sun in 1999 that he had finally paid off most of his debts. "I have a moral conscience that is real central," he told The Sun. "I didn't ask the federal government or anyone else to do me any favors."

A Baltimore native, Cummings was one of seven children in a working-class family. His mother and father had migrated from South Carolina where they were sharecroppers, and he recalls that "as a young boy in south Baltimore ... we did not have many opportunities. We did not play on grass. We played on asphalt." But he says he was set on a productive course by "two very strong parents," who scrimped and saved to buy their own home in a city neighborhood that was integrating.

Cummings pursues a strongly liberal course in the House, and he paints a vivid picture of the problems his constituents face, hoping to persuade the Republican-controlled Congress to lend a hand. He says communities in the 7th need lots of federal assistance to combat illegal drugs and violent crime, improve education and health care, and stimulate economic development that will put the unemployed to work. To that end, Cummings in 1999 introduced a bill to permanently authorize Healthy Start, a block grant program to aid mothers and infants. He also urged his colleagues to appropriate more money for domestic drug treatment programs instead of battling drug smuggling from countries such as Colombia. "Let me tell you something: If you don't have a demand [for drugs], you don't have to worry about Colombia," he said.

Cummings sits on the Government Reform Committee, where he is the ranking Democrat on the Criminal Justice, Drug Policy and Human Resources Subcommittee, and he has worked amicably with the GOP leadership on issues affecting federal workers and retirees. In the 105th Congress, he worked on legislation to revise regulations governing federal civil service jobs, including new restrictions on the employment of people who have been convicted of drug offenses.

In the 106th, Cummings won passage of a bill to give more paid leave to federal employees who donate bone marrow or organs. He said he hoped the legislation, intended to give federal employees adequate time to recover from such a procedure, would also encourage other public and private employers to provide similar benefits. He also won passage of a bill to enable a court to order federal workers to provide health insurance for their children.

Elected vice chairman of the Congressional Black Caucus in the 107th Congress, Cummings has fought hard for legislation to help minorities. He opposed Republican attempts to pare back programs that steer federal transportation contracts to companies owned by blacks, other minorities and women. He also cosponsored legislation in 1999 to direct the Justice Department to study traffic stop patterns to determine whether police target drivers based on race. "Thousands of people of color are the victims of DWB — driving while black," he said.

From his seat on the Transportation Committee, Cummings found common ground with the panel's former chairman, Republican Bud Shuster of Pennsylvania. In the 105th Congress, he concurred with Shuster's desire to spend more on transportation projects than the 1997 balanced-budget agreement had called for. Road-building, Cummings thinks, could offer the unemployed a chance for a paycheck.

Steering federal dollars to the 7th is a big priority for Cummings. In 1997, he had a hand in securing grants for a range of endeavors — making missile components for the Navy, improving public housing, providing more community policing, reducing infant mortality and establishing a technology center in Baltimore funded by the Department of Commerce and private foundations. "African-Americans, historically concentrated in agriculture, personal service and blue-collar occupations, are now disproportionately displaced in the emerging Information Age," Cummings has said. "Technological literacy is essential to succeed in the new economy."

When he served in the Maryland House, Cummings earned a reputation as a skilled consensus builder. But there he was part of a Democratic majority. In the Republican-run Congress, the point of consensus on most issues is well to the right of where Cummings stands, and often he can do little more than protest passage of bills he opposes. Back home in Baltimore, Cummings looks for ways to improve the lot of his constituents without relying on congressional action. He hosts job fairs. He organizes seminars to help constituents learn about various college aid programs. And he hosts an annual "How To Do Business With The Government" fair to help small businesses participate in the government procurement process.

Displaying his political skills at a young age, Cummings was president of his high school senior class. He graduated Phi Beta Kappa from Howard University and earned a law degree from the University of Maryland in 1976. Six years later, he was elected to the state House. During 13 years there, he rose to the chamber's second-ranking position, speaker pro tempore — the highest state office ever held by a black Maryland lawmaker. In 1996, he outpaced a field of 26 other Democrats and five Republicans to replace Democratic Rep. Kweisi Mfume, who resigned from the House to become president of the NAACP. In the overwhelmingly Democratic 7th District, his November election tally has never dropped below 80 percent.

KEY VOTES

2000

Yes Raise hourly minimum wage by $1 over two years

No Halt funding for U.S. mission in Kosovo unless European nations pay more

Yes Provide Medicare benefits to military retirees and their dependents

No Grant China permanent normal trade status

No Phase out estate, gift and trust taxes

No Prohibit implementation of president's national monument designations

No Approve GOP plan to provide prescription drug coverage for Medicare beneficiaries

+ Increase help for poor nations indebted to international financial institutions

1999

Yes Impose steel import quotas

No Kill proposal to take aviation trust funds off budget

No Require background checks on buyers only at gun shows with 10 or more vendors

No Remove barriers among banking, securities and insurance companies

Yes Authorize state grants to hire teachers and reduce class size

Yes Overhaul campaign finance law; ban "soft money" and restrict advocacy advertising

Yes Approve bipartisan plan to increase rights of patients in managed-care health plans

INTEREST GROUPS

	AFL-CIO	ADA	CCUS	ACU
2000	100%	85%	47%	4%
1999	89%	100%	21%	0%
1998	100%	100%	28%	4%
1997	100%	100%	30%	4%

CQ VOTE STUDIES

	PARTY UNITY		PRESIDENTIAL SUPPORT	
	Support	Oppose	Support	Oppose
2000	97%	3%	88%	12%
1999	98%	2%	85%	15%
1998	95%	5%	83%	17%
1997	94%	6%	77%	23%

MARYLAND 7

Inner-city Baltimore; western Baltimore County

The 7th includes the low-income neighborhoods of West Baltimore and follows the black migration west to include Baltimore County's middle-class, southwestern suburbs. The district's black majority gives Democrats a distinct advantage in both national and local contests.

The vast majority of the district's population resides in the city. Efforts to improve Baltimore's poor neighborhoods have been slow and urban problems, such as crime, drug abuse, teen pregnancy and unemployment, have prompted many of the city's middle-class residents to head to the suburbs.

But the picture within the city is not all bleak. Just north of the downtown business district is the gentrified Mount Vernon area, home of the Walters Art Gallery and the Peabody Music Academy. Farther north are Johns Hopkins University and the Baltimore Museum of Art.

Though overshadowed by Harborplace, the old retail section west of

the downtown hub still survives; the Lexington Food Market and Baltimore Arena are here. There are middle-class black communities along Liberty Heights Road in West Baltimore.

Black residents have a strong presence in the suburbs, even though the portion of Baltimore County in the 7th is about three-fifths white. The University of Maryland Baltimore County (UMBC) in Catonsville is located in the district, and its adjacent research area is attracting technology firms.

MAJOR INDUSTRY

Health care, manufacturing, technology

CITIES

Baltimore (pt.), 470,075 (1990); Catonsville (unincorporated) (pt.), 35,233 (1990); Woodlawn (unincorporated), 32,907 (1990)

UNUSUAL FEATURES

NAACP National Headquarters located in Baltimore; Great Blacks in Wax Museum celebrates significant achievements of black Americans.

Rep. Constance A. Morella (R)

Elected 1986; 8th term

CAPITOL OFFICE
225-5341; fax 225-1389; 2228 Rayburn Bldg. 20515

INTERNET
e-mail: rep.morella@mail.house.gov
web: www.house.gov/morella

COMMITTEES
Government Reform
  (District of Columbia - chairwoman)
Science

HOMETOWN
Bethesda

BORN
Feb. 12, 1931, Somerville, Mass.

RELIGION
Roman Catholic

FAMILY
Husband, Anthony C. Morella; nine children

EDUCATION
Boston U., B.A. 1954; American U., M.A. 1967

CAREER
Professor

POLITICAL HIGHLIGHTS
Candidate for Md. House, 1974; Md. House, 1979-87; sought Republican nomination for U.S. House, 1980

ELECTION RESULTS

2000 GENERAL

Constance A. Morella (R)	156,241	52.0%
Terry Lierman (D)	136,840	45.5%
Brian D. Saunders (CNSTP)	7,017	2.3%

2000 PRIMARY

Constance A. Morella (R)	unopposed

1998 GENERAL

Constance A. Morella (R)	133,145	60.3%
Ralph G. Neas (D)	87,497	39.6%

PREVIOUS WINNING PERCENTAGES
1996 (61%); 1994 (70%); 1992 (73%); 1990 (74%); 1988 (63%); 1986 (53%)

Despite being the House Republican with the least-loyal voting record in recent years, Morella remains tolerated, if not appreciated, by the Republican Party. GOP leaders are aware that, were it not for Morella's independent-minded, sometimes liberal voting record, they would likely lose her seat representing the affluent, Democratic-leaning Maryland suburbs of Washington, D.C. Her style is to help fellow Republicans when she can and to avoid rubbing salt in their wounds when she cannot.

The self-effacing, Shakespeare-quoting former community college English professor brings a personal note to many of the issues she embraces, especially women's health. These include the fight for a cure for breast cancer, which claimed the life of Morella's sister, Mary, in 1977. Morella and her husband, Anthony, a law professor, became guardians of Mary's six children and raised them with their own three children. Morella has quipped that her greatest feat thus far has been getting nine children through driver's education. An opera fan, she supports funding for the arts, noting her fantasy would be to sing the role of Mimi in "La Bohème."

Morella's pet issues range from the basic — such as increased spending on children's hospitals and programs to combat violence against women — to the more controversial, including a focus on domestic violence prevention and support for abortion rights. She opposes a ban on a procedure its opponents call "partial birth" abortion and has lobbied unsuccessfully to restore the U.S. contribution to the United Nations Fund for Population Activities, which conservatives have accused of supporting coercive family planning programs in China. She also has advocated providing unrestricted access to reproductive health clinics.

Morella was one of only nine House Republicans who did not support former Speaker Newt Gingrich, who faced an ethics investigation, when he sought re-election to that post at the opening of the 105th Congress. In 1998, Morella and only three other Republicans opposed all four articles of impeachment against President Clinton. Morella said Clinton would be remembered for "his sordid behavior and his failure to take responsibility for that behavior," but added it would be wrong to put the country through the turmoil and tumult of an impeachment trial.

While House leaders, mindful of the need to corral every GOP vote to ensure majority action, treat Morella with respect, they have not given her first-tier committee assignments. Still, the jurisdictions fit with the needs of her district.

She chaired the Science panel's Technology Subcommittee for six years, where she weighed in on issues of importance to the district's high-tech companies, as well as its huge government research institutions, which include the National Institutes of Health, the Food and Drug Administration and the National Institute for Standards and Technology. Morella and California Republican Steve Horn are credited with being among the first to warn of the potential vulnerability of computer software to the Y2K computer problem. Morella criticized the federal government for taking a lackadaisical approach in the matter.

In the 107th Congress, Morella took the reins of the Government Reform Committee's District of Columbia Subcommittee. The 8th District forms the northwest border of the District of Columbia, and the well-being of the city is of vital interest to her constituents.

In the past, while the full committee had been consumed with probes of alleged Clinton administration wrongdoing, Morella's seat on the panel's Civil Service Subcommittee proved to be a good post for a lawmaker whose constituents include a large number of federal employees. Morella fought elements of the 1995 GOP tax cut package that would have increased federal workers' contributions to their pension plans, and she later backed a higher cap on maximum federal contributions to the Thrift Savings Plan, a popular federal pension program. She successfully crafted language allowing federal agencies to subsidize daycare costs for low-income federal employees and has fought several GOP proposals to curb coverage of abortion services in federal workers' health plans.

She has fought for several pro-family issues, including use of child safety restraints in vehicles, child care tax credits for lower- and middle-income families, and a tougher line on enforcement of child support.

It is no surprise that Morella, as a former educator married to a college professor, also has strongly supported educational initiatives, including improved training and development for teachers and the creation of special savings accounts for educational use. Funds she has helped snare for her district include a $1.8 million technology grant for its public schools and a $3 million grant for magnet school programs. She also has pressured the Federal Communications Commission to require broadcasters to air more educational programs for children.

Morella's first taste of public life came in the early 1970s when she was appointed to a local commission for women. In that role she pushed to ensure that women could apply for credit without a spouse's signature.

She was involved in environmental and social issues during her eight years in the Maryland House, but the biggest factor in her 1986 victory for the open 8th District seat was her vivacious personality. She played up her family's immigrant heritage and her working-class upbringing, defeating Democratic state Sen. Stewart Bainum with 53 percent.

Morella's pleasant demeanor and independence from the conservative House GOP party line have enabled her to hold on to the otherwise strongly Democratic 8th District, generally winning re-election by comfortable margins. In 2000, however, she was hard-pressed to post a 6-point victory over Democrat Terry Lierman, whose campaign focused on the nationwide effort by Democrats to take back control of the House.

Her personal popularity has made her an oft-mentioned potential candidate for statewide office. However, she passed up challenges to Democratic Sen. Paul S. Sarbanes in 1994 and in 2000, citing her desire to continue to build seniority in the House.

KEY VOTES

2000
Yes Raise hourly minimum wage by $1 over two years
Yes Halt funding for U.S. mission in Kosovo unless European nations pay more
Yes Provide Medicare benefits to military retirees and their dependents
Yes Grant China permanent normal trade status
Yes Phase out estate, gift and trust taxes
No   Prohibit implementation of president's national monument designations
No   Approve GOP plan to provide prescription drug coverage for Medicare beneficiaries
Yes Increase help for poor nations indebted to international financial institutions

1999
No   Impose steel import quotas
Yes Kill proposal to take aviation trust funds off budget
No   Require background checks on buyers only at gun shows with 10 or more vendors
Yes Remove barriers among banking, securities and insurance companies
Yes Authorize state grants to hire teachers and reduce class size
Yes Overhaul campaign finance law; ban "soft money" and restrict advocacy advertising
Yes Approve bipartisan plan to increase rights of patients in managed-care health plans

INTEREST GROUPS

	AFL-CIO	ADA	CCUS	ACU
2000	50%	60%	71%	29%
1999	56%	80%	42%	12%
1998	70%	65%	56%	20%
1997	38%	65%	90%	20%

CQ VOTE STUDIES

	PARTY UNITY		PRESIDENTIAL SUPPORT	
	Support	Oppose	Support	Oppose
2000	50%	50%	63%	37%
1999	49%	51%	68%	32%
1998	40%	60%	71%	29%
1997	58%	42%	73%	27%

MARYLAND 8
Montgomery County

The 8th contains the northwestern Washington suburbs. Montgomery County, one of the nation's most affluent, leans Democratic but is winnable by liberal Republicans. The district's educated professionals help it thrive.

Although the suburbs just outside Washington contain mostly upper-income residents, the county's fastest-growing areas are the middle-income neighborhoods further north. Population growth has been spurred by development of the Interstate 270 "technology corridor," a hotbed for high-tech and biotechnology companies.

While Republican Rep. Morella has held the congressional seat since 1986, Democrats dominate local politics and have maintained a hold on the presidential contests. In 1992 and '96, Bill Clinton easily carried the county, and in 2000 Al Gore handily won the district by 24 percentage points. Voters, who include a large number of government employees, seek a socially conscious, fiscally conservative representative.

In the far northern and western areas of the county, officials struggle to preserve an agricultural heritage in an area with more conservative, Republican voting habits. The near-in suburbs include some working-class and low-income areas, home to many of the district's minorities.

MAJOR INDUSTRY
Technology, government, agriculture

MILITARY BASES
National Imagery and Mapping Agency, Bethesda, 4,500 (1998); National Naval Medical Center, 3,721 military, 1,025 civilian; Naval Surface Warfare Center, Carderock Division, 7 military, 1,700 civilian (2001)

CITIES
Bethesda (unincorporated), 62,936 (1990); Wheaton-Glenmont (unincorporated), 53,720 (1990); Gaithersburg, 48,395; Rockville, 48,160

UNUSUAL FEATURES
Author F. Scott Fitzgerald's gravesite in Rockville; Wheaton Metro station contains the longest escalator in the Northern Hemisphere – 230 feet.

Gov. Jane Swift (R)

First elected: Assumed office April 10, 2001, following the resignation of Gov. Paul Cellucci, R, who resigned to become U.S. ambassador to Canada

Length of term: 4 years

Term expires: 1/03

Salary: $135,000

Phone: (617) 727-6250

Hometown: Williamstown

Born: Feb. 24, 1965; North Adams, Mass.

Religion: Roman Catholic

Family: Husband, Chuck Hunt; one child

Education: Trinity College, B.A. 1987

Career: State consumer affairs director; state legislative aide

Political highlights: Mass. Senate, 1991-97; Republican nominee for U.S. House, 1996; lieutenant governor, 1999-2001

(The lieutenant governor position, left vacant by Lt. Gov. Swift, will not be filled until the 2002 election.)

STATE LEGISLATURE

General Court: Meeting time varies; usually year-round

House: 160 members, 2-year terms

2001 breakdown: 23R, 135D, 2 vacancies; 121 men, 37 women

Salary: $50,122

Phone: (617) 722-2356

Senate: 40 members, 2-year terms

2001 breakdown: 6R, 34D; 28 men, 12 women

Salary: $50,122

Phone: (617) 722-1276

STATE TERM LIMITS

Governor: 2 terms

Senate: No

House: No

URBAN STATISTICS

CITY	POPULATION
Boston	555,249
Worcester	167,132
Springfield	147,216
Lowell	101,103
New Bedford	94,780

REGISTERED VOTERS

Unenrolled	49%
Democrat	36%
Republican	14%

POPULATION

2000 population	6,349,097
1990 population	6,016,425
Percent change	+5.5%
Rank among states	13

Median age	35.8
Born in state	69%
Foreign born	10%
Urban/rural	84%/16%
Crime rate	644/100,000
Poverty level	8.7%
Federal workers	54,691
Military	24,278

REAPPORTIONMENT

Massachusetts retained its 10 House seats in reapportionment. The state legislature will draw new district lines in 2001.

MISCELLANEOUS

Web: www.state.ma.us

Capital: Boston

Land area: 7,838 sq. miles
Rank among states: 45

STATE ELECTION OFFICIAL
(617) 727-2828

DEMOCRATIC HEADQUARTERS
(617) 742-6770

REPUBLICAN HEADQUARTERS
(617) 423-2000

District Statistics

DIST.	D	2000 R	GREEN	D	1996 R	REF	D	1992 R	I	WHT	BLK	ASIAN	HISP	HOUSEHOLD INCOME	OVER 65+	UNDER 18	COLLEGE EDUCATION
1	57%	33%	9%	61%	26%	12%	48%	27%	25%	94%	2%	1%	5%	$31,903	14%	24%	21%
2	58	34	6	61	28	11	46	29	25	90	6	1	6	$33,401	14	24	19
3	58	35	6	60	30	10	45	31	23	95	2	2	4	$36,873	14	24	24
4	63	30	5	64	26	9	51	27	22	94	2	2	2	$39,005	14	23	31
5	56	36	6	58	31	10	42	32	26	90	2	4	8	$42,701	10	26	29
6	57	36	6	59	31	9	44	32	25	95	2	1	3	$40,836	14	23	27
7	63	29	6	64	27	7	50	29	21	94	2	3	3	$41,318	15	19	31
8	72	17	9	77	17	5	68	20	13	66	23	6	10	$30,417	11	18	36
9	62	31	6	62	29	8	48	31	21	88	7	3	5	$38,646	15	21	28
10	55	38	6	56	34	9	42	32	26	95	2	1	1	$37,489	16	23	26
STATE	60	33	6	61	28	9	48	29	23	90	5	2	5	$36,952	14	23	27

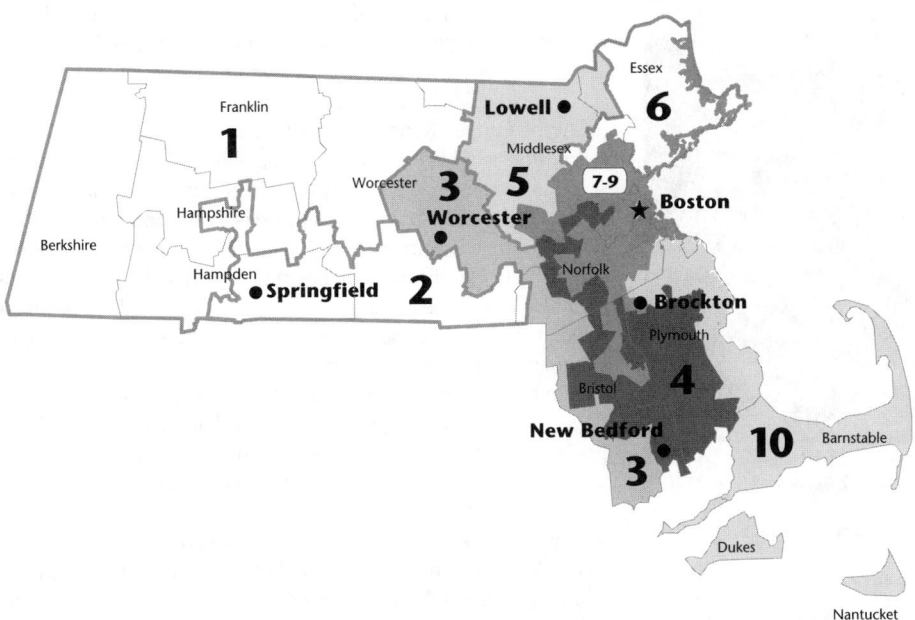

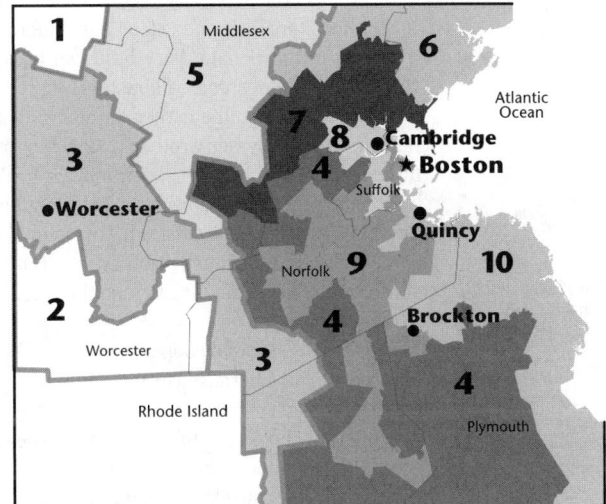

Sen. Edward M. Kennedy (D)

Elected 1962; 7th full term

The nation's image of Edward M. Kennedy has long been defined by family tragedy and political scandal: his stirring eulogies for family members, his embarrassing testimony at a nephew's rape trial, his tragic auto accident at Chappaquiddick three decades ago.

At the Capitol, Kennedy's reputation is more layered and nuanced. The earnestness of his tirades in favor of labor and environmental protections and for a stronger social safety net win grudging admiration even from colleagues who differ with him on those issues. And as the country's leading liberal, Kennedy remains an anchor for his party. Republicans call him the poster boy for discredited liberalism — labeling someone a "Teddy Kennedy liberal" is as dirty an epithet as they can sling — but for all their glee at denouncing him at fundraising dinners, Republicans have found Kennedy to be a Democrat with whom they can deal.

Kennedy is amenable to deal-making himself. His successful maneuvering with Republicans to pass legislation that expanded health benefits for the working disabled in 1999 showed he is no less effective under Republican rule of the Senate than he was as part of the Democratic majority.

As the 106th Congress began, Kennedy and Texas Republican Phil Gramm, a rock-ribbed conservative, hatched the compromise procedure that allowed the impeachment trial of President Clinton to get under way. "Stranger things have happened in politics, but the Kennedy-Gramm alliance is one of the strangest," John McCain, R-Ariz, said at the time.

A review of the legislative record suggests the deal might not have been so strange after all. Kennedy long ago understood what might be called the Iron Law of the Senate: Very little can be accomplished without the 60 votes needed to overcome filibusters.

"Kennedy has built a career on that understanding," New York Times reporter Adam Clymer wrote in a 1999 biography, "winning victories over three decades on civil rights, election law, health care, crime and other subjects, in a series of alliances with key Republicans from Howard Baker to Bob Dole to Hugh Scott to Strom Thurmond." Such partnerships continued in the 106th, when Kennedy worked with Bill Frist, R-Tenn., to broker a Senate compromise on how organs should be distributed to patients waiting for a transplant.

For all his sense that cooperation is an effective tool, Kennedy waves the tattered flag of liberalism in his endless efforts to expand the rights of patients in managed-care plans and increase the minimum wage. Standing at his desk at the rear of the Senate floor, the old lion wakes the sometimes somnolent chamber with his thunderous rhetoric, his face reddening and his voice needing no electronic amplification as he attacks school vouchers or rails about GOP proposals to change Medicare.

In the 106th, Kennedy pushed loudly and consistently for a sweeping "patients' bill of rights" that would have imposed many federal regulations on health insurers. While Republican opposition kept the plan from ever reaching a floor vote, Kennedy tried unsuccessfully to attach the measure to several 2000 spending bills. His constant badgering of the GOP leadership forced a showdown where Republicans brought their own managed-care legislation to the floor. While Kennedy's bill did not pass, he forced the GOP to change course, shaping the battleground for managed-care debates in the 107th.

It is impossible to talk about Kennedy's career without also recalling his

CAPITOL OFFICE
224-4543; fax 224-2417; 315 Russell Bldg. 20510

INTERNET
e-mail: senator@kennedy.senate.gov
web: kennedy.senate.gov

COMMITTEES
Armed Services
Health, Education, Labor & Pensions - ranking member
Judiciary
Joint Economic

HOMETOWN
Hyannis Port

BORN
Feb. 22, 1932, Boston, Mass.

RELIGION
Roman Catholic

FAMILY
Wife, Victoria Reggie Kennedy; three children, two stepchildren

EDUCATION
Harvard U., B.A. 1956; International Law School, The Hague (The Netherlands), attended 1958; U. of Virginia, LL.B. 1959

MILITARY SERVICE
Army, 1951-53

CAREER
Lawyer

POLITICAL HIGHLIGHTS
Suffolk County assistant district attorney, 1961-62; sought Democratic nomination for president, 1980

ELECTION RESULTS

2000 GENERAL

Edward M. Kennedy (D)	1,889,494	72.7%
Jack E. Robinson III (R)	334,341	12.9%
Carla Howell (LIBERT)	308,860	11.9%
Philip Lawler (CNSTP)	42,113	1.6%

2000 PRIMARY

Edward M. Kennedy (D)	unopposed

PREVIOUS WINNING PERCENTAGES
1994 (58%); 1988 (65%); 1982 (61%); 1976 (69%); 1970 (62%); 1964 (74%); 1962 Special Election (55%)

penchant for reckless behavior: the 1969 auto accident in which Mary Jo Kopechne drowned; his carousing at Capitol Hill restaurants in the 1980s; his humiliating 1992 testimony at the trial of William Kennedy Smith.

Kennedy's personal life had so tainted his image at the outset of the 1990s that he felt compelled to sit mute at the Supreme Court confirmation hearings of Clarence Thomas, who was accused of sexual harassment. The silence was a sharp disappointment to women and others who, in different days, would have counted on him. But his family life appears to have stabilized since 1992, when Kennedy was married for the second time, to Washington attorney Victoria Reggie.

Still, doubts about Kennedy's judgment revived Republican hopes of defeating him in 1994. Republican Mitt Romney, a venture capitalist, tapped into personal assets as the basis of his $7.6 million effort. He ran television spots portraying the senator, then 62, looking tired and haggard, and he questioned Kennedy's senatorial effectiveness. In response, the incumbent toured the state delivering federal checks and sought to paint Romney as unfamiliar with the legislative process. Bucking the GOP tide that year, Kennedy won with 58 percent. In 2000, he took 73 percent against another self-financing Republican businessman, Jack E. Robinson III.

For the past two decades, however, it has been clear that Kennedy never will fulfill the destiny that many had envisioned for him — namely, to take up the banner for his slain brothers and win the presidency. He ran only once, challenging President Carter for the Democratic nomination in 1980, but memories of Chappaquiddick were too fresh, and Kennedy launched his campaign without offering a clear idea of why he wanted to be president.

That campaign's most memorable moment came at the end, in a speech that secured his mantle as the leader of liberalism. "For me, a few hours ago, this campaign came to an end," he told a rapt audience at the Democratic convention. "For all those whose cares have been our concern, the work goes on, the cause endures, the hope still lives and the dream shall never die."

For all the ups and downs of his personal and political life, Kennedy's skill as a legislator constitutes an enduring legacy. Indeed, he achieved some of the greatest triumphs of his career after Republicans took control in 1995.

During the 104th Congress, he pushed to enact a minimum wage increase and a bill that mandated health insurance "portability." In the 105th, he proved during consideration of a bill to reauthorize the Food and Drug Administration that he could bend Congress to his will. Kennedy outlined a list of provisions he found egregious and set out to demolish them. He waved graphic photographs of hands and feet burned by bad lotions and of jaws deformed by faulty implants. In passionate speeches, he alleged that corporate greed was the root cause of those injuries. After weeks of such tactics, Republicans agreed to modify their bill.

Kennedy teamed up in the 105th with Judiciary Chairman Orrin G. Hatch, R-Utah, on tobacco and children's issues. When the two proposed an increase in the cigarette tax to extend health insurance to children whose low-income parents did not qualify for Medicaid, Majority Leader Trent Lott vowed: "A Kennedy big-government program is not going to be enacted." But Kennedy tapped into the growing anti-tobacco sentiment on Capitol Hill to help win approval of the $24 billion, five-year program.

As the 107th began, Kennedy was the fifth-longest-serving senator in U.S. history. In his first foray into electoral politics, in 1962, he was elected to fill the remaining two years of John F. Kennedy's Senate term. (The president had arranged for family friend Benjamin A. Smith to be appointed until his younger brother was old enough under the Constitution to serve.) First elected at age 30, Kennedy has spent more than half his life in Congress.

KEY VOTES

2000

No   Overhaul bankruptcy law and increase minimum wage
No   Limit fiscal 2001 discretionary spending to $600.3 billion
No   Override veto on nuclear waste disposal at Yucca Mountain site in Nevada
Yes Oppose effort to terminate Kosovo mission
Yes Include gender, sexual orientation and disability in federal hate crime protections
No   Approve GOP plan to restrict use of genetic information by health insurers
No   Kill amendment delaying implementation of an anti-missile defense system
No   Cut taxes for married couples
Yes Grant China permanent normal trade status

1999

No   Remove President Clinton from office for obstruction of justice
No   Kill amendment authorizing state grants to hire teachers and reduce class size
Yes Require criminal background checks for purchases at gun shows
No   Approve GOP proposal to increase rights of patients in managed-care health plans
?   Block effort to allow farm and medicine exports to Cuba
Yes Allow study of tougher automobile fuel efficiency standards
Yes Ratify nuclear weapons testing treaty
Yes Prohibit national political parties from collecting "soft money" donations
Yes Remove barriers among banking, securities and insurance companies

INTEREST GROUPS

	AFL-CIO	ADA	CCUS	ACU
2000	86%	90%	40%	12%
1999	88%	95%	47%	4%
1998	100%	95%	47%	0%
1997	100%	100%	40%	4%
1996	100%	90%	38%	0%
1995	100%	100%	33%	4%
1994	88%	90%	20%	0%
1993	82%	90%	36%	4%
1992	92%	100%	20%	0%
1991	83%	95%	20%	0%

CQ VOTE STUDIES

	PARTY UNITY		PRESIDENTIAL SUPPORT	
	Support	Oppose	Support	Oppose
2000	98%	2%	94%	6%
1999	97%	3%	93%	7%
1998	100%	0%	96%	4%
1997	97%	3%	88%	12%
1996	94%	6%	88%	12%
1995	96%	4%	92%	8%
1994	94%	6%	95%	5%
1993	96%	4%	97%	3%
1992	97%	3%	25%	75%
1991	93%	7%	32%	68%

Sen. John Kerry (D)

CAPITOL OFFICE
224-2742; fax 224-8525; 304 Russell Bldg. 20510

INTERNET
e-mail: john_kerry@kerry.senate.gov
web: kerry.senate.gov

COMMITTEES
Commerce, Science & Transportation
Finance
Foreign Relations
Small Business - ranking member

HOMETOWN
Boston

BORN
Dec. 11, 1943, Denver, Colo.

RELIGION
Roman Catholic

FAMILY
Wife, Teresa Heinz; two children, three
stepchildren

EDUCATION
Yale U., B.A. 1966; Boston College, J.D. 1976

MILITARY SERVICE
Navy, 1966-70

CAREER
Lawyer; county prosecutor

POLITICAL HIGHLIGHTS
Democratic nominee for U.S. House, 1972;
lieutenant governor, 1983-85

ELECTION RESULTS

1996 GENERAL

John Kerry (D)	1,334,135	52.2%
William F. Weld (R)	1,143,120	44.7%
Susan C. Gallagher (C)	70,007	2.7%

1996 PRIMARY

John Kerry (D)	221,213	98.6%
write-ins (D)	3,095	1.4%

PREVIOUS WINNING PERCENTAGES
1990 (57%); 1984 (55%)

Elected 1984; 3rd term

With a keen intellect, a penchant for self-promotion and an ability to project Kennedy-like charisma on television, Kerry has long been on political handicappers' lists of potential candidates for the Democratic presidential nomination. Having demurred after long and public ruminations both in 1992 and 2000 — when he ended up on Al Gore's shortlist of running mates — Kerry began the 107th Congress sending ample signals that he would at last make his bid for the White House in 2004.

To that end, Kerry made moves, both in and out of Congress, to get ready. He sought to position himself as the leading Democratic voice in the Senate against one of President Bush's most controversial proposals, opening the Arctic National Wildlife Refuge to oil exploration. He won a spot on the Finance Committee, affording him a prominent post from which to fight the president — or seek compromise with him — on tax, health care, trade, welfare and Social Security policy. And he raised his profile by joining the New Democrats, who are affiliated with the Democratic Leadership Council, a national centrist organization.

A decorated Vietnam veteran who gained publicity as an anti-war protester, Kerry has made his mark in Congress in foreign affairs, particularly on issues related to Vietnam. But he has also turned his 1960s activism into Senate policy positions on the environmental front. In recent years, Kerry has focused even more on domestic issues, sometimes staking out centrist positions, particularly on education and crime.

A leader of Vietnam Veterans Against the War, Kerry joined with other demonstrators in 1971 as they threw their medals over the White House fence. (He takes pains to explain that he opposed the returning of medals as a tactic and saved his own — three Purple Hearts, a Silver Star and a Bronze Star. He did toss over those of another veteran who could not travel to Washington.)

Kerry, who was a Naval officer in Vietnam, got front-page coverage when he asked the Senate Foreign Relations Committee, "How do you ask a man to be the last man to die for a mistake?" He tried to exploit the publicity by moving to Lowell and running for the House in the open 5th District in 1972. Kerry won his 10-way primary but lost in the fall to Republican Paul Cronin. During this period, Kerry received his first inquiry about a presidential run from CBS television reporter Morley Safer.

After his defeat, he went to law school and then worked as an assistant district attorney in Middlesex County. In 1982, he was elected lieutenant governor in a successful challenge of the Democratic establishment. Two years later, he beat Democratic Rep. James M. Shannon for the nomination to replace retiring Sen. Paul E. Tsongas. He won the general election over conservative businessman Raymond Shamie with 55 percent.

Twenty-five years after his service in Vietnam, the conflict still colored Kerry's actions and his life in Congress. In the mid-1990s, he teamed up with another decorated Vietnam veteran and ex-POW, Republican Sen. John McCain of Arizona, to push for normalized U.S. relations with Vietnam.

In 1994, Kerry and McCain sponsored an amendment that cleared the way for President Clinton to lift the longstanding trade embargo with Vietnam. "It's not a question of taking away leverage, but of giving leverage to us" in pursuing information about American soldiers unaccounted for in Vietnam, Kerry said. The action came a year after Kerry's Select Committee on POW-MIA Affairs concluded that there was "no compelling evidence" that any American remained alive in captivity in Southeast Asia.

More recently, Kerry has turned to domestic concerns. A participant in the original Earth Day in 1970, Kerry helped organize the 30th Earth Day celebration in 2000 and promoted environmentally friendly energy policies in Congress. He has undertaken difficult long-term assignments, such as building support in a skeptical Senate for the pollution restrictions of the 1997 Kyoto protocol on global warming.

In 1998, he drafted a comprehensive plan to overhaul public education that was heavy on ideas troublesome to traditional Democratic supporters. The plan would have transformed every public school into a charter school. It endorsed "public school choice," giving parents the option of sending children to public schools other than those in their geographic district.

Kerry also has embraced concepts at odds with powerful teachers unions, including raising teaching standards and making it easier for potential teachers with liberal arts degrees to get certified without many of the courses in education theory now required. He also has sought to change the tenure system, making it easier to fire bad teachers.

On crime, Kerry has drawn from his background as a federal prosecutor to back get-tough tactics. He has proposed a "two strikes and you're out" bill and a mandatory life sentence for crimes against children. In 1997, Kerry published a book tracing the increasing sophistication of organized crime.

In his role as the top Democrat on the Small Business Committee, Kerry has paid special attention to cutting federal red tape even while expanding some federal initiatives. He has touted the Small Business Administration's micro-loan program, which provides small loans to businesses that are having a hard time getting bank financing.

Kerry has a reputation as a lawmaker with a sharp mind who sometimes loses his focus. Though often charismatic in the legislative spotlight, he can come off as cold on a personal level.

He has been seen as overly aware of characteristics he shares with a legendary Massachusetts politician with the same initials. Like John F. Kennedy, Kerry is a product of privilege (his middle name is Forbes, after his mother's blue-blood family), was a decorated small-craft commander in wartime and then went quickly into politics. But in recent years, with his aborted presidential runs, Kerry's career has begun to resemble that of Edward M. Kennedy, his Democratic partner in the Massachusetts delegation.

Early in his Senate career, Kerry's reputation suffered somewhat from his apparent preoccupation with image. He got a reputation for caring about how things looked, and when he had corrective jaw surgery, it was regarded by some as an effort to improve his appearance.

He faced a tough re-election challenge in 1996 from William F. Weld, then the state's popular GOP governor. On the campaign trail, Weld's affable, down-to-earth style contrasted well with Kerry's stiff, aloof persona. And Kerry had to battle allegations of impropriety over his rent-free use of a lobbyist's apartment in Washington. But his late spending and solid performance in a series of debates carried him to victory by 7 percentage points.

Tabloids had a field day in 1997 when it was learned that Kerry and his wife, Teresa Heinz — an heir to the Heinz Foods fortune as the widow of Sen. John Heinz, R-Pa. — had obtained permission to move a fire hydrant from in front of their Boston townhouse. The couple applied for the move through regular channels in the fire department and had paid for the relocation themselves. Still, the Boston Herald labeled the project "The Little Dig" (a reference to Boston's "Big Dig" tunnel project) and implied that the move was the result of a published photo of Kerry's wife's vehicle parked illegally in front of the hydrant during the senator's 1996 re-election campaign.

KEY VOTES

2000

Yes Overhaul bankruptcy law and increase minimum wage

No Limit fiscal 2001 discretionary spending to $600.3 billion

No Override veto on nuclear waste disposal at Yucca Mountain site in Nevada

Yes Oppose effort to terminate Kosovo mission

Yes Include gender, sexual orientation and disability in federal hate crime protections

No Approve GOP plan to restrict use of genetic information by health insurers

No Kill amendment delaying implementation of an anti-missile defense system

? Cut taxes for married couples

Yes Grant China permanent normal trade status

1999

No Remove President Clinton from office for obstruction of justice

No Kill amendment authorizing state grants to hire teachers and reduce class size

Yes Require criminal background checks for purchases at gun shows

No Approve GOP proposal to increase rights of patients in managed-care health plans

No Block effort to allow farm and medicine exports to Cuba

Yes Allow study of tougher automobile fuel efficiency standards

Yes Ratify nuclear weapons testing treaty

Yes Prohibit national political parties from collecting "soft money" donations

Yes Remove barriers among banking, securities and insurance companies

INTEREST GROUPS

	AFL-CIO	ADA	CCUS	ACU
2000	75%	90%	53%	12%
1999	78%	95%	53%	0%
1998	100%	95%	50%	4%
1997	71%	95%	50%	0%
1996	86%	95%	31%	5%
1995	100%	95%	32%	4%
1994	88%	95%	30%	0%
1993	82%	90%	45%	12%
1992	83%	100%	10%	0%
1991	83%	95%	20%	5%

CQ VOTE STUDIES

	PARTY UNITY		PRESIDENTIAL SUPPORT	
	Support	Oppose	Support	Oppose
2000	96%	4%	97%	3%
1999	95%	5%	93%	7%
1998	95%	5%	94%	6%
1997	97%	3%	87%	13%
1996	92%	8%	92%	8%
1995	92%	8%	87%	13%
1994	94%	6%	90%	10%
1993	94%	6%	93%	7%
1992	92%	8%	23%	77%
1991	92%	8%	28%	72%

Rep. John W. Olver (D)

CAPITOL OFFICE
225-5335; fax 226-1224
1027 Longworth Bldg. 20515

INTERNET
e-mail: john.olver@mail.house.gov
web: www.house.gov/olver

COMMITTEES
Appropriations

HOMETOWN
Amherst

BORN
Sept. 3, 1936, Honesdale, Pa.

RELIGION
Unspecified

FAMILY
Wife, Rose Olver; one child

EDUCATION
Rensselaer Polytechnic Institute, B.S. 1955;
Tufts U., M.S. 1956; Massachusetts Institute of
Technology, Ph.D. 1961

CAREER
Professor

POLITICAL HIGHLIGHTS
Mass. House, 1969-73; Mass. Senate, 1973-91

ELECTION RESULTS

2000 GENERAL

John W. Olver (D)	169,375	68.2%
Pete Abair (R)	73,580	29.7%
Robert Potvin (I)	5,157	2.1%

2000 PRIMARY

John W. Olver (D)	unopposed

1998 GENERAL

John W. Olver (D)	121,863	71.7%
Gregory L. Morgan (R)	48,055	28.3%

PREVIOUS WINNING PERCENTAGES
1996 (53%); 1994 (99%); 1992 (52%); 1991 Special
Election (50%)

Elected June 1991; 5th full term

Olver has been in elective office for more than 30 years, demonstrating that brains — he earned a Ph.D. at the age of 24 — attention to detail and hard work can make for a successful political career.

Now in his fifth full term in the House, the former chemistry professor sits on the Appropriations Committee, where he is the top Democrat on the Military Construction Subcommittee and a member of his party's whip organization, as one of 12 deputy whips.

Olver's low-key personality — some would call him pleasantly professorial — seems an unlikely one for the campaign trail, yet he has never lost a race. And his election to the state Senate in 1972 and to the 1st District House seat in 1991 both represented successful challenges in historically GOP territory.

As the Bay State's lone member on the Appropriations Committee, Olver is expected not only to work for spending to benefit his western Massachusetts district, but also to carry water for his colleagues. Early in the 106th Congress, Democrat Joe Moakley, the dean of the state's House delegation, let it be known that he felt Olver should be doing more. Moakley suggested that Olver's personality was not suited to the give-and-take atmosphere of the Appropriations panel. "Some people are born salesmen, others are born librarians," Moakley told the Boston Herald. "He means well. He's a nice guy, bright enough, but he's not collegial," Moakley said.

There was some private talk within the delegation that Olver should be replaced on Appropriations, but Olver said that he took his obligations to the rest of the state seriously. Moakley later changed his tune, saying that "he's doing very well lately." In 2000, Olver used his Military Construction position to secure $20 million for Massachusetts projects.

In the committee, Olver is a hard worker with an eye for detail. Once, when he was trying to determine how the Pentagon sets priorities for spending on new National Guard and reserve facilities, he brought his own extensive worksheet to a committee meeting, passed out copies and provoked a lengthy discussion with the military officials who had come to testify.

When the Military Construction panel drafts its annual spending bill, Olver falls right in line with conservative colleagues who say not enough is spent to support the nation's military personnel. "We are spending billions on new weapons," he has said, "and we ought to spend enough to ensure that the servicemen and women who operate those sophisticated weapons are not left in substandard and in some cases deplorable living conditions."

But if he can sometimes find common ground with conservatives on quality-of-life issues, he remains a steadfast liberal and firm proponent of beating swords into plowshares. He notes that the Military Construction Subcommittee is not responsible for buying weapons; as for overall defense spending, he said, "We don't need the military budget at the level it is at. The Cold War is over."

Olver also sits on Appropriations' Transportation Subcommittee, where in 2000 he won approval of a provision in the annual spending bill that ensures that Boston's famously expensive "Big Dig" tunnel project will not eat up the state's entire allotment of highway spending; the provision requires that at least $400 million be spent on other projects.

Olver has been called the Massachusetts delegation's "most liberal liberal," which is saying something in a contingent that includes such pillars of the Democratic left as Rep. Barney Frank and Sen. Edward M. Kennedy. Olver's votes and speeches on the House floor lend credence to the characterization: It is rare to find him voting in agreement with anything the Republican leadership wants to do in economic or social policy. He is one of the most loyal Democratic lawmakers.

A member of the Progressive Caucus, which is the most liberal faction of House Democrats, he strongly believes in government's responsibility to solve society's problems and to play a part in economic development. On his Web page, Olver tells his constituents that his "chief priority as a member of Congress is to secure federal dollars that create opportunities for the people of the 1st District." He says he works "to ensure that western and central Massachusetts gets its fair share of federal attention and resources."

Olver fights to maintain federal aid for home heating fuel for low-income residents, a program important to New England, and he resists efforts to kill the Economic Development Administration, which he credits with fostering business growth in his district's struggling old industrial cities. As a member of the Rural Health Care Coalition, Olver worked in the 106th Congress to increase Medicare funding for home health care, hospitals and medical providers that were particularly affected by cuts in Medicare reimbursements in 1997.

His advocacy of government actions to protect the environment and to combat global warming, and his outdoor interests — cross-country skiing, hiking and rock climbing — endear him to the liberal precincts in the university communities around Amherst.

Born on a farm in Pennsylvania, Olver came to Massachusetts for graduate school. After receiving his Ph.D. from the Massachusetts Institute of Technology, he taught chemistry at the University of Massachusetts' Amherst campus for eight years before winning his first foray into elective politics — a state House race in 1968.

Four years later, he bucked the national GOP trend, unseating an incumbent Republican state senator. He stayed in the state Senate until 1991, when 17-term 1st District GOP Rep. Silvio O. Conte died.

Olver won a 10-way Democratic primary with surprising ease, and then he collected endorsements from his defeated rivals, as well as from union members, teachers, environmentalists, women's groups and abortion rights supporters. He won the special election by fewer than 2,000 votes — marking the first time since 1892 that the district had elected a Democrat to the House.

Since then, he has alternated close races, in 1992 and 1996, with re-election romps, in 1994 and 1998. The 2000 election broke that pattern, with Olver defeating the GOP challenger by 39 percentage points.

KEY VOTES

2000
Yes Raise hourly minimum wage by $1 over two years
No Halt funding for U.S. mission in Kosovo unless European nations pay more
Yes Provide Medicare benefits to military retirees and their dependents
No Grant China permanent normal trade status
No Phase out estate, gift and trust taxes
No Prohibit implementation of president's national monument designations
No Approve GOP plan to provide prescription drug coverage for Medicare beneficiaries
Yes Increase help for poor nations indebted to international financial institutions

1999
Yes Impose steel import quotas
Yes Kill proposal to take aviation trust funds off budget
No Require background checks on buyers only at gun shows with 10 or more vendors
No Remove barriers among banking, securities and insurance companies
Yes Authorize state grants to hire teachers and reduce class size
Yes Overhaul campaign finance law; ban "soft money" and restrict advocacy advertising
Yes Approve bipartisan plan to increase rights of patients in managed-care health plans

INTEREST GROUPS

	AFL-CIO	ADA	CCUS	ACU
2000	100%	90%	38%	4%
1999	89%	95%	13%	0%
1998	100%	95%	24%	0%
1997	100%	100%	30%	4%

CQ VOTE STUDIES

	PARTY UNITY		PRESIDENTIAL SUPPORT	
	Support	Oppose	Support	Oppose
2000	97%	3%	83%	17%
1999	96%	4%	88%	12%
1998	99%	1%	88%	12%
1997	97%	3%	80%	20%

MASSACHUSETTS 1
West — Berkshire Hills; Fitchburg; Amherst

The oranges of autumn, the whites of winter and the greens and Tanglewood music of spring and summer attract tourists from New York and eastern Massachusetts to the 1st. The Berkshire Mountains of western Massachusetts once protected American Indians from encroaching whites; 300 years later, the area serves as the home to a shrinking blue-collar and stable rural population. The district includes more than 40 percent of the state's land.

After decades as a dominant textile mill area and the world's top plastics producer, factory closures and downsizing decimated the region during the recession of the late 1980s and early 1990s. Pittsfield and Fitchburg suffered the most; General Electric reduced its defense-related workforce in Pittsfield from 11,000 in the 1980s to 2,000 a decade later. The population of many area cities continues to decline despite a modest recovery. A strong retail and plastics industry has spurred growth in Leominster.

Until the early 1990s, the 1st was a Republican stronghold. Now, rural areas east of Interstate 91 support Republicans, but the sparse population is overwhelmed by Democratic union voters in the northeast and university liberals around Amherst.

MAJOR INDUSTRY
Plastics, paper, tourism

MILITARY BASES
Barnes Air National Guard Base, 963 military, 277 civilian (1998)

CITIES
Pittsfield, 45,296; Holyoke, 40,677; Fitchburg, 40,407; Leominster, 40,358; Amherst (unincorporated), 35,288 (1990)

UNUSUAL FEATURES
John Chapman, known as Johnny Appleseed, born in Leominster; Famous native: W.E.B. DuBois (1868-1963), founder of the NAACP; First practical use in Great Barrington of alternating current transformer, which is used today.

Rep. Richard E. Neal (D)

Elected 1988; 7th term

CAPITOL OFFICE
225-5601; fax 225-8112; 2133 Rayburn Bldg. 20515

INTERNET
e-mail: www.house.gov/writerep
web: www.house.gov/neal

COMMITTEES
Ways & Means

HOMETOWN
Springfield

BORN
Feb. 14, 1949, Worcester, Mass.

RELIGION
Roman Catholic

FAMILY
Wife, Maureen Neal; four children

EDUCATION
American International College, B.A. 1972;
U. of Hartford, M.P.A. 1976

CAREER
College lecturer; teacher; mayoral aide

POLITICAL HIGHLIGHTS
Springfield City Council, 1978-84 (president, 1979);
mayor of Springfield, 1984-89

ELECTION RESULTS

2000 GENERAL

Richard E. Neal (D)	196,670	98.9%
write-ins	2,176	1.1%

2000 PRIMARY

Richard E. Neal (D)	20,253	86.5%
Joseph R. Fountain (D)	3,149	13.4%

1998 GENERAL

Richard E. Neal (D)	unopposed

PREVIOUS WINNING PERCENTAGES
1996 (72%); 1994 (59%); 1992 (53%); 1990 (100%);
1988 (80%)

Although Neal votes like a Democrat when it comes to environmental and labor causes, he has taken other positions that set him apart from most of his nine colleagues in the all-Democratic and liberal Massachusetts House delegation. He was one of only two in the state delegation to vote in 1997 for both the spending cut and tax cut components of a landmark balanced-budget agreement worked out between President Clinton and congressional Republicans.

Neal also was one of only two Bay Staters voting in 1997 to ban a procedure its opponents call "partial birth" abortion, and he backed GOP efforts in 1999 that sought to prevent pregnant teens from getting adult help to circumvent state abortion laws. He also supported another conservative favorite — a constitutional amendment allowing Congress to ban desecration of the U.S. flag.

Neal has made governing his life's work, going back to when he was a 24-year-old assistant to the mayor of Springfield. Now, in the House, he is just where a government junkie would want to be, shaping national tax policy from his seat on the powerful Ways and Means Committee and helping his party's cause as a member of the Democratic whip organization.

From his Ways and Means post, Neal focuses on tax issues with an eye to closing loopholes. In the 106th Congress, he cosponsored bipartisan legislation to prevent insurance companies from evading income taxes by setting up offices in Bermuda, a major concern to the Treasury because it could cost taxpayers several billion dollars every year. He also proposed simplifying tax forms through a variety of technical changes.

Another priority for Neal was to protect workers' pension plans when they left their jobs or when their company folded. He led opposition to a GOP pension and retirement bill in 2000 that Democrats contended would hurt lower-income Americans.

Neal sits on Ways and Means' Trade Subcommittee, and he casts a swing vote on trade issues. Siding with labor, he opposed the North American Free Trade Agreement in 1993 and Clinton's request in the 105th Congress for fast-track authority to negotiate trade agreements that Congress cannot amend. When it comes to China, however, he makes the case that sanctions would only aggravate that country's human rights situation. "In recent Chinese history, the worst human rights violations occurred in times of international isolation," he says.

He angered labor in 2000 by supporting a measure to grant China permanent normal trade status, again one of only two in the Massachusetts House delegation to do so. Amid concerns about China's human rights record, Neal described his vote to The Wall Street Journal as "a leap of faith," but he added: "Having said that, the Massachusetts economy is perfectly positioned to take advantage of this" move to open up trade with China. But his heart is usually with organized labor, as he said in 1998, "This booming economy that we are now experiencing will only continue to be stimulated by an expansion of unionized workers."

Although not prone to making long speeches, at times Neal has taken to the floor to sharply criticize the Republican majority. In 1998, he accused the GOP of "government by gimmick," arguing that the Republican leadership lacked "fundamental sincerity" and was pandering "to the lowest instincts of the American voter." Neal was peeved by a conservative proposal to scrap the tax code by 2002. He also objected to the GOP's persistent promotion of constitutional amendments to impose term limits, mandate a balanced budget and require approval by a two-thirds majority to increase taxes — all ideas that had failed before.

In the education arena, he opposes Republican ideas such as taxpayer-financed tuition vouchers and education savings accounts and accuses conservatives of "diverting resources from the public schools ... to the benefit of high-income Americans." Neal is interested in the federal government putting more muscle into school construction and repair. "I think it's important to note that everything in New England and the Northeast is old in many instances. ... There's lots more to do," he said in 1998.

Neal has attracted attention for his efforts to influence U.S. policy toward Cuba and Northern Ireland. Since traveling to Cuba in 1998, he has pressed for a softening of the U.S. embargo against the island nation. A grandson of Irish immigrants, Neal is co-chairman of the Ad Hoc Congressional Committee on Irish Affairs. In 1999, he urged a major restructuring of the predominantly Protestant Northern Ireland police force, the Royal Ulster Constabulary. In 1998, his name was floated as a potential candidate for ambassador to Ireland.

Neal began his political career in 1972 as co-chairman of George McGovern's presidential campaign in western Massachusetts. Neal then worked as an aide to Springfield Mayor William C. Sullivan and won three elections to the city council. He also taught history and government. In 1983, he won the first of three elections as Springfield mayor, drawing favorable notices for stimulating downtown rehabilitation and neighborhood revitalization.

Before veteran Democratic Rep. Edward P. Boland announced his retirement in 1988, he tipped off Neal to his plans, giving him a head start collecting signatures and dollars for his first congressional bid. By the time Boland made public his departure plans, Neal had toured the district's 38 towns and cities and amassed a $200,000 treasury. He won the nomination unopposed and crushed a weak GOP foe, but there was resentment from some politicians and voters who felt Neal had gotten an unfair break.

Those tensions crystallized in 1990 when Theodore E. Dimauro, mayor of Springfield before Neal, challenged him in the 1990 Democratic primary. But Dimauro's campaign collapsed after he admitted to spreading a rumor about one of the region's largest banks. Two years later, redistricting, anti-incumbent fever and Neal's 87 overdrafts at the private bank for House members led to an anemic showing by the incumbent: Neal won just 53 percent of the vote. Since then, however, he has had little trouble holding the seat.

KEY VOTES

2000
Yes Raise hourly minimum wage by $1 over two years
Yes Halt funding for U.S. mission in Kosovo unless European nations pay more
Yes Provide Medicare benefits to military retirees and their dependents
Yes Grant China permanent normal trade status
No Phase out estate, gift and trust taxes
No Prohibit implementation of president's national monument designations
No Approve GOP plan to provide prescription drug coverage for Medicare beneficiaries
Yes Increase help for poor nations indebted to international financial institutions

1999
Yes Impose steel import quotas
No Kill proposal to take aviation trust funds off budget
No Require background checks on buyers only at gun shows with 10 or more vendors
Yes Remove barriers among banking, securities and insurance companies
Yes Authorize state grants to hire teachers and reduce class size
Yes Overhaul campaign finance law; ban "soft money" and restrict advocacy advertising
Yes Approve bipartisan plan to increase rights of patients in managed-care health plans

INTEREST GROUPS

	AFL-CIO	ADA	CCUS	ACU
2000	90%	80%	38%	8%
1999	78%	95%	32%	4%
1998	100%	95%	35%	12%
1997	100%	90%	50%	25%

CQ VOTE STUDIES

	PARTY UNITY		PRESIDENTIAL SUPPORT	
	Support	Oppose	Support	Oppose
2000	92%	8%	83%	17%
1999	91%	9%	78%	22%
1998	95%	5%	80%	20%
1997	92%	8%	79%	21%

MASSACHUSETTS 2

South Central – Springfield; Northampton; Sturbridge

The rolling hills and thick forests of the 2nd extend from Springfield in the west to the Worcester suburbs in the east. Springfield dwarfs all other communities in the 2nd. Small, rural towns and intermittent farms dominate the rest of south-central Massachusetts.

Many of Springfield's successes of the 1990s were tied to its history as a hub for inventions, although the region's future rests with the insurance and financial services industries, which have replaced some of the city's shrinking manufacturing base. Springfield hopes to stem population loss with the construction of a new civic center and a new home for the Basketball Hall of Fame.

In the district's only multicultural region, Hispanics – many of whom moved to the 2nd in the 1950s to work in the tobacco fields – have gravitated to Springfield's North End, while African-Americans live near the city's center.

Residents in and around Springfield vote Democratic and dominate the district's elections. The city's blue-collar and Irish Catholic citizens support Rep. Neal's anti-abortion stance. Mount Holyoke College and Smith College provide a more liberal vote in Northampton. Well-to-do towns in the east are marginally Democratic but have voted some Republicans into state office.

MAJOR INDUSTRY
Telecommunications, insurance, health care

CITIES
Springfield, 147,216; Chicopee, 53,751; Northampton, 28,412; Agawam, 26,686

UNUSUAL FEATURES
First monkey wrench produced at Bemis & Call in Springfield in 1854; Basketball invented in Springfield in 1892; First U.S. Armory, built in 1794; First gasoline-powered car and first Pullman rail car invented in Springfield.

Rep. Jim McGovern (D)

CAPITOL OFFICE
225-6101; fax 225-5759; 430 Cannon Bldg. 20515

INTERNET
e-mail: www.house.gov/mcgovern/send.htm
web: www.house.gov/mcgovern

COMMITTEES
Resources
Transportation & Infrastructure

HOMETOWN
Worcester

BORN
Nov. 20, 1959, Worcester, Mass.

RELIGION
Roman Catholic

FAMILY
Wife, Lisa McGovern; one child

EDUCATION
American U., B.A. 1981, M.P.A. 1984

CAREER
Congressional aide

POLITICAL HIGHLIGHTS
Sought Democratic nomination for U.S. House, 1994

ELECTION RESULTS

2000 GENERAL

Jim McGovern (D)	213,065	98.8%
write-ins	2,496	1.2%

2000 PRIMARY

Jim McGovern (D)	unopposed

1998 GENERAL

Jim McGovern (D)	108,613	56.9%
Matthew J. Amorello (R)	79,174	41.5%
George Phillies (LIBERT)	2,887	1.5%

PREVIOUS WINNING PERCENTAGES
1996 (53%)

Elected 1996; 3rd term

McGovern arrived on Capitol Hill in 1997 well-versed in the ways of Congress and with a network of highly placed Democratic lawmakers to guide him as he moved onto the political stage after almost two decades behind the scenes.

As an aide to Sen. George McGovern (no relation), the former South Dakota senator and presidential candidate, and Rep. Joe Moakley, the former Rules Committee chairman and the dean of the Massachusetts House delegation, McGovern developed an appreciation for both idealism and pragmatism in politics. He told The Boston Globe: "McGovern taught me it was OK to be an idealist. Moakley taught me how to get things done."

A liberal Democrat, McGovern affiliates with the Progressive Caucus, the most left-leaning faction of House Democrats. But he teams up with lawmakers in both parties to work behind the scenes on nuts-and-bolts issues of economic development, education and health care. He has fought to improve Medicare payments for home health care, increase Pell Grants for college students and provide U.S. support for a United Nations program to provide school lunches.

In the 105th Congress, McGovern got a seat on the Transportation and Infrastructure Committee, a choice assignment for a freshman, and he was chosen for a spot in the Democratic whip organization. He also leapfrogged over 22 more-senior Democrats on the Transportation Committee in being appointed as one of the negotiators to craft the final version of a massive 1998 transportation authorization measure. He was able to win funding for a variety of Worcester-area highway, transit and bikeway projects.

Bay State lawmakers are concerned that the multibillion-dollar "Big Dig" tunnel project in Boston will eat up all the state's available transportation money, and McGovern, as the state's only member of the Transportation panel, has been in the middle of efforts to make sure other projects are also funded. He was active in federal and state negotiations to ensure what he called a "balanced statewide road and bridge program."

Also from his Transportation seat, McGovern has sought to upgrade Worcester's airport and attract more passenger traffic. And he joined a bipartisan effort to continue a ban on triple-trailer truck rigs on highways.

McGovern knows it is wise to keep in touch back home, and he convened an economic summit in Worcester to bring together local, state and federal government officials, academics and leaders of the private sector to discuss strategies to revitalize the 3rd District's economy.

He invited both President Clinton and Speaker J. Dennis Hastert to visit Worcester, the largest city in the 3rd District. Clinton went there several times, including to attend a memorial service for six Worcester firefighters who died battling a warehouse blaze. McGovern says he extended the invitation to Hastert, who has yet to visit, in an effort to heal the "rancor and divisiveness" in the House. In the same spirit, he asked his colleagues to mark "World Smile Day" in October 1999 on the occasion of the unveiling of a "Smiley Face" stamp in Worcester. The ubiquitous smiley face was designed in 1963 by a Worcester artist.

McGovern takes an interest in foreign affairs. He has traveled to Cuba twice; in 2000, he publicly urged Clinton to go to Cuba and announce he was normalizing diplomatic relations.

At the request of a group of high school students from his district, McGovern has become involved in conditions in East Timor, which is struggling to break away from Indonesia. In 1999, he traveled there to observe a plebiscite on independence. East Timor is of interest to McGovern's constituents because it was a Portuguese colony for hundreds of years. There is a substantial Portuguese community in the eastern portion of the 3rd.

In 1990, as a top aide to Moakley, McGovern was a key staff member on a House task force that looked into the 1989 murders of six Jesuit priests and two women in El Salvador. Several of the Salvadoran military officers who were implicated in the murders had graduated from the U.S. Army School of the Americas in Fort Benning, Ga., which trains Latin American military officers.

Since then, McGovern and Moakley have persistently tried to eliminate funding for the school, which McGovern says "continues to train military officers who harm and kill the innocent people of Latin America." The school was reorganized and renamed (the Defense Institute for Hemispheric Security Cooperation) in the 106th Congress but will remain in business at Fort Benning.

McGovern grew up in Worcester, where his father ran a liquor store and his mother was a dance teacher. His family followed politics closely, especially where the Kennedys were involved. He recalls that "when Robert Kennedy was killed, my father gathered us around the kitchen table and we wrote sympathy cards to Ethel."

McGovern had his first brush with politics when, as a student in junior high school, he found himself defending presidential candidate George McGovern because they shared the same last name. He then became involved in the campaign. Later, as an American University student, he worked in McGovern's Senate office. In 1984, when the South Dakotan launched another presidential bid, Jim McGovern was manager of the campaign in Massachusetts and made the nominating speech at the Democratic National Convention in San Francisco. The elder McGovern returned the favor in 1996 and campaigned for Jim McGovern in Massachusetts.

McGovern went to work for Moakley in 1981 and served on his personal staff and in the Rules Committee office until 1996.

He unsuccessfully sought the Democratic nomination for the 3rd District seat in 1994. In 1996, in an election considered something of an upset, McGovern defeated two-term GOP Rep. Peter I. Blute, 57 percent to 42 percent. In 1998, Republicans viewed McGovern as vulnerable and had high hopes for a victory by moderate state Sen. Matthew J. Amorello. But McGovern won re-election easily, 57 percent to 42 percent. In 2000, the GOP did not field a candidate.

KEY VOTES

2000
Yes Raise hourly minimum wage by $1 over two years
No Halt funding for U.S. mission in Kosovo unless European nations pay more
Yes Provide Medicare benefits to military retirees and their dependents
No Grant China permanent normal trade status
No Phase out estate, gift and trust taxes
No Prohibit implementation of president's national monument designations
No Approve GOP plan to provide prescription drug coverage for Medicare beneficiaries
Yes Increase help for poor nations indebted to international financial institutions

1999
Yes Impose steel import quotas
No Kill proposal to take aviation trust funds off budget
No Require background checks on buyers only at gun shows with 10 or more vendors
Yes Remove barriers among banking, securities and insurance companies
Yes Authorize state grants to hire teachers and reduce class size
Yes Overhaul campaign finance law; ban "soft money" and restrict advocacy advertising
Yes Approve bipartisan plan to increase rights of patients in managed-care health plans

INTEREST GROUPS

	AFL-CIO	ADA	CCUS	ACU
2000	100%	100%	33%	0%
1999	89%	100%	20%	0%
1998	100%	100%	39%	4%
1997	100%	100%	30%	4%

CQ VOTE STUDIES

	PARTY UNITY		PRESIDENTIAL SUPPORT	
	Support	Oppose	Support	Oppose
2000	98%	2%	86%	14%
1999	96%	4%	82%	18%
1998	97%	3%	80%	20%
1997	96%	4%	84%	16%

MASSACHUSETTS 3
Central and southeast — Worcester, coastal towns

From the mountains of Princeton to the ocean near Dartmouth, the 3rd cuts a diagonal sliver between the two towns that prompted the region's nickname, the "Ivy League" district, although neither school is in the state.

Worcester, a working-class city and the 3rd's population hub, dominates the district and plans to revitalize its downtown. A late-1990s project centralized its respected hospitals, research institutes and some drug manufacturing plants into an area called Medical City. Suburban communities to the north and south of Worcester have been filling up with suburbanites who commute to jobs in Boston or Providence, R.I.

After building a commuter rail, Franklin, to the southeast, has grown by 30 percent since 1990, the fastest in the state. Fall River (shared with the 4th District) is a fishing community at the southern end of the 3rd that has long been a bastion of blue-collar white ethnic Democrats.

The city also consistently has had one of the highest unemployment rates in Massachusetts, although the situation began to improve in the late 1990s.

After the 1990 census, then-Gov. William F. Weld forced a compromise with Democrats to draw the 3rd in a way that would give his Republicans a chance to win it. Democrats control the two tails of the district — the blue-collar bases in Worcester and Fall River. A ring of strong Republican support hovers in the towns surrounding Worcester, including Paxton, Holden, the Boylstons and Shrewsbury. However, Democrats can control the district unless urban voter turnout is especially low.

MAJOR INDUSTRY
Health care, heavy manufacturing, retail

CITIES
Worcester, 167,132; Fall River (pt.), 45,024 (1990); Attleboro, 39,902

UNUSUAL FEATURES
First American novel, William Hill Brown's "The Power of Sympathy," published in Worcester.

Rep. Barney Frank (D)

Elected 1980; 11th term

CAPITOL OFFICE
225-5931; fax 225-0182; 2252 Rayburn Bldg. 20515

INTERNET
e-mail: www.house.gov/writerep
web: www.house.gov/frank

COMMITTEES
Financial Services
Judiciary

HOMETOWN
Newton

BORN
March 31, 1940, Bayonne, N.J.

RELIGION
Jewish

FAMILY
Single

EDUCATION
Harvard U., B.A. 1962, J.D. 1977

CAREER
Lawyer; mayoral and congressional aide

POLITICAL HIGHLIGHTS
Mass. House, 1973-81

ELECTION RESULTS

2000 GENERAL

Barney Frank (D)	200,638	74.9%
Martin D. Travis (R)	56,553	21.1%
David J. Euchner (LIBERT)	10,553	3.9%

2000 PRIMARY

Barney Frank (D)	unopposed

1998 GENERAL

Barney Frank (D)	148,340	98.4%
write-ins	2,380	1.6%

PREVIOUS WINNING PERCENTAGES
1996 (72%); 1994 (99%); 1992 (68%); 1990 (66%);
1988 (70%); 1986 (89%); 1984 (74%); 1982 (60%);
1980 (52%)

Frank, more than any other House Democrat, has relished his role in the opposition since Republicans won control in 1994. "I'm used to being in the minority," he told The New York Times Magazine in 1996. "I'm a left-handed gay Jew. I've never felt, automatically, a member of any majority. So I started swinging from the opening bell of this Congress." And he has not let up.

The comment is quintessential Barney Frank: candid, self-deprecating and combative. After 20 years in the House, the quick-quipping Frank has amassed an encyclopedic knowledge of public policy issues and parliamentary rules, which he uses to wage his battles. And whatever their political stripes, people all over Washington listen to and enjoy his shtick. Frank was named funniest and smartest member of Congress in the 2000 Washingtonian magazine poll of Capitol Hill aides.

It is easy to see why. At a time when floor "debate" is often just members exchanging scripted speeches, Frank is spontaneous combustion, passionately making his liberal case in off-the-cuff — and carefully reasoned — arguments. Just one day before he had heart surgery in 1999, Frank was skirmishing on the floor with conservative Republican Ernest Istook of Oklahoma. "Yelling at Ernie Istook is, in fact, medically indicated," he told the Capitol Hill newspaper, Roll Call, afterward. "It's in Black's [medical] dictionary."

During debate in 1998 on a funding measure for the Department of Housing and Urban Development, Frank heaped scorn on what he said was GOP stinginess. "There is hardly an aspect of this important appropriations bill which comes close to being adequately funded," he said. "There simply is no way to improve this bill. ... We are reduced not even to robbing Peter to pay Paul, but to mugging Peter to pay Paul's burial expenses."

He frequently chides the GOP majority for dictating policy to the states in some areas, such as prison construction and gambling regulation, while posing as the party that champions states' rights. He savors opportunities to expose rifts within the Republican membership, gleefully remarking, "The right hand doesn't know what the far right hand is doing."

In 1998, Frank was center stage during Judiciary Committee impeachment proceedings against President Clinton. It was Frank who delivered one of the more memorable lines of the hearings, asking, "What did he touch, and when did he touch it?" as lawmakers were debating allegations of wrongdoing stemming from Clinton's attempt to cover up a relationship with a White House intern. Frank's question recalled a famous inquiry by GOP Sen. Howard H. Baker Jr. in the 1974 Watergate hearings: "What did the president know, and when did he know it?"

Frank, who was the first member of Congress to announce his homosexuality, pushed for a censure of the president, similar to the reprimand the House had levied on the congressman in 1990 after his own sex scandal. The punishment stemmed from revelations that a household employee Frank had hired was found to be running a prostitution business from Frank's apartment. The House voted 408-18 to reprimand Frank for bringing discredit on the House, rejecting moves to censure or to expel him.

Frank's willingness to use himself as an example illustrates the matter-of-fact way he has handled controversy about his personal life. "I answer every other question I'm asked," he said in disclosing his sexual orientation. In the 104th Congress, Frank led the opposition to a bill denouncing same-sex marriage. "If it bothers people, turn your head," he said. In the 107th, he introduced a bill to require the federal government to recognize such marriages if they are sanctioned by a state.

For all the attention Frank attracts by provoking the GOP, he also is willing to work with Republicans to reach compromise. "I think to be unrealistic and unpragmatic is to be disloyal to your ideology," he once said. While working with conservatives in 2000 to block a proposal to liberalize trade with China, he said, "If you're not able to work closely with people you despise, you can't really work here," he told The Boston Globe.

When Banking Committee Chairman Jim Leach, R-Iowa, was trying to line up support in the 105th Congress for legislation providing $17.9 billion for the International Monetary Fund, Frank agreed to round up Democratic votes in exchange for Leach's promise to place more emphasis on safeguarding human rights and promoting labor protections.

Frank became the top Democrat on the Banking panel's Subcommittee on Housing and Community Opportunity in the 106th Congress. He has been critical of Republican legislation to overhaul public housing law. He disliked the GOP plan to require that public housing tenants do community service, and he also objected to new rent payment provisions that aimed to open public housing to people besides the very poor. Frank's amendments to change those provisions lost by lopsided margins.

Republicans are not the only target of Frank's liberal wrath. After Clinton signed off on a budget agreement in May 1997 that promised to balance the books but also reduced spending on social programs and offered tax breaks that Frank deemed regressive, he complained that the president had betrayed party principles. "We addressed a letter to the Democratic president of the United States," Frank said, "and it came back 'addressee unknown.'"

Frank's belief that many domestic programs are underfunded leads him to take a skeptical view of overseas expenditures. For instance, he has been a vocal critic of the U.S. military mission in war-torn Bosnia and of U.S. financial support for expanding NATO.

A product of Bayonne, N.J., Frank went to Harvard University and stuck around to teach government, work for politicians and, eventually, launch a career in elective politics.

He worked for Boston Mayor Kevin White from 1968 to 1971 and then Massachusetts Democratic Rep. Michael Harrington until 1972, when the contacts he had made helped him win a seat in the state House. He served there for eight years before coming to Congress. Though he faced a tough re-election battle in 1982 after redistricting cost Massachusetts a seat, he has not faced major problems winning election since.

KEY VOTES

2000
Yes Raise hourly minimum wage by $1 over two years
Yes Halt funding for U.S. mission in Kosovo unless European nations pay more
Yes Provide Medicare benefits to military retirees and their dependents
No   Grant China permanent normal trade status
No   Phase out estate, gift and trust taxes
No   Prohibit implementation of president's national monument designations
No   Approve GOP plan to provide prescription drug coverage for Medicare beneficiaries
Yes Increase help for poor nations indebted to international financial institutions

1999
Yes Impose steel import quotas
No   Kill proposal to take aviation trust funds off budget
No   Require background checks on buyers only at gun shows with 10 or more vendors
No   Remove barriers among banking, securities and insurance companies
Yes Authorize state grants to hire teachers and reduce class size
Yes Overhaul campaign finance law; ban "soft money" and restrict advocacy advertising
Yes Approve bipartisan plan to increase rights of patients in managed-care health plans

INTEREST GROUPS

	AFL-CIO	ADA	CCUS	ACU
2000	100%	95%	33%	12%
1999	100%	100%	21%	0%
1998	100%	100%	33%	4%
1997	100%	100%	30%	4%

CQ VOTE STUDIES

	PARTY UNITY		PRESIDENTIAL SUPPORT	
	Support	Oppose	Support	Oppose
2000	94%	6%	84%	16%
1999	92%	8%	80%	20%
1998	94%	6%	81%	19%
1997	94%	6%	78%	22%

MASSACHUSETTS 4

Boston suburbs — Newton; New Bedford; part of Fall River

Downtowns replete with 18th- and 19th-century Town Hall buildings dot the Yankee communities in the 4th, several of which recently celebrated 300th or 350th anniversaries. The 4th's saxophone shape encompasses thickly settled Boston suburbs, rural cranberry bogs and urban New Bedford and Fall River (shared with the 3rd District).

While the northern well-to-do towns and Boston suburbs benefited from a strong economy in the 1990s, the southern fishing and former textile mill communities struggled to stave off double-digit unemployment. In Fall River and New Bedford, the textile industry declined to almost nothing in the early 1990s, while over-fishing idled commercial fishermen. In the 4th's center, cranberry bogs in Middleborough and biotechnology firms further north supplied that region with nearly full employment.

The blue-collar, immigrant-laden southern section of the district votes Democratic. Northeastern towns around Hanson and Pembroke had a Republican representative before the 1980 redistricting, but Democratic Rep. Frank's popularity and the large number of independent voters have obscured any GOP leanings. In the northwest, the wealthy towns of Wellesley, Dover and Sherborn tend to lean Republican, while well-to-do Newton and Brookline go for liberal Democrats.

MAJOR INDUSTRY
Fishing, cranberries, health care, textile manufacturing

CITIES
New Bedford, 94,780; Newton, 80,143; Brookline (unincorporated), 54,718 (1990)

UNUSUAL FEATURES
Fig Newtons originated in Newton, Mass.; Lizzie Borden hailed from Fall River; Former Gov. Michael S. Dukakis commuted downtown by trolley from his home in Brookline.

Rep. Martin T. Meehan (D)

Elected 1992; 5th term

CAPITOL OFFICE
225-3411; fax 226-0771; 2447 Rayburn Bldg. 20515

INTERNET
e-mail: martin.meehan@mail.house.gov
web: www.house.gov/meehan

COMMITTEES
Armed Services
Judiciary

HOMETOWN
Lowell

BORN
Dec. 30, 1956, Lowell, Mass.

RELIGION
Roman Catholic

FAMILY
Wife, Ellen T. Murphy; one child

EDUCATION
U. of Massachusetts, Lowell, B.S. 1978; Suffolk U.,
M.P.A. 1981, J.D. 1986

CAREER
County prosecutor; state securities investigator;
legislative aide

POLITICAL HIGHLIGHTS
No previous office

ELECTION RESULTS

2000 GENERAL

Martin T. Meehan (D)	199,601	98.0%
write-ins	4,040	2.0%

2000 PRIMARY

Martin T. Meehan (D)	16,394	73.0%
Thomas P. Tierney (D)	4,253	18.9%
Joseph F. Osbaldeston (D)	1,687	7.5%

1998 GENERAL

Martin T. Meehan (D)	127,418	70.7%
David E. Coleman (R)	52,725	29.3%

PREVIOUS WINNING PERCENTAGES
1996 (99%); 1994 (70%); 1992 (52%)

Meehan became a politics "junky" at an early age. His parents, who raised a large Irish-Catholic family, were active in grass-roots Democratic politics in Lowell. When "President Kennedy would come on the TV, there was silence in the house," he told the Lowell Sun.

Now in Congress, many of his legislative priorities, including campaign finance reform, his crusade against tobacco and even his interest in insurance coverage for fertility treatment, can be traced back to personal experience. Meehan's father, Martin T. Meehan Sr., was a typesetter for the Sun for more than 40 years. He had only a high school education himself but was well-read and politics was a passion — providing his son an early nudge in that direction. (The younger Meehan named his son Robert Francis, in honor of Bobby Kennedy.)

Meehan came to Congress promising to serve only eight years, but in 1999, saying that the pledge was a mistake in the absence of term limits for everyone, he announced he would seek a fifth term in 2000. Term limits advocates excoriated Meehan for his change of heart, but the issue did not resonate in his re-election campaign. He easily dispatched two Democratic primary foes, and the GOP was unable to qualify a candidate for the November ballot.

His record defies easy labeling, but he draws inspiration from the example of a previous 5th District lawmaker, the late Democrat Paul E. Tsongas, who made a name in the House, the Senate and in the 1992 presidential primaries as a social policy liberal and a budget-cutter.

Meehan serves on the Judiciary and Armed Services panels and has leadership roles in several unofficial Capitol Hill groups, including the Congressional Task Force on Tobacco and Health, the Northeast/Midwest Congressional Coalition and the Sustainable Development Caucus.

Meehan sides with the Democratic leadership on most issues, and he was a loyal supporter of President Clinton. But he is aggressively bipartisan on his signature issue — campaign finance overhaul — working so closely with cosponsor Christopher Shays that he says he trusts the Connecticut Republican "like a brother."

In the 105th and 106th Congresses, Meehan and Shays waged a marathon effort to overhaul the campaign finance system. The Shays-Meehan bill would bar national parties from receiving or spending "soft money" — unlimited contributions that are used for party-building activities and issue ads. State and local parties would no longer be able to use soft money for federal campaigns, and new restrictions would be imposed on campaign-related expenditures by third-party groups. Meehan told the Lowell Sun, "Do you think a working guy like my father would have ever been able to get in to see a member of Congress today? Fat chance. People like him ... should have as much right to influence the system as the fat cats."

Overcoming resistance from the House GOP leadership, Shays and Meehan finally pushed their bill to passage in August 1998, and again in September 1999. But the proposal died in the Senate both times.

In 2000, Congress did enact legislation to require certain nonprofit organizations to disclose their political spending. Meehan backed the effort, but he noted that "it is but a step."

On Armed Services, where he is the top Democrat on the Military Research and Development Subcommittee, Meehan gives close scrutiny to proposals for higher defense spending even as he tries to boost his district's economy by attracting defense-related work. He is a leading supporter of efforts to promote gender equity in the armed forces.

There is a personal story behind Meehan's antipathy toward the tobacco companies. He told The Boston Globe that his anti-tobacco fervor sprang in part from his father's 25-year smoking habit, which led to heart disease requiring surgery in 1967. "What really got me was that he was so addicted that he smoked a cigarette on the way home from being told he was going to die if he didn't stop," Meehan recalled. (His father, who eventually did stop smoking, died in October 2000.)

In 1994, after tobacco executives testified before a House hearing that nicotine was not addictive, Meehan was so outraged that he drafted a 111-page memo asking Attorney General Janet Reno to convene a grand jury to investigate perjury and fraud charges against the executives. Later, he paired with Utah Republican James V. Hansen to introduce a number of anti-smoking bills, including legislation to remove nicotine gradually from all tobacco products sold in the United States and to ban sales of tobacco over the Internet.

Meehan sponsored legislation to expand federal workers' health care insurance coverage to provide fertility treatment. He has a personal interest in the topic, as he and his wife sought help from a fertility clinic.

Concord, site of the famous early Revolutionary War battle, is in the 5th District, and that is where Tsongas and former New Hampshire GOP Sen. Warren B. Rudman met in 1992 to formulate their plans for a grass-roots group — the Concord Coalition — to press for a balanced federal budget. Meehan has upheld the town's honor, by rating among the most fiscally responsible members of Congress in the coalition's annual survey of members' votes.

After college, Meehan worked as an assistant to the mayor of Lowell, then as an aide to Democrat James M. Shannon, who had succeeded Tsongas as the 5th District's congressman. After his stint with Shannon, Meehan worked in state government, first as a state Senate aide, and then in the office of the secretary of state. He was a prosecuting attorney in the early 1990s, remaining active in local party politics, and in 1992 decided to challenge incumbent Democratic Rep. Chester G. Atkins, who had 127 overdrafts at the private bank for House members.

Meehan overwhelmed Atkins in the primary. Boosted by a large turnout from Lowell, Meehan beat former GOP Rep. Paul W. Cronin, in a district that had been drawn with a GOP edge. Meehan had a 15-point margin of victory that year; it was his last competitive election. His name crops up in speculation about candidates for the 2002 gubernatorial election in the Bay State.

KEY VOTES

2000
Yes Raise hourly minimum wage by $1 over two years
Yes Halt funding for U.S. mission in Kosovo unless European nations pay more
?   Provide Medicare benefits to military retirees and their dependents
Yes Grant China permanent normal trade status
No   Phase out estate, gift and trust taxes
No   Prohibit implementation of president's national monument designations
No   Approve GOP plan to provide prescription drug coverage for Medicare beneficiaries
Yes Increase help for poor nations indebted to international financial institutions

1999
Yes Impose steel import quotas
Yes Kill proposal to take aviation trust funds off budget
No   Require background checks on buyers only at gun shows with 10 or more vendors
No   Remove barriers among banking, securities and insurance companies
Yes Authorize state grants to hire teachers and reduce class size
Yes Overhaul campaign finance law; ban "soft money" and restrict advocacy advertising
Yes Approve bipartisan plan to increase rights of patients in managed-care health plans

INTEREST GROUPS

	AFL-CIO	ADA	CCUS	ACU
2000	90%	90%	45%	12%
1999	78%	100%	20%	0%
1998	100%	100%	31%	4%
1997	100%	90%	44%	20%

CQ VOTE STUDIES

	PARTY UNITY		PRESIDENTIAL SUPPORT	
	Support	Oppose	Support	Oppose
2000	92%	8%	81%	19%
1999	96%	4%	84%	16%
1998	97%	3%	88%	12%
1997	95%	5%	82%	18%

MASSACHUSETTS 5
North Central — Lawrence; Lowell

A generation ago, billowing smokestacks put Lawrence and Lowell among the nation's leading industrial centers. Today, the cities continue to be the population centers for the 5th, but the other wealthy suburbs and rural communities – home to some of the nation's most prestigious prep schools – give the district the highest median income in the state.

Lawrence's population has been declining as white flight carries many longtime residents to the suburbs, away from the growing Latino immigrant community. Residents left Lowell, too, in the early 1990s when a recession hobbled Digital Equipment Company and toppled computer giant Wang, which once employed 10,000. But a subsequent boom has attracted software and Internet companies, halting the decline.

Republicans controlled the 5th for most of the century until Paul Tsongas won the seat in 1974. Democrats have not let go since. The blue-collar and minority residents of Lowell and Lawrence vote strongly Democratic, as do many well-educated liberals in the suburbs. Other wealthy areas like Wayland, Carlisle, Acton and Andover lean Republican. District voters gave the edge to Al Gore in the 2000 presidential contest.

MAJOR INDUSTRY
Computer software, defense, textiles

CITIES
Lowell, 101,103; Lawrence, 69,794; Methuen, 42,364

UNUSUAL FEATURES
Concord, site of first day of fighting in the Revolutionary War on April 19, 1775 (now celebrated each year as Patriot's Day); Paul Revere's ride and the first Revolutionary battles in towns in the 5th and 7th districts are re-enacted every year; Walden Pond served as temporary home to Henry David Thoreau.

Rep. John F. Tierney (D)

CAPITOL OFFICE
225-8020; fax 225-5915; 120 Cannon Bldg. 20515

INTERNET
e-mail: www.house.gov/writerep
web: www.house.gov/tierney

COMMITTEES
Education & Workforce
Government Reform

HOMETOWN
Salem

BORN
Sept. 18, 1951, Salem, Mass.

RELIGION
Unspecified

FAMILY
Wife, Patrice Tierney

EDUCATION
Salem State College, B.A. 1973; Suffolk U., J.D. 1976

CAREER
Lawyer; chamber of commerce official

POLITICAL HIGHLIGHTS
Democratic nominee for U.S. House, 1994

ELECTION RESULTS

2000 GENERAL

John F. Tierney (D)	205,324	71.0%
Paul McCarthy (R)	83,501	28.9%

2000 PRIMARY

John F. Tierney (D)	unopposed

1998 GENERAL

John F. Tierney (D)	117,132	54.6%
Peter G. Torkildsen (R)	90,986	42.4%
Randal C. Fritz (I)	6,544	3.0%

PREVIOUS WINNING PERCENTAGES
1996 (48%)

Elected 1996; 3rd term

Tierney's legislative wish list includes such liberal agenda items as universal health insurance, public financing of political campaigns, and federal funds for hiring more public school teachers and for adult literacy programs. These are bold stances to take in his politically competitive district, which he won on his second try and then by just 371 votes.

He consistently hews to the party line, voting with his Democratic colleagues 95 percent of the time. He is a member of the Progressive Caucus, the most liberal faction of House Democrats.

From his seat on the Education and the Workforce Committee, he is a reliable critic of the GOP majority's proposals for the nation's schools and workers. He joins in the chorus of Democrats who accuse conservatives of seeking to boost private schools with programs such as tuition vouchers, instead of funding improvements in public schools.

"There is little or no evidence that there are enough private school slots for voucher students or that such programs are even remotely successful," he argues. Tierney has instead led the fight to provide federal funds to help local school districts hire more teachers — 100,000 more nationwide — so that class sizes can be reduced.

Praising the success of a federally supported education program in his hometown of Salem, Tierney said, "We did not make that school better by ... taking it out of the public school system and setting it aside. We did it by investing and providing resources." An opponent of GOP efforts to send federal dollars directly to states as education block grants, Tierney argues for preserving federal programs that help communities "raise the standard" for public schools.

On health care, Tierney would prefer a federally run "single-payer" health insurance system that would provide coverage for all Americans. Congress spent much of 1993 and 1994 debating such a proposal by President Clinton and failed to come anywhere near consensus. Tierney says such a plan would provide more services at a lower cost than the current system. But he has not pressed for federal health insurance legislation, saying he prefers to work on the issue incrementally.

In the 106th Congress, he authored a bill that would encourage individual states to develop their own universal coverage system for their residents. And he won House approval in 1999 for a federal study of ways to increase the number of people who have access to health care services.

Tierney has developed an interest in a specific health concern: the safety of genetically engineered food. In the 106th Congress, he sought to require the Department of Agriculture to study the health risks associated with genetically altered crops.

He also sits on the Government Reform Committee, where in the 105th Congress, he accused GOP Chairman Dan Burton of Indiana of gross partisanship and "serious misuse of taxpayer dollars" in his investigation of fundraising for Clinton's 1996 campaign. He has used his seat on the committee's National Security, Veterans Affairs and International Relations Subcommittee as a platform from which to seek better health care for veterans and to urge a slowdown in the march toward building a multibillion-dollar missile defense system.

In 2000, he sought, unsuccessfully, to shift money from a missile defense procurement account to pay for military health programs and prescription drug care for military retirees. He also gained funding for three community-based veterans health clinics in his district.

Tierney advocates a sweeping overhaul of the campaign finance system. He has championed a plan, which he calls the Clean Money, Clean Elections Act, that would provide public financing and free broadcast time for candidates who agree not to use personal funds or accept contributions. The bill would limit expenditures by political parties and include a prohibition on "soft money"— unlimited contributions used for party-building activities and issue ads.

Although Tierney served a year as president of the Salem Chamber of Commerce, he does not see eye-to-eye with the U.S. Chamber of Commerce, backing the business group's position only about 20 percent of the time. The National Federation of Independent Business rates his voting record at below 10 percent.

And, as is the case with other Northeastern lawmakers, Tierney has been a vigorous advocate of federal steps to increase the availability and hold down the price of home heating oil, a vital commodity in Massachusetts.

Tierney first became interested in politics as a boy growing up in Salem. His uncle served as a ward councilor in Peabody, and Tierney used to campaign with him door-to-door in the community. He worked to put himself through college, where he majored in political science. After law school, he worked for a private law practice and became active in Salem civic affairs.

Although the 6th District contains much of the territory of the oddly shaped district that spawned the term "gerrymander," it is now one of the most regularly shaped and compact of the state's 10 House districts. And since it was redrawn in 1992, it has been one of the most competitive, with Republican Peter G. Torkildsen holding it for two terms.

In 1994, Tierney launched his first political campaign and came within 4 percentage points of winning Torkildsen's seat in an otherwise good year for Republicans. Tierney tried again in 1996, and this time he pressed the point that Torkildsen was a reliable supporter of House Speaker Newt Gingrich, who was hugely unpopular in Massachusetts. With Clinton running up a 28 percentage point victory margin in the district's presidential voting, Tierney eked out a 371-vote win that was not official until a recount was completed in early December.

In 1998, Torkildsen was back for a rematch, stressing his moderate stands on such issues as abortion and gay rights and some gun control measures. GOP party strategists identified the 6th as a priority, but Tierney won with surprising ease, by 12 points.

In 2000, he breezed to re-election by a whopping 42-point margin.

www.cq.com

KEY VOTES

2000

Yes	Raise hourly minimum wage by $1 over two years
Yes	Halt funding for U.S. mission in Kosovo unless European nations pay more
Yes	Provide Medicare benefits to military retirees and their dependents
No	Grant China permanent normal trade status
No	Phase out estate, gift and trust taxes
No	Prohibit implementation of president's national monument designations
No	Approve GOP plan to provide prescription drug coverage for Medicare beneficiaries
Yes	Increase help for poor nations indebted to international financial institutions

1999

Yes	Impose steel import quotas
No	Kill proposal to take aviation trust funds off budget
No	Require background checks on buyers only at gun shows with 10 or more vendors
No	Remove barriers among banking, securities and insurance companies
Yes	Authorize state grants to hire teachers and reduce class size
Yes	Overhaul campaign finance law; ban "soft money" and restrict advocacy advertising
Yes	Approve bipartisan plan to increase rights of patients in managed-care health plans

INTEREST GROUPS

	AFL-CIO	ADA	CCUS	ACU
2000	100%	95%	28%	4%
1999	89%	100%	12%	4%
1998	100%	100%	22%	4%
1997	100%	100%	20%	12%

CQ VOTE STUDIES

	PARTY UNITY		PRESIDENTIAL SUPPORT	
	Support	Oppose	Support	Oppose
2000	97%	3%	81%	19%
1999	95%	5%	79%	21%
1998	98%	2%	83%	17%
1997	95%	5%	75%	25%

MASSACHUSETTS 6
North Shore — Lynn; Peabody

Pristine beaches line the cool ocean of Boston's North Shore, home to some of the most exclusive homes in the 6th and the state. Country clubs, fox hunting and polo matches are popular diversions for residents of the northern inland, where the population is sparse but wealthy.

The population is denser along the Route 128 high-tech corridor, which forms the district's southern border. Like much of Massachusetts in the 1990s, communities along Route 128 turned from a manufacturing- to an information-based economy. Fueled in part by Boston's universities, high-tech firms have flourished from Burlington to Gloucester, which also supports a major fishing industry.

Lynn, the 6th's largest community, is home to aerospace and defense contractors. Urban dwellers are concentrated mostly in Lynn, Haverhill and Peabody and furnish blue-collar and minority votes for Democrats. Northern well-to-do towns from Georgetown and Rowley to Gloucester

provide Republicans with local legislative seats. While the district has a clear Democratic tilt, Republicans can win here by attracting independents; nearly half of all voters are listed as "unenrolled" in either party. A Republican represented the 6th for four years in the 1990s, but the district supported the Democratic presidential candidate in 1992, '96 and 2000.

MAJOR INDUSTRY
Computer software, defense, fishing

MILITARY BASES
Hanscom Air Force Base, 1,561 military, 1,420 civilian (2000)

CITIES
Lynn 80,985; Haverhill 55,525; Peabody, 49,212

UNUSUAL FEATURES
Salem witch trials of 1692; This district holds most of the territory that spawned the original "gerrymandered" district, named after the 1812 governor, Elbridge Gerry.

Rep. Edward J. Markey (D)

Elected 1976; 13th full term

CAPITOL OFFICE
225-2836; fax 226-0092; 2108 Rayburn Bldg. 20515

INTERNET
e-mail: www.house.gov/writerep
web: www.house.gov/markey

COMMITTEES
Energy & Commerce
Resources

HOMETOWN
Malden

BORN
July 11, 1946, Malden, Mass.

RELIGION
Roman Catholic

FAMILY
Wife, Susan Blumenthal

EDUCATION
Boston College, B.A. 1968, J.D. 1972

MILITARY SERVICE
Army Reserve, 1968-73

CAREER
Lawyer

POLITICAL HIGHLIGHTS
Mass. House, 1973-77

ELECTION RESULTS

2000 GENERAL

Edward J. Markey (D)	211,543	98.9%
write-ins	2,268	1.1%

2000 PRIMARY

Edward J. Markey (D)	unopposed

1998 GENERAL

Edward J. Markey (D)	137,178	70.6%
Patricia H. Long (R)	56,977	29.3%

PREVIOUS WINNING PERCENTAGES
1996 (70%); 1994 (64%); 1992 (62%); 1990 (100%);
1988 (100%); 1986 (100%); 1984 (71%); 1982 (78%);
1980 (100%); 1978 (85%); 1976 Combined General
and Special Election (77%)

Markey's easy collegiality, ready wit and facility with the details of intricate legislation have enabled him to work across party lines to cut dozens of deals on energy, consumer protection and telecommunications bills during a quarter-century in the House. He is now the longest-tenured member on the Resources Committee and the third-most-senior Democrat on the powerful Energy and Commerce Committee.

Markey holds the ranking Democrat spot on Energy and Commerce's Telecommunications and the Internet Subcommittee, a position that affords him the chance to continue his pursuit of legislation to fine-tune federal regulation in the "new economy." The work seems suited to Markey's parochial interests — both political and personal.

His district's fortunes are tied to the high-tech Route 128 corridor, while his passion for Boston sports teams, the Red Sox in particular, is satisfied by the simulcasts on the Web that he monitors at the Capitol. Asked recently how the Internet had changed his life, he grinned and said, "Four words: Major League Baseball dot-com."

Markey passed up the opportunity to lead the Democratic side of the Resources Committee in the 107th Congress, so that he could remain the ranking Democrat on the Telecommunications panel.

The son of a milk truck driver, Markey mixes humor, biting sarcasm and literary allusion to enliven congressional debate. While reporters lap up his one-liners, critics have grumbled that he is almost too quick to summarize with a sound bite. Behind the scenes, however, Markey has proved himself consistently conversant on the mind-numbing minutia of the most complex regulatory questions.

His keen competitiveness manifests itself both in committee meetings and in the members' gym, where he is a basketball regular. And his willingness to deal is well-known to Republican Billy Tauzin of Louisiana, the new chairman of Energy and Commerce, who previously chaired the Telecommunications panel.

Markey takes particular pride in staying abreast of the ever-changing world of the Internet economy, where he focuses on consumer privacy. He favors legislation to require online retailers to get their customers' permission before sharing personal information with others. "The problem we face today isn't Big Brother, it's Big Browser," Markey said at a hearing on the issue in 2000. In the 106th, he launched the Congressional Privacy Caucus with a couple other lawmakers.

In 1999, Markey opposed the financial services overhaul, saying it wrongly allowed customers' personal information to be passed among the bank, brokerage and insurance affiliates in the expected new wave of financial service conglomerates. He won approval of language to erect some barriers to the exchange of information, but the provisions were deleted before the House passed the bill.

Markey takes a dim view of attempts to reopen key portions of the 1996 telecommunications act in the 107th Congress. He also opposes Tauzin's effort to allow Baby Bells to deliver high-speed data transmission over long-distance telephone lines even if they have not opened their local markets to competition. Consumers will benefit most, he says, if there is "ruthless Darwinian competition that would bring a smile to Adam Smith." (Markey helped draft the provision in the telecommunications law requiring "v-chip" circuitry in new televisions to allow parents to block programs rated as vio-

7th DISTRICT/**MASSACHUSETTS**

lent or sexually explicit.)

In the 106th, Markey worked with Tauzin to craft a law requiring the auto industry to provide the government with more information about product defects. The final bill included a provision by Markey directing the government to devise a crash test for rollovers. When fuel prices spiked, he won a 10-year effort to enact a law creating the Northeast Home Heating Oil Reserve. And he was an architect of the provision in a satellite television law making it possible for the first time for local broadcast stations to be part of a package of satellite-delivered TV service. But he also took part in negotiations, which ultimately ended in a standoff, aimed at crafting a compromise to deregulate the electric utility industry.

After a two-year leave to serve on the Budget Committee, Markey is back on Resources, where he tends to constituent concerns about the New England coast's ecology and the depleted Georges Bank fishing area. He is a champion of forest preservation and the Environmental Protection Agency, and he is expected to help lead the campaign to block President Bush's effort to open the Arctic National Wildlife Refuge to oil exploration.

In Markey's early days in Congress, he developed a minor national following because of his ardent opposition to domestic nuclear power and nuclear weaponry. He remains a leading congressional critic of nuclear proliferation. In 2000, he unsuccessfully pressed the Pentagon to take nuclear weapons off "hair trigger" alert in order to minimize the threat of mishaps, and he based his opposition to granting China permanent normal trade status on Beijing's role in the spread of nuclear arms.

Elected to the state House at 26, he served two terms, battling his party's leadership on occasion. Once, they retaliated by kicking him off the Judiciary Committee, and one opponent went so far as to throw the furniture from Markey's office into the hallway. He won election to Congress in 1976, capturing a seat that came open with the death of Democratic Rep. Torbert H. MacDonald. Markey's only tough campaign since was in 1984, when his opponent questioned his commitment to the job after Markey briefly ran for the Senate seat opening up with the departure of Democrat Paul E. Tsongas.

Markey was one of the more visible Democratic members of Congress who went to Florida during the disputed 2000 presidential election; he lobbied for a manual recount, hoping that would benefit the Democratic nominee, Vice President Al Gore. When that failed, Markey began pushing legislation to set a uniform poll closing time, which he says would lessen the impact on close races of television's election night projections.

KEY VOTES

2000
- Yes Raise hourly minimum wage by $1 over two years
- No Halt funding for U.S. mission in Kosovo unless European nations pay more
- Yes Provide Medicare benefits to military retirees and their dependents
- No Grant China permanent normal trade status
- ? Phase out estate, gift and trust taxes
- No Prohibit implementation of president's national monument designations
- ? Approve GOP plan to provide prescription drug coverage for Medicare beneficiaries
- Yes Increase help for poor nations indebted to international financial institutions

1999
- Yes Impose steel import quotas
- No Kill proposal to take aviation trust funds off budget
- No Require background checks on buyers only at gun shows with 10 or more vendors
- No Remove barriers among banking, securities and insurance companies
- Yes Authorize state grants to hire teachers and reduce class size
- Yes Overhaul campaign finance law; ban "soft money" and restrict advocacy advertising
- Yes Approve bipartisan plan to increase rights of patients in managed-care health plans

INTEREST GROUPS

	AFL-CIO	ADA	CCUS	ACU
2000	100%	85%	29%	4%
1999	100%	100%	16%	0%
1998	100%	90%	31%	4%
1997	100%	100%	20%	8%

CQ VOTE STUDIES

	PARTY UNITY		PRESIDENTIAL SUPPORT	
	Support	Oppose	Support	Oppose
2000	98%	2%	88%	12%
1999	96%	4%	79%	21%
1998	95%	5%	82%	18%
1997	96%	4%	76%	24%

MASSACHUSETTS 7
Northwest suburbs – Woburn; Framingham; Revere

The affluent northern tier of Route 128, a Silicon Valley of the East, shapes the 7th's character. Stretching east from the urban retail center of Route 9 in Framingham, along Route 128 and down to the middle-class coastal town of Revere, the district includes some of the state's most well-to-do communities. The area takes pride in its history; each year, Lexington re-enacts Paul Revere's ride and the first Revolutionary War battles (which took place in towns in both the 7th and 5th districts) on Patriot's Day.

A software and Internet industry arose from and replaced a high-tech manufacturing base that struggled in the early-1990s recession. Northwest of Boston, many Medford and Malden residents commute to blue-collar jobs in Boston. For decades, the North Shore coastal town of Revere has attracted middle-class vacationers to its beaches and now houses a growing Asian community.

The 7th's political roots are a dichotomy of Protestant, Yankee Republican and Irish Democrat. In the 1990s, the district leaned Democratic. The well-to-do sections of the 7th vary from Yankee conservative Weston to liberal Democratic Lincoln. Democrats also draw votes from a blue-collar, middle-class base in Framingham and the eastern part of the district.

MAJOR INDUSTRY
Computer software, telecommunications, defense

MILITARY
Natick Research and Development Laboratories (Army), 49 military, 903 civilian (1998)

CITIES
Framingham (unincorporated), 64,989 (1990); Waltham, 58,634; Medford, 55,559; Malden, 52,507

UNUSUAL FEATURES
James Pierpont wrote "Jingle Bells" in 1850 while sitting in Medford Square; Richard B. Fitzgibbon Jr. and Richard B. Fitzgibbon III of Stoneham, the only known American father-son duo to die in the Vietnam War.

Rep. Michael E. Capuano (D)

Elected 1998; 2nd term

CAPITOL OFFICE
225-5111; fax 225-9322
1232 Longworth Bldg. 20515

INTERNET
e-mail: www.house.gov/writerep
web: www.house.gov/capuano

COMMITTEES
Budget
Financial Services

HOMETOWN
Somerville

BORN
Jan. 9, 1952, Somerville, Mass.

RELIGION
Roman Catholic

FAMILY
Wife, Barbara Teebagy Capuano; two children

EDUCATION
Dartmouth College, B.A. 1973; Boston College, J.D. 1977

CAREER
Lawyer; Mass. legislative aide

POLITICAL HIGHLIGHTS
Somerville alderman, 1977-79; candidate for mayor of Somerville, 1979, 1981; Somerville alderman-at-large, 1985-89; mayor of Somerville, 1990-99; sought Democratic nomination for Mass. secretary of state, 1994

ELECTION RESULTS

2000 GENERAL

Michael E. Capuano (D)	unopposed	

2000 PRIMARY

Michael E. Capuano (D)	unopposed	

1998 GENERAL

Michael E. Capuano (D)	99,603	81.7%
Philip Hyde III (R)	14,125	11.6%
Andrea Morell (SW)	4,854	4.0%
Anthony Schinella (I)	3,129	2.6%

Like his predecessor, six-term Rep. Joseph P. Kennedy II, Capuano is a reliably Democratic vote. But unlike the liberal activism of that scion of the Kennedy clan, Capuano brings to the House a blue-collar pragmatism — honed during two decades in local politics, as an alderman and as mayor of working-class Somerville.

Capuano does not have the celebrity of Kennedy or of his uncle, President John F. Kennedy, whose political career began with his election to this Boston-based seat in 1946. And although Capuano (CAP-you-AH-no) is half Irish, his Italian-American surname is a change from the Irish identification of the Kennedys and of two others who have held the seat since World War II, James Michael Curley and former Speaker Thomas P. "Tip" O'Neill Jr.

Capuano has street smarts that belie his Ivy League education. And while he may occasionally use rough language that accentuates his brash personality, he is also one who carefully alphabetizes his files. Trained as a tax attorney, he is able to delve into the minutiae of budget and tax policy. In the 107th Congress, he will be able to use those skills in his new assignment to the Budget Committee. In his first term, his focus was on education and affordable housing. (He has a personal stake in the latter issue as his mother lives in housing for the elderly.)

Like many freshman legislators, Capuano in the 106th Congress had to adjust from being in charge to being one of the crowd. "I made more decisions in a day as mayor than all last year" in Congress, he told the Boston Herald early in 2000. But he is unambiguous in describing his plans to change that. Rather than rely on the congressional seniority system, he says, he wants to "find ways to short-circuit it." And in the 107th Congress he took a step in that direction by winning a seat on the Democratic Steering Committee, which makes the party's committee assignments.

Capuano's legislative approach is a pragmatic one: "I want to figure out what I think I can win and push the envelope a little." He adds that he tends to focus on "stuff that flies under the radar screen."

That strategy allowed Capuano to achieve some legislative success in his first term. A housing bill passed by the House in 2000 included his provision to allow teachers and uniformed municipal workers — even if their income is above the poverty level — to buy homes through federally subsidized housing programs.

In 1999, from his seat on the Banking Committee (renamed Financial Services), Capuano won approval of an amendment to require insurance companies bidding for federal contracts to show that they had not discriminated against poor or minority communities in selling insurance — or if they had, to prove that they were operating under an agreement designed to prevent such discrimination.

In the 106th Congress, he pushed for legislation to require Medicare coverage for services that encourage independence for senior citizens who lose their eyesight.

Capuano once joked that he wanted to be "the Democratic Tom DeLay," because his hard-driving, partisan style of campaigning is similar to that of the House GOP whip. But among his colleagues he is known for his wit. After renting his one-bedroom apartment on Capitol Hill, for instance, he challenged neighborhood thugs to come after him. "I'm tougher than most of those guys anyway," he quipped.

While describing himself as "a bit of a wise guy," he says he is discomfited by the discourse that takes place in Congress nowadays. "I'm regularly frustrated by the amount of rhetoric that we have. I understand it, I accept it as part of the reality, but I don't want to participate in it any more than I have to."

As far as getting legislation through, he says: "I personally have had a difficult time measuring my success, if you want the truth, because I have not yet solved the Medicare crisis. I'll get to it."

In the interim, in his first term he struck gold with an issue that resonated with constituents across class and racial lines when he declared his opposition to the Massachusetts Port Authority's plan for a new runway at Logan International Airport. Capuano argued that the authority should be concentrating instead on solving regional transportation ills.

While he criticized a $16 billion merger of two New England banks, Fleet Financial Group and BankBoston Corp., he fought to ensure that community banks in his district had a chance to bid on bank branches, automatic teller machines and other assets the two bank giants had to shed as a condition of their merger.

Capuano still must navigate a district where political tensions continually work their way to the surface. As mayor, he drew a steady flow of criticism from detractors who described his style as "tyrannical" and said he managed the city as a ward boss would, hiring friends and relatives for city jobs and running enemies out of city agencies. Capuano said the attacks on his leadership style were simply "a sign of a good executive."

Soon after taking office in Washington, Capuano criticized black leaders in the 8th District for not giving his 1998 campaign much support. Then, citing a need to save money and centralize operations, in 1999 he closed a district office in Boston's Roxbury neighborhood, which has a significant black population. After protests, he eventually reopened an office in the community.

Capuano triumphed in a 10-person Democratic donnybrook created by Kennedy's unexpected 1998 retirement in the staunchly Democratic 8th. Headlining the field was Raymond L. Flynn, a former Boston mayor and ambassador to the Vatican who had abandoned a flagging run for governor. But Capuano needled Flynn on his education and housing policies as mayor; others attacked Flynn's anti-abortion position.

Although greatly outspent by two other candidates, Capuano was lifted to victory by a strong turnout in Somerville. He breezed by a hapless Republican opponent that November, taking 82 percent of the vote. In 2000, the GOP did not field a candidate.

KEY VOTES

2000
Yes Raise hourly minimum wage by $1 over two years
No   Halt funding for U.S. mission in Kosovo unless European nations pay more
Yes Provide Medicare benefits to military retirees and their dependents
No   Grant China permanent normal trade status
No   Phase out estate, gift and trust taxes
No   Prohibit implementation of president's national monument designations
No   Approve GOP plan to provide prescription drug coverage for Medicare beneficiaries
Yes Increase help for poor nations indebted to international financial institutions

1999
Yes Impose steel import quotas
No   Kill proposal to take aviation trust funds off budget
No   Require background checks on buyers only at gun shows with 10 or more vendors
No   Remove barriers among banking, securities and insurance companies
Yes Authorize state grants to hire teachers and reduce class size
Yes Overhaul campaign finance law; ban "soft money" and restrict advocacy advertising
Yes Approve bipartisan plan to increase rights of patients in managed-care health plans

INTEREST GROUPS

	AFL-CIO	ADA	CCUS	ACU
2000	100%	100%	33%	0%
1999	100%	100%	16%	0%

CQ VOTE STUDIES

	PARTY UNITY		PRESIDENTIAL SUPPORT	
	Support	Oppose	Support	Oppose
2000	98%	2%	87%	13%
1999	95%	5%	81%	19%

MASSACHUSETTS 8

Parts of Boston and suburbs – Cambridge; Somerville

Boston and its suburbs in the 8th evoke an Olde Towne feel, from the upper-crust echelons of Beacon Hill to the grittier locales of Somerville. Always a hub for immigrants, locals say political rallies could be held in half a dozen languages. While the minority and immigrant population grows, whites have started to trickle into the suburbs from the city in search of more affordable housing.

Two of the world's most renowned universities – Harvard and the Massachusetts Institute of Technology – lie along the banks of the Charles River in Cambridge. The district also takes in more than 40 other colleges and universities, which drive much of the economy, whether through the blue-collar service employees who work at the schools and teaching hospitals or through the biotechnology software firms that employ local talent. There is a degree of tension in the 8th between these laborers and white-collar professionals who work at

the same institutions, but they coexist in reasonable peace partly because of their shared liberalism. The largest public transportation project in American history, the "Big Dig," to place the city's central highway underground, also has supplied thousands of construction jobs.

In a state dominated by Democrats, the 8th could be the safest seat. Carved to provide minorities a strong voice, the district combines the votes of well-to-do liberals and the more than 40 percent minority population to elect old-style Democrats in the tradition of Thomas P. "Tip" O'Neill Jr, who represented the area from 1953-87.

MAJOR INDUSTRY
Biotechnology, higher education, health care, tourism

CITIES
Boston (pt.), 342,917 (1990); Cambridge, 92,942; Somerville, 73,872

UNUSUAL FEATURES
The African-American 54th Regiment of Civil War fame was based in this district.

Rep. Joe Moakley (D)

CAPITOL OFFICE
225-8273; fax 225-3984; 235 Cannon Bldg. 20515

INTERNET
e-mail: jmoakley@mail.house.gov
web: www.house.gov/moakley

COMMITTEES
Rules - ranking member

HOMETOWN
South Boston

BORN
April 27, 1927, Boston, Mass.

RELIGION
Roman Catholic

FAMILY
Widowed

EDUCATION
U. of Miami, attended 1950-51; Suffolk U., J.D. 1956

MILITARY SERVICE
Navy, 1943-46

CAREER
Lawyer

POLITICAL HIGHLIGHTS
Mass. House, 1953-63; Mass. Senate, 1965-71; sought Democratic nomination for U.S. House, 1970; Boston City Council, 1971-73

ELECTION RESULTS

2000 GENERAL

Joe Moakley (D)	193,020	77.6%
Janet E. Jeghelian (R)	48,672	19.6%
David Rosa (I)	6,998	2.8%

2000 PRIMARY

Joe Moakley (D)	unopposed

1998 GENERAL

Joe Moakley (D)	unopposed

PREVIOUS WINNING PERCENTAGES
1996 (72%); 1994 (70%); 1992 (69%); 1990 (70%); 1988 (100%); 1986 (84%); 1984 (100%); 1982 (64%); 1980 (100%); 1978 (92%); 1976 (70%); 1974 (89%); 1972 (43%)

Elected 1972; 15th term

With his ever-ready smile, quick Irish wit and hearty handshake, Moakley embodies old-school politics, when lawmakers did not allow their partisan fervor to get in the way of friendship. "With enemies like that, who needs friends?" quipped Deborah Pryce, R-Ohio, of the genial man from "Southie."

While he is one of the House's most reliable liberal votes, never shy about taking the House floor to attack the policy stands of his GOP rivals, Moakley is respected and well-liked by members on both sides of the aisle. People continue to call him chairman six years after he lost the top post at the Rules Committee following the 1995 GOP takeover of the House.

Early in 2001, Moakley announced that he had been diagnosed with an incurable form of leukemia and would not seek re-election in 2002. Even in the face of the diagnosis, the congressman displayed his wit, reporting that the doctor had told him, "Don't buy any green bananas." In response, Rules Committee Chairman David Dreier, R-Calif., presented Moakley with a bunch of green bananas the day after his announcement. And his fellow House lawmakers, in an emotional vote, unanimously passed a bill naming the new federal courthouse in Boston after Moakley, waiving the rule that prohibits naming public works in honor of a sitting member.

Even before his leukemia diagnosis, Moakley had been plagued by a string of health problems in recent years, including a 1995 liver transplant necessitated by hepatitis B. Characteristically, he emerged from that ordeal to become a spokesman for transplant groups across the country and helped form the Congressional Task Force on Organ and Tissue Donation. He has sponsored legislation to require Medicare to pay for immunosuppressive drugs that keep donated organs from being rejected.

During five-plus years as Rules Committee chairman, Moakley was at the center of partisan politics, helping Democratic leaders decide which bills would come to the floor and how debate on them would be structured, usually at the expense of Republicans. Despite that role, Moakley was never seen as an iron-fisted ruler.

His foil on the committee for most of that time was former GOP Rep. Gerald B.H. Solomon of New York, a self-described "doctrinaire conservative" with a notoriously short temper. Moakley always let Solomon's harsh words slide by, using humor to defuse tense moments. In 1990, for instance, Solomon took to the floor to lambaste a rule that deprived Republicans of the right to offer any amendments, and in protest drew an X through a picture of Moakley. "I hope this does not mean that he takes me off his Christmas card list," Moakley said in response.

The congressman has occasionally sided with conservatives on specific issues. He voted to ban a procedure its opponents call "partial birth" abortion, and he supported a constitutional amendment allowing Congress to ban desecration of the U.S. flag.

But Moakley is best known for his old-fashioned liberalism. He was a leader of a long-running effort to close the U.S. Army School of the Americas in Fort Benning, Ga., which trains Latin American military leaders, some of whom have been implicated in torture and human rights abuses after their return to their home countries. In 2000, the House refused to close the school, instead renaming it and requiring a curriculum based on human rights and respect for democratic values. Moakley criticized the changes, saying they "don't amount to much more than a new coat of paint."

Moakley first became involved in Latin American issues in 1989 after six Jesuit priests were murdered in El Salvador. He was appointed by then-Speaker Tom Foley, D-Wash., to head a special task force to investigate the Salvadoran government's response to the killings. The Moakley Commission issued a report that revealed the involvement of several high-ranking Salvadoran military officials in the murders. The report helped lead to the termination of U.S. military aid to El Salvador. Moakley counts his work on the commission as "probably the highlight of my career. To cut off funds to stop a war. To stop people from getting killed."

Years later, Moakley visited El Salvador and was greeted in one village with crowds of singing and cheering fans. In gratitude, Moakley, who doesn't speak Spanish, responded in the only way he knew how: He stood before the crowd and sang his favorite ballad, "If You're Irish, Come Into the Parlor."

Moakley has traveled to Cuba numerous times in recent years and has met with Cuban President Fidel Castro to discuss human rights and the opening of trade relations. Moakley was an outspoken advocate of lifting the U.S. embargo on exports of food and medicine to the communist nation. In 2000, he voted for a series of amendments to the Treasury appropriations bill that blocked funding to implement the U.S. travel ban and economic sanctions against Cuba. Congress later passed a limited easing of sanctions in separate legislation.

During highly charged debate in 2000 over the return of young Cuban castaway Elián González, Moakley met with the boy's grandmothers and supported the child's return to his father in the communist country. Moakley attacked Vice President Al Gore's call to grant Elián permanent U.S. residency, saying such a move would tear apart the family and trample custody law.

Moakley was born, raised, and has lived his entire life in South Boston. He grew up in housing projects, an experience he credits with developing his liberal views and passion for social programs such as welfare and a decent minimum wage. At the age of 15, he forged a birth certificate and joined the Navy, serving in the South Pacific during World War II. "I'm still two years older as far as the Navy is concerned," he said.

After the war, Moakley was a champion boxer in college. He was elected to the state House at the age of 25 and later served in the state Senate. He won election to Congress in 1972, running as an independent against conservative Democratic Rep. Louise Day Hicks. Since then, only twice have Moakley's re-election numbers fallen below 70 percent.

KEY VOTES

2000

Yes Raise hourly minimum wage by $1 over two years
Yes Halt funding for U.S. mission in Kosovo unless European nations pay more
Yes Provide Medicare benefits to military retirees and their dependents
No   Grant China permanent normal trade status
No   Phase out estate, gift and trust taxes
No   Prohibit implementation of president's national monument designations
No   Approve GOP plan to provide prescription drug coverage for Medicare beneficiaries
Yes Increase help for poor nations indebted to international financial institutions

1999

Yes Impose steel import quotas
No   Kill proposal to take aviation trust funds off budget
No   Require background checks on buyers only at gun shows with 10 or more vendors
Yes Remove barriers among banking, securities and insurance companies
Yes Authorize state grants to hire teachers and reduce class size
Yes Overhaul campaign finance law; ban "soft money" and restrict advocacy advertising
Yes Approve bipartisan plan to increase rights of patients in managed-care health plans

INTEREST GROUPS

	AFL-CIO	ADA	CCUS	ACU
2000	100%	80%	30%	16%
1999	89%	90%	24%	4%
1998	100%	65%	33%	13%
1997	100%	85%	30%	8%

CQ VOTE STUDIES

	PARTY UNITY		PRESIDENTIAL SUPPORT	
	Support	Oppose	Support	Oppose
2000	92%	8%	81%	19%
1999	91%	9%	79%	21%
1998	94%	6%	79%	21%
1997	91%	9%	70%	30%

MASSACHUSETTS 9

Part of Boston, southern suburbs — Taunton; Braintree; part of Brockton

Boston's Italian North End and Irish "Southie" were encroached upon in the 1990s by young well-to-do professionals who choose to live in the 9th to take advantage of city life. The seaport in the northeast, long filled with vacant lots, is on the verge of a boom as the "Big Dig" central highway project creates the transportation infrastructure for growth. South of Boston, the cities are a mix of duplexes, old-money suburbs and new developments that attract white, middle-class residents from Boston.

Fidelity Investments' headquarters and smaller firms make the 9th one of the world's largest centers for mutual fund investing. Nearby, Faneuil Hall meeting and marketplace anchors the waterfront retail industry. South of the city, software development and medical-related industries have helped spur the economy.

The 9th's areas outside of Boston are conservative for Massachusetts. Some political observers think the district could be competitive for Republicans when Democratic Rep. Moakley retires. The growing suburban population helped elect Republican Gov. Paul Cellucci in 1998, and turnout among Boston liberals is low.

MAJOR INDUSTRY
Financial services, higher education, biotechnology, computer software

CITIES
Boston (pt.), 231,366 (1990); Taunton, 53,107; Brockton (pt.), 52,474 (1990)

UNUSUAL FEATURES
Patriots tossed boxes of tea into the district's Boston Harbor during the Boston Tea Party in 1773, a catalyst for the Revolutionary War.

Rep. Bill Delahunt (D)

Elected 1996; 3rd term

CAPITOL OFFICE
225-3111; fax 225-5658
1317 Longworth Bldg. 20515

INTERNET
e-mail: william.delahunt@mail.house.gov
web: www.house.gov/delahunt

COMMITTEES
International Relations
Judiciary

HOMETOWN
Quincy

BORN
July 18, 1941, Quincy, Mass.

RELIGION
Roman Catholic

FAMILY
Divorced; two children

EDUCATION
Middlebury College, B.A. 1963; Boston College,
J.D. 1967

MILITARY SERVICE
Coast Guard, 1963; Coast Guard Reserve, 1963-71

CAREER
Lawyer

POLITICAL HIGHLIGHTS
Quincy City Council, 1971-73; Mass. House, 1973-
75; Norfolk County district attorney, 1975-97

ELECTION RESULTS

2000 GENERAL

Bill Delahunt (D)	234,675	74.1%
Eric V. Bleicken (R)	81,192	25.7%

2000 PRIMARY

Bill Delahunt (D)	unopposed

1998 GENERAL

Bill Delahunt (D)	164,917	70.0%
Eric V. Bleicken (R)	70,466	29.9%

PREVIOUS WINNING PERCENTAGES
1996 (54%)

An outgoing and affable politician, Delahunt is a reliable liberal vote and a strong supporter of environmental and consumer causes. An aggressive partisan debater at times, he nevertheless has a knack for cultivating relationships with colleagues who don't share his ideological outlook. Former Judiciary Committee Chairman Henry J. Hyde of Illinois once said Delahunt brought "a maturity, leavened with a good sense of humor" to the committee.

Even before arriving on Capitol Hill, Delahunt (DELL-a-hunt) was a seasoned and able hand at the political game, serving on the Quincy City Council and in the Massachusetts House. He says he is part of the generation inspired to enter politics by fellow Bay Stater John F. Kennedy. At Middlebury College, Delahunt was co-chairman of a Vermont students-for-Kennedy group. The other chairman (and also a fraternity brother) was the late Ronald H. Brown, secretary of commerce under President Clinton.

After his service in the state House, Delahunt spent more than 20 years as a county district attorney, and his experience as a prosecutor has made him a key player for his party on Judiciary. Barney Frank of Massachusetts, the Judiciary panel's No. 2 Democrat, told The Boston Globe that Delahunt "makes it impossible for [Republicans] to say Democrats are soft on crime. Billy has locked up more people than everyone else on the committee put together. He is a liberal with his head on his shoulders."

Delahunt drew on his knowledge of juvenile crime when the House considered a GOP plan in the 105th Congress to award federal block grants to states that prosecuted more violent juvenile offenders as adults. He did not object to imprisoning "hard core" juvenile criminals, but he said, "If we are going to lock them up, let us not lock them up in an adult prison where they are going to receive the very best training in terms of violent crime. ... That is my experience as a prosecutor."

In debate with Republicans, Delahunt can be unsparing at times. "They do not know what they are talking about," he said of his GOP adversaries during action in the 105th on the juvenile crime bill. In the 106th, he scorned GOP efforts to ban gambling on high school and college sports, contending, "It won't make a damn bit of difference."

Delahunt criticized GOP efforts in the 106th to toughen bankruptcy laws, saying that a Republican-backed bill "goes after lower- and middle-class debtors" while making it easier for credit card companies to collect balances owed them. He pressed for an amendment placing a nationwide cap on homestead exemptions, to prevent wealthy debtors from evading their debts by buying expensive houses in states that exempt homes from bankruptcy proceedings.

Despite his heated rhetoric, Delahunt will collaborate with Republicans on occasion. He cosponsored bills with GOP lawmakers to make it easier for prisoners to secure DNA testing and to allow television cameras in federal courtrooms.

Delahunt, who adopted an abandoned Vietnamese baby girl in 1975, has been a force behind legislation to ease overseas adoptions. In the 106th, he won a major victory with passage of his bill to grant automatic citizenship to children adopted from abroad, as well as to foreign-born children of U.S. parents. "After what these parents have been through in bringing their children to the United States, the naturalization process is an extra burden they shouldn't have to bear," he said. He also won enactment of legislation allowing parents to get vaccinations for their adopted children in this country, instead of having to wait for shots overseas.

A member of the International Relations Committee, Delahunt pushed through a measure in 1999 to require the State Department to put greater focus on genocide and other crimes against humanity. "While we cannot police every problem, we will not passively watch atrocities unfold before our eyes," he said.

Delahunt is a staunch environmentalist. He proposed measures in the 106th Congress to toughen the Clean Air Act and maintain enforcement of environmental standards at military facilities. While serving on the Resources Committee in the 105th, he worked to address the plight of the New England fishing industry, which he said has "too many boats chasing too few fish" and is facing the prospect of more foreign competitors aggravating the problem of overfishing. He also harshly criticized the Japanese government for hunting whales.

Delahunt was a vocal critic of the GOP's move to impeach Clinton in late 1998, denouncing the decision to deny members a vote on censure as an alternative to impeachment. He and several other Democrats drafted a censure resolution — requiring the president's signature — declaring that Clinton had engaged in "reprehensible conduct" and had "egregiously failed" to set a moral standard for the nation. But the Judiciary Committee voted against the resolution on a party-line vote.

In 1971, Delahunt became a member of the city council in his native Quincy; in 1973, as a freshman in the Massachusetts House, he shared an office with a couple of other Beacon Hill rookies, Barney Frank and Edward J. Markey, now senior members of the state's congressional delegation. Sandwiched between his state and federal legislative jobs was his lengthy career as Norfolk County district attorney, prosecuting crimes in that metropolitan Boston jurisdiction.

When 12-term Democratic Rep. Gerry E. Studds announced his retirement from the 10th District in 1996, Delahunt was regarded as the Democratic front-runner. But in a hard-fought September primary contest, he trailed state Rep. Phil Johnston by about 300 votes. Delahunt went to court, charging that ballots that should have been counted for him were mistakenly counted as blank. A state Superior Court judge concurred, and Delahunt was certified the primary winner just 28 days before Election Day. He went on to win the general election by 13 percentage points.

He has had no trouble retaining his seat, winning in 1998 by 40 percentage points and increasing that margin to 48 points in 2000.

KEY VOTES

2000
Yes Raise hourly minimum wage by $1 over two years
Yes Halt funding for U.S. mission in Kosovo unless European nations pay more
Yes Provide Medicare benefits to military retirees and their dependents
No   Grant China permanent normal trade status
Yes Phase out estate, gift and trust taxes
No   Prohibit implementation of president's national monument designations
No   Approve GOP plan to provide prescription drug coverage for Medicare beneficiaries
Yes Increase help for poor nations indebted to international financial institutions

1999
Yes Impose steel import quotas
No   Kill proposal to take aviation trust funds off budget
No   Require background checks on buyers only at gun shows with 10 or more vendors
No   Remove barriers among banking, securities and insurance companies
Yes Authorize state grants to hire teachers and reduce class size
Yes Overhaul campaign finance law; ban "soft money" and restrict advocacy advertising
Yes Approve bipartisan plan to increase rights of patients in managed-care health plans

INTEREST GROUPS

	AFL-CIO	ADA	CCUS	ACU
2000	89%	85%	47%	8%
1999	100%	100%	24%	0%
1998	100%	100%	28%	8%
1997	100%	95%	20%	0%

CQ VOTE STUDIES

	PARTY UNITY		PRESIDENTIAL SUPPORT	
	Support	Oppose	Support	Oppose
2000	95%	5%	80%	20%
1999	95%	5%	81%	19%
1998	97%	3%	83%	17%
1997	94%	6%	76%	24%

MASSACHUSETTS 10
South Shore – Cape Cod; islands

Cool coastal breezes in the summer and warm ocean air in the winter attract retirees and seasonal tourists to the 10th, where most towns border the ocean. The area that spawned the nation's puritanical streak and Thanksgiving holiday still retains a Yankee flavor, but the northern part of the 10th has attracted residents from Boston's ethnic neighborhoods. A new rail line from Boston to several South Shore communities is contributing to the area's population boom.

Other than tourism, maritime technology and research are burgeoning industries along the Cape, especially in Woods Hole. In the district's north, a booming software industry helped the area recover from its early-1990s recession.

The mainland coastal towns of the 10th are commonly referred to as the South Shore. With the exception of a handful of thriving cranberry bogs, most of the South Shore towns consist of bedroom developments for Boston's professionals or Quincy's blue-collar

workers. The state's most liberal population lives on the far end of Cape Cod, where Provincetown, a predominately gay artists colony, thrives.

Although the 10th is one of the state's weaker Democratic districts, Republicans have failed to capture the area's congressional seat since 1970. Nearly half of the voters are "unenrolled," or independent, and the district has supported Republicans for other offices, including Paul Cellucci for governor in 1998.

MAJOR INDUSTRY
Marine technology, biotechnology, health care, tourism

CITIES
Quincy, 85,777; Weymouth (unincorporated), 54,063 (1990); Barnstable, 46,067; Plymouth (unincorporated), 45,608 (1990)

UNUSUAL FEATURES
Presidents John Adams and John Quincy Adams from Quincy; Ruth Wakefield first baked chocolate chip "Toll House" cookies in the 1930s in Whitman.

Gov. John Engler (R)

First elected: 1990
Length of term: 4 years
Term expires: 1/03
Salary: $172,000
Phone: (517) 373-3400
Hometown: Mt. Pleasant
Born: Oct. 12, 1948; Mt. Pleasant, Mich.
Religion: Roman Catholic
Family: Wife, Michelle Engler; three children
Education: Michigan State U., B.S. 1971; Thomas M. Dooley Law School, J.D. 1981
Career: Lawyer
Political highlights: Mich. House, 1971-79; Mich. Senate, 1979-91 (majority leader, 1985-91)

Election results:
1998 GENERAL

John Engler (R)	1,883,005	62.2%
Geoffrey Fieger (D)	1,143,574	37.8%

Lt. Gov. Dick Posthumus (R)

First elected: 1998
Length of term: 4 years
Term expires: 1/03
Salary: $102,000
Phone: (517) 373-6800

STATE LEGISLATURE

Legislature: Meets January-June and September-December
House: 110 members, 2-year terms
2001 breakdown: 57R, 52D, 1 vacancy; 83 men, 26 women
Salary: $77,400; $12,000/year expenses
Phone: (517) 373-0135
Senate: 38 members, 4-year terms
2001 breakdown: 23R, 15D; 32 men, 6 women
Salary: $77,400; $12,000/year expenses
Phone: (517) 373-2400

STATE TERM LIMITS

Governor: 2 terms (goes into effect in 2002; Engler cannot run again)
Senate: 2 terms
House: 3 terms

URBAN STATISTICS

CITY	POPULATION
Detroit	965,084
Grand Rapids	185,009
Warren	141,008
Flint	130,853
Lansing	127,716

REGISTERED VOTERS

Voters do not register by party.

POPULATION

2000 population	9,938,444
1990 population	9,295,297
Percent change	+6.9%
Rank among states	8
Median age	35.2
Born in state	75%
Foreign born	4%
Urban/rural	71%/29%
Crime rate	590/100,000
Poverty level	11.0%
Federal workers	56,255
Military	21,763

REAPPORTIONMENT

Michigan lost one House seat in reapportionment, dropping from 16 districts to 15. The state legislature will draw new district lines in 2001.

MISCELLANEOUS

Web: www.state.mi.us
Capital: Lansing
Land area: 56,809 sq. miles
 Rank among states: 22
STATE ELECTION OFFICIAL
(517) 373-2540
DEMOCRATIC HEADQUARTERS
(517) 371-5410
REPUBLICAN HEADQUARTERS
(517) 487-5413

District Statistics

DIST.	D	2000 R	GREEN	D	1996 R	REF	D	1992 R	I	WHT	BLK	ASIAN	HISP	HOUSEHOLD INCOME	OVER 65+	UNDER 18	COLLEGE EDUCATION
1	43%	53%	3%	47%	40%	12%	42%	35%	23%	96%	1%	0%	1%	$22,788	16%	26%	15%
2	38	59	2	41	50	9	34	45	21	93	4	1	3	$28,905	12	29	14
3	38	59	2	39	53	7	34	47	19	90	7	1	3	$31,917	11	28	19
4	45	53	2	47	41	12	37.9	37.5	25	97	1	0	2	$25,898	12	27	13
5	53	45	2	53	35	11	45	32	23	89	8	0	3	$26,312	13	28	11
6	46	52	2	46	44	9	40	38	22	88	10	1	2	$28,453	12	27	19
7	46	52	2	45	43	11	37.9	37.6	25	92	6	1	2	$29,976	12	27	14
8	50	47	2	49	41	9	41	36	24	90	6	2	3	$35,911	9	26	24
9	52	45	2	52	38	9	44	35	21	79	18	1	3	$34,737	9	28	18
10	48.6	48.9	2	48	40	11	36	42	22	97	2	1	1	$36,536	12	25	13
11	49.0	48.6	2	47	46	7	37	47	16	93	4	2	1	$49,021	12	24	34
12	54	43	2	53	38	9	42	41	18	93	4	2	1	$38,760	13	24	20
13	58	38	2	57	34	7	49	34	17	85	11	3	2	$36,596	9	24	27
14	88	11	1	86	11	3	81	13	6	29	69	1	1	$25,079	11	30	12
15	87	12	1	86	11	2	81	15	5	26	70	1	4	$15,264	14	28	11

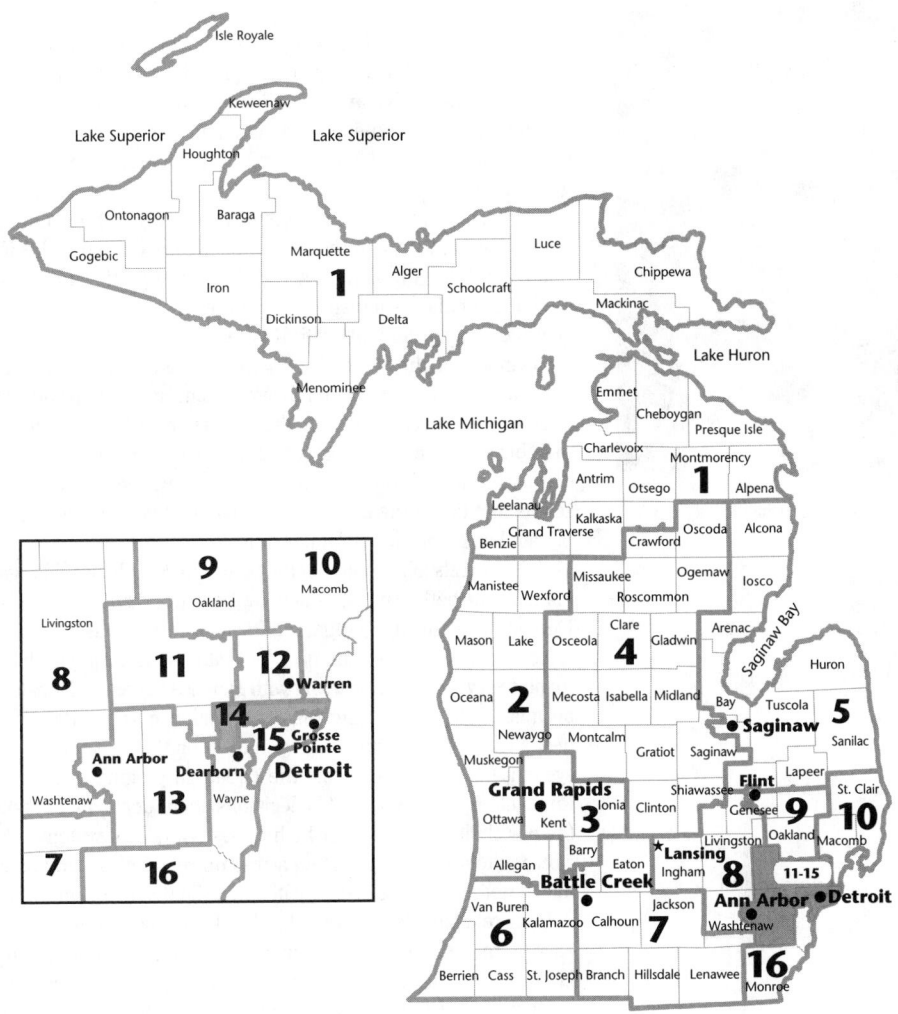

District Statistics

DIST.	VOTE FOR PRESIDENT									WHT	BLK	ASIAN	HISP	HOUSEHOLD INCOME	OVER 65+	UNDER 18	COLLEGE EDUCATION
	D	2000 R	GREEN	D	1996 R	REF	D	1992 R	I								
16	54%	44%	2%	54%	35%	11%	44%	36%	20%	97%	1%	1%	2%	$35,315	13%	25%	13%
STATE	51	46	2	52	39	9	44	36	19	83	14	1	2	$31,020	12	27	17

Sen. Carl Levin (D)

CAPITOL OFFICE
224-6221; fax 224-1388; 269 Russell Bldg. 20510

INTERNET
e-mail: senator@levin.senate.gov
web: levin.senate.gov

COMMITTEES
Armed Services - ranking member
Governmental Affairs
Small Business
Select Intelligence

HOMETOWN
Detroit

BORN
June 28, 1934, Detroit, Mich.

RELIGION
Jewish

FAMILY
Wife, Barbara Levin; three children

EDUCATION
Swarthmore College, B.A. 1956; Harvard U., LL.B. 1959

CAREER
Lawyer

POLITICAL HIGHLIGHTS
Michigan Civil Rights Commission general counsel, 1964-67; Detroit chief appellate defender, 1968-69; Detroit City Council, 1970-77 (president, 1974-77)

ELECTION RESULTS

1996 GENERAL

Carl Levin (D)	2,195,738	58.4%
Ronna Romney (R)	1,500,106	39.9%

1996 PRIMARY

Carl Levin (D)	unopposed

PREVIOUS WINNING PERCENTAGES
1990 (57%); 1984 (52%); 1978 (52%)

Elected 1978; 4th term

Whether the question is deployment of a national anti-missile defense system or the trial of an impeached president, Levin brings formidable talents to the legislative arena. He masters highly complex issues; he takes his opponents' arguments seriously and digs methodically for inconsistencies. And he does it with an amiable tenacity, making him a dogged but genial negotiator.

Furthermore, he can leverage his talents through institutional clout. As the senior Democrat on the Armed Services Committee, Levin is in a position to bird-dog the anti-missile defense system that President Bush has pledged to build — a plan Levin and other liberals fear could undermine arms control agreements with Russia.

Levin also is the senior Democrat on the Governmental Affairs panel's Permanent Subcommittee on Investigations, giving him considerable investigative authority — the panel's rules specifically recognize the right of members of the minority party to initiate investigations. Levin used the subcommittee to fashion a law that cracks down on mass-mail sweepstakes scams that target the elderly and to conduct hearings exposing the use of private banks for money laundering.

If Democrats take control of the Senate in 2003, he would regain the chairmanship of both panels, which he held during the Senate's 17 days of Democratic control in January 2001 before Bush was inaugurated.

Levin displayed his trademark legislative style during his brief stint at the Armed Services helm, sparring with Defense Secretary Donald H. Rumsfeld on missile defense during his confirmation hearing. Rather than butting heads with the incoming Pentagon chief on the wisdom of building such a system, Levin tried to recast the debate in pragmatic terms. He pressed Rumsfeld on whether Bush's decisions about deployment should consider the possibility that Russia, which opposes any U.S. system, might use it as a reason to drop out of existing arms control treaties, paradoxically making the United States less secure with a missile defense than without one.

Rumsfeld sidestepped the ploy, but Levin was aiming at a broader audience — moderates in the administration who, like Secretary of State Colin L. Powell, might be more receptive to the diplomatic consequences.

During the Clinton administration, many liberals openly grumbled that defense budgets were too high because the president's record of avoiding the draft during the Vietnam War made it politically risky for him to buck the top military leadership. By contrast, Levin said more spending was needed, provided Congress would allow the Pentagon to reduce its costs by closing some military bases.

President Clinton had undercut his own chances of winning a new round of base closures by maneuvering in 1995, before his re-election campaign, to save jobs at bases to be closed in Texas and California. Enraged Republicans vowed never to let the president preside over another round of base closures. Levin and Republican John McCain of Arizona, also on the Armed Services Committee, suggested that base closures resume after Clinton's term expired, but they were unsuccessful.

During Clinton's 1999 impeachment trial, Levin used his methodical, lawyerly approach to help set up the ground rules for the Senate procedure and then to argue for acquittal. He said the Republican House "managers," who served the role of prosecutors, had presented an ill-argued case based on flimsy evidence, testimony taken out of context and inferences.

Ironically, the impeachment trial was a result of one of Levin's earlier legislative initiatives as a member of the Governmental Affairs panel. In 1994, he was instrumental in getting Congress to reinstate the independent counsel system for investigating executive branch wrongdoing. The Independent Counsel Act had grown out of President Nixon's firing of Archibald Cox, the special counsel investigating Watergate. The aim of the law was to ensure that future investigations of high officials could be carried out without fear of interference from the president or his appointees at the Justice Department.

The independent counsel statute expired in 1992, amid GOP charges that the law had been used to harass Republican presidents. Two years later, Levin, with the help of then-Senate colleague William S. Cohen of Maine and an assist from the Clinton administration, got it reinstated. But Independent Counsel Kenneth W. Starr's lengthy investigation of Clinton turned Levin against the law, persuading him that it should be "radically reformed." When the legislation expired in 1999, Levin was one of four senators who proposed a bill that would have reauthorized the office but under much tighter controls that would make it very difficult for a special prosecutor to expand the scope of his inquiry. The bill failed.

On social issues, Levin clearly stands left of center. He voted against banning a procedure its opponents call "partial birth" abortion, and he opposes the ban on abortions at overseas military hospitals. But while he supported banning job discrimination on the basis of sexual orientation, he did vote to bar federal recognition of same-sex marriage.

After a bloody shooting spree in 1999 at Columbine High School in Colorado, Levin vowed to promote gun control legislation by speaking on gun crimes each week that the Senate was in session.

In the 1970s, Levin made a name for himself on the Detroit City Council, where he teamed with Mayor Coleman A. Young to demolish thousands of abandoned buildings. He and Young, a powerful presence among Michigan's black voters, strayed apart at times, but that probably helped Levin as a statewide candidate — it showed suburban voters he was not inextricably tied to Detroit's black majority.

That statewide run came in 1978, and Levin caught a big break when GOP Sen. Robert P. Griffin, disappointed at losing the contest for Senate Republican leader in 1977, announced that he would retire the next year and began skipping votes. Griffin eventually decided to run after all, but by that time, he had missed one-third of the Senate votes over an entire year. Levin said Griffin was obviously tired of the job, and the voters agreed that Griffin deserved a rest. Levin won by 4 percentage points.

Levin, whose older brother Sander serves in the House, has an avuncular manner, but he can and will play political hardball. In 1984, Carl Levin aired an ad showing his GOP opponent, former astronaut Jack Lousma, warming up a Japanese audience a year earlier by telling them about the Toyota he owned. In Michigan, where Japanese cars meant joblessness for autoworkers, the candidate's statement was a major embarrassment, and Levin made sure Michigan voters didn't miss it. President Reagan carried Michigan with 59 percent, but Levin held on to win with 52 percent.

In 1990, with national GOP leaders sharpening their knives for him, Levin amassed a daunting campaign treasury and early on aired television ads touting his accomplishments. Only after his opponent, GOP Rep. Bill Schuette, began attacking did Levin fire back, thereby preserving his "nice guy" image. Levin won a decisive 57 percent of the vote.

In 1996, running on a ticket headed by Clinton, Levin finally waged a campaign in a year favorable to the Democrats, and he won by a career-high 18 percentage points.

KEY VOTES

2000

Yes Overhaul bankruptcy law and increase minimum wage

No Limit fiscal 2001 discretionary spending to $600.3 billion

Yes Override veto on nuclear waste disposal at Yucca Mountain site in Nevada

Yes Oppose effort to terminate Kosovo mission

Yes Include gender, sexual orientation and disability in federal hate crime protections

No Approve GOP plan to restrict use of genetic information by health insurers

No Kill amendment delaying implementation of an anti-missile defense system

No Cut taxes for married couples

Yes Grant China permanent normal trade status

1999

No Remove President Clinton from office for obstruction of justice

No Kill amendment authorizing state grants to hire teachers and reduce class size

Yes Require criminal background checks for purchases at gun shows

No Approve GOP proposal to increase rights of patients in managed-care health plans

No Block effort to allow farm and medicine exports to Cuba

No Allow study of tougher automobile fuel efficiency standards

Yes Ratify nuclear weapons testing treaty

Yes Prohibit national political parties from collecting "soft money" donations

Yes Remove barriers among banking, securities and insurance companies

INTEREST GROUPS

	AFL-CIO	ADA	CCUS	ACU
2000	75%	90%	66%	12%
1999	89%	95%	53%	4%
1998	100%	90%	44%	0%
1997	86%	95%	50%	0%
1996	86%	85%	23%	5%
1995	100%	100%	26%	0%
1994	88%	95%	20%	0%
1993	91%	95%	18%	8%
1992	92%	100%	20%	0%
1991	75%	90%	0%	5%

CQ VOTE STUDIES

	PARTY UNITY		PRESIDENTIAL SUPPORT	
	Support	Oppose	Support	Oppose
2000	97%	3%	92%	8%
1999	97%	3%	89%	11%
1998	98%	2%	93%	7%
1997	95%	5%	90%	10%
1996	94%	6%	86%	14%
1995	97%	3%	89%	11%
1994	92%	8%	90%	10%
1993	97%	3%	93%	7%
1992	92%	8%	32%	68%
1991	90%	10%	37%	63%

Sen. Debbie Stabenow (D)

Elected 2000; 1st term

CAPITOL OFFICE
224-4822; fax 228-0325; 702 Hart Bldg. 20510

INTERNET
e-mail: senator@stabenow.senate.gov
web: stabenow.senate.gov

COMMITTEES
Agriculture, Nutrition & Forestry
Banking, Housing & Urban Affairs
Budget
Special Aging

HOMETOWN
Lansing

BORN
April 29, 1950, Clare, Mich.

RELIGION
United Methodist

FAMILY
Divorced; two children

EDUCATION
Michigan State U., B.A. 1972, M.S.W. 1975

CAREER
Leadership training consultant

POLITICAL HIGHLIGHTS
Ingham County Commission, 1975-78
(chairwoman, 1977-1978); Mich. House, 1979-91;
Mich. Senate, 1991-94; sought Democratic
nomination for governor, 1994; Democratic
nominee for lieutenant governor, 1994; U.S. House,
1997-2001

ELECTION RESULTS

2000 GENERAL

Debbie Stabenow (D)	2,061,952	49.5%
Spencer Abraham (R)	1,994,693	47.9%

2000 PRIMARY

Debbie Stabenow (D)	unopposed

PREVIOUS WINNING PERCENTAGES
1998 House Election (57%); 1996 House Election
(54%)

Stabenow's centrist views and pragmatic, problem-solving image position her to wield some influence in the 107th Congress' evenly split Senate. In two terms in the House, she showed her willingness to join with the GOP on a number of issues, while hewing to traditional Democratic positions on such matters as abortion rights, education, gun control and public funding for the arts.

Stabenow (STAB-uh-now) does not place much stock in party labels, once commenting during her House tenure, "What I hear from people back home is, 'Forget the ideology. What are you doing to make government work in a way that helps my family every day?'"

Stabenow affiliates with the coalition of centrist New Democrats in the Senate, as she did during her days in the House.

She has shown strong support for labor; in 2000, she opposed legislation granting China permanent normal trade status. But she also has voted for GOP-sponsored measures to restructure the nation's public housing system and to encourage states to prosecute violent juvenile offenders as adults. And she has supported a GOP-backed constitutional amendment to outlaw desecration of the U.S. flag.

Stabenow's first bill in the Senate was a measure to permit the reimportation of prescription drugs sold in other countries for a fraction of the cost consumers pay in the United States. She was one of several Democratic Senate candidates in 2000 who traveled by bus with senior citizens to pharmacies in Canada to illustrate the stark difference in prescription drug pricing.

One of Stabenow's first actions as a freshman senator was to introduce the man she had defeated for the post — Republican Spencer Abraham — in Senate Energy Committee hearings on Abraham's nomination to be secretary of energy. She urged Abraham's speedy confirmation.

Stabenow's narrow victory to unseat Abraham in 2000 was the latest progression in a successful political career that has spanned more than half her life. She established herself as a fixture in Michigan Democratic politics with three years on the Ingham County Commission (she first won in 1975 at age 25), 12 years in the Michigan House and four years in the state Senate.

She has had one down year in politics. In 1994, she lost the Democratic gubernatorial primary to veteran Democratic Rep. Howard Wolpe. She then accepted Wolpe's invitation to join him as a candidate for lieutenant governor, but their ticket was swamped as incumbent GOP Gov. John Engler swept to re-election in that strong Republican year.

Stabenow made a comeback in 1996, ending Republican Rep. Dick Chrysler's one-term hold on the politically competitive 8th District. She was easily re-elected in 1998.

That win set up Stabenow's Senate challenge to Abraham. Neither candidate had primary opposition. Stabenow was a vice chairwoman of the Democratic presidential convention in Los Angeles — an indication of the importance her party placed on her takeover bid.

Abraham launched a summertime campaign blitz that gave him a big lead in polls, and some Democratic strategists fretted that they might have to write off the race. But Stabenow and allied groups staged a late counteroffensive that enabled her campaign to peak at the right time. Benefiting from a strong turnout by blacks and union voters and a Michigan victory by Democratic presidential nominee Al Gore, Stabenow won by slightly more than 67,000 votes out of more than 4.1 million cast.

Rep. Bart Stupak (D)

Elected 1992; 5th term

CAPITOL OFFICE
225-4735; fax 225-4744; 2348 Rayburn Bldg. 20515

INTERNET
e-mail: stupak@mail.house.gov
web: www.house.gov/stupak

COMMITTEES
Energy & Commerce

HOMETOWN
Menominee

BORN
Feb. 29, 1952, Milwaukee, Wis.

RELIGION
Roman Catholic

FAMILY
Wife, Laurie Stupak; two children (one deceased)

EDUCATION
Northwestern Michigan Community College, A.A.
1972; Saginaw Valley State College, B.S. 1977;
Thomas M. Cooley Law School, J.D. 1981

CAREER
Lawyer; state trooper; patrolman

POLITICAL HIGHLIGHTS
Mich. House, 1989-91; sought Democratic
nomination for Mich. Senate, 1990

ELECTION RESULTS

2000 GENERAL

Bart Stupak (D)	169,649	58.4%
Chuck Yob (R)	117,300	40.4%

2000 PRIMARY

Bart Stupak (D)	40,601	88.9%
Sven Johnson (D)	5,051	11.1%

1998 GENERAL

Bart Stupak (D)	130,129	58.7%
Michelle A. McManus (R)	87,630	39.5%
John W. Loosemore (LIBERT)	2,306	1.0%

PREVIOUS WINNING PERCENTAGES
1996 (71%); 1994 (57%); 1992 (54%)

A former state trooper from Michigan's Upper Peninsula, Stupak's centrist New Democrat voting record and rough-and-ready style is a good fit for the mostly rural 1st District, where many people live far from the state's major population centers and regard themselves as rugged individualists.

An opponent of abortion, a supporter of gun owners' rights and a steadfast ally of organized labor, Stupak (STOO-pack) appeals to many social conservatives while also pleasing working-class, union-label Democrats with his populist views on trade and economic policy. On big votes, Stupak is often one of the last lawmakers to make up his mind.

He has bolstered his local political standing with his seat on the influential Energy and Commerce panel, where he works with the panel's top Democrat and his state colleague John D. Dingell.

Stupak suffered a personal tragedy in 2000, when his son committed suicide. He drew strength from the friendship of his congressional roommates in a Capitol Hill group house that seven of them share. When the sometimes gruff Stupak addressed his first remarks to the House after his son's funeral, his emotional eulogy to his son, with his expressions of gratitude to his colleagues, was a moving moment in House history.

Stupak's son, Bart Jr., was a popular high school athlete and student leader, who aspired to replace his father in the House. After Bart Jr.'s death, Stupak and his wife, Laurie, became suspicious that Accutane, an acne medicine their son was taking, may have been responsible for creating a suicidal depression. Stupak called for an independent study of the drug's effects and stronger warnings about its possible dangers. Later in the year, the House Government Reform panel held a hearing on the matter.

A law enforcement officer for 12 years before an injury in the line of duty forced him to retire in 1984, Stupak is the founder of the Congressional Law Enforcement Caucus. He often focuses on neighborhood crime prevention, including community and school policing. In the 106th Congress, he worked to limit public access to body armor, which emboldens some criminals to engage in shootouts with police. In 1999, he was named to a bipartisan task force to study school violence.

He also joined Tennessee Republican Zach Wamp, one of his housemates, in drafting a bill that sought to require the entertainment industry to develop a uniform ratings system for movies, television shows, video games and music that would include information about the content, particularly violence, and recommend a minimum age for viewing or playing.

Stupak is generally opposed to gun control, though he changed his mind somewhat after the shootings at Colorado's Columbine High School in 1999. He voted for the strictest of several proposals to require background checks at gun shows — a move that drew opposition from many in the 1st, where gun ownership is common and hunting is a popular pastime.

But Stupak said it was only a matter of fairness to treat gun shows the same as gun stores on the matter of background checks. He collected the names of constituents who called to complain and later called many of them back to explain his vote. He says he does that often on contentious votes. "When you take a tough vote, you don't run from it," he told the Wall Street Journal. The National Rifle Association, which had endorsed Stupak in the past, backed his 2000 challenger, Republican Chuck Yob.

Stupak's hometown of Menominee (his wife is mayor) is on the border with Wisconsin, only about 60 miles from Green Bay, and is almost 500 miles by car from Detroit. His district, which includes the entire Upper Peninsula and the northernmost part of the Lower Peninsula, is 22,766 square miles — 40 percent of the state's land area. It is the second-largest district east of the Mississippi River. Touching three of the Great Lakes, the 1st has 1,556 miles of shoreline — more than any other district in the continental United States.

Stupak walks a fine line on environmental issues. Economically struggling communities in the 1st District would like to attract more industry, but encouraging development threatens the quality of the natural environment, which attracts much-needed tourist dollars. During the past four years, Stupak voted with Republicans to continue road-building subsidies for the logging industry. But he also introduced legislation to ban oil drilling in the Great Lakes. And he criticized the National Park Service for proposing a ban on snowmobiles in many of its parks.

One of Stupak's top local priorities has been redevelopment of the K.I. Sawyer Air Force Base, which was his district's largest employer when the Pentagon slated it for shutdown on the 1993 base-closure list. Stupak got federal funds to help in converting the base to civilian use. The old base now includes the Marquette County Airport, an aircraft maintenance facility, a hotel, residences, and commercial and government offices. The success at Sawyer has been cited as a model for other military base conversion efforts.

As a lifelong resident of the Upper Peninsula (known by locals as the UP), Stupak prides himself on his "Yooper" background. He set out to be a police officer, earning associate and bachelor's degrees in criminal justice. While still a trooper, he obtained a law degree, which served him well after his forced retirement from the state police. He entered private law practice and got involved in local civic and political affairs. He won a state House seat in 1988 but gave it up in 1990 for a state Senate bid, in which he narrowly lost the Democratic primary.

Stupak's opportunity to try for Congress came in 1992 after GOP Rep. Robert W. Davis was revealed to be involved in the House bank scandal, with 878 overdrafts at the private bank for House members. Davis, who had been favored for re-election, decided to retire. In the November balloting against former GOP Rep. Philip E. Ruppe, Stupak won by 10 points, benefiting from a poor showing by GOP presidential candidate George Bush, who received only 35 percent of the district's votes. Buoyed by support from the National Rifle Association and Michigan Right to Life, Stupak improved to 57 percent in 1994. He has won re-election easily since then.

Despite a bad knee, Stupak is a star of the Democrats' baseball team.

KEY VOTES

2000

Yes	Raise hourly minimum wage by $1 over two years
?	Halt funding for U.S. mission in Kosovo unless European nations pay more
?	Provide Medicare benefits to military retirees and their dependents
No	Grant China permanent normal trade status
No	Phase out estate, gift and trust taxes
No	Prohibit implementation of president's national monument designations
No	Approve GOP plan to provide prescription drug coverage for Medicare beneficiaries
Yes	Increase help for poor nations indebted to international financial institutions

1999

Yes	Impose steel import quotas
No	Kill proposal to take aviation trust funds off budget
No	Require background checks on buyers only at gun shows with 10 or more vendors
No	Remove barriers among banking, securities and insurance companies
Yes	Authorize state grants to hire teachers and reduce class size
No	Overhaul campaign finance law; ban "soft money" and restrict advocacy advertising
Yes	Approve bipartisan plan to increase rights of patients in managed-care health plans

INTEREST GROUPS

	AFL-CIO	ADA	CCUS	ACU
2000	100%	65%	30%	22%
1999	100%	85%	16%	16%
1998	100%	90%	17%	20%
1997	100%	80%	40%	20%

CQ VOTE STUDIES

	PARTY UNITY		PRESIDENTIAL SUPPORT	
	Support	Oppose	Support	Oppose
2000	83%	17%	67%	33%
1999	83%	17%	70%	30%
1998	83%	17%	75%	25%
1997	83%	17%	71%	29%

MICHIGAN 1
Upper Peninsula; northern Lower Michigan

Rolling, forested hills and hundreds of inches of snow make the 1st one of the few places suited to skiing in the Midwest. Beaches and resorts around Traverse City and Petoskey also lure summer vacationers from Detroit, Chicago and Cleveland, feeding the area's tourist industry. But most of the 1st saw its economic foundations erode in the 1990s.

The Upper Peninsula (UP), surrounded by three of the Great Lakes and connected to the rest of the state by the Mackinac Bridge, is still recovering from two military base closures. Mining, which once drew immigrants to remote parts of the state, hasn't been a growth industry since the turn of the century. NAFTA has effectively killed most remaining copper, paper and iron production.

Tourism and timber products companies are the only growth industries. Paper, saw and veneer mills are scattered throughout the region, and snowmobiling makes up at least 40 percent of winter revenues for restaurants and hotels. Slow growth in northern

Michigan and the Upper Peninsula has gradually expanded this district's territory to encompass about 40 percent of the state's total land mass.

As a whole, the 1st backs Democratic candidates, but even the most liberal voters tend to be socially conservative. A strong tradition of union organization among miners and mill workers has left the western and central UP strongly Democratic, a preference shared by the eastern counties in the northern part of the state. At the top of the "mitten," the state's northwestern counties, with their growing population of retired executives, tend to go for Republicans.

MAJOR INDUSTRY
Mining, logging, tourism, auto parts

CITIES
Marquette, 19,634; Sault Ste. Marie, 15,283; Traverse City, 15,090

UNUSUAL FEATURES
Isle Royale National Park; National Ski Hall of Fame; Interlochen Center for the Arts.

Rep. Peter Hoekstra (R)

CAPITOL OFFICE
225-4401; fax 226-0779
1124 Longworth Bldg. 20515

INTERNET
e-mail: tellhoek@mail.house.gov
web: www.house.gov/hoekstra

COMMITTEES
Budget
Education & Workforce
(Select Education - chairman)
Select Intelligence

HOMETOWN
Holland

BORN
Oct. 30, 1953, Groningen, Netherlands

RELIGION
Christian Reformed Church

FAMILY
Wife, Diane Hoekstra; three children

EDUCATION
Hope College, B.A. 1975; U. of Michigan, M.B.A. 1977

CAREER
Furniture company executive

POLITICAL HIGHLIGHTS
No previous office

ELECTION RESULTS

2000 GENERAL

Peter Hoekstra (R)	186,762	64.4%
Bob Shrauger (D)	96,370	33.2%

2000 PRIMARY

Peter Hoekstra (R)	unopposed

1998 GENERAL

Peter Hoekstra (R)	146,854	68.7%
Bob Shrauger (D)	63,573	29.8%

PREVIOUS WINNING PERCENTAGES
1996 (65%); 1994 (75%); 1992 (63%)

Elected 1992; 5th term

Hoekstra has a vision — make the government run more like a business. And so on his website he publishes thematic essays, under the heading the "Myth of the Magical Bureaucracy," to make the point that the federal government cannot solve every problem. He also provides online examinations of specific issues, called "A Tale of Two Visions," in which he contrasts two ways of dealing with a specific topic, for example, teaching techniques — a government-centered approach (a vision of bureaucracy) and a community-based approach (a vision of opportunity).

Not surprisingly perhaps, Hoekstra (HOOK-struh) is not optimistic about the government successfully managing programs. In recent years, as chairman of an oversight subcommittee that came up with what he believed were damning tales of federal agencies unable to document how they were spending taxpayers' money, Hoekstra hoped that public outrage would bolster his efforts to reform government spending practices.

But with countless congressional investigations — many of them much sexier than his businesslike probes of the departments of Labor and Education — vying for public notice, Hoekstra found that his work was largely overlooked. A frustrated Hoekstra decided the GOP needed to do a better job of communicating its vision of a smaller federal government — one that was not expected to solve all of America's problems — and of reliance on individual and community initiative. In the 106th Congress, he got a chance to do just that, as chairman of the House Republican Conference's Communications Working Group, an advisory committee on marketing strategy.

Tapped by Conference Chairman J.C. Watts of Oklahoma, Hoekstra and 16 other GOP lawmakers met weekly to plan how best to keep Republicans focused on the party's legislative and policy priorities. In the communications post, Hoekstra was able to focus on the issues he had wanted to address when he ran, unsuccessfully, for the GOP Conference vice chairmanship in 1998. He came in third, losing to Tillie Fowler of Florida, partly because many conference members thought the GOP needed a woman in the leadership.

As chairman of Education and the Workforce's Oversight Subcommittee for six years, Hoekstra examined the books of the Labor and Education departments and of President Clinton's AmeriCorps community service program. He also headed a probe of election corruption within the Teamsters union for which he was criticized by members of both parties — Democrats argued that he was seeking partisan political advantage and Republicans contended that he wasn't being political enough. (In 2000, the Teamsters local in Michigan endorsed Hoekstra for re-election.)

Under the slogan "Education at a Crossroads," Hoekstra led his subcommittee in the 105th Congress through another oversight proceeding — a review of Education Department programs. His aim was to channel more money to local classrooms, and he notes that the hearings helped the GOP formulate the basis for its education agenda, highlighting basic academic work and local control. "Too few of our students are learning what they should be learning, despite the fact that the federal government spends more than $100 billion a year on education," he said.

Hoekstra sought to move up to a committee chairmanship in the 107th Congress, and he suggested splitting the Education and the Workforce panel into two committees. But GOP leaders decided against that plan, and the chairmanship of the full committee went to John A. Boehner of Ohio, who ranks just above Hoekstra in seniority. In the 107th, Hoekstra chairs the panel's Select Education Subcommittee, which focuses on at-risk children, juvenile justice and programs for the elderly.

Hoekstra is conscious of the bottom line: He spends modestly in his campaigns and he bunks in his Capitol Hill office rather than paying rent somewhere. From his Budget Committee seat and in frequent addresses on the House floor, he calls for a thrifty federal government, one that spends and taxes less. He was not pleased in the 105th Congress when his own party drafted a massive bill to authorize federal transportation programs and, at the end of the year, a catchall omnibus spending bill. Both bills, Hoekstra argued, spent too much money.

In keeping with his business background, Hoekstra is a determined foe of the Occupational Safety and Health Administration's efforts to impose new ergonomic regulations in the workplace. He also opposes what he believes is unfair competition from the government-owned Federal Prison Industries Inc., which pays inmates low wages to produce goods that compete with those made by private companies.

Attentive to an issue of concern in the Great Lakes region, Hoekstra is worried about the invasion of such species as the zebra mussel and sea lamprey, which hitch rides in seagoing vessels. He authored a bill in 2000 to require ships to cleanse their ballast tanks before entering Great Lakes waters.

Hoekstra was born in the Netherlands and emigrated to the United States with his family when he was three, settling in the town of Holland in a heavily Dutch part of Michigan. After receiving an M.B.A. from the University of Michigan, Hoekstra embarked on a career with Herman Miller Inc., an office-furniture maker whose headquarters is in the 2nd District.

In 1992, Hoekstra decided he could do a better job providing aggressive, reform-minded leadership than the district's 13-term congressman, Republican Guy Vander Jagt (for whom Hoekstra once interned). Hoekstra saved up his leave, set off on a bicycle tour of the 2nd (something he does annually), and overtook the incumbent in the GOP primary.

Hoekstra attacked Vander Jagt for neglecting his district in favor of national party fundraising — he was chairman of the National Republican Congressional Committee. Unable to afford television time, Hoekstra advertised on the radio and campaigned door-to-door. Helped by the fact that his home county was new to the district, whose map had just been redrawn, Hoekstra beat Vander Jagt by 6 percentage points.

That November, Hoekstra won with 63 percent of the vote, and he has since won easily in the solidly Republican district.

KEY VOTES

2000
No   Raise hourly minimum wage by $1 over two years
Yes   Halt funding for U.S. mission in Kosovo unless European nations pay more
Yes   Provide Medicare benefits to military retirees and their dependents
No   Grant China permanent normal trade status
Yes   Phase out estate, gift and trust taxes
No   Prohibit implementation of president's national monument designations
Yes   Approve GOP plan to provide prescription drug coverage for Medicare beneficiaries
No   Increase help for poor nations indebted to international financial institutions

1999
No   Impose steel import quotas
Yes   Kill proposal to take aviation trust funds off budget
Yes   Require background checks on buyers only at gun shows with 10 or more vendors
No   Remove barriers among banking, securities and insurance companies
No   Authorize state grants to hire teachers and reduce class size
No   Overhaul campaign finance law; ban "soft money" and restrict advocacy advertising
No   Approve bipartisan plan to increase rights of patients in managed-care health plans

INTEREST GROUPS

	AFL-CIO	ADA	CCUS	ACU
2000	10%	10%	90%	88%
1999	0%	5%	88%	88%
1998	10%	5%	82%	100%
1997	0%	15%	100%	88%

CQ VOTE STUDIES

	PARTY UNITY		PRESIDENTIAL SUPPORT	
	Support	Oppose	Support	Oppose
2000	93%	7%	23%	77%
1999	93%	7%	15%	85%
1998	93%	7%	24%	76%
1997	92%	8%	28%	72%

MICHIGAN 2

West — Holland; Muskegon

The 2nd stretches 140 miles along Lake Michigan, covering counties full of cherry trees and asparagus farms. Pioneers, most of them Dutch, were drawn to the region by rich logging opportunities. Now, heavy industrial manufacturing dominates the most populated counties, including Muskegon, Ottawa and Allegan, but the early settlers' pioneering spirit persists. Dutch independence has made the 2nd one of the most staunchly Republican districts in Michigan, rivaled only by the Grand Rapids district (the 3rd) just to the east.

Some support for Democratic candidates can be found among minority voters in the district's largest city, Muskegon, which is home to the 2nd's only Democratic representative in the state House. Muskegon has struggled to keep manufacturing jobs since the end of World War II. But local tax incentives have drawn in new automotive parts suppliers, helping the economy rebound. Western Michigan also hosts several of the nation's top office furniture makers, with both Herman

Miller and Haworth having their headquarters in the district.

South of Muskegon lies Holland, a conservative, Dutch-settled port town that draws tourists from all over the Midwest. Holland is the westernmost point of the "Dutch Triangle," formed by Holland, Grand Rapids and Kalamazoo. The turn-of-the-century Dutch lifestyle is recreated in Dutch Village, complete with wooden shoes and klompen dancers. The city's annual tulip festival draws about 500,000 visitors every May.

MAJOR INDUSTRY
Metal, furniture, tourism, agriculture

CITIES
Muskegon, 39,401; Holland, 33,652; Norton Shores, 23,138

UNUSUAL FEATURES
World's largest weather vane in Montague; National Asparagus Festival in Oceana County.

Rep. Vernon J. Ehlers (R)

Elected December 1993; 4th full term

CAPITOL OFFICE
225-3831; fax 225-5144
1714 Longworth Bldg. 20515

INTERNET
e-mail: rep.ehlers@mail.house.gov
web: www.house.gov/ehlers

COMMITTEES
Education & Workforce
House Administration
Science
(Environment, Technology & Standards -
chairman)
Transportation & Infrastructure
Joint Library - chairman

HOMETOWN
Grand Rapids

BORN
Feb. 6, 1934, Pipestone, Minn.

RELIGION
Christian Reformed Church

FAMILY
Wife, Johanna Meulink; four children

EDUCATION
Calvin College, attended 1952-55; U. of California,
Berkeley, A.B. 1956, Ph.D. 1960

CAREER
Professor; physicist

POLITICAL HIGHLIGHTS
Kent County Commission, 1975-83 (chairman, 1979-
82); Mich. House, 1983-85; Mich. Senate, 1985-93
(president pro tempore)

ELECTION RESULTS

2000 GENERAL

Vernon J. Ehlers (R)	179,539	65.0%
Tim Steele (D)	91,309	33.1%

2000 PRIMARY

Vernon J. Ehlers (R)	unopposed

1998 GENERAL

Vernon J. Ehlers (R)	146,364	73.1%
John Ferguson Jr. (D)	49,489	24.7%
Erwin J. Haas (LIBERT)	2,537	1.3%

PREVIOUS WINNING PERCENTAGES
1996 (69%); 1994 (74%); 1993 Special Election
(67%)

Thoughtful, low-key and polite, Ehlers has a demeanor befitting a former college physics professor. The lawmaker eagerly delves into weighty matters, such as national science policy and the sometimes conflicting interests of science and religion.

Ehlers (AY-lurz) lost the distinction of being the only research physicist in Congress in 1998, when Democrat Rush D. Holt of New Jersey was elected to the House, and in the 106th Congress the two joined forces to promote science education and expand research. In doing so, they filled a role occupied by California Democratic Rep. George E. Brown Jr., a champion of science during 17-plus terms, who died in 1999. "We're not trying to produce nerds — even though I still wear my plastic pocket protector," Ehlers told The Associated Press.

Legislation he sponsored in the 106th Congress to spend $235.3 million to train math and science teachers in grades K-8 was killed by House Democrats because it would have included private schools and their teachers. Opponents worried that private schools could influence teachers trained with the federal money, perhaps punishing them for teaching evolution.

Ehlers has a moderate voting record: conservative on fiscal matters, more liberal on social issues. He often breaks from the GOP majority on environmental issues and he has balked at the party's efforts to ban desecration of the U.S. flag and to prosecute violent juvenile offenders as adults. He was one of about 50 Republicans to join the Main Street Partnership, whose purpose is to "revitalize the political center in America" and promote civility in politics.

Regarded by colleagues as one of the smartest lawmakers, Ehlers is often called on by GOP leaders to employ his scientific expertise in the policy arena. As a college professor, he was a science adviser to then-Rep. Gerald R. Ford. When he came to Congress, Republican leaders asked him to help House members make use of the Internet. Ehlers offered lawmakers training, helped equip their offices with network software and new hardware, and advised them on how to set up websites to communicate with constituents.

In a report commissioned by the House leadership and issued in 1998, Ehlers recommended that federal support for basic research be given priority and that lawmakers consider privatizing the management of national laboratories doing non-defense-related research. In recognition of his efforts, Ehlers was designated the Science Committee's vice chairman in the 106th Congress, even though he ranked 11th in seniority among Republicans. In the 107th, he heads the panel's newly formed Subcommittee on Environment, Technology and Standards.

In the 106th, Ehlers supported his party's "eContract 2000," a package of initiatives for the high-tech industry that included proposals to grant tax breaks, prevent frivolous lawsuits and ease regulation to foster more growth. He also won House backing for an amendment to the Elementary and Secondary Education Act to make science a third priority — along with math and reading — in federal Title I programs for disadvantaged students.

Despite his non-confrontational mien, Ehlers has been drawn into partisan dust-ups. Known for his calm, deliberate manner, he was tapped to head a task force investigating the contested 1996 election victory of Democrat Loretta Sanchez over the Republican incumbent, Robert K. Dornan, in California's 46th District. Led by Ehlers, the three-member panel looked into charges by nine-term Rep. Dornan that voting by non-citizens had cost him the election against Sanchez. Ehlers issued massive subpoenas for documents from the

Immigration and Naturalization Service and Hispanic organizations, angering Sanchez and her supporters. Democrats said the task force's lengthy inquiry was racially tinged and called the probe a partisan witch hunt. The panel of two Republicans and one Democrat ruled early in 1998 that hundreds of illegal votes had been cast, but not enough to negate Sanchez's victory.

The son of a minister and a devout Christian himself, Ehlers is the co-author of several books that meld theology and science as guides to managing the environment. He chaired the National Conference of State Legislatures' Environment Committee while in the Michigan Legislature and in Congress he consistently has cast pro-environment votes.

Ehlers refers to his religious beliefs when he ponders the ethical issues surrounding cloning. While reluctant to place limits on scientific research, he nevertheless proposed legislation in the 105th outlawing the creation of a human embryo via cloning, saying it "crossed the line from experimentation and legitimate scientific work to an activity with profound moral repercussions." Other cloning research not involving the creation of a human life should continue, he said.

Due to severe asthma and allergies, both controlled somewhat now by medication, Ehlers was schooled at home until college. After receiving a doctorate in physics from the University of California at Berkeley when he was 26, Ehlers stayed at Berkeley as a lecturer and research physicist for six years. In 1966, he traded that liberal atmosphere for the conservative, religious-oriented campus of Calvin College in Grand Rapids, Mich., where he had spent three years as an undergraduate.

While teaching at Calvin, he took his first steps into public life in 1970 as a member of the West Michigan Environmental Action Council's board of directors. In 1982, Ehlers won election to the state House, succeeding Republican Paul B. Henry, who had moved to the state Senate. The two had become friends at Calvin College, where Henry taught political science. Over the next dozen years, Ehlers followed Henry up the political ladder, succeeding him in the state Senate and finally in Congress.

In mid-1993, Ehlers was president pro tempore of the Michigan Senate. Nearing 60, he was looking for new challenges and weighing a 1994 campaign for the Senate seat of Democrat Donald W. Riegle Jr. But when Henry died of brain cancer in July 1993, Ehlers launched a House bid, quickly moving to the head of an eight-person Republican pack. In a November 1993 special primary, Ehlers won the GOP nomination. The December special election was a waltz in the solidly conservative 3rd District, and Ehlers has posted landslide re-election victories since.

KEY VOTES

2000

Yes Raise hourly minimum wage by $1 over two years

Yes Halt funding for U.S. mission in Kosovo unless European nations pay more

Yes Provide Medicare benefits to military retirees and their dependents

Yes Grant China permanent normal trade status

Yes Phase out estate, gift and trust taxes

No Prohibit implementation of president's national monument designations

Yes Approve GOP plan to provide prescription drug coverage for Medicare beneficiaries

Yes Increase help for poor nations indebted to international financial institutions

1999

No Impose steel import quotas

No Kill proposal to take aviation trust funds off budget

Yes Require background checks on buyers only at gun shows with 10 or more vendors

Yes Remove barriers among banking, securities and insurance companies

No Authorize state grants to hire teachers and reduce class size

No Overhaul campaign finance law; ban "soft money" and restrict advocacy advertising

No Approve bipartisan plan to increase rights of patients in managed-care health plans

INTEREST GROUPS

	AFL-CIO	ADA	CCUS	ACU
2000	20%	20%	80%	64%
1999	0%	20%	96%	60%
1998	30%	25%	89%	56%
1997	13%	35%	90%	67%

CQ VOTE STUDIES

	PARTY UNITY		PRESIDENTIAL SUPPORT	
	Support	Oppose	Support	Oppose
2000	78%	22%	38%	62%
1999	83%	17%	29%	71%
1998	78%	22%	33%	67%
1997	83%	17%	42%	58%

MICHIGAN 3

West Central – Grand Rapids

Grand Rapids, Michigan's second-largest city, teems with auto plants and metals manufacturing, but it's a world away from Detroit. Conservative Dutch Republicans – not auto union Democrats – control the district, making the 3rd one of Michigan's most Republican regions. Its staunch conservatism is rivaled only by the neighboring 2nd District, based in Holland.

Also unlike Detroit, Grand Rapids has escaped complete dependence on the auto industry. The city is a leading producer of metal office furniture, in addition to making avionics systems, tools and home appliances. The city's economy prospered in the 1970s when modular furniture became popular, but it then suffered in the early 1990s when companies began to downsize their managerial staffs and cut back on office space. In a major effort to revitalize downtown Grand Rapids, the city built a new arena and recruited three minor league sports teams.

Gerald R. Ford made his way to the House and then the presidency

from Grand Rapids, and his brand of small-government Republicanism and fiscal restraint still holds sway in the 3rd. One of the district's largest employers, Amway Corp., consistently contributes to Republicans around the nation. This direct sales company, which markets personal- and home-care products, promotes its philosophy of private philanthropy by donating generously to Grand Rapids' universities, hospitals and churches.

MAJOR INDUSTRY
Office furniture, auto parts, metals manufacturing

CITIES
Grand Rapids, 185,009; Wyoming, 69,275; Kentwood, 42,893; Walker City, 20,381

UNUSUAL FEATURES
Norton Mound Group, one of the best preserved burial centers of Hopewell culture, which originated in Illinois and moved into Michigan some time between 500 and 300 B.C.

Rep. Dave Camp (R)

CAPITOL OFFICE
225-3561; fax 225-9679; 137 Cannon Bldg. 20515

INTERNET
e-mail: www.house.gov/writerep
web: www.house.gov/camp

COMMITTEES
Ways & Means

HOMETOWN
Midland

BORN
July 9, 1953, Midland, Mich.

RELIGION
Roman Catholic

FAMILY
Wife, Nancy Keil; three children

EDUCATION
Albion College, B.A. 1975; U. of San Diego, J.D. 1978

CAREER
Lawyer; congressional aide

POLITICAL HIGHLIGHTS
Mich. House, 1989-91

ELECTION RESULTS

2000 GENERAL

Dave Camp (R)	182,128	68.0%
Lawrence D. Hollenbeck (D)	78,019	29.1%
Alan Gamble (GREEN)	3,790	1.4%

2000 PRIMARY

Dave Camp (R)	unopposed

1998 GENERAL

Dave Camp (R)	155,343	91.3%
Dan Marsh (LIBERT)	10,404	6.1%
Stuart J. Goldberg (NL)	4,332	2.5%

PREVIOUS WINNING PERCENTAGES
1996 (66%); 1994 (73%); 1992 (63%); 1990 (65%)

Elected 1990; 6th term

Not yet 50, Camp has worked his way to the top row of the dais at the Ways and Means Committee, inching closer to a subcommittee chairmanship as he enters his second decade in the House. Despite his youthful appearance, Camp's demeanor on Capitol Hill more closely resembles the manner of many of the longtime members with whom he shares seniority than the manner of junior members closer to his age.

Elected to the House in 1990, Camp was on the leading edge of the wave of young conservative Republicans who have flooded the chamber in the past decade. But while a number of these members play the role of political outsider, Camp has made his mark the old-fashioned way, by landing a choice committee assignment, digging into some legislative issues and taking on a variety of chores for party leaders.

He ran J. Dennis Hastert's successful campaign for Speaker in the 106th Congress and is among Hastert's inner circle of advisers. The Speaker named him to a GOP task force formed to address the high cost of prescription drugs and put him on the House ethics committee — a dubious honor, but one that shows the leader's trust and a member's willingness to handle thankless tasks on behalf of the party.

Camp has several other, more formal leadership posts. He is a regional party whip and serves on the GOP Steering Committee, which makes Republicans' committee assignments.

In the 106th Congress, he chaired the executive committee of the National Republican Congressional Committee, which seeks to elect Republicans to the House. And he headed a leadership-appointed panel that recommends "corrections" bills for floor action. (The bills repeal federal regulations or laws that GOP leaders deem unnecessary.)

But it is on Ways and Means, where Camp has served since his second term, that he has been most influential. He has had a hand in writing bills to speed up adoptions and a key role in the enactment of a measure to overhaul the welfare system.

The GOP strategy in the 104th Congress had been to link welfare overhaul with big changes in the Medicaid system, and many Republicans (among them presidential candidate Bob Dole) argued for continued linkage. But Camp instigated a petition drive urging GOP leaders to move separately on welfare overhaul, improving its chances for enactment. That was the course ultimately taken, and after further compromise with the White House, Republicans finally agreed on a plan that President Clinton signed into law in August 1996.

In the 105th Congress, as the No. 2 Republican on Ways and Means' Human Resources Subcommittee, Camp played a leading role in passing legislation promoting the adoption of children in foster care. The law requires states to more aggressively pursue adoption for a child who has been placed in foster care after being abandoned or abused; it also makes family reunification a less compelling goal. That work led to Camp's induction into the National Council of Adoption's Hall of Fame. In the 106th Congress, Camp continued his work on adoption, playing a key role on a bill to ease adoptions of children from other countries.

While not as vocal as some young Republicans, Camp's point of departure on most issues is firmly conservative. And if the matter involves spending taxpayers' money, it's a good bet that he will come down on the side that costs the least. He takes his cost-cutting credo further than many Republicans, targeting both the Defense Department and NASA's International Space Station.

Camp has repeatedly joined Democrat Tim Roemer of Indiana in efforts to kill the International Space Station. Noting that cost estimates for the venture have continued to escalate, Camp argued that "while space is infinite, the generosity of the American taxpayer is not."

Camp and Roemer have also teamed up on another money-saving effort — legislation to apply any lawmaker's unused office and staff funds to deficit or debt reduction. Over the years, Camp has returned to the Treasury more than a half-million dollars from unused office account money, though lawmakers are not required to do so. He also donates his congressional pay increases to scholarships for college students.

In his Washington office, Camp features a rack of several dozen men's ties — a curiosity for his constituents visiting from the 4th District, who paw through the collection looking for ones that represent their school or organization. Camp began building the collection when The Detroit News published an article noting that Camp had come to Capitol Hill with just three ties. The article invited readers to send ties to Camp, which they continue to do.

Camp, whose interest in politics began at an early age, got hands-on experience when he volunteered on the local judicial campaign of the man in whose law office he was interning. Camp was childhood friends with GOP Rep. Bill Schuette, and he served as his friend's top aide after Schuette was elected to Congress in 1984.

Camp returned to Michigan in 1986 to manage Schuette's re-election campaign and resume his law career. But in 1988, Camp decided to run for an open Midland-based state House seat, which he won. Camp had barely found his chair in the legislature when GOP strategists began talking up Schuette to run against Democratic Sen. Carl Levin in 1990; almost in the same breath, they suggested Camp as a replacement for Schuette in the House.

When Schuette announced his campaign for the Senate, he also endorsed Camp to succeed him. Camp eked out a close GOP primary victory against four other candidates. He would have been favored in the November election in any case, but he lucked out when a sparsely contested Democratic primary produced an upset winner, Joan L. Dennison, who believed the public schools were run by atheists and who espoused support for some ideas of political extremist Lyndon H. LaRouche Jr. Camp coasted to victory, taking nearly two-thirds of the vote. His re-election contests have been easy. He ran without major-party opposition in 1998 and won with 68 percent of the vote in 2000.

KEY VOTES

2000

No Raise hourly minimum wage by $1 over two years

Yes Halt funding for U.S. mission in Kosovo unless European nations pay more

Yes Provide Medicare benefits to military retirees and their dependents

Yes Grant China permanent normal trade status

Yes Phase out estate, gift and trust taxes

Yes Prohibit implementation of president's national monument designations

Yes Approve GOP plan to provide prescription drug coverage for Medicare beneficiaries

No Increase help for poor nations indebted to international financial institutions

1999

No Impose steel import quotas

No Kill proposal to take aviation trust funds off budget

Yes Require background checks on buyers only at gun shows with 10 or more vendors

Yes Remove barriers among banking, securities and insurance companies

No Authorize state grants to hire teachers and reduce class size

No Overhaul campaign finance law; ban "soft money" and restrict advocacy advertising

No Approve bipartisan plan to increase rights of patients in managed-care health plans

INTEREST GROUPS

	AFL-CIO	ADA	CCUS	ACU
2000	0%	5%	90%	84%
1999	0%	15%	96%	79%
1998	0%	10%	100%	96%
1997	13%	20%	100%	84%

CQ VOTE STUDIES

	PARTY UNITY		PRESIDENTIAL SUPPORT	
	Support	Oppose	Support	Oppose
2000	91%	9%	24%	76%
1999	90%	10%	23%	77%
1998	92%	8%	27%	73%
1997	92%	8%	32%	68%

MICHIGAN 4
North Central – Midland

Forests and farms cover the 16 central Michigan counties that make up the 4th, Michigan's second-largest district. The white pine forests north of Midland, the district's largest town, were once some of the most bountiful logging lands in the state. Now, retirees and vacationers build second homes in the sparsely populated woods, and tourists come to ski, camp and hunt in these remote, north-central counties.

Midland, on the district's eastern border, is home to Dow Chemical and Dow Corning, producer of chemicals, plastics and silicone products. Dow Chemical's international headquarters sits on a 2,150-acre campus in Midland, giving the city more engineers, chemists and metallurgists per capita than any other city in the nation. The town finds itself vulnerable to Dow's corporate restructuring, but it also has benefited from Dow's generous philanthropy, with churches, schools and libraries built by the Dow fortune.

South of Midland, the district turns agricultural. Farmers, who till fields of sugar beets, dry beans, corn, wheat and oats, worry about free trade, price supports and crop insurance. The predominance of farms and small towns throughout the 4th makes it a reliably Republican district for congressional races, though Bill Clinton did well here. In 1992, Clinton eked out a victory by 1,200 votes, and in 1996, he won the district with 47 percent of the vote. The district returned to its GOP ways in 2000, however, when it gave the edge to President Bush.

MAJOR INDUSTRY
Tourism, agriculture, chemical and plastics manufacturing

CITIES
Midland, 40,769; Mount Pleasant, 23,638; Owosso, 15,418

UNUSUAL FEATURES
Ogemaw Hills Pathway, which runs through 15 miles of the AuSable State Forest, was created by a retreating glacier front 16,000 years ago.

Rep. James A. Barcia (D)

Elected 1992; 5th term

CAPITOL OFFICE
225-8171; fax 225-2168; 2419 Rayburn Bldg. 20515

INTERNET
e-mail: jim.barcia-pub@mail.house.gov
web: www.house.gov/barcia

COMMITTEES
Science
Transportation & Infrastructure

HOMETOWN
Bay City

BORN
Feb. 25, 1952, Bay City, Mich.

RELIGION
Roman Catholic

FAMILY
Wife, Vicki Bartlett; two stepchildren

EDUCATION
Saginaw Valley State U., B.A. 1974

CAREER
Congressional aide

POLITICAL HIGHLIGHTS
Mich. House, 1977-83 (majority whip, 1979-83);
Mich. Senate, 1983-93

ELECTION RESULTS

2000 GENERAL

James A. Barcia (D)	184,048	74.3%
Ronald G. Actis (R)	59,274	23.9%
Clint Foster (LIBERT)	3,070	1.2%

2000 PRIMARY

James A. Barcia (D)	unopposed

1998 GENERAL

James A. Barcia (D)	135,254	71.2%
Donald W. Brewster (R)	51,442	27.1%
Clint Foster (LIBERT)	2,179	1.1%

PREVIOUS WINNING PERCENTAGES
1996 (70%); 1994 (66%); 1992 (60%)

An avid bow hunter, Barcia aims his votes toward the center of the political spectrum, while he quietly goes about his work.

Barcia (BAR-sha) is one of the more conservative Northern Democrats in the House, voting less than two-thirds of the time in support of positions taken by the majority of House Democrats. In the 106th Congress, he opposed President Clinton 57 percent of the time, the sixth-lowest presidential support score among House Democrats. He is a member of the moderate New Democrat Coalition.

Barcia often backs the GOP position on fiscal and social policy matters. He has supported Republican-drafted legislation to cut the estate tax and to eliminate the "marriage penalty," a quirk in the tax code that results in some two-earner married couples paying higher taxes than they would if each partner were single.

The lawmaker is a co-chairman of the Pro-Life Caucus, voting against allowing abortion to be covered by federal employee health plans, opposing a procedure its opponents call "partial birth" abortion, and leading the Capitol Hill opposition to federal health research that involves the use of human embryos.

Barcia has strayed from Democrats on other issues. He has supported a number of bills to scale back environmental protections. In the 105th, he opposed a Clinton administration proposal for nationwide math and reading achievement tests. And in the 106th, he backed a proposal requiring that any increase in taxes be approved by a two-thirds majority.

Although Democratic leaders are sometimes troubled by Barcia's votes, they are grateful that he generally does not go out of his way to publicize his differences with the party. He usually keeps his rhetoric muted, as was his practice during 16 years in the state legislature, where he was known as a middle-of-the-road Democrat with open lines to both labor and management. In Congress, Barcia is generally a reliable vote in support of labor, opposing international trade agreements and backing union organizing efforts.

Barcia disagrees with Republicans who issue blanket condemnations about government tax rates. "If people want services from their government, then they have to be willing to pay the bills," Barcia once said about a 1993 budget plan that raised taxes.

The congressman's legislative agenda is based in equal measure on his committee assignments, his district's needs and his personal interests. He is the top Democrat on the Science panel's Technology Subcommittee, a post he took midway through the 105th. On the Science Committee, he literally tends to the nuts and bolts of lawmaking: One of the panel's bills in the 105th clarified standards for government testing of fasteners — nuts, bolts, screws, and the like. In the 106th Congress, Barcia focused his attention on whether U.S. industries, particularly small businesses, can cope with rapid changes in electronic commerce technologies.

Barcia's other committee is Transportation and Infrastructure. The panel crafted a massive transportation measure in the 105th Congress that authorized highway and mass transit funding increases for most states. Michigan did particularly well, as did Barcia's 5th District. In the 106th, the committee's focus shifted to aviation, where Barcia sought to improve service to small- and medium-size communities in his district that had seen a decline in air service.

Agriculture is important in the 5th — the district is a leading producer of navy beans and beet sugar and is the state's largest dairy producer. Barcia defends the federal sugar subsidy program from annual attempts to scuttle it. He tried in the 105th to win an exemption for farmers from regulations on the transport of hazardous materials, such as pesticides. He won House approval, but could not get the Senate to go along.

Barcia was a leader in the 106th Congress of an effort by lawmakers from Great Lakes states to step up the fight against encroachment by the zebra mussel, sea lamprey and other invasive species that have turned up in the Great Lakes.

In 1998, Barcia won approval of a resolution urging states to take steps to ensure that violent criminals serve at least 85 percent of their prison sentence. Barcia's measure was prompted by a 1989 attack on the daughter of a Bay City woman by a man who had been released from prison early. In addition to the attack on the daughter, which left her partially paralyzed, the offender committed two murders and six other violent crimes after his early prison release. Barcia also has backed legislation to address victims' rights and to expand the use of the death penalty.

Barcia is a fan of the Boys' and Girls' Clubs and has worked to obtain grants from anti-crime funding to support club activities that help keep young people busy and out of trouble.

Through his interest in bow hunting, Barcia has developed a friendship with longtime rock star Ted Nugent, who operates a sportsmen's club in Michigan. Barcia heads a task force on bow hunting for the Congressional Sportsmen's Caucus, and in 1999 he convinced TWA to stop charging a $50 fee to passengers taking their hunting bows on board a plane.

Born and raised in Bay City and educated at nearby Saginaw Valley State University, Barcia worked in Saginaw for state Rep. Don Albosta (who later served six years in the U.S. House). At age 24, after less than two years with Albosta, Barcia himself was elected to the state House. He served three terms, including two as majority whip, before moving up to the state Senate, where he stayed for a decade.

When nine-term Democratic Rep. Bob Traxler announced he would retire in 1992, Barcia launched his House bid. He made it through a three-way primary with 46 percent of the vote, receiving some criticism that he was a "career politician." The other Democratic hopefuls were to his left on the political spectrum, and only after he had the nomination in hand did organized labor get behind him. Barcia defeated GOP state Rep. Keith Muxlow, 60 percent to 38 percent, and his subsequent re-election contests have been uneventful.

KEY VOTES

2000

Yes   Raise hourly minimum wage by $1 over two years

Yes   Halt funding for U.S. mission in Kosovo unless European nations pay more

Yes   Provide Medicare benefits to military retirees and their dependents

No   Grant China permanent normal trade status

Yes   Phase out estate, gift and trust taxes

No   Prohibit implementation of president's national monument designations

No   Approve GOP plan to provide prescription drug coverage for Medicare beneficiaries

Yes   Increase help for poor nations indebted to international financial institutions

1999

Yes   Impose steel import quotas

No   Kill proposal to take aviation trust funds off budget

No   Require background checks on buyers only at gun shows with 10 or more vendors

Yes   Remove barriers among banking, securities and insurance companies

Yes   Authorize state grants to hire teachers and reduce class size

No   Overhaul campaign finance law; ban "soft money" and restrict advocacy advertising

Yes   Approve bipartisan plan to increase rights of patients in managed-care health plans

INTEREST GROUPS

	AFL-CIO	ADA	CCUS	ACU
2000	80%	40%	57%	56%
1999	100%	55%	52%	52%
1998	90%	90%	50%	40%
1997	88%	50%	60%	64%

CQ VOTE STUDIES

	PARTY UNITY		PRESIDENTIAL SUPPORT	
	Support	Oppose	Support	Oppose
2000	61%	39%	39%	61%
1999	62%	38%	46%	54%
1998	67%	33%	60%	40%
1997	61%	39%	45%	55%

MICHIGAN 5

East – Saginaw; Bay City

The 5th includes the 220 miles of shoreline along Lake Huron that form the Michigan Thumb. The district's population is concentrated in Saginaw, a small manufacturing hub, and Bay City, still a thriving port on Saginaw Bay. The 5th also takes in some of the working-class suburbs north of Flint. Although the district's industrial base includes plastics and sugar refining, the cities depend almost exclusively on General Motors auto parts plants, making the United Auto Workers union a formidable political force.

Union voters, however, are balanced by rural constituents in the district's northern counties and far reaches of the Thumb. The 5th has some of the most productive navy bean and sugar beet fields in the state. Sanilac County, at the base of the Thumb, leads Michigan in dairy production.

The district's blue-collar voters lean toward populist stances on economics, and rural voters hold conservative views on social issues, opposing both abortion and gun control. With its large population of auto workers, Saginaw, the district's largest city, is a Democratic stronghold. As a whole, the 5th supports Democrats in national elections but goes for Republicans locally.

MAJOR INDUSTRY

Auto parts manufacturing, agriculture, sugar processing

CITIES

Saginaw, 62,422; Bay City, 34,800

UNUSUAL FEATURES

Famous natives: Stevie Wonder (Saginaw), Madonna (Bay City); Monitor Sugar Co. in Bay City, largest sugar refinery east of the Mississippi River; Bay City once known as the "Lumber Capital of the World," with more than 50 lumber mills.

Rep. Fred Upton (R)

CAPITOL OFFICE
225-3761; fax 225-4986; 2333 Rayburn Bldg. 20515

INTERNET
e-mail: talk2.fsu@mail.house.gov
web: www.house.gov/upton

COMMITTEES
Education & Workforce
Energy & Commerce
(Telecommunications & the Internet - chairman)

HOMETOWN
St. Joseph

BORN
April 23, 1953, St. Joseph, Mich.

RELIGION
Protestant

FAMILY
Wife, Amey Upton; two children

EDUCATION
U. of Michigan, B.A. 1975

CAREER
Congressional aide; budget analyst

POLITICAL HIGHLIGHTS
No previous office

ELECTION RESULTS

2000 GENERAL

Fred Upton (R)	159,373	67.9%
James Bupp (D)	68,532	29.2%
William Bradley (LIBERT)	3,573	1.5%

2000 PRIMARY

Fred Upton (R)	unopposed

1998 GENERAL

Fred Upton (R)	113,292	70.1%
Clarence J. Annen (D)	45,358	28.1%
Glenn D. Whitt Jr. (LIBERT)	1,833	1.1%

PREVIOUS WINNING PERCENTAGES
1996 (68%); 1994 (74%); 1992 (62%); 1990 (58%);
1988 (71%); 1986 (62%)

Elected 1986; 8th term

Upton's blend of fiscal conservatism and more-liberal views on some social issues inspires confidence among moderates of both parties. A natural-born compromiser, he takes his time making decisions on almost everything, and so he has become an increasingly important presence in a House closely divided between Republicans and Democrats.

Upton says he even deliberates when trying to rent a movie with his wife, Amey: "We struggle when we go to Blockbuster," he told The Detroit News. "We spend an hour trying to decide."

Upton is low-key and friendly, telling people, "Just call me Fred." (President George W. Bush has nicknamed him "Freddy Boy," according to The New York Times.) Those who are weary of partisan battles look to Upton as a straight shooter, and the veteran legislator responds by looking for solutions that can be embraced by all sides. "I'm not going to vote party line," he once said. "I'm going to vote on the merits." Upton takes his votes seriously: At the beginning of the 107th Congress, he had not missed a roll call vote since 1997.

Upton arrived in Congress with solid credentials as a proponent of budget and tax cutting, because of his work with Reagan budget director David A. Stockman; and initially, he seemed to have a bright future in the rising conservative wing of the House GOP. He worked as a deputy whip for then-Speaker Newt Gingrich and in 1990 castigated President George Bush for agreeing to raise taxes. But he resigned from his deputy whip position in 1993 because Gingrich's confrontational style was not to his liking. After the GOP took power in 1995, the independent-minded Upton cast his lot with a loose coalition of mostly moderate Republicans.

Upton has emerged as a key power broker on issues ranging from tax cuts to consumer safety. Thanks in part to his strong working relationship with Speaker J. Dennis Hastert, he scored a key victory in the 106th Congress when he and other moderate Republicans forced the GOP leadership to accede to a "trigger" in a tax cut bill that would suspend the cuts if interest on the national debt increased. Although moderates had generally knuckled under to the leadership in the past, this time "we hung tough until we got what we wanted," Upton said.

When public outrage swelled in 2000 over the deaths of more than 100 people using vehicles equipped with Firestone tires, Upton, a member of the Commerce Committee, won speedy House passage of a landmark bill to impose prison terms on auto industry officials if they withhold information about defects. "We have lost more than 100 lives because of these tires," he said. "We have seen hundreds and hundreds of accidents, many serious injuries. And what this bill does is correct those problems."

Upton weighs in on some highly contentious political issues. He has joined a bipartisan coalition that wants to allow workers to invest a portion of their payroll taxes in the stock market, and he urges his colleagues to reform Social Security without engaging in partisan sniping. "Social Security should never be a partisan issue, and we need to work together on all sides," he said.

To the dismay of some conservatives, Upton sided with a minority of Republicans who voted for tighter restrictions on firearms purchases at gun shows, and he backs more health care spending and campaign finance changes. But he also remains committed to getting the federal budget under control. As he told The New York Times in 1999, "That's what drives me. ... That's why I chose to run [for Congress]. It's really everything."

In the 107th Congress, Upton is chairman of Energy and Commerce's

Telecommunications and the Internet Subcommittee. In the 106th, he had chaired the Oversight and Investigations Subcommittee, where he received national media attention during 1999 hearings into alleged abuses by the International Olympic Committee (IOC) over bidding by Atlanta and Salt Lake City to host the Olympics. When IOC officials pledged to reform the bidding process, Upton pledged to keep "staying on top of them. Our effort is not to trash the Olympics. We want to clean it up."

Upton's eclectic interests include a couple of other efforts that are not conventional fare for most conservatives. Breaking with anti-abortion forces, he is a vocal advocate of allowing research on fetal tissue, arguing that it can be helpful in finding a cure for many serious diseases. He does side with his party's conservative branch, however, on such issues as opposing federal recognition of same-sex marriage and pursuing a ban on a procedure its opponents call "partial birth" abortion.

Upton also has worked to improve race relations. When the Ku Klux Klan announced in 1998 that it was planning to march in the mostly white city of St. Joseph, in his 6th District, Upton went to a black church in neighboring Benton Harbor to get the message out that the people of St. Joseph did not welcome the Klan.

Though he is usually watchful of government spending, Upton has worked to save the Great Lakes foghorns. The U.S. Coast Guard wanted to dismantle the foghorn network to save money, but Upton blocked the effort. He said he owed the horns a debt of gratitude: Once, out sailing with friends when fog rolled in, Upton and his shipmates were led home by the foghorn blasts.

Upton was raised in Michigan in a wealthy Republican household (his grandfather helped found Whirlpool Corp., which is still based in the 6th). A sense of social responsibility was instilled in the young Upton early on. His parents took care of as many as two dozen foster children at various times, and one of Upton's first jobs was in a day care center.

Upton compiled a strong résumé before coming to Congress. He spent 10 years as an aide to Stockman during Stockman's tenures first as 4th District congressman and then at the Office of Management and Budget. After Stockman resigned his OMB post in 1985, Upton returned to the district and challenged GOP Rep. Mark D. Siljander.

Much of the local GOP establishment had long disliked Siljander, a Christian conservative activist. Upton generally avoided challenging Siljander's positions on issues, seeking instead to convince voters that he was simply a more appealing, less confrontational conservative. He won the race with 62 percent of the vote and has coasted to re-election since.

KEY VOTES

2000
Yes Raise hourly minimum wage by $1 over two years
Yes Halt funding for U.S. mission in Kosovo unless European nations pay more
Yes Provide Medicare benefits to military retirees and their dependents
Yes Grant China permanent normal trade status
Yes Phase out estate, gift and trust taxes
No Prohibit implementation of president's national monument designations
Yes Approve GOP plan to provide prescription drug coverage for Medicare beneficiaries
No Increase help for poor nations indebted to international financial institutions

1999
No Impose steel import quotas
No Kill proposal to take aviation trust funds off budget
No Require background checks on buyers only at gun shows with 10 or more vendors
Yes Remove barriers among banking, securities and insurance companies
No Authorize state grants to hire teachers and reduce class size
Yes Overhaul campaign finance law; ban "soft money" and restrict advocacy advertising
No Approve bipartisan plan to increase rights of patients in managed-care health plans

INTEREST GROUPS

	AFL-CIO	ADA	CCUS	ACU
2000	10%	25%	85%	60%
1999	0%	25%	92%	68%
1998	20%	15%	89%	56%
1997	13%	25%	90%	80%

CQ VOTE STUDIES

	PARTY UNITY		PRESIDENTIAL SUPPORT	
	Support	Oppose	Support	Oppose
2000	79%	21%	39%	61%
1999	80%	20%	32%	68%
1998	79%	21%	33%	67%
1997	83%	17%	37%	63%

MICHIGAN 6

Southwest – Kalamazoo; Benton Harbor; St. Joseph

Lush forests in Michigan's southwest corner make the 6th a prime spot for tourists and orchards. Cherries and peaches grow in the fruit belt that extends north from St. Joseph and Benton Harbor – once a stop on the Underground Railroad – through Van Buren County. Many affluent Chicagoans keep second homes in the wooded area along the Lake Michigan shoreline, which has become known as "Harbor County."

Kalamazoo, the 6th's most populous city, has a strong and diverse manufacturing economy. Cities throughout the district have escaped dependence on Detroit's auto-maker economy.

Both home appliance-manufacturer Whirlpool Corp., in Benton Harbor, and pharmaceutical-maker Pharmacia & Upjohn, in Portage, built their world headquarters in the district. Education is another economic

pillar, led by Western Michigan University's 28,000 students.

Kalamazoo's blue-collar workforce makes it one of the few Democratic parts of the 6th. But the city's voters are no match for the Republican influences in the district – Kalamazoo's conservative Dutch heritage, white-collar corporate managers and rural conservatives. All combine to make the 6th a moderate-to-conservative district.

Republicans still easily win local elections, and President Bush carried the district in 2000. But, like most of the state, the 6th voted for Bill Clinton by a small margin in 1992 and '96.

MAJOR INDUSTRY
Manufacturing, higher education, agriculture

CITIES
Kalamazoo, 75,660; Portage, 43,992; Benton Harbor, 11,719

UNUSUAL FEATURES
First outdoor pedestrian shopping mall in the United States built in Kalamazoo in 1959.

Rep. Nick Smith (R)

Elected 1992; 5th term

A former dairy farmer, Smith has a folksy manner and eclectic interests that range from scientific research to the long-term solvency of the Social Security system. He has been an elected official for close to 40 years, and he remains popular with district voters because of his plain-spoken and low-key ways.

A stalwart conservative, Smith pays great attention to nagging details and does not seem to mind if his concerns are not in vogue. His earthy style has helped him win re-election easily in the small towns and agricultural communities that are an important part of the 7th District.

Smith casts a dependably conservative vote on social issues. He would ban a procedure its opponents call "partial birth" abortion and favors constitutional amendments to outlaw flag burning and permit school prayer. He generally prefers to limit the federal government's reach and has joined with other Republicans to try to eliminate many government regulations.

However, he can also follow an independent course. Breaking with some in his party over the controversy surrounding Elián González, the six-year-old Cuban boy who spent months with his Miami relatives in 1999 and 2000, Smith said the father had the right of custody — even if he did live in a communist country. "I consider it very presumptuous to say that the family unit is less important than the country where one lives," Gannett News Service quoted him as saying.

Smith also departed from the majority of his party when he voted against giving the president the line-item veto. "I served under three governors while in the state legislature," he said. "Every one of these governors, liberal and conservative, used the leverage of the line-item veto to get the spending they wanted." He endorsed the presidential campaign of magazine publisher Steve Forbes in both 1996 and 2000 because of the long-shot candidate's strong stands. "It is so easy for politicians to gloss over tough issues with Congress being so stagnant," Smith said, according to The Associated Press.

Smith served on the Budget Committee for six years, from 1995 to 2001, and he sought the panel's chairmanship in the 107th Congress, promising to hold down spending to provide money for tax cuts. He lost out, in a four-way race, to Jim Nussle of Iowa. In the 107th, he left the committee and picked up a seat on International Relations.

From his Budget seat, Smith had involved himself in Capitol Hill balanced-budget debates and the long-term financial solvency of Social Security. He chaired a bipartisan task force on the nation's retirement system, and he sponsored legislation in the 106th Congress to allow workers to invest some of their payroll taxes in the stock market. Smith's plan also called for raising the retirement age and slowing the growth of benefits for higher-income recipients.

In the 106th, Smith took the gavel of the Science Committee's Basic Research Subcommittee (renamed Research in the 107th), putting him in a good position to protect research dollars for Michigan universities. In 2000, he helped win passage of a multibillion-dollar plan to expand government's role in computer and scientific research. "The current boom in information technology is based on the basic research carried out more than 15 years ago," he said. "There is an urgent need to replenish the knowledge base."

On the Agriculture Committee, Smith warns that U.S. government restrictions on farm exports and low-cost, foreign government-subsidized imports have placed farmers at a distinct competitive disadvantage.

CAPITOL OFFICE
225-6276; fax 225-6281; 2305 Rayburn Bldg. 20515

INTERNET
e-mail: rep.smith@mail.house.gov
web: www.house.gov/nicksmith

COMMITTEES
Agriculture
International Relations
Science
  (Research - chairman)

HOMETOWN
Addison

BORN
Nov. 5, 1934, Addison, Mich.

RELIGION
Congregationalist

FAMILY
Wife, Bonnalyn Smith; four children

EDUCATION
Michigan State U., B.A. 1957; U. of Delaware, M.S. 1959

MILITARY SERVICE
Air Force, 1959-61

CAREER
Dairy farmer

POLITICAL HIGHLIGHTS
Somerset Township Board of Trustees, 1962-66; Hillsdale County Board of Supervisors, 1966-68; Mich. House, 1979-83; Mich. Senate, 1983-93

ELECTION RESULTS

2000 GENERAL

Nick Smith (R)	147,369	61.2%
Jennie Crittendon (D)	86,080	35.7%

2000 PRIMARY

Nick Smith (R)	unopposed

1998 GENERAL

Nick Smith (R)	104,656	57.5%
Jim Berryman (D)	72,998	40.1%
Kenneth L. Proctor (LIBERT)	2,684	1.5%

PREVIOUS WINNING PERCENTAGES
1996 (55%); 1994 (65%); 1992 (88%)

He has also become a leading advocate for expanding the use of genetically modified crops. Although many environmentalists worry that changing the gene structure of plants can have unforeseen and potentially dangerous consequences, Smith plants genetically modified corn and soybeans on his own 1,400-acre farm, and he points out that the technology reduces his dependence on insecticides. "If these products don't gain acceptance, scientific research will stop, product development will stop, and it will limit science's ability to do great things in the world," he said in 2000. "It's important that we do what we can to ensure this technology ... does not get suppressed due to misinformation and misconceptions."

Just as he did during 14 years as a state legislator, Smith advocates tax cuts and spending restraint, backing conservative GOP plans to eliminate the current tax code and to require a two-thirds majority vote in both chambers to raise taxes. He was an early supporter of the flat tax idea. In 1995, he gave the Clinton White House fits when he tried to block an increase in the national debt limit even though the administration warned that it could cause the federal government to default on some payments. When the House finally approved an increase in the federal debt limit, Smith was one of just 30 Republicans voting "no."

Smith's frugality does not prevent him from steering federal money toward his district when he gets the chance. At the end of the 105th, for example, Smith cited excessive spending levels as his reason for voting against the massive catchall appropriations bill. But he also worked to include in the bill $322,000 to reimburse a county in his district for most of the cost of fighting an outbreak of hepatitis.

Smith has supported bipartisan legislation to ban the national parties from receiving or spending "soft money," the unlimited, largely unregulated contributions used for party-building activities and issue ads. Smith, who does not accept contributions from political action committees, won House approval of an amendment to increase penalties for candidates who knowingly accept illegal foreign contributions.

After four years in the Michigan House and a decade in the state Senate, Smith was one of four Republicans aiming at the open 7th District in 1992. He took 43 percent of the vote, nudging past his chief adversary, fellow state Sen. John Schwartz, by stressing his conservative credentials and winning the endorsement of Michigan Right to Life (even though Schwartz also opposed abortion). No Democrat filed to run, so Smith eased to victory over a minor challenger. He has since won re-election easily. He has promised to serve no more than 12 years in the House.

KEY VOTES

2000
No   Raise hourly minimum wage by $1 over two years
Yes   Halt funding for U.S. mission in Kosovo unless European nations pay more
Yes   Provide Medicare benefits to military retirees and their dependents
Yes   Grant China permanent normal trade status
?   Phase out estate, gift and trust taxes
Yes   Prohibit implementation of president's national monument designations
No   Approve GOP plan to provide prescription drug coverage for Medicare beneficiaries
No   Increase help for poor nations indebted to international financial institutions

1999
No   Impose steel import quotas
Yes   Kill proposal to take aviation trust funds off budget
Yes   Require background checks on buyers only at gun shows with 10 or more vendors
Yes   Remove barriers among banking, securities and insurance companies
No   Authorize state grants to hire teachers and reduce class size
Yes   Overhaul campaign finance law; ban "soft money" and restrict advocacy advertising
No   Approve bipartisan plan to increase rights of patients in managed-care health plans

INTEREST GROUPS

	AFL-CIO	ADA	CCUS	ACU
2000	10%	10%	84%	91%
1999	0%	10%	79%	84%
1998	30%	20%	83%	76%
1997	0%	15%	90%	88%

CQ VOTE STUDIES

	PARTY UNITY		PRESIDENTIAL SUPPORT	
	Support	Oppose	Support	Oppose
2000	93%	7%	24%	76%
1999	90%	10%	22%	78%
1998	88%	12%	26%	74%
1997	90%	10%	36%	64%

MICHIGAN 7
South central — Battle Creek; Jackson

The southern Michigan counties that make up the 7th take in small towns, farming communities and a few mid-size cities. Kellogg's Tony the Tiger makes his home in Battle Creek, the district's largest city, which has been dubbed "Cereal City." The cereal giant is not only one of the city's largest employers, but it also maintains one of the nation's top philanthropic organizations, donating some gifts to the Battle Creek area.

Outside Battle Creek, auto parts manufacturing drives small-town economies, especially in Jackson. Agriculture dominates most of the rest of the district, with soybeans and corn as the staple crops. The farming counties of Branch, Eaton, Hillsdale, Jackson and Lenawee have been fertile ground for the GOP, which has carried congressional elections. Rural and small-town voters tend to overwhelm the influence of the cities' blue-collar population, but even Democrats tend to be socially conservative. Unlike Detroit's autoworkers, many of

those living here have roots in the surrounding Republican countryside. When most of the state went for Bill Clinton in 1992, the 7th was evenly split. In 1996, Clinton won narrowly. But in 2000, district voters gave President Bush the edge, while the state as a whole voted for Al Gore.

The district's political and social culture has been shaped by Quaker settlements that made the area a station on the Underground Railroad and left many residents sensitive to issues such as racial segregation and the Vietnam War.

MAJOR INDUSTRY
Agriculture, food processing, auto parts manufacturing

CITIES
Battle Creek, 53,699; Jackson, 35,151; Adrian, 21,899

UNUSUAL FEATURES
Sojourner Truth lived in Battle Creek; Annual Cereal Festival, culminating in the world's longest breakfast table, in Battle Creek.

Rep. Mike Rogers (R)

CAPITOL OFFICE
225-4872; fax 225-5820; 509 Cannon Bldg. 20515

INTERNET
e-mail: mike.rogers@mail.house.gov
web: www.house.gov/mikerogers

COMMITTEES
Financial Services
Transportation & Infrastructure

HOMETOWN
Brighton

BORN
June 2, 1963, Livonia, Mich.

RELIGION
Methodist

FAMILY
Wife, Diane Rogers; two children

EDUCATION
Adrian College, B.A. 1985

MILITARY SERVICE
Army, 1985-88

CAREER
Home construction company owner; FBI agent

POLITICAL HIGHLIGHTS
Mich. Senate, 1995-2001 (majority floor leader, 1999-2001)

ELECTION RESULTS

2000 GENERAL

Mike Rogers (R)	145,190	48.8%
Dianne Byrum (D)	145,079	48.8%
Bonnie Bucqueroux (GREEN)	3,467	1.2%

2000 PRIMARY

Mike Rogers (R)	unopposed

Elected 2000; 1st term

Rogers — an Army veteran, former FBI special agent and co-founder of a modular home-building business — has a conservative bent on most issues. But his eclectic background, charming demeanor and positioning as a mainstream politician win votes from some independents and Democrats.

The freshman lawmaker needed all the support he could muster in his bid for the House: The contest, in one of the nation's premier "swing" districts, was the closest House race in 2000. Rogers' win was not official until mid-December, when the Democratic candidate, state Sen. Dianne Byrum, conceded after a partial recount failed to erase her opponent's slim lead. Roger gained the seat with an official margin of just 111 votes out of nearly 300,000 cast.

Still, Rogers' victory was impressive in a district — which includes the state capital of Lansing — that favored Democrats Al Gore for president and Debbie Stabenow over GOP incumbent Spencer Abraham for the Senate.

House Republican leaders in 2001 named Rogers — a former state Senate majority floor leader — a deputy whip, making him the only freshman in the GOP leadership in the 107th Congress. Rogers also was assigned to the Transportation and Financial Services committees.

But Rogers, who made education a key issue in his campaign and whose district includes Michigan State University, can also be expected to pursue his ideas for improving schools. As a state senator, he sponsored a bill — signed into law by Republican Gov. John Engler in 2000 — that allows parents to save money tax-free for their children's postsecondary education. In Congress, he has proposed legislation to provide federal tax incentives for families to save money for higher education.

Rogers said shortly after his victory in the 8th District that he had learned "what it feels like to lose an election and win an election on the same day." In the early morning hours following the election, Rogers drove home thinking he had lost to Byrum in their contest to succeed two-term Democratic Rep. Stabenow. Only when he got home was he informed that late-reporting precincts in his home county, Livingston, had put him on top.

MICHIGAN 8
Central — Lansing

Michigan's capital district, where Ransom Eli Olds founded Olds Motor Vehicle Co. in 1897, covers Lansing, East Lansing and some agricultural communities to the east. The dominance of General Motors, which makes Chevrolets, Cadillacs and Pontiacs in the district, is matched only by state government. Together, they employ thousands of people in the 8th.

Michigan State, the nation's first land-grant university, gave birth to the district's second-largest city, East Lansing. University students, faculty and auto workers make Ingham County strongly Democratic. They're joined by voters in the northeastern portion of the district, which covers the southern outskirts of Flint, where voters tend to follow Flint's Democratic voting habits.

But further east, in largely agricultural

Livingston County, the GOP holds sway. The county has been absorbing whites leaving area cities, including Detroit, Flint, Lansing and Pontiac.

The district supported Democratic presidential candidates in 1992, '96 and 2000. But the combination of strongly Democratic and Republicans areas has made the 8th a precarious place. On the congressional level, the district has been fickle – the seat has changed party hands three times since 1990.

MAJOR INDUSTRY
State government, auto manufacturing, higher education

CITIES
Lansing, 127,716; East Lansing, 46,565

UNUSUAL FEATURES
Basketball star Earvin "Magic" Johnson hails from Lansing; Howell celebrates the honeydew harvest with its annual Melon Festival.

Rep. Dale E. Kildee (D)

Elected 1976; 13th term

CAPITOL OFFICE
225-3611; fax 225-6393; 2107 Rayburn Bldg. 20515

INTERNET
e-mail: dale.kildee@mail.house.gov
web: www.house.gov/kildee

COMMITTEES
Education & Workforce
Resources

HOMETOWN
Flint

BORN
Sept. 16, 1929, Flint, Mich.

RELIGION
Roman Catholic

FAMILY
Wife, Gayle Heyn; three children

EDUCATION
Sacred Heart Seminary, B.A. 1952; U. of Detroit,
attended 1954; U. of Peshawar (Pakistan),
attended 1958-59; U. of Michigan, M.A. 1961

CAREER
Teacher

POLITICAL HIGHLIGHTS
Mich. House, 1965-75; Mich. Senate, 1975-77

ELECTION RESULTS

2000 GENERAL

Dale E. Kildee (D)	158,184	61.1%
Grant Garrett (R)	92,926	35.9%
Laurie M. Martin (LIBERT)	5,337	2.1%

2000 PRIMARY

Dale E. Kildee (D)	unopposed

1998 GENERAL

Dale E. Kildee (D)	105,457	55.9%
Tom McMillin (R)	79,062	41.9%
Malcolm Johnson (LIBERT)	4,006	2.1%

PREVIOUS WINNING PERCENTAGES
1996 (59%); 1994 (51%); 1992 (54%); 1990 (68%);
1988 (76%); 1986 (80%); 1984 (93%); 1982 (75%);
1980 (93%); 1978 (77%); 1976 (70%)

As the son of an autoworker who hails from the home of General Motors, Kildee's blue-collar credentials are rock solid, and his political views reflect his roots. He is a liberal Democrat with a belief in activist government and a strong pro-labor track record. He supports Democratic efforts to increase the minimum wage, expand federal funding for a variety of education programs and require more services from managed-care plans.

Such a disposition could have pushed Kildee to the margins politically in recent years as Republicans and even some moderate Democrats sought to halt, or even reverse, the reach of the federal government. But Kildee — who entered politics in 1964 in the heyday of Lyndon B. Johnson's Great Society war on poverty, civil rights crusades and other social reforms — has a pragmatic streak that steers him toward the center on some key votes.

A seminary graduate who became a Latin teacher after abandoning plans to become a Roman Catholic priest, Kildee generally presses for Washington to play an aggressive role in improving the lot of people in need.

Kildee is now the second-ranking Democrat on the Education and the Workforce Committee. In the 106th Congress, he was the ranking minority member on the panel's Early Childhood, Youth and Families Subcommittee, where he worked on a reauthorization of the Elementary and Secondary Education Act, but Congress made little progress on that front. The reauthorization is a top priority for lawmakers in the 107th Congress, and Kildee should be a key player in that debate, as the ranking Democrat on the newly formed Education Reform Subcommittee, which has jurisdiction over elementary and secondary education policy as well as Head Start and special education programs.

In the 105th, he played an active role in crafting a law that authorized more federal assistance to college students and a $300 million-a-year program of grants for teacher training and recruitment. The measure also reduced student loan rates to their lowest level in nearly two decades. Kildee praised the bill as a triumph of bipartisan cooperation.

While he remains a reliable ally of labor unions — in the 106th, he voted to impose steel import quotas, raise the minimum wage by $1 over two years and deny China permanent normal trade status — he has moved toward the center on some issues. In 1997, he differentiated himself from many on the Democratic left by voting for the two measures to implement the balanced-budget agreement between congressional Republicans and President Clinton, even though the deal curbed spending on Medicare and reduced the taxation of capital gains. In 1996, he voted for the final version of the welfare overhaul legislation, which likewise was anathema to most liberals. Kildee said Democrats had wrangled enough concessions from the GOP to make the measure acceptable.

Kildee opposes abortion and voted in the 105th to ban government approval of any drug that could induce abortion. In the 106th Congress, he backed a Republican fetal protection bill that opponents said would undermine the Supreme Court's 1973 *Roe v. Wade* decision.

But he gives no ground when it comes to the lot of American Indians. He first took notice of their plight as a child when he visited his father's hometown near the Grand Traverse reservation. A previous generation of Kildees had traded with the Indians, and Kildee said he was impressed with his father's concern for their condition. As a state legislator, Kildee wrote a law allowing Michigan's American Indians to attend its state colleges for free.

In his suit pocket are copies not only of the Constitution but of the landmark 1832 Supreme Court decision that gave the federal government exclusive jurisdiction over Indian affairs, and thus responsibility for Indians' welfare. In the House, that jurisdiction is generally exercised by the Resources Committee, where Kildee ranks third in Democratic seniority. When Congress in 1997 started talking about levying a tax on Indian-run gambling operations, he founded the Native American Caucus. In honor of all his efforts, the Grand Traverse Band of Ottawa and Chippewa Indians in 1998 named April 15 "Dale Kildee Day."

At the start of the 106th Congress, Kildee had the longest streak of consecutive votes cast of any active lawmaker — 6,961 — having missed no vote since 1985. By Congressional Quarterly's strict accounting, the streak ended on June 17, 1998, when he joined more than 60 lawmakers in voting "present" on an amendment to create an independent commission to study the campaign finance system. The Detroit News argues the streak did not end until Oct. 28, 2000, when Kildee missed a routine roll call vote to approve the congressional journal. He was engrossed in a meeting with Education Committee staffers and "boom, it was too late," Kildee told the News.

Kildee says his commitment to voting stems from a work ethic instilled in him as a child, when his father would trudge through the snow to get to his job at the Buick plant, and Kildee would do the same to get to school — sometimes to find that they were the only ones who showed up.

Kildee was elected to the Michigan House in 1964 and to the state Senate a decade later. He ran for Congress in 1976 to succeed Democrat Donald W. Riegle Jr., who was on his way to winning election to the Senate. Kildee won with 70 percent of the vote, starting a string of easy victories that ran through 1990.

But in the past decade Kildee became a target for Republicans looking for vulnerable Democratic incumbents. He had close calls in 1992 and 1994, when Republican Megan O'Neill, who had worked in the White House under President George Bush, ran strong campaigns.

In the 1992 race, Kildee had to answer for 100 overdrafts at the private bank for House members, and redistricting had dealt him a tough hand: Almost half the people in the redrawn 9th District were new to him. Kildee took 54 percent that year but was held to 51 percent in 1994, the year of the GOP sweep of Congress.

In 2000, Kildee was back up to 61 percent. But redistricting could again present a problem in 2002 — Michigan lost one House seat as a result of reapportionment.

KEY VOTES

2000
Yes Raise hourly minimum wage by $1 over two years
No Halt funding for U.S. mission in Kosovo unless European nations pay more
Yes Provide Medicare benefits to military retirees and their dependents
No Grant China permanent normal trade status
No Phase out estate, gift and trust taxes
No Prohibit implementation of president's national monument designations
No Approve GOP plan to provide prescription drug coverage for Medicare beneficiaries
Yes Increase help for poor nations indebted to international financial institutions

1999
Yes Impose steel import quotas
No Kill proposal to take aviation trust funds off budget
No Require background checks on buyers only at gun shows with 10 or more vendors
Yes Remove barriers among banking, securities and insurance companies
Yes Authorize state grants to hire teachers and reduce class size
Yes Overhaul campaign finance law; ban "soft money" and restrict advocacy advertising
Yes Approve bipartisan plan to increase rights of patients in managed-care health plans

INTEREST GROUPS

	AFL-CIO	ADA	CCUS	ACU
2000	100%	75%	42%	20%
1999	100%	90%	20%	12%
1998	100%	95%	33%	16%
1997	100%	80%	40%	24%

CQ VOTE STUDIES

	PARTY UNITY		PRESIDENTIAL SUPPORT	
	Support	Oppose	Support	Oppose
2000	87%	13%	72%	28%
1999	87%	13%	71%	29%
1998	84%	16%	74%	26%
1997	77%	23%	63%	37%

MICHIGAN 9
East Central — Flint; Pontiac

Flint, the birthplace of General Motors in 1908, gave rise to the modern labor movement 30 years later when sit-down strikes at two Flint plants forced the auto giant to recognize the power of the United Auto Workers union.

From the turn of the century until the late 1960s, both Flint and Pontiac, 30 miles south, grew along with the American auto industry. Then the 1970s oil shock and an increase in inexpensive imports undercut demand for GM cars and drove the district's economy into a downward spiral.

The U.S. auto industry has recovered from its 1970s slump, but jobs continue to be lost to automation and overseas production. Although GM jobs are not as plentiful, the auto industry has also given rise to a number of small, spin-off companies that employ a significant number of people in the district.

Both Flint and Pontiac, strongly influenced by the UAW, vote overwhelmingly Democratic. They're joined by Lapeer County, also Democratic but less strongly so. The 9th also includes 40 percent of Oakland County, one of the wealthiest counties in the nation and home to the American headquarters for DaimlerChrysler.

Voters in Oakland County, staunchly Republican, make the district competitive for the GOP, but even that does little to undermine the Democratic majority in the 9th. In the 2000 presidential contest, Al Gore edged out President Bush by 7 percentage points.

MAJOR INDUSTRY
Auto manufacturing, electronics

CITIES
Flint, 130,853; Pontiac, 68,149; Rochester Hills, 67,412; Waterford (unincorporated) (pt.), 66,692 (1990); Burton, 27,328

UNUSUAL FEATURES
Flint native Michael Moore's documentary film, "Roger & Me," chronicled the effect of GM's layoffs in the 1980s; Lapeer County Courthouse is the oldest working courthouse in Michigan.

Rep. David E. Bonior (D)

Elected 1976; 13th term

CAPITOL OFFICE
225-2106; fax 226-1169; 2207 Rayburn Bldg. 20515

INTERNET
e-mail: david.bonior@mail.house.gov
web: davidbonior.house.gov

COMMITTEES
Minority Whip — no committee assignments

HOMETOWN
Mount Clemens

BORN
June 6, 1945, Detroit, Mich.

RELIGION
Roman Catholic

FAMILY
Wife, Judy Bonior; three children

EDUCATION
U. of Iowa, B.A. 1967; Chapman College, M.A. 1972

MILITARY SERVICE
Air Force, 1968-72

CAREER
Probation officer; adoption caseworker

POLITICAL HIGHLIGHTS
Mich. House, 1973-77

ELECTION RESULTS

2000 GENERAL

David E. Bonior (D)	181,818	64.4%
Thomas Turner (R)	93,713	33.2%
Richard Friend (LIBERT)	4,412	1.6%

2000 PRIMARY

David E. Bonior (D)	31,835	88.2%
Mario Fundaro (D)	2,137	6.0%
Anthony America (D)	1,708	4.8%

1998 GENERAL

David E. Bonior (D)	108,770	52.4%
Brian Palmer (R)	94,027	45.3%
Richard Friend (LIBERT)	3,396	1.6%

PREVIOUS WINNING PERCENTAGES
1996 (54%); 1994 (62%); 1992 (53%); 1990 (65%);
1988 (54%); 1986 (66%); 1984 (58%); 1982 (66%);
1980 (55%); 1978 (55%); 1976 (52%)

When the Republicans took over the House in 1995, Bonior quickly earned a reputation as the Democrats' most ferociously partisan attack dog, relentlessly hounding Speaker Newt Gingrich with a long list of ethical misconduct allegations. It was an unlikely role for the introverted man who once studied for the priesthood — but one that Bonior has not shied away from since.

Still, that crusade has been over since Gingrich resigned at the end of the 105th Congress, and Bonior appears to have established an amicable relationship with the current Speaker, J. Dennis Hastert. The two have worked on several charities together, share an affinity for sports and have a similar soft-spoken manner. If Hastert's dealings with Minority Leader Richard A. Gephardt remain as frosty as they were in 1999-2000, Bonior could find himself the Democrats' main point of contact with the GOP leadership in the 107th Congress.

Bonior (BON-yer) had hoped that he would begin to play a far different role, but his dreams of becoming majority leader and working with a Speaker Gephardt were dashed when Republicans hung on to their majority in 2000. Early in the 107th Congress, Bonior said he would run for governor of Michigan in 2002.

A former high school football star who attended the University of Iowa on an athletic scholarship, Bonior has a scrappy political style that his friends say can be traced to his time on the gridiron, when he would readily throw his 175-pound, 5-foot-11-inch frame into far bigger players. As minority whip — the second-ranking spot in the party leadership — since 1995, Bonior has faithfully led the rhetorical charge against the GOP agenda, allowing Gephardt a measure of distance from the fray. "I can go both ways; I can be combative when I have to," Bonior says.

With his graying beard and penchant for sweaters, Bonior's professorial look can belie an all-out passion for his political causes. His strong liberal beliefs are grounded in his Roman Catholic upbringing and the need to pursue social justice, inculcated in him during a year in seminary. Another lesson learned then, he says, is that "being a leader in Congress is kind of like being a pastor."

He has blasted Republicans for, in his view, siding with health insurance companies over the needs of patients and for trying to cut taxes disproportionately for the rich. Taking aim at GOP fundraising practices, he once said, "There has been such a blatant, direct link between special-interest money and the Republican leadership's agenda that you might as well hang a sign out front that says 'Congress for Rent.'"

While he has long championed liberal causes — from stopping aid to the Nicaraguan contras in the 1980s to pushing for an expansion of federal hate crime laws in more recent years — Bonior does not walk in lock step with his Democratic colleagues. He opposes expansion of abortion rights, although he does not use his leadership position to advance that view.

He also consistently fought President Clinton's free-trade agenda, saying it failed to use U.S. leverage to promote environmental and human rights standards abroad. In the 103rd Congress, he opposed both the North American Free Trade Agreement and the General Agreement on Tariffs and Trade. In the 105th, he led the successful fight to deny the president fast-track authority to negotiate trade agreements that Congress cannot amend. In the 106th, he worked aggressively, though unsuccessfully, against the bill granting China permanent normal trade status. "One of our fastest-growing exports to China is American jobs," he said.

Bonior has a long history of pushing for environmental protection. In the Michigan House, he introduced the nation's first legislation to ban the class of chemicals known as PCBs, which are believed to cause cancer. During his first run for Congress in 1976, he handed out pine tree seedlings to voters.

Bonior is a loyal backer of organized labor, a politically beneficial stance in a district that takes in much of Detroit's blue-collar suburbs. In a gesture of solidarity with unions, for years Bonior refused to talk to reporters for Detroit's two daily newspapers, after they attempted in 1995 to break a strike by using replacement workers and employees who crossed the picket lines. Bonior entered The Detroit News in July 1997 and vowed not to leave until the paper agreed to rehire all of the strikers. He was arrested.

As a leader of Democratic efforts to increase the minimum wage, Bonior has cultivated alliances and friendships with such House Republicans as New Yorkers Jack Quinn and Amo Houghton, who also favor raising the federally guaranteed wage floor. In 2000, he worked with moderate Republican Tom Campbell of California to cut a symbolic $173,000 from appropriations legislation to protest the Immigration and Naturalization Service's practice of incarcerating immigrants suspected of terrorism without telling them of the charges or evidence against them.

In 1997, Bonior and his wife, Judy, spent their vacation hiking 300 miles across Michigan. He participates in Congress' annual baseball and basketball games. Bonior is also a sports fan, decorating his office with Detroit Tigers memorabilia and stealing away from the Capitol to attend the final baseball game at Tiger Stadium, which was torn down after the 1999 season.

Bonior inherited his political leanings from his father, Edward, a former city council member who later served as mayor of East Detroit. After a stint in the Air Force, as a cook, the younger Bonior returned home to Michigan, became an adoption caseworker and a probation officer, and won a seat in the Michigan House. In 1976, he jumped into the race for the congressional seat vacated when Democratic Rep. James G. O'Hara ran for the Senate. In the crowded Democratic primary, the unions were split and the Macomb County Democratic Party favored Bonior's main opponent, conservative state Sen. John T. Bowman. Bonior narrowly won the primary and the general election with an aggressive door-to-door campaign.

Bonior's liberal politics have kept him under 60 percent in seven of his 12 re-election bids. He has never won more than 66 percent of the vote.

KEY VOTES

2000
Yes Raise hourly minimum wage by $1 over two years
No   Halt funding for U.S. mission in Kosovo unless European nations pay more
Yes Provide Medicare benefits to military retirees and their dependents
No   Grant China permanent normal trade status
No   Phase out estate, gift and trust taxes
No   Prohibit implementation of president's national monument designations
No   Approve GOP plan to provide prescription drug coverage for Medicare beneficiaries
Yes Increase help for poor nations indebted to international financial institutions

1999
Yes Impose steel import quotas
No   Kill proposal to take aviation trust funds off budget
No   Require background checks on buyers only at gun shows with 10 or more vendors
Yes Remove barriers among banking, securities and insurance companies
Yes Authorize state grants to hire teachers and reduce class size
Yes Overhaul campaign finance law; ban "soft money" and restrict advocacy advertising
Yes Approve bipartisan plan to increase rights of patients in managed-care health plans

INTEREST GROUPS

	AFL-CIO	ADA	CCUS	ACU
2000	100%	100%	23%	8%
1999	100%	90%	16%	4%
1998	100%	95%	22%	16%
1997	100%	85%	40%	12%

CQ VOTE STUDIES

	PARTY UNITY		PRESIDENTIAL SUPPORT	
	Support	Oppose	Support	Oppose
2000	97%	3%	80%	20%
1999	94%	6%	79%	21%
1998	95%	5%	84%	16%
1997	92%	8%	73%	27%

MICHIGAN 10
Southeast – Macomb County; Port Huron

Situated northeast of Detroit at the base of the Michigan Thumb, the 10th covers most of Macomb and all of St. Clair counties. For years, Macomb County has been known as an electoral bellwether, attracting journalists and pollsters eager to predict election returns. In 18 of the past 21 elections for president, governor or senator, the Macomb County winner has taken the state.

Voters in Macomb's blue-collar suburban communities have strong union loyalties and socially conservative agendas, with a history of voting Democratic. But the county has steadily become more Republican since the late-1960s, supporting Nixon, Reagan and the first George Bush. Al Gore narrowly won the county in 2000.

The remainder of the district, including St. Clair County, covers rural Republican communities and farms, which are dependent on soybeans, fruit, corn and dairy products. Port Huron, a source of blue-collar Democratic votes, has grown with the expansion of the Detroit

metropolitan area. Residents along Lake Huron and Lake St. Clair tend to be concerned with water quality issues. The district also has a thriving small business community based on the boating industry. In general, the district leans more conservative than its longtime Democratic representative, Rep. Bonior.

MAJOR INDUSTRY
Auto manufacturing, agriculture, recreation

MILITARY BASES
Selfridge Air National Guard Base, 347 military, 1,753 civilian (1996)

CITIES
Clinton (unincorporated), 85,866 (1990); St. Clair Shores, 65,333; Roseville, 50,852; Port Huron, 32,337

UNUSUAL FEATURES
The 10th has the highest number of registered recreational boats per capita in the nation.

Rep. Joe Knollenberg (R)

CAPITOL OFFICE
225-5802; fax 226-2356; 2349 Rayburn Bldg. 20515

INTERNET
e-mail: rep.knollenberg@mail.house.gov
web: www.house.gov/knollenberg

COMMITTEES
Appropriations
(District of Columbia - chairman)

HOMETOWN
Bloomfield Township

BORN
Nov. 28, 1933, Mattoon, Ill.

RELIGION
Roman Catholic

FAMILY
Wife, Sandie Knollenberg; two children

EDUCATION
Eastern Illinois U., B.S. 1955

MILITARY SERVICE
Army, 1955-57

CAREER
Insurance broker

POLITICAL HIGHLIGHTS
Oakland County Republican Party chairman,
1978-86

ELECTION RESULTS

2000 GENERAL

Joe Knollenberg (R)	170,790	55.8%
Matthew Frumin (D)	124,053	40.5%
Marilyn MacDermaid (GREEN)	4,191	1.4%
Dick Gach (LIBERT)	3,371	1.1%

2000 PRIMARY

Joe Knollenberg (R)	unopposed

1998 GENERAL

Joe Knollenberg (R)	144,264	63.9%
Travis M. Reeds (D)	76,107	33.7%
Dick Gach (LIBERT)	5,433	2.4%

PREVIOUS WINNING PERCENTAGES
1996 (61%); 1994 (68%); 1992 (58%)

Elected 1992; 5th term

Knollenberg wants to get the government out of America's bathrooms — and a lot of other places as well.

He is best known for his crusade against federal standards that have limited post-1992 toilets to just 1.6 gallons per flush, less than half the volume of the previous standard, and also restricted the output of new showerheads.

But Knollenberg is equally opposed to fuel economy standards for Detroit's automakers; in fact, he distrusts most federal regulations. And he rails against the "exorbitant" federal tax burden.

Knollenberg's solid GOP voting record impressed his party leaders, and they gave him prime committee assignments — Appropriations and Budget, though he left the Budget Committee at the start of the 107th Congress.

While these assignments mark Knollenberg as a leadership ally, he was hoping to also gain the chairmanship of Appropriations' Energy and Water Subcommittee. But instead, he was given the gavel of the District of Columbia Subcommittee for the 107th.

Born into a large family (he was the fifth of 13 children) on a farm in central Illinois, Knollenberg attended college near home. But after graduation and two years in the Army, he moved to the Detroit area in 1959 to work for Allstate Insurance; he eventually opened his own Allstate branch office. His conservative views on regulatory, business, and environmental issues, reflecting his experiences as a small-business owner, are in line with the interests of the auto manufacturers and high-technology companies that fuel his affluent district's economy.

In keeping with his distrust of federal mandates and environmental programs, Knollenberg has been a keen opponent of the 1997 Kyoto climate change treaty, which he says would cost the United States as much as $300 billion a year to implement and cost the U.S. economy 2.4 million jobs. The pact has not been ratified by the Senate, but Knollenberg and his allies remained vigilant against what he termed "backdoor" attempts by the Clinton administration to implement certain aspects of the agreement. The pact would require the United States to reduce greenhouse gas emissions by 7 percent below 1990 levels, while developing nations would have no such mandate.

Knollenberg used his seat on Appropriations to attach language to several spending bills forbidding the Clinton administration from spending any money toward the implementation of the Kyoto pact. He also attached language to spending bills barring the administration from raising auto fuel economy standards, which would be a component of any effort to comply with the Kyoto agreement. "The idea of mandating carmakers to produce cars people don't want is silliness," Knollenberg said.

Although he has worked to prevent the Clinton administration from spending money on policies he dislikes, Knollenberg has used his Appropriations post to direct money to projects he does like. He has sought federal funds for artificial-kidney research at the University of Michigan, for a full-time customs agent at the Oakland-Pontiac Airport, for cleanup of the Rouge River, and for research on cheaper ways to remove snow and ice from highways.

Also on Appropriations, Knollenberg has championed U.S. aid to Lebanon to help that war-torn country build schools and hospitals. The Detroit area has a sizable Lebanese community. In 1999, Knollenberg served on a leadership-appointed task force that concluded that North Korea had not lived up to its agreement to discontinue its nuclear weapons program. The panel said no further aid should be provided to North Korea until it complied.

Knollenberg's toilet flush and showerhead volume bill has attracted the notice of headline writers and other punsters, who delight in the creative opportunities it affords. Knollenberg himself is not immune to the temptation — "We've had an overflow of complaints about these new toilets from consumers," he told the Detroit News — although he is serious about the legislation.

In the 106th Congress, he was able to convince the Commerce Committee's Energy and Power Subcommittee to schedule a vote on the bill. He lost, 12-13, but said he remained "committed to fighting frivolous federal laws and regulations" such as the mandate for toilets that often require two or three flushes.

Knollenberg's opposition to abortion and his backing of other conservative social policy initiatives earn him high ratings from groups such as the Christian Coalition and the American Conservative Union. And Knollenberg, whose son, Steve, is gay, earns low marks for his voting record from the Human Rights Campaign, an issue advocacy group for homosexuals. Knollenberg says his son's "sexual orientation is a personal matter" and that he "unequivocally" supports him "with all the love and respect that a family possibly can."

Knollenberg spent a number of years building an impressive civic and volunteer portfolio in his district, and all that work made him a known quantity when he ran for the House in 1992, seeking to replace retiring 18-term GOP Rep. William S. Broomfield. Though he campaigned as an outsider, he won his 11th District seat with an insider's skill, capitalizing on experience gained as Oakland County Republican Party chairman and as Broomfield's campaign chairman.

While two wealthy GOP candidates spent lots of time and money attacking each other, Knollenberg avoided much of the name-calling and emerged with a 13-point victory in the three-way race.

In the general election, Knollenberg faced Democrat Walter O. Briggs IV, nephew of respected former Democratic Sen. Philip A. Hart. Briggs had hoped that redistricting, which slightly diminished Republican strength in the 11th, would help him improve on his 1990 tally of 34 percent against Broomfield. But Knollenberg won with a solid 58 percent of the vote. His re-election victories since have come easily, although his 2000 percentage dipped to 56 percent, his lowest ever, against former State Department official Matthew Frumin, whose father had run against Knollenberg in 1996.

KEY VOTES

2000

No Raise hourly minimum wage by $1 over two years

No Halt funding for U.S. mission in Kosovo unless European nations pay more

Yes Provide Medicare benefits to military retirees and their dependents

Yes Grant China permanent normal trade status

Yes Phase out estate, gift and trust taxes

Yes Prohibit implementation of president's national monument designations

Yes Approve GOP plan to provide prescription drug coverage for Medicare beneficiaries

No Increase help for poor nations indebted to international financial institutions

1999

No Impose steel import quotas

Yes Kill proposal to take aviation trust funds off budget

Yes Require background checks on buyers only at gun shows with 10 or more vendors

Yes Remove barriers among banking, securities and insurance companies

No Authorize state grants to hire teachers and reduce class size

No Overhaul campaign finance law; ban "soft money" and restrict advocacy advertising

No Approve bipartisan plan to increase rights of patients in managed-care health plans

INTEREST GROUPS

	AFL-CIO	ADA	CCUS	ACU
2000	0%	0%	90%	80%
1999	0%	5%	92%	80%
1998	10%	0%	100%	96%
1997	13%	10%	100%	76%

CQ VOTE STUDIES

	PARTY UNITY		PRESIDENTIAL SUPPORT	
	Support	Oppose	Support	Oppose
2000	92%	8%	32%	68%
1999	90%	10%	30%	70%
1998	94%	6%	24%	76%
1997	90%	10%	31%	69%

MICHIGAN 11
Southeast – Part of Oakland County

Michigan's 11th – the most white-collar, best-educated and wealthiest district in the state – has historically stood apart from the rest of metropolitan Detroit as a lone free-market, Republican stronghold in a region renowned for its staunch support of pro-labor Democrats. But in recent years, this northern, suburban district has become more hospitable to Democrats, narrowly backing Bill Clinton in 1996 and Al Gore in 2000.

Covering the southwestern portion of Oakland County, the third-wealthiest county in the nation (according to 1990 Census Bureau statistics), the 11th houses the mansions of auto executives and the homes of Detroit's professionals. Communities such as Farmington Hills and Bloomfield, north of the northern Detroit boundary cut by 8 Mile Road, form a corridor between Grand River Avenue and the Northwestern Freeway that has served as one of the major routes for white exodus from Detroit. Southfield, a suburb just beyond the Detroit boundary, has become a haven for black urban professionals escaping Detroit's crime.

The northwestern part of the 11th is covered with lakes and golf courses. To the south, the district also includes the comfortable Wayne County communities of Redford and Livonia. Residents from the metropolitan Detroit Jewish community, mostly contained within the boundaries of the 11th, coupled with Southfield's black professionals, provide Democratic votes.

MAJOR INDUSTRY
Auto manufacturing, engineering, health care, insurance

CITIES
Livonia (pt.), 80,601 (1990); Farmington Hills, 79,693; Southfield (pt.), 67,949 (1990); Novi, 45,474

UNUSUAL FEATURES
First Holocaust museum in the United States in West Bloomfield – the Holocaust Memorial Center opened in 1984; The Woodward Dream Cruise is an annual celebration of the 1950s and '60 as motorists drive vintage cars up and down a 16-mile route along Woodward Avenue.

Rep. Sander M. Levin (D)

CAPITOL OFFICE
225-4961; fax 226-1033; 2300 Rayburn Bldg. 20515

INTERNET
e-mail: slevin@mail.house.gov
web: www.house.gov/levin

COMMITTEES
Ways & Means

HOMETOWN
Royal Oak

BORN
Sept. 6, 1931, Detroit, Mich.

RELIGION
Jewish

FAMILY
Wife, Victoria Levin; four children

EDUCATION
U. of Chicago, B.A. 1952; Columbia U., M.A. 1954;
Harvard U., LL.B. 1957

CAREER
Lawyer

POLITICAL HIGHLIGHTS
Oakland Board of Supervisors, 1961-64; Mich.
Senate, 1965-71 (minority leader, 1969-70);
Democratic nominee for governor, 1970, 1974

ELECTION RESULTS

2000 GENERAL

Sander M. Levin (D)	157,720	64.3%
Bart Baron (R)	78,795	32.1%
Thomas Ness (GREEN)	4,137	1.7%
Andrew Le Cureaux (LIBERT)	3,630	1.5%

2000 PRIMARY

Sander M. Levin (D)	unopposed

1998 GENERAL

Sander M. Levin (D)	105,824	55.9%
Leslie A. Touma (R)	79,619	42.0%
Albert J. Titran (LIBERT)	2,813	1.5%

PREVIOUS WINNING PERCENTAGES
1996 (57%); 1994 (52%); 1992 (53%); 1990 (70%);
1988 (70%); 1986 (76%); 1984 (100%); 1982 (67%)

Elected 1982; 10th term

A senior member of the Ways and Means Committee, Levin helps shape Democratic policy on trade. He is known for throwing himself into the details of legislation, determined to find what he sees as right answers even if they are complex. Sometimes, after a long day of thinking and fretting, he ends up looking so rumpled, with his hair strewn at wild angles, that he seems to have done physical, rather than intellectual, battle.

His strong support for organized labor and his liberal views on most issues repeatedly made him a top GOP target in the 1990s. Yet despite the distraction of having to wage million-dollar campaigns to stay in Congress, he has built a reputation as a pragmatist who can forge relationships with Republican colleagues and reach compromises.

Levin has survived challenges at the polls because he is a prolific fundraiser who can tout his influence on legislation on important topics — welfare and drugs, for instance — and because of long and close involvement in community affairs in the 12th District's north Detroit suburbs.

Levin serves as the ranking Democrat on Ways and Means' Trade Subcommittee, and he works hard to rally reluctant liberals behind some international trade agreements. In 2000, he played a critical role in securing House passage of legislation to grant China permanent normal trade status. To win over several dozen wavering lawmakers concerned by human rights abuses in China, Levin teamed with Doug Bereuter, R-Neb., to add language establishing a high-level commission to report annually to Congress on China's human rights and labor conditions.

The strategy, which succeeded in garnering the votes needed for passage, won Levin ringing praise from both Republicans and top Clinton administration officials. But it was not without risk: Levin had previously sided with labor by voting against the North American Free Trade Agreement in 1993, and his support of China trade drew fire from the powerful United Auto Workers (UAW) union, which has headquarters just a few miles from his district. But Levin downplayed the possibility of a labor backlash. "People don't vote over just one issue," he told USA Today. "In the end, UAW members won't abandon me." In 2000, Levin won re-election by his largest margin since 1990.

Levin votes a liberal line on most social policy issues, earning high marks from civil rights groups and proponents of environmental protection. He supports gun control and abortion rights, and voted against banning a procedure its opponents call "partial birth" abortion.

From his position on Ways and Means, Levin has repeatedly tried to strengthen the nation's welfare system. In the 104th Congress, he scored some success in modifying the GOP overhaul plan. Rather than try to defeat the plan, as some Democrats wanted, Levin quietly accepted the idea of ending the federal guarantee of providing welfare checks to eligible low-income mothers and children. He became an expert on the details and worked with the Clinton administration to pressure Republicans for certain revisions. When President Clinton signed the landmark bill in 1996, Levin was one of a handful of lawmakers who attended the Rose Garden ceremony that accompanied the bill signing. "I think we were able to press the Republicans in improving the bill as [it] relates to children," Levin said.

In the 105th, Levin played an important role in revising one aspect of the welfare law that Clinton and Democrats most disliked: its removal of benefits for sick and elderly legal immigrants. Although some conservatives groused at the change, Levin argued: "This is not about welfare reform, it is about community responsibility. It is not about moving a young parent from welfare to work, but about elderly people who cannot work."

In the 106th, Levin raised alarms about the number of low-income residents who were failing to apply for food stamps. "We fought to make sure food stamps and child care and health care were a part of welfare reform," Levin told The Wall Street Journal. "And now kids are hungry? What sense does that make?" He pressed for legislation that would require states to provide low-income residents with information about food stamp eligibility.

Levin has won considerable respect as a judicious legislator, and he looks for common ground with conservatives. He has been actively involved in legislation combating illegal drugs, including a bipartisan initiative, the Drug-Free Communities Act, that provides matching grants to localities that demonstrate a comprehensive approach to fighting drugs. With Ways and Means GOP colleague Sam Johnson of Texas, Levin has proposed establishing a tax credit for companies that conduct clinical testing research at U.S. medical schools and teaching hospitals.

Levin's political roots go back further than most. He first won elective office in 1964, taking a state Senate seat in the heavily Jewish Oakland County suburbs north of Detroit. He served as state Democratic Party chairman in the late 1960s and was viewed as a rising star when he ran for the governorship in 1970 and 1974. But his low-key, even-tempered manner did not shine in the statewide race, and he came up short in both gubernatorial bids.

After a stint as assistant administrator in the Agency for International Development, Levin announced for the House seat of retiring Democratic Rep. William M. Brodhead in 1982. With his well-known surname (his younger brother, Carl, had been in the U.S. Senate almost four years by then) and support from the party establishment, he overcame five primary opponents.

Although he coasted in the 1980s, Levin began facing tougher contests after a panel of federal judges redrew his district before the 1992 election. In three consecutive elections beginning in 1992, Levin won hard-fought and expensive contests against an Oakland County commissioner. In 1998, national GOP strategists threw their weight and cash behind a corporate public relations specialist, Leslie A. Touma, who criticized the incumbent for supporting several tax increases. But Levin waged another expensive defense of his record, and he prevailed with 56 percent of the vote. With redistricting in store for the 2002 election, Levin may once again face tough races, as Michigan loses one House seat to reapportionment.

KEY VOTES

2000
Yes Raise hourly minimum wage by $1 over two years
No   Halt funding for U.S. mission in Kosovo unless European nations pay more
Yes Provide Medicare benefits to military retirees and their dependents
Yes Grant China permanent normal trade status
No   Phase out estate, gift and trust taxes
No   Prohibit implementation of president's national monument designations
No   Approve GOP plan to provide prescription drug coverage for Medicare beneficiaries
Yes Increase help for poor nations indebted to international financial institutions

1999
No   Impose steel import quotas
Yes Kill proposal to take aviation trust funds off budget
No   Require background checks on buyers only at gun shows with 10 or more vendors
Yes Remove barriers among banking, securities and insurance companies
Yes Authorize state grants to hire teachers and reduce class size
Yes Overhaul campaign finance law; ban "soft money" and restrict advocacy advertising
Yes Approve bipartisan plan to increase rights of patients in managed-care health plans

INTEREST GROUPS

	AFL-CIO	ADA	CCUS	ACU
2000	90%	90%	52%	8%
1999	67%	95%	24%	4%
1998	100%	100%	33%	8%
1997	100%	100%	50%	4%

CQ VOTE STUDIES

	PARTY UNITY		PRESIDENTIAL SUPPORT	
	Support	Oppose	Support	Oppose
2000	93%	7%	90%	10%
1999	93%	7%	87%	13%
1998	93%	7%	83%	17%
1997	92%	8%	84%	16%

MICHIGAN 12
Suburban Detroit – Warren; Sterling Heights

A nearly square section of well-settled suburbs north of 8 Mile Road, Detroit's northern boundary, forms Michigan's 12th. The district is fertile ground for Democratic candidates and depends heavily on automobile manufacturing, making the United Auto Workers union a potent political force. But the influence of several wealthy towns keeps the district competitive for Republican candidates in some areas.

The western side of the district, along the Golden Corridor that runs from 8 Mile Road north to Utica, is lined with auto manufacturing facilities. Warren, the district's largest city and a traditional Democratic stronghold, is home to the GM Technical Center, a 330-acre design and engineering campus. Not far from there is the location of the former General Dynamics M-1 tank plant where Democratic presidential nominee Michael S. Dukakis took his ill-advised tank ride in 1988. The plant closed in the late 1990s although

General Dynamics still does considerable engineering and other work in their Sterling Heights Office, and the Army's Tank Automotive Command is still located in Warren.

Both Troy, in the southwestern corner of Oakland, Michigan's wealthiest county, and nearby Sterling Heights, lean toward the GOP. Both cities have benefited from growth in high-tech automotive research and design. Troy also has turned into a major office center, housing the world headquarters of Kmart.

MAJOR INDUSTRY
Auto and tank manufacturing, auto research and design

CITIES
Warren, 141,008; Sterling Heights, 124,571; Troy, 79,074

UNUSUAL FEATURES
Shrine of the Little Flower church in Royal Oak, where Father Charles Coughlin broadcast his controversial weekly radio programs in the 1930s.

Rep. Lynn Rivers (D)

Elected 1994; 4th term

Rivers entered politics at age 28 as a "mom who got mad at the system," serving first on the Ann Arbor school board and then in the Michigan House. A mother at 18, she worked at a number of low-paying jobs — she was a cook, a babysitter and a Tupperware sales representative — to help support her family.

Rivers tells her constituents she knows what it's like to have only the skills for a low-wage job or to be unable to afford health insurance. She worked her way through college, earning bachelor's and law degrees in her 30s.

In Congress, she votes a consistently liberal line, saying she wants "to bring the voice of ordinary people to Congress." She cited personal experience in objecting to a GOP proposal in the 104th Congress to require that federal student loans start accruing interest on the day a student entered school, rather than after graduation. "An education was only available to me because there were student loans," she said. She derided GOP colleagues who had benefited from the student loan program, yet were seeking to change it: "What hypocrisy. I guess it is easy to pull up the ladder of success once you and your children are safely on top."

Drawing on her eight years on the Ann Arbor school board, Rivers is an advocate for public schooling and an opponent of education initiatives such as providing parents with vouchers that can be used to pay tuition at private schools. She says that while the federal government must respect local control of schools, Washington should help set standards for education and help localities prepare students to compete in the global marketplace.

Named to the Budget Committee as a freshman, Rivers has weighed in strongly on the Social Security debate. She served on a bipartisan Social Security task force in the 106th Congress, but she concluded that Republicans were using the issue to try to score election-year points and warned that any progress on Social Security will be unlikely unless the parties learn to work together. "The Republican leadership has made it pretty clear we're not likely to move forward," she told Gannett News Service. "I don't think this task force is going to be able to have a bipartisan proposal because our views differ substantially."

She has also sought bipartisan consensus on the regulation of new technologies, as her 13th District adjoins an expanding software corridor in Ann Arbor. She is a member of the Congressional Internet Caucus, which seeks to bring together Republicans and Democrats to solve issues that have arisen with the booming use of the Internet. "Everybody is saying, 'Let's not regulate the Internet — except the way I want to.' ... It's going to be a very hard thing for us to develop reasonable policy around," Rivers told The Detroit News in 2000. "And I expect that we'll make some mistakes and end up having to go back and change early decisions."

In the 107th Congress, she rotated off the Budget Committee and took a seat on Education and the Workforce, where she is certain to be a strong voice for organized labor. She has balked at GOP proposals to allow companies to offer their employees compensatory time off in lieu of pay for overtime work. Proponents of the measure said it would enable employees to choose whether they want more money or more time. "Of course that is not true," Rivers scoffed in the 105th. "Employers can put ... pressure on an employee to choose time off rather than income, or they can pick and choose between employees about who will get the overtime [work], probably the one who will take time rather than money" as compensation.

CAPITOL OFFICE
225-6261; fax 225-3404
1724 Longworth Bldg. 20515

INTERNET
e-mail: www.house.gov/writerep
web: www.house.gov/rivers

COMMITTEES
Education & Workforce
Science

HOMETOWN
Ann Arbor

BORN
Dec. 19, 1956, Au Gres, Mich.

RELIGION
Protestant

FAMILY
Divorced; two children

EDUCATION
U. of Michigan, B.A. 1987; Wayne State U., J.D. 1992

CAREER
Law clerk

POLITICAL HIGHLIGHTS
Ann Arbor Board of Education, 1985-93 (vice president, 1986-87, president 1987-91); Mich. House, 1993-95

ELECTION RESULTS

2000 GENERAL

Lynn Rivers (D)	160,084	64.7%
Carl F. Barry (R)	79,445	32.1%
Karin R. Corliss (LIBERT)	4,578	1.9%

2000 PRIMARY

Lynn Rivers (D)	unopposed

1998 GENERAL

Lynn Rivers (D)	99,935	58.1%
Tom Hickey (R)	68,328	39.8%
Dean A. Hutyra (LIBERT)	2,873	1.7%

PREVIOUS WINNING PERCENTAGES
1996 (57%); 1994 (52%)

Rivers' other committee assignment is Science, where she tries to refute what she calls "junk science" — phony scientific findings used to justify the repeal of environmental protections. She balked in 1997 when news of successful sheep cloning experiments led some Republicans to push a bill banning federal funding of research into human cloning. Rivers weighed in on behalf of biotechnology companies, which argued that the legislation would interfere with legitimate genetic research into such areas as regeneration of diseased organ tissue and new forms of fertility treatment.

Although she agrees with Republican efforts to eliminate the "marriage penalty," a quirk in the tax code that results in some two-earner married couples paying higher taxes than they would if each partner were single, she disagreed with a GOP-drafted bill designed to take care of the problem. Calling the bill "poorly structured" and saying "it creates as many problems as it solves," Rivers said a better bill would target the tax relief to families that actually incur the marriage penalty. President Clinton ultimately vetoed the GOP bill, saying it would disproportionately benefit wealthier couples.

Rivers' willingness to slug it out rhetorically with Republicans helps explain why the House Democratic Class of 1994 — a tiny band hugely outnumbered by Republican freshmen — chose Rivers to serve as class president for 1996. Despite her scolding words about GOP fiscal policy proposals, she ended up supporting a landmark bipartisan balanced-budget agreement in the 105th after the White House wrung some late concessions from congressional Republicans.

For all her disagreements with the House's GOP conservatives, Rivers does have one thing in common with many of them: an interest in institutional reform issues, which she has called "the deimperialization of Congress." She lent support to Republican initiatives barring House members from receiving most gifts from lobbyists. During her three terms in Congress, Rivers said, she has saved more than $600,000 from her office budget, which she has returned to the U.S. Treasury.

Rivers managed to buck the national GOP trend in her 1994 House race, refusing to back down from her liberal positions and taking 52 percent against conservative Republican John A. Schall to keep the 13th in Democratic hands. She replaced William D. Ford, who retired after 15 terms.

She survived a well-financed challenge in 1996 from retired GOP businessman Joe Fitzsimmons. Countering charges that she was a big spender, Rivers pointed out that she returned nearly $200,000 of her office expense fund by not using franking privileges. She defeated Fitzsimmons with 57 percent of the vote and has since won re-election easily.

KEY VOTES

2000
Yes Raise hourly minimum wage by $1 over two years
Yes Halt funding for U.S. mission in Kosovo unless European nations pay more
Yes Provide Medicare benefits to military retirees and their dependents
No Grant China permanent normal trade status
No Phase out estate, gift and trust taxes
No Prohibit implementation of president's national monument designations
No Approve GOP plan to provide prescription drug coverage for Medicare beneficiaries
Yes Increase help for poor nations indebted to international financial institutions

1999
Yes Impose steel import quotas
No Kill proposal to take aviation trust funds off budget
No Require background checks on buyers only at gun shows with 10 or more vendors
No Remove barriers among banking, securities and insurance companies
Yes Authorize state grants to hire teachers and reduce class size
Yes Overhaul campaign finance law; ban "soft money" and restrict advocacy advertising
Yes Approve bipartisan plan to increase rights of patients in managed-care health plans

INTEREST GROUPS

	AFL-CIO	ADA	CCUS	ACU
2000	100%	95%	38%	8%
1999	78%	85%	28%	12%
1998	90%	100%	33%	12%
1997	100%	100%	30%	12%

CQ VOTE STUDIES

	PARTY UNITY		PRESIDENTIAL SUPPORT	
	Support	Oppose	Support	Oppose
2000	91%	9%	73%	27%
1999	86%	14%	62%	38%
1998	90%	10%	76%	24%
1997	89%	11%	83%	17%

MICHIGAN 13
Southeast — Ann Arbor; Westland; Ypsilanti

Michigan's 13th, situated on the flat land west of Detroit, contains a mix of auto workers, engineers and academics. Split between two counties, Wayne and Washtenaw, the district as a whole leans somewhat Democratic.

Interstate 94, joining the eastern and western ends of the 13th, has emerged as an engineering and research corridor where robotics companies, developing ways to automate auto manufacturing, have helped turn Detroit assembly line jobs into highly skilled, computerized work.

Blue-collar towns on the eastern edge of the 13th, which hold about one-third of the district's voters, depend on Detroit's car-making economy. Like most towns with strong ties to the United Auto Workers union, voters lean toward Democratic candidates. After flirting with support for GOP presidential candidates in the 1980s, this area returned to the Democratic fold in 1992, '96 and 2000. But

the towns in western Wayne County, including Canton, Northville and Plymouth, are more affluent and more Republican than their neighbors to the east.

At the district's far western reaches, voters again become Democratic. Both Ann Arbor, the district's largest city and home to the University of Michigan's academic community, and Ypsilanti, a working-class town southeast of Ann Arbor, vote reliably Democratic.

MAJOR INDUSTRY
Auto manufacturing, higher education, medical research

CITIES
Ann Arbor, 109,750; Westland, 86,369; Canton (unincorporated), 57,040 (1990); Ypsilanti township (unicorporated), 45,307 (1990); Garden City, 32,185

UNUSUAL FEATURES
Great Lakes Environmental Research Lab; Singer Iggy Pop, born in Ypsilanti.

Rep. John Conyers Jr. (D)

Elected 1964; 19th term

For Conyers, his six years as a leader of Democrats in the Republican-controlled House have given him a chance to reaffirm his basic convictions as an unreconstructed liberal. He still clings to the motto that first brought him to Congress in 1965: "Jobs, Justice and Peace."

He sees himself as the champion of the underdog, both at home and abroad, and he spends much of his time as the ranking Democrat on the Judiciary Committee thwarting what he considers to be efforts by the GOP to weaken individual rights to help business or law enforcement.

Conyers is the second-most-senior member of the House, ranking behind only his Michigan Democratic colleague John D. Dingell, for whom he once worked. After 18 terms in office, his manner has become at times erratic and a little unfocused. But while his delivery may be less fiery, the content of his remarks is still strongly partisan.

On Judiciary, Conyers won respect and gratitude from members in his party for his vociferous defense of President Clinton during the 1998 impeachment proceedings stemming from the president's relationship with former White House intern Monica Lewinsky. Conyers essentially accused Republicans of trying to stage a coup d'état to depose a twice-elected president.

Conyers was the only member of Judiciary in the 105th Congress who had also served on the committee in 1974 when the panel voted to impeach President Nixon. In defending Clinton, Conyers said there was no comparison between his conduct in the sex scandal and Nixon's in the Watergate affair. Clinton "can't be impeached without devaluing the rule of law and degrading [the meaning of] impeachable offenses," he said.

A co-founder (and now senior member) of the Congressional Black Caucus, Conyers has long advocated for civil rights, minorities and the poor. And his convictions can make things uncomfortable for his fellow Democrats. Conyers first introduced legislation to make the birthday of the Rev. Martin Luther King Jr. a national holiday just four days after the civil rights leader was assassinated in 1968, and he kept at it until he won enactment of the bill in 1983.

In each Congress during the past decade, Conyers has introduced legislation that would set up a commission to study whether the federal government owes reparations to African-American descendants of slaves. The bill has yet to receive a hearing, in either a Democratic- or Republican-controlled House.

After serving with the Army in Korea, Conyers enrolled at Wayne State University and got involved in politics while in law school there. The creation in 1964 of a second black-majority district in the city gave him an opening to try for Congress. He had a tough primary race, prevailing over accountant Richard H. Austin by just 108 votes; but he won easily in November in the Democratic district and has not faced serious opposition since.

Racial troubles in Conyers' district exploded in 1967, and rioting destroyed many blocks in the heart of his constituency. Conyers was booed when he stood atop a car telling rioters to return to their homes. Later, his office was gutted by fire.

For much of his House career, Conyers seemed less interested in being a legislative power broker than in being a liberal voice of protest. Twice in the early 1970s, he waged symbolic campaigns for Speaker against Carl Albert of Oklahoma, whom he accused of "stagnation and reaction." Both

CAPITOL OFFICE
225-5126; fax 225-0072; 2426 Rayburn Bldg. 20515

INTERNET
e-mail: john.conyers@mail.house.gov
web: www.house.gov/conyers

COMMITTEES
Judiciary - ranking member

HOMETOWN
Detroit

BORN
May 16, 1929, Detroit, Mich.

RELIGION
Baptist

FAMILY
Wife, Monica Conyers; two children

EDUCATION
Wayne State U., B.A. 1957, LL.B. 1958

MILITARY SERVICE
Mich. National Guard, 1948-50; Army, 1950-54; Army Reserve, 1954-57

CAREER
Lawyer; congressional aide

POLITICAL HIGHLIGHTS
Candidate for mayor of Detroit, 1989, 1993

ELECTION RESULTS

2000 GENERAL

John Conyers Jr. (D)	168,982	89.1%
William A. Ashe (R)	17,582	9.3%
Constance Catalfio (LIBERT)	2,113	1.1%

2000 PRIMARY

John Conyers Jr. (D)	unopposed

1998 GENERAL

John Conyers Jr. (D)	126,321	86.9%
Vendella M. Collins (R)	16,140	11.1%
Michael Freyman (LIBERT)	1,764	1.2%

PREVIOUS WINNING PERCENTAGES
1996 (86%); 1994 (82%); 1992 (82%); 1990 (89%); 1988 (91%); 1986 (89%); 1984 (89%); 1982 (97%); 1980 (95%); 1978 (93%); 1976 (92%); 1974 (91%); 1972 (88%); 1970 (88%); 1968 (100%); 1966 (84%); 1964 (84%)

times, Conyers lost overwhelmingly. He earned a reputation for being sarcastic and abrasive, which did not make it easy for him to assemble the alliances required to move legislation.

And his two quixotic bids to become the mayor of Detroit did not enhance his reputation. In 1989, he challenged Mayor Coleman A. Young and finished third in the primary. A 1993 run also failed.

But he gained ground with his colleagues in 1987 with his skillful handling of the impeachment of U.S. District Judge Alcee L. Hastings, who was accused of conspiring to solicit a bribe and leaking wiretap information. For Conyers, who was chairman of Judiciary's Criminal Justice Subcommittee, investigating a black judge who claimed the allegations against him were racially motivated presented a sticky political problem.

When Conyers began the proceedings, he said he too saw the possibility of racial bias in the charges. But as the investigation progressed, Conyers reached what he later called the most difficult conclusion of his House career — that Hastings was guilty and had fabricated his court defense. The Hastings impeachment resolution was easily approved by the subcommittee and full committee, and Conyers gave a floor speech on the case that brought him a standing ovation while helping deliver a vote of 413-3. (After being removed from office by the Senate, Hastings was elected to the House from South Florida in 1992.)

With the advent of the Republican majority in 1995, Conyers turned his attention to defeating the GOP agenda as measures came through the Judiciary Committee. He complained in 1996 that "The Republican Party is now completely led by extremists." He opposed the overhaul of welfare, the market-oriented 1996 farm law, a ban on a procedure its opponents call "partial birth" abortion, and a proposed constitutional amendment to limit congressional terms. In 1998, he resisted conservatives' attempt to overhaul the nation's bankruptcy laws. He argued that the GOP-backed bill was slanted in favor of creditors at the expense of consumers.

Conyers has a strong interest in jazz and frequently takes time out to listen to music in his office, where posters of various jazz artists are on display. In 1987, he successfully sponsored a House resolution declaring jazz a "rare and valuable national American treasure." He also sponsored legislation designating May 25 — the birthday of black tap artist Bill Robinson — National Tap Dance Day. Conyers' personal life made news in 1990 when, at age 61, he ended his lifelong bachelorhood and married a 25-year-old former aide, who gave birth to a son one month later. Conyers now has two sons.

KEY VOTES

2000

Yes Raise hourly minimum wage by $1 over two years
No Halt funding for U.S. mission in Kosovo unless European nations pay more
Yes Provide Medicare benefits to military retirees and their dependents
No Grant China permanent normal trade status
— Phase out estate, gift and trust taxes
No Prohibit implementation of president's national monument designations
No Approve GOP plan to provide prescription drug coverage for Medicare beneficiaries
Yes Increase help for poor nations indebted to international financial institutions

1999

Yes Impose steel import quotas
Yes Kill proposal to take aviation trust funds off budget
No Require background checks on buyers only at gun shows with 10 or more vendors
No Remove barriers among banking, securities and insurance companies
Yes Authorize state grants to hire teachers and reduce class size
Yes Overhaul campaign finance law; ban "soft money" and restrict advocacy advertising
Yes Approve bipartisan plan to increase rights of patients in managed-care health plans

INTEREST GROUPS

	AFL-CIO	ADA	CCUS	ACU
2000	100%	95%	30%	0%
1999	89%	100%	17%	8%
1998	100%	80%	20%	0%
1997	100%	95%	30%	4%

CQ VOTE STUDIES

	PARTY UNITY		PRESIDENTIAL SUPPORT	
	Support	Oppose	Support	Oppose
2000	98%	2%	85%	15%
1999	97%	3%	84%	16%
1998	95%	5%	90%	10%
1997	96%	4%	83%	17%

MICHIGAN 14

Parts of Detroit; Harper Woods; Highland Park

The auto industry kept Detroit humming for most of this century. The early factories drew people from rural Michigan, Appalachia, the South and Eastern Europe. Then race riots during the summer of 1967 and the oil crisis of the early 1970s sparked an evacuation of the Motor City. White residents fled to the suburbs, and auto makers moved to Mexico and non-union U.S. towns, leaving Detroit with some of the poorest and most crime-ridden neighborhoods in the nation. In 1960, 1.7 million people lived in Detroit. The city's population now hovers below 1 million.

The 14th, which covers the residential neighborhoods that sprang up north of Detroit's auto plants, has a few communities of professionals and white-collar city employees. It also has seen a few signs of economic renewal. Kmart built a new store in the district, the first national chain to move into the city in years. Property values are beginning to pick up, and crime rates are starting to fall – additional

signs that Detroit's worst days may be past.

Michigan's two Detroit districts, the 14th and 15th, deliver overwhelming Democratic margins, often offsetting the heavy Republican influence in the state's southeastern districts. The only Republican outposts in the 14th are a few small, affluent towns at the district's outskirts, including Grosse Pointe Woods and Grosse Pointe Shores.

MAJOR INDUSTRY
Auto and auto parts manufacturing, health care

CITIES
Detroit (pt.), 517,514 (1990); Highland Park, 19,192; Grosse Pointe Woods, 17,827

UNUSUAL FEATURES
Nation's first paved road: Woodward Avenue, between 6 Mile and 7 Mile roads (1909); Nation's first freeway: Davison Freeway, connecting Detroit and Highland Park (1942).

Rep. Carolyn Cheeks Kilpatrick (D)

Elected 1996; 3rd term

CAPITOL OFFICE
225-2261; fax 225-5730
1610 Longworth Bldg. 20515

INTERNET
e-mail: www.house.gov/writerep
web: www.house.gov/kilpatrick

COMMITTEES
Appropriations

HOMETOWN
Detroit

BORN
June 25, 1945, Detroit, Mich.

RELIGION
Baptist

FAMILY
Divorced; two children

EDUCATION
Ferris State U., A.A. 1965; Western Michigan U.,
B.S. 1968; U. of Michigan, M.S. 1972

CAREER
Teacher

POLITICAL HIGHLIGHTS
Mich. House, 1979-97; sought Democratic
nomination for Mich. Senate, 1994

ELECTION RESULTS

2000 GENERAL

Carolyn Cheeks Kilpatrick (D)	140,609	88.6%
Chrysanthea D. Boyd-Fields (R)	14,336	9.0%
Raymond H. Warner (LIBERT)	1,690	1.1%

2000 PRIMARY

Carolyn Cheeks Kilpatrick (D)	unopposed

1998 GENERAL

Carolyn Cheeks Kilpatrick (D)	108,582	87.0%
Chrysanthea D. Boyd-Fields (R)	12,887	10.3%
Linda S. Willey (LIBERT)	1,485	1.2%

PREVIOUS WINNING PERCENTAGES
1996 (88%)

Armed with a long agenda of district needs that call out for government attention, Kilpatrick in just two terms has put herself in a position to deliver. In the 106th Congress, she won a seat on the Appropriations Committee, where she has subcommittee posts on Transportation and Foreign Operations — positions she has used to address Detroit's transportation needs and to strengthen ties with African nations.

Kilpatrick is upfront about the challenges facing the center-city Detroit portion of her district, which "has the best and worst of America in it," as she told the Detroit News soon after her election. Kilpatrick's constituency is 70 percent African-American, and her district includes wide swaths of impoverished neighborhoods.

On her official website, Kilpatrick offers a look at her district, as many lawmakers do, highlighting its businesses, athletic teams, cultural attractions, and public and private institutions. But while most members simply brag about their districts, Kilpatrick also draws attention to her district's problems: highest infant mortality rate in the country; highest unemployment rate, highest school drop-out rate and lowest educational attainment in Michigan; and "some of the state's most blighted neighborhoods and substandard housing."

Mindful of her constituents' needs and their dependence on federal programs, Kilpatrick is one of Congress' more steadfast liberal voices. Her ideas about the role of the federal government have little in common with the prescriptions offered by the Republicans.

Yet in 1998, Kilpatrick did favor one GOP initiative — a renewal of federal highway and transit programs that authorized significantly more spending across the board. She proudly noted the inclusion of $24 million for an intermodal freight terminal in Detroit to link road, rail and marine freight delivery. In 2000, she hosted a regional transportation summit meeting with Transportation Secretary Rodney Slater and local officials to discuss public transportation needs in the area. That summit was in keeping with her desire to build broad coalitions of local and federal officials and constituents to develop solutions to problems.

Kilpatrick also joined with GOP Appropriations colleague Joe Knollenberg, who represents the nearby 11th District, in opposing congressional moves to increase mandated automobile fuel economy standards, anathema to the Detroit-area automobile industry. "I understand the concerns of my colleagues," she said, "but the industry has made some giant steps since 1996."

At Kilpatrick's behest, the Foreign Operations Subcommittee in 2000 approved $160 million in emergency assistance for flood relief to Mozambique. Kilpatrick traveled to Africa in both 1999 and 2000. The first trip was focused on the needs of children orphaned when their parents died of AIDS. On the second trip, she accompanied President Clinton to Nigeria, Tanzania and Egypt.

Kilpatrick also has undertaken a crusade to get corporate America and the federal government to spend more of their advertising dollars with women- and minority-owned media outlets and advertising agencies. As a member of the Banking Committee in the 105th Congress, she worked to get financial institutions to provide credit, insurance and other services to "underserved" communities.

In her freshman term, House Democratic leaders judged that Kilpatrick would reliably vote the party line and lend an assertive voice to floor debate, and they put her on a committee that was the scene of plenty of pitched partisan battles — House Oversight (renamed House Administration in the 106th). She performed up to their expectations, roundly denouncing the panel's move to thwart Democratic campaign finance overhaul proposals and its approval of additional money for the Judiciary and Government Reform committees to look into allegations of wrongdoing by Clinton and his re-election campaign team. In the 107th Congress, she was named to the Democratic Steering Committee, which makes committee assignments.

Kilpatrick holds a master's degree in education administration, and as a teacher in the Detroit public schools for eight years she taught business and vocational classes. Often in floor debate she makes her points by citing the needs of children. Arguing against a Republican proposal on juvenile justice, she said the legislation "only talks about enforcement. Nothing about hope. All studies show that children need to be educated, disciplined, counseled and loved. ... This bill puts more money into police and prisons, tactics that simply do not work without adequate prevention programs."

A Detroit native, Kilpatrick made education her career until 1978, when she won the first of nine terms in the state House, a full-time job. In Lansing, she mastered fiscal and appropriations issues and was known as a careful, thoughtful lawmaker with an ability to work across party lines. She once led a coalition of Democratic and Republican lawmakers seeking to block a proposal by popular Republican Gov. John Engler to halt state funding for local transportation programs.

Her predecessor in the 15th District, Democrat Barbara-Rose Collins, had not cut much of a legislative figure in Washington. But Kilpatrick, despite her stature in the Detroit community, was somewhat reluctant to challenge Collins, a one-time political ally. However, when Collins became the subject of separate investigations by the House ethics committee and the Justice Department into allegations of ethical and financial misconduct, Kilpatrick stepped forward.

Days before the primary, Collins helped ensure her own defeat when she held a fundraiser at a Detroit strip club that featured male and female exotic dancers. On primary day, Kilpatrick took a majority of the vote and beat Collins by 20 points. The November outcome was preordained in the heavily Democratic district, and Kilpatrick won re-election in 1998 and 2000 with ease.

Kilpatrick's son, Kwame, a school teacher like his mother, succeeded her in the state legislature upon her election to the House. In 2001, he became minority leader of the Michigan House.

KEY VOTES

2000
Yes Raise hourly minimum wage by $1 over two years
No   Halt funding for U.S. mission in Kosovo unless European nations pay more
Yes Provide Medicare benefits to military retirees and their dependents
No   Grant China permanent normal trade status
No   Phase out estate, gift and trust taxes
No   Prohibit implementation of president's national monument designations
No   Approve GOP plan to provide prescription drug coverage for Medicare beneficiaries
Yes Increase help for poor nations indebted to international financial institutions

1999
Yes Impose steel import quotas
Yes Kill proposal to take aviation trust funds off budget
No   Require background checks on buyers only at gun shows with 10 or more vendors
Yes Remove barriers among banking, securities and insurance companies
Yes Authorize state grants to hire teachers and reduce class size
Yes Overhaul campaign finance law; ban "soft money" and restrict advocacy advertising
Yes Approve bipartisan plan to increase rights of patients in managed-care health plans

INTEREST GROUPS

	AFL-CIO	ADA	CCUS	ACU
2000	100%	85%	42%	8%
1999	89%	100%	16%	0%
1998	100%	90%	28%	0%
1997	100%	100%	30%	12%

CQ VOTE STUDIES

	PARTY UNITY		PRESIDENTIAL SUPPORT	
	Support	Oppose	Support	Oppose
2000	96%	4%	83%	17%
1999	98%	2%	88%	12%
1998	96%	4%	88%	12%
1997	96%	4%	76%	24%

MICHIGAN 15

Parts of Detroit; Grosse Pointe; Hamtramck; River Rouge

General Motors built Detroit on a thriving American auto industry over the first half of the 20th century. Then riots in 1967 and the oil crisis of the 1970s decimated Detroit's economy and turned the city into a virtual war zone. The 15th suffered the worst of the 1967 riots in terms of property damage and deaths. For a time, Detroit was even known as the "Beirut of America."

The downtown and waterfront, covered by the 15th, have been a target for intensive redevelopment. The city soon will have two new sporting venues in downtown Detroit as part of a massive entertainment complex — Comerica Park opened in April 2000 for Major League Baseball's Detroit Tigers, and Ford Field is slated to open in 2002 for the National Football League's Detroit Lions. Three new casinos also were completed. It remains to be seen whether spill-over from these ventures will spur new businesses. The city still has relatively high taxes and a reputation for crime, while many of the affluent suburbs that surround Detroit have become regional office centers and have lured companies away from the city.

Even with the inclusion of a few wealthy, white communities — Grosse Pointe, Grosse Pointe Park and Grosse Pointe Farms — Michigan's 15th District is one of the poorest in the nation. It also has one of the highest rates of infant mortality in the nation. Along with the 14th, it delivers Democratic votes by huge margins, often offsetting the Republican influence in Michigan's southeast.

MAJOR INDUSTRY
Auto and auto parts manufacturing, county and municipal government

CITIES
Detroit (pt.), 510,460 (1990); Hamtramck, 17,801; Grosse Pointe Park, 12,883; Ecorse, 11,739; River Rouge, 10,722

UNUSUAL FEATURES
Belle Isle Zoo; Charles H. Wright Museum of African American History.

Rep. John D. Dingell (D)

Elected December 1955; 23rd full term

CAPITOL OFFICE
225-4071; 2328 Rayburn Bldg. 20515

INTERNET
e-mail: public.dingell@mail.house.gov
web: www.house.gov/dingell

COMMITTEES
Energy & Commerce - ranking member

HOMETOWN
Dearborn

BORN
July 8, 1926, Colorado Springs, Colo.

RELIGION
Roman Catholic

FAMILY
Wife, Deborah Dingell; four children

EDUCATION
Georgetown U., B.S. 1949, J.D. 1952

MILITARY SERVICE
Army, 1944-46

CAREER
County prosecutor

POLITICAL HIGHLIGHTS
No previous office

ELECTION RESULTS

2000 GENERAL

John D. Dingell (D)	167,142	71.0%
William Morse (R)	62,469	26.5%
Edward Hlavac (LIBERT)	2,814	1.2%

2000 PRIMARY

John D. Dingell (D)	unopposed

1998 GENERAL

John D. Dingell (D)	116,145	66.6%
William Morse (R)	54,121	31.0%
Edward Hlavac (LIBERT)	3,064	1.8%

PREVIOUS WINNING PERCENTAGES
1996 (62%); 1994 (59%); 1992 (65%); 1990 (67%);
1988 (97%); 1986 (78%); 1984 (64%); 1982 (74%);
1980 (70%); 1978 (77%); 1976 (76%); 1974 (78%);
1972 (68%); 1970 (79%); 1968 (74%); 1966 (63%);
1964 (73%); 1962 (83%); 1960 (79%); 1958 (79%);
1956 (74%); 1955 Special Election (76%)

If his imposing frame is not enough to intimidate any guileless visitors or political foes who wander into his office, a menagerie of the animals who once crossed Dingell's path might do the trick. He conquered many of the stuffed wild boar, deer, fish and birds on display, while others were gifts from those paying homage.

Dingell is the House's longest-serving member in the 107th Congress, but his tenure is far from his sole source of sway. The Republican retention of House control in 2000 denied him the chance to reclaim the gavel of the Energy and Commerce Committee, which he helped transform into what may be Capitol Hill's most influential regulatory committee. But, midway through his 70s and halfway through his fifth decade in the House, he still inspires fear among those whom he has in his sights.

Although he resigned from the National Rifle Association board in 1994 during debate on a crime bill, knowing that Dingell is an aggressive and successful hunter is key to understanding him as a cunning and sometimes merciless congressman. A complex man with a keenly honed political sense, he says he has adopted as his own the aphorism the Corleone family made famous in "The Godfather, Part II": "Keep your friends close, but your enemies closer."

In his 14 years as chairman of the Energy and Commerce Committee, Dingell built a remarkable fiefdom through a combination of ruthless expansionism and shrewd deal-cutting. He ran the committee with an iron fist and was a potent symbol of the Old Bull Democratic chairmen who made life miserable for the minority. Many Republicans hated Dingell's imperious manner and powerful leadership style when they were in the minority, but they saw him as a leadership model to emulate when they took control in the 104th Congress.

As his time in the minority began, Dingell signaled that he would take on a diminished role with élan. "There are other things than being committee chairman," he said. Since then, however, his frustration has appeared to grow. Asked what he had learned after nearly six years in the minority, Dingell responded: "Avoid it at all costs."

Dingell has a flair not only for tough talk but for disarming, sometimes folksy and colorful rhetoric. For instance, he has been known to call an opponent's comments as useful as "side pockets on a cow." He also refers to the Senate as "the cave of the winds."

On most issues, he stands with liberal Democrats, supporting civil rights, Great Society programs and expansion of the federal government's role. His bread-and-butter issues are automobiles and health care, details of which he learned from his father, John D. Dingell Sr., who represented the greater Detroit area in the House from 1933 until his death in 1955.

Dingell makes no apologies for his role as protector of the auto industry, saying, "That's what I'm sent here to do." To that end, Dingell fought a toughening of the Clean Air Act through much of the 1980s; in the end, he was credited with holding off action far longer than most lawmakers could have and then negotiating a decent deal for automakers.

Like his father, Dingell often is aligned with those who doggedly advocate more federal support for health care. In the 106th Congress, he joined forces with Charlie Norwood, a Republican dentist from Georgia, to create bipartisan patients' rights legislation. The House passed their bill overwhelmingly in 1999 when 68 Republicans bucked the GOP leadership to back it. As supporters rejoiced, Dingell reminded them to save their energy. "The time for rejoicing is really not here," he said, urging the crowd to "go back to work." Once President Clinton signs a bill, "we'll have a wingding." The 106th ended with Dingell still waiting.

Still, he has shepherded bills through Congress on a staggering array of subjects since he was elected to succeed his father in 1955. He amassed the broadest committee jurisdiction of any chairman in the postwar era, covering energy, health, communications, transportation, waste disposal and numerous regulatory agencies. He had a fairly good working relationship with the panel's Republican chairman from 1995 through 2000, Thomas J. Bliley Jr. of Virginia, now retired. But Dingell says he is likely to find a more kindred spirit in the new chairman, Billy Tauzin, R-La. "He and I will probably agree more than Bliley and I would," Dingell said in 2001.

While maintaining strong ties to industry, Dingell keeps working people in mind. And he always holds fast to certain liberal principles, including stoutly defending programs such as Medicare. He presided over the House in 1965 when the bill was passed that created that federal medical insurance program for the elderly and the disabled, and 30 years later he stood firm in his opposition to GOP attempts to curb its rate of growth. (He was on the 17-member commission that studied ways to ensure Medicare's solvency but disbanded in 1999 when it was unable to reach a consensus.)

As committee chairman, Dingell was known for bullying witnesses and badgering House members. But much of his reputation for ruthlessness came from his chairmanship of the Oversight Subcommittee, from which he zealously probed the propriety and performance of federal agencies. On occasion, he forced a sluggish federal regulator into action merely by threatening to call him before his subcommittee. And there were also "Dingell-grams," tart rebukes and testy inquiries penned by the chairman and his aggressive staff at a rate of hundreds per year. Even his Republican successor as chairman of the subcommittee lauded Dingell's accomplishments: "I don't believe too many people would dispute the fact that John Dingell had the most effective oversight" in Congress, said Texas Republican Joe L. Barton.

In 24 elections, Dingell has slipped below 60 percent only once (in the big GOP year of 1994). And the tradition of a Dingell representing the Detroit area in Congress is likely to continue beyond the incumbent's tenure, as the two most likely successors are his politically savvy wife Debbie, president of the General Motors Foundation and a Democratic national committeewoman, and his son Chris, a Michigan state senator since 1987.

KEY VOTES

2000
Yes Raise hourly minimum wage by $1 over two years
No   Halt funding for U.S. mission in Kosovo unless European nations pay more
Yes Provide Medicare benefits to military retirees and their dependents
No   Grant China permanent normal trade status
No   Phase out estate, gift and trust taxes
No   Prohibit implementation of president's national monument designations
No   Approve GOP plan to provide prescription drug coverage for Medicare beneficiaries
Yes Increase help for poor nations indebted to international financial institutions

1999
Yes Impose steel import quotas
No   Kill proposal to take aviation trust funds off budget
No   Require background checks on buyers only at gun shows with 10 or more vendors
No   Remove barriers among banking, securities and insurance companies
Yes Authorize state grants to hire teachers and reduce class size
Yes Overhaul campaign finance law; ban "soft money" and restrict advocacy advertising
Yes Approve bipartisan plan to increase rights of patients in managed-care health plans

INTEREST GROUPS

	AFL-CIO	ADA	CCUS	ACU
2000	100%	80%	33%	16%
1999	89%	80%	24%	12%
1998	100%	85%	28%	8%
1997	100%	80%	50%	8%

CQ VOTE STUDIES

	PARTY UNITY		PRESIDENTIAL SUPPORT	
	Support	Oppose	Support	Oppose
2000	89%	11%	81%	19%
1999	85%	15%	77%	23%
1998	89%	11%	82%	18%
1997	86%	14%	81%	19%

MICHIGAN 16
Southeast Wayne County; Monroe County

Henry Ford built the foundations of the 16th, which covers Monroe County, Dearborn and other communities downriver from Detroit. The district's largest city, Dearborn, is home to the Ford Motor Co. factory that was once the largest on earth. At capacity, the Rouge Plant employed 81,000 people and contained everything needed to build a car from the ground up, including a steel mill, glass factory and assembly line.

The district still is heavily industrial, but some factories stand vacant. An exception is the Flat Rock automotive plant, in southern Wayne County, a U.S.-Japanese joint venture and one of the 16th's largest employers.

The first wave of workers at plants lining the Detroit River came from Appalachia and the South, as well as Germany, Poland and Italy. Successive waves brought Arabs, including Shiite Moslems during World War I, and then Egyptians, Iraqis, Lebanese and others, leaving the district with the largest Arab-American population in the nation and a strong Arab business district along Warren Avenue.

Thoroughly unionized and mostly blue-collar, this district regularly elects Democrats by comfortable margins. There are only a few pockets of Republican affluence, mainly in the small towns of Riverview and Grosse Ile.

MAJOR INDUSTRY
Auto manufacturing, steel, chemical production

CITIES
Dearborn, 88,215; Taylor, 72,029; Dearborn Heights (pt.), 51,979 (1990); Lincoln Park, 41,898

UNUSUAL FEATURES
Henry Ford Museum, which houses the rocking chair that President Abraham Lincoln sat in when assassinated at Washington's Ford's Theatre on April 14, 1865, and the limousine that President John F. Kennedy rode in when shot on Nov. 22, 1963, in Dallas.

Complete Your Collection with CQ's Essential References on Congress

CQ's unique source for congressional voting information: a member-by-member survey and analysis of every roll call vote taken in the House and Senate during 2000.

Congressional Roll Call 2000, 106th Congress Second Session

June 2001 • 8 1/2 x 11 • 336 pages
Paperback • ISBN 1-56802-666-8 • $38.95

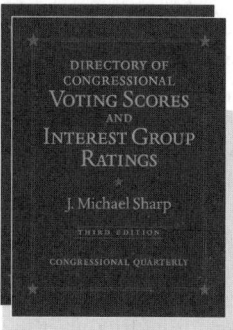

The most comprehensive and current compilation of voting-study and group-rating data for every legislator who has served in Congress from 1947 to 1999.

Directory of Congressional Voting Scores and Interest Group Ratings

2-Volume Set • 2000 • 8 1/2 x 11 • 1,712 pages
Hardbound • ISBN 1-5/6802-565-3 • $299.00

CQ's handy pocket guide to the 107th Congress includes must-have member information: biographies; photographs; contact information; staff; committee and subcommittee assignments; and 2000 election results and key votes.

Who's Who in Congress 2001: 107th Congress, Committee Edition

May 2001 • 4 x 9 • 368 pages
Paperback • ISBN 1-56802-725-7 • $17.95

The authoritative reference source for understanding Congress: the American institution where the most divisive public issues come for resolution.

CQ's Guide to Congress, 5th Edition

2-Volume Set • 1999 • 8 1/2 x 11 • 1,354 pages
Hardbound • ISBN 1-56802-477-0 • $315.00

CQ PRESS

TO ORDER:
Call Toll-Free: 800.638.1710 • Fax: 800.380.3810
Web: www.cqpress.com • E-mail: bookhelp@cq.com

Gov. Jesse Ventura (I)

First elected: 1998
Length of term: 4 years
Term expires: 1/03
Salary: $120,303
Phone: (651) 296-3391
Hometown: Maple Grove

Born: July 15, 1951; Minneapolis, Minn.
Religion: Unspecified
Family: Wife, Terry Ventura; two children
Education: North Hennepin Community College, attended 1974-75
Military Service: Navy, 1970-73; Naval Reserve, 1974-75
Career: Professional wrestler; actor; sports broadcaster; radio talk-show host
Political highlights: Mayor of Brooklyn Park, 1991-95

Election results:
1998 GENERAL

Jesse Ventura (REF)	773,713	37.0%
Norm Coleman (R)	717,350	34.3%
Hubert H. Humphrey III (D)	587,528	28.1%

Lt. Gov. Mae Schunk (I)

First elected: 1998
Length of term: 4 years
Term expires: 1/03
Salary: $66,169
Phone: (651) 296-3391

STATE LEGISLATURE

Legislature: Meets January-May in odd years; February-April in even years
House: 134 members, 2-year terms
2001 breakdown: 69R, 65D; 99 men, 35 women
Salary: $31,140
Phone: (651) 296-2146
Senate: 67 members, 4-year terms
2001 breakdown: 27R, 39D, 1I; 44 men, 23 women
Salary: $31,140
Phone: (651) 296-0504

STATE TERM LIMITS

Governor: No
Senate: No
House: No

URBAN STATISTICS

CITY	POPULATION
Minneapolis	353,395
St. Paul	256,213
Bloomington	86,226
Duluth	80,980
Rochester	80,768

REGISTERED VOTERS

Voters do not register by party.

POPULATION

2000 population	4,919,479
1990 population	4,375,099
Percent change	12.4%
Rank among states	21
Median age	34.9
Born in state	74%
Foreign born	3%
Urban/rural	70%/30%
Crime rate	338/100,000
Poverty level	10.4%
Federal workers	33,229
Military	20,084

REAPPORTIONMENT

Minnesota retained its eight House seats in reapportionment. The state legislature will draw new district lines in 2001.

MISCELLANEOUS

Web: www.state.mn.us
Capital: St. Paul
Land area: 79,617 sq. miles
  Rank among states: 14
STATE ELECTION OFFICIAL
(651) 215-1440
DEMOCRATIC HEADQUARTERS
(651) 293-1200
REPUBLICAN HEADQUARTERS
(651) 222-0022

District Statistics

DIST.	2000 D	2000 R	GREEN	1996 D	1996 R	REF	1992 D	1992 R	I	WHT	BLK	ASIAN	HISP	HOUSEHOLD INCOME	OVER 65+	UNDER 18	COLLEGE EDUCATION
1	46%	48%	5%	48%	37%	13%	39%	35%	26%	98%	0%	1%	1%	$28,403	14%	27%	19%
2	40	54	4	45	39	14	37	35	28	99	0	0	1	$26,937	16	29	13
3	45	50	4	46	41	10	38	37	25	96	2	2	1	$44,329	7	27	33
4	56	36	6	58	30	9	52	28	20	89	4	5	3	$32,287	13	25	28
5	63	28	8	64	25	8	58	24	18	84	9	4	2	$28,880	14	20	30
6	46	48	4	51	35	12	41	32	27	97	1	1	1	$42,161	5	31	22
7	39	54	5	45	40	13	38.3	38.1	24	97	0	0	1	$23,146	15	28	15
8	49	44	5	53	31	14	48	28	24	97	0	0	1	$24,472	16	27	14
STATE	**48**	**46**	**5**	**51**	**35**	**12**	**43**	**32**	**24**	**94**	**2**	**2**	**1**	**$30,909**	**13**	**27**	**22**

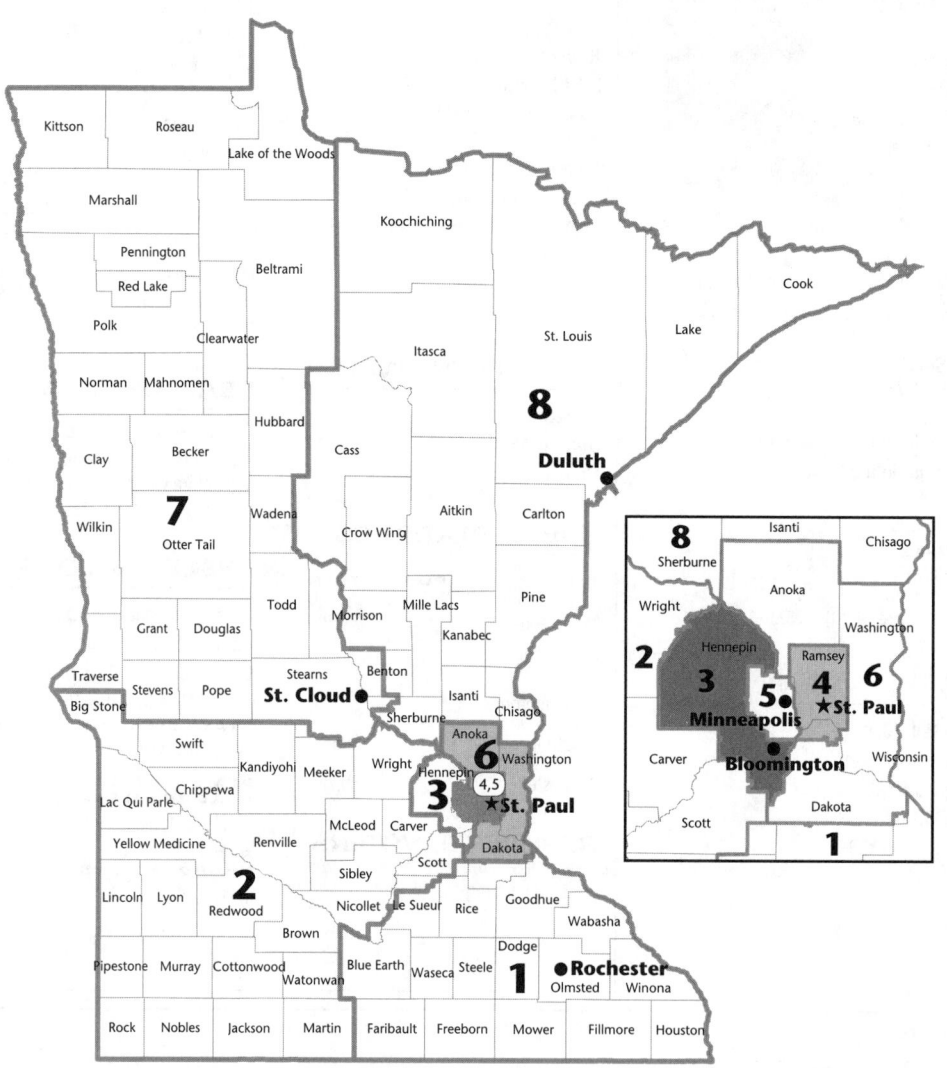

Sen. Paul Wellstone (D)

CAPITOL OFFICE
224-5641; fax 224-8438; 136 Hart Bldg. 20510

INTERNET
e-mail: senator@wellstone.senate.gov
web: wellstone.senate.gov

COMMITTEES
Foreign Relations
Health, Education, Labor & Pensions
Indian Affairs
Small Business
Veterans' Affairs

HOMETOWN
St. Paul

BORN
July 21, 1944, Washington, D.C.

RELIGION
Jewish

FAMILY
Wife, Sheila Ison Wellstone; three children

EDUCATION
U. of North Carolina, B.A. 1965, Ph.D. 1969

CAREER
Professor

POLITICAL HIGHLIGHTS
Democratic nominee for Minn. auditor, 1982;
Democratic National Committee, 1984-91

ELECTION RESULTS

1996 GENERAL

Paul Wellstone (D)	1,098,493	50.3%
Rudy Boschwitz (R)	901,282	41.3%
Dean Barkley (REF)	152,333	7.0%

1996 PRIMARY

Paul Wellstone (D)	194,699	86.2%
Dick Franson (D)	16,465	7.4%
Ed Hansen (D)	9,990	4.5%
Ole Savior (D)	4,180	1.9%

PREVIOUS WINNING PERCENTAGES
1990 (50%)

Elected 1990; 2nd term

One of the last of the unreconstructed liberals in Congress, Wellstone can seem like a walking anachronism. But he has grown to relish his role as a leading Senate voice for his party's core constituencies — the poor, the family farmer, the union worker. "I represent the Democratic wing of the Democratic Party," he proudly told audiences in Iowa as he considered a run for the presidency in 2000.

Wellstone cited his mission as a liberal advocate in January 2001, when he declared that he would run for re-election in 2002 and thereby break the pledge he had made, in his first Senate campaign in 1990, to serve only two terms. The onset of Republican control of both the White House and Congress had caused him to reconsider, he explained. And with an evenly divided Senate, he said, "I am in a position to make a huge difference," the Minneapolis Star Tribune reported.

Wellstone proudly emulates his Senate predecessors from Minnesota, Hubert H. Humphrey and Walter F. Mondale. He lists among his role models two other renowned liberal senators of the past generation, George McGovern and Robert F. Kennedy. And he appears unwavering in his belief that government can be a positive force in people's lives.

While other Democrats argue with the GOP over what kinds of tax cuts to enact, Wellstone is staking out his position well to the left — seeking expanded government aid to the poor, universal medical insurance, more federal spending on education and a higher minimum wage. Instead of accommodating business interests in an age of prosperity, Wellstone yearns for a new round of Theodore Roosevelt-style trust-busting, especially when it comes to industries such as agriculture.

And Wellstone rarely backs away from a fight. The champion 126-pound wrestler at the University of North Carolina has frequently tangled (only verbally) with Minnesota governor Jesse Ventura, the 250-pound former wrestling professional.

On farm issues, the libertarian Ventura has said that Wellstone's continued support of a type of farm subsidy that Congress ended in 1996 amounted to the endorsement of "a mild form of slavery," since the payments were conditioned on the production of certain crops. Wellstone countered that Ventura "profoundly misunderstands the agriculture debate," a charge that evoked cries of unfairness from the governor's spokesman.

The plight of Minnesota's family farmers has been an ongoing concern for Wellstone, who sees a direct connection between failing farms and the growth of agribusiness. Consolidation has made it impossible for small farms to compete, while having fewer food providers is bad for consumers, he argues.

Wellstone has taken a strong position on the nation's efforts to combat illegal drug use, especially against the package of military assistance to Colombia that Congress approved in 2000. He warned against sending weapons and advisers to a country with a poor record on human rights. He said the heavy aid to the military came at the expense of subsidies to coca farmers who might grow other crops. The likely result, he said, was that ruined farmers would join guerrilla or paramilitary groups. (During a visit by Wellstone to Colombia in December 2000, police defused two bombs near where the U.S. ambassador and Wellstone were scheduled to pass.)

Occasionally, Wellstone draws on his personal experience in framing an issue. He spoke out against Minnesota's statewide list of failing schools because it relied on test scores. Wellstone had been admitted to the University of North Carolina with an SAT score of less than 800 out of a possible 1600. "I don't want this report to cut off our teachers or our students at the knees," he told the Star Tribune. "I don't want this report to be about blame."

In the 106th Congress, and again early in the 107th, Wellstone took the lead in resisting an overhaul of bankruptcy laws, even after Republicans and Democrats agreed to a broad outline limiting debtors' use of the bankruptcy code to discharge their debts. For Wellstone, it was a classic cave-in to monied interests. He argued that many banks lobbying for the measure were trying to avoid their own responsibilities for overly aggressive credit card lending. Wellstone called President Clinton's veto of the bill in 2000 "a tremendous triumph for working families."

Wellstone went on the road in 1998, visiting Iowa, New Hampshire and other key primary states in a preliminary presidential campaign; he enjoyed his underdog status as pundits wrote off his campaign as the longest of long shots. His stump speech called for a return to party fundamental values — away from the New Democrat positions of Clinton and Vice President Al Gore. "People don't buy this philosophy that there is nothing government can or should do," he told a gathering of Iowa union members. "Good education, good health care and good jobs — that's what the Democrats stand for." He called off the campaign in 1999 after doctors told him the rigors of travel would aggravate a ruptured disk in his back.

Wellstone has found plenty of other opportunities to push the almost-forgotten liberal agenda. In the spring of 1997, for example, Wellstone launched a well-publicized "poverty tour" patterned after an RFK trip in 1967. Traveling through Mississippi, Appalachia, Chicago and Los Angeles, as well as his Twin Cities home base, he sought to publicize the plight of the poor, especially children, in the midst of a record period of economic growth.

On medical care, too, Wellstone harks back to an earlier era — the time before Clinton's failed 1994 plan to overhaul health care policy, when the nation seemed primed to do something about the 40 million who lack insurance. Wellstone has proposed a program to provide that insurance, at an annual cost of about $100 billion.

On a few issues, Wellstone has strayed from his liberal base. While he predictably opposed authorizing the war against Iraq in 1991, his peace activist supporters were dismayed when he supported the U.S. bombing of Iraq in December 1998. Wellstone said Iraqi President Saddam Hussein's refusal to abide by agreements left the United States without "any other choice."

Wellstone's style can rub some people the wrong way. Lobbyists named him one of the worst-dressed senators in a Washingtonian magazine survey. In another magazine survey of congressional staffers, he was named one of the Senate's "biggest windbags."

A political science professor at Carleton College for more than two decades, Wellstone gained visibility as a co-chairman of the Rev. Jesse Jackson's 1988 presidential campaign in Minnesota. Two years later, he took on GOP Sen. Rudy Boschwitz. In some of the most original campaign advertisements of the year, Wellstone starred in his own version of Michael Moore's sardonic documentary, "Roger and Me." Instead of stalking General Motors Corp. Chairman Roger Smith, Wellstone sought out Boschwitz.

With a 2 percentage point margin of victory, Wellstone was the only challenger to beat an incumbent that year. In 1996, he won a rematch against Boschwitz by 9 points.

The decision to break the term limits pledge could be a factor in 2002, with critics charging that Wellstone has abandoned his moral high ground.

KEY VOTES

2000

No   Overhaul bankruptcy law and increase minimum wage
No   Limit fiscal 2001 discretionary spending to $600.3 billion
No   Override veto on nuclear waste disposal at Yucca Mountain site in Nevada
Yes Oppose effort to terminate Kosovo mission
Yes Include gender, sexual orientation and disability in federal hate crime protections
No   Approve GOP plan to restrict use of genetic information by health insurers
No   Kill amendment delaying implementation of an anti-missile defense system
No   Cut taxes for married couples
No   Grant China permanent normal trade status

1999

No   Remove President Clinton from office for obstruction of justice
No   Kill amendment authorizing state grants to hire teachers and reduce class size
Yes Require criminal background checks for purchases at gun shows
No   Approve GOP proposal to increase rights of patients in managed-care health plans
No   Block effort to allow farm and medicine exports to Cuba
Yes Allow study of tougher automobile fuel efficiency standards
Yes Ratify nuclear weapons testing treaty
Yes Prohibit national political parties from collecting "soft money" donations
No   Remove barriers among banking, securities and insurance companies

INTEREST GROUPS

	AFL-CIO	ADA	CCUS	ACU
2000	88%	100%	20%	4%
1999	100%	90%	24%	8%
1998	100%	100%	22%	4%
1997	100%	100%	10%	4%
1996	100%	95%	31%	5%
1995	100%	100%	32%	4%
1994	100%	100%	10%	4%
1993	82%	100%	10%	4%
1992	92%	100%	10%	0%
1991	83%	95%	20%	5%

CQ VOTE STUDIES

	PARTY UNITY		PRESIDENTIAL SUPPORT	
	Support	Oppose	Support	Oppose
2000	97%	3%	90%	10%
1999	96%	4%	84%	16%
1998	99%	1%	87%	13%
1997	96%	4%	83%	17%
1996	92%	8%	85%	15%
1995	95%	5%	88%	12%
1994	94%	6%	82%	18%
1993	95%	5%	92%	8%
1992	95%	5%	24%	76%
1991	95%	5%	23%	77%

Sen. Mark Dayton (D)

Elected 2000; 1st term

Dayton's liberalism stands in sharp contrast to the strongly conservative ideology of his predecessor, Republican Sen. Rod Grams. The freshman's political beliefs resemble those of his senior colleague from Minnesota, Democrat Paul Wellstone, often called the Senate's most liberal member.

Dayton's liberal leanings go back to his college days. While his parents supported Republican Richard M. Nixon for president in 1960 and 1968, Dayton — who says Robert F. Kennedy is his political hero — was a vocal opponent of the Vietnam War and an advocate for liberal causes.

Dayton can claim a nearly lifelong commitment to public service and to Minnesota's arm of the Democratic Party. He worked as an aide to then-Sen. Walter F. Mondale, did a stint as state economic development commissioner, and from 1991 to 1995 was state auditor. Though he comes to the Senate without having held legislative office, Dayton credits that experience with giving him insight into the inner workings of the legislative process. He also spent time working as a public school teacher in New York City and as a counselor for a Boston social services agency.

Senior citizens, farmers and labor union members were the core constituencies that helped elect Dayton, who hopes to reciprocate by advocating their policy positions. A top priority for Dayton, whose committee assignments include the Agriculture panel, is helping to rewrite the 1996 "Freedom to Farm" law; he contends that the measure has failed farmers. Dayton also won seats on the Armed Services and Rules committees.

The senator favors requiring employers to provide health insurance for their workers, with an exception for companies that have fewer than 25 employees. He supports reducing the price of prescription drugs and ensuring that they are fully covered under the provisions of Medicare, and he advocates a "patients' bill of rights." Dayton also says he opposes privatizing Social Security.

Dayton is one of several candidates in the 2000 elections whose personal wealth helped them win Senate races. He is heir to a department store fortune; his great-grandfather founded Dayton Hudson Corp., which became the Target Corp., the retail giant.

The $12 million Dayton spent from his accounts enabled him to beat Grams — a politically vulnerable, one-term incumbent — netting the Democrat a seat he had first sought almost two decades before. (Dayton also spent freely in his narrow 1982 defeat by GOP Sen. David Durenberger and his failed 1998 bid in the Democratic primary for governor.)

Criticized for his heavy campaign spending in 2000, Dayton countered that because of his personal wealth, he is not beholden to special-interest groups. He backs overhauling the nation's campaign finance laws and has pledged to return all but $1 of his six-figure Senate salary to the U.S. Treasury.

Dayton benefited from facing a group of second-tier opponents in the September primary. Despite the lateness of the Democratic contest, Dayton's comfortable win gave him momentum and made him a solid favorite over Grams in the general election.

Grams, who had won his seat with less than a majority of the vote in the strong Republican year of 1994, had kept a low profile that depressed his popularity ratings. Dayton argued that Grams' voting record was too far right for Minnesota. The last straw for Grams may have been the media coverage of his son Morgan, who had run-ins with the law during the campaign. Dayton won by 6 percentage points.

CAPITOL OFFICE
224-3244; fax 228-2186; 346 Russell Bldg. 20510

INTERNET
web: dayton.senate.gov

COMMITTEES
Agriculture, Nutrition & Forestry
Armed Services
Rules & Administration

HOMETOWN
Minneapolis

BORN
Jan. 26, 1947, Minneapolis, Minn.

RELIGION
Presbyterian

FAMILY
Divorced; two children

EDUCATION
Yale U., B.A. 1969

CAREER
Investment company president; runaway youth home director; congressional and gubernatorial aide; social worker; science teacher

POLITICAL HIGHLIGHTS
Minn. commissioner of economic development, 1978; Democratic nominee for U.S. Senate, 1982; Minn. commissioner of energy and economic development, 1983-86; Minn. auditor, 1991-95; sought Democratic nomination for governor, 1998

ELECTION RESULTS

2000 GENERAL

Mark Dayton (D)	1,181,553	48.8%
Rod Grams (R)	1,047,474	43.3%
James Gibson (INDC)	140,583	5.8%

2000 PRIMARY

Mark Dayton (D)	178,972	41.3%
Michael Ciresi (D)	96,874	22.4%
Jerry R. Janezich (D)	90,074	20.8%
Rebecca Yanisch (D)	63,289	14.6%

Rep. Gil Gutknecht (R)

CAPITOL OFFICE
225-2472; fax 225-3246; 425 Cannon Bldg. 20515

INTERNET
e-mail: gil@mail.house.gov
web: www.house.gov/gutknecht

COMMITTEES
Agriculture
Budget
Science

HOMETOWN
Rochester

BORN
March 20, 1951, Cedar Falls, Iowa

RELIGION
Roman Catholic

FAMILY
Wife, Mary Gutknecht; three children

EDUCATION
U. of Northern Iowa, B.A. 1973

CAREER
Real estate broker; school supplies salesman;
auctioneer; computer software salesman

POLITICAL HIGHLIGHTS
Minn. House, 1983-95

ELECTION RESULTS

2000 GENERAL

Gil Gutknecht (R)	159,835	56.4%
Mary Rieder (D)	117,946	41.6%
Rich Osness (LIBERT)	5,440	1.9%

2000 PRIMARY

Gil Gutknecht (R)	unopposed

1998 GENERAL

Gil Gutknecht (R)	131,233	54.7%
Tracy L. Beckman (D)	108,420	45.2%

PREVIOUS WINNING PERCENTAGES
1996 (53%); 1994 (55%)

Elected 1994; 4th term

Gutknecht has an intellectual passion for history and a culinary passion for Spam. He likes to read military histories, and he can cite details from biographies on Abraham Lincoln and Winston Churchill. But he is also known for his weakness for Spam, a product of Hormel Foods Corp. in Austin, Minn., that he passes out to his colleagues. In 2000, he persuaded the Library of Congress to hold an exhibit on the popular lunch meat.

The outgoing Gutknecht (GOOT-neck) portrays himself as a common-sense fellow who doesn't put on airs. He has moderated his views since arriving in Washington as part of the Republican takeover in 1995, and he now focuses on Medicare funding and reducing drug costs as well as on such GOP favorites as cutting taxes. "Everyone who knows how democracies work knows how ultimately there is an ebb and flow to this business," he told the Minneapolis Star Tribune in 1999.

Gutknecht represents a swing district that voted twice for Bill Clinton and then for George W. Bush in 2000, so it can be a challenge for this conservative Republican to sell his voting record to the people in southeastern Minnesota. But Gutknecht is a skilled pitchman — for years he was a school-supply salesman, then an auctioneer — and in his four House elections, he has stayed a couple of strides ahead of the Democratic opposition.

Gutknecht, who likes to remind his constituents that his name means "good hired hand" in German, goes to great lengths to lobby for the agricultural interests in his district, home of the Jolly Green Giant of processed-vegetable fame. In 1999, he was so outraged by a year-end spending bill that granted higher subsidies to Northeastern dairy producers at the expense of those in the upper Midwest that he quit his position as GOP regional whip. In his resignation letter to top GOP leaders, he wrote: "I cannot, in good conscience, continue to be part of a leadership team that has trampled on the interests of thousands of dairy families in defiance of both sound policy and common sense."

In the 106th Congress, he picked up a seat on the Agriculture Committee to go with his Budget and Science panel assignments. He defends genetically modified food products that have come under fire from some consumer and environmental groups. He also votes for disaster assistance for farmers and, in 2000, supported legislation granting permanent normal trade status to China, an important market for U.S. agricultural products.

Gutknecht won election to the House in the 1994 flood of GOP victories that gave Republicans control of the chamber, and he happily joined his classmates in pushing the congressional debate on fiscal policy and social issues to the right. He is a firm opponent of abortion, and he calls for "empowering the states, local school districts and parents" by waiving federal education regulations that he says are "stifling innovation and creative thinking" in America's schools.

He supported a measure in 1999 that would have required background checks for purchases at gun shows, but only at events with 10 or more vendors. The vote came after a much-publicized school shooting at Columbine High School in Colorado. "This was an upper-middle-class school ... and the kids looked like my kids," he told the Star Tribune. Gun control advocates denounced the measure as a weak alternative to real gun control.

Gutknecht has talked a lot about cutting spending and taxes, but he has not always sided with his leadership. In 1998, he was one of only 11 Republicans to vote "no" when GOP leaders put forward a plan to cut taxes by $80 billion over five years because he worried that it would cut into funds needed to shore up Social Security. One year later, however, he supported a much larger tax cut and cited the swelling government surplus.

Compared with other conservatives, Gutknecht has been more skeptical about large increases in military spending. He says he believes in a strong defense, "but just look at the Defense Department and the amount of waste and duplication and mismanagement that we see." He has expressed annoyance with the number of Pentagon employees whose work is buying things. Gutknecht once said on the House floor, "I am told according to last count, we had something like 106,000 buyers" at the Pentagon.

In 2000, he won House passage of legislation opening U.S. borders to reimportation of U.S.-made prescription drugs because he was concerned that his constituents were being charged far more for pharmaceuticals than residents of Canada and other countries. "Once people realize that ... the world market price is a lot cheaper than ours, the pharmaceutical companies are going to have to rethink their marketing and pricing strategy," he said. "The drug companies simply cannot defend this indefensible pricing structure," the Star Tribune quoted him as saying.

Gutknecht has invested much energy in an effort that is politically appealing even if it irritates some of his colleagues: cutting back on House members' pensions. His idea is to bar members from accruing additional pension benefits after they have served six terms — providing incentive for members to leave after 12 years in office.

Born in Cedar Falls, Iowa, and educated at the University of Northern Iowa there, Gutknecht was active in Republican campaigns from an early age. After college, he worked as a salesman for a school-supply company that sent him to southeastern Minnesota. In 1982, he won election to the Minnesota House, and during a dozen years there, he was a loyal team player in the Independent-Republican caucus, attracting attention for his considerable oratorical ability and rising to the post of party floor leader.

After exploring a bid for a vacant U.S. Senate seat, he shifted his focus to the 1st District when Democratic Rep. Timothy J. Penny retired in 1994. With his base in the district's leading population center, Rochester, and his ties to the GOP hierarchy, Gutknecht easily won the party's endorsement and overwhelmed the comeback bid of former GOP Rep. Arlen I. Erdahl in the primary. In the hard-fought general election, which was targeted by both parties, Gutknecht won with 55 percent of the vote. He has fended off tough challenges since then by stressing his commitment to fiscal conservatism and his work for farmers.

KEY VOTES

2000

No Raise hourly minimum wage by $1 over two years
Yes Halt funding for U.S. mission in Kosovo unless European nations pay more
Yes Provide Medicare benefits to military retirees and their dependents
Yes Grant China permanent normal trade status
Yes Phase out estate, gift and trust taxes
Yes Prohibit implementation of president's national monument designations
Yes Approve GOP plan to provide prescription drug coverage for Medicare beneficiaries
No Increase help for poor nations indebted to international financial institutions

1999

Yes Impose steel import quotas
No Kill proposal to take aviation trust funds off budget
Yes Require background checks on buyers only at gun shows with 10 or more vendors
Yes Remove barriers among banking, securities and insurance companies
No Authorize state grants to hire teachers and reduce class size
No Overhaul campaign finance law; ban "soft money" and restrict advocacy advertising
No Approve bipartisan plan to increase rights of patients in managed-care health plans

INTEREST GROUPS

	AFL-CIO	ADA	CCUS	ACU
2000	0%	5%	80%	92%
1999	11%	15%	96%	92%
1998	10%	5%	94%	92%
1997	0%	15%	100%	92%

CQ VOTE STUDIES

	PARTY UNITY		PRESIDENTIAL SUPPORT	
	Support	Oppose	Support	Oppose
2000	92%	8%	24%	76%
1999	94%	6%	18%	82%
1998	92%	8%	24%	76%
1997	92%	8%	28%	72%

MINNESOTA 1
Southeast – Rochester, part of Mankato

A spirit of independence characterizes the 1st, which occupies Minnesota's southeastern corner and is bordered to the east by the Mississippi River. The district supported moderate, liberal, conservative and independent candidates simultaneously in the 1990s, electing a spectrum ranging from liberal Sen. Paul Wellstone to independent upstart Gov. Jesse Ventura. In 1992, 26 percent of voters supported Ross Perot.

Despite its strong independent streak, the 1st's mostly white and middle-class population leans Republican on the state and congressional levels. It has elected Republican Rep. Gutknecht for four consecutive terms. The GOP is heavily favored in Rochester, where the city's Mayo Clinic-centered health care industry draws a large professional population. Blue-collar residents who work for the meat-packing company Hormel in Mower County form the Democratic-Farmer-Labor Party stronghold. University town Winona also supports the DFL.

Corn, soybean and dairy farmers throughout the district lean Republican but are willing to exhibit an independent streak. The 1st's northern peak includes an array of colleges in Mankato and Northfield and reaches fractionally into metropolitan Minneapolis, where independent tendencies intensify.

MAJOR INDUSTRY
Agriculture, livestock, health care

CITIES
Rochester, 80,768; Mankato, 31,305; Winona, 24,965; Austin, 22,210

UNUSUAL FEATURES
Spam Jam observed in Austin, birthplace of Spam; Northfield hosts the "Defeat of Jesse James Days" to commemorate the James gang being driven off during an attempted robbery; World's largest ear of corn in Rochester.

Rep. Mark Kennedy (R)

CAPITOL OFFICE
225-2331; fax 225-6475
1415 Longworth Bldg. 20515

INTERNET
e-mail: mark.kennedy@mail.house.gov
web: markkennedy.house.gov

COMMITTEES
Agriculture
Transportation & Infrastructure

HOMETOWN
Watertown

BORN
April 11, 1957, Benson, Minn.

RELIGION
Roman Catholic

FAMILY
Wife, Debbie Kennedy; four children

EDUCATION
Saint John's U. (Minn.), B.A. 1978; U. of Michigan, M.B.A. 1983

CAREER
Giftware company financial executive; food company financial director; accountant

POLITICAL HIGHLIGHTS
No previous office

ELECTION RESULTS

2000 GENERAL

Mark Kennedy (R)	138,957	48.1%
David Minge (D)	138,802	48.0%
Gerald W. Brekke (INDC)	7,875	2.7%

2000 PRIMARY

Mark Kennedy (R)	13,779	79.3%
Joe Wagner (R)	3,598	20.7%

Elected 2000; 1st term

Kennedy, who unseated four-term Democratic Rep. David Minge in one of 2000's closest elections, had jokingly urged voters to send him to Congress to prove that there are Kennedys who are Republicans.

Kennedy shares some similarities with the House member who has the same surname, Rhode Island Democrat Patrick J. Kennedy. Both have a father and grandfather who were public officials, and both are members of large Roman Catholic families.

But there are big political differences between the GOP freshman from Minnesota's 2nd District and his colleague, the son of Massachusetts Sen. Edward M. Kennedy and a member of the famed liberal Democratic dynasty.

Mark Kennedy, a political newcomer, reflects his mostly conservative and rural constituency in southwest Minnesota. He sought and landed a seat on the Agriculture Committee, where he works to expand access to foreign markets for U.S. farm products and backs the use of ethanol, a corn-based fuel.

Kennedy, who also got a seat on the Transportation and Infrastructure Committee, wants to increase funding to build roads in his district. "Transportation dollars go to the urban areas, not to the rural areas," says Kennedy, whose district in the southwest quadrant of the state does not have a city with more than 20,000 residents.

Kennedy was an executive for the Pillsbury food products company and the giftware company Department 56. He was not involved in politics, although others in his family had held local office. His grandfather was mayor of Murdoch, in rural Swift County, and his father was on the county school board.

With minimal opposition for the GOP nomination, Kennedy was able to focus on Minge, who was seen as a Democratic moderate. Kennedy sought to puncture that reputation, painting Minge as more liberal than he let on.

Minge's incumbency almost rescued him, but the election night tally showed Kennedy the winner by 155 votes. Minge asked for a recount, but withdrew the request when it became clear he would not overcome Kennedy's advantage. The victory made Kennedy one of only two Republicans to unseat a House Democratic incumbent in 2000.

MINNESOTA 2
Southwest – Willmar

Tension between corporate and family farmers colors politics in Minnesota's traditionally Republican, but competitive southwestern quadrant, where corn, soybeans, sugar beets and hogs are staples of the economy.

Small farmers in the 2nd's hilly northwest and south-central areas vote for the Democratic-Farmer-Labor Party, while the district's Republican base is in its southern corners, where large tract farmers are reliant on export business.

Suburban migration from Minneapolis to the 2nd's rapidly growing northeastern counties has added to the number of affluent conservatives. These suburban, bedroom communities are more likely to vote for Republicans and conservative independents, as evidenced by their support for Gov. Jesse Ventura in 1998.

About 30 percent of the 2nd's population lives in these communities based on high-tech industry.

Casinos are big business for the Shakopee Mdewakanton Sioux tribe in Prior Lake, where rapid suburban growth became a conflict in the 1990s. With an overwhelmingly German, Norwegian and Swedish ancestry, the district's population is one of the most racially homogenous in the nation, although the number of Hispanic and African immigrants is growing in agricultural processing towns like Worthington and Willmar.

MAJOR INDUSTRY
Agriculture, food processing, manufacturing, casinos

CITIES
Chanhassen, 19,184; Willmar, 18,794; Chaska, 15,795

UNUSUAL FEATURES
Walnut Grove, childhood home of "Little House on the Prairie" series author Laura Ingalls Wilder.

Rep. Jim Ramstad (R)

Elected 1990; 6th term

On a range of issues, including abortion, the environment and gun control, Ramstad plots a more moderate course than most in his party, although he supports the party doctrine of free trade and tax reform.

He acknowledges that it isn't easy being a centrist in the often ideologically polarized House. "When controversial votes come up, I often get heat, especially when they deal with education and environment," he has said. But a genial personality and long experience in the workings of politics help him navigate the treacherous waters.

One of Ramstad's top interests in Congress is boosting treatment for people with drug and alcohol addictions. A recovering alcoholic, he speaks freely about his past struggles. Ramstad says he started drinking as a college senior, and he recognized that he needed to do something about his addiction in 1981 when he woke up in jail in Sioux Falls, S.D., after a night of drinking, fighting and a blackout. In an article for a Capitol Hill newspaper detailing his illness and recovery, he explained that he is "recovering, not recovered. ... Every day, I have to recover. Every day I do healthy, positive things so I won't take another drink."

He has repeatedly pressed for legislation that would ensure that insurance companies cover the costs of drug and alcohol treatment, and he favors expanded coverage for a range of mental disorders. Drawing on his personal experience, he urged Congress in 2000 to scrap a billion dollar-plus package to battle drug traffickers in Colombia and spend the money instead on treatment. "When will Congress and the president wake up to the basic fact that our nation's supply-side strategy does not address the underlying problem of addiction," he asked on the House floor.

Ramstad's district is home to numerous medical companies, and he has a strong interest in health issues. Concerned that Medicare sometimes takes years to approve reimbursement for new medical devices, he sponsored legislation in the 106th Congress to speed up the process. "These bureaucratic games are not fair to Medicare beneficiaries who need life-saving innovations," he told the Minneapolis Star Tribune. He also led efforts in the 106th to allow disabled people to earn more money without sacrificing medical benefits.

On the Ways and Means Committee, Ramstad lines up solidly behind his leadership on the issues of expanding trade and cutting taxes. In 2000, he helped rally Republicans behind legislation granting China permanent normal trade status, arguing, "We can't forfeit those markets or it would be an economic disaster for the United States," according to the Star Tribune.

In the 105th Congress, Ramstad supported efforts to make the Internal Revenue Service more user-friendly. He took on the agency again in 2000, assailing an IRS ruling, involving a family from Minnesota, that parents could not claim child deductions if their child was kidnapped. "It doesn't get any worse from out-of-touch Washington bureaucrats than to deny the family of a kidnapped child the dependency exemption, even though the family continues to spend thousands of dollars searching for their child and maintains the child's bedroom," he said. "No families' taxes will increase simply because a stranger abducted their child." The legislation became law in 2000.

Ramstad breaks with conservatives on many social issues. He seeks to steer a moderate course on abortion rights, backing legalized abortion but also supporting "reasonable limits" on access to the procedure. He agrees

CAPITOL OFFICE
225-2871; fax 225-6351; 103 Cannon Bldg. 20515

INTERNET
e-mail: mn03@mail.house.gov
web: www.house.gov/ramstad

COMMITTEES
Ways & Means

HOMETOWN
Minnetonka

BORN
May 6, 1946, Jamestown, N.D.

RELIGION
Protestant

FAMILY
Single

EDUCATION
U. of Minnesota, B.A. 1968; George Washington U., J.D. 1973

MILITARY SERVICE
Army Reserve, 1968-74

CAREER
Lawyer; professor; congressional and state House aide

POLITICAL HIGHLIGHTS
Minn. Senate, 1981-91

ELECTION RESULTS

2000 GENERAL

Jim Ramstad (R)	222,571	67.6%
Sue Shuff (D)	98,219	29.9%
Bob Odden (LIBERT)	5,302	1.6%

2000 PRIMARY

Jim Ramstad (R)	unopposed

1998 GENERAL

Jim Ramstad (R)	203,731	71.9%
Stanley J. Leino (D)	66,505	23.5%
Derek W. Schramm (MNTAX)	12,823	4.5%

PREVIOUS WINNING PERCENTAGES
1996 (70%); 1994 (73%); 1992 (64%); 1990 (67%)

with conservatives who want to ban a procedure its opponents call "partial birth" abortion, calling it "repulsive and extreme."

He also takes an independent tack on gun control. Ramstad was one of 54 Republicans in the 103rd Congress to support a five-day waiting period for handgun purchases. In 1999, he backed a series of gun control initiatives such as requiring background checks for purchases at gun shows, calling the proposals "common-sense gun measures."

Ramstad's effort to strike a balance between right and left was evident during the House's 1998 impeachment proceedings. He voted to authorize the Judiciary Committee to investigate whether sufficient grounds existed to impeach President Clinton, but he urged GOP colleagues to try to avoid the appearance of partisanship in the inquiry. After Judiciary presented the House with four articles of impeachment, Ramstad voted for two and against two.

Ramstad's upscale suburban district is solidly Republican, but there is considerable support for environmental protections, and Ramstad reflects that interest. After Republicans took control in 1994, he opposed GOP efforts to ease federal water pollution control regulations and to restrict the Environmental Protection Agency's regulatory authority. He also worked with a group of moderates to produce a milder rewrite of the Endangered Species Act, and he has battled against proposals to allow increased motor-boat traffic through northern Minnesota's Boundary Waters Canoe Area Wilderness.

Government has been an interest of Ramstad's since boyhood. His Web page carries the famous photo of a young Bill Clinton shaking hands with President Kennedy at the White House in 1963. Also in that photo is Ramstad, who was with Clinton in the American Legion Boys Nation contingent that was visiting Kennedy. Even all these years later, Ramstad has been known to brag that back in 1963, he beat Clinton in a basketball game.

Ramstad first came to Washington more than three decades ago to study law at George Washington University. In 1980, he won a seat in the Minnesota Senate, and he served there until he ran for the 3rd District seat vacated in 1990 by veteran Republican Rep. Bill Frenzel.

Although his abortion rights stance placed him at odds with many at the party convention, he won endorsements from prominent anti-abortion politicians, and he defeated four candidates after seven ballots. He won two-thirds of the vote in the general election against Democratic investment executive Lewis DeMars and has easily held the district since; only once in his five re-election victories has his share of the vote dropped below two-thirds.

KEY VOTES

2000
No Raise hourly minimum wage by $1 over two years
Yes Halt funding for U.S. mission in Kosovo unless European nations pay more
Yes Provide Medicare benefits to military retirees and their dependents
Yes Grant China permanent normal trade status
Yes Phase out estate, gift and trust taxes
No Prohibit implementation of president's national monument designations
Yes Approve GOP plan to provide prescription drug coverage for Medicare beneficiaries
Yes Increase help for poor nations indebted to international financial institutions

1999
No Impose steel import quotas
Yes Kill proposal to take aviation trust funds off budget
No Require background checks on buyers only at gun shows with 10 or more vendors
Yes Remove barriers among banking, securities and insurance companies
No Authorize state grants to hire teachers and reduce class size
Yes Overhaul campaign finance law; ban "soft money" and restrict advocacy advertising
No Approve bipartisan plan to increase rights of patients in managed-care health plans

INTEREST GROUPS

	AFL-CIO	ADA	CCUS	ACU
2000	10%	30%	90%	68%
1999	11%	40%	80%	72%
1998	0%	20%	94%	60%
1997	13%	40%	90%	64%

CQ VOTE STUDIES

	PARTY UNITY		PRESIDENTIAL SUPPORT	
	Support	Oppose	Support	Oppose
2000	78%	22%	41%	59%
1999	77%	23%	34%	66%
1998	68%	32%	43%	57%
1997	75%	25%	52%	48%

MINNESOTA 3

Western Twin Cities suburbs – Bloomington; Minnetonka

Minnesota's most affluent district, the 3rd encompasses Minneapolis' western suburbs, where large white-collar populations are grounded in fiscal conservatism but adhere to moderate social views on issues like abortion. The district also sometimes exhibits an independent streak.

With its abundance of high-tech industry, white-collar workers, golf courses and middle-class homes, the 3rd is a classic picture of suburban living. Several prominent Fortune 500 corporations have their headquarters in the district. Northwest Airlines, just outside the district (in the 6th), is another big employer.

The 3rd's second largest city, Brooklyn Park, was governed in the early 1990s by Mayor Jesse Ventura, who has since become governor with the 3rd's electoral blessing. The district has sent moderate

Republicans to Congress since 1970, but at the same time, it supported a conservative Republican for senator and Bill Clinton for president in 1992 and '96. In 2000, the district gave President Bush a 5 percentage point win.

Brooklyn Park, Bloomington and Brooklyn Center's blue-collar residents vote for the Democratic-Farmer-Labor Party, but the Republican and affluent south and west portions of the 3rd casts most of the vote, giving the 3rd a tilt to the right.

MAJOR INDUSTRY
Electronics, manufacturing, food processing

CITIES
Bloomington, 86,226; Brooklyn Park, 63,758; Plymouth, 62,152; Burnsville, 60,308; Minnetonka, 51,813

UNUSUAL FEATURES
The 4.2 million square-foot Mall of America in Bloomington, where between 30 and 40 million people visit annually.

Rep. Betty McCollum (D)

Elected 2000; 1st term

CAPITOL OFFICE
225-6631; fax 225-1968
1029 Longworth Bldg. 20515

INTERNET
e-mail: www.house.gov/writerep
web: www.house.gov/mccollum

COMMITTEES
Education & Workforce
Resources

HOMETOWN
St. Paul

BORN
July 12, 1954, Minneapolis, Minn.

RELIGION
Roman Catholic

FAMILY
Husband, Douglas McCollum; two children

EDUCATION
Inver Hills Community College, A.A. 1980; College of St. Catherine, B.A. 1987

CAREER
Substitute teacher; retail saleswoman

POLITICAL HIGHLIGHTS
North St. Paul City Council, 1987-92; Minn. House, 1993-2000

ELECTION RESULTS

2000 GENERAL

Betty McCollum (D)	130,403	48.0%
Linda Runbeck (R)	83,852	30.9%
Tom Foley (INDC)	55,899	20.6%

2000 PRIMARY

Betty McCollum (D)	35,911	50.4%
Steven G. Novak (D)	16,332	22.9%
Chris Coleman (D)	13,555	19.0%
Cathie Hartnett (D)	5,454	7.7%

Minnesota's history of electing liberal lions, such as past Sens. Hubert H. Humphrey and Walter Mondale and current Sen. Paul Wellstone, has given the state a politically progressive image. But McCollum's 2000 election win to succeed the late 12-term Democratic Rep. Bruce F. Vento made her only the second woman ever elected to represent Minnesota in Congress — the first, Democrat Coya Knutson, was unseated in 1958 after two House terms.

Vento, who had announced plans to retire but died of lung cancer in October 2000, was a popular liberal. McCollum, too, is strongly liberal and shares Vento's interest in environmental protection.

McCollum secured a spot on the Resources Committee, on which Vento was a senior member. She had served on the state House Environment Committee, where she worked to preserve wetlands and clean up abandoned, contaminated industrial sites known as "brownfields."

"Bruce Vento brought a clear and resounding voice to the preservation of our land and our lakes, our fields and streams," McCollum told The Associated Press soon after she won the Resources seat. "I sought this committee assignment because I wanted to carry on the congressman's legacy."

A former teacher, McCollum also sits on the Education and the Workforce Committee. And she was named the freshman class representative on the Democratic Congressional Campaign Committee, which advises and funds Democratic House candidates.

Though three other Democrats sought to succeed Vento, McCollum gained an essential edge for the September primary when she won the state Democratic Party's endorsement at its convention in June.

McCollum drew a seasoned Republican foe in state Sen. Linda Runbeck, but her biggest worry seemed to be the possible siphoning of Democratic votes by independent candidate Tom Foley, a former Democrat and longtime Ramsey County attorney. But Foley, who ran as a fiscal conservative, appeared to draw votes from both candidates. Though McCollum missed a majority with 48 percent of the vote, she easily outran Runbeck, who took 31 percent; Foley finished with 21 percent.

MINNESOTA 4

St. Paul and suburbs

St. Paul's liberal university communities, state government and labor populations provide a consistent stronghold for the Democratic-Farmer-Labor Party. Represented in Congress by a Democrat since 1949, voters in the 4th — about half of whom live in St. Paul — have elected DFL candidates at all levels of government. But as with most of central Minnesota, an independent streak is strong, as demonstrated by support for Ross Perot in 1992 and Gov. Jesse Ventura in 1998.

St. Paul is a traditionally Democratic city with a large German and Irish-Catholic population. The city developed as a major port and railroading center and still has a strong labor tradition. Today, blue-collar, black and Hispanic communities contribute to the city's Democratic flavor.

As the location of the state capital and headquarters of the Minnesota Mining and Manufacturing Co., or 3M, the district has a large percentage of white-collar workers who live in middle- and high-income neighborhoods. Several colleges, including the University of Minnesota agriculture school, are located in affluent communities north of St. Paul.

To the extent that Republicans have a base in the 4th, it's the growing suburbs to the north of the city, which have drawn city residents and a number of newcomers.

MAJOR INDUSTRY
State government, higher education, manufacturing

CITIES
St. Paul, 256,213; Maplewood, 34,920; Roseville, 34,391

UNUSUAL FEATURES
Supreme Court Justices Warren E. Burger and Harry A. Blackmun grew up in St. Paul; St. Paul's original name was Pig's Eye Landing, after bootlegger Pierre "Pig's Eye" Parrant.

Rep. Martin Olav Sabo (D)

CAPITOL OFFICE
225-4755; fax 225-4886; 2336 Rayburn Bldg. 20515

INTERNET
e-mail: martin.sabo@mail.house.gov
web: www.house.gov/sabo

COMMITTEES
Appropriations
Standards of Official Conduct

HOMETOWN
Minneapolis

BORN
Feb. 28, 1938, Crosby, N.D.

RELIGION
Lutheran

FAMILY
Wife, Sylvia Ann Lee; two children

EDUCATION
Augsburg College, B.A. 1959; U. of Minnesota, attended 1960

CAREER
Public official

POLITICAL HIGHLIGHTS
Minn. House, 1961-79 (minority leader, 1969-73; Speaker, 1973-79)

ELECTION RESULTS

2000 GENERAL

Martin Olav Sabo (D)	176,629	69.2%
Frank Taylor (R)	58,191	22.8%
Rob Tomich (INDC)	11,323	4.4%
Renee Lavoi (CNSTP)	4,522	1.8%
Chuck P. Charnstrom (LIBERT)	4,480	1.8%

2000 PRIMARY

Martin Olav Sabo (D)	unopposed

1998 GENERAL

Martin Olav Sabo (D)	145,535	66.9%
Frank Taylor (R)	60,035	27.6%
Kevin Houston (LIBERT)	7,378	3.4%
Michael Pennock (SW)	2,842	1.3%

PREVIOUS WINNING PERCENTAGES
1996 (64%); 1994 (62%); 1992 (63%); 1990 (73%); 1988 (72%); 1986 (73%); 1984 (70%); 1982 (66%); 1980 (70%); 1978 (62%)

Elected 1978; 12th term

Some of the policies that Sabo espouses are so liberal that it is hard to imagine them even getting a serious hearing from a Republican-controlled Congress, much less passing. He would like to change the tax laws to discourage "excessive executive pay." He has cosponsored a single-payer health care bill to guarantee all Americans health insurance through a taxpayer-financed system. And he backs public financing of political campaigns as a way to boost faith in the political system.

Yet while his proposals may seem bold or even radical in the existing political climate, Sabo is one of the House's most reserved and low-key legislators. He rarely seeks a public forum to advocate his views, preferring instead to work directly and quietly with other members. Reticence comes naturally to Sabo, whose low-key demeanor fits the stereotype of his Norwegian stock. In fact, he can be so reluctant to step into the spotlight that the Minneapolis Star Tribune once wrote, "Sabo's conduct as a legislator suggests a variation of an old Norwegian joke: He's a politician who cares so passionately about an issue that he'll almost speak out about it."

For a time, Sabo aspired to a starring role in the House leadership. He was chairman of the Democratic Study Group, a collection of liberal members, and he was a deputy whip. But when he sought the Democratic whip post for the 100th Congress, he ran a laconic campaign and ultimately gave it up when he figured he did not have the votes to win.

Sabo's community values and belief in an activist government are rooted in his upbringing. He was born in sparsely populated northwest North Dakota on the farm of his immigrant parents. Sabo's parents donated land for the community's school, where his mother volunteered as a cook and Sabo was valedictorian of a graduating class of three. In a 1994 interview with World Traveler Magazine, Sabo recalled how government helped his family. "I remember not having electricity and getting it from the federal government," he said, referring to the Roosevelt-era Rural Electrification Administration. "I've seen firsthand how government can help people."

Sabo keeps such a low profile that few beyond Capitol Hill are aware that he was an important contributor to the elimination of the budget deficit. As chairman of the Budget Committee in the 103rd Congress, Sabo was instrumental in building the case for President Clinton's controversial tax-raising, deficit-cutting budget plan. Its passage by the narrowest of margins in 1993 was a major factor in the declining deficits and robust economic growth that followed. Clinton hailed Sabo as a "chief architect" of the 1993 plan. Sabo said simply that it was "rewarding to have played a part in this process through my work on the Budget Committee."

That understatement is characteristic of Sabo. Republican Bill Frenzel, a former House colleague from Minnesota, says of Sabo, "He's a tease to understand, hard to get close to and yet so successful ... a guy who made it without huffing and puffing, who doesn't go around blowing his own horn, which is very rare, very refreshing in Congress."

Well-liked by Budget Committee staff members, Sabo was legendary for his quickness with numbers. He could leave the staff gaping when, after being handed a long table of numbers, Sabo would glance down the columns, hand it back, and say, "It doesn't add up."

After the Republicans took control of the House in 1995, Sabo served a term as Budget's ranking Democrat, fighting GOP spending cuts. He then left the committee, having served there the maximum time permitted under

Democratic rules. He returned to the Appropriations Committee.

Sabo has long pushed for expanding health care coverage for Americans, particularly children. In the 103rd Congress, he cosponsored Clinton's ill-fated proposal to substantially overhaul the nation's health care system as an alternative government-funded plan.

Sabo also is a staunch proponent of pay equity for workers. He was an early advocate in the 1990s of increasing the minimum wage. And while he supported 1996 legislation that raised the wage to $5.15 an hour, he thinks that it needs to be higher to keep low-wage workers out of poverty. He favors limiting the tax deductibility of an executive's salary to 25 times the amount paid to a company's lowest-paid worker. That step, Sabo says, would "send a message that those who work on the factory floor are as important to a company's success as those who work in the executive suite."

Sabo has used his seat on Appropriations to fight proposed budget cuts in low-income heating assistance, housing, education and environmental protection programs. He is a strong supporter of federal funding for mass transit and alternative modes of transportation such as bicycling, and he is adept at steering funds for federal projects to his district and state.

Sabo is consistently liberal on social issues. He opposed the welfare overhaul bill signed by Clinton in 1996, he voted against banning federal recognition of same-sex marriage, and he opposes conservatives' efforts to ban a procedure its opponents call "partial birth" abortion.

Sabo is a serious sports fan and, in particular, a devotee of baseball and the Minnesota Twins; he listens to broadcasts of Twins' games over the Internet on his office computer. Since the late 1980s, he has coached the Democratic squad in the annual congressional baseball game. After each election, he can be found reviewing congressional race results from across the nation, looking for promising new Democratic recruits for the team.

Sabo eschews flashy media campaigns by going door-to-door to meet voters in his district each election season. He is reluctant to criticize his opponents. But he has been a significant presence in Minnesota politics virtually all his adult life, having been first elected to the state House at age 22. He served there for 18 years, including six as Speaker.

When Democrat Donald Fraser left the House for an unsuccessful Senate bid in 1978, Sabo was seen as the logical successor. He easily won his party's nomination and won comfortably in the dependably Democratic 5th District. His re-election races have been routine, except for an intraparty challenge in 1992 when a faction of liberals complained that Sabo had opposed across-the-board defense cuts. Sabo won the primary with 67 percent.

KEY VOTES

2000
Yes	Raise hourly minimum wage by $1 over two years
No	Halt funding for U.S. mission in Kosovo unless European nations pay more
Yes	Provide Medicare benefits to military retirees and their dependents
No	Grant China permanent normal trade status
No	Phase out estate, gift and trust taxes
No	Prohibit implementation of president's national monument designations
No	Approve GOP plan to provide prescription drug coverage for Medicare beneficiaries
Yes	Increase help for poor nations indebted to international financial institutions

1999
Yes	Impose steel import quotas
Yes	Kill proposal to take aviation trust funds off budget
No	Require background checks on buyers only at gun shows with 10 or more vendors
Yes	Remove barriers among banking, securities and insurance companies
Yes	Authorize state grants to hire teachers and reduce class size
Yes	Overhaul campaign finance law; ban "soft money" and restrict advocacy advertising
+	Approve bipartisan plan to increase rights of patients in managed-care health plans

INTEREST GROUPS

	AFL-CIO	ADA	CCUS	ACU
2000	90%	100%	38%	0%
1999	75%	95%	13%	0%
1998	100%	90%	24%	0%
1997	100%	100%	30%	4%

CQ VOTE STUDIES

	PARTY UNITY		PRESIDENTIAL SUPPORT	
	Support	Oppose	Support	Oppose
2000	96%	4%	90%	10%
1999	92%	8%	86%	14%
1998	90%	10%	89%	11%
1997	92%	8%	87%	13%

MINNESOTA 5
Minneapolis and suburbs

Established at the northernmost navigable point on the Mississippi River, Minneapolis accounts for most of the 5th's vote and has supported liberal Rep. Sabo since 1978. Except for the affluent, white suburb of Edina in the southwest, the district elects Democratic-Farmer-Labor Party candidates at all levels.

The power of organized labor has waned as Minneapolis has evolved from a blue-collar mill town into a major business hub. However, the shift has yet to change the city's liberal orientation, which is bolstered by a strong arts community and the 50,000-student University of Minnesota in eastern Minneapolis. In the 2000 presidential election, Green Party candidate Ralph Nader received 8 percent of the 5th's vote – one of his highest percentages in the nation.

The presence of Fortune 500 companies could not halt a late-1980s downturn in the regional economy, but the Minneapolis economy performed well in the 1990s, attracting even more well-educated, white-collar workers.

Although Minneapolis is known for its Scandinavian heritage, the 5th is the state's most racially diverse district. Black and Asian communities contribute to the district's Democratic-Farmer-Labor voter rolls. Northwest of the downtown office towers are some poor neighborhoods, home to blacks and some of the city's Chippewa Indian population.

MAJOR INDUSTRY
Corporate administration, banking, higher education

CITIES
Minneapolis, 353,395; St. Louis Park, 42,456; Richfield, 33,699

UNUSUAL FEATURES
World's largest spoon in Minneapolis, the city that elected Hubert Humphrey mayor in 1945; Minneapolis is the hometown of music artist Prince; "Mary Tyler Moore Show" set in Minneapolis.

Rep. Bill Luther (D)

CAPITOL OFFICE
225-2271; fax 225-3368; 117 Cannon Bldg. 20515

INTERNET
e-mail: bill.luther@mail.house.gov
web: www.house.gov/luther

COMMITTEES
Energy & Commerce

HOMETOWN
Stillwater

BORN
June 27, 1945, Fergus Falls, Minn.

RELIGION
Roman Catholic

FAMILY
Wife, Darlene Luther; two children

EDUCATION
U. of Minnesota, B.S. 1967, J.D. 1970

CAREER
Lawyer

POLITICAL HIGHLIGHTS
Minn. House, 1975-77; Minn. Senate, 1977-95

ELECTION RESULTS

2000 GENERAL

Bill Luther (D)	176,340	49.6%
John Kline (R)	170,900	48.0%
Ralph A. Hubbard (CNSTP)	8,584	2.4%

2000 PRIMARY

Bill Luther (D)	unopposed

1998 GENERAL

Bill Luther (D)	148,728	50.0%
John Kline (R)	136,866	46.0%
Eric M. Johnson (LIBERT)	11,805	4.0%

PREVIOUS WINNING PERCENTAGES
1996 (56%); 1994 (50%)

Elected 1994; 4th term

Quiet and unassuming in manner, Luther is often bothered by the House's partisan nature. "Sometimes it feels more like we're in a sitcom than a deliberative body," he told the St. Paul Pioneer Press. "We seem to be continually diverted onto subjects other than the people's business."

The people's business, in Luther's view, includes balancing the budget while protecting the environment and enhancing educational opportunities. The range of his interests is illustrated by his membership in a number of congressional caucuses and task forces, on issues ranging from nuclear nonproliferation to missing and exploited children to education, the Internet, tobacco and health, and congressional reform.

Luther is a career legislator, a throwback to the time when Congress was dominated by Democrats with backgrounds in state and local government. He was 29 when he was first elected to the Minnesota House. Over the next two decades, he became a power in the state legislature, winning election to the state Senate in 1976 and rising to the No. 2 position in the Democratic leadership as assistant majority leader.

In Congress, he has emerged as an advocate for consumer privacy. He attempted unsuccessfully to attach a privacy provision to a sweeping financial services deregulation bill in 1999 that would have required companies to obtain permission from customers before passing on financial information about them to other companies. President Clinton signed the bill even though it lacked privacy safeguards, but Luther was heartened somewhat when he got a letter from Clinton agreeing that "consumers should have the right to decide whether their personal financial information can be shared."

Luther had more success on another consumer issue. Amid widespread concerns over Firestone tires that suffered blowouts and resulted in fatal accidents, he helped draft bipartisan legislation to require tire manufacturers to report foreign recalls of their products. "There was sufficient information out there so that these tragedies should never have occurred, and we need to immediately put in place a system that doesn't fail the American consumer again," Luther said after the bill was introduced.

Although he opposes much of the GOP agenda, Luther often works with the Republican majority and with the more conservative members of his own party to achieve legislative goals on issues such as restraining federal spending and revamping welfare.

He favors constitutional amendments mandating a balanced budget and imposing congressional term limits, and he voted for legislation granting the president line-item veto power over spending bills. He also backed GOP-drafted bills to deal more harshly with violent juvenile offenders and to restructure the nation's public housing program.

Despite these occasional votes for Republican-pushed measures, Luther remains a Democrat in good standing, backing his party almost 90 percent of the time. During the 104th Congress, he served as president of the outnumbered freshman Class of 1994, and he became a regional whip in the 106th. He has a seat on the powerful Energy and Commerce Committee.

He will side with more-liberal members of his party on issues such as abortion, gun control, trade and the environment. He has opposed efforts to ban a procedure its opponents call "partial birth" abortion. He took exception to a Republican move in 1996 to repeal the ban on certain semiautomatic assault-style weapons, and he backed gun control initiatives in 1999. Concerned about China's human rights record, Luther voted in 2000 against legislation that granted China permanent normal trade status.

Luther helped found a group of moderate Democrats in 1997 known as the New Democrat Coalition that seeks to find "mainstream, bipartisan solutions." Luther, who has heard Republicans attack him as a "tax-and-spend liberal," proudly points out that the Concord Coalition, a non-partisan, grass-roots organization that advocates fiscal responsibility, has cited him as a repeat member of its fiscal responsibility honor roll. In recent years, he has supported amendments seeking to freeze Pentagon spending at the previous year's levels.

He is well-connected within the Minneapolis legal establishment and is a prodigious fundraiser. His skills impressed a U.S. News & World Report reporter who watched him in action as he "bagged a donation" in less than two minutes. U.S. News reported that Luther has "gotten so good at working the phones that when new Democrats come to the House, party officials ask him to teach them how it's done."

But Luther also supports an overhaul of campaign finance laws. He prefers public financing of campaigns for candidates who agree to abide by voluntary spending limits. He sponsored such a law governing candidates for state office in Minnesota.

Luther came to Washington with scant experience at being part of a legislative minority. He was used to wielding power, developing what was known in St. Paul as the "Luther machine." One of his protégés became majority leader of the Minnesota House. And although he has an affable manner on the campaign trail, he had developed a reputation in the state Senate for sharp elbows and aggressive partisanship.

Shortly after his wife, Darlene, won an election of her own to the state House in 1993, Luther began laying the groundwork for a run for the suburban Twin Cities House seat that had belonged to a Democrat before being seized in 1992 by Republican Rod Grams. The seat opened up in 1994 when Grams announced he would run for the Senate.

Luther faced a difficult campaign. He lost more than 40 percent of the primary vote to a pair of little-known challengers, then weathered a nasty contest against Republican Tad Jude, a former state legislator and county commissioner. By trying to establish a moderate image and emphasizing jobs, crime and health care, Luther bucked a nationwide GOP tide and eked out a victory over Jude by a mere 550 votes out of nearly 227,000 ballots cast.

None of his re-election contests has been easy. He struggled to single-digit victories in both 1998 and 2000 against John Kline, a retired Marine colonel and White House aide under President Reagan.

KEY VOTES

2000

Yes Raise hourly minimum wage by $1 over two years
Yes Halt funding for U.S. mission in Kosovo unless European nations pay more
Yes Provide Medicare benefits to military retirees and their dependents
No Grant China permanent normal trade status
No Phase out estate, gift and trust taxes
No Prohibit implementation of president's national monument designations
No Approve GOP plan to provide prescription drug coverage for Medicare beneficiaries
Yes Increase help for poor nations indebted to international financial institutions

1999

Yes Impose steel import quotas
Yes Kill proposal to take aviation trust funds off budget
No Require background checks on buyers only at gun shows with 10 or more vendors
No Remove barriers among banking, securities and insurance companies
Yes Authorize state grants to hire teachers and reduce class size
Yes Overhaul campaign finance law; ban "soft money" and restrict advocacy advertising
Yes Approve bipartisan plan to increase rights of patients in managed-care health plans

INTEREST GROUPS

	AFL-CIO	ADA	CCUS	ACU
2000	90%	95%	42%	16%
1999	78%	100%	27%	8%
1998	90%	90%	56%	4%
1997	88%	85%	60%	24%

CQ VOTE STUDIES

	PARTY UNITY		PRESIDENTIAL SUPPORT	
	Support	Oppose	Support	Oppose
2000	88%	12%	75%	25%
1999	87%	13%	79%	21%
1998	89%	11%	75%	25%
1997	83%	17%	77%	23%

MINNESOTA 6
Eastern, southern Twin Cities suburbs

The 6th's semicircle of fast-growing Twin Cities suburbs has attracted one of the nation's largest concentrations of young families. Residents in the district's eastern suburbs build "starter castles" and pursue white-collar careers in the Twin Cities or in the growing employment base in the district.

Multiple redistrictings in the 1990s added affluent and Republican western suburbs and then removed them, leaving the 6th a highly competitive district, though the district's four-term Democratic House member, Rep. Luther, has managed to retain his seat.

Blue-collar communities in Anoka County in the north are faithful Democratic-Farmer-Labor Party supporters, as are working-class areas of Dakota County. But their political voice is competing with growing numbers of young professionals, who tend to be socially progressive but fiscally conservative. These newcomers are willing to split their ticket and have been attracted to independent candidates.

More than one-fourth of the district voted for Ross Perot in 1992, and the 6th solidly supported Gov. Jesse Ventura in 1998.

The 6th's economy is diversified and benefits from the presence of medical manufacturers, high-tech research and publishing companies. Northwest Airlines, headquartered in the area since 1952, is the district's economic linchpin, employing more than 20,000 people.

Washington County borders St. Paul on the east and, due to easy city access, these lakefront suburbs make up the state's fastest growing county.

MAJOR INDUSTRY
Corporate administration, air transportation

CITIES
Coon Rapids, 63,479; Eagan, 59,972; Apple Valley, 46,905; Blaine, 46,268

UNUSUAL FEATURES
Radio show host Garrison Keillor born in Anoka.

Rep. Collin C. Peterson (D)

Elected 1990; 6th term

CAPITOL OFFICE
225-2165; fax 225-1593; 2159 Rayburn Bldg. 20515

INTERNET
e-mail: www.house.gov/writerep
web: www.house.gov/collinpeterson

COMMITTEES
Agriculture
Select Intelligence

HOMETOWN
Detroit Lakes

BORN
June 29, 1944, Fargo, N.D.

RELIGION
Lutheran

FAMILY
Divorced; three children

EDUCATION
Moorhead State U., B.A. 1966

MILITARY SERVICE
Minn. National Guard, 1963-69

CAREER
Accountant

POLITICAL HIGHLIGHTS
Minn. Senate, 1977-87; sought Democratic
nomination for U.S. House, 1982; Democratic
nominee for U.S. House, 1984, 1986; sought
Democratic nomination for U.S. House, 1988

ELECTION RESULTS

2000 GENERAL

Collin C. Peterson (D)	185,771	68.7%
Glen Menze (R)	79,175	29.3%
Owen Sivertson (CNSTP)	5,550	2.1%

2000 PRIMARY

Collin C. Peterson (D)	unopposed

1998 GENERAL

Collin C. Peterson (D)	169,907	71.7%
Aleta Edin (R)	66,562	28.1%

PREVIOUS WINNING PERCENTAGES
1996 (68%); 1994 (51%); 1992 (50%); 1990 (54%)

As a founding member of the conservative caucus of House Democrats called the "Blue Dogs," Peterson often parts company with the more liberal members of his party. He draws high marks from both the National Right to Life Committee and the National Rifle Association, and he can sound like a Republican in his blistering attacks on the income tax system. An avid sportsman, he crosses swords with environmentalists over his proposals to expand game hunting.

With the House closely divided between the two parties, Peterson and his fellow Blue Dogs are in a position to play an important role in crafting fiscal policy. "We are the only people willing to work with the Republicans and actually legislate," Peterson once claimed. "The [other] Democrats just trash everything they are trying to do." The Blue Dogs' alternative budgets, respected by many on both sides of the aisle, helped to create momentum for a landmark balanced-budget package that President Clinton and congressional Republicans negotiated in 1997.

Peterson has a history of breaking with his party. In 1999, he was one of only two Democrats to vote against bipartisan legislation granting additional rights to managed-care patients and allowing them to sue their health care plans. Echoing the concerns of some on the right, he told the Minneapolis Star Tribune, "Injecting more lawsuits into the health care system does nothing to improve one's health."

Peterson's name was mentioned as a potential appointee to a high post in the Bush administration but, while he said he genuinely liked Bush — they talked about hunting when Peterson visited the White House early in 2001 — Peterson said he wasn't interested in an administration post, Democratic or Republican. "I'm not very good at taking orders," he told the Star Tribune.

He teamed up with Republican John Linder of Georgia in the 106th Congress to propose abolishing the Internal Revenue Service and replacing federal income and payroll taxes with a 23 percent national sales tax. A former accountant, Peterson blasted the tax code as overly complex, telling the Twin Cities' newspaper, "I can tell you that no one really understands the current tax system."

Peterson also supported conservative attempts to nullify Clinton's executive order prohibiting federal agencies from discriminating against gay people, to prevent the Food and Drug Administration from testing abortion-inducing drugs, and to advance a constitutional amendment on school prayer. He opposed a series of Clinton administration gun control initiatives in 1999, arguing that the government could do a better job of enforcing gun restrictions already in place. "Most of this stuff is just window dressing and politics," he said of the proposals, according to the Star Tribune.

Despite such positions, Peterson is able to maintain backing from traditional Democratic constituencies through his support of labor unions and his work protecting Minnesota farmers as the top Democrat on the Agriculture Committee's Livestock and Horticulture Subcommittee.

Peterson likes to share in the credit for defeating the perennial amendment to the agriculture spending bill to kill the sugar price-support program (the 7th District is home to many sugar beet farmers). But he has been less successful in protecting upper Midwestern dairy farmers from national pricing structures that favor producers in other regions.

A labor supporter, Peterson voted against a 1998 bill that would have curbed union organizing. He tends to follow the labor line on international trade, voting in 2000 against legislation granting China permanent normal trade status. He also opposed Republican moves to allow states to use certain grant funds to help low-income families send their children to private schools.

Peterson is the co-chairman of the Congressional Sportsmen's Caucus. (He told the Star Tribune he has "more dead animals on my wall than anybody in this Congress, except for Don Young," the Alaska Republican.) He stunned a reporter for Outdoor Life magazine (which in 2000 featured him as a friend of the sportsman in its voter guide) by pulling out two guns from the closet in his Capitol Hill office. He drew sharp criticism from environmentalists for pursuing a measure in the 106th Congress to allow states to establish hunting seasons for cormorants, which Peterson blamed for devastating populations of game fish. But he also worked with the Humane Society on a measure to ban the interstate transport of birds for cockfighting.

In an effort to focus attention on a fishing rights dispute, Peterson in 1998 introduced a constitutional amendment to allow part of his district to secede from the United States and be annexed by Manitoba, Canada. The 120-square-mile area, called the Northwest Angle, is held in trust for the Red Lake Band of Chippewa Indians, who took a dim view of the proposal. Peterson ended up proffering an apology to the Chippewas for acting without their consent or input. The proposed amendment gained a lot of publicity but never saw official action.

A pilot and a musician, Peterson was a trombonist in the Army National Guard band for six years and has made quite a name for himself in various appearances as a country-rock guitarist and singer. He often appears at fundraising events, including a joint appearance with country singer Willie Nelson at a Farm Aid concert.

Before his election to the House, Peterson served 10 years in the Minnesota Senate and owned an accounting firm. He ran for the House unsuccessfully four times — receiving the Democratic nomination in 1984 and 1986 and losing out to another Democrat in 1982 and 1988.

After the four setbacks, his political image was in disrepair. But he decided to run again in 1990 when the Republican incumbent, Arlan Stangeland, faced criticism over using his House credit card to charge several calls to or from the phone of a female Virginia lobbyist. Peterson was careful to present himself as a "new Collin Peterson," more mellow than in his previous campaigns, and he took 54 percent of the vote to oust Stangeland. After scratching out close re-election victories in 1992 and 1994, Peterson has since won easily.

KEY VOTES

2000
Yes Raise hourly minimum wage by $1 over two years
Yes Halt funding for U.S. mission in Kosovo unless European nations pay more
Yes Provide Medicare benefits to military retirees and their dependents
No Grant China permanent normal trade status
Yes Phase out estate, gift and trust taxes
Yes Prohibit implementation of president's national monument designations
Yes Approve GOP plan to provide prescription drug coverage for Medicare beneficiaries
Yes Increase help for poor nations indebted to international financial institutions

1999
Yes Impose steel import quotas
No Kill proposal to take aviation trust funds off budget
No Require background checks on buyers only at gun shows with 10 or more vendors
No Remove barriers among banking, securities and insurance companies
Yes Authorize state grants to hire teachers and reduce class size
No Overhaul campaign finance law; ban "soft money" and restrict advocacy advertising
No Approve bipartisan plan to increase rights of patients in managed-care health plans

INTEREST GROUPS

	AFL-CIO	ADA	CCUS	ACU
2000	60%	60%	52%	32%
1999	67%	40%	72%	52%
1998	80%	60%	56%	56%
1997	88%	65%	70%	52%

CQ VOTE STUDIES

	PARTY UNITY		PRESIDENTIAL SUPPORT	
	Support	Oppose	Support	Oppose
2000	60%	40%	49%	51%
1999	51%	49%	39%	61%
1998	54%	46%	55%	45%
1997	61%	39%	51%	49%

MINNESOTA 7
Northwest – Moorhead; part of St. Cloud

The vast 7th, which takes in the northwest quadrant of the state, includes the prairie wheat fields along the Red River and the hills, forests and lakes in the middle of the state. The district's major population center, St. Cloud, is former granite quarrying city and one of the fastest growing cities in the state. Apart from St. Cloud and Moorhead, a sister city to Fargo, N.D., there are few population centers. Farmers grow sugar beets around Moorhead in the Red River Valley, which has some of the 7th's most fertile farmland.

The Red River flood in 1997 capped nearly a decade of agricultural struggle in the rural northwestern third of Minnesota. Floods, drought, crop disease, diminishing federal safety nets and crop devaluation fatigued an already struggling economy. Although the 7th's light manufacturing and community colleges helped stabilize the situation, tourism and American Indian reservation gaming suffered when farmers could no longer afford the area's lake vacations or video slot machines.

Although a Democrat has held the congressional seat since 1990, the 7th has been one of the state's most politically marginal districts. In 1992 and '96 presidential elections, the district gave the edge to Bill Clinton. But in 2000, President Bush handily won the district by almost 15 percentage points. Residents tend to be socially conservative and fiscally moderate. The district's most conservative voters traditionally lived along the state's western border and within predominantly Catholic Stearns County, while St. Cloud has served as home to a mix of blue-collar Democrats and white-collar Republicans.

MAJOR INDUSTRY
Agriculture, light manufacturing, tourism, timber

CITIES
St. Cloud, 58,099; Moorhead, 33,395; Fergus Falls, 14,305

UNUSUAL FEATURES
Writer Sinclair Lewis, the first American to win the Nobel Prize for Literature, grew up in Sauk Centre, 40 miles northwest of St. Cloud; Little Falls was the boyhood home of aviator Charles Lindbergh.

Rep. James L. Oberstar (D)

Elected 1974; 14th term

CAPITOL OFFICE
225-6211; fax 225-0699; 2365 Rayburn Bldg. 20515

INTERNET
e-mail: www.house.gov/writerep
web: www.house.gov/oberstar

COMMITTEES
Transportation & Infrastructure - ranking member

HOMETOWN
Chisholm

BORN
Sept. 10, 1934, Chisholm, Minn.

RELIGION
Roman Catholic

FAMILY
Wife, Jean Oberstar; six children

EDUCATION
College of St. Thomas, B.A. 1956; College of
Europe (Bruges, Belgium), M.A. 1957

CAREER
Language teacher; congressional aide

POLITICAL HIGHLIGHTS
Sought Democratic nomination for U.S. Senate,
1984

ELECTION RESULTS

2000 GENERAL

James L. Oberstar (D)	210,094	67.9%
Robert Lemen (R)	79,890	25.8%
Mike Darling (I)	19,667	6.4%

2000 PRIMARY

James L. Oberstar (D)	unopposed

1998 GENERAL

James L. Oberstar (D)	173,734	66.0%
Jerry Shuster (R)	69,667	26.5%
Stan "The Man" Estes (REF)	15,137	5.7%
Larry Fuhol (LIBERT)	4,558	1.7%

PREVIOUS WINNING PERCENTAGES
1996 (67%); 1994 (66%); 1992 (59%); 1990 (73%);
1988 (75%); 1986 (73%); 1984 (67%); 1982 (77%);
1980 (70%); 1978 (87%); 1976 (100%); 1974 (62%)

Though he grew up in a blue-collar mining family in Minnesota's Iron Range, Oberstar often comes across as a policy wonk, waxing on about the elegance of his favorite legislative language. While he is a fierce ally of union causes, he also is one of the few congressmen who can articulate congressional policies in a couple of foreign languages, making him a favorite of the foreign press corps. And he has one of the longest records of service at the Capitol among the House Democrats, having spent 11 years as a top congressional aide before being elected in his own right in 1974.

All that experience has made him a savvy, hands-on legislator. His background, passions and style are well-suited to the Transportation and Infrastructure Committee, where he has been the ranking Democrat since 1995.

Oberstar's New Deal Democrat philosophy leads him to believe in the virtue of public works, and he was instrumental in the crafting of the massive 1998 law that dictated a historic level of federal investment in roads and mass transit. "That means highways. That means improvements. That means benefits to every congressional district in the country," he said at the time.

Oberstar and the committee's Republican chairman, Bud Shuster of Pennsylvania, worked tirelessly to persuade their colleagues to take both the Airport and Airway Trust Fund and the Highway Trust Fund "off-budget," meaning the money could only be spent on transportation and would not be counted toward a federal surplus or deficit. They did not succeed, but both funds are now protected — airline ticket tax revenue must be spent on aviation, motor fuel taxes on highway and transit programs.

Their work together on that issue was emblematic of their long-running partnership, which came to an end in 2001 when GOP term limit rules forced Shuster to step down as chairman. The panel has a history of bipartisanship extending back to the time Democrats were in control. (However, the new chairman, Republican Don Young of Alaska, is known for his aggressively partisan style.)

Oberstar's friendship with Shuster was evident when the powerful chairman was rebuked by the House ethics committee in 2000 for his relationship with a lobbyist. Oberstar took to the House floor to defend his colleague with near obsequiousness. "The gentleman has led the committee throughout all this ordeal with dignity and effectiveness," Oberstar said. "I know how pained the gentleman is over this report."

Oberstar often sounds verbose, expanding in great detail on a favorite congressional story or the beauty of certain legislation enacted in the past. Supporters say this is a result of Oberstar's desire to fully examine the substance of an issue so he can find common ground with opponents.

The Minnesota lawmaker has most frequently parted company with Republicans on the Transportation panel over labor issues. His father was an iron ore miner and union official who worked in both underground mines and open pits, where Oberstar labored as a teenager. His mother worked in a shirt factory to supplement the family's income.

While a loyal Democrat, Oberstar has squabbled with the liberal wing of the Democratic Party on the issues of abortion and gun owners' rights. A devout Roman Catholic, he proposed a constitutional amendment in the 105th Congress to ban abortions except in cases where the woman's life was in danger. But Oberstar refuses to get cozy with conservative Republican colleagues on the issue. "They call themselves the pro-life party, but that's not true," he said. "They don't support what is needed for the continuum of life — food stamps, the women and infant feeding program — for these same women they purport to care so much about."

Oberstar is also an advocate of adoption, as his oldest child was adopted. He has pushed for more federal funding for breast cancer research and education. His first wife died in 1991 after an eight-year battle with the disease, and he has since married a woman who had lost her first husband to cancer.

He generally sides with Democrats in fighting Republican efforts to scale back environmental protection laws — including the superfund hazardous waste cleanup program, and air and water quality laws — but Oberstar will oppose environmental groups if their positions clash with the interests of his constituents.

In 1998, for example, he strenuously opposed efforts to cut federal aid for construction of logging roads on federal lands, which environmentalists say damages forest ecosystems. Expressing frustration with urban interests that force policies that might hurt rural economies, Oberstar said, "This is not an issue between corporate giants and little guys. This is silk stocking environmentalists against us rural hicks from the sticks, and I am fed up with it."

A dedicated bicyclist who tries to ride regularly, Oberstar included in the 1998 highway law numerous provisions to encourage biking and enhance bicycle safety and education. In the 1991 highway law, he won an authorization of federal funds to convert abandoned railways into recreational bike paths.

Oberstar takes delight in demonstrating his facility with foreign languages, including French and Creole, which he taught to U.S. Navy personnel in Haiti in the early 1960s before coming to Washington. The congressman, who has a graduate degree from the College of Europe in Brussels, also speaks some Spanish, Italian, Slovenian and Serbo-Croatian.

Republicans have never caused Oberstar much trouble since he took over in the overwhelmingly Democratic 8th District in 1974, succeeding his mentor, Democratic Rep. John A. Blatnik. As an aide to Blatnik, the chairman of the Public Works and Transportation Committee, Oberstar learned how to bring Duluth and the Iron Range its share of federal public works. Blatnik was not shy about earmarking funds for projects to benefit individual members' districts.

As a congressman, Oberstar defended the practice. "Why should we accept that the center of all wisdom is in the state capital with the state Department of Transportation? Sometimes they don't divide money fairly. They tend to favor urban areas." Oberstar once said.

KEY VOTES

2000

Yes Raise hourly minimum wage by $1 over two years
No   Halt funding for U.S. mission in Kosovo unless European nations pay more
Yes Provide Medicare benefits to military retirees and their dependents
No   Grant China permanent normal trade status
No   Phase out estate, gift and trust taxes
No   Prohibit implementation of president's national monument designations
No   Approve GOP plan to provide prescription drug coverage for Medicare beneficiaries
Yes Increase help for poor nations indebted to international financial institutions

1999

Yes Impose steel import quotas
No   Kill proposal to take aviation trust funds off budget
No   Require background checks on buyers only at gun shows with 10 or more vendors
Yes Remove barriers among banking, securities and insurance companies
Yes Authorize state grants to hire teachers and reduce class size
Yes Overhaul campaign finance law; ban "soft money" and restrict advocacy advertising
Yes Approve bipartisan plan to increase rights of patients in managed-care health plans

INTEREST GROUPS

	AFL-CIO	ADA	CCUS	ACU
2000	100%	75%	25%	8%
1999	88%	75%	23%	12%
1998	100%	95%	24%	13%
1997	100%	80%	40%	17%

CQ VOTE STUDIES

	PARTY UNITY		PRESIDENTIAL SUPPORT	
	Support	Oppose	Support	Oppose
2000	92%	8%	80%	20%
1999	88%	12%	73%	27%
1998	90%	10%	85%	15%
1997	82%	18%	64%	36%

MINNESOTA 8

Northeast — Iron Range; Duluth

The expansive 8th covers about 26,000 square miles, encompassing Minnesota's entire northeastern quadrant. The mostly rural district stretches across land that includes flat farmland, bluffs and lakes. Its largest city, Duluth, is the shipping point for much of the grain from the Plains states.

Blue-collar Iron Range workers with strong ties to labor cement the 8th's long affiliation with the Democratic-Farmer-Labor Party. The 8th has not sent a Republican to Congress since 1945.

Tribulations of the steel and auto industries hurt the 8th in the 1980s, and populations continued to decline slightly in the 1990s. Increased mining productivity and the arrival of the aviation industry – including a Northwest Airlines maintenance base in shipping center Duluth – have helped the economy rebound.

The southern end of the district grew in the 1990s by attracting Twin Cities commuters. These residents are willing to stray from the 8th's solid DFL stance, more readily offering support to independent candidates. Swedes, Norwegians, Germans and American Indians add some diversity to the district, and American Indians enliven the economy with casinos. Huge tracts of the district's land are designated as state and national forests.

MAJOR INDUSTRY
Mining, timber, aviation, agriculture

CITIES
Duluth, 80,980; Hibbing, 17,305; Elk River, 16,975

UNUSUAL FEATURES
Actress Judy Garland from Grand Rapids; Singer Bob Dylan and former Boston Celtics basketball player Kevin McHale grew up in Hibbing; The nation's only gas station designed by Frank Lloyd Wright located in Cloque; World's largest hockey stick adorns Eveleth.

Gov. Ronnie Musgrove (D)

First elected: 2000
Length of term: 4 years
Term expires: 1/04
Salary: $101,800
Phone: (601) 359-3150
Hometown: Batesville
Born: July 29, 1956; Tocowa, Miss.
Religion: Baptist
Family: Wife, Melanie Musgrove; two children
Education: Northwest Mississippi Community College, A.A. 1976; U. of Mississippi, B.S. 1978; J.D. 1981
Career: Lawyer
Political highlights: Miss. Senate, 1988-96; lieutenant governor, 1996-2000;

Election results:

1999 GENERAL*

Ronnie Musgrove (D)	379,034	49.6%
Mike Parker (R)	370,691	48.5%

*Under the state constitution, since neither candidate received both a majority of popular votes and a majority of the 122 state House districts, the Mississippi House voted to elect Musgrove on Jan. 4, 2000.

Lt. Gov. Amy Tuck (D)

First elected: 1999
Length of term: 4 years
Term expires: 1/04
Salary: $60,000
Phone: (601) 359-3200

STATE LEGISLATURE

Legislature: Meets January-April
House: 122 members, 4-year terms
2001 breakdown: 33R, 86D, 3I; 106 men, 16 women
Salary: $10,000/year; $1,500/month out of session; $85/day in session; expenses during session
Phone: (601) 359-3360
Senate: 52 members, 4-year terms
2001 breakdown: 18R, 34D; 46 men, 6 women
Salary: $10,000/year; $1,500/month out of session; $85/day in session; expenses during session
Phone: (601) 359-3202

STATE TERM LIMITS

Governor: 2 terms
Senate: No
House: No

URBAN STATISTICS

CITY	POPULATION
Jackson	180,664
Gulfport	64,679
Hattiesburg	49,233
Biloxi	47,759
Greenville	41,731

REGISTERED VOTERS

Voters do not register by party.

POPULATION

2000 population	2,844,658
1990 population	2,573,216
Percent change	+10.5%
Rank among states	31
Median age	33.2
Born in state	77%
Foreign born	10%
Urban/rural	47%/53%
Crime rate	469/100,000
Poverty level	17.6%
Federal workers	26,375
Military	35,509

REAPPORTIONMENT

Mississippi lost one House seat in reapportionment, dropping from five districts to four. The state legislature will draw new district lines in 2001.

MISCELLANEOUS

Web: www.state.ms.us
Capital: Jackson
Land area: 46,914 sq. miles
 Rank among states: 31
STATE ELECTION OFFICIAL
(601) 359-6357
DEMOCRATIC HEADQUARTERS
(601) 969-2913
REPUBLICAN HEADQUARTERS
(601) 948-5191

District Statistics

DIST.	2000 D	2000 R	GREEN	1996 D	1996 R	REF	1992 D	1992 R	I	WHT	BLK	ASIAN	HISP	HOUSEHOLD INCOME	OVER 65+	UNDER 18	COLLEGE EDUCATION
1	38%	60%	1%	42%	49%	7%	42%	50%	9%	77%	23%	0%	0%	$20,867	13%	27%	11%
2	59	39	0	62	34	3	58	37	5	37	63	0	0	$15,530	13	33	13
3	33	66	1	36	58	5	34	58	8	67	31	0	0	$21,625	12	28	16
4	44	54	1	46	48	5	41	51	8	59	41	0	0	$20,234	13	28	18
5	32	66	1	35	56	8	32	54	14	78	20	1	1	$21,702	11	28	15
STATE	41	58	1	44	49	6	41	50	9	63	36	1	1	$20,136	12	29	15

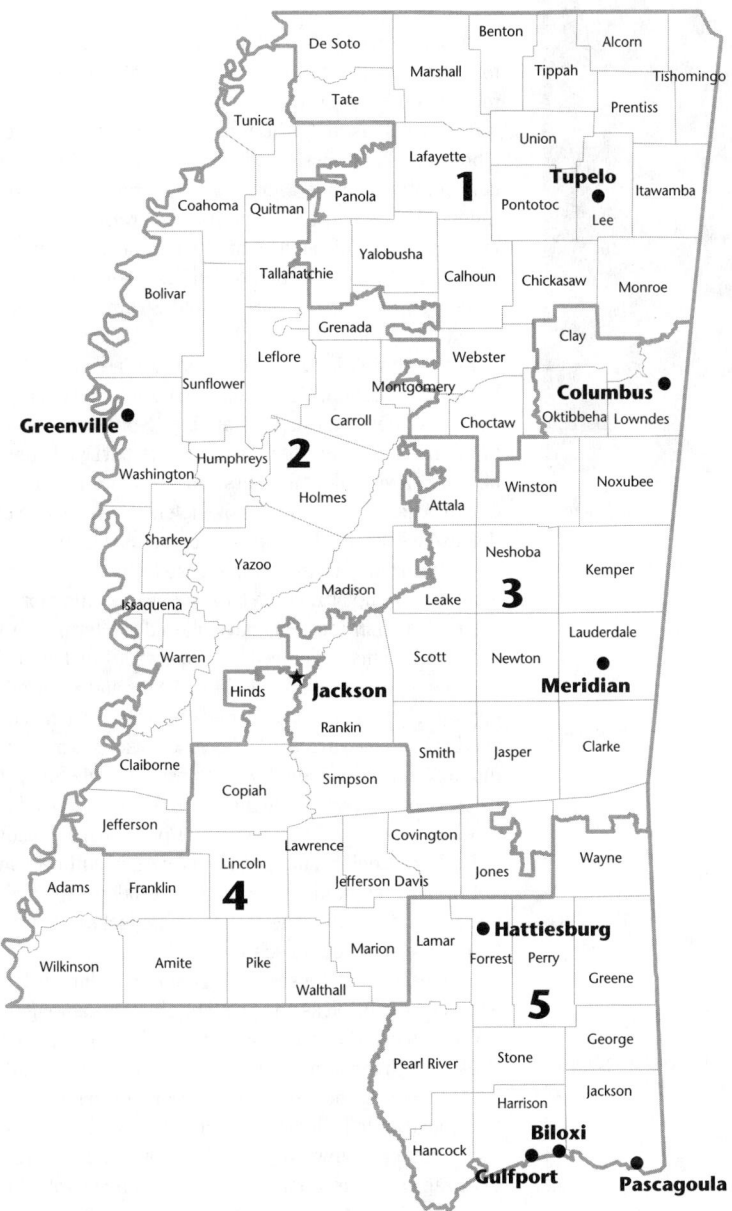

Sen. Thad Cochran (R)

CAPITOL OFFICE
224-5054; fax 224-9450; 326 Russell Bldg. 20510

INTERNET
e-mail: senator@cochran.senate.gov
web: cochran.senate.gov

COMMITTEES
Agriculture, Nutrition & Forestry
Appropriations
 (Agriculture, Rural Development & Related
 Agencies - chairman)
Governmental Affairs
 (International Security, Proliferation & Federal
 Services - chairman)
Rules & Administration
Joint Library
Joint Printing

HOMETOWN
Jackson

BORN
Dec. 7, 1937, Pontotoc, Miss.

RELIGION
Baptist

FAMILY
Wife, Rose Cochran; two children

EDUCATION
U. of Mississippi, B.A. 1959; Trinity College (U. of
Dublin, Ireland), attended 1963-64; U. of
Mississippi, J.D. 1965

MILITARY SERVICE
Navy, 1959-61

CAREER
Lawyer

POLITICAL HIGHLIGHTS
U.S. House, 1973-78

ELECTION RESULTS

1996 GENERAL

Thad Cochran (R)	624,154	71.0%
James W. "Bootie" Hunt (D)	240,647	27.4%

1996 PRIMARY

Thad Cochran (R)	138,813	95.3%
Richard O'Hara (R)	6,762	4.7%

PREVIOUS WINNING PERCENTAGES
1990 (100%); 1984 (61%); 1978 (45%); 1976 House
Election (76%); 1974 House Election (70%); 1972
House Election (48%)

Elected 1978; 4th term

Urbane, thoughtful and accessible, Cochran, with his courtly Southern manner, stands out in the modern Senate, where sharp, partisan rhetoric more often holds sway.

The soft-spoken Cochran has sometimes stepped back while his sharp-elbowed, fellow Mississippian, Trent Lott, and other, younger Republican conservatives bring their more confrontational style to the chamber. Indeed, Lott, Cochran's longtime rival within the state party, easily rolled over his senior colleague in the 1996 contest for Senate majority leader. And Cochran is the most-senior Republican senator without a committee chairmanship — other than 98-year-old Strom Thurmond, S.C., who surrendered the Armed Services chair at the start of the 106th Congress.

But Cochran's influence in the Senate and among Republicans should not be underestimated. He has played a pivotal role in agriculture policy since 1981 as either chairman or ranking Republican of the Agriculture Appropriations Subcommittee. He also has parlayed his chairmanship of an obscure Governmental Affairs subcommittee into leadership of the drive to deploy a nationwide anti-missile defense system, one of the signature GOP defense issues. Eschewing confrontation, which had not worked, Cochran won by carefully laying out the case for missile defense and then drafting a bill that would attract the largest possible number of Democrats.

And Cochran may also have altered the terms of the campaign finance debate when he announced in January 2001 that he had switched sides and would support an overhaul bill that Lott and most other Republicans had opposed. He said he was worried about the influence unregulated spending was having on lawmakers. "It became obvious to me that the influence of 'soft money' and independent groups was overwhelming the efforts of candidates," Cochran said. "Soft money" refers to unlimited contributions that are given to national political parties for party-building activities and issue ads.

In short, Cochran has acquired a certain authority in the Senate, though not of the magnitude that might have been expected from this Ole Miss honor student who made partner in his Jackson law firm when he was less than three years out of school.

Elected to the House in the Nixon landslide of 1972, Cochran quickly established himself as one of the bright lights among the new breed of GOP conservatives who were dissolving the Democrats' "Solid South." But while President Nixon's vaunted "Southern Strategy" included a none-too-subtle pitch to whites perturbed by the empowerment of African-Americans, Cochran avoided alienating blacks. Though his electoral base was the district's younger, upwardly mobile, urban and suburban white population, Cochran made an effort to maintain contact with the black community, which made up 43 percent of his constituency.

Yet Cochran is no liberal. In 1990, he was able to oust John H. Chafee of Rhode Island as secretary of the Senate Republican Conference — the third-ranking slot in the Senate GOP hierarchy — because the group's increasingly numerous conservatives were unhappy with Chafee's defection on such issues as allowing school prayer, banning flag desecration and adding a balanced-budget amendment to the Constitution, all of which Cochran supported.

Nor is Cochran loath to draw partisan lines. After Congress approved the use of military force against Iraq in January 1991, Cochran noted that most Democrats had voted "to the left of the United Nations — that's something the voters are going to have to consider." And during the Senate's trial of President Clinton in early 1999, Cochran favored having Monica Lewinsky testify before the chamber and voted to find Clinton guilty of both charges on which he had been impeached.

Still, Cochran's approach has been largely conciliatory as he focuses on the more-pragmatic business of legislating. He has plied his skills in the less-exotic business of parceling out federal money to Mississippi, particularly for agriculture programs. His easygoing manner has served him well in mediating the frequent conflicts between commodity interests and made him a natural for the collegial, bipartisan culture of the Appropriations Committee.

While still satisfying his colleagues from the Wheat Belt states of the Northern Plains and other regions, Cochran has fought for programs important to the South, including cotton, rice, peanuts and sugar. In 1999, for instance, he put into law a program supported by large-scale cotton growers that would let the nation's 2,600 largest farms circumvent the usual $150,000-per-producer cap on federal crop subsidies.

The rivalry between Cochran and Lott probably was inevitable, given that both are smart, attractive politicians in the same party in a relatively small state and that they are near contemporaries (Lott is four years younger). Cochran got to the Senate first, but Lott leapfrogged him in November 1994 by taking on, and beating, Alan K. Simpson of Wyoming for the second-ranking GOP job of whip. When Republican leader Bob Dole of Kansas resigned from the Senate in 1996 to run for president, Lott — who had a long head start in rounding up commitments of support for the top slot — easily bested Cochran, winning 44-8.

At that point, Cochran's Senate career seemed becalmed. Coincidentally, so did the 13-year-old, Republican-led effort to deploy an anti-missile defense system. At the start of 1997, Cochran took over the Governmental Affairs Subcommittee on International Security, Proliferation and Federal Services and set out to jump-start the anti-missile campaign. Cochran decided to lay out in detail the case for a missile defense system, holding 11 hearings during the year, and then shepherded to passage a bill declaring it to be national policy to deploy a nationwide defense as soon as technologically feasible.

Significantly, Cochran breaks ranks with conservative hard-liners on the next step in missile defense. If the country were forced to choose between deployment and continued observance of the ABM Treaty, he would deploy. But he favors trying to negotiate with Moscow changes in the treaty that would allow for deployment.

Cochran had been active in local party politics during his law career and was a key state figure in the 1968 presidential campaign of Richard M. Nixon. In 1972, when the retirement of Democratic Rep. Charles R. Griffin left the 4th District open, Cochran ran and won a narrow victory, thanks in large measure to the presence of a black independent candidate who siphoned off votes from the Democratic nominee.

After two easy House re-election wins, Cochran moved up to the Senate in 1978, becoming Mississippi's first Republican senator in a century, and succeeding Democrat James O. Eastland, who retired after 36 years. Capturing 45 percent of the vote, Cochran defeated Democrat Maurice Dantin and independent Charles Evers, who drew the black vote away from Dantin.

But in 1984, Cochran did not have to rely on someone taking the black vote away from the Democratic candidate. He won his second Senate term in a two-man race by sweeping all but a handful of Mississippi's 82 counties, including nearly half of those with black-majority populations. He was unopposed in 1990 (at a time when Democrats held all the top state offices and all five of Mississippi's House seats), and he cruised to victory in 1996 with 71 percent.

KEY VOTES

2000
Yes Overhaul bankruptcy law and increase minimum wage
Yes Limit fiscal 2001 discretionary spending to $600.3 billion
Yes Override veto on nuclear waste disposal at Yucca Mountain site in Nevada
Yes Oppose effort to terminate Kosovo mission
No Include gender, sexual orientation and disability in federal hate crime protections
Yes Approve GOP plan to restrict use of genetic information by health insurers
Yes Kill amendment delaying implementation of an anti-missile defense system
Yes Cut taxes for married couples
Yes Grant China permanent normal trade status

1999
Yes Remove President Clinton from office for obstruction of justice
Yes Kill amendment authorizing state grants to hire teachers and reduce class size
No Require criminal background checks for purchases at gun shows
Yes Approve GOP proposal to increase rights of patients in managed-care health plans
No Block effort to allow farm and medicine exports to Cuba
No Allow study of tougher automobile fuel efficiency standards
No Ratify nuclear weapons testing treaty
No Prohibit national political parties from collecting "soft money" donations
Yes Remove barriers among banking, securities and insurance companies

INTEREST GROUPS

	AFL-CIO	ADA	CCUS	ACU
2000	0%	0%	100%	92%
1999	0%	0%	88%	84%
1998	0%	0%	100%	76%
1997	0%	15%	90%	56%
1996	0%	5%	91%	94%
1995	8%	0%	95%	83%
1994	13%	10%	90%	92%
1993	9%	0%	91%	84%
1992	17%	10%	100%	85%
1991	25%	5%	80%	76%

CQ VOTE STUDIES

	PARTY UNITY		PRESIDENTIAL SUPPORT	
	Support	Oppose	Support	Oppose
2000	98%	2%	45%	55%
1999	94%	6%	38%	62%
1998	86%	14%	53%	47%
1997	82%	18%	68%	32%
1996	93%	7%	40%	60%
1995	93%	7%	34%	66%
1994	82%	18%	45%	55%
1993	91%	9%	26%	74%
1992	94%	6%	84%	16%
1991	90%	10%	91%	9%

Sen. Trent Lott (R)

CAPITOL OFFICE
224-6253; fax 224-2262; 487 Russell Bldg. 20510

INTERNET
e-mail: senatorlott@lott.senate.gov
web: lott.senate.gov

COMMITTEES
Commerce, Science & Transportation
Finance
Rules & Administration

HOMETOWN
Pascagoula

BORN
Oct. 9, 1941, Grenada County, Miss.

RELIGION
Baptist

FAMILY
Wife, Patricia Elizabeth Lott; two children

EDUCATION
U. of Mississippi, B.P.A. 1963, J.D. 1967

CAREER
Lawyer; congressional aide

POLITICAL HIGHLIGHTS
U.S. House, 1973-89

ELECTION RESULTS

2000 GENERAL

Trent Lott (R)	654,941	65.9%
Troy Brown (D)	314,090	31.6%

2000 PRIMARY

Trent Lott (R)	unopposed

PREVIOUS WINNING PERCENTAGES
1994 (69%); 1988 (54%); 1986 House Election (82%); 1984 House Election (85%); 1982 House Election (79%); 1980 House Election (74%); 1978 House Election (100%); 1976 House Election (68%); 1974 House Election (73%); 1972 House Election (55%)

Elected 1988; 3rd term

Since Lott had difficulty running the Senate with 55 Republican votes in the 106th Congress, it is no surprise that foe and friend alike question how he will manage with only 50 during the 107th.

Only the tie-breaking vote of Vice President Dick Cheney keeps Lott as the majority leader in 2001, after an election that was bittersweet for the Mississippian. He now has a Republican president to work with, but several close colleagues departed, some against their will. Lott's consigliere Slade Gorton of Washington lost a gut-wrenching race, and his friend and confidant Connie Mack of Florida has retired.

The evenly divided Senate yielded by those losses creates a seemingly impossible situation for Lott, who earned mixed grades at best for his stewardship of the body during the 106th Congress. He and his fellow Republicans acted as if they were running out the clock on a lame-duck president and counting down to the election. More often than not, Lott appeared more interested in shielding vulnerable incumbents from having to cast difficult votes than in passing legislation to burnish the record of the GOP Congress. To that end, he took frequent procedural steps that denied any senator the ability to offer amendments in the freewheeling fashion of the past. Gridlock ensued.

Lott began the 107th in only nominal control of the Senate. With several unreliable votes among Republican moderates, he faces the prospect of losing floor votes on topics such as patients' rights, gun control and education. And his GOP senatorial enemy, John McCain of Arizona, forced a campaign finance overhaul bill to the floor before any of President Bush's major proposals.

Lott unnerved many Republicans from the start by negotiating a Senate power-sharing agreement that gave Democrats equally divided committee ratios and equal staff resources and office space. Most Republican committee chairmen were unhappy with the arrangement, but Lott wanted to avoid a messy floor fight over inside-the-Senate issues just as Bush assumed office. "Different times call for different approaches," Lott said. "We have recognized that, and we're prepared to deal with that."

Lott is a study in contrasts. Generally genial and articulate, he can get into political hot water with occasional snappishness and off-the-cuff quips. The son of a shipyard worker, he favors tightly knotted silk ties and rarely allows a single hair out of place. A courtly Southerner, he talks faster than urban colleagues from the North. A committed conservative, he delights in a well-cut deal with Democrats. And not wanting to "waste time in useless gridlock," he prefers "cooperation on both sides of the aisle" — as long as it yields results.

Lott's relationship with President Clinton was never very good, and it deteriorated significantly after the 1997 bipartisan budget deal that Lott helped negotiate. But for Bush to advance his agenda, Lott must clearly make the Senate floor a place more amenable to debate. That means the prospect of losing some floor votes and the likelihood that his control over the proceedings will sometimes be broken. That would require a fundamental attitude adjustment for Lott, whose desire for order is legendary.

At the same time, his penchant for ad hoc decision-making has frustrated colleagues, who say he often makes important decisions with little consultation. That style has frayed some relationships, especially with GOP Whip Don Nickles of Oklahoma, who considered making a bid for majority leader when Lott was first elected to the job, in 1996, and may do so again.

With control of the chamber so tenuous, Lott will have to do much more consulting and consensus-building. Such an approach worked for him in 1999 during the greatest test of his career. In leading the Senate through Clinton's impeachment trial, he was credited with threading a difficult course between conservative Republicans and Democrats, tamping down the kind of lasting enmity that might have poisoned relations in the 106th Congress.

Lott came to the Senate in 1989 as part of a new and more aggressive breed, impatient with the clubby, bipartisan ways of the old Senate. His years as majority leader have been a constant struggle between his desire for orderly accomplishment and his fealty to conservatism. The guardians of the right have not always been pleased with the balance Lott has struck, such as his agreement to clear a catchall bill at the end of the 105th Congress that increased spending by billions of dollars and failed to cut taxes. When he endorsed ratification in 1997 of a treaty to ban the production and use of chemical weapons, Free Congress Foundation President Paul M. Weyrich blasted him as a "doormat for Bill Clinton."

He is often at odds with the chamber's free-spending appropriators. In 2000, he single-handedly blocked floor action on a $13 billion supplemental spending bill, saying it was too bloated. His victory was temporary; most of the legislation became law in piecemeal fashion as part of the regular appropriations bills.

Lott had the support of GOP conservatives in his 1996 campaign to become majority leader when Bob Dole of Kansas resigned to run for president. Lott cast Dole's departure as a chance for a more aggressive style of leadership. His opponent, fellow Mississippian Thad Cochran, presented it as an opportunity for GOP senators to vote against shrill politics and to rebuild public support of Congress. Lott won, 44-8.

But once he became majority leader, Lott worked with Democrats in the 104th Congress to help enact bills overhauling welfare, protecting people from losing their health insurance, improving the nation's drinking water systems and raising the minimum wage. "He probably would not like me to say this, but he's a pragmatist at heart," Minority Leader Tom Daschle said of Lott at the end of 1997.

While Lott and Daschle go out of their way to try to display a generally cooperative relationship, they often get frustrated with each other. Many times Lott cannot get GOP conservatives to agree with deals he has floated, Daschle complains; Lott makes the same complaints about Daschle and the liberals. But reaching agreement on the 50-50 power-sharing deal helped cement their relationship at the beginning of the 107th.

Lott did not become a Republican until the eve of his first House campaign, in 1972. He had come to Washington in 1968 as top aide to House Rules Committee Chairman William M. Colmer, D-Miss. When Colmer retired four years later, Lott filed for the GOP primary, saying he was "tired of the Muskies and the Kennedys and the Humphreys and the whole lot." Running that fall against Democrat Ben Stone, chairman of the state Senate Banking Committee, Lott captured 55 percent of the vote. In seven House re-election campaigns, he never failed to take at least two-thirds of the vote.

In the House, Lott was a key GOP strategist, first on the Rules Committee and, starting in 1981, as the first Republican whip ever from the deep South.

In 1988, Lott defeated Democratic Rep. Wayne Dowdy with 54 percent to win the Senate seat left open by the retirement of Democrat John C. Stennis. When the GOP won control of the Senate in 1994, Lott was elected party whip, 27-26, over Alan K. Simpson of Wyoming; Lott had promised Simpson before the election that he would not mount such a challenge.

KEY VOTES

2000

Yes	Overhaul bankruptcy law and increase minimum wage
Yes	Limit fiscal 2001 discretionary spending to $600.3 billion
No	Override veto on nuclear waste disposal at Yucca Mountain site in Nevada
No	Oppose effort to terminate Kosovo mission
No	Include gender, sexual orientation and disability in federal hate crime protections
Yes	Approve GOP plan to restrict use of genetic information by health insurers
Yes	Kill amendment delaying implementation of an anti-missile defense system
Yes	Cut taxes for married couples
Yes	Grant China permanent normal trade status

1999

Yes	Remove President Clinton from office for obstruction of justice
Yes	Kill amendment authorizing state grants to hire teachers and reduce class size
No	Require criminal background checks for purchases at gun shows
Yes	Approve GOP proposal to increase rights of patients in managed-care health plans
Yes	Block effort to allow farm and medicine exports to Cuba
No	Allow study of tougher automobile fuel efficiency standards
No	Ratify nuclear weapons testing treaty
No	Prohibit national political parties from collecting "soft money" donations
Yes	Remove barriers among banking, securities and insurance companies

INTEREST GROUPS

	AFL-CIO	ADA	CCUS	ACU
2000	0%	5%	93%	100%
1999	0%	0%	82%	96%
1998	0%	0%	94%	92%
1997	0%	5%	90%	72%
1996	0%	5%	85%	100%
1995	0%	0%	100%	96%
1994	0%	5%	90%	100%
1993	9%	5%	100%	92%
1992	17%	10%	90%	100%
1991	27%	5%	78%	86%

CQ VOTE STUDIES

	PARTY UNITY		PRESIDENTIAL SUPPORT	
	Support	Oppose	Support	Oppose
2000	98%	2%	45%	55%
1999	97%	3%	32%	68%
1998	96%	4%	39%	61%
1997	94%	6%	56%	44%
1996	97%	3%	34%	66%
1995	98%	2%	23%	77%
1994	97%	3%	40%	60%
1993	96%	4%	20%	80%
1992	96%	4%	83%	17%
1991	93%	7%	90%	10%

Rep. Roger Wicker (R)

CAPITOL OFFICE
225-4306; fax 225-3549; 206 Cannon Bldg. 20515

INTERNET
e-mail: roger.wicker@mail.house.gov
web: www.house.gov/wicker

COMMITTEES
Appropriations

HOMETOWN
Tupelo

BORN
July 5, 1951, Pontotoc, Miss.

RELIGION
Southern Baptist

FAMILY
Wife, Gayle Wicker; three children

EDUCATION
U. of Mississippi, B.A. 1973, J.D. 1975

MILITARY SERVICE
Air Force, 1976-80; Air Force Reserve, 1980-present

CAREER
County public defender; lawyer; congressional aide

POLITICAL HIGHLIGHTS
Miss. Senate, 1988-94

ELECTION RESULTS

2000 GENERAL

Roger Wicker (R)	145,967	69.8%
Joey Grist (D)	59,763	28.6%
Chris Lawrence (LIBERT)	3,310	1.6%

2000 PRIMARY

Roger Wicker (R)	unopposed

1998 GENERAL

Roger Wicker (R)	66,738	67.2%
Rex N. Weathers (D)	30,438	30.6%
John "Andy" Rouse (LIBERT)	2,157	2.2%

PREVIOUS WINNING PERCENTAGES
1996 (68%); 1994 (63%)

Elected 1994; 4th term

Wicker served as president of the 1994 GOP freshman class during the first blush of the "Republican revolution" but says, "I didn't come to Washington to burn all the buildings down." He takes issue with the portrayal of the Class of 1994 as pugnacious conservatives impatient for radical change. "We were all unfairly painted with the same brush," he said in 1998. "Most of us in our own ways are much more pragmatic and results-oriented."

Even now, he believes that many casual observers of Congress expect "us all to be a bunch of fire-breathers — and that's just not so and never has been." And it certainly does not describe Wicker, an easygoing, approachable man who sings in his church choir, acts in community theater groups and once chaired the Mississippi state Senate's Public Health and Welfare Committee even though the Democrats controlled the chamber.

Wicker is far from a political outsider. He first got a taste of Washington as a teenager when he served for a month as a congressional page. Later, he was an aide to Rep. Trent Lott on the House Rules Committee, and then he won election to the Mississippi Senate.

In his first House term, Wicker landed a place on the ultimate insider's committee, Appropriations. To that post he has since added an assignment as one of about 20 deputy whips and, in the 106th Congress, the chairmanship of the TVA (Tennessee Valley Authority) Caucus.

But just because Wicker is pragmatic does not mean he is not as conservative as any of his Class of '94 colleagues; he boasts a lifetime rating of 0 percent from both the Americans for Democratic Action and the AFL-CIO in their analyses of his voting record.

As might be expected from the man who succeeded Democratic Rep. Jamie L. Whitten, who served in the House for a record 53-plus years, Wicker does not support congressional term limits — one of the tenets of the "Contract With America" that House Republicans sought to implement when they assumed power in 1995. He points out that a small state such as Mississippi can hope to wield influence in Congress only if its lawmakers ascend to key positions — and that takes time.

On Appropriations, he has worked vigorously to see that Mississippi gets a goodly share of the federal spending pie. He strongly supports the Republican majority's efforts to reduce overall government spending and cut taxes, "but that doesn't mean all federal spending and all programs cease," he once said. Nevertheless, Wicker in 1999 backed a proposal to impose an across-the-board spending cut, declaring, "There are no winners and losers, and I don't know of any accounts that couldn't take a small hit."

In the 104th Congress, he convinced his fellow freshmen that the Appalachian Regional Commission (ARC) — an inviting target for some GOP budget-cutters — was vital to the development of areas such as northern Mississippi's 1st District, and the ARC was spared. In the 106th Congress, he backed a bipartisan plan to create a regional authority to foster economic development in the Mississippi Delta region. "It's unacceptable to me that a region of our state will not participate in this great economic expansion," he said.

Although Wicker does not have much seniority on Appropriations, he has powerful allies in the Senate who buttress his efforts to funnel federal dollars to Mississippi: Majority Leader Lott and senior Sen. Thad Cochran, an Appropriations subcommittee chairman. In addition to the ARC, Wicker has a long shopping list for Uncle Sam, including money for sewer construction, highway improvements, an industrial park and flood control initiatives. "Infrastructure spending enables the private sector to create jobs, and that has helped millions of Americans to become taxpayers," Wicker has said.

Wicker has used his Appropriations seat to win regulatory changes for the upholstered furniture industry, which employs thousands in factories scattered around the 1st District. At issue was whether a material used to fireproof furniture presents an even greater risk because of its carcinogenic properties.

As a member of Appropriations' Labor, Health and Human Services, and Education Subcommittee, he has an interest in health issues, including research into cancer, diabetes and cardiovascular diseases. Wicker says Mississippi's residents have a high incidence of cardiovascular disease.

Raised in a political family — his father was a county attorney, a member of the Mississippi Senate, and then a circuit judge for 20 years — Wicker organized the local Teenage Republican club in high school. Although his father was a Democrat — as virtually every office-holder in the South was in those days — Wicker says, "there's not a dime's worth of difference in his philosophy of government and mine."

Wicker earned undergraduate and law degrees from the University of Mississippi, where he was the first Republican ever to be elected student body president. While still in college, he was a delegate to the 1972 Republican National Convention and came to know a young Trent Lott as he was making his first run for Congress.

Wicker was in the Air Force ROTC and after law school served four years on active duty as a prosecutor before going to work for Lott in Washington. He came home to practice law and, in 1987, won a state Senate seat. There, he helped write Mississippi's strict abortion law and push through an education overhaul bill that included a controversial school-choice provision. He served with another young lawyer, who went on to become a successful author — John Grisham. He remembers Grisham selling his first novel out of the trunk of his car and so far has resisted his wife's entreaties that he also try his hand at writing.

When Whitten decided to retire from the 1st in 1994, the conservative-minded district was ripe for Republican picking. Wicker emphasized his legislative experience and ran a well-financed, tightly organized campaign, edging out Grant Fox, a former Cochran aide, for the GOP nomination.

In the general election, Wicker attracted significant support from conservative Democrats who warmed to his message of reducing the size of government and preserving small-town ideals. He won with 63 percent of the vote and has not been seriously challenged since.

KEY VOTES

2000

No	Raise hourly minimum wage by $1 over two years
Yes	Halt funding for U.S. mission in Kosovo unless European nations pay more
Yes	Provide Medicare benefits to military retirees and their dependents
Yes	Grant China permanent normal trade status
Yes	Phase out estate, gift and trust taxes
Yes	Prohibit implementation of president's national monument designations
Yes	Approve GOP plan to provide prescription drug coverage for Medicare beneficiaries
No	Increase help for poor nations indebted to international financial institutions

1999

No	Impose steel import quotas
Yes	Kill proposal to take aviation trust funds off budget
Yes	Require background checks on buyers only at gun shows with 10 or more vendors
Yes	Remove barriers among banking, securities and insurance companies
No	Authorize state grants to hire teachers and reduce class size
No	Overhaul campaign finance law; ban "soft money" and restrict advocacy advertising
No	Approve bipartisan plan to increase rights of patients in managed-care health plans

INTEREST GROUPS

	AFL-CIO	ADA	CCUS	ACU
2000	0%	0%	85%	84%
1999	0%	0%	96%	92%
1998	0%	0%	100%	96%
1997	0%	0%	100%	80%

CQ VOTE STUDIES

	PARTY UNITY		PRESIDENTIAL SUPPORT	
	Support	Oppose	Support	Oppose
2000	93%	7%	22%	78%
1999	95%	5%	22%	78%
1998	94%	6%	24%	76%
1997	95%	5%	28%	72%

MISSISSIPPI 1

North — Tupelo

The northeastern Hill Country and the rich farmland on the edge of the Delta region in northwestern Mississippi supports an agricultural economy in the 1st, while manufacturing dominates in Lee County and surrounding areas. De Soto, the district's most populous county, also is the fastest growing: its population expanded by nearly 50 percent between 1990 and 1999.

The region's largest city, Tupelo, is a national leader in upholstered furniture production. More than a dozen Fortune 500 companies are located in or near the city, drawing job seekers from poorer parts of the state. A national furniture market is held twice a year in Tupelo. In De Soto, the burgeoning businesses in Memphis, Tenn. – just north of the county – are attracting people into the less-taxed, less-expensive Mississippi. East of that area, Marshall and Benton counties serve as home to many of the district's African Americans.

The Tennessee-Tombigbee Waterway, which cuts through a handful of

counties in the northwestern corner of the 1st, connects the Tennessee and Tombigbee rivers to create an unbroken link to the Gulf of Mexico. Built in the 1980s, the waterway has spawned a boom of forestry-related business.

For most of the 20th century, Democrats dictated the politics of the 1st. But as the national Republican Party grew more socially conservative, voters turned away from Democrats in federal elections, favoring Republican presidential candidates in 1992, '96 and 2000. Democrats, however, dominate state and local elections, stemming from the party's provincial political monopoly since Reconstruction.

MAJOR INDUSTRY
Furniture, agriculture, textiles

CITIES
Tupelo, 36,817; Southaven, 27,454; Olive Branch, 17,460; Horn Lake, 14,430; Corinth, 13,868

UNUSUAL FEATURES
Jamie L. Whitten represented the district from 1941 to 1995 – the longest House service in the country's history at 53 years and two months.

Rep. Bennie Thompson (D)

Elected April 1993; 4th full term

CAPITOL OFFICE
225-5876; fax 225-5898; 2432 Rayburn Bldg. 20515

INTERNET
e-mail: thompsonms2nd@mail.house.gov
web: www.house.gov/thompson

COMMITTEES
Agriculture
Budget

HOMETOWN
Bolton

BORN
Jan. 28, 1948, Bolton, Miss.

RELIGION
Methodist

FAMILY
Wife, London Thompson; one child

EDUCATION
Tougaloo College, B.A. 1968; Jackson State U.,
M.S. 1972

CAREER
Teacher

POLITICAL HIGHLIGHTS
Bolton Board of Aldermen, 1969-73; mayor of
Bolton, 1973-79; Hinds County Board of
Supervisors, 1980-93

ELECTION RESULTS

2000 GENERAL

Bennie Thompson (D)	112,777	65.1%
Hardy Caraway (R)	54,090	31.2%
William G. Chipman (LIBERT)	4,305	2.5%
Lee F. Dilworth (REF)	2,135	1.2%

2000 PRIMARY

Bennie Thompson (D)	unopposed

1998 GENERAL

Bennie Thompson (D)	80,507	71.2%
William G. Chipman (LIBERT)	32,533	28.8%

PREVIOUS WINNING PERCENTAGES
1996 (60%); 1994 (54%); 1993 Special Runoff
Election (55%); 1993 Special Election (28%)

Many people have decided that the civil rights movement and the battle against racism in the United States is over, but for Thompson, that notion is most definitely premature. He sees discrimination against blacks in the hiring practices of government agencies, in economic opportunities, in de facto segregation of public schools and in countless other areas. For him, the civil rights struggle continues.

When Thompson entered politics three decades ago, the electoral system in Mississippi was bitterly divided over race, and black officeholders were few. In 1968, at age 20, he ran successfully for alderman in his native Bolton, but white officials prevented him from taking the seat until a court order forced the town to relent. The state's political landscape has changed much since then, with many blacks holding office. But in Thompson's view too much has stayed the same: He still feels that minorities wage an uphill battle against the wealthy and the powerful, and he calls for aggressive federal action to combat discrimination. His own Democratic Party does not escape; Thompson says African-Americans "have been taken for granted" in recent years.

When Thompson hears the conservative House GOP majority malign affirmative action, he bristles. He once told his colleagues, "For most of us who are over 45, we never had new textbooks in our community, we never had the opportunity to play in a public playground or swim in a public swimming pool, and so some of us take very seriously the notion of affirmative action because this was the only opportunity that many of us ever received."

The rural, black-majority 2nd District is one of the poorest in the nation. Farming has long been the dominant sector of the economy, and Thompson uses his seat on the Agriculture Committee to watch out for those interests. In recent years, however, riverboat casinos have sprung up in Tunica County and now are a leading source of jobs.

In the legislative arena, Thompson has been able to secure some federal funding to improve the infrastructure, rural housing and health care of the region, and while President Clinton was in the White House, he had success in working with the executive branch. As one of the top Democratic officials in the state, Thompson hosted Clinton and several Cabinet secretaries to make his case for federal assistance in the district. Each visit resulted in some kind of federal help, he says.

In the 106th Congress, Thompson spearheaded a Congressional Black Caucus effort, dubbed the "New Markets Initiative," to convince businesses that they should pay attention to the 38-member bloc of mostly liberal lawmakers. "Don't automatically assume that just because we're African-American that our interests don't go beyond civil rights and affirmative action," he said.

In 2000, Thompson, as the highest-ranking black member of the Budget Committee, was the chairman of the Black Caucus' Budget Task Force, which developed an alternative spending and tax blueprint that called for increased funding for a variety of social programs, including a big boost for education, and cuts in Pentagon spending. "For too long this economic upswing has missed a lot of the people we represent," Thompson told his colleagues.

He has harsh words for GOP budget priorities. "It makes no sense to force the poorest Americans to go without food stamps, school lunches and baby formula in order to balance the budget and then turn around and give wealthy campaign contributors ... a huge tax cut," he said in 1997.

He has joined other Black Caucus members from largely rural districts in protesting that the Agriculture Department has long been guilty of discriminating against blacks in the administration of federal farm and loan programs. "There just might be a conspiracy which our government is participating in to do away with African-American farmers in this country," he said in 1998.

In a similar vein, Thompson lodged a protest with the Mississippi Department of Wildlife, Fisheries and Parks about the dearth of minority employees in the agency, which receives federal funds. In both cases, agreements were reached, but Thompson continued to monitor what he felt was lagging compliance by the agencies.

He sponsored a resolution in 1999 commemorating the 45th anniversary of the Supreme Court's landmark *Brown v. Board of Education* decision outlawing segregation in schools, warning that "many of the freedoms won by the Brown decision have been rolled back or are currently under assault. White flight and a conspicuous attack on our public schools have facilitated the de facto segregation of our public schools."

Born in 1948, Thompson was educated in segregated elementary and secondary schools in Mississippi. At Tougaloo College, he met civil rights activist Fannie Lou Hamer, who inspired him to pursue a career in politics. Thompson graduated from Tougaloo in 1968 and that same year won a seat on the Bolton Board of Aldermen. Four years later, he was elected mayor of Bolton, and at age 32, he took a seat on the Board of Supervisors for Hinds County, which includes the state capital, Jackson.

The House seat that Thompson won in a 1993 special election had been held since 1987 by Mike Espy, Mississippi's first black in Congress since Reconstruction. Espy resigned in January 1993 to become Clinton's secretary of agriculture, a post he held through 1994.

In the special election to replace Espy, the first-place finisher in the initial balloting was Republican Hayes Dent, an adviser to GOP Gov. Kirk Fordice. Dent took 34 percent, while Thompson ran second with 28 percent. Coming in third, with 20 percent, was Espy's brother, Henry, the mayor of Clarksdale. Thompson prevailed in the runoff, 55 percent to 45 percent.

In his 1994 bid for a full term, Thompson faced Bill Jordan, a black attorney and ordained minister. Thompson was able to outspend Jordan and won by 15 percentage points. His subsequent re-election victories have been by even larger margins.

KEY VOTES

2000

Yes Raise hourly minimum wage by $1 over two years
No Halt funding for U.S. mission in Kosovo unless European nations pay more
Yes Provide Medicare benefits to military retirees and their dependents
No Grant China permanent normal trade status
No Phase out estate, gift and trust taxes
No Prohibit implementation of president's national monument designations
No Approve GOP plan to provide prescription drug coverage for Medicare beneficiaries
Yes Increase help for poor nations indebted to international financial institutions

1999

Yes Impose steel import quotas
Yes Kill proposal to take aviation trust funds off budget
No Require background checks on buyers only at gun shows with 10 or more vendors
Yes Remove barriers among banking, securities and insurance companies
Yes Authorize state grants to hire teachers and reduce class size
Yes Overhaul campaign finance law; ban "soft money" and restrict advocacy advertising
Yes Approve bipartisan plan to increase rights of patients in managed-care health plans

INTEREST GROUPS

	AFL-CIO	ADA	CCUS	ACU
2000	100%	90%	50%	8%
1999	100%	100%	17%	0%
1998	100%	95%	18%	13%
1997	100%	80%	40%	16%

CQ VOTE STUDIES

	PARTY UNITY		PRESIDENTIAL SUPPORT	
	Support	Oppose	Support	Oppose
2000	92%	8%	77%	23%
1999	94%	6%	82%	18%
1998	95%	5%	82%	18%
1997	89%	11%	70%	30%

MISSISSIPPI 2

West central – Mississippi Delta

The nutrient-rich flatlands of the Mississippi Delta and the agricultural economy stemming from it have promoted landowner/tenant relationships that have made the 2nd one of the poorest districts in the nation. Parts of the Delta still lack centralized running water. Traveling north from Vicksburg, the road drops 15 feet in Issaquena County, marking the beginning of the flat Delta, home of some of the nation's most fertile soil, which supports cotton and soybeans. Although some low-income white residents call the 2nd home, it is the only black-majority district in the state.

While casinos in Tunica County have helped erase its standing as the nation's poorest county, many casino workers don't live in the district and instead commute from the Memphis region. And to the extent that people move up, they move out – college graduates find few industries to support their skills. Vicksburg is the district's one bright spot, where a mixture of tourism, casinos and a Mississippi

River port have created prosperity.

Democratic since 1987, the 2nd's politics are dominated by the black vote. Republicans hold small areas around Jackson and the district's northeast, but Democrats hold most other local offices. Voters crave beneficial government programs, and lawmakers try to bring federal money to the area to build basics, like running water.

MAJOR INDUSTRY
Casinos, agriculture, fishing

CITIES
Greenville, 41,731; Jackson (pt.), 34,454 (1990); Vicksburg, 27,184

UNUSUAL FEATURES
The Delta was the real birthplace of blues music: Blues pioneer Muddy Waters born in Rolling Fork on April 4, 1915; Blues legend B.B. King born in Indianola on Sept. 16, 1925.

Rep. Charles W. 'Chip' Pickering Jr. (R)

CAPITOL OFFICE
225-5031; fax 225-5797; 427 Cannon Bldg. 20515

INTERNET
e-mail: www.house.gov/writerep
web: www.house.gov/pickering

COMMITTEES
Agriculture
Energy & Commerce

HOMETOWN
Laurel

BORN
Aug. 10, 1963, Laurel, Miss.

RELIGION
Baptist

FAMILY
Wife, Leisha Jane Pickering; five children

EDUCATION
Mississippi College, attended 1981-82; U. of Mississippi, B.A. 1986; Baylor U., M.B.A. 1989

CAREER
Congressional aide; USDA official

POLITICAL HIGHLIGHTS
No previous office

ELECTION RESULTS

2000 GENERAL

Charles Pickering Jr. (R)	153,899	73.2%
William Clay Thrash (D)	54,151	25.7%
Jonathan R. Golden (LIBERT)	2,313	1.1%

2000 PRIMARY

Charles Pickering Jr. (R)	unopposed

1998 GENERAL

Charles Pickering Jr. (R)	84,785	84.6%
C.T. Scarborough (LIBERT)	15,465	15.4%

PREVIOUS WINNING PERCENTAGES
1996 (61%)

Elected 1996; 3rd term

Pickering has quickly established himself in just two terms in Congress by combining the Capitol Hill savvy and legislative knowledge that he gained as a top staffer for Trent Lott with political support from the "Mississippi mafia" of Lott; Thad Cochran, the Magnolia State's senior senator; and Haley Barbour, the former Republican National Committee chairman.

Pickering won a spot on the House Republican Policy Committee as a freshman, and in his second term he got a Commerce Committee (now Energy and Commerce) assignment, giving him a chance to put his Senate staff expertise to work on issues such as telecommunications and energy policy.

The earnest, youthful-looking Pickering is still often taken for a staffer, but 3rd District voters know him as the son of a longtime political, religious and community leader, and House GOP leaders recognize him as a well-connected junior member who can be trusted to vote a dependably conservative line.

Pickering's principal work during more than four years as a legislative aide in Lott's Senate office and, briefly, on the Senate Commerce Committee involved the landmark telecommunications bill that became law in 1996. He now puts that background to use on the Energy and Commerce panel. Topping his agenda are measures to establish a uniform policy for taxing cellular telephone calls (by the jurisdiction where the cellular user is based rather than by the many jurisdictions through which a particular call may journey); to prohibit the Federal Communications Commission (FCC) from regulating the content, particularly the religious programming, of non-commercial educational television stations; and to speed up the FCC review of proposed telecommunications mergers.

Pickering's Washington connections may help explain his stand against two causes that draw strong support from Republicans hostile toward career politicians: He opposes term limits for members of Congress and has supported, on several occasions, cost of living pay raises for members.

He had sought a seat on Commerce when he first arrived, but competition for that committee is intense, and he had to wait two years to make use of his experience with Lott. To take the Commerce post, he gave up his seats on the Transportation, Agriculture, and Science panels, which had proved to be good secondary choices. He was able to return to the Agriculture panel in the 107th, while keeping his Energy and Commerce slot.

On the Science Committee, Pickering looked out for the varied aeronautical and scientific activities of the John C. Stennis Space Center in southern Mississippi and for federally supported research work at Mississippi colleges. In 1998, Pickering became chairman of the Science panel's Basic Research Subcommittee, replacing Steven H. Schiff, R-N.M., who died of cancer.

The continued health of defense contractors and military installations in the 3rd District is a major focus for Pickering. The Meridian Naval Air Station (which was spared after initially being included in the 1995 round of base closings) and Columbus Air Force Base are big contributors to the local economy, and the Lockheed Martin and Hughes Aircraft plants in the 3rd draw money from the Pentagon pot. In 2000, Lockheed Martin got a contract building the tail sections of the F-22 fighter.

Pickering, who says he is a seventh-generation Mississippian, comes from a prominent family in Jones County. His father, Charles Pickering Sr., is a federal judge. A generation ago the senior Pickering was a state legislator and a key player in the rebirth of the Mississippi Republican Party. He also headed the Mississippi chapter of the Southern Baptist Convention. When Charles Sr. chaired the state GOP, the executive director was Haley Barbour, who later chaired the RNC. The campaign manager for the younger Pickering's 1996 House bid was Henry Barbour, nephew of Haley.

But Pickering said he "kind of rebelled against" politics as a youth. He went to the small, Baptist-run Mississippi College for two years, where he played free safety on the football team — enough to "get it out of my system."

He worked for a year on the family dairy and catfish farm, which was run by his uncle and grandfather, and then went off to the University of Mississippi to study business. (Pickering wasn't a cheerleader like Lott and Cochran were, but he copes with that gap in his résumé by pointing out that his wife was.) After college, Pickering was a trailblazer in establishing a Baptist missionary presence beyond the Iron Curtain, in Hungary. Then it was back to another Baptist institution — Baylor University — for a master's degree with an emphasis on international business.

He came to Washington to work in the Bush administration's Agriculture Department (USDA), specializing in export promotion. He envisioned putting his missionary work, college training and USDA experience to good use in a career in international business.

But other events intervened: Pickering, who now has five boys, started a family (which he prominently features in his campaigns, telling constituents that if they can't give him their vote, they should at least offer their sympathy), and Lott, an old family friend, offered him a staff job. It was only then that a life in politics began to have an attraction for him.

There is a tradition in Mississippi of congressional aides moving into elective office, including 1st District GOP Rep. Roger Wicker and Lott himself, and so when 15-term Democratic Rep. G.V. "Sonny" Montgomery announced in 1995 that he would not run again, Pickering jumped at the chance. Over the years, while voters continued to re-elect Montgomery, the district's move toward the GOP made it apparent that a Republican had a good chance.

Pickering's political contacts and well-known name propelled him to first place in the nine-candidate GOP primary, and he won the runoff against former state Rep. Bill Crawford. In November, Pickering posted 61 percent against Democrat John Arthur Eaves Jr., a lawyer who also had grown up in a political family. Pickering has not been threatened since.

The 2002 election may be a different story, however. With Mississippi losing a seat in reapportionment, the new congressional map may throw Pickering into a race with another incumbent.

KEY VOTES

2000
No Raise hourly minimum wage by $1 over two years
Yes Halt funding for U.S. mission in Kosovo unless European nations pay more
Yes Provide Medicare benefits to military retirees and their dependents
Yes Grant China permanent normal trade status
Yes Phase out estate, gift and trust taxes
Yes Prohibit implementation of president's national monument designations
Yes Approve GOP plan to provide prescription drug coverage for Medicare beneficiaries
No Increase help for poor nations indebted to international financial institutions

1999
No Impose steel import quotas
Yes Kill proposal to take aviation trust funds off budget
Yes Require background checks on buyers only at gun shows with 10 or more vendors
Yes Remove barriers among banking, securities and insurance companies
No Authorize state grants to hire teachers and reduce class size
No Overhaul campaign finance law; ban "soft money" and restrict advocacy advertising
No Approve bipartisan plan to increase rights of patients in managed-care health plans

INTEREST GROUPS

	AFL-CIO	ADA	CCUS	ACU
2000	0%	0%	90%	100%
1999	22%	0%	88%	92%
1998	0%	0%	94%	100%
1997	0%	0%	90%	92%

CQ VOTE STUDIES

	PARTY UNITY		PRESIDENTIAL SUPPORT	
	Support	Oppose	Support	Oppose
2000	97%	3%	25%	75%
1999	95%	5%	21%	79%
1998	95%	5%	20%	80%
1997	96%	4%	23%	77%

MISSISSIPPI 3
East central — Meridian

From Oktibbeha County in the north to Jones County in the south, the timber industry dominates the central swath of the 3rd, a district changing from the Democratic stronghold it had been since the late 19th century to a reliably Republican voting bloc. With the exception of a few cities, the district is broken up into scores of rural communities.

Rankin County is one of the fastest-growing regions of the state, spurred by nearby Jackson residents seeking land in the suburbs. The county's unemployment rate is among Mississippi's lowest. Kemper and Noxubee counties on the state's eastern border include areas as poor as the Delta, with a sparse population that in some places does not have running water.

Republicans now control the federal politics of the 3rd, after being shut out for more than a century. The district provided Republican presidential candidates with overwhelming support in 1992, '96 and

2000. But most of the region's local elected officials are Democrats, likely – in part – due to the historic domination of that party through 1980.

MAJOR INDUSTRY
Timber, agriculture, higher education

MILITARY BASES
Meridian Naval Air Station, 189 military, 3,000 civilian; Columbus Air Force Base, 1,322 military, 430 civilian (1999)

CITIES
Meridian, 41,266; Columbus, 25,757; Pearl, 23,620; Starkville, 20,866

UNUSUAL FEATURES
Mississippi University for Women, established in 1884 in Columbus, was the first state college in the nation exclusively for women (it began admitting men in 1982); Jimmie Rodgers, often hailed as the "father of country music" hailed from Meridian, where there is now a museum in his honor.

Rep. Ronnie Shows (D)

CAPITOL OFFICE
225-5865; fax 225-5886
1408 Longworth Bldg. 20515

INTERNET
e-mail: www.house.gov/writerep
web: www.house.gov/shows

COMMITTEES
Agriculture
Financial Services
Veterans' Affairs

HOMETOWN
Bassfield

BORN
Jan. 26, 1947, Moselle, Miss.

RELIGION
Baptist

FAMILY
Wife, Johnnie Ruth Shows; four children

EDUCATION
Jones Junior College, attended 1965-66;
Southeastern Baptist College, attended 1967-69;
U. of Southern Mississippi, B.A. 1971

CAREER
Teacher; coach

POLITICAL HIGHLIGHTS
Jefferson Davis County circuit clerk, 1976-80;
Miss. Senate, 1980-88; Miss. District Highway
Commission, 1988-99

ELECTION RESULTS

2000 GENERAL

Ronnie Shows (D)	115,732	58.1%
Dunn Lampton (R)	79,218	39.8%
Ernie John Hopkins (LIBERT)	2,680	1.4%

2000 PRIMARY

Ronnie Shows (D)	unopposed

1998 GENERAL

Ronnie Shows (D)	73,252	53.4%
Delbert Hosemann (R)	61,551	44.9%

Elected 1998; 2nd term

In his first term, Shows joined the coterie of white Southern Democrats who support the GOP agenda almost as much as they side with their own party — establishing himself as one of the most conservative Democrats in the House.

In 1999, for example, Shows opposed his party 44 percent of the time in votes that pitted a majority of Democrats against a majority of Republicans. In 2000, he voted against his party 49 percent of the time, more often than all but just two other Democrats.

His maverick nature also led him to oppose President Clinton frequently. And like his party-unity score, his presidential-support score decreased the longer he was in office. In 1999, Shows opposed Clinton on 49 percent of the votes on which the president took a position; in 2000, his opposition to Clinton's stands increased to 66 percent.

His conservative streak has led some to wonder whether he might switch parties, but he dismisses such speculation and says he will always be a Democrat. "I'm going to be that way; I'm going to stay that way; and they're going to bury me that way," he says. Shows is much in the mold of his 5th District neighbor, Democrat Gene Taylor, who sides with his party on some issues but maintains a Southern conservatism.

Shows does back his party on certain high-profile votes. He has voted for his party's leader, Richard A. Gephardt, for House Speaker at the beginning of each Congress, even though he says Gephardt is too liberal. He also voted against approving the Republican "managers" from the Judiciary Committee who were chosen to present the impeachment case against Clinton before the Senate. Shows was critical of the president's behavior, but he said having all Republican "managers" made the effort too partisan for him to support.

Shows is a member of the coalition of conservative Democrats known as the "Blue Dogs," who hail mainly from the South and West, and in the 106th Congress he headed the group's education task force. He also has joined a more centrist group of Democrats, called the New Democrat Coalition.

The congressman stays close to his conservative roots when it comes to social issues. He supports legislation allowing the display of the Ten Commandments in schools. He opposes abortion and was a featured speaker at a January 2001 anti-abortion rally in Washington. And he votes consistently for gun owners' rights.

He cosponsored hundreds of bills in the 106th Congress, something critics said showed he was spreading himself too thin. But Shows says he signs onto legislation that is important to his district.

Among the measures he supported was a bill that would have allowed military retirees to join the same health care program available to federal employees. With military bases and their affiliated hospitals closing across the country, many military retirees are finding it difficult to get the free health care available at federal facilities. While more than 290 House members supported the bill, the costs were believed to be too high for the federal health care program to bear, and the GOP leadership would not schedule the measure for a vote.

Helping his constituents navigate the federal bureaucracy is one of Shows' priorities. To this end, in the 106th the congressman aided a veteran in getting a medal he had never received for his service in World War II. Shows also helped a local group secure federal funding for a program for drug-addicted parents.

Another of Shows' goals in Congress is to bring economic development to his southwestern Mississippi district, including those portions outside the Jackson area that are mainly poor and rural and have substantial black constituencies. He supports raising the minimum wage and will fight free-trade agreements that he thinks will hurt Mississippi workers.

Shows spent a decade as the state transportation commissioner for the southern portion of Mississippi — a useful background for his assignment to the Transportation Committee for the 106th Congress. In the 107th, Shows left Transportation after he won a seat on the Financial Services Committee, which oversees the banking, securities and insurance industries and housing programs. He also sits on the Veterans' Affairs and Agriculture panels.

Shows said that in his first term he was most surprised by the pervasive partisanship that exists in the House, adding that he once was prevented from offering an amendment on the floor because he was a Democrat.

A former junior high school basketball coach, Shows says he has made some valuable contacts in both parties in the House gymnasium. Open to current and former members of the House, the gym is a place where lawmakers can get to know one another on a more personal level, says Shows, and that helps build bridges across party lines. He is a regular player in pick-up basketball games at the gym, adding, "That's how I've met the Republicans I know."

He was one of a dozen House members from both parties who in 1999 played in a charity basketball game against a dozen lobbyists to raise money for the Hill Staffers for the Hungry program and Horton's Kids, a tutoring project for underprivileged children.

In 1998, Shows' 8 percentage point win over Republican lawyer Delbert Hosemann resulted from his deep roots in the 4th District's southern region and a heavy turnout of black voters. The seat came open when five-term Rep. Mike Parker retired. (Parker had won the district four times as a Democrat but jumped to the GOP in 1995.)

Shows was targeted early by the GOP for the 2000 elections. He said the campaign quickly became nasty and personal, and although a "win at all costs" character pervaded the race, he prevailed easily, defeating Republican Dunn Lampton, 58 percent to 40 percent.

The 2002 race may be a tough one for Shows. Mississippi lost a House seat as a result of reapportionment following the 2000 census, and the new district lines for the 2002 elections may throw Shows and Republican Charles W. "Chip" Pickering Jr. into the same district.

KEY VOTES

2000

Yes	Raise hourly minimum wage by $1 over two years
Yes	Halt funding for U.S. mission in Kosovo unless European nations pay more
Yes	Provide Medicare benefits to military retirees and their dependents
No	Grant China permanent normal trade status
Yes	Phase out estate, gift and trust taxes
+	Prohibit implementation of president's national monument designations
No	Approve GOP plan to provide prescription drug coverage for Medicare beneficiaries
No	Increase help for poor nations indebted to international financial institutions

1999

Yes	Impose steel import quotas
No	Kill proposal to take aviation trust funds off budget
No	Require background checks on buyers only at gun shows with 10 or more vendors
Yes	Remove barriers among banking, securities and insurance companies
Yes	Authorize state grants to hire teachers and reduce class size
Yes	Overhaul campaign finance law; ban "soft money" and restrict advocacy advertising
Yes	Approve bipartisan plan to increase rights of patients in managed-care health plans

INTEREST GROUPS

	AFL-CIO	ADA	CCUS	ACU
2000	60%	35%	61%	69%
1999	78%	55%	56%	52%

CQ VOTE STUDIES

	PARTY UNITY		PRESIDENTIAL SUPPORT	
	Support	Oppose	Support	Oppose
2000	51%	49%	34%	66%
1999	56%	44%	51%	49%

MISSISSIPPI 4
Southwest – Jackson

The most industrialized district in the state, the 4th combines small manufacturing with rural communities. Although the "big city," Jackson, is not that big, residents often look at the state capital the way others look at Washington – as a far-off place where people are more concerned about politics than anything else.

The recession of the late 1980s and early '90s decimated Natchez's oil and gas industry, but tourism helped the economy stay afloat; the small river city and its antebellum homes attract nearly 150,000 visitors per year. The timber industry also provides jobs, mostly in wood processing and paper production. Much of the district is racially split; in Jackson, blacks populate the south side, while more affluent whites live in the north.

The 4th leans Republican, and as in much of the South, whites have begun voting for Republicans on the federal level while continuing to elect conservative Democrats statewide and locally. The district's

sizable black population keeps the 4th's congressional seat competitive, and Democrats fare well when they turn out the African-American vote. President Bush won the 4th in 2000, but Democratic Rep. Shows was easily elected to a second term.

MAJOR INDUSTRY
Agriculture, meat processing, recreation

CITIES
Jackson (pt.), 161,452 (1990); Clinton (pt.), 20,252 (1990); Natchez 18,177

UNUSUAL FEATURES
Some call Natchez, the oldest settled city on the Mississippi River (1716), the "City of Five Flags" – Natchez has been controlled by the French, British, Spanish, the Confederacy and the United States; Jones County, called the "Free State of Jones," refused to join the Confederacy during the Civil War; MTV founder Bob Pittman a native of Brookhaven.

Rep. Gene Taylor (D)

CAPITOL OFFICE
225-5772; fax 225-7074; 2311 Rayburn Bldg. 20515

INTERNET
e-mail: www.house.gov/writerep
web: www.house.gov/genetaylor

COMMITTEES
Armed Services
Transportation & Infrastructure

HOMETOWN
Bay St. Louis

BORN
Sept. 17, 1953, New Orleans, La.

RELIGION
Roman Catholic

FAMILY
Wife, Margaret Taylor; three children

EDUCATION
Tulane U., B.A. 1976; U. of Southern Mississippi, Gulf Park, attended 1978-80

MILITARY SERVICE
Coast Guard Reserve, 1971-84

CAREER
Sales representative

POLITICAL HIGHLIGHTS
Bay St. Louis City Council, 1981-83; Miss. Senate, 1983-89; Democratic nominee for U.S. House, 1988

ELECTION RESULTS

2000 GENERAL

Gene Taylor (D)	153,264	78.8%
Randy McDonnell (R)	35,309	18.2%
Wayne Parker (LIBERT)	3,002	1.5%
Katie Perrone (REF)	2,820	1.5%

2000 PRIMARY

Gene Taylor (D)	unopposed

1998 GENERAL

Gene Taylor (D)	78,661	77.8%
Randy McDonnell (R)	19,341	19.1%
Ray Coffey (LIBERT)	1,530	1.5%
Robert Claunch (REF)	1,065	1.1%

PREVIOUS WINNING PERCENTAGES
1996 (58%); 1994 (60%); 1992 (63%); 1990 (81%); 1989 Special Runoff Election (65%); 1989 Special Election (42%)

Elected October 1989; 6th full term

Taylor is one of the most conservative Democrats in the House, and he annually ranks among the two or three members of his party who stray from the party line most often. He was the only House Democrat to vote "yes" on all four articles of impeachment against President Clinton late in 1998.

As the 107th Congress convened, Taylor declined to vote for Richard A. Gephardt, his party's nominee for Speaker, instead casting a protest ballot for Pennsylvania Democratic Rep. John P. Murtha. "I did my best to be respectful of my elders when I first started," he told the Biloxi Sun Herald. But "now it is my turn to say, 'hey guys, this is how you do it.' "

Taylor's decision not to support Gephardt came when House Democratic leaders declined to consider changes in the leadership after the party failed to win control of the House in the 2000 elections. "Someone's got to point out that when the coach keeps losing, you don't give him a bonus."

Listening to one of Taylor's relatively infrequent floor speeches, one would get the impression that he is an angry, humorless man who would just as soon fight lonely battles and remain aloof. But Taylor's personality is exactly the opposite. He is an easygoing, fun-loving guy, according to those who know him, particularly those who have attended his annual Mardi Gras party on Capitol Hill, complete with miniature floats, outlandish costumes, liquid refreshment and Taylor's homemade jambalaya.

Taylor's occasional floor speeches usually come only after he has become worked up over something — he uses the speeches as an outlet to vent his anger. As one staffer said, "If he was like he appears on TV, none of us would work for the S.O.B."

Taylor had strayed before on a leadership election, voting "present" in the election for Speaker in 1995; but in recent years, he had been generally much more sanguine about the role that conservatives such as himself can play in the party's inner councils.

Back in 1994, when Democrats lost control of the House, Taylor and many like-minded conservative Democrats were fed up with the way they felt they had been treated by the liberal majority of their party. "I'm sick and tired of being heard and not listened to," he said. Five of his colleagues switched to the GOP, and in early 1995, Taylor helped pull together a coalition of House Democrats with conservative views, known as the "Blue Dogs."

Taylor is an energetic champion of his district's military interests, its blue-collar factory workers and its socially conservative values. He is right in step with the House Republican majority on many high-profile issues — outlawing abortion, banning flag desecration, cutting off funds to the National Endowment for the Arts, protecting gun owners' rights, cracking down on violent crime by juveniles and curbing environmental regulations.

Taylor has gone after both House GOP leaders and President Clinton on the issue of trade, arguing that it is working people who are harmed by free-trade policies, while the monied establishment benefits. Taylor opposed granting China permanent normal trade status; and, as he sees it, the 1993 North American Free Trade Agreement has been a disaster, resulting in factory closings in many small towns in Mississippi.

In the 106th, as the top Democrat on Armed Services' Military Installations and Facilities Subcommittee, Taylor looked after the defense establishment in his district, which is home to Keesler Air Force Base, Naval Station Pascagoula and Ingalls Shipbuilding, the state's largest private employer. In the 107th, he took the top Democratic spot on the Military Procurement panel.

In the 105th, Taylor was the ranking Democrat on the Military Personnel Subcommittee, and in that role, he focused on improving health care for military retirees and increasing pay for lower-ranking service personnel, noting that thousands of military personnel were eligible for food stamps.

Taylor also sits on the Transportation and Infrastructure Committee, and he is an enthusiastic supporter of federal spending on highway construction, harbor dredging and other public works projects, especially those in Mississippi, where the growth of the casino industry along the Gulf Coast has exacerbated transportation problems.

Taylor served 13 years in the Coast Guard Reserves — twice winning commendations for his work skippering a 41-foot patrol boat on the Mississippi River, and he continues to have an abiding interest in things nautical. Earlier in his congressional career he lived on a boat while in Washington. Taylor protects the interests of his district's shrimpers and fishermen, urges increased Coast Guard funding, and promotes measures to help the U.S. shipbuilding and cruise ship industries compete against foreign companies.

Taylor went to Catholic schools, and he recalls the nuns wheeling in a television set so the students could watch the inauguration of the first Catholic president, John F. Kennedy. Taylor was only 7 years old, but he recalls that moment as the beginning of his interest in politics.

Taylor joined the Coast Guard after high school, and he remained in the reserves through his college days at Tulane, where he majored in political science and history, and during his career as a salesman for a box company.

His first foray into politics came in 1981, when he won a seat on the Bay St. Louis City Council. In 1983, he moved to the state Senate. During six years there, he focused on education issues, such as salary increases and merit pay for teachers, and earned a reputation as a maverick who had no use for lobbyists.

The Democratic Party was cool to Taylor in his first campaign for the 5th in 1988, when the district came open as Republican Trent Lott ran for the Senate. National party sources concluded that they could better spend their money elsewhere, but Taylor surprised with a strong, 45 percent showing against Republican Larkin Smith. Less than a year later, Smith died in a plane crash. In the special-election campaign, national Democratic Party support was once again slim, but Taylor prevailed over Lott's longtime Hill aide, Tom Anderson Jr., and Democratic Attorney General Mike Moore.

In 1990, Taylor won re-election with 81 percent against Smith's widow, Sheila. Since then, the GOP has periodically mounted a serious effort to topple him, but Taylor has prevailed with at least 58 percent each time.

KEY VOTES

2000
Yes Raise hourly minimum wage by $1 over two years
No   Halt funding for U.S. mission in Kosovo unless European nations pay more
Yes Provide Medicare benefits to military retirees and their dependents
No   Grant China permanent normal trade status
No   Phase out estate, gift and trust taxes
No   Prohibit implementation of president's national monument designations
No   Approve GOP plan to provide prescription drug coverage for Medicare beneficiaries
No   Increase help for poor nations indebted to international financial institutions

1999
Yes Impose steel import quotas
No   Kill proposal to take aviation trust funds off budget
Yes Require background checks on buyers only at gun shows with 10 or more vendors
No   Remove barriers among banking, securities and insurance companies
Yes Authorize state grants to hire teachers and reduce class size
Yes Overhaul campaign finance law; ban "soft money" and restrict advocacy advertising
Yes Approve bipartisan plan to increase rights of patients in managed-care health plans

INTEREST GROUPS

	AFL-CIO	ADA	CCUS	ACU
2000	60%	45%	38%	56%
1999	67%	50%	68%	72%
1998	33%	30%	41%	79%
1997	13%	20%	80%	80%

CQ VOTE STUDIES

	PARTY UNITY		PRESIDENTIAL SUPPORT	
	Support	Oppose	Support	Oppose
2000	57%	43%	40%	60%
1999	44%	56%	39%	61%
1998	41%	59%	33%	67%
1997	45%	55%	33%	67%

MISSISSIPPI 5
Southeast – Gulf Coast; Hattiesburg

The pristine white Gulf Coast beaches of the 5th are surrounded by casino resorts that have popped up since several counties changed their gaming laws in 1992. Every county in this conservative Democratic district grew between 1990 and '99, and more than half by double digits. Small forested rural communities predominate where strip malls and suburban sprawl do not. The district's healthy economy and general lack of poverty differentiate it from the rest of the state.

Defense-related businesses join casinos as the region's dominant industries. Unemployment statistics that fall below the state average reflect the region's relative prosperity. Hattiesburg has attracted a sizable retirement community, with new golf courses and a sprawling medical care facility at the University of Southern Mississippi.

The politics of the 5th mirror the voting patterns of an increasing portion of the South. A conservative Democrat holds the congressional seat, but the district tends to swing between Democratic and Republican on the local level. Republican presidential candidates garnered majority support in 1992, '96 and 2000. Most voters support conservative Democrats, but younger voters lean toward Republicans.

MAJOR INDUSTRY
Military, shipbuilding, casinos

MILITARY BASES
Keesler Air Force Base, 12,055 military, 3,619 civilian (1999); Gulfport Naval Construction Battalion Center, 3,574 military, 799 civilian (1997); Naval Meteorology and Oceanography Command, 36 military, 1,048 civilian (2000); Naval Station Pascagoula, 68 military, 130 civilian (1998)

CITIES
Gulfport 64,679; Hattiesburg 49,233; Biloxi 47,749; Pascagoula, 27,345

UNUSUAL FEATURES
Harrison County claims to have the largest manmade beach in the nation – 26 miles long.

Gov. Bob Holden (D)

First elected: 2000
Length of term: 4 years
Term expires: 1/05
Salary: $120,086
Phone: (573) 751-3222
Hometown: Jefferson City
Born: Aug. 24, 1949, Kansas City, Mo.
Religion: Disciples of Christ
Family: Wife, Lori Hauser Holden; two children
Education: Southwest Missouri State U., B.A. 1973
Military service: Mo. National Guard, 1971-75
Career: Congressional aide; assistant to the state treasurer
Political highlights: Mo. House, 1983-89; Mo. treasurer, 1993-2001

Election results:
2000 GENERAL

Bob Holden (D)	1,152,752	49.1%
James M. Talent (R)	1,131,307	48.2%

Lt. Gov. Joe Maxwell (D)

First elected: 2000
Length of term: 4 years
Term expires: 1/05
Salary: $77,184
Phone: (573) 751-4727

STATE LEGISLATURE

General Assembly: Meets January-May
House: 163 members, 2-year terms
2001 breakdown: 74R, 86D, 3 vacancies; 120 men, 40 women
Salary: $29,875
Phone: (573) 751-3659
Senate: 34 members, 4-year terms
2001 breakdown: 18R, 16D; 29 men, 5 women
Salary: $29,080
Phone: (573) 751-3766

STATE TERM LIMITS

Governor: 2 terms
Senate: 2 terms
House: 4 terms

URBAN STATISTICS

CITY	POPULATION
Kansas City	437,764
St. Louis	333,960
Springfield	142,669
Independence	117,545

REGISTERED VOTERS

Voters do not register by party.

POPULATION

2000 population	5,595,211
1990 population	5,117,073
Percent change	+9.3%
Rank among states	17

Median age	35.4
Born in state	70%
Foreign born	2%
Urban/rural	69%/31%
Crime rate	577/100,000
Poverty level	9.8%
Federal workers	58,899
Military	37,557

REAPPORTIONMENT

Missouri retained its nine House seats in reapportionment. The state legislature will draw new district lines.

MISCELLANEOUS

Web: www.state.mo.us
Capital: Jefferson City
Land area: 68,898 sq. miles
Rank among states: 18

STATE ELECTION OFFICIAL
(573) 751-2301

DEMOCRATIC HEADQUARTERS
(573) 636-5241

REPUBLICAN HEADQUARTERS
(573) 636-3146

District Statistics

DIST.	VOTE FOR PRESIDENT 2000 D	R	GREEN	1996 D	R	REF	1992 D	R	I	WHT	BLK	ASIAN	HISP	HOUSEHOLD INCOME	OVER 65+	UNDER 18	COLLEGE EDUCATION
1	78%	20%	1%	74%	20%	5%	69%	19%	13%	46%	52%	1%	1%	$24,963	14%	26%	20%
2	43	55	2	41	49	8	36	40	23	94	4	2	1	$43,957	10	26	34
3	51	46	2	49	39	11	44	32	24	96	2	1	1	$30,863	15	25	17
4	39	58	1	41	46	12	37	38	25	95	3	1	1	$23,064	15	26	13
5	61	36	2	58	33	8	52	26	22	73	24	1	3	$26,968	14	25	20
6	44	53	2	46	42	12	40	32	27	96	2	1	2	$27,165	14	26	16
7	35	62	2	37	51	11	37	45	19	97	1	0	1	$21,712	16	25	15
8	39	59	1	45	43	11	46	37	17	95	4	0	1	$18,207	16	26	10
9	43	54	2	44	42	12	41	34	25	95	4	1	1	$26,055	13	27	17
STATE	47	50	2	48	41	10	44	34	22	88	11	1	1	$26,362	14	26	18

Sen. Christopher S. Bond (R)

Elected 1986; 3rd term

CAPITOL OFFICE
224-5721; fax 224-8149; 274 Russell Bldg. 20510

INTERNET
e-mail: kit_bond@bond.senate.gov
web: bond.senate.gov

COMMITTEES
Appropriations
  (VA, HUD & Independent Agencies - chairman)
Budget
Environment & Public Works
Health, Education, Labor & Pensions
Small Business - chairman

HOMETOWN
Mexico

BORN
March 6, 1939, St. Louis, Mo.

RELIGION
Presbyterian

FAMILY
Divorced; one child

EDUCATION
Princeton U., A.B. 1960; U. of Virginia, LL.B. 1963

CAREER
Lawyer

POLITICAL HIGHLIGHTS
Republican nominee for U.S. House, 1968; Mo.
auditor, 1971-73; governor, 1973-77; Republican
nominee for governor, 1976; governor, 1981-85

ELECTION RESULTS

1998 GENERAL

Christopher S. Bond (R)	830,625	52.7%
Jay Nixon (D)	690,208	43.8%
Tamara A. Millay (LIBERT)	31,876	2.0%

1998 PRIMARY

Christopher S. Bond (R)	213,569	86.9%
Joyce P. Lea (R)	9,685	3.9%
Joseph "Joe" France (R)	6,178	2.5%
John R. Alsup (R)	5,824	2.4%
Douglas E. Jones (R)	5,596	2.3%
Joseph A. Schwan (R)	4,991	2.0%

PREVIOUS WINNING PERCENTAGES
1992 (52%); 1986 (53%)

Bond is a soft-edged conservative, happy to spend money on government programs that benefit his state and willing to cooperate with Democrats when he feels it is necessary to do so. He has a reputation as a low-key workhorse, yet his fellow Republicans have been reluctant to elect him to a leadership post — he has lost three attempts to become chairman of the Senate Republican Conference.

Still, as chairman of the Appropriations Subcommittee on Veterans Affairs, Housing and Urban Development, and Independent Agencies, he has responsibility for the third-largest of the 13 annual appropriations bills. He also champions the interests of small-business owners as head of the Small Business Committee.

Bond's pragmatic streak suits him well as chairman of the Appropriations subcommittee that oversees veterans, housing, space and environmental programs. He has managed to find consensus with the panel's ranking Democrat, Barbara A. Mikulski of Maryland, who like Bond is eager to deliver federal money back home.

When the watchdog group Citizens Against Government Waste gave Bond a "License to Pork" in 1999 for having brought home more than $50 million in federal dollars the year before, Bond was more proud than offended. "If they think it's pork, it's an awfully healthy diet for the people of Missouri, and I'm proud to participate in it," Bond told The Associated Press. "Just tell 'em, 'In the next batch, I'll bring along my own barbecue sauce.' "

During the Clinton administration, Bond was critical of several agencies under his subcommittee's jurisdiction, including the Department of Housing and Urban Development. In the 106th Congress, he proposed that HUD get out of the disaster aid business. "HUD has continued in its proud tradition of frittering away the funds, offering no accountability for where the money is being spent," he said. He later questioned HUD Secretary Andrew M. Cuomo over the agency's takeover of $60 million worth of federal grants to New York City for programs to help the homeless. Republicans saw the department's move as having been engineered by Cuomo to embarrass Republican Mayor Rudolph W. Giuliani and to help Hillary Rodham Clinton's New York Senate bid.

On the Small Business Committee, Bond has scrutinized federal agencies' "bundling" of contracts for different services into a single contract. The practice is intended to save administrative expenses, but critics, like Bond, say it makes the contracts too big for smaller businesses to make competitive bids.

He also has criticized how the Internal Revenue Service treats small businesses. "The tax code is just too difficult for people to understand," he said in 2000. "And the IRS has not operated in a way to serve small business effectively." When the agency moved in late 2000 to cut paperwork and penalties for about a million small entrepreneurs, Bond said he took it as a sign that the IRS was tuning in to his criticisms.

He has fought to exempt small businesses from increases in the minimum wage and in 2001 helped block the Occupational Safety and Health Administration from issuing new ergonomics regulations. And he has complained that strict clean air standards issued by the Environmental Protection Agency overburden small businesses.

In the interest of his state, he worked on a bill in the 106th to block the EPA from withholding federal highway funds from metropolitan areas that do not meet clean air standards. "Good highways are a matter of life and death," he said. "Cutting off highway construction doesn't solve the problems of air pollution." (St. Louis has never met the clean air test.)

Bond was involved in a major environmental dispute late in 2000 that had political ramifications — the Clinton administration's plans to alter water flows on the Missouri River to help endangered species, a move that threatened barge traffic on the river. The Senate, led by Bond, added language to a spending bill to prevent the Army Corps of Engineers from taking the step, but President Clinton vetoed the measure. Bond told the Kansas City Star that the veto would have "huge political ramifications all over Missouri." He added: "And I'm going to ramificate throughout the state." GOP presidential candidate George W. Bush carried Missouri by 3 percentage points.

Bond received international attention in 1998, when during a campaign debate he suggested repealing the 1976 ban on political assassinations. "One bullet at Hitler at the right time might have saved millions of people," he said at the debate, sponsored by the Jewish Community Relations Council of St. Louis. "I believe when you have a head of state, perhaps such as [Iraq's] Saddam Hussein, who is bent on carrying out evil and continues to do so, you may cause far less human suffering if you go after that leader."

In his six statewide races, Bond has never been an overwhelming favorite of Missouri voters. He has won by more than 10 percentage points only once — his first contest, in 1970, for state auditor. In five subsequent statewide runs, he reached 55 percent one time (his 1972 election as governor), and he lost one race (his 1976 gubernatorial re-election bid).

Bond broke into politics in 1968, seeking a seat in the House from northeastern Missouri. Although he lost, it was the year the modern GOP in Missouri was born. Richard M. Nixon carried the state, and John C. Danforth was elected attorney general. Bond took a job with Danforth, later his Senate colleague, and in 1970 won the office of state auditor. Two years later, Bond was elected the state's first GOP governor since World War II. In 1976, he lost a re-election bid to Democrat Joseph P. Teasdale, but he avenged that loss in 1980.

In 1986, Bond battled Democratic Lt. Gov. Harriett Woods in a bitter contest for the Senate seat vacated by retiring Democrat Thomas F. Eagleton. Bond offered himself as a budget-conscious conservative and painted Woods as a liberal with values out of sync with most Missourians. She called Bond a passive governor, an aloof aristocrat and a likely rubber stamp for President Reagan.

Woods' campaign foundered when she ran a television ad depicting a weeping farmer describing how he had been foreclosed by a company on whose board Bond served. Critics across the state branded the ad a crass attempt to put Missouri's farm troubles to political use. The ad provoked a backlash, damaging Woods' efforts to win support among conservative rural Democrats. Bond won with 53 percent.

In 1992, Bond's opponent, St. Louis County Council member Geri Rothman-Serot, sought to capitalize on the "Year of the Woman" tide. But Bond's campaign treasury was four times larger than Rothman-Serot's. His approval ratings remained healthy, and on Election Day, Bond was the Missouri GOP's only victorious statewide candidate. He took 52 percent of the vote, 7 percentage points ahead of Rothman-Serot.

In 1998, Democrats thought Missouri Attorney General Jay Nixon was a good bet to beat Bond. But Nixon couldn't make good — he angered black voters by moving to end a court-ordered school desegregation plan and attacked Bond as soft on crime for commuting sentences of murderers when he was governor. Those stands hurt Nixon, and Bond cruised to victory, 53 percent to 44 percent, with significant support from black voters.

KEY VOTES

2000
Yes Overhaul bankruptcy law and increase minimum wage
Yes Limit fiscal 2001 discretionary spending to $600.3 billion
Yes Override veto on nuclear waste disposal at Yucca Mountain site in Nevada
No Oppose effort to terminate Kosovo mission
No Include gender, sexual orientation and disability in federal hate crime protections
Yes Approve GOP plan to restrict use of genetic information by health insurers
Yes Kill amendment delaying implementation of an anti-missile defense system
Yes Cut taxes for married couples
Yes Grant China permanent normal trade status

1999
Yes Remove President Clinton from office for obstruction of justice
Yes Kill amendment authorizing state grants to hire teachers and reduce class size
No Require criminal background checks for purchases at gun shows
Yes Approve GOP proposal to increase rights of patients in managed-care health plans
No Block effort to allow farm and medicine exports to Cuba
No Allow study of tougher automobile fuel efficiency standards
No Ratify nuclear weapons testing treaty
No Prohibit national political parties from collecting "soft money" donations
Yes Remove barriers among banking, securities and insurance companies

INTEREST GROUPS

	AFL-CIO	ADA	CCUS	ACU
2000	0%	0%	100%	92%
1999	0%	0%	94%	84%
1998	13%	15%	89%	72%
1997	0%	15%	100%	76%
1996	29%	10%	100%	90%
1995	8%	5%	100%	70%
1994	13%	20%	100%	83%
1993	10%	25%	100%	80%
1992	33%	25%	100%	76%
1991	27%	20%	70%	81%

CQ VOTE STUDIES

	PARTY UNITY		PRESIDENTIAL SUPPORT	
	Support	Oppose	Support	Oppose
2000	96%	4%	46%	54%
1999	93%	7%	34%	66%
1998	88%	12%	38%	62%
1997	89%	11%	62%	38%
1996	95%	5%	37%	63%
1995	93%	7%	36%	64%
1994	78%	22%	49%	51%
1993	85%	15%	33%	67%
1992	84%	16%	75%	25%
1991	88%	12%	88%	12%

Sen. Jean Carnahan (D)

CAPITOL OFFICE
224-6154; fax 228-0043; 517 Hart Bldg. 20510

INTERNET
e-mail: senator_carnahan@carnahan.senate.gov
web: carnahan.senate.gov

COMMITTEES
Armed Services
Commerce, Science & Transportation
Governmental Affairs
Special Aging

HOMETOWN
Rolla

BORN
Dec. 20, 1933, Washington, D.C.

RELIGION
Baptist

FAMILY
Widowed; four children (one deceased)

EDUCATION
George Washington U., B.A. 1955

CAREER
Mo. first lady; homemaker

POLITICAL HIGHLIGHTS
No previous office

Appointed Jan. 2001; 1st term

Carnahan never planned to be a senator and will forever rue the circumstances that put her in that office. But she was sworn in at the start of the 107th Congress after one of the most unusual elections in U.S. history.

Carnahan's husband, two-term Democratic Gov. Mel Carnahan, was the career politician who in 2000 was engaged in a "battle of the titans" challenge to Republican Sen. John Ashcroft. But three weeks before the November election, Mel Carnahan, his son Roger and an aide died in a plane crash.

It was initially presumed that this tragedy would result in Ashcroft's re-election by default. But Democrats sparked a movement that asked voters to cast their ballots for the late governor, whose victory would enable his interim successor, Democratic former Lt. Gov. Roger Wilson, to appoint a senator until a 2002 special election.

The effort became a phenomenon after party officials persuaded Jean Carnahan, grieving over the loss of her husband and son, to agree to accept Wilson's appointment if Mel Carnahan were to receive more votes than Ashcroft.

Jean Carnahan refrained from campaigning, instead making one TV news program appearance and an ad introducing herself to voters. The voters then delivered their stunning verdict, giving Mel Carnahan 50 percent of the vote to Ashcroft's 48 percent and making him the first deceased candidate to win a Senate election. Two months later, Jean Carnahan was sworn in as Missouri's first woman senator.

Some Republican partisans urged Ashcroft to challenge the outcome — they raised a suggestion that Mel Carnahan, having died, no longer met the constitutional qualification that he be a resident of the state that elected him to the Senate — but Ashcroft quickly conceded.

Jean Carnahan responded in kind in January 2001 by introducing Ashcroft at the contentious Senate Judiciary Committee hearings into his nomination as attorney general in the Bush administration. But in a move that may have political consequences in 2002, she voted against his confirmation.

Though Carnahan had never pursued nor held public office, she is no political novice. Married to Mel Carnahan for 46 years — they began dating at age 15 — Carnahan campaigned and worked alongside her husband, often attending events on his behalf and once serving as his scheduler.

In her role as Missouri's first lady, the tireless and down-to-earth Carnahan was active in various areas, earning praise for her accomplishments on children's issues such as early education, day care and immunization. Holding a bachelor's degree in business and public administration, the Washington, D.C., native is also the author of three books, including a volume on the first families of Missouri, titled "If Walls Could Talk."

Carnahan has said her priorities in Congress are issues involving children, including education. She supports gun control measures that do not infringe on gun owners' rights, legislation to protect farmers during economic downturns, and efforts to use the federal budget surplus to bolster Medicare and Social Security.

Carnahan — who faces a decision on whether to run in the 2002 special election to fill out the remaining four years of the term won by her late husband — suggested she would not operate solely along party lines. She believes both parties must work together and told the St. Louis Post-Dispatch: "You just can't be philosophical about things and take hard positions. You've got to do things that work."

Rep. William Lacy Clay (D)

Elected 2000; 1st term

With his election as president of the Democrats' freshman Class of 2000, Clay took an immediate step toward living up to the legacy of his father, Democratic Rep. William L. Clay Sr., whom he replaced in the House.

The elder Clay, an African-American political pioneer, represented his St. Louis-based House district for 32 years and rose to serve as the senior Democrat on the Education and the Workforce Committee. Clay Jr. was exposed to the family tradition of public service at an early age; his father was first elected as a St. Louis alderman when Clay Jr. was 2. "The Clays are noted for being servants of the community — that's what we do and we do it well," the younger Clay says.

Clay Jr. shares his father's liberal agenda, but, as he politely but firmly reiterates, he is not his father. Known by his middle name, Lacy, he is widely regarded as mellower than his rough-edged and often contentious forebearer. He is an avid cook and a golf fanatic.

Clay first became aware of the Washington political scene in 1968, at age 12, when his father won election to Congress and moved the family to a suburb just outside Washington, D.C. As a college student, Clay Jr. worked on Capitol Hill as a doorman.

A win in a 1983 special election started Clay on a nearly eight-year tenure in the state House, followed by almost 10 years in the state Senate. He helped push through legislation benefiting welfare recipients, providing working-class homeowners with tax cuts and imposing new penalties for hate crimes.

Education and health care issues were main components of Clay's 2000 election campaign. Another priority for the lawmaker is spurring economic development in urban St. Louis County — where crime and a troubled public school system have contributed to a steady decline in population.

Clay has taken seats on the Financial Services and Government Reform committees.

Clay campaigned vigorously in the 2000 Democratic primary, easily fending off five challengers for the nomination; and, as was expected in the heavily Democratic 1st District, he won the seat by a landslide in November.

CAPITOL OFFICE
225-2406; fax 225-1725; 415 Cannon Bldg. 20515

INTERNET
e-mail: www.house.gov/writerep
web: www.house.gov/clay

COMMITTEES
Financial Services
Government Reform

HOMETOWN
St. Louis

BORN
July 27, 1956, St. Louis, Mo.

RELIGION
Roman Catholic

FAMILY
Wife, Ivie Lewellen Clay; one child

EDUCATION
U. of Maryland, B.S. 1983

CAREER
Congressional aide

POLITICAL HIGHLIGHTS
Mo. House, 1983-91; Mo. Senate, 1991-2000

ELECTION RESULTS

2000 GENERAL

William Lacy Clay (D)	149,173	75.2%
Zellner Dwight Billingsly (R)	42,730	21.5%
Brenda Reddick (GREEN)	3,099	1.6%
Tamara A. Millay (LIBERT)	2,253	1.1%

2000 PRIMARY

William Lacy Clay (D)	34,398	60.6%
Charlie Dooley (D)	15,612	27.5%
Eric E. Vickers (D)	3,543	6.2%
William C. Haas (D)	1,602	2.8%
Steven G. Bailey (D)	1,144	2.0%

MISSOURI 1

North St. Louis; Northeast St. Louis County

The majority of downtown St. Louis and the eastern portion of St. Louis County make up the 1st, a mixture of poor center-city communities and middle-class suburbs. While its suburbs have sprawled and prospered, the city of St. Louis has continued on a downward population spiral, and a portion of the city is filled with rundown, crime-ridden neighborhoods.

Most of St. Louis' popular attractions, such as Forest Park and the Gateway Arch, are included in the 1st, as are many of the area's larger companies. Washington University's hospital is a key piece of the health care industry. Large companies, including a Boeing plant near the St. Louis Airport that makes fighter planes, employ many city residents, but suburbanites in the 2nd and 3rd districts fill most of the higher-paying positions. A growing gambling industry also has developed along the Mississippi River.

Downtown St. Louis has remained fairly stable, while the areas just north and west have witnessed a sharp rise in crime. The city hopes a nearly $1 billion long-term revitalization plan and the renovated downtown convention center will help reverse the trend.

The 1st is the state's most Democratic district. Local and city races almost always favor Democratic candidates. The city and suburbs regularly battle for funding; education is a hot issue for center-city residents, whose public schools have been suffering for years.

MAJOR INDUSTRY
Manufacturing, airlines, higher education

CITIES
St. Louis (pt.), 221,526 (1990); University City (pt.), 40,058 (1990); Ferguson, 20,597

UNUSUAL FEATURES
Missouri Botanical Gardens.

Rep. Todd Akin (R)

CAPITOL OFFICE
225-2561; fax 225-2563; 501 Cannon Bldg. 20515

INTERNET
e-mail: rep.akin@mail.house.gov
web: www.house.gov/akin

COMMITTEES
Armed Services
Science
Small Business

HOMETOWN
Town & Country

BORN
July 5, 1947, Manhattan, N.Y.

RELIGION
Christian

FAMILY
Wife, Lulli Akin; six children

EDUCATION
Worcester Polytechnic Institute, B.S. 1971;
Covenant Theological Seminary, M.Div. 1985

MILITARY SERVICE
Army, 1972-80

CAREER
University lecturer; steel company manager;
computer company marketing executive

POLITICAL HIGHLIGHTS
Mo. House, 1989-2000

ELECTION RESULTS

2000 GENERAL

Todd Akin (R)	164,926	55.3%
Ted House (D)	126,441	42.4%

2000 PRIMARY

Todd Akin (R)	14,911	25.9%
Gene McNary (R)	14,855	25.8%
Francis E. Flotron Jr. (R)	12,362	21.5%
Barbara "Barb" Cooper (R)	10,538	18.3%
Jackie C. "Jack" Jackson (R)	4,955	8.6%

Elected 2000; 1st term

Akin's 12 years as a state legislator proved to be solid preparation for his transition to national politics. Elected by his colleagues as vice president of the House Republican Class of 2000, the freshman from suburban St. Louis angled for a seat on the Armed Services Committee — which he obtained.

His background as a former U.S. Army officer, his advocacy for shoring up the military, and the fact that Boeing Co. is a major St. Louis-region employer made Akin an obvious fit for Armed Services.

Akin stood out as one of the most outspoken conservative activists among Republicans elected in 2000. He is steadfastly opposed to abortion, same-sex marriage and gun control legislation. Akin, who home-schools his young children, advocates local control of schools and helping parents exercise choice over the schools their children attend.

Akin, who holds a divinity degree, claims a passion for the U.S. Constitution and has written and lectured on American history.

As a conservative's conservative, Akin has periodically found himself tilting at windmills. He unsuccessfully sued the state of Missouri after the state legislature approved the 1993 Outstanding Schools Act, a measure that included $310 million in tax increases.

But he has also scored some victories. Wary of the social impact of expanded gambling, he successfully pushed a voter initiative that ended riverboat gambling on docked boats.

Akin's image as doctrinaire spurred opponents to label him as ideologically isolated when he bid in 2000 for the 2nd District seat left open by four-term Rep. James M. Talent, that year's Republican nominee for governor. But the ardent grass-roots support of the district's numerous religious conservatives enabled Akin to narrowly prevail in a five-way primary, defeating former St. Louis County Executive Gene McNary by 56 votes.

Democrats hoped that the divisive GOP primary might provide an opening for their nominee, state Sen. Ted House, who espoused conservative views on social issues such as abortion. But an energetic campaign style and the district's Republican leanings carried Akin to a 13-point victory.

MISSOURI 2
Western St. Louis County; eastern St. Charles County

The Missouri and Mississippi rivers merge at the northeastern boundary of the 2nd, an affluent district composed mostly of upper middle-class suburbanites. Western St. Louis and St. Charles counties continue to prosper from a westward population boom started by mass departures from St. Louis in the 1980s.

Many residents in St. Louis County, where the overwhelming majority of the 2nd's residents live, commute to the St. Louis business district and enjoy some of the higher-paying jobs at companies such as Anheuser-Busch and DaimlerChrysler. Some workers also venture to Wentzville (in the 9th District) to a General Motors facility.

St. Charles County grew 50 percent in the 1980s and about 30 percent in the 1990s. A McDonnell Douglas missile facility in St. Charles merged with Boeing in the late 1990s, resulting in some job cuts, but the economy has been generally strong. A dwindling but diverse agricultural industry supports the northern fringes around the Mississippi-Missouri river junction.

Although Democrats held the 2nd during most of the latter part of the 20th century, Republicans have dominated in recent years. GOP presidential candidates won the district in 1992, '96 and 2000, and Republicans have a slight edge in state and local offices. Wealthy communities such as Ladue and Frontenac are as unshakably Republican as union-laden Florissant, St. Ann and Bridgeton are Democratic.

MAJOR INDUSTRY
Auto manufacturing, defense, agriculture

CITIES
St. Charles, 59,276; Chesterfield, 44,216; Florissant (pt.), 36,959 (1990)

UNUSUAL FEATURES
Times Beach, site of environmental disaster when soil became tainted with dioxin.

Rep. Richard A. Gephardt (D)

Elected 1976; 13th term

CAPITOL OFFICE
225-2671; fax 225-7452
1236 Longworth Bldg. 20515

INTERNET
e-mail: gephardt@mail.house.gov
web: www.house.gov/gephardt

COMMITTEES
Minority Leader - no committee assignments

HOMETOWN
St. Louis

BORN
Jan. 31, 1941, St. Louis, Mo.

RELIGION
Baptist

FAMILY
Wife, Jane Byrnes Gephardt; three children

EDUCATION
Northwestern U., B.S. 1962; U. of Michigan, J.D. 1965

MILITARY SERVICE
Mo. Air National Guard, 1965-71

CAREER
Lawyer

POLITICAL HIGHLIGHTS
St. Louis Board of Aldermen, 1971-76; sought Democratic nomination for president, 1988

ELECTION RESULTS

2000 GENERAL

Richard A. Gephardt (D)	147,222	57.8%
William J. Federer (R)	100,967	39.7%
Mary Maroney (GREEN)	3,266	1.3%

2000 PRIMARY

Richard A. Gephardt (D)	unopposed

1998 GENERAL

Richard A. Gephardt (D)	98,287	55.8%
William J. Federer (R)	74,005	42.0%
Michael H. Crist (LIBERT)	2,275	1.3%

PREVIOUS WINNING PERCENTAGES
1996 (59%); 1994 (58%); 1992 (64%); 1990 (57%); 1988 (63%); 1986 (69%); 1984 (100%); 1982 (78%); 1980 (78%); 1978 (82%); 1976 (64%)

For two intense and exhausting years, Gephardt made it his life's work to win back control of the House for the Democrats.

He put aside his planned campaign for the presidency, then forged a coordinated political front with an old nemesis, Al Gore, the party's nominee. He set to work raising a record $37 million for the Democratic Congressional Campaign Committee, then crisscrossed the country to stump with five dozen House candidates. He convinced a collection of senior Democrats to postpone retirement to take another shot at reclaiming the House majority, then publicly declined to be considered for the 2000 vice-presidential nomination. He engineered a scorched-earth legislative strategy, trying to block the majority Republicans at every turn. He arranged screenings of inspirational film clips for his troops. As a finale, he appeared before House Democrats in the war paint and breastplate of the Scottish freedom fighter William Wallace, protagonist of the movie "Braveheart."

But on Election Day, his campaign came up a hairsbreadth shy: A switch of 2,500 votes spread through five contests would have delivered the House to the Democrats — and made Gephardt the 52nd Speaker of the House.

Instead, in the 107th Congress, Gephardt remains the minority leader, a job he has held since the party's demoralizing loss of the majority in 1994. He is trying to galvanize dispirited Democrats yet again and convince them their chances in 2002 are at least as good as he said they were in 2000. It may be a tough sell, given the number of open seats Republicans had to defend the last time, the number of open seats the Democrats are expected to face this time, and the fact that the GOP holds more influence over congressional redistricting for this decade than it did in the 1990s.

The most common description colleagues give of Gephardt is "good listener." He is known for allowing all factions of the party to speak their minds in hopes of finding consensus on issues. He is not known as one who dictates from the top down, but instead looks to task forces and group meetings, where he solicits Democrats' views. This management style has given the growing number of moderate Democrats in the House a greater voice in policy decisions, despite Gephardt's generally liberal leanings. Even moderate Democrats who once strongly opposed Gephardt now generally praise his work as leader.

Some critics say his drive to find a House Democratic consensus can leave his party with a muddled stand, or no stand at all. The House passed a series of Republican tax cut bills in 2000 with unexpectedly large numbers of Democratic votes — a result of what some saw as Gephardt's failure to set a cohesive party strategy. And while Gephardt generally is credited with bringing Democrats of all ideological hues into the leadership fold, he has been excoriated by Republicans, who say his strategy in the 106th was to block Democrats from participating in bipartisan compromises so they could campaign against the GOP as a "do-nothing Congress."

Republicans portray Gephardt as not only unduly partisan, but also emotionally distant. Even those close to him say that Gephardt is not one to show his feelings publicly. It is rare to catch him in an unguarded moment, joking with colleagues or revealing anger. He and Speaker J. Dennis Hastert had minimal interaction during the 106th. When Gephardt called Hastert the day after the election to offer congratulations, it was the first time the two had spoken in months. Earlier in the fall, Hastert went to Missouri to campaign against Gephardt's re-election, a clear sign of their sour relationship and a blatant break from traditional leadership decorum.

As minority leader — and as majority leader from 1989 through 1994 — Gephardt has learned to make the most of the legislative process. With Democrats in the minority, he has used parliamentary maneuvers to try to force action on his party's proposals, and he has regularly engineered a solid bloc of votes against GOP bills to make legislating that much more difficult for the slim Republican majority. He has also been on the lookout to exploit breaks in the GOP ranks. During the debate on how to regulate managed-care plans in 1999, Gephardt facilitated negotiations between his side and renegade Republicans, resulting in a bill that the House passed despite an all-out campaign against it by GOP leaders.

Gephardt first was elected to Congress in 1976 on the strength of his rep-utation as a young activist on the machine-dominated St. Louis Board of Aldermen, where he served six years. After a hard-fought primary for an open seat — Democratic Rep. Leonor K. Sullivan was retiring — he won the general election with ease. But he has struggled some in recent years, fin-ishing below 60 percent in five of his last six elections.

Gephardt started his congressional career as a moderate-to-conservative Democrat. When he first came to the House in 1977, he supported consti-tutional amendments banning abortion and school busing. He led the fight in 1979 against President Carter's hospital cost control plan, opposed a 1977 minimum wage increase, and voted for President Reagan's 1981 tax cuts. He also was an original founder in 1984 of the Democratic Leadership Council, a group of moderates seeking to pull the party to the center.

But in preparation for his presidential run in 1988, Gephardt began to move his rhetoric to the left. Among other issue shifts, he dropped his sup-port of an anti-abortion constitutional amendment. Still, despite winning the Iowa caucuses, his campaign had foundered by early March.

Preparing for a second run in 2000, and anticipating Gore as his chief rival, Gephardt positioned himself not only as the senior liberal elected Democratic leader but also as one of President Clinton's most nettlesome Democratic critics. He opposed the welfare overhaul of 1996 as well as the budget-balancing plan of 1997 that Clinton brokered with the GOP. And he opposed most of Clinton's bids to expand trade. During the main trade debate of the 106th — on whether to grant China permanent normal trade status — Gephardt wavered in public for weeks before signaling that he would side with labor and environmental groups against the legislation. But he promised not to actively lobby against the bill, saying he wanted to avoid further splitting a party that was so strongly divided over the issue.

KEY VOTES

2000
Yes Raise hourly minimum wage by $1 over two years
No Halt funding for U.S. mission in Kosovo unless European nations pay more
Yes Provide Medicare benefits to military retirees and their dependents
No Grant China permanent normal trade status
No Phase out estate, gift and trust taxes
No Prohibit implementation of president's national monument designations
No Approve GOP plan to provide prescription drug coverage for Medicare beneficiaries
Yes Increase help for poor nations indebted to international financial institutions

1999
Yes Impose steel import quotas
No Kill proposal to take aviation trust funds off budget
No Require background checks on buyers only at gun shows with 10 or more vendors
Yes Remove barriers among banking, securities and insurance companies
Yes Authorize state grants to hire teachers and reduce class size
Yes Overhaul campaign finance law; ban "soft money" and restrict advocacy advertising
Yes Approve bipartisan plan to increase rights of patients in managed-care health plans

INTEREST GROUPS

	AFL-CIO	ADA	CCUS	ACU
2000	100%	90%	28%	13%
1999	89%	100%	24%	0%
1998	100%	90%	24%	12%
1997	100%	80%	11%	14%

CQ VOTE STUDIES

	PARTY UNITY		PRESIDENTIAL SUPPORT	
	Support	Oppose	Support	Oppose
2000	93%	7%	83%	17%
1999	94%	6%	88%	12%
1998	93%	7%	82%	18%
1997	91%	9%	76%	24%

MISSOURI 3

South St. Louis; southeast St. Louis County; Jefferson and Ste. Genevieve counties

Bordered on the east by the mighty Mississippi River, the 3rd includes older, established suburbs and newer, sprawling ones. Most of the middle-class constituents commute to St. Louis County's business district, although there are traces of small-scale farming, manufacturing and river trading.

Whereas St. Louis the city – politically separated from St. Louis County since 1876 – has declined in population in the past few decades, south St. Louis' residential areas have remained stable. Large Italian and German neighborhoods continue to present a strong voice. To the south, Jefferson County has been one of the state's fastest-growing areas since 1980. Bedroom communities such as Arnold and Imperial continue to prosper.

Most suburban residents work outside the district. Anheuser-Busch's headquarters and a relocated Defense Department mapping and imaging facility also provide jobs. On the fringes of Ste. Genevieve County, small farming complements a sizable river trading industry along the docks of the Mississippi, where chemical facilities also are located.

The district's blue-collar base favors Democrats, although the GOP finds significant support in middle-class communities such as St. Louis Hills and Arnold. A large Catholic contingent gives the district an anti-abortion tilt. The 3rd's communities often fight over education and economic development funding.

MAJOR INDUSTRY
Beer manufacturing, defense, health care

CITIES
St. Louis (pt.), 175,159 (1990); Oakville (unincorporated), 31,750 (1990); Mehlville (unincorporated), 27,557 (1990); Arnold, 21,352

UNUSUAL FEATURES
Catcher Yogi Berra and baseball player and announcer Joe Garagiola from St. Louis.

Rep. Ike Skelton (D)

CAPITOL OFFICE
225-2876; fax 225-2695; 2206 Rayburn Bldg. 20515

INTERNET
e-mail: ike.skelton@mail.house.gov
web: www.house.gov/skelton

COMMITTEES
Armed Services - ranking member

HOMETOWN
Lexington

BORN
Dec. 20, 1931, Lexington, Mo.

RELIGION
Christian Church

FAMILY
Wife, Susan Skelton; three children

EDUCATION
Wentworth Military Academy, A.A. 1951; U. of
Edinburgh (Scotland), attended 1953; U. of
Missouri, A.B. 1953, LL.B. 1956

CAREER
Lawyer; state prosecutor

POLITICAL HIGHLIGHTS
Lafayette County prosecuting attorney, 1957-60;
Mo. Senate, 1971-77

ELECTION RESULTS

2000 GENERAL

Ike Skelton (D)	180,634	66.9%
James A. Noland Jr. (R)	84,406	31.3%
Thomas L. Knapp (LIBERT)	2,878	1.1%

2000 PRIMARY

Ike Skelton (D)	unopposed

1998 GENERAL

Ike Skelton (D)	133,173	71.0%
Cecilia D. Noland (R)	51,005	27.2%
Edwin "Ed" Hoag (LIBERT)	3,438	1.8%

PREVIOUS WINNING PERCENTAGES
1996 (64%); 1994 (68%); 1992 (70%); 1990 (62%);
1988 (72%); 1986 (100%); 1984 (67%); 1982 (55%);
1980 (68%); 1978 (73%); 1976 (56%)

Elected 1976; 13th term

Skelton, the senior Democrat on the Armed Services Committee, may find it more comfortable with George W. Bush in the White House than Bill Clinton.

In two decades on the Armed Services panel, Skelton has been a reliable supporter of high defense budgets, particularly where the money improves the welfare of the troops and their combat-readiness. He also has kept an eye out for the interests of Missouri's two major military bases: the Army training center at Ft. Leonard Wood and Whiteman Air Force Base, home of the B-2 stealth bomber.

But Skelton also is a student of history who has pondered how peacetime militaries sometimes set the stage for future problems, and he has drawn on that knowledge to attack bureaucracies he sees as detrimental to the armed forces. In the 1980s, he reshaped the network of war colleges that prepare officers for higher rank. And in 1986, he was a leading proponent of the Goldwater-Nichols act, a sweeping reorganization of the U.S. military establishment that aimed to increase coordination among the services and provide the president with coherent military advice.

Skelton did not have much time to pursue that type of searching institutional reform during President Clinton's two terms in the White House. Instead, he devoted his energy to shaping the Democrats' defense policy. In Skelton's judgment, Clinton's defense budgets were too anemic and some of his policies too liberal either for the congressman or for his socially conservative central Missouri district. In 1996, for instance, Skelton proposed that Clinton boost his projected future defense budgets by at least $12 billion annually.

In 1993, as chairman of the Armed Services subcommittee dealing with personnel issues, Skelton — who had qualms about Clinton's proposal to revoke the military's ban on homosexuals — was one of the key Democrats who pushed the "don't ask, don't tell" compromise that Clinton accepted.

Skelton opposed some GOP attacks on Clinton's defense policies. Like many Republicans, he warned that Clinton was wearing out U.S. forces by frequently sending them overseas while cutting manpower. But Skelton opposed congressional efforts to force a pullout once troops were in the field. Similarly, when Republicans suggested that sexual harassment at Army training bases highlighted the peril of Clinton's policies broadening the role of women in the military, Skelton instead focused on the alleged transgressions of the drill instructors, noting the tremendous power they wield over recruits under their command.

Skelton likely will be able to stay out of that kind of partisan crossfire in the 107th Congress. The Bush administration has shown no interest in reopening the debates over women and gays in the military. On the only issue likely to arouse strong partisanship — missile defense — Skelton stands with centrist Democrats such as erstwhile vice-presidential nominee Sen. Joseph I. Lieberman, D-Conn., favoring deployment of a system but opposing a crash program of development.

That leaves Skelton free to focus on continuing to press for robust defense budgets and the sort of institutional changes he has promoted in the past. Although a childhood bout with polio kept Skelton from military service, he has had a lifelong interest in military history. And much of his desire to maintain military readiness stems from his study of the years between the World Wars — years that saw the allies disarm too much too soon. Convinced the military wasn't producing the kind of strategic thinkers who won World War II, Skelton helped push through a series of initiatives in the 1980s that changed the emphasis in war colleges from management skills to strategic thinking.

In the mid-1980s, Skelton was a key member of the small group of defense-minded Democrats on Armed Services who ousted the panel's aged and infirm chairman and replaced him with Les Aspin, D-Wis., who made the committee an active force in shaping defense policy. It was during that period that Skelton was a key player on the Goldwater-Nichols bill, which shifted power from the separate armed services to senior commanders responsible for military operations around the world. In later years, that law was widely credited with the smooth integration of forces from all the services for "joint" operations during the 1991 war with Iraq.

In 2000, Skelton endorsed a new challenge to conventional Pentagon thinking, calling on the Navy to supplement its current fleet of large, complex warships with smaller, less expensive vessels that could be built in greater numbers.

On most social issues, Skelton is in tune with his constituents and, thus, at odds with his more liberal Democratic colleagues, opposing abortion in most cases, voting to repeal the ban on certain semiautomatic assault-style weapons, and backing the overhaul of the welfare system. In the 106th Congress, he sided with Clinton only about three-fifths of the time.

Skelton was practically bred into politics. His father was a popular local prosecutor who lost races for state attorney general and Congress. A friend of Harry S. Truman, the elder Skelton brought his son to Washington for Truman's inauguration in 1949. Truman has continued to occupy a central role in Skelton's political life: He was endorsed by Truman's widow, chaired a joint session of Congress on the day it observed Truman's 100th birthday, fought the Smithsonian's original Enola Gay exhibit because he felt it unfairly questioned Truman's motives toward the Japanese, and cajoled the Navy into naming its newest aircraft carrier after the former president.

After six years in the Missouri Senate, Skelton ran for the House in 1976, seeking to succeed retiring Democratic Rep. William Randall. As a rural state legislator with a narrow political base, Skelton did not look particularly well-positioned when the campaign began, but he won with 56 percent. That was his closest race, except for a 1982 post-redistricting contest when he was forced to run against GOP freshman Rep. Wendell Bailey. Skelton benefited from greater familiarity with the new district's voters, and he won with 55 percent of the vote.

KEY VOTES

2000
Yes Raise hourly minimum wage by $1 over two years
No   Halt funding for U.S. mission in Kosovo unless European nations pay more
Yes Provide Medicare benefits to military retirees and their dependents
Yes Grant China permanent normal trade status
Yes Phase out estate, gift and trust taxes
No   Prohibit implementation of president's national monument designations
No   Approve GOP plan to provide prescription drug coverage for Medicare beneficiaries
Yes Increase help for poor nations indebted to international financial institutions

1999
Yes Impose steel import quotas
Yes Kill proposal to take aviation trust funds off budget
No   Require background checks on buyers only at gun shows with 10 or more vendors
Yes Remove barriers among banking, securities and insurance companies
Yes Authorize state grants to hire teachers and reduce class size
Yes Overhaul campaign finance law; ban "soft money" and restrict advocacy advertising
Yes Approve bipartisan plan to increase rights of patients in managed-care health plans

INTEREST GROUPS

	AFL-CIO	ADA	CCUS	ACU
2000	80%	40%	66%	40%
1999	78%	55%	52%	41%
1998	90%	65%	65%	36%
1997	75%	40%	78%	52%

CQ VOTE STUDIES

	PARTY UNITY		PRESIDENTIAL SUPPORT	
	Support	Oppose	Support	Oppose
2000	70%	30%	61%	39%
1999	61%	39%	64%	36%
1998	64%	36%	58%	42%
1997	62%	38%	47%	53%

MISSOURI 4
West central — Kansas City suburbs; Jefferson City

Laden with lakes, rivers and farmland, the 4th borders a large part of the Missouri River to the north. Besides portions of southeast Kansas City suburbs, state capital Jefferson City and moderately sized Sedalia and Belton, the district typifies rural and small-town Missouri.

Most of the 4th's residents work at small-scale farming or moderate-sized manufacturing. Some farming communities have been able to recuperate from severe flooding in 1993 and '95, but many residents were forced to search for more stable employment elsewhere. Tourism still helps the rural areas. In Miller and Camden counties, the more modern hotels and retail outlets of the Lake of the Ozarks region attract a different type of vacationer than the predominantly hunting, fishing and recreation waters of the Harry S. Truman and Stockton Lake areas.

The 4th's piece of the Kansas City suburbs hasn't grown as fast as the area north of the city (in the 6th) and the suburbs aren't as affluent, but

they provide some blue-collar manufacturing jobs. Across the district, in Jefferson City, state government employs more than 14,000 people.

Socially conservative voters in the 4th tend to favor moderate Democrats. Congressional elections heavily favor Democrats in the western counties while Republican votes can be tilled farther east, especially in Webster and Camden counties.

MAJOR INDUSTRY
State and federal government, defense, higher education, agriculture

MILITARY BASES
Fort Leonard Wood, 5,000 military, 1,879 civilian; Whiteman Air Force Base, 4,300 military, 402 civilian (1999)

CITIES
Jefferson City (pt.), 35,175 (1990); Belton, 22,684; Sedalia, 20,441

UNUSUAL FEATURES
Scott Joplin Ragtime Festival every June in Sedalia to honor the location where the famous ragtime composer got his start playing for railroad workers; Corn shucking championship and parade every fall in Marshall; The restored home of George Caleb Bingham in Arrow Rock honors the late American artist.

Rep. Karen McCarthy (D)

Elected 1994; 4th term

CAPITOL OFFICE
225-4535; fax 225-4403
1330 Longworth Bldg. 20515

INTERNET
e-mail: www.house.gov/writerep
web: www.house.gov/karenmccarthy

COMMITTEES
Energy & Commerce

HOMETOWN
Kansas City

BORN
March 18, 1947, Haverhill, Mass.

RELIGION
Roman Catholic

FAMILY
Divorced

EDUCATION
U. of Kansas, B.S. 1969; U. of Birmingham, England, attended 1974; U. of Missouri, Kansas City, M.A. 1976; U. of Kansas, M.B.A. 1986

CAREER
Investment banking analyst; teacher

POLITICAL HIGHLIGHTS
Mo. House, 1977-95

ELECTION RESULTS

2000 GENERAL
Karen McCarthy (D)	159,826	68.9%
Steve Gordon (R)	66,439	28.6%
Charles Reitz (GREEN)	2,548	1.1%
Alan Newberry (LIBERT)	2,350	1.0%

2000 PRIMARY
Karen McCarthy (D)	35,071	85.4%
Charles Lindsey (D)	6,013	14.6%

1998 GENERAL
Karen McCarthy (D)	101,313	65.9%
Penny Bennett (R)	47,582	31.0%
Grant S. Stauffer (LIBERT)	2,646	1.7%
Elizabeth Ann Dulaney (REF)	2,144	1.4%

PREVIOUS WINNING PERCENTAGES
1996 (67%); 1994 (57%)

McCarthy spent 18 years in the Missouri House, where she honed her political skills and her moderate positions — two elements she brought with her to the U.S. House. After watching her in action during her first term, in the 104th Congress, Democratic leaders promoted her to the influential Commerce Committee at the beginning of the 105th. And at the start of the 106th, she was appointed to the Democratic Steering Committee, which makes the party's committee assignments.

McCarthy says she likes the breadth of the Commerce Committee, and she has worked on matters ranging from environmental protections to telecommunications to energy issues. Brownfields, as polluted abandoned industrial or military sites are known, have been a particular interest, and McCarthy played a key role in 1997 in providing tax incentives for businesses to clean up the sites.

McCarthy's star has risen quickly in the House in part because her philosophy and voting record offer something appealing to each of the three main factions in the Democratic Caucus — the traditional liberals, the conservative "Blue Dogs," and a group of centrists who call themselves the New Democrat Coalition. McCarthy belongs to the New Democrat group, which says it seeks "mainstream, bipartisan solutions." She has joined this centrist group in backing measures that liberal Democrats rejected, such as the 1996 overhaul of the nation's welfare system.

But on some issues, McCarthy will slide to the left. She supports environmental protections, abortion rights and gun control. She has also staunchly opposed GOP budget priorities. Yet she joined with the GOP majority and the Democratic Blue Dogs in two of their constitutional amendment crusades — to mandate a balanced federal budget and to permit Congress to ban desecration of the U.S. flag.

Consensus is important to McCarthy: "You can't make progress — if you are serious about making the world a better place — unless you can work at compromise and consensus building," she told the Kansas City Star back in 1994. "You can't be an extreme anything and be successful. You must find that comfort zone in the middle."

As evidenced by her long tenure in the Missouri Legislature, McCarthy is interested in lawmaking, and she would rather form ad hoc alliances and work quietly to craft a bill than take to the House floor to engage in partisan debate.

In her first months in Congress, mindful that voters had given the GOP control of the House for the first time in 40 years, she told her constituents that she had heard their call for "more competent, more efficient government." Her long experience in state government gives her a measure of sympathy for the GOP view that state and local officials should have more authority. She backed Republican efforts to prevent Washington from imposing mandates on state and local governments without providing funds to meet them.

Although McCarthy shares the view of many Republicans that the government's role should be limited, "Government does have a responsibility to see that each individual has opportunity," she told the Kansas City Star. "And sometimes people need boots in order to pull themselves up by those bootstraps. I see government's role as getting out of the way once that's accomplished," she told the newspaper.

During her tenure in the Missouri House, she traveled to Japan for a two-month fellowship to study ozone depletion, and in 1997 Democratic leader

Richard A. Gephardt named her as one of six Democratic observers at a global climate change conference in Kyoto, Japan. She was the most-junior member Gephardt put in the group.

McCarthy is generally in favor of open international trade. But in 2000, she voted "no" on a measure to grant China permanent normal trade status, citing concerns about environmental and worker protections.

On Capitol Hill, she has continued the work she began as a state legislator in championing a compact between Missouri and Kansas that permits taxation in the Kansas City metropolitan area to fund cultural facilities and restore historic structures, such as Kansas City's historic Union Station, which has been transformed into a science museum and children's learning center. In 2000, she authored legislation to renew the state compact and worked to obtain federal grants to assist the local projects.

McCarthy was born in Massachusetts and lived on a farm there until she was 14, when her father, who worked for Western Electric, was transferred to a Kansas City suburb.

She can pinpoint the day she became interested in public service: It was on her 21st birthday in 1968 when Robert F. Kennedy spoke at the University of Kansas, where she was majoring in English. She told the Kansas City Star that the speech, talking of empowerment and opportunity for everyone, "stays with me even now. ... So I knew from that day forward I would work for him, and thus would be a Democrat."

After graduation, she got a job teaching high school English but remained interested in politics, and she won election to the Missouri House at the age of 29. For the next 18 years, she advanced in the legislature, becoming chairman of the Ways and Means Committee — while working as an analyst for an investment banking firm and later as a government affairs consultant.

McCarthy was regarded as the favorite to win the 5th District seat when African-American Democratic Rep. Alan Wheat left it in 1994 for an unsuccessful Senate campaign. Her status as front-runner did not discourage competition, however. Ten others ran in the Democratic primary, but McCarthy's well-financed and well-organized campaign stayed above the fray, and she won with 41 percent of the vote.

In the general election, she faced an appealing political outsider, conservative black Republican Ron Freeman, a former professional football player who worked for years as an urban youth coordinator. McCarthy took advantage of the overwhelmingly Democratic bent of the district to win by 14 percentage points. She has won subsequent elections by ratios of better than 2-to-1.

KEY VOTES

2000
Yes Raise hourly minimum wage by $1 over two years
No Halt funding for U.S. mission in Kosovo unless European nations pay more
Yes Provide Medicare benefits to military retirees and their dependents
No Grant China permanent normal trade status
No Phase out estate, gift and trust taxes
No Prohibit implementation of president's national monument designations
No Approve GOP plan to provide prescription drug coverage for Medicare beneficiaries
Yes Increase help for poor nations indebted to international financial institutions

1999
Yes Impose steel import quotas
No Kill proposal to take aviation trust funds off budget
No Require background checks on buyers only at gun shows with 10 or more vendors
No Remove barriers among banking, securities and insurance companies
Yes Authorize state grants to hire teachers and reduce class size
Yes Overhaul campaign finance law; ban "soft money" and restrict advocacy advertising
Yes Approve bipartisan plan to increase rights of patients in managed-care health plans

INTEREST GROUPS

	AFL-CIO	ADA	CCUS	ACU
2000	100%	95%	52%	4%
1999	75%	95%	44%	0%
1998	89%	100%	56%	0%
1997	88%	80%	60%	16%

CQ VOTE STUDIES

	PARTY UNITY		PRESIDENTIAL SUPPORT	
	Support	Oppose	Support	Oppose
2000	94%	6%	87%	13%
1999	94%	6%	80%	20%
1998	92%	8%	81%	19%
1997	90%	10%	82%	18%

MISSOURI 5
Kansas City and eastern suburbs

Mostly middle-class, Democratic residents live in Kansas City and the western Jackson County suburbs that make up the 5th. Although the city's suburban growth is greatest in its Kansas portion, Missouri communities have prospered.

A diverse economic base has enabled Kansas City to grow from a cow town. Transportation, telecommunications, steel and automobile production facilities highlight a solid industrial base. Many 5th District residents travel to Kansas or Missouri's 6th District to work at companies such as Sprint Communications or General Motors. The federal government also is a large employer. And although its influence is a far cry from what it once was, the city is a major market for feeder cattle and winter wheat.

Hallmark Cards, one of the city's largest employers, built a popular new entertainment complex in the downtown area. Refurbishing the City Market and Quality Hill communities has lured younger, well-to-do residents to the city. Still, the contrasting neighborhoods on opposite sides of Troost Avenue remind residents of the economic disparity in the city, which largely runs along racial lines. Offshoot cities Blue Springs and Lee's Summit experienced double-digit population growth during the first half of the 1990s, and although the city of Independence has not grown as much, it still accounts for about one-fifth of the district's vote.

The 5th's portion of Kansas City is solidly Democratic and socially moderate. Popular Rep. Alan Wheat, a black Democrat, represented the district from 1983-95, and the seat has remained Democratic.

MAJOR INDUSTRY
Auto manufacturing, agriculture

MILITARY BASES
Marine Corps Support Activity, 371 military, 242 civilian (2001)

CITIES
Kansas City (pt.), 341,179 (1990); Independence (pt.), 111,215 (1990); Lee's Summit (pt.), 45,985 (1990); Raytown, 28,911

UNUSUAL FEATURES
President Harry S. Truman from Independence.

Rep. Sam Graves (R)

Elected 2000; 1st term

CAPITOL OFFICE
225-7041; fax 225-8221
1407 Longworth Bldg. 20515

INTERNET
e-mail: sam.graves@mail.house.gov
web: www.house.gov/graves

COMMITTEES
Agriculture
Small Business
Transportation & Infrastructure

HOMETOWN
Tarkio

BORN
Nov. 7, 1963, Fairfax, Mo.

RELIGION
Baptist

FAMILY
Wife, Lesley Graves; three children

EDUCATION
U. of Missouri, B.S. 1986

CAREER
Farmer

POLITICAL HIGHLIGHTS
Mo. House, 1993-95; Mo. Senate, 1995-2000

ELECTION RESULTS

2000 GENERAL

Sam Graves (R)	138,925	50.9%
Steve Danner (D)	127,792	46.8%
James Dykes (LIBERT)	3,696	1.4%
Marie Richey (NL)	2,788	1.0%

2000 PRIMARY

Sam Graves (R)	30,014	68.1%
Teresa Anne Loar (R)	7,493	17.0%
Jeff Bailey (R)	4,575	10.4%
John Dady (R)	1,122	2.5%
Jack DeSelms (R)	901	2.0%

In his bid to capture the largely rural, northwest Missouri 6th District for the GOP in 2000, Graves was helped by the fact that he is a sixth-generation farmer. The freshman, who holds a bachelor's degree in agronomy, won a seat on the Agriculture Committee, where he seeks to increase exports of farm commodities.

In keeping with the fiscally conservative bent of his district, Graves gets behind business-friendly legislation. His other assignments are on the Small Business and the Transportation and Infrastructure committees.

An ardent and vocal critic of "big government" who reveres President Reagan, Graves advocates returning a portion of the budget surplus to taxpayers and supports giving local school districts control of federal education funding. The first bill he introduced in the House was a measure to give school officials more authority to discipline disabled students who pose risks to others.

Just six months before the 2000 election, Graves, then a state senator, appeared to be headed again to Jefferson City. He had no intention of running for Congress, because Pat Danner — a popular conservative Democrat who had represented the 6th District for four terms — had filed for re-election.

But Danner unexpectedly announced that May that she would retire. The filing period for candidates for the seat was reopened, and GOP officials coaxed eight-year state legislator Graves into entering the race. He quickly overshadowed several lesser-known Republican hopefuls.

The Democrats nominated the congresswoman's son, Steve Danner. But Graves' assertive campaign and conservative politics enabled him to gain momentum in a district that — outside of its portion of Kansas City — consists mainly of small towns and farms and is regarded as a swing district.

Graves' down-home image was enhanced by his habit of having Sunday dinner with his parents, siblings and their families. He was able to counter Democrats' campaign charges that he was too much of a conservative ideologue and prevailed over Danner by 4 percentage points.

MISSOURI 6
Northwest — St. Joseph

A mixture of suburbanites and farmers, the 6th is bordered by Iowa to the north, Nebraska and Kansas to the west, and the Missouri River to the south.

Kansas City's suburban boom in the 1980s provided steady growth for the middle-class residents of Platte, Clay, Jackson and Ray counties who work in the city's steel, transportation and communications companies. The export facilities at the Kansas City International Airport and Trans World Airlines' (now American Airlines) operation there also provide major employment. The area has attracted some insurance, financial services and agribusiness companies after losing people to Kansas City for decades.

Corn, soybean and livestock pervade the rest of the 6th, which is still suffering from 1980s agricultural crises and a series of natural disasters in the '90s. Many farmers who remained in the northern and eastern counties now moonlight for manufacturers.

The 6th is the state's most politically marginal district, and the parties alternated control throughout the 20th century, with the district changing hands in 2000. Bill Clinton took both 1990s elections, but GOP Senate candidates did well during the same period. In 2000, President Bush carried the district with 53 percent of the vote. Republicans for state office have fared better recently, especially in the northern, rural areas.

MAJOR INDUSTRY
Agriculture, international shipping, manufacturing

CITIES
Kansas City (pt.), 93,925 (1990); St. Joseph, 69,577; Blue Springs (pt.), 29,294 (1990)

UNUSUAL FEATURES
Plattsburg memorial honors former Sen. David Rice Atchison, who served as president for one day on March 4, 1849, in between the terms of Presidents Polk and Taylor; Jesse James raised near Kearney.

Rep. Roy Blunt (R)

CAPITOL OFFICE
225-6536; fax 225-5604; 217 Cannon Bldg. 20515

INTERNET
e-mail: www.house.gov/blunt/guest.htm
web: www.house.gov/blunt

COMMITTEES
Energy & Commerce

HOMETOWN
Strafford

BORN
Jan. 10, 1950, Niangua, Mo.

RELIGION
Baptist

FAMILY
Wife, Roseann Blunt; three children

EDUCATION
Southwest Baptist U., B.A. 1970; Southwest
Missouri State U., M.A. 1972

CAREER
University president; teacher

POLITICAL HIGHLIGHTS
Greene County clerk, 1973-84; Republican
nominee for lieutenant governor, 1980; Mo.
secretary of state, 1985-93; sought Republican
nomination for governor, 1992

ELECTION RESULTS

2000 GENERAL

Roy Blunt (R)	202,305	73.9%
Charles Christrup (D)	65,510	23.9%
Doug Burlison (LIBERT)	2,965	1.1%

2000 PRIMARY

Roy Blunt (R)	62,711	86.4%
Mike Harman (R)	9,856	13.6%

1998 GENERAL

Roy Blunt (R)	129,746	72.6%
Marc Perkel (D)	43,416	24.3%
Mike Harman (LIBERT)	5,639	3.2%

PREVIOUS WINNING PERCENTAGES
1996 (65%)

Elected 1996; 3rd term

After just two years in the House, Blunt's affable demeanor, listening skills, political savvy and willingness to work behind the scenes with all House Republican factions lifted him to a key post in the inner councils of the party: chief deputy whip. In 2001, as he began his third term, his standing on Capitol hill took another big step up.

As one of the earliest congressional backers of George W. Bush's presidential quest — and the chief liaison between the Texas governor and the House GOP during the campaign — Blunt is as well-positioned as anyone at the Capitol to play a key role in the relationship between the 43rd president and the 107th Congress.

Blunt continues in the top non-elective post in the House GOP leadership hierarchy; as chief deputy whip, he serves as a go-between, passing information both ways for the leadership and the rank-and-file with the bottom-line goal of advancing the GOP legislative agenda. In the 106th Congress, he often was detailed by the leadership to work with warring factions in the party to find a legislative middle ground. Those who saw him operate say he shares many of the attributes of the man he succeeded in that job, J. Dennis Hastert, who catapulted from chief deputy whip to the speakership in 1999.

In the 107th, Hastert appointed Blunt to head up a special panel to look into the voting system across the country, in the wake of widespread difficulties that were highlighted in the 2000 balloting.

Blunt is a fiscal conservative, slightly to the right even of his own party. He was one of 31 Republicans who voted against the spending portion of the 1997 balanced-budget plan, arguing that it permitted too much funding for President Clinton's favorite programs. In the 106th Congress, one of his major legislative priorities was "tax fairness." Of particular interest were bills to eliminate the estate tax and the "marriage penalty," a quirk in the tax code that results in some two-earner married couples paying more in taxes than they would if each partner were single. He also pushed to eliminate the 102-year-old telephone excise tax.

In 1999, Blunt won a coveted seat on the Commerce Committee (now Energy and Commerce). He had to relinquish seats he held in his first term on the Agriculture, Transportation and International Relations panels, but Commerce's far-reaching jurisdiction permitted him to continue working on many of the same issues, particularly agriculture, which is important to his constituents.

The son of a dairy farmer and a state legislator, Blunt was raised on a farm near Springfield. He now lives on another farm nearby, raising Angus cattle and a few horses, and doing many of the chores himself. Every summer he conducts an agricultural tour of the district, and his 2000 bus tour — which visited a dozen farms, ranches and agribusinesses — attracted trade representatives from Japan and Taiwan.

Although agriculture interests favor expanded trade, Blunt was conflicted in 2000 when faced with a vote on granting China permanent normal trade status. In the past, he had voted against opening trade, citing religious persecution and other human rights violations in China; but in 2000, he ultimately joined the majority that voted to enact the trade measure, saying that opening China to influences from the free world would improve conditions there.

In 1999, Blunt won a victory for the district's dairy industry when he was able to block a proposed new Department of Agriculture pricing system that would have reduced prices dairy farmers receive in most areas of the country. He also was able to prevent the Environmental Protection Agency from including propane — a major source of heating fuel in southwest Missouri — on its list of toxic substances.

Blunt is a frequent critic of federal regulations he sees as burdensome; one target is the Occupational Safety and Health Administration. In 1997, he tried to cut the agency's funding; and in 2000, he was a leading opponent of its plan to check home offices for unsafe working conditions, saying the agency had "given itself the keys to the front doors of millions of homes."

He also was a key player in the GOP move to prevent the implementation of new ergonomics rules issued in the final days of the Clinton administration, contending that the regulations aimed at preventing repetitive motion injuries would be particularly tough and expensive for small businesses to meet.

Blunt's leadership post and his Energy and Commerce Committee assignment both aid his fundraising efforts. With money from his political action committee, the Rely on Your Beliefs (RoyB for short) fund, he helped pay for Majority Whip Tom DeLay's operations at the 2000 Republican National Convention. Blunt's PAC also delivered $207,000 to Republican congressional candidates in the 2000 election cycle.

Blunt's first job after college was as a high school government and history teacher, but he was active in party politics at an early age, working in 1972 on an unsuccessful congressional bid by John Ashcroft, who went on to become governor, senator and now attorney general. A year later, Blunt was appointed Greene County Clerk by Republican Gov. Christopher S. Bond, now the state's senior senator. Blunt was re-elected to that post twice, and after an unsuccessful run for lieutenant governor in 1980, he won the first of two terms as secretary of state in 1984, serving under Ashcroft. (Blunt's oldest son, Matt, has continued the family's involvement in politics, serving in the legislature and winning election as secretary of state in 2000.)

After losing the Republican gubernatorial primary in 1992, Blunt accepted the presidency of his alma mater, Southwest Baptist University, seemingly finished with politics. But that changed in 1996, when GOP Rep. Mel Hancock announced his retirement. Blunt won a narrow primary victory over Gary Nodler, a former aide to GOP Rep. Gene Taylor, Hancock's predecessor in the 7th District. That November Blunt cruised to an easy win with 65 percent of the vote in the reliably Republican district. His re-election races have been cakewalks.

KEY VOTES

2000

No   Raise hourly minimum wage by $1 over two years
Yes   Halt funding for U.S. mission in Kosovo unless European nations pay more
Yes   Provide Medicare benefits to military retirees and their dependents
Yes   Grant China permanent normal trade status
Yes   Phase out estate, gift and trust taxes
Yes   Prohibit implementation of president's national monument designations
Yes   Approve GOP plan to provide prescription drug coverage for Medicare beneficiaries
No   Increase help for poor nations indebted to international financial institutions

1999

No   Impose steel import quotas
Yes   Kill proposal to take aviation trust funds off budget
Yes   Require background checks on buyers only at gun shows with 10 or more vendors
Yes   Remove barriers among banking, securities and insurance companies
No   Authorize state grants to hire teachers and reduce class size
No   Overhaul campaign finance law; ban "soft money" and restrict advocacy advertising
No   Approve bipartisan plan to increase rights of patients in managed-care health plans

INTEREST GROUPS

	AFL-CIO	ADA	CCUS	ACU
2000	0%	0%	90%	96%
1999	13%	10%	96%	87%
1998	0%	0%	82%	100%
1997	25%	10%	90%	80%

CQ VOTE STUDIES

	PARTY UNITY		PRESIDENTIAL SUPPORT	
	Support	Oppose	Support	Oppose
2000	98%	2%	25%	75%
1999	95%	5%	19%	81%
1998	95%	5%	17%	83%
1997	95%	5%	25%	75%

MISSOURI 7

Southwest — Springfield; Joplin

Two decades of rapid growth helped lift southwestern Missouri from a poor rural hideaway to a burgeoning resort region with a growing industrial base. Since the 1970s this part of Missouri has outpaced the rest of the state in population growth.

Springfield, the district's industrial and commercial center, has become a manufacturing hub. More than 40 percent of the 7th's residents live in Greene County, where Springfield is located, and neighboring Christian County. The district's other population center is Joplin. Once a lead and zinc mining town, it is now a manufacturing and trucking center. Tourism thrives in much of the district, especially in Branson, which has become a magnet for country music fans who are attracted to its theaters and studios.

In the southwestern corner of the district lies the more hilly Ozark region, which supports beef and dairy cattle, along with poultry. Many of the small, isolated communities in the Ozarks have not quite yielded

to development and remain legacies of the region's settlers — Scots-Irish mountaineers from eastern Tennessee, western Virginia and Kentucky. Many of these rural counties struggle economically.

The 7th has long been considered a Republican bastion. Springfield, the district's largest city, has become slightly more Democratic since the 1980s, partly because of the influx of new residents. However, the city still leans Republican. The 7th's conservatism also is reflected in its politically active religious organizations.

MAJOR INDUSTRY
Manufacturing, agriculture, tourism

CITIES
Springfield, 142,669; Joplin, 45,016; Carthage, 11,846

UNUSUAL FEATURES
President Harry S. Truman born in Lamar; Springfield is home to Fantastic Caverns, America's only ride-through cave; Branson, setting of Harold Bell Wright's novel, "The Shepherd of the Hills."

Rep. Jo Ann Emerson (R)

CAPITOL OFFICE
225-4404; fax 226-0326; 326 Cannon Bldg. 20515

INTERNET
e-mail: joann.emerson@mail.house.gov
web: www.house.gov/emerson

COMMITTEES
Appropriations

HOMETOWN
Cape Girardeau

BORN
Sept. 16, 1950, Bethesda, Md.

RELIGION
Presbyterian

FAMILY
Husband, Ron Gladney; two children, six stepchildren

EDUCATION
Ohio Wesleyan U., B.A. 1972

CAREER
Public affairs executive; lobbyist

POLITICAL HIGHLIGHTS
No previous office

ELECTION RESULTS

2000 GENERAL

Jo Ann Emerson (R)	162,239	69.3%
Bob Camp (D)	67,760	29.0%

2000 PRIMARY

Jo Ann Emerson (R)	unopposed

1998 GENERAL

Jo Ann Emerson (R)	104,271	62.6%
Anthony J. Heckemeyer (D)	59,426	35.7%
John B. Hendricks Jr. (LIBERT)	2,827	1.7%

PREVIOUS WINNING PERCENTAGES
1996 (51%); 1996 Special Election (63%)

Elected 1996; 3rd full term

In just two terms in the House, Emerson has quickly carved out a niche as a key advocate for rural America. She won a seat on the Appropriations Committee and its Agriculture Subcommittee in her second term, and in 2000 she was one of the guiding forces behind the revitalization of the dormant Rural Caucus, serving as one of its two co-chairmen.

Emerson succeeded her late husband, Bill Emerson, who died of lung cancer in June 1996. "I never sought this job. Fate put me here," she told The Washington Post soon after her election to Congress that fall.

Although she was born and raised in the Washington, D.C., suburbs and lived most of her life there, Emerson has worked to develop the same kind of bond her husband had with her southeast Missouri constituents. She continued her husband's annual summer agricultural tour of the district. She constantly points out that the 8th is the poorest of Missouri's nine congressional districts and told the St. Louis Post-Dispatch that she could not let her husband's work languish. "People like the way they were being represented, and I knew I could carry on in that manner," she said.

When district needs conflict with the GOP agenda, Emerson will go against the party's wishes. A tax cut, for example, is far down the list of priorities for her low- and middle-income constituents, she says, ranking below access to health care and healthy farm prices. Her interest in opening foreign markets to farm exports led her to join with Washington Republican George Nethercutt in pressing for an end to the U.S. food and medicine embargo against "terrorist" states, including Cuba.

But Emerson is no rebel. Her usual backing of the conservative agenda makes her a favorite of the Republican leadership, as does her gender, since the GOP is always looking for ways to counter analysts who say the party's ideology is less appealing to women voters. She is often tapped by the leadership for the visible role of presiding over the House.

Drawing on her 20 years of experience as a lobbyist — she worked for the American Insurance Association and the National Restaurant Association — Emerson has set about developing a wide range of friends and alliances. Soon after she took office, she played an active role in the House's March 1997 "civility" retreat in Hershey, Pa., where members from both parties got to know each other better, with an eye toward reducing rancor in the chamber.

She was the only congressional freshman named to the group of lawmakers who attended the 1997 conference on global warming in Kyoto, Japan. She opposes many of the actions agreed to by the U.S. negotiating team, arguing that they make unfair demands on U.S. producers and consumers. Since the conference, she has sponsored several amendments to prevent the executive branch from taking steps to adhere to the agreement, which has not been ratified by the Senate.

Emerson supports property owners' rights over efforts to increase environmental protections, and she believes that states should have primacy in land management decisions. She denounced President Clinton's plan to designate certain waterways as American Heritage Rivers and has opposed a number of wetlands protections measures.

On the Rural Caucus, Emerson deals with a range of issues important to her constituents. She believes that the 1996 "Freedom to Farm" law should be revisited to ensure that farmers have a better safety net to protect them during periods of low prices. The caucus also works to improve health care in rural areas, where low federal payments to hospitals and doctors endanger continued service. One of Emerson's priorities in the 106th Congress was to permit domestic pharmacies and other drug distributors to reimport U.S.-manufactured drugs from other countries, where they are sold much more cheaply. Rural lawmakers also are concerned about the so-called digital divide, complaining that rural areas often are bypassed when it comes to keeping pace with technological advances.

Emerson's undiluted conservatism is evident in the range of constitutional amendments she supports, including proposals to allow Congress to ban desecration of the U.S. flag, to require a balanced federal budget and to impose term limits on lawmakers. Her backing of a constitutional amendment to outlaw abortion sets her apart from some GOP women lawmakers. In 1999, she authored an amendment condemning the entertainment industry for its use of graphic brutality in movies, television, music, and video games.

Emerson was born in Bethesda, Md. Her father, Ab Hermann, was for many years the executive director of the Republican National Committee. After graduating from Ohio Wesleyan, Emerson returned to the Washington area, where she worked for the National Republican Congressional Committee (NRCC) and then began a career as a lobbyist. In Washington, she met Bill Emerson, who also was a lobbyist.

Her husband was a candidate for a ninth House term when he died. Although initially reluctant to jump into the race, Jo Ann told Good Housekeeping magazine that she "started getting comfortable with herself" halfway through her campaign, drawing inspiration from a family friend and former neighbor, Lindy Boggs, who had won a congressional seat in 1973 under similar circumstances, after the death of her husband, Hale Boggs, D-La.

Emerson had to run as an independent because the filing deadline for the primary had closed before her husband died, and the Missouri secretary of State said state law prohibited the reopening of the filing. However, she garnered the endorsements of the House Republican leadership, the NRCC (where she had served for a time as deputy director of communications) and the Missouri Republican Party.

Emerson wrapped herself in her husband's mantle — the campaign was called "Team Emerson" — and promised to continue his legacy. She won with 50 percent of the vote, finishing 13 points ahead of Democrat Emily Firebaugh and 39 points ahead of the official GOP candidate, Richard A. Kline. (The same day, she won a special election to fill the last two months of her husband's term.) Her re-election races since then have been routine. In 2000, she married St. Louis Democratic labor lawyer Ron Gladney.

KEY VOTES

2000

No Raise hourly minimum wage by $1 over two years

Yes Halt funding for U.S. mission in Kosovo unless European nations pay more

Yes Provide Medicare benefits to military retirees and their dependents

Yes Grant China permanent normal trade status

Yes Phase out estate, gift and trust taxes

Yes Prohibit implementation of president's national monument designations

Yes Approve GOP plan to provide prescription drug coverage for Medicare beneficiaries

No Increase help for poor nations indebted to international financial institutions

1999

Yes Impose steel import quotas

Yes Kill proposal to take aviation trust funds off budget

No Require background checks on buyers only at gun shows with 10 or more vendors

Yes Remove barriers among banking, securities and insurance companies

No Authorize state grants to hire teachers and reduce class size

No Overhaul campaign finance law; ban "soft money" and restrict advocacy advertising

No Approve bipartisan plan to increase rights of patients in managed-care health plans

INTEREST GROUPS

	AFL-CIO	ADA	CCUS	ACU
2000	10%	0%	80%	80%
1999	33%	10%	80%	80%
1998	10%	5%	83%	92%
1997	0%	5%	90%	88%

CQ VOTE STUDIES

	PARTY UNITY		PRESIDENTIAL SUPPORT	
	Support	Oppose	Support	Oppose
2000	91%	9%	24%	76%
1999	88%	12%	21%	79%
1998	92%	8%	22%	78%
1997	96%	4%	27%	73%

MISSOURI 8
Southeast – Cape Girardeau

Within the borders of the 8th is some of the state's most bountiful farmland, and the district's agricultural diversity is matched by its political breadth.

The 8th, which takes in Missouri's southeastern corner, spans the spectrum from solidly Republican counties in the west and northeast along the Mississippi River to "Yellow Dog" Democratic territory in the southeastern corner, known as the boot heel. District voters tend to be socially conservative on issues such as abortion and gun control and leary of environmental regulations.

The district often follows the Republican lead of its northeast counties, such as Cape Girardeau and Perry, in congressional contests. On the national level, the 8th gave Bill Clinton the edge in the 1992 and '96 presidential contests, but backed President Bush by a 20 percent margin in 2000.

The major growth centers in the district are its northern counties, Washington and St. Francois, which attract commuters to St. Louis. Both counties lean Democratic. The boot heel is a former wheat- and cotton-growing region which now produces soybeans and corn. Above the boot heel, along the Mississippi River, dairy production and beef cattle fuel the economy.

The district's varied agricultural economy, along with one of the world's richest lead supplies in the central counties, provide the 8th with unusual economic stability for a mostly rural area.

MAJOR INDUSTRY
Agriculture, mining, lumber

CITIES
Cape Girardeau, 36,687; Sikeston, 18,071; Poplar Bluff, 17,500

UNUSUAL FEATURES
U.S. population center near Edgar Springs; 1990 population center also was in the 8th, near Steelville; Laura Ingalls Wilder wrote her "Little House on the Prairie" books in Mansfield.

Rep. Kenny Hulshof (R)

CAPITOL OFFICE
225-2956; fax 225-5712; 412 Cannon Bldg. 20515

INTERNET
e-mail: www.house.gov/writerep
web: www.house.gov/hulshof

COMMITTEES
Ways & Means

HOMETOWN
Columbia

BORN
May 22, 1958, Sikeston, Mo.

RELIGION
Roman Catholic

FAMILY
Wife, Renee Hulshof; one child

EDUCATION
U. of Missouri, B.S. 1980; U. of Mississippi, J.D. 1983

CAREER
State and city prosecutor; public defender

POLITICAL HIGHLIGHTS
Sought Republican nomination for Boone County prosecutor, 1992; Republican nominee for U.S. House, 1994

ELECTION RESULTS

2000 GENERAL

Kenny Hulshof (R)	172,787	59.3%
Steven R. Carroll (D)	111,662	38.3%
Robert Hoffman (LIBERT)	3,608	1.2%

2000 PRIMARY

Kenny Hulshof (R)	unopposed

1998 GENERAL

Kenny Hulshof (R)	117,196	62.2%
Linda Vogt (D)	66,861	35.5%
Robert Hoffman (LIBERT)	4,248	2.3%

PREVIOUS WINNING PERCENTAGES
1996 (49%)

Elected 1996; 3rd term

One of the stars of the GOP freshman Class of 1996, Hulshof continued to shine in his second term on Capitol Hill, playing a major role in measures aimed at helping family farmers, an important constituency in the 9th District, and letting disabled people work while keeping their medical benefits.

When Hulshof (HULLZ-hoff) arrived in Washington in 1997, fresh from his election victory over veteran Democratic Rep. Harold L. Volkmer in a district that had last elected a Republican in 1920, he was rewarded by party leaders, who gave him a seat on the Ways and Means Committee. He was also honored by his fellow GOP freshmen, who elected him class president.

In his second term on Ways and Means, Hulshof was a key player on legislation, which became law, to permit disabled people to work and earn money without losing their medical benefits. "Rarely do we have a group of people coming to us in Washington and say, 'We want to be taxpayers,' " Hulshof said. He was also the principal sponsor of a bill to expand tax-free savings accounts devoted to educational expenses.

Also in the 106th Congress, Hulshof fought to win the repeal of the 1993 4.3-cents-per-gallon tax on fuel used by trains and boat traffic on inland waterways. And he continued his effort, begun in the 105th Congress, to permit farmers to set aside a portion of their income in tax-sheltered savings accounts for use during times of economic hardship. He also authored legislation that created a high-level government international trade position strictly devoted to looking out for the interests of agriculture — a matter of importance to his farm constituents in northeast Missouri.

Hulshof's post on Ways and Means also gave him the opportunity to fight Chairman Bill Archer's 1997 plan to phase out the tax break for ethanol — a plan that Archer quickly abandoned. In 1998, Hulshof was appointed as a conferee on the transportation authorization bill, and he and other farm-state lawmakers were able to win a seven-year extension of the ethanol credit. Farmers like ethanol because it is a corn-based fuel.

Hulshof is a loyal Republican vote across a range of economic and social policy issues, but he is not afraid to go his own way. "Generally, my goals do not conflict with those of the party," Hulshof said shortly after his arrival. But "there have been times when, in the interest of my constituents, I have bucked the Republican leadership."

As GOP freshman class president in the 105th Congress, Hulshof made a concerted effort to define himself and his peers as not only conservative but also pragmatic and cooperative, not given to the kind of ideological brinkmanship that characterized many in the confrontational House Republican Class of 1994. "We're a kinder, gentler freshman class," Hulshof said, adding that his classmates had "learned from the mistakes they [the GOP in the 104th Congress] made."

Hulshof told the Kansas City Star, just after he was first elected, "Two years ago, it was seen as a curse to have had any prior political experience. But we see it as an advantage because we know how to get things accomplished." Soon after the 105th Congress convened, Hulshof was a leading force behind a bipartisan "civility" retreat in Hershey, Pa., where the objective was for Republicans and Democrats to get acquainted with each other in a non-confrontational setting.

Also in the 105th, he joined with Florida Rep. Jim Davis, president of the freshman Democrats, to form a bipartisan freshman task force that explored changing the campaign finance system. Hulshof did not put himself on the task force when he appointed its Republican members, but he cosponsored an overhaul measure that the panel developed after holding hearings.

A former high school athlete, Hulshof stars as the first baseman for the GOP in the annual charity baseball game against the Democrats (he was the GOP's most valuable player in 2000), and as a guard and a forward on the congressional basketball team that plays a team of lobbyists in another charity event. Hulshof also sings and plays the drums in his church choir, and in the 105th Congress, he performed with three other Class of 1996 Republicans in a singing quartet called the Capitol Four.

Hulshof grew up on a southeastern Missouri farm, was active in Future Farmers of America and majored in agricultural economics at the University of Missouri. He recalls getting an uncomfortably personal lesson in how politics affects agriculture, when his parents almost lost their farm because of the 1980 U.S. grain embargo of the Soviet Union.

Hulshof moved from agriculture into law after taking a course in agricultural law at Missouri and then pursuing the specialty at the University of Mississippi law school. Upon graduation, Hulshof worked for three years as a public defender and three years as a prosecutor in southeast Missouri's Cape Girardeau County before moving to Columbia to work for the state attorney general.

He says his early political role models were Democratic Rep. Jerry Litton, who died in a 1976 plane crash just after winning a Senate primary, and Republican Bill Emerson, who represented southeast Missouri's 8th District from 1981 until his death in 1996.

Hulshof was a fill-in candidate in 1994 against Volkmer, tapped by party leaders to run after GOP front-runner Rick Hardy bowed out after the filing deadline. Hulshof traveled to Washington, D.C., to sign the "Contract With America" GOP campaign pledge and ran a good race despite his lack of political experience and name recognition. He lost by just 5 points, encouraging him to try again in 1996, when he was able to campaign full-time.

He had to overcome a stiff GOP primary challenge from wealthy ophthalmologist Harry Eggleston, who spent heavily from his own pocket. A glitch in vote reporting had Eggleston briefly believing he had won, but Hulshof prevailed. He went on to edge Volkmer by slightly less than 6,000 votes in November.

A significant benefit of Hulshof's Ways and Means post is that it has given a boost to his campaign fundraising. He has been able to amass a sizable campaign war chest that has discouraged serious challenges in 1998 and 2000.

KEY VOTES

2000
No — Raise hourly minimum wage by $1 over two years
Yes — Halt funding for U.S. mission in Kosovo unless European nations pay more
Yes — Provide Medicare benefits to military retirees and their dependents
Yes — Grant China permanent normal trade status
Yes — Phase out estate, gift and trust taxes
Yes — Prohibit implementation of president's national monument designations
Yes — Approve GOP plan to provide prescription drug coverage for Medicare beneficiaries
No — Increase help for poor nations indebted to international financial institutions

1999
No — Impose steel import quotas
Yes — Kill proposal to take aviation trust funds off budget
No — Require background checks on buyers only at gun shows with 10 or more vendors
Yes — Remove barriers among banking, securities and insurance companies
No — Authorize state grants to hire teachers and reduce class size
Yes — Overhaul campaign finance law; ban "soft money" and restrict advocacy advertising
— Approve bipartisan plan to increase rights of patients in managed-care health plans

INTEREST GROUPS

	AFL-CIO	ADA	CCUS	ACU
2000	0%	5%	85%	96%
1999	13%	25%	88%	84%
1998	0%	15%	100%	88%
1997	13%	15%	90%	92%

CQ VOTE STUDIES

	PARTY UNITY		PRESIDENTIAL SUPPORT	
	Support	Oppose	Support	Oppose
2000	96%	4%	19%	81%
1999	88%	12%	22%	78%
1998	89%	11%	25%	75%
1997	93%	7%	29%	71%

MISSOURI 9
Northeast – Columbia

Besides Columbia and the far western St. Louis suburbs, the 9th consists of small towns spread among farmlands. Residents include mostly middle-class and socially conservative Democrats, although rapid suburban growth is giving way to new wealth and the rise of some Republican sections.

The 9th includes about half of St. Charles County, booming with newcomers from St. Louis. Suburban growth is also swelling nearby Lincoln, Warren, Franklin and Gasconade counties. A General Motors plant in Wentzville and a Boeing hub in St. Charles (in the 2nd) provide lots of jobs, but most of the growth has come from small businesses. A wine industry that dates back more than 150 years provides income for Gasconade and Franklin counties.

Columbia, a steadily growing and mostly middle-class city, hosts the University of Missouri's flagship campus and a handful of medical facilities, including the Harry S. Truman Memorial Veterans Hospital.

Farther north, many rural communities have been unable to weather the agricultural depression of the 1980s and severe floods in the 1990s. Despite a huge exodus of young people from farming families, cattle, soybean, corn and winter wheat remain economic mainstays.

Traditionally Democratic, the 9th has become a swing district due to the growth of suburban St. Louis and the decline of "Yellow Dog" Democrats in rural communities. Prior to 1996, voters elected a Republican member of Congress just once in the 20th century, in 1920.

MAJOR INDUSTRY
Higher education, electronics, agriculture

CITIES
Columbia, 80,500; O'Fallon (pt.), 18,653 (1990); Hannibal, 17,854

UNUSUAL FEATURES
Samuel Clemens (Mark Twain) born in Hannibal, which attracts more than 250,000 people each year who pay tribute to "Tom Sawyer's fence;" Westminster College in Fulton, where Winston Churchill gave his "Iron Curtain" speech after World War II; Truman State University in Kirksville named for state icon Harry S. Truman; Annual "All-Star Mule and Donkey Show" in the Columbia area every August.

Gov. Judy Martz (R)

First elected: 2000
Length of term: 4 years
Term expires: 1/05
Salary: $83,672
Phone: (406) 444-3111
Hometown: Helena
Born: July 28, 1943, Big Timber, Mont.
Religion: Christian Church
Family: Husband, Harry Martz; two children
Education: Eastern Montana College, attended 1964-65
Career: Commercial solid waste disposal company owner; congressional aide; sporting goods retailer; Olympic athlete
Political highlights: Lieutenant governor, 1997-2001

Election results:

2000 GENERAL

Judy Martz (R)	209,135	51.0%
Mark O'Keefe (D)	193,131	47.1%
Stan Jones (LIBERT)	7,926	1.9%

Lt. Gov. Karl Ohs (R)

First elected: 2000
Length of term: 4 years
Term expires: 1/05
Salary: $58,962
Phone: (406) 444-3111

STATE LEGISLATURE

Legislature: Meets January-April
House: 100 members, 2-year terms
2001 breakdown: 58R, 42D; 73 men, 27 women
Salary: $71.83, 6 days per week while in session; $87.25/day in session allowance
Phone: (406) 444-4819
Senate: 50 members, 4-year terms
2001 breakdown: 31R, 19D; 43 men, 7 women
Salary: $71.83, 6 days per week while in session; $87.25/day in session allowance
Phone: (406) 444-4880

STATE TERM LIMITS

Governor: 2 terms in a 16-year period
Senate: 2 terms in a 16-year period
House: 4 terms in a 16-year period

URBAN STATISTICS

CITY	POPULATION
Billings	92,988
Missoula	58,460
Great Falls	56,340
Butte/Silver Bow	33,325
Bozeman	30,723

REGISTERED VOTERS

Voters do not register by party.

POPULATION

2000 population	902,195
1990 population	799,065
Percent change	+12.9%
Rank among states	44
Median age	36.9
Born in state	59%
Foreign born	2%
Urban/rural	53%/47%
Crime rate	132/100,000
Poverty level	16.6%
Federal workers	12,647
Military	8,474

REAPPORTIONMENT

Montana retained its one House seat in reapportionment.

MISCELLANEOUS

Web: www.state.mt.us
Capital: Helena
Land area: 145,556 sq. miles
Rank among states: 4
STATE ELECTION OFFICIAL
(406) 444-4732
DEMOCRATIC HEADQUARTERS
(406) 442-9520
REPUBLICAN HEADQUARTERS
(406) 442-6469

District Statistics

DIST.	VOTE FOR PRESIDENT 2000 D	R	GREEN	1996 D	R	REF	1992 D	R	I	WHT	BLK	ASIAN	HISP	HOUSEHOLD INCOME	OVER 65+	UNDER 18	COLLEGE EDUCATION
AL	33%	58%	6%	41%	44%	14%	38%	35%	26%	93%	<1%	1%	2%	$22,988	13%	28%	20%

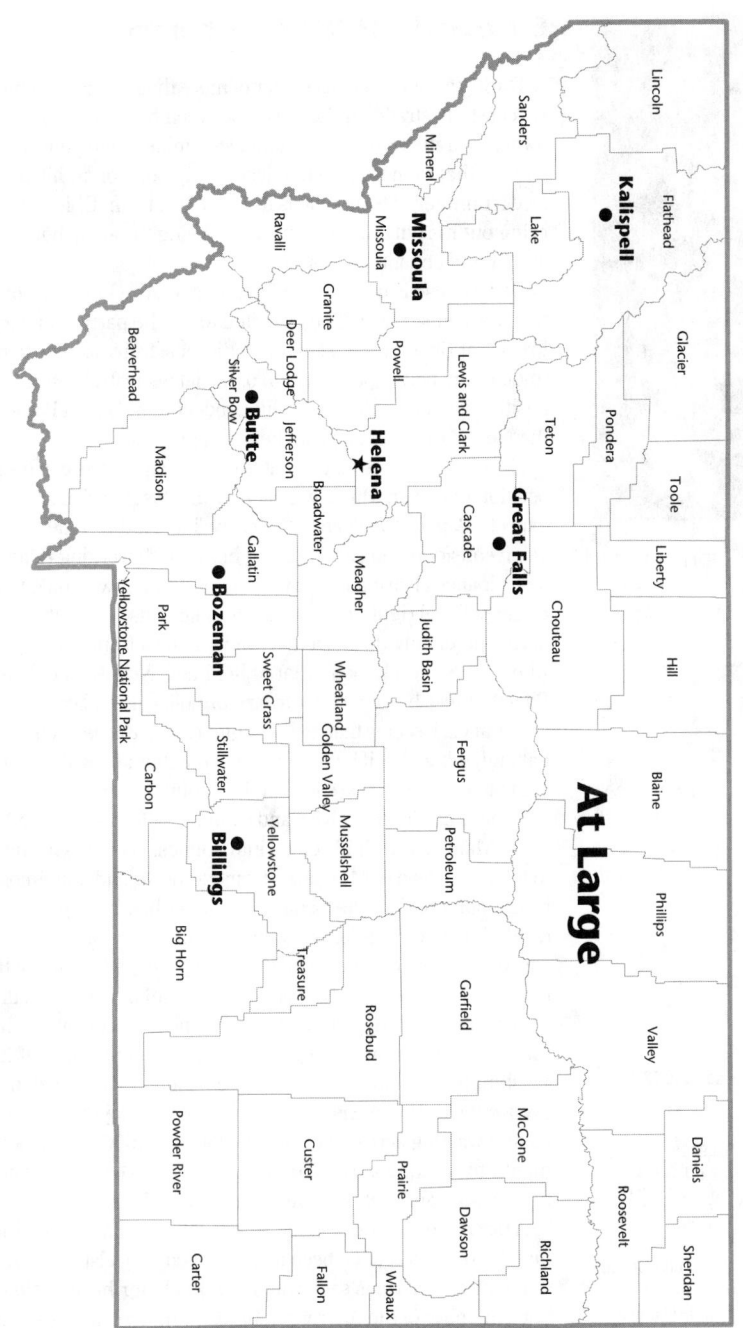

Sen. Max Baucus (D)

CAPITOL OFFICE
224-2651; fax 228-3687; 511 Hart Bldg. 20510

INTERNET
e-mail: max@baucus.senate.gov
web: baucus.senate.gov

COMMITTEES
Agriculture, Nutrition & Forestry
Environment & Public Works
Finance - ranking member
Joint Taxation

HOMETOWN
Helena

BORN
Dec. 11, 1941, Helena, Mont.

RELIGION
United Church of Christ

FAMILY
Wife, Wanda Minge; one child

EDUCATION
Stanford U., A.B. 1964, LL.B. 1967

CAREER
Lawyer

POLITICAL HIGHLIGHTS
Mont. House, 1973-75; U.S. House, 1975-78

ELECTION RESULTS

1996 GENERAL

Max Baucus (D)	201,935	49.6%
Denny Rehberg (R)	182,111	44.7%
Becky Shaw (REF)	19,276	4.7%
Stephen Heaton (NL)	4,168	1.0%

1996 PRIMARY

Max Baucus (D)	unopposed

PREVIOUS WINNING PERCENTAGES
1990 (68%); 1984 (57%); 1978 (56%); 1976 House Election (66%); 1974 House Election (55%)

Elected 1978; 4th term

During a congressional career of more than a quarter-century, Baucus has successfully straddled the divide between his state's farmers and business owners, on the right, and its unionized miners and educators, on the left.

Now that he has risen to a leadership position in his party, Baucus will face a number of tests if he is to win a fifth term. Chief among them is carrying out his duty to his party while trying to satisfy both his conservative and liberal constituencies.

Baucus also is the ranking Democrat on the Finance Committee, a position from which he will be expected to set the party's tone in responding to President Bush on a host of top-tier issues, from tax cuts to Medicare, from trade to the partial privatization of Social Security. He had long coveted the position and often filled in for his predecessor, Daniel Patrick Moynihan, in the New Yorker's final years before retirement.

Now Baucus faces considerable conflicting pressure in his newly acquired position of power. Minority Leader Tom Daschle also sits on the panel and expects Baucus to advance the party line. At the same time, Baucus' campaign considerations for 2002 and his smooth working relationship with the new Finance chairman, Charles E. Grassley, R-Iowa, could tempt him to veer to the political right on issues such as tax cuts.

As one of only three Democratic senators from a Rocky Mountain state (the others are Nevada's Harry Reid and New Mexico's Jeff Bingaman), Baucus must be constantly aware of political implications. From outward appearance, it seems that he is struggling with that burden. He tends to speak haltingly, almost as if he is thinking about the ramifications of what he is saying just as the words are leaving his mouth.

Baucus credits the advice and example of former Senate Majority Leader Mike Mansfield with his entry into politics. Baucus says he has attempted to follow the lead of Montana's Democratic legend, but times have changed in the state and in the Senate. Montana has become increasingly more divided; Democrats dominate in the stunningly picturesque mountainous western half, where the population is growing, while the GOP dominates in the more agrarian and economically struggling eastern half.

Baucus has tried to bridge the differences by convincing his constituents that he is just an average Joe, despite spending most of his adult life in Washington — and where he is often spotted jogging along the Potomac, even when the Senate is in recess. He has employed such homespun remedies as walking across the state in 1995 and 1996 and dedicating one day a month to working a "regular" job. He has served as a construction worker in Bozeman and a chili-serving waiter in Helena.

A placard on the desk in his Senate office declares that "Montana Comes First,"and that has often been true in Baucus' legislative efforts. He has spent much of his energies securing federal help for his constituents. Although not a member of the Appropriations Committee, he has steered tens of millions of dollars to Montana for projects, ranging from rural medical care to university research grants. In 2000, he sought to expedite disaster relief for Montanans affected by voracious forest fires. In the 105th Congress, as the top Democrat on the panel that wrote the law reauthorizing federal transportation programs, he helped push through a new funding formula that aided Western states. Montana's funding increased 60 percent.

In the 106th Congress, Baucus was a top Democrat on Finance's Trade Subcommittee, from which he helped to push to enactment several bills to expand world commerce. The highest-profile effort was the legislation granting China permanent normal trade status. It won 83 Senate votes, and its enactment promises enormous new export prospects for Baucus' farm constituents.

On many hot-button national issues, Baucus' vote cannot be easily predicted. He strongly supports abortion rights and in 1998 voted against overriding President Clinton's veto of legislation that would have barred a procedure its opponents call "partial birth" abortion. But he sided with Republicans in supporting politically popular constitutional amendments to prohibit flag burning and to require a balanced budget.

Baucus has faced much grief for reversing his career-long opposition to gun control by voting in 1993 for the Brady law, which mandated a waiting period and background check before the purchase of a handgun, and the 1994 crime law, which included a ban on certain semiautomatic assault-style weapons. But in 1999, Baucus was the only Senate Democrat who voted "no" on the key amendment to that year's gun control bill. It would have required mandatory background checks for firearms purchases at gun shows.

He was also the only Finance Committee Democrat in the 104th to vote for the controversial welfare overhaul package, which Clinton later signed, and the only Democrat on the Agriculture Committee to support legislation to cut food stamp spending.

Much of Baucus' legislative career has focused on environmental issues. It is on that subject that his fence-straddling can be most prevalent, in large part because his constituents share the sometimes conflicting goals of protecting the natural beauty around them while relying on natural resources for their livelihoods. He generally agreed with the Clinton administration's approach to revamping traditional pollution control laws, and he supported Clinton's moves to block property rights legislation. But on most land-use issues, Baucus has opposed environmentalists in recent years, most notably on the effort to increase grazing fees.

Baucus got much attention for his role in the enactment in 1990 of the first clean air law rewrite in 13 years. Under the guidance of Senate Majority Leader George J. Mitchell, Baucus — then chairman of the Environmental Protection Subcommittee — steered the bill through the Environment Committee, onto the floor and through negotiations with the House.

One of his challenges in the 106th Congress came not on legislation but on an allegation by Christine M. Niedermeier that she had been fired as his chief of staff for spurning the senator's advances. Baucus vehemently denied that, saying Niedermeier was dismissed because she treated his staff and constituents rudely. When mediation by the congressional Office of Compliance failed to resolve the dispute, she filed a federal lawsuit claiming discrimination. It was later dismissed.

The son of wealthy Helena ranchers, Baucus entered public life after finishing Stanford Law School in 1967 and serving as an attorney for the Securities and Exchange Commission in Washington for three years. His rise was swift after that. He returned home to Montana in 1971 to coordinate the state's constitutional convention. The next year, he won a seat in the state legislature.

Two years later, he won election to the House, dislodging a two-term Republican incumbent in the post-Watergate sweep of 1974. He was elected to the Senate in 1978, after winning a primary against Paul Hatfield, a Democrat who had recently been appointed to the seat.

Baucus has consistently faced tough challenges for re-election. His narrowest victory came in 1996, when he spent more than $3.7 million to eke out a win against Republican Lt. Gov. Dennis Rehberg. Baucus won by fewer than 20,000 votes, slightly less than 50 percent.

KEY VOTES

2000
Yes Overhaul bankruptcy law and increase minimum wage
No Limit fiscal 2001 discretionary spending to $600.3 billion
No Override veto on nuclear waste disposal at Yucca Mountain site in Nevada
Yes Oppose effort to terminate Kosovo mission
Yes Include gender, sexual orientation and disability in federal hate crime protections
No Approve GOP plan to restrict use of genetic information by health insurers
No Kill amendment delaying implementation of an anti-missile defense system
No Cut taxes for married couples
Yes Grant China permanent normal trade status

1999
No Remove President Clinton from office for obstruction of justice
No Kill amendment authorizing state grants to hire teachers and reduce class size
No Require criminal background checks for purchases at gun shows
No Approve GOP proposal to increase rights of patients in managed-care health plans
No Block effort to allow farm and medicine exports to Cuba
Yes Allow study of tougher automobile fuel efficiency standards
Yes Ratify nuclear weapons testing treaty
Yes Prohibit national political parties from collecting "soft money" donations
Yes Remove barriers among banking, securities and insurance companies

INTEREST GROUPS

	AFL-CIO	ADA	CCUS	ACU
2000	75%	85%	46%	16%
1999	78%	95%	59%	4%
1998	75%	80%	56%	5%
1997	29%	65%	70%	4%
1996	71%	85%	46%	20%
1995	83%	75%	47%	13%
1994	100%	85%	20%	0%
1993	73%	85%	20%	16%
1992	75%	95%	20%	4%
1991	58%	70%	20%	24%

CQ VOTE STUDIES

	PARTY UNITY		PRESIDENTIAL SUPPORT	
	Support	Oppose	Support	Oppose
2000	88%	12%	97%	3%
1999	87%	13%	81%	19%
1998	84%	16%	81%	19%
1997	73%	27%	87%	13%
1996	73%	27%	90%	10%
1995	68%	32%	79%	21%
1994	86%	14%	89%	11%
1993	85%	15%	90%	10%
1992	83%	17%	35%	65%
1991	83%	17%	41%	59%

Sen. Conrad Burns (R)

Elected 1988; 3rd term

The walls of Burns' office are filled with large color photos of cattle drives, cowboys and other scenes commonly associated with the Old West. But when Burns weighs in on issues, they are more likely to concern 21st century technologies such as satellite communications, reusable space launch vehicles and high-speed Internet access.

Burns is chairman of the Commerce Subcommittee on Communications, as well as Appropriations' Interior Subcommittee. From his Communications panel perch, he sponsored legislation and later helped broker a House-Senate conference to encourage privatization of the international satellite market and help aerospace giant Lockheed Martin Corp. acquire Comsat Corp., the U.S. signatory to the Intelsat international satellite consortium. He also was instrumental in crafting a federal loan guarantee program to subsidize direct-broadcast satellite companies and other telecommunications providers that expand services to improve television reception in rural areas.

Burns has been effective at steering federal dollars back to Montana and touts the state for a variety of high-tech causes, including as a possible launch site for the next generation of reusable spacecraft to replace NASA's shuttle. Despite this, some in the state worry that he is projecting too unsophisticated an image in Washington.

Following a tree-planting ceremony near the Lincoln Memorial soon after he joined the Senate, Burns walked over to a police horse and examined its mouth to see how old the animal was. A syndicated news story on the incident was carried by Burns' hometown newspaper, The Billings Gazette. "Thanks, Conrad, thanks for telling the world what hicks we are," the Gazette wrote. The harshest criticism came over Burns' glib remark that "there are awful good folks" in Montana, including some who "can read and write."

Burns embarrassed himself again in 1994 by telling the Bozeman Chronicle an anecdote about a rancher who used a racial epithet when referring to African-Americans. He also reported his own complaints about living in Washington, a city with a black-majority population.

The former rancher and livestock auctioneer still makes little effort to dispel the countrified persona he projected at a freshman orientation session — to which he wore old cowboy boots and a leather belt with a "C" on the buckle. During President Clinton's impeachment trial, Burns harked back to his time running auctions, saying his colleagues' body language told him more about what they were thinking than their speeches or legal lines of reasoning. "He's not telling me what he's saying," Burns would drawl to friends.

If Burns embarrasses his cowboy constituents — who expect a more refined representative — he earns kudos from the computer community, the so-called digerati, for his championing of the burgeoning telecommunications industry. Burns was praised by Clinton for promoting electronic commerce, but he also feuded with the administration over other digital issues, including Internet service rates and encryption technology, which allows digital information to be scrambled during computer transmission.

Burns has pushed for faster deployment of high-speed Internet services in outlying areas and criticizes the Federal Communications Commission (FCC) for not moving quickly enough to encourage the "build out" of the Internet backbone through deregulatory incentives. He favored cutting the telephone excise tax and joined with Commerce Chairman John

CAPITOL OFFICE
224-2644; fax 224-8594; 187 Dirksen Bldg. 20510

INTERNET
e-mail: conrad_burns@burns.senate.gov
web: burns.senate.gov

COMMITTEES
Appropriations
(Interior - chairman)
Commerce, Science & Transportation
(Communications - chairman)
Energy & Natural Resources
Small Business
Special Aging

HOMETOWN
Billings

BORN
Jan. 25, 1935, Gallatin, Mo.

RELIGION
Lutheran

FAMILY
Wife, Phyllis Burns; two children

EDUCATION
U. of Missouri, attended 1952-54

MILITARY SERVICE
Marine Corps, 1955-57

CAREER
Radio and television broadcaster

POLITICAL HIGHLIGHTS
Yellowstone County Commission, 1987-89

ELECTION RESULTS

2000 GENERAL

Conrad Burns (R)	208,082	50.6%
Brian Schweitzer (D)	194,430	47.2%
Gary Lee (REF)	9,089	2.2%

2000 PRIMARY

Conrad Burns (R)	unopposed

PREVIOUS WINNING PERCENTAGES
1994 (62%); 1988 (52%)

McCain, R-Ariz., to block FCC efforts to require broadcasters to provide free air time to political candidates.

Burns' other communications priorities include protecting privacy on the Internet, creating more competition in the satellite industry, improving the availability of government documents on the Internet and curbing "junk" e-mail.

Burns served for three years in the Marine Corps in Okinawa, Japan and Korea, often sleeping in sweltering Quonset huts. That left a lasting impression: He says the all-volunteer military, which competes with private industry for personnel, should upgrade family housing, especially given the increase in married recruits since his days as an $82-a-month corporal. One priority for Burns in the military construction spending bill in 1995 was $8.5 million for new latrines and a training support facility for the Army National Guard at Fort Harrison, Mont.

True to his Western heritage, Burns sides with the cattlemen of his state, who complain that large meatpackers do not offer them fair prices, and he pushed for stronger price-reporting requirements in 1998. He recalled on the Senate floor how he once had to auction off the farms of friends. With ranchers and farmers hit hard by low prices because of regional weather problems and decreased exports, he warned about conditions that might lead to further farm and ranch foreclosures. He voted against the agriculture spending bill in 1998, arguing that it did not meet farm needs.

Burns warred with the Clinton administration over land-use policies, siding with the many Westerners who see the federal government as an intrusive absentee landlord. He fought against an administration plan to reintroduce grizzly bears into sections of Idaho and Montana because ranchers feared the bears would harm their livestock.

Burns was a relative political novice when he entered the 1988 Senate race against Democratic Sen. John Melcher, having served less than two years as Yellowstone County commissioner. Despite being tagged as an underdog with no expertise on national or international issues, he had wide name recognition throughout the state thanks to his broadcasts on the Northern Agricultural Network, which he co-founded.

With strong backing from the National Republican Senatorial Committee and President Reagan's timely veto of a wilderness bill that Melcher authored — which gave credence to Burns' campaign claim that Melcher lacked clout on the Hill — Burns won with 52 percent of the vote. It was the biggest Senate upset of the year.

He won re-election in 1994 by stockpiling more than $3 million in campaign money while Democrats scrapped for the nomination. He defeated former University of Montana law school dean Jack Mudd, winning 62 percent of the vote.

Burns tossed his hat into the race for the only contested GOP Senate leadership slot heading into the 105th Congress, taking on Georgian Paul Coverdell for the opening as Republican Conference secretary. Burns sought to play up his regional appeal, arguing that he could help diversify the Senate's nearly all-Southern GOP leadership team, but he lost to Coverdell.

In 2000, Burns faced a stiff re-election challenge from farmer Brian Schweitzer, a political neophyte who focused his campaign on the high cost of prescription drugs. Schweitzer held Burns to a narrow, 3-point victory.

Burns' rough-hewn style and occasional political faux pas still get him in trouble. He drew heat back home in 2000 after initially supporting an asbestos lawsuit overhaul bill that could limit the size of injury claims. The bill was closely watched in Montana, where 200 residents in the town of Libby died from asbestos released by a closed W. R. Grace & Co. vermiculite mine. Burns later withdrew his support for the Senate version of the measure.

KEY VOTES

2000

+ Overhaul bankruptcy law and increase minimum wage
Yes Limit fiscal 2001 discretionary spending to $600.3 billion
Yes Override veto on nuclear waste disposal at Yucca Mountain site in Nevada
No Oppose effort to terminate Kosovo mission
Yes Include gender, sexual orientation and disability in federal hate crime protections
Yes Approve GOP plan to restrict use of genetic information by health insurers
Yes Kill amendment delaying implementation of an anti-missile defense system
Yes Cut taxes for married couples
Yes Grant China permanent normal trade status

1999

Yes Remove President Clinton from office for obstruction of justice
Yes Kill amendment authorizing state grants to hire teachers and reduce class size
No Require criminal background checks for purchases at gun shows
Yes Approve GOP proposal to increase rights of patients in managed-care health plans
No Block effort to allow farm and medicine exports to Cuba
No Allow study of tougher automobile fuel efficiency standards
No Ratify nuclear weapons testing treaty
No Prohibit national political parties from collecting "soft money" donations
Yes Remove barriers among banking, securities and insurance companies

INTEREST GROUPS

	AFL-CIO	ADA	CCUS	ACU
2000	0%	5%	93%	87%
1999	11%	0%	88%	96%
1998	0%	0%	100%	84%
1997	14%	15%	78%	88%
1996	0%	5%	85%	100%
1995	0%	0%	100%	83%
1994	13%	0%	70%	92%
1993	18%	20%	91%	96%
1992	25%	5%	100%	89%
1991	17%	5%	90%	86%

CQ VOTE STUDIES

	PARTY UNITY		PRESIDENTIAL SUPPORT	
	Support	Oppose	Support	Oppose
2000	90%	10%	51%	49%
1999	94%	6%	24%	76%
1998	94%	6%	38%	62%
1997	94%	6%	57%	43%
1996	97%	3%	29%	71%
1995	95%	5%	26%	74%
1994	84%	16%	43%	57%
1993	92%	8%	24%	76%
1992	94%	6%	85%	15%
1991	93%	7%	89%	11%

Rep. Denny Rehberg (R)

Elected 2000; 1st term

CAPITOL OFFICE
225-3211; fax 225-5687; 516 Cannon Bldg. 20515

INTERNET
e-mail: denny.rehberg@mail.house.gov
web: www.house.gov/rehberg

COMMITTEES
Agriculture
Resources
Transportation & Infrastructure

HOMETOWN
Billings

BORN
Oct. 5, 1955, Billings, Mont.

RELIGION
Episcopalian

FAMILY
Wife, Janice Lenhardt Rehberg; three children

EDUCATION
Montana State U., attended 1973-74; Washington State U., B.A. 1977

CAREER
Rancher; congressional aide; realtor

POLITICAL HIGHLIGHTS
Mont. House, 1985-91; lieutenant governor, 1991-97; Republican nominee for U.S. Senate, 1996

ELECTION RESULTS

2000 GENERAL

Denny Rehberg (R)	211,418	51.5%
Nancy Keenan (D)	189,971	46.3%
James J. Tikalsky (LIBERT)	9,132	2.2%

2000 PRIMARY

Denny Rehberg (R)	unopposed

A fifth-generation Montanan, Rehberg grew up on the cattle and goat ranch he now operates on the outskirts of Billings, high above town. He says the experience makes him familiar with the problems facing key constituents — the state's farmers and ranchers.

Like many Western Republicans, Rehberg is a conservative who wants to reduce the size of the federal government and limit its influence on property owners in Western states. "It seems as if the federal government does not see any farther than the Potomac," he says.

Rehberg (REE-berg), whose ranch has 500 head of cattle and 600 cashmere goats, scored a seat on the Agriculture Committee — a position he can use to look out for Montana farmers producing durum wheat and other crops and raising livestock. During his election campaign, he called for letting Montana residents form "forest advisory councils" to recommend whether to open up roadless lands to timber harvesting or protect them as wilderness areas. Rehberg also was given seats on the Resources and Transportation and Infrastructure panels.

The congressman has long had more than a casual interest in going to Washington, D.C. The one-time state Senate intern worked on Capitol Hill as an aide to Montana Republican Rep. Ron Marlenee before returning home in the mid-1980s to operate the family ranch and to launch his own political career.

After six years in the state House and six more as Montana's lieutenant governor (he was appointed in 1991 when Lt. Gov. Allen Kolstad quit to join the Bush administration), Rehberg ran a close but unsuccessful 1996 race to upset Democratic Sen. Max Baucus. Baucus wound up spending more than $3.7 million to defeat Rehberg by just 5 percentage points.

In 2000, he again sought a ticket to Congress when he entered the race for the state's only House seat, left open by GOP Rep. Rick Hill's retirement. At first, Rehberg looked to be the underdog in his contest with the Democratic nominee, state school superintendent Nancy Keenan. But Rehberg battled back in a campaign that was at times vitriolic, winning by 5 points.

MONTANA
At large

Montana's Big Sky country has long been a place where pioneers travel to strike it rich. Once explored by Lewis and Clark and later mined by fur trappers and gold seekers, Montana is now a prime destination for celebrities and telecommuters who want to own their own small piece of the frontier.

After the 1990 census, Montana lost one of its two congressional seats. The resulting district combines the state's politically independent halves into one unpredictable voting bloc. The western, mountainous half of the state leans Democratic, with a strong environmental base and a union tradition in mining and lumber mills. It's also home to the state's university community in Missoula. The eastern half, a flat plain used to raise wheat and cattle, follows a tradition of rural Republicanism.

Despite these differences, both halves can be conservative and independent. The state elected Jeannette Rankin, the first woman in Congress, in 1916. Ross Perot had some of his best showings in the nation here in both 1992 and '96. With an economy based on natural resources, Montana finds itself exploiting its terrain while also striving to protect it. In ballot initiatives, voters have rejected some environmental regulations. Yet Butte, the site of years of mining, is the center of a massive superfund clean-up effort.

MAJOR INDUSTRY
Agriculture, tourism, forestry

MILITARY BASES
Malmstrom Air Force Base, 3,577 military, 365 civilian (2000)

CITIES
Billings, 92,988; Missoula, 58,460; Great Falls, 56,340; Butte-Silver Bow, 33,325

UNUSUAL FEATURES
Glacier National Park; Jordan, site of a standoff in 1996 between federal authorities and an anti-tax group called The Freemen.

NEBRASKA

Gov. Mike Johanns (R)

First elected: 1998
Length of term: 4 years
Term expires: 1/03
Salary: $65,000
Phone: (402) 471-2244
Hometown: Lincoln
Born: June 18, 1950; Osage, Iowa
Religion: Roman Catholic
Family: Wife, Stephanie Johanns; two children
Education: St. Mary's College (Minn.), B.A. 1971; Creighton U., J.D. 1974
Career: Lawyer
Political highlights: Lancaster County Commission, 1982-86; Lincoln City Council, 1989-91; mayor of Lincoln, 1991-99

Election results:

1998 GENERAL

Mike Johanns (R)	293,910	53.9%
Bill Hoppner (D)	250,678	46.0%

Lt. Gov. David I. Maurstad (R)

First elected: 1998
Length of term: 4 years
Term expires: 1/03
Salary: $47,000
Phone: (402) 471-2256

STATE LEGISLATURE

Unicameral Legislature: Meets 90 days in odd years; 60 days in even years
Legislature: 49 nonpartisan members, 4-year terms
2001 breakdown: 40 men, 9 women
Salary: $12,000
Phone: (402) 471-2271

STATE TERM LIMITS

Governor: 2 consecutive terms
Legislature: 2 consecutive terms

URBAN STATISTICS

CITY	POPULATION
Omaha	386,742
Lincoln	215, 928
Bellevue	44,730
Grand Island	41,950
Kearney	28,381

REGISTERED VOTERS

Republican	50%
Democrat	36%
Nonpartisan	14%

POPULATION

2000 population	1,711,236
1990 population	1,578,385
Percent change	+8.4%
Rank among states	38
Median age	35.1
Born in state	70%
Foreign born	2%
Urban/rural	66%/34%
Crime rate	438/100,000
Poverty level	12.3%
Federal workers	15,840
Military	15,873

REAPPORTIONMENT

Nebraska retained its three House seats in reapportionment. The state legislature will draw new district lines in 2001.

MISCELLANEOUS

Web: www.state.ne.us
Capital: Lincoln
Land area: 76,878 sq. miles
  Rank among states: 15

STATE ELECTION OFFICIAL
(402) 471-3229

DEMOCRATIC HEADQUARTERS
(402) 434-2180

REPUBLICAN HEADQUARTERS
(402) 475-2122

District Statistics

DIST.	VOTE FOR PRESIDENT 2000 D	R	GREEN	1996 D	R	REF	1992 D	R	I	WHT	BLK	ASIAN	HISP	HOUSEHOLD INCOME	OVER 65+	UNDER 18	COLLEGE EDUCATION
1	36%	59%	4%	38%	50%	11%	33%	43%	24%	96%	1%	1%	1%	$25,763	15%	26%	18%
2	38	57	4	38	53	9	32	48	20	87	10	1	3	$30,889	10	28	25
3	25	71	3	29	59	12	24	50	27	98	0	0	3	$22,344	18	28	14
STATE	33	62	4	35	54	11	29	47	24	94	4	1	2	$26,016	14	27	19

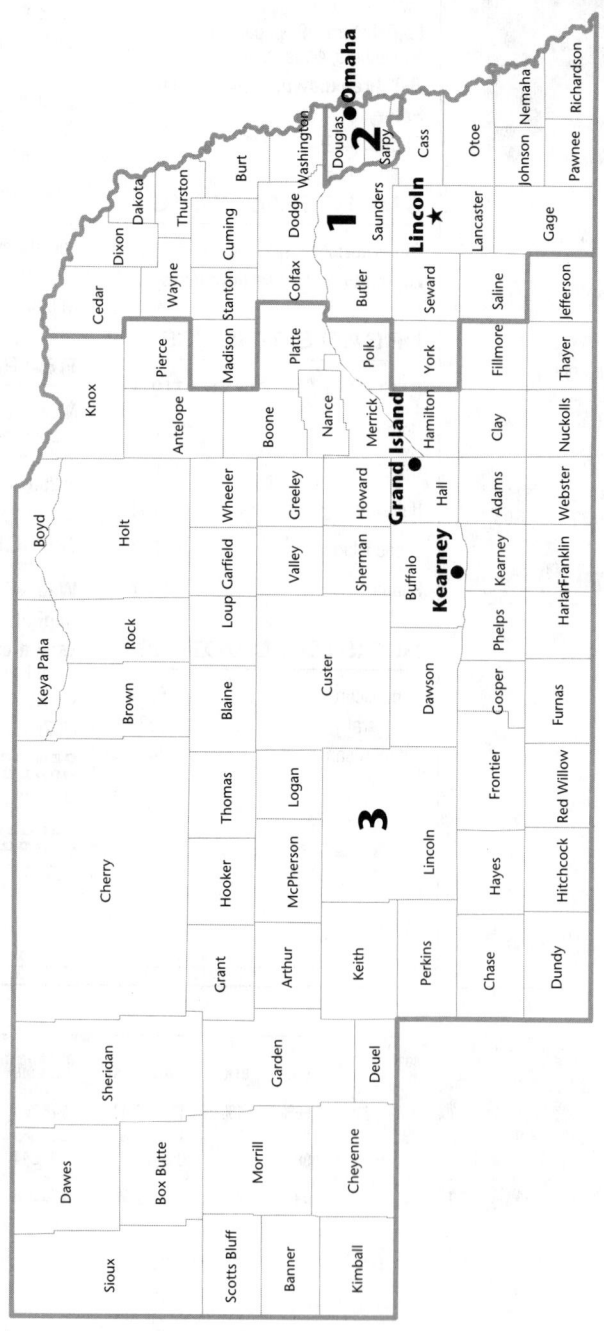

Sen. Chuck Hagel (R)

CAPITOL OFFICE
224-4224; fax 224-5213; 248 Russell Bldg. 20510

INTERNET
e-mail: chuck_hagel@hagel.senate.gov
web: hagel.senate.gov

COMMITTEES
Banking, Housing & Urban Affairs
    (International Trade & Finance - chairman)
Budget
Energy & Natural Resources
Foreign Relations
    (International Economic Policy, Export & Trade
    Promotion - chairman)

HOMETOWN
Omaha

BORN
Oct. 4, 1946, North Platte, Neb.

RELIGION
Episcopalian

FAMILY
Wife, Lilibet Hagel; two children

EDUCATION
U. of Nebraska, Omaha, B.A. 1971

MILITARY SERVICE
Army, 1967-68

CAREER
Investment bank executive; cellular phone
company founder; lobbyist; congressional aide;
radio talk show host

POLITICAL HIGHLIGHTS
Veterans Administration deputy administrator,
1981-82

ELECTION RESULTS

1996 GENERAL

Chuck Hagel (R)	379,933	56.1%
Ben Nelson (D)	281,904	41.7%
John DeCamp (LIBERT)	9,483	1.4%

1996 PRIMARY

Chuck Hagel (R)	112,953	62.2%
Don Stenberg (R)	67,974	37.5%

Elected 1996; 1st term

A business-oriented brand of conservatism, an occasional independence from Republican orthodoxy and a polished skill at media relations have combined to push Hagel to the national political forefront in his first Senate term.

An affable and articulate self-made millionaire and decorated Vietnam veteran, he had never held elective office before his stunning long-shot 1996 victory in a Senate race against popular Democratic Gov. Ben Nelson. (Nelson won the state's other Senate seat when it came open in 2000.) But Hagel got off to a fast start in Washington, earning high praise from his new colleagues.

In the summer of 2000, he was interviewed when George W. Bush was searching for a vice-presidential running mate, even though — or perhaps because — Hagel was an enthusiastic supporter of Arizona Sen. John McCain's bid for the Republican presidential nomination. Commentators noted that the two senators had much in common: heroic war service, plain-spoken candor and impatience with the status quo in government. What Hagel lacked, it was widely observed, was McCain's quick temper; he has been called "McCain without the attitude."

Hagel believes in a brand of pragmatic conservatism. He embraces the longstanding Republican tenets of tax cuts and reductions in federal government spending. But he has little patience for the foreign policy views of some on the GOP right who favor American isolationism and believe in unyielding economic sanctions on foreign nations guilty of human rights abuses. With a perspective rooted in business, Hagel stresses the importance of the global village and the virtues of internationalism. "The rest of the world keys off of America," he told CNN in November 2000. "Financial markets, foreign policy — everything works around us in many ways."

When Hagel arrived as a freshman in the 105th Congress, congressional ennui with international issues allowed him to grab the chairmanship of the Foreign Relations Subcommittee on International Economic Policy, Export and Trade Promotion. From that perch, he made his voice heard on nearly every foreign policy issue, from U.S. policy toward Iraq to granting China permanent normal trade status. "This is just so clearly in the interests of America, it's hardly even debatable anymore," he said of the China trade proposal, enacted in 2000.

Following the 2000 elections, many GOP lawmakers said that the closeness and murkiness of the results — the disputed presidential contest, the 50-50 partisan split in the Senate — could impair their work, but Hagel took a more upbeat view. "I actually think, and maybe because I am an optimist, that this might in fact force the next president to deal with some of the urgent challenges and issues of our time and develop a coalition agenda, a bipartisan agenda," he told The New York Times. "It might, in a strange way, unhook us from the special-interest groups."

Like McCain, Hagel makes no secret of his belief that the power of such groups needs to be held in check. He has been outspoken in criticizing the GOP's dependency on the unregulated and unlimited "soft money" that has financed the campaigns of the past decade. But he has sponsored campaign finance legislation that — in contrast to McCain's — would limit such contributions, not abolish them outright. Some advocates of overhauling the campaign finance system criticized Hagel's measure, contending it would open more loopholes than it attempted to close.

Hagel was among the first Senate Republicans to recognize the political popularity of creating a prescription drug benefit for Medicare recipients, introducing a bill to address the issue.

Hagel's independence and bluntness have made him a frequent talk-show guest. At the same time, those qualities have grated on some of his more-senior colleagues, including Majority Leader Trent Lott.

Lott chose Hagel as a deputy whip, one of three from the Class of 1996. But Hagel overstepped a bit when he decided in 1998 to challenge Mitch McConnell of Kentucky in his bid for re-election as chairman of the National Republican Senatorial Committee, the organization responsible for recruiting GOP candidates and raising the money to get them elected. Hagel noted that McConnell's efforts had failed to increase the Republican majority in the Senate for the 106th. "I come from the business world, where if you don't fulfill obligations, you're out," he said. Nevertheless, with Lott's tacit backing, McConnell trounced Hagel, 39-13.

In June 2000, Lott and Hagel battled again after Hagel's name began surfacing as a possible running mate for Bush. Weekly Standard Editor William Kristol said Lott "is doing everything he can to block Chuck Hagel from being the Republican vice-presidential nominee." Hagel, meanwhile, suggested in a conference call to reporters that changes in Senate leadership could occur if Republicans lost control of the Senate.

Hagel brings his business savvy to his seat on the Banking Committee, where in the 107th Congress he became chairman of the International Trade and Finance Subcommittee. He also gained slots on the Energy and Budget committees.

Hagel's compelling personal story has contributed to his rapid political rise. He grew up in a small town in Nebraska, where he started working as a carhop at a drive-in restaurant when he was 9 years old. In high school, he successfully ran for student council president, attracting attention through stunts such as tying a chicken to the hood of his car and driving around blaring out his positions as the chicken cackled.

Later, Hagel enlisted in the Army and spent a year as an infantryman in Vietnam, serving side-by-side with his brother, Tom. Hagel was seriously wounded twice and received two Purple Hearts, suffering burns so bad that they took a decade to heal completely.

After graduating from college in 1971, he landed a job with Rep. John Y. McCollister, R-Neb., and rose to be his top aide. Hagel became a lobbyist and campaigned heavily in 1980 for Ronald Reagan, who rewarded him with a top job at the Veterans Administration. He left government in 1982 to start a business on a shoestring, selling his seven-year-old Buick and two insurance bonds and investing his net worth of $5,000 in a cellular phone company he began with two partners. That company, Vanguard Cellular Systems Inc., eventually became the country's second-largest independent cell phone company and made Hagel a multimillionaire. In recognition of his efforts, Hagel was a recipient of the 2001 Horatio Alger Award, which recognizes self-made business leaders who have overcome adversity.

Hagel later spent two years in charge of the United Service Organizations, a nonprofit group providing assistance to military personnel, and in 1990 he became chief operating officer of the Economic Summit of Industrialized Nations. He entered the 1996 Senate primary as the underdog against Attorney General Don Stenberg but spent lavishly from his personal funds and swept the nomination with more than 60 percent of the vote.

In the fall, Hagel made the centerpiece of his bid the argument that federal tax cuts would stimulate economic growth, something he contended would do more to address problems in society than any government program. Helped by GOP criticism that Nelson was breaking an earlier pledge to serve out his term as governor, Hagel won by 14 percentage points.

KEY VOTES

2000

Yes Overhaul bankruptcy law and increase minimum wage
Yes Limit fiscal 2001 discretionary spending to $600.3 billion
Yes Override veto on nuclear waste disposal at Yucca Mountain site in Nevada
Yes Oppose effort to terminate Kosovo mission
No   Include gender, sexual orientation and disability in federal hate crime protections
Yes Approve GOP plan to restrict use of genetic information by health insurers
Yes Kill amendment delaying implementation of an anti-missile defense system
Yes Cut taxes for married couples
Yes Grant China permanent normal trade status

1999

Yes Remove President Clinton from office for obstruction of justice
Yes Kill amendment authorizing state grants to hire teachers and reduce class size
No   Require criminal background checks for purchases at gun shows
Yes Approve GOP proposal to increase rights of patients in managed-care health plans
No   Block effort to allow farm and medicine exports to Cuba
No   Allow study of tougher automobile fuel efficiency standards
No   Ratify nuclear weapons testing treaty
No   Prohibit national political parties from collecting "soft money" donations
Yes Remove barriers among banking, securities and insurance companies

INTEREST GROUPS

	AFL-CIO	ADA	CCUS	ACU
2000	0%	0%	100%	88%
1999	0%	5%	100%	88%
1998	0%	0%	94%	72%
1997	0%	5%	100%	80%

CQ VOTE STUDIES

	PARTY UNITY		PRESIDENTIAL SUPPORT	
	Support	Oppose	Support	Oppose
2000	94%	6%	49%	51%
1999	92%	8%	36%	64%
1998	89%	11%	42%	58%
1997	92%	8%	59%	41%

Sen. Ben Nelson (D)

Elected 2000; 1st term

Democratic officials welcomed Nelson's 2000 victory for the Nebraska Senate seat left open by retired two-term Democratic Sen. Bob Kerrey. Nelson's ability to hold the seat in a state that usually leans strongly Republican was a key to the Democrats' ability to gain a 50-50 partisan split in the Senate.

But Nelson, a self-described conservative Democrat, is certain to cause some uneasy moments for his party's Senate leadership. A Democrat has to be something of a maverick to succeed among Nebraska's mainly conservative electorate and Nelson, who served as Nebraska governor from 1991 to 1999, is one. The senator, for example, supports gun owners' rights and opposes abortion.

"Maybe that's not mainstream, but then I'm probably not a mainstream person. I have my own views. I happen to be a Democrat, but these are my views," he said during his Senate campaign.

That likely was one of the few times in the race that Nelson even mentioned his party affiliation. Instead, he touted his facility for fostering bipartisan cooperation as governor — a major theme in the presidential campaign of Republican George W. Bush as well.

Nelson exhibited this bipartisan tendency early in the 107th Congress when he was one of just eight Senate Democrats to vote for the confirmation of former Missouri GOP Sen. John Ashcroft as attorney general.

Yet on many issues, Nelson follows the Democratic line. One example is his stand on tax cuts. He stated during the 2000 campaign that any federal budget surplus should first be used to pay down the national debt, shore up Social Security and make prescription drugs more affordable.

A priority for the lawmaker is fighting any major changes to Social Security that he believes could threaten its solvency. Nelson takes a dim view of proposals to allow younger workers to invest a portion of their Social Security savings in equity or bond markets.

Much of Nebraska is farmland, and Nelson is likely to concentrate on agricultural issues. He vowed to change the 1996 "Freedom to Farm" law, which overhauled the nation's farm programs to make them more market-oriented but left farmers more vulnerable to economic downturns.

Upon his arrival in the Senate, Nelson was assigned to the Agriculture Committee. He also took seats on Armed Services — the Strategic Air Command is headquartered at Offutt Air Force base near Omaha — and Veterans' Affairs. He says that while he is not necessarily opposed to an anti-ballistic missile defense system, he has not been convinced of its relative importance.

Nelson was the Democrats' best — and perhaps only — hope of retaining the Senate seat Kerrey had vacated. He entered the 2000 race as the front-runner against state Attorney General Don Stenberg, who had survived a tough Republican primary.

Both candidates were seeking to redeem themselves after failed Senate bids in 1996. Stenberg had lost to upstart Republican businessman Chuck Hagel in the primary. And Nelson, who had entered the 1996 Senate race off his landslide 1994 re-election as governor, came into the general election the strong favorite, only to have Hagel surge to win with 56 percent.

But in 2000, Nelson overcame the state's Republican bent and hung on to win by just 2 percentage points — the closest Senate election in Nebraska's history.

CAPITOL OFFICE
224-6551; fax 228-0012; 720 Hart Bldg. 20510

INTERNET
e-mail: bennelson.senate.gov/email.html
web: bennelson.senate.gov

COMMITTEES
Agriculture, Nutrition & Forestry
Armed Services
Veterans' Affairs

HOMETOWN
Omaha

BORN
May 17, 1941, McCook, Neb.

RELIGION
Methodist

FAMILY
Wife, Diane Nelson; four children

EDUCATION
U. of Nebraska, B.A. 1963, M.A. 1965, J.D. 1970

CAREER
Lawyer

POLITICAL HIGHLIGHTS
Neb. director of insurance, 1975-76; governor, 1991-99; Democratic nominee for U.S. Senate, 1996

ELECTION RESULTS

2000 GENERAL

Ben Nelson (D)	353,093	51.0%
Don Stenberg (R)	337,977	48.8%

2000 PRIMARY

Ben Nelson (D)	105,661	92.1%
Al Hamburg (D)	8,482	7.4%

Rep. Doug Bereuter (R)

Elected 1978; 12th term

Now in his third decade in the House, Bereuter is among the chamber's most influential Republicans in the international policy arena. He advocates free trade, urges U.S. participation in international organizations and lobbies for a strong, but limited, role for the U.S. military abroad.

Bereuter had hoped to chair the International Relations Committee — he twice turned down home state GOP entreaties that he run for higher office, in hopes of winning the committee gavel — but that was not to be.

When GOP-imposed term limits on chairmanships forced International Relations Chairman Benjamin A. Gilman of New York to relinquish the post in the 107th Congress, Republican leaders gave the job to Henry J. Hyde of Illinois, who himself had to step down as Judiciary chairman.

Bereuter (BEE-right-er) did not come away empty-handed, however: He took the chairmanship of the Financial Services panel's International Monetary Policy and Trade Subcommittee. And he was named vice chairman of the Intelligence Committee, putting him in line to take the helm in two years.

Bereuter's generally internationalist views on issues — he supports the International Monetary Fund, for instance, and calls for U.S. payment of back dues owed to the United Nations — are not always in line with the majority of conservatives in his party. But the GOP leadership has long looked to Bereuter as a key adviser on foreign policy matters, particularly with regard to Sino-American relations.

In the 106th Congress, Bereuter, then-chairman of International Relations' Asia and the Pacific Subcommittee, used his knowledge on trade and his friendships with Democrats to broker a deal that was pivotal to enactment of a law granting China permanent normal trade status. When it became apparent that a House majority for the proposal was failing to solidify, Bereuter and Michigan Democrat Sander M. Levin developed legislation to assuage lawmakers' concerns about enhancing the trade status of a nation with a history of human rights violations, labor abuses and military posturing. Their package included mechanisms designed to protect domestic industries harmed by surges in Chinese imports and to monitor China's labor practices and human rights record.

Bereuter, who had assumed the Asia and the Pacific Subcommittee chairmanship in the 104th, said he chose the post because of the importance of the Pacific Rim to Nebraska. The state's agricultural exports amount to about $3.5 billion annually, and almost two-thirds goes to Asia, with Japan the largest customer.

Bereuter votes a centrist line on issues such as environmental protection, gun control and funding for the National Endowment for the Arts. His manner is thoughtful, low-key and non-confrontational; in debate, his focus is on substance, rather than rhetorical fireworks.

It was in this spirit that Bereuter urged the 1998 Nebraska Republican convention to exercise moderation in political debate. While he opposes abortion, he urged the delegates not to concentrate so much on the issue. "As important as that issue is," he said, "it is clear that the average Nebraska Republican voter does not believe this issue should absolutely predominate over all others."

The response from the party's right wing was immediate. One GOP county chairman condemned Bereuter and suggested he join the Democratic Party. But Bereuter did not back down. During the 2000 Republican National Convention in Philadelphia, where he served as a delegate, he said

CAPITOL OFFICE
225-4806; fax 225-5686; 2184 Rayburn Bldg. 20515

INTERNET
web: www.house.gov/bereuter

COMMITTEES
Financial Services
(International Monetary Policy & Trade -
chairman)
International Relations
Select Intelligence
(Intelligence Policy & National Security -
chairman)
Transportation & Infrastructure

HOMETOWN
Cedar Bluffs

BORN
Oct. 6, 1939, York, Neb.

RELIGION
Lutheran

FAMILY
Wife, Louise Bereuter; two children

EDUCATION
U. of Nebraska, B.A. 1961; Harvard U., M.C.P. 1966, M.P.A. 1973

MILITARY SERVICE
Army, 1963-65

CAREER
City planner; professor; state official

POLITICAL HIGHLIGHTS
Neb. Legislature, 1975-79

ELECTION RESULTS

2000 GENERAL

Doug Bereuter (R)	155,485	66.3%
Alan Jacobsen (D)	72,859	31.0%
David Oenbring (LIBERT)	6,147	2.6%

2000 PRIMARY

Doug Bereuter (R)	unopposed

1998 GENERAL

Doug Bereuter (R)	136,058	73.5%
Don Eret (D)	48,826	26.4%

PREVIOUS WINNING PERCENTAGES
1996 (70%); 1994 (63%); 1992 (60%); 1990 (65%);
1988 (67%); 1986 (64%); 1984 (74%); 1982 (75%);
1980 (79%); 1978 (58%)

the convention's broad tone and lack of rancor came close to the attitude of the party he envisions."I think the party is coming back to my ideal of an inclusive party," Bereuter told the Omaha World-Herald.

On the Financial Services Committee (formerly Banking), Bereuter's priorities, in addition to the international focus of his subcommittee, include housing, community development and the health of small banks. A city planner by profession, Bereuter was eager to put his expertise in urban affairs to use on the Banking Committee when he arrived in Washington. He did not get the assignment until his second term, but two years later he became the ranking Republican on the subcommittee with jurisdiction over international financial institutions, a close fit with his International Relations work.

Besides participating in dozens of international parliamentary exchanges, he occasionally leads congressional delegations abroad, teaching colleagues about foreign policy. (It was on a 1984 congressional trip to Eastern Europe that Bereuter befriended Levin, his collaborator on the compromise China trade proposal.)

While Bereuter backed President Clinton on lowering trade barriers with China, he had sharp disagreements with the president in other foreign policy areas. In the 105th Congress, he criticized the administration for providing missile technology to the Chinese and deploying troops in the Balkans, and he sought restrictions on U.S. companies using Chinese rockets to launch satellites.

Bereuter's background is unusual for a Nebraska politician. He held the state's top urban planning post under GOP Gov. Norbert Tiemann from 1968 to 1970. Later, he served one four-year term in the legislature, winning a reputation as one of the more liberal members by sponsoring a land-use planning bill opposed by farmers and ranchers.

Despite his conservative rhetoric during his first House campaign in 1978, Bereuter was still seen as a moderate in Lincoln. After besting a conservative state senator in the primary, he united Republican support and a large independent vote to win 58 percent against Hess Dyas, a former state Democratic Party chairman.

Since then, he has won re-election with ease.

In 2000, Bereuter had the inside track for a Senate seat when Bob Kerrey, the only Democrat in the state's five-man congressional delegation, announced his retirement. But as in 1998, when Nebraska Republicans sought a gubernatorial candidate, Bereuter stayed put, hoping re-election to a 12th term would bring the International Relations chairmanship.

KEY VOTES

2000
No Raise hourly minimum wage by $1 over two years
Yes Halt funding for U.S. mission in Kosovo unless European nations pay more
Yes Provide Medicare benefits to military retirees and their dependents
Yes Grant China permanent normal trade status
Yes Phase out estate, gift and trust taxes
Yes Prohibit implementation of president's national monument designations
Yes Approve GOP plan to provide prescription drug coverage for Medicare beneficiaries
No Increase help for poor nations indebted to international financial institutions

1999
No Impose steel import quotas
No Kill proposal to take aviation trust funds off budget
Yes Require background checks on buyers only at gun shows with 10 or more vendors
Yes Remove barriers among banking, securities and insurance companies
No Authorize state grants to hire teachers and reduce class size
Yes Overhaul campaign finance law; ban "soft money" and restrict advocacy advertising
No Approve bipartisan plan to increase rights of patients in managed-care health plans

INTEREST GROUPS

	AFL-CIO	ADA	CCUS	ACU
2000	10%	10%	90%	64%
1999	11%	35%	92%	62%
1998	0%	5%	100%	64%
1997	29%	20%	90%	68%

CQ VOTE STUDIES

	PARTY UNITY		PRESIDENTIAL SUPPORT	
	Support	Oppose	Support	Oppose
2000	82%	18%	32%	68%
1999	79%	21%	35%	65%
1998	84%	16%	28%	72%
1997	87%	13%	40%	60%

NEBRASKA 1
East – Lincoln; Norfolk

The 1st encompasses the eastern fifth of Nebraska, excluding Omaha and its suburbs. The region includes the state's capital, Lincoln, and the University of Nebraska's Memorial Stadium, which could qualify as the district's second-largest city when filled to its 74,031-seat capacity during a home football game. Despite the area's small-town reputation, growing industry in Omaha exurbs, including Lincoln, Norfolk and South Sioux City, is helping to make Nebraska a more urban state.

Lincoln, in particular, is thriving and has seen a major population increase – a boom led by the expanding state and city governments and by the university. Hospitals and a banking and insurance industry also help sustain the city's local economy.

Although the district was home to populist William Jennings Bryan and many supporters of his politics at the turn of the century, the 1st now votes consistently Republican at all levels. The University of Nebraska's main campus in Lincoln makes Lancaster County more liberal, but voter registration favors the GOP.

The strongest Democratic counties are at opposite corners of the district. In the northeast are Dakota County, with a large blue-collar contingent and some Hispanic and Asian residents, and Thurston County, made up almost entirely of Winnebago and Omaha Indian reservations. In the southwest is rural Saline County, dominated by people of Czech heritage with a longstanding Democratic tradition.

The region depends on agriculture but with a modern twist. Traditional crop and hog farming are supplemented by other agribusiness, such as meat processing, food packaging and fertilizer production. Telemarketing and polling companies, such as the Gallup Organization Inc., also are adding to white-collar job opportunities.

MAJOR INDUSTRY
Agriculture, meat processing, health care, government

CITIES
Lincoln, 215,928; Fremont, 24,591; Norfolk, 23,164

UNUSUAL FEATURES
Johnny Carson, former host of "The Tonight Show," grew up in Norfolk; Arbor Day first celebrated in Nebraska City in 1872.

Rep. Lee Terry (R)

CAPITOL OFFICE
225-4155; fax 226-5452
1513 Longworth Bldg. 20515

INTERNET
e-mail: Talk2Lee@mail.house.gov
web: www.house.gov/terry

COMMITTEES
Energy & Commerce

HOMETOWN
Omaha

BORN
Jan. 29, 1962, Omaha, Neb.

RELIGION
Methodist

FAMILY
Wife, Robyn Terry; three children

EDUCATION
U. of Nebraska, B.S. 1984; Creighton U., J.D. 1987

CAREER
Lawyer

POLITICAL HIGHLIGHTS
Omaha City Council, 1991-99

ELECTION RESULTS

2000 GENERAL

Lee Terry (R)	148,911	65.8%
Shelley Kiel (D)	70,268	31.1%
John J. Graziano (LIBERT)	6,856	3.0%

2000 PRIMARY

Lee Terry (R)	55,696	98.7%
write-ins (R)	758	1.3%

1998 GENERAL

Lee Terry (R)	106,782	65.5%
Michael Scott (D)	55,722	34.2%

Elected 1998; 2nd term

A stalwart conservative who reliably supports Republican priorities, Terry came by his political philosophy the old-fashioned way — from his parents. When his father, a onetime Douglas County election commissioner, won the Republican nomination for the 2nd District in 1976, the 14-year-old Lee worked on the campaign (his father lost the general election). His mother, another GOP loyalist, ran unsuccessfully for the Douglas County board in 1982.

"We didn't talk about Husker football at our table," Terry told the Omaha World-Herald. "My dad talked about what Congress was doing to us. He'd say, 'Don't they understand what that does to us?'"

Terry compiled a solidly conservative voting record in his first term, backing GOP leaders more than 90 percent of the time in both 1999 and 2000. His political views mirror those of President Bush. When Terry was asked during a 2000 debate whether there were any issues on which he disagreed with Bush, he said that he couldn't think of any except that he wished Bush would come out more strongly against abortion.

But unlike the more combative conservatives who came to the House in the mid-1990s, the smiling and fresh-faced Terry has positioned himself as a pragmatist. "I want to fight the good fight on abortion, but that doesn't mean I drag down an appropriations bill," he told the World-Herald after his 1998 election.

Terry was rewarded for his loyalty with a seat on the powerful Energy and Commerce Committee at the beginning of the 107th Congress. He had wanted an assignment to Ways and Means so he could focus on tax measures, but he also takes an interest in the business, energy, consumer protection and environmental issues under the purview of Energy and Commerce. "Local, statewide, national and global commerce are all important in my district, and I will be a strong advocate of free trade, as well as business development, on the committee," he said.

In the 106th, Terry devoted much of his time to tax issues. He signed on to at least two dozen tax-cutting proposals, and he pressed Ways and Means Chairman Bill Archer of Texas to do more to lower taxes on married couples. In one of his more notable floor maneuvers, Terry sought to embarrass Democrats by forcing a vote on $19 billion in tax increases that he lifted from President Clinton's budget in 1999. Democrats, put into the awkward position of opposing their own president, joined with Republicans in voting down the measure overwhelmingly. Minority Leader Richard A. Gephardt denounced Terry's maneuver as "another gimmick."

Early in the 107th Congress, Terry told supporters that he regarded Bush's proposed $1.6 trillion tax cut as "only a good start," according to the World-Herald.

Like other conservatives, Terry also makes an effort to cut government spending. He voted against a $13 billion emergency spending bill in 2000, contending that it amounted to "dishonesty in budgeting" because it mostly funded non-emergency items.

But he has supported federal spending for a variety of projects for his constituents, including a funding boost for Nebraska airports, grants for security officers in Omaha schools, and funds to build a fire and crash rescue station at Offutt Air Force Base. He got a lesson in the difficulties of cutting spending after criticizing Southerners for pressing for programs to help peanut farmers. "As one person from Georgia said to me, 'Our peanut is your corn,' " Terry told the World-Herald, speaking in a Southern drawl. "Point made."

Terry keeps a close eye on the needs of his district's farmers. He voted in 2000 to allow exports of food and medicine to Cuba and to grant China permanent normal trade status, both of which were top priorities for the agricultural lobby. He said he is willing to re-examine the "Freedom to Farm" act in the 107th, but he wants to retain the law's free-market philosophy. The 1996 law, which expires in 2002, has come under fire for cutting federal subsidies to farmers, even in times of tight market conditions.

Terry casts a conservative vote on social issues. He denounced a procedure its opponents call "partial birth" abortion, and he supports school vouchers, a high priority of the Bush administration.

He also voted in 2000 against an increase in the minimum wage. And he opposed a bipartisan campaign finance overhaul measure, saying it would violate the free speech rights of advocacy groups.

But Terry struggles with the question of gun owners' rights. Although he voted in 1999 against mandatory trigger locks, he said early in 2000 that he could support such a step, as well as waiting periods for purchases at gun shows, because he was dismayed by the nation's repeated school shootings. "You can't go through this last year without being touched in some way and at least say, 'Are there other reasonable steps we should be taking?' " he told the World-Herald.

Term limits is another issue that has given Terry pause. When he first ran for office, he pledged to serve no more than three terms, but he began backing away from that promise within a few months of arriving in Washington. He said he quickly realized the benefits that come with seniority.

Terry has taken an interest in politics since the age of 10, when he analyzed President Nixon's landslide victory on election night in 1972. After working on his father's congressional campaign, he mapped out a life plan in high school that emphasized involvement in politics.

In 1991, he won a seat on the Omaha City Council, where he served for eight years and played a role in lowering property taxes. He was considered the front-runner in the 1998 race for the 2nd District as soon as GOP Rep. Jon Christensen announced he would step down to run for governor.

In the GOP primary, Terry held off ex-Reagan administration budget official Steve Kupka and social conservative businessman Brad Kuiper. Though Democrats have at times run well in the 2nd, Terry breezed by newscaster Michael Scott, an underfinanced first-time candidate, in the general election. He won re-election in 2000 by better than 2-to-1.

KEY VOTES

2000

No Raise hourly minimum wage by $1 over two years

Yes Halt funding for U.S. mission in Kosovo unless European nations pay more

Yes Provide Medicare benefits to military retirees and their dependents

Yes Grant China permanent normal trade status

Yes Phase out estate, gift and trust taxes

Yes Prohibit implementation of president's national monument designations

Yes Approve GOP plan to provide prescription drug coverage for Medicare beneficiaries

No Increase help for poor nations indebted to international financial institutions

1999

No Impose steel import quotas

No Kill proposal to take aviation trust funds off budget

Yes Require background checks on buyers only at gun shows with 10 or more vendors

Yes Remove barriers among banking, securities and insurance companies

No Authorize state grants to hire teachers and reduce class size

No Overhaul campaign finance law; ban "soft money" and restrict advocacy advertising

No Approve bipartisan plan to increase rights of patients in managed-care health plans

INTEREST GROUPS

	AFL-CIO	ADA	CCUS	ACU
2000	0%	5%	95%	96%
1999	0%	5%	88%	83%

CQ VOTE STUDIES

	PARTY UNITY		PRESIDENTIAL SUPPORT	
	Support	Oppose	Support	Oppose
2000	96%	4%	25%	75%
1999	92%	8%	21%	79%

NEBRASKA 2
East – Omaha; Sarpy County suburbs

Built as the eastern terminus of the Union Pacific Railroad, Omaha is the heart of the 2nd. Omaha grew up as a blue-collar city; a railroad center, a Missouri River port and a place where cattle became steaks. To outsiders, this broad-shouldered, gritty image remains. But Omaha has become mainly a place of new downtown office buildings and white-collar jobs in agriculture and insurance businesses. Omaha also is known as the nation's "1-800 capital," thanks to more than two dozen telecommunications and credit processing companies.

As its core has filled with people through the years, the 2nd has become more compact. Located along the bluffs of the Missouri River, the 2nd now contains just Sarpy and Douglas counties and a tiny slice of Cass County, including the city of Plattsmouth.

Although the 2nd votes consistently Republican, Omaha's dwindling blue-collar base still sends a few Democrats to the state legislature, and victory in Omaha's south side is essential for Democrats to win

statewide. The district has always been anti-abortion, but social conservatives are gaining ground once held by more moderate European immigrants. Douglas County is reliably Republican, having voted for the GOP presidential candidate every time but once in the post-Roosevelt era. Omaha is home to three-fourths of Nebraska's growing black population, but the state's first black candidate for Congress lost the district by more than 30 percent in 1998.

MAJOR INDUSTRY
Toll-free service centers, food processing

MILITARY BASES
Offutt Air Force Base, 7,645 military, 1,256 civilian (1999)

CITIES
Omaha, 386,742; Bellevue, 44,730; Papillion, 20,048

UNUSUAL FEATURES
Gerald Ford and political activist Malcolm X born in Omaha; Father Flanagan's Boys' Town, incorporated 1936, the only village in the country completely run by children; Billionaire investor Warren Buffett lives in Omaha; his father, Howard Buffett, R, represented Omaha in the House from 1943-49 and 1951-53.

Rep. Tom Osborne (R)

Elected 2000; 1st term

Osborne made a rather late entry into politics at age 63 when he ran in 2000 for the 3rd District seat. Yet his past career — as the legendary head coach of the University of Nebraska's football team — gave him name recognition that most career politicians can only dream of.

So it was no surprise when Osborne became the heir apparent to five-term Republican Rep. Bill Barrett — who chose not to seek re-election — or that he coasted to victory with just token primary and general election opposition in the rural Republican stronghold.

Retired from coaching after the 1997 season, Osborne said he decided to run for office because he "still has some energy left." He also said he thought he could make a difference in the sprawling 3rd, a mainly agricultural area that he says has suffered from a recent downturn in the farm economy.

Osborne's committee assignments — Agriculture and Resources — reflect his district's interests. The congressman, who holds a doctorate in educational psychology, also took a place on the Education and the Workforce panel.

Osborne thinks an overhaul is in order for the landmark 1996 farm bill, which is up for reauthorization in 2002. In his view, the law's market-based provisions — aimed at giving farmers more flexibility in planting decisions — have worked well. But he contends the government needs to do a better job of providing adequate income protection for farmers when commodity prices drop. He supports expanded foreign trade to give Nebraska's farm goods wider market opportunities.

Osborne's interest in improving education led him to sponsor a youth mentoring program in Nebraska, called TeamMates. The program initially started with some of his school's football players mentoring 22 young people and developed into a statewide program that matches local middle-school students who are at risk with adult mentors in their communities. Osborne says that TeamMates is grounded in his belief that government spends too much money on prisons, halfway houses and other programs and not enough money to help young people avoid getting involved in crime.

CAPITOL OFFICE
225-6435; fax 226-1385; 507 Cannon Bldg. 20515

INTERNET
e-mail: www.house.gov/writerep
web: www.house.gov/osborne

COMMITTEES
Agriculture
Education & Workforce
Resources

HOMETOWN
Lemoyne

BORN
Feb. 23, 1937, Hastings, Neb.

RELIGION
Methodist

FAMILY
Wife, Nancy Osborne; three children

EDUCATION
Hastings College, B.A. 1959; U. of Nebraska, M.A. 1963, Ph.D. 1965

MILITARY SERVICE
Neb. National Guard, 1960-66

CAREER
College football coach; professional football player

POLITICAL HIGHLIGHTS
No previous office

ELECTION RESULTS

2000 GENERAL

Tom Osborne (R)	182,117	82.0%
Rollie Reynolds (D)	34,944	15.7%
Jerry Hickman (LIBERT)	4,909	2.2%

2000 PRIMARY

Tom Osborne (R)	52,438	70.7%
John Gale (R)	12,553	16.9%
Kathy Wilmot (R)	9,127	12.3%

NEBRASKA 3

Rural West – Grand Island, North Platte

Scouting what became the Oregon Trail in the 1820s, Maj. Stephen F. Long was the first to describe this section of the country as the "Great American Desert." Most of the 3rd's land is arid, and more than half the district's population lives along the meager Platte River.

Grand Island, Scottsbluff and North Platte each serve as regional centers, providing for the retail and health care needs of the surrounding counties. Industry and manufacturing also locate around these areas, as well as in Columbus, Hastings and Kearney. The rest of the district's 66 counties are left to cattle ranchers and sugar beet and wheat farmers.

The 3rd is fiercely independent politically – it gave more votes to Ross Perot than Bill

Clinton in 1992 – but the majority is strongly Republican. In the 2000 presidential contest, President Bush overwhelmingly carried the district, topping Al Gore by 46 percentage points. Reflecting the area's isolation, most voters are against government intervention. The 1st and 2nd districts dominate state politics, leaving the 3rd resentful that despite its massive land size, its interests, such as farm subsidies and property taxes, are not top priorities.

MAJOR INDUSTRY
Agriculture, tourism, food processing

CITIES
Grand Island, 41,950; Kearney, 28,381; North Platte, 23,708; Hastings, 21,263

UNUSUAL FEATURES
Pulitzer Prize-winning author Willa Cather grew up in Red Cloud and based many of her novels in the central-southern region of the state; Alliance is the home to Carhenge, a full-sized replica of Britain's Stonehenge made of cars; Fort Robinson served as a German prisoner-of-war camp during World War II.

Gov. Kenny Guinn (R)

First elected: 1998
Length of term: 4 years
Term expires: 1/03
Salary: $117,000
Phone: (775) 684-5670
Hometown: Las Vegas
Born: Aug. 24, 1936, Garland, Alaska
Religion: Protestant
Family: Wife, Dema Guinn; two children
Education: California State U., Fresno, B.A. 1957, M.A. 1958; Utah State U., Ph.D. 1970
Career: Bank chairman; interim university president; utility company chairman; school superintendent
Political highlights: No previous office
Election results:

1998 GENERAL
Kenny Guinn (R)	223,892	51.6%
Jan Laverty Jones (D)	182,281	42.0%
"None of these candidates"	12,641	2.9%
Chuck Horne (IA)	7,509	1.7%
Terry C. Savage (LIBERT)	7,307	1.7%

Lt. Gov. Lorraine Hunt (R)

First elected: 1998
Length of term: 4 years
Term expires: 1/03
Salary: $50,000
Phone: (775) 684-5637

STATE LEGISLATURE

Legislature: Meets February-June in odd years
House: 42 members, 2-year terms
2001 breakdown: 15R, 27D; 25 men, 17 women
Salary: $130/day while in session; $85/day allowance
Phone: (775) 684-8555
Senate: 21 members, 4-year terms
2001 breakdown: 12R, 9D; 16 men, 5 women
Salary: $130/day while in session; $85/day allowance
Phone: (775) 684-1437

STATE TERM LIMITS

Governor: 2 terms
Senate: 3 terms
House: 6 terms

URBAN STATISTICS

CITY	POPULATION
Las Vegas	418,658
Reno	166,650
Henderson	166,399
North Las Vegas	101,841

REGISTERED VOTERS

Democrat	41.7%
Republican	41.6%
Non-Partisan	14.0%
Independent American	1.7%
Other	1%

POPULATION

2000 population	1,998,257
1990 population	1,201,833
Percent change	+66.3%
Rank among states	35

Median age	35
Born in state	22%
Foreign born	9%
Urban/rural	88%/12%
Crime rate	799/100,000
Poverty level	10.6%
Federal workers	14,155
Military	11,329

REAPPORTIONMENT

Nevada gained one House seat in reapportionment, increasing from two districts to three. The state legislature will draw new district lines in 2001.

MISCELLANEOUS

Web: www.state.nv.us
Capital: Carson City
Land area: 109,806 sq. miles
Rank among states: 7
STATE ELECTION OFFICIAL
(775) 684-5705
DEMOCRATIC HEADQUARTERS
(702) 737-8683
REPUBLICAN HEADQUARTERS
(702) 258-9182

District Statistics

DIST.	VOTE FOR PRESIDENT 2000 D	R	GREEN	1996 D	R	REF	1992 D	R	I	WHT	BLK	ASIAN	HISP	HOUSEHOLD INCOME	OVER 65+	UNDER 18	COLLEGE EDUCATION
1	54%	42%	2%	51%	37%	9%	44%	31%	25%	80%	10%	4%	12%	$29,611	11%	24%	13%
2	41	55	3	40	47	10	33	39	28	89	3	3	8	$32,413	10	25	17
STATE	46	50	2	44	43	9	37	35	26	84	7	3	10	$31,011	11	25	15

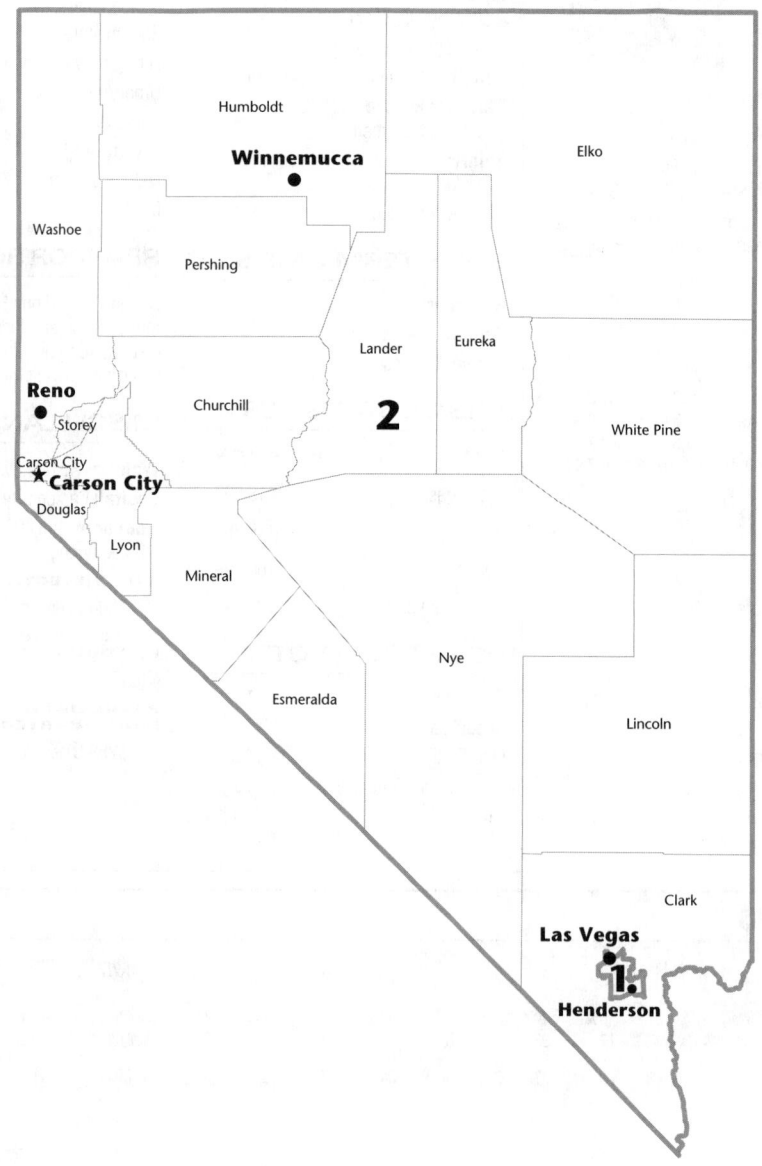

Sen. Harry Reid (D)

CAPITOL OFFICE
224-3542; fax 224-7327; 528 Hart Bldg. 20510

INTERNET
e-mail: senator_reid@reid.senate.gov
web: reid.senate.gov

COMMITTEES
Appropriations
Environment & Public Works - ranking member
Indian Affairs
Special Aging
Select Ethics - vice chairman

HOMETOWN
Searchlight

BORN
Dec. 2, 1939, Searchlight, Nev.

RELIGION
Mormon

FAMILY
Wife, Landra Reid; five children

EDUCATION
Southern Utah State College, A.S. 1959; Utah State U., B.A. 1961; George Washington U., J.D. 1964; U. of Nevada, Las Vegas, attended 1969-70

CAREER
Lawyer

POLITICAL HIGHLIGHTS
Nev. Assembly, 1969-71; lieutenant governor, 1971-75; Democratic nominee for U.S. Senate, 1974; candidate for mayor of Las Vegas, 1975; Nevada Gaming Commission chairman, 1977-81; U.S. House, 1983-87

ELECTION RESULTS

1998 GENERAL

Harry Reid (D)	208,650	47.9%
John Ensign (R)	208,222	47.8%
"None of the Above"	8,125	1.9%
Michael Cloud (LIBERT)	8,044	1.8%

1998 PRIMARY

Harry Reid (D)	unopposed

PREVIOUS WINNING PERCENTAGES
1992 (51%); 1986 (50%); 1984 House Election (56%); 1982 House Election (58%)

Elected 1986; 3rd term

Whenever the Senate is in session, the easiest way to reach Reid is to place a call to the Democratic cloakroom — a private meeting room just off the Senate floor. Reid spends more time on the floor than virtually any other senator, a natural outgrowth of the niche he has carved out as the minority whip, the chamber's No. 2 Democrat.

Under Reid, the job is much more than that of a vote-counter; he is also the Democrats' traffic cop, coordinating the flow of action on his side of the aisle. He is a loyal and trusted lieutenant to Minority Leader Tom Daschle, who routinely delegates to Reid many of the day-to-day responsibilities as floor leader. On any given day, the Nevadan will help line up speakers and coordinate with the GOP on the scheduling of debate on amendments. He also will fill in should the Democratic floor manager of a bill have to leave the chamber. Reid says his expanded duties are "a role I've developed for myself, and it's made the Senate work better."

The senator has only become more important with the 50-50 partisan split in the chamber. Reid has good relationships with many Republicans; if the Senate is to reach agreement on substantive legislation in the wake of the bitterly contested 2000 elections, it will require the kind of low-key comity that is a hallmark of Reid's style. Helping pressure Democrats to resist the temptation to offer politically charged amendments or to adopt delaying tactics on the floor may be among the tasks that fall to him.

"I really think that there's a good chance that this could turn out to be a productive Congress," Reid said as the 107th Congress was about to get under way. Predicting that Majority Leader Trent Lott will increase his tolerance for open-ended debate, Reid said that, in response, "there will be times when we're going to have to have our people just back off."

There was little backing off by Democrats in the battle-scarred 106th Congress, during which Daschle, Reid and a unified Democratic minority relentlessly pushed — with limited success — for repeated votes on Democratic agenda items such as a "patients' bill of rights," increasing the minimum wage and gun control. Lott was reluctant to expose his vulnerable incumbents to such votes, and he effectively brought floor action to a halt for extended stretches, which raised Democratic hackles.

The partisan battles took a toll on the relationship between Lott and Daschle, and Reid sometimes stepped in as a message-bearer when the two leaders were on bad terms.

In addition to his work as whip, Reid has several other duties in the 107th Congress. He remains the top Democrat on the Ethics Committee, and he has taken over the ranking minority position on the Environment and Public Works Committee, which has jurisdiction over highways, aviation and water projects as well as environmental issues. Environmentalists generally praise Reid's record, although his support for Nevada's mining industry has drawn their criticism; in the 106th, Reid unsuccessfully sought to ease proposed Interior Department rules to make mining companies cover cleanup costs and tighten waste disposal standards. As the ranking Democrat on Appropriations' Energy and Water Development Subcommittee, he has successfully pressed for additional resources for renewable energy research.

Reid is in his third term in the Senate after a difficult 1998 victory, which he won by just 428 votes over Republican John Ensign, then the congressman for Las Vegas. Their contest was bitter: Reid called Ensign "an embarrassment to the state," while Ensign's advertising described Reid as an "old card shark." But now the pair are in the Senate together — Ensign was elected in 2000 to succeed Democrat Richard H. Bryan, who retired — and as the 107th began, they appeared to have made amends.

There is one federal issue of paramount parochial importance in Nevada: keeping out nuclear waste. Reid and Bryan were able to stop legislation — a plan Reid once dubbed the "Screw Nevada Law" — to make Yucca Mountain, about 100 miles northwest of Las Vegas, the nation's temporary nuclear waste storage site. The pair worked together to convince their colleagues to sustain a veto by President Clinton in 2000.

As a practicing Mormon, Reid breaks from Democratic ranks on abortion. He is a steady vote for the GOP effort to ban a procedure its opponents call "partial birth" abortion. In 1999, he was one of only two Senate Democrats to oppose an amendment expressing support for the Supreme Court's 1973 *Roe v. Wade* decision to legalize abortion. And in 1998, he was one of two Democrats to back a bill that would have made it a federal crime to take a minor across state lines for an abortion to avoid parental consent or notification laws. The same year, however — when he was running for re-election — he was the most visible Senate supporter of a proposal to require federal workers' medical plans to offer coverage for contraceptives, a position supported by many women's groups.

Organized labor is an important Democratic constituency in Nevada, and Reid has been solicitous of unions' concerns. In 2000, he opposed enactment of the law granting China permanent normal trade status, though he voted against almost every floor amendment offered in an effort to derail the bill. Ranchers and miners also hold sway in his state, and Reid defends their interests on land-use issues.

Reid's self-made career has been part meteoric rise and part slow, hard climb. He was born into modest circumstances in the remote hamlet of Searchlight. He worked his way through school, including a stint as a policeman in the U.S. Capitol while in law school. He quickly became a successful attorney in booming Las Vegas, well on his way to becoming a millionaire, a state legislator and lieutenant governor — all by the age of 31. His political career stalled when the Democratic tide in the 1974 post-Watergate election failed to lift Reid past the state's Republican former governor, Paul Laxalt, in a close Senate race. In 1975, Reid lost a bid to be mayor of Las Vegas.

Reid was named chairman of the Nevada Gaming Commission in 1977. While in that job, the FBI uncovered evidence of the influence of organized crime in the Nevada gaming industry, and one reputed mobster accused Reid of being on the take. Reid was cleared of charges that he intervened on behalf of organized-crime figures before the gaming commission. And when he left the commission in 1981, Reid was praised for helping to eliminate criminal elements from the gaming industry. Politically, he was alive again.

Reid won a House seat in 1982 against former Republican state Rep. Peggy Cavnar. Four years later, he managed to win the first of three consecutive razor-thin victories in campaigns for the Senate. In one of the most closely watched races of 1986, Reid carried only two of the state's 16 counties against former Rep. Jim Santini, a Democrat turned Republican; but one of those was Clark County, Reid's political base and home to the majority of Nevada voters, who live in or near Las Vegas. Reid squeaked by with 50 percent of the vote.

In 1992, Reid struggled to win both the primary and the general election. Charles Woods, a wealthy, eccentric broadcast executive, held him to 53 percent in the primary. In the general election, Reid outspent GOP rancher Demar Dahl 5-to-1 and pulled off the win, with just 51 percent.

KEY VOTES

2000
Yes Overhaul bankruptcy law and increase minimum wage
No Limit fiscal 2001 discretionary spending to $600.3 billion
No Override veto on nuclear waste disposal at Yucca Mountain site in Nevada
Yes Oppose effort to terminate Kosovo mission
Yes Include gender, sexual orientation and disability in federal hate crime protections
No Approve GOP plan to restrict use of genetic information by health insurers
No Kill amendment delaying implementation of an anti-missile defense system
No Cut taxes for married couples
No Grant China permanent normal trade status

1999
No Remove President Clinton from office for obstruction of justice
No Kill amendment authorizing state grants to hire teachers and reduce class size
Yes Require criminal background checks for purchases at gun shows
No Approve GOP proposal to increase rights of patients in managed-care health plans
Yes Block effort to allow farm and medicine exports to Cuba
Yes Allow study of tougher automobile fuel efficiency standards
Yes Ratify nuclear weapons testing treaty
Yes Prohibit national political parties from collecting "soft money" donations
Yes Remove barriers among banking, securities and insurance companies

INTEREST GROUPS

	AFL-CIO	ADA	CCUS	ACU
2000	88%	90%	40%	12%
1999	100%	90%	35%	12%
1998	75%	90%	56%	20%
1997	86%	85%	50%	8%
1996	71%	85%	31%	15%
1995	100%	80%	37%	9%
1994	100%	85%	20%	4%
1993	82%	60%	18%	24%
1992	73%	80%	10%	23%
1991	92%	65%	10%	33%

CQ VOTE STUDIES

	PARTY UNITY		PRESIDENTIAL SUPPORT	
	Support	Oppose	Support	Oppose
2000	94%	6%	92%	8%
1999	92%	8%	82%	18%
1998	81%	19%	79%	21%
1997	83%	17%	84%	16%
1996	79%	21%	78%	22%
1995	74%	26%	75%	25%
1994	88%	12%	90%	10%
1993	86%	14%	88%	12%
1992	78%	22%	37%	63%
1991	75%	25%	51%	49%

Sen. John Ensign (R)

CAPITOL OFFICE
224-6244; fax 228-2193; 364 Russell Bldg. 20510

INTERNET
e-mail: ensign.senate.gov/contactjohn_email.html
web: ensign.senate.gov

COMMITTEES
Banking, Housing & Urban Affairs
Commerce, Science & Transportation
 (Manufacturing & Competitiveness - chairman)
Small Business
Special Aging

HOMETOWN
Las Vegas

BORN
March 25, 1958, Roseville, Calif.

RELIGION
Christian

FAMILY
Wife, Darlene Ensign; three children

EDUCATION
U. of Nevada, Las Vegas, attended 1976-79;
Oregon State U., B.S. 1981; Colorado State U.,
D.V.M. 1985

CAREER
Veterinarian; casino manager

POLITICAL HIGHLIGHTS
U.S. House, 1995-99; sought Republican
nomination for U.S. Senate, 1998

ELECTION RESULTS

2000 GENERAL

John Ensign (R)	330,687	55.1%
Ed Bernstein (D)	238,260	39.7%
write-ins	11,503	1.9%
Kathryn Rusco (GREEN)	10,286	1.7%

2000 PRIMARY

John Ensign (R)	95,904	88.0%
Richard Hamzik (R)	6,202	5.7%
write-ins (R)	5,290	4.9%
Fernando Platin (R)	1,543	1.4%

PREVIOUS WINNING PERCENTAGES
1996 House Election (50%); 1994 House Election
(49%)

Elected 2000; 1st term

Ensign's politics place him firmly in the conservative camp, and on many issues he finds himself opposing Nevada Democrat Harry Reid, his Senate colleague and former foe.

Ensign, who served four years in the House in the 1990s, left to challenge Reid for the Senate in the 1998 election, losing narrowly by just 428 votes. Soon after, in February 1999, Nevada's other senator, Democrat Richard H. Bryan, announced he would not seek re-election in 2000, and Ensign was primed for another race. A victory in November landed Ensign back on Capitol Hill after a two-year absence.

Ensign and Reid do agree on two matters of importance to their state — gambling and nuclear waste storage.

The gaming industry is Nevada's top employer, and Ensign joins Reid in defending the casinos' interests in Congress. Ensign has said his top priority is to stop efforts by Arizona Republican Sen. John McCain to bar betting on college sports. Ensign also is working to prohibit Internet gambling, a practice that has cut into casino revenues.

The senator's links to the industry go beyond political necessity. Ensign is a former casino manager and his stepfather is chairman of Mandalay Resort Group, the Las Vegas company that owns the Monte Carlo and Circus Circus.

Like all politicians who hope to win in Nevada, Ensign is an implacable foe of plans to build a permanent nuclear waste dump in Yucca Mountain, 100 miles outside Las Vegas. When the Democratic Party targeted Ensign in 2000 with television ads blaming the Republican majority in Congress for favoring the site, he countered by saying the state needed a senator in the majority party to fight against the waste dump.

On other matters, Ensign strongly opposes abortion rights — a somewhat risky position in Nevada, where voters in 1990 affirmed their abortion rights' stance by writing into state law the Supreme Court's 1973 *Roe v. Wade* decision that made abortion legal in the United States.

In the House, Ensign was a vocal backer of legislation to overhaul welfare. He noted that his biological father deserted the family. That made his mother eligible for welfare; instead, Ensign said, she earned $12 a day making change in a casino in Reno.

Ensign supports partial privatization of Social Security, which he believes would put younger workers in a better position to build wealth for their retirement. And he wants to see fundamental changes in the tax code: He supports provisions to scrap the current system and replace it with one that would minimize the role of the Internal Revenue Service.

Yet, even as he maintains his conservative stance, Ensign has proved that he can attract some Democratic support — and win elections.

As a House candidate in 1994, Ensign unseated Democratic Rep. James Bilbray to capture the 1st District for the GOP. The 1st, which takes in most of Las Vegas, leans Democratic, but Ensign ran with the national Republican tide to win by 1 percentage point. (President Clinton won the 1st by 13 percentage points in 1992 and by 14 points in 1996.) Ensign extended his victory margin to 7 points in his 1996 re-election bid.

In the 2000 Senate campaign, Ensign was immediately the GOP frontrunner, and the departure of Bryan made Ensign the favorite in November. Though Democrat Ed Bernstein, an attorney, was an aggressive opponent, he was outspent, and the better-known Ensign won with 55 percent.

Rep. Shelley Berkley (D)

Elected 1998; 2nd term

CAPITOL OFFICE
225-5965; fax 225-3119; 439 Cannon Bldg. 20515

INTERNET
e-mail: shelley.berkley@mail.house.gov
web: www.house.gov/berkley

COMMITTEES
International Relations
Transportation & Infrastructure
Veterans' Affairs

HOMETOWN
Las Vegas

BORN
Jan. 20, 1951, Manhattan, N.Y.

RELIGION
Jewish

FAMILY
Husband, Larry Lehrner; two children

EDUCATION
U. of Nevada, Las Vegas, B.A. 1972; U. of San Diego, J.D. 1976

CAREER
Lawyer; university regent

POLITICAL HIGHLIGHTS
Nev. Assembly, 1983-85

ELECTION RESULTS

2000 GENERAL

Shelley Berkley (D)	118,469	51.7%
Jon Porter (R)	101,276	44.2%
Charles Schneider (LIBERT)	4,011	1.8%
Christopher Hansen (IA)	3,933	1.7%

2000 PRIMARY

Shelley Berkley (D)	unopposed

1998 GENERAL

Shelley Berkley (D)	79,315	49.2%
Don Chairez (R)	73,540	45.7%
James Burns (LIBERT)	5,292	3.3%
Jess Howe (IA)	2,935	1.8%

Berkley's style in some ways reflects her hometown of Las Vegas — charismatic, fast-paced and eager to stand out in a crowd.

After she was first elected to Congress in 1998, Berkley quickly made her mark with her freshman Democratic colleagues, winning election as vice president of the Democratic class of 1998. The election was her first step toward validating the prediction of former Nevada Democratic Gov. Bob Miller that everyone on Capitol Hill would know about Berkley within a month of her arrival. Berkley took the comment as a compliment. "I tend to have a very effusive personality," she said.

Despite her desire to continue to make a name for herself, Berkley discovered in her early months in office that most reporters were less interested in her positions on issues than in her personal life. She drew publicity for showing up at a news conference wearing white tennis shoes with high heels and for her March 1999 wedding to a local physician at Bally's casino — an event that featured 19 bridesmaids.

As she settled into the job, Berkley worked hard to prove she was a serious legislator. She doggedly tended to constituents' concerns, most notably by joining in the Nevada congressional delegation's longstanding fight to keep nuclear waste out of the state. When the House failed in 2000 to pass a waste storage bill by a veto-proof margin, she regarded it a personal triumph. "That's when I realized for the first time I could do this and do it well," she said. "It gave me a lot of confidence."

Berkley also drew confidence from House Minority Leader Richard A. Gephardt and other senior Democrats who took her under their wing. The lawmakers steered millions of dollars in appropriations to projects in her rapidly growing district and offered her political counsel. "They give me advice on when to get in, when to back away, how to get the best reception for my ideas at a caucus," she told the Las Vegas Review-Journal in December 1999.

Berkley's longstanding interest in politics is fueled, she says, by her desire to give something back after her parents emigrated to the United States from Eastern Europe. She moved to Las Vegas at age 6, later attending the University of Nevada at Las Vegas, where she served as student body president before graduating with a political science degree.

After earning a law degree from the University of San Diego, Berkley returned to Las Vegas to start a career. She spent two years in the Nevada Assembly in the 1980s but became better known as a state university regent, a position that helped her become familiar with education issues. She also served on civic and legal boards before running for Congress.

Although Berkley was known in Nevada as a Democratic Party activist, she bills herself as a moderate who can work with members on both sides of the aisle. She is a member of the centrist New Democrat Coalition and has said she is an opponent of gun control, a position echoed by many Western politicians. However, some gun owners' rights activists criticized her in 1999 for voting in favor of a variety of gun-related proposals championed by Democrats, such as requiring background checks for gun purchases within three days. She responded that her support of such safety measures did not conflict with her belief that the federal government should not prevent citizens from owning guns.

Berkley, who was diagnosed with an advanced case of osteoporosis at about the time she won her first election in 1998, has championed legislation to require insurance coverage for bone mass measurements.

With the assistance of Gephardt and other senior House Democrats, Berkley was able to fend off a formidable challenge from Republican state Sen. Jon Porter and win re-election in 2000. Porter, who had earned a reputation for pragmatism and moderation during six years in the legislature, waged an aggressive campaign. He attacked Berkley in television ads for her opposition to Nevada Republican Gov. Kenny Guinn's prescription drug plan and for memos she had written several years earlier advising a client to make campaign contributions to judges as a way of currying favor.

The criticisms damaged Berkley's standing but failed to translate into any substantial support for Porter. Berkley stuck largely to a positive message and avoided direct confrontations with her opponent, winning with 52 percent of the vote. In declaring victory on election night, Berkley told supporters, "You like me, you really like me," borrowing from actress Sally Field's infamous Academy Award remarks.

Getting re-elected was a bit easier for Berkley than winning her initial House race. When Republican John Ensign left the 1st District in 1998 to run for the Senate, Berkley was regarded as the front-runner. But she squeaked by the Republican nominee, former county Judge Don Chairez, by just 3 percentage points, after battling the same ethics questions that Porter would later raise.

With one term under her belt, Berkley has vowed to continue her opposition to putting high-level spent fuel from commercial nuclear power plants at Yucca Mountain, located 100 miles northwest of Las Vegas. "I have said that along with other [delegation members], I will line up in front of the railroad ties to keep nuclear waste from going to Yucca Mountain," she said. She also promised to try to defeat legislation to ban betting on college sports, a proposal she said would have a devastating impact on the state's gambling industry.

At the same time, she promised to continue to stick up for her constituents, noting that voters in her district face a variety of special infrastructure needs, which her seat on the Transportation Committee may help her address. "They know I'm not afraid of anybody or anything," she said of her constituents. "I'm a lioness who takes care of her cubbies."

Berkley says that with more than 1 million residents in 2000, the 1st District was the nation's largest heading into redistricting. The addition of a third seat in Nevada for the 108th Congress could make life easier politically for Berkley by walling off her largely urban and Democratic constituency from rural and suburban Republican areas.

KEY VOTES

2000

Yes	Raise hourly minimum wage by $1 over two years
No	Halt funding for U.S. mission in Kosovo unless European nations pay more
Yes	Provide Medicare benefits to military retirees and their dependents
No	Grant China permanent normal trade status
Yes	Phase out estate, gift and trust taxes
No	Prohibit implementation of president's national monument designations
No	Approve GOP plan to provide prescription drug coverage for Medicare beneficiaries
Yes	Increase help for poor nations indebted to international financial institutions

1999

Yes	Impose steel import quotas
No	Kill proposal to take aviation trust funds off budget
No	Require background checks on buyers only at gun shows with 10 or more vendors
Yes	Remove barriers among banking, securities and insurance companies
Yes	Authorize state grants to hire teachers and reduce class size
Yes	Overhaul campaign finance law; ban "soft money" and restrict advocacy advertising
Yes	Approve bipartisan plan to increase rights of patients in managed-care health plans

INTEREST GROUPS

	AFL-CIO	ADA	CCUS	ACU
2000	80%	65%	57%	28%
1999	78%	100%	36%	4%

CQ VOTE STUDIES

	PARTY UNITY		PRESIDENTIAL SUPPORT	
	Support	Oppose	Support	Oppose
2000	81%	19%	63%	37%
1999	89%	11%	79%	21%

NEVADA 1

South – Las Vegas

The neon lights and chance of easy money continue to reel pleasure seekers into the 1st, which includes Las Vegas and surrounding areas. The state's largest city, Las Vegas, experienced phenomenal growth in the 1990s; the Las Vegas metropolitan area has been the fastest growing in the nation. The downside is that traffic congestion is now a major concern.

Gaming and tourists drive the 1st's economy. While the downtown hosts older casinos, Las Vegas Boulevard is home to the newer resorts. With a healthy economy, both large and small gaming companies have continued to set up shop. Even so, leaders are uncertain whether casinos will continue to see the growth they experienced in the early 1990s. California's discussion about opening more casinos of its own adds to the industry's worries. The district also attracts tourists to its surrounding national parks and desert topography.

The 1st is a competitive swing district that has attracted quite a bit of national attention and money in recent elections. Although it has a strong Democratic base in unionized service workers, newly arrived white-collar workers (many from California), Mormons in Henderson and high voter turnout by conservatives keep elections close. The area also has a strong independent streak; 25 percent voted for Ross Perot in 1992.

MAJOR INDUSTRY
Tourism, casinos, convention

CITIES
Las Vegas (pt.), 189,641 (1990); Henderson, 166,399; Paradise (unincorporated) (pt.), 124,656 (1990)

UNUSUAL FEATURES
At 30 stories, Luxor Casino is the biggest pyramid in the Western Hemisphere; Little White Chapel has a drive-through window for weddings.

Rep. Jim Gibbons (R)

CAPITOL OFFICE
225-6155; fax 225-5679; 100 Cannon Bldg. 20515

INTERNET
e-mail: mail.gibbons@mail.house.gov
web: www.house.gov/gibbons

COMMITTEES
Armed Services
Resources
Veterans' Affairs
Select Intelligence
  (Human Intelligence, Analysis &
  Counterintelligence - chairman)

HOMETOWN
Reno

BORN
Dec. 16, 1944, Sparks, Nev.

RELIGION
Protestant

FAMILY
Wife, Dawn Gibbons; three children

EDUCATION
U. of Nevada, Reno, B.S. 1967, M.S. 1973;
Southwestern U., J.D. 1979

MILITARY SERVICE
Air Force, 1967-71; Nev. Air National Guard,
1975-95

CAREER
Airline pilot; lawyer; geologist

POLITICAL HIGHLIGHTS
Nev. Assembly, 1989-94 (minority whip, 1993);
Republican nominee for governor, 1994

ELECTION RESULTS

2000 GENERAL

Jim Gibbons (R)	229,608	64.5%
Tierney Cahill (D)	106,379	29.9%
Dan Hansen (IA)	5,582	1.6%

2000 PRIMARY

Jim Gibbons (R)	68,917	89.6%
Mitchell T. Tracy (R)	7,986	10.4%

1998 GENERAL

Jim Gibbons (R)	201,623	81.1%
Christopher Horne (IA)	20,738	8.3%
Louis R. Tomburello (LIBERT)	18,561	7.5%

PREVIOUS WINNING PERCENTAGES
1996 (59%)

Elected 1996; 3rd term

Like the other elected officials from his state, Gibbons spends much of his time in Congress defending the state's gambling industry and trying to block construction of a nuclear waste storage site in the Nevada desert.

Fighting the nuclear waste storage site is good politics at home, but it is more awkward for Gibbons than for the Democrats in the Nevada delegation. The Republican-run Congress would like to allow temporary storage of nuclear waste above ground near Yucca Mountain in the Nevada desert until a permanent storage facility is ready — a plan the Nevada delegation strongly opposed.

A provision of the bill also would have weakened the authority of the Environmental Protection Agency to set radiation protection standards for Yucca Mountain — a proposal the Democrats and President Clinton opposed. They argued it was improper to encroach on the power of an agency that had wielded it for three decades. Gibbons and his Nevada colleagues were unable in 2000 to prevent Congress from passing a temporary storage bill, and Gibbons was one of only 18 Republicans to oppose it. But the measure died by a Clinton veto. Gibbons praised Clinton's action, one of the few times he had anything nice to say about the Democratic administration.

More typical were his comments about security at Los Alamos National Laboratory in New Mexico, which Gibbons referred to as the "irresponsible and dangerous security policies of this administration." On another occasion, he railed against "the disgraceful scandals and illegal coverups that have become an unfortunate characteristic of this administration."

Gibbons is not a hard man to find. Most days he is on the House floor as the chamber begins its daily session, wearing his trademark cowboy boots. He is one of the most dedicated of the five dozen or so GOP lawmakers who are on the party's "theme team." Team members take to the House floor for one-minute speeches, before the chamber begins its legislative business, to articulate Republican views of the world. In the 106th Congress, Gibbons gave 175 one-minute speeches — the most of any theme team member.

His committee assignments mesh well with his background, which includes degrees in mining and law and experience as a combat pilot. Gibbons sits on four committees — Resources, Armed Services, Veterans' Affairs, and Intelligence.

Although he has varied legislative interests, nuclear waste and gambling must top his House priorities. Since he first came to Washington in 1997, the battle to keep the nuclear waste site out of Nevada has consumed much of his time, and his training as a mining geologist lends a dose of authority to his argument that the waste dump would "expose the citizens of Nevada to the possibility of an environmental disaster of monumental proportions."

Yet Gibbons' "green" stance on nuclear waste was a departure from the norm — he usually sympathizes with property rights advocates and business interests in their disputes with environmentalists over matters such as enforcement of the Endangered Species Act. He is a co-chairman of the Congressional Mining Caucus, which lobbies in support of the mining industry. The 2nd District encompasses 99.8 percent of the state's land area, and almost 90 percent of it is owned by the federal government. Federal water and grazing regulations, and federal mining policies play key roles in the economic development of the state.

Gibbons chairs the Congressional Gaming Caucus in the 107th Congress. His support of Nevada's gambling industry kept him busy fighting proposals to outlaw gambling on college sports, to ban automated teller machines from casinos, to withhold a portion of bingo and keno winnings for federal income taxes, and to tax casino workers for the value of employer-provided meals. In many of those efforts, he found himself opposing fellow Republicans.

Gibbons also stands apart from the free-trade enthusiasts who are a majority in the House GOP. He voted against granting China permanent normal trade status, and he opposed giving the president fast-track authority to negotiate trade agreements that Congress cannot amend.

Gibbons was born in Sparks, just outside Reno. His father, who had only an eighth grade education, was a laborer for the Southern Pacific Railroad, and the family had little money. Their house was located in the flight path of the local airport, and Gibbons dreamt of being a pilot.

His father died the day he graduated from high school, and Gibbons says his mother pushed him to go to college, where he studied earth science and geology. Faced with a draft notice after graduation, Gibbons joined the Air Force. A combat pilot, he flew A-37 close air support planes during a tour in Vietnam. (Recalled to active duty during the Gulf War, Gibbons won a Distinguished Flying Cross.)

After the service, Gibbons was thwarted in his goal of becoming an airline pilot, as the airlines weren't hiring. Instead, he pursued geology, earning a master's degree, before deciding that he "didn't want to be packing rocks up a hill like my dad did." He entered law school and earned his degree about the same time that he was hired as a pilot. He spent most of the next two decades flying for Western Airlines and then for Delta.

In 1987, Gibbons helped his wife, Dawn, lobby the state legislature on a matter related to her business. That rekindled his interest in public affairs, which had begun years before when his mother ran for mayor of Sparks. In 1988, Gibbons won the first of three elections to the state Assembly.

Thanks to a race for governor in 1994, which he lost to incumbent Democrat Bob Miller, Gibbons was the best known of the Republicans who made a play for the 2nd in 1996 when veteran GOP Rep. Barbara F. Vucanovich retired. In the six-way Republican primary, Gibbons had the broadest background, and he took the nomination with 42 percent of the vote. He went on to win the Republican-leaning district by 23 percentage points.

It did Gibbons no harm that he shared the ballot with his own proposed amendment to the state constitution requiring a two-thirds vote of the legislature for any tax increase. The amendment, which was placed on the ballot via a petition drive led by Gibbons, also won.

KEY VOTES

2000
Yes Raise hourly minimum wage by $1 over two years
Yes Halt funding for U.S. mission in Kosovo unless European nations pay more
Yes Provide Medicare benefits to military retirees and their dependents
No   Grant China permanent normal trade status
Yes Phase out estate, gift and trust taxes
Yes Prohibit implementation of president's national monument designations
Yes Approve GOP plan to provide prescription drug coverage for Medicare beneficiaries
No   Increase help for poor nations indebted to international financial institutions

1999
Yes Impose steel import quotas
Yes Kill proposal to take aviation trust funds off budget
No   Require background checks on buyers only at gun shows with 10 or more vendors
Yes Remove barriers among banking, securities and insurance companies
No   Authorize state grants to hire teachers and reduce class size
No   Overhaul campaign finance law; ban "soft money" and restrict advocacy advertising
Yes Approve bipartisan plan to increase rights of patients in managed-care health plans

INTEREST GROUPS

	AFL-CIO	ADA	CCUS	ACU
2000	20%	30%	61%	88%
1999	44%	15%	68%	84%
1998	20%	20%	89%	92%
1997	0%	0%	80%	91%

CQ VOTE STUDIES

	PARTY UNITY		PRESIDENTIAL SUPPORT	
	Support	Oppose	Support	Oppose
2000	92%	8%	29%	71%
1999	91%	9%	20%	80%
1998	93%	7%	22%	78%
1997	92%	8%	30%	70%

NEVADA 2
Reno, the 'Cow Counties' and part of Clark County

The conservative-leaning 2nd takes in all of the state, except downtown Las Vegas and the town of Henderson. Reno and the capital, Carson City, anchor the 2nd in the west, while in the south the 1st District's Las Vegas dominates. In the district's "Cow Counties," agriculture, mining and ranching dominate. Nearly 90 percent of the district's land is federally owned.

In the 1800s, the gold rush attracted fortune seekers to Reno, the 2nd's largest city. Nowadays, fortune seekers are more inclined to try their luck in the city's glitzy casinos or head to Lake Tahoe. In recent years, though, gambling in Reno has not fared as well, and the industry is concerned that customers will flock to Indian reservation casinos in California. Yucca Mountain, the proposed national nuclear waste storage site located northwest of Las Vegas, also has been a contentious issue in the 2nd. The federal government is expected to make a decision about the proposed plan in 2001.

The 2nd has sent Republicans to Congress since 1983. Redistricting in 1991 increased the 2nd's land and gave it more GOP territory. The 2nd votes mostly Republican in local elections and is becoming increasingly conservative.

MAJOR INDUSTRY
Gaming, mining, manufacturing, warehousing

MILITARY BASES
Nellis Air Force Base, 6,408 military, 903 civilian (1999); Fallon Naval Air Station, 1,164 military, 1,478 civilian (1998)

CITIES
Reno, 166,650; Las Vegas (pt.), 68,654 (1990); Sparks, 64,338; Carson City, 50,046

UNUSUAL FEATURES
Nevada known for its "quickie divorces" – as long as one member of the couple is a Nevada resident, the couple need only wait six weeks to end a marriage; White King, a 10-foot, 4-inch tall polar bear on display in Elko, is said to be the world's largest polar bear.

Gov. Jeanne Shaheen (D)

First elected: 1996
Length of term: 2 years
Term expires: 1/03
Salary: $96,000
Phone: (603) 271-2121
Hometown: Madbury
Born: Jan. 28, 1947, St. Charles, Mo.
Religion: Protestant
Family: Husband, Bill Shaheen; three children
Education: Shippensburg U., B.A. 1969; U. of Mississippi, M.S.S. 1973
Career: Campaign manager; teacher
Political highlights: Democratic nominee for N.H. Senate, 1978; N.H. Senate, 1991-97

Election results:
2000 GENERAL

Jeanne Shaheen (D)	275,038	48.7%
Gordon Humphrey (R)	246,952	43.8%
Mary Brown (I)	35,904	6.4%

Senate President Arthur Klemm (R)

(no lieutenant governor)
Phone: (603) 271-2111

STATE LEGISLATURE

General Court: Meets January-June
House: 400 members, 2-year terms
2001 breakdown: 256R, 140D, 1L, 3 vacancies; 279 men, 118 women
Salary: $100/year
Phone: (603) 271-3661
Senate: 24 members, 2-year terms
2001 breakdown: 13R, 11D; 17 men, 7 women
Salary: $100/year
Phone: (603) 271-2111

STATE TERM LIMITS

Governor: No
Senate: No
House: No

URBAN STATISTICS

CITY	POPULATION
Manchester	102,830
Nashua	82,677
Concord	38,981
Rochester	28,241
Dover	26,586

REGISTERED VOTERS

Undeclared	38%
Republican	35%
Democrat	26%

POPULATION

2000 population	1,235,786
1990 population	1,109,252
Percent change	+11.4%
Rank among states	41
Median age	35.4
Born in state	44%
Foreign born	4%
Urban/rural	51%/49%
Crime rate	113/100,000
Poverty level	9.8%
Federal workers	8,083
Military	4,374

REAPPORTIONMENT

New Hampshire retained its two House seats in reapportionment. The state legislature will draw new district lines.

MISCELLANEOUS

Web: www.state.nh.us
Capital: Concord
Land area: 8,969 sq. miles
Rank among states: 44
STATE ELECTION OFFICIAL
(603) 271-3242
DEMOCRATIC HEADQUARTERS
(603) 225-6899
REPUBLICAN HEADQUARTERS
(603) 225-9341

District Statistics

DIST.	2000 D	2000 R	GREEN	1996 D	1996 R	REF	1992 D	1992 R	I	WHT	BLK	ASIAN	HISP	HOUSEHOLD INCOME	OVER 65+	UNDER 18	COLLEGE EDUCATION
				VOTE FOR PRESIDENT													
1	46%	49%	4%	49%	40%	10%	38%	39%	23%	98%	1%	1%	1%	$36,511	11%	25%	24%
2	48	47	4	50	38	10	41	37	23	98	1	1	1	$36,145	11	25	25
STATE	47	48	4	49	39	10	39	38	23	98	1	1	1	$36,329	11	25	24

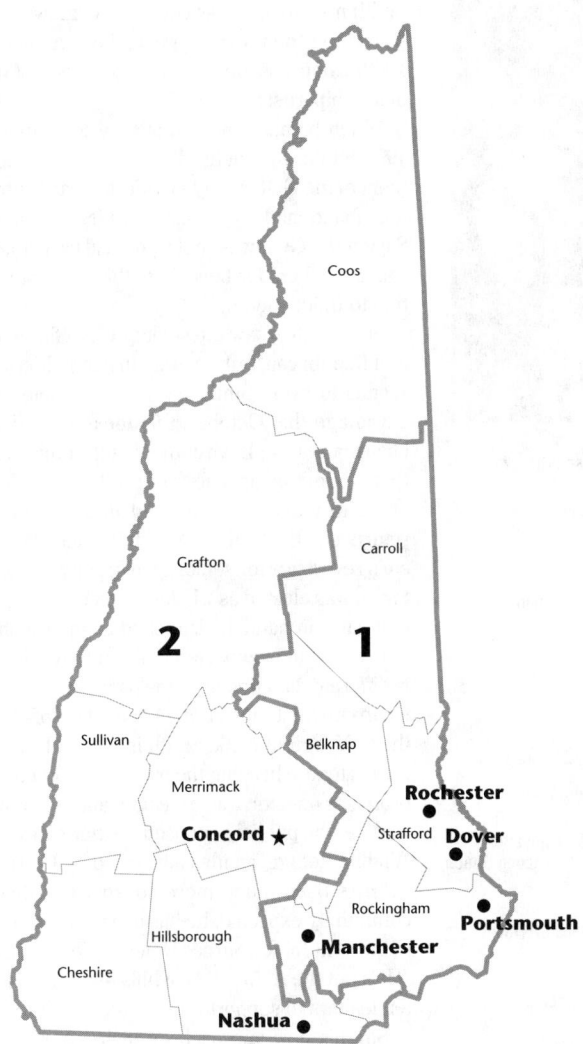

Sen. Robert C. Smith (R)

Elected 1990; 2nd term

CAPITOL OFFICE
224-2841; fax 224-1353; 307 Dirksen Bldg. 20510

INTERNET
e-mail: opinion@smith.senate.gov
web: smith.senate.gov

COMMITTEES
Armed Services
Environment & Public Works - chairman

HOMETOWN
Tuftonboro

BORN
March 30, 1941, Trenton, N.J.

RELIGION
Roman Catholic

FAMILY
Wife, Mary Jo Smith; three children

EDUCATION
Trenton Junior College, A.A. 1963; Lafayette
College, B.A. 1965; California State U., Long Beach,
attended 1968-69

MILITARY SERVICE
Naval Reserve, 1962-65; Navy, 1965-67; Naval
Reserve, 1967-69

CAREER
Real estate broker; high school teacher

POLITICAL HIGHLIGHTS
Gov. Wentworth Regional School Board
(Wolfeboro, N.H.), 1978-84; sought Republican
nomination for U.S. House, 1980; Republican
nominee for U.S. House, 1982; U.S. House, 1985-90

ELECTION RESULTS

1996 GENERAL

Robert C. Smith (R)	242,257	49.2%
Dick Swett (D)	227,355	46.2%
Ken Blevens (LIBERT)	22,261	4.5%

1996 PRIMARY

Robert C. Smith (R)	unopposed

PREVIOUS WINNING PERCENTAGES
1990 (65%); 1988 House Election (60%); 1986
House Election (56%); 1984 House Election (59%)

Amiable in person and unfailingly polite in one-on-one conversations, Smith nonetheless has come to be known for the rhetorical bombs he has thrown on the normally genteel Senate floor. Indeed, until midway in the 106th Congress, he may have been one of the last senators to be thought of as a bipartisan "player."

When he announced that he was quitting the Republican Party in July 1999, Smith stood at his desk on the Senate floor to deliver a sweeping indictment of the GOP as "hypocritical" — an "entrenched political industry" that had abandoned its principles on issues such as abortion and gun control. Saying the GOP was "not a political party that means anything" and that he was a "sucker" for believing otherwise, Smith switched his voter registration to Independent.

Some critics saw the soliloquy as a fitting end to Smith's quixotic career as a Republican, but several top party elders set to work quietly behind the scenes to bring Smith back into the fold. A Senate loss worked to their advantage that October: the unexpected death of John H. Chafee, R-R.I., chairman of the Environment and Public Works Committee. The gavel of that committee appears to have been the last enticement they needed in order to make a success out of their entreaties to Smith. He officially returned to the GOP on Nov. 1; the next day — taking advantage of the Senate's reverence for seniority to brush aside some Republican opposition — Smith was elected as Chafee's successor as committee chairman. And with that gavel in hand, he launched an improbable rehabilitation.

It was widely expected that Smith would take the panel in a dramatically different direction from the path charted by Chafee, who had championed environmental causes, often in the face of blunt attacks on regulations from the GOP's right flank, Smith included. But Smith has surprised many during his tenure heading the panel. He worked across party lines to strike compromises on toxic waste cleanup and restoration of the Florida Everglades. And he has publicly opposed further oil exploration in the Arctic National Wildlife Refuge, an idea advocated by President Bush.

"He's been much more constructive than many in the environmental community expected; he has been a pleasant surprise," said Greg Wetstone of the Natural Resources Defense Council, a leading environmental group. "He's put the right kinds of bills together, worked with Democrats and gotten leaders to support them. None of that is very easy."

Smith's new approach to environmental issues will be put to the test again in the 107th Congress, when he is expected to play a major role in the reauthorization of the Clean Air Act. In the winter of 2001, as the panel began considering legislation to clean up polluted industrial sites known as "brownfields," Smith counseled his colleagues: "Is this an ideal bill? Absolutely not. But continuing to delay enactment of this bill in search of a bill that will never pass is not the way to address the issues."

Prior to his chairmanship, Smith was best known for his passionate advocacy for conservative causes. He fought the Brady gun control law and restrictions on owning assault rifles and has called abortion "one of the great issues of the day, much as slavery was 100 years ago." His effort to restrict abortion rights has included graphic descriptions from the Senate floor of abortion procedures.

A Vietnam veteran who saw a year of active duty with the Navy in the Gulf of Tonkin, Smith is the Senate's most fervent believer that U.S. servicemen remained in captivity in Vietnam after the war ended in 1975. When John McCain, R-Ariz., a former prisoner of war in Vietnam, helped lead the Senate to vote in favor of normalizing diplomatic relations with Vietnam in 1995, Smith opposed him.

Smith sought the GOP presidential nomination in 2000, hoping "to reverse the cynicism in American politics." But his maverick campaign was greeted with puzzlement even in his home state, locale of the pivotal initial GOP primary. "One recent morning Bob Smith actually woke up, looked in the mirror and saw a president looking back," the Concord Monitor opined. "He should have splashed that vision away with a face full of cold water. ... Smith's decision is surprising for the ambition it reveals in this ambling man — and disturbing for the lack of perspective he demonstrates."

Still, the candidacy of a man whom opponents have called "Bumbling Bob" and the "abominable no-man" filled a void for some conservative activists, giving them a voice while most of the party establishment lined up behind the moderate Bush. The ultra-right John Birch Society once named Smith the nation's most conservative senator — edging out North Carolina Republican Jesse Helms for that distinction.

The burly former high school teacher's aggressive political style often has seemed out of place in the clubby hallways of the Senate. Smith's frustration with the GOP began to come to a head in 1998, when some party moderates maintained that the GOP would endanger its standing with big groups of voters in parts of the country if it came up with a slate of monolithically conservative congressional candidates.

"What the leadership ought to understand is, we win elections because of conservatives," Smith replied. "The party elite treats us like a force that has to be tolerated and not embraced. We expect to be embraced. If we are going to be merely tolerated, there are going to be serious problems. Then there will be a third party, and the bad news is, the Republican Party will be the third party."

On some occasions, however, Smith's down-the-line conservatism has given way to regional priorities. For example, while classic conservative support for free trade would seem to dictate a "yes" vote on the North American Free Trade Agreement in 1993, Smith opposed the pact, saying it was more important to protect the local industries and workers whose jobs might be threatened by competition south of the border.

A small-town real estate agent and one-time teacher, Smith has cultivated the image of a real-life "Mr. Smith Goes to Washington." He served on a school board for six years and then sought to move up to Capitol Hill, running unsuccessfully for the GOP nomination in New Hampshire's 1st District in 1980 and 1982. Smith won that seat in 1984 when Democratic incumbent Norman E. D'Amours ran for the Senate, and Smith served three terms in the House. He then ran successfully for the seat of retiring Republican Sen. Gordon J. Humphrey in 1990, easily defeating former Democratic Sen. John A. Durkin.

Smith had a tougher time of it in 1996 against Democratic Rep. Dick Swett, who accused Smith of holding views on issues such as abortion that were too far to the right even in New Hampshire. Swett also hectored Smith for voting for a Senate pay raise in 1991 after promising not to do so. On election night, early exit polls led networks to declare Swett the victor, but when all the votes were counted, Smith had won by 3 percentage points.

In early 2001, Smith was widely considered among the most vulnerable senators up for re-election in 2002. Former Gov. Steve Merrill and both of the state's House members, John E. Sununu and Charles Bass, have been urged by Republican factions to run against Smith. If he survives the GOP primary, he will likely face Democratic Gov. Jeanne Shaheen.

KEY VOTES

2000
Yes Overhaul bankruptcy law and increase minimum wage
Yes Limit fiscal 2001 discretionary spending to $600.3 billion
Yes Override veto on nuclear waste disposal at Yucca Mountain site in Nevada
No Oppose effort to terminate Kosovo mission
No Include gender, sexual orientation and disability in federal hate crime protections
Yes Approve GOP plan to restrict use of genetic information by health insurers
Yes Kill amendment delaying implementation of an anti-missile defense system
Yes Cut taxes for married couples
No Grant China permanent normal trade status

1999
Yes Remove President Clinton from office for obstruction of justice
Yes Kill amendment authorizing state grants to hire teachers and reduce class size
No Require criminal background checks for purchases at gun shows
Yes Approve GOP proposal to increase rights of patients in managed-care health plans
Yes Block effort to allow farm and medicine exports to Cuba
No Allow study of tougher automobile fuel efficiency standards
No Ratify nuclear weapons testing treaty
No Prohibit national political parties from collecting "soft money" donations
Yes Remove barriers among banking, securities and insurance companies

INTEREST GROUPS

	AFL-CIO	ADA	CCUS	ACU
2000	13%	10%	73%	100%
1999	22%	5%	82%	96%
1998	0%	5%	78%	100%
1997	14%	5%	50%	96%
1996	0%	5%	92%	100%
1995	0%	0%	100%	100%
1994	14%	5%	80%	100%
1993	9%	15%	91%	100%
1992	25%	5%	90%	96%
1991	17%	10%	70%	90%

CQ VOTE STUDIES

	PARTY UNITY		PRESIDENTIAL SUPPORT	
	Support	Oppose	Support	Oppose
2000	97%	3%	28%	72%
1999	94%	6%	16%	84%
1998	99%	1%	19%	81%
1997	97%	3%	51%	49%
1996	96%	4%	29%	71%
1995	97%	3%	18%	82%
1994	96%	4%	20%	80%
1993	96%	4%	11%	89%
1992	92%	8%	73%	27%
1991	94%	6%	86%	14%

Sen. Judd Gregg (R)

CAPITOL OFFICE
224-3324; fax 224-4952; 393 Russell Bldg. 20510

INTERNET
e-mail: mailbox@gregg.senate.gov
web: gregg.senate.gov

COMMITTEES
Appropriations
(Commerce, Justice, State & Judiciary -
chairman)
Budget
Governmental Affairs
Health, Education, Labor & Pensions
(Children & Families - chairman)

HOMETOWN
Rye

BORN
Feb. 14, 1947, Nashua, N.H.

RELIGION
Congregationalist

FAMILY
Wife, Kathleen Gregg; three children

EDUCATION
Columbia U., A.B. 1969; Boston U., J.D. 1972, LL.M.
1975

CAREER
Lawyer

POLITICAL HIGHLIGHTS
N.H. Governor's Executive Council, 1979-81; U.S.
House, 1981-89; governor, 1989-93

ELECTION RESULTS

1998 GENERAL

Judd Gregg (R)	213,477	67.8%
George Condodemetraky (D)	88,883	28.2%
Brian Christeson (LIBERT)	7,603	2.4%
Roy Kendel (IA)	4,733	1.5%

1998 PRIMARY

Judd Gregg (R)	64,121	85.6%
Phil Weber (R)	10,818	14.4%

PREVIOUS WINNING PERCENTAGES
1992 (48%); 1986 House Election (74%); 1984 House
Election (76%); 1982 House Election (71%); 1980
House Election (64%)

Elected 1992; 2nd term

When presidential candidate George W. Bush picked Gregg to play the part of his opponent, Al Gore, for debating practice in the fall of 2000, GOP campaign aides told The Washington Post that Gregg was the right person for the job because he was "smart ... stiff ... dour," characteristics many Republicans ascribed to Gore.

But even with his New England reserve, Gregg has managed to become something of a player in an institution known for its chumminess. His experience as a former House member and governor gives him a perspective that has proved useful to the Senate GOP leadership, particularly on the politically combustible issue of Social Security.

He is the GOP's chief deputy whip, and he enjoys a close relationship with Majority Leader Trent Lott, forged when they served together in the House Republican minority from 1981 through 1988. That year, Gregg ran for governor of New Hampshire and Lott for the Senate. During his House tenure, Gregg was an early participant in the Conservative Opportunity Society, a group founded by Republican Newt Gingrich of Georgia with the aim of toppling the House Democratic majority.

Gregg is a reliable conservative voice on fiscal and social policy matters ranging from cutting taxes to gun owners' rights. He has been a longtime ally of anti-abortion forces. As governor from 1989 to 1993, he vetoed bills that would have bolstered abortion rights provisions in New Hampshire law. In the Senate, he has voted to ban a procedure its opponents call "partial birth" abortion.

But while he is every bit as conservative as many of his Republican colleagues, in major ideological battles he is less likely to be out front in the rhetorical war. He tends to focus on the nitty-gritty details of large and complex issues, such as Social Security and other entitlement programs; he co-chairs a Budget Committee task force on Social Security. Unlike some of his party's conservative firebrands, Gregg is more prone to regard legislating as a give-and-take process that involves accommodating competing interests. His ability to work with Republicans and Democrats alike has made him valuable to the GOP leadership.

Early in the 106th Congress, Gregg emerged as a leading player in the debate over Social Security. He teamed with Democrat John B. Breaux of Louisiana to propose using a portion of the payroll tax for individual savings accounts. The senators contended it would enable the government to maintain the program's solvency without raising taxes or cutting benefits. But the proposal saw no action. Gregg warned that without a White House-congressional summit, agreement on a Social Security fix was "a long way off."

He occasionally follows his New Hampshire libertarian leanings, as when he broke party ranks in the 105th Congress over a tobacco bill. Pairing with Democrat Patrick J. Leahy of neighboring Vermont, he successfully opposed a liability cap in tobacco lawsuits on the grounds that it represented unwarranted government intervention. The cap would have limited the tobacco industry's overall liability in future lawsuits to $8 billion, in exchange for advertising restrictions and other concessions. Gregg assailed the plan as an "artificial, inappropriate legislative protection" that would be "totally outside the traditional manner in which we have managed our marketplace under our capitalist system."

Gregg also tried, unsuccessfully, to eliminate the federal crop insurance program for tobacco farmers. An opponent of tax breaks and subsidies for businesses, he led an unsuccessful fight in the 105th to rescind a tax break for hard-rock mining companies. He also opposes price supports for peanuts and sugar and an annual subsidy that helps U.S. companies market agricultural products overseas.

As chairman of Appropriations' Commerce, Justice and State Subcommittee, Gregg's ability to find compromises is tested annually when he attempts to move a spending bill through his panel without letting the measure get bogged down by hot-button policy debates. Nevertheless, Gregg's appropriations bill typically is one of the last to be completed because of the many controversial issues associated with it.

In 2000, debate focused on U.S. funding for U.N. international peacekeeping activities and on several high-tech policy matters. One provision, inserted by Gregg, blocked the Federal Communications Commission from moving forward with a plan to allow community groups to set up low-powered radio stations. Gregg argued that the FCC needed to better study the ramifications of the plan for other, established radio stations.

Sometimes the trouble with the spending bill is of Gregg's own making. In 1996, his panel's bill would have made a substantial cut in an administration-backed technology program and, under pressure to make a deal with the White House, the GOP leadership "unceremoniously removed" Gregg from negotiations, as he put it. "I was too disruptive to the process because I kept saying we should be concerned about our tax dollars," he said. "The American taxpayers were being fleeced."

He is not reluctant to use legislation to advance his causes. In 2000, for example, he turned to a legislative solution when a New Hampshire woman was killed by a man who had stalked her after obtaining her Social Security number from the Internet. Gregg's bill, signed by President Clinton in 2000, made it illegal for most companies or individuals to sell Social Security numbers.

Gregg has devoted almost his entire adult life to public service, and he comes from a political family — his father also was governor of New Hampshire. The younger Gregg practiced law only a short time before launching his political career in 1978, unseating a Republican incumbent to join the five-member state Executive Council. Two years later, he won the House seat of retiring GOP Rep. James C. Cleveland. Gregg's ascent in New Hampshire politics continued, with convincing wins in three more House elections and then a couple of two-year terms as governor. In each race, he took at least 60 percent of the vote.

When Gregg sought to return to Washington in 1992, however, he ran into stiff opposition. New Hampshire's economic woes fired up an angry electorate, helping Bill Clinton carry the state for president and putting pro-business Democrat John Rauh in a position to give Gregg his toughest electoral fight as they vied to replace retiring GOP Sen. Warren B. Rudman.

While acknowledging the state's economic hardships, Gregg frequently noted that he had kept a tight lid on spending and remained staunchly opposed to state income and sales taxes. The race went down to the wire. Gregg lost most of the counties in his old congressional district on the rural western side of New Hampshire, but he won the populous southeast corner of the state and the Republican "North Country" by enough votes to take the Senate seat by 3 percentage points.

Gregg won an easy re-election contest in 1998, even after his opponent, George Condodemetraky, accused him of draft dodging. Gregg vehemently denied the accusations (he received a valid medical deferment, he said) and refused to debate Condodemetraky on television. Gregg walked away with 68 percent of the vote.

KEY VOTES

2000

Yes Overhaul bankruptcy law and increase minimum wage
Yes Limit fiscal 2001 discretionary spending to $600.3 billion
Yes Override veto on nuclear waste disposal at Yucca Mountain site in Nevada
No Oppose effort to terminate Kosovo mission
No Include gender, sexual orientation and disability in federal hate crime protections
Yes Approve GOP plan to restrict use of genetic information by health insurers
Yes Kill amendment delaying implementation of an anti-missile defense system
Yes Cut taxes for married couples
Yes Grant China permanent normal trade status

1999

Yes Remove President Clinton from office for obstruction of justice
Yes Kill amendment authorizing state grants to hire teachers and reduce class size
No Require criminal background checks for purchases at gun shows
Yes Approve GOP proposal to increase rights of patients in managed-care health plans
Yes Block effort to allow farm and medicine exports to Cuba
Yes Allow study of tougher automobile fuel efficiency standards
No Ratify nuclear weapons testing treaty
No Prohibit national political parties from collecting "soft money" donations
Yes Remove barriers among banking, securities and insurance companies

INTEREST GROUPS

	AFL-CIO	ADA	CCUS	ACU
2000	0%	0%	86%	100%
1999	0%	0%	76%	91%
1998	0%	5%	89%	76%
1997	0%	10%	100%	76%
1996	0%	5%	92%	75%
1995	0%	0%	95%	87%
1994	0%	15%	90%	79%
1993	0%	10%	91%	92%
House Service:				
1988	13%	16%	93%	82%
1987	21%	20%	88%	80%

CQ VOTE STUDIES

	PARTY UNITY		PRESIDENTIAL SUPPORT	
	Support	Oppose	Support	Oppose
2000	98%	2%	38%	62%
1999	94%	6%	33%	67%
1998	91%	9%	43%	57%
1997	87%	13%	63%	37%
1996	91%	9%	34%	66%
1995	94%	6%	22%	78%
1994	84%	16%	42%	58%
1993	90%	10%	24%	76%
House Service:				
1988	90%	10%	69%	31%
1987	91%	9%	72%	28%

Rep. John E. Sununu (R)

CAPITOL OFFICE
225-5456; fax 225-5822; 316 Cannon Bldg. 20515

INTERNET
e-mail: rep.sununu@mail.house.gov
web: www.house.gov/sununu

COMMITTEES
Appropriations
Budget

HOMETOWN
Bedford

BORN
Sept. 10, 1964, Boston, Mass.

RELIGION
Roman Catholic

FAMILY
Wife, Catherine "Kitty" Sununu; three children

EDUCATION
Massachusetts Institute of Technology, B.S. 1986,
M.S. 1987; Harvard U., M.B.A. 1991

CAREER
Corporate financial officer; management
consultant; mechanical engineer

POLITICAL HIGHLIGHTS
No previous office

ELECTION RESULTS

2000 GENERAL

John E. Sununu (R)	150,609	51.9%
Martha Fuller Clark (D)	128,387	44.2%
Dan Belforti (LIB)	5,713	2.0%
Bob Bevill (I)	5,540	1.9%

2000 PRIMARY

John E. Sununu (R)	unopposed

1998 GENERAL

John E. Sununu (R)	104,430	66.8%
Peter Flood (D)	51,783	33.1%

PREVIOUS WINNING PERCENTAGES
1996 (50%)

Elected 1996; 3rd term

The son of a famously combative conservative — who gave up the governorship of New Hampshire in 1989 to be White House chief of staff in the Bush administration — John E. Sununu shares not only his father's name but also many of his political views. Still, the young congressman also traces his affinity for politics to his mother, Nancy, who has been involved in local politics for years.

His involvement in his parents' political activities seems to have left Sununu with not only an eagerness to be involved, but also useful knowledge about the nuts and bolts of campaigning — the importance of grass-roots support and personal interaction with voters, for instance.

Sununu has risen quickly in the House Republican ranks as a measured legislator of the rarest breed: He has been pressed to carry the GOP torch for saving federal resources, as a member of the Budget Committee; and he has been handed a seat at the table where those same federal resources are spent, the Appropriations Committee.

Soft-spoken, smart, pragmatic — and, at 36, the 12th youngest House member at the start of the 107th Congress — Sununu says his mechanical engineering background offers a useful, analytical approach to problem-solving and separates him from the lawyerly crowd in Washington. He regards former Rep. John R. Kasich, R-Ohio, as his mentor, a patient tutor on how to work respectfully with colleagues of varying views, seeking common ground and remaining cordial even in the face of disagreement. Sununu staged a long-shot bid to succeed the retiring Kasich as chairman of the Budget Committee in the 107th. He did not win the job, but observers noted that, not yet sworn in for his third term, Sununu was the most-junior House member running for a committee chairmanship.

Early in 2001, there was considerable discussion in New Hampshire GOP circles about the possibility of Sununu challenging the state's senior senator, Robert C. Smith, for the GOP Senate nomination in 2002.

Sununu is fiscally frugal and wants to reduce the scope and reach of federal government. But unlike some conservatives who have joined the House in recent years, he does not regard compromise as capitulation. In 2000, as lawmakers debated end-of-session spending bills and contemplated whether to exceed previously set spending limits, Sununu declared that, given the necessity of getting the bills signed by President Clinton, he would not insist on hewing to the budget cap. "I think there's nothing contradictory about being fiscally conservative and pragmatic," he said.

Earlier in the year, Sununu joined a small group of conservatives meeting in Chicago who decided to pursue more modest and realistic goals, particularly in seeking tax cuts.

Restraint in government taxation and spending is a bedrock belief of the New Hampshire GOP, and in his first term, Sununu was given a visible post from which to preach that gospel: a seat on the Budget Committee. Republican leaders also named him to the 39-member Republican Policy Committee, and in his second term, Sununu was given the Appropriations assignment as well. He led a Budget panel task force on "waste, fraud and abuse" in federal housing and infrastructure programs, and he also led a separate Republican working group on taxes in the 106th Congress.

Taking an Appropriations seat did not change Sununu's fiscal outlook. He says his goal continues to be "focusing on controlling the size of the federal bureaucracy" so that taxes can be cut. Sununu favors a flat tax, arguing that the federal government uses the current code to "engineer the way we live."

He has identified three priority areas for his Appropriations efforts: veterans' medical care (the government has a moral obligation to repay veterans for their service, he says); special education (which he calls the largest unfunded federal mandate on the state); and the basic science and medical research conducted by the National Science Foundation (NSF) and the National Institutes of Health.

His support for the NSF notwithstanding, Sununu says he does not back federal research directed toward product development. In 2000, he wrote an amendment to a spending bill shifting $157 million from a fuel research project to debt repayment and environmental programs. He argued that the research endeavor — a joint government and industry effort to develop a technology that could lead to cars getting 80 miles per gallon — was an inappropriate government expense amounting to "corporate welfare."

Sununu is generally a reliable vote for the Republican line. His voting record gets low ratings from environmental groups, but he does side with them occasionally. In 1997, he bucked the leadership to oppose legislation that would have rolled back endangered species regulations. He also introduced a bill to cut estate taxes for property owners who promise not to develop their land. In the 106th, he sponsored legislation to protect a 12-mile stretch of the Lamprey River in his district as a component of the Wild and Scenic Rivers System. And he is interested in energizing the process of cleaning up toxic waste sites covered by the superfund law.

As a junior high school student, Sununu observed firsthand his mother's work as a school board member, and her experiences in that capacity taught him the importance and difficulties of public service. He turned his aptitude for math and science into a degree in mechanical engineering and later, equipped with analytical skills honed in an engineering and business career, entered New Hampshire politics.

When GOP Rep. Bill Zeliff gave up his seat to run for governor in 1996, Sununu edged to a narrow victory in a seven-way battle for the Republican nomination. In the fall, he argued that his business background made him a better fit for the district than his opponent, state Democratic chairman Joseph F. Keefe, a lawyer. He came away with a 3-point victory.

Democrats in 1998 had trouble fielding a challenger, replacing the party's first choice, former state Rep. Cynthia McGovern, after criminal issues in her past were revealed. Sununu cruised to victory with 67 percent. In 2000, however, he was held to an 8-point margin by state Rep. Martha Fuller Clark.

KEY VOTES

2000

No Raise hourly minimum wage by $1 over two years
Yes Halt funding for U.S. mission in Kosovo unless European nations pay more
Yes Provide Medicare benefits to military retirees and their dependents
Yes Grant China permanent normal trade status
Yes Phase out estate, gift and trust taxes
Yes Prohibit implementation of president's national monument designations
Yes Approve GOP plan to provide prescription drug coverage for Medicare beneficiaries
Yes Increase help for poor nations indebted to international financial institutions

1999

No Impose steel import quotas
Yes Kill proposal to take aviation trust funds off budget
Yes Require background checks on buyers only at gun shows with 10 or more vendors
Yes Remove barriers among banking, securities and insurance companies
No Authorize state grants to hire teachers and reduce class size
No Overhaul campaign finance law; ban "soft money" and restrict advocacy advertising
No Approve bipartisan plan to increase rights of patients in managed-care health plans

INTEREST GROUPS

	AFL-CIO	ADA	CCUS	ACU
2000	10%	10%	85%	96%
1999	0%	0%	88%	100%
1998	0%	0%	94%	92%
1997	0%	5%	100%	92%

CQ VOTE STUDIES

	PARTY UNITY		PRESIDENTIAL SUPPORT	
	Support	Oppose	Support	Oppose
2000	95%	5%	28%	72%
1999	95%	5%	18%	82%
1998	91%	9%	25%	75%
1997	95%	5%	29%	71%

NEW HAMPSHIRE 1
East – Manchester

Located in the southeastern corner of the state, the 1st qualifies as New Hampshire's urban district. It covers barely one-fourth of the state's land yet contains seven of its 11 largest communities, including the largest, Manchester.

Recovering from an economic slump in the early 1990s, the district has been concentrating on attracting business. Most of the 1st's population resides in and around Manchester, which boasts many high-tech and manufacturing companies, and in Rockingham County along the coast. Towns in the southeastern part of the 1st, such as Exeter, Dover and Portsmouth are within commuting range to Boston.

The Portsmouth Naval Shipyard, across the state line in Kittery, Maine, employs residents from the 1st and has served as an economic anchor. Carroll County, in the northern end of the district, is more rural and thrives primarily on tourism and farming.

Historically, the 1st has been considered a safe Republican district, although economic uncertainties in the early 1990s helped Democrats garner more than their usual share of the district's presidential votes. In 2000, President Bush carried the district by only 3 percent. Its congressional seat has been safely Republican since the mid-1980s, and the district consistently has sent conservatives to the state legislature.

Manchester, which has a nominally Democratic Franco-American population, leans Republican with its high number of Catholic voters and the influence of the conservative daily newspaper, the Manchester Union Leader.

MAJOR INDUSTRY
Health care, insurance, computer manufacturing

CITIES
Manchester, 102,830; Rochester, 28,241; Dover, 26,586; Portsmouth, 25,798

UNUSUAL FEATURES
Birthplace of the 14th president, Franklin Pierce; Squam Lake, location for the film "On Golden Pond."

Rep. Charles Bass (R)

CAPITOL OFFICE
225-5206; fax 225-2946; 218 Cannon Bldg. 20515

INTERNET
e-mail: cbass@mail.house.gov
web: www.house.gov/bass

COMMITTEES
Budget
Energy & Commerce

HOMETOWN
Peterborough

BORN
Jan. 8, 1952, Boston, Mass.

RELIGION
Episcopalian

FAMILY
Wife, Lisa L. Bass; two children

EDUCATION
Dartmouth College, A.B. 1974

CAREER
Congressional aide; architectural products
executive

POLITICAL HIGHLIGHTS
Sought Republican nomination for U.S. House,
1980; N.H. House, 1983-89; N.H. Senate, 1989-93

ELECTION RESULTS

2000 GENERAL

Charles Bass (R)	152,581	56.2%
Barney Brannen (D)	110,367	40.6%
Brian Christeson (LIBERT)	6,188	2.3%

2000 PRIMARY

Charles Bass (R)	unopposed

1998 GENERAL

Charles Bass (R)	85,740	53.1%
Mary Rauh (D)	72,217	44.8%
Paula Werme (LIBERT)	3,338	2.1%

PREVIOUS WINNING PERCENTAGES
1996 (51%); 1994 (51%)

Elected 1994; 4th term

Bass was born into a Granite State political family and sought a career in politics at an early age.

His father, Perkins Bass, represented the same congressional district from 1955 to 1963, and his grandfather, Robert P. Bass, was the state's governor from 1911 to 1913. Charles Bass can recall tagging along with his father on the campaign trail and notes that he and his father were the same age, 42, when they first won election to the U.S. House.

Reserved and businesslike, Bass is serious about the nuts and bolts of legislation. He aligns himself with the Republican Main Street Partnership, whose members, mostly from the Northeast and Midwest, say they are "interested in moderate Republican policies, focusing on governance and on finding common sense solutions to national problems." In his House elections, Bass has sometimes faced intraparty challengers who assert he is not conservative enough.

Bass generally shares the view of GOP conservatives that the federal government discourages economic development by saddling business with too many regulations. But, as is the case with other Northeastern Republicans, he will sometimes back environmental protection measures. He opposed a GOP move in the 104th Congress to limit the powers of the Environmental Protection Agency, and he has proposed legislation to protect a large swath of forest in northern New England and New York.

In the 105th Congress, Bass voted against a Republican bill to make it easier for landowners to go to court to challenge federal environmental regulations that adversely affect the use of their land. But he does not always side with environmentalists. The League of Conservation Voters, for example, endorsed him in 1998, but his career voting score from that organization is just 46 percent.

Bass' qualified support for abortion rights also sets him apart from the GOP majority. Although he has voted in the past three Congresses to outlaw a procedure its opponents call "partial birth" abortion, he also voted to have contraceptives covered under the federal employees' insurance plan and to provide funding for family planning programs overseas. And he has backed legislation to allow abortions at overseas military hospitals if the woman paid for the procedure herself and to use Medicaid funds to finance abortion for pregnancies resulting from rape or incest.

One of Bass' top projects has been to seek full funding for federal programs for the education of disabled students. Education funding has been a potent issue in New Hampshire in recent years, and Bass believes that the federal government should regard helping the states with their special education programs as its top education priority.

Bass served on the Budget Committee in his first term and was a leader in the unsuccessful effort to move the federal government to a two-year budget and appropriations cycle. He joined with former Budget Committee Chairman John R. Kasich, R-Ohio, in urging Congress to make spending cuts beyond those agreed upon in the 1997 balanced-budget agreement. He has won plaudits from the Concord Coalition, a budget watchdog group, for his votes on budget matters. One pet peeve has been what he terms "cowboy welfare" — an Agriculture Department program that seeks to protect Western livestock by killing coyotes and other predators. "We have coyotes on my farm in New Hampshire, but nobody has given me a dime to get rid of them," he says.

But other spending programs gain his support. As a member of the Transportation and Infrastructure Committee, Bass supported the massive 1998 transportation authorization bill, which Kasich opposed. And he proudly notes the funding he has helped direct to New Hampshire for improvements to the Manchester airport, to U.S. 2 in the northern part of the state, and for a commuter rail line connecting Nashua to the Boston area.

In the 107th Congress, Bass won a coveted spot on the Energy and Commerce Committee, giving up his seats on Transportation and Intelligence.

Bass majored in electoral behavior and French at Dartmouth College and then worked as a congressional aide for two lawmakers from Maine before entering politics.

His first attempt to win the congressional seat once held by his father came in 1980 when GOP Rep. James C. Cleveland retired. Bass had gained some political experience during several years as chief of staff to Republican Rep. David F. Emery of Maine, but he was outmaneuvered by another New Hampshire "blue blood," Judd Gregg, whose father was a popular governor in the mid-1950s.

For the next dozen years, Bass ran a small manufacturing business in the southwest corner of the state while fashioning a political career in the New Hampshire General Court, the state legislative body. Bass spent a decade in the state legislature — six years in the House and four in the Senate. While he was in the Senate, he wrote New Hampshire's law on voluntary campaign spending limits. (In the U.S. House, he has been a strong backer of proposals to overhaul federal campaign finance laws.)

In 1992, he was beaten for re-election to his state Senate seat in the GOP primary by a conservative challenger. In 1994, when he decided to go for a congressional seat, Bass benefited from a split on the GOP right between two candidates who divided nearly half the primary vote. Bass easily outpolled a lesser-known rival for moderate Republican votes to win nomination with 29 percent. In the general election, the strong GOP tide that year helped sweep Bass to a 5 percentage point victory over Democratic Rep. Dick Swett.

In both 1996 and 1998, Bass drew a primary challenge from the conservative ranks of the GOP and went on to post narrow victories in November, collecting just 51 percent in 1996 and 53 percent in 1998. In 2000, he avoided a primary challenge. Faced with a well-funded Democratic challenge from political newcomer Barney Brannen, Bass nevertheless racked up his best margin, winning the election by a 56 percent to 41 percent tally.

KEY VOTES

2000

No   Raise hourly minimum wage by $1 over two years
Yes Halt funding for U.S. mission in Kosovo unless European nations pay more
Yes Provide Medicare benefits to military retirees and their dependents
Yes Grant China permanent normal trade status
Yes Phase out estate, gift and trust taxes
No   Prohibit implementation of president's national monument designations
Yes Approve GOP plan to provide prescription drug coverage for Medicare beneficiaries
No   Increase help for poor nations indebted to international financial institutions

1999

No   Impose steel import quotas
No   Kill proposal to take aviation trust funds off budget
Yes Require background checks on buyers only at gun shows with 10 or more vendors
Yes Remove barriers among banking, securities and insurance companies
No   Authorize state grants to hire teachers and reduce class size
Yes Overhaul campaign finance law; ban "soft money" and restrict advocacy advertising
No   Approve bipartisan plan to increase rights of patients in managed-care health plans

INTEREST GROUPS

	AFL-CIO	ADA	CCUS	ACU
2000	0%	20%	90%	75%
1999	0%	20%	88%	68%
1998	10%	10%	94%	63%
1997	0%	15%	90%	80%

CQ VOTE STUDIES

	PARTY UNITY		PRESIDENTIAL SUPPORT	
	Support	Oppose	Support	Oppose
2000	85%	15%	34%	66%
1999	83%	17%	27%	73%
1998	78%	22%	33%	67%
1997	87%	13%	39%	61%

NEW HAMPSHIRE 2
West – Concord; Nashua

The 2nd, which encompasses the entire western half of the state, spans from white-collar territory in the southern tier to the mountains and forests of the sparsely populated "North Country."

The district has an economy as varied as its population. Many of the upwardly mobile refugees from "Taxachusetts," who reside along the populous southern tier of the district in towns such as Salem, Windham and Atkinson, still work across the state line. Nashua, the 2nd's largest city, has experienced ups and downs with industries deeply involved in computers and defense electronics. The economy of the heavily forested "North Country" is closely tied to paper manufacturing and wood products. In between lie smaller blue-collar towns, many of which depend on tourist dollars from lake visitors and skiers.

Throughout most of the 20th century, the 2nd was regarded as one of the nation's most rock-ribbed Republican districts. But it has become more competitive in recent years. Not only did the district vote Democratic in the 1992, '96 and 2000 presidential elections, but it elected a Democrat to Congress in 1990 and '92. The liberal college towns of Hanover and Keene, as well as state capital Concord, provide reliable Democratic votes, while the northern counties tend to lean Republican. Prior to the 1998 election, the district consistently sent Republicans to the state legislature. But in 1998 the 2nd elected enough Democrats for the party to take control of the state Senate for the first time since 1912. Democratic control was short-lived, however, and in 2000 the GOP reclaimed the state legislature.

MAJOR INDUSTRY
Defense electronics, computer technology, health care

CITIES
Nashua, 82,677; Concord, 38,981; Keene 23,003

UNUSUAL FEATURES
"Old Man of the Mountain" stone profile – source for the state emblem – located in Franconia Notch in the White Mountains; New Hampshire's State House in Concord, oldest legislative building in America in which both houses continue to sit in their original chambers.

Gov. Donald T. DiFrancesco (R)

First elected:
Assumed office as acting governor Jan. 31, 2001, following the resignation of Gov. Christine Todd Whitman, R, to become administrator of the Environmental Protection Agency

Length of term: 4 years
Term expires: 1/02
Salary: $130,000
Phone: (609) 777-2500
Hometown: Scotch Plains
Born: Nov. 20, 1944; Scotch Plains, N.J.
Religion: Roman Catholic
Family: Wife, Diane DiFrancesco; three children
Education: Pennsylvania State U., B.S. 1966; Seton Hall U., J.D. 1969
Career: Lawyer
Political highlights: N.J. Assembly, 1976-79; N.J. Senate, 1979-present (president, 1992-present)

Senate President Donald T. DiFrancesco (R)

(no lieutenant governor)
Phone: (609) 292-5199

STATE LEGISLATURE

Legislature: Meets year-round
House: 80 members, 2-year terms
2001 breakdown: 45R, 35D; 65 men, 15 women
Salary: $35,000
Phone: (609) 292-5339
Senate: 40 members, 4-year terms
2001 breakdown: 25R, 15D; 36 men, 4 women
Salary: $35,000
Phone: (609) 292-5199

STATE TERM LIMITS

Governor: 2 consecutive terms
Senate: No
House: No

URBAN STATISTICS

CITY	POPULATION
Newark	263,087
Jersey City	230,458
Paterson	148,645
Elizabeth	110,586
Trenton	84,398

REGISTERED VOTERS

Unaffiliated	56%
Democrat	25%
Republican	19%

POPULATION

2000 population	8,414,350
1990 population	7,730,188
Percent change	+8.9%
Rank among states	9
Median age	36.4
Born in state	55%
Foreign born	13%
Urban/rural	89%/11%
Crime rate	493/100,000
Poverty level	8.6%
Federal workers	65,637
Military	30,205

REAPPORTIONMENT

New Jersey retained its 13 House seats in reapportionment. An independent commission will draw new district lines in 2001.

MISCELLANEOUS

Web: www.state.nj.us
Capital: Trenton
Land area: 7,419 sq. miles
  Rank among states: 46
STATE ELECTION OFFICIAL
(609) 292-3760
DEMOCRATIC HEADQUARTERS
(609) 392-3367
REPUBLICAN HEADQUARTERS
(609) 989-7300

District Statistics

DIST.	2000 D	2000 R	GREEN	1996 D	1996 R	REF	1992 D	1992 R	I	WHT	BLK	ASIAN	HISP	HOUSEHOLD INCOME	OVER 65+	UNDER 18	COLLEGE EDUCATION
1	64%	33%	3%	59%	27%	11%	48%	32%	20%	78%	16%	2%	6%	$35,250	12%	27%	17
2	54	42	3	50	36	12	41	39	20	81	14	1	6	$32,410	15	24	15
3	53	43	3	50	38	11	40.4	40.1	19	89	8	2	3	$41,257	15	24	24
4	52	44	3	51	37	11	40	41	19	84	12	1	5	$36,888	17	24	19
5	45	52	3	43	47	9	34	50	17	94	1	4	3	$53,433	13	24	33
6	57	38	4	55	33	10	44	39	17	82	11	5	6	$42,309	12	22	25
7	54	43	3	51	40	8	41	45	14	84	10	5	5	$50,996	14	21	32
8	61	36	3	58	34	6	46	43	12	75	13	4	17	$39,944	15	22	25
9	63	34	3	60	31	7	48	40	12	84	6	7	11	$40,816	16	19	25
10	84	14	2	82	13	3	71	20	8	33	60	2	12	$28,849	12	25	15
11	43	53	3	42	49	8	33	52	16	92	3	4	4	$57,219	11	23	37
12	51	45	4	48	42	8	40	43	17	90	5	4	3	$54,630	11	23	40
13	72	25	2	72	22	5	54	37	9	67	14	5	41	$28,721	12	24	16
STATE	**56**	**40**	**3**	**54**	**36**	**9**	**43**	**41**	**16**	**79**	**13**	**4**	**10**	**$40,927**	**13**	**23**	**25**

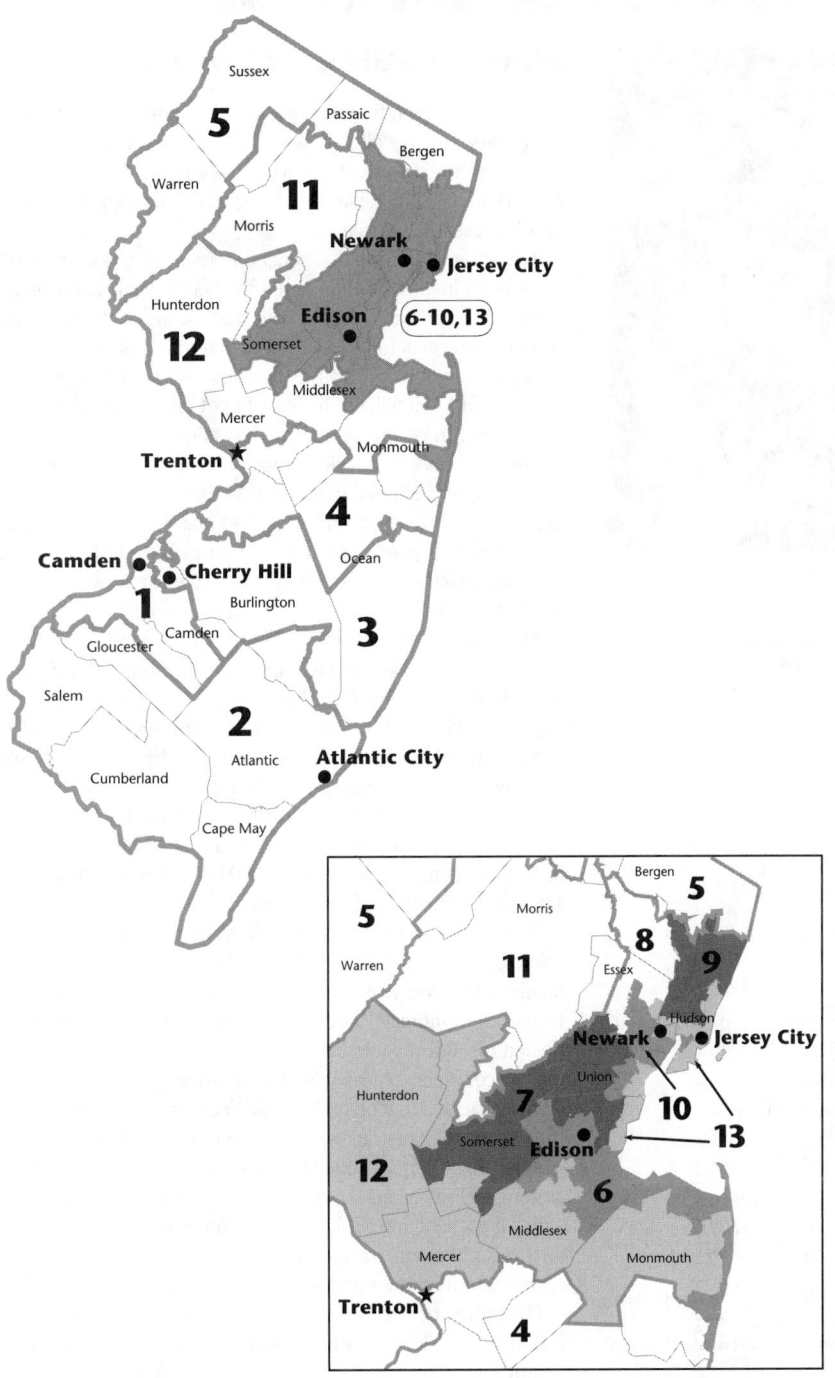

Sen. Robert G. Torricelli (D)

Elected 1996; 1st term

CAPITOL OFFICE
224-3224; fax 224-8567; 113 Dirksen Bldg. 20510

INTERNET
e-mail: senator_torricelli@torricelli.senate.com
web: torricelli.senate.gov

COMMITTEES
Finance
Foreign Relations
Governmental Affairs
Rules & Administration

HOMETOWN
Englewood

BORN
Aug. 26, 1951, Paterson, N.J.

RELIGION
Methodist

FAMILY
Divorced

EDUCATION
Rutgers U., A.B. 1974, J.D. 1977; Harvard U., M.P.A.
1980

CAREER
Lawyer; campaign aide

POLITICAL HIGHLIGHTS
U.S. House, 1983-97

ELECTION RESULTS

1996 GENERAL

Robert G. Torricelli (D)	1,519,154	52.7%
Dick Zimmer (R)	1,227,351	42.6%
Richard J. Pezzullo (NJC)	50,971	1.8%

1996 PRIMARY

Robert G. Torricelli (D)	unopposed

PREVIOUS WINNING PERCENTAGES
1994 House Election (63%); 1992 House Election
(58%); 1990 House Election (57%); 1988 House
Election (67%); 1986 House Election (69%); 1984
House Election (63%); 1982 House Election (53%)

Fast on his feet, first with a sound bite and phenomenally successful as a fundraiser, Torricelli has been well-armed for the political wars. But his hard-charging approach — which seems modeled on the old Oakland Raiders motto, "Just win, baby" — grates on fellow Democrats and generates increasing controversy.

A flair for the dramatic is only one reason he is known as "The Torch." Even in an institution dominated by media-savvy politicians, Torricelli has few peers in attracting news coverage, occasionally presenting himself to reporters to react to developments that have not yet occurred.

Some Democrats grumble that, however long his career lasts, Torricelli (tor-uh-SELL-ee) will not hesitate to put his own political fortunes ahead of the party's. In recent years, that has taken the form of an increasing willingness to break from Democratic positions on taxes. He has promoted tax cut packages designed to assist wealthier suburbanites, a core voting bloc in his state. As a new member of the Finance Committee in 2001, Torricelli maneuvered immediately to make himself central in the tax cut debate, pushing through the committee a package of education savings tax breaks more generous than those proposed by President Bush.

The seat on Finance was a reward for Torricelli's work as chairman of the Democratic Senatorial Campaign Committee, the party's candidate recruitment and fundraising arm, in the 2000 election cycle. Torricelli was appointed largely because of his own fundraising ability, which he had demonstrated in his first Senate campaign by raising $9.2 million.

As head of the Senate Democrats' campaign organization, Torricelli did not disappoint. He raised more than $100 million — a record amount — nearly doubling the party's war chest. All that money helped the Democrats pick up a net of four seats in the 2000 election, resulting in the 50-50 partisan split as the 107th Congress began.

But as he was winning plaudits among fellow Democrats for those efforts, a federal grand jury was investigating the way Torricelli had financed his own 1996 Senate campaign. Torricelli, who called the Justice Department inquiry "illogical," denied any wrongdoing and predicted that he and his aides would be cleared.

Torricelli seems incapable of walking away from a fight — even with a fellow Democrat. He took on National Security Adviser Samuel R. Berger over the Clinton administration's Kosovo policy and Attorney General Janet Reno over her handling of alleged Chinese espionage at U.S. nuclear weapons laboratories. He also joined forces with Sen. Fred Thompson, R-Tenn., in a failed attempt to sanction Chinese companies if they were caught exporting nuclear, chemical or biological weapons. The Clinton administration opposed him on the sanctions.

On many occasions, however, Torricelli's natural pugnacity serves Democrats well. "I know he rubs people the wrong way, but if I'm going into a fight I want Torricelli with me," said Sen. Mary L. Landrieu, D-La.

His intelligence, intensity and self-confidence have made him adept at floor debates and in the less-structured political brawls on television talk shows. And Torricelli is undaunted by the jibes and criticisms that come his way. "I went through boarding school, college and law school, and I never belonged to any clubs," he said in a 1999 interview. "I don't like clubs. My role in the United States Senate is not to go along to get along. ... If it frustrates people that I'm not easily defined, then who I am and what I'm about is starting to get through."

He has taken highly visible roles in the Senate, waging rhetorical war in 1999 against Republicans during the impeachment trial of President Clinton, and in 1997 during the Governmental Affairs Committee's inquiry into Democratic fundraising in the 1996 presidential campaign, including the influence of money from foreign nationals. It was during those hearings, however, that Torricelli learned the danger of being too quick to shoot off his verbal volleys. Warning his colleagues against Asian-bashing, he said he remembered watching Italian-bashing during the 1950-51 televised Senate hearings on organized crime. Reporters later noted that his impressions could not have been contemporaneous with the event, since the hearings ended when Torricelli was five days old.

Just three months into his Senate career, Torricelli thrust himself into the media spotlight when he mulled over how to vote on a constitutional amendment mandating a balanced budget. He had supported the proposal while in the House, but his vote had not been decisive. In the Senate, his vote would possibly determine the amendment's fate. Waiting until the last minute to announce his decision, he voted against the measure and it ultimately failed.

Back in New Jersey, Torricelli has had to work hard to mend fences with state Democrats. With typical bravado, he announced in the summer of 2000 that he would seek the Democratic nomination for New Jersey governor in 2001 — but he apparently had not done much to lay the foundation for such a campaign. Just 12 days later, he withdrew when it was clear that key state Democrats would instead be backing Jim McGreevey, the mayor of Woodbridge, guaranteeing a nasty primary fight.

At least part of the Democratic enmity could be traced to Torricelli's bitter rivalry with the state's senior senator, Democrat Frank R. Lautenberg, who retired after the 106th Congress. Their legendary mutual hostility climaxed in 1999, when Torricelli threatened his home state colleague in violent, vulgar language.

His personal life also has become rich newspaper fodder. His relationship with Patricia Duff, the former wife of billionaire Ronald O. Perelman, has landed him on the New York tabloid gossip pages. So did his relationship with Bianca Jagger, an ex-wife of the Rolling Stones' Mick Jagger.

The archetypal young man in a hurry, Torricelli was a political activist long before he was old enough to vote, working in the Democratic organization of his native Bergen County as a teenager. Watching how he works now, it is perhaps not surprising that when Torricelli was an undergraduate at Rutgers University, he won three campaigns for class president in part by using a sound truck to attract voters.

After law school, he was an aide to Democratic Gov. Brendan T. Byrne, worked briefly as executive director of the New Jersey Democratic Party, and came to Washington to join the staff of Vice President Walter F. Mondale. He ran the Carter-Mondale campaign for the 1980 Illinois primary and helped President Carter score a crucial victory. Also in 1980, Torricelli received a master's degree from Harvard.

In 1982, at age 31, he moved into a House district made more Democratic by redistricting and successfully challenged three-term GOP Rep. Harold C. Hollenbeck. During seven House terms, he rose to prominence on the International Relations Committee. But run-ins with House leaders helped thwart his ambition to chair the Democratic Congressional Campaign Committee, and in 1995, he said he would leave the House if he were picked to become national chairman of the Democratic Party. The offer never came.

Not surprisingly, he jumped when Democrat Bill Bradley announced his 1996 retirement from the Senate. After a nasty and expensive campaign, he defeated former GOP Rep. Dick Zimmer by 10 percentage points.

KEY VOTES

2000

Yes	Overhaul bankruptcy law and increase minimum wage
No	Limit fiscal 2001 discretionary spending to $600.3 billion
No	Override veto on nuclear waste disposal at Yucca Mountain site in Nevada
No	Oppose effort to terminate Kosovo mission
Yes	Include gender, sexual orientation and disability in federal hate crime protections
No	Approve GOP plan to restrict use of genetic information by health insurers
No	Kill amendment delaying implementation of an anti-missile defense system
Yes	Cut taxes for married couples
Yes	Grant China permanent normal trade status

1999

No	Remove President Clinton from office for obstruction of justice
No	Kill amendment authorizing state grants to hire teachers and reduce class size
Yes	Require criminal background checks for purchases at gun shows
No	Approve GOP proposal to increase rights of patients in managed-care health plans
Yes	Block effort to allow farm and medicine exports to Cuba
Yes	Allow study of tougher automobile fuel efficiency standards
Yes	Ratify nuclear weapons testing treaty
Yes	Prohibit national political parties from collecting "soft money" donations
Yes	Remove barriers among banking, securities and insurance companies

INTEREST GROUPS

	AFL-CIO	ADA	CCUS	ACU
2000	50%	75%	57%	29%
1999	78%	95%	41%	8%
1998	86%	85%	47%	8%
1997	86%	80%	40%	16%
House Service:				
1996	90%	70%	31%	21%
1995	83%	80%	25%	13%
1994	78%	65%	58%	6%
1993	100%	85%	20%	9%
1992	83%	85%	33%	16%
1991	92%	60%	30%	20%

CQ VOTE STUDIES

	PARTY UNITY		PRESIDENTIAL SUPPORT	
	Support	Oppose	Support	Oppose
2000	81%	19%	87%	13%
1999	91%	9%	84%	16%
1998	85%	15%	78%	22%
1997	90%	10%	89%	11%
House Service:				
1996	77%	23%	79%	21%
1995	85%	15%	82%	18%
1994	90%	10%	78%	22%
1993	90%	10%	94%	6%
1992	89%	11%	27%	73%
1991	89%	11%	36%	64%

Sen. Jon Corzine (D)

CAPITOL OFFICE
224-4744; fax 228-2197; 502 Hart Bldg. 20510

INTERNET
e-mail: corzine.senate.gov/comment.html
web: corzine.senate.gov

COMMITTEES
Banking, Housing & Urban Affairs
Environment & Public Works
Joint Economic

HOMETOWN
Summit

BORN
Jan. 1, 1947, Taylorville, Ill.

RELIGION
Christian non-denominational

FAMILY
Wife, Joanne Dougherty Corzine; three children

EDUCATION
U. of Illinois, B.A. 1969; U. of Chicago, M.B.A. 1973

MILITARY SERVICE
Marine Corps Reserve, 1969-75

CAREER
Investment bank CEO, manager; bond trader

POLITICAL HIGHLIGHTS
No previous office

ELECTION RESULTS

2000 GENERAL

Jon Corzine (D)	1,511,237	50.1%
Bob Franks (R)	1,420,267	47.1%
Bruce Afran (I)	32,841	1.1%

2000 PRIMARY

Jon Corzine (D)	251,216	58.0%
Jim Florio (D)	182,212	42.0%

Elected 2000; 1st term

Corzine's willingness to spend freely from his personal fortune is the reason he was able, as a first-time candidate, to win the 2000 race for New Jersey's open Senate seat. The former head of a major Wall Street brokerage firm, Corzine (cor-ZYNE) ran the most expensive self-financed campaign in history, spending more than $60 million of his own money to defeat Republican Rep. Bob Franks in the race for the seat left open by retired three-term Democratic Sen. Frank R. Lautenberg.

Yet it can be argued that Corzine's big spending also was a reason that Franks, who trailed badly in polls throughout much of the race, was able to make it a close contest. Franks' constant implications that Corzine was trying to "buy" a Senate seat gave him momentum in the campaign's closing weeks, though Corzine held on to win.

Corzine is not the product of inherited wealth. His father was a farmer and his mother a schoolteacher; Corzine said he took his first job at the age of 13 to help the family make ends meet.

He spent his career in the corporate world and worked his way up to be co-chairman of the investment banking company Goldman Sachs before leaving the firm in 1999. His outlook is shaped, he has said, by his desire to help ensure that others have the opportunity he had to achieve the American Dream.

Corzine holds strongly liberal views and ran in 2000 on a populist platform that included universal health care for children and a $3,000 tax credit for senior citizens and for families caring for an aging parent. Corzine also advocates rewarding high school students who earn at least a B average by using federal money to pay for their college tuition.

Also among the senator's liberal stands are his support for abortion rights and opposition to banning late-term abortions. And he favors legalizing same-sex marriage.

Like Lautenberg, his Senate predecessor, Corzine is a staunch supporter of gun control. He backs proposals to license and register all guns, ban sales of firearms at gun shows, impose safety standards on gun manufacturers and limit individuals' handgun purchases to one per month.

Corzine puts his business background to use in his position on the Banking Committee. He also has a seat on the Environment and Public Works panel and the Joint Economic Committee.

Though he had been a frequent Democratic Party contributor, Corzine was not known to New Jersey's voters when he entered the Senate race. Nor did he make an easy transition from business to politics: The plain-spoken Corzine often appeared ill at ease. Yet his appeal as a fresh face — along with his big spending — enabled him to soar past his Democratic primary rival, Jim Florio. The state's governor from 1990 to 1994, Florio never recovered politically from an unpopular tax increase that led to his 1993 defeat at the hands of Republican Christine Todd Whitman.

While Corzine was easily winning his nomination, four-term House member Franks barely squeaked by in the four-candidate Republican primary, winning by 1 percentage point.

Franks gained ground over his opponent by highlighting Corzine's reluctance to release his tax returns. He also claimed that he had experience as a public official that Corzine's millions could not buy. But Corzine was able to use his outsize campaign treasury to dominate the ad wars, and he prevailed in November, 50 percent to 47 percent.

Rep. Robert E. Andrews (D)

Elected 1990; 6th full term

CAPITOL OFFICE
225-6501; fax 225-6583; 2439 Rayburn Bldg. 20515

INTERNET
e-mail: rob.andrews@mail.house.gov
web: www.house.gov/andrews

COMMITTEES
Armed Services
Education & Workforce

HOMETOWN
Haddon Heights

BORN
Aug. 4, 1957, Camden, N.J.

RELIGION
Episcopalian

FAMILY
Wife, Camille Spinello Andrews; two children

EDUCATION
Bucknell U., B.A. 1979; Cornell U., J.D. 1982

CAREER
Professor

POLITICAL HIGHLIGHTS
Camden County Board of Freeholders, 1987-90
(director, 1988-90); sought Democratic nomination
for governor, 1997

ELECTION RESULTS

2000 GENERAL
Robert E. Andrews (D)	167,327	76.2%
Charlene Cathcart (R)	46,455	21.2%
Catherine L. Parrish (I)	3,090	1.4%

2000 PRIMARY
Robert E. Andrews (D)	unopposed

1998 GENERAL
Robert E. Andrews (D)	90,279	73.2%
Ronald L. Richards (R)	27,855	22.6%
David E. West Jr. (LIBERT)	1,684	1.4%
Joseph W. Stockman (PLP)	1,324	1.1%
Edward "Rob" Forchion (LMP)	1,257	1.0%

PREVIOUS WINNING PERCENTAGES
1996 (76%); 1994 (72%); 1992 (67%); 1990 (54%);
1990 Special Election (55%)

One of the first big splashes Andrews made in Congress was his cosponsorship, in 1994, of a spending-reduction plan known as "A-to-Z," named for its authors, Andrews and Republican Bill Zeliff of New Hampshire. That effort failed, but Andrews continues to employ an "A-to-Z" approach for his work in Congress, sponsoring a broad, soup-to-nuts range of legislative proposals.

Andrews is a smart, serious, hard-working legislator, and he is also the most prolific author of legislation in the House. In the 106th Congress, he introduced 98 bills, the most of any House member. Unlike many lawmakers whose legislative agendas are closely tied to their committee assignments, Andrews does not limit his focus. In the 106th, he offered bills dealing with matters ranging from foreign relations to agricultural marketing quotas, from tax policy to health care. Fifteen House committees had jurisdiction over bills he drafted. In the 107th, he kept up the pace.

But every lawmaker has priorities, and Andrews' top interests include overhaul of the managed-care system. He was a member of the House-Senate conference committee that sought to reach final agreement in 2000 on legislation to give patients more clout in their dealings with their HMOs. His appointment as one of the negotiators on the bill came as a result of his job as the top Democrat on the Education and the Workforce panel's Employer-Employee Relations Subcommittee. There, Andrews also sought to include more employees in company stock option plans.

Andrews is the son of a former shipyard worker and generally takes the side of organized labor, opposing free-trade agreements that he believes could cost U.S. workers their jobs. In fact, although Andrews has long had a reputation as something of a maverick, particularly on budget matters, he usually casts a dependable Democratic vote. He is a fairly conventional Northeastern Democrat, taking stands in support of environmental protection, abortion rights and gun control.

He proudly notes his 1993 success in pushing through a plan to have the federal government provide direct loans to college students. Previously, the government had only guaranteed loans students obtained from private banks. In 1998, the House backed Andrews' plan to make repayment of loans contingent on income. Lawmakers also approved his proposal to encourage vocational schools to train welfare recipients.

Andrews and other South Jersey lawmakers scored a coup in 2000 when they were able to convince the Navy to berth the retired battleship *New Jersey* in Camden, rather than in northern New Jersey. Another important local issue was a Delaware River dredging project, which Andrews opposed because it would have deposited most of the sludge in his district. "I guess they want to build a mud castle," he noted.

Earlier in his Capitol Hill career, Andrews' fiscal conservatism and aggressively independent behavior on issues such as the A-to-Z plan angered some Democrats, both in Congress and back home in Camden. In a 1994 Philadelphia Inquirer article, Democrat Robert Menendez of the 13th District called Andrews a "grandstander." In the same article, Democrat Donald M. Payne of the 10th District said Andrews was a "political opportunist."

In 1997, Andrews ran for governor, and those party rifts did not help him. A solid favorite to win the Democratic nomination, he was narrowly upset in the primary by state Sen. Jim McGreevey.

Andrews took the loss hard. He withdrew for a time from party politics and had harsh words not only for some party leaders but for the political system, saying that "people who control vast sums of money have undue leverage." But he has bounced back from the disappointment of 1997 and worked to build relations with other New Jersey Democrats.

Among his Capitol Hill colleagues, he is generally even-tempered; though not a backslapper, he is pleasant, approachable and displays a dry sense of humor. He usually takes the train home to Haddon Heights at night to be with his wife and two young daughters, who he says have been instrumental in toning down his former workaholic behavior.

Andrews says his childhood in the Jersey suburbs of Philadelphia holds the key to his views and goals as an adult. His father lost his shipyard job when Andrews was 14. His mother went to work as a secretary and his father eventually got a janitor's job. Andrews was the first in his family to go to college; he went on to earn a law degree and spend a half-dozen years practicing law in suburban Philadelphia.

In a 1997 interview with Gannett News Service, Andrews recalled that when his father lost his job, he said to him: "Maybe there's someone in the government who could help you." When his father dismissed the suggestion as unlikely, Andrews remembers thinking: "What were they doing, if not helping people like him?"

In 1986, at age 29, he ran for county government office and won election to a seat on the Camden County Board of Freeholders. He became known as a young reformer and two years later was chosen director of the board.

He was a protégé of Democratic Rep. James J. Florio, a liberal proponent of activist government who then represented the 1st District. After Florio was elected governor in 1989, Andrews moved to take his place in the House, winning a 1990 special-election race made more difficult by Florio's unpopularity over a big tax increase he had pushed through early in his tenure as governor. Andrews refrained from directly repudiating the governor, but he did take a "no new taxes" pledge for his first term. In the end, he prevailed by 11 percentage points. He won election to a full term on the same day.

Andrews won three easy re-election contests, making him the initial favorite in the 1997 gubernatorial race. His surprising and bitter loss had no carry-over effect in 1998: Andrews was unopposed for his party's nomination for re-election to the 1st District seat, and he prevailed in November by more than 50 points.

In 2000, he breezed to a similarly easy win.

KEY VOTES

2000
Yes Raise hourly minimum wage by $1 over two years
No   Halt funding for U.S. mission in Kosovo unless European nations pay more
Yes Provide Medicare benefits to military retirees and their dependents
No   Grant China permanent normal trade status
Yes Phase out estate, gift and trust taxes
No   Prohibit implementation of president's national monument designations
No   Approve GOP plan to provide prescription drug coverage for Medicare beneficiaries
Yes Increase help for poor nations indebted to international financial institutions

1999
Yes Impose steel import quotas
No   Kill proposal to take aviation trust funds off budget
No   Require background checks on buyers only at gun shows with 10 or more vendors
Yes Remove barriers among banking, securities and insurance companies
Yes Authorize state grants to hire teachers and reduce class size
Yes Overhaul campaign finance law; ban "soft money" and restrict advocacy advertising
Yes Approve bipartisan plan to increase rights of patients in managed-care health plans

INTEREST GROUPS

	AFL-CIO	ADA	CCUS	ACU
2000	90%	75%	38%	20%
1999	89%	95%	25%	20%
1998	90%	95%	44%	12%
1997	100%	85%	33%	22%

CQ VOTE STUDIES

	PARTY UNITY		PRESIDENTIAL SUPPORT	
	Support	Oppose	Support	Oppose
2000	88%	12%	75%	25%
1999	86%	14%	76%	24%
1998	86%	14%	77%	23%
1997	90%	10%	79%	21%

NEW JERSEY 1
Southwest — Camden

Across the Delaware River from Philadelphia, in southwestern New Jersey, the 1st is one of the state's most Democratic districts and one of the smallest in area. Much of the 1st's population is in the troubled city of Camden, one of the poorest cities in the nation.

For decades, Camden has been plagued by the departure of residents and businesses, a shrinking tax base, surging unemployment and crime, particularly drug trafficking. But the city appears to have turned a corner in recent years.

A new aquarium and a 25,000-seat outdoor amphitheater have attracted more tourists to Camden's waterfront. In 2000, the waterfront was the site of a welcoming ceremony for the Republican National Convention. The city also joined its port facilities with Philadelphia's to create one of the largest on the Eastern Seaboard, and EPA launched a redevelopment initiative to clean up industrial waste.

As distressed as the city is, the southern suburbs that fill out the 1st are flourishing with rapid development. Suburban towns such as Gloucester and Collingswood have benefited from urban flight. Vorhees Township also grew at a steady clip in the 1990s.

The voter base in Camden is largely black and employed in the public sector. In the surrounding areas, the voters are blue-collar, economically liberal and culturally conservative Reagan Democrats.

MAJOR INDUSTRY
Steel, education, shipping, manufacturing

CITIES
Camden, 82,402; Pennsauken (unincorporated), 34,733 (1990)

UNUSUAL FEATURES
Poet Walt Whitman grew up in Camden; Former Gov. James J. Florio served 15 years as the 1st's representative.

Rep. Frank A. LoBiondo (R)

Elected 1994; 4th term

CAPITOL OFFICE
225-6572; fax 225-3318; 225 Cannon Bldg. 20515

INTERNET
e-mail: lobiondo@mail.house.gov
web: www.house.gov/lobiondo

COMMITTEES
Small Business
Transportation & Infrastructure
(Coast Guard & Maritime Transportation -
chairman)

HOMETOWN
Vineland

BORN
May 12, 1946, Bridgeton, N.J.

RELIGION
Roman Catholic

FAMILY
Wife, Jan LoBiondo; two children

EDUCATION
St. Joseph's U., B.S. 1968

CAREER
Trucking company operations manager

POLITICAL HIGHLIGHTS
Cumberland County Board of Freeholders, 1984-87;
N.J. Assembly, 1988-94; Republican nominee for
U.S. House, 1992

ELECTION RESULTS

2000 GENERAL

Frank A. LoBiondo (R)	155,187	66.4%
Edward G. Janosik (D)	74,632	31.9%
Robert Gabrielsky (I)	3,252	1.4%

2000 PRIMARY

Frank A. LoBiondo (R)	unopposed

1998 GENERAL

Frank A. LoBiondo (R)	93,248	65.9%
Derek Hunsberger (D)	43,563	30.8%
Glenn E. Campbell (LIBERT)	2,955	2.1%
Mary A. Whittam (NJC)	1,748	1.2%

PREVIOUS WINNING PERCENTAGES
1996 (60%); 1994 (65%)

LoBiondo's grandfather and father, both immigrants, established a trucking company in South Jersey to transport farm produce to market, and today LoBiondo represents the district that accounts for more than 40 percent of the Garden State's agricultural production.

An economically diverse area, the 2nd District includes small truck farms and the beach communities of Cape May and Atlantic City, with its large hotels and casinos and its crime-ridden poorer sections. LoBiondo's legislative efforts are wide-ranging, in keeping with his district's diversity, and include coastal protections, tourism, gambling and agriculture. He is the only New Jersey member of the congressional Rural Caucus.

In some respects, LoBiondo (lo-bee-ON-dough) fits in well with his colleagues in the conservative House GOP Class of 1994. On fiscal policy, abortion and gun control, he hews to the right. (The National Rifle Association was a key backer of his first winning House bid.) He supports the GOP position about 80 percent of the time. Not one to seek a reputation as a party maverick, LoBiondo says his departures from the conservative line are simply in response to his district's interests.

His concern for the environment stems from the 2nd's considerable ocean frontage and wetlands areas, as well as residents' worries about pollution and preservation of natural resources. In the 107th Congress, he took the gavel of Transportation's Coast Guard and Maritime Transportation Subcommittee, whose purview includes the Coast Guard's base at Cape May.

LoBiondo is constantly on the alert for moves by New York to dump garbage off the Jersey coast, and he seeks federal dollars to restore storm-damaged Jersey beaches and to develop the state's Coastal Heritage Trail. In 1997, LoBiondo opposed conservatives who wanted to scale back enforcement of the Endangered Species Act. In 1995, he was among the minority of Republicans who voted "no" on a bill that would have relaxed regulations governing the discharge of wastes and storm water into waterways.

His stands on the environment, labor and on some social policy issues qualify him for membership in a small subset of the House GOP — moderates from the Northeast. In his last two re-election campaigns, he has received substantial support from labor unions, who like his record on increasing the minimum wage; backing the Davis-Bacon wage law, which requires federal construction contractors to pay workers the local prevailing wage; and opposing overseas trade agreements.

LoBiondo has championed the Meals on Wheels program, whose success he observed firsthand during his days as a county freeholder. He says the program will save the federal government money by lowering future Medicare and veterans health care costs. And he favors continued funding for the National Endowment for the Arts, saying that it is important to his district's efforts to extend tourism beyond the summer months.

One of LoBiondo's priorities in the 106th Congress was to obtain full funding for 20 empowerment zones that were designated in 1999 to receive federal aid targeted to distressed economic areas. One of the zones is located in the 2nd District's Cumberland County.

The 2nd also hosts the gambling mecca of Atlantic City, and LoBiondo is a co-founder of the Congressional Gaming Caucus, watching out for the interests of brick-and-mortar gambling establishments in the face of competition from Internet gambling. In the 106th, he authored legislation to require sweepstakes come-ons to clarify the relationship between winning and purchasing the sponsoring product. He said that many offers of prizes insinuate that the consumer will have a better chance of winning by making a purchase.

LoBiondo is strongly committed to spending restraint, and he can cite a host of votes against government programs that many Republicans support, including NASA's International Space Station. He also opposed the large tax cut sought by other House Republicans in 1999, favoring a smaller cut.

He votes against price supports for peanuts, sugar and tobacco; and he has criticized as "corporate welfare" the Market Promotion Program, which provides subsidies to commodity producers and food processors, many of which are large corporations, to help them advertise their products overseas.

LoBiondo grew up in the small South Jersey town of Rosenhayn in what would be a dream environment for many young boys — working around the trucks at LoBiondo Brothers Motor Express Inc., while also spending time on local farms owned by other members of his extended family.

His father was involved in local politics — for a time he was the mayor of Deerfield Township — and he instilled in his son the idea that public involvement, in civic organizations as well as in politics, is an important aspect of life. But the LoBiondo children also were expected to join the family business; for 26 years after college, LoBiondo worked in the family's trucking company.

In the early 1980s, LoBiondo ran for the Cumberland County Board of Freeholders. He served a three-year term and was ready to run for another stint when party leaders convinced him to run instead for a sudden opening in the General Assembly.

He served seven years there, trying for the 2nd District House seat in 1992 and winning just 41 percent of the vote against popular longtime Democratic Rep. William J. Hughes, whose moderate image and personal popularity offset the GOP's advantage in voter registration.

Two years later, Hughes retired, and LoBiondo entered the fray again. He easily overcame the better-funded William L. Gormley, longtime Atlantic County GOP boss and a member of the state Senate, by tagging him as a "closet Democrat." He then went on to defeat a little-known Democrat, Louis N. Magazzu, in the general election. LoBiondo has won re-election with ease since then; he says he will serve no more than 12 years in the House.

LoBiondo has been mentioned prominently as a potential candidate for statewide office. He seriously considered a run for the open U.S. Senate seat in 2000 but was dissuaded by national GOP leaders who were interested in fielding a strong team of House candidates in their bid to keep control of that chamber. His name is still in play, however, as a candidate for the 2002 Senate race, when Democrat Robert G. Torricelli is up for re-election.

KEY VOTES

2000

Yes	Raise hourly minimum wage by $1 over two years
Yes	Halt funding for U.S. mission in Kosovo unless European nations pay more
Yes	Provide Medicare benefits to military retirees and their dependents
No	Grant China permanent normal trade status
Yes	Phase out estate, gift and trust taxes
No	Prohibit implementation of president's national monument designations
Yes	Approve GOP plan to provide prescription drug coverage for Medicare beneficiaries
No	Increase help for poor nations indebted to international financial institutions

1999

Yes	Impose steel import quotas
No	Kill proposal to take aviation trust funds off budget
Yes	Require background checks on buyers only at gun shows with 10 or more vendors
Yes	Remove barriers among banking, securities and insurance companies
No	Authorize state grants to hire teachers and reduce class size
Yes	Overhaul campaign finance law; ban "soft money" and restrict advocacy advertising
Yes	Approve bipartisan plan to increase rights of patients in managed-care health plans

INTEREST GROUPS

	AFL-CIO	ADA	CCUS	ACU
2000	30%	20%	57%	64%
1999	67%	40%	68%	80%
1998	40%	30%	78%	68%
1997	63%	35%	67%	68%

CQ VOTE STUDIES

	PARTY UNITY		PRESIDENTIAL SUPPORT	
	Support	Oppose	Support	Oppose
2000	77%	23%	35%	65%
1999	80%	20%	18%	82%
1998	75%	25%	35%	65%
1997	83%	17%	36%	64%

NEW JERSEY 2
South — Atlantic City; Vineland

One of the state's most politically and economically diverse districts, the 2nd stretches from the Philadelphia suburbs in Gloucester County to the beach communities of Ocean City and Cape May. This is a Republican-leaning district, and locals generally support smaller government and oppose gun control. However, Democrats fare well in statewide elections and have a stronghold in south Cumberland County and in some of the district's more industrial towns.

The western corner of the 2nd is largely rural Salem County, home of a nuclear energy plant run by the Public Service Enterprise Group. The district's center includes Cumberland and Atlantic counties, where farmers' markets and small agrarian communities grow peaches, blueberries, cranberries and soybeans. South Cumberland County is the 2nd's most industrial area, although the economy is shifting from glass and plastic manufacturing to service. The area has been plagued with an unemployment rate higher than the state average.

Tourism is the cash crop in shore communities, where environmental and economic issues are one and the same; the local economy was hit hard when medical waste washed ashore in the late 1980s.

The 2nd includes one of the nation's most well-known gambling resorts, Atlantic City, where hotels and casinos create huge numbers of jobs, but where the poorer parts of the city are ravaged by crime and urban blight.

The Delaware River's busy port and one of the nation's largest petroleum centers also contribute to the economy.

MAJOR INDUSTRY
Gambling, tourism, farming

CITIES
Vineland, 55,360; Atlantic City, 37,708; Millville, 26,582

UNUSUAL FEATURES
Real estate mogul Donald Trump's boardwalk developments: The Taj Mahal, Plaza and Marina.

Rep. H. James Saxton (R)

Elected 1984; 9th full term

One of the GOP's most prominent "greens," the bespectacled, soft-spoken Saxton has been a champion of coastal protection and other environmental causes important to residents of his South Jersey district. When necessary, he has been willing to fight key Western Republicans who favor development and are critical of the Environmental Protection Agency.

Saxton also is a guardian of the 3rd District's military facilities — Fort Dix and McGuire Air Force Base. In the 107th Congress, he gained the chairmanship of the Armed Services Subcommittee on Military Installations and Facilities, a key post for looking out for the two bases. Early in 2001, Saxton proudly announced that the Air Force was going to make McGuire the home of a squadron of C-17 cargo planes and spend more than $30 million to ready the base for the mission.

Saxton has joined with other South Jersey lawmakers to compete more effectively with legislators from North Jersey, the more populous region of the state, for funds from the federal government. Saxton and his allies won a crucial victory in the 106th Congress when they helped persuade the Navy to pick Camden, rather than Bayonne, as the home of the mothballed battleship *USS New Jersey*, which is to become a floating museum.

Saxton's environmentalism is intertwined with his role as an advocate for South Jersey, which has suffered from pollution generated by large cities to its north and south. He has built a reputation as a strong steward of New Jersey's Atlantic coastline and its pristine Pine Barrens in the south. In the 106th, Saxton helped win passage of a measure directing the EPA to develop new standards for pollutants in coastal waters. The law also authorized $150 million for states to monitor coastal water quality.

Water quality is a sensitive issue in New Jersey, where, in the late 1980s, some state beaches were plagued by overflows of municipal sewage and medical waste. In 1995, Saxton fought his party's broad rewrite of the Clean Water Act. Saxton persuaded every member of the state's delegation except one — Republican Bob Franks — to oppose the GOP water bill on final passage. He offered an amendment that would have stripped the bill of some provisions that environmentalists most strongly opposed, but his proposal was rejected and the legislation ultimately passed.

In 1996, Saxton did win approval of an environmental provision in legislation aimed at protecting tap water. He and California Democrat Henry A. Waxman added "right to know" language requiring community water system officials to tell the public about the amount of pollutants in drinking water and the health effects when contaminant levels exceed EPA standards.

During his six-year tenure as chairman of the Resources Committee's Fisheries Conservation, Wildlife and Oceans Subcommittee, Saxton took on property rights activists — many of them from the West and South — who sought to scale back the Endangered Species Act. They argued that the law protects wildlife at great cost to landowners and the economy. But Saxton warned that proposals to compensate owners for any sharp drop in land values caused by protecting endangered species would bust the budget.

A conventional conservative on fiscal policy, Saxton sponsored a bill in the 106th Congress to exclude from an individual's taxable income up to $3,000 in mutual fund capital gains distributions. He also has questioned loans the International Monetary Fund has made to certain countries at below market rates. Saxton chairs the Joint Economic Committee in the 107th.

CAPITOL OFFICE
225-4765; fax 225-0778; 339 Cannon Bldg. 20515

INTERNET
e-mail: www.house.gov/writerep
web: www.house.gov/saxton

COMMITTEES
Armed Services
 (Military Installations & Facilities - chairman;
 Terrorism Oversight panel - chairman)
Resources
Joint Economic - chairman

HOMETOWN
Mount Holly

BORN
Jan. 22, 1943, Nicholson, Pa.

RELIGION
Methodist

FAMILY
Divorced; two children

EDUCATION
East Stroudsburg State College, B.A. 1965; Temple U., attended 1967-68

CAREER
Real estate broker; elementary school teacher

POLITICAL HIGHLIGHTS
N.J. Assembly, 1976-82; N.J. Senate, 1982-84

ELECTION RESULTS

2000 GENERAL

H. James Saxton (R)	157,053	57.3%
Susan Bass Levin (D)	112,848	41.2%

2000 PRIMARY

H. James Saxton (R)	unopposed

1998 GENERAL

H. James Saxton (R)	97,508	62.0%
Steven Polansky (D)	55,248	35.1%
Janice Presser (LIBERT)	2,527	1.6%

PREVIOUS WINNING PERCENTAGES
1996 (64%); 1994 (66%); 1992 (59%); 1990 (58%); 1988 (69%); 1986 (65%); 1984 (61%); 1984 Special Election (65%)

Saxton keeps to the middle on social policy issues. He generally opposes abortion and has backed legislation to ban a procedure its opponents call "partial birth" abortion. He also opposes allowing federal employees' health plans to cover abortions. But he has backed some gun control measures, including a ban on certain types of assault-style weapons. And he has opposed GOP efforts to eliminate funding for the National Endowment for the Arts.

A staunch advocate for Israel, Saxton led a House Task Force on Terrorism and Unconventional Warfare in the 106th Congress. Arab-American groups criticized Saxton in 1999 for opposing allied bombing in defense of Muslims in Kosovo. He said he was not taking sides in the dispute but contended that the United States should not aid the Kosovo Liberation Army (KLA), which he linked to terrorist elements in the Mideast.

Saxton argued that both Yugoslavian President Slobodan Milosevic and the KLA were to blame for the conflict in Kosovo. "There is no getting around the fact that Milosevic is a bad character. But there is also evidence the KLA are not nice guys, either," he told the Newark Star-Ledger.

Saxton backed a bill, passed by the House in 1996, aimed at limiting the president's ability to place U.S. troops under U.N. command. "When U.S. lives are at stake, the American public expects and demands that Americans are at the helm," Saxton said. In 1997, he supported setting a deadline for withdrawing U.S. troops from Bosnia.

A former real estate broker and elementary school teacher, Saxton served in the state legislature for eight years before making a bid for the House. In his first race, he struggled to win nomination for the seat left open in 1984 with the death of GOP Rep. Edwin B. Forsythe.

Saxton came into the campaign with support from the strong GOP organization in Burlington County but faced two Republicans from Ocean and Camden counties. Saxton ran ads on Philadelphia TV stations to attract voters in Camden County and drew support from his large state Senate constituency. After surviving the primary, he had little trouble winning the general election in the heavily Republican district.

Saxton had a tough contest in 1990, when he faced aggressive young Democrat John H. Adler, a former Cherry Hill City Council member. With many voters furious over Democratic Gov. James J. Florio'sz $2.8 billion tax package, the House race attracted a decade-high turnout. Although the state climate was hostile toward Democrats, Adler managed to hold Saxton to 58 percent.

Saxton inched up to 59 percent in 1992 and has won easily since then.

KEY VOTES

2000
Yes Raise hourly minimum wage by $1 over two years
Yes Halt funding for U.S. mission in Kosovo unless European nations pay more
Yes Provide Medicare benefits to military retirees and their dependents
No Grant China permanent normal trade status
Yes Phase out estate, gift and trust taxes
No Prohibit implementation of president's national monument designations
Yes Approve GOP plan to provide prescription drug coverage for Medicare beneficiaries
No Increase help for poor nations indebted to international financial institutions

1999
No Impose steel import quotas
No Kill proposal to take aviation trust funds off budget
Yes Require background checks on buyers only at gun shows with 10 or more vendors
Yes Remove barriers among banking, securities and insurance companies
No Authorize state grants to hire teachers and reduce class size
Yes Overhaul campaign finance law; ban "soft money" and restrict advocacy advertising
Yes Approve bipartisan plan to increase rights of patients in managed-care health plans

INTEREST GROUPS

	AFL-CIO	ADA	CCUS	ACU
2000	30%	20%	61%	56%
1999	22%	25%	68%	68%
1998	38%	25%	81%	63%
1997	38%	30%	80%	68%

CQ VOTE STUDIES

	PARTY UNITY		PRESIDENTIAL SUPPORT	
	Support	Oppose	Support	Oppose
2000	78%	22%	40%	60%
1999	80%	20%	32%	68%
1998	80%	20%	32%	68%
1997	85%	15%	35%	65%

NEW JERSEY 3
South Central – Cherry Hill

Covering one of New Jersey's oldest and wealthiest areas, the 3rd crosses the south-central section of the state, from the shores of Ocean County to the Pennsylvania border.

Industrial growth dominates the short strip of land that abuts the Delaware River and encompasses the affluent, Republican-leaning suburbs of Cinnaminson, Delran and Moorestown. In communities around Tom's River, dependent on beachcombers and tourists, offshore waste disposal and other environmental issues concern many voters. Local officials, most of whom are Republicans, emphasize their "green" credentials.

Military bases in Pemberton and Fort Dix make defense another salient issue. During the 1990s, the federal government funneled more than $500 million into modernization projects at McGuire Air Force Base, once slated to be closed, including $20 million for a new air terminal. The base now houses the East Coast's Air Mobility Wing.

With lots of wealthy, elderly voters, many of whom live in retirement communities along Route 70, the 3rd is becoming more safely Republican. The district also has the highest proportion of homeowners in the state. Municipal and school budgets, as well as tax rates, are among the lowest in the state – in part because of the high turnout by elderly voters.

MAJOR INDUSTRY
Retail sales, health care, farming

MILITARY BASES
McGuire Air Force Base, 8,385 military, 633 civilian (1999); Fort Dix (Army), 2,909 military, 2,553 civilian (1998)

CITIES
Cherry Hill (unincorporated), 69,319 (1990); Willingboro (unincorporated), 36,291 (1990); Holiday City-Berkeley (unincorporated), 14,293 (1990)

UNUSUAL FEATURES
Burlington County (shared with the 2nd and 4th districts) the second-largest cranberry-producing county in the nation; Olympian Carl Lewis from Willingboro.

Rep. Christopher H. Smith (R)

Elected 1980; 11th term

CAPITOL OFFICE
225-3765; fax 225-7768; 2373 Rayburn Bldg. 20515

INTERNET
e-mail: www.house.gov/writerep
web: www.house.gov/chrissmith

COMMITTEES
International Relations
Veterans' Affairs - chairman

HOMETOWN
Robbinsville

BORN
March 4, 1953, Rahway, N.J.

RELIGION
Roman Catholic

FAMILY
Wife, Marie Smith; four children

EDUCATION
Trenton State College, B.A. 1975

CAREER
Sporting goods executive; state anti-abortion
group director

POLITICAL HIGHLIGHTS
Republican nominee for U.S. House, 1978

ELECTION RESULTS

2000 GENERAL

Christopher H. Smith (R)	158,515	63.2%
Reed Gusciora (D)	87,956	35.1%
Stuart Chaifetz (I)	3,627	1.5%

2000 PRIMARY

Christopher H. Smith (R)	unopposed

1998 GENERAL

Christopher H. Smith (R)	92,991	62.2%
Larry Schneider (D)	52,281	35.0%
Keith Quarles (LIBERT)	1,753	1.2%

PREVIOUS WINNING PERCENTAGES
1996 (64%); 1994 (68%); 1992 (62%); 1990 (63%);
1988 (66%); 1986 (61%); 1984 (61%); 1982 (53%);
1980 (57%)

Smith's ticket to prominence in the House has been his energetic and steadfast opposition to abortion, an issue on which there are dozens of potential battles every year. He can be found, every time, manning the bulwarks, whether it be an effort to outlaw a particular abortion technique, to prevent the use of federal funds to pay for abortions for poor people or federal workers, or to protest foreign aid going to agencies that may perform or counsel women about abortions.

In the 107th Congress, he takes on a new role as chairman of the Veterans' Affairs Committee, where his top priority continues to be health care for veterans, a large constituency in New Jersey.

A telling indication of the New Jersey Republican's dedication to the anti-abortion cause came in 1999 when he suffered defeat in trying to bar government aid to the U.N. Population Fund, which Smith argues is used to support abortions, particularly in China, where he says the government's population control policies force some pregnant women to get abortions. After the loss, Smith told a reporter, "In 19 years in Congress, I have learned a lesson — I never stop fighting. This modest setback is just a prelude to the next win. Five minutes after, I was a little upset. Half an hour later, I was arguing another amendment."

The next week, Smith was back with an amendment reinstating Reagan and Bush administration restrictions barring U.S. aid for any international family planning organization unless it certified that it would not perform abortions or lobby to change abortion laws or government policies in other countries. He ultimately won inclusion of that proposal in the foreign operations appropriations bill by convincing House GOP leaders to link the amendment's adoption to the payment of nearly $1 billion in U.S. debts to the United Nations. President Clinton, eager to end a five-year standoff with the U.N., agreed to accept the provision for one year, though he exercised a waiver that kept it from having anything more than a symbolic effect.

In holding up the U.N. funds, Smith not only went toe-to-toe with the White House, he faced down Senate Foreign Relations Committee Chairman Jesse Helms, R-N.C., who shares Smith's anti-abortion views but was eager to see the U.N. reform legislation he had written become law.

The crowning moment of Smith's steadfast anti-abortion efforts came on Jan. 22, 2001, the 28th anniversary of *Roe v. Wade*, the Supreme Court decision that asserted a constitutional right to abortion. At a rally on the steps of the Supreme Court, Smith read a letter from newly inaugurated President Bush announcing that he would reinstate the abortion restrictions on international family planning groups.

Smith was executive director of the New Jersey Right to Life Committee before his election to Congress in 1980 at age 27. In most of his re-election battles, opponents have tried to convince voters that the congressman is so obsessed with abortion that he does not adequately represent other interests. But Smith has secured his position with diligent constituent work and careful attention to the interests of blue-collar workers and organized labor. On labor matters, the environment and gun control, Smith often breaks from his party's conservative majority.

But if moderation on those issues helps earn Smith easy re-election at home, what earns him headlines in Washington is his fight against abortion and for human rights. As chairman of the International Relations Subcommittee on International Operations and Human Rights from 1995 through

2000, Smith became well-known for his fight for human rights and his efforts to combat religious persecution abroad. In 1998, he won enactment of legislation establishing a federal program to help victims of torture both in the United States and abroad; in 1999, he won House approval of a bill to increase the authorized funding for the program.

In the 107th, as GOP-mandated term limits on committee chairmanships resulted in wholesale changes, Smith sought the gavel of either International Relations or Veterans' Affairs. The International Relations chairmanship was a long-shot bid — three other candidates had more seniority — but Smith had served 20 years on the veterans panel and was the No. 2 Republican in the 106th. On winning the gavel, Smith said he would work to achieve "world class" health care for veterans and to raise the visibility of the committee.

Smith also has focused on other health issues, including support for a coordinated federal role in researching and treating Lyme disease, a tick-borne ailment that is a problem in parts of New Jersey and neighboring states. He looked into possible causes of a cluster of autism cases in Brick, N.J., and he helped shepherd an asthmatic New Jersey boy through testimony at a House hearing on asthma inhalers.

Smith has a special interest in the rights of children and has sponsored legislation designed to monitor child labor conditions abroad and crack down on abuses. He often refers in conversation to his own four children, whose photographs are prominently featured in his congressional office. In the 106th, he won enactment of legislation to combat trafficking in women and children, who are often forced into prostitution. The law also doubled authorized funding for the Violence Against Women Act.

Smith is among the rare House Republicans who often side with organized labor. He opposed his party's effort to allow companies to offer employees compensatory time off instead of pay for overtime work. He was an early supporter of a minimum wage increase in 1996, and he opposed a GOP effort to exempt small businesses from paying the higher wage.

In the 106th, he sided with the GOP majority on House floor votes about three-fourths of the time, and he backed Clinton's position about a third of the time — a fairly high presidential-support score for a Republican.

Smith became ensconced in the 4th District with surprising ease, dismissing Democratic hopes of recapturing a district the party had long held before his election in 1980. That year Smith defeated 13-term Democratic Rep. Frank Thompson Jr., who had been caught up in the Abscam bribery scandal. After Thompson was indicted for bribery, Smith won with 57 percent and has won re-election easily since then.

KEY VOTES

2000
Yes Raise hourly minimum wage by $1 over two years
Yes Halt funding for U.S. mission in Kosovo unless European nations pay more
Yes Provide Medicare benefits to military retirees and their dependents
No   Grant China permanent normal trade status
Yes Phase out estate, gift and trust taxes
No   Prohibit implementation of president's national monument designations
Yes Approve GOP plan to provide prescription drug coverage for Medicare beneficiaries
Yes Increase help for poor nations indebted to international financial institutions

1999
Yes Impose steel import quotas
No   Kill proposal to take aviation trust funds off budget
No   Require background checks on buyers only at gun shows with 10 or more vendors
Yes Remove barriers among banking, securities and insurance companies
No   Authorize state grants to hire teachers and reduce class size
No   Overhaul campaign finance law; ban "soft money" and restrict advocacy advertising
Yes Approve bipartisan plan to increase rights of patients in managed-care health plans

INTEREST GROUPS

	AFL-CIO	ADA	CCUS	ACU
2000	50%	30%	47%	64%
1999	56%	40%	64%	79%
1998	30%	25%	61%	72%
1997	75%	30%	50%	64%

CQ VOTE STUDIES

	PARTY UNITY		PRESIDENTIAL SUPPORT	
	Support	Oppose	Support	Oppose
2000	73%	27%	42%	58%
1999	76%	24%	27%	73%
1998	79%	21%	27%	73%
1997	82%	18%	36%	64%

NEW JERSEY 4
Central — Trenton

The 4th spreads across the center of the state, from the Delaware River to the Jersey Shore, where the Garden State begins its transition from South to North Jersey.

The 4th's northwestern corner covers the capital, Trenton, and a Democratic demographic of government employees, African-Americans and Hispanics. Chambersburg, a large Italian neighborhood, is home to an old-fashioned Democratic machine.

But the 4th is balanced by more conservative suburbs in the eastern half of the district. Voters there tend to prefer Republicans for federal office but can exhibit an independent streak in local elections.

The Lakehurst Naval Air Warfare Center is a powerhouse in the local economy, but the district does not depend solely on defense. Trenton and its suburbs have a diverse range of businesses, and the small to midsize towns along the Jersey Shore in Ocean County depend heavily on tourism.

MAJOR INDUSTRY
State government, ceramics, tourism

MILITARY BASES
Naval Air Engineering Station Lakehurst, 300 military, 1,730 civilian (2000)

CITIES
Trenton, 84,398; Brick Township (unincorporated), 66,473 (1990); Mercerville-Hamilton Square (unincorporated), 26,873 (1990)

UNUSUAL FEATURES
Trenton was the site of two Revolutionary War battles and was temporarily the capital of the United States; John A. Roebling & Sons of Trenton made the cable for the Brooklyn Bridge and the Golden Gate Bridge; Lenox Inc. china company founded in Trenton; Bridge with illuminated sign proclaiming, "Trenton Makes, The World Takes."

Rep. Marge Roukema (R)

CAPITOL OFFICE
225-4465; fax 225-9048; 2469 Rayburn Bldg. 20515

INTERNET
e-mail: Rep.Roukema@mail.house.gov
web: www.house.gov/roukema

COMMITTEES
Education & Workforce
Financial Services
  (Housing & Community Opportunity -
  chairwoman)

HOMETOWN
Ridgewood

BORN
Sept. 19, 1929, West Orange, N.J.

RELIGION
Protestant

FAMILY
Husband, Richard Roukema; three children (one
deceased)

EDUCATION
Montclair State College, B.A. 1951, attended 1951-
53; Rutgers U., attended 1975-76

CAREER
High school history teacher

POLITICAL HIGHLIGHTS
Ridgewood Board of Education, 1970-73;
Republican nominee for U.S. House, 1978

ELECTION RESULTS

2000 GENERAL

Marge Roukema (R)	175,546	65.4%
Linda Mercurio (D)	81,715	30.4%
Michael "MJ" King (I)	5,329	2.0%
Robert J. McCafferty (I)	4,095	1.5%

2000 PRIMARY

Marge Roukema (R)	23,043	52.3%
E. Scott Garrett (R)	21,051	47.7%

1998 GENERAL

Marge Roukema (R)	106,304	63.7%
Mike Schneider (D)	55,487	33.3%
Thomas W. Wright (LIBERT)	2,395	1.4%

PREVIOUS WINNING PERCENTAGES
1996 (71%); 1994 (74%); 1992 (72%); 1990 (76%);
1988 (76%); 1986 (75%); 1984 (71%); 1982 (65%);
1980 (51%)

Elected 1980; 11th term

Although she is the longest-serving woman in the House, Roukema was rebuffed at the start of the 107th Congress in her bid to become the first woman to chair a major House committee.

Instead, Republicans picked Michael G. Oxley of Ohio to lead the new Financial Services Committee, formed by adding securities and insurance issues to the jurisdiction of the former Banking Committee, where Roukema (ROCK-ah-muh) had served since her arrival in Washington two decades ago. With characteristic hauteur, she refused a face-saving offer — arranged by Speaker J. Dennis Hastert — to leave Congress to be U.S. Treasurer in the new Bush administration. Instead, she took the chairmanship of Financial Services' Housing and Community Opportunity Subcommittee.

Some moderates were angered that one of their own had been the victim of a Solomonic move designed, at least in part, to settle a bitter turf battle at the Energy and Commerce Committee, which both Oxley and Billy Tauzin of Louisiana wanted to chair. But Roukema's unapologetic cultivation of her independent streak had used up much of her political capital within the GOP, whose leadership she has rarely been reluctant to criticize. She was often at odds with the previous GOP Speaker, Newt Gingrich, and continues to have a rocky relationship with Majority Leader Dick Armey.

"Quintessential adolescent behavior," she chided when Republican leaders kept the House in session through one night in the summer of 1995 as part of a parliamentary battle with the Democrats. "I don't have enough testosterone to deal with this."

Her views, and her style, continue to irritate many of her Republican constituents, as well, and they have nearly denied her renomination in her two most recent re-election races. In both, she was opposed by the far more conservative E. Scott Garrett, a member of the state Assembly; Roukema survived the GOP primary with 53 percent of the vote in 1998 and just 52 percent in 2000. In each case, however, she cruised to re-election in the fall in the affluent 5th District, where the majority of voters appear comfortable with her fiscal conservatism and her philosophy that consensus-building and compromise are essential to governing.

One high-point of that approach came in the 106th Congress, when Roukema, then chairwoman of the Banking Subcommittee on Financial Institutions and Consumer Credit, helped break a decades-long impasse to craft the law repealing Depression-era restrictions on affiliations between banks and insurance and securities firms. From her position on Banking, she also has had a significant hand in housing issues, particularly on mortgage financing for the elderly, disabled and homeless. A bill enacted at the end of 2000 included a version of her proposal to ensure the right of home owners to cancel their private mortgage insurance.

Perhaps her biggest legislative achievement, though, was her eight-year campaign for the Family and Medical Leave Act. Roukema, who had to drop her graduate studies in 1976 to care for a son, Todd, who was dying of leukemia, called the proposal "a bedrock family issue," but as its lead Republican sponsor she met with stiff conservative resistance. President George Bush vetoed the measure twice, and solid GOP voting in Congress sustained both vetoes.

The law's enactment in 1993 provided President Clinton with his first legislative trophy. The law requires large and medium-size businesses to provide unpaid leave to new parents, disabled workers and those caring for a seriously ill family member.

"What would I have done if not only did I have the tragedy and trauma of caring for my child, but also had to worry about losing a job and the roof over my head?" Roukema asked, in explaining her commitment to the idea.

She has broken with the Republican mainstream on several other prominent social issues. In the 106th, she voted for the mostly Democratic version of legislation to expand the rights of patients in managed-care plans.

She has long stood out as one of a few Republican women in the House to support abortion rights. She has voted to sustain requirements that states fund Medicaid abortions for poor women in some cases and has supported allowing federal employees' health care plans to cover abortions. In the 106th, she opposed a GOP bill to recognize a fetus as an entity distinct from a pregnant woman. But she has sided with efforts to ban a procedure its opponents call "partial birth" abortion.

A proponent of gun control, in 1999 Roukema opposed what she perceived as too-limited a package drafted after a shooting rampage at suburban Denver's Columbine High School.

While Roukema may still lean left on those issues, she has shifted to the right on others. She once backed affirmative action programs to assist minorities and women but now opposes them, having concluded that such initiatives can result in reverse discrimination. A former PTA president and high school teacher, she has used her seat on the Education and the Workforce Committee to concur with conservatives who call for more local control of public school funding. She has also been a tenacious advocate of helping parents collect the child support payments they are owed.

Her votes on spending bills often match the conservatism of many in her party; in 1998, for example, she was among the loudest critics of GOP leaders' deal with Clinton wrapping eight spending bills into a catchall measure that exceeded spending caps set out in the 1997 budget agreement. But like most members, she is not averse to using the appropriations process to try to bring money to her constituents. In 2000, she secured $3.5 million in a supplemental spending law for flood-control efforts in several areas in New Jersey affected by Hurricane Floyd.

Roukema was first elected to the House in 1980, on her second run against liberal Democratic Rep. Andrew Maguire. Aided by a strong showing by Ronald Reagan in northern New Jersey, she won with 51 percent and has not struggled in any general election since.

KEY VOTES

2000
No   Raise hourly minimum wage by $1 over two years
Yes Halt funding for U.S. mission in Kosovo unless European nations pay more
Yes Provide Medicare benefits to military retirees and their dependents
Yes Grant China permanent normal trade status
Yes Phase out estate, gift and trust taxes
No   Prohibit implementation of president's national monument designations
Yes Approve GOP plan to provide prescription drug coverage for Medicare beneficiaries
No   Increase help for poor nations indebted to international financial institutions

1999
Yes Impose steel import quotas
Yes Kill proposal to take aviation trust funds off budget
No   Require background checks on buyers only at gun shows with 10 or more vendors
Yes Remove barriers among banking, securities and insurance companies
No   Authorize state grants to hire teachers and reduce class size
Yes Overhaul campaign finance law; ban "soft money" and restrict advocacy advertising
Yes Approve bipartisan plan to increase rights of patients in managed-care health plans

INTEREST GROUPS

	AFL-CIO	ADA	CCUS	ACU
2000	0%	15%	76%	68%
1999	33%	45%	72%	60%
1998	20%	20%	78%	60%
1997	50%	50%	80%	42%

CQ VOTE STUDIES

	PARTY UNITY		PRESIDENTIAL SUPPORT	
	Support	Oppose	Support	Oppose
2000	82%	18%	44%	56%
1999	75%	25%	42%	58%
1998	74%	26%	34%	66%
1997	69%	31%	55%	45%

NEW JERSEY 5
North and West — Ridgewood

Encompassing the northernmost portion of New Jersey, the 5th is largely suburban and includes some of the most scenic and affluent areas of the state. It stretches from northern Bergen County west through Passaic and the hill-enclosed regions of Sussex County, crossing parts of the Appalachian Mountains and running south into Warren County.

Property values and income levels are among the highest in the state, and no municipality has more than 30,000 residents. Three-fifths of the district's population is in wealthy Bergen County, which includes Saddle River and its multimillion-dollar homes. The scenic back country of Sussex and Warren counties traditionally has been rural but grew about 10 percent in the 1990s as young professionals from New York City moved to the area. Warren County continues to experience significant housing development.

Politically, the 5th tends to vote Republican, although most voters are registered independent. Republican strength lies more in the growing areas to the west than in older areas in Bergen County. At the local level, pockets of Democratic strength include Phillipsburg in south Warren County and sections of Bergen County, where races are often close. Recent elections have resulted in some Democratic victories at the local level in Bergen and Warren counties.

MAJOR INDUSTRY
Pharmaceuticals, electronics, shipping

CITIES
Paramus, 25,877; West Milford (unincorporated), 25,430 (1990); Bergenfield, 24,584; Ridgewood, 24,488

UNUSUAL FEATURES
Richard Nixon retired to Park Ridge; Skylands Park, a minor league baseball stadium complex, is home to the New Jersey Cardinals and the nation's first minor league baseball museum.

Rep. Frank Pallone Jr. (D)

CAPITOL OFFICE
225-4671; fax 225-9665; 420 Cannon Bldg. 20515

INTERNET
e-mail: frank.pallone@mail.house.gov
web: www.house.gov/pallone

COMMITTEES
Energy & Commerce
Resources

HOMETOWN
Long Branch

BORN
Oct. 30, 1951, Long Branch, N.J.

RELIGION
Roman Catholic

FAMILY
Wife, Sarah Pallone; three children

EDUCATION
Middlebury College, B.A. 1973; Tufts U., M.A. 1974;
Rutgers U., J.D. 1978

CAREER
Lawyer

POLITICAL HIGHLIGHTS
Long Branch City Council, 1982-88; N.J. Senate,
1984-88

ELECTION RESULTS

2000 GENERAL

Frank Pallone Jr. (D)	141,698	67.5%
Brian T. Kennedy (R)	62,454	29.8%
Earl Gray (I)	4,252	2.0%

2000 PRIMARY

Frank Pallone Jr. (D)	unopposed

1998 GENERAL

Frank Pallone Jr. (D)	78,102	57.0%
Mike Ferguson (R)	55,180	40.3%

PREVIOUS WINNING PERCENTAGES
1996 (61%); 1994 (60%); 1992 (52%); 1990 (49%);
1988 (52%); 1988 Special Election (52%)

Elected 1988; 7th full term

Ambitious and sometimes aggressively partisan, Pallone's reputation in the House has evolved greatly during his six-plus terms on Capitol Hill. Once regarded as a lone wolf even by Democratic colleagues for his occasional votes and rhetoric against the party line, now he is a dogged promoter of his party's positions on health care and the environment. He is one of those most frequently found on the House floor at the end of the day's session speaking out on a wide range of topics.

In the 106th Congress, in the good graces of the Democratic leadership, Pallone (pa-LOAN) was named by Majority Leader Richard A. Gephardt to co-chair the party's health care task force and later was chosen as one of eight House Democratic negotiators on one of the most contentious bills of the 106th — a measure to give patients more leverage in dealing with managed health care organizations. And in the 107th, he serves on several party leadership committees, including posts on the Steering and Policy panels, which make committee assignments and advise the leadership on legislation.

As a freshman, Pallone had ruffled some in his home state delegation by criticizing a congressional pay raise. Not long afterward, when other New Jersey House Democrats got together to plot out a new congressional map for the 1990s, Pallone was conspicuously absent. So, too, was his district when a final plan was handed down in March 1992.

But Pallone found a way to win in 1992, and in the years since then he has become an energetic critic of the GOP majority. He sits on two committees that handle many controversial issues — Energy and Commerce and Resources — and he rails at what he sees as injustices done to consumers by big-business interests such as insurance companies and industrial polluters.

Pallone was active on the patients' rights issue in the 105th Congress, and his criticism of the GOP's proposals made him the target during the 1998 race of a $2 million negative advertising campaign paid for by a political action committee funded by insurance companies.

After winning another term by 17 percentage points, Pallone struck a defiant posture toward his critics. "I will tell the insurance industry right now, we're not scared at all. As far as I'm concerned ... you can spend $8 million or $10 million next time. I'm going to the floor of the House as soon as we get back and start working on HMO [health maintenance organization] reform."

As a native of the shore town of Long Branch, and as the representative of a significant swath of coastline, Pallone's legislative focus usually involves coastal environmental issues, a cause that he brought with him to Washington from his days as a member of the state Senate, where he sponsored bills to limit ocean dumping of garbage and sewage sludge.

In the House, Pallone continues to fight that battle. In 1995, he accused the GOP of wanting to undermine the federal ban against dumping trash and sludge at sea. A Republican-backed bill that year directed the National Oceanographic and Atmospheric Administration to evaluate and begin a demonstration project on the "deep ocean isolation of wastes," a provision Pallone said would "authorize the use of the ocean floor as a landfill."

Pallone has been among the Democrats most assertive in portraying the GOP as anti-environment, particularly in the 104th Congress when the Republicans tried, in Pallone's words, "to gut successful environmental laws," such as the Clean Water Act, the Clean Air Act, the superfund hazardous waste law and the Safe Drinking Water Act.

In the 106th Congress, he fought plans to dump sludge from harbor dredging operations. That stance drew the ire of longshoremen and at one hearing early in 2000, angry dockworkers erupted in boos and catcalls when Pallone spoke. He also sought money for beach replenishment projects, opposed plans to mine sand and gravel off the Jersey coast that he said would hurt marine life, and called for an end to the use of a gasoline additive — MTBE — that contaminated drinking water supplies.

Pallone has opposed a number of moves to liberalize international trade, citing environmental and labor concerns. He opposed the North American Free Trade Agreement in 1993, the General Agreement on Tariffs and Trade in 1994 and permanent normal trade relations with China in 2000.

A sizable Indian-American population in the 6th District prompted the congressman in 1993 to establish the House India Caucus, along with several other New Jersey lawmakers who also have large numbers of constituents with ties to India.

Pallone inherited his political interest from his father, who was a police officer in Long Branch and a longtime activist in local Democratic politics, including the campaigns of Democratic Rep. James J. Howard. Howard urged Pallone, a maritime lawyer, to run for the Long Branch City Council in 1982. Just one year later, Pallone won a state Senate seat in Monmouth County.

In March 1988, Howard, who was chairman of the Public Works Committee, died of a heart attack. Many Democratic insiders, including Howard's widow, lined up behind Pallone. In November, Pallone won two elections on the same day — a special election to fill the vacancy and a full term in his own right — each by 5 percentage points.

He has faced several other electoral challenges. In 1990, Democrats across New Jersey hunkered down, fearing the wrath of voters angry about Democratic Gov. James J. Florio's $2.8 billion tax increase. Pallone's little-known Republican challenger, lawyer Paul A. Kapalko, milked anti-tax fury for all it was worth, and Pallone survived by only 4,258 votes.

New Jersey lost a House seat in reapportionment for the 1990s, and Pallone in 1992 saw his Monmouth County-based "shore" district merged with Democratic Rep. Bernard J. Dwyer's 6th, anchored in Middlesex County where Pallone was not as well-known. Pallone got a break when Dwyer retired but had to defeat a state legislator that Dwyer had endorsed, before going on to notch a 7-point victory in November.

Since then, his re-election margins have been more comfortable. He seriously considered running for the Senate in 2000 but decided against it, partly at the behest of national Democratic leaders, who urged him to seek re-election as part of their push to regain control of the House.

KEY VOTES

2000
Yes Raise hourly minimum wage by $1 over two years
No Halt funding for U.S. mission in Kosovo unless European nations pay more
Yes Provide Medicare benefits to military retirees and their dependents
No Grant China permanent normal trade status
No Phase out estate, gift and trust taxes
No Prohibit implementation of president's national monument designations
No Approve GOP plan to provide prescription drug coverage for Medicare beneficiaries
Yes Increase help for poor nations indebted to international financial institutions

1999
Yes Impose steel import quotas
No Kill proposal to take aviation trust funds off budget
No Require background checks on buyers only at gun shows with 10 or more vendors
Yes Remove barriers among banking, securities and insurance companies
Yes Authorize state grants to hire teachers and reduce class size
Yes Overhaul campaign finance law; ban "soft money" and restrict advocacy advertising
Yes Approve bipartisan plan to increase rights of patients in managed-care health plans

INTEREST GROUPS

	AFL-CIO	ADA	CCUS	ACU
2000	100%	85%	30%	12%
1999	100%	95%	24%	8%
1998	100%	100%	28%	12%
1997	100%	95%	30%	12%

CQ VOTE STUDIES

	PARTY UNITY		PRESIDENTIAL SUPPORT	
	Support	Oppose	Support	Oppose
2000	91%	9%	77%	23%
1999	94%	6%	79%	21%
1998	92%	8%	78%	22%
1997	92%	8%	79%	21%

NEW JERSEY 6

Central — Part of Edison; New Brunswick; Long Branch

Wedged in the heart of the state's suburbs, the 6th is a competitive, bellwether district that has been leaning Democratic in recent years. Most of the district is in industrial Middlesex County, but a thin stretch incorporates the shore communities in Monmouth County. In the southwest corner, New Brunswick consolidates two Democratic voting blocs: young voters from Rutgers University, and blacks. Nearby Piscataway has shifted to Democrats and its wealthier suburbs of Highland Park have begun to vote Democratic.

Middle-class and independent-voting residents cluster around Edison (shared with the 7th), the district's largest city and home to corporate offices and some manufacturing. Issues such as the environment, Social Security and education are the bread and butter of local campaigns. The district also has one of the highest percentages of female voters in the state.

Exceptionally fast growth in this area after World War II established Middlesex County as the state's leader in industrial growth and earned it the nickname the "Sunbelt of New Jersey." The recent problems of Asbury Park are an exception to the generally sunny outlook. Once a vacation site made famous by rocker Bruce Springsteen, the town has seen crime grow as the economy has fallen apart.

MAJOR INDUSTRY
Education, communications technology, pharmaceuticals

CITIES
Edison (unincorporated) (pt.), 63,996 (1990); New Brunswick, 41,578; Sayreville, 38,626; Long Branch, 29,303

UNUSUAL FEATURES
Edison named after inventor Thomas Edison, whose workshop in Menlo Park is a local attraction and features the World's Largest Light Bulb, which is 65 years old, 13 feet tall, weighs eight tons, and is illuminated at night.

Rep. Mike Ferguson (R)

CAPITOL OFFICE
225-5361; fax 225-9460; 214 Cannon Bldg. 20515

INTERNET
e-mail: www.house.gov/writerep
web: www.house.gov/ferguson

COMMITTEES
Financial Services
Small Business
Transportation & Infrastructure

HOMETOWN
Warren

BORN
July 22, 1970, Ridgewood, N.J.

RELIGION
Roman Catholic

FAMILY
Wife, Maureen Ferguson; two children

EDUCATION
U. of Notre Dame, B.A. 1992; Georgetown U.,
M.P.P. 1995

CAREER
College instructor; education consulting firm
owner

POLITICAL HIGHLIGHTS
Republican nominee for U.S. House, 1998

ELECTION RESULTS

2000 GENERAL

Mike Ferguson (R)	128,434	51.6%
Maryanne S. Connelly (D)	113,479	45.6%
Jerry L. Coleman (I)	5,444	2.2%

2000 PRIMARY

Mike Ferguson (R)	10,748	40.6%
Tom Kean Jr. (R)	7,358	27.8%
Joel M. Weingarten (R)	6,089	23.0%
Patrick Morrisey (R)	2,284	8.6%

Elected 2000; 1st term

Although Ferguson majored in government as an undergraduate and later taught political science to college students, he says his inspiration to run for political office was his stint as a teacher at an inner-city high school in the Bronx while in his early twenties. That career trajectory once might have been associated with the making of a liberal Democrat. Instead, the experience solidified Ferguson's conservative views on what needs to be done to fix the nation's schools.

Ferguson, who holds a master's degree in education policy, has served as executive director of a national school reform advocacy group and is the founder of an educational consulting firm.

He is conservative on most social issues and strongly opposes abortion rights. He differs from many members of his party, though, in advocating gun control measures.

Although Ferguson was just 30 when he won election to the House (he is the second-youngest member of Congress), it was not his first attempt. In 1998, Ferguson was the Republican challenger to veteran Democratic Rep. Frank Pallone Jr. in the 6th District. But Pallone won, 57 percent to 40 percent, even though Ferguson's family wealth enabled him to spend a little more than $1 million on the race.

GOP Rep. Bob Franks' decision to run for the Senate in 2000 gave Ferguson a second chance to make a bid for the House, this time from the 7th District. Some Republicans questioned whether he was too conservative to win in a suburban New York City district, but Ferguson emphasized his more-centrist positions and defeated three rivals — including Tom Kean Jr., son of former New Jersey Gov. Thomas H. Kean — for the GOP nomination.

Ferguson's Democratic opponent was the former mayor of Fanwood, Maryanne S. Connelly, who had mounted a competitive House challenge to Franks in 1998. Democrats seized on Ferguson's anti-abortion stance to portray him as too far right. But he again stressed that his views were mainstream and won by 6 percentage points.

NEW JERSEY 7

North and Central – Parts of Woodbridge and Union

Redistricting in 1992 removed urban, industrial and Democratic Elizabeth from the 7th, a district that starts outside Newark and heads southwest into the middle of the state. Many expected the change would turn the district into reliable GOP territory. But despite the presence of many traditionally Republican communities and the election of a GOP representative, the 7th votes Democratic at the local level.

The central part of the 7th has a Democratic base in Woodbridge, Plainfield and Franklin, industrial towns with significant black populations. North of Plainfield, the towns are mostly suburban, white and Republican. Many are bedroom communities for commuters traveling to Newark and New York City.

A growing source of GOP strength can be found in southern Somerset County, where corporate and industrial growth has led to a small population boom. Much of Bridgewater, once dotted by horse farms, has been developed into office parks and shopping malls.

The Democratic strength is pushing westward from communities near Newark and making inroads at the local level. In 2000, the GOP regained the historically Republican towns of Westfield and Scotch Plains that fell to Democratic control in 1998. Prominent local issues include infrastructure, aircraft noise and the cleanup of superfund toxic waste sites.

MAJOR INDUSTRY
Pharmaceuticals, manufacturing, telecommunications

CITIES
Plainfield, 46,235; Union (pt.) 45,371 (1990); Westfield 29,265; South Plainfield, 21,184

UNUSUAL FEATURES
James E. McGreevey, the 1997 Democratic gubernatorial nominee, has been mayor of Woodbridge Township since 1992.

Rep. Bill Pascrell Jr. (D)

CAPITOL OFFICE
225-5751; fax 225-5782
1722 Longworth Bldg. 20515

INTERNET
e-mail: bill.pascrell@mail.house.gov
web: www.house.gov/pascrell

COMMITTEES
Small Business
Transportation & Infrastructure

HOMETOWN
Paterson

BORN
Jan. 25, 1937, Paterson, N.J.

RELIGION
Roman Catholic

FAMILY
Wife, Elsie Marie Pascrell; three children

EDUCATION
Fordham U., B.A. 1959, M.A. 1961

MILITARY SERVICE
Army, 1961; Army Reserve, 1962-67

CAREER
City official; teacher

POLITICAL HIGHLIGHTS
Paterson Board of Education, 1977-81 (president, 1981); N.J. Assembly, 1988-97; mayor of Paterson, 1990-97

ELECTION RESULTS

2000 GENERAL

Bill Pascrell Jr. (D)	134,074	67.0%
Anthony Fusco Jr. (R)	60,606	30.3%
Joseph A. Fortunato (I)	4,469	2.2%

2000 PRIMARY

Bill Pascrell Jr. (D)	unopposed

1998 GENERAL

Bill Pascrell Jr. (D)	81,068	62.1%
Matthew J. Kirnan (R)	46,289	35.4%

PREVIOUS WINNING PERCENTAGES
1996 (51%)

Elected 1996; 3rd term

Pascrell is in tune with the needs of his constituents in the diverse urban-suburban 8th District because he is one of them. He grew up in the working-class town of Paterson, the heart of the 8th, where his Italian immigrant grandparents had settled. He still lives in Paterson in a modest house in a middle-class neighborhood.

As the mayor of Paterson and as a member of the state General Assembly, Pascrell (pass-KRELL) devoted his attention to jobs, public safety and education. In the House, those issues remain at the top of his priority list, even if it means he must occasionally stray from the party line.

Pascrell steers a moderate course, mindful that in the 1990s the 8th District became a competitive arena after decades as solidly Democratic turf. His politics seem to resonate with voters, however, and as he entered his third term in the House, he had solidified his standing to the extent that he was being mentioned as a potential Democratic gubernatorial candidate in 2001.

He generally backs Democratic Party positions on matters such as funding for education, health care and gun control. But he has voted for tougher penalties for juvenile offenders, a GOP-drafted overhaul of the nation's public housing system, and a ban on a procedure its opponents call "partial birth" abortion.

And, citing studies that projected that liberalizing trade with China "would cost New Jersey 22,000 jobs," Pascrell in 2000 voted against a Clinton administration-backed bill to grant China permanent normal trade status. "We've permitted the hemorrhaging of American manufacturing for the past 20 years," Pascrell said, pointing out that Paterson is a prime example of the exodus of manufacturing jobs over the years. His China trade vote in the 106th Congress was in keeping with his views that the 1993 North American Free Trade Agreement has cost New Jersey thousands of jobs.

His top legislative priority in the 106th was a bill to provide a massive federal infusion of money — $5 billion over five years — to hire and train firefighters and to buy equipment. The initiative, patterned after the Community Oriented Policing (COPS) initiative that provided federal money to put 100,000 new police officers on the streets, was the brainchild of a citizen advisory committee that Pascrell established in the district shortly after his election. Pascrell's advisory panel noted that many towns have small volunteer fire departments that are ill-trained or equipped to deal with routine fires, much less incidents involving hazardous materials. And, Pascrell said, many departments in his district are having difficulty finding recruits because of lack of pay or training.

Acknowledging that the price tag was steep, Pascrell nevertheless collected well more than 200 cosponsors and noted that he had won a small preliminary victory when President Clinton recognized the need for added federal help for firefighting and proposed a small pilot program in his fiscal 2001 budget. Pascrell was overjoyed when the final 2000 spending bill included $100 million for the program.

On the Transportation Committee, he won funding for a pilot project to provide shuttle bus service in some towns in the 8th District, alleviating traffic congestion and eliminating the need for expensive new parking garages.

Pascrell also authored a bill that would lead eventually to a requirement that all new firearms be made with "smart" weapon technology, to prevent unauthorized users from firing them. His bill was aimed at making guns childproof. He also drafted legislation to improve outreach programs to inform veterans of all the benefits to which they are entitled.

Pascrell, whose father worked for the railroad, was the first member of his family to go to high school, and his neighborhood pals razzed him when he went off to college. He worked his way through Fordham, earning a bachelor's degree in journalism and a master's in philosophy.

Then he embarked on a 12-year career as a high school teacher in neighboring Paramus, interrupted by a stint in the Army. In 1974, he began working for the city of Paterson, first as director of the public works department and then heading up the planning and development office.

At the same time, he got involved in local politics, as a campaign volunteer for former Democratic Rep. Robert A. Roe and others. He was appointed to the Paterson Board of Education and was eventually elected its president.

He won a seat in the state General Assembly in 1987 and, as is permitted by New Jersey law, he simultaneously served as mayor of Paterson, beginning in 1990. As mayor, Pascrell promoted tough law enforcement measures, particularly in drug trafficking. To make it more difficult for dealers to communicate with their customers, he personally ripped out the lines and receivers of pay telephones that had not been issued a city permit and were not being monitored for drug traffic.

In 1996, his New Jersey mayoral colleagues elected him "mayor of the year," a bipartisan honor that he touted as proof of his record in helping Paterson rebound from the loss of manufacturing jobs. He also said his colleagues' support was evidence of his ability to go beyond party politics and work with lawmakers on both sides of the aisle to solve problems.

Pascrell was his party's choice to take on Rep. Bill Martini in 1996, two years after the freshman Republican's narrow victory ended 34 years of Democratic hegemony in the 8th District. (For 24 of those years, the district's congressman was Roe, who in the final two years of his tenure chaired the House Public Works and Transportation Committee.)

The national party gave Pascrell a boost, inviting him to speak at the 1996 Democratic National Convention, where he offered his views on the role of Congress: "Congress should be about giving people reason to have faith in their government again. It's not about taking from one group and giving to another." The AFL-CIO targeted the race as a key labor battlefield. Pascrell needed every bit of help he could get: He toppled Martini by a bare 51 percent to 48 percent margin. In acknowledgment of his tenuous hold on the seat, Pascrell immediately began amassing a war chest for 1998 and that dissuaded Martini from running. Pascrell's last two re-election contests have been routine.

KEY VOTES

2000

Yes	Raise hourly minimum wage by $1 over two years
No	Halt funding for U.S. mission in Kosovo unless European nations pay more
Yes	Provide Medicare benefits to military retirees and their dependents
No	Grant China permanent normal trade status
Yes	Phase out estate, gift and trust taxes
No	Prohibit implementation of president's national monument designations
No	Approve GOP plan to provide prescription drug coverage for Medicare beneficiaries
Yes	Increase help for poor nations indebted to international financial institutions

1999

Yes	Impose steel import quotas
No	Kill proposal to take aviation trust funds off budget
–	Require background checks on buyers only at gun shows with 10 or more vendors
Yes	Remove barriers among banking, securities and insurance companies
Yes	Authorize state grants to hire teachers and reduce class size
Yes	Overhaul campaign finance law; ban "soft money" and restrict advocacy advertising
Yes	Approve bipartisan plan to increase rights of patients in managed-care health plans

INTEREST GROUPS

	AFL-CIO	ADA	CCUS	ACU
2000	100%	75%	35%	20%
1999	100%	95%	25%	18%
1998	100%	95%	33%	16%
1997	100%	70%	40%	36%

CQ VOTE STUDIES

	PARTY UNITY		PRESIDENTIAL SUPPORT	
	Support	Oppose	Support	Oppose
2000	84%	16%	66%	34%
1999	86%	14%	80%	20%
1998	86%	14%	70%	30%
1997	81%	19%	68%	32%

NEW JERSEY 8

North – Paterson

The 8th consists of 21 communities in Passaic County and northern Essex County, including Paterson, the Garden State's third-largest. The district is a combination of urban centers and suburban towns extending from Pompton Lakes, in Passaic County in the north, to Maplewood, in Essex County, covering a total of 104 square miles.

Paterson, at the heart of the district, was once known for silk mills that made it a leading textile producer in the late 18th century. But after the introduction of rayon and other materials, Paterson experienced a serious economic downfall from which it never fully recovered. Today the city suffers from chronic unemployment and poverty.

The district's Essex County portion, by contrast, is mostly suburban, from wealthy Montclair and South Orange to the blue-collar and middle-class towns of Nutley and Belleville. Italian Catholics make up a large segment of this area and there are also pockets of Jewish voters.

Politically, the district leans Democratic but has become increasingly competitive. Three-fourths of Paterson's residents are black or Hispanic, and the city has a deep-seated labor tradition, making it voter-rich territory for Democratic candidates.

MAJOR INDUSTRY
Pharmaceutical research, medical supplies, communication equipment

CITIES
Paterson, 148,645; Clifton, 75,669; Passaic, 61,173

UNUSUAL FEATURES
George Washington and his army spent considerable time in Wayne, Pompton and Totowa during the Revolutionary War in the summer and fall of 1780; Samuel Colt lived in Paterson and made his first Colt revolver there; Domestic trendsetter Martha Stewart grew up in Nutley.

Rep. Steven R. Rothman (D)

Elected 1996; 3rd term

Although he has grown more comfortable in his role as a legislator and as a political figure, Rothman usually prefers to remain in the background, quietly studying the details of legislation and eschewing partisanship in favor of working toward a middle-ground solution. Colleagues describe him as soft-spoken and thoughtful.

In the 107th Congress, he will have more opportunity to find this middle ground with his new committee assignment — Appropriations — where members typically conduct business in a more bipartisan manner. He gave up his seats on the Judiciary and International Relations committees to take a place on the spending panel.

An assessment of Rothman offered midway through his first term by California Democratic Rep. Cal Dooley still applies. Dooley, a leader of the New Democrat Coalition of moderate Democrats, to which Rothman belongs, told the Bergen County-Hackensack Record that Rothman is the type of lawmaker who will "get underneath the hood and get their hands dirty and really get things done."

Rothman is a liberal vote on issues such as abortion, the environment, gun control and health care, but he has made an occasional foray into conservative territory. He was in the minority of Democrats who voted in favor of a constitutional amendment to ban desecration of the U.S. flag. "People can find plenty of ways to denigrate this country and still maintain their freedom of speech, but they can do it without desecrating the flag," Rothman told a veterans gathering.

Rothman, who served for three years as a Bergen County surrogate court judge, has voted with the GOP on occasion to require tougher treatment in the courts of violent juvenile offenders. He backs the death penalty.

Rothman's 1996 campaign included a pledge to balance the federal budget, and in 1997 he was among the minority of Democrats who supported the budget-balancing agreement worked out by the Clinton administration and Republican congressional leaders, saying it would "help bring about a smarter, more effective, more cost-efficient government."

But Rothman does not place budget frugality above what he views as essential government spending for such purposes as building and repairing schools, alleviating traffic congestion, cleaning up toxic waste sites, and taking care of veterans' health care needs. Arguing in 1997 for more highway and mass transit money for New Jersey, Rothman took a swipe at conservatives who begrudge those dollars but support spending that benefits their districts. "We don't have many military bases, we don't have hurricanes and other natural disasters, but we have traffic nightmares ... and a decaying infrastructure. Our roads and transit systems are our disasters, and the country has an obligation to support us in rebuilding them," he said.

In another instance, he complained about a funding formula for allocating veterans' health care dollars that he said discriminated against New Jersey. "Our veterans in New Jersey are becoming victims of a national scheme orchestrated by Southern and Western lawmakers to hoard federal aid to their states," Rothman said.

During the Judiciary Committee's impeachment proceedings against President Clinton in 1998, Rothman won kudos as a voice of calm and bipartisan reason. He did not excuse the president's behavior in the sex scandal that had led to the impeachment drive, but he was critical of the extensive investigation of the president by special counsel Kenneth W.

CAPITOL OFFICE
225-5061; fax 225-5851
1607 Longworth Bldg. 20515

INTERNET
e-mail: steven.rothman@mail.house.gov
web: www.house.gov/rothman

COMMITTEES
Appropriations

HOMETOWN
Fair Lawn

BORN
Oct. 14, 1952, Englewood, N.J.

RELIGION
Jewish

FAMILY
Divorced; two children

EDUCATION
Syracuse U., B.A. 1974; Washington U., J.D. 1977

CAREER
Judge; lawyer

POLITICAL HIGHLIGHTS
Mayor of Englewood, 1983-89; Democratic nominee for Bergen County Board of Freeholders, 1989; Bergen County surrogate court judge, 1993-96

ELECTION RESULTS

2000 GENERAL

Steven R. Rothman (D)	140,462	67.9%
Joseph Tedeschi (R)	61,984	30.0%
Lewis Pell (I)	2,273	1.1%

2000 PRIMARY

Steven R. Rothman (D)	unopposed

1998 GENERAL

Steven R. Rothman (D)	91,330	64.6%
Steve Lonegan (R)	47,817	33.8%

PREVIOUS WINNING PERCENTAGES
1996 (56%)

Starr. And he won plaudits from several panel Republicans for his low-key arguments against impeachment.

In the 106th Congress, Rothman authored legislation to establish a federal-local matching program to pay for metal detectors, security cameras or other safety precautions to keep guns out of schools. "The fact that we have to discuss metal detectors in schools at all sends a signal that our society has become too violent and that children have too easy access to guns," he said. "This is the sad reality. And until this Congress can agree on common-sense gun control legislation, we have an obligation to, at the very least, make sure our children are safe in their schools."

Rothman also sought to deny children access to cigarette vending machines, by banning them in establishments open to minors unless the proprietor agreed to perform thorough I.D. checks.

Back home in the densely populated North Jersey suburbs, just across the Hudson River from Manhattan, Rothman has joined the long-running local battle against aircraft noise at the busy Teterboro Airport. He has offered a range of solutions, including an evening curfew, requiring corporate jets to switch to new, quieter engines, and soundproofing in area schools.

In the international arena, Rothman looks out for the interests of the many ethnic groups in his diverse district, including Americans of Irish, Greek, Portuguese, Armenian and Indian ancestry. Israel's welfare is also a special concern for Rothman, who is Jewish.

Rothman was born in Englewood to working-class parents, and after leaving home for college and law school, he returned in 1978 to practice law. He immediately got involved in local Democratic Party politics. In 1983, he won the Englewood mayoralty and served in that post, working to balance the city's budget and reduce crime, until 1989, when he lost in a race for Bergen County freeholder.

His next campaign, in 1993 for the Bergen County Surrogate Court, was successful. He left that job early in 1996 to run for Congress, when Rep. Robert G. Torricelli launched his bid to succeed retiring Democratic Sen. Bill Bradley. Rothman won the Democratic nomination handily and faced off against Republican Kathleen A. Donovan, the Bergen County clerk.

Donovan is the kind of socially moderate, fiscally conservative Republican who usually runs well in New Jersey. But the 9th District, always difficult turf for GOP candidates, proved even tougher in 1996, as Bill Clinton carried it by a nearly 2-1 margin. Rothman won with 56 percent. The Democratic bent of the 9th has helped Rothman rack up two impressive re-election victories.

KEY VOTES

2000
Yes Raise hourly minimum wage by $1 over two years

No   Halt funding for U.S. mission in Kosovo unless European nations pay more

Yes Provide Medicare benefits to military retirees and their dependents

No   Grant China permanent normal trade status

No   Phase out estate, gift and trust taxes

No   Prohibit implementation of president's national monument designations

No   Approve GOP plan to provide prescription drug coverage for Medicare beneficiaries

Yes Increase help for poor nations indebted to international financial institutions

1999
Yes Impose steel import quotas

No   Kill proposal to take aviation trust funds off budget

No   Require background checks on buyers only at gun shows with 10 or more vendors

Yes Remove barriers among banking, securities and insurance companies

Yes Authorize state grants to hire teachers and reduce class size

Yes Overhaul campaign finance law; ban "soft money" and restrict advocacy advertising

Yes Approve bipartisan plan to increase rights of patients in managed-care health plans

INTEREST GROUPS

	AFL-CIO	ADA	CCUS	ACU
2000	100%	90%	38%	12%
1999	89%	100%	28%	4%
1998	100%	100%	29%	8%
1997	100%	90%	40%	13%

CQ VOTE STUDIES

	PARTY UNITY		PRESIDENTIAL SUPPORT	
	Support	Oppose	Support	Oppose
2000	89%	11%	80%	20%
1999	89%	11%	82%	18%
1998	87%	13%	83%	17%
1997	88%	12%	78%	22%

NEW JERSEY 9
North – Fort Lee; Hackensack

Across the Hudson River from Manhattan, the 9th ranks among the wealthier districts in the nation, but it falls in the middle of New Jersey's generally affluent suburbs. The most prestigious neighborhoods lie to the north, including Englewood and Fort Lee. High rises have sprung up along the river for New York City commuters. The district becomes more blue-collar as it runs south into Lyndhurst and Jersey City.

Redevelopment has strengthened this district's already solid economy. Anchored by the Giants' and Jets' Meadowlands stadium complex, the southern part of the district has seen increased commercial and residential development. Concerns about wetlands preservation have kept growth at a slow to moderate pace.

With a strong Hispanic population around Jersey City and a sizable proportion of black and Asian voters, Democrats far outnumber Republicans. In the district's southern areas, the working-class towns of North Arlington, Lyndhurst and Kearny provide a strong Democratic vote. The large population of Jewish voters in the western towns of Teaneck and Fairlawn also support Democrats. Bergen County, as a whole tends to support Republicans, however several of the older, affluent towns in the county have a long-running history of Democratic voting.

Republicans had been making inroads at the local level until 1998, when Democrats overturned some of those gains, scoring wins in formerly all-Republican town councils in Rutherford and Ridgefield.

MAJOR INDUSTRY
Health care, shipping, stadium events

CITIES
Jersey City (pt.), 52,668 (1990); Teaneck (unincorporated), 37,825 (1990); Hackensack, 37,656; Kearny (pt.), 34,603 (1990); Fort Lee, 33,854

UNUSUAL FEATURES
Actor John Travolta born in Englewood.

Rep. Donald M. Payne (D)

Elected 1988; 7th term

CAPITOL OFFICE
225-3436; fax 225-4160; 2209 Rayburn Bldg. 20515

INTERNET
e-mail: donald.payne@mail.house.gov
web: www.house.gov/payne

COMMITTEES
Education & Workforce
International Relations

HOMETOWN
Newark

BORN
July 16, 1934, Newark, N.J.

RELIGION
Baptist

FAMILY
Widowed; three children

EDUCATION
Seton Hall U., B.A. 1957

CAREER
Computer forms company executive; company community affairs director; high school teacher

POLITICAL HIGHLIGHTS
Essex County Board of Freeholders, 1972-78; sought Democratic nomination for Essex County executive, 1978; sought Democratic nomination for U.S. House, 1980; Newark Municipal Council, 1982-88; sought Democratic nomination for U.S. House, 1986

ELECTION RESULTS

2000 GENERAL

Donald M. Payne (D)	133,073	87.5%
Dirk B. Weber (R)	18,436	12.1%

2000 PRIMARY

Donald M. Payne (D)	unopposed

1998 GENERAL

Donald M. Payne (D)	82,244	83.5%
William Stanley Wnuck (R)	10,678	10.8%
Richard J. Pezzullo (NJC)	3,293	3.3%
Maurice Williams (SW)	2,279	2.3%

PREVIOUS WINNING PERCENTAGES
1996 (84%); 1994 (76%); 1992 (78%); 1990 (81%); 1988 (77%)

Payne is generally a low-key operator, working out of the spotlight on issues of importance to his Newark-based district and trying to chip away diligently at GOP legislation aimed at altering the shape of government programs for the poor such as welfare, Head Start, assistance in paying heating bills, and affirmative action.

And as the top Democrat on International Relations' Africa Subcommittee, he pushed the Clinton administration to pay more attention to relations with Africa.

Payne was a more visible presence in the 104th Congress, when he was chairman of the Congressional Black Caucus. He led the caucus through a difficult time, when public funding for the group and similar member organizations was discontinued by the new GOP-led House, intent on cutting congressional staff and expenses. During this period, Payne's quiet persuasiveness was tested. The caucus dealt with the funding cutoff by raising money privately to maintain its operations. The group also continued to offer alternative budget plans to those proposed by both parties and to support legislation of particular importance to African-Americans.

But since his two-year term as caucus chairman ended, Payne has once again slipped out of the limelight, although he still works patiently on traditional Democratic social programs such as education, labor and human rights, and on police treatment of minorities. He is one of the most liberal members of the House. "I would not call myself electrifying," he said a decade ago about his low-key style. "But I think there is a lot of dignity in being able to achieve things without having to create rapture."

During the spate of committee downsizing begun by the Democrats in the 103rd Congress and continued by the Republicans in the 104th, Payne was a key figure in the successful effort to retain the Africa Subcommittee as a separate entity.

He has pushed for development aid to African nations, noting that, "During the Cold War, the United States stayed engaged in Africa to fight off the threat of communism. Now we have a chance to help Africa eradicate the problems of health care, eradicate illiteracy, eradicate AIDS, fight disease and continue to move to democratization." He accompanied President Clinton on a six-nation Africa tour in 1998, and he has made several other visits to the continent, including trips to war-torn Congo and Rwanda.

Payne worked in the 106th Congress on legislation to expand trade ties between the United States and the nations of sub-Saharan Africa. He played a more prominent role on a number of human rights issues, sponsoring measures addressing genocide and slavery in the Sudan, civil war in Sierra Leone, famine in Ethiopia, and democratic elections in Senegal, among others. He brought a concern for human rights to domestic issues as well, deploring police brutality, racial profiling and the burning of black churches.

From his seat on the Education and the Workforce Committee, Payne also fought to continue the practice of targeting federal funds to low-income districts, in the face of Republican plans to give states more flexibility in deciding how to spend the money. He argues that the nation's great economic prosperity "has not spread to our inner cities," and that the government should not be abandoning its responsibilities to help all its citizens in the rush to balance the budget.

Payne credits much of his own success in life to an organization known as The Leaguers, and to its founders, Reynold and Mary Burch, both leading members of the Newark black community. Mrs. Burch used her contacts with Seton Hall University to help Payne win a four-year scholarship to the school. Payne was the first president of The Leaguers, which celebrated its 50th anniversary in 1999. The group's goals are to provide Newark inner-city teenagers with encouragement, education and work opportunities, and social outlets.

A high school history teacher and football coach after college, Payne moved into business in 1963 as community affairs director for the Newark-based Prudential Insurance Co. Later, he was vice president of a computer forms company founded by his brother.

The head of a "storefront YMCA" in inner-city Newark in the late 1950s, Payne became the first black president of the National Council of YMCAs in 1970 and later served two four-year terms as chairman of the YMCA's International Committee on Refugees. While participating in these activities, the widowed Payne was raising his three children and building his political career. He served six years as an Essex County freeholder and another six on the Newark Municipal Council.

Perseverance enabled Payne to pull himself up from poverty, and it also took perseverance — three campaigns — to win election in the black-majority 10th District. His path was blocked by the legendary Democratic Rep. Peter W. Rodino Jr., who had held the seat since 1949. Chairman of the Judiciary Committee, Rodino had achieved national fame during the 1974 Watergate impeachment hearings of President Nixon, but it was Rodino's steadfast advocacy of civil rights legislation that earned him the votes of blacks in the district.

Nevertheless, Payne tried twice — in 1980 and 1986 — to unseat Rodino, arguing that a black person could better represent the district, and that Rodino was a roadblock to black political advancement. The Rev. Jesse L. Jackson campaigned for Payne in 1986, arguing that Payne "has a kinship with this community [Rodino] does not have." But Rodino won the primary, 59 percent to 36 percent.

When Rodino said he would not run in 1988, party officials got behind Payne. Payne's only opposition came in the Democratic primary from city council colleague Ralph T. Grant Jr. But Payne's advantages — party support, a sizable campaign treasury and name recognition — easily brought him the nomination. Payne's November victory was a formality in this overwhelmingly Democratic district, making him the first black representative from New Jersey. He has won easily ever since.

KEY VOTES

2000

Yes Raise hourly minimum wage by $1 over two years

No Halt funding for U.S. mission in Kosovo unless European nations pay more

Yes Provide Medicare benefits to military retirees and their dependents

No Grant China permanent normal trade status

No Phase out estate, gift and trust taxes

No Prohibit implementation of president's national monument designations

No Approve GOP plan to provide prescription drug coverage for Medicare beneficiaries

Yes Increase help for poor nations indebted to international financial institutions

1999

Yes Impose steel import quotas

No Kill proposal to take aviation trust funds off budget

No Require background checks on buyers only at gun shows with 10 or more vendors

No Remove barriers among banking, securities and insurance companies

Yes Authorize state grants to hire teachers and reduce class size

Yes Overhaul campaign finance law; ban "soft money" and restrict advocacy advertising

Yes Approve bipartisan plan to increase rights of patients in managed-care health plans

INTEREST GROUPS

	AFL-CIO	ADA	CCUS	ACU
2000	100%	95%	33%	0%
1999	89%	100%	21%	0%
1998	100%	90%	20%	9%
1997	100%	85%	20%	5%

CQ VOTE STUDIES

	PARTY UNITY		PRESIDENTIAL SUPPORT	
	Support	Oppose	Support	Oppose
2000	97%	3%	86%	14%
1999	97%	3%	88%	12%
1998	97%	3%	89%	11%
1997	97%	3%	78%	22%

NEW JERSEY 10
Parts of Newark and Jersey City

Covering a multiracial, urban region centered on Newark, the 10th provides a solid base for Democrats. Outside Newark, the 10th extends into Essex County's working-class suburbs of Irvington and Montclair. Black, Hispanic and largely blue-collar, the district's large towns contribute to its Democratic leanings.

The 10th District portion of Newark is made up of the primarily black central, south and west wards and the racially mixed north section of the city. The central ward was decimated in the riots of 1967 and has never fully recovered.

The decade after the riots saw a steep decline in the number of jobs and an increase in the number of whites moving out of Newark. As the Irish and Italians who used to vie for political power fled to the suburbs, blacks became a majority and, accordingly, grabbed the reins of power at City Hall; African-Americans have held the mayoralty since 1970.

There have been efforts to revitalize the area, but the desperate living conditions and deep poverty continue. Recently, however, an infusion of new housing is helping some of Newark's worst neighborhoods, and the city's few major employers are starting to expand. A large new performing arts center also is helping, as are new retail outlets in Essex County.

The 10th votes consistently Democratic at all levels, although Rahway and Roselle sometimes vote Republican. Bill Clinton won by comfortable margins in the 1992 and '96 presidential contests and Al Gore received an overwhelming 84 percent of the vote in 2000.

MAJOR INDUSTRY
Aviation, higher education, pharmaceuticals

CITIES
Newark (pt.), 169,368 (1990); East Orange, 69,801; Elizabeth (pt.), 67,038 (1990); Rahway, 25,208

UNUSUAL FEATURES
West Orange was the longtime home of Thomas Edison.

Rep. Rodney Frelinghuysen (R)

CAPITOL OFFICE
225-5034; fax 225-3186; 2442 Rayburn Bldg. 20515

INTERNET
e-mail: rodney.frelinghuysen@mail.house.gov
web: www.house.gov/frelinghuysen

COMMITTEES
Appropriations

HOMETOWN
Harding

BORN
April 29, 1946, Manhattan, N.Y.

RELIGION
Episcopalian

FAMILY
Wife, Virginia T. Frelinghuysen; two children

EDUCATION
Hobart College, B.A. 1969; Trinity College (Conn.),
attended 1971

MILITARY SERVICE
Army, 1969-71

CAREER
County freeholder aide

POLITICAL HIGHLIGHTS
Morris County Board of Freeholders, 1974-83
(director, 1980); sought Republican nomination for
U.S. House, 1982; N.J. Assembly, 1983-95; sought
Republican nomination for U.S. House, 1990

ELECTION RESULTS

2000 GENERAL

Rodney Frelinghuysen (R)	186,140	68.0%
John P. Scollo (D)	80,958	29.6%
John Pickarski (I)	5,199	1.9%

2000 PRIMARY

Rodney Frelinghuysen (R)	unopposed

1998 GENERAL

Rodney Frelinghuysen (R)	100,910	67.7%
John P. Scollo (D)	44,160	29.6%
Austin S. Lett (LIBERT)	1,737	1.2%

PREVIOUS WINNING PERCENTAGES
1996 (66%); 1994 (71%)

Elected 1994; 4th term

Like many of his GOP colleagues, Frelinghuysen is a strong fiscal conservative. But he typically takes a moderate stance on many environmental and social policy issues, reflecting the views of his district's upscale suburbanites. More interested in governing than in ideological purity, he decries the practice of "damning the institution of Congress" and says, "Once you're in the majority, you now have a responsibility to govern."

Part of his respect for governing may be attributed to his background: The Frelinghuysen (FREE-ling-high-zen) family has a long record of public service stretching back to the Revolutionary War era. Six Frelinghuysens have served in Congress. The first was in the Continental Congress; another was secretary of state; one ran for vice president on a ticket with Henry Clay; and one was Frelinghuysen's father, Peter, who served in the House for 22 years, until 1975. Noting that he was 6 years old when his father first ran for Congress, Rodney Frelinghuysen observed in a newspaper interview that, "A lot of what you do in life is the direct result of those who bring you up. It either drives you toward this life, or drives you away."

During the late 1990s, Frelinghuysen's voting record placed him among President Clinton's top dozen or so House Republican supporters. But his views on fiscal matters, crime, welfare and labor issues leave no doubt that he is a Republican.

Frelinghuysen stresses fiscal prudence, urging that surpluses be used to pay down the federal debt. Evidence of his fiscal conservatism has included votes to end the federal road-building subsidy for timber companies and subsidies for tobacco farmers. He worked hard to eliminate the annual subsidy for the Tennessee Valley Authority (TVA), which was a target of cost-conscious members in the Northeast and Midwest whose constituents do not benefit from the low electric rates that the utility offers. In 1999, Congress finally ended the subsidy, which funded TVA's non-power activities such as management of recreation areas. But Frelinghuysen continued to criticize TVA's management and its long-term debt, which he says is a burden to taxpayers across the country.

As the only Republican from New Jersey on the Appropriations Committee, he is responsible for carrying water for his Garden State colleagues. A veteran of government funding battles who had previously chaired the New Jersey Assembly's Appropriations Committee, Frelinghuysen has pursued federal dollars for beach restoration, New York Harbor dredging, veterans hospitals, mass transit projects, and environmental cleanups. He also keeps a watchful eye on the Army's Picatinny Arsenal in the 11th District.

When he faced criticism from a watchdog group in 2000 for winning $55 million in beach replenishment projects, he insisted the funding was well-spent. "I make no apologies for fighting for New Jersey's fair share to ensure that our beaches are protected," he said. "Those who don't know our beautiful beaches have absolutely no idea how environmentally important they are to our state. ... Tourism is a $17 billion business, and it is highly dependent on beaches and waters that are clean and protected."

While some may ask how his service on the money-spending Appropriations Committee squares with his fiscal conservatism, Frelinghuysen argues that the panel has made the tough decisions on reducing the spending called for in the 1997 balanced-budget agreement. And he adds, "You can still be a fiscal conservative and have a heart."

In the 106th Congress, he backed a Clinton administration initiative to use

Medicare to pay for prescription drugs, saying, "Anything Congress and the president can do to lessen the burden on older Americans, so that they won't have to choose between putting food on the table or paying for important medication, will be a great help." He also backed a plan, opposed by GOP leaders, that would have allowed patients to sue their health plans in state court, and he sided with gun control advocates on a measure designed to require background checks for purchases at gun shows. He generally supports abortion rights, but he has voted to ban a procedure its opponents call "partial birth" abortion.

He joined with Clinton and most of his GOP colleagues in an effort to grant China permanent normal trade status. "It would be highly stupid to isolate China from America and prevent large and small American companies from trading with China," Frelinghuysen told The Star-Ledger in Newark. "It would put our own country at a huge disadvantage against the Europeans and Asians and Latin Americans who will be in there."

Frelinghuysen scored a victory in 2000 with House passage of a consumer bill to stop telemarketers from blocking consumers' caller identification devices. "Telemarketers know your name, your address and your telephone number," Frelinghuysen said. "It's only fair that they share the same information with consumers." The Senate did not act on the measure.

In the opening months of the 104th Congress, he voted for all the major tenets of the "Contract With America," including measures backing constitutional amendments for a balanced budget and term limits, overhauling welfare and scaling back the federal regulatory process.

Frelinghuysen started his political career after college and a stint in the Army during the Vietnam War by going to work for Dean Gallo, then a Morris County freeholder and later a member of the House. Frelinghuysen became a freeholder himself in 1974. In 1982, he lost a GOP primary for the 12th District House seat, but in 1983, he won a state Assembly seat. In 1990, he failed again in a contest for the 12th District. When he finally won election to the House in 1994, victory was bittersweet because it followed the death of friend and mentor Gallo. Ill health had forced Gallo in August 1994 to abandon his campaign for a sixth term. Gallo anointed Frelinghuysen, who had been managing the re-election bid, as his successor.

After New Jersey GOP insiders overwhelmingly ratified Gallo's choice at a special nominating convention, Frelinghuysen sailed to victory in the Republican-dominated 11th. Gallo died two days before the November election, which Frelinghuysen won with 71 percent over Democrat Frank Herbert, a former state senator. He has easily won re-election since.

KEY VOTES

2000
Yes Raise hourly minimum wage by $1 over two years
Yes Halt funding for U.S. mission in Kosovo unless European nations pay more
Yes Provide Medicare benefits to military retirees and their dependents
Yes Grant China permanent normal trade status
Yes Phase out estate, gift and trust taxes
No Prohibit implementation of president's national monument designations
Yes Approve GOP plan to provide prescription drug coverage for Medicare beneficiaries
No Increase help for poor nations indebted to international financial institutions

1999
No Impose steel import quotas
Yes Kill proposal to take aviation trust funds off budget
No Require background checks on buyers only at gun shows with 10 or more vendors
Yes Remove barriers among banking, securities and insurance companies
No Authorize state grants to hire teachers and reduce class size
Yes Overhaul campaign finance law; ban "soft money" and restrict advocacy advertising
Yes Approve bipartisan plan to increase rights of patients in managed-care health plans

INTEREST GROUPS

	AFL-CIO	ADA	CCUS	ACU
2000	10%	25%	71%	56%
1999	11%	40%	68%	48%
1998	10%	10%	83%	52%
1997	25%	40%	90%	52%

CQ VOTE STUDIES

	PARTY UNITY		PRESIDENTIAL SUPPORT	
	Support	Oppose	Support	Oppose
2000	73%	27%	48%	52%
1999	69%	31%	45%	55%
1998	77%	23%	37%	63%
1997	78%	22%	48%	52%

NEW JERSEY 11
North — Morris County

Exclusive, pastoral estates and Fortune 500 firms make the 11th one of the most privileged districts in the nation. Centrally located in northern New Jersey, with its population centered in Parsippany-Troy Hills, the 11th has one of the highest median household incomes in the nation. Its voters tend to be socially moderate, family-centered and ardently fiscally conservative, making the 11th one of the most solidly Republican districts in the northeast.

The recession of the early 1990s and that decade's bouts with corporate restructuring left the 11th with a glut of empty office space. But the office market has since picked up, and the 11th now hosts corporate giants, including AT&T, Nabisco and BASF.

Most of the district's residents used to commute to Manhattan, but with large employers springing up in eastern Morris County, fewer of the district's executives leave New Jersey for work.

Dover's Picatinny Arsenal experienced some defense cutbacks in the 1990s, however, it now appears to be safe from any further cuts. Housing costs rank among the highest in the nation and about 20 percent of Morris County's residents call themselves executives, according to 1990 Census Bureau statistics.

MAJOR INDUSTRY
Pharmaceuticals, electronics, chemicals

MILITARY BASES
Picatinny Arsenal (Army), 342 military, 2,699 civilian (1999)

CITIES
Parsippany-Troy Hills Township (unincorporated), 48,478 (1990); Livingston (unincorporated) (pt.), 26,609 (1990); Morristown, 16,472

UNUSUAL FEATURES
First national historic park established by the federal government – Morristown National Historical Park, which includes George Washington's Revolutionary War headquarters.

Rep. Rush D. Holt (D)

CAPITOL OFFICE
225-5801; fax 225-6025
1630 Longworth Bldg. 20515

INTERNET
e-mail: rush.holt@mail.house.gov
web: www.house.gov/rholt

COMMITTEES
Budget
Education & Workforce
Resources

HOMETOWN
Hopewell

BORN
Oct. 15, 1948, Weston, W.Va.

RELIGION
Quaker

FAMILY
Wife, Margaret Lancefield; three children

EDUCATION
Carleton College, B.A. 1970; New York U., M.S. 1980, Ph.D. 1981

CAREER
University research assistant director; physics professor

POLITICAL HIGHLIGHTS
Sought Democratic nomination for U.S. House, 1996

ELECTION RESULTS

2000 GENERAL

Rush D. Holt (D)	146,162	48.7%
Dick Zimmer (R)	145,511	48.5%
Carl J. Mayer (I)	5,811	1.9%

2000 PRIMARY

Rush D. Holt (D)	unopposed

1998 GENERAL

Rush D. Holt (D)	92,528	50.1%
Michael Pappas (R)	87,221	47.2%
Joseph A. Siano (LIBERT)	2,125	1.2%

Elected 1998; 2nd term

While the nation was consumed with the disputed 2000 presidential election, Holt was living out his own electoral drama. The plasma physicist was locked in a race with former Republican Rep. Dick Zimmer that brought charges of ballot irregularities and required three weeks of recounts. In the end, Holt won by 651 votes out of almost 300,000 cast.

The sprawling 12th District, with its affluent precincts and drug company headquarters, traditionally leans Republican, placing Holt at the top of the GOP's biannual list of the most endangered Democratic incumbents. To Republicans' chagrin, Holt has picked up swing voters by focusing on education and environmental issues that resonate with suburbanites, and by building a strong constituent service operation. His base remains the liberal-leaning bastion of Princeton, where he served as assistant director of the Princeton Plasma Physics Laboratory, which researches alternative energy sources.

Holt's background studying solar winds and his cerebral mien — he is a past champion on the TV quiz show "Jeopardy" — have made him something of a cult figure in the college town, where bumper stickers proclaim: "My congressman *is* a rocket scientist."

Holt says his scientific training sometimes enables him to look at issues on a larger scale and in the context of a longer time frame than is typical in Congress. But he rejects the notion that he is more intelligent than most of his colleagues. "Some people may think that a scientist is smarter than other members," he told the Newark Star-Ledger. "I just have a different background, different training. There are many very smart, very shrewd people here. This House is populated with very smart people."

Holt showed an independent streak in the 106th Congress by joining 23 other House Democrats in voting for the Republican-backed bill that would have given state and local authorities more control over federal funds for hiring and training teachers. The measure was offered as an alternative to President Clinton's much-touted effort to specifically designate funds to hire 100,000 new teachers. Holt defended breaking with the Democratic orthodoxy on education, saying the GOP plan would have given New Jersey more flexibility to spend the nearly $2 billion in aid that the state was slated to get under the measure.

The New Jersey lawmaker also crossed party lines to support GOP legislation that would have eliminated the estate tax and repealed the "marriage penalty," a quirk in the tax code that results in some two-earner couples paying higher income taxes. But he followed the Democratic line on most other occasions — voting with the party about 90 percent of the time in the 106th Congress. He backed proposals to license and register handguns as well as a measure that would have required federal health care plans to cover the costs of contraception. He voted against large-scale Republican tax cuts and opposed a constitutional amendment to ban flag desecration.

Holt, who has a seat on the Education and the Workforce Committee, wants to reduce class sizes and boost spending on after-school programs. He generally backs legislation that gives local school districts the authority to decide how to use their resources. And, as one of two physicists in Congress — Rep. Vernon J. Ehlers, R-Mich., is the other — Holt has been a vocal advocate of increased spending on math and science education.

Holt also sits on the Resources panel, where he has championed preserving open space and improving environmental protections for the

Delaware River. He favors congressional action to reduce global warming and protect biodiversity.

In the 107th Congress, Holt emerged as a prominent player on the potent consumer issue of electronic privacy. Holt believes it is unnerving that technology now allows marketers to track consumers' Internet surfing and phone-calling habits, and he says that strong disclosure and anti-spam laws would not deprive advertisers and others of reasonable expression. He sponsored legislation barring the transmission of unsolicited commercial messages to wireless phones and a separate bill prohibiting the use of information-collecting devices without proper notification and consent. "I know people who won't use the Web anymore because they feel they can't go anywhere without having a snooper on their tail," Holt said.

Holt's straightforward approach, intellect and political savvy led House Democrats early in the 107th Congress to elect him president of his Democratic sophomore class. The job puts him in the position of being an envoy between class members and the House Democratic leadership.

Holt's father, Rush Holt, was a Democratic senator from West Virginia from 1935 to 1941. Yet despite his political heritage, the younger Holt was not widely expected to seek elective office. The Democrat's 1998 victory over one-term GOP Rep. Michael Pappas in the 12th District was the year's biggest House upset. Holt was one of only six challengers to unseat an incumbent.

He won by portraying social conservative Pappas as too far to the right for the district. Pappas also inadvertently hurt his own cause by taking to the House floor to sing a song, set to the tune of "Twinkle Twinkle Little Star," in praise of Clinton's legal adversary, Independent Counsel Kenneth W. Starr. Holt turned the incident into a humorous, tide-turning campaign ad. He won by about 5,000 votes.

The victory made Holt one of the GOP's most-targeted Democratic incumbents in the 2000 elections. National Republican ads portrayed him as little more than a tax-and-spend liberal with Ivy League bona fides. But Holt blunted GOP contentions that he was fiscally irresponsible, pointing to his support of a plan that would keep surplus Social Security funds from being used for other government spending.

The campaign against moderate Republican Zimmer, who had held the district seat for three terms ending in 1996, turned bitter, particularly over 800 ballots that Middlesex County election workers had marked in pencil in an effort to make them more legible. Zimmer conceded after losing ground in recounts, and Holt said the experience would lead him to back measures in the 107th to standardize voting systems nationwide.

KEY VOTES

2000
Yes Raise hourly minimum wage by $1 over two years
No   Halt funding for U.S. mission in Kosovo unless European nations pay more
Yes Provide Medicare benefits to military retirees and their dependents
No   Grant China permanent normal trade status
Yes Phase out estate, gift and trust taxes
No   Prohibit implementation of president's national monument designations
No   Approve GOP plan to provide prescription drug coverage for Medicare beneficiaries
Yes Increase help for poor nations indebted to international financial institutions

1999
Yes Impose steel import quotas
Yes Kill proposal to take aviation trust funds off budget
No   Require background checks on buyers only at gun shows with 10 or more vendors
Yes Remove barriers among banking, securities and insurance companies
Yes Authorize state grants to hire teachers and reduce class size
Yes Overhaul campaign finance law; ban "soft money" and restrict advocacy advertising
Yes Approve bipartisan plan to increase rights of patients in managed-care health plans

INTEREST GROUPS

	AFL-CIO	ADA	CCUS	ACU
2000	80%	80%	47%	16%
1999	78%	95%	24%	4%

CQ VOTE STUDIES

	PARTY UNITY		PRESIDENTIAL SUPPORT	
	Support	Oppose	Support	Oppose
2000	88%	12%	67%	33%
1999	91%	9%	79%	21%

NEW JERSEY 12
North and Central – East Brunswick; Princeton

Compared with much of New Jersey, the 12th is wealthier, whiter and more educated. Occupying a western chunk in the middle of the state, the 12th meanders east almost to the coast. Taking in most of the wealthy and ethnically diverse town of East Brunswick and moving through Monmouth County, the 12th stops just short of the Jersey Shore communities on the Atlantic Ocean coast.

Despite its jagged shape, the district covers a swath of similar towns. Office parks dominate the landscape in these uniformly white-collar communities. Midsize towns, such as Ewing and Princeton, have benefited from economic growth but found themselves stuck with the side effects of suburban sprawl.

The river towns, such as Frenchtown and Lambertville, are filled with quaint antique shops and bed-and-breakfasts. Flemington, the Hunterdon County seat, has earned a reputation as a destination for outlet shopping and weekend getaways.

Towns built with old money, as well as growing suburban affluence, traditionally have made the district solidly Republican, except for a small Democratic constituency anchored by the academic community in Princeton. However, the district's sizable number of independent voters is helping to fuel a trend of electing Democrats at the congressional and presidential level. After supporting George Bush in 1992, the 12th gave the edge to the Democratic presidential candidate in 1996 and 2000.

MAJOR INDUSTRY
Education, military, pharmaceuticals

MILITARY BASES
Fort Monmouth (Army), 567 military, 5,245 civilian (2000)

CITIES
East Brunswick (unincorporated), 43,548 (1990); Ewing (unincorporated), 34,185 (1990); Princeton, 11,916

UNUSUAL FEATURES
Monmouth – site of the Lindbergh baby kidnapping trial and a major battle during the Revolutionary War.

Rep. Robert Menendez (D)

Elected 1992; 5th term

CAPITOL OFFICE
225-7919; fax 226-0792; 2238 Rayburn Bldg. 20515

INTERNET
e-mail: menendez@mail.house.gov
web: menendez.house.gov

COMMITTEES
International Relations
Transportation & Infrastructure

HOMETOWN
Union City

BORN
Jan. 1, 1954, Manhattan, N.Y.

RELIGION
Roman Catholic

FAMILY
Wife, Jane Menendez; two children

EDUCATION
St. Peter's College, B.A. 1976; Rutgers U., J.D. 1979

CAREER
Lawyer

POLITICAL HIGHLIGHTS
Union City Board of Education, 1974-82; mayor of Union City, 1986-92; N.J. Assembly, 1987-91; N.J. Senate, 1991-93

ELECTION RESULTS

2000 GENERAL

Robert Menendez (D)	117,856	78.7%
Theresa de Leon (R)	27,849	18.6%
Claudette C. Meliere (I)	2,741	1.8%

2000 PRIMARY

Robert Menendez (D)	unopposed

1998 GENERAL

Robert Menendez (D)	70,308	80.1%
Theresa de Leon (R)	14,615	16.6%
Richard S. Hester Sr. (PLC)	1,276	1.5%

PREVIOUS WINNING PERCENTAGES
1996 (79%); 1994 (71%); 1992 (64%)

Brash and ambitious, Menendez has turned his status as the only Cuban-American Democrat in Congress to great political advantage. He has served as a key adviser to a Democratic president and to a presidential nominee on the politics of the Cuban-American community while also acting as a voice for broader Hispanic interests.

The son of Cuban immigrants, Menendez often joins Congress' two other Cuban-American lawmakers — Ileana Ros-Lehtinen and Lincoln Diaz-Balart, both Florida Republicans — in rhetorical blasts at the regime of Cuban President Fidel Castro. Menendez stands out for his party identity, however, since Cuban-Americans have tended to vote Republican ever since President Reagan's anti-communist broadsides made them part of the GOP's electoral coalition.

Campaigning for the crucial swing states of Florida and New Jersey, both Bill Clinton and Al Gore sought to cut into this GOP support. They naturally turned to Menendez for advice when they faced tough choices on Cuba policy during their presidential election campaigns.

Clinton carried Florida in the 1996 campaign after Menendez helped broker a deal to modify and pass a bill designed to punish foreign companies that invest in Cuba.

Gore's historically close finish in Florida bears Menendez's fingerprints as well. In 1999, Menendez convinced Gore to squelch White House support for a proposal to establish an independent commission to review U.S. policy toward Cuba, including economic sanctions supported by Cuban-Americans. In 2000, Gore — at Menendez's suggestion — broke with the Clinton administration and urged that 6-year-old Cuban refugee Elián González be given permanent residency in the United States rather than returned to his father in Cuba.

Menendez's Hispanic background has served him well as he has climbed Democratic Party ranks. In a three-way contest for vice chairman of the House Democratic Caucus in 1999, Menendez emphasized his ability to unify the party's ideological, geographic and ethnic factions. He defeated Cal Dooley of California, who appealed to the conservative wing of the party, and Albert R. Wynn of Maryland, a liberal. The vice chairmanship was a step up from the appointed post he had held in the 105th Congress — one of four Democratic chief deputy whips.

Menendez has raised his profile by serving unofficially as the leadership's point man on issues of particular concern to Hispanics. In that capacity, he has persistently castigated Republicans for pursuing policies that he said showed a GOP bias against immigrant groups.

Menendez is a faithful liberal and a believer in activist government. He sides with organized labor, backs abortion rights, supports gun control and faults Republicans as proponents of tax breaks for the wealthy. Designated to make the Democrats' weekly radio address early in 2001, Menendez blasted President Bush's proposed $1.6 trillion tax cut, arguing that "families who depend on a paycheck — not an inheritance" would see little of the benefits. Menendez added that the typical Hispanic family would get only $223 and that "many lower- and middle-income families would receive nothing — not a dime."

In support of the Hispanic community, Menendez criticized the House GOP's investigation of Democrat Loretta Sanchez's narrow 1996 victory over Republican Robert K. Dornan in California's 46th District. He called the probe a "witch hunt" and a waste of taxpayer money. Dornan had insisted there was sufficient evidence of illegal voting in the Hispanic-majority district to invalidate Sanchez's victory. Menendez scoffed at Dornan's claims, saying, "This so-called evidence is useless and worthless and nothing more than an attack on Hispanic voters in the nation." The House Oversight Committee concluded that Dornan's complaint did not merit a call for a new election.

Menendez's intense engagement in the Sanchez-Dornan affair reflects his deep feelings of ethnic pride. He shows similar passion for the concerns of other ethnic groups in his district.

Many in the 13th District who immigrated to the United States remain actively interested in events in their countries of origin, and Menendez can keep abreast of those developments from his seat on the International Relations Committee, where he is the top Democrat on the Western Hemisphere Subcommittee.

Menendez won election to the Union City School Board in 1974, while still in college. He won the Union City mayoralty in 1986 and a state Assembly seat in 1987, serving in both offices simultaneously. He was appointed to fill a state Senate vacancy in early 1991 and that November was elected to the seat.

Redistricting for the 1990s nearly doubled the 13th's Hispanic population, and speculation arose that Menendez would be a good fit for the district. After seven-term Democratic Rep. Frank J. Guarini decided to retire in 1992, Menendez found himself with a clear path to election. He won the primary with 68 percent of the vote and the general election with 64 percent. Since then, he has coasted to re-election.

When New Jersey's senior senator, Democrat Frank R. Lautenberg, announced early in 1999 that he would not seek re-election in 2000, Menendez's name was at the top of the list of prospective Democratic successors. But he quickly scotched such talk, issuing a statement that his seniority and newly won post as vice chairman of the House Democratic Caucus were too important to give up. He is still viewed as a potential candidate for the Senate or for governor.

Menendez collects far more money than he needs to win re-election in the solidly Democratic 13th. He gave $425,000 of that excess cash to other Democrats in the 1998 election cycle, helping himself at the same time in gathering support for his successful campaign for the job in the party's leadership for the 106th Congress.

In the 2000 campaign cycle, he gave about $450,000 to candidates and to the Democratic Congressional Campaign Committee.

KEY VOTES

2000
Yes Raise hourly minimum wage by $1 over two years
No Halt funding for U.S. mission in Kosovo unless European nations pay more
Yes Provide Medicare benefits to military retirees and their dependents
No Grant China permanent normal trade status
No Phase out estate, gift and trust taxes
No Prohibit implementation of president's national monument designations
No Approve GOP plan to provide prescription drug coverage for Medicare beneficiaries
Yes Increase help for poor nations indebted to international financial institutions

1999
Yes Impose steel import quotas
No Kill proposal to take aviation trust funds off budget
No Require background checks on buyers only at gun shows with 10 or more vendors
Yes Remove barriers among banking, securities and insurance companies
Yes Authorize state grants to hire teachers and reduce class size
Yes Overhaul campaign finance law; ban "soft money" and restrict advocacy advertising
Yes Approve bipartisan plan to increase rights of patients in managed-care health plans

INTEREST GROUPS

	AFL-CIO	ADA	CCUS	ACU
2000	100%	95%	38%	8%
1999	100%	100%	24%	4%
1998	100%	95%	33%	12%
1997	100%	90%	40%	13%

CQ VOTE STUDIES

	PARTY UNITY		PRESIDENTIAL SUPPORT	
	Support	Oppose	Support	Oppose
2000	91%	9%	78%	22%
1999	91%	9%	81%	19%
1998	90%	10%	78%	22%
1997	90%	10%	76%	24%

NEW JERSEY 13
Parts of Jersey City and Newark

Within sight of some of the nation's best-known landmarks, including the Statue of Liberty and downtown Manhattan's gleaming office towers, the 13th now has a major landmark on its own turf – Ellis Island. After a protracted legal battle, the U.S. Supreme Court decided in 1998 that New Jersey can lay claim to 80 percent of the immigration gateway, whose lure has helped form the 13th's colorful character.

Covering the New Jersey shoreline, taking in parts of Jersey City and Newark, the 13th has a diverse community of Hispanics, many of whom came in a wave of immigration from countries all across Central and South America that followed a loosening of restrictions in 1965. The 13th was formed in 1992 to gather many of those scattered Hispanic neighborhoods, and, in 1992, the district elected the state's first Hispanic congressman. In five consecutive elections, Rep. Menendez has been re-elected handily – by a resounding 79 percent in 2000.

Russian, Indian, Korean and Filipino communities add to the district's diversity and its overwhelming Democratic vote. A few Republican presidential ballots are cast by Cuban communities in Union City, North Bergen, Guttenberg and West New York.

Although Newark's economy has struggled, much of the district is on stable ground. Both Jersey City and Hoboken have seen some neighborhoods gentrify, as young professionals and financial services companies have moved across the river from Manhattan. The district also is a transportation hub, with Newark International Airport and Port Newark-Elizabeth.

MAJOR INDUSTRY
Health care, retail, financial securities

CITIES
Jersey City (pt.), 122,374 (1990); Newark (pt.), 105,853 (1990); Union City, 56,946

UNUSUAL FEATURES
Frank Sinatra born and raised in Hoboken; Frank "I am the Law" Hague, a legendary Democratic machine politician, ruled Hudson County from 1917 to 1949.

Gov. Gary E. Johnson (R)

First elected: 1994
Length of term: 4 years
Term expires: 1/03
Salary: $90,000
Phone: (505) 827-3000
Hometown: Albuquerque
Born: Jan. 1, 1953; Minot, N.D.
Religion: Lutheran
Family: Wife, Dee Simms Johnson; two children
Education: U. of New Mexico, B.S. 1976
Career: Construction company owner
Political highlights: No previous office
Election results:
1998 GENERAL
Gary E. Johnson (R)	271,948	54.4%
Martin Chavez (D)	222,755	45.5%

Lt. Gov. Walter Bradley (R)

First elected: 1994
Length of term: 4 years
Term expires: 1/03
Salary: $65,000
Phone: (505) 827-3050

STATE LEGISLATURE

Legislature: Meets January-March in odd years; January-February in even years
House: 70 members, 2-year terms
2001 breakdown: 42R, 28D; 48 men, 22 women
Salary: $136/day
Phone: (505) 986-4751
Senate: 42 members, 4-year terms
2001 breakdown: 18R, 24D; 30 men, 12 women
Salary: $136/day
Phone: (505) 986-4714

STATE TERM LIMITS

Governor: 2 consecutive terms
Senate: No
House: No

URBAN STATISTICS

CITY	POPULATION
Albuquerque	420,578
Las Cruces	75,786
Santa Fe	69,299
Rio Rancho	52,012
Roswell	47,644

REGISTERED VOTERS

Democrat	52%
Republican	33%
No Party	12%
Other	3%

POPULATION

2000 population	1,819,046
1990 population	1,515,069
Percent change	+20.1%
Rank among states	36
Median age	33.8
Born in state	52%
Foreign born	5%
Urban/rural	73%/27%
Crime rate	853/100,000
Poverty level	20.4%
Federal workers	29,867
Military	18,427

REAPPORTIONMENT

New Mexico retained its three House seats in reapportionment. The state legislature will draw new district lines in 2002.

MISCELLANEOUS

Web: www.state.nm.us
Capital: Santa Fe
Land area: 121,364 sq. miles
   Rank among states: 5
STATE ELECTION OFFICIAL
(505) 827-3621
DEMOCRATIC HEADQUARTERS
(505) 830-3650
REPUBLICAN HEADQUARTERS
(505) 298-3662

District Statistics

		VOTE FOR PRESIDENT															
		2000			1996			1992									
DIST.	D	R	GREEN	D	R	REF	D	R	I	WHT	BLK	ASIAN	HISP	HOUSEHOLD INCOME	OVER 65+	UNDER 18	COLLEGE EDUCATION
1	49%	46%	4%	48%	43%	5%	46%	39%	16%	78%	3%	1%	38%	$27,074	10%	26%	26%
2	43	54	2	46	45	7	41	40	19	84	2	1	42	$21,456	12	31	15
3	52	43	4	53	38	6	51	34	15	66	1	1	34	$23,610	10	31	20
STATE	47.9	47.8	4	49	42	6	46	37	16	76	2	1	38	$24,087	11	30	20

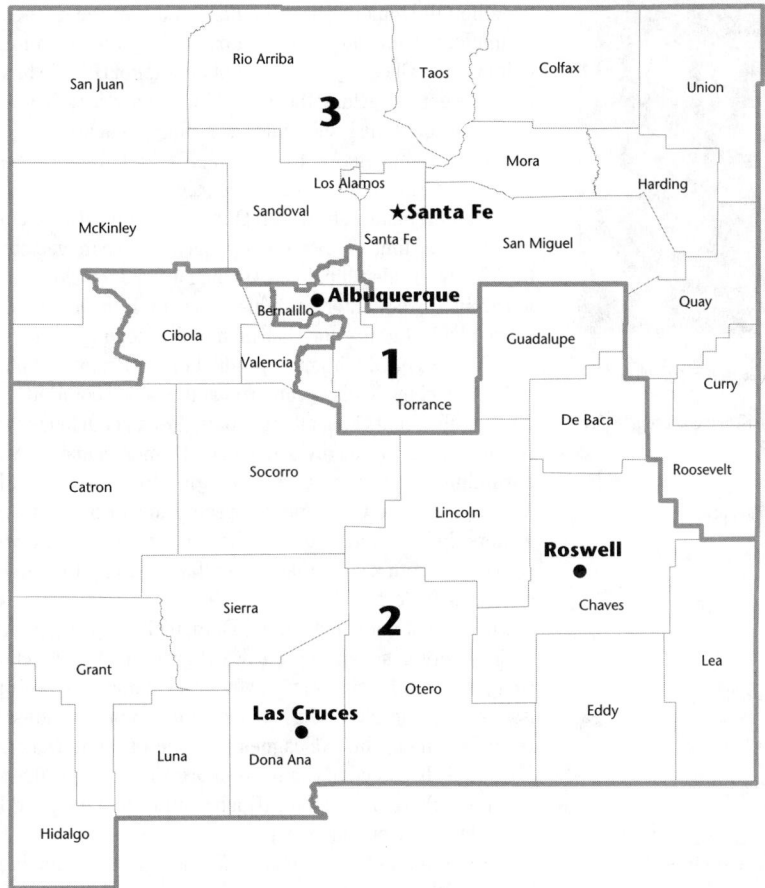

Sen. Pete V. Domenici (R)

Elected 1972; 5th term

CAPITOL OFFICE
224-6621; fax 228-0900; 328 Hart Bldg. 20510

INTERNET
e-mail: senator_domenici@domenici.senate.gov
web: domenici.senate.gov

COMMITTEES
Appropriations
   (Energy & Water Development - chairman)
Budget - chairman
Energy & Natural Resources
Governmental Affairs
Indian Affairs

HOMETOWN
Albuquerque

BORN
May 7, 1932, Albuquerque, N.M.

RELIGION
Roman Catholic

FAMILY
Wife, Nancy Domenici; eight children

EDUCATION
U. of Albuquerque, attended 1950-52; U. of New
Mexico, B.S. 1954; U. of Denver, LL.B. 1958

CAREER
Lawyer

POLITICAL HIGHLIGHTS
Albuquerque City Commission, 1966-70 (chairman
and ex-officio mayor, 1967-70); Republican
nominee for governor, 1970

ELECTION RESULTS

1996 GENERAL

Pete V. Domenici (R)	357,171	64.7%
Art Trujillo (D)	164,356	29.8%
Abraham Gutmann (GREEN)	24,230	4.4%
Bruce Bush (LIBERT)	6,064	1.1%

1996 PRIMARY

Pete V. Domenici (R)	unopposed

PREVIOUS WINNING PERCENTAGES
1990 (73%); 1984 (72%); 1978 (53%); 1972 (54%)

As the GOP's longtime field general in its budget wars with the White House — and as a hardworking devotee of finding common ground between Democrats and Republicans — the intense and influential Domenici commands as much bipartisan respect as anyone in Congress.

Although Domenici's advice has not always been heeded on fiscal policy matters, even within his own party, the Budget Committee chairman's opinions usually carry great weight on Capitol Hill. He has dedicated much of his career to tracking the federal budget and is widely regarded as knowing more about the issue's intricacies and political intrigues than just about anyone in Congress. "Pete Domenici is the budget process around here," Sen. Larry E. Craig, R-Idaho, once said.

For all his stature, however, Domenici (doh-MEN-ih-chee) has been left behind three times as Senate Republicans have moved steadily to the right to pick their leadership. In a 1984 bid for Senate majority leader, he finished fourth in a five-senator field; his close ally Bob Dole was elected. In 1990, Domenici lost a race for chairman of the Republican Policy Committee to Don Nickles of Oklahoma, a product of the Reagan revolution of 1980.

Domenici made his second run at the policy committee job at the end of 2000, challenging Craig after the party lost a net of four seats in the election, resulting in an evenly divided Senate. Domenici maintained that his party's shrinking Senate ranks were a signal that the GOP hierarchy should include someone with a proven record of working with Democrats. "Our leadership," he said, "needs a little bit of breadth and variety and needs somebody from a state that is less than a straight Republican state." Nevertheless, he lost, 26-24.

That defeat notwithstanding, Domenici has plenty to keep him busy. A tireless worker, he not only wields the gavel on the Budget panel in the 107th Congress, but he sits on virtually every committee with jurisdiction over issues affecting New Mexico, including Appropriations. He is so highly regarded among his colleagues that one of them, Majority Leader Trent Lott, publicly floated his name to George W. Bush in 2000 for consideration as a possible running mate. (Bush's father had included Domenici on *his* shortlist of vice-presidential prospects in 1988.)

Despite his influential status, Domenici has maintained a regular-guy image in Washington. A driven yet sensitive man, he appears genuinely distressed when a colleague is angry at him. He does not suffer criticism lightly and can bristle at those who question his actions. But he is deeply loyal to his staff, treating them like extended family members, and likewise displays considerable respect toward colleagues. "He understands that you don't do irreparable harm to relationships with anyone," former Sen. Warren B. Rudman, R-N.H., a close friend, once told The Washington Post. "If Pete has a fault, it's that he worries too much."

Domenici's fiscally conservative yet socially moderate approach has enabled him to work with a broad spectrum of lawmakers. He has teamed with conservative Phil Gramm, R-Texas, on Social Security legislation and worked with liberal Paul Wellstone, D-Minn., on mental health issues. (Both Domenici and Wellstone have watched close relatives struggle with mental illness.) At the same time, Domenici says he has been persistent in letting his GOP colleagues know when he thinks a bill is overly partisan: "I tell them not once but twice, and if I can tell them three times, I do."

Domenici's political acumen has not prevented him from tangling with some of his more conservative colleagues. Though he embraced President Bush's tax cut proposal in 2001, he did so only when surplus projections became so rosy that he was convinced the longstanding condition he had set for giving his support would be met: Taxes could be cut without tapping into the Social Security trust fund surplus. At the same time, Domenici suggested the surplus was big enough that discretionary spending should be allowed to grow by more than the 4 percent increase Bush called for in his first budget.

Domenici's advocacy of fiscal restraint was passed down by his father, an Italian immigrant grocer. When Domenici was accepted into law school, his father agreed to finance his education but demanded to be repaid if his son brought home an "F."

Domenici first was thrust into the limelight on budget issues in the 1980s, when the GOP controlled the Senate and he served his first stint as Budget Committee chairman, leading the panel in its three-way battles with the Reagan administration and the Democratic-controlled House. He was more interested in balancing the budget than in providing the fiscal stimulus sought by "supply side" conservatives — Reagan budget director David A. Stockman called him a "Hooverite."

During the 12 years that Republicans Ronald Reagan and George Bush held the White House, Domenici was expected at times to muffle his call to cut the budget. After spending four years criticizing President Clinton's administration, Domenici helped lead a team of GOP negotiators in May 1997 in producing an agreement to balance the budget by fiscal 2002. The sprawling pact bore Domenici's stamp of pragmatism by containing something for both sides — tax cuts along with limited new money for selected Democratic priorities such as health care for children.

Even as he has strived to reduce federal spending, Domenici has doggedly sought more money for New Mexico, something that has helped him become far and away his state's dominant political figure. He has been such an ardent protector of the Energy Department that some agency employees refer to him as "St. Pete." As chairman of the Appropriations Subcommittee on Energy and Water Development, he has repeatedly secured increases for the department, including hefty boosts in funding for nuclear weapons research at New Mexico's Los Alamos and Sandia national laboratories. He has been at the forefront of efforts to expand U.S. nuclear power production. He also has been aggressive in touting a variety of good-government proposals, such as moving to a two-year budget cycle.

Domenici is in a comfortable position politically. Enduringly popular with voters across the spectrum of his state's diverse population, he has not faced an even remotely difficult re-election race in more than 20 years. He goes to great lengths not to be perceived as an out-of-touch Beltway insider, a label that a number of opponents have tried unsuccessfully to pin on him.

Before entering politics, Domenici practiced law and played baseball; he was a good enough pitcher in college to receive a contract from a Brooklyn Dodgers farm team in 1954.

Domenici's background is in municipal government. As an Albuquerque city official in the late 1960s, he prided himself on holding neighborhood meetings to hear residents' complaints. After four years in city government, he ran for governor in 1970, losing to Democrat Bruce King by 5 points.

Undeterred, Domenici came back in 1972, this time running for the Senate seat being vacated by Democrat Clinton P. Anderson. He linked his Democratic foe, banker and former state Rep. Jack Daniels, to the unpopular presidential candidacy of George McGovern and won, with 54 percent. He struggled to win re-election in 1978, but since then, he has not faced a strong challenge for his seat.

KEY VOTES

2000

Yes Overhaul bankruptcy law and increase minimum wage
Yes Limit fiscal 2001 discretionary spending to $600.3 billion
Yes Override veto on nuclear waste disposal at Yucca Mountain site in Nevada
No Oppose effort to terminate Kosovo mission
No Include gender, sexual orientation and disability in federal hate crime protections
Yes Approve GOP plan to restrict use of genetic information by health insurers
Yes Kill amendment delaying implementation of an anti-missile defense system
Yes Cut taxes for married couples
Yes Grant China permanent normal trade status

1999

Yes Remove President Clinton from office for obstruction of justice
Yes Kill amendment authorizing state grants to hire teachers and reduce class size
No Require criminal background checks for purchases at gun shows
Yes Approve GOP proposal to increase rights of patients in managed-care health plans
? Block effort to allow farm and medicine exports to Cuba
No Allow study of tougher automobile fuel efficiency standards
No Ratify nuclear weapons testing treaty
No Prohibit national political parties from collecting "soft money" donations
Yes Remove barriers among banking, securities and insurance companies

INTEREST GROUPS

	AFL-CIO	ADA	CCUS	ACU
2000	0%	0%	100%	95%
1999	11%	5%	94%	88%
1998	13%	5%	100%	70%
1997	0%	25%	100%	60%
1996	14%	20%	83%	85%
1995	8%	5%	100%	78%
1994	13%	25%	90%	84%
1993	9%	20%	100%	80%
1992	17%	15%	78%	78%
1991	17%	10%	90%	76%

CQ VOTE STUDIES

	PARTY UNITY		PRESIDENTIAL SUPPORT	
	Support	Oppose	Support	Oppose
2000	94%	6%	51%	49%
1999	93%	7%	33%	67%
1998	83%	17%	57%	43%
1997	85%	15%	67%	33%
1996	90%	10%	42%	58%
1995	93%	7%	26%	74%
1994	78%	22%	53%	47%
1993	86%	14%	34%	66%
1992	89%	11%	82%	18%
1991	89%	11%	94%	6%

Sen. Jeff Bingaman (D)

Elected 1982; 4th term

In a Senate whose members so often resemble the hard-charging Captain Kirk of "Star Trek," Bingaman seems more like that show's Mr. Spock: cerebral, logical and seemingly without ego in his willingness to let others take credit for accomplishments.

Bingaman long has been regarded as one of the most studious — if least charismatic — senators, especially on complex topics such as technology, nuclear weapons and the domestic energy supply. But he has delved just as deeply into issues at the core of the Democratic agenda, including education and pensions.

For that reason, Bingaman has become a trusted adviser to Minority Leader Tom Daschle, and he belongs to a small "message group" that meets weekly with Daschle to shape the party's stands and priorities. Insiders credit Bingaman with persuading other Democratic senators to rally around such issues as school dropout prevention and teacher training. "When he speaks up to the [Democratic] caucus or policy committee or message group, he's very influential, because he's always thought it through," said Joel Johnson, a White House official under President Clinton who previously worked for Daschle.

Like former Sen. Bill Bradley of New Jersey — several of whose staffers now work for Bingaman — and former Vice President Al Gore, the party's 2000 presidential nominee, Bingaman is among those Democrats who appear more at home with the intricacies of policy than the glamour of politics. He avoids the television talk-show circuit, rarely takes part in news conferences and often lets other New Mexico lawmakers take the lead in putting out press releases about statewide matters. Although he is amiable in his relations with the media, he has maintained such a low profile during his nearly two decades in the Senate that some veteran Capitol Hill reporters have had trouble recognizing him.

Nevertheless, Bingaman has amassed a solid record of accomplishment as the top Democrat on the Energy and Natural Resources Committee. He took over the position in the 106th Congress and developed a good relationship with the panel's gruff chairman, Republican Frank H. Murkowski of Alaska. Bingaman's moderate views, his tendency not to automatically side with environmental groups, and his lack of interest in debating issues through the media have proved reassuring to Murkowski.

On measures ranging from forest preservation to rural electrification projects, Bingaman quietly found ways to make the legislation palatable to both sides, often by letting Murkowski know exactly what the Clinton administration could live with. The result was that 147 of the committee's bills were enacted in the 106th — a 75 percent increase over the 105th Congress and six times as many as in the 104th. The figure was the highest of any Senate committee.

Early in the 107th Congress, Bingaman continued to seek compromises over such contentious matters as nuclear waste storage and electricity deregulation. He criticized Republicans for being too interested in addressing California's electricity shortages by seeking to drill for oil in Alaska's Arctic National Wildlife Refuge, noting that less than 1 percent of California's electricity came from oil-fired plants.

He also remained devoted to furthering energy research: Since 1993, he has chaired the board of the Alliance to Save Energy, a nonprofit coalition promoting efficient energy use worldwide. "We have shortchanged our-

CAPITOL OFFICE
224-5521; fax 224-2852; 703 Hart Bldg. 20510

INTERNET
e-mail: senator_bingaman@bingaman.senate.gov
web: bingaman.senate.gov

COMMITTEES
Energy & Natural Resources - ranking member
Finance
Health, Education, Labor & Pensions
Joint Economic

HOMETOWN
Silver City

BORN
Oct. 3, 1943, El Paso, Texas

RELIGION
Methodist

FAMILY
Wife, Anne Kovacovich Bingaman; one child

EDUCATION
Harvard U., A.B. 1965; Stanford U., J.D. 1968

MILITARY SERVICE
Army Reserve, 1968-74

CAREER
Lawyer

POLITICAL HIGHLIGHTS
N.M. attorney general, 1979-83

ELECTION RESULTS

2000 GENERAL

Jeff Bingaman (D)	363,744	61.7%
Bill Redmond (R)	225,517	38.3%

2000 PRIMARY

Jeff Bingaman (D)	unopposed

PREVIOUS WINNING PERCENTAGES
1994 (54%); 1988 (63%); 1982 (54%)

selves in the past by cutting investment in R&D to meet other budget objectives," he said in 2001.

Bingaman augmented his portfolio in the 107th Congress with a seat on the Finance Committee, which writes tax, trade and health care legislation. Before joining Finance, Bingaman served on the Armed Services Committee, where his workmanlike devotion to detail earned him comparisons to the panel's venerated retired chairman, Democrat Sam Nunn of Georgia. Bingaman has been a proponent of putting defense technologies to use in the private sector.

That position is popular in New Mexico — home to two of the Energy Department's national laboratories, Sandia and Los Alamos, which have sought new missions with the end of the Cold War.

In the Senate, Bingaman has taken on a variety of unglamorous but important assignments. Daschle has appointed him to task forces studying high-wage job creation, Social Security and the settlement between the big tobacco companies and the states. Almost without exception, though, Bingaman has let other panel members grab the headlines on those issues. "He never seeks to advance himself; he never says, 'Look at me,'" said Kent Conrad, D-N.D., who chaired the tobacco group and notes that Bingaman is among those he turns to for advice on difficult issues. "I find him to be one of the colleagues I respect the most," Conrad said.

Bingaman also has won the respect of James M. Jeffords, R-Vt., chairman of the Health, Education, Labor and Pensions Committee. The two have worked together on pension issues, and Jeffords describes Bingaman as "sensible and non-partisan." New Mexico's far more media-savvy senator, Republican Pete V. Domenici, is equally respectful. The two generally stay out of each other's way, although a proposal by Domenici, Murkowski and Jon Kyl, R-Ariz., to set up a new nuclear weapons agency within the Energy Department was redrafted in 1999 in response to Bingaman's objections. He contended that the move to address lax security at nuclear weapons labs by establishing the agency encroached too much on the energy secretary's authority.

Like many of his colleagues, Bingaman has lamented the growing partisanship in the Senate. But he has remained persistent in pushing his ideas despite having less success, with Democrats in the minority. "Bitterness is not a word for him," his wife, Anne, once said. "It's not in his nature. His family is from Kansas, from Midwestern stock, and they're just very stoic."

Bingaman's family helped point him toward a political career. He grew up in the New Mexico mining town of Silver City, the son of a professor and nephew of John Bingaman, a confidant of the state's 24-year Democratic senator, Clinton Anderson. At Stanford Law School, Bingaman worked for Sen. Robert F. Kennedy's 1968 presidential campaign. Returning to New Mexico, he served as counsel to the 1969 state constitutional convention, joined a politically connected law firm and ran successfully for attorney general in 1978.

When he launched his 1982 Senate campaign, he was little-known outside the political and legal communities but politically unscarred. He won 54 percent to topple incumbent GOP Sen. Harrison H. Schmitt, a former Apollo astronaut, who appeared more interested in pet subjects such as 21st century technology than in the state's struggling economy.

In three re-election races since, only one has featured a serious challenger — Colin McMillan, a former Pentagon official, who used much of his own money in 1994 to aggressively attack Bingaman's stance regarding grazing fees on public lands and his support for President Clinton's budget policy. In the end, McMillan could not make sufficient inroads in Democratic counties, and Bingaman won with 54 percent.

KEY VOTES

2000

Yes Overhaul bankruptcy law and increase minimum wage

No Limit fiscal 2001 discretionary spending to $600.3 billion

No Override veto on nuclear waste disposal at Yucca Mountain site in Nevada

Yes Oppose effort to terminate Kosovo mission

Yes Include gender, sexual orientation and disability in federal hate crime protections

No Approve GOP plan to restrict use of genetic information by health insurers

No Kill amendment delaying implementation of an anti-missile defense system

No Cut taxes for married couples

Yes Grant China permanent normal trade status

1999

No Remove President Clinton from office for obstruction of justice

No Kill amendment authorizing state grants to hire teachers and reduce class size

Yes Require criminal background checks for purchases at gun shows

No Approve GOP proposal to increase rights of patients in managed-care health plans

No Block effort to allow farm and medicine exports to Cuba

Yes Allow study of tougher automobile fuel efficiency standards

Yes Ratify nuclear weapons testing treaty

Yes Prohibit national political parties from collecting "soft money" donations

Yes Remove barriers among banking, securities and insurance companies

INTEREST GROUPS

	AFL-CIO	ADA	CCUS	ACU
2000	75%	85%	64%	16%
1999	78%	100%	59%	4%
1998	75%	85%	56%	0%
1997	57%	90%	60%	0%
1996	100%	95%	15%	0%
1995	100%	90%	42%	0%
1994	75%	60%	50%	16%
1993	73%	70%	36%	20%
1992	92%	75%	20%	4%
1991	67%	65%	20%	19%

CQ VOTE STUDIES

	PARTY UNITY		PRESIDENTIAL SUPPORT	
	Support	Oppose	Support	Oppose
2000	87%	13%	95%	5%
1999	88%	12%	84%	16%
1998	87%	13%	87%	13%
1997	88%	12%	92%	8%
1996	88%	12%	84%	16%
1995	84%	16%	91%	9%
1994	84%	16%	89%	11%
1993	80%	20%	86%	14%
1992	75%	25%	44%	56%
1991	79%	21%	51%	49%

Rep. Heather A. Wilson (R)

Elected June 1998; 2nd full term

CAPITOL OFFICE
225-6316; fax 225-4975; 318 Cannon Bldg. 20515

INTERNET
e-mail: ask.heather@mail.house.gov
web: www.house.gov/wilson

COMMITTEES
Armed Services
Energy & Commerce

HOMETOWN
Albuquerque

BORN
Dec. 30, 1960, Keene, N.H.

RELIGION
Methodist

FAMILY
Husband, Jay Hone; three children

EDUCATION
Air Force Academy, B.S. 1982; Oxford U., M.Phil. 1984, D.Phil. 1985

MILITARY SERVICE
Air Force, 1978-89

CAREER
Management consultant; National Security Council staff member

POLITICAL HIGHLIGHTS
N.M. Children, Youth and Families secretary, 1995-98

ELECTION RESULTS

2000 GENERAL

Heather A. Wilson (R)	107,296	50.3%
John Kelly (D)	92,187	43.3%
Daniel Kerlinsky (GREEN)	13,656	6.4%

2000 PRIMARY

Heather A. Wilson (R)		unopposed

1998 GENERAL

Heather A. Wilson (R)	86,784	48.4%
Phillip J. Maloof (D)	75,040	41.9%
Robert L. Anderson (GREEN)	17,266	9.6%

1998 SPECIAL

Heather A. Wilson (R)	54,853	44.6%
Phillip J. Maloof (D)	48,747	39.6%
Robert L. Anderson (GREEN)	18,108	14.7%
Bruce Bush (LIBERT)	1,337	1.1%

A former Air Force officer, Wilson's military bearing and knowledge of the armed forces sets her apart from most women in Congress. Wilson, who says she is the first woman veteran to serve in Congress, is described by her hometown newspaper as someone who "with short-cropped hair and her back ramrod straight ... looks like she still would be at home in the Air Force blues she wore until 1989."

Always on the lookout for opportunities to showcase women, the House GOP leadership has seized on her background, giving her the spotlight to be a party spokesman on military issues, such as the United States' involvement in Kosovo. She says that she is often approached by young women who regard her as a role model for women in the military and politics.

Military matters still loom large for her. In the 107th Congress, she took a seat on the Armed Services Committee, where she can look out for the interests of Albuquerque's Kirtland Air Force Base and Sandia National Laboratories — two major employers in her district.

Wilson's other priorities include social issues such as health care and education. It was her interest in education that set her on the course to public service. She first gained notice in New Mexico when she applied to be superintendent of the Albuquerque school system in 1994. Although the job went to someone else, she caught the attention of GOP Gov. Gary E. Johnson, who soon extended Wilson an offer to join his administration, as secretary of the Department of Children, Youth and Families.

In the 106th Congress, Wilson authored a bill to provide college scholarships for as much as $10,000 annually to students who agree to become teachers. The measure stalled, but it remains a top priority in the 107th. She also wants to increase Medicare funding for New Mexico, which she says has been particularly hurt by changes in the formula for reimbursing health care providers.

On another home state matter, Wilson blasted the National Park Service, saying officials' ineptitude led to an out-of-control forest fire in 2000 that destroyed more than 400 homes and threatened the Los Alamos nuclear weapons lab. She defended scientists at Los Alamos who she believed were too broadly portrayed as security risks in the wake of reports of Chinese spying at the labs. "I believe that employees at the national laboratories are dedicated brilliant patriots who care as much about the security of this country" as anyone else, she said.

Although Wilson projects a reserved, even aloof image, she was sufficiently pleased with the House vote in 2000 to buy the 95,000-acre Baca Ranch in northern New Mexico that she planted a big kiss on the cheek of Utah GOP Rep. James V. Hansen, who resurrected the languishing bill. "I was real happy," she told the Albuquerque Journal. "You don't see that often on the House floor."

Wilson votes a reliably conservative line, with moderate tendencies on a few social issues. She supports requiring federal workers' health plans to offer contraceptive coverage, but she opposes using public funds to pay for abortions. She has voted to ban a procedure its opponents call "partial birth" abortion.

In 1998, Wilson was among a minority of Republicans who opposed a GOP-drafted prohibition on adoptions by non-married or non-related couples in the District of Columbia. Wilson, who has an adopted son, said that prospective adoptions should be reviewed on a case-by-case basis, not dictated by federal statute. And in 1999, she challenged the GOP leadership and forced the postponement of a bill that would have restructured the government's nuclear weapons program — a matter of key importance in New Mexico, home to Los Alamos and Sandia national laboratories. She blasted Republican leaders for not consulting her before bringing up the measure.

Wilson was a high school junior in New Hampshire when the Air Force Academy opened its doors to women, and she decided she wanted to be a pilot, like her father and grandfather. She graduated from the academy in 1982, the third class that included women. She never got around to getting a pilot's license, however, as she went to England as a Rhodes Scholar at Oxford. There she earned master's and doctoral degrees in international relations.

She served in the Air Force in Europe, leaving in 1989 to take a job with the National Security Council in the Bush White House. In 1991, she married Albuquerque lawyer Jay Hone and moved to New Mexico. She started a consulting firm and joined Gov. Johnson's Cabinet in 1995. She resigned that post early in 1998 to run for the House when Republican Steven H. Schiff, fighting a battle against skin cancer, said he would not seek re-election. Wilson entered the race with the endorsements of Schiff and GOP Sen. Pete V. Domenici.

Schiff's death in late March necessitated a special election to fill the remainder of the term, setting up double campaigns — one for the June 2 GOP primary for the November ballot and one for the June 23 special election. Wilson got a big boost from Domenici, becoming the GOP special-election nominee in a meeting of GOP party activists. That nomination also gave her a leg up in the regular-election primary battle, where she initially trailed conservative state Sen. William F. Davis.

Wilson handily beat Davis in the primary for the fall nomination, and three weeks later, in the special election, she prevailed with 45 percent of the vote. The Democrat, 31-year-old multimillionaire businessman and state Sen. Phillip J. Maloof, got 40 percent, and 15 percent went to liberal Green Party nominee Robert L. Anderson, who appeared to hurt Maloof more than he did Wilson. The trio went at it again in the fall, and Wilson again prevailed, with 48 percent.

Democrats in 2000 once again thought they had a good shot at grabbing the seat. In a rough-and-tumble campaign, Wilson narrowly edged Democrat John Kelly, who had resigned his post as U.S. Attorney to make the race. Kelly's tenure was marked by his role as the prosecutor of Chinese scientist Wen Ho Lee, who was eventually cleared of nuclear weapons security breaches at Los Alamos.

KEY VOTES

2000
Yes Raise hourly minimum wage by $1 over two years
Yes Halt funding for U.S. mission in Kosovo unless European nations pay more
Yes Provide Medicare benefits to military retirees and their dependents
Yes Grant China permanent normal trade status
Yes Phase out estate, gift and trust taxes
Yes Prohibit implementation of president's national monument designations
Yes Approve GOP plan to provide prescription drug coverage for Medicare beneficiaries
No Increase help for poor nations indebted to international financial institutions

1999
No Impose steel import quotas
No Kill proposal to take aviation trust funds off budget
Yes Require background checks on buyers only at gun shows with 10 or more vendors
Yes Remove barriers among banking, securities and insurance companies
No Authorize state grants to hire teachers and reduce class size
No Overhaul campaign finance law; ban "soft money" and restrict advocacy advertising
Yes Approve bipartisan plan to increase rights of patients in managed-care health plans

INTEREST GROUPS

	AFL-CIO	ADA	CCUS	ACU
2000	10%	10%	80%	80%
1999	11%	15%	88%	68%
1998	25%	0%	100%	83%

CQ VOTE STUDIES

	PARTY UNITY		PRESIDENTIAL SUPPORT	
	Support	Oppose	Support	Oppose
2000	87%	13%	33%	67%
1999	84%	16%	32%	68%
1998	87%	13%	22%	78%

NEW MEXICO 1
Central — Albuquerque

Built around Albuquerque, New Mexico's largest city, the 1st is the only urban district in a mostly desert state. Since the A-bomb was developed in 1945 in Los Alamos (less than 100 miles north in the 3rd District), Albuquerque has seen its population grow from 35,000 in 1940 to about 420,000 today as a scientific community grew up around military, research and aerospace industries.

While the defense industry declined around the nation during the 1990s, Albuquerque's research and defense sectors continued to prosper. Anchored with Sandia National Laboratories, which has been managed by Lockheed Martin since 1993, the 1st has attracted a slew of defense, biotechnology and semiconductor firms drawn to Albuquerque's 50-year history as a scientific community. The most recent businesses moving to the district include electronic and communication companies, most notably, Intel, which employs more than 5,000 workers in Rio Rancho (shared with the 3rd District).

The district tends to vote Democratic at the local level, and registered Democrats have an edge over Republicans. But most congressional representatives have been moderate Republicans with fiscally conservative, defense-oriented platforms. Reliably Democratic voters include the large state and local government workforce and residents of the Hispanic South Valley. Much of the district's Republican vote is cast in Albuquerque's upper middle-class Northeast Heights.

MAJOR INDUSTRIES
Higher education, scientific research, government

MILITARY BASES
Kirtland Air Force Base, 5,321 military, 2,019 civilian (1999)

CITIES
Albuquerque (pt.), 382,725 (1990); South Valley (unincorporated), 35,701 (1990); North Valley (unincorporated), 12,507 (1990)

UNUSUAL FEATURES
International Balloon Fiesta, world's largest hot air balloon event.

Rep. Joe Skeen (R)

CAPITOL OFFICE
225-2365; fax 225-9599; 2302 Rayburn Bldg. 20515

INTERNET
e-mail: www.house.gov/writerep
web: www.house.gov/skeen

COMMITTEES
Appropriations
(Interior - chairman)

HOMETOWN
Picacho

BORN
June 30, 1927, Roswell, N.M.

RELIGION
Roman Catholic

FAMILY
Wife, Mary Skeen; two children

EDUCATION
Texas A&M U., B.S. 1950

MILITARY SERVICE
Navy, 1945-46; Air Force Reserve, 1949-52

CAREER
Sheep rancher; soil and water engineer; flying service operator

POLITICAL HIGHLIGHTS
N.M. Senate, 1961-71 (minority leader, 1965-71); N.M. Republican Party chairman, 1962-65; Republican nominee for lieutenant governor, 1970; Republican nominee for governor, 1974, 1978

ELECTION RESULTS

2000 GENERAL

Joe Skeen (R)	100,742	58.1%
Michael A. Montoya (D)	72,614	41.9%

2000 PRIMARY

Joe Skeen (R)	unopposed

1998 GENERAL

Joe Skeen (R)	85,077	57.9%
E. Shirley Baca (D)	61,796	42.1%

PREVIOUS WINNING PERCENTAGES
1996 (56%); 1994 (63%); 1992 (56%); 1990 (100%); 1988 (100%); 1986 (63%); 1984 (74%); 1982 (58%); 1980 (38%)

Elected 1980; 11th term

Advancing age and Parkinson's disease have taken a noticeable physical toll on Skeen. His movements are slow and stiff, he speaks with considerably less force than he once did, and he relies increasingly on his staff for assistance. But time has done little to soften Skeen's hard-nosed posture on causes he holds dear.

In many ways, Skeen is a typical rural Western conservative — a rugged individualist who talks about respecting private property rights while lambasting Democratic policies directed at ranchers, loggers and other users of public lands. He is fond of asserting that environmentalists are "self-appointed saviors" and that they, along with most federal officials, "just don't understand" the problems of public land users.

Skeen's role in the House, however, separates him from most of the other GOP members hailing from the mountains and prairies: He is an appropriator, and an influential one. As a member of the exclusive "college of cardinals" — the 13 subcommittee chairmen of the House Appropriations Committee — he has set aside partisan differences and worked behind the scenes to keep the money flowing and members of both parties content.

In the 107th Congress, Skeen took the helm of the Interior Appropriations Subcommittee, giving him a platform for his hands-off views on federal public land management. Environmentalists and Skeen's Democratic critics say that the lawmaker's efforts on behalf of ranchers, miners and loggers reflect a desire to cling to the old ways of the West, in which decisions about the land were made by the few people who made a living from it.

But Skeen remains an unapologetic advocate of local control, noting that he practiced what he preaches when he obtained ownership over the public lands that once surrounded his 15,000-acre sheep ranch. "I bought the feds out and I bought the state out — it doesn't produce any more in terms of income, but it damn well belongs to me," he said. "We need to make our own determinations and not let our legislative systems do it."

Despite his belief that the federal government can be insensitive to rural Westerners' perspective on land management issues and other concerns, Skeen has nonetheless often looked to Uncle Sam for help for troubled mining industries in his home state. And on the Appropriations Committee, he works to bring home New Mexico's share of federal dollars, especially for agricultural research at New Mexico State University in Las Cruces. The college in 2000 named its arid lands research building after Skeen in recognition of his role in securing federal funds.

Skeen is one of the few House members who enthusiastically supports having a nuclear waste site in his district. The Waste Isolation Pilot Plant, located in underground salt caverns near the 2nd District town of Carlsbad, is the first permanent facility to store radioactive waste from nuclear weapons production factories in Colorado, Idaho and other states. After years of deadlock as well as political prodding from Skeen and other supporters of the project, the Energy Department began the first shipments to the site in 1999.

As chairman of the Appropriations panel on agriculture and rural development for six years, Skeen had to reconcile his job of funding farm programs with his responsibility to be a leader in the GOP's efforts to cut federal expenditures. He stressed his support for popular nutrition programs, such as food stamps and school lunches, while lamenting crusades by younger Republicans to prune back government. "You just can't keep chopping, chopping, chopping," he said of their efforts to cut spending.

Skeen's rough style has sometimes landed him in controversy. In 1997, when President Clinton discussed the possibility of a formal apology and financial restitution to black citizens as reparation for slavery, Skeen told an Albuquerque newspaper: "Anybody that wants to go back to Africa — or ethnic groups that want to go where they came from — we'll be happy to fund the fare." State Democratic Party and NAACP officials criticized his remarks, and Skeen apologized.

Skeen hasn't had too much trouble holding onto his seat in the largely rural 2nd District, even though Democratic strength in the 2nd has grown in recent years. One reason for his success is that many of the nominally Democratic older residents in the southeast oil-patch corner of the state known as "Little Texas" remain conservative and disposed to back Republicans such as Skeen. With his re-election in 2000 to an 11th term, he became New Mexico's longest-serving House member.

Skeen's longevity is all the more surprising considering the way in which he got to Washington — he is one of the few write-in candidates ever elected to Congress. Skeen's unusual victory came after Democratic Rep. Harold E. Runnels, who was unopposed for re-election, died on Aug. 5, 1980, after the ballot lineup was set with no Republican having filed. Skeen's write-in campaign yielded him 38 percent of the vote, enough to win the three-way contest.

In each of his re-election contests since then, Democrats generally have had trouble recruiting a candidate who posed a serious threat to Skeen. One of his opponents, Democratic state Rep. E. Shirley Baca of Las Cruces, ran against him twice, in 1996 and 1998. But Baca and others have been hampered by the fact that Skeen has refused since 1992 to debate any of his opponents. He says that voters know where he stands on the issues and that he doesn't want to give his foes any "free publicity."

Skeen's 2000 opponent, state Treasurer Michael A. Montoya, suggested that the congressman ducked debates because he does not want voters to see how badly he has been affected by Parkinson's disease. But Skeen scoffed at the accusation. "I live by myself, I drive myself, I walk myself, I talk myself," he told the Albuquerque Journal sarcastically in October 2000. "I attend all the committee hearings, sometimes two or three at a time. And just look at what I've done. Pretty good for someone with Parkinson's disease."

He could also have pointed out that he was one of only six House members who did not miss a vote in 2000. Skeen won re-election with 58 percent of the vote.

KEY VOTES

2000
No Raise hourly minimum wage by $1 over two years
Yes Halt funding for U.S. mission in Kosovo unless European nations pay more
Yes Provide Medicare benefits to military retirees and their dependents
Yes Grant China permanent normal trade status
Yes Phase out estate, gift and trust taxes
Yes Prohibit implementation of president's national monument designations
Yes Approve GOP plan to provide prescription drug coverage for Medicare beneficiaries
No Increase help for poor nations indebted to international financial institutions

1999
Yes Impose steel import quotas
Yes Kill proposal to take aviation trust funds off budget
Yes Require background checks on buyers only at gun shows with 10 or more vendors
Yes Remove barriers among banking, securities and insurance companies
No Authorize state grants to hire teachers and reduce class size
No Overhaul campaign finance law; ban "soft money" and restrict advocacy advertising
No Approve bipartisan plan to increase rights of patients in managed-care health plans

INTEREST GROUPS

	AFL-CIO	ADA	CCUS	ACU
2000	0%	0%	90%	84%
1999	22%	10%	88%	83%
1998	10%	10%	100%	84%
1997	13%	0%	100%	76%

CQ VOTE STUDIES

	PARTY UNITY		PRESIDENTIAL SUPPORT	
	Support	Oppose	Support	Oppose
2000	93%	7%	29%	71%
1999	89%	11%	23%	77%
1998	89%	11%	27%	73%
1997	91%	9%	32%	68%

NEW MEXICO 2
South – Little Texas; Las Cruces; Roswell

Covering the southern half of New Mexico, the 2nd earned the dubious distinction of having witnessed the first atomic bomb explosion in 1945. More than 50 years later, in 1999, the district opened the first permanent storage facility for radioactive waste from nuclear weapons production and defense-related research. Installed in deep salt beds near Carlsbad, it houses waste from numerous temporary sites throughout the nation.

Towns in the 2nd have built a stable economy on traditional Western industries. The Mexican highlands, along the Arizona border, are blanketed with copper and lead mines. In the southeastern corner of the state, "Little Texas," settled by Texans in the early 20th century, produces oil and gas, as well as cattle and sheep. This region also is home to one of the most prominent salt mines in the nation. While mining is on the decline, high-tech firms are on the rise and dairy farming has become the district's top agricultural product.

Although the 2nd's economy has remained stable, its voting habits have not. Beginning in the 1970s, ranchers and conservative Democrats steered away from a long Democratic tradition. Locally, the district has remained true to its roots, but is now more competitive at the national level.

MAJOR INDUSTRY
Agriculture, mining, oil and gas production

MILITARY BASES
Hollman Air Force Base, 4,008 military, 871 civilian (1999); White Sands Missile Range, 187 military, 2,147 civilian (1999)

CITIES
Las Cruces, 75,786; Roswell, 47,644; Alamogordo, 28,411; Hobbs, 26,898; Carlsbad, 26,262

UNUSUAL FEATURES
White Sands National Monument, world's largest gypsum dune field; Alleged UFO crash outside Roswell in 1947; Billy the Kid stood trial in Mesilla but escaped before being convicted; Very Large Array, grouping of huge telescope dishes that peer deep into space, near Socorro.

Rep. Tom Udall (D)

CAPITOL OFFICE
225-6190; fax 226-1331; 502 Cannon Bldg. 20515

INTERNET
e-mail: tom.udall@mail.house.gov
web: www.house.gov/tomudall

COMMITTEES
Resources
Small Business
Veterans' Affairs

HOMETOWN
Santa Fe

BORN
May 18, 1948, Tuscon, Ariz.

RELIGION
Mormon

FAMILY
Wife, Jill Z. Cooper; one stepchild

EDUCATION
Prescott College, B.A. 1970; Cambridge U., B.L.L.
1975; U. of New Mexico, J.D. 1977

CAREER
Lawyer

POLITICAL HIGHLIGHTS
Assistant U.S. attorney, 1978-81; sought
Democratic nomination for U.S. House, 1982;
Democratic nominee for U.S. House, 1988; N.M.
attorney general, 1991-99

ELECTION RESULTS

2000 GENERAL

Tom Udall (D)	135,040	67.2%
Lisa L. Lutz (R)	65,979	32.8%

2000 PRIMARY

Tom Udall (D)	49,585	82.6%
Francesca Lobato (D)	10,441	17.4%

1998 GENERAL

Tom Udall (D)	91,248	53.2%
Bill Redmond (R)	74,266	43.3%
Carol A. Miller (GREEN)	6,103	3.6%

Elected 1998; 2nd term

As the cousin of a current congressman, the nephew of a former congressman and the son of a former congressman and interior secretary, Udall can claim a family legacy of public service beyond practically anyone whose last name isn't Kennedy. It remains to be seen, though, whether he can transcend his backbencher status and become a substantive lawmaker in the mold of his father and uncle.

Udall and his Colorado cousin, Democrat Mark Udall, were elected to the House on the same day, bringing to Congress a second generation of their family. Tom's father, Stewart, was an Arizona congressman in the late 1950s and then secretary of interior to Presidents Kennedy and Johnson. Morris K. Udall, Tom's uncle and Mark's father, succeeded his brother, Stewart, in the House in 1961 and stayed there until 1991. "From the time I was 6, I heard my father and uncle talk about public service," Tom recalls.

Moving to the House after eight years as New Mexico's attorney general, Udall continues to focus on combating drunken driving, domestic violence, medical fraud and consumer abuse. His assignment to the Resources Committee befits a member of a family of environmentalists. He also serves on the Small Business panel and in 1999 — in an unusual move for a freshman — picked up a third committee assignment, on Veterans' Affairs.

The telegenic Udall, who carries himself with his father's straight-backed assurance and even talks like him, sees a silver lining in having to wait so long to come to Congress. "It deepened my understanding of New Mexico and the needs of its people," he said. "You're not playing the game of catch-up." Although he and his cousin Mark have similar personalities and interests — both are avid mountaineers — he believes his experience as attorney general "gives me a different perspective, a statewide perspective, on how the federal government interacts with the state." He has acknowledged, though, that it has not been easy making the transition from an attorney general's office with 150 employees to a congressional office with a staff of about 20.

Udall takes pains to stay in touch with his constituents, who range from nuclear scientists at Los Alamos National Laboratory to wealthy liberals in Santa Fe to rural Hispanics and Indians living in areas where unemployment remains fixed above 40 percent. He holds frequent town meetings across the district, which encompasses northern New Mexico and is roughly the size of Pennsylvania.

Udall has worked with his younger cousin Mark on legislation, including an effort to create a national environmental stewardship program encouraging volunteers to help preserve parks, forests and other sensitive tracts. Continuing a practice he started as attorney general, he has relied on his wife Jill Z. Cooper, also an attorney, as a close political confidante. Cooper, who was a consultant for the Presidential Commission on Holocaust Assets in 2000, stands in for her husband at events and serves as a sounding board for his ideas.

Udall spent much of his time in the 106th concentrating on matters of local interest, a practical approach for a House freshman in the minority. He worked with other members of the New Mexico delegation to have the federal government purchase the picturesque 95,000-acre Baca Ranch in his district. Udall, who speaks Spanish, reintroduced a measure his predecessor Republican Bill Redmond had sponsored creating a commission to review the claims of heirs to Hispanic land grants. He kept a relatively low profile in the political furor over alleged Chinese spying at Los Alamos, leaving the matter largely to his more senior New Mexico colleagues with greater experience on nuclear weapons issues. He has, however, joined other lawmakers in complaining about the polygraph program that the Energy Department instituted as a result of the scandal.

In response to concerns about online privacy from constituents starting Internet-related businesses, Udall teamed with Rep. Tom Campbell, R-Calif., in 2000 to introduce a bill that would create a government-sanctioned seal of approval for websites that protect privacy.

A reliable Democratic vote, Udall has aligned himself with his party's leaders in the House. He has become a cog in Minority Whip David E. Bonior's whip organization, working to round up votes for the leadership on key measures. He serves on three Democratic Caucus task forces — on education, energy, and health and Medicare.

In the 106th Congress, as chairman of a Democratic campaign finance task force, he urged Republicans to bring to the floor legislation sponsored by Reps. Christopher Shays, R-Conn., and Martin T. Meehan, D-Mass., that would ban "soft money," the unlimited contributions used for party-building activities and issue ads.

Udall also has worked on his party's other priorities, including education and health care, and released a study showing discrepancies in prescription drug prices in his district. He has expressed dissatisfaction with the congressional budget process and voted against the end-of-session catchall appropriations bill in 1999 because he said it contained too many gimmicks.

Udall's 1998 House campaign was his third try: He lost a 1982 Democratic primary for the 3rd District seat to Bill Richardson, who went on to win that year and served seven-plus terms. Then, in 1988, Udall was the Democratic nominee in the adjacent 1st District but lost to Republican Steven H. Schiff.

In 1998, Udall ran again in the 3rd, as local Democrats were eager to oust freshman Republican Redmond, a conservative minister who had won a three-way special election in May 1997 to replace Richardson (who left to become President Clinton's U.N. ambassador).

Udall won an eight-candidate Democratic primary; in the general election, he attacked Redmond as too conservative and won by a comfortable, 10 percentage point margin in the state's most Democratic district.

The Udall family's environmental credentials helped hold liberal Green Party nominee Carol A. Miller to just 4 percent of the vote after she had claimed 17 percent in the 1997 special election.

In 2000, Udall cruised to victory, by a ratio of more than 2-to-1.

KEY VOTES

2000
Yes Raise hourly minimum wage by $1 over two years
? Halt funding for U.S. mission in Kosovo unless European nations pay more
? Provide Medicare benefits to military retirees and their dependents
No Grant China permanent normal trade status
No Phase out estate, gift and trust taxes
No Prohibit implementation of president's national monument designations
No Approve GOP plan to provide prescription drug coverage for Medicare beneficiaries
Yes Increase help for poor nations indebted to international financial institutions

1999
Yes Impose steel import quotas
No Kill proposal to take aviation trust funds off budget
No Require background checks on buyers only at gun shows with 10 or more vendors
Yes Remove barriers among banking, securities and insurance companies
Yes Authorize state grants to hire teachers and reduce class size
Yes Overhaul campaign finance law; ban "soft money" and restrict advocacy advertising
Yes Approve bipartisan plan to increase rights of patients in managed-care health plans

INTEREST GROUPS

	AFL-CIO	ADA	CCUS	ACU
2000	90%	80%	35%	9%
1999	100%	95%	24%	0%

CQ VOTE STUDIES

	PARTY UNITY		PRESIDENTIAL SUPPORT	
	Support	Oppose	Support	Oppose
2000	91%	9%	77%	23%
1999	92%	8%	78%	22%

NEW MEXICO 3

North and East Central — Farmington; Santa Fe

In 1949, artist Georgia O'Keeffe made an adobe house in Abiquiu, a village northwest of Santa Fe, her permanent home. Painting until her death in 1986, O'Keeffe wove the New Mexican desert landscape into her work. Artists and tourists have since been drawn to Santa Fe and Taos to take in the breathtaking scenery and experience its Spanish and American Indian heritage. Art galleries and ski resorts have made the area a growing vacation destination.

But in the counties that ring the district's most populated areas, poverty persists at high rates. Largely Hispanic and American Indian populations struggle at farming and ranching. Alcoholism has a stranglehold on some western reservations. One economic oasis is Los Alamos, where the A-bomb was developed during World War II. A strong white-collar economy has grown up around the city's defense labs. The technology industry also has been growing in Rio Rancho (shared with the 1st District) where Intel has a large operation.

With large Hispanic and Native American populations – and a liberal, affluent base in Santa Fe – the district tilts toward Democratic candidates. Republicans can be found among Los Alamos' wealthy, conservative community, as well as San Juan County in the far northwest, an oil- and gas-producing region.

MAJOR INDUSTRY
State government, ranching, farming, tourism

MILITARY BASES
Cannon Air Force Base, 3,399 military, 393 civilian (1999)

CITIES
Santa Fe, 69,299; Farmington, 40,599; Clovis, 31,504; Rio Rancho (pt.), 30,658 (1990); Gallup, 19,977

UNUSUAL FEATURES
Santa Fe is the second oldest town in the nation, founded in 1607 by the Spanish, 13 years before the Pilgrims landed at Plymouth Rock; Camel Rock, natural formation that looks like a camel, between Santa Fe and Taos; Outdoor Santa Fe Opera; About 100 tribes exhibit at the Indian Market in Santa Fe every August.

Gov. George E. Pataki (R)

First elected: 1994
Length of term: 4 years
Term expires: 1/03
Salary: $178,389
Phone: (518) 474-8390
Hometown: Garrison
Born: June 24, 1945, Peekskill, N.Y.
Religion: Roman Catholic
Family: Wife, Elizabeth "Libby" Pataki; four children
Education: Yale U., B.A. 1967; Columbia U., J.D. 1970
Career: Lawyer; farm owner
Political highlights: Mayor of Peekskill, 1982-84; N.Y. Assembly, 1985-92; N.Y. Senate, 1993-95

Election results:
1998 GENERAL

George E. Pataki (R,C)	2,571,991	54.3%
Peter F. Vallone (D, WFM)	1,570,317	33.2%
Tom Golisano (INDC)	364,056	7.7%
Betsy McCaughey Ross (L)	77,915	1.6%
Michael Reynolds (RTL)	56,683	1.2%
Al Lewis (GREEN)	52,533	1.1%

Lt. Gov. Mary Donohue (R)

First elected: 1998
Length of term: 4 years
Term expires: 1/03
Salary: $151,000
Phone: (518) 474-4623

STATE LEGISLATURE

Legislature: Officially meets year-round; usually meets January-June
Assembly: 150 members, 2-year terms
2001 breakdown: 51R, 99D; 118 men, 32 women
Salary: $79,500
Phone: (518) 455-4218
Senate: 61 members, 2-year terms
2001 breakdown: 36R, 25D; 51 men, 10 women
Salary: $79,500
Phone: (518) 455-3216

STATE TERM LIMITS

Governor: No
Senate and House: No

URBAN STATISTICS

CITY	POPULATION
New York City	7,428,162
Buffalo	295,619
Rochester	214,470
Yonkers	191,458
Syracuse	150,563

REGISTERED VOTERS

Democrat	47%
Republican	28%
Other Parties/Unaffiliated	21%
Independence	2%
Conservative	1%
Liberal	1%

POPULATION

2000 population	18,976,457
1990 population	17,990,455
Percent change	+5.5%
Rank among states	3
Median age	35.5
Born in state	68%
Foreign born	16%
Urban/rural	84%/16%
Crime rate	689/100,000
Poverty level	16.7%
Federal workers	138,893
Military	57,885

REAPPORTIONMENT

New York lost two House seats in reapportionment, dropping from 31 districts to 29. The state legislature will draw new district lines.

MISCELLANEOUS

Web: www.state.ny.us
Capital: Albany
Land area: 47,224 sq. miles
Rank among states: 30
STATE ELECTION OFFICIAL
(518) 474-6220
DEMOCRATIC HEADQUARTERS
(212) 725-8825
REPUBLICAN HEADQUARTERS
(518) 462-2601

District Statistics

	VOTE FOR PRESIDENT																
		2000			1996			1992							HOUSEHOLD	OVER	UNDER	COLLEGE
DIST.	D	R	GREEN	D	R	REF	D	R	I	WHT	BLK	ASIAN	HISP	INCOME	65+	18	EDUCATION
1	52%	43%	3%	51%	36%	11%	38%	40%	21%	93%	4%	2%	4%	$45,464	12%	25%	23%
2	56	40	3	54	34	10	40.0	40.5	19	86	10	2	9	$50,076	10	25	19
3	55	41	3	53	38	7	44	42	14	94	2	3	4	$56,060	13	21	30
4	59	38	2	56	36	6	47	41	12	78	16	3	7	$50,887	15	22	26
5	62	35	3	60	32	6	52	35	12	84	3	11	7	$50,103	15	20	35
6	88	11	1	85	11	3	75	18	6	30	56	6	16	$36,223	11	25	15
7	71	25	3	69	24	5	56	35	9	70	10	12	21	$30,324	17	19	18
8	77	17	6	78	16	3	77	17	6	80	8	6	12	$32,784	15	16	42
9	67	29	3	65	28	5	59	33	9	88	3	6	8	$34,758	20	19	24
10	90	7	3	89	7	2	83	13	4	27	61	2	19	$23,164	10	29	17
11	89	7	3	90	7	1	87	10	3	19	74	3	11	$26,148	9	28	18
12	81	13	6	83	12	3	68	26	5	34	14	20	57	$20,444	8	28	10
13	53	44	3	51	40	7	39	48	13	87	6	6	7	$38,437	14	23	19
14	71	23	5	71	23	3	69	23	7	86	5	6	11	$42,184	16	11	51
15	90	6	4	89	5	2	86	11	3	28	47	2	45	$19,238	12	25	18

District Statistics

DIST.	2000 D	2000 R	GREEN	1996 D	1996 R	REF	1992 D	1992 R	I	WHT	BLK	ASIAN	HISP	HOUSEHOLD INCOME	OVER 65+	UNDER 18	COLLEGE EDUCATION
16	93%	6%	1%	94%	4%	2%	81%	15%	3%	20%	43%	2%	59%	$15,060	7%	34%	6%
17	87	11	2	85	11	3	76	19	5	40	42	4	28	$27,227	14	25	17
18	60	37	3	58	35	5	50	40	9	81	7	8	10	$43,754	17	19	33
19	50	45	4	48	41	9	40	42	17	89	7	2	5	$50,239	11	23	32
20	58	39	3	54	37	8	45	41	14	87	8	3	6	$47,107	11	26	30
21	57	37	5	58	30	10	48	34	18	91	6	2	2	$31,489	15	22	24
22	44	50	5	45	40	13	36	42	22	97	2	1	2	$33,306	13	25	20
23	45	50	4	46	40	13	37	40	23	96	3	1	1	$26,155	15	25	16
24	47.7	47.5	3	49	35	15	37.6	38.2	24	95	3	1	2	$25,687	12	27	14
25	53	42	4	51	38	10	41	36	22	91	7	1	1	$31,080	13	25	23
26	49	44	6	51	35	11	45	35	20	91	6	2	4	$30,335	13	23	23
27	42	53	4	44.3	44.2	11	33	42	25	96	2	1	1	$34,573	13	25	22
28	53	42	4	55	36	7	44	38	18	82	14	2	4	$33,899	13	24	27
29	52	43	4	51	35	12	40	33	27	93	4	1	3	$28,951	15	24	18
30	59	35	4	57	29	12	46	26	28	81	17	1	1	$26,263	15	24	15
31	42	53	4	44	41	14	34	40	26	96	2	1	1	$25,124	15	26	15
STATE	**60**	**35**	**4**	**60**	**31**	**8**	**50**	**34**	**16**	**74**	**16**	**4**	**12**	**$32,965**	**13**	**24**	**23**

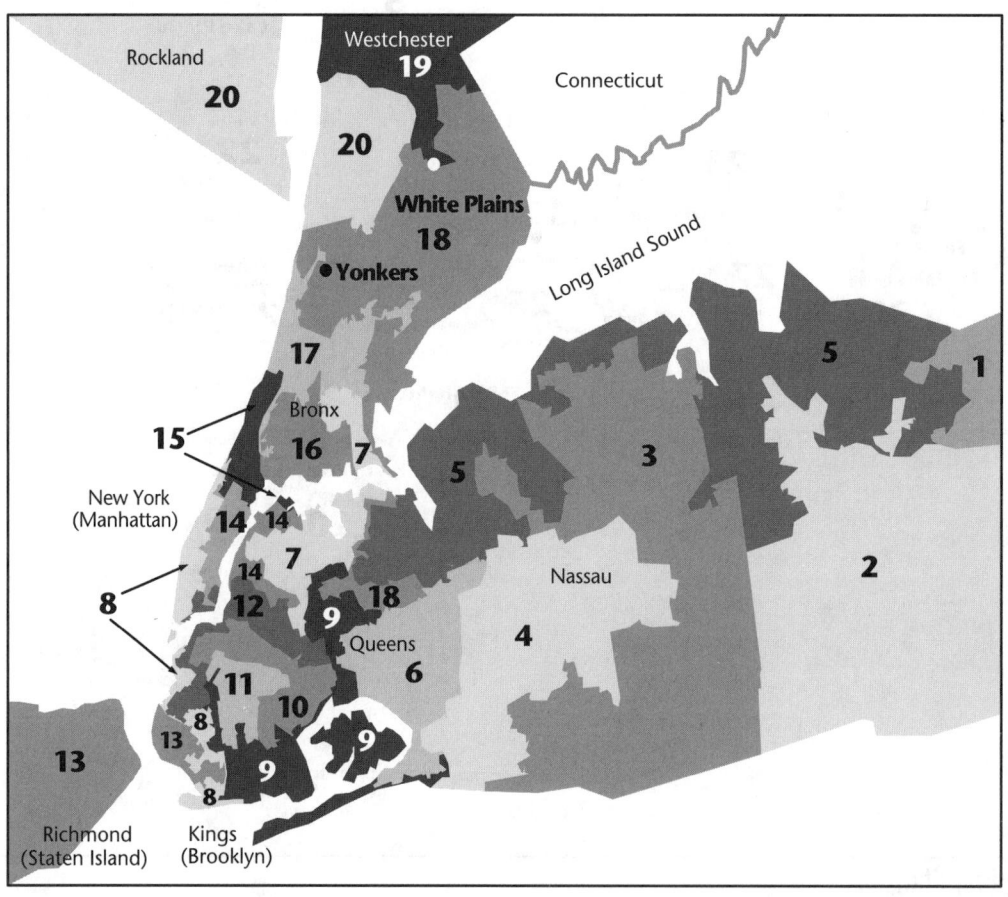

Sen. Charles E. Schumer (D)

CAPITOL OFFICE
224-6542; fax 228-3027; 313 Hart Bldg. 20510

INTERNET
e-mail: senator@schumer.senate.gov
web: schumer.senate.gov

COMMITTEES
Banking, Housing & Urban Affairs
Energy & Natural Resources
Judiciary
Rules & Administration

HOMETOWN
Brooklyn

BORN
Nov. 23, 1950, Brooklyn, N.Y.

RELIGION
Jewish

FAMILY
Wife, Iris Weinshall; two children

EDUCATION
Harvard U., B.A. 1971, J.D. 1974

CAREER
Lawyer

POLITICAL HIGHLIGHTS
N.Y. Assembly, 1975-81; U.S. House, 1981-99

ELECTION RESULTS

1998 GENERAL

Charles E. Schumer (D, INDC, L)	2,551,065	54.6%
Alfonse M. D'Amato (R, C, RTL)	2,058,988	44.1%

1998 PRIMARY

Charles E. Schumer (D)	388,701	50.8%
Geraldine A. Ferraro (D)	201,625	26.4%
Mark Green (D)	145,819	19.1%
Eric Ruano Melendez (D)	28,493	3.7%

PREVIOUS WINNING PERCENTAGES
1996 House Election (75%); 1994 House Election (73%); 1992 House Election (89%); 1990 House Election (80%); 1988 House Election (78%); 1986 House Election (93%); 1984 House Election (72%); 1982 House Election (79%); 1980 House Election (77%)

Elected 1998; 1st term

Schumer stands in proud defiance of those who would vilify "career politicians." The Brooklyn Democrat has spent his entire adult life in politics. "I believe in government. I've devoted my life to government," he says.

In 1998, he devoted his life to a knock-down, drag-out election contest with three-term Republican Sen. Alfonse M. D'Amato and emerged victorious in one of the year's most-watched races.

Many wondered how Schumer, who clearly enjoys his publicity, would deal with being eclipsed in name recognition by his state's junior senator, former first lady Hillary Rodham Clinton. Publicly, he has put on a happy face, praising her and even making a joint Super Bowl bet that forced the two New York senators to recite "The Raven" in front of the cameras after the Baltimore Ravens beat the New York Giants in January 2001. The two have a common ally in Howard Wolfson, who served as a top adviser to both in their Senate campaign. Still, Schumer didn't shy away from criticizing last-minute pardons made as President Clinton left office.

Schumer is an aggressive partisan, who is eager to make his liberal views known. Former Senate Republican leader Bob Dole of Kansas once joked that the most dangerous place to stand in Washington was between Schumer and a TV camera. But it is a measure of Schumer's intellect and hard work that he can talk knowledgeably on a wide range of public policy topics, always providing a dependable read on current liberal thinking.

He works hard to make sure people see him as not only a senator, but also as a working dad from Brooklyn with two daughters who attend public schools. Schumer, whose wife is New York City's transportation director, tries to spend only two nights a week in the Washington home he shares with Illinois Democratic Sen. Richard J. Durbin and California Democratic Rep. George Miller. On the weekend, in between bicycle rides, he races from event to event in New York and proudly states that he has visited each of New York's 62 counties in each of the years he has been a senator.

Upon his arrival in the Senate, Schumer landed seats on the Judiciary and Banking committees. Those are parallel assignments to the ones he had in the House, where he built a lengthy legislative record on such issues as gun control, crime prevention and protections for bank customers. In the 107th Congress, he added an assignment to the Energy Committee, just as soaring oil and gas prices made that a hot venue.

An active legislator by anyone's measurement, Schumer kicked off the 107th Congress at his usual frantic pace. He used his Judiciary Committee assignment to battle Attorney General John Ashcroft's nomination in the opening days of the Bush administration. "John Ashcroft's views and history of zealous advocacy on issues like civil rights, gun control and choice put him so far outside the mainstream that I am unconvinced even after the hearings that he will be the impartial, balanced decision-maker we need and deserve as our attorney general," Schumer said. He also said, in a remark widely quoted, that the fight against Ashcroft was "a shot across the bow" aimed at discouraging President Bush from making similarly divisive judicial nominations in the months and years ahead.

But Schumer also has reached across party lines. In the wake of the vote-counting problems in the 2000 presidential election, he introduced a bill in the 107th Congress with conservative Sen. Sam Brownback, R-Kan., that would establish a commission to examine voting procedures and provide $2.5 billion for states to modernize election systems. He has continued to work with Republican Susan M. Collins of Maine to try to deal with dwindling energy supplies in the Northeast. And he has collaborated with Texas Republican Phil Gramm on banking and energy issues, and with Judiciary Chairman Orrin G. Hatch on high-technology matters.

Schumer tries to serve both business interests and average New Yorkers when possible. After he helped advance a bill in the 106th to reduce securities transaction fees, and also argued for more protection for consumers with bad credit, the American Banker called Schumer "one of the few members of the often-polarized Senate Banking and Judiciary committees that can make both industry and community groups happy."

Schumer may have a national profile but he makes sure to address issues from a local perspective. He has been a sharp critic of Bush's budget priorities, arguing that they could lead to significant cuts in New York's drug treatment and housing programs. "If the president follows through with the cuts in these programs, the gains we've made across the state over the last eight years could become history," he said.

In 1998, Schumer was a familiar face on television as a defender of President Clinton during the impeachment proceedings against the president. Alone among the 435 House members and the 100 senators, Schumer cast votes on the matter in three venues — as a member of the House Judiciary Committee, then on the House floor in the December 1998 lame-duck session, and finally in February 1999 as a freshman senator.

He has long been a leader on gun control initiatives. When the National Rifle Association called him "the criminal's best friend," Schumer shot back: "I wear this like a badge of honor."

During his eight years in the House, Schumer carved out a middle-of-the-road record on other crime-related issues. He initially sided with House Judiciary Committee Republicans in 1997 on a juvenile crime bill aimed at encouraging states to try most juvenile offenders as adults.

On the Banking Committee, he defended consumer interests. In 1996, for instance, he promoted legislation to bolster regulations that require automatic teller machine operators to display notices about fees that are charged to their users.

An outspoken supporter of abortion rights, he helped push through the House a bill providing federal protection for clinics that perform abortions.

After graduating from Harvard University and Harvard Law School, Schumer became a New York state legislative aide, a state Assembly member for three terms, and a U.S. House member by age 29.

In 1998, Schumer decided the time was right to challenge D'Amato, but first he had to win a contentious primary against former Rep. Geraldine A. Ferraro and New York City Public Advocate Mark Green. Though Ferraro had celebrity status from her 1984 vice-presidential nomination, and Green was known statewide from his unsuccessful 1986 race against D'Amato, Schumer had the money; he won by a wide margin.

The general-election campaign between Schumer and D'Amato, two hard-knuckled political scrappers, was no holds barred. The incumbent branded the challenger as a liberal and attacked him for missing more than 100 floor votes while campaigning.

Schumer succeeded in deflecting D'Amato's charge that he was too liberal. He pointed to his anti-crime efforts as a Judiciary Committee member and put his gun control efforts in that context. Schumer cited the history of ethical allegations leveled against D'Amato and accused him of "too many lies for too long."

Though D'Amato spent more than $24 million, Schumer was competitive, spending almost $17 million. Schumer's campaign surged in the days before the election, and he won by almost 500,000 votes.

KEY VOTES

2000

No Overhaul bankruptcy law and increase minimum wage

No Limit fiscal 2001 discretionary spending to $600.3 billion

No Override veto on nuclear waste disposal at Yucca Mountain site in Nevada

Yes Oppose effort to terminate Kosovo mission

Yes Include gender, sexual orientation and disability in federal hate crime protections

No Approve GOP plan to restrict use of genetic information by health insurers

No Kill amendment delaying implementation of an anti-missile defense system

No Cut taxes for married couples

Yes Grant China permanent normal trade status

1999

No Remove President Clinton from office for obstruction of justice

No Kill amendment authorizing state grants to hire teachers and reduce class size

Yes Require criminal background checks for purchases at gun shows

No Approve GOP proposal to increase rights of patients in managed-care health plans

No Block effort to allow farm and medicine exports to Cuba

Yes Allow study of tougher automobile fuel efficiency standards

Yes Ratify nuclear weapons testing treaty

Yes Prohibit national political parties from collecting "soft money" donations

Yes Remove barriers among banking, securities and insurance companies

INTEREST GROUPS

	AFL-CIO	ADA	CCUS	ACU
2000	75%	95%	53%	12%
1999	89%	100%	53%	4%
House Service:				
1998	100%	100%	36%	9%
1997	100%	85%	40%	19%
1996	90%	90%	31%	5%
1995	100%	80%	32%	4%
1994	75%	90%	58%	5%
1993	100%	95%	9%	9%
1992	82%	95%	25%	0%
1991	92%	85%	20%	0%

CQ VOTE STUDIES

	PARTY UNITY		PRESIDENTIAL SUPPORT	
	Support	Oppose	Support	Oppose
2000	97%	3%	98%	2%
1999	94%	6%	91%	9%
House Service:				
1998	94%	6%	85%	15%
1997	90%	10%	83%	17%
1996	91%	9%	83%	17%
1995	89%	11%	87%	13%
1994	94%	6%	83%	17%
1993	97%	3%	83%	17%
1992	95%	5%	19%	81%
1991	93%	7%	28%	72%

Sen. Hillary Rodham Clinton (D)

Elected 2000; 1st term

CAPITOL OFFICE
224-4451; fax 228-0282; 476 Russell Bldg. 20510

INTERNET
e-mail: senator@clinton.senate.gov
web: clinton.senate.gov

COMMITTEES
Budget
Environment & Public Works
Health, Education, Labor & Pensions

HOMETOWN
Chappaqua

BORN
Oct. 26, 1947, Chicago, Ill.

RELIGION
Methodist

FAMILY
Husband, Bill Clinton; one child

EDUCATION
Wellesley College, B.A. 1969; Yale U., J.D. 1973

CAREER
First lady; lawyer; law school professor

POLITICAL HIGHLIGHTS
No previous office

ELECTION RESULTS

2000 GENERAL

Hillary R. Clinton (D, L, WFM)	3,747,310	55.3%
Rick A. Lazio (R, C)	2,915,730	43.0%

2000 PRIMARY

Hillary R. Clinton (D)	565,353	81.9%
Mark McMahon (D)	124,315	18.0%

It is hard to imagine a senator elected with as much fanfare as former first lady Clinton — hailed by her loyalists as a policy innovator and survivor of brutal conservative attacks against her and President Clinton, derided by critics as an overly ambitious, scandal-prone carpetbagger who had no business running for the Senate in New York.

Clinton secured her place in history in 2000, when she became the only first lady ever elected to a federal office, let alone the U.S. Senate. But that lofty distinction is balanced by a distinct disadvantage: She must operate, negotiate and legislate among many colleagues who long ago formed their opinions about her personality and politics.

Yet her strong name recognition plus her poise and persistence proved an asset on the campaign trail in her bid against Republican Rep. Rick A. Lazio. Her eight years in the White House had put her at the center of public attention and controversy. And her international celebrity certainly aided her campaign in a state where she had established residency only the previous year. She beat Lazio handily, by 12 percentage points.

But before election night 2000 even ended, her Senate GOP counterparts reacted to her joining them. "Getting a lot of attention and getting something done in the Senate don't always go hand in hand," said Majority Leader Trent Lott. "If she's smart, she'll keep a pretty low profile for a while."

Those who watched Clinton as the first lady of Arkansas and then of the United States caught healthy glimpses of her liberal views. She has emphasized her concern for the welfare of children ever since her days at Yale Law School and explains her positions on issues such as adoption, education, health care and gun control as extensions of that concern. In her 1996 book, "It Takes a Village," Clinton wrote, "In a democracy, government is not 'them' but 'us,' an endeavor that joins with volunteerism and the efforts of the private sector in sustaining our mutual obligations to our children, families and communities."

Her view of government has led some to describe her as a brilliant, practical political mind. But it has prompted others to decry her as a social engineer who would inject government into all realms of Americans' private lives — critics cite, for example, the sweeping but failed health care overhaul proposal she spearheaded during the first two years of the Clinton presidency.

As a Senate candidate, she focused on education proposals, including one to furnish high-needs schools with 75,000 teachers a year; health care efforts, including enactment of a "patients' bill of rights" and a Medicare prescription drug benefit; and economic revitalization measures such as tax incentives for technology investment.

Beyond her policy stances, Clinton has a reputation as a keen strategist, who excels at building consensus, and a tough and tenacious force, who seldom backs down from confrontation. Her formidable temper in private is well reported, but that is balanced by her remarkably unflappable manner in public. Many Americans will also continue to speculate about the impact on Clinton of her husband's past affair with White House intern Monica Lewinsky, which almost forced President Clinton from office.

Friends and aides have described Clinton's decision to run for the Senate when Democrat Daniel Patrick Moynihan retired as an eagerly awaited graduation of sorts. "I want independence. I want to be judged on my own merits," she said in a 1999 Talk magazine profile. "Now, for the first time, I'm making my own decisions. I can feel the difference. It's a great relief."

Rep. Felix J. Grucci Jr. (R)

Elected 2000; 1st term

CAPITOL OFFICE
225-3826; fax 225-3143
1505 Longworth Bldg. 20515

INTERNET
e-mail: www.house.gov/writerep
web: www.house.gov/grucci

COMMITTEES
Financial Services
Science
Small Business

HOMETOWN
Brookhaven

BORN
Nov. 25, 1951, Brookhaven, N.Y.

RELIGION
Roman Catholic

FAMILY
Wife, Madeline Grucci; two children

EDUCATION
Bellport High School, graduated 1970

CAREER
Fireworks company president

POLITICAL HIGHLIGHTS
Republican nominee for N.Y. Assembly, 1990;
Brookhaven Town Council, 1993-96; Brookhaven
town supervisor, 1996-2000

ELECTION RESULTS

2000 GENERAL

Felix Grucci (R, INDC, C, RTL)	133,020	55.5%
Regina Seltzer (D)	97,299	40.6%
Michael P. Forbes (WFM)	6,318	2.6%
William G. Holst (GREEN)	2,967	1.2%

2000 PRIMARY

Felix Grucci (R)	unopposed

Pundits often refer to partisan disagreements as "political pyrotechnics." But Grucci — a member of the family that owns and has its name on one of the world's largest fireworks firms — puts a new spin on that phrase.

Grucci, who landed seats on the Small Business, Financial Services and Science committees, touts his background in the private sector as a valuable asset. He says his experience as a businessman and local politician — he served eight years in the Brookhaven town government — educated him on how to keep small businesses alive and how to stimulate the economy.

Grucci closely follows the Republican line on most issues. He says his top priorities include protecting Social Security; ending the "marriage penalty," a quirk in the tax code that results in some two-earner married couples paying higher taxes; abolishing the estate tax; and guarding against federal spending sprees.

The congressman finds some room for agreement with Democrats on the environment, however — many residents of the 1st District rely on the ocean for the area's fishing and tourism industries. Grucci says that he supports continued federal investment in cleaning up the Long Island Sound.

Although Grucci's 2000 victory may not have been accompanied by sky-rockets, it did give Republicans something to celebrate: their quick recapture of the 1st District, which had turned over to the Democrats with the unexpected July 1999 party switch of three-term Rep. Michael P. Forbes.

Forbes said that his change of party was in response to the House GOP leadership's conservative "extremism." The switch spurred Republicans to vow revenge, yet it did not win over local Democrats who had been hostile to Forbes' conservative record — which included a vote to impeach President Clinton.

Grucci and the Republican Party geared up for an effort to oust Forbes, but the chance never came: Forbes did not make it to the general election, losing in the Democratic primary to party activist Regina Seltzer. The better-known and better-funded Grucci coasted to a 15 percentage point victory in November.

NEW YORK 1

Eastern Suffolk County — Brookhaven; Smithtown

Covering the eastern two-thirds of Long Island's Suffolk County, the 1st reaches out into the Atlantic Ocean. At its far eastern end, the 1st takes in the elite estates of some of New York's wealthiest in the Hamptons and Shelter Island. The rural end of the island has retained its pastoral character, with fishing villages, farms and wineries scattered throughout.

Moving west, the 1st takes in some blue-collar towns, populated by conservative Irish-Catholics and Italian-Americans. Towns at the district's far west, in Smithtown and Brookhaven, have boomed with suburban growth. Defense once dominated industry in the 1st, but scientific research has since replaced many of those jobs, attracted by the State University of New York in Stony Brook and Brookhaven

National Laboratory.

The 1st's lingering rural temperament and small-town feel make it one of the most conservative districts near New York City. Voter registration favors Republicans, but the district's brand of conservatism remains moderate, with many residents supporting more liberal views on abortion and gun control. Environmental issues rank high in the 1st, as many of the Island's towns depend on the ocean for fish and tourism. While Democrats represented the 1st for many of the past 30 years, the district has leaned Republican in recent years.

MAJOR INDUSTRY
Higher education, medicine, research

CITIES
Brookhaven (unincorporated), 407,779 (1990); Smithtown (pt.), 65,830 (1990); South Hampton (unincorporated), 44,976 (1990)

UNUSUAL FEATURES
The Big Duck, a 20-foot duck-shaped structure and museum in Flanders in South Hampton.

Rep. Steve Israel (D)

CAPITOL OFFICE
225-3335; fax 225-4669; 429 Cannon Bldg. 20515

INTERNET
e-mail: www.house.gov/writerep
web: www.house.gov/israel

COMMITTEES
Financial Services
Science

HOMETOWN
Dix Hills

BORN
May 30, 1958, Brooklyn, N.Y.

RELIGION
Jewish

FAMILY
Wife, Randi Israel; two children

EDUCATION
Nassau Community College, A.A. 1978; Syracuse U., attended 1978-79; George Washington U., B.A. 1982

CAREER
Public relations and marketing firm manager; assistant county executive; university fundraising director; Jewish advocacy group county director; congressional aide

POLITICAL HIGHLIGHTS
Huntington Town Board, 1993-2001 (majority leader, 1997-2001)

ELECTION RESULTS

2000 GENERAL

Steve Israel (D)	90,438	47.9%
Joan B. Johnson (R)	65,880	34.9%
Robert T. Walsh Sr. (RTL)	11,224	6.0%
Richard Thompson (C)	10,824	5.7%
D. Bishop (INDC, GREEN, WFM)	10,266	5.4%

2000 PRIMARY

Steve Israel (D)	6,004	45.4%
David Bishop (D)	5,449	41.2%
Ghenya B. Grant (D)	1,785	13.5%

Elected 2000; 1st term

Israel's takeover of Long Island's 2nd District seat in 2000 was a Democratic coup, but he will have to protect his flanks in the politically competitive district that elected Republican Rick A. Lazio four times.

So it was not surprising to see Israel sign on with the centrist New Democrat Coalition and take a seat on the Financial Services Committee upon his arrival in the 107th Congress. Israel — who had eyed a run for Congress ever since his years as an aide to New York Democratic Rep. Richard L. Ottinger in the early 1980s — also was chosen as the only freshman representative on the Democratic Steering Committee, which doles out committee assignments.

Israel characterizes himself as a fiscal conservative, calling for continued reduction of the national debt as a high priority. During his eight years on the Huntington Town Board, Israel had worked to cut the town's long-term debt in half. He objected during the 2000 campaign to the broad tax cuts that many Republicans advocate.

Placing health care at the top of his list of legislative concerns, Israel contends that many Long Island senior citizens have been rejected by their health maintenance organizations because reimbursement rates for Suffolk County were set too low in Medicare spending restraints approved in 1997.

The congressman opposes proposals that would permit people to divert some Social Security taxes to private investments.

Israel had to work hard and fast to win the House seat. Because of uncertainty over the popular Lazio's plans — he did not announce his Senate bid against Democrat Hillary Rodham Clinton until May 2000 — Israel got off to a late start. He then had to fight to a narrow win over Suffolk County legislator David Bishop in a three-way Sept. 12 Democratic primary.

Israel expected a tough race with the Republican nominee, Islip Town Clerk Joan Johnson. But Johnson proved to be a less-seasoned campaigner and lost votes to two conservative minor-party candidates, who opposed her moderate views on social issues.

In the end, Israel prevailed over Johnson by 13 percentage points.

NEW YORK 2
Western Suffolk County; Islip; Babylon

Taking in the central part of Long Island and covering western Suffolk County, the 2nd is full of suburban communities that popped up all over Suffolk County's potato fields during the post-World War II suburban boom. Now, the 2nd is home to a burgeoning computer sector and a waning defense industry.

Most of the district's white-collar workforce commutes to New York City. The district's indigenous industry has long been blue-collar. Defense plants hummed during the height of the Cold War, but the fall of the Iron Curtain brought job losses to the district. Computer and electronics firms have helped fill the void.

With some of the most affordable land on Long Island, the 2nd houses a solid middle class with a relatively large minority population in comparison to the adjacent 1st and 3rd districts. It's also home to Fire Island, a beach-side community where many of New York's affluent retreat for the summer.

With a 20 percent minority population, a significant Jewish community and a blue-collar base, the 2nd has a substantial Democratic vote, but the GOP has an edge in voter registration. A large number of independent voters makes this district competitive for centrist candidates of both parties. A Republican held the seat for most of the 1990s, but the 2nd went back to Democratic control in 2000.

MAJOR INDUSTRY
Computers, electronics, service

CITIES
Islip (unincorporated), 299,587 (1990); Babylon (unincorporated), 202,889 (1990); Huntington (pt.) (unincorporated), 67,733 (1990)

UNUSUAL FEATURES
Fire Island National Seashore separates the Atlantic Ocean from the Great South Bay.

Rep. Peter T. King (R)

Elected 1992; 5th term

King takes on all comers, both within and outside the Republican Party, and his pugilistic manner often draws headlines. During the 2000 presidential race, he denounced GOP candidate George W. Bush for speaking at Bob Jones University, a bastion of religious conservatism. In 1998, he sharply criticized Majority Whip Tom DeLay for blocking the House from voting to censure President Clinton as an alternative to impeachment. In 1997, he called Speaker Newt Gingrich "roadkill on the highway of American politics," saying the GOP leader was drifting to the political center.

King is difficult to categorize politically. He is conservative on some social policy matters, such as abortion. He favors making English the official language of the United States and urges tough measures to combat the smuggling of illegal aliens into the country.

But he voted for several high-profile Democratic initiatives in the 106th Congress, including a gun control bill and a plan to grant managed-care patients the right to sue their health care providers. Despite free-trade leanings, he sided with labor unions in 2000 by voting against granting China permanent normal trade status.

Yet he often shuns Democratic spending initiatives, preferring to cut taxes instead. And he favors giving states more authority over federal programs. Working well with members on both sides of the aisle, he has won federal dollars for district projects, including critical transportation routes.

A veteran of the rough-and-tumble politics in Nassau County, King says confrontation and partisanship are natural elements of the legislative and political business. "I really believe that democracy is a contact sport," he told Newsday. He has said that he places that sport "somewhere between roller derby and a 25-round fight."

Although King is one of the best-known members of the House because of his frequent television appearances and slashing commentary, he lacks major legislative accomplishments. He wants to cut taxes for married couples, beef up the nation's defense and shore up the long-term solvency of the Social Security system, but he has seldom introduced bills or held press conferences on such matters. "I'm not on the committees in question," he told Newsday. "I respect another member's turf. ... When it comes time for me to call in a favor for my district, I'm more inclined to get it."

When King has an opinion on an issue, however, he lets people know. A vigorous proponent of raising the minimum wage, he assailed Republicans in 1996 who portrayed the increase as a Democratic payoff to labor unions. "Instead of going for solid working people, people who work hard, are patriotic and put their kids through school, the people who would be role models for Republican campaign commercials, we're driving them away," King contended. "We're going to turn ourselves into a party of barefoot hillbillies who go to revival meetings."

King won national attention during the House's impeachment debate in 1998. He argued strenuously in the media that pursuing Clinton's impeachment was not the proper course. "The president should be tried and indicted after he leaves office, but we should not set a standard where a president can be subject to the whims of civil suit and independent counsel while he is in office," he said on NBC. He also told The Washington Post that GOP Whip DeLay intimidated party moderates skeptical of impeachment to get them to fall in with the party line. "There are a number of moderates who have spoken to me who are literally scared stiff," he said. King was one of

CAPITOL OFFICE
225-7896; fax 226-2279; 436 Cannon Bldg. 20515

INTERNET
e-mail: pete.king@mail.house.gov
web: www.house.gov/king

COMMITTEES
Financial Services
(Domestic Monetary Policy, Technology & Economic Growth - chairman)
International Relations

HOMETOWN
Seaford

BORN
April 5, 1944, Manhattan, N.Y.

RELIGION
Roman Catholic

FAMILY
Wife, Rosemary King; two children

EDUCATION
St. Francis College, B.A. 1965; U. of Notre Dame, J.D. 1968

MILITARY SERVICE
N.Y. National Guard, 1968-73

CAREER
Lawyer

POLITICAL HIGHLIGHTS
Hempstead Town Council, 1978-81; Nassau County comptroller, 1981-93

ELECTION RESULTS

2000 GENERAL

Peter T. King (R, INDC, C, RTL)	143,126	59.5%
Dal LaMagna (D, GREEN, WFM)	95,787	39.8%

2000 PRIMARY

Peter T. King (R)	8,651	77.6%
Robert Previdi (R)	2,495	22.4%

1998 GENERAL

Peter T. King (R, RTL)	117,258	64.3%
Kevin N. Langberg (D)	63,628	34.9%

PREVIOUS WINNING PERCENTAGES
1996 (55%); 1994 (59%); 1992 (50%)

only four Republicans who voted against all four articles of impeachment.

King had a series of high-profile run-ins and reconciliations with Speaker Gingrich. Late in the 104th, King said he would oppose Gingrich's re-election as Speaker because he felt that the focus on Gingrich's ethics problems would distract from the party's legislative goals. But after Gingrich won overwhelming support in the party conference, King fell in line behind the Speaker, and he even came to his defense during an aborted coup by GOP conservatives, saying disgruntled members should "stand behind their leader and give him the support that he needs."

In the 107th Congress, King chairs the Financial Services panel's Domestic Monetary Policy, Technology and Economic Growth Subcommittee.

On the International Relations Committee, King is best known as an avid and outspoken advocate of ending British rule in Northern Ireland. King is a confidant of Gerry Adams, the leader of Sinn Fein, the political wing of the Irish Republican Army (IRA). In 1997, he accused Senate Foreign Relations Committee Chairman Jesse Helms of "bigotry and ignorance" after the North Carolina Republican suggested that the IRA be labeled a terrorist organization under U.S. terrorism laws.

King, who has a sizable Irish-American constituency, also has worked on issues affecting Irish immigrants. He cosponsored a bill that set up a three-year program to allow 4,000 disadvantaged Irish citizens to come to the United States each year to learn job skills they could take back to Ireland.

Born to Irish immigrants, King grew up in a blue-collar Queens neighborhood and borrowed money to go to law school at Notre Dame. He first entered government in 1972 as a Nassau County deputy attorney and eventually became the county comptroller. When veteran GOP Rep. Norman F. Lent announced in June 1992 that he would not seek re-election, King moved with characteristic dispatch to establish himself as his successor, contending that his government experience would help him get things done in Washington.

After coasting through the primary, King faced a difficult general-election contest against Democrat Steve A. Orlins, a senior consultant to American Express who boasted a campaign treasury four times the size of King's. King accused Orlins of being "a carpetbagging millionaire" from Manhattan who was "trying to buy the election." Orlins, who grew up on Long Island, had lived in Manhattan until he rented a house in the 3rd District in July. King's long history of involvement in local civic and political affairs helped him hold the GOP-leaning district, and he beat Orlins by 4 percentage points. He has since cruised to re-election by comfortable margins.

KEY VOTES

2000
Yes	Raise hourly minimum wage by $1 over two years
No	Halt funding for U.S. mission in Kosovo unless European nations pay more
Yes	Provide Medicare benefits to military retirees and their dependents
No	Grant China permanent normal trade status
Yes	Phase out estate, gift and trust taxes
Yes	Prohibit implementation of president's national monument designations
Yes	Approve GOP plan to provide prescription drug coverage for Medicare beneficiaries
No	Increase help for poor nations indebted to international financial institutions

1999
Yes	Impose steel import quotas
No	Kill proposal to take aviation trust funds off budget
Yes	Require background checks on buyers only at gun shows with 10 or more vendors
Yes	Remove barriers among banking, securities and insurance companies
No	Authorize state grants to hire teachers and reduce class size
No	Overhaul campaign finance law; ban "soft money" and restrict advocacy advertising
Yes	Approve bipartisan plan to increase rights of patients in managed-care health plans

INTEREST GROUPS

	AFL-CIO	ADA	CCUS	ACU
2000	40%	15%	55%	64%
1999	44%	30%	54%	75%
1998	30%	10%	82%	76%
1997	75%	25%	40%	64%

CQ VOTE STUDIES

	PARTY UNITY		PRESIDENTIAL SUPPORT	
	Support	Oppose	Support	Oppose
2000	77%	23%	45%	55%
1999	79%	21%	32%	68%
1998	82%	18%	31%	69%
1997	83%	17%	32%	68%

NEW YORK 3

Eastern Nassau County — Oyster Bay

Most of Long Island's eastern Nassau County is included in the 3rd, where extravagant estates mingle with some of the nation's oldest suburbs. A wealthy district, the 3rd has New York's highest median income and the third-highest median income nationwide, according to 1990 Census Bureau statistics.

The Republican Party has long been a potent force in the 3rd, even with the district's significant labor presence from construction and professional unions. Most of the 3rd's elected officials are Republicans, but Democrats are gaining strength in Nassau County because of the county's recent financial problems, resulting in a changing of the guard.

Pockets of Democratic support exist in Plainview, Jericho and Long Beach, where many of the residents are Jewish. Bill Clinton won the district in 1992 and '96 and Al Gore won it in 2000, showcasing the 3rd's willingness to vote independent of party.

The 3rd's economy faltered when post-Cold War defense cutbacks in the 1980s caused major employer Northrop Grumman, an aircraft and electronics manufacturer, to scale back and later withdraw from the district. But the 3rd has since diversified its economy, expanding its base in information technology, and enjoying a low unemployment rate.

MAJOR INDUSTRY
Information technology, higher education

CITIES
Oyster Bay (unincorporated) (pt.), 267,080 (1990); Hempstead (unincorporated) (pt.) 239,536 (1990); Long Beach, 34,367

UNUSUAL FEATURES
President Theodore Roosevelt's Sagamore Hill estate in Cove Neck near Long Island Sound; Comedian Jerry Seinfeld grew up in Massapequa; Actor Billy Crystal from Long Beach; President Richard M. Nixon's dog Checkers buried at the Bide-a-Wee Association Pet Cemetery Memorial Park in Wantagh.

Rep. Carolyn McCarthy (D)

Elected 1996; 3rd term

CAPITOL OFFICE
225-5516; fax 225-5758
1224 Longworth Bldg. 20515

INTERNET
e-mail: www.house.gov/writerep
web: www.house.gov/carolynmccarthy

COMMITTEES
Budget
Education & Workforce

HOMETOWN
Mineola

BORN
Jan. 5, 1944, Brooklyn, N.Y.

RELIGION
Roman Catholic

FAMILY
Widowed; one child

EDUCATION
Glen Cove Nursing School, L.P.N. 1964

CAREER
Nurse

POLITICAL HIGHLIGHTS
No previous office

ELECTION RESULTS

2000 GENERAL

Carolyn McCarthy (D, INDC, WFM)	136,703	60.6%
Greg R. Becker (R, C, RTL)	87,830	38.9%

2000 PRIMARY

Carolyn McCarthy (D)	unopposed

1998 GENERAL

Carolyn McCarthy (D)	90,256	52.6%
Greg R. Becker (R)	79,984	46.6%

PREVIOUS WINNING PERCENTAGES
1996 (57%)

When McCarthy rose to speak on the House floor at 1 a.m. on June 18, 1999, a hush fell over the chamber. The widowed lawmaker, with tears flowing down her cheeks, implored her colleagues to support her amendment to toughen background check requirements for the purchase of a weapon at a gun show.

She told lawmakers that she had promised her slain husband and her seriously injured son that she would do anything she could to prevent more deaths from shootings. "I am Irish and I am not supposed to cry in front of anyone. But I made a promise a long time ago. ... If there was anything that I could do to prevent one family from going through what I have gone through then I have done my job," she said.

She knew that she had connected emotionally, particularly in the aftermath of a mass shooting in a Colorado high school. Minority Leader Richard A. Gephardt later said it was one of the most stirring speeches he had ever heard. But when the House voted, McCarthy once again found herself on the losing end of a gun control vote — the issue that propelled her into politics.

It all started in December 1993, when a deranged gunman opened fire on a Long Island Rail Road commuter train. Among the victims was McCarthy's husband, who was killed, and her adult son, who was seriously wounded. The "incident," as McCarthy calls it, spurred her to become an advocate for stricter gun control laws.

But when her representative in Congress — 4th District Republican Daniel Frisa — voted in 1996 to eliminate a 1994 ban on semiautomatic weapons, the suburban Long Island widow, a lifelong Republican, was incensed. When local party officials squelched her inquiries about mounting a primary challenge to Frisa, she gave up her GOP registration and launched a Democratic campaign to unseat him.

She raised more than $1 million and outspent Frisa, whom she tied to Speaker Newt Gingrich and the controversial House Republican effort to scale back projected spending increases in Medicaid and Medicare. Frisa seemed at a loss for an effective response to McCarthy, and in the final days of the campaign, he shunned appearances and interviews. McCarthy rolled to victory by 17 percentage points, taking 57 percent of the vote. In 2000, she bumped her victory margin up to 22 points.

The world of Washington politics initially was not altogether welcoming to McCarthy. The Republican majority, which supports gun owners' rights, has not given McCarthy many chances to shine (witness the 1 a.m. timing of her speech to wrap up the background check amendment), realizing the powerful gun control symbol that she has become. And Democrats assigned her to the Education and the Workforce and Small Business committees, rather than a high-profile assignment such as Commerce or Judiciary.

In the 106th Congress, McCarthy emerged as an important voice on health care issues — she is a licensed practical nurse — and she also weighed in on plans to make college more accessible and to increase the minimum wage. And in the 107th, she won a seat on the Budget panel, trading in her seat on Small Business. But she continues to focus her energies on reducing gun violence. "That is why I came to Congress," she says.

And so she presses her case whenever she can. A rare opportunity came for McCarthy in 1997, just a few months after she arrived on Capitol Hill, when a GOP-authored juvenile crime bill came to the floor. McCarthy and her gun control allies sought to add language to the measure requiring childproof trigger locks on all guns. The GOP leadership blocked the move. But the debate provoked enough public response for the Clinton administration to win concessions from eight major gun manufacturers, which agreed voluntarily to a White House call for trigger locks on all guns made in the United States.

Despite repeated legislative setbacks, McCarthy seems more determined than ever — especially after the birth of her first grandson, named for her slain husband. "I've come to the realization this is going to take a while," she told Newsday in 2000. Refocusing her efforts on incremental steps, she succeeded in the 106th in winning funding for 500 new federal agents to battle gun violations.

Critics accuse her of being a one-issue lawmaker, and McCarthy has acknowledged that her name will be forever linked to the issue of gun control. "I've come to peace with the fact that that will be in my obituary," she told The Associated Press.

Although her Democratic roots are shallow, she is comfortable among her new brethren. She is a backer of abortion rights and environmental protections, and she is a steady friend of labor. In 2000, she sided with labor by voting against legislation granting China permanent normal trade status.

McCarthy also strives to reach across the aisle, and there are some bows to conservatism in her voting record: She backed constitutional amendments outlawing desecration of the U.S. flag and requiring a two-thirds congressional majority to raise federal taxes. In the 106th, she voted to repeal the estate tax and the "marriage penalty"; she supported efforts to override President Clinton's vetoes of those bills.

Drawing on more than 30 years' experience as a nurse, McCarthy has become an important player on health-related bills, especially seeking more federal funds for breast cancer research. She supports efforts to give managed-care patients the right to sue their health care plans, pointing out that members of Congress and federal employees already have that right. "If it's good enough for us, why isn't it good enough for everyone else?"

And as one who struggled with dyslexia as a child, she has spoken for more federal aid for school districts to cope with the costs of educating learning-disabled children. She has backed multibillion-dollar Democratic plans to pay for new teachers and renovate aging schools, while opposing GOP proposals for school vouchers.

She has pledged to keep focusing on her signature issue. When longtime Democratic supporter Barbra Streisand wanted to produce a television movie based on her life, McCarthy agreed to cooperate with the making of the film — but only if it contained no scenes of gun violence.

KEY VOTES

2000
Yes Raise hourly minimum wage by $1 over two years
No Halt funding for U.S. mission in Kosovo unless European nations pay more
Yes Provide Medicare benefits to military retirees and their dependents
No Grant China permanent normal trade status
Yes Phase out estate, gift and trust taxes
No Prohibit implementation of president's national monument designations
No Approve GOP plan to provide prescription drug coverage for Medicare beneficiaries
Yes Increase help for poor nations indebted to international financial institutions

1999
Yes Impose steel import quotas
No Kill proposal to take aviation trust funds off budget
No Require background checks on buyers only at gun shows with 10 or more vendors
Yes Remove barriers among banking, securities and insurance companies
Yes Authorize state grants to hire teachers and reduce class size
Yes Overhaul campaign finance law; ban "soft money" and restrict advocacy advertising
Yes Approve bipartisan plan to increase rights of patients in managed-care health plans

INTEREST GROUPS

	AFL-CIO	ADA	CCUS	ACU
2000	70%	65%	65%	24%
1999	75%	90%	44%	8%
1998	80%	90%	61%	24%
1997	86%	80%	50%	16%

CQ VOTE STUDIES

	PARTY UNITY		PRESIDENTIAL SUPPORT	
	Support	Oppose	Support	Oppose
2000	84%	16%	68%	32%
1999	89%	11%	77%	23%
1998	82%	18%	68%	32%
1997	85%	15%	70%	30%

NEW YORK 4
Southwest Nassau County — Hempstead; Mineola

Wealthy New York City suburbanites and Wall Street commuters populate much of the 4th, which consumes the southwest corner of Long Island's Nassau County and borders eastern Queens. Median household income in the district is the second highest in New York, according to 1990 Census Bureau statistics.

With the largest minority population of Long Island's suburban congressional districts, Democrats have a base to draw on in the 4th, particularly in Hempstead and Uniondale, which include large black and Hispanic communities. The affluent and largely Jewish "Five Towns" (Inwood, Lawrence, Cedarhurst, Woodmere and Hewlett) are located in the 4th's southwestern corner and lean Democratic. But overall voter registration heavily favors the GOP.

District politics were competitive in the 1990s, with independent and socially moderate voters electing four different representatives during the decade. The district elected Republicans until 1996, when voters chose a pro-gun-control Democrat and then re-elected her to two more terms. The district voted for Bill Clinton in both of his presidential bids, overwhelmingly so in 1996. And in the 2000 presidential contest, Al Gore secured the district with 59 percent of the vote.

Some of the political upheaval may be tied to economic turmoil that began with the 1980s decline of the defense industry on which Long Island was heavily dependent. The district continues to rebuild and diversify, focusing on technology and small business. A number of working-class residents are employed by John F. Kennedy International Airport (across the district line in Queens' 6th District), Belmont Park race track, and large shopping centers such as Roosevelt Field and Green Acres.

MAJOR INDUSTRY
Health care, higher education

CITIES
Hempstead (unincorporated) (pt.), 486,103 (1990); North Hempstead (unincorporated) (pt.), 94,235 (1990)

UNUSUAL FEATURES
Charles Lindbergh departed for Paris from Roosevelt Field in Mineola.

Rep. Gary L. Ackerman (D)

CAPITOL OFFICE
225-2601; fax 225-1589; 2243 Rayburn Bldg. 20515

INTERNET
e-mail: gary_ackerman@mail.house.gov
web: www.house.gov/ackerman

COMMITTEES
Financial Services
International Relations

HOMETOWN
Queens

BORN
Nov. 19, 1942, Brooklyn, N.Y.

RELIGION
Jewish

FAMILY
Wife, Rita Ackerman; three children

EDUCATION
Queens College, B.A. 1965

CAREER
Teacher; publisher and editor; advertising executive

POLITICAL HIGHLIGHTS
Sought Democratic nomination for N.Y. City Council at large, 1977; N.Y. Senate, 1979-83

ELECTION RESULTS

2000 GENERAL

Ackerman (D, INDC, L, WFM)	137,684	68.0%
Edward Elkowitz (R, C)	61,084	30.2%
Anne T. Robinson (RTL)	3,846	1.9%

2000 PRIMARY

Ackerman (D)	unopposed

1998 GENERAL

Ackerman (D, INDC, L)	97,404	65.0%
David C. Pinzon (R, C)	49,586	33.1%
Anne T. Robinson (RTL)	2,872	1.9%

PREVIOUS WINNING PERCENTAGES
1996 (64%); 1994 (55%); 1992 (52%); 1990 (100%); 1988 (100%); 1986 (77%); 1984 (69%); 1983 Special Election (50%)

Elected March 1983; 9th full term

The quick-witted, boutonniere-sporting, liberal dean of New York's Long Island contingent, Ackerman is known for his sharp tongue and parliamentary stunts to get in his digs at the chamber's GOP majority.

In the 106th Congress, Ackerman's caustic broadsides were on full display. When the House took up a constitutional amendment in 1999 to ban desecration of the American flag, he came to the floor wearing a tie depicting the American flag and a red, white and blue badge. Such symbols, he argued, could be limited by the amendment. He also called the Howard Stern radio show, saying he was "naked and draped in the flag," according to his press secretary. "The real threat to our society is not the occasional burning of a flag, but the permanent banning of the burners," Ackerman said.

His staunchly liberal views on education, health care and the environment seldom prevail, but persistence (and some sarcasm) help Ackerman get his voice heard above the fray. During the tense moments before House members voted, late in 1998, on whether to launch an impeachment inquiry against President Clinton, Ackerman quipped: "I move that when the House adjourn, we do so to Salem, a quaint village in the Commonwealth of Massachusetts, whose history beckons us thence."

The remark — a reference to the site of the infamous 17th century witch trials — drew hisses from some Republicans on the floor but elicited a wry smile from House Speaker Newt Gingrich before he ruled Ackerman out of order.

Ackerman scoffs at pretension and convention. His residence in Washington is a houseboat on the Potomac called the Unsinkable II. (The original Unsinkable sank.)

A senior member of the International Relations Committee, Ackerman has become a respected voice on foreign policy, arguing that in the post-Cold War era, the United States should play an active role in promoting democracy abroad. Praised by Newsday for having "a thorough and nuanced grasp of foreign policy," he travels overseas often. He cites his first-hand experiences in foreign nations when urging measured responses to developments in India, North Korea, China and elsewhere.

He contends that to promote global security, the United States must remain actively engaged in dialogue even with nations such as China and North Korea that are allegedly involved in weapons proliferation. Breaking with his allies in labor, he voted in 2000 to grant China permanent normal trade status.

Similarly, he voted against a 1998 proposal to ban the export of U.S. satellites to China. The measure was pushed by Republicans — and embraced by many Democrats — in response to evidence that such technology transfers had helped China develop a nuclear arms capability. "If we don't deal with China, none of the issues that we believe are important will be addressed," Ackerman later said.

Ackerman first ventured into the realm of public policy in 1969. A social studies teacher and new father, he successfully sued the New York City Board of Education for the right of a father to receive unpaid leave to care for a newborn child. ("Maternity" leave was offered only to women.) He subsequently had run-ins with the Queens Democratic machine as a publisher of a weekly newspaper, and he lost as an independent in a 1977 challenge to a city council incumbent.

But he won a state Senate seat in 1978, and, after Democratic Rep.

Benjamin S. Rosenthal died in early 1983, Ackerman convinced Democratic leaders that he was the party's best hope in the special-election race against a wealthy independent, pollster Douglas Schoen, and a less competitive GOP candidate. He won the special election with 50 percent of the vote and cruised through four re-elections in the then-7th District, a mainly urban constituency that included many loyally Democratic Jewish and Hispanic voters.

After redistricting in 1992 removed much of his base in Queens and put him in the more conservative suburban Long Island 5th District, Ackerman faced a more difficult re-election battle. In addition to losing much of his base, he was caught up in the ruckus over the House's private bank for members, where he had 111 overdrafts. But he prevailed by 7 percentage points over GOP Suffolk County Legislator Allan E. Binder by rolling up a big margin in what remained of his Queens district. He has since won by comfortable margins.

Ackerman is an outspoken ally of India, and he has successfully battled repeated efforts by conservative Rep. Dan Burton, R-Ind., to cut aid to India. In the 105th, he dubbed such a Burton proposal "India bashing," adding, "It seems to me that the oldest democracy in the world should not be sanctioning the largest. That is not the way democracies treat each other."

Ackerman also succeeded in blocking a Republican proposal to ban most aid to nations that fail to support U.S. positions on at least one out of every four roll call votes at the United Nations General Assembly. He said it was a thinly disguised attempt to slash aid to India, one of four nations that did not meet that standard of support. (The other three — Cuba, Syria and North Korea — are already barred from U.S. aid in other ways.)

In addition to pursuing his international interests, Ackerman tackles many matters of parochial concern in the sprawling and diverse 5th. He saved the U.S. Coast Guard station at Eatons Neck from closing, he lobbies relentlessly for funds to clean up Long Island Sound, and he pushed for resolving the 1994 Long Island Rail Road strike.

Despite his liberal outlook, Ackerman has the capacity to work with ideological opposites, as he demonstrated in the 104th Congress when he joined conservative Tom Coburn, R-Okla., in passing a measure to provide that newborns be tested for AIDS and their mothers be told the results.

"You have to be willing to compromise," Ackerman told Newsday in the 105th. "Part of the problem is there is a group of Republicans down here who believe they are locked in a battle, not between good and bad, but between good and evil. Those who believe that way, they can't compromise with evil."

KEY VOTES

2000
Yes	Raise hourly minimum wage by $1 over two years
No	Halt funding for U.S. mission in Kosovo unless European nations pay more
?	Provide Medicare benefits to military retirees and their dependents
Yes	Grant China permanent normal trade status
No	Phase out estate, gift and trust taxes
No	Prohibit implementation of president's national monument designations
No	Approve GOP plan to provide prescription drug coverage for Medicare beneficiaries
Yes	Increase help for poor nations indebted to international financial institutions

1999
Yes	Impose steel import quotas
No	Kill proposal to take aviation trust funds off budget
No	Require background checks on buyers only at gun shows with 10 or more vendors
Yes	Remove barriers among banking, securities and insurance companies
Yes	Authorize state grants to hire teachers and reduce class size
Yes	Overhaul campaign finance law; ban "soft money" and restrict advocacy advertising
Yes	Approve bipartisan plan to increase rights of patients in managed-care health plans

INTEREST GROUPS

	AFL-CIO	ADA	CCUS	ACU
2000	90%	80%	41%	13%
1999	78%	100%	29%	0%
1998	100%	100%	35%	0%
1997	100%	80%	33%	13%

CQ VOTE STUDIES

	PARTY UNITY		PRESIDENTIAL SUPPORT	
	Support	Oppose	Support	Oppose
2000	96%	4%	94%	6%
1999	97%	3%	87%	13%
1998	97%	3%	86%	14%
1997	96%	4%	82%	18%

NEW YORK 5

Northeast Queens; northern Nassau and Suffolk counties

After redistricting in 1992, New York's Queens-based 7th transformed into the 5th, which skirts the North Shore from Queens to Suffolk County. Formerly a Democratic stronghold in multiracial Queens, the 5th became a competitive district that includes some of the nation's richest communities.

The 5th has a small minority population, most of which consists of Asian communities centered around Flushing. Numerous Jewish residents throughout the district contribute to the district's Democratic flavor. New York City Democrats have a slight edge in voter registration over Republican Suffolk County residents, and the 5th's longtime Democratic representative has easily won re-election. Bill Clinton won the 5th by nearly a 30 percent margin in 1996 and Al Gore carried the district with 62 percent of the vote in 2000.

Although pockets of low-income neighborhoods exist in the 5th, it remains one of New York's most affluent districts. Many of the district's residents commute to white-collar jobs outside the 5th, but the U.S. Merchant Marine Academy at Kings Point, Queens College in Flushing, Newsday in Melville and several major corporations contribute to the economy.

MAJOR INDUSTRY
Higher education, health care, small business

CITIES
New York (pt.), 292,475 (1990); Huntington (unincorporated) (pt.) 123,741 (1990); North Hempstead (unincorporated) (pt.) 90,776 (1990)

UNUSUAL FEATURES
Talk show host Rosie O'Donnell grew up in Commack; The 1954 original and 1995 remake of the movie "Sabrina" filmed in Glen Cove; In 1661, religious freedom advocate John Bowne allowed Quakers to worship in his Flushing home, one of the oldest structures in the state.

Rep. Gregory W. Meeks (D)

Elected February 1998; 2nd full term

Meeks owes his interest in public affairs to his mother, who resumed her education when her four children were in their teens and inspired him to become involved alongside her in community improvement projects. Raised in East Harlem public housing projects, Meeks believes that education and economic development are essential ingredients in helping his constituents improve their lot.

In Congress, Meeks' priorities include public education, affordable child care and the creation of jobs. A liberal who sometimes finds common cause with the business community, he is a fierce defender of affordable housing and a biting critic of police violence against minorities. Adept at winning funds for his constituents, he keeps an eye on the needs of John F. Kennedy International Airport, which is in his southeast Queens district.

A graduate of Howard University Law School, Meeks began his career as an assistant Queens County district attorney and as a narcotics crime prosecutor. After a brief stint on the State Investigation Commission, which probes wrongdoing by state officials and organized crime figures, Meeks gained an appointment as a state workers' compensation judge and subsequently moved up to the position of supervising law judge.

During those years, Meeks became involved in a variety of community matters — neighborhood cleanups, street repairs, traffic problems, street safety — in the working-class neighborhood of Far Rockaway where his parents were finally able to move.

Meeks says he always thought his involvement in politics would be behind the scenes, but community activist colleagues convinced him to run for office. In 1992, he won the first of three terms to the state Assembly, where he held seats on a range of committees that oversaw state codes, the judiciary, insurance, small business and government operations.

When Democrat Floyd H. Flake resigned his 6th District seat in 1997 to devote his time to the African Methodist Episcopal church in Queens, where he was a minister, he endorsed Meeks to be his successor. Propelled by additional key endorsements, Meeks got the Democratic nomination. He then captured 56 percent of the vote in a four-way general election that was marked by low voter turnout. He was unopposed in 1998 and 2000.

Meeks gained national attention in 2000 when he emerged as an important swing vote on high-profile legislation granting China permanent normal trade status. He was one of just two undecided Democrats who flew to China with Agriculture Secretary Dan Glickman to observe the Chinese economy. President Clinton repeatedly met with him to win his support. Although some lawmakers would revel in such attention, Meeks commented after a meeting with pro-trade business executives: "I can't take too much more of this."

Meeks announced his support for the measure just days before the floor vote. He said he made his decision partly because, when talking with people on the streets of Shanghai, he saw few signs of an oppressive society. "I did not expect them to be as open as they were," he said of the Chinese. He was also influenced by the prospect of increased trade going through JFK Airport and by a package of Clinton administration economic incentives that targeted both rural and urban areas of the United States.

Meeks has repeatedly expressed concerns about the legal rights of individuals. In 2000, after the National Collegiate Athletic Association investigated St. John's University in Queens, he introduced legislation that would

CAPITOL OFFICE
225-3461; fax 226-4169
1710 Longworth Bldg. 20515

INTERNET
e-mail: congmeeks@mail.house.gov
web: www.house.gov/meeks

COMMITTEES
Financial Services
International Relations

HOMETOWN
Far Rockaway

BORN
Sept. 25, 1953, Harlem, N.Y.

RELIGION
Baptist

FAMILY
Wife, Simone-Marie Meeks; three children

EDUCATION
Adelphi U., B.A. 1975; Howard U., J.D. 1978

CAREER
Workers' compensation board judge; city prosecutor

POLITICAL HIGHLIGHTS
N.Y. Assembly, 1993-98

ELECTION RESULTS

2000 GENERAL
Gregory W. Meeks (D, WFM)   unopposed
2000 PRIMARY
Gregory W. Meeks (D)   unopposed
1998 GENERAL
Gregory W. Meeks (D, L, INDC)   unopposed

PREVIOUS WINNING PERCENTAGES
1998 Special Election (56%)

give student-athletes certain legal rights and guarantee that they have independent legal counsel. "These young people are subjected to having their lives dissected before the public on mere allegations and without any independent legal representation during the investigation," Meeks warned.

He also wants to revamp the procedures of the Immigration and Naturalization Service, which he has called "archaic and ... in a large sense, prejudiced" against immigrants.

Meeks tends carefully to his district. In the 106th Congress, he pressed successfully for federal grants to boost economic development in parts of Queens. "I think we are well on our way to revitalizing the Rockaways," he said. When Republicans in 1999 pressed to cut the Department of Housing and Urban Development budget, Meeks blasted the plan as "a reprehensible act against the needy," and he warned that it would create a public housing emergency in his district and across the nation.

Meeks opposes vouchers to help parents pay private school tuition for their children. Subsidies for private schools diminish the commitment to public education, Meeks argues, and they provide help for only a handful of students. Instead, he says, more effort should be directed toward improving public education. In one of his few floor speeches in the 105th, Meeks told his colleagues, "We can build prisons, or we can build schools. ... We must, at all sacrifices, make sure that we build schools; therefore, we will not have to build prisons."

Although Meeks usually sides with the liberal wing of his party, he largely eschews the rhetoric that often defined the older generation of black political leaders. Beginning with his days as a community activist and a state assemblyman, he has tried to seek out allies wherever he can find them. In New York, that practice enabled him to develop ties to both the political and legal establishment and to community activists. In Washington, Meeks says he tries to seek common ground with members of both parties, and he will cast a pro-business vote if it means jobs for his district.

Nevertheless, Meeks is deeply involved with his party's black activist constituency. During his tenure as a state lawmaker, he was chairman of the statewide Council of Black Elected Democrats and claimed membership in four minority legislative caucuses.

Meeks made news in the fall of 1998 when he was one of more than a dozen black leaders arrested outside the Supreme Court as they protested the court's paucity of law clerks from minority groups. After four New York City police officers shot and killed a Guinean immigrant in 1999, he joined other black leaders in protesting police violence against minorities.

KEY VOTES

2000
Yes Raise hourly minimum wage by $1 over two years
No Halt funding for U.S. mission in Kosovo unless European nations pay more
Yes Provide Medicare benefits to military retirees and their dependents
Yes Grant China permanent normal trade status
No Phase out estate, gift and trust taxes
No Prohibit implementation of president's national monument designations
No Approve GOP plan to provide prescription drug coverage for Medicare beneficiaries
Yes Increase help for poor nations indebted to international financial institutions

1999
Yes Impose steel import quotas
No Kill proposal to take aviation trust funds off budget
No Require background checks on buyers only at gun shows with 10 or more vendors
Yes Remove barriers among banking, securities and insurance companies
Yes Authorize state grants to hire teachers and reduce class size
Yes Overhaul campaign finance law; ban "soft money" and restrict advocacy advertising
Yes Approve bipartisan plan to increase rights of patients in managed-care health plans

INTEREST GROUPS

	AFL-CIO	ADA	CCUS	ACU
2000	90%	95%	50%	8%
1999	89%	95%	29%	0%
1998	100%	85%	33%	5%

CQ VOTE STUDIES

	PARTY UNITY		PRESIDENTIAL SUPPORT	
	Support	Oppose	Support	Oppose
2000	95%	5%	92%	8%
1999	96%	4%	86%	14%
1998	97%	3%	90%	10%

NEW YORK 6
Southeast Queens – Jamaica; St. Albans

The 6th is economically centered around John F. Kennedy Airport on Jamaica Bay in southeastern Queens. This black-majority, middle-class district has elected black Democrats to the House since 1986. Bill Clinton took the 6th by more than three-fourths of the vote in both presidential bids, and the district gave Al Gore 88 percent in the 2000 contest. White, middle-class ethnic communities in the northeast and near the district's western border lean Democratic but are more willing to vote across party lines than the rest of the district.

The 6th's eastern border is formed by the line separating New York City's Queens from Nassau County. More than a generation ago, such communities as Springfield Gardens and St. Albans were settled by a burgeoning Irish and Italian Roman Catholic middle class. Today, while the economic profile of these areas is not much different, the demographics are completely changed – most of the residents are black.

The 6th is one of the most economically sound majority-minority districts. Its largest employer, JFK Airport, provides a steady job base and, combined with health care, municipal government and construction jobs, helps create a strong union constituency.

While most district residents are middle class, some southern Queens communities, including South Jamaica, have historically been troubled by unemployment and other urban ills, including a poor education system, persistent crime and drug abuse. In 2000, statistics showed violent crime declining significantly throughout the district.

MAJOR INDUSTRY
Aviation, health care, education

CITIES
New York (pt.) 580,337 (1990)

UNUSUAL FEATURES
Queens was home to singers Billie Holiday and James Brown.

Rep. Joseph Crowley (D)

Elected 1998; 2nd term

CAPITOL OFFICE
225-3965; fax 225-1909; 312 Cannon Bldg. 20515

INTERNET
e-mail: write2joecrowley@mail.house.gov
web: www.house.gov/crowley

COMMITTEES
Financial Services
International Relations

HOMETOWN
Elmhurst

BORN
March 16, 1962, Elmhurst, N.Y.

RELIGION
Roman Catholic

FAMILY
Wife, Kasey Crowley; two children

EDUCATION
Queens College, B.A. 1985

CAREER
State legislator

POLITICAL HIGHLIGHTS
N.Y. Assembly, 1986-99

ELECTION RESULTS

2000 GENERAL

Joseph Crowley (D)	78,207	71.7%
Rose Robles Birtley (R)	24,592	22.5%
Robert E. Hurley (C)	3,131	2.9%
Paul Gilman (GREEN)	1,999	1.8%
Garafalia Christea (RTL)	1,172	1.1%

2000 PRIMARY

Joseph Crowley (D)	unopposed

1998 GENERAL

Joseph Crowley (D)	50,924	69.0%
James J. Dillon (R)	18,896	25.6%
Richard Retcho (C)	3,960	5.4%

Crowley made it to Congress the easy way, and he has been trying ever since to prove that he belongs on Capitol Hill.

The previous incumbent, Thomas J. Manton, was a longtime friend of Crowley's father and uncle, both New York politicians. Manton surprised his fellow Democrats in 1998 when he announced his retirement several days after the primary filing deadline. That allowed party officials, including Manton, the Queens Democratic chairman, to handpick Crowley as the nominee. Crowley then swamped the Republican candidate, corporate security manager James J. Dillon, in the general election.

But rather than guaranteeing Crowley's entrenchment in this overwhelmingly Democratic district, Manton's tactics merely served to anger other Democrats who had wanted a shot at the seat. Several vowed to unseat Crowley in the 2000 Democratic primary, and in February 2000, after months of behind-the-scenes wrangling, they united behind Queens Councilman Walter McCaffrey.

But McCaffrey was fighting an uphill battle. During his first term in office, Crowley rarely stood still, seizing every opportunity to increase his stature and diminish the threat from potential opponents. He was so effective that it hardly seemed to matter when McCaffrey surprisingly pulled out of the race right before the September primary, citing fundraising difficulties and a mini-scandal involving allegations that he had overcharged for campaign expenses. Crowley coasted to victory in the general election, winning more than 70 percent of the vote against Republican Rose Robles Birtley, an airline sales manager.

Some say, however, that Crowley could get his payback in 2002, if Manton's political enemies in the state Assembly are able to influence the configuration of New York's congressional districts during remapping.

Yet Crowley displays a talent for cultivating other, and often more-senior, politicians. He scored a notable, and controversial, success in November 1999 when first lady Hillary Rodham Clinton — then on the verge of declaring her candidacy for the U.S. Senate from New York — hosted a fundraiser for him. That brought the first lady complaints from abortion rights groups because of Crowley's anti-abortion record. But it earned Crowley $150,000, part of a sizable war chest he accumulated to fend off opponents. A few months earlier, Mrs. Clinton had stayed overnight in his home.

Just as important, Crowley said, the first lady's visit gave him time with someone in a position to help him. Crowley said he encouraged her to urge President Clinton to renew his call for legislation that would help underwrite the cost of building or renovating schools. Schools in Crowley's district, flooded with immigrant children from around the world, are bursting at the seams. The president made such an appeal in his next State of the Union address, part of a more intense push by the Clinton administration in 2000 that netted some new school building funds.

Crowley used the political skills he gained in more than a decade as a state legislator in New York to maneuver his way into the presidency of the Democratic freshman class, a position that gave him stature in the district and greater access to top party officials. Crowley "has gained respect from his caucus for coalition-building and legislative know-how," the Capitol Hill newspaper Roll Call wrote in September 1999.

He also used his clout to goad lawmakers from the New York metropolitan area into joining him in opposing a relaxation of rules that limit the number and timing of flights at some of the nation's busiest airports, such as Queens' LaGuardia. Yet, in return for the support of upstate lawmakers in preventing more flights by large airliners until 2007, Crowley agreed to allow more flights by smaller commuter planes to LaGuardia from upstate districts. That decision later came back to haunt him when the new flights helped lead to record delays at the airport.

Crowley sought to deflect criticism for his anti-abortion stance by successfully sponsoring an amendment that renewed U.S. contributions to the United Nations Fund for Population Activities, despite accusations from anti-abortion Republicans that the organization condoned forced abortions in China.

As a member of the International Relations Committee, Crowley has plunged deeply into international politics, a longstanding personal interest and a concern of his constituents. He has traveled to Colombia, Israel and Kosovo since taking office. Crowley, whose mother is from Northern Ireland, has played a particularly large role in trying to keep the peace process in Northern Ireland moving forward.

In the 106th Congress, Crowley served on the Resources Committee, which is generally not concerned with issues relevant to his urban district; but from that post, he won funds to combat the Asian Longhorned Beetle ("the Beetles are coming back to Queens," joked Crowley), a pest that is devastating trees in the 7th District. In the 107th, Crowley left Resources to take a seat on the Financial Services Committee.

Crowley grew up in a political family. He said that one of his earliest political memories is handing out pamphlets with his family for Democrat Mario M. Cuomo after church. His uncle, Walter Crowley, was a well-known Queens politician who served on the New York City Council. The younger Crowley was first elected to the state Assembly just a year after his graduation from college.

The easygoing Crowley is popular with his fellow members and has formed a number of friendships across the aisle. He relaxes by playing basketball and guitar and singing in a band called "The Budget Blues" with three friends from his days in the New York Assembly. He has been known to perform a perfect imitation of Van Morrison singing "Wild Nights."

Crowley can justifiably claim that "family values" are part of his political life. Winning his first election in 1998 was a nice wedding gift: He married one week before he won. Almost a year later, his wife, Kasey, gave birth to the first baby of the freshman Class of 1998. And the family's second child was born about two weeks before the 2000 election.

KEY VOTES

2000

Yes Raise hourly minimum wage by $1 over two years

—   Halt funding for U.S. mission in Kosovo unless European nations pay more

Yes Provide Medicare benefits to military retirees and their dependents

No Grant China permanent normal trade status

No Phase out estate, gift and trust taxes

No Prohibit implementation of president's national monument designations

No Approve GOP plan to provide prescription drug coverage for Medicare beneficiaries

Yes Increase help for poor nations indebted to international financial institutions

1999

Yes Impose steel import quotas

No Kill proposal to take aviation trust funds off budget

No Require background checks on buyers only at gun shows with 10 or more vendors

Yes Remove barriers among banking, securities and insurance companies

Yes Authorize state grants to hire teachers and reduce class size

Yes Overhaul campaign finance law; ban "soft money" and restrict advocacy advertising

Yes Approve bipartisan plan to increase rights of patients in managed-care health plans

INTEREST GROUPS

	AFL-CIO	ADA	CCUS	ACU
2000	100%	85%	38%	20%
1999	89%	95%	32%	8%

CQ VOTE STUDIES

	PARTY UNITY		PRESIDENTIAL SUPPORT	
	Support	Oppose	Support	Oppose
2000	91%	9%	82%	18%
1999	91%	9%	81%	19%

NEW YORK 7

Parts of Queens and the Bronx — Long Island City

Democrats have long had an edge in the ethnically and racially diverse 7th, which rounds the northern tip of Queens and reaches across the Whitestone Bridge to grab a slice of the Bronx.

But the 7th's Democratic vote is somewhat less dependable than in most of New York City. Democratic-leaning Hispanics account for a substantial portion of the population, but non-Hispanic whites vote in greater numbers and tend to be socially conservative. The district includes a large Italian-American community based in the Bronx, as well as a sizable Chinese-American community in Flushing.

Jackson Heights, one of the fastest growing communities in New York City, lies at the center of the district. A middle- and working-class area, it experienced a significant increase in its Hispanic population in the 1990s.

The district is predominantly middle-class and residential, although

steady growth tied to New York City has spurred new businesses. Queens, which has about three-fourths of the district's population remains a bustling transportation hub. La Guardia Airport is in the 7th and employs more than 9,000 of the district's residents. The health care industry is a major employer in the Bronx.

At the district's western edge lies a portion of Long Island City, just north of the Queensboro Bridge. Once a longtime industrial center, the area has lost many of its factories and manufacturing jobs, but is now attracting some new high-tech companies.

MAJOR INDUSTRY

Service, aviation, manufacturing

CITIES

New York (pt.), 580,337 (1990)

UNUSUAL FEATURES

The 1970s TV show "All in the Family" set in the 7th; National Tennis Center (home of the U.S. Open); Mets' Shea Stadium.

Rep. Jerrold Nadler (D)

CAPITOL OFFICE
225-5635; fax 225-6923; 2334 Rayburn Bldg. 20515

INTERNET
e-mail: jerrold.nadler@mail.house.gov
web: www.house.gov/nadler

COMMITTEES
Judiciary
Transportation & Infrastructure

HOMETOWN
Manhattan

BORN
June 13, 1947, Brooklyn, N.Y.

RELIGION
Jewish

FAMILY
Wife, Joyce L. Miller; one child

EDUCATION
Columbia U., A.B. 1969; Fordham U., J.D. 1978

CAREER
Lawyer; state legislature aide

POLITICAL HIGHLIGHTS
N.Y. Assembly, 1976-92; candidate for Manhattan borough president, 1985; candidate for New York City comptroller, 1989

ELECTION RESULTS

2000 GENERAL

Jerrold Nadler (D, L, WFM)	150,273	81.2%
Marian S. Henry (R)	27,057	14.6%
Dan Wentzel (GREEN)	4,765	2.6%

2000 PRIMARY

Jerrold Nadler (D)	unopposed

1998 GENERAL

Jerrold Nadler (D, L)	112,948	86.0%
Theodore Howard (R)	18,383	14.0%

PREVIOUS WINNING PERCENTAGES
1996 (82%); 1994 (82%); 1992 (81%); 1992 Special Election (100%)

Elected 1992; 5th full term

One of the most liberal members of Congress, Nadler is a good fit for his district, which includes Manhattan's Upper West Side, Greenwich Village and parts of Brooklyn. The 8th has among the largest concentrations of liberal Jewish voters and gay and lesbian political activists in America, and few of them are happy that Republicans control Congress. Neither is Nadler.

He is a member of the Progressive Caucus, the most liberal faction of House Democrats; has close to a 100 percent career vote rating from the liberal Americans for Democratic Action — he is an honorary vice president of the ADA; and he has never been given a rating of higher than 8 percent by the American Conservative Union.

Nadler is quick on his feet in partisan debate, and he is eager to expound on his views, often in nugget-sized sound bites. He is one of the most prolific authors of legislation in the House, introducing stand-alone bills and penning countless amendments, both on the floor and in committee.

In the Judiciary Committee in particular, Nadler seems always at the ready with an amendment or an argument, or both, as the panel considers bills on guns, abortion, crime, consumer issues, and civil liberties. He is the top-ranking Democrat on Judiciary's Constitution Subcommittee, moving in the 107th Congress from the top Democratic spot on the Commercial and Administrative Law Subcommittee, whose jurisdiction includes such matters as bankruptcy law.

Nadler has strongly opposed Republican-backed legislation to overhaul the nation's bankruptcy laws, calling it "a bill of, by and for the credit card companies, which have waged a long and expensive campaign for it." The measure would require more bankruptcy filers to try to pay back at least some of their debt. Nadler and other consumer advocates contend that there would be fewer bankruptcies in the first place if credit card companies and banks would stop extending credit to poor risks.

Nadler takes a strong stand on issues of interest to the homosexual community. He has made it a priority to seek added funding for housing programs for people with AIDS, offering amendments to redirect funds from other programs, including NASA's International Space Station and National Science Foundation research.

He also criticized the Clinton administration's failure to lift the ban on gays in the military, saying, "The new 'don't ask, don't tell, don't get caught' policy represents a reaffirmation of the policy of official bigotry by the United States, with changes only in the methods by which that bigotry will be enforced."

But Nadler fervently defended President Clinton against Judiciary Republicans, who sought to impeach him for lying about his affair with a White House intern. Nadler accused the GOP of "running a lynch mob." In December 1998, Nadler chastised Robert L. Livingston, the Republicans' Speaker-designate for the 106th Congress, for resigning from office after admitting he had committed adultery. In Nadler's view, the Louisianan's resignation was as misguided as the impeachment effort. "It is a surrender to a developing sexual McCarthyism," Nadler said.

Nadler sits on the Transportation Committee and co-chairs the House Transit Caucus. One of his long-range goals is to increase freight rail service to New York City via a new freight line tunnel under New York Harbor. He says additional rail service would foster economic development, ease pollution and lower consumer costs in the city.

He has opposed several building proposals by New York developer Donald Trump, including one that would have cost the federal government $350 million, to move a highway. The proposed relocation of the West Side Highway would have allowed an unobstructed view of the Hudson River for residents of a Trump housing project. Nadler's opposition to the project earned him a derogatory mention in a Trump book, in which Nadler was described as "one of the most egregious hacks in contemporary politics." Nadler also has clashed with New York City's Republican Mayor Rudolph Giuliani, demanding investigations of violence by the city's police department.

Nadler made an immediate impression when he arrived in the House. He persuaded his Democratic colleagues to approve organizational reform that spreads out party power: The "Nadler rule" prohibits the top Democrat on a full committee from also holding the party's No. 1 seat on a subcommittee.

Brooklyn born, Nadler spent his early years on a New Jersey poultry farm. His family moved back to New York City after the farm failed. He earned a degree in government from Columbia University and a law degree from Fordham, which he attended at night while working at an off-track betting office during the day.

Politics has been a lifelong passion for Nadler. In high school, he became friends with Dick Morris — later to gain fame and then notoriety as a political consultant to Bill Clinton — and roomed with Morris at Columbia. Nadler organized students against the Vietnam War to campaign for Eugene J. McCarthy in the 1968 New Hampshire Democratic presidential primary. He was an aide to a New York state senator, and he campaigned for liberal Democratic Rep. Ted Weiss. In 1976, he won a seat in the New York state Assembly and served there for 16 years.

When Weiss died of a heart attack on the eve of the September 1992 Democratic primary, voters renominated him nonetheless, giving party officials the right to pick a successor. That set off a scramble among the district's ample cadre of Democratic activists, with six candidates jumping into the frenetic nine-day race for the nomination. While other hopefuls such as former Rep. Bella S. Abzug were better known to the public, Nadler had longstanding ties to the insiders who would cast the votes. He got the party's nomination and went on to win the special election and the general-election contest for a full term on the same day.

In the overwhelmingly Democratic 8th District, Nadler has since been re-elected with ease.

KEY VOTES

2000
Yes Raise hourly minimum wage by $1 over two years
No   Halt funding for U.S. mission in Kosovo unless European nations pay more
Yes Provide Medicare benefits to military retirees and their dependents
No   Grant China permanent normal trade status
No   Phase out estate, gift and trust taxes
No   Prohibit implementation of president's national monument designations
No   Approve GOP plan to provide prescription drug coverage for Medicare beneficiaries
Yes Increase help for poor nations indebted to international financial institutions

1999
Yes Impose steel import quotas
No   Kill proposal to take aviation trust funds off budget
No   Require background checks on buyers only at gun shows with 10 or more vendors
No   Remove barriers among banking, securities and insurance companies
Yes Authorize state grants to hire teachers and reduce class size
Yes Overhaul campaign finance law; ban "soft money" and restrict advocacy advertising
Yes Approve bipartisan plan to increase rights of patients in managed-care health plans

INTEREST GROUPS

	AFL-CIO	ADA	CCUS	ACU
2000	100%	95%	28%	4%
1999	100%	100%	12%	0%
1998	100%	100%	24%	8%
1997	100%	100%	20%	4%

CQ VOTE STUDIES

	PARTY UNITY		PRESIDENTIAL SUPPORT	
	Support	Oppose	Support	Oppose
2000	95%	5%	84%	16%
1999	98%	2%	84%	16%
1998	96%	4%	79%	21%
1997	96%	4%	82%	18%

NEW YORK 8
West Side Manhattan; parts of southwest Brooklyn

Starting at the southern tip of Manhattan, the 8th covers Wall Street and moves north through Manhattan's West Side, taking in Greenwich Village and Midtown to end up halfway up the west side of Central Park (the park itself is in the 14th District). The 8th also crosses the Brooklyn Bridge to skim Brooklyn's western waterfront and take in some of the borough's more impoverished neighborhoods.

The manufacturing industry that once sustained Brooklyn has been neglected in a surge of white-collar financial growth. Now officials are looking for ways to revitalize the decaying Brooklyn waterfront and Coney Island. Local leaders are championing a proposed rail-freight tunnel that would link Brooklyn to Staten Island or New Jersey.

Manhattan's heavily Democratic West Side has sent liberal representatives to Congress since 1970. Redistricting has combined

Manhattan's northwest, Midtown, Greenwich Village and financial districts with Brooklyn's Hasidic Jewish communities and minority neighborhoods in western and south Brooklyn and Coney Island.

The 8th's politically active communities – gay, Jewish, minority, art and student – supported Bill Clinton with at least 75 percent of the vote in 1992 and '96 and gave Al Gore 77 percent in 2000. The district's liberal Democratic representative has easily won re-election to five terms. The 8th's only conservative voters live in Brooklyn's upper middle-class Hasidic communities, like Boro Park, where residents are sometimes willing to back Republican candidates who share their socially conservative views.

MAJOR INDUSTRY
Finance, manufacturing, small business

CITIES
New York (pt.), 580,337 (1990)

UNUSUAL FEATURES
World Trade Center; Empire State Building; Coney Island, home to a century-old amusement park; Neil Simon's "Brighton Beach Memoirs" set near Coney Island.

Rep. Anthony Weiner (D)

Elected 1998; 2nd term

CAPITOL OFFICE
225-6616; fax 226-7253; 222 Cannon Bldg. 20515

INTERNET
e-mail: weiner@mail.house.gov
web: www.house.gov/weiner

COMMITTEES
Judiciary
Science

HOMETOWN
Brooklyn

BORN
Sept. 4, 1964, Brooklyn, N.Y.

RELIGION
Jewish

FAMILY
Single

EDUCATION
State U. of New York, Plattsburgh, B.A. 1985

CAREER
Congressional aide

POLITICAL HIGHLIGHTS
New York City Council, 1992-99

ELECTION RESULTS

2000 GENERAL

Anthony Weiner (D, L)	98,983	68.4%
Noach Dear (R, C)	45,649	31.6%

2000 PRIMARY

Anthony Weiner (D)	24,895	73.8%
Noach Dear (D)	8,847	26.2%

1998 GENERAL

Anthony Weiner (D, INDC)	69,439	66.4%
Louis Telano (R)	24,486	23.4%
Melinda Katz (L)	5,698	5.5%
Arthur J. Smith (C)	4,899	4.7%

Weiner is much like his mentor, Democratic Sen. Charles E. Schumer, the man he replaced in the House. Both have distinctive Brooklyn accents, liberal convictions and the ability to sum up quickly the day's events with a sound bite for the nightly news. Both are comfortable in the political environment; they even look a bit alike.

Young, energetic and ambitious, Weiner has had big shoes to fill since winning election in 1998 for the 9th District seat that Schumer left to run for the Senate. But, even as a freshman, Weiner (WEE-ner) seemed to find his feet quickly, winning approval in 1999 of $30 million over three years to encourage aircraft builders to design quieter engines. Airplane noise control is an important issue for his district, which must deal with flights from both LaGuardia and John F. Kennedy airports.

Weiner co-authored a study with New Jersey Democrat Rush D. Holt in early 2000 criticizing the Port Authority of New York and New Jersey for not using the money it raised from a $3-per-ticket charge to provide more help with soundproofing for area residents. The report found that LaGuardia and John F. Kennedy airports had done less on noise abatement than any other major airport surveyed.

Weiner was also part of a group of New York members who successfully fought back an attempt by the powerful Republican chairman of the House Transportation Committee, Bud Shuster of Pennsylvania, to open more slots for airplane takeoffs and landings at the two New York airports. Their success locked in the existing numbers until 2007.

Weiner came to politics early, with a run for student government at the State University of New York at Plattsburgh. His first campaign gave him an opportunity to hone a skill that has stood him in good stead: a self-deprecating sense of humor. He used slogans such as "Vote for Weiner. He'll be frank," "Weiner's on a roll," and "You'll relish Weiner," but he lost his bid.

He served for six years as a congressional aide in Schumer's Brooklyn and Washington, D.C., offices. Then in 1991, at age 27, he became the youngest person ever elected to the New York City Council. While on the city council, Weiner worked with at-risk teenagers to create an anti-graffiti cleanup group known as "Weiner's Cleaners."

Seven years later, he was among the youngest members of the 106th Congress. Upon his arrival on Capitol Hill, Weiner was given a seat on the Judiciary Committee, where he has been an active voice for the Democrats. During debate on legislation to create a federal system for asbestos litigation, which aligned asbestos victims against asbestos companies, Weiner said the companies "face enormous liability because they ought to. They've done harm to people." He won approval of an amendment that made it clear that any federal asbestos program would have to be funded — upfront — by the asbestos companies.

Weiner is a favorite of schedulers on the cable news shows, able to hold his own against any number of Republicans on a wide variety of issues. And he has been an active fundraiser for Democrats, especially in the campaign that elected first lady Hillary Rodham Clinton to the Senate.

On occasion, Weiner has reached across the aisle and worked with members of the Judiciary Committee's majority — a rarity among Democrats on that sharply partisan panel. Weiner joined with Arkansas Republican Asa Hutchinson, for example, to craft a compromise proposal designed to make it harder for the government to seize property from individuals. Their standard for confiscating property from suspected criminals was included in the measure signed into law.

And during committee action on legislation to renew federal grants for combating violence against women, Weiner joined with Ohio Republican Steve Chabot to win approval of an amendment requiring funds to be used to hire nurses specially trained in how to treat evidence collected from victims of sexual assault. Weiner said that evidence collected improperly can weaken a case against an alleged rapist.

He is also part of a bipartisan group of New York members who meet for lunch once a month to discuss issues of importance to their state. Other members include Democrats Joseph Crowley and Gregory W. Meeks and Republicans Vito J. Fossella, Thomas M. Reynolds and John E. Sweeney.

Weiner wants to protect Social Security cost of living increases and improve Medicare services for his district, which has a substantial elderly population. He has introduced legislation that would add a mechanism to adjust annual cost of living increases for Social Security based on where the recipient resides, arguing that the high cost of living in New York means retirees in his district get fewer benefits.

Education is also a top priority. Weiner, who is a product of the public school system and whose mother was a teacher, wants to increase the government's role in school construction and in bringing the Internet to all classrooms.

Weiner also has a seat on the Science Committee and was chosen by his colleagues in the Democratic Class of 1998 as their representative to the party's whip organization.

Though he was seen as the protégé of Schumer, Weiner did not have an easy path to his party's nomination in 1998. He won the Democratic nod for the 9th by fewer than 500 votes over state Assemblywoman Melinda Katz. But the November election was much easier: He coasted to a 43 percentage point victory in the overwhelmingly Democratic district.

In 2000, he won more than two-thirds of the vote in the general election. But his future is uncertain: The 9th is one district that may be carved up when New York redraws its congressional map for the 2002 elections.

Weiner has one claim to fame from his freshman term: He scored the only run for his team in the 1999 charity baseball game pitting House Republicans against House Democrats, which the GOP easily won. In a rare highlight for the Democratic team, Weiner did not just score the run, he forced it. After getting to first as a pinch runner, he stole second. On subsequent plays, he slid into third and then into home — head first.

KEY VOTES

2000

Yes Raise hourly minimum wage by $1 over two years
No   Halt funding for U.S. mission in Kosovo unless European nations pay more
Yes Provide Medicare benefits to military retirees and their dependents
Yes Grant China permanent normal trade status
No   Phase out estate, gift and trust taxes
No   Prohibit implementation of president's national monument designations
No   Approve GOP plan to provide prescription drug coverage for Medicare beneficiaries
Yes Increase help for poor nations indebted to international financial institutions

1999

Yes Impose steel import quotas
No   Kill proposal to take aviation trust funds off budget
No   Require background checks on buyers only at gun shows with 10 or more vendors
Yes Remove barriers among banking, securities and insurance companies
Yes Authorize state grants to hire teachers and reduce class size
Yes Overhaul campaign finance law; ban "soft money" and restrict advocacy advertising
Yes Approve bipartisan plan to increase rights of patients in managed-care health plans

INTEREST GROUPS

	AFL-CIO	ADA	CCUS	ACU
2000	90%	85%	40%	8%
1999	78%	100%	24%	0%

CQ VOTE STUDIES

	PARTY UNITY		PRESIDENTIAL SUPPORT	
	Support	Oppose	Support	Oppose
2000	94%	6%	90%	10%
1999	95%	5%	88%	12%

NEW YORK 9
Parts of Brooklyn and Queens — Sheepshead Bay; Forest Hills

Few districts are more geographically disparate than the 9th, which takes in widely separated parts of Brooklyn and Queens. The district was originally drawn to exclude concentrations of Hispanics in neighboring districts. But when the 12th District was ruled unconstitutional and redrawn in 1997, the 9th gained a larger portion of Queens. The district is now roughly split between Queens and Brooklyn.

The 9th is about 76 percent non-Hispanic white (according to 1990 Census Bureau statistics) and consistently votes Democratic. The district voted for Bill Clinton in 1992 and '96 and gave Al Gore a 38 percentage point margin of victory in the 2000 presidential contest.

Mostly middle class and residential, the 9th has a large Jewish population, and ethnic populations (mainly Italian- and Irish-American)

add to its strong Democratic flavor. The district's few social conservatives live in its wealthiest communities, Forest Hills and Kew Gardens, in the northeast corner.

Unemployment in Queens and Brooklyn is almost double that of Long Island counties to the east. To boost the area's economy, the region focused on revitalization along the waterfront community of Sheepshead Bay, which has spawned an economic turn-around.

MAJOR INDUSTRY
Service, finance, insurance, manufacturing

CITIES
New York (pt.), 580,338 (1990)

UNUSUAL FEATURES
Pip's Comedy Club, where Billy Crystal, Andrew "Dice" Clay, George Carlin and Adam Sandler started their careers; Queens Boulevard, termed the "Boulevard of Death" by local residents because 73 pedestrians have been killed on the busy six-lane roadway since 1973.

Rep. Edolphus Towns (D)

CAPITOL OFFICE
225-5936; fax 225-1018; 2232 Rayburn Bldg. 20515

INTERNET
e-mail: www.house.gov/writerep
web: www.house.gov/towns

COMMITTEES
Energy & Commerce
Government Reform

HOMETOWN
Brooklyn

BORN
July 21, 1934, Chadbourn, N.C.

RELIGION
Baptist

FAMILY
Wife, Gwendolyn Towns; two children

EDUCATION
North Carolina A&T State U., B.S. 1956; Adelphi U., M.S.W. 1973

MILITARY SERVICE
Army, 1956-58

CAREER
Professor; hospital administrator

POLITICAL HIGHLIGHTS
Brooklyn Borough deputy president, 1976-82

ELECTION RESULTS

2000 GENERAL

Edolphus Towns (D, L)	120,700	90.2%
Ernestine M. Brown (R)	6,852	5.1%
Barry Ford (WFM)	5,530	4.1%

2000 PRIMARY

Edolphus Towns (D)	25,735	57.5%
Barry Ford (D)	19,040	42.5%

1998 GENERAL

Edolphus Towns (D, L)	83,528	92.3%
Ernestine M. Brown (R)	5,577	6.2%
Ernest Johnson (C)	1,396	1.5%

PREVIOUS WINNING PERCENTAGES
1996 (91%); 1994 (89%); 1992 (96%); 1990 (93%); 1988 (89%); 1986 (89%); 1984 (85%); 1982 (84%)

Elected 1982; 10th term

Usually affable and low-key, Towns occasionally involves himself in controversy — such as when he endorsed Republican Rudolph Giuliani for re-election as mayor of New York City in 1997 — but he has not achieved as much of a presence on Capitol Hill as one might expect from a lawmaker now in his tenth term.

Towns has a seat on the Energy and Commerce Committee, and he has been the chairman or ranking minority member of a subcommittee, either on that panel or on the Government Reform Committee since the 103rd Congress. He was chairman of the Congressional Black Caucus in the 102nd Congress. Despite these positions, he has eluded the spotlight.

The New York Daily News in a 1998 survey rating the New York City congressional delegation ranked Towns near the bottom. His lowest scores came in the categories of "national presence" and "clout." His highest scores were for constituent service and work ethic.

Two years later, The New York Times endorsed his challenger in the Democratic primary, commenting that "after 18 years, [Towns'] record in Congress has been minimal and his support for tobacco and other special interests is troubling." In an overwhelmingly Democratic district such as the 10th, the Democratic primary is the real election, and the 10th has a long history of party infighting.

The 2000 primary, in which Towns rebuffed Harvard-trained lawyer Barry Ford by a 57 percent to 43 percent tally, was fought amid grumblings from some of Towns' critics that the congressman was going too far in trying to position his son, Darryl, a state assemblyman, as the heir to the district seat.

Towns' support for the tobacco industry may be rooted in his upbringing. The son of a sharecropper in North Carolina, where tobacco is a major crop, he notes that anti-tobacco legislation affects small farmers as well as the large manufacturers.

Thus, despite his background as a hospital administrator and his legislative interest in health issues, he has opposed legislation to ban smoking in public and to kill federally subsidized crop insurance for tobacco farmers. Until recently, Towns was a significant beneficiary of campaign donations from tobacco interests. He decided to stop taking contributions from tobacco companies in 2000.

In the 106th Congress, Towns' priorities included not only a range of preventive health and nutrition measures but also legislation to encourage teachers to live in the same communities where they work. He also backed a bill to narrow the "digital divide" — giving urban and rural communities access to new information technologies, and another to speed licensing of hydroelectric plants. On the latter bill, his Senate ally was conservative Republican Larry E. Craig of Idaho.

Towns also authored a bill to ban the sale of toys that resemble real guns. Later, after two teenagers were shot and killed when they pointed a real-looking toy gun at two police officers, he convinced a drug store chain to stop selling the toys.

In the 105th Congress, Towns was the top Democrat on Government Reform's Human Resources Subcommittee, where he paid special attention to health issues. He has expressed concern that changes in the nation's health care delivery system might impede pharmaceutical manufacturers' ability to develop new drugs. Preserving the profitability of that industry is of great importance to Towns because the Pfizer pharmaceutical company is in his district.

Another of Towns' interests has been the rights of student-athletes. In the 101st Congress, he won passage of the Student Athlete Right to Know Act. Towns worked with two former professional basketball players, Rep. Tom McMillen, D-Md., and Sen. Bill Bradley, D-N.J., in helping to enact the law requiring colleges to disclose the graduation rates of their athletes on scholarship.

Towns endured a spate of negative publicity as the House bank controversy unfolded in the 102nd Congress. He had 408 overdrafts at the private bank for House members; Towns explained, however, that his receptionist had embezzled $28,000 from his account to support a drug habit. But publicity from the incident — combined with 1991 news reports that the Black Caucus (which Towns chaired from 1991 to 1993) had used funds from the office account of a retiring member to pay delinquent taxes — gave a perception that Towns and the caucus should have paid closer attention to their financial affairs.

Towns was born in a small town in southeastern North Carolina and graduated from historically black North Carolina A & T in Greensboro. After a two-year Army stint, Towns came north and began the career that eventually led him into elective politics in Brooklyn. He worked as a teacher and hospital administrator and earned a master's degree in social work from Adelphi University. In 1976, he was appointed Brooklyn Borough deputy president, and while working at Borough Hall, he established links to numerous community organizations.

Towns' chance to run for the House came in 1982 after redistricting gave the 11th District an almost even split of blacks and Hispanics. The new district included some Brooklyn territory that had been represented by white Democratic Rep. Frederick W. Richmond. But Richmond, who had been indicted on charges of income tax evasion and possession of marijuana, resigned. (Richmond was later convicted.)

In the turbulent world of Brooklyn politics, Towns benefited from a lack of enemies. He drew support from party regulars as well as from a rival faction calling for reform. Towns fended off two Hispanic primary contenders to win nomination with 50 percent. He easily won in November, starting an unbroken string of general-election landslides in the Democratic stronghold. Redistricting in 1992 put him in a newly drawn but just as Democratic 10th District, where he has faced tough primary battles three times, including the 2000 contest.

KEY VOTES

2000
Yes Raise hourly minimum wage by $1 over two years
No Halt funding for U.S. mission in Kosovo unless European nations pay more
? Provide Medicare benefits to military retirees and their dependents
No Grant China permanent normal trade status
No Phase out estate, gift and trust taxes
No Prohibit implementation of president's national monument designations
No Approve GOP plan to provide prescription drug coverage for Medicare beneficiaries
Yes Increase help for poor nations indebted to international financial institutions

1999
Yes Impose steel import quotas
No Kill proposal to take aviation trust funds off budget
No Require background checks on buyers only at gun shows with 10 or more vendors
Yes Remove barriers among banking, securities and insurance companies
Yes Authorize state grants to hire teachers and reduce class size
Yes Overhaul campaign finance law; ban "soft money" and restrict advocacy advertising
Yes Approve bipartisan plan to increase rights of patients in managed-care health plans

INTEREST GROUPS

	AFL-CIO	ADA	CCUS	ACU
2000	100%	95%	50%	4%
1999	78%	95%	28%	4%
1998	100%	95%	31%	9%
1997	100%	85%	33%	9%

CQ VOTE STUDIES

	PARTY UNITY		PRESIDENTIAL SUPPORT	
	Support	Oppose	Support	Oppose
2000	97%	3%	89%	11%
1999	94%	6%	79%	21%
1998	93%	7%	85%	15%
1997	93%	7%	75%	25%

NEW YORK 10

Parts of Brooklyn — Bedford-Stuyvesant; Brooklyn Heights

The 10th arcs from just inland of Brooklyn's industrial waterfront to Jamaica Bay, encompassing one of New York's most economically and ethnically diverse constituencies. More than one-fourth of the district's residents live at or below the poverty line, but communities like Brooklyn Heights – partially included in the 10th's western portion – are some of the city's wealthiest. The 10th is homogeneously Democratic and gave Al Gore an overwhelming 90 percent of the vote in the 2000 presidential contest.

The 10th experienced a series of boundary changes in the 1990s due to redistricting challenges to the 12th District, formulated in 1992 to create a Hispanic-majority seat. That year, many of the 10th's Hispanic neighborhoods were moved to the 12th, and the 10th was left with a nearly two-thirds black majority. A federal court in 1997 ruled that the 12th was unconstitutionally gerrymandered, but the subsequent

redistricting changed the 10th only slightly and did not dilute the district's black majority.

Erosion in the 10th's manufacturing base has caused a scarcity of employment in the 10th. Joblessness has aggravated poverty, violent crime and racial tensions in some working-class and low-income communities like East New York, Bedford-Stuyvesant and Canarsie.

One of the biggest problems for the district is its aging infrastructure. One of the oldest areas of the city, its water and sewer lines are prone to collapse. Heavy truck traffic is eroding the Brooklyn-Queens Expressway and residential streets leading up to the Brooklyn and Manhattan bridges (both located in the 12th District).

MAJOR INDUSTRY
Government, higher education, small business, pharmaceuticals

CITIES
New York (pt.), 580,338 (1990)

UNUSUAL FEATURES
Spike Lee's film, "Do The Right Thing," set in Bedford-Stuyvesant.

Rep. Major R. Owens (D)

Elected 1982; 10th term

CAPITOL OFFICE
225-6231; fax 226-0112; 2309 Rayburn Bldg. 20515

INTERNET
e-mail: www.house.gov/writerep
web: www.house.gov/owens

COMMITTEES
Education & Workforce
Government Reform

HOMETOWN
Brooklyn

BORN
June 28, 1936, Memphis, Tenn.

RELIGION
Baptist

FAMILY
Wife, Maria Cuprill; five children

EDUCATION
Morehouse College, B.A. 1956; Atlanta U., M.L.S. 1957

CAREER
City community development commissioner; librarian

POLITICAL HIGHLIGHTS
N.Y. Senate, 1975-83

ELECTION RESULTS

2000 GENERAL

Major R. Owens (D, WFM)	112,050	87.0%
Susan Cleary (R)	8,406	6.5%
Una Clarke (L)	7,366	5.7%

2000 PRIMARY

Major R. Owens (D)	25,962	54.4%
Una Clarke (D)	21,769	45.6%

1998 GENERAL

Major R. Owens (D, L)	75,773	90.0%
David Greene (R, C)	7,284	8.7%
Phyllis Taliaferro (INDC)	1,144	1.4%

PREVIOUS WINNING PERCENTAGES
1996 (92%); 1994 (89%); 1992 (94%); 1990 (95%); 1988 (93%); 1986 (91%); 1984 (91%); 1982 (91%)

Owens is passionate, uncompromising and sometimes even belligerent about issues affecting people he believes are oppressed or discriminated against. "I am one of those who is not ashamed to be called a liberal," he says. "In fact, I am proud of it. I am a liberal, I am progressive, all of those kinds of things that people seem to shrink away from. Our group has not disappeared."

As ranking Democrat on the Education panel's Workforce Protections Subcommittee, Owens has tried to beat back Republican attacks on organized labor and efforts to relax health and safety regulations on business. For example, he opposed GOP legislation in 1998 allowing businesses to withhold from the Occupational Safety and Health Administration all records of safety and health assessments or audits they had conducted voluntarily. He argued that the bill encouraged employers to hide violations. "I cannot support legislation that rewards scofflaws," he said.

In the 106th Congress, Owens came at the issue from another angle: protecting whistleblowers. He introduced a bill that would have prevented retaliation against workers reporting injuries or unsafe working conditions. The bill also would have protected workers if they refused to perform duties they believed to be unsafe. As a member of the minority party, however, Owens had little power to advance his agenda, and the subcommittee never acted on the legislation.

At a time when many Democrats have pursued more centrist, achievable goals, Owens is still willing to push the envelope. In the 106th, he latched onto a Democratic priority — federal assistance to build new schools and repair aging and potentially hazardous ones. But while President Clinton and most Democrats sought a measure to subsidize the interest on school construction bonds, Owens advocated a bill that would have authorized $22 billion a year in direct federal payments over five years. He argued that poor communities would never be able to sell the construction bonds in the first place. Neither bill, however, succeeded.

Owens often focuses on symbolic protest rather than legislative maneuvering. Sometimes called "the rapping congressman," he pens poetry and rap lyrics to mock conservative initiatives by the GOP, saying this gives him "an outlet for political frustrations." Owens says he brings the rhythm of the streets to Congress with his rap poems, which are printed in the Congressional Record and displayed on his congressional website.

In the 105th Congress, Owens emerged as a strong defender of Clinton, denouncing the Clinton impeachment as a "religious lynching of a great president." Of the GOP move to impeach the president, Owens rapped: "Mice men gnawing/ At the core of the nation/ History will rate them/ The pompous petty generation/ Rodents feeding/ On the Monica sensation."

Owens is a strong supporter of federal aid for the disabled. He opposed a Republican plan in 1996 to make it easier to discipline unruly disabled students who are being educated under the Individuals with Disabilities Education Act. "This bill is an attack to establish a beachhead" for Republicans to "attempt a total annihilation of federal support for special education," he said. An irate colleague, Republican Randy "Duke" Cunningham of California, interrupted Owens to inquire pointedly, "Do we have to sit here and listen to this demagoguery?"

Owens is a leader of the Progressive Caucus, the most liberal faction of House Democrats. A staunch proponent of gun control, he has proposed rewriting or even repealing the Second Amendment, which guarantees the right of Americans to bear arms. "In order to safeguard our schools and make the environment more safe for our children ... the first thing we need to do is address the fact that we have a great proliferation of handguns in this nation, and we should end that proliferation of handguns," he said in a 1999 National Public Radio interview.

The 11th District is home to a large Caribbean immigrant population, and Owens advocates policies to aid Haitian transplants. In the 106th Congress, for instance, he introduced a bill to prevent the Immigration and Naturalization Service from deporting Haitians with American-born children under 18 and to allow children under 12 without parents to become U.S. citizens. "Elián González is one child," he said, referring to the 6-year-old Cuban boy who was temporarily housed by his relatives in Miami. "But there are thousands of children trapped in a situation that is cruel and inhumane — trapped by the laws of the U.S."

Born in Memphis, Tenn., and educated in the South as a librarian, Owens was a community organizer in Brooklyn's economically depressed Brownsville section in the mid-1960s when he was tapped by Mayor John V. Lindsay to head New York City's anti-poverty program. He made his first bid for elected office in 1974, winning a state Senate seat that he held for eight years.

When Owens set his sights on the House in 1982, he faced a tough opponent: state Sen. Vander Beatty, who as deputy Democratic leader in the state Senate had built a patronage empire in the Brooklyn black community. But Owens capitalized on Beatty's unsavory connections and his own reputation for honesty. He won by a narrow margin, a victory that Beatty challenged unsuccessfully in court.

Republicans have never posed a threat to Owens, whose solidly Democratic district is composed largely of African-Americans and other minorities. Only twice has Owens earned less than 90 percent of the vote in the general election, most recently in 2000, when he got 87 percent in a four-candidate race. But his tight hold on the 11th may be weakening. In 2000, with his district tilting increasingly toward West Indian immigrants, he barely survived a primary battle against City Councilwoman Una Clarke, who was born in Jamaica.

Clarke contended that Owens had failed to win a federal empowerment zone for the district and did not respond to constituents who needed help with immigration procedures or other matters. With the help of prominent Democrats, including first lady and New York Senate candidate Hillary Rodham Clinton, Owens won the primary by almost 9 percentage points.

KEY VOTES

2000

Yes   Raise hourly minimum wage by $1 over two years
No   Halt funding for U.S. mission in Kosovo unless European nations pay more
Yes   Provide Medicare benefits to military retirees and their dependents
No   Grant China permanent normal trade status
No   Phase out estate, gift and trust taxes
No   Prohibit implementation of president's national monument designations
No   Approve GOP plan to provide prescription drug coverage for Medicare beneficiaries
Yes   Increase help for poor nations indebted to international financial institutions

1999

Yes   Impose steel import quotas
No   Kill proposal to take aviation trust funds off budget
No   Require background checks on buyers only at gun shows with 10 or more vendors
Yes   Remove barriers among banking, securities and insurance companies
Yes   Authorize state grants to hire teachers and reduce class size
Yes   Overhaul campaign finance law; ban "soft money" and restrict advocacy advertising
Yes   Approve bipartisan plan to increase rights of patients in managed-care health plans

INTEREST GROUPS

	AFL-CIO	ADA	CCUS	ACU
2000	100%	90%	42%	0%
1999	89%	100%	21%	0%
1998	100%	100%	22%	0%
1997	100%	95%	20%	8%

CQ VOTE STUDIES

	PARTY UNITY		PRESIDENTIAL SUPPORT	
	Support	Oppose	Support	Oppose
2000	98%	2%	88%	12%
1999	97%	3%	85%	15%
1998	97%	3%	88%	12%
1997	96%	4%	76%	24%

NEW YORK 11

Central Brooklyn — Flatbush; Crown Heights; Brownsville

The 11th, a residential district in central Brooklyn with a black-majority population, covers some of the borough's best and worst neighborhoods. When the New York legislature in 1997 redrew the boundaries of the neighboring 12th — a Hispanic-majority district declared to be unconstitutionally gerrymandered — it changed the boundaries of the 11th only slightly. Some African-American residents in the north were replaced by residents of Park Slope in the northwest, increasing the district's white population and average income. But the change did not affect the district's reliably Democratic vote.

At the heart of the district is Flatbush, a working-class black and Hispanic neighborhood that has become home to Caribbean immigrants from Jamaica, Haiti, the Dominican Republic, Trinidad and Tobago. The district's West Indian Festival and parade attracts millions of visitors every year, a feature that economic development officials hope to exploit to draw tourists into Brooklyn.

North of Flatbush sits Crown Heights, made infamous in 1991 when a station wagon driven by an orthodox rabbi's assistant struck two children, killing one. The incident touched off four days of riots between African-Americans and Hasidic Jews and contributed to the defeat of then-mayor David Dinkins. The world headquarters of the Lubavitchers, an intellectual orthodox Jewish movement that began in the late 18th century, is located in Crown Heights.

MAJOR INDUSTRY
Health care, retail, tourism

CITIES
New York (pt.), 580,337 (1990)

UNUSUAL FEATURES
In 1947, Jackie Robinson became the first black major league baseball player at the Brooklyn Dodgers' Ebbets Field; Brooklyn Museum; Brooklyn Botanic Garden.

Rep. Nydia M. Velázquez (D)

Elected 1992; 5th term

CAPITOL OFFICE
225-2361; fax 226-0327; 2241 Rayburn Bldg. 20515

INTERNET
e-mail: www.house.gov/writerep
web: www.house.gov/velazquez

COMMITTEES
Financial Services
Small Business - ranking member

HOMETOWN
Brooklyn

BORN
March 28, 1953, Yabucoa, P.R.

RELIGION
Roman Catholic

FAMILY
Husband, Paul Bader

EDUCATION
U. of Puerto Rico, B.A. 1974; New York U., M.A. 1976

CAREER
Professor

POLITICAL HIGHLIGHTS
New York City Council, 1984-85; defeated for re-election to New York City Council, 1984

ELECTION RESULTS

2000 GENERAL

Nydia M. Velázquez (D, WFM)	81,699	86.5%
Rosemary Markgraf (R)	10,052	10.6%
Paul Pederson (SW)	1,025	1.1%

2000 PRIMARY

Nydia M. Velázquez (D)	15,894	77.1%
Mildred Rosario (D)	4,713	22.9%

1998 GENERAL

Nydia M. Velázquez (D)	53,269	83.6%
Rosemary Markgraf (R)	7,405	11.6%
Angel Diaz (C)	1,632	2.6%
Hector Cortes Jr. (L)	1,080	1.7%

PREVIOUS WINNING PERCENTAGES
1996 (85%); 1994 (92%); 1992 (77%)

The 12th District has the highest percentage of blue-collar workers in New York, and Velázquez says she wants to help "working men and women who want to go to work, raise and educate their children, and live in a clean environment."

She is in a good position to fulfill these goals as the top Democrat on the Small Business Committee — the first-ever Hispanic woman to serve as the ranking member of a full House committee. Velázquez (Veh-LASS-kez), who is also the first Puerto Rican woman ever elected to Congress, was brought up in the sugar cane region of the U.S. commonwealth. There, she and a twin sister and their seven siblings were raised by a cane-cutting father and a mother who helped the family make ends meet by selling food to the other cane workers. Her father also had a business that made cinder blocks, and he had to deal with the regulations, labor standards and taxes that confront all small businesses.

Velázquez says she takes inspiration from the hard work of her parents to keep their small businesses going. On Small Business, she has pushed to promote economic development in low-income areas and to increase the share of government business that goes to small firms. And she is a leader in the House, along with two other Puerto Rico-born lawmakers, on issues of importance to the island commonwealth.

A number of other House committees outrank Small Business in terms of prestige and clout, but if work on the low-visibility panel does not earn Velázquez a wealth of publicity, it does afford her the opportunity to promote entrepreneurship by women and minorities. In the 106th Congress, Velázquez introduced a number of bills with that goal, including a measure to help women-owned businesses win a bigger piece of the government procurement pie. She directed a Small Business Democratic staff study of the procurement practices at 21 government agencies that do substantial business with private industry. The study resulted in a "report card" that gave the agencies generally low marks with regard to using small firms.

One obstacle to small businesses winning more government contracts was the practice of "bundling" — combining several smaller contracts into a single, larger one, in an effort to obtain better terms for the government. Velázquez introduced a bill that would bar federal agencies from bundling contracts if that prevented them from meeting contracting goals negotiated by the Small Business Administration with each agency.

Another priority for Velázquez is to strengthen economic development programs for inner-city neighborhoods. She authored a portion of a "new markets" initiative in the 106th Congress designed to boost the economies of low- and middle-income areas that have not shared in the nation's economic prosperity. Her section of the bill called for a venture capital program tailored for small businesses.

On the Banking Committee (now Financial Services), Velázquez won House approval in the 106th Congress of her proposal to require greater participation by small businesses on the panel that determines how the resources of bankrupt companies will be distributed among various creditors. In the 105th, she sponsored a measure, which eventually became law, that directed the Treasury Department to devise a national strategy to fight money laundering and designate some parts of the country as "high intensity" money-laundering areas. One of those areas was a section of her district — Jackson Heights in Queens — known by federal prosecutors as

"Ground Zero" for money-laundering activity, with Colombian drug lords the major beneficiaries.

Velázquez has a keen interest in immigration issues. From 1986 until her election to the House, she worked as a liaison between the Puerto Rican government and Latino communities in the United States. Velázquez joined with other Puerto Rican lawmakers in demanding that the Navy stop using the small island of Vieques, just off Puerto Rico, for bombing practice. (She got herself arrested in a protest of the shelling.) The lawmakers supported President Clinton's offer of clemency to 16 Puerto Rican nationalists who had been imprisoned for terrorist acts in the late 1970s and early 1980s, although Velázquez had been urging an unconditional pardon.

After graduating from the University of Puerto Rico — the first person in her family to receive a college diploma — Velázquez came to New York City for graduate school. She then taught Puerto Rican studies at Hunter College and worked briefly as a special assistant to Democratic Rep. Edolphus Towns. She served briefly on the New York City Council before taking the Puerto Rico liaison job in 1986.

Her local name recognition increased dramatically shortly before her 1992 House race, when she ran a Hispanic voter registration effort financed by the Puerto Rican government. She said the effort registered 200,000 voters nationwide, but critics said she targeted the Brooklyn sections that later became part of her newly drawn Hispanic-majority congressional district.

During the campaign, an anonymous source faxed to the New York Post hospital records showing that Velázquez had attempted suicide in 1991. The records also revealed that she had been battling depression with alcohol and pills. Friends said her depression stemmed from being torn between her duty to her ailing parents in Puerto Rico and her work with the New York Hispanic community. She later sponsored legislation to protect patients' medical records.

Her biggest obstacle in the Democratic primary was nine-term Democratic Rep. Stephen J. Solarz, whose district had been dismantled in redistricting. Solarz hired Hispanic advisers and learned a few Spanish phrases, but as an unknown to many of his would-be constituents, he was branded a carpetbagger and a wealthy outsider. Velázquez defeated Solarz by 5 percentage points in the primary and crushed her Republican foe in the general election, capturing 77 percent.

Since 1992, Velázquez has won handily, even after 1997 court-ordered redistricting reduced the Hispanic population in the 12th District from 58 percent to 49 percent.

KEY VOTES

2000

Yes Raise hourly minimum wage by $1 over two years
No   Halt funding for U.S. mission in Kosovo unless European nations pay more
Yes Provide Medicare benefits to military retirees and their dependents
No   Grant China permanent normal trade status
Yes Phase out estate, gift and trust taxes
No   Prohibit implementation of president's national monument designations
No   Approve GOP plan to provide prescription drug coverage for Medicare beneficiaries
Yes Increase help for poor nations indebted to international financial institutions

1999

Yes Impose steel import quotas
No   Kill proposal to take aviation trust funds off budget
No   Require background checks on buyers only at gun shows with 10 or more vendors
Yes Remove barriers among banking, securities and insurance companies
Yes Authorize state grants to hire teachers and reduce class size
Yes Overhaul campaign finance law; ban "soft money" and restrict advocacy advertising
Yes Approve bipartisan plan to increase rights of patients in managed-care health plans

INTEREST GROUPS

	AFL-CIO	ADA	CCUS	ACU
2000	100%	90%	40%	4%
1999	100%	100%	24%	4%
1998	100%	95%	33%	8%
1997	100%	95%	20%	4%

CQ VOTE STUDIES

	PARTY UNITY		PRESIDENTIAL SUPPORT	
	Support	Oppose	Support	Oppose
2000	97%	3%	85%	15%
1999	95%	5%	76%	24%
1998	96%	4%	81%	19%
1997	98%	2%	80%	20%

NEW YORK 12

Lower East Side of Manhattan; parts of Brooklyn and Queens

The 12th was created in 1992 to form a Hispanic-majority district under the auspices of the Voting Rights Act. The district quickly came under scrutiny because its odd shape – many called it the Bullwinkle District because of its resemblance to the cartoon moose – suggesting it had been drawn unconstitutionally, with race as the predominant factor.

After a protracted battle, the state legislature redrew the district for the 1998 election, making it more compact. The new configuration had a minimal effect on neighboring districts but did change the 12th's racial makeup slightly. The Hispanic population dropped from 58 percent to 49 percent, more than doubling the non-Hispanic white population. The new 12th District kept two areas with large Asian and Hispanic populations – lower Manhattan, including Chinatown, and Sunset Park in Brooklyn. It also received the heavily Hispanic Brooklyn neighborhood of Williamsburg.

The redrawn 12th covers working-class and poor neighborhoods with industrial areas near Sunset Park, the Brooklyn Navy Yard, Greenpoint and East New York. The district's blue-collar and minority composition makes it firmly Democratic.

Even with a significant immigrant population that is disqualified from voting and low turnout among Hispanic voters, the 12th elected and continues to send a Puerto Rican representative to Congress. While it is unclear what will happen to the district in 2002 redistricting, current boundary lines have posed little electoral challenge to Rep. Velázquez.

MAJOR INDUSTRY
Health care, manufacturing, service

CITIES
New York (pt.), 580,337 (1990)

UNUSUAL FEATURES
Lower East Side Tenement Museum; Chinatown; Leaders have plans to build a 71-acre waterfront park across from Manhattan's downtown.

Rep. Vito J. Fossella (R)

CAPITOL OFFICE
225-3371; fax 226-1272
1239 Longworth Bldg. 20515

INTERNET
e-mail: vito.fossella@mail.house.gov
web: www.house.gov/fossella

COMMITTEES
Energy & Commerce
Financial Services

HOMETOWN
Great Kills

BORN
March 9, 1965, South Beach, N.Y.

RELIGION
Roman Catholic

FAMILY
Wife, Mary Pat Fossella; two children

EDUCATION
U. of Pennsylvania, B.S. 1987; Fordham U., J.D. 1993

CAREER
Management consultant; lawyer

POLITICAL HIGHLIGHTS
New York City Council, 1994-97

ELECTION RESULTS

2000 GENERAL

Vito J. Fossella (R, C, RTL)	109,806	64.6%
Katina M. Johnstone (D, WFM)	57,603	33.9%
Anita Lerman (INDC, GREEN)	2,653	1.6%

2000 PRIMARY

Vito J. Fossella (R)	unopposed

1998 GENERAL

Vito J. Fossella (R, C, RTL)	76,138	64.8%
Eugene V. "Gene" Prisco (D, L)	40,167	34.2%
Anita Lerman (INDC)	1,245	1.1%

PREVIOUS WINNING PERCENTAGES
1997 Special Election (61%)

Elected November 1997; 2nd full term

The easygoing Fossella has a regular-guy persona — described by the New York Daily News as a "self-deprecating, smart-aleck style" — that makes him approachable and personally popular in the district. In the few years since he took over the 13th District from well-known GOP Rep. Susan Molinari, Fossella has shown that he is likely to attract the same kind of national notice that Molinari once received.

Fossella not only followed Molinari's 1996 prime-time appearance at the Republican National Convention with an appearance of his own in 2000, he also played a leading role in the congressional debate over President Clinton's clemency offer to a group of Puerto Rican militant nationalists who were imprisoned for a string of bombings and robberies in the 1970s and 1980s.

In the 106th Congress, his first full term in Washington, Fossella (Fuh-SELL-ah) landed a seat on the Commerce Committee, where he was able to keep a sharp lookout for any moves that threatened to delay the closure of the Fresh Kills landfill on Staten Island — a matter of intense importance in the 13th, which includes Staten Island and a portion of Brooklyn.

Fossella votes a dependable conservative line, more so than most Republican lawmakers from the Northeast. He supported Clinton only about a quarter of the time, and his votes on most labor and social policy issues usually match up with the GOP majority.

Fossella's brief speech to the GOP convention in Philadelphia was, in part, payback from candidate George W. Bush for Fossella's early support of his candidacy. But Fossella also had an interesting tale to tell as he touted Bush's Social Security proposals: Fossella's great-grandfather, James O'Leary, was a Democratic member of Congress in the 1930s and 1940s and voted in favor of the creation of the Social Security system. "He had the foresight ... to act for my parents and my generation," Fossella said. "Now we need a leader who has the same foresight ... to act for future generations."

Although Fossella's family tree includes O'Leary and an uncle who was a New York City Council member, his mother says she never really expected her son to go into politics. Indeed, Fossella often points with pride to his work in the private sector as a real estate management consultant. He did not formally abandon his family's Democratic roots until 1990.

But Fossella's political instincts won out when the same New York City Council seat once held by his uncle Frank — and later by Molinari — came open in 1994. Fossella, by then a lawyer, took the council seat in a special election, and he won a full term later that same year.

As part of an overmatched GOP minority on the city council, Fossella managed to win notice in the conservative and insular borough of Staten Island by securing funding for the island's first new public schools in a decade and creating the Readers Are Leaders program that encourages fourth-graders to read — a program with which he still remains involved.

The landfill issue is another carryover from his city council days, when Fossella played a key role in mandating the closure of the landfill by the end of 2001. Now New York City must find another place to ship its garbage, and that is why his seat on what is now called Energy and Commerce matters. Lawmakers from other areas of the country want Congress to give local governments the power to restrict garbage shipments from out of state, and Fossella sought the Commerce post in order to fight that effort.

On the issue of clemency for the jailed Puerto Ricans, one of whose victims was a police officer who lives in his district, Fossella said he was outraged that convicted terrorists were negotiating the terms of their release from prison with high-ranking government officials, while the victims of their acts had no voice in the matter. Fossella introduced a resolution opposing the clemency offer, and the House voted overwhelmingly for it. He also drafted legislation that would require victims of crimes to be notified whenever the president considers clemency for the offenders.

When he arrived on Capitol Hill in late 1997 after his special-election victory, Fossella was given a seat on the Transportation and Infrastructure Committee, along with an assignment to Banking.

On Transportation, Fossella got $32 million for new ferries on the Staten Island-Manhattan run, the first new vessels in many years. He convinced state authorities to construct bus-only lanes on the Staten Island Expressway. Transportation is a big issue on Staten Island, linked to the rest of New York City by only one bridge and the storied ferry service. Fossella also worked to reduce noise from aircraft flying low over Staten Island after takeoff from Newark, New Jersey. The noise issue has been hotly contested for years and pits New York against New Jersey. Fossella's efforts continued in the 106th Congress, even though he left the Transportation panel.

He is also watchful for periodic efforts to alter funding formulas that determine allocation of education dollars. In 1999, he geared up to rebuff a plan to shift $20 million from Staten Island and Brooklyn to other New York boroughs.

Fossella drew attention in 1998 when he launched a fundraising campaign seeking $65,000 to back a USO show for troops in the Middle East. The campaign, the first ever for a member of Congress, arose from Fossella's discussions with Staten Island veterans who remembered the USO shows fondly. He also drew notice in 1999 when he protested a Brooklyn Museum of Art exhibit of the Virgin Mary in which elephant dung was used. "Nowhere does it say that the American taxpayer has to subsidize so-called art that desecrates one religion," he said.

When Susan Molinari announced in 1997 that she was resigning from the House to take a job with CBS, her father, Guy, a former House member himself and a force in Staten Island GOP politics as the borough president, immediately tapped Fossella as the heir apparent. Molinari referred to him as "my son." During the November 1997 special-election campaign, which coincided with the New York mayoral race, Fossella marched alongside GOP Mayor Rudolph W. Giuliani's re-election bandwagon. Giuliani's landslide margins within the district helped propel Fossella to an easy victory. His re-election contests since have been uneventful.

KEY VOTES

2000
No   Raise hourly minimum wage by $1 over two years
No   Halt funding for U.S. mission in Kosovo unless European nations pay more
Yes   Provide Medicare benefits to military retirees and their dependents
Yes   Grant China permanent normal trade status
Yes   Phase out estate, gift and trust taxes
Yes   Prohibit implementation of president's national monument designations
Yes   Approve GOP plan to provide prescription drug coverage for Medicare beneficiaries
No   Increase help for poor nations indebted to international financial institutions

1999
No   Impose steel import quotas
Yes   Kill proposal to take aviation trust funds off budget
Yes   Require background checks on buyers only at gun shows with 10 or more vendors
+   Remove barriers among banking, securities and insurance companies
No   Authorize state grants to hire teachers and reduce class size
No   Overhaul campaign finance law; ban "soft money" and restrict advocacy advertising
No   Approve bipartisan plan to increase rights of patients in managed-care health plans

INTEREST GROUPS

	AFL-CIO	ADA	CCUS	ACU
2000	0%	0%	80%	80%
1999	0%	15%	91%	83%
1998	0%	0%	100%	96%

CQ VOTE STUDIES

	PARTY UNITY		PRESIDENTIAL SUPPORT	
	Support	Oppose	Support	Oppose
2000	91%	9%	26%	74%
1999	89%	11%	26%	74%
1998	91%	9%	23%	77%
1997	100%	0%	13%	87%

NEW YORK 13
Staten Island; part of southwest Brooklyn

Although Democrats hold an edge in voter registration, Staten Island's large retired population and white, upper middle-class suburban residents are more amenable to Republicans than any of New York City's other districts. The 13th's predominantly Italian-American and Catholic conservatives — on both sides of the Verrazano-Narrows Bridge that connects Staten Island and Brooklyn — have elected a Republican representative since 1980.

Staten Island was so disenchanted with the city's Democratic leadership that in 1993 residents overwhelmingly approved a referendum to secede from the city. Enactment of the referendum was blocked by the state legislature, but grumbling and a court challenge likely would have continued if a newly elected Republican mayor and governor had not quelled concerns of Islanders. Chief among Staten Island's beefs had been the presence of the Fresh Kills landfill, a major dumping ground for the city. With the change in city leadership, the

dump has been scheduled to close by the end of 2001. In addition, the charge for the Verrazano-Narrows Bridge has been reduced and the Staten Island Ferry is now free — quieting talk of secession.

The largely Italian western Brooklyn portion of the 12th mirrors the much more populous Staten Island but earned unfavorable attention in 1989 when racial tension erupted after the murder of a black youth in Bensonhurst.

MAJOR INDUSTRY
Health care, retail, communications

MILITARY BASES
Fort Hamilton (Army), 1,146 military, 162 civilian (1998)

CITIES
New York (pt.), 580,337 (1990)

UNUSUAL FEATURES
Bay Ridge was the setting for the 1977 disco movie, "Saturday Night Fever;" Todt Hill, the highest point on the Eastern Seaboard.

Rep. Carolyn B. Maloney (D)

Elected 1992; 5th term

Maloney likes to speak her mind, whether by taking to the House floor or by writing scores of bills. And her views are firmly liberal, as she criticizes the Republican majority for meddling in the census or ignoring the rights of breast-feeding women or failing to protect the elderly from financial fraud.

As the co-chairwoman of the Congressional Caucus on Women's Issues and as the top Democrat on the subcommittee that oversaw the preparations for and administration of the 2000 census, Maloney in the 106th Congress was afforded platforms from which to voice her thoughts on women's issues and on how the census affects federal spending across the nation.

She is one of the most prolific authors of legislation in the House. In the 106th Congress, she introduced 53 bills and resolutions, more than all but nine lawmakers. Many of her bills represented priority issues for the women's caucus, which she co-chaired along with fellow New Yorker Sue W. Kelly, a Republican.

Some congressional observers say Maloney appears unfocused, in conversation and also in her legislative work. Clearly, her introduction of bills on a multitude of topics displays her varied interests. Her 53 bills in the past two years fell under the jurisdiction of 13 committees.

Newsday, in a 1998 assessment of Queens lawmakers (the 14th District includes the East Side of Manhattan and some neighborhoods in Queens), said Maloney "seemed surprisingly clueless when she arrived in Washington. ... But her stock has been rising." The New York Daily News was kinder in its own 1998 assessment, giving her high marks for work ethic and constituent service.

In the 105th Congress, Democratic leaders gave Maloney primary responsibility for making the case that the GOP was playing politics with the 2000 census. From her post as the ranking Democrat on the Census Subcommittee of the Government Reform panel, she waged battle with Chairman Dan Miller of Florida on whether the Census Bureau should be permitted to use statistical sampling to augment the traditional head count. Statistical sampling is a technique that scientifically estimates population in areas where traditional head-counting methods do not yield an accurate tally.

Calling it "the civil rights issue of the 1990s," Maloney accused the GOP of blocking sampling because it might boost the count of minorities and give Democrats an edge in redistricting. "The Republican leadership should not be afraid of counting blacks, Hispanics and Asians," she said.

The census count not only determines allocation of House seats in Congress, but also affects countless formulas for distributing federal dollars. Maloney argued that New York's population was significantly undercounted in 1990, costing the state billions of dollars. Her work on the census is tied in with a longstanding interest in what she sees as inequitable funding formulas that have cost both the state and the city federal dollars.

Maloney had her eye on a Government Reform seat even before she was elected, so she could put her New York City Council expertise on procurement and government contracting policies to use. She had been the city government's top watchdog against government waste, chairing the Committee on Contracts. She is the author of a number of provisions on contract oversight and federal debt collection.

Maloney also sits on the Financial Services Committee (formerly Banking), where she focuses on holding down credit card interest rates, pro-

CAPITOL OFFICE
225-7944; fax 225-4709; 2430 Rayburn Bldg. 20515

INTERNET
e-mail: rep.carolyn.maloney@mail.house.gov
web: www.house.gov/maloney

COMMITTEES
Financial Services
Government Reform
Joint Economic

HOMETOWN
Manhattan

BORN
Feb. 19, 1948, Greensboro, N.C.

RELIGION
Presbyterian

FAMILY
Husband, Clifton H.W. Maloney; two children

EDUCATION
Greensboro College, A.B. 1968

CAREER
Legislative aide; teacher

POLITICAL HIGHLIGHTS
New York City Council, 1982-93

ELECTION RESULTS

2000 GENERAL

Carolyn B. Maloney (D, L)	148,080	73.9%
Carla Rhodes (R)	45,453	22.7%
Sandra Stevens (GREEN)	4,869	2.4%

2000 PRIMARY

Carolyn B. Maloney (D)	unopposed

1998 GENERAL

Carolyn B. Maloney (D, L, INDC)	111,072	77.4%
Stephanie Kupferman (R)	32,458	22.6%

PREVIOUS WINNING PERCENTAGES
1996 (72%); 1994 (64%); 1992 (50%)

tecting the elderly from financial fraud and giving senior citizens in public housing the right to own household pets. In the 107th, she is the top Democrat on the Domestic Monetary Policy, Technology and Economic Growth Subcommittee.

Maloney's strong feminist streak is evident in her vocal defense of abortion rights and her interest in issues affecting women and children. She has introduced a number of bills to ensure the rights of women to breast-feed or express milk for their children while at work. "Breast-feeding is not a crime," she said. "But mothers ... have been made to feel as if they are engaging in some sort of lewd behavior." Her legislation to permit breast-feeding on federal property (after some nursing women were asked to leave the Capitol, federal museums and parks) was signed into law in 1999. In the past several Congresses, she has also introduced an equal rights amendment to the Constitution.

In 2000, she was able to win some money for work on a new Second Avenue subway line. She proudly notes her work to win continued funding for a United Nations family planning effort, and she co-founded a congressional task force on Parkinson's disease, which worked to give federal research efforts on the illness higher priority.

Maloney is a leading proponent of changing how political campaigns are run. She wants more funding for the Federal Election Commission to monitor campaign fundraising and investigate abuses. Maloney also has pushed for legislation to establish an independent commission to propose changes in the campaign finance system.

Maloney hails from Greensboro, N.C., where she was born and educated. She came to New York City for a visit in her early 20s and stayed, eventually embarking on a teaching career, which included an adult education class in East Harlem. She then took a series of jobs in the city's educational bureaucracy. Maloney says she realized that government had a larger impact than any teacher on the education of the city's youth, and she moved to Albany to work for the state legislature. Five years later, she was elected to the New York City Council, where she served 10 years.

When Maloney ran against seven-term GOP Rep. Bill Green in 1992, media hype about the "Year of the Woman" lent momentum to her underdog challenge. She also benefited from redistricting, which forced Green to campaign on some unfamiliar turf. She profited from name recognition built up during her time on the city council and beat Green narrowly, 50 percent to 48 percent.

Her re-election races since then have been runaways.

KEY VOTES

2000

Yes   Raise hourly minimum wage by $1 over two years

No   Halt funding for U.S. mission in Kosovo unless European nations pay more

Yes   Provide Medicare benefits to military retirees and their dependents

Yes   Grant China permanent normal trade status

No   Phase out estate, gift and trust taxes

No   Prohibit implementation of president's national monument designations

No   Approve GOP plan to provide prescription drug coverage for Medicare beneficiaries

Yes   Increase help for poor nations indebted to international financial institutions

1999

Yes   Impose steel import quotas

No   Kill proposal to take aviation trust funds off budget

No   Require background checks on buyers only at gun shows with 10 or more vendors

Yes   Remove barriers among banking, securities and insurance companies

Yes   Authorize state grants to hire teachers and reduce class size

Yes   Overhaul campaign finance law; ban "soft money" and restrict advocacy advertising

Yes   Approve bipartisan plan to increase rights of patients in managed-care health plans

INTEREST GROUPS

	AFL-CIO	ADA	CCUS	ACU
2000	90%	90%	45%	12%
1999	78%	100%	36%	4%
1998	100%	100%	33%	8%
1997	100%	95%	50%	8%

CQ VOTE STUDIES

	PARTY UNITY		PRESIDENTIAL SUPPORT	
	Support	Oppose	Support	Oppose
2000	92%	8%	82%	18%
1999	93%	7%	82%	18%
1998	93%	7%	82%	18%
1997	95%	5%	81%	19%

NEW YORK 14
East Side Manhattan; Parts of Queens

Republicans engineered politics on Manhattan's East Side when the mansions of aristocrats ruled this "Silk Stocking District." Beginning in the 1960s, the old-money elite were gradually supplanted by "limousine liberals," highly educated young professionals with a devotion to the arts. Some of the 14th's local leaders are still Republican and the 14th supported GOP Mayor Rudolph Giuliani in 1997, but the district elected a Democratic representative to Congress in 1992 and supported Democratic presidential candidates by huge margins in 1992, '96 and 2000.

In 1997, when a three-judge panel declared the nearby majority-Hispanic 12th District unconstitutionally gerrymandered, the boundaries of the 14th were redrawn to exclude its portion of Brooklyn. Although the district lost some working-class Democrats, it picked up new working-class neighborhoods in Queens. As a result, the changes caused no substantial shift in the 14th's political climate.

The 14th, which hosts some of New York City's most famous landmarks, including Central Park and Rockefeller Center, is a generally white, affluent district. Its Democratic base is supported by black populations near Harlem, Hispanic communities on the Lower East Side and a small part of Chinatown (most of the neighborhood is in the 12th District). Italian and Greek communities in Queens tend to be more socially conservative than their Manhattan neighbors but generally vote Democratic.

MAJOR INDUSTRY

Finance, publishing, communications, advertising, health care

CITIES

New York (pt.), 580,337 (1990)

UNUSUAL FEATURES

Central Park, Rockefeller Center, the Metropolitan Museum of Art, Grand Central Station, the United Nations and the Chrysler Building on Manhattan's East Side.

Rep. Charles B. Rangel (D)

CAPITOL OFFICE
225-4365; fax 225-0816; 2354 Rayburn Bldg. 20515

INTERNET
e-mail: www.house.gov/writerep
web: www.house.gov/rangel

COMMITTEES
Ways & Means - ranking member
Joint Taxation

HOMETOWN
Harlem

BORN
June 11, 1930, Harlem, N.Y.

RELIGION
Roman Catholic

FAMILY
Wife, Alma Rangel; two children

EDUCATION
New York U., B.S. 1957; St. John's U., LL.B. 1960

MILITARY SERVICE
Army, 1948-52

CAREER
Lawyer

POLITICAL HIGHLIGHTS
Assistant U.S. attorney, 1961-62; N.Y. Assembly, 1967-71; sought Democratic nomination for N.Y. City Council president, 1969

ELECTION RESULTS

2000 GENERAL

Charles B. Rangel (D, L, WFM)	130,161	91.9%
Jose A. Suero (R)	7,346	5.2%
Dean Loren (GREEN)	2,134	1.5%

2000 PRIMARY

Charles B. Rangel (D)	33,526	82.5%
Ruben Dario Vargas (D)	7,136	17.6%

1998 GENERAL

Charles B. Rangel (D, L)	90,424	93.1%
David E. Cunningham (R)	5,633	5.8%
Patrick McManus (C)	1,082	1.1%

PREVIOUS WINNING PERCENTAGES
1996 (91%); 1994 (97%); 1992 (95%); 1990 (97%); 1988 (97%); 1986 (96%); 1984 (97%); 1982 (97%); 1980 (96%); 1978 (96%); 1976 (97%); 1974 (97%); 1972 (96%); 1970 (87%)

Elected 1970; 16th term

Since dropping out of high school when he was 16, Rangel has overcome many obstacles to arrive at the pinnacle of power on Capitol Hill.

He survived firefights on the Korean peninsula that claimed much of his Army unit and eventually earned him the Purple Heart and Bronze Star. He returned to high school in his native Harlem at the age of 23 and continued on to earn bachelor's and law degrees under the G.I. Bill. And he recovered from setbacks in Congress, such as losing a race for majority whip in 1987, to become the ranking Democrat on the Ways and Means Committee and a key member of the party's leadership.

With the Democrats' failure to retake the House in the 2000 election, it appears Rangel may never reach the apex he has long sought: to chair Ways and Means, arguably the most powerful panel in Congress, which writes tax, trade, welfare, health care, Social Security and Medicare legislation.

He worked doggedly for the chance, transforming himself from a candidate with little modern campaign experience — largely because he hardly ever attracts more than token opposition in the 15th District — into a money-making machine, raising about $10 million for the party in the 1999-2000 election cycle. Only Minority Leader Richard A. Gephardt of Missouri and the chairman of the Democratic Congressional Campaign Committee, Patrick J. Kennedy of Rhode Island, raised more.

Rangel's efforts began in 1996, when his party first attempted to root out the Republicans who had come to power two years before. He spent much of his time on the road, offering to help Democrats in districts with substantial black populations and to conduct get-out-the-vote campaigns. By 2000, his national star had risen among Democrats and he raised much of his money at fêtes for himself, including a June birthday party at a Manhattan nightclub that netted more than $2 million for Democratic coffers. At the 2000 Democratic National Convention in Los Angeles, his autograph was highly sought by some of the entertainment celebrities in attendance.

Rangel attributed his lackluster convention speech to excessive scripting by party leaders; he does much better speaking off the cuff than reading a text. An energetic and aggressive partisan before the public, he defends the Democratic position with raspy-voiced glee. But he is described as friendly in private by many of the same people he publicly takes to task. In all situations, he relies on his sense of humor to smooth the way. His sly delivery and bombastic punch lines prompted one former aide to describe him as "a black Jackie Gleason."

Despite three decades in Washington, Rangel remains close to his Harlem roots. Raised by his seamstress mother and her family in the waning days of the Harlem Renaissance, Rangel's political career got its start when he appealed to the last of the Tammany Hall bosses to allow his grandfather to keep his job operating elevators at city hall. He succeeded, which convinced him to put his persuasive talents to work helping his friends and neighbors.

He first won election, to the state Assembly, in 1966. He won his House seat four years later. Rangel was among Harlem leaders who had tried to convince the legendary Adam Clayton Powell to spend more time watching over his district's interests in Congress and less time at a Caribbean vacation home. When Powell failed to clean up his act, Rangel defeated him in the Democratic primary — the main race in a district with few Republicans. The only significant challenger Rangel has faced since was Powell's son and namesake, in the 1994 primary.

Though Rangel has always assumed multiple roles in Congress, including founder and one-time chairman of the Congressional Black Caucus, he has remained heavily involved in district and New York City politics. That has not always made life easy. In 1999, he was entangled in a financial scandal at Harlem's historic Apollo Theater. He denied wrongdoing, and a lawsuit against Rangel and other members of the Apollo's board was dropped.

Rangel's legislative victories in Congress have also focused on his district. They have centered on providing tax incentives to bring retailers, housing and jobs to low-income districts such as his.

He worked with other lawmakers in 1978 to cut taxes for employers who hire hard-to-place workers. In 1986, he helped write a tax credit for developers who build low-income housing. In 1993, he joined with New York Republican Jack F. Kemp to enact a pilot project that offered businesses tax credits to move to blighted areas. As a result, Harlem has seen an economic resurgence, as chain retailers have located there. In 2001, he made a successful pitch to Bill Clinton to locate his post-presidential office in Harlem.

Rangel is a reliable liberal vote on social issues. He opposed the 1996 law that ended welfare's entitlement status and is a proponent of eliminating mandatory minimum penalties for drug possession.

On fiscal issues, he is a bit more pragmatic. Though he opposed much of the GOP's tax-cutting proposals on the grounds that they would do too little for lower-income Americans, he played a pivotal role in helping Republicans and President Clinton push a host of trade expansion measures through the 106th Congress. His support was considered integral to the enactment of laws granting China permanent normal trade status and further opening U.S. markets to goods made in Africa, Central America and the Caribbean. In both cases, Rangel brought along some Democrats who might have otherwise opposed bills anathema to organized labor. He is also a staunch advocate of re-establishing trade with Cuba.

While he worked with Republican Bill Archer of Texas on those issues and a few others during Archer's six years as Ways and Means chairman, the two did not always have a warm relationship, to the disappointment of the gregarious Rangel. He hopes to get along better with the new chairman, Bill Thomas of California, the successor to Archer, who retired.

Still, it may be difficult for Rangel to cede the long-coveted seat to yet another Republican. In 1996, after a grueling schedule of stumping in districts across the country, Rangel attributed much of his energy to his end goal: "I was campaigning to be chairman of Ways and Means. I don't know how well I would have done if I was campaigning to become the ranking member."

KEY VOTES

2000

Yes Raise hourly minimum wage by $1 over two years

No Halt funding for U.S. mission in Kosovo unless European nations pay more

? Provide Medicare benefits to military retirees and their dependents

Yes Grant China permanent normal trade status

No Phase out estate, gift and trust taxes

No Prohibit implementation of president's national monument designations

No Approve GOP plan to provide prescription drug coverage for Medicare beneficiaries

Yes Increase help for poor nations indebted to international financial institutions

1999

Yes Impose steel import quotas

No Kill proposal to take aviation trust funds off budget

No Require background checks on buyers only at gun shows with 10 or more vendors

Yes Remove barriers among banking, securities and insurance companies

Yes Authorize state grants to hire teachers and reduce class size

Yes Overhaul campaign finance law; ban "soft money" and restrict advocacy advertising

Yes Approve bipartisan plan to increase rights of patients in managed-care health plans

INTEREST GROUPS

	AFL-CIO	ADA	CCUS	ACU
2000	90%	90%	41%	4%
1999	78%	90%	29%	0%
1998	100%	90%	29%	9%
1997	100%	95%	30%	16%

CQ VOTE STUDIES

	PARTY UNITY		PRESIDENTIAL SUPPORT	
	Support	Oppose	Support	Oppose
2000	93%	7%	97%	3%
1999	96%	4%	81%	19%
1998	95%	5%	88%	12%
1997	96%	4%	82%	18%

NEW YORK 15

Northern Manhattan – Harlem; Washington Heights

This Harlem-centered district was a nexus of black political and cultural power during the heyday of the Harlem Renaissance in the 1920s. But by the time the district was created in 1944, the affluent black community had already attracted so many poor migrants that it had turned into a poverty-stricken district. Two highly popular black Democrats – Adam Clayton Powell Jr. and Rep. Rangel – have controlled the 15th since its creation, each serving more than 25 years. A solidly Democratic district, Bill Clinton won more than 85 percent of the vote here in 1992 and '96 and 90 percent chose Al Gore in 2000.

The past 20 years have brought substantial change to the 15th, with Puerto Rican and Dominican immigration supplanting the district's black majority. But low voter participation among Hispanics means the smaller non-Hispanic black population dominates the district's politics.

Harlem's 1996 designation as an federal empowerment zone has brought on the beginning of an economic resurgence. Refurbished brownstones, new restaurants, national retail chains and prominent corporations are moving into the area. In early 2001, Harlem also received a public relations boon when Clinton decided to lease office space in a building on 125th Street, the area's main thoroughfare.

Most of the 15th's jobs are provided by health care, higher education and small business sectors. But for most of the district's less-educated residents, those jobs are out of reach. The district's doctors, lawyers and other professionals reside in Harlem's affluent black neighborhoods like Strivers Row and the white, affluent Upper West Side and in Morningside Heights around Columbia University.

MAJOR INDUSTRY
Health care, higher education, retail

CITIES
New York (pt.), 580,337 (1990)

UNUSUAL FEATURES
The Apollo Theatre; Singers Lena Horne and Ella Fitzgerald, comedians Flip Wilson and Redd Foxx, heavyweight boxing champ Joe Lewis and baseball player Willie Mays hail from Harlem.

Rep. Jose E. Serrano (D)

CAPITOL OFFICE
225-4361; fax 225-6001; 2342 Rayburn Bldg. 20515

INTERNET
e-mail: jserrano@mail.house.gov
web: www.house.gov/serrano

COMMITTEES
Appropriations

HOMETOWN
Bronx

BORN
Oct. 24, 1943, Mayaguez, P.R.

RELIGION
Roman Catholic

FAMILY
Wife, Mary Staucet; five children

EDUCATION
Dodge Vocational H.S., graduated 1961; Lehman College, attended 1961

MILITARY SERVICE
Army Medical Corps, 1964-66

CAREER
School district administrator; banker

POLITICAL HIGHLIGHTS
N.Y. Assembly, 1975-90; sought Democratic nomination for Bronx borough president, 1985

ELECTION RESULTS

2000 GENERAL

Jose E. Serrano (D, L)	103,041	95.8%
Aaron Justice (R)	3,934	3.7%

2000 PRIMARY

Jose E. Serrano (D)	unopposed

1998 GENERAL

Jose E. Serrano (D, L)	67,367	95.4%
Thomas W. Bayley Jr. (R)	2,457	3.5%
Owen Camp (C)	756	1.1%

PREVIOUS WINNING PERCENTAGES
1996 (96%); 1994 (96%); 1992 (91%); 1990 (93%); 1990 Special Election (92%)

Elected March 1990; 6th full term

Serrano is an outspoken voice on two issues passionately debated within the Hispanic community: whether to end the U.S. embargo of Cuba, which he opposes, and whether to grant Puerto Rico statehood or independence, which he says the citizens of the island should decide. He has not been shy about engaging in high-profile activities that advance his case for each cause.

Serrano also has gone against his own party at times on federal spending matters. As a top Democrat on the Appropriations Committee, he has had to choose between siding with the panel on spending bills or rejecting measures that are opposed by the Democratic leadership. In 1999, for example, he voted for the bill funding the Commerce, Justice and State departments despite his party's opposition to its spending levels. And though he supported changes in immigration policy in 2000, he did not join with some other Democrats in urging President Clinton to veto any Commerce spending bill that did not include all the sought-after changes.

Serrano (sa-RAH-no, with a rolled 'R') gained the Appropriations post in 1993 when the Democratic leadership set out to make key panels "look more like America." In the 106th Congress, he became the top Democrat on the Commerce, Justice, State and Judiciary Subcommittee, which shepherds one of the most controversial annual spending measures through Congress.

As a panel member, Serrano has been able to obtain funding for a variety of South Bronx projects, including in social services, education, recreation, housing and cultural organizations.

But Serrano is best known for his high-profile battle to lift the decades-old U.S. trade embargo against Cuba. Of the 13 bills or resolutions he introduced in the 106th Congress, six dealt with the Cuba embargo. While Cuban-American critics of Fidel Castro's regime support increased economic sanctions, Serrano in the 106th reintroduced legislation to repeal the 1996 law that tightened the embargo against trade with Cuba. "It is inhumane to starve the Cuban people, punishing them with a trade embargo designed to bend their government to our political will," he has said.

In 2000, after a battle led by Republican George P. Nethercutt of Washington and other farm-state members, Congress did revise the law to allow some limited agricultural trade with Cuba and four other "rogue" nations, but the final measure fell far short of the changes Serrano sought.

He also introduced legislation to remove restrictions on American citizens traveling to Cuba and to allow the United States and Cuba to open news bureaus in each country. In this he was frustrated in 2000, as Congress tightened travel regulations. Serrano said that increased exchanges of information between Cubans and Americans will spur a peaceful democratic transition in the communist nation. He applauded Clinton's decision in March 1998 to reinstate direct flights to Cuba and to allow U.S.-based exiles to send money to family and friends living there.

His position on the Cuba embargo has led to bitter arguments with the two Cuban-American Republicans in the House: Lincoln Diaz-Balart and Ileana Ros-Lehtinen, both of whom represent parts of South Florida.

He tussled with Ros-Lehtinen in 1997 over a proposal requiring the State Department to notify Congress of all Cuban government complaints against U.S. citizens. The dispute got heated when he won approval of his amendment but Ros-Lehtinen forced a second vote, which he lost. His angry response was to call for recorded votes on every other amendment that had been agreed to over several days of debate, 21 in all. The resulting voting tied up floor action for hours, forced cancellation of committee meetings and kept lawmakers from other work.

The Puerto Rican-born Serrano broke with other Puerto Rican Democrats in 1998 to support legislation allowing the island's residents to vote on their political status. The bill, which passed the House by one vote, died in the Senate. It would have required that the people of Puerto Rico be given a choice between commonwealth status, which the island has now; statehood; or independence. He has called the commonwealth status "colonial" and said Puerto Ricans should choose either independence or statehood.

In 2000, Serrano was arrested outside the White House and led away in plastic handcuffs for protesting the Clinton administration's plan to continue to use the Puerto Rican beach of Vieques for training exercises using live bombs. His web page features a flashing banner proclaiming: "It's Time for the Navy to Leave Vieques."

Serrano represents a district that has been plagued by unemployment and crime, but his constituents can take hope from his up-from-poverty story. Serrano's parents emigrated to New York when he was 7. Raised in a housing project, he graduated from a vocational high school and served in the Army. He took a job with a New York City bank and began making political contacts in his work for a local school district in the Bronx.

Serrano's contacts in the school community helped him win a state Assembly seat in 1974. His tenure in Albany — including service as chairman of the Assembly Education Committee — made him a fixture in New York Hispanic politics.

When Democratic Rep. Robert Garcia resigned his seat in January 1990 after a defense contracting scandal, Serrano moved quickly to stake his claim. He breezed to victory with 92 percent of the vote in the special election against black Republican businessman Simeon Golar and won a full term with 93 percent that November.

In 1992, the already well-entrenched Serrano gained electoral insurance from a House redistricting plan that made his district more Hispanic. In elections since then, Serrano has gotten more than 90 percent of the vote.

He has tried to move up the ranks of the party leadership, but with no success. In the 105th Congress, he failed in his quest to be selected as one of his party's four chief deputy whips. Democratic leaders chose Robert Menendez of New Jersey, rather than Serrano, to succeed New Mexico Democrat Bill Richardson, who left Congress to work in the Clinton administration. Serrano had chaired the Hispanic Caucus in the 103rd Congress.

KEY VOTES

2000
Yes Raise hourly minimum wage by $1 over two years
No Halt funding for U.S. mission in Kosovo unless European nations pay more
Yes Provide Medicare benefits to military retirees and their dependents
Yes Grant China permanent normal trade status
No Phase out estate, gift and trust taxes
No Prohibit implementation of president's national monument designations
No Approve GOP plan to provide prescription drug coverage for Medicare beneficiaries
Yes Increase help for poor nations indebted to international financial institutions

1999
Yes Impose steel import quotas
Yes Kill proposal to take aviation trust funds off budget
No Require background checks on buyers only at gun shows with 10 or more vendors
No Remove barriers among banking, securities and insurance companies
Yes Authorize state grants to hire teachers and reduce class size
Yes Overhaul campaign finance law; ban "soft money" and restrict advocacy advertising
Yes Approve bipartisan plan to increase rights of patients in managed-care health plans

INTEREST GROUPS

	AFL-CIO	ADA	CCUS	ACU
2000	90%	90%	42%	0%
1999	89%	95%	12%	4%
1998	100%	90%	25%	0%
1997	100%	95%	30%	8%

CQ VOTE STUDIES

	PARTY UNITY		PRESIDENTIAL SUPPORT	
	Support	Oppose	Support	Oppose
2000	93%	7%	90%	10%
1999	93%	7%	70%	30%
1998	95%	5%	85%	15%
1997	97%	3%	80%	20%

NEW YORK 16

South Bronx

New York's 16th, covering the distressed neighborhoods of the South Bronx, is one of the poorest districts in the nation. Thirty percent of the area's residents live at or below the poverty line – well above the state average. But South Bronx's neighborhoods have started to turn around, thanks to grass-roots community work and a federally granted empowerment zone.

The South Bronx, overtaken by the post-World War II influx of Hispanics to New York City, has since 1970 elected Democrats of Puerto Rican origin to the House. The district is also home to many African, and South and Central American immigrants, and has one of the lowest non-Hispanic white populations in the nation.

Considered the most Democratic district in the nation, the 16th gave an astounding 94 percent of its vote to Bill Clinton in 1996 and 93 percent to Al Gore in 2000, their highest percentages in the nation. But like many districts with large minority and immigrant populations, voter turnout is low.

Like frontier settlements, several downtown developments of single-family homes and low-rise housing have been built on vacated lots by subsidized economic development organizations and occupied by people who grew up in the district and worked their way out, now returning to help rebuild the neighborhoods.

Light manufacturing firms also have set up shop, replacing some of the heavy industry that moved out decades ago. Yankee Stadium, just inside the district's boundaries, has so far survived threats from owner George Steinbrenner to move the team out of the borough.

MAJOR INDUSTRY
Health care, light manufacturing

CITIES
New York (pt.), 580,338 (1990)

UNUSUAL FEATURES
Bronx Zoo; New York Botanical Gardens.

Rep. Eliot L. Engel (D)

CAPITOL OFFICE
225-2464; fax 225-5513; 2303 Rayburn Bldg. 20515

INTERNET
e-mail: www.house.gov/writerep
web: www.house.gov/engel

COMMITTEES
Energy & Commerce
International Relations

HOMETOWN
Bronx

BORN
Feb. 18, 1947, Bronx, N.Y.

RELIGION
Jewish

FAMILY
Wife, Patricia Ennis Engel; three children

EDUCATION
Hunter-Lehman College, B.A. 1969; City U. of New York, Lehman College, M.A. 1973; New York Law School, J.D. 1987

CAREER
Teacher; guidance counselor

POLITICAL HIGHLIGHTS
Bronx Democratic district leader, 1974-77; N.Y. Assembly, 1977-88

ELECTION RESULTS

2000 GENERAL

Eliot L. Engel (D, L)	115,093	89.7%
Patrick McManus (C, R)	13,201	10.3%

2000 PRIMARY

Eliot L. Engel (D)	24,159	50.4%
Larry Seabrook (D)	19,629	41.0%
Sonia Zayas (D)	4,115	8.6%

1998 GENERAL

Eliot L. Engel (D, L)	80,947	88.0%
Peter Fiumefreddo (R, C, INDC)	11,037	12.0%

PREVIOUS WINNING PERCENTAGES
1996 (85%); 1994 (78%); 1992 (80%); 1990 (61%); 1988 (56%)

Elected 1988; 7th term

Looking at press releases from Engel's office, one might think he is a city councilman — notice of glaucoma screenings scheduled for Co-Op City, a high-rise complex; news about the construction of a new water filtration plant; and an announcement about the installation of a traffic light at a busy intersection. In his 22-square-mile congressional district, he has five offices. (Barbara Cubin, who represents the entire 97,000-plus square miles of Wyoming, has three district offices.)

Attention to local needs is second nature to Engel, who grew up in a Bronx middle-class housing project and earned his political spurs in local Democratic clubs. But it is also a political necessity now, as he must convince his constituents that he is still the man for them in Congress.

Engel is one of the few non-minority lawmakers who represent a district in which a majority of the populace belongs to a racial or ethnic minority, and in recent years he has been targeted by Hispanic and black challengers who have argued that he has lost touch with the needs of his district. As drawn for the 1990s, the 17th District is only 29 percent non-Hispanic white. A similar number of Engel's constituents are of Hispanic origin and almost 40 percent of the residents are black.

In 2000, Engel survived a nasty and racially tinged primary challenge from state Sen. Larry Seabrook, who is black and who received backing from Bronx Democratic Party leader Roberto Ramirez. Engel managed to win, 50 percent to 41 percent. Earlier, he had to withstand a serious challenge from salsa star Willie Colon in 1994 and less-organized challenges from another Hispanic candidate in 1996 and 1998.

Many political observers say that Engel's problems have stemmed not from anything he has or has not done in Congress, but from the fact that he is white in a majority-minority district. His political future depends, in large measure, on the shape of the district after the 2002 remapping.

Aside from local issues, Engel, who sits on the Energy and International Relations panels, has been active on a wide range of national matters, including policies related to mental health, illegal drugs, housing, and energy availability and price. His voting record is among the most liberal in the chamber. He supports the Democratic Party position more than 90 percent of the time.

Foreign affairs is one of Engel's principal interests in Washington. Such work is akin to constituent service: His district includes dozens of ethnic groups, including Irish, Italians and Eastern Europeans. (He co-chairs the Albanian Issues Caucus.) Like Engel, many of the district's residents are Jewish, and he is a strong supporter of Israel.

Engel is a liberal interventionist — he believes the United States should take steps to stop humanitarian tragedies. He was an early advocate of U.S. intervention in the civil war in Yugoslavia. In 1993, he joined a bipartisan group of lawmakers who urged the Clinton administration to take sides in Bosnia against the Serbs, who were being accused of perpetrating widespread atrocities in the name of "ethnic cleansing" — the forced removal of Muslims to create all-Serbian communities. Engel also supported limited airstrikes on Serbian positions.

In 2000, when the House voted on whether to start withdrawing from Kosovo unless U.S. allies bore more of the peacekeeping burden, Engel argued against it, saying: "What we have done in Kosovo is working. ... We have saved lives."

He opposed granting China normal trade status because of the country's human rights abuses. "Are we only for the almighty dollar or are we for morality and doing what's right?" he asked in 2000.

In keeping with his constituents' political inclinations, Engel follows a traditional Democratic course. He sides with labor unions, fights for civil rights, and defends such institutions as the United Nations, the Corporation for Public Broadcasting and the National Endowment for the Humanities against GOP attacks. He sometimes will cite his mother ("my best adviser in terms of health care, particularly the importance of prescription drug coverage and Medicare") or his constituents to explain his stand on controversial issues.

Engel is usually content to attend to constituent service and the nuts-and-bolts of legislation. But on one day every year, he has a brief moment on the national stage: He arrives early in the House chamber for the annual State of the Union address to be sure to grab an aisle seat so that he can greet the president and renew acquaintances with a number of ambassadors. He began the tradition as a freshman when he greeted President George Bush and continued in 2001 when he shook hands and chatted with George W. Bush as he walked down the aisle.

Engel's father was a welder, but father and son were both interested in politics and world affairs, and they walked picket lines together. The younger Engel was a political junkie growing up, even memorizing the names of all 100 senators as a youth, and he says that serving in Congress is like living a dream. He attended New York City public schools, where he later worked as a teacher and guidance counselor until his election to the state Assembly in 1977, when he defeated the candidate endorsed by the Democratic Party.

In the Assembly, he worked on housing and substance abuse issues and established his credentials in the "reform" wing of the Bronx Democratic organization. Thus, it was not completely unexpected when he announced in 1988 that he was giving up his Assembly seat to challenge Democratic Rep. Mario Biaggi, who was then on trial for bribery, conspiracy and extortion. Nevertheless, it was the gamble of his career. Biaggi remained highly popular, and most Democrats stood aside when Biaggi defiantly announced he would seek re-election in 1988.

But in August, Biaggi was convicted and resigned his seat. His name remained on the ballot, however, for both the primary and the general election (the latter because he regularly received the endorsement of district Republicans). Engel won both contests, taking 56 percent in the general election to Biaggi's 27 percent.

He easily rebuffed a Biaggi comeback attempt in 1992, but since then has felt growing pressure from Hispanic and black challengers.

KEY VOTES

2000
Yes	Raise hourly minimum wage by $1 over two years
No	Halt funding for U.S. mission in Kosovo unless European nations pay more
Yes	Provide Medicare benefits to military retirees and their dependents
No	Grant China permanent normal trade status
No	Phase out estate, gift and trust taxes
No	Prohibit implementation of president's national monument designations
No	Approve GOP plan to provide prescription drug coverage for Medicare beneficiaries
Yes	Increase help for poor nations indebted to international financial institutions

1999
Yes	Impose steel import quotas
No	Kill proposal to take aviation trust funds off budget
No	Require background checks on buyers only at gun shows with 10 or more vendors
Yes	Remove barriers among banking, securities and insurance companies
Yes	Authorize state grants to hire teachers and reduce class size
Yes	Overhaul campaign finance law; ban "soft money" and restrict advocacy advertising
Yes	Approve bipartisan plan to increase rights of patients in managed-care health plans

INTEREST GROUPS

	AFL-CIO	ADA	CCUS	ACU
2000	100%	85%	38%	22%
1999	89%	95%	24%	0%
1998	100%	95%	24%	4%
1997	100%	100%	30%	8%

CQ VOTE STUDIES

	PARTY UNITY		PRESIDENTIAL SUPPORT	
	Support	Oppose	Support	Oppose
2000	94%	6%	87%	13%
1999	94%	6%	84%	16%
1998	97%	3%	82%	18%
1997	92%	8%	77%	23%

NEW YORK 17
North Bronx; parts of southern Westchester

A middle- to working-class district where New York City runs into nearby suburbs, the 17th covers the North Bronx, with tentacles reaching into the South Bronx and Westchester County. It takes in the mammoth apartment complex known as Co-Op City that, with more than 50,000 residents, is a formidable voting bloc in itself.

Long a Democratic-voting district, the 17th consistently elects Democrats to all levels of government. Bill Clinton received 76 percent of the vote in the 1992 presidential contest and 85 percent in '96. And in 2000, the district gave Al Gore an overwhelming 87 percent.

The boundaries of the 17th were drawn to take in large tracts of minority residential neighborhoods, and the district is one of the state's most ethnically and racially diverse. On its east side, it covers a large portion of Mount Vernon that is almost two-thirds black. Farther north, it takes in part of New Rochelle, including its downtown, picking up more black voters. This leaves the 17th with a population that is divided

roughly evenly among blacks, whites and Hispanics.

Riverdale, a heavily Jewish neighborhood, sits at the western edge of the Bronx and is the 17th's most affluent and suburban community. But the district also includes some housing projects in the South Bronx and the poor, minority neighborhoods of Yonkers, which have been the site of a drawn-out court battle over housing and education discrimination. Yonkers is now under court supervision, remedying both problems.

MAJOR INDUSTRY
Health care, higher education, city government

CITIES
New York (pt.), 454,628 (1990); Yonkers (pt.), 68,968 (1990); Mount Vernon (pt.), 45,181 (1990)

UNUSUAL FEATURES
Duke Ellington, Elizabeth Cady Stanton, F.W. Woolworth, Nellie Bly and William Barclay 'Bat' Masterson are all buried in the Woodlawn Cemetery in the Bronx.

Rep. Nita M. Lowey (D)

Elected 1988; 7th term

After 12 years in the House, Lowey saw her plans to move up the political ladder in 2000 quashed when first lady Hillary Rodham Clinton jumped into the race to replace retiring New York Democratic Sen. Daniel Patrick Moynihan. Lowey had been patiently awaiting the opportunity for years, amassing campaign cash for a Senate run.

But after Clinton threw her hat into the ring, Lowey (LOW-ee) loyally and gracefully stepped aside. She seconded Clinton's nomination at the New York Democratic convention, and her chief of staff went on to become the press secretary for Clinton's Senate campaign. The classy way in which Lowey handled the awkward situation earned her praise from fellow Democrats and even a few Republicans.

Furthermore, for the 2000 elections, Lowey helped raise more than $6 million for the House Democrats' effort to recruit and elect women candidates. And she contributed more than $160,000 from her own campaign treasury to aid other Democrats. Her fundraising prowess gained notice from Democratic leaders, who rewarded her in the 107th Congress with the chairmanship of the Democratic Congressional Campaign Committee, House Democrats' political arm.

During her lengthy House career, the high-energy Lowey has established herself as a leading advocate for women's rights and other liberal causes. She has continually pushed family planning issues, fiercely opposing Republican efforts to eliminate appropriations for international family planning programs and to outlaw a procedure its opponents call "partial birth" abortion.

Although Lowey has frequently found herself on the losing end of abortion battles in the Republican-controlled House, she did enjoy an unexpected triumph in 1998 when she won contraceptive coverage for federal workers whose insurance plans cover pharmaceuticals. She called contraceptive coverage a "basic women's health benefit." Anti-abortion lawmakers, led by Christopher H. Smith, R-N.J., opposed Lowey, but she persevered during months of haggling and negotiating. Her provision finally was included in a spending bill, but only after she agreed to language that would exempt physicians with religious or moral objections to contraceptives from being required to prescribe them.

When claims of sexual harassment in the Army garnered attention during the 105th Congress, Lowey and other female members met with Army officials to suggest that the military set up a system outside the regular chain of command for soldiers to report allegations of misconduct. The group also discussed the problem with the other military services. "It is hard to believe that this activity ... has not occurred in the other branches as well," she said.

During the 106th, Lowey fought to give law enforcement three days to conduct background checks at gun shows. When the House took up a series of gun control amendments in 1999, Lowey used all of her powers of persuasion to drum up votes for a proposal by fellow New York Democrat Carolyn McCarthy to tighten federal regulation of gun shows.

She aggressively lobbied Gary A. Condit, D-Calif., seen as a conservative swing vote, arguing that a milder alternative bill under consideration at the time had been proposed to give Republicans political cover while voting down McCarthy's bill. After pleading with Condit just off the House floor, she turned to Connecticut Democrat Rosa DeLauro and said, "I think we got him." She was right, but in the end a weaker proposal prevailed.

CAPITOL OFFICE
225-6506; fax 225-0546; 2329 Rayburn Bldg. 20515

INTERNET
e-mail: nita.lowey@mail.house.gov
web: www.house.gov/lowey

COMMITTEES
Appropriations

HOMETOWN
Harrison

BORN
July 5, 1937, Bronx, N.Y.

RELIGION
Jewish

FAMILY
Husband, Stephen Lowey; three children

EDUCATION
Mount Holyoke College, B.A. 1959

CAREER
State government aide; homemaker

POLITICAL HIGHLIGHTS
N.Y. assistant secretary of state, 1985-87

ELECTION RESULTS

2000 GENERAL

Nita M. Lowey (D)	126,878	67.3%
John G. Vonglis (R, C)	58,022	30.8%
Florence T. O'Grady (RTL)	3,747	2.0%

2000 PRIMARY

Nita M. Lowey (D)	unopposed

1998 GENERAL

Nita M. Lowey (D)	91,623	82.8%
Daniel McMahon (C)	12,594	11.4%
Giulio A. Cavallo (INDC)	3,251	2.9%
Marion M. Connor (RTL)	3,234	2.9%

PREVIOUS WINNING PERCENTAGES
1996 (64%); 1994 (57%); 1992 (56%); 1990 (63%); 1988 (50%)

While Lowey proudly wears her liberal credentials, she also has become recognized as an inside player who maneuvers skillfully through the appropriations process. As a member of the Appropriations Committee, she knows how to deal, whether the issue is family planning funding, aid to Israel, or money for projects in New York. In recent years, Lowey has steered money to New York City for renovating Grant's Tomb and Penn Station. She initially won her seat on Appropriations in the 103rd Congress by aggressively lobbying the Democratic leadership.

While Lowey generally favors negotiation over confrontation, she went head-to-head with conservative Sen. Jesse Helms of North Carolina in 1999. Lowey joined a dozen House women who marched into a Senate hearing chaired by Helms to present him with a letter signed by more than 100 House members seeking action on an international treaty banning sexual discrimination, which Helms had held up. Helms had the women removed by the Capitol Police.

Lowey, a grandmother of four, got her start in politics a quarter-century ago. A graduate of Mount Holyoke College, she was a homemaker in Queens when she volunteered in a neighbor's 1974 campaign for lieutenant governor. That neighbor was Mario M. Cuomo. Though Cuomo lost the primary, new Democratic Gov. Hugh L. Carey appointed him as New York's secretary of state. Cuomo, in turn, hired Lowey to work in his department's anti-poverty division.

By the mid-1980s, Cuomo was governor and Lowey was the top aide to new Secretary of State Gail Shaffer. Lowey made an impressive debut in electoral politics in 1988 when she unseated two-term GOP Rep. Joseph J. DioGuardi in the then-20th District.

Lowey had survived a primary against Hamilton Fish III, publisher of The Nation magazine and son of a Republican House member, and against businessman Dennis Mehiel. She raised $1.3 million, a huge sum for a challenger. DioGuardi outspent her, but a newspaper reported in October that a New Rochelle auto dealer had funneled $57,000 in corporate contributions to DioGuardi's campaign through his employees. DioGuardi denied knowledge of the pass-through scheme, but the disclosures damaged him. Despite DioGuardi's effort to brand her as an extreme liberal, Lowey won narrowly.

DioGuardi returned for a rematch in 1990, but by then Lowey's personality, legislative work, constituent service and fundraising skills had established her as a strong favorite, and she won decisively. Since then, she has outdistanced all competition.

KEY VOTES

2000
Yes Raise hourly minimum wage by $1 over two years
No Halt funding for U.S. mission in Kosovo unless European nations pay more
Yes Provide Medicare benefits to military retirees and their dependents
Yes Grant China permanent normal trade status
No Phase out estate, gift and trust taxes
No Prohibit implementation of president's national monument designations
No Approve GOP plan to provide prescription drug coverage for Medicare beneficiaries
Yes Increase help for poor nations indebted to international financial institutions

1999
Yes Impose steel import quotas
Yes Kill proposal to take aviation trust funds off budget
No Require background checks on buyers only at gun shows with 10 or more vendors
Yes Remove barriers among banking, securities and insurance companies
Yes Authorize state grants to hire teachers and reduce class size
Yes Overhaul campaign finance law; ban "soft money" and restrict advocacy advertising
Yes Approve bipartisan plan to increase rights of patients in managed-care health plans

INTEREST GROUPS

	AFL-CIO	ADA	CCUS	ACU
2000	90%	75%	52%	9%
1999	78%	100%	16%	4%
1998	100%	100%	35%	8%
1997	100%	95%	40%	8%

CQ VOTE STUDIES

	PARTY UNITY		PRESIDENTIAL SUPPORT	
	Support	Oppose	Support	Oppose
2000	94%	6%	91%	9%
1999	94%	6%	86%	14%
1998	94%	6%	83%	17%
1997	95%	5%	85%	15%

NEW YORK 18
Parts of Westchester County — Bronx and Queens

This paisley-shaped district starts in southeastern Westchester County, which has two-thirds of the district's population and some of New York's most affluent communities. From there, it moves south and covers a part of the East Bronx that borders the Long Island Sound, making environmental issues salient to the 18th's constituents. The district then enters Queens via the Throgs Neck Bridge and follows a winding path through urban Flushing, which gives it much of its Asian population. After enveloping the southern part of Flushing Meadow Park, the district spreads west to take in the community of Rego Park and east to Utopia, site of St. John's University.

As a whole, the 18th is a residential district that leans Democratic, but not overwhelmingly. Westchester County has a Republican base but enough affluent Democratic voters to make it competitive. The 18th's most Democratic sections are the low- to middle-income portions of New York City and its other urban areas, including portions of New

Rochelle and White Plains, the county's seat and commercial center.

The 18th has the largest portion of Yonkers, Westchester's most populous city (which is split among three districts). Yonkers was involved in a lengthy federal court battle over housing and school discrimination that ended with a court-ordered plan to build scattered-site housing and magnet schools. The district excludes the minority neighborhoods of Yonkers, Mount Vernon and New Rochelle, all of which are in the minority-influenced 17th.

MAJOR INDUSTRY
Health care, higher education

CITIES
New York (pt.), 191,751 (1990); Yonkers (pt.), 114,743 (1990); New Rochelle (pt.), 56,570 (1990)

UNUSUAL FEATURES
Thomas Paine Cottage and Museum; Hudson River Museum; City Island.

Rep. Sue W. Kelly (R)

Elected 1994; 4th term

Elected as part of the 1994 Republican wave that swept the House, Kelly practices a more pragmatic brand of politics than many of the young conservatives who won seats in Congress that year. At age 58, she came to the House later in life — and with more than three decades of political and civic activism under her belt.

Before seeking a House seat, Kelly had helped in the campaigns of Republicans seeking local, state and national office. She co-founded a local chapter of the League of Women Voters, served as a PTA president, and volunteered as a rape crisis counselor and patients' advocate. She raised four children and taught junior high science and math, in addition to running a florist business.

Kelly has compiled a House voting record that is conservative overall but has moderate tinges on some issues such as abortion, which has rankled some of her conservative constituents. Unlike many in the GOP, she prefers targeted tax relief rather than across-the-board cuts. "I've never been about broad sweeping tax cuts," she said in 2000.

Belying her moderate reputation, Kelly waded into the hotly partisan battle over first lady Hillary Rodham Clinton's decision in 2000 to establish residency in New York state and run for the Senate. Kelly signed a searing letter distributed by a conservative group that described Clinton as "a dagger in the heart of any conservative idea" and claimed "there isn't a neo-socialist cause she won't shove down our throats." Although Democrats denounced the letter, Kelly stood her ground and told The Associated Press, "Hillary doesn't understand New York or New Yorkers."

In the 107th Congress, Kelly took the gavel of the Financial Services Subcommittee on Oversight and Investigations. She had sought the chairmanship of the Small Business Committee but lost out to the more-senior Donald Manzullo of Illinois. A former small-business woman, Kelly espouses anti-regulatory views popular with the business community.

As head of the Small Business Subcommittee on Regulatory Reform and Paperwork Reduction for four years, she sponsored legislation in the 105th to create a congressional agency to study the costs and benefits of major federal regulations. In 2000, she pressed for passage of a bill requiring the General Accounting Office to evaluate federal rules and regulations that affect the economy by more than $100 million. She said the measure would give Congress "the tools it needs to oversee the steady stream of new and often costly regulations coming from the federal government."

Women's health issues are a priority for Kelly. In the 105th, she was a sponsor of legislation to broaden insurance coverage for breast cancer treatments. She said requiring insurance companies to cover reconstructive surgery after mastectomies will "disabuse insurance companies of the notion that this procedure is merely cosmetic and therefore not always necessary." In 1999, Kelly pressed for more research into pregnancy-related complications, joining other women lawmakers in warning that African-American women are far more likely than white women to die during childbirth.

Of the seven women in the GOP Class of 1994, Kelly was the only one to join the Congressional Caucus on Women's Issues, a group identified with such legislative causes as family and medical leave, federal funding of abortion for low-income women and prevention of violence against women. At the start of the 106th, Kelly was named caucus co-chairwoman.

Seeing Kelly in that post did not sit well with members of some women's

CAPITOL OFFICE
225-5441; fax 225-3289; 1127 Longworth Bldg. 20515

INTERNET
e-mail: dearsue@mail.house.gov
web: www.house.gov/suekelly

COMMITTEES
Financial Services
(Oversight & Investigations - chairwoman)
Small Business
Transportation & Infrastructure

HOMETOWN
Katonah

BORN
Sept. 26, 1936, Lima, Ohio

RELIGION
Presbyterian

FAMILY
Husband, Edward W. Kelly; four children

EDUCATION
Denison U., B.A. 1958; Sarah Lawrence College, M.A. 1985

CAREER
Professor; teacher; hospital administrative aide; medical researcher; retailer

POLITICAL HIGHLIGHTS
No previous office

ELECTION RESULTS

2000 GENERAL

Sue W. Kelly (R, C)	145,532	60.9%
Larry Otis Graham (D, L, WFM)	85,871	35.9%
Frank X. Lloyd (RTL)	4,086	1.7%
Mark R. Jacobs (GREEN)	3,662	1.5%

2000 PRIMARY

Sue W. Kelly (R)	unopposed

1998 GENERAL

Sue W. Kelly (R, C)	104,467	62.2%
Dick Collins (D)	56,378	33.6%
Joseph J. DioGuardi (RTL)	5,941	3.5%

PREVIOUS WINNING PERCENTAGES
1996 (46%); 1994 (52%)

organizations in her district, who were unhappy with her 1997 vote to ban a procedure its opponents call "partial birth" abortion. Kelly had opposed the ban in 1996 but switched sides a year later. "Her position may be that she's pro-choice," Amy Paulin, co-chairman of the Westchester Women's Agenda, told The Journal News of Westchester County. "But she's not considered by the pro-choice community as pro-choice."

Kelly's change of mind on the "partial birth" abortion ban pleased conservatives, as did her vote to impeach President Clinton for grand jury perjury. She also sided with conservatives on the divisive issue of gun control, voting against New York Democrat Carolyn McCarthy's amendment in 1999 that would have required background checks for purchases at gun shows.

She drew fire from environmentalists in 1995 for supporting a bill revising the 1972 Clean Water Act. Defending her stand, Kelly said, "There are certain laws that become sacred cows, and it's very important that we sometimes address sacred cows." But she has also sided with the environmental community by voting to preserve the regulatory authority of the Environmental Protection Agency, pushing through legislation protecting Sterling Forest (a vast undeveloped parcel of land along the New York-New Jersey border) and urging the EPA to study contaminants in the Hudson River.

The 1994 retirement of moderate Republican Rep. Hamilton Fish Jr., longtime representative of the 19th District, opened the door to a stiff race between moderate and conservative elements in the local GOP. To win the primary, Kelly had to get past six conservative opponents, including former Rep. Joseph J. DioGuardi who had represented another district in the House from 1985 to 1989. Kelly won the GOP primary with 23 percent of the vote, and DioGuardi placed second, with 20 percent. He pressed on to November as the nominee of the Conservative and Right to Life parties, calling himself "the true conservative Republican in this race" and deriding Kelly as "a Democrat in disguise."

Fish chose family loyalty over party loyalty and endorsed the Democratic nominee, his son, Hamilton Fish III. Despite the divisions, Kelly benefited from the surging GOP gubernatorial campaign of George E. Pataki and won with 52 percent of the vote.

Kelly's 1996 race drew national attention when DioGuardi again ran as a third-party candidate, and anti-abortion GOP Reps. Christopher H. Smith of New Jersey and Robert K. Dornan of California backed him. Battling a well-funded Democratic challenger in addition to DioGuardi, Kelly won a plurality with 46 percent. She has since won re-election by comfortable margins.

KEY VOTES

2000

No Raise hourly minimum wage by $1 over two years
No Halt funding for U.S. mission in Kosovo unless European nations pay more
Yes Provide Medicare benefits to military retirees and their dependents
Yes Grant China permanent normal trade status
Yes Phase out estate, gift and trust taxes
No Prohibit implementation of president's national monument designations
Yes Approve GOP plan to provide prescription drug coverage for Medicare beneficiaries
Yes Increase help for poor nations indebted to international financial institutions

1999

Yes Impose steel import quotas
No Kill proposal to take aviation trust funds off budget
Yes Require background checks on buyers only at gun shows with 10 or more vendors
Yes Remove barriers among banking, securities and insurance companies
No Authorize state grants to hire teachers and reduce class size
Yes Overhaul campaign finance law; ban "soft money" and restrict advocacy advertising
Yes Approve bipartisan plan to increase rights of patients in managed-care health plans

INTEREST GROUPS

	AFL-CIO	ADA	CCUS	ACU
2000	20%	35%	76%	56%
1999	33%	50%	80%	56%
1998	50%	45%	83%	48%
1997	38%	40%	70%	64%

CQ VOTE STUDIES

	PARTY UNITY		PRESIDENTIAL SUPPORT	
	Support	Oppose	Support	Oppose
2000	75%	25%	46%	54%
1999	69%	31%	41%	59%
1998	66%	34%	41%	59%
1997	80%	20%	42%	58%

NEW YORK 19
Hudson Valley – Poughkeepsie

Despite its overall Republican tilt, the population in New York's 19th divides into two regions, each with its own political proclivities.

At the northern end is Poughkeepsie and its outlying suburbs, where IBM remains the major employer despite a major plant closing and layoffs in the mid-1990s. These northern counties, with small towns and dairy farms, provide a conservative voting base for Republican candidates.

At the district's southern end are the densely packed bedroom communities of northern Westchester County. Many residents in this area commute to jobs in New York City. Republicans outnumber Democrats in this region, but most of the county's voters are moderate, making Westchester County competitive ground. The county also includes Ossining, the site of the Sing Sing prison – its location on the Hudson gave rise to the euphemism about being "sent up the river."

Drawn by the groundwork built by IBM, technical and research firms have moved into the lower Hudson Valley. The district is also home to many of the nation's leading companies, including Reader's Digest and PepsiCo. The 19th also crosses the Hudson River to West Point, taking in the U.S. Military Academy.

MAJOR INDUSTRY
Computers, telecommunications, agriculture

MILITARY BASES
U.S. Military Academy, 1,416 military, 2,406 civilian (1999)

CITIES
Poughkeepsie, 27,748; Ossining Village, 22,724; Peekskill, 21,557

UNUSUAL FEATURES
Home and burial place of John Jay, president of the Continental Congress and first chief justice of the United States, in Katonah; Telegraph inventor Samuel F. B. Morse from Poughkeepsie; Sing Sing prison's chess club noted for its insightful commentary (delivered by telephone onto a television broadcast) during the famous 1972 chess match between American Bobby Fisher and Soviet Boris Spassky.

Rep. Benjamin A. Gilman (R)

CAPITOL OFFICE
225-3776; fax 225-2541; 2449 Rayburn Bldg. 20515

INTERNET
e-mail: www.house.gov/writerep
web: www.house.gov/gilman

COMMITTEES
Government Reform
International Relations
(Middle East & South Asia - chairman)

HOMETOWN
Middletown

BORN
Dec. 6, 1922, Poughkeepsie, N.Y.

RELIGION
Jewish

FAMILY
Wife, Georgia Nickles Tingus Gilman; three children, two stepchildren

EDUCATION
U. of Pennsylvania, B.S. 1946; New York Law School, LL.B. 1950

MILITARY SERVICE
Army, 1943-45

CAREER
Lawyer; state prosecutor

POLITICAL HIGHLIGHTS
N.Y. Assembly, 1967-73

ELECTION RESULTS

2000 GENERAL

Benjamin A. Gilman (R)	136,016	57.6%
Paul Feiner (D, L, GREEN, WFM)	94,646	40.1%
Christine M. Tighe (RTL)	5,371	2.3%

2000 PRIMARY

Benjamin A. Gilman (R)	unopposed

1998 GENERAL

Benjamin A. Gilman (R)	98,546	58.3%
Paul J. Feiner (D, INDC, L)	65,589	38.8%
Christine M. Tighe (RTL)	4,769	2.8%

PREVIOUS WINNING PERCENTAGES
1996 (57%); 1994 (68%); 1992 (66%); 1990 (69%);
1988 (71%); 1986 (69%); 1984 (69%); 1982 (53%);
1980 (74%); 1978 (62%); 1976 (65%); 1974 (54%);
1972 (48%)

Elected 1972; 15th term

Now the oldest member of the House, Gilman's years of public service and intraparty wars appear to have taken a physical toll. He tends to walk slightly stooped and wears a world-weary expression on his face. Yet Gilman, 78, is a friendly, low-key legislator, who is a serious conversationalist and a thoughtful listener. One of the few remaining "Rockefeller Republicans" in the New York House delegation, he holds liberal views on most social issues.

Gilman entered public service shortly after receiving a law degree in 1950, when he was appointed as a deputy assistant attorney general of New York. Two years later, he advanced to become an assistant attorney general and eventually went on to serve six years in the New York Assembly. Elected to the U.S. House in 1972, Gilman spent 22 years in a chamber controlled by the Democrats.

With the GOP takeover of the House in 1995, Gilman became chairman of the International Relations Committee. In panel debates, he adopted a formal style and rarely deviated from his written script. He often expressed exasperation at the tendency of some lawmakers to engage in meandering rhetorical bluster. At times, he was excluded from policy decisions by the more conservative House leadership. Gilman once acknowledged that his chairmanship was sometimes frustrating and disappointing, calling it a "test of diplomacy."

Yet his diplomatic efforts were not enough to keep him in his post after the 2000 elections. Republican leaders insisted on sticking to the pledge they made in 1994 to limit chairmanships to six years, and they turned down Gilman's request for a waiver to retain the post. He settled for the gavel of the Middle East and South Asia Subcommittee in the 107th Congress.

Gilman also sits on the Government Reform Committee, where he is the No. 2 Republican. He could take the helm of Government Reform in 2003, when that panel's chairman, Indiana Republican Dan Burton, will be forced to step down because of the GOP's term limit rule.

Gilman tends to have a more internationalist perspective than many of his younger GOP colleagues — a view that he attributes to his experiences in World War II. "The war left an indelible imprint upon all of us — that you can't afford to be isolationist in this small world of ours," he said.

His support for abortion rights occasionally puts him at odds with other members of his party, particularly in debates over restricting federal funding for international family planning organizations. He opposed the restriction not only on principle, but also out of concern that disputes over abortion would derail his committee's main piece of legislation — an authorization bill for State Department programs.

But in 1998, Republican leaders ignored Gilman's objection and added the abortion restrictions to the bill after it came out of his committee. True to his word, President Clinton vetoed the measure.

But at the end of the 105th Congress, Gilman achieved one of his major objectives: streamlining the foreign policy bureaucracy to make it more efficient. Clinton signed the legislation merging two independent foreign affairs agencies into the State Department and giving the secretary of state greater authority over the U.S. Agency for International Development.

Working with House Speaker J. Dennis Hastert, Gilman has helped direct billions of dollars in drug-fighting funds to Colombia. He has established close ties with Colombia's police and military. A small Colombian flag hangs near a U.S. flag in his office.

On a number of high-profile votes, Gilman has diverged from the majority of his party. In 1998, he was one of 30 Republicans to vote "no" on at least two articles of impeachment against Clinton. He then joined with other moderates in writing a letter to the Senate suggesting that it consider censuring the president instead of voting to remove him.

A supporter of organized labor, Gilman was one of only 42 Republicans who voted in 2000 to raise the minimum wage by $1 over two years. He opposed a GOP bill to allow companies to offer their employees compensatory time off in lieu of overtime pay. And in the 105th, Gilman was one of only eight Republicans to oppose a measure banning a procedure its opponents call "partial birth" abortion.

Gilman is part of a dwindling group of World War II veterans in Congress. During the war, he served as a staff sergeant in the Air Force, flying 35 missions over Japan and earning the Distinguished Flying Cross and the Air Medal with Oak Leaf Clusters. He is still an active colonel in the New York Guard, training several times a year.

Gilman earned his initial House victory after working his way through the ranks of appointive and elective office. He won an Assembly seat from Orange County in 1966, and after a six-year stint in the state legislature, he challenged Democratic Rep. John G. Dow for the House. Viewed as a moderate, Gilman defeated conservative builder Yale Rapkin in the Republican primary and went on to win in November with a comfortable plurality, even though Rapkin siphoned off 13 percent as the Conservative Party candidate.

After deflecting a 1974 comeback attempt by Dow, Gilman's re-election contests went smoothly until his district was combined with that of Democratic Rep. Peter A. Peyser's in 1982 redistricting. It was an angrier campaign than Gilman had been used to. Peyser criticized him for opposing a nuclear weapons freeze and for backing military aid to El Salvador. The usually soft-spoken Gilman fired back, calling Peyser — who had been a GOP House colleague of Gilman's before switching parties — an "ultra-liberal." Gilman's close ties to his geographically dominant Rockland-Orange base paid off, and he won handily.

Although many New York incumbents saw their districts redrawn in the redistricting that preceded the 1992 elections, Gilman got off lightly. Retaining his political base in exurban Rockland and Orange counties, he won with customary ease in both 1992 and 1994.

He continues to win easily, besting his Democratic challengers by close to 20 percentage points.

KEY VOTES

2000

Yes Raise hourly minimum wage by $1 over two years
No Halt funding for U.S. mission in Kosovo unless European nations pay more
Yes Provide Medicare benefits to military retirees and their dependents
No Grant China permanent normal trade status
? Phase out estate, gift and trust taxes
No Prohibit implementation of president's national monument designations
Yes Approve GOP plan to provide prescription drug coverage for Medicare beneficiaries
No Increase help for poor nations indebted to international financial institutions

1999

Yes Impose steel import quotas
No Kill proposal to take aviation trust funds off budget
No Require background checks on buyers only at gun shows with 10 or more vendors
Yes Remove barriers among banking, securities and insurance companies
No Authorize state grants to hire teachers and reduce class size
Yes Overhaul campaign finance law; ban "soft money" and restrict advocacy advertising
Yes Approve bipartisan plan to increase rights of patients in managed-care health plans

INTEREST GROUPS

	AFL-CIO	ADA	CCUS	ACU
2000	40%	35%	57%	43%
1999	56%	50%	48%	52%
1998	67%	45%	71%	38%
1997	75%	50%	60%	40%

CQ VOTE STUDIES

	PARTY UNITY		PRESIDENTIAL SUPPORT	
	Support	Oppose	Support	Oppose
2000	67%	33%	58%	42%
1999	62%	38%	48%	52%
1998	62%	38%	46%	54%
1997	70%	30%	49%	51%

NEW YORK 20

Rockland and parts of Westchester, Orange and Sullivan counties

The southern tip of the 20th sits just beyond New York City, taking in a far northeastern sliver of Yonkers and comfortable riverside communities such as Tarrytown, where Washington Irving wrote the classic tale of the headless horseman, the "Legend of Sleepy Hollow." This Westchester County portion of the 20th has a good number of Democratic voters, but overall, the district leans Republican.

From Westchester County, the 20th crosses the Hudson River and runs north, along the New Jersey and Pennsylvania borders, into rural upstate New York. Democratic-leaning Rockland County, full of small bedroom communities, has a relatively large Jewish population, including several established Hasidic communities. In the district's rural counties, Orange and Sullivan, farmers grow onions, lettuce and celery. This portion of the 20th also covers

some of the Catskill Mountains' Borscht Belt district, a Jewish resort area that has lost popularity over the past few decades. Locals have talked about replacing the resort with casinos in hopes of luring back tourists.

Economic development has become a key issue for this district, which has few major employers. Many residents make the long commute across the Tappan Zee Bridge, the widest point on the Hudson, into Westchester or New York City every morning.

MAJOR INDUSTRY
Health care, agriculture

CITIES
Ramapo (unincorporated), 93,861 (1990); Clarks (unincorporated), 79,346 (1990); Orange (unincorporated), 46,742 (1990)

UNUSUAL FEATURES
Woodstock music festival held in a field near Bethel in 1969; Brotherhood Winery, America's oldest winery, in Washingtonville; First section of the Appalachian Trail created in Bear Mountain State Park.

Rep. Michael R. McNulty (D)

Elected 1988; 7th term

The McNulty family is a virtual dynasty in its home base of Green Island, a municipality north of Albany. At 22, McNulty succeeded in his first try for public office, winning election as town supervisor — the same post his grandfather and father had held. He later became Green Island's mayor, then served in the state Assembly before winning election to the House in 1988.

McNulty spent his early years in the House toiling quietly as a vote-counter in the Democratic whip structure and was rewarded with a seat on the Ways and Means Committee at the start of his third term. Although he serves on the high-profile tax panel, McNulty keeps a low profile. He rarely speaks on the House floor, preferring to tend to business in committee and through constituent service.

McNulty has his differences with party doctrine on some social issues, but when it comes to matters important to organized labor, his Democratic stripes are bright. He is a firm believer in the need to increase the minimum wage. "You simply can't adequately support a family on $5.15 an hour," he said in 1999. He opposed legislation in the 104th Congress allowing employers to offer workers compensatory time off instead of overtime pay.

In the area of free trade as well, McNulty sides with unions, which fear loss of jobs to workers overseas. He opposed the 1993 North American Free Trade Agreement, and in 1998 he voted against giving the president fast-track authority to negotiate trade agreements that Congress must approve or reject without amendment. In 2000, he voted "no" on granting China permanent normal trade status.

On another trade issue, the congressman has been cool to legislation designed to increase trade with Vietnam. McNulty's brother was killed in the Vietnam War, and during debate in 2000 over a bill to provide incentives to U.S. companies doing business in Vietnam, McNulty said: "While the pain may subside, it never goes away."

McNulty has shown his independence on other occasions. He was one of only two Ways and Means members in 1996 to oppose legislation aimed at punishing foreign firms that aid the oil industries of Iran and Libya, saying that he favored a stronger version approved by the International Relations Committee. In the 106th Congress, he initially voted with the GOP (one of 65 Democrats to do so) to repeal the estate tax. Later, however, he returned to the Democratic fold when the House voted to sustain President Clinton's veto of the measure.

But McNulty strays from many in his party when it comes to abortion. He joined with Republicans in voting to ban a procedure its opponents call "partial birth" abortion and to prohibit federal workers' health plans from paying for abortions. He says he does not support an outright ban on abortion, but he opposes public funding of the procedure except in cases of rape, incest or danger to the life of the woman. In the 104th, he voted to require states to fund Medicaid abortions for poor women in those limited instances.

McNulty has backed the conservative Republican view on other contentious issues. In 1996, he supported a ban on federal recognition of same-sex marriage, and in 1997, he voted to limit congressional terms.

He joined with Rep. Amo Houghton, R-N.Y., in 1998 to sponsor a bill exempting from federal taxes the $1 million reward paid to David Kaczynski for turning in his brother, Theodore, better known as the Unabomber. David Kaczynski, a constituent of McNulty's, promised to donate the reward to the families of the Unabomber's victims but had to pay $300,000

CAPITOL OFFICE
225-5076; fax 225-5077; 2161 Rayburn Bldg. 20515

INTERNET
e-mail: mike.mcnulty@mail.house.gov
web: www.house.gov/mcnulty

COMMITTEES
Ways & Means

HOMETOWN
Green Island

BORN
Sept. 16, 1947, Troy, N.Y.

RELIGION
Roman Catholic

FAMILY
Wife, Nancy Ann McNulty; four children

EDUCATION
College of the Holy Cross, B.A. 1969

CAREER
Public official

POLITICAL HIGHLIGHTS
Green Island supervisor, 1970-77; Democratic nominee for N.Y. Assembly, 1976; mayor of Green Island, 1977-83; N.Y. Assembly, 1983-88

ELECTION RESULTS

2000 GENERAL

Michael R. McNulty (D, INDC, C)	175,339	74.4%
Thomas G. Pillsworth (R)	60,333	25.6%

2000 PRIMARY

Michael R. McNulty (D)	unopposed

1998 GENERAL

Michael R. McNulty (D, C, INDC)	146,639	74.2%
Lauren Ayers (R)	50,931	25.8%

PREVIOUS WINNING PERCENTAGES
1996 (66%); 1994 (67%); 1992 (63%); 1990 (64%); 1988 (62%)

in taxes, without enactment of special legislation. The measure was stripped out of the session-ending catchall spending bill at the last minute.

McNulty lines up from time to time with his party's most liberal elements. He voted in the 104th Congress against a welfare overhaul bill, against efforts to allow states to deny public education to illegal aliens, and against repeal of the ban on certain semiautomatic assault-style weapons. He supported Clinton's cherished AmeriCorps program, and he was on board for most of Clinton's early legislative endeavors, backing his budget, tax and economic stimulus bills in 1993 and voting for family and medical leave legislation.

McNulty grew up in a political family. His grandfather was elected Green Island tax collector in 1914 and went on to serve as town supervisor, county board chairman and county sheriff. McNulty's father, Jack, who served as town supervisor and mayor, bucked the Albany County Democratic organization by successfully challenging the official candidate in the primary for county sheriff. But party regulars retaliated by eliminating the sheriff's overtime budget for the county jail, forcing Jack McNulty to resign.

In his long political career, Congressman McNulty has waged only one unsuccessful campaign: a 1976 challenge to a Republican assemblyman. But he bounced back to win the first of three state Assembly terms in 1982. While a state legislator, McNulty once introduced legislation to make Uncle Sam the official state patriot. The real Uncle Sam is believed to have been Sam Wilson, a meatpacker from Troy, which is in McNulty's district.

McNulty's chance for a congressional seat came in 1988 with the sudden retirement of ailing Democratic Rep. Samuel S. Stratton. Within hours of the announcement, the district's Democratic leaders met and chose McNulty to replace him on the ballot.

With endorsements from Stratton and environmental groups, McNulty defeated local Republican official Peter Bakal with 62 percent. Two years later, he also won the Conservative Party's endorsement and topped GOP public relations consultant Margaret Buhrmaster with 64 percent.

Running in a district dominated by Albany, a Democratic stronghold, McNulty has since won each general election by a large margin. His one serious challenge came in the 1996 Democratic primary from environmental activist Lee H. Wasserman, who chided McNulty for his 63 percent support score for the House Republicans' "Contract With America" — the highest score among New York Democrats. McNulty won the primary, then cruised to victory in a three-way general-election contest against the GOP candidate and Wasserman, who ran as the nominee of the state's Liberal Party.

KEY VOTES

2000
Yes Raise hourly minimum wage by $1 over two years
No Halt funding for U.S. mission in Kosovo unless European nations pay more
Yes Provide Medicare benefits to military retirees and their dependents
No Grant China permanent normal trade status
Yes Phase out estate, gift and trust taxes
No Prohibit implementation of president's national monument designations
No Approve GOP plan to provide prescription drug coverage for Medicare beneficiaries
? Increase help for poor nations indebted to international financial institutions

1999
Yes Impose steel import quotas
No Kill proposal to take aviation trust funds off budget
No Require background checks on buyers only at gun shows with 10 or more vendors
Yes Remove barriers among banking, securities and insurance companies
Yes Authorize state grants to hire teachers and reduce class size
Yes Overhaul campaign finance law; ban "soft money" and restrict advocacy advertising
Yes Approve bipartisan plan to increase rights of patients in managed-care health plans

INTEREST GROUPS

	AFL-CIO	ADA	CCUS	ACU
2000	100%	55%	57%	17%
1999	88%	90%	21%	8%
1998	100%	75%	23%	21%
1997	100%	80%	30%	26%

CQ VOTE STUDIES

	PARTY UNITY		PRESIDENTIAL SUPPORT	
	Support	Oppose	Support	Oppose
2000	88%	12%	75%	25%
1999	89%	11%	77%	23%
1998	89%	11%	76%	24%
1997	87%	13%	67%	33%

NEW YORK 21

Capital District — Albany; Schenectady; Troy

As the terminus of the Erie Canal, which connects the Great Lakes to the Hudson River, New York's Capital District was one of the state's earliest industrial centers. Blue-collar workers and state employees give the Albany-Schenectady-Troy area a substantial union population and a solidly Democratic vote – unusual for an upstate district.

Albany is home to one of the nation's last big-city political machines, formed in 1921. During the heyday of Daniel O'Connell and Mayor Erastus Corning II, the Albany machine used to ensure Democratic victories throughout the area, but it now holds less sway over the area's ever-expanding suburbs. Few of the district's Democrats can be described as liberal. Most are quite conservative when it comes to social issues.

Despite large-scale industrial losses in the 1980s, manufacturing remains critical to the region. Job losses have been mitigated somewhat by an intensive effort to recruit small manufacturing and

high technology firms. The Rensselaer Technology Park was a vacant tract of land 20 years ago but now supports 2,000 jobs. Gone are the days, however, when residents could rely on life-long jobs at General Electric, which was one of the area's top employers until the 1980s, when the company substantially cut back on its operations in Schenectady. Now GE operates a much smaller research and development center on the same location.

MAJOR INDUSTRY
State government, manufacturing

MILITARY BASES
Watervliet Arsenal, 7 military, 834 civilian (1999)

CITIES
Albany, 93,994; Schenectady, 60,784; Troy, 51,201

UNUSUAL FEATURES
First railroad in America ran between Albany and Schenectady; Samuel Wilson, a meatpacker who provided the Army much of its rations during the War of 1812, is better known as Uncle Sam and is buried in Troy; Original U.S. Shaker settlement established in Watervliet in 1776.

Rep. John E. Sweeney (R)

CAPITOL OFFICE
225-5614; fax 225-6234; 416 Cannon Bldg. 20515

INTERNET
e-mail: john.sweeney@mail.house.gov
web: www.house.gov/sweeney

COMMITTEES
Appropriations

HOMETOWN
Troy

BORN
Aug. 9, 1955, Troy, N.Y.

RELIGION
Roman Catholic

FAMILY
Divorced; three children

EDUCATION
Hudson Valley Community College, A.A. 1978;
Russell Sage College, B.A. 1981; Western New
England College, J.D. 1991

CAREER
Gubernatorial adviser; lawyer; county public
safety program director

POLITICAL HIGHLIGHTS
N.Y. Republican Party executive director, 1992-95;
N.Y. labor commissioner, 1995-97

ELECTION RESULTS

2000 GENERAL

John E. Sweeney (R, C)	167,368	67.9%
Ken McCallion (D, GREEN, WFM)	79,111	32.1%

2000 PRIMARY

John E. Sweeney (R)	unopposed

1998 GENERAL

John E. Sweeney (R, C, INDC)	106,919	55.3%
Jean Parvin Bordewich (D)	81,296	42.1%
Francis A. "Fran" Giroux (RTL)	5,051	2.6%

Elected 1998; 2nd term

Having quickly learned how to use party loyalty and backroom navigational skills to his own benefit, Sweeney was rewarded at the start of his second term with one of the five open Republican seats on the Appropriations Committee for the 107th Congress. It was not the first time he won a plum assignment.

Arriving on Capitol Hill for his new-member orientation late in 1998, Sweeney was elected freshman class representative on the Republican Steering Committee, the panel that doles out GOP committee assignments. Sweeney himself got a seat on the Transportation Committee. But he told his party leaders that — since so many other freshmen wanted assignment to the same committee — he would be willing to remove himself from the panel, which controls billions of dollars' worth of construction projects.

Then-Transportation Chairman Bud Shuster, R-Pa., impressed with the gesture, insisted that Sweeney remain and made him vice chairman of the Aviation Subcommittee, which would oversee a massive airport construction bill during the 106th.

Out of public view, Sweeney served as one of the three-dozen assistant majority whips, corralling the votes of other freshmen and New York Republicans. He also introduced 43 bills during his first term — more than all but 16 other legislators and more than any other freshman, except his Empire State GOP colleague, Thomas M. Reynolds, who also put 43 measures into the hopper. (Sweeney started the 107th in similarly prolific fashion, on the first day introducing 22 bills on a wide range of subjects.)

After cruising to re-election in 2000 with better than two-thirds of the vote, Sweeney headed to Florida, where he played one of the more high-profile roles among the small army of House Republicans who were observing the recounts in critical counties and otherwise pressing George W. Bush's ultimately successful position in the disputed 2000 presidential election.

In his first term, Sweeney focused on cutting taxes and boosting the economy of his upstate New York district. He pushed tax breaks for small businesses as a way to stimulate economic development. And the Transportation panel assignment helped him deliver much-needed funding for the airport in Albany, a main link for many of his constituents to the rest of the world. Sweeney saw the airport as vital to reinvigorating the slumping economy of the region. In the 107th, Sweeney is in a position to continue his transportation pursuits as a member of the Appropriations panel's Transportation Subcommittee.

Sweeney has championed one environmental cause: limiting nitrogen oxide, sulfur dioxide and mercury emissions from Midwestern utility smokestacks, which contribute to the acid rain that has been blamed for killing plant and animal life in New York's Adirondack region and other Northeastern forests and lakes.

Yet Sweeney approached the issue in a surprisingly partisan way, frequently crossing swords with Democrats who appeared to be his natural allies. His acid rain bill in the 106th was cosponsored with New York Republicans Sherwood Boehlert and John M. McHugh, but it attracted no Democratic cosponsor from the region.

And when one environmental group's 2000 support scorecard contained poor marks for many Republicans, Sweeney declared that "the so-called League of Conservation voters is a political organization that places politics above the environment." He said the group had wrongly ignored many pro-environment actions taken by the GOP-controlled House while basing its ratings on measures opposed by Republicans, such as those designating national monuments.

Meanwhile, Sweeney has aggressively backed the General Electric Co. in one of the region's most controversial environmental issues — whether to dredge the Hudson River to eliminate toxic polychlorinated biphenyls, or PCBs. Over three decades ending in 1977, General Electric plants legally discharged approximately 1.1 million pounds of the suspected carcinogen into the river. The state Department of Environmental Conservation has prohibited human consumption of Hudson River fish since the 1970s.

Sweeney criticized Environmental Protection Agency Administrator Carol E. Browner for her decision late in the Clinton administration to proceed with a huge dredging operation. The agency said that without the dredging, the risk of cancer and other health problems would continue to exceed acceptable levels for at least 40 more years. Sweeney suggested that, by stirring up and moving contaminated sediment, the project "could do more harm than good to the people living along the river." Under the superfund law, General Electric could be forced to pay for the entire $460 million operation.

Sweeney had never held elective office before running to succeed retiring 10-term Republican Rep. Gerald B.H. Solomon in 1998. But Sweeney had been executive director of the state Republican Party in the early 1990s when a little-known GOP state legislator, George E. Pataki, upset Democratic icon Mario Cuomo's bid for a fourth term as governor. With Pataki in his corner, Sweeney's foray into elective politics was a breeze.

As Pataki's state labor commissioner from 1995 to 1997, Sweeney oversaw the state's welfare system, and he takes credit for lowering the number of people on public assistance. Ultimately, he says, his focus is "jobs, jobs and more jobs."

Solomon handpicked Sweeney as his successor, despite some policy differences. Sweeney is considered more moderate than his predecessor; he opposes a federal ban on abortion, for example, while Solomon was strongly against abortion rights. But they agreed on most issues, such as support for international trade and a constitutional amendment to protect the flag, and opposition to gun control.

With strong backing from Solomon, Pataki and the rest of the party leadership, Sweeney sailed through the four-candidate GOP primary. He took full advantage of the district's GOP leanings, winning comfortably over Democratic publisher and Red Hook Councilwoman Jean Parvin Bordewich. In 2000, he defeated Democratic attorney Kenneth McCallion by better than 2-to-1.

KEY VOTES

2000

No Raise hourly minimum wage by $1 over two years
Yes Halt funding for U.S. mission in Kosovo unless European nations pay more
Yes Provide Medicare benefits to military retirees and their dependents
Yes Grant China permanent normal trade status
Yes Phase out estate, gift and trust taxes
Yes Prohibit implementation of president's national monument designations
Yes Approve GOP plan to provide prescription drug coverage for Medicare beneficiaries
No Increase help for poor nations indebted to international financial institutions

1999

Yes Impose steel import quotas
No Kill proposal to take aviation trust funds off budget
Yes Require background checks on buyers only at gun shows with 10 or more vendors
Yes Remove barriers among banking, securities and insurance companies
No Authorize state grants to hire teachers and reduce class size
No Overhaul campaign finance law; ban "soft money" and restrict advocacy advertising
Yes Approve bipartisan plan to increase rights of patients in managed-care health plans

INTEREST GROUPS

	AFL-CIO	ADA	CCUS	ACU
2000	20%	10%	76%	72%
1999	56%	25%	76%	72%

CQ VOTE STUDIES

	PARTY UNITY		PRESIDENTIAL SUPPORT	
	Support	Oppose	Support	Oppose
2000	89%	11%	32%	68%
1999	86%	14%	25%	75%

NEW YORK 22
Rural East – Glens Falls; Saratoga Springs

New York's 22nd runs along the state's eastern border, starting just north of Poughkeepsie and stretching into the Adirondack mountains. It covers much of the primarily residential Hudson River valley, including the site of the Battle of Saratoga, America's first victory against the British in the Revolutionary War.

The district's population hub is in its center, in the Albany-Schenectady-Troy metropolitan area. This district has none of those cities, but much of their GOP suburbia. The three cities helped fuel a suburban boom in southern Saratoga County in the 1980s. Saratoga Springs, synonymous with world-class horse racing, attracts tourists during the summer months.

The district follows Interstate 87 into mountainous, scenic Adirondack Park and the resort areas of Lake George and Lake Champlain. Lake Placid, site of the 1932 and 1980 Winter Olympics, is in Essex County at the northern tip of the district.

The southern end of the district is made up of mainly rural territory in Schoharie, Greene, Columbia and northern Dutchess counties. It includes the Dutchess County estates – mansions built along the Hudson River by the nation's early millionaires, including the Vanderbilts, Martin Van Buren and Franklin Delano Roosevelt.

The suburbs outside industrial Troy provide the 22nd with a few Democratic voters, and the heavy presence of unionized state workers outside Albany makes labor an important issue. But, in general, the district's dairy farmers and small-town voters make the 22nd solidly Republican. In the 2000 presidential election, the 22nd was one of only four New York districts to support President Bush.

MAJOR INDUSTRY
Agriculture, tourism, paper manufacturing

CITIES
Saratoga Springs, 25,770; Glens Falls, 14,405

UNUSUAL FEATURES
Franklin Delano Roosevelt lost Dutchess County, site of his Hyde Park home, in seven of the nine general elections in which he competed; the two exceptions were his bids for N.Y. Senate in 1910 and '12.

Rep. Sherwood Boehlert (R)

CAPITOL OFFICE
225-3665; fax 225-1891; 2246 Rayburn Bldg. 20515

INTERNET
e-mail: rep.boehlert@mail.house.gov
web: www.house.gov/boehlert

COMMITTEES
Science - chairman
Transportation & Infrastructure
Select Intelligence

HOMETOWN
New Hartford

BORN
Sept. 28, 1936, Utica, N.Y.

RELIGION
Roman Catholic

FAMILY
Wife, Marianne Willey Boehlert; four children

EDUCATION
Utica College, A.B. 1961

MILITARY SERVICE
Army, 1956-58

CAREER
Congressional aide; public relations executive

POLITICAL HIGHLIGHTS
Sought Republican nomination for U.S. House,
1972; Oneida County executive, 1979-82

ELECTION RESULTS

2000 GENERAL

Sherwood Boehlert (R, INDC)	124,132	60.5%
David Vickers (C, RTL)	42,854	20.9%
Richard W. Englebrecht (D)	38,049	18.6%

2000 PRIMARY

Sherwood Boehlert (R)	15,269	57.3%
David Vickers (R)	11,382	42.7%

1998 GENERAL

Sherwood Boehlert (R)	111,242	80.8%
David Vickers (C, INDC)	26,493	19.2%

PREVIOUS WINNING PERCENTAGES
1996 (64%); 1994 (71%); 1992 (64%); 1990 (84%);
1988 (100%); 1986 (69%); 1984 (73%); 1982 (56%)

Elected 1982; 10th term

The only moderate Republican to be awarded a full committee chairmanship at the start of the 107th Congress, Boehlert is regarded as an important envoy between the House GOP leadership and the chamber's increasingly independent Republican swing voters.

Boehlert would like to use his new Science Committee chairmanship to promote math and science education, saying he is dismayed by studies showing that U.S. children have only average proficiency in those areas. The pro-environment lawmaker also wants the panel to help provide Congress with a sound scientific basis to make decisions on issues such as global climate change.

Boehlert has responsibility for overseeing NASA and the ongoing assembly of the International Space Station. Though the Science Committee traditionally is an enthusiastic backer of the space agency, relations between the panel's former chairman, F. James Sensenbrenner Jr., R-Wis., and NASA officials were sometimes testy.

Approachable and low-key, Boehlert has a ready command of the facts and is a forceful debater. He has long argued that "the overwhelming majority of Americans are moderates who want to get things done." To that end, he regularly departs from the Republican script and seeks alliances with Democrats on a range of issues. Annual vote surveys show Boehlert to be among the most independent-minded House Republicans, voting against his party about a third of the time.

Many of his defections come on environmental issues. Boehlert is regarded as one of the "greenest" House Republicans — he was one of only 10 Republicans endorsed in 2000 by the Sierra Club. He is remembered for rallying a coalition of moderate Republicans and Democrats against conservatives' efforts to scale back clean air and clean water laws in 1995. Boehlert helped remove 17 controversial provisions that had been attached to an appropriations bill funding the Environmental Protection Agency and that were designed to bar or restrict the agency's regulatory activities.

He warned Republican leaders that undermining environmental protections would alienate the public and hurt the GOP at the polls — advice that ultimately proved accurate. However, the episodes made him the scourge of anti-regulatory GOP Westerners, who still grouse about what they see as disloyalty to the party.

Boehlert continues to fight for more stringent standards to address the acid rain, smog and haze that plague his upstate New York district, pushing legislation mandating reductions to pollutants emitted by power plants in the Midwest. He has urged an overhaul of the federal superfund hazardous waste program to ensure that more money is spent on cleanup of the nation's worst toxic waste sites and less on litigation. His measure to revamp the superfund program won overwhelming approval from the Transportation Committee in 1999, but then stalled.

Though many in the modern-day GOP might wish it forgotten, Boehlert is a reminder that the national Republican Party once had a vibrant liberal wing. It was dominant in New York when Boehlert first entered public service in the 1960s, during the tenure of Gov. Nelson A. Rockefeller, a White House aspirant who later served as vice president.

Boehlert, known to practically everyone as "Sherry," is a member of a group of moderate Republicans — both on and off Capitol Hill — who call themselves the Republican Main Street Partnership. The group early in 1999 wrote to GOP leaders on Capitol Hill urging them to halt the "rhetoric of partisan hostility," arguing that "we must restore dignity to our debate, civility to our conversations and compassion to our perspective."

On fiscal policy matters, Boehlert generally concurs with his party's conservative majority, but in the 106th Congress he and a small band of moderates announced that they could not support the GOP's $792 billion tax cut.

"This tax cut is too large, and it's based upon totally optimistic assumptions," he declared. House GOP moderates have the reputation for quickly giving in to pressure from the leadership, but on the tax bill they held tough and forced the leaders to agree that any future reduction in income tax rates would be contingent on progress in reducing the national debt. The concession was not a huge one, and President Clinton still vetoed the bill, but moderates took it as evidence of their influence.

In other areas, Boehlert often votes with Democrats. He has favored increasing the minimum wage, sided with unions on labor matters and opposed banning a procedure its opponents call "partial birth" abortion. In 1999, he was among the minority of Republicans who voted in favor of a campaign finance overhaul bill and against an amendment to ease restrictions on the purchase of weapons at gun shows. In 2000, he supported a bipartisan measure, opposed by the GOP leadership, to give patients more clout with their HMOs.

Boehlert's left-of-center Republican philosophy has resulted in easy re-election wins over the years. This electoral security was hard-won for Boehlert, a 15-year congressional aide whose House ambitions were deferred for a decade after an initial defeat in 1972. That year, he had hoped to succeed his boss, retiring GOP Rep. Alexander Pirnie, but he lost to Donald J. Mitchell, an assemblyman, in a Republican primary. Boehlert swallowed his disappointment and went to work for Mitchell.

In 1979, he restarted his political career by winning the Oneida County executive post. By 1982, Mitchell was ready to retire. Boehlert was driving along an interstate highway in Oneida County when he heard the news. He pulled into a rest stop, called a radio station and announced his candidacy.

As county executive, he had earned high marks from labor unions, and he was one of only two New York Republicans to get the state AFL-CIO's endorsement in the 1982 elections. After winning the Republican primary comfortably, Boehlert capitalized on a huge organizational and financial advantage over Democrat Anita Maxwell, a dairy farmer who had lost badly to Mitchell in 1976. Boehlert won with 56 percent, and in every campaign since then, he has captured at least 60 percent of the vote.

KEY VOTES

2000
Yes Raise hourly minimum wage by $1 over two years
No Halt funding for U.S. mission in Kosovo unless European nations pay more
Yes Provide Medicare benefits to military retirees and their dependents
Yes Grant China permanent normal trade status
Yes Phase out estate, gift and trust taxes
No Prohibit implementation of president's national monument designations
Yes Approve GOP plan to provide prescription drug coverage for Medicare beneficiaries
Yes Increase help for poor nations indebted to international financial institutions

1999
Yes Impose steel import quotas
No Kill proposal to take aviation trust funds off budget
No Require background checks on buyers only at gun shows with 10 or more vendors
Yes Remove barriers among banking, securities and insurance companies
No Authorize state grants to hire teachers and reduce class size
Yes Overhaul campaign finance law; ban "soft money" and restrict advocacy advertising
Yes Approve bipartisan plan to increase rights of patients in managed-care health plans

INTEREST GROUPS

	AFL-CIO	ADA	CCUS	ACU
2000	30%	40%	80%	40%
1999	44%	65%	60%	40%
1998	90%	60%	61%	24%
1997	63%	55%	67%	32%

CQ VOTE STUDIES

	PARTY UNITY		PRESIDENTIAL SUPPORT	
	Support	Oppose	Support	Oppose
2000	68%	32%	61%	39%
1999	60%	40%	52%	48%
1998	59%	41%	60%	40%
1997	70%	30%	59%	41%

NEW YORK 23
Central – Utica; Rome

The 23rd covers the small towns and rural hamlets of central New York, where James Fenimore Cooper wrote tales of the frontier days that gave central New York its nickname, the "Leatherstocking Region." Despite its rural heritage, most of the district's population now lives around Utica and Rome, aging industrial cities on the Mohawk River that have suffered as heavy manufacturing leaves the state. Blue-collar jobs are still important to these cities, giving the 23rd a number of Democratic voters.

The district took a major hit when Griffiss Air Force Base closed in 1993, eliminating thousands of jobs. An effort to turn the Mohawk River Valley into a high-tech information center – aided by the Air Force's Rome Laboratory, which works with many of the state's universities – has helped replace some of those jobs. But attempts to utilize the base have not been successful.

The 23rd also is home to the Oneida Nation tribe, which runs a highly profitable casino in Verona and has a long-running lawsuit against the state to reclaim its native lands.

Chronic problems with acid rain in the Adirondacks have made environmental issues important to many of the district's residents. Aside from this proclivity for earth-friendly policies, the district's rural residents and dairy farmers are traditional Yankee Republicans. Combined with city voters, the district leans marginally Republican. The district has re-elected its Republican congressman since 1982 by large margins. On the presidential level, Bill Clinton carried the district in 1996, but President Bush won it in 2000 by 5 percentage points.

MAJOR INDUSTRY
Electronics, manufacturing, higher education

CITIES
Utica, 58,750; Rome, 39,696; Oneonta, 12,807

UNUSUAL FEATURES
National Baseball Hall of Fame in Cooperstown; National Soccer Hall of Fame in Oneonta; National Boxing Hall of Fame in Canastota; Former Sen. Daniel Patrick Moynihan owns a farm in Pindars Corners.

Rep. John M. McHugh (R)

CAPITOL OFFICE
225-4611; fax 226-0621; 2441 Rayburn Bldg. 20515

INTERNET
e-mail: www.house.gov/writerep
web: www.house.gov/mchugh

COMMITTEES
Armed Services
  (Military Personnel - chairman)
Government Reform
International Relations

HOMETOWN
Pierrepont Manor

BORN
Sept. 29, 1948, Watertown, N.Y.

RELIGION
Roman Catholic

FAMILY
Divorced

EDUCATION
Utica College of Syracuse U., B.A. 1970; State U. of
New York, Albany, M.P.A. 1977

CAREER
Legislative aide; city official; insurance broker

POLITICAL HIGHLIGHTS
N.Y. Senate, 1985-93

ELECTION RESULTS

2000 GENERAL

John M. McHugh (R, C)	138,322	74.3%
Neil P. Tallon (D)	42,698	22.9%
Willard Smith (INDC, GREEN)	5,167	2.8%

2000 PRIMARY

John M. McHugh (R)	unopposed

1998 GENERAL

John M. McHugh (R, C)	116,682	79.0%
Neil P. Tallon (D)	31,011	21.0%

PREVIOUS WINNING PERCENTAGES
1996 (71%); 1994 (79%); 1992 (61%)

Elected 1992; 5th term

Unlike many other Republicans who arrived on Capitol Hill in the early 1990s with little or no background in politics or government — and were proud of it — McHugh is a career politician. He began his service in government soon after graduating from college with a degree in political science. Along the way, he earned a master's degree in public administration.

While some of his colleagues work to significantly reduce the scope of the federal government, McHugh toils at making the government work better. His longstanding effort to reorganize the Postal Service is an apt metaphor: His six-year tenure as chairman of the Government Reform panel's Postal Service Subcommittee was marked by his struggle to piece together a consensus on how to help the Postal Service cope with developments in technology that profoundly changed the way Americans communicate with each other.

McHugh says that new communications technologies, including fax, e-mail and the Internet, have supplanted the Postal Service in transmitting many documents that had been the mainstay of the Postal Service's business. Electronic billing and competition from private mail and package delivery companies threaten the Postal Service's future unless it can adapt, McHugh argues. "Simply put, the current structure of the Postal Service is not suited for the dynamic communications marketplace of today," he said. In the 107th Congress, McHugh relinquished his Postal Service Subcommittee gavel because of GOP-imposed term limits on chairmanships, but he remains involved, as postal issues are being handled at the full committee level.

McHugh's vast upstate 24th District is one of the poorest in the state and its well-being is heavily dependent on defense spending at Fort Drum and on agriculture, particularly dairy farming — segments of the economy in which the federal government plays a key role. McHugh is well-positioned to look out for district interests. He is on the Armed Services Committee, where he chairs the Military Personnel Subcommittee. He also is co-chairman of the House Army Caucus. On agriculture issues, McHugh has been regarded as an expert on the dairy industry since his years as a state senator.

Fort Drum, home of the 10th Mountain Division, is a sizable civilian employer in the Watertown area. In the 106th, McHugh worked to obtain funds in the military construction spending bill to upgrade facilities there.

He was one of 10 Republicans in 1995 to vote against his party's massive deficit-reduction bill because he was upset with the way its agricultural provisions changed the federal dairy program. In 1998, when McHugh voted against giving the president fast-track trade negotiating authority, he explained that he did not think the bill provided sufficient protections for dairy farmers. "Under the president's trade proposal, it is clear that the interests of U.S. farmers could well be sacrificed again at the negotiating table," he said. "I simply cannot support a process that allows for yet another wholesale sellout of the dairy industry." In the 106th, McHugh was a leading opponent of the Clinton administration's proposed changes in dairy pricing policy.

Other priorities for McHugh in the 106th Congress were the price and availability of home heating oil (he was an early backer of legislation to establish a heating oil reserve), improved staffing and infrastructure at U.S.-Canadian border crossings, and a bill to permit hunting of the once-endangered double-breasted cormorant, whose population has exploded and now represents "a destructive force in the Great Lakes environment and in the local sport fishing economy," according to McHugh.

He was the principal sponsor of legislation, signed into law, to permit the

Postal Service to issue special stamps to aid in fundraising for worthy causes such as breast cancer research. The breast cancer stamp sells for 40 cents, with much of the markup over the cost of a regular stamp going to the federal government's research effort.

McHugh also raised an alarm about unscrupulous sweepstakes offers that use deceptive practices and often target the elderly. "Sweepstakes themselves are not evil, but experience teaches us that, where the law falls short, the dishonest will flock and honest people will suffer," he said.

McHugh was a top aide to the city manager of Watertown for five years and then worked for a state senator for nine years before seeking elective office. His background has shaped his approach to his job: He is at home with the behind-the-scenes, nuts-and-bolts work of governing and crafting legislation and doesn't need a lot of time in front of the television cameras.

As might be expected from someone who has made government work his career, McHugh seeks cooperation with Democrats and does not have a particularly ideological voting record. He supported President Clinton's position about a third of the time and voted against two of the articles of impeachment against him. McHugh also supports labor on a number of issues.

On most policy matters, however, McHugh fits comfortably into his party's conservative mold. He supports the rights of gun owners, and in 1996 he backed a GOP-led effort to repeal the 1994 ban on certain semiautomatic assault-style weapons. He has voted on several occasions to outlaw a procedure its opponents call "partial birth" abortion. And he voted against providing insurance coverage of contraceptives for federal workers.

McHugh grew up in a middle-class family in Watertown, majored in political science in college, and after a brief stint as an insurance broker, got his start in practical politics working as an assistant to the city manager in Watertown, the largest city in the 24th. He moved to the staff of state Sen. H. Douglas Barclay, where his duties included serving as a liaison to local governments in the district — a job that helped McHugh prepare for a successful run for the state Senate when Barclay retired in 1984.

During eight years in the state Senate, McHugh, as part of the Republican majority, worked to pass legislation to help farmers and pushed for a Northeastern dairy compact.

When GOP Rep. David O'B. Martin decided to retire from Congress in 1992, McHugh jumped into the race. He won the primary over a more conservative opponent, Morrison J. Hosley Jr., a local business owner and Hamilton town supervisor. Since winning his first House contest, McHugh has breezed to re-election in this historically Republican district.

KEY VOTES

2000
Yes Raise hourly minimum wage by $1 over two years
Yes Halt funding for U.S. mission in Kosovo unless European nations pay more
Yes Provide Medicare benefits to military retirees and their dependents
Yes Grant China permanent normal trade status
Yes Phase out estate, gift and trust taxes
Yes Prohibit implementation of president's national monument designations
Yes Approve GOP plan to provide prescription drug coverage for Medicare beneficiaries
No Increase help for poor nations indebted to international financial institutions

1999
Yes Impose steel import quotas
No Kill proposal to take aviation trust funds off budget
Yes Require background checks on buyers only at gun shows with 10 or more vendors
Yes Remove barriers among banking, securities and insurance companies
Yes Authorize state grants to hire teachers and reduce class size
Yes Overhaul campaign finance law; ban "soft money" and restrict advocacy advertising
Yes Approve bipartisan plan to increase rights of patients in managed-care health plans

INTEREST GROUPS

	AFL-CIO	ADA	CCUS	ACU
2000	20%	5%	80%	73%
1999	56%	35%	76%	72%
1998	40%	25%	89%	68%
1997	50%	15%	80%	60%

CQ VOTE STUDIES

	PARTY UNITY		PRESIDENTIAL SUPPORT	
	Support	Oppose	Support	Oppose
2000	87%	13%	34%	66%
1999	81%	19%	29%	71%
1998	80%	20%	35%	65%
1997	86%	14%	35%	65%

NEW YORK 24
North Country — Plattsburgh; Watertown; Oswego

One of the East's largest districts, the 24th covers more than one-fourth of the state, bordering Lake Champlain, the St. Lawrence Seaway and Lake Ontario. The waterways provide an inexpensive source of electricity, which has lured some heavy industry to the district and given it a number of blue-collar voters.

But the majority of the district is rural and Republican, full of small towns, dairy farmers and maple syrup producers. Concern for Fort Drum near Watertown, one of the district's economic mainstays, reinforces the 24th's tendency to support the GOP.

Although Fort Drum is one of the largest and most modern Army facilities on the East Coast and has thus far been safe from post-Cold War base closures, district residents experienced the economic hardship that comes with base closures when Plattsburgh Air Force

Base shut down in 1993. A "trade park" in the closed base's place has attracted 1,200 jobs, helping encourage the district's recovery.

Unemployment remains a problem throughout the district; harsh winters and high transportation costs make attracting jobs difficult. But the district also covers most of the Adirondack Mountains, making seasonal tourism a growing industry. In 1996, economic difficulties contributed to Clinton's victory in this otherwise Republican mainstay. And in 2000, Al Gore and President Bush nearly tied, receiving virtually the same number of votes. Clinton County, bordering independently minded Vermont, is the only county with a regular and substantial Democratic vote.

MAJOR INDUSTRY
Agriculture, manufacturing, tourism, defense

MILITARY BASES
Fort Drum, 10,343 military, 2,368 civilian (2000)

CITIES
Watertown, 27,440; Plattsburgh, 18,585; Oswego, 18,097

UNUSUAL FEATURES
Antique Boat Museum in Clayton.

Rep. James T. Walsh (R)

Elected 1988; 7th term

CAPITOL OFFICE
225-3701; fax 225-4042; 2351 Rayburn Bldg. 20515

INTERNET
e-mail: rep.james.walsh@mail.house.gov
web: www.house.gov/walsh

COMMITTEES
Appropriations
    (VA, HUD & Independent Agencies - chairman)

HOMETOWN
Syracuse

BORN
June 19, 1947, Syracuse, N.Y.

RELIGION
Roman Catholic

FAMILY
Wife, DeDe Ryan Walsh; three children

EDUCATION
St. Bonaventure U., B.A. 1970

CAREER
Marketing executive; social worker; Peace Corps volunteer

POLITICAL HIGHLIGHTS
Syracuse Common Council, 1978-88 (president, 1986-88); sought nomination for Onondaga County executive, 1987

ELECTION RESULTS

2000 GENERAL

James T. Walsh (R, INDC, C)	151,880	69.0%
Francis J. Gavin (D)	64,533	29.3%
Howie Hawkins (GREEN)	3,830	1.7%

2000 PRIMARY

James T. Walsh (R)	unopposed

1998 GENERAL

James T. Walsh (R, C)	121,204	69.4%
Yvonne Rothenberg (D, L, GREEN)	53,461	30.6%

PREVIOUS WINNING PERCENTAGES
1996 (55%); 1994 (58%); 1992 (56%); 1990 (63%); 1988 (57%)

Now in his second decade in Congress, the unassuming and occasionally moderate Walsh does not command even a fraction of the attention at the Capitol that now attends New York's new junior senator, Hillary Rodham Clinton. But he has become arguably the most important member of the Empire State's congressional delegation. Since 1999, he has chaired the Appropriations subcommittee that drafts the third-largest of the annual spending bills. No one else from New York, the nation's third-most-populous state, has such a prominent role in allocating federal dollars.

His subcommittee, known as VA-HUD, provides the funding for the Department of Housing and Urban Development (HUD), whose programs are of particular importance to New York City and upstate cities; the Department of Veterans Affairs (VA), which serves more than 1.3 million veterans in the state; the Environmental Protection Agency, which oversees the cleanup of the Hudson River and Onondaga Lake, a heavily polluted body of water in Walsh's hometown of Syracuse; as well as NASA, the Federal Emergency Management Agency and 19 other agencies. Walsh has used his position on Appropriations to steer hundreds of millions of dollars to New York, including nearly $40 million to his hometown alone in his panel's spending measure in 2000.

Aided in part by senior Republicans who knew his father, former Rep. William F. Walsh, the younger Walsh has formed friendships on both sides of the aisle. He is also known for having a sense of fairness. The subcommittee's top Democrat, Alan B. Mollohan of West Virginia, told the Syracuse Herald American, "You know Jim Walsh is in charge and, at the same time, you know you're a part of the process."

Walsh sees his chairmanship as important in aiding Syracuse and surrounding central New York, which has recently seen its share of economic decline. He answers critics of the appropriations process by pointing out that the practice of earmarking funds for local needs is a long-running tradition. "Does it have warts? Yes. Are there abuses? Yes, there are," he told the Herald American in 2000. "But it's as good a process as you can find because it gives members an opportunity to directly impact on problems and concerns they have in their districts."

As a reminder of the things he needs to accomplish, Walsh keeps a "things-to-do-this-year" list — a half sheet of paper — on his desk at all times. In 2000, in addition to the VA-HUD spending bill, that list included adding wool tariff provisions to a trade bill and securing a new generation of F-16 jet fighters for an Air National Guard unit in Syracuse.

Walsh also sits on the Agriculture Appropriations Subcommittee, which has jurisdiction over programs such as food stamps and milk price supports, crucial to upstate dairy farmers. In the 106th Congress, Walsh included a provision in an appropriations measure blocking new federal milk-pricing rules from taking effect, a move that protected upstate dairy farmers but infuriated lawmakers from the Upper Midwest. He also secured disaster aid for New York apple growers and helped write new food stamp rules allowing more people to qualify.

Before using his seniority to lay claim to the VA-HUD gavel, Walsh spent the 104th Congress as chairman of Appropriations' District of Columbia Subcommittee. He used that position to help write the 1995 law that created a financial control board to steer the capital city out of a longstanding fiscal morass. He also pressed the District to cut spending by imposing a limit on the local government's budget deficit. Republicans imposed other policy directives governing the use of federal and local funds for abortions for poor Washington, D.C., residents, but Walsh blocked efforts by fervent GOP budget-cutters who sought to reduce federal financial support for the city. "The Constitution placed responsibility for the District under the Congress," he said. "We should not shirk our responsibilities to our nation's capital."

Walsh has endorsed funding increases for the Peace Corps, in which he spent two years teaching rice-growing techniques in Nepal. "The only rice I'd ever seen was out of an Uncle Ben's box," he recalled 30 years later. He also has quietly opposed GOP efforts to eliminate AmeriCorps, the national service program modeled in some ways after the Peace Corps. The program's funding is covered by the VA-HUD bill, and when the House has voted to cut the appropriation, Walsh has worked to restore it later on.

While Walsh routinely sides with the Republican leadership at key moments, his vote cannot be taken for granted. He was among the GOP members who broke with their leaders and most of their colleagues to vote in both 1998 and 1999 for an overhaul of campaign finance law featuring a ban on "soft money" — the unlimited contributions used for party-building activities and issue ads. In 2000, he voted for a two-year increase in the minimum wage, which GOP leaders opposed.

A gun owner and hunter, Walsh is a member of the Congressional Sportsmen's Caucus. In 1999, he backed a measure to allow quick background checks for purchases at some gun shows, a proposal that was defeated in part because gun control advocates labeled it too weak. He also opposed a 1994 ban on certain semiautomatic assault-style weapons and voted to repeal the ban in 1996. But he did vote in 1993 for enactment of the Brady law, which mandated a five-day waiting period on handgun purchases until an instant check could be established.

Walsh is chairman of the Friends of Ireland congressional caucus and chaired a delegation that visited Northern Ireland with President Clinton in 1995. He is the sponsor of a law that allows individuals from disadvantaged areas in Northern Ireland to come to the United States for job training. The provision came to be called the "Walsh visa."

With a father who was mayor of Syracuse before serving in Congress, it was not surprising that Walsh became active in politics. He served more than a decade on the city council, including three years as council president. He entered Congress on his first try in 1988, when a four-term GOP incumbent, George C. Wortley, was nudged into retirement by party officials. He has won at least three-fifths of the vote in three of his six subsequent victories.

KEY VOTES

2000

Yes Raise hourly minimum wage by $1 over two years
Yes Halt funding for U.S. mission in Kosovo unless European nations pay more
Yes Provide Medicare benefits to military retirees and their dependents
Yes Grant China permanent normal trade status
Yes Phase out estate, gift and trust taxes
No   Prohibit implementation of president's national monument designations
Yes Approve GOP plan to provide prescription drug coverage for Medicare beneficiaries
No   Increase help for poor nations indebted to international financial institutions

1999

Yes Impose steel import quotas
Yes Kill proposal to take aviation trust funds off budget
Yes Require background checks on buyers only at gun shows with 10 or more vendors
Yes Remove barriers among banking, securities and insurance companies
No   Authorize state grants to hire teachers and reduce class size
Yes Overhaul campaign finance law; ban "soft money" and restrict advocacy advertising
Yes Approve bipartisan plan to increase rights of patients in managed-care health plans

INTEREST GROUPS

	AFL-CIO	ADA	CCUS	ACU
2000	10%	20%	85%	56%
1999	33%	35%	72%	64%
1998	40%	30%	89%	44%
1997	38%	35%	80%	75%

CQ VOTE STUDIES

	PARTY UNITY		PRESIDENTIAL SUPPORT	
	Support	Oppose	Support	Oppose
2000	79%	21%	43%	57%
1999	78%	22%	32%	68%
1998	73%	27%	36%	64%
1997	87%	13%	37%	63%

NEW YORK 25
Central — Syracuse

Located in the center of the state, Syracuse is the biggest city and economic hub of the 25th, which stretches from Lake Ontario to part of Broome County in the south. Small towns and farms fill out the area outside of Syracuse in this moderately conservative district.

Syracuse has not fully recovered from the departure of some big manufacturing plants in the 1980s and '90s, although the city has held on to some blue-collar jobs by encouraging light manufacturing firms. Other growth comes from service-related work in hospitals and universities. Outside of Syracuse, small towns rely on dairy farming.

Previously strong Republican territory, the 25th's GOP organization once held the loyalties of Irish, Italian, Polish and Jewish constituencies in and around Syracuse. The electorate's GOP leanings were reinforced by the typical upstate antipathy toward Democratic New York City. But the Republican machine has faded, and economic stagnation in the 1990s and the decline of the city's industrial sector

have helped the Democratic Party gain ground. In Syracuse, minorities and blue-collar workers contribute to the Democratic vote. So do upscale De Witt, which includes a sizable Jewish population, and lower-income areas in the city of Cortland. The 25th gave the edge to Al Gore and Sen. Hillary Rodham Clinton in 2000.

But the district's voter registration still favors the GOP, primarily because of the sizable Republican base that remains in Syracuse's suburbs and outlying areas. Cayuga County, along the 25th's northeastern border, and lightly populated Tioga County, at the southern end, are mainly Republican areas.

MAJOR INDUSTRY

Agriculture, service, manufacturing

CITIES

Syracuse, 150,563; Clay (unincorporated), 59,749 (1990); Salina (unincorporated), 35,145 (1990)

UNUSUAL FEATURES

First synthetic penicillin made in 1959 by Bristol Laboratories in Syracuse; The Brannock Device – used to measure feet for shoe size – invented by Syracusan Charles F. Brannock.

Rep. Maurice D. Hinchey (D)

CAPITOL OFFICE
225-6335; fax 226-0774; 2431 Rayburn Bldg. 20515

INTERNET
e-mail: mhinchey@mail.house.gov
web: www.house.gov/hinchey

COMMITTEES
Appropriations

HOMETOWN
Saugerties

BORN
Oct. 27, 1938, Manhattan, N.Y.

RELIGION
Roman Catholic

FAMILY
Wife, Ilene Marder; three children

EDUCATION
State U. of New York, New Paltz, B.S. 1968, M.A. 1970

MILITARY SERVICE
Navy, 1956-59

CAREER
State employee

POLITICAL HIGHLIGHTS
Democratic nominee for N.Y. Assembly, 1972; N.Y. Assembly, 1975-93

ELECTION RESULTS

2000 GENERAL

M. Hinchey (D, INDC, WFM, L)	140,395	62.0%
Bob Moppert (R, C)	83,856	37.0%
Paul J. Laux (RTL)	2,328	1.0%

2000 PRIMARY

M. Hinchey (D)	unopposed

1998 GENERAL

M. Hinchey (D, INDC, L)	108,204	61.8%
William H. "Bud" Walker (R, C)	54,776	31.3%
Randall Terry (RTL)	12,160	6.9%

PREVIOUS WINNING PERCENTAGES
1996 (55%); 1994 (49%); 1992 (50%)

Elected 1992; 5th term

Hinchey grew up in a working-class home, joined the Navy out of high school, worked in a local cement plant for five years and then paid his way through college by collecting tolls on the New York Thruway.

In Congress, he has traded his blue-collar garb for pin-stripe suits and elegant ties, and his silver-tinged hair is always in place. But while his sartorial preferences may have changed, Hinchey's politics are true to his roots: He boasts a 99 percent career rating from the AFL-CIO. He is in the Progressive Caucus, which is the most left-leaning of the Hill's policy groups, and he has never received less than a 95 percent rating from the liberal Americans for Democratic Action.

But he is not usually inclined to seek out partisan confrontation. He often teams with fellow upstate New York lawmakers on issues of common interest, joining Republican James T. Walsh of the neighboring 25th District, for instance, to secure $138 million in federal aid for apple growers, and working with the GOP's Amo Houghton of the 31st District to press for funding to upgrade the Southern Tier's principal east-west highway to interstate status.

Such an approach makes him a good fit for the Appropriations Committee, where bipartisan behavior is rewarded. But it is also indicative of Hinchey's pragmatism and his political background: He is one of just four Democrats among the 13 Upstate New York House members, and when he was first elected to the state Assembly in 1974, he was the first Democrat to represent that legislative district in 62 years.

Nevertheless, Hinchey is generally a dependable vote for Democratic Party positions, and he is a member of the Democratic whip team; in the 106th Congress, he was on Democratic task forces on education and health. He was rewarded for his loyalty with an appointment to the Appropriations Committee, where he can fight for programs that contribute to economic development in his district, which is still struggling to recover from massive layoffs by IBM in the early 1990s.

Funding for the new east-west Interstate 86 is important to the region's economic development, as was the aid to apple growers and a host of grants for specific development projects he was able to win in the 106th Congress. On the Agriculture Appropriations Subcommittee, Hinchey worked to open Cuba to agricultural exports from the United States.

To take the Appropriations assignment, Hinchey had to give up his seats on the Banking and Resources committees, but he still pursues those interests. In the 106th Congress, for instance, he offered bills to limit automated teller machine fees and to prohibit companies from offering checks as an enticement for people to take out loans.

Environmental policies remain Hinchey's principal concern outside of Appropriations, and it is on those issues that he is most likely to become embroiled in partisan disputes.

An environmental fight in the 1970s over the development of a huge power plant on the Hudson River was the primary impetus for Hinchey's entry into electoral politics. In the state Assembly, Hinchey chaired the Environmental Conservation Committee, investigating "Love Canal" and drafting bills to combat acid rain and to create the Hudson River Valley Greenway. Once in Congress, Hinchey followed up his efforts on the greenway by winning approval of his bill to designate much of the Hudson Valley as a National Heritage Area. He has been involved in a long-running effort to require General Electric to clean up toxic polychlorinated biphenyls, or PCBs, discharged into the Hudson River from its plant north of Albany.

Hinchey's liberalism was on display during his tenure on the Banking Committee, where he complained that the Republicans and moneyed interests protected the wealthy while overlooking the needs of average working people. "The disparity in income between those at the top and those at the bottom of the ladder is a cancer that will ultimately sap the vitality of our economic system, exacerbating the social problems that are already plaguing our society," he said in 1993.

Hinchey deviates from his traditional liberal line when it comes to gun owners' rights. He was the only New York Democrat voting in 1996 to repeal the ban on certain semiautomatic assault-style weapons and the only New York Democrat to vote against the ban in the first place in the 103rd Congress. He did support the Brady bill, which called for a five-day waiting period for handgun purchases. A member of the Congressional Sportsmen's Caucus, Hinchey received some unwelcome attention during his first House term when he was charged with carrying a loaded handgun in his baggage at Washington National Airport. He eventually pleaded no contest and was given a suspended sentence.

Hinchey's parents had been active in local party politics, and after his graduation from college, he was encouraged to get involved in behind-the-scenes political activities while starting a career in education. But soon, his environmental interests drew him into the electoral arena. He lost his first bid for the Assembly, in 1972, but came back two years later to begin an 18-year tenure in Albany.

In 1992, when nine-term Democratic Rep. Matthew F. McHugh retired, Hinchey sought to move up to Congress. He started as the underdog in the Democratic primary, facing Binghamton Mayor Juanita M. Crabb, who once had been talked about as a potential running mate for Democratic Gov. Mario M. Cuomo. But Hinchey prevailed by pushing a New Deal-like plan to revitalize the economy of the recession-hit region.

In November, Hinchey faced Republican Bob Moppert, a six-year county legislator. As Bill Clinton was carrying the 26th by 10 percentage points, Hinchey edged Moppert by 8,819 votes. The close race and competitive nature of the district made Hinchey a top GOP target for 1994, with Moppert back for a rematch. Hinchey survived again, winning by slightly more than 1,200 votes. In subsequent re-election bids, however, Hinchey has enjoyed more comfortable margins, winning in 2000 by 25 points.

With district lines due to be redrawn for 2002, Hinchey has hired a lobbyist to watch out for his interests in Albany.

KEY VOTES

2000
Yes Raise hourly minimum wage by $1 over two years
No   Halt funding for U.S. mission in Kosovo unless European nations pay more
Yes Provide Medicare benefits to military retirees and their dependents
No   Grant China permanent normal trade status
No   Phase out estate, gift and trust taxes
No   Prohibit implementation of president's national monument designations
No   Approve GOP plan to provide prescription drug coverage for Medicare beneficiaries
Yes Increase help for poor nations indebted to international financial institutions

1999
Yes Impose steel import quotas
Yes Kill proposal to take aviation trust funds off budget
No   Require background checks on buyers only at gun shows with 10 or more vendors
No   Remove barriers among banking, securities and insurance companies
?   Authorize state grants to hire teachers and reduce class size
Yes Overhaul campaign finance law; ban "soft money" and restrict advocacy advertising
Yes Approve bipartisan plan to increase rights of patients in managed-care health plans

INTEREST GROUPS

	AFL-CIO	ADA	CCUS	ACU
2000	100%	95%	23%	0%
1999	88%	95%	16%	4%
1998	100%	100%	22%	4%
1997	100%	95%	20%	8%

CQ VOTE STUDIES

	PARTY UNITY		PRESIDENTIAL SUPPORT	
	Support	Oppose	Support	Oppose
2000	98%	2%	94%	6%
1999	94%	6%	87%	13%
1998	96%	4%	83%	17%
1997	97%	3%	81%	19%

NEW YORK 26
South – Kingston; Binghamton; Ithaca

The elongated 26th reaches from high above Cayuga Lake's waters to the banks of the Hudson River. Most of the population is found in pockets at the district's extremes: the Ithaca and Binghamton areas to the west, and the Hudson Valley region, which includes the cities of Kingston, Newburgh and Beacon, on the eastern edge.

The 26th has been a casualty of changing times. IBM, a major employer in the district, laid off much of its workforce in the 1990s to regain its competitiveness in a quickly changing computer market, although it still maintains a strong presence. Defense contractors in Binghamton were hit hard by post-Cold War budget cuts. And the Catskills' once famous Borscht Belt resorts have declined, passed over by tourists who can now afford to vacation in more exotic locales. But the district has recovered by using Cornell University and SUNY-Binghamton to recruit new computer and electronics firms.

Ithaca, home to Cornell and Ithaca College, remains a haven for liberal activists. The town elected a Socialist mayor to three terms in the early 1990s and currently has an independent mayor. It also circulates its own currency, Ithaca HOURs, which is accepted in more than 350 locations. Broome County's Triple Cities – Binghamton, Johnson City and Endicott – have a mix of high-tech employees and blue-collar workers, making them marginal political territory.

The many rural residents in Tioga, Broome and Delaware counties provide a conservative foundation that favors the GOP, but the 26th's liberal-leaning towns in counties such as Tompkins (Ithaca) and Sullivan give the district a sizable Democratic base. Voter registration is split virtually evenly between Democrats and Republicans. The district has elected Democratic Rep. Hinchey since 1992 and supported Bill Clinton and Al Gore in 1992, '96 and 2000.

MAJOR INDUSTRY
Higher education, computers, manufacturing, agriculture

CITIES
Binghamton, 46,674; Ithaca, 29,401; Newburgh, 26,153

UNUSUAL FEATURES
Washington's Headquarters State Historic Site in Newburgh: military headquarters and residence for George Washington from 1782-83.

Rep. Thomas M. Reynolds (R)

Elected 1998; 2nd term

CAPITOL OFFICE
225-5265; fax 225-5910; 413 Cannon Bldg. 20515

INTERNET
e-mail: www.house.gov/writerep
web: www.house.gov/reynolds

COMMITTEES
House Administration
Rules

HOMETOWN
Springville

BORN
Sept. 3, 1950, Belfonte, Pa.

RELIGION
Presbyterian

FAMILY
Wife, Donna Reynolds; four children

EDUCATION
Springville Griffith Institute, attended; Kent State U., attended

MILITARY SERVICE
N.Y. Air National Guard, 1970-76

CAREER
Real estate and insurance broker; city legislative aide

POLITICAL HIGHLIGHTS
Concord Town Council, 1974-82; Erie County Legislature, 1982-88 (Republican leader, 1987-88); N.Y. Assembly, 1989-99 (minority leader, 1995-98)

ELECTION RESULTS

2000 GENERAL

Thomas M. Reynolds (R, C)	157,694	69.3%
Thomas W. Pecoraro (D)	69,870	30.7%

2000 PRIMARY

Thomas M. Reynolds (R)	unopposed

1998 GENERAL

Thomas M. Reynolds (R, C)	102,042	57.3%
Bill Cook (D, INDC, RTL)	75,978	42.7%

Considering his relative lack of seniority, Reynolds has been unusually successful at the inside game in the House. His initial triumph came soon after his election in 1998, when he was given a seat on the Rules Committee, only the second time a GOP freshman has won such an assignment in the past 75 years. As agents of the Speaker in setting the parameters for the House's legislative debates, members of the panel are viewed as a part of the extended leadership team.

Reynolds says that his seat on Rules — which sets the guidelines that govern floor action on individual bills — has afforded him a "great bird's-eye view of what's going on." The assignment also gave him more visibility than most freshmen, because senior House members come before the panel to pitch their legislative proposals.

In the 106th Congress, Reynolds also was the only freshman who was a deputy Republican whip. In addition to counting votes, whips are called on to persuade reluctant or undecided lawmakers to stick with the party on key votes. Reynolds said his work in Texan Tom DeLay's whip organization helped him understand the behind-the-scenes intricacies of passing legislation. That job, along with his Rules post, helped Reynolds get to know a significant number of his Republican colleagues.

So few were surprised when Speaker J. Dennis Hastert chose Reynolds as a co-chairman for Battleground 2000, an unprecedented effort by the National Republican Congressional Committee — the House GOP's candidate recruitment and fundraising organization — in which House members were to raise $16 million to help embattled colleagues, challengers and open-seat candidates. Reynolds pressed lawmakers with large cash reserves and safe seats to write checks; he talked others into conducting special fundraisers in their districts to bring in extra money. The drive brought in nearly $22 million.

Reynolds' success with Battleground 2000 earned him enough bonus points with the GOP leadership that he won another top insider's job for the 107th Congress — a seat on the House Administration Committee. That panel (whose majority members are also chosen by the Speaker) oversees the day-to-day logistics of the House, including the perquisites of the members, and also has jurisdiction over campaign finance legislation.

Reynolds won appointment to the Ways and Means Committee as well, although he immediately took a leave of absence for the 107th because House rules prohibit someone on Rules from serving on any other major committee. His reason for securing the assignment was farsighted and pragmatic: Were Democrats to win back the House in 2002, the GOP membership on Rules would shrink, and Reynolds would be forced off that panel because he is its junior GOP member. A seat waiting for him on the committee that writes tax, trade and health care legislation is the ideal fallback position.

In his first term, Reynolds focused on matters important to his constituents, including dairy pricing policy. Upstate dairy farmers vehemently opposed a new pricing method for milk proposed by the Clinton White House, and Reynolds was a key player in forcing the administration to choose another milk pricing plan in 1999. He also worked to get funds in the 2000 budget for marketing assistance for apple growers.

A major transportation route to and from Canada goes through the 27th District, and Reynolds was also involved in a deal to prevent traffic jams at the U.S.-Canadian border. At issue was a 1996 law that would have required the Immigration and Naturalization Service to keep track of everyone crossing the border. To avoid creating traffic backlogs, Reynolds in 1999 worked with other lawmakers to ease the requirement.

On trade matters, Reynolds favors a free-trade approach. In 2000, he supported the measure granting China permanent normal trade status. In the 107th, he is among those pushing to revive fast-track authority that would allow presidents to submit trade pacts that Congress must vote to either accept or reject, without amendment.

Reynolds has a keen interest in U.S.-Israeli relations, and in 2000, he introduced legislation to cut off aid to the Palestinian Authority if it unilaterally declared itself a state.

The New York lawmaker does not always follow the party line. In 1999, he voted for a patients' rights bill that the House Republican leadership opposed. "Giving the patient the right to sue their HMO, just as they already have the right to sue a hospital or a doctor, will increase accountability when it comes to treatment and care," he told the Buffalo News.

Reynolds' path up the inside lanes of the GOP hierarchy bears an unusual similarity to that of his predecessor and longtime ally, former GOP Rep. Bill Paxon. Indeed, Upstate Republicans called Reynolds the "perfect" successor to Paxon, when he quit the House in 1998; their careers before Congress followed almost identical, and rapid, upward trajectories.

Reynolds was just 23 when he won his first campaign, for the Concord Town Council. He later followed Paxon to the county legislature, then won election to fill Paxon's seat in the state legislature in 1988. During his decade in Albany, Reynolds earned a reputation as a hard-working conservative. He chaired the GOP's affordable housing task force and paid close attention to constituent service. In 1995, he was chosen leader of the Assembly's Republican minority, a position he held until he ran for the House in 1998.

Throughout Paxon's House career, Reynolds had served as Paxon's campaign manager, and Paxon returned the favor by managing Reynolds' House campaign. A shoo-in in the heavily Republican district, Reynolds was so flush with campaign cash that he was able to donate $50,000 to the House GOP campaign committee two weeks before his election, in which he won a 15 percentage point victory over college history professor Bill Cook.

In 2000, Reynolds breezed past Thomas W. Pecoraro, a partner in a vending machine business and one of the founders of the Erie County Independence Party, who was running on the Democratic ticket. Reynolds captured almost 70 percent of the vote.

KEY VOTES

2000
No   Raise hourly minimum wage by $1 over two years
Yes Halt funding for U.S. mission in Kosovo unless European nations pay more
Yes Provide Medicare benefits to military retirees and their dependents
Yes Grant China permanent normal trade status
Yes Phase out estate, gift and trust taxes
No   Prohibit implementation of president's national monument designations
Yes Approve GOP plan to provide prescription drug coverage for Medicare beneficiaries
No   Increase help for poor nations indebted to international financial institutions

1999
No   Impose steel import quotas
No   Kill proposal to take aviation trust funds off budget
Yes Require background checks on buyers only at gun shows with 10 or more vendors
Yes Remove barriers among banking, securities and insurance companies
No   Authorize state grants to hire teachers and reduce class size
No   Overhaul campaign finance law; ban "soft money" and restrict advocacy advertising
Yes Approve bipartisan plan to increase rights of patients in managed-care health plans

INTEREST GROUPS

	AFL-CIO	ADA	CCUS	ACU
2000	0%	0%	85%	84%
1999	11%	15%	92%	79%

CQ VOTE STUDIES

	PARTY UNITY		PRESIDENTIAL SUPPORT	
	Support	Oppose	Support	Oppose
2000	93%	7%	25%	75%
1999	88%	12%	25%	75%

NEW YORK 27
Suburban Buffalo and rural west — Amherst

New York's 27th starts in the Seneca Falls area and heads west through agriculture and manufacturing towns until reaching the Buffalo suburbs. Republican territory, the 27th was almost eliminated in 1992 redistricting but then-Rep. Bill Paxon's efforts to spare the seat paid off. The redrawn 27th takes in solidly GOP areas.

Although the district's manufacturing and farming sectors had their ups and downs in the 1990s, the economy held steady. The 27th's population is anchored in Amherst, a white-collar suburb of Buffalo and the 27th's largest city. The State University of New York at Buffalo and corporate office parks are mainstays.

The New York State Thruway links Erie County to the Rochester suburbs of Monroe County. Republicans usually carry these mainly middle-class suburbs. Between them and to the east are the dairy, vegetable and grain farms of rural western New York. Wyoming County is heavily agricultural, but it has a facility that is distinctly unbucolic:

the state penitentiary at Attica, the site in 1971 of one of the worst prison riots in U.S. history.

To the east are Ontario and Seneca counties, where the 27th moves into part of the Finger Lakes region, including some of its vineyards and the cities of Geneva and Seneca Falls. The western end of Wayne County (which borders Lake Ontario) is within Rochester's sphere.

Regarded as New York's most Republican district, the 27th gave President Bush 53 percent of the vote and his largest winning percentage in the state in 2000.

MAJOR INDUSTRY
Agriculture, manufacturing, service

CITIES
Amherst (unincorporated), 111,711 (1990); Chili (unincorporated), 25,178 (1990); Clarence (unincorporated), 20,041 (1990)

UNUSUAL FEATURES
First Women's Rights Convention held in 1848 in Seneca Falls; Joseph Smith, founder of the Mormon Church, grew up and had his first visions in Palmyra.

Rep. Louise M. Slaughter (D)

CAPITOL OFFICE
225-3615; fax 225-7822; 2347 Rayburn Bldg. 20515

INTERNET
e-mail: louiseny@mail.house.gov
web: www.house.gov/slaughter

COMMITTEES
Rules

HOMETOWN
Fairport

BORN
Aug. 14, 1929, Harlan County, Ky.

RELIGION
Episcopalian

FAMILY
Husband, Robert Slaughter; three children

EDUCATION
U. of Kentucky, B.S. 1951, M.P.H. 1953

CAREER
Legislative aide; market researcher; microbiologist

POLITICAL HIGHLIGHTS
Monroe County Legislature, 1975-79; N.Y.
Assembly, 1983-87

ELECTION RESULTS

2000 GENERAL

Louise M. Slaughter (D)	151,688	65.7%
Mark C. Johns (R, C)	75,348	32.6%

2000 PRIMARY

Louise M. Slaughter (D)	unopposed

1998 GENERAL

Louise M. Slaughter (D)	118,856	64.8%
Richard A. Kaplan (R, INDC)	56,443	30.8%
Paul Britton (C)	4,963	2.7%
Gerald D. Crawford (RTL)	3,196	1.7%

PREVIOUS WINNING PERCENTAGES
1996 (57%); 1994 (57%); 1992 (55%); 1990 (59%);
1988 (57%); 1986 (51%)

Elected 1986; 8th term

A staunch liberal on abortion policy, women's issues and gun control, Slaughter is a Southerner who represents a district in Upstate New York. Although she has lived most of her adult life in a suburb of Rochester, she was brought up in the mountains of Harlan County, Ky., a genuine coal miner's daughter.

Slaughter moved to Rochester from Kentucky in the 1950s, when her husband went to work as an executive with a local corporation. Her first brush with public policy came in 1971, when she joined with some neighbors to try to save a stand of trees from development. It was a losing battle. "I was so shy," Slaughter later told The Associated Press. "I thought in my best Kentucky fashion that if I would put on my best dress and go and be very nice and polite and ask them to save this forest that they would say, 'Well, why not?' And they just handed me my hat."

The episode sparked an interest in politics. She served as a Monroe County legislator and as an assistant to Mario M. Cuomo, then New York's secretary of state. In 1982, she ousted a GOP incumbent to move to the state Assembly, and she served four years there before taking on first-term GOP Rep. Fred J. Eckert, a conservative.

Slaughter told The Hill newspaper that actor Richard Gere, with whom she shared an interest in opposing Central American dictatorships, walked door-to-door with her in the campaign. Depicting Eckert as a right-wing obstructionist and parrying his efforts to portray her as an ultraliberal, Slaughter won with 51 percent.

She has since won by comfortable margins, despite being targeted during the 1990s by the National Republican Congressional Committee, the House GOP's campaign group.

When Slaughter came to Congress in 1987, House Democratic leaders quickly took a liking to her warmth, grit and liberal views. She was awarded a place on the Rules Committee in 1989, and she added a seat on the Budget Committee in 1991. But since then, Slaughter's aspirations for a bigger role in the party have been thwarted. She narrowly lost a race for the vice chairmanship of the Democratic Caucus in the 104th Congress, then failed in a bid to become ranking Democrat on the Budget Committee in the 105th Congress and rotated off the panel when her term expired.

A bacteriologist with a master's degree in public health, Slaughter often gets the job of arguing the Democratic case when women's health issues come to the House floor. In the 107th Congress, she is a vice chairwoman of the Congressional Caucus for Women's Issues.

Slaughter is front and center in opposing conservative initiatives to restrict abortion and family planning funds. She once called a GOP plan to curtail family planning aid to developing countries "inhumane," and she has attacked as "shameful" the GOP effort to ban a procedure its opponents call "partial birth" abortion. "In their war against a woman's right to choose," Slaughter said in the 105th, "anti-choice forces have shown that they are willing to sacrifice a woman's health and her future fertility to pursue an extreme agenda."

Slaughter is also concerned that advanced understanding of the human genome system, which offers promise of dramatic medical breakthroughs, could lead to discrimination against people with genetic disorders. In the 106th, she introduced a measure to protect people from being fired from their jobs or dropped by their insurers as the result of a genetic test. "Every human being has between five and 50 faulty genes," Slaughter said. "Genetic discrimination is not something that might happen to a hypothetical group of people. ... We are talking about ourselves."

Aggressive at winning federal funds for her district and looking out for the interests of local employers, Slaughter has been fiercely critical of the airline industry in the deregulated environment.

"This aeronautics structure was built with the tax dollars of the United States," she said in 2001. "Then deregulation came along, and we went from about 13 airlines in Rochester to about six. We can get service, but we pay the highest fares also in the country."

She introduced a bill in the 105th that would force greater competition by letting smaller carriers provide service to airports in small and midsize cities, and she helped lure a low-cost carrier, JetBlue, to Rochester.

In 2000, she criticized the proposed merger between United Airlines and US Airways, saying it could reduce airline competition; and in the 107th, she introduced legislation to impose a one-year moratorium on airline mergers. "I believe the flying public is as fed up as it's ever been," she said.

Slaughter raised some eyebrows in late 1998 when, responding to a reporter's question, Slaughter suggested that if President Clinton were impeached, it might be prudent for him not to fight to the bitter end, but rather to hand his office over to Vice President Al Gore. Later, Slaughter said she believed that Clinton should remain as president, since he had been able to carry on with his duties despite being impeached by the House.

Slaughter's legislative successes include a bill to increase education about the health risks of the anti-miscarriage drug DES, which has caused cancer and abnormalities in the offspring of some women who took the drug. In 1998, her plan to expand after-school programs received $200 million in funding as part of the education package that Clinton successfully lobbied to include in the end-of-session catchall appropriations bill.

True to her liberal leanings, Slaughter sided with labor unions in 2000 by voting against legislation granting China permanent normal trade status, even though Eastman Kodak, Xerox and other companies in her district are trying to expand into overseas markets.

Weighing in on a consumer issue, Slaughter introduced a measure in 1999 that would have limited credit card use by individuals younger than 21. "Madison Avenue and the credit card companies have convinced our college students that getting a credit card is a prerequisite for success, like good grades or a high SAT score," she said. "But upon graduation, many of these young people find themselves buried in debt."

KEY VOTES

2000
Yes Raise hourly minimum wage by $1 over two years
No   Halt funding for U.S. mission in Kosovo unless European nations pay more
Yes Provide Medicare benefits to military retirees and their dependents
No   Grant China permanent normal trade status
No   Phase out estate, gift and trust taxes
No   Prohibit implementation of president's national monument designations
No   Approve GOP plan to provide prescription drug coverage for Medicare beneficiaries
Yes Increase help for poor nations indebted to international financial institutions

1999
Yes Impose steel import quotas
No   Kill proposal to take aviation trust funds off budget
No   Require background checks on buyers only at gun shows with 10 or more vendors
Yes Remove barriers among banking, securities and insurance companies
Yes Authorize state grants to hire teachers and reduce class size
Yes Overhaul campaign finance law; ban "soft money" and restrict advocacy advertising
Yes Approve bipartisan plan to increase rights of patients in managed-care health plans

INTEREST GROUPS

	AFL-CIO	ADA	CCUS	ACU
2000	100%	90%	38%	4%
1999	100%	100%	21%	4%
1998	100%	100%	39%	8%
1997	100%	85%	30%	9%

CQ VOTE STUDIES

	PARTY UNITY		PRESIDENTIAL SUPPORT	
	Support	Oppose	Support	Oppose
2000	96%	4%	87%	13%
1999	96%	4%	81%	19%
1998	96%	4%	82%	18%
1997	96%	4%	79%	21%

NEW YORK 28

Rochester

A compact district, the 28th takes in the city of Rochester and surrounding Monroe County on Lake Ontario. Compared with Rochester, the Monroe County suburbs are relatively affluent. The most populous suburbs, Greece and Irondequoit, are north of the city; Pittsford, the wealthiest suburb, is southeast.

Optic and imaging manufacturing firms drive the 28th's economy, joined by high-tech startup companies that benefit from proximity to the district's major corporations (Eastman Kodak and Xerox Corp.) and the area's major academic institutions.

Rochester suffered from high unemployment during the 1990s, but the situation has been improving considerably. While much of the slack in the manufacturing sector has been picked up by the service industries, the lower salaries have exacerbated the problems of Rochester's low-income residents.

Unlike many northeastern cities with blue-collar bases, the Rochester area long held to a moderate Republican tradition typical of upstate New York. But it has begun to lean the other way. The district supported Bill Clinton in the 1992 and '96 presidential elections and Al Gore in 2000. The same Democrat has held the House seat since 1987.

Part of the Democrats' success has been tapping party members in Rochester, which has about two-fifths of the 28th's population and is the state's third-largest city. Overall, Democrats have a voter registration edge, but Republicans hold a plurality among registered voters in suburban Monroe County.

MAJOR INDUSTRY
Service, manufacturing, retail

CITIES
Rochester (pt.), 231,624 (1990); Greece (unincorporated), 90,106 (1990); Irondequoit (unincorporated), 52,377 (1990)

UNUSUAL FEATURES
Women's rights activist Susan B. Anthony's home in Rochester is now a museum; Abolitionist Frederick Douglas buried in Rochester.

Rep. John J. LaFalce (D)

Elected 1974; 14th term

CAPITOL OFFICE
225-3231; fax 225-8693; 2310 Rayburn Bldg. 20515

INTERNET
e-mail: www.house.gov/writerep
web: www.house.gov/lafalce

COMMITTEES
Financial Services - ranking member

HOMETOWN
Tonawanda

BORN
Oct. 6, 1939, Buffalo, N.Y.

RELIGION
Roman Catholic

FAMILY
Wife, Patricia LaFalce; one child

EDUCATION
Canisius College, B.S. 1961; Villanova U., J.D. 1964

MILITARY SERVICE
Army, 1965-67

CAREER
Lawyer

POLITICAL HIGHLIGHTS
N.Y. Senate, 1971-72; N.Y. Assembly, 1973-74

ELECTION RESULTS

2000 GENERAL
John J. LaFalce (D, INDC, L)	128,328	61.3%
Brett M. Sommer (R, C, RTL)	81,159	38.7%

2000 PRIMARY
John J. LaFalce (D)	unopposed

1998 GENERAL
John J. LaFalce (D, INDC, L)	97,235	57.0%
Chris Collins (R, C)	69,481	40.7%
David E. Denzel (RTL)	3,813	2.2%

PREVIOUS WINNING PERCENTAGES
1996 (62%); 1994 (55%); 1992 (54%); 1990 (55%);
1988 (73%); 1986 (91%); 1984 (69%); 1982 (91%);
1980 (72%); 1978 (74%); 1976 (67%); 1974 (60%)

As the ranking Democrat on the recently reconfigured Financial Services Committee — formerly the Banking Committee — LaFalce's principal challenge as the 107th Congress began was to develop a relationship with a chairman with whom he had never worked on committee matters. It was a tall order for someone not known to make congressional friends easily.

With Jim Leach of Iowa forced by GOP-imposed term limits to cede the gavel, LaFalce had expected to be working with one of two Republicans with whom he had built relationships, Richard H. Baker of Louisiana or Marge Roukema of New Jersey. But, to settle an intraparty turf battle, the GOP installed as chairman Michael G. Oxley of Ohio, sent over from the Energy and Commerce Committee and bringing that panel's past jurisdiction over insurance and securities legislation with him.

LaFalce has a reputation for seeking to craft bipartisan bills, often in consultation with GOP leaders and administration officials, that address the priorities of the financial services industry while also furthering Democratic goals of stronger consumer protection and improved banking services for the poor. During more than a quarter-century in the House, LaFalce has amassed a record as a reliable liberal — except on abortion, which he opposes. (He warns that Democrats risk losing ethnic and working-class voters by backing abortion rights.)

In promoting his ideas, he projects a firm and detailed grasp of the issues at hand. Many colleagues say the manner in which he wields his intellect is overbearing. LaFalce argues that his detractors misread his apparent certainty, and he contends that they would be "surprised at how seldom I think I'm right."

In the 107th, his legislative agenda centers on improving banking services for the poor. He also wants to review the effectiveness of the 1999 law that erased Depression-era walls among banks, insurers and securities firms. LaFalce sees the law as a success but has pushed to boost its privacy protection language, which allows consumers to block financial services conglomerates from sharing personal financial information with unaffiliated companies — but not from spreading such data among their own array of businesses.

In the 106th Congress, Republican Phil Gramm of Texas, chairman of the Senate Banking, Housing and Urban Affairs Committee, blocked a LaFalce proposal to offer public employees low down payments on mortgages. LaFalce did win language in a housing law enacted late in 2000 to ease the rules on reverse mortgages — those in which senior citizens borrow against their home equity to pay their living expenses — so that the money could be spent on long-term care.

LaFalce believes the banking industry has developed a two-tiered structure — one focusing on conventional loans and the other on sub-prime, or high-risk, loans with high interest rates and fees. He says that some lenders are taking advantage of the poor by offering such loans. To protect the poor, he would bar federally insured lenders from issuing "payday loans," those secured by a paycheck. And he staunchly defends the Community Reinvestment Act (CRA), which requires banks to document service to all segments of a community. LaFalce insists entry by banks into new activities under the 1999 overhaul "must be inextricably linked to a satisfactory performance on CRA."

Although he has rubbed some colleagues the wrong way, LaFalce made one pivotal move in his career to prove to his critics that he could win in the long run by being a gracious combatant. The time was 1996, when he challenged Henry B. Gonzalez's re-election as the ranking Democrat on Banking for the coming 105th Congress. LaFalce, who maintained that the octogenarian Texan had become ineffective, gained the backing of the House Democratic Steering Committee. But after Gonzalez made an emotional plea to the full party caucus, he won 82 votes, LaFalce got 62 and Bruce F. Vento of Minnesota got 47.

LaFalce then withdrew rather than face Gonzalez in a runoff, winning applause from his colleagues — and universal goodwill for his bid to move up once Gonzalez departed. He did not have long to wait for another chance. House Democrats installed him as their acting ranking member in 1998, when Gonzalez became ill; he formally took the post in 1999 after Gonzalez retired.

LaFalce traces his political views to his working-class childhood, when he aspired to be a baseball player, sports announcer, teacher or priest. His father, a laborer at General Mills, was a union steward, and his mother worked at a bakery. LaFalce worked his way through Buffalo's private Canisius High School, becoming his family's first high school graduate. In his first public speech as a student at the high school, he discussed two papal encyclicals that dealt with worker rights.

LaFalce later said that preparing that speech had convinced him of the need to ensure people the right to a job and a just wage. Echoes of that moral imperative can be heard in his approach to dealing with poverty. He cites religious leaders such as Pope John Paul II and the Rev. Billy Graham in backing Third World debt relief and aid to the poor.

From 1987 to 1995, LaFalce was chairman of the Small Business Committee and labored to change the panel's image as a backwater and give it a role in setting tax and regulatory policy.

LaFalce, who was in his fourth year in the state legislature, ran for the House in the post-Watergate year of 1974, seeking to replace retiring GOP Rep. Henry P. Smith. LaFalce captured 60 percent of the vote, becoming the area's first Democratic congressman in 62 years. He won re-election with ease through the 1980s but not so handily in the 1990s. William E. Miller, the namesake son of a longtime congressman in the area and the 1964 GOP vice-presidential nominee, held LaFalce to 54 percent in 1992 and 55 percent two years later.

LaFalce took just 61 percent in 2000 against Republican Brett M. Sommer, a high school history teacher.

KEY VOTES

2000
Yes	Raise hourly minimum wage by $1 over two years
?	Halt funding for U.S. mission in Kosovo unless European nations pay more
Yes	Provide Medicare benefits to military retirees and their dependents
Yes	Grant China permanent normal trade status
No	Phase out estate, gift and trust taxes
No	Prohibit implementation of president's national monument designations
No	Approve GOP plan to provide prescription drug coverage for Medicare beneficiaries
Yes	Increase help for poor nations indebted to international financial institutions

1999
Yes	Impose steel import quotas
Yes	Kill proposal to take aviation trust funds off budget
No	Require background checks on buyers only at gun shows with 10 or more vendors
Yes	Remove barriers among banking, securities and insurance companies
Yes	Authorize state grants to hire teachers and reduce class size
Yes	Overhaul campaign finance law; ban "soft money" and restrict advocacy advertising
Yes	Approve bipartisan plan to increase rights of patients in managed-care health plans

INTEREST GROUPS

	AFL-CIO	ADA	CCUS	ACU
2000	90%	65%	42%	12%
1999	78%	85%	24%	12%
1998	100%	85%	41%	8%
1997	100%	85%	40%	16%

CQ VOTE STUDIES

	PARTY UNITY		PRESIDENTIAL SUPPORT	
	Support	Oppose	Support	Oppose
2000	89%	11%	84%	16%
1999	84%	16%	78%	22%
1998	90%	10%	83%	17%
1997	86%	14%	79%	21%

NEW YORK 29
Northwest — Part of Buffalo; Niagara Falls

Niagara County, home to the world-famous Niagara Falls, is the 29th's centerpiece. The remainder of the district stretches east along Lake Ontario to the edge of Rochester. The district encompasses a full range of demographics, from the Italian-American community of Buffalo to the dairy farms of Orleans County.

The Niagara River powers the district's two main industries, tourism and manufacturing. The waterfall's romance attracts more than 10 million visitors annually. But the river also provides plentiful and inexpensive power for the region's significant manufacturing sector, which produces chemicals, auto parts and cereal, among other products.

Most residents live in the 29th's small portion of Erie County or in neighboring Niagara County (together they comprise 80 percent of the district's voting population). Their blue-collar base gives the

district its overall Democratic voter registration edge. But the 29th also has a piece of the Republican-leaning Rochester suburbs and some solid GOP turf in rural Orleans County, areas that help make the district politically competitive.

The 29th supported Bill Clinton in 1992 and '96 and Al Gore in 2000, and Democratic Rep. LaFalce has maintained his party's grasp on the seat, albeit with some difficulty during the 1990s.

MAJOR INDUSTRY
Chemical production, tourism, auto parts

CITIES
Buffalo (pt.), 113,145 (1990); Niagara Falls, 55,928; North Tonawanda, 32,443; Lockport, 22,277; Tonawanda, 15,653

UNUSUAL FEATURES
In 1980, President Jimmy Carter issued an emergency declaration in response to toxic pollution at Love Canal; An estimated 50,000 honeymooners visit Niagara Falls — negative ions generated by the falling water are thought to be a strong aphrodisiac and the reason for the city's honeymooning popularity.

Rep. Jack Quinn (R)

Elected 1992; 5th term

CAPITOL OFFICE
225-3306; fax 226-0347; 2448 Rayburn Bldg. 20515

INTERNET
e-mail: www.house.gov/writerep
web: www.house.gov/quinn

COMMITTEES
Transportation & Infrastructure
(Railroads - chairman)
Veterans' Affairs

HOMETOWN
Hamburg

BORN
April 13, 1951, Buffalo, N.Y.

RELIGION
Roman Catholic

FAMILY
Wife, Mary Beth McAndrews; two children

EDUCATION
Siena College, B.A. 1973; State U. of New York,
Buffalo, M.Ed. 1983

CAREER
Teacher

POLITICAL HIGHLIGHTS
Town of Hamburg Council, 1982-84; Hamburg town
supervisor, 1985-93

ELECTION RESULTS

2000 GENERAL

Jack Quinn (R, C, INDC)	138,452	67.1%
John Fee (D, L, WFM)	67,819	32.9%

2000 PRIMARY

Jack Quinn (R)	unopposed

1998 GENERAL

Jack Quinn (R, C, INDC)	116,093	67.8%
Crystal D. Peoples (D)	55,199	32.2%

PREVIOUS WINNING PERCENTAGES
1996 (55%); 1994 (67%); 1992 (52%)

Quinn is one of the few Republicans in the House who can lay undisputed claim to the title "champion of organized labor," and he has spent much of his first decade in Congress battling with the GOP leadership — and earning accolades from Democrats — not only on the minimum wage, trade and other labor issues, but also on campaign finance reform, gun control and the budget.

While this has caused many Republicans in Washington discomfort, Quinn's joviality in the clubby confines of the Speaker's Lobby just off the House floor has made him one of the more popular members on either side of the aisle. And his record has led to a string of electoral victories not expected by the first Republican in decades to represent the mostly Democratic, union-heavy precincts of downtown Buffalo. He has won re-election with two-thirds of the vote three times, including in 2000, when George W. Bush lost the district by 24 percentage points.

In the 107th Congress, Quinn continues to display his pro-labor bent by opposing the GOP move to repeal workplace ergonomics regulations issued in the final days of the Clinton administration. And he revived his long-running efforts to drive up the minimum wage, introducing legislation that calls for a $1 increase in the hourly wage over two years. Quinn was instrumental in forcing the Republican leaders of the 104th Congress to enact the most recent increase, to $5.15. At his urging, the House passed another wage hike in the 106th Congress, but it died in a series of disputes with the Senate.

Quinn comes from a union background — his father was a longtime engineer on the trains that served Buffalo's steel mills. "There are five sons in my family, and my mother jokes that all of our birthdays coincide with each time my father was on strike," he once said. Quinn says he became a Republican almost by chance: His uncle, a local GOP elections official, happened to be the one who sent him his voter registration papers while he was in college — with the box for Republican Party affiliation already checked off.

Quinn has been a dependable Republican vote in only two of his eight years in office. In 1993, his first year in the House, and 1995, when he backed the GOP "Contract With America," he voted with a majority of his party against a majority of Democrats about 85 percent of the time. Still, in the 106th, he backed the GOP three-quarters of the time on issues that divided the two parties, including several important matters such as prescription drug coverage for senior citizens, a ban on a procedure its opponents call "partial birth" abortion and an effort to withhold funding for peacekeeping operations in Kosovo.

As the 107th began, Quinn voted for the first three bills that would carry out President Bush's tax cut agenda: measures to cut income tax rates, repeal the estate tax and eliminate the "marriage penalty," a quirk in the tax code that results in some two-earner couples paying higher income taxes. He had supported the estate tax and marriage penalty bills that were cleared in 2000 but vetoed by President Clinton. But in 1999, Quinn was one of only four Republicans to vote against the GOP's $792 billion tax cut package. He argued that the bill was too big and would increase the national debt. "Most people in Buffalo aren't concerned about capital gains," he told The Buffalo News. "They're worried about putting food on the table."

Quinn butted heads — with both Clinton and GOP leaders — on the legislation, enacted in 2000, granting China permanent normal trade status. He said he agreed with union arguments that domestic jobs would be threatened by American companies moving their manufacturing to China, and that human rights abuses by China's government should not be tacitly overlooked. He hosted meetings with other House Republicans and union leaders in hopes of rallying more opposition to the measure in the weeks before the vote.

Since 1998, Quinn has been pushing legislation to increase benefits to railroad workers, their spouses and their widows. The House overwhelmingly passed the bill in 2000, but it died in the Senate. In the 107th, Quinn took the gavel of the Transportation Committee's Railroad Subcommittee, giving him new leverage for seeking enactment of the benefits increase.

Probably none of Quinn's votes have been as important to the GOP leadership as the three ballots he cast at the end of 1998 in favor of Clinton's impeachment. Quinn, who had developed a close friendship with the president — one year they watched the Super Bowl and ate pizza together at the White House — initially opposed impeachment. But he changed his mind a few days before the House vote. "The more I learn about the serious details of perjury and obstruction of justice, the more I am concerned about the president's failure to tell the truth under oath," he said.

That decision was widely regarded as a key factor in the pro-impeachment votes of several other moderate Republicans who had been undecided. Until then, it was not at all certain that the House would impeach the president. After the vote, an unidentified White House aide told the New York Daily News how Clinton had become the second president to be impeached: "Two words: Jack Quinn."

Democrats vowed to avenge Quinn's impeachment votes by working for his defeat in 2000. Their candidate, publisher and political novice John Fee, initially won the endorsement of the Buffalo AFL-CIO. The state union, however, backed Quinn and the local AFL-CIO later followed suit. Democratic anger toward Quinn faded, and he crushed Fee by a 2-to-1 ratio.

Before entering politics, Quinn taught high school English, coached basketball and track, and pursued a doctorate in education administration. In 1992, he was the Hamburg chief executive when he took on Erie County Executive Dennis Gorski for the House seat being vacated by Democrat Henry J. Nowak. Sensing that year's anti-incumbent mood, Quinn focused his campaign on proposals to limit congressional perquisites. He also described his opponent as a typical politician who represented "more of the same." Quinn won with 52 percent of the vote.

KEY VOTES

2000
Yes	Raise hourly minimum wage by $1 over two years
Yes	Halt funding for U.S. mission in Kosovo unless European nations pay more
?	Provide Medicare benefits to military retirees and their dependents
No	Grant China permanent normal trade status
Yes	Phase out estate, gift and trust taxes
No	Prohibit implementation of president's national monument designations
Yes	Approve GOP plan to provide prescription drug coverage for Medicare beneficiaries
No	Increase help for poor nations indebted to international financial institutions

1999
Yes	Impose steel import quotas
No	Kill proposal to take aviation trust funds off budget
Yes	Require background checks on buyers only at gun shows with 10 or more vendors
Yes	Remove barriers among banking, securities and insurance companies
No	Authorize state grants to hire teachers and reduce class size
Yes	Overhaul campaign finance law; ban "soft money" and restrict advocacy advertising
Yes	Approve bipartisan plan to increase rights of patients in managed-care health plans

INTEREST GROUPS

	AFL-CIO	ADA	CCUS	ACU
2000	40%	15%	70%	70%
1999	67%	50%	72%	60%
1998	40%	30%	76%	48%
1997	63%	30%	78%	58%

CQ VOTE STUDIES

	PARTY UNITY		PRESIDENTIAL SUPPORT	
	Support	Oppose	Support	Oppose
2000	76%	24%	43%	57%
1999	74%	26%	38%	62%
1998	76%	24%	32%	68%
1997	83%	17%	38%	62%

NEW YORK 30

West — Buffalo

Tucked on the shore of Lake Erie in western New York, the 30th contains most of the southern and eastern part of Buffalo and the portion of Erie County that lies south of the city.

The region went through a transition in the 1990s, struggling to shed its high unemployment and Rust Belt image of the previous decade. Trade agreements giving Canadian businesses access to Buffalo's skilled labor market and lower taxes have helped to revive Buffalo's manufacturing sector.

Sports teams, particularly the Buffalo Bills football franchise, are the pride of the city and bring together a diverse population. Buffalo has the highest concentration of black residents in the district and also is home to a large Polish-American population. South Buffalo has a large Irish population. Buffalo also is the center for the 30th's blue-collar workers.

The 30th is mostly Democratic but is willing to vote for a moderate Republican with union sympathies – as the district has done in sending Rep. Quinn to Congress for five terms. The lake shore is home to business executives, while the rural outskirts of Erie County are socially conservative. Residents gave Bill Clinton and Al Gore solid support in 1992, '96 and 2000.

MAJOR INDUSTRY
Pharmaceutical production, grain milling, automobile parts

CITIES
Buffalo (pt.), 214,978 (1990); Cheektowaga (unincorporated), 99,314 (1990); West Seneca (unincorporated), 47,830 (1990)

UNUSUAL FEATURES
Buffalo is the flour milling capital of the world, producing 6.6 million pounds per day; All major cities in the northeastern part of North America are within a 500-mile radius of Buffalo.

Rep. Amo Houghton (R)

Elected 1986; 8th term

Fifteen years ago, Houghton intended to step down as chief executive officer of Corning Glass and embark on a new career as a missionary to Zimbabwe. Those plans were altered when a seat in the House opened up, but in many ways, Houghton's work in Congress is similar to what he had in mind in Africa — promoting civility, faith and understanding between the races.

He is a driving force behind the semiannual civility retreats for members of the House and their families. He and Democrat John Lewis of Georgia are co-chairmen of the Faith & Politics Institute, an interfaith, nonpartisan organization that seeks to improve communication between the races and encourages lawmakers to apply spiritual values to political life.

In the past few years, Houghton (HO-tun) has joined Lewis in leading a congressional contingent to Selma, Ala., each March to commemorate the famous civil rights march across the Edmund Pettus Bridge. Early in 2000, Houghton invited the Episcopal bishop of Boston to join his staff for a monthlong unpaid fellowship.

In the day-to-day legislative work of Congress, Houghton displays the same interest in finding common ground. His voting record shows him to be an independent, moderate voice in the House GOP. He sided with President Clinton about half the time — one of the highest presidential support scores posted by any Republican. He was a founder and now serves as a member of the executive committee of the Republican Main Street Partnership, which seeks to promote centrist policymaking.

And he was one of only four House Republicans to vote against all four articles of impeachment against Clinton in 1998.

Houghton, a multimillionaire, is amiable and unassuming. Washingtonian magazine, in its annual survey of Capitol Hill staffers in 2000, reported that Houghton was considered the nicest member of Congress. He has been able to retain several of his top staffers for more than a decade — an eternity on Capitol Hill.

From his seat on the Ways and Means Committee, Houghton explains to his tax expert colleagues what their decisions on topics such as research and development tax credits would mean to businesses. He knows from experience: When he was at Corning, he was a strong supporter of the research that led to the firm's breakthroughs in fiber optics.

In the 106th Congress, Houghton took the gavel as chairman of the Ways and Means panel's Oversight Subcommittee. There, he authored what was designed to be the GOP response to Democratic efforts to require disclosure of political fundraising and spending by certain nonprofit organizations, known as "527s" — a reference to a section of the tax code. The debate was highly political. Although the Houghton measure eventually became law, it was narrowed in scope by GOP leaders and Houghton grumbled that he had wanted a more bipartisan bill.

Houghton sits on the International Relations Committee, where he continues to pursue his longstanding interest in Africa. Even though he never became a missionary, he provides financial assistance and other aid to a rural mission school in Zimbabwe and visits often. In 1999, the extent of the AIDS plague on the African continent hit home when he discovered that his friend, the superintendent of the school, had lost his son to the disease.

On transportation issues, he is a strong supporter of Amtrak, the national passenger railroad, and he has worked to upgrade Route 17, the main east-

CAPITOL OFFICE
225-3161; fax 225-5574
1111 Longworth Bldg. 20515

INTERNET
e-mail: www.house.gov/writerep
web: www.house.gov/houghton

COMMITTEES
International Relations
Ways & Means
  (Oversight - chairman)

HOMETOWN
Corning

BORN
Aug. 7, 1926, Corning, N.Y.

RELIGION
Episcopalian

FAMILY
Wife, Priscilla Houghton; four children, three stepchildren

EDUCATION
Harvard U., A.B. 1950, M.B.A. 1952

MILITARY SERVICE
Marine Corps, 1945-46

CAREER
Glassworks company executive

POLITICAL HIGHLIGHTS
No previous office

ELECTION RESULTS

2000 GENERAL

Amo Houghton (R, C)	154,238	77.3%
Kisun J. Peters (D)	45,193	22.7%

2000 PRIMARY

Amo Houghton (R)	unopposed

1998 GENERAL

Amo Houghton (R, C)	107,615	68.0%
Caleb Rossiter (D)	40,091	25.3%
James R. Pierce Sr. (RTL)	10,546	6.7%

PREVIOUS WINNING PERCENTAGES
1996 (72%); 1994 (85%); 1992 (71%); 1990 (70%); 1988 (96%); 1986 (60%)

west highway in the Southern Tier, designated as Interstate 86.

Despite his business background, Houghton often deviates from the conservative GOP script. "A lot of people out there don't have a home any more in the Republican Party," he has said. A supporter of abortion rights, he takes a dim view of social and religious conservatives who influence GOP leaders on many issues. "I don't think these people are Republicans," he once said. "The people who are posing as firefighters for the Republican Party, in a way, are really the pyromaniacs."

Houghton also has clashed with social and religious conservatives on free-trade issues. He is against efforts to impose economic sanctions on countries in an attempt to change their behavior. For example, he opposed legislation that would punish countries that persecute religious minorities. During debate on the bill, he said he had not heard from a single missionary group overseas that supported the measure.

Houghton is carrying on the traditions of a patrician family that for years has run Steuben County's Corning Inc. He served 19 years as chief executive officer of Corning, founded by the Houghton family in 1851, and on the boards of such firms as Procter & Gamble, IBM and Citibank. Then, at age 60, he entered the public sector, as had his father and grandfather. His father was ambassador to France; his grandfather served in the House for three years and then was ambassador to Germany and Great Britain.

Houghton's political opportunity arose in 1986, just as he was planning to devote his time to educational and religious work in Zimbabwe. New York Gov. Mario M. Cuomo tapped Democratic Rep. Stan Lundine to run for lieutenant governor, leaving what was then the 34th District seat open.

Houghton was popular in his hometown of Corning, where Corning Glass is the major employer. The company is involved in an array of local civic endeavors, and it helped finance the restoration of the city after a devastating flood in 1972. While he had never been particularly active in local Republican affairs, Houghton had little trouble securing the GOP nomination.

Houghton pointed to his experience creating jobs and was easily able to deflect criticism from his Democratic opponent, Cattaraugus County District Attorney Larry Himelein, who tried to portray Houghton as an elitist.

Houghton had planned to leave Congress in 2000, but he decided to seek re-election so that he would be in a position to protect the small-city, rural character of the 31st during redistricting. Houghton launched a save-the-district petition drive and raised considerable amounts of money for GOP candidates for the legislature, which will draw the new lines.

KEY VOTES

2000

Yes Raise hourly minimum wage by $1 over two years
No Halt funding for U.S. mission in Kosovo unless European nations pay more
No Provide Medicare benefits to military retirees and their dependents
Yes Grant China permanent normal trade status
Yes Phase out estate, gift and trust taxes
No Prohibit implementation of president's national monument designations
Yes Approve GOP plan to provide prescription drug coverage for Medicare beneficiaries
No Increase help for poor nations indebted to international financial institutions

1999

No Impose steel import quotas
? Kill proposal to take aviation trust funds off budget
Yes Require background checks on buyers only at gun shows with 10 or more vendors
Yes Remove barriers among banking, securities and insurance companies
No Authorize state grants to hire teachers and reduce class size
Yes Overhaul campaign finance law; ban "soft money" and restrict advocacy advertising
No Approve bipartisan plan to increase rights of patients in managed-care health plans

INTEREST GROUPS

	AFL-CIO	ADA	CCUS	ACU
2000	20%	20%	85%	52%
1999	11%	45%	87%	40%
1998	56%	30%	100%	29%
1997	50%	45%	90%	33%

CQ VOTE STUDIES

	PARTY UNITY		PRESIDENTIAL SUPPORT	
	Support	Oppose	Support	Oppose
2000	76%	24%	55%	45%
1999	70%	30%	49%	51%
1998	66%	34%	49%	51%
1997	72%	28%	60%	40%

NEW YORK 31
Southern Tier – Jamestown; Corning; Elmira

The 31st stretches more than 200 miles across the southwestern portion of the state – the Southern Tier – and encompasses a mix of forests, finger lakes and farms. Small towns and villages dot the countryside.

The district has a large number of blue-collar workers and is home to diverse manufacturing interests, including glassware, furniture and diesel engines. Agriculture accounts for more than 50 percent of the district's economy, mostly through dairy farms and wineries. Steuben County contains Corning, one of America's better-known company towns because of its glass products and costly crystal pieces. The Finger Lakes and surrounding parks draw thousands of visitors to the area each year.

Going back to the 1850s, this area has had a Republican representative for all but 12 years. Although Bill Clinton won the district in 1996, his margin of victory was not as large as elsewhere in the state. And, in

the 2000 presidential contest, the district supported President Bush by an 11 percentage point margin. Democrats rarely make inroads here, and those who do tend to be conservative.

Like much of the upstate region, the district's population declined in the 1990s – leaving its fate after redistricting uncertain. With New York losing two seats after the 2000 census, some believe that the 31st, which covers all or part of 10 counties, will be split up before the 2002 election. The population of Jamestown, the district's largest city, dropped by 8 percent in the 1990s.

MAJOR INDUSTRY
Dairy farming, tourism, furniture manufacturing

CITIES
Jamestown, 32,229; Elmira, 31,270; Olean, 15,943

UNUSUAL FEATURES
Lucy-Desi Museum in Jamestown commemorating longtime resident Lucille Ball; Corning Glass Center is a major tourist attraction.

Gov. Michael F. Easley (D)

First elected: 2000
Length of term: 4 years
Term expires: 1/05
Salary: $118,430
Phone: (919) 733-4240
Hometown: Rocky Mount
Born: March 23, 1950; Nash County, N.C.
Religion: Roman Catholic
Family: Wife, Mary Easley; one child
Education: U. of North Carolina, B.A. 1972; North Carolina Central U., J.D. 1976
Career: Lawyer
Political highlights: Brunswick, Bladen and Columbus County district attorney, 1982-92; sought Democratic nomination for U.S. Senate,1990; N.C. attorney general, 1993-2001

Election results:
2000 GENERAL

Michael F. Easley (D)	1,530,324	52.0%
Richard Vinroot (R)	1,360,960	46.3%
Barbara J. Howe (LIBERT)	42,674	1.5%

Lt. Gov. Beverly Perdue (D)

First elected: 2000
Length of term: 4 years
Term expires: 1/05
Salary: $104,523
Phone: (919) 733-7550

STATE LEGISLATURE

General Assembly: Meets January-June
House: 120 members, 2-year terms
2001 breakdown: 58R, 62D; 93 men, 27 women
Salary: $13,951
Phone: (919) 733-3451
Senate: 50 members, 2-year terms
2001 breakdown: 15R, 35D; 45 men, 5 women
Salary: $13,951
Phone: (919) 733-6854

STATE TERM LIMITS

Governor: 2 consecutive terms
Senate: No
House: No

URBAN STATISTICS

CITY	POPULATION
Charlotte	520,829
Raleigh	261,205
Greensboro	199,562
Durham	179,212
Winston-Salem	168,086

REGISTERED VOTERS

Democrat	50%
Republican	34%
Unaffiliated	16%

POPULATION

2000 population	8,049,313
1990 population	6,628,637
Percent change	+21.4%
Rank among states	11

Median age	35
Born in state	70%
Foreign born	2%
Urban/rural	50%/50%
Crime rate	607/100,000
Poverty level	14.0%
Federal workers	61,370
Military	120,100

REAPPORTIONMENT

North Carolina gained one House seat in reapportionment, increasing from 12 districts to 13. The state legislature will draw new district lines in 2001.

MISCELLANEOUS

Web: www.ncgov.com
Capital: Raleigh
Land area: 48,718 sq. miles
Rank among states: 29
STATE ELECTION OFFICIAL
(919) 733-7173
DEMOCRATIC HEADQUARTERS
(919) 821-2777
REPUBLICAN HEADQUARTERS
(919) 828-6423

District Statistics

DIST.	2000 D	2000 R	GREEN	1996 D	1996 R	REF	1992 D	1992 R	I	WHT	BLK	ASIAN	HISP	HOUSEHOLD INCOME	OVER 65+	UNDER 18	COLLEGE EDUCATION
1	57%	42%	0%	58	38	5				46%	50%	<1%	3%	$18,226	14%	28%	9%
2	44	55	0	45	49	6				66	27	1	7	$27,271	13	24	18
3	37	62	0	39	54	7				75	20	1	4	$24,553	12	25	14
4	51	48	0	51	44	5				72	20	4	5	$34,569	8	22	36
5	37	62	0							81	14	1	5				
6	34	65	0							84	11	1	4				
7	47	53	0	47	46	7				66	23	1	4	$24,708	9	25	16
8	43	56	0	46.0	46.2	8				65	26	1	6	$26,180	12	27	11
9	37	62	0							80	15	2	4				
10	33	67	0							90	6	1	4				
11	39	59	0	42	48	9				91	5	<1	3	$23,564	18	22	15
12	62	38	0							48	45	2	7				
STATE	43	56	0	44	49	7	42.7	43.4	14	72	22	1	5	$26,647	12	24	17

Note: Redistricting during the 1990s changed some districts substantially. The 1996 vote was recalculated. Racial and ethnic data is from the 2000 census.

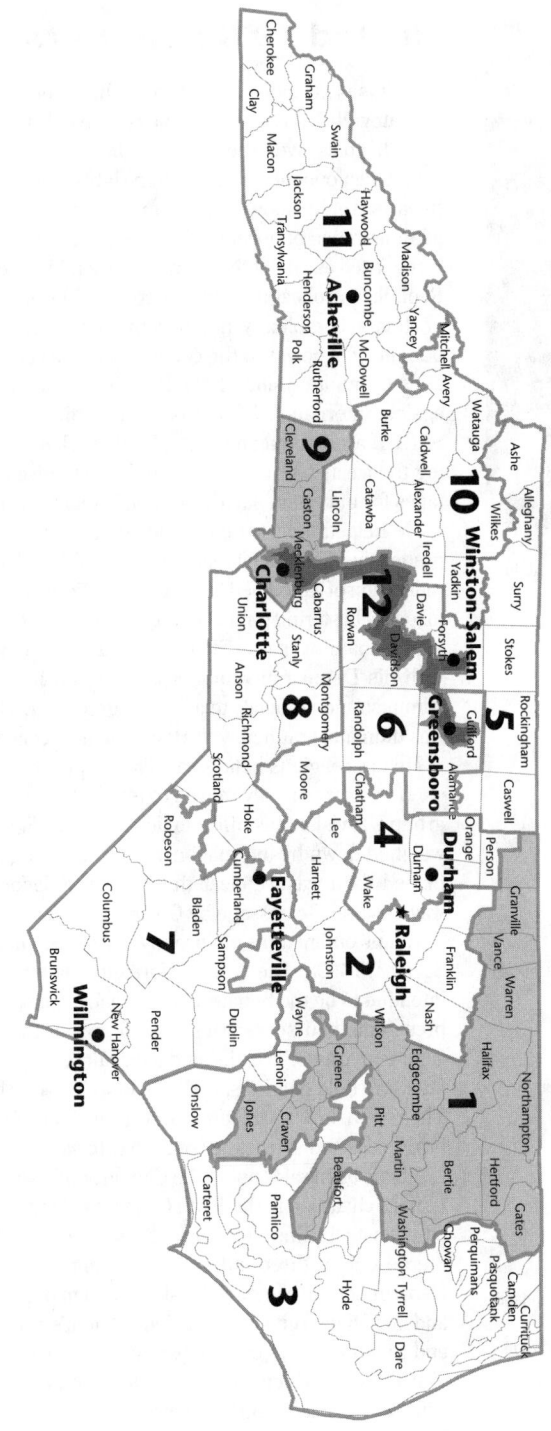

Sen. Jesse Helms (R)

CAPITOL OFFICE
224-6342; fax 228-1339; 403 Dirksen Bldg. 20510

INTERNET
e-mail: jesse_helms@helms.senate.gov
web: helms.senate.gov

COMMITTEES
Agriculture, Nutrition & Forestry
Foreign Relations - chairman
Rules & Administration

HOMETOWN
Raleigh

BORN
Oct. 18, 1921, Monroe, N.C.

RELIGION
Baptist

FAMILY
Wife, Dorothy Helms; three children

EDUCATION
Wingate College, attended 1938-39; Wake Forest
U., attended 1939-40

MILITARY SERVICE
Navy, 1942-45

CAREER
Journalist; broadcasting executive; banking
executive; congressional aide

POLITICAL HIGHLIGHTS
Raleigh City Council, 1957-61

ELECTION RESULTS

1996 GENERAL

Jesse Helms (R)	1,345,833	52.6%
Harvey B. Gantt (D)	1,173,875	45.9%

1996 PRIMARY

Jesse Helms (R)	unopposed

PREVIOUS WINNING PERCENTAGES
1990 (53%); 1984 (52%); 1978 (55%); 1972 (54%)

Elected 1972; 5th term

Helms is far more complex than his critics acknowledge. Described as "Senator No" for his willingness to block treaties and other executive branch goals over the years, Helms also remains one of the Senate's staunchest opponents of abortion rights, gay rights and federal funding of the arts. Yet he showed a pragmatic streak when dealing with the Clinton administration on foreign affairs. And despite his obstructionist tactics, he is regarded as one of the chamber's friendliest senators by Democratic and Republican colleagues and congressional staff.

Helms' complexity has become apparent as he has moved from the periphery of power to the center, serving as chairman of the Foreign Relations Committee since 1995. Before that, he often railed from the outside against international accords such as the Panama Canal Treaty and the SALT II arms reduction pact. He still is skeptical of such agreements, saying the treaties force the United States to give away clear strategic advantages for uncertain payoffs. But he is more open to compromise.

He helped defeat the Clinton administration's effort to ratify the Comprehensive Test Ban Treaty in 1999 and in 2000 doomed any prospect for ratification of a modified 1972 Anti-Ballistic Missile Treaty. But he sometimes follows a blistering public barrage with closed-door negotiations — as in the 1997 debate over the Chemical Weapons Convention, when he worked with his Democratic counterpart, Joseph R. Biden Jr. of Delaware, and administration officials to achieve agreement. The chemical weapons pact was ultimately ratified with Helms' acquiescence.

Helms' religious beliefs can lead him to embrace uncharacteristic causes. He was reportedly moved to tears when rock singer Bono, of the Irish group U2, visited his office to describe the plight of people in poor nations weighed down by international debts. Helms' support for a debt relief bill helped the measure clear the Foreign Relations Committee, paving the way for ultimate passage by Congress.

Helms outlined his philosophy in a speech to the U.S. Capitol Historical Society in 1998: The "Senate Foreign Relations Committee was, I believe, intended to be the Senate's brake on foreign policy. ... It is our job to say to presidents and secretaries of state, when they come demanding quick action on 'urgent' treaties and legislation, 'Slow down, let's think on this a little.' We hold hearings, we listen to witnesses with differing points of view. Then, sometimes, our job is to work with an administration to improve its proposals. And sometimes our job is to say 'no.' "

Helms often said "no" to the Clinton administration, particularly in his first term as chairman in the 104th Congress. For nearly six months, Helms halted almost all committee business to force consideration of his proposal to merge one of three independent foreign affairs agencies into the State Department. He contended that the foreign policy bureaucracy was too large and inefficient. But after President Clinton's re-election in 1996, both Helms and Biden were eager for bipartisan progress.

It became evident that even Democrats could work with Helms after Clinton replaced retiring Secretary of State Warren Christopher with Madeleine K. Albright, who shared Helms' strongly anti-communist views and feisty temperament. Albright won administration backing for Helms' proposal to reorganize the foreign affairs agencies. In return, she got not only Helms' qualified backing for the chemical weapons treaty but support for legislation repaying nearly $1 billion in U.S. debts to the United Nations. By the

www.cq.com

end of Albright's tenure, however, their relationship had soured: Helms concluded that Albright was unable to deliver on many of her promises.

A veteran crusader against the United Nations, Helms philosophically opposes commitments that cede U.S. authority to international organizations. Yet early in 2000, Helms, at the invitation of U.N. Representative Richard C. Holbrooke, addressed the Security Council, a visit Helms clearly enjoyed. He reciprocated by inviting Security Council members to Washington a few months later. Helms reported that he had seen progress in relations with the United Nations due in large part to that visit. "I'm surprised at how many friends that one little thing we did brought," he told the Winston-Salem Journal in 2001.

Helms' strong support for Israel and opposition to Castro's Cuba are partly rooted in home state politics. Helms doubted the wisdom of massive U.S. assistance to Israel until his 1984 re-election race with Democratic Gov. James B. Hunt Jr. During that campaign, Hunt received financial help from Israel's supporters, and ever since, Helms has been one of Israel's strongest backers.

He also has benefited from campaign contributions from Cuban-Americans. One of his early priorities as Foreign Relations chairman was a Cuba sanctions package he sponsored with Rep. Dan Burton, R-Ind. The bill was passed and signed by Clinton after Cuban fighter jets shot down two civilian aircraft, killing four Americans from an anti-Castro group.

Helms' critics portray him as an extremist, but time and again he has proven he knows the issues that energize the middle-class and the overwhelmingly white constituency that has carried him through many campaigns. He opposes abortion and affirmative action and has been unwavering in his support for school-sponsored prayer.

One of the centerpieces of Helms' lengthy social policy agenda is his crusade against homosexuality. He also has strong disdain for the National Endowment for the Arts. He repeatedly has offered proposals to kill the agency or at least bar funding for sexually explicit projects.

He also has left himself open to accusations of intolerance in other areas. In July 2000, Clinton told the NAACP annual convention that Helms' opposition to appointing a black judge to the all-white U.S. 4th Circuit Court of Appeals was "outrageous." James A. Wynn was the second black judge whose nomination to the court was effectively killed by Helms.

Similar charges of racism were leveled at Helms in his unsuccessful effort to block the nomination of the nation's first black female senator, Carol Moseley Braun of Illinois, to be U.S. ambassador to New Zealand. Helms ostensibly opposed the nomination because of Moseley Braun's alleged ethical violations while in the Senate, but the two had a history of personal tension. Helms also drew charges of sexism and the wrath of women lawmakers for not allowing his panel to consider a treaty banning discrimination against women.

For much of his adult life, Helms was a Democrat, even while he delivered conservative editorials for 12 years on WRAL-TV in Raleigh. He left the Democratic Party in 1970 and won his Senate seat as a Republican just two years later.

During his more than a quarter-century as one of the Senate's most fiery conservatives, Helms has received national attention in each of his re-election campaigns. His winning percentage has never been more than 55 percent in his five contests. What typically has played a crucial role in races is his fundraising; he has an extensive network of contributors, created by his pioneering use of direct mail.

Early in 2001, Helms sent out a fundraising letter, sparking speculation that, contrary to conventional wisdom, he may seek re-election in 2002, at the age of 81.

KEY VOTES

2000
Yes Overhaul bankruptcy law and increase minimum wage
Yes Limit fiscal 2001 discretionary spending to $600.3 billion
Yes Override veto on nuclear waste disposal at Yucca Mountain site in Nevada
No Oppose effort to terminate Kosovo mission
No Include gender, sexual orientation and disability in federal hate crime protections
Yes Approve GOP plan to restrict use of genetic information by health insurers
Yes Kill amendment delaying implementation of an anti-missile defense system
Yes Cut taxes for married couples
No Grant China permanent normal trade status

1999
Yes Remove President Clinton from office for obstruction of justice
Yes Kill amendment authorizing state grants to hire teachers and reduce class size
No Require criminal background checks for purchases at gun shows
Yes Approve GOP proposal to increase rights of patients in managed-care health plans
Yes Block effort to allow farm and medicine exports to Cuba
No Allow study of tougher automobile fuel efficiency standards
No Ratify nuclear weapons testing treaty
No Prohibit national political parties from collecting "soft money" donations
Yes Remove barriers among banking, securities and insurance companies

INTEREST GROUPS

	AFL-CIO	ADA	CCUS	ACU
2000	13%	5%	76%	100%
1999	22%	0%	82%	100%
1998	0%	0%	88%	100%
1997	14%	0%	70%	100%
1996	0%	5%	85%	100%
1995	0%	0%	100%	100%
1994	14%	0%	80%	100%
1993	18%	10%	80%	100%
1992	13%	5%	100%	100%
1991	20%	5%	88%	100%

CQ VOTE STUDIES

	PARTY UNITY		PRESIDENTIAL SUPPORT	
	Support	Oppose	Support	Oppose
2000	98%	2%	31%	69%
1999	94%	6%	18%	82%
1998	97%	3%	32%	68%
1997	99%	1%	47%	53%
1996	97%	3%	25%	75%
1995	97%	3%	20%	80%
1994	95%	5%	19%	81%
1993	97%	3%	12%	88%
1992	96%	4%	80%	20%
1991	94%	6%	88%	12%

Sen. John Edwards (D)

CAPITOL OFFICE
224-3154; fax 228-1374; 225 Dirksen Bldg. 20510

INTERNET
e-mail: senator@edwards.senate.gov
web: edwards.senate.gov

COMMITTEES
Commerce, Science & Transportation
Health, Education, Labor & Pensions
Small Business
Select Intelligence

HOMETOWN
Raleigh

BORN
June 10, 1953, Seneca, S.C.

RELIGION
Methodist

FAMILY
Wife, Elizabeth Anania Edwards; four children
(one deceased)

EDUCATION
North Carolina State U., B.S. 1974; U. of North
Carolina, J.D. 1977

CAREER
Lawyer

POLITICAL HIGHLIGHTS
No previous office

ELECTION RESULTS

1998 GENERAL

John Edwards (D)	1,029,237	51.2%
Lauch Faircloth (R)	945,943	47.0%
Barbara J. Howe (LIBERT)	36,963	1.8%

1998 PRIMARY

John Edwards (D)	277,468	51.4%
David Grier "D.G." Martin (D)	149,049	27.6%
Ella Scarborough (D)	55,486	10.3%
Robert Junior Ayers (D)	22,477	4.2%
Mike Robinson (D)	20,178	3.7%
James Everette Carmack (D)	8,200	1.5%
Gene Gay (D)	7,173	1.3%

Elected 1998; 1st term

With a seemingly perpetual smile on his face, Edwards has emerged from the Senate's 1998 freshman class as one of the chamber's rising stars. Although things have calmed down since his whirlwind first year, Edwards has impressed his colleagues with a felicitous combination of style and substance.

He is now trying to use his mounting supply of political capital to nudge the Senate closer to the middle. It is not that Edwards has a unique agenda. Along with just about every other lawmaker, he stresses the need to protect Social Security and Medicare, to improve public education and health care. But his willingness to work with Republicans while remaining a loyal Democrat on most issues, and a deft touch during debates that highlights his background as one of the nation's top trial lawyers, have won him friends and influenced colleagues.

Senate Minority Leader Tom Daschle and Edwards are on good terms, and many believe Edwards is being groomed for a move into a leadership position. He was also considered as a potential vice-presidential running mate for Democrat Al Gore in 2000. Now Edwards' name is among those mentioned as a possible candidate for the presidency in 2004.

Edwards says he sees the political middle as more representative of the public than conservative or liberal ideologies and talks frequently of the need to find a consensus on legislation. He affiliates with two moderate groups, the Senate New Democrats and the bipartisan Centrist Coalition, and he works closely with other like-minded senators, including Republican Olympia J. Snowe of Maine and Democrat Evan Bayh of Indiana, who is also a friend. (The two jog together regularly.)

Edwards switched his committee assignments in the 107th Congress, picking up slots on the Health, Education, Labor and Pensions Committee, the Commerce, Science and Transportation Committee, and the Intelligence panel while giving up seats on Banking and Governmental Affairs.

In 1999, Edwards' first order of business after he was sworn in was the impeachment trial of President Clinton. For a freshman senator with no political experience, the trial was a defining event — a chance to show off his skills as an orator and litigator.

Daschle chose Edwards for the three-person Democratic team that deposed key players in the impeachment saga, including former White House intern Monica Lewinsky. Edwards conducted about half of the Democratic deposition of Lewinsky, as well as the entire deposition of White House aide Sidney Blumenthal. The experience, coming on a weekend in which the nation was captivated by the trial, gave Edwards national exposure. But many senators say it was actually his speech behind closed doors that impressed them. In the speech, Edwards laid out the case for not removing the president from office.

"I think we saw firsthand why he made so much money talking to jurors," said Republican Gordon H. Smith of Oregon. "And why I had to make my money selling frozen peas." (Smith owns one of the largest frozen vegetable packaging companies in the country.)

Edwards' role in the impeachment trial was just the first exercise of his powers of persuasion. The North Carolinian was credited with upstaging Republican opponents in the 106th Congress when the chamber debated patient's rights legislation, one of his top priorities. Early in the 107th, he and Arizona Republican John McCain announced a bipartisan patients' rights proposal, which GOP leaders, including President Bush, quickly denounced. Edwards has continued to shine in floor debates on other topics as well.

But in his first term, Edwards also ran into roadblocks that proved frustrating. In 1999, he sought funding for emergency relief for constituents in the wake of Hurricane Floyd but was getting nowhere as the chamber rushed to close out the session. Edwards finally threatened to block action on the temporary appropriations measures needed to keep the government operating unless Senate leaders responded to his pleas. In the end, he did not get all the help he wanted, but he did get some.

Edwards says he did not like resorting to obstructionism during his first year in the Senate but felt he had no choice. Each weekend, as he traveled home to be with his family, which has since moved to Washington, he spent time with constituents who had lost their homes in the flooding.

Perhaps the most unlikely relationship Edwards has in the Senate is with his home state colleague, Republican Foreign Relations Committee Chairman Jesse Helms. The youthful Edwards, always sunny, always willing to compromise, seems to have little in common with the steadfastly conservative Senate veteran.

Even though Helms campaigned against Edwards during the 1998 Senate contest, it is an earlier event that has defined their relationship. In 1996, Edwards' 16-year-old son Wade traveled to Washington after being named a national finalist in an essay contest with the theme, "What it means to be an American." After a visit at the White House with first lady Hillary Rodham Clinton, Wade went on to Capitol Hill, where he met Helms, who invited him to talk for more than an hour.

Three weeks later, Wade died after he lost control of the car he was driving. Helms, who had never met John Edwards, called the family to offer his condolences and later paid tribute to the young man in a Senate floor speech. He described Wade as "one of the most impressive young men I have ever met" and went out of his way to make clear that Wade was not driving recklessly. He inserted Wade's essay, about the experience of going to the polls with his father, into the Congressional Record.

"I didn't know him at all, and he was just so extraordinarily kind that I sort of had a connection with him before I came here," Edwards says. "He and I, while we disagree on a lot of things, get along very well on a personal level."

Edwards grew up in Robbins, N.C., a small Piedmont town, where his father was a textile worker and his mother ran a small furniture refinishing shop. He was the first in his family to attend college, working his way through North Carolina State University and earning his law degree from the University of North Carolina. He graduated with honors from both schools.

Although Edwards was a political novice, he defeated one-term Republican Sen. Lauch Faircloth in 1998 — thus continuing a pattern going back five Senate elections. Not since Democratic Sen. Sam J. Ervin Jr. held the seat from 1954 through 1974 has anyone occupying it been able to last more than one term.

Edwards relied largely on his fortune amassed as a lawyer to fund his campaign while refusing contributions from political action committees. (He did, however, accept donations from the national Democratic Party, which receives money from PACs.)

Faircloth tried to attack Edwards' trial lawyer background, but the Democrat proudly pointed out that he had spent his adult life "being an advocate for people, mostly children and mostly families." Faircloth also declined to debate Edwards in person, drawing criticism.

Edwards painted himself as a political outsider and ran a well-scripted campaign. He defeated Faircloth by 4 percentage points, becoming one of only three challengers to unseat an incumbent that year.

KEY VOTES

2000

Yes Overhaul bankruptcy law and increase minimum wage

No Limit fiscal 2001 discretionary spending to $600.3 billion

Yes Override veto on nuclear waste disposal at Yucca Mountain site in Nevada

Yes Oppose effort to terminate Kosovo mission

Yes Include gender, sexual orientation and disability in federal hate crime protections

No Approve GOP plan to restrict use of genetic information by health insurers

No Kill amendment delaying implementation of an anti-missile defense system

No Cut taxes for married couples

Yes Grant China permanent normal trade status

1999

No Remove President Clinton from office for obstruction of justice

No Kill amendment authorizing state grants to hire teachers and reduce class size

Yes Require criminal background checks for purchases at gun shows

No Approve GOP proposal to increase rights of patients in managed-care health plans

No Block effort to allow farm and medicine exports to Cuba

Yes Allow study of tougher automobile fuel efficiency standards

Yes Ratify nuclear weapons testing treaty

Yes Prohibit national political parties from collecting "soft money" donations

Yes Remove barriers among banking, securities and insurance companies

INTEREST GROUPS

	AFL-CIO	ADA	CCUS	ACU
2000	75%	85%	40%	12%
1999	100%	90%	41%	8%

CQ VOTE STUDIES

	PARTY UNITY		PRESIDENTIAL SUPPORT	
	Support	Oppose	Support	Oppose
2000	94%	6%	92%	8%
1999	92%	8%	87%	13%

Rep. Eva Clayton (D)

CAPITOL OFFICE
225-3101; fax 225-3354; 2440 Rayburn Bldg. 20515

INTERNET
e-mail: nc01ima.pub@mail.house.gov
web: www.house.gov/clayton

COMMITTEES
Agriculture
Budget

HOMETOWN
Littleton

BORN
Sept. 16, 1934, Savannah, Ga.

RELIGION
Presbyterian

FAMILY
Husband, Theaoseus Clayton; four children

EDUCATION
Johnson C. Smith U., B.S. 1955; North Carolina
Central U., M.S. 1962; U. of North Carolina,
attended 1967

CAREER
Consulting firm owner; nonprofit executive; state
official; university official

POLITICAL HIGHLIGHTS
Sought Democratic nomination for U.S. House,
1968; N.C. assistant secretary of natural
resources, 1977-81; Warren County Commission,
1982-92 (chairman, 1982-90)

ELECTION RESULTS

2000 GENERAL

Eva Clayton (D)	124,171	65.6%
Duane E. Kratzer Jr. (R)	62,198	32.9%
Christopher Delaney (LIBERT)	2,799	1.5%

2000 PRIMARY

Eva Clayton (D)	unopposed

1998 GENERAL

Eva Clayton (D)	85,125	62.2%
Ted Tyler (R)	50,578	37.0%

PREVIOUS WINNING PERCENTAGES
1996 (66%); 1994 (61%); 1992 (67%); 1992 Special
Election (57%)

Elected 1992; 5th full term

In the aftermath of Hurricane Floyd, which devastated much of North Carolina in 1999, Clayton not only pressed for relief from the federal government, she provided her own relief from Washington. Clayton and New York Democratic Rep. Charles B. Rangel gathered together more than 500 volunteers, who fanned out across eastern North Carolina to help with the cleanup effort.

"We had everyone, from the White House to the elevator operators at the Capitol, helping us out with this," she told the Raleigh News and Observer. "It was a good idea that just grew."

Clayton herself donned work clothes and set to work removing a waterlogged carpet from a church in her mostly rural 1st District. The volunteer effort, which drew several of Clayton's fellow members of the Congressional Black Caucus and other North Carolina lawmakers, also included successful fundraising events that supplemented the federal disaster assistance she helped win.

A leader of the Rural Caucus, revitalized in 2000, and the top Democrat on the Agriculture Committee's Department Operations, Oversight, Nutrition and Forestry Subcommittee, Clayton says that poor and rural areas of the country have been largely bypassed by the nation's overall economic boom — and she wants to make sure that they are not forgotten.

Her voting record is generally in line with other members of the liberal wing of the Democratic Party. But because her focus is on rural needs, her priorities differ at times from those of most of her Black Caucus colleagues, who represent urban areas. She also splits with urban Democrats, with whom she generally agrees politically, when it comes to issues affecting her rural constituency.

When a major farm bill was debated on the House floor in 1996, Clayton was chagrined to find that crop subsidies helpful to her district were facing fire not only from free-market GOP conservatives but also from some urban liberals in her own party. In one debate, Clayton lectured Democrat Nita M. Lowey of New York, who had criticized the peanut program. "You may not know who those farmers are, but I do know, and many of them are minority farms, many of them are low-income farms."

Clayton was the first black woman elected to the House from North Carolina and one of two African-Americans elected from the state since 1901. (The second was Democrat Melvin Watt, who was also elected in 1992.)

She immediately attracted the attention of influential House Democrats and won a number of key party postings. With the backing of female peers and the Black Caucus, Clayton was elected president of her freshman class. In 1995, Democratic Leader Richard A. Gephardt tapped her for his new advisory Policy Committee. And in 1997, she was rewarded for her party work with a seat on the Budget Committee.

But the Agriculture panel remains her focus. She helped push legislation in 1998 to allow black farmers who had suffered discrimination at the hands of the Agriculture Department to seek legal redress. The measure lifted a statute of limitations on discrimination complaints, provided funding for compensation, and established expedited procedures for resolving cases.

Clayton disagrees with the majority in her party who criticize tobacco subsidies. She argues that penalizing growers would be unfair because they do not have the resources of tobacco companies and would have a hard time switching to other crops. "This is not about smoking," Clayton maintained in 1996. "This is about discriminating against the poorest of the poor of that industry. ... They really are attacking the small farmer." Clayton expects demand for tobacco products to decrease over the next few years. She therefore wants to see Congress explore ways of helping tobacco growers. "Farmers want financial security," she said, "and we have to find ways ... to help them transition to another crop or retirement."

Clayton is skeptical of most international trade agreements, arguing that they harm her district's economy, which includes the textile industry. Unlike many farm-state lawmakers, she does not view expanded exports as the cure for agriculture's woes. That anti-trade stance, along with her liberal stands on federal programs and social issues, makes her a favorite of organized labor.

Assertive, friendly and loquacious, Clayton nevertheless is largely disinterested in making television appearances, preferring instead to make her points in person, where the full force of her persuasiveness can be felt.

Clayton majored in biology in college, intending to become a doctor and do missionary work in Africa. But her life took her in another direction. She met the man who became her husband, attended law school and started a family. After her husband, Theaoseus, made three unsuccessful runs for the state House, Clayton was recruited in 1968 by politically active blacks to challenge a white incumbent, Rep. Lawrence H. Fountain, for the 2nd District seat. She failed to win the Democratic nomination but managed 31 percent against Fountain. A decade later, in 1982, she won her first elective office, a post on the Warren County Commission.

In 1992, with 10 years on the county commission under her belt, Clayton again ran for Congress, this time in the 1st District. Clayton, who was less well-known in the regional news media than were several of the other candidates, looked to grass-roots supporters, who were familiar with her work in the community as far back as the 1968 House race. With the help of organized labor, women's groups, ministers and minority activists, she made the runoff against then-Democratic state Rep. Walter B. Jones Jr., whose father had held the 1st District seat until his death in September 1992. She won by 10 percentage points over Jones and that victory paved the way to five wins over Republican Ted Tyler. (Jones, now a Republican, represents the 3rd District.)

She beat Tyler twice in 1992 — in a special election to fill out the remainder of the senior Jones' unexpired House term and then in the general election for a full term — and again in 1994, 1996 and 1998.

In 2000, the GOP fielded another candidate, Duane E. Kratzer Jr., but he fared no better; Clayton won with 66 percent.

KEY VOTES

2000
Yes   Raise hourly minimum wage by $1 over two years
Yes   Halt funding for U.S. mission in Kosovo unless European nations pay more
Yes   Provide Medicare benefits to military retirees and their dependents
No   Grant China permanent normal trade status
Yes   Phase out estate, gift and trust taxes
No   Prohibit implementation of president's national monument designations
No   Approve GOP plan to provide prescription drug coverage for Medicare beneficiaries
Yes   Increase help for poor nations indebted to international financial institutions

1999
Yes   Impose steel import quotas
Yes   Kill proposal to take aviation trust funds off budget
No   Require background checks on buyers only at gun shows with 10 or more vendors
Yes   Remove barriers among banking, securities and insurance companies
Yes   Authorize state grants to hire teachers and reduce class size
Yes   Overhaul campaign finance law; ban "soft money" and restrict advocacy advertising
Yes   Approve bipartisan plan to increase rights of patients in managed-care health plans

INTEREST GROUPS

	AFL-CIO	ADA	CCUS	ACU
2000	90%	70%	61%	16%
1999	89%	100%	21%	0%
1998	100%	100%	39%	0%
1997	100%	100%	40%	4%

CQ VOTE STUDIES

	PARTY UNITY		PRESIDENTIAL SUPPORT	
	Support	Oppose	Support	Oppose
2000	93%	7%	79%	21%
1999	94%	6%	83%	17%
1998	95%	5%	83%	17%
1997	94%	6%	75%	25%

NORTH CAROLINA 1

Northeast – Parts of Goldsboro, Greenville and Rocky Mount

Situated among the tobacco fields and Baptist churches of eastern North Carolina, the new 1st retains much of the flavor of its predecessor. Redrawn for the 1998 election and not affected by changes put in place for the 2000 election, the district's shape is more compact, but it remains a poor, rural, Democratic stronghold.

The main body of the district still rests along the Virginia border, with a stretch winding south to take in parts of several of the region's commercial centers – Goldsboro, Greenville and Kinston. But the 1st lost part of its southwestern leg, and with it Fayetteville and a substantial black population in the Wilmington area. The percentage of blacks has dropped slightly, but is still the highest of any district in the state at about 50 percent.

The 1st is one of the poorest districts in the nation. The area's economy is based overwhelmingly on manufacturing and agriculture. Cotton and peanut fields prevail in the northern counties, while tobacco, hogs and poultry dominate farther south. Manufacturing, primarily of textiles and lumber products, is scattered throughout.

Many white voters claim the Democratic roots of their forefathers but often support GOP candidates at the state and national level. A fair number are "Jessecrats," conservative Democratic supporters of Republican Sen. Jesse Helms. Republicans also find support in the increasingly affluent coastal turf of Beaufort and Craven counties.

MAJOR INDUSTRY
Agriculture, manufacturing, health care

CITIES
Wilson (pt.), 26,127 (1990); Goldsboro (pt.), 25,734 (1990); Greenville (pt.), 19,249 (1990); Rocky Mount (pt.), 17,057 (1990); Henderson, 16,661

UNUSUAL FEATURES
Caleb Bradham started selling "Brad's Drink" in 1898 at his New Bern drug store – the beverage is now known as Pepsi Cola; Crystal Lee Sutton, who inspired Sally Fields' role as a union organizer in "Norma Rae," (1979) worked at a J.P. Stevens textile factory in Roanoke Rapids.

Rep. Bob Etheridge (D)

Elected 1996; 3rd term

CAPITOL OFFICE
225-4531; fax 225-5662
1533 Longworth Bldg. 20515

INTERNET
e-mail: bob.etheridge@mail.house.gov
web: www.house.gov/etheridge

COMMITTEES
Agriculture
Science

HOMETOWN
Lillington

BORN
Aug. 7, 1941, Sampson County, N.C.

RELIGION
Presbyterian

FAMILY
Wife, Faye Cameron Etheridge; three children

EDUCATION
Campbell U., B.S. 1965

MILITARY SERVICE
Army, 1965-67

CAREER
Hardware store owner; tobacco farmer

POLITICAL HIGHLIGHTS
Harnett County Commission, 1973-77 (chairman, 1975-77); N.C. House, 1979-87; N.C. superintendent of Public Instruction, 1989-96

ELECTION RESULTS

2000 GENERAL

Bob Etheridge (D)	146,733	58.3%
Doug Haynes (R)	103,011	40.9%

2000 PRIMARY

Bob Etheridge (D)	unopposed

1998 GENERAL

Bob Etheridge (D)	100,550	57.4%
Dan Page (R)	72,997	41.7%

PREVIOUS WINNING PERCENTAGES
1996 (53%)

A former state superintendent of public schools and a part-time tobacco farmer, Etheridge has expertise in, and a high profile on, two modern-day policy dilemmas. On education, he sees eye-to-eye with those in his party who advocate an active role for the federal government in improving local schools. But on tobacco, Etheridge fights tooth and nail against many Democrats who seek to clamp down on the tobacco industry, warning that anti-tobacco initiatives may ruin "hard-working, God-fearing" family farmers.

Etheridge's floor votes rank him among the more moderate Southern House Democrats, but he must bear in mind that the 2nd District has conservative leanings; the district voted for Bob Dole in 1996 and George Bush in 2000.

When Etheridge attacks Republicans, it is generally over issues that resonate in his district, such as GOP attempts to restrict spending for disaster relief or schools. He is a member of the New Democrat Coalition, which hews to the political center.

House Democratic leaders, seeking to put Etheridge's experience to good use, gave him a seat on the Agriculture Committee and named him co-chairman of a party task force on education. He also sits on the Science panel.

Ever since arriving in Washington, Etheridge has vigorously defended tobacco farmers. In 1999, he denounced plans by the Clinton administration to sue the tobacco industry to recoup the costs of treating sick smokers. Noting that North Carolina tobacco farmers were already facing problems because of flooding from Hurricane Floyd, he said, "I guess we're going to go ahead and submerge them, finish drowning them," The Associated Press quoted him as saying.

Etheridge has fought against efforts to end the federal support program for tobacco, arguing that growers could not switch profitably to another crop and that land values in tobacco communities would plummet. People will continue to smoke, he says, but without the existing support system, small farmers will give way to large corporate farms owned and operated by cigarette manufacturers.

Etheridge employs that same theme — big corporations profiting while family farmers struggle — in opposing perennial efforts to curtail spending on the federal price-support program for peanuts, another key crop in North Carolina. Critics of the federal peanut program say it inflates the price of peanuts at the expense of consumers. "Hogwash," Etheridge said. "Candy manufacturers [who are big peanut buyers] have said they will not pass on any of the savings to consumers. Savings will be passed on to a few of the multibillion-dollar companies, and the price of candy bars will not go down."

Etheridge's focus on farming has led him to press for a trade agreement to allow tobacco farmers to export their produce to China. In 2000, Etheridge voted for legislation granting China permanent normal trade status, contending that it would provide the North Carolina economy with expanded markets. "Gaining access to China, the largest market in the world, will only help our state and our nation expand our economic leadership and extend our ideals of liberty, democracy and freedom to those who have been shut off from such basic rights and values for far too long," he said.

Before coming to Congress, Etheridge was the top man in North Carolina's public school system for almost eight years, and his wife and one of his three children are educators. Etheridge has spoken frequently and at length on the House floor of his desire to "build on what is working well in our public schools, rather than scapegoating public school principals, teachers, parents and children."

Etheridge favors proposals to develop voluntary national tests for elementary school students, but he opposes private school tuition voucher plans that "will only divert attention away from improving public schools." He believes the federal government should devote more dollars to the repair and construction of new schools. "I have seen multimillion-dollar prisons next door to crummy, crumbling, decaying public schools," Etheridge once said, "and then we have the gall to tell our children that education is important. They can see the difference in where we put our money."

Early in 2001, he was encouraged by President Bush's focus on education but lamented that Bush's voucher proposal was "dead on arrival as far as I am concerned."

On the Science Committee, Etheridge has a platform from which to watch out for the National Hurricane Center. With North Carolina repeatedly battered by hurricanes in recent years, he has focused on boosting disaster relief funding and improving hurricane forecasting, especially for inland areas where flooding can be a serious problem.

Born, raised and educated in east-central North Carolina, Etheridge was a hardware store owner and tobacco farmer when he first entered politics in 1972. He won election to the Harnett County Commission, serving for four years, the last two as chairman. In 1978, he won the first of four terms in the North Carolina General Assembly, where he rose to chair the Appropriations Committee. Then he moved to statewide office, holding the school superintendency for eight years.

That background made Etheridge the choice of 2nd District Democrats to contest the 1996 re-election of freshman Republican David Funderburk, who had been a zealous supporter of the House GOP's conservative agenda in the 104th Congress. Following the national Democratic script, Etheridge called Funderburk a threat to entitlement programs such as Social Security, Medicare and Medicaid. Etheridge's deep local roots helped him win with 53 percent of the vote.

In 1998, conservative state Sen. Dan Page and the national GOP went after Etheridge aggressively. Page was the first GOP candidate to air attack ads tying the Democratic candidate to President Clinton and his White House sex scandal. But Etheridge had given Republicans little opportunity to tag him as a liberal, and he won by 16 percentage points. He increased his victory margin in 2000.

KEY VOTES

2000

Yes	Raise hourly minimum wage by $1 over two years
No	Halt funding for U.S. mission in Kosovo unless European nations pay more
Yes	Provide Medicare benefits to military retirees and their dependents
Yes	Grant China permanent normal trade status
Yes	Phase out estate, gift and trust taxes
No	Prohibit implementation of president's national monument designations
No	Approve GOP plan to provide prescription drug coverage for Medicare beneficiaries
Yes	Increase help for poor nations indebted to international financial institutions

1999

Yes	Impose steel import quotas
Yes	Kill proposal to take aviation trust funds off budget
No	Require background checks on buyers only at gun shows with 10 or more vendors
Yes	Remove barriers among banking, securities and insurance companies
Yes	Authorize state grants to hire teachers and reduce class size
Yes	Overhaul campaign finance law; ban "soft money" and restrict advocacy advertising
Yes	Approve bipartisan plan to increase rights of patients in managed-care health plans

INTEREST GROUPS

	AFL-CIO	ADA	CCUS	ACU
2000	70%	60%	66%	28%
1999	89%	85%	48%	24%
1998	89%	80%	65%	28%
1997	88%	65%	70%	32%

CQ VOTE STUDIES

	PARTY UNITY		PRESIDENTIAL SUPPORT	
	Support	Oppose	Support	Oppose
2000	84%	16%	65%	35%
1999	79%	21%	67%	33%
1998	81%	19%	73%	27%
1997	80%	20%	66%	34%

NORTH CAROLINA 2

Central — Parts of Raleigh and Rocky Mount

Anchored in the thriving state capital of Raleigh, the 2nd fans eastward to take in several surrounding rural counties. While the area's economic hub, the high-tech Research Triangle Park, lies in the neighboring 4th, its influence radiates through the low hills of this eastern Piedmont district.

A mix of Research Triangle techies, university academics and government employees live in Raleigh and form the basis of the district's Democratic tilt. More than a third of voters are located here and in surrounding Wake County. The rest of the county holds booming and increasingly urban bedroom communities such as Knightdale and Garner. Sprawl has begun to infiltrate the surrounding counties as well, but they still rely primarily on tobacco farming (especially in Johnston, Nash and Harnett counties) and blue-collar manufacturing jobs.

Redrawn for the 1998 election but unchanged in the 2000 election, the district lost its share of Durham County but gained most of downtown

Raleigh and its eastern suburbs. The trade made the 2nd more suburban and a bit less Democratic but did slightly increase its percentage of blacks. The new 2nd also acquired part of hog-producing, politically swinging Sampson County. While Democratic registration remains high, many of the southern counties, notably Johnston, have begun to vote more Republican, especially at the state and national level.

MAJOR INDUSTRY
State government, higher education, agriculture

CITIES
Raleigh (pt.), 107,978 (1990); Rocky Mount (pt.), 31,940 (1990); Sanford, 21,825; Smithfield, 11,419; Wake Forest, 11,227

UNUSUAL FEATURES
Highway sign outside Sanford claims it is the brick capital of the United States; Sanford also home to Kendale Plaza, the world's longest strip mall connected by an unbroken roof; In Johnston County, Benson hosts a Mule Days harvest festival in September; Harnett County town of Erwin grew up around a denim plant and calls itself "Denim Capital of the World."

Rep. Walter B. Jones (R)

Elected 1994; 4th term

CAPITOL OFFICE
225-3415; fax 225-3286; 422 Cannon Bldg. 20515

INTERNET
e-mail: congjones@mail.house.gov
web: www.house.gov/jones

COMMITTEES
Armed Services
Financial Services
Resources

HOMETOWN
Farmville

BORN
Feb. 10, 1943, Farmville, N.C.

RELIGION
Roman Catholic

FAMILY
Wife, Joe Anne Jones; one child

EDUCATION
North Carolina State U., attended 1962-65; Atlantic
Christian College, B.A. 1967

MILITARY SERVICE
N.C. National Guard, 1967-71

CAREER
Lighting company executive; insurance benefits
company executive

POLITICAL HIGHLIGHTS
N.C. House, 1983-93; sought Democratic
nomination for U.S. House, 1992

ELECTION RESULTS

2000 GENERAL

Walter B. Jones (R)	121,940	61.4%
Leigh Harvey McNairy (D)	74,058	37.3%
David F. Russell (LIBERT)	2,457	1.2%

2000 PRIMARY

Walter B. Jones (R)	unopposed

1998 GENERAL

Walter B. Jones (R)	83,529	61.9%
Jon Williams (D)	50,041	37.1%

PREVIOUS WINNING PERCENTAGES
1996 (63%); 1994 (53%)

Jones, who grew up in a political household, followed in his father's footsteps, first into the family business and eventually into politics. However, the younger Jones, now in his fourth term representing the 3rd District, is blazing his own political career, far off the path of his father, who represented the neighboring 1st District for a quarter-century.

The most obvious departure is the fact that while his father was a Democrat, Jones is a Republican, switching parties in 1993 and winning election to the House in 1994 on his second try. A member of the House GOP's Conservative Action Team, a faction known as the CATs, he is more conservative than his father, annually garnering ratings of 100 percent or nearly so from the American Conservative Union. (Walter B. Jones Sr.'s scores were closer to 20 percent.)

And unlike the senior Jones, whose service with an earlier generation of lawmakers and whose post as a committee chairman served to promote pragmatic, result-oriented dealings, the younger Jones is one of the few unreconstructed "true believers" of the GOP Class of 1994. That class was marked by its members' uncompromising insistence that the party stand firm for the core conservative principles they espoused in their campaigns. Jones, in a gentlemanly, understated style, still holds to this course, even after many of his colleagues have decided that a dose of pragmatism and compromise is necessary.

After graduating from college in 1967, Jones became an executive with the family's office supply company, later moving on to other business ventures. It was not until he was almost 40 that Jones first sought elective office.

Walter B. Jones Sr. had begun his political career as mayor of the small town of Farmville, moving on to the state legislature before serving 25 years in the House. The younger Jones likewise started out small, winning a seat in the state House, where he served for a decade. And when he did try to follow his father in the national political arena — running for the 1st District seat in 1992 when his father decided to step down — he was rebuffed, losing a runoff in the Democratic primary to Eva Clayton in a district that had been redrawn as a black-majority district after the 1990 census. (Jones Sr. died in September of 1992, just a few weeks before Congress adjourned.)

Jones, who has dropped the Jr. from his name, comes down on the conservative side of most issues, including allowing prayer in public schools, providing school vouchers to help parents pay for private school tuition and increasing military spending. He frequently takes to the House floor to demand tax cuts and advocates a phaseout of the tax code.

Jones was a vocal supporter of the House GOP's "Contract With America" legislative agenda, and he votes a dependable Republican line, siding with his party more than 90 percent of the time.

On the Armed Services Committee, Jones looks out for the district's military installations and has authored a number of bills aimed at improving pay, benefits and housing for military personnel, including one in the 106th Congress to give a $500 tax credit to military families who are eligible for food stamps. He undertook a crusade in the 106th to block a Pentagon requirement that armed forces personnel be given an anthrax vaccination. Citing reports casting doubt on the safety of the vaccine, Jones proposed legislation to make the vaccination voluntary.

For all his conservative credentials, Jones, who represents a long swath of the Carolina coast, touts his concern for environmental protection when it comes to coastal matters. His district includes the tourist-rich barrier islands of the Outer Banks. During the 1998 campaign, he ran television ads in which he was featured walking on the beach saying, "It's everybody's responsibility to make sure that our rivers and waterways are clean now and for future generations." Jones succeeded during the 105th Congress with a bill designed to preserve the wild horses of Shackleford Banks, a part of the Cape Lookout National Seashore. The National Park Service had been studying the effect of the horses on area fauna, but Jones was not convinced that the park service was aggressive enough in protecting the animal. Jones' bill requires the agency to work with a local foundation to ensure that the equine population does not dip below 100.

Jones is a member of the Resources Committee and, in a show of bipartisanship, has joined with Democratic members who represent coastal districts to fight to retain the ban on offshore oil and gas drilling. He also was involved in the decade-long battle to preserve the 1870 lighthouse at Cape Hatteras. He pushed to build a stronger seawall to protect the landmark against beach erosion, but it was eventually decided that the lighthouse should be moved.

Jones is a fiscal conservative, often even more so than his party's leaders. He voted against the massive transportation authorization bill in 1998 and the even more massive end-of-year catchall spending bill, measures that were criticized by fiscal conservatives for breaking spending caps agreed to in 1997.

He has not been reticent, however, in speaking up for federal programs that are important to his district, such as the federal price-support program for peanut growers. He has also been vocal about protecting another important crop in his district — tobacco. Jones said that Clinton and the Food and Drug Administration (FDA) were conducting a "witch hunt" against the tobacco farmer. "This is big brother at its worst. What's next —prohibition of alcohol, caffeine, chocolate?" he railed on the House floor. "The government has no business in those decisions, and the FDA and commissioner have no authority to classify nicotine as a drug."

After switching to the GOP and setting his sights on the 3rd District, instead of his father's old 1st District seat, Jones in 1994 got the GOP nomination without a fight. In a close race, he bested four-term Democratic Rep. H. Martin Lancaster, 53 percent to 47 percent, linking the Democrat to the locally unpopular Clinton administration. He has won re-election easily since then and has harbored thoughts of running for the Senate in 2002 if Republican Jesse Helms decides to step down.

KEY VOTES

2000

No Raise hourly minimum wage by $1 over two years
Yes Halt funding for U.S. mission in Kosovo unless European nations pay more
Yes Provide Medicare benefits to military retirees and their dependents
No Grant China permanent normal trade status
Yes Phase out estate, gift and trust taxes
Yes Prohibit implementation of president's national monument designations
Yes Approve GOP plan to provide prescription drug coverage for Medicare beneficiaries
No Increase help for poor nations indebted to international financial institutions

1999

Yes Impose steel import quotas
Yes Kill proposal to take aviation trust funds off budget
No Require background checks on buyers only at gun shows with 10 or more vendors
Yes Remove barriers among banking, securities and insurance companies
No Authorize state grants to hire teachers and reduce class size
No Overhaul campaign finance law; ban "soft money" and restrict advocacy advertising
Yes Approve bipartisan plan to increase rights of patients in managed-care health plans

INTEREST GROUPS

	AFL-CIO	ADA	CCUS	ACU
2000	10%	5%	61%	96%
1999	50%	15%	72%	100%
1998	10%	5%	72%	100%
1997	0%	5%	80%	100%

CQ VOTE STUDIES

	PARTY UNITY		PRESIDENTIAL SUPPORT	
	Support	Oppose	Support	Oppose
2000	92%	8%	19%	81%
1999	91%	9%	19%	81%
1998	92%	8%	21%	79%
1997	96%	4%	24%	76%

NORTH CAROLINA 3

East — Parts of Greenville and Goldsboro; Outer Banks

The 3rd runs along the eastern shore from Virginia to north of Wilmington, sweeping from the fragile barrier islands of the Outer Banks to the tobacco and peanut fields of the coastal plain. It is a large swath of rural land inlaid with waterways, affluent vacation towns and military facilities; the closest thing to skyscrapers here are the historic lighthouses that dot the shoreline.

Redrawn for the 1998 election and unchanged in 2000, the district retained much of its character, gaining a handful of rural counties and Camp Lejeune Marine Corps Base, while sacrificing some livestock land in the southwest and a black-majority section of Goldsboro.

Historically a poor region, the district makes a living by fishing, farming, catering to tourists and working for the armed forces. At its southern end, two fingers of the district stretch west to take in parts of Pitt, Lenoir and Wayne counties, which are among the state's leading

counties in turkey, hog and wheat production.

The new 3rd is similar to the old in its racial and political makeup. Its black population fell only 1 percentage point, to 20 percent, and it still leans Republican. The 3rd had long been a Democratic stronghold, but dissatisfaction with Democrats at the state and national levels has translated into Republican gains since the early 1990s.

MAJOR INDUSTRY
Military, agriculture, tourism

MILITARY BASES
Camp Lejeune Marine Corps Base, 38,257 military, 4,294 civilian; Cherry Point Marine Corps Air Station and Naval Aviation Depot, 6,632 military, 5,619 civilian (1999); New River Marine Corps Air Station, 5,866 military, 135 civilian (1997); Elizabeth City Coast Guard Group Cape Hatteras, 450 military, 450 civilian (2000)

CITIES
Jacksonville, 68,554; Greenville (pt.), 25,723 (1990); Havelock, 20,539

UNUSUAL FEATURES
Wilbur and Orville Wright made their first flight on the Outer Banks.

Rep. David E. Price (D)

Elected 1986; 7th term
Did not serve 1995-97

CAPITOL OFFICE
225-1784; fax 225-2014; 2162 Rayburn Bldg. 20515

INTERNET
e-mail: david.price@mail.house.gov
web: www.house.gov/price

COMMITTEES
Appropriations
Budget

HOMETOWN
Chapel Hill

BORN
Aug. 17, 1940, Erwin, Tenn.

RELIGION
Baptist

FAMILY
Wife, Lisa Price; two children

EDUCATION
Mars Hill College, attended 1957-59; U. of North Carolina, B.A. 1961; Yale U., B.D. 1964, Ph.D. 1969

CAREER
Professor

POLITICAL HIGHLIGHTS
N.C. Democratic Party chairman, 1983-84; U.S. House, 1987-95; defeated for re-election to U.S. House, 1994

ELECTION RESULTS

2000 GENERAL

David E. Price (D)	200,885	61.7%
Jess Ward (R)	119,412	36.6%
C. Brian Towey (LIBERT)	5,573	1.7%

2000 PRIMARY

David E. Price (D)	56,886	89.2%
John W. Winters Jr. (D)	6,919	10.8%

1998 GENERAL

David E. Price (D)	129,157	57.4%
Tom Roberg (R)	93,469	41.6%
Gary Goodson (LIBERT)	2,284	1.0%

PREVIOUS WINNING PERCENTAGES
1996 (54%); 1992 (65%); 1990 (58%); 1988 (58%); 1986 (56%)

Price represents one of the South's more politically progressive districts and, on a wide range of issues, this professor-turned-politician votes with liberal Democrats in the House. The 4th District is home to the Raleigh-Durham-Chapel Hill Research Triangle Park, where many academics and Northern transplants have come to work.

Price was temporarily ousted from his seat in 1994 by a conservative Republican and, even though he promptly avenged that defeat two years later, he stays alert for further rumblings on his right. He tends to his district carefully through his work on the Appropriations Committee, and he takes a moderate position on such politically charged local issues as regulation of tobacco.

Born in East Tennessee to parents who both worked in education, Price got his undergraduate degree at the University of North Carolina and then went to Yale for graduate work, earning political science and divinity degrees. While teaching political science at Duke University in the 1970s, he became heavily involved in state Democratic politics. He served as chairman of the state party in 1983 and 1984.

The contacts Price made in his party work helped him raise money and attract supporters for a successful House race in 1986. After beating out three opponents for the Democratic nomination, Price ousted freshman GOP Rep. Bill Cobey by 12 percentage points. He won re-election three times by comfortable margins, but then he lost to former Raleigh Police Chief Fred Heineman by 1,215 votes in 1994, the year the GOP swept to majorities in both chambers of Congress.

Price quickly began plotting a comeback, even as some Democrats wondered whether the four-term congressman had set himself up for defeat by becoming too comfortable in office and forgetting about constituents' daily concerns. In his return engagement against Heineman, Price waged an aggressive grass-roots campaign, emphasizing door-to-door canvassing and plenty of personal contact with voters. On Election Day, Price prevailed comfortably, 54 percent to 44 percent. In the next two elections, Price has prevailed by ever increasing margins.

In ideological terms, Price could hardly be more different than the steadfastly conservative Heineman. Price has voted consistently with proponents of abortion rights and environmental protections, and he typically sides with organized labor. In the 106th Congress, he opposed GOP tax-cutting plans and voted with other Democrats for legislation that would have allowed patients to sue their health care plans.

But Price is also careful to stress the importance of bipartisanship. He has crossed party lines to join a fellow political science professor, Republican Steve Horn of California, in introducing a measure to bar federal candidates from broadcasting any campaign attack ad in which they did not appear.

One way Price keeps his constituents happy is by using his seat on Appropriations — where he also served in his first House stint — to funnel federal dollars into his district. In the 106th Congress, he battled for disaster relief funds in the wake of Hurricane Floyd, and he also landed $49 million for an Environmental Protection Agency facility in Research Triangle Park. The EPA funding "will keep North Carolina and the Research Triangle the pre-eminent environmental research area in the country," Price said.

An ardent free trader, Price voted for legislation in 2000 granting China permanent normal trade status. Although some worried about China's human rights violations, Price contended that the measure would bolster American jobs through increased exports. "This is simply an economic win for us, and we're really conceding nothing," he said. "Our markets are already largely open, so all the opening is on their side."

Price has tried to find a middle ground on tobacco, a touchy issue in a state where the leaf has long been hallowed. He backs tough restrictions on teenagers' access to tobacco products, but he calls for a "stabilization mechanism" so that local tobacco growers don't go belly-up.

In 1997, he voted against a Democratic amendment to eliminate the federal crop insurance subsidy for tobacco farmers. Price began his floor remarks by saying, "I am not a reflexive defender of the tobacco industry." Then he gave an academic analysis of his state's longtime cash cow and continued, "Denying crop insurance or disaster relief to these individuals will not change their geography or climate or the economic facts of life. It will not miraculously enable them to turn to some other crop or line of work. It will simply ruin many of them economically, especially those on the margin of profitability — those on the small farms."

Improving education is a personal interest for Price because of his past teaching experience. It is also good politics in the 4th District, with its concentration of universities, research facilities and high-technology firms. In 1997, Price scored a major legislative win when Congress passed education affordability legislation that he had been advocating for several years. The law made interest on student loans tax deductible and permitted penalty-free withdrawals from IRAs for education expenses.

Price has opposed GOP efforts to provide taxpayer-financed tuition vouchers that parents could use to send their children to private school. Vouchers, he says, would not raise standards at public schools. "The Republican voucher plan promises what it cannot deliver, and it would divert us from the challenge of making public education all that it can and must be," he said on the House floor.

Price is an advocate of generous funding for the National Science Foundation (NSF). During debate on an NSF authorization measure, he pointed out that in fiscal 1998, "more than 350 NSF-sponsored grants were awarded to residents of the Research Triangle counties of North Carolina." The awards have translated to about $44 million in projects for the three universities in and around the 4th District.

Democratic leaders called on Price's political science background early in the 107th Congress when he won appointment to an ad hoc committee to recommend improvements in election procedures.

KEY VOTES

2000
Yes Raise hourly minimum wage by $1 over two years
No   Halt funding for U.S. mission in Kosovo unless European nations pay more
Yes Provide Medicare benefits to military retirees and their dependents
Yes Grant China permanent normal trade status
No   Phase out estate, gift and trust taxes
No   Prohibit implementation of president's national monument designations
No   Approve GOP plan to provide prescription drug coverage for Medicare beneficiaries
Yes Increase help for poor nations indebted to international financial institutions

1999
Yes Impose steel import quotas
Yes Kill proposal to take aviation trust funds off budget
No   Require background checks on buyers only at gun shows with 10 or more vendors
Yes Remove barriers among banking, securities and insurance companies
Yes Authorize state grants to hire teachers and reduce class size
Yes Overhaul campaign finance law; ban "soft money" and restrict advocacy advertising
Yes Approve bipartisan plan to increase rights of patients in managed-care health plans

INTEREST GROUPS

	AFL-CIO	ADA	CCUS	ACU
2000	80%	85%	61%	4%
1999	89%	95%	40%	4%
1998	80%	95%	61%	8%
1997	100%	95%	50%	8%

CQ VOTE STUDIES

	PARTY UNITY		PRESIDENTIAL SUPPORT	
	Support	Oppose	Support	Oppose
2000	90%	10%	80%	20%
1999	87%	13%	74%	26%
1998	87%	13%	77%	23%
1997	86%	14%	76%	24%

NORTH CAROLINA 4
Central — Durham; Chapel Hill; part of Raleigh

With more than three-fourths of the district's population living in Durham and Wake counties, to understand Research Triangle Park is to understand the 4th. The medical and technological research park was created in the 1950s by a group of academics, politicians and businessmen who saw the need to diversify the state's economy beyond the traditional tobacco and textile industries. To tap the brainpower of the three surrounding universities – Duke University (Durham), the University of North Carolina (Chapel Hill) and North Carolina State University (Raleigh) – the park was located in the center of the triangle the schools create.

As the park grew, especially in the 1980s, the Durham of James B. Duke's Lucky Strike cigarettes largely disappeared. And as developers began converting tobacco warehouses into apartment buildings, concerns over quality-of-life issues arose. While the district leans strongly to the left, these highly educated voters can be independent-minded, especially on education and transportation issues.

Redistricting for the election that began the 106th Congress changed little of the 4th's political bent. Although it cut out the eastern, more Democratic, half of Raleigh's Wake County, it replaced it with all of Democratic Durham.

Based halfway between the ocean and the Blue Ridge mountains, the district spreads north and west from the Triangle, passing through rolling hills of evergreen forests to take in the rural, small-town speckled counties of Person, Chatham and Orange. Many upwardly mobile, politically swinging bedroom communities, such as Cary, also circle the Triangle.

MAJOR INDUSTRY
Technology research, higher education

CITIES
Durham, 179,212; Raleigh (pt.), 99,973 (1990); Cary, 91,213; Chapel Hill, 43,336; Apex 17,884

UNUSUAL FEATURES
Home to the Durham Bulls baseball team; The 1988 movie, "Bull Durham," starring Kevin Costner, was filmed here.

Rep. Richard M. Burr (R)

Elected 1994; 4th term

CAPITOL OFFICE
225-2071; fax 225-2995
1526 Longworth Bldg. 20515

INTERNET
e-mail: richard.burrnc05@mail.house.gov
web: www.house.gov/burr

COMMITTEES
Energy & Commerce
International Relations
Select Intelligence

HOMETOWN
Winston-Salem

BORN
Nov. 30, 1955, Charlottesville, Va.

RELIGION
Methodist

FAMILY
Wife, Brooke Burr; two children

EDUCATION
Wake Forest U., B.A. 1978

CAREER
Marketing manager

POLITICAL HIGHLIGHTS
Republican nominee for U.S. House, 1992

ELECTION RESULTS

2000 GENERAL

Richard M. Burr (R)	172,489	92.8%
Steven F. LeBoeuf (LIBERT)	13,366	7.2%

2000 PRIMARY

Richard M. Burr (R)	unopposed

1998 GENERAL

Richard M. Burr (R)	119,103	67.6%
Mike Robinson (D)	55,806	31.7%

PREVIOUS WINNING PERCENTAGES
1996 (62%); 1994 (57%)

The health care and technology sectors have supplanted tobacco as the dominant economic force in the 5th District, and Burr's legislative agenda reflects that.

Personable, telegenic, and with his sights set on higher office, Burr in the 106th Congress concentrated his efforts on prescription drug prices, rural health care, food safety warnings and biomedical research, as well as on trying to stem the defection of teachers and nurses from their professions into higher-paying high-tech jobs.

Burr's principal focus was his work on a GOP task force that developed a proposal to deal with the rising cost of prescription drugs for Medicare beneficiaries, declaring that matter to be "the single most important thing Congress can do" in the 106th.

He notes that the rising cost of drugs has forced some senior citizens who do not have prescription drug coverage as part of a supplemental insurance plan to make difficult economic choices about how to spend their limited dollars. And, he says, that's just the tip of the iceberg: High drug prices also threaten to force insurance companies to reduce or eliminate drug coverage for people who do have insurance. That could eventually lead to higher medical costs, as people who cannot or will not pay for the drugs themselves wind up hospitalized with serious medical problems the drugs would have prevented.

Burr is well-situated to deal with his health care priorities from his seat on the Energy and Commerce Committee's Health Subcommittee, a position he got as a freshman in the 104th Congress. From that post he is able to look out for his district's medical technology, medical education and pharmaceutical industries.

The lawmaker, who is from Winston-Salem, home to the R.J. Reynolds Tobacco Co., must continue to defend the interests of not only cigarette manufacturers but of the many farmers in the district who depend on tobacco for their livelihood. After the 105th Congress spent much of its time debating major tobacco-related legislation and failed to reach a consensus, tobacco fell off the front burner in the 106th, and that's the way Burr wanted it. (Burr quit smoking in 1998 after making a televised vow to do so.)

He also watches out for the textile industry and took issue in the 106th Congress with a bill to open markets to African goods. "Seldom on the House floor have I ever seen such a blatant attempt to eliminate U.S. jobs," he said.

Burr attracted favorable attention early in his congressional career when he was given a key role in the development of legislation to streamline the Food and Drug Administration's policies for approving drugs and medical devices, such as pacemakers. He began that work in the 104th Congress and was rewarded in the 105th when President Clinton signed into law FDA overhaul legislation that included his language to establish a fast-track approval process for drugs that treat life-threatening illnesses.

Although Burr is every bit as conservative as the typical member of the GOP Class of 1994, his patience and pragmatism in molding the FDA bill into something that could win congressional and presidential backing showed that he is more interested in the business of legislating than some of his classmates, who insist on adhering to their core conservative principles rather than compromising.

That interest in legislating, he says, was a major factor in his decision early in 1999 to pass on a run for governor in 2000, which a number of Tar Heel State Republicans had been urging. The governor's job is too administrative for his tastes, Burr said. He told the Greensboro News and Record the decision boiled down to goose bumps. According to the newspaper, Burr told a GOP audience about flying into Washington, D.C., with North Carolina Republican Howard Coble. Coble pointed to the lights of the Capitol Building and told him, "If you ever see that and you don't get goose bumps, it's time to leave." Burr told his supporters that he still gets goose bumps.

But Burr is ambitious and has been preparing himself for a run for the Senate — either in 2002 if Republican Jesse Helms decides to retire, or in 2004 against Democrat John Edwards. That preparation well in advance of a campaign is something new for Burr, who as a salesman for a wholesale distributor of consumer goods came home one day and announced to his wife that he was going to run for Congress. That was in 1991, and Burr recalls, "I'd never been active politically, and I certainly didn't even know how much a congressman made."

He lost that race, against Democrat Stephen L. Neal in 1992, but garnered 46 percent of the vote. After a stint as co-chairman of North Carolina Taxpayers United — and angered by the 1993 congressional vote to raise taxes — he was back in 1994. Neal decided to retire, and Burr won with 57 percent, his closest election.

His goal back then was to balance the federal budget. (Nevertheless, in 1997, when he got a chance to vote on the massive balanced-budget spending-cut bill, he was among the minority of Republicans to vote against it; he said the package cut too much from federal health care spending.)

Burr was born in Virginia and moved to Winston-Salem when he was 6. His father was a Presbyterian minister, and in retrospect, Burr believes his understanding of the importance personal contact and constituent service hold for a member of Congress dates back to his childhood.

He played football (strong safety) at Wake Forest and then took a sales job with a wholesale distributor — pushing Amana by day and teaching housewives how to cook with their new-fangled microwave ovens at night. Burr's outgoing personality and the skills he learned in the sales job are put to good use in his current occupation. He says he loves to campaign for re-election. One technique he favors is a periodic "take this job and try it" program, in which he asks constituents to invite him to work alongside them in their jobs. He's flipped hamburgers, delivered parcels and observed open-heart surgery.

KEY VOTES

2000

No	Raise hourly minimum wage by $1 over two years
Yes	Halt funding for U.S. mission in Kosovo unless European nations pay more
Yes	Provide Medicare benefits to military retirees and their dependents
No	Grant China permanent normal trade status
Yes	Phase out estate, gift and trust taxes
Yes	Prohibit implementation of president's national monument designations
Yes	Approve GOP plan to provide prescription drug coverage for Medicare beneficiaries
No	Increase help for poor nations indebted to international financial institutions

1999

No	Impose steel import quotas
Yes	Kill proposal to take aviation trust funds off budget
No	Require background checks on buyers only at gun shows with 10 or more vendors
Yes	Remove barriers among banking, securities and insurance companies
No	Authorize state grants to hire teachers and reduce class size
No	Overhaul campaign finance law; ban "soft money" and restrict advocacy advertising
No	Approve bipartisan plan to increase rights of patients in managed-care health plans

INTEREST GROUPS

	AFL-CIO	ADA	CCUS	ACU
2000	10%	5%	80%	88%
1999	33%	5%	84%	87%
1998	10%	5%	82%	92%
1997	13%	10%	90%	92%

CQ VOTE STUDIES

	PARTY UNITY		PRESIDENTIAL SUPPORT	
	Support	Oppose	Support	Oppose
2000	92%	8%	22%	78%
1999	93%	7%	17%	83%
1998	92%	8%	24%	76%
1997	94%	6%	28%	72%

NORTH CAROLINA 5
North Central – Part of Winston-Salem

In this northern Piedmont district, Mayberry meets R.J. Reynolds. The district's northern counties, which abut the Virginia border, are filled with small rural towns such as Mount Airy, the childhood home of Andy Griffith and the inspiration for the fictional setting of his 1960s television series. Many of the district's residents live to the south in Winston-Salem and surrounding Forsyth County, home to R.J. Reynolds Tobacco Co., which sits in the 12th District.

The economy of Forsyth County has changed over the past few years, veering away from the textile manufacturing and tobacco production that were once its bread and butter. While the leaf still employs several thousand, it is now second to the health care industry, due in part to the medical center at Wake Forest University. Banking also is on the rise. Textile and blue-collar manufacturing still prevail throughout the other counties, and grazing cattle wander over Surry County's low, rolling hills.

While Winston-Salem has a 37 percent black population, many of these residents live in the city's downtown area, which belongs to the neighboring 12th. This leaves the 5th as hearty Republican territory.

Court-ordered redistricting that took effect in the 2000 election did little to alter the district's political character. On its northern border, the 5th now takes in Ashe and Alleghany counties, which vote Republican in statewide and federal elections, but the district lost the northern portion of Republican-leaning Guilford County. Most counties lean Republican at all levels, except Caswell and Alleghany, which often favor Democratic candidates.

MAJOR INDUSTRY
Health care, tobacco, textiles, agriculture

CITIES
Winston-Salem (pt.), 89,215 (1990); Burlington (pt.), 36,339 (1990); Eden, 15,204; Reidsville, 14,118

UNUSUAL FEATURES
Surry County's Pilot Mountain known for the knob-shaped rock formation at its top.

Rep. Howard Coble (R)

Elected 1984; 9th term

As chairman of the Judiciary Committee's Courts, the Internet and Intellectual Property Subcommittee, Coble is a leading voice on issues central to the development of cutting-edge technology, such as providing copyright protection for digital information and computer software. But the cigar-smoking former prosecutor is anything but a high-tech whiz. Instead, he has the manner of an old-fashioned lawyer and describes himself as an "AM guy in an FM world." He refuses to use a computer and writes his speeches in longhand.

Coble's panel is at the center of debate over proposals to protect intellectual property distributed via the Internet, including popular music and databases. He has had some major successes in recent years, including his work in helping develop a landmark law in the 105th Congress to augment copyright protection for digital works such as computer software and compact discs. The measure was the first significant rewrite of the nation's copyright laws in two decades. And in 1999, he helped pass bills to allow delivery of local television channels via satellite and to move toward international standardization of patent applications.

In the 106th Congress, a stalemate blocked passage of Coble's proposal to establish tough criminal or civil penalties for the unauthorized distribution of information from private databases over the Internet. Commerce Committee Chairman Thomas J. Bliley Jr., who has since retired, argued for a looser approach that stressed enforcement by the Federal Trade Commission. Coble has vowed to continue pushing for a crackdown on database piracy in the 107th Congress. "This issue will not go away," he said. "Pirates still sail without fear."

Coble, who is a fan of bluegrass music, received praise in 2000 from musicians such as Bruce Springsteen and Bonnie Raitt for reversing himself on a key issue. He won passage of a law that nullified language he had authored in 1999 classifying sound recordings as "works for hire." The singers said that the 1999 language prevented them from taking ownership of popular songs from recording companies after copyrights expire. "Never in my wildest dreams did I think this would have become such a big deal," Coble said, explaining his change of heart.

Coble advocates legislation that would give franchise owners more leverage in disputes with corporate parents, including a ban on termination of franchise agreements without good cause. "I don't know of a single member of Congress who would stand by while their hard-working small-business owners are left buck-naked and defenseless against bad-faith tactics which have been used by a host of corporations," he said.

An amiable back-slapper, the North Carolina lawmaker can be blunt and uncompromising on issues that hit close to home, including his defense of the tobacco industry, a powerful presence in his state. When the Food and Drug Administration suggested regulating nicotine as a drug in 1995, he said, "It is lawfully grown, lawfully sold and lawfully consumed. It's a lawful product ... therefore, as a smoker, I assume the risks of consuming that lawful product."

As the son of a department store manager and a textile worker, Coble is also a strong defender of the textile and furniture industries, which play an important role in his district. He opposes abortion and takes a skeptical view of gun control and environmental regulation.

An enduring quest for Coble during his House career has been to end

CAPITOL OFFICE
225-3065; fax 225-8611; 2468 Rayburn Bldg. 20515

INTERNET
e-mail: howard.coble@mail.house.gov
web: www.house.gov/coble

COMMITTEES
Judiciary
(Courts, the Internet & Intellectual Property -
chairman)
Transportation & Infrastructure

HOMETOWN
Greensboro

BORN
March 18, 1931, Greensboro, N.C.

RELIGION
Presbyterian

FAMILY
Single

EDUCATION
Appalachian State U., attended 1949-50; Guilford
College, A.B. 1958; U. of North Carolina, J.D. 1962

MILITARY SERVICE
Coast Guard, 1952-56; Coast Guard Reserve,
1960-82; Coast Guard, 1977-78

CAREER
Lawyer; insurance claims supervisor

POLITICAL HIGHLIGHTS
N.C. House, 1969; assistant U.S. attorney, 1969-73;
N.C. Department of Revenue secretary, 1973-77;
Republican nominee for N.C. treasurer, 1976; N.C.
House, 1979-83

ELECTION RESULTS

2000 GENERAL

Howard Coble (R)	195,727	91.0%
Jeffrey D. Bentley (LIBERT)	18,726	8.7%

2000 PRIMARY

Howard Coble (R)	unopposed

1998 GENERAL

Howard Coble (R)	112,740	88.6%
Jeffrey D. Bentley (LIBERT)	14,454	11.4%

PREVIOUS WINNING PERCENTAGES
1996 (73%); 1994 (100%); 1992 (71%); 1990 (67%);
1988 (62%); 1986 (50%); 1984 (51%)

congressional and executive branch pensions. His effort dates back to legislation he introduced in 1985 to reduce retirement pay for House members, a move that some colleagues regarded as demagoguery. In a 1993 letter to White House Budget Director Leon E. Panetta, Coble suggested eliminating the federal contribution to the congressional pension plan as a further spending cut for the Clinton economic team to consider. He is one of the few members of Congress who does not participate in the pension program, calling it "a taxpayer ripoff."

His blunt talk won him media coverage in 1998, as the Judiciary Committee voted to recommend the impeachment of President Clinton. Coble criticized the president for committing perjury and took umbrage when former Democratic Rep. Robert F. Drinan of Massachusetts suggested that conservatives were looking for "vengeance" against a president who had bested them at the polls. "If anybody thinks vengeance is involved, I'll meet them in the parking lot," Coble retorted.

Coble began 1984 thinking about a run for governor. He had gained some notice among Republicans statewide, not only while in the state legislature but also as an assistant U.S. attorney and as secretary of the Department of Revenue under GOP Gov. James E. Holshouser Jr. in the mid-1970s.

But he bypassed a statewide bid to challenge freshman Democrat Robin Britt in the 6th District. Despite his previous experience, it took all of Coble's efforts to win the GOP nomination. Former state Sen. Walter C. Cockerham, a millionaire construction company owner, had been stumping in the district and courting Republican votes for several months before Coble entered the race. But armed with the support of most local GOP leaders, Coble pulled through the primary by a scant 164 votes.

Coble then stressed his fiscal conservatism against Britt, whom he sought to paint as an extravagant liberal. He criticized Britt for having gone against President Reagan on two of every three votes cast in 1983. Tapping into the flow of conservative Democrats who crossed party lines for Reagan, Coble won by 2,662 votes.

Britt immediately plotted a comeback. The 1986 results were even closer than those of 1984; only 79 votes separated the winner and the loser on Election Day. Britt appealed the election results, but his challenge proved unsuccessful.

Coble has had little to worry about since, cruising to huge victory margins every two years. In 1994, 1998 and 2000, Democrats did not field a challenger.

KEY VOTES

2000

No	Raise hourly minimum wage by $1 over two years
Yes	Halt funding for U.S. mission in Kosovo unless European nations pay more
Yes	Provide Medicare benefits to military retirees and their dependents
No	Grant China permanent normal trade status
Yes	Phase out estate, gift and trust taxes
Yes	Prohibit implementation of president's national monument designations
Yes	Approve GOP plan to provide prescription drug coverage for Medicare beneficiaries
No	Increase help for poor nations indebted to international financial institutions

1999

Yes	Impose steel import quotas
No	Kill proposal to take aviation trust funds off budget
Yes	Require background checks on buyers only at gun shows with 10 or more vendors
Yes	Remove barriers among banking, securities and insurance companies
No	Authorize state grants to hire teachers and reduce class size
No	Overhaul campaign finance law; ban "soft money" and restrict advocacy advertising
Yes	Approve bipartisan plan to increase rights of patients in managed-care health plans

INTEREST GROUPS

	AFL-CIO	ADA	CCUS	ACU
2000	10%	15%	76%	86%
1999	38%	15%	78%	100%
1998	11%	10%	89%	96%
1997	0%	5%	90%	88%

CQ VOTE STUDIES

	PARTY UNITY		PRESIDENTIAL SUPPORT	
	Support	Oppose	Support	Oppose
2000	96%	4%	21%	79%
1999	92%	8%	12%	88%
1998	93%	7%	16%	84%
1997	94%	6%	24%	76%

NORTH CAROLINA 6

Central — Greensboro and High Point

Located in the heart of the state, the 6th takes in part of the city of Greensboro and surrounding Guilford County and then heads south to include the famed golf course towns of Southern Pines and Pinehurst. Already firm GOP turf, boundary changes implemented for the 2000 election made the 6th even more solidly Republican.

The major boundary change between the 1998 and 2000 elections was to give downtown Greensboro and High Point, and its predominantly black residents, to the 12th District. The 6th picked up the northern third of Guilford County, and parts of conservative Alamance and Rowan counties, while losing a bit of Davidson County.

Greensboro, the third-largest city in the state, is home to a blend of manufacturing and service industries. Textiles, furniture and tobacco processing have long been the economic backbone of both the city and the district. Insurance companies, an American Express regional credit card service center and six colleges and universities have helped to diversify Greensboro's economy. The region has grown at a steady pace, and a proposal by Federal Express to create a hub at the Piedmont Triad International Airport in Greensboro could bring an influx of jobs, but some local residents have environmental concerns. Nearby High Point is a furniture manufacturing hub.

The 6th also includes the southern half of textile-influenced Alamance County, but the county's major city, Burlington, is in the 5th District. With a union-resistant textile industry, the county usually stays in the Republican fold. Southern Moore County includes Pinehurst and Southern Pines, upscale golf and retirement centers. The remainder of the district's land is mostly rural, tobacco country.

MAJOR INDUSTRY
Tobacco, furniture manufacturing, textiles

CITIES
Greensboro (pt.), 88,440 (1990); High Point (pt.), 37,200 (1990); Asheboro, 19,305; Southern Pines, 11,288

UNUSUAL FEATURES
Richard Petty Museum honors the NASCAR racing legend, who was an unsuccessful Republican candidate for secretary of state in 1996.

Rep. Mike McIntyre (D)

CAPITOL OFFICE
225-2731; fax 225-5773; 228 Cannon Bldg. 20515

INTERNET
e-mail: congmcintyre@mail.house.gov
web: www.house.gov/mcintyre

COMMITTEES
Agriculture
Armed Services

HOMETOWN
Lumberton

BORN
Aug. 6, 1956, Lumberton, N.C.

RELIGION
Presbyterian

FAMILY
Wife, Dee McIntyre; two children

EDUCATION
U. of North Carolina, B.A. 1978, J.D. 1981

CAREER
Lawyer

POLITICAL HIGHLIGHTS
No previous office

ELECTION RESULTS

2000 GENERAL

Mike McIntyre (D)	160,185	69.8%
James Adams (R)	66,463	28.9%
Bob Burns (LIBERT)	3,018	1.3%

2000 PRIMARY

Mike McIntyre (D)	63,520	93.5%
Randy Crow (D)	4,440	6.5%

1998 GENERAL

Mike McIntyre (D)	124,366	91.3%
Paul Meadows (LIBERT)	11,924	8.7%

PREVIOUS WINNING PERCENTAGES
1996 (53%)

Elected 1996; 3rd term

McIntyre is one of the most conservative Democrats in the House — conservative even by the standards of the "Blue Dogs," the group of Democrats who occupy their party's right flank. By any measure — how many times he crosses party lines, how often he opposed President Clinton, how he rates with interest groups such as the liberal Americans for Democratic Action and the conservative American Conservative Union — McIntyre is among the most conservative half-dozen House Democrats.

And that's right where the constituents in his conservative and politically competitive 7th District want him to be, looking out for tobacco farmers and the military and taking conservative stands on issues such as abortion, taxes, gun control, school prayer and protection of the flag.

McIntyre's voting record is so strongly conservative that there has periodically been talk of Republicans sounding him out about switching parties. But McIntyre's Democratic roots run deep. Coming of age in North Carolina in the 1970s, he was a Teen Democrat, a College Democrat and then a Young Democrat. So, instead of looking to leave the Democratic Party, McIntyre has worked, particularly through his membership in the Blue Dogs and the slightly less conservative New Democrat Coalition, to move the party's stance away from the left toward the center.

But while he is loath to join the Republicans officially, he often joins them on the House floor. He has backed constitutional amendments to require a two-thirds vote to raise taxes and to allow Congress to bar desecration of the U.S. flag. He angered the AFL-CIO by supporting a bill letting companies offer employees compensatory time off instead of pay for overtime work. He usually sides with anti-abortion forces. In the 106th Congress, he was among the minority of Democrats who crossed party lines to vote for GOP bills to scrap the tax code and to outlaw a procedure its opponents call "partial birth" abortion.

But McIntyre voted "no" on all four articles of impeachment against Clinton in 1998, and he holds traditional Democratic views on many topics. He believes that the federal government should play an important role in improving public schools, for example. "We all know we do not want ... the federal government telling us how to run our schools," he said in 1997. "But the local communities need help from [the] federal level."

McIntyre holds seats on the Agriculture and Armed Services panels — both committees that are useful to his district, where farming, especially tobacco, is big business and the military is a major influence. (Fort Bragg Army Base, Pope Air Force Base and Camp Lejeune Marine Corps Base are nearby in the 3rd and 8th districts.) He is active in the Rural Health Care Coalition and the Fatherhood Promotion Task Force on Capitol Hill.

In the 106th Congress, he was particularly venomous in his objections to Clinton administration moves against the tobacco industry, including a multibillion-dollar lawsuit and a proposal to increase cigarette taxes by 55 cents per pack. The Wilmington Morning Star reported that McIntyre called the move "political posturing at the expense of an economy that is reeling." Many tobacco farmers are small operators who would be hard-pressed to switch to another crop.

McIntyre is a stout defender of the federal tobacco program, which he says is essential to preserving small family farms that grow the leaf. When anti-smoking forces offered an amendment in 1997 to end the federal crop insurance subsidy for tobacco, McIntyre argued that without insurance, farmers would not be able to secure operating loans they need to plant their crop. "No loans means no tobacco crop. No crop means no income, no food, no future for their kids, no retirement. It means moving people from work to welfare — something I thought we were trying to get away from."

In the 106th, McIntyre played a role in winning approval of a massive dredging project to deepen the Cape Fear River channel to make the port of Wilmington accessible to fully loaded container ships.

After attending a November 1972 Fayetteville victory party for newly elected Democratic Rep. Charlie Rose, high school student McIntyre told his father that he wanted to be the next congressman from the 7th District. He served as an intern for Rose in 1974, but over the next decade did little on the political front to further his teenage vow.

He earned undergraduate and law degrees from the University of North Carolina, then returned to his home of Lumberton and built a law practice. He soon became deeply involved in local Democratic politics and in community affairs, ranging from the local PTA to service on the North Carolina Commission on Children and Youth, and then on the statewide Commission on the Family.

When Rose announced his retirement in 1996, McIntyre set about fulfilling his political dream of 24 years before. One of seven Democratic primary entrants, he took 23 percent of the vote, 7 percentage points behind leader Rose Marie Lowry-Townsend, a well-known American Indian and teachers union president who had been the presumed front-runner. Positioned to Lowry-Townsend's right in the runoff, McIntyre criss-crossed the 7th, stressing his years of community activism and arguing that he would be the Democrats' best choice to defend the seat. Shortly before the runoff, McIntyre won the backing of several influential leaders in the district's black community, and their support helped him win the nomination with 52 percent.

McIntyre's Republican opponent was Bill Caster, a New Hanover County (Wilmington) commissioner and retired Coast Guard officer, who was promised a subcommittee chairmanship by House Speaker Newt Gingrich if he captured the 7th for the GOP. McIntyre's conservative stance on issues such as abortion, gun owners' rights and military spending helped blunt GOP attacks, and McIntyre won with 53 percent even as Republican presidential candidate Bob Dole carried the district with 49 percent.

In 1998, McIntyre's conservative record convinced the political action committee headed by conservative Gary Bauer to make McIntyre one of the two Democrats it supported. He won without Republican opposition. In 2000, McIntyre cruised to another victory.

KEY VOTES

2000

Yes Raise hourly minimum wage by $1 over two years

No Halt funding for U.S. mission in Kosovo unless European nations pay more

Yes Provide Medicare benefits to military retirees and their dependents

No Grant China permanent normal trade status

Yes Phase out estate, gift and trust taxes

No Prohibit implementation of president's national monument designations

No Approve GOP plan to provide prescription drug coverage for Medicare beneficiaries

No Increase help for poor nations indebted to international financial institutions

1999

Yes Impose steel import quotas

No Kill proposal to take aviation trust funds off budget

No Require background checks on buyers only at gun shows with 10 or more vendors

Yes Remove barriers among banking, securities and insurance companies

Yes Authorize state grants to hire teachers and reduce class size

Yes Overhaul campaign finance law; ban "soft money" and restrict advocacy advertising

Yes Approve bipartisan plan to increase rights of patients in managed-care health plans

INTEREST GROUPS

	AFL-CIO	ADA	CCUS	ACU
2000	60%	35%	66%	48%
1999	89%	55%	52%	52%
1998	70%	60%	72%	52%
1997	50%	40%	80%	60%

CQ VOTE STUDIES

	PARTY UNITY		PRESIDENTIAL SUPPORT	
	Support	Oppose	Support	Oppose
2000	61%	39%	40%	60%
1999	54%	46%	46%	54%
1998	61%	39%	52%	48%
1997	54%	46%	44%	56%

NORTH CAROLINA 7
Southeast – Wilmington; part of Fayetteville

Based in the southern tip of the state, the 7th stretches from the well-off historic port city of Wilmington in the southeast to the military-based commercial hub of Fayetteville at its northern tip. In between lie tobacco fields, hog farms and manufacturing plants.

While the district lost all four of its military bases through redistricting for the 1998 election, Fort Bragg is just a few miles north, and much of Fayetteville's economy is based on its presence. In exchange for the losses, the district picked up the large swath of rural land at its center. The percentage of blacks in the district rose slightly to about 25 percent, mainly by taking in the southern portions of the old black-majority 1st.

While redistricting made the 7th more Democratic by removing Onslow County on the coast, the wealthy condo-dwellers of Wilmington and surrounding New Hanover County remain, pulling the district to the right. But the region's poor farmers, Lumbee Indians (mainly in

Robeson County), and most of Fayetteville's residents (especially its cohesive black community) contribute more left-leaning voters to create a conservative Democratic constituency that elects Democrats at the state and local levels but drifts toward the GOP in national elections. Accordingly, the 7th gave President Bush 53 percent of the vote in 2000.

MAJOR INDUSTRY
Agriculture, manufacturing, military, tourism

CITIES
Wilmington, 65,255; Fayetteville (pt.), 44,988 (1990); Lumberton, 20,413; Hope Mills, 9,776

UNUSUAL FEATURES
Wilmington is home to an emerging film production industry, with such movies as "Crimes of the Heart," "Blue Velvet," "Weekend at Bernie's," and "Sleeping with the Enemy," filmed there; Television show "Dawson's Creek" also filmed in Wilmington; Retired Chicago Bulls basketball star Michael Jordan grew up in Wilmington.

Rep. Robin Hayes (R)

CAPITOL OFFICE
225-3715; fax 225-4036; 130 Cannon Bldg. 20515

INTERNET
e-mail: www.house.gov/writerep
web: www.house.gov/hayes

COMMITTEES
Agriculture
Armed Services
Transportation & Infrastructure

HOMETOWN
Concord

BORN
Aug. 14, 1945, Concord, N.C.

RELIGION
Presbyterian

FAMILY
Wife, Barbara Hayes; two children

EDUCATION
Duke U., B.A. 1967

CAREER
Hosiery mill owner

POLITICAL HIGHLIGHTS
Concord Board of Aldermen, 1975-78; N.C. House, 1993-97; Republican nominee for governor, 1996

ELECTION RESULTS

2000 GENERAL

Robin Hayes (R)	111,950	55.0%
Mike Taylor (D)	89,505	44.0%

2000 PRIMARY

Robin Hayes (R)		unopposed

1998 GENERAL

Robin Hayes (R)	67,505	50.7%
Mike Taylor (D)	64,127	48.2%
Bob Burns (LIBERT)	1,492	1.1%

Elected 1998; 2nd term

A multimillionaire owner of a hosiery mill, Hayes is an affable, unpretentious and reliable Republican conservative. He champions tobacco interests, backs school vouchers and charter schools, and wants to boost the military's readiness for combat.

Hayes' committee assignments for the 107th Congress should help him hold on to his politically competitive district, which had elected a Democrat, Rep. W.G. "Bill" Hefner, for 24 years until his retirement in 1998. Hayes landed a seat on the Transportation Committee, enabling him to look out for his district's infrastructure needs. He also continues on Armed Services, a post important to the 8th District's Fort Bragg and Pope Air Force Base, and Agriculture, where tobacco interests get a sympathetic hearing.

Hayes has been one of the House's staunchest defenders of tobacco. He added an amendment to the agriculture appropriations bill in 2000 overturning an eight-year-old ban on using Agriculture Department funds to study medical uses for tobacco. In arguing in favor of the proposal, he pointed to recent developments that have allowed scientists to cultivate proteins in genetically modified tobacco plants for a vaccine to fight cervical cancer.

Hayes, who sits on Armed Services' Military Installations and Facilities Subcommittee, would like to see the Pentagon streamline its bidding processes and adopt other cost-saving innovations developed in the business world. He also wants to increase Pentagon spending and take steps to improve morale among U.S. troops. He authored a resolution declaring the American G.I. as the "Person of the Century," which won House approval in 2000. "It was an idea whose time had come," Hayes says. "The American G.I. had a strong sense of right and wrong; he wasn't willing to live where wrong prevailed."

Hayes' passion for hunting and fishing is well-known to his friends and colleagues. The walls in the basement of his Concord home are filled with animal trophies, and he has not let the demands of his job interfere with his hobby. "I've got to meet with a few more constituents, and then I'm headed for the woods," he told the Raleigh News & Observer in 2000. "I'm wearing my vest as we speak." In 2001, he took over as vice chairman of the Congressional Sportsmen's Caucus, a group representing nearly 200 fellow outdoors enthusiasts on Capitol Hill. Not surprisingly, he is a strong supporter of gun owners' rights.

Like many Carolinians, Hayes is a devout NASCAR fan. He is a part-owner of a car racing team and in February 2001 helped to arrange an Air Force flyover honoring the late NASCAR driver Dale Earnhardt before a race at North Carolina Speedway. In 1999, he also rewarded 20 campaign donors by taking them to a racing school for training to drive a Winston Cup car.

Growing up in Concord, Hayes says he was "a typical Southern conservative Democrat, raised in a family with a strong work ethic and family beliefs." After earning a history degree from Duke University, he began a business career that included jobs in the textile, trucking and highway contracting businesses. He eventually became a hosiery mill owner and heir to a textiles fortune; the Capitol Hill newspaper Roll Call estimated his wealth in 2001 at $35 million, third highest among House members.

Hayes became interested in politics by serving on his hometown's board of aldermen. By the time he ran for a seat in the North Carolina House in 1992, he had been a Republican for two years. "I realized that the [Democratic] party had left me; I hadn't left it," he said. "I believe in personal responsibility, limited government. The other side was just diametrically opposed to what I believed."

In 1994, just as the new Republican majority was winning control of Congress, Hayes played a key role in North Carolina's version of the "Republican revolution." He helped organize the Republican takeover of the state House, and his colleagues rewarded him by electing him whip.

In his initial bid for Congress, Hayes looked so strong in early 1998 that Democratic strategists essentially wrote off the seat after incumbent Democrat Hefner announced his retirement. In addition to his money, Hayes had made a name for himself across the district with a respectable though unsuccessful challenge to Democratic Gov. James B. Hunt in 1996.

Hayes outspent Democratic lawyer Mike Taylor by a 3-to-1 margin, but Taylor ran a strong campaign. Hayes prevailed narrowly, winning 51 percent to 48 percent.

The closeness of the race emboldened Democrats, prompting them two years later to pour hundreds of thousands of dollars into Taylor's second effort to recapture the seat for the party. The AFL-CIO ran ads attacking Hayes' record on senior citizens' health issues, while the Democratic Congressional Campaign Committee sponsored spots touting Taylor's plans for a Medicare-controlled prescription drug plan. Taylor criticized Hayes as a "textile baron" out of touch with the diversifying economy of the New South.

Hayes, however, fought back strongly. Prominent Republicans ranging from Arizona Sen. John McCain to the National Rifle Association's Charlton Heston campaigned on his behalf, and he diligently commuted home nearly every weekend to listen to voters. In Washington, he secured money for the district's needs. "We were able to help every county in our district and all the different problems they had," he said in 2001.

Hayes also demonstrated an interest in becoming involved with technology issues affecting poor rural areas. He introduced a measure in September 2000 to provide a tax credit for companies that install Internet lines in rural and low-income urban areas. Hayes beat Taylor in the rematch, with 55 percent of the vote.

Hayes' re-election put him among the ranks of North Carolina politicians who might seek to succeed longtime Republican Sen. Jesse Helms in 2002 if he retires. Although Hayes expressed hope in early 2001 that Helms would hold onto the seat, he said, "I've run statewide before; I would take a look if anything changes."

KEY VOTES

2000

No   Raise hourly minimum wage by $1 over two years
Yes Halt funding for U.S. mission in Kosovo unless European nations pay more
Yes Provide Medicare benefits to military retirees and their dependents
No   Grant China permanent normal trade status
Yes Phase out estate, gift and trust taxes
Yes Prohibit implementation of president's national monument designations
Yes Approve GOP plan to provide prescription drug coverage for Medicare beneficiaries
No   Increase help for poor nations indebted to international financial institutions

1999

Yes Impose steel import quotas
No   Kill proposal to take aviation trust funds off budget
No   Require background checks on buyers only at gun shows with 10 or more vendors
Yes Remove barriers among banking, securities and insurance companies
No   Authorize state grants to hire teachers and reduce class size
No   Overhaul campaign finance law; ban "soft money" and restrict advocacy advertising
No   Approve bipartisan plan to increase rights of patients in managed-care health plans

INTEREST GROUPS

	AFL-CIO	ADA	CCUS	ACU
2000	10%	5%	76%	76%
1999	33%	5%	88%	96%

CQ VOTE STUDIES

	PARTY UNITY		PRESIDENTIAL SUPPORT	
	Support	Oppose	Support	Oppose
2000	89%	11%	19%	81%
1999	94%	6%	17%	83%

NORTH CAROLINA 8

South Central – Parts of Kannapolis and Fayetteville

The 8th connects the worlds of eastern and western North Carolina, spanning from the Charlotte suburbs to military-dominated Fayetteville. It is a district split along geographic, economic and political lines.

To the west, the financially comfortable counties of Cabarrus and Stanly favor the GOP. The textile-based economies of the cities along Interstate 85, notably Concord and Kannapolis, are healthy. Union County is a Charlotte bedroom community with a religious bent.

In the east, the district becomes poorer and more rural as it reaches into the Sandhills region. The economy is based on poultry processing and manufacturing, as well as some mining and agriculture. Here, the district's black population and the Lumbee Indians of Robeson, Hoke and Scotland counties, provide a solid Democratic base.

The eastern part of the district has a strong military flavor. Although the 8th only has a small portion of Cumberland County, this area around Fayetteville includes two military bases and about 40 percent of the district's residents. Troop deployment for the Persian Gulf War so damaged the area's economy that the governor declared Cumberland and three other counties economic emergency areas.

While the eastern counties all vote strongly Democratic, almost 60 percent of voters live in the three western counties, giving GOP candidates an edge districtwide.

MAJOR INDUSTRY
Military, manufacturing, agriculture/livestock

MILITARY BASES
Fort Bragg (Army), 41,000 military, 4,029 civilian; Pope Air Force Base, 5,179 military, 313 civilian (1999)

CITIES
Concord, 50,258; Fayetteville (pt.), 30,707 (1990); Monroe, 22,337; Kannapolis (pt.), 21,220 (1990)

UNUSUAL FEATURES
North Carolina Speedway and Rockingham Dragway, known collectively as "The Rock," can draw 250,000 NASCAR fans to races.

Rep. Sue Myrick (R)

CAPITOL OFFICE
225-1976; fax 225-3389; 230 Cannon Bldg. 20515

INTERNET
e-mail: myrick@mail.house.gov
web: www.house.gov/myrick

COMMITTEES
Rules

HOMETOWN
Charlotte

BORN
Aug. 1, 1941, Tiffin, Ohio

RELIGION
Evangelical Methodist

FAMILY
Husband, Ed Myrick; two children, three stepchildren

EDUCATION
Heidelberg College, attended 1959-60

CAREER
Advertising executive

POLITICAL HIGHLIGHTS
Candidate for Charlotte City Council, 1981; Charlotte City Council, 1983-85; sought Republican nomination for mayor of Charlotte, 1985; mayor of Charlotte, 1987-91; sought Republican nomination for U.S. Senate, 1992

ELECTION RESULTS

2000 GENERAL

Sue Myrick (R)	181,161	68.6%
Ed McGuire (D)	79,382	30.0%

2000 PRIMARY

Sue Myrick (R)	unopposed

1998 GENERAL

Sue Myrick (R)	120,570	69.3%
Rory Blake (D)	51,345	29.5%
Alvin Jeffrey Taylor (LIBERT)	2,167	1.2%

PREVIOUS WINNING PERCENTAGES
1996 (63%); 1994 (65%)

Elected 1994; 4th term

After three terms, Myrick remains steadfast in her conviction that the GOP on Capitol Hill should stand firm for the core conservative principles she believes were responsible for the Republican victories of 1994.

Myrick is one of the members of the celebrated GOP Class of 1994 that helped Republicans take control of the House after 40 years of Democratic rule. She has tried to maintain that revolutionary spirit; she is a consistent conservative on both social and economic issues and, even as many of her Class of 1994 colleagues have come to embrace the virtues of pragmatism, she often has preferred confrontation to compromise.

But in the 106th Congress, Myrick also came to be known in another capacity, as a breast cancer patient and advocate of expanded federal help for low-income women who are diagnosed with breast or cervical cancer. She underwent surgery in December 1999 and continued treatments for about six months, cutting back on her workload and occasionally showing up for floor votes wearing a pink surgical mask to reduce the risk of catching an infection. She was embarrassed at first, she told the Charlotte Observer, "because everybody's looking at you." But soon she became accustomed to wearing the mask as well as a wig.

She said the experience had changed her, helping her keep things in perspective and convincing her to work "very hard not to get back in the same rat race." But it also led her to add to her priorities the task of educating women about the need for early detection and treatment of the disease.

Her ardent conservatism, and her distinct status as the only Southern Republican woman in the Class of 1994, brought her to the attention of party leaders when she first arrived in Congress, but her true-believer fervor later may have cost her a chance to move into the GOP's elected leadership.

Myrick got a seat on the Budget Committee in her first term and a post on the Rules Committee in her second. She also served as the Class of 1994 liaison to the leadership. But in 1997, she met with a small group of disgruntled conservatives, impatient with the pace of the "Republican revolution" and their leaders' willingness to compromise, who plotted to depose Newt Gingrich as Speaker.

The coup was foiled — coincidentally, about the same time that House Republicans met to elect two new leaders. Myrick was a candidate for secretary of the Republican Conference; but she finished second to Deborah Pryce of Ohio. Myrick tried for a leadership job again just before the beginning of the 106th, when the Republican Conference vice chairmanship opened up, but she finished fourth with 37 votes. During her leadership bids, Myrick argued that her experience as an advertising executive before and during her service in Charlotte city government would help her shape a successful GOP message.

In the 106th, Myrick was part of the GOP team designated to put out that message. As a member of the Republican Conference's Communications Working Group, Myrick is charged with articulating why the GOP agenda is in sync with the needs and wishes of the American people.

Her own agenda, in addition to a breast and cervical cancer treatment bill, includes legislation to create a national clearinghouse for information on missing adults, along the lines of an information clearinghouse for missing and exploited children. Other priorities include outlawing desecration of the U.S. flag, banning abortion and allowing religious expression in public places, including prayer in schools.

Myrick supported legislation during the 105th and 106th that sought to make it a crime to transport a minor across state lines to avoid state laws that require parental notification of abortions. "Right now a parent in Charlotte, N.C., must grant permission before the school nurse gives their child an aspirin, but a parent cannot prevent a stranger from taking their child out of school and up to New York City for an abortion," she said.

In 1999, she backed a resolution calling for a day of "solemn prayer, fasting and humiliation before God." She said that, "Inwardly, as a nation, we're falling apart."

Fiscal issues also are important to Myrick, who in 1999 blasted colleagues, including the GOP leadership, for approving an "emergency" spending bill loaded with millions of dollars for programs that were not emergencies, in her view. "Porking is rampant!" she said in a constituent newsletter.

Although her résumé includes just one year of college, Myrick is quick-witted and smart and exudes a cool professionalism that one observer describes as "executive demeanor," originating perhaps from her tenure as the chief executive of Charlotte.

She was born in Tiffin, Ohio, and attended Heidelberg College in her hometown for just a year before her parents decided that it was more important to use their limited financial resources to put her three brothers through school. They figured "I'd just get married," Myrick said.

Myrick entered the workforce without any real game plan, taking a series of jobs in Ohio, beginning with secretarial positions. She had no political aspirations before the early 1980s, when she and her husband had an unsatisfying experience with the Charlotte City Council over the purchase of a property for use as a combination home and business. Until then, Myrick says, she had never fully appreciated the impact of government on her life, and the experience kindled her interest in politics.

She ran for the city council in 1981 and lost but was victorious two years later. In 1985, she lost a bid to become mayor of Charlotte; but in 1987, she won the office, ousting Harvey B. Gantt. Myrick won re-election in 1989, though she feuded with conservative religious activists.

After five-term GOP Rep. Alex McMillan announced his retirement from the 9th District in 1994, Myrick's political experience gave her wide name recognition going into a five-way Republican primary. She struggled to win the nomination, prevailing only when news broke that her principal opponent, state House Minority Leader David Balmer, had falsified his résumé. In November, she met only modest Democratic resistance and has easily won re-election since then, with at least 63 percent of the vote.

KEY VOTES

2000

No Raise hourly minimum wage by $1 over two years

Yes Halt funding for U.S. mission in Kosovo unless European nations pay more

Yes Provide Medicare benefits to military retirees and their dependents

Yes Grant China permanent normal trade status

Yes Phase out estate, gift and trust taxes

Yes Prohibit implementation of president's national monument designations

Yes Approve GOP plan to provide prescription drug coverage for Medicare beneficiaries

No Increase help for poor nations indebted to international financial institutions

1999

\+ Impose steel import quotas

Yes Kill proposal to take aviation trust funds off budget

Yes Require background checks on buyers only at gun shows with 10 or more vendors

Yes Remove barriers among banking, securities and insurance companies

No Authorize state grants to hire teachers and reduce class size

No Overhaul campaign finance law; ban "soft money" and restrict advocacy advertising

No Approve bipartisan plan to increase rights of patients in managed-care health plans

INTEREST GROUPS

	AFL-CIO	ADA	CCUS	ACU
2000	0%	0%	90%	95%
1999	13%	5%	84%	91%
1998	10%	5%	83%	88%
1997	0%	5%	90%	100%

CQ VOTE STUDIES

	PARTY UNITY		PRESIDENTIAL SUPPORT	
	Support	Oppose	Support	Oppose
2000	96%	4%	26%	74%
1999	92%	8%	14%	86%
1998	94%	6%	19%	81%
1997	97%	3%	24%	76%

NORTH CAROLINA 9
Southwest — Gastonia; part of Charlotte

The 9th is more than just the suburbs around Charlotte, the largest metro area in the state. About half of the district's residents live in rural, textile-producing counties west of the city.

The primarily white suburbs on the southern side of Charlotte feed the city many of its bankers, brokers, accountants, health care professionals and other white-collar workers. The region's tremendous growth, much of it sparked by 1990's consolidation in the banking industry, has brought the traffic congestion, shopping malls and higher home values that usually accompany suburban sprawl.

To the west, life is different. The district encompasses the fields, barns, lakes and textile mills typical of rural North Carolina. Some factories have sprouted up as Charlotte has grown, and businesses have begun to use the outlying area as a distribution center.

Court-ordered redistricting for the 2000 election didn't change the district much politically. Remapping kept the Democratic registration at 52 percent, though the 9th votes solidly Republican at the state and federal level. The remap removed Lincoln County, a Republican-leaning area, and added areas surrounding Charlotte. Although the 9th leans Republican overall, at the the local level the counties differ: Mecklenburg is split politically, Cleveland is traditionally Democratic and Gaston is heavily Republican.

MAJOR INDUSTRY
Finance, service, retail, manufacturing

CITIES
Charlotte (pt.), 214,030 (1990); Gastonia, 62,106; Matthews 20,675; Shelby, 19,877; Mint Hill, 19,371

UNUSUAL FEATURES
After six years of planning, a Gaston County military veterans group in December 1998 succeeded in hoisting the largest flying American flag in the nation (114 by 65 feet), which can be seen from the tall office buildings in Charlotte more than 20 miles away; Cleveland County claims to produce more than half the world's supply of lithium.

Rep. Cass Ballenger (R)

CAPITOL OFFICE
225-2576; fax 225-0316; 2182 Rayburn Bldg. 20515

INTERNET
e-mail: cass.ballenger@mail.house.gov
web: www.house.gov/ballenger

COMMITTEES
Education & Workforce
International Relations
   (Western Hemisphere - chairman)

HOMETOWN
Hickory

BORN
Dec. 6, 1926, Hickory, N.C.

RELIGION
Episcopalian

FAMILY
Wife, Donna Ballenger; three children

EDUCATION
U. of North Carolina, attended 1944-45; Amherst
College, B.A. 1948

MILITARY SERVICE
Naval Air Corps, 1944-45

CAREER
Plastics company executive

POLITICAL HIGHLIGHTS
Catawba County Commission, 1966-74 (chairman,
1970-74); N.C. House, 1975-77; N.C. Senate, 1977-86

ELECTION RESULTS

2000 GENERAL

Cass Ballenger (R)	164,182	68.2%
Delmas Parker (D)	70,877	29.5%
Deborah G. Eddins (LIBERT)	5,599	2.3%

2000 PRIMARY

Cass Ballenger (R)	unopposed

1998 GENERAL

Cass Ballenger (R)	118,541	85.6%
Deborah G. Eddins (LIBERT)	19,970	14.4%

PREVIOUS WINNING PERCENTAGES
1996 (70%); 1994 (72%); 1992 (63%); 1990 (62%);
1988 (61%); 1986 (57%); 1986 Special Election
(58%)

Elected 1986; 8th full term

A businessman for almost 40 years before he entered the House at age 60, Ballenger has drawn on that background to push for changes in federal labor laws, some of which are almost as old as he is. The laws should be modernized, he says, to reflect dramatic changes in the work force since the Depression.

As chairman of the Education panel's Workforce Protections Subcommittee for six years, Ballenger was often the standard-bearer for the GOP on labor issues, pushing legislation to provide compensatory time off for workers instead of overtime pay and opposing Democratic efforts to increase the minimum wage.

But in the 107th Congress, Ballenger's legislative focus shifted to the international arena as he took on the chairmanship of International Relations' Western Hemisphere Subcommittee. The GOP leadership gave him the post to take advantage of his contacts in and knowledge of Latin America. Ballenger first traveled to Latin America more than 30 years ago when he joined his father-in-law on a trip for an organization that sent U.S. businessmen to help their South American counterparts.

Ballenger and his wife developed a deep interest in the region, and they have traveled extensively through South and Central America for charitable and humanitarian causes. The Ballengers have helped build homes in Nicaragua and Honduras, provided school furniture to Venezuela and Ecuador, and established a foundation to channel the aid. The congressman says he knows almost every leader in the region. Of particular interest to him lately has been Colombia, where the government is struggling to control the illegal drug trade.

A deputy whip for his party, Ballenger is conservative across the board, but rarely speaks out on social policy matters. When he does draw the spotlight on that front, he can surprise his colleagues. That was the case in the 105th Congress, when he was appointed by Speaker Newt Gingrich to the National Council on the Arts, which advises the National Endowment for the Arts. The NEA's budget has long been a target of conservative House members, and Ballenger had once voted to shut down the agency. But after several months on the arts council, he reported "that significant and positive changes have been made by this agency and Congress to ensure that taxpayers' funds are spent wisely and not on obscene and offensive art."

In the 106th Congress, he continued to tout the "new NEA." "I think everybody thought that the world would come to an end when they put me on [the council]," he said. Ballenger has long been a patron of the arts in North Carolina.

As chairman of the Workforce Protections panel, Ballenger had ambitions to enact pro-business legislation, but his plans met with stiff resistance from pro-labor Democrats. In response, he showed a willingness to shift to a more pragmatic approach, offering proposals for incremental change. Of special interest to Ballenger has been the Occupational Safety and Health Administration (OSHA), which he says places "excessive emphasis on penalties and citations." He says OSHA should act as a consultant to help business owners provide safe workplaces for their employees, rather than take an adversarial approach. After all, he says, complying with health and safety laws is in the employer's interest because a safe workplace is a more productive workplace.

In the 104th Congress, Ballenger introduced a bill that would have substantially curtailed OSHA's regulatory powers and shifted much of the agency's budget from enforcement to education. Labor activists picketed at Ballenger's district offices, arguing that the legislation would lead to unhealthful and unsafe workplaces, and the bill stalled.

Since then, he has sought smaller changes. In the 105th Congress, he introduced eight OSHA-related bills, each restricted in scope. The legislation called for the agency to emphasize voluntary consultations with businesses, rather than inspections and penalties. He won enactment of a measure to authorize a state consultancy program to advise companies on how to meet federal health and safety standards and to prohibit the agency from assessing penalties for violations the consultants discover, as well as another bill to end OSHA enforcement quotas. In the 106th Congress, he won approval of a bill to better protect workers who are exposed to HIV and other blood-borne risks through accidental needle pricks.

On home state matters, Ballenger is proud of his sponsorship of a bill to designate a segment of Wilson Creek in North Carolina as a component of the National Wild and Scenic Rivers System.

Ballenger served in the Navy in World War II, then went on to college. He returned home to Hickory, where he ran a company that made boxes and later founded Plastic Packaging Inc., which has become a substantial area employer and is still in the family.

He spent eight years in county government and nearly 12 years in the state legislature. Ballenger sought to advance to Congress in 1986 when the 10th District's veteran incumbent, Republican James T. Broyhill, announced his retirement. Both Ballenger and his chief GOP rival, George S. Robinson, promised to emulate Broyhill.

Ballenger overcame the 20-year age difference with his adversary — which Robinson cited in arguing that he would be better able to build seniority — and won the GOP primary by 11 percentage points. Then, Broyhill was appointed to the Senate to replace GOP Sen. John East, who died, setting up a special election for Broyhill's seat. In November, Ballenger comfortably won the special and general elections against Democrat Lester D. Roark, a former mayor of Shelby. In subsequent elections, Ballenger has prevailed easily, never falling below 61 percent.

A pleasant, low-profile man, Ballenger in years past could often be found in the Speaker's Lobby just off the House floor, cadging a cigarette from a doorman. With his wife badgering him to give up smoking, Ballenger never bought cigarettes, except when it came time to repay the doorman. He says he has finally been able to give up the habit.

KEY VOTES

2000

No Raise hourly minimum wage by $1 over two years

\+   Halt funding for U.S. mission in Kosovo unless European nations pay more

Yes Provide Medicare benefits to military retirees and their dependents

Yes Grant China permanent normal trade status

Yes Phase out estate, gift and trust taxes

Yes Prohibit implementation of president's national monument designations

Yes Approve GOP plan to provide prescription drug coverage for Medicare beneficiaries

No Increase help for poor nations indebted to international financial institutions

1999

No Impose steel import quotas

Yes Kill proposal to take aviation trust funds off budget

Yes Require background checks on buyers only at gun shows with 10 or more vendors

Yes Remove barriers among banking, securities and insurance companies

No Authorize state grants to hire teachers and reduce class size

No Overhaul campaign finance law; ban "soft money" and restrict advocacy advertising

No Approve bipartisan plan to increase rights of patients in managed-care health plans

INTEREST GROUPS

	AFL-CIO	ADA	CCUS	ACU
2000	0%	0%	94%	91%
1999	22%	5%	84%	80%
1998	0%	5%	82%	91%
1997	0%	10%	100%	83%

CQ VOTE STUDIES

	PARTY UNITY		PRESIDENTIAL SUPPORT	
	Support	Oppose	Support	Oppose
2000	96%	4%	23%	77%
1999	94%	6%	25%	75%
1998	94%	6%	22%	78%
1997	95%	5%	28%	72%

NORTH CAROLINA 10
Northwest – Hickory

The 10th is solid GOP country. Set among the small towns of the northwestern part of the state, the district has a rustic, hard-working, small-business flavor.

The district is among the most rural in the nation. While the economy of the southern counties is based largely on textile and furniture manufacturing, many northern residents get by growing Christmas trees and apples and raising poultry and cattle. High-tech manufacturing, especially fiber-optic cable, is increasing. Tourists visit the mountains near the Tennessee line and ski around Boone.

Court-ordered redistricting for the 2000 election changed the 10th's boundaries by removing the northern, Republican-leaning Ashe, Alleghany and Surry counties. In the south, the 10th gained the Republican bastion of Lincoln County. The new lines do little to change the strong Republican character of the 10th.

Catawba County is the district's most populous and votes solidly Republican. Some suburban sprawl has reached into the eastern and southern edges of the 10th, especially in the growing town of Hickory, the district's largest city. The furniture-making industry employs a large segment of the work force in Hickory. There also is production of cotton and synthetic yarns. Neighboring Iredell County is mostly rural and agricultural, with some manufacturing.

MAJOR INDUSTRY
Manufacturing, agriculture, livestock

CITIES
Hickory, 33,368; Lenoir, 16,702; Morganton, 15,695; Boone, 13,745; Statesville (pt.), 12,324 (1990)

UNUSUAL FEATURES
Stock-car racing legend Junior Johnson, dubbed "The Last American Hero" by writer Tom Wolfe in 1965, grew up on a farm in Wilkes County; Daniel Boone, one of the original settlers of Wilkesboro, built a home on the Yadkin River in the 1760s.

Rep. Charles H. Taylor (R)

Elected 1990; 6th term

CAPITOL OFFICE
225-6401; 231 Cannon Bldg. 20515

INTERNET
e-mail: repcharles.taylor@mail.house.gov
web: www.house.gov/charlestaylor

COMMITTEES
Appropriations
(Legislative Branch - chairman)

HOMETOWN
Brevard

BORN
Jan. 23, 1941, Brevard, N.C.

RELIGION
Baptist

FAMILY
Wife, Elizabeth Taylor; three children

EDUCATION
Wake Forest U., B.A. 1963, J.D. 1966

CAREER
Tree farmer; banker

POLITICAL HIGHLIGHTS
N.C. House, 1967-73 (minority leader, 1969-71);
N.C. Senate, 1973-75 (minority leader, 1973-75);
Republican nominee for U.S. House, 1988

ELECTION RESULTS

2000 GENERAL

Charles H. Taylor (R)	146,677	55.1%
Sam Neill (D)	112,234	42.1%
C. Barry Williams (LIBERT)	7,466	2.8%

2000 PRIMARY

Charles H. Taylor (R)	unopposed

1998 GENERAL

Charles H. Taylor (R)	112,908	56.6%
David Young (D)	84,256	42.2%
Chris Heckert (LIBERT)	2,259	1.1%

PREVIOUS WINNING PERCENTAGES
1996 (58%); 1994 (60%); 1992 (55%); 1990 (51%)

A tree farmer and a bank executive who is among the House's wealthier members, Taylor is strongly pro-business, anti-Washington and socially conservative. At least for the time being, his approach has played well enough among his notoriously fickle constituents. After switching House members five times during the 1980s, they have sent Taylor to Congress since 1990.

Still, controversy surrounding Taylor's financial dealings helped put his most recent re-election in jeopardy and it continued to hound him as the 107th Congress — and the redrawing of North Carolina's congressional map by a Democratic General Assembly — got under way.

To help him retain his seat, Republican leaders gave Taylor a spot on the Appropriations Committee in his second term, and he has used that platform to argue that an active federal effort was needed to promote economic growth in the 11th District, which encompasses the state's mountainous western tip. That effort included money to create an Alzheimer's care unit at the veterans hospital near Asheville, an initiative to bring the region additional high-speed Internet access and a proposal to boost tourism and add jobs.

But by 2000, he faced mounting criticism that he was out of touch with his constituents and had delivered too little back home. "Taylor's new programs and initiatives read more like a wish list, a to-do list rather than actual accomplishments that have dramatically benefited the region over the past two years," declared an Asheville Citizen-Times editorial in October 2000.

Initially elected on a "reform Congress" platform, in his first term Taylor and six other GOP freshmen formed the "Gang of Seven," which gained national attention for their rabble-rousing campaign against congressional perquisites and for full disclosure during the House bank overdraft scandal of the 102nd Congress. Taylor's conservatism and confrontational approach appear to reflect an independence and a dim view of Washington shared by many of his constituents. He once summed up his thoughts of federal bureaucrats by declaring on the House floor, "We know that the government will mess up a one-car funeral."

As an Appropriations subcommittee chairman since 1997, Taylor has not been known for intellectual rigor nor legislative acumen. Instead, he has tended to produce bills that his party leadership eventually saw fit to rewrite or otherwise rescue.

In the 107th Congress, Taylor retains the chairmanship of the Legislative Branch Subcommittee, which writes the bill that pays for congressional overhead — staff salaries, committee expenses, mail, security and upkeep of the Capitol — and an array of offices and agencies that serve Congress. It has been an uneasy fit for Taylor, who in his second term had unsuccessfully pushed for a 25 percent cut in funding for Congress.

The measure is generally among the least contentious of the 13 spending bills, but in 2000 Taylor stirred things up by proposing deep cuts in the budgets of several agencies, including the Capitol Police. (He considered, but did not add, a provision to require Capitol air conditioners to be turned off after July 1 to encourage adjournment each year by Independence Day.) House leaders later added money to the bill after members threatened to oppose it.

Taylor took his current post in 1998 after he was unable to outmaneuver a more junior appropriator, Republican David L. Hobson of Ohio, for the Military Construction Subcommittee gavel. His failure to win that job was attributed to his unhappy stewardship of the District of Columbia Subcommittee, which writes the smallest of the annual bills.

In both 1997 and 1998, that measure had become bogged down for months when Taylor sought to attach to it an array of "riders," legislative mandates reflecting his view that the city was poorly run and in need of strong federal guidance to put its house in order. Some riders would have required the District to reduce taxes by as much as $200 million and pay down its debt by $300 million, imposed caps on medical malpractice punitive damage awards, and required city workers to live in the District. Taylor's agenda provoked such intense opposition that House leaders ultimately took over negotiations on the bill and stripped most of the riders.

Taylor also has been known to spar with members of his own state's congressional delegation. During consideration of a supplemental appropriations bill in 2000, Eva Clayton, D-N.C., sought $1.5 million for a study of whether to reconstruct a dike breached by hurricane flooding in her district. When Taylor suggested the expense might not be justified, the Congressional Black Caucus mounted a protest; again, the GOP leadership took over and gave Clayton (a Black Caucus member) what she wanted.

Taylor won his first election, to a state House seat, fresh out of law school in 1966. He spent six years in the House and later served in the state Senate, becoming minority leader in each chamber. After losing to Democratic Rep. James McClure Clarke in 1988, Taylor won a 1990 rematch with 51 percent. Before 2000, he had won four re-election races with relative ease.

In 2000, the bad publicity from Taylor's financial woes was peaking. Tax collectors in two North Carolina counties had gone after him for almost $48,000 in overdue property taxes; when one threatened to garnish Taylor's House salary, the congressman paid some of the taxes under protest. The dust-up led House Majority Leader Dick Armey to issue a call at the state GOP convention: "Charlie Taylor, wherever you are — pay your taxes."

Taylor also faced criticism after revelations that he had extensive business ventures in Russia — including stakes in a potato warehouse, an apartment building and a chain of convenience stores — while he was cosponsoring a bill to create a program of U.S. aid for Russian home mortgages.

At the same time, Taylor learned that a federal grand jury had begun investigating loans by Blue Ridge Savings Bank, where he is the chairman of the board. The loans, made to a longtime political ally of the congressman, exceeded thrift loan limits.

Still, in 2000 Taylor defeated Democratic attorney Sam Neill, with 55 percent, as George W. Bush was carrying the district with 59 percent.

KEY VOTES

2000

No   Raise hourly minimum wage by $1 over two years

Yes   Halt funding for U.S. mission in Kosovo unless European nations pay more

Yes   Provide Medicare benefits to military retirees and their dependents

No   Grant China permanent normal trade status

Yes   Phase out estate, gift and trust taxes

Yes   Prohibit implementation of president's national monument designations

Yes   Approve GOP plan to provide prescription drug coverage for Medicare beneficiaries

No   Increase help for poor nations indebted to international financial institutions

1999

No   Impose steel import quotas

Yes   Kill proposal to take aviation trust funds off budget

Yes   Require background checks on buyers only at gun shows with 10 or more vendors

Yes   Remove barriers among banking, securities and insurance companies

No   Authorize state grants to hire teachers and reduce class size

No   Overhaul campaign finance law; ban "soft money" and restrict advocacy advertising

No   Approve bipartisan plan to increase rights of patients in managed-care health plans

INTEREST GROUPS

	AFL-CIO	ADA	CCUS	ACU
2000	11%	5%	72%	92%
1999	22%	5%	78%	100%
1998	20%	5%	88%	96%
1997	0%	0%	100%	91%

CQ VOTE STUDIES

	PARTY UNITY		PRESIDENTIAL SUPPORT	
	Support	Oppose	Support	Oppose
2000	94%	6%	21%	79%
1999	96%	4%	16%	84%
1998	95%	5%	18%	82%
1997	95%	5%	28%	72%

NORTH CAROLINA 11

West – Asheville

Based in the mountains and foothills of the Great Smoky Mountains, the 11th is a largely rural region dotted with tree farms, wood mills, and campgrounds. While agriculture and forestry have long played a major role in the region's economy, retail trade, health care and education have emerged as additional viable industries. Tourism also has a large role, with people flocking to the area to ski, hike the national park and Mount Mitchell (the highest peak east of the Mississippi) and tour the palatial Biltmore House, once home of Cornelius Vanderbilt's grandson.

Asheville, which along with surrounding Buncombe County takes in nearly a third of the district's residents, is the 11th's economic focal point. Residents recently spruced up its downtown, and efforts are under way to attract high-tech industry.

Long a hotly contested district, the 11th has moved toward the Republican column, thanks in part to a large influx of retirees. In state and national elections, it leans Republican, but at the local level it's more divided, with the southern counties voting Republican and the northern ones leaning Democrat. Redistricting for the 1998 had little effect, increasing Republican registration by only 1 percent. The 11th's boundaries were unchanged in 2000 redistricting.

MAJOR INDUSTRY
Retail trade, forest products, tourism, health care

CITIES
Asheville, 65,974; Waynesville, 9,506; Hendersonville, 9,125; Forest City, 7,632

UNUSUAL FEATURES
Many of the state's Cherokee Indians are the descendants of the estimated 1,000 Cherokees who hid in the mountains of western North Carolina to avoid the forced migration to Oklahoma along the path now known as the Trail of Tears; The Billy Graham Evangelistic Association operates a 1,500-acre training center called "The Cove" in Asheville; Several movies have been filmed at Asheville's Biltmore House, including "Being There" and "The Last of the Mohicans."

Rep. Melvin Watt (D)

CAPITOL OFFICE
225-1510; fax 225-1512; 2236 Rayburn Bldg. 20515

INTERNET
e-mail: nc12.public@mail.house.gov
web: www.house.gov/watt

COMMITTEES
Financial Services
Judiciary
Joint Economic

HOMETOWN
Charlotte

BORN
Aug. 26, 1945, Steele Creek, N.C.

RELIGION
Presbyterian

FAMILY
Wife, Eulada Watt; two children

EDUCATION
U. of North Carolina, B.S. 1967; Yale U., J.D. 1970

CAREER
Nursing home owner; campaign manager; lawyer

POLITICAL HIGHLIGHTS
N.C. Senate, 1985-86

ELECTION RESULTS

2000 GENERAL

Melvin Watt (D)	135,570	64.8%
Joshua "Chad" Mitchell (R)	69,596	33.3%
Anna Lyon (LIBERT)	3,978	1.9%

2000 PRIMARY

Melvin Watt (D)	unopposed

1998 GENERAL

Melvin Watt (D)	82,305	56.0%
Scott Keadle (R)	62,070	42.2%
Michael G. Smith (LIBERT)	2,713	1.8%

PREVIOUS WINNING PERCENTAGES
1996 (72%); 1994 (66%); 1992 (70%)

Elected 1992; 5th term

Watt combines a meticulous attention to the details of legislation with a knack for passionate liberal oratory. To win battles in a GOP-controlled Congress, the veteran civil rights lawyer and master debater immerses himself in arcane areas of law, such as banking regulation, then uses his Yale legal training to undo the opposition.

In 1999, for example, when the Judiciary Committee erupted in a partisan brawl over legislation to overhaul bankruptcy law, Watt steered clear of the uproar. While other liberal Democrats were blasting the GOP plan as anti-consumer and a sellout to the credit card industry, Watt quietly focused on the minutiae of the bill, line-by-line, phrase-by-phrase, to build a case against the Republican package.

But Watt also can match some of his better-known liberal colleagues in the verbal wars when he needs to. He is one of the most frequently heard Democratic voices in defense of civil liberties, both on the House floor and in the Judiciary Committee, where he is the ranking Democrat on the Commercial and Administrative Law Subcommittee.

When Republicans pushed for tougher sentences for juvenile offenders, Watt provided scathing opposition: "Lock up a 13-year-old with a murderer, a rapist and a robber," he said in 1999, "and guess what he'll want to be when he grows up?"

Despite his traditionally liberal voting record on many matters, Watt is on cordial terms with his district's large business community, and he takes into account its views on regulation and other issues in his work on the Financial Services Committee (formerly Banking). Charlotte's big financial services companies, including First Union, BankAmerica and Wachovia, would no doubt prefer to have a more conservative congressman, but Watt at least gives their opinions a fair hearing.

Watt is one of only two blacks elected to Congress from North Carolina in the 20th century (the other is his Democratic colleague, Eva Clayton), and his district's boundaries have been a continual subject of controversy. First drawn in 1992, the 12th District has been reconfigured three times since Watt came to Congress. A voter lawsuit, which claims that the 12th was illegally drawn to ensure the election of a black candidate, has challenged the district lines in court for more than eight years, during which time the Supreme Court has intervened four times.

Ultimately, the changing shape of Watt's district has proved more of a distraction than a threat to his seat in Congress: He won re-election in 1998 with 56 percent of the vote and in 2000 increased his total to 65 percent.

Watt's dogged determination is evident in a simple reading of his life story. Raised in a fatherless household, he grew up in a tin-roofed shack in rural Mecklenburg County that had no running water or electricity, but he went on to graduate Phi Beta Kappa from the University of North Carolina at Chapel Hill. Watt then got a law degree from Yale University and practiced civil rights law for 22 years before winning election to Congress.

In Washington, he has steadfastly focused on beating back GOP proposals to amend the Constitution. He relishes exposing what he considers to be flaws in the logic of Republican positions.

In the 105th Congress, he opposed a constitutional amendment proposed by Oklahoma Republican Ernest Istook that sought to expand protections for religious freedom. Supporters of Istook's measure said it was necessary because court interpretations of the First Amendment had curbed expression of religious beliefs. Watt sarcastically suggested repealing the entire portion of the First Amendment that protects religious freedom, saying: "The more words we give the Supreme Court to interpret, the more interpreting they are going to do."

In the same vein, Watt fought legislation to allow police officers to obtain evidence through illegal search and seizure if they were operating in good faith. He sought to nullify the bill by inserting the language of the Fourth Amendment, which protects Americans from unreasonable search and seizure. Watt's action left bill sponsor Bill McCollum, R-Fla., pleading with his colleagues: "Don't wipe out the bill by voting for the Constitution." (The bill passed without Watt's proposed change but did not become law.)

Watt's defense of civil liberties sometimes puts him in unexpected alliances with conservative Republicans. In 1996, he teamed up with Idaho Republican Helen Chenoweth to try to amend an anti-terrorism bill, contending that placing severe restrictions on death row appeals was a betrayal of the Founding Fathers' commitment to individual rights. "We can't sacrifice our constitutional principles because we're angry at people for bombing," he said.

Watt launched lonely crusades against a federal version of Megan's Law, which requires state and local law enforcement agencies to disclose information about sex offenders upon their release from prison. "An individual, having paid their debt to society by serving time and having complied with their sentence, ought to be able ... to get on with their lives," Watt said.

On the Financial Services Committee, Watt sees it as his job to stick up for the little guy. He voted against a comprehensive banking deregulatory measure in the 105th Congress because he was concerned that it could make financial services more expensive for consumers.

Watt also is actively involved in the panel's work on housing and urban affairs. In the 105th, he opposed a Republican-backed measure to overhaul public housing regulations. "What they want to do," he said on the House floor, "is to put more and more working poor in public housing, and that will be at the expense of the most poor people in this country and will deprive them of housing. And we are providing no funds for any additional housing under this bill. This is a paternalistic, inflexible, so-called reform bill."

Watt is a good athlete, and Democrats have relied heavily on him in the annual charity baseball game that pits his party against the GOP. As a star pitcher, Watt has had trouble controlling his curveball, but he was the Democrats' most valuable player in the 1995 and 1996 games, and he was the winning pitcher and co-MVP in 2000.

KEY VOTES

2000

Yes Raise hourly minimum wage by $1 over two years

Yes Halt funding for U.S. mission in Kosovo unless European nations pay more

Yes Provide Medicare benefits to military retirees and their dependents

No Grant China permanent normal trade status

? Phase out estate, gift and trust taxes

No Prohibit implementation of president's national monument designations

No Approve GOP plan to provide prescription drug coverage for Medicare beneficiaries

Yes Increase help for poor nations indebted to international financial institutions

1999

Yes Impose steel import quotas

Yes Kill proposal to take aviation trust funds off budget

No Require background checks on buyers only at gun shows with 10 or more vendors

Yes Remove barriers among banking, securities and insurance companies

Yes Authorize state grants to hire teachers and reduce class size

Yes Overhaul campaign finance law; ban "soft money" and restrict advocacy advertising

Yes Approve bipartisan plan to increase rights of patients in managed-care health plans

INTEREST GROUPS

	AFL-CIO	ADA	CCUS	ACU
2000	100%	85%	45%	8%
1999	100%	100%	12%	0%
1998	100%	100%	28%	4%
1997	100%	100%	30%	4%

CQ VOTE STUDIES

	PARTY UNITY		PRESIDENTIAL SUPPORT	
	Support	Oppose	Support	Oppose
2000	94%	6%	82%	18%
1999	94%	6%	83%	17%
1998	96%	4%	91%	9%
1997	94%	6%	77%	23%

NORTH CAROLINA 12

Central – Parts of Charlotte, Greensboro and Winston-Salem

Attacked in court as being an unconstitutional racial gerrymander since it was first drawn for the 1992 election, the 12th conducted the 2000 election with a 45 percent black population, up from a decade-low of 36 percent under the district's 1998 boundaries. The increase bolsters the district's solid Democratic credentials.

On its third and final set of boundaries for the decade, the 12th employed a shape the legislature approved in 1997 but was not used then because of court challenges. A zig-zag that begins in Charlotte, the 12th heads due north along Interstate 77 to Statesville, then swings southeast to pick up Interstate 85, poking into parts of Winston-Salem, High Point and Greensboro. The major change between the 1998 and 2000 elections was to flatten the wide middle (predominately conservative Rowan County), replacing the lost population there with an arm reaching into Greensboro and High Point.

The resulting district is on good economic footing. Charlotte's economy is booming. After a decade of consolidation among banks, the city surprised many by becoming the nation's biggest banking center outside of New York – the massive Bank of America is headquartered here. But the city's downtown (known as "uptown") also has its share of poverty and crime. The Biddleville neighborhood, to the west of the business district, is a hub of the black community and home to the predominately black Johnson C. Smith University. Outside of the city, transplants accustomed to New York City real estate prices have built upscale suburban neigborhoods with matching decorative street signs.

The 12th's portions of Winston-Salem and Greensboro are mainly black, lower- to middle-class neighborhoods.

MAJOR INDUSTRY
Finance, transportation, health care

CITIES
Charlotte (pt.), 181,904 (1990); Greensboro (pt.), 95,081 (1990); Winston-Salem (pt.), 54,270 (1990); High Point (pt.), 32,290 (1990)

UNUSUAL FEATURES
Evangelist Billy Graham born and reared in Charlotte.

Gov. John Hoeven (R)

First elected: 2000
Length of term: 4 years
Term expires: 12/04
Salary: $83,013
Phone: (701) 328-2200
Hometown: Bismarck
Born: March 13, 1957, Bismarck, N.D.
Religion: Roman Catholic
Family: Wife, Mical Hoeven; two children
Education: Dartmouth College, B.A. 1979; Northwestern U., M.B.A. 1981
Career: Bank CEO
Political highlights: No previous office
Election results:

2000 GENERAL

John Hoeven (R)	159,255	55.0%
Heidi Heitkamp (D)	130,1447	45.0%

Lt. Gov. Jack Dalrymple (R)

First elected: 2000
Length of term: 4 years
Term expires: 12/04
Salary: $64,452
Phone: (701) 328-2200

STATE LEGISLATURE

Legislative Assembly: Meets January-April in odd years
House: 98 members, 4-year terms
2001 breakdown: 69R, 29D; 79 men, 19 women
Salary: $3,000/year; $111/day in session
Phone: (701) 328-2916
Senate: 49 members, 4-year terms
2001 breakdown: 32R, 17D; 43 men, 6 women
Salary: $3,000/year; $111/day in session
Phone: (701) 328-2916

STATE TERM LIMITS

Governor: No
Senate: No
House: No

URBAN STATISTICS

CITY	POPULATION
Fargo	88,128
Bismarck	55,109
Grand Forks	45,967
Minot	35,673

REGISTERED VOTERS

Voters do not register by party.

POPULATION

2000 population	642,200
1990 population	638,800
Percent change	+0.5%
Rank among states	47
Median age	35.4
Born in state	73%
Foreign born	1%
Urban/rural	53%/47%
Crime rate	87/100,000
Poverty level	15.1%
Federal workers	8,985
Military	13,097

REAPPORTIONMENT

North Dakota retained its one House seat in reapportionment.

MISCELLANEOUS

Web: www.state.nd.us
Capital: Bismarck
Land area: 68,994 sq. miles
Rank among states: 17
STATE ELECTION OFFICIAL
(701) 328-4146
DEMOCRATIC HEADQUARTERS
(701) 255-0460
REPUBLICAN HEADQUARTERS
(701) 255-0030

District Statistics

DIST.	VOTE FOR PRESIDENT									WHT	BLK	ASIAN	HISP	HOUSEHOLD INCOME	OVER 65+	UNDER 18	COLLEGE EDUCATION
	2000 D	2000 R	GREEN	1996 D	1996 R	REF	1992 D	1992 R	I								
AL	33%	61%	3%	40%	47%	12%	32%	45%	23%	95%	1%	1%	1%	$23,213	14%	28%	18%

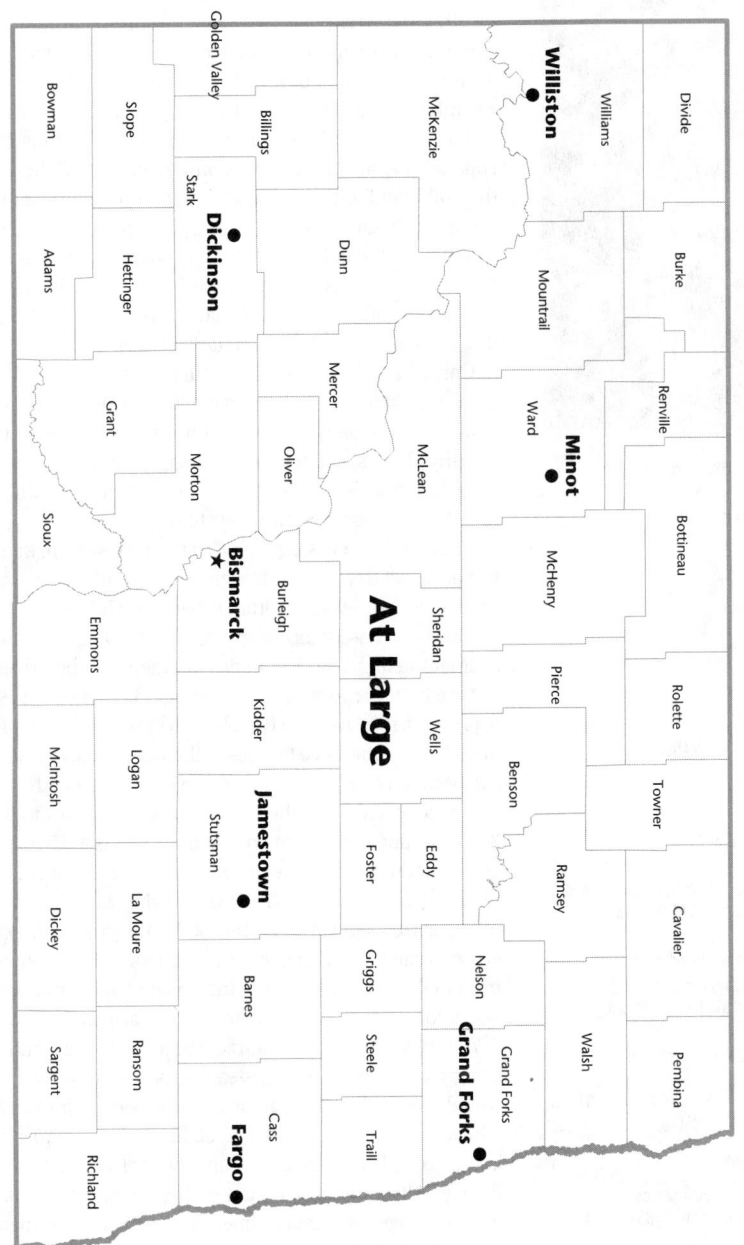

Sen. Kent Conrad (D)

CAPITOL OFFICE
224-2043; fax 224-7776; 530 Hart Bldg. 20510

INTERNET
e-mail: senator@conrad.senate.gov
web: conrad.senate.gov

COMMITTEES
Agriculture, Nutrition & Forestry
Budget - ranking member
Finance
Indian Affairs

HOMETOWN
Bismarck

BORN
March 12, 1948, Bismarck, N.D.

RELIGION
Unitarian

FAMILY
Wife, Lucy Calautti; one child

EDUCATION
U. of Missouri, attended 1967; Stanford U., A.B.
1971; George Washington U., M.B.A. 1975

CAREER
Management and personnel director

POLITICAL HIGHLIGHTS
Candidate for N.D. auditor, 1976; N.D. tax
commissioner, 1981-87

ELECTION RESULTS

2000 GENERAL

Kent Conrad (D)	176,470	61.5%
Duane Sand (R)	110,420	38.5%

2000 PRIMARY

Kent Conrad (D)	unopposed

PREVIOUS WINNING PERCENTAGES
1994 (58%); 1992 Special Election (63%); 1986
(50%)

Elected 1986; 3rd full term

Conrad is a relentless advocate for his state, battling for farmers and rural health providers. He strives to make sure that the people of North Dakota and other sparsely populated farming states are not ignored in Washington as they cope with floods, bad crop years and government policies that they say inhibit their ability to battle fairly for export markets.

With his bookish, junior executive looks and his background as North Dakota's top tax bureaucrat, Conrad does not fit the stereotype of a "son of the soil." And although he can be a fierce partisan, Conrad belongs to a group of Democratic moderates known as the Senate New Democrats, who hew to the political center and strive to reach across the aisle to try to break political deadlock. "What brings us together is a desire to get things done," Conrad told The Associated Press in 2000. "We have a shared view that things are pretty bogged down."

Conrad also has been a player in federal budget debates, both in the Budget Committee, where he became the top Democrat in the 107th Congress, and on the Senate floor. He chimes in steadily, with amendments and lengthy floor speeches, on a range of other issues that includes youth smoking, television programming, defense spending and the long-term health of the Social Security system.

Since the 1996 passage of GOP farm legislation, known as the "Freedom to Farm" act, that ended traditional crop subsidies, Conrad has repeatedly tried to create new agriculture programs while also voting for billions of dollars in disaster assistance to growers contending with low prices. Without government help, he says, countless farmers will be driven off the land. "Agriculture is on the verge of a depression," he warned in 1999. When Congress approved a massive disaster relief bill in 2000, he said, "This package is going to make the difference for tens of thousands of farm families all across America, between economic survival and economic death."

His concern about the farm economy led him to support legislation in 2000 granting permanent normal trade status to China. "It's in the best interest of America — and North Dakota — to have normal trade relations with the most populous country in the world," he said. Conrad also unsuccessfully pursued legislation in the 106th Congress to direct federal aid to farmers who can prove that agricultural imports hurt them economically, and he tried to draw attention to the increasing concentration of large agricultural operations, which he fears hurt family farms.

A moderate on taxes, Conrad rejected GOP tax-cutting plans in the 106th Congress as overly broad. Instead, he produced a $525 billion tax proposal that would have reduced estate taxes, provided tax breaks for family farms and education-related expenses and eliminated the "marriage penalty" — a quirk in the tax code that results in some two-earner married couples paying higher taxes. "It's carefully targeted so that we can provide tax relief without busting the budget," Conrad claimed. Yet his plan, like other tax proposals in the 106th, died amid partisan maneuvering.

Although Conrad can voice support for GOP proposals, he has often disappointed conservatives by opposing them at the last minute. In the 106th, he and North Dakota's junior senator, Democrat Byron L. Dorgan, decided after much deliberation to oppose a constitutional amendment barring flag desecration. The incident recalled debate in the 104th over a proposed balanced-budget constitutional amendment. At that time, Conrad, who had promised that the federal deficit would be the center of his political mission during his first Senate campaign in 1986, waited until the very end before opposing the balanced-budget amendment on the grounds that it could threaten Social Security. "I think we should be very reluctant to amend the Constitution of the United States," Conrad said in 2000.

Over the years, Conrad has offered a variety of ideas for reducing the deficit, such as a plan to freeze most domestic spending, while protecting agriculture, education, health care and veterans programs. Sometimes, he finds politically popular ways to save taxpayer money. For example, he introduced a successful amendment to a 1994 defense procurement bill that barred contractors from being reimbursed for their entertainment expenses.

Much of his time in the 105th was spent in the ultimately unsuccessful effort to convert a settlement between most of the states and tobacco companies into federal tobacco law. He sponsored the leading Democratic bill on the issue, pressing for tougher terms than the legal settlement, which aimed to reduce teen smoking and required tobacco companies to foot some of the bill for smokers' health costs.

Conrad also lobbied vigorously, with some success, to moderate GOP proposals to overhaul welfare. He especially opposed efforts to turn food stamps into a block grant program that would be run by the states. Facing opposition from rural lawmakers of both parties, GOP leaders agreed to keep food stamps a federal program.

More conservative than some Democrats on the issue of abortion, in 1998 Conrad voted to override President Clinton's veto of a ban on a procedure its opponents call "partial birth" abortion. He also opposes allowing federal employees' health care plans to cover abortion.

Conrad won approval in the 104th of a provision requiring "v-chip" circuitry in new televisions to allow parents to block programs rated as violent or sexually explicit. His plan became part of a broad telecommunications bill. "Parents are increasingly unhappy that they have limited ability to control what their children watch on television," he said.

Conrad's early years were marked by the death of his parents, who were killed by a drunk driver when he was 5. He and his brothers were raised by his grandparents. He went to high school at a U.S. military base in Libya, where he lived with family friends. Upon his return to North Dakota, still a teenager, he headed a statewide campaign to grant voting rights to 19-year-olds.

He was elected North Dakota tax commissioner in 1980 and re-elected in 1984, a post from which he took on big business. In 1986, he unseated GOP Sen. Mark Andrews in a narrow contest by linking the incumbent to the Reagan administration's unpopular farm policy. One of Conrad's pledges during that campaign was not to seek re-election unless the trade and budget deficits were dramatically reduced during his term in office. In April 1992, Conrad kept his promise by announcing his Senate retirement, even though he joked that he had written the pledge while suffering from a 104-degree fever.

But on Sept. 8, 1992, North Dakota's senior senator, Democrat Quentin N. Burdick, died — leaving two years in his Senate term, necessitating a special election in December. Democrats urged Conrad to run, and he was unchallenged for the party's nomination. He easily bested GOP state Rep. Jack Dalrymple, taking 63 percent of the vote.

In 1994, he won a full term — in part by covering his right flank with a TV ad in which he said, "A majority of the time, I vote with the Republican leader, Bob Dole." Conrad took 58 percent against Ben Clayburgh, a 70-year-old orthopedic surgeon, and chalked up another easy victory in 2000.

Both Conrad and his wife, Lucy Calautti, are avid baseball fans. She became Major League Baseball's Washington lobbyist in 2000.

KEY VOTES

2000

Yes	Overhaul bankruptcy law and increase minimum wage
No	Limit fiscal 2001 discretionary spending to $600.3 billion
No	Override veto on nuclear waste disposal at Yucca Mountain site in Nevada
Yes	Oppose effort to terminate Kosovo mission
Yes	Include gender, sexual orientation and disability in federal hate crime protections
No	Approve GOP plan to restrict use of genetic information by health insurers
No	Kill amendment delaying implementation of an anti-missile defense system
No	Cut taxes for married couples
Yes	Grant China permanent normal trade status

1999

No	Remove President Clinton from office for obstruction of justice
No	Kill amendment authorizing state grants to hire teachers and reduce class size
Yes	Require criminal background checks for purchases at gun shows
No	Approve GOP proposal to increase rights of patients in managed-care health plans
No	Block effort to allow farm and medicine exports to Cuba
No	Allow study of tougher automobile fuel efficiency standards
Yes	Ratify nuclear weapons testing treaty
Yes	Prohibit national political parties from collecting "soft money" donations
Yes	Remove barriers among banking, securities and insurance companies

INTEREST GROUPS

	AFL-CIO	ADA	CCUS	ACU
2000	71%	85%	42%	29%
1999	89%	90%	53%	16%
1998	88%	90%	61%	16%
1997	57%	65%	50%	16%
1996	71%	85%	23%	15%
1995	100%	90%	42%	9%
1994	75%	85%	40%	12%
1993	82%	80%	9%	24%
1992	75%	90%	20%	12%
1991	75%	75%	20%	43%

CQ VOTE STUDIES

	PARTY UNITY		PRESIDENTIAL SUPPORT	
	Support	Oppose	Support	Oppose
2000	87%	13%	90%	10%
1999	87%	13%	73%	27%
1998	87%	13%	75%	25%
1997	82%	18%	81%	19%
1996	87%	13%	83%	17%
1995	87%	13%	84%	16%
1994	85%	15%	89%	11%
1993	82%	18%	82%	18%
1992	71%	29%	32%	68%
1991	74%	26%	36%	64%

Sen. Byron L. Dorgan (D)

Elected 1992; 2nd term

Dorgan is a contemporary voice for the prairie populism that swept North Dakota in the early 1900s. The Senate's patience for long speeches gives him ample opportunity to rail at the large and distant forces — corporations, foreign governments, international financial institutions — that, he says, care not a whit for the common folk. "People feel powerless," Dorgan once said, "and they feel powerless because they're preyed upon by bigger interests."

The North Dakotan is a strong public speaker who also comes across in person as passionate about his beliefs, especially when it comes to helping struggling farmers. A true small-town boy, Dorgan was born in the farming community of Regent, where he grew up and where, he likes to say, he graduated in the top five in his high school class — of nine. Dorgan's political beliefs are rooted partly in his state's populist traditions and partly in the small-town values of his upbringing.

One of Dorgan's most passionate concerns is seeing to it that the government provides adequate aid to farmers. He won an appointment to the Appropriations panel's Agriculture Subcommittee in the 106th Congress, helping him steer more benefits to his rural constituents. With North Dakota farmers suffering from low commodity prices, he has led the charge for multibillion-dollar emergency aid packages.

Since the Republicans won enactment of "Freedom to Farm" legislation in the 104th Congress that ended traditional farm subsidies, Dorgan has sought to revive a system that boosts federal payments to farmers when crop prices are low. Chiding Republicans who resist subsidizing struggling farmers, he said in a speech at the 2000 Democratic National Convention, "Those who fail to stand up for American farm families have no claim to call themselves pro-family."

Dorgan is also concerned about boosting airline service to rural areas. At the beginning of the 106th, he teamed with West Virginia Democrat John D. Rockefeller IV to introduce legislation that would give grants to small communities to help them attract better air service. "While [airline] deregulation has been a wonderful success for the people who travel between the big cities of the country, it has been an unmitigated disaster for most rural areas and small communities," Dorgan said. Early in the 107th Congress, he demanded tough scrutiny of two proposed airline mergers.

Although his wheat farmers rely on foreign markets, Dorgan pursues an independent course on trade legislation. He reluctantly voted in 2000 to grant China permanent normal trade status. But he broke ranks with the Clinton administration in the 105th by fiercely opposing a renewal of fast-track authority that would have allowed the president to negotiate trade agreements that Congress cannot amend. Dorgan contended that such deals aggravated the trade deficit and weakened the economy. "We have the largest trade deficit in the history of the world right now, and it's getting worse, not better," he said in a 1997 floor speech. "My message to the administration and to Congress is simple. Fix the trade problems you've already created before you run off and negotiate new agreements that make new problems."

Dorgan also works to protect farm interests against international competition. In 1994, he agreed not to block Senate confirmation of several Clinton appointees for trade positions only after the administration made a deal with Canada to limit its wheat exports. American wheat farmers had complained that the Canadian government was unfairly subsidizing its shipments to the United States.

CAPITOL OFFICE
224-2551; fax 224-1193; 713 Hart Bldg. 20510

INTERNET
e-mail: senator@dorgan.senate.gov
web: dorgan.senate.gov

COMMITTEES
Appropriations
Commerce, Science & Transportation
Energy & Natural Resources
Indian Affairs

HOMETOWN
Bismarck

BORN
May 14, 1942, Regent, N.D.

RELIGION
Lutheran

FAMILY
Wife, Kimberly Olson Dorgan; four children (one deceased)

EDUCATION
U. of North Dakota, B.S. 1965; U. of Denver, M.B.A. 1966

CAREER
Aerospace company manager

POLITICAL HIGHLIGHTS
N.D. tax commissioner, 1969-80; Democratic nominee for U.S. House, 1974; U.S. House, 1981-92

ELECTION RESULTS

1998 GENERAL

Byron L. Dorgan (D)	134,747	63.2%
Donna Nalewaja (R)	75,013	35.2%
Harley McLain (REF)	3,598	1.7%

1998 PRIMARY

Byron L. Dorgan (D)	unopposed

PREVIOUS WINNING PERCENTAGES
1992 (59%); 1990 House Election (65%); 1988 House Election (71%); 1986 House Election (76%); 1984 House Election (79%); 1982 House Election (72%); 1980 House Election (57%)

Dorgan has been one of the Senate's most outspoken critics of the Federal Reserve Board, which he believes has not put enough emphasis on achieving economic growth but instead has been preoccupied with keeping a lid on inflation. The resulting higher interest rates, Dorgan argues, make credit more expensive for farmers, other businessmen and consumers who borrow money.

In 2000, he was one of just four senators to vote against President Clinton's nomination of Fed Chairman Alan Greenspan to a fourth term. Even though Greenspan had won glowing reviews on Wall Street for managing the economic expansion, Dorgan criticized him for repeatedly raising interest rates. "He was consistently wrong about how low unemployment could go, and he was consistently wrong about economic growth," Dorgan scoffed. "I think my Uncle Joe could have done a good job during this period," he said in a Washington Post interview.

Dorgan expressed interest in taking his populist outlook to a Senate leadership post in the 106th, when the retirement of Minority Whip Wendell H. Ford of Kentucky left an opening. But with Tom Daschle of neighboring South Dakota serving as minority leader, regional pressures worked against Dorgan for the whip position, which ultimately went to Harry Reid of Nevada. However, Daschle appointed Dorgan assistant Democratic leader for policy and co-chairman of the Democratic Policy Committee.

Republicans have branded Dorgan as too liberal for his state, although his voting record shows him to be toward the conservative end of the spectrum among Senate Democrats. For example, he joined Republicans in supporting a welfare overhaul measure that Clinton signed in 1996.

But conservatives who hoped he would side with them on a constitutional amendment to ban flag desecration were infuriated in 2000 when he announced his opposition to the measure. "Almost never have we passed constitutional amendments to take power away from people," Dorgan said, according to The Associated Press. "Most amendments have expanded the concept of freedom and liberty."

Dorgan's reaction to the flag desecration amendment reflected a much-publicized controversy in 1995 when the Senate debated a proposed balanced-budget constitutional amendment. Although Dorgan had voted for the amendment in 1994, both he and fellow North Dakota Democrat Kent Conrad made headlines by insisting that the amendment would have to be rewritten to include language to protect Social Security. Republicans would not agree to that, and both North Dakotans voted "no" as the amendment fell barely short of the two-thirds majority required for passage.

Other than a brief stint with a Denver-based aerospace firm, Dorgan has spent virtually all his career in government. He was working in the state tax department in 1969 when the governor appointed him state tax commissioner, making him the youngest constitutional officer in North Dakota history. By speaking out on an array of issues and suing out-of-state corporations to force them to pay taxes, he made a name for himself with voters.

Dorgan made it clear he had higher political ambitions by taking on GOP Rep. Mark Andrews in 1974. He held Andrews to 56 percent. When the House seat opened up in 1980, Dorgan won it in a campaign in which he tempered his liberal reputation by supporting an anti-abortion constitutional amendment and decrying government waste. After winning easy re-election victories, Dorgan took an open Senate seat in 1992, when Conrad announced he was retiring to fulfill an earlier pledge that he would not seek re-election unless the deficit was reduced. Dorgan easily defeated a Fargo city commissioner. He cruised to re-election in 1998 against his underfunded GOP foe by touting his success in winning aid for farmers and steering federal funds to North Dakota.

KEY VOTES

2000
Yes Overhaul bankruptcy law and increase minimum wage
No Limit fiscal 2001 discretionary spending to $600.3 billion
No Override veto on nuclear waste disposal at Yucca Mountain site in Nevada
Yes Oppose effort to terminate Kosovo mission
Yes Include gender, sexual orientation and disability in federal hate crime protections
No Approve GOP plan to restrict use of genetic information by health insurers
No Kill amendment delaying implementation of an anti-missile defense system
No Cut taxes for married couples
Yes Grant China permanent normal trade status

1999
No Remove President Clinton from office for obstruction of justice
No Kill amendment authorizing state grants to hire teachers and reduce class size
Yes Require criminal background checks for purchases at gun shows
No Approve GOP proposal to increase rights of patients in managed-care health plans
No Block effort to allow farm and medicine exports to Cuba
Yes Allow study of tougher automobile fuel efficiency standards
Yes Ratify nuclear weapons testing treaty
Yes Prohibit national political parties from collecting "soft money" donations
No Remove barriers among banking, securities and insurance companies

INTEREST GROUPS

	AFL-CIO	ADA	CCUS	ACU
2000	75%	90%	46%	16%
1999	100%	95%	35%	12%
1998	88%	90%	61%	12%
1997	86%	80%	50%	16%
1996	71%	85%	38%	20%
1995	100%	90%	47%	13%
1994	75%	85%	20%	8%
1993	78%	65%	10%	23%
House Service:				
1992	83%	70%	38%	28%
1991	75%	75%	40%	25%

CQ VOTE STUDIES

	PARTY UNITY		PRESIDENTIAL SUPPORT	
	Support	Oppose	Support	Oppose
2000	90%	10%	90%	10%
1999	88%	12%	73%	27%
1998	87%	13%	76%	24%
1997	87%	13%	81%	19%
1996	84%	16%	80%	20%
1995	89%	11%	86%	14%
1994	86%	14%	81%	19%
1993	83%	17%	81%	19%
House Service:				
1992	79%	21%	25%	75%
1991	76%	24%	30%	70%

Rep. Earl Pomeroy (D)

CAPITOL OFFICE
225-2611; fax 226-0893
1110 Longworth Bldg. 20515

INTERNET
e-mail: rep.earl.pomeroy@mail.house.gov
web: www.house.gov/pomeroy

COMMITTEES
Ways & Means

HOMETOWN
Bismarck

BORN
Sept. 2, 1952, Valley City, N.D.

RELIGION
Presbyterian

FAMILY
Wife, Laurie Kirby; two children

EDUCATION
U. of North Dakota, B.A. 1974; U. of Durham
(United Kingdom), attended 1975; U. of North
Dakota, J.D. 1979

CAREER
Lawyer

POLITICAL HIGHLIGHTS
N.D. House, 1981-85; N.D. insurance
commissioner, 1985-93

ELECTION RESULTS

2000 GENERAL

Earl Pomeroy (D)	151,173	52.9%
John Dorso (R)	127,251	44.6%
Jan Shelver (I)	4,731	1.7%

2000 PRIMARY

Earl Pomeroy (D)	unopposed

1998 GENERAL

Earl Pomeroy (D)	119,668	56.2%
Kevin Cramer (R)	87,511	41.1%
Kenneth R. Loughead (I)	5,709	2.7%

PREVIOUS WINNING PERCENTAGES
1996 (55%); 1994 (52%); 1992 (57%)

Elected 1992; 5th term

As the junior member of a trio of Democratic lawmakers who represent a state that has voted Republican in presidential elections for the past 35 years, Pomeroy holds his own in defending traditional Democratic values, using thoughtful, policy-wonkish arguments that are not readily captured in quotable, sound-bite snippets.

An attorney who served four years in the state legislature and eight as state insurance commissioner, Pomeroy understands the details of such complicated matters as pension law and Social Security. With a seat on the Ways and Means Committee in the 107th Congress, he is in a position to put that expertise to use.

But Pomeroy is also well-grounded in issues that are important to North Dakotans — agriculture and rural economic development. He grew up in a small town where his father ran a feed-and-fertilizer store and where he and his brother raised chickens on the family's small farm to make a few extra dollars. "I learned early on ... when farmers did well, we did well," he told The Hill newspaper. "And when they didn't do well, we didn't do well at all."

Agriculture, led by production of durum wheat (used for pasta), accounts for about half of North Dakota's economy, and Pomeroy was able to look out for farm interests from a seat on the Agriculture Committee, where he served during his first four terms before moving to Ways and Means. He favors liberalized trade laws to open foreign markets to farm exports, and he wants the GOP-drafted 1996 farm law rewritten to provide a better safety net for farmers.

Pomeroy opposes the use of embargoes on food exports as part of economic sanctions leveled against unfriendly countries. "Food should not be used as a weapon and farmers should not be used as fodder in international disputes," he says. In past years, to show his displeasure at what he said were inadequate administration efforts to guard against unfair imports of Canadian wheat, Pomeroy withheld his support for trade agreements. In 2000, however, he voted for the bill to grant China permanent normal trade status.

Rural lawmakers revived the defunct Rural Caucus in 2000, and Pomeroy was named one of the co-chairmen. He declared that "farmers and rural communities have been left behind in today's economic prosperity." That is particularly true in North Dakota, where the population in 2000 was less than it was in 1920, and where officials are trying to reverse, or at least slow down, the drain of young people to other states.

Pomeroy has a moderate voting record, backing his party about four-fifths of the time. He voted to ban on procedure its opponents call "partial birth" abortion, he supports gun owners' rights, and he usually backs frugal fiscal policies. He has voted for a conservative Democratic budget alternative every year that one has been offered.

Pomeroy is a bit more conservative than the senators from North Dakota, Kent Conrad and Byron L. Dorgan, but he shares the same serious, scholarly mien. The three men have a relationship that dates back to 1974, when Pomeroy was just out of college. That year, when Dorgan ran for the House, Conrad was his campaign manager and Pomeroy was a driver.

Pomeroy's years as insurance commissioner gave him expertise in a complex subject that is useful in Washington. He has taken the lead on the broad issue of retirement security, which includes personal savings, estate taxes, pensions, and Social Security.

Though Pomeroy is mild-mannered, he was quick to rush to the aid of three Clinton administration officials when a deranged man disrupted a hearing in early 2000. The man broke a glass bottle and waved the jagged piece around, apparently threatening to commit suicide, but standing close to the witness table where Agriculture Secretary Dan Glickman, Commerce Secretary William M. Daley and Trade Representative Charlene Barshefsky were seated. While most onlookers were stunned, Pomeroy dashed from his seat at the dais and, using his experience as a high school wrestler, helped subdue the man.

Pomeroy's demeanor is polite and self-deprecating. He says his parents instilled in him a sense of civic duty that was reinforced by missionary work in the South on behalf of the Methodist Church. His father died when he was a teenager, and the family relied on Social Security survivor's benefits to help him go to college — an experience Pomeroy recounts during debates over how to preserve the Social Security system.

Only a year out of law school, Pomeroy at age 28 bucked the 1980 Reagan Republican landslide and won election to North Dakota's state House. After two terms in the legislature, he moved on to the insurance commissioner's post in 1984.

In 1992, Pomeroy was wrapping up his second term as insurance commissioner, and he and his wife were making plans to move to Russia to work in the Peace Corps. He had long been interested in international affairs, inspired by a summer in Yugoslavia and a year as a student in England. But on the day of the state Democratic convention, the couple set aside their dreams of cultural exploration abroad.

Two days earlier, a political scramble had been touched off when Conrad announced that he was retiring from the Senate rather than renege on a 1986 campaign promise not to seek re-election unless the deficit was reduced. Dorgan, the state's six-term House member, jumped into the race to succeed him, leaving his House seat open. Hours before the nominations were to begin, Pomeroy accepted party entreaties to run for Dorgan's seat. (Conrad later ran for North Dakota's other Senate seat after Democrat Quentin N. Burdick died in September.)

North Dakotans displayed their usual penchant for split-ticket voting in November — casting ballots for GOP candidates for president, governor and most state legislative officers, but voting for Democrats Dorgan and Pomeroy for Congress. Pomeroy has had two close calls since then, in 1994, when his margin in that big Republican year was only 7 percentage points, and in 2000, when he defeated state Senate Majority Leader John Dorso by just 8 points.

KEY VOTES

2000

Yes	Raise hourly minimum wage by $1 over two years
No	Halt funding for U.S. mission in Kosovo unless European nations pay more
Yes	Provide Medicare benefits to military retirees and their dependents
Yes	Grant China permanent normal trade status
No	Phase out estate, gift and trust taxes
No	Prohibit implementation of president's national monument designations
No	Approve GOP plan to provide prescription drug coverage for Medicare beneficiaries
Yes	Increase help for poor nations indebted to international financial institutions

1999

Yes	Impose steel import quotas
No	Kill proposal to take aviation trust funds off budget
No	Require background checks on buyers only at gun shows with 10 or more vendors
Yes	Remove barriers among banking, securities and insurance companies
Yes	Authorize state grants to hire teachers and reduce class size
Yes	Overhaul campaign finance law; ban "soft money" and restrict advocacy advertising
Yes	Approve bipartisan plan to increase rights of patients in managed-care health plans

INTEREST GROUPS

	AFL-CIO	ADA	CCUS	ACU
2000	90%	85%	57%	8%
1999	78%	85%	44%	12%
1998	100%	90%	50%	21%
1997	88%	70%	60%	38%

CQ VOTE STUDIES

	PARTY UNITY		PRESIDENTIAL SUPPORT	
	Support	Oppose	Support	Oppose
2000	88%	12%	85%	15%
1999	80%	20%	73%	27%
1998	80%	20%	75%	25%
1997	78%	22%	71%	29%

NORTH DAKOTA
At Large

North Dakota includes fertile eastern Red River farmlands, wheat-covered plains, arid grasslands farther west, the Badlands and Teddy Roosevelt's beloved ranches near the western border.

The state's agriculture-based economy was shaken in the 1990s by floods, blizzards, foreign competition and the reduction of federal support systems. In 1997, agricultural income dropped drastically in the wake of devastating Red River floods and steep declines in the price of wheat. Economic trends intensified a migration of the state's young people away from rural farming communities and into the cities of Fargo and Grand Forks, where a diversified economy and several universities provide greater job choice.

Democrats have represented North Dakota in the House since 1981, and the state's congressional delegation was entirely Democratic in the 1990s. But prior to then, the state had elected only three Democratic representatives in 90 years and had supported only three Democratic presidents in the 20th century. Republicans are more numerous and unwavering in the western part of the state, while eastern communities and American Indian reservations are more supportive of Democrats. But Republican roots are strong throughout the state – the state legislature and governorship are GOP-controlled and President Bush handily carried the state in 2000.

MAJOR INDUSTRY
Agriculture, health care, higher education

MILITARY
Minot Air Force Base, 4,500 military, 1,200 civilian; Grand Forks Air Force Base, 2,618 military, 306 civilian (1999)

CITIES
Fargo, 88,128; Bismarck, 55,109; Grand Forks, 45,967; Minot, 35,673

UNUSUAL FEATURES
Lewis and Clark met Sakagawea, the Shoshone Indian woman who guided them to the Pacific Ocean, near the Mandan Indian village; Sitting Bull surrendered and spent two years imprisoned at Fort Buford; Gen. George Custer's home near Bismarck; World's largest concrete buffalo in Jamestown.

Gov. Bob Taft (R)

First elected: 1998
Length of term: 4 years
Term expires: 1/03
Salary: $126,496
Phone: (614) 466-3555
Hometown: Hilliard
Born: Jan. 8, 1942; Boston, Mass.
Religion: Methodist
Family: Wife, Hope Taft; one child
Education: Yale U., B.A. 1963; Princeton U., M.A. 1967; U. of Cincinnati, J.D. 1976
Career: State budget officer; U.S. State Department employee
Political highlights: Ohio House, 1976-80; Hamilton County Commission 1981-90; Ohio secretary of state, 1991-99

Election results:

1998 GENERAL

Bob Taft (R)	1,678,721	50.0%
Lee Fisher (D)	1,498,956	44.7%
John R. Mitchel (REF)	111,468	3.3%
Zanna Feitler (NL)	65,068	1.9%

Lt. Gov. Maureen O'Connor (R)

First elected: 1998
Length of term: 4 years
Term expires: 1/03
Salary: $66,306; but instead takes $116,563 from her other job as director of the Department of Public Safety
Phone: (614) 466-3396

STATE LEGISLATURE

General Assembly: Meets January-June in even-numbered years; January-July in odd-numbered years
House: 99 members, 2-year terms
2001 breakdown: 59R, 40D; 75 men, 24 women
Salary: $51,674
Phone: (614) 466-3357
Senate: 33 members, 4-year terms
2001 breakdown: 21R, 12D; 29 men, 4 women
Salary: $51,674
Phone: (614) 466-4900

STATE TERM LIMITS

Governor: 2 terms
Senate: 2 terms
House: 4 terms

URBAN STATISTICS

CITY	POPULATION
Columbus	671,247
Cleveland	501,662
Cincinnati	330,914
Toledo	307,946
Akron	211,822

REGISTERED VOTERS

Voters do not register by party.

POPULATION

2000 population	11,353,140
1990 population	10,847,115
Percent change	+4.7%
Rank among states	7
Median age	35.6
Born in state	74%
Foreign born	2%
Urban/rural	74%/26%
Crime rate	435/100,000
Poverty level	11.2%
Federal workers	83,126
Military	36,706

REAPPORTIONMENT

Ohio lost one House seat in reapportionment, dropping from 19 districts to 18. The state legislature will draw new district lines in 2001.

MISCELLANEOUS

Web: www.state.oh.us
Capital: Columbus
Land area: 40,953 sq. miles
Rank among states: 35
STATE ELECTION OFFICIAL
(614) 466-2585
DEMOCRATIC HEADQUARTERS
(614) 221-6563
REPUBLICAN HEADQUARTERS
(614) 228-2481

District Statistics

DIST.	VOTE FOR PRESIDENT 2000 D	2000 R	GREEN	1996 D	1996 R	REF	1992 D	1992 R	I	WHT	BLK	ASIAN	HISP	HOUSEHOLD INCOME	OVER 65+	UNDER 18	COLLEGE EDUCATION
1	50%	47%	2%	50%	43%	6%	42.9%	42.8%	14%	69%	30%	1%	1%	$25,405	13%	26%	19%
2	32	65	2	34	58	8	28	53	19	97	2	1	0	$34,688	11	27	24
3	50	47	2	50	41	8	41	40	18	81	18	1	1	$30,083	13	25	20
4	35	62	2	37	50	12	31	46	23	95	5	0	1	$27,312	13	27	11
5	39	57	2	42	44	13	33	41	25	96	2	0	3	$30,117	13	28	12
6	41	56	2	45	42	12	39.7	40.3	20	97	2	0	0	$21,761	13	26	11
7	39	58	2	41	48	10	34	45	22	93	5	1	1	$30,364	12	26	15
8	34	63	2	37	52	11	29	47	23	96	3	1	0	$31,171	12	27	15
9	55	42	2	55	34	10	47	33	20	85	12	1	3	$28,856	13	26	16
10	52	43	4	51	36	12	42	36	22	94	2	1	4	$30,323	15	24	19
11	82	15	2	79	15	5	73	16	10	40	59	1	1	$22,459	15	26	18
12	46	51	2	47	45	7	40	42	18	75	23	1	1	$30,859	9	27	24
13	46	50	3	46	39	14	38	36	27	94	4	0	3	$34,725	11	28	17
14	54	42	3	53	33	13	46	31	23	88	11	1	1	$28,184	13	24	20
15	44	52	3	44	48	7	36	45	20	92	5	2	1	$31,020	10	22	27

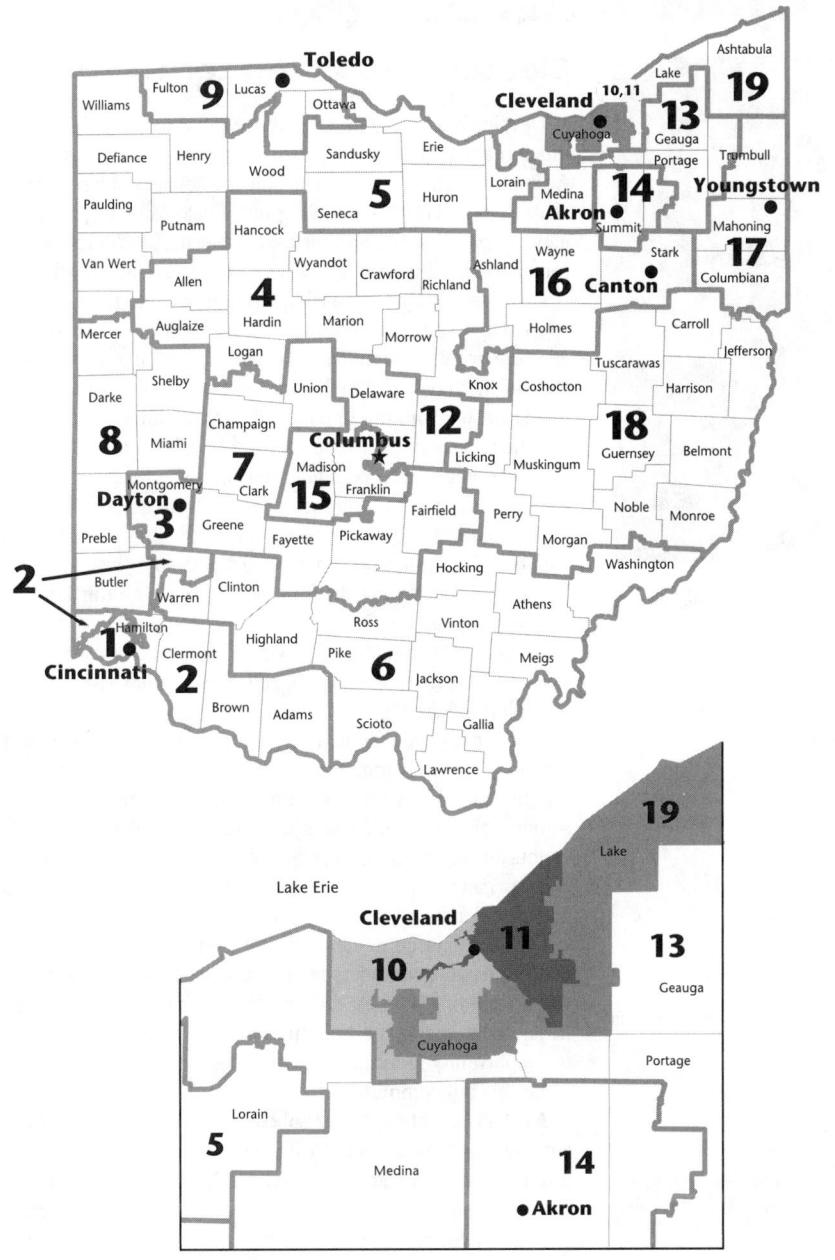

District Statistics

DIST.	VOTE FOR PRESIDENT									WHT	BLK	ASIAN	HISP	HOUSEHOLD INCOME	OVER 65+	UNDER 18	COLLEGE EDUCATION
	D	2000 R	GREEN	D	1996 R	REF	D	1992 R	I								
16	42%	54%	3%	43%	42%	14%	37%	39%	24%	94%	5%	0%	1%	$27,524	14%	26%	14%
17	58	38	3	58	28	13	50	26	24	89	10	0	1	$25,220	16	25	12
18	45	51	3	48	36	15	43	34	23	97	2	0	0	$22,808	15	26	9
19	50	46	3	48	39	12	40	37	23	97	2	1	1	$34,385	15	24	19
STATE	46	50	3	47	41	11	40	38	21	88	11	1	1	$28,706	13	26	17

Sen. Mike DeWine (R)

CAPITOL OFFICE
224-2315; fax 224-6519; 140 Russell Bldg. 20510

INTERNET
e-mail: senator_dewine@dewine.senate.gov
web: dewine.senate.gov

COMMITTEES
Appropriations
(District of Columbia - chairman)
Judiciary
(Antitrust, Business Rights & Competition -
chairman)
Select Intelligence

HOMETOWN
Cedarville

BORN
Jan. 5, 1947, Springfield, Ohio

RELIGION
Roman Catholic

FAMILY
Wife, Fran DeWine; eight children (one deceased)

EDUCATION
Miami U. (Ohio), B.S. 1969; Ohio Northern U., J.D.
1972

CAREER
Lawyer

POLITICAL HIGHLIGHTS
Greene County prosecuting attorney, 1977-81; Ohio
Senate, 1981-83; U.S. House, 1983-91; lieutenant
governor, 1991-95; Republican nominee for U.S.
Senate, 1992

ELECTION RESULTS

2000 GENERAL

Mike DeWine (R)	2,665,512	59.9%
Ted Celeste (D)	1,595,066	35.9%
John R. McAlister (LIBERT)	116,724	2.6%
John A. Eastman (NL)	70,713	1.6%

2000 PRIMARY

Mike DeWine (R)	1,029,860	79.5%
Ronald R. Dickson (R)	161,185	12.4%
Frank A. Cremeans (R)	104,219	8.1%

PREVIOUS WINNING PERCENTAGES
1994 (53%); 1988 House Election (74%); 1986 House
Election (100%); 1984 House Election (77%); 1982
House Election (56%)

Elected 1994; 2nd term

DeWine is a deliberate man whose legislative success usually comes after much reading and study. A lawmaker who actually reads detailed General Accounting Office reports, DeWine is known for diligently attending every class in law school, for pulling out a calculator to punch in numbers to gauge a bill's impact, and for asking his staff, "Will it work?" His wonkish reputation is enhanced by his wire-rim glasses and lopsided grin.

DeWine describes himself as "pragmatic and results-oriented." And he often gets results in an area that clearly motivates him — helping children. His concern for the welfare of children is behind much of the legislation DeWine has pushed, and that concern has led the usually conservative lawmaker to split with the Republican Party at times.

"There is nothing that impacts a legislator more than someone who comes to you with a personal, real-life experience," DeWine said during debate on his push to toughen laws on drunken driving.

DeWine's own experience includes the eight children he has fathered with his wife, Fran, who, if not the girl-next-door, was the girl-just-down-the-block whom DeWine called his sweetheart from third grade on. The two waited until Fran was 20 to marry so she would not be a teenage bride. Their third child, 22-year-old Becky, was killed in a car accident in 1993. DeWine said in a 1998 interview that he still doesn't know all the ways that Becky's death has affected him.

But he has devoted much of his career to such issues as drunken driving, mandatory sentencing, and adoption policy. He has long campaigned for tougher standards for legal intoxication, and in 2000 President Clinton signed a bill pressuring states to tighten the legal intoxication limit. DeWine counts among his biggest personal achievements a postage stamp encouraging organ and tissue donation. Becky's eyes were donated to two people after her death.

DeWine has cemented his hold on his Senate seat by pursuing a moderate-to-conservative agenda, and by winning funding for facilities in Ohio, including the NASA-Glenn Research Center. In the 107th Congress, he landed a seat on the Appropriations Committee, giving him an even better opportunity to funnel federal dollars to Ohio; he chairs the District of Columbia Subcommittee.

As chairman of the Aging Subcommittee of the Health, Education, Labor and Pensions Committee, DeWine in the 106th helped put together a compromise to reauthorize the 1965 Older Americans Act, which supports nutrition programs for the elderly such as Meals on Wheels. He continued his focus on children, teaming in 2000 with Sen. Christopher Dodd, D-Conn., on a measure that would require regulations to better protect children in medical research, and pursuing legislation to examine health insurance coverage of transplant-related anti-rejection drugs for children.

DeWine also won approval of a program to help courts identify mentally ill defendants. "Certainly, some mentally ill offenders must be incarcerated because of the severity of their crimes," he said. "But many others could receive appropriate care early on, reducing recidivism and unnecessary burdens on our police and corrections officials, as well as the mentally ill offender."

DeWine's involvement in issues affecting children stems not just from his family's experience, but also from some of the child-related cases that shook him up as a Greene County prosecutor in the late 1970s. He has successfully pushed legislation making it easier for states to get information about child-support payments, shifting the goal of adoption from preserving the family to protecting the children, and setting criminal penalties for parents who willfully evade paying child support.

His own child's use of an asthma inhaler convinced him that drug manufacturers do not know enough about drugs' effects on children. DeWine, who has asthma himself, also has argued that certain inhalers shouldn't be phased out for environmental reasons until there is a reasonable alternative.

DeWine's willingness to cross party lines on issues concerning children was most evident when the Senate in the 105th debated a comprehensive anti-smoking bill. DeWine successfully teamed with Illinois Democrat Richard J. Durbin to stiffen penalties on cigarette manufacturers who fail to reach goals for reducing youth smoking.

DeWine also weighed in on the perennial debate over campaign spending, as the Senate in the 107th adopted an amendment he authored along with Pete V. Domenici, R-N.M., and Durbin to increase limits on individual and political action committee contributions to Senate candidates facing wealthy and self-financed opponents. The amendment would use a formula based on each state's voting-age population to determine how much self-financing would trigger higher contribution limits. DeWine and Domenici argued that the proposal would help candidates of modest means remain competitive when they face extremely wealthy opponents.

Like many of his GOP colleagues, DeWine is a staunch opponent of abortion and voted to ban a procedure its opponents call "partial birth" abortion. In the 107th, he introduced a bill that would make it a federal crime to harm or kill a fetus during the commission of another federal crime.

DeWine is not reticent about seeking out liberal allies on certain issues. He worked with Wisconsin Democrat Russell D. Feingold on an Internet anti-pornography bill and with New York Democrat Daniel Patrick Moynihan on successful legislation to open Nazi war criminal records. His partnership with Democrats Paul Wellstone of Minnesota and Edward M. Kennedy of Massachusetts led to his biggest accomplishment in the 105th: a bill to consolidate more than 50 federal job training programs into three block grants to states while providing individuals with vouchers to pay for training.

DeWine's success in getting bipartisan bills passed made him a familiar figure at Clinton White House bill-signing ceremonies. He was present for the signing of bills facilitating adoptions, preserving the historic Underground Railroad, and overhauling Food and Drug Administration procedures — including giving drug-makers incentives to test medications for children, a provision DeWine had written.

Although he maintains a low-key profile, the Ohioan has never lacked drive or ambition. After law school, he worked as an assistant county prosecutor before running against his boss and beating him in 1976. In 1980, he won a seat in the Ohio Senate and, just two years later, won election to the House, where he served eight years. After becoming lieutenant governor under George V. Voinovich, he challenged Democratic Sen. John Glenn in 1992 but lost.

Undaunted, he ran again in 1994, this time for the seat being vacated by Democrat Howard M. Metzenbaum. DeWine faced political novice Joel Hyatt, a legal entrepreneur and Metzenbaum's son-in-law. Stressing his experience, DeWine won with 53 percent. With the victory, he seemed to verify an axiom of Ohio politics: You have to lose a statewide race before you can win one.

In 2000, DeWine cruised to an easy, 24-point win, over real estate broker Ted Celeste, younger brother of former Gov. Richard Celeste.

KEY VOTES

2000

Yes Overhaul bankruptcy law and increase minimum wage

Yes Limit fiscal 2001 discretionary spending to $600.3 billion

Yes Override veto on nuclear waste disposal at Yucca Mountain site in Nevada

Yes Oppose effort to terminate Kosovo mission

Yes Include gender, sexual orientation and disability in federal hate crime protections

Yes Approve GOP plan to restrict use of genetic information by health insurers

Yes Kill amendment delaying implementation of an anti-missile defense system

Yes Cut taxes for married couples

Yes Grant China permanent normal trade status

1999

Yes Remove President Clinton from office for obstruction of justice

Yes Kill amendment authorizing state grants to hire teachers and reduce class size

Yes Require criminal background checks for purchases at gun shows

Yes Approve GOP proposal to increase rights of patients in managed-care health plans

Yes Block effort to allow farm and medicine exports to Cuba

No Allow study of tougher automobile fuel efficiency standards

No Ratify nuclear weapons testing treaty

No Prohibit national political parties from collecting "soft money" donations

Yes Remove barriers among banking, securities and insurance companies

INTEREST GROUPS

	AFL-CIO	ADA	CCUS	ACU
2000	0%	10%	93%	80%
1999	22%	10%	82%	84%
1998	0%	10%	89%	64%
1997	0%	15%	80%	68%
1996	29%	15%	85%	85%
1995	8%	0%	89%	70%
House Service:				
1990	17%	17%	54%	83%
1989	17%	10%	90%	96%
1988	14%	5%	93%	100%
1987	13%	20%	93%	87%

CQ VOTE STUDIES

	PARTY UNITY		PRESIDENTIAL SUPPORT	
	Support	Oppose	Support	Oppose
2000	86%	14%	52%	48%
1999	84%	16%	38%	62%
1998	82%	18%	51%	49%
1997	81%	19%	62%	38%
1996	88%	12%	41%	59%
1995	87%	13%	30%	70%
House Service:				
1990	85%	15%	66%	34%
1989	89%	11%	71%	29%
1988	93%	7%	69%	31%
1987	83%	17%	71%	29%

Sen. George V. Voinovich (R)

Elected 1998; 1st term

After almost two decades as a government executive — including 10 years as Cleveland's mayor and eight as Ohio's governor — Voinovich is becoming acclimated to his role as one senator among 100. His job switch, he said, was akin to "going from being the orchestra leader to a member of the orchestra. And coming to the Senate, you're in the fourth chair, and sometimes you wonder whether or not your instrument is being heard."

Still, Voinovich (VOY-no-vitch) arrived in the Senate in 1999 as no stranger to Capitol Hill, having come to know many of his congressional contemporaries — and many of the byzantine ways of Congress — in his past life. "I've lobbied this place as president of the National League of Cities and chairman of the Governors Association," said Voinovich, who became Majority Leader Trent Lott's liaison to the nation's mayors and governors in the 106th Congress.

As he reached the midpoint of his first term, he had developed a reputation for moderation and alliance-building, an approach well-suited for thriving in the 50-50 Senate. Voinovich is seen as a mainstream Republican, but he has a history of breaking with his GOP colleagues, including on two top-tier issues — taxes and U.S. policy in the Balkans. That independent streak has threatened to leave him outside the deal-making process on occasion.

Voinovich was elected to the Senate in 1998 on a platform that included criticism of the Republicans' plans to cut taxes by tapping into projected budget surpluses, which he said should first be used to pay down the national debt and shore up Social Security. During the 106th Congress, his voting record consistently matched his campaign rhetoric. He was one of just two GOP senators to vote against a $792 billion, 10-year tax cut in 1999.

In 2000, he was one of two Republicans to oppose the Senate's initial budget resolution. He was one of four Senate Republicans who voted against a bill to end estate taxes and the only GOP senator to oppose a bill repealing the "marriage penalty," a quirk in the tax code that results in some married couples paying higher taxes. Those were not critical votes for the Republican Party, since it was always clear that the GOP could not overcome President Clinton's vetoes of the bills.

As 2001 began, however, Voinovich was the first GOP senator to publicly threaten to break with President Bush on his $1.6 trillion tax cut, putting the centerpiece of the new president's fiscal policies in peril in the evenly divided Senate. But Voinovich's long opposition to tax cuts came to an abrupt end in March when he urged Congress to clear a big tax cut retroactively as a way to ward off a possible recession. "If this economy goes into the dumpers and we sit here twiddling our thumbs, we'll pay a price for it," he said.

Voinovich also has displayed a maverick streak on Balkans policy. The grandson of a Serb, in his first year as a senator he took a politically risky stance as a vocal opponent of the NATO military action in Kosovo, which involved U.S. forces. He advocated continued diplomatic negotiations with Serb leader Slobodan Milosevic, saying that his own heritage had led him to conclude that U.S. efforts to isolate the Yugoslav president would only increase Milosevic's nationalist appeal. The view was unique in the Senate, where most opponents of the Kosovo mission were concerned with overextending American forces.

Voinovich's clout became evident after Milosevic was deposed in 2000. He enjoys a close relationship with Milosevic's successor, Vajislav Kostunica. While Voinovich is less demanding of the new regime than most senators,

CAPITOL OFFICE
224-3353; fax 228-1382; 317 Hart Bldg. 20510

INTERNET
e-mail: senator_voinovich@voinovich.senate.gov
web: voinovich.senate.gov

COMMITTEES
Environment & Public Works
(Clean Air, Wetlands, Private Property &
Nuclear Safety - chairman)
Governmental Affairs
(Oversight of Government Management -
chairman)
Select Ethics

HOMETOWN
Cleveland

BORN
July 15, 1936, Cleveland, Ohio

RELIGION
Roman Catholic

FAMILY
Wife, Janet Voinovich; four children (one deceased)

EDUCATION
Ohio U., B.A. 1958; Ohio State U., J.D. 1961

CAREER
Lawyer; state prosecutor

POLITICAL HIGHLIGHTS
Ohio House, 1967-71; Cuyahoga County auditor, 1971-76; Cuyahoga County Commission, 1977-78; lieutenant governor, 1979; mayor of Cleveland, 1979-89; Republican nominee for U.S. Senate, 1988; governor, 1991-98

ELECTION RESULTS

1998 GENERAL

George V. Voinovich (R)	1,922,087	56.5%
Mary O. Boyle (D)	1,482,054	43.5%

1998 PRIMARY

George V. Voinovich (R)	543,833	72.3%
David McCollough (R)	208,011	27.7%

the differences on Balkans policy have narrowed since the arrival of a democratic government.

In the 107th Congress, Voinovich chairs the Environment and Public Works subcommittee that has jurisdiction over air quality and wetlands and Governmental Affairs' Oversight of Government Management Subcommittee. On each, his background allows him to speak with authority about the effects of federal policy on states and localities.

Some of his positions on taxes clearly are linked to his time as governor. He has opposed Republican attempts to reduce federal gasoline taxes, saying they are needed to finance road-building back home. And he is a leader in the effort to craft legislation that would allow states to try to boost their collection of sales taxes on Internet transactions.

Voinovich's views on education today also echo his time in Columbus, where he was a strong believer in transferring federal power to the states. Now, he wants to weed out federal programs that duplicate state and local efforts, and he has sought to give states the flexibility to spend federal education money with fewer strings attached.

In his first two years in Congress, Voinovich worked to keep the federal government from claiming part of the $246 billion settlement agreed on by the states and the tobacco industry as compensation for smoking-related health care costs. He also helped craft a 1999 law allowing District of Columbia high school graduates to pay in-state tuition at any public college in the United States.

A white Republican from Cleveland's largely black and ethnic East Side, Voinovich is proficient at reaching across political, class and racial lines. He ranks among the more popular Ohio governors of the 20th century, winning acclaim for putting the state on a solid financial footing. A self-described management wonk, he is known for a detail-oriented approach to his work, and his personal frugality is legendary.

Despite his reputation as a moderate who is popular with Democrats, Voinovich does not always win bipartisan approval. As governor, he clashed with some traditional Democratic constituencies, drawing fire from environmentalists over air pollution standards and battling with labor leaders over a plan to overhaul the state workers' compensation system. A Roman Catholic, he aligns himself with social conservatives on issues such as abortion.

Voinovich's long climb up the governmental ladder began with a brief stint in the early 1960s as a state assistant attorney general. After serving in the state House and as auditor for Cuyahoga County, which encompasses Cleveland, he was elected lieutenant governor in 1978. The next year, he unseated Mayor Dennis J. Kucinich (now an Ohio congressman) after Cleveland's financial default. With the help of a financial control board, Voinovich reversed some of the city's problems and demonstrated his independence, as a critic of the Reagan administration's attacks on urban aid.

Voinovich's initial Senate bid failed miserably; he lost a highly promoted 1988 race to unseat Democratic Sen. Howard M. Metzenbaum, by 14 percentage points. But Voinovich rebounded two years later, defeating Ohio Attorney General Anthony Celebrezze to succeed Democrat Richard F. Celeste as governor.

In 1998, the timing was precisely right when Democratic Sen. John Glenn retired. Voinovich was immediately called the presumptive successor. He was not seriously challenged for the GOP nomination — although 27 percent of the primary vote went to a political unknown, and on primary day, a Voinovich initiative to raise sales taxes for education and property tax relief failed by a 4-1 ratio. In the general election, Voinovich won by 13 points over Mary O. Boyle, a former Cuyahoga County commissioner who had narrowly lost the 1994 Senate Democratic primary to succeed Metzenbaum.

KEY VOTES

2000

Yes Overhaul bankruptcy law and increase minimum wage

Yes Limit fiscal 2001 discretionary spending to $600.3 billion

Yes Override veto on nuclear waste disposal at Yucca Mountain site in Nevada

Yes Oppose effort to terminate Kosovo mission

Yes Include gender, sexual orientation and disability in federal hate crime protections

Yes Approve GOP plan to restrict use of genetic information by health insurers

Yes Kill amendment delaying implementation of an anti-missile defense system

No Cut taxes for married couples

Yes Grant China permanent normal trade status

1999

Yes Remove President Clinton from office for obstruction of justice

Yes Kill amendment authorizing state grants to hire teachers and reduce class size

Yes Require criminal background checks for purchases at gun shows

Yes Approve GOP proposal to increase rights of patients in managed-care health plans

No Block effort to allow farm and medicine exports to Cuba

No Allow study of tougher automobile fuel efficiency standards

No Ratify nuclear weapons testing treaty

No Prohibit national political parties from collecting "soft money" donations

Yes Remove barriers among banking, securities and insurance companies

INTEREST GROUPS

	AFL-CIO	ADA	CCUS	ACU
2000	13%	10%	80%	64%
1999	33%	20%	82%	88%

CQ VOTE STUDIES

	PARTY UNITY		PRESIDENTIAL SUPPORT	
	Support	Oppose	Support	Oppose
2000	78%	22%	59%	41%
1999	87%	13%	45%	55%

Rep. Steve Chabot (R)

CAPITOL OFFICE
225-2216; fax 225-3012; 129 Cannon Bldg. 20515

INTERNET
e-mail: www.house.gov/writerep
web: www.house.gov/chabot

COMMITTEES
International Relations
Judiciary
(Constitution - chairman)
Small Business

HOMETOWN
Cincinnati

BORN
Jan. 22, 1953, Cincinnati, Ohio

RELIGION
Roman Catholic

FAMILY
Wife, Donna Chabot; two children

EDUCATION
College of William and Mary, B.A. 1975; Northern
Kentucky U., J.D. 1978

CAREER
Lawyer

POLITICAL HIGHLIGHTS
Independent candidate for Cincinnati City Council,
1979; Republican candidate for Cincinnati City
Council, 1983; Cincinnati City Council, 1985-90;
Republican nominee for U.S. House, 1988;
Hamilton County commissioner, 1990-95

ELECTION RESULTS

2000 GENERAL

Steve Chabot (R)	116,768	53.0%
John Cranley (D)	98,328	44.6%
David A. Groshoff (LIBERT)	3,399	1.5%

2000 PRIMARY

Steve Chabot (R)	unopposed

1998 GENERAL

Steve Chabot (R)	92,421	53.0%
Roxanne Qualls (D)	82,003	47.0%

PREVIOUS WINNING PERCENTAGES
1996 (54%); 1994 (56%)

Elected 1994; 4th term

A hard-line conservative, Chabot generally stays on the fringes of congressional action. But he cast off his normally low-key persona when the spotlight fell on him in 1999 as one of the 13 "managers" who presented the House's case for removing President Clinton from office in the Senate impeachment trial.

Chabot (SHAB-utt) has been recognized by conservative groups for his consistent anti-tax voting record, at times showing more zeal than House GOP leaders for reducing the federal budget. He has stuck by his initial campaign pledge to restrain federal spending, even in some instances when the money would have benefited projects in his district. His record on social, environmental and labor issues is similarly conservative. In 2001, he was a featured speaker at the annual anti-abortion rally in Washington marking the anniversary of the Supreme Court's *Roe v. Wade* decision that legalized abortion.

Chabot has fended off charges of being too far to the right for the politically competitive 1st District, which is the more Democratic of the Cincinnati area's two districts. Although he has won election by respectable margins, his percentages have gradually decreased, from his initial 56 percentage point win in 1994 to 53 percent in both 1998 and 2000. But Republicans in the state legislature are expected to redraw the district before the 2002 elections and make it friendlier turf for conservatives.

In Congress, Chabot generally votes the GOP line, but he has crossed GOP leaders at times. He was one of about a dozen members who called for Speaker Newt Gingrich to step down after the GOP's net loss of five House seats in the 1998 elections. "It was clear to me that the Republican leadership — and by that I mean Newt Gingrich —had lost its direction," he told The Cincinnati Enquirer.

In 1999, he denounced a budget agreement negotiated by Clinton and the GOP leadership, saying it spent too much money. In 2000, he voted against a pair of costly appropriations bills, even though they funded projects in his district.

Chabot does not limit his opposition to government spending to social programs. He is a leading critic of tax breaks and subsidies for big business that he calls "corporate welfare," and he repeatedly tried to slash funding for the Market Access Program,which helps U.S. companies promote their products in overseas markets. In 1995, he tried to cut funding for mass transit grants, even though local civic leaders, including the mayor, wanted to use some of the money to study a possible light rail system for Cincinnati. Chabot voted against a massive highway funding bill in 1998, saying, "This bill is so full of pork, it squeals."

Chabot also has supported proposals to terminate the current tax code and to require approval by a two-thirds majority of Congress to raise taxes. He is a leading advocate of legislation to prevent state and local governments from taxing purchases and transactions on the Internet. When the House in 2000 extended for five years a federal ban on imposing Internet access fees, Chabot unsuccessfully sought a 99-year extension. "It's time to slam those gates shut, lock them tightly, and throw away the key," he said.

From his seat on the Judiciary Committee, Chabot seeks to ensure that his colleagues' plans to toughen enforcement of crime and immigration laws do not grant too much new power to the federal government. In the 106th Congress, he teamed up with Democratic Rep. Patrick J. Kennedy of Rhode Island on legislation to limit the government's ability to collect DNA samples for a national database, warning that the practice could infringe on Americans' privacy.

In the same vein, he was one of four Republicans on Judiciary to vote in 1995 against an anti-terrorism bill, opposing provisions that would have broadened federal jurisdiction over violent crimes. Faced with a proposal in an immigration bill that would have required employers to call the federal government to verify that prospective employees are legally eligible to work, he labeled the plan "1-800-BIG BROTHER." He has worked to toughen prison conditions and shorten death row appeals. In the 107th, he took the helm of the Constitution Subcommittee.

He emerged as one of the harshest critics of U.S. participation in the 1999 NATO bombing campaign in Yugoslavia and the subsequent peacekeeping operations. "It is like a bottomless pit ... going back again and again to fund these wars and peacekeeping forces all over the world," he said.

When the Judiciary Committee took up the matter of Clinton's impeachment in 1998, no one had to ask Chabot twice to climb on board the effort to oust the president. During his presentation to the Senate summarizing perjury law, Chabot said of Clinton: "He raised his right hand and swore to tell the truth, the whole truth and nothing but the truth. Then he lied."

Toward the end of the Senate proceedings, Chabot surprised colleagues by acknowledging that he had voted for Democrat Jimmy Carter in the 1976 presidential election. "This decision stemmed from my profound disappointment over Watergate," he said. Chabot's statement was an attempt to sway Democratic senators to vote to remove the president.

A Cincinnati native, Chabot taught elementary school during the day while taking law classes at night. His political career began on the Cincinnati City Council. After two failed bids for a seat on the council, Chabot finally won in 1985. He fell short in a congressional bid against Democrat Thomas A. Luken in 1988, then won an election in 1990 to the Hamilton County Board of Commissioners.

Chabot launched his second congressional campaign in 1994 against incumbent Democrat David Mann, who captured just 51 percent of the vote in the Democratic primary because of his opposition to some of Clinton's fiscal policy proposals. Chabot, emphasizing his blue-collar beginnings and Catholic roots, campaigned on a platform of lower taxes, less government and change in Washington. With national trends strongly favoring the GOP, Chabot won by 12 percentage points. He has since survived repeated Democratic attempts to unseat him, including a spirited challenge in 1998 by popular Cincinnati Mayor Roxanne Qualls.

KEY VOTES

2000
No   Raise hourly minimum wage by $1 over two years
Yes Halt funding for U.S. mission in Kosovo unless European nations pay more
Yes Provide Medicare benefits to military retirees and their dependents
Yes Grant China permanent normal trade status
Yes Phase out estate, gift and trust taxes
Yes Prohibit implementation of president's national monument designations
Yes Approve GOP plan to provide prescription drug coverage for Medicare beneficiaries
No   Increase help for poor nations indebted to international financial institutions

1999
No   Impose steel import quotas
Yes Kill proposal to take aviation trust funds off budget
No   Require background checks on buyers only at gun shows with 10 or more vendors
Yes Remove barriers among banking, securities and insurance companies
No   Authorize state grants to hire teachers and reduce class size
No   Overhaul campaign finance law; ban "soft money" and restrict advocacy advertising
No   Approve bipartisan plan to increase rights of patients in managed-care health plans

INTEREST GROUPS

	AFL-CIO	ADA	CCUS	ACU
2000	0%	5%	76%	100%
1999	0%	10%	84%	96%
1998	10%	0%	83%	96%
1997	0%	20%	100%	96%

CQ VOTE STUDIES

	PARTY UNITY		PRESIDENTIAL SUPPORT	
	Support	Oppose	Support	Oppose
2000	94%	6%	21%	79%
1999	89%	11%	22%	78%
1998	91%	9%	27%	73%
1997	87%	13%	27%	73%

OHIO 1

Hamilton County – Western Cincinnati and suburbs

Nestled in Ohio's southwestern corner, the 1st contains about 85 percent of Cincinnati's residents. The city's more than 40 percent black population is critical to Democrats, who have been muscled out in recent years by the city's traditional conservatives – German Catholics – and a growing suburban base.

The district sits in conservative, middle-class Hamilton County, which it shares with the 2nd District. Its southern border, the Ohio River, serves as a major thoroughfare for barges laden with cargo, helping Cincinnati earn its reputation as a regional center of commerce. The city's diverse economy prevented it from suffering the degree of hardship that hit other industrial cities in the 1980s, although the region has not been immune to defense cutbacks. Aircraft manufacturing and machine tool-making account for a large percentage of blue-collar jobs. The city also houses the headquarters of major U.S. companies

and is a magnet for research and development firms.

Racial tensions bubbled to the surface in April 2001 when a white police officer shot an unarmed black man, leading to several days of riots downtown. Blacks faulted the mostly white police force.

The 1st's mix of Democratic city dwellers and more conservative suburban residents gave Al Gore a 3 percent edge in 2000, but has elected Republican Rep. Chabot to four terms. With Republicans controlling the state's redistricting process, some believe that the district might be redrawn to become more safely Republican.

MAJOR INDUSTRY
Consumer products development and manufacturing, service

CITIES
Cincinnati (pt.), 311,159 (1990); Forest Park, 19,240; Finneytown (unincorporated), 13,096 (1990)

UNUSUAL FEATURES
Talk show host Jerry Springer, former council member and mayor of Cincinnati; The Red Stockings – now the Cincinnati Reds – were the nation's first professional baseball team; The National Underground Railroad Freedom Center set to open in Cincinnati in 2004.

Rep. Rob Portman (R)

CAPITOL OFFICE
225-3164; fax 225-1992; 238 Cannon Bldg. 20515

INTERNET
e-mail: portmail@mail.house.gov
web: www.house.gov/portman

COMMITTEES
Budget
Standards of Official Conduct
Ways & Means

HOMETOWN
Cincinnati

BORN
Dec. 19, 1955, Cincinnati, Ohio

RELIGION
Methodist

FAMILY
Wife, Jane Portman; three children

EDUCATION
Dartmouth College, B.A. 1979; U. of Michigan, J.D. 1984

CAREER
Lawyer

POLITICAL HIGHLIGHTS
White House associate counsel, 1989; White House Legislative Affairs director, 1989-91

ELECTION RESULTS

2000 GENERAL

Rob Portman (R)	204,184	73.6%
Charles W. Sanders (D)	64,091	23.1%
Robert E. Bidwell (LIBERT)	9,266	3.3%

2000 PRIMARY

Rob Portman (R)	unopposed

1998 GENERAL

Rob Portman (R)	154,344	75.8%
Charles W. Sanders (D)	49,293	24.2%

PREVIOUS WINNING PERCENTAGES
1996 (72%); 1994 (77%); 1993 Special Election (70%)

Elected May 1993; 4th full term

Since he arrived in Washington in 1984 to join a top-tier lobbying and law firm, Portman's political star has been steadily on the rise. The onset of the new administration puts him in the constellation of advisers — both to President Bush and to the Republican congressional leadership — key to moving the agenda of the 107th Congress. Speaker J. Dennis Hastert has formalized that role, appointing Portman to chair meetings of the House GOP leadership and to serve as its chief liaison to the White House. Portman also secured a spot on the Budget Committee in the 107th.

The Republican leadership assignment bodes well not only for the GOP, which has come to rely on Portman's steady hand and intelligence, but also for Democrats. Portman has been one of the most bipartisan members of the Ways and Means Committee, where tackling the intricacies of the tax code has become his specialty. The main tax measures he sponsored in the 106th Congress — plans to increase tax incentives for retirement savings and to repeal a 102-year-old tax on telephone service — were cosponsored by prominent Democrats. He worked with Sen. Bob Kerrey, D-Neb., to overhaul the IRS in 1998, and Portman's chief tax aide once worked for the Democrats.

He knows the Democratic line so well, in fact, that he was chosen to play the part of Democratic vice-presidential candidate Joseph I. Lieberman during Dick Cheney's debate preparations in 2000.

During the presidential campaign, Portman served as a leading spokesman for Bush's proposal to establish private Social Security accounts for younger Americans. In the 107th, he has a key role in promoting Bush's tax cut agenda and continues to be a strong voice for trade expansion.

Portman's skill in navigating the Washington establishment is both obvious and well-practiced. He is often among the few members involved in final negotiations over Ways and Means matters, even though he is 14th in seniority on the GOP side of the committee. He earned his insider stripes through extensive involvement in both the executive branch and the big-money world of Washington's K Street corridor.

After graduating from the University of Michigan law school in 1984, Portman joined the prominent and politically well-connected Washington law firm Patton, Boggs and Blow. In 1988, he spent many hours volunteering for the elder George Bush's presidential campaign. The work paid off when Bush tapped Portman to be a liaison to Congress. He eventually rose to become director of the Office of Legislative Affairs.

Portman was back in his native Cincinnati working as a lawyer when the 2nd District seat came open early in 1993 with the resignation of GOP Rep. Bill Gradison, in whose office Portman once interned. He won a tight three-way primary against former Rep. Bob McEwen and home builder Jay Buchert. He cruised to victory in the general election seven weeks later and has had no trouble holding the solidly Republican district since. Portman's 2000 race drew attention when the Democratic challenger, Charles W. Sanders, was removed from office as mayor of Waynesville, in a recall election the same day he lost to Portman by 51 percentage points.

Public policy has long been Portman's primary focus, and the favorable impression he made on House GOP leaders upon his arrival on Capitol Hill earned him a seat on Ways and Means less than two years later. Portman quickly made his presence felt by winning enactment of a plank in the "Contract With America," the 1994 House GOP campaign manifesto. His measure, which garnered bipartisan backing, put some restrictions on unfunded federal mandates — costly requirements Congress imposes on state and local governments.

Portman has a talent for reaching across the aisle and compromising, when necessary, with those who do not share his conservative philosophy. This served him well in the 106th, when he teamed up with Benjamin L. Cardin, D-Md., on legislation that aimed to increase workers' retirement security by allowing them to set aside more money in IRAs. Although the House passed the bill by a wide margin in 2000, the Clinton administration and some Democrats protested that Portman's plan would disproportionately benefit the well-off. But he insisted that critics were focusing on "unrealistic scenarios," and the measure was part of the end-of-session GOP tax package. That bill died under the threat of a veto by President Clinton.

Portman also took aim at a 3 percent telephone excise tax first imposed during the Spanish-American War. His measure to repeal the tax, cosponsored by Robert T. Matsui, D-Calif., was passed overwhelmingly in the House, but it ran into a Clinton veto.

As Portman's stature in the GOP ranks has grown, he has taken on increasingly high-profile assignments. Appointed by Hastert to a task force on youth violence in the 106th, Portman called on lawmakers to examine violence in entertainment and to make it more difficult for teens to obtain firearms illegally.

GOP leaders tapped Portman, a stalwart free-trader, to persuade fellow Republicans to support legislation — eventually enacted — granting China permanent normal trade status. He argued that open trade would help liberalize China's domestic policies.

Portman's overall voting record is solidly conservative, and in some instances he has been more tight-fisted about spending money than many in his party. During debate in the 105th Congress on the $218 billion transportation authorization measure, for instance, he criticized the legislation for going beyond the limitations of the 1997 balanced-budget agreement. He told The Cincinnati Post that the bill was "a budget-buster produced by the same kind of inside-the-Beltway politics we were elected to change."

Portman is a bit of a policy wonk, but his eyes also light up when the conversation turns to a very different subject: whitewater kayaking. When he was a student at Dartmouth, he navigated the entire 1,800-plus miles of the Rio Grande, and he and a companion are believed to be the first Westerners to kayak China's Yangtze River. He told Paddler magazine he keeps his skills sharp by maneuvering his kayak in the House swimming pool.

KEY VOTES

2000
No Raise hourly minimum wage by $1 over two years
Yes Halt funding for U.S. mission in Kosovo unless European nations pay more
Yes Provide Medicare benefits to military retirees and their dependents
Yes Grant China permanent normal trade status
Yes Phase out estate, gift and trust taxes
Yes Prohibit implementation of president's national monument designations
Yes Approve GOP plan to provide prescription drug coverage for Medicare beneficiaries
No Increase help for poor nations indebted to international financial institutions

1999
No Impose steel import quotas
Yes Kill proposal to take aviation trust funds off budget
Yes Require background checks on buyers only at gun shows with 10 or more vendors
Yes Remove barriers among banking, securities and insurance companies
No Authorize state grants to hire teachers and reduce class size
No Overhaul campaign finance law; ban "soft money" and restrict advocacy advertising
-   Approve bipartisan plan to increase rights of patients in managed-care health plans

INTEREST GROUPS

	AFL-CIO	ADA	CCUS	ACU
2000	0%	0%	85%	87%
1999	0%	5%	92%	76%
1998	0%	5%	78%	88%
1997	0%	20%	90%	92%

CQ VOTE STUDIES

	PARTY UNITY		PRESIDENTIAL SUPPORT	
	Support	Oppose	Support	Oppose
2000	91%	9%	31%	69%
1999	89%	11%	30%	70%
1998	91%	9%	29%	71%
1997	90%	10%	31%	69%

OHIO 2
Southwest and eastern Cincinnati and suburbs

The 2nd includes a stretch of four counties along Ohio's southwestern border and extends north to hook a portion of a fifth. It is one of the most solidly Republican districts in the state and one with a distinct split between its suburban and rural elements. While Cincinnati's wealthy Republican establishment – including the Taft family – has had significant political influence over the years, the district's rural counties have considerably less political pull.

The 2nd includes about 15 percent of Cincinnati's residents. The majority of the district's vote is cast there and in surrounding Hamilton County, which is hearty Republican territory.

To the east, fast-growing Clermont County has become more Republican as it has edged closer to Cincinnati's metropolitan orbit, while to the north, conservative Warren County is filling up with Dayton-area commuters.

Economically, rural Adams County has suffered the most, with the third highest unemployment in the state. But the rest of the 2nd has remained strong. The economy revolves around light manufacturing and the retail and service industries, and the district's economic health has been boosted by construction around Cincinnati's downtown.

MAJOR INDUSTRY
Manufacturing, service, retail

CITIES
Cincinnati (pt.), 52,881 (1990); Norwood, 21,651; Blue Ash, 12,093; Reading, 11,218

UNUSUAL FEATURES
Underground Railroad landmark in Ripley: the Rev. John Rankin House, where Harriet Beecher Stowe is believed to have obtained ideas for "Uncle Tom's Cabin;" President Ulysses S. Grant born in Point Pleasant; The Serpent Mound, the oldest raised-earth mound in North America, built by the Adena people (800 B.C. to 100 A.D.).

Rep. Tony P. Hall (D)

CAPITOL OFFICE
225-6465; fax 225-9272
1432 Longworth Bldg. 20515

INTERNET
e-mail: www.house.gov/writerep
web: www.house.gov/tonyhall

COMMITTEES
Rules

HOMETOWN
Dayton

BORN
Jan. 16, 1942, Dayton, Ohio

RELIGION
Presbyterian

FAMILY
Wife, Janet Hall; two children (one deceased)

EDUCATION
Denison U., A.B. 1964

CAREER
Real estate broker; Peace Corps volunteer

POLITICAL HIGHLIGHTS
Ohio House, 1969-73; Ohio Senate, 1973-79; Democratic nominee for Ohio secretary of state, 1974

ELECTION RESULTS

2000 GENERAL

Tony P. Hall (D)	177,731	83.0%
Regina Burch (NL)	36,516	17.0%

2000 PRIMARY

Tony P. Hall (D)	unopposed

1998 GENERAL

Tony P. Hall (D)	114,198	69.3%
John Shondel (R)	50,544	30.7%

PREVIOUS WINNING PERCENTAGES
1996 (64%); 1994 (59%); 1992 (60%); 1990 (100%); 1988 (77%); 1986 (74%); 1984 (100%); 1982 (88%); 1980 (57%); 1978 (54%)

Elected 1978; 12th term

Known internationally for his humanitarian work, Hall's Capitol Hill colleagues call him "Mr. Hunger." As a leading activist on providing the poor with nourishment, he insists that everyone on the planet has a "right to food" and asks the United States to act assertively to feed the hungry and comfort the afflicted in places such as Ethiopia, Rwanda, Sudan and North Korea.

Hall travels extensively to developing nations — including Iraq in 2000 — to assess their plight and bring international attention to their needs. Sharply critical of his fellow lawmakers, he gave Congress a D+ grade in 1999 on nutrition issues because it "posted a miserable record of responding to the needs of miserable people in our country." Hall has twice been nominated for the Nobel Peace Prize by Republican colleague Frank R. Wolf of Virginia, who is in a Bible study group with Hall.

A born-again Christian, Hall's deeply held religious beliefs inform both his concern for the poor and his opposition to abortion and the death penalty. "If you sit back and do nothing, you've already lost," he told the Dayton Daily News in 1998. In the 107th Congress, he endorsed President Bush's faith-based charities program, in which religious groups would be eligible for federal money to provide community services.

Hall's interest in human rights dates to his two-year service with the Peace Corps in Thailand soon after his graduation from college. His image as a human rights advocate was reinforced in the 106th Congress by his proposal to restrict diamond imports from such groups as the Sierra Leone rebels who had killed and maimed thousands of people. "Whether Congress likes it or not, American consumers will not be a party to this blood trade," he said. His proposal won some bipartisan support in 2000, and he continued the effort in 2001.

Hall voted against a 2000 measure to grant permanent normal trade status to China, because he was concerned about China's human rights record. Hall said "this legislation is a dog, and it smells." Despite his pacifist leanings, he supported the 1999 air campaign against Yugoslavia, which he believed would relieve the suffering of refugees fleeing the forces of Yugoslav President Slobodan Milosevic.

In addition to his crusade to alleviate hunger, Hall is best known for sponsoring a resolution in both the 105th and 106th to officially apologize for slavery. Although President Clinton eventually expressed regret for the role the United States played in slavery, Hall believes that a more formal apology is warranted. He has faced scorching criticism over the issue from both whites and blacks, with some contending that an apology is unwarranted and others saying it is a hollow gesture. But Hall responds: "You have to do the first thing. I always felt the first thing was to apologize," he told The Associated Press.

An independent-minded lawmaker, he can work well across the aisle and will side with conservatives on such issues as abortion. In 1996, a group led by Hall asked for — and won — a key abortion clause to the Democratic Party's national convention platform that said, "We respect the individual conscience of each American on this difficult issue." Hall, who spoke at the convention, talked about "the needs of the vulnerable in our nation — the poor and the sick, the elderly, the children and the unborn."

Hall's name is so closely connected to international humanitarian efforts that he is sometimes criticized by opponents at home who assert that he neglects somewhat the needs of Ohio's 3rd District. But he reminds his critics that hunger exists in the United States as well. He has been active in a host of Dayton-area projects to find food for the hungry, organizing campaigns to collect food and raise money for community food banks, senior citizen centers and homeless shelters. He has also successfully boosted health care services in the Dayton area.

His work on behalf of his district also includes more-traditional efforts. Hall joins with Republican David L. Hobson of the neighboring 7th District in looking out for Wright-Patterson Air Force Base, which is the Dayton area's leading employer. He also won passage of 1992 legislation to establish the Dayton Aviation Heritage National Historical Park.

Hall's humanitarian agenda took a hit in the mid-1990s when the GOP took control of Congress and moved to curtail spending on social programs, including the welfare system. He won back some ground in the 105th Congress, when lawmakers voted to restore to legal immigrants food stamp benefits that had been eliminated. The GOP majority was initially against the restoration, causing Hall to observe, "The Statue of Liberty must be weeping." In the 106th, he cosponsored legislation that would have required states to track the effects of the 1996 welfare overhaul law.

In 1989, Hall became chairman of the Select Committee on Hunger, and when it was eliminated in 1993, he went on a 22-day hunger strike, losing 23 pounds but gaining intense media attention. He ended his protest after the Agriculture Department and the World Bank promised to call conferences on the hunger issue. His fast also led to creation of the Congressional Hunger Center, a nonpartisan clearinghouse that helps direct aid and develop policy.

Hall first made a name for himself as a small-college football all-star at Denison University, where he played tailback in the early 1960s. His father had served as Dayton's Republican mayor for five years, and the younger Hall continued the family's political tradition by representing Dayton in the Ohio legislature for nearly a decade, as well as mounting an unsuccessful campaign for Ohio secretary of state.

When liberal GOP Rep. Charles W. Whalen decided to retire in 1978, Hall was the clear choice of organized labor and the Montgomery County Democratic Party. Hall defeated Republican Dudley P. Kircher, a former Chamber of Commerce official, by emphasizing his legislative experience and calling Kircher the "voice of big business." Hall took 70 percent of the vote in Dayton and won narrowly districtwide. He easily won re-election throughout the 1980s.

In 1992, Republicans waged a serious campaign behind Persian Gulf War veteran Peter Davis, hoping to capitalize on Hall's 1991 opposition to using force against Iraq. But Hall took 60 percent, and he has won easily since.

KEY VOTES

2000

Yes	Raise hourly minimum wage by $1 over two years
?	Halt funding for U.S. mission in Kosovo unless European nations pay more
Yes	Provide Medicare benefits to military retirees and their dependents
No	Grant China permanent normal trade status
No	Phase out estate, gift and trust taxes
No	Prohibit implementation of president's national monument designations
No	Approve GOP plan to provide prescription drug coverage for Medicare beneficiaries
Yes	Increase help for poor nations indebted to international financial institutions

1999

Yes	Impose steel import quotas
Yes	Kill proposal to take aviation trust funds off budget
No	Require background checks on buyers only at gun shows with 10 or more vendors
Yes	Remove barriers among banking, securities and insurance companies
Yes	Authorize state grants to hire teachers and reduce class size
Yes	Overhaul campaign finance law; ban "soft money" and restrict advocacy advertising
Yes	Approve bipartisan plan to increase rights of patients in managed-care health plans

INTEREST GROUPS

	AFL-CIO	ADA	CCUS	ACU
2000	100%	75%	52%	21%
1999	89%	80%	25%	12%
1998	80%	75%	44%	21%
1997	88%	70%	50%	21%

CQ VOTE STUDIES

	PARTY UNITY		PRESIDENTIAL SUPPORT	
	Support	Oppose	Support	Oppose
2000	84%	16%	70%	30%
1999	76%	24%	71%	29%
1998	76%	24%	66%	34%
1997	72%	28%	64%	36%

OHIO 3
Southwest – Dayton

The 3rd encompasses Dayton and nearly all of surrounding Montgomery County. While most of Dayton's suburbs yield Republican majorities, the urban vote – driven by Dayton's black population and large blue-collar workforce – has kept the 3rd Democratic in most elections.

About one-third of district residents live in Dayton, a struggling city surrounded by better-off suburbs. These include the fast-growing and largely blue-collar suburban townships to the north, and GOP-inclined, white-collar suburbs, such as Kettering, to the south.

Once one of the state's most successful manufacturing centers, Dayton has suffered bitter economic setbacks. A torrent of departures has displaced its manufacturing base, and its landlocked setting has made further expansion difficult. Still, the 3rd's defense industry, centered around the Wright-Patterson Air Force Base, has had some success in attracting aerospace and technology research companies.

MAJOR INDUSTRY
Auto manufacturing, defense, service

MILITARY BASES
Wright-Patterson Air Force Base (shared with the 7th District), 8,270 military, 10,391 civilian (1999)

CITIES
Dayton, 169,338; Kettering, 57,156; Huber Heights (pt.), 38,686 (1990); Trotwood, 28,070

UNUSUAL FEATURES
Dayton Peace Agreement, ending hostilities in the former Yugoslavia, signed in 1995 at the Wright-Patterson Air Force Base; Dayton was the lifelong home of the Wright brothers, who designed and tested several airplanes at Huffman Prairie, now part of Wright-Patterson Air Force Base; Montgomery County has been called the "Cradle of Creativity" and claims to be birthplace of the refrigerator, the ice cream cone and the stepladder.

Rep. Michael G. Oxley (R)

Elected June 1981; 10th full term

CAPITOL OFFICE
225-2676; 2233 Rayburn Bldg. 20515

INTERNET
e-mail: mike.oxley@mail.house.gov
web: www.house.gov/oxley

COMMITTEES
Financial Services - chairman

HOMETOWN
Findlay

BORN
Feb. 11, 1944, Findlay, Ohio

RELIGION
Lutheran

FAMILY
Wife, Patricia Oxley; one child

EDUCATION
Miami U. (Ohio), B.A. 1966; Ohio State U., J.D. 1969

CAREER
FBI agent; lawyer

POLITICAL HIGHLIGHTS
Ohio House, 1973-81

ELECTION RESULTS

2000 GENERAL

Michael G. Oxley (R)	156,510	67.4%
Daniel L. Dickman (D)	67,330	29.0%
Ralph Mullinger (LIBERT)	8,278	3.6%

2000 PRIMARY

Michael G. Oxley (R)	unopposed

1998 GENERAL

Michael G. Oxley (R)	112,011	63.8%
Paul McClain (D)	63,529	36.2%

PREVIOUS WINNING PERCENTAGES
1996 (65%); 1994 (100%); 1992 (61%); 1990 (62%);
1988 (100%); 1986 (75%); 1984 (78%); 1982 (65%);
1981 Special Election (50%)

Whether on the baseball diamond or in the political arena, the gregarious but fiercely competitive Oxley is not afraid to suffer some bumps and bruises in the pursuit of victory. As a result, he is no stranger to winning in either venue.

Probably his most important congressional victory came at the opening of the 107th Congress, when fellow House Republicans chose Oxley to be chairman of a committee on which he had never served and expanded the panel's jurisdiction to include his areas of expertise: securities and insurance. He paved the way for his election as chairman of the refashioned Financial Services Committee by refusing to concede the gavel of the Energy and Commerce Committee to Billy Tauzin of Louisiana.

Tauzin was considered the favorite throughout their long rivalry for that chairmanship, and many others might have sought a way to save face early on. Instead, Oxley tried to raise as much in campaign cash for Republicans as Tauzin had done; he threw a 1950s theme party to compete with Tauzin's Cajun-flavored events at the 2000 Republican National Convention; and he refused to concede that Tauzin's nearly 14 years as a Democrat on the Commerce panel (he switched to the GOP in 1995) should count when the chairmanship was decided. A lifelong Republican, Oxley had sat on the committee since 1983.

When it came time to choose between the two, Speaker J. Dennis Hastert and other GOP leaders decided to give each an important chairmanship. Accommodating Oxley required the GOP to deny its longest-serving woman member, Marge Roukema of New Jersey, and a skilled financial leader, Richard H. Baker of Louisiana, their bids for the chairmanship of what had been called the Banking Committee. (To bolster Oxley's power on his new committee, four of his GOP allies were given special permission to serve under him on Financial Services while also keeping their seats on Energy and Commerce.)

The motto "To the victor goes the spoils" is one with which Oxley has long been familiar. He is one of the most unabashed defenders of many of the perquisites of membership in Congress. At his annual fundraising weekend in Vail, Colo., the invited lobbyists may ski at reduced costs but spend much of their time at social events. Oxley is often one of the best-traveled members, appearing frequently on the annual list of lawmakers who have taken the most trips paid for by private groups, and he offers no apology for those travels.

Though a tough competitor, he is also one of the more jovial members of Congress, known for his quick laugh and megawatt smile. He was a jock in high school, and many of his congressional colleagues know him through the many sporting events in which he still takes part.

Oxley became the manager of the GOP team for the annual charity congressional baseball game in 1999. A team mainstay for years, he retired as a player a few years after breaking his wrist so severely in the 1994 game — in a collision at first base with Democrat Sherrod Brown, another Ohio representative — that steel pins had to be inserted in Oxley's arm.

An avid golfer, he opted to tee off in California at the annual pro-am tournament at Pebble Beach instead of attending a retreat for House Republicans in Williamsburg, Va., in February 2001. Just a few months earlier, Oxley and Tauzin had set aside their differences to play in an Alexandria, Va., golf and tennis tournament that benefited a children's charity started by Rep. Deborah Pryce, R-Ohio.

Oxley is also a big basketball fan and shoots hoops in the House gym. He won the House free-throw shooting contest in 1998, hitting 47 out of 50 from the foul line, defending the title he shared in 1997 with Jay Dickey, R-Ark.

For the U.S. Chamber of Commerce and other business groups, Oxley's voting record is nearly as perfect. A solid fiscal conservative, he will now and then cast a vote with the Democrats. He was an FBI agent for three years after law school, and he sometimes has responded to calls for gun control. In the 103rd Congress, he voted to enact the five-day waiting period for handgun purchases. And he opposed an amendment to a 1996 anti-terrorism bill that stripped the measure of several new law enforcement powers.

One of the GOP's top lieutenants on the Commerce panel since the party took control of Congress in the 104th Congress, Oxley played a significant role in winning enactment of the 1999 law repealing Depression-era barriers to mergers among banks, insurance companies and securities firms. He also helped shepherd to passage a 1995 measure — one of just two enacted despite a veto by President Clinton — insulating companies from securities fraud lawsuits when they distributed erroneous but good-faith profit projections.

Oxley traces his conservative roots to his rural Midwestern upbringing. Born in rural Findlay, Ohio, he sported a flat-top haircut in high school and excelled in athletics. As a student at Ohio's Miami University in the mid-1960s, he recalls jousting with the liberal professors. Barry Goldwater's "The Conscience of a Conservative" and free-market economist Milton Friedman were important influences. "In college," Oxley said in a 1995 interview, "I became the class conservative."

While many of his generation were protesting the Vietnam War or participating in the social revolution, Oxley, the son of a county prosecutor, went to law school and signed on with the FBI. He later received a commendation for his role in a tense, high-profile arrest of two suspected bank robbers who were members of the Black Panthers.

In 1972, at age 28, he won a seat in the Ohio House. He got an opening to run for Congress in April 1981, when GOP Rep. Tennyson Guyer died. Oxley was an early favorite in the special election, but he had stiff primary competition and won narrowly. In the general election, he faced a tough Democratic candidate — state Rep. Dale Locker — but spent $275,000 to flood the district with ads. Oxley struggled to a 341-vote victory. A recount delayed his swearing-in for nearly a month. Oxley handily won a rematch in 1982 and has not been challenged seriously since.

KEY VOTES

2000

No	Raise hourly minimum wage by $1 over two years
Yes	Halt funding for U.S. mission in Kosovo unless European nations pay more
Yes	Provide Medicare benefits to military retirees and their dependents
Yes	Grant China permanent normal trade status
Yes	Phase out estate, gift and trust taxes
Yes	Prohibit implementation of president's national monument designations
Yes	Approve GOP plan to provide prescription drug coverage for Medicare beneficiaries
No	Increase help for poor nations indebted to international financial institutions

1999

No	Impose steel import quotas
Yes	Kill proposal to take aviation trust funds off budget
Yes	Require background checks on buyers only at gun shows with 10 or more vendors
Yes	Remove barriers among banking, securities and insurance companies
No	Authorize state grants to hire teachers and reduce class size
No	Overhaul campaign finance law; ban "soft money" and restrict advocacy advertising
No	Approve bipartisan plan to increase rights of patients in managed-care health plans

INTEREST GROUPS

	AFL-CIO	ADA	CCUS	ACU
2000	0%	0%	95%	81%
1999	0%	5%	96%	76%
1998	11%	5%	100%	96%
1997	13%	10%	100%	68%

CQ VOTE STUDIES

	PARTY UNITY		PRESIDENTIAL SUPPORT	
	Support	Oppose	Support	Oppose
2000	96%	4%	30%	70%
1999	89%	11%	28%	72%
1998	91%	9%	25%	75%
1997	89%	11%	35%	65%

OHIO 4

West Central — Mansfield; Lima; Findlay

The 4th is a solid block of Ohio Corn Belt counties. The land supports soybeans, corn, livestock and Republicans. Not one of the 11 counties in the 4th has supported a Democratic presidential candidate since 1964. Two of the three largest, Allen and Hancock counties, have backed the GOP national ticket since the Roosevelt-Landon contest of 1936.

Democrats have oases of support, but they are few and far between. Democrats can normally count on votes in Mansfield, the district's largest city, and in surrounding Richland County, which has a sizable black constituency. While those votes occasionally help a Democrat get elected to local office, they are rarely enough to swing the district in national elections.

Along with corn and soybeans, manufacturing is important to the 4th. While declines in the automobile industry in the 1980s and defense cutbacks in the 1990s caused economic hardships throughout some parts of the district, the 4th's three large auto manufacturing plants and small industrial companies continue to spur the economy. Findlay, headquarters of the joint venture Marathon Ashland Petroleum, is the 4th's most prosperous city.

MAJOR INDUSTRY
Agriculture, auto manufacturing, oil

CITIES
Mansfield, 51,326; Lima, 42,635; Findlay, 38,509; Marion, 36,362

UNUSUAL FEATURES
Lima was one of the original refinery centers for John D. Rockefeller's Standard Oil; Carousel Park in downtown Mansfield boasts one of the world's largest carousels; Gen. William Tecumseh Sherman lived in Mansfield; Neil Armstrong born in Wapakoneta, where there is a museum named in his honor; Marion was the home of President Warren G. Harding.

Rep. Paul E. Gillmor (R)

Elected 1988; 7th term

A state legislator who comes to Congress is usually regarded as having received a promotion, but Gillmor had to give up a good deal of power when he joined the House in 1989. He had served 22 years in the Ohio Senate — the last 10 of them as either minority leader or Senate president.

Because of that background, Gillmor knows that a legislative body can't have effective leaders unless it also has loyal followers. He has made a point of being one of the latter, reliably toeing the line laid down by the party's leadership and serving as deputy whip.

In the 107th Congress, Gillmor has moved into the echelon of leaders, taking the gavel of Energy and Commerce's Environment and Hazardous Materials Subcommittee. And he is one of four Energy and Commerce members who were also given seats on the newly constituted Financial Services Committee (formerly Banking), which was given some of the jurisdiction that had resided with the former Commerce Committee.

An Air Force veteran and graduate of the University of Michigan Law School, Gillmor keeps a low profile in Washington, tending to concentrate on lesser-known issues. He rarely draws notice in the national media and does not even get much coverage in Ohio. He is a solid conservative but not so ideological that he balks when party leaders say it is time to negotiate and compromise. Yet he will often wait until the final days before announcing his position on a hot-button issue.

In the 106th Congress, Gillmor focused on financial issues from his Commerce seat. He pressed for legislation requiring mutual funds to show the impact of taxes on performance results, contending that this would help investors identify the funds best for them. "It's very difficult to make an intelligent investment decision without it," Gillmor said just before the House passed the measure overwhelmingly. The Ohioan also played a role on a sweeping rewrite of financial services laws. He worked with Democrat Edward J. Markey of Massachusetts on legislation that placed restrictions on businesses selling a customer's financial and medical information.

Gillmor has taken aim at corporate gift-giving. He sponsored controversial bills in both the 105th and 106th to require corporations to disclose charitable donations. Business leaders worry that the measure could discourage donations, but Gillmor contends that shareholders should be informed. "This is an issue of shareholder rights," he said. "Whose money is it?" Gillmor's concern is that corporate heads can make donations to organizations with whom they have personal connections, even though such donations are not in the best interest of shareholders.

Like many in his party, Gillmor backed sweeping tax cuts in the 106th and opposed a bipartisan plan to give patients greater rights to sue their managed-care plans. A swing vote in 2000 on granting China permanent normal trade status, he ultimately backed the bill, contending that "open engagement" would lead to improvements in human rights conditions in China. GOP leaders can usually count on Gillmor to answer the call when they push measures to lower international trade barriers.

He also supported the GOP leadership when they reached a balanced-budget agreement with the White House in 1997, even though some on the GOP right felt it did not cut taxes and spending enough. And he backed continued funding for two big-ticket items targeted by budget-cutters — NASA's space station and the B-2 stealth bomber.

But Gillmor made a rare break with party leaders in the 106th, cospon-

CAPITOL OFFICE
225-6405; fax 225-1985
1203 Longworth Bldg. 20515

INTERNET
e-mail: www.house.gov/writerep
web: www.house.gov/gillmor

COMMITTEES
Energy & Commerce
   (Environment & Hazardous Materials -
   chairman)
Financial Services

HOMETOWN
Old Fort

BORN
Feb. 1, 1939, Tiffin, Ohio

RELIGION
Methodist

FAMILY
Wife, Karen L. Gillmor; five children

EDUCATION
Ohio Wesleyan U., B.A. 1961; U. of Michigan, J.D. 1964

MILITARY SERVICE
Air Force, 1965-66

CAREER
Lawyer

POLITICAL HIGHLIGHTS
Ohio Senate, 1967-89 (minority leader, 1978-80, 1983-84, president, 1981-82, 1985-88); sought Republican nomination for governor, 1986

ELECTION RESULTS

2000 GENERAL

Paul E. Gillmor (R)	169,857	69.8%
Dannie Edmon (D)	62,138	25.5%
David J. Schaffer (NL)	5,881	2.4%
John F. Green (LIBERT)	5,464	2.3%

2000 PRIMARY

Paul E. Gillmor (R)	unopposed

1998 GENERAL

Paul E. Gillmor (R)	123,979	66.7%
Susan Davenport Darrow (D)	61,926	33.3%

PREVIOUS WINNING PERCENTAGES
1996 (61%); 1994 (73%); 1992 (100%); 1990 (69%); 1988 (61%)

soring campaign finance legislation that would have banned "soft money," which are the unlimited contributions used for party-building activities and issue ads.

A social conservative, Gillmor opposes abortion and voted against a plan in the 106th to allow gay couples in the District of Columbia to adopt children. He supports the rights of gun owners, resisting efforts in 1999 to tighten restrictions on gun purchases. Gillmor also favors constitutional amendments to limit congressional terms and to prohibit desecration of the U.S. flag. He voted to eliminate the National Endowment for the Arts, preferring to issue block grants for the arts to states instead.

Gillmor is a proponent of GOP education initiatives. After introducing legislation in the 104th to create education savings accounts modeled after IRAs, he voted in the 105th to expand that initiative, as well as to let parents use taxpayer-financed vouchers to pay private school tuition.

Gillmor's dedication to parochial concerns was on display in 1997, when he went to bat for a local charter aircraft company, Griffing Flying Service, that was threatened by a proposed tax. And, as lawmakers grappled with electric utility deregulation, Gillmor — mindful of the Davis-Besse nuclear power plant along his district's shoreline — said efforts must not harm companies that haven't yet recovered the construction costs of such facilities.

Gillmor brags about a number of superlatives in the 5th District — world's tallest wooden roller coaster; world's largest ketchup, washing machine and baking soda plants. And he proudly notes that it is the birthplace of inventor Thomas Alva Edison. After several years of attempting to honor Edison, Gillmor finally won passage of a bill in the 105th to mint a special half-dollar coin in 2004 to mark the 125th anniversary of the invention of the light bulb.

Elected to the state Senate at 27, Gillmor served 22 years in that chamber, eventually wielding considerable clout as president of the Senate and as the highest-ranking Republican in state government. He lost a 1986 bid for the gubernatorial nomination, and two years later he decided to seek the seat of retiring GOP Rep. Delbert L. Latta.

But Gillmor's primary opponent turned out to be Latta's son, Robert, a 32-year-old lawyer. In a bitter contest, Gillmor towered over the newcomer in personal recognition, stressing his fiscal conservatism and successes in the Senate. But Latta campaigned aggressively, aided by his father's ready-made organization.

Despite his advantages, Gillmor won the primary by just 27 votes — the smallest margin in any 1988 House contest. He went on to top 60 percent in the general election, just as he has in every re-election bid since.

KEY VOTES

2000

No   Raise hourly minimum wage by $1 over two years
Yes Halt funding for U.S. mission in Kosovo unless European nations pay more
Yes Provide Medicare benefits to military retirees and their dependents
Yes Grant China permanent normal trade status
?   Phase out estate, gift and trust taxes
Yes Prohibit implementation of president's national monument designations
Yes Approve GOP plan to provide prescription drug coverage for Medicare beneficiaries
No   Increase help for poor nations indebted to international financial institutions

1999

Yes Impose steel import quotas
Yes Kill proposal to take aviation trust funds off budget
Yes Require background checks on buyers only at gun shows with 10 or more vendors
Yes Remove barriers among banking, securities and insurance companies
No   Authorize state grants to hire teachers and reduce class size
Yes Overhaul campaign finance law; ban "soft money" and restrict advocacy advertising
No   Approve bipartisan plan to increase rights of patients in managed-care health plans

INTEREST GROUPS

	AFL-CIO	ADA	CCUS	ACU
2000	0%	10%	80%	76%
1999	11%	15%	88%	80%
1998	0%	5%	100%	68%
1997	13%	10%	89%	84%

CQ VOTE STUDIES

	PARTY UNITY		PRESIDENTIAL SUPPORT	
	Support	Oppose	Support	Oppose
2000	91%	9%	32%	68%
1999	88%	12%	24%	76%
1998	87%	13%	29%	71%
1997	91%	9%	32%	68%

OHIO 5

Northwest — Sandusky; Bowling Green

The 5th is shaped like a big bow tie and runs from Ohio's northwest corner across to the middle of the state. At its center, forming part of the knot, is the university town of Bowling Green (shared with the 9th). In the district's northeast is Sandusky, a Lake Erie port and the district's largest town. The district is a mixture of fertile, flat farmland, limestone plains and small towns.

In the eastern counties of Erie and Sandusky, the economy's strength rests largely on manufacturing. Wineries and sugar beet production also are key features of the local economy, as is tourism around Lake Erie.

The 5th's western counties are almost exclusively devoted to agriculture and food packaging. Migrant workers who live in farm camps during the harvesting months help boost this district's Hispanic population to 3 percent, three times the state's average of about 1 percent, according to 1990 Census Bureau statistics.

Historically strong GOP territory, the 5th supported GOP presidential candidates in 1992, '96 and 2000 and support for congressional and state Republicans has remained solid. One of the few Democratic-leaning areas is Sandusky, a fishing market and coal port. Erie County casts the largest share of the district's vote, and its sizable blue-collar element occasionally pushes the county into the Democratic column.

MAJOR INDUSTRY
Manufacturing, agriculture, tourism

CITIES
Sandusky, 27,932; Tiffin, 17,991; Bowling Green (pt.) 12,929

UNUSUAL FEATURES
Cedar Point Amusement Park in Sandusky attracts 3.5 million visitors a year; Birthplace of Thomas A. Edison in Milan; President Rutherford B. Hayes lived in Fremont, and the Hayes Presidential Center is located there.

Rep. Ted Strickland (D)

CAPITOL OFFICE
225-5705; fax 225-5907; 336 Cannon Bldg. 20515

INTERNET
e-mail: www.house.gov/writerep
web: www.house.gov/strickland

COMMITTEES
Energy & Commerce

HOMETOWN
Lucasville

BORN
Aug. 4, 1941, Lucasville, Ohio

RELIGION
Methodist

FAMILY
Wife, Frances Smith Strickland

EDUCATION
Asbury College, B.A. 1963; U. of Kentucky, M.A. 1966; Asbury Theological Seminary, M.A. 1967; U. of Kentucky, Ph.D. 1980

CAREER
Professor; psychologist; minister

POLITICAL HIGHLIGHTS
Democratic nominee for U.S. House, 1976, 1978, 1980; U.S. House, 1993-95; defeated for re-election to U.S. House, 1994

ELECTION RESULTS

2000 GENERAL

Ted Strickland (D)	138,849	57.7%
Michael Azinger (R)	96,966	40.3%
Ken MacCutcheon (LIBERT)	4,759	2.0%

2000 PRIMARY

Ted Strickland (D)	unopposed

1998 GENERAL

Ted Strickland (D)	102,852	57.0%
Nancy P. Hollister (R)	77,711	43.0%

PREVIOUS WINNING PERCENTAGES
1996 (51%); 1992 (51%)

Elected 1992; 4th term
Did not serve 1995-97

House members typically keep close tabs on their constituents' views, but Strickland has special cause to weigh his district's concerns heavily: He has lost as many congressional campaigns as he has won, and a prior Washington engagement — serving in the 103rd Congress — ended with voters tossing him from office in 1994. Since narrowly winning back his seat in 1996, Strickland has established himself by luring federal dollars to impoverished areas of his rural district and curbing his liberal inclinations on environmental and some social policy issues.

The son of a steelworker and one of nine siblings, Strickland has an eclectic professional background. He holds a divinity degree and a doctorate in counseling psychology, and he has worked as a minister, prison psychologist, college professor and director of a Methodist children's home.

Strickland ran unsuccessfully for Congress in 1976, 1978 and 1980 before hitting pay dirt in 1992. That victory resulted in part from post-census redistricting that put two veteran GOP incumbents — Bob McEwen and Clarence E. Miller — in the same district. Strickland narrowly defeated the eventual GOP nominee, McEwen, who had gone through a tough primary and was damaged by publicity about his 166 overdrafts at the private bank for House members.

That was just the beginning of Strickland's political seesaw. After winning by fewer than 4,000 votes in 1992, he narrowly lost the 1994 race to conservative Republican businessman Frank A. Cremeans, again by fewer than 4,000 votes. He climbed back into the ring in 1996, winning a nationally watched rematch with Cremeans that was viewed as something of a referendum on the 104th Congress. Strickland's margin of victory was a comparatively luxurious 6,000 votes, and he has won by comfortable margins since.

Strickland hurt himself with voters by following a moderately liberal line during his first term. He supported abortion rights and voted for President Clinton's controversial 1993 budget, which raised taxes to cut the deficit. During a 1994 debate with Cremeans, he opened himself up to conservative criticism by saying the government might have to raise some taxes for universal health care, an idea he supported.

Even though he represents a closely divided electorate, Strickland is a reliable Democratic vote on a number of issues, including education and taxes, and he backs efforts to give managed-care patients the right to sue their health care providers. A staunch ally of labor, he voted against 2000 legislation granting China permanent normal trade status. He said the plan was "primarily being driven by large multinational corporations that have no particular loyalty to a country or a set of political, economic or environmental values."

However, Strickland sometimes breaks with his party in deference to majority opinion in the 6th District, which is an economically struggling and culturally conservative swath of Appalachia in southeastern Ohio. A case in point was his opposition in 1997 to tougher clean air standards proposed by the Environmental Protection Agency (EPA). "I've got to look at these kinds of issues in terms of 'What's it mean to the people that I'm here to represent?' " Strickland said. "If I represented a different region of the country, I would probably be tempted to take a different position." But since high-sulfur coal mines, a uranium-enrichment facility and other heavy industries are among the relatively few large employers in the 6th, Strickland cited "an obligation to try to protect my district" from stiffer EPA standards.

In the 106th, Strickland spent much of his time battling for a compensation package to help government workers who were exposed to dangerous levels of radiation while building the nation's nuclear arsenal. The issue resonated in the 6th, home of the Portsmouth Gaseous Diffusion Plant in Piketon, where hundreds of workers may be eligible for the benefits.

Such workers "played a crucial and sometimes overlooked role in winning the Cold War," Strickland said. "We now know that, despite their heroic and patriotic effort, the government and its contractors used their labor, exposed them to deadly substances and then avoided the truth when they fell in the grip of unexplained illness. ... We can never truly repay these men and women for their sacrifice, but this compensation package will ensure them some amount of comfort and dignity in their future years."

He has also followed his constituents' bent in backing a constitutional amendment to ban flag desecration, despite his irritation with colleagues "who try to solve every problem by changing the Constitution." Seeking a middle ground on what he calls "socially divisive issues," he has supported funds for family planning but voted to ban a procedure its opponents call "partial birth" abortion. Strickland opposes conservatives' efforts to end federal funding of the National Endowment for the Arts, but he usually sides with them in opposing gun control initiatives.

Drawing on his experience as a psychologist in a maximum security prison, Strickland introduced legislation in the 106th to prohibit the privatization of prisons. He warns that such institutions would focus on profits rather than safety. "Short of execution, incarceration is the ultimate expression of society's power over the individual, and it must remain the responsibility of the public," he wrote in a 1999 Washington Post column.

Strickland breaks with some Democrats on the Energy and Commerce panel (formerly Commerce) over tobacco issues. Concerned about the future economic prospects of the small-scale tobacco growers in the 6th District's Gallia County on the West Virginia border, he has voted against eliminating the federal crop insurance subsidy for tobacco. He also backs farmers on other issues, pressing his colleagues in 1999 to provide emergency drought assistance for growers struggling with low yields and depressed prices.

Strickland says he would not seek to serve in the House more than eight or 10 years, but he opposes a constitutional amendment mandating term limits, citing the electoral history of the 6th as proof that voters have sufficient power to affect turnover. "My district has shown that it is capable of making a decision to elect someone and turn them out and turn them back in," he said. "Why interfere with that?"

KEY VOTES

2000

Yes Raise hourly minimum wage by $1 over two years
No Halt funding for U.S. mission in Kosovo unless European nations pay more
Yes Provide Medicare benefits to military retirees and their dependents
No Grant China permanent normal trade status
No Phase out estate, gift and trust taxes
No Prohibit implementation of president's national monument designations
No Approve GOP plan to provide prescription drug coverage for Medicare beneficiaries
Yes Increase help for poor nations indebted to international financial institutions

1999

Yes Impose steel import quotas
No Kill proposal to take aviation trust funds off budget
No Require background checks on buyers only at gun shows with 10 or more vendors
Yes Remove barriers among banking, securities and insurance companies
Yes Authorize state grants to hire teachers and reduce class size
Yes Overhaul campaign finance law; ban "soft money" and restrict advocacy advertising
Yes Approve bipartisan plan to increase rights of patients in managed-care health plans

INTEREST GROUPS

	AFL-CIO	ADA	CCUS	ACU
2000	100%	90%	31%	12%
1999	100%	85%	20%	12%
1998	100%	85%	33%	32%
1997	100%	75%	44%	24%

CQ VOTE STUDIES

	PARTY UNITY		PRESIDENTIAL SUPPORT	
	Support	Oppose	Support	Oppose
2000	85%	15%	67%	33%
1999	84%	16%	63%	37%
1998	85%	15%	66%	34%
1997	83%	17%	70%	30%

OHIO 6

South – Portsmouth; Chillicothe; Athens

The 6th is an economically struggling and culturally conservative swath of Appalachia that encompasses some of Ohio's poorest rural areas. Taking in all of Ohio's southeast corner, the district reaches across to fast-growing Warren County in Ohio's southwest.

The 6th's poor but socially conservative population makes the district a battleground in congressional and presidential races. Residents want the federal government out of their lives on issues like gun control, but can be of a different mind when it comes to the economy. On the federal level, Bill Clinton narrowly won the district in 1996, but in 2000 President Bush was able to carry the 6th by 15 percentage points. Athens – home to Ohio University – is traditionally one of the state's most Democratic counties.

Many of the district's counties, especially those along the Ohio River in old coal mining territory, suffer high unemployment – approaching 13 percent in some areas. Among these is Scioto County, the 6th's most

populous, which also contains Portsmouth, the district's largest city. While Portsmouth's steel and bricks have long sustained the region, the district's economic linchpin is the nearby uranium-enrichment facility located in Pike County.

The economic picture brightens in the 6th's portion of Warren County, where Cincinnati bedroom communities were a center of growth for the state in the 1990s.

MAJOR INDUSTRY
Service, manufacturing

CITIES
Portsmouth, 22,996; Athens, 21,967; Chillicothe (pt.), 19,913 (1990)

UNUSUAL FEATURES
Portsmouth city flood wall known for its elaborate historic murals painted by prominent mural artist Robert Dafford; Opera singer Kathleen Battle, native of Portsmouth; Marietta was the first European settlement in the Northwest Territories; Wilmington claims to be home of the banana split – reportedly invented at Hazzard's Drug Store in 1907 – and hosts an annual Banana Split Festival.

Rep. David L. Hobson (R)

CAPITOL OFFICE
225-4324; fax 225-1984
1514 Longworth Bldg. 20515

INTERNET
e-mail: www.house.gov/writerep
web: www.house.gov/hobson

COMMITTEES
Appropriations
(Military Construction - chairman)

HOMETOWN
Springfield

BORN
Oct. 17, 1936, Cincinnati, Ohio

RELIGION
Methodist

FAMILY
Wife, Carolyn Hobson; three children

EDUCATION
Ohio Wesleyan U., B.A. 1958; Ohio State U., J.D.
1963

MILITARY SERVICE
Ohio Air National Guard, 1958-63

CAREER
Financial executive

POLITICAL HIGHLIGHTS
Candidate for Ohio House, 1982; Ohio Senate,
1982-90 (majority whip, 1986-88, president pro
tempore, 1988-90)

ELECTION RESULTS

2000 GENERAL

David L. Hobson (R)	163,646	67.6%
Donald E. Minor Jr. (D)	60,755	25.1%
John R. Mitchel (I)	13,983	5.8%
Jack Null (LIBERT)	3,802	1.6%

2000 PRIMARY

David L. Hobson (R)	unopposed

1998 GENERAL

David L. Hobson (R)	120,765	67.2%
Donald E. Minor Jr. (D)	49,780	27.7%
James Schrader (LIBERT)	9,146	5.1%

PREVIOUS WINNING PERCENTAGES
1996 (68%); 1994 (100%); 1992 (71%); 1990 (62%)

Elected 1990; 6th term

Known as "Uncle Dave" around Capitol Hill, Hobson has made himself an indispensable behind-the-scenes adviser to the Republican leadership, including Speaker J. Dennis Hastert. He also has won high marks from members of both parties for his easygoing personality and trustworthiness. Those traits are particularly useful on the Appropriations Committee, where he is now beginning his second term as one of the 13 "cardinals," or subcommittee chairmen.

Since 1999, he has run the panel that drafts the military construction spending bill, a measure that is rarely controversial but that nonetheless requires the chairman to mediate among dozens of members clamoring to bring home money for their forts and bases. On appropriations and other matters, Hobson often serves as the "fixer" in dicey negotiations, insisting that both sides come away with something of value.

Hobson arrived in Washington in 1990 with years of experience in politics and business. Not only had he risen to a leadership position in the Ohio General Assembly, but he had served as chairman of a financial services company and on the boards of a bank, an oil company and a restaurant concern. And, at 54, he was older than many of the other GOP lawmakers then starting their careers, giving him a different perspective than his younger, more ambitious and less patient colleagues.

His congressional résumé shows how much the GOP leadership has trusted him since his arrival. Appointed to the Rules Committee as a freshman, he won posts on the Budget and Appropriations panels as a sophomore and he was Speaker Newt Gingrich's personal appointee to the Budget Committee in the 104th and 105th Congresses. In that role, he served as a conduit between the Speaker and Ohio Republican John R. Kasich, the chairman of the Budget Committee who retired after the 106th Congress.

Hobson is regarded as a moderate, but that view has less to do with how he votes than with his willingness to accept compromise as part of lawmaking. He does claim membership in the Republican Main Street Partnership, a group of top business leaders, state government officials and moderate GOP members of Congress that works to "revitalize the political center in America" and "provide a means for those who share centrist values to shape political debate."

He was one of the last Republicans to make known how he would vote on President Clinton's impeachment in 1998, and his votes then mirrored the action of the House. He voted for the two articles that were adopted and against the two articles that were rejected.

Hobson supported Clinton 33 percent of the time in 2000 (the average House GOP score was 27 percent), although he voted with most Republicans 90 percent of the time on votes that pitted them against most Democrats (the average House GOP party-unity score was 88 percent). His few dissenting votes in the 106th Congress came on matters such as withholding authorization for Kosovo military operations, imposing steel import restrictions — an issue important to the significant labor interests in the 7th District — and allowing the Interior Department to spend money on the management of some federal lands designated as national monuments in 1999.

He broke with GOP hard-liners in 1996 when he expressed a willingness to negotiate with Clinton on a balanced-budget plan, rather than risk a government shutdown over the controversy. The next year, when Congress and the White House struck a balanced-budget agreement, he fought to keep lawmakers on that course. He voted against a massive highway bill that authorized more spending than the agreement called for and counseled against tax cuts that might endanger the plan.

A former member of the Ohio Air National Guard, Hobson says that in the 107th Congress, he will steer the military construction bill toward improving the quality of life of military personnel, a Bush administration priority as well. In the 106th, he got the Pentagon to reverse a new system for calculating off-base housing allowances when it became evident the formula was paying some military personnel too much for housing and others not enough. He also tucked $470 million into a supplemental spending bill in 2000 to improve American bases worldwide.

Hobson has a history of bringing money home, mostly to Wright-Patterson Air Force Base, much of which lies in the 7th District. In recent years, he has obtained money for more family housing and an upgrade of the base hospital and kept the Air Force's Institute of Technology on the base. He also worked to save Springfield Air National Guard Base from elimination.

In the 106th, he made a parochially difficult decision to back a move by the House to suspend production of the new F-22 fighter. (The project is managed at Wright-Patterson.) In the end, however, not only did the fighter survive but the complicated deal to save it produced an additional $94 million for technology programs at the base.

While in Congress, Hobson has continued to focus on health care issues, an interest he developed as a state senator. In the 105th, he was on a GOP task force that drafted legislation to help patients deal with managed-care health insurers. He also worked to require that military doctors have current and unrestricted licenses to practice, a move that came after the Dayton Daily News discovered some military doctors were working with revoked or suspended licenses. And with other Ohio lawmakers, Hobson convinced the Department of Health and Human Services to permit hospitals to continue restocking the supplies of volunteer ambulance squads that have brought in patients. Hobson maintained that many volunteer rescue squads could not afford supplies.

In 1982, a month after losing respectably in a state House race, Hobson was appointed to the state Senate seat that Republican Mike DeWine gave up in a successful bid for the U.S. House. Hobson's election to the House came eight years later, when DeWine (now Ohio's senior senator) ran for lieutenant governor. Hobson won 62 percent of the vote and has been re-elected since with ease.

KEY VOTES

2000

No	Raise hourly minimum wage by $1 over two years
No	Halt funding for U.S. mission in Kosovo unless European nations pay more
Yes	Provide Medicare benefits to military retirees and their dependents
Yes	Grant China permanent normal trade status
Yes	Phase out estate, gift and trust taxes
No	Prohibit implementation of president's national monument designations
Yes	Approve GOP plan to provide prescription drug coverage for Medicare beneficiaries
No	Increase help for poor nations indebted to international financial institutions

1999

Yes	Impose steel import quotas
Yes	Kill proposal to take aviation trust funds off budget
Yes	Require background checks on buyers only at gun shows with 10 or more vendors
Yes	Remove barriers among banking, securities and insurance companies
No	Authorize state grants to hire teachers and reduce class size
No	Overhaul campaign finance law; ban "soft money" and restrict advocacy advertising
No	Approve bipartisan plan to increase rights of patients in managed-care health plans

INTEREST GROUPS

	AFL-CIO	ADA	CCUS	ACU
2000	0%	0%	90%	72%
1999	38%	20%	83%	80%
1998	20%	5%	82%	88%
1997	13%	5%	90%	80%

CQ VOTE STUDIES

	PARTY UNITY		PRESIDENTIAL SUPPORT	
	Support	Oppose	Support	Oppose
2000	90%	10%	33%	67%
1999	85%	15%	29%	71%
1998	91%	9%	28%	72%
1997	90%	10%	33%	67%

OHIO 7
West central – Springfield; Lancaster

The 7th resembles a gaping mouth ready to swallow Columbus whole. Its nine counties surround Columbus, albeit from afar, on three sides. In the north, the 7th's rural counties – Union and Champaign – have been GOP strongholds for generations. The rest of the district, including Clark County and the city of Springfield, is more politically competitive but maintains a strong Republican presence.

Residential growth around Columbus has especially affected Clark and Fairfield counties, which serve as bedroom communities and are filling up with white-collar commuters.

Clark and its county seat, Springfield, suffered economically in the early 1980s but have seen a dramatic turnaround. New companies, including trucking and auto manufacturing plants and distribution firms, now call the area home. Elsewhere in the district, agribusiness and the defense industry contribute to the economy's strength. The Wright-Patterson Air Force Base in Greene County is the largest single-site employer in Ohio.

MAJOR INDUSTRY
Auto manufacturing, military, technology research, agriculture

MILITARY BASES
Wright-Patterson Air Force Base (shared with the 3rd District), 8,270 military; 10,391 civilian (1999)

CITIES
Springfield, 65,154; Beavercreek, 40,861; Lancaster, 36,714; Fairborn, 33,775; Xenia, 25,598

UNUSUAL FEATURES
Gen. William Tecumseh Sherman born in Lancaster; Modern combine, invented in Springfield, helped revolutionize harvesting and the agriculture industry; Bellefontaine home to the first cement street.

Rep. John A. Boehner (R)

Elected 1990; 6th term

CAPITOL OFFICE
225-6205; fax 225-0704
1011 Longworth Bldg. 20515

INTERNET
e-mail: john.boehner@mail.house.gov
web: www.house.gov/boehner

COMMITTEES
Agriculture
Education & Workforce - chairman

HOMETOWN
West Chester

BORN
Nov. 17, 1949, Cincinnati, Ohio

RELIGION
Roman Catholic

FAMILY
Wife, Debbie Boehner; two children

EDUCATION
Xavier U., B.S. 1977

MILITARY SERVICE
Navy, 1968

CAREER
Plastics and packaging executive

POLITICAL HIGHLIGHTS
Ohio House, 1985-91

ELECTION RESULTS

2000 GENERAL

John A. Boehner (R)	179,756	71.0%
John G. Parks (D)	66,293	26.2%
David R. Shock (LIBERT)	7,254	2.9%

2000 PRIMARY

John A. Boehner (R)	unopposed

1998 GENERAL

John A. Boehner (R)	127,979	70.7%
John W. Griffin (D)	52,912	29.3%

PREVIOUS WINNING PERCENTAGES
1996 (70%); 1994 (100%); 1992 (74%); 1990 (61%)

He gives the outward impression that he is simply happy to go along to get along, answering even the most pointed questions with a shrug or a nod as he puffs on an ever-present cigarette. Beneath Boehner's calm exterior, though, beats the heart of an ambitious politician and a formidable competitor.

Boehner (BAY-ner) entered Congress in 1991 and was one of the rabble-rousing Gang of Seven, minority party freshmen in the 102nd Congress eager to rein in — or at least rail against — what they saw as the excesses of the House that culminated in its internal bank scandal. Four years later, he was chairman of the Republican Conference, the fourth-highest position in the new House majority hierarchy.

With the fall of Speaker Newt Gingrich after the GOP's poor showing in the 1998 elections, Boehner also tumbled, losing his chairmanship to Oklahoma's J.C. Watts Jr. His opponents said Boehner was ineffective in articulating the House Republicans' controversial positions on issues such as the government shutdowns of 1995-96, but his supporters said he was simply a scapegoat for the GOP's inability to stick to a plan.

Unable to play the role of one of the party's public faces — which seemed to come naturally to the son of tavern owners — Boehner shifted tactics and focused instead on seeking legislative opportunities. As chairman of a subcommittee on employer-employee relations, he inserted himself into hot-button debates on health care and pension overhaul.

The tactic paid off. As the 107th Congress convened, he was chosen chairman of the Education and the Workforce Committee, defeating two tough opponents — the more-senior Tom Petri of Wisconsin and the more aggressive Peter Hoekstra of Michigan. Boehner happily settled for the gavel, despite his clear desire to return to the elected leadership.

But he got off to a rocky start when panel Democrats initially boycotted committee meetings to protest his plans to shift authority over historically black, Hispanic and Indian colleges to a new subcommittee. Democrats said the change split jurisdiction over higher education issues along racial lines. Boehner, who argued that minority schools would receive more attention through the new structure, eventually agreed to a compromise.

The chairmanship gives Boehner heightened visibility, as the panel has a lead role in turning President Bush's education overhaul plan into law. The job is also sure to highlight Boehner's almost religious allegiance to free enterprise. He and a partner built a small plastics and packaging firm — Nucite Sales Inc. — into a multimillion-dollar business soon after his graduation from Xavier University.

He says one of his proudest legislative accomplishments was enactment of the 1996 "Freedom to Farm" act — a sweeping overhaul to bring farm policy more in line with free-market principles. Boehner, whose district is mostly made up of corn, soybean, poultry and livestock farms, is the second-ranking Republican on the Agriculture Committee, where he continues to press for a more free-market approach to farming. And, despite the fact that the head of the world's largest dairy cooperative lives in the 8th District, Boehner has sought to abolish the federal milk-pricing system.

The congressman took on a major legislative task in the 105th, when his business contacts prompted Republican leaders to appoint him liaison to the financial services industry. He helped shepherd through the House a controversial bill to rewrite the complex web of laws that govern banks, stock brokerages and insurance firms, but the bill died in the Senate. (A revised measure was enacted in the 106th.)

In 1999, Boehner sponsored a version of health care overhaul that closely tracked legislation Republican leaders had pushed through the House the year before. It would have prohibited health insurance plans from preventing doctors from discussing expensive treatments with patients and would have created a new process for patients to appeal grievances. The measure did not advance, however.

In addition to focusing on scoring legislative victories after his leadership loss, Boehner kept up his record as a prolific fundraiser for the party and continued to maintain contacts with the business community.

A prime venue for communication with Boehner has always been the golf course. A low handicapper (three or four), he is as passionate about the game as he is skilled. He spends much of his free time in Florida, maintaining not only his stroke but also the deep tan he sports all year.

It was one such trip to Florida, at the end of 1996, that inadvertently led to a legal entanglement between Boehner and another House member. During a family vacation, Boehner joined a telephone conference call in which GOP leaders discussed strategy for dealing with their Speaker's ethical troubles. A Florida couple intercepted the call and taped it. They said they gave a copy of the tape to Jim McDermott of Washington, then the ranking Democrat on the House ethics committee. Excerpts were soon cited in newspaper stories. Boehner sued in 1998, alleging that his privacy had been violated. McDermott maintains that he was within his First Amendment rights. The matter is before the Supreme Court, which must decide whether to hear or dismiss the case.

The oldest of 11 children, Boehner put himself through college over an eight-year period through a variety of jobs, one as a janitor for a company at which his future wife worked. Boehner's experiences dealing with government regulations as a businessman sparked his interest in public office.

After six years in the state House, he was an underdog when he joined the 1990 GOP field against incumbent Donald E. "Buz" Lukens. Lukens had been convicted of a misdemeanor charge stemming from a sexual liaison with a 16-year-old girl, and former Rep. Thomas N. Kindness was favored to oust him in the primary. But Boehner, capitalizing on business and community support and outspending Kindness by more than 5-to-1, won the primary with 49 percent. In the general election, he swept every county, besting former Hamilton Mayor Gregory V. Jolivette, the Democratic nominee. Boehner has easily dispatched all opponents since.

KEY VOTES

2000

No	Raise hourly minimum wage by $1 over two years
Yes	Halt funding for U.S. mission in Kosovo unless European nations pay more
Yes	Provide Medicare benefits to military retirees and their dependents
Yes	Grant China permanent normal trade status
?	Phase out estate, gift and trust taxes
Yes	Prohibit implementation of president's national monument designations
Yes	Approve GOP plan to provide prescription drug coverage for Medicare beneficiaries
No	Increase help for poor nations indebted to international financial institutions

1999

No	Impose steel import quotas
Yes	Kill proposal to take aviation trust funds off budget
Yes	Require background checks on buyers only at gun shows with 10 or more vendors
Yes	Remove barriers among banking, securities and insurance companies
No	Authorize state grants to hire teachers and reduce class size
No	Overhaul campaign finance law; ban "soft money" and restrict advocacy advertising
No	Approve bipartisan plan to increase rights of patients in managed-care health plans

INTEREST GROUPS

	AFL-CIO	ADA	CCUS	ACU
2000	0%	5%	85%	87%
1999	0%	10%	92%	91%
1998	0%	0%	89%	96%
1997	0%	0%	100%	87%

CQ VOTE STUDIES

	PARTY UNITY		PRESIDENTIAL SUPPORT	
	Support	Oppose	Support	Oppose
2000	95%	5%	30%	70%
1999	93%	7%	27%	73%
1998	96%	4%	25%	75%
1997	96%	4%	26%	74%

OHIO 8
Southwest – Hamilton; Middletown

Running along the state's western border, the 8th is anchored by Butler County, home to the district's two largest cities, Hamilton and Middletown. Butler has long voted solidly Republican, but the expansion of its suburbs has escalated a rightward trend. The county is known for electing some of Ohio's more conservative state and congressional legislators. The 8th gave Republican presidential candidates solid victories in 1992, '96 and 2000.

About half of the 8th's residents live outside Butler County in a string of fertile Corn Belt counties. Corn and soybeans are the major cash crops here, and poultry and livestock also are moneymakers. While the more rural Darke and Mercer counties had been trending Democratic, both voted solidly Republican in 2000.

Overall, the district has seen significant growth, especially in Butler and Miami counties. Union Township, in Butler County, is one of the state's fastest-growing suburbs, and many residents here commute to

Cincinnati or Dayton. While bad weather and low pork prices hurt the 8th's dominant agriculture industry in the late 1990s, the district's strong manufacturing base, along with new construction and commercial development, helped prevent economic hardship.

MAJOR INDUSTRY
Agriculture, manufacturing, higher education

CITIES
Hamilton, 60,901; Middletown (pt.), 45,991 (1990); Fairfield, 42,242

UNUSUAL FEATURES
Hamilton once known as the "Safe Capital of the World" for the burglar-resistant safes made there; Darke County hosts an Annie Oakley festival each year in honor of their homegrown sharpshooter; Annual pork festival in Preble County features a troupe of racing pigs; The Great Outdoor Underwear Festival is held each year in Piqua.

Rep. Marcy Kaptur (D)

Elected 1982; 10th term

Nearing the end of her second decade in the House, Kaptur has reached several positions of institutional prominence. She is the chamber's senior Democratic woman and the senior woman of either party on the Appropriations Committee, where she has been the ranking Democrat on the Agriculture Subcommittee since 1997.

Still, her longevity has not regularly brought with it either influence or legislative success. Indeed, on two key issues Kaptur often finds herself at odds with her fellow Democrats. Unlike most of her party colleagues in the House — especially the women — Kaptur is not an abortion rights advocate and opposes using federal funds to pay for abortions. And her congressional career has been marked by a steady but often unsuccessful effort to prevent the lowering of international trade barriers. In both areas, her views reflect the concerns of Kaptur's white ethnic constituency, many of whom put stock in the Catholic Church's teachings on abortion or fear losing their well-paying blue-collar jobs to low-wage competitors abroad.

Kaptur is emblematic of these people. She lives with her brother, Stephen, in the same small house where they were raised, and she attends mass at the same church where she was baptized. Their parents ran grocery stores in Toledo and nearby Rossford and worked in local auto plants; Kaptur also was an autoworker to help pay for college. Although she is one of the first children of the Baby Boom, some of her domestic practices are from a bygone era. She maintains the family garden and cans some of the produce; she bakes Polish coffeecakes and makes Polish sausages at the holidays; she paints watercolors; she sews her own curtains.

From her seat on Appropriations, Kaptur engages in the familiar pastime of trying to funnel federal dollars home. Agriculture is Ohio's biggest industry, and as a reminder of that, she sometimes gives her colleagues samples of items — Hirzel spaghetti sauce, Heritage seeds — produced in the state. She also looks out for the interests of the sugar beet growers who are a major farming presence in her district.

She was a leading player in the campaign to save federal sugar subsidies when the current federal farm law was written in the 104th Congress — it is set for reauthorization in the 107th Congress — arguing that without the government's help domestic farmers could lose out to imports from Mexico. It is only fair, in her view, to help U.S. industries survive when they have to comply (appropriately, in her view) with labor, environmental and health standards that are higher than in other nations.

Using similar arguments, Kaptur was a leader in the campaigns against all the major trade expansion initiatives of the Clinton administration. She fought enactment of the 1993 law to carry out the North American Free Trade Agreement and the 1994 law that created the World Trade Organization, as well as President Clinton's requests to revive fast-track authority to negotiate trade agreements that Congress cannot amend. Her high profile in opposing a president of her own party on trade issues led independent presidential candidate Ross Perot to ask her to be his running mate in 1996. Kaptur declined and supported Clinton's re-election.

In 2000, when the House debated whether to grant China permanent normal trade status, Kaptur was eager to rebut Clinton's argument that doing so would open a giant new market for U.S. goods and services. The real result, she said, would be a continued lowering of the standard of living. "Americans are running like gerbils in a cage because of the pressure of the

CAPITOL OFFICE
225-4146; fax 225-7711; 2366 Rayburn Bldg. 20515

INTERNET
e-mail: rep.kaptur@mail.house.gov
web: www.house.gov/kaptur

COMMITTEES
Appropriations

HOMETOWN
Toledo

BORN
June 17, 1946, Toledo, Ohio

RELIGION
Roman Catholic

FAMILY
Single

EDUCATION
U. of Wisconsin, B.A. 1968; U. of Michigan, M.U.P. 1974; Massachusetts Institute of Technology, attended 1981

CAREER
White House aide; urban planner

POLITICAL HIGHLIGHTS
No previous office

ELECTION RESULTS

2000 GENERAL

Marcy Kaptur (D)	168,547	74.8%
Dwight E. Bryan (R)	49,446	21.9%
Galen Fries (LIBERT)	4,239	1.9%
Dennis Slotnick (NL)	3,096	1.4%

2000 PRIMARY

Marcy Kaptur (D)	unopposed

1998 GENERAL

Marcy Kaptur (D)	130,793	81.2%
Edward Emery (R)	30,312	18.8%

PREVIOUS WINNING PERCENTAGES
1996 (77%); 1994 (75%); 1992 (74%); 1990 (78%); 1988 (81%); 1986 (78%); 1984 (55%); 1982 (58%)

multinational corporate ethic on the way production is organized and distributed in the world," she said.

As the 107th began, Kaptur showed that she would be equally quick to challenge the new president. She joined eight other Ohio members in protesting an Export-Import Bank loan guarantee for modernization of a Chinese steel mill. Though the financing was approved in the final month of the Clinton administration, Kaptur's warning was aimed squarely at incoming President Bush: "The executive branch better get its ducks in order," she said. "We do not in a coherent way stand up for America's manufacturing industries."

Kaptur took a weeklong trip to Russia and Ukraine in 2001 to investigate steel and farming issues, as well as a trip to Iowa to talk about domestic farm policy — fueling talk in Washington (which her aides moved to tamp down) that she might seek the Democratic presidential nomination in 2004.

After the 1997 death of her mother, Anastasia, Kaptur and her brother founded the nonprofit Anastasia Fund to promote liberty, community development and free religious expression in the face of political and economic pressures. The fund has helped support groups in Ukraine, China and Mexico. Kaptur also has established the Kaptur Community Fund, which makes charitable donations in Toledo; she regularly contributes her congressional pay raise to the fund.

A staunch defender of the War Powers Act, Kaptur was a plaintiff in a federal lawsuit, which ultimately failed, alleging that Clinton did not obey the law by bombing Yugoslavia in 1999.

She had better success in her quest for a national memorial to the veterans of World War II. She first introduced a bill on the issue in 1987, inspired by a constituent, Roger Durbin, who was a veteran of the war. The measure, enacted in 1993, is supposed to yield a memorial in Washington by 2003.

Kaptur was the first member of her family to attend college. She then worked as a city planner, helping to create community development corporations to revitalize low-income areas of Toledo. That led to a job in the Carter administration as an adviser on urban policy.

Kaptur was working on her doctorate in urban planning at the Massachusetts Institute of Technology when she was recruited to challenge first-term GOP Rep. Ed Weber in 1982. With northwest Ohio in a deep recession, Weber's support for President Reagan's economic agenda proved politically fatal; Kaptur won by 19 percentage points.

She was held to 55 percent in 1984 but has won more than 70 percent of the vote in every re-election race since.

KEY VOTES

2000

Yes Raise hourly minimum wage by $1 over two years

No Halt funding for U.S. mission in Kosovo unless European nations pay more

Yes Provide Medicare benefits to military retirees and their dependents

No Grant China permanent normal trade status

No Phase out estate, gift and trust taxes

No Prohibit implementation of president's national monument designations

No Approve GOP plan to provide prescription drug coverage for Medicare beneficiaries

Yes Increase help for poor nations indebted to international financial institutions

1999

Yes Impose steel import quotas

Yes Kill proposal to take aviation trust funds off budget

No Require background checks on buyers only at gun shows with 10 or more vendors

No Remove barriers among banking, securities and insurance companies

Yes Authorize state grants to hire teachers and reduce class size

Yes Overhaul campaign finance law; ban "soft money" and restrict advocacy advertising

? Approve bipartisan plan to increase rights of patients in managed-care health plans

INTEREST GROUPS

	AFL-CIO	ADA	CCUS	ACU
2000	100%	75%	30%	18%
1999	100%	85%	26%	4%
1998	100%	80%	17%	28%
1997	100%	75%	22%	32%

CQ VOTE STUDIES

	PARTY UNITY		PRESIDENTIAL SUPPORT	
	Support	Oppose	Support	Oppose
2000	91%	9%	73%	27%
1999	87%	13%	68%	32%
1998	85%	15%	71%	29%
1997	79%	21%	49%	51%

OHIO 9
Northwest — Toledo

The 9th revolves around Toledo, stretching along the Michigan border to take in Fulton County in the west. Almost three-fifths of the district's residents live in Toledo, which sits at the mouth of the Maumee River, the largest river flowing into the Great Lakes. Toledo's large concentrations of blue-collar ethnics – Germans, Irish, Poles and Hungarians – make it a lonely Democratic outpost in rural, Republican northwestern Ohio.

Republicans are concentrated in the more affluent suburbs on Toledo's west side, such as upscale Ottawa Hills. The 9th's westernmost county, Fulton, is one of the most Republican counties in Ohio, but Toledo's Democratic voters overwhelm Republicans elsewhere in the district.

Toledo's economy has long depended on the auto industry, which closed several Toledo factories in the 1980s. But the industry is back, albeit in smaller form, with a major Jeep assembly line and a

General Motors parts factory. Growth in the city's petroleum and manufacturing industries, including glass and machinery, also has sped the city's recovery. Outside Toledo, wheat, soybeans and corn are the district's lifeblood. About 50 percent of the district's land mass is agricultural.

MAJOR INDUSTRY
Auto manufacturing, agriculture, health care

CITIES
Toledo, 307,946; Sylvania, 19,274; Oregon, 19,102

UNUSUAL FEATURES
Ohio Baseball Hall of Fame in Lucas County; Toledo known to television viewers as the home of Cpl. Max Klinger, a character in the series "M*A*S*H;" Toledo's historic "Old West End" known for its Victorian homes and claims to have been the nation's largest residential neighborhood at the turn of the century.

Rep. Dennis J. Kucinich (D)

Elected 1996; 3rd term

CAPITOL OFFICE
225-5871; fax 225-5745
1730 Longworth Bldg. 20515

INTERNET
e-mail: www.house.gov/writerep
web: www.house.gov/kucinich

COMMITTEES
Education & Workforce
Government Reform

HOMETOWN
Cleveland

BORN
Oct. 8, 1946, Cleveland, Ohio

RELIGION
Roman Catholic

FAMILY
Divorced; one child

EDUCATION
Case Western Reserve U., B.A. 1973, M.A. 1973

CAREER
Video producer; public power consultant

POLITICAL HIGHLIGHTS
Cleveland City Council, 1969-75; Democratic
nominee for U.S. House, 1972; independent
candidate for U.S. House, 1974; mayor of
Cleveland, 1977-79; Cleveland City Council, 1983;
sought Democratic nomination for U.S. House,
1988, 1992; Ohio Senate, 1995-97

ELECTION RESULTS

2000 GENERAL

Dennis J. Kucinich (D)	167,063	75.0%
Bill Smith (R)	48,930	22.0%
Ron Petrie (LIBERT)	6,762	3.0%

2000 PRIMARY

Dennis J. Kucinich (D)	56,781	93.2%
C. River Smith (D)	4,145	6.8%

1998 GENERAL

Dennis J. Kucinich (D)	110,552	66.8%
Joseph J. Slovenec (R)	55,015	33.2%

PREVIOUS WINNING PERCENTAGES
1996 (49%)

A hard-charging, pro-union lawmaker, Kucinich is a master at reducing public policy debates into easy-to-understand terms. Faced with a federal proposal to ship nuclear waste across Ohio, he responded dryly, according to The Associated Press: "I think people will want to know if they are getting hundreds of free X-rays as they are sitting in traffic."

Kucinich first drew national notice more than two decades ago as the flamboyant, controversial — and short-tenured — "boy mayor" of Cleveland. Although he has toned down his style somewhat, Kucinich (ku-SIN-itch) continues to stand out in the staid legislative arena. When he established a congressional website in 2000, he included links to polka, bowling and kielbasa, prompting some to joke about his "sausage links."

A master at winning attention, Kucinich stood on railroad tracks outside Cleveland to denounce a railroad merger, and he held up a black umbrella full of holes to illustrate the potential flaws of a missile defense system. He burst into a Polish song at the funeral of a fellow Cleveland politician, explaining that the deceased used to sing it at ward meetings.

Upon his arrival in Washington in 1997, Kucinich quickly proved that he was no longer the cocksure "bad boy" of the 1970s. At a high-profile Washington insiders' banquet, he won over the audience of lawmakers, journalists and lobbyists with self-deprecating jokes. And as chairman of a charity fundraising "funniest celebrity in Washington" contest in 1999, Kucinich performed the entire Gettysburg Address in a Donald Duck voice, reported The Washington Post.

On the political front, Kucinich rarely leaves much doubt about where he stands. In the 107th Congress, he is chairman of the Progressive Caucus, the most liberal faction of House Democrats. A frequent speaker on the House floor, he is a strongly pro-labor Democrat, finding much common ground on economic and trade issues with Minority Leader Richard A. Gephardt. He is a harsh critic of international trade pacts that he believes send American jobs overseas.

True to his labor roots, Kucinich opposed President Clinton's call in 2000 to grant permanent normal trade status to China, criticizing that country's human rights record. In 1997, he explained: "I am not opposed to trade, but we should not let free trade mean that we trade away jobs in this country, we trade away the level of wages which people have worked a lifetime for, we trade away our basic political rights, we trade away our environment."

A member of the Education and the Workforce Committee, Kucinich is concerned that workers will be exploited in the economy of the future. He voted against a GOP proposal to let companies offer employees compensatory time off in lieu of pay for overtime work, warning that employers would coerce workers to accept time off instead of money.

On some social issues, however, Kucinich votes a more conservative line than the majority of Democrats. He opposes abortion and voted for a constitutional amendment barring U.S. flag desecration.

One of Kucinich's legislative passions is warning Americans about genetically modified foods. Even though many scientists insist there is no danger in altering the gene structures of corn and other foods, Kucinich contends that there has not been enough research on the issue. He proposed legislation in the 106th Congress mandating labels on "biotech" foods. "If we are what we eat, shouldn't we know what is in our food, so we know what we will become?" he said.

Practicing what he preaches, Kucinich has made a radical change in his own diet. Even though he grew up on kielbasa, kishkes (stuffed beef casings) and other rich Eastern European fare, he became a vegetarian in 1995. Now his meals feature rice, tofu and green tea. "Once I was able to make the transition, I've had enormous amounts of energy, I sleep better, and I don't get tired as much," he said in 2000.

In the international arena, Kucinich criticized the NATO bombing campaign in Yugoslavia in 1999. He joined with two dozen other lawmakers in an unsuccessful federal court case that accused Clinton of violating the 1973 War Powers Resolution and committing U.S. troops for more than 60 days without Hill approval. "The war in which the United States is involved under the participation of NATO is an illegal war," he said. "The Constitution provides for Congress alone to have the power to declare war," the Cleveland Plain Dealer quoted him as saying.

Even though Kucinich is partly of Croatian descent, and he represents a sizable Serbian constituency, he said that had little to do with his anti-bombing stance. In a 1999 interview with The Plain Dealer, he identified himself as a pacifist who carries a prayer in his wallet that begins, "Make me a channel of your peace." He has been skeptical of other military initiatives, including efforts to develop a national missile defense system. Because of a heart murmur, he did not serve in the military.

The son of a truck driver, and one of seven siblings, Kucinich earned a master's degree in communications at Case Western University and has worked as a copy editor, sportswriter and political commentator. He launched his political career by winning a seat on the Cleveland City Council in 1969.

By the age of 31, he was mayor. But Kucinich's fall was as spectacular as his rise. During his brief, stormy service as mayor of Cleveland, the city fell into financial default, and his popularity sank so low that he wore a bulletproof vest when he threw out the first pitch of the Cleveland Indians' 1978 season.

Kucinich lost his 1979 mayoral re-election bid to George V. Voinovich (who went on to become governor and was elected to the Senate in 1998). But then both Cleveland and its former mayor rebounded. Kucinich seized a state Senate seat from a GOP incumbent in 1994. And in 1996 — after four previous failed bids to win a U.S. House seat, dating as far back as 1972 — he took aim at two-term Republican Rep. Martin R. Hoke. Kucinich won the seat by linking Hoke to unpopular House Speaker Newt Gingrich. He won by less than 3 percentage points but breezed through his two re-elections, expanding his margin to 34 and then 53 percentage points.

KEY VOTES

2000
Yes Raise hourly minimum wage by $1 over two years
Yes Halt funding for U.S. mission in Kosovo unless European nations pay more
Yes Provide Medicare benefits to military retirees and their dependents
No   Grant China permanent normal trade status
No   Phase out estate, gift and trust taxes
No   Prohibit implementation of president's national monument designations
No   Approve GOP plan to provide prescription drug coverage for Medicare beneficiaries
No   Increase help for poor nations indebted to international financial institutions

1999
Yes Impose steel import quotas
No   Kill proposal to take aviation trust funds off budget
No   Require background checks on buyers only at gun shows with 10 or more vendors
No   Remove barriers among banking, securities and insurance companies
Yes Authorize state grants to hire teachers and reduce class size
Yes Overhaul campaign finance law; ban "soft money" and restrict advocacy advertising
Yes Approve bipartisan plan to increase rights of patients in managed-care health plans

INTEREST GROUPS

	AFL-CIO	ADA	CCUS	ACU
2000	90%	80%	28%	16%
1999	100%	90%	12%	20%
1998	100%	90%	22%	20%
1997	100%	90%	20%	16%

CQ VOTE STUDIES

	PARTY UNITY		PRESIDENTIAL SUPPORT	
	Support	Oppose	Support	Oppose
2000	89%	11%	76%	24%
1999	83%	17%	63%	37%
1998	84%	16%	78%	22%
1997	81%	19%	65%	35%

OHIO 10
Cleveland — West Side and suburbs

The 10th includes the western portion of Cleveland and follows the migration of its ethnic residents into the western and southern suburbs. The district, composed mainly of Reagan Democrats, has successfully navigated the transition from an industrial to a service economy.

The line between the 10th and 11th districts generally divides Cleveland's white and black neighborhoods. The 10th contains the state's largest concentration of ethnic voters, mostly Poles, Czechs, Italians, Irish and Germans. Although industry still provides the backbone of the city's economy, the 10th has attracted smaller, high-tech companies and undergone a downtown restoration, helping the district maintain its steady employment base.

The immediate suburbs have a strong union presence and a Democratic leaning. At the 10th's western edge, it contains more conservative, white-collar residents who commute from the affluent communities of such towns as Bay Village. Democrats dominate the state legislature from this district, but some other local offices are split evenly. On the federal level, the 10th supported Bill Clinton in 1992 and '96 and Al Gore in 2000. Although the congressional seat was designed with Democratic candidates in mind, a large population of Reagan Democrats makes it winnable by Republicans.

MAJOR INDUSTRY
Manufacturing, banking, high technology

CITIES
Cleveland (pt.), 219,243 (1990); Parma, 81,207; Lakewood, 54,222; North Olmsted, 32,978; Westlake, 29,570

UNUSUAL FEATURES
Rock and Roll Hall of Fame; A publisher dropped an "a" from city founder Moses Cleaveland's name so that it would fit neatly on his page, giving the city's name its current spelling; NASA's Lewis Research Center.

Rep. Stephanie Tubbs Jones (D)

Elected 1998; 2nd term

The first African-American woman elected to Congress from Ohio, Jones has a wide-ranging résumé that could allow her to develop into a rising star in the Democratic Party. Although her political leanings are decidedly liberal, she has shown a willingness to work across party lines and through established channels of power in the pursuit of her legislative goals. As a result, Jones enjoys growing clout in Congress and increasing popularity in her home state.

The situation is a substantial departure from the first time Jones injected herself into national affairs. As a student at Case Western Reserve University, she was among a group of anti-Vietnam War demonstrators who forced the university to shut down in the spring of 1970. "My goal at the time was curing the ills of society," she told the Cleveland Plain Dealer in 2000. "At that time, I never wanted to be a public official, but ultimately I made the decision that I could do more from within than without."

Still, Jones does not hesitate to take politically risky positions. She has expressed concern that users of crack cocaine, many of whom are members of minority groups, often serve longer sentences than users of powdered cocaine, who are more often white. She opposes mandatory minimum sentencing, saying it "takes away, in my opinion, the need for a judge."

In 2000, she was one of only 27 members of the House who voted against a symbolic expression of support for her own home state's motto, "With God, all things are possible." A federal appeals court had declared the motto unconstitutional, and 333 lawmakers voted to express disapproval of that decision. Jones said she respected and supported the ruling. That same year, she was on the losing side of a lopsided House vote (380-19) on a bill to give rape victims the power to demand HIV tests for any arrested suspect. Opponents said that would inappropriately compel people to submit to a test before they had a chance to prove their innocence.

In 1999, Jones supported a proposal to allow as long as three days for background checks of would-be buyers at gun shows. When that amendment was narrowly defeated, she voted against the bill, which limited the checks to 24 hours. The measure was defeated by a small band of Republicans who objected to any gun control laws and an overwhelming majority of Democrats, many of whom contended the proposal was so porous it could weaken current law. "As a former prosecutor, I know that it's difficult to do a gun check in 24 hours," Jones said.

Jones can be pragmatic in her approach, and she takes pride in her ability to pursue her agenda in ways that do not always grab the spotlight. She has used her seats on the Financial Services and Small Business panels to help boost economic development in her district and to attack predatory lending practices that she says are more often targeted at minorities. She also has pursued those goals as chairman of the Congressional Black Caucus's Housing Task Force, where she held hearings on alleged abuses by some lenders who make sub-prime, or high-risk, loans with high interest rates and fees. "Not every sub-prime lender is predatory, but every predatory lender is a sub-prime lender," Jones said.

But — noting that her district includes both parts of inner-city Cleveland and some of its affluent suburbs — Jones says she does not want to be considered a one-track legislator: "My vision is larger than just issues that affect minorities."

Jones believes any federal surpluses should be used to bolster the finan-

CAPITOL OFFICE
225-7032; fax 225-1339
1516 Longworth Bldg. 20515

INTERNET
e-mail: stephanie.tubbs.jones@mail.house.gov
web: www.house.gov/tubbsjones

COMMITTEES
Financial Services
Small Business
Standards of Official Conduct

HOMETOWN
Cleveland

BORN
Sept. 10, 1949, Cleveland, Ohio

RELIGION
Baptist

FAMILY
Husband, Mervyn Jones; one child

EDUCATION
Case Western Reserve U., B.A. 1971, J.D. 1974

CAREER
Lawyer; municipal judge

POLITICAL HIGHLIGHTS
Cuyahoga County judge, 1983-91; Cuyahoga County prosecutor, 1991-99

ELECTION RESULTS

2000 GENERAL
Stephanie Tubbs Jones (D)	164,134	84.8%
James Sykora (R)	21,630	11.2%
Joel C. Turner (LIBERT)	4,230	2.2%
Sonja K. Glavina (NL)	3,525	1.8%

2000 PRIMARY
Stephanie Tubbs Jones (D)	67,680	91.5%
Gerald C. Henley (D)	6,286	8.5%

1998 GENERAL
Stephanie Tubbs Jones (D)	115,226	80.4%
James D. Hereford (R)	18,592	13.0%
Jean Murrell Capers (I)	9,477	6.6%

cial soundness of Social Security, and she opposes raising the program's retirement age. She also wants to make day care more available and less expensive for working families and to invest more money in early childhood education programs.

Jones usually votes the Democratic line, and she campaigned for her party's presidential candidate, Al Gore, in 2000. However, she will publicly split with party leaders on occasion. She joined other Democratic lawmakers and actress Goldie Hawn in 2000 at an event to denounce President Clinton's pursuit of granting China permanent normal trade status.

In her committees, Jones is one of the few lawmakers who is not afraid to acknowledge when she is unclear about something. During debate in the 106th Congress on overhauling financial services law, Jones would ask witnesses before the Banking Committee (renamed Financial Services in the 107th) to clarify basic concepts or define terms. "As a trial lawyer, you learn to be very succinct," she said.

Jones had planned a career in social work but instead became a lawyer. Her first job after law school was as a trial attorney for the Equal Employment Opportunity Commission. In 1981, she was elected to a Cleveland municipal judgeship, and two years later, she was a gubernatorial appointee to a judgeship that handled felony cases.

Jones was elected in 1991 as the Cuyahoga County prosecutor, overseeing a staff of about 300. She received nationwide attention in 1998 for refusing to re-open the case of the late Dr. Sam Sheppard, the basis for "The Fugitive" television series and movie. He was convicted in 1954 of murdering his wife and served 10 years in prison before being acquitted in a retrial.

In 1998, Jones won a convincing primary victory and four-fifths of the general-election vote to succeed Democrat Louis Stokes, who retired after serving 15 terms. She calls Stokes, the state's first black congressman, a "mentor and close friend."

In 2000, Jones trounced her Republican opponent, taking 85 percent of the vote in the overwhelmingly Democratic 11th District.

Jones' stature continues to grow at home. Endorsing her for a second term in 2000, the Plain Dealer praised Jones' attention to social issues and her ability to work with Republican members of the Ohio congressional delegation. The newspaper also conducted a poll that year suggesting that Jones would be the most formidable challenger to Cleveland's Democratic mayor, Michael R. White, in 2001.

Jones expressed little interest in the post for now, although she did not rule out a bid someday.

KEY VOTES

2000
Yes Raise hourly minimum wage by $1 over two years
No Halt funding for U.S. mission in Kosovo unless European nations pay more
Yes Provide Medicare benefits to military retirees and their dependents
No Grant China permanent normal trade status
No Phase out estate, gift and trust taxes
? Prohibit implementation of president's national monument designations
No Approve GOP plan to provide prescription drug coverage for Medicare beneficiaries
Yes Increase help for poor nations indebted to international financial institutions

1999
Yes Impose steel import quotas
No Kill proposal to take aviation trust funds off budget
No Require background checks on buyers only at gun shows with 10 or more vendors
Yes Remove barriers among banking, securities and insurance companies
Yes Authorize state grants to hire teachers and reduce class size
Yes Overhaul campaign finance law; ban "soft money" and restrict advocacy advertising
Yes Approve bipartisan plan to increase rights of patients in managed-care health plans

INTEREST GROUPS

	AFL-CIO	ADA	CCUS	ACU
2000	100%	100%	47%	0%
1999	89%	90%	25%	0%

CQ VOTE STUDIES

	PARTY UNITY		PRESIDENTIAL SUPPORT	
	Support	Oppose	Support	Oppose
2000	98%	2%	89%	11%
1999	96%	4%	87%	13%

OHIO 11
Cleveland – East Side and suburbs

One of the smallest districts in the state, the 11th consists of the poor, inner-city areas of Cleveland's East Side and fans out to the east to include the city's upper middle-class suburbs. The combination of the district's black majority and its liberal suburbanites makes it heavily Democratic in both local and national contests. Democratic presidential candidates usually win their highest percentage in the state in the 11th.

Although suburban growth has lured many of Cleveland's businesses and residents outside the city, there has been a smattering of new commercial and residential developments in the downtown area.

The district's inner-city neighborhoods, containing much of the district's black majority, live mostly below the poverty line. Toward Lake Erie are some middle-class neighborhoods, inhabited mostly by Italians and Eastern Europeans.

The upper middle-class suburbs of Cleveland Heights, Shaker Heights and University Heights to the east contain a large proportion of Jews and young professionals, forming some of Ohio's most liberal and racially integrated communities. Case Western Reserve University is located in University Circle, Cleveland's cultural center.

From the circle area, commuters drive along historic Euclid Avenue to their jobs downtown. While the avenue now bears the marks of poverty, it was known as "Millionaire's Row" at the turn of the century. Few of the old mansions remain. The one belonging to John D. Rockefeller, founder of Standard Oil, was razed after his death in 1937.

MAJOR INDUSTRY
Health care, manufacturing, utilities

CITIES
Cleveland (pt.), 286,373 (1990); Cleveland Heights, 53,277; Euclid, 49,498; East Cleveland, 29,077; Shaker Heights, 28,297

UNUSUAL FEATURES
Shaker Historical Museum; First indoor shopping mall in the nation, built in 1890.

Rep. Pat Tiberi (R)

CAPITOL OFFICE
225-5355; fax 226-4523; 508 Cannon Bldg. 20515

INTERNET
e-mail: www.house.gov/writerep
web: www.house.gov/tiberi

COMMITTEES
Education & Workforce
Financial Services

HOMETOWN
Columbus

BORN
Oct. 21, 1962, Columbus, Ohio

RELIGION
Roman Catholic

FAMILY
Wife, Denice Tiberi

EDUCATION
Ohio State U., B.A. 1985

CAREER
Realtor; congressional aide

POLITICAL HIGHLIGHTS
Ohio House, 1993-2001 (majority leader, 1999-2001)

ELECTION RESULTS

2000 GENERAL

Pat Tiberi (R)	139,242	52.9%
Maryellen O'Shaughnessy (D)	115,432	43.8%
Lawrence N. Hogan (LIBERT)	4,546	1.7%

2000 PRIMARY

Pat Tiberi (R)	57,548	73.0%
Eugene J. Watts (R)	16,331	20.7%
Ramona Whisler (R)	3,481	4.4%
Andrew George Zuckowski (R)	1,469	1.9%

Elected 2000; 1st term

During his eight years in the Ohio House, Tiberi developed an image as a conservative Republican who was willing and able to work with Democrats. In fact, Tiberi approaches government much like the man he succeeded: nine-term Republican Rep. John R. Kasich, who was the House Budget Committee chairman before his retirement.

Tiberi's bipartisan tendencies crystallized in his role as state House majority leader. He said he expected to be able to "cross the [partisan] divide much like John Kasich has been able to do in the past 18 years."

The similarity is not coincidental. Tiberi (TEA-berry) worked as a House aide to Kasich for eight years before running for office in his own right. And during his re-election campaign for the Ohio House in 1994, the Columbus Dispatch, in endorsing Tiberi, praised him for "exhibiting bipartisan ingenuity" by getting three of his bills approved as amendments to other bills.

In the state House, Tiberi established a DNA database to track violent criminals and was a prime mover of "tort reform" legislation that limited large jury awards but later was ruled unconstitutional.

Tiberi also authored legislation requiring performance audits for schools. In Congress, his assignment to the Education and the Workforce Committee allows him to pursue his interest in this issue; he was named vice chairman of the Select Education Subcommittee. He also got a seat on the Financial Services panel.

But Tiberi's chief thrust is pursuing policies that aim to reduce the size and scope of the federal government. He supports replacing the tax code with a simpler system and using budget surplus money to cut taxes and reduce the national debt. He favors adapting Social Security to allow private investment accounts for individuals.

Tiberi, who was barred by an Ohio term-limit law from seeking re-election to the state House in 2000, needed little coaxing to enter the race to succeed Kasich. He trounced state Sen. Eugene J. Watts in the GOP primary, then bested a formidable Democratic opponent, Columbus City Councilwoman Maryellen O'Shaughnessy, by 9 percentage points in the general election.

OHIO 12
Central — Eastern Columbus and suburbs

The 12th includes the eastern half of Columbus and the suburban counties to the north and east of the city. The city has become primarily white collar, and its thriving service economy has led to significant growth in both the city and its adjacent areas. While the urban areas of the district lean Democratic, the GOP influence in the suburbs tends to overwhelm the district.

For Democrats to be successful in the 12th, they must command the urban portion of the district, which is heavily black and poorer than the surrounding areas. Bill Clinton barely won the district in 1996, the first time a Democratic presidential candidate had won the district in 20 years. Traveling from the State Capitol building along Broad Street and into the suburbs,

black Democratic support goes down and Republican support goes up.

The suburbs, especially Delaware County to the north, have experienced enormous growth and startlingly low unemployment rates in recent years. The influx of white-collar, upper middle-class residents has allowed Republicans to lay claim to the district. Most local officials in the suburban areas also are Republican. Western Licking County is experiencing its own share of growth, but Licking becomes more blue collar east of the city.

MAJOR INDUSTRY
Financial services, manufacturing

CITIES
Columbus (pt.), 284,281 (1990); Westerville, 34,295; Reynoldsburg, 30,282

UNUSUAL FEATURES
Full-scale replica of Christopher Columbus' ship, the Santa Maria; World's largest building in the shape of a basket, serves as headquarters for Longaberger Basket Co.

Rep. Sherrod Brown (D)

CAPITOL OFFICE
225-3401; fax 225-2266; 2438 Rayburn Bldg. 20515

INTERNET
e-mail: sherrod@mail.house.gov
web: www.house.gov/sherrodbrown

COMMITTEES
Energy & Commerce
International Relations

HOMETOWN
Lorain

BORN
Nov. 9, 1952, Mansfield, Ohio

RELIGION
Lutheran

FAMILY
Divorced; two children

EDUCATION
Yale U., B.A. 1974; Ohio State U., M.A. 1979, M.A. 1981

CAREER
Teacher

POLITICAL HIGHLIGHTS
Ohio House, 1975-83; Ohio secretary of state, 1983-91; defeated for re-election as Ohio secretary of state, 1990

ELECTION RESULTS

2000 GENERAL

Sherrod Brown (D)	170,058	64.6%
Rick H. Jeric (R)	84,295	32.0%
Michael A. Chmura (LIBERT)	5,837	2.2%
David Kluter (NL)	3,108	1.2%

2000 PRIMARY

Sherrod Brown (D)	unopposed

1998 GENERAL

Sherrod Brown (D)	116,309	61.5%
Grace L. Drake (R)	72,666	38.5%

PREVIOUS WINNING PERCENTAGES
1996 (61%); 1994 (49%); 1992 (53%)

Elected 1992; 5th term

Brown has carved out a solid niche for himself by taking on health care issues with down-to-earth, no-nonsense populist fervor. He has an astute political ear for the issues of the moment — everything from prescription drug benefits under Medicare to tighter regulation of health maintenance organizations to health coverage for the uninsured. By placing himself at the center of those debates, Brown has earned a future in House Democratic circles as long and bright as a college professor who has just earned tenure.

Brown had big shoes to fill when he became the ranking Democrat on the Commerce panel's Health Subcommittee in the 105th Congress. He succeeded Henry A. Waxman of California, who had mastered the intricate details of health care programs and was known for his hard-nosed questioning of witnesses he thought were not giving him straight answers.

The Ohio lawmaker may be more low-key and affable than Waxman in his personal style, but he ultimately ends up in the same place, sticking up for the Democratic Party line by advocating step-by-step expansions of health coverage while needling Republicans over hot-button political issues such as prescription drug coverage for senior citizens. He says his interest in health issues stems from his father, who was a physician.

In the 106th Congress, Brown played the prescription drug issue deftly, taking senior citizens into Canada to buy medications at lower prices. The point of the exercise, he said, was to illustrate how the same prescription drugs cost less in Canada, where the government negotiates prices with drug companies to make sure seniors can afford life-saving medications, than in the United States, where drug companies can "unilaterally and monopolistically set drug prices at whatever level they want."

Congress did not add a prescription drug benefit to Medicare, as Democrats proposed, but lawmakers did pass a narrower backup plan that Brown advocated that lets pharmacies reimport American prescription drugs from countries where they are less expensive.

Brown had less success in advancing two other health care proposals he cosponsored in the 106th: letting early retirees between the ages of 55 and 64 buy into Medicare, and giving states incentives to cover low-income parents as well as their children under Medicaid and the State Children's Health Insurance Program.

Brown was educated at Yale and holds two graduate degrees, but few can match his populist tone when he thinks jobs are at risk in his labor-dominated industrial district. He persistently argued against free-trade agreements pushed by the Clinton administration, maintaining that the pacts prevent the United States from responding to trade practices that are unfair or immoral.

As a freshman in the 103rd, Brown work tirelessly to defeat the North American Free Trade Agreement (NAFTA) — lobbying fellow freshmen, taking the House floor time and again to detail the pact's flaws, and publishing a newsletter that kept track of anti-NAFTA activities.

In the 104th, he became a standard-bearer for those in the House who believed China was not entitled to normal trade relations because of its human rights record. When Congress eventually approved normal trade relations in 2000, under heavy lobbying from the Clinton administration, Brown was one of the dissenters.

Brown normally finds himself in agreement with his party peers in Congress, siding with Democrats on more than 90 percent of the votes that pit one party against the other. On occasion, though, he will break from the majority of House Democrats, as when he backed constitutional amendments to balance the budget and limit congressional terms.

His occasional straying from the Democratic line hasn't hurt his relations with Minority Leader Richard A. Gephardt, who put him on the Democratic Congressional Campaign Committee to make use of his fundraising talents. Gephardt told the Cleveland Plain Dealer that "there are some people here who like politics, but they don't like policy. There are others who like policy but really don't like politics. He likes both, and that's a real gift."

In a 1999 television interview in which Brown discussed the book he had just written about his congressional experiences entitled, "Congress from the Inside," Brown listed four important steps for freshmen. Leading the list, he said, was to get on the right committee.

Brown won his coveted seat on the Energy and Commerce Committee in his first term, after campaigning hard for the assignment. He even parted with a favored baseball card — that of 1950s Boston Red Sox outfielder Jimmy Piersall, who suffered from mental illness. Brown gave the card to influential California Democrat Vic Fazio, with the note: "Don't be crazy. Vote for Sherrod Brown for Energy and Commerce."

His first House victory in 1992 marked a successful return for the one-time "boy wonder" of Ohio politics. In 1974, just before his 22nd birthday, Brown was elected to the state House, where he served four terms. In 1982, he was elected secretary of state, a post to which he was re-elected in 1986 and from which he was expected to vault to higher office.

But Brown lost a re-election bid in 1990 to Republican Bob Taft, the latest in a long line of politically successful Ohio Tafts. (Taft was elected governor in 1998.) Brown had proposed a two-month, unpaid leave of absence from his job to take an educational trip to Japan, and Taft hammered him with ads that proclaimed: "Sayonara, Sherrod."

In 1992, Brown made a bid for the House, joining seven other Democrats in the race for the open 13th District. He was his party's front-runner, though he had moved into the 13th to run, and he easily won the Democratic nomination. In the November election, he handily defeated Republican Margaret R. Mueller, a millionaire social worker who had lost three times to Democrat Dennis E. Eckart in the old 11th District. Brown prevailed with just a plurality of the vote in 1994 — a bad year for Ohio Democrats — but has won with ease since then. However, with the GOP in control of the redistricting process, Brown's safe perch may be shaken when district lines are redrawn to reflect Ohio's loss of one House seat.

KEY VOTES

2000
Yes Raise hourly minimum wage by $1 over two years
Yes Halt funding for U.S. mission in Kosovo unless European nations pay more
Yes Provide Medicare benefits to military retirees and their dependents
No Grant China permanent normal trade status
No Phase out estate, gift and trust taxes
No Prohibit implementation of president's national monument designations
No Approve GOP plan to provide prescription drug coverage for Medicare beneficiaries
Yes Increase help for poor nations indebted to international financial institutions

1999
Yes Impose steel import quotas
Yes Kill proposal to take aviation trust funds off budget
No Require background checks on buyers only at gun shows with 10 or more vendors
No Remove barriers among banking, securities and insurance companies
Yes Authorize state grants to hire teachers and reduce class size
Yes Overhaul campaign finance law; ban "soft money" and restrict advocacy advertising
Yes Approve bipartisan plan to increase rights of patients in managed-care health plans

INTEREST GROUPS

	AFL-CIO	ADA	CCUS	ACU
2000	100%	90%	25%	4%
1999	100%	100%	0%	0%
1998	100%	100%	17%	4%
1997	100%	100%	22%	12%

CQ VOTE STUDIES

	PARTY UNITY		PRESIDENTIAL SUPPORT	
	Support	Oppose	Support	Oppose
2000	97%	3%	81%	19%
1999	95%	5%	80%	20%
1998	97%	3%	83%	17%
1997	96%	4%	82%	18%

OHIO 13

Northeast — Cleveland, Akron and Youngstown suburbs

The 13th, an odd, H-shaped district in the northeast, borders both the Akron and Cleveland metropolitan areas. The western stem of the "H" contains part of Lorain and Medina counties, while the eastern stem covers Geauga and parts of Portage and Trumbull counties. Those two strips are connected by a band of suburbs along the Ohio Turnpike.

Although Cleveland's rapid growth has seeped into surrounding suburbs and rural Portage County to the east, industrial areas in Lorain County have struggled to replace jobs as automobile and steel plants there shut down.

An industrial, blue-collar heritage in Lorain County and the suburban neighborhoods nearest to Cleveland gives the 13th an overall Democratic lean. Reagan Democrats dominate the heavily ethnic Lorain County and the suburban band to the south of Cleveland. In more rural counties to the south and east, voters lean Republican both locally and nationally, yet their sparse populations make them less influential in congressional contests.

The urban Catholic Democrats and rural Protestant Republicans are roughly divided by the liberal area around Oberlin College, in Lorain County, whose residents took a strong anti-slavery stance in the 19th century and continue to crusade for social reforms.

MAJOR INDUSTRY
Auto and auto parts manufacturing, steel, agriculture

CITIES
Lorain, 67,377; Elyria, 55,826; Brunswick, 32,849

UNUSUAL FEATURES
Sea World of Ohio; Oberlin College, founded in 1833, the first coeducational institution of higher learning in the United States.

Rep. Tom Sawyer (D)

CAPITOL OFFICE
225-5231; fax 225-5278
1414 Longworth Bldg. 20515

INTERNET
e-mail: www.house.gov/writerep
web: www.house.gov/sawyer

COMMITTEES
Energy & Commerce

HOMETOWN
Akron

BORN
Aug. 15, 1945, Akron, Ohio

RELIGION
Presbyterian

FAMILY
Wife, Joyce Handler; one child

EDUCATION
U. of Akron, B.A. 1968, M.A. 1970

CAREER
Teacher

POLITICAL HIGHLIGHTS
Ohio House, 1977-83; mayor of Akron, 1984-86

ELECTION RESULTS

2000 GENERAL

Tom Sawyer (D)	149,184	64.8%
Rick Wood (R)	71,432	31.1%
William McDaniel Jr. (LIBERT)	5,603	2.4%
Walter P. Keith (NL)	3,869	1.7%

2000 PRIMARY

Tom Sawyer (D)	unopposed

1998 GENERAL

Tom Sawyer (D)	106,046	62.7%
Tom Watkins (R)	63,027	37.3%

PREVIOUS WINNING PERCENTAGES
1996 (54%); 1994 (52%); 1992 (68%); 1990 (60%);
1988 (75%); 1986 (54%)

Elected 1986; 8th term

Sawyer works diligently and speaks in measured tones, like the teacher he once was, eschewing the kind of polarizing partisan rhetoric often heard in the House. He weighs issues with care and tries to resolve disagreements with civility. Explaining his strategy for gaining influence in the legislative process, Sawyer once said, "You've got to be patient. You get into a position where you're trusted by sufficient numbers of others in those areas where you hope to make a difference."

Although Sawyer has a generally liberal voting record and serves as an at-large whip for the Democrats, he is no ideologue. On international trade, for example, he has broken with his labor supporters despite threats of a backlash at the polls.

And while Republicans and Democrats often square off in bitter partisan battles, Sawyer tries to promote a greater spirit of cooperation. He helped organize bipartisan retreats for House members and their families in 1997 and 1999 in Hershey, Pa., and in 2001 at The Greenbrier resort in West Virginia, in the hope that lawmakers who establish friendships will be less likely to feud when conducting legislative business.

Since landing his Energy and Commerce Committee (formerly Commerce) seat in 1997, Sawyer has placed a strong emphasis on energy issues. In the 106th Congress, he sponsored a measure to spur the expansion of electricity transmission networks between producers and suppliers as part of the larger matter of deregulation, aiming to ensure the reliability of electricity transmission.

Sawyer's interest in maintaining reliable electric power was prompted by a health emergency involving his mother. A power outage shut off the oxygen pump Sawyer's mother was using to help her breathe, and she could not get up from her electric recliner to reach a manually operated tank; she had to call 911 for help. Sawyer said the incident underscored that "people depend in a life-and-death way on electricity, and we can't have a bumpy transition," as the once tightly regulated industry is opened to competition.

When the Commerce panel wrestled in the 105th with legislation on transporting nuclear waste to a temporary storage site in Nevada, Sawyer got Energy and Power Subcommittee Chairman Dan Schaefer, R-Colo., to accept a proposal stating that when nuclear waste is removed from plants, it should be transported to the national storage site along routes that limit exposure in heavily populated areas. "If the unforeseeable or improbable [accident] does happen somehow," Sawyer said, "we all want the risks to human life or health to be as low as can possibly be."

Sawyer also has been active in another area where Energy and Commerce legislates — health care policy. In the 106th Congress, Sawyer backed a bipartisan proposal to give patients greater rights, including the ability to sue their health care providers. In the 104th, he and Ohio Republican David L. Hobson persuaded the House to add a provision to a health insurance bill that sought to speed the transmission of insurance data to doctors and hospitals by electronic means, thus eliminating paperwork and reducing opportunities for fraud.

When Sawyer was born in Akron in 1945, the city was known as "the rubber center of the universe," with a huge blue-collar work force employed in tire making. But in his lifetime, tire manufacturing has moved away to lower-wage venues in the South and abroad, and many in the district now work in the polymer industry, which benefits from increased international trade. That helps explain why, despite pressure from union leaders who feared the loss of jobs to overseas companies, Sawyer voted in 2000 to grant China permanent normal trade status.

"The truth is we have not made a passenger car tire in Akron since 1979," said Sawyer, who also supported other trade pacts such as the 1993 North American Free Trade Agreement. "You've got two choices," he told Knight-Ridder. "Are we going to struggle ... to try to recapture again what we once were? Or are we going to do our very best to become outstanding at those things that are going to be in our future?"

When Democrats had the House majority, Sawyer headed the Post Office and Civil Service Committee's Census and Population Subcommittee. When data pointed to an undercount in the 1990 census, with a bias against minorities, Sawyer pressed for a statistical adjustment of the head count, but he was rebuffed by the Bush administration and by the courts.

Although Republicans disbanded the Post Office Committee in 1995, Sawyer has continued to work on census issues and to push for statistical sampling in the 2000 census, to compensate for those likely to be missed by traditional counting methods. Rejecting Republican arguments that such sampling invites politically motivated tampering with the count, an unusually adamant Sawyer said in 1998: "It is absolutely irresponsible for Congress to force the Census Bureau to continue to use counting methods that have proven decade after decade to yield poor results at high costs, when sound science will allow us to do better."

Sawyer, who makes his own gumbo for some Akron campaign events, has not lost a single election in a political career that spans more than two decades and includes stints as mayor of Akron and as a state legislator, as well as his House service. His hold on the 14th District, though, has been tested at times.

Sawyer first won the district in 1986, after surviving a primary battle against Democratic state Sen. Oliver Ocasek — a 60-year-old, pro-labor war horse. While Ocasek was garrulous and emotional, and boasted ties to old-time labor leaders, Sawyer was reserved, methodical and adept at nuts-and-bolts organizing. Sawyer won by 10 percentage points, then took the general election with 54 percent over Republican Lynn Slaby, the Summit County prosecutor.

Sawyer has generally won re-election since by comfortable margins, although he was held to 52 percent in a 1994 rematch with Slaby. His re-election counts continue to rise — he earned 54 percent in 1996, 63 percent in 1998, and 65 percent in 2000.

KEY VOTES

2000
Yes Raise hourly minimum wage by $1 over two years
No Halt funding for U.S. mission in Kosovo unless European nations pay more
Yes Provide Medicare benefits to military retirees and their dependents
Yes Grant China permanent normal trade status
No Phase out estate, gift and trust taxes
No Prohibit implementation of president's national monument designations
No Approve GOP plan to provide prescription drug coverage for Medicare beneficiaries
Yes Increase help for poor nations indebted to international financial institutions

1999
Yes Impose steel import quotas
Yes Kill proposal to take aviation trust funds off budget
No Require background checks on buyers only at gun shows with 10 or more vendors
Yes Remove barriers among banking, securities and insurance companies
Yes Authorize state grants to hire teachers and reduce class size
Yes Overhaul campaign finance law; ban "soft money" and restrict advocacy advertising
Yes Approve bipartisan plan to increase rights of patients in managed-care health plans

INTEREST GROUPS

	AFL-CIO	ADA	CCUS	ACU
2000	90%	90%	47%	4%
1999	78%	100%	24%	0%
1998	90%	95%	44%	0%
1997	100%	95%	50%	8%

CQ VOTE STUDIES

	PARTY UNITY		PRESIDENTIAL SUPPORT	
	Support	Oppose	Support	Oppose
2000	95%	5%	93%	7%
1999	95%	5%	89%	11%
1998	94%	6%	88%	12%
1997	95%	5%	88%	12%

OHIO 14

Northeast – Akron

Located in northeastern Ohio, the 14th includes the city of Akron and its surroundings. Akron's history as a blue-collar factory town makes the district heavily Democratic. At one time, 90 percent of the nation's tires were manufactured in this district and it was referred to as the "premier factory town in America." As the major tire companies have cut back manufacturing operations in the 14th, the population has decreased, and the economy is trying to make the shift from industrial to white-collar jobs.

Although the tire companies have moved many of their factories, many of their corporate headquarters and research facilities remain in Akron, keeping they city alive through tough years by providing steady employment and economic strength for the city. The city also has been renovating its downtown and recreational areas along the Ohio & Erie Canal. Blue-collar descendants combined with blacks, ethnic whites and the academic community at the University of Akron help the city

retain its Democratic character from its blue-collar past.

North of Akron, suburbs and farmland in northern Summit County and western Portage County provide a Republican presence in the district. However, they are too sparse to overcome Akron's Democratic advantage. Although Democratic presidential candidates have a strong hold on the 14th, local officials in the state legislature are split between the two parties.

MAJOR INDUSTRY
Manufacturing, polymer research, agriculture

CITIES
Akron, 211,822; Cuyahoga Falls, 49,193; Stow, 32,162; Barberton, 27,360; Kent, 25,780

UNUSUAL FEATURES
Inventure Place (the National Inventors Hall of Fame) and Dr. Bob's Home (birthplace of Alcoholics Anonymous) in Akron; In 1970, Ohio National Guardsmen opened fire on anti-Vietnam protesters at Kent State University, killing four students; The guardsmen were later acquitted.

Rep. Deborah Pryce (R)

CAPITOL OFFICE
225-2015; fax 225-3529; 221 Cannon Bldg. 20515

INTERNET
e-mail: pryce.oh15@mail.house.gov
web: www.house.gov/pryce

COMMITTEES
Rules
  (Legislative & Budget Process - chairwoman)

HOMETOWN
Perry Township

BORN
July 29, 1951, Warren, Ohio

RELIGION
Presbyterian

FAMILY
Husband, Randy Walker; one child (deceased),
one stepchild

EDUCATION
Ohio State U., B.A. 1973; Capital U., J.D. 1976

CAREER
City prosecutor

POLITICAL HIGHLIGHTS
Franklin County Municipal Court judge, 1985-92

ELECTION RESULTS

2000 GENERAL

Deborah Pryce (R)	156,792	67.5%
Bill Buckel (D)	64,805	27.9%
Scott T. Smith (LIBERT)	10,700	4.6%

2000 PRIMARY

Deborah Pryce (R)	61,931	88.1%
Craig Z. Lortz (R)	8,400	11.9%

1998 GENERAL

Deborah Pryce (R)	113,846	65.7%
Adam Clay Miller (D)	49,334	28.5%
Kevin Nestor (I)	9,996	5.8%

PREVIOUS WINNING PERCENTAGES
1996 (71%); 1994 (71%); 1992 (44%)

Elected 1992; 5th term

As the 107th Congress began, Pryce was the highest-ranking woman in the House. A prosecutor and judge before her arrival in Washington, Pryce's ability to mediate conflicts has aided her rapid rise in the GOP ranks, where in November 2000 she became the new vice chairman of the Republican Conference.

As one of only three Republican women elected to the House in the Class of 1992, Pryce was a star from the start. Her first-term colleagues named her their "interim leader" for the early weeks of the 103rd Congress, and when Republicans became the House majority in 1995, she was assigned to the Rules Committee, which sets the guidelines that govern floor action on individual bills. In 1997, Pryce continued her climb in the GOP by winning election as Republican Conference secretary, an entry-level rung on the leadership ladder.

In 2000, she was unopposed for the conference vice chairmanship. In the 107th Congress, she heads the Rules panel's Legislative and Budget Process Subcommittee, which oversees the congressional budget process.

Pryce's political success has been clouded by personal tragedy. Her 9-year-old daughter, Caroline, died in September 1999 after a battle with cancer. Pryce has since taken a more active role on family and health care issues, including efforts to raise federal funding for cancer research. She has indicated that she may try to build on the Family and Medical Leave Act, which requires businesses to give employees time off to care for relatives. Pryce, who took leave from the House during her daughter's illness, voted against the original legislation in 1993, fearing it would put a costly burden on employers. She supports proposals that would help families but that she says "are compatible with good, conservative principles."

Pryce is among Speaker J. Dennis Hastert's inner circle, where she can be counted on to give him the "straight line about what members are thinking and what will fly," according to one leadership aide.

While she generally votes the party line, there have been notable exceptions. In 1999, she opposed two impeachment articles brought against President Clinton — the only elected GOP leader who did not vote "yes" on all four charges. She has voted in some instances with gun control proponents and abortion rights advocates. In 2000, she was one of a minority of House Republicans to support funding for the Clinton administration effort to sue the tobacco industry, and she backed enactment of the law to require disclosure by certain political fundraising groups.

The Speaker in the 105th Congress, Newt Gingrich, selected Pryce to lead a GOP task force on tobacco policy. The task force proposal would not have imposed new taxes on cigarettes; rather, it would have redefined the Food and Drug Administration's role in regulating nicotine, established an anti-tobacco public service campaign and encouraged states to impose penalties on minors who smoke.

The proposal drew fire from all sides, including from within the GOP, with some conservatives saying the regulations went too far and several moderates saying the measure did not go far enough to reduce smoking. The task force's proposal was never formally introduced.

Gingrich also chose Pryce for the 12-member group that designed legislation, passed by the House in 1998, to give consumers more clout in dealing with their managed-care plans. Though the bill contained patient protections sought by Democrats, including expanded rights to appeal coverage decisions to an outside panel, it did not let consumers sue their health plans, as Democrats wanted. The measure died in the Senate.

Pryce has been a leader on children's issues, sponsoring a law enacted in 2000 that increased funding to prevent child abuse and to investigate such crimes. An adoptive mother, she has worked to make adoption easier for qualified applicants. She cosponsored the 1996 law that streamlined adoption procedures for children in foster care. The bill altered a 1980 law, putting more emphasis on placing children in safe homes as opposed to reuniting them with relatives, who may not provide a stable environment.

During consideration of the adoption bill, Pryce found out that a family in her district could lose their adopted twin girls, who were part Indian. The Pomo tribe had learned of the girls' heritage after the adoption was complete and had sued to have the adoption revoked and to obtain custody of the children. In response, Pryce sought — unsuccessfully — to bar a tribe from getting involved in an adoption process unless one of the child's biological parents had a significant relationship with the tribe; ancestry alone would not be enough for a tribe to claim rights to a child.

In 1994, Pryce drew widespread publicity with her proposal to bar federal prison inmates from training on free weights or studying martial arts. "Taxpayer dollars," she said, "are being used to build bigger and better thugs."

Having studied, worked and lived in the Columbus area for three decades, Pryce is well-versed in the nuances of her congressional district. After attending Ohio State University for her undergraduate degree and Capital University for her law degree, she worked for the state government and as a city prosecutor before being elected as a judge on the Franklin County Municipal Court in 1985.

Shortly after she began her second six-year term on the bench, she resigned in 1992 to enter the crowded GOP field vying for the seat of veteran GOP Rep. Chalmers P. Wylie, who was retiring. She won the party's endorsement and then prevailed in a tight, three-way general-election race by just 6 percentage points. Since then, she has been re-elected by large margins.

Abortion has been a tough issue for Pryce since that first campaign, when some abortion foes complained that they had been deceived into believing Pryce sided with them. (Their support at the time was pivotal to her securing the GOP nomination.) Pryce supports family planning programs, favors allowing federal employees' health care plans to cover abortions, and has voted to lift the ban on abortions in overseas military hospitals. But she wants to prohibit a procedure its opponents call "partial birth" abortion.

KEY VOTES

2000

No   Raise hourly minimum wage by $1 over two years

Yes   Halt funding for U.S. mission in Kosovo unless European nations pay more

Yes   Provide Medicare benefits to military retirees and their dependents

Yes   Grant China permanent normal trade status

Yes   Phase out estate, gift and trust taxes

Yes   Prohibit implementation of president's national monument designations

Yes   Approve GOP plan to provide prescription drug coverage for Medicare beneficiaries

No   Increase help for poor nations indebted to international financial institutions

1999

No   Impose steel import quotas

?   Kill proposal to take aviation trust funds off budget

Yes   Require background checks on buyers only at gun shows with 10 or more vendors

Yes   Remove barriers among banking, securities and insurance companies

No   Authorize state grants to hire teachers and reduce class size

?   Overhaul campaign finance law; ban "soft money" and restrict advocacy advertising

No   Approve bipartisan plan to increase rights of patients in managed-care health plans

INTEREST GROUPS

	AFL-CIO	ADA	CCUS	ACU
2000	0%	15%	90%	80%
1999	0%	20%	100%	56%
1998	25%	5%	100%	83%
1997	0%	15%	100%	72%

CQ VOTE STUDIES

	PARTY UNITY		PRESIDENTIAL SUPPORT	
	Support	Oppose	Support	Oppose
2000	90%	10%	35%	65%
1999	84%	16%	38%	62%
1998	88%	12%	30%	70%
1997	90%	10%	41%	59%

OHIO 15
Central — Western Columbus and suburbs

The 15th includes most of Columbus, the state's centrally located capital, and spans part of Franklin and all of Madison counties to the south and west of the city. It also takes in the northwestern corner of Pickaway County. While it does not include the heart of downtown Columbus (in the neighboring 12th), the district encompasses Ohio State University and most of the academic community.

Columbus is not known as a tourist attraction except in August, when the Ohio State Fair opens, and on Saturdays in autumn when the Ohio State Buckeyes play football at home. However, the region is generally regarded as a good place to raise a family. Covering much of Franklin County's expanding service sector, which includes several large high-tech research centers, the district has a steady employment base. Madison County, although comparable to Franklin in size, is much more rural and less densely populated.

The district traditionally has been the more Republican of the two that

divide the capital — the nearby 12th includes most of the heavily black East Side of Columbus. The university's academic community and neighborhoods in the nearby West Side of Columbus support Democrats, but they are more than offset by the rock-ribbed Republican suburbs west of the Olentangy and Scioto Rivers. GOP presidential candidates do very well in Upper Arlington and other affluent suburbs to the west.

MAJOR INDUSTRY
Retail trade, health care, research

CITIES
Columbus (pt.), 347,989 (1990); Upper Arlington, 31,553; Grove City, 27,856

UNUSUAL FEATURES
Ohio State Fair held every August at the Ohio Expo Center; Historic German Village reflects architecture and character of a 19th-century German neighborhood.

Rep. Ralph Regula (R)

Elected 1972; 15th term

Behind Regula's kind face and easy manner is a shrewd politician who has built a reputation over three decades in Congress as a powerful pragmatist. Regula excels at his job as chairman of one of the House's 13 Appropriations subcommittees by walking a fine line between compromise and capitulation. He usually looks for the middle ground on controversial matters rather than digging in his heels, and he is respected for his ability to maneuver deftly among GOP factions and across party lines to reach workable solutions.

In the 107th Congress, after six years at the helm of the Interior Appropriations Subcommittee, he was forced by GOP-imposed term limits to give up that gavel. As the second-ranking Republican on the Appropriations Committee, Regula (REG-you-luh) had his pick among six other subcommittees, and he chose the panel in charge of the largest of the 13 spending bills — Labor, Health and Human Services and Education.

Regula's diplomacy and negotiating skills proved vital during his tenure on Interior Appropriations, where many fights over land and natural resources policy are waged. One of the smaller of the 13 annual spending measures, the Interior bill has nonetheless provided more than its share of clashes over spending levels for timber harvesting, mining, offshore oil drilling and the National Endowment for the Arts, which is funded under the legislation.

"He constantly has a battle within his committee between the Westerners and the Greens," fellow appropriator and Ohio Republican David L. Hobson told The Associated Press in 1999. "Ralph is one of those rare people who can move between both of them and not have them mad at him." At a committee meeting in 2000, the ranking Democrat on the Appropriations panel, David R. Obey of Wisconsin, who is not known for his kind words for Republicans in the heat of spending battles, called Regula "one of the most laid-back members" of the House.

That political facility has at times provoked suspicion among some Republicans and conservative groups who have pegged Regula, a former state legislator who lives on an Ohio farm and calls himself a "tree-hugger," as too liberal. Regula has handled the charges — hurled most violently by Western private property rights advocates after he took over the Interior chairmanship in 1995 — with disarming candor. He met with his detractors to listen to their criticism, traveled to the West to witness the roots of their concerns and attended meetings of the Western Caucus.

Some conservative GOP lawmakers have raised concerns not only about Regula's willingness to compromise on environmental issues but also about a few other moderate streaks in his record: He has supported a minimum wage increase and family planning programs and resisted proposals for taxpayer-financed private school vouchers.

Regula describes himself as "an advocate of environmental protections within the context of practical economic realities." While his voting record generally receives low marks from environmental interest groups — the League of Conservation Voters gave him a score of only 13 percent for the 106th Congress — he has done enough environmental preservation work to receive awards from a variety of organizations. He can be found on Capitol Hill wearing a tie covered with turtles, especially when the House is debating the Interior bill.

The son of an Ohio farmer, Regula, as a young lawyer in the early 1960s, was instrumental in saving a wooded area from developers and turning it into a nature preserve. In the 104th Congress, he opposed an effort by con-

CAPITOL OFFICE
225-3876; fax 225-3059; 2306 Rayburn Bldg. 20515

INTERNET
e-mail: www.house.gov/writerep
web: www.house.gov/regula

COMMITTEES
Appropriations
(Labor, Health & Human Services & Education - chairman)

HOMETOWN
Navarre

BORN
Dec. 3, 1924, Beach City, Ohio

RELIGION
Episcopalian

FAMILY
Wife, Mary Regula; three children

EDUCATION
Mount Union College, B.A. 1948; William McKinley School of Law, LL.B. 1952

MILITARY SERVICE
Navy, 1944-46

CAREER
Lawyer; high school teacher; principal

POLITICAL HIGHLIGHTS
Ohio Board of Education, 1960-64; Ohio House, 1965-67; Ohio Senate, 1967-73

ELECTION RESULTS

2000 GENERAL

Ralph Regula (R)	162,294	69.2%
William Smith (D)	62,709	26.8%
Richard L. Shetler (LIBERT)	6,166	2.6%
Brad Graef (NL)	3,231	1.4%

2000 PRIMARY

Ralph Regula (R)	unopposed

1998 GENERAL

Ralph Regula (R)	117,426	64.0%
Peter D. Ferguson (D)	66,047	36.0%

PREVIOUS WINNING PERCENTAGES
1996 (69%); 1994 (75%); 1992 (64%); 1990 (59%); 1988 (79%); 1986 (76%); 1984 (72%); 1982 (66%); 1980 (79%); 1978 (78%); 1976 (67%); 1974 (66%); 1972 (57%)

servatives to limit the Environmental Protection Agency's authority, and he strongly backed funding for Everglades restoration. In the 105th, to the delight of environmental groups, he cut from the Interior bill an annual subsidy to timber companies logging on public lands.

Despite his penchant for preservation, Regula opposed Clinton administration requests to buy more land to expand the national park system, arguing that the government cannot afford to maintain the facilities it already has.

The dean of the Ohio GOP delegation, Regula's personal popularity among colleagues and his preference for seeking areas of common agreement have proved useful in bipartisan efforts by Ohio lawmakers on such issues as highway funding and the merger of the Conrail and Norfolk Southern railroads. Regula also defends federal support of clean coal technology research, a program of particular interest in his area, where most electricity is produced by coal-fired plants.

The steel industry is important to the 16th District, and Regula, as chairman of the Steel Caucus, has argued vociferously before several international bodies that Japan, Brazil and Russia are taking advantage of their government subsidies to dump their steel imports onto the U.S. market.

His hometown causes also include preserving the memory of President McKinley, Canton's most famous son. Regula, who graduated from a now-defunct law school named after the 25th president, undertook an effort in 1991 to spend federal money to buy a house in Canton where McKinley once lived. The home, purchased and renovated with private funds, became the site of a First Ladies' Library founded by Regula's wife, Mary. In 1998, Regula got $300,000 in federal funding to help the library hire a professional staff.

He preserves McKinley's memory in other ways as well: For years, he gave red carnations to his House colleagues on McKinley's birthday. And at the start of every Congress, he introduces a bill to bar Alaskans from changing the name of Mount McKinley — the nation's tallest peak, situated in Alaska — to Denali, its Indian name.

Regula was a schoolteacher and principal and served on the state board of education for four years before he was elected to the state legislature, where he represented a large swath of Stark County — the heart of the 16th District. So when GOP Rep. Frank Bow retired in 1972 after 22 years in the House, Regula was viewed as the logical choice to succeed him.

Regula won his first election with 57 percent of the vote and has been a force in northeast Ohio since. Even between 1978 and 1988, a period of economic upheaval for the industrial areas of his district, he always won at least 66 percent of the vote.

KEY VOTES

2000

No Raise hourly minimum wage by $1 over two years

Yes Halt funding for U.S. mission in Kosovo unless European nations pay more

Yes Provide Medicare benefits to military retirees and their dependents

Yes Grant China permanent normal trade status

Yes Phase out estate, gift and trust taxes

Yes Prohibit implementation of president's national monument designations

Yes Approve GOP plan to provide prescription drug coverage for Medicare beneficiaries

No Increase help for poor nations indebted to international financial institutions

1999

Yes Impose steel import quotas

Yes Kill proposal to take aviation trust funds off budget

Yes Require background checks on buyers only at gun shows with 10 or more vendors

Yes Remove barriers among banking, securities and insurance companies

No Authorize state grants to hire teachers and reduce class size

Yes Overhaul campaign finance law; ban "soft money" and restrict advocacy advertising

No Approve bipartisan plan to increase rights of patients in managed-care health plans

INTEREST GROUPS

	AFL-CIO	ADA	CCUS	ACU
2000	10%	10%	80%	76%
1999	22%	25%	84%	64%
1998	40%	20%	89%	64%
1997	38%	30%	90%	56%

CQ VOTE STUDIES

	PARTY UNITY		PRESIDENTIAL SUPPORT	
	Support	Oppose	Support	Oppose
2000	88%	12%	36%	64%
1999	83%	17%	32%	68%
1998	87%	13%	28%	72%
1997	86%	14%	39%	61%

OHIO 16
Northeast – Canton

A region of traditional Midwestern values and work ethic, the 16th centers on Canton in northeastern Ohio's Stark County and includes three-and-a-half neighboring counties to the west.

Although the boundaries have changed somewhat, the Canton-based 16th was represented by William McKinley more than a century ago. McKinley launched his governorship from the district and conducted his 1896 presidential campaign from a front porch in Canton.

Canton has a rich manufacturing and steel-producing history, and high-skill manufacturing remains at the core of the region's steadily prosperous economy today. West of Stark County, the district becomes more rural and agricultural, although the importance of manufacturing is still evident. Holmes County has a sizable Amish population and is a popular Ohio tourist destination.

This basically Republican district has a few Democratic parts. Like nearby Akron and Youngstown, Canton is a working-class city that often votes Democratic in local elections, but it does not share in the solidly Democratic tradition of the rest of northeastern Ohio. Since 1920, only four Democratic presidential candidates have carried Stark County, which accounts for nearly two-thirds of the district's population. Outside Stark County, the district tends to be even more Republican and conservative.

MAJOR INDUSTRY
Steel, bearings manufacturing, health care

CITIES
Canton, 78,582; Massillon, 30,634; Wooster, 24,308

UNUSUAL FEATURES
Professional Football Hall of Fame in Canton; President William McKinley's burial site in a Canton park.

Rep. James A. Traficant Jr. (D)

CAPITOL OFFICE
225-5261; fax 225-3719; 2446 Rayburn Bldg. 20515

INTERNET
e-mail: telljim@mail.house.gov
web: www.house.gov/traficant

COMMITTEES
No assignments

HOMETOWN
Poland

BORN
May 8, 1941, Youngstown, Ohio

RELIGION
Roman Catholic

FAMILY
Wife, Patricia Choppa; two children

EDUCATION
U. of Pittsburgh, B.S. 1963; Youngstown State U., M.S. 1973, M.S. 1976

CAREER
County drug program director

POLITICAL HIGHLIGHTS
Mahoning County sheriff, 1981-85

ELECTION RESULTS

2000 GENERAL

James A. Traficant Jr. (D)	120,333	50.0%
Paul Alberty (R)	54,751	22.7%
Randy D. Walter (I)	51,793	21.5%
Lou D'Apolito (I)	9,568	4.0%
Carol Ann McCoy (NL)	3,154	1.3%

2000 PRIMARY

James A. Traficant Jr. (D)	59,415	50.5%
Robert Hagan (D)	40,079	34.1%
George Tablack (D)	16,203	13.8%
Christopher C. Doutt (D)	1,988	1.7%

1998 GENERAL

James A. Traficant Jr. (D)	123,718	68.2%
Paul Alberty (R)	57,703	31.8%

PREVIOUS WINNING PERCENTAGES
1996 (91%); 1994 (77%); 1992 (84%); 1990 (78%); 1988 (77%); 1986 (72%); 1984 (53%)

Elected 1984; 9th term

One of the most colorful figures on Capitol Hill, Traficant has long been known for his daily policy tirades and his constant call on the House floor to "Beam me up" — the Star Trek-inspired phrase he regularly uses to voice his indignation and befuddlement. Behind Traficant's carefully cultivated populist shtick is a consummate politician whose theatrical style has proved very popular with the folks back home.

Long regarded as little more than an eccentric representative of a depressed steel region, he began the 107th Congress by abandoning his party and voting for Republican J. Dennis Hastert for Speaker. Traficant contended that many Democrats had worked against his bid for re-election. He also said he owed Hastert a debt of gratitude for his help with legislation to make it more difficult for the IRS to seize taxpayers' property.

Democrats were furious. "He's toast," said Ohioan Tony P. Hall. Democrats refused to give Traficant any committee assignments, and Republicans said they could not give him any GOP committee slots unless he joined the Republican Conference. Traficant, who said he regarded himself as an "independent Democrat," refused to do so, and he became a man without a committee.

By threatening in 2000 to leave his party just as it appeared that the Democrats might retake the House by a narrow margin, he forced both parties to court his vote — a strategy he used to win bipartisan support for a $25 million grant for a new community center in Youngstown.

The former sheriff, who more than once has faced federal corruption probes into his own dealings, stands out among his navy-suited colleagues by wearing checked suits and cream ties — a clothing style that, according to USA Today, "only a racetrack tout could love." With arms waving and hair askew, Traficant takes to the floor nearly every day with a message of working-class economic anxiety. He vents profound — and often profane — unhappiness on matters such as foreign aid, trade and immigration, skewering his targets with memorable attack lines. Not one to tiptoe around an issue, he suggested that an environmental regulator "go to a proctologist for a brain scan" and rejected a proposed budget deal in 1993 by telling President Clinton to "shove this big tax increase up your compromise."

Politically, Traficant is difficult to characterize. He votes with the GOP more often than almost any other House Democrat, and he takes conservative positions on issues ranging from environmental regulations to illegal immigration. Early in the 107th, he was one of only 10 Democrats who voted for a GOP bill to cut income taxes. But he also is a stalwart ally of union causes, opposing trade bills and pressing for tougher anti-dumping regulations.

Before 2000, Traficant enjoyed a lock on the heavily Democratic 17th District, cruising to re-election with at least two-thirds of the vote. But he faced new scrutiny by federal investigators during the 106th amid media reports that he may have broken tax laws or House rules by accepting gifts. Shortly before the March Democratic primary, in which the suddenly vulnerable incumbent faced state Sen. Robert F. Hagan and two other challengers, Traficant predicted he would be indicted. Nevertheless, he took the primary with 50 percent of the vote, then easily won re-election. In May 2001, a federal grand jury handed down a 10-count indictment charging him with bribery, tax evasion and obstruction of justice.

Despite his iconoclastic nature, Traficant had risen to the senior ranks of the Transportation Committee, where he aggressively pursued federal grants and loans for the Mahoning Valley. "I was called the king of pork because I got five bridges funded," he said in 1998. "I don't apologize for a damn thing."

When talk turns to the global economy, Traficant has an earful for anyone in either party who favors lowering international trade barriers, especially with China. He voices the outrage of working-class constituents — many of whom once had high-paying factory jobs — who feel left behind by corporations that have shifted jobs abroad to take advantage of cheaper labor. A passionate defender of U.S.-made goods, he frequently attaches "buy American" language to appropriations bills.

He supports GOP-led efforts to crack down on illegal immigration. Endorsing a measure in 1997 to allow deployment of U.S. troops along the U.S.-Mexico border, Traficant said, "We have got millions of illegal immigrants, many of them running over our borders with backpacks full of cocaine and heroin. Beam me up. Whoever created this immigration policy is in fact smoking dope."

No friend of the IRS, Traficant added a provision to a 1998 tax bill that severely restricts the ability of the agency to seize the property of tax evaders. "I've seen the other side of that One-Eyed Jack," he told U.S. News & World Report. It was on that provision that Hastert provided the help that won him Traficant's vote for Speaker two years later.

While Traficant is known for his anger and passion on the House floor, offstage he is a friend to all in the House — members, doorkeepers and cops alike. He calls everyone "chairman," the Capitol Hill expression usually reserved for those in actual positions of power.

A former football star at the University of Pittsburgh, Traficant ran an anti-drug program in Mahoning County before being elected sheriff in 1980. He became a hero to the district's hard-hit factory workers, but he quickly alienated virtually every government official in the area by claiming that most were controlled by organized crime.

Those allegations took on an ironic cast when Traficant was indicted for bribery, with the FBI obtaining recordings of him accepting money from underworld figures. Traficant, despite a lack of legal training, defended himself in court, put on a stunning performance and said he took the money to get evidence against the mobsters. The jury believed him, voting to acquit after a seven-week trial.

In 1984, Traficant's popularity spurred him to challenge the incumbent Republican representative. Although Traficant was underfinanced and had to overcome the hostility of Democratic leaders — one of whom sought to get him committed to a mental institution — Traficant drew large crowds with his attacks on banks, big business and the IRS. He won with 53 percent.

KEY VOTES

2000

Yes Raise hourly minimum wage by $1 over two years
Yes Halt funding for U.S. mission in Kosovo unless European nations pay more
Yes Provide Medicare benefits to military retirees and their dependents
No Grant China permanent normal trade status
Yes Phase out estate, gift and trust taxes
Yes Prohibit implementation of president's national monument designations
Yes Approve GOP plan to provide prescription drug coverage for Medicare beneficiaries
Yes Increase help for poor nations indebted to international financial institutions

1999

Yes Impose steel import quotas
No Kill proposal to take aviation trust funds off budget
Yes Require background checks on buyers only at gun shows with 10 or more vendors
Yes Remove barriers among banking, securities and insurance companies
Yes Authorize state grants to hire teachers and reduce class size
No Overhaul campaign finance law; ban "soft money" and restrict advocacy advertising
Yes Approve bipartisan plan to increase rights of patients in managed-care health plans

INTEREST GROUPS

	AFL-CIO	ADA	CCUS	ACU
2000	40%	30%	52%	60%
1999	100%	60%	36%	52%
1998	90%	45%	61%	64%
1997	75%	25%	60%	76%

CQ VOTE STUDIES

	PARTY UNITY		PRESIDENTIAL SUPPORT	
	Support	Oppose	Support	Oppose
2000	22%	78%	32%	68%
1999	43%	57%	44%	56%
1998	33%	67%	47%	53%
1997	23%	77%	36%	64%

OHIO 17
Northeast – Youngstown, Warren

The 17th, bordering Pennsylvania in the northeastern part of the state, includes all of Mahoning and most of Columbiana and Trumbull counties. Once a leading steel-producing area, the Mahoning Valley now symbolizes industrial decline; the steel mills that remain are silent and abandoned.

Despite some economic diversification, young people searching for opportunities often look elsewhere, and the population of most cities has declined. However, local leaders are hoping that the manufacturing industry in the region is starting to turn around. The regional airport, which houses a large Air Force Reserve base, is undergoing an expansion project that is expected to turn it into an air cargo hub.

The 17th was one of Ohio's most Democratic districts for much of the 20th century, and it cast Ohio's second-highest district vote for Al Gore in the 2000 presidential contest. The 17th's remaining blue-collar base, ethnic communities and black populations in Youngstown and Warren are important Democratic forces. Although the Republican vote increases south of the industrial Mahoning Valley, the GOP's numbers are too small to make much of a difference overall.

MAJOR INDUSTRY
Automobile assembly and wiring, manufacturing

MILITARY BASES
Youngstown Municipal Airport Air Force Reserve Station, 1,392 military, 273 civilian (1999)

CITIES
Youngstown, 82,757; Warren, 47,845; Boardman (unincorporated), 38,596 (1990)

UNUSUAL FEATURES
Mill Creek Park in Youngstown is one of the nation's largest urban parks at 2,530 acres; Salem was a Quaker center of anti-slavery activity in the 1800s.

Rep. Bob Ney (R)

CAPITOL OFFICE
225-6265; fax 225-3394
1024 Longworth Bldg. 20515

INTERNET
e-mail: www.house.gov/writerep
web: www.house.gov/ney

COMMITTEES
Financial Services
House Administration - chairman
Joint Library
Joint Printing

HOMETOWN
St. Clairsville

BORN
July 5, 1954, Wheeling, W.Va.

RELIGION
Roman Catholic

FAMILY
Engaged to Elizabeth Mikropoulos; two children

EDUCATION
Ohio U., attended 1972-74; Ohio State U., B.S. 1976

CAREER
State health and education program manager;
local safety director; educator

POLITICAL HIGHLIGHTS
Ohio House, 1981-83; defeated for re-election to
Ohio House, 1982; Ohio Senate, 1984-95

ELECTION RESULTS

2000 GENERAL

Bob Ney (R)	152,325	64.4%
Marc D. Guthrie (D)	79,232	33.5%
John R. Bargar Sr. (LIBERT)	4,948	2.1%

2000 PRIMARY

Bob Ney (R)	unopposed

1998 GENERAL

Bob Ney (R)	113,119	60.3%
Robert L. Burch (D)	74,571	39.7%

PREVIOUS WINNING PERCENTAGES
1996 (50%); 1994 (54%)

Elected 1994; 4th term

In an odd twist of fate, Ney took over the chairmanship of the House Administration Committee in the 107th Congress, a position that was held for years by another representative from Ohio's 18th District — Democrat Wayne L. Hays. Hays was forced to resign from Congress in 1976 after news broke that his secretary was primarily his mistress. But Ohio voters forgave his indiscretions, and Hays won a seat in the Ohio House in 1978. Two years later, he lost that seat to Republican Bob Ney.

Ney now sits at the helm of the panel that not only oversees the operations of the House and Capitol Hill support agencies but also deals with campaign finance law. A man who resists easy categorization, Ney is a dependably conservative Republican on most issues, but he breaks party ranks to aggressively defend labor interests.

Ney may be the only member of Congress who speaks Farsi, and he also speaks better-than-average French and knows a fair amount of Italian — a language he picked up from his melting-pot district, which contains much of what is left of Ohio's coal and steel industries.

He assiduously looks out for those industries and their workers, whether by blocking tougher air emission regulations, opposing international trade agreements or opposing more visas for foreign high-technology workers — all of which he believes can threaten jobs. His attention to such issues is one reason he has won election three times in a working-class district that previously had not elected a Republican in 48 years.

In 2000, Ney was the only Republican among 71 congressional incumbents who received a promise of financial aid from the AFL-CIO. He sided with unions in the 106th Congress by leading GOP opposition to legislation granting China permanent normal trade status. "I don't want to shut off relationships and markets," Ney told The Columbus Dispatch. "But this is a hideous agreement. I am a fair trader ... and right now, we don't have fair trade" with China.

Ney's stand on China put him in the unusual position of being targeted by U.S. Chamber of Commerce ads for "turning his back on the working families of Ohio" — even as the chamber endorsed his re-election bid based on his record of supporting business 92 percent of the time in 1999.

The congressman often tries to appeal directly to the considerable organized labor contingent in his district. In the 105th and 106th, he helped push a proposal that was a top priority of police unions to give state public safety employees the right to join a union, bargain collectively and seek mediation for labor disputes. In the 104th, Ney helped thwart an effort to eliminate federal labor protection for mass transit workers. He has also been a consistent advocate for minimum wage increases, and he battled in the 106th to impose quotas on steel imports.

On social issues, however, Ney's conservative views are never in doubt. He opposes abortion and gun control, and he voted for sweeping welfare overhaul legislation in the 105th.

Ney is a strong foe of federal regulations, especially those that require businesses to undertake costly efforts to reduce pollution. In 2000, he won passage of an amendment to cut the Environmental Protection Agency's administrative budget by $5 million and transfer the funds to veterans' health care programs. "For too long, the EPA's irrational air regulations have brutalized working families in this country, and it is time for them to tighten their belts by spending $5 million less on their travel and management budget," he said.

Over-regulation of the coal industry, Ney has said, has "taken food off of the tables of people in southern Ohio." He contends that Ohioans and other Midwesterners have "suffered tremendously" under the Clean Air Act, specifically its provisions targeting emissions that cause acid rain.

Ney attracted a fair amount of media attention while making up his mind on the impeachment of President Clinton in 1998. He was a high-profile hold-out who, unlike other undeclared Ohioans, was willing to discuss his inde-cision on national television. As a result, he received a huge amount of out-side advice, including 8,500 e-mail messages in just one day. In the end, he voted "yes" on two of the four impeachment articles that passed the House, saying Clinton "has shattered the trust of the American people."

Ney doesn't hesitate to use emotional appeals, especially when it comes to bread-and-butter issues of his district. At a steel rally outside the White House in 1999, a pumped-up Ney, sporting a black leather jacket and black jeans, addressed industry supporters. After his speech, he marched to the White House gates and ostentatiously demanded to talk with an adminis-tration official. Ney was then invited inside for a meeting.

He shows some imagination in personal matters as well. Early in 2001, he proposed to his girlfriend in the Capitol dome. (USA Today reported that he had wanted to pop the question atop the dome, but she was afraid of heights and didn't make it all the way to the top.)

Raised in a middle-class family — his father was a camera operator for a TV station and his mother worked in a liquor store — Ney worked his way through Ohio State University. He taught English in Iran in 1978 but had to return home when the revolution that toppled the shah broke out.

Ney got his start in elective politics at age 26, winning a seat in the Ohio House in 1980 by toppling Hays. In 1984, Ney won election to the state Sen-ate, where he eventually rose to become chairman of the Ohio Senate's Finance Committee. He won a reputation as a bipartisan player and worked with Democrats on a major health care overhaul bill. The measure, which was designed to make it easier for workers to get insurance even if they switched jobs, became law.

After nine-term Democratic Rep. Douglas Applegate's retirement left the 18th District seat open in 1994, the well-funded Ney easily dispatched five rivals in the GOP primary. In the general election, he defeated Demo-cratic state Rep. Greg L. DiDonato, a conservative, by calling for a balanced-budget amendment and term limits for members. He had a close call in 1996 but has won his last two elections by comfortable margins.

KEY VOTES

2000

Yes Raise hourly minimum wage by $1 over two years
Yes Halt funding for U.S. mission in Kosovo unless European nations pay more
Yes Provide Medicare benefits to military retirees and their dependents
No   Grant China permanent normal trade status
Yes Phase out estate, gift and trust taxes
Yes Prohibit implementation of president's national monument designations
Yes Approve GOP plan to provide prescription drug coverage for Medicare beneficiaries
No   Increase help for poor nations indebted to international financial institutions

1999

Yes Impose steel import quotas
No   Kill proposal to take aviation trust funds off budget
No   Require background checks on buyers only at gun shows with 10 or more vendors
Yes Remove barriers among banking, securities and insurance companies
No   Authorize state grants to hire teachers and reduce class size
No   Overhaul campaign finance law; ban "soft money" and restrict advocacy advertising
No   Approve bipartisan plan to increase rights of patients in managed-care health plans

INTEREST GROUPS

	AFL-CIO	ADA	CCUS	ACU
2000	40%	20%	61%	83%
1999	44%	10%	92%	84%
1998	30%	15%	83%	80%
1997	38%	20%	80%	71%

CQ VOTE STUDIES

	PARTY UNITY		PRESIDENTIAL SUPPORT	
	Support	Oppose	Support	Oppose
2000	88%	12%	29%	71%
1999	89%	11%	16%	84%
1998	85%	15%	27%	73%
1997	91%	9%	34%	66%

OHIO 18

East — Steubenville, Zanesville

The 18th, in the eastern half of Ohio, borders the West Virginia panhandle and includes 12 full counties, half of Licking and a sliver of Columbiana. This mostly rural district, spanning land along the Ohio River, contains most of Ohio's remaining steel and coal producers. Those industries have been declining for decades, which has led to high unemployment and low pay for workers in the 18th. The area faces harsh competition in steel from abroad, and Clean Air Act regulations threaten local high-sulfur coal.

While much of the district has started to redevelop, Licking County is a pocket of prosperity, with Newark as a growing manufacturing and research center. Although the Newark Air Force Base was closed in 1995, the impact was softened as most of its workers successfully moved to private companies, where they continue to work primarily on missile guidance systems.

In Jefferson, Belmont and Monroe counties, the steelworking and coal-mining Democrats of the district generally show strong party allegiance, though they tend to shy away from supporting liberals. This part of Ohio resembles West Virginia and eastern Kentucky. Locals raise some cattle, but the hilly terrain makes farming generally unprofitable.

The district's industrial character and ethnic diversity, including a large Catholic population of Eastern European and Greek immigrants, have made it primarily Democratic in the past half-century. However, the western part of the district is more Republican, and redistricting in 1992 added more farmers and more GOP-leaning voters to the mix. In 1994, voters elected a Republican to the House for the first time in 48 years and have continued to do so.

MAJOR INDUSTRY
Steel, manufacturing, coal

CITIES
Newark (pt.), 28,642 (1990); Zanesville, 26,989; Steubenville, 21,970

UNUSUAL FEATURES
Underground Railroad stop in Leesville; Astronaut and former Sen. John Glenn born in New Concord.

Rep. Steven C. LaTourette (R)

Elected 1994; 4th term

CAPITOL OFFICE
225-5731; fax 225-3307; 2453 Rayburn Bldg. 20515

INTERNET
e-mail: www.house.gov/writerep
web: www.house.gov/latourette

COMMITTEES
Financial Services
Government Reform
Transportation & Infrastructure
 (Economic Development, Public Buildings &
 Emergency Management - chairman)

HOMETOWN
Madison

BORN
July 22, 1954, Cleveland, Ohio

RELIGION
Methodist

FAMILY
Divorced; four children

EDUCATION
U. of Michigan, B.A. 1976; Cleveland State U., J.D.
1979

CAREER
Lawyer

POLITICAL HIGHLIGHTS
Candidate for Lake County prosecutor, 1984; Lake
County prosecutor, 1989-94

ELECTION RESULTS

2000 GENERAL

Steven C. LaTourette (R)	206,639	64.8%
Dale Virgil Blanchard (D)	101,842	31.9%
Sid Stone (LIBERT)	10,367	3.3%

2000 PRIMARY

Steven C. LaTourette (R)	unopposed

1998 GENERAL

Steven C. LaTourette (R)	126,786	66.4%
Elizabeth Kelley (D)	64,090	33.6%

PREVIOUS WINNING PERCENTAGES
1996 (55%); 1994 (49%)

With a moderate voting record and a willingness to work with Democrats on a wide range of issues, LaTourette stands apart from most of his colleagues in the GOP Class of 1994.

Perhaps it was growing up in the progressive Cleveland suburb of Cleveland Heights (which declared itself a "nuclear free" zone) that taught him to be inclusive. Or perhaps it is the character of the 19th District he now represents, where blue-collar Democrats are a powerful presence and voters twice backed Bill Clinton for president.

LaTourette (la-TUR-et) says that the conservative politics of the many "true believers" of the GOP Class of 1994 "is not my politics." He adds that sometimes he wishes those colleagues would not be so strident with their demands and rhetoric. That is the same advice he used to give the young, gung-ho prosecutors who worked for him when he was Lake County's prosecuting attorney.

LaTourette's brand of moderate Republicanism goes over well in the 19th, where Tom Coyne Jr., the Democrat he beat in 1996, declared before the 1998 election, "I think he has done a good job," according to the Cleveland Plain Dealer.

LaTourette typically concurs with GOP conservatives on social policy issues. He consistently votes with anti-abortion forces, he supported repeal of the ban on certain semiautomatic assault-style weapons, and he backed welfare overhaul. House Republican leaders still turn to him to preside over contentious floor debates, a role reserved for unflappable members who have a knack for House rules and an understanding of leadership objectives.

But he has strayed from the party line often, including supporting some Democratic initiatives to raise the minimum wage and to set tough standards for the managed health care industry. In the 1998 debate on managed-care legislation, LaTourette was a highly visible defector to the Democrats' patients' rights bill, one of only 10 Republicans siding with the minority.

He was also partly responsible for killing a GOP bill to overhaul the ailing Amtrak rail system that would have ended significant labor protections for Amtrak workers. These and other key pro-labor votes in the 105th Congress prompted the AFL-CIO, which had spent heavily to try to defeat LaTourette in 1996, to back him for re-election in 1998; the union even ran radio ads thanking LaTourette for his votes on issues important to organized labor.

When LaTourette first arrived in the House, he was hoping for a seat on the Judiciary Committee, where he could make use of his background as a private attorney, public defender and prosecutor. But Ralph Regula, the dean of the Ohio GOP delegation, told him that he would be of more use to the state on the Transportation Committee, where he was the only Ohio Republican in the 104th. On a panel where bipartisan inclinations such as LaTourette's are valued, he has been able to ensure that his district gets its share of highway money. In the 107th, he chairs the panel's Economic Development, Public Buildings and Emergency Management Subcommittee.

LaTourette also sits on the Financial Services (formerly Banking) Committee, where to the displeasure of the big Cleveland banks, he was a prime mover, along with Democrat Paul E. Kanjorski of Pennsylvania, of legislation loosening restrictions on credit union membership. Big financial institutions objected to the legislation, arguing that it would give credit unions an unfair advantage when competing for customers. But LaTourette, a 20-

year credit union member who recalls that his credit union offered him over-draft protection and welcomed his business when he was a $13,000-a-year public defender, was among the credit unions' strongest allies in the House, and the bill was signed into law in 1998.

LaTourette was raised in a politically active home. Both his mother and grandmother were active volunteers for the Cleveland area's longtime Republican congresswoman, Frances Payne Bolton. He recalls, as a 6-year-old, loading Bolton campaign literature on his little red wagon, which bore a Nixon-Lodge bumper sticker. His grandmother has been the inspiration for several legislative efforts, including a bill to require sweepstakes mailers to disclose the slim odds of winning. He cites the example of his grandmother, in her mid-80s, who subscribed to Field and Stream magazine because she thought it would boost her chances of winning a mail-order sweepstakes.

Even as a youth, LaTourette wasn't afraid to rock the boat a bit. In high school, he led a petition drive to permit students to wear jeans and grow facial hair. According to The Plain Dealer, LaTourette grew lamb-chop side-burns that made him look "sort of like an Elvis impersonator." He has sported a beard since he was 18 "because I've always thought my face looked better that way."

After law school, LaTourette worked as a public defender, a job he says taught him what it was like to have "nobody like you." He was in his second term as Lake County prosecutor when he decided to run for Congress. The determining factor was Democratic freshman Eric Fingerhut's vote for the 1993 tax hike, which LaTourette says convinced him that Fingerhut was too liberal for the district.

Dubbing Fingerhut an out-of-touch liberal, LaTourette hammered him for supporting President Clinton's 1993 budget, which reduced the deficit but also raised taxes. LaTourette won by 5 percentage points and has increased that margin in all his re-election races.

LaTourette is approachable and self-deprecating. Early in his House career, he allowed funny-man columnist Dave Barry to do a volunteer stint as a press assistant in his office. Barry's influence was noticeable in a 1995 speech LaTourette gave on tort reform: "As a lawyer, I am the last person to suggest that everybody in my profession is a money-grubbing, scum-sucking toad. The actual figure is only about 73 percent," LaTourette told the House. "I am, of course, just pulling the Speaker's honorable leg. The vast majority of lawyers are responsible professionals, as well as, in many ways, human beings."

LaTourette's long-range aspiration — with no timetable attached — is to be a judge.

KEY VOTES

2000

No	Raise hourly minimum wage by $1 over two years
Yes	Halt funding for U.S. mission in Kosovo unless European nations pay more
Yes	Provide Medicare benefits to military retirees and their dependents
No	Grant China permanent normal trade status
Yes	Phase out estate, gift and trust taxes
Yes	Prohibit implementation of president's national monument designations
Yes	Approve GOP plan to provide prescription drug coverage for Medicare beneficiaries
Yes	Increase help for poor nations indebted to international financial institutions

1999

Yes	Impose steel import quotas
No	Kill proposal to take aviation trust funds off budget
Yes	Require background checks on buyers only at gun shows with 10 or more vendors
Yes	Remove barriers among banking, securities and insurance companies
No	Authorize state grants to hire teachers and reduce class size
Yes	Overhaul campaign finance law; ban "soft money" and restrict advocacy advertising
Yes	Approve bipartisan plan to increase rights of patients in managed-care health plans

INTEREST GROUPS

	AFL-CIO	ADA	CCUS	ACU
2000	30%	25%	80%	68%
1999	33%	35%	79%	64%
1998	60%	40%	78%	52%
1997	50%	30%	90%	71%

CQ VOTE STUDIES

	PARTY UNITY		PRESIDENTIAL SUPPORT	
	Support	Oppose	Support	Oppose
2000	84%	16%	35%	65%
1999	77%	23%	31%	69%
1998	78%	22%	38%	62%
1997	84%	16%	35%	65%

OHIO 19

Cleveland suburbs – Ashtabula and Lake counties

The 19th reaches into a group of Cleveland suburbs in Cuyahoga County and snakes up along the Lake Erie shoreline to include all of Lake and Ashtabula counties in Ohio's far northeastern corner. Republicans, Democrats, autoworkers, farmers and suburbanites are all included in this diverse district.

The 19th's economy is a mixed bag. Brook Park, the district's westernmost city, is a usually Democratic, blue-collar autoworkers' community, sensitive to the ups and downs of the car-making industry. To the east are the wealthy Republican suburbs of eastern Cleveland, which are relatively better off than their western suburban counterparts.

The depressed far northeastern communities remain reliant on the ailing steel, chemical and automobile manufacturing industries but have seen some new life from migrants from Cleveland. Plants along Lake Erie have been particularly hurt by increased foreign competition

in steel and chemicals. Finally, about 17 percent of the district's votes are cast in agricultural Ashtabula County, which borders Pennsylvania.

The district leaned Democratic both locally and nationally for much of the past half-century but since the late 1980s has elected an increasing number of Republicans and become intensely competitive. Mentor, the district's largest city and a traditionally industrial, swing area, has seen an influx of Republicans with its recent growth.

MAJOR INDUSTRY
Auto manufacturing, chemicals, health care

CITIES
Mentor, 51,686; Garfield Heights (pt.), 26,798 (1990); Brook Park, 21,600

UNUSUAL FEATURES
Holden Arboretum, largest in the United States; President James A. Garfield Historic Site.

Gov. Frank Keating (R)

First elected: 1994
Length of term: 4 years
Term expires: 1/03
Salary: $101,139.96
Phone: (405) 521-2342
Hometown: Oklahoma City
Born: Feb. 10, 1944; St. Louis, Mo.
Religion: Roman Catholic
Family: Wife, Cathy Keating; three children
Education: Georgetown U., A.B. 1966; U. of Oklahoma, J.D. 1969
Military service: Air Force, 1952-53
Career: Lawyer, FBI agent
Political highlights: Okla. House, 1972-74; Okla. Senate, 1974-81; U.S. attorney, 1981-84; Republican nominee for U.S. House, 1984; assistant secretary of the Treasury, 1985-88; associate attorney general, 1988-89; acting deputy secretary of the Department of Housing and Urban Development, 1989-93

Election results:

1998 GENERAL

Frank Keating (R)	505,498	57.9%
Laura Boyd (D)	357,552	40.9%

Lt. Gov. Mary Fallin (R)

First elected: 1994
Length of term: 4 years
Term expires: 1/03
Salary: $75,530
Phone: (405) 521-2161

STATE LEGISLATURE

Legislature: meets February-May yearly
House: 101 members, 2-year terms
2001 breakdown: 48R, 53D; 92 men, 9 women
Salary: $38,400
Phone: (405) 521-2711
Senate: 48 members, 4-year terms
2001 breakdown: 18R, 30D; 42 men, 6 women
Salary: $38,400
Phone: (405) 524-0126

STATE TERM LIMITS

Governor: 2 terms
Senate: No more than 12 years combined
House: No more than 12 years combined

URBAN STATISTICS

CITY	POPULATION
Oklahoma City	475,322
Tulsa	381,579
Norman	94,193
Lawton	79,927

REGISTERED VOTERS

Democrat	55%
Republican	36%
Other	9%

POPULATION

2000 population	3,450,654
1990 population	3,145,585
Percent change	+9.7%
Rank among states	27
Median age	35.2
Born in state	64%
Foreign born	2%
Urban/rural	68%/32%
Crime rate	560/100,000
Poverty level	14.1%
Federal workers	44,493
Military	41,819

REAPPORTIONMENT

Oklahoma lost one House seat in reapportionment, dropping from six districts to five. The state legislature will draw new district lines in 2001.

MISCELLANEOUS

Web: www.state.ok.us
Capital: Oklahoma City
Land area: 68,679 sq. miles
Rank among states: 19
STATE ELECTION OFFICIAL
(405) 521-2391
DEMOCRATIC HEADQUARTERS
(405) 239-2700
REPUBLICAN HEADQUARTERS
(405) 528-3501

District Statistics

DIST.	2000 D	2000 R	GREEN	1996 D	1996 R	REF	1992 D	1992 R	I	WHT	BLK	ASIAN	HISP	HOUSEHOLD INCOME	OVER 65+	UNDER 18	COLLEGE EDUCATION
1	37%	62%	0%	37%	54%	9%	30%	49%	21%	83%	10%	1%	2%	$27,472	11%	26%	23%
2	46	53	0	47	40	13	43	36	22	77	5	0	1	$20,633	15	27	12
3	42	56	0	47	40	13	42	34	24	84	4	1	1	$18,394	16	26	13
4	38	61	0	40	49	11	33	41	25	84	7	2	4	$25,391	11	27	19
5	30	68	0	31	59	10	25	51	24	87	6	2	3	$28,348	13	26	26
6	38	61	0	41	47	11	34	43	23	78	13	1	4	$21,797	15	27	13
STATE	38	60	0	40	48	11	34	43	23	82	7	1	3	$23,577	13	27	19

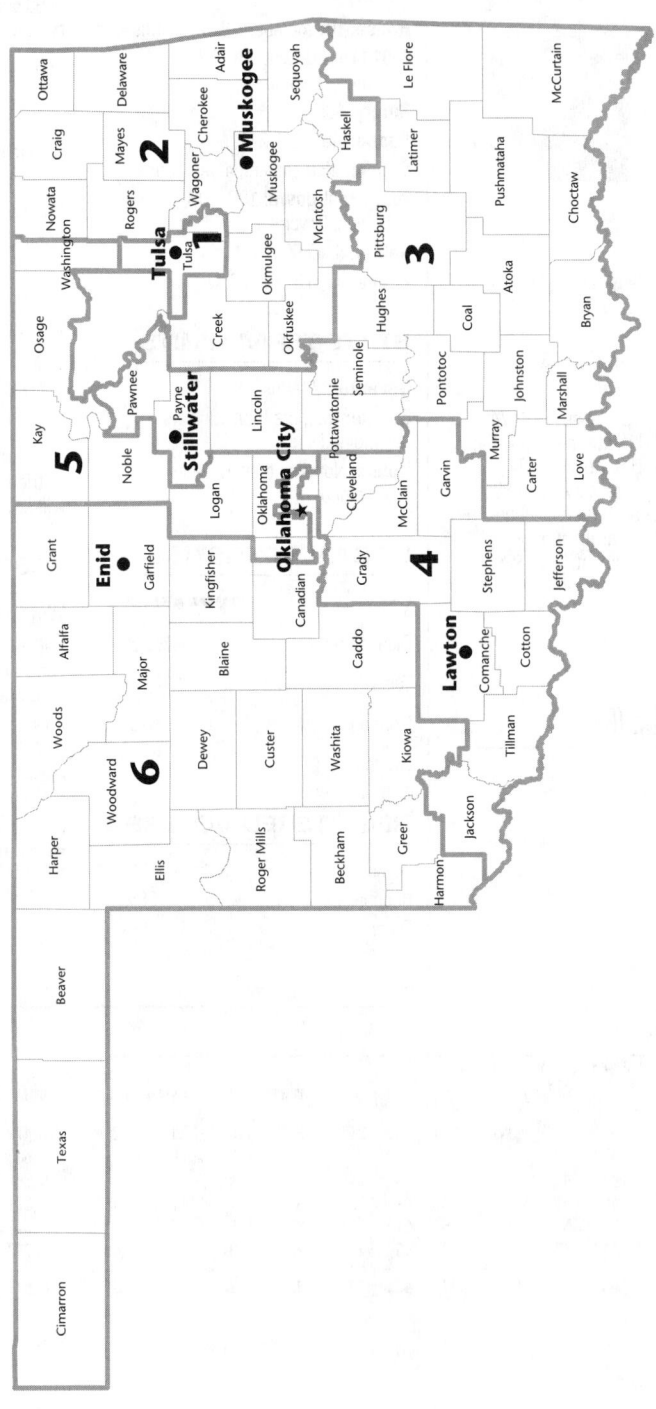

Sen. Don Nickles (R)

CAPITOL OFFICE
224-5754; fax 224-6008; 133 Hart Bldg. 20510

INTERNET
e-mail: senator@nickles.senate.gov
web: nickles.senate.gov

COMMITTEES
Budget
Energy & Natural Resources
 (Energy Research, Development, Production &
 Regulation - chairman)
Finance
 (Taxation & IRS Oversight - chairman)
Rules & Administration

HOMETOWN
Ponca City

BORN
Dec. 6, 1948, Ponca City, Okla.

RELIGION
Roman Catholic

FAMILY
Wife, Linda Nickles; four children

EDUCATION
Oklahoma State U., B.B.A. 1971

MILITARY SERVICE
Okla. National Guard, 1970-76

CAREER
Machine company executive

POLITICAL HIGHLIGHTS
Okla. Senate, 1979-81

ELECTION RESULTS

1998 GENERAL
Don Nickles (R)	570,682	66.4%
Don E. Carroll (D)	268,898	31.3%
Mike Morris (I)	15,516	1.8%

1998 PRIMARY
Don Nickles (R)	unopposed

PREVIOUS WINNING PERCENTAGES
1992 (59%); 1986 (55%); 1980 (54%)

Elected 1980; 4th term

In the 106th Congress, Nickles seemed like a one-man Senate bomb squad, defusing shells dropped by Democrats on issues such as health care and the minimum wage. But in the 107th Congress — with the Senate split down the middle and the White House in Republican hands — his role is anybody's guess.

A self-described policy wonk, Nickles holds the potential to be President Bush's detail man, helping to fill in the essential nuts and bolts of the new president's broad policy goals. On the other hand, he could just as easily end up being pigeonholed as yet another down-the-line conservative, and someone to be taken for granted if Bush reaches toward the political center to fashion a governing coalition.

Nickles is the Senate's No. 2 Republican, officially the assistant majority leader. But his real job is basically that of whip, responsible for counting votes and rallying GOP support for party initiatives while blocking Democrats from winning support for their proposals. In addition to collecting votes, in the 106th Congress, it often fell to Nickles to build consensus among Republicans.

Easily the most visible example was the "patients' bill of rights." Democrats relentlessly pushed the idea, aiming to give people more clout in challenging the medical decisions of their managed-care plans. Polls showed that the public strongly favored such a proposal. Majority Leader Trent Lott — with whom Nickles has a sometimes uneasy relationship — handed the issue off to the Oklahoman, and Nickles pulled together conservatives and moderates alike behind an approach more narrowly targeted than the Democrats' plan, then masterfully shepherded it through the Senate in 1999.

After getting the bill to a conference committee, which he chaired, Nickles was at the center of an impasse that pitted the House against the Senate and doomed the measure. House Republicans signaled a willingness to accept most of what the Democrats wanted, but Nickles held firm, declaring the House-passed bill bad legislation that would drive up health care costs and prompt companies to drop coverage for their employees.

In retrospect, it was probably a long shot that Nickles, who has spent two decades in the Senate fighting costly regulations on business, would reach agreement on a managed-care bill with President Clinton or liberal Sen. Edward M. Kennedy, D-Mass.

As the bill died, Nickles' lieutenants insisted that the issue would not hurt Republican incumbents on Election Day. Democrats, however, said that the issue helped to unseat GOP senators in Michigan, Washington, Minnesota and Missouri.

Nickles also took the lead in blocking a bid by Kennedy to raise the minimum wage by $1 over two years, instead winning passage of a three-year phase-in accompanied by a big package of business-related tax breaks. Like almost everything else in the hyperpolarized 106th, that bill also died.

The medical insurance and minimum wage episodes illustrate Nickles' strength: rallying Republicans around a common approach. He is far less successful at reaching out to Democrats, at least on high-profile issues. And Nickles' critics say he shows a lot more interest in devising policy than in running a vote-counting operation.

Unlike Lott and the top two Senate Democrats — party leader Tom Daschle and whip Harry Reid — Nickles did not serve in the House. He arrived in the Senate two decades ago as a baby-faced 32-year-old, and he has lamented the bitterness that has influenced the way Lott and Daschle have handled the Senate floor for much of the past several years.

When the majority leader's job came open with Bob Dole's departure to run for president in 1996, Nickles — popular and respected among Republican conservatives — considered challenging Lott for the position. Instead, he negotiated with Lott for a suite of offices just off the floor and a bigger staff budget.

After Republicans failed to add to their majority in the 1998 elections, it was widely rumored that Nickles might challenge Lott, but that did not happen, either. His office quickly disavowed any talk of such a challenge in the wake of the disastrous 2000 cycle, which saw five GOP incumbents ousted.

Instead, speculation is that Nickles — who must relinquish the whip position after 2002 under Senate GOP rules — will make a run at Lott then. That potential threat puts considerable pressure on Lott not to stray too far from his own conservative base in his decision-making as majority leader.

Nickles reluctantly backed Lott's methods in recent years. The majority leader has been quick to try to cut off debate and has used parliamentary tactics to restrict Democrats' ability to force votes on their issues. Nickles would welcome a return to more freewheeling debate. As a conservative backbencher, he was sometimes a patron of lost causes, forcing votes, for example, to attack the law that effectively requires federal contractors to pay union wages.

Still, in the 106th, Nickles was not above using a legislative shortcut to try to pass legislation to thwart Oregon's law permitting physician-assisted suicide. Facing a filibuster threat by Oregon Democrat Ron Wyden, Nickles inserted his bill in a year-end tax measure, which died amid a veto threat and under a Wyden filibuster.

Nickles also was a leader in crafting the Senate's version of a bill to erase the "marriage penalty," a quirk in the tax code that results in some two-earner couples paying higher income taxes. He and other Finance Committee conservatives, including Lott and Phil Gramm, R-Texas, pressured Chairman William V. Roth Jr., R-Del., to drop a bipartisan approach and go with a more generous plan — strongly backed by pro-family groups — that not only addressed the marriage penalty but also increased the marriage "bonus" received by single-earner married couples. In the end, Roth's approach prevailed, but the bill was vetoed by Clinton.

The marriage penalty case demonstrated one of Nickles' roles in the Senate Republican Conference: to push the party as far in the conservative direction as possible. That often means he is unhappy with the final results. For example, he was among the conservatives who voted against a massive catchall spending bill in 1998. He also backed — in opposition to Lott and House Speaker J. Dennis Hastert — a "veto strategy," as Republicans struggled in late 2000 to complete action on annual spending bills in their final budget endgame with Clinton.

Nickles has been active in Republican politics since graduating from Oklahoma State University in 1971, first running for public office in 1978, when he won a seat in the state Senate. Just two years later, he entered the Republican primary to replace retiring GOP Sen. Henry Bellmon. He attracted the support of the Moral Majority and other conservative Christian groups, which came to his aid with volunteers and voter registration drives. Nickles won a close, five-way Republican battle.

Then, drawing on the electoral strength of Republican presidential candidate Ronald Reagan, Nickles captured a 10 percentage point victory in November. He has been re-elected three times by steadily increasing margins.

KEY VOTES

2000
Yes Overhaul bankruptcy law and increase minimum wage
Yes Limit fiscal 2001 discretionary spending to $600.3 billion
Yes Override veto on nuclear waste disposal at Yucca Mountain site in Nevada
No Oppose effort to terminate Kosovo mission
No Include gender, sexual orientation and disability in federal hate crime protections
Yes Approve GOP plan to restrict use of genetic information by health insurers
Yes Kill amendment delaying implementation of an anti-missile defense system
Yes Cut taxes for married couples
Yes Grant China permanent normal trade status

1999
Yes Remove President Clinton from office for obstruction of justice
Yes Kill amendment authorizing state grants to hire teachers and reduce class size
No Require criminal background checks for purchases at gun shows
Yes Approve GOP proposal to increase rights of patients in managed-care health plans
No Block effort to allow farm and medicine exports to Cuba
No Allow study of tougher automobile fuel efficiency standards
No Ratify nuclear weapons testing treaty
No Prohibit national political parties from collecting "soft money" donations
Yes Remove barriers among banking, securities and insurance companies

INTEREST GROUPS

	AFL-CIO	ADA	CCUS	ACU
2000	0%	0%	86%	100%
1999	0%	0%	88%	96%
1998	0%	0%	83%	96%
1997	0%	0%	100%	96%
1996	0%	0%	100%	100%
1995	0%	0%	100%	100%
1994	0%	5%	90%	100%
1993	0%	5%	91%	96%
1992	8%	0%	89%	96%
1991	25%	0%	100%	95%

CQ VOTE STUDIES

	PARTY UNITY		PRESIDENTIAL SUPPORT	
	Support	Oppose	Support	Oppose
2000	97%	3%	40%	60%
1999	98%	2%	27%	73%
1998	98%	2%	23%	77%
1997	97%	3%	59%	41%
1996	99%	1%	34%	66%
1995	98%	2%	22%	78%
1994	94%	6%	25%	75%
1993	95%	5%	18%	82%
1992	95%	5%	79%	21%
1991	90%	10%	91%	9%

Sen. James M. Inhofe (R)

Elected 1994; 1st full term

Few lawmakers exemplify the Senate's evolution from a collegial chamber into an openly partisan body more than Inhofe. Brash and blunt-spoken, he is brutally honest about his conservatism in a place that prides itself on its ability to bridge political divides.

In clashing with liberal Minnesota Democrat Paul Wellstone, Inhofe once remarked: "There probably are not two members of the U.S. Senate who are further apart philosophically than the senior senator from Minnesota and myself. I would probably believe him to be an extreme left-wing radical liberal, and he believes me to be an extreme right-wing radical conservative. And I think maybe we are both right."

More than most Senate Republicans, Inhofe (IN-hoff) did little to hide his contempt for President Clinton and his policies. He cast the only vote in 2000 against a popular water projects bill sought by the Clinton administration to restore Florida's Everglades, arguing that it cost too much. Late in 1999, after Clinton made several recess appointments of judges, Inhofe unsuccessfully tried to block all of the president's future judicial nominations.

Two years earlier, Inhofe had quietly slipped through an amendment on the Senate floor that would have blocked tough new Clinton-backed clean air regulations. But his action, accomplished in a virtually empty chamber, angered Democrats, who said that Inhofe had not followed the custom of informing them of his intentions. Majority Leader Trent Lott said he supported the amendment but not the tactic, and he reversed the Senate's approval of the amendment the next day.

Inhofe can come across as somewhat stiff in person, especially in contrast to his more personable conservative colleague from Oklahoma, Assistant Majority Leader Don Nickles. Inhofe has feuded for years with the editorial page of his hometown newspaper, the Tulsa World, and he remains suspicious of what he believes to be the national news media's liberal bias. "Don't look for any fair treatment — we're not going to get it," he told Oklahoma GOP delegates at a 2000 Republican National Convention breakfast. Clinton's departure likely will diminish Inhofe's aggressiveness, but it could resurface if he perceives his party is too prone to compromise with Democrats.

After chairing the Environment and Public Works panel's Clean Air Subcommittee, he decided in the 107th Congress to switch jobs with Ohio Republican George V. Voinovich and take over the committee's Transportation and Infrastructure Subcommittee. Inhofe said he had accomplished his goals as head of the Clean Air panel by protecting Oklahoma counties against what he believed were unnecessarily stringent air quality standards. "With George W. Bush entering the White House, I think the right things are going to be done there," Inhofe told the Tulsa newspaper, adding that if Al Gore had been elected, "I would be keeping that job."

Inhofe says his main goal at his new subcommittee is to seek a repeal of the law that sends state transportation dollars through the federal government before they are routed back to the states. "It's an unnecessary process," he says.

A staunch proponent of cutting the federal budget, Inhofe voted against a massive catchall appropriations bill at the end of the 105th Congress and assailed GOP leaders for striking a deal with Clinton that increased spending by billions of dollars. In his typically blunt style, Inhofe said: "By caving in to so many of the demands of this dishonest president, Republicans are

CAPITOL OFFICE
224-4721; fax 228-0380; 453 Russell Bldg. 20510

INTERNET
e-mail: jim_inhofe@inhofe.senate.gov
web: inhofe.senate.gov

COMMITTEES
Armed Services
(Readiness & Management Support - chairman)
Environment & Public Works
(Transportation & Infrastructure - chairman)
Indian Affairs
Select Intelligence

HOMETOWN
Tulsa

BORN
Nov. 17, 1934, Des Moines, Iowa

RELIGION
Presbyterian

FAMILY
Wife, Kay Inhofe; four children

EDUCATION
U. of Tulsa, B.A. 1973

MILITARY SERVICE
Army, 1956-58

CAREER
Real estate developer; insurance executive

POLITICAL HIGHLIGHTS
Okla. House, 1967-69; Okla. Senate, 1969-77; Republican nominee for governor, 1974; Republican nominee for U.S. House, 1976; mayor of Tulsa, 1978-84; defeated for re-election as mayor of Tulsa, 1984; U.S. House, 1987-94

ELECTION RESULTS

1996 GENERAL

James M. Inhofe (R)	670,610	56.7%
Jim Boren (D)	474,162	40.1%
Bill Maguire (I)	15,092	1.3%
Agnes Marie Regier (LIBERT)	14,595	1.2%

1996 PRIMARY

James M. Inhofe (R)	116,241	75.3%
Dan Lowe (R)	38,044	24.7%

PREVIOUS WINNING PERCENTAGES
1994 Special Election (55%); 1992 House Election (53%); 1990 House Election (56%); 1988 House Election (53%); 1986 House Election (55%)

not adequately representing grass-roots America."

Inhofe's main interest, however, lies with the Armed Services Committee, where he chairs the Military Readiness and Management Support Subcommittee. A staunchly pro-defense lawmaker whose state has several military installations, Inhofe has been a strong advocate of a national missile defense system. He also wants to boost spending to improve the military's readiness for combat. He led the criticism of the Clinton administration's handling of the military base-closure process. In 1998, Inhofe was able to make it more difficult for the Pentagon to close or scale back bases without congressional approval.

An Army veteran and experienced pilot, Inhofe has had his share of brushes with danger. While traveling to Oklahoma City in 1999, his private plane lost its propeller, forcing him to glide about seven miles to make an emergency high-speed landing. He said it was his third forced landing in 41 years of flying. A National Transportation Safety Board investigation found no evidence of anything suspicious that could have caused the mishap.

Inhofe's fiery conservatism has made him a hero to Tulsa's hard-core conservatives, including important energy interests and religious fundamentalists. Inhofe predicted in a 1999 speech that Clinton's affair with White House intern Monica Lewinsky would trigger a moral revolution and end an "age of perversion." His conservative base of support was enough to help him through 10 years in the state legislature, a mayoral career and four close House election victories, but it did not look sufficient to sustain a statewide campaign until 1994.

While serving in the state Senate, he lost a 1974 campaign for governor (won by Democrat David L. Boren) and a 1976 campaign for Congress, before being elected mayor of Tulsa in 1978. He lost a re-election bid for mayor in an upset in 1984, then bounced back just two years later to win election to the House district dominated by Tulsa.

In four House campaigns in the state's most Republican district, Inhofe never got more than 56 percent of the vote. In 1988, his campaign for re-election was complicated when he sued his brother over a stock sale involving the family insurance business. In 1992, there was more litigation and a court-ordered payment to the Federal Deposit Insurance Corporation. Inhofe appealed the ruling, which was reversed.

In the 1994 Senate contest, Democratic Rep. Dave McCurdy had been the favorite since Boren, who had gone on to serve as senator, announced he would retire in midterm to become president of the University of Oklahoma. McCurdy fit the general mold of conservative Democratic politics, in equal parts a populist and a friend to business. But in all his years of positioning, McCurdy had made one error that proved to be fatal: He became associated with Bill Clinton. That bolstered the Republican strategy, which was to run the race as a referendum on Clinton. No matter what McCurdy said about having differences with the president, Inhofe could top it. Inhofe had opposed virtually every move Clinton had made and could recite the list.

McCurdy tried to chip away at Inhofe's integrity by making an issue of a fine that Inhofe had paid on a 1986 election law violation. Inhofe also had to overcome disclosures that he graduated from college 14 years later than he had claimed. But nothing seemed to matter except the Republican tide and the TV ads that showed McCurdy's face changing into Clinton's. Inhofe won by 15 percentage points.

Inhofe continued to benefit from the crushing defeat he delivered to McCurdy when he ran for re-election to a full six-year term in 1996. Strong Democratic opposition did not emerge, and he defeated Jim Boren, a cousin of the former senator, by 17 percentage points.

KEY VOTES

2000
Yes   Overhaul bankruptcy law and increase minimum wage
Yes   Limit fiscal 2001 discretionary spending to $600.3 billion
Yes   Override veto on nuclear waste disposal at Yucca Mountain site in Nevada
No   Oppose effort to terminate Kosovo mission
?   Include gender, sexual orientation and disability in federal hate crime protections
Yes   Approve GOP plan to restrict use of genetic information by health insurers
Yes   Kill amendment delaying implementation of an anti-missile defense system
Yes   Cut taxes for married couples
No   Grant China permanent normal trade status

1999
Yes   Remove President Clinton from office for obstruction of justice
Yes   Kill amendment authorizing state grants to hire teachers and reduce class size
No   Require criminal background checks for purchases at gun shows
Yes   Approve GOP proposal to increase rights of patients in managed-care health plans
No   Block effort to allow farm and medicine exports to Cuba
No   Allow study of tougher automobile fuel efficiency standards
No   Ratify nuclear weapons testing treaty
No   Prohibit national political parties from collecting "soft money" donations
Yes   Remove barriers among banking, securities and insurance companies

INTEREST GROUPS

	AFL-CIO	ADA	CCUS	ACU
2000	13%	5%	85%	100%
1999	11%	0%	94%	100%
1998	0%	5%	76%	100%
1997	14%	5%	50%	100%
1996	0%	0%	100%	100%
1995	0%	0%	100%	100%
House Service:				
1994	0%	0%	0%	100%
1993	8%	10%	91%	100%
1992	36%	10%	75%	96%
1991	9%	5%	90%	100%

CQ VOTE STUDIES

	PARTY UNITY		PRESIDENTIAL SUPPORT	
	Support	Oppose	Support	Oppose
2000	100%	0%	30%	70%
1999	95%	5%	23%	77%
1998	97%	3%	14%	86%
1997	99%	1%	49%	51%
1996	100%	0%	28%	72%
1995	98%	2%	24%	76%
House Service:				
1994	99%	1%	45%	55%
1993	97%	3%	31%	69%
1992	96%	4%	83%	17%
1991	93%	7%	72%	28%

Rep. Steve Largent (R)

Elected 1994; 4th full term

Largent is one of a select group of Republicans, which includes Sen. Jim Bunning of Kentucky and Rep. Jim Ryun of Kansas, who have graduated from the sporting world to Congress to press for traditional family values and reduced government spending.

A telegenic former football player — his pass-receiving records in a 14-year career with the Seattle Seahawks earned him a place in the Pro Football Hall of Fame — Largent sides with the most conservative elements of his party on such issues as trying to eliminate the tax code and battling gay rights. But he has tempered his views somewhat and will work across the aisle on certain bipartisan proposals, backing budget plans that increase some spending and breaking with his party over the Elián González case.

Largent, an impatient lawmaker who seems to yearn for a congressional equivalent of the hurry-up offense in pro football, once said he wanted his House career to be remembered as "brilliant, but brief." Early in 2001, he confirmed that he intends to run for governor of Oklahoma in 2002, bringing his House career to a close.

Largent drew national media notice as a "star quality" freshman in the conservative Class of 1994, many of whom expected Congress' new Republican majority to make dramatic policy changes. As it turned out, the degree of change didn't meet Largent's expectations, and he repeatedly rebelled against GOP leaders who he felt were too timid. At the beginning of the 106th Congress, he mounted a stiff challenge to Majority Leader Dick Armey's bid for re-election to his leadership post, pushing the Texan to a third ballot before succumbing, 127-95.

On most issues, Largent hews to strongly conservative positions. Continuing a longtime crusade against gay rights, he tried to amend legislation in the 106th Congress to ban unmarried couples from adopting children in the District of Columbia. An advocate of gun owners' rights, he said during a gun control debate in 1999: "There are many contributing factors to the problems of juvenile crime, including parental responsibility and cultural influences such as television and movies that glorify a culture of death and violence. ... Adding new laws to crack down on law-abiding citizens by limiting their right to bear arms is counter-intuitive and wrong."

He has also repeatedly tried to eliminate the tax code and cut federal funding for public broadcasting, and he assailed the Clinton administration for failing to crack down on pornography. His fiscal conservatism led him to object to the practice of requesting specific road funds for his district during reauthorization of a massive highway bill in the 105th, telling aides, "My vote was not for sale."

Largent, however, surprised some of his conservative allies in 2000 during the international custody dispute over 6-year-old Elián González. At a time when many Republicans wanted to keep Elián in Miami, Largent said the boy should be returned to Cuba and reunited with his father. Even though he objected to Cuba's communist government, "Elián is a little boy who has lost his mother and desperately needs his father," he wrote in a New York Times column.

He has also taken a bipartisan tack on the issue of electricity deregulation. In the 106th, Largent teamed up with Democrat Edward J. Markey of Massachusetts on legislation, similar to that proposed by the Clinton administration, that would give states a flexible mandate to adopt retail competition structures for their power markets. Although some of the nation's

CAPITOL OFFICE
225-2211; fax 225-9187; 106 Cannon Bldg. 20515

INTERNET
e-mail: ok01.largent@mail.house.gov
web: www.house.gov/largent

COMMITTEES
Energy & Commerce

HOMETOWN
Tulsa

BORN
Sept. 28, 1954, Tulsa, Okla.

RELIGION
Christian

FAMILY
Wife, Terry Largent; four children

EDUCATION
U. of Tulsa, B.S. 1976

CAREER
Marketing consultant; professional football player

POLITICAL HIGHLIGHTS
No previous office

ELECTION RESULTS

2000 GENERAL

Steve Largent (R)	138,528	69.3%
Dan Lowe (D)	58,493	29.3%
Michael Clem (LIBERT)	2,984	1.5%

2000 PRIMARY

Steve Largent (R)	38,206	87.7%
Evelyn L. Rogers (R)	5,355	12.3%

1998 GENERAL

Steve Largent (R)	91,031	61.8%
Howard Plowman (D)	56,309	38.2%

PREVIOUS WINNING PERCENTAGES
1996 (68%); 1994 (63%)

largest utilities successfully lobbied against the proposal, Largent contended, "There are no losers in this bill." He also took aim at some conservative activists who sided with the utilities.

Still, more often than not, Largent rejects political compromise. He joined just 25 other Republicans in voting against the blueprint for a landmark balanced-budget deal in 1997 because he felt it failed to cut taxes or spending significantly. "I've just never been a person who could accept mediocrity as the best we could do," he told The Daily Oklahoman. In 1999, however, he supported a bipartisan budget bill that protected Social Security funding, even though it boosted spending for many programs. "If you step back and look at the forest for the trees, it's a positive trend," he told The Washington Post.

An evangelical Christian who credits religion for helping him recover from a difficult childhood, Largent faced controversy in 2000 when House leaders struggled to pick a new chaplain. Eyeing the collar of a priest who was under consideration for the post, Largent reportedly said: "Tell me about that thing you're wearing." His comments drew fire from Democratic Rep. Anna G. Eshoo of California, a Catholic, but Largent denied any anti-Catholic bias. He told the New York Daily News that he was just trying to learn "when and where does a priest wear a collar."

Largent's chaotic childhood began when his father left home, and his mother married an abusive alcoholic. Largent, who traces his emphasis on family values to his upbringing, would later tell The New York Times: "I can remember crying myself to sleep many times saying my family will never be like this." He was a quiet boy who worried his teachers by staring out the window. To give him more of a male perspective, his mother signed him up for Little League baseball, which turned out to be the genesis of highly successful college and professional sports careers.

Though Largent's 1994 House campaign was his first bid for public office, he had started building relationships with conservative political and business leaders, including former professional quarterback and New York Republican Rep. Jack Kemp, even before his 1989 retirement from football. When 1st District GOP Rep. James M. Inhofe decided to run for the Senate in 1994, GOP Sen. Don Nickles and Largent's wife, Terry, urged Largent to go for the seat.

With strong backing from Christian activists, Largent won the primary with 51 percent of the vote, then cruised to victory over Tulsa oilman Stuart Price. He has had a lock on his district since and has been able to devote time to fundraising and campaigning for GOP candidates and conservative causes.

KEY VOTES

2000
No Raise hourly minimum wage by $1 over two years
?   Halt funding for U.S. mission in Kosovo unless European nations pay more
Yes Provide Medicare benefits to military retirees and their dependents
Yes Grant China permanent normal trade status
Yes Phase out estate, gift and trust taxes
Yes Prohibit implementation of president's national monument designations
Yes Approve GOP plan to provide prescription drug coverage for Medicare beneficiaries
No Increase help for poor nations indebted to international financial institutions

1999
Yes Impose steel import quotas
No Kill proposal to take aviation trust funds off budget
Yes Require background checks on buyers only at gun shows with 10 or more vendors
Yes Remove barriers among banking, securities and insurance companies
No Authorize state grants to hire teachers and reduce class size
No Overhaul campaign finance law; ban "soft money" and restrict advocacy advertising
No Approve bipartisan plan to increase rights of patients in managed-care health plans

INTEREST GROUPS

	AFL-CIO	ADA	CCUS	ACU
2000	0%	0%	90%	95%
1999	13%	15%	87%	91%
1998	11%	10%	82%	92%
1997	0%	5%	90%	96%

CQ VOTE STUDIES

	PARTY UNITY		PRESIDENTIAL SUPPORT	
	Support	Oppose	Support	Oppose
2000	95%	5%	23%	77%
1999	94%	6%	21%	79%
1998	91%	9%	27%	73%
1997	93%	7%	23%	77%

OKLAHOMA 1
Tulsa; part of Wagoner County

Wooden homes on small plots of land in the city's outskirts contrast with the skyscrapers of downtown Tulsa, the heart of the 1st and one of the most solidly Republican enclaves in Oklahoma. Once the "Oil Capital of the World," Tulsa thrived on digging for "black gold" until the market dried up in the 1980s. At the same time, farms fought to survive the drought conditions.

The economy struggled until the late 1980s, when an effort to attract a diverse range of businesses through tax breaks and other incentives started to pay off. Tulsa has become a manufacturing hub of flight simulators. While aviation and aerospace manufacturing have remained productive, the telecommunications and financial services industries have helped prolong growth.

With the local economy on the mend, real estate prices are beginning to rise as Tulsa expands to the east and south. Young professionals are moving into the more established sections of the city's center. South

Tulsa is sprinkled with executive homes, and new subdivisions are springing up in the bedroom communities of Broken Arrow, Owasso and Jenks.

Although Democrats split the votes in the 1st's local elections, Republicans dominate the federal level. The region has voted for a Democratic presidential candidate only twice since 1920. Socially conservative issues play well here, the home of Oral Roberts University.

MAJOR INDUSTRY
Airline, defense manufacturing, oil

CITIES
Tulsa (pt.), 361,628 (1990); Broken Arrow (pt.), 56,871 (1990); Sand Springs (pt.), 15,015 (1990)

UNUSUAL FEATURES
One of the deadliest race riots in American history took place in the Tulsa neighborhood of Greenwood in June 1921 – nearly 300 people died; Oral Roberts University, known for its 200-foot prayer tower and "Praying Hands" sculpture.

Rep. Brad Carson (D)

CAPITOL OFFICE
225-2701; fax 225-3038; 317 Cannon Bldg. 20515

INTERNET
e-mail: brad.carson@mail.house.gov
web: www.house.gov/bradcarson

COMMITTEES
Resources
Small Business
Transportation & Infrastructure

HOMETOWN
Claremore

BORN
March 11, 1967, Winslow, Ariz.

RELIGION
Baptist

FAMILY
Wife, Julie Carson

EDUCATION
Baylor U., B.A. 1989; Oxford U., M.A. 1991; U. of Oklahoma, J.D. 1994

CAREER
Lawyer; Defense Department aide

POLITICAL HIGHLIGHTS
No previous office

ELECTION RESULTS

2000 GENERAL

Brad Carson (D)	107,273	54.9%
Andy Ewing (R)	81,672	41.8%
Neil Mavis (LIBERT)	6,467	3.3%

2000 PRIMARY RUNOFF

Brad Carson (D)	35,410	56.8%
Bill Settle (D)	26,981	43.3%

2000 PRIMARY

Brad Carson (D)	39,837	44.9%
Bill Settle (D)	34,964	39.4%
James R. Wilson (D)	13,949	15.7%

Elected 2000; 1st term

Carson's capture of the open 2nd District seat brought the district, long a conservative Democratic stronghold, back to Democratic hands after a six-year flirtation with the GOP. The seat had been held by Republican Rep. Tom Coburn, who had agreed to limit his term in office.

So a warm reception awaited Carson, a former Rhodes Scholar with an engaging personality, moderate Democratic agenda and deep local roots. A member of the Cherokee tribe, he says he is a sixth-generation northeastern Oklahoman.

Carson subscribes to many Democratic standards, such as creating a Medicare-controlled prescription drug program and shoring up Social Security. But he also backs more military spending and expanded international trade, and he opposes gun control measures — stands that place him toward the conservative side of the Democratic spectrum. Upon his arrival in the 107th Congress, Carson joined the centrist New Democrat Coalition in the House.

Carson describes Oklahoma's farmers as "the backbone of this state" and advocates increasing exports of American agricultural products. The congressman's interest in upgrading the road network in his primarily rural district led him to seek a seat on the Transportation and Infrastructure Committee. Carson also was assigned to the Resources and Small Business committees.

An attorney who taught law at the University of Tulsa, Carson spent a year as a Defense Department aide, working on special projects, including military readiness and gender-integrated training.

Carson showed an ease on the campaign trail in 2000 that belied his status as a first-time candidate. But he had to make up for lost time in the general-election campaign. He was nominated in a September runoff over a political veteran, state Rep. Bill Settle, while car dealer Andy Ewing had won the Republican nomination outright in the primary four weeks earlier. Even though Ewing had the endorsement of popular incumbent Coburn, Carson coasted to a surprising 13 percentage point win.

OKLAHOMA 2
Northeast — Muskogee

In the foothills of the Ozark Mountains, the thickly forested section of the 2nd provides northeast Oklahoma with its nickname, the "Green Country." It is a poor rural area with Democratic sympathies. Although Oklahoma does not include any reservations, American Indians make up a larger portion of the population than in any other state, totaling nearly 30 percent.

The lakes and waterways, the state's most extensive, attract tourists and the elderly, helping to boost the economy. Agriculture dominates the region, but low commodity prices in the mid-1990s hurt the economy, especially the markets for soybeans, wheat, milk and beef. Rogers and Wagoner counties have become two of the fastest-growing regions in the state as some Tulsa residents move out for the comfort of the suburbs. Delaware County, which contains most of Grand Lake O' The Cherokees, was one of the state's fastest-growing regions in the 1980s and through the 1990s.

The 2nd's poor, rural base has a long tradition of voting Democratic, but the district did elect a socially conservative Republican to Congress for three terms before Rep. Carson won the district in 2000. Most local government officials are Democrats, and Bill Clinton won in both 1992 and '96 with percentages nearly matching the rest of the nation. However, in the 2000 presidential contest, President Bush carried the district with 53 percent.

MAJOR INDUSTRY
Paper products, small manufacturing, health care

CITIES
Muskogee 38,432; Claremore, 21,781; Sapulpa 20,114;

UNUSUAL FEATURES
The American Indian "Trail of Tears" of 1838-39 ended in Tahlequah, and nearly 20 percent of the Cherokee Nation died en route.

Rep. Wes Watkins (R)

CAPITOL OFFICE
225-4565; fax 225-5966
1401 Longworth Bldg. 20515

INTERNET
e-mail: wes.watkins@mail.house.gov
web: www.house.gov/watkins

COMMITTEES
Budget
Ways & Means

HOMETOWN
Stillwater

BORN
Dec. 15, 1938, DeQueen, Ark.

RELIGION
Presbyterian

FAMILY
Wife, Lou Watkins; three children

EDUCATION
Oklahoma State U., B.S. 1960, M.S. 1961

MILITARY SERVICE
Okla. National Guard, 1960-67

CAREER
Communications executive; homebuilding
contractor; economic developer

POLITICAL HIGHLIGHTS
Okla. Senate (served as a Democrat), 1975-77;
U.S. House, 1977-91 (served as a Democrat);
sought Democratic nomination for governor, 1990;
independent candidate for governor, 1994

ELECTION RESULTS

2000 GENERAL

Wes Watkins (R)	137,826	86.6%
Argus W. Yandell Jr. (I)	14,660	9.2%
R.C. Sevier White (LIBERT)	6,730	4.2%

2000 PRIMARY

Wes Watkins (R)	unopposed

1998 GENERAL

Wes Watkins (R)	89,832	62.0%
Walt Roberts (D)	55,163	38.0%

PREVIOUS WINNING PERCENTAGES
1996 (51%); 1988 (100%); 1986 (78%); 1984 (78%);
1982 (82%); 1980 (100%); 1978 (100%); 1976 (82%)
* Elected as a Democrat 1976-88

Elected 1996; 10th term
Also served 1977-91

An affable, old-school politician, Watkins mostly stays out of the media spotlight, preferring instead to cultivate personal relationships and work behind the scenes to win his legislative goals, most of which focus on improving the lot of his constituents.

Although he is relatively new to the GOP fold (he served in the House as a Democrat from 1977 to 1991), Watkins is loyal to party leaders and casts a reliably Republican vote on such issues as tax cuts and gun owners' rights. Unlike some on the Republican right, however, he does not hesitate to vote for increased spending if his district will benefit. Breaking ranks with more conservative Oklahoma representatives such as Steve Largent, Watkins voted for a costly disaster relief bill in 1999 that helped his constituents rebuild from deadly storms. "I cannot turn my back on them," he said.

Watkins, who was born just across the Oklahoma border in DeQueen, Ark., is the product of a classic "Okie" Depression childhood. Before he was 10 years old, his family had traveled west three times from Arkansas to California, trying to scratch out a living in the Golden State. After college, he ran a land development and real estate company and served a term in the state Senate. Beginning in 1977, he served 14 years as a Democrat in the House, left for two unsuccessful gubernatorial campaigns, then captured his old House seat as a Republican in 1996.

Neck surgery and chronic pain from an unrelated back problem briefly led Watkins to announce his retirement in April 1998. But after a speedy recovery, he changed his mind and won re-election; he won easily again in 2000. Redistricting may play a role in his decision to seek another term: Oklahoma lost one seat in reapportionment.

Watkins is an ardent tax-cutter. He voted repeatedly in the 106th Congress to override President Clinton's vetoes of Republican tax legislation. After Clinton vetoed a $792 billion tax cut measure, saying it was too large, Watkins said, "This was the most pro-family, pro-economic growth tax relief bill I have seen in all my years in Congress," The Daily Oklahoman reported. In the 107th, his new post on the Budget Committee gives him a platform to advance his fiscal beliefs.

As demonstrated by his vote for disaster relief, Watkins will put his district's interests ahead of ideology. When he was a Democrat in the House, he endeared himself to constituents by using his seat on the Appropriations Committee to bring home millions in federal dollars to boost his rural district's economy.

Although he has switched political parties, Watkins' objective is unchanged. He wants to get help from Washington to expand economic prosperity in his district and state. He speaks from personal experience about the economic plight of rural Americans. In a 1988 newspaper interview, he recalled, "Some of my first memories were the days around World War II when my family went to California looking for a job."

In exchange for running under the Republican banner in 1996, Watkins won a promise from GOP leaders for an assignment to the Ways and Means Committee. Watkins has used his seat on that panel to win two large tax breaks for his constituents. In the 105th, he met privately with Ways and Means Chairman Bill Archer of Texas to persuade him to retain a tax break that encouraged development on Indian reservations and to include specifically businesses on former Indian land in Oklahoma, a move that the Internal Revenue Service and even Oklahoma's senior Republican Sen. Don Nickles opposed.

In the 106th, Watkins added a provision to tax legislation allowing oil and gas producers to deduct more costs from their income taxes. He also introduced a measure that would grant more incentives to domestic oil and gas producers in order to reduce U.S. dependence on imported oil.

Part of Watkins' secret for getting federal money for his district has been his willingness to go for small slices of the pie — little projects that fly in beneath the budget-cutters' radar. Over time, these incremental efforts add up. At one point during Watkins' service as a Democrat, his office sported a map of the 3rd District marked with yellow and green dots. The yellow dots stood for unfinished federal projects; the green dots symbolized those that had been completed. The map was thick with dots.

Watkins keeps an eye out for his district in other ways as well. In the 106th, he worked with moderates in both parties on environmental legislation that sought to protect wilderness and other undeveloped land, figuring it would boost recreational opportunities in Oklahoma. "I am cosponsoring the legislation because I support the principles of wildlife conservation and wildlife education, and this bill gives the states some flexibility to target the funds in ways that best meet their needs. This is a plus for gaming states like Oklahoma," he said.

Watkins first won election to the House in 1976 by succeeding House Speaker Carl Albert who retired after 30 years in Congress. Albert favored his longtime chief aide, Charles Ward, but Watkins had a stronger organization. In 1990, Watkins set his sights on the governor's mansion. But he narrowly lost the nomination in a runoff, an experience that left him embittered toward the Democratic Party. He made a repeat run for governor as an independent in 1994, finishing third and, in the view of some Democrats, taking enough votes from the Democratic nominee to give the election to Republican Frank Keating.

When Democratic Rep. Bill Brewster, who had succeeded Watkins in the House, announced at the end of 1995 that he would not seek re-election, Watkins decided to run as a Republican despite the Democratic tilt of the 3rd District. "If I were a political opportunist, I would be running as a Democrat," Watkins said. "But the national Democratic Party is controlled by extreme liberals and does not represent Oklahoma's traditional and conservative moral values." His wife Lou, who represented Oklahoma on the Democratic National Committee for four years, followed Watkins in his party switch.

KEY VOTES

2000

No Raise hourly minimum wage by $1 over two years
Yes Halt funding for U.S. mission in Kosovo unless European nations pay more
Yes Provide Medicare benefits to military retirees and their dependents
Yes Grant China permanent normal trade status
Yes Phase out estate, gift and trust taxes
Yes Prohibit implementation of president's national monument designations
Yes Approve GOP plan to provide prescription drug coverage for Medicare beneficiaries
No Increase help for poor nations indebted to international financial institutions

1999

No Impose steel import quotas
Yes Kill proposal to take aviation trust funds off budget
Yes Require background checks on buyers only at gun shows with 10 or more vendors
Yes Remove barriers among banking, securities and insurance companies
No Authorize state grants to hire teachers and reduce class size
No Overhaul campaign finance law; ban "soft money" and restrict advocacy advertising
No Approve bipartisan plan to increase rights of patients in managed-care health plans

INTEREST GROUPS

	AFL-CIO	ADA	CCUS	ACU
2000	0%	0%	95%	87%
1999	0%	0%	96%	96%
1998	10%	5%	100%	92%
1997	0%	0%	89%	96%

CQ VOTE STUDIES

	PARTY UNITY		PRESIDENTIAL SUPPORT	
	Support	Oppose	Support	Oppose
2000	94%	6%	28%	72%
1999	94%	6%	21%	79%
1998	94%	6%	24%	76%
1997	97%	3%	26%	74%

OKLAHOMA 3
Southeast – 'Little Dixie'

Known as "Little Dixie" for its heavy Southern influence, the 3rd relies on farming and is more than 70 percent Democratic. The rolling hills flatten and the forest thins as one moves west through Love and Carter counties. American Indians, some of whose ancestors ended their "Trail of Tears" march in the area, have a sizable presence in the district.

A 1998 drought was as severe as any in the dust bowl era of the 1930s, but conservation techniques prevented similar sandstorms. The economy, however, did suffer. Farmers were forced to use feed for grazing animals by mid-summer, several months earlier than normal, padding their expenses. In addition to beef and poultry, farmers cultivate peanuts and wheat, and in rocky southeastern McCurtain County, the timber industry thrives. Marginal oil and natural gas wells compose the energy businesses that survived the 1980s industry depression.

The district is the most heavily Democratic in the state – conservative "Yellow Dog" Democrat territory – and Republicans might not have fielded a candidate in 1996 if Rep. Watkins hadn't run as a Republican. The district is now willing to stray from its Democratic roots. Watkins secured re-election in 2000 with an overwhelming 87 percent of the vote. And the 3rd supported President Bush in the 2000 contest after backing Bill Clinton – although without a majority – in 1992 and '96. Democrats dominate local elective offices.

MAJOR INDUSTRY
Timber, ranching, oil and gas

MILITARY BASES
McAlester Army Ammunition Plant, 4 military, 909 civilian (2001)

CITIES
Stillwater, 38,444; Shawnee, 27,979; Ardmore, 24,095; McAlester, 17,416

UNUSUAL FEATURES
Athlete Jim Thorpe born in Gordon Grove in 1887; Astronaut Gordon Cooper grew up in Shawnee.

Rep. J.C. Watts Jr. (R)

CAPITOL OFFICE
225-6165; fax 225-3512
1007 Longworth Bldg. 20515

INTERNET
e-mail: rep.jcwatts@mail.house.gov
web: www.house.gov/watts

COMMITTEES
Armed Services

HOMETOWN
Norman

BORN
Nov. 18, 1957, Eufaula, Okla.

RELIGION
Southern Baptist

FAMILY
Wife, Frankie Watts; five children

EDUCATION
U. of Oklahoma, B.S. 1981

CAREER
Property management company owner;
professional football player; youth minister

POLITICAL HIGHLIGHTS
Okla. Corporation Commission, 1991-95

ELECTION RESULTS

2000 GENERAL

J.C. Watts Jr. (R)	114,000	64.9%
Larry Weatherford (D)	54,808	31.2%
Susan Ducey (REF)	4,897	2.8%
Keith B. Johnson (LIBERT)	1,979	1.1%

2000 PRIMARY

J.C. Watts Jr. (R)	21,960	81.0%
James Odom (R)	5,163	19.0%

1998 GENERAL

J.C. Watts Jr. (R)	83,272	61.5%
Ben Odom (D)	52,107	38.5%

PREVIOUS WINNING PERCENTAGES
1996 (58%); 1994 (52%)

Elected 1994; 4th term

Watts' career threatens to become a cautionary tale about what happens when a rapidly rising political star lacks a solid power base. Late in 1998, going into just his third term, Watts was elected GOP Conference chairman, the fourth-ranking spot in the House leadership. But he has struggled in that role and verged on quitting politics altogether.

He is a celebrated orator, known for moving gatherings of Republicans, church groups and young people. But he sometimes has struggled to sound authoritative away from the lectern, and other members of the leadership quickly took over the communications role that had been a traditional part of the conference chairman's job. (As the 106th Congress wore on, Watts began holding regular news conferences and worked to become more accessible to the media.) Also missing from Watts' portfolio are the weekly meetings with lobbyists that his predecessor presided over.

Watts grew so frustrated with his diminished leadership role, which largely revolved around serving as liaison between leaders and unhappy committee chairmen and rank-and-file members, that he gave serious consideration in 1999 to not seeking a fourth term, telling the Tulsa World that he was thinking of honoring a pledge he made in 1994 to serve only three terms. When CBS reported that he was considering resigning his seat before the end of the 106th, however, Watts assured the numerous party elders who called him that he would run again.

Watts, a former football star, is the only black Republican in the House. Though he consistently rejects any assertion that he owes his celebrity and high office to that fact — "My skin color is just a byproduct," he says — his party has trotted him out at countless conventions and rallies to highlight its own "diversity." Watts has authored no more and no less legislation than the average junior member; most of his bills that have drawn serious attention have revolved around social issues, including race.

Although he has been involved in general strategy sessions with Speaker J. Dennis Hastert and other leaders, he has been much less consumed by policy development than by his efforts to improve services and deliver information to Republican colleagues. That has meant focusing on aspects of the job that are less glamorous but nonetheless close to members' hearts: making slides and other visual aids that members use at town hall meetings in their districts, for example.

Watts is a fixture at high-profile legislative and political rallies and extremely popular with the party's grass-roots followers, who admire his homilies in favor of the GOP gospel of tax cuts, a strong national defense, free-market changes to the Social Security system and gun owners' rights.

Watts' name is still bandied about during quadrennial vice-presidential selection discussions, but his biography probably has a bit too much of the tabloid in it for him to be put on a national ticket. He fathered two children out of wedlock, both born in 1986. He married the mother of one child. The other child was raised by his aunt and uncle, and Watts says that the fact that the child was not aborted and was raised without "one dime of government assistance" is proof of the consistency of his beliefs. He dismisses as old news charges that his political opponents make about his frequent tax difficulties and his role as state corporation commissioner in a bribery case investigated by the FBI.

For all of his drawing power within Republican circles, Watts has been no star legislatively, and he has antagonized other black leaders. His father ran for state labor commissioner in 1998 as a Democrat, saying, "I'm not like my boy. I told him that running for the Republican ticket is like a chicken voting for Colonel Sanders." J.C. Watts Sr. was the first black policeman in Eufaula, Okla.; the street where the younger Watts was raised has since been named for the congressman.

Outside the GOP, Watts seldom has been credited with bravery for taking stances that are not traditionally associated with black leaders. "The same values that I espouse today — hard work, personal responsibility, sacrifice, commitment, discipline — I got those things from my athletic background, my faith and my upbringing," he wrote to readers via a sports website "chat." "I could talk about those things when I was a minister or as a football player ... and it was fine. I was considered a hero and a great role model. But once you get into politics and declare a party affiliation, all of a sudden you become a 'sellout.' "

Watts' major legislative concern during the 106th was a bill to offer financial incentives in so-called renewal communities. Working with Small Business Committee Chairman James M. Talent, R-Mo., and others, Watts was able to win approval of the legislation to give tax credits and deductions to businesses in troubled neighborhoods, as well as to allow federal funds to pay for drug counseling and rehabilitation performed by religious organizations. "They take a much more comprehensive approach to healing," Watts said. "They try to deal with the mental and physical and spiritual person."

He is best known for counseling a "go slow" approach to revising affirmative action laws, preferring a purely merit-based approach but recognizing that discrimination is not dead.

Raised in a poor black neighborhood in a rural community, Julius Caesar Watts won fame as a star quarterback for the University of Oklahoma. After six years in the Canadian Football League, Watts and his family settled in Norman, where he worked in real estate and petroleum marketing. Watts became a Republican in 1989, then won election in 1990 to the state's Corporation Commission, which regulates the energy industry. That made him the first black elected to statewide office in Oklahoma history.

Watts entered the 1994 House race to succeed Democrat Dave McCurdy (who ran for the Senate), with high name recognition and good access to campaign funds. He was the leading vote-getter in the five-candidate GOP primary and won the runoff by 4 percentage points. That November, the Republican tide swept through Oklahoma, where GOP candidates won the Senate, the governorship and five of six House seats. Watts took 52 percent of the vote and has increased his winning percentage in subsequent elections.

KEY VOTES

2000

No Raise hourly minimum wage by $1 over two years
Yes Halt funding for U.S. mission in Kosovo unless European nations pay more
Yes Provide Medicare benefits to military retirees and their dependents
Yes Grant China permanent normal trade status
Yes Phase out estate, gift and trust taxes
Yes Prohibit implementation of president's national monument designations
Yes Approve GOP plan to provide prescription drug coverage for Medicare beneficiaries
No Increase help for poor nations indebted to international financial institutions

1999

No Impose steel import quotas
No Kill proposal to take aviation trust funds off budget
Yes Require background checks on buyers only at gun shows with 10 or more vendors
Yes Remove barriers among banking, securities and insurance companies
No Authorize state grants to hire teachers and reduce class size
No Overhaul campaign finance law; ban "soft money" and restrict advocacy advertising
No Approve bipartisan plan to increase rights of patients in managed-care health plans

INTEREST GROUPS

	AFL-CIO	ADA	CCUS	ACU
2000	0%	0%	90%	88%
1999	0%	0%	100%	92%
1998	10%	10%	94%	84%
1997	0%	0%	89%	100%

CQ VOTE STUDIES

	PARTY UNITY		PRESIDENTIAL SUPPORT	
	Support	Oppose	Support	Oppose
2000	98%	2%	25%	75%
1999	94%	6%	22%	78%
1998	92%	8%	21%	79%
1997	96%	4%	25%	75%

OKLAHOMA 4
Southwest; part of Oklahoma City

Home to the state's largest university and several military bases, the 4th occupies a portion of the southwest corner of the state from Oklahoma City through Lawton to the Texas border. Its residents, mostly conservative on social and fiscal issues, live in college towns like Norman and more rural areas like Cotton and Jefferson counties.

The 4th's once-booming oil economy suffered from the low prices of the 1990s, and a concurrent drought helped decimate the southwest. Two of the smaller counties in the 4th lost population in the early 1990s. But, overall, the district's population increased about 9 percent by the close of the decade, as the military maintained its ubiquitous presence. With about 46,000 personnel, the military bases inject the region with plenty of retail dollars. Still, even after the drought, agriculture remains an essential economic cog. Soybeans, cotton, wheat and peanuts fill many of the district's family farms.

The 4th has epitomized the Oklahoman trend toward voting for

Republicans in national elections. Although once confined to presidential elections, district votes for the GOP have swung behind congressional candidates and trickled down to some state legislators. The Christian Coalition and other groups have attracted socially conservative voters who grew up voting for Democrats.

MAJOR INDUSTRY
Military, higher education, oil production

MILITARY BASES
Tinker Air Force Base, 6,870 military, 15,356 civilian; Fort Sill (Army), 14,567 military, 5,376 civilian (2000); Altus Air Force Base, 2,503 military, 2,143 civilian (2001)

CITIES
Norman, 94,193; Lawton, 79,927; Oklahoma City (pt.), 45,448 (1990); Moore, 45,431

UNUSUAL FEATURES
Apache warrior Geronimo was imprisoned at Ft. Sill Military Reservation near Lawton.

Rep. Ernest Istook (R)

Elected 1992; 5th term

CAPITOL OFFICE
225-2132; fax 226-1463; 2404 Rayburn Bldg. 20515

INTERNET
e-mail: istook@mail.house.gov
web: www.house.gov/istook

COMMITTEES
Appropriations
(Treasury, Postal Service & General
Government - chairman)

HOMETOWN
Oklahoma City

BORN
Feb. 11, 1950, Fort Worth, Texas

RELIGION
Mormon

FAMILY
Wife, Judy Lee Istook; five children

EDUCATION
Baylor U., B.A. 1971; Oklahoma City U., J.D. 1976

CAREER
Lawyer; gubernatorial aide; journalist

POLITICAL HIGHLIGHTS
Warr Acres City Council, 1983-87; Okla. House,
1987-93

ELECTION RESULTS

2000 GENERAL

Ernest Istook (R)	134,159	68.4%
Garland McWatters (D)	53,275	27.2%
Bill Maguire (I)	5,930	3.0%
Robert T. Murphy (LIBERT)	2,658	1.4%

2000 PRIMARY

Ernest Istook (R)	39,976	84.8%
Phillip A. Hillian (R)	7,179	15.2%

1998 GENERAL

Ernest Istook (R)	103,217	68.2%
M.C. Smothermon (D)	48,182	31.8%

PREVIOUS WINNING PERCENTAGES
1996 (70%); 1994 (78%); 1992 (53%)

Istook skillfully straddles the line that divides ideological firebrands and legislative pragmatists in the House GOP. He is an ally of Christian conservatives, but he has also diligently chaired a subcommittee on the ultimate insider panel, Appropriations.

On issues such as abortion and gun owners' rights, school prayer and policies affecting homosexuals, Istook (IZ-took) takes up the banner of the most conservative elements of the Republican Party. He also doesn't hesitate to take shots at the political left. Defending the Boy Scouts in 2000 for their policy of prohibiting openly gay scoutmasters, he denounced the "mean-spirited bigotry of the far left. It's wrong for them to abuse government by saying that all groups must endorse and embrace homosexuality."

Istook helped found the Conservative Action Team, now known as the Republican Study Group, a caucus of members on the GOP's right wing that is devoted to restraining government spending and regulation and promoting a conservative ideal of family and social life. Instead of using his Appropriations seat to secure funds for his district — the traditional tack — he has concentrated most of his efforts on blocking spending that he views as unnecessary, or on trying to attach conservative policy language to appropriations bills.

Such endeavors have often made Istook a thorn in the side of the GOP leadership. But he seems to have a sense of just how far he can press his case without earning a reputation as an unreasonable pest. He once said that he and his staunchly conservative allies expected to be allowed votes on their priorities, but he acknowledged that their positions might not prevail. "The expectation should be an opportunity rather than a guarantee of success," he said.

At the beginning of the 107th Congress, Istook landed the chairmanship of the Treasury, Postal Service and General Government Appropriations Subcommittee. In that position, he has authority over an annual spending bill that typically draws conservative amendments and sparks battles over issues as diverse as funding anti-drug programs, granting congressional pay raises and providing abortion coverage for federal workers.

Istook gained experience with policy disputes over spending measures during the 106th, when he chaired the Appropriations Subcommittee for the District of Columbia. Siding with conservatives, he worked to prohibit the city from spending public funds on abortions, operating a needle-exchange program or legalizing marijuana for medical purposes. But he left the District's budget largely intact and softened some conservative provisions, winning grudging praise from Democrats who had feared a more heavy-handed approach. "Here is an example of a right-wing ideologue maturing to the point where he should rightfully be considered a serious legislator," Rep. James P. Moran, D-Va., the ranking Democrat on the District of Columbia panel in the 106th Congress, told The Washington Post.

Istook pursued several socially conservative initiatives in the 106th. He sponsored legislation, which became law, to cut off federal funding to schools and libraries that failed to block objectionable Internet sites, and he supported funding school programs that stress the importance of sexual abstinence. "Teens need to hear a clear message that abstinence is the right thing, and it's the only sure way to prevent teen pregnancy and avoid sexually transmitted diseases," he said. Another priority for Istook over the years has been a constitutional amendment that would guarantee the right to pray in public schools. GOP leaders have brought the proposal to the House floor several times, but while a majority of members support it, it has fallen short of the two-thirds majority vote needed for approval.

In the late 1990s, Istook emerged as a biting critic of President Clinton. Complaining about the price tag of the omnibus appropriations bill that passed at the end of the 105th, Istook implied that Clinton had demanded extra spending so he could secure the backing of congressional liberals in his looming impeachment battle. "Because his future depends on their support," Istook said, "he made it clear that he would veto anything that didn't give the most liberal of the Democrats what they want in exchange. This is 'protection money,' and that's wrong."

Members of the Appropriations Committee — even the conservative ones — typically see it as part of their job to deliver a generous share of federal largesse to their home districts and states. Istook is not immune to that impulse, but he has worked more to curb federal spending than to funnel it to his district. While he did secure funds to help rebuild the area of Oklahoma City surrounding the federal building that was destroyed in a 1995 bomb blast, he wanted the money spent just in that part of town, not more widely, so he added limiting language to that effect. Also, he opposed granting a federal subsidy to Oklahoma City for a city trolley system.

Istook learned about the legislative process before he came to Congress. After graduating from Baylor University with a journalism degree, he covered the Capitol in Oklahoma City as a radio reporter, went to law school at night, got married and started a family that grew to five children. After earning his law degree, he worked as an aide to Democratic Gov. David L. Boren and then went into private practice. His first elective office was to the city council in the Oklahoma City suburb of Warr Acres. In 1986, he won a seat in the state House, where he rose to assistant minority leader.

Campaigning for the House in 1992 on an anti-pork platform, Istook won the 5th District after denying renomination to eight-term GOP Rep. Mickey Edwards, who was damaged by having 386 House bank overdrafts.

He also had to defeat former U.S. Attorney Bill Price, who had been the GOP's 1990 nominee for governor. Most of the primary attention went to Edwards and Price, while Istook ran a ground-level campaign that relied less on media ads and more on targeting likely GOP voters through direct mail and phone banks. Price ran first in the primary, but Istook survived and in the runoff, his surging campaign scored a 12 percentage point victory over Price.

The Republican tilt of the 5th allowed Istook to win with 53 percent in the general election. Re-election victories have come easily since then.

KEY VOTES

2000
No Raise hourly minimum wage by $1 over two years
Yes Halt funding for U.S. mission in Kosovo unless European nations pay more
Yes Provide Medicare benefits to military retirees and their dependents
Yes Grant China permanent normal trade status
+ Phase out estate, gift and trust taxes
Yes Prohibit implementation of president's national monument designations
No Approve GOP plan to provide prescription drug coverage for Medicare beneficiaries
No Increase help for poor nations indebted to international financial institutions

1999
No Impose steel import quotas
Yes Kill proposal to take aviation trust funds off budget
No Require background checks on buyers only at gun shows with 10 or more vendors
Yes Remove barriers among banking, securities and insurance companies
No Authorize state grants to hire teachers and reduce class size
No Overhaul campaign finance law; ban "soft money" and restrict advocacy advertising
No Approve bipartisan plan to increase rights of patients in managed-care health plans

INTEREST GROUPS

	AFL-CIO	ADA	CCUS	ACU
2000	10%	5%	73%	90%
1999	0%	0%	83%	92%
1998	0%	0%	94%	95%
1997	0%	5%	89%	100%

CQ VOTE STUDIES

	PARTY UNITY		PRESIDENTIAL SUPPORT	
	Support	Oppose	Support	Oppose
2000	93%	7%	25%	75%
1999	96%	4%	19%	81%
1998	96%	4%	17%	83%
1997	97%	3%	18%	82%

OKLAHOMA 5
North Central — Part of Oklahoma City

North of Oklahoma City and running to the Kansas border, the rolling Midwestern plains become more evident in the 5th — an area comfortably clasped by Bible Belt conservatism. Starting in the state capital, the district wraps up and over Stillwater and Tulsa to Washington County, where lush forests and vegetation cover the land.

The boom of the early 1980s brought large population increases to parts of the district, but after the economy landed with a thud by decade's end, corporations scaled back and the population declined in some sections.

By the early 1990s, the 5th's economy diversified out of necessity. While oil and gas still compose a large chunk of the economy, along with some agriculture, energy corporations have had to expand their businesses to plastics and other industries. Telecommunications companies such as Lucent Technologies are also taking hold in the district.

Republicans control the federal elections in the 5th, the most Republican district in the state. While other Oklahoma districts are increasingly voting for Republicans in presidential elections, voters in the 5th have consistently favored Republicans for decades. In the 2000 presidential contest, President Bush secured his highest vote margin in the state from 5th District voters.

MAJOR INDUSTRY
Oil, computer hardware, state government

CITIES
Oklahoma City, (pt.) 239,397 (1990); Edmond, 66,757; Bartlesville, 33,693; Ponca City, 26,052

UNUSUAL FEATURES
Guthrie was the original state capital, and Oklahoma City became the capital in 1910; Osage Indians discovered oil on their reservation in the late 19th century, and by the turn of the century, they were the richest people per capita in the United States.

Rep. Frank D. Lucas (R)

CAPITOL OFFICE
225-5565; fax 225-8698; 438 Cannon Bldg. 20515

INTERNET
e-mail: www.house.gov/writerep
web: www.house.gov/lucas

COMMITTEES
Agriculture
(Conservation, Credit, Rural Development &
Research - chairman)
Financial Services
Science

HOMETOWN
Cheyenne

BORN
Jan. 6, 1960, Cheyenne, Okla.

RELIGION
Baptist

FAMILY
Wife, Lynda Lucas; three children

EDUCATION
Oklahoma State U., B.S. 1982

CAREER
Farmer; rancher

POLITICAL HIGHLIGHTS
Republican nominee for Okla. House, 1984, 1986;
Okla. House, 1989-94

ELECTION RESULTS

2000 GENERAL

Frank D. Lucas (R)	95,635	59.3%
Randy Beutler (D)	63,106	39.2%
Joseph V. Cristiano (LIBERT)	2,435	1.5%

2000 PRIMARY

Frank D. Lucas (R)	unopposed

1998 GENERAL

Frank D. Lucas (R)	85,261	65.0%
Paul M. Barby (D)	43,555	33.2%
Ralph B. Finkle Jr. (I)	2,455	1.9%

PREVIOUS WINNING PERCENTAGES
1996 (64%); 1994 (70%); 1994 Special Election
(54%)

Elected May 1994; 4th full term

Lucas' style is low-key and informal, and he is a persistent advocate for government aid to farmers. Although he has been an elected official for more than a decade, Lucas likes to say he "still tries to earn an honest living" as a farmer and rancher in western Oklahoma, where his family has worked the land for more than 100 years.

In his work on the Agriculture and Financial Services committees, Lucas' comments often are rooted in observations he makes as he "tromp[s] around on my own farm and on the fields of farmers all over the district."

As chairman of the Agriculture Committee's Subcommittee on Conservation, Credit, Rural Development and Research, Lucas may find himself playing a significant role on omnibus farm legislation in the 107th Congress. He voted for the 1996 "Freedom to Farm" bill, one of the GOP's major deregulatory triumphs. But the law, which expires in 2002, has drawn intense criticism from Democrats and some farmers because it fails to compensate growers during times of low commodity prices. Lucas, who is extremely loyal to his leaders and serves as an assistant party whip, has praised the farm law as "a bold step" and said Congress should "fine-tune the farm bill."

But with farmers facing catastrophe because of drought and low prices, Lucas has become a cheerleader for bills that rescue farmers with cash. When House leaders announced an aid package of almost $4 billion in 1998, Lucas said he wouldn't mind seeing more, and he ultimately voted for a $5.9 billion bill. "If we have $5 billion to help our [agricultural] producers, that's a very strong pull for me," he said.

And when Congress passed a multibillion-dollar drought emergency bill in 2000, Lucas predicted that farmers might need still more help. "Until it rains, the costs that are out there will continue to mount," The Associated Press quoted him as saying.

With an eye to his rural constituents, Lucas pursued legislation in the 106th to fix thousands of aging dams and to protect farms from floodwaters. He also focuses on private property rights and supports international trade. Lucas backed a measure in 2000 to grant permanent normal trade status to China, a major market for U.S. farmers.

Although a steadfast conservative on most issues, Lucas is willing to look for middle ground. After the 1996 election, when congressional Republicans were facing negotiations with President Clinton on a balanced-budget plan, he called for compromise. "The American people gave us a second term to control Congress," Lucas said, "but they also gave us a Democratic president." When the final budget plan drew catcalls from some on the GOP right as a capitulation to the White House, Lucas differed. "We are going to balance the federal budget for the first time since 1969 and grant broad tax cuts to Americans who haven't seen them since 1981. I call it a home run — make that a grand slam," he said.

Lucas supported another big spending measure in the 105th that irritated some on his party's right wing: a $218 billion transportation reauthorization bill. Included in it was more than $100 million to begin reconstruction of a heavily traveled segment of Interstate 40 in Oklahoma City. Lucas' district, though largely rural, also includes parts of the city. Another Oklahoma Republican, Tom Coburn, said he was "embarrassed and disgusted" by the amount of pork-barrel spending in the transportation bill, but Lucas was part of the overwhelming majority that passed it.

Lucas has spent a lot of time working on legislation stemming from the

April 1995 bombing in downtown Oklahoma City that destroyed the Alfred P. Murrah Federal Building, located in the 6th, and killed 168 people. The House passed a resolution offered by Lucas that condemned the bombing and offered condolences to the victims' families.

After two suspects were indicted for the bombing, the judge in the case moved the trial to Denver, ruling that the two could not get a fair trial in Oklahoma. Lucas added a provision to an anti-terrorism bill then moving through the House to provide closed-circuit television access to any trial that has been moved more than 350 miles from where the original trial would have taken place. He said it was a burden to the survivors and victims' families in Oklahoma City to have to travel so far to see the accused stand trial. He also won passage of language allowing survivors of the bombing to watch the trial and still testify in the penalty phase.

Members of the 105th Congress approved a measure sponsored by Lucas to establish on the site of the bombing a national memorial as part of the National Park System. In 1998, he and neighboring GOP Rep. Ernest Istook, with a strong assist from Appropriations Chairman Robert L. Livingston, got additional federal funds to cover bomb-repair costs in Oklahoma City.

A fifth-generation Oklahoman, Lucas became interested in politics while at Oklahoma State University. He was president of the College Republicans while working on a degree in agricultural economics. After graduating, he returned home to Cheyenne and soon entered politics. He made two unsuccessful bids for a state House seat in a mostly Democratic area, before capturing a seat in a sprawling district in 1988. In the legislature, he served on committees that dealt with taxes, agriculture, energy, small business and government reform, and he chaired the state House Republican Caucus.

After 10-term Democratic Rep. Glenn English resigned the 6th District seat in early 1994 to head a rural electric lobbying association in Washington, Lucas had to outpoll four other Republicans in the primary and runoff. By stressing his work in agriculture and lifelong residency in the 6th, he won 54 percent of the vote in the general election against Democrat Dan Webber Jr., who had spent years in Washington as an aide to Oklahoma Democratic Sen. David L. Boren.

In 1996 and again in 1998, Lucas easily defeated Democrat Paul M. Barby, the son of a prominent ranching family and a member of the board of regents for Oklahoma colleges. The races attracted national attention because the openly homosexual Barby said he wanted to protest "the three Gs" slogan that conservative Republican James M. Inhofe employed in his successful 1994 Senate bid — "God, gays and guns."

KEY VOTES

2000

No	Raise hourly minimum wage by $1 over two years
Yes	Halt funding for U.S. mission in Kosovo unless European nations pay more
Yes	Provide Medicare benefits to military retirees and their dependents
Yes	Grant China permanent normal trade status
Yes	Phase out estate, gift and trust taxes
Yes	Prohibit implementation of president's national monument designations
Yes	Approve GOP plan to provide prescription drug coverage for Medicare beneficiaries
No	Increase help for poor nations indebted to international financial institutions

1999

No	Impose steel import quotas
No	Kill proposal to take aviation trust funds off budget
No	Require background checks on buyers only at gun shows with 10 or more vendors
Yes	Remove barriers among banking, securities and insurance companies
No	Authorize state grants to hire teachers and reduce class size
No	Overhaul campaign finance law; ban "soft money" and restrict advocacy advertising
No	Approve bipartisan plan to increase rights of patients in managed-care health plans

INTEREST GROUPS

	AFL-CIO	ADA	CCUS	ACU
2000	0%	0%	85%	91%
1999	11%	0%	96%	96%
1998	0%	0%	100%	100%
1997	0%	0%	90%	92%

CQ VOTE STUDIES

	PARTY UNITY		PRESIDENTIAL SUPPORT	
	Support	Oppose	Support	Oppose
2000	97%	3%	22%	78%
1999	93%	7%	17%	83%
1998	95%	5%	22%	78%
1997	97%	3%	29%	71%

OKLAHOMA 6
West and Panhandle; part of Oklahoma City

With nothing to stop it on the flat plains, the wind blows with constant force in the 6th, an area devastated by the Dust Bowl of the 1930s. In the 1990s, the district became best known as home of the Alfred P. Murrah Federal Building, site of the 1995 Oklahoma City bombing that killed 168 people. A memorial to those who died and the Institution for Prevention of Terrorism commemorate the site.

Few areas felt the boom or the bust of the 1980s oil market more than the 6th. More than half of the district's counties lost population in the first half of the 1990s because of the downturn. Locals are striving to diversify their economic base beyond agriculture and oil. Guymon in Texas County voted to allow large-scale hog farming; it is now the only county nearby with significantly increasing population. Still, some residents are aggravated by the smell.

Although the 6th is overwhelmingly Republican, Interstate 40 provides a dividing line, south of which the district is primarily

Democratic. Northern settlers from Kansas and Nebraska brought their Republican leanings, while the southeastern part of the district is home to conservative Democrats whose families settled from Texas.

MAJOR INDUSTRY
Agriculture, oil, aviation manufacturing

MILITARY BASES
Vance Air Force Base, 1,367 military, 201 civilian (2000)

CITIES
Oklahoma City (pt.); 159,810 (1990); Enid, 45,196; Del City, 23,683

UNUSUAL FEATURES
The shopping cart and parking meter were invented in Oklahoma City; On Nov. 27, 1868, Gen. George A. Custer led an Army contingent in the Battle of Washita, which is also referred to as the "Black Kettle Massacre," in which 103 men, women and children died.

Gov. John Kitzhaber (D)

First elected: 1994
Length of term: 4 years
Term expires: 1/03
Salary: $88,300
Phone: (503) 378-3111
Hometown: Eugene
Born: March 5, 1947; Colfax, Wash.
Religion: Unspecified
Family: Wife, Sharon Kitzhaber; one child
Education: Dartmouth College, B.A. 1969; U. of Oregon, M.D. 1973
Career: Physician
Political highlights: Ore. House, 1979-81; Ore. Senate, 1981-93 (president, 1985-93)

Election results:

1998 GENERAL

John Kitzhaber (D)	717,061	64.4%
Bill Sizemore (R)	334,001	30.0%
Richard P. Burke (LIBERT)	20,200	1.8%
Blair Bobier (PACIFIC)	15,843	1.4%

Secretary of State Bill Bradbury (D)

(no lieutenant governor)
First elected: Appointed 1999; elected 2000
Length of term: 4 years
Term expires: 1/05
Salary: $67,900
Phone: (503) 986-1523

STATE LEGISLATURE

General Assembly: Meets January-May
House: 60 members, 2-year terms
2001 breakdown: 33R, 27D; 39 men, 21 women
Salary: $1,283/month, $85/day in session
Phone: (503) 986-1187
Senate: 30 members, 4-year terms
2001 breakdown: 16R, 14D; 22 men, 8 women
Salary: $1,283/month, $85/day in session
Phone: (503) 986-1187

STATE TERM LIMITS

Governor: 2 terms
Senate: 2 terms; no more than 12 years combined
House: 3 terms; no more than 12 years combined

URBAN STATISTICS

CITY	POPULATION
Portland	503,637
Eugene	130,501
Salem	129,650
Gresham	87,106

REGISTERED VOTERS

Democrat	39%
Repubican	36%
Other	25%

POPULATION

2000 population	3,421,399
1990 population	2,842,321
Percent change	+20.4%
Rank among states	28

Median age	36.6
Born in state	47%
Foreign born	5%
Urban/rural	70%/30%
Crime rate	444/100,000
Poverty level	15.0%
Federal workers	29,971
Military	12,704

REAPPORTIONMENT

Oregon retained its five House seats in reapportionment. The state legislature will draw new district lines in 2001.

MISCELLANEOUS

Web: www.state.or.us
Capital: Salem
Land area: 96,002 sq. miles
  Rank among states: 10
STATE ELECTION OFFICIAL
(503) 986-1518
DEMOCRATIC HEADQUARTERS
(503) 224-8200
REPUBLICAN HEADQUARTERS
(503) 520-1996

District Statistics

DIST.	VOTE FOR PRESIDENT 2000 D	R	GREEN	1996 D	R	REF	1992 D	R	I	WHT	BLK	ASIAN	HISP	HOUSEHOLD INCOME	OVER 65+	UNDER 18	COLLEGE EDUCATION
1	51%	44%	4%	50%	38%	7%	44%	32%	24%	93%	1%	3%	4%	$33,227	12%	25%	31%
2	34	59	4	38	48	11	35	38	27	94	0	1	5	$23,949	16	26	15
3	61	31	7	57	28	7	53	26	21	87	6	4	3	$27,150	13	25	19
4	44	49	5	45	40	10	42	32	26	96	0	1	2	$24,593	15	25	17
5	46	48	4	47	41	9	40	35	25	94	1	2	5	$28,608	13	26	21
STATE	47.0	46.5	5	47	39	9	42	33	24	93	2	2	4	$27,250	14	26	21

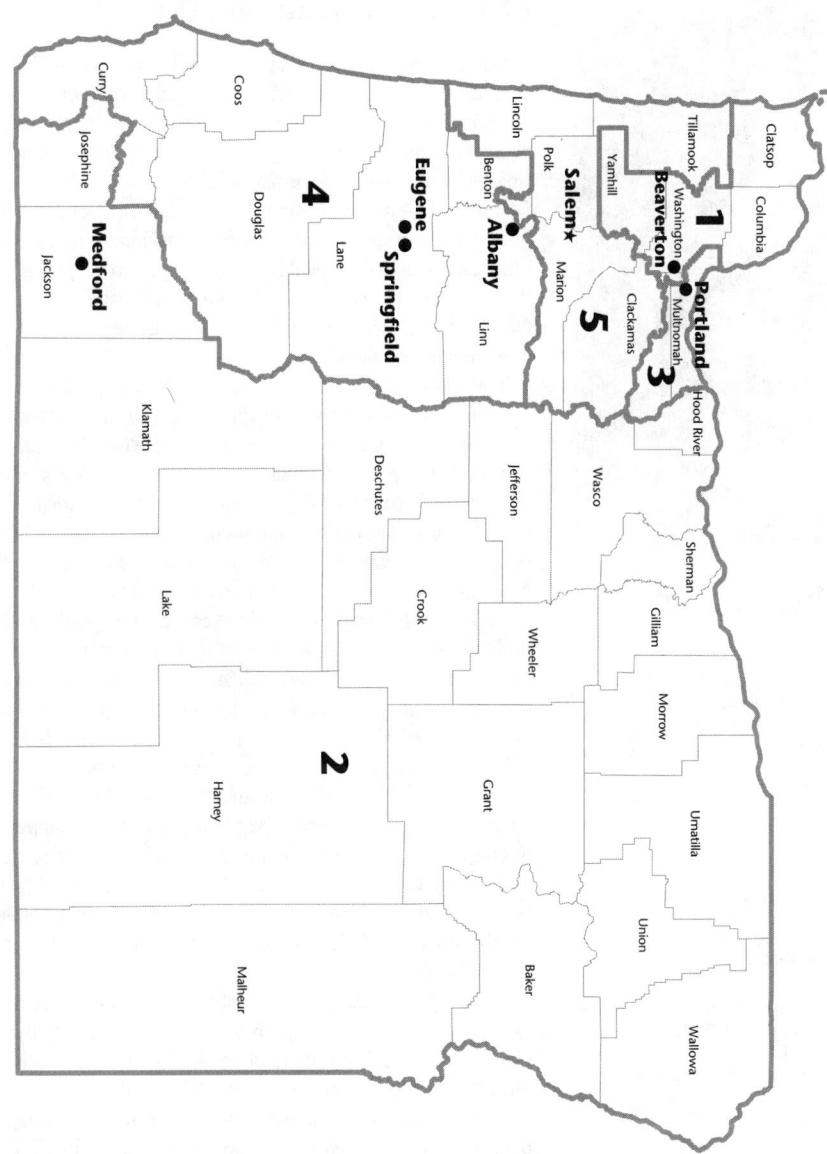

Sen. Ron Wyden (D)

Elected January 1996; 1st full term

Gangly and rumpled, Wyden hardly cuts the typical figure of a U.S. senator. But he has emerged as a powerful and shrewd deal-maker, negotiating skillfully across the aisle to advance education and health programs and to head off repeated efforts by more-senior senators to override Oregon's physician-assisted suicide law.

Although Wyden came to the Senate with a liberal reputation, he has displayed a strong pragmatic streak by working with Republicans to limit tax hikes and to help curb health care costs. "There's nothing important you can do in Washington without working in a bipartisan way," he told the Portland Oregonian. "It's that simple." Yet on such issues as consumer protection and gun control, he takes a liberal stance.

The Oregon Democrat seems equally comfortable discussing the intricate policy details of social programs or standing in front of a microphone denouncing the GOP agenda. Shunning the usual trappings of a senator, he refused to trade in his wrinkled sweaters for natty suits on the campaign trail in 1996, despite the urgings of his staff. But the former high school basketball star is competitive and focused, and he has dedicated his adult life to progressive causes. His idea of relaxation is to browse through wonkish magazines such as The Nation or The Atlantic Monthly.

In the 106th Congress, Wyden scored some legislative wins by teaming up with Republicans in an attempt to find common ground on contentious issues. He worked with Republican Bill Frist of Tennessee on legislation to give local school districts more flexibility in meeting federal standards, and he wrote a bill with Republican John McCain of Arizona to limit liability for failures related to year 2000 computer problems.

Joining with House Republican Christopher Cox of California, he also pursued a worldwide ban on Internet taxation. "What happens when someone in Oregon uses America Online in Virginia to order perfume from France and ships it to her friend in Canada?" Wyden asked. "The temptation to tax is just too great," The Oregonian reported. The plan built on 1998 legislation by Wyden and Cox to impose a three-year moratorium on taxing products sold online.

In the eyes of many of his constituents, Wyden's greatest triumph in the 106th Congress was his vigorous defense of Oregon's physician-assisted suicide law. He faced an uphill fight after House conservatives easily passed a bill prohibiting doctors from prescribing drugs to deliberately cause a patient's death, and many senators, including Majority Whip Don Nickles of Oklahoma, signaled support for the measure. But Wyden waged a furious battle to run out the legislative clock in 2000, threatening to filibuster the measure, enlisting the support of influential groups such as the American Cancer Society and combing through other pieces of legislation to make sure Nickles did not slip in the House plan.

Wyden's argument that the federal government should defer to the states on such medical matters ultimately swayed most of his Democratic colleagues, and Nickles was unable to overcome Wyden's delaying tactics. "This is incredible," Wyden said. "With the dust settling on the 106th Congress, a battle the experts said couldn't be won to preserve Oregon's vote has indeed been won." But he conceded that Senate Republicans or the Bush White House might pursue the matter again during the 107th.

A staunch consumer advocate, Wyden has proposed "bill of rights" protections for airline passengers and health care consumers. At the beginning

CAPITOL OFFICE
224-5244; fax 228-2717; 516 Hart Bldg. 20510

INTERNET
e-mail: wyden.senate.gov/mail2.htm
web: wyden.senate.gov

COMMITTEES
Budget
Commerce, Science & Transportation
Energy & Natural Resources
Environment & Public Works
Select Intelligence
Special Aging

HOMETOWN
Portland

BORN
May 3, 1949, Wichita, Kan.

RELIGION
Jewish

FAMILY
Divorced; two children

EDUCATION
U. of California, Santa Barbara, attended 1967-69; Stanford U., A.B. 1971; U. of Oregon, J.D. 1974

CAREER
Senior citizen advocacy group state director; lawyer; professor

POLITICAL HIGHLIGHTS
U.S. House, 1981-96

ELECTION RESULTS

1998 GENERAL

Ron Wyden (D)	682,425	61.1%
John Lim (R)	377,739	33.8%
Karyn Moskowitz (PACIFIC)	22,024	2.0%
Jim Brewster (LIBERT)	18,221	1.6%

1998 PRIMARY

Ron Wyden (D)	283,654	91.8%
John Sweeney (D)	25,456	8.2%

PREVIOUS WINNING PERCENTAGES
1996 Special Election (48%); 1994 House Election (73%); 1992 House Election (77%); 1990 House Election (81%); 1988 House Election (99%); 1986 House Election (86%); 1984 House Election (72%); 1982 House Election (78%); 1980 House Election (72%)

of the 106th, he joined with McCain in backing a measure to give greater consumer protections to airline passengers. "Customer service must be a bigger priority for airlines," he said.

One of Wyden's top priorities is expanding Medicare to cover the costs of prescription drugs for seniors. In the 106th, he worked with Republican Olympia Snowe of Maine on an ambitious measure to use tobacco taxes to cover the costs of prescription drugs. Although the measure did not pass, it helped define the debate over changing Medicare and drew some support from major drug companies.

By working with Republicans, Wyden has occasionally drawn criticism from liberal groups. In the 106th, for example, he teamed up with Republican Larry E. Craig of Idaho to pass legislation to guarantee federal payments to rural counties that have lost revenue because of reduced logging on federal lands. "The new relationship between the counties and the federal government means that the 21st century relationship is not just going to be about cutting trees," Wyden said. But environmentalists objected, fearing that the plan would encourage logging by requiring counties to divert money to forest projects.

But on most issues, Wyden is a reliable liberal vote. A longtime critic of managed care, he has repeatedly taken aim at the so-called gag rules that restrict doctors from discussing with their patients certain treatment options that might fall outside the scope of health plans. He also is an outspoken critic of the tobacco industry, a position that gained him notoriety in 1994 when he asked tobacco executives testifying before the House Energy and Commerce Committee whether they considered tobacco addictive — an assertion they all denied. He repeated the question in 1998 during Senate Commerce hearings, and four of the five CEOs recanted. Wyden was quick to point out the irony.

The Oregon lawmaker's crusades are not limited to national issues. He is a persistent critic of Senate traditions he finds stifling or unfair. Early in 1999, Wyden celebrated success in his longstanding campaign to end the secrecy of an informal Senate procedure that had allowed any one senator to hold up action on a measure anonymously, without stating the reason.

Wyden has forged an unusually close working relationship with Oregon's junior senator, Republican Gordon H. Smith, as the two men put aside the bitterness of their 1996 Senate contest. "We just decided that out of this crucible we had learned a lot about each other," Wyden said. "If anything, we respected each other more for what we had been through." The two have joined on several bills, including one that would have required students who take guns to school to be held temporarily and to undergo a psychological evaluation.

Wyden was Oregon executive director for the Gray Panthers, an organization promoting senior citizens' interests, when he first ran for the House in 1980. He ousted Democratic Rep. Robert Duncan in the primary and easily defeated GOP foe Darrell R. Conger in the decidedly Democratic Portland-based 3rd District. Wyden was re-elected seven times, never falling below 70 percent of the vote; he worked his way up the seniority ladder on the House Energy and Commerce panel and by the mid-1980s, was being discussed as a possible candidate for statewide office.

When GOP Sen. Bob Packwood resigned under fire in late 1995, Wyden jumped into the special-election race. Despite some stumbles — most notably on a televised quiz show in which he failed to quote the price of common grocery items — he edged fellow Democratic Rep. Peter A. DeFazio in the primary. In the nationally watched general election, Wyden defeated Smith, state Senate president, by 2 points, portraying himself as a reasonable-minded alternative to the conservative Smith on such issues as education, the environment, revamping Medicare, and balancing the budget.

KEY VOTES

2000

Yes   Overhaul bankruptcy law and increase minimum wage

No   Limit fiscal 2001 discretionary spending to $600.3 billion

No   Override veto on nuclear waste disposal at Yucca Mountain site in Nevada

Yes   Oppose effort to terminate Kosovo mission

Yes   Include gender, sexual orientation and disability in federal hate crime protections

No   Approve GOP plan to restrict use of genetic information by health insurers

No   Kill amendment delaying implementation of an anti-missile defense system

No   Cut taxes for married couples

Yes   Grant China permanent normal trade status

1999

No   Remove President Clinton from office for obstruction of justice

No   Kill amendment authorizing state grants to hire teachers and reduce class size

Yes   Require criminal background checks for purchases at gun shows

No   Approve GOP proposal to increase rights of patients in managed-care health plans

No   Block effort to allow farm and medicine exports to Cuba

Yes   Allow study of tougher automobile fuel efficiency standards

Yes   Ratify nuclear weapons testing treaty

Yes   Prohibit national political parties from collecting "soft money" donations

Yes   Remove barriers among banking, securities and insurance companies

INTEREST GROUPS

	AFL-CIO	ADA	CCUS	ACU
2000	63%	90%	60%	8%
1999	78%	100%	59%	4%
1998	75%	100%	56%	4%
1997	71%	80%	70%	8%
1996	86%	95%	38%	15%
House Service:				
1995	100%	90%	29%	12%
1994	78%	80%	58%	0%
1993	92%	95%	18%	4%
1992	73%	95%	25%	0%
1991	83%	85%	30%	5%

CQ VOTE STUDIES

	PARTY UNITY		PRESIDENTIAL SUPPORT	
	Support	Oppose	Support	Oppose
2000	97%	3%	95%	5%
1999	91%	9%	91%	9%
1998	88%	12%	85%	15%
1997	83%	17%	86%	14%
1996	92%	8%	95%	5%
House Service:				
1995	90%	10%	83%	17%
1994	96%	4%	81%	19%
1993	96%	4%	78%	22%
1992	92%	8%	17%	83%
1991	95%	5%	31%	69%

Sen. Gordon H. Smith (R)

CAPITOL OFFICE
224-3753; fax 228-3997; 404 Russell Bldg. 20510

INTERNET
e-mail: oregon@gsmith.senate.gov
web: gsmith.senate.gov

COMMITTEES
Budget
Commerce, Science & Transportation
(Surface Transportation & Merchant Marine - chairman)
Energy & Natural Resources
(Water & Power - chairman)
Foreign Relations
(European Affairs - chairman)

HOMETOWN
Pendleton

BORN
May 25, 1952, Pendleton, Ore.

RELIGION
Mormon

FAMILY
Wife, Sharon Smith; three children

EDUCATION
Brigham Young U., B.A. 1976; Southwestern U., J.D. 1979

CAREER
Frozen food company owner; lawyer

POLITICAL HIGHLIGHTS
Ore. Senate, 1993-97 (president, 1995-97);
Republican nominee for U.S. Senate, 1996
(special election)

ELECTION RESULTS

1996 GENERAL

Gordon H. Smith (R)	677,336	49.8%
Tom Bruggere (D)	624,370	45.9%
Brent Thompson (REF)	20,381	1.5%
Gary Kutcher (PACIFIC)	14,193	1.0%

1996 PRIMARY

Gordon H. Smith (R)	224,428	78.1%
Lon Mabon (R)	23,479	8.2%
Kirby Brumfield (R)	15,744	5.5%
Jeff Lewis (R)	13,359	4.6%
Robert J. Fenton (R)	8,958	3.1%

Elected 1996; 1st term

A deeply conservative man who represents a state with liberal leanings, Smith works hard to find centrist compromises, sometimes breaking party ranks on high-profile issues. The former Mormon bishop acknowledges that he has strong moral opinions about such socially charged matters as abortion and homosexuality. But he takes care not to inject his personal beliefs into the political arena. "If you want to talk to me about sin, go with me to church," he told the Portland Oregonian. "If you want to talk about public policy, then go with me to the U.S. Senate."

Smith is difficult to categorize politically. He earns top marks from business groups and casts a frugal vote on fiscal matters. But he reaches across the aisle to forge alliances with Democrats on such divisive issues as gun control and hate crimes legislation, and he has worked to bolster funding for education. In many respects, he seeks to emulate the political independence of the man he replaced: Republican Mark O. Hatfield.

Smith may be one of the most resilient members of the Senate. Even though he lost a grueling race for one Oregon Senate seat to Democrat Ron Wyden in January 1996, he bounced back immediately to run for a second, tightly contested open seat, winning that race in November 1996. His office proclaims proudly that Smith is the first person ever to run for two Senate seats in the same year.

Personable, telegenic and noted for his eye-catching suits that stand out from the traditional Senate garb, Smith is a self-made millionaire who transformed his family's unprofitable Eastern Oregon frozen vegetable processing company into one of the largest frozen vegetable packers in the country. He calls himself "the biggest pea-picker in American politics."

Smith made national headlines in 1999 when he led a successful uprising against GOP leaders who attempted to block gun control legislation. He originally voted with his leadership against a Democratic plan to require background checks on people who buy firearms at gun shows but threatened to change his vote when the GOP failed to offer a compromise plan. "If a gun is transacted at a gun show, there should be a background check," he said in a rare moment of anger. "That is not a huge imposition upon the Second Amendment." At Smith's behest, Republicans put forward an alternative.

On other issues, Smith's attempts to represent his constituents have steered him into unlikely alliances with Democrats. He teamed up with Massachusetts Democratic Sen. Edward M. Kennedy to pass hate crimes legislation that makes attacks on homosexuals a federal crime, saying, "We should ... teach that some crime is so odious that an extra measure of prosecution is demanded by us, so that it will never again be repeated among us." He also backed a $516 billion liability settlement with the tobacco industry, breaking ranks with GOP leaders.

Smith sought a bipartisan approach to address the nation's problems in education, which he called "the most important issue before this Congress." He joined Massachusetts Democrat John Kerry in the 106th Congress to propose funding to help local school districts recruit principals and to offer special programs for troubled students. The measure also sought to give parents more choice over where their children attend public school. The approach won backing from several Democrats and moderate Republicans. "We're trying to be comprehensive but avoid the hot buttons like vouchers and school construction," Smith told The Oregonian.

Smith has an especially good working relationship with his Oregon colleague, Wyden, now that the bitterness of their 1996 contest has passed. The two crisscrossed Oregon together after the 1999 impeachment trial of President Clinton — Wyden voted to acquit, Smith to convict — to give their constituents a real-life demonstration of bipartisanship. "Our natures are to find solutions, not just confrontations," Smith said. "He simply starts from the left. I start from the right." (Smith, who spent part of his childhood in Maryland, later discovered that he and Wyden had attended the same high school in Bethesda.)

But Smith found himself at odds with Wyden and others in the Oregon delegation when Oregon's physician-assisted suicide law came under fire in the 106th Congress. Torn between representing the will of his constituents, who had voted for the law, and his own belief that human life should not be cut short, Smith announced in 2000 that he would back a bill forbidding doctors to deliberately cause a patient's death. "I admit to having wrestled for a different conclusion on this issue in order that I might once again take comfort in the crowd," an emotional Smith told the Judiciary Committee. "But on a matter of this magnitude — a matter of life and death — I have failed to find comfort with a troubled conscience."

Despite his willingness to seek bipartisan solutions, Smith has proved a loyal Republican when GOP leaders need his support, such as when he switched his vote in 1998 to back an amendment capping fees that attorneys may collect from tobacco litigation. With Smith's switch, the GOP won by one vote.

Smith, who chairs the Energy panel's Water and Power Subcommittee, also sides with conservatives on some environmental issues. He opposes a plan to breach four dams on the Snake River in order to restore populations of endangered salmon.

In the foreign policy arena, Smith supported the U.S. military intervention in early 1999 in Kosovo, the rebellious Serbian province largely populated by ethnic Albanians. A sharp critic of former Yugoslav President Slobodan Milosevic, he won approval of legislation in the 105th that required congressional action before Clinton could lift economic sanctions against Serbia. Smith is chairman of Foreign Relations' European Affairs Subcommittee.

In 1997, Smith successfully pushed a measure to impose sanctions on Russia if that country implemented a law allowing religious persecution. The following year, with an eye to Oregon farmers, Smith pressed successfully for legislation exempting farm products from overseas sanctions.

Smith entered politics in 1992, winning a seat in the state Senate and ascending to the position of Senate president in just two years. But he lost a narrow and bitter race to Wyden in the special election to fill the Senate vacancy created by Republican Bob Packwood's resignation. Wyden, a veteran House Democrat, attacked Smith for receiving support from groups opposed to abortion and homosexual rights, for environmental violations at his food processing plant and for his lavish personal spending. Wyden won the election by 2 percentage points.

When Hatfield, Oregon's senior senator, announced his retirement later that year, Smith initially said he would not run again. But national Republicans urged him into the fray. Easily winning the GOP nomination, Smith redoubled his efforts to portray himself as a reasonable centrist in the general election against Democratic businessman Tom Bruggere. Smith reached out to moderate voters in the Portland area, vowing to support federal funding for abortions for low-income women in cases of rape or incest or to save the life of the woman. He eked out a victory, by a slim, 4-point margin.

KEY VOTES

2000
Yes Overhaul bankruptcy law and increase minimum wage

Yes Limit fiscal 2001 discretionary spending to $600.3 billion

Yes Override veto on nuclear waste disposal at Yucca Mountain site in Nevada

Yes Oppose effort to terminate Kosovo mission

Yes Include gender, sexual orientation and disability in federal hate crime protections

Yes Approve GOP plan to restrict use of genetic information by health insurers

Yes Kill amendment delaying implementation of an anti-missile defense system

Yes Cut taxes for married couples

Yes Grant China permanent normal trade status

1999
Yes Remove President Clinton from office for obstruction of justice

Yes Kill amendment authorizing state grants to hire teachers and reduce class size

No Require criminal background checks for purchases at gun shows

Yes Approve GOP proposal to increase rights of patients in managed-care health plans

No Block effort to allow farm and medicine exports to Cuba

Yes Allow study of tougher automobile fuel efficiency standards

Yes Ratify nuclear weapons testing treaty

No Prohibit national political parties from collecting "soft money" donations

Yes Remove barriers among banking, securities and insurance companies

INTEREST GROUPS

	AFL-CIO	ADA	CCUS	ACU
2000	0%	10%	100%	84%
1999	11%	15%	94%	76%
1998	0%	5%	94%	72%
1997	0%	25%	100%	72%

CQ VOTE STUDIES

	PARTY UNITY		PRESIDENTIAL SUPPORT	
	Support	Oppose	Support	Oppose
2000	89%	11%	62%	38%
1999	86%	14%	43%	57%
1998	85%	15%	55%	45%
1997	83%	17%	65%	35%

Rep. David Wu (D)

CAPITOL OFFICE
225-0855; fax 225-9497
1023 Longworth Bldg. 20515

INTERNET
e-mail: david.wu@mail.house.gov
web: www.house.gov/wu

COMMITTEES
Education & Workforce
Science

HOMETOWN
Portland

BORN
April 8, 1955, Taiwan

RELIGION
Presbyterian

FAMILY
Wife, Michelle Wu; two children

EDUCATION
Stanford U., B.S. 1977; Harvard Medical School,
attended 1978; Yale U., J.D. 1982

CAREER
Lawyer

POLITICAL HIGHLIGHTS
No previous office

ELECTION RESULTS

2000 GENERAL

David Wu (D)	176,902	58.3%
Charles Starr (R)	115,303	38.0%
Beth King (LIBERT)	10,858	3.6%

2000 PRIMARY

David Wu (D)	unopposed

1998 GENERAL

David Wu (D)	119,993	50.1%
Molly Bordonaro (R)	112,827	47.1%
Michael De Paulo (LIBERT)	4,218	1.8%

Elected 1998; 2nd term

As a freshman, Wu faced what may have been the most difficult policy decision of his career and — despite angering many powerful forces in his district — he emerged stronger. With such a test behind him and a solid record of support for his party, Wu appeared to be well-positioned to move up in the Democratic ranks in his second term.

Just 16 months after Wu was first elected to the House with 50.1 percent of the vote, President Clinton submitted a bill to the House in March 2000 to permanently grant China the same low tariff rates as most other nations. The proposal posed conflicting pressures for dozens of lawmakers; none faced the particular external and internal forces that Wu did.

Born in Taiwan and the first person of full Chinese ancestry to serve in the House, Wu told voters when he was campaigning in 1998 that he would vote against granting such a trade privilege to China if human rights abuses did not abate there.

Many appeared to doubt he would stick to that position. After all, he had been elected to represent part of Oregon's "Silicon Forest," which is heavily dependent on the success of Pacific Rim trade by such corporate giants as Nike and Intel. And he had helped advocate for such companies' interests as a partner of a law firm that represented high-technology businesses on issues including trade. In addition, many of the ethnic Chinese who hailed his victory as a great advance for Asian-Americans wanted to see their homeland move back into the world trading system. (The China bill abolished an annual congressional review of U.S. treatment of Chinese imports, thus paving the way for that country to enter the World Trade Organization and for U.S. producers to reap the benefits of greater access to 1 billion Chinese consumers.)

Though Wu was pushed hard, he stuck by his campaign promise. Not only did he vote against the legislation, but he also helped the measure's opponents, led by Minority Whip David E. Bonior of Michigan, round up votes in an ultimately unsuccessful bid to defeat it.

In an impassioned floor speech that won applause from House colleagues, Wu recalled the difficulties his family had endured to emigrate from Taiwan. "I will refuse to turn my back on the sacrifice of my parents and countless other Americans who have stood and fought in the cause of freedom," he said. "This is a bad trade agreement. This is bad policy, and this is counter to fundamental American values."

Wu's decision so angered the computer-chip behemoth Intel Corp. that it began hosting fundraisers for his opponent in 2000, Republican state Sen. Charles Starr. The athletic shoe giant Nike Inc. also gave money to Starr, as did some Chinese-American activists. Wu had anticipated such difficulties early on, however, and had maintained a sizable campaign war chest. In addition, the funding he lost from business and ethnic contacts was largely replaced with increased contributions from the AFL-CIO, teachers unions and others who saw a kindred spirit. Wu outspent Starr, launched a drive to register new Asian-American voters and won his second term by 20 percentage points.

With the exception of the China measure, much of Wu's agenda in the House has centered on education policy. A member of the Education and the Workforce Committee and the husband of a Head Start teacher, Wu has been on the front lines in trying to increase funding for public education. He allied himself closely with the Clinton administration in such efforts and attempted to attach $11.4 billion to a Republican education bill in 1999 to fully fund a Clinton plan to hire 100,000 new teachers. The amendment was blocked from coming to the floor by House leaders.

Wu has hewed to the party line on most issues. His vote in 2000 for a Republican measure to repeal the tax code's "marriage penalty" was a rare break with the Democratic leadership. He affiliates with the burgeoning New Democrat Coalition, a group of pro-business, centrist Democrats.

His handling of the China issue and his evident intellectual capacity — Wu attended Harvard Medical School and graduated from Yale Law School — suggest he may have what it takes to move up the ladder in Congress. But his initial efforts have not borne fruit. Upon entering the House, he fought for a seat on the Appropriations Committee but was unsuccessful. He also lost a bid to join the Energy and Commerce panel in the 107th.

The congressman was still in the throes of a newcomer's excitement when Clinton invited him and his wife, Michelle, to watch the 2000 Super Bowl at the White House. Wu had his traditional game-time snack — ribs from a Tigard, Ore., restaurant — delivered; his favorite team, the St. Louis Rams, won.

He had followed the Rams, then based in Los Angeles, as a child in California in the 1960s. Wu arrived in the United States with his mother and sisters when he was 7 years old. The family joined Wu's father, who had come to this country to study when Wu was four months old.

Back in Los Angeles to address the Democratic National Convention in 2000, Wu said he had become involved in public life because of the difference government decisions had made in his own future. He said his family had been able to move to the United States because President Kennedy had updated quotas that had been used to limit Chinese immigrants. "Public decisions make a difference," he said. "Elections change the course of nations."

In another homage to his adopted homeland, Wu has made a habit of naming those in his household after famous Americans. His son, born on the Fourth of July 1997, is Matthew Jefferson Adams Wu. Family dogs have included Sam Rayburn and Teddy Roosevelt; a cat was named Lyndon Johnson.

Wu had never held public office when Democrat Elizabeth Furse's retirement opened up the 1st District in 1998. He was well-known in the Portland legal and business community and was able to edge past Washington County Commission Chairman Linda Peters in the Democratic primary. In the general election, the district's Democratic tendencies lifted Wu to a 3 percentage point victory over public relations consultant Molly Bordonaro.

KEY VOTES

2000

Yes Raise hourly minimum wage by $1 over two years
Yes Halt funding for U.S. mission in Kosovo unless European nations pay more
Yes Provide Medicare benefits to military retirees and their dependents
No Grant China permanent normal trade status
No Phase out estate, gift and trust taxes
No Prohibit implementation of president's national monument designations
No Approve GOP plan to provide prescription drug coverage for Medicare beneficiaries
Yes Increase help for poor nations indebted to international financial institutions

1999

Yes Impose steel import quotas
Yes Kill proposal to take aviation trust funds off budget
No Require background checks on buyers only at gun shows with 10 or more vendors
Yes Remove barriers among banking, securities and insurance companies
Yes Authorize state grants to hire teachers and reduce class size
Yes Overhaul campaign finance law; ban "soft money" and restrict advocacy advertising
Yes Approve bipartisan plan to increase rights of patients in managed-care health plans

INTEREST GROUPS

	AFL-CIO	ADA	CCUS	ACU
2000	90%	90%	52%	20%
1999	89%	100%	24%	4%

CQ VOTE STUDIES

	PARTY UNITY		PRESIDENTIAL SUPPORT	
	Support	Oppose	Support	Oppose
2000	83%	17%	67%	33%
1999	87%	13%	78%	22%

OREGON 1

Western Portland and suburbs

Nestled into the west bank of the Willamette River, Portland's Silicon Forest hums with new companies assembling computer chips. Californians and other migrants have come to Portland in droves, looking for an urban economy with a leisurely lifestyle.

Many of the most affluent urbanites have settled in the city; others are filling up suburban Washington and Yamhill counties. Aided by a western light rail that stretches to Hillsboro, towns that were once bedroom communities have turned into satellite cities with their own streams of commuters.

Outside the Portland metro area, the 1st is struggling to keep its traditional industries intact. A highly public battle between loggers and environmentalists over the fate of the spotted owl has dampened forestry. Salmon stocks are dwindling due to excessive harvests and hydroelectric dams. Tourism and a modest wine industry have helped fill some of the void.

Politically, the 1st is one of the most competitive battlegrounds in the state. Affluent voters inside Portland's city limits, about 15 percent of the district's residents, back liberal Democrats. But voters in the suburban counties are strongly Republican. In the far northwest counties of Clatsop and Columbia, voters become more Democratic, but most are more socially conservative than their counterparts in Portland. With a number of big businesses in the district, international trade has become a hot issue in congressional contests.

MAJOR INDUSTRY

Electronics, computer manufacturing

CITIES

Portland (pt.), 85,310 (1990); Hillsboro, 65,835; Beaverton, 64,563; Tigard, 38,212; McMinnville, 24,440

UNUSUAL FEATURES

Nike Inc. world headquarters in Beaverton; Columbia River Maritime Museum.

Rep. Greg Walden (R)

CAPITOL OFFICE
225-6730; fax 225-5774
1404 Longworth Bldg. 20515

INTERNET
e-mail: greg.walden@mail.house.gov
web: www.house.gov/walden

COMMITTEES
Energy & Commerce
Resources

HOMETOWN
Hood River

BORN
Jan. 10, 1957, The Dalles, Ore.

RELIGION
Episcopalian

FAMILY
Wife, Mylene Walden; one child

EDUCATION
U. of Oregon, B.S. 1981

CAREER
Radio station owner; congressional aide

POLITICAL HIGHLIGHTS
Ore. House, 1989-95 (majority leader, 1991-93);
Ore. Senate, 1995-97 (assistant majority leader,
1995-97)

ELECTION RESULTS

2000 GENERAL

Greg Walden (R)	220,086	73.6%
Walter A. Ponsford (D)	78,101	26.1%

2000 PRIMARY

Greg Walden (R)	unopposed

1998 GENERAL

Greg Walden (R)	132,316	61.5%
Kevin M. Campbell (D)	74,924	34.8%
Lindsey Bradshaw (LIBERT)	4,729	2.2%
Rohn "Grandpa" Webb (S)	2,773	1.3%

Elected 1998; 2nd term

Walden arrived in Congress with a reputation as a dealmaker, a talent honed during eight years in the Oregon legislature, five of those as a party leader. In Washington, he continues to prove his ability to win over Democratic votes, even while staunchly defending the interests of the farming and logging industries so vital to the 2nd District.

During his first year in office in 1999, he won enactment of a bill to permit export of pears with slight flaws that do not affect taste or shelf life — a major victory for the fruit farmers of eastern Oregon.

In the 107th Congress, Walden landed a plum committee assignment on the Energy and Commerce Committee, adding it to the post on the Resources panel that he held during the 106th. He had to relinquish spots on the Agriculture and Government Reform committees.

The Resources panel deals with issues of great importance to the 2nd District. The federal government owns more than half of the district's territory, including 10 national forests, and Walden is a strong critic of federal land-use regulations. "This is a district under siege by federal policies," he has said. He supports an easing of federal regulations under the Endangered Species Act, he opposes the removal of dams on the Snake River to save salmon, and he wants to make it easier for property owners to challenge zoning decisions that adversely affect the use of their land.

In his first term, Walden pushed for legislation to prevent the Steens Mountain area, a physical landmark used by ranchers for grazing, from being declared a national monument by the Clinton administration. He argued that such a designation would draw thousands of tourists to a pristine area and "throw a wrench in the century-old public-private management of the mountain."

But while he opposes environmental groups on such issues as dam removal and land-use restrictions, the former Eagle Scout supports initiatives to encourage the use of alternative fuels and recycling. He is the co-chairman of the bipartisan 150-member House Renewable Energy Caucus, which supports the use of wind, solar and geothermal power to reduce air pollution and reliance on foreign oil.

Reared on a cherry orchard, Walden has said that expansion of trade is vital to the survival of family-owned farms. He was an enthusiastic supporter of making permanent the normal trade relations status the United States has afforded China.

Walden opposes new gun control laws but has adopted a moderate position on abortion: he opposes federal funding for abortion but does not support laws that would ban it outright. He says his views on abortion were shaped by personal experience: in 1993, he and his wife, Mylene, considered but rejected aborting a fetus diagnosed with a congenital heart defect. The baby boy was born prematurely and died.

Walden opposes the procedure known by opponents as "partial birth" abortion but does not advocate a repeal of the Supreme Court's *Roe v. Wade* decision establishing the right to abortion. He says that the decision on whether to have an abortion should be left to parents.

Days after his election to the House in 1998, Walden was tapped by Majority Leader Dick Armey to deliver the GOP response to one of President Clinton's weekly radio addresses. Walden used the opportunity to urge bipartisan compromise on plans to reduce the debt, cut taxes for those of middle income, shore up Social Security and improve education and health care.

Walden often speaks of the need for better education and health care and environmental policies that nurture growth in small towns "far from America's booming e-cities." While agriculture dominates the economy of the district, the region also is becoming a magnet for wind-surfing and snow-boarding tourists. Walden himself enjoys downhill skiing at Mount Hood and sailing on the Columbia River.

As a youth, he worked at his father's radio station in Hood River. Walden, who developed his own broadcast voice as a one-time disc jockey and talk-show host, later bought the family business with his wife. Their company, Columbia Gorge Broadcasters, now operates four popular music and news radio stations.

Walden got his introduction to politics during a seven-year stint as an aide to former Republican Rep. Denny Smith of Oregon, who was noted for being a political maverick. But Walden's low-key consensus-building style is similar to another Republican from Oregon named Smith: his predecessor, Bob Smith, who retired as chairman of the Agriculture Committee. (He also considers himself close to a third politically prominent Republican from Oregon named Smith: Sen. Gordon H. Smith, who served with Walden in the legislature and is a 2nd District constituent.)

Walden served eight years at the state capital in Salem, including nearly three years as House majority leader and two years as assistant Senate majority leader. He was a key supporter of Oregon's health insurance changes for Medicaid recipients, which called for setting medical priorities, or rationing, to cut costs.

Walden threatened to run for Congress as an independent in 1996 to challenge Republican Rep. Wes Cooley, who had been accused of lying about his military record in a voter pamphlet after winning the 1994 GOP primary. But Speaker Newt Gingrich lured Bob Smith out of retirement to run again for the GOP nomination, promising him the chairmanship of the Agriculture Committee if he won. When Smith agreed to run, both Walden and Cooley bowed out. (In 1997, Cooley was found guilty and ordered to pay fines and perform community service.)

When Smith decided to retire once again in 1998, Walden quickly established himself as the front-runner. He breezed to victory in the GOP primary and easily defeated Democrat Kevin M. Campbell, a former county judge, in the heavily Republican district. In 2000, he romped to re-election, by a 3-to-1 ratio. He is regarded as a potential statewide candidate some day, but he took himself out of the early speculation for the governor's race in 2002, when Democratic Gov. John Kitzhaber will have to step down.

KEY VOTES

2000
No — Raise hourly minimum wage by $1 over two years
Yes — Halt funding for U.S. mission in Kosovo unless European nations pay more
Yes — Provide Medicare benefits to military retirees and their dependents
Yes — Grant China permanent normal trade status
Yes — Phase out estate, gift and trust taxes
Yes — Prohibit implementation of president's national monument designations
Yes — Approve GOP plan to provide prescription drug coverage for Medicare beneficiaries
No — Increase help for poor nations indebted to international financial institutions

1999
No — Impose steel import quotas
No — Kill proposal to take aviation trust funds off budget
Yes — Require background checks on buyers only at gun shows with 10 or more vendors
Yes — Remove barriers among banking, securities and insurance companies
No — Authorize state grants to hire teachers and reduce class size
No — Overhaul campaign finance law; ban "soft money" and restrict advocacy advertising
No — Approve bipartisan plan to increase rights of patients in managed-care health plans

INTEREST GROUPS

	AFL-CIO	ADA	CCUS	ACU
2000	20%	5%	90%	88%
1999	22%	10%	96%	80%

CQ VOTE STUDIES

	PARTY UNITY		PRESIDENTIAL SUPPORT	
	Support	Oppose	Support	Oppose
2000	96%	4%	25%	75%
1999	90%	10%	22%	78%

OREGON 2
East and Southwest — Medford; Bend

Oregon's 2nd covers two-thirds of the state, bordering Washington, Idaho, Nevada and California. About 60 percent of that land is owned by the federal government, causing considerable strife with the district's residents, who depend on fishing, farming and logging to make a living.

The 2nd lost timber jobs when the spotted owl was deemed an endangered species and its Oregon forest habitat protected from clear-cutting. Those jobs have been difficult to replace in a district with few urban areas. Farmers produce fruit, wheat and hay in the district's plateaus and river valleys, but cattle farmers have seen their access to public grazing lands limited. At the same time, the Columbia River's fishing industry has faced restrictions on salmon under the Endangered Species Act. During the 1980s, economic pains drove enough people from the district that it declined in population, but numbers rebounded in the 1990s as retired couples moved to the area.

With almost 60,000 people, Medford is the largest city in the 2nd. Medford is surrounded by pear, cherry and apple orchards of the fruit-growing Rogue River Valley. Less than 20 miles southeast of Medford is Ashland, which has hosted the Oregon Shakespeare Festival since 1935.

Hostility toward the federal government makes the 2nd Oregon's most reliably Republican district, voting for the Republican presidential candidate in 1992, '96 and 2000. Democrats are scattered through parts of Ashland and Bend, but they are too few to swing the district.

MAJOR INDUSTRY
Agriculture, forestry, tourism

CITIES
Medford, 59,937; Bend, 36,210; Grants Pass, 22,717; Ashland, 18,659; Klamath Falls, 18,561

UNUSUAL FEATURES
Crater Lake National Park; Warm Springs Indian Reservation.

Rep. Earl Blumenauer (D)

CAPITOL OFFICE
225-4811; fax 225-8941
1406 Longworth Bldg. 20515

INTERNET
e-mail: write.earl@mail.house.gov
web: www.house.gov/blumenauer

COMMITTEES
International Relations
Transportation & Infrastructure

HOMETOWN
Portland

BORN
Aug. 16, 1948, Portland, Ore.

RELIGION
Unspecified

FAMILY
Divorced; two children

EDUCATION
Lewis and Clark College, B.A. 1970, J.D. 1976

CAREER
Public official

POLITICAL HIGHLIGHTS
Ore. House, 1973-77; Multnomah County
Commission, 1978-86; candidate for Portland City
Council, 1980; Portland City Council, 1986-96;
candidate for mayor of Portland, 1992

ELECTION RESULTS

2000 GENERAL

Earl Blumenauer (D)	181,049	66.8%
Jeffrey L. Pollock (R)	64,128	23.7%
Tre Arrow (GREEN)	15,763	5.8%
Bruce A. Knight (LIBERT)	4,942	1.8%
Walter F. "Walt" Brown (S)	4,703	1.7%

2000 PRIMARY

Earl Blumenauer (D)	70,388	88.1%
John Sweeney (D)	9,237	11.6%

1998 GENERAL

Earl Blumenauer (D)	153,889	83.9%
Bruce A. Knight (LIBERT)	16,930	9.2%
Walter F. "Walt" Brown (S)	10,199	5.6%
write-ins	2,333	1.3%

PREVIOUS WINNING PERCENTAGES
1996 (67%); 1996 Special Election (70%)

Elected May 1996; 3rd full term

As a liberal Democrat in a Republican-controlled House, Blumenauer has had his share of frustration inside the halls of the Capitol. But he gets national attention by espousing the view that government should help people promote what he calls "livability" in their communities.

An avid bicyclist and runner, Blumenauer (BLUE-men-hour) pursues this goal in ways both great and small: by cajoling the U.S. Postal Service not to close old downtown facilities that are community gathering spots; by calling on the House to add showers and lockers for staffers who bike to work; by lobbying from his Transportation Committee seat to spend billions on mass transit, bicycle trails, historic preservation and other community enhancement projects; and by proposing legislation making it harder for owners of professional sports teams to pull their franchises out of a city with little or no notice.

After being advised by former Oregon GOP Sen. Mark O. Hatfield about the need for freshmen to stand out, he decided to wear a bow tie and start a bow tie caucus. He has won admiring profiles in USA Today and other widely read publications for refusing to own a car in Washington. He bikes to his Capitol Hill office from his nearby apartment and cycles to meetings at the White House. He hangs a T-shirt in his office that gives advice on creating "an American Renaissance" — eat at diners, shop on Main Street, put a porch on your house, live in a walkable community.

Blumenauer's livability agenda resonated with the Clinton administration, and Al Gore adopted some of the proposals in his 2000 campaign for the presidency. But his ideas are received less enthusiastically by Republicans wary of proposals that resemble 1960s-style "social engineering."

Looking for common ground with conservatives, Blumenauer tries to tap into the GOP's desire to shift decision-making away from Washington to states and localities. He talks of "the power of the collaborative process — sitting down at the table and allowing local voices to be heard"; and he tries to cast his concerns in a non-partisan light. "Local officials dealing with police and parks and people's backyards ... can't afford to be gratuitously partisan," he says.

Blumenauer has gotten considerable media mileage out of some of his livability initiatives, such as his legislation requiring the Postal Service to abide by local land-use and zoning regulations, which could discourage it from closing downtown offices. "Citizens have had more choices over which Elvis stamp they prefer than over the future of their local post office," he said. "Relocations can end up tearing the heart out of historic downtowns."

Another headline-grabber was Blumenauer's attempt to discourage pro sports teams from relocating. He proposed legislation, dubbed the "Give Fans a Chance" act, to revoke the National Football League provision that generally prohibits public ownership of franchises. Citing the example of the publicly owned Green Bay Packers, he said: "A community which owns its own team is a community investing in its own livability — defining what it wants of and for itself."

In the 106th Congress, Blumenauer teamed up with GOP Rep. Doug Bereuter of Nebraska on "Two Floods and You're Out" legislation. The bill aimed to discourage homeowners from rebuilding in flood-ravaged areas, which can be a costly proposition for the government's flood insurance program. "This is one issue where the fiscal conservatives can join with the environmental protection folks," he said, according to the Los Angeles Times.

As the Transportation Committee worked in the 105th on legislation reauthorizing the nation's transportation programs, Blumenauer stressed the importance of giving communities a strong voice in deciding how money should be spent. "Our citizens, our constituents, know what they need," he said. "If we engage them in the process of planning for our future, they will respond with innovation and non-traditional solutions." He scored a major success by winning federal funding for the Portland area's planned 21-mile South/North Light Rail Project.

In keeping with the majority sentiment among his liberal Portland constituents, Blumenauer is a consistent vote to protect the environment, preserve abortion rights and defend federal funding of the arts. He supports gun control efforts and opposes a constitutional amendment allowing Congress to prohibit flag desecration.

But, breaking with labor unions and many in his party, Blumenauer is a stalwart supporter of lowering international trade barriers, a reflection of Portland's growing economic ties to Pacific Rim countries. In the 3rd District, he says, "one out of every five jobs depends on trade." Accordingly, he supported granting China permanent normal trade status in 2000. Although critics of the trade deal raised concerns about China's human rights record, Blumenauer countered: "The most progress is going to be made by actually engaging the Chinese."

An activist since his teenage years in the late 1960s, Blumenauer was just one year out of Lewis and Clark College in 1971 when he testified before a congressional subcommittee in support of a constitutional amendment to lower the voting age to 18. Elected to the Oregon House at the age of 24, he quickly rose to prominence as chairman of the Revenue Committee. He won a seat on the Multnomah County Board of Commissioners in 1978, then election in 1986 to the Portland City Council. In those jobs, he was instrumental in establishing the ambitious and much-praised land-use planning procedures that Portland uses to control metropolitan sprawl.

Although Blumenauer had had some political stumbles — he failed in a 1980 city council bid and ran unsuccessfully for mayor of Portland in 1992 — his widespread name recognition and broad appeal put him in a good position to try for the 3rd in early 1996. The House seat was vacant because Democratic Rep. Ron Wyden won a January 1996 Senate special election to replace disgraced Republican Bob Packwood, who resigned. Blumenauer easily won the three-way Democratic primary and sailed past GOP nominee Mark Brunelle, winning the right to serve through the end of the 104th Congress. He has since won re-election with ease.

KEY VOTES

2000

Yes	Raise hourly minimum wage by $1 over two years
No	Halt funding for U.S. mission in Kosovo unless European nations pay more
Yes	Provide Medicare benefits to military retirees and their dependents
Yes	Grant China permanent normal trade status
?	Phase out estate, gift and trust taxes
No	Prohibit implementation of president's national monument designations
No	Approve GOP plan to provide prescription drug coverage for Medicare beneficiaries
Yes	Increase help for poor nations indebted to international financial institutions

1999

Yes	Impose steel import quotas
No	Kill proposal to take aviation trust funds off budget
No	Require background checks on buyers only at gun shows with 10 or more vendors
Yes	Remove barriers among banking, securities and insurance companies
Yes	Authorize state grants to hire teachers and reduce class size
Yes	Overhaul campaign finance law; ban "soft money" and restrict advocacy advertising
Yes	Approve bipartisan plan to increase rights of patients in managed-care health plans

INTEREST GROUPS

	AFL-CIO	ADA	CCUS	ACU
2000	90%	90%	42%	0%
1999	78%	95%	40%	4%
1998	100%	95%	41%	4%
1997	100%	95%	40%	4%

CQ VOTE STUDIES

	PARTY UNITY		PRESIDENTIAL SUPPORT	
	Support	Oppose	Support	Oppose
2000	93%	7%	88%	12%
1999	90%	10%	80%	20%
1998	92%	8%	85%	15%
1997	93%	7%	82%	18%

OREGON 3
East and North Portland and eastern suburbs

Split by the Willamette River, the city of Portland has two personalities. The eastern portion, covered by the 3rd, still depends on the blue-collar economy that made Portland a thriving international port for lumber and fruit. The Portland Port and Portland International Airport make the city a leading center of trade and distribution. Computer chips and cappuccino drive the city's western side, which is in the 1st.

Compared to the rest of Portland, the 3rd is a multicultural haven. Most of the city's minorities, both African- and Asian-American, live in the far northeastern and southeastern sections of the city.

The 3rd's second-largest city, Gresham, was once a thriving farm community. It's now the easternmost stop on Portland's light rail system and growing rapidly. Beyond the towns at Portland's edge, the district quickly turns rural. Mount Hood National Forest covers the far eastern part of the district.

The 3rd's residents in Portland tend to be less liberal than their counterparts in the 1st but nevertheless produce comfortable Democratic margins. East of the city, the district turns more conservative, but Republicans are few and far between.

The district voted for Bill Clinton in both 1992 and '96 and gave Al Gore a 30 percentage point win over President Bush in 2000.

MAJOR INDUSTRY
Wholesale trade and distribution, health care, forestry

CITIES
Portland (pt.), 352,009 (1990); Gresham, 87,106; Powellhurst-Centennial (unincorporated), 28,756 (1990); Milwaukie, 19,770

UNUSUAL FEATURES
Forest Park, one of the largest urban parks in the nation; Mount Hood, Oregon's highest peak at 11,235 feet.

Rep. Peter A. DeFazio (D)

Elected 1986; 8th term

CAPITOL OFFICE
225-6416; fax 225-0032; 2134 Rayburn Bldg. 20515

INTERNET
e-mail: peter.defazio@mail.house.gov
web: www.house.gov/defazio

COMMITTEES
Resources
Transportation & Infrastructure

HOMETOWN
Springfield

BORN
May 27, 1947, Needham, Mass.

RELIGION
Roman Catholic

FAMILY
Wife, Myrnie L. Daut

EDUCATION
Tufts U., B.A. 1969; U. of Oregon, attended 1969-71,
M.S. 1977

MILITARY SERVICE
Air Force, 1967-71

CAREER
Congressional aide

POLITICAL HIGHLIGHTS
Lane County Commission, 1982-86; sought
Democratic nomination for U.S. Senate (special
election), 1996

ELECTION RESULTS

2000 GENERAL

Peter A. DeFazio (D)	197,998	68.0%
John Lindsey (R)	88,950	30.6%
David G. Duemler (S)	3,696	1.3%

2000 PRIMARY

Peter A. DeFazio (D)	unopposed

1998 GENERAL

Peter A. DeFazio (D)	157,524	70.1%
Steve J. Webb (R)	64,143	28.6%
Karl G. Sorg (S)	2,694	1.2%

PREVIOUS WINNING PERCENTAGES
1996 (66%); 1994 (67%); 1992 (71%); 1990 (86%);
1988 (72%); 1986 (54%)

Pick almost any topic, particularly those high on the GOP leadership's legislative agenda, and the chances are good that DeFazio has made a loud, emotional and sometimes sarcastic House floor speech on the subject.

A profile in the Eugene Register-Guard dubbed DeFazio a "populist and pit bull." The congressman thinks it is a fair description, although he says he has mellowed since he came to Congress in 1987. But he told a Portland reporter in 1997, "I don't think I've lost my fire or anything. I'm still down on the floor waving my fist ... and pounding on the dais."

DeFazio (da-FAH-zee-o) keeps busy in the House, jabbing at GOP policies as the chairman in the 106th Congress of the Progressive Caucus, a group of the chamber's most liberal Democrats that is particularly keen on cutting defense spending. He also will take shots at Democrats, such as in 2000 when he called President Clinton's steps to reduce oil prices "pathetic."

DeFazio's career has been shaped by a populist philosophy and the belief that his constituents appreciate his straight talk even more than they might appreciate a few extra federal dollars. He has encouraged his independent image by driving a 1963 Dodge Dart around the district and offering up a recipe for home-brewed beer on his website. A dog lover, he owns two Chesapeake Bay retrievers — "they make great watchdogs," he says.

On the Transportation Committee, DeFazio is active in aviation and surface transportation matters and on a broad range of consumer issues that arise in legislation dealing with trade and government regulation. He is the top Democrat on the panel's Water Resources and Environment Subcommittee.

In the 106th Congress, he pressed for legislation to force airlines to improve customer service. When airlines instead proposed voluntary steps to address growing numbers of consumer complaints, DeFazio shot back, "The flying public has seen these promises made and then broken time and time again and won't be fooled by the latest blast of hot air."

In the 105th, while preparing for a fight over proposals to deregulate the electricity business, DeFazio pointed out that reduced safety standards, poor service and increased costs had arisen in industries that Congress already had largely set free from federal regulation — aviation, railroads, telecommunications, and cable television. And he warned against the trend toward airline alliances that "look like mergers to me." In each instance, consumers are getting a raw deal, DeFazio says.

On the electricity deregulation front, DeFazio counsels Congress to take a go-slow approach. He has made himself the region's expert on energy policy, and he opposes electricity deregulation, saying that retail electricity is a natural monopoly. But he also is against deregulation for the practical reason that Northwest ratepayers, who benefit from low-cost power from the Bonneville Power Administration, would likely see their electric bills increase under deregulation. His go-slow approach proved prescient as Californians faced rolling blackouts in January 2001 after the state deregulated its electricity market.

DeFazio shares with many of his constituents a skepticism about international entanglements, particularly in the trade arena. U.S. trade policy, he believes, "exports our jobs, drives down wages and destroys the environment." He voted against granting China permanent normal trade status in 2000, and he was the only Oregonian in the House in the 103rd to vote against both the 1993 North American Free Trade Agreement and legislation to implement the 1994 General Agreement on Tariffs and Trade.

DeFazio also sits on the Resources Committee, where he finds it harder to make headway on legislation. He has a tough juggling act when it comes to forest and resource management questions. His district and state include strongly conflicting interests on those issues — the loggers who oppose restrictions on timber cutting and the environmentalists who want restrictions. He notes wryly that he has been blasted, on a case-by-case basis, by both the timber industry and environmentalists.

In 1999, DeFazio proposed that the government make stable annual payments to rural counties that have lost revenue because of reduced logging in federal forests. The plan, which would have ended a system of linking federal payments to timber sales receipts, drew support from the Clinton administration, but many Westerners preferred to continue tying federal payments to timber sales.

DeFazio's sarcasm can soar during floor debates. When GOP Rep. Randy "Duke" Cunningham charged in a 2000 debate over military spending that the Democratic Socialists of America's website has a link to the Progressive Caucus, DeFazio threatened to invoke "a point of personal privilege very soon if the gentleman continues with his bizarre and inaccurate accusations because he cannot operate a computer properly." He acknowledges that his choice of words sometimes annoys his colleagues, and he admits that his sarcasm may have cost him a seat on the Appropriations Committee in the 103rd Congress.

DeFazio's first taste of politics came as a youth in Massachusetts at the knee of his great-uncle, a classic Boston pol who followed the word Republican with the Boston-accented epithet "bastud" so often that it sounded like one word to the young DeFazio. After earning a graduate degree in gerontology from the University of Oregon, DeFazio went to work for Oregon Democratic Rep. Jim Weaver, a hot-tempered populist. He then struck out on his own, winning election to the Lane County Commission in 1982 and earning a reputation for being aggressive by suing to nullify contracts between Oregon utilities and the Washington Public Power Supply System, whose failed nuclear projects had resulted in utility rate increases.

When Weaver announced he would not seek re-election in 1986, DeFazio stepped in. By portraying himself as heir to Weaver's populist appeal, he narrowly won the Democratic primary. Deflecting criticism that he was too close to Weaver, he won the general election with 54 percent and has subsequently held his district with ease. He fell short in a special-election bid for the Senate, however, losing to Democratic Rep. Ron Wyden in a hard-fought December 1995 primary. Wyden went on to win the seat.

KEY VOTES

2000

Yes	Raise hourly minimum wage by $1 over two years
Yes	Halt funding for U.S. mission in Kosovo unless European nations pay more
Yes	Provide Medicare benefits to military retirees and their dependents
No	Grant China permanent normal trade status
No	Phase out estate, gift and trust taxes
No	Prohibit implementation of president's national monument designations
No	Approve GOP plan to provide prescription drug coverage for Medicare beneficiaries
Yes	Increase help for poor nations indebted to international financial institutions

1999

Yes	Impose steel import quotas
No	Kill proposal to take aviation trust funds off budget
No	Require background checks on buyers only at gun shows with 10 or more vendors
No	Remove barriers among banking, securities and insurance companies
Yes	Authorize state grants to hire teachers and reduce class size
Yes	Overhaul campaign finance law; ban "soft money" and restrict advocacy advertising
Yes	Approve bipartisan plan to increase rights of patients in managed-care health plans

INTEREST GROUPS

	AFL-CIO	ADA	CCUS	ACU
2000	100%	90%	25%	8%
1999	100%	100%	12%	8%
1998	100%	95%	12%	16%
1997	100%	85%	20%	28%

CQ VOTE STUDIES

	PARTY UNITY		PRESIDENTIAL SUPPORT	
	Support	Oppose	Support	Oppose
2000	86%	14%	67%	33%
1999	92%	8%	73%	27%
1998	93%	7%	80%	20%
1997	90%	10%	68%	32%

OREGON 4
Southwest – Eugene

Loggers, fishermen and environmentalists combine to give the 4th a potentially combustible political mix. In the early 1990s, the district was a prime battleground in the fight between lumber mills and environmentalists over the fate of the spotted owl. The brouhaha has since quieted down, and most of the unionized mills have been forced to close.

Fishing, another of the district's economic mainstays, also has dwindled. Most commercial fishermen – in towns such as Charleston, Bandon and Port Orford – are looking for a way out, having been harmed by frequent run closings, short seasons and low prices. While this rural region's unemployment has been steadily improving, it is still higher than average. The district has been counting on tourists and retirement communities to revitalize its economy.

Eugene and Springfield, the district's most populous cities, have fared better. Research at the University of Oregon, still a hotbed of

environmentalism, has lured high-tech companies. Computer manufacturers and software developers now vie with lumber and paper producers to dominate the economy.

Voters in the 4th support Democratic statewide candidates, but their behavior is less certain at the local level. Eugene and Springfield vote reliably Democratic, but voters in Linn and Douglas counties occasionally support Republicans in the legislature. Coos and Curry counties, which once had a strong union tradition, now lean Republican.

MAJOR INDUSTRY
Forestry, agriculture, fishing, tourism

CITIES
Eugene, 130,501; Springfield, 50,744; Albany, 38,773; Roseburg, 19,874

UNUSUAL FEATURES
Movie "Stand by Me" filmed in Lane County; Curry County is the nation's leading producer of Easter lilies.

Rep. Darlene Hooley (D)

Elected 1996; 3rd term

Hooley can be spotted hurrying through the halls of the Capitol wearing running shoes to complement her regular business attire. The sneakers offer a hint about Hooley's get-down-to-work legislative style.

A former teacher whose duties included coaching girls' sports teams, she arrived in Congress with a reputation gained during two decades in state and local government as a serious and conciliatory lawmaker, more interested in formulating policy than engaging in partisan and ideological confrontation. She attributed her narrow 1996 election to the House, in part, to her bipartisan, consensus-building style. "I think that's what people are looking for," she said.

Hooley represents a swing district, and she works hard to cultivate a moderate image. A member of the New Democrat Coalition, which hews toward the political center, she presses for limited tax cuts and supports trade initiatives. But she sides with the left when it comes to politically charged social issues such as abortion.

Hooley's interests in Congress include many of the same issues she dealt with as a local official, including improving access to education — for preschool students through programs such as Head Start and for college students through tuition tax credits and increased student loan availability. Like many in her party, she opposes vouchers for private school tuition, contending that the government instead should focus on improving public schools.

Hooley advocates requiring drug companies to make prescription medications available to all consumers at the same prices that they offer to their largest buyers. Her position angered the drug industry, which launched an ad campaign in 1999 that accused her of "playing politics" with prescription drugs. But Hooley said the legislation would help senior citizens struggling to afford medication.

Another priority is children's health issues. In a 1997 floor speech, Hooley empathized with "the parents who lay awake each night wondering what they can do when their kids get sick." Most of those parents have jobs, she said, but do not have employer-provided health insurance. Later that year, the House passed legislation that included $24 billion to expand children's health care.

On environmental issues, Hooley says she adamantly opposes any efforts to weaken clean air and clean water regulations. But, cognizant of the district economy's heavy reliance on logging, agriculture and fishing, Hooley contends that the federal government should set standards but not dictate to local governments and industry how to meet those standards.

Ever since arriving on Capitol Hill, Hooley has pressed for cutting certain taxes — especially the estate tax and taxes on married couples. The first bill she introduced was a joint effort with Republican freshman John Cooksey of Louisiana that called for reduced estate taxes on family-owned small businesses and farms. "Fiscal discipline and common sense tell us we should provide targeted tax relief that helps families and fuels the economic engine of the nation," she said in 1999. In 2000, she was among the minority of Democrats who joined with Republicans on bills to phase out the estate tax and eliminate the "marriage penalty," and later she voted to override President Clinton's vetoes of the measures.

But Hooley, a member of the Budget Committee, opposed GOP legislation in the 106th Congress to cut taxes by $792 billion, criticizing the plan as a budget-buster.

CAPITOL OFFICE
225-5711; fax 225-5699
1130 Longworth Bldg. 20515

INTERNET
e-mail: darlene@mail.house.gov
web: www.house.gov/hooley

COMMITTEES
Budget
Financial Services

HOMETOWN
West Linn

BORN
April 4, 1939, Williston, N.D.

RELIGION
Lutheran

FAMILY
Divorced; two children

EDUCATION
Pasadena Nazarene College, attended 1957-59;
Oregon State U., B.S. 1961

CAREER
Teacher

POLITICAL HIGHLIGHTS
West Linn City Council, 1977-81; Ore. House, 1981-87; Clackamas County Commission, 1987-97

ELECTION RESULTS

2000 GENERAL

Darlene Hooley (D)	156,315	56.8%
Brian Boquist (R)	118,631	43.1%

2000 PRIMARY

Darlene Hooley (D)		unopposed
write-ins (D)	623	1.1%

1998 GENERAL

Darlene Hooley (D)	124,916	54.9%
Marylin Shannon (R)	92,215	40.5%
Michael Donnelly (PACIFIC)	3,637	1.6%
Blaine Thallheimer (LIBERT)	2,979	1.3%

PREVIOUS WINNING PERCENTAGES
1996 (51%)

From her seat on the Financial Services Committee (formerly Banking), Hooley campaigns for greater consumer protections. In the 106th, she introduced legislation to require credit card companies to provide customers with the date by which a payment must be postmarked to avoid a late fee. Concerned about "identify theft," she also pursued a plan that would require banks and credit agencies to confirm address changes with customers so the customers would know if their accounts were being used illegally by someone else.

Early in the 105th, Hooley was involved in a bipartisan freshman task force that worked to develop a compromise campaign finance bill. The measure would have banned "soft money" — unlimited contributions used for party-building activities and issue ads — and required more disclosure by candidates about the source of their funds. Hooley, acknowledging that the proposal did not represent a comprehensive overhaul, told her colleagues, "I guess I am just practical enough that I want something that I can pass."

Generally a dependable Democratic vote, Hooley does break ranks occasionally. For example, in 1997 she was in the minority of Democrats to vote for a bill to overhaul the nation's public housing system. She supported the measure despite the fact that, as a member of the Banking Committee that drafted the bill, she saw the demise of a long list of Democratic amendments intended to soften the proposal's impact on the poor. Only three Banking panel Democrats voted for the bill on the House floor.

A former reading, music and physical education teacher, Hooley decided to run for a seat on the West Linn City Council in 1977 because she was unhappy with its response to her son's fall onto concrete under playground equipment. According to the Corvallis Gazette-Times, when she talked to the council members about the accident, they said, "Sorry, but that's the cheapest way to maintain the equipment." Soon afterward, she sought and won a seat on the city council.

After four years as a councilwoman, Hooley served in the Oregon House and on the Clackamas County Commission, focusing on issues ranging from recycling to welfare.

In her 1996 House race, she easily outpaced two lesser-known Democrats to claim the party's nomination and the right to take on conservative GOP freshman Rep. Jim Bunn, who had narrowly won in 1994. Hooley quickly won the support of national Democrats, and Bunn found himself assailed in a barrage of negative ads that portrayed him as too conservative for the district and sought to tie him to House Speaker Newt Gingrich. Hooley won with 51 percent of the vote, and she has been re-elected by comfortable margins since.

KEY VOTES

2000

Yes	Raise hourly minimum wage by $1 over two years
Yes	Halt funding for U.S. mission in Kosovo unless European nations pay more
Yes	Provide Medicare benefits to military retirees and their dependents
Yes	Grant China permanent normal trade status
Yes	Phase out estate, gift and trust taxes
No	Prohibit implementation of president's national monument designations
No	Approve GOP plan to provide prescription drug coverage for Medicare beneficiaries
Yes	Increase help for poor nations indebted to international financial institutions

1999

Yes	Impose steel import quotas
No	Kill proposal to take aviation trust funds off budget
No	Require background checks on buyers only at gun shows with 10 or more vendors
Yes	Remove barriers among banking, securities and insurance companies
Yes	Authorize state grants to hire teachers and reduce class size
Yes	Overhaul campaign finance law; ban "soft money" and restrict advocacy advertising
Yes	Approve bipartisan plan to increase rights of patients in managed-care health plans

INTEREST GROUPS

	AFL-CIO	ADA	CCUS	ACU
2000	80%	70%	61%	16%
1999	78%	100%	40%	4%
1998	80%	95%	59%	12%
1997	88%	90%	50%	16%

CQ VOTE STUDIES

	PARTY UNITY		PRESIDENTIAL SUPPORT	
	Support	Oppose	Support	Oppose
2000	85%	15%	67%	33%
1999	87%	13%	79%	21%
1998	88%	12%	78%	22%
1997	88%	12%	80%	20%

OREGON 5

Willamette Valley, Pacific Coast – Salem; Corvallis

Oregon City, the western terminus of the 2,000-mile Oregon Trail, in 1844 became the first incorporated city west of the Mississippi River. For settlers who made the five-month journey from Independence, Mo., the town marked the end of an arduous trek to Oregon's fertile Willamette Valley. The 5th covers the northern part of that valley, then spills over the Coast Ranges to cover two Pacific counties, Tillamook and Lincoln.

Clackamas, Marion and Polk counties are at the heart of the Willamette Valley, Oregon's most fertile farmland. The valley is the center of the state's profitable trade in greenhouse crops, seeds and berries. Hops from Marion and Clackamas counties go into some of the nation's finest beers. Polk County grows cherries and wine grapes; wineries dot Polk and Marion counties.

Once exclusively dependent on agriculture and timber, the district's economy has diversified and now supports environmental research, high-tech manufacturing and tourism. Although bound by urban growth limits, Portland's residential suburbs are expanding into Clackamas County.

In the 1990s, the 5th had four different House members, alternating between Republicans and Democrats. However, the district has settled down slightly and has elected Democratic Rep. Hooley for three terms. Corvallis, home to Oregon State University, is the district's most liberal region. Its Democratic voters are joined by the left-leaning coastal counties. Polk County votes generally Republican. But more than 70 percent of the district's residents live in two unpredictable counties, Clackamas and Marion, that have a large number of independent, swing voters.

MAJOR INDUSTRY
Agriculture, lumber, paper, food processing

CITIES
Salem, 129,650; Corvallis (pt.), 44,737 (1990); Keizer, 29,822; Oregon City; 24,417; West Linn, 22,432

UNUSUAL FEATURES
End of the Oregon Trail museum; Oregon Coast Aquarium.

PENNSYLVANIA

Gov. Tom Ridge (R)

First elected: 1994
Length of term: 4 years
Term expires: 1/03
Salary: $138,270
Phone: (717) 787-2500
Hometown: Erie
Born: Aug. 26, 1945; Munhall, Pa.
Religion: Roman Catholic
Family: Wife, Michele Moore Ridge; two children
Education: Harvard U., B.A. 1967; Dickinson School of Law, J.D. 1972
Military service: Army, 1968-70
Career: Lawyer
Political highlights: Erie assistant district attorney, 1979-82; U.S. House, 1983-95

Election results:

1998 GENERAL

Tom Ridge (R)	1,736,844	57.4%
Ivan Itkin (D)	938,745	31.0%
Peg Luksik (CONSTL)	315,761	10.4%
Ken V. Krawchuk (LIBERT)	33,591	1.1%

Lt. Gov. Mark Schweiker (R)

First elected: 1994
Length of term: 4 years
Term expires: 1/03
Salary: $116,147
Phone: (717) 787-3300

STATE LEGISLATURE

General Assembly: Meets year-round
House: 203 members, 2-year terms
2001 breakdown: 104R, 99D; 175 men, 28 women
Salary: $61,889
Phone: (717) 787-2372
Senate: 50 members, 4-year terms
2001 breakdown: 30R, 20D; 45 men, 5 women
Salary: $61,889
Phone: (717) 787-5920

STATE TERM LIMITS

Governor: 2 consecutive terms
Senate: No
House: No

URBAN STATISTICS

CITY	POPULATION
Philadelphia	1,417,601
Pittsburgh	336,882
Erie	101,474
Allentown	100,160
Reading	73,778

REGISTERED VOTERS

Democrat	48%
Republican	42%
Other	10%

POPULATION

2000 population	12,281,054
1990 population	11,881,643
Percent change	+3.4%
Rank among states	6
Median age	37.3
Born in state	80%
Foreign born	3%
Urban/rural	69%/31%
Crime rate	442/100,000
Poverty level	11.2%
Federal workers	111,517
Military	45,066

REAPPORTIONMENT

Pennsylvania lost two House seats in reapportionment, dropping from 21 districts to 19. The state legislature will draw new district lines.

MISCELLANEOUS

Web: www.state.pa.us
Capital: Harrisburg
Land area: 44,820 sq. miles
Rank among states: 32
STATE ELECTION OFFICIAL
(717) 787-5280
DEMOCRATIC HEADQUARTERS
(717) 238-9381
REPUBLICAN HEADQUARTERS
(717) 234-4901

District Statistics

DIST.	2000 D	2000 R	GREEN	1996 D	1996 R	REF	1992 D	1992 R	I	WHT	BLK	ASIAN	HISP	HOUSEHOLD INCOME	OVER 65+	UNDER 18	COLLEGE EDUCATION
1	85%	13%	1%	83%	12%	4%	73%	19%	8%	38%	52%	2%	9%	$20,372	13%	27%	10%
2	88	11	1	86	10	3	80	14	6	35	62	2	1	$24,880	15	22	22
3	66	31	2	61	28	10	52	31	17	89	5	3	4	$29,157	18	23	13
4	47	50	2	47	42	10	48	31	21	96	3	0	0	$26,792	16	24	15
5	38	58	3	40	46	13	36	42	22	98	1	1	1	$23,934	14	24	15
6	44	53	3	42	45	13	36	41	23	95	2	1	3	$28,766	17	23	13
7	50	47	2	45	44	9	39	44	18	94	4	2	1	$41,710	15	22	31
8	50	46	2	45	42	11	40	39	22	95	3	2	2	$43,483	11	26	25
9	32	65	2	36	53	11	33	48	20	98	1	0	0	$24,309	15	25	10
10	47	50	3	45	43	11	38	42	20	98	1	0	1	$25,648	17	24	14
11	49	47	3	48	38	13	42	39	20	98	1	0	1	$24,310	19	22	13
12	45	52	2	46	40	13	47	33	20	98	1	0	0	$22,024	17	24	11
13	54	43	2	50	41	8	44	40	16	91	6	2	1	$44,764	15	22	33
14	62	35	2	59	33	7	58	26	15	81	18	1	1	$24,751	17	21	23
15	49	47	3	47	41	11	42	37	22	94	2	1	5	$33,049	15	23	18

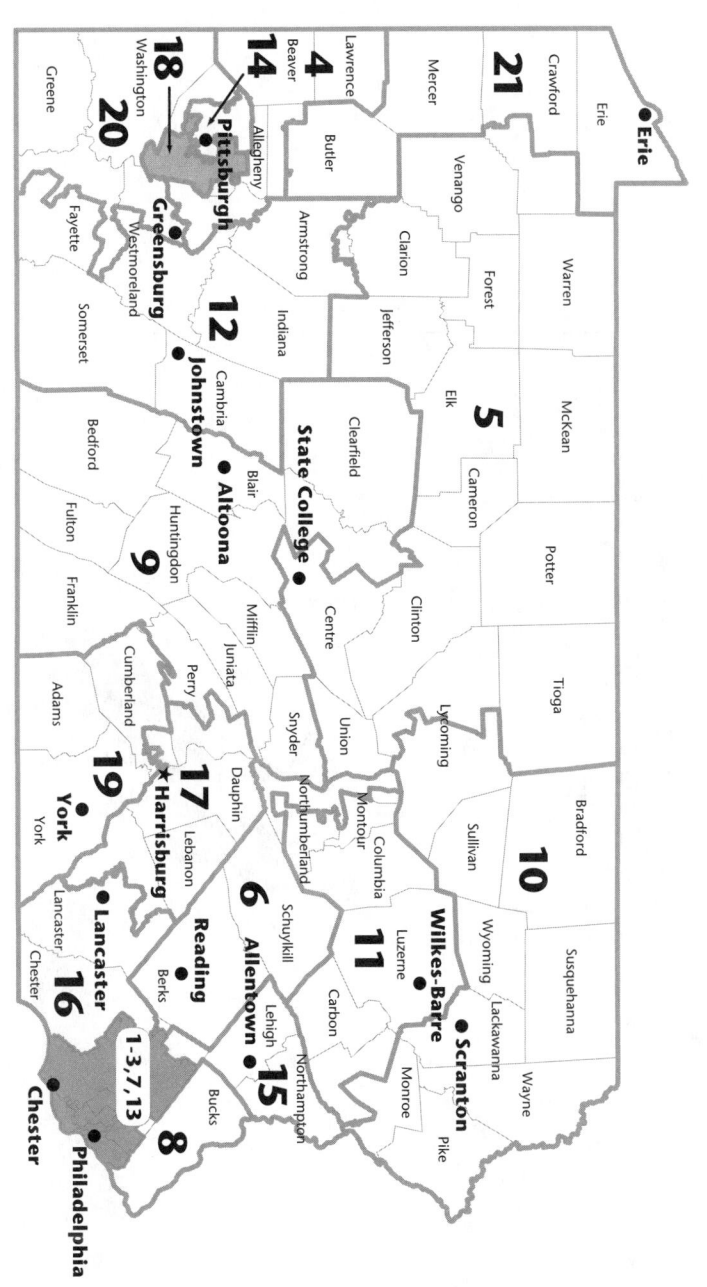

District Statistics

| DIST. | VOTE FOR PRESIDENT 2000 | | | 1996 | | | 1992 | | | WHT | BLK | ASIAN | HISP | HOUSEHOLD INCOME | OVER 65+ | UNDER 18 | COLLEGE EDUCATION |
	D	R	GREEN	D	R	REF	D	R	I								
16	39%	58%	2%	37%	53%	8%	32%	49%	19%	92%	5%	1%	4%	$37,553	12%	26%	24%
17	37	60	2	37	54	8	32	50	18	91	7	1	2	$31,841	13	24	16
18	57	41	2	52	39	9	52	31	18	91	8	1	0	$29,003	19	21	21
19	36	61	2	38	52	9	34	47	20	96	3	1	1	$32,424	13	24	16
20	51	47	2	50	39	11	51	29	20	96	3	0	0	$26,294	17	23	17
21	48	49	2	49	40	10	45	35	20	95	4	0	1	$25,845	15	25	15
STATE	51	46	2	49	40	10	45	36	18	89	9	1	2	$29,069	15	24	18

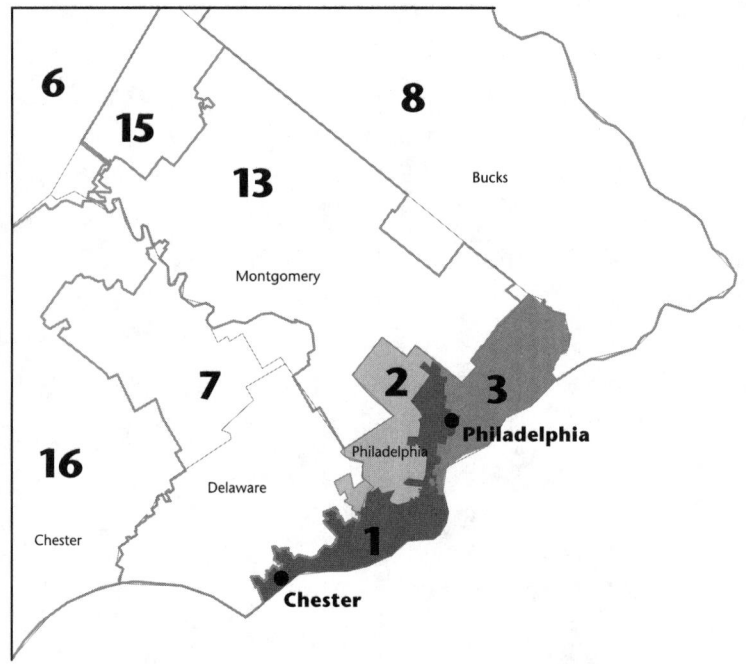

Sen. Arlen Specter (R)

Elected 1980; 4th term

CAPITOL OFFICE
224-4254; fax 228-1229; 711 Hart Bldg. 20510

INTERNET
e-mail: senator_specter@specter.senate.gov
web: specter.senate.gov

COMMITTEES
Appropriations
(Labor, Health & Human Services &
Education - chairman)
Environment & Public Works
Judiciary
Veterans' Affairs - chairman

HOMETOWN
Philadelphia

BORN
Feb. 12, 1930, Wichita, Kan.

RELIGION
Jewish

FAMILY
Wife, Joan Specter; two children

EDUCATION
U. of Pennsylvania, B.A. 1951; Yale U., LL.B. 1956

MILITARY SERVICE
Air Force, 1951-53

CAREER
Lawyer; professor

POLITICAL HIGHLIGHTS
Philadelphia district attorney, 1966-74; Republican
nominee for mayor of Philadelphia, 1967; defeated
for re-election as Philadelphia district attorney,
1973; sought Republican nomination for U.S.
Senate, 1976; sought Republican nomination for
governor, 1978

ELECTION RESULTS

1998 GENERAL

Arlen Specter (R)	1,814,180	61.3%
Bill Lloyd (D)	1,028,839	34.8%
Dean Snyder (CONSTL)	68,377	2.3%
Jack Iannantuono (LIBERT)	46,103	1.6%

1998 PRIMARY

Arlen Specter (R)	376,322	67.2%
Larry Murphy (R)	101,120	18.1%
Tom Lingenfelter (R)	82,168	14.7%

PREVIOUS WINNING PERCENTAGES
1992 (49%); 1986 (56%); 1980 (51%)

Sometimes it is hard to remember that this is the same man who grilled Anita Hill so aggressively during the 1991 confirmation hearing of Supreme Court nominee Clarence Thomas. Back then, Specter struck many women voters as coldhearted and insensitive and he had to fight to keep his Senate seat the next year. Now, Specter fights to soften anti-abortion language in the GOP platform, tries to outdo Democrats on education spending and not infrequently votes with Democrats on such matters as legislation that would allow patients to sue their managed-care plans.

This is the moderate face Specter believes the Republican Party will have to project if it wants to regain strength in the largely Democratic Northeast. When the party approved a platform for the 2000 elections that called for a constitutional amendment to ban abortion, Specter tried to get the platform committee to back off its stance and told reporters that this was not the way to win elections. In 1999, he became one of the first Republicans to endorse hate crimes legislation, joining liberal Democrats Edward M. Kennedy of Massachusetts and Ron Wyden of Oregon in sponsoring a bill to provide greater protections against such crimes. He affiliates with the bipartisan Centrist Coalition.

As chairman of the Appropriations subcommittee that funds the departments of Labor, Health and Human Services, and Education, Specter is in a position to affect the party's legislative face and makes full use of it. In 2000, he put together a bill that gave the Department of Education more money than President Clinton had requested. He also made sure the bill provided more than double the increase Clinton sought for biomedical research, one of Specter's biggest health care priorities.

He even made peace with Anita Hill — sort of. Passing through the Oklahoma City airport in late 1997, the two ran into each other as they waited for the same flight. Hill listened with a mixture of anger and amazement as Specter "spoke to me as if the bad thing that happened at his hand didn't really happen." Specter, who had accused Hill of "flat-out perjury" in connection with her sexual harassment charge against Thomas, was now asking Hill if he could stay in touch with her about women's issues. "For me, the hearings were a learning experience," Specter later told The Washington Post. "Out of those hearings came a lot of progress in respecting women."

Specter's performance in those hearings likely had little to do with disrespect for women; that is just the way he is around people. The senator has a reputation for being abrasive and difficult, especially with staffers who he believes have come to briefings less than fully prepared. He is just as likely to lecture visitors on constitutional issues — showing off his knowledge and testing theirs — as he is to throw obscure facts about international law into his speeches. (When he voted in 1999 to acquit Clinton on both articles of impeachment presented to the Senate, he noted that Scottish law gave senators three options — guilty, not guilty or not proved — and opted for the third.)

Specter can get away with a lot, however, because even senators who do not like dealing with him personally do not want to get on the wrong side of the Labor-HHS Subcommittee chairman. There is simply too much money at stake for critical education, health care and job training programs. That is also why he does not endure the kinds of challenges that other moderate Republicans face from conservatives and the GOP leadership.

Furthermore, Specter holds the line on GOP policies that he believes are most important. He included money in the 2000 education spending bill for two key Clinton proposals — school repairs and smaller class sizes — but he made it clear that the funds should come in the form of block grants that states could spend on other things. That was his way of acknowledging the importance of those initiatives without dictating education policy to the states, which he said would have violated a fundamental GOP principle: letting states and school districts decide how to educate children.

On other occasions, Specter was just as willing as any other Republican to pick fights with Clinton. He decried the last-minute negotiations between the GOP leadership and the Clinton administration that shaped the Labor-HHS spending bills in 1998 and 1999, saying the Constitution puts Congress in charge of appropriations, not the White House.

When Republicans put appropriations on a faster timetable in 2000, Specter jumped at the chance to lay out a bill that reflected GOP priorities, even if it ended in a Clinton veto. By October 2000, Specter had become a genuine obstacle, refusing to budge on the spending total of his bill as the Clinton administration insisted on more money to cover its education and health care priorities.

Eventually, Specter walked out on the talks, declaring that if GOP leaders wanted to add money in, that would be their decision, not his. He framed it as a principled stand to swing the constitutional power of appropriations back to Congress, but he also noted that he had already fought conservatives in his party to boost the bill's funding as much as he had. It was time for a moderate Republican to protect himself.

In 1993, Specter had surgery to remove a brain tumor. The problem was not diagnosed until a procedure known as magnetic resonance imaging was used — prompting Specter to become an outspoken proponent of health tests no matter what the expense. In 1997, he pressed Health and Human Services Secretary Donna E. Shalala to issue new guidelines advising that women in their 40s get mammography screening to detect breast cancer.

Another example of Specter's tendency to draw from personal experience in developing national policy was the bitter memory of his own father's anger at never receiving a bonus he was promised for his military service. The experience fueled Specter's push in the 105th, as chairman of the Veterans' Affairs Committee, for the Pentagon to do more to help ailing veterans of the Persian Gulf War.

Specter's roots in Philadelphia politics reach to the early 1960s, when he was an assistant district attorney. He made a name for himself serving on the Warren Commission, which investigated the 1963 John F. Kennedy assassination, and went on to become Philadelphia district attorney. A bright young star in Pennsylvania GOP politics, he lost his momentum by suffering a string of electoral defeats, including a race for mayor of Philadelphia.

He decided to make one more attempt when GOP Sen. Richard S. Schweiker announced he would retire in 1980. Luckily for Specter, his Democratic opponent, Pittsburgh Mayor Pete Flaherty, was also a two-time statewide loser. A slim margin in Philadelphia and large tallies in the Philadelphia suburbs overcame Flaherty's strength in the west.

Specter's next tough race came in 1992, the year after the Clarence Thomas hearings. Democratic challenger Lynn Yeakel, president of a Philadelphia-based women's fundraising organization, looked formidable, especially in light of the anger among women's groups toward Specter for his performance in the hearings. However, Yeakel squandered her momentum over the summer while Specter returned to his moderate roots and campaigned energetically. He won by 3 percentage points.

By 1998, Specter had come back; he won 61 percent of the vote over state Rep. Bill Lloyd.

KEY VOTES

2000
Yes Overhaul bankruptcy law and increase minimum wage
No Limit fiscal 2001 discretionary spending to $600.3 billion
Yes Override veto on nuclear waste disposal at Yucca Mountain site in Nevada
No Oppose effort to terminate Kosovo mission
Yes Include gender, sexual orientation and disability in federal hate crime protections
Yes Approve GOP plan to restrict use of genetic information by health insurers
Yes Kill amendment delaying implementation of an anti-missile defense system
Yes Cut taxes for married couples
No Grant China permanent normal trade status

1999
No Remove President Clinton from office for obstruction of justice
Yes Kill amendment authorizing state grants to hire teachers and reduce class size
No Require criminal background checks for purchases at gun shows
Yes Approve GOP proposal to increase rights of patients in managed-care health plans
No Block effort to allow farm and medicine exports to Cuba
No Allow study of tougher automobile fuel efficiency standards
Yes Ratify nuclear weapons testing treaty
No Prohibit national political parties from collecting "soft money" donations
Yes Remove barriers among banking, securities and insurance companies

INTEREST GROUPS

	AFL-CIO	ADA	CCUS	ACU
2000	50%	40%	53%	62%
1999	44%	40%	47%	48%
1998	83%	45%	60%	33%
1997	57%	70%	50%	32%
1996	57%	50%	77%	50%
1995	33%	55%	79%	36%
1994	38%	55%	60%	46%
1993	45%	45%	100%	57%
1992	83%	65%	60%	30%
1991	58%	40%	50%	71%

CQ VOTE STUDIES

	PARTY UNITY		PRESIDENTIAL SUPPORT	
	Support	Oppose	Support	Oppose
2000	67%	33%	59%	41%
1999	64%	36%	53%	47%
1998	49%	51%	60%	40%
1997	50%	50%	71%	29%
1996	64%	36%	59%	41%
1995	65%	35%	49%	51%
1994	56%	44%	56%	44%
1993	64%	36%	47%	53%
1992	41%	59%	45%	55%
1991	67%	33%	68%	32%

Sen. Rick Santorum (R)

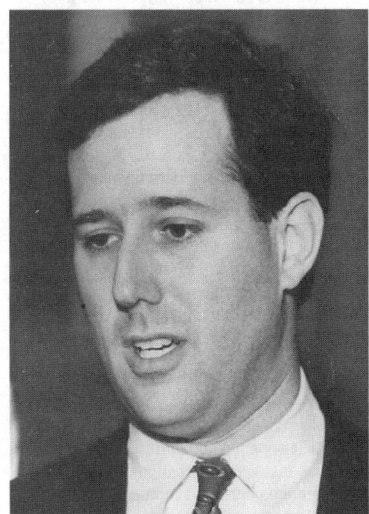

CAPITOL OFFICE
224-6324; fax 228-0604; 120 Russell Bldg. 20510

INTERNET
e-mail: senator@santorum.senate.gov
web: santorum.senate.gov

COMMITTEES
Armed Services
  (Airland Forces - chairman)
Banking, Housing & Urban Affairs
Rules & Administration
Special Aging

HOMETOWN
Pittsburgh

BORN
May 10, 1958, Winchester, Va.

RELIGION
Roman Catholic

FAMILY
Wife, Karen Garver Santorum; five children

EDUCATION
Pennsylvania State U., B.A. 1980; U. of Pittsburgh,
M.B.A. 1981; Dickinson School of Law, J.D. 1986

CAREER
Lawyer; legislative aide

POLITICAL HIGHLIGHTS
U.S. House, 1991-95

ELECTION RESULTS

2000 GENERAL

Rick Santorum (R)	2,481,962	52.4%
Ron Klink (D)	2,154,908	45.5%

2000 PRIMARY

Rick Santorum (R)	unopposed

PREVIOUS WINNING PERCENTAGES
1994 (49%); 1992 House Election (61%); 1990 House Election (51%)

Elected 1994; 2nd term

Santorum is unusually blunt-spoken for a politician, and he has an impatient manner that can sometimes come across as arrogant. But he can also be focused and engaging. He came to the Senate in 1995 with the reputation of being a brash young conservative.

"I am someone who sticks to my principles. It concerned me that that meant that I came across to some as confrontational or a rebel," he said in a 2000 interview with The Associated Press. "I've worked hard to have people see me as someone who is trying to work very hard to follow through to fulfill the promises I made."

But Santorum has learned to moderate his approach — an adjustment that helped him win a hard-fought re-election campaign in 2000 and also secure the post of GOP Conference chairman, the third-ranking leadership post, at the beginning of his second term. A fellow member of the GOP leadership team, Mitch McConnell of Kentucky, told the Philadelphia Inquirer, "He's very bright and he has a very high energy level. Those are the two things I think of when I think of Rick."

The son of an Italian immigrant, the boyish-faced Santorum stresses individual responsibility and self-reliance, not government assistance programs. He can draw on his own experience of holding down a full-time job while attending law school. Santorum also takes care to tend to his constituents' needs, pressing for programs to help farmers and supporting some labor causes such as an increase in the minimum wage.

A skillful politician, he has strengthened his hold on the state by pressing for federal funds for roads and other public works, despite his distaste for government spending. "Whether you vote with them on the 'patients' bill of rights' is probably less important to people than whether you helped them get their sewer grant," he told The Washington Post. He works hard to stay in touch with his constituents, visiting each of Pennsylvania's 67 counties every year.

A stalwart conservative on social issues, he saves his harshest rhetoric for the issue of abortion. He remains a leader in the fight to outlaw a procedure its opponents call "partial birth" abortion, which he has called "barbaric" and "the calculated killing of the nearly born." His legislation repeatedly won a majority in the Senate but fell short of enough votes to override President Clinton's vetoes. He is certain to revisit the issue in the 107th Congress, now that a like-minded Republican is in the White House.

Abortion for Santorum is a personal issue. He keeps a photograph on his desk of an underdeveloped baby, which is his own late son, Gabriel Michael. The baby was born after only five months of gestation when complications forced an early delivery, and he died two hours later. The Santorums rejected any thought of an abortion, firm in the belief that such a move would constitute murdering their son.

Santorum has been a leading Republican voice on health care issues. A member of the Republican Health Care Task Force, he favors the establishment of tax-free accounts, known as medical savings accounts (MSAs), into which people or their employers can deposit money for the uninsured portions of their health costs. "You are the payer, not the insurance company," he said. "We believe that MSAs will drive down costs." Like most conservatives, he opposed a bill in the 106th to allow patients to sue their health maintenance organizations.

On a more limited health care issue, Santorum helped win passage of a bill in 1998 to ensure Supplemental Security Income (SSI) payments for children with life-threatening illnesses. Under the new law, stricken children would not see a reduction in their SSI benefits when they received gifts from foundations.

Santorum also weighs in on Social Security. Like President Bush, he favors allowing people to invest a portion of their retirement funds in the market. In the 106th, he helped spearhead a GOP effort to protect Social Security funds from being raided to pay for other programs by severing Social Security from the rest of the budget. The nation's retirement system is a top priority to Santorum's constituents, as Pennsylvania has the second-highest concentration of senior citizens in the country.

As a member of the Agriculture Committee, Santorum in 2000 proposed direct federal payments to dairy farmers to help them in times of low prices, and he has joined with environmentalists to seek to protect farms from urban sprawl. With an eye to holding down costs for food manufacturers such as Pennsylvania-based Hershey Foods Corp., he tried to eliminate peanut and sugar price supports during debate over the 1996 farm bill. He briefly blocked committee approval of the bill, but he ultimately settled for a compromise that would pare back the supports somewhat. "You got to get what you can get," Santorum said later.

When he went from the House to the other side of the Capitol, conservatives viewed Santorum as a breath of fresh air, since he brought hard-nosed tactics and a sense of urgency to the more discursive Senate. But to many Senate veterans, Santorum simply seemed a boor. When he accused Clinton of telling "bald-faced untruths" to the American public during last-minute budget negotiations in 1995, veteran Democratic Sen. Robert C. Byrd of West Virginia mourned that such talk would lead the Senate to be seen as "just a miserable lot of bickering juveniles."

Nevertheless, the freshman put his sharp tongue to work in 1995 as GOP leaders tapped him to help as floor manager of a sweeping welfare overhaul bill. Despite his youth and relative inexperience, he went toe-to-toe with veteran Democrats, tossing off detailed explanations of welfare's woes and working with GOP moderates to ensure passage the next year. He regards welfare reform as one of his proudest accomplishments. In 2000, he told the Pittsburgh Post-Gazette: "If there's any piece of legislation that I'm going to stake my claim to, there's more of me in [that legislation] than any other member of the Senate or House, and I believe it's been the most successful piece of legislation passed not just in the last six years but in the last 30 years."

Santorum was smitten by politics as a student at Penn State University, working in GOP congressional campaigns and winning election as state chairman of the College Republicans. After working as an aide in the state legislature for several years, he mounted a long-shot effort in 1990 to unseat Democratic Rep. Doug Walgren, organizing a textbook grass-roots campaign and upsetting the incumbent by 2 percentage points.

In 1994, he took on Democratic Sen. Harris Wofford, who had won a special election in 1991. Santorum ran a fiery campaign that fed on widespread voter discontent with Washington, painting his opponent as an out-of-date liberal and assailing him for supporting gun control measures. He won with 49 percent to Wofford's 47 percent.

Democrats targeted Santorum as one of the Senate's most vulnerable incumbents in 2000. They contended he was too conservative for moderate Pennsylvania voters. But a divisive Democratic primary weakened their cause, and the eventual nominee, Rep. Ron Klink, struggled to raise money from deep-pocket Democratic donors. By moderating his image and emphasizing his work on a range of issues, including welfare reform and Social Security, Santorum won re-election by 7 percentage points.

KEY VOTES

2000
Yes Overhaul bankruptcy law and increase minimum wage
Yes Limit fiscal 2001 discretionary spending to $600.3 billion
Yes Override veto on nuclear waste disposal at Yucca Mountain site in Nevada
No Oppose effort to terminate Kosovo mission
No Include gender, sexual orientation and disability in federal hate crime protections
Yes Approve GOP plan to restrict use of genetic information by health insurers
Yes Kill amendment delaying implementation of an anti-missile defense system
Yes Cut taxes for married couples
Yes Grant China permanent normal trade status

1999
Yes Remove President Clinton from office for obstruction of justice
Yes Kill amendment authorizing state grants to hire teachers and reduce class size
No Require criminal background checks for purchases at gun shows
Yes Approve GOP proposal to increase rights of patients in managed-care health plans
Yes Block effort to allow farm and medicine exports to Cuba
No Allow study of tougher automobile fuel efficiency standards
No Ratify nuclear weapons testing treaty
No Prohibit national political parties from collecting "soft money" donations
Yes Remove barriers among banking, securities and insurance companies

INTEREST GROUPS

	AFL-CIO	ADA	CCUS	ACU
2000	0%	0%	93%	100%
1999	25%	5%	81%	88%
1998	0%	0%	89%	84%
1997	14%	15%	90%	84%
1996	43%	15%	77%	95%
1995	8%	5%	100%	83%
House Service:				
1994	22%	15%	100%	81%
1993	50%	20%	73%	70%
1992	58%	20%	88%	83%
1991	42%	15%	80%	80%

CQ VOTE STUDIES

	PARTY UNITY		PRESIDENTIAL SUPPORT	
	Support	Oppose	Support	Oppose
2000	96%	4%	49%	51%
1999	91%	9%	30%	70%
1998	91%	9%	40%	60%
1997	91%	9%	61%	39%
1996	93%	7%	40%	60%
1995	96%	4%	24%	76%
House Service:				
1994	83%	17%	56%	44%
1993	83%	17%	46%	54%
1992	83%	17%	72%	28%
1991	88%	12%	72%	28%

Rep. Robert A. Brady (D)

Elected May 1998; 2nd full term

CAPITOL OFFICE
225-4731; fax 225-0088; 216 Cannon Bldg. 20515

INTERNET
e-mail: www.house.gov/writerep
web: www.house.gov/robertbrady

COMMITTEES
Armed Services
Small Business

HOMETOWN
Philadelphia

BORN
April 7, 1945, Philadelphia, Pa.

RELIGION
Roman Catholic

FAMILY
Wife, Debra Brady; two children

EDUCATION
St. Thomas More H.S., graduated 1963

CAREER
Union lobbyist; carpenter

POLITICAL HIGHLIGHTS
34th Ward Democratic Executive Committee, 1967-present (leader, 1980-present); candidate for Philadelphia City Council, 1983; Philadelphia Democratic Party chairman, 1986-present

ELECTION RESULTS

2000 GENERAL

Robert A. Brady (D)	149,621	88.3%
Steven N. Kush (R)	19,920	11.8%

2000 PRIMARY

Robert A. Brady (D)	28,333	77.4%
Andrew J. Carn (D)	6,346	17.3%
Timothy Hannah (D)	1,943	5.3%

1998 GENERAL

Robert A. Brady (D)	77,788	81.2%
William M. Harrison (R)	15,898	16.6%
John J. Featherman (LIBERT)	1,198	1.2%

PREVIOUS WINNING PERCENTAGES
1998 Special Election (74%)

Brady gives added meaning to former Speaker Thomas P. "Tip" O'Neill's observation that "all politics is local." Now in his second full term in Congress, Brady still serves as chairman of the Philadelphia Democratic Party and as Democratic Party leader in Philadelphia's 34th Ward.

He is a throwback to a different era of politics, when voters were accustomed to legislators who catered to their immediate needs and left national issues to the party leaders.

In Washington, he pays strict attention to the everyday needs of his mostly ethnic, working-class constituents (the 1st is the country's only black-majority district represented by a white lawmaker). Of all the issues he has dealt with since his election to Congress, the only one mentioned in his official biography is his central role in ending a transit strike in Philadelphia.

When he was first elected to the House in a 1998 special election, Brady acknowledged that he hadn't paid much attention to a number of national issues, but that was OK with the folks back home. In endorsing him for re-election in 2000, The Philadelphia Inquirer noted, "It is true that Mr. Brady is more the party boss and deal-maker than the keen analyst of policy. But it takes more than wonks to make a Congress."

Brady grew up in a working-class family. He was an athlete of note (he proudly recalls teaming with Wilt Chamberlain in a neighborhood pickup game) but had to forgo scholarship offers, instead going to work as a carpenter to help support his family. After 12 years as a carpenter, he moved into a full-time post with the carpenter's union.

Brady, who says that he is a "roll-up-your-sleeves guy," may be a bit rough around the edges, but he is well-versed in the workings of a powerful political machine that is nearly the last of its kind.

He still takes to heart a lesson he learned years ago — an event that served to propel him into politics. He recalls that he decided to become involved when his mother felt the local party boss was insufficiently attentive to her request for a new bulb in a streetlight. Brady was 22 when he was elected to the 34th Ward Democratic Executive Committee, and he has been in the local party organization ever since. He held a variety of posts in city hall, the Pennsylvania Turnpike Authority and the city's redevelopment agency. Many of the positions enabled him to find jobs for people; the Inquirer reported that Brady once dubbed himself "the largest employment agency in Pennsylvania."

His congressional Web page proudly notes that while he is not particularly comfortable at center stage, "he is most at home at the negotiating table." Building on his years of union negotiating experience, Brady hosted a fence-mending session after the bitter 1999 Philadelphia Democratic mayoral primary and brokered the end to the transit strike in 1998.

His secret is not complicated: "All I did was get them talking," said Brady when a deal had been reached in the transit strike. "If good people keep talking, they'll get it done," he said, according to the Inquirer.

It doesn't hurt that, in his years of work for the Democratic Party, Brady has built personal relationships with the movers and shakers of the city and accumulated a large core of political supporters.

As a longtime labor union member, Brady can be expected to come to labor's defense in Washington. Not surprisingly, the AFL-CIO, in its ratings of lawmakers' voting records, has given Brady a lifetime mark of 100 percent.

Brady seldom speaks on the House floor, but when he does it usually has to do with a labor issue. In debate over a bill in 1999 dealing with ergonomics and workplace injuries, Brady said, "I heard that we can trust business to take care of its workers. If it did, we would not need collective bargaining ... grievance procedures." He continued, "It is the unions ... that take care of employees, not management."

Brady comes to the aid of the steel industry in its effort to limit the import of foreign government-subsidized steel, and he opposes normal trade relations with China. In 1999, he opposed a bill to allow satellite television companies to deliver local programming, citing concerns that local stations with union workers might lose viewers.

He says his top priority on Capitol Hill is to bring home the bacon for his constituents. "I would like to bring back some federal monies that I believe are due this city," Brady said. As a member of the Armed Services Committee, he strives to direct a fair share of Pentagon spending toward Philadelphia contractors and the scaled-down Navy facility that is what is left of the former Philadelphia Naval Shipyard.

He also has pushed for federal assistance to relocate residents of Philadelphia's Logan neighborhood, where more than 1,000 homes had to be demolished because the land was sinking.

Before his 1998 House race, Brady had run just once for elective office, losing his bid for a seat on the Philadelphia City Council in 1983. But Brady's grasp of city politics — as well as nominating rules that favored the candidate with the backing of the party machinery — made him a formidable candidate in the May 1998 special election after his predecessor, Democrat Thomas M. Foglietta, resigned to become ambassador to Italy. He easily got the Democratic nod for the special primary, which practically ensured his victory in the overwhelmingly Democratic district.

Several would-be contenders, including former Foglietta aide Stanley White, dropped out after learning of Brady's candidacy. Brady won the special election with 74 percent of the vote and has been re-elected with increasingly healthy tallies.

Despite his large victory margins, Brady could not vote for himself because he did not live in the 1st District but rather the neighboring 2nd. Brady said he spent his first 37 years as a resident of the 1st until its lines were redrawn in 1982. "I didn't move, the district moved," he said.

Redistricting after the 2000 census may hurt Brady; Pennsylvania will lose two seats in reapportionment, and one Philadelphia-area seat is expected to be dropped when the GOP-run legislature redraws the lines.

KEY VOTES

2000
Yes Raise hourly minimum wage by $1 over two years
No Halt funding for U.S. mission in Kosovo unless European nations pay more
Yes Provide Medicare benefits to military retirees and their dependents
No Grant China permanent normal trade status
No Phase out estate, gift and trust taxes
No Prohibit implementation of president's national monument designations
No Approve GOP plan to provide prescription drug coverage for Medicare beneficiaries
Yes Increase help for poor nations indebted to international financial institutions

1999
Yes Impose steel import quotas
No Kill proposal to take aviation trust funds off budget
No Require background checks on buyers only at gun shows with 10 or more vendors
No Remove barriers among banking, securities and insurance companies
Yes Authorize state grants to hire teachers and reduce class size
Yes Overhaul campaign finance law; ban "soft money" and restrict advocacy advertising
Yes Approve bipartisan plan to increase rights of patients in managed-care health plans

INTEREST GROUPS

	AFL-CIO	ADA	CCUS	ACU
2000	100%	90%	42%	12%
1999	100%	95%	20%	8%
1998	100%	50%	25%	0%

CQ VOTE STUDIES

	PARTY UNITY		PRESIDENTIAL SUPPORT	
	Support	Oppose	Support	Oppose
2000	95%	5%	86%	14%
1999	94%	6%	82%	18%
1998	97%	3%	88%	12%

PENNSYLVANIA 1
South and central Philadelphia; part of Chester

Home of the Philly Cheesesteak, the 1st is known for its patriotic attractions, including the Liberty Bell and Independence Hall, the birthplace of the Constitution. Its thriving Italian population supports a famous market where vendors sell produce, meat and cheese. Many Catholic churches still hold mass in Italian, and bocce ball courts can be found at Marconi Plaza park. The 1st also hosts Veterans Stadium and First Union Center, home to the city's major-league sports teams.

Once home to factory workers and a large ethnic, blue-collar workforce, factory shut-downs have left swaths of the 1st with a bleak economic landscape. The district has the lowest median income of all Pennsylvania districts, according to 1990 Census Bureau statistics. While Philadelphia overall won notice for substantial economic recovery in the 1990s and is seeing a surge of construction jobs, major sections of this area have yet to recover from a long period of industrial decay.

Chester and the nearby closed Philadelphia Naval Shipyard comprise one of the poorest, and most Democratic, areas of the district. More than three-fourths black, Chester has only a fraction of the jobs it used to and unemployment runs high. The city suffers from a school system that regularly ranks as one of the worst in the state. In early 2001, it became the first school district in Pennsylvania to privatize in an effort to improve student performance.

The black-majority 1st is solidly Democratic. A strong union presence and a large black population make this district a shoo-in for most Democratic nominees.

MAJOR INDUSTRY
Government, service, health care

CITIES
Philadelphia (pt.), 488,897 (1990); Chester (pt.), 41,729 (1990)

UNUSUAL FEATURES
Republican National Convention at the First Union Center in 2000; Comedian Bill Cosby graduated from Temple University in 1977; The Liberty Bell has "Pennsylvania" spelled as "Pensylvania"; Sylvester Stallone's "Rocky" movies filmed in south Philadelphia.

Rep. Chaka Fattah (D)

CAPITOL OFFICE
225-4001; fax 225-5392
1205 Longworth Bldg. 20515

INTERNET
e-mail: www.house.gov/writerep
web: www.house.gov/fattah

COMMITTEES
Appropriations
House Administration

HOMETOWN
Philadelphia

BORN
Nov. 21, 1956, Philadelphia, Pa.

RELIGION
Baptist

FAMILY
Wife, Renee Chenault; two children

EDUCATION
Community College of Philadelphia, attended 1976;
U. of Pennsylvania, M.A. 1986

CAREER
Public official

POLITICAL HIGHLIGHTS
Democratic candidate for Philadelphia City
Commission, 1978; Pa. House, 1983-89;
Pa. Senate, 1989-95; Consumer Party nominee for
U.S. House (special election), 1991

ELECTION RESULTS

2000 GENERAL

Chaka Fattah (D)	180,021	98.0%
Ken V. Krawchuk (LIBERT)	3,673	2.0%

2000 PRIMARY

Chaka Fattah (D)	unopposed

1998 GENERAL

Chaka Fattah (D)	102,763	86.5%
Anne Marie Mulligan (R)	16,001	13.5%

PREVIOUS WINNING PERCENTAGES
1996 (88%); 1994 (86%)

Elected 1994; 4th term

Combining an ambitious liberal agenda, a longstanding willingness to challenge the powers-that-be and the savvy he has gained during almost two decades in elective office, Fattah is a self-described "practical idealist."

Fattah (SHOCK-ah fa-TAH), whose roots in public life stretch back to his youthful days as a community activist inspired by his mother, is full of ideas about things that government can do to make the American dream come true for his inner-city constituents. He acknowledges that many of them have little chance for success — now. But "you have to put your ideas out there, so that people know where you're coming from and so, when you're in the majority, folks will have an idea of where you want to go."

And he notes, occasionally those ideas can come to fruition.

Also a pragmatist, Fattah is able to form bipartisan alliances and willing to compromise when legislative success is in sight. The best example of that may be his effort, in the 105th Congress, to expand nationwide a motivational tool used by private citizens in a number of cities to encourage low-income youths to set their sights on college. Fattah's proposal, which he dubbed "high hopes for college," is designed to let children know that, regardless of family income, college is within their reach if they achieve academically. The program provides low-income children with support such as tutoring, mentoring and counseling as early as sixth or seventh grade and gives schools incentives to offer courses that prepare the students for college.

Fattah initially wanted to provide guaranteed Pell Grants to the students but toned that down to attract Republican backing. The final version promised students some financial support, but not necessarily in grants. "I told them, 'Here's a social program you don't have to pay for unless it works,'" Fattah recalled. He joined with conservative Republican Mark Souder of Indiana and won key support from the Clinton administration. The proposal, dubbed GEAR UP, became law in 1998.

In the 107th Congress, Fattah got a seat on the Appropriations Committee and immediately became the ranking Democrat on the District of Columbia Subcommittee. He had originally sought the assignment two years earlier, hoping to restore to Pennsylvania the seat that had been held by fellow Philadelphian Thomas M. Foglietta, who resigned in 1997.

Although he had to leave the Education and the Workforce panel to take the Appropriations assignment, education is Fattah's top priority, dating back to his years in the Pennsylvania General Assembly. In the 106th, Fattah continued his effort to require states to fund all their public schools equally or to prove that students throughout the state have equal achievement levels. Fattah also introduced legislation to give colleges incentives to keep students in school through graduation.

Fattah is not averse to using non-legislative approaches to important issues. He founded and backs an annual three-day seminar at which students are encouraged to consider attending graduate school.

But he recalls advice given to him by former Democratic Rep. Louis Stokes of Ohio: Many people can give speeches and do good civic deeds, but only the 535 members of Congress can introduce bills and pass laws. And so, Fattah's emphasis is on legislation. His priorities in the 106th Congress included bills to encourage states to afford all residents access to at least a minimum standard of health care and to prohibit stores from insisting that customers have a credit card as a condition of doing business.

Fattah arrived in Congress in 1995, just as Republicans assumed control. He took the post of whip for the Congressional Black Caucus and wasted no time denouncing the new majority's ideas. During a debate early in the 104th on a GOP proposal to overhaul the welfare system, he said: "We have some tough cowboys here on the floor of the House. This is a new, interesting kind of wagon train in which the cowboys have decided to throw the women and infants and the children and the senior citizens out of the wagon train so they can get where they are going faster. It is cruel."

Born Arthur Davenport, one of six boys in an inner-city household headed by his widowed mother, Fattah's name was changed when his mother married community activist David Fattah. According to an extensive Philadelphia Inquirer personality profile that he displays in his office, Fattah's mother named him "Chaka" in honor of a Zulu warrior. Fattah's parents produced a magazine for the black community and established the House of Umoja, which became a neighborhood gathering place and haven for youths trying to work their way out of gang life.

Fattah remembers political discussions and his family's efforts to improve housing in the area. He met Democratic Rep. William H. Gray III and worked on one of his campaigns, and then, at age 22, ran for the Philadelphia City Commission, which was responsible for voter registration. He came in fourth in a field of 24. In 1982, he successfully challenged a Democratic Party-backed incumbent for a state House seat, becoming, at 25, the youngest person ever elected to the state legislature.

It was not the last time he bucked the party. After six years in the state House and two in the state Senate, Fattah entered the 1991 special-election race to succeed Gray, who had resigned to become president of the United Negro College Fund. But the Democratic Party backed longtime City Councilman Lucien E. Blackwell, and Fattah temporarily quit the party to run on the Consumer Party ticket. Blackwell won with 39 percent to Fattah's 28 percent.

Redistricting for the 1990s — in which Fattah had a hand as a member of the state Senate — reduced the 2nd District's black population from 80 percent of the total to 62 percent. That put Blackwell at risk because his appeal was strongest among West Philly's poor and working-class blacks, and in 1994, Fattah challenged Blackwell's renomination. The incumbent had the backing of Philadelphia Mayor Ed Rendell and City Council President John Street. But Fattah outworked Blackwell and claimed the primary victory with an impressive 58 percent. In the overwhelmingly Democratic 2nd, Fattah has not been seriously challenged since.

KEY VOTES

2000
Yes Raise hourly minimum wage by $1 over two years
No Halt funding for U.S. mission in Kosovo unless European nations pay more
Yes Provide Medicare benefits to military retirees and their dependents
No Grant China permanent normal trade status
No Phase out estate, gift and trust taxes
No Prohibit implementation of president's national monument designations
No Approve GOP plan to provide prescription drug coverage for Medicare beneficiaries
Yes Increase help for poor nations indebted to international financial institutions

1999
Yes Impose steel import quotas
No Kill proposal to take aviation trust funds off budget
No Require background checks on buyers only at gun shows with 10 or more vendors
No Remove barriers among banking, securities and insurance companies
Yes Authorize state grants to hire teachers and reduce class size
Yes Overhaul campaign finance law; ban "soft money" and restrict advocacy advertising
Yes Approve bipartisan plan to increase rights of patients in managed-care health plans

INTEREST GROUPS

	AFL-CIO	ADA	CCUS	ACU
2000	100%	95%	40%	0%
1999	78%	95%	24%	0%
1998	100%	95%	25%	0%
1997	100%	100%	50%	0%

CQ VOTE STUDIES

	PARTY UNITY		PRESIDENTIAL SUPPORT	
	Support	Oppose	Support	Oppose
2000	97%	3%	94%	6%
1999	97%	3%	86%	14%
1998	96%	4%	88%	12%
1997	96%	4%	86%	14%

PENNSYLVANIA 2

West Philadelphia; Chestnut Hill

From the vantage point of the William Penn statue atop City Hall, the 2nd stretches west and north over some of Philadelphia's long-established neighborhoods. The district encompasses the Center City skyscrapers, then moves west across the Schuylkill River past the University of Pennsylvania. West Philadelphia, once Irish, Greek and Jewish, is now nearly all black with pockets of middle-class and poor communities. The soaring 30th Street train station is in West Philly.

North of City Hall, the 2nd incorporates the affluent city neighborhood of Overbrook and runs against the posh Main Line communities outside the city. It also includes Fairmount Park, flanking the Schuylkill River, which houses the city's art museum, zoo and "Boathouse Row." The park runs north along diverse, middle-class neighborhoods, some of which have seen some recent gentrification, and ends in Chestnut Hill.

The 2nd's many blue-collar workers and substantial minority population make its Democratic majority overwhelming; it one of Pennsylvania's highest numbers of registered Democrats. The most competitive races are Democratic primaries, and in presidential and congressional elections, Democrats routinely receive 80 percent of the vote.

This is the district where Bill Clinton and Al Gore received their highest district tallies in the Keystone State in 1992, '96 and 2000. Gore captured an overwhelming 88 percent of the vote, to President Bush's 11 percent, in 2000.

MAJOR INDUSTRY
Education, health care, tourism

CITIES
Philadelphia (pt.), 530,814 (1990); Yeadon, 11,344; Lansdowne, 11,037

UNUSUAL FEATURES
Eastern State Penitentiary, the most expensive upon its opening in 1829, held the infamous gangster Al Capone; The Philadelphia Zoo is home to America's only giant river otters.

Rep. Robert A. Borski (D)

CAPITOL OFFICE
225-8251; fax 225-4628; 2409 Rayburn Bldg. 20515

INTERNET
e-mail:
wwwa.house.gov/borski/ima/get_address.htm
web: www.house.gov/borski

COMMITTEES
Transportation & Infrastructure

HOMETOWN
Philadelphia

BORN
Oct. 20, 1948, Philadelphia, Pa.

RELIGION
Roman Catholic

FAMILY
Wife, Karen Lloyd; five children

EDUCATION
U. of Baltimore, B.A. 1972

CAREER
Stockbroker

POLITICAL HIGHLIGHTS
Pa. House, 1977-83

ELECTION RESULTS

2000 GENERAL
Robert A. Borski (D)	130,528	68.8%
Charles F. Dougherty (R)	59,343	31.3%

2000 PRIMARY
Robert A. Borski (D)	unopposed

1998 GENERAL
Robert A. Borski (D)	66,270	59.3%
Charles F. Dougherty (R)	45,390	40.7%

PREVIOUS WINNING PERCENTAGES
1996 (69%); 1994 (63%); 1992 (59%); 1990 (60%);
1988 (63%); 1986 (62%); 1984 (64%); 1982 (50%)

Elected 1982; 10th term

Borski, not one to seek out the camera, has a style well-suited to the Transportation and Infrastructure Committee, where members typically work behind the scenes and in bipartisan fashion. Now that he is approaching the end of his second decade in the House, the seniority system has lifted him to the No. 3 Democratic seat on Transportation.

As a teenager in Northeast Philadelphia, Borski was a standout athlete for the Frankford High Pioneers, captaining the basketball and baseball teams. He is not that kind of high-profile leader in Congress, but he still gives his all for the community where he grew up, devoting most of his energies to the parochial needs and concerns of the 3rd District. He votes a mostly liberal, pro-labor line and remains a loyal ally of the Democratic leadership.

As a high-ranking member on Transportation, Borski formed a good working relationship with Pennsylvania Republican Bud Shuster, who chaired the panel until the 107th Congress. Borski backed a controversial bill by Shuster in the 105th to boost funding for highways, mass transit and other transportation-related projects across the nation. Although some criticized the plan as a budget buster, Borski praised its funding for mass transit. "People in my city of Philadelphia know all too well that, as companies abandon our cities for the suburbs, they take their jobs and opportunities with them, leaving unemployed city dwellers," he said. City dwellers without cars "must rely on transit systems to get them to work."

Borski is in a good position to lobby for Philadelphia's wide range of public works wants: money for improvements to Interstate 95 and local highways, funding for mass transit systems, dollars for dredging waterways and beefing up port and rail facilities, and support for expanding airport services. In the 107th, he took the top Democratic post on the new Highways and Transit Subcommittee, moving from his previous post as the ranking Democrat on the Water Resources and Environment Subcommittee.

In the 106th Congress, in his former subcommittee slot, he pressed for a bill, backed by port officials, that would require the government to pay for dredging deep-water port channels, rather than raising the money through a tax on vessel operators or other port users.

His subcommittee position pulled him at times well beyond his customary focus on Philadelphia into issues such as government response to natural disasters and desalination efforts in communities short of fresh water. When the panel wrestled with environmental issues, Borski's duty was to draw a bright green line, positioning Democrats as environmentally friendly and Republicans as too cozy with business and development interests.

As the subcommittee began debate in the 105th Congress on legislation to overhaul the superfund hazardous waste cleanup program, Borski warned Republicans about pushing a bill that would go easy on polluters. "I will not support any legislation that fails to ensure the protection of human health and the environment," he said. "The nearly 70 million Americans, including 10 million children, who live within four miles of a superfund site do not want hazardous waste left in their neighborhoods, threatening their water supplies and their health."

Borski waves the environmentalist banner on another issue debated in the Water Resources panel — wetlands conservation. When Republicans proposed changing the guidelines that govern development in wetlands areas, Borski said their plan "unfairly tilts the field towards further loss of wetlands." He also backs efforts to promote cleanup of "brownfields" — abandoned industrial sites where pollution discourages redevelopment.

Borski delivers a solid Democratic vote on fiscal and health care issues. He strongly backed a bipartisan plan in the 106th Congress to allow managed-care patients to sue their health care plans, and he introduced legislation designed to prevent senior citizens from being kicked off insurance policies. "These managed-care companies have cut a path of destruction that has been devastating to our seniors' health care," he said in 2000.

Borski has repeatedly voted against GOP tax-cutting proposals. He rebuked a balanced-budget plan passed by Congress in 1997, saying it delivered a "crushing blow ... to the sick, the needy and the elderly in my district." Borski says his constituency includes more than 100,000 senior citizens, and that more than half of the people admitted to hospitals in the 3rd District depend entirely on Medicare or Medicaid.

Borski's record on abortion has generally been in step with the culturally conservative ethnic Catholics who are a political force in the 3rd. But he is cold to other conservative "hot-button" proposals, such as a constitutional amendment to ban desecration of the U.S. flag.

A staunch ally of labor, Borski supports an increase in the minimum wage. He opposes trade agreements that union leaders believe could cost American jobs, and he voted against legislation in 2000 to grant China permanent normal trade status. "China will deserve [permanent trade] status when it fully opens its markets to foreign competition, abides by international human rights standards and ceases military support for terrorist nations," he said.

After graduating from the University of Baltimore, where he had an athletic scholarship, and returning home to a job at the Philadelphia Stock Exchange, Borski began his political career by winning a seat in the state House in 1976. He took a step toward Congress by managing another congressional candidate's campaign — the unsuccessful 1981 special-election effort of Philadelphia Democratic Party Chairman David Glancey in the old 3rd District.

One year later, Borski decided to launch his own campaign when redistricting grafted his state legislative base in the blue-collar "river ward" of Bridesburg onto GOP Rep. Charles F. Dougherty's territory in Philadelphia's semi-suburban Northeast. With economic discontent strong in blue-collar Philadelphia, the clean-cut Borski seemed a good vehicle for protesting hard times. He won a surprise victory with 2,664 votes. He has held the district easily since then, despite several comeback attempts by Dougherty.

KEY VOTES

2000
Yes Raise hourly minimum wage by $1 over two years
No Halt funding for U.S. mission in Kosovo unless European nations pay more
Yes Provide Medicare benefits to military retirees and their dependents
No Grant China permanent normal trade status
No Phase out estate, gift and trust taxes
No Prohibit implementation of president's national monument designations
No Approve GOP plan to provide prescription drug coverage for Medicare beneficiaries
Yes Increase help for poor nations indebted to international financial institutions

1999
Yes Impose steel import quotas
No Kill proposal to take aviation trust funds off budget
No Require background checks on buyers only at gun shows with 10 or more vendors
Yes Remove barriers among banking, securities and insurance companies
Yes Authorize state grants to hire teachers and reduce class size
Yes Overhaul campaign finance law; ban "soft money" and restrict advocacy advertising
Yes Approve bipartisan plan to increase rights of patients in managed-care health plans

INTEREST GROUPS

	AFL-CIO	ADA	CCUS	ACU
2000	100%	75%	47%	16%
1999	89%	85%	24%	12%
1998	100%	90%	22%	12%
1997	100%	75%	30%	17%

CQ VOTE STUDIES

	PARTY UNITY		PRESIDENTIAL SUPPORT	
	Support	Oppose	Support	Oppose
2000	89%	11%	84%	16%
1999	87%	13%	78%	22%
1998	91%	9%	79%	21%
1997	84%	16%	61%	39%

PENNSYLVANIA 3
Northeast Philadelphia

Of the three districts that include parts of Philadelphia, the 3rd is the only district completely within city limits. To the east of the 3rd lies the Delaware River, where three bridges join the 3rd to neighboring New Jersey. The 3rd is a mostly residential district with a suburban feel, where many local firefighters and police officers choose to live. Closer to the center of Philadelphia, the back yards become smaller and the buildings taller.

Despite having more white-collar workers than other parts of the state, the 3rd was hit by job losses during the 1990s at the industrial centers of Port Richmond and Kensington. But economic troubles are tempered by the presence of several hospitals and major transportation arteries. The popular outlet shopping center, Franklin Mills, also is located in the 3rd.

Democrats fare well in the 3rd, although the district is more socially conservative than its Philadelphia neighbors, the 1st and 2nd districts.

The presence of the Philadelphia Police Academy and the lingering influence of Holmesburg Prison, which closed in 1995, tends to reinforce conservative attitudes on law enforcement issues. The 3rd backed Ronald Reagan in the 1980s, but Democrats regained control in presidential contests in the 1990s and 2000. Al Gore won the district by 35 percentage points in 2000. Irish and Polish populations around the 3rd's southern tip are a key part of its Democratic base.

MAJOR INDUSTRY
Manufacturing, law enforcement, service

CITIES
Philadelphia (pt.), 565,866 (1990)

UNUSUAL FEATURES
Betsy Ross House, where the first American flags were made; Penn's Landing, near Philadelphia's famous South Street, where William Penn first arrived in Pennsylvania.

Rep. Melissa A. Hart (R)

Elected 2000; 1st term

Elected three times to the state Senate from a heavily Democratic area, Hart has long been regarded by GOP officials as a rising star, and when four-term Democratic Rep. Ron Klink left the 4th District open to run for the Senate, party leaders cleared the way for Hart's candidacy.

First elected to the state Senate at 28, Hart made a name for herself during her 10 years in the chamber; she chaired the Finance Committee, where she sponsored a measure to eliminate Pennsylvania's tax on computer company services, such as software design, and offered legislation to facilitate electronic commerce in the state. She mentored Phil English, who was her chief of staff and also worked for the Finance Committee before he was elected to the House from the 21st District in 1994.

A business and German major in college who went on to earn a law degree, Hart won seats on the Judiciary and Financial Services panels that appear to mesh with her background. She also has a Science Committee post.

She has expressed support for simplifying the tax code and eliminating the estate tax, the capital gains tax, and the tax code's "marriage penalty." One of her top priorities is stimulating economic development and job growth.

Hart opposes abortion rights and strongly supports gun owners' rights, positions that are in sync with the socially conservative district she represents.

In the 2000 campaign, Hart's unopposed nomination gave her an advantage over state Rep. Terry Van Horne, who won the eight-candidate Democratic primary with 24 percent of the vote.

Hart's campaign benefited from the Republican Party's relentless targeting of Van Horne. The day after he won the primary, the National Republican Congressional Committee circulated newspaper reports of a 1994 incident in which Van Horne was overheard using a racial epithet in referring to a black state legislator. Though Van Horne explained that he had apologized for the incident, the 2000 contest remained highly negative.

Dispelling doubts that a conservative Republican could carry the 4th, Hart sprinted to a 59 percent win — in a district where GOP presidential nominee George W. Bush edged Democrat Al Gore by 3 percentage points.

CAPITOL OFFICE
225-2565; fax 226-2274
1508 Longworth Bldg. 20515

INTERNET
e-mail: melissa.hart@mail.house.gov
web: www.house.gov/hart

COMMITTEES
Financial Services
Judiciary
Science

HOMETOWN
Bradford Woods

BORN
April 4, 1962, Pittsburgh, Pa.

RELIGION
Roman Catholic

FAMILY
Single

EDUCATION
Washington & Jefferson College, B.A. 1984;
U. of Pittsburgh, J.D. 1987

CAREER
Lawyer

POLITICAL HIGHLIGHTS
Pa. Senate, 1991-2001

ELECTION RESULTS

2000 GENERAL

Melissa A. Hart (R)	145,390	59.0%
Terry Van Horne (D)	100,995	41.0%

2000 PRIMARY

Melissa A. Hart (R)	unopposed

PENNSYLVANIA 4

West — Beaver County; part of Westmoreland County

The 4th starts at the western Pennsylvania border in Beaver and Lawrence counties and wraps around the northern and eastern sides of Pittsburgh. Once a top producer of iron and steel, this traditionally blue-collar district is struggling to bounce back from hard economic times.

The area's major highways and proximity to Pittsburgh make the 4th attractive to commuters and expanding companies. Although abandoned steel mills still line the rivers, other sectors are beginning to prosper, bringing some much-needed diversity to the economy. Along with the health care industry, which is a major employer, the 4th has a growing number of computer firms. Larger companies, such as U.S. Gypsum and National Gypsum, are bringing more jobs to the area. The district has yet to regain the population of its booming steel days, but some areas, including parts of Butler County, are experiencing rapid residential growth.

Although union tradition has long kept the 4th Democratic from the township level to the presidency, socially conservative Republicans who oppose gun control can break union strength. Just that happened in 2000, when President Bush captured the 4th and Republican Rep. Hart wrested control of the House seat from Democrats. Much of the district's GOP base can be found in small farming communities and the southern tier of Butler County.

MAJOR INDUSTRY
Health care, steel, manufacturing

CITIES
Plum, 26,465; New Castle, 25,841; New Kensington, 14,703; Aliquippa, 12,320

UNUSUAL FEATURES
Once inhabited by the Delaware, Shawnee and Ohio River Iroquois Indian tribes; French trading post in Revolutionary times.

Rep. John E. Peterson (R)

CAPITOL OFFICE
225-5121; fax 225-5796; 307 Cannon Bldg. 20515

INTERNET
e-mail: john.peterson@mail.house.gov
web: www.house.gov/johnpeterson

COMMITTEES
Appropriations
Resources

HOMETOWN
Pleasantville

BORN
Dec. 25, 1938, Titusville, Pa.

RELIGION
Methodist

FAMILY
Wife, Saundra Peterson; one child

EDUCATION
Titusville H.S., graduated 1956

MILITARY SERVICE
Army Reserve, 1957-63

CAREER
Supermarket owner

POLITICAL HIGHLIGHTS
Pleasantville Borough Council, 1969-77; Pa. House, 1977-85; Pa. Senate, 1985-97

ELECTION RESULTS

2000 GENERAL

John E. Peterson (R)	147,570	82.7%
Thomas A. Martin (LIBERT)	17,020	9.5%
William M. Belitskus (GREEN)	13,857	7.8%

2000 PRIMARY

John E. Peterson (R)	unopposed

1998 GENERAL

John E. Peterson (R)	99,502	84.9%
William M. Belitskus (GREEN)	17,734	15.1%

PREVIOUS WINNING PERCENTAGES
1996 (60%)

Elected 1996; 3rd term

"I come from rural Pennsylvania" is Peterson's political calling card, his starting point whenever he rises to speak on behalf of his constituents. The 5th District, comprising almost a quarter of the state of Pennsylvania and sprawling across more than 10,000 square miles of mountains, valleys, hamlets and a sizable national forest, has a decidedly rural character. It is the birthplace of America's oil industry and the home of Punxsutawney Phil, the famous groundhog. The largest urban area is a college town — State College, the site of Pennsylvania State University.

Peterson's legislative agenda, tailored to his district's needs, includes rural health care, economic development, multiple use of the Allegheny National Forest and development of the 5th's remaining fossil energy reserves.

His priorities also reflect his upbringing: Born and raised in the small town of Titusville near where Edwin Drake drilled the country's first oil well, Peterson grew up in a low-income household headed by a steelworker father who never went to high school and who was a recovering alcoholic. The four children went to work to help with family expenses; college was never an option for Peterson. (In his 30s, he attended a rural leadership training program at Penn State.)

What emerged from that childhood was a strong work ethic, an aversion to alcohol that led to his work to combat substance abuse among rural youths, and an interest in improving the educational prospects of the district's children through expanded vocational education and college financial aid.

Government has a role in those matters, Peterson argues, but on certain levels Washington bureaucrats should not be involved. In the 105th Congress, when he served on the Education and the Workforce Committee, Peterson contended that federal education mandates distract local schools from teaching students, and he was an outspoken opponent of a proposal to implement nationwide educational progress tests. "What happens when we have too many federal rules?" he asks. "Less money to the classroom, more money for bureaucrats."

And from his seat on the Resources Committee in the 105th, Peterson warned that environmental extremism tramples the rights of private property owners. "Regulations and laws and declarations have a huge impact on rural life," threatening rural people's "very ability to earn a living and to exist and live where they want to live," he says.

Still, in Peterson's worldview the feds don't always wear black hats. He often pleads for help from Washington to boost the economy of the 5th, with its struggling small towns and pockets of rural Appalachian poverty. Starting in the 106th Congress, Peterson's assignment on the Appropriations panel put him in a better position to direct federal dollars to the district. Peterson replaced the retiring Joseph M. McDade, beating out Joseph R. Pitts to become the Keystone State's only Republican on the committee in the 106th.

In 1997, when budget-cutters targeted the Economic Development Administration, Peterson sprang to its defense: "We look at EDA as the doctor who can give us a transfusion to help us maintain economic life." Peterson went on to paint a picture of "what happens in a small town in America when you lose the only factory ... and there [are] no other job opportunities within 40 miles. ... I will never forget the look on those people's faces," he said, "and I sure do not want to tell them that there is not an Economic Development Administration to help them." Peterson is similarly assertive in his advocacy of federal funding for vocational education in rural areas.

His top priority in the 106th Congress was rural health care. As a member of the bipartisan House Rural Health Care Coalition, and in alliance with the House GOP's Western Caucus (to which he belongs), he has pushed for legislation to give health care providers financial incentives to serve rural regions, including tax breaks for primary-care physicians and higher Medicare payments to rural hospitals and health maintenance organizations.

Peterson has badgered the Forest Service to make sure that the Allegheny National Forest is kept open for logging and other uses and that local communities are helped in providing fire and emergency services.

When it comes to his role in the House Republican Conference, Peterson is a two-sided coin. He can operate in the fashion of his party's pragmatic legislative dealmakers, but he also has a foot in the camp of its most committed conservative stalwarts. On a broad range of issues, Peterson is as conservative as they come in the House GOP. He opposes abortion, supports gun owners' rights, and wants to give parents taxpayer-financed vouchers to pay tuition at private schools.

A year after completing high school, Peterson joined the Army Reserves and then opened a small grocery store in nearby Pleasantville with his brother and a family friend, who put up the money. Peterson eventually bought out his partners and expanded the store, which he sold in 1984.

In 1969, at the urging of other local businessmen in Pleasantville, he entered politics, winning a seat on the borough council and serving there eight years.

In 1976, Peterson won election to the state House, and in 1984 he moved to the state Senate, where he chaired the Public Health and Welfare Committee and the Republican Policy Committee. Concerns of rural Pennsylvanians and small-business owners were his focus in Harrisburg.

When Republican Rep. William F. Clinger did not seek re-election in 1996, Peterson was well-situated to succeed him: His state Senate district covered roughly the western half of the big 5th. Peterson's winning tally in November was 60 percent, but his victory did not come easily. In the spring, he had to fight off three opponents in the Republican primary, including surgeon Daniel S. Gordeux and Bob Shuster, the son of GOP Rep. Bud Shuster, the powerful chairman of the House Transportation and Infrastructure Committee who represented the neighboring 9th District for almost three decades.

His GOP base secure, Peterson has had no re-election difficulty. In both 1998 and 2000, Democrats did not even field a challenger.

KEY VOTES

2000

No Raise hourly minimum wage by $1 over two years

Yes Halt funding for U.S. mission in Kosovo unless European nations pay more

Yes Provide Medicare benefits to military retirees and their dependents

Yes Grant China permanent normal trade status

Yes Phase out estate, gift and trust taxes

Yes Prohibit implementation of president's national monument designations

Yes Approve GOP plan to provide prescription drug coverage for Medicare beneficiaries

No Increase help for poor nations indebted to international financial institutions

1999

Yes Impose steel import quotas

No Kill proposal to take aviation trust funds off budget

No Require background checks on buyers only at gun shows with 10 or more vendors

Yes Remove barriers among banking, securities and insurance companies

? Authorize state grants to hire teachers and reduce class size

No Overhaul campaign finance law; ban "soft money" and restrict advocacy advertising

No Approve bipartisan plan to increase rights of patients in managed-care health plans

INTEREST GROUPS

	AFL-CIO	ADA	CCUS	ACU
2000	0%	0%	90%	96%
1999	25%	5%	100%	80%
1998	0%	0%	100%	96%
1997	0%	5%	100%	96%

CQ VOTE STUDIES

	PARTY UNITY		PRESIDENTIAL SUPPORT	
	Support	Oppose	Support	Oppose
2000	94%	6%	27%	73%
1999	91%	9%	19%	81%
1998	95%	5%	24%	76%
1997	96%	4%	28%	72%

PENNSYLVANIA 5
Northwest, Central – State College

The largest of all the Pennsylvania districts, the 5th encompasses 16 counties and the state's largest university, Pennsylvania State. The district's upper counties share a border with New York state, and the 5th's western counties sit less than 30 miles from the Ohio border. In sprawling land framed by the Appalachian Mountains sit struggling towns and pockets of poverty.

State College, the district's largest city, has hopped on the high-tech bandwagon, bringing in manufacturing firms that specialize in electronics and computer products. Its technology-driven development mimics the tide that brought Silicon Valley to prominence, though on a much smaller scale. The district also boasts a contingent of more than 200 meteorologists. While State College's workforce is technologically advanced, the 5th's other counties remain tied to timber production, manufacturing and oil refinement.

Much of the 5th – particularly its northern counties – votes Republican but exceptions exist. The university keeps Centre County competitive for Democrats. Neighboring Clinton County and, to the west, Elk County have a Democratic lean, while Jefferson County remains staunchly Republican. Republicans in this district tend to be both economically and socially conservative.

MAJOR INDUSTRY
Manufacturing, higher education, timber

CITIES
State College, 39,017; Oil City, 11,159; Warren, 10,175

UNUSUAL FEATURE
Town of Punxsutawney holds a yearly celebration for groundhog "Punxsutawney Phil," who becomes a national media star on Groundhog Day; Pennsylvania's smaller version of the Grand Canyon located in Tioga County.

Rep. Tim Holden (D)

CAPITOL OFFICE
225-5546; fax 226-0996; 2417 Rayburn Bldg. 20515

INTERNET
e-mail: www.house.gov/writerep
web: www.house.gov/holden

COMMITTEES
Agriculture
Transportation & Infrastructure

HOMETOWN
St. Clair

BORN
March 5, 1957, St. Clair, Pa.

RELIGION
Roman Catholic

FAMILY
Wife, Gwen Holden

EDUCATION
Bloomsburg U., B.A. 1980

CAREER
Probation officer; insurance broker; realtor

POLITICAL HIGHLIGHTS
Schuylkill County sheriff, 1985-93

ELECTION RESULTS

2000 GENERAL

Tim Holden (D)	140,084	66.3%
Thomas G. Kopel (R)	71,227	33.7%

2000 PRIMARY

Tim Holden (D)	unopposed

1998 GENERAL

Tim Holden (D)	85,374	61.0%
John Meckley (R)	54,579	39.0%

PREVIOUS WINNING PERCENTAGES
1996 (59%); 1994 (57%); 1992 (52%)

Elected 1992; 5th term

One of the more conservative Northern Democrats, Holden disagrees with many in his party on social and fiscal issues. The burly former sheriff hails from a tradition of working-class Democrats who focus on the basics — holding on to their jobs and their guns, and keeping the tax man out of their wallets. His low-key demeanor, moderate-to-conservative voting record and attention to local needs suit the home folks just fine.

Holden opposes abortion and supports gun owners' and private property rights, as well as a constitutional amendment to ban U.S. flag desecration. But he moves closer to the left side of the party on health care issues, such as expanding Medicare to include a prescription drug benefit, and he votes a pro-union line by opposing international trade deals.

Holden sits on the Transportation and Agriculture committees, and he is also active in the Congressional Mining Caucus. From those posts, he works quietly to secure funding for local highway and transit projects, to protect the interests of the local dairy industry, and to make the district's large reserves of coal more marketable by spurring researchers to develop technology to burn it more cleanly.

Holden delivers remarks on the House floor only a handful of times each year, but he will speak out when he feels Pennsylvania's interests are threatened. In 2000, he battled efforts by the Environmental Protection Agency to regulate ash and other waste from coal-burning power plants as hazardous substances, pointing out that ash is often used to reclaim Pennsylvania mines. "If this ash were to be regulated as hazardous, it would have been a fatal blow to reclamation efforts in our Pennsylvania," he said. Joining several other Pennsylvania lawmakers, he backed a plan to use federal dollars to help clean up mining residue.

In the 105th Congress, he opposed a move to cut funding for research into clean coal technology. His district sits atop the largest deposit of anthracite coal in the country, and finding ways to make better use of it would not only boost the local economy but also contribute to U.S. energy self-sufficiency, he says. The proposal to slash coal research "presents a clear choice between investing in the future or just giving up and remaining dependent on foreign oil," Holden argued.

Holden is a member of the "Blue Dogs," a coalition of conservative Democrats hailing mainly from the South and West. On welfare, the budget and other issues, they have sought a middle course — to the right of the party's liberals but more centrist than the majority of Republicans. Although Holden casts a skeptical eye on government spending programs, he voted against a GOP-backed $792 billion tax cut in the 106th because he felt the government should focus instead on paying down the national debt. As the 107th Congress began, he found fault with President Bush's tax cut proposal, arguing, according to the Reading Eagle-Times, that it "is too big if Bush hopes to keep his campaign promise of increasing military pay and defense spending."

Holden's Democratic stripes are most visible on issues important to organized labor. He typically sides with labor unions in their disputes with the pro-business GOP leadership — supporting a higher minimum wage and opposing Republican efforts to curb union organizing methods.

Trade issues for Holden are complicated by the fact that his district's interests include not only union workers, who worry about the loss of jobs to foreign countries, but also export-minded industries such as communications and steel, as well as a number of firms that must import chemicals for use in their manufacturing processes. On most trade votes, however, he sides with labor. He opposed the North American Free Trade Agreement in the 103rd, and in the 105th, voted against a bill to give the president fast-track authority to negotiate trade agreements that Congress cannot amend. In 2000, he opposed granting China permanent trade status, saying it could hurt the local economy. "If we enter into this agreement," he told the Allentown Morning Call, "we'll lose."

In the 105th, Holden left the Government Reform and Oversight Committee to take a seat on Transportation and Infrastructure, just in time to help draft a massive transportation funding bill. Pennsylvania fared well in the bill — no coincidence as the committee's chairman was Pennsylvania Republican Bud Shuster. The bill funded a variety of highway and transit projects for the 6th District, and Holden could boast of securing $75 million for work on a Reading-to-Philadelphia commuter rail project.

Holden's family has a tradition of public service. His father, Joseph "Sox" Holden, was a Schuylkill County commissioner for almost two decades. And his great-grandfather, John Siney, founded the Miner's Benevolent Association, the forerunner of the United Mine Workers union.

When Holden shows up at a fire hall barbecue or a high school football game in the district, he moves with the easy affability of someone who has spent most of his life at such events.

He was born in St. Clair, just north of Pottsville in Schuylkill County. A star linebacker, he started college in Virginia on a football scholarship, but returned home after a year to recuperate from a bout of tuberculosis and completed his college education about an hour north of his hometown.

Holden worked in the insurance and real estate businesses and then was a probation officer and sergeant-at-arms in the Pennsylvania House. At age 28, he won the first of two four-year terms as Schuylkill County sheriff.

In 1992, he won a three-way Democratic primary to succeed retiring 12-term Democratic Rep. Gus Yatron. In the general election against John E. Jones, a Republican lawyer and judge, Holden emphasized his "man of the people" roots. "I'm not an elitist. I'm not personally wealthy, and I don't just come around when I'm running for office," he said. Despite being outspent by more than $150,000, Holden squeaked by with a 4 percentage point victory, and he has won by comfortable margins since.

Holden is the catcher on the congressional Democrats' baseball team, giving a gritty performance in blocking errant pitches and hustling after foul balls in the annual charity game against the Republicans.

KEY VOTES

2000
Yes Raise hourly minimum wage by $1 over two years
No Halt funding for U.S. mission in Kosovo unless European nations pay more
Yes Provide Medicare benefits to military retirees and their dependents
No Grant China permanent normal trade status
No Phase out estate, gift and trust taxes
No Prohibit implementation of president's national monument designations
No Approve GOP plan to provide prescription drug coverage for Medicare beneficiaries
No Increase help for poor nations indebted to international financial institutions

1999
Yes Impose steel import quotas
No Kill proposal to take aviation trust funds off budget
No Require background checks on buyers only at gun shows with 10 or more vendors
Yes Remove barriers among banking, securities and insurance companies
? Authorize state grants to hire teachers and reduce class size
Yes Overhaul campaign finance law; ban "soft money" and restrict advocacy advertising
Yes Approve bipartisan plan to increase rights of patients in managed-care health plans

INTEREST GROUPS

	AFL-CIO	ADA	CCUS	ACU
2000	90%	55%	50%	32%
1999	88%	65%	58%	28%
1998	90%	70%	56%	24%
1997	86%	50%	70%	54%

CQ VOTE STUDIES

	PARTY UNITY		PRESIDENTIAL SUPPORT	
	Support	Oppose	Support	Oppose
2000	75%	25%	68%	32%
1999	68%	32%	54%	46%
1998	73%	27%	61%	39%
1997	63%	37%	50%	50%

PENNSYLVANIA 6
Southeast – Reading

The rural neighbor of northwest Philadelphia, the 6th is situated on the ridge-and-valley section of the Appalachian Mountains. The Schuylkill River meanders through the heart of the district.

As in much of Pennsylvania, Berks and Schuylkill counties have struggled to move the focus of their economies from steel, textiles and coal to other industries. Berks County, with the help of Reading's shopping outlets, is no longer recognized as a major railroad or manufacturing center. It now features a large and diverse economic base where no single employer dominates the work force.

Berks also reaps tourist revenue from its popular historical sites, including covered-bridge tours. Schuylkill County, with an ever-declining mining economy, has been less successful in its efforts to diversify.

Republicans hold a slim margin in voter registration but have nevertheless supported the conservative Democratic incumbent, who has won by large margins. While some residents vote Democratic, following the party's traditional links to labor unions and work issues, others align with the GOP for its positions on gun laws and abortion. Presidential elections were tight in this district in the 1990s, with George Bush prevailing in 1992 and Bob Dole in '96. President Bush had an easier time in 2000, carrying the district by 9 percentage points.

MAJOR INDUSTRY
Manufacturing, tourism, retail

CITIES
Reading, 73,778; Pottstown (pt.), 18,623 (1990); Pottsville, 15,438

UNUSUAL FEATURES
Birthplace of Daniel Boone in Exeter Township; Pottsville is home to America's oldest active brewery, the Yuengling brewery.

Rep. Curt Weldon (R)

CAPITOL OFFICE
225-2011; fax 225-8137; 2466 Rayburn Bldg. 20515

INTERNET
e-mail: curtpa07@mail.house.gov
web: www.house.gov/curtweldon

COMMITTEES
Armed Services
  (Military Readiness - chairman)
Science

HOMETOWN
Aston

BORN
July 22, 1947, Marcus Hook, Pa.

RELIGION
Protestant

FAMILY
Wife, Mary Gallagher Weldon; five children

EDUCATION
West Chester State College, B.A. 1969

CAREER
Teacher; consultant

POLITICAL HIGHLIGHTS
Mayor of Marcus Hook, 1977-82; Delaware County
Council, 1981-86 (chairman, 1982-86); Republican
nominee for U.S. House, 1984

ELECTION RESULTS

2000 GENERAL

Curt Weldon (R)	172,569	64.8%
Peter A. Lennon (D)	93,687	35.2%

2000 PRIMARY

Curt Weldon (R)	unopposed

1998 GENERAL

Curt Weldon (R)	119,491	71.8%
Martin J. D'Urso (D)	46,920	28.2%

PREVIOUS WINNING PERCENTAGES
1996 (67%); 1994 (70%); 1992 (66%); 1990 (65%);
1988 (68%); 1986 (61%)

Elected 1986; 8th term

When it comes to national defense, no member of Congress has fought more aggressively to establish a U.S. anti-missile program than Weldon. But while his hard-charging persona may have helped put missile defense at the top of the national security agenda, it did not appear to serve him as well in the fight to take over the helm of the Armed Services Committee in the 107th Congress.

Weldon waged a vigorous, though unsuccessful, campaign to win the Armed Services chair, spending $17,000 on a 35-page glossy booklet, for example, to show what his priorities would be for the committee. "When I do something, I go all the way," he said.

Weldon lost out to Republican Bob Stump of Arizona, the more-senior member of the committee. Though seniority played a role in the selection, some Republican lawmakers said that Weldon's aggressive, sometimes abrasive style was a factor in his loss.

For the 107th, Weldon was chosen as chairman of the Military Readiness Subcommittee, a much less prominent role than he had played as head of the Military Research and Development Subcommittee for six years. (He had to give up his top spot on the Military Research panel because of GOP-imposed term limits on chairmanships.)

National security issues are Weldon's passion, and there is not much that is moderate about his views on the topic. He frequently and fervently criticized President Clinton for not spending more on defense even as the U.S. military's commitment in overseas trouble spots expanded. "It's an impossible situation," Weldon said in the 105th. "We have a president with an internationalist foreign policy and an isolationist defense budget."

Despite his loss to Stump, Weldon is expected to continue his front-and-center role in defense debates and issues involving U.S.-Russia relations. In 1999, he saw some successes on those two fronts. Congress approved his bill declaring it a national policy to deploy an anti-missile defense system "as soon as technologically possible." The legislation was the culmination of years of work for Weldon, who had to convince not only the Clinton administration, but many skeptical Republicans, that such a system was needed, feasible and worth the billions of dollars it will cost.

It was not an easy cause to sell: Democratic liberals and some fiscal conservatives in Weldon's own party blanch at the multibillion-dollar cost and the technical problems in developing a national missile defense system. When a Pentagon official expressed cost concerns at a 1997 meeting of Weldon's Military Research Subcommittee, he bristled: "I don't care about the budgetary impact. That's not my responsibility, and it shouldn't be yours."

Weldon was able to cite new evidence that North Korea, Iran and possibly other nations had long-range missiles that could threaten American troops abroad or even U.S. territory. Early in 1999, the Clinton administration cited the same study in announcing its new assessment of the risk.

"Congressman Weldon and others like him played a key part in pushing the debate, especially at a time when missile defense was a fringe issue," Steven M. Kosiak of the Center for Strategic and Budgetary Assessments told The Washington Post in 2000. "They kept the flame going to some extent and made it almost a mainstream position."

In 1999, Weldon led a delegation of lawmakers to a series of meetings in Vienna with members of the Duma, Russia's parliament, in which the parties agreed on the basic principles of a peace settlement in Kosovo. The agreement later became the blueprint for negotiations between NATO and Yugoslavian strongman Slobodan Milosevic.

Weldon's interest in carving out these policy niches dates to his life before coming to Congress. A Russian studies major in college, he devotes much of his time to helping the Russians establish a capitalist economy and democratic institutions. Fluent in Russian, he also runs what amounts to a personal diplomatic shuttle service between Washington and Moscow, regularly traveling to Russia and hosting Russian visitors in United States. "I want to help Russia stabilize itself," he says. "I want to help them have a middle class."

In recent years, Weldon has added China to his portfolio of overseas interests. He has spoken at the National Defense University of the People's Liberation Army and lectured at other Chinese universities (including two that named him an honorary faculty member). While he believes that China, like Russia, poses a threat to U.S. security, he said in the 105th Congress that "an isolationist approach [toward China] advocated by some of my conservative colleagues is the wrong approach." In the 106th, Weldon favored granting China permanent normal trade status, despite often backing organized labor's position.

His blue-collar background makes him more sympathetic than many Republicans to the views of organized labor. Weldon has sided with labor on key votes: He opposed the 1993 North American Free Trade Agreement and fast-track authority for the president to negotiate trade agreements that Congress cannot amend, and supported bills to ban the permanent replacement of striking workers and to raise the minimum wage.

As a former volunteer firefighter, Weldon founded the Congressional Fire Services Caucus, which now has several hundred members.

The youngest of nine children, he grew up in a small, working-class town south of Philadelphia, went into teaching, joined the volunteer fire department, and became mayor of his hometown, Marcus Hook, in 1977. He rose to prominence by reviving the town, which was gripped by economic decline and gang warfare. His accomplishments caught the eye of the powerful Delaware County GOP, and in 1981 he won a seat on the Delaware County Council.

In 1984, local Republicans saw Weldon as a good fit for the district's conservative mix of blue- and white-collar workers and nominated him for a run against Democratic Rep. Bob Edgar. His near-win (he lost by only 412 votes) made him the favorite two years later when Edgar ran for the Senate and the seat came open. Weldon prevailed with 61 percent of the vote that year and has won re-election easily since then.

KEY VOTES

2000
Yes Raise hourly minimum wage by $1 over two years
Yes Halt funding for U.S. mission in Kosovo unless European nations pay more
Yes Provide Medicare benefits to military retirees and their dependents
Yes Grant China permanent normal trade status
Yes Phase out estate, gift and trust taxes
No Prohibit implementation of president's national monument designations
Yes Approve GOP plan to provide prescription drug coverage for Medicare beneficiaries
No Increase help for poor nations indebted to international financial institutions

1999
Yes Impose steel import quotas
No Kill proposal to take aviation trust funds off budget
Yes Require background checks on buyers only at gun shows with 10 or more vendors
Yes Remove barriers among banking, securities and insurance companies
No Authorize state grants to hire teachers and reduce class size
Yes Overhaul campaign finance law; ban "soft money" and restrict advocacy advertising
Yes Approve bipartisan plan to increase rights of patients in managed-care health plans

INTEREST GROUPS

	AFL-CIO	ADA	CCUS	ACU
2000	20%	5%	80%	76%
1999	44%	20%	68%	73%
1998	40%	25%	78%	60%
1997	50%	30%	89%	60%

CQ VOTE STUDIES

	PARTY UNITY		PRESIDENTIAL SUPPORT	
	Support	Oppose	Support	Oppose
2000	85%	15%	33%	67%
1999	84%	16%	29%	71%
1998	81%	19%	28%	72%
1997	83%	17%	37%	63%

PENNSYLVANIA 7
Suburban Philadelphia – Part of Delaware County

Located west of Philadelphia, the 7th takes in vast tracts of middle-class suburbia, including most of Delaware County and a small portion of Montgomery and Chester counties. The district is known as a Republican machine, and its conservative voting record makes the 7th an important stop for statewide GOP candidates. That's why local Republican officials breathed hard when Bill Clinton won Delaware County in 1992 and went on to win the whole district in 1996. After heavy campaigning around Philadelphia by both candidates in 2000, Al Gore widened Clinton's 1996 margin, beating President Bush by 3 percent. Capturing the Philadelphia suburbs was a key to Gore's statewide success. But, at the same time, the 7th's voters sent a Republican senator and representative to Congress.

The 7th attracted significant economic growth in the 1990s. Its defense industry, driven by Lockheed Martin and Boeing, is a large employer, as are the pharmaceutical and high-tech sectors. The area's new developments, many of which are springing up in the less populated areas of Chester County, are attracting Philadelphia residents.

Upper Merion Township in Montgomery County has been expanding rapidly since the opening of the Blue Route, a highway linking Interstate 95, along the Delaware River, with the Schuylkill Expressway near King of Prussia.

Closer to Philadelphia, older suburbs such as Norwood, Ridley Park and Upper Darby are mostly white and working class. Marcus Hook, an old refinery town along the Delaware River, also fits that description. Nearby Chester, and its black population, is in the 1st.

MAJOR INDUSTRY
Health care, pharmaceuticals, defense

CITIES
Drexel Hill (unincorporated), 29,744 (1990); Upper Merion (pt.), 25,613 (1990); King of Prussia (unincorporated), 18,406 (1990); Phoenixville, 15,425

UNUSUAL FEATURES
Thomas Massey House, one of the state's oldest English Quaker homes; King of Prussia Mall, largest East Coast shopping center.

Rep. James C. Greenwood (R)

Elected 1992; 5th term

CAPITOL OFFICE
225-4276; fax 225-9511; 2436 Rayburn Bldg. 20515

INTERNET
e-mail: www.house.gov/writerep
web: www.house.gov/greenwood

COMMITTEES
Education & Workforce
Energy & Commerce
  (Oversight & Investigations - chairman)

HOMETOWN
Erwinna

BORN
May 4, 1951, Philadelphia, Pa.

RELIGION
Presbyterian

FAMILY
Wife, Christina Greenwood; three children

EDUCATION
Dickinson College, B.A. 1973

CAREER
Social services agency caseworker; state
legislative aide

POLITICAL HIGHLIGHTS
Pa. House, 1981-87; Pa. Senate, 1987-93

ELECTION RESULTS

2000 GENERAL

James C. Greenwood (R)	154,090	59.2%
Ron Strouse (D)	100,617	38.7%
Philip C. Holmen (REF)	5,394	2.1%

2000 PRIMARY

James C. Greenwood (R)	25,170	67.2%
Tom Lingenfelter (R)	12,278	32.8%

1998 GENERAL

James C. Greenwood (R)	93,697	63.2%
Bill Tuthill (D)	48,320	32.6%
Scott Wolfertz (CONSTL)	3,917	2.6%

PREVIOUS WINNING PERCENTAGES
1996 (59%); 1994 (66%); 1992 (52%)

Greenwood is a social worker, not just in training and past work experience but in his current role as a bridge-building GOP moderate. His efforts to bring together disparate factions range from fostering agreement among lawmakers of all persuasions to reaching out to alienated youth.

In a Republican Party that rules the House by a slim margin, Greenwood is often called upon to serve as a liaison between the moderate wing of the GOP, to which he belongs, and the party's leaders or the larger conservative faction of the House GOP.

In the 106th Congress, Greenwood was the representative of the moderate Tuesday Group in the councils of the GOP leadership. He also was part of the GOP's Communications Working Group, which sought to shape the GOP message to emphasize how the party's agenda meshes with the day-to-day interests of the electorate. With bipartisan ties strained and the public perception of congressional Republicans diminished by the sharply partisan debate over the impeachment of President Clinton, Greenwood counseled his fellow Republicans that they must show they care for Americans in their daily lives. In the 106th, he helped organize a bipartisan group of lawmakers, The Members Forum on Public Policy, to foster discussions "where all sides of an issue can be discussed in a less politically competitive venue than the House floor or committee meetings."

In the course of his congressional career, Greenwood has been called on to participate in a number of ad hoc working groups whose goal was to reach agreement on difficult policy issues, including legislation to overhaul the welfare and Medicare systems, streamline Food and Drug Administration drug-approval regulations, and develop a GOP proposal for Medicare prescription drug coverage. He has also sought to bring moderate and conservative Republicans together on GOP policy toward environmental issues, and he participated in a bipartisan working group on youth violence.

On the latter task force, Greenwood, who authored language in a 1999 law directing the National Academy of Sciences to study violence in schools, noted that "school personnel ... need to identify the children in their schools who are bullied and ostracized and reach out to them."

Greenwood sometimes feels a bit ostracized himself in the ranks of the GOP, as the party's moderates express ongoing concern about whether their views are being given due respect. Even though he is on the leadership's message team, he is not afraid to voice personal dissent. Early in 2000, after the GOP Rules Committee refused to permit moderate Republicans to offer alternate language on a bill to outlaw a procedure its opponents call "partial birth" abortion, Greenwood objected. "I got stiffed and I don't like it. It makes me reluctant to bend over backwards the next time somebody needs me," he told Roll Call, a Capitol Hill newspaper.

Greenwood's voting record shows him to be one of the most liberal members of the GOP, particularly on social issues such as abortion rights, family planning, gun control, environmental protections and funding for the National Endowment for the Arts. He was one of 30 House Republicans who voted to support Clinton on at least two of the four articles of impeachment before the House in 1998. After the vote, he and three other moderate Republicans announced they favored Clinton's censure by the Senate, rather than conviction and removal from office. The four Republicans noted that censure was not an option when they cast their ballots on the House floor.

Although he is a moderate on social issues, Greenwood hews to a conservative line on fiscal policy. He supports a balanced-budget constitutional amendment.

Most of his legislative interests are tied to his committee assignments — Energy and Commerce and Education and the Workforce — which have given him the chance to weigh in on issues such as cleanup of superfund toxic waste sites and of polluted industrial areas, known as brownfields; managed health care; and oversight of the Food and Drug Administration. On the latter issue, Greenwood played a key role in 1997 legislation to revamp the way in which the FDA reviews new prescription drugs. In the 107th Congress, he chairs the Energy panel's Oversight and Investigations Subcommittee.

In the 106th Congress, Greenwood expanded his legislative interests to nuclear proliferation. As co-chairman of the India Caucus, Greenwood in 2000 accompanied Clinton on a trip to South Asia and said he would urge leaders of the region to "take concrete steps to stem the tide of the spread of [nuclear weapons]" and "to work cooperatively to reduce tensions in the region." Also in the 106th, Greenwood sought insurance coverage for prescription contraceptives and worked to increase funding for research into autism.

It was romance that got Greenwood into politics: His girlfriend's father was a state legislator, and Greenwood worked for him as a legislative assistant and campaign manager. After spending four years as a Bucks County social worker — where he met his wife, also a social worker — he won a seat in the state House in 1980 and moved to the state Senate in 1986.

Greenwood was an activist state legislator. He helped pass a collective bargaining law that addressed a state problem with teacher strikes. He played a large role in passing a solid waste act that mandated recycling and set up a state superfund for compensation for hazardous waste cleanups. And he pursued legislation on housing and children's issues.

In 1992, Greenwood ran successfully for the House on a platform of change against 14-year incumbent Democrat Peter H. Kostmayer, despite his own 12-year political career. Greenwood lumped Kostmayer with a Congress whose "me first" attitude was symbolized by "bounced checks [Kostmayer had 50 overdrafts at the private bank for House members], international junkets [and] deluxe perks." Greenwood won with 52 percent. Kostmayer pondered a rematch in 1994 but did not run, and Greenwood easily won re-election.

Since then, his toughest challenges have come from within the GOP, from candidates who argued that he was too liberal.

KEY VOTES

2000

Yes	Raise hourly minimum wage by $1 over two years
Yes	Halt funding for U.S. mission in Kosovo unless European nations pay more
Yes	Provide Medicare benefits to military retirees and their dependents
Yes	Grant China permanent normal trade status
Yes	Phase out estate, gift and trust taxes
?	Prohibit implementation of president's national monument designations
Yes	Approve GOP plan to provide prescription drug coverage for Medicare beneficiaries
No	Increase help for poor nations indebted to international financial institutions

1999

Yes	Impose steel import quotas
No	Kill proposal to take aviation trust funds off budget
Yes	Require background checks on buyers only at gun shows with 10 or more vendors
Yes	Remove barriers among banking, securities and insurance companies
No	Authorize state grants to hire teachers and reduce class size
Yes	Overhaul campaign finance law; ban "soft money" and restrict advocacy advertising
Yes	Approve bipartisan plan to increase rights of patients in managed-care health plans

INTEREST GROUPS

	AFL-CIO	ADA	CCUS	ACU
2000	11%	25%	77%	60%
1999	33%	70%	76%	41%
1998	20%	25%	94%	48%
1997	13%	55%	90%	50%

CQ VOTE STUDIES

	PARTY UNITY		PRESIDENTIAL SUPPORT	
	Support	Oppose	Support	Oppose
2000	73%	27%	54%	46%
1999	71%	29%	44%	56%
1998	68%	32%	38%	62%
1997	79%	21%	49%	51%

PENNSYLVANIA 8
Northern Philadelphia suburbs — Bucks County

Nestled between Philadelphia and Trenton, N.J., the 8th includes all of Bucks and a small portion of Montgomery counties. Established in 1682 by William Penn as one of the three original counties in Pennsylvania, Bucks features stately mansions such as Pennsbury Manor, Penn's home. The scenery and country charm attracted wealthy new residents in the 1990s.

Bucks County grew about 10 percent in the 1990s, on par with its suburban neighbor, Montgomery County. The area's healthy, white-collar economy claims to support more than 20,000 small businesses. The decade was not without economic problems. Blue-collar workers faced cutbacks in the steel industry, once a significant employer in Bucks County. A new deep-water port has helped, making the 8th something of a distribution and warehouse center.

Voters in the 8th tend to be fiscally conservative but support environmentalism and hold moderate stances on some social issues.

Residents of upper Bucks are heavily Republican, while central and lower Bucks tend to be more Democratic or independent. Republicans hold an edge in overall voter registration. In 1992, voters tossed out the longtime Democratic incumbent representative in favor of a moderate Republican. At the same time, the 8th narrowly endorsed Bill Clinton in 1992 and repeated the favor in 1996. In 2000, the district gave Al Gore a 4 percentage point edge.

MAJOR INDUSTRY
Health care, wholesale and retail trade, tourism

MILITARY BASES
Willow Grove Naval Air Station, 6,260 military, 615 civilian (1999)

CITIES
Bristol, 10,101; Morrisville, 9,765 (1990)

UNUSUAL FEATURES
George Washington crossing the Delaware River re-enacted in Washington Crossing each Christmas Day; Former GOP Reps. Susan Molinari and Bill Paxon were married in artsy New Hope – the New Yorkers didn't want to choose between their districts for the ceremony; Nobel Prize winning author Pearl S. Buck lived in Bucks County.

Vacant Seat

Rep. Bud Shuster, R
Resigned Feb. 2, 2001

Republican Rep. Bud Shuster resigned his seat Feb. 2, 2001, ending a House career of more than 28 years in which he played a central role in advocating increased federal funding for the nation's transportation infrastructure.

A day after he was sworn in for his 15th term in Congress, Shuster stunned residents of Pennsylvania's 9th District with his announcement that he would soon resign from the House. He cited "health scares" — his own and his wife's — and the realization that he had "reached the pinnacle of my congressional career" during six years at the helm of the Transportation and Infrastructure Committee. The GOP's self-imposed term limits on chairmanships forced Shuster to relinquish the gavel in 2001.

His resignation drew about a dozen Republican contenders for the May 15 special election to replace him. Shuster's son, Bill, a first-time candidate, was chosen by district Republican officials as the nominee at a special convention in February. Democrats picked Centre County Commissioner H. Scott Conklin as their nominee.

Shuster was a force to be reckoned with in the House. As the driver of the juggernaut 75-member Transportation Committee, he insisted on big increases in spending for the nation's highway, mass transit and aviation infrastructure and steamrolled the opposition — even when it included the leadership of his own party.

His ability to promote increased public works spending and to set aside generous projects for his district earned him the reputation as the "king of asphalt" on Capitol Hill. Back home, the results of his wheeling and dealing can be found all over the district. Most prominent is Interstate 99, the Bud Shuster Highway, a north-south route in the western part of the 9th.

The 106th Congress had its ups and downs for Shuster. The House reprimanded him in 2000 for his relationship with longtime aide Ann M. Eppard. An ethics panel found that for 18 months after she became a lobbyist, Eppard continued to play a major role in Shuster's office, including scheduling and advisory services.

But Shuster also had his high moments. He left a major mark in the 106th Congress by succeeding in greatly increasing the amount of money spent on transportation through his 2000 aviation bill. That followed an earlier triumph in the 105th Congress — a massive authorization of federal highway and transit programs.

As the May 15th special election approached, Bill Shuster, an autodealer, was a big favorite to win in the heavily Republican district. But there was a contentious behind-the-scenes battle for the GOP nomination. One candidate accused the elder Shuster of planning his retirement in the latter part of 2000 and preparing his son to enter the race, while withholding his plans from other prospective candidates.

The younger Shuster received degrees in political science and history from Dickinson College and an M.B.A. from American University. Like his father, Shuster takes a conservative stance on social issues. Both Shusters oppose gun control and abortion and support tax cuts.

The Democratic candidate, Conklin, also holds conservative views on social issues, such as gun control and abortion. In 1998, Conklin unsuccessfully ran against Republican Jake Corman for the state Senate seat vacated by J. Doyle Corman, Jake's father.

PENNSYLVANIA 9
South Central – Altoona

Situated in the south-central part of Pennsylvania, the 9th contains no booming metropolis — Altoona, the largest city, is nestled in the Allegheny Mountains and maintains a small-town feel. Most of the towns have populations under 5,000, making this one of the most rural districts in the nation.

After decades of decline brought about by waning railroad and mining industries, the area has begun to rebound. Once again residents can thank transportation-related industry for the growth. Bedford County saw its job creation rate shoot up as improvements began on the aging Pennsylvania Turnpike (which opened as the nation's first superhighway in 1940). And the city of Breezewood continues to draw in travelers with its garish display of neon signs adorning hotels and fast-food restaurants at the turnpike interchange.

Still, the bulk of the district's land is rural and dependent on agriculture. The 9th also includes some of Centre County, home of Pennsylvania State University. Although State College is in the 5th, outlying towns such as Port Matilda and Philipsburg are in the 9th.

The district has a religious population, one of the most conservative in the state. Voters oppose most gun control and other "big government" policies. The 9th's small business owners and farmers tend also to be fiscally conservative. Voters went solidly for Republican presidential candidates in 1992, '96 and 2000. The GOP controls most local offices.

MAJOR INDUSTRY
Agriculture, manufacturing, services

MILITARY BASES
Letterkenny Army Depot, 157 military, 1,136 civilian (1999)

CITIES
Altoona, 49,363; Chambersburg, 17,760; Waynesboro, 10,007

UNUSUAL FEATURES
President James Buchanan, a native of Mercersburg, vacationed in Bedford Springs.

RECENT ELECTION RESULTS

2000 GENERAL		
Bud Shuster (R)		unopposed
1998 GENERAL		
Bud Shuster (R)		unopposed
1996 GENERAL		
Bud Shuster (R)	142,105	73.7%
Monte Kemmler (D)	50,650	26.3%
1994 GENERAL		
Bud Shuster (R)		unopposed
1992 GENERAL		
Bud Shuster (R)		unopposed

Rep. Donald L. Sherwood (R)

Elected 1998; 2nd term

CAPITOL OFFICE
225-3731; fax 225-9594
1223 Longworth Bldg. 20515

INTERNET
e-mail: www.house.gov/writerep
web: www.house.gov/sherwood

COMMITTEES
Appropriations

HOMETOWN
Tunkhannock

BORN
March 5, 1941, Nicholson, Pa.

RELIGION
Methodist

FAMILY
Wife, Carol Sherwood; three children

EDUCATION
Dartmouth College, B.A. 1963

MILITARY SERVICE
Army, 1964-66

CAREER
Automobile dealer; bank executive; horse farm owner; forestry equipment company owner

POLITICAL HIGHLIGHTS
Tunkhannock Area School Board, 1975-99 (president, 1992-98)

ELECTION RESULTS

2000 GENERAL

Donald L. Sherwood (R)	124,830	52.6%
Patrick Casey (D)	112,580	47.4%

2000 PRIMARY

Donald L. Sherwood (R)	unopposed

1998 GENERAL

Donald L. Sherwood (R)	84,275	48.7%
Patrick Casey (D)	83,760	48.4%
Thomas J. McLaughlin (REF)	4,998	2.9%

Sherwood spent his first term in Congress working feverishly to prove that he could deliver the goods to his district, and his constituents rewarded him with another close victory that helped keep the House under Republican control.

The congressman has deep roots in the 10th District — he is a sixth-generation resident of northeastern Pennsylvania. Older than most members newly elected to Congress in recent years, he boasts a varied background in business, local school board service and volunteer activities — all of which helped when he first ran for the House in 1998.

Sherwood's hopes of following his predecessor, veteran Republican Joseph M. McDade, onto the Appropriations Committee in his freshman term were dashed when Speaker Newt Gingrich stepped down after the GOP's disappointing showing at the polls in 1998. Gingrich had promised him the Appropriations slot a few weeks before the election, but with Gingrich no longer on hand, Sherwood wound up on the Transportation, Resources and Armed Services committees instead.

He tried again at the start of the 107th Congress, succeeding after Republican leaders agreed to enlarge the committee's membership on both sides to placate Democrats demanding additional seats. He sits on three subcommittees whose jurisdictions include the departments of Treasury, Health and Human Services, Labor and Education and the legislative branch of government.

From the start of his House service, Sherwood focused on getting federal help for residents of his economically troubled district. After oil prices spiked in the summer of 2000, for example, he worked with other Northeastern lawmakers to get money in the Interior appropriations bill to fund a Northeastern home heating oil reserve of up to two million barrels, to be used in emergencies, including severe price increases or interruptions in supply.

Using his position on the Resources Committee in the 106th, Sherwood also got a bill through the House that designated Lackawanna Valley, the former coal-producing region, as a historic preservation area and authorized as much as $1 million to run preservation programs there.

Sherwood continued to press for a bill that McDade had championed to give the families of some airline crash victims additional legal recourse. The issue took on local importance because a group of tourists from the town of Montoursville, in Sherwood's district, were among those killed when TWA Flight 800 exploded off the coast of Long Island in July 1996. Under maritime laws, when a plane crashed over water, family members could sue only in federal court and were barred from seeking damages for anything other than lost income. The bill would have given crash victims' families the same rights regardless of whether a plane crashed over land or water.

The Pennsylvania lawmaker keeps close tabs on issues that affect military bases, as the largest employer in his district is the sprawling Tobyhanna Army Depot, where the army repairs and maintains communications and electronic equipment. In 2000, he used his position on the Armed Services Committee to help secure $6.7 million to bring a new missile maintenance facility to Tobyhanna.

Sherwood and other members of that panel were instrumental in blocking the Defense Department from initiating a new round of military base closures. Previous rounds of base closures, they argued, hadn't saved as much money as the Pentagon first projected.

As a Republican, Sherwood often faces difficult decisions because his district has a large number of elderly people and because labor unions historically have had a strong influence in the blue-collar city of Scranton. He was one of a handful of Republicans who held out until the last minute before voting in favor of a measure in 2000 that granted China permanent normal trade status. At the same time, Sherwood bucked his party leadership and supported a minimum wage increase in the 106th Congress. He also was one of 68 House Republicans to go against party leaders by voting for a bipartisan "patients' bill of rights" measure in 1999.

Sherwood served more than 20 years on the local school board, including six years as its president, and he owned several Chevrolet dealerships in northeastern Pennsylvania. He said that watching many young people move out of the area in search of economic opportunity sparked his interest in national politics.

In 1998, when McDade decided to retire after 36 years in the House, Sherwood jumped into the fray, along with seven other Republicans. He easily outdistanced the GOP field, winning almost half the votes cast.

With McDade's departure, Democrats saw an opportunity, and they tapped attorney Patrick Casey, the 32-year-old son of former Democratic Gov. Robert P. Casey, hoping the younger Casey's mix of social conservatism and economic populism would dovetail with the district.

Sherwood stressed his varied business experience and spent more than $770,000 of his own money on his campaign. He won by just 515 votes out of more than 173,000 cast.

During the 2000 rematch against Casey, the budget stalemate that dragged on through the election campaign made life difficult for Sherwood, as it did for many other Republican incumbents. With the campaign in full swing and Congress still in session, he raced back and forth between Scranton and Washington, D.C., in his Chevy pickup truck.

Casey began his campaign shortly after the 1998 contest ended. He criticized Sherwood's stances on health care and Social Security, referring to him in advertisements as "millionaire Don Sherwood." The Sierra Club also put Sherwood on its list of incumbents to unseat, airing radio ads that attacked the Republican for "putting our natural heritage at risk."

But Sherwood emphasized his experience and legislative accomplishments during his first term. His campaign got a funding boost from House Speaker J. Dennis Hastert's Retain Our Majority Program. In the close race, Sherwood prevailed by about 5 percentage points.

KEY VOTES

2000

Yes Raise hourly minimum wage by $1 over two years
Yes Halt funding for U.S. mission in Kosovo unless European nations pay more
Yes Provide Medicare benefits to military retirees and their dependents
Yes Grant China permanent normal trade status
Yes Phase out estate, gift and trust taxes
Yes Prohibit implementation of president's national monument designations
Yes Approve GOP plan to provide prescription drug coverage for Medicare beneficiaries
No Increase help for poor nations indebted to international financial institutions

1999

Yes Impose steel import quotas
No Kill proposal to take aviation trust funds off budget
No Require background checks on buyers only at gun shows with 10 or more vendors
Yes Remove barriers among banking, securities and insurance companies
No Authorize state grants to hire teachers and reduce class size
No Overhaul campaign finance law; ban "soft money" and restrict advocacy advertising
Yes Approve bipartisan plan to increase rights of patients in managed-care health plans

INTEREST GROUPS

	AFL-CIO	ADA	CCUS	ACU
2000	20%	10%	85%	75%
1999	33%	10%	88%	80%

CQ VOTE STUDIES

	PARTY UNITY		PRESIDENTIAL SUPPORT	
	Support	Oppose	Support	Oppose
2000	86%	14%	38%	62%
1999	88%	12%	20%	80%

PENNSYLVANIA 10

Northeast – Scranton

Situated in the upper northeast corner of Pennsylvania, the 10th is home to the Pocono Mountains, a popular honeymoon retreat known for its skiing, fishing and golfing. Nestled in these mountains is Scranton, one of the state's larger cities but a diminishing economic influence with the long decline of coal, steel and railroads.

New industries, including technology, have moved into the 10th, but the labor force hasn't always kept pace, forcing officials to develop retraining programs. Tourism remains strong, especially during the summer months.

The district's major city, Scranton, is similar to other hardscrabble eastern Pennsylvania industrial towns like Allentown, 75 miles to the south. Traditional Democratic constituencies – blue-collar, union and ethnic workers – are aging yet still a factor. The area's economic development needs and elderly population help drive its penchant for federal dollars. Health care is an important campaign issue.

But unlike Allentown's 15th District, the 10th has large swaths of rural, socially conservative heartland. When these rural voters are combined with Democrats who oppose abortion and gun control, then added to the district's modest population of newcomers – who tend to be white-collar, pro-business types – it adds up to Republican electoral success.

Scranton was a presidential battleground in the high-stakes 2000 contest to win Pennsylvania. The 10th had backed George Bush in the 1992 contest, then switched to narrowly support Bill Clinton in 1996. After a campaign that featured multiple visits by the candidates and a barrage of television advertising, President Bush won a 3 point victory.

MAJOR INDUSTRY
Manufacturing, health care, tourism

MILITARY BASES
Tobyhanna Army Depot, 347 military, 3,969 civilian (1999)

CITIES
Scranton, 73,766; Williamsport, 29,922; Dunmore, 13,983

UNUSUAL FEATURES
Little League World Series in Williamsport; Former Rep. Joseph M. McDade, R, obtained $80 million for Steamtown, a railroad museum.

Rep. Paul E. Kanjorski (D)

CAPITOL OFFICE
225-6511; fax 225-0764; 2353 Rayburn Bldg. 20515

INTERNET
e-mail: paul.kanjorski@mail.house.gov
web: www.house.gov/kanjorski

COMMITTEES
Financial Services
Government Reform

HOMETOWN
Nanticoke

BORN
April 2, 1937, Nanticoke, Pa.

RELIGION
Roman Catholic

FAMILY
Wife, Nancy Kanjorski; one child

EDUCATION
Temple U., attended 1957-62; Dickinson School of Law, attended 1962-65

MILITARY SERVICE
Army, 1960-61

CAREER
Lawyer

POLITICAL HIGHLIGHTS
Sought Democratic nomination for U.S. House (special election), 1980; sought Democratic nomination for U.S. House, 1980

ELECTION RESULTS

2000 GENERAL

Paul E. Kanjorski (D)	131,948	66.4%
Stephen A. Urban (R)	66,699	33.6%

2000 PRIMARY

Paul E. Kanjorski (D)	unopposed

1998 GENERAL

Paul E. Kanjorski (D)	88,933	66.8%
Stephen A. Urban (R)	44,123	33.2%

PREVIOUS WINNING PERCENTAGES
1996 (68%); 1994 (67%); 1992 (67%); 1990 (100%); 1988 (100%); 1986 (71%); 1984 (59%)

Elected 1984; 9th term

A Polish Catholic, Kanjorski reflects the views and concerns of the white, ethnic, working-class people who still dominate politics in his part of Pennsylvania. A social conservative who opposes abortion, Kanjorski is also a fierce defender of his district's interests.

Some of his top priorities include securing federal funding to help clean up Pennsylvania's mines and winning Department of Energy compensation for local weapons workers exposed to contamination during the Cold War. He battles against the drive to lower international trade barriers, worrying about how it will affect local blue-collar employment.

He also focuses on poverty issues. "I am worried about having a two-tiered or three-tiered society," he told The Associated Press in 1999. "We put a lot of things in jeopardy if we ever get into difficult times. You run the risk of having destabilization." To help combat poverty, he sponsored legislation in the 106th Congress to encourage private investment companies to invest in economically distressed areas.

Despite his moderate bent, Kanjorski can get down in the partisan trenches. In the 105th, he sharply criticized GOP investigations of Democratic campaign fundraising practices, and he was one of only five Democrats who voted against any impeachment inquiry of President Clinton.

But he has also warned his own leaders about taking partisan warfare too far. In 2000, he publicly criticized top Democrats for deciding to file a racketeering lawsuit against GOP Whip Tom DeLay of Texas. "This is almost the criminalization of politics," Kanjorski said in Roll Call. "Right now it's just the leadership boys that are doing this. But their sandbox is going to fall over into the sandbox of all members one of these days." Indeed, Kanjorski, who first came to Congress as a Capitol page in 1954, says he laments modern-day lapses in the congressional tradition of comity among members.

In one of the most closely watched votes of 2000, Kanjorski reluctantly voted against Clinton's bid to grant China permanent normal trade status. He announced his opposition just hours before the floor vote, after failing to win legislation to help workers bypassed by the high-technology revolution. He said he could not assure his constituents that "sufficient protections are in place to preserve their economic security. We must promote economic growth that will benefit both current workers and future generations in northeastern and central Pennsylvania."

Kanjorski joins with many in his party in criticizing Republican efforts to cut taxes. In the 106th, he voted to uphold Clinton's vetoes of bills to eliminate the estate tax and "marriage penalty," contending that such plans could interfere with efforts to pay down the national debt. "Retiring the debt and dealing with the financial challenges confronting Social Security and Medicare are critical to protecting our children and grandchildren from facing a crushing tax burden in future years," he said.

He also prodded the federal government to compensate thousands of American workers (including some who worked at a plant in northeastern Pennsylvania), who were sickened by exposure to the metal beryllium and other hazardous substances in the rush to produce nuclear weapons during the Cold War. The House voted in 2000 to include the compensation package in a defense authorization bill. "This compensation is long overdue," Kanjorski said. "These Americans helped us win the Cold War and were put at risk without their knowledge."

On the Financial Services Committee (formerly Banking), Kanjorski is the ranking member of the Capital Markets, Insurance, and Government-Sponsored Enterprises Subcommittee, which in the 107th Congress was given additional jurisdiction over securities issues that formerly were handled by the Commerce Committee. On Financial Services, Kanjorski has worked with no great strife on bills to benefit credit unions and to promote home ownership. In the 105th, he was actively involved in the passage of a bill to give credit unions broad leeway to seek new members.

But on the Government Reform Committee, Kanjorski has tangled repeatedly with GOP Chairman Dan Burton of Indiana. During an investigation in the 105th into alleged Democratic campaign fundraising abuses, Kanjorski helped mobilize committee Democrats to deny Burton the two-thirds vote he needed to grant immunity to witnesses he wanted to question. "I have now come to the conclusion that the entire committee should be conducting its investigation in a chamber with padded walls," Kanjorski said. "We're starting to embarrass the American people."

Kanjorski is always looking for ways to breathe new life into his district's struggling economy. He had a role in helping transform a former brewery in Wilkes-Barre into office space for several federal agencies, and he successfully lobbied Clinton to include the Upper Susquehanna River when he unveiled his American Heritage Rivers initiative. Kanjorski said the designation would spur communities along the river to cooperate in cleaning it up and would promote tourism and economic development.

Kanjorski was born and grew up in Nanticoke, near Wilkes-Barre. After waging a pair of unsuccessful House campaigns in 1980 (one in a special election), he owed his 1984 House victory to an intestinal parasite and a sunny beach. The outcome of his primary challenge to Democratic Rep. Frank Harrison might have been different if not for the discovery that water supplies in parts of the 11th District were contaminated with the giardia parasite. As people boiled their water to make it drinkable, Harrison flew off on a congressional excursion to Central America.

Kanjorski pounced on Harrison with a largely self-financed blitz of clever ads portraying the incumbent as an aloof globe-trotter. One ad showed a picture of a sunny Costa Rican beach and noted Harrison's visit there, then switched to a shot of a tea kettle on a stove and concluded, "It's enough to make you boil." Harrison tried to ignore Kanjorski and stressed his experience in Washington, but Kanjorski leaped from long shot to victor.

In November, Kanjorski handily defeated Republican Robert P. Hudock with 59 percent of the vote. With his conservative view of social issues, Kanjorski remains attractive to district voters and continues to win easily.

KEY VOTES

2000
Yes Raise hourly minimum wage by $1 over two years
No Halt funding for U.S. mission in Kosovo unless European nations pay more
Yes Provide Medicare benefits to military retirees and their dependents
No Grant China permanent normal trade status
No Phase out estate, gift and trust taxes
No Prohibit implementation of president's national monument designations
No Approve GOP plan to provide prescription drug coverage for Medicare beneficiaries
Yes Increase help for poor nations indebted to international financial institutions

1999
Yes Impose steel import quotas
No Kill proposal to take aviation trust funds off budget
No Require background checks on buyers only at gun shows with 10 or more vendors
Yes Remove barriers among banking, securities and insurance companies
Yes Authorize state grants to hire teachers and reduce class size
Yes Overhaul campaign finance law; ban "soft money" and restrict advocacy advertising
Yes Approve bipartisan plan to increase rights of patients in managed-care health plans

INTEREST GROUPS

	AFL-CIO	ADA	CCUS	ACU
2000	100%	65%	42%	16%
1999	89%	75%	24%	16%
1998	100%	85%	22%	12%
1997	100%	90%	40%	12%

CQ VOTE STUDIES

	PARTY UNITY		PRESIDENTIAL SUPPORT	
	Support	Oppose	Support	Oppose
2000	82%	18%	80%	20%
1999	83%	17%	72%	28%
1998	86%	14%	82%	18%
1997	78%	22%	68%	32%

PENNSYLVANIA 11
Northeast – Wilkes-Barre

Since the turn of the century, the health of the 11th District has been inextricably linked to the production, manufacture and sale of coal. Demand for the district's anthracite coal peaked in the 1910s and '20s. Since then, a few cities in this district have disappeared with the long decline of the coal industry and the rise of oil and natural gas. Centralia, site of a still-burning underground mine, turned into a ghost town after a federally ordered evacuation.

Other towns, such as Jim Thorpe and Wilkes-Barre, have been more prosperous. Jim Thorpe, given that moniker in 1954 for the decathlon Olympic gold medalist who is buried in town, was a haven for millionaires and has maintained its historic charm as a preservation project of the Department of the Interior. To the north, Wilkes-Barre attracted attention during the 2000 presidential contest, as both candidates sought to pick up votes toward winning the state from the competitive northeast Pennsylvania area.

This district historically has had a knack for picking winning presidential candidates and supporting them at percentages uncannily close to the nation as a whole. In 2000, district voters came close to the correct percentage, but chose the wrong winner. Al Gore carried the district with 49 percent, to President Bush's 47 percent.

At other levels, the district has loyal ties to the Democrat Party, the result of a large Irish population and a strong union tradition. The departure of coal and the influx of technology have led to an increase in registered Republicans but not enough to challenge the Democratic status quo. Although the 11th has plenty of Reagan Democrats who could swing to support a Republican, it has elected a Democrat to its congressional seat since 1982.

MAJOR INDUSTRY
Manufacturing, retail trade, tourism

CITIES
Wilkes-Barre, 42,358; Hazleton, 22,981; Kingston, 13,216

UNUSUAL FEATURES
Berwick prides itself on its high school football team, a perennial power in Pennsylvania that has produced several NFL players.

Rep. John P. Murtha (D)

CAPITOL OFFICE
225-2065; fax 225-5709; 2423 Rayburn Bldg. 20515

INTERNET
e-mail: murtha@mail.house.gov
web: www.house.gov/murtha

COMMITTEES
Appropriations

HOMETOWN
Johnstown

BORN
June 17, 1932, New Martinsville, W.Va.

RELIGION
Roman Catholic

FAMILY
Wife, Joyce Murtha; three children

EDUCATION
U. of Pittsburgh, B.A. 1962

MILITARY SERVICE
Marine Corps, 1952-55, 1966-67; Marine Corps Reserve, 1967-90

CAREER
Car wash owner and operator

POLITICAL HIGHLIGHTS
Democratic nominee for U.S. House, 1968; Pa. House, 1969-74

ELECTION RESULTS

2000 GENERAL

John P. Murtha (D)	145,538	70.8%
Bill Choby (R)	56,575	27.5%
James N. O'Neil (REF)	3,324	1.6%

2000 PRIMARY

John P. Murtha (D)	unopposed

1998 GENERAL

John P. Murtha (D)	100,528	68.5%
Timothy E. Holloway (R)	46,239	31.5%

PREVIOUS WINNING PERCENTAGES
1996 (70%); 1994 (69%); 1992 (100%); 1990 (62%);
1988 (100%); 1986 (67%); 1984 (69%); 1982 (61%);
1980 (59%); 1978 (69%); 1976 (68%); 1974 (58%);
1974 Special Election (50%)

Elected February 1974; 14th full term

Few lawmakers match — and none surpasses — Murtha's prowess for drafting appropriations legislation and putting behind it a broad, bipartisan coalition of House members, many of whom have a concrete stake in the bill's enactment.

Murtha and the other senior members of the Appropriations Committee see themselves as indispensible to keeping the wheels of federal spending turning through compromise and judicious application of legislative lubricant — modest additions to presidential budgets for specific projects of great importance to individual members.

To the GOP "revolutionaries" who took control of the Capitol in 1995, Murtha and his ilk are a political fifth column, who have too often used public largess to lure even some Republicans into not only preserving the federal colossus, but expanding it. Statesmen or saboteurs, the appropriators have prevailed. In the closely divided 107th Congress, many erstwhile leaders of the revolution are gone or marginalized. Unless the House divides sharply along party lines, appropriators should have a field day, and none more so than Murtha, who has been either chairman or the ranking minority member of the Defense Appropriations Subcommittee since 1989.

Murtha's effectiveness hinges on finding out what his colleagues want, touching base with all interested parties to determine what he realistically can get and delivering on his commitments. This requires personal attention, which Murtha invests prodigally. During roll call votes, members who need a sympathetic hearing for some hometown priority usually can find him sitting in a corner of the House chamber, holding court among a coterie of Democrats from other Rust Belt districts.

Besides shoring up support for defense bills with this type of retail politics, Murtha has amassed considerable goodwill among his colleagues on a wholesale basis by his consistent efforts to increase congressional pay, a task with no constituency (and many critics) off Capitol Hill.

Beyond his mastery of the legislative process, Murtha brings special assets into the arena when the subject is defense. For one thing, the former Marine can plausibly claim to speak for several dozen Democratic defense hawks, most from Southern or border states, who may be predisposed to support the type of larger Pentagon budgets that many Republicans advocate. These Democrats could hold the balance of power if enough of the remaining Republican budget watchdogs balk at increased defense spending.

On a more personal level, Murtha speaks on military affairs with the moral authority of a decorated veteran of Vietnam ground combat, one of the few to serve in the House. While some congressional veterans use their military experience to rhetorically bludgeon their opponents, Murtha rarely mentions his in public, but his colleagues are well aware of it. That background is the root of his strong focus on military personnel issues. He was an early leader in the successful drive by military brass in 1998-99 to liberalize military pensions. By the same token, he opposed some of the peacekeeping deployments ordered by President Clinton because he felt U.S. forces were being spread too thin, and thus were overworked.

Murtha's views on defense also have credibility because he works the military establishment the way he works the House: face to face, so he can look his interlocutor in the eye. Impatient with the Viewgraph extravaganzas beloved by Pentagon briefers, Murtha frequently and without fanfare travels to deployments in far-off regions to assess the situation.

Like the other Appropriations heavyweights, Murtha does not merely grease the legislative wheels for his bills; he tries to use appropriations legislation to shape policy, with mixed results. In 2000, for instance, it was easy for Murtha and Defense Subcommittee Chairman Jerry Lewis, R-Calif., to boost the Army's plan to develop a new type of lightweight, easily deployable combat vehicle: They put into their bill twice as much money as the Pentagon had requested for the project.

Despite their clout, the two were less successful a year earlier when they tried to use the defense spending bill for leverage on a much broader issue. With Murtha's backing, Lewis tried to eliminate production funds for the Air Force's new F-22 fighter, arguing both that the program had some serious problems and that the Pentagon was planning to spend more money than it could afford on three different combat jets in the coming years. But the F-22 had too many supporters for it to be held as a policy hostage, so while House appropriators won some concessions on the management of the program, they failed to stop the plane's production.

In his voting record, Murtha is something of a political throwback: a latter-day version of the lunch-pail liberals who made up a large bloc of the House Democratic membership from the New Deal until the late 1960s, when the party splintered over Vietnam. The coal and steel industries that once were the 12th District's economic lifeblood were decimated by the recessions of the 1980s, but the area's economy is rebounding as high-tech industries move in — many in response to the economic development programs Murtha has squirreled into appropriations laws over the years.

The 12th remains a working-class Democratic stronghold, and Murtha is a reliable ally of organized labor, regularly pressing to raise the minimum wage and protect workers against adverse impacts of trade agreements. Once a car-wash operator, he supports small-business priorities, such as a larger health insurance tax deduction for the self-employed. Reflecting his district's conservatism, Murtha supports gun owners' rights; like some other leading, liberal Democrats who are Catholic, he opposes abortion.

When longtime GOP Rep. John P. Saylor died in 1973, Murtha, then a state legislator, won narrowly over Harry M. Fox, a former Saylor aide, in a special election that focused on the Republicans' Watergate problems. His toughest re-election challenge since was in 1990, when he was almost blindsided in the Democratic primary by lawyer Kenneth B. Burkley, who made the contest a referendum on Murtha's use of congressional power to benefit himself. Murtha won by 8 percentage points.

KEY VOTES

2000
Yes   Raise hourly minimum wage by $1 over two years
No   Halt funding for U.S. mission in Kosovo unless European nations pay more
?   Provide Medicare benefits to military retirees and their dependents
No   Grant China permanent normal trade status
No   Phase out estate, gift and trust taxes
No   Prohibit implementation of president's national monument designations
No   Approve GOP plan to provide prescription drug coverage for Medicare beneficiaries
Yes   Increase help for poor nations indebted to international financial institutions

1999
Yes   Impose steel import quotas
Yes   Kill proposal to take aviation trust funds off budget
No   Require background checks on buyers only at gun shows with 10 or more vendors
Yes   Remove barriers among banking, securities and insurance companies
Yes   Authorize state grants to hire teachers and reduce class size
No   Overhaul campaign finance law; ban "soft money" and restrict advocacy advertising
Yes   Approve bipartisan plan to increase rights of patients in managed-care health plans

INTEREST GROUPS

	AFL-CIO	ADA	CCUS	ACU
2000	100%	55%	45%	24%
1999	89%	60%	43%	24%
1998	100%	75%	47%	21%
1997	100%	50%	56%	32%

CQ VOTE STUDIES

	PARTY UNITY		PRESIDENTIAL SUPPORT	
	Support	Oppose	Support	Oppose
2000	70%	30%	74%	26%
1999	67%	33%	58%	42%
1998	73%	27%	73%	27%
1997	62%	38%	65%	35%

PENNSYLVANIA 12
Southwest – Johnstown

Some 100 miles east of Pittsburgh, the 12th includes most of the six counties between Mt. Davis and the Allegheny River. This once-booming center of coal, steel and iron production is diversifying its economy to escape economic distress and industrial loss.

The 12th has been the unfortunate victim of floods that devastated Johnstown, the district's largest city, three times in modern history. The Great Flood of 1889, the most severe, destroyed the town and killed 2,200 people. Again in 1936 and 1977, floods took additional lives and caused significant damage. The 1980s recession had a similar devastating effect on the economy. Coal and steel industries fell and the unemployment rate skyrocketed to more than 27 percent.

More recently, the district has bounced back, in part by attracting some high-tech industry, including a Sony plant in Westmoreland. Capitalizing on past hardships, the Johnstown Flood Museum also draws tourists to the area. The city's large health care base has

remained stable, and the home health care industry is growing.

This working-class district has been a Democratic stronghold from the township to the presidency since the dawn of the New Deal. Like other Pennsylvania towns with an industrial past and aging population, Johnstown wants federal economic help but many voters are more socially conservative than the national Democratic Party.

After supporting Bill Clinton in 1992 and '96, the district strayed from its Democratic roots in the 2000 presidential contest when it gave President Bush a 7 percentage point win over Al Gore. Johnstown's Cambria County was the only central Pennsylvania county to back Gore, albeit narrowly, but it wasn't enough to overcome the district's rural voters, who strongly oppose gun control.

MAJOR INDUSTRY
Manufacturing, service, health care

CITIES
Johnstown, 24,998; Indiana, 14,674

UNUSUAL FEATURES
National Drug Intelligence Center in Johnstown tracks illegal drugs across the nation; Architect Frank Lloyd Wright's Fallingwater house.

Rep. Joseph M. Hoeffel (D)

Elected 1998; 2nd term

CAPITOL OFFICE
225-6111; fax 226-0611
1229 Longworth Bldg. 20515

INTERNET
e-mail: www.house.gov/writerep
web: www.house.gov/hoeffel

COMMITTEES
Budget
International Relations
Science

HOMETOWN
Abington

BORN
Sept. 3, 1950, Philadelphia, Pa.

RELIGION
Protestant

FAMILY
Wife, Francesca Hoeffel; two children

EDUCATION
Boston U., B.S. 1972; Temple U., J.D. 1986

MILITARY SERVICE
Army Reserve, 1970-76

CAREER
Lawyer

POLITICAL HIGHLIGHTS
Democratic nominee for Pa. House, 1974; Pa. House, 1977-85; Democratic nominee for U.S. House, 1984, 1986; Montgomery County Commission, 1992-98; Democratic nominee for U.S. House, 1996

ELECTION RESULTS

2000 GENERAL

Joseph M. Hoeffel (D)	146,026	52.8%
Stewart Greenleaf (R)	126,501	45.7%
Ken Cavanaugh (LIBERT)	4,224	1.5%

2000 PRIMARY

Joseph M. Hoeffel (D)	unopposed

1998 GENERAL

Joseph M. Hoeffel (D)	95,105	51.6%
Jon D. Fox (R)	85,915	46.6%
Thomas P. Burke (LIBERT)	3,470	1.9%

Cautious, calculating and smart, Hoeffel has a personality that is well-suited to his educated, affluent suburban district, which in the past eight years has changed its mind three times about its House member.

Calling himself "a moderate Democrat in a moderate Republican district," Hoeffel (HUFF-el) takes care that his record in Congress hugs the center. He is moderate on social issues and more conservative fiscally. He affiliates with the New Democrat Coalition, although he breaks with them on some issues — trade with China, for example.

In the House, Hoeffel has made it a point to be diligent about constituent concerns and to go after government funds for projects such as the Schuylkill River Heritage Area, intended to preserve the region's heritage as a leading coal producer. "When you are new here you don't get a lot of attention," Hoeffel says, and that seems to be fine with him.

A member of the Budget Committee, Hoeffel tends to be conservative about spending, but early in the 107th Congress, he also cautioned against GOP plans for a $1.6 trillion tax cut. "There is such a thing as too many tax cuts. It's just as fiscally irresponsible as too much spending," he said.

Hoeffel told the Allentown Morning Call that he favors an annual tax rebate that would be based on the state of the economy and the federal budget surplus. He also argues against tax breaks and subsidies for big business that he calls "corporate welfare" and major new government spending initiatives.

A member of the International Relations Committee, Hoeffel is a strong supporter of Israel, where he traveled during his first term. He also went to Russia early in 2001. He says that, while relations had been strained by U.S. plans for a missile defense system, Russia is a "strategic partner and potentially strong ally." Hoeffel told the Allentown Morning Call that Western nations should support restructuring and forgiveness of Russian debt. But, he cautioned, "there's plenty in Russia we don't like. We always have to maintain our military strength and keep our eyes wide open," he told the newspaper.

Hoeffel is also interested in tackling the national dilemma over education policy. He says he is part of a group of lawmakers seeking a "third way" on education, promoting a plan that would provide more money for teachers and technology in schools in return for higher standards. Hoeffel says he holds "socially progressive" positions, including support for abortion rights and gun control measures. Hoeffel's wife is a registered nurse, and he advocates regulating health maintenance organizations to allow doctors more leeway and patients more choices.

If Hoeffel seems reserved in Washington, he is quite the opposite in his Montgomery County district. In 2000, Hoeffel visited 40 of the district's communities on a walking tour that coincided with the Republican National Convention in Philadelphia. He holds numerous press conferences at home to explain his votes in the House.

His outreach techniques include "Saturdays with Joe," a series of town meetings and supermarket visits he conducts twice a month. In 2001, he launched "Joe's Job Days," in which he will work at a different job in his district one day each month — a program he patterned after that of Florida Democratic Sen. Bob Graham.

Hoeffel is straightforward in explaining his high level of activity. "Left to their own devices, people will vote Republican," he said. "So at home I have to be a very visible, very aggressive advocate for what I believe in."

While maintaining a moderate voting record, Hoeffel has been careful to find ways to tend to key Democratic constituencies, such as environmental and labor groups, which have rewarded him with fundraising dollars and campaign support. For example, he wants to strengthen the Endangered Species Act, and he sided with labor in 2000 by voting against granting China permanent normal trade status.

Hoeffel says that his interest in running for public office began with a college course on diplomatic history and the fact that he attended college during the Vietnam War. He made his first run for public office soon after, losing in a bid for the Pennsylvania House in 1974.

Two years later, he ran again and won, serving in the state House for eight years. In 1984 and 1986, he ran unsuccessfully for Congress, mounting respectable challenges to Republican Rep. Lawrence Coughlin.

After finishing his law degree and taking a five-year hiatus from politics, Hoeffel won a race for Montgomery County commissioner in 1991, serving there until 1998. In between, he mounted his third run for Congress, suffering an 84-vote near miss against Republican Rep. Jon D. Fox in 1996.

In 1998, Hoeffel came armed with an ample campaign treasury, and he won by 5 percentage points in a rematch with Fox, who had limped out of a divisive four-way GOP primary with less than a majority of votes. Hoeffel convinced 13th District voters that he was the moderate, independent voice they wanted in Congress. His victory was also impressive, in that two Republican statewide candidates — Gov. Tom Ridge and Sen. Arlen Specter — both carried the 13th District overwhelmingly.

Hoeffel's ability to stick to a moderate course was frustrating to Stewart Greenleaf, his challenger in the 2000 election. Republicans had turned to Greenleaf, a veteran state senator who supports abortion rights, as their best shot at returning the district to its GOP roots. (Republicans had controlled the district for 76 years until 1992, when Democrat Marjorie Margolies Mezvinksy was elected, only to lose to Republican Fox two years later.)

In the 2000 campaign, Greenleaf tried to lay claim to the moderate label, attacking Hoeffel as "liberal" for such actions as voting against overriding President Clinton's veto of GOP-backed legislation to repeal the tax code's "marriage penalty." But the attacks did not stick.

At the same time, Hoeffel benefited from Democratic presidential candidate Al Gore's coattails, in particular his mobilization of traditional Democratic voters. While Gore took 54 percent to George W. Bush's 43 percent, Hoeffel beat Greenleaf 53 percent to 46 percent.

KEY VOTES

2000
Yes Raise hourly minimum wage by $1 over two years
No Halt funding for U.S. mission in Kosovo unless European nations pay more
Yes Provide Medicare benefits to military retirees and their dependents
No Grant China permanent normal trade status
No Phase out estate, gift and trust taxes
No Prohibit implementation of president's national monument designations
No Approve GOP plan to provide prescription drug coverage for Medicare beneficiaries
Yes Increase help for poor nations indebted to international financial institutions

1999
Yes Impose steel import quotas
Yes Kill proposal to take aviation trust funds off budget
No Require background checks on buyers only at gun shows with 10 or more vendors
Yes Remove barriers among banking, securities and insurance companies
Yes Authorize state grants to hire teachers and reduce class size
Yes Overhaul campaign finance law; ban "soft money" and restrict advocacy advertising
Yes Approve bipartisan plan to increase rights of patients in managed-care health plans

INTEREST GROUPS

	AFL-CIO	ADA	CCUS	ACU
2000	100%	90%	42%	8%
1999	78%	100%	20%	4%

CQ VOTE STUDIES

	PARTY UNITY		PRESIDENTIAL SUPPORT	
	Support	Oppose	Support	Oppose
2000	91%	9%	87%	13%
1999	91%	9%	85%	15%

PENNSYLVANIA 13
Northwest Philadelphia suburbs — the Main Line

Taking in most of Montgomery County, 20 miles west of Philadelphia, the 13th is the wealthiest district in the state. This area is known as the Main Line, after the Pennsylvania Railroad's Main Line, the railway along which doctors, lawyers and old-money families built their estates. But suburban growth has been changing this once-Republican stronghold.

The 13th was somewhat of a battleground at the federal level in the 1990s. Republican Sen. Arlen Specter remains a district favorite, but Democrats captured the House seat in 1992, '98 and 2000. Al Gore spent a lot of time campaigning here in 2000. Analysts say he was seeking to depict President Bush as a hard-line conservative in front of suburban voters. In the end, Gore was rewarded with an 11 point victory in the district. His success in Philadelphia and many of its suburbs helped offset losses in rural, anti-gun control counties and was key to his statewide win. Bill Clinton also won the 13th in 1992

and '96, but by smaller margins than Gore.

The 13th is growing both residentially and commercially. Many workers still commute to Philadelphia, but new office parks support an expanding employment base. Housing units have sprouted along Route 422, occupied by employees of pharmaceutical firms that relocated to Upper Providence Township. Overall, the county grew 11 percent in the 1990s — on par with its suburban neighbor, Bucks County — forcing Montgomery County to address typical suburban sprawl issues. Areas closer to the city like Plymouth Meeting and Abington are more Democratic than the outlying older boroughs.

MAJOR INDUSTRY
Health and business services, chemicals

CITIES
Norristown, 29,276; Lansdale, 15,768; Lower Moreland (pt.), 9,051 (1990)

UNUSUAL FEATURES
Valley Forge Historic National Park, where George Washington and the Continental Army survived a harsh winter in 1777-78; Lancaster Pike, first turnpike in the state.

Rep. William J. Coyne (D)

CAPITOL OFFICE
225-2301; fax 225-1844; 2455 Rayburn Bldg. 20515

INTERNET
web: www.house.gov/coyne

COMMITTEES
Ways & Means

HOMETOWN
Pittsburgh

BORN
Aug. 24, 1936, Pittsburgh, Pa.

RELIGION
Roman Catholic

FAMILY
Single

EDUCATION
Robert Morris College, B.S. 1965

MILITARY SERVICE
Army, 1955-57

CAREER
Accountant

POLITICAL HIGHLIGHTS
Pa. House, 1971-73; sought Democratic nomination for Pa. Senate, 1972; Pittsburgh City Council, 1974-81; Pittsburgh Democratic Party chairman, 1978-84

ELECTION RESULTS

2000 GENERAL

William J. Coyne (D)		unopposed

2000 PRIMARY

William J. Coyne (D)		unopposed

1998 GENERAL

William J. Coyne (D)	83,355	60.5%
Bill Ravotti (R)	52,745	38.3%
Dorothy L. Kolis (SW)	1,625	1.2%

PREVIOUS WINNING PERCENTAGES
1996 (61%); 1994 (64%); 1992 (72%); 1990 (72%); 1988 (79%); 1986 (90%); 1984 (77%); 1982 (75%); 1980 (69%)

Elected 1980; 11th term

A corporate accountant before he entered politics, Coyne is one of the quieter members of the House, where he is a low-key and unobtrusive ally of the Democratic leadership. Coyne reliably votes with the House's most liberal members but never joins in their rhetorical tirades against conservative policies. While he occasionally will make his disapproval known in a brief floor speech, he normally submits a prepared text to be printed in the Congressional Record.

Now in his third decade in Congress, Coyne has risen into his party's upper ranks on the powerful Ways and Means Committee — he is the panel's No. 4 Democrat.

Few House Democrats are as predictable as Coyne in their opposition to proposals put forward by the GOP majority. He stands the liberal ground, opposing such conservative mainstays as a constitutional amendment that would prohibit desecration of the U.S. flag and a ban on a procedure its opponents call "partial birth" abortion. Siding with labor unions, he is cool to expanding trade agreements.

Coyne is a reliable opponent of GOP tax-cutting proposals. In 2000, he warned his colleagues that repealing the estate tax "reduces the progressivity of the tax code. ... This bill would cause the gap between low-income people and the wealthy to grow even faster."

But Coyne has embraced some proposals put forward by Republican colleagues on Ways and Means. He joined Philip M. Crane, R-Ill., in proposing tax relief for more people who donate to charity. Amid widespread calls for tax simplification, he teamed up with fellow Ways and Means Democrat Richard E. Neal of Massachusetts in the 106th Congress to propose a package of reforms that would cut tax returns by about 200 lines.

Although many Ways and Means Committee members support free trade, Coyne's views are shaped by his pro-labor and pro-steel attitudes. In 2000, he voted against legislation granting China permanent normal trade status, contending that Congress instead should continue to revisit China's trade status each year. "Ending the United States' right to review the terms of trade with China yearly will only slow the pace of reform and remove a powerful deterrent to the most flagrant, visible abuses of human rights in China," he said.

Similarly, he voted in the 105th against a bill to give the president fast-track authority to negotiate trade agreements that Congress cannot amend. He warned that the resulting pacts "would destroy U.S. jobs and drive down American workers' wages." In 1998, he joined the chorus of voices from the Congressional Steel Caucus decrying the "dumping" of below-cost foreign steel in the United States, particularly by Asian nations that Coyne argued were trying to "export their way out of financial calamity."

Coyne's background in accounting helped him perform valuable service to his party on a prominent issue in the 105th: restructuring the Internal Revenue Service. Conservative Republicans expressed sympathy for taxpayers who told harrowing tales of harassment at the hands of overzealous IRS agents. While acknowledging the need for changes, Coyne argued that broad-brush vilification of the IRS was not warranted. He said some of the public's animosity should be directed at Congress for creating a complex and confusing tax code.

Coyne was one of four members of Congress on the 17-member IRS Restructuring Commission. Ways and Means took the commission's advice into consideration when drafting the IRS legislation that became law in 1998. Coyne praised the bill for the most part, but he did note that it included some tax law changes that would cost the federal government substantial revenue starting in 2008 — "just when the baby boom generation will place additional burdens on Social Security and Medicare," he warned.

Coyne looks out for the business and financial interests of Pittsburgh. In the 103rd, he won a permanent tax exemption for industrial development bonds, which state and local governments use to attract new manufacturing businesses.

On social issues, Coyne is usually in the liberal camp. He voted against a GOP-drafted measure in the 106th that would have allowed patients to sue their health plans for damages in state courts. In the 104th, he was one of only 67 members who opposed a bill to prohibit federal recognition of same-sex marriages and to allow states to refuse to recognize such marriages even if they were sanctioned by other states. He also opposed a GOP welfare overhaul plan even after Republicans revised it enough to get President Clinton's promise to sign it. Concerned about eroding federal benefits to the poor, he pressed for legislation in the 106th that would require greater efforts to reach out to low-income people who may be eligible for food stamps. Hunger is "actually getting worse," he contended.

But Coyne is not always in lock step with the party's most stalwart liberals, as he demonstrated in 1997 by voting for balanced-budget legislation that congressional Republicans hashed out with the Clinton administration. He said a bad GOP tax bill had been rendered worthy of support because his party had successfully pushed for education tax breaks and other concessions from the GOP. "Democrats are responsible for shifting the benefits of this bill from the wealthy to middle-class American families," he said.

In his long political career, Coyne has never strayed far from his inner-city Pittsburgh roots. After high school, he was in the Army for two years, serving in Korea. He earned a degree from Pittsburgh's Robert Morris College in 1965 and five years later won election to the state House. He lost a state Senate bid in 1972 but in 1973 was elected to the Pittsburgh City Council. While on the council, he also served as chairman of the Pittsburgh Democratic Party.

When the 14th District seat came open in 1980 with the retirement of longtime Democratic Rep. William S. Moorhead, Coyne had the connections to claim it. The city Democratic organization helped him easily defeat Moorhead's son in the primary. Coyne cruised past the GOP nominee that fall and has never been in jeopardy since.

KEY VOTES

2000

Yes Raise hourly minimum wage by $1 over two years
No Halt funding for U.S. mission in Kosovo unless European nations pay more
Yes Provide Medicare benefits to military retirees and their dependents
No Grant China permanent normal trade status
No Phase out estate, gift and trust taxes
No Prohibit implementation of president's national monument designations
No Approve GOP plan to provide prescription drug coverage for Medicare beneficiaries
Yes Increase help for poor nations indebted to international financial institutions

1999

Yes Impose steel import quotas
No Kill proposal to take aviation trust funds off budget
No Require background checks on buyers only at gun shows with 10 or more vendors
No Remove barriers among banking, securities and insurance companies
Yes Authorize state grants to hire teachers and reduce class size
Yes Overhaul campaign finance law; ban "soft money" and restrict advocacy advertising
Yes Approve bipartisan plan to increase rights of patients in managed-care health plans

INTEREST GROUPS

	AFL-CIO	ADA	CCUS	ACU
2000	100%	90%	30%	8%
1999	89%	95%	24%	0%
1998	100%	80%	22%	4%
1997	100%	100%	20%	0%

CQ VOTE STUDIES

	PARTY UNITY		PRESIDENTIAL SUPPORT	
	Support	Oppose	Support	Oppose
2000	98%	2%	85%	15%
1999	97%	3%	83%	17%
1998	95%	5%	83%	17%
1997	97%	3%	83%	17%

PENNSYLVANIA 14

Pittsburgh and suburbs

The 14th, which includes Pittsburgh and its suburbs from Edgewood to McCandless, has undergone an economic transformation while maintaining its Democratic tradition and ethnic character.

Medical centers and universities, parks, skyscrapers and high-tech industry have replaced the smoke stacks from the steel industry once nestled between the Allegheny, Monongahela and Ohio rivers. A thriving, corporate downtown has grown up in the "Golden Triangle," where the Allegheny and Monongahela rivers meet. Major League Baseball's Pittsburgh Pirates played their first game in a new stadium in April 2001, and the National Football League's Pittsburgh Steelers also are slated to get a new stadium in 2001. While this economic renaissance has opened white-collar and service-oriented jobs, there are fewer high-wage manufacturing jobs available for the working class.

Even with the diversification of the 14th's economy, the district has remained true to its Democratic roots. Union strength translates into lopsided Democratic margins, and Democrats far outnumber Republicans. Republicans can be found in a thorough search of the 14th, particularly in the northern and western suburbs. Republican candidates have begun to make inroads at the local level.

The city's unique international quality also remains intact, with distinct neighborhoods dotting its landscape. Among the numerous enclaves are Bloomfield, home to many Italians; Lawrenceville, with Germans and Poles; and Squirrel Hill, which has a sizable Jewish population.

MAJOR INDUSTRY
Banking, government, health care

CITIES
Pittsburgh, 336,882; Franklin Park, 11,034; Bellevue, 9,126

UNUSUAL FEATURES
Andy Warhol born in Pittsburgh: "In the future, everybody will be world-famous for 15 minutes."

Rep. Patrick J. Toomey (R)

Elected 1998; 2nd term

CAPITOL OFFICE
225-6411; fax 226-0778; 224 Cannon Bldg. 20515

INTERNET
e-mail: rep.toomey.pa15@mail.house.gov
web: www.house.gov/toomey

COMMITTEES
Budget
Financial Services
Small Business
    (Tax, Finance & Exports - chairman)

HOMETOWN
Allentown

BORN
Nov. 17, 1961, Providence, R.I.

RELIGION
Roman Catholic

FAMILY
Wife, Kris Toomey; one child

EDUCATION
Harvard U., B.A. 1984

CAREER
Restaurateur; investment banker

POLITICAL HIGHLIGHTS
Allentown Government Study Commission,
1994-96

ELECTION RESULTS

2000 GENERAL

Patrick J. Toomey (R)	118,307	53.3%
Ed O'Brien (D)	103,864	46.8%

2000 PRIMARY

Patrick J. Toomey (R)	unopposed

1998 GENERAL

Patrick J. Toomey (R)	81,755	55.0%
Roy C. Afflerbach (D)	66,930	45.0%

At a time when Republican congressional leaders have pushed their budget priorities to the political center by favoring more spending on education, health and science, Toomey remains one of his party's "true believers" — an unabashed fiscal conservative who argues the GOP should do more to shrink government and maintain fiscal discipline.

The former restaurateur and international investment banker raised his profile during his first term from his seat on the Budget Committee. In 2000, Toomey included language in the annual congressional budget resolution to block passage of a supplemental appropriations bill that year unless its spending was matched with offsetting cuts. The move angered senior members of the Appropriations Committee and for a time threatened funding for peacekeeping operations in Kosovo, drug-fighting efforts in Colombia and disaster aid for hurricane victims.

Toomey backed down and agreed to drop his proposal after GOP leaders promised to support his future efforts to set aside specific portions of the newfound budget surplus to pay down the national debt. To mollify a half-dozen or so like-minded conservatives who were convinced the surplus was weakening their party's commitment to cut spending, Republican leaders included Toomey's proposal in a military construction spending bill that reserved $4 billion of the surplus to pay off the national debt.

"Some of us are very concerned that [Republicans] have neglected to make the principled argument about excessive spending," Toomey said at the time. "I think the government spends too much money."

These and other actions put Toomey at the fulcrum of a widening intra-party rift between conservative hard-liners and Republican pragmatists, who are more likely to strike deals with Democrats on government programs. Enough defections from mavericks like Toomey, combined with a united Democratic front, could defeat Republican leadership initiatives on issues such as tax reductions in the closely divided 107th Congress. But Toomey is just as likely to be ignored on votes carried by large bipartisan majorities. Such was the case at the end of the 106th Congress, when his complaints about increases in education spending and other initiatives contained in a final budget package went unheeded.

Despite his sometimes provocative stands, Toomey has earned colleagues' respect on certain financial issues, using his background in investment banking to illuminate debates before the Financial Services Committee (formerly Banking). During consideration in 2000 of legislation to rewrite the nation's commodities laws, Toomey offered a lengthy amendment that attempted to define what a futures contract is.

This seemingly semantic exercise, in Toomey's view, could have helped Congress draw up clear ground rules for the trading of a complicated class of investments known as derivatives, which account for a multitrillion-dollar worldwide market but whose legal status was uncertain under existing laws. The panel's chairman, Republican Jim Leach of Iowa, praised Toomey's effort as constructive but persuaded him to withdraw the amendment, saying it would make the committee's bill diverge from versions approved by the Commerce and Agriculture committees.

Toomey's scholarly brand of fiscal conservatism plays well in his politically competitive Lehigh Valley district. However, his stands on trade and entitlement programs such as Social Security have put him at odds with some constituencies in a district that tends to lean Democratic. His vote in 2000 to grant China permanent normal trade status drew fierce criticism from unions in an area where some blame imports for the closure of a large Bethlehem Steel Corp. plant. And Toomey's support of a Republican measure to privatize parts of Social Security and establish personal savings accounts that operate similarly to mutual funds rankled some voters, who feared the proposal would work against them and imperil the national pension system.

Toomey says his careers in the restaurant business and investment banking taught him firsthand how government agencies can pose a "real headache" for small-business owners. He favors legislation that would make it easier for small and medium-size firms to buy insurance for their employees. He also has called for abolishing the Internal Revenue Service and instituting a flat-tax system. On social policy issues, he is viewed as a moderate — supporting, for example, abortion rights.

Toomey spent seven years in the high-pressure world of international finance, trading futures contracts, swaps and other sophisticated, often volatile financial instruments. In 1990, he invested in a chain of sports-themed restaurants in Allentown and Lancaster called Rookies. Despite majoring in political philosophy in college, Toomey had little political experience other than a summer internship in the office of Republican Sen. John H. Chafee of Rhode Island.

But Toomey said the results of the 1994 elections convinced him there was an "opportunity to change the direction of government" and make it more responsive to the citizenry. In 1994, he was elected to a two-year stint on the Allentown Government Study Commission, where he won enactment of a plan making it harder for the city council to raise taxes.

In 1998, Toomey jumped into the open-seat race created by the retirement of three-term moderate Democrat Paul McHale. In a tight six-candidate GOP primary, Toomey edged past the 1996 nominee, Bob Kilbanks, by less than 3 percentage points. He then faced veteran Democratic state Sen. Roy C. Afflerbach, who accused Toomey of having tenuous ties to the district. But the well-funded Toomey portrayed Afflerbach as a tax-raising career politician and won comfortably.

In 2000, Toomey faced a well-financed challenge from former United Steelworkers local president Ed O'Brien, who attacked Toomey's support of the China trade deal and his stand on Social Security and generally depicted him as too conservative for the district. Toomey, benefiting from strong support from business groups, ran ads calling O'Brien an "old-fashioned liberal" and charging that his opponent was in the pocket of labor bosses and trial attorneys. In the end, Toomey captured 53 percent of the vote.

KEY VOTES

2000

No	Raise hourly minimum wage by $1 over two years
Yes	Halt funding for U.S. mission in Kosovo unless European nations pay more
Yes	Provide Medicare benefits to military retirees and their dependents
Yes	Grant China permanent normal trade status
Yes	Phase out estate, gift and trust taxes
Yes	Prohibit implementation of president's national monument designations
Yes	Approve GOP plan to provide prescription drug coverage for Medicare beneficiaries
No	Increase help for poor nations indebted to international financial institutions

1999

Yes	Impose steel import quotas
Yes	Kill proposal to take aviation trust funds off budget
Yes	Require background checks on buyers only at gun shows with 10 or more vendors
Yes	Remove barriers among banking, securities and insurance companies
No	Authorize state grants to hire teachers and reduce class size
No	Overhaul campaign finance law; ban "soft money" and restrict advocacy advertising
No	Approve bipartisan plan to increase rights of patients in managed-care health plans

INTEREST GROUPS

	AFL-CIO	ADA	CCUS	ACU
2000	0%	10%	80%	95%
1999	11%	5%	88%	92%

CQ VOTE STUDIES

	PARTY UNITY		PRESIDENTIAL SUPPORT	
	Support	Oppose	Support	Oppose
2000	92%	8%	29%	71%
1999	91%	9%	28%	72%

PENNSYLVANIA 15
East – Allentown; Bethlehem

Sixty miles north of Philadelphia and bordering New Jersey to the east, the 15th takes in the rolling Lehigh Valley, including the cities of Allentown, Bethlehem and Easton. The district's economy finally has started to turn around after a long struggle to regain its pre-World War II economic status, built on a powerful steel industry.

Technology office parks now cover the landscape where factories were once the mainstay. With the departure of Mack Trucks in the 1980s, firms such as Lucent Technologies have moved in and rejuvenated the economy. Many of the district's towns date back to colonial times, some with well-established Pennsylvania Dutch heritage. But the 250-year-old German influence has been diluted by westward migration into the region from New Jersey and New York.

President Bush and Al Gore made multiple trips to the 15th's Lehigh Valley during the 2000 campaign, prompting Gov. Tom Ridge to declare, "If Pennsylvania is a battleground state, the Lehigh Valley is the bull's

eye." Ultimately, Gore prevailed, capturing the district by just 2 percentage points. The win was an important part of his statewide victory. Bill Clinton narrowly carried the 15th in 1992 and '96.

Blue-collar, ethnic workers provide a dwindling but – as Gore's victory shows – still powerful base for Democrats. But incoming white-collar workers and socially conservative Democrats sent a Republican to the House in 1998 and 2000, as well as from 1979 to '93. As analysts note, the challenge is that area Democrats are more socially conservative than their national counterparts – especially on gun control – while local Republicans are more economically liberal than the national GOP.

MAJOR INDUSTRY
Manufacturing, technology, health care

CITIES
Allentown, 100,160; Bethlehem, 69,511; Easton, 25,292

UNUSUAL FEATURES
The Liberty Bell was hidden from the British in an Allentown church for a year during the Revolutionary War; Easton is home to the Crayola Crayon factory; Just Born Inc. in Bethlehem makes more than 600 million Peeps (brightly colored marshmallow candies) around Easter.

Rep. Joseph R. Pitts (R)

CAPITOL OFFICE
225-2411; fax 225-2013; 204 Cannon Bldg. 20515

INTERNET
e-mail: pitts.pa16@mail.house.gov
web: www.house.gov/pitts

COMMITTEES
Energy & Commerce
International Relations

HOMETOWN
Kennett Square

BORN
Oct. 10, 1939, Lexington, Ky.

RELIGION
Protestant

FAMILY
Wife, Virginia M. Pitts; three children

EDUCATION
Asbury College, A.B. 1961; West Chester U., M.Ed.
1972

MILITARY SERVICE
Air Force, 1963-69

CAREER
Nursery owner; teacher

POLITICAL HIGHLIGHTS
Pa. House, 1972-96

ELECTION RESULTS

2000 GENERAL

Joseph R. Pitts (R)	162,403	67.0%
Robert S. Yorczyk (D)	80,177	33.1%

2000 PRIMARY

Joseph R. Pitts (R)	unopposed

1998 GENERAL

Joseph R. Pitts (R)	95,979	70.5%
Robert S. Yorczyk (D)	40,092	29.5%

PREVIOUS WINNING PERCENTAGES
1996 (59%)

Elected 1996; 3rd term

Pitts follows the same road in Congress that he traveled during 24 years in the Pennsylvania legislature — one with few left turns. He is a strong proponent of cutting taxes and limiting the scope of the federal government, and he is a fervent opponent of abortion.

As he launched his 2000 re-election bid, the three-term lawmaker was lauded by the Lancaster New Era, a newspaper in his district, as "a tax cutter, budget balancer and moral crusader."

His agenda on Capitol Hill extends well beyond the purview of his committee assignments, reflecting his varied background and his understanding that, as a relatively junior member, the chances of advancing his goals solely through the legislative process are slim. In fact, in the 107th Congress, he completely changed his committees, swapping his former posts on Armed Services, Budget and Small Business for new ones on Energy and Commerce and International Relations.

To further his agenda, Pitts takes another tack, forging alliances that advocate a larger role in civic life for families, businesses and religious and non-profit groups. These organizations include the Conservative Action Team (known as the CATs), the Renewal Alliance, the Fatherhood Promotion Task Force, the Pro-Life Caucus, the Religious Prisoners Congressional Task Force and the Values Action Team, which he leads. He even serves as a liaison between two of the groups, delivering weekly reports to the CATs on what the Values Action Team is doing.

Under fire in 1998 for not aggressively pursuing a conservative agenda on social issues, GOP leaders created the Values Action Team, an ad hoc task force, and named Pitts its head. The group's priorities included congressional action on measures that would restrict abortion, abolish federal arts funding and eliminate the "marriage penalty," a quirk in the tax code that results in some two-earner married couples paying higher taxes than they would if each partner were single.

Pitts in 1998 helped organize an effort by Republican freshmen to overhaul the federal tax code. He and about 20 GOP freshmen proposed a tax cut package that included reductions in the marriage penalty, exclusion from taxation of some interest and dividend income, and deductibility of all health insurance premiums paid by self-employed workers.

Many of Pitts' priorities derive from his experiences as a child of missionaries and as a young father. Pitts spent most of his youth in the back country of the Philippines, where his parents were engaged in missionary work. He witnessed poverty and devastation close up as well as the personal satisfaction that a life in public service can bring.

After returning to his native Kentucky, marrying and earning a college degree in philosophy and religion, Pitts embarked on a teaching career along with his wife. When his wife became pregnant, he discovered that the family could not live on his lone teaching salary.

He joined the Air Force, where he spent five and a half years, including three tours of duty in Southeast Asia in which he flew 116 combat missions as the navigator and electronic warfare officer of a B-52. He considered an Air Force career but discarded the idea when, returning home after an active duty tour, his 3-year-old son did not recognize him.

Pitts drew on his military experience in his work on Armed Services, where he carved out a niche as an advocate for increasing the United States' electronic warfare capabilities, which were stretched thin during the

1999 bombing campaign in Kosovo, he said.

After leaving the Air Force, Pitts moved the family to Pennsylvania, where he earned a master's degree and went back to teaching — high school math and science. (He has sponsored legislation to require that 95 percent of federal education dollars reach the classroom and are not lost in the bureaucracy.) Pitts eventually joined his wife's family's landscape and nursery business and then started his own landscaping firm.

He is active in a number of human rights organizations, including the Helsinki Commission. But unlike many lawmakers with strong human rights agendas, Pitts favored opening trade with China, arguing that increased involvement in international affairs would spur China to improve its human rights record. In 2000, as the issue heated up, Pitts hosted briefings for lawmakers where academics and religious leaders made the case for trade with China.

Social policy conservatives have a vocal ally in Pitts. He gives no quarter on the abortion issue; in fact, his anti-abortion ardor earned him serious opposition from pro-abortion rights Republicans in his 1992 and 1994 state House primaries and in his 1996 congressional bid. He also wants to boost prosecutions for violations of obscenity and child exploitation laws.

In the 105th, he helped found the Fatherhood Promotion Task Force, a group seeking to promote parental responsibility (formed in the wake of a study indicating almost a quarter of U.S. children live without fathers at home). He made news in 1999 when he blamed Homer Simpson, Hank Hill and other bumbling TV cartoon fathers for contributing to the decline of fatherhood.

Pitts' affiliation with a number of non-legislative organizations on the Hill once also included his membership in a singing group called the Capitol Four, but it disbanded after the 105th Congress when one of the quartet, Republican Michael Pappas of New Jersey, was defeated.

Pitts got into politics soon after he moved to Pennsylvania, working on local political campaigns, but did not think of running for office himself until colleagues convinced him to run for an open state House seat in 1972. He upset the party-endorsed candidate and served in the House for 24 years, including eight years as chairman of the Appropriations Committee.

In 1996, longtime GOP Rep. Robert S. Walker decided to retire, and Pitts entered the fray. He won a hard-fought five-way primary race and, given the GOP's more than 2-to-1 edge in registered voters, won election by 22 percentage points. He has not been challenged seriously in either of his re-election bids.

KEY VOTES

2000

No	Raise hourly minimum wage by $1 over two years
Yes	Halt funding for U.S. mission in Kosovo unless European nations pay more
Yes	Provide Medicare benefits to military retirees and their dependents
Yes	Grant China permanent normal trade status
Yes	Phase out estate, gift and trust taxes
Yes	Prohibit implementation of president's national monument designations
Yes	Approve GOP plan to provide prescription drug coverage for Medicare beneficiaries
No	Increase help for poor nations indebted to international financial institutions

1999

?	Impose steel import quotas
Yes	Kill proposal to take aviation trust funds off budget
Yes	Require background checks on buyers only at gun shows with 10 or more vendors
Yes	Remove barriers among banking, securities and insurance companies
No	Authorize state grants to hire teachers and reduce class size
No	Overhaul campaign finance law; ban "soft money" and restrict advocacy advertising
No	Approve bipartisan plan to increase rights of patients in managed-care health plans

INTEREST GROUPS

	AFL-CIO	ADA	CCUS	ACU
2000	0%	0%	85%	100%
1999	0%	0%	92%	92%
1998	0%	0%	100%	96%
1997	0%	5%	100%	96%

CQ VOTE STUDIES

	PARTY UNITY		PRESIDENTIAL SUPPORT	
	Support	Oppose	Support	Oppose
2000	98%	2%	19%	81%
1999	97%	3%	17%	83%
1998	96%	4%	21%	79%
1997	96%	4%	28%	72%

PENNSYLVANIA 16

Southeastern — Lancaster

Located in southeastern Pennsylvania and bordering Delaware and Maryland to the south, the 16th includes almost all of Lancaster and part of Chester counties. Commonly referred to as "Pennsylvania Dutch Country," the 16th is reliably Republican.

The strong work ethic of the local labor force and the district's proximity to major roadways attract companies to the area, which is central to the mid-Atlantic's major markets. Economic expansion has brought in new residents, and some of the area's farmland has been built over with tract housing. Rolling and pastoral Chester County became Pennsylvania's seventh-fastest growing county in the 1990s.

Although the 16th welcomes the development, farm preservation remains a major concern, especially in Lancaster, an area ranked among the top nationally in agricultural product sales. Tourism also enhances the 16th's robust economy. Some 4.5 million tourists

annually flock to Dutch Country to gaze at Amish horse-drawn carriages, browse at quilt shops and dine in family style restaurants.

Lancaster, with its Amish heritage, sets the district's conservative political tone. Since the dawn of the Civil War, the area included in the 16th has favored the Republican Party at the national and local levels. Voters in Chester County tend to be more socially moderate than their counterparts in Lancaster County.

MAJOR INDUSTRY
Agriculture, tourism, manufacturing

CITIES
Lancaster, 52,712; West Chester, 17,858; Coatesville, 12,945

UNUSUAL FEATURES
Longwood Gardens, a 1,050-acre horticultural park created by the du Pont family in "chateau country," an area filled with country estates; Kennett Square in Chester County is known for its mushroom farms, which rely on a large migrant workforce; One of the architects of the U.S. Capitol designed the Chester County Courthouse.

Rep. George W. Gekas (R)

CAPITOL OFFICE
225-4315; fax 225-8440; 2109 Rayburn Bldg. 20515

INTERNET
e-mail: askgeorge@mail.house.gov
web: www.house.gov/gekas

COMMITTEES
Judiciary
(Immigration & Claims - chairman)

HOMETOWN
Harrisburg

BORN
April 14, 1930, Harrisburg, Pa.

RELIGION
Greek Orthodox

FAMILY
Wife, Evangeline Charas Gekas

EDUCATION
Dickinson College, B.A. 1952; Dickinson School of
Law, J.D. 1958

MILITARY SERVICE
Army, 1953-55

CAREER
Lawyer; county prosecutor

POLITICAL HIGHLIGHTS
Pa. House, 1967-75; defeated for re-election to
Pa. House, 1974; Pa. Senate, 1977-83

ELECTION RESULTS

2000 GENERAL

George W. Gekas (R)	166,236	71.5%
Leslye Hess Herrmann (D)	66,190	28.5%

2000 PRIMARY

George W. Gekas (R)	unopposed

1998 GENERAL

George W. Gekas (R)	unopposed

PREVIOUS WINNING PERCENTAGES
1996 (72%); 1994 (100%); 1992 (70%); 1990 (100%);
1988 (100%); 1986 (74%); 1984 (73%); 1982 (58%)

Elected 1982; 10th term

In his early years in Congress, Gekas' long-running crusade in favor of the death penalty was the issue that invariably served to characterize the former prosecutor. Today, he is still adamant that capital punishment should be more broadly employed as a deterrent to violent crime.

But since the GOP takeover of the House in 1995 elevated him to a Judiciary subcommittee chairmanship, Gekas' horizons have been expanded, and in recent years his focus has shifted to issues such as bankruptcy, the independent counsel statute and federal agency rule-making procedures — matters that had been small blips on his radar screen in the past.

In the 107th Congress, Gekas sought to broaden his horizons further, offering himself as a candidate for Judiciary Committee chairman, to replace Henry J. Hyde of Illinois, who had to step down because of GOP-imposed term limits. Gekas lost out to the more senior F. James Sensenbrenner of Wisconsin, but was able to claim the Immigration and Claims Subcommittee chairmanship.

When the Democrats controlled the House, Gekas (GEE-kus) was best known for his involvement in crime and punishment issues, which were his priorities in the Pennsylvania legislature and which are under the purview of Judiciary's Crime Subcommittee, where he has served. The man who once vowed to use "every parliamentary maneuver known to mankind" to ensure enactment of a death penalty bill has made capital punishment a personal crusade. At every twist and turn of the legislative process — particularly when he was in the minority — Gekas was there with a fistful of amendments, seeking to add the death penalty as punishment for an array of crimes.

Then, in the 104th, Gekas took the helm of Judiciary's Commercial and Administrative Law Subcommittee, which had been overshadowed in the past, but which was given a meatier role in the GOP "Contract With America" effort to rein in federal regulators. He entered the fray enthusiastically, offering legislation to require federal agencies to follow an elaborate cost-benefit analysis when proposing new regulations. He also delved into the complicated issue of bankruptcy law, which lawmakers have struggled, unsuccessfully, to overhaul for years. When Congress had last dealt with the subject, in 1994, Gekas' involvement was minimal. But in his role as chairman, Gekas pushed measures to prevent all but the lowest-income people from avoiding repayment of their debts by declaring bankruptcy.

On that, and on some of the other contentious issues before his subcommittee, Gekas' latitude to craft legislation that suits him is restricted by the wishes of higher-ups in the committee and in the GOP leadership.

Gekas is a staunch conservative and a reliable party man on fiscal and social policy issues, reflecting the ingrained conservatism of his central Pennsylvania district. Yet more than once during recent years he has worked to tone down proposals from the Republican right that he regards as overzealous.

In one case, he agreed with some of his GOP colleagues who maintained that the Legal Services Corporation (LSC) was not a legal aid organization for the poor but a tool of the left that spent taxpayers' money on class-action lawsuits and other efforts to advance a leftist agenda. Nevertheless, he opposed the outright and immediate elimination of the organization, as demanded by many conservatives. After one meeting with a group of fervent LSC critics, Gekas lamented, "I failed to get through to them."

In the 105th, Gekas broke with most fellow Judiciary panel Republicans when he successfully moved to kill a sweeping bill that would have ended federal racial and gender preferences in hiring. He said he wanted to end "policies which favor people on the basis of immutable characteristics," but he felt the bill went too far and he feared that "forcing the issue at this time could jeopardize the daily progress being made in ensuring equality."

In 1998 and 1999, Gekas played a prominent role in the impeachment of President Clinton. He was one of 13 "managers" who argued the House's case for Clinton's removal from office in the Senate impeachment trial.

Gekas is not the most polished public speaker, and his tangled syntax can leave his audience bemused, but his performance during the impeachment trial impressed many observers. He departed from his prepared text, which laid out an overview of the crimes of obstruction of justice and perjury, to tell the story of his immigrant mother attending naturalization classes when he was a child, studying long and hard for the right to become an American citizen. Clinton's actions struck at the very heart of the legal system his mother studied, Gekas said. "Can anyone say that purposefully trying to destroy someone's case in the courtroom is not an attack of our system of government?" he asked.

Gekas is the co-founder of the Congressional Biomedical Research Caucus. His support of such research has led him to back tough penalties for protesters — "animal rights terrorists," he calls them — who destroy animal research facilities.

For more than a decade, he has pushed for legislation that would prevent a government shutdown if Congress and the president failed to complete action on appropriations bills on time. In 1997, after partial government shutdowns in 1995 and 1996 brought the proposal more attention, Congress approved the bill, but it was vetoed by Clinton. Gekas has refused to give up.

A member of Harrisburg's small but influential Greek community, Gekas took the traditional path to political success in central Pennsylvania. He went to a local college and law school, became an assistant district attorney, then moved on to the state Capitol for 14 years in the legislature. Gekas fashioned his state legislative career around a hard-line stance on crime.

Gekas encountered remarkably few obstacles on his path to Congress in 1982. He launched his campaign after Democratic Rep. Allen Ertel announced for governor and after the GOP-controlled General Assembly approved new district lines favoring the election of a Republican. He captured 58 percent of the vote in that first race and has always racked up more than 70 percent in his re-election races, often running unopposed.

KEY VOTES

2000

No Raise hourly minimum wage by $1 over two years

Yes Halt funding for U.S. mission in Kosovo unless European nations pay more

Yes Provide Medicare benefits to military retirees and their dependents

Yes Grant China permanent normal trade status

Yes Phase out estate, gift and trust taxes

Yes Prohibit implementation of president's national monument designations

Yes Approve GOP plan to provide prescription drug coverage for Medicare beneficiaries

No Increase help for poor nations indebted to international financial institutions

1999

Yes Impose steel import quotas

No Kill proposal to take aviation trust funds off budget

Yes Require background checks on buyers only at gun shows with 10 or more vendors

Yes Remove barriers among banking, securities and insurance companies

No Authorize state grants to hire teachers and reduce class size

No Overhaul campaign finance law; ban "soft money" and restrict advocacy advertising

No Approve bipartisan plan to increase rights of patients in managed-care health plans

INTEREST GROUPS

	AFL-CIO	ADA	CCUS	ACU
2000	0%	0%	95%	87%
1999	11%	5%	100%	84%
1998	0%	10%	100%	84%
1997	25%	15%	100%	88%

CQ VOTE STUDIES

	PARTY UNITY		PRESIDENTIAL SUPPORT	
	Support	Oppose	Support	Oppose
2000	92%	8%	28%	72%
1999	91%	9%	24%	76%
1998	93%	7%	21%	79%
1997	90%	10%	29%	71%

PENNSYLVANIA 17
South Central — Harrisburg

Anchored in south-central Pennsylvania, the 17th is home to Harrisburg, the state capital, which sits 100 miles west of Philadelphia and 200 miles east of Pittsburgh. Here, in Republican-minded central Pennsylvania, state government and manufacturing remain king.

Harrisburg's skyline is dominated by the capitol building, topped with a dome inspired by St. Peter's Basilica in Rome. Inside these walls are many Democratic state government workers and legislative staffers, the only reliably Democratic stronghold in the district. Those wanting a real taste of Dauphin County skip Harrisburg and go to Hershey, also know as "Chocolatetown, U.S.A." The chocolate factory stands at the center of town, emanating the most pleasant of industrial odors.

Not only in Dauphin, but in Lebanon County as well, computer and electrical components manufacturing helps run the economy. The construction of distribution centers that store office supplies, hardware and computer parts is also on the rise. The economy is

thriving in the 17th, and the work force is practically not large enough to satisfy the demand for labor.

MAJOR INDUSTRY
Light manufacturing, government, tourism

MILITARY BASES
Fort Indiantown Gap, 454 military, 873 civilian; Carlisle Barracks, 460 military, 537 civilian (1999)

CITIES
Harrisburg, 48,619; Lebanon, 23,463; Ephrata, 13,341; Columbia, 10,492

UNUSUAL FEATURES
Street lights in the town of Hershey are shaped like Hershey Kisses; The Milton Hershey School's Founders Hall has the largest unsupported dome in the Western Hemisphere; Wilt Chamberlain scored NBA-record 100 points in a single game in Hershey.

Rep. Mike Doyle (D)

Elected 1994; 4th term

Doyle won election to the House in 1994 by using some of the "time for a change" rhetoric popularized by GOP conservatives. He was one of just four Democrats who swam against the national GOP tide that year to capture a House seat that had been in Republican hands.

Doyle said the voters who elected him were sending "a clear message: They wanted government waste and inefficiency eliminated; they wanted the pork-barrel, spendthrift ways of the past to change; they wanted our deficit brought down."

In Congress, Doyle's voting record places him in league with the Republicans about a quarter of the time — a relatively high percentage for a Northern Democrat. He sided with conservatives in the 106th Congress on such issues as cutting taxes on married couples, banning a procedure its opponents call "partial birth" abortion and taking a hard line on cutting government spending.

But Doyle shows his Democratic stripes by voting with organized labor, and in 1999, he joined gun control advocates in pressing for background checks of gun purchasers. He displayed sufficient party loyalty that he was able to win a coveted seat on the Energy and Commerce Committee in the 107th.

If Doyle is more comfortable with the GOP majority than most Democrats, it may be because he once was one of them. For 16 years, he was chief of staff to a Republican in the Pennsylvania Senate. He himself was a Republican for many of those years, converting to the other party in 1992.

Doyle's positions on economic and environmental matters reflect the priorities of the 18th, a blue-collar district built around the steel industry of Pittsburgh, which has recently seen hard times. "Everybody in western Pennsylvania is concerned about restoring a sense of economic security in our region. We've seen so much heavy industry leave, which has been devastating for the region," he told a Penn State publication.

Amid concerns about mounting energy prices in 2000, Doyle won passage of legislation establishing a $47.5 million program to examine the potential of tapping arctic deposits of frozen methane as an energy source. Although scientists are uncertain about the environmental impact of releasing methane hydrates, Doyle contended that it could help wean the United States from foreign energy supplies. "If only 1 percent of the methane hydrate resource could be made recoverable, the United States could more than double its domestic natural gas resource base," he said as the House passed his bill.

To take the post on Energy and Commerce, Doyle had to give up his seats on the Science and Veterans' Affairs committees. On those panels, he had worked to further the interests of the advanced medical research companies and hospitals in the 18th District as well as the numerous veterans in "The Deer Hunter" country of the Monongahela Valley. He proposed legislation in the 106th to establish a national veterans cemetery in the Pittsburgh area. In 1997, he obtained $12.4 million for renovations at the veterans hospital in Pittsburgh.

In a bid to help revitalize western Pennsylvania's troubled steel towns, Doyle has pressed for legislation creating a national historic park outside Pittsburgh that would highlight the historic role of the steel industry. He also pushed for an expansion of empowerment zones, which offer tax incentives for businesses locating in designated distressed areas; for federal aid for local sewerage system improvements; and for funds to maintain locks and

CAPITOL OFFICE
225-2135; fax 225-3084; 133 Cannon Bldg. 20515

INTERNET
e-mail: rep.doyle@mail.house.gov
web: www.house.gov/doyle

COMMITTEES
Energy & Commerce

HOMETOWN
Swissvale

BORN
Aug. 5, 1953, Pittsburgh, Pa.

RELIGION
Roman Catholic

FAMILY
Wife, Susan Doyle; four children

EDUCATION
Pennsylvania State U., B.S. 1975

CAREER
Insurance company executive; state legislative aide

POLITICAL HIGHLIGHTS
Swissvale Borough Council, 1977-81

ELECTION RESULTS

2000 GENERAL

Mike Doyle (D)	156,131	69.4%
Craig C. Stephens (R)	68,798	30.6%

2000 PRIMARY

Mike Doyle (D)	unopposed

1998 GENERAL

Mike Doyle (D)	98,363	67.7%
Dick Walker (R)	46,945	32.3%

PREVIOUS WINNING PERCENTAGES
1996 (56%); 1994 (55%)

dams on the Monongahela River.

On the Science Committee, Doyle was a frequent and vocal critic of proposed stricter Environmental Protection Agency clean air standards, saying that the multibillion-dollar cost to business to comply with the new pollution limits "is quite a burden to place on our economy, given the very questionable scientific basis EPA has presented. ... Now is the time for research, not regulation," he argued. In blasting a 1997 international accord to curb global warming by reducing industrial emissions, he said the Clinton administration should "look at emissions reduction as a challenge to our scientific and technological know-how, not as an opportunity to burden major segments of the economy."

He supports federal energy research programs, particularly fossil fuels research, and has worked hard to defend them periodically against lawmakers who would rather spend the money elsewhere. After losing a series of funding battles, Doyle and other Science Committee members introduced legislation in the 105th to merge the Energy Department's fossil energy programs with the energy efficiency and renewable energy divisions, saving administrative costs while preserving research activities.

Before coming to Congress, Doyle had a long record of involvement in suburban Pittsburgh politics. He earned a degree in community development from Penn State, then returned to his hometown of Swissvale (just east of Pittsburgh) in the mid-1970s. He entered the insurance business, got involved in community affairs as executive director of the Turtle Creek Valley Citizens Union and was elected to the Swissvale Borough Council, serving as finance and recreation chairman.

He worked for GOP state Sen. Frank A. Pecora for years. In 1992, Pecora became a Democrat and fought through a crowded House Democratic primary to win the right to challenge freshman GOP Rep. Rick Santorum, only to lose decisively in November. Doyle jumped to the Democratic Party that same year.

In 1994, with Santorum running statewide for senator, Doyle tried his hand at the open 18th, surviving a seven-person primary and winning the Democratic nomination with 20 percent of the vote. In the general election, Doyle was not well-known across the district, but neither was GOP nominee John McCarty, and Doyle capitalized on the district's Democratic lean to win by 10 percentage points.

Doyle won re-election by 16 points in 1996, even though the Pittsburgh Post-Gazette endorsed the GOP candidate, lawyer David B. Fawcett. In the past two elections, Doyle has prevailed by margins of more than 30 points.

KEY VOTES

2000

Yes	Raise hourly minimum wage by $1 over two years
+	Halt funding for U.S. mission in Kosovo unless European nations pay more
Yes	Provide Medicare benefits to military retirees and their dependents
No	Grant China permanent normal trade status
No	Phase out estate, gift and trust taxes
No	Prohibit implementation of president's national monument designations
No	Approve GOP plan to provide prescription drug coverage for Medicare beneficiaries
Yes	Increase help for poor nations indebted to international financial institutions

1999

Yes	Impose steel import quotas
No	Kill proposal to take aviation trust funds off budget
No	Require background checks on buyers only at gun shows with 10 or more vendors
Yes	Remove barriers among banking, securities and insurance companies
Yes	Authorize state grants to hire teachers and reduce class size
Yes	Overhaul campaign finance law; ban "soft money" and restrict advocacy advertising
Yes	Approve bipartisan plan to increase rights of patients in managed-care health plans

INTEREST GROUPS

	AFL-CIO	ADA	CCUS	ACU
2000	100%	65%	47%	20%
1999	100%	85%	32%	16%
1998	100%	80%	50%	25%
1997	88%	65%	70%	36%

CQ VOTE STUDIES

	PARTY UNITY		PRESIDENTIAL SUPPORT	
	Support	Oppose	Support	Oppose
2000	79%	21%	70%	30%
1999	77%	23%	67%	33%
1998	79%	21%	68%	32%
1997	68%	32%	61%	39%

PENNSYLVANIA 18

Pittsburgh suburbs; Clairton; McKeesport

Home to "Steel Valley," the 18th is completely contained within western Pennsylvania's densely populated Allegheny County. The district wraps around the city of Pittsburgh, and two major rivers, the Allegheny and Monongahela, weave through the 18th. Access to major waterways made the first half of the 20th century prosperous for the 18th – it was the most important and largest producer of steel in the United States.

But the days when Pittsburgh suburbs were thriving communities have long passed. While the city of Pittsburgh is making an economic comeback, the suburbs are not experiencing the same prosperity. Few have recovered from steel's decline. Monroeville and Penn Hills have seen commercial development and some technology businesses move in, but towns such as West Mifflin and Clairton find it difficult to break out of their "Steel Valley" stereotype.

Just as steel is king in the 18th, the Democrats rule politics. During the 1980s, residents backed Democrats, allowing presidential underdogs Walter Mondale and Michael Dukakis to fare quite well. This trend continued into the 1990s when former Republican governor and Allegheny County native Dick Thornburgh lost in a special Senate election in 1991. Bill Clinton won the district in both 1992 and '96 and Al Gore secured it in 2000. Although small, there are Republican sections, most notably in the affluent neighborhood of Fox Chapel.

MAJOR INDUSTRY
Health care, manufacturing, air cargo, steel

CITIES
Monroeville, 27,667; McKeesport, 22,698; West Mifflin, 22,024; Baldwin, 20,031; Wilkinsburg, 18,736

UNUSUAL FEATURES
In the 1980s, a bad economy forced Clairton, setting for the movie, "The Deer Hunter," to furlough its police and turn off street lights.

Rep. Todd R. Platts (R)

CAPITOL OFFICE
225-5836; fax 226-1000
1032 Longworth Bldg. 20515

INTERNET
e-mail: www.house.gov/writerep
web: www.house.gov/platts

COMMITTEES
Education & Workforce
Government Reform
Transportation & Infrastructure

HOMETOWN
York

BORN
March 5, 1962, York, Pa.

RELIGION
Episcopalian

FAMILY
Wife, Leslie Platts; two children

EDUCATION
Shippensburg U., B.S. 1984; Pepperdine U., J.D. 1991

CAREER
Lawyer; gubernatorial and state legislative aide

POLITICAL HIGHLIGHTS
Pa. Republican Party finance director, 1988; Pa. House, 1993-2000

ELECTION RESULTS

2000 GENERAL

Todd R. Platts (R)	168,722	72.6%
Jeff Sanders (D)	61,538	26.5%

2000 PRIMARY

Todd R. Platts (R)	21,448	33.3%
Albert Masland (R)	18,674	29.0%
Dick Stewart (R)	11,973	18.6%
Charles Gerow (R)	8,314	12.9%
Christopher Reilly (R)	3,948	6.1%

Elected 2000; 1st term

Having an upright image is usually a good thing in politics — maybe more so in a congressional district such as the 19th, packed with Republican-voting conservatives. So it was a grace note for Platts when a local newspaper, the York Daily Record, described him during his 2000 House campaign as "so clean he squeaks when he walks."

But the eight-year state House representative had little need of the extra boost to win the open 19th District seat. Having already prevailed in a tight five-way GOP primary, his election was assured, since the district is a Republican stronghold.

When Platts was 14 years old, he volunteered for Republican Rep. Bill Goodling's first re-election campaign. Goodling would serve 13 terms and rise to the chairmanship of the Education and the Workforce Committee before retiring in 2001. (Goodling's departure left the House without a member of the Goodling family for the first time since 1966; Goodling's father held the seat from 1961 to 1965 and 1967 to 1975.)

When Platts got a seat on the Education panel for the 107th Congress, he was doing more than just following in Goodling's footsteps. Platts brings his own expertise to the table, having chaired the state House Education panel's Subcommittee on Basic Education. He says that more resources should go directly to schools and that localities should decide how to allocate the money. And though he is a fiscal conservative, Platts favors more federal funding to ensure smaller class sizes in kindergarten through third grade.

Platts is the freshman class representative on the Republican Policy Committee. He sought and won an assignment to the Transportation panel and was given a Government Reform Committee post. He made changing campaign finance law a central theme in his campaign and says he declined "special interest" contributions.

Though greatly outspent in the 2000 GOP primary, Platts won with 33 percent of the vote, 4 percentage points ahead of fellow state Rep. Albert Masland. The district's Republican leanings ensured his victory; he defeated Democrat Jeff Sanders, a college professor, by a nearly 3-to-1 ratio.

PENNSYLVANIA 19
South Central — York

Located in south-central Pennsylvania, the 19th includes all of York and Adams counties and all but a small portion of Cumberland County. At the edge of Pennsylvania Dutch country, the 19th's historic landscape has a reliably Republican constituency and flourishing agricultural and manufacturing industries. In Adams County, a largely agricultural area, 1.8 million tourists visit the site of the 1863 Battle of Gettysburg each year. Many come for the annual reenactment of one of the Civil War's most significant battles.

Even as Democratic presidential candidates captured the Keystone State in 1992, '96 and 2000, the counties of the 19th stayed true to their Republican roots. Democrats in the 19th find sanctuary in the counties' more urban areas, such as Gettysburg and York.

This GOP enclave continues to attract tourists and business. Located at the crossroads of several major highways, the 19th is a prime location for manufacturing and distribution centers, including depots and logistical support facilities for the Department of Defense. York County serves as the district's industrial hub. Residential growth, a more recent trend in the district, also can be attributed to the district's location, making the area attractive to Marylanders in search of lower taxes and affordable real estate.

MAJOR INDUSTRY
Agriculture, manufacturing, distribution

MILITARY BASES
Defense Distribution Depot Susquehanna, 22 military, 2,199 civilian (1999)

CITIES
York, 39,704; Carlisle, 17,504; Hanover, 14,478

UNUSUAL FEATURES
Birthplace of the Articles of Confederation; York served as the U.S. Capitol from 1777-78 while the British occupied Philadelphia; Harley Davidson motorcycle factory in York.

Rep. Frank R. Mascara (D)

CAPITOL OFFICE
225-4665; fax 225-3377; 314 Cannon Bldg. 20515

INTERNET
e-mail: www.house.gov/writerep
web: www.house.gov/mascara

COMMITTEES
Financial Services
Transportation & Infrastructure

HOMETOWN
Charleroi

BORN
Jan. 19, 1930, Belle Vernon, Pa.

RELIGION
Roman Catholic

FAMILY
Wife, Dolores Mascara; four children

EDUCATION
California U. of Pennsylvania, B.S. 1972

MILITARY SERVICE
Army, 1946-47

CAREER
Accountant; educator

POLITICAL HIGHLIGHTS
Washington County controller, 1974-79;
Washington County Commission chairman, 1980-95; sought Democratic nomination for U.S. House, 1992

ELECTION RESULTS

2000 GENERAL

Frank R. Mascara (D)	145,131	64.4%
Ronald J. Davis (R)	80,312	35.6%

2000 PRIMARY

Frank R. Mascara (D)	unopposed

1998 GENERAL

Frank R. Mascara (D)	unopposed

PREVIOUS WINNING PERCENTAGES
1996 (54%); 1994 (53%)

Elected 1994; 4th term

Mascara first won his House seat at an age when most people are planning their retirement. He is a generation older than most of the members first elected with him in 1994, and many of his beliefs are shaped by his working-class roots. Mascara's father was injured in a steel mill accident, and his grandfather died in a mining accident. Mascara paid for the headstone on his grandfather's grave in Belle Vernon, Pa., which carries the epitaph "Coal Miner."

Mascara serves to remind his party's leadership that House Democrats still include a contingent of culturally conservative, ethnic New Deal Democrats from districts that are hard-pressed to adapt to new economic realities. His blue-collar constituents, who have been hurt by declining employment in the steel and coal industries, are struggling to find a role in the global marketplace.

Mascara often agrees with conservative Republicans on social policy issues. He opposes abortion, voted to repeal the ban on certain semiautomatic assault-style weapons and favors a constitutional amendment to prohibit flag desecration. In the 104th Congress, he was one of the few Democrats giving early backing to the GOP's welfare overhaul plan, and during debate on changing immigration laws, he voted for a GOP measure denying public education to illegal immigrants. In 1997, he supported a constitutional amendment imposing a 12-year limit on congressional terms.

When Democrats pressed for gun control measures in the 106th, Mascara broke with party liberals by insisting that social problems, not access to guns, were responsible for violence. "The pillars of the church have been shaken with a steady moral decline; parents are often forced to be absent when their children return home from school; school teachers are reluctant or no longer have the authority to discipline students; and the violence on television, movies and video games is outrageous," he wrote in a 1999 column in the Pittsburgh Post-Gazette. "Since society is reluctant to confront these issues, some argue that the passage of gun control legislation will make all of these problems disappear. I don't think so."

Mascara doesn't speak a lot on the House floor, but when he does, it is often to lament his district's economic woes. Once, when expressing support for increasing the minimum wage, he said, "I represent southwestern Pennsylvania, an area of the country that lost 200,000 jobs in the 1980s when the winds of change blew through the steel mills and the coal mines. Many of my constituents are now left to subsist on $4.25 per hour, or $8,840 per year, hardly a living wage and nowhere near enough to raise a family."

Loyal to organized labor, Mascara votes against trade agreements that he worries can hurt U.S. workers. In 1997, he was against giving the president fast-track authority to negotiate trade agreements that Congress cannot amend, and in 2000, he voted against granting China permanent normal trade status. "Like many others, I am concerned for the well-being of Chinese workers," he said. "But it is unreasonable to expect trade to bring more freedom to China. Moreover, I will not ask my constituents to accept lower paying jobs to improve social and political conditions in China."

Mascara takes a moderate approach on fiscal issues. After initially opposing a sweeping balanced-budget agreement in 1997, he swung around to support it after Republicans gave ground on several issues in negotiations with the Clinton White House. In the 106th, he supported some GOP-backed tax cuts, such as a measure reducing taxes on married couples.

But he reacts viscerally against conservative proposals that he believes could weaken workplace safety regulations. In the 104th, he joined Democrat Bob Wise of West Virginia in seeking to exempt aircraft, mine and nuclear safety regulations from a GOP-backed regulatory moratorium. "We know firsthand about one of the world's most dangerous occupations, working in the mines," Mascara told the House. "While in good times our communities have benefited economically from the mining industry, they have also experienced the tragedy of mining accidents and poor health that can result from years of breathing coal dust." Mascara said passage of his amendment with Wise was a matter of "life and death," but the House rejected it.

Mascara believes in federal spending on public works. On the Transportation Committee, one of Mascara's causes is pushing for completion of a local highway project, the Mon-Fayette Expressway. Mascara said he and his constituents believe that once the highway is built, "like the playing field in the movie 'Field of Dreams,' ... businesses and jobs will follow."

In the 106th Congress, Mascara took a seat on the Banking Committee, renamed Financial Services in the 107th. To take that assignment, he had to relinquish his post on Veterans' Affairs, where he was a stout defender of benefits for all present and former military personnel. "I come from a family with a long history of serving in the military," he once told his colleagues in a floor speech. "I myself am an Army veteran. I have four brothers who served in World War II, and my immigrant father earned a Silver Star for valiant and heroic service in World War I. Thus, it is no secret that I strongly feel that our country owes a deep obligation to all active duty military personnel and veterans."

Mascara built his political career in Washington County, where more than one-third of the people in the 20th District live. After serving in the Army and working as an accountant, he became Washington County controller in 1974 and served as chairman of the county board of commissioners from 1980 until he took his House seat in 1995.

Mascara first tried for the House in 1992, losing by just 2 percentage points in a primary challenge to veteran Democratic incumbent Austin J. Murphy. When Murphy decided to step down in 1994, Mascara tried again, stressing his experience as a mediator between management and labor, and defeated two opponents in the Democratic primary. In a year when Republicans ran strong nationally, Mascara defeated GOP nominee Mike McCormick, an investment adviser and political newcomer, by 6 points. He has had little trouble since.

KEY VOTES

2000

Yes	Raise hourly minimum wage by $1 over two years
No	Halt funding for U.S. mission in Kosovo unless European nations pay more
Yes	Provide Medicare benefits to military retirees and their dependents
No	Grant China permanent normal trade status
No	Phase out estate, gift and trust taxes
No	Prohibit implementation of president's national monument designations
No	Approve GOP plan to provide prescription drug coverage for Medicare beneficiaries
Yes	Increase help for poor nations indebted to international financial institutions

1999

Yes	Impose steel import quotas
No	Kill proposal to take aviation trust funds off budget
No	Require background checks on buyers only at gun shows with 10 or more vendors
Yes	Remove barriers among banking, securities and insurance companies
Yes	Authorize state grants to hire teachers and reduce class size
Yes	Overhaul campaign finance law; ban "soft money" and restrict advocacy advertising
Yes	Approve bipartisan plan to increase rights of patients in managed-care health plans

INTEREST GROUPS

	AFL-CIO	ADA	CCUS	ACU
2000	100%	65%	47%	28%
1999	100%	70%	20%	21%
1998	100%	85%	33%	20%
1997	100%	65%	50%	32%

CQ VOTE STUDIES

	PARTY UNITY		PRESIDENTIAL SUPPORT	
	Support	Oppose	Support	Oppose
2000	79%	21%	65%	35%
1999	76%	24%	65%	35%
1998	80%	20%	73%	27%
1997	71%	29%	61%	39%

PENNSYLVANIA 20
Southwest – The Mon Valley; Washington

Located south of Pittsburgh, the 20th includes all of Washington and Greene counties and part of Allegheny, Westmoreland and Fayette. This region's past is marked by the boom-and-bust cycles of the coal and steel industries, while its recent history has been marked by repeated efforts to move into the economy of the 21st century.

The demise of the district's traditional industries led to massive job losses. In the coal towns of Fayette and Greene counties and the steel towns of Donora and Brownsville along the Monongahela River, unemployment soared, reaching as high as 200,000 in the 1980s. Now, economic development is visible, especially in Washington County with the construction of Southpointe, a 600-acre industrial park near Canonsburg.

The 20th clings to the Democratic tradition of its industrialized past. Democrats far outnumber Republicans. The GOP has a foothold in Peters Township in Allegheny County and in parts of Westmoreland County. Conservative political financier Richard Mellon Scaife operates the Pittsburgh Tribune-Review down Route 30 in Greensburg. Despite the presence of a few Republican voters, the 20th is known as the most reliably Democratic region in the state outside the cities of Pittsburgh and Philadelphia. In the 2000 presidential election, Al Gore won all but Westmoreland County in the 20th. Interestingly, however, that translated to only a 4 percent margin of victory in the district, perhaps owing to the area's socially conservative residents, who oppose gun control.

MAJOR INDUSTRY
Agriculture, health care, manufacturing

CITIES
Bethel Park, 33,627; Greensburg, 15,357; Washington, 14,727; Uniontown, 11,263

UNUSUAL FEATURES
George Washington fought at Fort Necessity, site of the opening battle of the French and Indian War.

Rep. Phil English (R)

CAPITOL OFFICE
225-5406; fax 225-3103
1410 Longworth Bldg. 20515

INTERNET
e-mail: phil.english@mail.house.gov
web: www.house.gov/english

COMMITTEES
Ways & Means
Joint Economic

HOMETOWN
Erie

BORN
June 20, 1956, Erie, Pa.

RELIGION
Roman Catholic

FAMILY
Wife, Christiane English

EDUCATION
U. of Pennsylvania, B.A. 1979

CAREER
State legislative aide

POLITICAL HIGHLIGHTS
Erie City controller, 1986-89; Republican nominee
for Pa. treasurer, 1988

ELECTION RESULTS

2000 GENERAL

Phil English (R)	135,164	60.8%
Marc Flitter (D)	87,018	39.2%

2000 PRIMARY

Phil English (R)	unopposed

1998 GENERAL

Phil English (R)	94,518	63.4%
Larry Klemens (D)	54,591	36.6%

PREVIOUS WINNING PERCENTAGES
1996 (51%); 1994 (50%)

Elected 1994; 4th term

English's interest in politics was evident at an early age. The son of an Erie lawyer who was active in community affairs, English was a political science major in college and an alternate delegate, at age 20, to the Republican National Convention in 1976. After college, he spent eight years as a legislative aide for a closely divided Pennsylvania state legislature — specializing in tax and social welfare issues — sandwiched around a term as the elected controller of the Democratic-run city of Erie.

English seemed to be content with his behind-the-scenes career as a top legislative staff member and never really considered running for Congress until an open-seat opportunity presented itself in 1994. His moderate tendencies have served him well in winning four House elections as a Republican in a competitive, blue-collar district.

His expertise on tax matters and his track record in dealing with the imperative of bipartisan cooperation gave him a leg up when he arrived on Capitol Hill as part of the massive GOP Class of 1994.

His moderate political philosophy and experience in government placed him outside the norm in a class dominated by conservatives who proudly trumpeted their "outsider" status. English, nevertheless, had the credentials that convinced GOP leaders to put him on the Ways and Means Committee, the first GOP freshman in decades to win a seat on the powerful tax-writing panel.

He arrived brimming with ideas, from wide-ranging plans to simplify the tax code, provide tax incentives for a variety of education savings plans, and cut government spending to more-focused proposals, such as his bills reducing the excise tax on beer and permitting clergymen to join in the Social Security and Medicare systems late in their careers. As would be expected from a former legislative staffer, English is conversant with the details of his bills and is a voracious reader who often tests the mettle of his own staff in keeping up with the myriad details of congressional action.

The political composition of the 21st District requires English to use his wealth of political experience and pay careful attention to his voting record. Bill Clinton was a comfortable winner in the district in both of his presidential races, while George W. Bush carried the district by just 1 percentage point. Organized labor has substantial electoral clout in the district, and in English's first two winning House campaigns, he didn't have many votes to spare.

English exhibits a moderate streak on issues of importance to the district, such as increasing the minimum wage and defending the steel industry against low-cost imports. He attended the World Trade Organization meetings in Seattle in 1999 to warn against any softening of anti-dumping regulations that are important to the steel business. He backs trade adjustment assistance programs, which help workers who lose their jobs to foreign competition. In the 104th Congress, he was in the minority of Republicans who backed measures to protect the collective bargaining rights of mass transit workers.

But he does not always take the side of labor. He generally favors open trade and in 1996 voted for a GOP-backed (and labor-opposed) bill to allow businesses to offer their employees compensatory time off instead of overtime pay.

English is a reliable GOP vote on other issues, and his seat on the Ways and Means panel allows him to influence policy rather than rely on rhetorical warfare like some of his Class of 1994 colleagues. "I'm certainly less inclined to throw bombs than someone who is strictly on the sidelines of the process," he said.

Early in 2000, English's tax plan, the Simplified USA Tax (USA stands for unlimited savings allowance), won a hearing before the Ways and Means Committee. In 1998, he tried to take on the entire tax code. In front of constituents in Erie, he attempted to cut through the 5,000-page U.S. tax code with a chainsaw. But the chainsaw knocked the book off the table twice. Even after putting the code on the sidewalk, he was just able to nick it with the chainsaw. English finally joked about how tough it was to enact tax reform.

In 2000, English was named to the House GOP leadership's task force on Medicare coverage for prescription drugs. Another priority for English in the 106th Congress was his proposal to provide tax benefits for saving money not only for college expenses but also for job training and primary and secondary education.

In 1998, he voted "no" on three of four articles of impeachment against President Clinton. He voted for the fourth article, charging perjury, but with reluctance, he told his constituents.

After working for four years as a staffer in the state legislature, English in 1985 won election as Erie City controller, on a pledge to be a watchdog over the Democratic-dominated government. In 1988, at the midpoint of his four-year term, English ran for state treasurer. While he impressed GOP officials with his knowledge of state fiscal issues, he lost by nearly 500,000 votes.

When his term as controller was over, he switched roles, moving from candidate to strategist. He traveled to the Pittsburgh suburbs to help a little-known underdog, Rick Santorum, organize his 1990 upset of Democratic Rep. Doug Walgren. English then returned to Harrisburg as a legislative staffer, including a stint as chief of staff to state Sen. Melissa A. Hart (now a House freshman from the neighboring 4th District).

In 1994, when GOP Rep. Tom Ridge left the 21st District seat open, English was presented with a golden opportunity to return to elective politics, and he jumped at the chance. He had little trouble winning the Republican nomination. Santorum returned English's 1990 favor, helping with the campaign.

Come November, the one-two punch of the national Republican tide and a top-of-the-ticket boost from Ridge's successful gubernatorial campaign helped English prevail by 2 percentage points. He had another close race in 1996, but his past two contests have been easier.

KEY VOTES

2000
Yes Raise hourly minimum wage by $1 over two years
Yes Halt funding for U.S. mission in Kosovo unless European nations pay more
Yes Provide Medicare benefits to military retirees and their dependents
Yes Grant China permanent normal trade status
Yes Phase out estate, gift and trust taxes
No   Prohibit implementation of president's national monument designations
Yes Approve GOP plan to provide prescription drug coverage for Medicare beneficiaries
Yes Increase help for poor nations indebted to international financial institutions

1999
Yes Impose steel import quotas
No   Kill proposal to take aviation trust funds off budget
Yes Require background checks on buyers only at gun shows with 10 or more vendors
Yes Remove barriers among banking, securities and insurance companies
?   Authorize state grants to hire teachers and reduce class size
No   Overhaul campaign finance law; ban "soft money" and restrict advocacy advertising
No   Approve bipartisan plan to increase rights of patients in managed-care health plans

INTEREST GROUPS

	AFL-CIO	ADA	CCUS	ACU
2000	30%	25%	76%	56%
1999	38%	25%	76%	72%
1998	50%	35%	89%	68%
1997	75%	20%	70%	76%

CQ VOTE STUDIES

	PARTY UNITY		PRESIDENTIAL SUPPORT	
	Support	Oppose	Support	Oppose
2000	83%	17%	38%	62%
1999	84%	16%	24%	76%
1998	81%	19%	36%	64%
1997	86%	14%	38%	62%

PENNSYLVANIA 21
Northwest – Erie

Located in the northwest corner of the state, the 21st includes all of Erie and Mercer counties and portions of Butler and Crawford. This historically blue-collar center is home to Erie, the third-largest city in the state. A port on the Great Lakes, Erie has been an industrial center for more than a century.

Although the 21st was hard hit by economic restructuring in the 1980s, it remained an industrial area. Fewer steel mills line Mercer County; those that remain now operate with a smaller employment base.

Despite these changes, Mercer boasts the largest concentration of pipe and tube production in the nation. In Crawford, nearly 150 tooling and machining shops dominate the county's landscape. Industrial expansion in Erie is also on the rise with a one-million-square-foot facility housing a distribution center and a manufacturing plant.

With Erie and Mercer voting Democratic and Butler and Crawford

voting Republican, the 21st is a classic swing district. Although Erie is traditionally Democratic, with Italians and Poles vying for political power, its surrounding areas are becoming politically competitive. Many of Mercer's residents tend to cross party lines, even though more of Mercer's voters are registered Democrats.

Al Gore won two of the district's four counties – Erie and Mercer – in the 2000 presidential election, but he lost the district overall by 1 percentage point. The 12th had solidly backed Bill Clinton in 1992 and '96.

MAJOR INDUSTRY
Manufacturing, agriculture, health care

CITIES
Erie, 101,474; Hermitage, 16,343; Sharon, 16,154; Butler, 14,778; Meadville,13,900

UNUSUAL FEATURES
Gov. Tom Ridge hails from Erie; U.S. Brig Niagra, the only remaining fighting ship of its kind from the War of 1812, docked in the district.

RHODE ISLAND

Gov. Lincoln C. Almond (R)

First elected: 1994
Length of term: 4 years
Term expires: 1/03
Salary: $95,000
Phone: (401) 222-2080
Hometown: Lincoln
Born: June 16, 1936, Central Falls, R.I.
Religion: Episcopalian
Family: Wife, Marilyn Almond; two children
Education: U. of Rhode Island, B.S. 1958; Boston U., J.D. 1961
Military service: Naval Reserve, Submarine Service, 1953-61
Career: Lawyer
Political highlights: Lincoln town administrator, 1963-69; Republican nominee for U.S. House, 1968; U.S. attorney, 1969-78; Republican nominee for governor, 1978; U.S. attorney, 1981-93

Election results:
1998 GENERAL

Lincoln C. Almond (R)	156,180	51.0%
Myrth York (D)	129,105	42.1%
Robert J. Healey Jr. (CMO)	19,250	6.3%

Lt. Gov. Charles J. Fogarty (D)

First elected: 1998
Length of term: 4 years
Term expires: 1/03
Salary: $80,000
Phone: (401) 222-2371

STATE LEGISLATURE

Legislature: Meets January-June
House: 100 members, 2-year terms
2001 breakdown: 15R, 84D, 1 vacancy; 75 men, 24 women
Salary: $11,236
Phone: (401) 222-2466
Senate: 50 members, 2-year terms
2001 breakdown: 6R, 44D; 40 men, 10 women
Salary: $11,236
Phone: (401) 222-6655

STATE TERM LIMITS

Governor: 2 terms
Senate: No
House: No

URBAN STATISTICS

CITY	POPULATION
Providence	149,887
Warwick	83,994
Cranston	75,009
Pawtucket	67,662
East Providence	47,835

REGISTERED VOTERS

Voters do not register by party.

POPULATION

2000 population	1,048,319
1990 population	1,003,464
Percent change	+4.5%
Rank among states	43
Median age	36.2
Born in state	63%
Foreign born	9%
Urban/rural	86%/14%
Crime rate	334/100,000
Poverty level	11.6%
Federal workers	10,591
Military	9,676

REAPPORTIONMENT

Rhode Island retained its two House seats in reapportionment. The state legislature will draw new district lines.

MISCELLANEOUS

Web: www.state.ri.us
Capital: Providence
Land area: 1,045 sq. miles
 Rank among states: 50
STATE ELECTION OFFICIAL
(401) 222-2345
DEMOCRATIC HEADQUARTERS
(401) 721-9900
REPUBLICAN HEADQUARTERS
(401) 453-4100

District Statistics

DIST.	2000 D	2000 R	GREEN	1996 D	1996 R	REF	1992 D	1992 R	I	WHT	BLK	ASIAN	HISP	HOUSEHOLD INCOME	OVER 65+	UNDER 18	COLLEGE EDUCATION
1	62%	31%	6%	61%	26%	11%	50%	28%	22%	93%	3%	1%	4%	$31,675	16%	22%	22%
2	60	33	6	59	28	12	45	30	25	90	4	2	5	$32,729	14	23	21
STATE	61	32	6	60	27	11	47	29	23	91	4	2	5	$32,181	15	23	21

Sen. Jack Reed (D)

CAPITOL OFFICE
224-4642; fax 224-4680; 320 Hart Bldg. 20510

INTERNET
e-mail: jack@reed.senate.gov
web: reed.senate.gov

COMMITTEES
Armed Services
Banking, Housing & Urban Affairs
Health, Education, Labor & Pensions
Joint Economic - ranking member

HOMETOWN
Cranston

BORN
Nov. 12, 1949, Providence, R.I.

RELIGION
Roman Catholic

FAMILY
Single

EDUCATION
U.S. Military Academy, B.S. 1971; Harvard U.,
M.P.P. 1973, J.D. 1982

MILITARY SERVICE
Army, 1971-79; Army Reserve, 1979-91

CAREER
Lawyer

POLITICAL HIGHLIGHTS
R.I. Senate, 1985-91; U.S. House, 1991-97

ELECTION RESULTS

1996 GENERAL
Jack Reed (D)	230,676	63.5%
Nancy J. Mayer (R)	127,368	35.1%
Donald W. Lovejoy (I)	5,327	1.5%

1996 PRIMARY
Jack Reed (D)	59,336	86.1%
Don Gil (D)	9,554	13.9%

PREVIOUS WINNING PERCENTAGES
1994 House Election (68%); 1992 House Election
(71%); 1990 House Election (59%)

Elected 1996; 1st term

Rhode Islanders have the son of Massachusetts Sen. Edward M. Kennedy representing them in the House, and, in Reed, they have a senator who is an ideological soul mate of the Massachusetts liberal.

But while the Kennedys are Democratic royalty, Reed comes from common-man stock. His father was a custodian and his mother a factory worker in South Providence. At his Catholic prep school, he was an over-achieving, 124-pound defensive back who won admission to West Point in 1967. After graduation, he commanded a company of the Army's 82nd Airborne Division. He left the Army at age 29 to attend Harvard Law School and then took a job in Rhode Island's biggest corporate law firm. In 1984, he won a seat in the state Senate, and in 1990 he was elected to the House.

In three terms in the House and part of one in the Senate, Reed has built a reputation as a nice guy who delivers crackerjack constituent service.

In the 106th Congress, he landed a seat on the Armed Services panel. He used the post to push for new programs at two Rhode Island facilities, the Naval Undersea Warfare Center and the Naval Education Training Center, and for more submarine construction. Rhode Island is home to Electric Boat, one of the last two submarine builders in the nation, and in 1997, Reed was quick with the proud announcement when the Armed Services Committee voted to allow Electric Boat and the other sub manufacturer, Newport News Shipbuilding, to construct jointly the next generation of nuclear-powered submarines.

Reed has immersed himself in defense policy, noting that military pay and benefits are not the only factors in determining whether the armed services can attract and retain personnel. He has said that experienced personnel are leaving the service for many reasons, including fewer opportunities for promotion in the smaller post-Cold War military and greater opportunities in the booming civilian economy for skilled leaders and technicians. "We have a very profound problem here that will not be easily remedied simply by raising pay and allowances," he warned.

Reed also is taking an increasingly visible role on social issues. He took the lead among Senate Democrats in efforts to close the so-called gun show loophole, calling for legislation requiring background checks for people who buy guns from private dealers. Supporters of the effort say current laws can be exploited by criminals, who can make purchases at gun shows and avoid the background checks required at gun stores by the 1993 Brady Act. Such legislation has been opposed by Republicans and the National Rifle Association, which say it will impose too many restrictions on law-abiding gun buyers and dealers. The Senate passed one such measure, with then-Vice President Al Gore casting the tie-breaking vote, in 1999 following the massacre at Colorado's Columbine High School. However, the legislation stalled in the House.

Reed attracted attention in the 106th by blocking a bill to grant a group of Syrian Jews permanent residency in the United States until Congress granted 10,000 Liberians the same status. The Liberians, 4,000 of whom live in Rhode Island, were given temporary protected status in 1991 when they fled civil war in their West African nation. Though they received annual extensions, their temporary status did not make them eligible to seek U.S. citizenship. The standoff was resolved when the Clinton administration threatened to veto a spending bill unless the Liberians were allowed to become residents.

Reed also weighed in on technology issues in 2000. With Vermont's senators, Democrat Patrick J. Leahy and Republican James M. Jeffords, he urged appropriators not to include language in the education spending bill requiring schools to use filtering technology to block children's access to pornography on the Internet. The senators argued it was preferable to enforce existing laws on Internet pornography and recommend programs to inform parents.

Reed and Sen. Kennedy have found themselves on the same side of a number of battles over social policy. In 1997, they were the only two senators to oppose legislation overhauling the Food and Drug Administration, arguing that the measure did not provide enough safeguards in the approval of medical devices. The two men were on the same side a month later when they opposed a bill to shift the focus of the Occupational Safety and Health Administration from enforcing workplace health and safety laws to working with employers to fix problems. Among the lawmakers' objections: The measure would give employers two years of freedom from citations if private consultants certified that their workplaces met OSHA standards. The shift, Reed said, would allow employers to "write a check and buy themselves two years of immunity."

Reed and Sen. Kennedy's son, 1st District Democratic Rep. Patrick J. Kennedy, found themselves on opposite sides of a dispute over whether the Narragansett Indians should be allowed to open a casino in the state. Kennedy supported the tribe's right to offer gambling on tribal lands, but Reed and the rest of the Rhode Island congressional delegation opposed it. In 1998, Reed, Democratic Rep. Robert Weygand and GOP Sen. John H. Chafee urged the House Resources Committee to reject Kennedy-sponsored legislation that would have paved the way for Indian gaming in the state.

Reed also has an interest in foreign affairs. In May 1998, he traveled to the Middle East for Israel's 50th anniversary, using the trip to meet with Israeli Prime Minister Benjamin Netanyahu and Syrian President Hafez al-Assad. Reed said he delivered a message from Netanyahu to al-Assad, inviting a resumption of peace talks between the two nations.

The senator provided strong support for President Clinton's decision in August 1998 to attack suspected terrorist sites in Afghanistan and Sudan following the bombings of two American embassies in Africa. "Taking military action ... is essential to maintaining both our national security and our responsibility as the world superpower," Reed said.

After six years in the state Senate, Reed ran for the House in 1990, emerging from a pack of Democratic hopefuls to defeat Republican Gertrude M. "Trudy" Coxe, a well-known environmentalist. He took the 2nd District seat that GOP Rep. Claudine Schneider gave up to wage an ultimately unsuccessful challenge to Democratic Sen. Claiborne Pell.

Before long, Reed was widely regarded as heir-apparent to Pell, whose health was failing. When Pell announced that he would retire in 1996 after 36 years in office, Reed was well-prepared to expand his campaign into the state's other district, where, because of Rhode Island's small size, his name recognition already was high. He avoided a potentially contentious primary when Joseph Paolino Jr., a former Providence mayor and former U.S. ambassador to Malta, passed up the race and ran for Reed's open House seat. Reed wound up with token opposition in the Senate primary.

Republicans nominated state Treasurer Nancy J. Mayer, a moderate who said she would bring the fiscal acumen she had demonstrated at the state level to Washington and put it to work trying to eliminate the federal deficit. Reed stayed well ahead in the race despite negative advertising paid for by the National Republican Senatorial Committee, which sought to convince voters that he was a tax-and-spend liberal. The final outcome was a rout for Reed, who took 64 percent of the vote.

KEY VOTES

2000

No Overhaul bankruptcy law and increase minimum wage

No Limit fiscal 2001 discretionary spending to $600.3 billion

No Override veto on nuclear waste disposal at Yucca Mountain site in Nevada

Yes Oppose effort to terminate Kosovo mission

Yes Include gender, sexual orientation and disability in federal hate crime protections

No Approve GOP plan to restrict use of genetic information by health insurers

No Kill amendment delaying implementation of an anti-missile defense system

No Cut taxes for married couples

Yes Grant China permanent normal trade status

1999

No Remove President Clinton from office for obstruction of justice

No Kill amendment authorizing state grants to hire teachers and reduce class size

Yes Require criminal background checks for purchases at gun shows

No Approve GOP proposal to increase rights of patients in managed-care health plans

No Block effort to allow farm and medicine exports to Cuba

Yes Allow study of tougher automobile fuel efficiency standards

Yes Ratify nuclear weapons testing treaty

Yes Prohibit national political parties from collecting "soft money" donations

Yes Remove barriers among banking, securities and insurance companies

INTEREST GROUPS

	AFL-CIO	ADA	CCUS	ACU
2000	75%	95%	46%	12%
1999	100%	100%	47%	4%
1998	88%	95%	56%	0%
1997	100%	100%	44%	0%
House Service:				
1996	82%	80%	31%	5%
1995	100%	90%	25%	12%
1994	78%	85%	50%	5%
1993	100%	90%	18%	9%
1992	92%	90%	13%	4%
1991	92%	95%	20%	0%

CQ VOTE STUDIES

	PARTY UNITY		PRESIDENTIAL SUPPORT	
	Support	Oppose	Support	Oppose
2000	97%	3%	95%	5%
1999	96%	4%	89%	11%
1998	98%	2%	90%	10%
1997	99%	1%	86%	14%
House Service:				
1996	88%	12%	81%	19%
1995	92%	8%	82%	18%
1994	97%	3%	91%	9%
1993	96%	4%	83%	17%
1992	95%	5%	14%	86%
1991	93%	7%	29%	71%

Sen. Lincoln Chafee (R)

CAPITOL OFFICE
224-2921; fax 228-2853; 141 Russell Bldg. 20510

INTERNET
e-mail: senator_chafee@chafee.senate.gov
web: chafee.senate.gov

COMMITTEES
Environment & Public Works
(Superfund, Waste Control & Risk
Assessment - chairman)
Foreign Relations
(Western Hemisphere - chairman)
Joint Economic

HOMETOWN
Warwick

BORN
March 26, 1953, Warwick, R.I.

RELIGION
Episcopalian

FAMILY
Wife, Stephanie Chafee; three children

EDUCATION
Brown U., B.A. 1975

CAREER
Defense company machine shop planner;
blacksmith

POLITICAL HIGHLIGHTS
Warwick City Council, 1986-91; Republican
nominee for mayor of Warwick, 1990; mayor of
Warwick, 1992-99

ELECTION RESULTS

2000 GENERAL

Lincoln Chafee (R)	222,588	56.9%
Bob Weygand (D)	161,023	41.2%
Christopher Young (REF)	4,107	1.1%

2000 PRIMARY

Lincoln Chafee (R)	unopposed

Elected 2000; 1st full term
Appointed November 1999

Chafee's brief Senate career is noteworthy chiefly for the remarkable consistency with which he has abandoned his party on major votes. Yet GOP leaders did not put heavy pressure on Chafee as he assembled the liberal voting record that helped seal his election in 2000. He was able to keep the Senate seat that his father, John, had occupied from 1977 until his death in October 1999. The younger Chafee initially had been appointed to the seat by Rhode Island's GOP Gov. Lincoln C. Almond.

From the congressional budget to a Democratic-led drive to create a "patients' bill of rights" to efforts to eliminate estate taxes, Chafee has cut against the GOP grain. In 2000, he sided with President Clinton on 88 percent of the votes on which Clinton had staked out a clear position — more than many loyal Democrats. And when Republicans and Democrats lined up on opposite sides of an issue in 2000, Chafee voted with the Democrats almost two-thirds of the time.

Chafee said he gave Majority Leader Trent Lott and Republican Whip Don Nickles credit for being understanding of his votes. But the GOP leaders' patience may be sorely tested in the 107th Congress since, in a 50-50 Senate, Republicans do not have any votes to spare.

Chafee's recommendations in late 2000 to the incoming Bush administration sounded like talking points from the Democratic playbook. "My advice is to just start working with Democratic issues like minimum wage, a patients' bill of rights and campaign finance reform," he said, according to The Associated Press. "These are Democratic issues that it seems we can make accomplishments on."

At a meeting with Vice President-elect Dick Cheney, however, Chafee said he got a chilly response when he inquired about the Bush administration's willingness to accept new gun control measures. Chafee bridled when Cheney said the new administration would pursue a conservative agenda. "My eyes widened and I just said in this partisan climate where Democrats are going to come at us with guns blazing, we're going to get off to a rocky start," Chafee said, according to The Associated Press. "I think when I said I was for gun safety I lost him."

The Rhode Island lawmaker said he read the results of the 2000 elections as a mandate for moderates in both parties to assert themselves. At the start of the 107th Congress, he voted to shake up the Senate GOP leadership by backing Pete V. Domenici of New Mexico in his challenge to Republican Policy Committee Chairman Larry E. Craig of Idaho. Domenici lost in a close vote, a result that angered Chafee, who said the message was, "we're sticking with the really hard-core conservatives for our leadership."

Chafee went on to blast GOP leaders, telling the Providence Journal, "They're not hearing any other voices in that leadership. ... We just came out of a bad election, so more than ever, you would think they should be willing to change."

On his arrival in Congress, Chafee took seats on the Environment and Public Works Committee, which his father had chaired, and the Foreign Relations panel. On Environment, he heads the Superfund Subcommittee, where one of his priorities is legislation to promote the redevelopment of brownfields — abandoned, contaminated industrial sites that pose problems for developers under existing toxic-waste laws.

In the foreign policy arena, he cast a key vote in 1999 against a measure to kill funding for U.S. peacekeeping troops in Kosovo unless Congress authorized their presence.

Labor groups have praised Chafee's support for increasing the minimum wage but were unhappy when he voted for a bill in 2000 to grant China permanent normal trade status.

Chafee, whose ancestors were among Rhode Island's earliest settlers, has an eclectic background. While studying the classics at Brown University, he spent summers sweeping up after carpenters and bricklayers at construction sites. After graduating, he set off for horseshoeing school at Montana State University. Inspired by a James A. Michener article, "Go Waste, Young Man," that urged young men to explore the world before settling down, he apprenticed in Kentucky and Florida before heading to the harness tracks of Edmonton and Calgary.

Chafee is quite likely the most prominent politician ever mentioned in Hoofcare & Lameness: The Journal of Equine Foot Science. Its August 1999 issue wished the farrier-politician good luck on the hustings. "I wanted to see something of life," Chafee said. "And I enjoyed working at a trade."

After seven years in northwestern Canada, Chafee returned to Rhode Island and worked as a machine shop planner for General Dynamics Corp. He followed his father into elective office in 1986 by winning a seat on the Warwick City Council. He lost his first bid for Warwick mayor in 1990 but won the job two years later, becoming the first GOP mayor in 32 years of Rhode Island's second-most-populous city — where Democrats outnumber Republicans by more than 10-to-1.

Chafee began campaigning in March 1999 to succeed his father, who had announced he would not run for a fifth term. But after the elder Chafee died that fall, GOP Gov. Almond appointed Lincoln Chafee to the post, giving him a leg up in the race.

Chafee also benefited in 2000 from a bruising Democratic primary between Rep. Bob Weygand and former Lt. Gov. Richard A. Licht, the party's 1988 nominee against the late Sen. Chafee. Weygand won the Democratic primary, but his opposition to abortion cost him support among abortion rights Democrats in the general election. Exit polls showed Chafee got support from about half of Rhode Island's Democrats. Chafee was also a sentimental favorite — his father, who had represented Rhode Island for more than two decades, was a highly respected lawmaker known for his bipartisanship.

Weygand tried to link Chafee to conservative GOP leaders, criticized his plans to reduce the costs of prescription drugs and to preserve Social Security, and said that Chafee had accomplished little during his months as an appointed senator. Chafee countered with ads promoting his moderate stance on issues such as gun control and abortion rights and his support for the environment. He was among the very few Republicans to pick up the endorsement of the League of Conservation Voters, which ran $250,000 worth of television ads on his behalf.

In an unusual move, the National Republican Senatorial Committee produced and funded a television spot touting Chafee's votes in support of a patients' rights measure and Medicare coverage of prescription drugs, even though GOP leaders opposed both proposals. The announcer said, "Tell Senator Lincoln Chafee to keep up his independent fight for Rhode Island."

One issue that apparently did not hurt Chafee was his admission — offered as Bush was being pressed on questions of illegal drug use — that he had used cocaine while in college. In fact, his poll numbers even jumped a few points. "People said, 'Good for him, he tells the truth,' " Chafee said. He won with 57 percent of the vote.

Chafee is the 42nd person to follow his father into the Senate, but only the seventh to immediately succeed his father.

KEY VOTES

2000

Yes Overhaul bankruptcy law and increase minimum wage

No Limit fiscal 2001 discretionary spending to $600.3 billion

No Override veto on nuclear waste disposal at Yucca Mountain site in Nevada

Yes Oppose effort to terminate Kosovo mission

Yes Include gender, sexual orientation and disability in federal hate crime protections

Yes Approve GOP plan to restrict use of genetic information by health insurers

Yes Kill amendment delaying implementation of an anti-missile defense system

Yes Cut taxes for married couples

Yes Grant China permanent normal trade status

1999

Yes Remove barriers among banking, securities and insurance companies

INTEREST GROUPS

	AFL-CIO	ADA	CCUS	ACU
2000	50%	70%	66%	44%

CQ VOTE STUDIES

	PARTY UNITY		PRESIDENTIAL SUPPORT	
	Support	Oppose	Support	Oppose
2000	37%	63%	88%	12%
1999	56%	44%	100%	0%

Rep. Patrick J. Kennedy (D)

CAPITOL OFFICE
225-4911; fax 225-3290; 407 Cannon Bldg. 20515

INTERNET
e-mail: patrick.kennedy@mail.house.gov
web: www.house.gov/patrickkennedy

COMMITTEES
Appropriations

HOMETOWN
Providence

BORN
July 14, 1967, Brighton, Mass.

RELIGION
Roman Catholic

FAMILY
Single

EDUCATION
Providence College, B.A. 1991

CAREER
Public official

POLITICAL HIGHLIGHTS
R.I. House, 1989-95

ELECTION RESULTS

2000 GENERAL

Patrick J. Kennedy (D)	123,442	66.7%
Steve Cabral (R)	61,522	33.3%

2000 PRIMARY

Patrick J. Kennedy (D)	unopposed

1998 GENERAL

Patrick J. Kennedy (D)	92,788	66.8%
Ronald G. Santa (R)	38,460	27.7%
James C. Sheehan (REF)	6,202	4.5%

PREVIOUS WINNING PERCENTAGES
1996 (69%); 1994 (54%)

Elected 1994; 4th term

The famous Kennedy name has been both a blessing and a curse for the youngest member of the political dynasty now serving in Congress.

At the start of his third term in 1999, at the age of 31, Kennedy was appointed as the top fundraiser for House Democrats. As chairman of the Democratic Congressional Campaign Committee (DCCC) during the 2000 election cycle, Kennedy used his name to bring in record amounts of political donations. He more than doubled the amount of money raised from the previous cycle, from $40 million to $100 million. "When we're going around the country, it helps get your calls returned," Kennedy said of his family name.

Kennedy is the son of Sen. Edward M. Kennedy of Massachusetts, cousin of former Rep. Joseph P. Kennedy II, nephew of the late President John F. Kennedy and the late Sen. Robert F. Kennedy, and great-grandson of John Francis Fitzgerald, who represented Massachusetts in the House 100 years ago.

To help raise money for the Democrats during the 2000 elections, Kennedy rewarded big donors with visits to the dynasty's fabled compound in Hyannis Port, Mass., and entertained others at the grand oceanfront mansions of Newport, R.I., that are part of his district. Early in Kennedy's congressional career, his father, noting his son's attractiveness on the fundraising circuit, grumbled in jest, "He's crowding me. I was always measured by my brothers. Now, I'm being measured by my son."

But the younger Kennedy's fundraising success did not help in keeping his name out of the tabloids. He made headlines in March 2000 when he shoved a Los Angeles International Airport security guard after she told him his carry-on bag was too big. The woman filed a battery suit, but the Los Angeles district attorney's office declined to bring charges. Later that year, Kennedy was again in the papers after the Coast Guard was called to take his distraught date off his chartered yacht following an argument. Kennedy's office blamed much of the attention on the famous family name.

After Democrats failed in their bid to capture control of the House in 2000, Kennedy told his leadership he would step down as DCCC chairman, saying he wanted to spend more time back home. For several weeks, House Democratic Leader Richard A. Gephardt tried to change Kennedy's mind, but failed. "I've done my share," Kennedy told The Associated Press. However, even without the official post, he remained active on the fundraising circuit.

After leaving the DCCC, Kennedy won back his seat on the Appropriations Committee. He was appointed to the panel in 1998 but immediately took a leave of absence to chair the campaign committee. Because of the seniority he racked up during his leave of absence, he ranks above nine other Democrats on Appropriations.

Kennedy votes dependably with his party, but he has proven slightly more conservative than his father on some issues, including defense spending and abortion. Defense dollars help fuel the economy of Kennedy's district, which is home to naval facilities in and around Newport that employ about 7,000 people. In 1996, he opposed an effort to freeze defense spending for fiscal 1997 at the prior year's level.

In the 104th and 105th Congresses, Kennedy sided with a majority of Republicans to outlaw a procedure its opponents call "partial birth" abortion. His father and cousin both voted against the ban. But on other matters relating to abortion policy, Kennedy consistently sides with proponents of abortion rights.

In 2000, Kennedy cast a controversial vote to repeal the federal charter of the Boy Scouts of America, a response to the Scouts' ban on homosexuals as troop leaders. He was one of just 12 House members voting in favor of the repeal, and Republicans hoped to use the vote against him in November. But Kennedy easily won a fourth term with 67 percent of the vote.

Kennedy voices the concerns of his generation about the affordability of higher education. He criticized Republicans in the 104th for supporting lower taxes while at the same time proposing cutbacks in student loans. "The Republicans offer a tax cut to the rich and then try to pay for it on the backs of students," he said. In the 105th, Kennedy sponsored legislation to make interest payments on student loans deductible.

Kennedy's experience as an asthmatic placed him in the center of a battle in 1997 over a Food and Drug Administration (FDA) proposal to phase out inhalers used by asthmatics to treat their symptoms. The FDA said it had to take the metered dose inhalers off the market because the chlorofluorocarbons they contain damage the ozone layer. The agency said suitable replacements were available, but Kennedy sharply disputed that fact. He called on a powerful ally — his father — to include language in an FDA overhaul bill to block the agency from taking the action. That language failed to make the final version, but he received assurances from the FDA that the phase-out would not occur until an adequate replacement was available.

Kennedy was at his most fervent during the 1996 debate on repealing a ban on certain semiautomatic assault-style weapons. Taking on House proponents of repeal, a choked-up Kennedy, whose two uncles were killed by assassins, said, "Families like mine know all too well what the damage of weapons can do. All I have to say to you is: you play with the devil, you die with the devil. You will never know what it's like because you don't have someone in your family killed. It's not the person who's killed. It's the whole family that's affected."

His speech provoked an equally heated response from New York Republican Gerald B.H. Solomon. "My wife lives alone five days a week in a rural area of Upstate New York," Solomon shouted. "She has a right to defend herself when I'm not there, son. And don't you ever forget it."

Kennedy got an early start in politics. He moved to Rhode Island to attend Providence College and while still in school, at the age of 21, he was elected to the state's House of Representatives. Six years later, he was elected to Congress, one of just 13 freshman Democrats elected to the House during the 1994 GOP sweep. At 27, he was the youngest person elected to the 104th Congress.

KEY VOTES

2000
Yes	Raise hourly minimum wage by $1 over two years
No	Halt funding for U.S. mission in Kosovo unless European nations pay more
Yes	Provide Medicare benefits to military retirees and their dependents
No	Grant China permanent normal trade status
No	Phase out estate, gift and trust taxes
No	Prohibit implementation of president's national monument designations
No	Approve GOP plan to provide prescription drug coverage for Medicare beneficiaries
Yes	Increase help for poor nations indebted to international financial institutions

1999
Yes	Impose steel import quotas
No	Kill proposal to take aviation trust funds off budget
No	Require background checks on buyers only at gun shows with 10 or more vendors
Yes	Remove barriers among banking, securities and insurance companies
+	Authorize state grants to hire teachers and reduce class size
Yes	Overhaul campaign finance law; ban "soft money" and restrict advocacy advertising
Yes	Approve bipartisan plan to increase rights of patients in managed-care health plans

INTEREST GROUPS

	AFL-CIO	ADA	CCUS	ACU
2000	100%	90%	15%	16%
1999	100%	90%	25%	4%
1998	100%	95%	33%	12%
1997	100%	80%	20%	17%

CQ VOTE STUDIES

	PARTY UNITY		PRESIDENTIAL SUPPORT	
	Support	Oppose	Support	Oppose
2000	97%	3%	81%	19%
1999	96%	4%	78%	22%
1998	91%	9%	79%	21%
1997	94%	6%	77%	23%

RHODE ISLAND 1
East – Part of Providence; Pawtucket; Newport

The 1st occupies the top of Rhode Island, along the Massachusetts border, and then moves south to take in the northeastern part of the capital, Providence, and the Newport and island communities in the southeast. While the district is solidly Democratic, it also has a long-standing independent streak. On May 4, 1776, Rhode Island was the first colony to renounce allegiance to Great Britain and declare independence.

The district's industry is mostly centered in the northern Blackstone Valley. Woonsocket, a manufacturing city, hosts the headquarters of CVS, now the largest drugstore in the nation. The coastal economy south of Providence relies largely on maritime defense, with companies like Raytheon (which makes sonar components for Navy submarines) and a large Naval base and training center, which has been the district's top employer since the 1970s. The district's population has been stagnant since the 1980s.

Democrats dominate the district, getting support from ethnic minorities as well as the area's large Catholic majority. Republicans have made inroads only when Democrats have been weakened by scandal or internal conflict. Some small, wealthy, coastal towns support the GOP, but larger towns lean Democratic.

MAJOR INDUSTRY
Defense, education, manufacturing

MILITARY BASES
Naval Station Newport, 3,299 military, 3,751 civilian (2000)

CITIES
Pawtucket, 67,662; Providence (pt.), 56,023 (1990); East Providence, 47,835; Woonsocket, 41,409; Newport, 24,232

UNUSUAL FEATURES
Providence Mayor Vincent A. "Buddy" Cianci Jr. perhaps the nation's only mayor with his own line of marinara sauce (The Mayor's Own Marinara Sauce); One of the nation's oldest taverns, the White Horse Tavern, opened in Newport before 1673.

Rep. Jim Langevin (D)

CAPITOL OFFICE
225-2735; fax 225-5976; 109 Cannon Bldg. 20515

INTERNET
e-mail: james.langevin@mail.house.gov
web: www.house.gov/langevin

COMMITTEES
Armed Services
Small Business

HOMETOWN
Warwick

BORN
April 22, 1964, Warwick, R.I.

RELIGION
Roman Catholic

FAMILY
Single

EDUCATION
Rhode Island College, B.A. 1990; Harvard U.,
M.P.A. 1994

CAREER
Public official

POLITICAL HIGHLIGHTS
Delegate to R.I. Constitutional Convention, 1986;
R.I. House, 1989-95; R.I. secretary of state, 1995-
2001

ELECTION RESULTS

2000 GENERAL

Jim Langevin (D)	123,805	62.3%
Rodney D. Driver (CFC)	42,625	21.4%
Robert G. Tingle (R)	27,932	14.0%
Dorman J. Hayes Jr. (GREEN)	4,536	2.3%

2000 PRIMARY

Jim Langevin (D)	22,955	47.2%
Kathleen Coyne-McCoy (D)	14,219	29.3%
Angel Taveras (D)	5,803	11.9%
Kevin J. McAllister (D)	5,633	11.6%

Elected 2000; 1st term

Langevin had a boyhood dream to be a police officer. In 1980, when he was 16 years old, Langevin enrolled in a police department cadet program in his hometown of Warwick, R.I. But his life and ambitions changed forever on Aug. 22, 1980, when a police officer's gun accidentally discharged a bullet that struck Langevin in the neck, leaving him paralyzed for life.

The people of Warwick rallied to Langevin's aid. And despite his disability, Langevin (LAN-juh-vin) earned a master's degree in public administration from Harvard and devoted himself to a career in public service.

The result has been a meteoric political career that sent Langevin to Congress with his easy 2000 victory in the 2nd District, a seat that Democratic Rep. Bob Weygand left open to run, unsuccessfully, for the Senate.

Langevin was just 22 when he did a one-year stint in 1986 as a delegate to the state constitutional convention. Two years later he was elected to the state House. In 1994, he won the first of two terms as Rhode Island secretary of state, a position in which he built a reputation as an advocate of greater access to government. He released a scathing report in 1998 that slammed the legislature for repeatedly violating the state's open meetings law. He also was a force behind the state's upgrading of its voting machines.

His concern for Rhode Island's large elderly population, coupled with his own lengthy hospital stay after the gun accident, has made health care a top priority. He backs an incremental approach to universal health care and supports allowing individuals age 55 to 64 to buy into the Medicare program. Like Weygand, Langevin opposes abortion rights and supports gun control.

Langevin may be more fiscally conservative than most Democrats. In the Rhode Island House, he was the author of a law that slowed state spending.

He would like to use federal budget surplus money to reduce the national debt, arguing that interest on the debt eats up hundreds of billions of dollars that could be spent on education and health care.

In the solidly Democratic 2nd District, Langevin's 62 percent easily outpaced, Rodney D. Driver, running on the Conscience for Congress ticket. The GOP candidate, casino supervisor Robert G. Tingle, got only 14 percent.

RHODE ISLAND 2

West – Western Providence; Warwick

Bordering Connecticut on one side and the Narragansett Bay on the other, the 2nd occupies the western half of Rhode Island, covering the upstate rolling hills and most of the metropolitan area around Providence. Washington County, the southernmost part of the district, has beaches and lakes that attract tourists and residents alike. Twelve miles off the southern coast lies Block Island, a scenic vacation spot with more than 365 ponds.

Like many parts of the nation, the 2nd's economy is shifting from manufacturing to service. The change has caused a shift in population, with people leaving Providence for Washington County, attracted by the growing businesses centered in the county's idyllic landscape. As white residents have departed the Providence

area, more blacks and Hispanics have moved in, increasing the city's already Democratic tendency.

The 2nd is home to many working- and middle-class towns, with a substantial union population that votes Democratic. The 2nd has voted for a Republican president only once since the 1980s, when voters supported Ronald Reagan in 1984. Despite that, the district's large Catholic population has made abortion a key issue.

MAJOR INDUSTRY
Defense, tourism, banking

CITIES
Providence (pt.), 104,705 (1990); Warwick, 83,994; Cranston, 75,009; Westerly (unincorporated), 21,605 (1990)

UNUSUAL FEATURES
The first armed conflict of the American Revolution took place in Rhode Island in 1772 when patriots in eight longboats captured and burned two British revenue ships.

SOUTH CAROLINA

Gov. Jim Hodges (D)

First elected: 1998
Length of term: 4 years
Term expires: 1/03
Salary: $106,078
Phone: (803) 734-9400
Hometown: Lancaster
Born: Nov. 19, 1956, Lancaster, S.C.
Religion: Methodist
Family: Wife, Rachel Hodges; two children
Education: Davidson College, attended; U. of South Carolina, B.S. 1979; J.D. 1982
Career: Lawyer
Political highlights: Lancaster County attorney, 1983-86; Lancaster County Democratic Committee vice chairman, 1986; S.C. House, 1987-99 (minority leader, 1995-99)
Election results:

1998 GENERAL		
Jim Hodges (D)	570,070	53.2%
David Beasley (R)	484,088	45.2%

Lt. Gov. Bob Peeler (R)

First elected: 1994
Length of term: 4 years
Term expires: 1/03
Salary: $46,545 (accepts $44,736)
Phone: (803) 734-2080

STATE LEGISLATURE

General Assembly: Meets January-June
House: 124 members, 2-year terms
2001 breakdown: 70R, 54D; 109 men, 15 women
Salary: $10,400/year, $95/day in session, $1,000/month expenses
Phone: (803) 734-2010
Senate: 46 members, 4-year terms
2001 breakdown: 24R, 22D; 44 men, 2 women
Salary: $10,400/year, $95/day in session, $1,000/month expenses
Phone: (803) 212-6200

STATE TERM LIMITS

Governor: 2 consecutive terms
Senate: No
House: No

URBAN STATISTICS

CITY	POPULATION
Columbia	111,821
Charleston	89,063
North Charleston	84,106
Greenville	56,873
Rock Hill	48,474

REGISTERED VOTERS

Voters do not register by party.

POPULATION

2000 population	4,012,012
1990 population	3,486,703
Percent change	+15.1%
Rank among states	26
Median age	34.7
Born in state	68%
Foreign born	1%
Urban/rural	55%/45%
Crime rate	990/100,000
Poverty level	13.7%
Federal workers	29,258
Military	56,340

REAPPORTIONMENT

South Carolina retained its six House seats in reapportionment. The state legislature will draw new district lines in 2001.

MISCELLANEOUS

Web: www.myscgov.com
Capital: Columbia
Land area: 30,111 sq. miles
Rank among states: 40

STATE ELECTION OFFICIAL
(803) 734-9060

DEMOCRATIC HEADQUARTERS
(803) 799-7798

REPUBLICAN HEADQUARTERS
(803) 988-8440

District Statistics

	VOTE FOR PRESIDENT																
	2000			1996			1992										
DIST.	D	R	GREEN	D	R	REF	D	R	I	WHT	BLK	ASIAN	HISP	HOUSEHOLD INCOME	OVER 65+	UNDER 18	COLLEGE EDUCATION
1	38%	60%	2%	37%	56%	6%	33%	53%	14%	78%	20%	1%	1%	$28,765	9%	26%	20%
2	40	58	2	41	54	5	36	52	11	73	25	1	1	$30,693	10	26	24
3	35	63	1	39	54	7	35	52	13	78	21	0	0	$25,693	13	25	14
4	33	64	2	37	56	6	33	55	12	79	20	1	1	$27,703	12	25	18
5	42	56	1	46	47	7	43	45	12	68	31	0	0	$25,215	12	27	13
6	63	36	1	66	30	3	62	31	7	37	62	0	1	$19,189	12	29	12
STATE	**41**	**57**	**1**	**44**	**50**	**6**	**40**	**48**	**12**	**69**	**30**	**1**	**1**	**$28,705**	**11**	**27**	**17**

Sen. Strom Thurmond (R)

CAPITOL OFFICE
224-5972; fax 224-1300; 217 Russell Bldg. 20510

INTERNET
e-mail: senator@thurmond.senate.gov
web: thurmond.senate.gov

COMMITTEES
Armed Services
Judiciary
(Constitution, Federalism & Property Rights -
chairman)
Veterans' Affairs

HOMETOWN
Aiken

BORN
Dec. 5, 1902, Edgefield, S.C.

RELIGION
Baptist

FAMILY
Separated; four children (one deceased)

EDUCATION
Clemson U., B.S. 1923

MILITARY SERVICE
Army Reserve, 1924-41; Army, 1942-46; Army
Reserve, 1947-65

CAREER
Lawyer; teacher

POLITICAL HIGHLIGHTS
Edgefield superintendent of education, 1929-33;
S.C. Senate, 1933-38; S.C. Circuit Court of Appeals,
1938-46; governor, 1947-51; States' Rights nominee
for president, 1948; sought Democratic nomination
for U.S. Senate, 1950

ELECTION RESULTS

1996 GENERAL

Strom Thurmond (R)	619,739	53.4%
Elliott Close (D)	510,810	44.0%

1996 PRIMARY

Strom Thurmond (R)	132,157	60.3%
Harold Worley (R)	65,670	30.1%
Charles E. Thompson (R)	20,188	9.5%

PREVIOUS WINNING PERCENTAGES
1990 (64%); 1984 (67%); 1978 (56%); 1972 (64%);
1966 (62%); 1960 (100%); 1956 Special Election
(100%); 1954 (63%)
* Elected as a Democrat 1956-60

Elected 1954; 7th full term
Did not serve April-November 1956

Ninety-eight years old as the 107th Congress began, Thurmond is the oldest person ever to serve in Congress and the longest-serving member in Senate history. The 107th will be Thurmond's last Congress; should he complete his term, he will be 100 years old when he leaves the Senate. In 1998, he became the second senator in history, behind Democrat Robert C. Byrd of West Virginia, to cast 15,000 votes.

Thurmond's life in the Senate now echoes his early political career as a Southern judge, more ceremonial than substantive. Still, his longevity is remarkable, aided in some measure by his legendary constituent service operation.

But his long tenure in the Senate has not always won accolades. In 1998, some worried conservatives suggested that Thurmond step down in time for South Carolina's outgoing Republican governor to appoint a GOP replacement. The Wall Street Journal and the National Review, both conservative in their editorial policy, called on Thurmond to retire. The Journal editorialized, "It is time for Senator Thurmond to consider the example of [former House Speaker] Newt Gingrich [who resigned] in realizing the moment has come to give his successors an opportunity to carry the country's politics onward."

The conservatives' concern was that Thurmond would not be able to complete his term, which ends in January 2003, affording incoming Democratic Gov. Jim Hodges the power of appointment. (Hodges had defeated incumbent David Beasley in the 1998 election.) Their concern was heightened when the 2000 elections produced a 50-50 partisan split in the Senate. In early 2001, Washington buzzed when Thurmond was hospitalized for exhaustion and he stopped his customary practice of opening each day's session of the Senate.

In early 1999, as he began his 44th year in the Senate, Thurmond handed the chairmanship of the Armed Services Committee over to Republican John W. Warner of Virginia, who told his colleague, "You've been like a big brother to me." Committee members gave the two lawmakers a standing ovation. Thurmond says he was not pressured to give up the post, but that the time had come to give someone else a chance. "If I reach a point where I can't give 100 percent to the job, I'll get out," he said. "Unlike old generals, I do not intend to fade away."

But Thurmond had heard rumblings from his Senate colleagues that they might take away the chairmanship, and so he announced that he would step down from the post at the end of the 105th Congress. "I think the time has come for me to turn the reins of the committee over to the next generation of leadership," he said in 1997.

After leaving the committee chair, Thurmond said he would focus on raising the profile of the largely honorary job of Senate president pro tempore, a position that puts him third in line to succeed the president. By tradition, the post has been held by the senator in the majority party with the longest tenure. The position mainly involves gaveling the Senate into session and receiving formal communications to the chamber.

As president pro tem, Thurmond stood on the Senate dais as the impeachment trial of President Clinton began in early 1999. Thurmond greeted Chief Justice William H. Rehnquist as a phalanx of senators escorted the nation's top jurist into a hushed Senate chamber. Reading from a note card, as he does in virtually all of his public remarks, Thurmond greeted the chief justice and swore him in as presiding officer for the trial of the president.

Aside from his ceremonial duties, Thurmond in the 106th Congress undertook an effort to reverse a new federal rule permitting vintners to put on their wine labels assertions about the possible medical advantages of moderate consumption of wine, including cardiovascular benefits. He blocked several Treasury Department nominations until the Clinton administration promised to revise the labeling rules. The move was in line with Thurmond's long attempt to require tougher health warnings on alcoholic beverage containers and advertisements. Though a champion of this cause for decades, his effort became more intense at the beginning of the 103rd Congress, when his eldest daughter was killed by a drunken driver while crossing a street in Columbia, S.C.

In 2000, Thurmond demonstrated that he still has clout in South Carolina. He was among the members of the state's GOP establishment who helped George W. Bush win a bruising primary that buoyed Bush's bid for the presidency in the wake of a drubbing in the New Hampshire primary. In a recorded call sent out to thousands of Palmetto State voters, Thurmond promised that Bush would "restore integrity to the White House."

In 1948, when Thurmond ran for president on the Dixiecrat ticket, he epitomized the Southern, states' rights, segregationist politician. He holds the record for the longest filibuster in Senate history, 24 hours and 18 minutes, in opposition to 1957 civil rights legislation. He has punctuated his long political career with turns and reversals, but he has always seemed to carry his constituents with him.

After starting out in 1929 as superintendent of education in the town of Edgefield, Thurmond moved up to the state Senate during the Depression. In 1946, after returning from World War II, he was elected governor.

He was in his second year in office when the Democratic National Convention decided to adopt a strong civil rights plank, and Thurmond decided to offer himself as a regional candidate for president on the States' Rights Democratic ticket. He carried South Carolina, Alabama, Mississippi and Louisiana, capturing 39 electoral votes.

Thurmond made a first try for the Senate in 1950 but lost the Democratic primary to incumbent Olin D. Johnston. In 1954, however, he won, becoming the first and, so far, the only politician elected to the Senate as a write-in candidate. Sen. Burnet R. Maybank had died, and the 31-member State Democratic Committee froze Thurmond out by choosing state Sen. Edgar A. Brown. Thurmond focused his campaign on whether "31 men" or the voters should make the decision. He defeated Brown by nearly 60,000 votes with his write-in campaign. True to a 1954 promise, Thurmond resigned in the spring of 1956 and ran for re-election that fall without the benefit of incumbency. No one filed against him — a circumstance that repeated itself in 1960, when he ran for a full six-year term.

In September 1964, Thurmond announced he was joining the GOP because the Democrats were "leading the evolution of our nation to a socialistic dictatorship." He easily won as a Republican two years later. Thurmond has had mostly smooth rides to re-election.

In his bid for a seventh full term in 1996, however, he faced a well-financed Democratic foe in Elliott Close, a real estate developer and textile heir. Spending lavishly from his own pocket, Close called himself a "new conservative" for the next century, and in one of his TV ads, the message on Thurmond was, "It's about time for him to come home." Close criticized the incumbent for refusing to debate, but Thurmond said he didn't want to give his challenger any free publicity. Thurmond came out on top with 53 percent of the vote.

KEY VOTES

2000

Yes Overhaul bankruptcy law and increase minimum wage
Yes Limit fiscal 2001 discretionary spending to $600.3 billion
Yes Override veto on nuclear waste disposal at Yucca Mountain site in Nevada
No   Oppose effort to terminate Kosovo mission
No   Include gender, sexual orientation and disability in federal hate crime protections
Yes Approve GOP plan to restrict use of genetic information by health insurers
Yes Kill amendment delaying implementation of an anti-missile defense system
Yes Cut taxes for married couples
Yes Grant China permanent normal trade status

1999

Yes Remove President Clinton from office for obstruction of justice
Yes Kill amendment authorizing state grants to hire teachers and reduce class size
No   Require criminal background checks for purchases at gun shows
Yes Approve GOP proposal to increase rights of patients in managed-care health plans
Yes Block effort to allow farm and medicine exports to Cuba
No   Allow study of tougher automobile fuel efficiency standards
No   Ratify nuclear weapons testing treaty
No   Prohibit national political parties from collecting "soft money" donations
Yes Remove barriers among banking, securities and insurance companies

INTEREST GROUPS

	AFL-CIO	ADA	CCUS	ACU
2000	0%	0%	86%	100%
1999	22%	0%	76%	100%
1998	0%	0%	94%	76%
1997	14%	5%	80%	96%
1996	0%	5%	92%	95%
1995	0%	0%	100%	96%
1994	13%	5%	80%	96%
1993	10%	10%	82%	83%
1992	25%	10%	100%	89%
1991	25%	10%	70%	90%

CQ VOTE STUDIES

	PARTY UNITY		PRESIDENTIAL SUPPORT	
	Support	Oppose	Support	Oppose
2000	98%	2%	45%	55%
1999	92%	8%	24%	76%
1998	91%	9%	44%	56%
1997	95%	5%	58%	42%
1996	97%	3%	39%	61%
1995	97%	3%	26%	74%
1994	93%	7%	39%	61%
1993	93%	7%	28%	72%
1992	94%	6%	78%	22%
1991	93%	7%	90%	10%

Sen. Ernest F. Hollings (D)

CAPITOL OFFICE
224-6121; fax 224-4293; 125 Russell Bldg. 20510

INTERNET
e-mail: senator@hollings.senate.gov
web: hollings.senate.gov

COMMITTEES
Appropriations
Budget
Commerce, Science & Transportation - ranking member

HOMETOWN
Charleston

BORN
Jan. 1, 1922, Charleston, S.C.

RELIGION
Lutheran

FAMILY
Wife, Rita "Peatsy" Liddy; four children

EDUCATION
The Citadel, B.A. 1942; U. of South Carolina, LL.B. 1947

MILITARY SERVICE
Army, 1942-45

CAREER
Lawyer

POLITICAL HIGHLIGHTS
S.C. House, 1949-55; lieutenant governor, 1955-59; governor, 1959-63; sought Democratic nomination for U.S. Senate, 1962; sought Democratic nomination for president, 1984

ELECTION RESULTS

1998 GENERAL

Ernest F. Hollings (D)	562,791	52.7%
Bob Inglis (R)	488,132	45.7%
Richard T. Quillian (LIBERT)	16,987	1.6%

1998 PRIMARY

Ernest F. Hollings (D)	unopposed

PREVIOUS WINNING PERCENTAGES
1992 (50%); 1986 (63%); 1980 (70%); 1974 (70%); 1968 (62%); 1966 Special Election (51%)

Elected 1966; 6th full term

With his ramrod-straight posture and his rumbling baritone, Hollings sounds and looks like a powerhouse senator from an earlier era. The lawmaker known universally as "Fritz" is a bridge to a time when Southern Democratic legends such as Mississippi's John Stennis and James Eastland ruled the institution. Hollings has served more than a third of a century in the Senate, but he is still the junior senator from his home state, surpassed by the longest-serving senator of all, Republican and fellow South Carolinian Strom Thurmond, who was first elected in 1954.

At times, Hollings' Southern drawl can be utterly incomprehensible. But he can be sharp as a razor in debate, using historical allusions and humor to drive home his points. And in an age when politicians conduct focus panels before they utter a word, Hollings is not afraid to speak his mind.

He holds the top Democratic spot on the Commerce, Justice, State Appropriations Subcommittee. He chaired the Commerce, Science and Transportation Committee from 1987 to 1995 and remains its top-ranking Democrat. He and panel Chairman John McCain, R-Ariz., disagree fundamentally on the major issues before their committee, with McCain favoring sweeping deregulation and free trade and Hollings taking a more cautious stance. McCain was a strong opponent of the 1996 telecommunications overhaul, believing it did not go far enough, while Hollings was one of its architects.

When the two men clash, stalemate sometimes results. That happened in 2000, when Hollings helped quash a bid by McCain and other lawmakers to extend a moratorium on Internet-specific taxes. McCain sided with online businesses that argued taxes could stifle the Internet's growth; Hollings championed states and Main Street retailers, who wanted a deal to give states more authority to collect sales taxes on online purchases.

Hollings describes himself as a champion of trial lawyers and consumers. A former trial lawyer himself, he links his feelings for the underdog to family hardships endured in the Depression, when his father's dry goods store went out of business. "The little people need representation. That's why I've always been for the trial lawyers," Hollings said.

He is also a staunch supporter of efforts to develop new technology and set rules of the road for the Internet, while arguing that high-tech companies must protect consumers and workers. He waged a fierce but futile fight in 1999 against legislation to limit companies' liability for any year 2000 computer problems, calling it a "get out of jail free card."

A key consumer issue for Hollings is Internet privacy. He wants to require online vendors to get a consumer's consent before collecting or sharing personal information. Hollings also favors close oversight of a new law requiring the auto industry to make more disclosures to the government about potential safety problems, in the wake of deaths linked to Ford Explorer sport-utility vehicles and Firestone tires.

A master of debate, Hollings is not shy about standing alone, as he did in 2000, when he cast the only vote against a proposal to raise the visa quota for skilled foreign workers. He called instead for better training and education to fill high-tech jobs domestically. "What we are really facing is a foot race for the high-tech political money," he said. "I am not joining in this charade."

Hollings also opposed the North American Free Trade Agreement in 1993. He argues that trade restrictions have helped South Carolina lure manufacturers such as BMW and Hitachi. In opposing permanent normal trade status for China in 2000, he warned that the United States was trading full-time manufacturing jobs for part-time jobs. "When are we going to sober up and get a competitive trade policy?" he asked.

He has been a prominent player in several important policy debates of his era: poverty, civil rights, the budget deficit, arms control, the defense buildup in the 1980s and the defense retrenchment of the 1990s.

Modern times have brought new issues to the fore, but Hollings has continued to appeal to a cross-section of voters in a state that has become a GOP bastion. If anything, Hollings now seems more of a throwback than Thurmond. While Thurmond has mostly shed his Dixiecrat ways, Hollings remains one of the few old-style white Southern Democrats, progressive on education and civil rights and conservative on fiscal and defense policy.

He advocates paying down the federal debt and opposes using the Social Security trust fund to pay for other programs. He has been associated with some major legislative endeavors aimed at balancing the budget, chief among them the 1985 Gramm-Rudman-Hollings law, which set up a mechanism for automatic spending cuts if deficit targets were not met.

Hollings is a liberal on some social issues. He supports abortion rights and is a strong backer of nutritional programs and public health centers. He opposed the 1993 Brady gun control law but has supported some gun restrictions, including mandatory handgun safety locks. He also advocates a proposal to bar graphic violence in television programs at times when children make up a "substantial portion" of the audience. And he has been a leader in pushing to protect coastal lands.

As an appropriator, Hollings has backed efforts by the Justice Department to pursue a lawsuit against the nation's largest tobacco companies to recoup the federal cost of smoking-related illness, and he has supported federal matching funds for private research into advanced technology.

Despite his deep streak of fiscal conservatism, he proudly plays the old insider game of scoring projects and money for South Carolina. He happily owned up to securing $45 million to bring a BMW plant to South Carolina, saying once the overall budget is set, "ol Fritz" is going to get his share.

On foreign policy, Hollings has questioned the U.S. role in global peacekeeping operations. In 1991, he opposed the use of military force against Iraq, which had just conquered Kuwait. He has advocated a limited national missile defense system and more spending to modernize the military, including the National Guard.

In the heat of battle, Hollings can be intemperate. In his 1998 re-election campaign, he brushed aside a request by his foe, GOP Rep. Bob Inglis, to sign a pledge to run a courteous campaign. He called Inglis a "goddamned skunk" and said he could "kiss my fanny." Such vignettes created the image of Hollings as impolitic and diverted attention from his legislative triumphs. Still, Hollings prevailed by 7 percentage points over Inglis.

A former Army captain who won a Bronze Star in World War II, Hollings won election to the South Carolina House in 1948 when he was 26; a decade later, he won election as governor. As a candidate in the late 1950s, Hollings firmly espoused states' rights and condemned school integration. But as governor, he quietly integrated the public schools.

In 1962, he challenged Democratic Sen. Olin D. Johnston and lost. Johnston died in 1965, however, and Democratic Gov. Donald Russell appointed himself to the seat. In 1966, Hollings ousted Russell in the special primary to finish Johnston's term. He won a full term two years later and rolled over weak opponents in 1974, 1980 and 1986. In 1992, former GOP Rep. Thomas F. Hartnett portrayed him as an arrogant, entrenched incumbent, but Hollings won with 50 percent, 3 points ahead of Hartnett.

KEY VOTES

2000

Yes   Overhaul bankruptcy law and increase minimum wage

No   Limit fiscal 2001 discretionary spending to $600.3 billion

Yes   Override veto on nuclear waste disposal at Yucca Mountain site in Nevada

No   Oppose effort to terminate Kosovo mission

Yes   Include gender, sexual orientation and disability in federal hate crime protections

No   Approve GOP plan to restrict use of genetic information by health insurers

No   Kill amendment delaying implementation of an anti-missile defense system

No   Cut taxes for married couples

No   Grant China permanent normal trade status

1999

No   Remove President Clinton from office for obstruction of justice

No   Kill amendment authorizing state grants to hire teachers and reduce class size

Yes   Require criminal background checks for purchases at gun shows

No   Approve GOP proposal to increase rights of patients in managed-care health plans

No   Block effort to allow farm and medicine exports to Cuba

Yes   Allow study of tougher automobile fuel efficiency standards

Yes   Ratify nuclear weapons testing treaty

Yes   Prohibit national political parties from collecting "soft money" donations

Yes   Remove barriers among banking, securities and insurance companies

INTEREST GROUPS

	AFL-CIO	ADA	CCUS	ACU
2000	88%	85%	33%	20%
1999	100%	85%	27%	12%
1998	29%	55%	71%	33%
1997	83%	75%	20%	8%
1996	57%	70%	46%	20%
1995	75%	75%	37%	35%
1994	71%	50%	40%	22%
1993	91%	55%	27%	42%
1992	50%	35%	60%	63%
1991	75%	55%	40%	62%

CQ VOTE STUDIES

	PARTY UNITY		PRESIDENTIAL SUPPORT	
	Support	Oppose	Support	Oppose
2000	90%	10%	82%	18%
1999	89%	11%	80%	20%
1998	81%	19%	74%	26%
1997	74%	26%	75%	25%
1996	82%	18%	82%	18%
1995	76%	24%	76%	24%
1994	80%	20%	86%	14%
1993	79%	21%	73%	27%
1992	58%	42%	38%	62%
1991	63%	37%	56%	44%

Rep. Henry E. Brown Jr. (R)

CAPITOL OFFICE
225-3176; fax 225-3407
1017 Longworth Bldg. 20515

INTERNET
e-mail: www.house.gov/writerep
web: www.house.gov/henrybrown

COMMITTEES
Budget
Transportation & Infrastructure
Veterans' Affairs

HOMETOWN
Hanahan

BORN
Dec. 20, 1935, Bishopville, S.C.

RELIGION
Baptist

FAMILY
Wife, Billye Brown; three children

EDUCATION
Berkeley High School, graduated 1953

MILITARY SERVICE
S.C. National Guard, 1953-62

CAREER
Grocery chain executive; grocery store data processor; shipyard worker; convenience store employee

POLITICAL HIGHLIGHTS
Hanahan City Council, 1981-85; S.C. House, 1985-2000

ELECTION RESULTS

2000 GENERAL

Henry E. Brown Jr. (R)	139,597	60.3%
Andy Brack (D)	82,622	35.7%
Bill Woolsey (LIBERT)	6,010	2.6%

2000 PRIMARY RUNOFF

Henry E. Brown Jr. (R)	21,631	54.6%
Buck Limehouse (R)	17,990	45.4%

2000 PRIMARY

Henry E. Brown Jr. (R)	22,072	43.6%
Buck Limehouse (R)	17,171	33.9%
Van Jenerette (R)	4,269	8.4%
Wheeler Tillman (R)	2,627	5.2%
Michael Seekings (R)	2,470	4.9%
Charlie E. Thompson (R)	1,998	4.0%

Elected 2000; 1st term

Brown's record during 16 years in the state House and his business background as a grocery company executive show that he is conservative — a solid credential for a member from the Republican-leaning 1st District.

Brown won the 2000 race to succeed Republican Rep. Mark Sanford, who had limited himself to three terms, on a platform that included ardent advocacy for tax cuts, opposition to increasing the federal minimum wage and support for a prescription drug benefit program based in the private sector.

Yet Brown — who at age 65 when sworn in is the oldest member of the House Class of 2000 — is a seasoned lawmaker with a pragmatic streak. Noting the near-even division of Republicans and Democrats in the House, he told Dow Jones News Service, "It's too close to get caught up in partisanship." Brown had a reputation for working across party lines as the first Republican chairman of the South Carolina House Ways and Means Committee in more than 100 years.

Brown told voters in 2000 that his experience in business and his budget work as a legislator would help him expand local economic prosperity in his role as a congressman. He can put his conservative fiscal beliefs to work with his assignment to the Budget Committee, while he also watches out for the interests of the port of Charleston — a mainstay of his home region's economy — on the Transportation and Infrastructure Committee.

A one-time shipyard worker, Brown worked his way up from data processor to the top rungs of the Piggly Wiggly grocery chain. He began his political career on the Hanahan City Council and in 1984 won the state legislative seat that he would keep until his election to Congress.

Running against five opponents in the 2000 GOP primary, Brown drew attention to his name by mailing 20,000 O'Henry candy bars to voters. He finished first in the primary and took 55 percent of the vote to defeat former state transportation official Buck Limehouse in the GOP runoff two weeks later. Although Democrats nominated a credible candidate in Internet entrepreneur Andy Brack — a longtime aide to Democratic Sen. Ernest F. Hollings — Brown coasted to a 60 percent victory.

SOUTH CAROLINA 1

East – Part of Charleston; Myrtle Beach

Encompassing the northeastern half of the state's coastline, the 1st is marked by two of South Carolina's landmark tourism cities, Charleston and Myrtle Beach.

Once a hub for military installations, defense downsizing hit Charleston with a vengeance in the early 1990s. But the city has since shifted its economy to manufacturing, shipping and health care, and the closed Charleston Naval Base has been redeveloped and now supports about 4,000 jobs. Myrtle Beach's economy is less diverse but no less thriving. The tourist resort welcomes 13 million visitors a year, fueling the growth of restaurants, motels, golf courses, marinas and vacation resorts.

Charleston is an icon of the New South but retains its traditional, conservative base.

Surrounded by reminders of antebellum history, the city is nicknamed the "Holy City" for the church steeples marking its skyline. Myrtle Beach is less traditional. The district's demographics – white, affluent, and suburban – make it predictable Republican territory. An exception is the strong environmental and anti-development sentiment shared by many coastal residents.

MAJOR INDUSTRY
Tourism, shipping, health care

MILITARY BASES
Charleston Air Force Base, 5,290 military, 623 civilian; Charleston Naval Weapons Station, 181 military, 284 civilian (1998)

CITIES
North Charleston (pt.), 54,324 (1990); Charleston (pt.), 47,513 (1990); Mount Pleasant, 44,785; Goose Creek, 28,818; Myrtle Beach, 25,495

UNUSUAL FEATURES
Charleston Harbor home to Fort Sumter, where the Civil War began in April 1861.

Rep. Floyd D. Spence (R)

Elected 1970; 16th term

As Spence wrapped up his six-year stint as head of the Armed Services Committee late in 2000, he gave one more speech in his long series of jeremiads warning that President Clinton was undermining the U.S. military by giving it too many jobs and too few dollars.

"Either we accept our role as the sole global superpower and ... provide our military with the associated necessary resources, or we decline this difficult responsibility," he declared. "Continuing to attempt to fulfill our superpower responsibilities on the cheap is simply no longer an option."

There has been an undertone of frustrated resignation to Spence's crusade for higher defense budgets: In the mid-1990s, GOP budget-cutters were nearly as big an obstacle as were Clinton and liberal Democrats, and Spence believed that the Clinton administration had lulled the public into a false sense of national security.

In the 107th Congress, Spence, who gave up the full committee chairmanship due to GOP-imposed term limits, took the gavel of the panel's Military Procurement Subcommittee. As he settles into his new, less influential post, Spence can take some credit for having reshaped the political debate on defense in a way that gives his side the upper hand. By doggedly highlighting concrete problems faced by forces in the field with an earnest ferocity that belied his amiable demeanor, and by setting the stage for acknowledged experts to make the case, Spence gave the pro-defense forces on Capitol Hill powerful political momentum.

Though a reliable Pentagon supporter, Spence had climbed to the top of Armed Services' GOP ranks without establishing a very high profile. This was due, in part, to a devastating illness that slowed him in the mid-1980s. Though an athlete in his youth, by his late 50s emphysema had so obstructed his breathing that, by early 1988, he had to be rolled into the House chamber in a wheelchair equipped with portable oxygen. In May 1988, Spence became only the fourth person in North America to undergo a complete lung transplant. (Anti-rejection drugs eventually weakened his kidneys so much that he needed a kidney transplant in 2000. The donor was his son, David.)

Spence's 13 years on the House ethics panel also kept him out of the limelight on defense issues, as did the contrast between his low-key style and the flamboyance of Les Aspin of Wisconsin and Ronald V. Dellums of California, the two Democratic Armed Services chairmen with whom he worked as ranking Republican.

But in the months before the 1994 elections, Spence performed what amounted to a dry run for the job he would take on. It was a politically bleak time for traditional defense hawks like Spence. The end of the Cold War left the public apathetic about military affairs. But Spence directed the Armed Services panel's Republican staff to turn up the heat on a reluctant administration. Fanning out to military bases around the country, the aides documented instances of air squadrons grounded, Army training maneuvers canceled and Navy ships left unready. The preparedness problems stressed by Spence's 1994 report, reinforced by a follow-up study in 1997, set the tone for GOP attacks on Clinton's defense spending plans.

Spence began routinely asking military service chiefs to list priority programs left out of Clinton's budget requests. Since most of the money Congress then added to the budget came from these lists, Republicans could frame the issue as a choice between Clinton's judgment and that of the military chiefs.

Spence played a similar role in the debate on national missile defense. Con-

CAPITOL OFFICE
225-2452; fax 225-2455; 2405 Rayburn Bldg. 20515

INTERNET
e-mail: www.house.gov/writerep
web: www.house.gov/spence

COMMITTEES
Armed Services
(Military Procurement - chairman)
Veterans' Affairs

HOMETOWN
Lexington

BORN
April 9, 1928, Columbia, S.C.

RELIGION
Lutheran

FAMILY
Wife, Deborah Williams; four children

EDUCATION
U. of South Carolina, A.B. 1952, LL.B. 1956

MILITARY SERVICE
Naval Reserve, 1947-88

CAREER
Lawyer

POLITICAL HIGHLIGHTS
S.C. House, 1957-63 (served as a Democrat);
Republican nominee for U.S. House, 1962; S.C.
Senate, 1967-71 (minority leader, 1967-71)

ELECTION RESULTS

2000 GENERAL

Floyd D. Spence (R)	154,338	57.0%
Jane Frederick (D)	110,672	40.8%
Timothy Moultrie (LIBERT)	3,622	1.3%

2000 PRIMARY

Floyd D. Spence (R)	unopposed

1998 GENERAL

Floyd D. Spence (R)	119,583	57.8%
Jane Frederick (D)	84,864	41.0%
Maurice T. Raiford (NL)	2,276	1.1%

PREVIOUS WINNING PERCENTAGES
1996 (90%); 1994 (100%); 1992 (88%); 1990 (89%);
1988 (53%); 1986 (54%); 1984 (62%); 1982 (59%);
1980 (56%); 1978 (57%); 1976 (58%); 1974 (56%);
1972 (100%); 1970 (53%)

vinced that the public had a false sense of security about the missile threat — buttressed by a 1995 administration report saying the country would face no new missile threats for at least 15 years — Spence added a provision to the 1996 defense authorization bill for a commission to assess the missile threat. Chaired by former, and future, Defense Secretary Donald H. Rumsfeld, the commission reported in July 1998 that the United States might face a missile threat from North Korea and other hostile regimes within five years. The report gave a huge boost to missile defense proponents in Congress.

Spence repeatedly accused the Clinton administration of undermining the Energy Department's ability to maintain and modernize the U.S. nuclear stockpile. In 1997, he collaborated with Dellums to tighten restrictions on the export of super-computers that might help Russia and China develop nuclear weapons. In 1998, he and other Republicans pushed legislation aimed at barring the export of U.S.-built space satellites to China for launch. And he has tried to keep a tight rein on U.S. aid intended to help Russia dispose of nuclear, chemical and biological weapons, warning that the program might facilitate Russian weapons development efforts.

Spence makes sure the defense bills he writes take care of his district, which has three major bases as well as the Energy Department's Savannah River Site, a nuclear material production facility that is South Carolina's largest industrial employer.

Outside the defense arena, Spence is an old-style, conservative Southern Republican. He has supported a ban on a procedure its opponents call "partial birth" abortion, voted against a measure to grant the president fast-track authority to negotiate trade agreements Congress cannot amend, and backed a constitutional amendment to grant individuals the right to express their religious beliefs on public property.

A star athlete at the University of South Carolina, Spence later practiced law and in 1957 won a state House seat as a Democrat. He switched parties in 1962, saying the Democratic Party was too liberal. Spence was first elected to the House in 1970, stressing his opposition to the U.S. Supreme Court's busing decisions and collecting 53 percent of the vote.

In 1998, running for his 15th term, Spence encountered a serious challenge from Democrat Jane Frederick, an architect and mother of two, who blasted Spence for opposing the Family and Medical Leave Act. Spence won with 58 percent. Frederick tried again in 2000 when Spence's need for a kidney transplant highlighted the 72-year-old incumbent's history of medical problems. But there was no sign during the campaign that the operation slowed him down or cut into his support.

KEY VOTES

2000

? Raise hourly minimum wage by $1 over two years

Yes Halt funding for U.S. mission in Kosovo unless European nations pay more

Yes Provide Medicare benefits to military retirees and their dependents

No Grant China permanent normal trade status

Yes Phase out estate, gift and trust taxes

Yes Prohibit implementation of president's national monument designations

Yes Approve GOP plan to provide prescription drug coverage for Medicare beneficiaries

No Increase help for poor nations indebted to international financial institutions

1999

No Impose steel import quotas

No Kill proposal to take aviation trust funds off budget

Yes Require background checks on buyers only at gun shows with 10 or more vendors

Yes Remove barriers among banking, securities and insurance companies

No Authorize state grants to hire teachers and reduce class size

No Overhaul campaign finance law; ban "soft money" and restrict advocacy advertising

Yes Approve bipartisan plan to increase rights of patients in managed-care health plans

INTEREST GROUPS

	AFL-CIO	ADA	CCUS	ACU
2000	13%	5%	93%	85%
1999	33%	10%	80%	88%
1998	10%	5%	78%	100%
1997	0%	0%	90%	88%

CQ VOTE STUDIES

	PARTY UNITY		PRESIDENTIAL SUPPORT	
	Support	Oppose	Support	Oppose
2000	95%	5%	19%	81%
1999	93%	7%	22%	78%
1998	95%	5%	18%	82%
1997	97%	3%	27%	73%

SOUTH CAROLINA 2

Central and South — Columbia suburbs; Hilton Head

The oddly shaped 2nd winds from the state capital of Columbia down through the middle of the state to a sandy stretch along the coast. The two ends of the district encapsulate some of the state's wealthiest communities: the suburbs of Columbia (in Richland and Lexington counties) and Beaufort and Hilton Head Island on the southern tip.

Columbia's suburbs grew steadily in the 1990s. While state and local government are still the city's largest employers, its private sector is becoming more of a force. At the southern end of the 2nd, retirees and tourists are drawn to Hilton Head Island, which grew more than 30 percent in the 1990s. Just up the shore from the swanky resorts, recruits sweat at the Parris Island Marine Corps camp.

The areas between Columbia and Hilton Head are considerably poorer. More than a fourth of Allendale, Hampton and Jasper counties residents live below the poverty line, relying on tenant farming and sharecropping. While this area votes heavily Democratic, overall, the wealth of white-collar professionals in the north and south pushes the 2nd firmly into the Republican column. Even in the less well-off suburbs, the blue-collar working class retains socially conservative roots.

MAJOR INDUSTRY
Tourism, government, military, agriculture

MILITARY BASES
Fort Jackson (Army), 5,706 military, 2,009 civilian; Marine Corps Recruitment Depot (Parris Island), 2,041 military, 785 civilian (1999); Beaufort Marine Corps Air Station, 3,462 military, 692 civilian (1999)

CITIES
Columbia (pt.), 53,117 (1990); Hilton Head Island, 31,181; St. Andrews (unincorporated), 25,692 (1990)

UNUSUAL FEATURES
The first federally authorized black unit to fight for the Union, the First South Carolina Volunteers, camped in Beaufort; Hilton Head Island, site of the largest naval engagement of the Civil War.

Rep. Lindsey Graham (R)

Elected 1994; 4th term

Graham is a straight-talking, independent sort, who moves aggressively along his own path regardless of the direction signs posted by his party leadership.

In the early months of the 2000 presidential election campaign, Graham took a high-profile position by supporting Arizona Sen. John McCain instead of backing his party's front-runner, Texas Gov. George W. Bush. Graham became one of McCain's most ardent and quoted supporters, despite the fact that the South Carolina Republican Party establishment was behind Bush.

"They're trying to divide the party," Carroll Campbell, former South Carolina GOP governor and Bush supporter, complained to The Washington Post. "They're the hot Young Turks; they want to run things now," he said of Graham and the other conservatives who flooded the House in 1994. But Graham is not likely to alienate the state party establishment further, as he has decided to run for Sen. Strom Thurmond's seat in 2002 when the South Carolina Republican icon retires.

Graham came to Washington as part of the rebel GOP Class of 1994, a large bloc of conservatives who vowed to change the way business was conducted in the nation's capital and who helped the Republicans win control of the House for the first time in 40 years. But he says three terms in office have matured his thinking. "I'm a practical conservative now," Graham told The New York Times in 2000. "I'll vote for bills that I wouldn't have voted for two years ago."

That does not mean he has completely given up on challenging his party. Graham was one of just 21 Republicans who signed on to Democratic-backed legislation to broaden regulation of managed-care health plans in 1999. And he was one of two Judiciary Committee Republicans who voted against a GOP bill to set up a federal system to compensate those who have been exposed to asbestos, a measure opponents argued was an attempt to provide a government bailout for asbestos companies.

Graham hews to a strict conservatism, wavering only rarely. He opposes abortion. He voted to repeal the ban on certain semiautomatic assault-style weapons. He favors amending the Constitution to outlaw flag desecration. He opposes federal funding of the National Endowment for the Arts, calling it an "elitist organization out of touch with the American people."

True to his conservative leanings, Graham typically seeks to limit the scope of the federal government, but in one area he is a proponent of increased spending. During debate in 1998 on the annual defense authorization bill, Graham fought to require the Energy Department to produce tritium — a radioactive form of hydrogen gas that is a critical element of nuclear warheads — at the Savannah River nuclear complex in his district. He was defeated not by fiscal conservatives but by the efforts of Alabama Republican Sen. Jeff Sessions, who wanted the multibillion-dollar project to go to an Alabama nuclear reactor run by the Tennessee Valley Authority, the site eventually chosen.

Graham has been front and center on many of the more dramatic events in the House. In the six months that President Clinton's impeachment preoccupied Capitol Hill and the nation's media, Graham became a fixture on the television news programs that provided coverage of the controversy. Even the status of his love life became fodder for gossip columnists eager to cash in on public curiosity about the blue-eyed bachelor with boyish charm.

Graham was a central figure in the proceedings, and he annoyed many

CAPITOL OFFICE
225-5301; fax 225-3216
1429 Longworth Bldg. 20515

INTERNET
e-mail: www.house.gov/writerep
web: www.house.gov/graham

COMMITTEES
Armed Services
Education & Workforce
Judiciary

HOMETOWN
Seneca

BORN
July 9, 1955, Seneca, S.C.

RELIGION
Southern Baptist

FAMILY
Single

EDUCATION
U. of South Carolina, B.A. 1977, attended 1977-78, J.D. 1981

MILITARY SERVICE
Air Force, 1982-88, 1990; S.C. Air National Guard, 1989-94; Air Force Reserve, 1995-present

CAREER
Lawyer

POLITICAL HIGHLIGHTS
S.C. House, 1993-95

ELECTION RESULTS

2000 GENERAL
Lindsey Graham (R)	150,176	67.8%
George Brightharp (D, UC)	67,174	30.3%
Adrian Banks (LIBERT)	3,116	1.4%

2000 PRIMARY
Lindsey Graham (R)	unopposed

1998 GENERAL
Lindsey Graham (R)	unopposed

PREVIOUS WINNING PERCENTAGES
1996 (60%); 1994 (60%)

in his party by suggesting early on that Clinton's offenses might not rise to the level of impeachment. "Is this Watergate or Peyton Place?" was his question. But Graham became persuaded that Clinton did deserve to be impeached. He was one of the 13 House Republicans in 1999 who presented the case against Clinton to the Senate, though he was lower in seniority than most members of the Judiciary Committee.

Graham knows that Clinton's impeachment will forever be part of his story, no matter what else happens. "I don't want to be remembered as the impeachment boy. That shortchanges who I am," Graham told The New York Times in 2000. "I know that the first line of my obituary is going to be that. Bill Clinton's obituary will mention it, too. I'm no more happy about it than he is."

Graham also was one of the leaders of the 1997 abortive coup against Speaker Newt Gingrich. Graham became de facto leader of the coup attempt against Gingrich the way leaders often do: He was the one who took the initiative to gather together Republican dissidents to air grievances and discuss removing Gingrich as Speaker because of concerns that he was compromising with the Democratic White House too much. When word of the insurrection reached Gingrich, other top GOP leaders — some of whom had participated in Graham's group — denied they had supported an uprising, and the coup fizzled.

Yet the affair did not make Graham a pariah in the party, perhaps because many in the GOP harbored reservations about whether Gingrich was an effective leader. Also, Graham humbly admitted that his involvement in the intrigue had taught him a thing or two about the difficulty of leading the GOP majority. "I understand a little bit more about the dynamics that he faced," he acknowledged in 1998. "This is a hard crowd to manage on a good day."

Despite his youthful appearance and aw-shucks manner, Graham is no greenhorn. He holds two academic degrees and studied for a third, worked for two years in the legal office of Shaw Air Force Base in Sumter, S.C., and then was a chief prosecutor for the Air Force in Europe for four years. As a member of the Air National Guard, he was called to active duty and served as a military lawyer during the 1991 Persian Gulf War.

In 1992, he won a seat in the state House and stayed one term. He saw an opportunity for advancement early in 1994, when 10-term Democratic Rep. Butler Derrick decided to retire. Graham won easily that fall, beating Democratic state Sen. James Bryan with 60 percent of the vote. He earned the same tally in 1996 against Democratic lawyer Debbie Dorn, was unopposed in 1998, and won with 68 percent in 2000.

KEY VOTES

2000

No Raise hourly minimum wage by $1 over two years
Yes Halt funding for U.S. mission in Kosovo unless European nations pay more
Yes Provide Medicare benefits to military retirees and their dependents
No Grant China permanent normal trade status
Yes Phase out estate, gift and trust taxes
Yes Prohibit implementation of president's national monument designations
Yes Approve GOP plan to provide prescription drug coverage for Medicare beneficiaries
No Increase help for poor nations indebted to international financial institutions

1999

Yes Impose steel import quotas
Yes Kill proposal to take aviation trust funds off budget
Yes Require background checks on buyers only at gun shows with 10 or more vendors
Yes Remove barriers among banking, securities and insurance companies
No Authorize state grants to hire teachers and reduce class size
Yes Overhaul campaign finance law; ban "soft money" and restrict advocacy advertising
Yes Approve bipartisan plan to increase rights of patients in managed-care health plans

INTEREST GROUPS

	AFL-CIO	ADA	CCUS	ACU
2000	10%	5%	70%	100%
1999	56%	20%	50%	88%
1998	10%	15%	76%	88%
1997	0%	5%	90%	92%

CQ VOTE STUDIES

	PARTY UNITY		PRESIDENTIAL SUPPORT	
	Support	Oppose	Support	Oppose
2000	98%	2%	17%	83%
1999	89%	11%	18%	82%
1998	92%	8%	22%	78%
1997	95%	5%	25%	75%

SOUTH CAROLINA 3
West — Anderson; Aiken

Encompassing the northwestern corner of the state, the 3rd is one of South Carolina's most uniform and rural districts. Many voters in this area are converts to the Republican Party, having shifted over from "Yellow Dog" Democrat status. Rep. Graham is the first Republican to hold this seat since Reconstruction. Local races are competitive, ultimately turning into a battle between the socially conservative, pro-business candidates of both parties. Most communities enjoy a reputation as homes of old-fashioned Southern gentility.

The brimming economy has further boosted opportunities for the GOP. The base of engineers surrounding the Savannah River Nuclear Complex in Aiken, the district's largest employer, has helped attract Fortune 500 firms to the area, as well as several U.S. divisions of international companies. To the northwest, Anderson has built a more industrial economy, moving away from its rural roots. Many area textile mills have successfully shifted to high-tech fiber

manufacturing. Clemson University provides the economic and social nexus for Pickens County at the 3rd's northern tip.

The district is solidly Republican at the federal level, although it still elects a few Democrats locally. The 3rd's most populous voting jurisdictions — Anderson, Aiken and Pickens counties — are heavily Republican. Pickens County gave President Bush 71 percent of its vote in 2000. Counties in the 3rd's midsection are more rural, less prosperous, and less Republican-leaning. This area includes McCormick County, where the majority of the population is black.

MAJOR INDUSTRY
Manufacturing, textiles, cotton

CITIES
Anderson, 26,166; Greenwood, 19,278; Easley, 17,998; Aiken (pt.), 16,461 (1990); North Augusta, 16,369

UNUSUAL FEATURES
The 70,000-acre Lake Thurmond (previously known as Clarks Hill Lake, renamed after Republican Sen. Strom Thurmond); In Anderson, Clarks Schwabel produces the radar-invisible "skin" of F-117 Stealth Fighters; Aiken known as the polo center of the South.

Rep. Jim DeMint (R)

CAPITOL OFFICE
225-6030; fax 226-1177; 504 Cannon Bldg. 20515

INTERNET
e-mail: www.house.gov/writerep
web: www.demint.house.gov

COMMITTEES
Education & Workforce
Small Business
  (Workforce, Empowerment & Government
  Programs - chairman)
Transportation & Infrastructure

HOMETOWN
Greenville

BORN
Sept. 2, 1951, Greenville, S.C.

RELIGION
Presbyterian

FAMILY
Wife, Debbie DeMint; four children

EDUCATION
U. of Tennessee, B.S. 1973; Clemson U., M.B.A. 1981

CAREER
Market research company owner

POLITICAL HIGHLIGHTS
No previous office

ELECTION RESULTS

2000 GENERAL

Jim DeMint (R)	150,436	79.6%
Ted Adams (CNSTP)	16,532	8.7%
April Bishop (LIBERT)	12,757	6.8%
Peter J. Ashy (REF, UC)	6,210	3.3%
C. Faye Walters (NL)	2,640	1.4%

2000 PRIMARY

Jim DeMint (R)	41,851	77.3%
Frank Delano Raddish (R)	12,279	22.7%

1998 GENERAL

Jim DeMint (R)	105,264	57.7%
Glenn Gilbert Reese (D)	73,314	40.2%
C. Faye Walters (NL)	1,988	1.1%

Elected 1998; 2nd term

As much as any member, DeMint exemplifies a new brand of conservatism among House Republicans. While he tends to vote with social conservatives on such issues as abortion and school vouchers, he does not like to take a high profile on these stands and prefers to accent his positions on economic issues. His favorite subjects are small government, low taxes, free trade and the infusion of jobs into his western South Carolina district.

The owner of a Greenville market research firm, DeMint (da-MENT) became an expert in positioning a product in a crowded marketplace — be it motor oil or St. Pauli Girl beer. DeMint turned his talent to the political arena after meeting Bob Inglis, who was gearing up for a run for the House in 1992. The two hit it off, and DeMint, looking for a new challenge, became an unpaid adviser to Inglis, also a political neophyte. The campaign was successful.

Six years later, when Inglis left the House for what proved to be an unsuccessful bid for the Senate, DeMint won the 4th District seat for himself. DeMint recalls that until meeting Inglis he had no interest in politics other than a general frustration with government. But, he told The Associated Press, working with Inglis "allowed me to see that mortal people can do this job."

DeMint's marketing background has served him well in Washington. He focused much of his early attention on marketing GOP ideas, as freshman class president and as a member of working groups aiming to hone the Republican message. He is an effective speaker who chooses his words carefully and is a great proponent of staying on point. He produced a concise list of Republican themes on a laminated card and distributed it to his colleagues to help them spread the GOP message, "secure the future."

He argues that what the Republican Party needs are spokesmen who "can take the Republican message and communicate it persuasively to swing voters — someone who can say Republicans have a heart and soul, as well as good logic."

In the 107th Congress, with a Republican in the White House, DeMint says that GOP conservatives can project a positive image. "We found ourselves in the Clinton administration always being against something. ... That put us in a position on the sidelines always saying, 'No, no, no.' ... Our greatest accomplishment was minimizing the damage."

DeMint's politics can be described in four words: smaller government, lower taxes. "I'm under the umbrella of individual freedom," he says. "Too much of our money and power has been taken out of the hands of the individual and moved to Washington." He expresses concern that the more citizens come to depend on federal programs, the closer the country will move toward a "socialistic state." "Reliance on government takes away personal freedom," he argues.

He is an advocate of fairly substantial changes to entitlement programs such as Social Security and Medicare. He backs individual Social Security investment accounts and personal medical savings accounts. He also wants to scrap the income tax in favor of a national sales tax.

He sometimes takes a libertarian tone. During his 1998 campaign, DeMint asked: "When government takes half of what you earn, runs your schools, owns your retirement plan and controls health care ... are you really free?"

DeMint is viewed with some suspicion back home. Social conservatives see him as a "country club" Republican, while the district's more moderate and liberal constituents consider his anti-tax and anti-Washington positions to be stereotypical right-wing dogma.

This dichotomy reflects the political realities of his district, which is changing dramatically as the result of a growing manufacturing base. Social conservatism runs deep in the 4th, which is squarely in the Bible Belt and home to Bob Jones University, a bastion of evangelicalism. Yet the centerpiece of the district's economy, a sprawling BMW plant outside Spartanburg, manufactures some of the most prized symbols of upward mobility, particularly the trendy Z3 roadster and the X5 sport utility vehicle. Interstate 85, linking Greenville and Spartanburg, is sometimes referred to as the "autobahn."

The district is also home to the remnants of a textile industry, which takes a position on international trade that is considerably different from BMW's. BMW and the other new plants generally favor free-trade policies, unlike the textile industry. DeMint has had to walk a fine line on the trade issue, but he has made his free-trade proclivities clear.

In the 107th Congress, DeMint chairs the Small Business panel's Workforce, Benefits and Empowerment Subcommittee, which focuses on helping small businesses attract and retain top-quality workers.

He has taken some positions designed to distinguish himself from run-of-the-mill pro-business conservatives and to underscore his standing as a citizen legislator. He has vowed to retire after three terms, a stance that was fairly common at the height of the term limits movement in 1994 but that made him stand out somewhat in 1998. In the 106th Congress, he co-founded the Citizen Legislators Caucus, made up of lawmakers who have agreed to limit their terms voluntarily. He told The Associated Press that the group hoped to keep the notion alive, but "not to be negative about all those who don't limit their terms."

DeMint meets weekly in an interdenominational Bible study group of about 10 men, a practice he's followed for more than 20 years. He says he relies on those meetings to keep him focused on matters that are larger than he is.

In an odd twist, DeMint was first elected in part by subtly running against religious conservatives. The standard-bearers of the right, such as the Christian Coalition and the Family Research Council, lined up behind DeMint's main opponent in the primary, state Sen. Mike Fair. But DeMint won by uniting Republicans who thought Fair was a bit too strident, even for a conservative district like South Carolina's 4th. In his second election, in 2000, DeMint easily turned back a primary challenge and had no Democratic foe in November.

KEY VOTES

2000

No Raise hourly minimum wage by $1 over two years

Yes Halt funding for U.S. mission in Kosovo unless European nations pay more

Yes Provide Medicare benefits to military retirees and their dependents

Yes Grant China permanent normal trade status

Yes Phase out estate, gift and trust taxes

Yes Prohibit implementation of president's national monument designations

Yes Approve GOP plan to provide prescription drug coverage for Medicare beneficiaries

No Increase help for poor nations indebted to international financial institutions

1999

No Impose steel import quotas

No Kill proposal to take aviation trust funds off budget

Yes Require background checks on buyers only at gun shows with 10 or more vendors

Yes Remove barriers among banking, securities and insurance companies

No Authorize state grants to hire teachers and reduce class size

No Overhaul campaign finance law; ban "soft money" and restrict advocacy advertising

No Approve bipartisan plan to increase rights of patients in managed-care health plans

INTEREST GROUPS

	AFL-CIO	ADA	CCUS	ACU
2000	0%	0%	90%	100%
1999	11%	0%	92%	91%

CQ VOTE STUDIES

	PARTY UNITY		PRESIDENTIAL SUPPORT	
	Support	Oppose	Support	Oppose
2000	98%	2%	22%	78%
1999	97%	3%	11%	89%

SOUTH CAROLINA 4
Northwest – Greenville; Spartanburg

Located in northwestern South Carolina, the 4th is centered on Greenville County, the state's most populous. Successful manufacturing and warehousing ventures have transformed the area from its textile past of 30 years ago. Greenville now claims to have more engineers per capita than any other county in the nation.

Similar patterns of economic growth have helped Spartanburg to the northeast. More than 90 international firms have located in the city. The best-known example is BMW, which began production in 1994 at its first North American assembly plant in Spartanburg, now the sole producer of the Z3 Roadster. Agriculture also plays a role in the Spartanburg area; its sprawling orchards yield one of the biggest peach crops in the South.

Spreading wealth has helped keep this district solidly Republican. But the local GOP has two distinct camps: mainstream, business-oriented conservatives and intensely conservative Christian fundamentalists

focused around Greenville-based Bob Jones University. President Bush sparked a controversy during the 2000 campaign when he spoke at the school, which banned interracial dating at the time.

With its rank-and-file textile workers and farm laborers, Spartanburg is less heavily Republican than Greenville. While surrounding Spartanburg County has developed a Democratic-leaning base with its German, Swiss, Japanese, Indian and British immigrants, many still opt for the GOP.

MAJOR INDUSTRY
Engineering, manufacturing, textiles

CITIES
Greenville, 56,873; Spartanburg, 40,704; Wade Hampton (unincorporated), 20,014 (1990); Greer, 15,222

UNUSUAL FEATURES
Cowpens National Battlefield, near Chesnee, where in 1781 American forces outwitted a larger British contingent by passing around both flanks at the same time, the first and only time the double envelopment maneuver had been successfully executed on American soil; Vietnam War Gen. William C. Westmoreland born in Spartanburg County.

Rep. John M. Spratt Jr. (D)

Elected 1982; 10th term

CAPITOL OFFICE
225-5501; fax 225-0464
1536 Longworth Bldg. 20515

INTERNET
e-mail: john.spratt@mail.house.gov
web: www.house.gov/spratt

COMMITTEES
Armed Services
Budget - ranking member

HOMETOWN
York

BORN
Nov. 1, 1942, Charlotte, N.C.

RELIGION
Presbyterian

FAMILY
Wife, Jane Stacy; three children

EDUCATION
Davidson College, A.B. 1964; Oxford U., M.A. 1966;
Yale U., LL.B. 1969

MILITARY SERVICE
Army, 1969-71

CAREER
Lawyer; community bank executive; insurance
agency owner; farmer

POLITICAL HIGHLIGHTS
No previous office

ELECTION RESULTS

2000 GENERAL

John M. Spratt Jr. (D)	126,877	58.8%
Carl Gullick (R)	85,247	39.5%
Tom Campbell (LIBERT)	3,665	1.7%

2000 PRIMARY

John M. Spratt Jr. (D)	unopposed

1998 GENERAL

John M. Spratt Jr. (D)	95,696	58.0%
Mike Burkhold Jr. (R)	66,367	40.2%
Dianne Nevins (NL)	2,765	1.7%

PREVIOUS WINNING PERCENTAGES
1996 (54%); 1994 (52%); 1992 (61%); 1990 (100%);
1988 (70%); 1986 (100%); 1984 (92%); 1982 (68%)

Spratt is among the most amiable Democrats in Congress, and a battle-tested leader for the party on fiscal matters. He rarely raises his voice or pounds a fist to make a point. And no matter how strongly he might disagree with an opponent, he does not allow anger or partisan fervor to alter his professorial delivery of statistics and history lessons.

Such qualities inevitably helped him when he was a lead negotiator and salesman for the 1997 budget-balancing deal that President Clinton had struck with the congressional leadership. Newly installed as the ranking Democrat on the Budget Committee, Spratt's most important role was to lobby Minority Leader Richard A. Gephardt to help staunch Democrats' opposition to the proposal, which had been worked out primarily between GOP leaders and the Clinton White House. He has called the budget deal "the biggest achievement that I can lay any claim to."

After that, Spratt continued to serve as a point man in Congress for Clinton's budget initiatives. He delivered a speech at the 2000 Democratic National Convention in Los Angeles in which he credited Clinton and Vice President Al Gore with eliminating the deficit and keeping the economy humming.

With a Republican in the White House, Spratt likely will be an increasingly prominent voice for his party on budget issues. At the start of the 107th Congress, he hammered President Bush's proposed plan to cut taxes by $1.6 trillion over the coming decade as an irresponsible commitment of ephemeral resources — money that exists only in the form of uncertain budget surplus projections for the next 10 years.

Former Budget Committee Chairman John R. Kasich, R-Ohio, who retired at the end of the 106th Congress, generally produced partisan budget blueprints despite Spratt's pleas for compromise. In 2000, Spratt's oft-repeated warning that the GOP could never live within its own budget resolution turned out to be on the mark; appropriations shattered the budget's limit of $600.3 billion in discretionary spending authority by $37 billion, or 6 percent.

Spratt says he has a cordial relationship with the Budget panel chairman for the 107th, Republican Jim Nussle of Iowa, who he says will take a "more methodical, more institutional" approach. But Spratt doesn't expect the results to change much. "I'm not deluding myself," he said as the year began. "He's been pleasant, he's been cordial ... but nobody has any illusions about where this leads."

Despite his spirited jousting with Republicans on the Budget Committee, Spratt's fiscal attitude has historically been to the right of many in his party. He supported a constitutional amendment to balance the federal budget in both 1994 and 1995 and got behind the GOP move to enact the 1996 law that gave the president line-item veto power. He even sought, unsuccessfully, to extend the veto power to tax incentives. (The Supreme Court struck down the line-item veto law as unconstitutional in 1998.)

Spratt also sits on the Armed Services Committee, where he has long been an influential moderating force on national security issues, and he remains a heavy-hitter for Democrats when defense takes center stage. He upset Republican plans in the 104th to create a nationwide anti-missile defense system, handing the GOP its first major defeat after the party won control of Congress. But in the 106th, he cosponsored the law, enacted in 1999, calling for deployment of a missile defense system "as soon as is technologically feasible." Spratt said this was acceptable because it required no timetable or other particulars and reduced the risk of antagonizing the Russians.

The South Carolina lawmaker has shown a conservative tilt on some issues outside the defense arena as well, such as his efforts to shield children from unsuitable programming on television. When a more ambitious idea of his — to yank the federal licenses of television stations that aired violent programs during prime viewing hours for children — went nowhere, Spratt cosponsored the 1996 law requiring that most new TV sets come with a "v-chip" to allow parents to block objectionable programming. He is nevertheless a reliable vote for the Democratic leadership on most bread-and-butter social issues.

Spratt has been a leading advocate for the textile industry, which helps fuel the 5th District's economy. He voted for the North American Free Trade Agreement in 1993 after the Clinton administration got the Philippines and some other developing countries to accept a longer phaseout of U.S. quotas limiting textile imports. However, in 2000 he voted against granting China permanent normal trade status.

In 1998, Spratt broke his right arm in two places after slipping on some of the Senate's famous bean soup that had spilled on some steps inside the Capitol. Spratt said he had a cousin who was hiking around the Himalayan mountains at the time when he heard the BBC report: "We have a story about a congressman by the name of Jack Spratt, believe it or not. It seems he could stay away from the fat, but not the bean soup. He slipped in a puddle of it and broke his arm."

Spratt has had to work hard to convince his conservative-leaning constituency that he remains perceptibly to the right of the bulk of House Democrats. With his lofty academic credentials (from Davidson, Oxford and Yale) and his background as a lawyer and community bank president, Spratt is not the obvious choice for a district where many of the Democratic voters come from poor textile towns and dusty farms.

Winning his first House race in 1982 — on the retirement of Democratic Rep. Ken Holland — Spratt persuasively argued that his work with small-town law clients and bank depositors had given him an understanding of their circumstances. He won re-election with ease throughout the 1980s, but in the past decade he has often been targeted for defeat by the national GOP. He survived the Republican sweep of 1994 by a slim, 4 percentage point margin, and his tally has edged up in subsequent ballots; his 59 percent in 2000 gave him a 19-point victory.

KEY VOTES

2000
Yes Raise hourly minimum wage by $1 over two years
No   Halt funding for U.S. mission in Kosovo unless European nations pay more
Yes Provide Medicare benefits to military retirees and their dependents
No   Grant China permanent normal trade status
No   Phase out estate, gift and trust taxes
No   Prohibit implementation of president's national monument designations
No   Approve GOP plan to provide prescription drug coverage for Medicare beneficiaries
Yes Increase help for poor nations indebted to international financial institutions

1999
Yes Impose steel import quotas
Yes Kill proposal to take aviation trust funds off budget
No   Require background checks on buyers only at gun shows with 10 or more vendors
Yes Remove barriers among banking, securities and insurance companies
Yes Authorize state grants to hire teachers and reduce class size
Yes Overhaul campaign finance law; ban "soft money" and restrict advocacy advertising
Yes Approve bipartisan plan to increase rights of patients in managed-care health plans

INTEREST GROUPS

	AFL-CIO	ADA	CCUS	ACU
2000	78%	70%	52%	20%
1999	100%	80%	26%	12%
1998	90%	85%	50%	17%
1997	88%	70%	50%	17%

CQ VOTE STUDIES

	PARTY UNITY		PRESIDENTIAL SUPPORT	
	Support	Oppose	Support	Oppose
2000	82%	18%	59%	41%
1999	82%	18%	74%	26%
1998	81%	19%	73%	27%
1997	83%	17%	73%	27%

SOUTH CAROLINA 5
North Central — Rock Hill

The 5th spans 13 mostly rural counties in the north-central part of the state, stretching from near Charlotte, N.C., to the Columbia suburbs, then spreading east and west. The combination of tobacco farmers, white-collar Charlotte commuters and textile workers makes this a conservative district, still clinging to its traditional Southern Democrat roots.

In the midsection and west, rural counties such as Newberry, Chester, Lancaster and Kershaw produce cotton for the textile mills that historically have dominated this region's economy. The two largest cities, Rock Hill and Sumter, add immigrants from the North. Rock Hill, once dependent on the textile industry, now serves as a home for white-collar commuters and Winthrop University.

The city of Sumter, once the center of a large agricultural area, is now shifting towards industry. Seven miles west of Sumter, Shaw Air Force Base makes up one-third of the area's economy. In the east, residents of Darlington, Dillon and Marlboro counties depend heavily on tobacco farming.

Politically, the district is dominated by poorer, rural, "Yellow Dog" Democrats. Taxes, economic growth and agricultural policies are dominant issues in the 5th, which also has a significant contingent of union workers.

MAJOR INDUSTRY
Cotton, textiles, tobacco

MILITARY BASES
Shaw Air Force Base, 5,209 military, 488 civilian (1999)

CITIES
Rock Hill, 48,474; Sumter (pt.), 27,863 (1990); Gaffney, 13,665

UNUSUAL FEATURES
Lee County Cotton Festival, held every October, celebrates the agricultural history of "King Cotton;" Televangelist Jim Bakker's PTL ministry headquarters were located in Fort Mill.

Rep. James E. Clyburn (D)

Elected 1992; 5th term

CAPITOL OFFICE
225-3315; fax 225-2313; 319 Cannon Bldg. 20515

INTERNET
e-mail: jclyburn@mail.house.gov
web: www.house.gov/clyburn

COMMITTEES
Appropriations

HOMETOWN
Columbia

BORN
July 21, 1940, Sumter, S.C.

RELIGION
African Methodist Episcopal

FAMILY
Wife, Emily England; three children

EDUCATION
South Carolina State College, B.S. 1962

CAREER
State official; teacher

POLITICAL HIGHLIGHTS
S.C. human affairs commissioner, 1974-92; sought
Democratic nomination for S.C. secretary of state,
1978, 1986

ELECTION RESULTS

2000 GENERAL

James E. Clyburn (D)	138,053	71.8%
Vince Ellison (R)	50,005	26.0%
Dianne Nevins (NL)	2,339	1.2%
Lynwood Earl Hines (LIBERT)	1,934	1.0%

2000 PRIMARY

James E. Clyburn (D)	unopposed

1998 GENERAL

James E. Clyburn (D)	116,507	72.6%
Gary McLeod (R)	41,421	25.8%
George C. Taylor (NL)	2,496	1.6%

PREVIOUS WINNING PERCENTAGES
1996 (69%); 1994 (64%); 1992 (65%)

A pragmatist, Clyburn usually works behind the scenes on his priority projects, which include bringing federal dollars home to his district — the poorest in South Carolina and one of the poorest in the nation. From his Appropriations Committee seat, he seeks federal funds to help the 6th District pay for bridges, roads, new water systems, housing, and economic development. He uses his post on the Transportation Appropriations Subcommittee to boost highway funding for all of South Carolina.

In 2000, Clyburn helped broker a deal between President Clinton and Speaker J. Dennis Hastert on a plan to increase investment in low-income and rural areas. During the Clinton years in the White House, Clyburn enlisted the assistance of executive branch officials to highlight particular district needs. Clinton came to the 6th in 1996 to inspect a black church that was one of a number destroyed in a series of fire bombings.

The first black representative elected from South Carolina since 1896 (when his great-uncle, George Washington Murray, served), Clyburn received some help from the start from House Democratic leaders. In his first term, he won a spot on the Transportation and Infrastructure Committee and was named as one of 18 regional whips. He also was president of his freshman class in the second half of the 103rd Congress.

Clyburn generally votes with the liberal wing of his party. He presses for more rights for managed-care patients while criticizing GOP efforts to cut taxes and institute school vouchers. He voted against granting China permanent normal trade status, saying the measure would hurt the "average Joes" in his district unless it was amended to protect the textile industry.

In the 106th Congress, Clyburn served as chairman of the Congressional Black Caucus, and he played a role in negotiating a purchase of Martin Luther King Jr.'s personal papers by the Library of Congress. He also oversaw hearings on police brutality and pressed for appointments of more black judges, especially in the 4th Circuit Court of Appeals, which includes South Carolina. "I would suggest that the principle of judgment by one's peers is seriously impaired" in the 4th Circuit, he said.

But Clyburn can moderate his liberal views. He has voted for a constitutional amendment to ban flag desecration, and in the 104th he supported two Republican-backed constitutional amendments: one to mandate a balanced budget and another to impose congressional term limits.

Clyburn was the state's only member of the Transportation Committee when Congress passed a sweeping transportation bill in the 105th. He was proud to report that the measure authorized a huge increase in spending for the Palmetto State. He was also instrumental in continuing the program that seeks to give 10 percent of construction contracts to disadvantaged businesses. Leapfrogging several more-senior colleagues, Clyburn was named as one of eight House Democratic members who negotiated the final version of the bill with the Senate.

Some critics said the funding increase was the result of unseemly congressional pork-barreling, but Clyburn retorted that many of the projects were directed toward communities like his own, "which have been historically neglected. ... They, [and] I, do not take kindly to efforts to improve their quality of life being labeled pork."

The 6th District is home to a number of historically black colleges, including South Carolina State, and Clyburn has been in the forefront of efforts to obtain federal assistance in restoring and preserving campus buildings, a massive undertaking, according to a General Accounting Office review.

Clyburn also looks out for the small tobacco farmers in his district. He opposed proposals for big increases in the cigarette tax and urged Congress to protect the interests of farmers in any comprehensive tobacco legislation. He acknowledged, "All of us know there's no future in tobacco," but he vowed that "until alternative crops are developed, I feel compelled to advocate fair treatment for ... the affected families, many of whom have little hope for a decent living otherwise."

In 1999, Clyburn stepped down temporarily from Appropriations to make room for New York Rep. Michael P. Forbes, who had been stripped of his Appropriations seat by Republicans after switching to the Democratic Party. Clyburn returned in the 107th after Forbes lost his re-election bid.

An avid golfer (his current handicap is hovering near 11), Clyburn says you can tell a lot about a person by the way he or she plays golf. He told The Hill newspaper, "You watch a guy who takes risks, or a guy who will lay up rather than going for it. ... You can tell whether or not he's timid or aggressive."

When Democratic Gov. John West named him as a special assistant for human resources in 1971, Clyburn, who had taught school and headed the state's Commission for Farm Workers, was the first black to serve as a gubernatorial appointee in the state in more than 70 years. Three years later, he became the state's Human Affairs commissioner, where he earned a reputation as an able conciliator and established close ties with those in the political power structure.

The son of a minister and a member of one of the most prominent black families in South Carolina politics, Clyburn always had his eye on moving up. In 1978 and 1986, he unsuccessfully sought the Democratic nomination for secretary of state. During his political career in South Carolina, Clyburn saw "the system" become more open to blacks, an evolution confirmed when 1992 redistricting created the black-majority 6th District.

White Democratic incumbent Robin Tallon at first said he would seek re-election. But he backed out, saying he did not want to provoke a racially divisive campaign. Clyburn and four other black Democrats ran in the primary. While all had some political experience, none could match Clyburn's name recognition in the black community or his high-level contacts in the white Democratic Party establishment. Clyburn took 56 percent of the primary vote and rolled up 65 percent in the general election. He has won by large margins since then, and his name has been mentioned as a possible Senate candidate in 2002.

KEY VOTES

2000

Yes Raise hourly minimum wage by $1 over two years

No Halt funding for U.S. mission in Kosovo unless European nations pay more

Yes Provide Medicare benefits to military retirees and their dependents

No Grant China permanent normal trade status

No Phase out estate, gift and trust taxes

No Prohibit implementation of president's national monument designations

No Approve GOP plan to provide prescription drug coverage for Medicare beneficiaries

Yes Increase help for poor nations indebted to international financial institutions

1999

Yes Impose steel import quotas

Yes Kill proposal to take aviation trust funds off budget

No Require background checks on buyers only at gun shows with 10 or more vendors

Yes Remove barriers among banking, securities and insurance companies

Yes Authorize state grants to hire teachers and reduce class size

Yes Overhaul campaign finance law; ban "soft money" and restrict advocacy advertising

+ Approve bipartisan plan to increase rights of patients in managed-care health plans

INTEREST GROUPS

	AFL-CIO	ADA	CCUS	ACU
2000	100%	85%	57%	8%
1999	100%	85%	13%	0%
1998	100%	95%	28%	4%
1997	100%	90%	30%	16%

CQ VOTE STUDIES

	PARTY UNITY		PRESIDENTIAL SUPPORT	
	Support	Oppose	Support	Oppose
2000	91%	9%	75%	25%
1999	95%	5%	85%	15%
1998	95%	5%	83%	17%
1997	89%	11%	75%	25%

SOUTH CAROLINA 6

Central and South – Florence; parts of Columbia and Charleston

A black-majority district, the 6th winds its way through 16 counties in the eastern half of the state, starting near the North Carolina border and reaching south of Charleston. With five of South Carolina's six poorest counties, the 6th is the state's poorest district.

Roughly 40 percent of the district's families depend on tobacco and related industries for their income. In the 1980s, Lee, Bamberg, Marion and Williamsburg counties lost population as residents left farms and textile jobs disappeared. For those who stayed, agriculture remains an important part of life.

Other sectors of the district's economy have fared better. Pharmaceuticals contribute to Florence County, while metalworking and plastics manufacturing, paperboard and textiles

sustain the economy in the city of Florence. Nearly 12,000 retired military personnel call the district home, and many residents who live around Columbia commute to state government jobs.

The 6th gives solid and consistent support to Democrats at all levels of government. Strong turnout among the district's many black-majority communities makes this seat a virtual Democratic lock, although some Republican support exists in the suburbs of Charleston and Columbia.

MAJOR INDUSTRY
Agriculture, health care, government, textiles

CITIES
Columbia (pt.), 44,935 (1990); Charleston (pt.), 32,901 (1990); Florence, 30,053

UNUSUAL FEATURES
All of the state's historically black colleges and universities are within the district; Clarendon County (pop. 32,502) can claim five South Carolina governors – and all were related.

SOUTH DAKOTA

Gov. William J. Janklow (R)

First elected: 1978, 1994
Length of term: 4 years
Term expires: 1/03
Salary: $92,602
Phone: (605) 773-3212
Hometown: Brandon
Born: Sept. 13, 1939, Chicago, Ill.
Religion: Lutheran
Family: Wife, Mary Dean Janklow; three children
Education: U. of South Dakota, B.A. 1964, J.D. 1966
Military service: Marine Corps, 1956-59
Career: Lawyer
Political highlights: S.D. attorney general, 1975-79; governor, 1979-87; sought Republican nomination for U.S. Senate, 1986

Election results:

1998 GENERAL

William J. Janklow (R)	166,621	64.0%
Bernie Hunhoff (D)	85,473	32.9%
Bob Newand (LIBERT)	4,389	1.7%
Ronald Wieczorek (I)	3,704	1.4%

Lt. Gov. Carole Hillard (R)

First elected: 1994
Length of term: 4 years
Term expires: 1/03
Salary: $12,635 for legislative duties, plus $54,590 executive salary based on full-time employment
Phone: (605) 773-3661

STATE LEGISLATURE

Legislature: Meets January-February in even numbered years, January-March in odd-numbered years
House: 70 members, 2-year terms
2001 breakdown: 50R, 20D; 59 men, 11 women
Salary: $12,000 for 2-year term; $110/day in session
Phone: (605) 773-3661
Senate: 35 members, 2-year terms
2001 breakdown: 24R, 11D; 30 men, 5 women
Salary: $12,000 for 2-year term; $110/day in session
Phone: (605) 773-3251

STATE TERM LIMITS

Governor: 2 consecutive terms
Senate: 4 consecutive terms
House: 4 consecutive terms

URBAN STATISTICS

CITY	POPULATION
Sioux Falls	116,720
Rapid City	58,268
Aberdeen	25,019
Watertown	20,063

REGISTERED VOTERS

Republican	48%
Democrat	39%
Other	13%

POPULATION

2000 population	754,844
1990 population	696,004
Percent change	+8.5%
Rank among states	46
Median age	35.2
Born in state	70%
Foreign born	1%
Urban/rural	50%/50%
Crime rate	197/100,000
Poverty level	10.8%
Federal workers	10,767
Military	8,260

REAPPORTIONMENT

South Dakota retained its one House seat in reapportionment.

MISCELLANEOUS

Web: www.state.sd.us
Capital: Pierre
Land area: 75,896 sq. miles
Rank among states: 16
STATE ELECTION OFFICIAL
(605) 773-3537
DEMOCRATIC HEADQUARTERS
(605) 335-7337
REPUBLICAN HEADQUARTERS
(605) 224-7347

District Statistics

DIST.	VOTE FOR PRESIDENT 2000 D	2000 R	GREEN	1996 D	1996 R	REF	1992 D	1992 R	I	WHT	BLK	ASIAN	HISP	HOUSEHOLD INCOME	OVER 65+	UNDER 18	COLLEGE EDUCATION
AL	38%	60%	0%	43%	47%	10%	37%	41%	22%	92%	<1%	<1%	1%	$22,503	15%	29%	17%

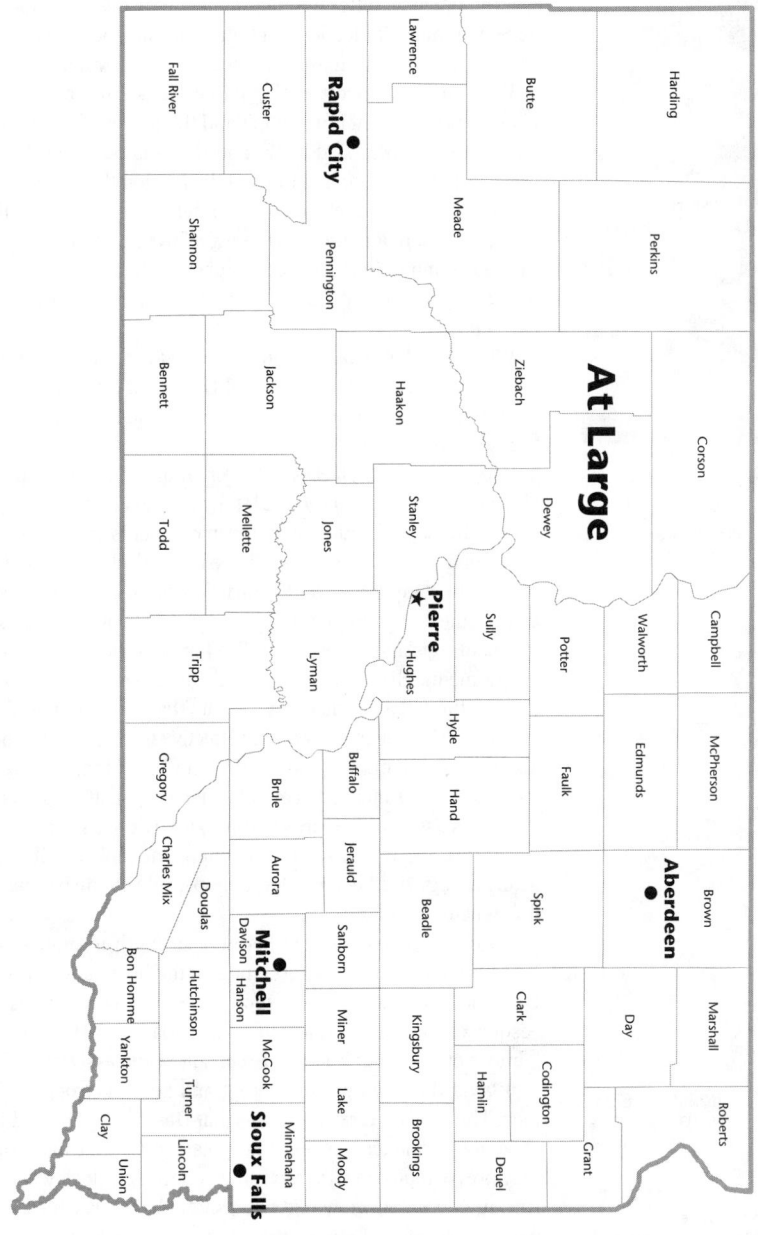

Sen. Tom Daschle (D)

CAPITOL OFFICE
224-2321; fax 224-2047; 509 Hart Bldg. 20510

INTERNET
e-mail: tom_daschle@daschle.senate.gov
web: daschle.senate.gov

COMMITTEES
Agriculture, Nutrition & Forestry
Finance
Rules & Administration

HOMETOWN
Aberdeen

BORN
Dec. 9, 1947, Aberdeen, S.D.

RELIGION
Roman Catholic

FAMILY
Wife, Linda Hall Daschle; three children

EDUCATION
South Dakota State U., B.A. 1969

MILITARY SERVICE
Air Force, 1969-72

CAREER
Congressional aide

POLITICAL HIGHLIGHTS
U.S. House, 1979-87

ELECTION RESULTS

1998 GENERAL

Tom Daschle (D)	162,884	62.1%
Ron Schmidt (R)	95,431	36.4%
Byron Dale (LIBERT)	3,796	1.4%

1998 PRIMARY

Tom Daschle (D)	unopposed

PREVIOUS WINNING PERCENTAGES
1992 (65%); 1986 (52%); 1984 House Election (57%);
1982 House Election (52%); 1980 House Election
(66%); 1978 House Election (50%)

Elected 1986; 3rd term

Even his most bitter enemies concede that Daschle has performed ably as Senate minority leader since Republicans took over Congress in 1995. The 107th Congress may be his toughest leadership challenge yet.

Without a Democrat in the White House, the party has lost both the nation's pre-eminent bully pulpit and the power of the veto. So it has fallen largely to Daschle (DASH-ull) and the Democrats of the Senate to carry their party's message and to block legislation they oppose from becoming law. Despite Democrats' disappointment at losing the White House, their gain of four additional seats, creating a 50-50 partisan split in the Senate, had them beginning the 107th on an upbeat note. And they are already talking of retaking the majority in 2002, when the midterm dynamic favors the party out of power.

With President Clinton and Vice President Al Gore off the Washington stage, Daschle's role as a national Democratic spokesman is more prominent than it has ever been. His name is mentioned as a possible challenger to President Bush in 2004.

Early in the 107th, Democrats were mulling over what mix of cooperation and confrontation with the GOP they should aim for. The split on the north side of the Capitol, unprecedented in recent history, raised tantalizing questions about how the Senate would be run and whether some of the traditions of freewheeling debate and centrist coalition-building would be resurrected over the long haul. In the first major debate of 2001, on campaign finance overhaul legislation, Daschle rallied his troops to defeat several "poison pill" amendments. He also held all but one of the Democrats together in an effort to deny the full $1.6 trillion in tax cuts that Bush proposed.

Daschle had been remarkably effective in keeping Democrats unified for six years, a task made easier by the simple fact that they were in the minority — and by the tactics Majority Leader Trent Lott employed to run the Senate. Lott's use of procedures that frequently froze Democrats out of the legislative process both angered and united the rank-and-file. Now, that Republican strategy has been rendered inoperable by the precise partisan split in the Senate.

Daschle was able to use his new strength in numbers to negotiate a landmark power-sharing agreement at the beginning of the 107th that gave Democrats equal representation on Senate committees and equal staff resources and office space. The negotiation with Lott offered a telling glimpse of the Daschle style. He consulted endlessly with fellow Democrats, took a hard line on power-sharing and kept his troops united behind the idea. The general perception was that Daschle had bested Lott in the talks.

Many lawmakers believe the polarization that has gripped Congress may prove impossible to overcome and that gridlock will inevitably return. Any such breakdown would put a spotlight on Daschle to act as one of his party's pre-eminent statesmen, because if he is not perceived as reaching across the aisle to Republicans, he will surely be accused by them of engineering deadlock.

In the past, Daschle has been a harsh critic of Lott for being too quick to try to cut off debate; the two have had an uneasy relationship off the floor. But Daschle has not always been consistent in this regard, supporting comprehensive spending packages negotiated by Clinton that gave Democrats legislative wins but upended Senate procedure. Democratic delaying tactics helped create the dynamics that yielded such "omnibus" bills. Under Senate rules, unity among 41 Democrats can prevent a final vote indefinitely on almost anything. Like a commander of an outmanned guerrilla force, Daschle has often used this power to tie the GOP majority in knots.

Daschle also knows how to maneuver in a crisis, such as the first presidential impeachment trial in 131 years. He aggressively objected to GOP trial procedures, which he saw as unfair to Clinton, yet his tone never turned bitter and he worked intensively with Lott to avoid a replay of the partisan impeachment brawl in the House. He emerged with his stature enhanced and his political standing stronger than ever — and not a single Democrat voted to convict on either article of impeachment.

The onset of his tenure as Senate Democratic leader was underwhelming: a 24-23 victory over Connecticut's Christopher J. Dodd at the end of 1994, when Majority Leader George J. Mitchell of Maine retired. Making his victory even sweeter was the fact that Robert C. Byrd of West Virginia — a former Democratic leader and a Daschle critic early in the 104th — nominated Daschle for re-election two years later. "I am here today to tell you that I was totally wrong about this young man," Byrd said. "He has steel in his spine, despite his reasonable and modest demeanor."

Since arriving in Congress in 1979, the unassuming and soft-spoken Daschle has been consistently underrated. In a Senate full of famous faces and outsize egos, the former altar boy strolls through the Capitol unrecognized as tourists gawk at the Kennedys and McCains around him.

Not so, of course, in South Dakota. Daschle is relentless in promoting his state's interests. For months, he single-handedly thwarted enactment of the otherwise non-controversial energy and water appropriations bill in 2000; he objected to language that would have stopped the Army Corps of Engineers from revising its Missouri River management plan to emphasize wildlife preservation upriver (including South Dakota) at the potential expense of barge traffic downriver. Daschle enlisted Clinton's veto pen to win the fight, to the consternation of House Democratic Leader Richard A. Gephardt of Missouri — usually a close Daschle ally.

Daschle's legislative specialties have hewed closely to home state interests and political needs: agriculture, which is a requirement, not an elective, for farm state lawmakers; veterans issues, a cause that tends to transcend ideology; American Indian affairs, important in South Dakota because of its population; and health care, particularly the special concerns of rural regions.

Daschle returned to the Finance Committee in the 107th Congress, reclaiming a seat he gave up in 1994 to Carol Moseley Braun, D-Ill., a pivotal ally in his race for leader. He also helped to fill four Democratic vacancies on the panel, raising the odds that he will be a major force when the committee drafts tax, health, welfare and trade legislation.

Daschle's Capitol career began as an aide to South Dakota Democratic Sen. James G. Abourezk, in the mid-1970s. He moved back home in 1976 to become field director for Abourezk and to start running for a House seat two years later. At age 30, Daschle won the 1978 open House seat campaign on sheer energy. He and his first wife rang more than 40,000 doorbells in a year, and Daschle prevailed by just 139 votes, and only after a final canvass reversed the apparent result on Election Day. Daschle delighted in telling this story during the contested 2000 presidential election.

Having secured a reputation in the House as a diligent defender of his state's agriculture interests, he won 52 percent in 1986 to oust GOP Sen. James Abdnor, who had a reputation as ineffective. Daschle's re-elections in 1992 and 1998 against modest competition were nonetheless impressive in a state that has become increasingly Republican, and in 1996, he played a key role in helping South Dakota Democrat Tim Johnson oust GOP Sen. Larry Pressler. He has a big personal stake in seeing Johnson win re-election in 2002.

KEY VOTES

2000

Yes	Overhaul bankruptcy law and increase minimum wage
No	Limit fiscal 2001 discretionary spending to $600.3 billion
No	Override veto on nuclear waste disposal at Yucca Mountain site in Nevada
Yes	Oppose effort to terminate Kosovo mission
Yes	Include gender, sexual orientation and disability in federal hate crime protections
No	Approve GOP plan to restrict use of genetic information by health insurers
No	Kill amendment delaying implementation of an anti-missile defense system
No	Cut taxes for married couples
Yes	Grant China permanent normal trade status

1999

No	Remove President Clinton from office for obstruction of justice
No	Kill amendment authorizing state grants to hire teachers and reduce class size
Yes	Require criminal background checks for purchases at gun shows
No	Approve GOP proposal to increase rights of patients in managed-care health plans
No	Block effort to allow farm and medicine exports to Cuba
?	Allow study of tougher automobile fuel efficiency standards
Yes	Ratify nuclear weapons testing treaty
Yes	Prohibit national political parties from collecting "soft money" donations
Yes	Remove barriers among banking, securities and insurance companies

INTEREST GROUPS

	AFL-CIO	ADA	CCUS	ACU
2000	71%	85%	71%	8%
1999	89%	90%	56%	8%
1998	88%	90%	61%	4%
1997	71%	80%	60%	4%
1996	86%	90%	38%	0%
1995	100%	95%	37%	4%
1994	63%	80%	40%	4%
1993	91%	75%	20%	12%
1992	75%	95%	20%	22%
1991	83%	85%	10%	24%

CQ VOTE STUDIES

	PARTY UNITY		PRESIDENTIAL SUPPORT	
	Support	Oppose	Support	Oppose
2000	93%	7%	95%	5%
1999	93%	7%	84%	16%
1998	90%	10%	90%	10%
1997	92%	8%	92%	8%
1996	94%	6%	93%	7%
1995	93%	7%	92%	8%
1994	91%	9%	94%	6%
1993	90%	10%	93%	7%
1992	82%	18%	25%	75%
1991	91%	9%	27%	73%

Sen. Tim Johnson (D)

CAPITOL OFFICE
224-5842; fax 228-5765; 324 Hart Bldg. 20510

INTERNET
e-mail: tim@johnson.senate.gov
web: johnson.senate.gov

COMMITTEES
Appropriations
Banking, Housing & Urban Affairs
Budget
Energy & Natural Resources
Indian Affairs

HOMETOWN
Vermillion

BORN
Dec. 28, 1946, Canton, S.D.

RELIGION
Lutheran

FAMILY
Wife, Barbara Johnson; three children

EDUCATION
U. of South Dakota, B.A. 1969, M.A. 1970; Michigan
State U., attended 1970-71; U. of South Dakota,
J.D. 1975

MILITARY SERVICE
Army, 1969

CAREER
Lawyer; county prosecutor; legislative aide

POLITICAL HIGHLIGHTS
S.D. House, 1979-83; S.D. Senate, 1983-87; U.S.
House, 1987-97

ELECTION RESULTS

1996 GENERAL

Tim Johnson (D)	166,533	51.3%
Larry Pressler (R)	157,954	48.7%

1996 PRIMARY

Tim Johnson (D)	unopposed

PREVIOUS WINNING PERCENTAGES
1994 House Election (60%); 1992 House Election
(69%); 1990 House Election (68%); 1988 House
Election (72%); 1986 House Election (59%)

Elected 1996; 1st term

A legislator with a low-key, cerebral manner, Johnson takes positions slightly to the right of South Dakota's other, better-known senator, Democratic Leader Tom Daschle.

Johnson, who calls himself a centrist and political bridge-builder, belongs to the moderate Senate New Democrats and the bipartisan Centrist Coalition. "Each party has its share of good ideas and bad ideas," he told The Associated Press in 2000. "I want to cut through the clutter of partisanship to truly resolve the problems facing our state and nation."

At the start of the 107th Congress, he was given a seat on the Appropriations Committee, from which he will be better able to help his rural state. To take the prestigious Appropriations post, he had to give up his seat on the Agriculture Committee, but agricultural issues continue to occupy much of his attention. He says that in the 107th he wants to overhaul the system of federal payments to farmers.

Johnson generally takes the side of small farmers over food processors. He sponsored a measure in 1999 to ban livestock ownership by large meatpackers, with the goal of helping small producers compete in the marketplace. He has also led efforts to require country-of-origin labels for meat products — an idea supported by farmers but opposed by meatpackers. "American consumers have the right to know the origin of the meat products they are buying," Johnson said in 2000. "And foreign-born beef should not be able to take advantage of the high regard consumers have for domestically produced meat."

With an eye to his state's farmers, Johnson voted for legislation in 2000 granting China permanent normal trade status. Although some members raised concerns about China's human rights record, Johnson said, "I guarantee that if Congress ratifies this trade agreement, South Dakota producers and businesses will see tremendous new trade opportunities available to them in China."

Like many Democrats, Johnson is highly critical of the 1996 "Freedom to Farm" act, a GOP-written law that authorized fixed annual payments to farmers regardless of conditions in the marketplace. The law is due to expire in 2002, and Johnson wants to amend it to provide farmers with more of a safety net instead of passing emergency disaster relief legislation when commodity prices drop. Under current law, "we are forced to throw more money at a bad farm policy that provides no safety net for farmers and ranchers," he said in 1999. "Frankly, I would think that Republicans who preach that they want to shore up the budget would agree that this is not sound policy."

Johnson is generally content to tend to issues of importance to his South Dakota constituents. On occasion, he will venture into areas of national controversy, such as seeking to curb violence in the entertainment industry.

In the 106th Congress, Johnson urged the industry to refrain from marketing violent products to minors, and he supported an initiative to limit violent programming during hours when children are likely watching television. "While parents have the ultimate responsibility to control what their children view, families deserve a safe harbor during the evening to have the opportunity to watch programs which do not contain violence," he said.

Johnson's moderate bent is exhibited in his mixed record on gun control proposals and his opposition to federal funding of abortion. He backed a five-day waiting period requirement for handgun purchases, saying the wait created "only negligible inconvenience to law-abiding handgun owners, but he also voted to repeal the ban on semiautomatic assault-style weapons. He wants to reduce the estate tax but voted against a GOP plan to cut taxes by $792 billion in the 106th Congress, arguing that it could take money away from government programs for rural residents. "It would bring virtually to a close our rural development initiatives that have attempted to try to develop off-farm income opportunities in small and large towns all across South Dakota," he warned.

Johnson scored a victory in 2000 when he sponsored legislation, signed into law by President Clinton, requiring federal prison inmates to pay a small co-payment when seeing a doctor. "At a time when ordinary South Dakota families have to make co-payments, prisoners ought to make co-payments if they have the resources to do so," he said.

His ties to the minority leader — and his dedication to protecting Social Security — paid off for Democrats early in the 105th Congress, when Republicans attempted to pass a balanced-budget constitutional amendment. Johnson was one of four freshman Democrats — along with Robert G. Torricelli of New Jersey, Mary L. Landrieu of Louisiana and Max Cleland of Georgia — who had supported the idea in their 1996 Senate campaigns and initially signaled to Daschle that they were not inclined to change their positions. But Daschle, Clinton administration officials and senior Senate Democrats patiently led Johnson and Torricelli into the opposition camp.

In a 1997 announcement, Johnson cited the issue of "protecting" Social Security as his reason for opposing the balanced-budget amendment before the Senate. "In the past I have supported a version similar to this amendment," Johnson said in a statement, "but I cannot [support this version] knowing that it will jeopardize Social Security, as well as the ability of the government to set aside funds for disasters, recessions or other crises."

Proponents of the amendment were stung by Johnson's decision to oppose it. "This is a question of honesty," Majority Leader Trent Lott said on the Senate floor. "When you give your word ... during the election campaign ... and then six months later you say, 'Gee whiz, I have learned something new,' it is hard to take." Johnson dismissed Lott's criticisms, saying he had cast a vote of conscience and didn't need a Mississippian lecturing him about how to represent South Dakotans.

Johnson spent his years in the House as a tenacious advocate for his state's farmers, aggressively seeking federal funds for local water projects, bridges and roads. He also focused on matters affecting senior citizens, an important constituency in South Dakota. He sponsored legislation in the House that would have penalized companies found to charge excessive prices for prescription drugs. In the Senate in the 106th, he pressed for expanded health care benefits for military retirees.

A fourth-generation South Dakotan, Johnson became familiar with the legislative process by working as a budget analyst in the Michigan state Senate. After returning to his home state and starting a law practice, he ran for the legislature in 1978, serving two terms in the state House and two in the Senate. He ran for Congress in 1986 when Daschle decided to give up South Dakota's lone House seat to run for the Senate. After narrowly beating a folksy state senator with longstanding farm credentials in the primary, Johnson cruised in the general election and easily won re-election four times.

In 1996, he challenged three-term Republican Sen. Larry Pressler, enduring a hard-fought, closely contested battle in which he was the target of relentless television ads branding him a liberal. Johnson responded by characterizing Pressler as out of touch and captive to special interests. Johnson prevailed in an expensive race by fewer than 10,000 votes out of more than 300,000 ballots cast.

KEY VOTES

2000

Yes Overhaul bankruptcy law and increase minimum wage
No Limit fiscal 2001 discretionary spending to $600.3 billion
No Override veto on nuclear waste disposal at Yucca Mountain site in Nevada
Yes Oppose effort to terminate Kosovo mission
Yes Include gender, sexual orientation and disability in federal hate crime protections
No Approve GOP plan to restrict use of genetic information by health insurers
No Kill amendment delaying implementation of an anti-missile defense system
No Cut taxes for married couples
Yes Grant China permanent normal trade status

1999

No Remove President Clinton from office for obstruction of justice
No Kill amendment authorizing state grants to hire teachers and reduce class size
Yes Require criminal background checks for purchases at gun shows
No Approve GOP proposal to increase rights of patients in managed-care health plans
No Block effort to allow farm and medicine exports to Cuba
Yes Allow study of tougher automobile fuel efficiency standards
Yes Ratify nuclear weapons testing treaty
Yes Prohibit national political parties from collecting "soft money" donations
Yes Remove barriers among banking, securities and insurance companies

INTEREST GROUPS

	AFL-CIO	ADA	CCUS	ACU
2000	75%	80%	60%	16%
1999	89%	95%	47%	8%
1998	88%	90%	56%	4%
1997	71%	80%	70%	12%
House Service:				
1996	73%	55%	33%	37%
1995	75%	85%	50%	28%
1994	67%	55%	75%	24%
1993	92%	65%	36%	21%
1992	67%	70%	50%	32%
1991	83%	65%	40%	20%

CQ VOTE STUDIES

	PARTY UNITY		PRESIDENTIAL SUPPORT	
	Support	Oppose	Support	Oppose
2000	91%	9%	98%	2%
1999	93%	7%	78%	22%
1998	93%	7%	89%	11%
1997	86%	14%	87%	13%
House Service:				
1996	80%	20%	69%	31%
1995	82%	18%	77%	23%
1994	90%	10%	82%	18%
1993	87%	13%	73%	27%
1992	83%	17%	29%	71%
1991	80%	20%	34%	66%

Rep. John Thune (R)

CAPITOL OFFICE
225-2801; fax 225-5823
1005 Longworth Bldg. 20515

INTERNET
e-mail: jthune@mail.house.gov
web: www.house.gov/thune

COMMITTEES
Agriculture
Small Business
(Rural Enterprises & Agricultural Policy -
chairman)
Transportation & Infrastructure

HOMETOWN
Pierre

BORN
Jan. 7, 1961, Pierre, S.D.

RELIGION
Protestant

FAMILY
Wife, Kimberley Thune; two children

EDUCATION
Biola U., B.S. 1983; U. of South Dakota, M.B.A.
1984

CAREER
Municipal league executive; congressional aide

POLITICAL HIGHLIGHTS
S.D. Republican Party executive director, 1989-91;
S.D. railroad director, 1991-93

ELECTION RESULTS

2000 GENERAL
John Thune (R)	231,083	73.4%
Curt M. Hohn (D)	78,321	24.9%
Brian Lerohl (LIBERT)	5,357	1.7%

2000 PRIMARY
John Thune (R)	unopposed

1998 GENERAL
John Thune (R)	194,157	75.1%
Jeff Moser (D)	64,433	24.9%

PREVIOUS WINNING PERCENTAGES
1996 (58%)

Elected 1996; 3rd term

Politically savvy and ambitious, Thune is regarded as someone with a strong political future. Yet his political advancement is not likely to be in the House, as he has repeatedly stated that he will not seek more than three terms. If that pledge holds, Thune is now in his last term.

The House is Thune's first elective office, but he arrived on Capitol Hill in 1997 with experience in several jobs that gave him a solid grounding in federal, state and local government. Sensing his political smarts, his peers in the Republican Class of 1996 selected him as their liaison to the party leadership.

Thune (THOON) sits on the Agriculture and Transportation committees. He gained a seat on the Small Business Committee in the 106th Congress and became chairman of the Rural Enterprises and Agricultural Policy Subcommittee in the 107th.

In the 106th Congress, Thune worked to shore up the federal crop insurance program and to increase overseas markets for South Dakota's agricultural producers, for him a solution to the problem of the shaky farm economy that is preferable to increasing federal farm supports. He wants to pave the way for more exports through international trade agreements, including opening up trade with China, and to end the policy of withholding food exports to selected nations as part of punitive sanctions.

Thune attended meetings of the World Trade Organization in Seattle in 1999, as a congressional observer to make sure U.S. farm interests were considered. Because of widespread protests by environmentalists and union organizers, Thune spent much of his time confined to his hotel. Thune told home state reporters that having grown up in the small town of Murdo, "I kind of missed the whole '60s thing, so this is new to me."

In the 106th Congress, Thune worked hard to win congressional approval of an important South Dakota water project that had been on the state's priority list for years. The Lewis and Clark rural water system project calls for the construction of a pipeline to bring Missouri River water hundreds of miles to Sioux Falls and surrounding communities in South Dakota, Minnesota and Iowa. The project received initial funding in 2000, along with about $60 million for several other South Dakota flood control and drinking water projects.

Thune was placed in a tricky position in 1997, when he had to weigh the interests of GOP leaders against the needs of his home state, which was being overwhelmed by flood waters. Republican leaders got into a standoff with the Clinton administration over providing emergency disaster relief funds for flood-ravaged areas of the Dakotas and Minnesota. Seeing the aid measure as a "must-pass" bill, top GOP strategists sought to use that leverage to win concessions from the White House on other matters.

Thune, who is South Dakota's only House member, decided that loyalty to his state came first. He argued against the strategy of confrontation that served to delay the disaster aid for several months, but his advice was ignored. "We have made a crucial mistake in putting politics and process in front of people," he said. The GOP gambit failed, however. Thune eventually won approval for the emergency funds to be disbursed directly to the states rather than through the Federal Emergency Management Agency, to speed their distribution. Thune's stance on the flood relief issue won him plaudits at home.

In the 106th Congress, Thune was his class representative to the Republican Policy Committee, and he was part of many GOP press conferences providing the party's view on taxes, spending bills and Social Security. Thune generally backs his party's leaders, and his tally for support of the GOP position is better than 90 percent. He votes for conservative social policies such as restricting abortion and banning desecration of the U.S. flag. But his national priorities include revamping the tax code and attacking wasteful government spending.

On the Transportation Committee, Thune in 1998 worked to increase South Dakota's highway funding and to designate the north-south Interstate 29 as a high-priority route, raising its chances for increased funding. In 2000, he worked for additional federal grants to many small South Dakota airports.

Thune grew up in the small town of Murdo, about 40 miles south of the capital city of Pierre. His parents were educators, and he was a star athlete in both high school and college. (In Congress, Thune plays in both the congressional baseball and basketball games.)

Years ago, a spectator who first saw Thune as a freshman member of the high school basketball team wound up having a great influence on his life. That spectator was South Dakota Rep. James Abdnor. Abdnor struck up a conversation with Thune, and they stayed in touch over the years. After Thune completed graduate school, he moved to Washington to work for then-Sen. Abdnor, specializing in tax and small-business issues. After Abdnor was defeated for re-election in 1986, Thune followed him to the Small Business Administration, where Abdnor served as administrator.

Later, Thune was deputy staff director of the Senate Small Business Committee. In 1989, he returned to South Dakota, where he served as executive director of the state GOP and then as state railroad director under Republican Gov. George Mickelson. In 1993, Thune was named executive director of the South Dakota Municipal League, an association of local governments.

In 1996, Democratic Rep. Tim Johnson left South Dakota's lone House seat open to mount a successful challenge to Republican Sen. Larry Pressler. At Mickelson's urging, Thune made a bid for the House seat, and scored a convincing primary victory over Lt. Gov. Carole Hillard to win the GOP nomination. In November, Thune handily defeated Rick Weiland, a longtime aide to Democratic Sen. Tom Daschle, by 21 percentage points. He was re-elected by impressive margins in 1998 and 2000. If he leaves the House after three terms, Thune is expected to be a candidate for South Dakota governor or senator in 2002.

KEY VOTES

2000

Yes Raise hourly minimum wage by $1 over two years
Yes Halt funding for U.S. mission in Kosovo unless European nations pay more
Yes Provide Medicare benefits to military retirees and their dependents
Yes Grant China permanent normal trade status
Yes Phase out estate, gift and trust taxes
Yes Prohibit implementation of president's national monument designations
Yes Approve GOP plan to provide prescription drug coverage for Medicare beneficiaries
No   Increase help for poor nations indebted to international financial institutions

1999

No   Impose steel import quotas
No   Kill proposal to take aviation trust funds off budget
No   Require background checks on buyers only at gun shows with 10 or more vendors
Yes Remove barriers among banking, securities and insurance companies
No   Authorize state grants to hire teachers and reduce class size
Yes Overhaul campaign finance law; ban "soft money" and restrict advocacy advertising
No   Approve bipartisan plan to increase rights of patients in managed-care health plans

INTEREST GROUPS

	AFL-CIO	ADA	CCUS	ACU
2000	10%	5%	85%	76%
1999	11%	10%	92%	80%
1998	0%	5%	100%	92%
1997	13%	5%	90%	88%

CQ VOTE STUDIES

	PARTY UNITY		PRESIDENTIAL SUPPORT	
	Support	Oppose	Support	Oppose
2000	91%	9%	29%	71%
1999	91%	9%	22%	78%
1998	95%	5%	23%	77%
1997	95%	5%	27%	73%

SOUTH DAKOTA

At Large

Low crop prices wounded eastern South Dakota's agriculture-based economy in the 1990s, adding to a steady migration into cities, where finance, computers and health care have gradually overtaken meat packing as the primary industries. Citibank, Gateway and others moved into South Dakota during the 1990s to take advantage of low taxes and wages. Moving west, away from the more populated areas, the arid, hilly portion of the state relies on ranching, mining and tourism – Mount Rushmore, the Black Hills and the Badlands are located there.

South Dakota has one of the nation's highest percentages of American Indians, at just more than 8 percent of the state's population. Traditionally poor, the Indian communities found a bright spot in casinos in the 1990s; all nine of the state's Indian reservations grew in population over the decade. But poverty is still a major problem. Unemployment nears 80 percent in Shannon County in the southwest, home of the Pine Ridge Indian Reservation. It is considered the poorest county in the nation.

Divided by the Missouri River, the eastern and western parts of the state vote opposite one another. Western, ranching Republicans outnumber eastern urban and agricultural Democrats by about 46,000 registered voters. American Indians, found predominantly in the west, also traditionally have supported Democrats. With only three exceptions – 1932, 1936 and 1964 – Republican presidential candidates won the state during the 20th century.

MAJOR INDUSTRY
Agriculture, finance

MILITARY
Ellsworth Air Force Base, 3,349 military, 413 civilian (1999)

CITIES
Sioux Falls, 116,720; Rapid City, 58,268; Aberdeen, 25,019; Watertown, 20,063; Brookings, 17,286

UNUSUAL FEATURES
Wounded Knee, where more than 200 Sioux were massacred in one day in 1890; NBC News anchor Tom Brokaw born in Webster.

Gov. Don Sundquist (R)

First elected: 1994
Length of term: 4 years
Term expires: 1/03
Salary: $85,000
Phone: (615) 741-2001
Hometown: Nashville
Born: March 15, 1936, Moline, Ill.
Religion: Lutheran
Family: Wife, Martha Sundquist; three children
Education: Augustana College (Rock Island, Ill.), B.A. 1957
Military Service: Navy, 1957-59
Career: Printing, advertising and marketing executive
Political highlights: U.S. House, 1983-95

Election results:

1998 GENERAL
Don Sundquist (R)	669,973	68.6%
John Jay Hooker (D)	287,750	29.5%

Lt. Gov. John S. Wilder (D)

(elected by the state Senate)
First elected: 1971
Length of term: 2 years
Term expires: 1/03
Salary: $49,500
Phone: (615) 741-2368

STATE LEGISLATURE

General Assembly: Meets for 90 days over 2 years, beginning in January
House: 99 members, 2-year terms
2001 breakdown: 41R, 58D; 83 men, 16 women
Salary: $16,500/year, $114/day in session, $525/month expenses
Phone: (615) 741-2901
Senate: 33 members, 4-year terms
2001 breakdown: 15R, 18D; 28 men, 5 women
Salary: $16,500/year, $114/day in session, $525/month expenses
Phone: (615) 741-2730

STATE TERM LIMITS

Governor: 2 terms
Senate: No
House: No

URBAN STATISTICS

CITY	POPULATION
Memphis	606,109
Nashville-Davidson	506,385
Knoxville	174,860
Chattanooga	147,110
Clarksville	99,049

REGISTERED VOTERS

Voters do not register by party.

POPULATION

2000 population	5,689,283
1990 population	4,877,185
Percent change	+16.7%
Rank among states	16

Median age	35.6
Born in state	69%
Foreign born	1%
Urban/rural	61%/39%
Crime rate	790/100,000
Poverty level	13.4%
Federal workers	50,308
Military	23,782

REAPPORTIONMENT

Tennessee retained its nine House seats in reapportionment. The state legislature will draw new district lines.

MISCELLANEOUS

Web: ww.state.tn.us
Capital: Nashville
Land area: 41,219 sq. miles
   Rank among states: 34
STATE ELECTION OFFICIAL
(615) 741-7956
DEMOCRATIC HEADQUARTERS
(615) 327-9779
REPUBLICAN HEADQUARTERS
(615) 292-9497

District Statistics

DIST.	2000 D	2000 R	GREEN	1996 D	1996 R	REF	1992 D	1992 R	I	WHT	BLK	ASIAN	HISP	HOUSEHOLD INCOME	OVER 65+	UNDER 18	COLLEGE EDUCATION
1	37%	61%	1%	37%	55%	7%	37%	52%	12%	98%	2%	0%	0%	$21,952	14%	23%	13%
2	39	59	1	42	51	6	41	48	11	92	6	1	1	$25,267	13	23	19
3	45	54	1	46	47	7	44.1	44.2	12	87	12	1	1	$24,687	14	24	16
4	46	53	1	46	45	8	48	40	12	96	4	0	0	$20,685	14	25	9
5	58	40	1	55	39	5	53	37	10	75	23	1	1	$28,208	12	23	23
6	45	54	1	45	47	7	48	40	12	93	6	1	1	$29,234	11	26	17
7	41	58	1	41	54	5	40	50	10	86	12	1	1	$29,242	10	27	19
8	49	50	1	51	44	6	48	43	9	80	20	0	1	$22,622	14	26	10
9	74	24	1	71	26	2	66	30	4	40	59	1	1	$22,117	12	27	17
STATE	47	51	1	48	46	6	47	42	10	83	16	1	1	$24,807	13	25	16

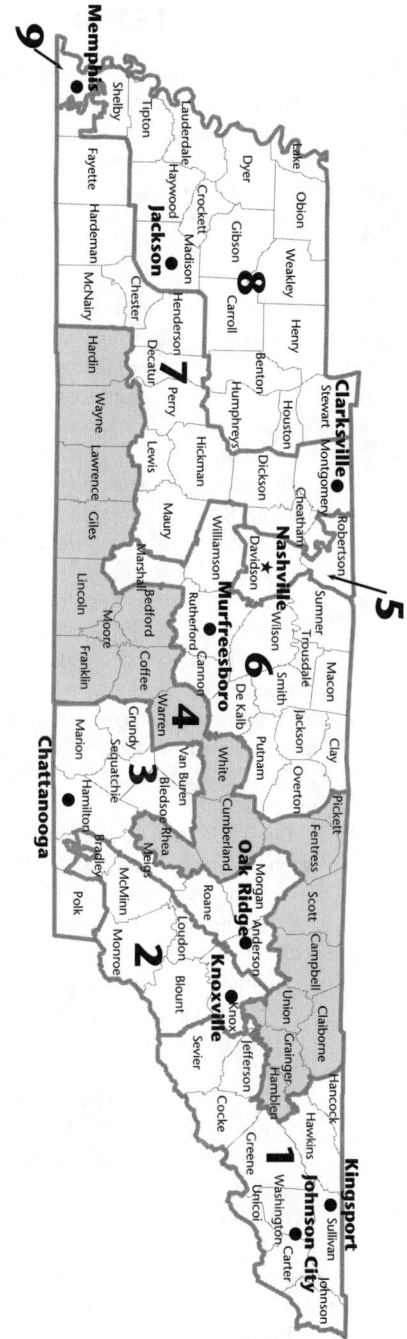

Sen. Fred Thompson (R)

CAPITOL OFFICE
224-4944; fax 228-3679; 511 Dirksen Bldg. 20510

INTERNET
e-mail: senator_thompson@thompson.senate.gov
web: thompson.senate.gov

COMMITTEES
Finance
Governmental Affairs - chairman
Select Intelligence

HOMETOWN
Nashville

BORN
Aug. 19, 1942, Sheffield, Ala.

RELIGION
Protestant

FAMILY
Divorced; three children

EDUCATION
Memphis State U., B.S. 1964; Vanderbilt U., J.D. 1967

CAREER
Lawyer; actor; congressional aide

POLITICAL HIGHLIGHTS
Assistant U.S. attorney, 1969-72

ELECTION RESULTS

1996 GENERAL

Fred Thompson (R)	1,091,554	61.4%
Houston Gordon (D)	654,937	36.8%

1996 PRIMARY

Fred Thompson (R)	266,549	94.1%
Jim Counts (R)	16,715	5.9%

PREVIOUS WINNING PERCENTAGES
1994 Special Election (60%)

Elected 1994; 1st full term

Thompson spent his first three years in the Senate rising to a position of influence. He spent the next three years struggling to solidify that position.

In the 105th Congress, he came under sharp criticism from leaders of his own party for his handling of high-profile hearings into alleged campaign fundraising abuses by the Democrats during the 1996 presidential campaign. He was less visible in the 106th Congress, although he tried to interest the Senate in legislation to reduce arms proliferation. When he was unable to get the measure considered on its own, he threatened to attach it to a bill liberalizing trade with China.

A former movie actor, Thompson is one of the most recognizable members of the Senate. He is a sought-after speaker at GOP political fundraisers. In the 107th Congress, he added a seat on the Intelligence Committee to his posts on Governmental Affairs, which he chairs, and Finance. His high profile in the Senate and decisive way of speaking made some in his party mention him as a potential presidential candidate in 2000, but Thompson never moved in that direction. "Why would one want to run for president — that's the real question," said Thompson. "Not, why does one not run for president."

Thompson spent much of 2000 focusing on his non-proliferation bill. Unable to persuade Majority Leader Trent Lott to call up the measure on its own, Thompson decided to wage his fight during the Senate's consideration of the House-passed bill to grant China permanent normal trade status. That strategy angered many of the trade bill's supporters, who wanted the Senate to pass that legislation quickly. Some business lobbyists and key Republicans argued that a vote for Thompson's measure was a vote to kill the trade bill.

But Thompson, a self-described free-trader, was adamant, saying he wanted to curb China's role in the spread of nuclear weapons. "I see a lot of opportunity to keep some bad things from happening and at the end of the day raising the awareness level of people," he said. "It may not result in legislation but it might."

Thompson seems to be getting used to the slow and methodical ways of the Senate. "I guess what happened is I narrowed my focus somewhat and I've tried to have a sense of priorities and have a little longer game plan," he said. While he still gets frustrated at times, Thompson said he has learned that the Senate "is a place where things have to slow down and you have got to get a fairly good consensus to get anything done. ... All in all the system has served us very well."

During his first three years in the Senate, Thompson was tapped by GOP leaders to spearhead the 1997 investigations into the Clinton presidential campaign because of his clean-but-tough image and because he had played a significant role in the Watergate hearings more than two decades earlier. He had been the top staff lawyer to then-Sen. Howard H. Baker Jr., R-Tenn., the Watergate Committee's vice chairman, and sometimes had interrogated witnesses.

The 1997 investigation was to be Thompson's day in the sun. But with public attention waning and no "smoking gun" to be found, the proceedings were dismissed as partisan political theater and were largely ignored by the media. Thompson came under fire from Democrats for initially requesting $6.5 million for the investigation — far more money than they thought necessary. He also drew criticism from some Republicans for proposing to scrutinize fundraising practices by congressional campaigns.

Thompson is an outspoken critic of the current campaign financing system. In 2001, he was one of 12 Republicans to support sweeping legislation to overhaul campaign funding rules and outlaw "soft money" — unlimited contributions intended for party-building activities and issue ads.

In the 106th Congress, Thompson helped broker a deal with the House to pass legislation providing compensation for thousands of ailing uranium mine workers, including those who work at the Oak Ridge National Laboratory in Tennessee.

Thompson generally advocates limited federal government, lauding bills that seek to shift power from Washington to state and local authorities. He once opposed a popular bill to help local police departments purchase bulletproof vests, saying it would "encourage people in communities all across the country to drive on past city hall, drive on past the state capitol, drive to the airport, fly to Washington and ask the Congress to help them solve a local problem."

A reliably conservative vote, Thompson voted to ban a procedure its opponents call "partial birth" abortion, terminate the tax code and eliminate funding for the National Endowment for the Arts. He advocates a shift to a biennial budget system, rather than the existing annual system. "There are important things that we ought to be spending 70 percent of our time on and it's backwards," he said. "We don't have time enough for oversight and what I call the real issues."

Early in 1999, Thompson cast one of 10 GOP "no" votes on one of the two impeachment charges brought against President Clinton. However, he joined most of his Republican colleagues in voting to oust Clinton from office on the other charge. "The pattern of disrespect for the law exhibited by the president, as well as the harm it caused to the federal courts, warrants his conviction," Thompson said.

After watching his name bounced around as a potential running mate for George W. Bush, Thompson joined the list of passed-over senators. As the 107th Congress began, Thompson was the subject of speculation about his own political future. He called a press conference to announce he had decided not to run for governor in 2002 but left some question as to whether he would seek re-election to the Senate that year. One thing is clear, he said, "I won't be here for the rest of my life."

Thompson had a lengthy career as an actor before his election to the Senate in 1994. In his movie roles — which include appearances in "The Hunt for Red October" and "In the Line of Fire" — Thompson often played the role of a determined and sometimes impatient authority figure with a firm handshake and a pronounced Southern accent.

During his first bid for office in a 1994 special election, he played the role of an outsider, driving around Tennessee in a pickup truck and sporting a flannel shirt. He contrasted his background as a one-time night-shift worker in a bicycle factory and the son of a used-car salesman with that of his Democratic opponent, Rep. Jim Cooper, a Rhodes scholar and Harvard law graduate and the son of a former governor.

Cooper began the campaign as the clear favorite to succeed Democratic Sen. Harlan Mathews in the seat Al Gore had held until 1993. But Cooper saw his initial edge in fundraising (he had nearly $4 million) all but erased by a late influx of dollars for Thompson, who wound up winning 60 percent of the vote.

In 1996, Thompson used his formidable campaign treasury to run feel-good TV ads and captured 61 percent, defeating Democratic lawyer Houston Gordon. He was only the second statewide candidate to tally more than one million votes.

KEY VOTES

2000

Yes Overhaul bankruptcy law and increase minimum wage

Yes Limit fiscal 2001 discretionary spending to $600.3 billion

Yes Override veto on nuclear waste disposal at Yucca Mountain site in Nevada

Yes Oppose effort to terminate Kosovo mission

No Include gender, sexual orientation and disability in federal hate crime protections

Yes Approve GOP plan to restrict use of genetic information by health insurers

Yes Kill amendment delaying implementation of an anti-missile defense system

Yes Cut taxes for married couples

Yes Grant China permanent normal trade status

1999

Yes Remove President Clinton from office for obstruction of justice

Yes Kill amendment authorizing state grants to hire teachers and reduce class size

No Require criminal background checks for purchases at gun shows

Yes Approve GOP proposal to increase rights of patients in managed-care health plans

Yes Block effort to allow farm and medicine exports to Cuba

No Allow study of tougher automobile fuel efficiency standards

No Ratify nuclear weapons testing treaty

Yes Prohibit national political parties from collecting "soft money" donations

Yes Remove barriers among banking, securities and insurance companies

INTEREST GROUPS

	AFL-CIO	ADA	CCUS	ACU
2000	0%	0%	93%	92%
1999	0%	5%	71%	84%
1998	13%	10%	89%	84%
1997	0%	0%	60%	88%
1996	0%	0%	100%	85%
1995	8%	5%	89%	83%

CQ VOTE STUDIES

	PARTY UNITY		PRESIDENTIAL SUPPORT	
	Support	Oppose	Support	Oppose
2000	93%	7%	50%	50%
1999	94%	6%	40%	60%
1998	87%	13%	42%	58%
1997	89%	11%	59%	41%
1996	96%	4%	36%	64%
1995	92%	8%	31%	69%

Sen. Bill Frist (R)

Elected 1994; 2nd term

Senate Republicans consistently look to Frist for guidance on health issues, and the heart and lung transplant surgeon — the only physician in the Senate — has not disappointed his colleagues.

In the 106th Congress, Frist helped guide the Republican Party to its position on expanding the federal Medicare program to provide prescription drugs for senior citizens. He was a key member of the conference committee that unsuccessfully sought to reconcile two vastly different House and Senate bills to give patients more clout with their health insurers. He also served as an influential adviser to George W. Bush's presidential campaign — first on health issues, and later as the candidate's chief liaison to Senate Republicans.

Whether the issue is health care, education or taxes, he has consistently followed the Republican Party tenet that less government is better government. But Frist — who is proud of his efforts to get bipartisan backing for his policy proposals — is also adept at forming alliances with Democrats to push initiatives.

In the 106th, for example, he worked with Edward M. Kennedy, D-Mass., to fashion legislation that would more fairly distribute hearts, lungs, livers and other organs to thousands of patients awaiting a transplant. And with Ron Wyden, D-Ore., he successfully pushed the Senate to pass legislation that would give states more freedom in spending federal education funds. A version of the measure became law in 1999.

In hopes of shoring up the financially troubled Medicare system, Frist teamed up with another Democrat, John B. Breaux of Louisiana, to develop a bill that would revamp the federal health care insurance program for nearly 40 million elderly and disabled recipients by having the private sector play a broader role in delivering medical care. While Frist knew the ambitious legislation would not become law, he said it was important to start a discussion about future changes. The pair reintroduced similar legislation at the start of the 107th Congress. (The partnership had begun in 1997, when the two served on a 17-member commission created to study long-term changes to Medicare. The panel disbanded early in 1999, unable to reach a consensus.)

Although he has a solidly conservative voting record, Frist is not as aggressive as some newer Senate members. Like most in his party, he opposes abortion and favors tax and spending cuts. His primary focus, however, is on health and education programs, as well as a range of science issues, including broadening the government's oversight of experimental medical technologies such as gene therapy.

Frist's lifesaving medical activities on the Hill occasionally have overshadowed his legislative work. After a gun battle in July 1998 left two Capitol Police officers dead and two other people wounded, Frist rushed to the scene to assist emergency medical personnel and helped save the life of the man who had shot the officers, Russell Eugene Weston Jr. Earlier, in 1995, he gave constituent service new meaning by administering cardio-pulmonary resuscitation to a heart attack victim from Tennessee.

Drawing on Frist's medical credentials, GOP leaders have given him a high-profile role on almost all health-related legislation, with an eye toward enhancing the party's credibility on matters as varied as medical research, tobacco policy and even road-building through a protected Alaska wilderness area. (Proponents argued that the proposed road would have given a

CAPITOL OFFICE
224-3344; fax 228-1264; 416 Russell Bldg. 20510

INTERNET
e-mail: senator_frist@frist.senate.gov
web: frist.senate.gov

COMMITTEES
Budget
Foreign Relations
 (African Affairs - chairman)
Health, Education, Labor & Pensions
 (Public Health - chairman)

HOMETOWN
Nashville

BORN
Feb. 22, 1952, Nashville, Tenn.

RELIGION
Presbyterian

FAMILY
Wife, Karyn Frist; three children

EDUCATION
Princeton U., B.A. 1974; Harvard U., M.D. 1978

CAREER
Surgeon

POLITICAL HIGHLIGHTS
No previous office

ELECTION RESULTS

2000 GENERAL
Bill Frist (R)	1,255,444	65.1%
Jeff Clark (D)	621,152	32.2%
Tom Burrell (GREEN)	25,815	1.3%

2000 PRIMARY
Bill Frist (R)	unopposed

PREVIOUS WINNING PERCENTAGES
1994 (56%)

remote town better access to emergency health care.)

Since the 105th Congress, Frist has chaired the Public Health Subcommittee on what is now called the Health, Education, Labor and Pensions Committee. In the 105th, he helped develop the Senate GOP version of legislation to give patients more protection in dealing with managed-care health plans. Frist — whose father founded the large health care conglomerate Hospital Corporation of America — opposes broad federal mandates as well as Democratic proposals to allow patients to sue their health plans for damages.

Frist's significant role in drafting the GOP's anti-tobacco legislation in the 105th Congress included designing the sections establishing Food and Drug Administration authority over tobacco products; he argued that the agency could not regulate tobacco under existing law, a view later upheld by the federal courts.

From his arrival in 1995 through his re-election in 2000 (he defeated Democrat Jeff Clark, a computer science professor, with 65 percent), Frist missed only 1 percent of Senate roll call votes. But despite all his time in the Capitol he is not a Washington insider and appears uncomfortable with some of the trappings of Congress. He sponsored legislation to end free airport parking and other traditional perks for senators.

Frist makes time for fun. He and Tennessee's other senator, Republican Fred Thompson, have waged what Frist calls an "epic battle" each of the past six summers. Led by the senators themselves, aides from the two offices face off on the softball diamond for the "coveted" Davy Crockett Spittoon. When Frist's office first captured the title in 1998, color photos of the team's triumph were posted on his website.

Frist may have less time for such pursuits in the next two years, because he is the new chairman of the National Republican Senatorial Committee, the Senate GOP's political arm. In 2002, the Republicans will be defending 20 seats; the Democrats, just 14. Frist ultimately was unopposed for the post, which is a part of the formal GOP leadership. Mitch McConnell of Kentucky stepped aside after four years in the job. Frist has promised to serve in the Senate only until his second term ends, in 2007.

Before entering politics, Frist founded and ran Vanderbilt University's transplant center and performed the first successful hear-lung transplant in the South. He is a licensed pilot. An interest in public policy, which he studied in college, and public service, which he practiced as a physician, enticed him to seek public office. As a doctor, Frist could help just one person at a time. But as a lawmaker, he reasoned, he could help a greater number of people in a far more sweeping manner.

As a student at Princeton University, he interned in 1972 with Rep. Joe Evins, D-Tenn. When Frist told the congressman he might want to be a lawmaker someday, Evins urged Frist to go do something else for about 20 years and then give Washington a try. Frist followed his mentor's advice.

Frist spent $9.5 million, most of it from his own pocket, to defeat three-term Democratic Sen. James R. Sasser in 1994. But it was neither his wealth nor his medical fame that spurred his victory. Frist won because he was unmistakably a political outsider, and because Sasser could not stop looking like the sort of Democratic career politician that provoked many voters' wrath in 1994. An earnest campaigner, Frist was an ideal messenger for an electorate angry at Washington: He had never sought office before and had gone much of his adult life without even voting.

A lack of political polish seemed to work to Frist's benefit. As a famous doctor with ample personal resources, he could plausibly deny interest in politics as a career. And, he would say to audiences on the stump, "Who better than a heart surgeon to take out the bleeding-heart liberal, Jim Sasser?"

KEY VOTES

2000

Yes Overhaul bankruptcy law and increase minimum wage
Yes Limit fiscal 2001 discretionary spending to $600.3 billion
Yes Override veto on nuclear waste disposal at Yucca Mountain site in Nevada
Yes Oppose effort to terminate Kosovo mission
No   Include gender, sexual orientation and disability in federal hate crime protections
Yes Approve GOP plan to restrict use of genetic information by health insurers
Yes Kill amendment delaying implementation of an anti-missile defense system
Yes Cut taxes for married couples
Yes Grant China permanent normal trade status

1999

Yes Remove President Clinton from office for obstruction of justice
Yes Kill amendment authorizing state grants to hire teachers and reduce class size
No   Require criminal background checks for purchases at gun shows
Yes Approve GOP proposal to increase rights of patients in managed-care health plans
No   Block effort to allow farm and medicine exports to Cuba
No   Allow study of tougher automobile fuel efficiency standards
No   Ratify nuclear weapons testing treaty
No   Prohibit national political parties from collecting "soft money" donations
Yes Remove barriers among banking, securities and insurance companies

INTEREST GROUPS

	AFL-CIO	ADA	CCUS	ACU
2000	0%	0%	86%	92%
1999	0%	0%	100%	92%
1998	0%	5%	94%	80%
1997	0%	10%	100%	72%
1996	0%	0%	100%	95%
1995	0%	0%	100%	83%

CQ VOTE STUDIES

	PARTY UNITY		PRESIDENTIAL SUPPORT	
	Support	Oppose	Support	Oppose
2000	95%	5%	50%	50%
1999	96%	4%	33%	67%
1998	94%	6%	45%	55%
1997	89%	11%	59%	41%
1996	96%	4%	40%	60%
1995	96%	4%	25%	75%

Rep. Bill Jenkins (R)

CAPITOL OFFICE
225-6356; fax 225-5714
1708 Longworth Bldg. 20515

INTERNET
e-mail: www.house.gov/writerep
web: www.house.gov/jenkins

COMMITTEES
Agriculture
Judiciary

HOMETOWN
Rogersville

BORN
Nov. 29, 1936, Detroit, Mich.

RELIGION
Baptist

FAMILY
Wife, Kathryn Jenkins; four children

EDUCATION
Tennessee Technological U., B.B.A. 1958;
U. of Tennessee, J.D. 1961

MILITARY SERVICE
Army, 1960-62

CAREER
Lawyer; farmer; state conservation department commissioner

POLITICAL HIGHLIGHTS
Tenn. House, 1963-71 (Speaker, 1969-71); sought Republican nomination for governor, 1970; circuit court judge, 1990-96

ELECTION RESULTS

2000 GENERAL

Bill Jenkins (R)		unopposed

2000 PRIMARY

Bill Jenkins (R)		unopposed

1998 GENERAL

Bill Jenkins (R)	68,904	69.1%
Kay C. White (D)	30,710	30.8%

PREVIOUS WINNING PERCENTAGES
1996 (65%)

Elected 1996; 3rd term

Jenkins rarely speaks on the House floor, issues few press releases and refrains from sending his constituents taxpayer-funded newsletters. While many lawmakers believe they must deliver clever sound bites for the evening news or the C-SPAN audience, Jenkins does none of that.

His reticence is just fine with East Tennessee voters. After winning the Republican nomination in 1996 with just 18 percent of the vote in an 11-candidate field, Jenkins won re-election in 1998 with 69 percent. In 2000, Democrats did not even field a challenger.

Jenkins unfailingly attends to the top-notch constituent service operation he inherited from his predecessor, GOP Rep. James H. Quillen. He holds numerous town hall meetings to let the voters know he is listening to their concerns. In his overwhelmingly Republican district (which hasn't elected a Democrat in more than a century), Jenkins has little need for self-promotion as long as he pays attention to the folks back home.

On the Agriculture and Judiciary committees, he stands vigilant against legislation that would harm the small tobacco farmers in his district. He backs trade agreements that would open world markets to agricultural exports from the district. He is watchful that any move to deregulate the electricity industry does not harm customers of the Tennessee Valley Authority's power grid. And he casts a fiscally frugal vote, with the exception of backing increased defense spending.

Jenkins' style among his House colleagues is low-key as well. During committee debate, he will usually sit quietly and listen, and when he does speak, it is often to utter a folksy expression that stands in contrast to the legal language of Capitol Hill. In his 1996 campaign, he promised that he would offer Washington a "fresh dose of Appalachian straight talk."

Jenkins introduces few bills. In his first two terms in Congress, he was the primary sponsor of just 15 bills, including one to name a court house after Quillen, and 10 to suspend the duty on the import of chemicals and other materials used by a large manufacturing plant in his district.

His top goal when he arrived in Washington was to see Congress balance the federal budget. His frugality also extends to his own spending. He spends considerably less than allowed for his staff and travel expenses and returns the unspent portion to the Treasury.

Jenkins is also up-front about embracing federal involvement in some aspects of his constituents' lives. "I think there are things that every congressional district is entitled to," he told the Knoxville News-Sentinel in 1996. "Water projects, sewer projects, highway projects that will be needed. I certainly think it is legitimate to try to obtain those."

On Judiciary, he remained below the public radar screen during its impeachment probe of President Clinton in 1998, when several other committee members took advantage of the spotlight to become regulars on the Sunday morning talk shows.

But when it came time to consider articles of impeachment against Clinton, Jenkins was a solid supporter of all four articles. He rejected Democrats' arguments that the alleged offenses did not warrant the disruption that a Senate trial would cause. "The Congress did not initiate or encourage the conduct that brought us here," he said. Impeachment "will not be the end of our republic."

Protecting his district's farmers involves walking something of a fine line for Jenkins. He has complained that farmers face "difficult and expensive" federal regulatory burdens, but he also argued for a continued federal role when anti-tobacco forces sought to end the federal crop insurance subsidy to tobacco growers — a program that benefits many small farming operations in the 1st District.

He says many tobacco farmers have no economically feasible alternative to growing tobacco. In 1999, he joined with Tennessee's GOP Sen. Bill Frist in sending a letter to Clinton urging him not to pursue federal litigation against the tobacco industry. "Continued attempts by the federal government to attack the tobacco industry will surely end tobacco farming as a way of life for thousands of small farmers, with serious repercussions for their families and communities," the letter stated.

Four decades ago, Jenkins was a boy wonder in Tennessee politics. He had been out of law school just one year when he won election to the state House in 1962. Before the decade was out, when the House was split 49-49 and at odds over whom to elect as Speaker, Jenkins persuaded a black Democrat to switch to his side in the leadership race and, at 32, Jenkins was elected Speaker — the only Republican to be elected to that post in the 20th century.

His tenure in the job was brief. In 1970, he tried for the Republican gubernatorial nomination but ran third in the primary with 21 percent. The man who defeated him for governor, Winfield Dunn, named Jenkins to head the state Department of Conservation, and President Nixon appointed him to the Tennessee Valley Authority board, where he served until 1978.

For the next dozen years, Jenkins focused on the law and his beef cattle and burley tobacco farm in Rogersville. But he stayed involved in GOP circles and in 1990 got back into public life, entering the judicial arena with an appointment as a circuit court judge.

In 1996, Quillen's retirement after 17 terms unleashed a lot of pent-up political ambition in the 1st District. Jenkins touted his status as the only farmer among the leading candidates in the huge GOP field, and he claimed to be the only "dyed-in-the-wool, card-carrying bona fide hillbilly" in the race.

Thanks to his many years of political involvement, Jenkins proved to have a few more friends spread across the district. He won nomination with 18 percent of the vote, besting conservative state Sen. Jim Holcomb by only 331 votes. Despite that slim margin, the 1st stuck to its record of not sending a Democrat to Congress in this century, and Jenkins rolled to victory in November, taking 65 percent of the vote.

Jenkins cruised to re-election in 1998 and ran unopposed in 2000.

KEY VOTES

2000

No Raise hourly minimum wage by $1 over two years

Yes Halt funding for U.S. mission in Kosovo unless European nations pay more

Yes Provide Medicare benefits to military retirees and their dependents

Yes Grant China permanent normal trade status

Yes Phase out estate, gift and trust taxes

Yes Prohibit implementation of president's national monument designations

Yes Approve GOP plan to provide prescription drug coverage for Medicare beneficiaries

No Increase help for poor nations indebted to international financial institutions

1999

Yes Impose steel import quotas

No Kill proposal to take aviation trust funds off budget

No Require background checks on buyers only at gun shows with 10 or more vendors

Yes Remove barriers among banking, securities and insurance companies

No Authorize state grants to hire teachers and reduce class size

No Overhaul campaign finance law; ban "soft money" and restrict advocacy advertising

Yes Approve bipartisan plan to increase rights of patients in managed-care health plans

INTEREST GROUPS

	AFL-CIO	ADA	CCUS	ACU
2000	0%	0%	80%	91%
1999	33%	15%	84%	87%
1998	10%	5%	89%	100%
1997	13%	5%	100%	88%

CQ VOTE STUDIES

	PARTY UNITY		PRESIDENTIAL SUPPORT	
	Support	Oppose	Support	Oppose
2000	94%	6%	22%	78%
1999	91%	9%	16%	84%
1998	95%	5%	20%	80%
1997	94%	6%	29%	71%

TENNESSEE 1

Northeast – Tri-cities

Rolling hills and mountains cover the 1st, which borders Virginia and North Carolina. Thanks to Tennessee Valley Authority power, what were once isolated highland towns and tobacco patches are now scattered small cities with moderate economic growth.

Kingsport, Johnson City and Bristol, known collectively as the Tri-cities, center around plastics and paper manufacturing. East Tennessee State University, a major employer in Johnson City, is a regional medical hub for much of the lower Appalachian region.

Campers, hikers and other visitors seeking the serenity of the Great Smoky Mountains National Park must pass through an area jam-packed with large hotels, outlet shopping malls and neon amusement parks. Neighboring Pigeon Forge and Gatlinburg bring in millions of dollars each year through a booming tourist industry.

To the west, counties such as Hancock and Hawkins have been unable to provide sustainable incomes, and much of the area is severely impoverished. Farmers here raise tobacco, poultry and livestock; there is also zinc and limestone mining.

The 1st votes overwhelmingly Republican in most federal elections, having sent a Republican to the House for more than a century. The rural areas almost always elect Republican state representatives, and the urban areas only sporadically send a Democrat to Nashville. However, mayoral and other local elections are usually nonpartisan.

MAJOR INDUSTRY
Manufacturing, tourism, tobacco

CITIES
Johnson City, 59,160; Kingsport, 42,769; Bristol, 24,564; Greeneville, 15,657

UNUSUAL FEATURES
Dollywood, theme park of country music star Dolly Parton; President Andrew Jackson was a circuit riding judge in the 1st District; Bristol has been recognized as the birthplace of country music.

Rep. John J. 'Jimmy' Duncan Jr. (R)

Elected 1988; 7th full term

CAPITOL OFFICE
225-5435; fax 225-6440; 2400 Rayburn Bldg. 20515

INTERNET
e-mail: www.house.gov/writerep
web: www.house.gov/duncan

COMMITTEES
Resources
Transportation & Infrastructure
(Water Resources & Environment - chairman)

HOMETOWN
Knoxville

BORN
July 21, 1947, Lebanon, Tenn.

RELIGION
Presbyterian

FAMILY
Wife, Lynn Duncan; four children

EDUCATION
U. of Tennessee, B.S. 1969; George Washington U.,
J.D. 1973

MILITARY SERVICE
Tenn. National Guard and Army Reserve, 1970-87

CAREER
Judge; lawyer

POLITICAL HIGHLIGHTS
Knox County Criminal Court judge, 1981-88

ELECTION RESULTS

2000 GENERAL

John J. "Jimmy" Duncan Jr. (R)	187,154	89.3%
Kevin J. Rowland (LIBERT)	22,304	10.7%

2000 PRIMARY

John J. "Jimmy" Duncan Jr. (R)	unopposed

1998 GENERAL

John J. "Jimmy" Duncan Jr. (R)	90,860	88.6%
Robert O. Watson (I)	4,372	4.3%
Greg Samples (I)	4,332	4.2%
George Njezic (I)	2,920	2.8%

PREVIOUS WINNING PERCENTAGES
1996 (71%); 1994 (90%); 1992 (72%); 1990 (81%);
1988 (56%); 1988 Special Election (56%)

Duncan was at the center of one of the major legislative achievements of the 106th Congress — the enactment of a bill to increase significantly federal support for aviation programs.

As chairman of Transportation's Aviation Subcommittee, Duncan was an influential participant in drafting and negotiating the bill, helping fulfill Transportation Chairman Bud Shuster's declaration that 1999 would be the committee's "year of aviation." As with most things congressional, it took longer than a year, but by the time the measure was completed in 2000, Duncan was able to include a number of provisions that had been on his agenda for years, including improving passenger airline service to small and medium-size cities such as his hometown of Knoxville.

In his three terms as subcommittee chairman, Duncan often found himself involved in the top news of the day, steadily increasing his influence within the aviation community and gaining visibility beyond East Tennessee. But, constrained by GOP-imposed term limits on chairmanships, Duncan had to give up the Aviation Subcommittee in the 107th Congress. He now chairs the Water Resources and Environment Subcommittee.

Conservative on fiscal policy and social issues, Duncan votes much like the younger GOP firebrands who came to the House in the 1990s. But he has a higher regard for the House as an institution than some of the younger conservatives, a reflection of the fact that his father, John J. Duncan, held the seat before him. He says he seeks to emulate his father, who made himself a popular congressman for more than twenty years by tending to local concerns and eschewing the national spotlight.

The Transportation Committee as a whole operates in a bipartisan manner, and Duncan ran the Aviation Subcommittee with the fair-handed demeanor of a judge, which he once was, fostering a collegial atmosphere in which even the most partisan Democrat feels he will get a fair shake.

Duncan was determined to use the broad aviation bill to improve air service to small communities, which he says have endured high fares and poor service since airline deregulation. He included provisions to increase funding for the Essential Air Service program, which subsidizes airline passenger service in small communities, and to help airlines buy smaller jet airplanes if they promised to use them to fly to underserved communities. Duncan also added proposals to establish guidelines for air tours over national parks and to increase penalties for unruly behavior by airline passengers.

Duncan in the 105th Congress persuaded the Federal Aviation Administration to fund testing of new explosives-detection equipment at Knoxville's McGhee Tyson Airport. And he worked with fellow Tennesseean Van Hilleary to obtain $20 million for expansion and upgrading of Air National Guard facilities at the Knoxville airport. Duncan played a key role in seeking reimbursement from Egypt of half of the estimated $19 million spent by the U.S. government in its investigation of the 1999 crash of Egypt Air Flight 990.

Beyond his aviation interests, Duncan also pays close attention to two local institutions — the Tennessee Valley Authority, headquartered in Knoxville, and Great Smoky Mountains National Park, the country's most-visited national park, part of which lies in his district.

In accordance with the law creating it, Great Smoky is one of the few national parks that may not charge an entrance fee. In the 105th, Duncan won approval of legislation to let the park keep all other fees it collects.

Duncan also sits on the Resources Committee, where he has opposed

www.cq.com

expanding the national park system, arguing that the Park Service cannot afford to maintain existing parks properly. In the 106th Congress, he offered legislation to include on federal income tax forms a line allowing taxpayers to donate one or more dollars to benefit the national parks.

On Resources, Duncan contends that out-of-control preservationists "will absolutely destroy our standard of living. Unfortunately, we cannot turn our entire nation into a giant tourist attraction." Responding to the Clinton administration's policy of no net loss of wetlands, Duncan said, "What we need now is no net loss of private property."

Duncan is also dedicated to cutting federal spending. He says the first thing he asks his staff when they discuss a proposal is: "How much does it cost?" In the 106th, he voted to kill NASA's International Space Station and said that the federal purchase of a 95,000-acre ranch in New Mexico was a "rip-off." In the 105th, Duncan voted to abolish crop insurance subsidies for tobacco, even though tobacco is the largest cash crop in the 2nd District.

Duncan followed his father into politics, and he occasionally wonders what his life would have been like if the senior Duncan had chosen another path. His father was part of a group that brought minor league baseball to Knoxville in 1956, and young Duncan spent five-and-a-half seasons as the Smokies batboy and was the public address announcer during his first year in college. "I wanted to play baseball, but when I realized I wasn't good enough to make it as a player, I wanted to go into baseball full time," he told the Knoxville News-Sentinel. He said he believes he would have followed his father into baseball, but John Duncan turned down a chance to be president of the South Atlantic League. Instead, his father ran for mayor, leading to a long career in politics.

John Duncan was mayor of Knoxville from 1959 to 1964 and then served a generation in Congress (1965-88). Duncan Jr.'s uncle was a judge. The younger Duncan also took the courtroom route into politics. He served seven years as a criminal court judge in Knox County.

The years on the bench helped Duncan build enough of a reputation to be a strong candidate in his own right in 1988 when his father, in failing health, decided the 100th Congress would be his last. (The elder Duncan died shortly after making his retirement announcement.)

In his first congressional campaign, though, there was little doubt that Duncan campaigned primarily as his father's son. Although he is generally known as "Jimmy," he appeared on the ballot as John J. Duncan. He won 56 percent of the vote in both the special and general elections that year and has not been seriously challenged since.

KEY VOTES

2000

No	Raise hourly minimum wage by $1 over two years
Yes	Halt funding for U.S. mission in Kosovo unless European nations pay more
Yes	Provide Medicare benefits to military retirees and their dependents
No	Grant China permanent normal trade status
Yes	Phase out estate, gift and trust taxes
Yes	Prohibit implementation of president's national monument designations
Yes	Approve GOP plan to provide prescription drug coverage for Medicare beneficiaries
No	Increase help for poor nations indebted to international financial institutions

1999

Yes	Impose steel import quotas
No	Kill proposal to take aviation trust funds off budget
Yes	Require background checks on buyers only at gun shows with 10 or more vendors
Yes	Remove barriers among banking, securities and insurance companies
No	Authorize state grants to hire teachers and reduce class size
Yes	Overhaul campaign finance law; ban "soft money" and restrict advocacy advertising
Yes	Approve bipartisan plan to increase rights of patients in managed-care health plans

INTEREST GROUPS

	AFL-CIO	ADA	CCUS	ACU
2000	10%	15%	71%	84%
1999	44%	25%	56%	92%
1998	10%	15%	78%	84%
1997	0%	10%	80%	88%

CQ VOTE STUDIES

	PARTY UNITY		PRESIDENTIAL SUPPORT	
	Support	Oppose	Support	Oppose
2000	89%	11%	12%	88%
1999	85%	15%	16%	84%
1998	88%	12%	22%	78%
1997	90%	10%	30%	70%

TENNESSEE 2

East – Knoxville

Nestled in the valley of the Great Smoky Mountains at the mouth of the Tennessee River, the 2nd wraps around Knoxville and stretches south to include some Chattanooga suburbs.

State and federal jobs in the district are abundant for residents who tend to criticize big government year after year. The Tennessee Valley Authority is headquartered in Knoxville, and the Pellissippi Parkway enables commuters to quickly travel west of Knoxville to the Oak Ridge National Laboratory (in the 3rd District).

But Knoxvillians will tell you their pride and joy is University of Tennessee athletics. Restaurants, hotels and other businesses thrive on the fans who flock to the university's gargantuan football stadium and basketball arena each year. Continuing with the theme, Knoxville opened a Women's Basketball Hall of Fame along the river in 1999. It has helped draw tourists to the downtown area, which suffered from the departure of businesses seeking the economic prosperity of the

city's western end.

The GOP is entrenched in the 2nd, which has not sent a Democrat to Congress since pre-Civil War days. In fact, rarely does the Republican incumbent sweat an election.

The GOP's standard playbook does well in the 2nd: support for a strong defense, frugality in federal spending (especially on welfare programs), and traditional "family values." Local politics are much less partisan and the state seats are usually split evenly between parties.

MAJOR INDUSTRY
Higher education, aluminum, electronics

CITIES
Knoxville, 174,860; Maryville, 24,906; Farragut, 17,146; Athens, 13,949

UNUSUAL FEATURES
On home football game days, the University of Tennessee's Neyland stadium becomes the state's fifth largest city, with more than 106,000 in attendance; Knoxville is the birthplace of film director Quentin Tarantino; Knoxville hosted the World's Fair in 1982.

Rep. Zach Wamp (R)

Elected 1994; 4th term

CAPITOL OFFICE
225-3271; fax 225-3494; 423 Cannon Bldg. 20515

INTERNET
e-mail: www.house.gov/writerep
web: www.house.gov/wamp

COMMITTEES
Appropriations

HOMETOWN
Chattanooga

BORN
Oct. 28, 1957, Fort Benning, Ga.

RELIGION
Baptist

FAMILY
Wife, Kim Wamp; two children

EDUCATION
U. of North Carolina, attended 1977-78; U. of Tennessee, attended 1978-79; U. of North Carolina, attended 1979-80

CAREER
Real estate broker

POLITICAL HIGHLIGHTS
Republican nominee for U.S. House, 1992

ELECTION RESULTS

2000 GENERAL

Zach Wamp (R)	139,840	63.9%
Will Callaway (D)	75,785	34.6%
Trudy A. Austin (LIBERT)	3,235	1.5%

2000 PRIMARY

Zach Wamp (R)	unopposed

1998 GENERAL

Zach Wamp (R)	75,100	66.0%
James M. Lewis Jr. (D)	37,144	32.6%
Richard M. Sims (I)	1,468	1.3%

PREVIOUS WINNING PERCENTAGES
1996 (56%); 1994 (52%)

On the way to winning his House seat in 1994, Wamp pledged allegiance to the conservatives' creed of balancing the budget and reining in "big government." But when he arrived in Congress, Wamp found that the budget ax often was aimed squarely at programs of particular importance to his constituents in the economically struggling 3rd District.

In some cases, Wamp (WOMP) defended Uncle Sam's role and complained that other federal programs were not singled out for the same scrutiny as those that help Tennessee. "The Tennessee Valley Authority is not perfect," he conceded on the House floor early in his House career, but "neither is the Pentagon perfect, neither are the Centers for Disease Control perfect, neither is the White House perfect. ... I have not seen any amendments to zero these core functions out."

Wamp got a seat on the Appropriations Committee in his second term, the first Tennessee Republican to serve on the panel since 1910. He sits on the Energy and Water Development and Interior subcommittees. Wamp says he is one of the more fiscally conservative members of the panel, pointing to his 1997 vote opposing the implementation of a balanced-budget agreement worked out between congressional Republicans and the White House. He wanted the measure to include a tough enforcement mechanism to curtail spending. In 1998, he also voted against a huge, end-of-year spending measure.

But the Tennessee lawmaker says he also recognizes that service on the committee requires compromise in order to advance the annual appropriations measures. He and other one-time GOP revolutionaries are "not so dogmatic anymore. Most of us are more pragmatic," Wamp said in 1999. "You can't be a strident ideologue on Appropriations," he says.

Wamp demonstrates his pragmatism by agreeing to trim funding for agencies such as the Economic Development Agency (EDA) and the Appalachian Regional Commission (ARC), which help rural areas, as long as funding for other federal agencies is also cut back. But he fought those who sought to abolish the agencies entirely. Wamp credited the EDA and ARC for helping spur economic growth in East Tennessee. "There is a role for the federal government," he says.

While the Tennessee Valley Authority (TVA) was once a catalyst for economic development in the region, it is now simply the local power company, Wamp says. The region needs to find other ways to spur economic growth, he notes, either through research at the Oak Ridge National Laboratories in his district or the Marshall Space Flight Center in nearby Huntsville, Ala.

TVA's annual federal subsidy for non-power programs, such as flood control and maintenance of recreational facilities, was a perennial target of budget-cutters. In 1998, as the chairman of the TVA Caucus, Wamp helped work out an agreement to end the federal subsidy in exchange for refinancing TVA's debt with federal banks, at a savings for TVA of $1.2 billion.

In the 106th Congress, he supported funding for Oak Ridge research projects and voted for legislation to compensate thousands of ailing uranium mine workers, including those who worked at Oak Ridge labs.

Wamp casts a reliably conservative vote in favor of gun owners' rights and tax cuts. He contends that gun control laws would do little to curb youth violence. "The No. 1 common denominator among youths that commit violence is abuse, neglect and violence in the home before the age of 5," Wamp said in 2000. "Guns is just one piece of this very complex puzzle."

In the 106th Congress, he pressed, unsuccessfully, for a proposal requiring the labeling of entertainment products, such as video games, that contain violent scenes. Wamp was named vice chairman of a Bipartisan Working Group on Youth Violence in the 106th. He also worked with North Carolina Democrat Bob Etheridge on a "Character Counts" bill that would authorize federal grants to schools to create character education programs to help children "view the world through a moral lens."

Wamp will usually defer to his constituents on issues that come before the House. When the Clinton administration moved in 1995 to prop up the sagging Mexican currency, a skeptical Wamp received a briefing from Federal Reserve Board Chairman Alan Greenspan. "Sitting and listening to Mr. Greenspan last night," Wamp said, "I couldn't help but realize that he's a whole lot more intelligent than I am. As a matter of fact, he's a whole lot smarter than the people of East Tennessee who I was elected to represent. But I'm going to vote with them this time and not with Mr. Greenspan."

Every Tuesday evening that the House is in session, Wamp meets with a handful of other lawmakers to pray and talk about the spiritual and moral challenges they face as husbands, fathers and congressmen. Early in 2001, he chaired the annual National Prayer Breakfast.

Wamp is among the minority of lawmakers who does not have a college degree, telling the newspaper Roll Call that he attended the University of North Carolina but left to seek help for drug and alcohol abuse problems. Wamp recalls the day in February 1984 that he took the first step to "clean my life up." After that, he immersed himself in community and church activities, drawing inspiration from a comment by golfer Chi Chi Rodriguez: "Takers eat well, but givers sleep well."

Community leaders urged him to run for public office, but he demurred, telling them he'd "been through too many mud puddles in my life." But when his wife joined in, he decided to run.

Wamp came within 3,000 votes of unseating Democratic Rep. Marilyn Lloyd in 1992. He tried again in 1994 when Lloyd announced that she would not seek an 11th term. He was aggressively challenged for the party's nomination by state Rep. Kenneth J. Meyer, who made use of Wamp's admitted past cocaine addiction. Wamp still took 67 percent of the primary vote and went on to a 6 percentage point victory in November against Democratic property assessor Randy Button. Seeking re-election in 1996, Wamp won Lloyd's endorsement, and he cruised to a 14-point win. In subsequent elections, he has won by about 30 points. Wamp has said he will serve no more than 12 years in the House.

KEY VOTES

2000

No Raise hourly minimum wage by $1 over two years

? Halt funding for U.S. mission in Kosovo unless European nations pay more

Yes Provide Medicare benefits to military retirees and their dependents

No Grant China permanent normal trade status

Yes Phase out estate, gift and trust taxes

Yes Prohibit implementation of president's national monument designations

Yes Approve GOP plan to provide prescription drug coverage for Medicare beneficiaries

No Increase help for poor nations indebted to international financial institutions

1999

Yes Impose steel import quotas

Yes Kill proposal to take aviation trust funds off budget

No Require background checks on buyers only at gun shows with 10 or more vendors

Yes Remove barriers among banking, securities and insurance companies

No Authorize state grants to hire teachers and reduce class size

Yes Overhaul campaign finance law; ban "soft money" and restrict advocacy advertising

Yes Approve bipartisan plan to increase rights of patients in managed-care health plans

INTEREST GROUPS

	AFL-CIO	ADA	CCUS	ACU
2000	10%	10%	71%	87%
1999	44%	20%	60%	96%
1998	10%	15%	76%	84%
1997	0%	5%	80%	92%

CQ VOTE STUDIES

	PARTY UNITY		PRESIDENTIAL SUPPORT	
	Support	Oppose	Support	Oppose
2000	93%	7%	19%	81%
1999	90%	10%	14%	86%
1998	89%	11%	18%	82%
1997	93%	7%	28%	72%

TENNESSEE 3
Southeast – Chattanooga; Oak Ridge

Stretching from just north of Knoxville to the Georgia border, the 3rd mixes rolling hills with two major cities, Oak Ridge and Chattanooga.

Once mostly industrial, Chattanooga is attempting to attract high-tech jobs with a "Technology Corridor" similar to Research Triangle Park in North Carolina. The plan encourages collaboration among high-tech companies in Knoxville, Chattanooga and Oak Ridge. A recently completed highway linking the Knoxville airport to Oak Ridge – home of nuclear laboratories where World War II weapons were created – has boosted growth.

Chattanooga has worked on projects along the Tennessee River to inject life into its downtown. The Tennessee Aquarium, the world's largest freshwater aquarium, has paved the way for new downtown apartments, nightlife and museums. Since the aquarium opened in 1992, the city has attracted $450 million in downtown investments. Economic struggles in isolated rural areas such as Morgan and

Grundy counties – where water and electricity are sometimes unreliable – contrast with steady economic growth throughout the rest of the district.

The 3rd historically gives its representatives long tenures in Washington. Republican dominance in the 1960s and early '70s gave way to Watergate-era disillusionment that led to a 10-term hold for Democrats. But in 1994 Republicans won the House seat and continue to win re-election by large margins. Ronald Reagan and George Bush won easily in the 1980s, but Bill Clinton ran close races in the 1990s, losing the district by only a few dozen votes in 1992. In 2000, President Bush won the district with a 9 percentage point margin of victory.

MAJOR INDUSTRY
Nuclear research, high-tech research

CITIES
Chattanooga, 147,110; Cleveland (pt.), 28,220 (1990); Oak Ridge, 26,788

UNUSUAL FEATURES
Popularized by the Glenn Miller song, the Chattanooga Choo-Choo has been restored as a historic landmark.

Rep. Van Hilleary (R)

CAPITOL OFFICE
225-6831; fax 225-3272; 114 Cannon Bldg. 20515

INTERNET
e-mail: van.hilleary@mail.house.gov
web: www.house.gov/hilleary

COMMITTEES
Armed Services
Budget
Education & Workforce

HOMETOWN
Spring City

BORN
June 20, 1959, Dayton, Tenn.

RELIGION
Presbyterian

FAMILY
Wife, Meredith Hilleary

EDUCATION
U. of Tennessee, B.S. 1981, attended 1985-87;
Samford U., J.D. 1990

MILITARY SERVICE
Air Force, 1982; Air Force Reserve, 1982-present

CAREER
Textile industry executive

POLITICAL HIGHLIGHTS
Republican nominee for Tenn. Senate, 1992

ELECTION RESULTS

2000 GENERAL

Van Hilleary (R)	133,622	65.8%
David H. Dunaway (D)	67,165	33.1%
J. Patrick Lyons (I)	2,418	1.2%

2000 PRIMARY

Van Hilleary (R)	unopposed

1998 GENERAL

Van Hilleary (R)	62,829	59.6%
Jerry W. Cooper (D)	42,627	40.4%

PREVIOUS WINNING PERCENTAGES
1996 (58%); 1994 (57%)

Elected 1994; 4th term

Hilleary decided to run for the House after watching Congress vote to raise taxes in 1993 — a vote that he said made him feel almost physically ill. A staunchly conservative advocate of smaller government and lower taxes, Hilleary has retained the revolutionary fervor that he brought to Capitol Hill in 1994.

He embodies the spirit of the Class of 1994, which wrenched control of the House from the Democrats after 40 years. In fact, Hilleary (HILL-ary) was the central character in a 1998 book about the class called "The Freshmen." He told author Linda Killian about the day in 1993 when he watched on C-SPAN as the House narrowly approved President Clinton's budget plan, with its attendant $250 billion tax increase.

As he saw it, Clinton and the Democrats stood for "bigger government, more taxes, more regulation and more intrusion into people's lives." He decided that night to run for Congress himself. "At least a Republican Congress would help keep the country from going pell-mell in that direction," he said.

In the 106th Congress, Hilleary remained just as passionate about cutting taxes. In a newsletter to constituents, he told them that deficit spending and higher taxes represented "two great travesties imposed on them by their federal government." He is a leader of the Republican Study Group (formerly known as the Conservative Action Team), a caucus of House Republicans who advocate a conservative agenda. In the 106th, he opposed Clinton administration positions more than any other member of Congress.

A lawyer by training, Hilleary says his proudest achievement came during his military service. Serving as a C-130 navigator, Hilleary volunteered for two tours of duty in the Persian Gulf War and earned honors for helping rescue two injured Marines from a smoky, nearly inaccessible runway. The lessons of military service permeate Hilleary's view of the world; themes of discipline and traditional values echo throughout his speeches. His experiences in the gulf helped him deal with the disappointment he had felt earlier when he failed to make the grade as a pilot. "It was really a blow to my self-esteem. I had never failed at anything," he told the Nashville Tennessean. But after his Desert Storm service, "I came back a new person. I was ready to tackle the world," he recalled.

As a member of the House, Hilleary has tackled a host of conservative causes, including fights against government spending, abortion and desecration of the U.S. flag. He may be best known, however, in the fight to impose term limits on members of Congress. He touted congressional term limits as the most important plank of the House GOP's 1994 "Contract With America," and he became the first freshman since 1897 to offer a constitutional amendment that advanced as far as the House floor. Hilleary has promised to serve no more than six terms.

Despite his zeal to cut federal spending, Hilleary also looks out for his constituents. He was able to win extra federal money in the 106th Congress for rural school systems, including 47 in Tennessee, which usually do not have as much expertise in applying for federal grants. He also worked for legislation to improve satellite TV service for rural areas.

Hilleary sponsored a bill to block a federal regulation requiring banks to "profile" their customers. The measure sought to improve enforcement of money laundering laws, but he argued it could result in a "big brother" prying into the private financial matters of people not accused of crimes.

Like many of his Class of 1994 colleagues who came to Washington and hoped to change the federal government in a hurry, Hilleary has at times been frustrated by his party's leadership. He complains they are too willing to seek out compromise instead of standing fast for conservative principles. He was irked early in 1997 when Republican leaders scheduled action on a bill to restore $2.7 billion in airline ticket, cargo and fuel taxes that had expired. "Is this what the conservative 105th Congress is going to stand for, if the first substantive bill we vote on is a tax increase?" Hilleary asked.

Later that year, Hilleary was one of about two dozen House Republicans who took part in secret meetings that eventually led to a short-lived coup attempt against Speaker Newt Gingrich. Hilleary told the Knoxville News-Sentinel, "There is a leadership vacuum. No agenda. No message. We are losing the gains we made." After the 1998 elections led to Republican losses in the House, he increased his criticism of Gingrich's leadership and publicly urged him to step down.

Hilleary was in the ROTC during his days at the University of Tennessee, and he entered the Air Force aiming to be a pilot. But he did not make the cut. This disappointment made Hilleary rethink his future, and he opted for a spot in the Air Force Reserves and a job in his family's textile business.

He earned a law degree and in 1992 decided to run for the state Senate, when he heard Democratic Gov. Ned McWherter talking about implementing a state income tax. No other Republican was willing to challenge incumbent Democrat Anna Belle Clement O'Brien, and Hilleary recalls waging a fumbling, naive campaign, but he worked hard and won a respectable 48 percent of the vote.

Two years later, with six-term Democrat Jim Cooper leaving the 4th District in 1994 for an ultimately unsuccessful Senate bid, Hilleary was back on the campaign trail. Former GOP Sen. Howard H. Baker Jr., whose family base in Huntsville is in the 4th, was impressed by Hilleary's 1992 campaign and his status as a Persian Gulf veteran. Baker held a fundraiser for Hilleary at his Scott County home.

Hilleary won the GOP primary handily and caught a break when the Democratic nominee, Jeff Whorley, a former top aide to Tennessee Rep. Bart Gordon, did not win enthusiastic backing in November from his defeated party rivals. Hilleary's strong grass-roots organization was indispensable in the rural, sprawling district, which has no central media market. Whorley got no help from Cooper's resounding Senate defeat, and Hilleary soared to a solid 57 percent to 42 percent victory. His winning margins have crept up since then.

KEY VOTES

2000

No Raise hourly minimum wage by $1 over two years
Yes Halt funding for U.S. mission in Kosovo unless European nations pay more
Yes Provide Medicare benefits to military retirees and their dependents
Yes Grant China permanent normal trade status
Yes Phase out estate, gift and trust taxes
Yes Prohibit implementation of president's national monument designations
Yes Approve GOP plan to provide prescription drug coverage for Medicare beneficiaries
No Increase help for poor nations indebted to international financial institutions

1999

Yes Impose steel import quotas
No Kill proposal to take aviation trust funds off budget
No Require background checks on buyers only at gun shows with 10 or more vendors
Yes Remove barriers among banking, securities and insurance companies
No Authorize state grants to hire teachers and reduce class size
No Overhaul campaign finance law; ban "soft money" and restrict advocacy advertising
No Approve bipartisan plan to increase rights of patients in managed-care health plans

INTEREST GROUPS

	AFL-CIO	ADA	CCUS	ACU
2000	0%	0%	80%	92%
1999	33%	15%	83%	96%
1998	10%	5%	83%	96%
1997	0%	5%	90%	100%

CQ VOTE STUDIES

	PARTY UNITY		PRESIDENTIAL SUPPORT	
	Support	Oppose	Support	Oppose
2000	96%	4%	14%	86%
1999	93%	7%	9%	91%
1998	93%	7%	20%	80%
1997	96%	4%	21%	79%

TENNESSEE 4
Northeast and south central

Nearly as long as the state itself, the 4th extends 300 miles and borders five other districts. Traveling from west to east, plains turn into rolling hills that merge with the Cumberland Plateau and eventually the Appalachian Mountains.

Besides being consistently rural, the only similarity among the district's 22 counties is that local needs almost always take precedence over national issues. Although four media markets serve the district, stores, churches and schools are the main forums for political discussion. Opposition to gun control and gays in the military typifies the socially conservative constituency.

Commercial centers are rare in the 4th; Morristown, the largest city, has a population of just about 23,000. Scattered automobile parts factories and air flight research provide employment, but small-scale farming is predominant. The Tennessee Valley Authority provides low-cost power to the district, one of the poorest in the nation.

In 1994, the 4th sent its second Republican representative since Reconstruction to Washington, due in part to 1992 redistricting that removed some Democratic votes. Democratic populism prevails in the central counties, while the western, northern and eastern counties remain strongly Republican. In the 2000 presidential contest, President Bush carried the district with 53 percent of the vote.

MAJOR INDUSTRY
Agriculture, surface mining, auto parts, manufacturing

MILITARY BASES
Arnold Air Force Base, 100 military, 171 civilian (1999)

CITIES
Morristown, 23,299; Tullahoma, 19,815; Shelbyville, 17,003

UNUSUAL FEATURES
Scopes "Monkey" Trial in Dayton in 1925 upheld a ruling making it illegal to teach evolution; Jack Daniels sour mash whiskey distillery in Lynchburg is located in a dry county (Moore).

Rep. Bob Clement (D)

Elected January 1988; 7th full term

CAPITOL OFFICE
225-4311; fax 226-1035; 2229 Rayburn Bldg. 20515

INTERNET
e-mail: bob.clement@mail.house.gov
web: www.house.gov/clement

COMMITTEES
Budget
Transportation & Infrastructure

HOMETOWN
Nashville

BORN
Sept. 23, 1943, Nashville, Tenn.

RELIGION
Methodist

FAMILY
Wife, Mary Clement; two children, two stepchildren

EDUCATION
U. of Tennessee, B.S. 1967; Memphis State U., M.B.A. 1968

MILITARY SERVICE
Army, 1969-71; Tenn. National Guard, 1971-2000

CAREER
College president; marketing, management and real estate executive

POLITICAL HIGHLIGHTS
Tenn. Public Service Commission, 1973-79; sought Democratic nomination for governor, 1978; Democratic nominee for U.S. House, 1982

ELECTION RESULTS

2000 GENERAL

Bob Clement (D)	149,277	72.5%
Stan Scott (R)	50,386	24.5%
David Carew (LIBERT)	6,268	3.0%

2000 PRIMARY

Bob Clement (D)	unopposed

1998 GENERAL

Bob Clement (D)	74,611	82.8%
William M. Lancaster (I)	6,162	6.8%
Al Borgman (I)	4,983	5.5%
Gary I. Worden (I)	4,345	4.8%

PREVIOUS WINNING PERCENTAGES
1996 (72%); 1994 (60%); 1992 (67%); 1990 (72%); 1988 (100%); 1988 Special Election (62%)

Politics has long been the family business in the Clement household. But unlike the heirs to other well-known Tennessee political families, such as the Bakers, Gores, Fords and Duncans, Clement had to strive for more than two decades after his father left office to translate his family name into sustained electoral success.

Once seen as a fiery populist and ambitious self-promoter, Clement now has an image in the House as a quiet and generally loyal party man whose eyes stay firmly fixed on constituent service. Like many white Southern Democrats, he has a moderate to conservative bent on both fiscal and social issues. A member of the moderate New Democrat Coalition, Clement has bucked the majority of his party to back GOP-drafted spending reduction and tax cut bills. He was one of 10 Democrats to vote for President Bush's income tax cut plan early in the 107th Congress.

He has also voted to crack down on juvenile offenders, scale back some environmental protections and amend the Constitution to permit Congress to outlaw desecration of the U.S. flag. Of the last proposal, Clement said, "I am not a legal scholar. I simply say, if the Supreme Court holds that our Constitution permits flag burning, it is time to change our Constitution."

Like many centrist Democrats, Clement supports free-trade initiatives, voting for the 1993 North American Free Trade Agreement and for a proposal to extend the president's fast-track authority to negotiate trade agreements that Congress cannot amend. In 2000, however, he opposed legislation granting permanent normal trade status to China. "I cannot, in good conscience, award China ... when there are serious national security concerns, when China's record of compliance with past agreements leaves much to be desired, and when China's progress in economic power and technological development has overlooked progress on human rights and religious freedom," he said.

Overseas human rights violations are a major concern for Clement. In the 105th, he helped win enactment of legislation promoting religious freedom around the world by creating an independent commission to make policy recommendations and establishing an ambassador-at-large to advocate for worldwide religious freedom. "This is a stand for the most precious freedom, the right dearest to every human heart," he said. "This is an historic stand for the freedom of the people of God in every nation to worship Him in freedom and in truth."

In 1999, he led a group of Democrats who urged President Clinton to order a 72-hour halt in the bombing campaign against Yugoslavia in the hope that Yugoslavia President Slobodan Milosevic would respond with a troop withdrawal. He also said that Congress should consider lifting a ban on political assassinations, contending that it would be better for the armed forces to target one dangerous leader than to bomb an entire nation. "In future conflicts, we're going to have to revisit our policy of going after a country and not an individual," he said. "Maybe we'd make these terrorists think twice."

Clement, whose official biography brags that he has "helped thousands of Tennesseans during his career," keeps a careful eye in Washington on the state's interests, including highway funding and a new commuter rail line serving Nashville and its suburbs. In the 107th Congress, he is the top Democrat on the Transportation Committee's Railroads Subcommittee.

Clement and other Tennessee lawmakers fought hard in the 105th Congress to keep some federal funding for the Tennessee Valley Authority

(TVA), the massive Depression-era public works project that provides the state with low-cost electricity and other benefits such as flood control and recreation areas. Clement served on the TVA board of directors from 1979 to 1981, and he opposed efforts by Northeastern and Midwestern lawmakers to kill funding for TVA's non-power activities.

Clement was chagrined in 1997 when TVA Chairman Craven Crowell proposed that the agency do without the annual funding. With energy deregulation on the horizon, Crowell contended that TVA should concentrate on its profitable power generation work and give up the economic development and research activities subsidized by its federal appropriation. "It's like he's put us in a boxing match blindfolded, tied our hands behind us and is still expecting us to support and defend TVA," Clement complained. Yet funding for the non-power activities was ultimately ended.

Clement is a big booster of the industry that is Nashville's main claim to fame: country music. In the 105th, he opposed a section of a copyright bill that would exempt some small businesses from paying royalties when they played music. "As the representative from Music City, U.S.A.," Clement said, he was concerned that the proposal would "compromise the intellectual property rights of our songwriters. ... Songwriters write songs for a living. Are we telling them they should work for free?" His argument did not prevail, however.

Clement's father, Frank G. Clement, served as Tennessee's governor for three terms in the 1950s and 1960s. The son was hailed as a political "boy wonder" in 1972 when he won a seat on the state Public Service Commission. Then 29, he was the youngest candidate ever elected statewide in Tennessee. But when he sought the nomination for governor in 1978, he lost to wealthy businessman Jake Butcher. And in 1982, he narrowly lost a race for the 7th District seat to Republican Don Sundquist (who is now governor).

Clement then withdrew from politics, becoming president of Cumberland College in Lebanon, just east of Nashville. But when Democratic Rep. Bill Boner became Nashville's mayor, Clement made a bid to fill the open seat in the 5th. He won a hard-fought nomination battle against wealthy businessman Phil Bredesen, winning by 4 percentage points, then went on to claim 62 percent of the vote in the special general election in January 1988.

Although he has a firm hold on the Democratic 5th, Clement has repeatedly been mentioned as a strong contender for statewide office. A 2000 poll released by the Knoxville News-Sentinel showed that he would be the front-runner for his party's nomination in the 2002 governor's race.

KEY VOTES

2000
Yes Raise hourly minimum wage by $1 over two years
No Halt funding for U.S. mission in Kosovo unless European nations pay more
Yes Provide Medicare benefits to military retirees and their dependents
No Grant China permanent normal trade status
Yes Phase out estate, gift and trust taxes
No Prohibit implementation of president's national monument designations
No Approve GOP plan to provide prescription drug coverage for Medicare beneficiaries
Yes Increase help for poor nations indebted to international financial institutions

1999
Yes Impose steel import quotas
No Kill proposal to take aviation trust funds off budget
Yes Require background checks on buyers only at gun shows with 10 or more vendors
Yes Remove barriers among banking, securities and insurance companies
Yes Authorize state grants to hire teachers and reduce class size
Yes Overhaul campaign finance law; ban "soft money" and restrict advocacy advertising
Yes Approve bipartisan plan to increase rights of patients in managed-care health plans

INTEREST GROUPS

	AFL-CIO	ADA	CCUS	ACU
2000	80%	60%	76%	40%
1999	67%	85%	68%	32%
1998	67%	85%	72%	24%
1997	75%	55%	80%	25%

CQ VOTE STUDIES

	PARTY UNITY		PRESIDENTIAL SUPPORT	
	Support	Oppose	Support	Oppose
2000	74%	26%	57%	43%
1999	72%	28%	63%	37%
1998	76%	24%	65%	35%
1997	74%	26%	67%	33%

TENNESSEE 5

Nashville

Home to state capital Nashville, the 5th is Tennessee's second-smallest district, but it looms large in economic, political and cultural value.

"Music City U.S.A." is known for the Grand Ole Opry and homes of country music stars. And while country music is unquestionably Nashville's most famous industry, state government is its top employer with more than 17,000 jobs. Vanderbilt and 16 other schools make the district a hub for higher education in the state. And, as a national health care center, the district hosts several insurance companies and research facilities, including the Vanderbilt University Medical Center.

While bargain retail stores and country music theme park Opryland have drawn hordes of tourists and locals to suburban Nashville, the downtown area has struggled. Nashvillians see their new downtown hockey arena and football stadium – home of the National Hockey League's Predators and the National Football League's Titans – as the future of the city.

The area's recent economic boom has attracted many young, Republican-leaning upper-class couples to neighborhoods such as Bellvue and the Hermitage. But the rural, tobacco-farming base in northern Robertson County remains staunchly Democratic, and the district's abundance of government employees, academics and labor unions favors moderate Democrats. Not a single Republican captured Nashville's congressional seat in the 20th century.

MAJOR INDUSTRY
Country music, religious publishing, auto manufacturing, government

CITIES
Nashville-Davidson (pt.), 484,823 (1990); Springfield (pt.), 9,443 (1990)

UNUSUAL FEATURES
"The Hermitage," home of President Andrew Jackson; The only life-size reproduction of the Parthenon in Nashville.

Rep. Bart Gordon (D)

CAPITOL OFFICE
225-4231; fax 225-6887; 2368 Rayburn Bldg. 20515

INTERNET
e-mail: bart.gordon@mail.house.gov
web: www.house.gov/gordon

COMMITTEES
Energy & Commerce
Science

HOMETOWN
Murfreesboro

BORN
Jan. 24, 1949, Murfreesboro, Tenn.

RELIGION
Methodist

FAMILY
Wife, Leslie Gordon

EDUCATION
Middle Tennessee State U., B.S. 1971; U. of
Tennessee, J.D. 1973

MILITARY SERVICE
Army Reserve, 1971-72

CAREER
Lawyer

POLITICAL HIGHLIGHTS
Tenn. Democratic Party chairman, 1981-83

ELECTION RESULTS

2000 GENERAL

Bart Gordon (D)	168,861	62.1%
David Charles (R)	97,169	35.7%
Jim Coffer (I)	4,685	1.7%

2000 PRIMARY

Bart Gordon (D)	unopposed

1998 GENERAL

Bart Gordon (D)	75,055	54.6%
Walt R. Massey Jr. (R)	62,277	45.3%

PREVIOUS WINNING PERCENTAGES
1996 (54%); 1994 (51%); 1992 (57%); 1990 (67%);
1988 (76%); 1986 (77%); 1984 (63%)

Elected 1984; 9th term

Gordon's political career, which once looked like it might soar, has slowed down as he tends to the earthbound problems of his Middle Tennessee constituency. He also charts a course that often diverges from the national Democratic line. His once strongly Democratic district "is becoming more of a suburban, independent district, and the Republican leanings are increasing, without question," he noted in 1996.

Gordon had a close call during his 1994 re-election race, when his Republican challenger tied him to President Clinton, who was wildly unpopular in Tennessee at the time. Gordon squeaked by with just 2,000 votes.

He is well known in the House for being the fastest man in Congress. He has finished first among lawmakers in the annual three-mile Capital Challenge road race 12 times, beating out such athletes as GOP Rep. Jim Ryun of Kansas, a one-time Olympic silver medalist. "Every year I get one year older, and the competition seems one year younger, so I have to train that much harder," Gordon said of his road running.

Gordon runs three to four times a week to keep ahead of his racing foes, and he has moderated his politics to stave off electoral challenges. Like many conservatives, he supports tax cuts and gun owners' rights, and he is a fierce critic of efforts to regulate tobacco.

Gordon has strayed from the party line more often since the GOP takeover of the House. He has supported the Republicans on a number of key initiatives, including measures to overhaul the welfare system and to toughen immigration laws. Early in 2001, he was one of only 10 Democrats to vote for President Bush's income tax cut. In 1999, he opposed a Democratic initiative to impose a 72-hour background check on gun show purchases, saying that such a requirement would be "unreasonable."

But Gordon sides with organized labor in pressing for an increase in the minimum wage and opposing such trade measures as legislation in 2000 to grant China permanent normal trade status.

Mostly, Gordon pays attention to matters of concern to his district. During the 106th, he urged his colleagues not to prejudge hearings into a massive tire recall by Firestone, which has a plant in his district. "I think we should be looking for the facts and not be trying to have a showboat operation here," Gordon said.

Gordon reaches across the aisle to work with GOP members on issues that involve space technology and computer security, sponsoring legislation to establish a national policy on digital signatures, which are used to verify the source of an electronic communication and determine whether it has been altered in transit. After a series of NASA mission failures, he urged colleagues in 1999 to study the agency's goals carefully before committing more money to space ventures. "Maybe money is needed," he told The Associated Press. "But we have a responsibility to the taxpayers to give them a little more assurance before we give [NASA] more money."

He sharply criticized Republicans in the 106th for wanting to eliminate funding for NASA's Triana project, a camera-equipped satellite. Vice President Al Gore was a strong supporter of the project. GOP lawmakers were engaging in "a misguided partisan effort" to hurt Gore's presidential campaign, Gordon charged, and he contended that the project "would be a tremendous education tool that all schools would have access to and be a treasure chest of resources" for scientists.

In his first decade on Capitol Hill, Gordon earned a place in the

Democratic leadership's heart and the party's whip organization with occasional liberal votes on social issues and loyal work on the Rules Committee. He was an architect of compromises in 1990 and 1991 that would ultimately lead to the Family and Medical Leave Act, requiring businesses to give workers unpaid time off to be with newborn children or ill family members.

But after his 1994 scare at the polls, Gordon became more mindful of his constituents' conservative impulses on certain issues. He fought Clinton's regulations aimed at limiting tobacco's appeal to minors, and he introduced a bill that would have stripped the Food and Drug Administration of its authority to restrict tobacco ads at auto races. "I also oppose trying to treat tobacco as a drug because that's just a backdoor approach to going back to the old Prohibition days. We know that doesn't work," Gordon said.

Gordon earned perhaps his greatest fame in March 1991, when at the request of NBC News, he posed as a prospective vocational education student. He was encouraged at a school in Memphis to sign up for a truck-driving course, using student loans to pay his way. "They were more interested in getting me to sign up for the school than they were in seeing that I would be placed in a good job later or got good training," Gordon said on the NBC show "Exposé." He has since sought to cut off access to the student loan program for schools that have high loan default rates.

Gordon picked up a lasting taste for congressional politics as a college student, when he went to work in the 1968 congressional campaign of Democratic state Rep. John Bragg, who lost the race. Fresh out of law school, Gordon won a seat on the state Democratic Executive Committee, and in 1979, he parlayed his contacts into a position as the party's executive director. Two years later, he won the party chairmanship, attracting notice with his computerized mailing lists and fundraising efforts.

When Democratic Rep. Al Gore gave up his 6th District seat in 1984 to run for the Senate, Gordon was ready. He set himself apart in the six-way primary with a sophisticated phone bank and direct-mail operation and won with 28 percent. Despite facing the potentially explosive issue of a paternity suit that had been brought against him and was later dismissed, Gordon won all but two counties on Election Day against Williamson County construction executive Joe Simkins.

Gordon generally won re-election by comfortable margins until 1994, when GOP lawyer Steve Gill attempted to tie him to Clinton. Gordon fought back aggressively and won narrowly. Gordon and Gill squared off again in 1996, but this time Gordon won by 12 percentage points. He has held onto his seat easily since then.

www.cq.com

KEY VOTES

2000

Yes Raise hourly minimum wage by $1 over two years
Yes Halt funding for U.S. mission in Kosovo unless European nations pay more
Yes Provide Medicare benefits to military retirees and their dependents
No   Grant China permanent normal trade status
Yes Phase out estate, gift and trust taxes
No   Prohibit implementation of president's national monument designations
No   Approve GOP plan to provide prescription drug coverage for Medicare beneficiaries
Yes Increase help for poor nations indebted to international financial institutions

1999

Yes Impose steel import quotas
No   Kill proposal to take aviation trust funds off budget
No   Require background checks on buyers only at gun shows with 10 or more vendors
Yes Remove barriers among banking, securities and insurance companies
Yes Authorize state grants to hire teachers and reduce class size
Yes Overhaul campaign finance law; ban "soft money" and restrict advocacy advertising
Yes Approve bipartisan plan to increase rights of patients in managed-care health plans

INTEREST GROUPS

	AFL-CIO	ADA	CCUS	ACU
2000	80%	60%	71%	44%
1999	88%	70%	71%	36%
1998	80%	90%	72%	36%
1997	75%	60%	70%	36%

CQ VOTE STUDIES

	PARTY UNITY		PRESIDENTIAL SUPPORT	
	Support	Oppose	Support	Oppose
2000	71%	29%	50%	50%
1999	68%	32%	62%	38%
1998	74%	26%	62%	38%
1997	69%	31%	65%	35%

TENNESSEE 6

North central — Murfreesboro

The hilly countryside of the 6th includes some Nashville suburbs and two university communities, Murfreesboro (Middle Tennessee State University) and Cookeville (Tennessee Tech University). The district has been loyal to the Democratic Party since the days of Andrew Jackson, who built his political career in the area. The only exception is in the wealthy Nashville suburbs of Williamson County, which increasingly back the GOP.

The neighboring 5th houses most of Nashville's country music attractions, but the 6th enjoys a slightly higher median income. In the Nashville area's orbit, the economy was strong in the 1990s. Some residents have government jobs in the city, but the 6th relies more on automobile parts spin-offs created by a nearby Saturn facility (in the 7th District) and a Nissan plant. Tobacco farming and book distribution also are big businesses.

Rural and small-town areas on the western side of the 6th are less well off. Textile producers and other small-scale manufacturers here offer primarily lower-wage jobs, and remoteness from urban areas means the service-sector economy is not large.

The 6th is overwhelmingly Protestant, supporting a socially conservative constituency that favors prayer in schools. Al Gore represented this area, which has faithfully sent Democrats to Congress. But the district's Democratic tradition has been fading on the presidential level. Native son Gore lost the district in 2000, and the 6th narrowly favored Bob Dole in 1996, as the growing suburban population agreed with the GOP's attacks on Bill Clinton's character.

MAJOR INDUSTRY
Auto and textile manufacturing, book and video distribution

CITIES
Murfreesboro, 61,177; Hendersonville, 39,728; Franklin, 33,656; Cookeville, 26,071, Smyrna, 25,162

UNUSUAL FEATURES
Carthage, home of former Vice President Al Gore; Cordell Hull practiced law in Celina before becoming President Franklin Delano Roosevelt's secretary of state from 1933 until the end of World War II.

Rep. Ed Bryant (R)

CAPITOL OFFICE
225-2811; fax 225-2989; 408 Cannon Bldg. 20515

INTERNET
e-mail: www.house.gov/writerep
web: www.house.gov/bryant

COMMITTEES
Energy & Commerce

HOMETOWN
Henderson

BORN
Sept. 7, 1948, Jackson, Tenn.

RELIGION
Protestant

FAMILY
Wife, Cynthia Bryant; three children

EDUCATION
U. of Mississippi, B.A. 1970, J.D. 1972

MILITARY SERVICE
Army, 1970-78

CAREER
Lawyer

POLITICAL HIGHLIGHTS
Republican nominee for U.S. House, 1988; U.S.
attorney, 1991-93

ELECTION RESULTS

2000 GENERAL

Ed Bryant (R)	171,056	69.6%
Richard P. Sims (D)	71,587	29.1%
Denis Solee (I)	2,941	1.2%

2000 PRIMARY

Ed Bryant (R)	unopposed

1998 GENERAL

Ed Bryant (R)	unopposed

PREVIOUS WINNING PERCENTAGES
1996 (64%); 1994 (60%)

Elected 1994; 4th term

Bryant was one of 13 House lawmakers from the Judiciary Committee who argued the case for President Clinton's removal from office in the 1999 Senate impeachment trial. No friend to Clinton, he was a forceful supporter of all four articles of impeachment leveled against the president. "I believe the president committed crimes, and I think the evidence is there," Bryant said. "Lying, especially under oath, is not permissible."

Bryant's views and voting record are dependably Republican, yet, despite his vigorous prosecution of Clinton, he is not viewed as stridently partisan. He is soft-spoken, with a Southern drawl. As Bryant prepared to take a deposition from former White House intern Monica Lewinsky in the impeachment case, his GOP colleague, Lindsay Graham of South Carolina, told the Nashville Tennessean: "He's just got a very low-key, easy-to-listen-to approach. ... His personality won't get in the way."

Before his election to the House, Bryant served as U.S. attorney for the Western District of Tennessee, so he was a natural choice to gain a seat on Judiciary. But he gave up that assignment as well as a post on the Agriculture panel to take a seat on the Commerce Committee (now Energy and Commerce) in the 106th Congress. While on Commerce, Bryant was named to a GOP task force that developed a plan for offering insurance coverage to Medicare recipients to help them cope with the high price of prescription drugs.

He also was put in charge of drafting a portion of a bill to deregulate the electricity industry. Bryant's task was to watch out for the interests of the Tennessee Valley Authority (TVA) and its customers, who have been accustomed to low-cost electricity and worry that electricity deregulation would cause their rates to rise.

Bryant also authored a bill to shield car rental companies from liability should a customer cause an accident. His involvement in this tort reform measure was a continuation of his interest in similar legislation that was debated in Judiciary.

Throughout his time on Judiciary, Bryant was a faithful advocate of the Republican line. He argued for stiffer sentences for criminals, and he criticized "renegade" federal judges whom conservatives see as activist liberals. In the 105th Congress, he won enactment of a law giving the military justice system another sentencing option: life without parole.

The interests of the 7th District's tobacco growers played a part in Bryant's breaking from the GOP line to oppose the spending portion of the 1997 balanced-budget agreement. He was one of only 32 Republicans voting "no" on the legislation, which included higher taxes on cigarettes. Later in the 105th, Bryant warned that a proposed legal settlement between state attorneys general and the tobacco industry could yield vast sums in attorneys' fees and little financial compensation for tobacco growers. Bryant introduced legislation to impose a 95 percent income tax rate on attorneys' fees paid in connection with the proposed $369 billion settlement.

Bryant is a vigilant booster of Fort Campbell, located on the Tennessee-Kentucky border, and has sought to upgrade aging facilities there. In the 105th Congress, he was successful in prohibiting Kentucky from levying state income taxes on Tennessee residents who work on the Kentucky side of the base. About four-fifths of the base is in Tennessee, which does not have an income tax.

On another matter of local interest, Bryant has worked with Mississippi

GOP Rep. Roger Wicker to create a large industrial park in the bordering jurisdictions of Fayette County, Tenn., and Marshall County, Miss. And Bryant sponsored legislation to give drug manufacturers — including Schering-Plough Corp., which has a large facility just outside Bryant's district and produces the allergy medicine Claritin — a better chance to win an extension on drug patents.

Bryant says he was an apolitical person who first cast a vote in a presidential election at age 28 — for Democrat Jimmy Carter, because he wanted to be loyal to a fellow Southerner. And Bryant became interested in politics, he says, only when he went to work for a west Tennessee law firm that had close ties to the Republican Party. He says he began studying the issues and soon decided that the GOP was a closer fit to his own philosophy and values.

Bryant's father was an electrician who worked on a number of TVA jobs until he was disabled in an electrical accident. Bryant's mother was a nurse. He was in the ROTC in college and, figuring he was going to be drafted, decided to volunteer and enter the Army as an officer. The Army permitted him to delay his active duty until after he had completed law school. He joined the Judge Advocate General's Corps, where he served as a prosecutor and as an instructor at West Point.

After Bryant completed his military service and returned to Tennessee, his law firm asked him to help on the 1984 Senate campaign of Republican Victor "Bulldog" Ashe against Democratic Rep. Al Gore. Bryant says one of his major duties included cleaning up after Ashe's campaign mascot bulldog, but he also helped run Ashe's campaign in several counties. Ashe lost in a rout (he subsequently was elected mayor of Knoxville), but for Bryant, the political seeds were sown.

He worked on Pat Robertson's 1988 GOP presidential campaign and that November lost an 8th District House race to Democrat John Tanner. Bryant went back to private law practice until 1991, when he was named U.S. attorney for western Tennessee. During his tenure there, he prosecuted then-Rep. Harold E. Ford Sr. on bank, mail and tax fraud charges. Bryant resigned from the Justice Department after his superiors supported Ford's request for a new jury. Ultimately, Ford was acquitted.

When GOP Rep. Don Sundquist left the 7th District in 1994 to run for governor, Bryant decided to give elective politics another try. His superior organization in the district's rural counties propelled him to victory in a seven-way GOP primary, and he has had little trouble since in the increasingly Republican district.

KEY VOTES

2000

No	Raise hourly minimum wage by $1 over two years
Yes	Halt funding for U.S. mission in Kosovo unless European nations pay more
Yes	Provide Medicare benefits to military retirees and their dependents
Yes	Grant China permanent normal trade status
Yes	Phase out estate, gift and trust taxes
Yes	Prohibit implementation of president's national monument designations
Yes	Approve GOP plan to provide prescription drug coverage for Medicare beneficiaries
No	Increase help for poor nations indebted to international financial institutions

1999

Yes	Impose steel import quotas
No	Kill proposal to take aviation trust funds off budget
Yes	Require background checks on buyers only at gun shows with 10 or more vendors
Yes	Remove barriers among banking, securities and insurance companies
No	Authorize state grants to hire teachers and reduce class size
No	Overhaul campaign finance law; ban "soft money" and restrict advocacy advertising
No	Approve bipartisan plan to increase rights of patients in managed-care health plans

INTEREST GROUPS

	AFL-CIO	ADA	CCUS	ACU
2000	0%	0%	80%	95%
1999	22%	5%	92%	88%
1998	0%	0%	100%	100%
1997	0%	5%	100%	100%

CQ VOTE STUDIES

	PARTY UNITY		PRESIDENTIAL SUPPORT	
	Support	Oppose	Support	Oppose
2000	96%	4%	24%	76%
1999	96%	4%	17%	83%
1998	96%	4%	20%	80%
1997	96%	4%	26%	74%

TENNESSEE 7

West Central — Clarksville; part of Shelby County

Bordering Kentucky to the north and Mississippi to the south, the 7th begins with the wealthy suburbs of eastern Memphis and moves north to include two moderately sized cities, Clarksville and Columbia.

Inner-city decay and white flight have depopulated Memphis (in the 9th District) over the last few decades. Wealthy suburban bedroom communities in eastern Shelby and Fayette counties consequently grew, attracting Memphis commuters. Heading east and north, agriculture provides for rural counties, where corn, tobacco, hogs and cattle dominate.

At the northern end of the district, a few miles from the Kentucky border, Clarksville has benefited from diverse manufacturing and the expansion of Fort Campbell, one-fifth of which is in Kentucky.

Democratic until the 1970s, the 7th now leans slightly toward the GOP. The 7th's Shelby County is solid Republican territory, but "Yellow Dog"

Democrats outweigh Republican voters in Clarksville and surrounding rural sectors. In state elections, voters favor Democrats, but the district tends to vote for Republican presidential candidates. The GOP has held the congressional seat since the early 1970s, with support from socially conservative suburban, rural and military contingents.

MAJOR INDUSTRY
Tobacco, cattle, auto manufacturing

MILITARY BASES
Fort Campbell, 25,719 military, 2,802 civilian (2001) (Shared with Kentucky's 1st District)

CITIES
Clarksville, 99,049; Germantown, 37,781; Columbia, 32,308

UNUSUAL FEATURES
Home of President James K. Polk in Columbia; Mule Day in Columbia attracts 250,000 every April; Gov. Don Sundquist from Clarksville; Shiloh Park (mostly in the 4th) memorializes those who died during one of the bloodiest battles during the Civil War.

Rep. John Tanner (D)

CAPITOL OFFICE
225-4714; fax 225-1765
1226 Longworth Bldg. 20515

INTERNET
e-mail: john.tanner@mail.house.gov
web: www.house.gov/tanner

COMMITTEES
Ways & Means

HOMETOWN
Union City

BORN
Sept. 22, 1944, Halls, Tenn.

RELIGION
Disciples of Christ

FAMILY
Wife, Betty Ann Tanner; two children

EDUCATION
U. of Tennessee, B.S. 1966, J.D. 1968

MILITARY SERVICE
Navy, 1968-72; Tenn. National Guard, 1974-2000

CAREER
Lawyer; insurance company owner

POLITICAL HIGHLIGHTS
Tenn. House, 1977-89

ELECTION RESULTS

2000 GENERAL

John Tanner (D)	143,127	72.3%
Billy Yancy (R)	54,929	27.7%

2000 PRIMARY

John Tanner (D)	32,078	86.7%
Marvin Williams (D)	4,914	13.3%

1998 GENERAL

John Tanner (D)	unopposed

PREVIOUS WINNING PERCENTAGES
1996 (67%); 1994 (64%); 1992 (84%); 1990 (100%); 1988 (62%)

Elected 1988; 7th term

Tanner is the most conservative Democrat on the Ways and Means Committee, and he may also be the most bipartisan. His willingness to work across the aisle has made him a player on a host of bills, including welfare and tax reform.

Tanner rarely speaks on the House floor and is seldom the subject of media features. But he has quietly used his seat on Ways and Means and his leadership role in the "Blue Dogs," a coalition of conservative Democrats, to try to pull the Democratic Party to the political center — the ground preferred by his rural and small-town West Tennessee constituents.

In the 106th Congress, he teamed with conservative Washington Republican Jennifer Dunn on a bill to phase out the estate tax and with liberal New York Democrat Charles B. Rangel, the top Ways and Means Democrat, on a package of small-business tax breaks to sweeten a proposed hike in the minimum wage. In the 104th, he worked with moderate Delaware Republican Michael N. Castle to introduce a bipartisan bill overhauling the welfare system. President Clinton endorsed the Tanner-Castle measure, and elements of the bill eventually became law.

Tanner's voting record in the 106th was conservative enough to attract an endorsement from the U.S. Chamber of Commerce. Yet he was thought to be enough of a loyal Democrat to win appointment to a party task force brainstorming on how to win a Democratic House majority. "The perception in the land is that the Democrats are too liberal, the Republicans are too rigid and too conservative, and the Blue Dogs or some group like them are where to go in terms of governing," Tanner once said.

Tanner's votes place him squarely in the midst of the Blue Dogs. The group was formed in 1994, when many conservative Democrats were chafing at what they viewed as indifference to their views by the liberal majority in the Democratic Caucus. Tanner says Democratic leaders now realize they must include a broader range of ideologies, if they hope to regain control of the House. Tanner has been a leader in drafting the Blue Dogs' alternative budget proposals, which have served as a basis for compromise between more-liberal Democrats and the GOP. He called the 1997 balanced-budget deal a "constructive middle ground" that included "significant parts of the Blue Dog budget."

With his district's farmers in mind, Tanner's top legislative priority in the 106th Congress was a bill that called for a phase-out of the estate tax over a 10-year period. The measure sought to help keep family farms in the family. Tanner was also active in pushing his "debt reduction lockbox" bill to require that half of the on-budget surplus be dedicated to paying off the national debt. "Where I come from, it's considered to be very poor form if you owe a fellow some money and if you come into some money and you don't pay him, and you do something else with it," he said.

Tanner supported legislation in 2000 to grant China permanent normal trade status, arguing that, "The only way to keep and create American jobs here is by expanding markets abroad," he told the Memphis Commercial Appeal. The China trade vote and an earlier one giving employers the option of offering their workers time off instead of overtime pay, cost Tanner support from some labor groups. But Tanner defended the votes, saying he was looking at the long-term potential for job creation. "I try to reflect the district, and if that's upsetting to them [labor unions], I can't help it," Tanner said.

Tanner also is a leader in the Congressional Sportsmen's Caucus, and in the 105th he helped enact a law that establishes hunting and fishing, along with wildlife observation and environmental education, as legitimate uses of the national wildlife refuge system. Tanner's district includes all or part of five national wildlife refuges.

Tanner was also successful in 2000 in getting through legislation to transfer about 1,900 acres of a Naval air station north of Memphis to local authorities. A runway on the land will be used as an alternative to the Memphis airport, he said, with emphasis on air cargo operations.

Tanner's father was a farmer, and he also worked in the family's long-established insurance business. His mother taught school. Tanner attended the University of Tennessee, playing guard on the freshman basketball team and earning bachelor's and law degrees. He then served four years in the Navy as a lawyer, prosecuting court-martials.

After his Naval service, Tanner joined a private law practice back in his hometown of Union City. In 1976, he ran for the state House at the urgings of colleagues in the American Legion, where he was a state officer. He was also encouraged by Tennessee House Speaker Ned Ray McWherter, who is distantly related to Tanner by marriage. Tanner served in the Tennessee House for 12 years.

In 1988, when Democratic Rep. Ed Jones, a longtime family friend, retired after nearly two decades in the House, Tanner came out of the blocks fast. He quickly assembled an enviable organization and financial base, boosted by his connections to Jones and McWherter. His relaxed, "good ol' boy" style helped him win over rural and small-town voters. He handily defeated GOP nominee Ed Bryant, a Jackson lawyer.

Bryant argued that Tanner would be controlled by the liberal Democratic Party leadership in Washington. "Bull," said Tanner. "Ed Jones has been his own man and John Tanner will be his own man." He won with more than 60 percent of the vote and has rolled to re-election ever since. (Bryant went on to win the neighboring 7th District House seat in 1994.)

Early in his House career, Tanner had a chance for more visibility. In 1992, after Sen. Al Gore was elected vice president on the ticket with Bill Clinton, the Tennessee governor, who happened to be McWherter, needed to appoint an interim replacement to fill Gore's Senate seat. Although the job was said to be Tanner's for the asking, he told McWherter he preferred to stay on in the House. The Senate appointment went to Harlan Mathews.

Many Tennessee Democrats, including McWherter, think Tanner would be a strong candidate for governor in 2002, but he has demurred.

KEY VOTES

2000
Yes Raise hourly minimum wage by $1 over two years
Yes Halt funding for U.S. mission in Kosovo unless European nations pay more
Yes Provide Medicare benefits to military retirees and their dependents
Yes Grant China permanent normal trade status
Yes Phase out estate, gift and trust taxes
No Prohibit implementation of president's national monument designations
No Approve GOP plan to provide prescription drug coverage for Medicare beneficiaries
Yes Increase help for poor nations indebted to international financial institutions

1999
Yes Impose steel import quotas
No Kill proposal to take aviation trust funds off budget
Yes Require background checks on buyers only at gun shows with 10 or more vendors
Yes Remove barriers among banking, securities and insurance companies
Yes Authorize state grants to hire teachers and reduce class size
Yes Overhaul campaign finance law; ban "soft money" and restrict advocacy advertising
Yes Approve bipartisan plan to increase rights of patients in managed-care health plans

INTEREST GROUPS

	AFL-CIO	ADA	CCUS	ACU
2000	60%	45%	85%	36%
1999	78%	70%	76%	29%
1998	60%	60%	88%	41%
1997	63%	40%	80%	40%

CQ VOTE STUDIES

	PARTY UNITY		PRESIDENTIAL SUPPORT	
	Support	Oppose	Support	Oppose
2000	71%	29%	56%	44%
1999	67%	33%	62%	38%
1998	69%	31%	58%	42%
1997	66%	34%	59%	41%

TENNESSEE 8
West – Jackson; part of Shelby County

The mighty Mississippi to the west and the Tennessee and Cumberland rivers to the east frame the rolling hills and flat farmland that make up the 8th. Except for Memphis' northern suburbs and Jackson, the district is overwhelmingly rural, Democratic and working class. Democrats have held this seat since Reconstruction. The sole Republican oasis is the district's slice of Shelby County, where young couples are moving in at a steady pace. Bill Clinton carried the district in the 1990s, but President Bush narrowly edged out native son Al Gore in 2000, winning by about 700 votes.

The district is among the nation's poorest, but a few manufacturing plants prevent the economy from slipping further. A Pringles potato chip plant employs more than 1,300 in Jackson, and tire, auto and textile manufacturers are scattered throughout less-populated sectors. Mechanization has decreased factory employment but increased production on small farms. State and federal government also provide much-needed jobs via three large state prisons and a downsized, but still significant, naval air station in Millington.

The northern section of the Tennessee River feeds into Kentucky Lake in the northeast of the district. Besides hosting Tennessee Valley Authority dams and power plants, these large waterways draw many avid hunters and fisherman to the district. Also, thousands of bird watchers flock to Reelfoot Lake each winter to view the migration of hundreds of bald eagles.

MAJOR INDUSTRY
Manufacturing, agriculture, government

MILITARY BASES
Mid-South Naval Support Activity, 3,703 military, 2,005 civilian (1999)

CITIES
Memphis (pt.), 60,834 (1990); Jackson, 54,036; Millington, 19,281; Dyersburg, 16,939

UNUSUAL FEATURES
Civil War battles fought at Fort Donelson, Fort Henry and Fort Pillow; Reelfoot Lake, one of the nation's largest freshwater lakes, born out of an earthquake in 1811; 65-foot tall replica Eiffel Tower in Paris.

Rep. Harold E. Ford Jr. (D)

Elected 1996; 3rd term

CAPITOL OFFICE
225-3265; fax 225-5663; 325 Cannon Bldg. 20515

INTERNET
e-mail: rep.harold.ford.jr@mail.house.gov
web: www.house.gov/ford

COMMITTEES
Education & Workforce
Financial Services

HOMETOWN
Memphis

BORN
May 11, 1970, Memphis, Tenn.

RELIGION
Baptist

FAMILY
Single

EDUCATION
U. of Pennsylvania, B.A. 1992; U. of Michigan, J.D. 1996

CAREER
Law clerk; congressional aide

POLITICAL HIGHLIGHTS
No previous office

ELECTION RESULTS

2000 GENERAL

Harold E. Ford Jr. (D)		unopposed

2000 PRIMARY

Harold E. Ford Jr. (D)		unopposed

1998 GENERAL

Harold E. Ford Jr. (D)	75,428	78.7%
Claude Burdikoff (R)	18,078	18.9%

PREVIOUS WINNING PERCENTAGES
1996 (61%)

Sworn into office at the precocious age of 26, Ford has established himself as a rising political star, especially after being tapped by his party to deliver the keynote address at the 2000 Democratic National Convention. He makes no secret of his ambition to win a statewide, or even national, office. In an interview with The Associated Press in 2000, he lifted his arm toward the ceiling and said, "If this is the trajectory I'm on, I like where I'm going."

Savvy and articulate, Ford follows in the footsteps of his father, Democrat Harold E. Ford Sr., who represented the 9th District for 11 terms. But in reaching for the political center, the younger Ford represents a new generation of black leaders. A member of both the conservative "Blue Dogs" and the moderate New Democratic Coalition, he supports such conservative causes as capital gains tax cuts and a constitutional amendment protecting school prayer. But he also focuses on such Democratic priorities as increasing the minimum wage and boosting education funding.

Ford has been politically active since the tender age of 4, when he made a radio ad for his father's first campaign. His script: "If you want better housing, better jobs and lower cookie prices, go to the polls and vote for my daddy for Congress." Ford family lore has it that when Harold Sr. was sworn into Congress in 1975, the 4-year-old son, who was in the chamber with his father, raised his hand along with the members and announced, "This is what I want to do when I grow up."

Over the next 20 years, Ford earned a history degree from the University of Pennsylvania, worked on President Clinton's first transition team, was an aide to the Senate Budget Committee under former Tennessee Democratic Sen. James Sasser and served in the Economic Development Administration of Clinton's Commerce Department.

At times, Ford's conservative leanings have irritated his Democratic colleagues. He skirmished with Minority Leader Richard A. Gephardt, at one point questioning whether Gephardt's leadership style was outdated. In 1998, he sharply criticized Clinton's behavior in the Monica Lewinsky scandal. Despite White House lobbying efforts, he joined with Republicans in the 106th Congress in voting to override a Clinton veto of legislation to end the estate tax, calling the levy "unfair and senseless."

But Ford weighs in with Democrats on some of the party's signature issues, including providing Medicare recipients with prescription drug benefits. In 2000, he called on lawmakers to "help seniors avoid having to choose between buying groceries or taking the medication their doctors prescribe. We cannot wait any longer."

A member of the Education and the Workforce Committee, Ford makes the case for additional federal funding for education. He has pointed to various problems facing public schools in his district, where, he said in 1997, "many of our students even today are being let out at noon because they have no air conditioning in their schools. At 7 a.m., classrooms where they are trying to teach algebra and basic English and basic science, the temperature is stifling, 96, 97 and 98 degrees."

He faults the GOP majority for spending too much effort developing "ways to punish and sentence kids." And he prods Congress to support projects, such as wiring schools to the Internet, that he says will help students succeed "in the skills-dependent and technology-driven economy of the 21st century." But he has also shown interest in a controversial Republican priority: creating a school voucher program. "I have not seen a voucher plan that works," he told The Washington Post. "But if you show me one, I'll support it."

Ford sides with liberals on some gun control measures, such as requiring trigger locks and background checks for gun purchases. "If we make it impossible for ex-cons to ever vote again and difficult to work, we should make it impossible for them to own guns," he told Gannett News Service. But he opposes broader steps such as registration of gun owners.

Although he sometimes votes with Republicans, Ford can also be sharply critical of them. In 1997, he rapped Senate Majority Leader Trent Lott for saying that business political action committees such as the one run by Federal Express (which is headquartered in Ford's district) would "squirm considerably" if they continued to donate to Democratic campaigns. "I am deeply concerned about the willingness of people in power to pressure potential contributors," Ford said.

He also could not summon up much bipartisan spirit in his 1997 work on the Government Reform Committee (which he left in the 107th to join the Financial Services Committee). He joined the chorus of Democrats complaining that the GOP majority was running a one-sided investigation of alleged 1996 campaign finance irregularities. From his perspective as "a member of Generation X," Ford said the conduct of the hearings had reinforced "the cynicism, the skepticism, the suspicion that young people have" about the political process.

Ford also donned the "Generation X" mantle in 1997, when he asked Clinton to include younger people on his advisory board for the administration's "Initiative on Race." Ford said any discussion on racial issues needs to include "someone who never sat in the back of the bus, someone who has never been denied the right to vote, someone who has never been denied the right to lodge at his or her hotel choice. ... We're hoping to talk about some of the new challenges ... and a new dimension of solutions that may present themselves," Ford told Fox TV News.

After running his father's 1992 and 1994 House campaigns, Ford launched his own 1996 campaign shortly before his graduation from law school at the University of Michigan. His campaign buttons and T-shirts simply said "Jr." Voters in the Memphis-based 9th knew the candidate sought to succeed his father, who served as his son's campaign coordinator.

Memphis Mayor W.W. Herenton, a political rival of the Ford family, openly shopped for a heavy-hitting politician he could back for a run against the younger Ford. But Ford rolled to victory in the three-way Democratic primary with 60 percent of the vote. He crushed GOP candidate Rod DeBerry in the general election and has easily won re-election.

KEY VOTES

2000

Yes Raise hourly minimum wage by $1 over two years

Yes Halt funding for U.S. mission in Kosovo unless European nations pay more

? Provide Medicare benefits to military retirees and their dependents

Yes Grant China permanent normal trade status

Yes Phase out estate, gift and trust taxes

No Prohibit implementation of president's national monument designations

No Approve GOP plan to provide prescription drug coverage for Medicare beneficiaries

Yes Increase help for poor nations indebted to international financial institutions

1999

Yes Impose steel import quotas

No Kill proposal to take aviation trust funds off budget

No Require background checks on buyers only at gun shows with 10 or more vendors

Yes Remove barriers among banking, securities and insurance companies

Yes Authorize state grants to hire teachers and reduce class size

Yes Overhaul campaign finance law; ban "soft money" and restrict advocacy advertising

Yes Approve bipartisan plan to increase rights of patients in managed-care health plans

INTEREST GROUPS

	AFL-CIO	ADA	CCUS	ACU
2000	80%	60%	70%	24%
1999	78%	100%	40%	4%
1998	88%	80%	62%	14%
1997	100%	85%	60%	8%

CQ VOTE STUDIES

	PARTY UNITY		PRESIDENTIAL SUPPORT	
	Support	Oppose	Support	Oppose
2000	89%	11%	74%	26%
1999	90%	10%	81%	19%
1998	91%	9%	75%	25%
1997	93%	7%	80%	20%

TENNESSEE 9

Memphis

The 9th includes most of Tennessee's largest city, Memphis, which sits atop the bluffs of the Mississippi River. Memphis continues to struggle with racial tension that has hindered its growth since the civil rights movement of the 1960s. Most of its majority-black population lives downtown, while much of the white population has moved to the eastern suburbs. However, revitalization efforts have paved the way for inner-city economic development and integrated downtown residences such as Harbourtown and South Bluffs.

Memphis is a key distribution center. Federal Express is based at the Memphis International Airport, making it the world's busiest cargo airport and attracting international companies to the area. The economy also depends on St. Jude Children's Research Hospital, one of the nation's top pediatric-care centers.

It remains to be seen whether Memphis has fully recovered from industrial decline that began in the 1970s, but tourism has remained an economic mainstay, with people flocking to honor two American icons – Elvis Presley and Martin Luther King Jr. The hotel where King was assassinated is now a museum.

The area first sent an African-American to Congress in 1974, initiating the reign of Democratic, black political power in Memphis. Republicans usually capture the white vote and Democrats receive the black vote at all levels. However, in 1998, more than 40 percent of white voters sent Rep. Ford, a black Democrat, back to Congress, possibly signaling a change. Ford was unopposed in 2000.

MAJOR INDUSTRY
Distribution, health care, government

CITIES
Memphis (pt.), 519,594 (1990)

UNUSUAL FEATURES
Graceland, home of Elvis Presley; W.C. Handy developed the blues musical style on Beale Street; The Great American Pyramid, a 32-story downtown arena, seats 22,000 spectators; Memphis takes its name from the Egyptian city with ports on the banks of another meandering waterway, the Nile.

TEXAS

Gov. Rick Perry (R)

First elected: Assumed office Dec. 21, 2000, following the resignation of Gov. George W. Bush, R, as he prepared to assume the presidency

Length of term: 4 years

Term expires: 1/03

Salary: $118,345

Phone: (512) 463-2000

Hometown: Austin

Born: March 4, 1950, Paint Creek, Texas

Religion: Methodist

Family: Wife, Anita Perry; two children

Education: Texas A&M U., B.S. 1972

Military Service: Air Force, 1972-77

Career: Farmer; rancher

Political highlights: Texas House, 1984-90; Texas commissioner of agriculture, 1990-98; lieutenant governor, 1999-2000

Lt. Gov. Bill Ratliff (R)

First elected: Elected by the state Senate on Dec. 28, 2000, to fill the vacancy left when Lt. Gov. Rick Perry, R, became governor

Length of term: 4 years

Term expires: 1/03

Salary: $7,200/year; $95/day in session (receives his salary as state senator)

Phone: (512) 463-0001

STATE LEGISLATURE

Legislature: Meets January-May in odd-numbered years

House: 150 members, 2-year terms

2001 breakdown: 72R, 78D; 120 men, 30 women

Salary: $7,200/year; $95/day when in session

Phone: (512) 463-0845

Senate: 31 members, 4-year terms

2001 breakdown: 16R, 15D; 27 men, 4 women

Salary: $7,200/year; $95/day when in session

Phone: (512) 463-0001

STATE TERM LIMITS

Governor: No
Senate: No
House: No

URBAN STATISTICS

CITY	POPULATION
Houston	1,845,967
San Antonio	1,147,213
Dallas	1,076,214
El Paso	612,770
Austin	587,873

REGISTERED VOTERS

Voters do not register by party.

POPULATION

2000 population	20,851,820
1990 population	16,986,510
Percent change	+22.8%
Rank among states	2
Median age	32.7
Born in state	65%
Foreign born	9%
Urban/rural	91%/9%
Crime rate	603/100,000
Poverty level	15.0%
Federal workers	184,577
Military	165,408

REAPPORTIONMENT

Texas gained two House seats in reapportionment, increasing from 30 districts to 32. The state legislature will draw new district lines in 2001.

MISCELLANEOUS

Web: www.state.tx.us

Capital: Austin

Land area: 261,914 sq. miles
Rank among states: 2

STATE ELECTION OFFICIAL
(512) 463-5650

DEMOCRATIC HEADQUARTERS
(512) 478-9800

REPUBLICAN HEADQUARTERS
(512) 477-9821

District Statistics

	VOTE FOR PRESIDENT																
DIST.	2000 D	R	GREEN	1996 D	R	REF	1992 D	R	I	WHT	BLK	ASIAN	HISP	HOUSEHOLD INCOME	OVER 65+	UNDER 18	COLLEGE EDUCATION
1	36%	63%	1%	45%	46%	9%	39%	38%	23%	79%	18%	0%	3%	$21,697	16%	26%	13%
2	37	61	1	45.3	45.0	10	43	35	22	79	17	0	5	$21,216	14	27	10
3	29	68	2	32	59	8	22	45	33	84	7	4	8	$41,683	5	29	36
4	27	71	1	35	56	9	28	41	30	88	8	0	4	$26,974	14	27	16
5	41	57	2	46	45	8	37.1	37.3	26	75	16	1	14	$25,817	13	25	19
6	28	69	2	33	60	7	24	46	30	90	5	2	6	$40,930	6	27	33
7	26	71	2	28	66	5	22	58	20	80	6	5	16	$40,331	6	27	41
8	22	76	2	27	67	6	22	55	23	90	5	2	7	$35,809	7	28	29
9	44	54	2	48	44	7	44	36	21	72	22	2	9	$29,406	11	27	19
10	42	46	11	53	39	6	48	32	20	73	11	3	21	$27,280	7	24	35
11	33	65	1	42	50	8	36	41	23	76	16	2	12	$22,283	13	27	15
12	40	58	2	46	45	8	38	35	28	80	8	2	16	$27,366	12	27	15
13	31	68	1	39	52	8	36	43	20	79	8	1	19	$20,907	14	28	14
14	34	63	3	42	50	8	37	41	22	78	11	1	23	$23,812	13	28	14
15	54	45	1	60	34	5	53	33	14	76	1	0	74	$17,866	11	35	12

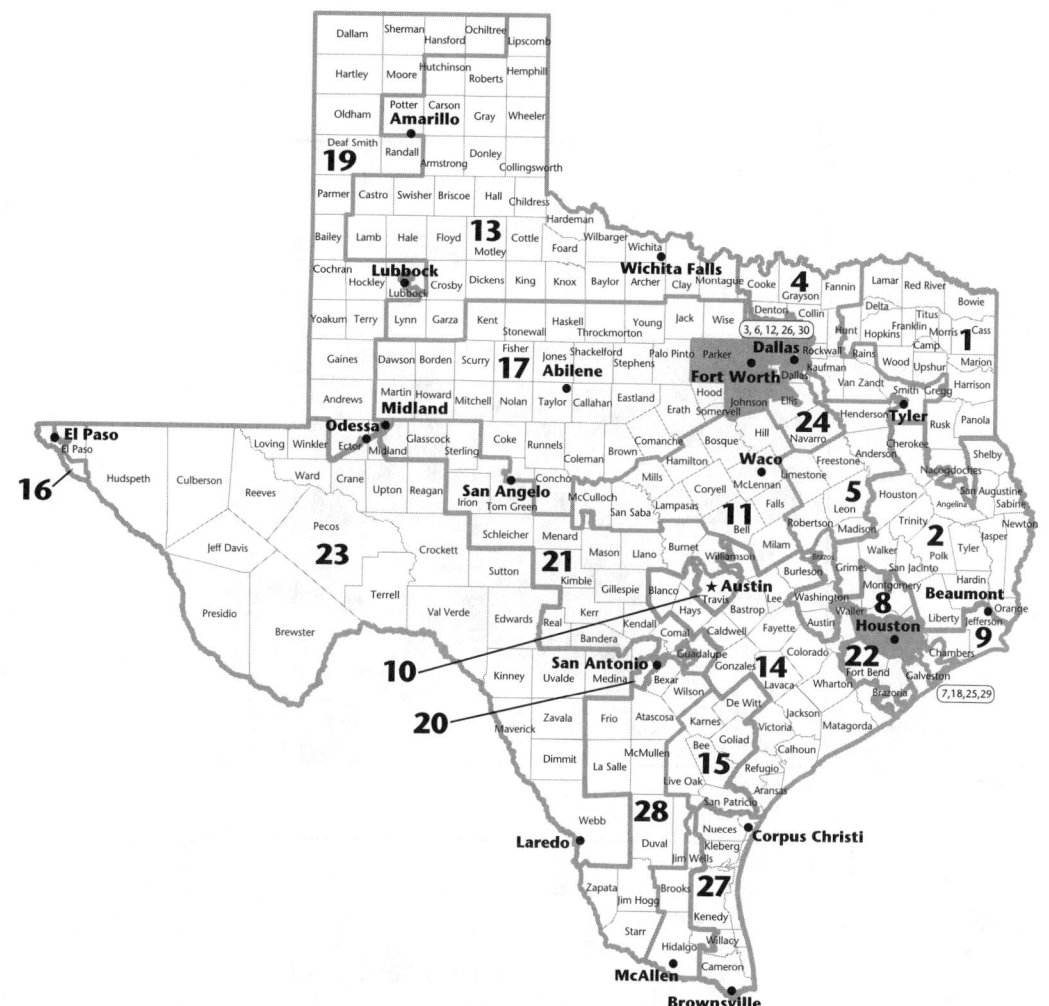

District Statistics

DIST.	D	2000 R	GREEN	D	1996 R	REF	D	1992 R	I	WHT	BLK	ASIAN	HISP	HOUSEHOLD INCOME	OVER 65+	UNDER 18	COLLEGE EDUCATION
16	58%	39%	2%	63%	32%	5%	51%	35%	14%	77%	4%	1%	70%	$22,632	8%	32%	15%
17	28	70	1	39	51	10	34	39	27	86	4	1	17	$21,532	16	27	13
18	71	26	3	73	23	4	66	22	12	40	45	3	23	$22,240	9	27	16
19	19	79	1	26	67	6	23	60	17	86	2	1	19	$27,267	10	29	21
20	55	42	3	59	35	5	48	34	17	72	6	1	60	$22,372	10	30	16
21	24	73	3	30	63	7	25	52	23	91	3	1	14	$32,103	13	26	28
22	36	62	2	38	56	6	30	48	22	72	13	7	17	$40,160	6	29	30
23	41	56	2	50	44	6	42	41	17	74	3	1	62	$21,555	9	34	17
24	51	47	1	53	39	7	42	33	26	64	20	2	21	$27,091	9	30	15
25	49	47	3	51	44	5	42	39	18	63	23	4	18	$29,611	8	28	26
26	27	70	2	30	62	7	22	48	30	87	5	3	9	$40,269	8	23	41
27	49.3	48.7	1	57	37	5	48	36	17	79	2	1	66	$21,552	10	33	15
28	56	42	1	62	32	6	55	30	16	69	9	1	60	$20,276	11	32	8
29	60	38	1	61	33	6	49	33	18	58	15	2	45	$23,808	7	33	9
30	70	29	1	69	25	5	59	23	18	42	45	2	18	$24,775	8	29	14
STATE	**38**	**59**	**2**	**44**	**49**	**7**	**37**	**41**	**22**	**75**	**12**	**2**	**26**	**$27,016**	**10**	**29**	**20**

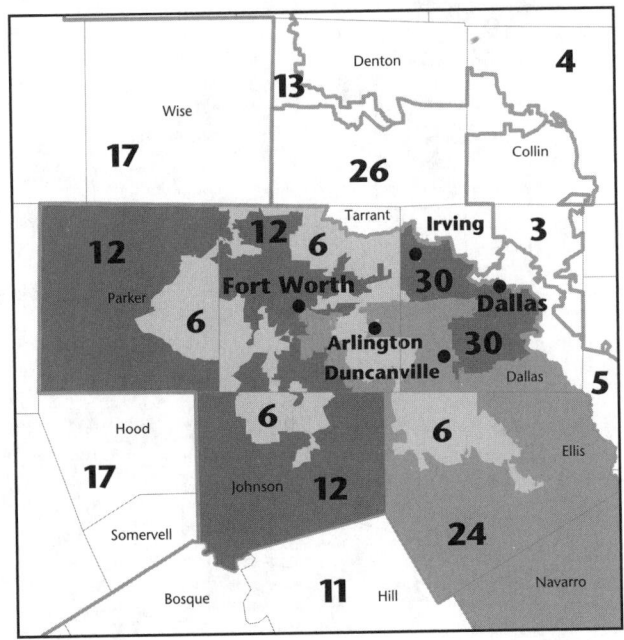

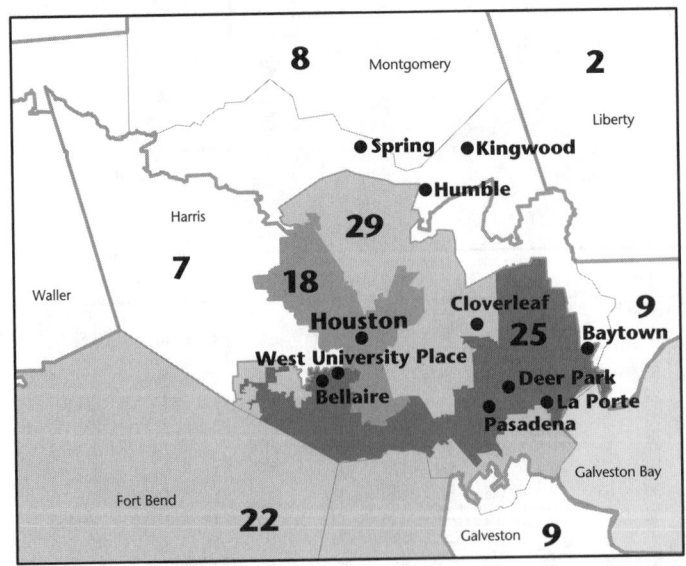

Sen. Phil Gramm (R)

CAPITOL OFFICE
224-2934; fax 228-2856; 370 Russell Bldg. 20510

INTERNET
e-mail: phil_gramm@gramm.senate.gov
web: gramm.senate.gov

COMMITTEES
Banking, Housing & Urban Affairs - chairman
Budget
Finance

HOMETOWN
College Station

BORN
July 8, 1942, Fort Benning, Ga.

RELIGION
Episcopalian

FAMILY
Wife, Wendy Lee Gramm; two children

EDUCATION
U. of Georgia, B.B.A. 1964, Ph.D. 1967

CAREER
Professor

POLITICAL HIGHLIGHTS
Sought Democratic nomination for U.S. Senate,
1976; U.S. House, 1979-85 (served as a Democrat
1979-Jan. 1983); sought Republican nomination for
president, 1996

ELECTION RESULTS

1996 GENERAL

Phil Gramm (R)	3,027,680	54.8%
Victor M. Morales (D)	2,428,776	43.9%

1996 PRIMARY

Phil Gramm (R)	838,339	85.0%
David Young (R)	75,463	7.7%
Henry C. "Hank" Grover (R)	72,400	7.3%

PREVIOUS WINNING PERCENTAGES
1990 (60%); 1984 (59%); 1983 Special House
Election (55%); 1982 House Election (95%); 1980
House Election (71%); 1978 House Election (65%)
* Elected as a Democrat 1978-82

Elected 1984; 3rd term

Gramm has a reputation as one of the most partisan and divisive members of the Senate. He angers many Democrats, and even moderate Republicans sometimes find themselves bickering with Gramm over his relentless pursuit of conservative ideals. His critics view him as arrogant and obstinate, someone who would rather let important legislation founder than accept compromise.

Gramm admits to possessing a considerable ego, and he shows no signs of doubt that his views are right and his course correct. Yet he also has a folksy Southern manner that helps soften his hard edges.

His rigid reputation had Wall Street nervous when Gramm took the gavel of the Banking Committee in the 106th Congress. The financial services industries — which had been pushing unsuccessfully for years to clear an overhaul of the laws regulating banks, brokerages and insurers — viewed Gramm's ascension to the chairmanship as a potential setback for their cause.

Not surprisingly, Gramm got off to a rocky start as chairman. When the committee took up a financial services overhaul bill, Gramm wrangled with Democrats and the White House over a community lending law that requires banks to make loans in poor neighborhoods. Gramm said the law amounted to government-backed "extortion" and was being used by community groups to extract grants and questionable loans from banks. Democrats countered that Gramm was trying to gut a law that had worked well for decades without hurting bank profits.

The initial result was a bill that emerged from the committee with no Democratic support, drew a veto threat and passed the Senate on a near party-line vote. GOP leaders eager for a legislative achievement pressed Gramm to compromise, and he rose to the occasion, striking a deal with President Clinton on the community lending issue and other matters. The final statute repeals restrictions on cross-ownership among banks, brokerages and insurers and creates a new regulatory structure for large financial conglomerates.

Still, Gramm relishes his roles as spoiler and partisan bulldog and did not want that deal to tarnish his reputation. "Somehow people have gotten this idea — and I've got to dispel it because it could have an impact on me as a future legislator — that somehow I've become sweet and lovable," he said. "I'd like to reject that outright."

Gramm reinforced this point later in 2000 when he and a handful of other tight-fisted Budget Committee Republicans stalled the panel's work on the budget resolution for weeks. Gramm sought a one-year freeze in spending, excluding Social Security and Medicare, and provisions to make it more difficult for appropriators to exceed the budget's spending limits. Although he did not get the freeze, the committee bent his way and settled on a level of spending lower than what GOP leaders wanted. Gramm also won approval of several spending restraint mechanisms.

As the 107th Congress began, Gramm was quick off the mark with a tax cut bill that embodied President Bush's campaign-trail proposal — not waiting for the president to send up his own detailed plans. Gramm was an early supporter of Bush's presidential bid but said he would not be interested in a Cabinet post. In the Senate, "I'm ... trying to do the Lord's work in the Devil's city," Gramm told The Hill, a Capitol Hill newspaper.

Though deeply immersed in policymaking on matters of high finance, he is not in the Senate's large club of millionaires. He jokes that instead of investing in stocks and bonds, he invests in "tuition and groceries." He often employs homespun phraseology to make his case and to beat down his opponents; invoking lessons from "my momma" is an old standard.

Gramm's father, a staff sergeant in the Army, was disabled while on duty and died when Gramm was a teenager. As a result, Gramm's mother often worked double shifts to support the family. During his youth in Georgia, he helped bring in money by delivering newspapers.

Gramm is a party stalwart on social issues. He opposes abortion rights and gun control, for instance, and he routinely attacks federal programs to benefit people who are unwilling, in his words, to "pull the wagon." But his two decades in Congress have been marked since the outset by a focus on fiscal policy, in which he has long preached the virtues of balancing the budget and cutting taxes. In his second House term, in the 97th Congress, he developed the package of spending cuts that formed the basis of President Reagan's attack on the size and growth of the federal government. Four years later, after just eight months as a senator, he was the driving force behind a major rewrite of the federal budget process.

Gramm also has been active in the debate over how to shore up Social Security and Medicare, the government-sponsored health insurance program for the elderly. In the 105th, he was named to a 17-member commission studying long-term changes to Medicare, such as raising the eligibility age or requiring wealthier seniors to pay higher premiums. He backed a comprehensive plan to rescue Medicare offered in 1999 by the commission's co-chairman, Democratic Sen. John B. Breaux of Louisiana, but the proposal fell one vote short of the majority needed to make it a formal recommendation to Congress.

In 1998, Gramm played a key role in defeating sweeping tobacco legislation by Sen. John McCain, R-Ariz. Gramm argued that the bill was more about a huge tax increase than it was about combating underage smoking.

While teaching economics at Texas A & M University, Gramm began his political career with an unsuccessful 1976 primary challenge to Democratic Sen. Lloyd Bentsen. Two years later, Gramm won election to the House as a Democrat, displaying formidable fundraising abilities. But soon after he arrived in Washington, his conservative views brought him into conflict with the House Democratic leadership.

When he campaigned for a position on the House Budget Committee, Democratic leaders asked for and received a written pledge that he would be loyal to the party's budget. Yet in 1981, he secretly collaborated with Republicans on the Reagan budget; he would sit in on Democratic budget caucuses, then report back to the White House. Democrats found this out and barred him from meetings. But Reagan's budget ultimately passed, and voters at home seemed indifferent to the Democrats' intramural dispute.

At the start of the next Congress, Gramm was ejected from the Budget Committee. He then left the Democratic Party, resigned his House seat and won easy re-election to it as a Republican. That 1983 election marked the first time in Texas history that the 6th District had gone to the GOP.

When GOP Sen. John Tower announced that he would retire at the conclusion of the 98th Congress, Gramm was ready to run, and he was the favorite from the outset. In the GOP primary, he easily defeated Ron Paul (who now represents the 14th District in the House). In the general election, he took 59 percent of the vote against state Sen. Lloyd Doggett (who now represents the 10th District). He has won re-election since by margins that were comfortable, if not always overwhelming.

In 1996, Gramm made a run at the 1996 Republican presidential nomination. He placed fifth in the Iowa caucuses, however, and dropped out before the New Hampshire primary.

KEY VOTES

2000

Yes Overhaul bankruptcy law and increase minimum wage
Yes Limit fiscal 2001 discretionary spending to $600.3 billion
Yes Override veto on nuclear waste disposal at Yucca Mountain site in Nevada
No Oppose effort to terminate Kosovo mission
No Include gender, sexual orientation and disability in federal hate crime protections
Yes Approve GOP plan to restrict use of genetic information by health insurers
Yes Kill amendment delaying implementation of an anti-missile defense system
Yes Cut taxes for married couples
Yes Grant China permanent normal trade status

1999

Yes Remove President Clinton from office for obstruction of justice
Yes Kill amendment authorizing state grants to hire teachers and reduce class size
No Require criminal background checks for purchases at gun shows
Yes Approve GOP proposal to increase rights of patients in managed-care health plans
Yes Block effort to allow farm and medicine exports to Cuba
No Allow study of tougher automobile fuel efficiency standards
No Ratify nuclear weapons testing treaty
No Prohibit national political parties from collecting "soft money" donations
Yes Remove barriers among banking, securities and insurance companies

INTEREST GROUPS

	AFL-CIO	ADA	CCUS	ACU
2000	0%	0%	86%	100%
1999	0%	0%	94%	96%
1998	0%	0%	94%	96%
1997	14%	0%	80%	100%
1996	0%	0%	100%	100%
1995	0%	0%	100%	100%
1994	0%	5%	100%	100%
1993	0%	5%	100%	92%
1992	8%	0%	100%	93%
1991	17%	0%	89%	95%

CQ VOTE STUDIES

	PARTY UNITY		PRESIDENTIAL SUPPORT	
	Support	Oppose	Support	Oppose
2000	97%	3%	35%	65%
1999	97%	3%	29%	71%
1998	97%	3%	33%	67%
1997	99%	1%	56%	44%
1996	99%	1%	25%	75%
1995	96%	4%	19%	81%
1994	94%	6%	36%	64%
1993	98%	2%	22%	78%
1992	98%	2%	90%	10%
1991	95%	5%	96%	4%

Sen. Kay Bailey Hutchison (R)

Elected June 1993; 2nd full term

Capitol Hill reporters in search of a juicy quote from a Texas senator may generally seek out the more unrestrained Phil Gramm, but Texans looking for a legislative helping hand know Hutchison is a better bet. Determined and focused on home state issues, she has used her growing influence — and her choice seat on the Appropriations Committee — to guard her state's interests as she enters her second full term.

Hutchison's focus may be expected to change and broaden in the 107th Congress now that she has broken into what had been an all-male Senate GOP leadership team. After avoiding a potential fight with Rick Santorum of Pennsylvania for the position of Republican Conference chairman, Hutchison set her sights on becoming the conference secretary, a post left vacant in the summer of 2000 by the death of the respected and influential Paul Coverdell of Georgia. She had no opposition for the position.

Hutchison won the support of colleagues by stressing the party's need to better defend its priorities and explain its motives to the public. "We need to talk about why we are doing all the things we are doing," she said.

While she has sometimes been dismissed as more fluff than substance, her move into the leadership solidifies Hutchison's reputation as a person of influence in the party. It also highlights her working relationship with Majority Leader Trent Lott, who has asked her on numerous occasions to represent the party's position. Her role in the leadership, says one member of her inner circle, is to be a conservative with a friendly face. And her fellow lawmakers know she is happy to share the spotlight.

This is not Hutchison's first foray into issues of national import. Earlier, she carved out a niche in national security matters, becoming a respected voice on foreign policy; and she has been a leading GOP advocate of repealing the "marriage penalty," a quirk in the tax code that results in some two-earner married couples paying higher income taxes. But she spends most of her time fighting for Texas' farmers, military bases, historic sites and oil industry.

Hutchison says she simply looks for middle ground on politically thorny issues. "People are saying they want coalition government, they want bipartisan cooperation, and if we are going to succeed, we are going to have to find those areas where we agree," she told the Houston Chronicle in 2000.

The question many now have is whether Hutchison will stick around the Senate and continue to move up the leadership ladder, or return to Texas in 2002 to run for governor. After easily winning a second full Senate term in 2000 — garnering more votes than any candidate in Texas history — Hutchison stoked the speculation by saying she had not "closed the door" on the notion. Later she quickly sought to put a damper on such talk.

Hutchison blithely cultivates her image as the University of Texas cheerleader she once was — preening for the cameras the night before President Bush's inauguration, for example, wearing heavily tooled red cowboy boots under her floor-length gown at the Texas State Society's Black Tie and Boots Ball. But during legislative deal-making she can display an iron will, pursuing such matters as increased road funding with a single-minded tenacity. Those who have followed her career say she makes sure to be an expert on the issues she is involved with but does not like to go off message or off subject.

Although she generally sides with conservatives, Hutchison has expressed some moderate leanings. She opposes a procedure its oppo-

CAPITOL OFFICE
224-5922; fax 224-0776; 284 Russell Bldg. 20510

INTERNET
e-mail: senator@hutchison.senate.gov
web: hutchison.senate.gov

COMMITTEES
Appropriations
  (Military Construction - chairwoman)
Commerce, Science & Transportation
  (Aviation - chairwoman)
Rules & Administration

HOMETOWN
Dallas

BORN
July 22, 1943, Galveston, Texas

RELIGION
Episcopalian

FAMILY
Husband, Ray Hutchison

EDUCATION
U. of Texas, J.D. 1967, B.A. 1992

CAREER
Broadcast journalist; lawyer; banking executive; candy manufacturer

POLITICAL HIGHLIGHTS
Texas House, 1973-77; sought Republican nomination for U.S. House, 1982; Texas treasurer, 1991-93

ELECTION RESULTS

2000 GENERAL

Kay Bailey Hutchison (R)	4,082,091	65.0%
Gene Kelly (D)	2,030,315	32.4%
Douglas Sandage (GREEN)	91,448	1.5%
Mary Ruwart (LIBERT)	72,798	1.2%

2000 PRIMARY

Kay Bailey Hutchison (R)	unopposed

PREVIOUS WINNING PERCENTAGES
1994 (61%); 1993 Special Runoff Election (67%); 1993 Special Election (29%)

nents call "partial birth" abortion, but says she supports abortion rights. She has drawn criticism from conservatives for voting in favor of criminal and civil penalties for people who block access to abortion clinics. Along with many other conservatives, she wants to repeal the federal tax code and start fresh, but she also opposed efforts to cut funding for the National Endowment for the Arts.

Hutchison had a busy, if not flashy, 106th Congress. Along with running for re-election and laying the groundwork for her election to the leadership, she pushed through legislation to increase airport security and sponsored a measure to make "cyberstalking" a federal crime. She led a delegation to visit a Texas National Guard unit serving in the Bosnia region in 2000 and urged the federal government to address Gulf War syndrome more seriously. Continuing her work on behalf of home state oil companies, she fought against Interior Department efforts to create a new formula for determining royalties that companies must pay for pumping oil on federal land, and she pushed another bill calling for tax credits for small oil companies.

As chairman of the D.C. Appropriations Subcommittee, Hutchison, according to a District official, was "tough, very tough" on financial stability issues. "She was a little too strident at times but it was a pleasure to work with someone who knew what was going on," the official said. (She switched assignments to chair the Military Construction Subcommittee in the 107th.)

Hutchison arrived in Washington in 1993 in the midst of a wide-ranging career both in and out of public life. After graduating from the University of Texas School of Law in 1967, she found herself unable to get a job. In the book "Nine and Counting," written by the nine female senators serving in the 106th Congress, Hutchison said about 30 law firms made clear they could not risk hiring a woman. "I had all of the confidence in the world, and suddenly it was meaningless because I couldn't get a job," she said in the book.

The lack of a job led Hutchison into journalism. She worked for a Texas television station until voters sent her to the state legislature from Houston in 1972 at the age of 29. While in Austin, she teamed up with Democratic legislator Sarah Weddington (the lawyer who filed the suit that became *Roe v. Wade*) on bills protecting victims of sex offenses, including a ban on publishing the names of rape victims.

Hutchison moved to Dallas and unsuccessfully sought the GOP nomination for an open House seat in 1982, then spent much of the next decade in the business world as a banking executive and candy manufacturer. She won a race to become state treasurer in 1990 and came to the Senate in 1993 after winning a special election called after President Clinton chose Democrat Lloyd Bentsen to be his first Treasury secretary.

In 1993, Hutchison was indicted on charges that she had abused her office as Texas treasurer. She was acquitted in February 1994 after the state prosecutor declined to proceed with a case that many said was politically motivated. Hutchison then won a full six-year term to the Senate with three-fifths of the vote. Despite the potentially damaging allegations, Hutchison said the incident made it easier to deal with the ups and downs of politics. And if Texas Gov. George W. Bush had not been the Republican presidential nominee, Hutchison's supporters say her big-state residency and gender would have earned her a certain spot on the shortlist of prospective 2000 vice-presidential candidates.

Hutchison says her style has been shaped by her experiences as a woman in business and politics. "There was always the feeling that because I was a woman maybe I wouldn't be tough enough," she recalled in "Nine and Counting." "Overcoming that kind of undercurrent was one of my greatest challenges."

KEY VOTES

2000

No   Overhaul bankruptcy law and increase minimum wage

Yes   Limit fiscal 2001 discretionary spending to $600.3 billion

Yes   Override veto on nuclear waste disposal at Yucca Mountain site in Nevada

No   Oppose effort to terminate Kosovo mission

No   Include gender, sexual orientation and disability in federal hate crime protections

Yes   Approve GOP plan to restrict use of genetic information by health insurers

Yes   Kill amendment delaying implementation of an anti-missile defense system

Yes   Cut taxes for married couples

Yes   Grant China permanent normal trade status

1999

Yes   Remove President Clinton from office for obstruction of justice

Yes   Kill amendment authorizing state grants to hire teachers and reduce class size

No   Require criminal background checks for purchases at gun shows

Yes   Approve GOP proposal to increase rights of patients in managed-care health plans

No   Block effort to allow farm and medicine exports to Cuba

No   Allow study of tougher automobile fuel efficiency standards

No   Ratify nuclear weapons testing treaty

No   Prohibit national political parties from collecting "soft money" donations

Yes   Remove barriers among banking, securities and insurance companies

INTEREST GROUPS

	AFL-CIO	ADA	CCUS	ACU
2000	0%	0%	93%	96%
1999	0%	0%	94%	88%
1998	0%	0%	100%	88%
1997	0%	5%	100%	92%
1996	0%	5%	92%	100%
1995	8%	0%	100%	87%
1994	0%	10%	100%	96%
1993	0%	13%	100%	94%

CQ VOTE STUDIES

	PARTY UNITY		PRESIDENTIAL SUPPORT	
	Support	Oppose	Support	Oppose
2000	96%	4%	45%	55%
1999	90%	10%	29%	71%
1998	92%	8%	37%	63%
1997	95%	5%	63%	37%
1996	98%	2%	34%	66%
1995	96%	4%	29%	71%
1994	94%	6%	38%	62%
1993	88%	12%	46%	54%

Rep. Max Sandlin (D)

CAPITOL OFFICE
225-3035; fax 225-5866; 324 Cannon Bldg. 20515

INTERNET
e-mail: www.house.gov/writerep
web: www.house.gov/sandlin

COMMITTEES
Financial Services
Transportation & Infrastructure

HOMETOWN
Marshall

BORN
Sept. 29, 1952, Texarkana, Texas

RELIGION
Baptist

FAMILY
Wife, Leslie Howell; four children

EDUCATION
Baylor U., B.A. 1975, J.D. 1978

CAREER
Lawyer; fuel company executive

POLITICAL HIGHLIGHTS
Harrison County Democratic Party chairman,
1984-86; Harrison County judge, 1986-89; Harrison
County Court at law judge, 1989-96

ELECTION RESULTS

2000 GENERAL

Max Sandlin (D)	118,157	55.8%
Noble Willingham (R)	91,912	43.4%

2000 PRIMARY

Max Sandlin (D)	56,207	84.6%
B.D. Blount (D)	10,265	15.4%

1998 GENERAL

Max Sandlin (D)	80,788	59.4%
Dennis Boerner (R)	55,191	40.6%

PREVIOUS WINNING PERCENTAGES
1996 (52%)

Elected 1996; 3rd term

Commerce and government have long been closely intertwined in the Lone Star State, and Sandlin — an energy executive, lawyer and judge — fits the mold of Democratic businessman-politician with the ability to appeal to a range of Texas voters.

After getting his law degree from Baylor, Sandlin set up shop as an attorney, eventually making a small fortune in the oil, gas and gasoline distribution business and, in 1986, moving into the first of two county-level judgeships. He has established himself in the largely rural and politically centrist 1st District by supporting popular conservative causes while staying faithful to Democratic efforts to help senior citizens and lower-income workers.

Sandlin's freshman Democratic colleagues in the 105th Congress chose him to be part of the party's House whip structure, and in the 106th he became an at-large whip. He also serves on the Democratic Steering Committee, which makes committee assignments. Sandlin also sought the company of House Democrats who share his interest in moving the party toward the center. He joined the conservative "Blue Dog" coalition and the moderate New Democrat Coalition, which says it seeks "mainstream, bipartisan solutions."

From his early days as a freshman, Sandlin talked of a "spirit of cooperation" with Republicans. "This class has learned from the mistakes and the polarization" of the 104th Congress, he said.

Several Republican initiatives have won Sandlin's endorsement. He is one of the few Democrats to support a constitutional amendment requiring a two-thirds congressional majority to raise federal taxes, and he also favors repealing the estate tax. He backs a constitutional amendment to outlaw desecration of the U.S. flag, votes to ban a procedure its opponents call "partial birth" abortion, opposes congressional pay raises and often seeks to scale back environmental regulations.

A member of the Congressional Sportsmen's Caucus, Sandlin is an enthusiastic hunter and opposes gun control. He told the Fort Worth Star-Telegram in 1999 that he owned about 15 guns and had already begun to teach his 4-year-old son how to shoot.

But on other issues, Sandlin sides with the more liberal members of his party. He is a staunch supporter of patients' rights legislation that would allow managed-care patients to sue their health care providers. "As we increase access to health care, we must not allow unqualified parties to make critical decisions about patient treatment," he said in the 106th. "Patients need to feel confident that their doctors are giving them all necessary information, without concern of retaliation by a health insurance provider."

A member of the Congressional Arts Caucus, Sandlin resists GOP efforts to cut federal funding for the National Endowment for the Arts. He allies himself with organized labor in its fight against a GOP measure allowing companies to offer their employees compensatory time off instead of pay for overtime work. He also supports such Democratic priorities as increasing the minimum wage and approving funds to hire 100,000 new teachers.

One of Sandlin's most difficult decisions in 2000 was whether to vote for legislation granting China permanent normal trade status. After being heavily lobbied by unions opposed to the measure and businesses that supported it, Sandlin waited until the final 10 seconds of voting on the House floor before supporting the measure. He told reporters afterward that the United States would be in a better position to improve human rights in China than "if we shut our door" to trading opportunities. He also said the measure could help spur economic growth in the 1st.

In the 105th, Sandlin cited personal experience in criticizing a GOP juvenile justice bill intended to encourage states to prosecute juveniles accused of violent crimes in the adult justice system. "I rise as the father of four children, a youth baseball, basketball, softball coach, a former judge," he said in 1997. "I have heard thousands of juvenile cases. ... Some children absolutely must be incarcerated ... [but] spending more and more and more tax dollars to prosecute children and locking them up ... simply will not work." Sandlin and most Democrats voted to amend the GOP bill to channel more federal dollars toward locally run prevention and early intervention programs. He joined 76 other Democrats in supporting the amended GOP bill, but the proposal fell to nearly united Republican opposition.

After voting for a landmark balanced-budget agreement in 1997, Sandlin called it "a victory for the Democratic Party," bragging that Republicans were thwarted in their attempts to increase the age for Medicare eligibility, introduce a co-payment for services and raise premiums for wealthier seniors. "Republicans say Medicare is welfare, and we see it as a promise to the American people that needs to be kept," Sandlin said.

Sandlin sits on the Transportation Committee, where he has worked hard to fund highway construction projects in his district. He advocates continued funding for Amtrak's Texas Eagle route, which runs through the 1st.

A member of the Financial Services Committee, Sandlin wants to improve access to capital in rural America. In the 106th, he voted for legislation, known as the Community Renewal and New Markets Act, that was designed to provide tax breaks and other incentives for companies that do business in economically distressed areas. "Rural America still lags behind the rest of the country when it comes to earnings, employment, education and other key economic indicators," he said. "We still have a lot of work to do to ensure that places like East Texas are not left on the outside looking in at this strong national economy."

When Democratic Rep. Jim Chapman left the 1st in 1996 for an ultimately unsuccessful Senate bid, Sandlin sought the open seat, stressing his community involvement and promising to be "the chief marketing agent for the district." Aided by Chapman's backing, Sandlin won the nomination with 56 percent. He outspent the GOP nominee, attorney Ed Merritt, and won the general election by 5 percentage points, even as GOP presidential candidate Bob Dole narrowly carried the district. In 2000, Sandlin fended off a spirited challenge by actor Noble Willingham and posted a 12-point victory.

KEY VOTES

2000
Yes Raise hourly minimum wage by $1 over two years
No Halt funding for U.S. mission in Kosovo unless European nations pay more
Yes Provide Medicare benefits to military retirees and their dependents
Yes Grant China permanent normal trade status
Yes Phase out estate, gift and trust taxes
No Prohibit implementation of president's national monument designations
No Approve GOP plan to provide prescription drug coverage for Medicare beneficiaries
Yes Increase help for poor nations indebted to international financial institutions

1999
Yes Impose steel import quotas
No Kill proposal to take aviation trust funds off budget
No Require background checks on buyers only at gun shows with 10 or more vendors
Yes Remove barriers among banking, securities and insurance companies
Yes Authorize state grants to hire teachers and reduce class size
Yes Overhaul campaign finance law; ban "soft money" and restrict advocacy advertising
Yes Approve bipartisan plan to increase rights of patients in managed-care health plans

INTEREST GROUPS

	AFL-CIO	ADA	CCUS	ACU
2000	80%	60%	71%	33%
1999	78%	70%	60%	24%
1998	80%	80%	61%	40%
1997	88%	60%	70%	36%

CQ VOTE STUDIES

	PARTY UNITY		PRESIDENTIAL SUPPORT	
	Support	Oppose	Support	Oppose
2000	75%	25%	57%	43%
1999	74%	26%	68%	32%
1998	72%	28%	63%	37%
1997	74%	26%	67%	33%

TEXAS 1

Northeast — Texarkana; Marshall

The 1st wraps around Texas' northeastern corner along the Oklahoma and Arkansas borders near the city of Texarkana, then stretches south along the Louisiana border to include parts of Nacogdoches County. Mostly removed from the Dallas-Fort Worth suburbs, the district has a rural landscape and a Southern feel that's harder to find in the rest of the state. Nearly three-fourths of its population are native Texans; the state average stands at 65 percent.

The economic dominance of natural resources – timber, oil and natural gas – has diminished since the oil bust of the 1980s and the rise of the manufacturing sector, which now drives the economy. The 1st still faces some economic challenges from foreign timber companies and cattle ranchers who can sell their products at lower prices. A small but significant defense industry is centered around Greenville, which is shared with the 4th. Slow population growth and miles of forests and agricultural land are hallmarks of the district but do less to improve its

economic shape than the highways that connect the district to the outside world.

Residents of the 1st tend to be conservative, even among Democrats, and the region has been called the "buckle of the Bible Belt." A bastion of political populism, the district has the highest percentage of elderly residents in the state (based on 1990 Census Bureau statistics) and provides strong support for the GOP in the western portions of the 1st. Conservative Democrats still run well along the eastern border near Arkansas and Louisiana.

MAJOR INDUSTRY
Timber, light manufacturing, agriculture

MILITARY BASES
Red River Army Depot, 177 military, 1,859 civilian (1999)

CITIES
Longview (pt.), 33,710 (1990); Texarkana, 32,285; Marshall, 24,338

UNUSUAL FEATURES
The city of Texarkana is split between Texas and Arkansas – it has two mayors, two police forces and two school systems; It's also the birthplace of Ross Perot.

Rep. Jim Turner (D)

CAPITOL OFFICE
225-2401; fax 225-5955; 208 Cannon Bldg. 20515

INTERNET
e-mail: www.house.gov/writerep
web: www.house.gov/turner

COMMITTEES
Armed Services
Government Reform

HOMETOWN
Crockett

BORN
Feb. 6, 1946, Fort Lewis, Wash.

RELIGION
Baptist

FAMILY
Wife, Ginny Turner; two children

EDUCATION
U. of Texas, B.B.A 1968, M.B.A. 1971, J.D. 1971

MILITARY SERVICE
Army, 1970-78

CAREER
Lawyer; gubernatorial aide

POLITICAL HIGHLIGHTS
Texas House, 1981-84; mayor of Crockett, 1989-91; Texas Senate, 1991-96

ELECTION RESULTS

2000 GENERAL

Jim Turner (D)	162,891	91.1%
Gary Lyndon Dye (LIBERT)	15,939	8.9%

2000 PRIMARY

Jim Turner (D)	unopposed

1998 GENERAL

Jim Turner (D)	81,556	58.4%
Brian Babin (R)	56,891	40.8%

PREVIOUS WINNING PERCENTAGES
1996 (52%)

Elected 1996; 3rd term

Reared in East Texas, the son of an Army man who returned home to the small town of Crockett to start a small business, Turner's political bent is exactly what you would expect — conservative and Democratic.

He affiliates with the conservative "Blue Dogs" (he is one of three co-chairmen of the group in the 107th Congress) and the more centrist New Democrat Coalition, and he exhibits the pragmatism that both groups say they want to foster in Congress.

Turner — a serious-minded lawyer, and a deacon and Sunday school teacher in his church — is quite a contrast to the man he replaced, "Good-time Charlie" Wilson, a wisecracking, backslapping, womanizing divorcee, but his political views are the same in many respects.

On key issues, Turner's votes are difficult to peg politically. He supports federal funding for the National Endowment for the Arts and generally takes a pro-labor line. While he has sided with abortion rights proponents, he voted to ban a procedure its opponents call "partial birth" abortion. And he opposes gun control efforts. He supported President Clinton only about 60 percent of the time and bucks the majority of House Democrats with regularity.

Many of Turner's priorities on Capitol Hill are the same issues that were important to him during his 10 years in the Texas Legislature — as a Texas state senator, he served on the Education and Criminal Justice committees, and from 1993 to 1994, he was chairman of the Texas Commission on Children and Youth. On Capitol Hill, Turner helped found the bipartisan Congressional Fatherhood Promotion Task Force in response to a study indicating that about a quarter of U.S. children are living without fathers in the household.

In the 105th Congress, Turner had significant objections to GOP-proposed juvenile justice legislation, calling it one-dimensional for its emphasis on punishment rather than prevention. But in the 106th, he was one of the small band of Democrats who voted with Republicans to crack down on those who sold or provided sexually explicit material to minors. The proposal, drafted in the wake of a mass shooting at Columbine High School in Colorado, was designed to address what backers termed the "root causes" of youth violence.

Another priority drawn from Turner's days in the state legislature is a plan, backed by his fellow Texans in the House, Republican Kevin Brady and Democrat Lloyd Doggett, to review most federal programs every 10 years with an eye toward eliminating those that have outlived their purpose. (In Texas, a state sunset law resulted in the closure of dozens of state agencies and the merger of many others, Turner says, saving millions of dollars.) The proposal failed in the 105th Congress, but Turner, Brady and Doggett returned in the 106th with their "Abolishment of Obsolete Agencies and Federal Sunset Act of 1999."

As the price of prescription drugs became a concern nationwide, Turner in the 106th was at the forefront on the issue, cosponsoring legislation with Democrat Tom Allen of Maine to ensure that senior citizens can buy drugs at the same discounted prices afforded the federal government and HMOs, which have the muscle to negotiate lower prices.

Environmentalists find Turner's vote tough to get. In 1997, he was one of only 33 Democrats opposing an amendment to curtail funding for construction of logging roads in the nation's Forest Service system. Turner rose on the House floor to speak "on behalf of the loggers and the small sawmill owners in my district." And in 2000, Turner warily viewed the Environmental Protection Agency's move to increase regulation of timber harvesting — a significant industry in East Texas. More than 1,700 timber farmers turned out in Lufkin to hear details of the plan, and Turner, along with Democrats Max Sandlin of Texas and Marion Berry of Arkansas, who represent neighboring districts, prepared legislation to protect the timber industry.

Turner was born in Fort Lewis, Wash., where his father was serving in the Army. The family returned to its original home in East Texas when Turner was 5, and his father started a construction business and opened a hardware store. Turner recalls being interested in politics at an early age — he was in student government in school and at the University of Texas. While he was still in college, he worked for a state lawmaker and for Democratic Govs. John Connally and Preston Smith.

Turner was in the ROTC in college and served an active duty stint with the Army after graduate school, where he had earned a law degree and an M.B.A. After his discharge from the Army, Turner practiced law, always with the idea of getting involved in politics.

The opportunity came in 1980, when he made a successful run for the Texas House. Turner served four years there, leaving to work for Democratic Gov. Mark White. After a two-year stint as mayor of Crockett, he returned to Austin in 1991 when he won election to the state Senate.

In Turner's many campaigns, he was noted for his unusual campaign literature — a cookbook containing his wife Ginny's favorite recipes. Through the years, the cookbook's offerings have expanded beyond the Turner kitchen, but it remains a popular, and collectible, campaign tool.

When Wilson decided to retire in 1996, Turner got the Democratic nomination without much trouble, boosted by his political experience in the state House and Senate and as mayor of Crockett, as well as his church and civic involvement. The Republican nominee, dentist Brian Babin, hoped to become the first Republican in more than a century to represent the areas that make up the 2nd District. Babin tried to appeal to conservative and blue-collar voters by portraying Turner as an "elitist liberal." Turner prevailed by 6 percentage points, however, and handily defeated Babin in a 1998 rematch, increasing his margin to 18 points. In 2000, Turner had no major party opposition.

Back home in Crockett, Turner and his father still frequent a favorite diner, spending hours swapping stories with customers — rather than making the rounds to visit with local officials.

KEY VOTES

2000
Yes Raise hourly minimum wage by $1 over two years
No   Halt funding for U.S. mission in Kosovo unless European nations pay more
Yes Provide Medicare benefits to military retirees and their dependents
Yes Grant China permanent normal trade status
No   Phase out estate, gift and trust taxes
No   Prohibit implementation of president's national monument designations
No   Approve GOP plan to provide prescription drug coverage for Medicare beneficiaries
Yes Increase help for poor nations indebted to international financial institutions

1999
Yes Impose steel import quotas
No   Kill proposal to take aviation trust funds off budget
No   Require background checks on buyers only at gun shows with 10 or more vendors
No   Remove barriers among banking, securities and insurance companies
Yes Authorize state grants to hire teachers and reduce class size
Yes Overhaul campaign finance law; ban "soft money" and restrict advocacy advertising
Yes Approve bipartisan plan to increase rights of patients in managed-care health plans

INTEREST GROUPS

	AFL-CIO	ADA	CCUS	ACU
2000	80%	75%	61%	29%
1999	67%	75%	60%	28%
1998	60%	65%	72%	48%
1997	75%	50%	80%	48%

CQ VOTE STUDIES

	PARTY UNITY		PRESIDENTIAL SUPPORT	
	Support	Oppose	Support	Oppose
2000	75%	25%	68%	32%
1999	64%	36%	60%	40%
1998	58%	42%	53%	47%
1997	68%	32%	64%	36%

TEXAS 2
East – Lufkin; Orange

A sprawling mass of east Texas territory, the hardscrabble 2nd borders Louisiana to the east and reaches west to near Bryan. Its southern border skirts the oil city of Beaumont (in the 9th District) and suburbs northeast of Houston. A mostly rural district, the 2nd's largest city is Lufkin, located in the northern end of the district and surrounded by vast timber forests.

The 2nd's economy has been split between the eastern and southern portions, which rely on the chemical and shipping industries based in Orange and nearby Beaumont and Port Arthur, and the northern and western sections, where timber still reigns. Government jobs and contracts became increasingly important to the region as its industrial and manufacturing economies slipped somewhat during the late 1980s and early '90s. Slow population growth and a high percentage of blue-collar workers have made it difficult to attract higher-paying service jobs.

In some ways, the 2nd's political situation hasn't changed much since populist Democrat Charles Wilson began his 24 years in Congress in 1972. Although religious conservatives have garnered a base of support, the region's distance from the GOP-solid suburbs of Houston and Dallas makes it an important swing area for Democrats, provided they aren't too liberal. When Wilson retired in 1996, a conservative Democrat won the seat, although he lost the counties closest to Houston. On the presidential level, the 2nd went for Bill Clinton in 1992 and – by just a hair – in 1996 but gave President Bush 61 percent of its vote in 2000.

MAJOR INDUSTRY
Timber, petrochemicals, shipping

CITIES
Lufkin, 33,482; Huntsville, 32,148; Orange, 19,754

UNUSUAL FEATURES
Huntsville's favorite son is Sam Houston, the first president of the Republic of Texas; Houston died on his way to visit the "medicinal baths" of Sour Lake, a town north of Beaumont that got its name when crude oil seeped into the waters of a nearby lake.

Rep. Sam Johnson (R)

CAPITOL OFFICE
225-4201; fax 225-1485
1030 Longworth Bldg. 20515

INTERNET
e-mail: www.house.gov/writerep
web: www.house.gov/samjohnson

COMMITTEES
Education & Workforce
(Employer-Employee Relations - chairman)
Ways & Means

HOMETOWN
Plano

BORN
Oct. 11, 1930, San Antonio, Texas

RELIGION
Methodist

FAMILY
Wife, Shirley Melton; three children

EDUCATION
Southern Methodist U., B.B.A. 1951; George
Washington U., M.S.I.A. 1974

MILITARY SERVICE
Air Force, 1951-79

CAREER
Home builder; Air Force pilot

POLITICAL HIGHLIGHTS
Texas House, 1985-91

ELECTION RESULTS

2000 GENERAL

Sam Johnson (R)	187,486	71.6%
Billy Wayne Zachary (D)	67,233	25.7%
Lance Flores (LIBERT)	7,178	2.7%

2000 PRIMARY

Sam Johnson (R)	40,802	93.5%
J.A. Gonnell (R)	2,843	6.5%

1998 GENERAL

Sam Johnson (R)	106,690	91.2%
Ken Ashby (LIBERT)	10,288	8.8%

PREVIOUS WINNING PERCENTAGES
1996 (73%); 1994 (91%); 1992 (86%); 1991 Special
Runoff Election (53%); 1991 Special Election (20%)

Elected May 1991; 5th full term

Solid, steady and unassuming, Johnson is a dependable anchor for the conservative faction of House Republicans, offering his younger compatriots the lessons of his experience while helping them to remain focused on their goal of limiting federal government.

Born in 1930, Johnson is older but every bit as conservative as the younger-generation hard-liners who compose the chamber's right wing.

Johnson was a career Air Force pilot who spent seven years as a prisoner of war in Vietnam. He came to Congress in 1991, four years before the large conservative Class of 1994 took office. His conservative views are unchanging. That background, combined with his seniority and dependability, wins him the respect, and the attention, of his colleagues.

Everyone seems to like Johnson, even those with whom he disagrees. That is fortunate, because Johnson's brand of conservatism often puts him at odds on policy matters not only with most Democrats, but also with many moderate Republicans. He is one of the four founders of the Conservative Action Team, known as the CATs, a group of the most conservative House members.

The goals of the CATs are most often associated with the large and assertive Class of 1994, and Johnson takes no offense that, despite his founding member status, he is often overlooked as a conservative spokesman. In fact, Johnson would just as soon remain in the background.

That's not to say he's a shrinking violet: He was particularly outspoken in his criticism of President Clinton, dating back to the 1992 presidential campaign, when he characterized Clinton's post-college trip to Moscow and his avoidance of military service as un-American. And he had run-ins with fellow Republican Newt Gingrich as well, participating in an abortive attempt to topple the Speaker when he thought that the GOP leadership was too willing to compromise its principles in dealing with Clinton.

But Johnson praises Speaker J. Dennis Hastert for trying to accommodate the competing desires of factions in the party while being mindful of the GOP's slim margin of control. Because Johnson feels he and other conservatives receive a fair hearing, he says he's more inclined to cut Hastert some slack to deal with the political reality of a small margin. Johnson reports that most of the CATs seem to agree, although some of the more militant members occasionally "have to be leaned on" to be more pragmatic.

Johnson remains committed to reducing the size of federal government and its reach into citizens' lives. Although years of experience on Capitol Hill have tempered his short-term expectations, he has remained confident that his views will ultimately prevail. He says it takes a term or two in Congress to develop a full appreciation of the way things work in Washington — particularly the role of the Senate and the White House. For that reason, he is sorry to see some lawmakers voluntarily limit their terms in Congress.

Johnson's staff reports he is perpetually optimistic, even while pursuing some seemingly endless campaigns such as the one he waged to eliminate the so-called Social Security earning test, in which the benefits of some senior citizens were reduced if they continued to earn a salary. He finally saw victory on that front in 2000.

From his post on the Ways and Means Committee, Johnson has been a leader in the CATs' push for big tax cuts, including elimination of the inheritance tax, cuts in the capital gains rate and a fix of the "marriage penalty," a quirk in the tax code that results in some two-earner married couples paying higher taxes than they would if each partner were single. Johnson says he would favor repealing the 16th Amendment, which authorized the collection of federal income tax.

Johnson is on the board of regents of the Smithsonian Institution, and he is particularly enthusiastic about the National Air and Space Museum annex under construction near Dulles International Airport in Virginia. He originally won appointment to the Smithsonian board in 1995 when he and other lawmakers protested an exhibit on the "Enola Gay" — the plane that dropped the first atomic bomb on Japan — because it depicted Japan as a victim. Johnson got Gingrich to appoint him to the board, and a scaled-back exhibit focused on the mechanics of the plane rather than the morality of its mission.

Johnson doesn't talk much about his days as a POW, which included almost three years in solitary confinement, but he did write a book about his experience, "Captive Warriors." After his solitary confinement ended, he roomed with Sen. John McCain at the prison camp. Although Johnson was tortured and sustained permanent injuries, he never despaired of being freed.

Johnson did not plan on a military career. He recalls that participation in the ROTC was mandatory when he went to high school toward the end of World War II. He continued ROTC at Southern Methodist University in his hometown of Dallas but was aiming at a career in business and law.

The Korean War intervened, however, and his entire ROTC class was called to duty. Johnson was quickly accepted into flight training, and he fell in love with flying. That's what sold him on a career in the Air Force.

He flew combat missions in Korea and Vietnam, was a member of the precision flying team, the Thunderbirds, for two years, and served as the Air Force's "Top Gun" — director of the Air Force Fighter Weapons School.

Johnson's plane was shot down over North Vietnam in 1966, and he was held prisoner nearly seven years. While in prison, he began thinking about a future in politics. Upon his release, he had three operations on his right hand, including a tendon transplant, and was able to resume flying.

After retiring from the Air Force in 1979 as a colonel, Johnson went into the home-building business in Dallas. He became active in local Republican Party affairs and, in 1984, he won a seat in the Texas House representing the suburbs of Collin County, where he built a reputation as a law-and-order conservative. He broadened his contacts in the Dallas area as co-chairman of George Bush's north Texas 1988 presidential campaign and as chairman of 3rd District GOP Rep. Steve Bartlett's campaigns in 1988 and 1990.

Bartlett resigned in March 1991 to run for mayor of Dallas. Johnson overcame a tough scramble to win the GOP nomination, but in the wealthy, solidly Republican 3rd District, has had no electoral difficulty since.

KEY VOTES

2000
No	Raise hourly minimum wage by $1 over two years
Yes	Halt funding for U.S. mission in Kosovo unless European nations pay more
Yes	Provide Medicare benefits to military retirees and their dependents
Yes	Grant China permanent normal trade status
Yes	Phase out estate, gift and trust taxes
Yes	Prohibit implementation of president's national monument designations
Yes	Approve GOP plan to provide prescription drug coverage for Medicare beneficiaries
No	Increase help for poor nations indebted to international financial institutions

1999
No	Impose steel import quotas
Yes	Kill proposal to take aviation trust funds off budget
No	Require background checks on buyers only at gun shows with 10 or more vendors
Yes	Remove barriers among banking, securities and insurance companies
No	Authorize state grants to hire teachers and reduce class size
No	Overhaul campaign finance law; ban "soft money" and restrict advocacy advertising
No	Approve bipartisan plan to increase rights of patients in managed-care health plans

INTEREST GROUPS

	AFL-CIO	ADA	CCUS	ACU
2000	0%	0%	85%	100%
1999	0%	0%	88%	96%
1998	0%	0%	88%	100%
1997	0%	10%	100%	96%

CQ VOTE STUDIES

	PARTY UNITY		PRESIDENTIAL SUPPORT	
	Support	Oppose	Support	Oppose
2000	98%	2%	25%	75%
1999	97%	3%	17%	83%
1998	96%	4%	20%	80%
1997	95%	5%	29%	71%

TEXAS 3
Northeast Dallas suburbs; Plano

Most of the 3rd's population comes from suburban Dallas, but the district extends northward to take in much of Collin County as well. Before its boundaries were altered by a federal court in 1996, the 3rd was a bastion of affluence and power. Although the alterations removed wealthy areas like Highland Park and University Park and added a section of Plano's black neighborhoods, the district remains economically well-off, white and Republican.

Collin continues to see tremendous growth as Dallas sprawls northward. Many corporate headquarters have moved into the Plano area, and wealthy executives have built half-million-dollar homes in sections like Deerfield. The concentration of electronic and telecommunications firms along U.S. Highway 75 has earned that area the name, "Telecom Corridor." Texas Instruments and Electronic Data Systems are a major presence along the corridor. Just off the Lyndon B. Johnson Freeway along U.S. 75, Richardson has benefited greatly from high-tech firms and is growing at a rapid rate. Frisco also is undergoing a population and development boom.

The district has middle-class areas like Mesquite, which has just over 100,000 residents, and Garland, which grew at a steady pace in the 1980s and '90s. Virtually all of Garland and about half of Mesquite are in the 3rd. Although downtown Dallas is in the 30th, its white-collar companies rely heavily on the 3rd for their workforce.

The district is solidly Republican – Collin County is filled with young, upwardly mobile professionals and is even more Republican than the Dallas suburbs. The district, which in general is fiscally conservative and holds traditional views, votes Republican at local, state and national levels.

MAJOR INDUSTRY
Telecommunications, transportation, banking

CITIES
Garland (pt.), 189,415 (1990); Plano (pt.), 158,396 (1990); Richardson, 87,517; Dallas (pt.), 83,768 (1990); Allen, 42,075

UNUSUAL FEATURES
Annual hot air balloon festival in Plano.

Rep. Ralph M. Hall (D)

Elected 1980; 11th term

CAPITOL OFFICE
225-6673; fax 225-3332; 2221 Rayburn Bldg. 20515

INTERNET
e-mail: rmhall@mail.house.gov
web: www.house.gov/ralphhall

COMMITTEES
Energy & Commerce
Science - ranking member

HOMETOWN
Rockwall

BORN
May 3, 1923, Fate, Texas

RELIGION
Methodist

FAMILY
Wife, Mary Ellen Hall; three children

EDUCATION
Texas Christian U., attended 1943; U. of Texas, attended 1946-47; Southern Methodist U., LL.B. 1951

MILITARY SERVICE
Navy, 1942-45

CAREER
Lawyer; aluminum company president

POLITICAL HIGHLIGHTS
Rockwall County judge, 1951-63; Texas Senate, 1963-73 (president pro tempore, 1968-69); sought Democratic nomination for lieutenant governor, 1972

ELECTION RESULTS

2000 GENERAL

Ralph M. Hall (D)	145,887	60.3%
Jon Newton (R)	91,574	37.9%
Joe Turner (LIBERT)	4,417	1.8%

2000 PRIMARY

Ralph M. Hall (D)	unopposed

1998 GENERAL

Ralph M. Hall (D)	82,989	57.6%
Jim Lohmeyer (R)	58,954	40.9%
Jim Simon (LIBERT)	2,137	1.5%

PREVIOUS WINNING PERCENTAGES
1996 (64%); 1994 (59%); 1992 (58%); 1990 (100%); 1988 (66%); 1986 (72%); 1984 (58%); 1982 (74%); 1980 (52%)

Courtly and soft-spoken, Hall is one of the last examples of the old-fashioned conservative Southern Democrat, a breed whose numbers in Congress are dwindling as Republicans capture more and more ground in the South's traditionally Democratic strongholds.

The septuagenarian's voting record could easily be mistaken for that of one of his younger conservative Republican colleagues. In the 106th Congress, Hall advocated scrapping most of the existing tax code and replacing it with a national sales tax or a flat tax. He also voted to phase out the federal estate tax and was a leading supporter of legislation to prohibit the Federal Communications Commission from regulating the content of public broadcasting — a move designed to make it easier for religious broadcasters to obtain non-commercial educational broadcast licenses.

In the 106th, he voted against his party and against President Clinton's position more often than any other House Democrat. Hall also was one of only five Democrats to break ranks with the party and support impeaching Clinton on the critical first charge of lying to a federal grand jury. And in the 107th Congress, he was one of only 10 Democrats to back President Bush's income tax cut.

Hall's northeast Texas district was represented for nearly half a century by Democratic Speaker Sam Rayburn. Today, however, the national Democratic Party has big image problems in this part of the country, which helps explain why Hall so reliably sides with the GOP, even when hardly any other Democrat does so. Not only does he back Republicans on policy, Hall often sides with them on procedure. As far back as 1985, he voted "present" rather than support Democrat Thomas P. "Tip" O'Neill Jr. of Massachusetts for Speaker.

Still, Hall has no plans to switch parties."I'm an old-time Democrat. I'm pro-family, pro-national defense, pro-jobs, and I haven't changed. ... It's my duty to stay in that party and pull them back toward the center," he said in 1997.

After Democrats fell into minority status in the House in 1995, Hall helped start the "Blue Dog" coalition, a group of about 30 conservative House Democrats that seeks to pull the party to the right.

Stylistically, Hall is anything but a firebrand. An infrequent sponsor of legislation, he prefers to quietly look after the interests of his home state's oil and gas industry as the No. 2 Democrat on the Energy and Commerce panel's Energy and Air Quality Subcommittee. "I don't have any pride of authorship ... and I'll take somebody else's bill if it gives me what I want," he says.

Hall also is a strong advocate for NASA and has championed the space agency's biomedical and basic science programs from his seat as ranking Democrat on the Science Committee. Hall was visibly disappointed when NASA scrapped a planned shuttle mission devoted to microgravity experiments in early 2000 so the agency could direct more money to the $60 billion International Space Station. But, characteristically, he declined to publicly chastise NASA officials at an oversight hearing.

The fourth-ranking Democrat on the Energy and Commerce panel, Hall is a favorite of ranking minority member John D. Dingell of Michigan, even if the two do not always see eye-to-eye. Hall's folksy humor and encyclopedic supply of rural Texas stories can defuse tension, and his political acumen gives him influence when he decides to weigh in.

Hall generally eschews quick legislative fixes. He was pleased that lawmakers did not move rapidly in drafting legislation to deregulate electric utilities during the 105th and 106th Congresses, saying states were better positioned to take the lead. He says he places more of a premium on "doing it right, rather than doing it now."

In the 106th, Hall and Texas Republican Joe L. Barton sponsored a reauthorization of the nation's pipeline laws. The measure contained modest safety changes, such as a requirement that the government study the use of remotely controlled shut-off valves that could halt the flow of gas when a leak occurs. The topic gained national attention when three Washington state youths were killed in a natural gas pipeline explosion in 1999, and other lawmakers advocated a tougher overhaul of pipeline rules.

In 1998, Hall was a key player in reversing a 1997 mandate to sell oil from the Strategic Petroleum Reserve, an underground cache of millions of barrels of oil that is supposed to be used to stabilize oil prices during an energy crisis. He opposed selling oil from the reserve in any instance, but particularly when oil prices dropped far below what the oil had originally cost Uncle Sam.

During intense deliberations over the 1990 Clean Air Act, Hall and Texas Republican Jack Fields succeeded in scaling back proposed requirements for auto companies to build alternatively fueled vehicles. Hall and others said the change would create a level playing field for alternative fuels other than methanol, but critics saw it as a major victory for the auto and oil industries.

Hall created a minor stir in 1999 by introducing legislation to restrict the use of tax-exempt bonds by certain governmental entities. Nevada lawmakers said the bill would make it harder for the Las Vegas Convention and Visitors Authority to float $150 million in tax-exempt bonds to build an addition to the Las Vegas Convention Center. Hall later retreated, saying the bill could have affected financing of municipal electric projects.

Hall got an early start in politics. He was elected a judge in his home county of Rockwall in 1950 while still attending law school at Southern Methodist University. After 12 years on the bench, he moved up to the state Senate and spent a decade there, rising to become president pro tempore. In 1972, Hall ran for lieutenant governor on a conservative platform and finished fourth in the Democratic primary, leading him to quit public life and concentrate on business. But when 4th District Democrat Ray Roberts announced his retirement in 1980 after 18 years, Hall re-entered politics, defeating Republican John H. Wright, a Tyler business manager, with 52 percent of the vote. Republicans have not mounted a comparable challenge since.

KEY VOTES

2000
No Raise hourly minimum wage by $1 over two years
Yes Halt funding for U.S. mission in Kosovo unless European nations pay more
Yes Provide Medicare benefits to military retirees and their dependents
Yes Grant China permanent normal trade status
Yes Phase out estate, gift and trust taxes
Yes Prohibit implementation of president's national monument designations
Yes Approve GOP plan to provide prescription drug coverage for Medicare beneficiaries
No Increase help for poor nations indebted to international financial institutions

1999
No Impose steel import quotas
Yes Kill proposal to take aviation trust funds off budget
No Require background checks on buyers only at gun shows with 10 or more vendors
Yes Remove barriers among banking, securities and insurance companies
No Authorize state grants to hire teachers and reduce class size
No Overhaul campaign finance law; ban "soft money" and restrict advocacy advertising
Yes Approve bipartisan plan to increase rights of patients in managed-care health plans

INTEREST GROUPS

	AFL-CIO	ADA	CCUS	ACU
2000	10%	20%	80%	88%
1999	22%	20%	71%	84%
1998	20%	15%	76%	96%
1997	25%	10%	80%	96%

CQ VOTE STUDIES

	PARTY UNITY		PRESIDENTIAL SUPPORT	
	Support	Oppose	Support	Oppose
2000	35%	65%	22%	78%
1999	30%	70%	31%	69%
1998	23%	77%	30%	70%
1997	39%	61%	27%	73%

TEXAS 4
Northeast – Sherman; part of Tyler

The 4th covers a wide swath of the Red River Valley area north and east of Dallas, which was once represented by former Democratic House Speaker Sam Rayburn but now is increasingly familiar territory for the GOP. The district extends from the Oklahoma border to the oil cities of Tyler and Longview to the east. It has an older, more rural and more blue-collar population than most other Texas districts, and many residents espouse economic conservatism and gun rights.

Voters in the 4th elect conservatives of both parties to local and national offices, but the GOP has made dramatic inroads since the 1980s. Republican presidential candidates easily won the 4th in 1992 and '96, giving Bob Dole 56 percent of the vote, 7 points higher than the state average. And in 2000, President Bush garnered 71 percent of the district vote, his sixth highest percentage in Texas. Although Democrats have held this seat for decades, experts say the 4th will probably elect a Republican when Rep. Hall steps down.

Many Rockwall County residents commute to jobs in Dallas, while those in other counties farm the land for peanuts and other crops that became popular after the cotton industry's decline. The oil bust in the mid-1980s hurt the economy near Tyler and Longview, but other areas have rebounded with the help of several electronics manufacturing plants located in or near the district. Since the mid-1980s, both the agricultural and manufacturing sectors have posted large gains, offsetting the oil decline.

MAJOR INDUSTRY
Health care, electronics manufacturing, agriculture

CITIES
Tyler (pt.), 47,377 (1990); Longview (pt.), 39,544 (1990); Sherman, 34,105

UNUSUAL FEATURES
Tyler bills itself as the "Rose Capital of the World" and hosts a week-long festival each October; Former House Speaker Rayburn hailed from Bonham, in Fannin County.

Rep. Pete Sessions (R)

CAPITOL OFFICE
225-2231; fax 225-5878
1318 Longworth Bldg. 20515

INTERNET
e-mail: petes@mail.house.gov
web: www.house.gov/sessions

COMMITTEES
Rules

HOMETOWN
Dallas

BORN
March 22, 1955, Waco, Texas

RELIGION
United Methodist

FAMILY
Wife, Nete Sessions; two children

EDUCATION
Southwestern U., B.S. 1978

CAREER
Public policy analyst; phone company executive

POLITICAL HIGHLIGHTS
Sought Republican nomination for U.S. House
(special election), 1991; Republican nominee for
U.S. House, 1994

ELECTION RESULTS

2000 GENERAL

Pete Sessions (R)	100,487	54.0%
Regina Montoya Coggins (D)	82,629	44.4%
Ken Ashby (LIBERT)	2,842	1.5%

2000 PRIMARY

Pete Sessions (R)	unopposed

1998 GENERAL

Pete Sessions (R)	61,714	55.8%
Victor M. Morales (D)	48,073	43.4%

PREVIOUS WINNING PERCENTAGES
1996 (53%)

Elected 1996; 3rd term

A former businessman and executive at a conservative think tank, Sessions is in tune with GOP efforts to cut federal spending and reduce taxes. He says his predominantly middle-class constituents want a representative who will lighten their tax load and increase their take-home pay.

Sounding many of the same themes as President Bush, Sessions favors allowing people to privately invest a portion of their Social Security payments, and he would increase local control over education. In the 106th Congress, his party loyalty was rewarded with an appointment to the Rules Committee, an arm of the leadership that sets the guidelines for action on individual bills.

Although the conservative views that Sessions espouses are popular throughout much of Texas, the 5th District is closely split between Republicans and Democrats. The congressman, who is the son of former FBI Director William S. Sessions, had to overcome a strong Democratic challenge in 2000, and he has taken some criticism for his partisan approach. In a tepid endorsement of his 2000 re-election bid, The Dallas Morning News said in an editorial that he "could be more effective if he were to present a less partisan style."

Sessions is a vocal supporter of the GOP's tax-cutting efforts and in the 106th Congress sought a constitutional amendment to require approval by a two-thirds majority of Congress to raise taxes. "If a tax increase were truly a good idea, certainly two-thirds of the Congress could agree on it," he said. Opponents, however, warned that the plan could stymie government attempts to raise needed revenue. But Sessions renewed his push for the amendment in the 107th.

Sessions has a prominent role in the House Results Caucus, a group whose motto is: "Give the government the money it needs, but not a penny more." The caucus's aim is to make the federal government more efficient. Its members take a hard look at the funding of government programs that show a high incidence of waste, fraud and abuse as identified by the General Accounting Office. The caucus contends, for example, that poor inventory management results in $15 billion a year wasted on unneeded stock; Sessions has looked into improving inventory management in the defense sector.

The Texas lawmaker has backed legislation to create a Congressional Office of Regulatory Analysis to study the financial impact of major government regulations rather than relying on executive branch analyses. And he is critical of the Internal Revenue Service and current tax laws, favoring a plan to replace the tax code with a simpler system.

On trade matters, Sessions generally backs a free-trade approach. He voted in 2000 to grant China permanent normal trade status. He also favored giving President Clinton fast-track authority to negotiate trade agreements that Congress cannot amend — a leadership-endorsed position that drew resistance from a number of GOP conservatives.

But Sessions says that his support of expanded trade does not extend to situations in which the United States is at an unfair disadvantage. He has expressed concern that the 1993 North American Free Trade Agreement (NAFTA) and the 1994 General Agreement on Tariffs and Trade created an "uneven playing field" for Americans, and he has backed legislation calling for an assessment of NAFTA's impact to ensure that American workers and businesses are benefiting from the pact. He has said, however, that "people who are anti-NAFTA are many times isolationists. I am not an isolationist."

As the father of a boy with Down syndrome, Sessions has joined with liberal Democratic Sen. Edward M. Kennedy of Massachusetts in an effort to help families care for children with special needs. The lawmakers sponsored a measure in the 106th to allow the parents of a child with special needs to keep working and still receive Medicaid benefits for their child. "Our family has been fortunate in that Alex has been able to receive the care that he has needed," Sessions said. "However, many families face similar situations, without the ability to access the critical health care coverage that their child's disabilities require."

A leading critic of the Clinton administration, Sessions was among the first group of Republican lawmakers calling for a congressional inquiry into possible impeachment proceedings against Clinton over campaign fundraising practices. In the 106th, he said Attorney General Janet Reno should resign because of allegations that the FBI mishandled its 1993 raid on the Branch Davidian compound near Waco.

Born in Waco and educated at Southwestern University in Georgetown, Texas, Sessions went to work after college at Southwestern Bell Telephone Co. and Bell Communications Research. (He says he never missed a day of work in 16 years at the company.)

It took Sessions three tries to get to Congress. His first campaign was in 1991, when he entered the House special-election contest to succeed 3rd District Rep. Steve Bartlett, who had resigned to run for mayor of Dallas. Sessions finished sixth. In 1994, after leaving his job at Bell, Sessions ran in the 5th District and gave incumbent Democrat John Bryant a tough fight but lost, 50 percent to 47 percent. After his defeat, he served as vice president for public policy at the National Center for Policy Analysis, a Dallas-based conservative think tank.

In 1996, redistricting gave the 5th District a slightly more Republican tilt. With Bryant running for the Senate, Sessions was able to end his losing streak, with a 53 percent to 47 percent victory over John Pouland, a lawyer and former chairman of the Dallas County Democratic Party.

Democrats thought they had a good chance to retake the 5th in 1998 and nominated Victor M. Morales, a high school teacher who had come from nowhere to give Republican Sen. Phil Gramm an unexpectedly tough race in 1994. But Morales, the grandson of Mexican immigrants, never regained the magic of that campaign, and Sessions cruised to victory with 56 percent.

In 2000, Democrats chose Regina Montoya Coggins, a political commentator and lawyer who had worked in the Clinton White House. Sessions prevailed, winning by 10 percentage points.

KEY VOTES

2000
No Raise hourly minimum wage by $1 over two years
Yes Halt funding for U.S. mission in Kosovo unless European nations pay more
Yes Provide Medicare benefits to military retirees and their dependents
Yes Grant China permanent normal trade status
Yes Phase out estate, gift and trust taxes
Yes Prohibit implementation of president's national monument designations
Yes Approve GOP plan to provide prescription drug coverage for Medicare beneficiaries
No Increase help for poor nations indebted to international financial institutions

1999
No Impose steel import quotas
Yes Kill proposal to take aviation trust funds off budget
Yes Require background checks on buyers only at gun shows with 10 or more vendors
Yes Remove barriers among banking, securities and insurance companies
No Authorize state grants to hire teachers and reduce class size
No Overhaul campaign finance law; ban "soft money" and restrict advocacy advertising
Yes Approve bipartisan plan to increase rights of patients in managed-care health plans

INTEREST GROUPS

	AFL-CIO	ADA	CCUS	ACU
2000	0%	0%	76%	96%
1999	11%	5%	84%	96%
1998	0%	0%	89%	100%
1997	0%	0%	90%	100%

CQ VOTE STUDIES

	PARTY UNITY		PRESIDENTIAL SUPPORT	
	Support	Oppose	Support	Oppose
2000	98%	2%	26%	74%
1999	96%	4%	21%	79%
1998	97%	3%	20%	80%
1997	96%	4%	26%	74%

TEXAS 5

East Central — Part of Dallas; eastern and southern suburbs

The 5th encompasses several neighborhoods to the north and east of Dallas, then stretches 200 miles south to draw in seven counties and parts of three other counties. About 55 percent of the district's residents live in Dallas County.

The economy of Dallas and its surrounding suburbs is strong and on the rise, with new businesses constantly appearing and high-tech jobs increasing. Many of the suburbs outside the city have growing populations and provide easy access to a bustling metropolis while supplying the benefits of small-town life. Mesquite (shared with the 3rd District) was once predominantly farmland but is now a popular residential area.

Prisons are a large employer in rural parts of the district. Cattle, natural gas and coal continue to be big industries as well. Many of the smaller towns previously relied on steel or lumber and were hard hit when those fell. Today, however, there are brownfield revitalization efforts taking place in the 5th.

The 5th leans toward the GOP in most elections, although it has favored Democrats in some tight statewide contests. After redistricting in 1996, the district picked up some reliably Republican territory in the northeast neighborhoods of Dallas. Still, Tyler (Smith County) and Bryan (Brazos County) have large black populations and vote heavily Democratic, making the district more competitive. President Bush won the 5th in 2000, but by 2 points less than his 59 percent statewide average.

MAJOR INDUSTRY
High-tech, prisons, service

CITIES
Dallas (pt.), 230,225 (1990); Mesquite (pt.), 69,369 (1990); Tyler (pt.), 32,827; Bryan (pt.), 20,998 (1990)

UNUSUAL FEATURES
Joe Kool, reputedly one of the most difficult bulls to ride in the world, appeared regularly for a decade at the renowned Mesquite Rodeo.

Rep. Joe L. Barton (R)

CAPITOL OFFICE
225-2002; fax 225-3052; 2264 Rayburn Bldg. 20515

INTERNET
e-mail: rep.barton@mail.house.gov
web: www.house.gov/barton

COMMITTEES
Energy & Commerce
(Energy & Air Quality - chairman)
Science

HOMETOWN
Ennis

BORN
Sept. 15, 1949, Waco, Texas

RELIGION
Methodist

FAMILY
Wife, Janet Barton; three children

EDUCATION
Texas A&M U., B.S. 1972; Purdue U., M.S. 1973

CAREER
Engineering consultant

POLITICAL HIGHLIGHTS
Sought Republican nomination for U.S. Senate
(special election), 1993

ELECTION RESULTS

2000 GENERAL

Joe L. Barton (R)	222,685	88.1%
Frank Brady (LIBERT)	30,056	11.9%

2000 PRIMARY

Joe L. Barton (R)	unopposed

1998 GENERAL

Joe L. Barton (R)	112,957	72.9%
Ben B. Boothe (D)	40,112	25.9%
Richard A. Bandlow (LIBERT)	1,817	1.2%

PREVIOUS WINNING PERCENTAGES
1996 (77%); 1994 (76%); 1992 (72%); 1990 (66%);
1988 (68%); 1986 (56%); 1984 (57%)

Elected 1984; 9th term

In recognition of Barton's four years as chairman of the Commerce Committee's Oversight and Investigations Subcommittee, his staff still likes to call him the "waste watchdog." But the canine analogy also could describe the dogged persistence of the congressman, who has sunk his teeth into a few issues and refused to let go — even in the face of repeated disappointments and seemingly lengthening odds.

In the 107th Congress, Barton wields the gavel at another subcommittee, Energy and Air Quality, of what is now called the Energy and Commerce Committee. The job puts him in a prime position to influence the congressional response to the energy crunch — prompted by California's electricity woes and the soaring prices for oil and natural gas — that has resurfaced near the top of the national agenda. As the debate got under way, Barton signaled that his participation would come in close coordination with the fellow Texan in the White House, George W. Bush. Despite cultivating a reputation as a loyal, free-market conservative, he has shown a capacity to work with the other side to get what he wants.

Barton took over the energy subcommittee in 1999 and spent much of the next two years in a futile effort to move legislation that would foster competition in the electric power industry, the last major regulated monopoly in the nation. Republicans have been advocating deregulation of the industry since they took control of Congress in 1995, but they never have reached accord on the myriad issues involved. And the new energy crunch quickly forced the matter onto the agenda for the 107th.

Barton's conservatism is especially strong on fiscal matters. For years he has called for a constitutional amendment requiring three-fifths majority approval in Congress to raise taxes. He is concerned that House GOP leaders are not sufficiently firm in their commitment to limiting taxes and spending, and he wants a formal structure in place.

Yet when it comes to home state projects, such as the now-defunct superconducting super collider and NASA's work on the International Space Station, Barton sings a different tune. Support for these big-ticket items leaves him open to charges of inconsistency, and in one House debate over funding for the collider, a Democrat observed that Barton "is obviously a contortionist, being on two sides of fiscal policy at the same time."

Barton's campaign for the tax limitation amendment is just one manifestation of his fiscal conservatism. In 1996, after Republican budget confrontations with the White House had led to two government shutdowns, Barton was one of the last GOP holdouts resisting a compromise with the Clinton administration to break the impasse. In 1998, he opposed a massive transportation authorization bill, even though his "no" vote cost him some money for projects in his district.

Barton is just as persistent on cutting government waste as he is in keeping watch over government spending. When the GOP won control of the House, Barton took over the Oversight panel from Democrat John D. Dingell of Michigan, who has a reputation as a merciless investigator. Barton's reputation is not so fearsome, but he pursued an energetic agenda that included some high-profile partisan skirmishes.

His subcommittee investigated Clinton administration Energy Secretary Hazel R. O'Leary's travel expenses, the cleanup of radioactive waste at a site in Washington state, efficiency at national laboratories, waste in the Medicare program, the Federal Communications Commission's move to an office complex developed by a political ally of Vice President Al Gore, and a related matter involving links between Energy Department contracts and campaign donations.

Barton was proudest of the subcommittee's work on the Food and Drug Administration drug approval process. In 1997, Barton was a key player on legislation to overhaul the agency. He and Anna G. Eshoo, D-Calif., brokered an agreement on how the agency should approve medical devices — items ranging from thermometers to pacemakers. That agreement was regarded as a major factor in enactment of the legislation to streamline FDA regulation.

Barton's agenda has not always been politically popular. For example, he favors mandatory random drug testing for members of Congress and their staffs, a requirement for his own aides. In 1998, Barton irked GOP leaders when he demanded a vote on legislation — which he opposed — to restore food stamp benefits to legal immigrants, who had lost the benefits in the 1996 welfare overhaul law. Barton's move also angered many farmers and a good number of his colleagues because it held up a bill that also funded a crop insurance program. Barton only postponed the inevitable: The bill was sent to the White House two weeks later.

Barton also has received some heat at home for missing floor votes; he attributes a spate of absences in part to family obligations when a younger brother died. In 2000, nine days before Texas judge Jon Barton died of liver cancer, the congressman took to the House floor to appeal to the public for information about new forms of treatment.

An engineering consultant for Atlantic Richfield Co., Barton had never run for office before 1984, when he won the seat that fellow Republican Phil Gramm left to run for the Senate. Barton was secure enough in his House seat that he ran for the Senate himself in 1993, when Democrat Lloyd Bentsen left to become Treasury secretary. Portraying himself as the foremost proponent of "family values" among the candidates, he took 14 percent to finish third in a 24-person, all-party special-election primary. That defeat did not affect his stature in the 6th District; he won re-election the next year with 76 percent.

In 1998, American Airlines, angered that Barton had supported the lifting of some restrictions on the use of Love Field near downtown Dallas — bringing more competition to American's hub at Dallas-Fort Worth International — bankrolled a serious primary challenger, attorney Greg Mullanax. But Barton took 73 percent of the primary vote and cruised to re-election in the fall. In 2000, he had no Democratic opponent.

KEY VOTES

2000

No	Raise hourly minimum wage by $1 over two years
Yes	Halt funding for U.S. mission in Kosovo unless European nations pay more
Yes	Provide Medicare benefits to military retirees and their dependents
No	Grant China permanent normal trade status
Yes	Phase out estate, gift and trust taxes
Yes	Prohibit implementation of president's national monument designations
Yes	Approve GOP plan to provide prescription drug coverage for Medicare beneficiaries
No	Increase help for poor nations indebted to international financial institutions

1999

No	Impose steel import quotas
Yes	Kill proposal to take aviation trust funds off budget
No	Require background checks on buyers only at gun shows with 10 or more vendors
No	Remove barriers among banking, securities and insurance companies
No	Authorize state grants to hire teachers and reduce class size
No	Overhaul campaign finance law; ban "soft money" and restrict advocacy advertising
No	Approve bipartisan plan to increase rights of patients in managed-care health plans

INTEREST GROUPS

	AFL-CIO	ADA	CCUS	ACU
2000	11%	10%	83%	100%
1999	11%	5%	86%	91%
1998	0%	5%	78%	100%
1997	0%	10%	78%	92%

CQ VOTE STUDIES

	PARTY UNITY		PRESIDENTIAL SUPPORT	
	Support	Oppose	Support	Oppose
2000	93%	7%	23%	77%
1999	95%	5%	16%	84%
1998	94%	6%	20%	80%
1997	92%	8%	25%	75%

TEXAS 6

Suburban Dallas – Part of Fort Worth; part of Arlington

The 6th consists of parts of Johnson, Parker, Tarrant, Dallas and Ellis counties, with more than 80 percent of the district's population concentrated in Arlington and Fort Worth. The two parts of the snake-shaped district are connected only by Eagle Mountain Lake in northwestern Tarrant.

Population growth in Arlington has leveled out in recent years after a tremendous boom from the 1950s through the '90s. There are black and Hispanic communities in the district, and the Vietnamese and Samoan populations have increased, but the 6th is generally white, financially secure and suburban.

Arlington used to have mostly blue-collar workers employed by General Motors, but the area now has become an entertainment center with amusement parks, hotels and the Ballpark at Arlington,

which is in the 24th District.

Fort Worth's economy also has diversified and expanded in recent years. Many businesses have been attracted to the northern Tarrant County area by its climate, housing and proximity to the Dallas-Fort Worth International Airport, shared with the 30th District.

The 6th is Republican at both the national and local levels. Residents of Fort Worth and Arlington tend to be fiscally conservative and socially moderate. But the suburbs north of Arlington are made up largely of middle- to upper-class families that tend to be more conservative on social issues.

MAJOR INDUSTRY
Transportation, technology, financial services

CITIES
Arlington (pt.), 170,745 (1990); Fort Worth (pt.), 102,612 (1990); Bedford, 50,451

UNUSUAL FEATURES
Dallas/Fort Worth area known as the Aviation Capital of the World; the cities' airport has more than 2,800 takeoffs and landings per day.

Rep. John Culberson (R)

CAPITOL OFFICE
225-2571; fax 225-4381
1728 Longworth Bldg. 20515

INTERNET
e-mail: john.culberson@mail.house.gov
web: www.house.gov/culberson

COMMITTEES
Budget
Education & Workforce
Science

HOMETOWN
Houston

BORN
Aug. 24, 1956, Houston, Texas

RELIGION
Methodist

FAMILY
Wife, Belinda Culberson; one child

EDUCATION
Southern Methodist U., B.A. 1981; South Texas
College of Law, J.D. 1988

CAREER
Lawyer; political advertising agency employee;
oil rig mud logger

POLITICAL HIGHLIGHTS
Texas House, 1986-2000

ELECTION RESULTS

2000 GENERAL

John Culberson (R)	183,712	73.9%
Jeff Sell (D)	60,694	24.4%
Drew Parks (LIBERT)	4,182	1.7%

2000 PRIMARY RUNOFF

John Culberson (R)	29,968	60.0%
Peter Wareing (R)	20,017	40.0%

2000 PRIMARY

John Culberson (R)	23,894	37.7%
Peter Wareing (R)	16,837	26.6%
Cathy McConn (R)	8,488	13.4%
Mark Brewer (R)	4,865	7.7%
Wallace Henley (R)	4,649	7.3%
Ron Kapche (R)	3,107	4.9%
Eugene Y. Hsiao (R)	1,063	1.7%

Elected 2000; 1st term

Texas' 7th District was constituted as an affluent suburban Houston Republican stronghold under a 1966 redistricting plan, but freshman Culberson is only the third lawmaker to hold its House seat. He succeeded retired Ways and Means Chairman Bill Archer, who held the seat for 30 years. Archer's predecessor, George Bush, held the seat for four years and went on to become both president and the father of a president.

State legislative veteran Culberson survived an expensive 2000 primary runoff against businessman Peter Wareing. But once he did, his election was assured: The 7th is one of the most Republican districts in the nation.

Culberson moved to the U.S. House after 14 years in the Texas House, where he was Republican whip and a member of the Environmental Regulation, Natural Resources, Public Education and Corrections committees. As a congressional newcomer, he received assignments to the Budget, Education and the Workforce, and Science panels.

Culberson calls himself a "stainless steel conservative." Like Archer, the words "cut," "abolish" and "repeal" come up frequently when Culberson talks about fiscal policy. He favors a national sales tax to offset cuts in or revocation of the income tax, elimination of the capital gains tax, and a reduction in Social Security taxes. He also backs legislation to phase out all federal agencies unless they can justify their existence.

A career defense attorney specializing in civil law, Culberson calls himself a "passionate tort reformer," and he worked in the state House to limit lawsuits and damage claims under product liability law. He also focused on reducing federal oversight of the state's prison system.

"I have deep-seated convictions that I am very passionate about," he says, "and I'm not a good spectator when it comes to government and protecting our way of life."

Culberson also believes that he has a distinct advantage over other members of Congress, saying, "As a former Texas state legislator, I will be the only member of Congress that has had a working relationship with President George W. Bush and his staff."

TEXAS 7

Western Houston; northwestern suburbs

Mostly white, wealthy Houston suburbs and western Harris County make up the 7th, one of the most highly educated districts in the state. From the southwest Houston suburbs, the district extends 30 miles west along Interstate 10 to Katy and includes smaller towns north and west of Houston. About half the district's residents live within Houston city limits, but the city's suburbs continue to expand. Katy has seen steady population growth, adding to the Republican advantage.

Removed from downtown Houston's oil and gas companies, the 7th nonetheless has several important corporate residents, including Compaq Computer Corp. The Galleria, a huge shopping and office complex, provides jobs and a major retail presence. Like other areas around

Houston, the district rebounded slowly after the oil industry's troubles in the 1980s. But an increasing emphasis on high-tech firms and corporate headquarters enabled the 7th to enjoy sustained economic growth during the 1990s.

One of the most reliably Republican districts in the nation, the 7th is typified by white-collar executives, good schools and religious conservatism. The district's Republican character runs deep: GOP candidates at all levels routinely rack up 70 percent or more of the vote in general elections. Those Democrats who do mount challenges – not a universal occurrence – receive scant electoral support.

MAJOR INDUSTRY
Technology, retail, health care

CITIES
Houston (pt.), 295,117 (1990); Mission Bend (unincorporated), 10,750 (1990); Katy (pt.), 6,982 (1990)

UNUSUAL FEATURES
Former President George Bush represented the 7th from 1967 to 1971.

Rep. Kevin Brady (R)

Elected December 1996; 3rd term

CAPITOL OFFICE
225-4901; fax 225-5524; 428 Cannon Bldg. 20515

INTERNET
e-mail: rep.brady@mail.house.gov
web: www.house.gov/brady

COMMITTEES
Ways & Means

HOMETOWN
The Woodlands

BORN
April 11, 1955, Vermillion, S.D.

RELIGION
Roman Catholic

FAMILY
Wife, Cathy Brady; one child

EDUCATION
U. of South Dakota, B.S. 1990

CAREER
Chamber of commerce executive

POLITICAL HIGHLIGHTS
Texas House, 1991-96

ELECTION RESULTS

2000 GENERAL

Kevin Brady (R)	233,848	91.6%
Gil Guillory (LIBERT)	21,368	8.4%

2000 PRIMARY

Kevin Brady (R)	unopposed

1998 GENERAL

Kevin Brady (R)	123,372	92.8%
Don L. Richards (LIBERT)	9,576	7.2%

PREVIOUS WINNING PERCENTAGES
1996 General Runoff Election (59%); 1996 General Election (42%)

Born into a family of Democrats (his uncle was a state senator, his father a county party official), Brady's early experiences with a host of civic groups and his 18 years as a chamber of commerce executive molded his pro-business, solidly Republican political philosophy.

Brady's father, a lawyer, was shot and killed in a South Dakota courtroom by the deranged spouse of a client. His mother, in raising her five children, urged them to become involved in school and community activities. Brady, who was 12 when his father died, ran for the student council, played sports year-round, and joined the Boy Scouts and other local civic organizations. In so doing, he says, he developed an appreciation of the important role the private sector plays in the civic well-being of a community.

That view was reinforced after college when he took a series of chamber of commerce jobs — first in Rapid City, and later in Beaumont and The Woodlands, Texas. He says he has observed countless business leaders who are role models for civic involvement and who have shown that private sector solutions to community problems are often more effective than government programs.

The unassuming Brady comes across as a regular guy — a dad who sometimes brings his young son to his congressional office; a baseball lover who relishes the annual charity ballgame against the Democrats — and those who know him say that's exactly right.

But Brady is also a fast-rising lawmaker whose interests range from international trade to the nation's space industry, from extradition treaties to campaign finance reform. In the 107th Congress, he won a seat on the powerful Ways and Means Committee, maintaining a Houston presence on the panel in the wake of the departure of his mentor and Houston-area neighbor, Bill Archer. Although the new assignment required him to give up his seat on the Science panel, he continues to look out for the interests of the space industry, important to the local economy. The 8th District includes two high-tech research parks, and the Johnson Space Center is in the neighboring 9th.

Brady sides with his party more than 90 percent of the time, but he has bucked the leadership on occasion. In 1998, he was one of 12 Republicans who voted against a GOP bill to increase consumer protections for those with managed-care health plans. Brady argued that the measure would not permit states to continue to regulate certain group health plans. He also maintains that GOP leaders should support campaign finance restrictions on "soft money" — the unlimited contributions used for party-building activities and issue ads.

In 1997, he protested when House GOP leaders manipulated the parliamentary process to make it extremely difficult to stop an automatic cost of living pay adjustment for lawmakers. "Rather than standing on the principle of honest, open government, we hid behind a procedure," he said.

Because of the circumstances of his father's death, Brady, as a Texas House member, refused to vote for a bill to allow Texans to carry concealed weapons, and he says he still opposes such a measure today. He says many of his legislative priorities have been inspired by comments from constituents at cracker-barrel gatherings, including a bill to protect teachers from frivolous lawsuits and his proposal to apply the longstanding Texas state agency sunset law to the federal government.

Brady says such legislation, requiring that every federal agency justify its existence on a regular basis or face consolidation, privatization or elimination, is essential to contain the scope of government. He began to push for the measure in the 105th Congress, when he was assigned to the Government Reform panel, and has continued the effort even though he left the committee after just a few weeks to take the International Relations post.

On International Relations, (which he also gave up for his Ways and Means seat), Brady focused his efforts in the 106th on updating and expanding the scope of extradition treaties. "Those engaged in drug trafficking, terrorism, violent crime, fraud and corruption are taking advantage of outdated treaties," he argues, adding that the United States has no extradition agreements at all with many nations.

As the only Texan on the International Relations panel, he found himself the conduit for letters to then-Gov. George W. Bush from overseas groups protesting the state's liberal use of the death penalty. In 1997, Brady introduced a resolution urging the Clinton administration to oppose attempts by any U.N. agency to investigate capital punishment in the United States.

Brady attended the University of South Dakota, where he was the center fielder on the baseball team. He sheepishly acknowledges that, although he left college in 1978, he didn't actually graduate until 1990 because he had neglected to complete the paperwork for a work-study class. After an opponent in his first Texas House race unearthed that fact, Brady dug out the old course work to clear up the incomplete grade.

Brady spent six years in the Texas House, where he says politics did not get in the way of policy nearly as much as it seems to in Washington. In 1996, GOP Rep. Jack Fields announced he would not seek re-election in the 8th District. It took Brady an arduous four elections, but he eventually vanquished his chief rival for the seat, wealthy Republican physician Gene Fontenot.

Fontenot emerged on top in the March primary for the GOP nomination, but he did not capture a majority of the vote. Brady had much stronger ties to the district and defeated Fontenot in the April runoff. But a three-judge federal panel redrew the 8th as well as 12 other Texas congressional districts in response to a Supreme Court ruling that found illegal "racial gerrymandering" at play in the Texas map. The federal court threw out the primary results from those districts and ordered new elections. In November, Fontenot forced Brady into a December runoff. Brady finally won the seat, taking 59 percent.

He is safely ensconced in the district, not having had to face a Democratic challenger since 1996.

KEY VOTES

2000

No	Raise hourly minimum wage by $1 over two years
Yes	Halt funding for U.S. mission in Kosovo unless European nations pay more
Yes	Provide Medicare benefits to military retirees and their dependents
Yes	Grant China permanent normal trade status
Yes	Phase out estate, gift and trust taxes
Yes	Prohibit implementation of president's national monument designations
Yes	Approve GOP plan to provide prescription drug coverage for Medicare beneficiaries
No	Increase help for poor nations indebted to international financial institutions

1999

No	Impose steel import quotas
No	Kill proposal to take aviation trust funds off budget
No	Require background checks on buyers only at gun shows with 10 or more vendors
No	Remove barriers among banking, securities and insurance companies
No	Authorize state grants to hire teachers and reduce class size
No	Overhaul campaign finance law; ban "soft money" and restrict advocacy advertising
Yes	Approve bipartisan plan to increase rights of patients in managed-care health plans

INTEREST GROUPS

	AFL-CIO	ADA	CCUS	ACU
2000	0%	0%	80%	100%
1999	11%	15%	95%	88%
1998	0%	0%	94%	96%
1997	0%	5%	100%	100%

CQ VOTE STUDIES

	PARTY UNITY		PRESIDENTIAL SUPPORT	
	Support	Oppose	Support	Oppose
2000	97%	3%	24%	76%
1999	94%	6%	21%	79%
1998	94%	6%	20%	80%
1997	97%	3%	28%	72%

TEXAS 8

Northern Houston suburbs; College Station

A thin strip of land connects the two bulbous portions of the 8th — suburban areas north of Houston and land surrounding the cities of Bryan and College Station. A Republican bastion, the district resembles a lopsided barbell and contains not only the vast oil fields that characterize much of Texas, but also dairy farms and Texas A&M University, the state's oldest public institution of higher education.

Unlike the more liberal University of Texas at Austin, Texas A&M has a conservative military and agricultural tradition that complements many of the 8th's values — free market economics and defense hawkishness. As a result, voters have given Republicans some of their largest margins in the state at every level.

Republican presidential nominee Bob Dole garnered two-thirds of the vote in 1996, much more than the 49 percent he gathered statewide. And in 2000, native son President Bush carried the district overwhelmingly with 76 percent of the vote — 17 percentage points

above his statewide average.

The two land masses of the 8th differ widely in economic character. At the eastern end, the more populous of the barbell's two ends, the northern Houston suburbs have planned communities that house executives from the Houston Advanced Research Center and the region's many medical facilities. The area nearer to College Station, however, depends more on farming. While benefiting from Houston's oil and gas industries, the steadying influence of Texas A&M and the dairy industry helps keep the district economy healthy.

MAJOR INDUSTRY
Health care, agriculture, education

CITIES
College Station, 61,121; Bryan (pt.), 37,779 (1990); Kingwood (unincorporated), 37,397 (1990)

UNUSUAL FEATURES
George Bush Presidential Library at Texas A&M; Town of Chappell Hill was the first in Texas planned by a woman.

Rep. Nick Lampson (D)

CAPITOL OFFICE
225-6565; fax 225-5547; 417 Cannon Bldg. 20515

INTERNET
e-mail: nick.lampson@mail.house.gov
web: www.house.gov/lampson

COMMITTEES
Science
Transportation & Infrastructure

HOMETOWN
Beaumont

BORN
Feb. 14, 1945, Beaumont, Texas

RELIGION
Roman Catholic

FAMILY
Wife, Susan Lampson; two children

EDUCATION
Lamar U., B.S. 1968, M.Ed. 1971

CAREER
Teacher; home health care business owner

POLITICAL HIGHLIGHTS
Jefferson County tax assessor, 1977-95

ELECTION RESULTS

2000 GENERAL

Nick Lampson (D)	130,143	59.2%
Paul Williams (R)	87,165	39.7%
Chuck Knipp (LIBERT)	2,508	1.1%

2000 PRIMARY

Nick Lampson (D)	unopposed

1998 GENERAL

Nick Lampson (D)	86,055	63.7%
Tom Cottar (R)	49,107	36.3%

PREVIOUS WINNING PERCENTAGES
1996 General Runoff Election (53%); 1996 General Election (46%)

Elected December 1996; 3rd term

Lampson came to Congress with a solid background in local government — he served as Jefferson County tax assessor for 18 years — and experience as a science teacher and the owner of a home health care business. But he has had limited experience outside of Texas. He was born, raised, educated and worked in the Beaumont area. Other than trips to Mexico, he had never left the United States until his second year in Congress. "Let's just say I had a big learning curve on many issues," Lampson says.

But he found a niche in Congress soon after his arrival in 1997 when, following a rash of child abductions in Texas, including that of a 12-year-old girl from his district who was later found dead, he co-founded the Missing and Exploited Children's Caucus. The bipartisan caucus, which presses for legislation to help families protect their children and aid communities and law enforcement agencies searching for missing children, now has more than 150 members. His involvement with the caucus broadened his legislative perspective, Lampson says.

He had entered the House with some fame as the man who toppled Republican Steve Stockman — a top target of Democrats in the 1996 elections. Lampson's victory did not come until Dec. 10, when he defeated Stockman in an election delayed by court-ordered redistricting that threw off the election timetable. That late election put the national spotlight on three races in Texas, and Lampson's victory over Stockman (who had unseated longtime incumbent Democratic Rep. Jack Brooks two years earlier), was widely acclaimed by the national Democratic Party.

The Democratic leadership gave him a seat on the Science Committee — a logical assignment for Lampson, whose district includes the Johnson Space Center south of Houston and many energy-related industries. He also gained a seat on the Transportation and Infrastructure Committee.

On Science, Lampson is a stout defender of the International Space Station, a perennial target of congressional budget-cutters. He says he supports the project "because of what America learned about its future in 1969," when Americans first landed on the moon. "I saw firsthand how our progress in space, culminating in the lunar landing, encouraged and inspired students," he says.

By and large, Democratic leaders are satisfied with Lampson's voting record in the House. Typically, he takes the side of organized labor in its disputes with the GOP on worker-management issues, and he opposes Republican efforts to rein in environmental protections. A member of the moderate New Democrat Coalition, Lampson says he is a bit more liberal than some of his East Texas Democratic colleagues who have aligned with the more conservative "Blue Dog" coalition. "I tell them it's hard to break me out of the moderate mold."

His moderate voting record is a good match for the 9th District, where he has lived his entire life. Lampson's grandparents came to Texas from Sicily. He has five brothers and sisters, and gatherings of the extended family in southeast Texas would often attract 30 or more people. Lampson says he is continually inspired by his older sister, who was stricken with polio when she was 12 and is confined to a wheelchair. She has served as her brother's campaign manager in most of his political campaigns.

Lampson was 12 when his father died. He took a janitorial job in the local school to help out the family. He attended Lamar University, just three blocks from his high school, working his way through college.

He also earned some money playing the saxophone professionally for six years, which included stints with a number of local bands. He says he gave up professional music when he had to make a choice between a six-week gig in Las Vegas with the Boogie Kings or finishing college. He later played backup sax on a country music CD produced as a fundraising project for the National Center for Missing and Exploited Children.

Lampson was an intern for the local congressman, Democrat Brooks, and was involved in student government throughout college. He wanted to be a dentist but was stymied by organic chemistry, so he took a biology degree and got a job teaching high school science. He likes to recall a lesson in community activism learned by one of his science classes. In investigating the contents of a stagnant pond near the school, the students found three harmful organisms, and the class then badgered local authorities to clean up the pond.

Lampson himself was active in local Democratic Party affairs, and after three unsuccessful bids for elective office, he was elected Jefferson County tax assessor in 1976.

He decided in 1996 to make a run at Stockman, who had ousted Brooks in 1994 with the strong backing of supporters of gun owners' rights. Stockman was thought to be one of the most vulnerable GOP incumbents because of his contacts with militia groups and his staunchly conservative voting record. Lampson had little trouble defeating his four competitors for the Democratic nomination, and he moved quickly to attack Stockman's voting record and to label him a right-wing extremist.

But in August, it appeared as if Stockman was getting something of a break when a three-judge federal panel redrew the district's map, along with 12 other Texas districts, in response to a Supreme Court redistricting decision. After remapping, the judges threw out the results of the state's March primary in the affected districts, reopened candidate filing and ordered that an all-candidate primary be held in conjunction with the November general election.

The campaign leading to the December runoff was a slugfest. The Justice Department sent a team of observers to monitor voting in Beaumont and Galveston and to investigate charges that white poll watchers linked to Stockman had intimidated minorities. Stockman accused Lampson of fraudulently collecting Medicare payments made to a home health care company operated by his wife. Each national party put on a full-court press for its candidate, but the Democratic effort proved superior. Lampson prevailed with 53 percent of the vote. He has won two easy re-elections since.

KEY VOTES

2000

Yes Raise hourly minimum wage by $1 over two years
No Halt funding for U.S. mission in Kosovo unless European nations pay more
Yes Provide Medicare benefits to military retirees and their dependents
No Grant China permanent normal trade status
Yes Phase out estate, gift and trust taxes
No Prohibit implementation of president's national monument designations
No Approve GOP plan to provide prescription drug coverage for Medicare beneficiaries
Yes Increase help for poor nations indebted to international financial institutions

1999

Yes Impose steel import quotas
No Kill proposal to take aviation trust funds off budget
No Require background checks on buyers only at gun shows with 10 or more vendors
No Remove barriers among banking, securities and insurance companies
Yes Authorize state grants to hire teachers and reduce class size
Yes Overhaul campaign finance law; ban "soft money" and restrict advocacy advertising
Yes Approve bipartisan plan to increase rights of patients in managed-care health plans

INTEREST GROUPS

	AFL-CIO	ADA	CCUS	ACU
2000	90%	75%	57%	24%
1999	78%	90%	32%	16%
1998	100%	90%	33%	16%
1997	88%	75%	50%	24%

CQ VOTE STUDIES

	PARTY UNITY		PRESIDENTIAL SUPPORT	
	Support	Oppose	Support	Oppose
2000	82%	18%	69%	31%
1999	84%	16%	77%	23%
1998	86%	14%	81%	19%
1997	86%	14%	77%	23%

TEXAS 9
Southeast — Beaumont; Galveston

From the suburbs east of Houston to the Gulf of Mexico, the 9th is oil country. Its largest cities, Beaumont, Galveston and Port Arthur, are heavily involved in the production and distribution of petroleum products. When the bottom fell out of the oil industry in the 1980s, unemployment skyrocketed. Many of the district's towns lost population, though they slowly regained people throughout the 1990s.

The 9th's large number of factory jobs make it one of the few Texas districts where unions wield significant political power. While the unions underpin the area's economically liberal outlook, residents also tend to be socially conservative. Republicans have attracted votes from Galveston and the "Golden Triangle" – the area bounded by Beaumont, Port Arthur and Orange (in the 2nd District) – by appealing to issues like voters' opposition to gun control. The GOP also picks up some votes in the 9th's section of the Houston suburbs, but it has too few residents to swing the district by itself.

The sometimes marshy land between Houston and the coast doesn't yield many crops but instead contains NASA's Lyndon B. Johnson Space Center, refineries and shipbuilding facilities. The 9th also relies on coastal industries, including ship repair and commercial fishing.

Although the oil bust of the 1980s hurt the 9th's economy, the rapid growth of the petrochemical industry in the 1990s helped the district grow. Shipbuilders rely on the government, as does the Space Center, located 20 miles southeast of Houston. A growing service sector near Galveston has helped diversify the economy. Galveston, with its nearby beaches, also has emerged as a tourist destination.

MAJOR INDUSTRY
Petrochemicals, shipbuilding, health care

CITIES
Beaumont, 109,697; Galveston, 59,790; Port Arthur, 56,574; League City, 44,966

UNUSUAL FEATURES
Galveston is the site of many Texas firsts, including the first post office (1836) and first law firm west of the Mississippi River (1846); Nederland maintains its Dutch roots with a windmill and annual Heritage Festival.

Rep. Lloyd Doggett (D)

CAPITOL OFFICE
225-4865; fax 225-3073; 328 Cannon Bldg. 20515

INTERNET
e-mail: lloyd.doggett@mail.house.gov
web: www.house.gov/doggett

COMMITTEES
Ways & Means

HOMETOWN
Austin

BORN
Oct. 6, 1946, Austin, Texas

RELIGION
Methodist

FAMILY
Wife, Libby Belk; two children

EDUCATION
U. of Texas, B.B.A. 1967, J.D. 1970

CAREER
Lawyer

POLITICAL HIGHLIGHTS
Texas Senate, 1973-85; Democratic nominee for
U.S. Senate, 1984; Texas Supreme Court judge,
1989-94

ELECTION RESULTS

2000 GENERAL

Lloyd Doggett (D)	203,628	84.6%
Michael Davis (LIBERT)	37,203	15.5%

2000 PRIMARY

Lloyd Doggett (D)	unopposed

1998 GENERAL

Lloyd Doggett (D)	116,127	85.2%
Vincent J. May (LIBERT)	20,155	14.8%

PREVIOUS WINNING PERCENTAGES
1996 (56%); 1994 (56%)

Elected 1994; 4th term

Partisan and confrontational, Doggett, in his first years in the House, made a name for himself as a Democratic "attack dog" challenging every GOP policy decision. Although he still enjoys taking to the House floor to unleash his verbal barrages, his barbs are now directed at a wider range of targets, including tobacco companies and corporations that make creative use of tax shelters.

Doggett, assigned to the Ways and Means Committee in the 106th Congress, focuses his efforts on doing away with what he terms abusive tax shelters and pushing the Democratic effort to increase the minimum wage. He is scornful of corporations' use of tax shelters, citing such examples as U.S. drug companies donating outdated or inappropriate drugs to other countries and then getting tax deductions. "The dumping of useless drugs is actually worse than no help at all, since such toxic junk must be destroyed by those most in need," Doggett said.

When Doggett first came to Congress, the rhetoric he used to describe Speaker Newt Gingrich produced heated arguments in the House. In one incident in late 1995, Doggett was admonished by the presiding officer in the House not to call Gingrich a "crybaby" on the floor. Doggett assumed the role of partisan inquisitor soon after arriving in Congress. He and a small group of his Democratic colleagues used the same parliamentary guerrilla warfare tactics that Republicans once employed to challenge the Democratic House majority.

Doggett still relishes his role as GOP critic. Early in the 106th Congress, he complained that the GOP-run House had conducted little business. "The same brand of zealotry" that "insisted on shutting down the government" in 1995 and 1996 "has once again shut down a large part of our American government. During the month of January, the Congress of the United States did not approve one single bill," he said.

Later in the year, Doggett added: "House Republicans have made an art form this year of doing nothing. ... But there is one thing worse, and that is doing wrong," he raged when the Ways and Means panel approved a GOP-drafted tax cut measure. Even when he supports a Republican proposal, Doggett cannot resist a verbal dart. When the House passed a bill in 2000 to repeal the so-called Social Security earnings test, Doggett said that the measure, which he voted for, represented an "eat dessert first" approach rather than dealing with the long-term solvency of Social Security.

Such partisanship would be politically risky for many Southern Democrats, whose districts typically contain a number of conservative voters. But Doggett's Austin constituency includes many left-leaning academics and government workers, and their support makes Doggett one of the most liberal of the white Southern Democrats in the House.

Doggett's legislative interests include prohibiting U.S. promotion of the sale of American tobacco products abroad. "The government should not be in the business of exporting death," Doggett said. In the 106th Congress, he authored a bill designed to deter the smuggling of tobacco products into the United States and fought subsidies for tobacco exporters. And he was a key player in action in the 106th to require nonprofit groups that run issue-advocacy efforts during political campaigns to disclose their donors and their expenditures.

Doggett has urged Congress to take greater interest in determining whether existing federal programs are working as intended. For several years he has sponsored or cosponsored legislation calling for periodic congressional review of federal programs. The legislation is based on a Texas law that he authored when he was a state senator, which he says has saved the state more than $600 million by terminating inefficient or unneeded programs. Doggett's commitment to fighting government waste has caused the Concord Coalition, a balanced-budget advocacy group, to include him on its deficit-reduction honor roll.

Austin has become a center for many high-technology firms (the locals refer to it as "Silicon Hills"), and Doggett is a co-founder, with Republican Thomas M. Davis III of Virginia, of the congressional Information Technology Working Group. The group conducts periodic informational programs on technology issues that do not lend themselves to discussion in a partisan committee atmosphere, Doggett explains. One priority is to ensure a continued availability of skilled workers by easing immigration restrictions on trained foreigners and by beefing up training for domestic high-tech workers.

From his hillside apartment in Austin, Doggett can view all the key landmarks of his life. Born and raised in Austin and educated at the University of Texas, Doggett has been politically active in the city ever since his 1960s service in student government.

Within two years of taking his law degree in 1970, he won election to the state Senate. He served there until 1985, compiling a record of support for consumers and civil rights while backing the death penalty and tough criminal sanctions against drug traffickers and violent criminals. In 1984, he ran for the U.S. Senate, but he was mowed down in November by GOP nominee Phil Gramm, who was buoyed by Ronald Reagan's immense popularity in the Lone Star State.

In 1988, Doggett returned to public office by winning a seat on the state Supreme Court, and he was serving there when 81-year-old Democratic Rep. J.J. Pickle announced he would not seek another term in 1994. Doggett was the first Democrat to announce his candidacy, and his quick start spared him primary competition.

In November, he faced GOP real estate consultant A. Jo Baylor, who was hindered by her inexperience on the stump and a lack of funds in her bid to become the first black Republican woman elected to Congress.

Doggett, by contrast, was flush, taking in more than $1.2 million by the end of the campaign. The conservative tide that rolled over much of the country in 1994 did not reach Austin, and Doggett won comfortably. He has been re-elected easily ever since.

KEY VOTES

2000
Yes Raise hourly minimum wage by $1 over two years
Yes Halt funding for U.S. mission in Kosovo unless European nations pay more
Yes Provide Medicare benefits to military retirees and their dependents
Yes Grant China permanent normal trade status
No Phase out estate, gift and trust taxes
No Prohibit implementation of president's national monument designations
No Approve GOP plan to provide prescription drug coverage for Medicare beneficiaries
Yes Increase help for poor nations indebted to international financial institutions

1999
Yes Impose steel import quotas
Yes Kill proposal to take aviation trust funds off budget
No Require background checks on buyers only at gun shows with 10 or more vendors
Yes Remove barriers among banking, securities and insurance companies
Yes Authorize state grants to hire teachers and reduce class size
Yes Overhaul campaign finance law; ban "soft money" and restrict advocacy advertising
Yes Approve bipartisan plan to increase rights of patients in managed-care health plans

INTEREST GROUPS

	AFL-CIO	ADA	CCUS	ACU
2000	80%	85%	33%	12%
1999	67%	100%	24%	4%
1998	90%	100%	39%	8%
1997	100%	95%	40%	16%

CQ VOTE STUDIES

	PARTY UNITY		PRESIDENTIAL SUPPORT	
	Support	Oppose	Support	Oppose
2000	90%	10%	86%	14%
1999	90%	10%	82%	18%
1998	92%	8%	81%	19%
1997	92%	8%	81%	19%

TEXAS 10
Central — Austin

The once expansive rural district that Lyndon B. Johnson represented in the House (1937-49) has been shrinking in size and growing in population ever since he left. Today, the 10th is limited to Austin and surrounding Travis County, where the population explosion has brought new inhabitants, many drawn to the area's burgeoning computer industry.

Austin is largely considered a Democratic island in the vast Republican sea of the Lone Star State. A kind of Seattle for the South, Austin has been attracting music-lovers and computer programmers in search of a hip, youthful place in a warm climate. State government workers and the University of Texas at Austin add to the city's liberal political bent.

Austin's Travis County was one of the few large counties in Texas to hand Bill Clinton a solid majority in 1996 (he also won the 10th in 1992). But the 10th backed its resident governor, now-President

Bush, in 2000, giving him a 4 percentage point edge over Al Gore.

A troubled oil industry in the mid-1980s did not permanently wound the 10th's economy, which was buoyed by its university and state government employers. In the '90s, the area became a hub for high-tech startup firms, and its technology sector has been growing rapidly. In 1998, Fortune magazine proclaimed Austin the nation's No. 1 business city. In 1999, the city opened a new municipal airport on the site of the former Bergstrom Air Force Base — Austin-Bergstrom International Airport.

MAJOR INDUSTRY
Software development, high-tech, service, state government

CITIES
Austin (pt.), 511,349 (1990)

UNUSUAL FEATURES
The city's country music scene gets national exposure on the weekly public television show "Austin City Limits"; South by Southwest, a huge pop and rock music festival in Austin, is held each spring; Austin is home to North America's largest urban colony of Mexican free-tailed bats.

Rep. Chet Edwards (D)

CAPITOL OFFICE
225-6105; fax 225-0350; 2459 Rayburn Bldg. 20515

INTERNET
e-mail: www.house.gov/writerep
web: www.house.gov/edwards

COMMITTEES
Appropriations

HOMETOWN
Waco

BORN
Nov. 24, 1951, Corpus Christi, Texas

RELIGION
Methodist

FAMILY
Wife, Lea Ann Edwards; two children

EDUCATION
Texas A&M U., B.A. 1974; Harvard U., M.B.A. 1981

CAREER
Radio station executive; congressional aide

POLITICAL HIGHLIGHTS
Sought Democratic nomination for U.S. House,
1978; Texas Senate, 1983-91

ELECTION RESULTS

2000 GENERAL

Chet Edwards (D)	105,782	54.8%
Ramsey W. Farley (R)	85,546	44.3%

2000 PRIMARY

Chet Edwards (D)	unopposed

1998 GENERAL

Chet Edwards (D)	71,142	82.4%
Vince Hanke (LIBERT)	15,161	17.6%

PREVIOUS WINNING PERCENTAGES
1996 (57%); 1994 (59%); 1992 (67%); 1990 (53%)

Elected 1990; 6th term

Edwards serves as a bridge-builder between the liberal and conservative wings of the Democratic Party. His own political philosophy places him squarely in the party's center.

His middle-of-the-road politics, coupled with his friendly, easygoing nature, made Edwards an obvious choice for a chief deputy whip post when Democratic leaders were looking to bring conservatives back into the fold in the 104th Congress. The conservative wing of the party was feeling ignored by the end of the 104th; five Southern Democrats soon switched to the GOP. After six years of an outreach effort, Edwards says that although there still are problems on occasion, House Democrats are now "a family that is respectful of its members."

Edwards' principal legislative concern is to preserve the separation of church and state. He argues against proposals put forth by conservatives such as a national day of prayer and a proposed constitutional amendment to guarantee the right to prayer and other religious expression on public property. He also opposes federal funding for religious groups. "The best way to ruin religion is to politicize it," he says. And he argues that government involvement could "destroy religious tolerance."

When proponents of the constitutional amendment to allow prayer on public property, led by Oklahoma Republican Ernest Istook, prepared to bring the measure to the House floor in 1998, Edwards and his allies mobilized months in advance by organizing a whip organization to rally votes against the measure.

The proposed amendment fell far short of the required two-thirds majority, but Edwards has remained vigilant as the religious freedom debate has moved to other fronts, including a bid to display the Ten Commandments on public property and so-called charitable choice proposals that would make religious groups eligible for certain government grants. "Think what is going to happen when we have Baptists and Methodists and Jews and Muslims and Hindus and all of the 2,000 religious sects in America all competing for the almighty federal dollar?" Edwards argued in 1999.

Edwards follows his leadership on most votes, supporting public education initiatives and opposing efforts to prohibit affirmative action in higher education admissions. He also is against providing taxpayer-funded vouchers for private school education. And he opposes another effort pushed by conservatives, a bill to outlaw a procedure its opponents call "partial birth" abortion; Edwards argues that under the measure a physician could be sent to jail for trying to save a woman's life. But he does vote with most Republicans to toughen judicial treatment of violent juveniles and to scale back federal authority in environmental and land-use matters.

As the only Texas Democrat on the Appropriations Committee, Edwards is the go-to guy for his colleagues in securing funding for Texas priorities. The 11th District hosts the massive Army base at Fort Hood, and Edwards is particularly watchful of defense interests, including Texas-based aerospace firms, military retirement benefits and education for the children of military personnel.

During Edwards' tenure in the House, there have been two mass killings in his district that stirred strong feelings on the issue of restricting gun owners' rights. While the House in 1991 debated a crime bill that included a ban on certain semiautomatic assault-style weapons, news broke that a man with an automatic pistol had killed 22 people and wounded at least 20 more in a

Killeen cafeteria before killing himself.

In early 1993, Edwards' district again was the focus of national attention during a 51-day standoff between federal agents and the Branch Davidian religious sect just outside Waco that started with the killing of four law enforcement officers and ended with the fiery deaths of Branch Davidian leader David Koresh and nearly all the members of his sect. These events were on Edwards' mind when he voted in 1994 to ban 19 types of assault-style weapons.

Edwards was in high school during the height of the civil rights movement. He says two books — "Black Like Me" and "To Kill a Mockingbird" — convinced him that government should play a vital role in righting social wrongs. At Texas A & M University, he was a leader in the Student Conference on National Affairs, where he got to know the local congressman, Olin E. "Tiger" Teague. As his college days wound down, Edwards asked for Teague's help in landing a job with Democratic Sen. Lloyd Bentsen. That fell through, but Teague gave him a job, which Edwards intended to give up after a year to continue his education at Harvard Business School.

But in 1976, after two years with Teague, Edwards was told by the veteran lawmaker that he wasn't going to seek re-election in 1978. Teague urged Edwards to try for the seat.

The crowded Democratic primary included 36-year-old Texas A & M Economics Professor Phil Gramm. Edwards says that Gramm, now a U.S. senator from Texas, in those days had long hair and wore sandals. He was a brilliant professor who never had to use notes in his lectures, Edward says. Gramm barely edged by Edwards, by fewer than 200 votes, to get into a runoff that led to Gramm's first election to Congress.

Edwards went off to Harvard, then returned to Texas to enter the business world. But he spotted an opportunity to run for the state Senate and in 1982 became, at 31, the youngest senator elected to the state legislature. His ambition did not go unnoticed, and it was no big surprise when he started campaigning for lieutenant governor in 1989. But when Democratic Rep. Marvin Leath announced he would step down in 1990, Edwards moved to the 11th to run for the House.

The GOP nominee, state Rep. Hugh D. Shine, outspent Edwards and tried to tar him as a carpetbagger, although his state Senate district did overlap some with the House district. But voters took notice of Edwards' chit, secured from House Speaker Thomas S. Foley, for Leath's seat on Armed Services. Edwards won with 53 percent of the vote. He has had little trouble since.

KEY VOTES

2000

Yes	Raise hourly minimum wage by $1 over two years
No	Halt funding for U.S. mission in Kosovo unless European nations pay more
Yes	Provide Medicare benefits to military retirees and their dependents
Yes	Grant China permanent normal trade status
No	Phase out estate, gift and trust taxes
No	Prohibit implementation of president's national monument designations
No	Approve GOP plan to provide prescription drug coverage for Medicare beneficiaries
Yes	Increase help for poor nations indebted to international financial institutions

1999

Yes	Impose steel import quotas
Yes	Kill proposal to take aviation trust funds off budget
No	Require background checks on buyers only at gun shows with 10 or more vendors
No	Remove barriers among banking, securities and insurance companies
Yes	Authorize state grants to hire teachers and reduce class size
Yes	Overhaul campaign finance law; ban "soft money" and restrict advocacy advertising
Yes	Approve bipartisan plan to increase rights of patients in managed-care health plans

INTEREST GROUPS

	AFL-CIO	ADA	CCUS	ACU
2000	70%	80%	52%	8%
1999	78%	85%	42%	8%
1998	90%	90%	44%	8%
1997	88%	60%	70%	28%

CQ VOTE STUDIES

	PARTY UNITY		PRESIDENTIAL SUPPORT	
	Support	Oppose	Support	Oppose
2000	84%	16%	78%	22%
1999	80%	20%	79%	21%
1998	84%	16%	81%	19%
1997	78%	22%	73%	27%

TEXAS 11

Central – Waco

The 11th's residents are not party-line voters, and they do not embrace change – in 64 years, the district has had just three congressmen. While longtime Democratic Rep. Edwards carried all but one of the district's 12 counties in 2000, the 11th is trending Republican. President Bush won every county in 2000 in this rural district set between Dallas and Austin. Four years earlier, Bob Dole won all but two counties, Milam and Falls.

About one-third of the district's residents reside in each of Bell and McLennan counties, which together provide the bulk of Democratic votes. Waco, in McLennan County, is the 11th's core and is considered the educational, cultural and economic lifeblood of central Texas. It is also the largest marketing center between Austin and Dallas. The district was largely insulated from the energy bust of the 1980s and has seen steady economic growth.

Fort Hood, the district's massive military base in Bell County, is an economic mainstay that has yet to be substantially affected by defense cutbacks. It has drawn retired veterans – more than any other district in the nation – who come to the 11th largely for its mild climate and three veterans' medical centers.

MAJOR INDUSTRY
Military, agriculture, light manufacturing

MILITARY BASES
Fort Hood (Army), 42,384 military, 3,047 civilian (1999)

CITIES
Waco, 108,520; Killeen, 81,405; Temple, 52,154

UNUSUAL FEATURES
President George W. Bush's ranch in Crawford, outside of Waco; Texas Ranger Museum in Waco includes Billy the Kid's rifle and guns used on both sides of the Bonnie and Clyde ambush; Waco is home to Baylor University, the world's largest Baptist-affiliated university; In 1993, a complex outside Waco known as Ranch Apocalypse was the scene of a deadly standoff between federal agents and members of the Branch Davidian group.

Rep. Kay Granger (R)

CAPITOL OFFICE
225-5071; fax 225-5683; 435 Cannon Bldg. 20515

INTERNET
e-mail: texas.granger@mail.house.gov
web: www.house.gov/granger

COMMITTEES
Appropriations
Budget

HOMETOWN
Fort Worth

BORN
Jan. 18, 1943, Greenville, Texas

RELIGION
Methodist

FAMILY
Divorced; three children

EDUCATION
Texas Wesleyan U., B.S. 1965

CAREER
Insurance agent; teacher

POLITICAL HIGHLIGHTS
Fort Worth City Council, 1989-91; mayor of Fort
Worth, 1991-95

ELECTION RESULTS

2000 GENERAL

Kay Granger (R)	117,739	62.7%
Mark Greene (D)	67,612	36.0%
Rick L. Clay (LIBERT)	2,565	1.4%

2000 PRIMARY

Kay Granger (R)	unopposed

1998 GENERAL

Kay Granger (R)	66,740	61.9%
Tom Hall (D)	39,084	36.3%
Paul Barthel (LIBERT)	1,917	1.8%

PREVIOUS WINNING PERCENTAGES
1996 (58%)

Elected 1996; 3rd term

Granger is viewed by her party's leaders as someone to promote. Smart and ambitious, she confronts the challenge that Republicans have faced in translating their legislative agenda into terms that will resonate with voters, particularly women.

Granger is the first Republican woman to represent Texas in the House. She can speak with authority from the perspective of a businesswoman, a working parent and a local elected official. A divorced mother of three, she started her own insurance agency and served as mayor of Fort Worth, a non-partisan post.

Granger was wooed by both parties when she indicated interest in running for the 12th District seat in 1996, and Republican leaders have tried to make sure she is happy about choosing their side. Granger made it clear, even as a freshman, that she had aspirations for a broader role in the party, and she was given a position as an assistant whip. In the 106th Congress, she received a seat on the Appropriations Committee.

She still has her sights set on a role in the House leadership and considered a bid for a low-level rung on the Republican Caucus leadership ladder for the 107th Congress before dropping out at the last moment. She did win a seat on the Budget Committee, however.

Granger's legislative priorities are shaped by her background. Her interest in championing tax-free education savings accounts for college can be traced to her own experience working her way through school and to the difficulties a favorite niece had in saving enough money to pay for her daughter's education. Granger persuaded Ways and Means Committee Chairman Bill Archer, R-Texas, to include her educational savings account plan in a 1997 tax cut bill. Granger has sponsored legislation to authorize tax-deferred prepaid college tuition plans.

GOP leaders were also happy to give Granger a prominent role in arguing for legislation that would allow companies to offer employees compensatory time off in lieu of pay for overtime work. Democrats slammed the measure as a sop to business that would lead to workers being coerced to forgo overtime pay. But Granger, who raised three children on her own, said the bill would give people flexibility to take time off to deal with family concerns.

In the 106th Congress, Granger was vice chairwoman of the bipartisan Women's Caucus, which works to redefine "women's issues" to include matters such as retirement security, workplace issues and the economy.

She is also involved with a group that calls itself the Renewal Alliance, a coalition of about 20 House and Senate Republicans who promote public-private partnerships to address social ills. The group got started to counter Democratic rhetoric about Republicans being hard-hearted toward the nation's less fortunate. "When I heard there was a group in Washington talking about how we can encourage community renewal and taking our community into our own hands, I thought, well that's me," Granger said. She likes to say that she wants to "lower voices while raising the sights" of her Republican colleagues.

Although Granger supports abortion rights, she says that changing the Republican Party's official line against abortion is not a top priority. "To some, I think it's the most important issue, but that's not really where I'm coming from," she said. And in fact, Granger in 1997 voted to ban a procedure its opponents call "partial birth" abortion. She also opposed the early

www.cq.com

release of $385 million for international family planning programs, which critics say promote abortion overseas.

Granger does what she can to keep federal dollars flowing to her district's defense manufacturers, which include Lockheed Martin and Bell Helicopter Textron. She has supported continued federal funding of the F-16, the F-22 and the V-22 Osprey aircraft.

She was an early supporter of fellow Texas Republican George W. Bush's presidential bid. Two of her staff members joined the Bush campaign, and she was mentioned as a possibility for a Cabinet-level job in the Bush administration.

Granger was born in Greenville, Texas, to two public school teachers who divorced when she was 13. Her mother taught in the Fort Worth area for 45 years. Granger told the Fort Worth Star-Telegram that her mother never told her that she could be anything she wanted; rather, that she *had* to be whatever she wanted. "I was not self-made," Granger says. "I was made by my mother." Granger followed her mother and became a teacher in the same Birdville school district that named an elementary school after her mother. Granger taught literature and journalism for 10 years. But then she decided to switch careers.

She went into the insurance business in 1978, eventually founding her own agency. In 1981, she was appointed to the Fort Worth Zoning Commission, where she served until she was elected to the city council in 1989. Two years later, she was elected mayor.

During her mayoral tenure, citizen patrol initiatives and other anti-gang efforts helped cut crime by 50 percent. She lured new businesses to the city, and she was able to reduce property taxes for the first time in 11 years. Her pro-business stands endeared her to the Fort Worth business community, which in 1999 made her the first woman chosen as outstanding business executive of the year. Both Democrats and Republicans courted her as a House candidate when Democratic Rep. Pete Geren decided not to seek re-election in 1996.

After choosing to run under the Republican banner and resigning as mayor, Granger heard grumbling from some on the GOP right. She was attacked by two primary opponents as a liberal and was opposed by the Tarrant County Republican chairman. But she won nomination with a whopping 69 percent of the GOP primary vote.

In November, she defeated another former Fort Worth mayor, Hugh Parmer, by 17 percentage points. She has not been seriously challenged since.

KEY VOTES

2000

?	Raise hourly minimum wage by $1 over two years
Yes	Halt funding for U.S. mission in Kosovo unless European nations pay more
Yes	Provide Medicare benefits to military retirees and their dependents
Yes	Grant China permanent normal trade status
Yes	Phase out estate, gift and trust taxes
Yes	Prohibit implementation of president's national monument designations
Yes	Approve GOP plan to provide prescription drug coverage for Medicare beneficiaries
No	Increase help for poor nations indebted to international financial institutions

1999

No	Impose steel import quotas
Yes	Kill proposal to take aviation trust funds off budget
Yes	Require background checks on buyers only at gun shows with 10 or more vendors
No	Remove barriers among banking, securities and insurance companies
No	Authorize state grants to hire teachers and reduce class size
No	Overhaul campaign finance law; ban "soft money" and restrict advocacy advertising
?	Approve bipartisan plan to increase rights of patients in managed-care health plans

INTEREST GROUPS

	AFL-CIO	ADA	CCUS	ACU
2000	0%	5%	84%	84%
1999	0%	5%	95%	78%
1998	10%	5%	100%	84%
1997	0%	0%	100%	92%

CQ VOTE STUDIES

	PARTY UNITY		PRESIDENTIAL SUPPORT	
	Support	Oppose	Support	Oppose
2000	93%	7%	25%	75%
1999	92%	8%	26%	74%
1998	91%	9%	28%	72%
1997	95%	5%	29%	71%

TEXAS 12

Northwest Tarrant County; part of Fort Worth

The 12th is made up of parts of Johnson and Parker counties, the northwest section of Tarrant County and a segment of Fort Worth. The district is mostly white, middle-class and a mix of rural and suburban. Tarrant County is by far the most populous of the three counties, but new housing developments are appearing in some sections of traditionally rural Johnson and Parker counties.

The economic strength of the 12th depends heavily on transportation. Within or adjacent to the Fort Worth-based district are three major airports, an Air Force base, three railroad lines, several interstate highways and a myriad of businesses that depend on one or more of these conveyances. The Union Pacific and now-combined Burlington Northern Santa Fe railroads are both active in the district, but the air industry has far surpassed rail. Large government defense contracts have helped create jobs and fuel economic growth.

Politically, the 12th is competitive terrain. In the past, Democratic

candidates have received robust percentages here. But the district appears to be leaning Republican, electing a Republican representative in 1996, then solidly re-electing her in 1998 and 2000. In general, Parker and Johnson counties tend to vote Republican and are more conservative on social issues.

MAJOR INDUSTRY
Defense technology, transportation, medicine

MILITARY BASES
Naval Air Station Fort Worth, Joint Reserve Base, Fort Worth, 2,062 active duty, 1,646 civilian (2000)

CITIES
Fort Worth (pt.), 275,808 (1990); Haltom City (pt.), 27,789 (1990); Cleburne, 26,198

UNUSUAL FEATURES
National Cowgirl Museum in Fort Worth showcases women rodeo riders and contributors to Western heritage, including painter Georgia O'Keeffe and sharpshooter Annie Oakley; Cowtown Coliseum, in the historic Stockyards district of Fort Worth, was the site of the world's first indoor rodeo and the world's first live radio broadcast of a rodeo.

Rep. William M. 'Mac' Thornberry (R)

CAPITOL OFFICE
225-3706; fax 225-3486; 131 Cannon Bldg. 20515

INTERNET
e-mail: www.house.gov/writerep
web: www.house.gov/thornberry

COMMITTEES
Armed Services
(Special DOE Reorganization panel - chairman)
Budget
Resources

HOMETOWN
Clarendon

BORN
July 15, 1958, Clarendon, Texas

RELIGION
Presbyterian

FAMILY
Wife, Sally Adams; two children

EDUCATION
Texas Tech U., B.A. 1980; U. of Texas, J.D. 1983

CAREER
Lawyer; cattleman; State Department official;
congressional aide

POLITICAL HIGHLIGHTS
No previous office

ELECTION RESULTS

2000 GENERAL

William Thornberry (R)	117,995	67.6%
Curtis Clinesmith (D)	54,343	31.2%
Brad Clardy (LIBERT)	2,137	1.2%

2000 PRIMARY

William Thornberry (R)	30,867	91.5%
David Morris (R)	2,863	8.5%

1998 GENERAL

William Thornberry (R)	81,141	67.9%
Mark Harmon (D)	37,027	31.0%
Georganne Payne (LIBERT)	1,298	1.1%

PREVIOUS WINNING PERCENTAGES
1996 (67%); 1994 (55%)

Elected 1994; 4th term

Thornberry will never be mistaken for a moderate, but his style does differ from that of many other younger conservatives who have made headlines by demanding that the Republican Party hold firm to a hard-right course without compromise. The Texan says an effective lawmaker must have "energy, patience and persistence."

Although Thornberry never held elected office before winning his congressional seat, he worked as chief of staff to Texas GOP Rep. Larry Combest. Like his former boss, Thornberry can temper his conservatism with a bit of pragmatism when the need arises.

For instance, while he called for an outright abolition of the estate tax in the 105th Congress, Thornberry was willing to settle for half a loaf — a big increase in the amount that is exempt from taxation. "The reality last year on the estate tax was we were not going to get rid of it," he said in 1998. "So if you can make it a little better and then come back the next year, that's the way to get it abolished."

Thornberry traces his conservatism to his upbringing on the Texas ranch that has been in the family for more than 70 years. He grew up in a modest house built by his grandfather in the 1930s. "I was taught at a very young age the importance of doing a good job and putting in an honest day's work," he told the Texas Tech University alumni magazine in 1997. "I also learned how much a person can accomplish if they're just left alone to do it. In many respects, these are two foreign concepts in Washington."

After graduating from the University of Texas law school in 1983, Thornberry spent six years in and around Capitol Hill and ultimately served as a deputy assistant secretary of state for legislative affairs in the Reagan administration. Back in Texas in 1989, he worked in an Amarillo law firm while helping run his family's cattle ranch. In his successful 1994 challenge to Democratic Rep. Bill Sarpalius, who had supported raising taxes as part of President Clinton's unpopular 1993 budget plan, Thornberry played up his family's close ties to the land. Since beating Sarpalius with 55 percent of the vote, Thornberry has had no problem winning re-election.

Thornberry gained notice in the 106th Congress by helping to write legislation restructuring the Energy Department's nuclear weapons programs and putting them under a largely autonomous new agency, the National Nuclear Security Administration (NNSA). For his efforts, he landed the chairmanship of the Special Oversight Panel on Department of Energy Reorganization, established by the Armed Services Committee in 1999 to help implement the new law.

Congress created the new nuclear administration in reaction to reports detailing China's alleged attempts to steal highly classified information from the Energy Department's nuclear weapons laboratories. The legislation sparked considerable controversy because of concerns that the agency could operate outside of the reach of environmental, health and safety regulations, but Thornberry said it was necessary to protect national security. "With the NNSA," he declared, "we are going to make sure that the nation's nuclear weapons facilities are run with a clear, military-like chain of command."

Thornberry's interest in national security hardly stops with nuclear issues. "Defense is the first priority of the federal government, and we need to take care of that before we address other issues," he says. While some lawmakers contemplate other uses for a projected federal budget surplus, Thornberry insists that any "excess" money go to increase defense spending. He is a leading advocate for the construction of a U.S. anti-missile defense system.

The Texan looks out for the interests of the 13th District's Sheppard Air Force Base, just north of Wichita Falls. He also has an interest in V-22 Osprey tilt-rotor aircraft, which are assembled by Bell Helicopter in Amarillo.

On issues before the Resources panel, Thornberry sides squarely with the concerns of ranchers. He is a staunch proponent of property owners' rights and believes that federal laws and regulations impinge unduly on farmers' land-use decisions. "Property rights," he says, "become the foundation for quality of life." Accordingly, he regularly supports bills to overhaul the Endangered Species Act, which allows the government to block development on private lands. In the 106th Congress, he denounced the law as "an example of how the federal government has crossed the line between responsible conservation and overzealous regulation."

Coming from a district where cotton is big business, Thornberry has a keen interest in federal policies affecting that crop, as well as other agricultural commodities. He supported measures in the 106th to strengthen the Federal Crop Insurance Program and grant drought-stricken farmers $5.4 billion in aid. In the 104th Congress, he voted for the GOP "Freedom to Farm" bill, a broad rewrite of agriculture programs that sought to replace New Deal-era crop subsidies with a system more in line with free-market principles. But he also bucked House leaders by working with Combest — now chairman of the Agriculture Committee — to preserve the federal support system for cotton. "It makes more sense for cotton," Thornberry told The Dallas Morning News. "We have less flexibility than other parts of the country, like Iowa and Illinois, that have rain and rich soil."

While others in his class balked at their leadership's compromises with Clinton in the 1995, '96 and '97 budget battles and plotted to remove Newt Gingrich as Speaker in 1997 because they found him too conciliatory, Thornberry stayed apart from the coup.

Although he favors a leaner government, Thornberry is not averse to supporting funding that helps his district. Like his Democratic predecessor, Thornberry spoke up for the Amarillo-based Helium Reserve program, which employed about 200 people overseeing the federal government's stockpile of helium gas. In 1996, when the House considered a measure to end the program, Thornberry was a lonely voice arguing for privatizing it to help provide more financial return for taxpayers and protect workers in Amarillo.

Thornberry joins many fellow Lone Star State representatives, including Majority Leader Dick Armey, as an active member of the Boot Caucus, an informal Hill coalition of boot-wearing lawmakers.

KEY VOTES

2000
No Raise hourly minimum wage by $1 over two years
Yes Halt funding for U.S. mission in Kosovo unless European nations pay more
Yes Provide Medicare benefits to military retirees and their dependents
Yes Grant China permanent normal trade status
Yes Phase out estate, gift and trust taxes
Yes Prohibit implementation of president's national monument designations
Yes Approve GOP plan to provide prescription drug coverage for Medicare beneficiaries
No Increase help for poor nations indebted to international financial institutions

1999
No Impose steel import quotas
Yes Kill proposal to take aviation trust funds off budget
No Require background checks on buyers only at gun shows with 10 or more vendors
No Remove barriers among banking, securities and insurance companies
No Authorize state grants to hire teachers and reduce class size
No Overhaul campaign finance law; ban "soft money" and restrict advocacy advertising
Yes Approve bipartisan plan to increase rights of patients in managed-care health plans

INTEREST GROUPS

	AFL-CIO	ADA	CCUS	ACU
2000	0%	0%	76%	88%
1999	22%	5%	76%	88%
1998	0%	5%	89%	100%
1997	0%	5%	100%	96%

CQ VOTE STUDIES

	PARTY UNITY		PRESIDENTIAL SUPPORT	
	Support	Oppose	Support	Oppose
2000	97%	3%	25%	75%
1999	93%	7%	20%	80%
1998	92%	8%	23%	77%
1997	96%	4%	32%	68%

TEXAS 13

Eastern Panhandle – Wichita Falls; part of Amarillo

The conservative 13th starts at the Oklahoma border, runs through the Panhandle below Lubbock in the west and then heads east, covering the South Plains, the Red River Valley and taking in a bit of Denton. A monstrous and mainly rural district, the 13th includes all or part of 38 sparsely settled counties.

Oil and cotton dominate the district's economy, and both suffered during the 1980s and early '90s as oil prices dropped and droughts starved the land. Thanks to other industries, the main cities weathered the difficulties. In Amarillo, Pantex is the nation's only nuclear weapons assembly and disassembly plant. The city also has a hand in producing the military's V-22 Osprey, which takes off like a helicopter but flies like a plane. After several crashes during testing, the aircraft's future is uncertain.

In Wichita Falls, factories are rampant, but the jewel of the economy is Sheppard Air Force Base, which has so far escaped downsizing. Many

of the district's rural counties depend on the Ogallala Aquifer to grow wheat, sorghum, sugar beets, corn and hay.

Republicans took the House seat from Democrats in 1994, the result of a growing conservative trend. Locally, Republicans do well in many of the rural small towns that dot the district, particularly around Amarillo. The portion of Lubbock that's in the 13th favors Democrats. Closer to blue-collar Wichita Falls, voters traditionally favored Democrats, but elections are getting more competitive.

MAJOR INDUSTRY
Agriculture, oil, defense

MILITARY BASES
Sheppard Air Force Base, 3,486 military, 1,294 civilian (1999)

CITIES
Wichita Falls, 98,919; Amarillo (pt.), 95,803 (1990); Denton (pt.), 44,170 (1990); Lubbock (pt.), 39,774 (1990)

UNUSUAL FEATURES
Singer Buddy Holly born and raised in Lubbock; A stretch of Route 66, made famous by songs and television, cuts through the 13th.

Rep. Ron Paul (R)

CAPITOL OFFICE
225-2831; fax 226-4871; 203 Cannon Bldg. 20515

INTERNET
e-mail: rep.paul@mail.house.gov
web: www.house.gov/paul

COMMITTEES
Financial Services
International Relations

HOMETOWN
Surfside

BORN
Aug. 20, 1935, Pittsburgh, Pa.

RELIGION
Protestant

FAMILY
Wife, Carol Wells; five children

EDUCATION
Gettysburg College, B.S. 1957; Duke U., M.D. 1961

MILITARY SERVICE
Air Force, 1963-65; Pa. Air National Guard, 1965-68

CAREER
Physician

POLITICAL HIGHLIGHTS
Republican nominee for U.S. House, 1974; U.S.
House, 1976-77, 1979-85; sought Republican
nomination for U.S. Senate, 1984; Libertarian
candidate for president, 1988

ELECTION RESULTS

2000 GENERAL

Ron Paul (R)	137,370	59.7%
Loy Sneary (D)	92,689	40.3%

2000 PRIMARY

Ron Paul (R)	unopposed

1998 GENERAL

Ron Paul (R)	84,459	55.3%
Loy Sneary (D)	68,014	44.5%

PREVIOUS WINNING PERCENTAGES
1996 (51%); 1982 (99%); 1980 (51%); 1978 (51%);
1976 Special Runoff Election (56%); 1976 Special
Election (40%)

Elected 1996; 6th full term
Also served 1976-77, 1979-85

Paul is not the type of politician to jump on the bandwagon. When the House agreed in 2000 to award a gold medal to popular Peanuts cartoonist Charles M. Schulz by a resounding vote of 410-1, Paul cast the lone dissenting vote. He also was the only "no" when the House voted 400-1 to urge Haiti to conduct free, fair and peaceful elections and 423-1 to increase criminal penalties for so-called date rape drugs. All told, he cast the solitary "no" vote in the House 28 times in the 106th Congress.

The Texas physician, often called "Dr. No," votes against such measures because he believes they represent an unwarranted extension of federal authority. The one-time Libertarian candidate for president argues that the government has no right to take any action that is not specifically authorized by the Constitution, and he would like to return the country to the days when states held most of the power and the value of the dollar was pegged to gold. He once wrote: "The government perpetually takes our money, lies to us and makes our lives worse."

Such absolutist views mean that Paul casts solo dissenting votes far more often than any other member of the House, and his refusal to compromise limits his effectiveness. But Paul has gained a national following of sorts though his devotion to principle, and he receives campaign contributions from like-minded people across the country.

Marching to a different drummer is not new for Paul. After starting to develop his political theories in medical school and working as an obstetrician, he served two stints in the House during the late 1970s and early 1980s, when there were just a few Republicans in Texas' overwhelmingly Democratic delegation. Then he left the GOP to run as the Libertarian Party's 1988 nominee for president. He got about 432,000 votes (about 0.5 percent) in a campaign in which he renounced the Republican Party, spoke out against foreign aid and "corporate welfare" — certain tax breaks and subsidies for big business — and advocated the legalization of drugs.

When he returned to the House in 1996 (defeating the preferred GOP candidate in a hard-fought primary), he received a lukewarm reception from his party. Still, top Republicans appear content — or perhaps resigned — to let Paul be Paul. "So far, he's been for us more than 'agin' us," House Majority Whip Tom DeLay of Texas told the Austin American-Statesman.

Paul maintains that members of Congress should be required to document the constitutional authority for every bill they introduce. He votes "no" on virtually every appropriations bill that comes to the House floor. He nixed resolutions condemning a coup in Sierra Leone and terrorist bombings in Jerusalem. "While we as individuals have a moral obligation to express our concerns about the philosophies in the world around us and the treatment of our fellow man," Paul says, "the federal government does not."

When he opposed a gold medal for Mother Teresa in 1997, he challenged his 434 colleagues to contribute $100 each toward the minting of the gold medal. Paul, noting that no one took him up on his offer, observed: "Of course, it is easier to be generous with other people's money." Consistent with his beliefs, he argues that money for more bike trails should come from private donors, not the federal treasury — even though he is an avid bicyclist who would like to see more trails constructed.

Paul takes a dim view of U.S. aid to foreign countries. "Under our Constitution, the government has no right to send the taxpayers' money overseas," he says. He has backed efforts to end U.S. support for the International Monetary Fund and to force the United States to pull out of the World Trade Organization. He also opposes "so-called peacekeeping missions" and sponsored legislation that would have required the United States to withdraw from the United Nations. In the 107th Congress, he was given a seat on the International Relations Committee.

Although he typically votes for free-trade measures, he opposed a bill in 2000 granting China permanent normal trade status because it would have created a commission to make annual reports on human rights abuses.

Paul's Libertarian beliefs make him an erratic ally of GOP causes. He opposes legislation that would prohibit same-sex marriage, saying "everyone is an individual and ought to be treated equally." He also opposes a constitutional amendment to ban flag burning and brands federal efforts to combat illegal drugs "an absolute failure." But he parts company with his former Libertarian brethren in advocating an anti-abortion stand. Paul has said that "whether a civilized society treats human life with dignity or contempt will determine the outcome of that civilization."

At times, Paul has shown a bit of flexibility with the GOP leadership. When his party was struggling in 1997 to pass a District of Columbia spending bill, he changed his vote from "no" to "present," allowing the measure to pass 203-202. Paul's distaste for what he perceives to be "corporate welfare" also made him the only Texas Republican voting in 1997 to terminate the International Space Station program, which is funded by NASA, an important employer in the Houston area. He votes against farm subsidies, but he says the farmers in his district like him "because I protect their right to have a gun and I keep the EPA off their back," he told the St. Petersburg Times.

Paul was first elected to Congress in an April 1976 special election to replace Democratic Rep. Bob Casey, who had resigned to join the Federal Maritime Commission. Paul defeated Democrat Bob Gammage, who in the general election seven months later felled Paul by 268 votes. But in 1978, Paul got the upper hand again, edging Gammage by 1,200 votes.

In 1984, Paul relinquished his House seat to run, unsuccessfully, for the Senate; he lost the primary. Twelve years later, he won election to the 14th District, which includes some areas he represented in his earlier House career. In winning, he beat the preferred candidate of the GOP establishment, Rep. Greg Laughlin, who had represented the district as a Democrat but switched to the GOP in 1995. Paul prevailed in the primary by pressing his anti-tax and anti-government message; he won the general election by just 3 percentage points, in spite of criticism that he supported the legalization of drugs. He has since won re-election by comfortable margins.

KEY VOTES

2000
No Raise hourly minimum wage by $1 over two years

Yes Halt funding for U.S. mission in Kosovo unless European nations pay more

Yes Provide Medicare benefits to military retirees and their dependents

No Grant China permanent normal trade status

Yes Phase out estate, gift and trust taxes

Yes Prohibit implementation of president's national monument designations

No Approve GOP plan to provide prescription drug coverage for Medicare beneficiaries

No Increase help for poor nations indebted to international financial institutions

1999
No Impose steel import quotas

No Kill proposal to take aviation trust funds off budget

No Require background checks on buyers only at gun shows with 10 or more vendors

No Remove barriers among banking, securities and insurance companies

No Authorize state grants to hire teachers and reduce class size

No Overhaul campaign finance law; ban "soft money" and restrict advocacy advertising

No Approve bipartisan plan to increase rights of patients in managed-care health plans

INTEREST GROUPS

	AFL-CIO	ADA	CCUS	ACU
2000	44%	30%	45%	76%
1999	38%	10%	60%	92%
1998	40%	20%	65%	88%
1997	25%	30%	60%	80%

CQ VOTE STUDIES

	PARTY UNITY		PRESIDENTIAL SUPPORT	
	Support	Oppose	Support	Oppose
2000	80%	20%	27%	73%
1999	75%	25%	30%	70%
1998	76%	24%	31%	69%
1997	81%	19%	41%	59%

TEXAS 14
Southeast – Victoria; San Marcos

Spanning a 15,000-square-mile area between Houston and San Antonio, the 14th contains a stretch of coastal land from south of Galveston to near Corpus Christi and then spreads inland to wrap around Austin. The district has only two cities with relatively large populations, and nearly 80 percent of its residents are native-born Texans. Dominated by farms and petrochemical plants, the 14th leans Republican but has Democratic roots and a sizable minority population.

Chemical companies like Dow Chemical have their facilities near the Gulf Coast, where they rode the 1980s oil glut to success by making antifreeze and other products. Victoria, the district's largest city, is a leading oil and chemical center. Mingled with the chemical-producers on the coast are fishermen who haul in boatloads of shrimp.

Farmers in the 14th's interior grow rice, grain and sorghum, while the northwestern reaches of the district benefit from Austin's health care and government sectors. The district also holds attraction for nature lovers, who can visit Goose Island State Park, the Aransas National Wildlife Refuge and several bird sanctuaries.

Politically, the 14th tends to elect Republicans but not by the overwhelming margins that some suburban Houston districts rack up, especially at the national level. Locally, Republicans tend to do very well in the southern portions of the 14th, while the areas around Austin have taken on some of that city's more liberal leanings.

MAJOR INDUSTRY
Petrochemicals, agriculture, health care

CITIES
Victoria, 61,699; San Marcos, 40,538; Bay City, 18,896

UNUSUAL FEATURES
Former President Lyndon B. Johnson born in Blanco County; Stephen F. Austin, Texas' founder, from Jones Creek, near the city of Freeport.

Rep. Rubén Hinojosa (D)

Elected 1996; 3rd term

CAPITOL OFFICE
225-2531; fax 225-5688
1535 Longworth Bldg. 20515

INTERNET
e-mail: rep.hinojosa@mail.house.gov
web: www.house.gov/hinojosa

COMMITTEES
Education & Workforce
Financial Services

HOMETOWN
Mercedes

BORN
Aug. 20, 1940, Edcouch, Texas

RELIGION
Roman Catholic

FAMILY
Wife, Martha Hinojosa; five children

EDUCATION
U. of Texas, B.B.A. 1962; U. of Texas, Pan
American, M.B.A. 1980

CAREER
Food processing executive

POLITICAL HIGHLIGHTS
Texas State Board of Education, 1974-84
(chairman of special populations)

ELECTION RESULTS

2000 GENERAL

Ruben Hinojosa (D)	106,570	88.5%
Frank L. Jones (LIBERT)	13,167	10.9%

2000 PRIMARY

Ruben Hinojosa (D)	46,247	73.5%
Diana Rivera-Martinez (D)	12,710	20.2%
Mel Buentello Hawkins (D)	3,928	6.2%

1998 GENERAL

Ruben Hinojosa (D)	47,957	58.4%
Tom Haughey (R)	34,221	41.6%

PREVIOUS WINNING PERCENTAGES
1996 (62%)

The eighth of 11 children born to parents who had immigrated to the United States from Mexico, Hinojosa grew up in an agricultural community in South Texas and attended an elementary school where Mexican-American children were segregated from Anglo students. His priorities in Congress — expanding educational opportunities and promoting small-business development in his heavily Hispanic district — are strongly influenced by his life experience.

From his modest beginnings, he rose to become president of a family-owned food-processing company with more than 400 employees. He served for a decade on the state board of education and was instrumental in creating the South Texas Community College system in the upper Rio Grande Valley.

Hinojosa (ee-na-HO-suh) serves on the Education and the Workforce Committee and became chairman of the Congressional Hispanic Caucus's education task force shortly after he arrived in Washington. In those positions, he lobbies for federal dollars to address "the disparity in educational opportunity between Hispanics and other Americans." He has helped direct millions of dollars to Hispanic colleges and universities and fund efforts to connect schools and libraries to the Internet.

After a 1999 study showed that many qualified Hispanics fail to attend college, Hinojosa said Hispanics need to take responsibility in pushing for better schools and more college opportunities. He favors legislation to bolster programs that seek to reduce the high school dropout rate and provide more education opportunities for migrant workers.

In the 107th Congress, Hinojosa was among the vocal Democrats who complained about new Education Chairman John A. Boehner's plan to shift authority over historically black, Hispanic and Indian colleges to a new subcommittee. Democrats said the change split jurisdiction over higher education issues along racial lines. Boehner, who argued that minority schools would receive more attention through the new structure, eventually agreed to a compromise.

In the 105th Congress, Hinojosa praised a landmark budget agreement that included funding for scholarships to help middle-class students attend college. However, he maintained that more had to be done. In 1997, he joined with Hispanic Caucus members and others in introducing legislation seeking to redirect existing Higher Education Act programs to "pointedly target" resources to "those most in need," including Hispanics and American Indians.

The following year, he won a substantial increase in federal aid to colleges that serve large numbers of Hispanic students. Funding also was increased for bilingual and migrant education and for Head Start — all Hinojosa priorities.

Hinojosa broke from the Clinton administration on one of its high-profile education proposals: introducing voluntary national tests to track and improve the performance of elementary school students. Recalling his own struggles as a student — Spanish was his first language, and he says he "took years" to master English — Hinojosa argued that a "national test should not be used as a basis for making high-stakes educational decisions" because of "enormous inequalities" between the resources available to schools attended primarily by poor and minority students and schools with more affluent populations.

Hinojosa joined the Financial Services Committee in the 107th, giving up his seat on Small Business. On the latter, Hinojosa had helped create a Women's Business Center at the University of Texas-Edinburg.

He supports efforts to cut taxes and regulations. But he assailed a GOP proposal in 1999 for $792 billion in tax cuts, contending that it would threaten Social Security and Medicare. "This is by far the most irresponsible and reckless chicanery I've ever witnessed in my political tenure," he said.

The Texan was in the spotlight in the 106th Congress during the debate over granting China permanent normal trade status. With Hinojosa undecided on the issue, the Clinton administration took the extraordinary step of sending him and another member (New York Democrat Gregory W. Meeks) on a fact-finding tour of China. In the end, Hinojosa backed the administration's plea to open up trade with China — after holding out for funding for an information technology center in South Texas.

With an eye to his rural constituents, Hinojosa also supported legislation in the 106th allowing satellite companies to carry local television programming. "Broadening consumer choice is what my constituents have said they want," he said. "Fair access is now what they will receive."

Hinojosa's overall voting record is liberal, but he has sided with conservatives on occasion. He supported congressional term limits, backed a constitutional amendment to prohibit flag desecration and voted to ban a procedure its opponents call "partial birth" abortion. He affiliates with the moderate New Democrat Coalition.

Hinojosa has lobbied for a new interstate highway in the 15th District that would serve as a trade route from Mexico and would help relieve local traffic bottlenecks occurring from increased cross-border commercial traffic, a result of the North American Free Trade Agreement. The massive 1998 transportation measure included money to connect U.S. 281 with Interstate 37.

The Hinojosa family's prominence and his own community involvement helped Hinojosa win the open 15th District seat in 1996. He succeeded Democratic Rep. E. "Kika" de la Garza, who retired after more than three decades in the House. Given the 15th's strong one-party voting tradition — it is a Democratic bulwark in the Lone Star State — Hinojosa's biggest challenge in taking the seat was winning his party's nomination. In a hotly contested five-way battle for the Democratic nod, he edged out Anglo lawyer Jim Selman.

Against Republican minister Tom Haughey, Hinojosa won by 26 percentage points in 1996 and by 17 points in a 1998 rematch. The GOP did not field a candidate against him in 2000.

KEY VOTES

2000
Yes Raise hourly minimum wage by $1 over two years
No Halt funding for U.S. mission in Kosovo unless European nations pay more
Yes Provide Medicare benefits to military retirees and their dependents
Yes Grant China permanent normal trade status
No Phase out estate, gift and trust taxes
– Prohibit implementation of president's national monument designations
No Approve GOP plan to provide prescription drug coverage for Medicare beneficiaries
Yes Increase help for poor nations indebted to international financial institutions

1999
Yes Impose steel import quotas
No Kill proposal to take aviation trust funds off budget
No Require background checks on buyers only at gun shows with 10 or more vendors
Yes Remove barriers among banking, securities and insurance companies
Yes Authorize state grants to hire teachers and reduce class size
Yes Overhaul campaign finance law; ban "soft money" and restrict advocacy advertising
Yes Approve bipartisan plan to increase rights of patients in managed-care health plans

INTEREST GROUPS

	AFL-CIO	ADA	CCUS	ACU
2000	90%	80%	50%	8%
1999	78%	100%	40%	4%
1998	89%	95%	59%	16%
1997	100%	75%	60%	29%

CQ VOTE STUDIES

	PARTY UNITY		PRESIDENTIAL SUPPORT	
	Support	Oppose	Support	Oppose
2000	92%	8%	88%	12%
1999	89%	11%	78%	22%
1998	91%	9%	79%	21%
1997	84%	16%	73%	27%

TEXAS 15

South – Bee, Brooks, Hidalgo and San Patricio counties; McAllen

Situated in southern Texas, the convoluted boundaries of the 15th take in the agricultural and cattle areas north of Corpus Christi and then dip down to the Texas-Mexico border. The 15th includes Texas' largest Hispanic population (according to 1990 Census Bureau statistics), which contributes to the district's overall Democratic leaning.

The 15th is one of the poorest districts in the nation. Community leaders struggle to bring jobs to the region and to provide job training to residents. Hidalgo, an agriculture area, is the most populous and fastest growing county in the district. Along the U.S.-Mexico border, *maquiladoras* – assembly or manufacturing plants that use low-cost labor and import many parts from the United States – are the mainstay. Trade with Mexican border cities like Reynosa also has helped boost the economy.

The 15th's congressional seat has never been held by a Republican. While Republicans became more competitive in the 1990s, Democrats continue to dominate. Despite losing the state, Bill Clinton won the 15th with 53 percent of the vote in 1992, his highest tally in any non-urban district in Texas. In '96, Clinton raised that number to 60 percent. And despite making his home a few hundred miles away in Austin and carrying the state with 59 percent, President Bush captured only 45 percent of the district vote in 2000. It was one of the 10 Texas congressional districts in which Al Gore won.

MAJOR INDUSTRY
Small business, trade, manufacturing

MILITARY BASES
Naval Station Ingleside, 4,703 military, 235 civilian (1999)

CITIES
McAllen, 110,292; Pharr, 45,844; Edinburg, 45,454; Mission, 43,947

UNUSUAL FEATURES
In 1836, Colonel James Walker Fannin of the Texas independence movement was executed with members of his troop in what was known as the "Goliad Massacre."

Rep. Silvestre Reyes (D)

Elected 1996; 3rd term

CAPITOL OFFICE
225-4831; fax 225-2016
1527 Longworth Bldg. 20515

INTERNET
e-mail: www.house.gov/writerep
web: www.house.gov/reyes

COMMITTEES
Armed Services
Veterans' Affairs
Select Intelligence

HOMETOWN
El Paso

BORN
Nov. 10, 1944, Canutillo, Texas

RELIGION
Roman Catholic

FAMILY
Wife, Carolina Gaytan; three children

EDUCATION
U. of Texas, attended 1964-65; Texas Western
College, attended 1965-66; El Paso Community
College, A.A. 1977

MILITARY SERVICE
Army, 1966-68

CAREER
U.S. Border Patrol agent

POLITICAL HIGHLIGHTS
Canutillo School Board, 1968-70

ELECTION RESULTS

2000 GENERAL

Silvestre Reyes (D)	92,649	68.3%
Daniel Power (R)	40,921	30.2%
Dan Moser (LIBERT)	2,080	1.5%

2000 PRIMARY

Silvestre Reyes (D)	unopposed

1998 GENERAL

Silvestre Reyes (D)	67,486	87.9%
Stu Nance (LIBERT)	5,329	6.9%
Lorenzo Morales (I)	3,952	5.1%

PREVIOUS WINNING PERCENTAGES
1996 (71%)

Reyes came to Congress after more than a quarter-century with the U.S. Border Patrol, a background that has made him an important player on immigration issues. In the 106th Congress, he helped shape legislation to reorganize the Immigration and Naturalization Service (INS), contending that the agency was failing to fulfill its responsibilities.

Reyes (sil-VES-truh RAY-ess, with rolled R's) was the main Democratic sponsor of a controversial bill to disband the INS and divide its authority between two new agencies. Although some immigration advocates contended the measure would further undermine services for immigrants, Reyes said it was essential to restructure the INS because it was poorly administered. Citing a backlog of almost 2 million people waiting to become citizens, Reyes said, "I would say we don't have any place to go but up," according to California's Orange County Register. He also criticized the INS for failing to hire 1,000 border patrol agents as called for in the budget.

Reyes contends that the INS suffers from what he calls a "conflicting mission" — trying to keep out illegal immigrants while trying to help legal immigrants gain services and seek citizenship. In the 105th Congress, Reyes sponsored a bill that would have established the Border Patrol as a stand-alone enforcement agency within the Justice Department.

Reyes has regularly found himself at odds with House colleagues on border issues. Early in his first House term, he objected as the House voted to reverse President Clinton's certification of Mexico as a drug-fighting ally. And he protested as the House also voted to allow the deployment of up to 10,000 U.S. military personnel to help patrol the border.

When the House in the 105th weighed in on Mexico's fitness to be certified as a drug-fighting ally, Reyes defended that country's performance, saying, "I have been on the front lines in the so-called war on drugs. ... I have personally observed Mexico's commitment to stem the tide of drug trafficking." Predicting that a vote to decertify would be "an affront" to Mexicans, he added: "Drug trafficking is not just a Mexican problem or issue. We on the northern side of the border must do more to stem the demand for illicit drugs."

Reyes was even more indignant about the prospect of 10,000 U.S. troops guarding the border, a proposal offered by Ohio Democrat James A. Traficant Jr. "The military mission is combat. ... This body should focus its time and energy on giving the Border Patrol the resources they need," he said. "We need professional, bilingual ... law enforcement officers, properly trained to deal with situations and problems along our border." But nearly all Republicans and more than one-third of Democrats voted with Traficant.

A strong voice on Hispanic issues, Reyes is chairman of the Congressional Hispanic Caucus in the 107th Congress. He is also a member of the Democratic Steering Committee, which makes committee assignments.

Called "Silver" by his friends, Reyes is the first Hispanic to represent the 16th District, where Hispanics make up 70 percent of the population. Reyes calls it "one of the poorest districts in the country," and he seeks federal funding for better roads and bridges to handle increased commercial traffic and retraining programs for workers in El Paso's garment industry whose jobs shifted to lower-wage Mexico. In 1999, he helped land $51 million in funding for programs aimed at helping the Army's Fort Bliss in the district, and millions more for housing and water projects.

In the 106th Congress, in a bid to help low-income students gain access to new technology, Reyes introduced legislation to provide schools with $400 million in computers and computer training. "In our digital economy, the access to technology is now a fundamental civil right," he said. "It is a fact that those who have access to technology and who know how to use it will have bright and prosperous futures, while those who don't will be techno-logically illiterate and left behind."

Reyes has a seat on the Armed Services Committee, where he is wary of military downsizing and base closings. The 16th has a sizable population of military retirees, whose needs Reyes monitors from Veterans' Affairs, where he is the top-ranking Democrat on the Benefits Subcommittee. In the 107th, he also won appointment to the Intelligence Committee.

Reyes, who lost the hearing in his right ear in Vietnam, has objected to "stonewalling" by military officials in addressing various health complaints of Persian Gulf War veterans. He has pressed for an official acknowledgment "that in fact a Gulf War syndrome does exist."

On floor votes, Reyes normally sides with the majority in his party. After voting against an appropriations package in 1999, he said, "The Republican leadership has given us a fiscally irresponsible budget." But he has sup-ported a few measures pushed by conservatives, including a ban on a pro-cedure its opponents call "partial birth" abortion and constitutional amend-ments limiting congressional terms and outlawing U.S. flag desecration.

Reyes began his career with the U.S. Immigration and Naturalization Ser-vice in 1969 upon returning from Army service in Vietnam. After serving as assistant regional commissioner in Dallas, he oversaw the Border Patrol in McAllen and El Paso. He instituted "Operation Hold the Line" in El Paso, stationing more officers at the border to prevent unauthorized crossings into the United States — a shift from the previous emphasis on rounding up people already in the country illegally.

Reyes retired from the Border Patrol in the fall of 1995 to launch a bid for the House seat representing the district where he was born and raised. The 16th was held by seven-term Democrat Ronald D. Coleman, who decided to retire amid negative publicity that stemmed in part from his 673 over-drafts at the private bank for House members.

Reyes, citing the need to restore integrity to the district, enjoyed a surge of popularity because of his Border Patrol leadership. In the primary and subsequent runoff, he narrowly defeated a former Coleman aide, Jose Luis Sanchez, before easily dispatching a Republican insurance agent in the general election. In the solidly Democratic 16th, Reyes has had no difficul-ty in his two re-election bids.

KEY VOTES

2000
Yes Raise hourly minimum wage by $1 over two years
No Halt funding for U.S. mission in Kosovo unless European nations pay more
Yes Provide Medicare benefits to military retirees and their dependents
Yes Grant China permanent normal trade status
No Phase out estate, gift and trust taxes
No Prohibit implementation of president's national monument designations
No Approve GOP plan to provide prescription drug coverage for Medicare beneficiaries
Yes Increase help for poor nations indebted to international financial institutions

1999
Yes Impose steel import quotas
No Kill proposal to take aviation trust funds off budget
No Require background checks on buyers only at gun shows with 10 or more vendors
Yes Remove barriers among banking, securities and insurance companies
Yes Authorize state grants to hire teachers and reduce class size
Yes Overhaul campaign finance law; ban "soft money" and restrict advocacy advertising
Yes Approve bipartisan plan to increase rights of patients in managed-care health plans

INTEREST GROUPS

	AFL-CIO	ADA	CCUS	ACU
2000	90%	80%	42%	16%
1999	78%	85%	33%	26%
1998	100%	80%	47%	13%
1997	100%	65%	40%	38%

CQ VOTE STUDIES

	PARTY UNITY		PRESIDENTIAL SUPPORT	
	Support	Oppose	Support	Oppose
2000	88%	12%	88%	12%
1999	83%	17%	78%	22%
1998	87%	13%	78%	22%
1997	80%	20%	71%	29%

TEXAS 16
West – El Paso and suburbs

Looking more toward Mexico than Texas, the solidly Democratic 16th includes most of El Paso and some suburbs. Joined to Mexico by the Bridge of the Americas, the 16th has a 70 percent Hispanic population (according to 1990 Census Bureau statistics), with many of those residents speaking Spanish and celebrating Mexican holidays.

Mexico has had a long and deep affect on the 16th's economy – El Paso's growth was credited to trade with Mexico long before free trade zones and global markets flourished. Companies on the U.S. side of the border provide supplies and services to manufacturing plants in Mexico, and residents from El Paso's sister city, Ciudad Juarez, often cross the border to spend money in El Paso's stores. In recent years, leaders have been concerned with the effects of NAFTA, which they blame for displacing American workers. The trade agreement has been partially responsible for an explosion of *maquiladoras*, twin plants in which Mexican workers do the bulk of the manufacturing labor and Americans complete the products with final details.

Democrats held the 16th's congressional seat for all but two years in the 20th century, often unchallenged by Republicans since the 1960s. The 16th gave Bill Clinton more than 63 percent of its vote in 1996, nearly 20 points higher than the state average. In 2000, President Bush captured only 39 percent of the district vote, 20 percentage points below his statewide average. The pattern of Democratic domination also applies to local races.

MAJOR INDUSTRY
Manufacturing, apparel, defense

MILITARY BASES
Fort Bliss (Army), 9,881 military; 2,262 civilian (1999) (shared with the 23rd District)

CITIES
El Paso (pt.), 565,024 (1990); Socorro, 27,530; Fort Bliss (pt.), 11,316 (1990)

UNUSUAL FEATURES
The Border Patrol Museum features displays of aircraft and vehicles used by the patrol as well as surveillance equipment and confiscated items; Fort Bliss, the largest air defense artillery training center in the world, occupies an area larger than the entire state of Rhode Island.

Rep. Charles W. Stenholm (D)

Elected 1978; 12th term

Stenholm has spent his career forging a socially and fiscally conservative path that often meanders far outside the House Democratic mainstream. But rather than undermining his position, that independence has raised Stenholm's stock in both parties and given him a measure of bipartisan respect enjoyed by few on Capitol Hill.

A farmer in background and temperament, Stenholm is soft-spoken and courteous, and he often attributes his optimistic nature to the fact that farmers constantly must weather tough odds to get their jobs done. His style and views have established him as a leader both among House Democrats generally and among centrists specifically — he has been named a deputy whip and has served as co-chairman of the Democratic Policy Committee.

At the same time, during the disputed presidential election of 2000 his name was mentioned at least as often by Republicans, as a candidate for secretary of agriculture in a Bush administration, as it was by Democrats pondering who might serve in a Gore administration.

Stenholm, who wears cowboy boots in the halls of Congress and speaks with a distinct Texas drawl, is constantly challenged to reflect the politics of his increasingly Republican-leaning district. He deviates from the party line about half the time but maintains: "I'm a Democrat, period," as he put it in 1986. "Philosophically, I am what I am, and that's a conservative Democrat. I believe that philosophy, tempered with the liberal and moderate viewpoints, is best for the country."

Still, Stenholm says he recognizes the pivotal role that can be played by compromisers like him. He told a financial group three days after the 2000 election: "Americans want a radical center, not a radical left or right."

Stenholm has been a figure to whom like-minded Democrats gravitate for leadership in their particular brand of activism. In the 1980s, he was a leader of the "Boll Weevil" Southern Democrats, who joined with Republicans to back the opening budget proposals of President Reagan. In 1995, he co-founded the "Blue Dogs," a group of fiscally conservative Democrats; and over the past six years he developed a series of budget and tax proposals that were politically viable middle grounds between the positions of President Clinton and the GOP.

He says leading the centrist charge was his hope from the day he arrived in Washington. "My goal was to become more than one vote on those issues that are important to the 17th District and to the country," he said in 2000. "I would like for people to be able to follow my vote and then to feel comfortable that they have voted the right way."

And they do follow. In 2000, his Blue Dog budget came the closest to a bipartisan consensus, garnering 138 Democratic and 33 Republican votes. By contrast, the Democratic leadership's plan received no GOP support; and the GOP blueprint that ultimately prevailed picked up just two Democratic votes.

Stenholm began playing an important role in the budget debate soon after his arrival in the House in 1979, and he never wavered from his homey fiscal mantra: "Peas before dessert," meaning no tax cuts or spending increases until the budget is balanced. With the books now balanced, he advocates using any surplus to reduce the national debt and strengthen the Social Security system.

Stenholm has placed particular emphasis on a bill he introduced with Rep. Jim Kolbe, R-Ariz., in 1998 to overhaul Social Security based on a plan by the National Commission for Retirement Policy, which they co-chaired with

CAPITOL OFFICE
225-6605; fax 225-2234
1211 Longworth Bldg. 20515

INTERNET
e-mail: texas17@mail.house.gov
web: www.house.gov/stenholm

COMMITTEES
Agriculture - ranking member

HOMETOWN
Abilene

BORN
Oct. 26, 1938, Stamford, Texas

RELIGION
Lutheran

FAMILY
Wife, Cindy Stenholm; three children

EDUCATION
Tarleton State Junior College, A.A. 1959; Texas Tech U., B.S. 1961, M.S. 1962

CAREER
Cotton farmer; teacher

POLITICAL HIGHLIGHTS
No previous office

ELECTION RESULTS

2000 GENERAL

Charles W. Stenholm (D)	120,670	59.0%
Darrell Clements (R)	72,535	35.5%
Debra Monde (LIBERT)	11,180	5.5%

2000 PRIMARY

Charles W. Stenholm (D)	unopposed

1998 GENERAL

Charles W. Stenholm (D)	75,367	53.6%
Rudy Izzard (R)	63,700	45.3%
Gordon Mobley (LIBERT)	1,618	1.2%

PREVIOUS WINNING PERCENTAGES
1996 (52%); 1994 (54%); 1992 (66%); 1990 (100%); 1988 (100%); 1986 (100%); 1984 (100%); 1982 (97%); 1980 (100%); 1978 (68%)

Sens. John B. Breaux, D-La., and Judd Gregg, R-N.H.

Stenholm also has sought a middle ground on tax cuts. He railed against the $792 billion Republican tax cut of 1999, calling it fiscally irresponsible to consider tax relief that depended on anticipated future surpluses. He supports reductions in the estate tax and elimination of the tax code's "marriage penalty," but he voted against the GOP versions of the legislation in 2000.

The top Democrat on the Agriculture Committee, Stenholm's hands-on experience keeps him passionate about helping rural farmers. His support of government assistance for agriculture has been unwavering, despite his general fiscal austerity, and he is respected for his mastery of highly technical legislative matters. Stenholm and GOP Chairman Larry Combest, a fellow Texan with whom he gets along well, run the panel as a true bipartisan arena, where crop insurance and farm assistance legislation usually emerge by consensus.

The Clinton administration followed Stenholm's lead on some farm proposals, such as his plan in the 106th Congress to create farm subsidies that would take effect when commodity prices are low. On other farm issues, Stenholm was willing to part with the administration, such as when he and Combest in 2000 opposed clean water regulations that they saw as hurting farmers.

Stenholm enjoyed success early in life. In high school, he earned the highest honor of the Future Farmers of America and played on two state championship football teams. He first experienced the national political scene in 1966, when the U.S. Agriculture Department issued a ruling that did not go over well in his cotton-growing plains section of Texas. As executive vice president of the Rolling Plains Cotton Growers Association, Stenholm visited Washington to lobby against the ruling and had partial success in changing it.

In 1977, President Carter named Stenholm to a panel that advises the Agricultural and Conservation Service. He resigned the next year to run for the House when Democrat Omar Burleson retired after 16 terms. Winning with 68 percent in what was then a solidly Democratic district, Stenholm was re-elected the next six times without a GOP opponent.

As Stenholm's prominence in Washington grew, his political troubles at home intensified, and formidable election competition surfaced in the 1990s as GOP strength increased throughout the South. He had his first true taste of trouble in 1994, when Phil Boone, an unheralded time management consultant, held him to 54 percent. Then, Rudy Izzard, a businessman and dentist, held him to 52 percent in 1996 and 54 percent in 1998. Stenholm's tally grew to 59 percent in 2000 against Judge Darrell Clements.

KEY VOTES

2000

No	Raise hourly minimum wage by $1 over two years
No	Halt funding for U.S. mission in Kosovo unless European nations pay more
Yes	Provide Medicare benefits to military retirees and their dependents
Yes	Grant China permanent normal trade status
No	Phase out estate, gift and trust taxes
Yes	Prohibit implementation of president's national monument designations
No	Approve GOP plan to provide prescription drug coverage for Medicare beneficiaries
Yes	Increase help for poor nations indebted to international financial institutions

1999

Yes	Impose steel import quotas
Yes	Kill proposal to take aviation trust funds off budget
No	Require background checks on buyers only at gun shows with 10 or more vendors
No	Remove barriers among banking, securities and insurance companies
Yes	Authorize state grants to hire teachers and reduce class size
Yes	Overhaul campaign finance law; ban "soft money" and restrict advocacy advertising
Yes	Approve bipartisan plan to increase rights of patients in managed-care health plans

INTEREST GROUPS

	AFL-CIO	ADA	CCUS	ACU
2000	50%	45%	70%	52%
1999	67%	55%	68%	54%
1998	60%	40%	76%	48%
1997	29%	40%	90%	58%

CQ VOTE STUDIES

	PARTY UNITY		PRESIDENTIAL SUPPORT	
	Support	Oppose	Support	Oppose
2000	59%	41%	52%	48%
1999	49%	51%	53%	47%
1998	50%	50%	49%	51%
1997	53%	47%	53%	47%

TEXAS 17
West Central – Abilene

Starting west of Fort Worth, the conservative 17th takes in the central Texas plains and heads through Abilene until reaching Midland in western Texas. The culture of the old West lingers in this part of the Lone Star State with ranches, cotton and cowboys.

When the 1980s oil glut hit home in Texas, refineries covered the 17th's prairie. Today, there are only a fraction of the rigs that once blanketed the area, and some of those oil-producing towns have disappeared. Abilene, the district's largest city, has made an effort to revitalize its downtown. Three church-sponsored colleges also nurture a powerful evangelical community.

Cattle and cotton are still big in the 17th, but low cattle prices and droughts have jeopardized both. Adding a measure of stability to the economy, however, are Air Force bases near Abilene and in the neighboring 21st District. The prison industry has also done well, with facilities in Abilene, Snyder and Big Spring.

The 17th is represented by a conservative Democrat. While the district is socially conservative, its economic hardships have sent it in search of government assistance in agriculture. At the local level, Republicans tend to be favored, but in some areas north and west of Abilene, conservative Democrats do well. In 2000, President Bush received 70 percent of the district vote – 11 percentage points above his Texas average.

MAJOR INDUSTRY
Cattle, cotton, defense, oil

MILITARY BASES
Dyess Air Force Base, 4,986 military, 345 civilian (1999)

CITIES
Abilene, 108,995; San Angelo (pt.), 50,955 (1990); Big Spring, 21,995

UNUSUAL FEATURES
Abilene named after the famous cattle shipping center in Abilene, Kan.; First Hilton Hotel in Cisco.

Rep. Sheila Jackson-Lee (D)

Elected 1994; 4th term

CAPITOL OFFICE
225-3816; fax 225-3317; 403 Cannon Bldg. 20515

INTERNET
e-mail: tx18@mail.house.gov
web: www.house.gov/jacksonlee

COMMITTEES
Judiciary
Science

HOMETOWN
Houston

BORN
Jan. 12, 1950, Queens, N.Y.

RELIGION
Seventh-Day Adventist

FAMILY
Husband, Elwyn Lee; two children

EDUCATION
Yale U., B.A. 1972; U. of Virginia, J.D. 1975

CAREER
Lawyer; congressional aide

POLITICAL HIGHLIGHTS
Houston municipal judge, 1987-89; Houston City
Council, 1990-95

ELECTION RESULTS

2000 GENERAL

Sheila Jackson-Lee (D)	131,857	76.5%
Bob Levy (R)	38,191	22.2%
Colin Nankervis (LIBERT)	2,330	1.4%

2000 PRIMARY

Sheila Jackson-Lee (D)	unopposed

1998 GENERAL

Sheila Jackson-Lee (D)	82,091	89.9%
James Galvan (LIBERT)	9,176	10.1%

PREVIOUS WINNING PERCENTAGES
1996 (77%); 1994 (73%)

If there's a bill being debated on the floor of the House, odds are high that at some point Jackson-Lee will speak. The four-term Texas Democrat has become renowned in the halls of Congress for taking to the floor to address forcefully almost any topic, from civil rights and health issues to the naming of post office buildings. She is a determined advocate for the poor and disadvantaged.

When President Clinton appeared at a Houston fundraiser for Jackson-Lee in early 1998, he praised her as a "fireball" with "enormous energy," and he drew laughter with his description of her forceful manner. "When I see her coming at me with that look in her eye," Clinton said, "I don't even want to hear what she has to say. I just say, 'Yes, yes.' "

Jackson-Lee often finds that the House Republican majority says "No, no" to her proposals, but she seems undaunted by her party's minority status. She wages ceaseless rhetorical battle — speaking out for women, minorities and the poor, skewering the GOP relentlessly and castigating conservatives' proposals as "shameless," "a disgrace" or "an outrage."

While she has won praise for her ability to fight any verbal battle, she has also been criticized by supporters who have cautioned her to pick her fights so that her arguments and speeches get more attention. Jackson-Lee has ignored such advice. Her verbal proclivities have established her as a standard by which to rate other members' loquaciousness. When ranking Democrat David R. Obey of Wisconsin spoke at length during a long Appropriations Committee meeting, Republican Whip Tom DeLay of Texas called him the "Sheila Jackson-Lee of the Appropriations Committee." And a number of her long-winded colleagues, when trying to play down their own propensity to talk, have argued, "but I'm no Sheila Jackson-Lee."

In the 106th Congress, Jackson-Lee continued her focus on social issues. Reaching across the aisle, she sponsored a bill with DeLay to strengthen child protective services and give law enforcement and social workers more tools to handle child abuse cases. Jackson-Lee said the measure would help millions of children "who suffer in silence ... due to child abuse."

A member of the Judiciary Committee, Jackson-Lee is the top Democrat on the Immigration and Claims Subcommittee. She is quick to join the fray on a wide range of Judiciary topics, including abortion rights, affirmative action and assisted suicide. In the 106th, she sought to exempt Oregon's assisted-suicide law from a Republican-backed bill that would have barred physicians from helping patients kill themselves with prescription drugs. "We come in with this Big Brother attitude that we should overcome the Oregon law," Jackson-Lee said. "I believe what we will do is increase suicide. ... [Patients] will use their own means."

Responding to criticism of affirmative action, she said that without it, "institutions are left to favor the privileged as they did in the past. We are all familiar with the 'good old boy' system. ...There still is systemic bias in our society favoring certain groups over others, and many still do not want to accept that fact."

Jackson-Lee says many of her views were molded by former Democratic Rep. Barbara Jordan, a Houstonian who served in the House from 1973 to 1979 and became a nationally known voice for liberalism. When Jackson-Lee was a young staff member on Capitol Hill in 1975, she sought out Jordan for advice on how to make a difference in society. In the style of Jordan, Jackson-Lee's voting record marks her as one of the Texas delegation's most liberal Democrats, siding with her party more than 90 percent of the time.

But Jackson-Lee broke with some on the left when she backed legislation in 2000 to grant China permanent normal trade status. She said the economic engagement would do more to improve human rights conditions in China than trying to isolate the country. Jackson-Lee also noted that the trade pact would help her constituents. "This has to mean something more than just a good deal for corporations and big businesses," she told Knight-Ridder. "I do believe that we in Houston benefit by the economic fallout."

Jackson-Lee pays attention to parochial needs. On the Science Committee she is a stout defender of NASA, whose Houston facility is in an adjoining district. Her 1997 vote against eliminating funding for additional B-2 stealth bombers indicates her appreciation for the economic importance of the defense-industrial complex in Texas. In 2000, she lobbied the administration to designate parts of Houston as an empowerment zone, thereby making low-income areas eligible for millions of dollars in federal grants.

Active on education issues, Jackson-Lee won approval of a proposal enabling the Federal Aviation Administration to issue research and engineering grants to colleges and universities that are historically black or have largely Latino student bodies. The House also approved a Jackson-Lee plan that would allow the National Science Foundation to donate excess computers to schools.

Born in New York and educated at Yale and the University of Virginia law school, Jackson-Lee ended up in Texas when her husband took a job with the University of Houston. She had two children and made three unsuccessful bids for local judgeships in Houston before becoming a municipal judge in 1987.

In 1990, she won an at-large seat on the City Council, where she earned a reputation as a tireless worker who rarely missed a political or community event. She sponsored and won unanimous support for a gun safety law establishing penalties for parents who failed to keep guns in their homes locked up safely out of reach of children. She pushed for expanded summer hours at city parks and recreation centers as a way to reduce gang activity.

Jackson-Lee sought a promotion to Congress in 1994, challenging Rep. Craig Washington in the Democratic primary. She benefited from his opposition to funding for the superconducting super collider and the space station. That, combined with Washington's brash personal style, tilted the balance in Jackson-Lee's favor, and she won with 63 percent to 37 percent.

In the heavily Democratic 18th, that primary victory was tantamount to election, and she has never faced a serious re-election challenge.

KEY VOTES

2000
Yes Raise hourly minimum wage by $1 over two years
No Halt funding for U.S. mission in Kosovo unless European nations pay more
Yes Provide Medicare benefits to military retirees and their dependents
Yes Grant China permanent normal trade status
No Phase out estate, gift and trust taxes
No Prohibit implementation of president's national monument designations
No Approve GOP plan to provide prescription drug coverage for Medicare beneficiaries
Yes Increase help for poor nations indebted to international financial institutions

1999
Yes Impose steel import quotas
No Kill proposal to take aviation trust funds off budget
No Require background checks on buyers only at gun shows with 10 or more vendors
Yes Remove barriers among banking, securities and insurance companies
Yes Authorize state grants to hire teachers and reduce class size
Yes Overhaul campaign finance law; ban "soft money" and restrict advocacy advertising
Yes Approve bipartisan plan to increase rights of patients in managed-care health plans

INTEREST GROUPS

	AFL-CIO	ADA	CCUS	ACU
2000	90%	80%	50%	4%
1999	78%	100%	29%	0%
1998	100%	95%	44%	4%
1997	100%	80%	44%	13%

CQ VOTE STUDIES

	PARTY UNITY		PRESIDENTIAL SUPPORT	
	Support	Oppose	Support	Oppose
2000	92%	8%	88%	12%
1999	96%	4%	78%	22%
1998	94%	6%	83%	17%
1997	92%	8%	76%	24%

TEXAS 18
Downtown Houston

Downtown Houston's older black neighborhoods and its more progressive residents make up the 18th, one of the poorest areas of the city. The 18th was one of three Texas districts created after the 1990 census to be declared racially gerrymandered by the courts. The new 18th is roughly Y-shaped and centered on downtown Houston. Redistricting in 1996 stripped the 18th of its suburban areas and of its black majority – African-Americans now represent 45 percent of the population, down from 51 percent before redistricting (calculated with 1990 Census Bureau statistics). Staunchly Democratic, the district includes a significant portion of Houston's gay and lesbian population.

In stark contrast to the conservative 7th District immediately to the west, the 18th often gives two-thirds of its votes to Democratic candidates in elections at all levels. In the 2000 presidential contest, the 18th gave President Bush his lowest percentage among the state's congressional districts – 26 percent. The populations around Texas

Southern University and the University of Houston add to the Democratic total. The 18th has a few middle-class neighborhoods and also includes the Heights, a trendier area attracting some young professionals.

Downtown office buildings are filled with the employees of oil and gas companies and other white-collar executives. Many of these workers, however, commute from outside the district. The oil bust of the 1980s dealt downtown a blow, but the area has slowly been rebuilding its economic strength by adding financial services companies. And in 2000, the city opened a new downtown baseball stadium, Enron Field. Still, the 18th has some of the poorest areas in southeast Texas.

MAJOR INDUSTRY
Energy, government, business services

CITIES
Houston (pt.), 528,117 (1990)

UNUSUAL FEATURES
The Houston Livestock Show and Rodeo is the world's largest rodeo; Houston officials estimate that more than 2,000 corporations have headquarters in the city's downtown.

Rep. Larry Combest (R)

CAPITOL OFFICE
225-4005; fax 225-9615
1026 Longworth Bldg. 20515

INTERNET
e-mail: www.house.gov/writerep
web: www.house.gov/combest

COMMITTEES
Agriculture - chairman
Small Business

HOMETOWN
Lubbock

BORN
March 20, 1945, Memphis, Texas

RELIGION
Methodist

FAMILY
Wife, Sharon Combest; two children (one deceased)

EDUCATION
West Texas State U., B.B.A. 1969

CAREER
Electronics wholesaler; congressional aide; farmer

POLITICAL HIGHLIGHTS
No previous office

ELECTION RESULTS

2000 GENERAL

Larry Combest (R)	170,319	91.6%
John M. Turnbow (LIBERT)	15,579	8.4%

2000 PRIMARY

Larry Combest (R)	unopposed

1998 GENERAL

Larry Combest (R)	108,266	83.6%
Sidney Blankenship (D)	21,162	16.4%

PREVIOUS WINNING PERCENTAGES
1996 (80%); 1994 (100%); 1992 (77%); 1990 (100%); 1988 (68%); 1986 (62%); 1984 (58%)

Elected 1984; 9th term

Combest's Capitol Hill office is a portrait of political experience tinged with what he calls "a Western flair" — drafts of bills and policy files mingle with chaps and spurs, a cowhide rug and a cow skull in "the bunkhouse," as he has dubbed it. The decor befits the fourth-generation family farmer and Agriculture Committee chairman, who has spent his career as a staunch advocate for farmers and believes the government should provide a safety net for the agricultural economy.

Combest tends to mirror his rural district's, and much of his party's, conservative stances against government regulations and taxes. At the same time, he welcomes the government's financial help for farmers and its protection of agricultural interests when it comes to trade pacts. He put his career on the line in 1995 when he rebelled against a GOP-drafted farm bill that he felt shortchanged cotton growers and did not include strong enough protections for the farmers it sought to wean off government subsidies.

While he is a reliable conservative who almost always votes with the GOP right, Combest routinely seeks bipartisan compromise and will break with his party on agriculture and trade issues if his constituents' interests are at stake. Known for his close attention to legislative detail, Combest attributes his willingness to work hard and stand up for his constituency to his days growing up on a cotton farm in Texas' Northern Panhandle. "It's where you get your work ethic. If you make a deal and shake hands on it, it's a deal."

His farming experience also emboldens him to take strong stances when he believes they are necessary. He says his background has helped tremendously in his work on the Agriculture panel because it has given him an appreciation of the difficulties farmers face.

Combest's worldview is not unlike that of Agriculture's top Democrat, fellow Texan Charles W. Stenholm, whose 17th District adjoins Combest's 19th. They have worked closely together on crop insurance reform and federal farm assistance, and — while their approaches are different — the two have collaborated to begin a rewrite of the 1996 farm policy law, which expires in 2002. That 1996 law, which replaced crop subsidies with a seven-year schedule of fixed payments, was designed to move farmers toward a free-market system, but Congress in 1998-2000 ended up providing $25 billion in bailouts for farmers facing record low commodities prices. Of the 1996 law Combest says: "Something is broken."

He says bipartisanship makes sense when writing agriculture policy, where regional and commodity-specific considerations are usually more important than party affiliation. During his tenure, the Agriculture panel has returned to the bipartisan cooperation it enjoyed before the bitterness that followed the GOP takeover of the House in 1995.

Combest was an area president of the Future Farmers of America while in high school and active in the student senate in college; he took a job with the U.S. Agricultural Stabilization Service shortly after graduating. His political career began in earnest when Texas Republican Sen. John Tower summoned him in 1971 for what Combest now calls "an opportunity too great to pass up" — a position as an agriculture specialist in his office.

Combest worked his way up in the office and, after a brief return to the private sector, sought a House seat when Democratic Rep. Kent Hance (who later switched to the GOP) announced for the Senate in 1984. The district had not elected a Republican in its 50-year history but voted regularly for GOP state and national candidates and seemed ripe to switch. After a bitter primary battle with hard-right conservative Ron Fleming, Combest defeated former Hance aide Don Richards in the general election with 58 percent of the vote. He has never fallen below 62 percent since then in eight re-election campaigns and ran unopposed in 1990 and 1994.

Beyond agriculture policy, Combest says his experience as an aide to Tower instilled in him an appreciation for interparty comity. During those years, Combest recalls, he developed great respect for Minnesota Democrat Hubert H. Humphrey Jr., who would engage in bitter debates with Tower, only to leave the Senate floor arm-in-arm with the Texas Republican. "You respect another's right to differ, and you respect where you're both coming from, if it's done honestly," Combest says.

Given the premium he says he places on honesty, it is not surprising that Combest was particularly upset to learn from a news report in 1996 that his dream of becoming chairman of the Agriculture Committee in the 105th Congress had fallen victim to larger political machinations. Republican leaders, worried about losing the Oregon seat of embattled freshman Rep. Wes Cooley, persuaded Cooley to drop his bid for re-election to make way for a comeback by his House predecessor, Bob Smith, who had retired at the end of the 104th. The GOP leadership promised Smith, who had joined Agriculture at the same time as Combest, the chairmanship if he ran — which he did, winning easily.

"I was devastated at the time," said Combest, who was put in charge of the Forestry, Resource Conservation and Research Subcommittee. At the end of 1997, Smith announced that he would not run again — giving Combest a clear path to take over the committee in the 106th.

He got the gavel despite his efforts during the 104th to undermine the GOP "Freedom to Farm" bill. Breaking with conservative Republicans who were pushing a free-market approach that would eventually do away with farm subsidy programs, Combest worked with Democrats on a plan that would scale back farm programs to meet budget-cutting targets but keep their structure intact. He signed onto the GOP measure only after being assured by leaders that the cotton and rice programs would survive.

Still, he has worked ever since to "fix" the 1996 law, which he maintains caused more problems for farmers than it solved. Later in 1996, Combest gained House passage of a measure permitting farmers receiving subsidies to plant a second crop of fruits or vegetables if an earlier one failed. He has played key roles in increasing crop insurance coverage and aid to farmers, successfully shepherding through legislation in 2000 that encouraged growers to buy crop insurance by subsidizing a greater share of the annual premium.

KEY VOTES

2000

No   Raise hourly minimum wage by $1 over two years

Yes   Halt funding for U.S. mission in Kosovo unless European nations pay more

Yes   Provide Medicare benefits to military retirees and their dependents

Yes   Grant China permanent normal trade status

Yes   Phase out estate, gift and trust taxes

Yes   Prohibit implementation of president's national monument designations

Yes   Approve GOP plan to provide prescription drug coverage for Medicare beneficiaries

No   Increase help for poor nations indebted to international financial institutions

1999

No   Impose steel import quotas

No   Kill proposal to take aviation trust funds off budget

No   Require background checks on buyers only at gun shows with 10 or more vendors

No   Remove barriers among banking, securities and insurance companies

No   Authorize state grants to hire teachers and reduce class size

No   Overhaul campaign finance law; ban "soft money" and restrict advocacy advertising

No   Approve bipartisan plan to increase rights of patients in managed-care health plans

INTEREST GROUPS

	AFL-CIO	ADA	CCUS	ACU
2000	0%	0%	100%	88%
1999	11%	5%	92%	96%
1998	0%	0%	94%	100%
1997	0%	10%	100%	92%

CQ VOTE STUDIES

	PARTY UNITY		PRESIDENTIAL SUPPORT	
	Support	Oppose	Support	Oppose
2000	97%	3%	22%	78%
1999	95%	5%	19%	81%
1998	95%	5%	22%	78%
1997	96%	4%	29%	71%

TEXAS 19

Western Panhandle – Parts of Lubbock and Amarillo

The conservative 19th starts in the Panhandle and travels south through cattle and cotton country until reaching oil field operations near Odessa. With ranches, cattle and remnants of the cowboy lifestyle, the 19th offers a taste of the wild West and feels little like the "Old South," which never really reached this far west.

Lubbock, which is shared with the 13th District, is the largest city in the 19th and thrives on the acres upon acres of cotton surrounding the city. Lubbock calls itself the world's largest cottonseed processing center and is home to Texas Tech University.

Besides cotton, the 19th also takes in cattle ranches to the north and oil in the south. Because the 19th's economy is so dependent on agriculture and oil, it was nearly devastated during the worldwide oil glut of the 1980s and bad weather in the 1990s. Famine and drought

have been detrimental to cattle and cotton, and continued low oil prices have dampened the oil industry. Reese Air Force Base was another major employer, but it was shut down under the 1995 military restructuring.

Before the current Republican representative won the 19th in 1984, only Democrats had held the seat during its 50-year history. More recently, Republicans have done well at all levels and routinely receive between 60 and 70 percent of the vote. In the 2000 presidential contest, the 19th gave President Bush his highest percentage among the state's congressional districts, 79 percent.

MAJOR INDUSTRY
Cattle, agriculture, oil and gas

CITIES
Lubbock (pt.), 154,625 (1990); Amarillo (pt.), 69,220 (1990); Odessa (pt.), 61,817 (1990)

UNUSUAL FEATURES
George W. Bush ran for the seat in 1978, but was defeated by former Democratic Rep. Kent Hance; Odessa boasts the world's largest barbecue pit, big enough to grill 16,500 pounds of beef.

Rep. Charlie Gonzalez (D)

Elected 1998; 2nd term

CAPITOL OFFICE
225-3236; fax 225-1915; 327 Cannon Bldg. 20515

INTERNET
e-mail: www.house.gov/writerep
web: www.house.gov/gonzalez

COMMITTEES
Financial Services
Small Business

HOMETOWN
San Antonio

BORN
May 5, 1945, San Antonio, Texas

RELIGION
Roman Catholic

FAMILY
Wife, Becky Whetstone; one child, two
stepchildren

EDUCATION
U. of Texas, B.A. 1969; St. Mary's U. (Texas), J.D.
1972

MILITARY SERVICE
Texas Air National Guard, 1969-75

CAREER
Lawyer

POLITICAL HIGHLIGHTS
Bexar County judge, 1982-87; Texas District Court
judge, 1988-97

ELECTION RESULTS

2000 GENERAL
Charlie Gonzalez (D)	107,487	87.7%
Alejandro DePena (LIBERT)	15,087	12.3%

2000 PRIMARY
Charlie Gonzalez (D)	unopposed

1998 GENERAL
Charlie Gonzalez (D)	50,356	63.2%
James D. Walker (R)	28,347	35.6%
Alejandro DePena (LIBERT)	1,010	1.3%

1998 PRIMARY RUNOFF
Charlie Gonzalez (D)	13,439	62.1%
Maria A. Berriozabal (D)	8,189	37.9%

He lives in the same Capitol Hill apartment that his father occupied, but that — and a famous last name — could be all Charlie Gonzalez shares with his legendary father, the late Henry B. Gonzalez.

Henry B., as he was known, became a powerhouse in San Antonio's Democratic politics during his 37 years in the House. That has now given way to the son's pragmatic, New Democrat style, which contrasts with his father's passionate and often stubborn brand of classic populism.

Many political analysts believed the younger Gonzalez — known in some parts of his central and west-side San Antonio district as *"el hijo"* (the son) — could credit his initial victory to his last name, citing the father's legendary prominence in the heavily Democratic, Hispanic-majority district. While the current congressman, the third oldest of eight children, has said that his father's reputation was hard to live up to, he had developed a public resumé of his own, including 15 years in elected office as a local judge and state district judge.

He says that he is proudest of his work from the bench to speed the resolution of domestic violence cases and promote mediation as an alternative to litigation — a signal that his is a style different from the irascible, occasionally pugilistic senior Gonzalez.

Since the night of his election in 1998, Charlie Gonzalez has indicated he would not hesitate to try to make his mark in Washington by taking positions different from those of his father. "Dad doesn't give advice unless he's asked," he said that evening. But in his first term, carving out his own identity has sometimes been difficult. He bears a strong physical resemblance to his father as a young congressman — so strong that Rep. Henry J. Hyde, R-Ill., once greeted Charlie Gonzalez as "Henry" while Gonzalez was sharing lunch in the members' dining room with a friend from law school. "So much for impressing a constituent," Gonzalez said.

Even so, Gonzalez has made a different mark in trade, specifically in the aftermath of the 1993 North American Free Trade Agreement (NAFTA). While his father virulently opposed the legislation to implement that pact, the younger Gonzalez stands by it. "I believe NAFTA was necessary for the stability of Mexico," he told the San Antonio Express-News.

In his first term, Gonzalez sought to facilitate international trade by sponsoring legislation establishing a U.S. Customs Service processing area at the San Antonio International Airport and an amendment setting up a toll-free, safety violation hotline to address concerns about the increase in Mexican truck traffic in the United States as a result of NAFTA.

While he says he understands the concerns that unions, environmentalists and human rights advocates have with the globalization of trade, he argues that these are outweighed by the benefits of more open trade at home, touting statistics that show a majority of manufacturing sales in his district are exports. Over the objections of labor unions, which supported his election, Gonzalez backed President Clinton's bid to grant China permanent normal trade status.

Gonzalez's assignment to the Financial Services Committee is partly attributable to the legacy of his father, who served on the panel (then known as Banking) throughout his House tenure and was its chairman for six years. Gonzalez also has a seat on the Small Business Committee. A teenager when his father was first elected to the House, he says he has a realistic perspective of what he can accomplish as a junior member.

In general, Gonzalez has taken a different tack than his father in dealing with the Democratic Party hierarchy. While his father's independent streak often upset party leaders, the younger Gonzalez has positioned himself as a team player — he held fundraisers and made appearances with Clinton and Vice President Al Gore, for example. His party credentials and experience helped him lead the 23-member Democratic freshman class of the 106th Congress, which voted him vice president for the second half of 1999.

On the Hill, he has become a participant in the Congressional Hispanic Caucus — another difference from his father, who declined to join — and has pushed for increased funding to combat diabetes, AIDS and mental illness among Latinos. He emerged as the caucus' point person on increasing Hispanic response to the 2000 census, and he was a staunch defender of the statistical sampling techniques the Census Bureau and the Clinton administration sought for the 2000 population count. Advocates of sampling argued that it was a way to limit the census undercount, most notable among ethnic minorities.

In the 106th Congress, Gonzalez pushed a measure to extend for five years tax credits for companies hiring young people living in poor areas or members of low-income families. The bill was aimed at benefiting his district, which has not shared in much of San Antonio's economic boom.

With a population of more than 1.1 million, San Antonio is one of the nation's largest cities and a burgeoning insurance, technology and telecommunications center. Gonzalez is trying to address issues that threaten the economic well-being of his district, which includes portions of downtown and west San Antonio's working-class neighborhoods. His leading parochial concerns have been improving the standing of San Antonio's public schools and redevelopment of Kelly Air Force Base, where maintenance operations have been privatized.

In his first race for Congress, he had to survive a seven-way Democratic primary that included former San Antonio council member Maria A. Berriozabal and a runoff election to win the party's nomination.

In the general contest, he took 63 percent against GOP research scientist James D. Walker, who had hoped his anti-abortion, fiscal conservatism platform would play well with the district's Catholics and conservative voters. Gonzalez won, in part, by combining support from San Antonio lawyers with the backing of some of Henry B.'s old political patrons, including organized labor.

In 2000, Gonzalez was unopposed in the primary and had no Republican opponent in the general election.

KEY VOTES

2000
Yes Raise hourly minimum wage by $1 over two years
No Halt funding for U.S. mission in Kosovo unless European nations pay more
Yes Provide Medicare benefits to military retirees and their dependents
Yes Grant China permanent normal trade status
No Phase out estate, gift and trust taxes
No Prohibit implementation of president's national monument designations
No Approve GOP plan to provide prescription drug coverage for Medicare beneficiaries
Yes Increase help for poor nations indebted to international financial institutions

1999
Yes Impose steel import quotas
No Kill proposal to take aviation trust funds off budget
No Require background checks on buyers only at gun shows with 10 or more vendors
Yes Remove barriers among banking, securities and insurance companies
Yes Authorize state grants to hire teachers and reduce class size
Yes Overhaul campaign finance law; ban "soft money" and restrict advocacy advertising
Yes Approve bipartisan plan to increase rights of patients in managed-care health plans

INTEREST GROUPS

	AFL-CIO	ADA	CCUS	ACU
2000	90%	80%	50%	8%
1999	78%	100%	36%	0%

CQ VOTE STUDIES

	PARTY UNITY		PRESIDENTIAL SUPPORT	
	Support	Oppose	Support	Oppose
2000	93%	7%	88%	12%
1999	94%	6%	84%	16%

TEXAS 20
Downtown San Antonio

A city rich in history, San Antonio witnessed the death of Davy Crockett and the famed fall of the Alamo. Since those rugged days in the early 1800s, San Antonio has grown into the nation's ninth largest city. The strongly Democratic 20th takes in the city, including the heavily Hispanic West Side, and some surrounding communities.

A huge military presence in San Antonio makes up the biggest chunk of the economy, but mid-1990s downsizing caused the city some economic pains, and more problems are on the immediate horizon. Kelly Air Force Base, one of the city's largest employers, has been downsizing and is scheduled to completely shut down in 2001. Local leaders are working to recruit private industry to the closing base, which is set to become a business park.

Although tourism does not make up for the defense industry's losses, it continues to be a reliable moneymaker. The Alamo, site of the 1836 battle with Mexico, is in the heart of downtown. The city's scenic

Paseo del Rio, or Riverwalk, also is a popular draw with its shops, restaurants and hotels winding along the San Antonio River. The most urban of San Antonio's four districts, the 20th has felt pressure on its roads, courts and schools as trade has increased due to NAFTA.

Democrats dominate most of this Hispanic-majority district. Republicans are clustered in the largely white, higher-income areas northwest and northeast of San Antonio.

MAJOR INDUSTRY
Military, tourism, government

MILITARY BASES
Kelly Air Force Base, 9,393 military, 4,592 civilian; Fort Sam Houston (Army), 8,099 military, 3,312 civilian; Lackland Air Force Base, 7,009 military, 2,478 civilian (1999)

CITIES
San Antonio (pt.), 522,893 (1990)

UNUSUAL FEATURES
Sculptor Gutzon Borglum designed Mt. Rushmore presidential carvings in a studio in San Antonio; St. Anthony Hotel in San Antonio, reportedly became the first fully air conditioned hotel in the world in 1941.

Rep. Lamar Smith (R)

CAPITOL OFFICE
225-4236; fax 225-8628; 2231 Rayburn Bldg. 20515

INTERNET
e-mail: www.house.gov/writerep
web: www.house.gov/lamarsmith

COMMITTEES
Judiciary
 (Crime - chairman)
Science

HOMETOWN
San Antonio

BORN
Nov. 19, 1947, San Antonio, Texas

RELIGION
Christian Scientist

FAMILY
Wife, Elizabeth Smith; two children

EDUCATION
Yale U., B.A. 1969; Southern Methodist U., J.D.
1975

CAREER
Lawyer; rancher

POLITICAL HIGHLIGHTS
Texas House, 1981-82; Bexar County
Commissioners Court, 1983-85

ELECTION RESULTS

2000 GENERAL

Lamar Smith (R)	251,049	75.9%
Jim Green (D)	73,326	22.2%
C. W. Steinbrecher (LIBERT)	6,503	2.0%

2000 PRIMARY

Lamar Smith (R)	unopposed

1998 GENERAL

Lamar Smith (R)	165,047	91.4%
Jeffrey C. Blunt (LIBERT)	15,561	8.6%

PREVIOUS WINNING PERCENTAGES
1996 (76%); 1994 (90%); 1992 (72%); 1990 (75%);
1988 (93%); 1986 (61%)

Elected 1986; 8th term

A soft-spoken conservative, Smith has made a name for himself as the House's most ardent crusader against illegal immigration. For six years he sat at the helm of Judiciary's Immigration Subcommittee, a post he had to relinquish in 2001 because of GOP-imposed term limits on chairmanships. Even as his tenure as Immigration chairman was coming to an end, Smith continued his hard-line attacks on illegal immigration, going so far as to sub-poena Attorney General Janet Reno in October 2000 to gather government records on illegal immigrants in the United States.

In the 107th Congress, Smith took the gavel of the Crime Subcommittee, acing out George W. Gekas of Pennsylvania, who had wanted the job and had more seniority. One of Smith's priorities is legislation to deal more strongly with juvenile offenders, including building more detention facilities and hiring more staff for the juvenile justice system.

Smith's genial personality blunts the hard edge of his conservatism, and he has enjoyed warm relations with many Democrats, including the ranking members on the Immigration and Crime subcommittees.

In the 106th Congress, Smith was active on immigration matters on several fronts. He clashed with U.S. business leaders in 2000 over how many special visas should be made available for highly skilled workers. High-technology businesses wanted to increase the number of H1-B visas to hire workers from overseas. Smith, seeking to protect U.S. technology employees from layoffs and overseas competition, drafted several proposals boosting the number of H-1Bs significantly, but with the requirement that employers show they had first tried to recruit U.S. workers. "Today, there is still no objective, credible study that documents a shortage of American high-tech workers," Smith said.

But House Republican leaders, friendly to business groups, never allowed Smith's proposals to come to the floor. Instead, they brought up a bill that gave the business community the increase it sought without Smith's restrictions.

Smith was more successful in fighting a Democratic attempt to provide amnesty for illegal immigrants in the United States since 1986. President Clinton had threatened to veto an end-of-year catchall appropriations bill unless it included amnesty language. Smith called on GOP leaders to hold firm in opposition.

"Amnesty is bad policy," he said. "It rewards lawbreakers, is unfair to law-abiding legal immigrants, makes a mockery of our laws, and encourages new waves of illegal immigration." After gaining immigration records from Reno's office, Smith released a report late in 2000 showing that illegal immigration had remained almost the same before and after the 1986 amnesty.

Smith shepherded to passage one of the signal accomplishments of the Republican-majority Congress: a 1996 crackdown on illegal immigration. The legislation, enacted in the 104th Congress, increased penalties for document fraud and the smuggling of aliens and made it easier for illegal immigrants to be detained at the border or deported after arrival.

Smith originally had introduced a much tougher measure, addressing legal as well as illegal immigration, but he gave up parts of it as specific provisions ran into opposition from Democrats, the Senate or pro-business Republicans. Smith reasoned that getting a chunk of what he wanted was better than nothing. "Three-fourths of a loaf tastes pretty good," he said.

The Texas lawmaker has also worked unsuccessfully over the years to clarify the 14th Amendment's constitutional guarantee of citizenship to anyone born in this country. He would deny citizenship to children born to parents who are in the country illegally. "The 14th Amendment is being enforced in ways for which it was not intended," Smith says.

Despite Smith's aggressive fights with Democrats on immigration matters, he has crossed party lines on other issues. He worked with Democratic Sen. Joseph I. Lieberman of Connecticut to increase family television programming for children.

Smith's congenial demeanor did not always suit his position as chairman of the House ethics committee, a post he left at the start of the 107th Congress. In October 2000, the ethics panel issued a formal Letter of Reproval against Rep. Bud Shuster, R-Pa., saying the chairman of the Transportation Committee "engaged in serious official misconduct" and "committed substantial violations" of House rules. The letter, which concluded a three-year probe, faulted Shuster for questionable dealings with a former staff member-turned-lobbyist, improperly accepting gifts, and spending campaign contributions on travel and meals at fancy restaurants.

Smith joined the ethics panel, formally known as the Committee on Standards of Official Conduct, in 1997 during an investigation of Speaker Newt Gingrich. Smith was the only panel member to vote against the $300,000 penalty that was ultimately assessed against Gingrich for supplying the committee with incorrect information about his use of tax-exempt organizations for political gain.

"There's some suggestion that if he didn't break the law, he came very close," Smith said of Gingrich. But, citing a comment from the ethics committee counsel that Gingrich had "run some very yellow lights," Smith said, "[Y]ou do not get ticketed, or you should not, for running a very yellow light, no matter how close it is to being a red one."

A graduate of Yale University, Smith, a fifth-generation Texan, spent a year in the Texas House and two years as a Bexar County commissioner, before making a run for Congress in 1986. When GOP Rep. Tom Loeffler declared plans to seek the governorship, Smith quickly announced that he would run for his 21st District seat.

After defeating a more conservative Republican in the primary, Smith went on to face former state Sen. Pete Snelson in the general election. Snelson's base in Midland, at the district's west end, positioned him to play to rural perceptions of Smith as an elitist, big-city lawyer. But Smith won the support of rural voters and rolled to victory with 61 percent. Now any electoral worries are a distant memory.

KEY VOTES

2000

No	Raise hourly minimum wage by $1 over two years
Yes	Halt funding for U.S. mission in Kosovo unless European nations pay more
Yes	Provide Medicare benefits to military retirees and their dependents
Yes	Grant China permanent normal trade status
Yes	Phase out estate, gift and trust taxes
Yes	Prohibit implementation of president's national monument designations
Yes	Approve GOP plan to provide prescription drug coverage for Medicare beneficiaries
No	Increase help for poor nations indebted to international financial institutions

1999

No	Impose steel import quotas
Yes	Kill proposal to take aviation trust funds off budget
Yes	Require background checks on buyers only at gun shows with 10 or more vendors
Yes	Remove barriers among banking, securities and insurance companies
No	Authorize state grants to hire teachers and reduce class size
No	Overhaul campaign finance law; ban "soft money" and restrict advocacy advertising
No	Approve bipartisan plan to increase rights of patients in managed-care health plans

INTEREST GROUPS

	AFL-CIO	ADA	CCUS	ACU
2000	0%	5%	85%	96%
1999	13%	0%	88%	84%
1998	0%	0%	100%	92%
1997	0%	0%	100%	88%

CQ VOTE STUDIES

	PARTY UNITY		PRESIDENTIAL SUPPORT	
	Support	Oppose	Support	Oppose
2000	99%	1%	25%	75%
1999	96%	4%	19%	81%
1998	95%	5%	23%	77%
1997	94%	6%	31%	69%

TEXAS 21

South Central – Northern Bexar County; Austin suburbs

The 21st's odd shape reflects the lengths to which Texas mapmakers went in 1992 to divide Democratic and Republican neighborhoods. Because of their efforts, the district remains largely conservative territory. Its huge land mass takes in all or part of 21 counties, from oil-rich Midland County in the northwest, to the northeastern Austin suburbs in Williamson County and San Antonio's metro area in the southeast.

Almost one-fourth of the district's population lives in Bexar County, most in the middle- and upper-class neighborhoods of San Antonio. The 21st also takes in San Angelo's wealthier neighborhoods where the mostly white residents are well-educated professionals, many of whom work in the high-tech industry. The district's military and farming populations deliver a consistently Republican vote at the local and national levels.

Nearby military bases contribute to the 21st's economy and account for the district's large numbers of active and retired military personnel. While the diverse economy has remained relatively strong, the late 1990s brought signs of an economic slow-down in Midland County's oil industry and elsewhere in the district as ranchers and farmers applied for federal drought and flood assistance.

MAJOR INDUSTRY
Agriculture, high-tech, government

MILITARY BASES
Goodfellow Air Force Base, San Angelo, 1,247 military, 504 civilian (1999)

CITIES
San Antonio (pt.), 132,681 (1990); Round Rock, 67,173; San Angelo (pt.), 37,742 (1990); Cedar Park, 27,115

UNUSUAL FEATURES
Tom Green County is the self-proclaimed "sheep and wool capital" of the nation; The Admiral Nimitz Museum and Historical Center in Fredericksburg has a major collection of Allied and Japanese aircraft, guns and other artifacts from World War II.

Rep. Tom DeLay (R)

CAPITOL OFFICE
225-5951; fax 225-5241; 2370 Rayburn Bldg. 20515

INTERNET
e-mail: www.house.gov/writerep
web: www.majoritywhip.house.gov

COMMITTEES
Appropriations

HOMETOWN
Sugar Land

BORN
April 8, 1947, Laredo, Texas

RELIGION
Baptist

FAMILY
Wife, Christine DeLay; one child

EDUCATION
Baylor U., attended 1965-67; U. of Houston, B.S. 1970

CAREER
Pest control business owner

POLITICAL HIGHLIGHTS
Texas House, 1979-85

ELECTION RESULTS

2000 GENERAL

Tom DeLay (R)	154,662	60.4%
Jo Ann Matranga (D)	92,645	36.2%
Bob Schneider (REF)	5,577	2.2%
Kent J. Probst (LIBERT)	3,383	1.3%

2000 PRIMARY

Tom DeLay (R)	41,901	83.3%
Michael "Fjet" Fjetland (R)	8,385	16.7%

1998 GENERAL

Tom DeLay (R)	87,840	65.2%
Hill Kemp (D)	45,386	33.7%
Steve Grupe (LIBERT)	1,494	1.1%

PREVIOUS WINNING PERCENTAGES
1996 (68%); 1994 (74%); 1992 (69%); 1990 (71%); 1988 (67%); 1986 (72%); 1984 (65%)

Elected 1984; 9th term

A copy of the Ten Commandments and a leather bullwhip are among the items adorning DeLay's office — totems that capture the essence of the man who holds the No. 3 position in the House Republican leadership, but whom many view as the most powerful person in Congress.

DeLay revels in the reputation that has brought him the nickname "The Hammer," and friends and foes alike agree he is the most effective whip in recent memory. With their diminished majority in the 107th Congress, House Republicans' success is likely to depend as heavily as ever on DeLay's ability to deliver votes. At the same time, any attempt to bridge the partisan divide will have to get past him.

DeLay's style is a mixture of anger and persuasiveness, partisan fervor and political practicality. While he can be combative in pursuit of a majority on even a minor measure, he wants it known that he will do nearly anything to keep fellow Republicans happy, from plying them with Texas barbecue during nighttime sessions to ensuring they are not cheated out of their share of pet projects in appropriations bills.

Despite his conservative zeal, which has led him to push the GOP against the popular tide on an array of issues, one of DeLay's campaign goals in 2000 was to help re-elect GOP moderates in order to hold the party's narrow margin. His political action committee raised $3.1 million, 70 percent more than what Speaker J. Dennis Hastert raised through his PAC. But his fundraising acumen also earned him a share of controversy. The Democratic Congressional Campaign Committee sued DeLay, accusing him of evading federal campaign finance disclosure laws and extorting contributions from lobbyists. "I know they're after me," DeLay has said of Democrats. "They monitor my every move, my every step." The suit was settled in 2001.

His relationship with the nation's most prominent Texas Republican, President Bush, has not always been smooth. When DeLay proposed saving $9 billion in 1999 by delaying payment of a tax credit for low-income workers, then-candidate Bush warned Congress not to "balance their budget on the backs of the poor." DeLay shot back: Bush "needs a little education on how Congress works." (Still, his idea was soon abandoned.)

Congressional Democrats made the demonization of DeLay part of their 2000 electoral strategy, not only because of his conservative views but also because he remained better known nationally than Hastert, whose promotion from chief deputy whip to Speaker in 1998 was engineered largely by DeLay. Their generally close relationship, and the broad latitude Hastert has usually given DeLay, have left the impression with many that the whip is the true power behind the throne. Both men strongly deny this is so.

DeLay had a tumultuous relationship with the previous GOP Speaker, plotting with other restless conservatives to oust Newt Gingrich in 1997. After the coup attempt fizzled, DeLay publicly apologized to the rank-and-file and subtly pointed at other conspirators who had denied complicity, Majority Leader Dick Armey among them. DeLay's confession cemented the respect and loyalty he receives from other House Republicans; after the GOP unexpectedly lost five House seats in the 1998 election, he was the only member of the leadership not challenged for his post.

Many members say DeLay does not use fear tactics to instill loyalty, but rather, tries to cultivate a bond of trust with every House Republican. Though he is known to respect a difference of opinion on issues, he has little use for those who promise to vote with the leadership and then switch sides without warning.

While he avoids intimidating his GOP colleagues, DeLay never shies away from a fight with a Democrat. During the disputed 2000 presidential election, he charged that "the Democratic Party is prosecuting a war to reverse the results of a fair, free election. ... Make no mistake, we are witnessing nothing less than a theft in progress." Two years before, DeLay made it his cause to insist on President Clinton's removal from office, rather than congressional censure. His denunciations of the president gave DeLay folk hero status among social conservatives.

Bare-knuckled partisanship led to a fabled altercation on the House floor in 1997 after Wisconsin Democrat David R. Obey brandished a Washington Post story maintaining that business lobbyists helped write a key deregulation bill in DeLay's office. The two argued, inches apart. Each pointed a finger at the other. After DeLay shoved Obey, the two were separated by an aide. "Everybody is scared of me for some reason," DeLay said at a news conference the next day.

DeLay won his "Hammer" nickname soon after Republicans won House control in 1994 for his efforts to squeeze more contributions out of Washington lobbyists and to press trade associations to hire only Republicans for top positions. In 1999, he was admonished by the House ethics committee for threatening to punish a trade association because it had hired a former House Democrat as its president.

DeLay adamantly opposes efforts to overhaul campaign finance laws, attacking proposals to curb political spending as threats to free speech. He has instead called for increasing and even abolishing limits on direct campaign contributions to federal candidates.

DeLay's solid conservative credentials are buttressed by his efforts against federal regulation. He wrote the planks of the House GOP's 1994 "Contract With America" that called for rolling back federal regulations. He has sought the repeal of the 1990 Clean Air Act revisions. And he led the Republican effort to block the Labor Department from issuing new ergonomics regulations in 2000 and — when that initial effort failed — to overturn the rules early in 2001.

Having spent much of his childhood in Venezuela with his father, an oil drilling contractor, DeLay first entered politics out of frustration with regulations affecting his pest extermination business. "I was struggling to build a company and the government was getting in my way every time I turned around," he said. After six years in the Texas House, he won a GOP-leaning seat in Congress in 1984 with 65 percent and has since won re-election easily.

KEY VOTES

2000

No Raise hourly minimum wage by $1 over two years
Yes Halt funding for U.S. mission in Kosovo unless European nations pay more
Yes Provide Medicare benefits to military retirees and their dependents
Yes Grant China permanent normal trade status
Yes Phase out estate, gift and trust taxes
Yes Prohibit implementation of president's national monument designations
Yes Approve GOP plan to provide prescription drug coverage for Medicare beneficiaries
No Increase help for poor nations indebted to international financial institutions

1999

No Impose steel import quotas
Yes Kill proposal to take aviation trust funds off budget
Yes Require background checks on buyers only at gun shows with 10 or more vendors
Yes Remove barriers among banking, securities and insurance companies
No Authorize state grants to hire teachers and reduce class size
No Overhaul campaign finance law; ban "soft money" and restrict advocacy advertising
No Approve bipartisan plan to increase rights of patients in managed-care health plans

INTEREST GROUPS

	AFL-CIO	ADA	CCUS	ACU
2000	0%	0%	84%	88%
1999	0%	0%	92%	92%
1998	0%	0%	100%	96%
1997	0%	0%	100%	88%

CQ VOTE STUDIES

	PARTY UNITY		PRESIDENTIAL SUPPORT	
	Support	Oppose	Support	Oppose
2000	99%	1%	23%	77%
1999	97%	3%	23%	77%
1998	95%	5%	20%	80%
1997	96%	4%	27%	73%

TEXAS 22

Southwest Houston and suburbs; Fort Bend and Brazoria counties

The conservative 22nd includes nearly all of two counties southwest of Houston, plus a small slice of the city itself. The majority of its residents live in fast-growing Houston suburbs outside Harris County or in more rural settings. The district contains booming communities like Sugar Land and upscale homes surrounding the Lyndon B. Johnson Space Center, where many NASA scientists and astronauts live. The 22nd's communities have lower crime rates and higher incomes than other Houston-area cities.

The northern section of Fort Bend County, shifted into the 22nd in 1996 redistricting, brought a heavily black area into the district, but the electoral impact has been small. The 22nd hasn't voted for a Democratic presidential candidate since 1964. President Bush racked up a 26 percent margin of victory in 2000, and GOP presidential candidates won with 18 percent margins in both 1992 and '96.

Many residents commute to work at the Lyndon B. Johnson Space Center, located in the neighboring 9th District. Fort Bend County, which includes Sugar Land, has turned from a sugar-growing area to suburbia since the 1960s. Sugar refiner Imperial Holly still maintains its presence in Sugar Land, but the city has welcomed new planned developments and a range of corporations. Brazoria County has retained much of its agrarian feel, as residents grow rice and sorghum and raise cattle.

MAJOR INDUSTRY
Aerospace, agriculture, retail

CITIES
Houston (pt.), 194,857 (1990); Sugar Land, 68,442; Pearland, 34,936; Lake Jackson (pt.), 25,098 (1990)

UNUSUAL FEATURES
The annual "Texian Market Days" in Fort Bend County include re-enactments of 1830s pioneer life, when the area was settled by some of the "Old 300" families led by Stephen F. Austin; George Observatory includes a memorial to the seven astronauts who died aboard the space shuttle Challenger in 1986.

Rep. Henry Bonilla (R)

CAPITOL OFFICE
225-4511; fax 225-2237; 2458 Rayburn Bldg. 20515

INTERNET
e-mail: www.house.gov/writerep
web: www.house.gov/bonilla

COMMITTEES
Appropriations
(Agriculture, Rural Development, FDA & Related
Agencies - chairman)

HOMETOWN
San Antonio

BORN
Jan. 2, 1954, San Antonio, Texas

RELIGION
Baptist

FAMILY
Wife, Deborah Knapp; two children

EDUCATION
U. of Texas, B.A. 1976

CAREER
Television reporter, producer and executive;
gubernatorial aide

POLITICAL HIGHLIGHTS
No previous office

ELECTION RESULTS

2000 GENERAL

Henry Bonilla (R)	119,679	59.3%
Isidro Garza Jr. (D)	78,274	38.8%
Jeffrey C. Blunt (LIBERT)	3,801	1.9%

2000 PRIMARY

Henry Bonilla (R)	unopposed

1998 GENERAL

Henry Bonilla (R)	73,177	63.8%
Charles Urbina Jones (D)	40,281	35.1%
William Stallknecht (LIBERT)	1,262	1.1%

PREVIOUS WINNING PERCENTAGES
1996 (62%); 1994 (63%); 1992 (59%)

Elected 1992; 5th term

As one of three Hispanic House Republicans, Bonilla plays a high-profile role as his party tries to appeal to minority groups. The former TV news broadcaster says that the GOP and Hispanics speak the same political language — favoring small businesses and a strong military, opposing high taxes and intrusive government.

Party leaders have made a point of showcasing Bonilla (bo-NEE-uh), who has risen from a childhood in a San Antonio housing project to become a potential candidate for statewide office. He got a seat on the Appropriations Committee in his first term. In 2000, he was one of three co-chairmen of the Republican National Convention that nominated George W. Bush for president. And he was frequently mentioned as a Bush Cabinet prospect, although the possibility that his Democratic-tilting district might have slipped back into opposition hands may have worked against him.

Bonilla is a leader of the Republican National Committee's New Majority Council, which seeks to recruit minority voters and candidates. So far, a key aim is yet to be met: No new Republican minority member has been elected to the House since its only black Republican, J.C. Watts Jr. of Oklahoma, in 1994.

As a legislator, Bonilla is a doctrinaire conservative. But he will be pressed to take a more pragmatic approach as the new chairman of the Agriculture Appropriations Subcommittee in the 107th Congress. He is not known for successfully working with Democrats, a must if his panel's annual spending bill is to advance smoothly.

Until his rise to a subcommittee chairmanship, Bonilla was best known on Appropriations for fighting often-futile battles against President Clinton's efforts to impose new regulations on businesses. For years, he helped hold up the annual funding bill for the departments of Labor, Health and Human Services, and Education in a bid to block the implementation of workplace standards to minimize repetitive-motion injuries. In 2000, Clinton issued new ergonomics rules in the final days of his administration, but GOP lawmakers succeeded in repealing the regulations in 2001.

Bonilla also tried unsuccessfully in 1998 to block the House from requiring tougher anti-flammability standards on sleepwear for infants.

On environmental issues, Bonilla is usually friendly to business interests and private property owners. "All too often we see the rights of weeds and bugs placed above the rights of landowners in Texas," he once said. When a drought in Texas in 2000 forced water rationing, Bonilla's response was hyperbolic: "The plain fact is that the source of all the pain inflicted on this region is the Endangered Species Act."

Bonilla wants to enact a federal law requiring compensation for property owners when environmental restrictions limit use of their property. He opposed a moratorium on Forest Service road-building. And in 1998, he joined with most House Republicans to block the Clinton administration from taking any preliminary steps to implement the international pact on climate change worked out in Kyoto, Japan.

Bonilla represents more of the U.S.-Mexico border than any House member — some 800 miles. When Mexico's government in 1999 proposed requiring refundable cash deposits of up to $800 as a condition of driving into Mexico, he worked with Democrat Solomon P. Ortiz of Texas and the Clinton administration to successfully pressure the Mexican government to back down.

Although in his first term he was a proponent of the 1993 North American Free Trade Agreement, Bonilla told a Texas newspaper he wanted more assurances about the safety of Mexican trucks that are allowed to cross the border under the agreement. In 2000, he voted for the measure granting China permanent normal trade status.

Bonilla has only occasionally voted against the GOP line. In the 106th, for example, he opposed a Republican-led effort to cut off funding for peacekeeping operations in Kosovo. In the 105th, he was one of 55 Republicans to vote against a ban on affirmative action in public college admissions.

The Texan's conservative stripes showed in the welfare overhaul debate of 1996, when he was the only member of the Hispanic Caucus to vote for the law's enactment. He also supported the unsuccessful effort by California Republican Elton Gallegly to bar the children of illegal immigrants from attending public schools.

Bonilla has criticized the Department of Education's bilingual education requirements, arguing that schools should be able to adopt a more English-centered approach. He was the only Hispanic in the House to back a move later that year to make it easier for states to devise their own bilingual education programs. He has opposed efforts to designate English as the nation's official language, however. "For those fear-mongers who think we need some kind of amendment ... to help us promote English, English is already the official language of the world," he said. "We do not need an amendment to tell us that."

Bonilla worked at several TV stations across the country and served as press secretary to Pennsylvania Gov. Richard Thornburgh before returning to his native San Antonio in 1986 to work as a public affairs executive at the local CBS affiliate. At the time, four-term Democratic incumbent Albert G. Bustamante was suddenly being viewed as out of touch. He had moved into a mansion outside his district, which includes some of the poorest neighborhoods in the country, and his 30 overdrafts at the private bank for House members offended those struggling to balance their own books each month.

In his first bid for elective office in 1992, Bonilla drove across the district, shaking hands in stores and coffee shops, introducing himself as an agent of change and chatting in Spanish. It was an appealing strategy in a district that was five-eighths Hispanic. So, too, was the presence of his wife, anchor of the region's highest-rated TV newscast.

Bonilla won by 21 percentage points and has not been seriously challenged since.

KEY VOTES

2000
No   Raise hourly minimum wage by $1 over two years
No   Halt funding for U.S. mission in Kosovo unless European nations pay more
Yes   Provide Medicare benefits to military retirees and their dependents
Yes   Grant China permanent normal trade status
Yes   Phase out estate, gift and trust taxes
Yes   Prohibit implementation of president's national monument designations
Yes   Approve GOP plan to provide prescription drug coverage for Medicare beneficiaries
No   Increase help for poor nations indebted to international financial institutions

1999
No   Impose steel import quotas
Yes   Kill proposal to take aviation trust funds off budget
?   Require background checks on buyers only at gun shows with 10 or more vendors
No   Remove barriers among banking, securities and insurance companies
No   Authorize state grants to hire teachers and reduce class size
No   Overhaul campaign finance law; ban "soft money" and restrict advocacy advertising
No   Approve bipartisan plan to increase rights of patients in managed-care health plans

INTEREST GROUPS

	AFL-CIO	ADA	CCUS	ACU
2000	0%	0%	90%	82%
1999	11%	0%	84%	91%
1998	11%	10%	88%	92%
1997	0%	5%	90%	95%

CQ VOTE STUDIES

	PARTY UNITY		PRESIDENTIAL SUPPORT	
	Support	Oppose	Support	Oppose
2000	92%	8%	30%	70%
1999	90%	10%	20%	80%
1998	85%	15%	30%	70%
1997	93%	7%	34%	66%

TEXAS 23
Southwest – Laredo; San Antonio suburbs

The politically moderate 23rd skims El Paso in the west, heads over to San Antonio in the east and borders Mexico to the south. The largest district in a state that boasts of doing everything bigger and better, the 23rd includes 29 counties, following the Rio Grande River to include the bulk of Texas' border with Mexico. The district's Hispanic population reaches 62 percent, according to 1990 Census Bureau statistics.

The 23rd includes some of the nation's poorest counties along its southern border. Seasonal employment, the influx of legal and illegal immigrants and an abundance of cheaper Mexican labor contribute to high unemployment. Manufacturing operations along the border known as *maquiladoras* are an integral part of the economy. While it may be too early to gauge the long-term effects of NAFTA, an increase in trade and manufacturing has been of immediate benefit to the area.

The border communities often seem to have more in common with their Mexican neighbors than with the rest of Texas. Laredo celebrates

Mexican Independence Day, and three bridges connect it to its Mexican sister city, Nuevo Laredo.

In 1992, the 23rd elected a Republican who has since held onto the seat. While most of the district's rural residents lean Democratic, a majority of the 23rd's voters come from the Republican hub of Bexar County. Locally, most areas outside Bexar County continue to elect Democrats, but Republicans have made inroads in swaying conservative Democrats. The district supported Bill Clinton in 1992 and '96, however, it gave native son President Bush the edge in 2000.

MAJOR INDUSTRY
Agriculture, trade, tourism

MILITARY BASES
Fort Bliss, 9,881 military, 2,262 civilian (shared with the 16th District); Laughlin Air Force Base, 1,053 military, 898 civilian (1999)

CITIES
Laredo, 183,160; San Antonio (pt.), 64,720 (1990); Del Rio, 35,728

UNUSUAL FEATURES
Texas' largest county, Brewster, is 6,208 square miles, about the size of Connecticut and Rhode Island combined.

Rep. Martin Frost (D)

CAPITOL OFFICE
225-3605; fax 225-4951; 2256 Rayburn Bldg. 20515

INTERNET
e-mail: martin.frost@mail.house.gov
web: www.house.gov/frost

COMMITTEES
Rules

HOMETOWN
Dallas

BORN
Jan. 1, 1942, Glendale, Calif.

RELIGION
Jewish

FAMILY
Wife, Kathy George Frost; three children

EDUCATION
U. of Missouri, B.A., B.J. 1964; Georgetown U., J.D.
1970

MILITARY SERVICE
Army Reserve, 1966-72

CAREER
Lawyer; reporter

POLITICAL HIGHLIGHTS
Sought Democratic nomination for U.S. House,
1974

ELECTION RESULTS

2000 GENERAL

Martin Frost (D)	103,152	61.8%
Bryndan Wright (R)	61,235	36.7%
Robert Worthington (LIBERT)	2,561	1.5%

2000 PRIMARY

Martin Frost (D)	unopposed

1998 GENERAL

Martin Frost (D)	56,321	57.5%
Shawn Terry (R)	40,105	40.9%

PREVIOUS WINNING PERCENTAGES
1996 (56%); 1994 (53%); 1992 (60%); 1990 (100%);
1988 (93%); 1986 (67%); 1984 (59%); 1982 (73%);
1980 (61%); 1978 (54%)

Elected 1978; 12th term

In the halls of the Capitol, the bespectacled Frost can often be seen walking quickly and frowning to himself. It is the expression of a theorist busily trying to figure out a formula in his head.

Anybody who is familiar with the stereotype of a Texas politico — a back-slapping fellow of grandiose gestures — knows that Frost is not your typical Lone Star State legislator. As reserved as he is focused, Frost has built a reputation as a powerful intellect in the personality-driven world of Washington, compensating for a lack of charisma with an acute command of the details that decide political campaigns, policy disputes and partisan battles.

Frost, who is chairman of the Democratic Caucus and is leading the Democratic effort to come out on top in post-census redistricting by the states, has a wonkish zeal for grappling with politics and policy that has helped propel him to the No. 2 Democratic slot on the Rules Committee. He has also demonstrated a keen understanding of political redistricting and a talent for fundraising that is largely self-taught.

Frost is regarded as an effective pragmatist. That measured approach extends to his political style, which is fiercely partisan without being ultra-liberal. "You don't have to be ideological to be partisan," one top aide observes. "He looks at the world from the middle."

For Frost, the devil — and the key to any task — is always in the details. Minority Leader Richard A. Gephardt calls Frost "the most focused human being I've ever met." Frost owes his post as Democratic Caucus chairman, the third-ranking Democrat in the House, largely to his performance as chairman of the Democratic Congressional Campaign Committee (DCCC). There, he was the architect of a strategy that led Democrats in 1998 to a historic midterm election gain of five seats in the House — the first midterm gain by the party holding the presidency since 1934 — and that drove Speaker Newt Gingrich from Congress.

Frost set about the job of transforming the DCCC into a modern political operation, recruiting candidates who were themselves fundraisers, teaching them how to run better campaigns and instituting strict rules for incumbents that required them to contribute to colleagues and other candidates. Fundraising, he lectured them, is in the details and is the key to the Democrats' all-important goal of winning back the House and being in a position to set the agenda.

Democrats fell just short of that target in 1998, but the party rewarded Frost for the unexpected House gains with the caucus post, where he concentrated on honing the Democratic message, often providing rhetorical cover for members and seeking to act as a conduit to other leaders for the concerns of various factions. He also tried to broaden the caucus's reach, hoping to balance Democrats' traditionally strong ties with labor by planning bagel breakfasts and "get to know you" sessions with the business community.

Frost studied journalism as an undergraduate at the University of Missouri and worked for a time in his youth at Congressional Quarterly, where he first mastered redistricting and covered agriculture and the environment.

Not long after earning a law degree from Georgetown University in 1970, he entered politics. He challenged Democratic Rep. Dale Milford for the party nomination in 1974, contending the incumbent was too supportive of the Nixon administration. He lost that bid, but in 1978 he was back and with the help of organized labor, beat Milford and went on to win the general election with 54 percent of the vote.

Once in Congress, Frost got an inside track early with the help of Majority Leader and then Speaker Jim Wright, a fellow Texan who helped the younger man land a spot on the Rules Committee when he was a freshman.

As a Jewish Southern white male, Frost represents a variety of constituencies that are important to the Democratic Party. Coming from a politically competitive district, Frost has learned in his own campaigns — particularly in recent years as aggressive Republican challengers have tried to paint him as a tax-and-spend, left-wing liberal — that a Democrat locked in battle with a GOP foe is wise to stress centrist themes that have broad voter appeal. As DCCC chairman, Frost encouraged many candidates to adopt that approach, being careful to recruit candidates that fit the political makeup of their districts.

Frost's politics are more liberal than those of most of his fellow white Southern Democrats, although after taking a career-low 53 percent at the polls in 1994, he shifted to the right during the 104th Congress on some hot-button issues, and his subsequent victories have been by slightly more comfortable margins. In the main, though, Frost talks about the staple centrist Democratic issues — education, health care and Social Security — and votes loyally with the party leadership.

Frost also courts his local constituency with work on projects near and dear to them. Having refrained for months from announcing his position on granting China permanent normal trade status — a top Clinton administration priority in the 106th — Frost bargained with the White House for a deal that would allow defense contractor Northrop Grumman Corp. to keep two plants the company had considered moving from his district. He has also lobbied for funds to widen Interstate 30, a crucial Texas traffic artery, and for the Dallas area's light rail system. For more than a decade he has pushed to secure funding for the first veterans cemetery in Texas.

A Texas tragedy led Frost to take up a cause that became one of his biggest legislative successes. During House debate on a crime bill in May 1996, he won passage of an amendment expanding federal jurisdiction over repeat child molesters, establishing a sentence of life without parole for anyone convicted of a second sex crime against a child. The impetus for the measure was the kidnapping and murder of 9-year-old Amber Hagerman of Arlington, Texas.

Since his marriage in August 1998 to his fourth wife, Kathy — the adjutant general of the Army — colleagues who know Frost well insist that while he's still deep in thought, the frown has faded a bit.

KEY VOTES

2000

Yes Raise hourly minimum wage by $1 over two years

No Halt funding for U.S. mission in Kosovo unless European nations pay more

Yes Provide Medicare benefits to military retirees and their dependents

Yes Grant China permanent normal trade status

No Phase out estate, gift and trust taxes

No Prohibit implementation of president's national monument designations

No Approve GOP plan to provide prescription drug coverage for Medicare beneficiaries

Yes Increase help for poor nations indebted to international financial institutions

1999

Yes Impose steel import quotas

No Kill proposal to take aviation trust funds off budget

No Require background checks on buyers only at gun shows with 10 or more vendors

Yes Remove barriers among banking, securities and insurance companies

Yes Authorize state grants to hire teachers and reduce class size

Yes Overhaul campaign finance law; ban "soft money" and restrict advocacy advertising

Yes Approve bipartisan plan to increase rights of patients in managed-care health plans

INTEREST GROUPS

	AFL-CIO	ADA	CCUS	ACU
2000	90%	80%	47%	12%
1999	88%	85%	42%	4%
1998	100%	95%	56%	8%
1997	100%	80%	60%	20%

CQ VOTE STUDIES

	PARTY UNITY		PRESIDENTIAL SUPPORT	
	Support	Oppose	Support	Oppose
2000	87%	13%	81%	19%
1999	85%	15%	76%	24%
1998	84%	16%	73%	27%
1997	85%	15%	78%	22%

TEXAS 24
Parts of Dallas and Tarrant counties

The 24th draws much of its population from Fort Worth and Arlington in Tarrant County, and the city of Dallas. It extends to take in most of Ellis and part of Navarro counties, mostly Democratic-leaning rural areas.

Blue-collar workers in the 24th have borne the brunt of military cutbacks and defense contractor layoffs. The city was dealt a setback in 1998 when Dallas Naval Air Station was shut down. An aircraft repair company briefly took over the base but has since declared bankruptcy. The 24th also produces components for the V-22 Osprey, which takes off like a helicopter but flies like a plane. After several crashes during testing, it was unclear whether the program would survive. But the area still has some major defense contractors, including Northrop Grumman Corp. and Lockheed Martin Corp.

Arlington's entertainment venues – including the Ballpark at Arlington, home of the Texas Rangers – are large employers in the district, and the University of Texas at Arlington to the southwest benefits the local economy as well. South of Dallas, the residential area of Oak Cliff will be the site of a large business center called Pinnacle Park, which is expected to create 2,000 new jobs and boost the local economy.

The district leans Democratic, and 1996 redistricting increased its Democratic tilt by drawing in more of the Grand Prairie area, which is mostly middle class. The district also includes some predominantly black and Democratic areas of southeast Fort Worth. Overall, blacks and Hispanics each represent about 20 percent of the district's population (according to 1990 Census Bureau statistics), and the Hispanic population is increasing.

MAJOR INDUSTRY
Defense, transportation, entertainment

CITIES
Arlington (pt.), 116,101 (1990); Dallas (pt.), 107,960 (1990); Fort Worth (pt.), 73,277 (1990)

UNUSUAL FEATURES
Six Flags over Texas amusement park is home to the Texas Giant, consistently named the No. 1 wooden roller coaster in the world.

Rep. Ken Bentsen (D)

Elected 1994; 4th term

Bentsen is a business-friendly politician in the mold of his Uncle Lloyd, the longtime Texas senator and former Treasury secretary. He believes the federal government should play an active role in promoting economic activity by investing in infrastructure, education and other domestic needs and by helping U.S. companies compete in the global marketplace.

Bentsen is also careful to tend to business interests in his district, including the Port of Houston, NASA, the oil and gas industry, and the hospital and research facilities that make up the Texas Medical Center.

He affiliates with the moderate New Democrat Coalition, and on social policy issues, he is one of the more liberal white Southern Democrats. Bentsen has a low-key manner and inspires descriptions such as "brainy" and "wonkish."

The Texan has been more critical of Republican tax-cutting efforts than some Southern Democrats, and he warned that a GOP budget plan in the 106th Congress that called for almost $800 billion in tax cuts "tests the bounds of fiscal reality, while failing the test of fiscal prudence and priorities." He also criticized the first budget proposed by President Bush: "I am concerned that the president may be engaging in the time-honored tradition of sending us a budget loaded with spending cuts the Congress can't swallow."

A former Capitol Hill staff member and Houston investment banker, Bentsen is a natural to serve on the Financial Services Committee (formerly Banking); he also has a seat on the Budget Committee.

Bentsen weighed in on sweeping bankruptcy legislation in the 106th, adding his support for an amendment to retain a Texas law that enables debtors to protect their homes from seizure. He criticized federal efforts to override the state's homestead exemption as an "egregious" incursion into a historic Texas practice. The legislation was ultimately vetoed, but a similar provision was included in a bankruptcy bill passed by the House at the start of the 107th.

Bentsen pressed for several modest health care measures in the 106th, including eliminating disparities in the amount teaching hospitals are reimbursed by Medicare for training young doctors, lifting some restrictions on international patients who receive health care in the United States, and giving states the authority to allow schools, homeless shelters and health care clinics to enroll children in Medicaid. Of the latter plan, he said: "Our responsibility is to try and figure out how to make the system work more efficiently."

Although he may side with Republicans on business-related matters, Bentsen usually opposes conservative social policies. On abortion, education, the environment, and worker-management disputes, his vote is squarely in the Democratic column.

Foreign trade has been of particular interest to Bentsen. He has opposed budget-cutters' efforts to reduce funding for the Overseas Private Investment Corporation (OPIC) and other federally backed trade development agencies. In response to critics who call the program "corporate welfare," Bentsen says that OPIC, which provides credit and risk insurance to U.S. exporters, is necessary for helping U.S. businesses tap new foreign markets.

He emerged as a swing vote in 2000 when the House took up a controversial measure granting China permanent normal trade status. Breaking with labor unions that warned the measure could cost American jobs, Bentsen announced he would vote for it — but only after supporters agreed

CAPITOL OFFICE
225-7508; fax 225-2947; 405 Cannon Bldg. 20515

INTERNET
e-mail: ken.bentsen@mail.house.gov
web: www.house.gov/bentsen

COMMITTEES
Budget
Financial Services

HOMETOWN
Houston

BORN
June 3, 1959, Houston, Texas

RELIGION
Presbyterian

FAMILY
Wife, Tamra Bentsen; two children

EDUCATION
U. of St. Thomas, B.A. 1982; American U., M.P.A. 1985

CAREER
Investment banker; congressional aide

POLITICAL HIGHLIGHTS
Harris County Democratic Party chairman, 1990-93

ELECTION RESULTS

2000 GENERAL

Ken Bentsen (D)	106,112	60.1%
Phil Sudan (R)	68,010	38.5%
Clifford Lee Messina (LIBERT)	2,400	1.4%

2000 PRIMARY

Ken Bentsen (D)	unopposed

1998 GENERAL

Ken Bentsen (D)	58,591	57.9%
John M. Sanchez (R)	41,848	41.3%

PREVIOUS WINNING PERCENTAGES
1996 General Runoff Election (57%); 1996 (34%); 1994 (52%)

to create a commission that would report on programs to help workers who lose their jobs because of increased imports. "It's not enough to say there are more winners than losers and move on," Bentsen said. "We must strengthen the safety net for American workers in less-competitive industries who lose their jobs due to trade."

One cause taken on by Bentsen that is popular with the oil industry is his effort to eliminate a federal tax subsidy given to producers of ethanol, a corn-based alcohol fuel championed by lawmakers from corn-producing states. Bentsen argues that ethanol yields less energy per gallon than gasoline, and he contends that "ethanol subsidies artificially inflate the price of corn food products, costing American consumers millions each year."

Although Bentsen doesn't sit on the Appropriations Committee, he knows how to funnel federal money to his district. With some regularity, his office puts out word of federal dollars flowing to the Houston area, including funds to widen the Houston Ship Channel, to build a variety of bayou flood-control projects, and to conduct research at the Texas Medical Center sponsored by the National Institutes of Health. He is also a strong supporter of NASA's International Space Station, which is part of the work of Houston's Johnson Space Center. Critics of the orbiting laboratory call it "pork in space," and each year, they try to kill its funding. So far, they have failed.

After working for Texas Democratic Rep. Ronald D. Coleman while he was in his 20s, Bentsen went on to become an investment banker and used his chairmanship of the Harris County Democratic Party to lay a foundation for election to Congress.

When he first ran for the open 25th District seat in 1994, Bentsen was regarded as something of an underdog to replace Democratic Rep. Mike Andrews, who gave up the seat to run, unsuccessfully, for the Senate. Texas and the nation were trending Republican, and Bentsen's GOP opponent, Gene Fontenot, spent more than $4.6 million (much of it his own money) on the race.

After winning a hard-fought five-way contest for the nomination, Bentsen, with the aid of the national Democratic Party, portrayed Fontenot as part of the "radical right," noting his opposition to abortion even to protect the life of the woman. Bentsen won with 52 percent of the vote.

He has appeared vulnerable at times, especially in 1996 when he was forced into an unusual runoff against his Republican challenger. He won the runoff by 15 percentage points. But Bentsen seems to have strengthened his hold on the district, winning 58 percent in 1998 and 60 percent in 2000.

KEY VOTES

2000
Yes	Raise hourly minimum wage by $1 over two years
No	Halt funding for U.S. mission in Kosovo unless European nations pay more
Yes	Provide Medicare benefits to military retirees and their dependents
Yes	Grant China permanent normal trade status
No	Phase out estate, gift and trust taxes
No	Prohibit implementation of president's national monument designations
No	Approve GOP plan to provide prescription drug coverage for Medicare beneficiaries
Yes	Increase help for poor nations indebted to international financial institutions

1999
Yes	Impose steel import quotas
Yes	Kill proposal to take aviation trust funds off budget
No	Require background checks on buyers only at gun shows with 10 or more vendors
Yes	Remove barriers among banking, securities and insurance companies
Yes	Authorize state grants to hire teachers and reduce class size
Yes	Overhaul campaign finance law; ban "soft money" and restrict advocacy advertising
Yes	Approve bipartisan plan to increase rights of patients in managed-care health plans

INTEREST GROUPS

	AFL-CIO	ADA	CCUS	ACU
2000	80%	90%	47%	8%
1999	78%	95%	40%	8%
1998	80%	95%	50%	4%
1997	88%	75%	60%	13%

CQ VOTE STUDIES

	PARTY UNITY		PRESIDENTIAL SUPPORT	
	Support	Oppose	Support	Oppose
2000	88%	12%	86%	14%
1999	84%	16%	79%	21%
1998	85%	15%	78%	22%
1997	85%	15%	80%	20%

TEXAS 25
South Houston and suburbs

The 25th covers the southern portions of Houston from its west end through Pasadena and Baytown east of the city. It takes in much of the land around the port of Houston, including the cities of Morgan's Point and Deer Park. One of the few swing districts in the Houston area, the 25th has a mix of upscale neighborhoods, Reagan Democrats and suburban black areas. It also has a sizable portion of Houston's Jewish population. Stances on issues, not party affiliation, often decide close elections, although 1996 redistricting made the 25th more competitive by trimming some of its Democratic edge.

The 25th's voters tend to be fiscally conservative but socially progressive, evidenced by their support for abortion rights. The eastern edges of the district have refineries, cowboy bars along with union Democrats who went for Ronald Reagan in 1980 but also helped Al Gore win the district by a 2 percentage point margin in 2000. It was one of the 10 Texas congressional districts that Gore won. The western,

more suburban portion of the 25th lies next to the 7th District, one of the most conservative in the area.

Once mostly agricultural, the district's land has long since been converted to industrial purposes, including refining and plastics production. The 25th's proximity to the Houston Ship Channel and the presence of the Texas Medical Center, which has an estimated $10 billion impact on the region, helped boost the economy during the 1990s. Many residents commute to the nearby Lyndon B. Johnson Space Center.

MAJOR INDUSTRY
Energy, shipping, health care

CITIES
Houston (pt.), 347,315 (1990); Pasadena (pt.), 84,596 (1990); Baytown (pt.), 43,304 (1990); Deer Park, 30,804

UNUSUAL FEATURES
The original "Yellow Rose of Texas," a slave from Morgan's Point named Emily, is credited with helping Texans win the battle of San Jacinto in 1836 by detaining Mexican Gen. Santa Anna.

Rep. Dick Armey (R)

CAPITOL OFFICE
225-7772; fax 226-8101; 301 Cannon Bldg. 20515

INTERNET
e-mail: www.house.gov/writerep
web: armey.house.gov

COMMITTEES
Majority Leader — no committee assignments

HOMETOWN
Irving

BORN
July 7, 1940, Cando, N.D.

RELIGION
Presbyterian

FAMILY
Wife, Susan Byrd; five children

EDUCATION
Jamestown College, B.A. 1963; U. of North Dakota,
M.A. 1964; U. of Oklahoma, Ph.D. 1969

CAREER
Economist; professor

POLITICAL HIGHLIGHTS
No previous office

ELECTION RESULTS

2000 GENERAL

Dick Armey (R)	214,025	72.5%
Steve Love (D)	75,601	25.6%
Fred E. Badagnani (LIBERT)	5,646	1.9%

2000 PRIMARY

Dick Armey (R)	48,179	87.6%
Larry Thompson (R)	6,806	12.4%

1998 GENERAL

Dick Armey (R)	120,332	88.1%
Joe Turner (LIBERT)	16,182	11.9%

PREVIOUS WINNING PERCENTAGES
1996 (74%); 1994 (76%); 1992 (73%); 1990 (70%);
1988 (69%); 1986 (68%); 1984 (51%)

Elected 1984; 9th term

Armey spent much of the 106th Congress rehabilitating his image within his party, and by one important measure he had succeeded at the start of the 107th Congress: He was unopposed in his bid for a fourth term as House majority leader, the No. 2 position in the GOP hierarchy.

Two years before, by contrast, he barely held onto the job as fellow Republicans — angry at their unexpected losses in the 1998 election — sought to purge most of their top-tier leadership. Armey survived only because the vote against him was splintered. More than half of his GOP colleagues voted for someone else on the first ballot; he was not re-elected until the third ballot.

Chastened by the experience, Armey retreated behind the scenes, eschewing the television talk-show circuit to concentrate on the mechanics of running the House and mending fences with the rank-and-file. He also worked tirelessly to raise money for fellow Republicans, holding 20 fundraisers in Washington in 1999 alone. His political action committee, the Majority Leader's Fund, raised $2.2 million for candidates during the 2000 election cycle, as much as Speaker J. Dennis Hastert's PAC.

By the start of 2001, Armey's supporters say, he had succeeded in regaining the trust of his colleagues, and many of his allies predicted that he would return to a much more active role in policy decisions — and a more visible profile — in the 107th Congress. Physically, he is hard to miss, with his barrel-chested stature, his armadillo-skin cowboy boots, and his slow and occasionally slurred speech, in which the inflections of his native North Dakota compete with the drawl of his adopted home state.

Armey began 2001 eager to take a lead role in turning President Bush's tax proposals into law, and despite his somewhat diminished leadership role in the 106th, he remained the House GOP point man on tax cuts. In 2000, Congress cleared a repeal of the estate tax and the tax code's "marriage penalty," but both died under President Clinton's veto pen. Armey had no better success with a catchall package that he hoped would end the 106th with a tax-cutting flourish. He tried to negotiate with the lame-duck administration, but in the end, Clinton spurned the legislation and it died after the House passed it. Armey also was key in shaping the $792 billion GOP tax package of 1999, but Clinton vetoed that, too.

For years he has gotten essentially nowhere with his proposal for scrapping the graduated federal income tax and replacing it with a flat tax with almost no exemptions.

A free-market conservative, Armey consistently opposes government intervention. His congressional website offers weekly "Armey Axioms," which include such insights as "The market is rational and the government is dumb," and "Liberals don't see anything good happen unless the government does it."

Armey is a leading spokesman for conservative causes, particularly those of the religious right. He is a prime proponent of school vouchers, although in 1999 the House handily rejected his proposal to create a $100 million program of federally funded vouchers for private school tuition. Also that year, he led a church revival on Capitol Hill to celebrate the reintroduction of a school prayer constitutional amendment that failed to win approval in the 105th Congress. "Our laws should at every turn be a complement to and encouragement for those laws of the Lord God Almighty," Armey declared. The amendment — to allow the posting of the Ten Commandments and other religious teachings in government buildings — went nowhere in the 106th, either.

Armey's chief responsibility as majority leader is to decide which bills are to be brought before the House, and when — a task requiring considerable political and tactical skill in an era of narrow GOP majorities. His trial by fire came in 1995, when he orchestrated the 100-day drive to consider all the legislation promised in the "Contract With America," the campaign manifesto that had propelled Republicans into the majority the year before. He had been one of the principal authors of the contract.

Armey's personal style belies his background as a former college professor with a doctoral degree in economics. During his weekly press briefings, he spends almost as much time dropping Texas-style aphorisms as he does discussing policy — he likes to talk about bass fishing or riff on the lyrics of his favorite country singer, Jerry Jeff Walker. And he is not widely viewed as a reliable "big picture" spokesman for the GOP. He has sought advice to improve his TV appearances, but his flat delivery and sometimes garbled syntax remain less than ideal for the medium.

Some have pointed to his questionable communication skills as one reason he was almost demoted in 1998. He was challenged by Steve Largent of Oklahoma and Jennifer Dunn of Washington. A bid to recruit a potentially more dangerous opponent, Hastert, fizzled when Armey declined to release his fishing buddy from a previous commitment of support. (That decision left Hastert available when the Speaker's position opened up unexpectedly at the end of 1998.)

Armey's shaky hold on power dated to July 1997, when he denied that he had encouraged a group of conservative GOP lawmakers who were planning an insurrection against Speaker Newt Gingrich. Armey insisted that he was not complicit because he had done nothing beyond participating in "what-if" scenarios about who might advance to the Speaker's chair. In the end, he helped stop the coup by announcing his support for Gingrich. But Armey's protestations of innocence did not convince a number of his colleagues, some of whom theorized that Armey had decided to support Gingrich only when he realized that he would not be the one to replace the dethroned Speaker.

However tenuous his position in Washington circles of power has been in recent years, Armey has had nothing to worry about at home. Since winning his initial race by less than 3 percentage points against one-term Democratic Rep. Tom Vandergriff, he has never gotten less than 68 percent of the vote.

KEY VOTES

2000
No Raise hourly minimum wage by $1 over two years
Yes Halt funding for U.S. mission in Kosovo unless European nations pay more
Yes Provide Medicare benefits to military retirees and their dependents
Yes Grant China permanent normal trade status
Yes Phase out estate, gift and trust taxes
Yes Prohibit implementation of president's national monument designations
Yes Approve GOP plan to provide prescription drug coverage for Medicare beneficiaries
No Increase help for poor nations indebted to international financial institutions

1999
No Impose steel import quotas
Yes Kill proposal to take aviation trust funds off budget
Yes Require background checks on buyers only at gun shows with 10 or more vendors
Yes Remove barriers among banking, securities and insurance companies
No Authorize state grants to hire teachers and reduce class size
No Overhaul campaign finance law; ban "soft money" and restrict advocacy advertising
No Approve bipartisan plan to increase rights of patients in managed-care health plans

INTEREST GROUPS

	AFL-CIO	ADA	CCUS	ACU
2000	0%	0%	90%	92%
1999	0%	0%	92%	96%
1998	0%	0%	100%	100%
1997	0%	0%	100%	88%

CQ VOTE STUDIES

	PARTY UNITY		PRESIDENTIAL SUPPORT	
	Support	Oppose	Support	Oppose
2000	99%	1%	23%	77%
1999	97%	3%	23%	77%
1998	97%	3%	22%	78%
1997	96%	4%	25%	75%

TEXAS 26
Suburban Dallas; part of Irving

The 26th consists of parts of four counties that cover the suburbs north of Dallas, with the majority of its population coming from Dallas County. Redistricting in the 1990s moved the district south and west – originally its northern edge almost touched the Oklahoma border.

As the population of Dallas expanded in the 1990s, it stretched north into rural Denton and Collin counties. Denton's population has boomed since the 1970s and continues to grow today as upper middle-class families build large homes in the area. In Collin, once-rural towns like Frisco and McKinney have caught the overgrowth from the Plano area. However, the entire northern section and much of the western edge of the district remain rural and depend on cotton, eggs, cattle and corn.

Like the rest of the Dallas-Fort Worth area districts, the 26th's economic wealth is derived mainly from its infrastructure. Some residents depend on Love Field and nearby Dallas-Fort Worth International Airport (in the 6th and 20th districts) for their paychecks.

The city of Irving was removed from the district during 1996 redistricting. The 26th now includes the wealthy communities of Highland Park and University Park, home to Southern Methodist University.

Overall, the district is predominantly white, upper-class and suburban. Residents of the 26th voted more than 2-to-1 for President Bush in the 2000 presidential election and overwhelmingly re-elected their Republican representative. The area tends to be conservative both fiscally and socially, but local issues – such as highway transportation – remain the top priority to many.

MAJOR INDUSTRY
Transportation, telecommunications, education

CITIES
Dallas (pt.), 217,436 (1990); Carrollton, 103,311; Lewisville, 77,355; Flower Mound, 49,164

UNUSUAL FEATURES
Ross Perot lives in north Dallas; The $110-million Texas Motor Speedway, the second-largest sports facility in the nation, just north of Fort Worth in Denton County.

Rep. Solomon P. Ortiz (D)

CAPITOL OFFICE
225-7742; fax 226-1134; 2304 Rayburn Bldg. 20515

INTERNET
e-mail: www.house.gov/writerep
web: www.house.gov/ortiz

COMMITTEES
Armed Services
Resources

HOMETOWN
Corpus Christi

BORN
June 3, 1937, Robstown, Texas

RELIGION
Methodist

FAMILY
Divorced; two children

EDUCATION
Institute of Applied Science, attended 1962;
Del Mar College, attended 1965-67

MILITARY SERVICE
Army, 1960-62

CAREER
Law enforcement official

POLITICAL HIGHLIGHTS
Nueces County constable, 1965-69; Nueces
County Commission, 1969-77; Nueces County
sheriff, 1977-83

ELECTION RESULTS

2000 GENERAL

Solomon P. Ortiz (D)	102,088	63.4%
Pat Ahumada (R)	54,660	33.9%
William Bunch (LIBERT)	4,324	2.7%

2000 PRIMARY

Solomon P. Ortiz (D)	unopposed

1998 GENERAL

Solomon P. Ortiz (D)	61,638	63.3%
Erol A. Stone (R)	34,284	35.2%
Mark G. Pretz (LIBERT)	1,476	1.5%

PREVIOUS WINNING PERCENTAGES
1996 (65%); 1994 (59%); 1992 (55%); 1990 (100%);
1988 (100%); 1986 (100%); 1984 (64%); 1982 (64%)

Elected 1982; 10th term

Defense issues are Ortiz's major focus, and though he is not a high-profile personality, his voice is amplified by seniority, which has lifted him to the No. 4 Democratic seat on the Armed Services Committee. There, and as co-chairman of the congressional Depot Caucus, he looks after the interests of South Texas' military bases and the troops' quality of life.

Befitting a lawmaker whose district borders Mexico, and whose constituency is two-thirds Hispanic, Ortiz is active on issues such as cross-border trade and tourism, immigration, drug smuggling and what he regards as the entertainment industry's woeful record in presenting positive portrayals of Hispanics. He is helping to lay the groundwork for South Texas to play a key role in the commercialization of space, perhaps playing host to a launch facility.

Ortiz's overall voting record is less liberal than those of other Hispanic Democrats in the House; his votes would place him comfortably with the centrist New Democrat Coalition of House Democrats, although he has declined to join the group. Through the last six years of President Clinton's tenure, Ortiz supported the president only slightly more than 60 percent of the time.

Ortiz's legislative agenda is driven much more by the economic and social needs of the low-income, relatively poorly educated 27th District than by ideology or party. Perhaps for that reason, he was better situated than many Democrats to deal with the shock of the GOP takeover in 1995. And because of his personal relationships with many Republicans, he was able to gain a favorable hearing for many of his proposals. "He worms his way into their hearts," said one longtime aide.

As the top ranking Democrat on the Military Readiness Subcommittee, Ortiz has warned that defense downsizing and spending cuts have threatened the quality of life of military personnel. "Morale is bad," Ortiz said at a 1998 hearing on defense restructuring. "We have thousands of our young [military] families receiving food stamps because we don't pay them adequately."

Ortiz's concern for the troops' quality of life is smart politics in the 27th District, with its large population of enlisted personnel. Also, his personal experience has led to the conviction that military personnel should be given a chance at upward mobility, as he was.

The child of a migrant family, Ortiz grew up poor near Corpus Christi, working a variety of odd jobs to help out his family. When he was 16, his father died. He dropped out of high school and soon after that joined the Army. "It was the one place that would give me free room and board and let me send my check back home to my mother," he recalls.

Ortiz served in the military police, which put him on the path to a trailblazing career in law enforcement and local government. He mounted his first electoral bid in 1964, defeating the incumbent Nueces County constable. Four years later, he became the first Hispanic elected to the county commission, and then in 1976 he was the first Hispanic to win election as county sheriff, his springboard to the House in 1982.

In his work on the Military Readiness panel, Ortiz is concerned that unhappiness over pay, benefits and the overall quality of life makes it difficult to keep trained and experienced military personnel, and he sometimes wonders whether the United States will have to reinstitute the draft.

The military presence in the 27th includes two naval air stations and an Army depot. The facilities survived the cutbacks mandated in the 1990s by the Defense Base Realignment and Closure Commission. Still, Ortiz remains wary of further defense downsizing proposals. "I think that we have cut too much, too soon, too quick. And we're going to regret it," he said in 1998.

Ortiz particularly opposes Pentagon proposals to privatize repair work done at large military maintenance depots, such as the one in Corpus Christi that services Army helicopters. He and other members of the Depot Caucus pressure decision-makers to keep work flowing to the depots. "We are like the CIA" in keeping tabs on depot work, Ortiz told The Associated Press.

Ortiz was a key player in the enactment of legislation in 1988 requiring at least 60 percent of depot-maintenance work to be performed by federal employees. That "60-40" law — since amended to 50-50 — has been instrumental in preventing further cuts in depot work forces across the country.

In the 106th Congress, Ortiz played a key role in calling attention to a short-lived proposal by Mexican authorities to require payment of a deposit, of as much as $800, on each car that entered Mexico. The plan, designed to discourage people from illegally selling U.S. cars in Mexico, would have harmed trade, Ortiz and his allies argued. He also helped convince the Mexican government not to levy a tax on the manufacturing plants in northern Mexico known as *maquiladoras*, which use low-cost labor and U.S. parts, and which are often owned by U.S. companies.

Ortiz is concerned about the treatment of Hispanics in the United States. In 1998, he chafed at a Republican amendment to require Puerto Rico to adopt English as its official language as a condition for being accepted as a state. As chairman of the Congressional Hispanic Caucus in the 102nd Congress, he helped push through legislation increasing access to voting materials in languages other than English.

He criticized a 1997 proposal to send 10,000 U.S. troops to the Mexican border to fight drug trafficking. "Mexico is our neighbor, friend and economic partner. It would be a mistake to station troops who have been trained to kill the enemy on the international border," he said.

During the 1996 House debate on overhauling immigration laws, Ortiz argued against further restricting legal immigration by the relatives of U.S. citizens and legal permanent residents. Ortiz says he hopes that increased trade will stimulate economic growth in countries such as Mexico, reducing the number of illegal immigrants seeking work in the United States.

Redistricting in 1982 gave Ortiz an opening to Washington. As drawn by a three-judge federal panel, the 27th was good territory for a Mexican-American Democrat, and Ortiz took advantage of his 18 years in elective office in Nueces County to defeat four other Democrats in the primary and easily prevail in the general election. Only twice has his tally fallen below 60 percent.

KEY VOTES

2000
Yes Raise hourly minimum wage by $1 over two years
No   Halt funding for U.S. mission in Kosovo unless European nations pay more
Yes Provide Medicare benefits to military retirees and their dependents
Yes Grant China permanent normal trade status
No   Phase out estate, gift and trust taxes
Yes Prohibit implementation of president's national monument designations
No   Approve GOP plan to provide prescription drug coverage for Medicare beneficiaries
Yes Increase help for poor nations indebted to international financial institutions

1999
Yes Impose steel import quotas
No   Kill proposal to take aviation trust funds off budget
No   Require background checks on buyers only at gun shows with 10 or more vendors
No   Remove barriers among banking, securities and insurance companies
Yes Authorize state grants to hire teachers and reduce class size
Yes Overhaul campaign finance law; ban "soft money" and restrict advocacy advertising
Yes Approve bipartisan plan to increase rights of patients in managed-care health plans

INTEREST GROUPS

	AFL-CIO	ADA	CCUS	ACU
2000	90%	65%	45%	24%
1999	88%	60%	33%	32%
1998	90%	70%	56%	17%
1997	100%	60%	60%	35%

CQ VOTE STUDIES

	PARTY UNITY		PRESIDENTIAL SUPPORT	
	Support	Oppose	Support	Oppose
2000	76%	24%	71%	29%
1999	70%	30%	65%	35%
1998	76%	24%	68%	32%
1997	64%	36%	56%	44%

TEXAS 27

Gulf Coast — Corpus Christi; Brownsville

Anchored by the tourist hub of Corpus Christi in the north, the mostly urban 27th runs south to the Rio Grande River, with the Gulf of Mexico on its eastern coast. Ranches are the mainstay between the two largest cities, Corpus Christi and Brownsville, which together contain more than half the 27th's population.

A port city, Corpus Christi has a solid economy fueled by its reliable tourism industry and a military presence that grew in the 1990s. Oil and gas used to be among the biggest industries in the city in the 1980s, but now petrochemical refining, which is also found up and down the coast, is more common. Farther south, the port city of Brownsville ails from an influx of illegal immigrants and high poverty, but new manufacturing plants and *maquiladoras* (assembly or manufacturing plants that use low-cost labor and import many parts from the United States) have brightened the area. Visitors coming from Mexico boost Brownsville's retail industry. "Eco-tourism" also adds to the economy

by drawing bird and turtle watchers to the area's wetlands.

The 27th was created by redistricting in 1982 and has been held by the same Democrat since. While most local areas are comfortably Democratic, some affluent areas in Harlingen and Corpus Christi lean Republican.

MAJOR INDUSTRY
Manufacturing, trade, tourism

MILITARY BASES
Corpus Christi Naval Air Station, 2,159 military, 1,241 civilian (2000); Corpus Christi Army Depot, 10 military, 2,700 civilian (2001); Naval Air Station Kingsville, 840 military, 350 civilian (1999)

CITIES
Corpus Christi, 281,791; Brownsville, 147,701; Harlingen, 57,139

UNUSUAL FEATURES
Padre Island, popular college spring break location; Port Isabel served as a supply depot during the U.S.-Mexican War (1846-48).

Rep. Ciro D. Rodriguez (D)

Elected April 1997; 2nd full term

One of the more liberal members of the Texas House delegation, Rodriguez has made education and preserving jobs at local military installations his chief focus on Capitol Hill.

Inspired by the civil rights struggle of the 1960s to switch his career from pharmacology to social work, Rodriguez tries to fight what he sees as disparities in educational and economic opportunities for minorities. His district is 60 percent Hispanic, and is one of the poorest and least-educated areas of the nation. The 28th District, Rodriguez says, "has a lot of diversity and a lot of poverty."

Rodriguez's voting record places him to the left of the other five Hispanics in the state delegation. His votes supporting abortion rights and gun control have led his opponents to argue that he is too liberal for the district. He told the Fort Worth Star-Telegram that he once bought a shotgun after his home had twice been burglarized. But burglars returned for a third time, and that time they stole the shotgun. He told the newspaper he no longer owns a gun, saying that now, "I don't feel I need one in my house."

In the 106th Congress, Rodriguez served on a leadership-appointed education task force, which worked to develop a party agenda on education initiatives for the 107th Congress. In the 105th, Rodriguez sided with Republicans and other Hispanic Democrats in opposing standardized testing of fourth- and eighth-graders to measure their progress in reading and math. Referring to his 12 years of experience on a local school board, Rodriguez argued that Texas schoolchildren are already tested enough and that a nationwide test would be unfair to students with limited English skills who may be learning at a different pace.

But on most education issues, Rodriguez is squarely in the Democratic mainstream, voicing strong opposition to a GOP plan to provide some parents with vouchers to help pay their child's tuition at a school of their choice. "Vouchers are not the answer. Abandoning our public schools will only make it worse," he said. Instead, he said, Congress should concentrate on ensuring that teachers are well-trained and have the resources that enable them to do their jobs. Rodriguez's wife is an elementary school librarian in San Antonio.

Rodriguez has seats on the Armed Services and Veterans' Affairs committees, where he can look out for the military bases and personnel in his district. Rodriguez met privately with Defense Secretary William S. Cohen in 2000 as they flew to San Antonio, where Cohen announced that the Pentagon would not require local officials to make a $103 million payment to acquire portions of the soon-to-be-closed Kelly Air Force Base.

Many of Rodriguez's constituents work at Kelly's aircraft maintenance depot, which is just across district lines in the neighboring 20th District. The base was ordered closed in the 1995 round of military base closings. Rodriguez and his Texas allies were generally dissatisfied in the 105th Congress with plans for privatization of the base, although President Clinton did promise a package of economic aid for San Antonio to help soften the impact.

In the 106th Congress, Rodriguez continued his efforts to help local officials convert Kelly's military work to jobs in the private sector. Rodriguez says he hopes to replace the 10,000-plus military jobs with even better-paying civilian ones for such aerospace firms as Boeing, Lockheed Martin and Pratt and Whitney.

CAPITOL OFFICE
225-1640; fax 225-1641; 323 Cannon Bldg. 20515

INTERNET
e-mail: www.house.gov/writerep
web: www.house.gov/rodriguez

COMMITTEES
Armed Services
Veterans' Affairs

HOMETOWN
San Antonio

BORN
Dec. 9, 1946, Piedras Negras, Mexico

RELIGION
Roman Catholic

FAMILY
Wife, Carolina Pena; one child

EDUCATION
St. Mary's U. (Texas), B.A. 1973; Our Lady of the Lake U., M.S.W. 1978

CAREER
Social worker; social work instructor

POLITICAL HIGHLIGHTS
Harlandale School Board, 1975-87; Texas House, 1987-97

ELECTION RESULTS

2000 GENERAL

Ciro D. Rodriguez (D)	123,104	89.0%
William Stallknecht (LIBERT)	15,156	11.0%

2000 PRIMARY

Ciro D. Rodriguez (D)	unopposed

1998 GENERAL

Ciro D. Rodriguez (D)	71,849	90.5%
Edward Elmer (LIBERT)	7,504	9.5%

PREVIOUS WINNING PERCENTAGES
1997 Special Runoff Election (67%); 1997 Special Election (46%)

In the 106th Congress, Rodriguez came to the defense of the Immigration and Naturalization Service and the Customs Service in light of law enforcement probes of corruption and bribe-taking among border officials. Rodriguez laid much of the blame on Congress for refusing to provide adequate funding for both agencies and said that the actions of a few border guards should not tar the entire work force.

Rodriguez was born in Mexico to a family that often moved back and forth across the border as his father took a series of jobs working on large industrial refrigeration units. The family settled in the San Antonio area when Rodriguez was 3 years old. He became a U.S. citizen when he was 18. Of the six children in the family, he is the only one who attended college.

He entered college intending to be a pharmacist but soon turned to social work. He has held jobs helping heroin addicts and patients in mental health clinics. Rodriguez ran for the local school board because he felt that not enough was being done to help schools in poor areas. He served 12 years on the Harlandale school board and in 1987 moved up to the Texas House, where he continued to work to equalize school funding.

In 1997, when the 28th District's Democratic Rep. Frank Tejeda died after a two-year battle with brain cancer, Rodriguez decided to run for the seat. Tejeda's death provoked a scramble among 15 prospective successors, including nine Democrats. Rodriguez dominated the voting in the March special election, but his 46 percent share of the vote fell short of the majority required to win the seat outright.

In the April runoff, Rodriguez faced former San Antonio City Councilman Juan Solis, also a Democrat, who launched an aggressive challenge to Rodriguez, characterizing himself as Tejeda's true heir because he shared the former member's anti-abortion position.

But Rodriguez, who attended the same high school and college as Tejeda, attracted most of the support from fellow state legislators and prominent Democrats in city government. Rodriguez won the Democratic runoff handily, tantamount to election in the overwhelmingly Democratic stronghold.

In his 1998 re-election bid, Rodriguez easily defeated two Democratic primary opponents. The Republican Party did not field a candidate.

A long-running political feud between the Rodriguez and Tejeda families continued to simmer, however. For a while in 1999, Bexar County Commissioner Robert Tejeda, the late congressman's cousin, considered a challenge to Rodriguez in 2000. In the end, however, Rodriguez had no major party opposition.

KEY VOTES

2000

Yes Raise hourly minimum wage by $1 over two years

Yes Halt funding for U.S. mission in Kosovo unless European nations pay more

Yes Provide Medicare benefits to military retirees and their dependents

No Grant China permanent normal trade status

No Phase out estate, gift and trust taxes

No Prohibit implementation of president's national monument designations

No Approve GOP plan to provide prescription drug coverage for Medicare beneficiaries

Yes Increase help for poor nations indebted to international financial institutions

1999

Yes Impose steel import quotas

Yes Kill proposal to take aviation trust funds off budget

No Require background checks on buyers only at gun shows with 10 or more vendors

No Remove barriers among banking, securities and insurance companies

Yes Authorize state grants to hire teachers and reduce class size

Yes Overhaul campaign finance law; ban "soft money" and restrict advocacy advertising

Yes Approve bipartisan plan to increase rights of patients in managed-care health plans

INTEREST GROUPS

	AFL-CIO	ADA	CCUS	ACU
2000	100%	85%	50%	12%
1999	89%	100%	21%	8%
1998	100%	100%	39%	4%
1997	100%	75%	56%	26%

CQ VOTE STUDIES

	PARTY UNITY		PRESIDENTIAL SUPPORT	
	Support	Oppose	Support	Oppose
2000	94%	6%	84%	16%
1999	90%	10%	79%	21%
1998	92%	8%	81%	19%
1997	87%	13%	74%	26%

TEXAS 28
South San Antonio; Zapata

The 28th starts in southern San Antonio and heads south through brush country to the Mexico border. The district's population center is in the low- and middle-class communities of San Antonio, while the southern part of the district is mostly sparsely populated agricultural land. Residents in this Hispanic-majority district are among the least-educated in the nation and among the poorest in the state.

San Antonio's five military bases sustain the economy in the northern part of the 28th. The area faces a significant blow from the scheduled 2001 closure of Kelly Air Force Base, the largest base in the 20th and a major employer for the 28th's Hispanic residents.

But while other industries help keep San Antonio afloat, there is not much in the way of enterprise in the south, where the unemployment rate remains high.

Democrats do well in the 28th at every level. However, Republicans

have been elected in the white, middle-class suburbs of the northeast section of San Antonio. A large Catholic influence gives the 28th a socially conservative bent.

MAJOR INDUSTRY
Defense, agriculture, tourism

MILITARY BASES
Randolph Air Force Base, 4,164 military, 4,382 civilian; Brooks Air Force Base, 1,352 military, 1,342 civilian (1999)

CITIES
San Antonio (pt.), 279,283 (1990); Seguin (pt.), 15,890 (1990); Alice (pt.), 15,419 (1990)

UNUSUAL FEATURES
San Antonio Missions National Historical Park; Caro Brown, the first woman to win a Pulitzer Prize for journalism, worked at the Alice Daily News during the 1940s and '50s.

Rep. Gene Green (D)

CAPITOL OFFICE
225-1688; fax 225-9903; 2335 Rayburn Bldg. 20515

INTERNET
e-mail: ask.gene@mail.house.gov
web: www.house.gov/green

COMMITTEES
Energy & Commerce

HOMETOWN
Houston

BORN
Oct. 17, 1947, Houston, Texas

RELIGION
Methodist

FAMILY
Wife, Helen Albers Green; two children

EDUCATION
U. of Houston, B.B.A. 1971; Bates College of Law, attended 1971-77

CAREER
Lawyer

POLITICAL HIGHLIGHTS
Texas House, 1973-85; Texas Senate, 1985-92

ELECTION RESULTS

2000 GENERAL

Gene Green (D)	84,665	73.3%
Joe Vu (R)	29,606	25.6%
Ray E. Dittmar (LIBERT)	1,204	1.0%

2000 PRIMARY

Gene Green (D)	unopposed

1998 GENERAL

Gene Green (D)	44,179	92.8%
Lea Sherman (I)	2,013	4.2%
James P. Chudleigh (LIBERT)	1,439	3.0%

PREVIOUS WINNING PERCENTAGES
1996 (68%); 1994 (73%); 1992 (65%)

Elected 1992; 5th term

Green focuses his rhetoric on core Democratic issues: support for public education, expanded health care for senior citizens, federal programs to provide opportunities for minorities and the disadvantaged, and pocketbook concerns of the working class. Although he strays from the party line when it is time to vote on the environment, gun control, juvenile crime and public housing, he enjoys good relations with Democratic leaders, in part because he doesn't trumpet his differences with the party.

Green is part of a dwindling breed on Capitol Hill — the white Southern Democrat, whose numbers have dropped in the House from 62 in the 103rd Congress to just 34 as the 107th began.

He was given a seat on the Commerce (now Energy and Commerce) Committee in the 105th Congress, and Green uses that perch to look out for Texas interests in communications, health care and energy development. He also serves as a deputy whip, and he sits on the Democratic Steering Committee, which makes committee assignments.

Green grew up in a part of the 29th District called "Redneck Alley," home mostly to working-class whites. He represented the area in the Texas Legislature from 1973 until his run for Congress in a newly drawn 29th in 1992. As an Anglo representative of a largely Hispanic district (it had a Hispanic-majority population until 1996, when the Supreme Court ordered that it be redrawn), Green has to pay strict attention to constituent needs.

In the 106th, he pressed unsuccessfully for the Census Bureau to use statistical data to ensure that Hispanics and other minorities were not undercounted in the 2000 census. He has also derided efforts to declare English the official language of the United States. "This is a solution in search of a problem," he said of such an initiative in the 104th.

Green is a stalwart supporter of expanded health care. Signing on to a measure in the 106th to provide Medicaid and other benefits for pregnant women and children who are legal immigrants, he said: "Investing in the preventive services Medicaid provides saves taxpayers money in the long run." He also backs legislation to give managed-care patients more rights, including the power to sue their health care providers.

In his first two terms, he had a seat on the committee with jurisdiction over education, and that still ranks as his top priority. He is a strong defender of public education, often noting that his wife is a public school math teacher. Vouchers to help parents pay tuition for their children at private schools would do little good in his district, Green says: "We need to fix the problems of the millions and not the few." Instead, Green favors devoting federal funds to expand Head Start, to assist in the construction of new facilities and to train more teachers.

Unlike some of the more conservative members of his party, Green stands against GOP tax-cutting efforts. He voted against a popular Republican measure in the 106th that would have reduced taxes on married couples, saying that it "only benefits the wealthiest of Americans and does nothing to help the working folks in my district."

Trade issues are of particular interest to workers in his blue-collar district. Green voted against the North American Free Trade Agreement in the 103rd, despite support for the pact by Houston's business community. He also opposed a measure in 2000 granting China permanent normal trade status. Green has sided with organized labor by voting against legislation allowing employers to offer their workers compensatory time off instead of pay for overtime work.

But his support for Democratic positions stops just short of the level that would permit party leaders to take him for granted. He voted for GOP-sponsored legislation to toughen criminal penalties for violent juvenile offenders and to overhaul public housing policies. On environmental matters, Green often has sided with the Republican majority by opposing new Environmental Protection Agency clean air standards and backing bills to aid landowners in challenging zoning decisions.

He generally votes in favor of gun owners' rights, contending in 1999 that "adding more gun laws may sound good, but it is not necessarily effective." During a series of votes on regulating gun purchases and curbing youth violence in the 106th, he weighed in with social conservatives by supporting a measure that would have allowed the display of the Ten Commandments in public schools and government buildings.

The 29th is home to Houston's port and airport, and Green has worked to obtain funds for widening the Houston Ship Channel to the Gulf of Mexico and to secure expanded air service, particularly to Latin America. He is a strong supporter of NASA, an important Houston-area employer, and of its International Space Station project.

On the issue of abortion, Green's current view differs from his earlier position. In February 1992, a month before his first House primary, he dropped his longstanding opposition to abortion when he came under attack for having sponsored anti-abortion bills in the state legislature. Green said he had gradually come to alter his views on abortion, but critics said he had changed his mind to enhance his prospects of winning the 29th. In Congress, he has opposed Republican-led attempts to ban a procedure its opponents call "partial birth" abortion.

Green's district was created in 1992 after reapportionment gave Texas three more seats. The 29th's boundaries were drawn with an eye toward increasing Hispanic representation by crafting a map that had a 61 percent Hispanic population. In his first three campaigns, Green faced primary challenges from Hispanics who felt they could better represent the district.

He won a hard-fought five-way primary in 1992, besting Houston City Council member Ben Reyes in two runoffs — the first was voided after election officials discovered that some Republicans had illegally crossed over and cast ballots. Green then cruised to victory in the general election with 65 percent in the largely Democratic 29th. He has continued to strengthen his hold on the district, especially after the court-ordered redrawing of the 29th in 1996 reduced the number of Hispanic voters.

KEY VOTES

2000
Yes Raise hourly minimum wage by $1 over two years
Yes Halt funding for U.S. mission in Kosovo unless European nations pay more
Yes Provide Medicare benefits to military retirees and their dependents
No Grant China permanent normal trade status
No Phase out estate, gift and trust taxes
No Prohibit implementation of president's national monument designations
No Approve GOP plan to provide prescription drug coverage for Medicare beneficiaries
Yes Increase help for poor nations indebted to international financial institutions

1999
Yes Impose steel import quotas
No Kill proposal to take aviation trust funds off budget
No Require background checks on buyers only at gun shows with 10 or more vendors
+ Remove barriers among banking, securities and insurance companies
Yes Authorize state grants to hire teachers and reduce class size
Yes Overhaul campaign finance law; ban "soft money" and restrict advocacy advertising
Yes Approve bipartisan plan to increase rights of patients in managed-care health plans

INTEREST GROUPS

	AFL-CIO	ADA	CCUS	ACU
2000	100%	90%	33%	20%
1999	89%	70%	24%	26%
1998	100%	95%	47%	16%
1997	100%	75%	60%	42%

CQ VOTE STUDIES

	PARTY UNITY		PRESIDENTIAL SUPPORT	
	Support	Oppose	Support	Oppose
2000	81%	19%	69%	31%
1999	80%	20%	69%	31%
1998	86%	14%	71%	29%
1997	77%	23%	64%	36%

TEXAS 29

Southeast – Parts of Houston; Pasadena

Located on the eastern side of Houston's downtown, the 29th is a blue-collar, working-class district near refineries and factories that employ many union members. Beginning near Interstate 45, south of downtown, the district wraps around the city's core until it again reaches I-45 north of the downtown area.

Originally created as a Hispanic-majority district, the 29th has since been pared down so that Hispanics make up less than half of the population (as calculated with 1990 Census Bureau statistics). Plenty of traditionally Hispanic neighborhoods remain, however, along with a strip of suburbia north of Houston. Although turnout is usually low, the 29th's voters fall solidly in the Democratic column, usually giving Democrats a 20-percent margin in elections.

In the bottom half of the district, near Interstate 10, are working-class areas such as Jacinto City, Galena Park and most of Channelview. Communities along the district's southern border include South

Houston and part of Pasadena. The Houston Ship Channel, a major shipping route that has seen increased business since the introduction of the NAFTA and GATT trade agreements, is also partially included in the district.

The 29th's northern chunk, which is generally bound by the road FM 1960, includes the George Bush Intercontinental Aiport, a source of employment for many district residents. The 29th rivals the neighboring 18th in poverty and has one of the lowest percentages of college-educated residents in the state.

MAJOR INDUSTRY
Chemicals, energy, construction

CITIES
Houston (pt.), 317,907 (1990); Pasadena (pt.), 42,141 (1990); Cloverleaf (unincorporated), 18,230 (1990)

UNUSUAL FEATURES
The Port of Houston is the eighth-busiest in the nation; More than 40 percent of the district's residents speak a language other than English.

Rep. Eddie Bernice Johnson (D)

Elected 1992; 5th term

CAPITOL OFFICE
225-8885; fax 226-1477
1511 Longworth Bldg. 20515

INTERNET
e-mail: rep.e.b.johnson@mail.house.gov
web: www.house.gov/ebjohnson

COMMITTEES
Science
Transportation & Infrastructure

HOMETOWN
Dallas

BORN
Dec. 3, 1935, Waco, Texas

RELIGION
Baptist

FAMILY
Divorced; one child

EDUCATION
Texas Christian U., B.S. 1967; Southern Methodist
U., M.P.A. 1976

CAREER
Business relocation company owner; nurse; U.S.
Health, Education & Welfare Department official

POLITICAL HIGHLIGHTS
Texas House, 1973-77; Texas Senate, 1987-93

ELECTION RESULTS

2000 GENERAL

Eddie Bernice Johnson (D)	109,163	91.8%
Kelly Rush (LIBERT)	9,798	8.2%

2000 PRIMARY

Eddie Bernice Johnson (D)	unopposed

1998 GENERAL

Eddie Bernice Johnson (D)	57,603	72.2%
Carrie Kelleher (R)	21,338	26.8%
Barbara L. Robinson (LIBERT)	811	1.0%

PREVIOUS WINNING PERCENTAGES
1996 (55%); 1994 (73%); 1992 (72%)

Johnson is a strong-minded veteran of Texas politics. A trailblazer for women and blacks in the 1970s, she became adept enough at wielding power in the state legislature that she moved up to the U.S. House in 1992 by drawing a district preordained to elect her. She is the first black elected official to represent Dallas in Congress.

At the beginning of the 107th Congress, she was elected to chair the 38-member Congressional Black Caucus. With many caucus members openly questioning whether George W. Bush fairly won the closely contested 2000 presidential election, Johnson immediately pledged to focus on voting issues. "We saw a real travesty that occurred this election," Johnson said at the beginning of her term. "We will continue to make sure people can vote without intimidation."

Johnson's views on many social policy issues — such as abortion rights, welfare and health care — are typically liberal. But her votes on trade and economic development, issues important to her district, are more in line with centrist Democrats and Republicans.

Johnson was trained as a nurse, and she worked for a time as the chief psychiatric nurse at the Veteran's Administration Hospital in Dallas. She won her first state House election in 1972, serving as a legislator until she resigned in 1977 to work as regional director for the Department of Health, Education and Welfare in the Carter administration. Next she turned to private business, setting up Eddie Bernice Johnson and Associates, which helped businesses expand or relocate in the Dallas-Fort Worth area. She continued to operate the business after her 1986 election to the state Senate, and she expanded it in 1988 to include airport concessions management.

Perhaps because of her business background, Johnson has cast some significant pro-business votes in Congress. Breaking ranks with organized labor, she supported legislation in 2000 granting China permanent normal trade status. "If America is serious about helping the Chinese people, we must engage China through a variety of avenues, including commerce," Johnson contended. "Trade with China means jobs for North Texas, growth for Dallas-Fort Worth and the export of American values to the world's most populous nation."

Johnson also came to the defense of Microsoft Corp. in 2000 as the company was battling a government antitrust plan to split it in two. "Instead of focusing on bringing down [Microsoft founder] Bill Gates, we need to invest in resources to create more Bill Gateses," she said. Johnson's comments drew some media attention because Gates had donated vast sums for minority scholarships and Microsoft made a contribution to the Congressional Black Caucus Foundation. But the congresswoman denied any quid pro quo.

Johnson has yet to make it to a top House committee, even after a vigorous effort to gain a spot on Ways and Means in the 105th. But she busies herself on other committees that give her opportunities to fight for projects important to her district.

When the Transportation Committee took up a massive public works bill in the 105th, she won many projects important to the 30th District, including widening a stretch of Interstate 30 and repairing the Houston Street Viaduct, a historic bridge over the Trinity River in Dallas. Critics charged that the bill was stuffed with special projects that pandered to narrow constituencies. Johnson, however, defended projects such as those she was touting for the

Dallas area, saying, "That is not pork. That is working and listening to people at home who know best what their communities want and need."

Spurring economic development and job growth is a priority for Johnson, as minority unemployment is a big concern. The jobs argument helped sway her to support production of additional B-2 stealth bombers, a stand that united her with many Republicans and put her at odds with fellow liberals in the Black Caucus. Johnson argued that the B-2 is a cost-effective way to save lives, and she noted that during production of the first set of B-2 bombers, Northrop Grumman employed about 6,000 people at a plant in her district.

On most matters, though, Johnson sees little to like in the GOP agenda. She opposes conservatives' efforts to ban a procedure its opponents call "partial birth" abortion, and she has fought a number of GOP proposals she felt would limit or repeal labor protections. In the 106th, she pressed for a number of gun safety plans, including mandating that child safety locks be included in all gun sales. "It's so simple, but it's a long distance between having these and having a life lost," she said.

She has spoken out on shortcomings in Medicare and in the nation's health care system as a whole. In 1998, she hosted a forum in her district to help constituents cope with sometimes misleading information about changes in Medicare policies. Also, she joined several women in Congress in sponsoring a bill calling for more research funding for osteoporosis, a bone density deficiency that affects elderly women. On the Science Committee, she has lobbied for a federal grant program to encourage children to study math and science.

During the 104th, Johnson received some unfavorable publicity about staffing and campaign finance problems. She was fined $44,000 by the Federal Election Commission for failing to file timely and accurate disclosure statements during her 1992 campaign. Her top aide quit, alleging that Johnson required the staff to perform personal errands and engage in campaign activities during office hours. Another staffer sued the House and settled for $28,000, alleging she was terminated because of her pregnancy.

Johnson easily won her 1992 and 1994 House campaigns, but then her electoral fate was caught up in the judicial and legislative wrangling at the state and national level over minority-majority House districts, including the 30th. After the U.S. Supreme Court in 1996 threw out certain House districts in Texas as "racial gerrymanders," Johnson landed in a substantially redrawn district that was 42 percent new to her. But she captured a 55 percent majority in an eight-person contest and her last two re-elections have been by huge margins.

KEY VOTES

2000

?	Raise hourly minimum wage by $1 over two years
No	Halt funding for U.S. mission in Kosovo unless European nations pay more
Yes	Provide Medicare benefits to military retirees and their dependents
Yes	Grant China permanent normal trade status
No	Phase out estate, gift and trust taxes
No	Prohibit implementation of president's national monument designations
No	Approve GOP plan to provide prescription drug coverage for Medicare beneficiaries
Yes	Increase help for poor nations indebted to international financial institutions

1999

Yes	Impose steel import quotas
No	Kill proposal to take aviation trust funds off budget
No	Require background checks on buyers only at gun shows with 10 or more vendors
Yes	Remove barriers among banking, securities and insurance companies
Yes	Authorize state grants to hire teachers and reduce class size
Yes	Overhaul campaign finance law; ban "soft money" and restrict advocacy advertising
Yes	Approve bipartisan plan to increase rights of patients in managed-care health plans

INTEREST GROUPS

	AFL-CIO	ADA	CCUS	ACU
2000	88%	75%	57%	9%
1999	78%	90%	36%	0%
1998	89%	90%	47%	4%
1997	100%	85%	40%	16%

CQ VOTE STUDIES

	PARTY UNITY		PRESIDENTIAL SUPPORT	
	Support	Oppose	Support	Oppose
2000	95%	5%	88%	12%
1999	93%	7%	81%	19%
1998	93%	7%	86%	14%
1997	89%	11%	79%	21%

TEXAS 30
Downtown Dallas; part of Irving

After it was declared unconstitutionally gerrymandered by a federal court, the 30th was redrawn in 1996 and is now confined to Dallas County. Shaped like a tilted "S," the 30th now stretches from the Dallas-Fort Worth International Airport southeast through Irving and downtown Dallas, then curves southwest to take in Lancaster, part of Grand Prairie and the DeSoto suburbs.

The area lost some of its black population during redistricting but, at 45 percent, blacks still hold a plurality in the 30th (as calculated with 1990 Census Bureau statistics). There has been a rise in Asian and Indian populations due to corporate expansions. As the population grows, road congestion and air pollution have become concerns. Leaders hope that a recent expansion of the city's light rail system into the suburbs will alleviate some of the problems.

Once a quiet suburb, Irving boomed in the 1980s and '90s. The massive Exxon Mobil Corp. made its corporate home here in late 1999 when

Irving-based Exxon completed the biggest corporate union ever, with revenues of $171 billion in 1998. The city has been growing fast enough that officials decided in 1999 to overturn Irving's more than 20-year refusal of public housing money, which had been based on concerns over what federal strings would accompany the funds.

The 30th is overwhelmingly Democratic at both national and local levels. Despite a large blue-collar population in Dallas, the city's banking industry and corporations make it fiscally conservative on many issues. Downtown Dallas tends to be moderate to liberal on social issues, while suburbs like Irving are more conservative.

MAJOR INDUSTRY
Banking, technology, transportation

CITIES
Dallas (pt.), 382,478 (1990); Irving (pt.), 155,589 (1990)

UNUSUAL FEATURES
Dealey Plaza and Texas School Book Depository, where President Kennedy was assassinated in 1963; State Fair of Texas attracts 3 million people and features Big Tex – the world's only 52-foot-tall talking cowboy.

UTAH

Gov. Michael O. Leavitt (R)

First elected: 1992
Length of term: 4 years
Term expires: 1/05
Salary: $96,700
Phone: (801) 538-1000
Hometown: Cedar City
Born: Feb. 11, 1951; Cedar City, Utah
Religion: Mormon
Family: Wife, Jacalyn Leavitt; five children
Education: Southern Utah U., B.A. 1978
Military Service: Utah National Guard, 1969-75
Career: Insurance executive
Political highlights: Utah Board of Regents, 1989-92

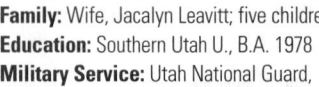

Election results:

2000 GENERAL

Michael O. Leavitt (R)	424,837	55.8%
Bill Orton (D)	321,979	42.3%
Jeremy Friedbaum (IA)	14,990	2.0%

Lt. Gov. Olene S. Walker (R)

First elected: 1992
Length of term: 4 years
Term expires: 1/05
Salary: $75,200
Phone: (801) 538-1040

STATE LEGISLATURE

Legislature: Meets 45 days yearly, January-March
House: 75 members, 2-year terms
2001 breakdown: 51R, 24D; 57 men, 18 women
Salary: $120/day in session
Phone: (801) 538-1029
Senate: 29 members, 4-year terms
2001 breakdown: 20R, 9D; 24 men, 5 women
Salary: $120/day in session
Phone: (801) 538-1035

STATE TERM LIMITS

Governor: 3 consecutive terms (beginning with the 1996 election; Leavitt can run in 2004)
Senate: 3 terms
House: 6 terms

URBAN STATISTICS

CITY	POPULATION
Salt Lake City	171,151
Provo	110,690
West Valley City	102,718
Sandy	101,853
Orem	82,965

REGISTERED VOTERS

Voters do not register by party.

POPULATION

2000 population	2,233,169
1990 population	1,722,850
Percent change	+29.6%
Rank among states	34

Median age	26.9
Born in state	67%
Foreign born	3%
Urban/rural	87%/13%
Crime rate	334/100,000
Poverty level	9.0%
Federal workers	30,620
Military	16,037

REAPPORTIONMENT

Utah retained its three House seats in reapportionment. The state legislature will draw new district lines.

MISCELLANEOUS

Web: www.state.ut.us
Capital: Salt Lake City
Land area: 82,168 sq. miles
Rank among states: 12
STATE ELECTION OFFICIAL
(801) 538-1041
DEMOCRATIC HEADQUARTERS
(801) 328-1212
REPUBLICAN HEADQUARTERS
(801) 533-9777

District Statistics

DIST.	VOTE FOR PRESIDENT 2000 D	2000 R	GREEN	1996 D	1996 R	REF	1992 D	1992 R	I	WHT	BLK	ASIAN	HISP	HOUSEHOLD INCOME	OVER 65+	UNDER 18	COLLEGE EDUCATION
1	22%	72%	3%	29%	59%	10%	22%	49%	29%	94%	1%	2%	5%	$30,563	9%	37%	21%
2	34	57	7	41	47	9	31	39	29	94	1	2	5	$30,960	9	34	27
3	23	72	3	29	58	10	24	49	27	93	0	2	5	$26,570	8	38	19
STATE	26	67	5	33	54	10	25	43	27	94	1	2	5	$29,470	9	37	22

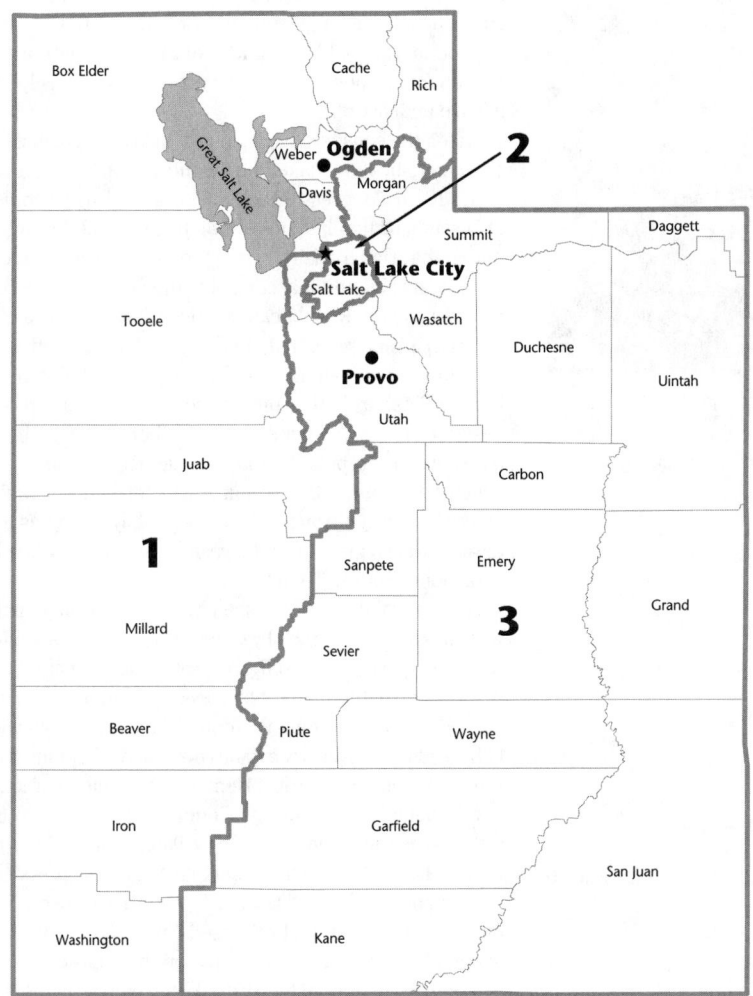

Sen. Orrin G. Hatch (R)

CAPITOL OFFICE
224-5251; fax 224-6331; 104 Hart Bldg. 20510

INTERNET
e-mail: senator_hatch@hatch.senate.gov
web: hatch.senate.gov

COMMITTEES
Finance
 (International Trade - chairman)
Indian Affairs
Judiciary - chairman
Select Intelligence
Joint Taxation

HOMETOWN
Salt Lake City

BORN
March 22, 1934, Pittsburgh, Pa.

RELIGION
Mormon

FAMILY
Wife, Elaine Hatch; six children

EDUCATION
Brigham Young U., B.S. 1959; U. of Pittsburgh, J.D. 1962

CAREER
Lawyer

POLITICAL HIGHLIGHTS
Sought Republican nomination for president, 2000

ELECTION RESULTS

2000 GENERAL

Orrin G. Hatch (R)	504,803	65.6%
Scott N. Howell (D)	242,569	31.5%
Carlton E. Bowen (AMI)	11,938	1.6%
Jim Dexter (LIBERT)	10,394	1.4%

2000 PRIMARY

Orrin G. Hatch (R)	unopposed

PREVIOUS WINNING PERCENTAGES
1994 (69%); 1988 (67%); 1982 (58%); 1976 (54%)

Elected 1976; 5th term

His high-collared shirts and his nearly perfect voting record on the issues conservative groups watch intently give Hatch the outward appearance of rigid ideologue, someone unlikely to look for compromise. But Hatch also has a longstanding friendship with the Senate's leading liberal Democrat, Edward M. Kennedy of Massachusetts, a relationship that confounds many conservatives in part because it has led to several joint legislative endeavors.

Hatch the conservative is, in fact, also a pragmatist by nature. The latter characteristic may make him a central figure in the evenly divided Senate of the 107th Congress. Much of President Bush's domestic agenda — and all his judicial nominations — will be funneled through the Judiciary Committee that Hatch chairs. Except for 17 days at the start of 2001, when the Democrats had nominal control of the Senate, Hatch has chaired the committee since the Republican takeover of Congress in 1995.

Hatch is more tolerant than many GOP conservatives of government support for the poor, an outlook that may be rooted in his childhood. He was born in Pittsburgh, the son of a metal lather. His Senate website biography describes the Hatch family losing its home during the Depression and his father having to build another house using lumber retrieved from a fire. Hatch remembers that a dairy sign formed one wall of the house. He worked his way through school, variously toiling as a janitor, an all-night desk clerk in a girls' dormitory, and a metal lather like his father. As a lather, he joined the AFL-CIO.

As an adult, the straight-laced Mormon is a singer and songwriter whose work has been performed by Gladys Knight. He has produced or co-produced seven compact discs of religious, romantic and patriotic songs, and he even hawked one of them on cable television's Home Shopping Network in 1997. He dedicated a love song to Kennedy and his second wife, Victoria, on their fifth wedding anniversary and has dedicated other tunes to Mother Teresa and Princess Diana. Hatch's involvement in the entertainment business has given him a unique perspective as Congress grapples with intellectual property rights issues, including the free availability of music over the Internet.

In 1999, Hatch launched a quixotic bid for the presidency. Lacking money and support, he finished last in Iowa's GOP caucuses. He dropped out of the race the next week and endorsed Bush. Some maintain that his run was intended to position him for a spot on the Supreme Court in a Bush administration. At the start of the 107th, Hatch enhanced his standing with the new president by shepherding to confirmation Bush's most controversial Cabinet nominee, Attorney General John Ashcroft, a staunch conservative.

As Judiciary chairman, Hatch has shown a talent for finding compromise on thorny legislative questions, such as how Congress should rewrite the rules by which law enforcement officers seize property they believe was used in a crime. Rep. Henry J. Hyde, R-Ill., who was House Judiciary Committee chairman from 1995 through 2000, had made the issue a personal crusade for more than seven years, believing it should be more difficult for the government to seize private property. Hatch helped bridge the divide between Hyde and the Clinton administration, which did not want to weaken the law enforcement tool, and found a compromise that became law in 2000.

But sometimes, walking the line between different points of view has cost the lawmaker. During the last six years of President Clinton's tenure, Hatch was criticized by other Republicans, who said he was allowing too many liberals to take seats on federal district and appeals courts. Hatch seldom voted against a nominee and often lectured from the committee dais about the need for an independent judiciary that included liberal thinkers as well as conservative ones. In 1997, Republican hard-liners intent on limiting Clinton's influence over the judiciary tried, but ultimately failed, to strip Hatch of many of his powers in considering judicial nominees. But Democrats attacked him on this issue as well, saying Hatch unfairly delayed scores of nominations, particularly those of minorities and women, a charge that Hatch angrily denied.

Hatch's divergence from the Republican mainstream has frequently annoyed his colleagues. After Kenneth W. Starr, an independent counsel, submitted a report to Congress in 1998 outlining 11 possible grounds for impeaching Clinton, Hatch suggested censure or rebuke as a preferable punishment, directly contravening Republican Party orthodoxy. In the end, Hatch voted in 1999 to convict Clinton on both articles of impeachment considered by the Senate.

One 1997 partnership with Kennedy — a proposal to provide insurance to children whose low-income parents did not qualify for Medicaid, and to pay for the plan with a 43-cent-a-pack cigarette tax increase — really provoked Republicans' ire. American Conservative Union Chairman David Keene accused Hatch of "helping liberals derail the conservative agenda" and said the proposal "offers more evidence that, unfortunately, [Hatch's] reputation as a bona fide conservative is slowly eroding."

Hatch and Kennedy boiled their argument down to a choice between tobacco companies and a boy named Joey, whose photo appeared on materials they used to buttress their pitch. "Who do you stand with, Joe Camel or Joey?" Hatch asked. Ultimately, their proposal was killed.

In this and other instances, Hatch's tendency to reach across party lines rankles some GOP activists. They question whether he has been too quick to strike deals and too slow to go to the mat for their most cherished causes. Hatch dismisses the criticisms, showing a personality trait one does not associate with ideologues. "One of my biggest failings is that ... I can't hold a grudge," he told the National Review in 1997. "I can't stay mad."

Before becoming Judiciary chairman, Hatch typically struck a more aggressively partisan posture on legal matters, as he demonstrated during the 1991 confirmation of Clarence Thomas for the Supreme Court. Hatch argued against reopening the panel's hearings even after the sexual harassment accusation against Thomas was made public. Once Anita Hill's allegations were aired, Hatch and Arlen Specter of Pennsylvania led the hard-hitting Republican assault on the charges before a national television audience.

Hatch's first Senate campaign in 1976 was a textbook example of anti-Washington politics, in which his lack of government experience at any level almost certainly helped. In his legal practice, he had represented clients fighting federal regulations and sensed that Utah was fed up with Washington's rulemaking; this became the centerpiece of a campaign in which he first won the GOP nomination over Jack W. Carlson, a former assistant secretary of interior, and then defeated incumbent Democrat Frank E. Moss with 54 percent.

Although he came under attack for being rigid in both his conservative views and his personal style, he won re-election in 1982 with 58 percent against Ted Wilson, a two-term mayor of Salt Lake City. He took 67 percent in 1988 against Brian Moss, son of the senator he had ousted, even though he drew national attention with a speech in which he said Democrats were "the party that has, basically, I think, denigrated a lot of the values that have made this country the greatest country in the world." His two subsequent re-elections have been by similarly large margins.

KEY VOTES

2000
Yes Overhaul bankruptcy law and increase minimum wage
Yes Limit fiscal 2001 discretionary spending to $600.3 billion
Yes Override veto on nuclear waste disposal at Yucca Mountain site in Nevada
Yes Oppose effort to terminate Kosovo mission
No   Include gender, sexual orientation and disability in federal hate crime protections
Yes Approve GOP plan to restrict use of genetic information by health insurers
Yes Kill amendment delaying implementation of an anti-missile defense system
Yes Cut taxes for married couples
Yes Grant China permanent normal trade status

1999
Yes Remove President Clinton from office for obstruction of justice
Yes Kill amendment authorizing state grants to hire teachers and reduce class size
No   Require criminal background checks for purchases at gun shows
Yes Approve GOP proposal to increase rights of patients in managed-care health plans
No   Block effort to allow farm and medicine exports to Cuba
No   Allow study of tougher automobile fuel efficiency standards
No   Ratify nuclear weapons testing treaty
No   Prohibit national political parties from collecting "soft money" donations
Yes Remove barriers among banking, securities and insurance companies

INTEREST GROUPS

	AFL-CIO	ADA	CCUS	ACU
2000	0%	0%	100%	95%
1999	11%	0%	88%	84%
1998	0%	5%	94%	80%
1997	0%	15%	100%	68%
1996	0%	5%	92%	100%
1995	0%	0%	100%	83%
1994	0%	5%	90%	100%
1993	0%	5%	100%	88%
1992	17%	5%	100%	96%
1991	25%	10%	90%	86%

CQ VOTE STUDIES

	PARTY UNITY		PRESIDENTIAL SUPPORT	
	Support	Oppose	Support	Oppose
2000	94%	6%	55%	45%
1999	92%	8%	30%	70%
1998	87%	13%	48%	52%
1997	87%	13%	63%	37%
1996	94%	6%	32%	68%
1995	95%	5%	27%	73%
1994	95%	5%	37%	63%
1993	96%	4%	28%	72%
1992	95%	5%	88%	12%
1991	93%	7%	92%	8%

Sen. Robert F. Bennett (R)

Elected 1992; 2nd term

Bennett bears an uncanny resemblance to a man who was in the Senate 30 years ago — his father, Wallace F. Bennett, who served from 1951 through 1974. The son is taller, but otherwise looks and acts in much the same manner as his father. He is a deliberate speaker who measures his words carefully, often using homespun humor to get his point across. He tends to be a reserved and quiet man.

Bennett's slow and steady approach has made him a trusted adviser to top Senate leaders. His thoughtful demeanor also helps him reach across party lines. Although he failed in a bid to join the GOP leadership in the shuffle that came about when Majority Leader Bob Dole departed in 1996, Bennett won appointments to chair both the seven-member Senate Special Committee on the Year 2000 Technology Problem and a task force on congressional reorganization.

And in the 106th Congress, Majority Leader Trent Lott appointed the Utahn to head the Senate GOP's High Tech Task Force, to advise other senators on technology issues. In 2000, Bennett proudly displayed his new, high-tech car, a gasoline-electric hybrid that gets more than 60 miles per gallon with low emissions.

Although a staunch conservative, especially on regulatory and fiscal issues, Bennett breaks party ranks on occasion. He supports funding for the National Endowment for the Arts and opposes a constitutional amendment to ban desecration of the U.S. flag. On the latter issue, he contends, "If we start the precedent of amending the Constitution every time there is a Supreme Court decision with which we disagree, we run the risk of seeing the Constitution turned into something other than basic law."

But Bennett joins with other conservative Western Republicans who accuse federal land-management agencies and environmentalists of waging a "war on the West." He expressed outrage in the late 1990s and 2000 when President Clinton repeatedly used his executive authority to create national monuments in Utah and other Western states, thereby blocking mining and ranching on those lands.

Although usually amiable, Bennett has engaged in some pointed exchanges with Arizona Republican John McCain. When McCain in 1999 alleged that campaign contributions had corrupted the political system, Bennett said that McCain had accused him of corruption in seeking federal funds for Utah. "I am unaware of any money given that influenced my action here," he said. "I have been accused of being corrupt. ... I take personal offense."

Joining with GOP leaders in the 106th Congress, Bennett also battled McCain's efforts to pass legislation overhauling campaign laws. He cast his arguments in highly personal terms, saying his father, also a senator from Utah, was not corrupt even though he had accepted an envelope with $5,000 of cash as a campaign donation. "Those who are corrupt will be corrupt regardless of the system," he said. "And those who are not corrupt will not be corrupt regardless of the system."

But Bennett had one abiding focus late in 1998 and 1999 — the conversion of computer systems for the new millennium. "I've become immersed in this," he said in a 1998 speech. "It has become my obsession."

Bennett saw his task as ensuring that government agencies and private companies did everything possible to revamp their technological systems before Jan. 1, 2000, when the much-anticipated Y2K problem threatened to

CAPITOL OFFICE
224-5444; fax 224-4908; 431 Dirksen Bldg. 20510

INTERNET
e-mail: senator@bennett.senate.gov
web: bennett.senate.gov

COMMITTEES
Appropriations
  (Legislative Branch - chairman)
Banking, Housing & Urban Affairs
  (Financial Institutions - chairman)
Governmental Affairs
Small Business
Joint Economic

HOMETOWN
Salt Lake City

BORN
Sept. 18, 1933, Salt Lake City, Utah

RELIGION
Mormon

FAMILY
Wife, Joyce Bennett; six children

EDUCATION
U. of Utah, B.S. 1957

CAREER
Time management company CEO; management consultant

POLITICAL HIGHLIGHTS
No previous office

ELECTION RESULTS

1998 GENERAL

Robert F. Bennett (R)	316,652	64.0%
Scott Leckman (D)	163,172	33.0%
Gary R. Van Horn (IA)	15,073	3.0%

1998 PRIMARY

Robert F. Bennett (R)	unopposed

PREVIOUS WINNING PERCENTAGES
1992 (55%)

cause computer systems to fail.

To that end, he won enactment of legislation in 1998 that encouraged U.S. businesses to share information about year 2000 solutions and established a government year 2000 website on the matter.

Although he tried not to be alarmist (the year 2000 conversion "will not be the end of the world as we know it," he said), he urged people to take all possible precautions. His own website included tips such as checking with police, doctors, pharmacists and grocers about their services, and keeping batteries, warm blankets and "a couple of extra cans of food" on hand.

Since Y2K came and went with few problems, Bennett has continued his focus on computers. In 2000, Lott named him to head up a cyber security working group. After a virus known as the "love bug" played havoc with computer systems in 2000, he urged that the government beef up security measures. The virus "demonstrates several weaknesses in our government's ability to detect and respond to fast-moving cyber events in a coordinated and efficient manner," he said.

Bennett also has become an advocate for medical privacy. He introduced a bill in the 106th Congress to give patients the right to inspect and copy their health and treatment information, and to clarify that they can revoke the permission to use their medical records. The federal standard would pre-empt state laws. "There is an increasingly urgent need for uniformity in our laws that govern access to and disclosure of personal health information," he said.

On the Appropriations Committee, Bennett is adept at looking out for his state. He struck gold in the 105th Congress by winning $640 million for light rail, park-and-ride lots and buses for the 2002 Winter Olympics in Salt Lake City, plus additional funding for security planning. He also scored a victory with the enactment of legislation that provides $50 million for Utah public schools in exchange for federal government acquisition of more than 363,000 acres of state-owned land. In the 107th, he continued to ensure the flow of federal aid to Utah as the Olympics approached.

Bennett, who became head of a task force on congressional reorganization in the 105th, has an interest in administrative issues. In 1993, he proposed legislation, which was never acted on, to reorganize congressional committees, adopt a two-year budget cycle and establish congressional task forces to set priorities for legislative action.

Although Bennett's successful 1992 Senate bid at age 59 was his first campaign, he was no political naif. He had previously worked in Washington as a White House adviser to President Nixon and had run some of his father's Senate campaigns. He also was a millionaire businessman who made his fortune with the Franklin Day Planner, a schedule organizer, when he launched his first electoral bid.

He edged past steel company executive Joe Cannon (brother of 3rd District Rep. Christopher B. Cannon) by 3 percentage points in the GOP primary and faced Democratic Rep. Wayne Owens in the general election. Bennett's connection with the 1972 Watergate break-in became an issue because he bought a public relations firm that employed E. Howard Hunt, who was indicted in the Watergate burglary. Bennett said he fired Hunt after the scandal. He also denied rumors that he was "Deep Throat," the informant who guided Washington Post reporters to the heart of the Watergate issue.

Bennett raised $4.5 million and outspent Owens, by a ratio of more than 2-to-1, en route to a 15-point victory. In fact, Bennett overdid his 1992 fundraising. In 1996, he agreed to pay a $55,000 fine to the Federal Election Commission for what he called "unintentional violations" during the 1992 campaign.

In 1998, he raised more than five times as much as the Democrat, surgeon Scott Leckman, and won with 64 percent of the vote.

KEY VOTES

2000
Yes Overhaul bankruptcy law and increase minimum wage
Yes Limit fiscal 2001 discretionary spending to $600.3 billion
Yes Override veto on nuclear waste disposal at Yucca Mountain site in Nevada
No Oppose effort to terminate Kosovo mission
No Include gender, sexual orientation and disability in federal hate crime protections
Yes Approve GOP plan to restrict use of genetic information by health insurers
Yes Kill amendment delaying implementation of an anti-missile defense system
Yes Cut taxes for married couples
Yes Grant China permanent normal trade status

1999
Yes Remove President Clinton from office for obstruction of justice
Yes Kill amendment authorizing state grants to hire teachers and reduce class size
No Require criminal background checks for purchases at gun shows
Yes Approve GOP proposal to increase rights of patients in managed-care health plans
No Block effort to allow farm and medicine exports to Cuba
No Allow study of tougher automobile fuel efficiency standards
No Ratify nuclear weapons testing treaty
No Prohibit national political parties from collecting "soft money" donations
Yes Remove barriers among banking, securities and insurance companies

INTEREST GROUPS

	AFL-CIO	ADA	CCUS	ACU
2000	0%	5%	100%	95%
1999	11%	0%	94%	84%
1998	0%	10%	89%	64%
1997	0%	10%	100%	68%
1996	0%	5%	92%	95%
1995	0%	0%	100%	81%
1994	0%	5%	90%	100%
1993	0%	5%	100%	88%

CQ VOTE STUDIES

	PARTY UNITY		PRESIDENTIAL SUPPORT	
	Support	Oppose	Support	Oppose
2000	92%	8%	52%	48%
1999	93%	7%	31%	69%
1998	84%	16%	53%	47%
1997	87%	13%	62%	38%
1996	92%	8%	36%	64%
1995	96%	4%	27%	73%
1994	91%	9%	38%	62%
1993	94%	6%	32%	68%

Rep. James V. Hansen (R)

Elected 1980; 11th term

CAPITOL OFFICE
225-0453; fax 225-5857; 242 Cannon Bldg. 20515

INTERNET
e-mail: www.house.gov/writerep
web: www.house.gov/hansen

COMMITTEES
Armed Services
Resources - chairman

HOMETOWN
Farmington

BORN
Aug. 14, 1932, Salt Lake City, Utah

RELIGION
Mormon

FAMILY
Wife, Ann Hansen; five children

EDUCATION
U. of Utah, B.S. 1960

MILITARY SERVICE
Navy, 1951-53

CAREER
Insurance executive; developer

POLITICAL HIGHLIGHTS
Farmington City Council, 1960-72; Utah House, 1973-81 (Speaker, 1979-81)

ELECTION RESULTS

2000 GENERAL

James V. Hansen (R)	180,591	69.0%
Kathleen McConkie (D)	71,229	27.2%
Hartley D. Anderson (IA)	5,131	2.0%
Dave S. Seely (LIBERT)	3,151	1.2%

2000 PRIMARY

James V. Hansen (R)	unopposed

1998 GENERAL

James V. Hansen (R)	109,708	67.7%
Steve Beierlein (D)	49,307	30.4%
Gerard A. Arthus (LIBERT)	3,070	1.9%

PREVIOUS WINNING PERCENTAGES
1996 (68%); 1994 (65%); 1992 (65%); 1990 (52%); 1988 (60%); 1986 (52%); 1984 (71%); 1982 (63%); 1980 (52%)

Mild-mannered yet blunt-talking at times, Hansen easily switches between his status as a respected consensus builder and his role as a fierce advocate for Westerners' land-use concerns. He has been trusted by GOP leaders over the years to handle tough jobs, including several stints on the House ethics committee.

Hansen took up the Resources Committee gavel at the start of the 107th Congress and with it the responsibility for presiding over debates that pit Western property rights defenders and resource-based businesses against conservation-minded Democrats and moderate Republicans. A former chairman of the Western Caucus, Hansen has backed efforts to ease environmental restrictions on the timber and mining industries, and he generally supports reducing government regulation of business.

His views on environmental policy are similar to those of Republican Don Young of Alaska, the Resources panel's former chairman, although the two men have had a prickly relationship, rooted in part in past struggles over strategy. Both lawmakers are prone to confront environmentalists and to produce legislation that is popular with rural, Western constituents but not always palatable to House and Senate leaders.

Hansen was infuriated with President Clinton's 1996 decision to invoke the Antiquities Act of 1906 and declare 1.7 million acres of southern Utah canyon lands a national monument. "He's just trying to appease Eastern environmentalists," Hansen told USA Today. "And he's hurting the area, the economy, taking away private property rights and hurting schoolchildren."

But Hansen had difficulty winning support for his efforts to restrict Clinton's authority. In the 106th Congress, he sought unsuccessfully to limit the president's power to unilaterally set aside lands for preservation. "The Constitution is abundantly clear that Congress is the organization that handles the public lands of America, not the executive branch," he said. His bill requiring the president to consult with a state's governor and congressional delegation before invoking the Antiquities Act won House approval but died in the Senate.

In the 107th Congress, with President Bush in the White House, Hansen wants to test congressional support for reversing some of Clinton's actions, including opening some areas designated as national monuments to activities such as hunting, mining and off-road vehicle use — or even rescinding a monument designation.

"For the first time in eight years, the people of the West feel like they have a listening ear in the White House," Hansen said in 2001. "After the bruising treatment of recent years, that's a wonderful feeling." Like Bush, Hansen favors allowing oil exploration in Alaska's Arctic National Wildlife Refuge.

Hansen has had some luck in cutting bipartisan deals on narrow measures to improve the management of federal property. In 2000, for instance, he helped win enactment of a law that requires film crews to pay fees for the use of public lands during filming, and he pushed successfully for reauthorization of the National Historic Preservation Fund. In the 105th, he helped win passage of a Senate bill that limited the term of national park concession contractors to no more than 20 years and barred preferential treatment for large contractors.

Hansen is embroiled in an ongoing battle with environmentalists and Democrats who want large tracts of Utah designated as Red Rock wilderness areas. He has argued for a middle course. But critics attacked as a "wilder-less" bill a proposal he backed in 2000 to create a San Rafael Swell conservation area and to develop a land management plan that allows recreational and other activities on the land.

Hansen, an avid bird hunter and former Mormon bishop with strong moral views, has occasionally gone against his party to back restrictions on the tobacco, liquor and gambling industries. In 2000, he won a key vote when the House narrowly passed language he sponsored with Henry A. Waxman, D-Calif., to allow the Justice Department to use money from other Cabinet agencies to pursue a lawsuit against the tobacco industry to recover the federal health care costs of smoking-related illnesses. In the 105th, he supported cutting tax deductions for gambling losses and restricting liquor advertising. He is a staunch conservative on such social issues as abortion and gun control.

A former insurance broker and developer, Hansen took an unusual turn as a consumer crusader in 1998 by leading the push for bipartisan legislation to require mortgage insurers to cancel coverage when a homeowner's equity reaches 22 percent. His original proposal was inspired by his own difficulties in trying to cancel mortgage insurance on a condominium he owned in Crystal City, Va.

In the 105th, Hansen accepted the invitation of Majority Leader Dick Armey to chair the ethics panel, formally called the Committee on Standards of Official Conduct. The committee had become embroiled in partisanship and public finger-pointing during its probe in the 104th of Speaker Newt Gingrich's political fundraising. The recruitment of Hansen, who had served on the panel for 12 years, reflected a desire to restore the bipartisan and discreet manner in which the panel used to operate. He won praise for an even-handed approach as chairman, stressing terse public comments and informal inquiries. His term ended in 1999.

On the Armed Services Committee, Hansen sides with efforts to boost military funding. A Navy veteran, he has been a staunch advocate for veterans programs on the Veterans' Affairs panel, where he served until the 107th.

Hansen, who holds the record as the longest-serving House member from Utah, has seen a few bumpy elections but now appears to be firmly in command. Riding President Reagan's coattails in 1980, Hansen, then Speaker of the Utah House, defeated an incumbent, Democrat Gunn McKay, winning 52 percent of the vote. He won rematches with McKay in 1986 and 1988. In 1990, Hansen defeated Democrat Kenley Brunsdale, chief aide to then-2nd District Democratic Rep. Wayne Owens, winning with 52 percent. That was his last tough race.

KEY VOTES

2000

No	Raise hourly minimum wage by $1 over two years
Yes	Halt funding for U.S. mission in Kosovo unless European nations pay more
Yes	Provide Medicare benefits to military retirees and their dependents
Yes	Grant China permanent normal trade status
Yes	Phase out estate, gift and trust taxes
Yes	Prohibit implementation of president's national monument designations
Yes	Approve GOP plan to provide prescription drug coverage for Medicare beneficiaries
No	Increase help for poor nations indebted to international financial institutions

1999

Yes	Impose steel import quotas
No	Kill proposal to take aviation trust funds off budget
Yes	Require background checks on buyers only at gun shows with 10 or more vendors
Yes	Remove barriers among banking, securities and insurance companies
No	Authorize state grants to hire teachers and reduce class size
No	Overhaul campaign finance law; ban "soft money" and restrict advocacy advertising
No	Approve bipartisan plan to increase rights of patients in managed-care health plans

INTEREST GROUPS

	AFL-CIO	ADA	CCUS	ACU
2000	0%	0%	85%	95%
1999	13%	10%	96%	84%
1998	0%	5%	100%	100%
1997	0%	0%	90%	91%

CQ VOTE STUDIES

	PARTY UNITY		PRESIDENTIAL SUPPORT	
	Support	Oppose	Support	Oppose
2000	95%	5%	25%	75%
1999	93%	7%	24%	76%
1998	96%	4%	20%	80%
1997	96%	4%	27%	73%

UTAH 1

West – Salt Lake City suburbs; Odgen; Logan; rural Utah

In the 1840s, Mormon pioneers journeyed into the mountainous terrain of northern Utah. Today, the 1st, stretching from the far northern tip of Utah to the growing retirement hub in the state's southwestern edge, retains that Mormon influence. A strong emphasis on family is found in these parts – the 1st has one of the nation's highest proportions of married couples and couples with children.

The 1st saw its population grow in the 1990s as residents flocked to areas near Salt Lake City and into small towns in the south. Ogden, the 1st's largest city, was once a lively railroad town but today looks more toward defense. Hill Air Force Base is one of the state's largest employers. The 1st received a boost in the 1990s from an influx of high-tech companies to Salt Lake City (in the 2nd District) and its surroundings. However, about one-fourth of the 1st is rural, making agriculture, the environment and property rights major issues.

Over the past century, the territory that is now the 1st has exchanged party hands several times. But Mormons began to identify solidly with the GOP in the 1970s, and a Republican has represented most of the 1st's area since 1977. Locally, most areas favor Republicans, although Democrats pick up some votes in Weber County, once a center of railroad-related work.

MAJOR INDUSTRY
Manufacturing, defense, high-tech

MILITARY BASES
Hill Air Force Base, 6,456 military, 9,418 civilian; Tooele Army Depot, 55 military, 846 civilian; Deseret Chemical Depot, 1 military, 523 civilian; Dugway Proving Ground, 33 military, 443 civilian (1999)

CITIES
Ogden, 68,210; Layton, 56,469; St. George, 47,994; Bountiful, 41,169; Logan, 40,778

UNUSUAL FEATURES
Great Salt Lake, world's second-largest saltwater lake; Bingham Canyon Mine, biggest manmade pit in the world.

Rep. Jim Matheson (D)

CAPITOL OFFICE
225-3011; fax 225-5638; 410 Cannon Bldg. 20515

INTERNET
e-mail: www.house.gov/writerep
web: www.house.gov/matheson

COMMITTEES
Budget
Science
Transportation & Infrastructure

HOMETOWN
Salt Lake City

BORN
March 21, 1960, Salt Lake City, Utah

RELIGION
Mormon

FAMILY
Wife, Amy Herbener; one child

EDUCATION
Harvard U., B.A. 1982; U. of California, Los
Angeles, M.B.A. 1987

CAREER
Energy consulting firm owner; energy company
project manager; environmental group advocate

POLITICAL HIGHLIGHTS
No previous office

ELECTION RESULTS

2000 GENERAL

Jim Matheson (D)	145,021	55.9%
Derek W. Smith (R)	107,114	41.3%
Bruce Bangerter (IA)	4,704	1.8%

2000 PRIMARY

Jim Matheson (D)	unopposed

Elected 2000; 1st term

Democrats hope that Matheson can bring some order to the chaos that has marked congressional politics in the 2nd District, which has sent nine different representatives to the House over the past 30 years, with five shifts of party control and several scandals along the way.

Matheson is an energy consultant with a centrist agenda and a familiar name as the son of the late Democratic Gov. Scott M. Matheson, a popular figure who served two terms, from 1977 to 1985.

The mild-mannered Matheson has affiliated himself with the "Blue Dogs" and the New Democrats, two groups that advocate centrist policies and bipartisan cooperation and that are generally at the right end of the Democratic political spectrum on Capitol Hill. His advocacy of bipartisan approaches was reflected in his selection as the Democrats' liaison to the House Republican freshmen.

In his 2000 campaign, Matheson avoided identifying himself as a Democrat and touted himself as a fiscal conservative. He said he supports paying down the national debt, using part of the budget surplus to shore up Social Security and Medicare and providing "reasonable tax relief where it is needed most."

On other issues, Matheson, who has seats on the Budget, Transportation and Science panels, sounds like many fellow Democrats. He says preserving open space is a priority, and he favors strict enforcement of air and water quality standards. He also stresses the need to lower prescription drug costs.

Matheson would have been a first-rate Democratic recruit even under normal circumstances, but he benefited greatly from the turmoil surrounding the two-term tenure of his predecessor, Republican Merrill Cook.

The combative Cook — whose own predecessor, Republican Enid Greene, had to retire after one term because of a scandal involving her then-husband's handling of her finances — received reams of bad publicity over his temperamental outbursts. That set the stage for Cook's June primary defeat by a wealthy political newcomer, Internet executive Derek W. Smith.

But Smith got his own dose of bad press, over his past business practices, and Matheson sailed to an easy, 15 percentage point win.

UTAH 2
Central — Parts of Salt Lake City

Southeast of the world's second-largest saltwater lake lies Salt Lake City, the capital of Utah and the core of the 2nd. Taking in most of the city and surrounding county, the 2nd is home to a well-educated, white-collar workforce. The Historic Temple Square in downtown Salt Lake City serves as a reminder that this is the heart of the Mormon church but, ironically, the city's diversity makes it the least Mormon part of Utah.

The 1990s brought growth — more than 100,000 people moved into Salt Lake County, many of them settling in the city's southwestern suburbs. Companies, attracted to the city's low cost of living, right-to-work laws and well-educated workers, also have been gravitating to the area. Financial services play a dominant role in the economy, with computer and biotechnology firms also making their

presence felt. Preparations for the 2002 Winter Olympics also are providing a boost. Democrats held the 2nd in the late 1980s and early '90s, losing the seat in 1994. Mormons provide reliable support for the GOP, but the district has enough cultural and racial diversity to keep conservative Democrats competitive, as reflected in the 2000 election of Rep. Matheson. At the local level Democrats do well in Salt Lake City proper. Suburbs to the south and southwest remain more Republican.

MAJOR INDUSTRY
Financial services, manufacturing, tourism

CITIES
Salt Lake City (pt.), 120,669 (1990); Sandy, 101,853; West Jordan, 65,139

UNUSUAL FEATURES
Downtown's Temple Square includes the Tabernacle and Latter-Day Saints headquarters; University of Utah science professor James W. Cronin won the Nobel Prize in physics in 1980; Alta and Snowbird ski resorts — "the greatest snow on earth" — are right outside the city.

Rep. Christopher B. Cannon (R)

CAPITOL OFFICE
225-7751; fax 225-5629; 118 Cannon Bldg. 20515

INTERNET
e-mail: cannon.ut03@mail.house.gov
web: www.house.gov/cannon

COMMITTEES
Government Reform
Judiciary
Resources
Science

HOMETOWN
Mapleton

BORN
Oct. 20, 1950, Salt Lake City, Utah

RELIGION
Mormon

FAMILY
Wife, Claudia Fox Cannon; eight children

EDUCATION
Brigham Young U., B.S. 1974; Harvard Business School, attended 1975-76; Brigham Young U., J.D. 1980

CAREER
Venture capital executive; steel company executive; Cabinet department lawyer; lawyer

POLITICAL HIGHLIGHTS
Utah Republican Party finance chairman, 1992-94

ELECTION RESULTS

2000 GENERAL

Christopher B. Cannon (R)	138,943	58.5%
Donald Dunn (D)	88,547	37.3%
Michael J. Lehman (IA)	5,436	2.3%
Kitty K. Burton (LIBERT)	3,570	1.5%

2000 PRIMARY

Christopher B. Cannon (R)	unopposed

1998 GENERAL

Christopher B. Cannon (R)	100,830	76.9%
Will Christensen (IA)	20,720	15.8%
Kitty K. Burton (LIBERT)	9,553	7.3%

PREVIOUS WINNING PERCENTAGES
1996 (51%)

Elected 1996; 3rd term

Cannon is the most dependable GOP vote in the congressional delegation of what is arguably the most dependably Republican state in the union, supporting the party line more than 95 percent of the time.

Toward the end of the 105th Congress and throughout the 106th, he was best known for his impeachment crusade against President Clinton and for his continuing feud with his former Republican colleague, 2nd District Rep. Merrill Cook, which culminated in Cannon endorsing Cook's Republican primary challenger.

On Capitol Hill, Cannon, aside from his role in impeachment, has been largely a quiet presence who is generally heard from only when the topic is one of his priority issues. Cannon's legislative interests range from land-use policies (two-thirds of his district is owned by the federal government), to full disclosure to consumers of information on their credit reports, to high-tech issues, such as a ban on Internet dissemination of recipes for making methamphetamines. He also has authored broader legislation to help in the battle against abuse of methamphetamines.

In the 106th Congress, he was vice chairman of the Western Caucus, a group of about 60 lawmakers, mostly Republicans, who work to advance issues that are of importance to Western states, where the federal government owns huge tracts of land and water is precious. Cook also was named to head a GOP task force aimed at helping lawmakers make full use of modern technology in their offices.

During his first term, in the 105th Congress, Cannon devoted most of his time to matters involving the development and preservation of land. Not only are such issues paramount in the district, but Cannon undoubtedly owed his 1996 election victory to local outrage over Clinton's unilateral creation of a 1.7 million-acre national monument — Grand Staircase-Escalante — that largely precluded the development of rich mineral reserves.

Upon his arrival in Congress, Cannon joined fellow Utah Republican James V. Hansen on the Resources Committee, embarking on a multi-pronged counterattack on the monument issue. Contending that Clinton made his decision without consultation or even notification of local officials, and that his motives were purely political, Cannon even claimed that Clinton's move was related to the receipt of campaign funds from an overseas group that stood to benefit if Utah coal lands were not developed.

Given his dim view of Clinton, it was no surprise in 1998 when he was one of the president's harshest critics on the Judiciary Committee as the panel drew up articles of impeachment. In early 1999, he was one of the 13 "managers" who presented the House case for impeachment before the Senate. When Clinton was acquitted, Cannon was outraged.

Cannon and Cook, whose personal behavior was the main reason for his primary defeat in 2000, began feuding early in their freshman terms, and although the two Utahns initially said they had patched up their differences, it was not for long. Cook accused Cannon of involvement in a wiretapping, to which Cannon said, "I don't know how to respond to these recent rants from Merrill Cook." Finally, in 2000, Cannon endorsed Cook's GOP foe, Derek Smith, saying that Cook could not win in November.

The Provo-Orem area of the 3rd District is the birthplace of Word Perfect and home to a significant computer software industry, including Novell and hundreds of other firms, and Cannon has been active on the Judiciary panel in technology issues, including a move to increase the number of skilled immigrants permitted to enter the country to take jobs. He worked on legislation that would protect the Mormon Church's massive collection of genealogy data from being downloaded from the Internet and sold by other companies.

In the 106th Congress, Cannon continued his work on public lands issues. He authored a bill to create a Western Legacy district to offer some environmental protections to almost 3 million acres of southern Utah land, known as the San Rafael Swell. He got the Clinton administration to sign on, but the bill was abruptly pulled from the House floor in June when it ran afoul of last-minute lobbying by conservation groups, which said it did not provide enough protection, such as prohibitions on off-road vehicles.

Cannon, who has sponsored a number of bills dealing with Utah's public lands, ranks low in the eyes of conservation groups such as the League of Conservation Voters and the Sierra Club, which say his bills allow for development of wilderness areas and preclude more comprehensive preservation efforts.

Cannon serves on the governing board of the National Holocaust Museum. A member of the Church of Jesus Christ of Latter-day Saints, Cannon believes that Mormons feel a strong kinship with Jews because Mormons also were persecuted for their beliefs for much of their early history.

Cannon got an economics degree from Brigham Young University, taking time during college to serve a church mission in Guatemala. He flunked out of Harvard Business School but returned to BYU to earn a law degree.

In the mid-1980s, he served three years as associate solicitor in the Interior Department and as a Commerce Department attorney during the Reagan administration before returning to Utah to reap success in the business world. He teamed up with his brother, Joe, to buy and reopen Geneva Steel Co. in 1987. After a falling-out with his brother, Cannon started his own venture capital company, Cannon Industries. He became active in local party politics, and in 1996 he headed up Lamar Alexander's presidential campaign in Utah.

Cannon returned the 3rd District to GOP hands in 1996, thwarting Democrat Bill Orton's bid for a fourth term. The victory was regarded as a mild upset and was fueled by Clinton's Escalante wilderness announcement just seven weeks before the election. Cannon dipped into his sizable personal fortune — his financial statements put his worth at more than $10 million — to help fund his bid against Orton. In both 1996 and 1998, Cannon had to defeat a more conservative Republican foe in the primary to win his party's nomination.

KEY VOTES

2000

No Raise hourly minimum wage by $1 over two years

Yes Halt funding for U.S. mission in Kosovo unless European nations pay more

Yes Provide Medicare benefits to military retirees and their dependents

Yes Grant China permanent normal trade status

Yes Phase out estate, gift and trust taxes

Yes Prohibit implementation of president's national monument designations

Yes Approve GOP plan to provide prescription drug coverage for Medicare beneficiaries

No Increase help for poor nations indebted to international financial institutions

1999

Yes Impose steel import quotas

No Kill proposal to take aviation trust funds off budget

Yes Require background checks on buyers only at gun shows with 10 or more vendors

Yes Remove barriers among banking, securities and insurance companies

No Authorize state grants to hire teachers and reduce class size

No Overhaul campaign finance law; ban "soft money" and restrict advocacy advertising

Yes Approve bipartisan plan to increase rights of patients in managed-care health plans

INTEREST GROUPS

	AFL-CIO	ADA	CCUS	ACU
2000	0%	0%	95%	100%
1999	22%	10%	92%	92%
1998	0%	5%	100%	95%
1997	13%	10%	90%	96%

CQ VOTE STUDIES

	PARTY UNITY		PRESIDENTIAL SUPPORT	
	Support	Oppose	Support	Oppose
2000	99%	1%	24%	76%
1999	96%	4%	15%	85%
1998	94%	6%	19%	81%
1997	94%	6%	31%	69%

UTAH 3

East – Provo; Orem; rural Utah

Utah's conservative 3rd takes in the eastern part of the state, skimming Salt Lake City to include some Democrat-leaning areas. Heading south of Salt Lake City on Interstate 15 takes one to Provo and Orem, the 3rd's economic centers. A heavily Mormon-influenced district, the 3rd has one of the nation's highest concentrations of married couples.

With a flourishing computer industry, the Provo/Orem area is akin to a mini-Silicon Valley. Newly minted graduates from the 3rd's four colleges have helped make the area attractive to some of the computer industry's big-name companies. Outside Utah County, cattle ranching, mining and tourism sustain small-town life. The north-central part of Utah, noted for its abundance of natural beauty, is ski country.

While some of the 3rd's rural eastern communities saw sharp population declines during the 1980s, these areas have begun to rebound. Grand County, once devastated by the collapse of the uranium mining industry, has seen new life since telecommuter and

artist communities have sprung up in the town of Moab. However, the area has not yet fully recovered – it is still losing some of its population and umemployment is high. Tourism is important in these parts – Arches and Canyonlands national parks are nearby.

The 3rd is now considered safe Republican territory, but a Democratic stint from 1991-97 showed the GOP that cracks in the party could be dangerous. Locally, most areas vote for Republicans, although the western part of Salt Lake County and blue-collar workers in Carbon and Summit counties lean Democratic. Since about two-thirds of the district is federal land, voters tend to be very concerned with land use issues and private property rights.

MAJOR INDUSTRY
Computer software, tourism, manufacturing

CITIES
Provo, 110,690; West Valley City (pt.), 86,539 (1990); Orem, 82,965

UNUSUAL FEATURES
Actor Robert Redford's Sundance Film Festival in Park City; Philo T. Farnsworth, credited with inventing TV, lived in Provo; Dinosaurland in Vernal, with life-size dinosaurs.

Gov. Howard Dean (D)

First elected:
Succeeded Richard A.
Snelling, R, on Aug. 14,
1991; elected 1992
Length of term: 2
years
Term expires: 1/03
Salary: $96,678
Phone: (802) 828-3333
Hometown: Burlington
Born: Nov. 17, 1948, East Hampton, N.Y.
Religion: Congregationalist
Family: Wife, Judy Steinberg; two
children
Education: Yale U., B.A. 1971; Albert
Einstein College of Medicine, M.D. 1978
Career: Physician
Political highlights: Vt. House, 1983-87
(assistant majority leader, 1985-86);
lieutenant governor, 1987-91

Election results:

2000 GENERAL
Howard Dean (D)	148,059	50.5%
Ruth Dwyer (R)	111,359	38.0%
Anthony Pollina (PRO)	28,116	9.6%

Lt. Gov. Douglas Racine (D)

First elected: 1996
Length of term: 2 years
Term expires: 1/03
Salary: $48,256
Phone: (802) 828-2226

STATE LEGISLATURE

General Assembly: Meets
biennially, January-April; session
often extended
House: 150 members, 2-year terms
2001 breakdown: 83R, 62D, 4P, 1I;
107 men, 43 women
Salary: $536/week
Phone: (802) 828-2247
Senate: 30 members, 2-year terms
2001 breakdown: 14R, 16D;
21 men, 9 women
Salary: $536/week
Phone: (802) 828-2231

STATE TERM LIMITS

Governor: No
Senate: No
House: No

URBAN STATISTICS

CITY	POPULATION
Burlington	38,332
Rutland	16,649
South Burlington	14,257

REGISTERED VOTERS

Voters do not register by party.

POPULATION

2000 population	608,827
1990 population	562,758
Percent change	+8.2%
Rank among states	49
Median age	36.1
Born in state	57%
Foreign born	3%
Urban/rural	32%/68%
Crime rate	120/100,000
Poverty level	9.9%
Federal workers	5,478
Military	4,501

REAPPORTIONMENT

Vermont retained its one House seat
in reapportionment.

MISCELLANEOUS

Web: www.state.vt.us
Capital: Montpelier
Land area: 9,249 sq. miles
Rank among states: 43
STATE ELECTION OFFICIAL
(802) 828-2304
**DEMOCRATIC
HEADQUARTERS**
(802) 229-1783
**REPUBLICAN
HEADQUARTERS**
(802) 223-3411

District Statistics

DIST.	VOTE FOR PRESIDENT 2000 D	R	GREEN	1996 D	R	REF	1992 D	R	I	WHT	BLK	ASIAN	HISP	HOUSEHOLD INCOME	OVER 65+	UNDER 18	COLLEGE EDUCATION
AL	51%	41%	7%	53%	31%	12%	46%	31%	23%	99%	<1%	1%	1%	$29,792	12%	27%	24%

Sen. Patrick J. Leahy (D)

CAPITOL OFFICE
224-4242; fax 224-3479; 433 Russell Bldg. 20510

INTERNET
e-mail: senator_leahy@leahy.senate.gov
web: leahy.senate.gov

COMMITTEES
Agriculture, Nutrition & Forestry
Appropriations
Judiciary - ranking member

HOMETOWN
Middlesex

BORN
March 31, 1940, Montpelier, Vt.

RELIGION
Roman Catholic

FAMILY
Wife, Marcelle Leahy; three children

EDUCATION
St. Michael's College, B.A. 1961; Georgetown U.,
J.D. 1964

CAREER
Lawyer

POLITICAL HIGHLIGHTS
Chittenden County state's attorney, 1966-75

ELECTION RESULTS

1998 GENERAL

Patrick J. Leahy (D)	154,567	72.2%
Fred Tuttle (R)	48,051	22.4%
Hugh Douglas (LIBERT)	4,199	2.0%
Barry M. Nelson (I)	2,893	1.4%
Robert Melamede (VG)	2,459	1.1%

1998 PRIMARY

Patrick J. Leahy (D)	18,643	96.6%
write-ins (D)	647	3.4%

PREVIOUS WINNING PERCENTAGES
1992 (54%); 1986 (63%); 1980 (50%); 1974 (50%)

Elected 1974; 5th term

Midway through his fifth term in the Senate, the smart and articulate Leahy is continuing his long-running practice of pursuing a wide variety of causes with national and international ramifications — from the protection of personal information to the banning of anti-personnel land mines to the regulation of computer encryption technology.

As the sixth-most-senior Democratic senator, he is able to pursue his eclectic agenda from three positions of power. He is the ranking Democrat on the Judiciary Committee, which has jurisdiction over a broad swath of business and social policy matters, from the bankruptcy code to gun control; he is the senior Democrat on the Appropriations subcommittee that sets foreign aid spending and policy; and he is a senior member on Agriculture, which he chaired for eight years until the GOP won control of the Senate in 1995.

Generally, Leahy operates with purse-lipped determination, following a liberal Democratic line. Yet he never seems to forget the concerns of his rural and agricultural state, and he has shown a willingness to deal with Republicans to protect Vermont's interests, whether that means helping the agricultural economy or trying to combat a growing drug epidemic among the state's teenagers.

He sees his parochial focus as an obligation handed to him by those who wrote the Constitution. "We are such a small state," Leahy has said about Vermont, now the second-least-populated state after Wyoming. "The only place we have an equal voice with the rest of the country is in the U.S. Senate."

That responsibility includes fighting for Northeastern dairy farmers as lawmakers rewrite the farm law in the 107th Congress. Another priority is federal funding to fight teenage drug use. In the past, Leahy has joined forces with Judiciary Committee Chairman Orrin G. Hatch, R-Utah, to help increase treatment funds for rural states that are often overlooked in federal programs to combat narcotics.

Another focus for Leahy is the death penalty. In the 106th Congress, he sought unsuccessfully to win passage of his bill to make it easier for prisoners to secure DNA testing and to improve the quality of counsel in death penalty cases by establishing national minimum standards for the defense of those accused of capital crimes.

Leahy also cultivates an image of a senator who is plugged in to pop culture. He is an enthusiastic fan of both Batman and the Grateful Dead, and in 1996, he was one of the first Capitol Hill lawmakers to launch a website; he dubbed himself the "cyber-senator."

Leahy won accolades for his tough but fair handling of the Judiciary Committee's confirmation hearings on the nomination of John Ashcroft to be attorney general. (With the Senate technically under the control of the Democrats for the first two weeks of the 107th, Leahy initially wielded the gavel at Judiciary.) Still, the former prosecutor did not hesitate to try to defeat the nomination.

Leahy was the first to raise the issue of the "Ashcroft standard" — the contention by the nominee's opponents that, during his one term as a GOP senator from Missouri, Ashcroft had applied an unfair standard for confirming President Clinton's nominees. Leahy specifically criticized Ashcroft's reasons for opposing Bill Lann Lee to run the Justice Department's Civil Rights Division. The Vermonter cited Ashcroft's remarks stating that he did not believe Lee could set aside his personal views on affirmative action and enforce the law. Leahy and other Democrats asked whether Ashcroft, a conservative, would have difficulty living up to his own pledge to enforce the laws that he personally disagreed with. Ashcroft eventually won confirmation, but Leahy's pointed questioning put his party's arguments against the nominee into sharp focus.

In the 105th Congress, Leahy regularly accused Republicans of subjecting Clinton's judicial nominees to political litmus tests on controversial issues such as abortion, affirmative action and judicial activism. But when the Democrats were in the majority, Leahy took a different approach. During the 1991 confirmation hearings on Supreme Court nominee Clarence Thomas, the senator ignored a tradition of refraining from pressing nominees for their views on issues that could come before the high court. Leahy sought Thomas' position on several issues, most notably abortion, and elicited Thomas' assertions that he had never discussed the landmark *Roe v. Wade* decision — statements that Thomas' opponents exhibited as proof the nominee was being deliberately evasive.

Leahy generally supports abortion rights, but he has voted to ban a procedure its opponents call "partial birth" abortion, a stand that cost him the endorsement of the National Organization for Women in his 1998 re-election race. Yet he has also fought to keep international family planning funding free of abortion restrictions.

He may be best known for championing a worldwide ban on land mines. His work on the issue began in 1989, when he started a fund — the Leahy War Victims Fund — to supply medical aid to land mine victims. By the 1990s, he was clashing openly with the Clinton administration, which opposed an all-out ban on the weapons. Leahy introduced legislation to ban U.S.-made land mines and aggressively lobbied the White House at every turn, confessing on more than one occasion that "they are sick of me." In 1998, he secured more than $35 million for research and development of alternatives to land mines and new techniques to remove or render them impotent.

Leahy has sought to update copyright law to reflect the advent of the Internet, and he is also an avid supporter of the effort to ease export restrictions on encryption software, which allows digital information to be scrambled during computer transmission to prevent the data from being intercepted. In 2000, he was tapped to head the Senate Democratic Task Force on Privacy, which focuses on medical records, financial transactions and Internet security. That same year, he helped win enactment of the law that established a framework for making electronic signatures as binding as pen-and-ink ones on some contracts and records, while preserving essential safeguards to protect consumers.

Leahy was just 26 when he was elected Chittenden County prosecutor in 1966. Eight years later, the post-Watergate mood helped him score an upset to win the seat vacated by Republican George D. Aiken, who was 82. He was the youngest elected senator in the state's history, and Vermont's first Democratic senator since the Republican Party was founded in 1854.

In the GOP landslide of 1980, he emphasized his Vermont roots and won by just 2,500 votes against New York native Stewart Ledbetter, a former state banking commissioner. That close call lured former GOP Gov. Richard A. Snelling out of retirement six years later, but Leahy was well-financed and won with 63 percent. The anti-incumbent mood of 1992 did not help Secretary of State James H. Douglas, who fell 11 percentage points short of beating Leahy. In 1998, Leahy faced one of the year's most talked-about opponents, 79-year-old dairy farmer Fred Tuttle. The star of a 1996 mock documentary about an unlikely congressional candidate, Tuttle turned fiction into fact when he won the GOP nomination. He pledged to spend just $251, a dollar for each Vermont town. That drew national media attention, but just 22 percent of the vote.

KEY VOTES

2000

Yes Overhaul bankruptcy law and increase minimum wage
No   Limit fiscal 2001 discretionary spending to $600.3 billion
Yes Override veto on nuclear waste disposal at Yucca Mountain site in Nevada
Yes Oppose effort to terminate Kosovo mission
Yes Include gender, sexual orientation and disability in federal hate crime protections
?   Approve GOP plan to restrict use of genetic information by health insurers
No   Kill amendment delaying implementation of an anti-missile defense system
No   Cut taxes for married couples
Yes Grant China permanent normal trade status

1999

No   Remove President Clinton from office for obstruction of justice
No   Kill amendment authorizing state grants to hire teachers and reduce class size
Yes Require criminal background checks for purchases at gun shows
No   Approve GOP proposal to increase rights of patients in managed-care health plans
No   Block effort to allow farm and medicine exports to Cuba
Yes Allow study of tougher automobile fuel efficiency standards
Yes Ratify nuclear weapons testing treaty
Yes Prohibit national political parties from collecting "soft money" donations
Yes Remove barriers among banking, securities and insurance companies

INTEREST GROUPS

	AFL-CIO	ADA	CCUS	ACU
2000	75%	85%	58%	8%
1999	100%	95%	41%	4%
1998	88%	90%	56%	12%
1997	67%	80%	60%	13%
1996	100%	90%	23%	5%
1995	100%	100%	16%	0%
1994	100%	95%	20%	0%
1993	82%	95%	27%	8%
1992	100%	100%	10%	0%
1991	92%	95%	20%	5%

CQ VOTE STUDIES

	PARTY UNITY		PRESIDENTIAL SUPPORT	
	Support	Oppose	Support	Oppose
2000	94%	6%	89%	11%
1999	94%	6%	82%	18%
1998	87%	13%	83%	17%
1997	89%	11%	87%	13%
1996	88%	12%	75%	25%
1995	96%	4%	89%	11%
1994	96%	4%	89%	11%
1993	94%	6%	93%	7%
1992	96%	4%	24%	76%
1991	90%	10%	28%	72%

Sen. James M. Jeffords (R)

Elected 1988; 3rd term

Jeffords is one of the most mild-mannered, ultra-polite members of the Senate, but he is also a black belt in tae kwon do. He is a moderate Republican who rarely sees eye to eye with Majority Leader Trent Lott. Yet away from the Senate floor, Jeffords found harmony with Lott and two other conservative senators — Larry E. Craig of Idaho and John Ashcroft of Missouri, now the attorney general — as they belted out Oak Ridge Boys songs under the banner of the "Singing Senators." (With Ashcroft's departure, the group has stopped performing, for now.)

And while Vermont's junior senator bucks his party more often than nearly any other Republican, he is just as likely to be a good soldier on major issues. He has been a reliable spokesman for the Senate GOP approach to health care, faithfully opposing any expansion of the right to sue managed-care plans until political pressure forced Senate Republicans to endorse broader legal rights for patients in 2000. At the same time, he has balked at some of his party's education proposals and voted against one of its major initiatives, a bill that would have let families save up to $2,000 a year in tax-preferred accounts for elementary and secondary education expenses.

Jeffords cannot be pigeonholed. It is safe to call him a moderate, though, and it is safe to say that his conservative Republican colleagues treat him with suspicion. (Lott was known to introduce Jeffords at Singing Senators performances with the line, "And over on my left — my *far* left ...")

In recent years, he has voted with Democrats almost as often as he has sided with Republicans. In 2000, Jeffords supported his party's position only 55 percent of the time. In 1999, he backed the GOP on two-thirds of the floor votes — his highest party loyalty score since he joined the Senate in 1989. In the 106th Congress, he supported President Clinton more often than any Republican senator except Lincoln Chafee of Rhode Island.

In 2000, Jeffords was one of only 10 Republicans to win an election endorsement from the Sierra Club. And early in the 107th, Jeffords made it known that he opposed President Bush's proposal for a $1.6 trillion tax cut, arguing that it was too costly and tilted toward the rich.

Jeffords' views sometimes work against him on the issues where he should be most effective. As chairman of the Health, Education, Labor and Pensions Committee, Jeffords should have taken center stage in 2000 when the Senate tried to reauthorize and rewrite the 1965 Elementary and Secondary Education Act, the main federal education law. Instead, he took a back seat to Republican Judd Gregg of New Hampshire, who reshaped Jeffords' bill in committee so that it was more to the liking of the panel's conservative Republican members. With their support, Gregg added a block grant demonstration project that would have let 15 states use federal funds for any educational purpose.

Jeffords thought that approach threw too much control to the states without demanding anything in return; his original bill would have allowed states to combine federal funds designated for specific programs — but with more oversight by the Department of Education and a guarantee that Title I funds for disadvantaged students would continue to go to low-income school districts. Rather than oppose Gregg, Jeffords voted "present," allowing the bill to move forward and reach the Senate floor. It never got any further: Lott pulled the measure from the floor after a week of debate when he could not round up enough votes to block a proposed Democratic gun control amendment.

CAPITOL OFFICE
224-5141; fax 228-0776; 728 Hart Bldg. 20510

INTERNET
e-mail: vermont@jeffords.senate.gov
web: jeffords.senate.gov

COMMITTEES
Finance
Health, Education, Labor & Pensions - chairman
Veterans' Affairs
Special Aging

HOMETOWN
Shrewsbury

BORN
May 11, 1934, Rutland, Vt.

RELIGION
Congregationalist

FAMILY
Wife, Elizabeth Daley; two children

EDUCATION
Yale U., B.S.I.A. 1956; Harvard U., LL.B. 1962

MILITARY SERVICE
Navy, 1956-59; Naval Reserve, 1959-90

CAREER
Lawyer

POLITICAL HIGHLIGHTS
Vt. Senate, 1967-69; Vt. attorney general, 1969-73; sought Republican nomination for governor, 1972; U.S. House, 1975-89

ELECTION RESULTS

2000 GENERAL

James M. Jeffords (R)	189,133	65.6%
Ed Flanagan (D)	73,352	25.4%
Charles W. Russell (CNSTP)	10,079	3.5%
Rick Hubbard (I)	5,366	1.9%
Billy Greer (VG)	4,889	1.7%
Hugh Douglas (LIBERT)	3,843	1.3%

2000 PRIMARY

James M. Jeffords (R)	60,234	77.8%
Rick Hubbard (R)	15,991	20.7%

PREVIOUS WINNING PERCENTAGES
1994 (50%); 1988 (68%); 1986 House Election (89%); 1984 House Election (65%); 1982 House Election (69%); 1980 House Election (79%); 1978 House Election (75%); 1976 House Election (67%); 1974 House Election (53%)

In 1998, Jeffords had suffered another embarrassing defeat when he was unable to corral enough votes in his committee to advance legislation that would have subjected the tobacco industry to tougher regulation by the Food and Drug Administration. Stymied by Republicans, a clearly upset Jeffords took the unusual step of pulling the bill from consideration.

Still, the Vermont lawmaker has had moments of triumph in recent years, notably with legislation affecting people with disabilities. He and Democrat Edward M. Kennedy of Massachusetts teamed up in 1999 to win passage of legislation to help individuals with disabilities go to work without losing their health care coverage. The law allows workers with disabilities to stay on Medicare longer and lets states create an option for them to buy into Medicaid. In doing so, it tackles one of the biggest factors — the fear of losing insurance for expensive health care needs — that contributes to a nearly 70 percent unemployment rate among people with disabilities.

When Jeffords was next in line to chair the Labor and Human Resources Committee in the 105th Congress after the retirement of Nancy Landon Kassebaum, R-Kan., there were rumblings of a possible challenge from the right. It would not have been the first time: In 1983, Jeffords' fifth term in the House, conservative opposition kept him from becoming the top Republican on the Agriculture Committee. In 1997, however, Lott backed the Vermonter despite calls to give the post to someone more conservative.

Jeffords most often attracts notice when he goes against the GOP on social issues. In 1994, he was the only Republican senator to cosponsor Clinton's proposed overhaul of the nation's health care system. The plan was so completely discredited by attacks from other Republicans that it was a major factor in the GOP's takeover of Congress that year.

His interest in education programs has manifested itself not just in legislation, but through a Washington, D.C., literacy program he created that now involves 1,500 students, 10 senators and the sponsorship of major Washington corporations. As part of the initiative, Jeffords tutors at a Capitol Hill school every week.

Jeffords has deep roots in his state. His father was the chief justice of the Vermont Supreme Court, and the family's presence reaches back to 1792. After serving a term in the Vermont Senate and four years as the state's attorney general, Jeffords suffered his sole political defeat, losing a GOP gubernatorial primary in 1972. The party hierarchy viewed him as too liberal, and he lost by less than 5,000 votes.

Jeffords bounced back in 1974, winning a three-way primary for Vermont's lone House seat. He went on to win the general election with 53 percent of the vote over former Burlington Mayor Francis Cain — a seat he held for 14 years. In 1988, he decided to cash in on his status as heir apparent to the Senate seat held by Republican Robert T. Stafford, who was retiring. Jeffords entered the general election an overwhelming favorite and was never threatened, winning 68 percent of the vote.

In 1994, he faced a tough challenge for a second term from Democratic opponent Jan Backus, an underfunded liberal who had scored an upset victory in the primary. Jeffords eventually won the general election by 10 percentage points.

By 2000, Jeffords faced a new challenge: a politically sensitive run against Democrat Ed Flanagan, the first openly gay Senate candidate ever nominated by a major party. It came in the same year that Vermont became the first state to enact a civil union law, allowing gay couples to receive benefits similar to those available under marriage — provoking a backlash in the form of a "Take Back Vermont" movement. Still, neither candidate made an issue of either the law or Flanagan's sexual orientation, and Jeffords retained the backing of gay rights groups. He won re-election with 66 percent of the vote.

KEY VOTES

2000

Yes Overhaul bankruptcy law and increase minimum wage

No Limit fiscal 2001 discretionary spending to $600.3 billion

Yes Override veto on nuclear waste disposal at Yucca Mountain site in Nevada

Yes Oppose effort to terminate Kosovo mission

Yes Include gender, sexual orientation and disability in federal hate crime protections

Yes Approve GOP plan to restrict use of genetic information by health insurers

No Kill amendment delaying implementation of an anti-missile defense system

Yes Cut taxes for married couples

No Grant China permanent normal trade status

1999

No Remove President Clinton from office for obstruction of justice

Yes Kill amendment authorizing state grants to hire teachers and reduce class size

No Require criminal background checks for purchases at gun shows

Yes Approve GOP proposal to increase rights of patients in managed-care health plans

No Block effort to allow farm and medicine exports to Cuba

Yes Allow study of tougher automobile fuel efficiency standards

Yes Ratify nuclear weapons testing treaty

Yes Prohibit national political parties from collecting "soft money" donations

Yes Remove barriers among banking, securities and insurance companies

INTEREST GROUPS

	AFL-CIO	ADA	CCUS	ACU
2000	38%	55%	73%	36%
1999	22%	45%	76%	40%
1998	38%	55%	89%	24%
1997	0%	45%	100%	21%
1996	43%	50%	62%	45%
1995	36%	55%	76%	23%
1994	50%	85%	50%	12%
1993	40%	60%	64%	38%
1992	56%	65%	60%	27%
1991	50%	65%	22%	10%

CQ VOTE STUDIES

	PARTY UNITY		PRESIDENTIAL SUPPORT	
	Support	Oppose	Support	Oppose
2000	55%	45%	75%	25%
1999	67%	33%	56%	44%
1998	49%	51%	69%	31%
1997	53%	47%	78%	22%
1996	58%	42%	53%	47%
1995	59%	41%	51%	49%
1994	32%	68%	79%	21%
1993	46%	54%	57%	43%
1992	39%	61%	47%	53%
1991	38%	62%	56%	44%

Rep. Bernard Sanders (I)

Elected 1990; 6th term

Having spent most of his 10 years in Congress blazing his own path between the aisles as the institution's only Independent, Sanders — a self-described "Democratic socialist" — is an idealist who incorporates a healthy dose of pragmatism in his style. His allegiance to Democrats on social issues has allowed him to accumulate considerable seniority; but his willingness to forge unlikely alliances with libertarians and even the most conservative of Republicans on trade measures has kept the wild-haired Brooklyn native in a class by himself.

His rumpled appearance and informal demeanor — he calls himself "Bernie" and encourages others to do the same — can give the impression that Sanders is a softie, but under his laid-back surface lurks a passionate activist who often speaks gruffly and never hesitates to make himself heard for a cause he feels is just. In the 106th Congress, that meant accompanying buses filled with senior citizens to Canada to highlight the low cost of prescription drugs across the border and push for Medicare coverage of such medication.

His maverick streak has been reflected in his willingness to join forces with conservative Republicans in opposing the economic policies of the International Monetary Fund (IMF), which he said were "only protecting foreign speculators, international banks and crooks in Russia, creating misery for millions of ordinary people." His rhetoric, combined with GOP mistrust of President Clinton's foreign policies, helped stall IMF funding for months in 1998. In the 107th Congress, he is the ranking minority member on the Financial Services panel's International Monetary Policy and Trade Subcommittee, giving him a platform to advance his views.

His relations with House Democrats have not always been so friendly. When he arrived, Sanders was blocked from joining the Democratic Caucus by conservative Democrats and even some liberals, who thought a socialist member would harm the party's image. In a compromise, he stayed out of the caucus but was given committee assignments by the Democrats. Over the years, he has managed to accrue enough clout to be taken seriously.

As his stock in Congress has risen, Sanders says he has become more attuned to the need to build coalitions — even with the least likely allies — on such tough issues as demanding an overhaul of the IMF and opposing trade with China. "When I came here, I would have said that probably the likelihood of my working with conservatives ... was nil. I would not have thought to do that," he said in 2000. But "when you see people like [Republicans] Dana Rohrabacher or Chris Smith or Spencer Bachus making the right critiques ... and if you're seeing moderate Democrats saying the opposite, you start to say, 'Why not? Let's work together.' "

The former college professor frets over the decline in voter turnout in the United States, which he says illustrates just how out of touch lawmakers have become. "I ran for Congress because in my view, [it] does not do an effective job in representing the needs of working people, low-income people," Sanders says. He worries that economic policies pursued by both parties are making life harder for middle-income Americans. "Congress today is principally concerned with representing the wealthy and the powerful," he added.

Sanders has always gone his own way, from the time he left New York in 1968, part of a wave of liberals abandoning urban life for Vermont's green acres. While many of his fellow transplants flocked to the Democratic Party,

CAPITOL OFFICE
225-4115; fax 225-6790; 2135 Rayburn Bldg. 20515

INTERNET
e-mail: bernie@mail.house.gov
web: bernie.house.gov

COMMITTEES
Financial Services
Government Reform

HOMETOWN
Burlington

BORN
Sept. 8, 1941, Brooklyn, N.Y.

RELIGION
Jewish

FAMILY
Wife, Jane O'Meara Sanders; one child, three stepchildren

EDUCATION
U. of Chicago, B.A. 1964

CAREER
Professor; free-lance writer; documentary filmmaker

POLITICAL HIGHLIGHTS
Independent candidate for U.S. Senate, 1972, 1974; independent candidate for governor, 1972, 1976, 1986; mayor of Burlington, 1981-89; independent candidate for U.S. House, 1988

ELECTION RESULTS

2000 GENERAL

Bernard Sanders (I)	196,118	69.2%
Karen Kerin (R)	51,977	18.3%
Peter Diamondstone (D)	14,918	5.3%
Stewart Skrill (I)	11,816	4.2%
Jack "Buck" Rogers (VG)	4,799	1.7%
Daniel Krymkowski (LIBERT)	2,978	1.1%

1998 GENERAL

Bernard Sanders (I)	136,403	63.4%
Mark Candon (R)	70,740	32.9%
Matthew S. Mulligan (VG)	3,464	1.6%

PREVIOUS WINNING PERCENTAGES
1996 (55%); 1994 (50%); 1992 (58%); 1990 (56%)

Sanders helped found Vermont's anti-capitalist, anti-Vietnam War Liberty Union Party, from which he ran in four statewide campaigns in the early 1970s. He never captured more than 4 percent of the vote, but the strong grass-roots base he built finally paid off in 1981 when he unseated the Democratic incumbent by 10 votes to become Burlington's first socialist mayor. He won three more terms by increasing margins, pursuing populist goals while presiding over the revitalization of the city's downtown.

These days, Sanders pays homage to his progressive roots with a plaque on the wall of his Capitol Hill office honoring Eugene V. Debs, founder of the American Socialist Party. An advocate of a universal health care system, Sanders is the founder and chairman of the Progressive Caucus, the most liberal members of the House. He is the chamber's first identifiable socialist since Victor L. Berger of Wisconsin, who served four terms in the 1910s and '20s.

Sanders' good standing among Democrats stems largely from his history of supporting that party's initiatives on such issues as patient-friendly health care plans, environmental protection, affordable housing and a higher minimum wage. But he resists the "liberal" label, insisting instead on being known as a progressive who opposes tax breaks and subsidies for big business that he considers "corporate welfare" and big spending for defense and intelligence activities.

Sanders also works on home state issues. He has been a staunch proponent of federal heating assistance for low-income residents and fought hard to guarantee that Vermont gets its share of the aid, helping to win $1 billion more for the program in late 1998. He also worked with other Northeastern legislators to delay an Agriculture Department proposal that would have aided Midwestern dairy farmers at the expense of Northeastern milk producers.

Sanders was viewed as a spoiler when he ran in 1988 for Vermont's lone House seat, vacated when GOP Rep. James M. Jeffords left to run for the Senate. Still, his defeat by Republican Peter Smith was by only 4 percent. When the two squared off two years later, Smith's efforts in the last weeks of the race to paint Sanders as an admirer of communist Cuban dictator Fidel Castro backfired, and Sanders won with 56 percent.

In 1992, he comfortably won re-election against Tim Philbin, a favorite of the state GOP's conservative wing, but he barely held on in 1994, a banner year for Republicans nationwide. In 1996, he prevailed over two major-party opponents with 55 percent, and his winning tallies rose above 60 percent in 1998 and 2000.

KEY VOTES

2000

Yes Raise hourly minimum wage by $1 over two years

Yes Halt funding for U.S. mission in Kosovo unless European nations pay more

Yes Provide Medicare benefits to military retirees and their dependents

No Grant China permanent normal trade status

No Phase out estate, gift and trust taxes

No Prohibit implementation of president's national monument designations

No Approve GOP plan to provide prescription drug coverage for Medicare beneficiaries

Yes Increase help for poor nations indebted to international financial institutions

1999

Yes Impose steel import quotas

No Kill proposal to take aviation trust funds off budget

No Require background checks on buyers only at gun shows with 10 or more vendors

No Remove barriers among banking, securities and insurance companies

Yes Authorize state grants to hire teachers and reduce class size

Yes Overhaul campaign finance law; ban "soft money" and restrict advocacy advertising

Yes Approve bipartisan plan to increase rights of patients in managed-care health plans

INTEREST GROUPS

	AFL-CIO	ADA	CCUS	ACU
2000	100%	95%	23%	4%
1999	100%	100%	8%	12%
1998	100%	100%	18%	8%
1997	100%	100%	20%	12%

CQ VOTE STUDIES

	PARTY UNITY		PRESIDENTIAL SUPPORT	
	Support	Oppose	Support	Oppose
2000	96%	4%	78%	22%
1999	96%	4%	76%	24%
1998	95%	5%	85%	15%
1997	94%	6%	73%	27%

VERMONT

At large

Resting on the shores of Lake Champlain and rolling through the rustic Green Mountains, the second-least populous state in the nation feels like a good, small-town neighbor.

This is the land of Ben & Jerry's, started when two friends converted an old gas station into an ice cream shop in Burlington. Small businesses mix with dairy farms and manufacturing plants, as well as with the electronics companies that arrived in the 1980s. While the high-tech boom fizzled in the early 1990s, the state is working to reignite it. There also is an effort to attract tourists, so prevalent on the ski slopes in winter, to visit the state year round, although none of Vermont's attractions are advertised on roadside billboards – state law prohibits them.

A growth spurt that began in the early 1960s, when people outnumbered cows for the first time, has altered the state's political profile. Once the bastion of Yankee Republicanism, the state moved solidly to the left with the 1980s and '90s influx of young liberal urbanites, who joined the remnants of the late 1960's counterculture settlers. In state and federal elections, the strong progressive contingency based in Burlington and surrounding Chittenden County usually out-votes the numerous Yankee libertarian conservatives, based mostly in East Montpelier and some of the Burlington suburbs. Rural areas of the state, especially the northeastern corner, also hold a few Republican votes. Democrats dominate the central swath of land along Interstates 89 and 91, as well as the southeastern corner. Many small urban centers, like Montpelier and Rutland, once reliably Republican, now have more Democrats.

MAJOR INDUSTRY
Manufacturing, tourism, dairy farming

CITIES
Burlington, 38,332; Rutland, 16,649; South Burlington, 14,257

UNUSUAL FEATURES
In Bristol, the Lord's Prayer Rock stands beside a road – Dr. Joseph Greene had the prayer carved into the rock in 1891, hoping it would prevent wagon drivers from cursing their horses during the muddy season.

Gov. James S. Gilmore III (R)

First elected: 1997
Length of term: 4 years
Term expires: 1/02
Salary: $124,855
Phone: (804) 786-2211
Hometown: Richmond
Born: Oct. 6, 1949; Richmond, Va.
Religion: Methodist
Family: Wife, Roxane Gilmore; two children
Education: U. of Virginia, B.A. 1971; J.D. 1977
Military Service: Army 1971-74
Career: Lawyer
Political highlights: Republican candidate for Va. House, 1981; Henrico County Republican Party chairman, 1982-86; Henrico County attorney, 1988-94; Va. attorney general, 1994-97; Republican National Committee chairman, 2001-present

Election results:

1997 GENERAL

James S. Gilmore III (R)	969,062	55.8%
Donald S. Beyer Jr. (D)	738,971	42.6%

Lt. Gov. John H. Hager (R)

First elected: 1997
Length of term: 4 years
Term expires: 1/02
Salary: $36,321
Phone: (804) 786-2078

STATE LEGISLATURE

General Assembly: Meets January-February in odd-numbered years; January-March in even-numbered years
House: 100 members, 2-year terms
2001 breakdown: 52R, 47D, 1I; 85 men, 15 women
Salary: $17,640
Phone: (804) 698-1527
Senate: 40 members, 4-year terms
2001 breakdown: 22R, 18D; 32 men, 8 women
Salary: $18,000
Phone: (804) 698-7410

STATE TERM LIMITS

Governor: Cannot serve consecutive terms
Senate: No
House: No

URBAN STATISTICS

CITY	POPULATION
Virginia Beach	433,461
Norfolk	225,875
Chesapeake	202,759
Richmond	189,700
Newport News	179,138

REGISTERED VOTERS

Voters do not register by party.

POPULATION

2000 population	7,078,515
1990 population	6,187,358
Percent change	+14.4%
Rank among states	12
Median age	34.8
Born in state	54%
Foreign born	5%
Urban/rural	69%/31%
Crime rate	345/100,000
Poverty level	8.8%
Federal workers	163,596
Military	164,865

REAPPORTIONMENT

Virginia retained its 11 House seats in reapportionment. The state legislature will draw new district lines in 2001.

MISCELLANEOUS

Web: www.state.va.us
Capital: Richmond
Land area: 39,598 sq. miles
Rank among states: 37
STATE ELECTION OFFICIAL
(804) 786-6551
DEMOCRATIC HEADQUARTERS
(804) 644-1966
REPUBLICAN HEADQUARTERS
(804) 780-0111

District Statistics

DIST.	2000 D	2000 R	GREEN	1996 D	1996 R	REF	1992 D	1992 R	I	WHT	BLK	ASIAN	HISP	HOUSEHOLD INCOME	OVER 65+	UNDER 18	COLLEGE EDUCATION
1	39%	58%	2%	41%	51%	7%				75%	20%	2%	3%				
2	45	53	2	45	47	7				67	23	5	4				
3	65	32	2	65	29	5				38	57	1	3				
4	49.0	49.2	1	50	42	7				57	39	1	2				
5	40	56	2	43	48	8	41%	47%	12%	73	24	1	2	$24,807	14%	23%	13%
6	39	58	2	41	50	8	37	50	13	85	12	1	2	$27,155	15	22	17
7	35	62	2	34	59	6				82	13	2	2				
8	55	40	4	55	40	4	51	37	11	67	14	9	14	$48,839	9	19	48
9	42	55	2	46	43	10	45	43	12	95	3	1	1	$20,857	13	23	12
10	39	58	2	38	54	6	33	50	17	83	7	5	6	$46,205	7	27	30
11	49	47	3	48	46	5	42.6	43.1	14	67	11	12	13	$54,369	6	25	44
STATE	**44**	**52**	**2**	**45**	**47**	**7**	**41**	**45**	**14**	**72**	**20**	**4**	**5**	**$33,328**	**11**	**24**	**25**

Note: 1998 redistricting changed some districts substantially. The 1996 presidential vote was recalculated. Racial and ethnic data is from the 2000 census.

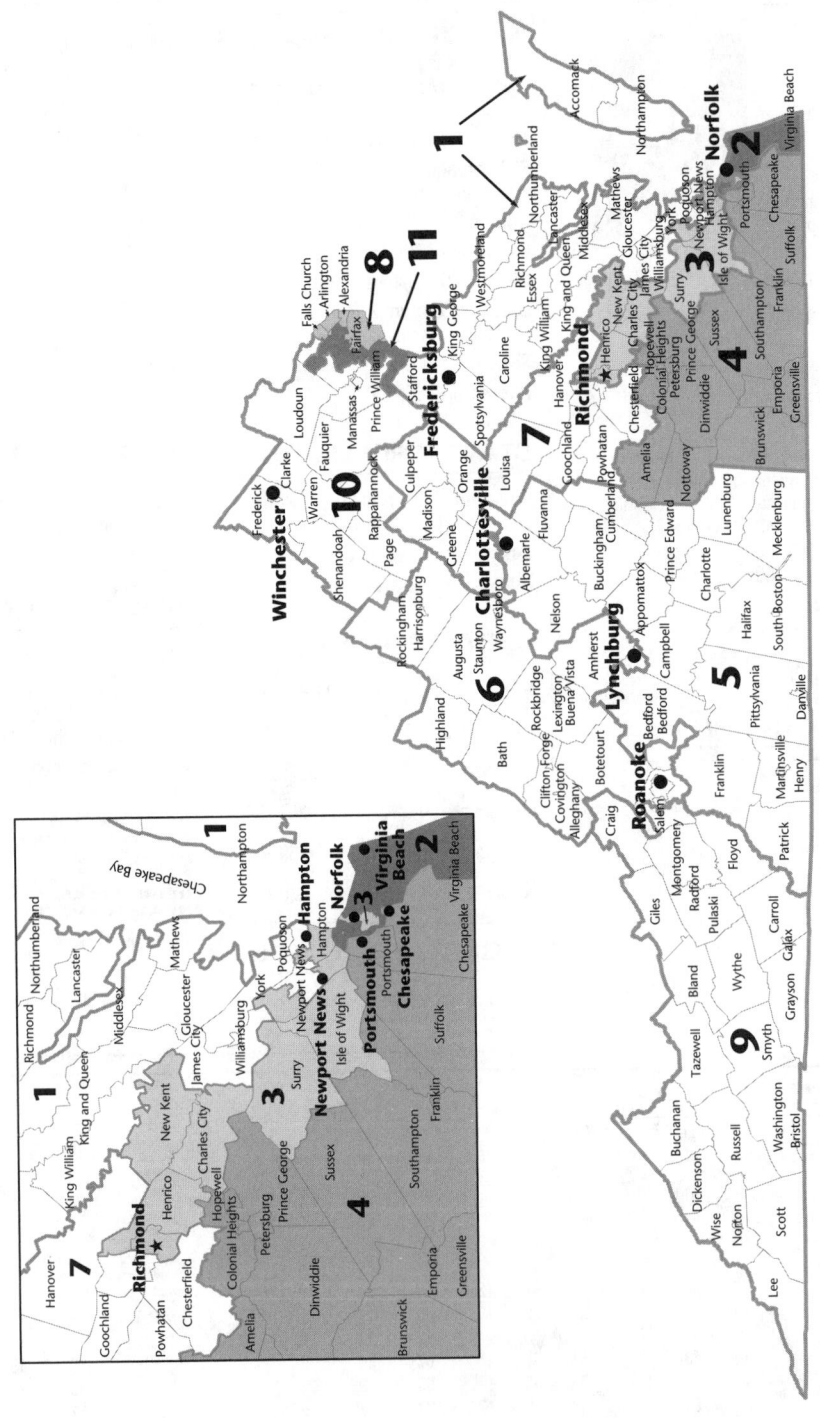

Sen. John W. Warner (R)

CAPITOL OFFICE
224-2023; fax 224-6295; 225 Russell Bldg. 20510

INTERNET
e-mail: senator@warner.senate.gov
web: warner.senate.gov

COMMITTEES
Armed Services - chairman
Environment & Public Works
Health, Education, Labor & Pensions
Rules & Administration

HOMETOWN
Alexandria

BORN
Feb. 18, 1927, Washington, D.C.

RELIGION
Episcopalian

FAMILY
Divorced; three children

EDUCATION
Washington and Lee U., B.S. 1949; U. of Virginia,
LL.B. 1953

MILITARY SERVICE
Navy, 1944-46; Marine Corps, 1950-52; Marine
Corps Reserve, 1952-64

CAREER
Lawyer; farmer

POLITICAL HIGHLIGHTS
Assistant U.S. attorney, 1956-60; under secretary
of the Navy, 1969-72; secretary of the Navy,
1972-74

ELECTION RESULTS

1996 GENERAL

John W. Warner (R)	1,235,744	52.5%
Mark Warner (D)	1,115,982	47.4%

1996 PRIMARY

John W. Warner (R)	323,520	65.5%
James C. Miller III (R)	170,015	34.5%

PREVIOUS WINNING PERCENTAGES
1990 (81%); 1984 (70%); 1978 (50%)

Elected 1978; 4th term

In more than two decades at the center of congressional action on national security and foreign affairs, Warner has demonstrated a grasp of the issues, an instinctive preference for consensus solutions and an aptitude for the political stoop labor needed to hammer them out.

For trying to bridge partisan disagreements that more-combative Republicans wanted to highlight, Warner has paid a hefty political price at times, both in the Senate and back home. But as the 107th Congress began — and Warner entered his third year as chairman of the Armed Services Committee — his political flanks were secure. Moreover, with George W. Bush in the White House, the debate over defense spending may take place in a climate congenial to Warner's pragmatic style — one that emphasizes solving problems rather than dramatizing disputes.

GOP animosity toward President Clinton ruled out bipartisan approaches, even on some ideologically neutral defense issues. Now, there is at least the possibility of significant bipartisanship on key defense issues, since President Bush is being guided by the type of internationalist Republicans who worked in his father's administration. While such an approach would resonate in the Senate with a significant number of Democrats as well as most Republicans, neither group's support may be taken for granted, so Warner's skill and diligence in working with colleagues is particularly important.

Though his overall voting record has been in the Senate Republican mainstream, Warner has displayed an independent streak since his arrival in 1979. He has been particularly confident of his own judgment on defense issues, lacing his speeches with references to his experience as undersecretary and then secretary of the Navy in the Nixon administration.

Early in his Senate career, Warner was discounted by some as a wealthy dilettante whose ruggedly handsome aspect, piercing gaze and sometimes florid rhetoric invited parody as Hollywood's version of a senator. That image was heightened by his marriage to movie star Elizabeth Taylor and, later, by his relationship with TV personality Barbara Walters. When Republicans took control of the Senate in 1981, however, Warner began demonstrating the attention to detail and legislative savvy that are now seen as his forte.

Warner informs himself and influences his colleagues through personal observation and face-to-face conversation rather than through think-tank seminars and academic analyses. He often visits gritty backwaters where U.S. forces are deployed or where U.S. strategic and commercial interests are involved. More routinely, he visits the Pentagon to sound out senior officers, some of whom he has dealt with for years.

On key defense issues that divide the two parties, Warner has been a loyal soldier in the GOP ranks. Indeed, during nearly two decades of largely inconclusive partisan sparring over the Republican-led effort to develop a national anti-missile defense, Warner had a pivotal role in the two initiatives that came closest to accelerating the program. But the deal he helped broker in 1995 was thwarted by conservatives, typifying a decade of clashes over his handling of issues ranging from anti-satellite weapons to the deployment of U.S. ships in the Persian Gulf.

His critics repeatedly charged that Warner's search for compromise blurred partisan differences that should have been highlighted to mobilize public support for the GOP cause. And they still say Warner failed to do enough to salvage the 1989 nomination of former Armed Services Committee Chairman John G. Tower, R-Texas, to be secretary of defense.

In a move widely regarded as payback, Strom Thurmond, R-S.C., who had yielded the senior Republican slot on Armed Services to Warner, reasserted his seniority in 1993. Warner's contentious relationship with conservatives was further exacerbated later that year when he refused to back a conservative Christian activist nominated by the Virginia Republican Party for lieutenant governor. And in 1994, he denounced the state GOP's Senate nominee, Oliver L. North, a central figure in the Iran-contra scandal, as unfit to serve in the Senate.

Conservatives retaliated by challenging Warner's own re-nomination in 1996, but the effort fizzled and Warner began assiduously shoring up his party standing. His most dramatic initiative to that end came in 1997, when, as Rules Committee chairman, he doggedly pursued for 10 months allegations that Sen. Mary L. Landrieu, D-La., had won in 1996 as a result of massive vote fraud. Ultimately, the Rules panel dropped the probe for want of evidence.

When Thurmond became Armed Services chairman in 1995, at age 92, Warner took on the delicate task of quietly keeping the panel on course. When Thurmond stepped down in 1999, there was no challenge to Warner's succession, but the job he acquired has much less clout than it did in the 1980s, when Warner was working his way up the committee ladder. With the Soviet Union a rapidly fading memory, defense issues have less prestige on Capitol Hill.

Moreover, the aura of importance surrounding the annual defense authorization bill — the panel's chief means of influencing military policy — has dimmed in the more than six years of Republican control of Capitol Hill. Because GOP hard-liners have used the measure to press an agenda with minimal chance of becoming law, the bill has often been overtaken, some say rendered almost superfluous, by the companion defense appropriations bill.

With Foreign Relations Committee Chairman Jesse Helms, R-N.C., so staunchly conservative on many issues, Warner has extended his role as a potential broker for bipartisan compromise into the foreign policy arena. In the 106th, for instance, he tried to loosen the embargo on food and medical shipments to Cuba and to end a long-running standoff with the United Nations over the arrears in U.S. dues.

Because of Warner's background — service in the Navy and Marines, and five years as a top Navy Department official — and because of his state's economic stake in the Atlantic Fleet base at Norfolk and in nearby Newport News Shipbuilding Inc., some Army officers worried that he would shill for the Navy as chairman. But Newport News' future as a supplier of aircraft carriers and submarines now seems secure, and Warner has been able to focus on shoring up the panel's clout on non-parochial issues, including preparation for such non-traditional threats as terrorist attacks with nuclear, chemical or biological weapons.

Warner has never been the choice of conservatives among Virginia's Republicans. Despite his in-state education, he was looked upon as an outsider. Some voters saw him as a socialite and fortune hunter: Before his marriage to Taylor, he was married to heiress Catherine Mellon and received a reported $7 million from her in their divorce settlement.

He became the party's Senate nominee in 1978 only after their pick, Richard Obenshain, died in a plane crash two months after defeating Warner at the state convention. Aided by his celebrity marriage to Taylor, whose presence guaranteed large crowds on the campaign trail, Warner won by fewer than 5,000 votes in the closest Senate election in Virginia history.

He won re-election handily in 1984 and 1990, but in 1996, after fending off the intraparty challenge, he was held to 52 percent by Democrat Mark Warner (no relation), a cellular telephone entrepreneur, who spent more than $10 million of his own money to challenge the incumbent.

KEY VOTES

2000
Yes Overhaul bankruptcy law and increase minimum wage
Yes Limit fiscal 2001 discretionary spending to $600.3 billion
Yes Override veto on nuclear waste disposal at Yucca Mountain site in Nevada
No Oppose effort to terminate Kosovo mission
No Include gender, sexual orientation and disability in federal hate crime protections
Yes Approve GOP plan to restrict use of genetic information by health insurers
Yes Kill amendment delaying implementation of an anti-missile defense system
Yes Cut taxes for married couples
Yes Grant China permanent normal trade status

1999
Yes Remove President Clinton from office for obstruction of justice
Yes Kill amendment authorizing state grants to hire teachers and reduce class size
Yes Require criminal background checks for purchases at gun shows
Yes Approve GOP proposal to increase rights of patients in managed-care health plans
No Block effort to allow farm and medicine exports to Cuba
X Allow study of tougher automobile fuel efficiency standards
No Ratify nuclear weapons testing treaty
No Prohibit national political parties from collecting "soft money" donations
Yes Remove barriers among banking, securities and insurance companies

INTEREST GROUPS

	AFL-CIO	ADA	CCUS	ACU
2000	0%	0%	100%	92%
1999	0%	10%	100%	84%
1998	13%	20%	100%	79%
1997	0%	10%	100%	80%
1996	0%	5%	85%	95%
1995	0%	5%	100%	91%
1994	25%	20%	90%	80%
1993	9%	10%	91%	84%
1992	17%	20%	100%	74%
1991	25%	20%	80%	76%

CQ VOTE STUDIES

	PARTY UNITY		PRESIDENTIAL SUPPORT	
	Support	Oppose	Support	Oppose
2000	92%	8%	52%	48%
1999	87%	13%	39%	61%
1998	85%	15%	39%	61%
1997	89%	11%	67%	33%
1996	93%	7%	42%	58%
1995	94%	6%	26%	74%
1994	77%	23%	60%	40%
1993	80%	20%	28%	72%
1992	87%	13%	73%	27%
1991	82%	18%	89%	11%

Sen. George F. Allen (R)

CAPITOL OFFICE
224-4024; fax 224-5432; 204 Russell Bldg. 20510

INTERNET
e-mail: senator_allen@allen.senate.gov
web: allen.senate.gov

COMMITTEES
Commerce, Science & Transportation
(Science, Technology & Space - chairman)
Foreign Relations
(International Operations & Terrorism -
chairman)
Small Business

HOMETOWN
Midlothian

BORN
March 8, 1952, Whittier, Calif.

RELIGION
Presbyterian

FAMILY
Wife, Susan Allen; three children

EDUCATION
U. of Virginia, B.A. 1974, J.D. 1977

CAREER
Lawyer

POLITICAL HIGHLIGHTS
Republican nominee for Va. House, 1979; Va.
House, 1982-91; U.S. House, 1991-93; governor,
1994-98

ELECTION RESULTS

2000 GENERAL

George F. Allen (R)	1,420,460	52.3%
Charles S. Robb (D)	1,296,093	47.7%

2000 PRIMARY

George F. Allen (R)	unopposed

PREVIOUS WINNING PERCENTAGES
1991 Special House Election (62%)

Elected 2000; 1st term

Allen said during his 2000 campaign that the best predictor of what someone will do in the future is what he or she did in the past. If that is true, Allen will be a vote for conservative tenets such as increased military spending, anti-crime initiatives, local control of education and tax reduction.

He styles himself a "common-sense conservative" in the mode of Thomas Jefferson, the intellectual third president of the United States and founder of the University of Virginia, Allen's alma mater.

Allen appears as comfortable in jeans and cowboy boots as in a business suit. And even critics who accuse him of glibness concede that he is a likeable figure. Some observers compare Allen's persona to that of former President Reagan, his political hero. (Allen co-chaired Young Virginians for Reagan during Reagan's 1976 challenge to President Ford.)

Despite his conservative orientation, the Virginian has expressed a desire to work with Democrats in Congress. He has modulated his tone since the 1994 state Republican convention. As Virginia's governor at the time, he said of Democrats, "Let's enjoy knocking their soft teeth down their whiny throats" — a line that brought to mind his victory-driven father, the late George Allen Sr., who coached the NFL's Los Angeles Rams and Washington Redskins.

One of Allen's bipartisan priorities is expanding the already large high-technology sector of Virginia's economy. He chairs the Senate Republican High Tech Task Force as well as the Commerce panel's Science, Technology and Space Subcommittee.

Along with a seat on Commerce, Allen won assignment to the Foreign Relations Committee. The post is a good match for a state with a large military presence. (Virginia's senior senator, Republican John W. Warner, chairs the Armed Services Committee.)

Not yet 50, Allen has a gold-plated political résumé. In 1982, he won a seat to the Virginia House, beating the Democratic incumbent who had defeated him in his initial political foray three years earlier. After serving nine years in the state legislature, in November 1991 Allen easily won a special election to replace ailing GOP Rep. D. French Slaughter Jr., who resigned.

Allen did not seek re-election in 1992 after a Democratic-drawn redistricting plan put him in the same district as veteran Republican Rep. Thomas J. Bliley Jr. But that left Allen free to run a long campaign for governor, which ended with his easy 1993 victory over Democratic state Attorney General Mary Sue Terry. As governor, he concentrated on abolishing parole and attracting high-tech industry to Virginia. His popularity helped spark a surge that carried the Republican Party to its current dominance in Virginia politics.

Limited by state law to one term as governor, Allen left office in 1998. But he quickly geared up for a campaign to unseat two-term Democratic Sen. Charles S. Robb in 2000. Once a towering political figure, Robb never recovered from questions about his personal life that forced him in 1994 to battle for re-election over the controversial GOP nominee, Iran-contra figure Oliver L. North. Robb's low-key demeanor also contrasted poorly with Allen's backslapping fellowship.

Allen gained an early advantage in campaign fundraising and moved quickly to secure support in populous Northern Virginia, Robb's home base. Though Robb managed a late upswing, Allen won, 52 percent to 48 percent. The Republican leadership showed its gratitude by naming Allen a deputy whip in the 107th Congress.

Rep. Jo Ann Davis (R)

CAPITOL OFFICE
225-4261; fax 225-4382
1123 Longworth Bldg. 20515

INTERNET
e-mail: joanndavis@mail.house.gov
web: www.house.gov/joanndavis

COMMITTEES
Armed Services
Government Reform
International Relations

HOMETOWN
Yorktown

BORN
June 29, 1950, Rowan, N.C.

RELIGION
Assemblies of God

FAMILY
Husband, Chuck Davis; two children

EDUCATION
Hampton Roads Business College, attended 1971

CAREER
Realtor; administrative assistant

POLITICAL HIGHLIGHTS
Va. House, 1998-2001

ELECTION RESULTS

2000 GENERAL

Jo Ann Davis (R)	151,344	57.5%
Lawrence Davies (D)	97,399	37.0%
Sharon Wood (LIBERT)	9,652	3.7%
Josh Billings (I)	4,082	1.6%

2000 PRIMARY

Jo Ann Davis (R)	14,274	35.2%
Paul Jost (R)	12,171	30.0%
Mike Rothfeld (R)	8,932	22.0%
Robert Cunningham (R)	2,686	6.6%
Philip G. Short (R)	2,535	6.2%

Elected 2000; 1st term

Davis made state political history with her 2000 victory, becoming the first Republican woman to represent Virginia in Congress. She succeeded nine-term Republican Rep. Herbert H. Bateman, who had planned to retire but died in September.

Unlike most Republican women in Congress — who tend to be moderates, especially on social issues such as abortion — Davis espouses solidly conservative positions on both fiscal and social issues.

Davis is a strong opponent of both abortion and gun control: Her campaign touted an "A" rating she received from the National Rifle Association. But if Davis' views are firmly right-of-center, they are not manifested in the fiery floor speeches that are a staple of some of her conservative colleagues. Davis has a low-key and soft-spoken demeanor.

Representing a Tidewater district with a large military constituency, Davis is following an agenda set by Bateman, who chaired the Armed Services Subcommittee on Military Readiness. Saying that her chief priority is strengthening the military, Davis landed a hoped-for seat on the Armed Services Committee, along with assignments to the Government Reform and International Relations panels.

Davis diverges from her predecessor in her career trajectory. Bateman was a practicing lawyer and longtime elected official. Davis grew up poor and quit college after just one day because she was homesick. She became an executive secretary, then later earned a real estate license and opened her own firm. She first ran for elective office in 1997, upsetting a veteran Democratic incumbent for a seat in the state House.

Davis' 2000 U.S. House victory testified to the strength of her grassroots appeal to conservative voters. She won the five-candidate Republican primary despite spending less than $40,000. The runner-up, businessman Paul Jost, spent more than $1 million.

In the general election — practically a formality in the solidly conservative 1st District — Davis easily beat Democrat Lawrence Davies, an African-American pastor and former Fredericksburg mayor.

VIRGINIA 1
East – Parts of Newport News and Hampton; Fredericksburg

The Republican-friendly 1st lies along Virginia's coast, swinging inland to pick up Fredericksburg in the north and sweeping around to take in Williamsburg and parts of the shipbuilding cities of Hampton and Newport News in the south. The district also stretches across the Chesapeake Bay to include Accomack and Northampton counties on Virginia's Eastern Shore.

After a court-ordered remapping of the neighboring 3rd District in 1998, the 1st had to adjust its lines, losing parts of Hampton and Richmond suburbs and regaining some of the inland counties it lost in a 1992 redrawing, including Essex and King and Queen. But the remapping had little political impact on this district where GOP candidates perform well on the state level.

Industry in the 1st revolves around its military installations and NASA sites, which have attracted a growing high-tech private sector. Colleges and universities also contribute to the district's economic base, as do shipbuilding and tourism. The most popular tourist destinations – Williamsburg, Jamestown and Yorktown – recall Virginia's Colonial past. Inland, agriculture and chickens help drive the economy.

MAJOR INDUSTRY
Defense, technology, agriculture

MILITARY BASES
Langley Air Force Base, 9,024 military, 1,721 civilian; Dahlgren Naval Surface Warfare Center, 893 military, 3,092 civilian; Yorktown Naval Weapons Station (Naval In-Service Engineering), 2,500; Fort A.P. Hill (Army), 777 military, 207 civilian (1999)

CITIES
Newport News (pt.), 76,003 (1990); Hampton (pt.), 54,518 (1990); Fredericksburg, 18,826

UNUSUAL FEATURES
Jamestown, the first English settlement in North America.

Rep. Ed Schrock (R)

CAPITOL OFFICE
225-4215; fax 225-4218; 128 Cannon Bldg. 20515

INTERNET
e-mail: ed.schrock@mail.house.gov

COMMITTEES
Armed Services
Budget
Government Reform
Small Business

HOMETOWN
Virginia Beach

BORN
April 6, 1941, Middletown, Ohio

RELIGION
Baptist

FAMILY
Wife, Judy Schrock; one child

EDUCATION
Alderson-Broaddus College, B.A. 1964; American U., M.A. 1975

MILITARY SERVICE
Navy, 1964-88

CAREER
Stockbroker; Navy officer

POLITICAL HIGHLIGHTS
Va. Senate, 1996-2001

ELECTION RESULTS

2000 GENERAL

Ed Schrock (R)	97,856	52.0%
Jody Wagner (D)	90,328	48.0%

2000 PRIMARY

Ed Schrock (R)	unopposed

Elected 2000; 1st term

Schrock is a conservative who spent 24 years in the Navy, retiring as a captain, and then began his political career in the state Senate. His views and military background made him a strong front-runner in 2000 when he ran to succeed seven-term Democratic Rep. Owen B. Pickett in the Republican-leaning 2nd District, home to the world's largest naval base — Norfolk Naval Base —and other military installations.

Yet Schrock needed all the help his credentials could give him. Faced with an unexpectedly strong Democratic opponent — securities lawyer Jody Wagner, a first-time candidate with a long record of community involvement and strong fundraising skills — Schrock just held on to win with 52 percent.

Schrock's congressional tenure got off to a promising start. He received the seat on the Armed Services Committee that House Republican leaders had promised him — the retired Pickett was a senior member on that panel — and was chosen president of the 28-member GOP freshman class.

Schrock advocates increased military spending and has expressed concern about difficulties the armed forces have had in recruiting and retaining personnel. Schrock also says he wants to improve delivery of health care services to veterans, and he is a proponent of the federal impact aid program that helps educate children who belong to military families.

An adherent of conservative Republican orthodoxy on social and fiscal issues, Schrock is an abortion opponent and as a state senator voted to ban a procedure its opponents call "partial birth" abortion. He backs tax credits to help parents save for their children's education.

As a state senator, Schrock sponsored a law that created a Cabinet-level technology secretary position in Virginia. He also helped secure funding for a technology center in Virginia Beach.

In addition to his Armed Services assignment, Schrock got seats on the Budget, Government Reform, and Small Business committees.

A 25-year survivor of cancer, Schrock says he is sensitive to the need for a strong health care system. He supports tax-free medical savings accounts and provision of a $2,000 health insurance credit to low-income families.

VIRGINIA 2

Virginia Beach and parts of Norfolk

Redistricting for the 1998 election gave the 2nd all of Virginia Beach, a center for white-collar, suburban military families and retirees. Although the added population should fit right in with the 2nd's conservative bent, the district retains parts of blue-collar Norfolk, and the district as a whole is willing to support Democrats who look after military interests.

Virginia Beach's tourism-driven population boom of the 1980s is over, but the area has held its ground in the face of military base closings. The Norfolk Naval Base continues to dominate the economy, which also is bolstered by shipbuilding and shipping companies. The Hampton Roads port is the world's biggest shipper of coal.

The 2nd is home to Pat Robertson's religious broadcast network, but the

district's conservatism derives more from military and economic issues than social questions. Although the district was represented by a Democrat for 14 years prior to the 2000 election, Republican presidential candidates fare well. Locally, Republicans hold the state House seats.

MAJOR INDUSTRY
Military, tourism, agriculture

MILITARY BASES
Norfolk Naval Base, 82,432 military, 28,125 civilian (2000); Oceana Naval Air Station, 8,624 military, 1,776 civilian; Little Creek Naval Amphibious Base, 6,298 military, 2,641 civilian; Fort Story (Army), 2,395 military, 29 civilian (1999); Atlantic Fleet Combat Training Center, Dam Neck, 2,355 military, 950 civilian (1998)

CITIES
Virginia Beach, 433,461; Norfolk (pt.), 169,702 (1990)

UNUSUAL FEATURES
Cape Henry Lighthouse in Virginia Beach is the oldest federal building in the United States, finished circa 1791.

Rep. Robert C. Scott (D)

Elected 1992; 5th term

CAPITOL OFFICE
225-8351; fax 225-8354; 2464 Rayburn Bldg. 20515

INTERNET
e-mail: www.house.gov/writerep
web: www.house.gov/scott

COMMITTEES
Education & Workforce
Judiciary

HOMETOWN
Newport News

BORN
April 30, 1947, Washington, D.C.

RELIGION
Episcopalian

FAMILY
Divorced

EDUCATION
Harvard U., A.B. 1969; Boston College, J.D. 1973

MILITARY SERVICE
Army Reserve, 1970-74; Mass. National Guard, 1974-76

CAREER
Lawyer

POLITICAL HIGHLIGHTS
Va. House, 1979-83; Va. Senate, 1983-93; Democratic nominee for U.S. House, 1986

ELECTION RESULTS

2000 GENERAL

Robert C. Scott (D)	137,527	97.7%
write-ins	3,226	2.3%

2000 PRIMARY

Robert C. Scott (D)	unopposed

1998 GENERAL

Robert C. Scott (D)	48,129	76.0%
Robert S. Barnett (I)	14,453	22.8%
write-ins	772	1.2%

PREVIOUS WINNING PERCENTAGES
1996 (82%); 1994 (79%); 1992 (79%)

Scott is a pillar of the Democratic left, challenging a wide range of conservative initiatives. The first black to represent Virginia in the House since 1891, Scott is a dependable voice for the liberal position, supporting abortion rights, opposing the death penalty and faulting Republicans for lavishing resources on punishment for crimes while starving social programs that he says will help prevent crime.

As the top-ranking Democrat on Judiciary's Crime Subcommittee, Scott has been a persistent and vocal obstacle to GOP crime measures, questioning whether the Republican proposals violate the rights of defendants, consumers and poor people. Scott is also a leading critic of GOP plans to provide federal funding for faith-based organizations that provide social services. He argues that funding such groups would be unconstitutional because sponsors of these faith-based programs would be permitted to discriminate in hiring.

When Republicans try to pass constitutional amendments to protect the flag, promote school prayer, limit taxation or extend rights to crime victims, Scott admonishes members that they took an oath to "support and defend" the Constitution, not "support and amend" it, as he said in 1997. During debate on a constitutional amendment to ban desecration of the U.S. flag, Scott argued that the whole point of the First Amendment is to protect unpopular forms of expression, even flag burning, from a "tyranny of the majority." He said, "We have not, in this 200 years, amended our Constitution to stop cross burnings, racial epithets, or pornography, despite the fact that these forms of speech are also offensive to many."

On a host of Republican crime bills, Scott has argued that the GOP's "tough on crime" approach does not work. He says education and jobs are the answer. "It makes no sense, waiting for the children to mess up and then lock them up, when it is cheaper to invest in crime prevention programs and prevent them from getting in trouble in the first place," he said. Scott says that some, but not all, of his views are based on the racial inequity of the criminal justice system. He points out that the death penalty is disproportionately imposed on black defendants and that racial profiling in police work is a serious issue. Scott says that "justice is not dispensed equally. If you have money, you get by. If you don't, you don't."

Although he argues against many of the GOP crime initiatives, Scott was generally able to work well with Crime Subcommittee Chairman Bill McCollum of Florida.

From his seat on the Education and the Workforce Committee, Scott advances the argument that standardized test scores (he calls it "high stakes testing") should not be viewed as the benchmark for determining whether schools are doing their job. Scott says that standardized tests place low-income school districts and their students at a disadvantage. If the government requires students to pass such tests before they can graduate, Scott argues: "If you find a school where you have people not passing, you ought not punish the students; you ought to fix the school."

But Scott will leave behind his liberal roots when it comes to looking out for southeast Virginia's military establishment and its tobacco growers and producers. And Scott has found himself allied with Republicans on some issues that he believes would subvert the Constitution, including campaign finance restrictions and measures to protect property owners from government actions that adversely affect their use of the land.

A former member of the Army Reserve and the National Guard, Scott is a leading pro-Pentagon voice in the Congressional Black Caucus. He seeks to advance the interests of the military bases and shipbuilding facilities in the 3rd District, where Newport News Shipbuilding and the Army's Fort Eustis are major employers. Scott's district is also home to one of the nation's largest cigarette plants, a south Richmond facility operated by Philip Morris. In 1997, he opposed efforts to eliminate the crop insurance subsidy for tobacco farmers.

Scott was a leading critic of Republican efforts in late 1998 to impeach President Clinton. On Judiciary, he argued that "historians and constitutional scholars have said that these allegations [against Clinton], even if they were true, do not constitute impeachable offenses." While the rest of the Democrats on Judiciary were ready to censure the president for his actions related to his relationship with a White House intern, Scott opposed even that step. He said that co-equal branches of government should not censure one another.

Scott is the son of a surgeon and a teacher. When local white officials resisted court-ordered integration of the Richmond schools, the Scotts, along with other well-to-do black families, sent their son to a Massachusetts prep school. He graduated from Harvard University and earned his law degree from Boston College. He returned home to Newport News after law school and became active in local civic groups and political organizations.

Scott won a seat in the state House in 1978 and moved up to the state Senate in 1983. He first ran for the U.S. House in 1986, but failed to unseat 1st District GOP Rep. Herbert H. Bateman. Scott nevertheless captured 44 percent of the vote and broadened his name recognition.

In 1992, with a newly drawn 3rd District that was 64 percent black, Scott tried again. He easily won the Democratic primary, and his victory in the general election was a forgone conclusion, given the district's demographics.

In 1997, his political future was jeopardized when a three-judge federal panel struck down the 3rd District's boundaries. But Virginia lawmakers agreed upon a plan, passed by the General Assembly in February 1998 and approved by the Justice Department a month later, that redrew the lines without harming Scott's prospects for re-election.

The 3rd's black population was cut to 54 percent, largely by removing black neighborhoods in Petersburg and Portsmouth, but Scott was re-elected in November with 76 percent of the vote. In 2000, Republicans did not field a candidate.

KEY VOTES

2000

Yes Raise hourly minimum wage by $1 over two years
No   Halt funding for U.S. mission in Kosovo unless European nations pay more
Yes Provide Medicare benefits to military retirees and their dependents
No   Grant China permanent normal trade status
No   Phase out estate, gift and trust taxes
No   Prohibit implementation of president's national monument designations
No   Approve GOP plan to provide prescription drug coverage for Medicare beneficiaries
Yes Increase help for poor nations indebted to international financial institutions

1999

Yes Impose steel import quotas
No   Kill proposal to take aviation trust funds off budget
No   Require background checks on buyers only at gun shows with 10 or more vendors
Yes Remove barriers among banking, securities and insurance companies
Yes Authorize state grants to hire teachers and reduce class size
No   Overhaul campaign finance law; ban "soft money" and restrict advocacy advertising
Yes Approve bipartisan plan to increase rights of patients in managed-care health plans

INTEREST GROUPS

	AFL-CIO	ADA	CCUS	ACU
2000	100%	95%	42%	4%
1999	89%	90%	28%	4%
1998	100%	95%	28%	20%
1997	100%	90%	40%	8%

CQ VOTE STUDIES

	PARTY UNITY		PRESIDENTIAL SUPPORT	
	Support	Oppose	Support	Oppose
2000	93%	7%	81%	19%
1999	91%	9%	83%	17%
1998	91%	9%	89%	11%
1997	89%	11%	72%	28%

VIRGINIA 3

Southeast — Parts of Richmond, Newport News and Norfolk

Court-ordered redistricting for the 1998 election reduced the 3rd's black population from 64 to nearly 54 percent, but the move did not diminish the district's Democratic loyalties, which are easily the strongest in the state. The remapping also did little to change the economic character of the district, the boundaries of which begin in historic Richmond and reach southeast into military and shipbuilding territory, including parts of Newport News, Hampton and Norfolk.

In the 1990s, the 3rd continued to benefit from one of the nation's largest ports at Hampton Roads and from growing financial firms in Richmond. State government is another major component driving the economy of Richmond and its vicinity, as is manufacturing. Richmond boasts one of the largest cigarette plants in the nation.

The Hampton Roads area has a heavy concentration of naval installations as well as shipbuilding and ship repair companies. Among these is the nation's largest privately owned shipyard – Newport News Shipbuilding – which builds Navy carriers and submarines. The 3rd has not been immune to military cutbacks. Fort Eustis experienced sizable downsizing in the 1990s, and the industrial city of Norfolk suffered population loss, which also was blamed on military downsizing.

Democratic Rep. Scott has won by wide margins, and the 3rd voted strongly in favor of Al Gore in 2000. Locally, Democrats are favored in elections, although there are some Republican-leaning areas, particularly near Richmond.

MAJOR INDUSTRY
Defense, shipbuilding and repair, shipping

MILITARY BASES
Fort Eustis (Army), 6,137 military, 2,249 civilian; Fort Monroe (Army), 770 military, 1,425 civilian (1999)

CITIES
Richmond (pt.), 167,776 (1990); Newport News (pt.), 94,042 (1990); Norfolk (pt.), 91,527 (1990); Hampton (pt.), 79,275 (1990)

UNUSUAL FEATURES
Edgar Allen Poe Museum; The author spent much of his childhood in Richmond.

Vacant Seat

Rep. Norman Sisisky, D
Died March 29, 2001

Democratic Rep. Norman Sisisky, a genial and persistent man who was a key figure for his Virginia Tidewater district on the Armed Services Committee, died March 29, 2001. He had surgery for lung cancer only days before his death. He had survived a bout with colon cancer in 1995.

Sisisky was the second-ranking Democrat on Armed Services — an important post for a district with a heavy military presence, including the Army's Fort Lee and the Norfolk Naval Shipyard, a repair facility for much of the fleet.

A special election to fill the remainder of Sisisky's term was scheduled for June 19, 2001.

After initially winning his seat in 1982, Sisisky easily prevailed in his subsequent re-election contests. The GOP did not even field a candidate against him in 1998 or 2000.

Yet Republicans were optimistic of winning the special election to succeed Sisisky. GOP officials said the 4th District is typical of the conservative-leaning Southern districts that their candidates have won following the departures of popular Democratic incumbents, but the 2000 presidential election showed that the 4th can be a political battleground. George W. Bush carried the district by a margin of just 473 votes in 2000.

Sisisky's death followed the departures of two other Tidewater lawmakers who served on Armed Services. Democrat Owen B. Pickett of Virginia's 2nd District did not seek re-election in 2000; Republican Herbert H. Bateman of the 1st District, who planned to retire, died on Sept. 11, 2000.

Since his first day in Congress, Sisisky's main work was on defense issues. His Armed Services duties were so important to him that in early 1998, when he had the chance to become ranking Democrat on the full Small Business Committee, he turned down the post because he would have had to relinquish his ranking minority spot on the Armed Services Military Procurement Subcommittee. Sisisky used every opportunity to promote the Navy, and especially the big aircraft carriers built in Newport News, just across the James River from his district.

The military's influence lends a conservative flavor to politics in the 4th District, and Sisisky reflected its leanings. A member of the "Blue Dogs," a coalition of center-right Democrats, Sisisky's habitual seat on the House floor was next to the center aisle that divides Democrats and Republicans, symbolizing his readiness for compromise.

He supported a constitutional amendment to ban desecration of the U.S. flag and backed gun owners' rights. On environmental issues, he was sympathetic to the business community's concerns about regulations it viewed as burdensome. He looked out for programs important to the district's many peanut and tobacco farms.

But Sisisky's voting record also had some liberal and populist elements, reflecting the fact that the 4th District includes a sizable black population and many working-class whites. He opposed taxpayer-financed vouchers to pay for private school tuition and a plan to require a two-thirds majority vote of Congress to raise taxes. Siding with organized labor, he voted in 2000 against granting China permanent normal trade status, citing concerns about that country's "proliferation of weapons."

Sisisky built a small soft-drink bottling firm into a successful beverage distributorship and was a millionaire before he entered politics, winning a state assembly seat in 1973 and a U.S. House seat in 1982.

VIRGINIA 4
Southeast — Chesapeake; Portsmouth

Located in the southeastern part of the state, the 4th takes in both rural tobacco growing areas and the military towns of Chesapeake and Portsmouth. The district's boundaries were redrawn in 1998 for the election that began the 106th Congress; it picked up urban areas from the neighboring 3rd, a black-majority district, which increased the 4th's black population from 32 to 39 percent.

Although the 4th's military installations lost civilian employees in the 1990s wave of downsizing, the overall effect on the district was small. The district's largest city, Chesapeake, compensated by attracting new manufacturing businesses. Outside of the 4th's urban areas, tobacco and peanut farming play a central role, especially in counties along the North Carolina border.

A politically competitive district, the 4th elected a Democrat in 1982 after the seat had been held by a Republican for 10 years. Redistricting in 1998 might have given the 4th a more liberal streak, but it is expected not to have much of an effect overall. Local seats are shared by both parties.

MAJOR INDUSTRY
Military, agriculture, health care

MILITARY BASES
Fort Lee (Army), 3,684 military, 1,873 civilian; Naval Security Group Activity Northwest, 654 military, 231 civilian; Naval Medical Center Portsmouth, 3,900 military, 900 civilian (1999); Norfolk Naval Shipyard at Portsmouth, 50 military, 3,315 civilian (2000); U.S. Atlantic Command's Joint Warfighting Center, 176 military, 145 civilian; Coast Guard Atlantic Area and 5th District Headquarters, 4,300 military (total number including personnel at other bases, civilian number not available) (1998)

CITIES
Chesapeake, 202,759; Portsmouth, 98,305; Suffolk, 64,805; Petersburg, 34,398

UNUSUAL FEATURES
Planters Mr. Peanut statue in Suffolk.

RECENT ELECTION RESULTS

2000 GENERAL		
Norman Sisisky (D)	189,787	98.9%
write-ins	2,108	1.1%
1998 GENERAL		
Norman Sisisky (D)	64,563	97.0%
write-ins	2,016	3.0%
1996 GENERAL		
Norman Sisisky (D)	160,100	78.6%
A.J. "Tony" Zevgolis (R)	43,516	21.4%
1994 GENERAL		
Norman Sisisky (D)	115,055	61.6%
George Sweet (R)	71,678	38.4%
1992 GENERAL		
Norman Sisisky (D)	147,649	68.4%
A.J. "Tony" Zevgolis (R)	68,286	31.6%

Rep. Virgil H. Goode Jr. (I)

Elected 1996; 3rd term

CAPITOL OFFICE
225-4711; fax 225-5681
1520 Longworth Bldg. 20515

INTERNET
e-mail: rep.goode@mail.house.gov
web: www.house.gov/goode

COMMITTEES
Appropriations

HOMETOWN
Rocky Mount

BORN
Oct. 17, 1946, Richmond, Va.

RELIGION
Baptist

FAMILY
Wife, Lucy D. Goode; one child

EDUCATION
U. of Richmond, B.A. 1969; U. of Virginia, J.D. 1973

MILITARY SERVICE
Va. National Guard, 1969-75

CAREER
Lawyer

POLITICAL HIGHLIGHTS
Va. Senate, 1973-97; sought Democratic
nomination for U.S. Senate, 1982, 1994

ELECTION RESULTS

2000 GENERAL

Virgil H. Goode Jr. (I)	143,312	67.4%
John Boyd (D)	65,387	30.7%
Joseph S. Spence (I)	3,936	1.9%

1998 GENERAL

Virgil H. Goode Jr. (D)	73,097	98.9%
write-ins	785	1.1%

PREVIOUS WINNING PERCENTAGES
1996 (60%)
* Elected as a Democrat 1996-98

Early in 2000, Goode took a step that, based on his voting record, was hardly a surprise — he left the Democratic Party and declared himself an Independent. He joined the Republican Caucus and voted for Republican J. Dennis Hastert for Speaker when the 107th Congress convened.

To many observers, Goode's move was long overdue. Ever since he came to Capitol Hill in 1997, his votes and views showed him to be more comfortable with the GOP. But his ancestral Democratic ties kept him from making the switch.

Democrats in Washington "treated me OK," Goode said. "But the majority view of the national party was not in tune with the views" of the folks back home. Goode (rhymes with food) said that the switch would allow him to vote his conscience without betraying his constituents. "I will be voting as I have been in the past," he told The Washington Post.

Goode agrees with Republicans on such issues as gun control, abortion and constitutional amendments to set term limits and ban desecration of the flag. He opposes tougher environmental controls on businesses. Even in 1999, when he was still a Democrat, he opposed the Clinton administration on roll call votes more often than such Republican stalwarts as Dick Armey and Tom DeLay of Texas and Henry J. Hyde of Illinois, and he supported the GOP party line more often than more than two dozen Republicans. For years, that kind of voting pattern prompted speculation that Goode was a good bet to leave the Democratic Party. But he would always reply that he was born and raised a Democrat and would remain in the party.

A number of other conservative Democrats, such as Texans Ralph Hall and Charles W. Stenholm, owe their Democratic allegiance more to historical roots than agreement on issues, and they formed the "Blue Dog" coalition in 1995 to give voice to their conservative philosophy. Since then, many Blue Dogs report, the Democratic Party has become more accepting of the conservative branch of the party. But Goode, who joined the Blue Dogs upon his arrival in Congress, remained uncomfortable, and speculation that he was about to leave the Democratic Party was always in the air.

In 1998, he was one of just five House Democrats who voted to impeach President Clinton. That action brought retaliation from local Democratic officials, who passed a motion expressing deep concern about his votes and declined to invite him to co-host the annual Jefferson-Jackson Day fundraising dinner. They later backed off their criticism, but when Goode switched, a number of campaign donors asked for their money back.

In aligning with the GOP on Capitol Hill, Goode found that Republicans treated him well. They immediately gave him a seat on the Appropriations Committee, which Goode used to press for funds for economic development in his district, known locally as Southside.

Goode's legislative priorities center on improving the economy in the relatively poor 5th District, which has been hurt by closures of textile plants and downsizing of the tobacco industry. In 2000, he voted against granting China permanent normal trade status, citing the loss of textile jobs to Asia.

He fought a congressional move to end crop insurance subsidies to tobacco farmers. "If we destroy the American tobacco farmer, 350,000 good jobs will be lost. We will be buying Chinese cigarettes, we will be buying Brazilian cigarettes, and we will be wrecking our trade surplus that agriculture so richly provides this nation," he warned.

He opposes the idea of subjecting tobacco to regulation by the Food and

Drug Administration. "If it regulates tobacco, is the [Food and Drug Administration] going to regulate sunshine next?" he asked. "People get skin cancer from too much sun."

Goode has often said, when asked why he didn't become a Republican: "My Daddy was a Democrat." So were his uncle and his grandfather, and most of the people around him when he was growing up in Rocky Mount.

Virgil Sr. was in the state legislature and also served as a commonwealth's attorney, and a stretch of highway in Rocky Mount is named after him. Virgil Jr. recalls tagging along with his father to local meetings and gatherings around wood stoves at the country stores that were the public meeting places in many small towns in the district. "If you could get the country store vote, you had it made," Goode recalls.

Upon his graduation from law school, Goode quickly jumped into politics when an opening developed in the state Senate. He made no secret of having higher ambitions, and in 1982 and 1994, unsuccessfully pursued his party's nomination for the U.S. Senate.

Goode's reputation as a maverick had been cemented after the state legislative elections of 1995, when the state Senate was deadlocked. Democrats retained effective control because the Democratic lieutenant governor held a tie-breaking vote. But Goode insisted on an "equitable division" of power in the committee system, and he forced a power-sharing arrangement in which the GOP gained control of four committees. Goode himself surrendered a gavel to a Republican to help grease the deal. (He did get a slot on the conference committee that determined the state budget.) Goode reportedly disapproved of the Democrats who were in line to chair some committees, thinking them hostile to gun owners' rights and the tobacco industry.

In 1996, the day after Democratic Rep. L. F. Payne Jr. announced he would not seek another term from the 5th, Goode launched his bid for Congress, boasting strong support from Democratic elected officials in the district and a core of faithful followers built up over his six terms in the state Senate. Goode campaigned in his trademark down-home style, reminiscent of his father's, driving around the district to small-town events where he winged most of his speeches and habitually handed out emery boards and pencils embossed with his name. (His father used to give out small kitchen implements.) He won by 24 percentage points. In 1998, he drew no GOP foe.

After he left the Democratic Party, local party officials vowed to mount a serious election challenge in 2000, but the party did little to aid its candidate, black farmer and activist John Boyd, and Goode cruised to an easy victory.

KEY VOTES

2000

No Raise hourly minimum wage by $1 over two years

Yes Halt funding for U.S. mission in Kosovo unless European nations pay more

Yes Provide Medicare benefits to military retirees and their dependents

No Grant China permanent normal trade status

Yes Phase out estate, gift and trust taxes

Yes Prohibit implementation of president's national monument designations

Yes Approve GOP plan to provide prescription drug coverage for Medicare beneficiaries

No Increase help for poor nations indebted to international financial institutions

1999

Yes Impose steel import quotas

No Kill proposal to take aviation trust funds off budget

No Require background checks on buyers only at gun shows with 10 or more vendors

Yes Remove barriers among banking, securities and insurance companies

No Authorize state grants to hire teachers and reduce class size

No Overhaul campaign finance law; ban "soft money" and restrict advocacy advertising

No Approve bipartisan plan to increase rights of patients in managed-care health plans

INTEREST GROUPS

	AFL-CIO	ADA	CCUS	ACU
2000	10%	10%	66%	100%
1999	44%	25%	84%	92%
1998	30%	30%	72%	83%
1997	13%	25%	80%	84%

CQ VOTE STUDIES

	PARTY UNITY		PRESIDENTIAL SUPPORT	
	Support	Oppose	Support	Oppose
2000	94%	6%	14%	86%
1999	22%	78%	16%	84%
1998	28%	72%	26%	74%
1997	38%	62%	29%	71%

VIRGINIA 5
South — Danville; Charlottesville

Rich in Civil War landmarks, the 5th extends from Charlottesville, in the central part of the state, to the south-central tier bordering North Carolina, an area known as "Southside." Protecting tobacco growers is important in the rural 5th, as are issues that affect the district's elderly.

A relatively poor district, the 5th relies heavily on agriculture and textiles. Known as the heart of tobacco country, the 5th still supports a vast tobacco industry, but in recent years manufacturing has taken a more prominent role. Danville, the district's largest city, is a tobacco and textile center on the North Carolina border. To the west is Henry County, which surrounds the textile and furniture town of Martinsville.

The seasonal nature of the economy led to above-average unemployment during some of the 1990s in the district's southwestern corner — Danville and the area west of it. But the district's economy also saw some strong performances during the decade. Bedford

County, between Roanoke and Lynchburg, and Fluvanna County, in the orbit of Charlottesville, have grown by attracting commuters as well as many small businesses.

The 5th is politically mixed: It has supported Democrats in Congress but went for GOP presidential candidates in 1992, '96 and 2000. Suburban Charlottesville, home of the University of Virginia, stands out for its near-universal support of Democrats. Overall, the district tends to elect conservative Democrats, who survive in spite of Republican strength in local and presidential races.

MAJOR INDUSTRY
Agriculture, manufacturing, service

CITIES
Danville, 50,795; Charlottesville, 36,815; Martinsville, 14,996

UNUSUAL FEATURES
Appomattox Court House, where Gen. Robert E. Lee surrendered to Gen. Ulysses S. Grant, ending the Civil War; Thomas Jefferson's home, Monticello, just south of Charlottesville.

Rep. Robert W. Goodlatte (R)

Elected 1992; 5th term

CAPITOL OFFICE
225-5431; fax 225-9681; 2240 Rayburn Bldg. 20515

INTERNET
e-mail: talk2bob@mail.house.gov
web: www.house.gov/goodlatte

COMMITTEES
Agriculture
   (Department Operations, Oversight, Nutrition &
   Forestry - chairman)
Education & Workforce
Judiciary

HOMETOWN
Roanoke

BORN
Sept. 22, 1952, Holyoke, Mass.

RELIGION
Christian Scientist

FAMILY
Wife, Maryellen Goodlatte; two children

EDUCATION
Bates College, B.A. 1974; Washington and Lee U.,
J.D. 1977

CAREER
Lawyer; congressional aide

POLITICAL HIGHLIGHTS
Roanoke City Republican Committee chairman,
1980-83; 6th Congressional District Republican
Party chairman, 1983-88

ELECTION RESULTS

2000 GENERAL

Robert W. Goodlatte (R)		unopposed

2000 PRIMARY

Robert W. Goodlatte (R)		unopposed

1998 GENERAL

Robert W. Goodlatte (R)	89,177	69.3%
David Bowers (D)	39,487	30.7%

PREVIOUS WINNING PERCENTAGES
1996 (67%); 1994 (100%); 1992 (60%)

As a lawyer in Roanoke, Goodlatte took advantage of the latest communications and information technology to build a competitive practice that included a specialty in immigration law. "Using technology, I was able to compete with lawyers from Washington and New York," he recalls.

Goodlatte believes his own experience offers a broader lesson: If areas such as the rural, agricultural 6th District are to participate in the nation's economic progress, they must be part of the ongoing technological revolution with its new means of communicating and sharing information. He draws a comparison with the railroad in the 19th century: "If the railroad came through your town, and connected you with the rest of the country, you'd boom. If it didn't, you'd go bust."

New technologies can actually give bucolic areas such as the 6th an advantage over big cities, Goodlatte says. The region's natural beauty, relatively low cost of living, low crime and unclogged roads are a powerful draw, particularly if 21st century jobs are available.

To this end, Goodlatte (GOOD-lat) has been a key player in almost every major computer-related bill before Congress, including measures aimed at protecting users' privacy, preserving intellectual copyright protections for artists and creators of software, shielding children from indecent material and safeguarding consumers from fraud. He was the principal House sponsor of legislation in the 106th Congress to provide loan guarantees to help rural satellite and cable television systems deliver local broadcast stations to viewers who would otherwise have no reception.

And to ensure that the modern-day Internet "railroad" and other means of communication do not bypass rural areas, Goodlatte has been a key player in a number of initiatives to encourage and provide incentives for the industry to bring new technologies to sparsely populated areas where the profit potential is less.

Along with his Virginia neighbor, Democrat Rick Boucher, who represents the rural 9th, Goodlatte co-chairs the bipartisan Congressional Internet Caucus. He also heads up the House Republican High Technology Working Group. In those roles, he strives to educate his fellow members about new technology issues and to advance the philosophy that the government should largely stay out of the way of innovators and entrepreneurs.

Goodlatte says that the GOP's philosophy about the limited role of government is more in tune with the needs and desires of high-tech industries than that of the Democratic Party. But he also notes that, thus far, most Internet-related issues have lent themselves to bipartisan cooperation in Congress. He cites as a prime example his partnership with California Democrat Zoe Lofgren on legislation to permit the export of software encryption technology, which allows digital information to be scrambled during computer transmission. While he seeks out bipartisan cooperation, Goodlatte's political philosophy and voting record matches his constituents' conservative views, on both fiscal and social issues.

Although Goodlatte is best known for his work on high-tech issues, he also holds a key post on the Agriculture Committee. As chairman of the Department Operations Subcommittee, Goodlatte is in a position to look out for the poultry and dairy farms that dominate the 6th District. In the 106th Congress, his subcommittee was given added jurisdiction over national forests, a matter of some consequence in this Shenandoah Valley district, where about a third of the acreage is national forest land.

Goodlatte also has a longstanding interest in the food stamp program and proudly notes that a number of GOP-authored changes in the program (along with an improved national economy) have reduced federal spending on food stamps by more than $10 billion annually.

He has been in the forefront of measures to ban convicted food stamp traffickers from ever receiving food stamp benefits; to ensure that prison inmates, who are provided "three square meals a day," are not also receiving food stamps; to improve record-keeping to ensure that dead people are not still listed on the rolls; and to require able-bodied food stamp recipients to work. And he touts food banks, which, with a relatively small amount of federal money, make use of volunteers from community groups to distribute food to needy people.

The information superhighway is not the only highway in which Goodlatte is interested. He obtained funds in the 1998 transportation bill for an upgrade of Interstate 81 and for preliminary work on a proposed new highway in his district, Interstate 73. And in 2000, he and Boucher teamed up to seek passenger rail service for southwest Virginia.

Goodlatte is low-key and prefers to work on the details of legislation rather than engage in partisan jousting. He says it is important for the GOP to trumpet its message and its accomplishments, but before it can do that, lawmakers first must do the hard work of passing legislation.

Goodlatte had a middle-class upbringing in western Massachusetts; his father managed a Friendly's ice cream store and his mother worked part time in a department store. They were not politically active, but Goodlatte remembers being fascinated by current affairs and politics at an early age.

His involvement in GOP activities dates back to his days as president of the College Republicans at Bates College in Maine. After getting a law degree at Washington & Lee College in Lexington, Va., Goodlatte went to work for the area's GOP congressman, M. Caldwell Butler. He served two years as the district office manager before starting his own law practice. He later joined a private law firm in Roanoke, all the while remaining active in a variety of local party posts.

Unlike in many other regions of Virginia, the GOP had long been competitive in the 6th. Goodlatte thought about running for Congress in 1986, but the arrival of his second child at the start of the campaign season kept him from entering the race. In 1992, however, when Democratic Rep. Jim Olin retired, Goodlatte decided the time was right. He won easily, with 60 percent of the vote, and has not been seriously challenged since.

KEY VOTES

2000

No Raise hourly minimum wage by $1 over two years
Yes Halt funding for U.S. mission in Kosovo unless European nations pay more
Yes Provide Medicare benefits to military retirees and their dependents
Yes Grant China permanent normal trade status
Yes Phase out estate, gift and trust taxes
Yes Prohibit implementation of president's national monument designations
Yes Approve GOP plan to provide prescription drug coverage for Medicare beneficiaries
No Increase help for poor nations indebted to international financial institutions

1999

No Impose steel import quotas
Yes Kill proposal to take aviation trust funds off budget
Yes Require background checks on buyers only at gun shows with 10 or more vendors
Yes Remove barriers among banking, securities and insurance companies
No Authorize state grants to hire teachers and reduce class size
No Overhaul campaign finance law; ban "soft money" and restrict advocacy advertising
No Approve bipartisan plan to increase rights of patients in managed-care health plans

INTEREST GROUPS

	AFL-CIO	ADA	CCUS	ACU
2000	0%	0%	85%	100%
1999	22%	5%	88%	96%
1998	0%	0%	100%	100%
1997	13%	10%	100%	80%

CQ VOTE STUDIES

	PARTY UNITY		PRESIDENTIAL SUPPORT	
	Support	Oppose	Support	Oppose
2000	97%	3%	22%	78%
1999	95%	5%	16%	84%
1998	92%	8%	23%	77%
1997	94%	6%	29%	71%

VIRGINIA 6

West – Roanoke; Lynchburg

Running along the Shenandoah Valley, the conservative 6th is a collage of mountainous terrain, small towns, medium-sized cities and natural beauty. The 6th has one of the largest populations of senior citizens in the state, a mostly white-collar work force and a generous dose of Republicans.

The brand of Republicanism in the rural valley has traditionally been a moderate one. The 1992 election of Republican Rep. Goodlatte ended the Democrats' decade-long domination of the 6th seat, but Democrats still won in local elections in the 1990s and remain competitive in towns north of Roanoke such as Covington and Clifton Forge. Chemical plants and pulpwood and paper mills are in this area. While Roanoke, the district's major population center, has a strong Democratic base with union ties, Republicans have done well in Roanoke's suburbs, in Lynchburg and in most rural areas.

Roanoke has a variety of industries, including furniture and electrical

products manufacturing. Both Roanoke and Lynchburg saw their populations shrink slighly in the 1990s, but the manufacturing economy was generally solid. Outside the Roanoke and Lynchburg metropolitan areas, the 6th depends mainly on dairy farming, livestock and poultry. In the north, Rockingham County leads the state in livestock and hay production. Tourists traveling to the district's national parks and numerous caverns also help boost the local economy.

MAJOR INDUSTRY
Agriculture, livestock, manufacturing

CITIES
Roanoke, 93,357; Lynchburg, 63,926; Harrisonburg, 34,129; Staunton, 24,496; Salem, 24,037

UNUSUAL FEATURES
Lynchburg is the home of evangelist Jerry Falwell's Liberty University and Thomas Road Baptist Church; President Woodrow Wilson born in Staunton (pronounced "Stanton").

Rep. Eric Cantor (R)

CAPITOL OFFICE
225-2815; fax 225-0011; 329 Cannon Bldg. 20515

INTERNET
e-mail: eric.cantor@mail.house.gov
web: www.house.gov/cantor

COMMITTEES
Financial Services
International Relations

HOMETOWN
Glen Allen

BORN
June 6, 1963, Richmond, Va.

RELIGION
Jewish

FAMILY
Wife, Diana Cantor; three children

EDUCATION
George Washington U., B.A. 1985; College of
William & Mary, J.D. 1988; Columbia U., M.S. 1989

CAREER
Lawyer

POLITICAL HIGHLIGHTS
Va. House, 1992-2001

ELECTION RESULTS

2000 GENERAL

Eric Cantor (R)	192,652	66.9%
Warren A. Stewart (D)	94,935	33.0%

2000 PRIMARY

Eric Cantor (R)	20,902	50.3%
Stephen H. Martin (R)	20,639	49.7%

Elected 2000; 1st term

Cantor was 37 years old when he won the 2000 race for the open seat in Virginia's 7th District. Though he is one of the younger members of the Class of 2000, his nine years in the Virginia House mark him as one of the most politically experienced.

Cantor brings to the 107th Congress a background in law and real estate, as well as a long association with the man he succeeded, 10-term Republican Rep. Thomas J. Bliley Jr., the chairman of the House Commerce Committee, who retired.

As a teenager, Cantor worked on Bliley's first House re-election campaign, in 1982. He would later serve as Bliley's campaign chairman.

Like Bliley, Cantor advocates limited government, lower taxes and a stronger military. Yet his conservative bearing does not prevent Cantor from describing himself as "someone who likes to work toward consensus, somebody who desires to work with all different types of people."

Given his business background and past service on the state House Corporations, Insurance and Banking Committee, Cantor likely welcomed his 107th Congress assignment to the Financial Services Committee.

Cantor backs spending restraint and tax reductions. He unsuccessfully pushed for a state constitutional amendment to require that some budget surplus money be returned to taxpayers. A $1,000 educational tax credit that could be used for books, computers or other educational needs is one of his top legislative priorities. He says the credit "would provide an incentive for parents to get involved in their children's education."

Also assigned to the International Relations Committee, Cantor is a strong supporter of Israel. He and New York's Benjamin A. Gilman currently are the only Jewish Republicans in the House.

Cantor essentially clinched his 2000 election in the primary. Running with Bliley's backing and a huge fundraising advantage, Cantor edged state Sen. Stephen H. Martin by just 263 votes. As the 7th is Virginia's most heavily Republican district, Cantor's one-sided win over Democratic educator Warren A. Stewart surprised no one.

VIRGINIA 7
Central – Part of Richmond and western suburbs

With some of the fastest growing areas in the state, the comfortably Republican 7th contains parts of Richmond, including its affluent old-money suburbs, and reaches north into farmlands. Redistricted for the 1998 election, the 7th traded some close-in Richmond suburbs for fast-growing areas to the west and north of the city.

Most of the 7th's residents work in Richmond, which grew steadily in the 1990s on the strength of banking and manufacturing. Richmond, the longtime center of state government and commerce, also was one of the South's early manufacturing centers, concentrating on tobacco processing. Nearby Philip Morris continues to employ thousands of employees who live in the district.

The northern stretch of the 7th is home to traditional farming communities that are gradually being taken over by people who drive or ride long-distance commuter buses or trains to jobs in metropolitan Washington. To the northwest, Greene County grew 48 percent in the 1990s by attracting Charlottesville commuters.

The 7th is a Republican bastion, with Republicans winning at every level of government. Republican presidential candidates won overwhelmingly in the 7th in 1992, '96 and 2000.

MAJOR INDUSTRY
Agriculture, government, manufacturing

MILITARY BASES
Defense Supply Center, Richmond, 52 military, 3,015 civilian (2001)

CITIES
Richmond (pt.), 58,511 (1990); Culpeper (unincorporated), 8,581 (1990); Ashland (unincorporated), 5,864 (1990)

UNUSUAL FEATURES
Tennis star Arthur Ashe born in Richmond in 1943.

Rep. James P. Moran (D)

Elected 1990; 6th term

CAPITOL OFFICE
225-4376; fax 225-0017; 2239 Rayburn Bldg. 20515

INTERNET
e-mail: www.house.gov/writerep
web: www.house.gov/moran

COMMITTEES
Appropriations
Budget

HOMETOWN
Arlington

BORN
May 16, 1945, Buffalo, N.Y.

RELIGION
Roman Catholic

FAMILY
Divorced; four children

EDUCATION
College of the Holy Cross, B.A. 1967; City U. of
New York, Bernard M. Baruch School of Finance,
attended 1967-68; U. of Pittsburgh, M.P.A. 1970

CAREER
Investment broker

POLITICAL HIGHLIGHTS
Alexandria City Council, 1979-84 (vice mayor, 1982-
84); mayor of Alexandria, 1985-90

ELECTION RESULTS

2000 GENERAL

James P. Moran (D)	164,178	63.3%
Demaris Miller (R)	88,262	34.1%
Ron Crickenberger (I)	3,483	1.3%
Rick Herron (I)	2,805	1.1%

2000 PRIMARY

James P. Moran (D)	unopposed

1998 GENERAL

James P. Moran (D)	97,545	66.7%
Demaris Miller (R)	48,352	33.1%

PREVIOUS WINNING PERCENTAGES
1996 (66%); 1994 (59%); 1992 (56%); 1990 (52%)

A former amateur boxer, Moran has spent much of his political career leading with his chin. He seems to relish his reputation as a pugilistic pol, but in the House he has also earned a reputation for working across party lines. He made headlines for a number of personal travails during the 106th Congress.

Moran has repeatedly spoken of wanting to break the noses of other politicians — even President Clinton's. After the president admitted to a relationship with a White House intern, Moran told Hillary Rodham Clinton that if he were the first lady's older brother, he would have taken the president outside and broken his nose.

Despite the rhetorical haymakers, he usually works amicably with his GOP colleague from the neighboring 11th District, Thomas M. Davis III. Moran and Davis have collaborated successfully to close the District of Columbia's troubled prison in the Virginia suburb of Lorton and to get funds for the replacement of the deteriorating and overcrowded Woodrow Wilson Bridge, which carries tens of thousands of suburban Virginia commuters across the Potomac River daily.

Moran regained his seat on the Appropriations Committee at the start of the 105th Congress — a position he had temporarily lost after the Republican takeover of Congress in 1995 reduced the number of committee seats assigned to Democrats. In the 107th, he took the top Democratic post on the Legislative Branch Subcommittee, relinquishing the ranking minority slot on the District of Columbia Subcommittee that he held in the 106th.

In an effort to steer toward the political middle, Moran in 1997 joined with two fellow Democrats to found the moderate New Democrat Coalition, which seeks "mainstream, bipartisan solutions" and which now numbers more than 70. Moran's own voting record is eclectic. Like most Democrats, he supported the effort to increase the minimum wage in 2000, and he joins his party in advocating environmental protection, gun control and, in most cases, abortion rights. But he sides with many conservatives in consistently voting for legislation to ban a procedure its opponents call "partial birth" abortion. He has also backed GOP efforts to gain approval of a balanced-budget constitutional amendment.

One of Moran's priorities is providing a skilled work force for the high-tech industry — a strong presence in Northern Virginia. He favors legislation to create regional alliances among industry, colleges and the federal government for developing high-tech training programs. Moran also has pushed tax credits for companies that provide high-tech training for their employees.

An ardent believer in free trade, Moran in 2000 joined with the majority of the New Democrats to go against the party grain and support a bill granting China permanent normal trade status. In 1998, he voted to give the president fast-track authority to negotiate trade agreements that Congress must approve or reject without amendment. He also backed approval of the 1993 North American Free Trade Agreement and the 1994 General Agreement on Tariffs and Trade.

Despite Moran's ability to work with members of both parties, he can display a partisan temper. As the House debated whether U.S. troops should be sent to Bosnia in 1995, Moran got into a tussle with California Republican Randy "Duke" Cunningham. As he was leaving the House floor, Moran gave Cunningham a stiff push, initiating a partisan shoving match among other lawmakers. (Cunningham had said Moran, who had voted against committing U.S. forces to the Persian Gulf in 1991, had "turned his back" on Desert Storm.)

A few months earlier, during consideration of a foreign aid bill, Moran had threatened to punch Indiana Republican Dan Burton. During an International Relations meeting, Burton had walked over to an official for the Agency for International Development to say he would try to cut the agency's budget. Moran, whose Northern Virginia district includes a substantial number of federal workers, called Burton's behavior "bullying" and warned: "You pull that again and I'll break your nose. Don't you ever do that to a federal worker again."

Moran's temper also was on display at home. His wife of 11 years, Mary, filed for divorce one day after placing an emergency call to police during a domestic argument. No charges were filed, and Moran brought his own divorce complaint three weeks later. Court filings showed the couple had lost a considerable amount of money: Moran blamed his wife for profligate spending; she blamed him for losing $120,000 in speculative stock trading.

In October 2000, The Washington Post reported that Moran had accepted a $25,000 low-interest loan from a lobbyist who was a close friend and was also running for a House seat in neighboring Montgomery County, Md.

First elected to the Alexandria City Council in 1979, Moran saw his career derail briefly in 1984 when, after pleading no contest to a misdemeanor conflict-of-interest charge, he resigned as vice mayor as part of a plea agreement. He ran as an independent in 1985 and beat the incumbent mayor. He was still serving as mayor in 1990 when he decided to mount a challenge to the 8th District's six-term GOP Rep. Stan Parris, one of the scrappiest street-fighters in Washington-area politics.

Moran and Parris clearly did not like each other. Parris compared Moran to Iraqi leader Saddam Hussein; Moran called Parris a "racist" and a "fatuous jerk" and professed a desire to "break his nose." Moran castigated Parris for his longstanding opposition to abortion. One television ad depicted women locked in jail cells, warning that Parris wanted to make abortion illegal. The ad ended with an image of the Statue of Liberty behind bars. Boosted by the abortion issue, Moran carried the election with 52 percent.

Redistricting in late 1991 transformed the 8th into a Democratic stronghold. Even within his new friendly confines, Moran had a fight on his hands in 1992. Arlington lawyer Kyle McSlarrow, a political newcomer, ran a nettlesome campaign. Moran touted his support for abortion rights and McSlarrow's opposition. He outspent McSlarrow by a 2-to-1 margin and earned 56 percent. Moran has never dipped below that percentage since.

KEY VOTES

2000
Yes Raise hourly minimum wage by $1 over two years
No   Halt funding for U.S. mission in Kosovo unless European nations pay more
Yes Provide Medicare benefits to military retirees and their dependents
Yes Grant China permanent normal trade status
Yes Phase out estate, gift and trust taxes
No   Prohibit implementation of president's national monument designations
No   Approve GOP plan to provide prescription drug coverage for Medicare beneficiaries
Yes Increase help for poor nations indebted to international financial institutions

1999
No   Impose steel import quotas
Yes Kill proposal to take aviation trust funds off budget
No   Require background checks on buyers only at gun shows with 10 or more vendors
Yes Remove barriers among banking, securities and insurance companies
Yes Authorize state grants to hire teachers and reduce class size
Yes Overhaul campaign finance law; ban "soft money" and restrict advocacy advertising
Yes Approve bipartisan plan to increase rights of patients in managed-care health plans

INTEREST GROUPS

	AFL-CIO	ADA	CCUS	ACU
2000	60%	70%	66%	12%
1999	67%	90%	64%	12%
1998	70%	75%	61%	8%
1997	88%	65%	50%	13%

CQ VOTE STUDIES

	PARTY UNITY		PRESIDENTIAL SUPPORT	
	Support	Oppose	Support	Oppose
2000	83%	17%	77%	23%
1999	79%	21%	75%	25%
1998	79%	21%	81%	19%
1997	80%	20%	75%	25%

VIRGINIA 8

D.C. suburbs — Part of Fairfax County; Arlington; Alexandria

An arc-shaped area in Northern Virginia, the Democratic 8th is one of the wealthiest districts in the state, although there are poorer pockets along the U.S. Route 1 corridor. The 8th is mostly white, but ethnic diversity has increased over time, especially in Arlington County and Alexandria. A smattering of landmarks gives the district a colonial flavor, but the area is far from old-fashioned. The 8th bustles with technology businesses and defense contractors, drawn to the district's substantial military presence, including the Pentagon.

Fairfax County is Virginia's most populous jurisdiction, and in the 1990s it led the district in growth. The trend continued elsewhere in the 8th. While government and defense-related employment is important to the economy, high-tech took off as the hot industry of the 1990s.

The 8th votes overwhelmingly Democratic in congressional and

presidential elections. Away from the Democratic base in Arlington and Alexandria, affluent voters in McLean elect a few Republicans locally.

MAJOR INDUSTRY
Government, high-tech, service

MILITARY BASES
Pentagon, 23,000 total (2001); Fort Belvoir (Army), 2,686 military, 4,488 civilian; Fort Myer (Army), 2,007 military, 808 civilian (1999); Naval Sea Systems Command, 350 military, 3,750 civilian (includes other naval employees); Henderson Hall, 1,910 military, 200 civilian (2001)

CITIES
Arlington, 174,838; Alexandria, 117,390; McLean (pt.) (unincorporated) 33,896 (1990)

UNUSUAL FEATURES
After losing the 2000 presidential election, Al Gore moved back into his suburban Arlington house, which he had rented out while serving as vice president; The U.S. Capitol could fit into any one of the Pentagon's five wedge-shaped sections; Despite the Pentagon's 17.5 miles of corridors, it takes only seven minutes to walk between any two points.

Rep. Rick Boucher (D)

Elected 1982; 10th term

CAPITOL OFFICE
225-3861; fax 225-0442; 2187 Rayburn Bldg. 20515

INTERNET
e-mail: ninthnet@mail.house.gov
web: www.house.gov/boucher

COMMITTEES
Energy & Commerce
Judiciary

HOMETOWN
Abingdon

BORN
Aug. 1, 1946, Abingdon, Va.

RELIGION
Methodist

FAMILY
Single

EDUCATION
Roanoke College, B.A. 1968; U. of Virginia, J.D. 1971

CAREER
Lawyer

POLITICAL HIGHLIGHTS
Va. Senate, 1976-82

ELECTION RESULTS

2000 GENERAL

Rick Boucher (D)	137,488	69.8%
Michael D. "Oz" Osborne (R)	59,335	30.1%

2000 PRIMARY

Rick Boucher (D)	unopposed

1998 GENERAL

Rick Boucher (D)	87,163	60.9%
Joe Barta (R)	55,918	39.1%

PREVIOUS WINNING PERCENTAGES
1996 (65%); 1994 (59%); 1992 (63%); 1990 (97%);
1988 (63%); 1986 (99%); 1984 (52%); 1982 (50%)

Boucher's interest in all things digital might seem to make him a bit of a mismatch with his rural, coal-mining constituency, but he has assiduously tended to the legislative needs of his district's small-town, cattle-raising, tobacco-growing residents. His leadership on Internet issues is not at all inappropriate for the economic hopes of his district.

Precise and wonkish, Boucher (BOUGH-cher) comes naturally to his job. His father was a Republican commonwealth's attorney in Washington County, and both his grandfather and great-grandfather were Democratic state delegates. "By the time I was 11 or 12, I made the decision to be an attorney and made the decision to be a part of public life," Boucher told The Roanoke Times & World News in 1997.

Boucher's views on Internet issues carry special weight because he is a member of both the Energy and Commerce and Judiciary committees. The two panels share jurisdiction over regulation of the new online economy. On Energy and Commerce, Boucher focuses on technology matters, a subject that has engrossed him since he tried to improve satellite TV service for his constituents in the 1980s. A co-founder of the Congressional Internet Caucus, Boucher tries to combine his interest in digital technology with his plans for economic development in the 9th. He dreams of electronic classrooms and envisions a linkage of all the high schools and colleges in southwest Virginia via fiber optics.

Boucher has secured grants from the Agriculture Department's Rural Utilities Service and such private concerns as GTE and Sprint to help link up area schools. He believes that electronic communication permits rural areas to be competitive with urban areas in many segments of the economy. "I see telecommunications as a bridge from any rural district to the American economic mainstream," Boucher said.

A key player on satellite, digital copyright and intellectual property issues, Boucher worked in the 106th Congress on legislation to set standards for the Internet. The ambitious measure aimed to establish privacy safeguards and regulate bulk commercial e-mail, as well as require cable TV companies to allow competing companies to use their cable wires for high-speed Internet access. Boucher also advocated an "e-sign" bill that would provide national recognition of digital signatures, thereby enabling contracts to be executed online.

In the 107th, he wants to amend federal copyright laws in order to make it legal to store music digitally and listen to songs over the Internet. It is important to "educate members of Congress about the potential for using the Internet in a manner that does not cost copyright owners anything but at the same time adds an enormous amount of convenience to users," he told The Associated Press. Boucher has been trying to foster the growth of the Internet since sponsoring legislation in the 103rd that would have accelerated development of the high-performance computer networks that provide the foundation for the "information superhighway." He also won passage of legislative provisions helping to ensure that rural phone customers have access to the latest technologies.

In his own House office, Boucher has eliminated the interoffice memo and decreed that all staff communication be done by e-mail or phone. He has a grand vision of the future, one in which members carry tiny, wireless "personal digital assistants" onto the House floor with Internet access and e-mail. When legislation is debated, a stream of information literally would be at members' fingertips. "I hope it would make lawmakers better at what they do," Boucher said.

On the Energy side of Energy and Commerce, a priority of Boucher's in the 107th is to emphasize the advantages of coal and pursue tax credits to aid in the use of cleaner coal-burning technologies. The committee will need to deal with with the issue of the nation's dwindling energy supplies.

On Judiciary, Boucher usually takes a bipartisan role. He often is the only Democrat joining with Republicans in supporting tough immigration policies and a prohibition on the recognition of same-sex marriage. He fought the Clinton administration on tobacco regulations, and he supports the rights of gun owners. Since the 105th Congress, he has joined with Republicans in an effort to toughen bankruptcy law, although he would soften some of the GOP's proposals. "Bankruptcy has become a financial planning tool for many who could repay their debts," he says.

Yet when the Judiciary Committee in 1998 took up its most high-profile debate of the decade — launching an inquiry into alleged impeachable offenses committed by President Clinton — Boucher took a more partisan tack. He was the Democrat who offered the party's resolution to conduct a narrower inquiry, hoping, he said during a rare floor appearance, to avoid a long-running spectacle that could harm the country.

He also backs his party's efforts to raise the minimum wage and opposes many GOP tax-cutting proposals. Organized labor is a strong presence in his district's coal counties, and Boucher has taken its side on trade issues. He voted against granting China permanent normal trade status in 2000, and in 1993, opposed the North American Free Trade Agreement.

Boucher has sought to validate his district's musical heritage. He sponsored a 1998 resolution recognizing the twin cities of Bristol, Va., and Bristol, Tenn., as the birthplace of country music. Some historians point to the Bristol area as launching the genre because of the famed "Bristol sessions" of 1927, with country music legends Jimmie Rodgers and the Carter family.

After graduating from the University of Virginia Law School, Boucher joined a Wall Street firm, worked as an advance man for George McGovern's 1972 presidential campaign, and ultimately joined his family's law firm in 1978. He won a seat in the state Senate, then took on GOP Rep. William C. Wampler in 1982. With high unemployment plaguing the district's coal fields, Boucher won the hard-fought contest by just 1,123 votes out of more than 150,000 cast. Two years later, he edged to a 4 percentage point victory over state Rep. Jefferson Stafford. He has had little trouble since, only once falling below 60 percent.

KEY VOTES

2000

Yes Raise hourly minimum wage by $1 over two years

Yes Halt funding for U.S. mission in Kosovo unless European nations pay more

Yes Provide Medicare benefits to military retirees and their dependents

No Grant China permanent normal trade status

Yes Phase out estate, gift and trust taxes

No Prohibit implementation of president's national monument designations

No Approve GOP plan to provide prescription drug coverage for Medicare beneficiaries

Yes Increase help for poor nations indebted to international financial institutions

1999

Yes Impose steel import quotas

? Kill proposal to take aviation trust funds off budget

No Require background checks on buyers only at gun shows with 10 or more vendors

Yes Remove barriers among banking, securities and insurance companies

Yes Authorize state grants to hire teachers and reduce class size

Yes Overhaul campaign finance law; ban "soft money" and restrict advocacy advertising

Yes Approve bipartisan plan to increase rights of patients in managed-care health plans

INTEREST GROUPS

	AFL-CIO	ADA	CCUS	ACU
2000	80%	75%	55%	29%
1999	88%	70%	48%	21%
1998	100%	95%	35%	4%
1997	100%	85%	40%	8%

CQ VOTE STUDIES

	PARTY UNITY		PRESIDENTIAL SUPPORT	
	Support	Oppose	Support	Oppose
2000	80%	20%	61%	39%
1999	75%	25%	67%	33%
1998	81%	19%	79%	21%
1997	82%	18%	76%	24%

VIRGINIA 9
Southwest – Blacksburg; Bristol

Covered with forests, mountainous terrain and a slew of small factory and coal towns, the Democratic-leaning 9th is rich in beauty but also is one of Virginia's poorest districts. Located in the southwestern part of the state, the 9th has struggled with high poverty rates and a weak economic base.

Coal mining provides jobs in counties at the western tip of the 9th, which also is the most economically depressed part of the district. Elsewhere, manufacturing is the major industry.

Diversifying the economy and ensuring clean drinking water for thousands of residents who lack it are priorities in the 9th. Leaders have targeted the Internet as a way to get community exposure and to offer residents new learning opportunities. Although the district's overall population was stagnant in the 1990s, Craig County grew with Salem and Roanoke commuters. Blacksburg, home to the state's largest university – Virginia Tech – remains the 9th's largest city.

Surrounding Montgomery County is economically atypical of the 9th.

The district is known as the "Fighting 9th," a name that reflects the area's fiercely competitive politics and its ornery isolation from the political establishment in Richmond. In the post-World War II era, when Democrats routinely dominated Virginia politics, the 9th was the one of the only areas in which Republicans were consistently strong. Since then, the GOP has lost ground, and Democrats have held the 9th since 1983. At the local level, members of both parties hold elected seats.

MAJOR INDUSTRY
Manufacturing, coal mining, agriculture

CITIES
Blacksburg, 34,458; Bristol, 16,709; Christiansburg, 16,615; Radford, 15,668

UNUSUAL FEATURES
Brass markers placed through the city of Bristol mark the Virginia-Tennessee state line.

Rep. Frank R. Wolf (R)

CAPITOL OFFICE
225-5136; fax 225-0437; 241 Cannon Bldg. 20515

INTERNET
e-mail: www.house.gov/writerep
web: www.house.gov/wolf

COMMITTEES
Appropriations
(Commerce, Justice, State & Judiciary -
chairman)

HOMETOWN
Vienna

BORN
Jan. 30, 1939, Philadelphia, Pa.

RELIGION
Presbyterian

FAMILY
Wife, Carolyn Wolf; five children

EDUCATION
Pennsylvania State U., B.A. 1961; Georgetown U.,
LL.B. 1965

MILITARY SERVICE
Army Reserve, 1962-63

CAREER
Lawyer; lobbyist; congressional aide

POLITICAL HIGHLIGHTS
Sought Republican nomination for U.S. House,
1976; Republican nominee for U.S. House, 1978

ELECTION RESULTS

2000 GENERAL

Frank R. Wolf (R)	238,817	84.2%
Brian M. Brown (LIBERT)	28,107	9.9%
Marc A. Rossi (I)	16,031	5.7%

2000 PRIMARY

Frank R. Wolf (R)	unopposed

1998 GENERAL

Frank R. Wolf (R)	103,648	71.6%
Cornell W. Brooks (D)	36,476	25.2%
Robert A. Buchanan (I)	4,506	3.1%

PREVIOUS WINNING PERCENTAGES
1996 (72%); 1994 (87%); 1992 (64%); 1990 (61%);
1988 (68%); 1986 (60%); 1984 (63%); 1982 (53%);
1980 (51%)

Elected 1980; 11th term

Wolf arrived in Congress two decades ago, long on conservative principles but short on legislative know-how. Over the years, he has learned how to pick his fights and make his presence felt.

Since the GOP takeover of Congress in 1995, Wolf has been one of the House's 13 "cardinals" — Appropriations subcommittee chairmen. From the helm of the Transportation Subcommittee, he shepherded the annual transportation spending bill through the process for six years with a minimum of controversy. He took the gavel of the Commerce, Justice, State and the Judiciary Subcommittee in the 107th Congress.

While low-key and deliberate as an appropriator, he can be passionate when it comes to his pet concerns, delivering heartfelt, and at times angry, speeches on the floor on issues ranging from human rights abuses in Tibet to the menace of large trucks on the highways.

Wolf's religious faith is a driving force in his work, especially in the foreign policy arena. He has been adamant in his criticism of some countries, including Iraq, China and Sudan, for human rights violations and religious persecution. In 2000, Wolf was among the 57 Republicans who voted against granting China permanent normal trade status, calling China an "evil empire" and citing allegations that the Chinese government imprisons religious leaders and has a one-child policy that critics say leads to forced abortions.

He has traveled widely to look into reports of human rights problems, and he maintains a feature on his website titled, "Congressman Wolf Investigates." His bill to establish a State Department office of religious persecution met with resistance from the Clinton administration, but it became law in 1998, though with milder language that the Senate had insisted upon. In the 107th, he and Democrat Tom Lantos of California are co-chairmen of the congressional Human Rights Caucus.

Wolf was the chief author of a law to create a national gambling commission to study the burgeoning industry and its impact on American society. He maintains that an increase in casinos has led to a higher incidence of compulsive gambling, and he faults the gambling industry for not taking the problem seriously. Of particular concern have been reports that some casinos run by American Indians have not benefited members of their tribes.

As Transportation Appropriations chairman, Wolf's legislative skills were often tested in battles with Bud Shuster, R-Pa., who chaired the authorizing Transportation Committee for the same six years. The two lawmakers clashed over guaranteed funding mechanisms in the massive 1998 highway and transit authorization law and again in 2000, during the writing of a law setting policy for aviation programs. Shuster bested Wolf on both measures, locking in funding for road and airport construction and limiting appropriators' options. Wolf had argued that not enough transportation funding would be available for other priorities, such as the Coast Guard, rail programs and air traffic control.

Wolf has shared GOP leaders' desire to contain transportation spending. In 1995, he backed the leadership's effort to reduce funding for transportation programs in pursuit of smaller deficits and reduced government. He initially succeeded in banning lawmakers' special "demonstration" projects, which he said would "liberate" his colleagues from having to deliver funding back home. But lawmakers' urge to spend money on home state projects could not be held back once fiscal forecasts showed the budget deficit disappearing.

Despite his rhetoric against "outright pork," Wolf has never short-changed his own district. One of the ways he has made himself electorally secure has been by working to ease the daily commuting grind for his constituents in the sprawling suburbs of Washington. In 2000, Wolf made sure there was ample funding for a replacement to the aging Woodrow Wilson bridge that spans the Potomac River, $50 million for improvements to a highway serving Dulles International Airport and $2 million to study proposals for an additional Potomac bridge to reduce congestion between the technology corridors of Northern Virginia and Maryland.

During the 106th Congress, Wolf showed he had learned enough legislative tricks to outmaneuver his powerful foes on transportation issues. He overcame the reluctance of Shuster and Senate Commerce Committee Chairman John McCain, R-Ariz., to address the issue of truck safety. He had been rebuffed by the two powerful chairmen in 1998 when he tried to toughen truck safety inspections by transferring the Federal Highway Administration's Office of Motor Carriers, which regulates long-haul carriers, to the National Highway Traffic Safety Administration. Wolf said the Office of Motor Carriers had become too cozy with the trucking industry.

Over the next year, Wolf helped to stoke publicity about the rising toll of truck-related highway deaths — convening hearings, allying himself with consumer groups, going out on truck inspections and beating the drum with media interviews. At the end of 1999, McCain and Shuster combined to pass legislation creating a new Motor Carrier Safety Administration.

In 2000, Wolf also reversed a previous defeat and orchestrated congressional approval of a new national .08 blood alcohol content standard. The beer, wine and spirits industries, with the backing of Shuster, had defeated a similar proposal in 1998.

It was with similar persistence that Wolf first won election to the House. Barely a year after Democrat Joseph L. Fisher won his House seat in 1974, Wolf began campaigning to defeat him. His 1976 effort had the backing of activists in the most conservative wing of the local GOP, but he did not survive the primary. In 1978, with greater name recognition and better financing, Wolf won the Republican nomination but lost to Fisher in November. In 1980, Wolf benefited from a national GOP surge, and capping a five-year effort, he won a narrow victory over Fisher.

Before his election to Congress, Wolf was an aide to Rep. Edward G. Biester, R-Pa., deputy assistant secretary of interior, and a lobbyist for baby food and farm implement manufacturers. He has enjoyed mostly smooth rides to re-election.

KEY VOTES

2000
No Raise hourly minimum wage by $1 over two years
No Halt funding for U.S. mission in Kosovo unless European nations pay more
Yes Provide Medicare benefits to military retirees and their dependents
No Grant China permanent normal trade status
Yes Phase out estate, gift and trust taxes
Yes Prohibit implementation of president's national monument designations
Yes Approve GOP plan to provide prescription drug coverage for Medicare beneficiaries
Yes Increase help for poor nations indebted to international financial institutions

1999
No Impose steel import quotas
Yes Kill proposal to take aviation trust funds off budget
Yes Require background checks on buyers only at gun shows with 10 or more vendors
Yes Remove barriers among banking, securities and insurance companies
No Authorize state grants to hire teachers and reduce class size
Yes Overhaul campaign finance law; ban "soft money" and restrict advocacy advertising
Yes Approve bipartisan plan to increase rights of patients in managed-care health plans

INTEREST GROUPS

	AFL-CIO	ADA	CCUS	ACU
2000	20%	10%	71%	72%
1999	22%	20%	68%	68%
1998	20%	10%	72%	80%
1997	25%	15%	90%	84%

CQ VOTE STUDIES

	PARTY UNITY		PRESIDENTIAL SUPPORT	
	Support	Oppose	Support	Oppose
2000	85%	15%	30%	70%
1999	84%	16%	32%	68%
1998	88%	12%	24%	76%
1997	88%	12%	28%	72%

VIRGINIA 10
North — Part of Fairfax County

Located in the northern part of Virginia, the Republican-oriented 10th bridges a dizzying range of economies and lifestyles, with mountains and farmland at one end and the congested Washington suburbs at the other. A hotbed of economic activity in the 1990s, the 10th is a mostly white-collar area that includes some of the state's wealthiest counties – Loudoun, Fauquier and part of Fairfax.

A majority of the district's population resides in suburban Northern Virginia, and many residents commute to jobs in the District of Columbia. The growth of the Washington metropolitan area has heavily affected the 10th. All of the district's counties grew substantially in the 1990s – newfound high-tech magnet Loudoun County nearly doubled in population. About one-sixth of Fairfax County is in the 10th, accounting for one-fourth of the district's population. Most of the remaining suburbanites live in Prince William and Loudoun counties.

Beyond suburbia, agriculture and manufacturing fuel the economy.

Clarke and Frederick counties produce about half of Virginia's apples and peaches. Winchester (Frederick County), the center of the state's apple-growing industry, also is home to the state's Democratic political dynasty, the Byrd family. But with few exceptions, the district has long since abandoned its Democratic roots.

The 10th voted overwhelmingly in favor of Republican presidential candidates in 1992, '96 and 2000. It long has been represented by a Republican congressman, and the GOP also dominated local state House seats in the 1990s.

MAJOR INDUSTRY
Federal government, high-tech, manufacturing

CITIES
Manassas, 33,498; Chantilly (unincorporated), 29,337 (1990); Leesburg, 26,820; Centreville (unincorportated), 26,553 (1990); Winchester, 22,477

UNUSUAL FEATURES
Luray Caverns; Manassas National Battlefield Park, site of Civil War battles of First and Second Bull Run.

Rep. Thomas M. Davis III (R)

Elected 1994; 4th term

CAPITOL OFFICE
225-1492; fax 225-3071; 306 Cannon Bldg. 20515

INTERNET
e-mail: tom.davis@mail.house.gov
web: www.house.gov/tomdavis

COMMITTEES
Energy & Commerce
Government Reform
(Technology & Procurement Policy - chairman)

HOMETOWN
Falls Church

BORN
Jan. 5, 1949, Minot, N.D.

RELIGION
Christian Scientist

FAMILY
Wife, Margaret "Peggy" Davis; three children

EDUCATION
Amherst College, B.A. 1971; U. of Virginia, J.D. 1975

MILITARY SERVICE
Army, 1971-72; Va. National Guard, 1972-79; Army Reserve, 1972-79

CAREER
Lawyer; professional services firm executive; state legislative aide

POLITICAL HIGHLIGHTS
Fairfax County Board of Supervisors, 1980-94 (chairman, 1991-94)

ELECTION RESULTS

2000 GENERAL

Thomas M. Davis III (R)	150,395	61.9%
Mike Corrigan (D)	83,455	34.4%
Robert McBride (LIBERT)	4,774	2.0%
C.W. "Levi" Levy (I)	4,059	1.7%

2000 PRIMARY

Thomas M. Davis III (R)	unopposed

1998 GENERAL

Thomas M. Davis III (R)	91,603	81.7%
C.W. "Levi" Levy (I)	18,807	16.8%
write-ins	1,701	1.5%

PREVIOUS WINNING PERCENTAGES
1996 (64%); 1994 (53%)

Davis is in his second term as chairman of the National Republican Congressional Committee, the political arm of the House GOP, and he began 2001 by setting expectations at least as high as he had the year before.

With the midterm elections more than a year and a half in the future, Davis was predicting that reapportionment and redistricting would enable Republicans to pick up at least 10 House seats in 2002. That would allow President Bush to buck a powerful historical trend: In each of the past nine administrations, the first election after a president took office brought losses for his party in the House.

Davis got a heaping share of the credit when the GOP overcame an array of obstacles — among them, a surge in Democratic fundraising and an unusually large number of Republican open seats to defend — and retained control of the House for the 107th Congress. The main work of the NRCC is recruiting candidates and then raising the money to help them win. Davis threw himself into both tasks as he took over what he has described as his dream job.

The Virginia lawmaker has been a political junkie since his youth; he was a Senate page for four years in the mid-1960s and wrote a college honors thesis on "The Political Realignment of the Outer South." He can readily recall reams of political trivia from memory, much the way ardent baseball fans can rattle off the career statistics of their favorite players.

Davis put his encyclopedic knowledge of local political dynamics and regional demographics to work finding candidates whose views made them electable at home — even if those same positions might deviate somewhat from House GOP orthodoxy. Under his direction, the NRCC raised a record amount of more than $130 million for the 2000 election, about one-sixth of it brought in by other House Republicans, who were pressed to donate extra campaign cash or raise funds for "battleground" races.

While Davis was able to raise a substantial amount himself from his own constituents in Northern Virginia's thriving technology sector, he also crisscrossed the country to promote GOP candidates. He made a concerted effort not to fuse the House elections into a national contest, a tactic the GOP used in 1998 when it lost five seats to the Democrats.

In all these ways, Davis was consistent with his own pragmatic, "big tent" views about the GOP's best chance for long-term success. It was an approach that melded together his fiercely competitive instincts — sometimes hidden behind his rumpled appearance — and his own ideology. He is one of the more moderate surviving members from the "revolutionary" GOP Class of 1994 when it comes to legislating, and he has been quicker than most of his classmates to compromise with Democrats.

As he prepared his campaign to keep the House in GOP hands in 2002, Davis worked to bolster his own political security early on, reportedly cutting a deal with his colleagues in the two neighboring House districts that should preserve all of their bases of support in redistricting — even though one of them, James P. Moran, is a Democrat.

Unlike some of his GOP peers who came to Congress from the private sector, Davis has made a career in government, serving as chairman of the Board of Supervisors in Fairfax County, the fastest-growing suburb of Washington, D.C. Davis earned a reputation for working in a low-key and non-confrontational manner and harmonizing diverse constituencies.

Hoping to benefit his high-technology constituency, Davis pushed legislation, enacted in the 106th Congress, expanding the number of special, H1-B visas for highly-skilled workers, giving legal standing to electronic signatures used in online transactions, and granting China permanent normal trade status.

In the 107th Congress, Davis has two new committee assignments that will be helpful in advancing his high-technology agenda. He is chairman of the new Government Reform Subcommittee on Technology and Procurement Policy, and he has added an appointment to the powerful Energy and Commerce Committee, where he sits on the Telecommunications and the Internet Subcommittee.

Davis also uses his growing clout to address more parochial concerns in Northern Virginia. Chief among them has been securing federal funds to replace the aging Woodrow Wilson Bridge, which spans the Potomac River below Washington, connecting Virginia and Maryland. In 2000, Davis helped obtain the final $600 million needed for a new 12-lane bridge; he and other Virginia lawmakers won the first $900 million two years before.

When Davis has split with the Republican leadership, it has often been to champion the interests of the thousands of government workers who live in his district. He called federal employees "hostages" to the government shutdowns of 1995-96 as he pressured GOP leaders to end their standoff with President Clinton. And he was one of only 11 Republicans in the 104th who opposed a GOP tax cut because it would have been paid for, in part, by requiring federal employees to contribute more to their pension funds.

Davis also chaired Government Reform's District of Columbia Subcommittee from 1995 through 2000. Taking the gavel as a freshman, he worked closely with Democrats on the panel to create a new financial oversight board to deal with the city's financial crisis. In 2000, the D.C. government passed its fourth consecutive balanced budget, an achievement that will allow local officials to retake control of the city's finances in 2001. Dealing with the District's operations at times brought Davis into conflict with Democratic proponents of D.C. home rule, but he has a collegial relationship with Democrat Eleanor Holmes Norton, the District's non-voting delegate.

Davis was first elected to the Fairfax County Board of Supervisors in 1979, and he upset an incumbent Democrat in 1991 to become chairman. During his tenure he worked to cut business taxes and liberalize land-use rules. He cultivated a non-ideological image in his winning 1994 campaign against freshman Democratic Rep. Leslie L. Byrne, who was a member of the Democratic leadership's whip organization and an aggressive partisan. Davis has had no difficulty winning re-election since then.

VIRGINIA 11
D.C. suburbs — Parts of Fairfax and Prince William counties

A politically competitive district, the 11th is a thin, erratically shaped sliver that is home to well-educated, middle- and upper-class suburbanites. One of the wealthiest districts in the state and nation, the 11th has a mostly white population, although eastern Fairfax County is more diverse.

The 11th grew steadily in the 1990s, with Prince William County posting 30 percent growth. The district contains the largest portion of Fairfax County, the most populous jurisdiction in Virginia. Many residents work in downtown Washington, either for the federal government or for companies whose business is linked to the government. While the government remains a major employer, high-tech is the fastest growing industry, and dozens of companies have put down roots in office-park developments in Fairfax. The district's abundance of land also has made it attractive to businesses.

KEY VOTES

2000
No Raise hourly minimum wage by $1 over two years
Yes Halt funding for U.S. mission in Kosovo unless European nations pay more
Yes Provide Medicare benefits to military retirees and their dependents
Yes Grant China permanent normal trade status
Yes Phase out estate, gift and trust taxes
No Prohibit implementation of president's national monument designations
Yes Approve GOP plan to provide prescription drug coverage for Medicare beneficiaries
No Increase help for poor nations indebted to international financial institutions

1999
No Impose steel import quotas
No Kill proposal to take aviation trust funds off budget
Yes Require background checks on buyers only at gun shows with 10 or more vendors
Yes Remove barriers among banking, securities and insurance companies
No Authorize state grants to hire teachers and reduce class size
No Overhaul campaign finance law; ban "soft money" and restrict advocacy advertising
Yes Approve bipartisan plan to increase rights of patients in managed-care health plans

INTEREST GROUPS

	AFL-CIO	ADA	CCUS	ACU
2000	0%	5%	80%	70%
1999	22%	35%	88%	56%
1998	30%	15%	100%	64%
1997	38%	25%	100%	72%

CQ VOTE STUDIES

	PARTY UNITY		PRESIDENTIAL SUPPORT	
	Support	Oppose	Support	Oppose
2000	87%	13%	36%	64%
1999	79%	21%	39%	61%
1998	81%	19%	34%	66%
1997	82%	18%	39%	61%

The 11th is a swing district, electing a Democrat in 1992, then replacing her with a Republican in 1994. Democrats have gone neck and neck with Republicans in presidential elections, losing by less than a point in 1992 but coming back to win in 1996 and in 2000, when Al Gore managed a 2 percentage point margin over President Bush.

MAJOR INDUSTRY
Federal government, high-tech, service

MILITARY BASES
Marine Corp. Base, Quantico, 6,805 military; 2,232 civilian (1999)

CITIES
Annandale (unincorporated), 50,975 (1990); Reston (unincorporated), 48,509 (1990); Fairfax, 20,697; Herndon, 19,195; Vienna, 17,226

UNUSUAL FEATURES
Fairfax Court House where George and Martha Washington's wills were recorded and are still kept.

WASHINGTON

Gov. Gary Locke (D)

First elected: 1996
Length of term: 4 years
Term expires: 1/05
Salary: $135,960
Phone: (360) 902-4111
Hometown: Seattle
Born: Jan. 21, 1950, Seattle, Wash.
Religion: Chinese Baptist
Family: Wife, Mona Lee Locke; two children
Education: Yale U., B.A. 1972; Boston U., J.D. 1975
Career: Lawyer; deputy county prosecuter
Political highlights: Wash. House, 1982-93; King County executive, 1993-96

Election results:

2000 GENERAL

Gary Locke (D)	1,441,973	58.4%
John Carson (R)	980,060	39.7%
Steve LaPage (LIBERT)	47,819	1.9%

Lt. Gov. Brad Owen (D)

First elected: 1996
Length of term: 4 years
Term expires: 1/05
Salary: $71,070
Phone: (360) 786-7700

STATE LEGISLATURE

Legislature: Meets January-May in odd-numbered years; January-March in even-numbered years
House: 98 members, 2-year terms
2001 breakdown: 49R, 49D; 65 men, 33 women
Salary: $32,064
Phone: (360) 786-7750
Senate: 49 members, 4-year terms
2001 breakdown: 24R, 25D; 27 men, 22 women
Salary: $32,064
Phone: (360) 786-7550

STATE TERM LIMITS

Governor: 2 terms
Senate: No
House: No

URBAN STATISTICS

CITY	POPULATION
Seattle	537,150
Spokane	184,323
Tacoma	180,020
Vancouver	118,743
Bellevue	105,521

REGISTERED VOTERS

Voters do not register by party.

POPULATION

2000 population	5,894,121
1990 population	4,866,692
Percent change	+21.1%
Rank among states	15
Median age	35.1
Born in state	48%
Foreign born	7%
Urban/rural	76%/24%
Crime rate	441/100,000
Poverty level	8.9%
Federal workers	66,840
Military	73,524

REAPPORTIONMENT

Washington retained its nine House seats in reapportionment. An independent commission will draw new district lines in 2001.

MISCELLANEOUS

Web: access.wa.gov
Capital: Olympia
Land area: 66,581 sq. miles
Rank among states: 20
STATE ELECTION OFFICIAL
(360) 902-4151
DEMOCRATIC HEADQUARTERS
(206) 583-0664
REPUBLICAN HEADQUARTERS
(206) 575-2900

District Statistics

DIST.	2000 D	2000 R	GREEN	1996 D	1996 R	REF	1992 D	1992 R	I	WHT	BLK	ASIAN	HISP	HOUSEHOLD INCOME	OVER 65+	UNDER 18	COLLEGE EDUCATION
1	54%	42%	4%	51%	37%	8%	41%	32%	27%	92%	1%	5%	2%	$40,390	9%	26%	31%
2	48	46	5	47	39	10	41	33	26	94	1	2	3	$31,305	12	27	18
3	47	48	5	49	38	10	42	33	25	95	1	2	2	$29,154	13	27	17
4	34	62	3	40	48	10	35	43	22	83	1	1	16	$25,055	12	30	16
5	40	55	3	44	43	11	40	37	23	93	1	2	3	$25,107	13	26	20
6	51	43	4	50	36	10	44	32	25	87	5	4	3	$27,882	14	25	18
7	72	20	7	69	20	5	66	19	16	76	10	12	3	$29,707	15	17	37
8	49	47	3	47	40	9	38	35	27	92	2	5	2	$42,379	8	28	29
9	53	42	3	51	36	10	42	31	26	86	5	6	4	$32,194	9	27	18
STATE	50	45	4	50	37	9	42	32	24	89	3	4	4	$31,183	12	26	23

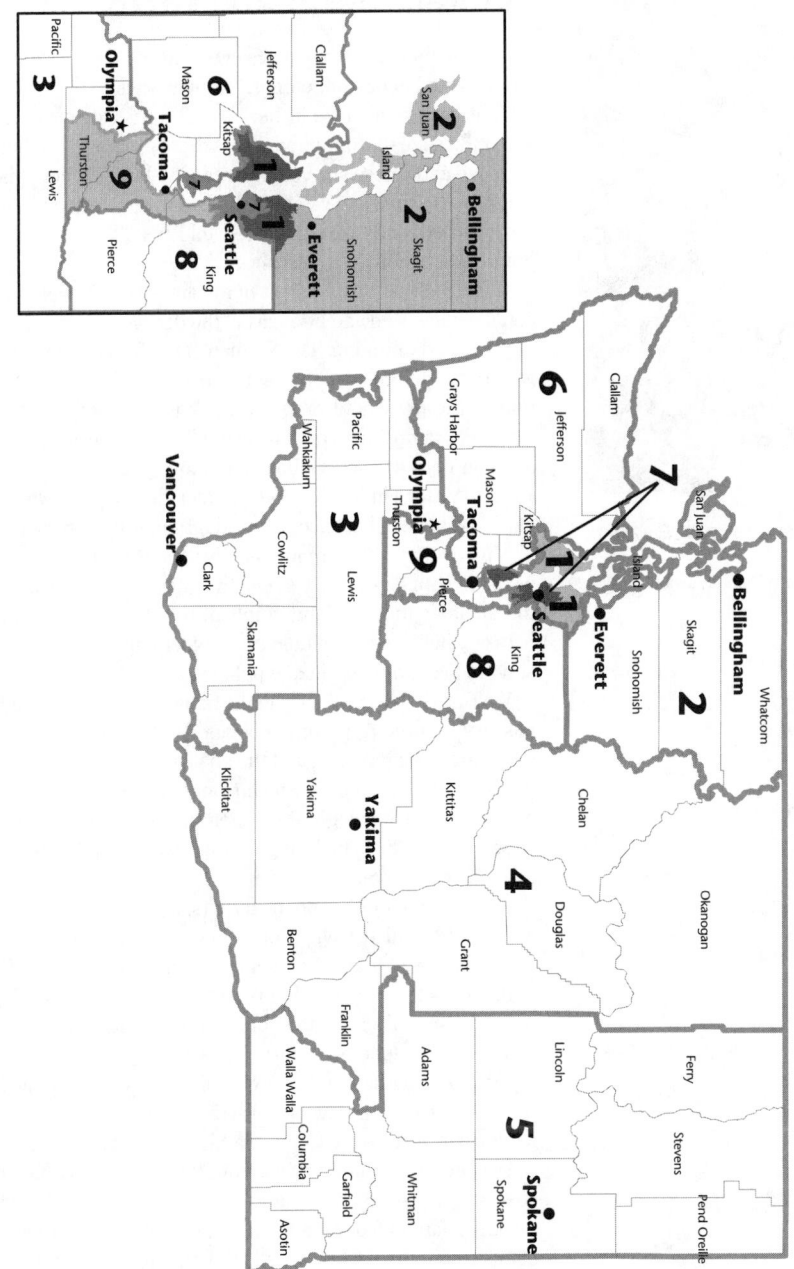

Sen. Patty Murray (D)

CAPITOL OFFICE
224-2621; fax 224-0238; 173 Russell Bldg. 20510

INTERNET
e-mail: senator_murray@murray.senate.gov
web: murray.senate.gov

COMMITTEES
Appropriations
Budget
Health, Education, Labor & Pensions
Veterans' Affairs

HOMETOWN
Seattle

BORN
Oct. 11, 1950, Seattle, Wash.

RELIGION
Roman Catholic

FAMILY
Husband, Rob Murray; two children

EDUCATION
Washington State U., B.A. 1972

CAREER
Parenting class instructor

POLITICAL HIGHLIGHTS
Shoreline School Board, 1983-89; Wash. Senate, 1989-93

ELECTION RESULTS

1998 GENERAL

Patty Murray (D)	1,103,184	58.4%
Linda Smith (R)	785,377	41.6%

1998 PRIMARY (OPEN)

Patty Murray (D)	479,009	45.9%
Linda Smith (R)	337,407	32.3%
Chris Bayley (R)	155,864	14.9%
Warren E. Hanson (R)	22,411	2.2%

PREVIOUS WINNING PERCENTAGES
1992 (54%)

Elected 1992; 2nd term

"Just about every woman I've ever known in politics got involved because she was mad about something," Murray says.

That is certainly true in her case. Two decades ago she was outraged when the state discontinued a preschool program that her young children attended and where she volunteered. She bundled her children into the car and drove to the state capital to lobby for restoration of the funds. She was further riled when one lawmaker told her: "You can't make a difference. You're just a mom in tennis shoes."

"I figured that I could sit at home and say, 'Oh, well, that's too bad,' or I could get involved and be a part of the decision-making process," she wrote in "Nine and Counting: The Women of the Senate," a book she co-authored with the eight other women senators of the 106th Congress. The cancellation of the preschool program back in 1980 led her first to organize a statewide campaign of parents to get the funds restored, then to a four-year term on her local school board and four years in the state Senate, and in 1992, to victory in her U.S. Senate race during what was termed the "Year of the Woman." (The elections brought four new women to the Senate.)

Murray turned that mom-in-tennis-shoes insult into a campaign symbol in 1992. With eight years of elective office under her belt, she was hardly the amateur that the label implied, but it helped her draw comparisons between her real-life, middle-class experiences and the men "in dark suits and red ties" who dominated politics.

Well into her second term in the Senate, and now a grandmother, Murray has seats on the Appropriations and Budget committees among her four committee assignments, and the chairmanship of the Democratic Senatorial Campaign Committee. She no longer presents herself as a novice in tennis shoes, but her legislative agenda still reflects the everyday, middle-class concerns that she brought to Washington in 1993 — education, health care, the environment.

As a reminder of her political roots, Murray displays a number of tennis shoes in her office. Civic groups often present her with awards that build on the theme — a telephone in the shape of a tennis shoe, for instance.

In the 106th Congress, her priorities included decreasing the size of elementary school classes, a long-running battle of Murray's; improving pipeline safety (she was spurred to action by an explosion in her state that killed three youths in 1999); expanding the federal family leave law to give parents time off to participate in activities at their children's school; and protecting a stretch of the Columbia River known as the Hanford Reach.

Despite broadening party commitments, Murray has not strayed from attending to issues important to her constituents. She seeks to gather a healthy share of federal dollars for her state as a member of the Appropriations Committee, where she is the ranking Democrat on the Transportation Subcommittee. Among her other Appropriations subcommittees is Interior. During debates on national forests and logging practices, Murray argues for environmental protection.

She also serves on the Health, Education, Labor and Pensions Committee. Much of her effort there has been focused on obtaining federal money to help school districts hire 100,000 additional teachers, with the goal of reducing the size of classes in grades one through three. "I am a former teacher. I am a former school board member. I am a parent of two students who went through our public schools. I have been out there as a PTA member. I have been a state legislator dealing with education. I have seen education from every angle," she said during a Senate debate on the issue.

In 1998, Congress approved $1.2 billion as the first installment in the Clinton administration's seven-year program to hire the additional teachers. In the 106th, Murray battled with home state colleague Slade Gorton, a Republican, who championed the GOP's plan to disburse the money in block grants to states, allowing them to decide how to spend the funds — and not necessarily on additional teachers. Murray argued that "a block grant cannot teach a single child to read. A block grant cannot teach a single child the basics."

Murray's crusade to enact a bill to improve pipeline safety was inspired by the 1999 blast in Bellingham, near where her sister teaches school. Another legislative priority — a measure to prevent schools from using certain pesticides and lawn care additives — also comes from personal experience. According to The Seattle Times, when Murray's son was 4 or 5, he was playing outside when a cloud of chemicals drifted over the fence from where a pesticide sprayer was working. She testified before state legislators, urging them to pass a bill requiring sprayers to notify neighbors about their plans.

Her children, now young adults, have not been shy about challenging their mother. She recalls in "Nine and Counting" that when she was in the state Senate, her daughter editorialized in the school paper against one of her stands. And her son organized a petition drive against his mother's bill to require bicycle helmets for youths.

Like many women leaders of the Democratic Party, Murray refrained from sharply criticizing President Clinton during his 1999 impeachment trial. That restraint was a departure from an earlier stance in her Senate career: Murray was one of five women senators in the 104th who pressured the Ethics Committee to hold public hearings on sexual misconduct charges against Oregon GOP Sen. Bob Packwood.

Murray grew up in a Seattle suburb, helping out, along with her six siblings, in the five-and-dime store her father ran. Murray's father developed multiple sclerosis when she was a teenager, and the children had to work to put themselves through college. Murray got a degree in recreation, with the intention of working with children. That is what she was doing when she ran into the legislator who passed on the "mom in tennis shoes" sobriquet.

Two early breaks gave Murray a decisive boost in her 1992 Senate race, which she originally entered with the goal of knocking off Democratic incumbent Brock Adams. He dropped out in March after a newspaper article detailed accounts by eight unidentified women who said Adams had made unwanted and inappropriate sexual advances toward them.

Murray got another break when the popular Democratic Gov. Booth Gardner, who was leaving office, decided against seeking the Senate seat. Still, to win the primary and the general election, Murray had to get past two better-known and popular moderates who had years of congressional experience — former Democratic Rep. Don Bonker and GOP Rep. Rod Chandler. She was able to portray both as Washington insiders.

She came in first in the all-candidate primary, with 28 percent. Chandler won the GOP nomination, with 20 percent. Murray held that early lead — condescending comments from Chandler only served to reinforce Murray's campaign theme — and she won on Election Day with 54 percent.

Described early in the 1998 election cycle as one of the Senate's most vulnerable incumbents, Murray talked more about close-to-home issues, such as increasing education funding and protecting the Hanford Reach from development, while her Republican opponent, Rep. Linda Smith, campaigned on opposing abortion and impeaching Clinton. Murray won re-election with a decisive 58 percent of the vote.

KEY VOTES

2000

Yes Overhaul bankruptcy law and increase minimum wage
No Limit fiscal 2001 discretionary spending to $600.3 billion
Yes Override veto on nuclear waste disposal at Yucca Mountain site in Nevada
Yes Oppose effort to terminate Kosovo mission
Yes Include gender, sexual orientation and disability in federal hate crime protections
No Approve GOP plan to restrict use of genetic information by health insurers
No Kill amendment delaying implementation of an anti-missile defense system
? Cut taxes for married couples
Yes Grant China permanent normal trade status

1999

No Remove President Clinton from office for obstruction of justice
? Kill amendment authorizing state grants to hire teachers and reduce class size
Yes Require criminal background checks for purchases at gun shows
No Approve GOP proposal to increase rights of patients in managed-care health plans
No Block effort to allow farm and medicine exports to Cuba
Yes Allow study of tougher automobile fuel efficiency standards
Yes Ratify nuclear weapons testing treaty
Yes Prohibit national political parties from collecting "soft money" donations
Yes Remove barriers among banking, securities and insurance companies

INTEREST GROUPS

	AFL-CIO	ADA	CCUS	ACU
2000	63%	90%	64%	8%
1999	88%	100%	59%	4%
1998	88%	90%	56%	4%
1997	71%	90%	70%	0%
1996	100%	90%	17%	0%
1995	100%	95%	33%	0%
1994	88%	90%	20%	0%
1993	91%	90%	14%	0%

CQ VOTE STUDIES

	PARTY UNITY		PRESIDENTIAL SUPPORT	
	Support	Oppose	Support	Oppose
2000	94%	6%	87%	13%
1999	93%	7%	88%	12%
1998	91%	9%	82%	18%
1997	93%	7%	87%	13%
1996	95%	5%	89%	11%
1995	93%	7%	91%	9%
1994	98%	2%	94%	6%
1993	94%	6%	96%	4%

Sen. Maria Cantwell (D)

CAPITOL OFFICE
224-3441; fax 228-0514; 717 Hart Bldg. 20510

INTERNET
e-mail: maria@cantwell.senate.gov
web: cantwell.senate.gov

COMMITTEES
Energy & Natural Resources
Judiciary
Small Business

HOMETOWN
Mountlake Terrace

BORN
Oct. 13, 1958, Indianapolis, Ind.

RELIGION
Roman Catholic

FAMILY
Single

EDUCATION
Miami U. (Ohio), B.A. 1981

CAREER
Internet audio company executive; public
relations consultant

POLITICAL HIGHLIGHTS
Wash. House, 1987-92; U.S. House, 1993-95;
defeated for re-election to U.S. House, 1994

ELECTION RESULTS

2000 GENERAL

Maria Cantwell (D)	1,199,437	48.7%
Slade Gorton (R)	1,197,208	48.6%
Jeff Jared (LIBERT)	64,734	2.6%

2000 PRIMARY (OPEN)

Slade Gorton (R)	560,787	43.6%
Maria Cantwell (D)	472,609	36.7%
Deborah Senn (D)	168,110	13.1%
Warren E. Hanson (R)	17,782	1.4%
Jeff Jared (LIBERT)	16,247	1.3%
Barbara Lampert (D)	15,150	1.2%
Robert Tilden Medley (D)	14,009	1.1%

PREVIOUS WINNING PERCENTAGES
1992 House Election (55%)

Elected 2000; 1st term

Cantwell's late-decision victory — she was not declared the winner in her hard-fought match with Republican incumbent Slade Gorton until Dec. 1 — brought the total of women in the Senate in the 107th Congress to 13, a new record over the previous high of nine in the 106th.

Her win also ensured that the Senate would start the 107th Congress in a flat-footed, 50-50 tie between Republicans and Democrats.

But Cantwell's performance, during six years in the state House and two years in the U.S. House (1993-95), suggests that her moderate views may help bridge the divide between the two parties. In representing the 1st District (mostly the northern Seattle suburbs), she took a pro-business stance while holding fast to traditional Democratic views on core social issues such as abortion rights.

A native of Indiana, Cantwell first came to the Seattle area as a political organizer for Democratic presidential candidate Alan Cranston in the early 1980s. She stayed on, starting her own public relations firm, and was elected to the state legislature at the age of 28. In the state House, she was noted for her work on balancing environmental concerns and economic growth. Cantwell won election to Congress in 1992 but lost her re-election bid two years later, swept aside by that year's Republican tide, in the person of Rick White.

Between her tenure in the House and her election to the Senate, Cantwell became wealthy as a marketing executive for RealNetworks, a computer software company that sells products designed to send and receive audio and video via the Internet. In launching her political comeback bid in 2000, Cantwell's ability to sell off $10 million in RealNetworks stock options to finance her Senate campaign enabled her to blow past her once-favored Democratic primary opponent, state Insurance Commissioner Deborah Senn, and gain an even footing with incumbent Gorton.

Cantwell made technology issues a centerpiece of her campaign. She opposed Justice Department efforts to break up Microsoft — a leading employer in her state. She differed with some industry figures, however, in supporting efforts to require companies that do business on the Internet to divulge how personal data is collected and used.

On most issues, she hews to the Democratic Party line. She champions requiring trigger locks for guns, closing the "gun show loophole" that lets people buy guns without background checks, and covering prescription drug costs under Medicare.

Cantwell's image as a high-technology advocate and Democratic stalwart was both her political strength and weakness in the campaign. She won big in the Seattle area. But Gorton's efforts to pigeonhole her as Seattle's candidate hindered her in the state's more-conservative rural areas: Cantwell managed to win despite carrying only five of the state's 39 counties. She narrowly won the year's closest Senate race, defeating Gorton by 2,229 votes, a margin of less than one-tenth of 1 percent.

Cantwell did not get a hoped-for seat on the Commerce Committee, which oversees many technology-related matters. She did get slots on Judiciary, which handles high-tech intellectual property issues, and on Small Business.

She also replaced Gorton on the Energy and Natural Resources Committee, where she can deal with home state matters involving hydroelectric power and resource development, including timber production.

Rep. Jay Inslee (D)

CAPITOL OFFICE
225-6311; fax 226-1606; 308 Cannon Bldg. 20515

INTERNET
e-mail: jay.inslee@mail.house.gov
web: www.house.gov/inslee

COMMITTEES
Financial Services
Resources

HOMETOWN
Bainbridge Island

BORN
Feb. 9, 1951, Seattle, Wash.

RELIGION
Protestant

FAMILY
Wife, Trudi Inslee; three children

EDUCATION
Stanford U., attended 1969-70; U. of Washington,
B.A. 1973; Willamette U., J.D. 1976

CAREER
Lawyer

POLITICAL HIGHLIGHTS
Wash. House, 1989-93; U.S. House, 1993-95;
defeated for re-election to U.S. House, 1994;
sought Democratic nomination for governor, 1996

ELECTION RESULTS

2000 GENERAL

Jay Inslee (D)	155,820	54.6%
Dan McDonald (R)	121,823	42.7%
Bruce Newman (LIBERT)	7,993	2.8%

2000 PRIMARY (OPEN)

Jay Inslee (D)	80,362	55.6%
Dan McDonald (R)	60,303	41.7%
Bruce Newman (LIBERT)	3,950	2.7%

1998 GENERAL

Jay Inslee (D)	112,726	49.8%
Rick White (R)	99,910	44.1%
Bruce Craswell (AMH)	13,837	6.1%

PREVIOUS WINNING PERCENTAGES
1992 (51%)

Elected 1998; 3rd term
Also served 1993-95

Having won one of the bigger upsets of 1992, Inslee was swept out by the Republican tide two years later, his voting record too liberal for a GOP-leaning district in the center of the state. But he was back in 1998, after moving to the Seattle suburbs and winning in a more middle-of-the-road district — one that appears willing to let Inslee display his party stripes more openly.

Within months of his return for the 106th Congress, he was kayaking the waterways of the 1st District with the PBS "Science Guy," Bill Nye — a well-known educator who has pressed for greater environmental protections. Inslee, who sits on the Resources Committee, later used the trip to underscore his own pro-environment stance and his support for legislation to guarantee nearly $3 billion a year in spending to buy park land, protect environmentally sensitive lands, preserve wildlife, prevent urban sprawl and restore historic buildings.

"I spent four days in a kayak going all across the waterways in my district," Inslee told his colleagues in a floor speech. "I came away impressed with one thing: It is about time that the U.S. Congress makes this commitment." The legislation Inslee was backing was stymied by Republicans, although President Clinton got the GOP to agree to a major expansion of environmental protection spending in 2000.

He backs the Democratic line on key issues, supporting his party's failed efforts in 2000 to boost the minimum wage by $1 an hour over two years. He also supports abortion rights and opposes a ban on a procedure its opponents call "partial birth" abortion.

On gun control, one of the issues that fueled Inslee's political trouble in his first term, he has stayed in the Democratic camp. In 1999, he voted for an unsuccessful Democratic alternative to a GOP provision regulating background checks for firearms sales at gun shows. Democrats said the GOP language was flimsy.

Still, Inslee casts himself as a political moderate and has aligned himself with the New Democrat Coalition, a group of pro-business Democrats. In 2000, when Inslee was facing a stiff challenge to his first re-election in his new district, he shifted a bit toward the center politically. His party-unity score (the frequency with which he sided with Democrats on votes that pitted the two parties against each other) fell from 88 percent to 80 percent, while his presidential-support score (how often he backed Clinton) dropped from 78 percent to 67 percent.

Inslee voted in the 106th for a bill to make it more difficult for consumers to seek bankruptcy protection — a measure that many Democrats said was tilted too far in favor of business interests. He supports free trade and strongly defends the business practices of the software giant Microsoft Corp., which employs thousands at its 1st District headquarters.

He also looks out for the Boeing Co., another major Seattle-area employer. He supports robust funding for the Export-Import Bank, which helps Boeing compete for international sales against foreign competitors that are subsidized by their governments.

Perhaps ironically, Inslee made a name for himself in the 106th by hammering on a problem created — albeit unintentionally — by computer-related companies such as Microsoft, whose technological innovations have made it easy for businesses to amass, sort, and exchange vast amounts of data about their customers. Inslee maintains that the privacy of citizens is under serious assault by those seeking to profit from the use, sale or trading of databases containing personal information.

As a member of the Banking Committee (now called Financial Services), Inslee pushed for inclusion of a privacy amendment in legislation that repealed barriers to cross-affiliation among banks, insurance companies and brokerage firms. Inslee wanted to require that banks notify customers before releasing transaction data and give them the ability to block such actions. When the committee approved weaker privacy protections, Inslee voted against the bill. That measure was enacted in 2000.

Inslee practiced law in the small town of Selah, near Yakima in south central Washington, until winning a state House seat in 1988. There, he served as vice chairman of the Appropriations Committee and of the panel that helped negotiate a budget deal that reduced the state's deficit.

When 4th District GOP Rep. Sid Morrison declared that he was giving up his seat to run for governor in 1992, Inslee wavered on whether to run, first announcing that he was thinking about a bid, then saying he wasn't interested, and finally, in April, deciding to make the run.

Inslee's folksy style and tireless campaigning lifted him to a narrow primary victory and to an equally narrow victory in November over Republican Doc Hastings.

As a member of the 103rd Congress, he cast two votes that were unpopular with his rural, Republican-leaning constituents: one supporting Clinton's deficit-reduction package, which raised taxes, the other banning some types of assault weapons. With the National Rifle Association targeting him for defeat in 1994, Inslee lost by 6 percentage points in a rematch with Hastings.

After the loss, Inslee moved to the Seattle area, where he had grown up. He waged an unsuccessful primary bid for governor in 1996, but then unseated two-term Republican Rep. Rick White in 1998 in the suburban Seattle 1st District. Inslee attacked White's support for the impeachment proceedings against Clinton. Inslee's victory was aided by the third-party candidacy of Bruce Craswell, whose 6 percent tally was regarded as coming largely from White's Republican base.

In 2000, in a race that was heavily funded by both sides, Inslee dueled with Republican state Sen. Dan McDonald over who was more beholden to the special interests financing their campaigns. Inslee stressed his independence and his centrist views by pointing to his votes in favor of overriding Clinton's veto of Republican measures to repeal the tax code's "marriage penalty" and to do away with the estate tax. Inslee won by 12 percentage points.

KEY VOTES

2000

Yes Raise hourly minimum wage by $1 over two years
Yes Halt funding for U.S. mission in Kosovo unless European nations pay more
Yes Provide Medicare benefits to military retirees and their dependents
Yes Grant China permanent normal trade status
Yes Phase out estate, gift and trust taxes
No Prohibit implementation of president's national monument designations
No Approve GOP plan to provide prescription drug coverage for Medicare beneficiaries
Yes Increase help for poor nations indebted to international financial institutions

1999

Yes Impose steel import quotas
No Kill proposal to take aviation trust funds off budget
No Require background checks on buyers only at gun shows with 10 or more vendors
No Remove barriers among banking, securities and insurance companies
Yes Authorize state grants to hire teachers and reduce class size
Yes Overhaul campaign finance law; ban "soft money" and restrict advocacy advertising
Yes Approve bipartisan plan to increase rights of patients in managed-care health plans

INTEREST GROUPS

	AFL-CIO	ADA	CCUS	ACU
2000	70%	70%	71%	28%
1999	78%	100%	32%	8%
1994	56%	70%	n/a%	10%
1993	67%	75%	36%	17%

CQ VOTE STUDIES

	PARTY UNITY		PRESIDENTIAL SUPPORT	
	Support	Oppose	Support	Oppose
2000	80%	20%	67%	33%
1999	88%	12%	78%	22%
1994	83%	17%	78%	22%
1993	87%	13%	71%	29%

WASHINGTON 1

Puget Sound (west and east) – North Seattle suburbs

On the banks of Puget Sound, the Information Age shines with increasing power. Microsoft, the 1st's largest employer, makes its home in the former farming area of Redmond. In the 1980s and '90s, the region suburbanized and the population exploded, with many of the "Microsoft Millionaires" moving into the crescent north of Seattle.

The region's military bases help spur the economy, but it's the high-tech boom – especially along Interstate 5 – that has attracted newcomers. Most residents live on the east side of Puget Sound, in King and Snohomish counties; the military bases are on the west side.

The district's blue-collar roots remain strong as nearby Boeing plants provide well-paying union jobs. Boeing, the state's largest private employer, announced in March 2001 that it would move its corporate headquarters out of Washington, but most manufacturing jobs

appeared safe for the time being.

The 1st was Republican until redistricting after the 1990 census. Now the district could go either way, as demonstrated by the flip-flops in party control during the 1990s. Well-to-do young professionals provide the area with a heavy contingent of fiscally conservative, socially moderate voters who can support moderates from either party. But the strong union presence weighs heavily, as does the more liberal northern Seattle constituency.

MAJOR INDUSTRY
Software, military, aviation construction

MILITARY BASES
Bangor Naval Submarine Base, 5,068 military, 2,287 civilian (2000); Naval Undersea Warfare Engineering Station, 24 military, 1,399 civilian (1998)

CITIES
Kirkland, 45,635; Edmonds, 40,751; Lynnwood, 34,034; Bothell, 30,335

UNUSUAL FEATURES
Bainbridge Island, a 30 minute ferry ride from downtown Seattle.

Rep. Rick Larsen (D)

CAPITOL OFFICE
225-2605; fax 225-4420
1529 Longworth Bldg. 20515

INTERNET
e-mail: rick.larsen@mail.house.gov
web: www.house.gov/larsen

COMMITTEES
Agriculture
Transportation & Infrastructure

HOMETOWN
Lake Stevens

BORN
June 15, 1965, Arlington, Wash.

RELIGION
Methodist

FAMILY
Wife, Tiia Karlen; two children

EDUCATION
Pacific Lutheran U., B.A. 1987; U. of Minnesota,
M.P.A. 1990

CAREER
Dental association lobbyist; port economic
development official

POLITICAL HIGHLIGHTS
Snohomish County Council, 1998-2000 (chairman,
1999)

ELECTION RESULTS

2000 GENERAL

Rick Larsen (D)	146,617	50.0%
John Koster (R)	134,660	45.9%
Stuart Andrews (LIBERT)	7,672	2.6%
Glen Johnson (NL)	4,231	1.4%

2000 PRIMARY (OPEN)

John Koster (R)	72,244	49.1%
Rick Larsen (D)	68,315	46.4%
Stuart Andrews (LIBERT)	4,274	2.9%
Glen Johnson (NL)	2,412	1.6%

Elected 2000; 1st term

Although Larsen had held political office only since 1998 (as a Snohomish County councilman), local Democratic Party strategists saw enough promise in him in 2000 to persuade a potential rival, state Rep. Jeff Morris, to stay out of the open-seat 2nd District contest and avoid a divisive primary. Running under the moderate New Democrat banner, Larsen scored something of a coup by returning the politically split district to Democratic hands.

Once in Congress, the low-key Larsen joined the House New Democrat Coalition. He won a seat on the Transportation and Infrastructure Committee, which fits well with his district's priorities — the Boeing Company and B.F. Goodrich Aerospace are major employers in the 2nd. His other assignment, to the Agriculture Committee, enables him to look out for 2nd District interests such as dairy and timber.

High-technology industries are big in Washington, and Larsen is conversant in issues that concern them. He says his top priority is to make sure there are safeguards in place to prevent companies and others from gaining access to and improperly using an individual's medical and financial records.

On a local hot-button issue, Larsen says the government needs to find ways to ensure oil pipeline safety. In June 1999, three people were killed when a pipeline ruptured in the 2nd District city of Bellingham. Larsen wants to boost community awareness of pipeline locations.

The retirement of three-term GOP Rep. Jack Metcalf created an opening in the 2nd, a competitive swing district in which each of the elections in the 1990s had been decided by 10 percentage points or fewer.

Although Larsen supports expanded international trade, he received campaign help from organized labor, as well as other traditional Democratic backers such as abortion rights advocates and environmental groups, all of which mounted ground or mail campaigns on Larsen's behalf in the final weeks of the race. The result was a Democratic takeover, with Larsen prevailing, 50 percent to 46 percent, over Republican state Rep. John Koster, who had run on a strongly conservative platform.

WASHINGTON 2

Puget Sound — Everett; Bellingham

West of the Cascade Mountains in the northwest corner of the state, the 2nd covers an area that is mostly rural in its topography and socially moderate in its politics. Most of the district's population lives along Interstate 5, while the rural areas just west of the forested mountains provide residents with large plots of land and plenty of room to ride their horses.

During the last several decades, the older economic mainstays of farming, logging and paper began long declines that affected the economies of many of the communities. But in the 1980s and '90s, the economy and population exploded with growth in the technology industry. Infrastructure improvements have not kept pace, so traffic is an issue. Thousands of Boeing workers live in the district; the firm's March 2001 decision to move its corporate headquarters, and about 1,000 jobs, out of state caused concern.

The 2nd was a Democratic district, but it is now fiercely contested. Labor plays a crucial role in elections, and its endorsement can be pivotal. Environmental concerns motivate many voters in Whatcom County. The western urban centers of Everett and Bellingham are liberal, while the eastern rural sections are highly independent with conservative tendencies and suspicions about western urban interests.

MAJOR INDUSTRY
Aviation, computer software, shipping

MILITARY BASES
Everett Naval Station, 5,465 military, 448 civilian; Whidbey Island Naval Air Station, 7,632 military, 1,428 civilian (1998)

CITIES
Everett, 87,352; Bellingham, 63,019

UNUSUAL FEATURES
Tulip festival in Skagit County every April.

Rep. Brian Baird (D)

CAPITOL OFFICE
225-3536; fax 225-3478
1721 Longworth Bldg. 20515

INTERNET
e-mail: brian.baird@mail.house.gov
web: www.house.gov/baird

COMMITTEES
Science
Small Business
Transportation & Infrastructure

HOMETOWN
Vancouver

BORN
March 7, 1956, Chama, N.M.

RELIGION
Protestant

FAMILY
Wife, Rachel Nugent

EDUCATION
U. of Utah, B.S. 1977; U. of Wyoming, M.S. 1980, Ph.D. 1984

CAREER
Professor; psychologist

POLITICAL HIGHLIGHTS
Democratic nominee for U.S. House, 1996

ELECTION RESULTS

2000 GENERAL

Brian Baird (D)	159,428	56.4%
Trent Matson (R)	114,861	40.6%
Erne Lewis (LIBERT)	8,375	3.0%

2000 PRIMARY (OPEN)

Brian Baird (D)	81,240	56.2%
Trent Matson (R)	58,077	40.2%
Erne Lewis (LIBERT)	5,332	3.7%

1998 GENERAL

Brian Baird (D)	120,364	54.7%
Don Benton (R)	99,855	45.3%

Elected 1998; 2nd term

Baird has an earnestness that borders at times on idealism. Ask him, for instance, about the issue of campaign financing, and he'll tell you that his colleagues are "literally killing" themselves by spending so much time on the phone raising money. Like many would-be reformers, he believes everyday people are losing out because of the need for politicians to raise money. "People they elected to represent them are spending so much time chasing money, they can't work together on the issues," he says.

Most of Baird's attention has been devoted to helping settle local disputes and otherwise attend to the parochial needs of his politically competitive district. He is a classic New Democrat, progressive on many issues such as education and health care, but eager to help businesses (particularly high-tech companies) that provide jobs and make the economy hum. He voted to override President Clinton's vetoes of Republican legislation to ease the tax burden on married couples and to abolish the estate tax. "I don't believe government is the source of all solutions," Baird says, "but I don't think the solution is to blame government for all the problems."

Baird gained his sense of activism from his parents. His father, who was a school principal, also owned a small business and was a classic small-town community activist — a member of the Lion's Club who served on the city council. Baird began his career as a clinical psychologist but remained politically active.

When no other Democrat opted to run against Republican Rep. Linda Smith in 1996, Baird put together an underfunded, grass-roots campaign that nearly unseated her. Smith later ran unsuccessfully for the Senate in 1998, opening the way for Baird.

Serving as Democratic freshman class president at the beginning of his congressional career, Baird strived to help Democrats and Republicans become friends. He and the GOP's class president, Jim DeMint of South Carolina, organized a wine tasting, a barbecue and other social events. But such efforts quickly fell by the board, in part because of the demands of heavy schedules. A larger inhibiting factor was the partisan nature of politics, Baird said, which makes it difficult to socialize with a colleague when his party is running attack ads against you.

Baird himself tries to maintain a bipartisan approach, seeking to secure at least one Republican cosponsor for each piece of legislation he introduces. He joined with DeMint, for instance, on a bill designed to promote small businesses.

On national issues, Baird's top legislative priority is education, including smaller class and school sizes and increased aid to college students. He sponsored legislation seeking to create pilot aid programs for part-time college and vocational school students. Another of his priorities is to increase support for mental health programs, which the former psychology professor says are greatly underfunded.

Most of Baird's activities have centered on matters of concern to southwestern Washington. The 3rd District is home to high-tech workers in Olympia and its suburbs, whose concerns are expanding trade and improving schools, and it also includes rural communities struggling with more basic infrastructure problems. Baird has sought more federal help for these communities to fight illegal production of methamphetamines, a problem in his district and many other rural areas.

In his first term, Baird won passage of legislation to transfer ownership of the Vancouver Barracks from the military to that city. He also worked with the Federal Emergency Management Agency to provide disaster assistance to 130 district families whose homes were destroyed by mudslides. He convinced the Army Corps of Engineers to bolster a sewage treatment plant, which was under threat from a rising river, in the small community of Pe Ell. And he secured some government surplus computers for use in a senior citizens' apartment building. The computer area, he said, has since become the social center of the complex. "That's pretty neat," he noted. "That's pretty rewarding."

While Baird concedes that following former Speaker Thomas P. "Tip" O'Neill's dictum that all politics is local "makes sense politically," he argues that looking out for his constituents is the job he was elected to do.

He has a seat on the Transportation and Infrastructure Committee, where he is working to get federal funds for a $196 million project to deepen portions of the Columbia River to increase shipping traffic. He also serves on the Small Business Committee.

Baird is an active outdoorsman. A coffee-table book about the Lewis and Clark expedition is one of the first items to greet visitors to his Capitol Hill office. In 1999, he was able to change the federal designation of the Lewis and Clark National Historic Trail to reflect its ending in Oregon and Washington, not just Oregon.

Baird came close enough to winning the 3rd District seat in 1996 that he went through freshman orientation that year. He led incumbent Smith in the ballot box tally, but when absentee ballots were added to the count, Baird had lost by 887 votes. He had not received significant help from the Democratic Congressional Campaign Committee (DCCC) or labor unions until he came close to beating Smith in an all-party primary. Washington holds its primaries in September, so by the time national help came for Baird, it was too little, too late.

But he was well-positioned for a run in 1998 and received major support from the DCCC that year. He beat GOP state Sen. Don Benton by 10 percentage points. In 2000, he got a break when Rick Jackson, a doctor and a highly touted Republican challenger, dropped out of the race, and Baird went on to post a 16-point victory.

Baird supported Clinton administration policies aimed at stopping Serbian aggression and ending the violence in Yugoslavia, including the deployment of U.S. peacekeeping troops. For three years, he had housed a Bosnian teenager who had lost his leg at age 14 in a Serbian mortar attack. Baird recalled teaching the teenager how to ski and rock climb.

KEY VOTES

2000
Yes Raise hourly minimum wage by $1 over two years
No   Halt funding for U.S. mission in Kosovo unless European nations pay more
Yes Provide Medicare benefits to military retirees and their dependents
Yes Grant China permanent normal trade status
Yes Phase out estate, gift and trust taxes
No   Prohibit implementation of president's national monument designations
No   Approve GOP plan to provide prescription drug coverage for Medicare beneficiaries
Yes Increase help for poor nations indebted to international financial institutions

1999
Yes Impose steel import quotas
No   Kill proposal to take aviation trust funds off budget
No   Require background checks on buyers only at gun shows with 10 or more vendors
Yes Remove barriers among banking, securities and insurance companies
Yes Authorize state grants to hire teachers and reduce class size
Yes Overhaul campaign finance law; ban "soft money" and restrict advocacy advertising
Yes Approve bipartisan plan to increase rights of patients in managed-care health plans

INTEREST GROUPS

	AFL-CIO	ADA	CCUS	ACU
2000	80%	70%	75%	12%
1999	88%	95%	33%	4%

CQ VOTE STUDIES

	PARTY UNITY		PRESIDENTIAL SUPPORT	
	Support	Oppose	Support	Oppose
2000	89%	11%	75%	25%
1999	89%	11%	77%	23%

WASHINGTON 3
Southwest — Olympia; Vancouver

The Lewis and Clark expedition used the Columbia River, which snakes west along the 3rd's southern boundary, to reach the Pacific Ocean in November 1805. The Cascade Mountains and surrounding forests provided this southwest region of the state with a once-booming timber industry. But as the area's explosive growth continues, trees and farmland are being cleared to make way for suburban developments.

The 3rd still has vast stretches of woodlands, including the scenic Coastal Range and much of the Cascade Mountains, with Mount Ranier just outside the northern border. Timber used to dominate the economy, but when the timber industry suffered severe cutbacks in the 1990s, many of the workers eventually transferred into non-union jobs with high-tech companies.

Clark County's population grew 45 percent from 1990 to 2000 as many Portland, Ore., workers prefer cheaper land prices in Washington. In some parts of the district, however, home prices tripled in 10 years.

The 3rd has been Democratic since 1961 with only a brief hiatus in the GOP camp when a Republican held the district for two terms in the 1990s. The rural communities tend to vote Republican, and Olympia's state government dependent Thurston County votes Democratic, leaving Clark County as the battleground for the district. With rates of growth in the double digits, voters have demanded infrastructure improvements to relieve traffic congestion and overcrowding in schools.

MAJOR INDUSTRY
Timber, mining, computer hardware

CITIES
Vancouver 118,743; Olympia 39,904; Longview 34,256

UNUSUAL FEATURES
Mount St. Helens erupted May 18, 1980, killing 57 people and destroying enough lumber for 300,000 two-bedroom homes.

Rep. Doc Hastings (R)

Elected 1994; 4th term

A former owner of a small paper supply business, Hastings has quickly become a significant player in the Republican hierarchy by being fiercely conservative and loyal to party leaders. Known as "Doc," a nickname his family game him when he was a boy, he resembles the local pharmacist rather than a congressman. His phrasing can be awkward instead of sound-bite ready, and he prefers to keep out of the spotlight.

But GOP leaders value his allegiance and, in the 105th Congress, they appointed him to the powerful Rules Committee, which determines the guidelines for considering legislation on the House floor. Hastings gained another feather in his cap in the 106th when he was appointed an assistant majority whip. "Doc's behind-the-scenes, common-sense-style leadership is just what's needed," said Majority Whip Tom DeLay of Texas in announcing the appointment. Then in the 107th, the leadership gave him a seat on the Budget Committee.

Hastings uses his influential posts to advance conservative causes and the agricultural interests of his district. And when the 4th District's needs clash with the Republican agenda, such as cutting the size of government and reducing spending, his constituents' concerns often prevail.

Hastings, for example, has been a strong supporter of providing billions of federal dollars to clean up radioactive waste at the Hanford nuclear reservation in the 4th, where the government produced plutonium for the nation's nuclear arsenal from World War II until the 1980s. While the congressman has criticized government mismanagement and called for more local involvement and privatization of the cleanup project, he also has worked to make sure that federal dollars keep flowing for the undertaking, which will take years. He drafted language in 2000 to provide compensation to workers made ill by exposure to dangerous substances at Hanford and other nuclear weapons sites.

In 2000, Hastings voted for legislation granting China permanent normal trade status, saying that opening trade markets is a priority for his district's producers. "As one of the most trade-dependent states in the nation, the best thing we can do for our farmers and farm communities is to open up new export markets and help level the playing field," he said. He also wants to boost federal spending for the Market Access Program, a controversial initiative that pays for the overseas marketing of U.S. agricultural products.

In the 106th, Hastings pressed for legislation to exempt certain housing for farm workers from the federal Migrant and Seasonal Worker Protection Act, thereby allowing Washington growers to house migrant workers in licensed tent camps for the short cherry-picking season. He argued that the state's laws and inspectors should take precedence in regulating the temporary housing. "My legislation would remove the federal strings that are complicating the migrant-worker housing issue and allow the problem to be addressed where it should be — locally," he said in 1999.

He often portrays himself as a buffer between an overly meddlesome federal government and local officials who know best how to run their affairs. For example, he advocates giving state and local officials primary authority over management of the Hanford Reach, a 51-mile section of the Columbia River in his district that is one of the largest undisturbed river stretches in the country and a critical spawning ground for salmon. Environmentalists want to designate the Hanford Reach as federally protected and off-

CAPITOL OFFICE
225-5816; fax 225-3251
1323 Longworth Bldg. 20515

INTERNET
e-mail: www.house.gov/hastings/get_address.htm
web: www.house.gov/hastings

COMMITTEES
Budget
Rules
Standards of Official Conduct

HOMETOWN
Pasco

BORN
Feb. 7, 1941, Spokane, Wash.

RELIGION
Protestant

FAMILY
Wife, Claire Hastings; three children

EDUCATION
Columbia Basin College, attended 1959-61;
Central Washington U., attended 1964

MILITARY SERVICE
Army Reserve, 1964-69

CAREER
Paper supply business owner

POLITICAL HIGHLIGHTS
Wash. House, 1979-87; Republican nominee for
U.S. House, 1992

ELECTION RESULTS

2000 GENERAL

Doc Hastings (R)	143,259	60.9%
Jim Davis (D)	87,585	37.3%
Fred Krauss (LIBERT)	4,260	1.8%

2000 PRIMARY (OPEN)

Doc Hastings (R)	79,683	60.8%
Jim Davis (D)	42,337	32.3%
Gordon Allen Pross (R)	5,420	4.1%
Fred Krauss (LIBERT)	3,684	2.8%

1998 GENERAL

Doc Hastings (R)	121,684	69.1%
Gordon Allen Pross (D)	43,043	24.4%
Peggy McKerlie (REF)	11,363	6.5%

PREVIOUS WINNING PERCENTAGES
1996 (53%); 1994 (53%)

limits to development.

On another environmental issue, Hastings opposes efforts to breach four dams on the Snake River in order to restore the runs of endangered species of salmon. "Losing the flood control, irrigation, clean power generation and transportation benefits of these dams would be a grave mistake, and one not easily corrected," he said in the 106th Congress.

In the 105th Congress, Hastings took up the fight for Kennewick Man, a 9,300-year-old skeleton, found in the 4th District, that is one of the oldest sets of human bones discovered in North America and may be the continent's earliest evidence of humans with Caucasian features. The Army Corps of Engineers prompted an international debate when it announced plans to hand over the skeleton for reburial to local tribes that claimed Kennewick Man as one of their ancestors. Scientists filed suit to prevent the exchange temporarily, and Hastings proposed a bill that would have ensured that they could study the bones. The matter remains in court.

Beyond local concerns, Hastings' issues are GOP issues, and he sides with his party most of the time. He had established himself as a friend of social policy conservatives during his tenure in the state House.

Hastings has joined with party leaders in advocating a heavy dose of tax cuts, starting with reducing capital gains taxes, repealing the estate tax, and ending the "marriage penalty," a quirk in the tax code that results in some two-earner married couples paying higher taxes than they would if each partner were single.

Before his arrival in Washington, Hastings ran his family's paper supply business in Pasco for years and was active in civic affairs and local Republican politics. He was chairman of the Franklin County GOP central committee and a delegate to two national Republican conventions. He served eight years in the Washington House, winning leadership posts as assistant majority leader and chairman of the GOP caucus.

In 1992, Hastings drew solid backing from GOP religious activists and was considered the most conservative of the four Republicans running to succeed GOP Rep. Sid Morrison, a moderate who ran unsuccessfully for governor that year. Though Hastings won his party's nomination handily, he narrowly lost to Democrat Jay Inslee.

In a 1994 rematch, Hastings cast the campaign as a referendum on Inslee's support for the agenda of President Clinton, whose popularity was then at a low ebb in the GOP-leaning district. Hastings ousted Inslee, and he has held on to his seat easily since then. (Inslee returned to the House in the 106th Congress after moving to the Seattle area and winning election in the 1st District.)

KEY VOTES

2000

No Raise hourly minimum wage by $1 over two years

Yes Halt funding for U.S. mission in Kosovo unless European nations pay more

Yes Provide Medicare benefits to military retirees and their dependents

Yes Grant China permanent normal trade status

Yes Phase out estate, gift and trust taxes

Yes Prohibit implementation of president's national monument designations

Yes Approve GOP plan to provide prescription drug coverage for Medicare beneficiaries

No Increase help for poor nations indebted to international financial institutions

1999

No Impose steel import quotas

No Kill proposal to take aviation trust funds off budget

No Require background checks on buyers only at gun shows with 10 or more vendors

Yes Remove barriers among banking, securities and insurance companies

No Authorize state grants to hire teachers and reduce class size

No Overhaul campaign finance law; ban "soft money" and restrict advocacy advertising

No Approve bipartisan plan to increase rights of patients in managed-care health plans

INTEREST GROUPS

	AFL-CIO	ADA	CCUS	ACU
2000	0%	0%	94%	92%
1999	0%	0%	100%	92%
1998	0%	0%	94%	100%
1997	0%	0%	100%	92%

CQ VOTE STUDIES

	PARTY UNITY		PRESIDENTIAL SUPPORT	
	Support	Oppose	Support	Oppose
2000	98%	2%	23%	77%
1999	97%	3%	16%	84%
1998	97%	3%	23%	77%
1997	98%	2%	29%	71%

WASHINGTON 4
Central — Yakima and Tri-Cities

Lying just east of the Cascade Mountains, the 4th is a big chunk of central Washington, bordering Canada on the north and Oregon on the south. Included within its borders area are Yakima, the district's largest city, and the Tri-Cities area of Pasco, Kennewick and Richland.

The district's economy revolves around agriculture. Yakima County was largely desert before a huge irrigation project helped make it one of the nation's premier apple-growing areas. Columbia Crest uses grapes grown in the Yakima Valley for its wines. The district's residents care for and want to protect the environment but bristle at federal regulations that hamper the region's businesses.

Hanford Nuclear Reservation, a 570 square mile tract next to the Columbia River, was a major supplier of jobs throughout the Cold War. In 1988 the plutonium plant was shut down and employment declined precipitously. Hanford is now the nation's most

contaminated nuclear site with 54 million gallons of deadly material stored in aging underground tanks.

The 4th is a battleground between Democrats and Republicans, except in recent presidential elections, when Republicans carried the district. (The 4th was the only district in the state to back Republican presidential candidates in 1992 and '96.) While the north has been favorable to Democrats, the most populous area – the southeast Tri-City area – is staunchly Republican.

MAJOR INDUSTRY
Scientific research, timber, apple orchards

CITIES
Yakima, 72,483; Kennewick, 50,727; Richland, 37,553; Pasco, 27,779

UNUSUAL FEATURES
The oldest skeleton ever found in North America was discovered along the banks of the Columbia River in Richland in August 1996 – dubbed the "Kennewick Man," he is believed to be more than 9,300 years old.

Rep. George Nethercutt (R)

Elected 1994; 4th term

CAPITOL OFFICE
225-2006; fax 225-3392; 223 Cannon Bldg. 20515

INTERNET
e-mail: george.nethercutt-pub@mail.house.gov
web: www.house.gov/nethercutt

COMMITTEES
Appropriations
Science

HOMETOWN
Spokane

BORN
Oct. 7, 1944, Spokane, Wash.

RELIGION
Presbyterian

FAMILY
Wife, Mary Beth Nethercutt; two children

EDUCATION
Washington State U., B.A. 1967; Gonzaga U., J.D. 1971

CAREER
Lawyer; congressional aide

POLITICAL HIGHLIGHTS
Spokane County Republican Party chairman, 1990-94

ELECTION RESULTS

2000 GENERAL

George Nethercutt (R)	144,038	57.3%
Tom Keefe (D)	97,703	38.9%
Greg Holmes (LIBERT)	9,473	3.8%

2000 PRIMARY (OPEN)

George Nethercutt (R)	64,341	45.4%
Tom Keefe (D)	30,263	21.4%
Richard Clear (R)	28,373	20.0%
Thomas Flynn (D)	15,609	11.0%
Greg Holmes (LIBERT)	3,129	2.2%

1998 GENERAL

George Nethercutt (R)	110,040	56.9%
Brad Lyons (D)	73,545	38.1%
John Beal (AMH)	9,673	5.0%

PREVIOUS WINNING PERCENTAGES
1996 (56%); 1994 (51%)

Nethercutt, who won national attention in 1994 for his stunning defeat of Democratic House Speaker Thomas S. Foley, found himself in an uncomfortable spotlight during the 106th Congress for a different reason. He was the most prominent of a handful of Republican House members who reneged on their pledges to voluntarily limit their service in the House.

Publicly pained by the issue, Nethercutt as early as 1997 said, "I know I said six [years in office], but 12 is more realistic. I think 12 years is a more comfortable time to accomplish your objectives." Two years later, he made it official: "I've changed my mind. I made a mistake when I chose to set a limit on my service. The work I've done will not be finished by the end of this term."

Because he had made term limits a key issue in his 1994 campaign, Nethercutt faced national criticism for his about-face; cartoonist Garry Trudeau labeled him "Weasel King" in his Doonesbury strip. Term limits advocates, who had spent $300,000 in 1994 to help Nethercutt topple Foley, felt so betrayed that they vowed to spend a considerable sum in the 2000 election to oust their former standard-bearer. But Nethercutt dismissed term limits groups as "outside agitators" and stressed his work for farmers and other constituents. Praised by Republican leaders for his decision to stay in Congress, he cruised to victory in the 2000 GOP primary and crushed Democratic activist Tom Keefe in the general election.

Although his defeat of Foley made him something of a symbol for the new Republican order, Nethercutt is hardly a revolutionary. Rather, he is like Foley in his penchant to protect the federal dollars that flow to his home state. In fact, one of Nethercutt's first proposals in 1999 was to rename Spokane's federal building the "Thomas S. Foley Federal Building and United States Courthouse." In introducing the measure, he praised the former House Speaker for being "a gentleman who sought consensus."

An amiable and soft-spoken man, Nethercutt too seeks consensus, especially when it comes to his efforts on the Appropriations Committee. He gained a position on the committee when he first came to Congress, a rare honor for a freshman, but one that GOP leaders deemed an appropriate reward for toppling Foley. His approach on Appropriations has been to work quietly and collegially.

Nethercutt comes across as a moderate in person, but his conservative credentials are rarely in doubt. An opponent of abortion rights and gun control, he also has voted with the GOP majority to limit the regulatory authority of the Environmental Protection Agency. He has opposed race- and sex-based preferences in higher education, the restoration of food stamps for legal immigrants and legislation to overhaul the campaign finance system. In the 105th Congress, he was among the first group of Republicans to call for President Clinton's resignation after the president admitted a sexual relationship with former White House intern Monica Lewinsky.

But Nethercutt found himself in the company of some liberals on a high-profile issue in the 106th: breaching the economic embargo against Cuba and five other "rogue" nations. Breaking with many in his own party, he emerged in 2000 as the leading House sponsor of a measure to prevent the administration from imposing unilateral sanctions on countries, including Cuba, barring trade in food and medical products. "America's foreign competitors have been undercutting our domestic producers and selling their agricultural goods to these sanctioned nations," he said. "Unilateral sanctions mean lost sales, diminished reputation as a reliable supplier and depressed commodity prices."

In pressing successfully for limited agricultural trade with Cuba and the other five countries, Nethercutt had his district in mind. "Cuba would buy rice, peas and lentils that come from our state of Washington, wheat and other commodities, but our farmers are prohibited from selling it to them," he said at the time. "Food and medicine shouldn't be used as weapons. All these embargoes hurt is our farmers."

Nethercutt's district is heavily agricultural, and he has fought for his farmers by battling other international sanctions. When it appeared that winter wheat exports might suffer in 1998 because the United States had imposed sanctions against India and Pakistan over their nuclear weapons tests, Nethercutt helped win passage of legislation that exempted agricultural exports from the sanctions. In a tribute to the congressman's efforts, Pakistan Ambassador Riaz H. Khokhar called him when Pakistan decided to purchase 300,000 metric tons of wheat in the summer of 1998.

Nethercutt has tangled with environmentalists by trying to block federal land-use regulations in the Columbia River Basin. And he is a leading opponent of plans to breach four Snake River dams in his district that environmentalists blame for blocking runs of endangered species of salmon. "I don't believe dam removal is the silver-bullet answer, and I won't support a proposal that restores salmon on the backs of those who depend on the system: the agriculture, natural resources, small communities and residents of my Eastern Washington district," he said in 2000.

In the 1970s, Nethercutt worked on Capitol Hill for Sen. Ted Stevens of Alaska, then went into private law practice with his father, specializing in estate planning and probate and adoption law. He was active in civic affairs, founding a nursery for victims of child abuse and raising money to combat juvenile diabetes. Although he was a former Spokane County GOP chairman, he never held public office before he entered the 1994 House race against Foley.

With Foley struggling to hold on to the increasingly conservative district, Nethercutt spent more than $1 million, and he was aided by conservative groups making independent expenditures to defeat the incumbent. By campaigning for less government, Nethercutt carried the district's nine rural counties and prevailed overall, 51 percent to 49 percent.

In 1996, Democrats fielded farmer Judy Olson, a former president of the National Association of Wheat Growers; but Nethercutt prevailed with 56 percent. In 1998, he coasted to victory over Democrat Brad Lyons, a farmer.

KEY VOTES

2000

No   Raise hourly minimum wage by $1 over two years

Yes   Halt funding for U.S. mission in Kosovo unless European nations pay more

Yes   Provide Medicare benefits to military retirees and their dependents

Yes   Grant China permanent normal trade status

Yes   Phase out estate, gift and trust taxes

Yes   Prohibit implementation of president's national monument designations

Yes   Approve GOP plan to provide prescription drug coverage for Medicare beneficiaries

No   Increase help for poor nations indebted to international financial institutions

1999

No   Impose steel import quotas

Yes   Kill proposal to take aviation trust funds off budget

No   Require background checks on buyers only at gun shows with 10 or more vendors

Yes   Remove barriers among banking, securities and insurance companies

No   Authorize state grants to hire teachers and reduce class size

No   Overhaul campaign finance law; ban "soft money" and restrict advocacy advertising

No   Approve bipartisan plan to increase rights of patients in managed-care health plans

INTEREST GROUPS

	AFL-CIO	ADA	CCUS	ACU
2000	0%	5%	80%	88%
1999	0%	10%	88%	84%
1998	0%	0%	89%	96%
1997	13%	5%	100%	92%

CQ VOTE STUDIES

	PARTY UNITY		PRESIDENTIAL SUPPORT	
	Support	Oppose	Support	Oppose
2000	93%	7%	25%	75%
1999	92%	8%	23%	77%
1998	95%	5%	27%	73%
1997	96%	4%	29%	71%

WASHINGTON 5

East – Spokane

The fertile soil and rolling hills of eastern Washington make the 5th's protein-rich wheat some of the most desired in the world. Politically conservative, the district remains dependent on markets for its natural resources, including timber and precious metals.

The 5th takes up the eastern third of the state, with Spokane as the district's population center. Largely dependent on manufacturing, the area has suffered intermittent layoffs, but a sharp rise in demand in the electronics manufacturing industry offered opportunities for workers to retrain. Also known as the "Inland Empire," Spokane serves as the retail and industrial center for eastern Washington, northeastern Oregon and western Idaho.

The 5th's politics are closer to Idaho than western Washington. The rural communities and natural resource-dependent economy make for people who like to keep federal interference to a minimum and advocate private property rights. Democratic

majorities cannot be counted on in Spokane, one of the nation's more conservative cities. Democrats do get elected in the southeast, where the population around Washington State University in Pullman provides some liberal support. The district voted for Bill Clinton in the 1992 and '96 presidential contests, but gave the edge to President Bush in 2000.

MAJOR INDUSTRY
Agriculture, timber, electronics manufacturing

MILITARY BASES
Fairchild Air Force Base, 4,675 military, 1,021 civilian (1998)

CITIES
Spokane, 184,323; Walla Walla, 28,862; Pullman, 24,096

UNUSUAL FEATURES
Sonora Smart Dodd, of Spokane, thought up the idea for Father's Day while listening to a Mother's Day sermon in 1909, and in 1924 President Calvin Coolidge proclaimed the third Sunday in June as Father's Day.

Rep. Norm Dicks (D)

CAPITOL OFFICE
225-5916; fax 226-1176; 2467 Rayburn Bldg. 20515

INTERNET
e-mail: www.house.gov/writerep
web: www.house.gov/dicks

COMMITTEES
Appropriations

HOMETOWN
Bremerton

BORN
Dec. 16, 1940, Bremerton, Wash.

RELIGION
Lutheran

FAMILY
Wife, Suzanne Dicks; two children

EDUCATION
U. of Washington, B.A. 1963, J.D. 1968

CAREER
Congressional aide

POLITICAL HIGHLIGHTS
No previous office

ELECTION RESULTS

2000 GENERAL

Norm Dicks (D)	164,853	64.7%
Bob Lawrence (R)	79,215	31.1%
John Bennett (LIBERT)	10,645	4.2%

2000 PRIMARY (OPEN)

Norm Dicks (D)	103,131	66.1%
Bob Lawrence (R)	38,817	24.9%
William Edward Chovil (R)	7,882	5.0%
John Bennett (LIBERT)	6,311	4.0%

1998 GENERAL

Norm Dicks (D)	143,308	68.4%
Bob Lawrence (R)	66,291	31.6%

PREVIOUS WINNING PERCENTAGES
1996 (66%); 1994 (58%); 1992 (64%); 1990 (61%); 1988 (68%); 1986 (71%); 1984 (66%); 1982 (63%); 1980 (54%); 1978 (61%); 1976 (74%)

Elected 1976; 13th term

Dicks is a master of the legislative game who wins battles in the House the way he won a mixed doubles tennis tournament a couple years ago: Before the final match, the one-time University of Washington football star got himself and his partner psyched up by clenching his fists and bellowing, "Huskies!" He then won by demonstrating that, despite his linebacker's build, he is a highly skilled tennis player.

Dicks cuts a vivid figure on Capitol Hill with his boisterous bonhomie and a persistence in working his issues that verges on bullheadedness. On the normally collegial Appropriations Committee, he is aggressive and full of bluster. On the House floor, he makes his case bluntly and repeatedly with handshakes, pats on the back and even bear hugs, sometimes annoying his opponents but frequently wearing them down. His Capitol Hill mentor, the legendary Washington Democratic Sen. Warren Magnuson, used to skewer his protégé's exuberance by joking that when Dicks was a linebacker, he was always five yards offside.

But that flamboyant manner complements finely honed political skills. Dicks' three years as an aide to Magnuson, then a senior member of the Appropriations Committee, amounted to a master class in the art of legislating, both to shape national policy and to bring home the bacon. With the powerful backing of fellow Washingtonian and then-Democratic Caucus Chairman Tom Foley, Dicks got onto Appropriations in his freshman term, with seats on the Interior Subcommittee and, two years later, the Defense panel. He followed Magnuson's footsteps in focusing on defense and natural resources issues crucial to his state, quickly establishing himself as a serious player in both policy fields.

By 1982, Dicks was collaborating with Democratic defense policy heavyweights Rep. Les Aspin of Wisconsin and Sen. Sam Nunn of Georgia to pressure the Reagan administration toward a more moderate negotiating stance in nuclear arms reduction talks with the Soviet Union. By the late 1980s, he was Capitol Hill's leading proponent of the B-2 stealth bomber — a position that had a strong parochial dimension; aerospace giant Boeing, a key element of Washington's economy, was a major subcontractor on the B-2. But there also was a serious argument on policy grounds for Dicks' position, and he made the case knowledgeably.

Still, he is not remotely self-conscious about simply delivering the goods to his state, nor are his efforts narrowly focused on his own district: He boasted in 1998 that defense spending in Washington remained at a steady $5 billion to $6 billion per year even though nationwide defense spending was down 40 percent in the past decade. Many of his initiatives are far less cosmic in scope than his arms control and B-2 crusades. His additions to the defense spending bill in 2000 included $4 million to buy software from a Bellevue company for the National Guard and $4 million for a Seattle firm's research on water-jet propulsion, as well as $100 million to improve the 21 existing B-2s.

Because Dicks was in tune with Republican efforts to spend more on defense than President Clinton requested, the GOP takeover of the House in 1995 was less traumatic for him than for many other senior Democrats. Moreover, the Appropriations Committee has retained its collegial, bipartisan ways, to the outrage of some GOP conservatives. So Dicks has been able to do well, helping to enlarge the Pentagon's spending pie and making sure that Washington state got at least its fair share of the increase.

On the other hand, a Republican majority has made Dicks' life more complicated in dealing with natural resources issues important to his state, and particularly to his district with its significant fishing, timber and tourism interests. With his influence over the Interior spending bill — he became the Interior Subcommittee's senior Democrat in 1997 — Dicks has been able to direct dollars to the Northwest to preserve national forests, boost recovery of depleted salmon stock and, in general, balance competing environmental and commercial concerns.

Since 1995, Republicans from Western states with huge tracts of public land, who take a dim view of federal land-use restrictions, have tried to use the Interior spending bill as a weapon in their war with the federal government. In the 105th and 106th Congresses, for example, Dicks had to fend off attacks on a Clinton administration study of endangered salmon populations and other environmental problems in the Columbia River Basin in seven Western states.

In 2000, he melded his interest in environmental protection with his desire to preserve the Appropriations panel's clout by helping to sidetrack a bill that would have provided $3 billion a year, for 15 years, for conservation programs — outside the appropriations process. In its place, Dicks added to the Interior spending bill a program earmarking $12 billion for federal land acquisition over a six-year period but making annual expenditures from the fund subject to the appropriations process.

Partisan battles over the Interior bill are intensified by the fact that the measure also includes federal funding for the National Endowment for the Arts — a constant target of conservatives. Dicks is a staunch defender of federal funding for the arts, and he also falls in line with his party's liberal wing on other social policy issues. He opposes Republican efforts to offer school vouchers, to repeal a ban on certain semiautomatic assault-style weapons and to prohibit a procedure its opponents call "partial birth" abortion.

Dicks decided to run for Congress in 1976, when the 6th District seat came open. He tapped into the resources of labor and other interest groups to win the primary and had no trouble against a weak Republican that fall.

In 1980, he was held to 54 percent by Republican James Beaver, a conservative law professor. His challenger in 1982, GOP state Sen. Ted Haley, painted Dicks as a profligate spender too friendly with military contractors. But that charge gave Dicks an excuse to talk about projects he had brought home. Dicks' 63 percent indicated that he was gaining security. Since then, he has dropped below 60 percent only once — in the GOP year of 1994.

KEY VOTES

2000

Yes Raise hourly minimum wage by $1 over two years
No   Halt funding for U.S. mission in Kosovo unless European nations pay more
Yes Provide Medicare benefits to military retirees and their dependents
Yes Grant China permanent normal trade status
No   Phase out estate, gift and trust taxes
No   Prohibit implementation of president's national monument designations
No   Approve GOP plan to provide prescription drug coverage for Medicare beneficiaries
No   Increase help for poor nations indebted to international financial institutions

1999

No   Impose steel import quotas
Yes Kill proposal to take aviation trust funds off budget
No   Require background checks on buyers only at gun shows with 10 or more vendors
Yes Remove barriers among banking, securities and insurance companies
Yes Authorize state grants to hire teachers and reduce class size
Yes Overhaul campaign finance law; ban "soft money" and restrict advocacy advertising
Yes Approve bipartisan plan to increase rights of patients in managed-care health plans

INTEREST GROUPS

	AFL-CIO	ADA	CCUS	ACU
2000	80%	80%	45%	8%
1999	67%	90%	28%	0%
1998	90%	95%	39%	0%
1997	88%	70%	60%	17%

CQ VOTE STUDIES

	PARTY UNITY		PRESIDENTIAL SUPPORT	
	Support	Oppose	Support	Oppose
2000	89%	11%	88%	12%
1999	90%	10%	84%	16%
1998	85%	15%	85%	15%
1997	81%	19%	78%	22%

WASHINGTON 6
West — Bremerton; Tacoma

The green, lush habitation of the 6th is part of what gives Washington its nickname, the "Evergreen State." Olympic National Park and Olympic National Forest constitute more than half the district's land. Along the coast, the mountains drop to the Pacific Ocean.

Logging and fishing remain major industries in the west, but fights over environmental protections for the spotted owl and other endangered species have forced some companies to cut back their work forces.

Communities are trying to diversify their economies and have been successful, for the most part, in attracting high-tech companies. Bremerton, with the Puget Sound Naval Shipyard and Naval Station Bremerton, depends heavily on the military.

The 6th includes northern Tacoma, where the industrial city's blue-collar, heavily unionized electorate generally tilts Pierce County to the Democrats. The district gave Bill Clinton 50 percent of its vote in 1996,

with roughly equal percentages in the 6th's portions of Pierce and Kitsap counties. In the 2000 presidential contest, Al Gore secured the district with 51 percent of the vote.

MAJOR INDUSTRY
Lumber, fishing, shipping, health care

MILITARY BASES
Puget Sound Naval Shipyard, 33 military, 7,600 civilian; Naval Station Bremerton, 211 military (7,587 military on home-ported ships), 23 civilian (2001)

CITIES
Tacoma (pt.), 146,425 (1990); Bremerton, 40,612; Lakewood (pt.), 39,940 (1990); University Place, 26,358

UNUSUAL FEATURES
The U.S.S. Missouri, the battleship on which the Japanese signed their surrender ending World War II, was based in Bremerton from the end of the war until 1998, when it was moved to Hawaii.

Rep. Jim McDermott (D)

CAPITOL OFFICE
225-3106; fax 225-6197
1035 Longworth Bldg. 20515

INTERNET
e-mail: www.house.gov/writerep
web: www.house.gov/mcdermott

COMMITTEES
Budget
Ways & Means

HOMETOWN
Seattle

BORN
Dec. 28, 1936, Chicago, Ill.

RELIGION
Episcopalian

FAMILY
Wife, Therese Hansen; two children

EDUCATION
Wheaton College, B.S. 1958; U. of Illinois, M.D.
1963

MILITARY SERVICE
Navy Medical Corps, 1968-70

CAREER
Psychiatrist

POLITICAL HIGHLIGHTS
Wash. House, 1971-73; sought Democratic
nomination for governor, 1972; Wash. Senate,
1975-87; Democratic nominee for governor, 1980;
sought Democratic nomination for governor, 1984

ELECTION RESULTS

2000 GENERAL

Jim McDermott (D)	193,470	72.8%
Joe Szwaja (GREEN)	52,142	19.6%
Joel Grus (LIBERT)	20,197	7.6%

2000 PRIMARY (OPEN)

Jim McDermott (D)	94,450	77.9%
Joe Szwaja (GREEN)	16,214	13.4%
Joel Grus (LIBERT)	10,546	8.7%

1998 GENERAL

Jim McDermott (D)	183,076	88.2%
Stan Lippmann (REF)	19,545	9.4%
Jeff Powers (SW)	4,921	2.4%

PREVIOUS WINNING PERCENTAGES
1996 (81%); 1994 (75%); 1992 (78%); 1990 (72%);
1988 (76%)

Elected 1988; 7th term

McDermott is the only psychiatrist in Congress, and as such, fellow Democrats have looked to him when developing strategy on health care matters, such as curbing the growing power of managed-care insurers, overhauling the federal Medicare program and providing prescription drug coverage for senior citizens.

McDermott has been willing to oblige, and his medical background gives him credibility to do so. But he has never moderated the decidedly independent streak he exercises on the Ways and Means Committee; on health care he is often to the left of most Democrats, and on trade he frequently takes positions to the right of his party. And he is not shy about giving his opinion, even when it reflects unfavorably on his own party or its leadership.

He called 2000 "the most unproductive public policy year I've spent in my life," adding that blame should be spread equally between the parties. "Everything was crafted on their side to win the election. And everything we tried to do was [to] derail them from winning the election." That sort of rhetorical potency has made McDermott, known for his quick laugh and backslapping manner, one of the most prominently featured Democratic critics of Republican budget and tax proposals.

More often than not, McDermott comes off as an outspoken liberal of the old school: blunt, confrontational and eager to wave a flag for the Democratic cause. His voting record is solidly Democratic, and he remains devoted to the historically liberal tilt of his party, even as some insist it must move to the center. "We could stand with a little packaging work, but the basic thrust of what we did the last 60 years is not wrong," he said.

As evidence that he is rarely afraid to step out of the mainstream in pursuit of that agenda, early in the 107th Congress McDermott formed an alliance with a Republican Ways and Means colleague, Louisiana's Jim McCrery, to develop a universal health insurance bill that would replace employer-based coverage with mandatory individual policies subsidized for low-income families.

The move was a continuation of a crusade that gained prominence in the 103rd Congress, when McDermott proposed — and pushed vigorously for — a single-payer health-care plan under which all Americans would be guaranteed health insurance benefits through a taxpayer-financed system. He ignored his own leadership's requests that lawmakers delay introducing health care bills until President Clinton had unveiled his health care overhaul plan. He also helped worsen the Clinton plan's dismal prospects, by rallying support among House liberals for his own proposal and using the clout of his forces to hold the president and congressional Democratic leaders to core demands, including coverage for all Americans and tight limits on cost increases.

In the 105th Congress, McDermott worked on a number of narrower health care bills, such as one to establish federal privacy standards for individual medical records. In the 106th, he took some heat for pushing legislation to set up a patent-review process for the antihistamine Claritin. The drug is manufactured by Schering-Plough Corp., which was trying to extend its patent. Neither bill was enacted.

McDermott landed on Ways and Means in the 102nd Congress with a combination of qualifications. He had chaired the Washington State Senate's Ways and Means panel. He had the backing of fellow Washingtonian Thomas S. Foley, who was then Speaker. And his medical degree made his candidacy attractive to Pete Stark of California, who chaired the Health Sub-committee and was looking for a doctor to match expertise with the Ener-gy and Commerce panel's resident physician at the time, J. Roy Rowland, D-Ga. (The two panels share jurisdiction over health care.)

McDermott also has an expertise in trade — of critical importance to Seattle-area businesses, including aircraft manufacturer Boeing, one of the country's largest exporters. McDermott backed the measure that granted China permanent normal trade status in the 106th, and he was one of just four Democrats on Ways and Means to endorse legislation in the 105th giv-ing the president fast-track authority to negotiate trade agreements that Con-gress cannot amend.

McDermott's mid-career turn as a Foreign Service medical officer in Africa (in 1987-88, after he left the state legislature) honed his interest in international affairs. In 1998, he accompanied Clinton on the first presi-dential trip to Africa in 20 years. That same year, he introduced a bill to encourage trade and investment in Northern Ireland and the counties that border the Irish Republic. In the 107th, he is co-chairman of a congressional caucus on India and Indian Americans.

After setting up a practice in Seattle in 1966, McDermott left for a stint as a Navy psychiatrist in Long Beach, Calif. In 1970, he came back and won a state House race, starting a lengthy legislative career punctuated by three losing bids for governor. He served in the state House for two years, and after a two-year break, won three four-year terms in the state Senate. Since his election to Congress in 1988, his re-election races have all been run-aways, and McDermott's seat is considered one of the state's safest for the Democratic Party.

Perhaps his most controversial period in Congress came during his tenure as the top Democrat on the House ethics committee in the 103rd and 104th, when the panel was investigating the propriety of Speaker Newt Gingrich's fundraising activities. McDermott resigned amid allegations that he had leaked a tape concerning Gingrich to the media. The tape was a recording of a conference call, intercepted by a Florida couple, in which GOP leaders discussed strategy for dealing with their Speaker's ethical troubles.

After the tape worked its way to McDermott, excerpts were cited in news-paper stories. One of the call's participants, Rep. John A. Boehner of Ohio, sued in 1998, alleging that his privacy had been violated. McDermott main-tains that he was within his First Amendment rights. The matter is before the Supreme Court, which must decide whether to hear or dismiss the case.

KEY VOTES

2000

Yes Raise hourly minimum wage by $1 over two years

No Halt funding for U.S. mission in Kosovo unless European nations pay more

Yes Provide Medicare benefits to military retirees and their dependents

Yes Grant China permanent normal trade status

– Phase out estate, gift and trust taxes

No Prohibit implementation of president's national monument designations

No Approve GOP plan to provide prescription drug coverage for Medicare beneficiaries

Yes Increase help for poor nations indebted to international financial institutions

1999

No Impose steel import quotas

No Kill proposal to take aviation trust funds off budget

No Require background checks on buyers only at gun shows with 10 or more vendors

No Remove barriers among banking, securities and insurance companies

+ Authorize state grants to hire teachers and reduce class size

Yes Overhaul campaign finance law; ban "soft money" and restrict advocacy advertising

Yes Approve bipartisan plan to increase rights of patients in managed-care health plans

INTEREST GROUPS

	AFL-CIO	ADA	CCUS	ACU
2000	90%	80%	42%	0%
1999	75%	55%	12%	5%
1998	89%	90%	38%	0%
1997	100%	90%	20%	4%

CQ VOTE STUDIES

	PARTY UNITY		PRESIDENTIAL SUPPORT	
	Support	Oppose	Support	Oppose
2000	97%	3%	94%	6%
1999	96%	4%	87%	13%
1998	96%	4%	95%	5%
1997	98%	2%	85%	15%

WASHINGTON 7

Seattle and suburbs

Framed by mountains, lakes and Puget Sound, the 7th provides a serene atmosphere for Seattle. Although more rain falls in Seattle than almost any other part of the nation, the region is considered one of the most desirable places to live. The 7th's diversity and liberal political leanings help inspire a cultural scene recognized for creating 1990s social trends like grunge music.

The Seattle region has become a home to high-tech startups and industry leaders. Software behemoth Microsoft, in nearby Redmond (1st District), is only one of more than 3,000 computer firms in the area. Aviation also provides thousands of jobs, as does the area's biotechnology industry. Boeing's March 2001 decision to move its corporate headquarters out of the state was a blow, although it was expected to cost the area only about 1,000 jobs in the short term. Boeing is the state's largest private employer, with more than 78,000 workers around Seattle.

Although the city's population growth has not kept pace with the state as a whole, Seattle's suburbs, especially in the north, form one of the fastest growing regions in the country. The Port of Seattle is one of the nation's major gateways to Asian markets and makes the 7th's economy dependent on trade. The late-1990s Asian economic crisis affected some large, multinational corporations in the area, but the technology boom kept the economy prosperous.

The 7th is one of the nation's most liberal bastions. Democrats often face no opposition in elections. The community cares mostly about health care, sustaining the environment, education and, most recently, traffic and urban sprawl; the population growth in suburbs outside the 7th has created long delays on the area's roadways.

MAJOR INDUSTRY
Aviation, computer software, health care

CITIES
Seattle (pt.), 484,527 (1990)

UNUSUAL FEATURES
In 1971, the first Starbucks Coffee opened at Pike's Place Market.

Rep. Jennifer Dunn (R)

Elected 1992; 5th term

Dunn's avocation is gardening. But with the election of her political ally George W. Bush to the White House, it is unlikely that she will find much time to tend to the rhododendrons and other plants in her Bellevue yard. Instead, she is reprising her role as a spokeswoman for her party and pouring much of her creative energy into arranging the Republican legislative agenda in the most attractive and presentable way possible.

Through a combination of her own political skill and the GOP desire to counter its image as the party of white men in dark suits, Dunn rose rapidly to prominence in House Republican ranks after her arrival in 1993, aided by the accession of her ally Newt Gingrich. Her bid for the majority leader post in 1998, though unsuccessful, marked the first time a woman had run for such a senior leadership position in Congress. (J. Dennis Hastert's belated entry into the race upset Dunn's calculations about her own candidacy, and neither of them was able to unseat Dick Armey, who still retains the position.) But Dunn's prestige slid sharply when Hastert succeeded Gingrich as Speaker in the 106th Congress.

With President Bush's election, Dunn's fortunes are back on the rise. She campaigned energetically for Bush and was mentioned as a possible secretary of the Commerce or Labor departments. She lost out in large part because her party could ill afford to put any GOP seat at risk in the closely divided 107th Congress. Still, Dunn will likely be in the thick of many of the administration's legislative endeavors.

Dunn's voting record has been consistently conservative, but she usually takes care to couch GOP arguments in positive, non-threatening language. "I have always been a proponent of softening our rhetoric," she said before the 1996 elections. "I believe we can pursue the same positions we have been, but we don't need to be as harsh and scary about it."

Dunn helps to put a warm face on Republican efforts to overhaul federal social programs, injecting her personal history into policy debates. During consideration of welfare or labor legislation, she can be heard describing her empathy, "as a single mother who raised two sons," for the difficulties experienced by working parents.

She nonetheless votes a loyal Republican line on fiscal policy and social issues. As a freshman in 1993, she surprised some of her more-senior female colleagues by voting against the Family and Medical Leave Act, enacted that year. She supports gun owners' rights, voted to overturn President Clinton's ban on discrimination based on sexual orientation, and supported a "religious freedom" constitutional amendment propounded by advocates of school prayer.

Solidly pro-business and a proponent of lowering international trade barriers, she uses her Ways and Means seat to look out for the interests of Seattle-area businesses, including aircraft manufacturer Boeing, one of the country's largest exporters.

Dunn got her seat on the powerful Ways and Means Committee in 1995, and in 1997, she was elected to an entry-level party leadership post, Republican Conference secretary. Later the same year, she won promotion to conference vice chairman. She became a regular presence on the podium at Republican news conferences and rallies, striving to help her party appeal to more women voters. In the 106th Congress, she co-chaired a House Bipartisan Working Group on Youth Violence.

Dunn's highest-profile legislative initiatives have been on tax issues. In

CAPITOL OFFICE
225-7761; fax 225-8673
1501 Longworth Bldg. 20515

INTERNET
e-mail: dunnwa08@mail.house.gov
web: www.house.gov/dunn

COMMITTEES
Ways & Means

HOMETOWN
Bellevue

BORN
July 29, 1941, Seattle, Wash.

RELIGION
Episcopalian

FAMILY
Divorced; two children

EDUCATION
Stanford U., attended 1959; U. of Washington, attended 1960-62; Stanford U., B.A. 1963

CAREER
State party official

POLITICAL HIGHLIGHTS
Wash. Republican Party chairwoman, 1980-92

ELECTION RESULTS

2000 GENERAL

Jennifer Dunn (R)	183,255	62.2%
Heidi Behrens-Benedict (D)	104,944	35.6%
Bernard McIlroy (LIBERT)	6,269	2.1%

2000 PRIMARY (OPEN)

Jennifer Dunn (R)	89,133	60.8%
Heidi Behrens-Benedict (D)	54,449	37.1%
Bernard McIlroy (LIBERT)	3,059	2.1%

1998 GENERAL

Jennifer Dunn (R)	135,539	59.7%
Heidi Behrens-Benedict (D)	91,371	40.3%

PREVIOUS WINNING PERCENTAGES
1996 (65%); 1994 (76%); 1992 (60%)

the 106th, she introduced a bill to repeal taxes on estates, gifts and trust funds. Working with moderate Democrats such as John Tanner of Tennessee and associations representing farmers, small businesses and manufacturers, she built a broad coalition of support for the measure, which even drew backing from some of the House's more liberal Democrats.

Though many observers initially gave the bill little chance, the House passed it soundly in 2000 — with 65 Democratic supporters — but with fewer votes than were needed to override Clinton's veto. In the 107th Congress, Dunn remains a leading proponent of estate tax repeal.

Since she defeated her 6th grade boyfriend in an election for student body president, Dunn has had a passion for politics. She continued her involvement in student government through high school and at Stanford University. In 1964, she became aware of an upstart Republican politician named Ronald Reagan; he became her political idol. When she moved back to her home state, she poured much of her free time into campaigning for him and even named her second son Reagan.

When her marriage to King County's Republican Party chairman dissolved, Dunn worked in the county's tax assessing office before testing her own political ambitions. In 1980, she won the chairmanship of Washington state's Republican Party with the help of her contacts in the Reagan campaigns and in King County Republican circles. The job was perfect for Dunn. It allowed her to advance her career while providing enough money to support her two sons and enough flexibility to raise them on her own.

The position, and her fundraising prowess, put her in good standing with both of Reagan's successful presidential campaigns and with his successor, George Bush. She was at one point vice chairman of the Republican National Committee's executive board.

Dunn made her first bid for public office in 1992. She eked out a Republican primary victory in the open 8th District over Pam Roach, a first-term state senator and ardent abortion opponent who cast Dunn as a denizen of the established and more affluent suburbs of King County. Dunn had an easier time in the general election, taking 60 percent against her Democratic opponent, George O. Tamblyn, a Mercer Island businessman. Tamblyn, who had switched parties, was unable to make a case against her conservative fiscal views and more moderate image on social issues. Since then, she has easily won re-election.

Dunn was seen as a hot prospect to run for the Senate in 1998 against Democratic incumbent Patty Murray, but she declined to take the risk; the chance of continued advancement in the House looked like a better bet.

KEY VOTES

2000

No Raise hourly minimum wage by $1 over two years

Yes Halt funding for U.S. mission in Kosovo unless European nations pay more

Yes Provide Medicare benefits to military retirees and their dependents

Yes Grant China permanent normal trade status

Yes Phase out estate, gift and trust taxes

Yes Prohibit implementation of president's national monument designations

Yes Approve GOP plan to provide prescription drug coverage for Medicare beneficiaries

No Increase help for poor nations indebted to international financial institutions

1999

No Impose steel import quotas

Yes Kill proposal to take aviation trust funds off budget

Yes Require background checks on buyers only at gun shows with 10 or more vendors

Yes Remove barriers among banking, securities and insurance companies

No Authorize state grants to hire teachers and reduce class size

No Overhaul campaign finance law; ban "soft money" and restrict advocacy advertising

No Approve bipartisan plan to increase rights of patients in managed-care health plans

INTEREST GROUPS

	AFL-CIO	ADA	CCUS	ACU
2000	0%	0%	95%	88%
1999	0%	10%	96%	80%
1998	0%	0%	100%	96%
1997	0%	0%	100%	92%

CQ VOTE STUDIES

	PARTY UNITY		PRESIDENTIAL SUPPORT	
	Support	Oppose	Support	Oppose
2000	92%	8%	28%	72%
1999	88%	12%	28%	72%
1998	94%	6%	23%	77%
1997	95%	5%	31%	69%

WASHINGTON 8

Puget Sound (east) – King County suburbs; Bellevue

The allure of Mt. Rainier's snow-capped peaks and picturesque towns within reach of Seattle helped the 8th become the state's fastest growing district in the 1980s. Now some of Seattle's most prosperous suburbs are here. But the fiscally conservative, mostly Republican area could be undergoing a second transformation as demographic changes erode once-solid support for the GOP.

Attracting residents who work for the area's high-tech companies, including Microsoft (whose Redmond headquarters is over the district line in the 1st), the 8th nonetheless has a blue-collar working base because of aircraft-maker Boeing. The company's March 2001 decision to move its headquarters – and about 1,000 jobs – out of the state was a blow, although the firm's area plants were expected to be unaffected by the change. It wasn't the first time Boeing, the state's biggest private employer, had cut back; major layoffs as recent as 1998

and '99 caused some workers to leave the district.

In addition to its near-in Seattle suburbs, the 8th continues east to the border of King County and heads south to take in a mostly rural part of Pierce County, which includes Mt. Rainier National Park.

While Republicans have won for years, the 8th's politics are slowly changing. Fiscally conservative suburbanites vote for like-minded candidates, but many of the 8th's voters, particularly women, shy away from social conservatives. Vietnamese, Russian and Cambodian immigrants are diversifying the area and could have a bigger influence on future elections. Democratic presidential candidates captured the district in 1992, '96 and 2000, albeit not always by very large margins.

MAJOR INDUSTRY
Logging, aviation manufacturing, software

CITIES
Bellevue (pt.), 69,085 (1990); East Hill-Meridian (unincorporated), 42,696 (1990); Cascade-Fairwood (unincorporated) (pt.), 27,700 (1990)

UNUSUAL FEATURES
First pontoon bridge made of reinforced concrete was finished on July 2, 1940, connecting Mercer Island and Seattle.

Rep. Adam Smith (D)

CAPITOL OFFICE
225-8901; fax 225-5893; 116 Cannon Bldg. 20515

INTERNET
e-mail: adam.smith@mail.house.gov
web: www.house.gov/adamsmith

COMMITTEES
Armed Services
Resources

HOMETOWN
Tacoma

BORN
June 15, 1965, Washington, D.C.

RELIGION
Christian

FAMILY
Wife, Sara Smith; one child

EDUCATION
Fordham U., B.A. 1987; U. of Washington, J.D. 1990

CAREER
City prosecutor; lawyer

POLITICAL HIGHLIGHTS
Wash. Senate, 1991-97

ELECTION RESULTS

2000 GENERAL

Adam Smith (D)	135,452	61.7%
Chris Vance (R)	76,766	35.0%
Jonathan V. Wright (LIBERT)	7,405	3.4%

2000 PRIMARY (OPEN)

Adam Smith (D)	70,901	59.8%
Chris Vance (R)	34,861	29.4%
Gary Snell (R)	9,322	7.9%
Jonathan V. Wright (LIBERT)	3,569	3.0%

1998 GENERAL

Adam Smith (D)	111,948	64.7%
Ron Taber (R)	61,108	35.3%

PREVIOUS WINNING PERCENTAGES
1996 (50%)

Elected 1996; 3rd term

Smith has the distinction of being the first person ever re-elected in the 9th District. The district was created in 1992, after population growth during the 1980s earned Washington a ninth House seat. The 9th was drawn right where the growth had been the greatest: in the suburbs and exurbs east and south of Seattle.

The 9th is a district that will change its mind. The first two men elected (one a Democrat, the other a Republican) each lost after one House term — party allegiance is not a big factor in many residents' voting decisions. Smith has survived by presenting himself as a pragmatic centrist who is pro-business and fiscally conservative, but also mindful of such liberal causes as abortion rights. Just 31 when he won election to Congress, Smith entered the House with significant legislative experience — a half-dozen years in the Washington Senate.

A member of the moderate New Democrat Coalition, he has joined with conservatives on such issues as banning desecration of the U.S. flag and encouraging states to prosecute violent juvenile offenders in adult courts.

On domestic policy issues, Smith takes a more liberal line, favoring environmental protections, abortion rights and federal arts funding. But he makes a point of putting some rhetorical distance between himself and the House Democratic leadership, which he once called "out of touch" with average Americans.

When Republican George W. Bush moved into the White House in 2001, Smith said he was willing to "work with him on everything." He told the Tacoma News Tribune he was "not about to join those who demonize Bush." But he also warned that if Bush "thinks he can 'aw shucks' us and do whatever he wants, he is mistaken."

One of Smith's top priorities is supporting the many high-technology companies in his district. In the 106th Congress, he backed legislation allowing more skilled foreign workers to take jobs in the United States. He also worked with the New Democrat Coalition on a technological agenda dubbed "e-genda 2.0" that stressed increased access to overseas markets and improved technology education.

On the Armed Services Committee, Smith battled efforts to restrict data-scrambling encryption technology, which makes information stored in computers more secure. Other members of the committee worried that wider private sector use of encryption could hamper U.S. efforts at intelligence gathering and predicting military attacks; but Smith in the 105th Congress argued that restricting encryption would force U.S. software companies to move overseas to keep up with foreign developers of the technology.

Smith also uses his Armed Services seat to look out for the interests of Boeing, his district's largest employer, by supporting construction of the F-22 stealth fighter plane. He was able to include money in the 1998 defense authorization bill for a new health care facility at a military base in his district, and he backed federal funding for nuclear-waste cleanup at the Hanford Nuclear Facility in the state.

Timber giant Weyerhaeuser Co. has its headquarters in the 9th, but Smith usually aligns with fellow Resources Committee Democrats from similarly urbanized Western districts, who are sympathetic to calls for environmental protections. He opposed a GOP plan in 1999 that would have allowed the removal of damaged trees from national forests without lengthy environmental impact reviews.

Smith favors limited tax cuts, and he introduced legislation in the 106th Congress to eliminate estate taxes on family-owned businesses and farms. But he opposed a GOP bill in the 106th to cut taxes by $792 billion, warning that such a plan could endanger the budget surplus and interfere with efforts to shore up Social Security and Medicare. "I support tax cuts. I think we need tax cuts. But this was just too much," he said in a Gannett News Service article. "The problem is it's 10 pounds of manure in a 5-pound bag." Early in the 107th, Smith voted against a bill to lower income tax rates, the first element of President Bush's $1.6 trillion tax cut plan.

Smith's father was in the International Association of Machinists and Aerospace Workers as a baggage handler at the Seattle-Tacoma airport. Smith himself was a member of the Teamsters Union while working for the United Parcel Service (UPS) during college, and union support played a big role in his 1996 election. Not surprisingly, Smith typically sides with organized labor on floor votes involving worker-management issues.

However, many jobs in the 9th are tied to businesses engaged in import-export activities, and Smith broke with labor by voting in 2000 for a measure granting China permanent normal trade status. But in 1998, he voted against Clinton's request for fast-track authority to negotiate trade agreements that Congress cannot amend, citing concern that worker rights and environmental safeguards would not be ensured.

Smith likes to point out that he is a lifelong resident of the area he represents in Congress, but he actually was born "inside the Beltway," in Washington, D.C. He was adopted when he was one week old and brought West to his new parents' home in the "other Washington." Smith's adoptive father died shortly before Smith headed East to attend Fordham University. He worked for UPS through his undergraduate years, then earned a law degree from the University of Washington in Seattle.

His upset victory in the 1990 state Senate election made Smith, at 25, the youngest state senator in the country. Four years later, when many Democratic officeholders in the state were swept out of office by the 1994 Republican tide, Smith won election to a second term.

By then, Smith was well-known as a tireless campaigner who had made repeat visits to many of the 40,000 homes in his legislative district. So he was considered a rising star among Washington Democrats when he announced that he would challenge freshman GOP Rep. Randy Tate in the 1996 election. Aided by a barrage of AFL-CIO television and radio ads, Smith pulled off the win, 50 percent to 47 percent. In 1998, he won by 30 percentage points and in 2000, his margin was 27 points.

KEY VOTES

2000
+ Raise hourly minimum wage by $1 over two years
No Halt funding for U.S. mission in Kosovo unless European nations pay more
Yes Provide Medicare benefits to military retirees and their dependents
Yes Grant China permanent normal trade status
+ Phase out estate, gift and trust taxes
No Prohibit implementation of president's national monument designations
No Approve GOP plan to provide prescription drug coverage for Medicare beneficiaries
+ Increase help for poor nations indebted to international financial institutions

1999
No Impose steel import quotas
Yes Kill proposal to take aviation trust funds off budget
Yes Require background checks on buyers only at gun shows with 10 or more vendors
Yes Remove barriers among banking, securities and insurance companies
Yes Authorize state grants to hire teachers and reduce class size
Yes Overhaul campaign finance law; ban "soft money" and restrict advocacy advertising
Yes Approve bipartisan plan to increase rights of patients in managed-care health plans

INTEREST GROUPS

	AFL-CIO	ADA	CCUS	ACU
2000	67%	45%	80%	21%
1999	56%	85%	56%	20%
1998	100%	100%	39%	0%
1997	88%	80%	50%	20%

CQ VOTE STUDIES

	PARTY UNITY		PRESIDENTIAL SUPPORT	
	Support	Oppose	Support	Oppose
2000	80%	20%	78%	22%
1999	75%	25%	75%	25%
1998	83%	17%	80%	20%
1997	84%	16%	83%	17%

WASHINGTON 9
Puget Sound – Tacoma

After the population of Seattle's suburbs jumped dramatically in the 1980s, leaders carved the area south of the city into a new district, the 9th. The district consists mostly of sprawling suburban communities, following Interstate 5 south from Seattle, through Tacoma (shared with the 6th) and on toward Olympia (in the 3rd). The district also reaches south to pick up a more sparsely populated piece of Thurston County.

The 9th is a Boeing district. The aircraft company employs more than 78,000 workers in the Seattle region and has major operations in the 9th, forming the backbone of a strong local economy. Boeing's March 2001 annoucement that it would move its headquarters, and about 1,000 jobs, out of state was a blow. But the firm, the state's largest private employer, plans to keep its Seattle factories in operation.

As with the city's northern suburbs, the corridor along Interstate 5 has become a magnet for high-tech companies that provide high-paying jobs for the well-educated residents. A large military presence and the

headquarters of paper giant Weyerhaeuser also add to the economy.

Politically, the 9th is as evenly split a district as they come; a 1992 poll found Democrats and Republicans within one percentage point of each other. But 41 percent of those voters considered themselves independents. Blue-collar workers from Boeing form a solid Democratic base, while the well-to-do and fiscally conservative suburbanites tend to vote Republican. Political observers predict that no incumbent will rest easy in this district.

MAJOR INDUSTRY
Timber, aviation manufacturing, computer software

MILITARY BASES
Fort Lewis (Army), 20,000 military, 5,000 civilian (1999); McChord Air Force Base, 3,631 military, 1,999 civilian (2000)

CITIES
Federal Way, 74,398; Tacoma (pt.), 30,239 (1990); Des Moines, 26,588; Burien (pt.), 23,788 (1990)

UNUSUAL FEATURES
Before becoming commander of the American forces in the Persian Gulf, Gen. Norman Schwarzkopf was commander of Fort Lewis.

WEST VIRGINIA

Gov. Bob Wise (D)

First elected: 2000
Length of term: 4 years
Term expires: 1/05
Salary: $90,000
Phone: (304) 558-2000
Hometown: Clendenin
Born: Jan. 6, 1948; Washington, D.C.
Religion: Episcopalian
Family: Wife, Sandra Wise; two children
Education: Duke U., A.B. 1970; Tulane U., J.D. 1975
Career: Lawyer
Political highlights: W.Va. Senate, 1981-83; U.S. House, 1983-2001

Election results:
2000 GENERAL
Bob Wise (D)	324,822	50.1%
Cecil H. Underwood (R)	305,926	47.2%
Denise Giardina (MOUNT)	10,416	1.6%

Senate President
Earl Ray Tomblin (D)

(no lieutenant governor)
Phone: (304) 357-7801

STATE LEGISLATURE

General Assembly: Meets January-March
House: 100 members, 2-year terms
2001 breakdown: 25R, 75D; 80 men, 20 women
Salary: $15,000
Phone: (304) 340-3200
Senate: 34 members, 4-year terms
2001 breakdown: 6R, 28D; 29 men, 5 women
Salary: $15,000
Phone: (304) 357-7800

STATE TERM LIMITS

Governor: 2 consecutive terms
Senate: No
House: No

URBAN STATISTICS

CITY	POPULATION
Charleston	54,598
Huntington	52,273
Wheeling	32,526
Parkersburg	32,212
Morgantown	29,017

REGISTERED VOTERS

Democrat	63%
Republican	29%
Other	8%

POPULATION

2000 population	1,808,344
1990 population	1,793,477
Percent change	+0.8%
Rank among states	37
Median age	38.1
Born in state	77%
Foreign born	1%
Urban/rural	36%/64%
Crime rate	219/100,000
Poverty level	17.8%
Federal workers	21,583
Military	9,662

REAPPORTIONMENT

West Virginia retained its three House seats in reapportionment. The state legislature will draw new district lines.

MISCELLANEOUS

Web: www.state.wv.us
Capital: Charleston
Land area: 24,087 sq. miles
Rank among states: 41
STATE ELECTION OFFICIAL
(304) 558-6000
DEMOCRATIC HEADQUARTERS
(304) 342-8121
REPUBLICAN HEADQUARTERS
(304) 344-3446

District Statistics

DIST.	VOTE FOR PRESIDENT 2000 D	2000 R	GREEN	1996 D	1996 R	REF	1992 D	1992 R	I	WHT	BLK	ASIAN	HISP	HOUSEHOLD INCOME	OVER 65+	UNDER 18	COLLEGE EDUCATION
1	43%	54%	2%	49%	38%	13%	46%	35%	19%	98%	2%	1%	1%	$21,903	16%	24%	14%
2	44	54	2	49	40	11	45	39	16	96	3	0	0	$22,253	14	25	13
3	51	47	1	58	32	10	55	32	13	95	4	0	0	$18,166	15	26	10
STATE	46	52	2	52	37	11	48	35	16	96	3	<1	<1	$20,795	15	25	12

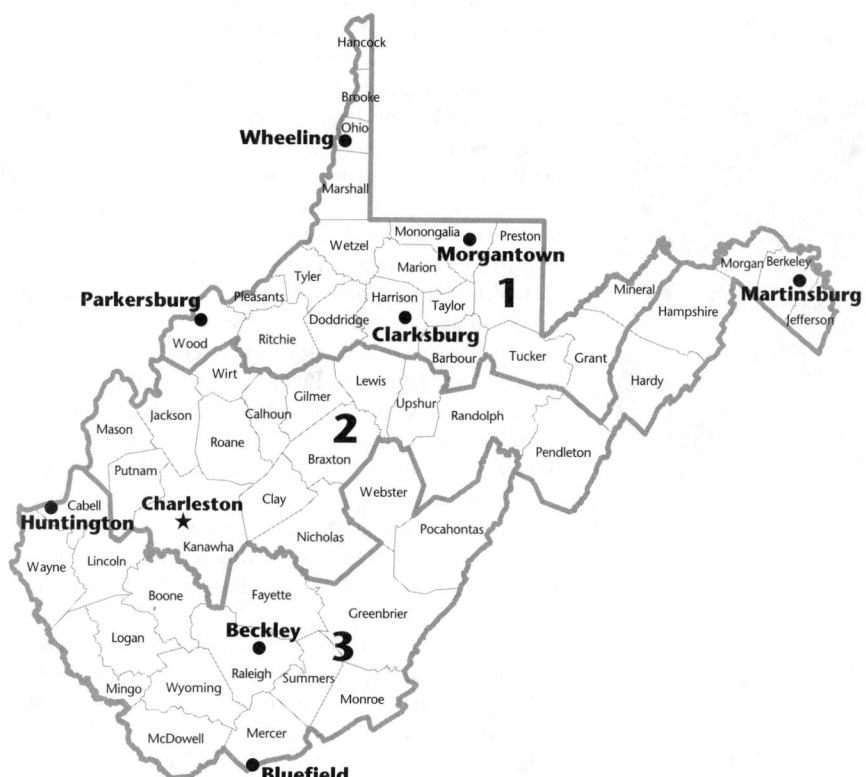

Sen. Robert C. Byrd (D)

Elected 1958; 8th term

Someday the Senate will exist without Robert C. Byrd. But it will be a very different place. The West Virginia Democrat is the Senate's self-appointed guardian, its reverential historian, the master of its rules and procedures.

Byrd wrote the book on the Senate, literally. He is the author of a handsomely bound, four-volume history of the institution, a project that grew out of a series of speeches he delivered on the Senate floor. His devotion to the Senate, and the Constitution, is legendary. When House Republicans championed their "Contract With America," the legislative game plan that helped propel them into power in 1994, Byrd was dismissive. Pulling out a well-worn copy of the Constitution, he said: "This is *my* contract with America."

Byrd has been derided for his flowery, long-winded speeches and his relentless (and generally successful) crusade as senior Democrat on the Appropriations Committee to funnel federal funds to his home state. He can be prickly and imperious. But no one questions his respect and admiration for the institution he has served for more than 40 years. "He has taken on the role of protector of this institution the likes of which no one has before or probably will in the future," Senate Democratic Leader Tom Daschle told The Washington Post.

In turn, Byrd's colleagues show him extraordinary deference on matters of precedent and procedure. During the impeachment trial of President Clinton, which was unlike anything the Senate had seen in 131 years, Republicans and Democrats alike looked to Byrd for guidance. Before the trial began, Republican Mitch McConnell of Kentucky, a fierce partisan, said, "I'm going to take my cues from Sen. Byrd. I think he's the expert."

Byrd's life story could have been written by Horatio Alger. The senator was born Cornelius Calvin Sale Jr. When he was 1, his mother died and his father gave him to an aunt and uncle, Vlurma and Titus Byrd; they raised him in the hardscrabble coal country of southern West Virginia. Byrd graduated first in his high school class, but it took him 12 years before he could afford to start college. He worked as a gas station attendant, grocery store clerk, shipyard welder and butcher before his talents as a fiddle player helped him win a seat in the state legislature in 1946. Friends drove Byrd around the hills and hollows, where he brought the voters out by playing "Cripple Creek" and "Rye Whiskey."

From then on, he never lost an election. As Byrd once put it, "There are four things people believe in in West Virginia: God Almighty; Sears, Roebuck; Carter's Little Liver Pills; and Robert C. Byrd."

Although a loyal Democrat, Byrd places at least as great an emphasis on the prerogatives of the Senate and the needs of his home state as he does on political ideology. He has drawn fire from environmentalists for his support of the coal industry and from free-traders for legislation to help U.S. steel companies combat dumping practices by foreign rivals. At the start of the 107th Congress, he was one of only eight Democrats to vote for President Bush's controversial choice for attorney general, former Missouri Sen. John Ashcroft — a staunch conservative. Byrd said it is a president's prerogative to name his Cabinet.

But he rallied his party after Republicans swept to power in the 104th. He emerged as a formidable force in blocking GOP proposals he found offensive or pernicious, notably the line-item veto and a balanced-budget constitutional amendment. In 2000, he cast a key vote against a constitutional amendment banning flag desecration, even though he had previously sup-

CAPITOL OFFICE
224-3954; fax 228-0002; 311 Hart Bldg. 20510

INTERNET
e-mail: senator_byrd@byrd.senate.gov
web: byrd.senate.gov

COMMITTEES
Appropriations - ranking member
Armed Services
Budget
Rules & Administration

HOMETOWN
Sophia

BORN
Nov. 20, 1917, North Wilkesboro, N.C.

RELIGION
Baptist

FAMILY
Wife, Erma Ora Byrd; two children

EDUCATION
American U., J.D. 1963; Marshall U., B.A. 1994

CAREER
Lawyer

POLITICAL HIGHLIGHTS
W.Va. House, 1947-51; W.Va. Senate, 1951-53; U.S. House, 1953-59

ELECTION RESULTS

2000 GENERAL

Robert C. Byrd (D)	469,215	77.8%
David T. Gallaher (R)	121,635	20.2%
Joe Whelan (LIBERT)	12,627	2.1%

2000 PRIMARY

Robert C. Byrd (D)	unopposed

PREVIOUS WINNING PERCENTAGES
1994 (69%); 1988 (65%); 1982 (69%); 1976 (100%); 1970 (78%); 1964 (68%); 1958 (59%); 1956 House Election (57%); 1954 House Election (63%); 1952 House Election (56%)

ported the idea. "The foolish and the dead alone never change their minds," he said on the floor.

Fiercely protective of the Senate, Byrd frequently accused the Clinton White House of overstepping its authority. In 2000, he tried to force a withdrawal of U.S. troops from Kosovo unless Congress voted to continue its peacekeeping mission. "This is about ... the arrogance of power and a White House that insists on putting our men and women in harm's way," he said. Angered that Energy Secretary Bill Richardson failed to show up for a Senate hearing on security breaches at his department, Byrd dressed him down. "You have shown an extreme contempt ... of this Congress," he lectured Richardson at a 2000 hearing. "You've had a bright and brilliant career. But you will never again receive the support of the Senate of the United States for any office to which you might be appointed."

Byrd was a pivotal figure in the 1999 impeachment trial of Clinton. He was highly critical of the president in the months leading up to the trial and said during it that he had become convinced that Clinton had lied under oath about his affair with a White House intern. Yet Byrd felt the lack of public support for removing Clinton from office meant that convicting the president would cause greater damage than allowing him to finish his term, even though he described having to say the words "not guilty" as like having a bone caught in his throat. He offered a motion to dismiss the trial — a clear sign, the president's lawyers later said, that Clinton had won.

There have been indications that age is beginning to take its toll on the 83-year-old Byrd. A tremor causes his hands to shake, sometimes quite noticeably. In 1999, he was involved in a minor fender-bender that grew into something of a contretemps after Byrd was given congressional immunity, a privilege granted by the Constitution. He eventually waived immunity, pleaded no contest and paid a small fine.

But it is still dangerous to underestimate Byrd, particularly when it comes to matters related to appropriations. Indeed, no less a figure than House Speaker J. Dennis Hastert learned that lesson — when he tangled with Byrd in the 106th Congress over a provision aiding steel companies (including one in West Virginia) that Byrd had slipped into a supplemental appropriations bill. As House and Senate negotiators worked late one evening on the bill, Hastert sent word that he wanted Byrd's "pork" provision removed. Byrd sat silently until just before midnight, and when he finally spoke, his words dripped with indignation. "I must say I'm offended when I'm told that we can't have this in this bill, and when I'm told that if it's in this bill it won't be taken up," he said. "Run over me, that's all right. But tell the good Speaker I'm not dropping anything." His provision eventually passed as a separate bill.

Such triumphs make up the core of Byrd's legislative legacy. He stepped down as Senate majority leader in 1989 to head the Appropriations Committee, bragging that he would use the post to become West Virginia's leading industry. He promised $1 billion in federal funds for his state, a goal he reached in less than two years.

Byrd's political career has featured its share of mistakes, some quite spectacular. As a young man, he joined the Ku Klux Klan, a decision he came to publicly regret. In 1964, he filibustered the landmark Civil Rights Act, at one point holding the floor with a 14-hour speech that is among the longest on record. He also has lamented that chapter of his career.

But Byrd has served long enough to learn from some past mistakes. In 1993, when the U.S. military mission in Somalia started going badly, he recalled his decision to stick with President Johnson's expansion of the war in Vietnam. Never again, Byrd told his colleagues, and he succeeded in forging a bipartisan agreement that forced Clinton to wind down the Somalia operation.

KEY VOTES

2000
Yes Overhaul bankruptcy law and increase minimum wage
No Limit fiscal 2001 discretionary spending to $600.3 billion
No Override veto on nuclear waste disposal at Yucca Mountain site in Nevada
No Oppose effort to terminate Kosovo mission
No Include gender, sexual orientation and disability in federal hate crime protections
Yes Approve GOP plan to restrict use of genetic information by health insurers
No Kill amendment delaying implementation of an anti-missile defense system
Yes Cut taxes for married couples
No Grant China permanent normal trade status

1999
No Remove President Clinton from office for obstruction of justice
No Kill amendment authorizing state grants to hire teachers and reduce class size
Yes Require criminal background checks for purchases at gun shows
No Approve GOP proposal to increase rights of patients in managed-care health plans
Yes Block effort to allow farm and medicine exports to Cuba
No Allow study of tougher automobile fuel efficiency standards
P Ratify nuclear weapons testing treaty
Yes Prohibit national political parties from collecting "soft money" donations
Yes Remove barriers among banking, securities and insurance companies

INTEREST GROUPS

	AFL-CIO	ADA	CCUS	ACU
2000	63%	75%	40%	28%
1999	100%	80%	47%	20%
1998	88%	80%	44%	16%
1997	100%	70%	40%	16%
1996	86%	70%	23%	15%
1995	92%	85%	26%	26%
1994	75%	75%	30%	40%
1993	100%	55%	18%	24%
1992	92%	100%	20%	19%
1991	83%	65%	10%	33%

CQ VOTE STUDIES

	PARTY UNITY		PRESIDENTIAL SUPPORT	
	Support	Oppose	Support	Oppose
2000	72%	28%	75%	25%
1999	80%	20%	70%	30%
1998	72%	28%	74%	26%
1997	81%	19%	81%	19%
1996	82%	18%	81%	19%
1995	82%	18%	82%	18%
1994	73%	27%	74%	26%
1993	87%	13%	80%	20%
1992	75%	25%	27%	73%
1991	76%	24%	49%	51%

Sen. John D. Rockefeller IV (D)

Elected 1984; 3rd term

Given his family fortune and his upbringing, it may seem odd that Rockefeller represents a state with one of the nation's lowest per capita personal incomes. But Rockefeller relies on a self-deprecating sense of humor to come across as an ordinary man, and West Virginia voters usually refer to him as just plain "Jay."

Rockefeller has worked hard at gaining the confidence of West Virginia residents from the day he arrived in the state in 1964 as a 27-year-old VISTA anti-poverty volunteer, who planned to stay for a year. Working for the Action for Appalachia Youth program seemed a strange choice for Rockefeller, a Harvard graduate who had spent three years in Tokyo studying Japanese. But the experience was transformational, and two years later he had not only found a permanent home, but had won election to the state House of Delegates. And in one way, his family wealth has insulated him from suspicion back home. With no need to curry favor or campaign cash from special interests, Rockefeller can devote all of his energies to helping his hard-pressed constituents.

He has a long way to go, however, before he can hope to match the largess of his home state colleague Robert C. Byrd, the dean of Senate Democrats. As top Democrat on the Appropriations Committee, Byrd long ago brought more than $1 billion in federal projects to West Virginia.

Still, Rockefeller does his part to protect West Virginia's interests, using his seniority on the Finance and Commerce committees to fight for state causes. He is well-positioned to influence some of the major debates of the 107th Congress, including tax cuts and a Medicare overhaul. He is the No. 2 Democrat on Finance and the ranking member of its Health Care Subcommittee. He also is the ranking Democrat on Veterans' Affairs and the top Democrat on Commerce's Aviation Subcommittee. In the 107th, he added an assignment to the Intelligence Committee.

West Virginians surprised many poll watchers by voting for George W. Bush in the 2000 election. Rockefeller said he was not fazed by the outcome in his state. "It was an election that was lost by [Democratic presidential candidate Al] Gore as much as anything else. It doesn't change what people are worried about in my state. It doesn't change who they are. I will agree with Bush on some things, and I will disagree with him on other things."

Early in 2001, Rockefeller did disagree with President Bush's $1.6 trillion, 10-year package of tax cuts. "When you look at the surplus and you look at the tax plan, they equal each other," he said. "And there won't be anything left for anything else."

Rockefeller has been a tireless advocate of comprehensive health coverage for all. He served as chairman in 1989 of the so-called Pepper Commission, a bipartisan panel that tried to promote long-term care for the elderly and health coverage for the uninsured. Although the commission made recommendations in both areas, its members failed to agree on how to pay for the proposals and the package died.

A decade later, Rockefeller was a member of another blue-ribbon commission studying ways to ensure the long-term solvency of Medicare. This time, he was one of seven members (of 17) to oppose an overhaul plan offered by Sen. John B. Breaux, D-La., the panel's co-chairman. Rockefeller argued, among other things, that Breaux's proposed prescription drug benefits were too stingy. The "no" votes were enough to block a formal recommendation and essentially killed the issue for the 106th Congress.

CAPITOL OFFICE
224-6472; fax 224-7665; 531 Hart Bldg. 20510

INTERNET
e-mail: senator@rockefeller.senate.gov
web: rockefeller.senate.gov

COMMITTEES
Commerce, Science & Transportation
Finance
Veterans' Affairs - ranking member
Select Intelligence
Joint Taxation

HOMETOWN
Charleston

BORN
June 18, 1937, Manhattan, N.Y.

RELIGION
Presbyterian

FAMILY
Wife, Sharon Percy; four children

EDUCATION
International Christian U. (Tokyo), attended 1957-60; Harvard U., A.B. 1961

CAREER
College president; public official

POLITICAL HIGHLIGHTS
W.Va. House, 1967-69; W.Va. secretary of state, 1969-73; Democratic nominee for governor, 1972; governor, 1977-85

ELECTION RESULTS

1996 GENERAL

John D. Rockefeller IV (D)	456,526	76.6%
Betty A. Burks (R)	139,088	23.4%

1996 PRIMARY

John D. Rockefeller IV (D)	280,303	88.4%
Bruce Barilla (D)	36,637	11.6%

PREVIOUS WINNING PERCENTAGES
1990 (68%); 1984 (52%)

Breaux is pushing a modified version of his plan in the 107th, and Rockefeller is ready to do battle again.

One priority for Rockefeller in the 107th is enactment of a Medicare prescription drug benefit — he says it is "outrageous" that the program doesn't already cover drug costs. And he says he will fight against any changes in Medicare that could hurt lower-income beneficiaries.

Rockefeller also goes to bat for his state's steel industry. He was often critical of the Clinton administration's handling of steel industry concerns. On the first day of the 1999 session, he introduced legislation to curb dumping of below-cost imported steel in U.S. markets and to require better monitoring of steel imports. The administration shot back, saying the bill would violate international trade agreements and "could spark a round of destructive protectionism."

Because of the fight, Rockefeller said he "nearly lost my relationship with Clinton. But it didn't matter because steel was more important to me than the relationship." Rockefeller, co-chairman of the Senate Steel Caucus, says he will continue to fight for steel in the 107th. He pushed the subject with Bush administration officials, and Bush himself, early in 2001.

On Capitol Hill, Rockefeller's affable personality and strong command of legislative details help him win support on many issues. He can be the most partisan of Democrats, arguing that Republicans are out to hurt the little guy, or the pragmatist willing to do what it takes to strike a deal. And since Republicans took control of the Senate in the 104th Congress, he has played both roles, working with his own party's liberal wing to push for broader health care coverage while lining up with the GOP in an effort to overhaul product liability laws.

Rockefeller has continued to move up the Senate seniority ladder while waiting for a return to the power he held briefly when Democrats were in control in the early 1990s. In the 103rd Congress, he not only chaired the Finance Committee's health panel, he also was chairman of the Veterans' Affairs Committee. In the latter role, he won enactment of a number of significant bills, including one authorizing the Department of Veterans Affairs to pay benefits to veterans disabled by the so-called Persian Gulf syndrome, a multitude of ailments stemming from service in the Gulf War.

After Rockefeller's 1964 stint as a VISTA volunteer stretched into two years, he decided to make his home in West Virginia and enter politics. He served in the state House and as secretary of state, then lost a race for the governor's office in 1972. He strengthened his ties to the state by serving as president of West Virginia Wesleyan College and ran for governor again in 1976, this time successfully. Along the way, he married Sharon Percy, daughter of then-Sen. Charles H. Percy, R-Ill.

In winning his 1976 bid, Rockefeller trounced former GOP Gov. Cecil Underwood, who was seeking a return to the statehouse after a 16-year absence. Rockefeller won a second gubernatorial term in 1980. Barred from seeking a third term by West Virginia law, he ran for the Senate in 1984 and defeated a wealthy, young political neophyte, John Raese — spending $12 million to do so. He has easily won re-election twice since then.

Given his name recognition, wealth and political experience, Rockefeller has been mentioned as a potential presidential contender for 2004. But he told the Charleston Daily Mail in 2001 that he was not interested. "If I'd wanted to do it, I would have in 1991," he told the newspaper. He tested the waters that year, traveling to Iowa and New Hampshire before pulling back.

Rockefeller concedes that there is a personal element to his decision not to seek the presidency in 2004. "I am sufficiently private to not want to do this," he told the newspaper. "There's a point where I've decided to say, 'You can't have all of me.'"

KEY VOTES

2000

- Yes Overhaul bankruptcy law and increase minimum wage
- No Limit fiscal 2001 discretionary spending to $600.3 billion
- No Override veto on nuclear waste disposal at Yucca Mountain site in Nevada
- Yes Oppose effort to terminate Kosovo mission
- Yes Include gender, sexual orientation and disability in federal hate crime protections
- No Approve GOP plan to restrict use of genetic information by health insurers
- No Kill amendment delaying implementation of an anti-missile defense system
- No Cut taxes for married couples
- Yes Grant China permanent normal trade status

1999

- No Remove President Clinton from office for obstruction of justice
- No Kill amendment authorizing state grants to hire teachers and reduce class size
- Yes Require criminal background checks for purchases at gun shows
- No Approve GOP proposal to increase rights of patients in managed-care health plans
- No Block effort to allow farm and medicine exports to Cuba
- Yes Allow study of tougher automobile fuel efficiency standards
- Yes Ratify nuclear weapons testing treaty
- Yes Prohibit national political parties from collecting "soft money" donations
- Yes Remove barriers among banking, securities and insurance companies

INTEREST GROUPS

	AFL-CIO	ADA	CCUS	ACU
2000	75%	85%	60%	4%
1999	89%	100%	41%	4%
1998	100%	90%	56%	0%
1997	71%	70%	67%	8%
1996	86%	85%	46%	16%
1995	100%	90%	42%	9%
1994	75%	95%	22%	0%
1993	91%	70%	18%	12%
1992	91%	100%	20%	7%
1991	75%	90%	10%	5%

CQ VOTE STUDIES

	PARTY UNITY		PRESIDENTIAL SUPPORT	
	Support	Oppose	Support	Oppose
2000	96%	4%	97%	3%
1999	94%	6%	89%	11%
1998	93%	7%	94%	6%
1997	88%	12%	86%	14%
1996	93%	7%	93%	7%
1995	88%	12%	88%	12%
1994	90%	10%	97%	3%
1993	94%	6%	95%	5%
1992	89%	11%	28%	72%
1991	92%	8%	36%	64%

Rep. Alan B. Mollohan (D)

Elected 1982; 10th term

CAPITOL OFFICE
225-4172; fax 225-7564; 2346 Rayburn Bldg. 20515

INTERNET
e-mail: www.house.gov/writerep
web: www.house.gov/mollohan

COMMITTEES
Appropriations

HOMETOWN
Fairmont

BORN
May 14, 1943, Fairmont, W.Va.

RELIGION
Baptist

FAMILY
Wife, Barbara Whiting; five children

EDUCATION
College of William and Mary, A.B. 1966; West
Virginia U., J.D. 1970

MILITARY SERVICE
Army Reserve, 1970-83

CAREER
Lawyer

POLITICAL HIGHLIGHTS
No previous office

ELECTION RESULTS

2000 GENERAL

Alan B. Mollohan (D)	170,974	87.8%
Richard Kerr (LIBERT)	23,797	12.2%

2000 PRIMARY

Alan B. Mollohan (D)	unopposed

1998 GENERAL

Alan B. Mollohan (D)	105,101	84.7%
Richard Kerr (LIBERT)	19,013	15.3%

PREVIOUS WINNING PERCENTAGES
1996 (100%); 1994 (70%); 1992 (100%); 1990 (67%);
1988 (75%); 1986 (100%); 1984 (54%); 1982 (53%)

The son of a congressman, Mollohan worked as a Washington, D.C., lawyer before succeeding his father in the House, and he has risen into the top Democratic ranks on the Appropriations Committee. As you would expect of one with a family background in politics and the credentials of a political "insider," Mollohan sees the legislative process as a give-and-take business, one in which people with opposing opinions work quietly to reach compromise.

When Republicans took control of the House in 1995, Mollohan lost out on a coveted chairmanship of an Appropriations subcommittee. In the 106th Congress, he assumed the top Democratic position on Appropriations' Veterans Affairs, Housing and Urban Development, and Independent Agencies Subcommittee, and he remained in that post in the 107th Congress.

The subcommittee, known as VA-HUD, funds a complex group of federal agencies, and veterans groups, low-income housing advocates, the space industry and environmentalists must all compete for the same pool of federal dollars. But membership on the panel provides plenty of opportunities to secure funding for home state projects. NASA may not launch rockets from West Virginia, but it has located small segments of the vast space industry in the state. Mollohan has been a strong backer of space exploration.

In floor debate, Mollohan's manner is always respectful, but he is plainly unhappy with dogmatic lawmakers who, in his view, make all-or-nothing demands and employ obstructionist tactics. He complains that the appropriations process is sometimes held hostage by "budget extremists." But he is able to work closely with his panel's chairman, Republican James T. Walsh of New York, who also looks for bipartisanship and accommodation.

In many ways, Mollohan reflects his blue-collar constituents, with his moderate views on economic policy and his more conservative stance on social issues. An outdoorsman and hunter, he has consistently supported gun owners' rights. In 1996, he voted to repeal a ban on certain semi-automatic assault-style weapons.

Mollohan takes a strong stand against abortion, but his views on that subject do not hamper his ability to work with liberal Democrats in other areas. Indeed, most liberals are in agreement with him on another sensitive issue — capital punishment, which he opposes.

Mollohan has sided with conservatives on some issues of environmental regulation, a stance that grows out of his state's dependence on coal mining, steel-making and other heavy industries. His opposition to what he called "unsound" acid rain legislation that penalized coal-burning plants and factories made him one of only 21 House members in 1990 to vote against reauthorizing the Clean Air Act.

In 1998, Mollohan joined Appropriations panel Republicans in limiting the Clinton administration's authority to "develop, propose or issue rules, regulations, decrees or orders" designed to implement the 1997 Kyoto global climate change treaty, which would require the United States to make substantial reductions in "greenhouse" gas emissions.

With steel mills in his district struggling for profitability, Mollohan has backed foreign "anti-dumping" measures. Low-priced imported steel, he contends, has contributed to the industry's decline in his district and across the nation. Mollohan is also a reliable vote for organized labor.

Over the years, Mollohan and his West Virginia colleague on the Senate

Appropriations Committee, Democrat Robert C. Byrd, have worked diligently to steer money to their home state. Evidence of their efforts is rife in the 1st District, including prisons, clinics, federal office and research centers, and road and water projects. Byrd and Mollohan, two institutionalists, have a common outlook on the role of the federal government.

As a member of the Appropriations panel's Commerce, Justice, State Subcommittee, Mollohan secured almost $9 million in 2000 for the Justice Department to operate the national White Collar Crime Center in his district. The federal "cybercop" center, which was created to lead the nation's fight against Internet fraud will be in his hometown of Fairmont.

Mollohan has longstanding ties to the more formal world of Washington. He was 9 years old when his father, Robert H. Mollohan, was first elected to the House. Robert Mollohan served from 1953 to 1957 and then again from 1969 to 1983.

In the 1982 campaign to succeed his father, some voters questioned whether Mollohan's West Virginia roots ran deep enough. For the previous decade, he had been a Washington lawyer who counted Pittsburgh-based Consolidation Coal Co. as a major client. Rank-and-file miners in the 1st District were leery of a corporate lawyer representing them; many lined up behind Mollohan's pro-labor primary opponent, state Sen. Dan Tonkovich.

But the elder Mollohan had close connections with party officials and business and labor leaders. Their support proved crucial to his son, who narrowly won the primary. In the fall, Mollohan took 53 percent against GOP state Rep. John F. McCuskey.

In 1984, Mollohan bucked a Republican tide and fended off GOP state Rep. Jim Altmeyer with a late media barrage focusing on Altmeyer's spotty attendance record in the state House. He won with 54 percent and has not struggled in any general election since.

Mollohan's only competitive contest for renomination came in a 1992 primary following redistricting. He faced fellow Democratic Rep. Harley O. Staggers Jr. after reapportionment cost the state one of its four House seats. Both men had followed their fathers to Congress, but Staggers portrayed himself as an "outsider," criticizing Mollohan for writing overdrafts at the private bank for House members. Mollohan highlighted the importance to the district of his seat on the Appropriations Committee. Much more of the reshaped 1st was Mollohan's old territory, and he won the primary with better than 60 percent of the vote.

In the past three elections, the GOP has not bothered to field a candidate against Mollohan.

KEY VOTES

2000
Yes Raise hourly minimum wage by $1 over two years
No Halt funding for U.S. mission in Kosovo unless European nations pay more
Yes Provide Medicare benefits to military retirees and their dependents
No Grant China permanent normal trade status
Yes Phase out estate, gift and trust taxes
No Prohibit implementation of president's national monument designations
No Approve GOP plan to provide prescription drug coverage for Medicare beneficiaries
Yes Increase help for poor nations indebted to international financial institutions

1999
Yes Impose steel import quotas
Yes Kill proposal to take aviation trust funds off budget
No Require background checks on buyers only at gun shows with 10 or more vendors
Yes Remove barriers among banking, securities and insurance companies
Yes Authorize state grants to hire teachers and reduce class size
No Overhaul campaign finance law; ban "soft money" and restrict advocacy advertising
Yes Approve bipartisan plan to increase rights of patients in managed-care health plans

INTEREST GROUPS

	AFL-CIO	ADA	CCUS	ACU
2000	90%	60%	52%	28%
1999	88%	60%	36%	31%
1998	100%	70%	27%	32%
1997	100%	70%	30%	33%

CQ VOTE STUDIES

	PARTY UNITY		PRESIDENTIAL SUPPORT	
	Support	Oppose	Support	Oppose
2000	70%	30%	69%	31%
1999	64%	36%	58%	42%
1998	74%	26%	69%	31%
1997	71%	29%	62%	38%

WEST VIRGINIA 1
North – Wheeling; Parkersburg; Morgantown

Located in the northernmost part of the state, the Democratic-leaning 1st is a predominantly rural region but the most urban of West Virginia's three districts. It contains six of the state's 10 largest cities and its largest university. Wheeling, an industrial town and commercial center in the north, and Parkersburg, a regional trade center in the west, are two of the main urban areas.

The district was hit hard by economic depression in the 1980s, losing population as factories shut down and coal mines mechanized. Unemployment remained high in the 1990s – topping 10 percent in some counties – and 11 of 19 counties lost population. But a budding technology sector has brightened economic prospects. FBI and NASA facilities have opened in the district, and Morgantown, home to West Virginia University, is attracting high-tech firms. Located amid the coal fields of Monongalia County (one of the state's leading coal-producing counties), Morgantown also is home to Software Valley, an

organization that promotes regional computer-oriented business and research activity.

Although the 1st has long elected Democrats to Congress and has more registered Democrats than Republicans, Parkersburg and Wheeling have some Republican-leaning state House districts.

MAJOR INDUSTRIES
Metals, high-tech, chemical

CITIES
Wheeling, 32,526; Parkersburg, 32,212; Morgantown, 29,017; Weirton, 21,080; Fairmont, 20,029

UNUSUAL FEATURES
Prabhupada's Palace of Gold, built by the International Society for Krishna Consciousness, in Moundsville; Don Knotts of "The Andy Griffith Show" born in Morgantown in 1924.

Rep. Shelley Moore Capito (R)

Elected 2000; 1st term

Friends and family were convinced that Capito, an affable and energetic mother of three, had what it took to win the 2nd District contest in 2000. In so doing, Capito (CAP-ih-toe) broke a long Republican congressional losing streak in the state, narrowly winning the seat left open when nine-term Democratic Rep. Bob Wise embarked on his successful bid for governor.

Capito is the first West Virginia Republican to win a House seat since 1980. And she is only the second woman to represent the Mountaineer State in Congress. In the 107th Congress, she was selected vice chairwoman of the bipartisan Congressional Caucus for Women's Issues.

Capito supports abortion rights and gun owners' rights, as did her Democratic predecessor. Her priorities are economic growth, job creation and affordable prescription drugs. And she firmly backs President Bush's tax cut plan. The freshman won a hoped-for seat on the Transportation and Infrastructure panel; she also serves on Financial Services.

Capito has strong political bloodlines in West Virginia as the daughter of Republican Arch A. Moore Jr., who served the state for 12 years in the House and another 12 as governor, in a political career that spanned more than three decades. (Moore's career ended in scandal when he pled guilty to a five-count federal indictment that included taking illegal campaign contributions for his gubernatorial campaign.)

Though raised in a political home, Capito did not seek elective office until she was 42. But the former college official was a familiar presence in Charleston, as a community volunteer and a spectator at her children's sporting events. After four years in the state House, Capito emerged in 2000 as a highly touted Republican recruit in the race for the 2nd District seat. Unopposed for the GOP nod, Capito faced Democrat Jim Humphreys, a wealthy lawyer and former state senator who spent more than $6 million of his own money on the race. Capito edged Humphreys by 2 1/2 percentage points with help from a blizzard of ads by the National Republican Congressional Committee criticizing Humphreys' legislative record and his alleged failure to pay his taxes on time.

CAPITOL OFFICE
225-2711; fax 225-7856
1431 Longworth Bldg. 20515

INTERNET
e-mail: www.house.gov/writerep
web: www.house.gov/capito

COMMITTEES
Financial Services
Small Business
Transportation & Infrastructure

HOMETOWN
Charleston

BORN
Nov. 26, 1953, Glen Dale, W.Va.

RELIGION
Presbyterian

FAMILY
Husband, Charles L. Capito Jr.; three children

EDUCATION
Duke U., B.S. 1975; U. of Virginia, M.Ed. 1976

CAREER
University system information center director; college career counselor

POLITICAL HIGHLIGHTS
W.Va. House, 1997-2001

ELECTION RESULTS

2000 GENERAL
Shelley Moore Capito (R)	108,769	48.5%
Jim Humphreys (D)	103,003	45.9%
John Brown (LIBERT)	12,543	5.6%

2000 PRIMARY
Shelley Moore Capito (R) unopposed

WEST VIRGINIA 2
Center – Charleston; Eastern Panhandle

An economically diverse district, the 2nd stretches across the mountainous state from the Ohio border and ends in the Eastern Panhandle at Harper's Ferry. The 2nd is home to poor coal mining areas and isolated towns, as well as the more prosperous capital city and a commuting class in the Eastern Panhandle.

Charleston, the district's dominant city, is a center for chemical plants, state employees and retail shopping. Surrounding Charleston is Kanawha, the state's largest county, which retains its industrial character and leans Democratic despite being socially conservative. The chemical plants that provide jobs in "Chemical Valley" along the Kanawha River have raised environmental concerns. The mainly Democratic mountain regions

north and east of Kanawha remain heavily dependent on coal.

Economic depression during the 1980s drove residents from the 2nd. But during the 1990s, eastern counties within commuting distance of Washington, D.C., grew rapidly. On the other end of the district, in Putnam County, a Toyota plant is expanding to support more than 900 jobs.

The 2nd was loyal to Democrats in congressional elections for 18 years before electing a Republican in 2000. Pockets of Republicans dot the district, particularly in the Panhandle, where they register in strong numbers.

MAJOR INDUSTRY
Chemicals, lumber, manufacturing

CITIES
Charleston, 54,598; Martinsburg, 15,754; South Charleston, 14,203

UNUSUAL FEATURES
Abolitionist John Brown hanged after attempting to incite a slave revolt in Harper's Ferry in 1859.

Rep. Nick J. Rahall II (D)

Elected 1976; 13th term

CAPITOL OFFICE
225-3452; fax 225-9061; 2307 Rayburn Bldg. 20515

INTERNET
e-mail: nrahall@mail.house.gov
web: www.house.gov/rahall

COMMITTEES
Resources - ranking member
Transportation & Infrastructure

HOMETOWN
Beckley

BORN
May 20, 1949, Beckley, W.Va.

RELIGION
Presbyterian

FAMILY
Divorced; three children

EDUCATION
Duke U., A.B. 1971; George Washington U.,
attended 1972

CAREER
Broadcasting executive; travel agent

POLITICAL HIGHLIGHTS
No previous office

ELECTION RESULTS

2000 GENERAL

Nick J. Rahall II (D)	146,807	91.3%
Jeff Robinson (LIBERT)	13,979	8.7%

2000 PRIMARY

Nick J. Rahall II (D)	unopposed

1998 GENERAL

Nick J. Rahall II (D)	78,814	86.6%
Joe Whelan (LIBERT)	12,196	13.4%

PREVIOUS WINNING PERCENTAGES
1996 (100%); 1994 (64%); 1992 (66%); 1990 (52%);
1988 (61%); 1986 (71%); 1984 (67%); 1982 (81%);
1980 (77%); 1978 (100%); 1976 (46%)

Rahall got an early start in Congress and even now, in his 13th term, is still slightly younger than the average member of the House — a combination that gives him a good shot at a committee chairmanship some day, if the Democratic Party regains its majority status in the House.

He is among the top 5 percent in House seniority, holds the ranking Democrat position on the Resources panel, and has climbed to the No. 2 Democratic spot on the Transportation Committee.

Rahall (RAY-haul) has not made as big a name for himself inside the party as some of his peers in the Class of 1976 — a group that includes Minority Leader Richard A. Gephardt and Minority Whip David E. Bonior. This is partly because his star was tarnished some years back by negative publicity about his personal behavior, and partly because the liberal majority in the House Democratic Caucus takes issue with his opposition to abortion and his support for gun owners' rights. But organized labor values Rahall, and most of the time, Democratic leadership can count on his support.

And, although he is not among the party's leaders on Capitol Hill, he has carved out a niche for himself as one of the "Big Four" on the Transportation panel, where he can direct federal infrastructure dollars to his home state in the fashion of his long-ago boss, veteran Democratic Sen. Robert C. Byrd.

Rahall's main work has been to develop considerable expertise in subjects under his committees' purview. In his early years, his agenda was almost solely aimed at promoting and protecting the West Virginia coal industry. When Democrats ran the House, he chaired, at different times, subcommittees on both Resources and Transportation.

Of Lebanese heritage, Rahall has been a frequent critic of Israel and an advocate of closer ties to Arab states.

In the Republican-majority 105th Congress, he was one of the key players in the Transportation Committee as it worked on a mammoth bill to reauthorize federal highway programs. As one of the "Big Four" — along with full committee Chairman Bud Shuster of Pennsylvania, Surface Transportation Subcommittee Chairman Tom Petri of Wisconsin, and the full committee's ranking Democrat, James L. Oberstar of Minnesota — he was involved in the key House decisions on the bill, which passed in 1998 and included plenty of goodies for West Virginia. During the debate on that bill, which got caught up in the congressional effort to balance the federal budget, Rahall defended Shuster from attacks by fiscally conservative Republicans, calling them "right-wing wacko kids."

In the 106th Congress, with the highway bill behind them for another six years, the panel dropped from the spotlight, but Rahall still found much to do, on issues such as truck safety, passenger air service to small communities, and complaints about poor Amtrak and rail freight service in the aftermath of large rail mergers. He strongly opposed a GOP plan to repeal 4.3 cents of the federal gasoline tax in the wake of rapidly increasing prices at the pump, calling it "a simply stupid idea."

On the Resources panel, Rahall continues to wage his longstanding battle to overhaul an 1872 mining law. His plan would require hard-rock miners to pay royalties for their extractions from public lands, a policy that would make West Virginia mining operations, on mostly private lands, more competitive with mines on public lands in the West. He has been unsuccessful in his overhaul bids but has played a role in imposing a year-by-year moratorium on the issuance of any new low-cost mining claims on federal lands.

Rahall's voting record is in line with the attitudes of his coal-mining, blue-collar, low-income district, which is culturally conservative while at the same time welcoming of federal help in local economic development and social services, particularly with the demise of coal.

His record on environmental regulation is mixed. He has obtained funds to clean up abandoned coal mines. In 1999, he authored an amendment to uphold an Interior Department ruling that limited the size of mining waste disposal sites on federal lands to five acres. Western lawmakers objected because many mining operations require large tracts. Just a few months later, the Westerners accused Rahall of hypocrisy when he led an effort by the West Virginia delegation to overturn a court decision that disposal of waste from mountaintop coal mining operations in West Virginia violated the Clean Water Act.

Rahall comes from an affluent West Virginia family that owns broadcasting properties. He had his first job on Capitol Hill when he was 20, working the summer delivering mail. He earned his undergraduate degree at Duke University, then became an aide to Sen. Byrd before returning to West Virginia to work in the family businesses.

His break into politics came in 1976, when Democratic Rep. Ken Hechler decided to run for governor. Rahall, then 27, was far from the best-known contender in the Democratic House field, but he had family money and he spent it on a media campaign none of his foes could match, winning the nomination with 37 percent of the vote. After the primary, Hechler, who did not get the gubernatorial nomination, mounted a write-in drive to keep his House seat. Rahall never could have beaten Hechler in a primary, but the general-election write-in effort was too difficult even for a popular incumbent and Rahall won with a 46 percent tally.

His only re-election difficulties have come when he was periodically caught up in criticism about his personal behavior. He racked up thousands of dollars in gambling debts in the mid-1980s, got divorced, took many trips financed by taxpayers or lobbyists (often with female companions) and pleaded guilty to alcohol-related reckless driving charges. The criticism has been more muted in recent years — news reports of his congressional travel in 1999 noted that he had cut back significantly — although the Charleston Gazette noted disapprovingly that Rahall had reported he owed at least $70,000 in credit card debt.

Nevertheless, in the overwhelmingly Democratic 3rd District, Rahall has not faced a Republican opponent since 1994.

KEY VOTES

2000
Yes Raise hourly minimum wage by $1 over two years
No Halt funding for U.S. mission in Kosovo unless European nations pay more
Yes Provide Medicare benefits to military retirees and their dependents
No Grant China permanent normal trade status
Yes Phase out estate, gift and trust taxes
No Prohibit implementation of president's national monument designations
No Approve GOP plan to provide prescription drug coverage for Medicare beneficiaries
Yes Increase help for poor nations indebted to international financial institutions

1999
Yes Impose steel import quotas
No Kill proposal to take aviation trust funds off budget
Yes Require background checks on buyers only at gun shows with 10 or more vendors
Yes Remove barriers among banking, securities and insurance companies
Yes Authorize state grants to hire teachers and reduce class size
No Overhaul campaign finance law; ban "soft money" and restrict advocacy advertising
Yes Approve bipartisan plan to increase rights of patients in managed-care health plans

INTEREST GROUPS

	AFL-CIO	ADA	CCUS	ACU
2000	90%	70%	42%	28%
1999	100%	65%	24%	20%
1998	100%	85%	28%	24%
1997	100%	80%	20%	21%

CQ VOTE STUDIES

	PARTY UNITY		PRESIDENTIAL SUPPORT	
	Support	Oppose	Support	Oppose
2000	79%	21%	71%	29%
1999	75%	25%	69%	31%
1998	78%	22%	77%	23%
1997	72%	28%	61%	39%

WEST VIRGINIA 3

South — Huntington; Beckley

The 3rd is a predominately rural region taking in the state's southern counties. Known as the "coal district," the 3rd is home to six of the state's 10 leading coal-producing counties, including the top two: Boone and Mingo.

In the 1980s, technological advances in coal mining sharply reduced the need for manpower, and the 3rd has struggled to create new jobs. The decline, which also took a toll on the 3rd's population, added misery to a region that has always had pockets of Appalachian poverty. The situation improved in the 1990s as some counties grew slightly, although other counties continued to see residents leave, and unemployment rates remained high. The 3rd does, however, contribute to the state's tourism industry with its ski resorts, white water rafting areas and The Greenbrier, a five-star hotel in White Sulphur Springs.

Huntington, the district's largest city, is cushioned by its location on the Ohio River and a diversified economy that includes tobacco growers

as well as oil and steel companies.

While Huntington's white-collar sector and tobacco growers help make Cabell County the most Republican part of the 3rd, Democrats historically have held a lock on both local and federal offices and continue to register in large numbers.

MAJOR INDUSTRY
Coal, wood products, tourism

CITIES
Huntington, 52,273; Beckley, 19,228; Bluefield, 12,361

UNUSUAL FEATURES
Now-closed nuclear bomb shelter for Congress under The Greenbrier resort; Sunshine Farm and Gardens, one of the nation's most extensive plant collections; Mingo County, site of the "West Virginia Mine Wars" of the 1920s depicted in the movie "Matewan;" "Bloody Mingo" also the site of part of the feuding between the Hatfields and McCoys.

Gov. Scott McCallum (R)

First elected: Assumed office Feb. 1, 2001, following the resignation of Gov. Tommy G. Thompson, R, who left to become secretary of Health and Human Services

Length of term: 4 years

Term expires: 1/03

Salary: $122,407

Phone: (608) 266-1212

Hometown: Madison

Born: May 2, 1950; Fond du Lac, Wis.

Religion: Christian Scientist

Family: Wife Laurie McCallum; three children

Education: Macalester College, B.A. 1972; Johns Hopkins U., M.A. 1974

Career: Property development and management firm owner; local YMCA program director; congressional aide

Political highlights: Wis. Senate, 1977-87; Republican nominee for U.S. Senate, 1982; lieutenant governor, 1987-2001

(State Sen. Margaret A. Farrow, R, was nominted to be lieutenant governor on Feb. 28, 2001, by Gov. Scott McCallum, R. As of April 20, 2001, her nomination was awaiting state Senate approval.)

STATE LEGISLATURE

General Assembly: Meets for five floor periods of varying length over two-year session

State Assembly: 99 members, 2-year terms

2001 breakdown: 56R, 43D; 77 men, 22 women

Salary: $44,233

Phone: (608) 266-1501

Senate: 33 members, 4-year terms

2001 breakdown: 15R, 18D; 22 men, 11 women

Salary: $44,233

Phone: (608) 266-2517

STATE TERM LIMITS

Governor: No

Senate: No

House: No

URBAN STATISTICS

CITY	POPULATION
Milwaukee	572,424
Madison	210,674
Green Bay	98,362
Kenosha	89,447
Racine	80,902

REGISTERED VOTERS

Voters do not register by party.

POPULATION

2000 population	5,363,675
1990 population	4,891,769
Percent change	9.6%
Rank among states	18
Median age	35.3
Born in state	76%
Foreign born	2%
Urban/rural	66%/34%
Crime rate	271/100,000
Poverty level	8.8%
Federal workers	29,494
Military	19,338

REAPPORTIONMENT

Wisconsin lost one House seat in reapportionment, dropping from nine districts to eight. The state legislature will draw new district lines.

MISCELLANEOUS

Web: www.wisconsin.gov

Capital: Madison

Land area: 54,314 sq. miles
Rank among states: 25

STATE ELECTION OFFICIAL
(608) 266-8005

DEMOCRATIC HEADQUARTERS
(608) 255-5172

REPUBLICAN HEADQUARTERS
(608) 257-4765

District Statistics

DIST.	2000 D	2000 R	GREEN	1996 D	1996 R	REF	1992 D	1992 R	I	WHT	BLK	ASIAN	HISP	HOUSEHOLD INCOME	OVER 65+	UNDER 18	COLLEGE EDUCATION
1	49%	47%	3%	50%	38%	11%	41%	36%	23%	92%	5%	1%	3%	$31,431	12%	27%	15%
2	58	36	5	55	33	8	50	32	18	96	2	2	1	$30,625	11	24	27
3	49	46	5	50	34	14	43	33	24	98	0	1	0	$25,758	14	27	16
4	46	50	3	49	40	9	41	38	21	94	1	1	6	$32,260	13	25	17
5	65	31	3	63	29	5	57	31	13	61	35	2	2	$26,267	13	27	24
6	43	53	3	45	41	12	35	41	25	98	0	1	1	$28,038	15	26	13
7	48	46	4	49	35	14	42	34	24	97	0	1	0	$25,277	15	27	13
8	44	52	3	46	42	11	36	40	24	96	0	1	1	$28,169	14	27	15
9	34	63	3	37	52	9	30	48	22	98	0	1	1	$37,579	12	27	21
STATE	47.8	47.6	4	49	39	10	41	37	22	92	5	1	2	$29,442	12	26	18

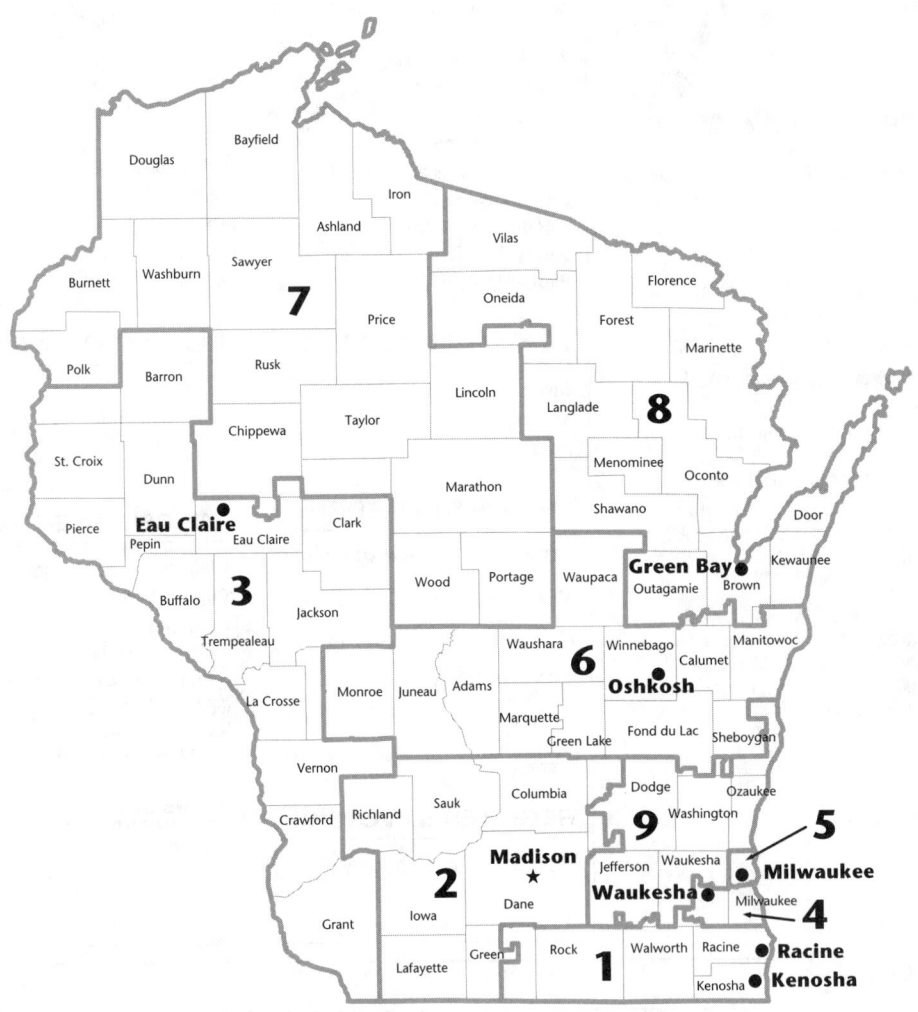

Sen. Herb Kohl (D)

CAPITOL OFFICE
224-5653; fax 224-9787; 330 Hart Bldg. 20510

INTERNET
e-mail: senator_kohl@kohl.senate.gov
web: kohl.senate.gov

COMMITTEES
Appropriations
Judiciary
Special Aging

HOMETOWN
Milwaukee

BORN
Feb. 7, 1935, Milwaukee, Wis.

RELIGION
Jewish

FAMILY
Single

EDUCATION
U. of Wisconsin, B.A. 1956; Harvard U., M.B.A. 1958

MILITARY SERVICE
Army Reserve, 1958-64

CAREER
Professional basketball team owner; department and grocery store owner

POLITICAL HIGHLIGHTS
Wis. Democratic Party chairman, 1975-77

ELECTION RESULTS

2000 GENERAL
Herb Kohl (D)	1,563,238	61.5%
John Gillespie (R)	940,744	37.0%

2000 PRIMARY
Herb Kohl (D)	184,920	89.8%
Jim Sigl (D)	20,858	10.1%

PREVIOUS WINNING PERCENTAGES
1994 (58%); 1988 (52%)

Elected 1988; 3rd term

One of the wealthiest members of Congress, Kohl funds his own campaigns and spends his own money lavishly on popular projects in his state. He donated $25 million to his alma mater, the University of Wisconsin, to build the Kohl Center sports arena in Madison, which opened in 1998. In 1985, he won plaudits for buying the Milwaukee Bucks to prevent the basketball team's relocation out of state.

A quiet and unobtrusive man, Kohl, who often travels the halls of Congress casually chewing gum, is persistent on issues of importance to him, particularly fiscal matters. Although he is profligate with his own money, he is frugal with Uncle Sam's. He has won high marks from such budget watchdog groups as the Concord Coalition and Taxpayers for Common Sense. He voted against the giant catchall spending bill that passed at the end of the 105th Congress, and another enacted in 1999.

In 1997, 1998 and 1999, Kohl and his Wisconsin colleague, Russell D. Feingold, were among only a handful of Democrats to vote against supplemental spending bills that ostensibly provided money for emergency needs. Kohl argued that some of the spending was not for true emergencies and so should have been offset by cuts elsewhere.

Kohl, who affiliates with the moderate Senate New Democrats, has been a solid vote for a constitutional amendment to require a balanced federal budget, and he supported the short-lived presidential line-item veto law. Even after the government began running surpluses, he continued to press for fiscal restraint, warning against actions that could plunge the government's books back into the red. He cautioned in 1998 that, "Our economy is strong right now, but we can't afford to be shortsighted." In 1998, Kohl helped make sure that Congress did not get a cost of living increase, birddogging legislation that would prevent the pay hike.

On the Appropriations Committee, Kohl has a long history of opposing spending. In the 103rd Congress, for example, Kohl was out front in challenging the Clinton administration's economic stimulus package, arguing that about $11 billion of new spending needed to be balanced by cuts in other areas.

Kohl hews closer to traditional Democratic positions on social issues and generally follows the party line on the environment, student loans, drug prevention programs and gun control. He supports abortion rights and voted against banning a procedure its opponents call "partial birth" abortion.

Kohl has fought to defend Wisconsin's dairy industry and to overturn what he considers unfair milk-pricing policies, but his efforts have been overwhelmed by resistance from other regions. Kohl and Feingold briefly delayed adjournment in November 1999 by threatening to filibuster the year-end catchall spending bill, saying it contained provisions harmful to Midwestern dairy farmers. They gave up only after losing a test vote and settling for a promise that the issue would be revisited in the future.

Kohl's emphasis on fiscal discipline has at times taken a back seat to home state interests. In 2000, as the ranking Democrat on the Agriculture Appropriations Committee, he added $473 million in emergency aid for dairy farmers to the agriculture spending bill, of which about $100 million was targeted at small-scale Wisconsin dairy farms. Kohl helped secure another $50 million to assist cranberry growers — a large contingent of whom reside in Wisconsin.

Drawing on his experiences in business, Kohl has been willing to offer advice on commerce issues, especially when the Judiciary Committee's Antitrust, Business Rights and Competition Subcommittee looked at some major mergers. In 1998, Kohl, as ranking Democrat on the subcommittee, joined with its chairman, Ohio Republican Mike DeWine, to ask the Justice Department and the Federal Communications Commission not to approve mergers between telecommunications companies without setting conditions aimed at ensuring that consumers see more benefits.

Kohl also has tangled with trial lawyers. In 1999, he introduced legislation with Republican Charles E. Grassley of Iowa to penalize "frivolous filings" by basing lawyers' fees on a percentage of the damages actually paid to members of the plaintiffs' "class" in class action suits.

Because of his popularity in the state and his proven ability to run an effective self-financed campaign, Kohl is sometimes mentioned as a possible future candidate for governor. But he has brushed aside such suggestions, insisting he is happy as a senator.

Kohl's fortune was derived mostly from a family chain of grocery and department stores. Still, he has long been known for a low-key lifestyle. When in Wisconsin, he is often sighted eating breakfast at inexpensive diners near his home in Milwaukee.

He spent much of his pre-congressional adult life running his family's business and involving himself in politics as a behind-the-scenes financier and briefly as state Democratic Party chairman in the mid-1970s.

Reporter Kenneth Lamke of the Milwaukee Journal Sentinel said Kohl's political approach has been consistently low-key for decades. In the middle 1970s, Lamke recalls, he was covering the annual state Democratic Party Convention, and Kohl was the state party chairman. Still, Kohl asked if he could catch a ride when the reporter had to leave the gathering early to drive back to Milwaukee. "He didn't want to hang around and do all that small talk. He wasn't comfortable with it," said Lamke, amazed decades later that the state chairman would duck out of his own convention early.

Although the family sold the Kohl department stores in 1979, the chain kept the name. When he began his Senate race in 1988, he already had high name recognition. Not that it mattered much, as he spent nearly $7.5 million (most of it his own money) in the campaign — enough to buy plenty of name recognition.

Kohl used his status as one of the state's richest men to stress his independence, based on his ability to self-finance his campaigns. In the primary, facing former Gov. Anthony S. Earl and 1986 Senate nominee Ed Garvey, Kohl deflected their jabs with a simple message: "Nobody's senator but yours." He won an easy plurality.

In the general election, Kohl faced Susan Engeleiter, the moderate Republican leader of the state Senate. His saturation television advertising emphasized his private sector success and commitment to service. It was a campaign on a scale unlike any the state had seen. Kohl's total outlay was double the previous state record.

Engeleiter tried to compete with the continuing deluge of Kohl ads on TV by portraying herself as more in tune with ordinary people's problems. She downplayed ideology by labeling herself "A Wisconsin Original." In the campaign's closing weeks, polls found Engeleiter gaining on Kohl. But time ran out before she could find an issue or other means of closing the gap. Kohl won by 4 percentage points.

In 1994, Kohl's GOP challenger was state Rep. Robert T. Welch. Kohl moved quickly to cast himself as a centrist in contrast to his staunchly conservative opponent and won with 58 percent of the vote. In 2000, he took 62 percent against Republican John Gillespie, the head of Rawhide Boys Ranch, a nonprofit facility to which Wisconsin courts assign juvenile delinquents.

KEY VOTES

2000

Yes Overhaul bankruptcy law and increase minimum wage
No Limit fiscal 2001 discretionary spending to $600.3 billion
Yes Override veto on nuclear waste disposal at Yucca Mountain site in Nevada
No Oppose effort to terminate Kosovo mission
Yes Include gender, sexual orientation and disability in federal hate crime protections
No Approve GOP plan to restrict use of genetic information by health insurers
No Kill amendment delaying implementation of an anti-missile defense system
Yes Cut taxes for married couples
Yes Grant China permanent normal trade status

1999

No Remove President Clinton from office for obstruction of justice
No Kill amendment authorizing state grants to hire teachers and reduce class size
Yes Require criminal background checks for purchases at gun shows
No Approve GOP proposal to increase rights of patients in managed-care health plans
Yes Block effort to allow farm and medicine exports to Cuba
No Allow study of tougher automobile fuel efficiency standards
Yes Ratify nuclear weapons testing treaty
Yes Prohibit national political parties from collecting "soft money" donations
Yes Remove barriers among banking, securities and insurance companies

INTEREST GROUPS

	AFL-CIO	ADA	CCUS	ACU
2000	63%	85%	60%	20%
1999	78%	100%	41%	4%
1998	88%	85%	44%	4%
1997	29%	70%	80%	20%
1996	86%	75%	69%	20%
1995	92%	95%	47%	17%
1994	63%	90%	50%	12%
1993	73%	95%	45%	24%
1992	83%	95%	30%	11%
1991	58%	90%	20%	24%

CQ VOTE STUDIES

	PARTY UNITY		PRESIDENTIAL SUPPORT	
	Support	Oppose	Support	Oppose
2000	87%	13%	79%	21%
1999	90%	10%	91%	9%
1998	87%	13%	86%	14%
1997	74%	26%	90%	10%
1996	84%	16%	88%	12%
1995	84%	16%	84%	16%
1994	75%	25%	81%	19%
1993	84%	16%	81%	19%
1992	79%	21%	30%	70%
1991	83%	17%	41%	59%

Sen. Russell D. Feingold (D)

Elected 1992; 2nd term

CAPITOL OFFICE
224-5323; fax 224-2725; 506 Hart Bldg. 20510

INTERNET
e-mail: senator@feingold.senate.gov
web: feingold.senate.gov

COMMITTEES
Budget
Foreign Relations
Judiciary
Special Aging

HOMETOWN
Middleton

BORN
March 2, 1953, Janesville, Wis.

RELIGION
Jewish

FAMILY
Wife, Mary Feingold; two children, two stepchildren

EDUCATION
U. of Wisconsin, B.A. 1975; Oxford U., B.A. 1977; Harvard U., J.D. 1979

CAREER
Lawyer

POLITICAL HIGHLIGHTS
Wis. Senate, 1983-93

ELECTION RESULTS

1998 GENERAL

Russell D. Feingold (D)	890,059	50.5%
Mark W. Neumann (R)	852,272	48.4%

1998 PRIMARY

Russell D. Feingold (D)	unopposed

PREVIOUS WINNING PERCENTAGES
1992 (53%)

In the final hours before Congress adjourned in 1999, Feingold and a handful of other angry Midwesterners refused to let their colleagues go home. All that was standing between the Senate and the Thanksgiving dinner table was a vote to clear the session-ending appropriations deal. But first, Feingold wanted to harangue senators about dairy policy. He stalked the Senate floor with books of cheese recipes, among other potential filibuster reading materials, threatening to slow the consideration of the spending package for days to protest provisions he saw as harmful to his region's dairy farmers. He gave up only after overwhelmingly losing a test vote and settling for a promise that the issue would be revisited in the future.

It was not an unusual situation for Feingold (FINE-gold), who has a reputation for bucking the establishment. While his maverick style has served him well at times, it also has hurt him in other situations, and it nearly cost him his seat in 1998.

Feingold is among the more socially liberal members of the Senate. He favors abolishing the death penalty, he supports abortion rights, and he backs labor interests. But unlike many of his liberal colleagues, Feingold has had a long-running passion for balancing the budget. A member of the Budget Committee, Feingold was harping about reducing the national debt long before the idea was made easy by the booming economy and mushrooming tax collections.

Feingold supported the ill-fated line-item veto, and in 1998 he voted to sustain President Clinton's veto of a list of military construction projects even though a $4.2 million training facility in Milwaukee was on the list. Clinton's vetoes were overturned by Congress, and the line-item veto was later struck down by the Supreme Court.

Still, the senator is not a hard-core fiscal conservative. Before the budget was balanced, Feingold's deficit reduction efforts often took the form of support for tax increases rather than for scaling back social programs. He voted in 1993 for the Clinton deficit-reduction bill, which raised taxes, and he opposed the 1997 balanced-budget agreement, which called for tax relief and discretionary spending cuts.

Feingold is best known for his crusade, in partnership with Arizona Republican John McCain, to overhaul the nation's campaign finance system. In the 107th Congress, Feingold and McCain renewed their longtime effort and, for the first time, got a bill through the Senate. The two lawmakers insist that Congress must change the way political campaigns are funded. Their legislation would ban unregulated "soft money," which goes to political parties rather than candidates, and it would place restrictions on so-called issue advocacy advertising, the ads designed to influence the outcome of an election without specifically endorsing a candidate.

A dependable friend of labor, Feingold has frequently opposed business-backed measures. He was against Republican-sought revisions to the bankruptcy code that would make it harder for people declaring bankruptcy to walk away from their debts. The legislation was pushed by credit card companies and other creditors concerned about the increased rate of bankruptcy filings, but Feingold believed the GOP was pushing for changes that would be too hard on debtors.

He voted against a bill, opposed by organized labor, that would have permitted entry into the United States of additional highly skilled workers to fill high-tech jobs, and against another measure that would have authorized companies to offer their employees compensatory time off instead of pay for overtime work. He also objected to limiting punitive damages in product liability lawsuits.

Feingold opposed a bill that would have given the president fast-track authority to negotiate trade agreements that Congress could accept or reject, but not amend. A 1999 study by the libertarian Cato Institute of how members voted on trade issues categorized him as an "isolationist."

Feingold ranked among those Senate Democrats most likely to oppose Clinton's policy positions. As a member of the Foreign Relations Committee, Feingold is concerned with human rights abuses overseas, and he criticized the Clinton administration for not taking a harder line with China over its human rights policies.

Feingold's most famous break with Clinton and his party was in January 1999, when he was the only Democratic senator to vote against a proposal to dismiss the impeachment charges against Clinton before the trial began. His decision provoked an avalanche of media attention, but Feingold largely shunned the notoriety, which perhaps helped soothe the anger of some of his Democratic colleagues. In the end, he joined every other Democratic senator in voting to acquit Clinton of perjury and obstruction of justice, concluding that the charges were insufficient to warrant the president's removal.

Feingold is attentive and energetic when it comes to home state concerns, and he appears to have a genuine affection for campaigning and constituent service. He has kept a pledge he made in his first Senate campaign in 1992 to visit all 72 counties in the state every year he is in office. He has vowed to spend most of his time in Wisconsin and send his children to school there. In Washington, he keeps an eye out for home state interests, especially the concerns of dairy farmers. To help U.S. ranchers, he supports a labeling law that would identify the country of origin of meat products.

Feingold has been unconventional on the campaign trail, a trait that has both fueled and endangered his runs for office. In 1992, he was a little-known state senator woefully short on campaign funds who scored a stunning long-shot primary victory and then knocked off a GOP incumbent. He steered clear of the mud-slinging going on between the other Democratic candidates and ran a series of humorous, offbeat television ads that gained him national attention. One of his more memorable sight gags was to use the back of his left hand as the map in his TV spots to illustrate his travels across Wisconsin; he boasted, of course, that he knew his home state like the back of his hand.

But six years later, Feingold's buck-the-system style nearly cost him his seat. He was thought to be the clear front-runner in his effort against Republican Rep. Mark W. Neumann, but Feingold refused to accept outside money to help fund his campaign. He wrote stern letters to groups such as the AFL-CIO and the Sierra Club demanding that they pull any "issue ads" aimed at helping him win.

Feingold even took umbrage when national Democrats tried to run an independent-expenditure ad directly calling for Feingold's election — and funded by regulated "hard" money, rather than unregulated soft money — and he demanded that the ad be taken off the airwaves. Heavily outspent by Neumann and a Republican-backed soft money campaign, Feingold barely held on, winning by about 2 percentage points.

Feingold's stubborn adherence to principle irritated some in his own party who feared losing the seat to a Republican, but he also won grudging admiration from some of his colleagues for his willingness to put his political career on the line for his beliefs.

KEY VOTES

2000

No Overhaul bankruptcy law and increase minimum wage
No Limit fiscal 2001 discretionary spending to $600.3 billion
No Override veto on nuclear waste disposal at Yucca Mountain site in Nevada
No Oppose effort to terminate Kosovo mission
Yes Include gender, sexual orientation and disability in federal hate crime protections
No Approve GOP plan to restrict use of genetic information by health insurers
No Kill amendment delaying implementation of an anti-missile defense system
No Cut taxes for married couples
No Grant China permanent normal trade status

1999

No Remove President Clinton from office for obstruction of justice
No Kill amendment authorizing state grants to hire teachers and reduce class size
Yes Require criminal background checks for purchases at gun shows
No Approve GOP proposal to increase rights of patients in managed-care health plans
No Block effort to allow farm and medicine exports to Cuba
Yes Allow study of tougher automobile fuel efficiency standards
Yes Ratify nuclear weapons testing treaty
Yes Prohibit national political parties from collecting "soft money" donations
No Remove barriers among banking, securities and insurance companies

INTEREST GROUPS

	AFL-CIO	ADA	CCUS	ACU
2000	88%	100%	20%	8%
1999	100%	100%	24%	8%
1998	100%	90%	28%	12%
1997	86%	95%	20%	8%
1996	86%	95%	31%	10%
1995	100%	100%	42%	13%
1994	100%	100%	10%	4%
1993	91%	100%	0%	12%

CQ VOTE STUDIES

	PARTY UNITY		PRESIDENTIAL SUPPORT	
	Support	Oppose	Support	Oppose
2000	92%	8%	90%	10%
1999	88%	12%	82%	18%
1998	86%	14%	83%	17%
1997	86%	14%	86%	14%
1996	87%	13%	86%	14%
1995	90%	10%	79%	21%
1994	84%	16%	65%	35%
1993	94%	6%	85%	15%

Rep. Paul D. Ryan (R)

CAPITOL OFFICE
225-3031; fax 225-3393
1217 Longworth Bldg. 20515

INTERNET
e-mail: www.house.gov/writerep
web: www.house.gov/ryan

COMMITTEES
Ways & Means
Joint Economic

HOMETOWN
Janesville

BORN
Jan. 29, 1970, Janesville, Wis.

RELIGION
Roman Catholic

FAMILY
Wife, Janna Little

EDUCATION
Miami U. (Ohio), B.A. 1992

CAREER
Congressional aide; economic policy analyst

POLITICAL HIGHLIGHTS
No previous office

ELECTION RESULTS

2000 GENERAL

Paul D. Ryan (R)	177,612	66.6%
Jeffrey C. Thomas (D)	88,885	33.3%

2000 PRIMARY

Paul D. Ryan (R)	unopposed

1998 GENERAL

Paul D. Ryan (R)	108,475	57.1%
Lydia Spottswood (D)	81,164	42.7%

Elected 1998; 2nd term

As the youngest freshman member of the 106th Congress, the energetic and genuinely boyish-looking Ryan was determined to do everything he could to solidify his hold on the politically competitive southeast corner of Wisconsin while earning his stripes as a serious legislator back in Washington.

He raised plenty of campaign money, toured the 1st District constantly and used a seat on the Budget Committee to latch onto an issue with broad appeal among voters: a much-ballyhooed "lockbox" in which Social Security surpluses could theoretically be shielded from those who would use them for other purposes. The combination paid off: Ryan evaded a serious challenge to his re-election, winning with 67 percent in 2000 against Democratic physician Jeffrey C. Thomas, even as Vice President Al Gore carried the district, 49 percent to 47 percent, over George W. Bush.

The reward for Ryan when he returned to the Capitol was substantial. He was given one of the two available GOP seats on the Ways and Means Committee, which is called on to write the bulk of the legislation — on taxes, health care, Social Security, welfare and trade — that turns into law the policies that the Budget panel lays out in its annual budget resolution.

Ryan devoted the bulk of his efforts in his first term to constituent service and familiarizing himself with the 1st District. He even toured the district in a mobile office made from a converted moving truck. "I'm new to a lot of the people I represent, so I think it's important to get to know" them, he said in early 2000. As a former congressional staff aide, Ryan was already schooled on the issues, so he kept his Washington staff small and opened more field offices in Wisconsin than his predecessor, Republican Mark W. Neumann.

Perhaps Ryan's biggest success in his first term came after several private managed-care plans funded by the Medicare system pulled out of Racine County in the 1st, which would have forced thousands of senior citizens to join the traditional government-run Medicare system. As a result, seniors would have been required to pay higher out-of-pocket costs or buy "Medigap" insurance.

In response, Ryan successfully pushed to make Racine eligible for higher hospital reimbursement rates as Congress enacted a measure in 1999 to ease Medicare cuts enacted two years earlier. In the district, he helped put together a deal between an insurance company and a hospital health care provider to keep a managed-care option available and won speedy approval of the plan by federal health care regulators.

At the same time, Ryan was an active member of the Budget Committee, giving him a platform to push core GOP issues such as tax cuts and curbs on federal spending. He was a key sponsor of legislation that aimed to halt the practice of "raiding" the Social Security trust funds to pay for other federal programs; the bill was never considered by the Senate. During the 2000 debate on the budget resolution, the articulate Ryan played an unusually active role for a freshman — performing well in what turned out to be an audition for the Ways and Means seat that he was already eyeing.

Ryan had less success in a 1999 battle over dairy policy. Wisconsin stood to benefit from new milk-pricing rules proposed by the Clinton administration, but members from other dairy states united to block the rules. Ryan and fellow Wisconsin Republican Mark Green won a two-month delay in congressional action, but lost in the end as House leaders blocked the White House-proposed changes as part of a deal on the year's wrap-up spending package.

A Roman Catholic, Ryan was initially among the Republicans concerned over the way their own leadership handled the selection of a new House chaplain in the 106th. A Wisconsin priest, Timothy J. O'Brien, had received the most support from a bipartisan panel of lawmakers set up to recommend candidates, but House Speaker J. Dennis Hastert and Majority Leader Dick Armey preferred another candidate, a non-Catholic.

Their decision spawned charges that the House GOP was prejudiced against Catholics and had Catholic Republican leaders in Wisconsin "literally yelling at me over this issue," Ryan told the Chicago Tribune. He and Green pressed Hastert and Armey to rethink the decision, though Ryan later accepted the Speaker's pledge that no anti-Catholic bias was involved. Ultimately, Hastert defused the situation by choosing a Catholic chaplain, although not O'Brien.

Although just 28 when he became a congressman, Ryan was no political novice. He had done more than five years of economic policy work in Washington — as a staffer on the Small Business Committee for Wisconsin GOP Sen. Robert W. Kasten, an adviser and speechwriter for the conservative think tank Empower America, and a top aide to Kansas Republican Sam Brownback in both the House and Senate.

He returned to Wisconsin late in 1997 to work for his family's earth-moving business and to prepare for his foray into electoral politics. When Neumann decided to run, unsuccessfully, for the Senate, it appeared Ryan would have to fight for the GOP nomination. But his strongest potential rivals dropped out. His opponent in the general election was Democrat Lydia Spottswood, a former Kenosha City Council president who nearly beat Neumann in 1996. Ryan proved to have much stronger campaign skills — he earned the nickname "robocandidate" — and he won by more than 27,000 votes, a surprisingly large margin given that the previous three races in the district had been won by margins of 4,000 votes or less.

Ryan has boasted of working seven-day, 120-hour weeks, with eight hours set aside for pursuits such as hunting and fishing. In his first term, however, he evidently found time for at least one additional personal pursuit: In April 2000, he announced his engagement to Janna Little, an Oklahoman whom he met at one of his fundraisers. They were married that December.

Despite his zest for politics, Ryan does not anticipate a lengthy career in Congress, though he views his current job as a good primer for his ultimate goal of a business career.

KEY VOTES

2000

No	Raise hourly minimum wage by $1 over two years
Yes	Halt funding for U.S. mission in Kosovo unless European nations pay more
Yes	Provide Medicare benefits to military retirees and their dependents
Yes	Grant China permanent normal trade status
Yes	Phase out estate, gift and trust taxes
Yes	Prohibit implementation of president's national monument designations
Yes	Approve GOP plan to provide prescription drug coverage for Medicare beneficiaries
No	Increase help for poor nations indebted to international financial institutions

1999

Yes	Impose steel import quotas
Yes	Kill proposal to take aviation trust funds off budget
Yes	Require background checks on buyers only at gun shows with 10 or more vendors
Yes	Remove barriers among banking, securities and insurance companies
No	Authorize state grants to hire teachers and reduce class size
No	Overhaul campaign finance law; ban "soft money" and restrict advocacy advertising
No	Approve bipartisan plan to increase rights of patients in managed-care health plans

INTEREST GROUPS

	AFL-CIO	ADA	CCUS	ACU
2000	0%	5%	90%	88%
1999	22%	10%	92%	92%

CQ VOTE STUDIES

	PARTY UNITY		PRESIDENTIAL SUPPORT	
	Support	Oppose	Support	Oppose
2000	95%	5%	22%	78%
1999	90%	10%	21%	79%

WISCONSIN 1
Southeast – Racine; Kenosha

From the shores of Lake Michigan to the center of Green County, the 1st blends rural communities with some of the state's largest industrial areas. The district's two largest cities are sandwiched between Milwaukee and Chicago along Lake Michigan: Racine, originally settled by Danish immigrants, and Kenosha, with a sizable Italian community.

After losing a Chrysler plant in 1988, Kenosha's economy diversified, and its affordable real estate prices began to attract more Chicago commuters. Kenosha County and neighboring Walworth County grew about twice as fast as the state average in the 1990s. Several corporate parks are located in nearby Pleasant Prairie, and visitors are lured to the city to visit Dairyland, the nation's largest greyhound dog racing track. Locals are proud of Kenosha's ranking in a 1997 Reader's Digest survey as the nation's second best city for raising families.

Farms dot the rural areas, but crop growers outnumber dairy farmers,

a rarity in Wisconsin. Resort complexes around Lake Geneva and Lake Delavan cater to wealthy vacationers from Milwaukee and Chicago. In the west-central part of the district are the smaller industrial cities of Janesville and Beloit, in Democratic-leaning Rock County. Beloit was settled by a group of immigrants from New Hampshire who founded Beloit College in 1846. Janesville's economy has hit some rough patches as the number of manufacturing jobs has declined, and demand for trucks from its General Motors plant has softened.

A socially diverse population has made this once firmly Republican district the most contested in the state. While Democrats draw a firm level of support from the four manufacturing cities, Republicans look to the suburban and rural areas for a conservative base. In 2000, Al Gore narrowly won the district, capturing 49 percent of the vote.

MAJOR INDUSTRY
Automotive manufacturing, heavy machine manufacturing, farming

CITIES
Kenosha, 89,447; Racine, 80,902; Janesville, 60,255; Beloit, 35,728

UNUSUAL FEATURES
Racine's Salmon-A-Rama fishing match; Orson Welles born in Kenosha.

Rep. Tammy Baldwin (D)

Elected 1998; 2nd term

CAPITOL OFFICE
225-2906; fax 225-6942
1022 Longworth Bldg. 20515

INTERNET
e-mail: tammy.baldwin@mail.house.gov
web: www.house.gov/baldwin

COMMITTEES
Budget
Judiciary

HOMETOWN
Madison

BORN
Feb. 11, 1962, Madison, Wis.

RELIGION
Unspecified

FAMILY
Partner, Lauren Azar

EDUCATION
Smith College, A.B. 1984; U. of Wisconsin, J.D. 1989

CAREER
Lawyer; public policy analyst

POLITICAL HIGHLIGHTS
Madison City Council, 1986; Dane County Board, 1986-94; Wis. Assembly, 1993-99

ELECTION RESULTS

2000 GENERAL

Tammy Baldwin (D)	163,534	51.4%
John Sharpless (R)	154,632	48.6%

2000 PRIMARY

Tammy Baldwin (D)	unopposed

1998 GENERAL

Tammy Baldwin (D)	116,377	52.5%
Josephine Musser (R)	103,528	46.7%

Baldwin made history in 1998 not only as the first woman elected to Congress from Wisconsin, but also as the first openly gay woman to win a congressional election. She takes pride in her trailblazing achievement: "No one can say it can't happen anymore."

But Baldwin also wants to make sure she is not a one-note lawmaker, known only for her sexual orientation. "That's of course the challenge when you are a pathmaker, not to be seen as a single issue," she says.

Perhaps because she has spent most of her adult life in politics, Baldwin seemed to adjust to Congress fairly easily, balancing her liberal policy agenda with a pragmatic willingness to work with Republicans on the Judiciary Committee, where she serves, to achieve her objectives. "I can't get legislation passed without Republicans," she notes.

When the panel worked on the reauthorization of the Violence Against Women Act in 2000, for example, Democrats and Republicans found little they could agree on, and most Democrats saw their amendments fail. But Baldwin worked with Crime Subcommittee Chairman Bill McCollum, R-Fla., and won approval of her proposal to create a $10 million grant program to help disabled women who are victims of violence.

Baldwin said one of the reasons she is more inclined to reach across the aisle is that she was not in Congress during the 1998 impeachment deliberations by the Judiciary Committee, which left bitter feelings between the parties. In addition, she spent time in the minority when she served in the Wisconsin Legislature — good preparation for her role in the GOP-controlled House, she says.

Her self-deprecating humor has made it easier for her to connect on a personal level with other lawmakers, especially conservatives who might have been uncomfortable with her lifestyle. (Though same-sex marriages are not legal in Wisconsin, Baldwin wears a wedding ring and exchanged vows in 1998 with Lauren Azar, a lawyer.) Baldwin was a hit with her speech in 1999 at the annual Congressional Dinner of the Washington Press Club. "You invited me because I'm one of the first elected officials who represents a group historically discriminated against," she said. "A group that has been kept out of jobs, harassed at the workplace. A group that's been unfairly stereotyped and made the object of rude and base humor. Of course, I'm talking about blondes ... especially blondes named Tammy."

In her first year in Congress, Baldwin, who also sits on the Budget Committee, won plaudits from the National Taxpayers Union, which said she voted for less spending than all but one of her Badger State colleagues in 1999.

But Baldwin also is a member of the Progressive Caucus, the most liberal faction of House Democrats, which seeks higher unemployment benefits, increased social spending and a hike in the minimum wage. The group advocates universal health care — the issue Baldwin made the centerpiece of her 1998 election campaign. She presses for traditional liberal programs such as child nutrition initiatives and expansions of both Head Start and the Family and Medical Leave Act.

Baldwin supported legislation, signed into law in 1999, that made it easier for the disabled to work without losing their health care benefits. She also favored a Democratic-backed measure allowing patients to sue their health care plans for denial of coverage. And she cosponsored the Democrats' plan to provide prescription drug coverage for senior citizens on Medicare.

On Judiciary, she was one of several Democrats in the 106th who called for the panel to consider legislation to toughen penalties for hate crimes. She also urged extension of a section of the bankruptcy code that permits farmers to continue operating while they reorganize their debts.

She was an active participant in the milk-pricing battles of 1999. Wisconsin members, backed by the Clinton administration, tried to revamp the Depression-era milk marketing system, which pays farmers more for milk the farther they are from Eau Claire, Wis. Powerful farming interests from the Northeast and South, which benefit from the existing system, derailed the administration's plans, but Baldwin took heart from the ability of Wisconsin members to block efforts to form new dairy compacts. Those agreements, in force in several states, make it much more difficult for out-of-state milk farmers to sell their products in states belonging to a compact.

Senior issues are also important to Baldwin, who has a close relationship with her grandmother who helped raise her. And she wants to help restore veterans' faith in government, especially those vets who served during the Persian Gulf War and returned ill, with a disease doctors could not identify, now known as Gulf War syndrome. It is important, she says, to "rebuild trust with a group of veterans who have been told 'it's all in your head.' "

She has a favorite saying, framed in her office, by anthropologist Margaret Mead. "Never doubt that a small group of thoughtful, committed citizens can change the world. Indeed, it is the only thing that ever has."

Baldwin got on the Madison City Council when she was 24 and has been in office ever since. She served in the Wisconsin Assembly for six years before coming to Congress. Her predecessor, moderate Republican Scott L. Klug, had held the 2nd District for four terms despite its pronounced Democratic leaning. Klug's decision not to run again in 1998 created a takeover opportunity for the Democrats.

Baldwin's impressive fundraising operation helped her win a September primary over two well-known opponents, Dane County Executive Rick Phelps and state Sen. Joe Wineke. Her Republican opponent, former state Insurance Commissioner Josephine Musser, won her six-way primary with just 21 percent of the vote and antagonized conservatives with her support of abortion rights. Nonetheless, Baldwin had to make the most of her effective television ads and grass-roots organization to win the general election by 6 percentage points.

The district was a battleground again in 2000, with Baldwin eking out a 3-point victory over moderate Republican John Sharpless, a University of Wisconsin history professor.

KEY VOTES

2000

Yes Raise hourly minimum wage by $1 over two years
Yes Halt funding for U.S. mission in Kosovo unless European nations pay more
Yes Provide Medicare benefits to military retirees and their dependents
No Grant China permanent normal trade status
No Phase out estate, gift and trust taxes
No Prohibit implementation of president's national monument designations
No Approve GOP plan to provide prescription drug coverage for Medicare beneficiaries
Yes Increase help for poor nations indebted to international financial institutions

1999

Yes Impose steel import quotas
Yes Kill proposal to take aviation trust funds off budget
No Require background checks on buyers only at gun shows with 10 or more vendors
No Remove barriers among banking, securities and insurance companies
Yes Authorize state grants to hire teachers and reduce class size
Yes Overhaul campaign finance law; ban "soft money" and restrict advocacy advertising
Yes Approve bipartisan plan to increase rights of patients in managed-care health plans

INTEREST GROUPS

	AFL-CIO	ADA	CCUS	ACU
2000	100%	90%	23%	4%
1999	100%	90%	4%	4%

CQ VOTE STUDIES

	PARTY UNITY		PRESIDENTIAL SUPPORT	
	Support	Oppose	Support	Oppose
2000	96%	4%	78%	22%
1999	96%	4%	79%	21%

WISCONSIN 2
South — Madison

Once described by former GOP Gov. Lee Dreyfus as "23 square miles surrounded by reality," the 2nd's Madison has long been Wisconsin's liberal centerpiece. But the 2nd is more than university- and state government-dominated Madison, and that helps explain how Republican Scott Klug managed to topple a 32-year Democratic incumbent in 1990 and then go on to complete an eight-year stint in Congress. After Klug retired, the 2nd went back to its Democratic roots and elected a liberal gay woman to the post.

With two-thirds of the district's voters living in Madison's Dane County, Klug succeeded by tapping the suburbs for support. Towns like Fitchburg, Sun Prairie and Middleton are growing briskly with young professionals who tend to be socially liberal but fiscally conservative. Outside the city, Dane County's corn stalks and cows make it the second-largest farming region in the state.

Most of the district's land lies outside of Dane and is solidly

Republican. Dairy and beef farms are struggling in the western part of the 2nd, where rolling hills make most large scale farming impractical. The Lands' End clothing catalog company is here, in Dodgeville. To the north, the natural wonders of the Wisconsin Dells lure tourists to the Wisconsin River.

Madison's stable economy is built around an educated population of white-collar professionals. In addition to the University of Wisconsin's main campus and the state government, there are several insurance companies and a growing biotechnology sector. The city has been cited by magazines as one of the most livable in the nation.

MAJOR INDUSTRY
Higher education, farming, insurance

MILITARY BASES
Truax Field, 75 military, 268 civilian (2000)

CITIES
Madison, 210,674; Sun Prairie, 20,391; Fitchburg, 20,149

UNUSUAL FEATURES
Taliesin, Frank Lloyd Wright's studio and home, now a thriving artist community.

Rep. Ron Kind (D)

CAPITOL OFFICE
225-5506; fax 225-5739
1713 Longworth Bldg. 20515

INTERNET
e-mail: ron.kind@mail.house.gov
web: www.house.gov/kind

COMMITTEES
Agriculture
Education & Workforce
Resources

HOMETOWN
La Crosse

BORN
March 16, 1963, La Crosse, Wis.

RELIGION
Lutheran

FAMILY
Wife, Tawni Zappa; two children

EDUCATION
Harvard U., B.A. 1985; London School of
Economics, M.A. 1986; U. of Minnesota, J.D. 1990

CAREER
County prosecutor; lawyer

POLITICAL HIGHLIGHTS
No previous office

ELECTION RESULTS

2000 GENERAL

Ron Kind (D)	173,505	63.7%
Susan Tully (R)	97,741	35.9%

2000 PRIMARY

Ron Kind (D)	unopposed

1998 GENERAL

Ron Kind (D)	128,256	71.5%
Troy A. Brechler (R)	51,001	28.4%

PREVIOUS WINNING PERCENTAGES
1996 (52%)

Elected 1996; 3rd term

Kind draws his inspiration from the thousands of college students in Eastern Europe who helped bring down their communist governments in the late 1980s and from former Wisconsin Democratic Sen. William O. Proxmire, who showcased wasteful government spending with his "Golden Fleece" awards.

Backpacking through Eastern Europe as communism was crumbling, Kind witnessed the fall of the Berlin Wall (wielding a sledgehammer himself at one point), shook hands with new Czechoslovakian president Vaclav Havel, and met with many students. "These were average people, like me, trying to make a difference," he told the Wisconsin State Journal. Kind says he saw firsthand the power that can be achieved when disparate factions come together for a common purpose.

As a summer intern for Proxmire, Kind helped with the research for many of the senator's famous "Golden Fleece" awards and came away from that experience with an appreciation for fiscal frugality. He says he strives to carry on Proxmire's legacy, and he regularly wins kudos from the Concord Coalition, a budget watchdog group, for his votes on fiscal matters.

Only the third Democrat to represent the western Wisconsin district in the past 90 years, Kind insists that bipartisanship is essential to legislative success in Washington and electoral success back home. Upon his arrival in Washington in 1997, he solicited the advice of his Republican predecessor, Steve Gunderson, and hired two members of Gunderson's staff.

Kind has joined with Republicans to bring attention to the needs of rural health care providers and nursing homes, and he was the co-founder of the bipartisan Upper Mississippi River Congressional Caucus. He has also sided with Republicans on a number of key votes, including measures to limit congressional terms and ban a procedure its opponents call "partial birth" abortion.

Bipartisanship may sit more easily with Kind than it does with many lawmakers. One supporter told the La Crosse Tribune that he didn't know whether Kind was a Democrat or Republican when they first met. Kind is a member of the New Democrat Coalition, a group of about 70 moderate Democrats who say they seek "mainstream, bipartisan solutions."

He is a dependable Democratic vote on education and social policy, although, as a former prosecutor, he sides on occasion with the GOP in support of tougher treatment of criminals. At the same time, he believes government could help local communities reach children before they turn to crime by continuing federal funding for programs such as Head Start.

He is generally pro-labor (his father, who was a union leader, lost his phone company job after a strike), but he angered labor leaders in 2000 when he voted to grant China permanent normal trade status.

Coming from one of the leading dairy regions in the country, Kind's first priority on reaching Washington was to contact Agriculture Secretary Dan Glickman to discuss dairy prices. In 2000, with milk prices at a two-decade low, Kind urged Glickman to release $125 million in federal aid immediately. Beyond that, Kind urges a comprehensive dialogue on dairy policy, to end the battle that pits farmer against farmer and region against region.

He opposes the Depression-era milk marketing system, which pays dairy farmers more for milk the farther they are from Eau Claire, Wis., the historical center of the dairy industry, which is in Kind's district. The system was intended to ensure farmers a minimum price for their milk by addressing different production and transportation costs. To call attention to what he says is the absurdity and unfairness of that policy, Kind in 2000 introduced legislation to authorize fines for gasoline price-gouging that would be higher in areas closer to Eau Claire. In the 107th, he won a seat on the Agriculture panel.

The Mississippi River runs along the western boundary of the 3rd District for more than 200 miles — farther than any other congressional district — and Kind has been involved in several efforts to clean up the river, including reducing sediment and dealing with nitrogen fertilizer runoff from farms, which has created serious problems downstream. "I feel a certain moral responsibility," he told the St. Louis Post-Dispatch.

Inspired by the stories his father and uncle told about their military service during the Korean War and World War II, Kind in the 106th Congress was the leading sponsor of legislation authorizing the Library of Congress to undertake a major effort to collect videotaped oral histories from veterans.

Kind is a local success story. He grew up in a blue-collar neighborhood. A high school football and basketball star, he won an academic scholarship to Harvard University, where he supplemented his income with a number of work-study jobs. ("I think I still probably hold the record for most toilets cleaned," he told the Milwaukee Journal Sentinel.) Kind quarterbacked the football team before suffering a career-ending shoulder injury in his junior year. The next summer, in 1984, he worked with Proxmire on Capitol Hill.

After receiving a law degree and working two years for a Milwaukee law firm, Kind returned home to La Crosse to become a county prosecutor.

With the Republican takeover of the House in 1995, Kind began thinking about politics, and when Gunderson announced his retirement, Kind quickly entered the 3rd District race. With little money, he waged a grass-roots campaign, drawing on his experience working on the campaign of Wisconsin Democrat Russell D. Feingold — though significantly outspent, Feingold had managed to win election to the Senate in 1992.

Gunderson expressed an interest in reversing his retirement, particularly as circumstances put him in line to chair the Agriculture Committee. When the GOP nominee, Jim Harsdorf, did not step aside, however, Gunderson honored his commitment to retire but did not endorse Harsdorf. Kind beat Harsdorf, 52 percent to 48 percent. In 1998 and 2000, Kind won re-election easily, and his name is mentioned as a possible candidate for governor in 2002.

KEY VOTES

2000
Yes Raise hourly minimum wage by $1 over two years
No   Halt funding for U.S. mission in Kosovo unless European nations pay more
Yes Provide Medicare benefits to military retirees and their dependents
Yes Grant China permanent normal trade status
?   Phase out estate, gift and trust taxes
No   Prohibit implementation of president's national monument designations
No   Approve GOP plan to provide prescription drug coverage for Medicare beneficiaries
Yes Increase help for poor nations indebted to international financial institutions

1999
No   Impose steel import quotas
Yes Kill proposal to take aviation trust funds off budget
No   Require background checks on buyers only at gun shows with 10 or more vendors
Yes Remove barriers among banking, securities and insurance companies
Yes Authorize state grants to hire teachers and reduce class size
Yes Overhaul campaign finance law; ban "soft money" and restrict advocacy advertising
Yes Approve bipartisan plan to increase rights of patients in managed-care health plans

INTEREST GROUPS

	AFL-CIO	ADA	CCUS	ACU
2000	80%	80%	50%	8%
1999	56%	90%	44%	4%
1998	90%	85%	56%	20%
1997	100%	85%	50%	28%

CQ VOTE STUDIES

	PARTY UNITY		PRESIDENTIAL SUPPORT	
	Support	Oppose	Support	Oppose
2000	86%	14%	81%	19%
1999	82%	18%	76%	24%
1998	86%	14%	77%	23%
1997	89%	11%	79%	21%

WISCONSIN 3
West – Eau Claire; La Crosse

In a state that bills itself as "America's Dairyland," the 3rd stands at the head of the herd. It has more cows than people and is one of the nation's leading milk-producing districts. Following Wisconsin's western boundary with Minnesota and Iowa, the 3rd borders about 200 miles of the Mississippi River, more than any other district in the nation.

The flat prairie land and nutrient-rich soil in the south contribute to ideal milk-producing conditions. But smaller farms have struggled, and heavy manufacturing in the district's two largest cities – La Crosse and Eau Claire – isn't what it used to be, keeping population growth below the state average (which itself is below the national average). Suburban expansion from Minneapolis-St. Paul, just across the state line, is driving the district's main growth area, St. Croix County. Tourism also is important. A dozen lakes in the northwest attract vacationers and retirees.

The sparsely populated southwest, with relatively stable farms, has forged more conservative and Republican voters, while in the north, the manufacturing jobs and unsettled farmers have produced Democratic sympathizers. In 1992, nearly one-fourth of the voters picked Ross Perot, and in 2000 Al Gore just barely secured the district by 3 percentage points. The 3rd's congressional seat is not considered safe for either party, but individual incumbents – a Republican in the early 1990s and a Democrat in the late 1990s – have easily won re-election.

MAJOR INDUSTRY
Dairy farming, heavy manufacturing, tourism

CITIES
Eau Claire (pt.), 55,180 (1990); La Crosse, 49,409; Menomonie, 15,304

UNUSUAL FEATURES
Laura Ingalls Wilder lived in northwest part of district; the NFL's Kansas City Chiefs and Chicago Bears have summer training sites at universities in the district; Milk prices paid to farmers nationwide are determined by a region's distance from Eau Claire, the historic center of the dairy industry.

Rep. Gerald D. Kleczka (D)

CAPITOL OFFICE
225-4572; fax 225-8135; 2301 Rayburn Bldg. 20515

INTERNET
e-mail: www.house.gov/writerep
web: www.house.gov/kleczka

COMMITTEES
Budget
Ways & Means

HOMETOWN
Milwaukee

BORN
Nov. 26, 1943, Milwaukee, Wis.

RELIGION
Roman Catholic

FAMILY
Wife, Bonnie Kleczka

EDUCATION
U. of Wisconsin, attended 1961-62, attended 1967, attended 1970

MILITARY SERVICE
Wis. Air National Guard, 1963-69

CAREER
Accountant

POLITICAL HIGHLIGHTS
Wis. Assembly, 1969-74; Wis. Senate, 1975-84

ELECTION RESULTS

2000 GENERAL

Gerald D. Kleczka (D)	163,622	60.8%
Tim Riener (R)	101,811	37.8%
Nikola Rajnovic (LIBERT)	3,705	1.4%

2000 PRIMARY

Gerald D. Kleczka (D)	unopposed

1998 GENERAL

Gerald D. Kleczka (D)	105,841	57.9%
Tom Reynolds (R)	76,666	42.0%

PREVIOUS WINNING PERCENTAGES
1996 (58%); 1994 (54%); 1992 (66%); 1990 (69%); 1988 (100%); 1986 (100%); 1984 (67%); 1984 Special Election (65%)

Elected April 1984; 9th full term

Born and raised in Milwaukee, Kleczka is a Catholic of Polish descent who represents the large Central and Eastern European ethnic population in the city's South Side neighborhoods. Kleczka works on issues that matter most in his constituents' daily lives, including health care, taxes, jobs, community development and consumer protection.

Kleczka (KLETCH-kuh) is a pro-union voice for his blue-collar district, where manufacturing is a dwindling but still important factor in the economy. His constituents usually vote Democratic, but they often hold conservative views on social issues, such as abortion.

Although he has aligned himself with the GOP on some issues, such as cutting government spending, Kleczka can lob partisan grenades. He took offense when Republicans in 2000 brought up a resolution praising Catholic schools after they passed over a Catholic priest to be the new House chaplain. "One could ask, is this a way that some can clear their conscience?" he asked. "Is this resolution before us because maybe it is an attempt to repair some of the damage done to the Catholic vote in this country?"

Slightly more conservative than other Midwestern Democrats, Kleczka on occasion will subjugate his personal views when House Democratic leaders really need his vote. In 1992, as Democratic leaders scrambled to round up support to defeat the balanced-budget constitutional amendment, Kleczka answered their call for help, even though he had cosponsored the proposal and would later return to the ranks of amendment supporters.

Being a good soldier for the Democratic leadership was key to helping Kleczka win his Ways and Means seat, although he had to wait nine years for it. He got the choice assignment in 1993, claiming the "Wisconsin seat" on the panel that had been held by Democrat Jim Moody, who left the House. In the 106th Congress, the Democratic leadership added a seat on the Budget Committee to Kleczka's portfolio.

Although Kleczka supports limited tax cuts, he faulted Republican plans in the 106th as favoring the wealthy and endangering the government's budget surplus. In 1999, he warned that an approximately $800 billion tax cut proposal could spawn budget deficits. "Know that the estimated surplus is based on unrealistic economic assumptions," he said. "To think that our unprecedented growth and prosperity will continue forever is pure folly."

In 1997, he attracted attention for his attempt to tax lawmakers who sleep in their Capitol Hill offices for that "employer-sponsored benefit." The amendment was defeated, but Kleczka offered it to make the point that some Republicans were not observing their "Contract With America" pledge that members of Congress should abide by the same laws as all Americans.

One of Kleczka's main interests is protecting individual privacy rights. In the 106th Congress, he teamed with Ways and Means colleague E. Clay Shaw Jr., R-Fla., in an attempt to prohibit federal, state and local government agencies from selling Social Security numbers or displaying the numbers on such documents as driver's licenses. His concern is that criminals who obtain Social Security numbers can use them to get credit cards and run up big debts. Bringing the issue home to Kleczka was the fact that two of his staffers were victimized by such identity theft. "Social Security numbers were never intended to be national identifiers," he said.

Health care is another major concern of Kleczka's, whose brother received a lung transplant in 1993. On Ways and Means, he works on the Democrats' version of legislation to protect patients' rights in disputes with

HMOs. He also proposed legislation that would prohibit well-to-do Medicare beneficiaries from entering into private contracts with doctors for services currently covered by Medicare. He argued that allowing such arrangements could lead to a two-tiered system of health care for senior citizens and "continue the withering of the Medicare program."

His ties to organized labor have caused him to break with most Ways and Means members on issues involving expanded trade. In 2000, he voted against legislation granting China permanent normal trade status, contending that Congress instead should continue the practice of regularly reviewing trade relations with that country. "It's not that we don't want to trade with China," he said. "We just don't want to fling open the doors of this country to trade with China and never have it reviewed again," he told the Los Angeles Times.

Kleczka will, however, vote with Republicans on certain social issues. In the 105th, for instance, he voted for GOP bills to crack down on violent juvenile offenders and to prevent the Food and Drug Administration from approving certain abortion-inducing drugs. He opposes federal funding of abortions and voted to ban a procedure its opponents call "partial birth" abortion, but he supports federal funding for family planning efforts. Kleczka also backed the GOP-led overhaul of the welfare system, which he criticized as rife with fraud. He said Congress should disabuse welfare recipients of the notion that welfare is a "permanent refuge from the world of work."

A dog lover who sometimes brings his shelty to the office, Kleczka in 2000 won passage of a measure that bans the import of products made with the fur of dogs or cats. He was spurred into action by investigations revealing that as many as 2 million dogs and cats each year are killed overseas so their pelts can be used for such products as clothes and novelty items. "This serves as a loud and clear message that the United States will have no part in supporting this horrific trade," he said.

Kleczka launched his political career at the age of 24, winning election to the state Assembly. He later served in the state Senate, rising to become one of the most influential lawmakers on tax and budget matters while retaining his reputation as a down-to-earth deal-maker and a hard-nosed campaigner. When Democratic Rep. Clement J. Zablocki, the Foreign Affairs Committee chairman, died in late 1983, Kleczka was the front-runner to replace him and won an April 1984 special election by a healthy 65 percent.

He has won re-election since by generally comfortable margins, although he faced a stiff challenge in the GOP banner year of 1994, winning by just 9 percentage points.

KEY VOTES

2000
Yes Raise hourly minimum wage by $1 over two years
Yes Halt funding for U.S. mission in Kosovo unless European nations pay more
Yes Provide Medicare benefits to military retirees and their dependents
No Grant China permanent normal trade status
No Phase out estate, gift and trust taxes
No Prohibit implementation of president's national monument designations
No Approve GOP plan to provide prescription drug coverage for Medicare beneficiaries
Yes Increase help for poor nations indebted to international financial institutions

1999
Yes Impose steel import quotas
No Kill proposal to take aviation trust funds off budget
No Require background checks on buyers only at gun shows with 10 or more vendors
No Remove barriers among banking, securities and insurance companies
Yes Authorize state grants to hire teachers and reduce class size
Yes Overhaul campaign finance law; ban "soft money" and restrict advocacy advertising
Yes Approve bipartisan plan to increase rights of patients in managed-care health plans

INTEREST GROUPS

	AFL-CIO	ADA	CCUS	ACU
2000	100%	85%	30%	20%
1999	89%	95%	24%	16%
1998	100%	90%	39%	20%
1997	88%	70%	50%	25%

CQ VOTE STUDIES

	PARTY UNITY		PRESIDENTIAL SUPPORT	
	Support	Oppose	Support	Oppose
2000	88%	12%	78%	22%
1999	87%	13%	75%	25%
1998	85%	15%	75%	25%
1997	81%	19%	65%	35%

WISCONSIN 4

Southern Milwaukee and Milwaukee County suburbs; southeast Waukesha County

Densely packed Polish flats in the northern part of the 4th and sprawling suburbs to the west make this district one of the most politically and physically diverse in the state.

The heart of Milwaukee has long been its South Side bungalow belt, whose plain but sturdy houses evoke the 1950s. Television viewers still associate the city with the setting for "Laverne and Shirley." Since the turn of the century, the city's huge Polish community has been based on its South Side, and the area remains predominantly Polish and German. However, the region also houses the state's largest concentration of Hispanic residents, a growing constituency.

With Wisconsin losing a congressional seat in the 2000 reapportionment, there is a strong possibility that the 4th might be combined with Milwaukee's other, less wealthy district, the 5th. Suburban sprawl has continued to drain white residents out of the city;

Milwaukee lost 5 percent of its population in the 1990s. Nonetheless, the local economy is better off than it was in the 1980s, when the area's job base suffered from de-industrialization. West of the city, Waukesha County gained 56,000 residents in the 1990s, attracting white-collar businesses as well as residential development.

The loss of union jobs and general urban flight have eroded the Democratic base of support in Milwaukee's south. While the core of city voters in southern Milwaukee County vote Democratic, Waukesha County to the west votes Republican. The 4th now behaves like a suburban swing district. It voted for Bill Clinton in 1992 and '96, but it supported President Bush in 2000 by 4 percentage points.

MAJOR INDUSTRY
Machinery manufacturing, service

CITIES
Milwaukee (pt.), 202,167 (1990); Waukesha, 63,261; West Allis, 59,332; New Berlin, 38,360; Greenfield, 35,246

UNUSUAL FEATURES
World's largest four-sided analog clock on Allen-Bradley building; Holler House, oldest sanctioned bowling alley in the United States.

Rep. Thomas M. Barrett (D)

Elected 1992; 5th term

CAPITOL OFFICE
225-3571; fax 225-2185
1214 Longworth Bldg. 20515

INTERNET
e-mail: telltom@mail.house.gov
web: www.house.gov/barrett

COMMITTEES
Energy & Commerce

HOMETOWN
Milwaukee

BORN
Dec. 8, 1953, Milwaukee, Wis.

RELIGION
Roman Catholic

FAMILY
Wife, Kristine Barrett; four children

EDUCATION
U. of Wisconsin, B.A. 1976, J.D. 1980

CAREER
Lawyer

POLITICAL HIGHLIGHTS
Candidate for Wis. Assembly, 1982; Wis.
Assembly, 1984-89; Wis. Senate, 1989-93

ELECTION RESULTS

2000 GENERAL

Thomas M. Barrett (D)	173,893	77.7%
Jonathan Smith (R)	49,296	22.0%

2000 PRIMARY

Thomas M. Barrett (D)	unopposed

1998 GENERAL

Thomas M. Barrett (D)	121,129	78.2%
Jack Melvin (R)	33,506	21.6%

PREVIOUS WINNING PERCENTAGES
1996 (73%); 1994 (62%); 1992 (69%)

A Milwaukeean born and bred, Barrett put himself through school working on loading docks and at a local Harley-Davidson plant. His preferred method of campaigning in this blue-collar district has always been door-to-door visiting. And so neighborhood issues — child care, education, crime, housing, community development, health care — occupy the top spot on Barrett's congressional priority list.

In the 106th Congress, after a quick four-month stint on the Judiciary Committee late in the 105th while that panel was considering the impeachment of President Clinton, Barrett moved to the Commerce panel (now Energy and Commerce), a prize post where he has continued his work on health care issues while trying to prevent businesses from overlooking poor neighborhoods.

Many of Barrett's legislative concerns stem from sweeping changes in Wisconsin's welfare system and the state's new health care system for the poor. Both initiatives are viewed as likely models for nationwide policy, especially now that former Wisconsin Gov. Tommy G. Thompson is serving as secretary of health and human services in the Bush administration. Barrett's 5th District, which has most of the state's minority population and many of its poorest neighborhoods, has much at stake in the welfare and health care policy debates. Although Barrett has failed to block major GOP welfare initiatives, he argues for increased federal and state aid to provide child care for welfare recipients thrust back into the work force.

Barrett is an outspoken supporter of expanding Medicare to include prescription drug benefits, which he says is a top concern of seniors in his district. In the 106th, he worked to boost Medicaid payments to Wisconsin and retain children's health insurance funds. "These provisions will help provide health care for the people who need it most," he said. "It is particularly important that Wisconsin continue to reach out to underserved populations and ensure that they have access to both hospitals and health care."

Barrett also has sought to broaden business opportunities in economically distressed areas. In the 106th, he pressed unsuccessfully for an amendment to expand the Community Reinvestment Act, or CRA, which requires banks to try to make loans to all areas in which they collect deposits. Although some conservatives wanted to scale back the law, Barrett contended, "I've seen no evidence that it's forced them [banks] to make bad loans. ... It allows them to be good corporate citizens." He also proposed a measure that would have required insurers to compile and make public data on the race, gender, income and location of their policyholders and applicants.

Barrett touts his fiscal conservatism and points to accolades he has received from several federal spending watchdog organizations, including the Concord Coalition. He supported the short-lived presidential line-item veto authority and would have preferred it extend further to apply to special-interest tax breaks. He voted against the massive transportation reauthorization bill in 1998, arguing that its funding total was far more than what Congress had agreed to just a year before in its balanced-budget deal. Late in the 105th, he voted against the end-of-session catchall spending bill, telling his constituents that it spent too much money and that its cobbled-together nature made it impossible to know what it contained.

As a member of the Government Reform Committee in the 105th, Barrett was sharply critical of GOP Chairman Dan Burton's inquiry into allegations of wrongdoing in Democratic campaign fundraising. He said Burton was running a "kangaroo court," with the primary objective of launching political attacks against the president, "with no element of fairness and no effort to find the truth."

His performance on that panel indicated he was willing and able to mix it up with Republicans, but he was not viewed as overly partisan — attributes that attracted the notice of Democratic leaders when they had a vacancy to fill on the Judiciary Committee. During the impeachment hearings in late 1998, Barrett decided that "President Clinton's conduct was wrong, and he must be held accountable" for lying about an affair with a White House intern, but he argued that censure was the preferable alternative. "Our Constitution does not allow us, no, it does not allow you, to remove a president from office because you can't stand him," Barrett told Republicans.

Barrett is usually a reliable vote for his party, and like many Democrats, he has taken aim at Republican tax-cutting plans, warning in 1999 that major cuts could "start the nation back down the road of inflated federal budget deficits." He sided with organized labor in 2000 by voting against a Clinton plan to grant China permanent normal trade status.

On domestic policy issues, Barrett favors gun control but opposes abortion. He wants to outlaw a procedure its opponents call "partial birth" abortion. In the 106th Congress, he endorsed gun control regulations such as trigger lock requirements and mandatory background checks for purchases of firearms at gun shows, calling the plans "no-brainers that did not affect anybody's right to hunt or own a gun."

Barrett's district is about 35 percent black, and he joined in the 105th with a few other lawmakers in a series of "congressional conversations on race," seeking to promote a dialogue of the sort spurred by Clinton's town-hall meeting initiative on race relations.

Barrett grew up in Milwaukee, and, before his 1992 election to the House, he had ventured from his hometown only as far as the state capital — first to go to college and law school and later to serve in the state legislature. He is comfortable with his blue-collar constituents, and his campaigns rely more on door-to-door canvassing than on media coverage or expensive advertising campaigns. "I find it relaxing, and it's something I'm very comfortable doing," he once said. "And when you talk to someone at their home, they're relaxed." Part of his enjoyment may result from the fact that his constituents do not need much convincing. Barrett easily won a crowded primary in 1992 to replace Democrat Jim Moody, who made an unsuccessful run for the Senate, and he trounced the Republican nominee by better than 2-to-1. He has had no re-election difficulties since.

KEY VOTES

2000

Yes Raise hourly minimum wage by $1 over two years
Yes Halt funding for U.S. mission in Kosovo unless European nations pay more
Yes Provide Medicare benefits to military retirees and their dependents
No Grant China permanent normal trade status
No Phase out estate, gift and trust taxes
No Prohibit implementation of president's national monument designations
No Approve GOP plan to provide prescription drug coverage for Medicare beneficiaries
Yes Increase help for poor nations indebted to international financial institutions

1999

Yes Impose steel import quotas
Yes Kill proposal to take aviation trust funds off budget
No Require background checks on buyers only at gun shows with 10 or more vendors
No Remove barriers among banking, securities and insurance companies
Yes Authorize state grants to hire teachers and reduce class size
Yes Overhaul campaign finance law; ban "soft money" and restrict advocacy advertising
Yes Approve bipartisan plan to increase rights of patients in managed-care health plans

INTEREST GROUPS

	AFL-CIO	ADA	CCUS	ACU
2000	100%	100%	38%	8%
1999	78%	100%	12%	4%
1998	100%	95%	17%	4%
1997	100%	90%	40%	20%

CQ VOTE STUDIES

	PARTY UNITY		PRESIDENTIAL SUPPORT	
	Support	Oppose	Support	Oppose
2000	93%	7%	79%	21%
1999	93%	7%	85%	15%
1998	93%	7%	89%	11%
1997	91%	9%	84%	16%

WISCONSIN 5
Northern Milwaukee, Milwaukee County suburbs

The compact 5th takes in Milwaukee's North Side and its suburbs. The district encompasses most of the city's traditional German neighborhoods, its black neighborhoods and the affluent East Side.

The northern half of Milwaukee County had long been defined by the beer breweries that are now largely gone, but heavy manufacturing helped keep the 5th's blue-collar base.

Some of the richest and poorest Wisconsinites live in the 5th's Milwaukee, which remains one of the nation's most racially segregated cities. Mansions on Lake Michigan's shore have little in common with the inner-city African-American neighborhoods with double-digit unemployment. The city's population decrease in the 1990s came from white residents moving from the heart of Milwaukee to middle-class suburbs north and west of the city. What remains is Wisconsin's most diverse city; more Milwaukee residents now classify themselves as minority than as white.

With Wisconsin losing a congressional seat in the 2000 reapportionment, there is a strong possibility that the 5th might be combined with its southside neighbor, Milwaukee's 4th. The 5th is the nation's second least populated district, according to the 2000 Census.

Overall, the 5th is solidly Democratic and draws support from its substantial Democratic base of union workers and minorities. In recent years, Democratic federal candidates won with large majorities. Republicans entice a modicum of support from the well-to-do northeastern shore and western suburbs.

MAJOR INDUSTRY
Heavy manufacturing, education, service

CITIES
Milwaukee (pt.), 425,921 (1990); Wauwatosa, 45,405

UNUSUAL FEATURES
Home to Harley-Davidson; Last district in the nation to elect a Socialist Party member – Victor L. Berger, (1911-13, 1923-29); Milwaukee also has had three Socialist Party mayors, including the nation's first in a major city in 1910; Schlitz, "the beer that made Milwaukee famous," closed its Milwaukee brewery in 1981.

Rep. Tom Petri (R)

CAPITOL OFFICE
225-2476; fax 225-2356; 2462 Rayburn Bldg. 20515

INTERNET
e-mail: tompetri@mail.house.gov
web: www.house.gov/petri

COMMITTEES
Education & Workforce
Transportation & Infrastructure
(Highways & Transit - chairman)

HOMETOWN
Fond du Lac

BORN
May 28, 1940, Marinette, Wis.

RELIGION
Lutheran

FAMILY
Wife, Anne Neal Petri; one child

EDUCATION
Harvard U., A.B. 1962, J.D. 1965

CAREER
Lawyer; Peace Corps volunteer

POLITICAL HIGHLIGHTS
White House aide, 1969-70; Wis. Senate, 1973-79;
Republican nominee for U.S. Senate, 1974

ELECTION RESULTS

2000 GENERAL		
Tom Petri (R)	179,205	65.0%
Daniel Flaherty (D)	96,125	34.9%
2000 PRIMARY		
Tom Petri (R)	31,113	86.8%
John Moder (R)	4,713	13.2%
1998 GENERAL		
Tom Petri (R)	144,144	92.6%
Timothy Farness (TAX)	11,267	7.2%

PREVIOUS WINNING PERCENTAGES
1996 (73%); 1994 (100%); 1992 (53%); 1990 (100%);
1988 (74%); 1986 (97%); 1984 (76%); 1982 (65%);
1980 (59%); 1979 Special Election (50%)

Elected April 1979; 11th full term

Having lost his bid to become chairman of a full committee — Education and the Workforce — Petri must settle into another term wielding the gavel of a significant subcommittee at Transportation and Infrastructure. In a way, it is an odd post for Petri, who has cultivated a reputation as a critic of wasteful Washington spending.

Petri (PEA-try) is the second-ranking Republican on the Transportation Committee, which has become renowned for delivering billions of dollars in construction projects to congressional districts in the last half-decade, even while the GOP majority was espousing its commitment to governmental belt-tightening. In the 107th Congress, Petri finds himself at the helm of the Highways and Transit Subcommittee, a dream job for anyone who enjoys bringing home the federal bacon and helping colleagues do the same.

Petri, however, has made a practice of bestowing "Porker Awards" to highlight "waste resulting from federal activity," and he has been a prominent opponent of some proposed federal water projects in the West that have strong backing within his own party.

But if Petri is frugal, he also is amicable and pragmatic, a legislator willing to compromise. The dean of Wisconsin's delegation, Democratic Rep. David R. Obey, once commended Petri for sticking to his principles without translating "conservatism into meanness or zealousness." Petri has a reputation for eschewing the limelight and digging into the details of legislating.

Had seniority been the determining factor, Petri would have become chairman of Education and the Workforce in 2001, as the panel takes a lead role in turning into law President Bush's ambitious plans for overhauling federal education policy. Instead, House leaders decided to choose chairmen based on interviews and presentations. While several aspirants arrived for their interviews bearing gifts ranging from bags of peanuts to fancy lunch boxes, Petri came armed only with a six-point plan. "He's resisting that kind of razzmatazz," Petri's spokesman explained. The leadership picked John A. Boehner of Ohio.

Despite the setback, Petri can be expected to work diligently behind the scenes. He is a chairman's dream lieutenant, willing to take on the legislative legwork while giving the credit to his colleague with the gavel. He is also something of an institutionalist and one of the few members who have ever volunteered to sit on the House ethics committee. (He was on the panel when it considered the case that led to Speaker Jim Wright's resignation in 1989.)

As chairman of the Surface Transportation Subcommittee from 1995 through 2000, Petri worked in harness with full Transportation Committee Chairman Bud Shuster, R-Pa., to craft the most expensive transportation funding bill in U.S. history. It was enacted in 1998. A legion of House members endorsed what Shuster and Petri proposed, many of them hoping to get a generous slice of the bacon for their districts. Shuster and Petri overcame stiff resistance from House GOP leaders and fiscal conservatives, who argued that the bill cost $34 billion more than its allowance in the 1997 balanced-budget agreement.

As Shuster pressured GOP leaders for the funding level he wanted, he was portrayed as both persistent and obstinate. Petri made it through the negotiations with his reputation for mild-manneredness intact. And Wisconsin received a 48 percent boost in road funding, erasing its status as a "donor" state, one that contributes more in gasoline tax receipts than it gets back in federal aid. Considering his insider role, Petri did not secure all that much for his own constituents, just $22 million for a bypass near his home of Fond du Lac.

Even as he lobbied for the bill, Petri's penny-pinching side was evident as he kept up his quest to kill funding for the Auburn Dam in California, which at $950 million would be the most expensive American dam ever built, and for the Animas-La Plata water project in Colorado and New Mexico. He has aggressively monitored other big construction projects, decrying cost overruns on Boston's "Big Dig" highway project and on the replacement for the aging Woodrow Wilson Bridge, which spans the Potomac just south of Washington. His most successful attack on a pet project may have come in 1988, however, when he led an effort killing a bill that would have written off a federal loan for a library in honor of former Speaker Thomas P. "Tip" O'Neill Jr.

Petri's votes on education are in step with the conservative Republican line; he backs the school-choice agenda, which includes providing parents with taxpayer-financed vouchers to pay private school tuition for students in grades K-12. But he is one of the most vocal advocates among House Republicans for increasing the federal commitment to loans for higher education.

Petri votes with his party's anti-abortion majority and is a supporter of gun owners' rights. One of his most notable departures from the GOP has been his effort to expand the earned-income tax credit, a tax break for the working poor.

The congressman helps wage the Wisconsin delegation's perennial battle against federal milk price supports. He has called the program "an outdated relic of 1930s agriculture policy" and says that it helps milk producers in the Northeast and Southeast while hurting those in the Upper Midwest. The program was set up to encourage regional dairy production at a time when refrigeration was not advanced enough to permit long-distance transport.

Petri was born in northern Wisconsin, but he ranged far afield — to college and law school at Harvard, and to Somalia with the Peace Corps — before starting a law practice in Fond du Lac and winning a state Senate seat in 1972. He was the sacrificial GOP Senate nominee against Democrat Gaylord Nelson in 1974, a terrible year for Republicans after President Nixon's resignation. But the exposure helped him win a close contest for the House in a 1979 special election to replace GOP Rep. William A. Steiger, who had died. He has had mostly easy victories since then. But in 1992, Petri was hampered by negative publicity about his 77 overdrafts at the private bank for House members, and he garnered only 53 percent.

KEY VOTES

2000
No Raise hourly minimum wage by $1 over two years
Yes Halt funding for U.S. mission in Kosovo unless European nations pay more
Yes Provide Medicare benefits to military retirees and their dependents
Yes Grant China permanent normal trade status
Yes Phase out estate, gift and trust taxes
No Prohibit implementation of president's national monument designations
Yes Approve GOP plan to provide prescription drug coverage for Medicare beneficiaries
No Increase help for poor nations indebted to international financial institutions

1999
Yes Impose steel import quotas
No Kill proposal to take aviation trust funds off budget
Yes Require background checks on buyers only at gun shows with 10 or more vendors
Yes Remove barriers among banking, securities and insurance companies
No Authorize state grants to hire teachers and reduce class size
Yes Overhaul campaign finance law; ban "soft money" and restrict advocacy advertising
No Approve bipartisan plan to increase rights of patients in managed-care health plans

INTEREST GROUPS

	AFL-CIO	ADA	CCUS	ACU
2000	0%	10%	76%	84%
1999	22%	20%	88%	80%
1998	10%	15%	94%	88%
1997	38%	25%	80%	80%

CQ VOTE STUDIES

	PARTY UNITY		PRESIDENTIAL SUPPORT	
	Support	Oppose	Support	Oppose
2000	89%	11%	32%	68%
1999	86%	14%	22%	78%
1998	86%	14%	31%	69%
1997	84%	16%	29%	71%

WISCONSIN 6
Central – Oshkosh; Fond du Lac; Manitowoc

The 6th carves a swath across the middle of Wisconsin from Lake Michigan to a point 30 miles east of the Mississippi River, encompassing industrial parks, rural small towns, farmland and the state's largest inland body of water, Lake Winnebego.

Politically, the 6th is unusual. Although it has a higher percentage of blue-collar workers than any other district in the state, many vote Republican. Socially conservative Catholics and Lutherans, many with German ancestry, and a historical dominance by the local chambers of commerce forged a conservative region. Yet the 6th is still considered somewhat of a swing district. Voters chose George Bush for president in 1992, Bill Clinton in 1996 and President Bush in 2000.

The most Democratic county is Manitowoc, a prominent Lake Michigan ship-building center in the days when wooden vessels plied the seas. More than a third of the jobs in Manitowoc County are involved in manufacturing and processing, well above the statewide average, and unions are a significant force. Tourism also is important, with ferry service across the lake to Ludington, Mich.

The paper industry remains a dominant employer to the north and east, and towns like Oshkosh, Fond du Lac and Manitowoc form a scattered industrial corridor. Manufacturing is the backbone for much of the district, but farming also has a strong presence. After all-important dairying, output from the district's farms is diverse, including corn, peas, beans and cranberries.

MAJOR INDUSTRY
Paper, dairy, cranberries, tourism

MILITARY BASES
Fort McCoy (Army), 322 military, 1,669 civilian (1999)

CITIES
Oshkosh, 60,333; Fond du Lac, 40,987; Manitowoc, 33,491

UNUSUAL FEATURES
Ripon was one of the birthplaces of the Republican Party in 1854; Meeting of the Experimental Aircraft Association draws 750,000 people and 12,000 airplanes to Oshkosh each year.

Rep. David R. Obey (D)

Elected April 1969; 16th full term

During three decades, seven presidencies and countless battles for liberal causes, Obey has gained a reputation as a complex man of undisputed intelligence, occasionally irascible disposition and formidable legislative skill. His combustible manner and brutal honesty on the House floor are matched by his deep understanding of the policy preferences, procedures and politics at work behind the scenes.

Obey (OH-bee) considers himself an institutionalist, someone with respect for the House's ideals of civilized debate and collegiality. (He directed a rewrite of the House ethics code after a series of scandals in the 1970s.) Yet his pugnacity and partisanship are legendary on Capitol Hill, and with Republicans running not only Congress but also the White House, some of what he sees is simply more than he can bear.

Quite often, he seems close to boiling over, the array of long pencils in his shirt pocket threatening to topple out as he wags his finger in disgust at any number of GOP maneuvers. But he also shows a genial side, playing the harmonica in a bluegrass band and occasionally displaying a sense of humor. Asked, during a particularly tense moment in the 2000 budget negotiations, to predict when the 106th Congress would adjourn, Obey began warbling "Silent Night." (The session ended Dec. 15.)

Even as a member of the minority, where much of the game is making the majority look bad, Obey manifests a feeling of responsibility to the institution. When debate opened in 1998 on whether to conduct a full-scale impeachment inquiry of President Clinton, Obey took note of the many empty seats in the House chamber, spoke of the historical importance of the moment and urged both parties' leaders to direct their members to "get their tails here."

Obey spent a quarter-century in the House majority, and for the final nine months of 1994, he chaired the Appropriations Committee. While some long-tenured Democrats have retired rather than endure life in the minority, Obey still seems to relish the fight — framing it in unusually personal terms. Asked in 1998 if he might move on, he said with a grin, "I just wouldn't give the bastards the satisfaction."

Obey has remained in the spotlight because he is the ranking Democrat on Appropriations, where he takes a hands-on approach to managing each of the 13 spending bills. During the Clinton administration, he used the annual spending wars to sharpen his party's message to the public, all the while maneuvering to ensure the bills received Clinton's approval. With George W. Bush as president, he is positioned to take a lead role in opposing the White House's spending priorities.

Many Obey dust-ups have attracted attention. In 1997, he and Majority Whip Tom DeLay stood nearly toe-to-toe, shouting and jabbing fingers toward each other until an aide separated them. (DeLay was incensed that Obey had suggested lobbyists were improperly helping to draft GOP legislation.) But Republicans are not the only ones who have felt Obey's wrath. His temper was an issue in his failed campaign to chair the Budget Committee two decades ago, and once, after a policy dispute, he referred to Clinton as a "goddamn liar." Still, Obey resisted the GOP drive to impeach Clinton, saying he doubted the House had the "capacity to handle a parking case fairly, much less something of this importance."

Although he lists his occupation as real estate broker, Obey has been a legislator almost all his adult life. He was elected to the Wisconsin state

CAPITOL OFFICE
225-3365; fax 225-3240; 2314 Rayburn Bldg. 20515

INTERNET
e-mail: www.house.gov/writerep
web: www.house.gov/obey

COMMITTEES
Appropriations - ranking member

HOMETOWN
Wausau

BORN
Oct. 3, 1938, Okmulgee, Okla.

RELIGION
Roman Catholic

FAMILY
Wife, Joan Obey; two children

EDUCATION
U. of Wisconsin, B.S. 1960, M.A. 1962

CAREER
Real estate broker

POLITICAL HIGHLIGHTS
Wis. Assembly, 1963-69

ELECTION RESULTS

2000 GENERAL

David R. Obey (D)	173,007	63.3%
Sean Cronin (R)	100,264	36.7%

2000 PRIMARY

David R. Obey (D)	unopposed

1998 GENERAL

David R. Obey (D)	115,613	60.6%
Scott West (R)	75,049	39.3%

PREVIOUS WINNING PERCENTAGES
1996 (57%); 1994 (54%); 1992 (64%); 1990 (62%); 1988 (62%); 1986 (62%); 1984 (61%); 1982 (68%); 1980 (65%); 1978 (62%); 1976 (73%); 1974 (71%); 1972 (63%); 1970 (68%); 1969 Special Election (52%)

House when he was 24 and won election to the U.S. House at age 30, in a 1969 special election to succeed Melvin R. Laird, the first defense secretary of the Nixon administration. Obey was the first Democrat ever to represent the 7th District, and he has won at least 60 percent in all but two of his 16 re-election races. And for all his liberal passion, he understands that law-making involves compromise. "There's a distinction between what you believe as an individual member ... the philosophy that drives you, versus what your obligation is to the House as a whole to try to solve problems and bridge differences," he said while chairing Appropriations.

During that brief period, Obey worked as a troubleshooter, speeding enactment of spending bills by seeking out GOP members and resolving problems before they caused delays. As a result, all 13 measures became law by the start of the fiscal year, a rare occurrence in recent years.

In the minority, he has been prescient on several fiscal matters. In 1997, he warned that Congress could not stay within the budget "caps" central to that year's balanced-budget agreement; they have been repeatedly broken. As the 105th ended, he thanked Republicans for taking a hard line, pre-dicting — accurately, as it turned out — that as a consequence, the Demo-crats would do well in the year-end appropriations battle.

"I get a great release and I find it very relaxing to simply be able to tell peo-ple what I know is the reality and not have to dance around a dozen fictions," Obey once said. "Time has a way of demonstrating whether you know what you're talking about or whether you're a damn fool," he added.

Obey's reputation as a liberal stalwart stems from his tussles with Repub-licans over fiscal policy. But, mindful of sentiment in his largely rural and small-town district, he supports gun owners' rights and votes a restrictive line on some abortion issues; for example, he supported a ban of a proce-dure its opponents call "partial birth" abortion.

Obey, who grew up in a staunchly Republican family, once hitched a wagon to his bicycle and campaigned door to door in his hometown of Wausau for GOP Sen. Joseph R. McCarthy and presidential candidate Dwight D. Eisenhower. But he says that he reconsidered when McCarthy followers on the local school board tried to have his high school history teacher "canned for being a Bolshevik" — actually, for teaching that the polit-ical platform of the U.S. Chamber of Commerce and the U.S. Constitution were not necessarily the same thing. "When I saw what McCarthyism did to the best teacher I ever had," he said, "it showed me that if you had any dedication to individual liberty and freedom of speech, that at that time in that county, there was no room for you in the local Republican Party."

KEY VOTES

2000
Yes Raise hourly minimum wage by $1 over two years
No Halt funding for U.S. mission in Kosovo unless European nations pay more
Yes Provide Medicare benefits to military retirees and their dependents
No Grant China permanent normal trade status
No Phase out estate, gift and trust taxes
No Prohibit implementation of president's national monument designations
No Approve GOP plan to provide prescription drug coverage for Medicare beneficiaries
Yes Increase help for poor nations indebted to international financial institutions

1999
Yes Impose steel import quotas
Yes Kill proposal to take aviation trust funds off budget
No Require background checks on buyers only at gun shows with 10 or more vendors
No Remove barriers among banking, securities and insurance companies
Yes Authorize state grants to hire teachers and reduce class size
Yes Overhaul campaign finance law; ban "soft money" and restrict advocacy advertising
Yes Approve bipartisan plan to increase rights of patients in managed-care health plans

INTEREST GROUPS

	AFL-CIO	ADA	CCUS	ACU
2000	100%	95%	15%	4%
1999	100%	90%	4%	4%
1998	100%	95%	11%	16%
1997	100%	80%	30%	21%

CQ VOTE STUDIES

	PARTY UNITY		PRESIDENTIAL SUPPORT	
	Support	Oppose	Support	Oppose
2000	94%	6%	82%	18%
1999	87%	13%	80%	20%
1998	92%	8%	89%	11%
1997	90%	10%	71%	29%

WISCONSIN 7
Northwest — Wausau; Superior; Stevens Point

Encompassing more than one-fourth of the state, the 7th is the most rural district in Wisconsin. Small towns and villages, not farms, dominate the district's northern counties, where the weather makes the growing season 30 days shorter than at the Illinois border. Hundreds of lakes in the north create a tranquil lifestyle that draws more senior citizens than any other region in the state.

In the south, nutrient rich soil engenders ideal farming, although the once-dominant dairy industry has declined since the 1980s. Smaller farms, which once thrived here, are shutting down, causing farmers to sell their land to large farms or developers building suburban homes. But cities along the Wisconsin River have enjoyed a small boom in recent years from paper production and some service industries.

While the same Democrat has held the 7th's congressional seat since 1969, without strong Democratic candidates at the top of the district's ticket, some observers think the region could lean Republican.

Democrats lure strong support from the blue-collar centers of Wausau and Stevens Point in the mostly Polish south, and in Superior to the north. But the mostly Scandinavian descendants of the rural north, as well as the more recently vocal Christian Right, make some areas of the district more competitive.

MAJOR INDUSTRY
Paper, manufacturing, dairy farming

CITIES
Wausau, 36,726; Superior, 27,339; Stevens Point, 23,266; Wisconsin Rapids, 18,718

UNUSUAL FEATURES
Marathon County is the nation's largest producer of ginseng; Poniatowski is exact center of the northern half of the western hemisphere; Colby cheese named after a district town; Hayward is home to the National Fresh Water Fishing Hall of Fame.

Rep. Mark Green (R)

CAPITOL OFFICE
225-5665; fax 225-5729
1218 Longworth Bldg. 20515

INTERNET
e-mail: mark.green@mail.house.gov
web: www.house.gov/markgreen

COMMITTEES
Financial Services
Judiciary

HOMETOWN
Green Bay

BORN
June 1, 1960, Boston, Mass.

RELIGION
Roman Catholic

FAMILY
Wife, Susan Green; three children

EDUCATION
U. of Wisconsin, Eau Claire, B.A. 1983; U. of
Wisconsin, Madison, J.D. 1987

CAREER
Lawyer; teacher

POLITICAL HIGHLIGHTS
Wis. Assembly, 1993-99

ELECTION RESULTS

2000 GENERAL

Mark Green (R)	211,388	74.6%
Dean Reich (D)	71,575	25.3%

2000 PRIMARY

Mark Green (R)	unopposed

1998 GENERAL

Mark Green (R)	112,418	54.6%
Jay W. Johnson (D)	93,441	45.4%

Elected 1998; 2nd term

Green says a teaching stint with his wife in a remote Kenyan village helped shape his views and started him thinking about a career in politics — a career that began before his immigrant parents were even eligible to vote. He says the Kenyan experience "sensitized me to the problems of the human condition," but he also came away with the belief that government policies can stifle economic opportunity.

Green calls himself a "bleeding heart conservative," saying he has a commitment to social policy, but moderates it with the belief that government should get out of the way. Yet Green does not subscribe to the anti-government rhetoric that some conservatives spout. "I believe in limited government, not in getting rid of it," he told the Milwaukee Journal Sentinel.

As a freshman in the 106th Congress, Green led some members of the Class of 1998 in developing legislation to make it easier for state governments to win federal approval to try innovative approaches to solving social problems. Wisconsin has been a leader in experimenting with ways to improve programs such as welfare. Green had a front-row seat in those efforts as a three-term member of the state Assembly before winning election to Congress.

When he arrived in Washington, Green announced that he intended to focus on taxes, and he did push for the Republican tax agenda from his seat on the Budget Committee. But Green made his biggest splash on the social policy front.

Foremost was his proposal to impose life prison sentences on second-time sex offenders. He based his "two strikes — they're out" bill on similar legislation he had written in the Wisconsin legislature. The measure, which gained House passage in 2000, was predicated on studies indicating that sex offenders usually repeat their crime. "The sad reality is that pedophiles re-offend over and over again until they are removed from society once and for all," he said on the House floor. "This bill is not ... about deterrence. It is about removing bad people from society." In the 107th Congress, Green gained a seat on the Judiciary Committee, where he will continue to pursue his "two strikes" bill. He also received an assignment on the Financial Services Committee (formerly Banking).

In his first term, Green drafted several other legislative proposals, including a bill to give financial assistance to law enforcement officers who purchase homes in high-crime areas and another to help disabled people buy homes.

As the only Republican to knock off an incumbent House Democrat in 1998, Green was well-treated by party leaders when he arrived in Washington. He received a spot in the GOP whip organization and a place on the Republican Policy Committee and is a member of the executive board of the National Republican Campaign Committee. Green's first-term voting record will give the GOP leadership no cause to regret its confidence in him.

Green also tends to the home fires. Lawmakers from Wisconsin must involve themselves in dairy policy, and Green was in the midst of a significant battle in the 106th Congress. Green and other Badger State lawmakers favored an administration proposal to rewrite the Depression-era milk-pricing policy that had given milk producers in other regions a better deal in order to help them compete with producers in the Upper Midwest.

Lawmakers from other regions were able to block the milk-pricing changes, leading Green to declare: "This place is locked in a time warp. This place is using a milk-pricing mechanism that was created in the era of the manual typewriter." He said he was disappointed that the Clinton administration had not fought harder for the proposed policy. Green also sought to help Wisconsin farmers by pushing to liberalize the income-averaging provisions of the tax code and by supporting better tax treatment for the sale of a family farm to another member of the same family.

On one issue of particular interest to his state, Green urged that Wisconsin prisoners who are housed in out-of-state prisons be counted as Wisconsin residents. Green said he was concerned that a reduction in the state's population would cost Wisconsin millions of dollars in federal spending. As it turned out, Green's proposal would not have enabled Wisconsin to retain its nine House seats in the post-census reapportionment.

For the 107th Congress, Green said he wants President Bush to declare a national mission — similar to President Kennedy's challenge to put a man on the moon — to develop cures for diseases such as cancer and diabetes.

Green's family moved to Green Bay when he was 5 years old, ending a long journey for both his parents. His father, a physician, was born in South Africa and grew up in Kenya. His mother, who trained as a nurse, is from England. They did not become U.S. citizens until 1995.

Green was a champion swimmer in college. After graduation, he went to law school and worked in the office of the state's attorney general. When he finished law school, Green and his wife took teaching assignments in Kenya, as Green wanted to visit his father's former home.

When they returned from Africa, Green joined a law firm in Green Bay and became active in local party politics. In 1992, he won the first of three two-year terms in the Assembly, where he chaired the Judiciary Committee and the Republican Caucus. He was called a "rising star" in a survey of state capital insiders conducted by Madison Magazine.

He declined to run for the 8th District seat in 1996, when longtime GOP Rep. Toby Roth retired, but he was fast out of the blocks in the 1998 election as the GOP sought to prove that Democrat Jay Johnson's 1996 victory was a fluke in a district that had sent a Democrat to Washington just four times in the 20th century.

Green focused on the philosophical differences between himself and Johnson. He kept pace with Johnson in fundraising and portrayed the incumbent as too liberal for the district, and voters agreed. The final tally gave Green a 9 percentage point victory, the second-largest margin of victory over an incumbent in 1998. In 2000, he cruised to re-election, winning about three-fourths of the votes.

KEY VOTES

2000
No Raise hourly minimum wage by $1 over two years
Yes Halt funding for U.S. mission in Kosovo unless European nations pay more
Yes Provide Medicare benefits to military retirees and their dependents
Yes Grant China permanent normal trade status
Yes Phase out estate, gift and trust taxes
Yes Prohibit implementation of president's national monument designations
Yes Approve GOP plan to provide prescription drug coverage for Medicare beneficiaries
No Increase help for poor nations indebted to international financial institutions

1999
No Impose steel import quotas
Yes Kill proposal to take aviation trust funds off budget
Yes Require background checks on buyers only at gun shows with 10 or more vendors
Yes Remove barriers among banking, securities and insurance companies
No Authorize state grants to hire teachers and reduce class size
No Overhaul campaign finance law; ban "soft money" and restrict advocacy advertising
No Approve bipartisan plan to increase rights of patients in managed-care health plans

INTEREST GROUPS

	AFL-CIO	ADA	CCUS	ACU
2000	10%	5%	85%	84%
1999	0%	5%	92%	87%

CQ VOTE STUDIES

	PARTY UNITY		PRESIDENTIAL SUPPORT	
	Support	Oppose	Support	Oppose
2000	93%	7%	22%	78%
1999	90%	10%	21%	79%

WISCONSIN 8
Northeast – Green Bay; Appleton

The emotional heart of Wisconsin beats in the 8th at the southern end of a bay – Green Bay. The Green Bay Packers football team has focused international attention on the region and pulled in millions of dollars. But it's the paper industry along Green Bay and around Appleton – and the surrounding Fox River Valley – that solidifies the area as blue collar.

The sparsely populated north holds the state's largest tracts of forests, supplying the local paper industry. The natural resources-dependent economy here is generally stable, and the land also supports grain and dairy farming. Nature-loving tourists and vacation homeowners flock to the hundreds of lakes nearby in Vilas County, in a lakes region on the Michigan border. But the wealthiest residents head for Wisconsin's northeast peninsula, Door County, which is rich with apple orchards and second homes.

The 8th is a swing district and in 1998 saw a Republican

congressman elected after a one-term Democrat. On the presidential level, the district voted for George Bush in 1992, Bill Clinton in 1996 and President Bush in 2000. Republicans dominate except in a densely populated blue-collar pocket centered in Green Bay. In the north, the GOP taps into a traditional small government attitude. To the south, with the exception of the Appleton region, the Fox River Valley favors conservative Democrats.

Historically, Appleton has welcomed right-wing sympathizers and is the home of the conservative John Birch Society and the late GOP Sen. Joseph R. McCarthy.

MAJOR INDUSTRY
Casinos, paper products, health care

CITIES
Green Bay, 98,362; Appleton (pt.), 59,422 (1990); De Pere, 19,978

UNUSUAL FEATURES
Seven of 11 Indian reservations in Wisconsin; More than 50-year wait for season tickets to the Packers – 56,000 people are in line before you.

Rep. F. James Sensenbrenner Jr. (R)

Elected 1978; 12th term

CAPITOL OFFICE
225-5101; fax 225-3190; 2332 Rayburn Bldg. 20515

INTERNET
e-mail: sensen09@mail.house.gov
web: www.house.gov/sensenbrenner

COMMITTEES
Judiciary - chairman

HOMETOWN
Menomonee Falls

BORN
June 14, 1943, Chicago, Ill.

RELIGION
Episcopalian

FAMILY
Wife, Cheryl Warren; two children

EDUCATION
Stanford U., A.B. 1965; U. of Wisconsin, J.D. 1968

CAREER
Lawyer

POLITICAL HIGHLIGHTS
Wis. Assembly, 1969-75; Wis. Senate, 1975-79

ELECTION RESULTS

2000 GENERAL

James Sensenbrenner (R)	239,498	74.0%
Mike Clawson (D)	83,720	25.9%

2000 PRIMARY

James Sensenbrenner (R)	unopposed

1998 GENERAL

James Sensenbrenner (R)	175,533	91.4%
Jeffrey M. Gonyo (INDC)	16,419	8.6%

PREVIOUS WINNING PERCENTAGES
1996 (74%); 1994 (100%); 1992 (70%); 1990 (100%);
1988 (75%); 1986 (78%); 1984 (73%); 1982 (100%);
1980 (78%); 1978 (61%)

A blunt-spoken conservative with a quick temper, Sensenbrenner reached a milestone in a long legislative career by being named chairman of the Judiciary Committee at the start of the 107th Congress. But he nearly did not get the job, as Republican leaders first considered offering former Chairman Henry J. Hyde of Illinois a waiver from GOP term limit rules so he could keep the post he had held for six years. Then, Sensenbrenner had to win a Steering Committee vote over a challenge from George W. Gekas of Pennsylvania.

Sensenbrenner's ascent represented a vindication of sorts. During the 104th Congress, he was passed over for a Judiciary subcommittee chairmanship despite being the third-most-senior Republican of the entire committee. At the time, it was noted that even some in his own party found Sensenbrenner's personality less than endearing. In 1997, he was given the chairmanship of the Science Committee, where he fostered cooperative relations with the top-ranking Democrat, George E. Brown Jr. of California, and after Brown's death, Ralph M. Hall of Texas.

Sensenbrenner, who was one of the House prosecutors in the 1999 Senate impeachment trial of President Clinton, and who has not shied away from partisan behavior, nevertheless put the new Bush administration on notice that he planned to conduct vigorous oversight of the Republican administration's actions.

Sensenbrenner is a staunch foe of abortion and opposes most restrictions on gun ownership. However, he supports a five-day waiting period for handgun purchases, citing the success of Wisconsin's 48-hour "cooling off" period. Sensenbrenner was an original cosponsor of the 1996 "Defense of Marriage Act," which barred federal recognition of same-sex marriage. He also has introduced legislation on several occasions that would clarify the role of federal courts in class-action lawsuits.

At the helm of the Science Committee, Sensenbrenner had to contend with inevitable turf battles with other House committees and indifference to science bills from the Senate — problems that traditionally plague the Science panel. His major accomplishment in the 106th Congress was shepherding the first reauthorization bill for NASA since 1992.

The measure, which authorized $42.4 billion over three years for the space agency, was the product of nearly two years of on-and-off negotiations that stalled over such issues as the cost and scope of the International Space Station and an earth observation satellite that would beam images of Earth to the Internet. The impasse was broken after Sensenbrenner and House negotiators dropped their opposition to the satellite in exchange for cost controls on the space station.

Under Sensenbrenner, the Science Committee showed bipartisan support for NASA and the space station, even in the face of cost overruns and delays. However, Sensenbrenner's personal relationship with NASA Administrator Daniel Goldin was rocky. Sensenbrenner questioned Goldin's oversight of the space station project after Russia failed to deliver a critical service module on time, and relations between the two men were so chilly that they did not exchange the customary handshake or even acknowledge each other before the start of one oversight hearing.

Sensenbrenner has been skeptical of other "big science" projects, as evidenced by his 1993 vote to halt funding for the atom-smashing superconducting super collider. And there was a more partisan edge to another of his causes as Science chairman: opposing ratification of the Kyoto international climate-control treaty, which calls on the United States and other developed nations to reduce greenhouse gas emissions by 2012. Sensenbrenner criticized the Clinton administration for not including developing nations in the pact — an omission that he and many Republicans said could push U.S. manufacturing jobs to less-industrialized Third World nations.

One of the wealthiest members of Congress, Sensenbrenner is heir to a paper and cellulose manufacturing fortune, most of which stems from his great-grandfather's invention of the sanitary napkin shortly after World War I. Marketing it under the brand name Kotex, Sensenbrenner's ancestor went on to become the chairman of Kimberly-Clark.

Sensenbrenner added to his wealth late in 1997, when he won $250,000 in the District of Columbia's lottery. He purchased the ticket while buying beer for an office Christmas party and then left town for the holidays. Two weeks later, he returned to cash the ticket, thinking he had just won $10. He gave some of the winnings to charity and invested the rest.

Sensenbrenner has held public office practically since his 1968 graduation from law school. His personal resources and conservative views have earned him an undefeated record at the polls — even though his personality rubs some the wrong way.

To reach Congress in 1978, Sensenbrenner had to dip into the family coffers to overcome a strong GOP primary challenge. With Republican Bob Kasten giving up the 9th District seat to run for governor, Sensenbrenner was viewed as the obvious successor. He had been elected to four terms in the state Assembly before moving in 1975 to the state Senate, where he rose to be assistant minority leader. He had a solid political base in the older, more affluent lakeside suburbs, and his conservative bent reminded voters of the popular Kasten.

But his opponent in the primary was Susan Engeleiter, a state legislator who would later become state Senate GOP leader, the Republican nominee for U.S. Senate in 1988 and then director of the Small Business Administration. Sensenbrenner was familiar enough to voters in the most Republican of Milwaukee's suburbs that he managed to squeak by in the primary by 589 votes.

The 1978 Democratic nominee, Milwaukee lawyer Matthew J. Flynn, was also on his way to higher visibility in statewide politics as Democratic Party chairman and U.S. Senate candidate. But he could not raise enough money to compete successfully. Sensenbrenner stressed his support for cutting taxes and defeated Flynn by a solid margin. Re-election has come easily since and in some elections, he has not had Democratic opposition.

KEY VOTES

2000

No	Raise hourly minimum wage by $1 over two years
Yes	Halt funding for U.S. mission in Kosovo unless European nations pay more
No	Provide Medicare benefits to military retirees and their dependents
No	Grant China permanent normal trade status
Yes	Phase out estate, gift and trust taxes
Yes	Prohibit implementation of president's national monument designations
Yes	Approve GOP plan to provide prescription drug coverage for Medicare beneficiaries
Yes	Increase help for poor nations indebted to international financial institutions

1999

No	Impose steel import quotas
Yes	Kill proposal to take aviation trust funds off budget
Yes	Require background checks on buyers only at gun shows with 10 or more vendors
Yes	Remove barriers among banking, securities and insurance companies
No	Authorize state grants to hire teachers and reduce class size
No	Overhaul campaign finance law; ban "soft money" and restrict advocacy advertising
No	Approve bipartisan plan to increase rights of patients in managed-care health plans

INTEREST GROUPS

	AFL-CIO	ADA	CCUS	ACU
2000	22%	20%	70%	88%
1999	11%	10%	80%	96%
1998	0%	5%	78%	92%
1997	13%	20%	80%	88%

CQ VOTE STUDIES

	PARTY UNITY		PRESIDENTIAL SUPPORT	
	Support	Oppose	Support	Oppose
2000	91%	9%	20%	80%
1999	92%	8%	21%	79%
1998	86%	14%	22%	78%
1997	88%	12%	32%	68%

WISCONSIN 9

Milwaukee suburbs; part of Waukesha County; Sheboygan

Wisconsin's most suburban and well-to-do district, the 9th attracts middle managers moving out of Milwaukee County and those transferred into the state. Rising property values have provided lifelong dairy farmers with retirement nest eggs as they sell land to housing developers. Where dairy once dominated, a suburban ring has formed along Ozaukee County, West Bend and northern Waukesha County.

A growing manufacturing base, led by the expanding Quad Graphics Inc. (which prints Time and Newsweek, among other titles), attracts blue-collar workers to the area. In the west, the district also includes Dodge and Jefferson counties, where small towns and dairy farms dominate but are being encroached upon by suburban sprawl. In Dodge County, Waupun is a major state prison site, Beaver Dam is a resort community, and the Horicon Marsh is a federal and state preserve for geese and ducks.

Republicans hold a firm grip on the 9th, where Democratic presidential candidates have failed to muster 40 percent of the vote since before 1980. With the highest median income in the state (calculated against 1990 Census Bureau statistics) and a religious fervor, the 9th votes conservatively on pocketbook issues and prefers its lawmakers to concur with the Christian Coalition. The strongest concentration of Democrats is in the district's portion of Waukesha County, in the Milwaukee sphere. But most of the county's Democratic areas are in the neighboring 4th.

MAJOR INDUSTRY
Printing, manufacturing, agriculture

CITIES
Sheboygan, 49,558; Brookfield, 38,290; Menomonee Falls, 31,925; West Bend, 29,095; Mequon, 22,321

UNUSUAL FEATURES
Waubeka, the birthplace of Flag Day; Sheboygan considered the bratwurst capital of the world.

WYOMING

Gov. Jim Geringer (R)

First elected: 1994
Length of term: 4 years
Term expires: 1/03
Salary: $95,000
Phone: (307) 777-7434
Hometown: Wheatland
Born: April 24, 1944; Wheatland, Wyo.
Religion: Lutheran
Family: Wife, Sherri Geringer; five children
Education: Kansas State U., B.S. 1967
Military service: Air Force, 1967-77; Air Force Reserve, 1977-91
Career: Farmer
Political highlights: Wyo. House, 1982-88; Wyo. Senate, 1988-94

Election results:

1998 GENERAL

Jim Geringer (R)	97,235	55.6%
John P. Vinich (D)	70,754	40.5%
Dave Dawson (LIBERT)	6,899	3.9%

Secretary of State Joe Meyer (R)

(no lieutenant governor)
First elected: 1998
Length of term: 4 years
Term expires: 1/03
Salary: $77,000
Phone: (307) 777-7378

STATE LEGISLATURE

General Assembly: Meets January-March in odd-numbered years, February-March in even-numbered years
House: 60 members, 2-year terms
2001 breakdown: 46R, 14D; 51 men, 9 women
Salary: $125/day in session
Phone: (307) 777-7852
Senate: 30 members, 4-year terms
2001 breakdown: 20R, 10D; 25 men, 5 women
Salary: $125/day in session
Phone: (307) 777-7711

STATE TERM LIMITS

Governor: 2 terms
Senate: 3 terms
House: 3 terms

URBAN STATISTICS

CITY	POPULATION
Cheyenne	53,925
Casper	48,233
Laramie	24,905

REGISTERED VOTERS

Republican	60%
Democrat	30%
Other	10%

POPULATION

2000 population	493,782
1990 population	453,588
Percent change	+8.9%
Rank among states	50
Median age	35.2
Born in state	43%
Foreign born	2%
Urban/rural	65%/35%
Crime rate	255/100,000
Poverty level	10.6%
Federal workers	7,034
Military	6,349

REAPPORTIONMENT

Wyoming retained its one House seat in reapportionment.

MISCELLANEOUS

Web: www.state.wy.us
Capital: Cheyenne
Land area: 97,105 sq. miles
Rank among states: 9
STATE ELECTION OFFICIAL
(307) 777-7186
DEMOCRATIC HEADQUARTERS
(307) 637-8940
REPUBLICAN HEADQUARTERS
(307) 234-9166

District Statistics

DIST.	2000 D	2000 R	GREEN	1996 D	1996 R	REF	1992 D	1992 R	I	WHT	BLK	ASIAN	HISP	HOUSEHOLD INCOME	OVER 65+	UNDER 18	COLLEGE EDUCATION
AL	28%	68%	2%	37%	50%	12%	34%	40%	26%	94%	1%	1%	6%	$27,096	10%	30%	19%

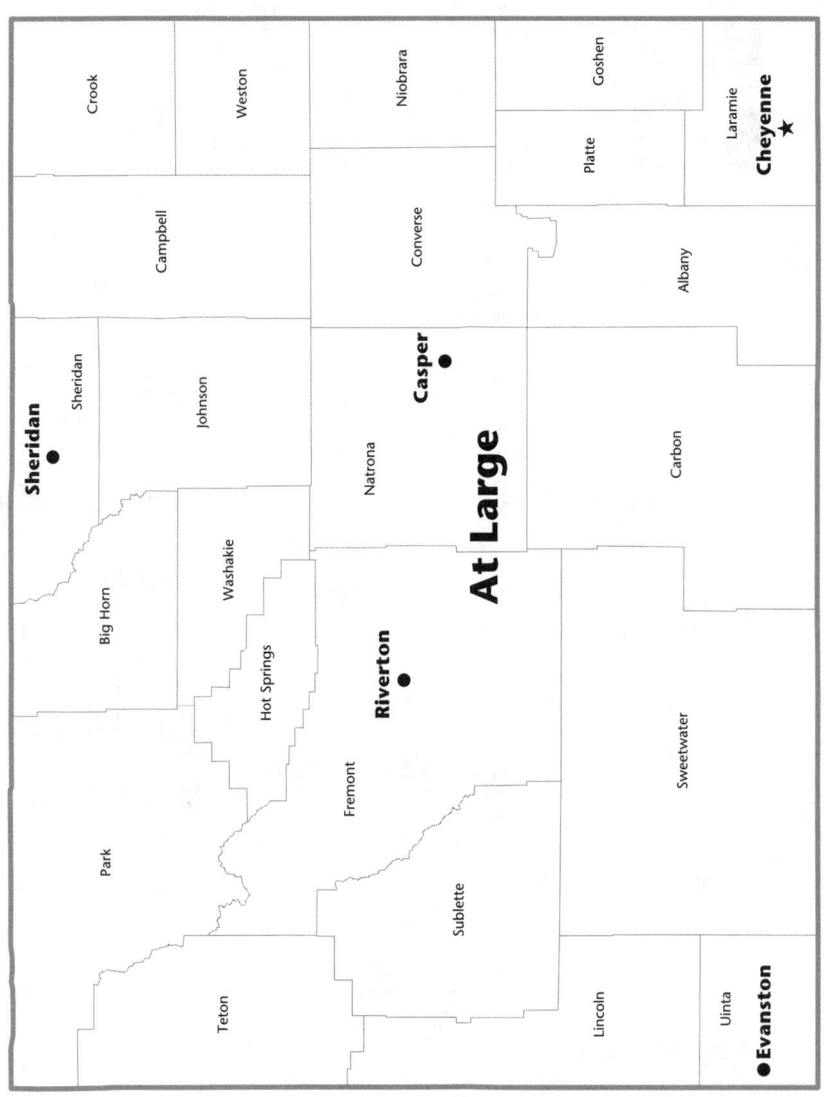

www.cq.com

Sen. Craig Thomas (R)

CAPITOL OFFICE
224-6441; fax 224-1724; 109 Hart Bldg. 20510

INTERNET
e-mail: craig@thomas.senate.gov
web: thomas.senate.gov

COMMITTEES
Agriculture, Nutrition & Forestry
Energy & Natural Resources
  (National Parks, Historic Preservation &
  Recreation - chairman)
Foreign Relations
  (East Asian & Pacific Affairs - chairman)
Indian Affairs
Select Ethics

HOMETOWN
Casper

BORN
Feb. 17, 1933, Cody, Wyo.

RELIGION
Methodist

FAMILY
Wife, Susan Thomas; four children

EDUCATION
U. of Wyoming, B.A. 1955; La Salle U., LL.B. 1963

MILITARY SERVICE
Marine Corps, 1955-59

CAREER
Power company executive

POLITICAL HIGHLIGHTS
Sought Republican nomination for Wyo. treasurer,
1978, 1982; Wyo. House, 1985-89; U.S. House,
1989-95

ELECTION RESULTS

2000 GENERAL
Craig Thomas (R)	157,622	73.8%
Mel Logan (D)	47,087	22.0%
Margaret Dawson (LIBERT)	8,950	4.2%

2000 PRIMARY
Craig Thomas (R)	unopposed

PREVIOUS WINNING PERCENTAGES
1994 (59%); 1992 House Election (58%);
1990 House Election (55%); 1989 Special
House Election (52%)

Elected 1994; 2nd term

Thomas' job, as he sees it, is to watch out for Wyoming's farmers and ranchers. Few senators focus on their home state interests as ardently as Thomas. Yet he also takes a diplomatic approach to politics, striving to maintain good communication with Senate Democrats. "Being able to communicate with them allows you to have some input without confrontation," he says.

An affable man with a low-key legislative approach, Thomas is a former Marine Corps captain and power company executive. He grew up on a ranch outside Cody and has maintained close ties to his state's ranchers, once serving as vice president of the Wyoming Farm Bureau. He has devoted himself to defending Wyoming's oil and agriculture industries, as well as trying to wrest control of public lands from the federal government.

About half the land in Wyoming is controlled by the federal government, and Thomas is adept at using his seat on the Energy and Natural Resources Committee to try to prevent the government from shortchanging commercial interests.

He tangled repeatedly with the Clinton administration, denouncing President Clinton's decisions during the 106th Congress to set aside land in national monuments without seeking approval from Congress and warning that limiting access to the lands could set back local economies. Like President Bush, he wants to expand oil and gas production. Thomas also gained a seat on the Agriculture Committee in the 107th Congress.

In the 106th, Thomas successfully delayed a Clinton administration initiative to ban snowmobiles in Yellowstone and other national parks, an issue that is likely to resurface in the 107th Congress. "A unilateral move to simply force visitors out is counter to the very nature of what our parks were established for, in favor of a 'look but do not touch' policy," Thomas said. "The repercussions of this action go well beyond just sticking it to snow machine users and will be opposed vigorously in Congress."

In 1999, Thomas introduced a measure to restrict federal control over land-use policies by giving more input to local officials. "By mandating that local communities be consulted, decisions ultimately will better reflect the needs of the people who depend on these areas for economic survival," he said. When Congress weighed legislation to spend billions of dollars on land purchases to create parks and protect wildlife habitat, he insisted that the federal government focus instead on improving maintenance of the land it already owned rather than acquire more.

The National Park Service's maintenance backlog has been a major concern for Thomas. He successfully pushed an extension of an experimental fee program that allowed more than 300 federal parks and recreation areas to collect $180 million in new money in 1998. He also won passage of a bill allowing the Park Service to ultimately earn an 8 percent royalty from all concession sales, rather than an average 3 percent, and won passage of legislation to create a Yellowstone National Park commemorative silver dollar to raise money for parks.

Although Thomas' parks legislation had bipartisan backing, his proposals have at times earned Republicans something of a black eye on environmental issues. In the 104th Congress, for example, he took the lead on a high-profile measure that would have allowed 12 Western states to take control of 270 million acres of federal land, including wilderness areas that are among the nation's few remaining pristine ecosystems. Thomas said the states could do a better job overseeing the lands than the federal Bureau of Land Management. But his advocacy of the proposal earned a lot of press attention at a time when Republicans were under pressure to prove they cared about protecting the environment. Thomas reluctantly delayed the bill, saying, "This is a concept, a fundamental change that should be talked about in the next few years."

Rural health care is another top concern for Thomas. In 1999, he won a $500,000 grant to build Wyoming's first community health care center. The co-chairman of the Senate Rural Health Caucus, Thomas has pressed for legislation that would increase physician recruitment incentives, equalize Medicare payments between rural and urban programs and help fund "telemedicine" programs. He also supports measures to increase high-speed Internet access to rural areas and boost funding for rural airports.

When he is not thinking about Wyoming and Western land issues, Thomas turns his attention to the Far East. As chairman of Foreign Relations' East Asian and Pacific Affairs Subcommittee, he says he has learned to appreciate the sensitivity that diplomacy requires. "People tend to think that we're all on the Internet, therefore we understand each other, and that's not true," he says. "The cultures and, in many ways, the values are still quite different."

He voted in 2000 to grant China permanent normal trade status, though many religious conservatives favored sanctioning China for its human rights practices. "Wyoming is an exporting state," he said. "Nearly 50 percent of our products are sold outside the U.S. So when the most populous country in the world is forced to take down its protectionist walls, our producers will sell more goods and our workers will benefit."

Thomas is a reliable advocate of GOP tax cutting plans. He is particularly focused on doing away with the estate tax, which has forced many ranchers and farmers to sell their lands. "When they are forced to sell to pay the tax man these open spaces are sometimes lost forever," Thomas said. He looks skeptically on government spending programs, and he broke ranks with GOP leaders in late 1998 to vote against a massive, end-of-session appropriations measure because it would have increased spending by billions of dollars.

A boyhood friend of former GOP Wyoming Sen. Alan K. Simpson, Thomas was initially viewed as something less than a juggernaut in Wyoming politics. He twice sought the GOP nomination for state treasurer, losing both times.

But in 1984, at age 51, he was elected to the Wyoming House, where he was serving four years later when GOP Rep. Dick Cheney was picked by President George Bush to be secretary of defense. Thomas got the nod from the party's state central committee and won the special election to succeed Cheney with 52 percent.

One of the safest places for a Republican senator is in Wyoming, where Democrats have not won a Senate election since 1970. Thomas' 1994 campaign to succeed retiring Republican Sen. Malcolm Wallop banked on the idea that Wyoming voters would want another senator just as ready and willing to fight the Democratic Clinton administration as Wallop was.

As it turned out, Thomas had read the tea leaves and the voters' mood pretty well. The Democrats nominated popular Gov. Mike Sullivan, but it made no difference. While Sullivan was hardly a liberal, he had a link to Clinton that dated from their service together in the National Governors Association, and he was the first sitting governor to endorse Clinton for the presidency. Thomas won handily by almost 20 percentage points.

In 2000, he did even better, swamping his Democratic foe by a better than 3-1 ratio.

KEY VOTES

2000

Yes Overhaul bankruptcy law and increase minimum wage

Yes Limit fiscal 2001 discretionary spending to $600.3 billion

Yes Override veto on nuclear waste disposal at Yucca Mountain site in Nevada

No Oppose effort to terminate Kosovo mission

No Include gender, sexual orientation and disability in federal hate crime protections

Yes Approve GOP plan to restrict use of genetic information by health insurers

Yes Kill amendment delaying implementation of an anti-missile defense system

Yes Cut taxes for married couples

Yes Grant China permanent normal trade status

1999

Yes Remove President Clinton from office for obstruction of justice

Yes Kill amendment authorizing state grants to hire teachers and reduce class size

No Require criminal background checks for purchases at gun shows

Yes Approve GOP proposal to increase rights of patients in managed-care health plans

No Block effort to allow farm and medicine exports to Cuba

No Allow study of tougher automobile fuel efficiency standards

No Ratify nuclear weapons testing treaty

No Prohibit national political parties from collecting "soft money" donations

Yes Remove barriers among banking, securities and insurance companies

INTEREST GROUPS

	AFL-CIO	ADA	CCUS	ACU
2000	0%	0%	92%	92%
1999	0%	0%	100%	87%
1998	13%	5%	89%	84%
1997	0%	10%	90%	84%
1996	0%	5%	92%	100%
1995	0%	5%	100%	83%
House Service:				
1994	0%	5%	100%	89%
1993	17%	10%	91%	87%
1992	45%	20%	88%	79%
1991	0%	0%	100%	95%

CQ VOTE STUDIES

	PARTY UNITY		PRESIDENTIAL SUPPORT	
	Support	Oppose	Support	Oppose
2000	97%	3%	40%	60%
1999	96%	4%	31%	69%
1998	95%	5%	39%	61%
1997	98%	2%	57%	43%
1996	98%	2%	29%	71%
1995	96%	4%	22%	78%
House Service:				
1994	92%	8%	42%	58%
1993	93%	7%	33%	67%
1992	87%	13%	78%	22%
1991	94%	6%	83%	17%

Sen. Michael B. Enzi (R)

Elected 1996; 1st term

CAPITOL OFFICE
224-3424; fax 228-0359; 290 Russell Bldg. 20510

INTERNET
e-mail: senator@enzi.senate.gov
web: enzi.senate.gov

COMMITTEES
Banking, Housing & Urban Affairs
 (Securities & Investment - chairman)
Health, Education, Labor & Pensions
 (Employment, Safety & Training - chairman)
Small Business
Special Aging

HOMETOWN
Gillette

BORN
Feb. 1, 1944, Bremerton, Wash.

RELIGION
Presbyterian

FAMILY
Wife, Diana Enzi; three children

EDUCATION
George Washington U., B.S. 1966; U. of Denver,
M.S. 1968

MILITARY SERVICE
Wyo. Air National Guard, 1967-73

CAREER
Accountant; shoe store owner

POLITICAL HIGHLIGHTS
Mayor of Gillette, 1975-82; Wyo. House, 1987-91;
Wyo. Senate, 1991-96

ELECTION RESULTS

1996 GENERAL

Michael B. Enzi (R)	114,116	54.1%
Kathy Karpan (D)	89,103	42.2%
W. David Herbert (LIBERT)	5,289	2.5%
Lloyd Marsden (NL)	2,569	1.2%

1996 PRIMARY

Michael B. Enzi (R)	27,056	32.5%
John Barrasso (R)	24,918	29.9%
Curt Meier (R)	14,739	17.7%
Nimi McConigley (R)	6,005	7.2%
Kevin P. Meenan (R)	6,000	7.2%
Kathleen P. Jachowski (R)	2,269	2.7%
Brian E. Coen (R)	943	1.1%
Cleveland B. Holloway (R)	874	1.0%

In many respects, Enzi is a man of traditional values. A former Eagle Scout, he taught Sunday school for 10 years, coached youth soccer and served on his hometown bank's board of directors. He favors initiatives to move power from Washington to the states, increase the role of religion in public schools and promote traditional values through the tax code.

Enzi (EN-zee) explained his support of a plan in the 106th Congress to reduce taxes on married couples by saying, "It's very important that we examine our tax policy and restructure it so that we encourage things like marriage, purchasing health insurance, saving for retirement, higher education and home buying. ...These actions will lead to stronger families, higher-quality living, self-reliance and solid communities." Similarly, in pressing for legislation to allow public schools to post the Ten Commandments, he wrote in a 1999 letter to Judiciary Chairman Orrin G. Hatch: "There is nothing wrong with posting a document that says it is wrong to kill people, to steal from other people and that you should respect your parents."

Enzi and other Western Republicans often want to tug the Senate to the right. Like Wayne Allard of Colorado and Jon Kyl of Arizona, among others, Enzi is strongly anti-tax and fiercely opposed to government regulations, especially those that affect the livelihoods of Western miners and ranchers. In the tradition of many Westerners, he is an avid hunter and fisherman.

But Enzi leaves tradition behind when it comes to computers. A former computer programmer for an oil well servicing company, he created a stir in his first year by announcing his intention to bring his laptop computer onto the Senate floor, where there has been a longtime ban on mechanical devices that might prove distracting. "It's only proper that those charged with making sensible laws regarding the Internet, information access, computer use and other areas actually use computers and know what they're all about," he said. But Senate tradition prevailed, and the Rules Committee voted in 1997 to specifically ban laptop computers from the floor.

More recently, Enzi has strived to overhaul regulations governing exports of sensitive high-technology products. In the 106th, he tried unsuccessfully to reauthorize the Export Administration Act and streamline the process by which the government regulates the export of "dual-use" products that have both military and commercial uses. When the legislation bogged down in 2000, he conceded to the Newsbytes News Network: "I feel like we're trying to achieve a Utopia. And Utopia is something which just won't work or pass around here." But he continued to pursue the issue in the 107th Congress.

Enzi chairs the Health, Education, Labor and Pensions panel's Subcommittee on Employment, Safety and Training, which enables him to work on changing Occupational Safety and Health Administration (OSHA) policies that he says are too burdensome, particularly for small businesses. He opposed ergonomics regulations imposed in the final days of the Clinton administration and backed congressional action in the 107th Congress to overturn them. He introduced a bill in 1999 that would give businesses leeway to use independent advisers to evaluate the safety of their operations, and he sharply criticized an OSHA statement, which was quickly withdrawn, that companies should be responsible for the safety of employees who work out of their homes.

Looking out for Wyoming's mining companies, Enzi also took aim at a Clinton administration initiative to require that mine operators protect workers from noise by rotating them or using quieter machines. "I have read through this rule several times now, and I have to say that it makes no sense to me," he said in an article by The Associated Press. "I seriously question whether those who wrote this rule have ever actually been to a mine."

Enzi favors increased access to public lands despite warnings by environmentalists that logging, mining and motorized vehicles can cause lasting harm. Making the case to increase logging, he blamed devastating wildfires in 2000 in part on government regulations that prevented timber companies from thinning out trees. He has also worked to keep Yellowstone and other national parks open to snowmobilers. In the 106th Congress, when the Clinton administration tried to ban snowmobiles in national parks, Enzi reacted angrily: "What and who is next in line to be banned? Automobiles? Horses? Bicycles?"

Enzi clashes with environmentalists over other issues. He is an outspoken opponent of the 1997 Kyoto global warming treaty. Although environmentalists praised the Kyoto treaty as a first step toward reversing potentially catastrophic worldwide weather changes, Enzi derided it as an empty gesture that would hurt the U.S. economy. He said it could lead to the loss of more than 5,000 Wyoming coal mining jobs while many less-developed nations would be free to continue polluting the atmosphere.

Much of Enzi's legislative focus has been to get the federal government to spend less. His first speech on the Senate floor was to urge passage of a balanced-budget amendment to the Constitution. At the end of the 105th Congress, he joined a conservative minority in opposing an omnibus appropriations bill that contained billions of dollars in emergency spending.

With the federal government finally showing a surplus in 1998, thanks in part to Congress' preoccupation during the previous decade with reducing the deficit, Enzi set his sights on another long-term goal: paying down the federal debt. In the 106th, he pressed for legislation that would require the government to retire its debt within 30 years, with federal revenues required to exceed spending every year beginning in fiscal 2000. "The federal government cannot continue handing out money and pretending it's everyone's best friend," he said.

As chairman of the Banking Committee's International Trade and Finance Subcommittee in the 106th Congress, Enzi was an important voice on export issues. He tends to support free-trade initiatives, supporting legislation in 2000 granting China permanent normal trade status despite concerns about that country's human rights record. "The United States should not isolate the people of China from the exchange of information and products," he said on the Senate floor. "We should not impede the efforts of Chinese citizens to trade and exchange property, which is an essential aspect of a free society." In the 107th Congress, Enzi moved from the Trade panel to the top spot on the Securities and Investment Subcommittee.

Enzi, who ran a shoe-store business (NZ Shoes) with his wife, began his political climb in 1974 at age 30, winning election as mayor of Gillette, in northeastern Wyoming. He served a pair of four-year terms in that job and was credited with guiding the city through a population explosion that more than doubled its size. In 1986, he won a seat in the Wyoming House, where he served four years; and in 1991, he moved up to the state Senate, where he served as chairman of the Revenue Committee.

When he launched his 1996 Senate campaign to replace retiring veteran Republican Sen. Alan K. Simpson, Enzi appeared to face long odds against several high-profile Republican opponents. But by building a network of supporters drawn in part from the Wyoming Christian Coalition and stressing his opposition to abortion, he narrowly won the GOP primary. He won the general election by 12 percentage points over Kathy Karpan, a former two-term Wyoming secretary of state.

KEY VOTES

2000
Yes Overhaul bankruptcy law and increase minimum wage
Yes Limit fiscal 2001 discretionary spending to $600.3 billion
Yes Override veto on nuclear waste disposal at Yucca Mountain site in Nevada
No Oppose effort to terminate Kosovo mission
No Include gender, sexual orientation and disability in federal hate crime protections
Yes Approve GOP plan to restrict use of genetic information by health insurers
Yes Kill amendment delaying implementation of an anti-missile defense system
Yes Cut taxes for married couples
Yes Grant China permanent normal trade status

1999
Yes Remove President Clinton from office for obstruction of justice
Yes Kill amendment authorizing state grants to hire teachers and reduce class size
No Require criminal background checks for purchases at gun shows
Yes Approve GOP proposal to increase rights of patients in managed-care health plans
No Block effort to allow farm and medicine exports to Cuba
No Allow study of tougher automobile fuel efficiency standards
No Ratify nuclear weapons testing treaty
No Prohibit national political parties from collecting "soft money" donations
Yes Remove barriers among banking, securities and insurance companies

INTEREST GROUPS

	AFL-CIO	ADA	CCUS	ACU
2000	0%	0%	100%	92%
1999	0%	0%	94%	92%
1998	0%	0%	94%	92%
1997	14%	10%	70%	88%

CQ VOTE STUDIES

	PARTY UNITY		PRESIDENTIAL SUPPORT	
	Support	Oppose	Support	Oppose
2000	97%	3%	35%	65%
1999	95%	5%	24%	76%
1998	96%	4%	31%	69%
1997	98%	2%	51%	49%

Rep. Barbara Cubin (R)

CAPITOL OFFICE
225-2311; fax 225-3057
1114 Longworth Bldg. 20515

INTERNET
e-mail: barbara.cubin@mail.house.gov
web: www.house.gov/cubin

COMMITTEES
Energy & Commerce
Resources
   (Energy & Mineral Resources - chairwoman)

HOMETOWN
Casper

BORN
Nov. 30, 1946, Salinas, Calif.

RELIGION
Episcopalian

FAMILY
Husband, Frederick William Cubin III; two children

EDUCATION
Creighton U., B.S. 1969; Casper College, attended 1993

CAREER
Medical office manager; realtor; chemist

POLITICAL HIGHLIGHTS
Wyo. House, 1987-93; Wyo. Senate, 1993-95

ELECTION RESULTS

2000 GENERAL

Barbara Cubin (R)	141,848	66.8%
Michael Allen Green (D)	60,638	28.6%
Lewis Stock (LIBERT)	6,411	3.0%
Victor Raymond (NL)	3,415	1.6%

2000 PRIMARY

Barbara Cubin (R)	54,946	77.8%
Larry Jay Herdt (R)	10,148	14.4%
Dino Wenino (R)	5,515	7.8%

1998 GENERAL

Barbara Cubin (R)	100,687	57.8%
Scott Farris (D)	67,399	38.7%
Steve Richardson (LIBERT)	6,133	3.5%

PREVIOUS WINNING PERCENTAGES
1996 (55%); 1994 (53%)

Elected 1994; 4th term

About half of Wyoming is owned by the federal government — an important factor in the daily lives of residents of the Cowboy State, which is rich in natural resources and whose economy is heavily dependent on the harvesting of those resources.

Cubin (CUE-bin), who is a descendant of early homesteaders in the state, grew up sensitized to the relationship between Wyoming residents and their federal landlord. She believes that many Easterners do not understand the problems of those who live in the water-starved, federally dominated West, where environmentalists' proposals to place large tracts of land off-limits from development threaten residents' economic livelihood.

Those views come across loud and clear in her work on Capitol Hill, and her chairmanship of the Resources panel's Energy and Mineral Resources Subcommittee gives her clout to influence federal lands policies and a soapbox to make her concerns known. One of the founders of the Congressional Mining Caucus, Cubin has made it a priority to promote two of Wyoming's resource-based industries — mining of coal and trona, a type of soda ash used in glassware, detergents and baking soda.

In the 107th Congress, Cubin won a place in the GOP leadership, defeating Judy Biggert of Illinois, 123-76, for Republican Conference secretary, a post vacated when Deborah Pryce of Ohio moved up to vice chairman. Cubin also is a member of the Steering Committee, which makes recommendations to the Republican Conference on committee assignments. She sits on the influential Energy and Commerce panel as well.

Cubin comes down squarely on the side of private property interests, ranchers and miners, which puts her at odds with environmental groups. But while this member of the House Class of 1994 is an ardent conservative, she will occasionally take a stand that sets her apart from the GOP's right wing.

In the 105th Congress, for example, she pushed an initiative condemning the widely publicized beating death of University of Wyoming student Matthew Shepard, who was a homosexual. "We cannot lie down, we cannot bury our heads, and we cannot sit on our hands," she said. The measure won approval overwhelmingly.

But Cubin's views on most social policy issues, including gun owners' rights, are conservative. In 2000, she was elected to a three-year term on the National Rifle Association's board of directors.

While steadfast in her defense of private property rights, Cubin can be diplomatic and restrained in her remarks, perhaps because of her previous experience in public office — she served in the Wyoming Legislature for eight years before coming to Washington. Still, she is no shrinking violet. Cubin blasted the Clinton administration's land policies, saying, "Bill Clinton and Al Gore do not want people to make a living off the public lands, other than to be here and serve the folks who want to come and see the place."

Nor is she shy about taking on a fellow Republican, even the former chairman of the Resources Committee, the crusty Don Young of Alaska. In the 106th Congress, she fought Young's bill to provide billions of dollars for the federal government to buy environmentally sensitive land. "Our lands are currently being locked away from public use ... at an alarming pace," she said. "The last thing we need in Wyoming is more federal land when the government can't adequately manage the property it has now."

Cubin in 1998 bristled at opponents of a bill to allow clearing of underbrush and diseased trees on federal forest lands. Conservatives said the measure would promote forest health and discourage fires, while critics called the bill a thinly disguised attempt to increase logging. Cubin, who said most of the forests in her state are at risk of catastrophic fires, called Eastern moderates' attempt to modify the bill part of an "extreme, radical environmental agenda." Because of their efforts, she said, "people will be killed, and property will be lost, and habitat will be destroyed."

In 2000, Cubin's subcommittee investigated payments by the independent watchdog Project on Government Oversight to Interior and Energy department officials for serving as advisers on oil royalty lawsuits. Her panel sought to cite the project's officials for contempt of Congress for refusing to answer questions under subpoena.

That was not the first time she played hardball in a subcommittee investigation. In 1998, her panel investigated how the Interior Department arrived at a new rule on hard-rock mining. She clashed with Interior Secretary Bruce Babbitt when he said he would not turn over documents pertaining to the regulation, which was being challenged in court. Cubin's subcommittee, which ultimately subpoenaed the documents, issued a report that accused Interior of bypassing the required public comment period for a proposed regulation. A federal court later ordered the department to rescind the regulation.

In a 1999 House floor speech, outlining why she is a Republican, Cubin noted that the GOP was best at translating the ideals of personal responsibility and individual freedom. "It is time to restore the American precept that each individual is accountable for his actions," she said. Speaking just weeks after the mass killings of students at a Colorado high school, she said, "As a wife, a woman, a mother of two sons, I believe that only a return to values and personal responsibility will end this sort of violence."

Cubin sought in 1999 to focus attention on a concern of women by taking a lead role in the distribution of cellular telephones to domestic violence prevention groups, in hopes of enhancing the security of victims and potential victims of domestic violence.

Cubin grew up in Casper, earned a degree in chemistry, and worked as a teacher, social worker, chemist and realtor. She was active in local party politics and various civic groups, including the Wyoming State Choir, the PTA, a suicide prevention organization and a homeless shelter. She served in the Wyoming Legislature, specializing in energy-related matters, before seeking Wyoming's at-large House seat in 1994, which became open when the GOP incumbent, Craig Thomas, ran for the Senate. She prevailed in a five-way primary and went on to trounce Democratic lawyer Bob Schuster by 12 percentage points in November. She has won re-election easily.

KEY VOTES

2000

No	Raise hourly minimum wage by $1 over two years
Yes	Halt funding for U.S. mission in Kosovo unless European nations pay more
Yes	Provide Medicare benefits to military retirees and their dependents
Yes	Grant China permanent normal trade status
Yes	Phase out estate, gift and trust taxes
Yes	Prohibit implementation of president's national monument designations
Yes	Approve GOP plan to provide prescription drug coverage for Medicare beneficiaries
Yes	Increase help for poor nations indebted to international financial institutions

1999

No	Impose steel import quotas
No	Kill proposal to take aviation trust funds off budget
No	Require background checks on buyers only at gun shows with 10 or more vendors
Yes	Remove barriers among banking, securities and insurance companies
No	Authorize state grants to hire teachers and reduce class size
No	Overhaul campaign finance law; ban "soft money" and restrict advocacy advertising
No	Approve bipartisan plan to increase rights of patients in managed-care health plans

INTEREST GROUPS

	AFL-CIO	ADA	CCUS	ACU
2000	10%	5%	80%	100%
1999	22%	5%	91%	88%
1998	0%	5%	94%	100%
1997	0%	0%	71%	100%

CQ VOTE STUDIES

	PARTY UNITY		PRESIDENTIAL SUPPORT	
	Support	Oppose	Support	Oppose
2000	97%	3%	24%	76%
1999	94%	6%	18%	82%
1998	96%	4%	21%	79%
1997	97%	3%	27%	73%

WYOMING
At Large

The jagged peaks of the Grand Tetons rise more than 5,000 feet from the Jackson Hole Valley to their 13,000-foot apex, less than 10 miles from the nation's steepest ski slopes at Jackson Hole Mountain. With the smallest population of any state, Wyoming basks in its wide open spaces, which define its libertarian politics and natural resource-based economy.

Yellowstone National Park is one of the most visited parks in the nation, and tourism is an essential part of Wyoming's economy. The state also relies on mining and commodities sales, so booms and busts coincide with market prices for those goods. After several years of budget shortfalls, the state had a substantial surplus in 2000 due to rising oil prices. However, the population is stagnant – increasing only 5 percent since 1980 – and most oil jobs are only temporary. Many of the state's most skilled workers leave the state, with more than 50 percent of college graduates moving away for lack of employment.

Wyoming is a primarily Republican state. Residents savor their land and resources and abhor government intrusion of any kind, especially in dictating how land must be used. In most regions, residents are happy with the state's relative seclusion and tranquil lifestyle and are not particularly warm to population growth. Although income from natural resources has decreased in terms of the amount it contributes to the budget, the state's lawmakers are loath to raise taxes and dare not entertain a dreaded income tax.

MAJOR INDUSTRY
Mining, tourism, railroads

MILITARY BASES
Francis E. Warren Air Force Base, 3,253 military, 456 civilian (1999)

CITIES
Cheyenne 53,925, Casper 48,233, Laramie 24,905

UNUSUAL FEATURES
Yellowstone National Park became the first national park in 1872; In 1920, Jackson became the first town in the nation to elect an all-female slate – mayor, council and marshal.

Delegates/Resident Commissioner

Puerto Rico sends a "resident commissioner" to the House for a four-year term, while the District of Columbia, the Virgin Islands, Guam and American Samoa elect delegates who serve two-year terms.

The delegates and resident commissioner can introduce legislation, speak on the House floor and vote in committee. But they cannot vote on the House floor — a circumstance that has led the District of Columbia government to issue license plates reading, "Taxation Without Representation."

The five non-voting representatives were given floor voting rights under certain circumstances in the 103rd Congress, which was controlled by the Democrats.

But the privilege was largely symbolic — if any vote was so close that the participation of the delegates and resident commissioner could affect the outcome, there was another vote in which they were not permitted to participate.

That limited voting privilege was revoked when the GOP took control in the 104th Congress.

Because the Resources Committee has jurisdiction over U.S. territorial affairs, all of the overseas representatives serve there.

AMERICAN SAMOA
Del. Eni F.H. Faleomavaega (D)
Elected 1988; 7th term

CAPITOL OFFICE
225-8577; fax 225-8757; 2422 Rayburn Bldg. 20515

INTERNET
e-mail: faleomavaega@mail.house.gov
web: www.house.gov/faleomavaega

COMMITTEES
International Relations
Resources

HOMETOWN
Pago Pago

BORN
Aug. 15, 1943, Vailoatai, Am. Samoa

RELIGION
Mormon

FAMILY
Wife, Hinanui Bambridge Cave; five children

EDUCATION
Brigham Young U., A.A. 1964, B.A. 1966; Texas Southern U., attended 1969; U. of Houston, J.D. 1972; U. of California, Berkeley, LL.M. 1973

MILITARY SERVICE
Army, 1966-69; Army Reserve, 1983-present

CAREER
Lawyer; territorial prosecutor; congressional aide

POLITICAL HIGHLIGHTS
Democratic candidate for U.S. House, 1984; lieutenant governor, 1985-89

PRONUNCIATION
EN-ee FOL-ee-oh-mav-ah-ENG-uh

DISTRICT OF COLUMBIA
Del. Eleanor Holmes Norton (D)
Elected 1990; 6th term

CAPITOL OFFICE
225-8050; fax 225-3002; 2136 Rayburn Bldg. 20515

INTERNET
e-mail: www.house.gov/writerep
web: www.house.gov/norton

COMMITTEES
Government Reform
Transportation & Infrastructure

HOMETOWN
Washington

BORN
June 13, 1937, Washington, D.C.

RELIGION
Episcopalian

FAMILY
Divorced; two children

EDUCATION
Antioch College, B.A. 1960; Yale U., M.A. 1963, LL.B. 1964

CAREER
Professor; lawyer

POLITICAL HIGHLIGHTS
New York City Human Rights Commission, 1971-77; Equal Employment Opportunity Commission chairman, 1977-81

GUAM
Del. Robert A. Underwood (D)
Elected 1992; 5th term

CAPITOL OFFICE
225-1188; fax 226-0341; 2428 Rayburn Bldg. 20515

INTERNET
e-mail: guamtodc@mail.house.gov
web: www.house.gov/underwood

COMMITTEES
Armed Services
Resources

HOMETOWN
Baza Gardens

BORN
July 13, 1948, Tamuning, Guam

RELIGION
Roman Catholic

FAMILY
Wife, Lorraine Aguilar; five children

EDUCATION
California State U., Los Angeles, B.A. 1969, M.A. 1971; U. of Southern California, Ph.D. 1987

CAREER
Professor; college administrator

POLITICAL HIGHLIGHTS
No previous office

VIRGIN ISLANDS
Del. Donna M.C. Christensen (D)
Elected 1996; 3rd term

CAPITOL OFFICE
225-1790; fax 225-5517; 1510 Longworth Bldg. 20515

INTERNET
e-mail: donna.christensen@mail.house.gov
web: www.house.gov/christian-christensen

COMMITTEES
Resources
Small Business

HOMETOWN
St. Croix

BORN
Sept. 19, 1945, Teaneck, N.J.

RELIGION
Moravian

FAMILY
Husband, Chris Christensen; two children, four stepchildren

EDUCATION
St. Mary's College (Ind.), B.S. 1966; George Washington U., M.D. 1970

CAREER
Physician; health official

POLITICAL HIGHLIGHTS
Virgin Is. Democratic Territorial Committee, 1980-97 (chairwoman, 1980-82); Virgin Is. Board of Education, 1984-86; Virgin Is. acting commissioner of health, 1993-94

PUERTO RICO
Res. Cmmsr. Anibal Acevedo-Vila (D)
Elected 2000; 1st term

CAPITOL OFFICE
225-2615; fax 225-2154; 126 Cannon Bldg. 20515

INTERNET
e-mail: anibal@mail.house.gov
web: www.house.gov/acevedo-vila

COMMITTEES
Agriculture
Resources
Small Business

HOMETOWN
San Juan

BORN
Feb. 13, 1962, Hato Rey, P.R.

RELIGION
Roman Catholic

FAMILY
Wife, Luisa Gandara; two children

EDUCATION
U. of Puerto Rico, B.A. 1982, J.D. 1985; Harvard U., LL.M. 1987

CAREER
Lawyer; gubernatorial aide

POLITICAL HIGHLIGHTS
Puerto Rico House, 1993-2000 (minority leader, 1997-2000)

Did You Know?

Knowing a lawmaker's political party or what state he or she is from can be helpful in understanding a member of Congress.

But there are many other factors that contribute to a member's priorities and interests and to their standing in the congressional universe. Seniority or committee assignments, for example, can provide some insight into a member's clout and areas of expertise. Which informal congressional groups they belong to, and how they vote with respect to the wishes of their party or the president, or how various interest groups view their voting records, can also be useful in getting a handle on a particular member.

Each member's background contains unique experiences and interests that often provide some insight into their behavior as a member of Congress. And sometimes these personal tidbits can offer a fascinating humanizing touch.

For example, did you know that:

Neil Abercrombie, D-Hawaii, wrote a novel in which 125 members of the House were killed.

Gary L. Ackerman, D-N.Y., used to live on a houseboat named the "Unsinkable." It sank.

Georgia Republican **Bob Barr's** mother thinks he is a flaming liberal.

Roscoe G. Bartlett, R-Md., holds 20 patents.

The father of Texas Republican **Kevin Brady,** was murdered in a South Dakota courtroom.

Jim Bunning, R-Ky., is a member of the Baseball Hall of Fame.

Ben Nighthorse Campbell, R-Colo., was a member of the 1964 Olympic team.

Michael N. Castle, R-Del., is the only former governor in the House.

James E. Clyburn, D-S.C., is the first black elected from South Carolina since 1896. That person was his great uncle, George Washington Murray.

Elijah E. Cummings, D-Md., was burdened with thousands of dollars in debt when he arrived in the House. He spent two winters without heat because he couldn't afford to fix his furnace.

Randy "Duke" Cunningham, R-Calif., was the first air ace of the Vietnam War. Later he was a "top gun" flight instructor.

Florida Republican **Lincoln Diaz-Balart's** aunt was once married to Fidel Castro.

John D. Dingell, D-Mich., is the dean of the House. A Dingell has represented Michigan in the House since 1932.

David Dreier, R-Calif., is the youngest-ever chairman of the Rules Committee.

Robert L. Ehrlich Jr., R-Md., was the captain of the Princeton football team.

When **Anna G. Eshoo,** D-Calif., was a school girl in Connecticut, President Truman gave her a ride home from school.

Chaka Fattah, D-Pa., was born Arthur Davenport.

Rodney Frelinghuysen, R-N.J., is the sixth member of his family to serve in Congress.

The favorite sandwich of Maryland Republican **Wayne T. Gilchrest** is peanut butter and mayonnaise on rye.

Bart Gordon, R-Tenn., can run 3 miles in about 17 minutes.

Bob Graham, R-Fla., has saved the more than 2,000 notebooks that he has filled with notes and reminders to himself.

Gil Gutknecht, R-Minn., has a culinary passion for Spam and persuaded the Library of Congress to hold an exhibit on the lunch meat.

In 1997, **Tony P. Hall,** D-Ohio, was nominated for the Nobel Peace Prize (by Rep. Frank R. Wolf, R-Va.)

A former federal judge, **Alcee L. Hastings,** D-Fla., was impeached and removed from office.

"Doc" Hastings, R-Wash., did not graduate from college.

Orrin G. Hatch, R-Utah, is a songwriter, with a repertoire ranging from bossa nova to rock and rap.

Joel Hefley, R-Colo., won a coin flip with a colleague in the state legislature to determine which of them would run for Congress.

Rush D. Holt, D-N.J., a physicist, is a former champion on the TV quiz show, "Jeopardy."

As a staffer, **Steve Horn,** R-Calif., was on the Senate floor when the Tonkin Gulf Resolution passed in 1964.

Asa Hutchinson, R-Ark., once prosecuted Roger Clinton (Bill's brother) on drug charges.

Jesse L. Jackson Jr., D-Ill., vacuums his office carpet for relaxation.

James M. Jeffords, R-Vt., holds a black belt in Tae Kwon Do.

Sam Johnson, R-Texas, spent almost seven years in a North Vietnamese prison camp. For a brief stretch, he roomed with John McCain.

Ron Kind, D-Wis., helped former Wisconsin Sen. William Proxmire with his "Golden Fleece" awards.

Dennis J. Kucinich, D-Ohio, was so unpopular as mayor of Cleveland that he wore a bullet-proof vest to throw out the first pitch at an Indians game.

Tom Lantos, D-Calif., fought with the Hungarian resistance against the Nazis. He escaped from a Nazi work camp.

Steve Largent, R-Okla., is a member of the Pro Football Hall of Fame.

John Lewis, D-Ga., was a leader of the famous civil rights march in Selma, Ala., in 1965.

A 24-year-old Yale law student named Bill Clinton campaigned for **Joseph I. Lieberman,** D-Conn., in 1970, as Lieberman ran for the state Senate.

Trent Lott, R-Miss., was an aide to a Democratic member of the House.

Carolyn McCarthy, D-N.Y., was propelled into politics by her husband's murder.

The grandparents of **Carrie P. Meek,** D-Fla., were slaves.

John L. Mica, R-Fla., is a long-time Republican; his brother, Dan, served in the House as a Democrat.

Barbara A. Mikulski, D-Md., is the fifth most senior woman in congressional history.

Constance A. Morella, R-Md., is an opera afficionado; her dream is to sing in "La Boheme."

Jim Nussle, R-Iowa, once spoke on the House floor with a paper bag over his head.

As a youth, **David R. Obey,** D-Wis., campaigned for Sen. Joseph R. McCarthy.

John W. Olver, D-Mass., earned a master's degree at age 19.

Major R. Owens, D-N.Y., writes rap lyrics and poetry.

Of the 56 House votes in the 106th Congress on which there was a solitary nay, **Ron Paul,** R-Texas, cast that vote 28 times.

Collin C. Peterson, D-Minn., plays guitar in a country rock band.

The Oak Ridge Boys have recorded some of Illinois Democrat **David Phelps'** gospel songs.

Ralph Regula, R-Ohio, works to preserve the memory of William McKinley.

Ileana Ros-Lehtinen, R-Fla., is the first Hispanic woman elected to Congress.

Bobby L. Rush, D-Ill., is a former Black Panther. He served six months in prison on a weapons charge.

Jim Ryun, R-Kan., made the cover of Sports Illustrated when he was still in high school.

Joe Scarborough, R-Fla., has written more than 300 songs.

F. James Sensenbrenner Jr., R-Wis., was one of the wealthiest members of Congress even before he won $250,000 in the D.C. lottery.

As a freshman in the 105th Congress, **John Shimkus,** R-Ill., collected the autographs of every other member of Congress.

Joe Skeen, R-N.M., was first elected to Congress as a write-in candidate.

Vic Snyder, D-Ark., has degrees in medicine and law.

Floyd D. Spence, R-S.C, underwent an experimental double-lung transplant and later had a kidney transplant. (His son was the donor.)

John M. Spratt Jr., D-S.C., broke his arm when he slipped in some Senate bean soup.

A former teacher, **Tom Tancredo,** R-Colo., first ran for office on a dare from his students.

Strom Thurmond, R-S.C., participated in the invasion of Normandy (at the age of 41).

James A. Traficant Jr., D-Ohio, uttered the phrase "beam me up" on the House floor 178 times during the 106th Congress.

J.C. Watts Jr., R-Okla., was twice named most valuable player of the Orange Bowl.

Lynn Woolsey, D-Calif., went on welfare after a divorce left her on her own with three young children and no job skills.

Fastest Members of Congress

Each year a number of members of Congress participate in a three-mile footrace in East Potomac Park in Washington, D.C. Here are the best times posted by current members of Congress in the 2000 race.

Member	Time	Member	Time
Rep. Bart Gordon, D-Tenn.	17:14	Sen. Jack Reed, D-R.I.	23:11
Rep. Jim Ryun, R-Kan.	19:56	Rep. Asa Hutchinson, R-Ark.	24:53
Rep. Earl Pomeroy, D-N.D.	20:09	Rep. Kenny Hulshof, R-Mo.	25:02
Rep. Steve Largent, R-Okla.	20:50	Rep. Thomas M. Barrett, D-Wis.	25:18
Rep. Zack Wamp, R-Tenn.	21:56	Rep. George Nethercutt, R-Wash.	25:21
Sen. Tim Hutchinson, R-Ark.	22:36	Sen. Bill Frist, R-Tenn.	25:29
Rep. Baron P. Hill, D-Ind.	22:40	Sen. Jeff Bingaman, D-N.M.	25:44
Sen. Don Nickles, R-Okla.	22:56	Sen. Tom Daschle, D-S.D.	26:08
Rep. Earl Blumenauer, D-Ore.	22:58	Rep. James P. Moran, D-Va.	27:08
Rep. Mark Udall, D-Colo.	23:03	Sen. Charles E. Grassley, R-Iowa	28:36

Congressional Half-Life

The following is a list of the current members who have served more than half of their life in Congress. Length of service is as of Jan. 3, 2001.

Name	Party-State	Age at Swearing-in	Length of Service	% of Life In Congress
Rep. John D. Dingell	D-Mich.	29 years, 158 days	45 years, 21days	60
Sen. Robert C. Byrd	D-W.Va.	35 years, 44 days	48 years	58
Sen. Edward M. Kennedy	D-Mass.	30 years, 258 days	38 years, 57 days	55
Sen. Daniel K. Inouye	D-Hawaii	34 years, 348 days	41 years, 135 days	54
Rep. David R. Obey	D-Wis.	30 years, 180 days	31 years, 277 days	51
Rep. John Conyers Jr.	D-Mich.	35 years, 233 days	36 years	50

Note: Sen. John B. Breaux, D-La., who began serving in the House of Representatives in 1972, was scheduled to join the list April 28, 2001, when he will have served 28 years, 213 days.

10 Oldest Members of Congress

Member	Birthdate
Sen. Strom Thurmond, R-S.C.	Dec. 5, 1902
Sen. Robert C. Byrd, D-W.Va.	Nov. 20, 1917
Sen. Jesse Helms, R-N.C.	Oct. 18, 1921
Sen. Ernest F. Hollings, D-S.C.	Jan. 1, 1922
Rep. Benjamin A. Gilman, R-N.Y.	Dec. 6, 1922
Rep. Ralph M. Hall, D-Texas	May 3, 1923
Sen. Ted Stevens, R-Alaska	Nov. 18, 1923
Rep. Henry J. Hyde, R-Ill.	April 18, 1924
Sen. Daniel K. Inouye, D-Hawaii	Sept. 7, 1924
Sen. Daniel K. Akaka, D-Hawaii	Sept. 11, 1924

10 Youngest Members of Congress

Member	Birthdate
Rep. Adam H. Putnam, R-Fla.	July 31, 1974
Rep. Mike Ferguson, R-N.J.	July 22, 1970
Rep. Harold E. Ford Jr., D-Tenn.	May 11, 1970
Rep. Paul D. Ryan, R-Wis.	Jan. 29, 1970
Rep. Patrick J. Kennedy, D-R.I.	July 14, 1967
Rep. Brad Carson, D-Okla.	March 11, 1967
Rep. Robert B. Aderholt, R-Ala.	July 22, 1965
Rep. Rick Larsen, D-Wash.	June 15, 1965
Rep. Adam Smith, D-Wash.	June 15, 1965
Rep. Jesse L. Jackson Jr., D-Ill.	March 11, 1965

Members' Occupations
107th Congress

	House			Senate			Congress
	Democrat	Republican	Total	Democrat	Republican	Total	Total
Actor/Entertainer		1	1		1	1	2
Aeronautics		1	1	1		1	2
Agriculture	8	17	25	1	5	6	31
Artistic/Creative		1	2*				2*
Business/Banking	56	103	159	8	16	24	183
Clergy	1	1	2		1	1	3
Education	53	38	92*	8	8	16	108*
Engineering	1	8	9				9
Health Care	3	1	4				4
Homemaker/Domestic	1	1	2	1		1	3
Journalism	1	7	9*	1	6	7	16*
Labor	1	1	2		1	1	3
Law	84	71	156†	28	25	53	210†
Law Enforcement	7	3	10				10
Medicine	6	8	14		3	3	17
Military		2	2		1	1	3
Professional Sports		3	3		1	1	4
Public Service/Politics	70	56	126	18	10	28	154
Real Estate	2	22	24	2	2	4	28
Secretarial/Clerical		2	2				2
Technical/Trade	1	2	3				3
Miscellaneous	1	5	6				6

* Total includes Independent Bernard Sanders of Vermont; † Total includes Independent Virgil H. Goode Jr. of Virginia.
Note: Some members have more than one occupation.

Members' Religious Affiliations
107th Congress

	House			Senate			Congress
	Democrat	Republican	Total	Democrat	Republican	Total	Total
African Methodist Episcopal	2		2				2
Baptist	33	30	64†	2	7	9	73†
Christian Church	3		3				3
Christian Reformed Church		2	2				2
Christian Scientist		5	5				5
Disciples of Christ	1		1				1
Eastern Orthodox	1	3	4	1	1	2	6
Episcopalian	7	23	30	3	7	10	40
Jewish	24	2	27*	9	1	10	37*
Lutheran	8	8	16	3	1	4	20
Methodist	16	34	50	10	6	16	66
Mormon	3	8	11	1	4	5	16
Pentecostal		3	3				3
Presbyterian	15	23	38	3	7	10	48
Roman Catholic	76	49	125	14	10	24	149
Seventh-day Adventist	1	2	3				3
Unitarian	1	1	2	1		1	3
United Church of Christ/ Congregationalist		3	3	3	2	5	8
Unspecified Protestant	13	25	38		3	3	41
Unspecified, other	7		7		1	1	8

* Total includes Independent Bernard Sanders of Vermont; † Total includes Independent Virgil H. Goode Jr. of Virginia.

www.cq.com

Party Switchers

The following members of Congress changed their party affiliations after their election to Congress. A number of other members switched parties before coming to Congress.

Name	Old Party	New Party	Date Switched
Sen. Strom Thurmond, S.C.	D	R	Sept. 16, 1964
Rep. Bob Stump, Ariz.	D	R	Sept. 24, 1981
Sen. Phil Gramm, Texas	D	R	Jan. 5, 1983
Sen. Richard C. Shelby, Ala.	D	R	Nov. 9, 1994
Sen. Ben Nighthorse Campbell, Colo.	D	R	March 3, 1995
Rep. Nathan Deal, Ga.	D	R	April 10, 1995
Rep. Billy Tauzin, La.	D	R	Aug. 6, 1995
Rep. Wes Watkins, Okla.	D	R	Jan. 5. 1996*
Rep. Virgil H. Goode Jr., Va.	D	I	Jan. 24, 2000

* Watkins retired from the House in January 1991, announced his party switch in 1996 and later that year was elected again to the House.

Note: Sen. Robert C. Smith, N.H., announced in July 1999 he was leaving the Republican Party and becoming an independent. In November 1999, he rejoined the GOP.

Senators Up for Re-election in 2002

20 Republicans, 14 Democrats

Allard, Wayne	R-Colo.	Johnson, Tim	D-S.D.
Baucus, Max	D-Mont.	Kerry, John	D-Mass.
Biden, Joseph R. Jr.	D-Del.	Landrieu, Mary L.	D-La.
Carnahan, Jean	D-Mo.	Levin, Carl	D-Mich.
Cleland, Max	D-Ga.	McConnell, Mitch	R-Ky.
Cochran, Thad	R-Miss.	Reed, Jack	D-R.I.
Collins, Susan	R-Maine	Roberts, Pat	R-Kan.
Craig, Larry E.	R-Idaho	Rockefeller, John D. IV	D-W.Va.
Domenici, Pete V.	R-N.M.	Sessions, Jeff	R-Ala.
Durbin, Richard J.	D-Ill.	Smith, Gordon H.	R-Ore.
Enzi, Michael B.	R-Wyo.	Smith, Robert C.	R-N.H.
Gramm, Phil	R-Texas	Stevens, Ted	R-Alaska
Hagel, Chuck	R-Neb.	Thompson, Fred	R-Tenn.
Harkin, Tom	D-Iowa	Thurmond, Strom	R-S.C.
Helms, Jesse	R-N.C.	Torricelli, Robert G.	D-N.J.
Hutchinson, Tim	R-Ark.	Warner, John W.	R-Va.
Inhofe, James M.	R-Okla.	Wellstone, Paul	D-Minn.

Born Abroad

These members of Congress were born outside the 50 states and the District of Columbia:

Name	Country
Rep. Diana DeGette, D-Colo.	Japan
Rep. Lincoln Diaz-Balart, R-Fla.	Cuba
Rep. Peter Hoekstra, R-Mich.	Netherlands
Rep. Tom Lantos, D-Calif.	Hungary
Sen. John McCain, R-Ariz.	Panama Canal Zone
Rep. Ciro D. Rodriguez, D-Texas	Mexico
Rep. Ileana Ros-Lehtinen, R-Fla.	Cuba
Rep. Jose E. Serrano, D-N.Y.	Puerto Rico
Rep. Nydia M. Velázquez, D-N.Y.	Puerto Rico
Rep. David Wu, D-Ore.	Taiwan

The Dakota Connection

The combined population of North Dakota and South Dakota is less than 1.4 million, yet the two states are the birth place of 15 current members of Congress. By way of contrast, Florida, with a population of almost 16 million, is the birthplace of just 10 members. Members of Congress who were born in North Dakota or South Dakota:

Member	Birthplace
Rep. Dick Armey, R-Texas	Cando, N.D.
Rep. Kevin Brady, R-Texas	Vermillion, S.D.
Sen. Kent Conrad, D-N.D.	Bismarck, N.D.
Sen. Tom Daschle, D-S.D.	Aberdeen, S.D.
Rep. Thomas M. Davis III, R-Va.	Minot, N.D.
Sen. Byron L. Dorgan, D-N.D.	Regent, N.D.
Rep. Darlene Hooley, D-Ore.	Williston, N.D.
Sen. Tim Johnson, D-S.D.	Canton, S.D.
Rep. Collin C. Peterson, D-Minn.	Fargo, N.D.
Rep. Earl Pomeroy, D-N.D.	Valley City, N.D.
Rep. Jim Ramstad, R-Minn.	Jamestown, N.D.
Rep. Martin Olav Sabo, D-Minn.	Crosby, N.D.
Rep. Todd Tiahrt, R-Kan.	Vermillion, S.D.
Rep. John Thune, R-S.D.	Pierre, S.D.
Rep. Karen L. Thurman, D-Fla.	Rapid City, S.D.

No Blacks or Women

States that have never been represented in Congress by either a black person or a woman:

Alaska   **Delaware**
Iowa   **New Hampshire**
Vermont

Former Representatives in Senate

25 Republicans, 24 Democrats

Name	Party, State	Served in House
Daniel K. Akaka	D-Hawaii	1977-90
Wayne Allard	R-Colo.	1991-97
George F. Allen	R-Va.	1991-93
Max Baucus	D-Mont.	1975-78
Barbara Boxer	D-Calif.	1983-93
John B. Breaux	D-La.	1972-87
Sam Brownback	R-Kan.	1995-96
Jim Bunning	R-Ky.	1987-99
Robert C. Byrd	D-W.Va.	1953-59
Ben Nighthorse Campbell	R-Colo.	1987-93
Maria Cantwell	D-Wash.	1993-95
Thomas R. Carper	D-Del.	1983-93
Thad Cochran	R-Miss.	1973-78
Larry E. Craig	R-Idaho	1981-91
Michael D. Crapo	R-Idaho	1993-99
Tom Daschle	D-S.D.	1979-87
Mike DeWine	R-Ohio	1983-91
Christopher J. Dodd	D-Conn.	1975-81
Byron L. Dorgan	D-N.D.	1981-93
Richard J. Durbin	D-Ill.	1983-97
John Ensign	R-Nev.	1995-99
Phil Gramm	R-Texas	1979-85
Charles E. Grassley	R-Iowa	1975-81
Judd Gregg	R-N.H.	1981-89
Tom Harkin	D-Iowa	1975-85
Tim Hutchinson	R-Ark.	1993-97
James M. Inhofe	R-Okla.	1987-94
Daniel K. Inouye	D-Hawaii	1959-63
James M. Jeffords	R-Vt.	1975-89
Tim Johnson	D-S.D.	1987-97
Jon Kyl	R-Ariz.	1987-95
Blanche Lincoln	D-Ark.	1993-97
Trent Lott	R-Miss.	1973-89
John McCain	R-Ariz.	1983-87
Barbara A. Mikulski	D-Md.	1977-87
Bill Nelson	D-Fla.	1979-91
Jack Reed	D-R.I.	1991-97
Harry Reid	D-Nev.	1983-87
Pat Roberts	R-Kan.	1981-97
Rick Santorum	R-Pa.	1991-95
Paul S. Sarbanes	D-Md.	1971-77
Charles E. Schumer	D-N.Y.	1981-99
Richard C. Shelby	R-Ala.	1979-87
Robert C. Smith	R-N.H.	1985-91
Olympia J. Snowe	R-Maine	1979-95
Debbie Stabenow	D-Mich.	1997-2001
Craig Thomas	R-Wyo.	1989-95
Robert G. Torricelli	D-N.J.	1983-97
Ron Wyden	D-Ore.	1981-96

Senate Presidential Support and Opposition

Support scores represent those who voted most often in support of President Clinton in 1999 and 2000. Opposition scores represent those who most often voted against the president's position. Scores are represented in percentages. Only members of the 107th Congress are listed.

106th Congress

Support — Republicans

Lincoln Chafee, R.I.	88
James M. Jeffords, Vt.	65
Arlen Specter, Pa.	56
Olympia J. Snowe, Maine	55
Susan Collins, Maine	53
Gordon H. Smith, Ore.	52
George V. Voinovich, Ohio	52
Richard G. Lugar, Ind.	52
Ted Stevens, Alaska	45
John W. Warner, Va.	45
Fred Thompson, Tenn.	45
Mike DeWine, Ohio	45
Peter G. Fitzgerald, Ill.	44
Orrin G. Hatch, Utah	42
Chuck Hagel, Neb.	42
Pete V. Domenici, N.M.	41
Thad Cochran, Miss.	41
Richard C. Shelby, Ala.	41
Robert F. Bennett, Utah	41
Bill Frist, Tenn.	41

Support — Democrats

John Kerry, Mass.	95
Bob Graham, Fla.	94
Charles E. Schumer, N.Y.	94
Edward M. Kennedy, Mass.	94
Evan Bayh, Ind.	93
Ron Wyden, Ore.	93
John D. Rockefeller IV, W.Va.	93
Daniel K. Akaka, Hawaii	93
Richard J. Durbin, Ill.	92
Christopher J. Dodd, Conn.	92
Jack Reed, R.I.	92
Tom Harkin, Iowa	92
Joseph I. Lieberman, Conn.	91
Carl Levin, Mich.	90
Paul S. Sarbanes, Md.	90
Joseph R. Biden Jr., Del.	90
John Edwards, N.C.	89
Jeff Bingaman, N.M.	89
Daniel K. Inouye, Hawaii	89
Tom Daschle, S.D.	89

Opposition — Republicans

Robert C. Smith, N.H.	79
Jesse Helms, N.C.	76
James M. Inhofe, Okla.	74
Jim Bunning, Ky.	71
Wayne Allard, Colo.	71
Michael B. Enzi, Wyo.	71
Tim Hutchinson, Ark.	69
Phil Gramm, Texas	68
Don Nickles, Okla.	67
Jeff Sessions, Ala.	67
Pat Roberts, Kan.	67
Larry E. Craig, Idaho	66
Strom Thurmond, S.C.	66
Craig Thomas, Wyo.	65
Sam Brownback, Kan.	65
Judd Gregg, N.H.	65
Michael D.Crapo, Idaho	65
Frank H. Murkowski, Alaska	64
Kay Bailey Hutchison, Texas	64
Conrad Burns, Mont.	63

Opposition — Democrats

Robert C. Byrd, W.Va.	27
Byron L. Dorgan, N.D.	19
John B. Breaux, La.	19
Max Cleland, Ga.	19
Kent Conrad, N.D.	19
Ernest F. Hollings, S.C.	19
Blanche Lincoln, Ark.	18
Dianne Feinstein, Calif.	15
Mary L. Landrieu, La.	15
Patrick J. Leahy, Vt.	14
Robert G. Torricelli, N.J.	14
Herb Kohl, Wis.	14
Russell D. Feingold, Wis.	14
Paul Wellstone, Minn.	13
Tim Johnson, S.D.	13
Harry Reid, Nev.	13
Patty Murray, Wash.	13
Barbara Boxer, Calif.	12
Max Baucus, Mont.	11
Barbara A. Mikulski, Md.	11

Senate Party Unity and Opposition

Support scores represent those who voted most often with their party's majority against the other party in 1999 and 2000. Opposition scores represent those who most often voted against their party's majority. Scores are represented in percentages. Only members of the 107th Congress are listed.

106th Congress

Support — Republicans

Larry E. Craig, Idaho	98
Michael D. Crapo, Idaho	98
Frank H. Murkowski, Alaska	98
Jon Kyl, Ariz.	98
Trent Lott, Miss.	98
Don Nickles, Okla.	97
Wayne Allard, Colo.	97
Phil Gramm, Texas	97
James M. Inhofe, Okla.	97
Mitch McConnell, Ky.	97
Sam Brownback, Kan.	96
Jim Bunning, Ky.	96
Michael B. Enzi, Wyo.	96
Craig Thomas, Wyo.	96
Tim Hutchinson, Ark.	96
Bill Frist, Tenn.	95
Thad Cochran, Miss.	95
Judd Gregg, N.H.	95
Jesse Helms, N.C.	95
Pat Roberts, Kan.	95

Support — Democrats

Barbara Boxer, Calif.	98
Paul S. Sarbanes, Md.	98
Edward M. Kennedy, Mass.	97
Carl Levin, Mich.	97
Tom Harkin, Iowa	97
Richard J. Durbin, Ill.	97
Daniel K. Akaka, Hawaii	97
Jack Reed, R.I.	96
Barbara A. Mikulski, Md.	96
Paul Wellstone, Minn.	96
John Kerry, Mass.	95
John D. Rockefeller IV, W.Va.	95
Charles E. Schumer, N.Y.	95
Patrick J. Leahy, Vt.	94
Ron Wyden, Ore.	93
Patty Murray, Wash.	93
Harry Reid, Nev.	93
Tom Daschle, S.D.	93
John Edwards, N.C.	93
Tim Johnson, S.D.	92

Opposition — Republicans

Lincoln Chafee, R.I.	62
James M. Jeffords, Vt.	37
Arlen Specter, Pa.	35
Olympia J. Snowe, Maine	30
Susan Collins, Maine	26
George V. Voinovich, Ohio	17
Peter G. Fitzgerald, Ill.	15
Mike DeWine, Ohio	15
John McCain, Ariz.	13
Gordon H. Smith, Ore.	13
Richard G. Lugar, Ind.	13

Opposition — Democrats

Zell Miller, Ga.	75
John B. Breaux, La.	26
Robert C. Byrd, W.Va.	23
Blanche Lincoln, Ark.	18
Mary L. Landrieu, La.	16
Kent Conrad, N.D.	13
Jeff Bingaman, N.M.	13
Max Baucus, Mont.	13
Robert G. Torricelli, N.J.	13
Joseph I. Lieberman, Conn.	12
Herb Kohl, Wis.	12

House Presidential Support and Opposition

Support scores represent those who voted most often in support of President Clinton in 1999 and 2000. Opposition scores represent those who most often voted against the president's position. Scores are represented in percentages. Only members of the 107th Congress are listed.

106th Congress

Support — Republicans

Constance A. Morella, Md.	66
Sherwood Boehlert, N.Y.	56
Nancy L. Johnson, Conn.	52
Amo Houghton, N.Y.	52
Benjamin A. Gilman, N.Y.	52
Michael N. Castle, Del.	49
Christopher Shays, Conn.	49
James C. Greenwood, Pa.	49
Rodney Frelinghuysen, N.J.	46
Wayne T. Gilchrest, Md.	45
Sue W. Kelly, N.Y.	44
Marge Roukema, N.J.	43
Steve Horn, Calif.	42
Jim Leach, Iowa	41
Jack Quinn, N.Y.	40
Judy Biggert, Ill.	39
Jim Kolbe, Ariz.	39
Greg Ganske, Iowa	39
Peter T. King, N.Y.	38
Thomas M. Davis III., Va.	38

Support — Democrats

Howard L. Berman, Calif.	92
Tom Sawyer, Ohio	91
Jim McDermott, Wash.	91
Maurice D. Hinchey, N.Y.	90
Gary L. Ackerman, N.Y.	90
Chaka Fattah, Pa.	90
Robert T. Matsui, Calif.	89
Juanita Millender-McDonald, Calif.	89
Gregory W. Meeks, N.Y.	89
Anthony D. Weiner, N.Y.	89
Nita M. Lowey, N.Y.	88
Lucille Roybal-Allard, Calif.	88
Bobby L. Rush, Ill.	88
Benjamin L. Cardin, Md.	88
Sander M. Levin, Mich.	88
Xavier Becerra, Calif.	88
Martin Olav Sabo, Minn.	88
Stephanie Tubbs Jones, Ohio	88
Charles B. Rangel, N.Y.	88
Donald M. Payne, N.J.	87

Opposition — Republicans

Van Hilleary, Tenn.	89
Roscoe G. Bartlett, Md.	87
Dana Rohrabacher, Calif.	86
John J. "Jimmy" Duncan Jr., Tenn.	86
John Hostettler, Ind.	86
Terry Everett, Ala.	85
Dan Burton, Ind.	85
Charlie Norwood, Ga.	85
Richard W. Pombo, Calif.	85
Jack Kingston, Ga.	84
Nathan Deal, Ga.	84
Jim DeMint, S.C.	84
Joel Hefley, Colo.	84
Zack Wamp, Tenn.	84
Mac Collins, Ga.	84
Howard Coble, N.C.	84
Bob Barr, Ga.	83
Robert B. Aderholt, Ala.	83
J.D. Hayworth, Ariz.	83
Lindsey Graham, S.C.	83

Opposition — Democrats

Ralph M. Hall, Texas	73
James A. Traficant Jr., Ohio	62
Gene Taylor, Miss.	61
Ken Lucas, Ky.	59
Mike McIntyre, N.C.	57
James A. Barcia, Mich.	57
Ronnie Shows, Miss.	57
Collin C. Peterson, Minn.	56
Robert E. "Bud" Cramer, Ala.	48
Charles W. Stenholm, Texas	47
Chris John, La.	46
David Phelps, Ill.	46
William O. Lipinski, Ill.	45
Norman Sisisky, Va.	45
Bard Gordon, Tenn.	44
Gary A. Condit, Calif.	44
Marion Berry, Ark.	42
Jerry F. Costello, Ill.	42
John Tanner, Tenn.	41
Sanford D. Bishop Jr., Ga.	40

House Party Unity and Opposition

Support scores represent those who voted most often with their party's majority against the other party in 1999 and 2000. Opposition scores represent those who most often voted against their party's majority. Scores are represented in percentages. Only members of the 107th Congress are listed.

106th Congress

Support — Republicans

Dick Armey, Texas	98
Tom DeLay, Texas	98
Lamar Smith, Texas	98
Jim Ryun, Kan.	97
Pete Sessions, Texas	97
Joseph R. Pitts, Pa.	97
Sam Johnson, Texas	97
Christopher B. Cannon, Utah	97
Bob Stump, Ariz.	97
Doc Hastings, Wash.	97
Jim DeMint, S.C.	97
J. Dennis Hastert, Ill.	97
Gary G. Miller, Calif.	97
Roy Blunt, Mo.	96
Wally Herger, Calif.	96
Terry Everett, Ala.	96
Ed Bryant, Tenn.	96
J.D. Hayworth, Ariz.	96
Larry Combest, Texas	96
Charles W. "Chip" Pickering Jr., Miss.	96

Support — Democrats

Bob Filner, Calif.	98
Juanita Millender-McDonald, Calif.	98
William J. Coyne, Pa.	98
Lucille Roybal-Allard, Calif.	98
Major R. Owens, N.Y.	97
Bobby L. Rush, Ill.	97
Elijah E. Cummings, Md.	97
Stephanie Tubbs Jones, Ohio	97
Tom Lantos, Calif.	97
Danny K. Davis, Ill.	97
John Conyers Jr. , Mich.	97
Henry A. Waxman, Calif.	97
Lynn Woolsey, Calif.	97
Donald M. Payne, N.J.	97
Rosa DeLauro, Conn.	97
Jim McGovern, Mass.	97
Edward J. Markey, Mass.	97
Jerrold Nadler, N.Y.	97
MIchael E. Capuano, Mass.	97
John W. Olver, Mass.	97

Opposition — Republicans

Constance A. Morella, Md.	50
Sherwood Boehlert, N.Y.	36
Benjamin A. Gilman, N.Y.	36
Christopher Shays, Conn.	31
Steve Horn, Calif.	31
Nancy L. Johnson, Conn.	31
Rodney Frelinghuysen, N.J.	29
Jim Leach, Iowa	29
Michael N. Castle, Del.	28
James C. Greenwood, Pa.	28
Sue W. Kelly, N.Y.	28
Amo Houghton, N.Y.	27
Greg Ganske, Iowa	26
Christopher H. Smith, N.J.	25
Jack Quinn, N.Y.	25
Wayne T. Gilchrest, Md.	25
Ron Paul, Texas	23
Jim Ramstad, Minn.	22
Peter T. King, N.Y.	22
Frank A. LoBiondo, N.J.	22

Opposition — Democrats

Ralph M. Hall, Texas	68
James A. Traficant Jr., Ohio	67
Gene Taylor, Miss.	50
Ken Lucas, Ky.	50
Ronnie Shows, Miss.	46
Charles W. Stenholm, Texas	46
Collin C. Peterson, Minn.	45
Mike McIntyre, N.C.	43
Chris John, La.	41
Robert E. "Bud" Cramer, Ala.	41
James A. Barcia, Mich.	38
Norman Sisisky, Va.	37
Ike Skelton, Mo.	35
Gary A. Condit, Calif.	34
Alan B. Mollohan, W.Va.	33
Marion Berry, Ark.	33
John P. Murtha, Pa.	32
John Tanner, Tenn.	31
Jim Turner, Texas	31
Leonard L. Boswell, Iowa	31

House "Blue Dog" Coalition

Co-chairmen **Allen Boyd, Fla.** **Chris John, La.** **Jim Turner, Texas**

Joe Baca, Calif.
Marion Berry, Ark.
Sanford D. Bishop Jr., Ga.
Leonard L. Boswell, Iowa
Brad Carson, Okla.
Gary A. Condit, Calif.
Robert E. "Bud" Cramer, Ala.
Harold E. Ford Jr., Tenn.
Ralph M. Hall, Texas
Jane Harman, Calif.

Baron P. Hill, Ind.
Tim Holden, Pa.
William O. Lipinski, Ill.
Ken Lucas, Ky.
Jim Matheson, Utah
Mike McIntyre, N.C.
Dennis Moore, Kan.
Collin C. Peterson, Minn.
David Phelps, Ill.
Mike Ross, Ark.

Loretta Sanchez, Calif.
Max Sandlin, Texas
Adam B. Schiff, Calif.
Ronnie Shows, Miss.
Charles W. Stenholm, Texas
John Tanner, Tenn.
Ellen O. Tauscher, Calif.
Gene Taylor, Miss.
Mike Thompson, Calif.

House New Democrat Coalition

Co-chairmen **Cal Dooley, Calif.** **James P. Moran, Va.** **Tim Roemer, Ind.**

Tom Allen, Maine
Brian Baird, Wash.
James A. Barcia, Mich.
Ken Bentsen, Texas
Shelley Berkley, Nev.
Marion Berry, Ark.
Earl Blumenauer, Ore.
Lois Capps, Calif.
Brad Carson, Okla.
Bob Clement, Tenn.
Robert E. "Bud" Cramer, Ala.
Joseph Crowley, N.Y.
Jim Davis, Fla.
Susan A. Davis, Calif.
Peter Deutsch, Fla.
Anna G. Eshoo, Calif.
Bob Etheridge, N.C.
Harold E. Ford Jr., Tenn.
Charlie Gonzalez, Texas
Jane Harman, Calif.
Baron P. Hill, Ind.
Rubén Hinojosa, Texas
Joseph M. Hoeffel, Pa.
Rush D. Holt, N.J.

Michael M. Honda, Calif.
Darlene Hooley, Ore.
Jay Inslee, Wash.
Steve Israel, N.Y.
Chris John, La.
Ron Kind, Wis.
John J. LaFalce, N.Y.
Nick Lampson, Texas
Jim Langevin, R.I.
Rick Larsen, Wash.
John B. Larson, Conn.
Ken Lucas, Ky.
Bill Luther, Minn.
Carolyn B. Maloney, N.Y.
Jim Maloney, Conn.
Jim Matheson, Utah
Robert T. Matsui, Calif.
Carolyn McCarthy, N.Y.
Karen McCarthy, Mo.
Mike McIntyre, N.C.
Juanita Millender-McDonald, Calif.
Dennis Moore, Kan.
Grace F. Napolitano, Calif.

David Phelps, Ill.
David E. Price, N.C.
Silvestre Reyes, Texas
Mike Ross, Ark.
Steven R. Rothman, N.J.
Loretta Sanchez, Calif.
Max Sandlin, Texas
Adam B. Schiff, Calif.
Brad Sherman, Calif.
Ronnie Shows, Miss.
Adam Smith, Wash.
Vic Snyder, Ark.
John M. Spratt Jr., S.C.
Charles W. Stenholm, Texas
Bart Stupak, Mich.
John Tanner, Tenn
Ellen O. Tauscher, Calif.
Mike Thompson, Calif.
Jim Turner, Texas
Tom Udall, N.M.
Robert Wexler, Fla.
David Wu, Ore.

Progressive Caucus

Officers
Rep. Dennis J. Kucinich, Ohio – chairman
Rep. Barbara Lee, Calif. – vice chairwoman
Rep. Cynthia A. McKinney, Ga.
Rep. Major R. Owens, N.Y.
Rep. Bernard Sanders, Vt.
Sen. Paul Wellstone, Minn.

Members
Rep. Neil Abercrombie, Hawaii
Rep. Tammy Baldwin, Wis.
Rep. Xavier Becerra, Calif.
Rep. David E. Bonior, Mich.
Rep. Corrine Brown, Fla.
Rep. Sherrod Brown, Ohio
Rep. Michael E. Capuano, Mass.
Rep. Julia Carson, Ind.
Rep. John Conyers Jr., Mich.
Rep. Danny K. Davis, Ill.
Rep. Peter A. DeFazio, Ore.
Rep. Rosa DeLauro, Conn.
Rep. Lane Evans, Ill.
Del. Eni F.H. Faleomavaega, Am. Samoa
Rep. Sam Farr, Calif.
Rep. Chaka Fattah, Pa.
Rep. Bob Filner, Calif.
Rep. Barney Frank, Mass.
Rep. Luis V. Gutierrez, Ill.
Rep. Earl F. Hilliard, Ala.

Rep. Maurice D. Hinchey, N.Y.
Rep. Jesse L. Jackson Jr., Ill.
Rep. Stephanie Tubbs Jones, Ohio
Rep. Marcy Kaptur, Ohio
Rep. Tom Lantos, Calif.
Rep. John Lewis, Ga.
Rep. Jim McDermott, Wash.
Rep. Jim McGovern, Mass.
Rep. Carrie P. Meek, Fla.
Rep. George Miller, Calif.
Rep. Patsy T. Mink, Hawaii
Rep. Jerrold Nadler, N.Y.
Del. Eleanor Holmes Norton, D.C.
Rep. John W. Olver, Mass.
Rep. Ed Pastor, Ariz.
Rep. Donald M. Payne, N.J.
Rep. Nancy Pelosi, Calif.
Rep. Jan Schakowsky, Ill.
Rep. Jose E. Serrano, N.Y.
Rep. Pete Stark, Calif.
Rep. Bennie Thompson, Miss.
Rep. John F. Tierney, Mass.
Rep. Tom Udall, N.M.
Rep. Nydia M. Velazquez, N.Y.
Rep. Maxine Waters, Calif.
Rep. Melvin Watt, N.C.
Rep. Henry A. Waxman, Calif.
Rep. Lynn Woolsey, Calif.

Republican Main Street Partnership

Members of Congress who are members of the partnership, which also includes several governors and former elected officials. All members are Republicans.

Rep. Charles Bass, N. H.
Rep. Doug Bereuter, Neb.
Rep. Judy Biggert, Ill.
Rep. Sherwood Boehlert, N.Y.
Rep. Ken Calvert, Calif.
Rep. Dave Camp, Mich.
Sen. Lincoln Chafee, R.I
Rep. Michael N. Castle, Del., president of the board
Sen. Susan Collins, Maine, board member
Rep. Thomas M. Davis III, Va.
Rep. Vernon J. Ehlers, Mich.
Rep. Jo Ann Emerson, Mo.
Rep. Phil English, Pa.
Rep. Mark Foley, Fla.
Rep. Rodney Frelinghuysen, N.J.
Rep. Greg Ganske, Iowa
Rep. Paul E. Gillmor, Ohio
Rep. Benjamin A. Gilman, N.Y.
Rep. Porter J. Goss, Fla.
Rep. James C. Greenwood, Pa.
Rep. David L. Hobson, Ohio
Rep. Steve Horn, Calif.
Rep. Amo Houghton, N.Y., founder and board member
Rep. Johnny Isakson, Ga.
Sen. James M. Jeffords, Vt.

Rep. Nancy L. Johnson, Conn.
Rep. Sue W. Kelly, N.Y.
Rep. Jim Kolbe, Ariz.
Rep. Ray LaHood, Ill.
Rep. Steven C. LaTourette, Ohio
Rep. Jim Leach, Iowa
Rep. Jerry Lewis, Calif.
Sen. John McCain, Ariz.
Rep. Jim McCrery, La.
Rep. Constance A. Morella, Md.
Rep. George Nethercutt, Wash.
Rep. Doug Ose, Calif.
Rep. Tom Petri, Wis.
Rep. Deborah Pryce, Ohio
Rep. Jack Quinn, N.Y.
Rep. Jim Ramstad, Minn.
Rep. Ralph Regula, Ohio
Rep. Marge Roukema, N.J.
Rep. E. Clay Shaw, Jr., Fla.
Rep. Christopher Shays, Conn.
Sen. Gordon H. Smith, Ore.
Sen. Olympia J. Snowe, Maine, board member
Rep. Fred Upton, Mich., board member
Rep. James T. Walsh, N.Y.

CAMPAIGN FINANCE

Winners Outspent by Opponents

(in order of spending margin)

Senate

Name, Party, State	Expenditures	Opponent	Expenditures
Debbie Stabenow, D-Mich.	$8,194,394	Spencer Abraham, R	$13,028,636
Thomas R. Carper, D-Del.	2,608,942	William V. Roth Jr., R	4,366,884
Mel Carnahan, D-Mo.	8,800,864	John Ashcroft, R	9,378,581
Bill Nelson, D-Fla.	8,603,249	Bill McCollum, R	8,658,246
Lincoln Chafee, R-R.I.	2,265,221	Bob Weygand, D	2,297,885

House

Name, Party, State	Expenditures	Opponent	Expenditures
Shelley Moore Capito, R-W.Va.	$1,288,226	James F. Humphrey, D	$6,969,933
Adam B. Schiff, D-Calif.	4,351,025	James E. Rogan, R	6,889,947
Ken Bentsen, D-Texas	1,354,444	Phil Sudan, R	3,247,033
Ric Keller, R-Fla.	1,322,044	Linda Chapin, D	2,329,165
Anthony Weiner, D-N.Y.	528,367	Noach Dear, R	1,521,320
John Hostettler, R-Ind.	743,755	Paul Perry, D	1,567,499
Rob Simmons, R-Conn.	1,063,147	Sam Gejdenson, D	1,816,863
Jim Matheson, D-Utah	1,027,543	Derek Smith, R	1,681,135
Corrine Brown, D-Fla.	483,828	Jennifer Carroll, R	1,049,195
Constance A. Morella, R-Md.	1,715,940	Terry Lierman, D	2,217,488
John E. Sununu, R-N.H.	578,633	Martha Clark, D	1,055,513
Bob Barr, R-Ga.	3,495,641	Roger F. Kahn, D	3,959,860
Tim Roemer, D-Ind.	734,206	Chris Chocola, R	1,109,616
Steve Horn, R-Calif.	580,445	Gerrie Schipske, D	737,929
Mike Ross, D-Ark.	1,638,414	Jay Dickey, R	1,754,085
Roscoe G. Bartlett, R-Md.	445,919	Donald Dearmon, D	509,509
Ed Schrock, R-Va.	1,097,074	Jody Wagner, D	1,157,345
Charles Bass, R-N.H.	812,727	Barney L. Brannen III, D	872,733
Shelley Berkley, D-Nev.	2,062,803	Jon Porter, R	2,110,996
Christopher B. Cannon, R-Utah	340,723	Donald Dunn, D	378,565

CAMPAIGN FINANCE

10 Least-Expensive Winning House Campaigns

Name	Expenditures
Norman Sisisky, D-Va.	$56,828
Bill Jenkins, R-Tenn.	92,463
Joel Hefley, R-Colo.	127,282
Jim Turner, D-Texas	138,491
William J. Coyne, D-Pa.	142,754
Nick Smith, R-Mich.	152,467
Ralph Regula, R-Ohio	166,663
Louise M. Slaughter, D-N.Y.	167,851
Ileana Ros-Lehtinen, R-Fla.	186,363
Tony P. Hall, D-Ohio	192,835

CAMPAIGN FINANCE
Top 10 Senate Spenders

Name, Party, State	Expenditures	Opponent	Expenditures
Jon Corzine, D-N.J.	$63,209,506	Bob Franks, R	$6,394,936
Hillary Rodham Clinton, D-N.Y.	41,469,898	Rick A. Lazio, R	40,576,273
Mark Dayton, D-Minn.	11,955,330	Rod Grams, R	6,024,866
Maria Cantwell, D-Wash.	11,533,295	Slade Gorton, R	6,402,488
George F. Allen, R-Va.	10,887,124	Charles S. Robb, D	6,810,252
Rick Santorum, R-Pa.	10,616,262	Ron Klink, D	3,941,166
Dianne Feinstein, D-Calif.	10,346,170	Tom Campbell, R	4,378,283
Bill Nelson, D-Fla.	8,603,249	Bill McCollum, R	8,658,246
Debbie Stabenow, D-Mich.	8,194,394	Spencer Abraham, R	13,028,636
Bill Frist, R-Tenn.	6,105,303	William Clark, D	273,406

CAMPAIGN FINANCE
Top 10 House Spenders

Name, Party, State	Expenditures	Opponent	Expenditures
Richard A. Gephardt, D-Mo.	$5,580,964	William Federer, R	$2,319,819
Adam B. Schiff, D-Calif.	4,351,025	James E. Rogan Jr., R	6,889,947
Darrell Issa, R-Calif.	3,600,907	Peter Kouvelis, D	20,319
Bob Barr, R-Ga.	3,495,641	Roger F. Kahn, D	3,959,860
E. Clay Shaw Jr., R-Fla.	3,078,008	Elaine Bloom, D	2,378,327
Anne M. Northup, R-Ky.	2,916,818	Eleanor Jordan, D	1,700,171
Donald L. Sherwood, R-Pa.	2,751,597	Patrick Casey, D	1,619,801
Bill Luther, D-Minn.	2,597,244	John Kline, R	1,205,449
Rush D. Holt, D-N.J.	2,595,067	Dick Zimmer, R	2,196,588
Henry J. Hyde, R-Ill.	2,436,839	Brent Christensen, D	279,108

Closest Elections of 2000

Race	Winner	Votes	Loser	Votes	Margin
Mich. 8	Mike Rogers, R	145,190	Dianne Byrum, D	145,079	111
Minn. 2	Mark Kennedy, R	138,957	David Minge, D	138,802	155
Fla. 22	E. Clay Shaw Jr., R	105,855	Elaine Bloom, D	105,256	599
N.J. 12	Rush D. Holt, D	146,162	Dick Zimmer, R	145,511	651
Calif. 38	Steve Horn, R	87,266	Gerrie Schipske, D	85,498	1,768
Wash. Senate	Maria Cantwell, D	1,199,437	Slade Gorton, R	1,197,208	2,229
Conn. 2	Rob Simmons, R	114,380	Sam Gejdenson, D	111,520	2,860
Fla. 8	Ric Keller, R	125,253	Linda Chapin, D	121,295	3,958
Ark. 4	Mike Ross, D	108,143	Jay Dickey, R	104,017	4,126
Calif. 36	Jane Harman, D	115,651	Steven T. Kuykendall, R	111.199	4,452

Delegation Deans

South Carolina Democratic Sen. Ernest F. Hollings notes that, despite his 34-plus years in the Senate, he is still the state's junior senator. That length of service would make him the most senior member in 45 of the states. Arkansas is the only state that has no lawmaker with at least 10 years of service.

Here are the senior members in each state, based on total length of service in Congress as of Jan. 3, 2001:

State	Most Senior Member	Years of Service	State	Most Senior Member	Years of Service
Ala.	Richard C. Shelby, R	22	Mont.	Max Baucus, D	26
Alaska	Ted Stevens, R	32 / 10 days	Neb.	Doug Bereuter, R	22
Ariz.	Bob Stump, R	24	Nev.	Harry Reid, D	18
Ark.	Tim Hutchinson, R	8	N.H.	Robert C. Smith, R	16
Calif.	Pete Stark, D	28		Judd Gregg, R	16
Colo.	Joel Hefley, R	14	N.J.	Marge Roukema, R	20
	Ben Nighthorse Campbell, R	14		Christopher H. Smith, R	20
Conn.	Christopher J. Dodd, D	26	N.M.	Pete V. Domenici, R	28
Del.	Joseph R. Biden Jr., D	28	N.Y.	Charles B. Rangel, D	30
Fla.	C.W. Bill Young, R	30	N.C.	Jesse Helms, R	28
Ga.	John Lewis, D	14	N.D.	Byron L. Dorgan, D	20
Hawaii	Daniel K. Inouye, D	41 / 135 days	Ohio	Ralph Regula, R	28
Idaho	Larry E. Craig, R	20	Okla.	Don Nickles, R	20
Ill.	Philip M. Crane, R	31 / 39 days	Ore.	Ron Wyden, D	20
Ind.	Richard G. Lugar, R	24	Pa.	John P. Murtha, D	26 / 332 days
Iowa	Charles E. Grassley, R	26	R.I.	Jack Reed, D	10
	Tom Harkin, D	26	S.C.	Strom Thurmond, R	45 / 159 days
Kan.	Pat Roberts, R	20	S.D.	Tom Daschle, D	22
Ky.	Harold Rogers, R	20	Tenn.	Bart Gordon, D	16
La.	John B. Breaux, D	28 / 95 days	Texas	Charles W. Stenholm, D	22
Maine	Olympia J. Snowe, R	22		Martin Frost, D	22
Md.	Paul S. Sarbanes, D	30	Utah	Orrin G. Hatch, R	24
Mass.	Edward M. Kennedy, D	38 / 57 days	Vt.	Patrick J. Leahy, D	26
Mich.	John D. Dingell, D	45 / 21 days		James M. Jeffords, R	26
Minn.	James L. Oberstar, D	26	Va.	John W. Warner, R	22 / 1 day
Miss.	Thad Cochran, R	28	Wash.	Norm Dicks, D	24
	Trent Lott, D	28	W. Va.	Robert C. Byrd, D	48
Mo.	Richard A. Gephardt, D	24	Wis.	David R. Obey, D	31 / 277 days
	Ike Skelton, D	24	Wyo.	Craig Thomas, R	11 / 246 days

Campaign Finance

Figures are given for all members of Congress and their general election opponents as reported by the Federal Election Commission (FEC). If only one candidate is listed, either that candidate was unopposed or the second-leading vote-getter did not raise at least $5,000.

For House members, figures are for the 2000 elections. For senators, figures are for their most recent election.

The campaign finance data covers the receipts and expenditures of each candidate during the two-year election cycle. Data for 2000 covers the period Jan. 1, 1999, to Dec. 31, 2000. Data for 1998 covers the period Jan. 1, 1997, to Dec. 31, 1998. Data for 1996 covers the period Jan. 1, 1995, to Dec. 31, 1996.

The figures for political action committee (PAC) receipts are based on the FEC summary report for each candidate. Amounts designated include contributions from both PACs and candidate committees, but not party committees.

Where CQ was able to determine that a member does not accept PAC contributions, a zero appears.

The FEC updates its information regularly. See the FEC website at www.fec.gov.

Candidates who ran in special elections in the two-year cycle are marked with †. In these cases, campaign finance figures include money spent on the special elections.

Some New York candidates who were defeated in the primary ran in the general election on another party ticket.

Alabama

	RECEIPTS	FROM PACS	EXPENDITURES
SENIOR SENATOR - 1998			
Shelby (R)	$3,544,147	$1,167,950 (33%)	$1,890,484
Suddith (D)	$16,058	$500 (3%)	$15,723
JUNIOR SENATOR - 1996			
Sessions (R)	$3,905,870	$936,673 (24%)	$3,862,359
Bedford (D)	$3,216,772	$447,820 (14%)	$3,088,324
DISTRICT 1			
Callahan (R)	$335,839	$197,872 (59%)	$344,493
DISTRICT 2			
Everett (R)	$1,242,951	$270,985 (22%)	$1,424,354
DISTRICT 3			
Riley (R)	$766,990	$358,164 (47%)	$637,222
DISTRICT 4			
Aderholt (R)	$1,739,251	$646,969 (37%)	$1,683,278
Folsom (D)	$1,211,915	$313,775 (26%)	$1,134,694
DISTRICT 5			
Cramer (D)	$1,262,741	$538,486 (43%)	$512,728
DISTRICT 6			
Bachus (R)	$672,429	$351,503 (52%)	$577,565
DISTRICT 7			
Hilliard (D)	$483,046	$137,150 (28%)	$484,630
Martin (R)	$18,665	$1,000 (5%)	$18,431

Alaska

	RECEIPTS	FROM PACS	EXPENDITURES
SENIOR SENATOR - 1996			
Stevens (R)	$3,271,582	$1,203,797 (37%)	$2,711,710
JUNIOR SENATOR - 1998			
Murkowski (R)	$1,433,941	$752,735 (52%)	$911,926
Sonneman (D)	$26,606	$0 (0%)	$26,091
AT LARGE			
Young (R)	$1,297,578	$657,013 (51%)	$1,030,168

Arizona

	RECEIPTS	FROM PACS	EXPENDITURES
SENIOR SENATOR - 1998			
McCain (R)	$4,450,544	$1,146,419 (26%)	$2,461,900
Ranger (D)	$375,463	$25,100 (7%)	$371,439
JUNIOR SENATOR - 2000			
Kyl (R)	$2,985,612	$880,280 (29%)	$2,503,674
DISTRICT 1			
Flake (R)	$558,483	$129,869 (23%)	$505,210
Mendoza (D)	$78,017	$59,500 (76%)	$74,451
DISTRICT 2			
Pastor (D)	$743,176	$419,050 (56%)	$569,648
Barenholtz (R)	$87,727	$2,000 (2%)	$85,066
DISTRICT 3			
Stump (R)	$419,796	$227,679 (54%)	$377,426
Scharer (D)	$7,265	$1,200 (17%)	$7,233
DISTRICT 4			
Shadegg (R)	$706,496	$345,218 (49%)	$572,248
DISTRICT 5			
Kolbe (R)	$1,652,089	$681,773 (41%)	$1,541,478
Cunningham (D)	$554,578	$90,384 (16%)	$553,098
DISTRICT 6			
Hayworth (R)	$1,355,402	$598,049 (44%)	$1,183,832
Nelson (D)	$52,184	$11,500 (22%)	$48,522

Arkansas

	RECEIPTS	FROM PACS	EXPENDITURES
SENIOR SENATOR - 1996			
Hutchinson (R)	$1,691,276	$482,175 (29%)	$1,604,014
Bryant (D)	$1,606,053	$474,056 (30%)	$1,577,838
JUNIOR SENATOR - 1998			
Lincoln (D)	$3,056,184	$1,133,856 (37%)	$3,122,776
Boozman (R)	$1,099,108	$162,300 (15%)	$1,093,007
DISTRICT 1			
Berry (D)	$1,147,693	$421,800 (37%)	$1,169,274
Myshka (R)	$298,618	$15,362 (5%)	$298,491
DISTRICT 2			
Snyder (D)	$634,016	$217,172 (34%)	$624,989
Thomas (R)	$261,970	$22,500 (9%)	$261,969
DISTRICT 3			
Hutchinson (R)	$1,151,689	$284,229 (25%)	$949,743
DISTRICT 4			
Ross (D)	$1,671,793	$674,362 (40%)	$1,641,164
Dickey (R)	$1,710,294	$8,000 (0.5%)	$1,786,307

California

	RECEIPTS	FROM PACS	EXPENDITURES
SENIOR SENATOR - 2000			
Feinstein (D)	$10,464,194	$1,245,727 (12%)	$10,346,170
Campbell (R)	$4,733,507	$11,600 (0.2%)	$4,378,283
JUNIOR SENATOR - 1998			
Boxer (D)	$12,828,962	$1,214,649 (9%)	$13,737,548
Fong (R)	$10,818,417	$1,510,264 (14%)	$10,764,892
DISTRICT 1			
Thompson (D)	$932,639	$361,798 (39%)	$851,612
Chase (R)	$17,130	$299 (2%)	$17,730
DISTRICT 2			
Herger (R)	$692,904	$331,836 (48%)	$664,374
DISTRICT 3			
Ose (R)	$857,443	$341,436 (40%)	$593,164
Kent (D)	$306,128	$47,836 (16%)	$303,024
DISTRICT 4			
Doolittle (R)	$555,081	$190,121 (34%)	$587,722
Norberg (D)	$15,140	$3,600 (24%)	$14,540
DISTRICT 5			
Matsui (D)	$744,254	$527,490 (71%)	$769,342
Payne (R)	$45,517	$150 (0%)	$44,395
DISTRICT 6			
Woolsey (D)	$634,080	$247,235 (39%)	$576,539
McAuliffe (R)	$17,835	$0 (0%)	$17,979
DISTRICT 7			
Miller (D)	$382,248	$227,032 (59%)	$443,578
Hoffman (R)	$6,699	$100 (1%)	$5,388
DISTRICT 8			
Pelosi (D)	$410,465	$280,979 (68%)	$608,318
DISTRICT 9			
Lee (D)	$492,132	$215,983 (44%)	$452,812
DISTRICT 10			
Tauscher (D)	$1,566,172	$831,376 (53%)	$1,540,830
Hutchison (R)	$1,138,999	$94,860 (8%)	$1,127,901
DISTRICT 11			
Pombo (R)	$460,171	$229,216 (50%)	$451,956
Santos (D)	$12,980	$7,500 (58%)	$12,980
DISTRICT 12			
Lantos (D)	$510,024	$119,350 (23%)	$310,957
DISTRICT 13			
Stark (D)	$446,284	$298,938 (67%)	$414,879
DISTRICT 14			
Eshoo (D)	$807,567	$374,897 (46%)	$642,146
DISTRICT 15			
Honda (D)	$2,153,003	$595,609 (28%)	$2,125,541
Cunneen (R)	$1,451,184	$541,936 (37%)	$1,429,904
DISTRICT 16			
Lofgren (D)	$522,757	$260,459 (50%)	$486,365
DISTRICT 17			
Farr (D)	$587,265	$324,280 (55%)	$692,932
Engler (R)	$30,608	$278 (1%)	$31,107
DISTRICT 18			
Condit (D)	$785,996	$394,678 (50%)	$686,683
Wilson (R)	$32,185	$0 (0%)	$31,087

DISTRICT 19			
Radanovich (R)	$692,161	$203,583 (29%)	$659,104
Rosenberg (D)	$221,775	$22,185 (10%)	$219,555
DISTRICT 20			
Dooley (D)	$1,758,417	$1,099,483 (63%)	$1,793,089
Rodriguez (R)	$1,163,341	$344,300 (30%)	$1,257,145
DISTRICT 21			
Thomas (R)	$1,327,203	$857,933 (65%)	$1,529,664
DISTRICT 22			
Capps (D)	$1,639,838	$594,859 (36%)	$1,498,955
Stoker (R)	$822,009	$226,365 (28%)	$815,000
DISTRICT 23			
Gallegly (R)	$1,060,307	$303,217 (29%)	$1,022,565
Case (D)	$728,584	$134,750 (18%)	$726,953
DISTRICT 24			
Sherman (D)	$1,187,710	$432,548 (36%)	$1,064,622
Doyle (R)	$168,743	$29,295 (17%)	$166,148
DISTRICT 25			
McKeon (R)	$703,354	$217,929 (31%)	$674,238
Gold (D)	$35,596	$0 (0%)	$34,112
DISTRICT 26			
Berman (D)	$887,309	$293,694 (33%)	$521,478
DISTRICT 27			
Schiff (D)	$4,352,754	$722,324 (17%)	$4,351,025
Rogan (R)	$6,871,077	$1,012,593 (15%)	$6,889,947
DISTRICT 28			
Dreier (R)	$805,446	$369,377 (46%)	$1,130,755
Nelson (D)	$188,387	$25,850 (14%)	$188,122
DISTRICT 29			
Waxman (D)	$517,643	$335,450 (65%)	$389,766
DISTRICT 30			
Becerra (D)	$864,056	$459,547 (53%)	$1,046,470
DISTRICT 31			
Solis (D)	$1,106,090	$298,085 (27%)	$978,263
DISTRICT 33			
Roybal-Allard (D)	$303,188	$192,821 (64%)	$292,932
DISTRICT 34			
Napolitano (D)	$435,723	$307,649 (71%)	$356,984
Canales (R)	$1,789	$0 (0%)	$1,839
DISTRICT 35			
Waters (D)	$251,256	$147,300 (59%)	$266,309
McGill (R)	$7,906	$1,500 (19%)	$10,178
DISTRICT 36			
Harman (D)	$2,003,735	$532,691 (27%)	$1,998,739
Kuykendall (R)	$2,031,073	$1,119,862 (55%)	$1,988,938
DISTRICT 37			
Millender-McDonald (D)	$210,761	$167,844 (80%)	$194,214
DISTRICT 38			
Horn (R)	$516,518	$0 (0%)	$580,445
Schipske (D)	$738,812	$246,210 (33%)	$738,427
DISTRICT 39			
Royce (R)	$904,893	$328,699 (36%)	$327,284
Kanel (D)	$33,760	$10,500 (31%)	$24,805
DISTRICT 40			
Lewis (R)	$751,501	$394,824 (53%)	$805,526

DISTRICT 41

Miller (R)	$496,670	$296,131 (60%)	$514,991
Favila (D)	$75,158	$27,100 (36%)	$81,937

DISTRICT 42

Baca (D) †	$1,407,031	$897,077 (64%)	$1,347,431
Pirozzi (R) †	$872,094	$319,513 (37%)	$991,679

DISTRICT 43

Calvert (R)	$467,080	$226,879 (49%)	$421,029

DISTRICT 44

Bono (R)	$596,807	$194,664 (33%)	$582,684
Oden (D)	$127,416	$2,206 (2%)	$125,866

DISTRICT 45

Rohrabacher (R)	$279,346	$100,249 (36%)	$307,431
Crisell (D)	$53,254	$28,900 (54%)	$52,674

DISTRICT 46

Sanchez (D)	$2,055,613	$477,191 (23%)	$1,640,175
Tuchman (R)	$299,578	$61,987 (21%)	$296,060

DISTRICT 47

Cox (R)	$1,566,875	$268,048 (17%)	$1,171,803
Graham (D)	$18,744	$0 (0%)	$17,922

DISTRICT 48

Issa (R)	$3,612,764	$191,806 (5%)	$3,600,907
Kouvelis (D)	$21,685	$0 (0%)	$20,319

DISTRICT 49

Davis (D)	$1,953,863	$512,045 (26%)	$1,926,497
Bilbray (R)	$1,946,608	$990,366 (51%)	$1,846,574

DISTRICT 50

Filner (D)	$670,149	$317,075 (47%)	$400,015
Divine (R)	$11,112	$1,000 (9%)	$11,002

DISTRICT 51

Cunningham (R)	$607,657	$282,451 (46%)	$572,440
Barraza (D)	$5,810	$0 (0%)	$0

DISTRICT 52

Hunter (R)	$822,324	$280,889 (34%)	$856,691
Barkacs (D)	$270,887	$50 (0%)	$270,663

Colorado

	RECEIPTS	FROM PACS	EXPENDITURES
SENIOR SENATOR - 1998			
Campbell (R)	$3,224,271	$1,120,303 (35%)	$3,045,982
Lamm (D)	$1,836,621	$187,343 (10%)	$1,818,801
JUNIOR SENATOR - 1996			
Allard (R)	$2,198,131	$1,061,594 (48%)	$2,233,429
Strickland (D)	$3,313,065	$395,145 (12%)	$3,294,915
DISTRICT 1			
DeGette (D)	$661,596	$309,212 (47%)	$542,495
Thomas (R)	$58,875	$7,250 (12%)	$63,514
DISTRICT 2			
Udall (D)	$1,403,136	$391,185 (28%)	$1,330,529
Cox (R)	$510,189	$4,000 (1%)	$513,495
DISTRICT 3			
McInnis (R)	$939,920	$373,378 (40%)	$545,836
DISTRICT 4			
Schaffer (R)	$288,181	$115,441 (40%)	$248,736
DISTRICT 5			
Hefley (R)	$134,966	$84,579 (63%)	$127,282

DISTRICT 6

Tancredo (R)	$1,311,576	$510,352 (39%)	$1,123,854
Toltz (D)	$1,019,650	$192,083 (19%)	$1,019,651

Connecticut

	RECEIPTS	FROM PACS	EXPENDITURES
SENIOR SENATOR - 1998			
Dodd (D)	$4,102,172	$1,192,570 (29%)	$4,442,567
Franks (R)	$1,501,937	$71,602 (5%)	$1,478,307
JUNIOR SENATOR - 2000			
Lieberman (D)	$3,666,873	$975,344 (27%)	$3,786,665
Giordano (R)	$1,278,539	$0 (0%)	$1,276,376
DISTRICT 1			
Larson (D)	$768,612	$310,504 (40%)	$755,392
Backlund (R)	$82,824	$200 (0.2%)	$69,042
DISTRICT 2			
Simmons (R)	$1,077,563	$282,775 (26%)	$1,063,147
Gejdenson (D)	$1,899,575	$556,943 (29%)	$1,816,863
DISTRICT 3			
DeLauro (D)	$567,334	$265,024 (47%)	$680,778
Gold (R)	$74,312	$0 (0%)	$73,864
DISTRICT 4			
Shays (R)	$941,684	$68,052 (7%)	$1,039,573
Sanchez (D)	$176,121	$15,470 (9%)	$172,155
DISTRICT 5			
Maloney (D)	$2,106,496	$1,130,622 (54%)	$2,104,091
Nielsen (R)	$1,435,385	$300,785 (21%)	$1,426,019
DISTRICT 6			
Johnson (R)	$1,583,962	$902,306 (57%)	$1,163,610
Valenti (D)	$15,676	$0 (0%)	$11,642

Delaware

	RECEIPTS	FROM PACS	EXPENDITURES
SENIOR SENATOR - 1996			
Biden (D)	$1,636,013	$0 (0%)	$1,966,313
Clatworthy (R)	$1,332,167	$71,734 (5%)	$1,326,427
JUNIOR SENATOR - 2000			
Carper (D)	$2,629,812	$599,245 (23%)	$2,608,942
Roth (R)	$4,256,984	$1,727,178 (41%)	$4,366,884
AT LARGE			
Castle (R)	$675,048	$227,675 (34%)	$588,911
Miller (D)	$32,705	$0 (0%)	$28,831

Florida

	RECEIPTS	FROM PACS	EXPENDITURES
SENIOR SENATOR - 1998			
Graham (D)	$4,341,972	$1,164,317 (27%)	$5,094,581
Crist (R)	$1,337,307	$94,841 (7%)	$1,487,498
JUNIOR SENATOR - 2000			
Nelson (D)	$6,639,259	$1,195,617 (18%)	$6,635,832
McCollum (R)	$7,936,639	$1,391,571 (18%)	$8,664,112
DISTRICT 1			
Scarborough (R)	$755,055	$261,899 (35%)	$772,995

DISTRICT 2

Boyd (D)	$520,985	$396,093 (76%)	$378,202
Dodd (R)	$16,332	$0 (0%)	$16,227

DISTRICT 3

Brown (D)	$729,079	$407,100 (56%)	$483,828
Carroll (R)	$1,145,303	$258,887 (23%)	$1,049,195

DISTRICT 4

Crenshaw (R)	$921,042	$221,626 (24%)	$863,422
Sullivan (D)	$143,250	$12,475 (9%)	$143,350

DISTRICT 5

Thurman (D)	$660,533	$523,150 (79%)	$643,355
Enwall (R)	$301,621	$6,000 (2%)	$297,977

DISTRICT 6

Stearns (R)	$521,213	$308,674 (59%)	$228,628

DISTRICT 7

Mica (R)	$478,265	$169,629 (35%)	$206,125
Vaughen (D)	$39,382	$3,500 (9%)	$40,088

DISTRICT 8

Keller (R)	$1,345,241	$626,041 (47%)	$1,322,044
Chapin (D)	$1,686,848	$560,018 (33%)	$1,669,191

DISTRICT 9

Bilirakis (R)	$528,472	$370,396 (70%)	$518,118

DISTRICT 10

Young (R)	$489,893	$363,900 (74%)	$336,372

DISTRICT 11

Davis (D)	$446,981	$293,141 (66%)	$447,707

DISTRICT 12

Putnam (R)	$1,077,949	$561,233 (52%)	$1,047,257
Stedem (D)	$653,223	$367,962 (56%)	$650,578

DISTRICT 13

Miller (R)	$369,108	$89,229 (24%)	$369,407
Dunn (D)	$49,614	$11,000 (22%)	$50,948

DISTRICT 14

Goss (R)	$225,014	$105,829 (47%)	$259,684

DISTRICT 15

Weldon (R)	$831,459	$285,422 (34%)	$910,906
Kurth (D)	$573,636	$216,550 (38%)	$698,292

DISTRICT 16

Foley (R)	$1,874,407	$808,535 (43%)	$1,544,903
Brown (D)	$652,191	$96,968 (15%)	$626,210

DISTRICT 17

Meek (D)	$270,937	$140,267 (52%)	$298,389

DISTRICT 18

Ros-Lehtinen (R)	$425,695	$146,965 (35%)	$192,368

DISTRICT 19

Wexler (D)	$908,618	$273,141 (30%)	$447,274
Thompson (R)	$11,095	$0 (0%)	$10,620

DISTRICT 20

Deutsch (D)	$1,372,669	$291,935 (21%)	$558,259

DISTRICT 21

Diaz-Balart (R)	$483,016	$217,232 (45%)	$294,122

DISTRICT 22

Shaw (R)	$2,755,056	$1,316,733 (48%)	$3,086,708
Bloom (D)	$2,391,453	$406,279 (17%)	$2,378,327

DISTRICT 23

Hastings (D)	$377,839	$133,250 (35%)	$375,037

Georgia

	RECEIPTS	FROM PACS	EXPENDITURES
SENIOR SENATOR - 1996			
Cleland (D)	$2,944,283	$710,670 (24%)	$2,926,391
Millner (R)	$9,917,102	$563,120 (6%)	$9,858,955
JUNIOR SENATOR - 2000			
Miller (D)	$2,684,514	$765,150 (29%)	$2,533,746
Mattingly (R)	$1,114,900	$135,549 (12%)	$1,093,408
DISTRICT 1			
Kingston (R)	$839,391	$282,957 (34%)	$652,186
Griggs (D)	$70,127	$2,000 (3%)	$70,119
DISTRICT 2			
Bishop (D)	$1,003,852	$579,306 (58%)	$1,069,838
Glenn (R)	$925,427	$92,700 (10%)	$953,867
DISTRICT 3			
Collins (R)	$616,089	$320,621 (52%)	$697,766
Notti (D)	$146,581	$600 (0.4%)	$131,447
DISTRICT 4			
McKinney (D)	$480,336	$191,560 (40%)	$410,270
Warren (R)	$315,385	$26,133 (8%)	$315,512
DISTRICT 5			
Lewis (D)	$682,137	$356,200 (52%)	$811,850
Schwab (R)	$32,174	$1,000 (3%)	$28,253
DISTRICT 6			
Isakson (R) †	$1,721,066	$496,532 (29%)	$1,601,856
Jeffrey (R) †	$240,910	$9,046 (4%)	$215,737
DeHart (D)	$36,466	$0 (0%)	$36,463
DISTRICT 7			
Barr (R)	$3,442,211	$489,450 (14%)	$3,495,641
Kahn (D)	$4,004,704	$125,566 (3%)	$3,859,860
DISTRICT 8			
Chambliss (R)	$1,805,868	$610,714 (34%)	$1,841,653
Marshall (D)	$978,213	$271,749 (28%)	$896,654
DISTRICT 9			
Deal (R)	$375,557	$225,411 (60%)	$429,979
Harrington (D)	$109,674	$0 (0%)	$69,884
DISTRICT 10			
Norwood (R)	$1,274,505	$441,125 (35%)	$787,855
Freeman (D)	$24,687	$600 (2%)	$26,713
DISTRICT 11			
Linder (R)	$636,115	$256,637 (40%)	$418,105

Hawaii

	RECEIPTS	FROM PACS	EXPENDITURES
SENIOR SENATOR - 1998			
Inouye (D)	$1,743,520	$571,755 (33%)	$1,375,601
JUNIOR SENATOR - 2000			
Akaka (D)	$601,881	$316,415 (53%)	$428,516
Carroll (R)	$107,253	$300 (0.3%)	$97,407
DISTRICT 1			
Abercrombie (D)	$805,055	$489,279 (61%)	$722,133
Meyers (R)	$22,892	$13,000 (57%)	$22,042
DISTRICT 2			
Mink (D)	$348,363	$211,680 (61%)	$337,420
Francis (R)	$200,038	$29,500 (15%)	$195,390

Idaho

	RECEIPTS	FROM PACS	EXPENDITURES
SENIOR SENATOR - 1996			
Craig (R)	$2,695,939	$1,027,626 (38%)	$2,809,897
Minnick (D)	$2,179,155	$86,377 (4%)	$2,140,878
JUNIOR SENATOR - 1998			
Crapo (R)	$1,803,195	$794,715 (44%)	$1,563,811
Mauk (D)	$243,284	$29,200 (12%)	$241,443
DISTRICT 1			
Otter (R)	$1,212,820	$309,206 (25%)	$1,212,580
Pall (D)	$72,266	$10,300 (14%)	$72,061
DISTRICT 2			
Simpson (R)	$720,232	$377,370 (52%)	$731,554

Illinois

	RECEIPTS	FROM PACS	EXPENDITURES
SENIOR SENATOR - 1996			
Durbin (D)	$4,767,940	$1,153,210 (24%)	$4,966,804
Salvi (R)	$4,754,916	$522,330 (11%)	$4,752,025
JUNIOR SENATOR - 1998			
Fitzgerald (R)	$17,897,956	$1,003,452 (6%)	$17,677,698
Moseley-Braun (D)	$7,222,013	$1,260,576 (17%)	$7,200,895
DISTRICT 1			
Rush (D)	$722,452	$356,381 (49%)	$656,599
DISTRICT 2			
Jackson (D)	$545,037	$214,250 (39%)	$304,619
DISTRICT 3			
Lipinski (D)	$438,979	$284,409 (65%)	$387,674
Groth (R)	$18,466	$1,110 (6%)	$18,073
DISTRICT 4			
Gutierrez (D)	$448,374	$202,600 (45%)	$454,558
DISTRICT 5			
Blagojevich (D)	$819,335	$248,300 (30%)	$277,035
DISTRICT 6			
Hyde (R)	$2,744,677	$414,363 (15%)	$2,436,839
Christensen (D)	$280,143	$6,636 (2%)	$279,108
DISTRICT 7			
Davis (D)	$318,845	$167,350 (52%)	$251,566
DISTRICT 8			
Crane (R)	$1,064,989	$679,930 (64%)	$970,024
Pressl (D)	$286,279	$45,600 (16%)	$281,881
DISTRICT 9			
Schakowsky (D)	$849,837	$183,803 (22%)	$694,724
Driscoll (R)	$95,360	$12 (0%)	$98,852
DISTRICT 10			
Kirk (R)	$2,083,719	$573,967 (28%)	$2,030,292
Gash (D)	$1,975,304	$515,761 (26%)	$1,967,426
DISTRICT 11			
Weller (R)	$1,514,988	$692,357 (46%)	$976,795
Stevenson (D)	$146,091	$450 (0.3%)	$144,916
DISTRICT 12			
Costello (D)	$673,465	$261,006 (39%)	$373,057
DISTRICT 13			
Biggert (R)	$544,312	$259,974 (48%)	$395,773

DISTRICT 14			
Hastert (R)	$2,385,649	$1,307,648 (55%)	$2,299,072
DISTRICT 15			
Johnson (R)	$1,926,919	$399,793 (21%)	$1,760,128
Kelleher (D)	$958,618	$316,930 (33%)	$953,233
DISTRICT 16			
Manzullo (R)	$703,280	$220,364 (31%)	$682,309
Hendrickson (D)	$54,043	$15,920 (29%)	$54,882
DISTRICT 17			
Evans (D)	$1,204,520	$660,134 (55%)	$1,270,267
Baker (R)	$946,942	$380,431 (40%)	$984,857
DISTRICT 18			
LaHood (R)	$1,060,668	$320,542 (30%)	$974,251
Harant (D)	$86,431	$15,005 (17%)	$86,262
DISTRICT 19			
Phelps (D)	$531,961	$362,401 (68%)	$300,056
Eatherly (R)	$34,674	$0 (0%)	$32,428
DISTRICT 20			
Shimkus (R)	$843,987	$474,617 (56%)	$645,920
Cooper (D)	$248,965	$61,450 (25%)	$249,049

Indiana

	RECEIPTS	FROM PACS	EXPENDITURES
SENIOR SENATOR - 2000			
Lugar (R)	$3,593,294	$863,899 (24%)	$4,251,603
Johnson (D)	$1,451,828	$138,900 (10%)	$1,451,786
JUNIOR SENATOR - 1998			
Bayh (D)	$4,158,990	$1,078,856 (26%)	$3,914,375
Helmke (R)	$646,906	$34,850 (5%)	$645,999
DISTRICT 1			
Visclosky (D)	$447,337	$215,322 (48%)	$390,320
Reynolds (R)	$12,457	$0 (0%)	$12,457
DISTRICT 2			
Pence (R)	$1,109,916	$357,854 (32%)	$1,106,140
Rock (D)	$369,095	$128,450 (35%)	$369,888
DISTRICT 3			
Roemer (D)	$679,009	$457,960 (67%)	$734,206
Chocola (R)	$1,127,274	$47,496 (4%)	$1,109,616
DISTRICT 4			
Souder (R)	$245,471	$84,029 (34%)	$288,827
Foster (D)	$31,188	$5,100 (16%)	$30,685
DISTRICT 5			
Buyer (R)	$705,633	$353,517 (50%)	$720,714
Goodnight (D)	$459,132	$212,300 (46%)	$455,147
DISTRICT 6			
Burton (R)	$713,472	$258,025 (36%)	$622,401
Griesey (D)	$9,165	$0 (0%)	$9,123
DISTRICT 7			
Kerns (R)	$677,556	$278,354 (41%)	$571,791
Graf (D)	$8,846	$200 (2%)	$11,302
DISTRICT 8			
Hostettler (R)	$730,355	$83,968 (11%)	$743,755
Perry (D)	$1,571,743	$471,970 (30%)	$1,568,521
DISTRICT 9			
Hill (D)	$1,028,137	$536,061 (52%)	$981,802
Bailey (R)	$245,631	$3,500 (1%)	$245,202

DISTRICT 10

Carson (D)	$507,667	$269,944 (53%)	$340,203
Scott (R)	$84,525	$6,150 (7%)	$84,108

Iowa

	RECEIPTS	FROM PACS	EXPENDITURES
SENIOR SENATOR - 1998			
Grassley (R)	$3,291,469	$1,339,266 (41%)	$2,781,940
Osterberg (D)	$165,655	$25,200 (15%)	$165,429
JUNIOR SENATOR - 1996			
Harkin (D)	$4,665,182	$1,061,573 (23%)	$5,276,708
Lightfoot (R)	$2,474,871	$553,512 (22%)	$2,439,679
DISTRICT 1			
Leach (R)	$389,098	$0 (0%)	$375,143
Simpson (D)	$29,129	$4,750 (16%)	$28,536
DISTRICT 2			
Nussle (R)	$822,867	$482,871 (59%)	$907,935
Smith (D)	$92,952	$31,247 (34%)	$92,577
DISTRICT 3			
Boswell (D)	$757,498	$416,100 (55%)	$710,518
Marcus (R)	$243,223	$4,210 (2%)	$245,972
DISTRICT 4			
Ganske (R)	$1,055,301	$379,747 (36%)	$841,115
Huston (D)	$128,422	$27,500 (21%)	$125,658
DISTRICT 5			
Latham (R)	$489,182	$254,006 (52%)	$375,152
Palecek (D)	$5,935	$212 (4%)	$5,933

Kansas

	RECEIPTS	FROM PACS	EXPENDITURES
SENIOR SENATOR - 1998			
Brownback (R)	$2,147,205	$918,278 (43%)	$1,719,612
Feleciano (D)	$39,450	$12,650 (32%)	$39,500
JUNIOR SENATOR - 1996			
Roberts (R)	$2,297,886	$1,216,831 (53%)	$2,305,898
Thompson (D)	$662,523	$203,024 (31%)	$659,066
DISTRICT 1			
Moran (R)	$540,019	$231,479 (43%)	$358,597
DISTRICT 2			
Ryun (R)	$443,593	$222,404 (50%)	$284,064
DISTRICT 3			
Moore (D)	$1,784,800	$683,385 (38%)	$1,759,414
Kline (R)	$1,062,841	$293,451 (28%)	$1,054,489
DISTRICT 4			
Tiahrt (R)	$960,600	$384,667 (40%)	$854,357
Nolla (D)	$326,284	$83,500 (26%)	$315,524

Kentucky

	RECEIPTS	FROM PACS	EXPENDITURES
SENIOR SENATOR - 1996			
McConnell (R)	$3,840,374	$1,293,151 (34%)	$4,669,642
Beshear (D)	$1,879,343	$229,780 (12%)	$2,073,794

JUNIOR SENATOR - 1998			
Bunning (R)	$3,597,425	$1,363,896 (38%)	$3,746,540
Baesler (D)	$3,855,690	$771,022 (20%)	$3,825,731
DISTRICT 1			
Whitfield (R)	$1,426,748	$744,989 (52%)	$1,495,305
Roy (D)	$716,066	$303,337 (42%)	$716,066
DISTRICT 2			
Lewis (R)	$437,636	$250,915 (57%)	$225,008
DISTRICT 3			
Northup (R)	$2,896,393	$1,102,290 (38%)	$2,916,818
Jordan (D)	$1,727,126	$485,112 (28%)	$1,700,171
DISTRICT 4			
Lucas (D)	$942,239	$565,569 (60%)	$854,357
Bell (R)	$62,966	$2,000 (3%)	$62,817
DISTRICT 5			
Rogers (R)	$647,861	$336,712 (52%)	$459,993
DISTRICT 6			
Fletcher (R)	$2,493,053	$1,139,810 (46%)	$2,300,940
Baesler (D)	$1,719,303	$576,136 (34%)	$1,484,436
Galbraith (I)	$12,988	$0 (0%)	$12,594

Louisiana

	RECEIPTS	FROM PACS	EXPENDITURES
SENIOR SENATOR - 1998			
Breaux (D)	$3,992,303	$1,533,040 (38%)	$3,858,472
Donelon (R)	$364,056	$19,845 (5%)	$364,073
JUNIOR SENATOR - 1996			
Landrieu (D)	$2,899,684	$535,736 (18%)	$2,715,287
Jenkins (R)	$1,969,175	$479,543 (24%)	$1,967,742
DISTRICT 1			
Vitter (R) †	$2,493,055	$403,400 (16%)	$1,956,948
Treen (R) †	$1,116,499	$93,900 (8%)	$1,147,601
DISTRICT 2			
Jefferson (D)	$393,367	$279,421 (71%)	$563,238
DISTRICT 3			
Tauzin (R)	$1,194,679	$812,025 (68%)	$1,477,133
DISTRICT 4			
McCrery (R)	$628,850	$282,662 (45%)	$574,127
DISTRICT 5			
Cooksey (R)	$630,524	$180,078 (29%)	$513,769
DISTRICT 6			
Baker (R)	$919,564	$559,495 (61%)	$916,205
DISTRICT 7			
John (D)	$643,915	$378,651 (59%)	$627,685

Maine

	RECEIPTS	FROM PACS	EXPENDITURES
SENIOR SENATOR - 2000			
Snowe (R)	$2,236,146	$817,009 (37%)	$1,981,504
Lawrence (D)	$739,637	$145,703 (20%)	$727,655
JUNIOR SENATOR - 1996			
Collins (R)	$1,721,825	$598,836 (35%)	$1,621,475
Brennan (D)	$978,848	$321,757 (33%)	$976,805

DISTRICT 1

Allen (D)	$667,259	$210,455 (32%)	$639,119
Amero (R)	$478,724	$77,542 (16%)	$478,817

DISTRICT 2

Baldacci (D)	$505,992	$315,042 (62%)	$508,966
Campbell (R)	$70,867	$200 (0.3%)	$69,343

Maryland

	RECEIPTS	FROM PACS	EXPENDITURES
SENIOR SENATOR - 2000			
Sarbanes (D)	$1,851,731	$748,964 (40%)	$1,837,286
Rappaport (R)	$147,024	$2,510 (2%)	$146,866
JUNIOR SENATOR - 1998			
Mikulski (D)	$2,908,352	$925,021 (32%)	$3,014,312
Pierpont (R)	$297,770	$0 (0%)	$297,768
DISTRICT 1			
Gilchrest (R)	$224,978	$2,400 (1%)	$225,166
Bozman (D)	$72,736	$9,100 (13%)	$52,987
DISTRICT 2			
Ehrlich (R)	$1,001,036	$415,441 (42%)	$871,393
DISTRICT 3			
Cardin (D)	$740,708	$472,055 (64%)	$564,687
DISTRICT 4			
Wynn (D)	$588,183	$372,669 (63%)	$465,471
DISTRICT 5			
Hoyer (D)	$1,259,484	$796,089 (63%)	$1,268,702
Hutchins (R)	$77,202	$5,500 (7%)	$64,208
DISTRICT 6			
Bartlett (R)	$232,299	$65,025 (28%)	$445,919
DeArmon (D)	$466,503	$59,100 (13%)	$509,509
DISTRICT 7			
Cummings (D)	$369,229	$71,800 (19%)	$444,442
DISTRICT 8			
Morella (R)	$1,101,894	$474,095 (43%)	$1,154,410
Lierman (D)	$2,226,442	$111,194 (5%)	$2,217,488

Massachusetts

	RECEIPTS	FROM PACS	EXPENDITURES
SENIOR SENATOR - 2000			
Kennedy (D)	$6,623,179	$864,078 (13%)	$3,662,652
Robinson (R)	$163,929	$0 (0%)	$163,927
JUNIOR SENATOR - 1996			
Kerry (D)	$10,342,115	$14,591 (0%)	$10,962,607
Weld (R)	$8,074,417	$816,495 (10%)	$8,002,123
DISTRICT 1			
Olver (D)	$662,275	$260,099 (39%)	$646,363
Abair (R)	$161,464	$6,490 (4%)	$170,442
DISTRICT 2			
Neal (D)	$720,715	$416,952 (58%)	$369,098
DISTRICT 3			
McGovern (D)	$848,573	$301,253 (36%)	$550,240
DISTRICT 4			
Frank (D)	$464,795	$140,813 (30%)	$471,381
Travis (R)	$24,701	$500 (2%)	$24,553

DISTRICT 5

Meehan (D)	$1,410,673	$0 (0%)	$508,730

DISTRICT 6

Tierney (D)	$739,050	$188,704 (26%)	$426,934
McCarthy (R)	$55,248	$3,160 (6%)	$54,403

DISTRICT 7

Markey (D)	$591,089	$0 (0%)	$584,630

DISTRICT 8

Capuano (D)	$661,252	$245,375 (37%)	$443,990

DISTRICT 9

Moakley (D)	$1,435,113	$479,550 (33%)	$1,127,856
Jeghelian (R)	$22,405	$0 (0%)	$19,796

DISTRICT 10

Delahunt (D)	$755,389	$246,377 (33%)	$231,526

Michigan

	RECEIPTS	FROM PACS	EXPENDITURES
SENIOR SENATOR - 1996			
Levin (D)	$6,021,723	$889,738 (15%)	$5,965,017
Romney (R)	$3,258,351	$3,269,294(100%)	$3,287,547
JUNIOR SENATOR - 2000			
Stabenow (D)	$8,297,375	$955,856 (12%)	$8,194,394
Abraham (R)	$11,838,542	$2,485,419 (21%)	$13,028,636
DISTRICT 1			
Stupak (D)	$1,029,162	$761,147 (74%)	$971,337
Yob (R)	$691,469	$150,556 (22%)	$691,468
DISTRICT 2			
Hoekstra (R)	$335,258	$11,228 (3%)	$291,642
Shrauger (D)	$182,984	$33,650 (18%)	$175,328
DISTRICT 3			
Ehlers (R)	$374,505	$102,210 (27%)	$302,826
Steele (D)	$28,091	$11,000 (39%)	$28,090
DISTRICT 4			
Camp (R)	$1,072,422	$365,444 (34%)	$1,026,361
Hollenbeck (D)	$5,975	$1,500 (25%)	$6,099
DISTRICT 5			
Barcia (D)	$299,898	$190,105 (63%)	$202,688
Actis (R)	$24,637	$0 (0%)	$18,089
DISTRICT 6			
Upton (R)	$771,231	$346,064 (45%)	$620,512
DISTRICT 7			
Smith (R)	$212,697	$79 (0%)	$152,467
DISTRICT 8			
Rogers (R)	$2,224,233	$937,385 (42%)	$2,195,500
Byrum (D)	$2,114,471	$702,738 (33%)	$2,147,131
DISTRICT 9			
Kildee (D)	$570,758	$328,179 (57%)	$307,376
Garrett (R)	$107,367	$4,075 (4%)	$107,366
DISTRICT 10			
Bonior (D)	$2,336,205	$997,301 (43%)	$2,312,101
Turner (R)	$23,197	$0 (0%)	$23,263
DISTRICT 11			
Knollenberg (R)	$1,210,801	$332,690 (27%)	$1,104,909
Frumin (D)	$209,727	$10,983 (5%)	$207,948

DISTRICT 12			
Levin (D)	$1,178,217	$624,241 (53%)	$1,054,666
Baron (R)	$48,174	$5,000 (10%)	$43,657
DISTRICT 13			
Rivers (D)	$440,702	$132,584 (30%)	$408,014
Barry (R)	$14,111	$0 (0%)	$11,926
DISTRICT 14			
Conyers (D)	$451,606	$277,450 (61%)	$272,976
DISTRICT 15			
Kilpatrick (D)	$455,496	$239,875 (53%)	$357,453
DISTRICT 16			
Dingell (D)	$1,124,214	$847,208 (75%)	$1,048,787

Minnesota

	RECEIPTS	FROM PACS	EXPENDITURES
SENIOR SENATOR - 1996			
Wellstone (D)	$5,991,013	$571,723 (10%)	$5,979,224
Boschwitz (R)	$4,450,625	$1,033,247 (23%)	$4,409,982
JUNIOR SENATOR - 2000			
Dayton (D)	$12,040,466	$0 (0%)	$11,957,114
Grams (R)	$5,902,543	$1,623,289 (28%)	$6,024,866
DISTRICT 1			
Gutknecht (R)	$979,145	$288,365 (29%)	$969,598
Rieder (D)	$373,939	$133,855 (36%)	$372,636
DISTRICT 2			
Kennedy (R)	$912,385	$180,501 (20%)	$896,993
Minge (D)	$845,799	$506,218 (60%)	$848,795
DISTRICT 3			
Ramstad (R)	$762,585	$314,119 (41%)	$747,976
Shuff (D)	$23,138	$3,500 (15%)	$22,824
DISTRICT 4			
McCollum (D)	$1,180,499	$401,857 (34%)	$1,090,046
Runbeck (R)	$913,510	$290,518 (32%)	$900,795
Foley (INDC)	$311,703	$21,200 (7%)	$274,287
DISTRICT 5			
Sabo (D)	$441,092	$252,309 (57%)	$467,849
Taylor (R)	$57,585	$2,600 (5%)	$53,641
DISTRICT 6			
Luther (D)	$1,400,988	$526,688 (38%)	$2,597,244
Kline (R)	$1,236,301	$440,379 (36%)	$1,205,449
DISTRICT 7			
Peterson (D)	$337,941	$254,150 (75%)	$207,292
Menze (R)	$53,918	$1,150 (2%)	$60,721
DISTRICT 8			
Oberstar (D)	$884,424	$642,918 (73%)	$1,032,070
Lemen (R)	$28,040	$0 (0%)	$22,253

Mississippi

	RECEIPTS	FROM PACS	EXPENDITURES
SENIOR SENATOR - 1996			
Cochran (R)	$787,233	$540,354 (69%)	$828,693
JUNIOR SENATOR - 2000			
Lott (R)	$4,241,819	$791,025 (19%)	$3,663,052
Brown (D)	$51,716	$7,500 (15%)	$40,349

DISTRICT 1			
Wicker (R)	$1,254,306	$318,718 (25%)	$1,283,515
DISTRICT 2			
Thompson (D)	$536,455	$259,900 (48%)	$409,852
DISTRICT 3			
Pickering (R)	$918,030	$497,752 (54%)	$519,957
DISTRICT 4			
Shows (D)	$1,187,682	$655,674 (55%)	$1,196,099
Lampton (R)	$481,318	$118,196 (25%)	$479,540
DISTRICT 5			
Taylor (D)	$317,625	$172,600 (54%)	$287,750

Missouri

	RECEIPTS	FROM PACS	EXPENDITURES
SENIOR SENATOR - 1998			
Bond (R)	$5,848,137	$1,919,491 (33%)	$6,229,649
Nixon (D)	$2,573,843	$413,937 (16%)	$2,568,879
DISTRICT 1			
Clay (D)	$720,617	$357,675 (50%)	$679,776
Billingsly (R)	$11,352	$0 (0%)	$3,787
DISTRICT 2			
Akin (R)	$1,062,818	$341,269 (32%)	$1,015,568
House (D)	$869,953	$433,232 (50%)	$858,204
DISTRICT 3			
Gephardt (D)	$3,816,891	$838,109 (22%)	$5,580,964
Federer (R)	$2,377,050	$35,550 (1%)	$2,319,819
DISTRICT 4			
Skelton (D)	$651,285	$383,299 (59%)	$624,593
Noland (R)	$11,256	$413 (4%)	$11,256
DISTRICT 5			
McCarthy (D)	$433,185	$282,694 (65%)	$331,907
Gordon (R)	$9,066	$1,100 (12%)	$10,060
DISTRICT 6			
Graves (R)	$1,111,218	$625,348 (56%)	$1,115,338
Danner (D)	$805,554	$393,826 (49%)	$811,060
DISTRICT 7			
Blunt (R)	$1,616,797	$940,446 (58%)	$1,177,456
DISTRICT 8			
Emerson (R)	$772,620	$420,837 (54%)	$794,800
DISTRICT 9			
Hulshof (R)	$1,122,368	$554,708 (49%)	$1,202,235
Carroll (D)	$369,821	$156,500 (42%)	$362,876

Montana

	RECEIPTS	FROM PACS	EXPENDITURES
SENIOR SENATOR - 1996			
Baucus (D)	$3,449,478	$1,352,466 (39%)	$3,748,502
Rehberg (R)	$1,369,530	$333,744 (24%)	$1,358,165
JUNIOR SENATOR - 2000			
Burns (R)	$3,931,267	$1,683,501 (43%)	$4,337,961
Schweitzer (D)	$2,103,712	$354,574 (17%)	$2,033,530
AT LARGE			
Rehberg (R)	$2,153,239	$758,515 (35%)	$2,132,364
Keenan (D)	$1,923,295	$564,163 (29%)	$1,932,099

Nebraska

	RECEIPTS	FROM PACS	EXPENDITURES
SENIOR SENATOR - 1996			
Hagel (R)	$3,612,338	$486,034 (13%)	$3,564,316
Nelson (D)	$2,179,131	$926,268 (43%)	$2,159,653
JUNIOR SENATOR - 2000			
Nelson (D)	$2,782,642	$1,298,059 (47%)	$2,794,887
Stenberg (R)	$1,871,463	$456,076 (24%)	$1,859,252
DISTRICT 1			
Bereuter (R)	$349,613	$245,750 (70%)	$380,036
Jacobsen (D)	$111,863	$18,000 (16%)	$107,256
DISTRICT 2			
Terry (R)	$888,202	$360,177 (41%)	$858,465
Kiel (D)	$358,029	$121,328 (34%)	$345,347
DISTRICT 3			
Osborne (R)	$493,356	$0 (0%)	$484,797
Reynolds (D)	$13,919	$250 (2%)	$12,857

Nevada

	RECEIPTS	FROM PACS	EXPENDITURES
SENIOR SENATOR - 1998			
Reid (D)	$3,905,324	$1,219,324 (31%)	$4,939,010
Ensign (R)	$3,454,820	$1,295,185 (37%)	$3,490,256
JUNIOR SENATOR - 2000			
Ensign (R)	$4,878,526	$1,715,992 (35%)	$4,872,176
Bernstein (D)	$2,483,512	$333,766 (13%)	$2,449,093
DISTRICT 1			
Berkley (D)	$2,067,764	$879,780 (43%)	$2,062,803
Porter (R)	$1,394,975	$388,612 (28%)	$1,386,081
DISTRICT 2			
Gibbons (R)	$592,777	$243,819 (41%)	$320,019

New Hampshire

	RECEIPTS	FROM PACS	EXPENDITURES
SENIOR SENATOR - 1996			
Smith (R)	$1,708,376	$875,951 (51%)	$1,718,413
Swett (D)	$1,759,089	$348,388 (20%)	$1,558,563
JUNIOR SENATOR - 1998			
Gregg (R)	$1,183,131	$685,620 (58%)	$904,448
Condodemetraky (D)	$35,827	$7,350 (21%)	$28,547
DISTRICT 1			
Sununu (R)	$544,265	$178,568 (33%)	$578,633
Clark (D)	$1,151,998	$26,375 (2%)	$1,055,513
DISTRICT 2			
Bass (R)	$782,025	$349,497 (45%)	$812,727
Brannen (D)	$881,376	$299,384 (34%)	$872,115

New Jersey

	RECEIPTS	FROM PACS	EXPENDITURES
SENIOR SENATOR - 1996			
Torricelli (D)	$9,211,508	$952,153 (10%)	$9,134,854
Zimmer (R)	$8,212,612	$1,197,917 (15%)	$8,238,181
JUNIOR SENATOR - 2000			
Corzine (D)	$63,253,520	$235,909 (0.4%)	$63,209,506
Franks (R)	$6,428,214	$1,221,491 (19%)	$6,394,936
DISTRICT 1			
Andrews (D)	$920,729	$475,199 (52%)	$444,224
Cathcart (R)	$10,865	$710 (7%)	$7,162
DISTRICT 2			
LoBiondo (R)	$813,562	$339,392 (42%)	$779,831
Janosik (D)	$76,374	$5,190 (7%)	$75,622
DISTRICT 3			
Saxton (R)	$1,716,664	$564,187 (33%)	$2,143,518
Levin (D)	$1,772,649	$338,429 (19%)	$1,760,625
DISTRICT 4			
Smith (R)	$506,195	$157,332 (31%)	$611,785
Gusciora (D)	$118,755	$27,000 (23%)	$115,392
DISTRICT 5			
Roukema (R)	$1,003,004	$558,705 (56%)	$1,005,148
Mercurio (D)	$70,030	$38,280 (55%)	$65,607
DISTRICT 6			
Pallone (D)	$1,114,908	$578,505 (52%)	$863,186
Kennedy (R)	$36,085	$0 (0%)	$37,021
DISTRICT 7			
Ferguson (R)	$2,398,279	$590,098 (25%)	$2,412,820
Connelly (D)	$1,984,266	$494,838 (25%)	$2,028,816
DISTRICT 8			
Pascrell (D)	$987,841	$330,065 (33%)	$1,081,808
Fusco (R)	$247,519	$1,250 (1%)	$279,545
DISTRICT 9			
Rothman (D)	$1,083,837	$430,680 (40%)	$880,283
Tedeschi (R)	$45,150	$0 (0%)	$30,099
DISTRICT 10			
Payne (D)	$448,257	$227,765 (51%)	$347,319
DISTRICT 11			
Frelinghuysen (R)	$726,873	$263,756 (36%)	$557,937
Scollo (D)	$10,400	$5,100 (49%)	$9,161
DISTRICT 12			
Holt (D)	$2,659,446	$806,006 (30%)	$2,595,080
Zimmer (R)	$2,223,722	$610,745 (27%)	$2,196,588
DISTRICT 13			
Menendez (D)	$2,188,542	$578,130 (26%)	$1,713,018
de Leon (R)	$13,119	$2,340 (18%)	$19,822

New Mexico

	RECEIPTS	FROM PACS	EXPENDITURES
SENIOR SENATOR - 1996			
Domenici (R)	$3,264,601	$1,154,329 (35%)	$3,110,548
Trujillo (D)	$163,728	$12,800 (8%)	$163,613
JUNIOR SENATOR - 2000			
Bingaman (D)	$2,730,680	$1,192,335 (44%)	$2,568,649
Redmond (R)	$718,772	$75,409 (10%)	$706,424
DISTRICT 1			
Wilson (R)	$2,241,534	$884,156 (39%)	$2,203,322
Kelly (D)	$1,601,069	$282,276 (18%)	$1,635,633
DISTRICT 2			
Skeen (R)	$697,423	$381,889 (55%)	$699,299
Montoya (D)	$291,446	$46,450 (16%)	$292,955

DISTRICT 3

Udall (D)	$772,927	$268,136 (35%)	$376,174
Lutz (R)	$38,761	$1,900 (5%)	$39,120

New York

	RECEIPTS	FROM PACS	EXPENDITURES
SENIOR SENATOR - 1998			
Schumer (D)	$16,825,671	$560,446 (3%)	$16,671,877
D'Amato (R)	$17,760,311	$1,926,518 (11%)	$24,195,287
JUNIOR SENATOR - 2000			
Clinton (D)	$41,752,247	$930,192 (2%)	$41,469,898
Lazio (R)	$39,020,511	$2,346,311 (6%)	$40,576,273
DISTRICT 1			
Grucci (R)	$1,603,505	$577,178 (36%)	$1,565,346
Forbes (D/WFM)	$1,369,329	$597,650 (44%)	$1,455,171
Seltzer (D)	$364,046	$52,972 (15%)	$357,158
DISTRICT 2			
Israel (D)	$1,124,208	$398,697 (35%)	$1,055,977
Johnson (R)	$1,072,856	$408,490 (38%)	$1,015,225
Bishop (D/GREEN)	$389,064	$98,900 (25%)	$353,153
DISTRICT 3			
King (R)	$791,425	$337,809 (43%)	$455,110
LaMagna (D)	$391,896	$2,500 (1%)	$387,966
DISTRICT 4			
McCarthy (D)	$2,003,462	$513,254 (26%)	$1,923,299
Becker (R)	$282,183	$41,250 (15%)	$269,062
DISTRICT 5			
Ackerman (D)	$1,053,194	$283,894 (27%)	$686,913
DISTRICT 6			
Meeks (D)	$358,780	$143,405 (40%)	$313,591
DISTRICT 7			
Crowley (D)	$778,327	$340,640 (44%)	$657,359
Birtley (R)	$120,577	$500 (0.4%)	$120,776
DISTRICT 8			
Nadler (D)	$907,858	$269,494 (30%)	$485,835
DISTRICT 9			
Weiner (D)	$1,147,670	$362,296 (32%)	$528,367
Dear (D/R)	$1,493,665	$4,000 (0.3%)	$1,521,320
DISTRICT 10			
Towns (D)	$1,183,139	$671,799 (57%)	$1,187,226
Ford (D/WFM)	$299,903	$1,250 (0.4%)	$300,304
DISTRICT 11			
Owens (D)	$543,228	$249,290 (46%)	$549,071
Cleary (R)	$24,605	$0 (0%)	$22,790
Clarke (D/L)	$260,337	$0 (0%)	$265,208
DISTRICT 12			
Velázquez (D)	$473,816	$282,350 (60%)	$437,579
Markgraf (R)	$11,079	$0 (0%)	$11,078
DISTRICT 13			
Fossella (R)	$1,020,821	$428,203 (42%)	$767,582
Johnstone (D)	$41,045	$0 (0%)	$39,475
DISTRICT 14			
Maloney (D)	$1,077,125	$363,950 (34%)	$802,053
Rhodes (R)	$47,878	$0 (0%)	$36,949
DISTRICT 15			
Rangel (D)	$1,970,428	$1,081,195 (55%)	$2,032,835

DISTRICT 16

Serrano (D)	$202,394	$157,419 (78%)	$210,037
DISTRICT 17			
Engel (D)	$920,986	$479,547 (52%)	$1,028,928
DISTRICT 18			
Lowey (D)	$1,758,439	$263,598 (15%)	$1,055,962
DISTRICT 19			
Kelly (R)	$896,434	$389,004 (43%)	$980,892
Graham (D)	$456,357	$16,875 (4%)	$374,199
DISTRICT 20			
Gilman (R)	$1,203,093	$327,784 (27%)	$1,177,222
Feiner (D)	$434,357	$8,250 (2%)	$431,215
DISTRICT 21			
McNulty (D)	$537,609	$267,675 (50%)	$334,030
Pillsworth (R)	$27,913	$400 (1%)	$12,402
DISTRICT 22			
Sweeney (R)	$1,073,578	$466,253 (43%)	$807,676
McCallion (D)	$76,469	$2,250 (3%)	$72,122
DISTRICT 23			
Boehlert (R)	$669,267	$357,186 (53%)	$808,371
Englebrecht (D)	$14,522	$0 (0%)	$14,129
Vickers (C, RTL)	$30,798	$1,100 (4%)	$29,583
DISTRICT 24			
McHugh (R)	$275,615	$169,244 (61%)	$300,643
DISTRICT 25			
Walsh (R)	$695,412	$387,639 (56%)	$580,767
DISTRICT 26			
Hinchey (D)	$808,516	$308,901 (38%)	$795,829
Moppert (R)	$177,774	$10,525 (6%)	$176,395
DISTRICT 27			
Reynolds (R)	$1,249,224	$419,820 (34%)	$832,254
Pecoraro (D)	$31,741	$3,700 (12%)	$31,441
DISTRICT 28			
Slaughter (D)	$454,036	$171,136 (38%)	$167,851
DISTRICT 29			
LaFalce (D)	$869,981	$506,744 (58%)	$487,016
Sommer (R)	$22,970	$100 (0.4%)	$21,595
DISTRICT 30			
Quinn (R)	$962,425	$450,428 (47%)	$615,608
Fee (D)	$189,661	$9,000 (5%)	$220,267
DISTRICT 31			
Houghton (R)	$909,760	$410,881 (45%)	$851,505

North Carolina

	RECEIPTS	FROM PACS	EXPENDITURES
SENIOR SENATOR - 1996			
Helms (R)	$7,808,820	$1,021,560 (13%)	$7,798,520
Gantt (D)	$8,128,548	$406,338 (5%)	$8,012,980
JUNIOR SENATOR - 1998			
Edwards (D)	$8,420,983	$0 (0%)	$8,331,382
Faircloth (R)	$9,370,462	$1,963,934 (21%)	$9,375,771
DISTRICT 1			
Clayton (D)	$395,864	$228,350 (58%)	$393,413
Kratzer (R)	$6,554	$1,000 (15%)	$6,290
DISTRICT 2			
Etheridge (D)	$1,110,249	$494,973 (45%)	$911,578

	RECEIPTS	FROM PACS	EXPENDITURES
Haynes (R)	$281,927	$24,250 (9%)	$281,926

DISTRICT 3

Jones (R)	$1,199,430	$579,019 (48%)	$1,266,779
McNairy (D)	$1,178,387	$54,000 (5%)	$1,176,161

DISTRICT 4

Price (D)	$813,309	$301,645 (37%)	$686,476
Ward (R)	$43,722	$1,000 (2%)	$41,009

DISTRICT 5

Burr (R)	$967,970	$330,366 (34%)	$421,060

DISTRICT 6

Coble (R)	$566,281	$454,626 (80%)	$301,790

DISTRICT 7

McIntyre (D)	$774,868	$321,875 (42%)	$428,263

DISTRICT 8

Hayes (R)	$1,962,007	$810,938 (41%)	$1,942,592
Taylor (D)	$842,453	$424,861 (50%)	$817,077

DISTRICT 9

Myrick (R)	$961,261	$331,576 (34%)	$959,304
McGuire (D)	$65,543	$23,750 (36%)	$71,375

DISTRICT 10

Ballenger (R)	$238,648	$128,201 (54%)	$266,557

DISTRICT 11

Taylor (R)	$1,487,737	$171,600 (12%)	$1,880,039
Neill (D)	$1,084,056	$230,954 (21%)	$1,030,634

DISTRICT 12

Watt (D)	$310,866	$232,400 (75%)	$361,869
Mitchell (R)	$25,417	$1,100 (4%)	$25,254

North Dakota

	RECEIPTS	FROM PACS	EXPENDITURES
SENIOR SENATOR - 2000			
Conrad (D)	$2,256,475	$1,443,306 (64%)	$2,312,543
Sand (R)	$399,590	$49,500 (12%)	$399,584
JUNIOR SENATOR - 1998			
Dorgan (D)	$1,855,934	$1,085,014 (58%)	$1,680,613
Nalewaja (R)	$151,448	$2,750 (2%)	$152,183
AT LARGE			
Pomeroy (D)	$997,280	$728,580 (73%)	$1,052,831
Dorso (R)	$452,768	$144,544 (32%)	$448,823

Ohio

	RECEIPTS	FROM PACS	EXPENDITURES
SENIOR SENATOR - 2000			
DeWine (R)	$5,583,868	$1,218,826 (22%)	$5,699,889
Celeste (D)	$477,784	$91,402 (19%)	$477,176
JUNIOR SENATOR - 1998			
Voinovich (R)	$6,098,620	$1,311,653 (22%)	$6,756,712
Boyle (D)	$2,233,970	$347,585 (16%)	$2,236,137

DISTRICT 1

Chabot (R)	$1,083,178	$535,980 (49%)	$1,099,555
Cranley (D)	$469,001	$151,404 (32%)	$465,561

DISTRICT 2

Portman (R)	$675,656	$4,150 (1%)	$406,952
Sanders (D)	$12,483	$3,500 (28%)	$12,599

DISTRICT 3

Hall (D)	$149,734	$124,050 (83%)	$192,835

DISTRICT 4

Oxley (R)	$910,740	$685,960 (75%)	$790,624
Dickman (D)	$31,281	$4,800 (15%)	$29,528

DISTRICT 5

Gillmor (R)	$407,286	$295,189 (72%)	$245,036

DISTRICT 6

Strickland (D)	$745,991	$466,398 (63%)	$544,415
Azinger (R)	$213,802	$7,829 (4%)	$214,745

DISTRICT 7

Hobson (R)	$576,253	$224,845 (39%)	$706,884

DISTRICT 8

Boehner (R)	$1,006,503	$461,030 (46%)	$1,042,008
Parks (D)	$31,553	$15,690 (50%)	$31,295

DISTRICT 9

Kaptur (D)	$510,801	$269,150 (53%)	$285,239
Bryan (R)	$86,971	$4,000 (5%)	$86,815

DISTRICT 10

Kucinich (D)	$453,499	$222,127 (49%)	$550,063

DISTRICT 11

Jones (D)	$259,299	$153,100 (59%)	$245,018

DISTRICT 12

Tiberi (R)	$2,374,205	$954,423 (40%)	$2,349,872
O'Shaughnessy (D)	$1,341,532	$532,327 (40%)	$1,340,688

DISTRICT 13

Brown (D)	$1,125,871	$545,956 (48%)	$789,866
Jeric (R)	$28,603	$600 (2%)	$28,276

DISTRICT 14

Sawyer (D)	$539,071	$370,005 (69%)	$515,026
Wood (R)	$34,985	$100 (0%)	$34,102

DISTRICT 15

Pryce (R)	$587,530	$431,888 (74%)	$589,675

DISTRICT 16

Regula (R)	$154,831	$0 (0%)	$166,663

DISTRICT 17

Traficant (D)	$196,979	$96,566 (49%)	$285,165
Alberty (R)	$173,858	$0 (0%)	$173,068
Walter (I)	$479,053	$0 (0%)	$476,871

DISTRICT 18

Ney (R)	$900,553	$554,651 (62%)	$725,334
Guthrie (D)	$229,209	$107,625 (47%)	$226,429

DISTRICT 19

LaTourette (R)	$652,707	$345,479 (53%)	$332,893

Oklahoma

	RECEIPTS	FROM PACS	EXPENDITURES
SENIOR SENATOR - 1998			
Nickles (R)	$2,718,188	$1,058,146 (39%)	$2,415,565
Carroll (D)	$8,619	$0 (0%)	$8,618
JUNIOR SENATOR - 1996			
Inhofe (R)	$2,706,849	$1,117,944 (41%)	$2,510,946
Boren (D)	$312,183	$0 (0%)	$311,171

DISTRICT 1

Largent (R)	$539,999	$275,263 (51%)	$401,666
Lowe (D)	$24,599	$1,000 (4%)	$24,468

DISTRICT 2
Carson (D) | $1,299,849 | $420,066 (32%) | $1,287,378
Ewing (R) | $999,392 | $306,753 (31%) | $998,403

DISTRICT 3
Watkins (R) | $707,712 | $303,754 (43%) | $288,397

DISTRICT 4
Watts (R) | $1,674,695 | $578,338 (35%) | $1,546,659
Weatherford (D) | $57,494 | $4,100 (7%) | $57,455

DISTRICT 5
Istook (R) | $620,352 | $237,735 (38%) | $520,608
McWatters (D) | $21,531 | $3,000 (14%) | $22,801

DISTRICT 6
Lucas (R) | $633,934 | $293,581 (46%) | $700,850
Beutler (D) | $601,449 | $77,508 (13%) | $599,785

Oregon

	RECEIPTS	FROM PACS	EXPENDITURES
SENIOR SENATOR - 1998			
Wyden (D)	$3,300,468	$1,019,403 (31%)	$2,866,368
Lim (R)	$413,449	$2,000 (0.5%)	$413,187
JUNIOR SENATOR - 1996			
Smith (R)	$3,840,273	$757,905 (20%)	$3,764,272
Bruggere (D)	$3,318,883	$406,731 (12%)	$3,301,736
DISTRICT 1			
Wu (D)	$1,670,733	$487,555 (29%)	$1,500,974
Starr (R)	$285,143	$34,626 (12%)	$283,345
DISTRICT 2			
Walden (R)	$712,720	$312,083 (44%)	$523,820
DISTRICT 3			
Blumenauer (D)	$466,414	$227,914 (49%)	$404,807
Pollock (R)	$100,649	$0 (0%)	$92,005
DISTRICT 4			
DeFazio (D)	$461,781	$260,066 (56%)	$332,650
Lindsey (R)	$36,982	$0 (0%)	$36,969
DISTRICT 5			
Hooley (D)	$881,163	$439,945 (50%)	$762,764
Boquist (R)	$182,567	$20,500 (11%)	$197,061

Pennsylvania

	RECEIPTS	FROM PACS	EXPENDITURES
SENIOR SENATOR - 1998			
Specter (R)	$6,255,657	$1,399,922 (22%)	$4,535,887
Lloyd (D)	$188,384	$20,594 (11%)	$187,157
JUNIOR SENATOR - 2000			
Santorum (R)	$9,126,046	$1,878,625 (21%)	$10,616,262
Klink (D)	$3,960,955	$923,833 (23%)	$3,941,166
DISTRICT 1			
Brady (D)	$658,468	$234,650 (36%)	$411,375
DISTRICT 2			
Fattah (D)	$330,321	$162,601 (49%)	$296,851
DISTRICT 3			
Borski (D)	$518,662	$293,198 (57%)	$474,626
Dougherty (R)	$106,910	$9,000 (8%)	$106,908
DISTRICT 4			
Hart (R)	$1,729,673	$871,124 (50%)	$1,724,048

Van Horne (D) | $694,704 | $371,879 (54%) | $694,846

DISTRICT 5
Peterson (R) | $429,260 | $175,157 (41%) | $413,790

DISTRICT 6
Holden (D) | $537,708 | $337,540 (63%) | $417,147
Kopel (R) | $31,379 | $2,240 (7%) | $30,913

DISTRICT 7
Weldon (R) | $535,713 | $222,650 (42%) | $618,319
Lennon (D) | $31,478 | $0 (0%) | $22,578

DISTRICT 8
Greenwood (R) | $892,054 | $0 (0%) | $889,821
Strouse (D) | $196,566 | $0 (0%) | $196,563

DISTRICT 10
Sherwood (R) | $2,820,653 | $962,656 (34%) | $2,751,597
Casey (D) | $1,615,787 | $497,560 (31%) | $1,619,801

DISTRICT 11
Kanjorski (D) | $382,004 | $235,021 (62%) | $271,258
Urban (R) | $28,857 | $1,544 (5%) | $18,760

DISTRICT 12
Murtha (D) | $918,066 | $482,650 (53%) | $968,531
Choby (R) | $8,312 | $0 (0%) | $8,310

DISTRICT 13
Hoeffel (D) | $1,770,988 | $666,002 (38%) | $1,772,923
Greenleaf (R) | $1,493,863 | $376,011 (25%) | $1,488,942

DISTRICT 14
Coyne (D) | $191,231 | $152,750 (80%) | $142,754

DISTRICT 15
Toomey (R) | $1,073,207 | $500,287 (47%) | $1,025,795
O'Brien (D) | $777,263 | $361,233 (46%) | $774,388

DISTRICT 16
Pitts (R) | $374,573 | $123,976 (33%) | $366,418
Yorczyk (D) | $9,850 | $0 (0%) | $9,809

DISTRICT 17
Gekas (R) | $218,161 | $153,629 (70%) | $206,666
Herrmann (D) | $25,557 | $7,675 (30%) | $22,090

DISTRICT 18
Doyle (D) | $509,159 | $342,334 (67%) | $455,391
Stephens (R) | $8,382 | $0 (0%) | $7,729

DISTRICT 19
Platts (R) | $315,089 | $0 (0%) | $308,158
Sanders (D) | $62,997 | $5,900 (9%) | $36,209

DISTRICT 20
Mascara (D) | $454,325 | $317,500 (70%) | $509,444

DISTRICT 21
English (R) | $1,212,981 | $672,566 (55%) | $1,219,501
Flitter (D) | $573,454 | $40,815 (7%) | $573,378

Rhode Island

	RECEIPTS	FROM PACS	EXPENDITURES
SENIOR SENATOR - 1996			
Reed (D)	$2,688,136	$1,031,702 (38%)	$2,732,011
Mayer (R)	$787,231	$132,368 (17%)	$773,789
JUNIOR SENATOR - 2000			
Chafee (R)	$2,531,413	$699,056 (28%)	$2,265,221
Weygand (D)	$2,420,479	$836,823 (35%)	$2,297,885

DISTRICT 1

Kennedy (D)	$1,687,712	$499,619 (30%)	$1,263,102
Cabral (R)	$9,704	$1,500 (15%)	$8,902

DISTRICT 2

Langevin (D)	$1,109,472	$281,017 (25%)	$1,091,752
Driver (CFC)	$325,983	$147 (0.4%)	$321,183

South Carolina

	RECEIPTS	FROM PACS	EXPENDITURES
SENIOR SENATOR - 1996			
Thurmond (R)	$2,335,746	$782,308 (33%)	$2,385,185
Close (D)	$1,919,735	$0 (0%)	$1,913,574
JUNIOR SENATOR - 1998			
Hollings (D)	$4,547,251	$1,231,069 (27%)	$4,968,456
Inglis (R)	$2,210,434	$17,500 (1%)	$2,143,278
DISTRICT 1			
Brown (R)	$629,817	$197,990 (31%)	$606,776
Brack (D)	$486,323	$81,000 (17%)	$485,733
DISTRICT 2			
Spence (R)	$621,713	$390,698 (63%)	$618,718
Frederick (D)	$412,670	$79,720 (19%)	$406,753
DISTRICT 3			
Graham (R)	$1,153,517	$322,616 (28%)	$750,013
Brightharp (D)	$57,425	$0 (0%)	$57,232
DISTRICT 4			
DeMint (R)	$308,041	$0 (0%)	$303,967
DISTRICT 5			
Spratt (D)	$1,153,841	$663,900 (58%)	$1,136,157
Gullick (R)	$342,558	$25,090 (7%)	$342,397
DISTRICT 6			
Clyburn (D)	$581,459	$314,750 (54%)	$449,439
Ellison (R)	$32,550	$0 (0%)	$39,945

South Dakota

	RECEIPTS	FROM PACS	EXPENDITURES
SENIOR SENATOR - 1998			
Daschle (D)	$5,614,668	$1,901,170 (34%)	$4,861,541
Schmidt (R)	$540,728	$56,201 (10%)	$492,854
JUNIOR SENATOR - 1996			
Johnson (D)	$2,866,518	$847,621 (30%)	$2,990,554
Pressler (R)	$4,091,490	$1,513,835 (37%)	$4,468,434
AT LARGE			
Thune (R)	$1,221,843	$278,001 (23%)	$953,757

Tennessee

	RECEIPTS	FROM PACS	EXPENDITURES
SENIOR SENATOR - 1996			
Thompson (R)	$4,232,418	$1,080,345 (26%)	$3,469,369
Gordon (D)	$800,607	$88,600 (11%)	$795,969
JUNIOR SENATOR - 2000			
Frist (R)	$5,825,454	$1,022,063 (18%)	$6,105,303
Clark (D)	$286,469	$85,000 (30%)	$273,406
DISTRICT 1			
Jenkins (R)	$168,879	$141,200 (84%)	$92,463

DISTRICT 2

Duncan (R)	$583,772	$288,288 (49%)	$342,829

DISTRICT 3

Wamp (R)	$826,283	$0 (0%)	$737,216
Callaway (D)	$188,033	$21,100 (11%)	$232,095

DISTRICT 4

Hilleary (R)	$1,415,020	$11,552 (1%)	$1,355,924
Dunaway (D)	$1,009,951	$58,500 (6%)	$1,017,105

DISTRICT 5

Clement (D)	$671,553	$276,200 (41%)	$715,189

DISTRICT 6

Gordon (D)	$1,212,006	$652,447 (54%)	$1,135,811
Charles (R)	$175,911	$14,500 (8%)	$174,937

DISTRICT 7

Bryant (R)	$827,549	$401,438 (49%)	$727,131
Sims (D)	$13,685	$2,500 (18%)	$12,101

DISTRICT 8

Tanner (D)	$668,140	$472,114 (71%)	$621,357

DISTRICT 9

Ford (D)	$558,502	$210,534 (38%)	$475,376

Texas

	RECEIPTS	FROM PACS	EXPENDITURES
SENIOR SENATOR - 1996			
Gramm (R)	$3,802,167	$1,107,961 (29%)	$6,289,591
Morales (D)	$991,290	$4,539 (0.5%)	$978,862
JUNIOR SENATOR - 2000			
Hutchison (R)	$3,410,444	$642,467 (19%)	$3,518,862
Kelly (D)	$4,654	$0 (0%)	$4,602
DISTRICT 1			
Sandlin (D)	$1,667,970	$740,029 (44%)	$1,628,926
Willingham (R)	$250,608	$19,121 (8%)	$246,791
DISTRICT 2			
Turner (D)	$527,533	$347,075 (66%)	$138,491
DISTRICT 3			
Johnson (R)	$942,535	$414,031 (44%)	$892,324
Zachary (D)	$6,776	$1,000 (15%)	$6,702
DISTRICT 4			
Hall (D)	$732,869	$460,507 (63%)	$739,496
Newton (R)	$137,313	$11,239 (8%)	$136,484
DISTRICT 5			
Sessions (R)	$1,986,465	$833,569 (42%)	$1,826,456
Coggins (D)	$1,642,494	$330,044 (20%)	$1,636,875
DISTRICT 6			
Barton (R)	$1,004,946	$566,116 (56%)	$944,244
DISTRICT 7			
Culberson (R)	$1,092,972	$320,639 (29%)	$1,085,071
Sell (D)	$16,637	$2,500 (15%)	$13,122
DISTRICT 8			
Brady (R)	$361,532	$224,954 (62%)	$370,246
DISTRICT 9			
Lampson (D)	$1,347,420	$497,169 (37%)	$1,373,927
Williams (R)	$127,531	$5,519 (4%)	$104,570
DISTRICT 10			
Doggett (D)	$582,856	$289,352 (50%)	$232,268

DISTRICT 11

Edwards (D)	$1,131,273	$577,707 (51%)	$1,281,637
Farley (R)	$563,085	$8,335 (1%)	$558,727

DISTRICT 12

Granger (R)	$803,593	$305,817 (38%)	$671,838
Greene (D)	$82,656	$9,950 (12%)	$83,280

DISTRICT 13

Thornberry (R)	$714,078	$215,028 (30%)	$741,039
Clinesmith (D)	$313,487	$63,750 (20%)	$306,776

DISTRICT 14

Paul (R)	$2,413,684	$109,065 (5%)	$2,353,816
Sneary (D)	$1,148,186	$414,494 (36%)	$1,145,842

DISTRICT 15

Hinojosa (D)	$496,742	$135,608 (27%)	$470,513

DISTRICT 16

Reyes (D)	$423,147	$135,905 (32%)	$406,530
Power (R)	$30,625	$1,300 (4%)	$30,621

DISTRICT 17

Stenholm (D)	$1,064,609	$711,366 (67%)	$871,201
Clements (R)	$95,861	$2,150 (2%)	$89,888

DISTRICT 18

Jackson-Lee (D)	$462,043	$220,225 (48%)	$409,631
Levy (R)	$20,272	$0 (0%)	$20,272

DISTRICT 19

Combest (R)	$720,317	$454,427 (63%)	$556,470

DISTRICT 20

Gonzalez (D)	$661,255	$358,429 (54%)	$619,173

DISTRICT 21

Smith (R)	$536,635	$96,779 (18%)	$543,754

DISTRICT 22

DeLay (R)	$1,342,920	$863,586 (64%)	$1,298,995
Matranga (D)	$9,993	$1,000 (10%)	$6,597

DISTRICT 23

Bonilla (R)	$1,156,942	$517,880 (45%)	$1,050,250
Garza (D)	$369,635	$39,000 (11%)	$364,440

DISTRICT 24

Frost (D)	$2,016,162	$1,101,824 (55%)	$1,983,181
Wright (R)	$213,049	$7,000 (3%)	$200,359

DISTRICT 25

Bentsen (D)	$1,325,707	$687,048 (52%)	$1,354,444
Sudan (R)	$3,216,793	$32,851 (1%)	$3,247,033

DISTRICT 26

Armey (R)	$1,373,930	$575,994 (42%)	$1,325,516
Love (D)	$8,414	$200 (2%)	$8,040

DISTRICT 27

Ortiz (D)	$528,349	$154,850 (29%)	$428,480
Ahumada (R)	$39,689	$0 (0%)	$39,068

DISTRICT 28

Rodriguez (D)	$347,888	$215,869 (62%)	$294,228

DISTRICT 29

Green (D)	$649,362	$473,067 (73%)	$626,951
Vu (R)	$68,996	$500 (1%)	$50,896

DISTRICT 30

Johnson (D)	$304,363	$192,906 (63%)	$243,072

Utah

	RECEIPTS	FROM PACS	EXPENDITURES
SENIOR SENATOR - 2000			
Hatch (R)	$3,082,208	$1,220,662 (40%)	$3,130,550
Howell (D)	$299,747	$14,000 (5%)	$299,239
JUNIOR SENATOR - 1998			
Bennett (R)	$1,560,616	$774,405 (50%)	$1,546,219
Leckman (D)	$274,075	$10,750 (4%)	$265,494
DISTRICT 1			
Hansen (R)	$378,034	$156,081 (41%)	$338,572
McConkie (D)	$78,166	$2,125 (3%)	$75,137
DISTRICT 2			
Matheson (D)	$1,366,631	$470,335 (34%)	$1,305,202
Smith (R)	$1,692,241	$275,601 (16%)	$1,681,135
DISTRICT 3			
Cannon (R)	$344,855	$216,288 (63%)	$340,723
Dunn (D)	$379,269	$87,189 (23%)	$378,565

Vermont

	RECEIPTS	FROM PACS	EXPENDITURES
SENIOR SENATOR - 1998			
Leahy (D)	$1,153,672	$0 (0%)	$1,014,751
JUNIOR SENATOR - 2000			
Jeffords (R)	$2,087,965	$1,112,558 (53%)	$1,889,243
Flanagan (D)	$1,093,161	$67,434 (6%)	$1,054,977
AT LARGE			
Sanders (I)	$656,270	$137,744 (21%)	$323,561
Skrill (I)	$21,501	$0 (0%)	$21,501

Virginia

	RECEIPTS	FROM PACS	EXPENDITURES
SENIOR SENATOR - 1996			
Warner (R)	$5,033,390	$1,601,460 (32%)	$5,196,091
Warner (D)	$11,625,483	$1,250 (0%)	$11,600,424
JUNIOR SENATOR - 2000			
Allen (R)	$10,073,255	$1,581,172 (16%)	$9,995,980
Robb (D)	$6,737,158	$1,622,753 (24%)	$6,810,252
DISTRICT 1			
Davis (R)	$427,805	$202,917 (47%)	$407,945
Davies (D)	$176,317	$28,800 (16%)	$152,592
DISTRICT 2			
Schrock (R)	$1,122,070	$550,233 (49%)	$1,097,074
Wagner (D)	$1,163,000	$244,900 (21%)	$1,157,345
DISTRICT 3			
Scott (D)	$255,440	$154,300 (60%)	$250,417
DISTRICT 5			
Goode (I)	$642,701	$258,285 (40%)	$581,016
Boyd (D)	$59,795	$6,000 (10%)	$38,455
DISTRICT 6			
Goodlatte (R)	$684,097	$274,524 (40%)	$395,342
DISTRICT 7			
Cantor (R)	$1,583,311	$388,928 (25%)	$1,500,482
Stewart (D)	$71,085	$6,350 (9%)	$70,430

DISTRICT 8

	RECEIPTS	FROM PACS	EXPENDITURES
Moran (D)	$1,027,091	$489,954 (48%)	$1,203,058
Miller (R)	$216,105	$14,833 (7%)	$210,573

DISTRICT 9

Boucher (D)	$871,124	$622,910 (72%)	$676,127
Osborne (R)	$33,964	$0 (0%)	$33,501

DISTRICT 10

Wolf (R)	$529,482	$258,663 (49%)	$465,729

DISTRICT 11

Davis (R)	$1,737,138	$669,775 (39%)	$1,515,583
Corrigan (D)	$75,190	$5,000 (7%)	$72,833

Washington

	RECEIPTS	FROM PACS	EXPENDITURES
SENIOR SENATOR - 1998			
Murray (D)	$5,341,967	$861,629 (16%)	$5,600,592
Smith (R)	$5,234,596	$687 (0%)	$5,159,527
JUNIOR SENATOR - 2000			
Cantwell (D)	$11,538,665	$0 (0%)	$11,533,295
Gorton (R)	$6,384,256	$1,770,339 (28%)	$6,402,488
DISTRICT 1			
Inslee (D)	$2,009,904	$630,359 (31%)	$2,009,131
McDonald (R)	$1,468,550	$417,076 (28%)	$1,462,965
DISTRICT 2			
Larsen (D)	$1,584,392	$648,501 (41%)	$1,579,101
Koster (R)	$1,118,046	$463,033 (41%)	$1,092,585
DISTRICT 3			
Baird (D)	$1,382,509	$512,906 (37%)	$1,368,592
Matson (R)	$494,972	$114,041 (23%)	$487,812
DISTRICT 4			
Hastings (R)	$696,310	$267,257 (38%)	$766,774
Davis (D)	$441,427	$154,100 (35%)	$433,054
DISTRICT 5			
Nethercutt (R)	$1,666,604	$818,992 (49%)	$1,749,203
Keefe (D)	$652,505	$301,961 (46%)	$651,225
DISTRICT 6			
Dicks (D)	$688,723	$356,125 (52%)	$596,375
Lawrence (R)	$116,991	$3,500 (3%)	$117,547
DISTRICT 7			
McDermott (D)	$368,032	$131,273 (36%)	$322,022
Szwaja (GREEN)	$33,331	$0 (0%)	$33,331
DISTRICT 8			
Dunn (R)	$1,735,156	$724,081 (42%)	$1,731,507
Behrens-Benedict (D)	$372,903	$49,594 (13%)	$377,825
DISTRICT 9			
Smith (D)	$1,076,886	$518,222 (48%)	$1,046,195
Vance (R)	$633,799	$150,499 (24%)	$634,816

West Virginia

	RECEIPTS	FROM PACS	EXPENDITURES
SENIOR SENATOR - 2000			
Byrd (D)	$1,127,278	$509,530 (45%)	$1,045,993
JUNIOR SENATOR - 1996			
Rockefeller (D)	$3,004,275	$987,319 (33%)	$2,538,473

DISTRICT 1

Mollohan (D)	$294,750	$204,850 (69%)	$335,864

DISTRICT 2

Capito (R)	$1,367,504	$587,209 (43%)	$1,288,226
Humphreys (D)	$6,982,393	$307,600 (4%)	$6,969,933

DISTRICT 3

Rahall (D)	$668,423	$344,613 (52%)	$354,164

Wisconsin

	RECEIPTS	FROM PACS	EXPENDITURES
SENIOR SENATOR - 2000			
Kohl (D)	$4,986,165	$0 (0%)	$4,991,364
Gillespie (R)	$584,877	$13,500 (2%)	$582,221
JUNIOR SENATOR - 1998			
Feingold (D)	$4,072,878	$398,762 (10%)	$3,846,089
Neumann (R)	$4,409,161	$592,890 (13%)	$4,373,953
DISTRICT 1			
Ryan (R)	$1,343,419	$522,026 (39%)	$1,059,963
Thomas (D)	$13,311	$0 (0%)	$13,379
DISTRICT 2			
Baldwin (D)	$1,600,964	$427,947 (27%)	$1,680,093
Sharpless (R)	$654,743	$122,150 (19%)	$647,530
DISTRICT 3			
Kind (D)	$637,925	$276,469 (43%)	$564,246
Tully (R)	$125,052	$4,000 (3%)	$124,818
DISTRICT 4			
Kleczka (D)	$662,442	$445,989 (67%)	$632,355
Riener (R)	$47,120	$4,000 (8%)	$47,119
DISTRICT 5			
Barrett (D)	$553,864	$270,316 (49%)	$221,766
Smith (R)	$16,342	$50 (0.3%)	$16,339
DISTRICT 6			
Petri (R)	$643,944	$330,764 (51%)	$703,496
Flaherty (D)	$217,836	$39,350 (18%)	$213,059
DISTRICT 7			
Obey (D)	$1,075,642	$644,519 (60%)	$1,085,618
Cronin (R)	$192,613	$600 (0.3%)	$192,479
DISTRICT 8			
Green (R)	$778,560	$389,972 (50%)	$553,153
Reich (D)	$15,235	$550 (4%)	$13,904
DISTRICT 9			
Sensenbrenner (R)	$501,176	$244,379 (49%)	$464,515
Clawson (D)	$9,940	$100 (1%)	$6,717

Wyoming

	RECEIPTS	FROM PACS	EXPENDITURES
SENIOR SENATOR - 2000			
Thomas (R)	$958,656	$483,343 (50%)	$762,833
Logan (D)	$7,979	$5,700 (71%)	$4,187
JUNIOR SENATOR - 1996			
Enzi (R)	$984,906	$476,177 (48%)	$953,572
Karpan (D)	$819,417	$277,930 (34%)	$814,258
AT LARGE			
Cubin (R)	$644,416	$363,037 (56%)	$640,700

Senate Committees

The standing and select committees of the U.S. Senate are listed below in alphabetical order. The listings include a telephone number, room number and party ratio for each full committee. Membership is given in order of seniority on the committee. Subcommittee membership is listed in order of seniority.

On full committee rosters, members of the majority party, Republicans, are shown in roman type; members of the minority party, Democrats, are shown in *italic* type.

The word "vacancy" indicates that a committee or subcommittee seat had not been filled at press time. Subcommittee vacancies do not necessarily indicate vacancies on full committees, or vice versa.

Partisan committees are listed on page 1163.

The telephone area code for Washington, D.C., is 202. Abbreviations for Senate office buildings are: SD — Dirksen Building, SH — Hart Building, SR — Russell Building. The ZIP code for all Senate offices is 20510.

AGRICULTURE, NUTRITION & FORESTRY
224-2035 328A SR
Party Ratio: R 10-D 10
Richard G. Lugar, R-Ind., chairman

Jesse Helms, N.C.	*Tom Harkin, Iowa*
Thad Cochran, Miss.	*Patrick J. Leahy, Vt.*
Mitch McConnell, Ky.	*Kent Conrad, N.D.*
Pat Roberts, Kan.	*Tom Daschle, S.D.*
Peter G. Fitzgerald, Ill.	*Max Baucus, Mont.*
Craig Thomas, Wyo.	*Blanche Lincoln, Ark.*
Wayne Allard, Colo.	*Zell Miller, Ga.*
Tim Hutchinson, Ark.	*Debbie Stabenow, Mich.*
Michael D. Crapo, Idaho	*Ben Nelson, Neb.*
	Mark Dayton, Minn.

FORESTRY, CONSERVATION & RURAL REVITALIZATION
224-2035 328A SR
Crapo, chairman

Republicans: McConnell, Thomas, Allard, Hutchinson
Democrats: Lincoln, Leahy, Daschle, Stabenow, Dayton

MARKETING, INSPECTION & PRODUCT PROMOTION
224-2035 328A SR
Fitzgerald, chairman

Republicans: Helms, Cochran, Roberts, Thomas
Democrats: Baucus, Leahy, Conrad, Nelson (Neb.), Dayton

PRODUCTION & PRICE COMPETITIVENESS
224-2035 328A SR
Roberts, chairman

Republicans: Helms, Cochran, Fitzgerald, McConnell
Democrats: Conrad, Daschle, Baucus, Lincoln, Miller

RESEARCH, NUTRITION & GENERAL LEGISLATION
224-2035 328A SR
McConnell, chairman

Republicans: Allard, Hutchinson, Crapo, Helms
Democrats: Leahy, Conrad, Miller, Stabenow, Nelson (Neb.)

APPROPRIATIONS
224-3471 S-128 Capitol
Party Ratio: R 14-D 14
Ted Stevens, R-Alaska, chairman

Thad Cochran, Miss.	*Robert C. Byrd, W.Va.*
Arlen Specter, Pa.	*Daniel K. Inouye, Hawaii*
Pete V. Domenici, N.M.	*Ernest F. Hollings, S.C.*
Christopher S. Bond, Mo.	*Patrick J. Leahy, Vt.*
Mitch McConnell, Ky.	*Tom Harkin, Iowa*
Conrad Burns, Mont.	*Barbara A. Mikulski, Md.*
Richard C. Shelby, Ala.	*Harry Reid, Nev.*
Judd Gregg, N.H.	*Herb Kohl, Wis.*
Robert F. Bennett, Utah	*Patty Murray, Wash.*
Ben Nighthorse Campbell, Colo.	*Byron L. Dorgan, N.D.*
Larry E. Craig, Idaho	*Dianne Feinstein, Calif.*
Kay Bailey Hutchison, Texas	*Richard J. Durbin, Ill.*
Mike DeWine, Ohio	*Tim Johnson, S.D.*
	Mary L. Landrieu, La.

AGRICULTURE, RURAL DEVELOPMENT & RELATED AGENCIES
224-5270 136 SD
Cochran, chairman

Republicans: Specter, Bond, McConnell, Burns, Craig
Democrats: Kohl, Harkin, Dorgan, Feinstein, Durbin, Johnson

COMMERCE, JUSTICE, STATE & JUDICIARY
224-7277 S-146A Capitol
Gregg, chairman

Republicans: Stevens, Domenici, McConnell, Hutchison, Campbell
Democrats: Hollings, Inouye, Mikulski, Leahy, Kohl, Murray

DEFENSE
224-7255 119 SD
Stevens, chairman

Republicans: Cochran, Specter, Domenici, Bond, McConnell, Shelby, Gregg, Hutchison
Democrats: Inouye, Hollings, Byrd, Leahy, Harkin, Dorgan, Durbin, Reid, Feinstein

DISTRICT OF COLUMBIA
224-1526 S-128 Capitol
DeWine, chairman

Republican: Hutchison
Democrats: Landrieu, Durbin

ENERGY & WATER DEVELOPMENT
224-7260   127 SD
Domenici, chairman

Republicans: Cochran, McConnell, Bennett, Burns, Craig
Democrats: Reid, Byrd, Hollings, Murray, Dorgan, Feinstein

FOREIGN OPERATIONS
224-2104   142 SD
McConnell, chairman

Republicans: Specter, Gregg, Shelby, Bennett, Campbell, Bond
Democrats: Leahy, Inouye, Harkin, Mikulski, Durbin, Johnson, Landrieu

INTERIOR
224-7233   131 SD
Burns, chairman

Republicans: Stevens, Cochran, Domenici, Bennett, Gregg, Campbell
Democrats: Byrd, Leahy, Hollings, Reid, Dorgan, Feinstein, Murray

LABOR, HEALTH & HUMAN SERVICES & EDUCATION
224-7230   186 SD
Specter, chairman

Republicans: Cochran, Gregg, Craig, Hutchison, Stevens, DeWine
Democrats: Harkin, Hollings, Inouye, Reid, Kohl, Murray, Landrieu

LEGISLATIVE BRANCH
224-8921   S-125 Capitol
Bennett, chairman

Republican: Stevens
Democrats: Durbin, Johnson

MILITARY CONSTRUCTION
224-7204   140 SD
Hutchison, chairwoman

Republicans: Burns, Craig, DeWine
Democrats: Feinstein, Inouye, Johnson, Landrieu

TRANSPORTATION
224-2175   133 SD
Shelby, chairman

Republicans: Specter, Bond, Bennett, Campbell, Hutchison
Democrats: Murray, Byrd, Mikulski, Reid, Kohl, Durbin

TREASURY & GENERAL GOVERNMENT
224-7337   188 SD
Campbell, chairman

Republicans: Shelby, DeWine
Democrats: Dorgan, Mikulski, Landrieu

VA, HUD & INDEPENDENT AGENCIES
224-7211   130 SD
Bond, chairman

Republicans: Burns, Shelby, Craig, Domenici, DeWine
Democrats: Mikulski, Leahy, Harkin, Byrd, Kohl, Johnson

ARMED SERVICES
224-3871   228 SR
Party Ratio: R 12-D 12
John W. Warner, R-Va., chairman

Strom Thurmond, S.C.	Carl Levin, Mich.
John McCain, Ariz.	Edward M. Kennedy, Mass.
Robert C. Smith, N.H.	Robert C. Byrd, W.Va.
James M. Inhofe, Okla.	Joseph I. Lieberman, Conn.
Rick Santorum, Pa.	Max Cleland, Ga.
Pat Roberts, Kan.	Mary L. Landrieu, La.
Wayne Allard, Colo.	Jack Reed, R.I.
Tim Hutchinson, Ark.	Daniel K. Akaka, Hawaii
Jeff Sessions, Ala.	Bill Nelson, Fla.
Susan Collins, Maine	Ben Nelson, Neb.
Jim Bunning, Ky.	Jean Carnahan, Mo.
	Mark Dayton, Minn.

AIRLAND
224-3871   228 SR
Santorum, chairman

Republicans: Inhofe, Roberts, Hutchinson, Sessions, Bunning
Democrats: Lieberman, Cleland, Nelson (Fla.), Nelson (Neb.), Carnahan, Dayton

EMERGING THREATS & CAPABILITIES
224-3871   228 SR
Roberts, chairman

Republicans: Smith (N.H.), Santorum, Allard, Hutchinson, Collins
Democrats: Landrieu, Kennedy, Byrd, Lieberman, Nelson (Fla.), Dayton

PERSONNEL
224-3871   228 SR
Hutchinson, chairman

Republicans: Thurmond, McCain, Allard, Collins
Democrats: Cleland, Kennedy, Reed, Akaka, Carnahan

READINESS & MANAGEMENT SUPPORT
224-3871   228 SR
Inhofe, chairman

Republicans: Thurmond, McCain, Santorum, Roberts, Bunning
Democrats: Akaka, Byrd, Cleland, Landrieu, Nelson (Neb.), Dayton

SEAPOWER
224-3871   228 SR
Sessions, chairman

Republicans: McCain, Smith (N.H.), Collins, Bunning
Democrats: Kennedy, Lieberman, Landrieu, Reed, Carnahan

STRATEGIC
224-3871   228 SR
Allard, chairman

Republicans: Thurmond, Smith (N.H.), Inhofe, Sessions
Democrats: Reed, Byrd, Akaka, Nelson (Fla.), Nelson (Neb.)

BANKING, HOUSING & URBAN AFFAIRS

224-7391 534 SD
Party Ratio: R 10-D 10
Phil Gramm, R-Texas, chairman

Richard C. Shelby, Ala.	Paul S. Sarbanes, Md.
Robert F. Bennett, Utah	Christopher J. Dodd, Conn.
Wayne Allard, Colo.	Tim Johnson, S.D.
Michael B. Enzi, Wyo.	Jack Reed, R.I.
Chuck Hagel, Neb.	Charles E. Schumer, N.Y.
Rick Santorum, Pa.	Evan Bayh, Ind.
Jim Bunning, Ky.	Zell Miller, Ga.
Michael D. Crapo, Idaho	Thomas R. Carper, Del.
John Ensign, Nev.	Debbie Stabenow, Mich.
	Jon Corzine, N.J.

ECONOMIC POLICY
224-7391 534 SD
Bunning, chairman

Republicans: Bennett, Ensign
Democrats: Schumer, Miller, Corzine

FINANCIAL INSTITUTIONS
224-7391 534 SD
Bennett, chairman

Republicans: Ensign, Shelby, Allard, Santorum, Bunning, Crapo
Democrats: Johnson, Miller, Carper, Stabenow, Dodd, Reed, Bayh

HOUSING & TRANSPORTATION
224-7391 534 SD
Allard, chairman

Republicans: Santorum, Ensign, Shelby, Enzi, Hagel
Democrats: Reed, Carper, Stabenow, Corzine, Dodd, Schumer

INTERNATIONAL TRADE & FINANCE
224-7391 534 SD
Hagel, chairman

Republicans: Enzi, Crapo
Democrats: Bayh, Miller, Johnson

SECURITIES & INVESTMENT
224-7391 534 SD
Enzi, chairman

Republicans: Shelby, Crapo, Bennett, Allard, Hagel, Santorum, Bunning
Democrats: Dodd, Johnson, Reed, Schumer, Bayh, Corzine, Carper, Stabenow

BUDGET

224-0642 621 SD
Party Ratio: R 11-D 11
Pete V. Domenici, R-N.M., chairman

Charles E. Grassley, Iowa	Kent Conrad, N.D.
Don Nickles, Okla.	Ernest F. Hollings, S.C.
Phil Gramm, Texas	Paul S. Sarbanes, Md.
Christopher S. Bond, Mo.	Patty Murray, Wash.
Judd Gregg, N.H.	Ron Wyden, Ore.
Olympia J. Snowe, Maine	Russell D. Feingold, Wis.
Bill Frist, Tenn.	Tim Johnson, S.D.
Gordon H. Smith, Ore.	Robert C. Byrd, W.Va.
Wayne Allard, Colo.	Bill Nelson, Fla.
Chuck Hagel, Neb.	Debbie Stabenow, Mich.
	Hillary Rodham Clinton, N.Y.

COMMERCE, SCIENCE & TRANSPORTATION

224-5115 508 SD
Party Ratio: R 11-D 11
John McCain, R-Ariz., chairman

Ted Stevens, Alaska	Ernest F. Hollings, S.C.
Conrad Burns, Mont.	Daniel K. Inouye, Hawaii
Trent Lott, Miss.	John D. Rockefeller IV, W.Va.
Kay Bailey Hutchison, Texas	John Kerry, Mass.
Olympia J. Snowe, Maine	John B. Breaux, La.
Sam Brownback, Kan.	Byron L. Dorgan, N.D.
Gordon H. Smith, Ore.	Ron Wyden, Ore.
Peter G. Fitzgerald, Ill.	Max Cleland, Ga.
John Ensign, Nev.	Barbara Boxer, Calif.
George F. Allen, Va.	John Edwards, N.C.
	Jean Carnahan, Mo.

AVIATION
224-4852 427 SH
Hutchison, chairwoman

Republicans: Stevens, Burns, Lott, Snowe, Brownback, Smith (Ore.), Fitzgerald, Ensign
Democrats: Rockefeller, Hollings, Inouye, Breaux, Dorgan, Wyden, Cleland, Edwards, Carnahan

COMMUNICATIONS
224-5184 227 SH
Burns, chairman

Republicans: Stevens, Lott, Hutchison, Snowe, Brownback, Smith (Ore.), Fitzgerald, Ensign, Allen
Democrats: Hollings, Inouye, Kerry, Breaux, Rockefeller, Dorgan, Wyden, Cleland, Boxer, Edwards

CONSUMER AFFAIRS, FOREIGN COMMERCE & TOURISM
224-5183 425 SH
Fitzgerald, chairman

Republicans: Burns, Brownback, Smith (Ore.), Ensign, Allen
Democrats: Dorgan, Rockefeller, Wyden, Boxer, Edwards, Carnahan

MANUFACTURING & COMPETITIVENESS
224-1745 508 SD
Ensign, chairman

Republicans: Brownback, Fitzgerald
Democrats: Wyden, Hollings, Rockefeller

OCEANS & FISHERIES
224-8172 428 SH
Snowe, chairwoman

Republicans: Stevens, Hutchison, Smith (Ore.), Fitzgerald
Democrats: Kerry, Hollings, Inouye, Breaux, Boxer

SCIENCE, TECHNOLOGY & SPACE
224-8172 428 SH
Allen, chairman

Republicans: Stevens, Burns, Lott, Hutchison, Brownback, Fitzgerald
Democrats: Breaux, Rockefeller, Kerry, Dorgan, Cleland, Edwards, Carnahan

SURFACE TRANSPORTATION & MERCHANT MARINE
224-4852 427 SH
Smith (Ore.), chairman

Republicans: Stevens, Burns, Lott, Hutchison, Snowe, Brownback, Fitzgerald, Ensign
Democrats: Inouye, Rockefeller, Kerry, Breaux, Dorgan, Wyden, Cleland, Boxer, Carnahan

ENERGY & NATURAL RESOURCES
224-4971 364 SD
Party Ratio: R 11-D 11
Frank H. Murkowski, R-Alaska, chairman

Pete V. Domenici, N.M.	*Jeff Bingaman, N.M.*
Don Nickles, Okla.	*Daniel K. Akaka, Hawaii*
Larry E. Craig, Idaho	*Byron L. Dorgan, N.D.*
Ben Nighthorse Campbell, Colo.	*Bob Graham, Fla.*
Craig Thomas, Wyo.	*Ron Wyden, Ore.*
Richard C. Shelby, Ala.	*Tim Johnson, S.D.*
Conrad Burns, Mont.	*Mary L. Landrieu, La.*
Jon Kyl, Ariz.	*Evan Bayh, Ind.*
Chuck Hagel, Neb.	*Dianne Feinstein, Calif.*
Gordon H. Smith, Ore.	*Charles E. Schumer, N.Y.*
	Maria Cantwell, Wash.

ENERGY RESEARCH, DEVELOPMENT, PRODUCTION & REGULATION
224-6567 312 SH
Nickles, chairman

Republicans: Domenici, vice chairman, Shelby, Hagel, Thomas, Kyl, Craig, Campbell, Burns
Democrats: Graham, Akaka, Wyden, Johnson, Landrieu, Bayh, Feinstein, Schumer, Cantwell

FORESTS & PUBLIC LAND MANAGEMENT
224-6170 317 SD
Craig, chairman

Republicans: Burns, vice chairman, Domenici, Nickles, Smith (Ore.), Thomas, Kyl, Shelby
Democrats: Wyden, Akaka, Johnson, Landrieu, Bayh, Feinstein, Schumer, Cantwell

NATIONAL PARKS, HISTORIC PRESERVATION & RECREATION
224-6969 354 SD
Thomas, chairman

Republicans: Campbell, vice chairman, Burns, Smith (Ore.), Hagel, Domenici
Democrats: Akaka, Dorgan, Graham, Landrieu, Bayh, Schumer

WATER & POWER
224-8115 312 SH
Smith (Ore.), chairman

Republicans: Kyl, vice chairman, Craig, Campbell, Shelby, Hagel
Democrats: Dorgan, Graham, Wyden, Johnson, Feinstein, Cantwell

ENVIRONMENT & PUBLIC WORKS
224-6176 410 SD
Party Ratio: R 9-D 9
Robert C. Smith, R-N.H., chairman

John W. Warner, Va.	*Harry Reid, Nev.*
James M. Inhofe, Okla.	*Max Baucus, Mont.*
Christopher S. Bond, Mo.	*Bob Graham, Fla.*
George V. Voinovich, Ohio	*Joseph I. Lieberman, Conn.*
Michael D. Crapo, Idaho	*Barbara Boxer, Calif.*
Lincoln Chafee, R.I.	*Ron Wyden, Ore.*
Arlen Specter, Pa.	*Thomas R. Carper, Del.*
Ben Nighthorse Campbell, Colo.	*Hillary Rodham Clinton, N.Y.*
	Jon Corzine, N.J.

CLEAN AIR, WETLANDS, PRIVATE PROPERTY & NUCLEAR SAFETY
224-6176 410 SD
Voinovich, chairman

Republicans: Inhofe, Crapo, Campbell
Democrats: Lieberman, Carper, Clinton, Corzine

FISHERIES, WILDLIFE & WATER
224-6176 410 SD
Crapo, chairman

Republicans: Bond, Warner, Chafee, Campbell
Democrats: Graham, Baucus, Wyden, Clinton, Corzine

SUPERFUND, WASTE CONTROL & RISK ASSESSMENT
224-6176 410 SD
Chafee, chairman

Republicans: Warner, Inhofe, Crapo, Specter
Democrats: Boxer, Wyden, Carper, Clinton, Corzine

TRANSPORTATION & INFRASTRUCTURE
224-6176 410 SD
Inhofe, chairman

Republicans: Warner, Bond, Voinovich, Chafee
Democrats: Baucus, Graham, Lieberman, Boxer, Wyden

FINANCE
224-4515 219 SD
Party Ratio: R 10-D 10
Charles E. Grassley, R-Iowa, chairman

Orrin G. Hatch, Utah	*Max Baucus, Mont.*
Frank H. Murkowski, Alaska	*John D. Rockefeller IV, W.Va.*
Don Nickles, Okla.	*Tom Daschle, S.D.*
Phil Gramm, Texas	*John B. Breaux, La.*
Trent Lott, Miss.	*Kent Conrad, N.D.*
James M. Jeffords, Vt.	*Bob Graham, Fla.*
Fred Thompson, Tenn.	*Jeff Bingaman, N.M.*
Olympia J. Snowe, Maine	*John Kerry, Mass.*
Jon Kyl, Ariz.	*Robert G. Torricelli, N.J.*
	Blanche Lincoln, Ark.

HEALTH CARE
224-4515 219 SD
Snowe, chairwoman

Republicans: Gramm, Jeffords, Grassley, Kyl, Hatch, Nickles, Thompson
Democrats: Rockefeller, Daschle, Bingaman, Kerry, Torricelli, Lincoln, Breaux, Graham

INTERNATIONAL TRADE
224-4515   219 SD
Hatch, chairman

Republicans: Grassley, Thompson, Murkowski, Gramm, Lott, Jeffords, Snowe
Democrats: Baucus, Rockefeller, Daschle, Conrad, Kerry, Lincoln, Graham, Torricelli

LONG-TERM GROWTH & DEBT REDUCTION
224-4515   219 SD
Murkowski, chairman

Republicans: Grassley, Kyl
Democrats: Graham, Baucus, Conrad

SOCIAL SECURITY & FAMILY POLICY
224-4515   219 SD
Kyl, chairman

Republicans: Nickles, Lott, Jeffords, Gramm
Democrats: Breaux, Rockefeller, Bingaman, Daschle, Kerry

TAXATION & IRS OVERSIGHT
224-4515   219 SD
Nickles, chairman

Republicans: Lott, Hatch, Thompson, Snowe, Murkowski
Democrats: Conrad, Torricelli, Breaux, Bingaman, Lincoln, Baucus

FOREIGN RELATIONS
224-4651   450 SD
Party Ratio: R 9-D 9
Jesse Helms, R-N.C., chairman

Richard G. Lugar, Ind.	*Joseph R. Biden Jr., Del.*
Chuck Hagel, Neb.	*Paul S. Sarbanes, Md.*
Gordon H. Smith, Ore.	*Christopher J. Dodd, Conn.*
Craig Thomas, Wyo.	*John Kerry, Mass.*
Bill Frist, Tenn.	*Russell D. Feingold, Wis.*
Lincoln Chafee, R.I.	*Paul Wellstone, Minn.*
George F. Allen, Va.	*Barbara Boxer, Calif.*
Sam Brownback, Kan.	*Robert G. Torricelli, N.J.*
	Bill Nelson, Fla.

AFRICAN AFFAIRS
224-4651   450 SD
Frist, chairman

Republicans: Brownback, Smith (Ore.)
Democrats: Feingold, Dodd, Boxer

EAST ASIAN & PACIFIC AFFAIRS
224-4651   450 SD
Thomas, chairman

Republicans: Helms, Lugar, Hagel
Democrats: Kerry, Torricelli, Feingold, Biden

EUROPEAN AFFAIRS
224-4651   450 SD
Smith (Ore.), chairman

Republicans: Lugar, Chafee, Hagel
Democrats: Biden, Sarbanes, Dodd, Wellstone

INTERNATIONAL ECONOMIC POLICY, EXPORT & TRADE PROMOTION
224-4651   450 SD
Hagel, chairman

Republicans: Thomas, Chafee, Allen
Democrats: Sarbanes, Nelson (Fla.), Wellstone, Torricelli

INTERNATIONAL OPERATIONS & TERRORISM
224-4651   450 SD
Allen, chairman

Republicans: Helms, Frist, Brownback
Democrats: Boxer, Kerry, Nelson (Fla.), Biden

NEAR EASTERN & SOUTH ASIAN AFFAIRS
224-4651   450 SD
Brownback, chairman

Republicans: Smith (Ore.), Thomas, Frist
Democrats: Wellstone, Torricelli, Boxer, Sarbanes

WESTERN HEMISPHERE
224-4651   450 SD
Chafee, chairman

Republicans: Allen, Helms, Lugar
Democrats: Dodd, Nelson (Fla.), Kerry, Feingold

GOVERNMENTAL AFFAIRS
224-4751   340 SD
Party Ratio: R 8-D 8
Fred Thompson, R-Tenn., chairman

Ted Stevens, Alaska	*Joseph I. Lieberman, Conn.*
Susan Collins, Maine	*Carl Levin, Mich.*
George V. Voinovich, Ohio	*Daniel K. Akaka, Hawaii*
Pete V. Domenici, N.M.	*Richard J. Durbin, Ill.*
Thad Cochran, Miss.	*Robert G. Torricelli, N.J.*
Judd Gregg, N.H.	*Max Cleland, Ga.*
Robert F. Bennett, Utah	*Thomas R. Carper, Del.*
	Jean Carnahan, Mo.

INTERNATIONAL SECURITY, PROLIFERATION & FEDERAL SERVICES
224-2254   442 SH
Cochran, chairman

Republicans: Stevens, Collins, Domenici, Gregg, Bennett
Democrats: Akaka, Levin, Torricelli, Cleland, Carper, Carnahan

INVESTIGATIONS
224-3721   100 SR
Collins, chairwoman

Republicans: Stevens, Voinovich, Domenici, Cochran, Gregg, Bennett
Democrats: Levin, Akaka, Durbin, Torricelli, Cleland, Carper, Carnahan

OVERSIGHT OF GOVERNMENT MANAGEMENT
224-3682   601 SH
Voinovich, chairman

Republicans: Stevens, Collins, Domenici, Cochran
Democrats: Durbin, Akaka, Torricelli, Carper, Carnahan

HEALTH, EDUCATION, LABOR & PENSIONS

224-5375 428 SD
Party Ratio: R 10-D 10
James M. Jeffords, R-Vt., chairman

Judd Gregg, N.H.	*Edward M. Kennedy, Mass.*
Bill Frist, Tenn.	*Christopher J. Dodd, Conn.*
Michael B. Enzi, Wyo.	*Tom Harkin, Iowa*
Tim Hutchinson, Ark.	*Barbara A. Mikulski, Md.*
John W. Warner, Va.	*Jeff Bingaman, N.M.*
Christopher S. Bond, Mo.	*Paul Wellstone, Minn.*
Pat Roberts, Kan.	*Patty Murray, Wash.*
Susan Collins, Maine	*Jack Reed, R.I.*
Jeff Sessions, Ala.	*John Edwards, N.C.*
	Hillary Rodham Clinton, N.Y.

AGING
224-2962 608 SH
Hutchinson, chairman

Republicans: Jeffords, Warner, Bond, Roberts
Democrats: Mikulski, Dodd, Murray, Edwards, Clinton

CHILDREN & FAMILIES
224-5800 615 SH
Gregg, chairman

Republicans: Frist, Warner, Bond, Collins
Democrats: Dodd, Bingaman, Wellstone, Murray, Reed

EMPLOYMENT, SAFETY & TRAINING
224-7229 607 SH
Enzi, chairman

Republicans: Jeffords, Gregg, Sessions
Democrats: Wellstone, Kennedy, Dodd, Harkin

PUBLIC HEALTH
224-7139 424 SD
Frist, chairman

Republicans: Gregg, Enzi, Hutchinson, Roberts, Collins, Sessions
Democrats: Kennedy, Harkin, Mikulski, Bingaman, Reed, Edwards, Clinton

INDIAN AFFAIRS

224-2251 838 SH
Party Ratio: R 7-D 7
Ben Nighthorse Campbell, R-Colo., chairman

Frank H. Murkowski, Alaska	*Daniel K. Inouye, Hawaii*
John McCain, Ariz.	*Kent Conrad, N.D.*
Pete V. Domenici, N.M.	*Harry Reid, Nev.*
Craig Thomas, Wyo.	*Daniel K. Akaka, Hawaii*
Orrin G. Hatch, Utah	*Paul Wellstone, Minn.*
James M. Inhofe, Okla.	*Byron L. Dorgan, N.D.*
	Tim Johnson, S.D.

JUDICIARY

224-5225 224 SD
Party Ratio: R 9-D 9
Orrin G. Hatch, R-Utah, chairman

Strom Thurmond, S.C.	*Patrick J. Leahy, Vt.*
Charles E. Grassley, Iowa	*Edward M. Kennedy, Mass.*
Arlen Specter, Pa.	*Joseph R. Biden Jr., Del.*
Jon Kyl, Ariz.	*Herb Kohl, Wis.*
Mike DeWine, Ohio	*Dianne Feinstein, Calif.*
Jeff Sessions, Ala.	*Russell D. Feingold, Wis.*
Sam Brownback, Kan.	*Charles E. Schumer, N.Y.*
Mitch McConnell, Ky.	*Richard J. Durbin, Ill.*
	Maria Cantwell, Wash.

ADMINISTRATIVE OVERSIGHT & THE COURTS
224-7572 308 SH
Sessions, chairman

Republicans: Grassley, Thurmond, Specter
Democrats: Schumer, Kennedy, Feingold, Durbin

ANTITRUST, BUSINESS RIGHTS & COMPETITION
224-9494 161 SD
DeWine, chairman

Republicans: Hatch, Specter, Thurmond, Brownback
Democrats: Kohl, Leahy, Feingold, Schumer, Cantwell

CONSTITUTION, FEDERALISM & PROPERTY RIGHTS
224-4135 524 SD
Thurmond, chairman

Republicans: Hatch, Kyl, McConnell
Democrats: Feingold, Leahy, Kennedy, Durbin

IMMIGRATION
224-6098 323 SD
Brownback, chairman

Republicans: Specter, Grassley, Kyl, DeWine
Democrats: Kennedy, Feinstein, Schumer, Durbin, Cantwell

TECHNOLOGY, TERRORISM & GOVERNMENT INFORMATION
224-6791 325 SH
Kyl, chairman

Republicans: DeWine, Sessions, McConnell
Democrats: Feinstein, Biden, Kohl, Cantwell

YOUTH VIOLENCE
224-5564 224 SD
Grassley, chairman

Republicans: Hatch, Sessions, Brownback, McConnell
Democrats: Biden, Kohl, Feinstein, Durbin, Cantwell

RULES & ADMINISTRATION
224-6352 305 SR
Party Ratio: R 9-D 9
Mitch McConnell, R-Ky., chairman

John W. Warner, Va.	*Christopher J. Dodd, Conn.*
Jesse Helms, N.C.	*Robert C. Byrd, W.Va.*
Ted Stevens, Alaska	*Daniel K. Inouye, Hawaii*
Thad Cochran, Miss.	*Dianne Feinstein, Calif.*
Rick Santorum, Pa.	*Robert G. Torricelli, N.J.*
Don Nickles, Okla.	*Charles E. Schumer, N.Y.*
Trent Lott, Miss.	*John B. Breaux, La.*
Kay Bailey Hutchison, Texas	*Tom Daschle, S.D.*
	Mark Dayton, Minn.

SELECT ETHICS
224-2981 220 SH
Party Ratio: R 3-D 3
Pat Roberts, R-Kan., chairman

George V. Voinovich, Ohio	*Harry Reid, Nev.*
Craig Thomas, Wyo.	*Daniel K. Akaka, Hawaii*
	Blanche Lincoln, Ark.

SELECT INTELLIGENCE
224-1700 211 SH
Party Ratio: R 8-D 8
Richard C. Shelby, R-Ala., chairman

Jon Kyl, Ariz.	*Bob Graham, Fla.*
James M. Inhofe, Okla.	*Carl Levin, Mich.*
Orrin G. Hatch, Utah	*John D. Rockefeller IV, W.Va.*
Pat Roberts, Kan.	*Dianne Feinstein, Calif.*
Mike DeWine, Ohio	*Ron Wyden, Ore.*
Fred Thompson, Tenn.	*Richard J. Durbin, Ill.*
Richard G. Lugar, Ind.	*Evan Bayh, Ind.*
	John Edwards, N.C.

SMALL BUSINESS
224-5175 428A SR
Party Ratio: R 9-D 9
Christopher S. Bond, R-Mo., chairman

Conrad Burns, Mont.	*John Kerry, Mass.*
Robert F. Bennett, Utah	*Carl Levin, Mich.*
Olympia J. Snowe, Maine	*Tom Harkin, Iowa*
Michael B. Enzi, Wyo.	*Joseph I. Lieberman, Conn.*
Peter G. Fitzgerald, Ill.	*Paul Wellstone, Minn.*
Michael D. Crapo, Idaho	*Max Cleland, Ga.*
George F. Allen, Va.	*Mary L. Landrieu, La.*
John Ensign, Nev.	*John Edwards, N.C.*
	Maria Cantwell, Wash.

SPECIAL AGING
224-5364 G31 SD
Party Ratio: R 10-D 10
Larry E. Craig, R-Idaho, chairman

James M. Jeffords, Vt.	*John B. Breaux, La.*
Conrad Burns, Mont.	*Harry Reid, Nev.*
Richard C. Shelby, Ala.	*Herb Kohl, Wis.*
Rick Santorum, Pa.	*Russell D. Feingold, Wis.*
Susan Collins, Maine	*Ron Wyden, Ore.*
Michael B. Enzi, Wyo.	*Evan Bayh, Ind.*
Tim Hutchinson, Ark.	*Blanche Lincoln, Ark.*
Peter G. Fitzgerald, Ill.	*Thomas R. Carper, Del.*
John Ensign, Nev.	*Debbie Stabenow, Mich.*
	Jean Carnahan, Mo.

VETERANS' AFFAIRS
224-9126 412 SR
Party Ratio: R 7-D 7
Arlen Specter, R-Pa., chairman

Strom Thurmond, S.C.	*John D. Rockefeller IV, W.Va.*
Frank H. Murkowski, Alaska	*Bob Graham, Fla.*
James M. Jeffords, Vt.	*Daniel K. Akaka, Hawaii*
Ben Nighthorse Campbell, Colo.	*Paul Wellstone, Minn.*
Larry E. Craig, Idaho	*Patty Murray, Wash.*
Tim Hutchinson, Ark.	*Zell Miller, Ga.*
	Ben Nelson, Neb.

Partisan Senate Committees

REPUBLICAN LEADERS

President . . . . Vice President Dick Cheney
President Pro Tempore . . . . Strom Thurmond
Majority Leader . . . . Trent Lott
Assistant Majority Leader . . . . Don Nickles
Conference Chairman . . . . Rick Santorum
Conference Vice Chairwoman . . . . Kay Bailey Hutchison
Chief Deputy Whip . . . . Judd Gregg
Deputy Whip . . . . George F. Allen
. . . . Jim Bunning
. . . . Susan Collins
. . . . Michael D. Crapo
. . . . Chuck Hagel
. . . . Tim Hutchinson
. . . . Jon Kyl
. . . . Jeff Sessions
. . . . Gordon H. Smith
. . . . Craig Thomas

NATIONAL REPUBLICAN SENATORIAL COMMITTEE
(202) 675-6000 425 Second St. N.E. 20002

Chairman . . . . Bill Frist

Governing Committee: Christopher S. Bond; Sam Brownback; John Ensign; Peter G. Fitzgerald; Judd Gregg; Rick Santorum

COMMITTEE ON COMMITTEES
(202) 224-4521 SH-730

Chairman . . . . Jon Kyl

POLICY COMMITTEE
(202) 224-2946 SR-347

Chairman . . . . Larry E. Craig

Members: Richard G. Lugar; Ted Stevens; John W. Warner; Phil Gramm; Pete V. Domenici; John McCain; Frank H. Murkowski; Robert C. Smith; Charles E. Grassley; Jesse Helms; Fred Thompson; James M. Jeffords; Ben Nighthorse Campbell; Orrin G. Hatch; Mitch McConnell; Pat Roberts; Richard C. Shelby; Christopher H. Bond; Arlen Specter

DEMOCRATIC LEADERS

Minority Leader . . . . Tom Daschle
Assistant Minority Leader . . . . Harry Reid
Conference Chairman . . . . Tom Daschle
Conference Secretary . . . . Barbara A. Mikulski
Chief Deputy Whip . . . . John B. Breaux
Assistant Floor Leader . . . . Richard J. Durbin
Chief Deputy for Strategic Outreach . . . . Barbara Boxer
Technology and Communications
    Committee Chairman . . . . John D. Rockefeller IV
Deputy Whip . . . . Jeff Bingaman
. . . . Jack Reed
. . . . Barbara Boxer
. . . . Max Cleland

DEMOCRATIC SENATORIAL CAMPAIGN COMMITTEE
(202) 224-2447 430 S. Capitol St. S.E. 20003

Chairwoman . . . . Patty Murray
Vice Chairman . . . . Bill Nelson

Committee co-chairmen: Charles E. Schumer; Dianne Feinstein; John B. Breaux; Jon Corzine; Blanche Lincoln; Thomas R. Carper; Jack Reed, Ben Nelson; Edward M. Kennedy; Mark Dayton; Harry Reid; John Edwards; Patrick J. Leahy; Jeff Bingaman; Ron Wyden; Debbie Stabenow; Barbara A. Mikulski; Daniel K. Inouye, Tim Johnson

POLICY COMMITTEE
(202) 224-3232 SH-419

Chairman . . . . Byron L. Dorgan
Regional Chairwoman . . . . Patty Murray
Regional Chairman . . . . Jack Reed
Regional Chairwoman . . . . Mary L. Landrieu
Regional Chairman . . . . Evan Bayh

Members: Tom Daschle; Dianne Feinstein; Joseph I. Lieberman; Daniel K. Akaka; Paul Wellstone; Blanche Lincoln; Robert G. Torricelli; Russell D. Feingold; Charles E. Schumer; Ron Wyden; Ernest F. Hollings; John D. Rockefeller IV; Tim Johnson; Zell Miller; Bill Nelson; Thomas R. Carper; Hillary Rodham Clinton; Jon Corzine; Jean Carnahan; Barbara A. Mikulski; Harry Reid

STEERING AND COORDINATION COMMITTEE
(202) 224-9048 SH-712

Chairman . . . . John Kerry

Members: Max Baucus; Tom Harkin; Jeff Bingaman; Christopher J. Dodd; John B. Breaux; Kent Conrad; Joseph R. Biden Jr.; Barbara Boxer; Tom Daschle; Bob Graham; Carl Levin; Patrick J. Leahy; Daniel K. Inouye; Herb Kohl; Robert C. Byrd; Edward M. Kennedy; Max Cleland; Paul S. Sarbanes; Harry Reid; Richard J. Durbin; John Edwards

House Committees

The standing and select committees of the U.S. House are listed below in alphabetical order. Membership is given in order of seniority on the committee. If a non-voting delegate or the resident commissioner is a member of the committee, the party ratio reflects that membership. Non-voting representatives, while they cannot vote on the House floor, enjoy status equal to that of their voting colleagues on committees. Subcommittees membership is listed in order of seniority.

On full commitee rosters, members of the majority party, Republicans, are shown in roman type; members of the minority party, Democrats, are shown in *italic* type. Independents are labeled. The word "vacancy" indicates that a committee or subcommittee seat had not been filled at press time. Subcommittee vacancies do not necessarily indicate vacancies on full committees, or vice versa.

The telephone area code for Washington, D.C., is 202. Abbreviations for House office buildings are: CHOB – Cannon House Office Building, LHOB – Longworth House Office Building, RHOB – Rayburn House Office Building, OHOB – O'Neill House Office Building, and FHOB – Ford House Office Building. The ZIP code is 20515.

AGRICULTURE
225-2171 1301 LHOB
Party Ratio: R 27-D 24
Larry Combest, R-Texas, chairman

John A. Boehner, Ohio, vice chairman	*Charles W. Stenholm, Texas*
Robert W. Goodlatte, Va.	*Gary A. Condit, Calif.*
Richard W. Pombo, Calif.	*Collin C. Peterson, Minn.*
Nick Smith, Mich.	*Cal Dooley, Calif.*
Terry Everett, Ala.	*Eva Clayton, N.C.*
Frank D. Lucas, Okla.	*Earl F. Hilliard, Ala.*
Saxby Chambliss, Ga.	*Tim Holden, Pa.*
Jerry Moran, Kan.	*Sanford D. Bishop Jr., Ga.*
Bob Schaffer, Colo.	*Bennie Thompson, Miss.*
John Thune, S.D.	*John Baldacci, Maine*
Bill Jenkins, Tenn.	*Marion Berry, Ark.*
John Cooksey, La.	*Mike McIntyre, N.C.*
Gil Gutknecht, Minn.	*Bob Etheridge, N.C.*
Bob Riley, Ala.	*Leonard L. Boswell, Iowa*
Mike Simpson, Idaho	*David Phelps, Ill.*
Doug Ose, Calif.	*Ken Lucas, Ky.*
Robin Hayes, N.C.	*Mike Thompson, Calif.*
Ernie Fletcher, Ky.	*Baron P. Hill, Ind.*
Charles W. "Chip" Pickering Jr., Miss.	*Joe Baca, Calif.*
Timothy V. Johnson, Ill.	*Rick Larsen, Wash.*
Tom Osborne, Neb.	*Mike Ross, Ark.*
Mike Pence, Ind.	*Anibal Acevedo-Vila, P.R.*
Denny Rehberg, Mont.	*Ron Kind, Wis.*
Sam Graves, Mo.	*Ronnie Shows, Miss.*
Adam H. Putnam, Fla.	
Mark Kennedy, Minn.	

CONSERVATION, CREDIT, RURAL DEVELOPMENT & RESEARCH
225-2171 1301 LHOB
Lucas (Okla.), chairman

Republicans: Moran (Kan.), vice chairman, Thune, Ose, Osborne, Graves, Putnam, Kennedy (Minn.)
Democrats: Hilliard, Baldacci, Phelps, Thompson (Calif.), Baca, Peterson (Minn.), Clayton

DEPARTMENT OPERATIONS, OVERSIGHT, NUTRITION & FORESTRY
225-4913 1430 LHOB
Goodlatte, chairman

Republicans: Pombo, Moran (Kan.), Cooksey, Simpson, Rehberg, Putnam
Democrats: Clayton, Berry, Acevedo-Vila, Hilliard, Holden, Baldacci

GENERAL FARM COMMODITIES
225-2171 1301 LHOB
Chambliss, chairman

Republicans: Boehner, Smith (Mich.), Everett, Lucas (Okla.), Moran (Kan.), Thune, Jenkins, Gutknecht, Riley, Ose, Hayes, Pickering, Johnson (Ill.), Pence, Rehberg, Graves, Kennedy (Minn.)
Democrats: Dooley, Thompson (Miss.), Bishop, Berry, McIntyre, Boswell, Phelps, Lucas (Ky.), Hill, Baca, Ross, Acevedo-Vila, Larsen, Kind, Shows, Thompson (Calif.), Peterson (Minn.)

LIVESTOCK & HORTICULTURE
225-2171 1432P LHOB
Pombo, chairman

Republicans: Boehner, vice chairman, Goodlatte, Gutknecht, Riley, Pickering, Osborne, Pence, Putnam
Democrats: Peterson (Minn.), Holden, Boswell, Larsen, Ross, Condit, Dooley, Etheridge

SPECIALTY CROPS & FOREIGN AGRICULTURE
225-2171 1301 LHOB
Everett, chairman

Republicans: Chambliss, vice chairman, Schaffer, Jenkins, Simpson, Hayes, Fletcher, Rehberg, Putnam
Democrats: Condit, Bishop, McIntyre, Etheridge, Lucas (Ky.), Hill, Thompson (Miss.), Thompson (Calif.)

APPROPRIATIONS
225-2771 H-218 Capitol
Party Ratio: R 35 D 29 I 1
C.W. Bill Young, R-Fla., chairman

Ralph Regula, Ohio	*David R. Obey, Wis.*
Jerry Lewis, Calif.	*John P. Murtha, Pa.*
Harold Rogers, Ky.	*Norm Dicks, Wash.*
Joe Skeen, N.M.	*Martin Olav Sabo, Minn.*
Frank R. Wolf, Va.	*Steny H. Hoyer, Md.*
Tom DeLay, Texas	*Alan B. Mollohan, W.Va.*
Jim Kolbe, Ariz.	*Marcy Kaptur, Ohio*
Sonny Callahan, Ala.	*Nancy Pelosi, Calif.*
James T. Walsh, N.Y.	*Peter J. Visclosky, Ind.*
Charles H. Taylor, N.C.	*Nita M. Lowey, N.Y.*
David L. Hobson, Ohio	*Jose E. Serrano, N.Y.*
Ernest Istook, Okla.	*Rosa DeLauro, Conn.*
Henry Bonilla, Texas	*James P. Moran, Va.*
Joe Knollenberg, Mich.	*John W. Olver, Mass.*
Dan Miller, Fla.	*Ed Pastor, Ariz.*
Jack Kingston, Ga.	*Carrie P. Meek, Fla.*

Rodney Frelinghuysen, N.J.
Roger Wicker, Miss.
George Nethercutt, Wash.
Randy "Duke" Cunningham, Calif.
Todd Tiahrt, Kan.
Zach Wamp, Tenn.
Tom Latham, Iowa
Anne M. Northup, Ky.
Robert B. Aderholt, Ala.
Jo Ann Emerson, Mo.
John E. Sununu, N.H.
Kay Granger, Texas
John E. Peterson, Pa.
Virgil H. Goode Jr., I-Va.
John T. Doolittle, Calif.
Ray LaHood, Ill.
John E. Sweeney, N.Y.
David Vitter, La.
Donald L. Sherwood, Pa.

David E. Price, N.C.
Chet Edwards, Texas
Robert E. "Bud" Cramer, Ala.
Patrick J. Kennedy, R.I.
James E. Clyburn, S.C.
Maurice D. Hinchey, N.Y.
Lucille Roybal-Allard, Calif.
Sam Farr, Calif.
Jesse L. Jackson Jr., Ill.
Carolyn Cheeks Kilpatrick, Mich.
Allen Boyd, Fla.
Chaka Fattah, Pa.
Steven R. Rothman, N.J.

AGRICULTURE, RURAL DEVELOPMENT, FDA & RELATED AGENCIES
225-2638 2362 RHOB
Bonilla, chairman

Republicans: Walsh, Kingston, Nethercutt, Latham, Emerson, Goode (I), LaHood
Democrats: Kaptur, DeLauro, Hinchey, Farr, Boyd

COMMERCE, JUSTICE, STATE & JUDICIARY
225-3351 H-309 Capitol
Wolf, chairman

Republicans: Rogers (Ky.), Kolbe, Taylor (N.C.), Regula, Latham, Miller (Fla.), Vitter
Democrats: Serrano, Mollohan, Roybal-Allard, Cramer, Kennedy (R.I.)

DEFENSE
225-2847 H-149 Capitol
Lewis (Calif.), chairman

Republicans: Young (Fla.), Skeen, Hobson, Bonilla, Nethercutt, Cunningham, Frelinghuysen, Tiahrt
Democrats: Murtha, Dicks, Sabo, Visclosky, Moran (Va.)

DISTRICT OF COLUMBIA
225-5338 H-147 Capitol
Knollenberg, chairman

Republicans: Istook, Cunningham, Doolittle, Sweeney, Vitter
Democrats: Fattah, Mollohan, Olver

ENERGY & WATER DEVELOPMENT
225-3421 2362 RHOB
Callahan, chairman

Republicans: Rogers (Ky.), Frelinghuysen, Latham, Wicker, Wamp, Emerson, Doolittle
Democrats: Visclosky, Edwards, Pastor, Clyburn, Roybal-Allard

FOREIGN OPERATIONS & EXPORT FINANCING
225-2041 H-150 Capitol
Kolbe, chairman

Republicans: Callahan, Knollenberg, Kingston, Lewis (Calif.), Wicker, Bonilla, Sununu
Democrats: Lowey, Pelosi, Jackson, Kilpatrick, Rothman

INTERIOR
225-3081 B-308 RHOB
Skeen, chairman

Republicans: Regula, Kolbe, Taylor (N.C.), Nethercutt, Wamp, Kingston, Peterson (Pa.)
Democrats: Dicks, Murtha, Moran (Va.), Hinchey, Sabo

LABOR, HEALTH & HUMAN SERVICES & EDUCATION
225-3508 2358 RHOB
Regula, chairman

Republicans: Young (Fla.), Istook, Miller (Fla.), Wicker, Northup, Cunningham, Granger, Peterson (Pa.), Sherwood
Democrats: Obey, Hoyer, Pelosi, Lowey, DeLauro, Jackson, Kennedy (R.I.)

LEGISLATIVE BRANCH
225-5338 H-147 Capitol
Taylor (N.C.), chairman

Republicans: Wamp, Lewis (Calif.), LaHood, Sherwood
Democrats: Moran (Va.), Hoyer, Kaptur

MILITARY CONSTRUCTION
225-3047 B-300 RHOB
Hobson, chairman

Republicans: Walsh, Miller (Fla.), Aderholt, Granger, Goode (I), Skeen, Vitter
Democrats: Olver, Edwards, Farr, Boyd, Dicks

TRANSPORTATION
225-2141 2358 RHOB
Rogers (Ky.), chairman

Republicans: Wolf, DeLay, Callahan, Tiahrt, Aderholt, Granger, Emerson, Sweeney
Democrats: Sabo, Olver, Pastor, Kilpatrick, Serrano, Clyburn

TREASURY, POSTAL SERVICE & GENERAL GOVERNMENT
225-5834 B-307 RHOB
Istook, chairman

Republicans: Wolf, Northup, Sununu, Peterson (Pa.), Tiahrt, Sweeney, Sherwood
Democrats: Hoyer, Meek, Price, Rothman, Visclosky

VA, HUD & INDEPENDENT AGENCIES
225-3241 H-143 Capitol
Walsh, chairman

Republicans: DeLay, Hobson, Knollenberg, Frelinghuysen, Northup, Sununu, Goode (I), Aderholt
Democrats: Mollohan, Kaptur, Meek, Price, Cramer, Fattah

ARMED SERVICES
225-4151 2120 RHOB
Party Ratio: R 32-D 28
Bob Stump, R-Ariz., chairman

Floyd D. Spence, S.C.,
 vice chairman
Duncan Hunter, Calif.
James V. Hansen, Utah
Curt Weldon, Pa.
Joel Hefley, Colo.
H. James Saxton, N.J.
John M. McHugh, N.Y.

Ike Skelton, Mo.
John M. Spratt Jr., S.C.
Solomon P. Ortiz, Texas
Lane Evans, Ill.
Gene Taylor, Miss.
Neil Abercrombie, Hawaii
Martin T. Meehan, Mass.
Robert A. Underwood, Guam

Terry Everett, Ala.
Roscoe G. Bartlett, Md.
Howard P. "Buck" McKeon, Calif.
J.C. Watts Jr., Okla.
William M. "Mac"
  Thornberry, Texas
John Hostettler, Ind.
Saxby Chambliss, Ga.
Van Hilleary, Tenn.
Joe Scarborough, Fla.
Walter B. Jones, N.C.
Lindsey Graham, S.C.
Jim Ryun, Kan.
Bob Riley, Ala.
Jim Gibbons, Nev.
Robin Hayes, N.C.
Heather A. Wilson, N.M.
Ken Calvert, Calif.
Rob Simmons, Conn.
Ander Crenshaw, Fla.
Mark Steven Kirk, Ill.
Jo Ann Davis, Va.
Ed Schrock, Va.
Todd Akin, Mo.
Vacancy

Rod R. Blagojevich, Ill.
Silvestre Reyes, Texas
Tom Allen, Maine
Vic Snyder, Ark.
Jim Turner, Texas
Adam Smith, Wash.
Loretta Sanchez, Calif.
Jim Maloney, Conn.
Mike McIntyre, N.C.
Ciro D. Rodriguez, Texas
Cynthia A. McKinney, Ga.
Ellen O. Tauscher, Calif.
Robert A. Brady, Pa.
Robert E. Andrews, N.J.
Baron P. Hill, Ind.
Mike Thompson, Calif.
John B. Larson, Conn.
Susan A. Davis, Calif.
Jim Langevin, R.I.
Vacancy

MILITARY INSTALLATIONS & FACILITIES
225-7120 2340 RHOB
Saxton, chairman

Republicans: Hostettler, Scarborough, Hayes, vice chairman, Calvert, Crenshaw, Schrock, Hefley, McHugh, Everett
Democrats: Abercrombie, Taylor (Miss.), Ortiz, Underwood, Reyes, Snyder, Rodriguez, Thompson (Calif.)

MILITARY PERSONNEL
225-7560 2340 RHOB
McHugh, chairman

Republicans: Thornberry, Graham, Ryun, vice chairman, Wilson, Simmons, Kirk, J. Davis (Va.), Schrock, Akin
Democrats: Meehan, Sanchez, McKinney, Tauscher, Andrews, Hill, Davis (Calif.), Langevin

MILITARY PROCUREMENT
225-4440 2340 RHOB
Spence, chairman

Republicans: Hansen, Hefley, Everett, McKeon, Watts, Thornberry, Graham, vice chairman, Ryun, Gibbons, Wilson, Simmons, Kirk, J. Davis (Va.), Vacancy
Democrats: Taylor (Miss.), Skelton, Spratt, Evans, Blagojevich, Allen, Turner, Smith (Wash.), Maloney (Conn.), McIntyre, McKinney, Tauscher, Brady (Pa.)

MILITARY READINESS
225-6288 2117 RHOB
Weldon (Pa.), chairman

Republicans: Bartlett, Chambliss, Jones (N.C.), Riley, vice chairman, Hunter, Hansen, McKeon, Watts, Hilleary, Gibbons, Vacancy
Democrats: Ortiz, Evans, Underwood, Maloney (Conn.), McIntyre, Rodriguez, Brady (Pa.), Hill, Davis (Calif.), Vacancy

MILITARY RESEARCH & DEVELOPMENT
225-1967 2340 RHOB
Hunter, chairman

Republicans: Hilleary, vice chairman, Akin, Weldon (Pa.),

Saxton, Bartlett, Hostettler, Chambliss, Scarborough, Jones (N.C.), Riley, Hayes, Calvert, Crenshaw, Schrock
Democrats: Meehan, Abercrombie, Spratt, Taylor (Miss.), Reyes, Allen, Snyder, Turner, Smith (Wash.), Sanchez, Andrews, Larson, Langevin

MERCHANT MARINE PANEL
225-2891 2117 RHOB
Hunter, chairman

Republicans: Weldon (Pa.), Saxton, Jones (N.C.), vice chairman, Crenshaw, J. Davis (Va.)
Democrats: Allen, Taylor (Miss.), Smith (Wash.), Maloney (Conn.)

MORALE, WELFARE & RECREATION PANEL
226-2843 2340 RHOB
Bartlett, chairman

Republicans: McHugh, Chambliss, vice chairman, Scarborough, Jones (N.C.), Riley, Hayes, Crenshaw, Kirk, Schrock
Democrats: Underwood, Ortiz, Abercrombie, Meehan, Reyes, Andrews, Davis (Calif.), Vacancy

DOE REORGANIZATION PANEL
225-3040 2340 RHOB
Thornberry, chairman

Republicans: Spence, Hunter, Graham, Ryun, Gibbons, Wilson, Calvert, vice chairman
Democrats: Tauscher, Spratt, McKinney, Larson, Langevin, Vacancy

TERRORISM PANEL
226-0532 2117 RHOB
Saxton, chairman

Republicans: Hunter, Hansen, Weldon (Pa.), Everett, Bartlett, Watts, Hostettler, vice chairman, Gibbons, Hayes, Calvert, Simmons
Democrats: Snyder, Reyes, Turner, Sanchez, Maloney (Conn.), McIntyre, Rodriguez, McKinney, Hill, Langevin

BUDGET
226-7270 309 CHOB
Party Ratio: R 24-D 19
Jim Nussle, R-Iowa, chairman

John E. Sununu, N.H.,
  vice chairman
Peter Hoekstra, Mich.,
  vice chairman
Charles Bass, N.H.
Gil Gutknecht, Minn.
Van Hilleary, Tenn.
William M. "Mac"
  Thornberry, Texas
Jim Ryun, Kan.
Mac Collins, Ga.
Ernie Fletcher, Ky.
Gary G. Miller, Calif.
Patrick J. Toomey, Pa.
Wes Watkins, Okla.
Doc Hastings, Wash.
John T. Doolittle, Calif.
Rob Portman, Ohio
Ray LaHood, Ill.
Kay Granger, Texas
Ed Schrock, Va.

John M. Spratt Jr., S.C.
Jim McDermott, Wash.
Bennie Thompson, Miss.
Ken Bentsen, Texas
Jim Davis, Fla.
Eva Clayton, N.C.
David E. Price, N.C.
Gerald D. Kleczka, Wis.
Bob Clement, Tenn.
James P. Moran, Va.
Darlene Hooley, Ore.
Tammy Baldwin, Wis.
Carolyn McCarthy, N.Y.
Dennis Moore, Kan.
Michael E. Capuano, Mass.
Michael M. Honda, Calif.
Joseph M. Hoeffel, Pa.
Rush D. Holt, N.J.
Jim Matheson, Utah

John Culberson, Texas
Henry E. Brown Jr., S.C.
Ander Crenshaw, Fla.
Adam H. Putnam, Fla.
Mark Steven Kirk, Ill.

EDUCATION & WORKFORCE

225-4527 2181 RHOB
Party Ratio: R 27-D 22
John A. Boehner, R-Ohio, chairman

Tom Petri, Wis., vice chairman	*George Miller, Calif.*
Marge Roukema, N.J.	*Dale E. Kildee, Mich.*
Cass Ballenger, N.C.	*Major R. Owens, N.Y.*
Peter Hoekstra, Mich.	*Donald M. Payne, N.J.*
Howard P. "Buck" McKeon, Calif.	*Patsy T. Mink, Hawaii*
Michael N. Castle, Del.	*Robert E. Andrews, N.J.*
Sam Johnson, Texas	*Tim Roemer, Ind.*
James C. Greenwood, Pa.	*Robert C. Scott, Va.*
Lindsey Graham, S.C.	*Lynn Woolsey, Calif.*
Mark Souder, Ind.	*Lynn Rivers, Mich.*
Charlie Norwood, Ga.	*Ruben Hinojosa, Texas*
Bob Schaffer, Colo.	*Carolyn McCarthy, N.Y.*
Fred Upton, Mich.	*John F. Tierney, Mass.*
Van Hilleary, Tenn.	*Ron Kind, Wis.*
Vernon J. Ehlers, Mich.	*Loretta Sanchez, Calif.*
Tom Tancredo, Colo.	*Harold E. Ford Jr., Tenn.*
Ernie Fletcher, Ky.	*Dennis J. Kucinich, Ohio*
Jim DeMint, S.C.	*David Wu, Ore.*
Johnny Isakson, Ga.	*Rush D. Holt, N.J.*
Robert W. Goodlatte, Va.	*Hilda L. Solis, Calif.*
Judy Biggert, Ill.	*Susan A. Davis, Calif.*
Todd R. Platts, Pa.	*Betty McCollum, Minn.*
Pat Tiberi, Ohio	
Ric Keller, Fla.	
Tom Osborne, Neb.	
John Culberson, Texas	

21ST CENTURY COMPETITIVENESS

225-4527 2181 RHOB
McKeon, chairman

Republicans: Isakson, vice chairman, Boehner, Castle, Johnson (Texas), Graham, Souder, Upton, Ehlers, Goodlatte, Osborne
Democrats: Mink, Tierney, Kind, Holt, Wu, Rivers, McCollum, Andrews, Hinojosa

EDUCATION REFORM

225-4527 2181 RHOB
Castle, chairman

Republicans: Schaffer, vice chairman, Petri, Roukema, Greenwood, Souder, Upton, Hilleary, Ehlers, Tancredo, Fletcher, DeMint, Biggert, Platts, Keller, Osborne, Culberson
Democrats: Kildee, Scott, Woolsey, Hinojosa, McCarthy (N.Y.), Sanchez, Ford, Solis, Davis (Calif.), Owens, Payne, Roemer, Kind, Kucinich

EMPLOYER-EMPLOYEE RELATIONS

225-4527 2181 RHOB
Johnson (Texas), chairman

Republicans: Fletcher, vice chairman, Boehner, Roukema, Ballenger, Hoekstra, McKeon, Tancredo, DeMint, Tiberi
Democrats: Andrews, Payne, Kildee, Rivers, McCarthy (N.Y.), Tierney, Ford

SELECT EDUCATION

225-4527 2181 RHOB
Hoekstra, chairman

Republicans: Tiberi, vice chairman, Petri, Greenwood, Norwood, Schaffer, Hilleary, Platts
Democrats: Roemer, Scott, Holt, Davis (Calif.), McCollum, Sanchez

WORKFORCE PROTECTIONS

225-4527 2181 RHOB
Norwood, chairman

Republicans: Biggert, vice chairwoman, Ballenger, Graham, Isakson, Goodlatte, Keller, Culberson
Democrats: Owens, Kucinich, Mink, Woolsey, Sanchez, Solis

ENERGY & COMMERCE

225-2927 2125 RHOB
Party Ratio: R 31-D 26
Billy Tauzin, R-La., chairman

Michael Bilirakis, Fla.	*John D. Dingell, Mich.*
Joe L. Barton, Texas	*Henry A. Waxman, Calif.*
Fred Upton, Mich.	*Edward J. Markey, Mass.*
Cliff Stearns, Fla.	*Ralph M. Hall, Texas*
Paul E. Gillmor, Ohio	*Rick Boucher, Va.*
James C. Greenwood, Pa.	*Edolphus Towns, N.Y.*
Christopher Cox, Calif.	*Frank Pallone Jr., N.J.*
Nathan Deal, Ga.	*Sherrod Brown, Ohio*
Steve Largent, Okla.,	*Bart Gordon, Tenn.*
vice chairman	*Peter Deutsch, Fla.*
Richard M. Burr, N.C.	*Bobby L. Rush, Ill.*
Edward Whitfield, Ky.	*Anna G. Eshoo, Calif.*
Greg Ganske, Iowa	*Bart Stupak, Mich.*
Charlie Norwood, Ga.	*Eliot L. Engel, N.Y.*
Barbara Cubin, Wyo.	*Tom Sawyer, Ohio*
John Shimkus, Ill.	*Albert R. Wynn, Md.*
Heather A. Wilson, N.M.	*Gene Green, Texas*
John Shadegg, Ariz.	*Karen McCarthy, Mo.*
Charles W. "Chip"	*Ted Strickland, Ohio*
Pickering Jr., Miss.	*Diana DeGette, Colo.*
Vito J. Fossella, N.Y.	*Thomas M. Barrett, Wis.*
Roy Blunt, Mo.	*Bill Luther, Minn.*
Thomas M. Davis III, Va.	*Lois Capps, Calif.*
Ed Bryant, Tenn.	*Mike Doyle, Pa.*
Robert L. Ehrlich Jr., Md.	*Chris John, La.*
Steve Buyer, Ind.	*Jane Harman, Calif.*
George P. Radanovich, Calif.	
Joseph R. Pitts, Pa.	
Mary Bono, Calif.	
Greg Walden, Ore.	
Lee Terry, Neb.	
Charles Bass, N.H.	

COMMERCE, TRADE & CONSUMER PROTECTION

225-2927 2125 RHOB
Stearns, chairman

Republicans: Upton, Deal, vice chairman, Whitfield, Cubin, Shimkus, Shadegg, Bryant, Buyer, Radanovich, Bass, Pitts, Bono, Walden, Terry
Democrats: Towns, DeGette, Capps, Doyle, John, Harman, Waxman, Markey, Gordon, Deutsch, Rush, Eshoo

ENERGY & AIR QUALITY
225-2927 2125 RHOB
Barton, chairman

Republicans: Cox, Largent, vice chairman, Burr, Whitfield, Ganske, Norwood, Shimkus, Wilson, Shadegg, Pickering, Fossella, Blunt, Bryant, Radanovich, Bono, Walden
Democrats: Boucher, Hall (Texas), Sawyer, Wynn, Doyle, John, Waxman, Markey, Gordon, Rush, McCarthy (Mo.), Strickland, Barrett, Luther

ENVIRONMENT & HAZARDOUS MATERIALS
225-2927 2125 RHOB
Gillmor, chairman

Republicans: Greenwood, Largent, Ganske, Shimkus, vice chairman, Wilson, Fossella, Ehrlich, Buyer, Radanovich, Bass, Pitts, Bono, Walden, Terry
Democrats: Pallone, Towns, Brown (Ohio), Green (Texas), McCarthy (Mo.), Barrett, Luther, Capps, Doyle, Harman, Waxman, Deutsch

HEALTH
225-2927 2125 RHOB
Bilirakis, chairman

Republicans: Barton, Upton, Greenwood, Deal, Burr, Whitfield, Ganske, Norwood, vice chairman, Cubin, Wilson, Shadegg, Pickering, Bryant, Ehrlich, Buyer, Pitts
Democrats: Brown (Ohio), Waxman, Strickland, Barrett, Capps, Hall (Texas), Towns, Pallone, Deutsch, Eshoo, Stupak, Engel, Wynn, Green (Texas)

OVERSIGHT & INVESTIGATIONS
225-2927 2125 RHOB
Greenwood, chairman

Republicans: Bilirakis, Stearns, Gillmor, Largent, Burr, Whitfield, vice chairman, Bass
Democrats: Deutsch, Stupak, Strickland, DeGette, John, Rush

TELECOMMUNICATIONS & THE INTERNET
225-2927 2125 RHOB
Upton, chairman

Republicans: Bilirakis, Barton, Stearns, vice chairman, Gillmor, Cox, Deal, Largent, Cubin, Shimkus, Wilson, Pickering, Fossella, Blunt, T. Davis (Va.), Ehrlich, Terry
Democrats: Markey, Gordon, Rush, Eshoo, Engel, Green (Texas), McCarthy (Mo.), Luther, Stupak, DeGette, Harman, Boucher, Brown (Ohio), Sawyer

FINANCIAL SERVICES
225-7502 2129 RHOB
Party Ratio: R 37 D 32 I 1
Michael G. Oxley, R-Ohio, chairman

Jim Leach, Iowa	*John J. LaFalce, N.Y.*
Marge Roukema, N.J., vice chairwoman	*Barney Frank, Mass.*
	Paul E. Kanjorski, Pa.
Doug Bereuter, Neb.	*Maxine Waters, Calif.*
Richard H. Baker, La.	*Bernard Sanders, I-Vt.*
Spencer Bachus, Ala.	*Carolyn B. Maloney, N.Y.*
Michael N. Castle, Del.	*Luis V. Gutierrez, Ill.*
Peter T. King, N.Y.	*Nydia M. Velázquez, N.Y.*
Ed Royce, Calif.	*Melvin Watt, N.C.*
Frank D. Lucas, Okla.	*Gary L. Ackerman, N.Y.*
Bob Ney, Ohio	*Ken Bentsen, Texas*
Bob Barr, Ga.	*Jim Maloney, Conn.*

Sue W. Kelly, N.Y.	*Darlene Hooley, Ore.*
Ron Paul, Texas	*Julia Carson, Ind.*
Paul E. Gillmor, Ohio	*Brad Sherman, Calif.*
Christopher Cox, Calif.	*Max Sandlin, Texas*
Dave Weldon, Fla.	*Gregory W. Meeks, N.Y.*
Jim Ryun, Kan.	*Barbara Lee, Calif.*
Bob Riley, Ala.	*Frank R. Mascara, Pa.*
Steven C. LaTourette, Ohio	*Jay Inslee, Wash.*
Donald Manzullo, Ill.	*Jan Schakowsky, Ill.*
Walter B. Jones, N.C.	*Dennis Moore, Kan.*
Doug Ose, Calif.	*Charlie Gonzalez, Texas*
Judy Biggert, Ill.	*Stephanie Tubbs Jones, Ohio*
Mark Green, Wis.	*Michael E. Capuano, Mass.*
Patrick J. Toomey, Pa.	*Harold E. Ford Jr., Tenn.*
Christopher Shays, Conn.	*Ruben Hinojosa, Texas*
John Shadegg, Ariz.	*Ken Lucas, Ky.*
Vito J. Fossella, N.Y.	*Ronnie Shows, Miss.*
Gary G. Miller, Calif.	*Joseph Crowley, N.Y.*
Eric Cantor, Va.	*William Lacy Clay, Mo.*
Felix J. Grucci Jr., N.Y.	*Steve Israel, N.Y.*
Melissa A. Hart, Pa.	*Mike Ross, Ark.*
Shelley Moore Capito, W.Va.	
Mike Ferguson, N.J.	
Mike Rogers, Mich.	
Pat Tiberi, Ohio	

CAPITAL MARKETS, INSURANCE & GSEs
226-0469 2129 RHOB
Baker, chairman

Republicans: Ney, vice chairman, Shays, Cox, Gillmor, Paul, Bachus, Castle, Royce, Lucas (Okla.), Barr, Jones (N.C.), LaTourette, Shadegg, Weldon (Fla.), Ryun, Riley, Fossella, Biggert, Miller (Calif.), Ose, Toomey, Ferguson, Hart, Rogers (Mich.)
Democrats: Kanjorski, Ackerman, Velázquez, Bentsen, Sandlin, Maloney (Conn.), Hooley, Mascara, Jones (Ohio), Capuano, Sherman, Meeks, Inslee, Moore, Gonzalez, Ford, Hinojosa, Lucas (Ky.), Shows, Crowley, Israel, Ross

DOMESTIC MONETARY POLICY, TECHNOLOGY & ECONOMIC GROWTH
226-0473 B-303 RHOB
King, chairman

Republicans: Leach, vice chairman, Royce, Lucas (Okla.), Paul, LaTourette, Ose, Green (Wis.), Shays, Shadegg, Fossella, Grucci, Hart, Capito
Democrats: Maloney (N.Y.), Frank, Meeks, Sanders (I), Maloney (Conn.), Hooley, Sandlin, Gonzalez, Capuano, Hinojosa, Clay, Ross

FINANCIAL INSTITUTIONS & CONSUMER CREDIT
225-2258 2129 RHOB
Bachus, chairman

Republicans: Weldon (Fla.), vice chairman, Roukema, Bereuter, Baker, Castle, Royce, Lucas (Okla.), Barr, Kelly, Gillmor, Ryun, Riley, LaTourette, Manzullo, Jones (N.C.), Biggert, Toomey, Cantor, Grucci, Hart, Capito, Ferguson, Rogers (Mich.), Tiberi
Democrats: Waters, Maloney (N.Y.), Watt, Ackerman, Bentsen, Sherman, Sandlin, Meeks, Gutierrez, Mascara, Moore, Gonzalez, Kanjorski, Maloney (Conn.), Hooley, Carson (Ind.), Lee, Ford, Hinojosa, Lucas (Ky.), Shows, Crowley

HOUSING & COMMUNITY OPPORTUNITY
225-6634 B-303 RHOB
Roukema, chairwoman

Republicans: Green (Wis.), vice chairman, Bereuter, Bachus, King, Ney, Barr, Kelly, Riley, Miller (Calif.), Cantor, Grucci, Rogers (Mich.), Tiberi
Democrats: Frank, Velázquez, Carson (Ind.), Lee, Schakowsky, Jones (Ohio), Capuano, Waters, Sanders (I), Watt, Clay, Israel

INTERNATIONAL MONETARY POLICY & TRADE
226-0473 B-304 RHOB
Bereuter, chairman

Republicans: Ose, vice chairman, Roukema, Baker, Castle, Ryun, Manzullo, Biggert, Green (Wis.), Toomey, Shays, Miller (Calif.), Capito, Ferguson
Democrats: Sanders (I), Waters, Frank, Watt, Carson (Ind.), Kanjorski, Sherman, Schakowsky, Maloney (N.Y.), Gutierrez, Velázquez, Bentsen

OVERSIGHT & INVESTIGATIONS
226-3280 212 OHOB
Kelly, chairwoman

Republicans: Paul, vice chairman, King, Ney, Cox, Weldon (Fla.), Jones (N.C.), Shadegg, Fossella, Cantor, Tiberi
Democrats: Gutierrez, Bentsen, Inslee, Schakowsky, Moore, Capuano, Shows, Crowley, Clay

GOVERNMENT REFORM
225-5074 2157 RHOB
Party Ratio: R 24 D 19 I 1
Dan Burton, R-Ind., chairman

Benjamin A. Gilman, N.Y.	*Henry A. Waxman, Calif.*
Constance A. Morella, Md.	*Tom Lantos, Calif.*
Christopher Shays, Conn.	*Major R. Owens, N.Y.*
Ileana Ros-Lehtinen, Fla.	*Edolphus Towns, N.Y.*
John M. McHugh, N.Y.	*Paul E. Kanjorski, Pa.*
Steve Horn, Calif.	*Patsy T. Mink, Hawaii*
John L. Mica, Fla.	*Bernard Sanders, I-Vt.*
Thomas M. Davis III, Va.	*Carolyn B. Maloney, N.Y.*
Mark Souder, Ind.	*Eleanor Holmes Norton, D.C.*
Joe Scarborough, Fla.	*Elijah E. Cummings, Md.*
Steven C. LaTourette, Ohio	*Dennis J. Kucinich, Ohio*
Bob Barr, Ga., vice chairman	*Rod R. Blagojevich, Ill.*
Dan Miller, Fla.	*Danny K. Davis, Ill.*
Doug Ose, Calif.	*John F. Tierney, Mass.*
Ron Lewis, Ky.	*Jim Turner, Texas*
Jo Ann Davis, Va.	*Tom Allen, Maine*
Todd R. Platts, Pa.	*Jan Schakowsky, Ill.*
Dave Weldon, Fla.	*William Lacy Clay, Mo.*
Christopher B. Cannon, Utah	*Vacancy*
Adam H. Putnam, Fla.	*Vacancy*
C. L. "Butch" Otter, Idaho	
Ed Schrock, Va.	
Vacancy	

CENSUS
226-1973 114 OHOB
Miller (Fla.), chairman

Republicans: Cannon, vice chairman, Souder, Barr, Vacancy
Democrats: Clay, Maloney (N.Y.), Davis (Ill.)

CIVIL SERVICE
225-6427 B-371C RHOB
Scarborough, chairman

Republicans: Weldon (Fla.), vice chairman, Morella, Mica, Souder, Otter
Democrats: Davis (Ill.), Owens, Norton, Cummings

CRIMINAL JUSTICE, DRUG POLICY & HUMAN RESOURCES
225-2577 B-372 RHOB
Souder, chairman

Republicans: Gilman, vice chairman, Ros-Lehtinen, Mica, Barr, Miller (Fla.), Ose, J. Davis (Va.), Weldon (Fla.)
Democrats: Cummings, Blagojevich, Sanders (I), Davis (Ill.), Turner, Allen, Vacancy

DISTRICT OF COLUMBIA
225-3741 B-349A RHOB
Morella, chairwoman

Republicans: Platts, vice chairman, T. Davis (Va.), Scarborough
Democrats: Norton, Vacancy, Vacancy

ENERGY POLICY, NATURAL RESOURCES & REGULATORY AFFAIRS
225-4407 B-377 RHOB
Ose, chairman

Republicans: Otter, vice chairman, Shays, McHugh, LaTourette, Cannon, Vacancy, Vacancy
Democrats: Tierney, Lantos, Towns, Mink, Kucinich, Blagojevich

GOVERNMENT EFFICIENCY, FINANCIAL MANAGEMENT & INTERGOVERNMENTAL RELATIONS
225-5147 B-373 RHOB
Horn, chairman

Republicans: Lewis (Ky.), vice chairman, Miller (Fla.), Ose, Putnam
Democrats: Schakowsky, Owens, Kanjorski, Maloney (N.Y.)

NATIONAL SECURITY & VETERANS AFFAIRS
225-2548 B-372 RHOB
Shays, chairman

Republicans: Putnam, vice chairman, Gilman, Ros-Lehtinen, McHugh, LaTourette, Lewis (Ky.), Platts, Weldon (Fla.), Otter, Schrock
Democrats: Kucinich, Sanders (I), Allen, Lantos, Tierney, Schakowsky, Clay, Maloney (N.Y.), Vacancy

TECHNOLOGY & PROCUREMENT POLICY
225-6751 B-349A RHOB
T. Davis (Va.), chairman

Republicans: J. Davis (Va.), vice chairwoman, Horn, Ose, Schrock
Democrats: Turner, Kanjorski, Mink

HOUSE ADMINISTRATION

225-8281 1309 LHOB
Party Ratio: R 6-D 3
Bob Ney, R-Ohio, chairman

Vernon J. Ehlers, Mich.	*Steny H. Hoyer, Md.*
John L. Mica, Fla.	*Chaka Fattah, Pa.*
John Linder, Ga.	*Jim Davis, Fla.*
John T. Doolittle, Calif.	
Thomas M. Reynolds, N.Y.	

INTERNATIONAL RELATIONS

225-5021 2170 RHOB
Party Ratio: R 26-D 23
Henry J. Hyde, R-Ill., chairman

Benjamin A. Gilman, N.Y.	*Tom Lantos, Calif.*
Jim Leach, Iowa	*Howard L. Berman, Calif.*
Doug Bereuter, Neb.	*Gary L. Ackerman, N.Y.*
Christopher H. Smith, N.J.,	*Eni F.H. Faleomavaega,*
vice chairman	*Am. Samoa*
Dan Burton, Ind.	*Donald M. Payne, N.J.*
Elton Gallegly, Calif.	*Robert Menendez, N.J.*
Ileana Ros-Lehtinen, Fla.	*Sherrod Brown, Ohio*
Cass Ballenger, N.C.	*Cynthia A. McKinney, Ga.*
Dana Rohrabacher, Calif.	*Alcee L. Hastings, Fla.*
Ed Royce, Calif.	*Earl F. Hilliard, Ala.*
Peter T. King, N.Y.	*Brad Sherman, Calif.*
Steve Chabot, Ohio	*Robert Wexler, Fla.*
Amo Houghton, N.Y.	*Jim Davis, Fla.*
John M. McHugh, N.Y.	*Eliot L. Engel, N.Y.*
Richard M. Burr, N.C.	*Bill Delahunt, Mass.*
John Cooksey, La.	*Gregory W. Meeks, N.Y.*
Tom Tancredo, Colo.	*Barbara Lee, Calif.*
Ron Paul, Texas	*Joseph Crowley, N.Y.*
Nick Smith, Mich.	*Joseph M. Hoeffel, Pa.*
Joseph R. Pitts, Pa.	*Earl Blumenauer, Ore.*
Darrell Issa, Calif.	*Shelley Berkley, Nev.*
Eric Cantor, Va.	*Grace F. Napolitano, Calif.*
Jeff Flake, Ariz.	*Adam B. Schiff, Calif.*
Brian Kerns, Ind.	
Jo Ann Davis, Va.	

AFRICA
226-7812 255 FHOB
Royce, chairman

Republicans: Houghton, Tancredo, Flake, Kerns
Democrats: Payne, Meeks, Lee, Hilliard

EAST ASIA & THE PACIFIC
226-7825 B-359 RHOB
Leach, chairman

Republicans: Rohrabacher, Kerns, Smith (N.J.), Royce, Chabot, Burr, Issa, Flake
Democrats: Faleomavaega, Brown (Ohio), Davis (Fla.), Blumenauer, Ackerman, Hastings (Fla.), Meeks

EUROPE
226-7820 2401A RHOB
Gallegly, chairman

Republicans: Bereuter, King, Burr, Cooksey, Smith (Mich.), Gilman, Leach, Burton, Cantor
Democrats: Hastings (Fla.), Sherman, Wexler, Davis (Fla.), Engel, Delahunt, Lee, Crowley

INTERNATIONAL OPERATIONS & HUMAN RIGHTS
225-5748 B-358 RHOB
Ros-Lehtinen, chairwoman

Republicans: Smith (N.J.), Paul, Ballenger, Tancredo, Pitts
Democrats: McKinney, Menendez, Napolitano, Schiff

MIDDLE EAST & SOUTH ASIA
226-9940 B-359 RHOB
Gilman, chairman

Republicans: Burton, Chabot, McHugh, Pitts, Issa, Cantor, J. Davis (Va.), Rohrabacher, King, Cooksey
Democrats: Ackerman, Berman, Sherman, Wexler, Engel, Crowley, Hoeffel, Berkley, Schiff

WESTERN HEMISPHERE
226-7820 2401-A RHOB
Ballenger, chairman

Republicans: Gallegly, Ros-Lehtinen, Paul, Smith (Mich.), J. Davis (Va.)
Democrats: Menendez, Delahunt, Napolitano, Faleomavaega, Payne

JUDICIARY

225-3951 2138 RHOB
Party Ratio: R 21-D 16
F. James Sensenbrenner Jr., R-Wis., chairman

Henry J. Hyde, Ill.	*John Conyers Jr., Mich.*
George W. Gekas, Pa.	*Barney Frank, Mass.*
Howard Coble, N.C.	*Howard L. Berman, Calif.*
Lamar Smith, Texas	*Rick Boucher, Va.*
Elton Gallegly, Calif.	*Jerrold Nadler, N.Y.*
Robert W. Goodlatte, Va.	*Robert C. Scott, Va.*
Steve Chabot, Ohio	*Melvin Watt, N.C.*
Bob Barr, Ga.	*Zoe Lofgren, Calif.*
Bill Jenkins, Tenn.	*Sheila Jackson-Lee, Texas*
Asa Hutchinson, Ark.	*Maxine Waters, Calif.*
Christopher B. Cannon, Utah	*Martin T. Meehan, Mass.*
Lindsey Graham, S.C.	*Bill Delahunt, Mass.*
Spencer Bachus, Ala.	*Robert Wexler, Fla.*
Joe Scarborough, Fla.	*Tammy Baldwin, Wis.*
John Hostettler, Ind.	*Anthony Weiner, N.Y.*
Mark Green, Wis.	*Adam B. Schiff, Calif.*
Ric Keller, Fla.	
Darrell Issa, Calif.	
Melissa A. Hart, Pa.	
Jeff Flake, Ariz.	

COMMERCIAL & ADMINISTRATIVE LAW
225-2825 B-353 RHOB
Barr, chairman

Republicans: Flake, Gekas, Green (Wis.), Issa, Chabot, Hart
Democrats: Watt, Nadler, Baldwin, Weiner, Waters

CONSTITUTION
226-7680 H2-362 FHOB
Chabot, chairman

Republicans: Jenkins, Graham, Bachus, Hostettler, Hart, Smith (Texas), Hutchinson
Democrats: Nadler, Frank, Conyers, Scott, Watt

COURTS, THE INTERNET & INTELLECTUAL PROPERTY
225-5741 B-351A RHOB
Coble, chairman

Republicans: Hyde, Gallegly, Goodlatte, Jenkins, Hutchinson, Cannon, Graham, Bachus, Scarborough, Hostettler, Keller
Democrats: Berman, Conyers, Boucher, Lofgren, Delahunt, Wexler, Waters, Meehan, Baldwin, Vacancy

CRIME
225-3926 207 CHOB
Smith (Texas), chairman

Republicans: Green (Wis.), Coble, Goodlatte, Chabot, Barr, Hutchinson, Keller
Democrats: Scott, Weiner, Jackson-Lee, Meehan, Delahunt

IMMIGRATION & CLAIMS
225-5727 B-370B RHOB
Gekas, chairman

Republicans: Issa, Hart, Smith (Texas), Gallegly, Cannon, Flake
Democrats: Jackson-Lee, Frank, Berman, Lofgren, Meehan

RESOURCES
225-2761 1324 LHOB
Party Ratio: R 28-D 24
James V. Hansen, R-Utah, chairman

Don Young, Alaska, vice chairman	Nick J. Rahall II, W.Va.
Billy Tauzin, La.	George Miller, Calif.
H. James Saxton, N.J.	Edward J. Markey, Mass.
Elton Gallegly, Calif.	Dale E. Kildee, Mich.
John J. "Jimmy" Duncan Jr., Tenn.	Peter A. DeFazio, Ore.
Joel Hefley, Colo.	Eni F.H. Faleomavaega, Am. Samoa
Wayne T. Gilchrest, Md.	Neil Abercrombie, Hawaii
Ken Calvert, Calif.	Solomon P. Ortiz, Texas
Scott McInnis, Colo.	Frank Pallone Jr., N.J.
Richard W. Pombo, Calif.	Cal Dooley, Calif.
Barbara Cubin, Wyo.	Robert A. Underwood, Guam
George P. Radanovich, Calif.	Adam Smith, Wash.
Walter B. Jones, N.C.	Donna M.C. Christensen, Virgin Is.
William M. "Mac" Thornberry, Texas	Ron Kind, Wis.
Christopher B. Cannon, Utah	Jay Inslee, Wash.
John E. Peterson, Pa.	Grace F. Napolitano, Calif.
Bob Schaffer, Colo.	Tom Udall, N.M.
Jim Gibbons, Nev.	Mark Udall, Colo.
Mark Souder, Ind.	Rush D. Holt, N.J.
Greg Walden, Ore.	Jim McGovern, Mass.
Mike Simpson, Idaho	Anibal Acevedo-Vila, P.R.
Tom Tancredo, Colo.	Hilda L. Solis, Calif.
C. L. "Butch" Otter, Idaho	Brad Carson, Okla.
Tom Osborne, Neb.	Betty McCollum, Minn.
Jeff Flake, Ariz.	
Denny Rehberg, Mont.	
Vacancy	

ENERGY & MINERAL RESOURCES
225-9297 1626 LHOB
Cubin, chairwoman

Republicans: Tauzin, Thornberry, Cannon, Gibbons, vice chairman, Tancredo, Otter, Flake, Rehberg
Democrats: Kind, Rahall, Markey, Ortiz, Dooley, Inslee, Napolitano, Carson (Okla.)

FISHERIES CONSERVATION, WILDLIFE & OCEANS
226-0200 H2-188 FHOB
Gilchrest, chairman

Republicans: Young (Alaska), Tauzin, Saxton, vice chairman, Pombo, Jones (N.C.)
Democrats: Underwood, Faleomavaega, Abercrombie, Ortiz, Pallone

FORESTS & FOREST HEALTH
225-0691 1337 LHOB
McInnis, chairman

Republicans: Duncan, Peterson (Pa.), vice chairman, Souder, Simpson, Tancredo, Otter, Hansen
Democrats: Inslee, Kildee, Udall (N.M.), Udall (Colo.), Holt, Acevedo-Vila, McCollum

NATIONAL PARKS, RECREATION & PUBLIC LANDS
226-7736 1333 LHOB
Hefley, chairman

Republicans: Gallegly, Duncan, Gilchrest, Radanovich, Jones (N.C.), vice chairman, Thornberry, Cannon, Schaffer, Gibbons, Souder, Simpson, Tancredo
Democrats: Christensen, Kildee, Faleomavaega, Pallone, Udall (N.M.), Udall (Colo.), Holt, McGovern, Acevedo-Vila, Solis, McCollum

WATER & POWER
225-8331 1522 LHOB
Calvert, chairman

Republicans: Pombo, Radanovich, vice chairman, Walden, Simpson, Otter, Osborne, Flake
Democrats: Smith (Wash.), DeFazio, Dooley, Napolitano, McGovern, Solis, Carson (Okla.)

RULES
225-9191 H-312 Capitol
Party Ratio: R 9-D 4
David Dreier, R-Calif., chairman

Porter J. Goss, Fla.	Joe Moakley, Mass.
John Linder, Ga.	Martin Frost, Texas
Deborah Pryce, Ohio	Tony P. Hall, Ohio
Lincoln Diaz-Balart, Fla.	Louise M. Slaughter, N.Y.
Doc Hastings, Wash.	
Sue Myrick, N.C.	
Pete Sessions, Texas	
Thomas M. Reynolds, N.Y.	

LEGISLATIVE & BUDGET PROCESS
225-1547 421 CHOB
Pryce, chairwoman

Republicans: Goss, vice chairman, Hastings (Wash.), Myrick, Dreier
Democrats: Frost, Moakley

TECHNOLOGY & THE HOUSE
225-8925 421 CHOB
Linder, chairman

Republicans: Diaz-Balart, vice chairman, Sessions, Reynolds, Dreier
Democrats: Hall (Ohio), Slaughter

SCIENCE
225-6371 2320 RHOB
Party Ratio: R 25-D 22
Sherwood Boehlert, R-N.Y., chairman

Lamar Smith, Texas	Ralph M. Hall, Texas
Constance A. Morella, Md.	Bart Gordon, Tenn.
Christopher Shays, Conn.	Jerry F. Costello, Ill.
Curt Weldon, Pa.	James A. Barcia, Mich.
Dana Rohrabacher, Calif.	Eddie Bernice Johnson, Texas
Joe L. Barton, Texas	Lynn Woolsey, Calif.
Ken Calvert, Calif.	Lynn Rivers, Mich.
Nick Smith, Mich.	Zoe Lofgren, Calif.
Roscoe G. Bartlett, Md.	Sheila Jackson-Lee, Texas
Vernon J. Ehlers, Mich.	Bob Etheridge, N.C.
Dave Weldon, Fla.	Nick Lampson, Texas
Gil Gutknecht, Minn.,	John B. Larson, Conn.
vice chairman	Mark Udall, Colo.
Christopher B. Cannon, Utah	David Wu, Ore.
George Nethercutt, Wash.	Anthony Weiner, N.Y.
Frank D. Lucas, Okla.	Brian Baird, Wash.
Gary G. Miller, Calif.	Joseph M. Hoeffel, Pa.
Judy Biggert, Ill.	Joe Baca, Calif.
John Culberson, Texas	Jim Matheson, Utah
Todd Akin, Mo.	Steve Israel, N.Y.
Timothy V. Johnson, Ill.	Dennis Moore, Kan.
Mike Pence, Ind.	Michael M. Honda, Calif.
Felix J. Grucci Jr., N.Y.	
Melissa A. Hart, Pa.	
Vacancy	

ENERGY
225-9662 390 FHOB
Bartlett, chairman

Republicans: Rohrabacher, Calvert, Ehlers, Nethercutt, Biggert, Akin, Hart, vice chairwoman
Democrats: Woolsey, Costello, Jackson-Lee, Wu, Matheson, Lampson

ENVIRONMENT, TECHNOLOGY & STANDARDS
225-8844 2319 RHOB
Ehlers, chairman

Republicans: Morella, Shays, Weldon (Pa.), Smith (Mich.), Gutknecht, Cannon, Culberson, Grucci, vice chairman, Hart
Democrats: Barcia, Rivers, Lofgren, Udall (Colo.), Weiner, Baird, Hoeffel, Baca

RESEARCH
225-7858 B-374 RHOB
Smith (Mich.), chairman

Republicans: Smith (Texas), Weldon (Pa.), Gutknecht, Lucas (Okla.), Miller (Calif.), Biggert, Akin, Johnson (Ill.), vice chairman, Grucci, Hart
Democrats: Johnson (Texas), Etheridge, Israel, Rivers, Larson, Baird, Baca, Moore, Woolsey

SPACE & AERONAUTICS
225-7858 B-374 RHOB
Rohrabacher, chairman

Republicans: Smith (Texas), Barton, Calvert, Bartlett, Weldon (Fla.), vice chairman, Cannon, Nethercutt, Lucas (Okla.), Miller (Calif.), Culberson, Pence
Democrats: Gordon, Lampson, Larson, Moore, Lofgren, Jackson-Lee, Etheridge, Udall (Colo.), Wu, Weiner

SELECT INTELLIGENCE
225-4121 H-405 Capitol
Party Ratio: R 11-D 9
Porter J. Goss, R-Fla., chairman

Doug Bereuter, Neb.,	Nancy Pelosi, Calif.
vice chairman	Sanford D. Bishop Jr., Ga.
Michael N. Castle, Del.	Jane Harman, Calif.
Sherwood Boehlert, N.Y.	Gary A. Condit, Calif.
Jim Gibbons, Nev.	Tim Roemer, Ind.
Ray LaHood, Ill.	Alcee L. Hastings, Fla.
Randy "Duke"	Silvestre Reyes, Texas
Cunningham, Calif.	Leonard L. Boswell, Iowa
Peter Hoekstra, Mich.	Collin C. Peterson, Minn.
Richard M. Burr, N.C.	
Saxby Chambliss, Ga.	
Asa Hutchinson, Ark.	

HUMAN INTELLIGENCE, ANALYSIS & COUNTERINTELLIGENCE
225-4121 H-405 Capitol
Gibbons, chairman

Membership to be announced.

INTELLIGENCE POLICY & NATIONAL SECURITY
225-4121 H-405 Capitol
Bereuter, chairman

Membership to be announced.

TECHNICAL & TACTICAL INTELLIGENCE
225-4121 H-405 Capitol
Castle, chairman

Membership to be announced.

SMALL BUSINESS
225-5821 2361 RHOB
Party Ratio: R 19-D 17
Donald Manzullo, R-Ill., chairman

Larry Combest, Texas	Nydia M. Velázquez, N.Y.
Joel Hefley, Colo.	Juanita Millender-McDonald,
Roscoe G. Bartlett, Md.	Calif.
Frank A. LoBiondo, N.J.	Danny K. Davis, Ill.
Sue W. Kelly, N.Y.	Bill Pascrell Jr., N.J.
Steve Chabot, Ohio	Donna M.C. Christensen,
Patrick J. Toomey, Pa.	Virgin Is.
Jim DeMint, S.C.	Robert A. Brady, Pa.
John Thune, S.D.	Tom Udall, N.M.
Mike Pence, Ind.	Stephanie Tubbs Jones, Ohio
Mike Ferguson, N.J.	Charlie Gonzalez, Texas
Darrell Issa, Calif.	David Phelps, Ill.
Sam Graves, Mo.	Grace F. Napolitano, Calif.
Ed Schrock, Va.	Brian Baird, Wash.
Felix J. Grucci Jr., N.Y.	Mark Udall, Colo.
Todd Akin, Mo.	Jim Langevin, R.I.
Shelley Moore Capito, W.Va.	Mike Ross, Ark.
Vacancy	Brad Carson, Okla.
	Anibal Acevedo-Vila, P.R.

REGULATORY REFORM & OVERSIGHT
226-2630 B-363 RHOB
Pence, chairman

Republicans: Combest, Kelly, Graves, Bartlett, Akin, Toomey
Democrats: Brady (Pa.), Pascrell, Gonzalez, Phelps, Langevin, Acevedo-Vila

RURAL ENTERPRISES, AGRICULTURE & TECHNOLOGY
226-2630 B-363 RHOB
Thune, chairman

Republicans: Bartlett, Grucci, Pence, Vacancy
Democrats: Udall (N.M.), Christensen, Phelps, Carson (Okla.)

TAX, FINANCE & EXPORTS
226-2630 B-363 RHOB
Toomey, chairman

Republicans: Chabot, Issa, Schrock, Akin, LoBiondo, DeMint, Thune
Democrats: Pascrell, Langevin, Napolitano, Acevedo-Vila, Davis (Ill.), Brady (Pa.), Ross

WORKFORCE, EMPOWERMENT & GOVERNMENT PROGRAMS
226-2630 B-363 RHOB
DeMint, chairman

Republicans: LoBiondo, Ferguson, Grucci, Issa, Schrock, Capito
Democrats: Millender-McDonald, Davis (Ill.), Jones (Ohio), Gonzalez, Ross, Christensen

STANDARDS OF OFFICIAL CONDUCT
225-7103 HT-2 Capitol
Party Ratio: R 5-D 5
Joel Hefley, R-Colo., chairman

Rob Portman, Ohio	*Howard L. Berman, Calif.*
Doc Hastings, Wash.	*Martin Olav Sabo, Minn.*
Asa Hutchinson, Ark.	*Ed Pastor, Ariz.*
Judy Biggert, Ill.	*Zoe Lofgren, Calif.*
	Stephanie Tubbs Jones, Ohio

TRANSPORTATION & INFRASTRUCTURE
225-9446 2165 RHOB
Party Ratio: R 41-D 34
Don Young, R-Alaska, chairman

Tom Petri, Wis., vice chairman	*James L. Oberstar, Minn.*
Sherwood Boehlert, N.Y.	*Nick J. Rahall II, W.Va.*
Howard Coble, N.C.	*Robert A. Borski, Pa.*
John J. "Jimmy" Duncan Jr., Tenn.	*William O. Lipinski, Ill.*
Wayne T. Gilchrest, Md.	*Peter A. DeFazio, Ore.*
Steve Horn, Calif.	*Bob Clement, Tenn.*
John L. Mica, Fla.	*Jerry F. Costello, Ill.*
Jack Quinn, N.Y.	*Eleanor Holmes Norton, D.C.*
Vernon J. Ehlers, Mich.	*Jerrold Nadler, N.Y.*
Spencer Bachus, Ala.	*Robert Menendez, N.J.*
Steven C. LaTourette, Ohio	*Corrine Brown, Fla.*
Sue W. Kelly, N.Y.	*James A. Barcia, Mich.*
Richard H. Baker, La.	*Bob Filner, Calif.*
Asa Hutchinson, Ark.	*Eddie Bernice Johnson, Texas*
John Cooksey, La.	*Frank R. Mascara, Pa.*
John Thune, S.D.	*Gene Taylor, Miss.*
Frank A. LoBiondo, N.J.	*Juanita Millender-McDonald, Calif.*
Jerry Moran, Kan.	*Elijah E. Cummings, Md.*
Richard W. Pombo, Calif.	*Earl Blumenauer, Ore.*
Jim DeMint, S.C.	*Max Sandlin, Texas*
Doug Bereuter, Neb.	*Ellen O. Tauscher, Calif.*
Mike Simpson, Idaho	*Bill Pascrell Jr., N.J.*
Johnny Isakson, Ga.	*Leonard L. Boswell, Iowa*
Robin Hayes, N.C.	*Jim McGovern, Mass.*
Rob Simmons, Conn.	*Tim Holden, Pa.*
Mike Rogers, Mich.	*Nick Lampson, Texas*
Shelley Moore Capito, W.Va.	*John Baldacci, Maine*
Mark Steven Kirk, Ill.	*Marion Berry, Ark.*
Henry E. Brown Jr., S.C.	*Brian Baird, Wash.*
Timothy V. Johnson, Ill.	*Shelley Berkley, Nev.*
Brian Kerns, Ind.	*Brad Carson, Okla.*
Denny Rehberg, Mont.	*Jim Matheson, Utah*
Todd R. Platts, Pa.	*Michael M. Honda, Calif.*
Mike Ferguson, N.J.	*Rick Larsen, Wash.*
Sam Graves, Mo.	
C. L. "Butch" Otter, Idaho	
Mark Kennedy, Minn.	
Three Vacancies	

AVIATION
226-3220 2251 RHOB
Mica, chairman

Republicans: Petri, Duncan, Horn, Quinn, Ehlers, Bachus, Kelly, Baker, Hutchinson, Cooksey, vice chairman, Thune, LoBiondo, Moran (Kan.), Simpson, Isakson, Hayes, Kirk, Johnson (Ill.), Rehberg, Graves, Kennedy (Minn.), Vacancy, Vacancy
Democrats: Lipinski, Norton, Johnson (Texas), Boswell, Baldacci, DeFazio, Costello, Menendez, Brown (Fla.), Millender-McDonald, Sandlin, Tauscher, Pascrell, Holden, Lampson, Berkley, Carson (Okla.), Matheson, Honda, Rahall

COAST GUARD & MARITIME TRANSPORTATION
226-3552 507 FHOB
LoBiondo, chairman

Republicans: Coble, Gilchrest, DeMint, Simmons, vice chairman
Democrats: Brown (Fla.), Barcia, Taylor (Miss.), DeFazio

ECONOMIC DEVELOPMENT, PUBLIC BUILDINGS & EMERGENCY MANAGEMENT
225-3014 586 FHOB
LaTourette, chairman

Republicans: Cooksey, Rogers (Mich.), Capito, vice chairwoman, Vacancy
Democrats: Costello, Berry, Norton, Barcia

HIGHWAYS & TRANSIT
226-0727 B-376 RHOB
Petri, chairman

Republicans: Boehlert, Coble, Duncan, Mica, Quinn, LaTourette, Kelly, Baker, Thune, Moran (Kan.), Pombo, DeMint, Bereuter, Isakson, Hayes, Simmons, Rogers (Mich.), Capito, Kirk, Brown (S.C.), Johnson (Ill.), Kerns, Rehberg, Platts, Ferguson, Graves, Otter, Kennedy (Minn.), vice chairman, Vacancy
Democrats: Borski, Rahall, Barcia, Filner, Mascara, Millender-McDonald, Cummings, Sandlin, Pascrell, Holden, Berkley, Tauscher, Carson (Okla.), Matheson, Honda, Larsen, Lipinski, Clement, Nadler, Johnson (Texas), Boswell, McGovern, Baird, Costello, Brown (Fla.)

RAILROADS
225-5504 589 FHOB
Quinn, chairman

Republicans: Petri, Boehlert, Coble, Mica, Bachus, Moran (Kan.), DeMint, Simmons, Capito, Platts, Ferguson, vice chairman

Democrats: Clement, Nadler, Rahall, Borski, Filner, Cummings, Blumenauer, Baldacci, Larsen, Lipinski

WATER RESOURCES & ENVIRONMENT
225-4360 B-375 RHOB
Duncan, chairman

Republicans: Boehlert, Gilchrest, Horn, Ehlers, LaTourette, Kelly, Baker, Hutchinson, Pombo, Bereuter, Simpson, Brown (S.C.), Kerns, Rehberg, vice chairman, Otter, Vacancy, Vacancy, Vacancy
Democrats: DeFazio, Menendez, Taylor (Miss.), Blumenauer, McGovern, Lampson, Baird, Mascara, Berry, Borski, Filner, Johnson (Texas), Millender-McDonald, Pascrell, Honda

VETERANS' AFFAIRS
225-3527 335 CHOB
Party Ratio: R 17-D 14
Christopher H. Smith, R-N.J., chairman

Bob Stump, Ariz.	*Lane Evans, Ill.*
Michael Bilirakis, Fla.,	*Bob Filner, Calif.*
vice chairman	*Luis V. Gutierrez, Ill.*
Floyd D. Spence, S.C.	*Corrine Brown, Fla.*
Terry Everett, Ala.	*Julia Carson, Ind.*
Steve Buyer, Ind.	*Silvestre Reyes, Texas*
Jack Quinn, N.Y.	*Vic Snyder, Ark.*
Cliff Stearns, Fla.	*Ciro D. Rodriguez, Texas*
Jerry Moran, Kan.	*Ronnie Shows, Miss.*
J.D. Hayworth, Ariz.	*Shelley Berkley, Nev.*
Howard P. "Buck"	*Baron P. Hill, Ind.*
McKeon, Calif.	*Tom Udall, N.M.*
Jim Gibbons, Nev.	*Vacancy*
Mike Simpson, Idaho	*Vacancy*
Richard H. Baker, La.	
Rob Simmons, Conn.	
Ander Crenshaw, Fla.	
Henry E. Brown Jr., S.C.	

BENEFITS
225-9164 337 CHOB
Hayworth, chairman

Republicans: Spence, vice chairman, Quinn, Crenshaw, Smith
Democrats: Reyes, Brown (Fla.), Evans, Vacancy

HEALTH
225-9154 338 CHOB
Moran (Kan.), chairman

Republicans: Stearns, vice chairman, McKeon, Gibbons, Simpson, Baker, Simmons, Crenshaw, Brown (S.C.)
Democrats: Filner, Shows, Berkley, Rodriguez, Gutierrez, Carson (Ind.), Vacancy

OVERSIGHT & INVESTIGATIONS
225-3569 335 CHOB
Buyer, chairman

Republicans: Stump, vice chairman, Bilirakis, Everett
Democrats: Snyder, Hill, Udall (N.M.)

WAYS & MEANS
225-3625 1102 LHOB
Party Ratio: R 24-D 17
Bill Thomas, R-Calif., chairman

Philip M. Crane, Ill.	*Charles B. Rangel, N.Y.*
E. Clay Shaw Jr., Fla.	*Pete Stark, Calif.*
Nancy L. Johnson, Conn.	*Robert T. Matsui, Calif.*
Amo Houghton, N.Y.	*William J. Coyne, Pa.*
Wally Herger, Calif.	*Sander M. Levin, Mich.*
Jim McCrery, La.	*Benjamin L. Cardin, Md.*
Dave Camp, Mich.	*Jim McDermott, Wash.*
Jim Ramstad, Minn.	*Gerald D. Kleczka, Wis.*
Jim Nussle, Iowa	*John Lewis, Ga.*
Sam Johnson, Texas	*Richard E. Neal, Mass.*
Jennifer Dunn, Wash.	*Michael R. McNulty, N.Y.*
Mac Collins, Ga.	*William J. Jefferson, La.*
Rob Portman, Ohio	*John Tanner, Tenn.*
Phil English, Pa.	*Xavier Becerra, Calif.*
Wes Watkins, Okla.	*Karen L. Thurman, Fla.*
J.D. Hayworth, Ariz.	*Lloyd Doggett, Texas*
Jerry Weller, Ill.	*Earl Pomeroy, N.D.*
Kenny Hulshof, Mo.	
Scott McInnis, Colo.	
Ron Lewis, Ky.	
Mark Foley, Fla.	
Kevin Brady, Texas	
Paul D. Ryan, Wis.	

HEALTH
225-3943 1136 LHOB
Johnson (Conn.), chairwoman

Republicans: McCrery, Crane, Johnson (Texas), Camp, Ramstad, English, Dunn
Democrats: Stark, Kleczka, Lewis (Ga.), McDermott, Thurman

HUMAN RESOURCES
225-1025 B-317 RHOB
Herger, chairman

Republicans: Johnson (Conn.), Watkins, McInnis, McCrery, Camp, English, Lewis (Ky.)
Democrats: Cardin, Stark, Levin, McDermott, Doggett

OVERSIGHT
225-7601 1136 LHOB
Houghton, chairman

Republicans: Portman, Weller, Hulshof, McInnis, Foley, Johnson (Texas), Dunn
Democrats: Coyne, McNulty, Lewis (Ga.), Thurman, Pomeroy

SELECT REVENUE MEASURES
226-5911 1135 LHOB
McCrery, chairman

Republicans: Hayworth, Weller, Lewis (Ky.), Foley, Brady (Texas), Ryan
Democrats: McNulty, Neal, Jefferson, Tanner

SOCIAL SECURITY
225-9263 B-316 RHOB
Shaw, chairman

Republicans: Johnson (Texas), Collins, Hayworth, Hulshof, Lewis (Ky.), Brady (Texas), Ryan
Democrats: Matsui, Doggett, Cardin, Pomeroy, Becerra

TRADE
225-6649 1104 LHOB
Crane, chairman

Republicans: Shaw, Houghton, Camp, Ramstad, Dunn, Herger, English, Nussle
Democrats: Levin, Rangel, Neal, Jefferson, Becerra, Tanner

Partisan House Committees

REPUBLICAN LEADERS

Speaker of the House . . . . J. Dennis Hastert
Majority Leader. . . . . Dick Armey
Majority Whip. . . . . Tom DeLay
Conference Chairman . . . . J.C. Watts Jr.
Conference Vice Chairwoman . . . . Deborah Pryce
Conference Secretary . . . . Barbara Cubin

Deputy Whips: Roy Blunt (Chief); Cass Ballenger; Mac Collins; Barbara Cubin; John T. Doolittle; Robert L. Ehrlich Jr.; Mark Foley; Paul E. Gillmor; Porter J. Goss; Van Hilleary; Sam Johnson; Bob Ney; Deborah Pryce; Thomas M. Reynolds; Mike Rogers, Billy Tauzin; Todd Tiahrt; Roger Wicker

NATIONAL REPUBLICAN CONGRESSIONAL COMMITTEE
479-7070 320 First St. S.E. 20003

Chairman . . . . Thomas M. Davis III
Executive Committee Chairman . . . . . . Thomas M. Reynolds
Vice Chairman. . . . . John T. Doolittle
Vice Chairman. . . . . Jim McCrery
Vice Chairman. . . . . Jerry Weller
Vice Chairwoman. . . . . Anne M. Northup
Vice Chairman. . . . . John Culberson
Redistricting Task Force. . . . . John Linder

Members: Roy Blunt; John A. Boehner; Henry Bonilla; Ander Crenshaw; David Dreier; Jo Ann Emerson; Phil English; Mark Green; Doc Hastings; David L. Hobson; Johnny Isakson; Jerry Moran; Bob Ney; Rob Portman; Adam H. Putnam; Ed Royce; Pete Sessions; Donald L. Sherwood; John E. Sununu; John E. Sweeney; Fred Upton; Greg Walden; Roger Wicker

POLICY COMMITTEE
225-6168 2471 RHOB

Chairman . . . . Christopher Cox

Subcommittee chairmen: Lincoln Diaz-Balart; Jerry Weller; Doug Ose; Ernie Fletcher; Heather A. Wilson; David Vitter; John E. Sununu

Members: J. Dennis Hastert; Dick Armey; Tom DeLay; J.C. Watts; Deborah Pryce; Barbara Cubin; Thomas M. Davis III; Rob Portman; John Thune; Ander Crenshaw; Bill Thomas; Billy Tauzin; David Dreier; Jim Nussle; C.W. Bill Young; Shelley Moore Capito; Benjamin A. Gilman; Brian Kerns; Todd Tiahrt; Darrell Issa; Floyd D. Spence; Patrick J. Toomey; Roger Wicker; Kenny Hulshof; Mark Green; Todd R. Platts; Vito J. Fossella; Felix J. Grucci Jr., Joe Knollenburg; John Shadegg; Cliff Stearns; Robert W. Goodlatte; Henry J. Hyde; Ron Lewis; Bob Schaffer; Nick Smith; Bob Stump; Dave Weldon

STEERING COMMITTEE
225-0600 H-232 Capitol

Chairman . . . . J. Dennis Hastert

Members: Dick Armey; Tom DeLay; Boy Blunt, J.C. Watts Jr.; Christopher Cox; Deborah Pryce; Barbara Cubin; Thomas M. Davis III; C.W. Bill Young; David Dreier; Bill Thomas; Ken Calvert; Sonny Callahan; Dave Camp; Tom Latham; Ralph Regula; John M. McHugh; John Linder; Cass Ballenger; Joe L. Barton; Bob Stump; Don Young; Jerry Moran; John E. Sweeney; John Culberson

DEMOCRATIC LEADERS

Minority Leader . . . . Richard A. Gephardt
Minority Whip . . . . David E. Bonior
Caucus Chairman . . . . Martin Frost
Caucus Vice Chairman. . . . . Robert Menendez
Assistant to the Leader . . . . Rosa DeLauro
Ex-Officio. . . . . Joe Moakley

Deputy Whips: Chet Edwards (Chief); John Lewis (Chief); Ed Pastor (Chief); Maxine Waters (Chief); Gene Green; Eddie Bernice Johnson; Robert T. Matsui; John W. Olver; Charles B. Rangel; Bobby L. Rush; Martin Olav Sabo; Charles W. Stenholm; Bart Stupak; Nydia M. Velázquez; Lynn Woolsey; Albert R. Wynn

DEMOCRATIC CONGRESSIONAL CAMPAIGN COMMITTEE
863-1500 430 S. Capitol St. S.E. 20003

Chairwoman. . . . . Nita M. Lowey
Other leaders not available at press time.

STEERING COMMITTEE
225-0100 H-204 Capitol

Chairman . . . . Richard A. Gephardt
Co-Chairman . . . . Steny H. Hoyer
Vice Chairman. . . . . Jose E. Serrano
Vice Chairwoman . . . . Maxine Waters
Vice Chairman. . . . . John Tanner

Members: David E. Bonior, Martin Frost; Robert Menendez; Rosa DeLauro; Nita M. Lowey; Chet Edwards; John Lewis; Ed Pastor; Brad Sherman; Mike Thompson; Collin C. Peterson; William O. Lipinski; Darlene Hooley; Max Sandlin; Bart Gordon; Nick J. Rahall II; John P. Murtha; Eliot L. Engel; David R. Obey; John M. Spratt Jr.; Joe Moakley; Charles B. Rangel; John D. Dingell; Benjamin L. Cardin; Michael E. Capuano; James E. Clyburn; Elijah E. Cummings; Jim Davis; Gene Green; Steven Israel; William J. Jefferson; Carolyn Cheeks Kilpatrick; Karen McCarthy; Frank Pallone Jr.; Nancy Pelosi; Silvestre Reyes; Tim Roemer; Lucille Roybal-Allard; Bennie Thompson; Peter J. Visclosky; Lynn Woolsey

Joint Committees

JOINT ECONOMIC
224-5171 G01 SD

SENATE MEMBERS
Robert F. Bennett, R-Utah, vice chairman

Sam Brownback, Kan.
Jeff Sessions, Ala.
Michael D. Crapo, Idaho
Lincoln Chafee, R.I.

Jack Reed, R.I.
Jeff Bingaman, N.M.
Edward M. Kennedy, Mass.
Paul S. Sarbanes, Md.
Jon Corzine, N.J.

HOUSE MEMBERS
H. James Saxton, R-N.J., chairman

Paul D. Ryan, Wis.
Lamar Smith, Texas
Jennifer Dunn, Wash.
Phil English, Pa.
Adam H. Putnam, Fla.

Pete Stark, Calif.
Carolyn B. Maloney, N.Y.
Melvin Watt, N.C.
Vacancy

JOINT TAXATION
225-3621 1015 LHOB

SENATE MEMBERS
Charles E. Grassley, R-Iowa, vice chairman

Orrin G. Hatch, Utah
Frank H. Murkowski, Alaska

Max Baucus, Mont.
John D. Rockefeller IV, W. Va.

HOUSE MEMBERS
Bill Thomas, R-Calif., chairman

Philip M. Crane, Ill.
E. Clay Shaw Jr., Fla.

Charles B. Rangel, N.Y.
Pete Stark, Calif.

JOINT LIBRARY
225-8281 1309 LHOB

Membership to be announced.

JOINT PRINTING
225-8281 1309 LHOB

Membership to be announced.

Senate Seniority

Senate rank is first determined by the length of consecutive service in the Senate.

For senators who entered the Senate on the same day, several tie-breaking procedures determine seniority.

In order of precedence, these factors are: previous Senate service, service as the vice president, previous House service; service in the Cabinet, service as a state governor. If a tie still exists, senators are ranked according to the population of their state at the time of swearing in.

Republican Sens. Strom Thurmond, Richard C. Shelby and Ben Nighthorse Campbell all began their service as Democrats. The Republican Conference credited their service as Democrats toward their seniority.

REPUBLICANS

1.	Strom Thurmond, S.C.	Nov. 7, 1956
2.	Ted Stevens, Alaska	Dec. 24, 1968
3.	Jesse Helms, N.C.	Jan. 3, 1973
4.	Pete V. Domenici, N.M.	Jan. 3, 1973
5.	Richard G. Lugar, Ind.	Jan. 4, 1977
6.	Orrin G. Hatch, Utah	Jan. 4, 1977
7.	Thad Cochran, Miss.	Dec. 27, 1978
8.	John W. Warner, Va.	Jan. 2, 1979
9.	Charles E. Grassley, Iowa	Jan. 5, 1981
10.	Arlen Specter, Pa.	Jan. 5, 1981
11.	Don Nickles, Okla.	Jan. 5, 1981
12.	Frank H. Murkowski, Alaska	Jan. 5, 1981
13.	Phil Gramm, Texas	Jan. 3, 1985
14.	Mitch McConnell, Ky.	Jan. 3, 1985
15.	Richard C. Shelby, Ala.	Jan. 6, 1987
16.	John McCain, Ariz.	Jan. 6, 1987
17.	Christopher S. Bond, Mo.	Jan. 6, 1987
18.	Trent Lott, Miss.	Jan. 3, 1989
19.	James M. Jeffords, Vt.	Jan. 3, 1989
20.	Conrad Burns, Mont.	Jan. 3, 1989
21.	Robert C. Smith, N.H.	Dec. 7, 1990
22.	Larry E. Craig, Idaho	Jan. 3, 1991
23.	Judd Gregg, N.H.	Jan. 5, 1993
24.	Ben Nighthorse Campbell, Colo.	Jan. 5, 1993
25.	Robert F. Bennett, Utah	Jan. 5, 1993
26.	Kay Bailey Hutchison, Texas	June 14, 1993
27.	James M. Inhofe, Okla.	Nov. 30, 1994
28.	Fred Thompson, Tenn.	Dec. 9, 1994
29.	Olympia J. Snowe, Maine	Jan. 4, 1995
30.	Mike DeWine, Ohio	Jan. 4, 1995
31.	Jon Kyl, Ariz.	Jan. 4, 1995
32.	Craig Thomas, Wyo.	Jan. 4, 1995
33.	Rick Santorum, Pa.	Jan. 4, 1995
34.	Bill Frist, Tenn.	Jan. 4, 1995
35.	Sam Brownback, Kan.	Nov. 27, 1996
36.	Pat Roberts, Kan.	Jan. 7, 1997
37.	Wayne Allard, Colo.	Jan. 7, 1997
38.	Tim Hutchinson, Ark.	Jan. 7, 1997
39.	Jeff Sessions, Ala.	Jan. 7, 1997
40.	Gordon H. Smith, Ore.	Jan. 7, 1997
41.	Chuck Hagel, Neb.	Jan. 7, 1997
42.	Susan Collins, Maine	Jan. 7, 1997
43.	Michael B. Enzi, Wyo.	Jan. 7, 1997
44.	Jim Bunning, Ky.	Jan. 6, 1999
45.	Michael D. Crapo, Idaho	Jan. 6, 1999
46.	George V. Voinovich, Ohio	Jan. 6, 1999
47.	Peter G. Fitzgerald, Ill.	Jan. 6, 1999
48.	Lincoln Chafee, R.I.	Nov. 4, 1999
49.	John Ensign, Nev.	Jan. 3, 2001
50.	George F. Allen, Va.	Jan. 3, 2001

DEMOCRATS

1.	Robert C. Byrd, W.Va.	Jan. 7, 1959
2.	Edward M. Kennedy, Mass.	Nov. 7, 1962
3.	Daniel K. Inouye, Hawaii	Jan. 9, 1963
4.	Ernest F. Hollings, S.C.	Nov. 9, 1966
5.	Joseph R. Biden Jr., Del.	Jan. 3, 1973
6.	Patrick J. Leahy, Vt.	Jan. 14, 1975
7.	Paul S. Sarbanes, Md.	Jan. 4, 1977
8.	Max Baucus, Mont.	Dec. 15, 1978
9.	Carl Levin, Mich.	Jan. 15, 1979
10.	Christopher J. Dodd, Conn.	Jan. 5, 1981
11.	Jeff Bingaman, N.M.	Jan. 3, 1983
12.	John Kerry, Mass.	Jan. 2, 1985
13.	Tom Harkin, Iowa	Jan. 3, 1985
14.	John D. Rockefeller IV, W.Va.	Jan. 15, 1985
15.	John B. Breaux, La.	Jan. 6, 1987
16.	Barbara A. Mikulski, Md.	Jan. 6, 1987
17.	Tom Daschle, S.D.	Jan. 6, 1987
18.	Harry Reid, Nev.	Jan. 6, 1987
19.	Bob Graham, Fla.	Jan. 6, 1987
20.	Kent Conrad, N.D.	Jan. 6, 1987
21.	Herb Kohl, Wis.	Jan. 3, 1989
22.	Joseph I. Lieberman, Conn.	Jan. 3, 1989
23.	Daniel K. Akaka, Hawaii	April 28, 1990
24.	Paul Wellstone, Minn.	Jan. 3, 1991
25.	Dianne Feinstein, Calif.	Nov. 10, 1992
26.	Byron L. Dorgan, N.D.	Dec. 15, 1992
27.	Barbara Boxer, Calif.	Jan. 5, 1993
28.	Russell D. Feingold, Wis.	Jan. 5, 1993
29.	Patty Murray, Wash.	Jan. 5, 1993
30.	Ron Wyden, Ore.	Feb. 6, 1996
31.	Richard J. Durbin, Ill.	Jan. 7, 1997
32.	Robert G. Torricelli, N.J.	Jan. 7, 1997
33.	Tim Johnson, S.D.	Jan. 7, 1997
34.	Jack Reed, R.I.	Jan. 7, 1997
35.	Max Cleland, Ga.	Jan. 7, 1997
36.	Mary L. Landrieu, La.	Jan. 7, 1997
37.	Charles E. Schumer, N.Y.	Jan. 6, 1999
38.	Blanche Lincoln, Ark.	Jan. 6, 1999
39.	Evan Bayh, Ind.	Jan. 6, 1999
40.	John Edwards, N.C.	Jan. 6, 1999
41.	Zell Miller, Ga.	July 27, 2000
42.	Bill Nelson, Fla.	Jan. 3, 2001
43.	Thomas R. Carper, Del.	Jan. 3, 2001
44.	Debbie Stabenow, Mich.	Jan. 3, 2001
45.	Maria Cantwell, Wash.	Jan. 3, 2001
46.	Ben Nelson, Neb.	Jan. 3, 2001
47.	Hillary Rodham Clinton, N.Y.	Jan. 3, 2001
48.	Jon Corzine, N.J.	Jan. 3, 2001
49.	Jean Carnahan, Mo.	Jan. 3, 2001
50.	Mark Dayton, Minn.	Jan. 3, 2001

House Seniority

REPUBLICANS

House Republicans determine seniority by length of service. Members who previously served in the House are given credit for most of that service.

For members who joined at the beginning of a Congress, service is credited from the first day of the session. Seniority for members who won special elections is credited from the date of the election.

Reps. Bob Stump, Billy Tauzin and Nathan Deal began their service as Democrats. The Republican Conference has credited their service as Democrats toward their seniority. No credit is given for other previous service, such as a senator or governor.

1. Philip M. Crane, Ill.	Nov. 25, 1969
2. Floyd D. Spence, S.C.	Jan. 21, 1971
3. C.W. Bill Young, Fla.	Jan. 21, 1971
4. Benjamin A. Gilman, N.Y.	Jan. 3, 1973
5. Ralph Regula, Ohio	Jan. 3, 1973
6. Don Young, Alaska	March 6, 1973
7. Henry J. Hyde, Ill.	Jan. 14, 1975
8. Jim Leach, Iowa	Jan. 4, 1977
9. Bob Stump, Ariz.	Jan. 4, 1977
10. Doug Bereuter, Neb.	Jan. 15, 1979
11. Jerry Lewis, Calif.	Jan. 15, 1979
12. F. James Sensenbrenner Jr., Wis.	Jan. 15, 1979
13. Bill Thomas, Calif.	Jan. 15, 1979
14. Tom Petri, Wis.	April 3, 1979
15. Billy Tauzin, La.	May 17, 1980
16. David Dreier, Calif.	Jan. 5, 1981
17. James V. Hansen, Utah	Jan. 5, 1981
18. Duncan Hunter, Calif.	Jan. 5, 1981
19. Harold Rogers, Ky.	Jan. 5, 1981
20. Marge Roukema, N.J.	Jan. 5, 1981
21. E. Clay Shaw Jr., Fla.	Jan. 5, 1981
22. Joe Skeen, N.M.	Jan. 5, 1981
23. Christopher H. Smith, N.J.	Jan. 5, 1981
24. Frank R. Wolf, Va.	Jan. 5, 1981
25. Michael G. Oxley, Ohio	June 25, 1981
26. Michael Bilirakis, Fla.	Jan. 3, 1983
27. Sherwood Boehlert, N.Y.	Jan. 3, 1983
28. Dan Burton, Ind.	Jan. 3, 1983
29. George W. Gekas, Pa.	Jan. 3, 1983
30. Nancy L. Johnson, Conn.	Jan. 3, 1983
31. H. James Saxton, N.J.	Nov. 6, 1984
32. Wes Watkins, Okla.	Jan. 7, 1997
Also served 1977-91	
33. Dick Armey, Texas	Jan. 3, 1985
34. Joe L. Barton, Texas	Jan. 3, 1985
35. Sonny Callahan, Ala.	Jan. 3, 1985
36. Howard Coble, N.C.	Jan. 3, 1985
37. Larry Combest, Texas	Jan. 3, 1985
38. Tom DeLay, Texas	Jan. 3, 1985
39. Jim Kolbe, Ariz.	Jan. 3, 1985
40. Cass Ballenger, N.C.	Nov. 4, 1986
41. Richard H. Baker, La.	Jan. 6, 1987
42. Elton Gallegly, Calif.	Jan. 6, 1987
43. J. Dennis Hastert, Ill.	Jan. 6, 1987
44. Joel Hefley, Colo.	Jan. 6, 1987
45. Wally Herger, Calif.	Jan. 6, 1987
46. Amo Houghton, N.Y.	Jan. 6, 1987
47. Constance A. Morella, Md.	Jan. 6, 1987
48. Lamar Smith, Texas	Jan. 6, 1987
49. Fred Upton, Mich.	Jan. 6, 1987
50. Curt Weldon, Pa.	Jan. 6, 1987
51. Christopher Shays, Conn.	Aug. 18, 1987
52. Jim McCrery, La.	April 16, 1988
53. John J. "Jimmy" Duncan Jr., Tenn.	Nov. 8, 1988
54. Christopher Cox, Calif.	Jan. 3, 1989
55. Paul E. Gillmor, Ohio	Jan. 3, 1989
56. Porter J. Goss, Fla.	Jan. 3, 1989
57. Dana Rohrabacher, Calif.	Jan. 3, 1989
58. Cliff Stearns, Fla.	Jan. 3, 1989
59. James T. Walsh, N.Y.	Jan. 3, 1989
60. Ileana Ros-Lehtinen, Fla.	Aug. 29, 1989
61. Ron Paul, Texas	Jan. 7, 1997
Also served 1976-77, 1979-85	
62. John A. Boehner, Ohio	Jan. 3, 1991
63. Dave Camp, Mich.	Jan. 3, 1991
64. Randy "Duke" Cunningham, Calif.	Jan. 3, 1991
65. John T. Doolittle, Calif.	Jan. 3, 1991
66. Wayne T. Gilchrest, Md.	Jan. 3, 1991
67. David L. Hobson, Ohio	Jan. 3, 1991
68. Jim Nussle, Iowa	Jan. 3, 1991
69. Jim Ramstad, Minn.	Jan. 3, 1991
70. Charles H. Taylor, N.C.	Jan. 3, 1991
71. Sam Johnson, Texas	May 18, 1991
72. Spencer Bachus, Ala.	Jan. 5, 1993
73. Roscoe G. Bartlett, Md.	Jan. 5, 1993
74. Henry Bonilla, Texas	Jan. 5, 1993
75. Steve Buyer, Ind.	Jan. 5, 1993
76. Ken Calvert, Calif.	Jan. 5, 1993
77. Michael N. Castle, Del.	Jan. 5, 1993
78. Mac Collins, Ga.	Jan. 5, 1993
79. Nathan Deal, Ga.	Jan. 5, 1993
80. Lincoln Diaz-Balart, Fla.	Jan. 5, 1993
81. Jennifer Dunn, Wash.	Jan. 5, 1993
82. Terry Everett, Ala.	Jan. 5, 1993
83. Robert W. Goodlatte, Va.	Jan. 5, 1993
84. James C. Greenwood, Pa.	Jan. 5, 1993
85. Peter Hoekstra, Mich.	Jan. 5, 1993
86. Steve Horn, Calif.	Jan. 5, 1993
87. Ernest Istook, Okla.	Jan. 5, 1993
88. Peter T. King, N.Y.	Jan. 5, 1993
89. Jack Kingston, Ga.	Jan. 5, 1993
90. Joe Knollenberg, Mich.	Jan. 5, 1993
91. John Linder, Ga.	Jan. 5, 1993
92. Donald Manzullo, Ill.	Jan. 5, 1993
93. John M. McHugh, N.Y.	Jan. 5, 1993
94. Scott McInnis, Colo.	Jan. 5, 1993
95. Howard P. "Buck" McKeon, Calif.	Jan. 5, 1993
96. John L. Mica, Fla.	Jan. 5, 1993
97. Dan Miller, Fla.	Jan. 5, 1993
98. Richard W. Pombo, Calif.	Jan. 5, 1993
99. Deborah Pryce, Ohio	Jan. 5, 1993
100. Jack Quinn, N.Y.	Jan. 5, 1993

101. Ed Royce, Calif.	Jan. 5, 1993	
102. Nick Smith, Mich.	Jan. 5, 1993	
103. Rob Portman, Ohio	May 4, 1993	
104. Vernon J. Ehlers, Mich.	Dec. 7, 1993	
105. Frank D. Lucas, Okla.	May 10, 1994	
106. Ron Lewis, Ky.	May 24, 1994	
107. Steve Largent, Okla.	Nov. 16, 1994	
108. Bob Barr, Ga.	Jan. 4, 1995	
109. Charles Bass, N.H.	Jan. 4, 1995	
110. Ed Bryant, Tenn.	Jan. 4, 1995	
111. Richard M. Burr, N.C.	Jan. 4, 1995	
112. Steve Chabot, Ohio	Jan. 4, 1995	
113. Saxby Chambliss, Ga.	Jan. 4, 1995	
114. Barbara Cubin, Wyo.	Jan. 4, 1995	
115. Thomas M. Davis III, Va.	Jan. 4, 1995	
116. Robert L. Ehrlich Jr., Md.	Jan. 4, 1995	
117. Phil English, Pa.	Jan. 4, 1995	
118. Mark Foley, Fla.	Jan. 4, 1995	
119. Rodney Frelinghuysen, N.J.	Jan. 4, 1995	
120. Greg Ganske, Iowa	Jan. 4, 1995	
121. Lindsey Graham, S.C.	Jan. 4, 1995	
122. Gil Gutknecht, Minn.	Jan. 4, 1995	
123. Doc Hastings, Wash.	Jan. 4, 1995	
124. J.D. Hayworth, Ariz.	Jan. 4, 1995	
125. Van Hilleary, Tenn.	Jan. 4, 1995	
126. John Hostettler, Ind.	Jan. 4, 1995	
127. Walter B. Jones, N.C.	Jan. 4, 1995	
128. Sue W. Kelly, N.Y.	Jan. 4, 1995	
129. Ray LaHood, Ill.	Jan. 4, 1995	
130. Tom Latham, Iowa	Jan. 4, 1995	
131. Steven C. LaTourette, Ohio	Jan. 4, 1995	
132. Frank A. LoBiondo, N.J.	Jan. 4, 1995	
133. Sue Myrick, N.C.	Jan. 4, 1995	
134. George Nethercutt, Wash.	Jan. 4, 1995	
135. Bob Ney, Ohio	Jan. 4, 1995	
136. Charlie Norwood, Ga.	Jan. 4, 1995	
137. George P. Radanovich, Calif.	Jan. 4, 1995	
138. Joe Scarborough, Fla.	Jan. 4, 1995	
139. John Shadegg, Ariz.	Jan. 4, 1995	
140. Mark Souder, Ind.	Jan. 4, 1995	
141. William M. "Mac" Thornberry, Texas	Jan. 4, 1995	
142. Todd Tiahrt, Kan.	Jan. 4, 1995	
143. Zach Wamp, Tenn.	Jan. 4, 1995	
144. Dave Weldon, Fla.	Jan. 4, 1995	
145. Jerry Weller, Ill.	Jan. 4, 1995	
146. Edward Whitfield, Ky.	Jan. 4, 1995	
147. Roger Wicker, Miss.	Jan. 4, 1995	
148. J.C. Watts Jr., Okla.	Jan. 9, 1995	
149. Jo Ann Emerson, Mo.	Nov. 5, 1996	
150. Jim Ryun, Kan.	Nov. 27, 1996	
151. Robert B. Aderholt, Ala.	Jan. 7, 1997	
152. Roy Blunt, Mo.	Jan. 7, 1997	
153. Kevin Brady, Texas	Jan. 7, 1997	
154. Christopher B. Cannon, Utah	Jan. 7, 1997	
155. John Cooksey, La.	Jan. 7, 1997	
156. Jim Gibbons, Nev.	Jan. 7, 1997	
157. Kay Granger, Texas	Jan. 7, 1997	
158. Kenny Hulshof, Mo.	Jan. 7, 1997	
159. Asa Hutchinson, Ark.	Jan. 7, 1997	
160. Bill Jenkins, Tenn.	Jan. 7, 1997	
161. Jerry Moran, Kan.	Jan. 7, 1997	
162. Anne M. Northup, Ky.	Jan. 7, 1997	
163. John E. Peterson, Pa.	Jan. 7, 1997	
164. Charles W. "Chip" Pickering Jr., Miss.	Jan. 7, 1997	
165. Joseph R. Pitts, Pa.	Jan. 7, 1997	
166. Bob Riley, Ala.	Jan. 7, 1997	
167. Bob Schaffer, Colo.	Jan. 7, 1997	
168. Pete Sessions, Texas	Jan. 7, 1997	
169. John Shimkus, Ill.	Jan. 7, 1997	
170. John E. Sununu, N.H.	Jan. 7, 1997	
171. John Thune, S.D.	Jan. 7, 1997	
172. Vito J. Fossella, N.Y.	Nov. 4, 1997	
173. Mary Bono, Calif.	April 7, 1998	
174. Heather A. Wilson, N.M.	June 23, 1998	
175. Judy Biggert, Ill.	Jan. 6, 1999	
176. Jim DeMint, S.C.	Jan. 6, 1999	
177. Ernie Fletcher, Ky.	Jan. 6, 1999	
178. Mark Green, Wis.	Jan. 6, 1999	
179. Robin Hayes, N.C.	Jan. 6, 1999	
180. Gary G. Miller, Calif.	Jan. 6, 1999	
181. Doug Ose, Calif.	Jan. 6, 1999	
182. Thomas M. Reynolds, N.Y.	Jan. 6, 1999	
183. Paul D. Ryan, Wis.	Jan. 6, 1999	
184. Donald L. Sherwood, Pa.	Jan. 6, 1999	
185. Mike Simpson, Idaho	Jan. 6, 1999	
186. John E. Sweeney, N.Y.	Jan. 6, 1999	
187. Tom Tancredo, Colo.	Jan. 6, 1999	
188. Lee Terry, Neb.	Jan. 6, 1999	
189. Patrick J. Toomey, Pa.	Jan. 6, 1999	
190. Greg Walden, Ore.	Jan. 6, 1999	
191. Johnny Isakson, Ga.	Feb. 23, 1999	
192. David Vitter, La.	May 29, 1999	
193. Todd Akin, Mo.	Jan. 3, 2001	
194. Henry E. Brown Jr., S.C.	Jan. 3, 2001	
195. Eric Cantor, Va.	Jan. 3, 2001	
196. Shelley Moore Capito, W.Va.	Jan. 3, 2001	
197. Ander Crenshaw, Fla.	Jan. 3, 2001	
198. John Culberson, Texas	Jan. 3, 2001	
199. Jo Ann Davis, Va.	Jan. 3, 2001	
200. Mike Ferguson, N.J.	Jan. 3, 2001	
201. Jeff Flake, Ariz.	Jan. 3, 2001	
202. Sam Graves, Mo.	Jan. 3, 2001	
203. Felix J. Grucci Jr., N.Y.	Jan. 3, 2001	
204. Melissa A. Hart, Pa.	Jan. 3, 2001	
205. Darrell Issa, Calif.	Jan. 3, 2001	
206. Timothy V. Johnson, Ill.	Jan. 3, 2001	
207. Ric Keller, Fla.	Jan. 3, 2001	
208. Mark Kennedy, Minn.	Jan. 3, 2001	
209. Brian Kerns, Ind.	Jan. 3, 2001	
210. Mark Steven Kirk, Ill.	Jan. 3, 2001	
211. Tom Osborne, Neb.	Jan. 3, 2001	
212. C. L. "Butch" Otter, Idaho	Jan. 3, 2001	
213. Mike Pence, Ind.	Jan. 3, 2001	
214. Todd R. Platts, Pa.	Jan. 3, 2001	
215. Adam H. Putnam, Fla.	Jan. 3, 2001	
216. Denny Rehberg, Mont.	Jan. 3, 2001	
217. Mike Rogers, Mich.	Jan. 3, 2001	
218. Ed Schrock, Va.	Jan. 3, 2001	
219. Rob Simmons, Conn.	Jan. 3, 2001	
220. Pat Tiberi, Ohio	Jan. 3, 2001	

DEMOCRATS

House Democrats determine seniority by length of service. Members who previously served in the House are given some credit for that service — when they return, they are ranked above other members of that entering class.

For members who joined at the beginning of a Congress, service is credited from the first day of the session. Seniority for members who won special elections is credited from the date of the election. No credit is given for other previous service, such as a senator or governor.

1. John D. Dingell, Mich.	Dec. 13, 1955
2. John Conyers Jr., Mich.	Jan. 4, 1965
3. David R. Obey, Wis.	April 1, 1969
4. Charles B. Rangel, N.Y.	Jan. 21, 1971
5. Joe Moakley, Mass.	Jan. 3, 1973
6. Pete Stark, Calif.	Jan. 3, 1973
7. John P. Murtha, Pa.	Feb. 5, 1974
8. John J. LaFalce, N.Y.	Jan. 14, 1975
9. George Miller, Calif.	Jan. 14, 1975
10. James L. Oberstar, Minn.	Jan. 14, 1975
11. Henry A. Waxman, Calif.	Jan. 14, 1975
12. Edward J. Markey, Mass.	Nov. 2, 1976
13. David E. Bonior, Mich.	Jan. 4, 1977
14. Norm Dicks, Wash.	Jan. 4, 1977
15. Richard A. Gephardt, Mo.	Jan. 4, 1977
16. Dale E. Kildee, Mich.	Jan. 4, 1977
17. Nick J. Rahall II, W.Va.	Jan. 4, 1977
18. Ike Skelton, Mo.	Jan. 4, 1977
19. Martin Frost, Texas	Jan. 15, 1979
20. Tony P. Hall, Ohio	Jan. 15, 1979
21. Robert T. Matsui, Calif.	Jan. 15, 1979
22. Martin Olav Sabo, Minn.	Jan. 15, 1979
23. Charles W. Stenholm, Texas	Jan. 15, 1979
24. William J. Coyne, Pa.	Jan. 5, 1981
25. Barney Frank, Mass.	Jan. 5, 1981
26. Ralph M. Hall, Texas	Jan. 5, 1981
27. Tom Lantos, Calif.	Jan. 5, 1981
28. Steny H. Hoyer, Md.	May 19, 1981
29. Howard L. Berman, Calif.	Jan. 3, 1983
30. Robert A. Borski, Pa.	Jan. 3, 1983
31. Rick Boucher, Va.	Jan. 3, 1983
32. Lane Evans, Ill.	Jan. 3, 1983
33. Marcy Kaptur, Ohio	Jan. 3, 1983
34. Sander M. Levin, Mich.	Jan. 3, 1983
35. William O. Lipinski, Ill.	Jan. 3, 1983
36. Alan B. Mollohan, W.Va.	Jan. 3, 1983
37. Solomon P. Ortiz, Texas	Jan. 3, 1983
38. Major R. Owens, N.Y.	Jan. 3, 1983
39. John M. Spratt Jr., S.C.	Jan. 3, 1983
40. Edolphus Towns, N.Y.	Jan. 3, 1983
41. Gary L. Ackerman, N.Y.	March 1, 1983
42. Gerald D. Kleczka, Wis.	April 3, 1984
43. Bart Gordon, Tenn.	Jan. 3, 1985
44. Paul E. Kanjorski, Pa.	Jan. 3, 1985
45. James A. Traficant Jr., Ohio	Jan. 3, 1985
46. Peter J. Visclosky, Ind.	Jan. 3, 1985
47. Benjamin L. Cardin, Md.	Jan. 6, 1987
48. Peter A. DeFazio, Ore.	Jan. 6, 1987
49. John Lewis, Ga.	Jan. 6, 1987
50. Tom Sawyer, Ohio	Jan. 6, 1987
51. Louise M. Slaughter, N.Y.	Jan. 6, 1987
52. Nancy Pelosi, Calif.	June 2, 1987
53. Bob Clement, Tenn.	Jan. 19, 1988

54. Jerry F. Costello, Ill.	Aug. 9, 1988
55. Frank Pallone Jr., N.J.	Nov. 8, 1988
56. Eliot L. Engel, N.Y.	Jan. 3, 1989
57. Nita M. Lowey, N.Y.	Jan. 3, 1989
58. Jim McDermott, Wash.	Jan. 3, 1989
59. Michael R. McNulty, N.Y.	Jan. 3, 1989
60. Richard E. Neal, Mass.	Jan. 3, 1989
61. Donald M. Payne, N.J.	Jan. 3, 1989
62. John Tanner, Tenn.	Jan. 3, 1989
63. Gary A. Condit, Calif.	Sept. 12, 1989
64. Gene Taylor, Miss.	Oct. 17, 1989
65. Jose E. Serrano, N.Y.	March 20, 1990
66. Patsy T. Mink, Hawaii	Sept. 22, 1990
Also served 1965-77	
67. Robert E. Andrews, N.J.	Nov. 6, 1990
68. Neil Abercrombie, Hawaii	Jan. 3, 1991
Also served Sept. 1986-Jan. 1987	
69. Robert E. "Bud" Cramer, Ala.	Jan. 3, 1991
70. Rosa DeLauro, Conn.	Jan. 3, 1991
71. Cal Dooley, Calif.	Jan. 3, 1991
72. Chet Edwards, Texas	Jan. 3, 1991
73. William J. Jefferson, La.	Jan. 3, 1991
74. James P. Moran, Va.	Jan. 3, 1991
75. Collin C. Peterson, Minn.	Jan. 3, 1991
76. Tim Roemer, Ind.	Jan. 3, 1991
77. Maxine Waters, Calif.	Jan. 3, 1991
78. John W. Olver, Mass.	June 4, 1991
79. Ed Pastor, Ariz.	Sept. 24, 1991
80. Eva Clayton, N.C.	Nov. 3, 1992
81. Jerrold Nadler, N.Y.	Nov. 3, 1992
82. James A. Barcia, Mich.	Jan. 5, 1993
83. Thomas M. Barrett, Wis.	Jan. 5, 1993
84. Xavier Becerra, Calif.	Jan. 5, 1993
85. Sanford D. Bishop Jr., Ga.	Jan. 5, 1993
86. Corrine Brown, Fla.	Jan. 5, 1993
87. Sherrod Brown, Ohio	Jan. 5, 1993
88. James E. Clyburn, S.C.	Jan. 5, 1993
89. Peter Deutsch, Fla.	Jan. 5, 1993
90. Anna G. Eshoo, Calif.	Jan. 5, 1993
91. Bob Filner, Calif.	Jan. 5, 1993
92. Gene Green, Texas	Jan. 5, 1993
93. Luis V. Gutierrez, Ill.	Jan. 5, 1993
94. Alcee L. Hastings, Fla.	Jan. 5, 1993
95. Earl F. Hilliard, Ala.	Jan. 5, 1993
96. Maurice D. Hinchey, N.Y.	Jan. 5, 1993
97. Tim Holden, Pa.	Jan. 5, 1993
98. Eddie Bernice Johnson, Texas	Jan. 5, 1993
99. Carolyn B. Maloney, N.Y.	Jan. 5, 1993
100. Cynthia A. McKinney, Ga.	Jan. 5, 1993
101. Martin T. Meehan, Mass.	Jan. 5, 1993
102. Carrie P. Meek, Fla.	Jan. 5, 1993
103. Robert Menendez, N.J.	Jan. 5, 1993
104. Earl Pomeroy, N.D.	Jan. 5, 1993

105. Lucille Roybal-Allard, Calif.	Jan. 5, 1993
106. Bobby L. Rush, Ill.	Jan. 5, 1993
107. Robert C. Scott, Va.	Jan. 5, 1993
108. Bart Stupak, Mich.	Jan. 5, 1993
109. Karen L. Thurman, Fla.	Jan. 5, 1993
110. Nydia M. Velazquez, N.Y.	Jan. 5, 1993
111. Melvin Watt, N.C.	Jan. 5, 1993
112. Lynn Woolsey, Calif.	Jan. 5, 1993
113. Albert R. Wynn, Md.	Jan. 5, 1993
114. Bennie Thompson, Miss.	April 13, 1993
115. Sam Farr, Calif.	June 8, 1993
116. John Baldacci, Maine	Jan. 4, 1995
117. Ken Bentsen, Texas	Jan. 4, 1995
118. Lloyd Doggett, Texas	Jan. 4, 1995
119. Mike Doyle, Pa.	Jan. 4, 1995
120. Chaka Fattah, Pa.	Jan. 4, 1995
121. Sheila Jackson-Lee, Texas	Jan. 4, 1995
122. Patrick J. Kennedy, R.I.	Jan. 4, 1995
123. Zoe Lofgren, Calif.	Jan. 4, 1995
124. Bill Luther, Minn.	Jan. 4, 1995
125. Frank R. Mascara, Pa.	Jan. 4, 1995
126. Karen McCarthy, Mo.	Jan. 4, 1995
127. Lynn Rivers, Mich.	Jan. 4, 1995
128. Jesse L. Jackson Jr., Ill.	Dec. 12, 1995
129. Juanita Millender-McDonald, Calif.	March 26, 1996
130. Elijah E. Cummings, Md.	April 16, 1996
131. Earl Blumenauer, Ore.	May 21, 1996
132. David E. Price, N.C.	Jan. 7, 1997
Also served 1987-95	
133. Ted Strickland, Ohio	Jan. 7, 1997
Also served 1993-95	
134. Tom Allen, Maine	Jan. 7, 1997
135. Marion Berry, Ark.	Jan. 7, 1997
136. Rod R. Blagojevich, Ill.	Jan. 7, 1997
137. Leonard L. Boswell, Iowa	Jan. 7, 1997
138. Allen Boyd, Fla.	Jan. 7, 1997
139. Julia Carson, Ind.	Jan. 7, 1997
140. Jim Davis, Fla.	Jan. 7, 1997
141. Danny K. Davis, Ill.	Jan. 7, 1997
142. Diana DeGette, Colo.	Jan. 7, 1997
143. Bill Delahunt, Mass.	Jan. 7, 1997
144. Bob Etheridge, N.C.	Jan. 7, 1997
145. Harold E. Ford Jr., Tenn.	Jan. 7, 1997
146. Ruben Hinojosa, Texas	Jan. 7, 1997
147. Darlene Hooley, Ore.	Jan. 7, 1997
148. Chris John, La.	Jan. 7, 1997
149. Carolyn Cheeks Kilpatrick, Mich.	Jan. 7, 1997
150. Ron Kind, Wis.	Jan. 7, 1997
151. Dennis J. Kucinich, Ohio	Jan. 7, 1997
152. Nick Lampson, Texas	Jan. 7, 1997
153. Jim Maloney, Conn.	Jan. 7, 1997
154. Carolyn McCarthy, N.Y.	Jan. 7, 1997
155. Jim McGovern, Mass.	Jan. 7, 1997
156. Mike McIntyre, N.C.	Jan. 7, 1997
157. Bill Pascrell Jr., N.J.	Jan. 7, 1997
158. Silvestre Reyes, Texas	Jan. 7, 1997
159. Steven R. Rothman, N.J.	Jan. 7, 1997
160. Loretta Sanchez, Calif.	Jan. 7, 1997
161. Max Sandlin, Texas	Jan. 7, 1997
162. Brad Sherman, Calif.	Jan. 7, 1997
163. Adam Smith, Wash.	Jan. 7, 1997
164. Vic Snyder, Ark.	Jan. 7, 1997

165. Ellen O. Tauscher, Calif.	Jan. 7, 1997
166. John F. Tierney, Mass.	Jan. 7, 1997
167. Jim Turner, Texas	Jan. 7, 1997
168. Robert Wexler, Fla.	Jan. 7, 1997
169. Ciro D. Rodriguez, Texas	April 12, 1997
170. Gregory W. Meeks, N.Y.	Feb. 3, 1998
171. Lois Capps, Calif.	March 10, 1998
172. Barbara Lee, Calif.	April 7, 1998
173. Robert A. Brady, Pa.	May 19, 1998
174. Jay Inslee, Wash.	Jan. 6, 1999
Also served 1993-95	
175. Brian Baird, Wash.	Jan. 6, 1999
176. Tammy Baldwin, Wis.	Jan. 6, 1999
177. Shelley Berkley, Nev.	Jan. 6, 1999
178. Michael E. Capuano, Mass.	Jan. 6, 1999
179. Joseph Crowley, N.Y.	Jan. 6, 1999
180. Charlie Gonzalez, Texas	Jan. 6, 1999
181. Baron P. Hill, Ind.	Jan. 6, 1999
182. Joseph M. Hoeffel, Pa.	Jan. 6, 1999
183. Rush D. Holt, N.J.	Jan. 6, 1999
184. Stephanie Tubbs Jones, Ohio	Jan. 6, 1999
185. John B. Larson, Conn.	Jan. 6, 1999
186. Ken Lucas, Ky.	Jan. 6, 1999
187. Dennis Moore, Kan.	Jan. 6, 1999
188. Grace F. Napolitano, Calif.	Jan. 6, 1999
189. David Phelps, Ill.	Jan. 6, 1999
190. Jan Schakowsky, Ill.	Jan. 6, 1999
191. Ronnie Shows, Miss.	Jan. 6, 1999
192. Mike Thompson, Calif.	Jan. 6, 1999
193. Mark Udall, Colo.	Jan. 6, 1999
194. Tom Udall, N.M.	Jan. 6, 1999
195. Anthony Weiner, N.Y.	Jan. 6, 1999
196. David Wu, Ore.	Jan. 6, 1999
197. Joe Baca, Calif.	Nov. 16, 1999
198. Jane Harman, Calif.	Jan. 3, 2001
Also served 1993-99	
199. Brad Carson, Okla.	Jan. 3, 2001
200. William Lacy Clay, Mo.	Jan. 3, 2001
201. Susan A. Davis, Calif.	Jan. 3, 2001
202. Michael M. Honda, Calif.	Jan. 3, 2001
203. Steve Israel, N.Y.	Jan. 3, 2001
204. Jim Langevin, R.I.	Jan. 3, 2001
205. Rick Larsen, Wash.	Jan. 3, 2001
206. Jim Matheson, Utah	Jan. 3, 2001
207. Betty McCollum, Minn.	Jan. 3, 2001
208. Mike Ross, Ark.	Jan. 3, 2001
209. Adam B. Schiff, Calif.	Jan. 3, 2001
210. Hilda L. Solis, Calif.	Jan. 3, 2001

Index

A

Abercrombie, Neil, D-Hawaii (1), **288**
Acevedo-Vila, Anibal, D-P.R. (AL), **1124**
Ackerman, Gary L., D-N.Y. (5), **678**
Aderholt, Robert B., R-Ala. (4), **13**
Akaka, Daniel K., D-Hawaii, **286**, 291
Akin, Todd, R-Mo. (2), **574**
Allard, Wayne, R-Colo., **168**, 172, 177, 179, 1119
Allen, George F., R-Va., **1039**
Allen, Tom, D-Maine (1), **444**, 959
Andrews, Robert E., D-N.J. (1), **629**
Armey, Dick, R-Texas (26), 140, 204, 260, 274, 332, 377, 383, 429, 432, 637, 742, 759, 838, 882, 981, 998, **1006**, 1023, 1045, 1076, 1098

B

Baca, Joe, D-Calif. (42), **144**
Bachus, Spencer, R-Ala. (6), **17**, 20, 1033
Baird, Brian, D-Wash. (3), 367, **1066**
Baker, Richard H., R-La. (6), **434**, 726, 782
Baldacci, John, D-Maine (2), 444, **446**
Baldwin, Tammy, D-Wis. (2), 272, **1099**
Ballenger, Cass, R-N.C. (10), **756**
Barcia, James A., D-Mich. (5), **509**
Barr, Bob, R-Ga. (7), 180, **272**
Barrett, Thomas M., D-Wis. (5), **1105**
Bartlett, Roscoe G., R-Md. (6), **464**
Barton, Joe L., R-Texas (6), 3, 531, 964, **967**
Bass, Charles, R-N.H. (2), 617, **622**
Baucus, Max, D-Mont., 287, 372, **590**, 594
Bayh, Evan, D-Ind., **350**, 736
Becerra, Xavier, D-Calif. (30), **123**, 242
Bennett, Robert F., R-Utah, 920, **1020**
Bentsen, Ken, D-Texas (25), **1004**
Bereuter, Doug, R-Neb. (1), 522, **600**, 840
Berkley, Shelley, D-Nev. (1), **610**
Berman, Howard L., D-Calif. (26), **116**, 122
Berry, Marion, D-Ark. (1), **52**, 960
Biden, Joseph R. Jr., D-Del., **201**, 372, 734
Biggert, Judy, R-Ill. (13), **331**, 1121
Bilirakis, Michael, R-Fla. (9), **225**, 246, 346
Bingaman, Jeff, D-N.M., 25, 590, **658**
Bishop, Sanford D. Jr., D-Ga. (2), **262**
Blagojevich, Rod R., D-Ill. (5), **316**
Blumenauer, Earl, D-Ore. (3), **840**
Blunt, Roy, R-Mo. (7), **582**
Boehlert, Sherwood, R-N.Y. (23), 87, 712, **714**
Boehner, John A., R-Ohio (8), 162, 177, 270, 503, **790**, 1075, 1107
Bond, Christopher S., R-Mo., 452, **570**, 578, 583
Bonilla, Henry, R-Texas (23), **1000**
Bonior, David E., D-Mich. (10), 81, 463, **518**, 836, 1089
Bono, Mary, R-Calif. (44), 108, **148**
Borski, Robert A., D-Pa. (3), **857**
Boswell, Leonard L., D-Iowa (3), **380**
Boucher, Rick, D-Va. (9), 1047, **1052**
Boxer, Barbara, D-Calif., 63, **65**, 78, 125, 156, 159, 453
Boyd, Allen, D-Fla. (2), **213**
Brady, Kevin, R-Texas (8), 959, **970**
Brady, Robert A., D-Pa. (1), **853**

C

Callahan, Sonny, R-Ala. (1), **7**
Calvert, Ken, R-Calif. (43), **146**
Camp, Dave, R-Mich. (4), **507**
Campbell, Ben Nighthorse, R-Colo., **166**, 174
Cannon, Christopher B., R-Utah (3), 1021, **1025**
Cantor, Eric, R-Va. (7), **1049**
Cantwell, Maria, D-Wash., **1062**
Capito, Shelley Moore, R-W.Va. (2), **1088**
Capps, Lois, D-Calif. (22), **108**, 149
Capuano, Michael E., D-Mass. (8), **490**
Cardin, Benjamin L., D-Md. (3), 379, **458**, 779
Carnahan, Jean, D-Mo., **572**
Carper, Thomas R., D-Del., **203**, 205
Carson, Brad, D-Okla. (2), **821**
Carson, Julia, D-Ind. (10), **368**
Castle, Michael N., R-Del. (AL), **204**, 946
Chabot, Steve, R-Ohio (1), 687, **776**
Chafee, Lincoln, R-R.I., **896**, 1031
Chambliss, Saxby, R-Ga. (8), 262, **274**
Christensen, Donna M.C., D-Virgin Is. (AL), **1124**
Clay, William Lacy, D-Mo. (1), **573**
Clayton, Eva, D-N.C. (1), **738**, 742, 759, 760
Cleland, Max, D-Ga., **256**, 258, 391, 923
Clement, Bob, D-Tenn. (5), **940**
Clinton, Hillary Rodham, D-N.Y., 42, 319, 669, **671**, 673, 674, 682, 686, 691, 704, 718, 719, 725, 737, 1050
Clyburn, James E., D-S.C. (6), **916**
Coble, Howard, R-N.C. (6), 151, 747, **748**, 1026
Cochran, Thad, R-Miss., **554**, 557, 558, 562
Collins, Mac, R-Ga. (3), **264**
Collins, Susan, R-Maine, 440, 441, **442**, 445
Combest, Larry, R-Texas (19), 980, 989, **992**
Condit, Gary A., D-Calif. (18), **100**, 704
Conrad, Kent, D-N.D., 659, **764**, 767, 768
Conyers, John Jr., D-Mich. (14), **526**
Cooksey, John, R-La. (5), **432**, 683, 844
Corzine, Jon, D-N.J., **628**
Costello, Jerry F., D-Ill. (12), **329**
Cox, Christopher, R-Calif. (47), 42, **154**, 832
Coyne, William J., D-Pa. (14), **877**
Craig, Larry E., R-Idaho, 64, **294**, 423, 656, 688, 833, 896, 1031
Cramer, Robert E. "Bud", D-Ala. (5) **15**
Crane, Philip M., R-Ill. (8), 106, 307, **322**, 877
Crapo, Michael D., R-Idaho, **296**, 300

Breaux, John B., D-La., 43, **420**, 422, 437, 618, 930, 954, 989, 1084
Brown, Corrine, D-Fla. (3), **215**, 241
Brown, Henry E. Jr., R-S.C. (1), **907**
Brown, Sherrod, D-Ohio (13), 782, **799**
Brownback, Sam, R-Kan., 186, **388**, 390, 394, 669, 1098
Bryant, Ed, R-Tenn. (7), **944**, 947
Bunning, Jim, R-Ky., **404**, 413, 819
Burns, Conrad, R-Mont., **592**
Burr, Richard M., R-N.C. (5), **746**
Burton, Dan, R-Ind. (6), 121, **361**, 466, 486, 679, 708, 735, 872, 1051
Buyer, Steve, R-Ind. (5), 145, 315, **359**, 578
Byrd, Robert C., D-W.Va., 23, 852, 903, 921, **1082**, 1084, 1087, 1089

Pronunciation Guide for Congress

The following is an informal pronunciation guide for some members of Congress whose names are frequently mispronounced:

SENATE

Evan Bayh, D-Ind. — BY
John B. Breaux, D-La. — BRO
Lincoln Chafee, R-R.I. — CHAY-fee
Max Cleland, D-Ga. — CLEE-lend
Jon Corzine, D-N.J. — cor-ZYNE
Michael D. Crapo, R-Idaho — CRAY-poe
Tom Daschle, D-S.D. — DASH-el
Pete V. Domenici, R-N.M. — da-MEN-ih-chee
Michael B. Enzi, R-Wyo. — EN-zee
Russell D. Feingold, D-Wis. — FINE-gold
Dianne Feinstein, D-Calif. — FINE-stine
James M. Inhofe, R-Okla. — IN-hoff
Daniel K. Inouye, D-Hawaii — in-NO-ay
Mary L. Landrieu, D-La. — LAN-drew
Rick Santorum, R-Pa. — san-TORE-um
Debbie Stabenow, D-Mich. — STAB-uh-now
Robert G. Torricelli, D-N.J. — tor-uh-SELL-ee

HOUSE

Robert B. Aderholt, R-Ala. — ADD-er-holt
Spencer Bachus, R-Ala. — BACK-us
John Baldacci, D-Maine — Ball-DA-chee
James A. Barcia, D-Mich. — BAR-sha
Xavier Becerra, D-Calif. — HAH-vee-air beh-SEH-ra
Doug Bereuter, R-Neb. — BEE-right-er
Michael Bilirakis, R-Fla. — bil-lee-RACK-us
Rod R. Blagojevich, D-Ill. — bla-GOY-a-vich
Earl Blumenauer, D-Ore. — BLUM-men-hour
Sherwood Boehlert, R-N.Y. — BO-lert
John A. Boehner, R-Ohio — BAY-ner
Henry Bonilla, R-Texas — bo-NEE-uh
David E. Bonior, D-Mich. — BON-yer
Rick Boucher, D-Va. — BOUGH-cher
Steve Buyer, R-Ind. — BOO-yer
Michael E. Capuano, D-Mass. — KAP-you-AH-no
Steve Chabot, R-Ohio — SHAB-butt
Saxby Chambliss, R-Ga. — SAX-bee CHAM-bliss
Joseph Crowley, D-N.Y. — KRAU-lee
Barbara Cubin, R-Wyo. — CUE-bin
Peter A. DeFazio, D-Ore. — da-FAH-zee-o
Diana DeGette, D-Colo. — de-GET
Bill Delahunt, D-Mass. — DELL-a-hunt
Rosa DeLauro, D-Conn. — da-LAUR-o
Peter Deutsch, D-Fla. — DOYCH
Lincoln Diaz-Balart, R-Fla. — DEE-az baa-LART
Vernon J. Ehlers, R-Mich. — AY-lurz
Robert L. Ehrlich Jr., R-Md. — ER-lick
Anna G. Eshoo, D-Calif. — EH-shoo
Eni F.H. Faleomavaega, D-Am. Samoa —
   EN-ee FOL-ee-oh-mav-ah-ENG-uh
Chaka Fattah, D-Pa. — SHOCK-ah fa-TAH
Vito J. Fossella, R-N.Y. — VEE-toe Fuh-SELL-ah
Rodney Frelinghuysen, R-N.J. — FREE-ling-high-zen
Elton Gallegly, R-Calif. — GAL-uh-glee
Greg Ganske, R-Iowa — GAN-skee
Virgil H. Goode Jr., I-Va. — GOOD (rhymes with 'food')
Robert W. Goodlatte, R-Va. — GOOD-lat

Luis V. Gutierrez, D-Ill. — loo-EES goo-tee-AIR-ez
Gil Gutknecht, R-Minn. — GOOT-neck
Van Hilleary, R-Tenn. — HILL-ary
Rubén Hinojosa, D-Texas — ru-BEN ee-na-HO-suh
Joseph M. Hoeffel, D-Pa. — HUFF-ull
Peter Hoekstra, R-Mich. — HOOK-struh
John Hostettler, R-Ind. — HO-stet-lur
Amo Houghton, R-N.Y. — HO-tun
Kenny Hulshof, R-Mo. — HULLZ-hoff
Darrell Issa, R-Calif. — EYE-sah
Ernest Istook, R-Okla. — IZ-took
Gerald D. Kleczka, D-Wis. — KLETCH-kuh
Jim Kolbe, R-Ariz. — COLE-bee
Dennis J. Kucinich, D-Ohio — ku-SIN-itch
Jim Langevin, D-R.I. — LANN-juh-vinn
Steven C. LaTourette, R-Ohio — la-TUR-et
Frank A. LoBiondo, R-N.J. — lo-bee-ON-dough
Zoe Lofgren, D-Calif. — ZO
Nita M. Lowey, D-N.Y. — LOW-ee
Donald Manzullo, R-Ill. — man-ZOO-low
Jerrold Nadler, D-N.Y. — NAD-ler
Bob Ney, R-Ohio — NAY
David R. Obey, D-Wis. — OH-bee
Doug Ose, R-Calif. — OH-see
Frank Pallone Jr., D-N.J. — pa-LOAN
Bill Pascrell Jr., D-N.J. — pas-KRELL
Ed Pastor, D-Ariz. — pas-TORE
Nancy Pelosi, D-Calif. — pa-LOH-see
Tom Petri, R-Wis. — PEE-try
Richard W. Pombo, R-Calif. — POM-bo
George P. Radanovich, R-Calif. — Ruh-DON-o-vitch
Ralph Regula, R-Ohio — REG-you-luh
Denny Rehberg, R-Mont. — REE-berg
Silvestre Reyes, D-Texas — sil-VES-treh RAY-ess (rolled 'R')
Dana Rohrabacher, R-Calif. — ROAR-ah-BAH-ker
Ileana Ros-Lehtinen, R-Fla. — il-ee-AH-na ross-LAY-tin-nen
Marge Roukema, R-N.J. — ROCK-ah-muh
Joe Scarborough, R-Fla. — SCAR-burro
Bob Schaffer, R-Colo. — SHAY-fer
Jan Schakowsky, D-Ill. — shuh-KOW-ski
Jose E. Serrano, D-N.Y. — ho-ZAY sa-RAH-no (rolled 'R')
John Shadegg, R-Ariz. — SHAD-egg
John Shimkus, R-Ill. — SHIM-kus
Ronnie Shows, D-Miss. — rhymes with 'cows'
Hilda L. Solis, D-Calif. — soh-LEEZ
Mark Souder, R-Ind. — SOW (rhymes with 'now')-dur
Bart Stupak, D-Mich. — STEW-pack
Tom Tancredo, R-Colo. — tan-CRAY-doe
Ellen O. Tauscher, D-Calif. — TAU (rhymes with 'how')-sher
Billy Tauzin, R-La. — TOE-zan
John Thune, R-S.D. — THOON
Todd Tiahrt, R-Kan. — TEE-hart
Pat Tiberi, R-Ohio — TEA-berry
Nydia M. Velázquez, D-N.Y. — NID-ee-uh veh-LASS-kez
Peter J. Visclosky, D-Ind. — vis-KLOSS-key
Anthony Weiner, D-N.Y. — WEE-ner
Lynn Woolsey, D-Calif. — WOOL-zee